P9-AQL-777

I consider a story merely as a frame on which to stretch my materials. It is the play of thought, and sentiment, and language; the weaving in of characters . . . these are among what I aim at.
■ **WASHINGTON IRVING**

I have the writer's healthy selfish instinct to keep open the multiple vision that the fly's eye of the writer had brought me.
■ **NADINE GORDIMER**

The poet's mission on earth is to inspire and to illuminate; and to leave behind to our glorious descendants an intricate and varied map of humanity.
■ **MARILYN CHIN**

I think a little menace is fine to have in a story. For one thing, it's good for the circulation. There has to be tension, a sense that something is imminent, that certain things are in relentless motion, or else, most often, there simply won't be a story.
■ **RAYMOND CARVER**

Fiction is obliged to stick to possibilities. Truth isn't.
■ **MARK TWAIN**

The great and only possible dignity of man lies in his power to deliberately choose certain moral values by which to live as steadfastly as if he too, like a character in a play, were immured against the corrupting rush of time.
■ **TENNESSEE WILLIAMS**

www.bedfordstmartins.com/charters

Visit the Charters Web site with book-specific materials for *Literature and Its Writers,* Second Edition, and *Literature and Its Writers,* Compact Second Edition

Our exciting new Web site for *Literature and Its Writers,* Second Edition, and *Literature and Its Writers,* Compact Second Edition, offers students and instructors a variety of accessible and helpful resources that complement the texts and provide additional opportunities to think and write about the literature in the books. Key features of our Web site include —

- ***Study questions and writing suggestions*** to accompany the selections in the books.
- ***Sample syllabi and assignment ideas*** for instructors.
- ***Annotated research links*** for hundreds of authors in the books.

www.bedfordstmartins.com

On the Bedford/St. Martin's Web site, you will find many helpful resources, including —

LitLinks **www.bedfordstmartins.com/literature/litlinks**
Clear, concise annotations and links to over 500 professionally maintained sites help students browse with direction, whether they're looking for a favorite text, additional biographical information about an author, critical articles, or conversation with other students and scholars.

The English Research Room **www.bedfordstmartins.com/english_research**
Serving as both a general resource and a central location for book-specific content, this area provides reference information, interactive tutorials, practice exercises, and additional assignments that help students conduct research and write research projects, along with links to the most useful search engines, research guides, and primary sources.

Research and Documentation Online **www.bedfordstmartins.com/hacker/resdoc**
Citing sources correctly in a final paper is often a challenge, and the Web has made it even more complex. This online version of the popular booklet *Research and Documentation in the Electronic Age,* by Diana Hacker, provides clear, authoritative advice on documentation in every discipline. It also covers conducting library and online research and includes links to Internet research sources.

LITERATURE AND ITS WRITERS

An Introduction to Fiction, Poetry, and Drama

■ Books Written or Edited by Ann Charters

The Story and Its Writer: An Introduction to Short Fiction
The American Short Story and Its Writer: An Anthology
Major Writers of Short Fiction: Stories and Commentaries
Beats & Company: Portrait of a Literary Generation
Kerouac: A Biography
The Portable Beat Reader
The Portable Jack Kerouac
Selected Letters of Jack Kerouac, 1940–1956
Selected Letters of Jack Kerouac, 1957–1969
Nobody: The Story of Bert Williams

■ Books Written by Samuel Charters

Some Poems/Poets: Studies in American Underground Poetry
Elvis Presley Calls His Mother After the Ed Sullivan Show
Mr. Jabi and Mr. Smythe
Jelly Roll Morton's Last Night at the Jungle Inn: An Imaginary Memoir
Louisiana Black: A Novel
A Country Year: A Chronicle
From a Swedish Notebook
Robert Johnson
Sweet as the Showers of Rain
The Country Blues
The Day Is So Long and the Wages So Small: Music on a Summer Island
The Legacy of the Blues: A Glimpse into the Art and the Lives of Twelve Great Bluesmen
The Roots of the Blues: An African Search
The Bluesmen: The Story and the Music of the Men Who Made the Blues

■ Books Written by Ann Charters and Samuel Charters

I Love: The Story of Vladimir Mayakovsky and Lili Brik
Blues Faces

Second Edition

LITERATURE AND ITS WRITERS

An Introduction to Fiction, Poetry, and Drama

Ann Charters
UNIVERSITY OF CONNECTICUT

Samuel Charters

BEDFORD / ST. MARTIN'S
Boston ■ New York

For Bedford / St. Martin's
Developmental Editor: Maura Shea
Production Editor: Lori Chong Roncka
Production Supervisors: Donna Peterson and Joe Ford
Director of Marketing: Karen Melton
Editorial Assistant: Tracey Finch
Production Assistant: Thomas P. Crehan
Copyeditors: Paula Woolley and Jane Zanichkowsky
Text Design: Anna George
Cover Design: Donna Lee Dennison
Cover Art: Author Jamaica Kincaid at her home office in Bennington, Vermont. Photograph by Taro Yamasaki / PEOPLE Weekly.
Composition: Stratford Publishing Services
Printing and Binding: Quebecor Printing Hawkins

President: Charles H. Christensen
Editorial Director: Joan E. Feinberg
Editor in Chief: Karen S. Henry
Director of Editing, Design, and Production: Marcia Cohen
Managing Editor: Elizabeth M. Schaaf

Library of Congress Control Number: 00–103096

Copyright © 2001 by Bedford / St. Martin's
All rights reserved. No part of this book may be reproduced, stored in a retrieval system, or transmitted in any form or by any means, electronic, mechanical, photocopying, recording, or otherwise, except as may be expressly permitted by the applicable copyright statutes or in writing by the Publisher.

Manufactured in the United States of America.

5 4 3 2 1 0
f e d c b a

For information, write: Bedford / St. Martin's, 75 Arlington Street, Boston, MA 02116 (617-399-4000)

ISBN: 0–312–20979–7

Acknowledgments

FICTION

Chinua Achebe. "Marriage Is a Private Affair" from *Girls at War and Other Stories*. Copyright © 1972, 1973 by Chinua Achebe. Reprinted by permission of Doubleday, a division of Random House, Inc., and Harold Ober Associates.

Sherman Alexie. "The Lone Ranger and Tonto Fistfight in Heaven" from *The Lone Ranger and Tonto Fistfight in Heaven*. Copyright © 1993 by Sherman Alexie. Reprinted by permission of Grove / Atlantic, Inc.

Isabel Allende. "An Act of Vengeance" from *Short Stories by Latin American Women: The Magic and the Real*, ed. Celia Correas de Zapata (Houston: Arte Publico–U of Houston, 1990). Reprinted by permission of the publisher.

Acknowledgments and copyrights are continued at the back of the book on pages 2120–33, which constitute an extension of the copyright page. It is a violation of the law to reproduce these selections by any means whatsoever without the written permission of the copyright holder.

PREFACE FOR INSTRUCTORS

Introductory literature anthologies are designed to help students explore the many ways to read, think, and write about literature. This is what *Literature and Its Writers* does, but with an important difference: As much as possible, it lets the words of writers themselves — the storytellers, the poets, the dramatists whose work appears in the anthology — lead the exploration.

A DISTINCTIVE EMPHASIS ON WRITERS AND WRITING

Writers, we believe, offer the best insights on the literature they create, and on the writing they perform. Accordingly, *Literature and Its Writers* is threaded with writer talk: with quotations that clarify, with examples that enlighten, and especially with *commentaries* that show how writers think and write about literature. We have found that students respond readily to these voices in the text. They are more willing to raise their own voices to enter the conversation. They listen more attentively to what is being said. They express themselves more confidently. Having before them examples of writers speaking plainly, or colorfully, or profoundly, or provokingly, they are better able to speak and write that way themselves. Through the weave of literary works and literary voices, students comprehend what a human enterprise literature is; they come to see it as the work of talented, questing people like themselves. Not only do students explore *what* literature means and *how* it derives meaning — interpretation and analysis — but they also ask two fundamental questions about it: How is it made, and how is it related to us?

In our anthology, the seventy stories, 329 poems, and fifteen plays are complemented by 140 commentaries that discuss specific literary works, literary form and influence, and the creative process. Students encounter not only "A Rose for Emily," but also what William Faulkner had to say about his famous story; not just the poetry of Emily Dickinson, but also Dickinson's remarks about her poetry in letters to Thomas Wentworth Higginson; not just Lorraine Hansberry's *A Raisin in the Sun,* but also Hansberry's admiring tributes to William Shakespeare and Arthur Miller. The commentaries provide numerous discussion and writing opportunities, as well as models of how writers think, read, and write about literature. But the focus on writers does not stop with the commentaries. Words of the writers themselves are interwoven throughout the uncommonly full biographical headnotes for individual authors, and in our definitions and discussions of the traditional elements of literary genres. Students hear from Margaret Atwood on a writer's voice, Robert Frost on rhyme, and Edward Albee on playwriting.

Finally, we have shifted all questions and selection-specific writing suggestions from the book itself to the Instructor's Manual and to a Web site, which students can access. We do this so that our prompts neither interfere with what the writers have to say about the literature, nor influence how students interpret it. The choice of assigning or not assigning our apparatus remains the instructor's.

HOW THIS BOOK IS ORGANIZED

Literature and Its Writers, Second Edition, is divided into five parts. Parts One and Five are devoted to all aspects of reading and writing, and to understanding literary theory. Parts Two, Three, and Four are devoted to short fiction, poetry, and drama. Within each of these parts, introductory chapters discuss the genre, its elements, and how to read, think, and write about a work in a particular genre. Then comes the literature — the fiction and drama sections prepared by Ann Charters and the poetry section prepared by Samuel Charters. Seventy stories, arranged alphabetically by author, represent the most extensive and diverse selection of the type of literature students most enjoy. Three hundred twenty-nine poems, appearing within the discussion chapters and in an alphabetically arranged anthology of forty-six poets, include familiar classics and fresh poems from contemporary poets. Fifteen plays, from enduring works by Sophocles and Tennessee Williams to contemporary plays by August Wilson and Caryl Churchill, are arranged chronologically so the headnotes can trace the development of dramatic tradition.

Following the literature in each section are the commentaries: Forty-seven on stories and storytellers, fifty-five on poetry and poets, and thirty-eight on plays and playwrights. Although they mainly present the remarks of the writers themselves, the commentaries also include a sampling of contemporary criticism, which is discussed in detail in Part Five. Each section closes with casebooks of commentaries that provide an in-depth look — in the authors' own words and the words of other writers, scholars, and critics — at three storytellers (Raymond Carver, Zora Neale Hurston, and Flannery O'Connor), four poets (Emily Dickinson, Robert Frost, Langston Hughes, and Sharon Olds), and three playwrights (William Shakespeare, Arthur Miller, and Lorraine Hansberry).

NEW TO THIS EDITION

In addition to the many new selections, what sets the second edition of *Literature and Its Writers* apart from the first is our focus on showing students *how to use* what storytellers, poets, and playwrights have to say about the art and craft of literature to shape and define their own interpretations.

New Stories, Poems, and Plays

The twenty-five new stories, 119 new poems, and six new plays encompass a greater array of writers than ever before, striking a balance between classic works and less canonical but highly teachable ones. In the fiction section, the new stories include much-anthologized works by Raymond Carver and Kate Chopin, American multicultural stories by Sandra Cisneros and Sherman Alexie, international stories by Nadine Gordimer and Chinua Achebe, and contemporary stories by John Edgar Wideman and Edwidge Danticat. The poetry section continues to provide a balance of familiar and less familiar works on compelling themes by classic and contemporary poets. Several of the new selections in the poetry section are collected in a new thematic chapter, Poets Speaking Out, which brings together for study poems about politics, society, and the environment. Also new are special sections on song and rhyme and literary limericks. In the drama section, we now offer instructors more options than ever before to teach classic works — such as Sophocles' *Antigone* (in addition to *Oedipus the King*), Shakespeare's *The Tempest* (in addition to *Hamlet*) — and contemporary works by American multicultural playwrights including August Wilson, Philip Kan Gotanda, and Milcha Sanchez-Scott.

New Commentaries and Casebooks

The thirty-four new commentaries, including selections by Joseph Conrad, Amy Tan, Langston Hughes, Louise Glück, William Carlos Williams, Caryl Churchill, and Aimé Césaire, provide students with more opportunities for discussion and writing than ever before. Three new casebooks (one for each genre) allow students to study the lives and works of fiction writer Zora Neale Hurston, poet Sharon Olds, and playwright Arthur Miller. The fiction casebook on Raymond Carver now encourages students to consider Carver as a writer who frequently revised the works he had already published. Each casebook author in the book is represented with a compelling photograph.

Expanded Instruction on Reading, Thinking, and Writing about Literature

In the second edition, we have provided more ways for student writers to enter the conversation about literature and to discover the writing process that works for them. Now prominently positioned at the front of the book in Part One on Reading, Thinking, and Writing about Literature, the writing instruction has been newly shaped to show students how to use the commentaries to think and write about literature. Part One reveals one student's process of reading a short story, thinking about it in her journal, reading a related commentary, generating new ideas about the story, creating an essay topic from those thoughts, writing several drafts of an essay, and participating in a peer review.

Situated in all five parts of the book, ten student papers provide realistic models for writing different types of essays. Four of these essays are grouped together in Part Five in a new chapter on basic types of literary papers. Also in Part Five is a greatly expanded section on the research paper with detailed and up-to-date information on finding a topic, evaluating online sources, drafting the essay, and documenting sources.

A new chapter in Part Five introduces students to the basic schools of literary theory and references several commentaries throughout the book as examples of each critical approach.

INSTRUCTOR'S MANUAL AND WEB SITE

Resources for Teaching Literature and Its Writers, Second Edition, presents a wide range of teaching resources, including essays that offer interpretations of individual works to explore in the classroom, selected bibliographies for many writers, questions to prompt student discussion, writing topics, an extensive list of audiovisual resources, and a thematic table of contents.

In addition, we now have a companion Web site located at **www.bedfordstmartins.com/charters**. The site provides annotated links to hundreds of authors in the book, study questions and writing suggestions for students and instructors, and sample syllabi and assignment ideas.

CD AND VIDEOTAPES

Speaking of Literature, a CD with readings of selected poems, stories, scenes from plays, and commentaries from writers is available to instructors who adopt *Literature and Its Writers,* Second Edition. This rich resource for instructors and students brings literature to life through the compelling voices of celebrated writers and actors. Instructors may also obtain a selection of videotapes of stories and poems in the book.

COMPACT EDITION

Literature and Its Writers, Second Edition, is also available in a compact paperback edition containing forty-nine stories, 264 poems, ten plays, and ninety-eight commentaries. The compact edition retains all of the longer book's editorial features for those who want a smaller, less expensive anthology.

ACKNOWLEDGMENTS

In this second edition, we consider ourselves fortunate to have had the opportunity to work with our most responsive and resourceful editor, Maura Shea, whose dedication to the project has helped us through many bumpy patches. We would also like to acknowledge the steadfast support of the president of Bedford/St. Martin's, Charles Christensen, who originally came to us with the idea for this anthology. In shaping the direction of the book, we worked closely with executive editor Steve Scipione for the first edition, and he has continued to offer useful insights and suggestions throughout the revision process. Our patient production editor, Lori Roncka, attentively saw the book through its final stages. Also at Bedford/St. Martin's, we would like to thank Joan Feinberg, Kathy Retan, and Elizabeth Schaaf for their encouragement; Tracey Finch for her tireless library research and assistance on the Web site; Jose Quesada for his help in translating Spanish phrases; and Nicole Simonsen for a variety of editorial tasks. We thank Janet Gardner of the University of Massachusetts, Dartmouth, and Barbara Fister of Gustavus Adolphus College, who helped write and update the chapter on the research paper. For assistance with the Instructor's Manual, we are grateful to Susan Abbotson of the University of Connecticut, who wrote the entries in the Drama section; William Sheidley of the University of Southern Colorado, who wrote many of the entries in the Fiction section; and Joanne Diaz for her work on the list of audiovisual resources.

In addition, professors who used the previous edition of the anthology and generously took time to share their ideas about it include: Janice M. Alberghene, Fitchburg State College; Homer Arrington, Santa Barbara City College; Crystal Bacon, Gloucester County College; Anne Carr, Southeast Community College; Mary Jane Chaffee, Campbellsville College; Seamus Cooney, Western Michigan University; Benjamin B. Edwards, Tulsa Community College; Stephen Ersinghaus, Tunxis Community-Technical College; Luis Gámez, Western Michigan University; Laurie Glover, University of California–Davis; Sally Harrold, Southwestern Oregon Community College; Diana Joseph, Mesa State College; Robert Judd, Columbia-Greene Community College; Carol King, Rensselaer Polytechnic Institute; David A. Kossy, De Paul University; Joellen Masters, Boston University; Teresa Melnick, Onondaga Community College; Clara L. Metzmeier, Campbellsville University; Angela Morris, Hawaii Pacific University; Keith Neilson, California State University; Elyse O'Connor, Boston University; Randy Rudder, Nashville State Technical Institute; Andrea Sanelli, Chabot College and Evergreen Valley College; William Schikora, Bay State College; Michael Schultz, Washburn University of

Topeka; Grant T. Smith,Viterbo College; Gwen Sorrell Sell, Macon State College; Anthony Turner, Wallace Community College; Steven Weibe, Merced College; Nancy Weingart, John Carroll University; Jane Whorton, Pearl River Community College.

We would also like to thank our reviewers: Brian Anderson, Central Piedmont Community College; Lee Barnes, Community College of Southern Nevada; Elizabeth Flores, College of Lake County; Deborah Ford, University of Southern Mississippi; Katie Hanson, Augustana College; Marilyn Roberts, Waynesburg College; Sue Ann Schatz, University of New Mexico; Richard Spiese, California State University–Long Beach; Martin Trapp, Northwestern Michigan College; Tom Zaniello, Northern Kentucky University.

Ann Charters
University of Connecticut

Samuel Charters

(Photo by Reenie Barrow)

ABOUT THE EDITORS

ANN CHARTERS *(Ph.D., Columbia University) is the editor of* The Story and Its Writer, *Fifth Edition (Bedford/St. Martin's, 1999), the best-selling introduction to fiction. She is a professor of English at the University of Connecticut and has taught introduction to literature courses for many years. A preeminent authority on the Beat writers, Charters has written a critically acclaimed biography of Jack Kerouac; compiled* Beats & Company, *a collection of her own photographs of Beat writers; and edited the best-selling* Portable Beat Reader. *Her most recent books are* The Kerouac Reader, Selected Letters of Jack Kerouac, 1957–1969, *and* The American Short Story and Its Writer.

■

SAMUEL CHARTERS *has taught creative writing and published widely in a variety of genres, including eleven books of poetry, four novels, a book of criticism on contemporary American poetry, a biography (coauthored with Ann Charters) of the poet Vladimir Mayakovsky, and translations of the poetry of Tomas Tranströmer and Edith Södergran. An ethnomusicologist, he produces blues and jazz recordings and has published ten books about music, among them a study of Robert Johnson and histories of New York and New Orleans jazz.*

BRIEF CONTENTS

CONTENTS

4 STORIES AND STORYTELLERS *55*

INTRODUCTION

CONNECTING WITH LITERATURE

> Writing, for me, is an act of faith, a hope that I will discover what I mean by "truth." I also think of reading as an act of faith, a hope that I will discover something remarkable about ordinary life, about myself. And if the writer and the reader discover the same thing, if they have that connection, the act of faith has resulted in an act of magic. To me, that's the mystery and the wonder of both life and fiction — the connection between two individuals who discover in the end that they are more the same than they are different.
>
> – Amy Tan, "In the Canon, For All the Wrong Reasons"

Why study literature? We read stories, poems, and plays for many reasons. When you allow yourself to become fully immersed in an author's words and ideas, you can bring to life an imaginary world that can tell you something about your own everyday reality. As a student of literature, you will find that the stories, poems, and plays in this anthology will often enable you to view life with a new clarity as you relate what you have read to your own experience.

The novelist Vladimir Nabokov proposed a quiz for students of literature that would give ten definitions of a reader and ask them to choose any four definitions that added up to what they considered the necessary qualities of a *good* reader. In Nabokov's essay "Good Readers and Good Writers," his quiz went as follows:

1. The reader should belong to a book club.
2. The reader should identify himself or herself with the hero or heroine.
3. The reader should concentrate on the social-economic or historical angle.
4. The reader should prefer a story with action and dialogue to one with none.
5. The reader should have seen the book in a movie.
6. The reader should be a budding author.
7. The reader should have imagination.

8. The reader should have memory.
9. The reader should have a dictionary.
10. The reader should have some artistic sense.

Nabokov predicted that most students would choose items 2 and 3 as essential to being a good reader, but he insisted that only the last four items were necessary. You don't always have to identify with the hero or heroine of a literary work, using the text as a mirror to project an image of yourself playing out different roles. And if you anxiously expect your instructor to teach you that there is only one correct interpretation of a complex poem, story, or play — or if you lazily prefer to approach a text with a preconceived notion of its meaning, which you copy down in the classroom before you read the assignment for yourself — then you will not start out as a good student of literature.

A good reader possesses an active imagination, a retentive memory, a college dictionary, and a rudimentary artistic sense. Furthermore, if you hope to become a great reader, you will also need to bring to the course — along with your imagination and memory — a strong desire to refine and develop your critical sense. This quality will evolve naturally from your close reading and writing about literary texts.

The process of making a close connection with literature and becoming a great reader always helps you to become a better writer. The American poet Robert Frost aptly described this process when he said, "To learn to write is to learn to have ideas." Reading closely and thinking critically about the literature in this anthology will suggest ideas that you can develop in class discussions and in your essays.

At first you may suppose that you have little in common with the distinguished authors gathered here, but bear in mind that each of them was once a beginner. The short story writer Raymond Carver described taking his first college course in "Creative Writing 101." After reading his commentary, one student recognized a connection with Carver's experience in this short essay.

STUDENT ESSAY

Raymond Carver's "Creative Writing 101"

We all have several turning points in our life. These turning points may include getting married, losing loved ones, having children, and changing jobs. However, we can have other turning points which exert more subtle effects on us and are no less significant.

The American writer Raymond Carver married young and had two children. He eked out a living to support his family, but he wanted to go to college because of his desire to be a writer. He felt in his bones that he had to get an education in order to learn more about being a writer. When he finally could enroll in a college writing course, he was fortunate to have John Gardner, a young novelist, as his teacher.

Studying with Gardner was a significant turning point in Carver's life. Gardener became aware of Carver's difficulty in finding a place to work, so he offered his student the key to his office, where Carver could begin what he remembered as his "first serious attempts at writing." Just as important, Gardner read Carver's first stories seriously. Sometimes Carver had to revise a sentence several times to satisfy his teacher. Gardner insisted that a writer must be honest. He couldn't "fake it" by writing about something he didn't believe in.

Carver learned what he called "a writer's values and craft" from his first writing teacher. These were what Gardner taught him in Creative Writing 101, Carver's most important turning point as a writer.

Understanding Carver's experience in Creative Writing 101 as an important turning point is the connection the student makes between her own knowledge of life and Carver's essay. Going on to analyze the "values and craft" exemplified by works of literature will help you to develop your own skills as a reader and writer. For example, you can read about the American playwright Lorraine Hansberry's "Shakespearean Experience" and compare it in an essay with your own response to *Hamlet* or *The Tempest*. You can analyze the dazzling sparks of ideas about the themes of love and death in the works of Emily Dickinson or Sylvia Plath, or interpret the genius of Langston Hughes as he translates the pain of racism into poetry accessible to everyone.

In the essay "Good Readers and Good Writers," Nabokov understood the complexity of our responses to literature. He believed that every author "may be considered as a storyteller, as a teacher, and as an enchanter. A major writer combines these three — storyteller, teacher, enchanter — but it is the enchanter in him that predominates and makes him a major writer."

Initially we all turn to storytellers for mental and emotional stimulation, the pleasure of entering an alternative universe to our own, evoked in our minds from our connection with the words of a literary text. Not only does great literature entertain us — it also provokes our thought. If we think about what we have read after we have finished a story, poem, or play, we realize that authors are often teachers — their words contribute to the development of our own sense of values and remind us of the inexorable brevity and essential mystery of our everyday lives. Finally, we can return to the story, poem, or play for what many readers consider the most enchanting connection with literature: We can use our artistic sense to study what Nabokov called "the individual magic" of each writer's genius — the beauty resulting from the style, the imagery, and the pattern of the literary text.

READING LITERATURE

Regardless of where you start to read and write about literature — whether you begin with short stories, poems, or plays — the important thing to remember is that you must try to read your assignments slowly and carefully. When you become a student of literature, you do not read in the same casual way that you pick up a newspaper or a magazine, or even in the way that you concentrate on the pages of the assignments for your other courses, trying to find and underline passages in which the author has stated the meaning or main ideas about the subject in words that you then memorize for a quiz or an exam.

The way you read this so-called objective prose in history or science textbooks can be described as linear, in that the objectivity of the text evokes a similar objectivity in your attention to the words on the page. You read along sentence by sentence, following the linear development of the author's thesis or argument. Works of literature, on the other hand, create meaning differently. Literary texts have an additional dimension of *significance* as well as meaning.

Significance is expressed through your personal response to the story, poem, or play. It is how you connect with what the author as storyteller, teacher, and enchanter has created in the text — what *you* make of it. As you read, your comprehension arises from your experience of life, which also includes your study of literature. Reading the author headnotes and commentaries in *Literature and Its Writers* will help you expand your literary background by adding to your knowledge of the writers' lives, historical times, and cultural tradition.

The English critic Cyril Connolly once said, "Literature is the art of writing something that will be read twice." Try to read your assignments twice, the first time enjoying the experience of *arriving* at the end of the text, seeing how the author resolves the plot of a story or play or develops the subject of a poem. The second time you read a text, you can focus on *getting there*, becoming aware of how authors create the world evoked on the page by using the elements of their craft. This is called **close reading**. It is essential for understanding what an author has created in the text. This process will assist you in interpreting accurately what you have read. Close reading will also reveal the writer's creation of design and pattern in the literary work, as distinctive to each author as his or her fingerprints. Through this process of careful reading, you are taking the first steps toward thinking critically about the text and discovering its significance for you.

THINKING AND WRITING ABOUT LITERATURE

With literature, *you* help to create meaning. The way you interpret what you read determines the significance of a story, poem, or play for you. Literature becomes meaningful when you read actively. Slow down. Take the time to think about the text. Relate the author's personal vision to your own experiences of life and literature and the questions you ask of them.

To help you connect with literature so that you can develop your critical thinking and express your ideas effectively in essays, this anthology opens with a chapter on writing about a short story by the American author Eudora Welty. This discussion shows how reading Welty's commentary on her story in the early stages of the writing process can stimulate your critical thinking about its significance. This first part of the book describes the step-by-step process of composing a short essay about literature. The chapter concludes with a list of general guidelines on how to write papers.

Just as one student understood that there was a parallel between Raymond Carver's commentary "Creative Writing 101" and her experience of life's "turning points," you create the significance that a story, poem, or play has for you as you refine your thoughts about it. Expressing your ideas in an essay will help you to clarify your response for yourself and others. You write to discover what you know, hoping "to find truth at the end of a pencil," as Ernest Hemingway described it.

To facilitate your progress in *Literature and Its Writers,* detailed suggestions to help you think and write about what you read are included, along with short student essays, in the introductory chapters to each of the literary genres of fiction, poetry, and drama. Part Five, the last section of the textbook, offers strategies for developing your ideas about your reading into essays. Various critical approaches to literature are presented, followed by several rhetorical methods useful in writing longer essays, each with an accompanying student paper. The research paper is the topic of the final chapter of the anthology.

PART ONE

READING, THINKING, AND WRITING ABOUT LITERATURE

- *. . . a combination of the artistic and scientific [temperament]. The enthusiastic artist alone is apt to be too subjective in his attitude toward a book, and so a scientific coolness of judgment will temper the intuitive heat.*

  – Vladimir Nabokov (on the qualities of the ideal reader)

- *I now know and trust completely that writing happens long before I ever type a word; that my best thinking and writing will happen before and after the first draft but not necessarily during it.*

  – Alex Johnson

- *A story writer is more than happy to be read by students; the fact that these serious readers think and feel something in response to his work he finds life-giving.*

  – Eudora Welty (on her readers' response to "A Worn Path")

READING, THINKING, AND WRITING ABOUT LITERATURE

> Literature is our conversation between the past and present out of which we articulate ourselves.
>
> –DANA GIOIA, "Fallen Star," *Hungry Mind Review* 52

Read literature for the pleasure of it, Ernest Hemingway once told an interviewer, adding that "whatever else you find will be the measure of what you brought to the reading." Literature expands your view of the world, by inviting you to share the perspective of gifted storytellers, poets, and dramatists who can entertain, instruct, and perhaps enchant you. An assignment to create an essay about literature gives you the opportunity to explain how you have been affected by what you have read. In your essay, you explore your connection with the text and clarify your ideas about its significance. The writing process begins as soon as you ask the smallest question about the meaning or the structure of a literary work.

Good ideas are essential to a successful essay. How do you develop your initial emotional response to a story, poem, or play into ideas for a paper? There is no magic formula that guarantees a good essay, since all writers must find their own way and learn to do it for themselves. If you understand the various steps involved, the writing process can become much easier. As the essayist Alex Johnson has observed, writing is always a challenge, but it does not always have to be a chore. In "Having a Bad Morning," she confessed uncertainty as to "how to get the thinking out."

> It took me years of trial and error to learn the obvious: writing is best and most satisfying done in stages. . . . I now know and trust completely that writing happens long before I ever type a word; that my best thinking and writing will happen before and after the first draft but not necessarily during it; that by seeing writing as a process, I now

> know the pleasure of making connections: ruminating on a subject, seeing patterns emerge, watching an argument evolve, evidence cohere. In short, that glorious territoriality of staking and claiming a subject as my own.

The best way to write an essay about literature is to proceed in stages, understanding that good writing is as much a process as it is an end result. When you are fully engaged in this endeavor, you will discover that the process also turns you into a better reader. Both as a reader and a writer, you will exercise your sensitivity and intelligence if you work conscientiously through the various stages toward the final draft of your paper.

Assume, for example, that your first writing assignment will be a two- to three-page paper (500 to 750 words) on Eudora Welty's story "A Worn Path." You have one week to turn in your essay. Everyone works differently, but here is a description of how you might budget your time most efficiently during the week by taking the writing process in stages. This process is a lot easier than procrastinating until the day before your paper is due and then pulling a hectic all-nighter in a desperate effort to get the work finished on time.

First, before you start to write, you must read the story carefully at least twice. In "Good Readers and Good Writers," Vladimir Nabokov suggested that the ideal reader should develop "a combination of the artistic and the scientific [temperament]. The enthusiastic artist alone is apt to be too subjective in his attitude toward a book, and so a scientific coolness of judgment will temper the intuitive heat." Read Welty's story the first time for pleasure; bring out your "scientific coolness" when you study it the second time.

EUDORA WELTY

A Worn Path

1941

It was December — a bright frozen day in the early morning. Far out in the country there was an old Negro woman with her head tied in a red rag, coming along a path through the pinewoods. Her name was Phoenix Jackson. She was very old and small and she walked slowly in the dark pine shadows, moving a little from side to side in her steps, with the balanced heaviness and lightness of a pendulum in a grandfather clock. She carried a thin, small cane made from an umbrella, and with this she kept tapping the frozen earth in front of her. This made a grave and persistent noise in the still air, that seemed meditative like the chirping of a solitary little bird.

She wore a dark striped dress reaching down to her shoe tops, and an equally long apron of bleached sugar sacks, with a full pocket: all neat and tidy, but every time she took a step she might have fallen over her shoelaces, which dragged from her unlaced shoes. She looked straight ahead. Her eyes were blue with age. Her skin had a pattern all its own of numberless branching wrinkles and as though a whole little tree stood in the middle of her forehead, but a golden color ran underneath, and the two knobs of her cheeks were illumined by a yellow burning under the dark. Under the red rag her hair came down on her neck in the frailest of ringlets, still black, and with an odor like copper.

Now and then there was a quivering in the thicket. Old Phoenix said, "Out of my way, all you foxes, owls, beetles, jack rabbits, coons and wild animals! . . . Keep out from under these feet, little bobwhites. . . . Keep the big wild hogs out of my path. Don't let none of those come running my direction. I got a long way." Under her small black-freckled hand her cane, limber as a buggy whip, would switch at the brush as if to rouse up any hiding things.

On she went. The woods were deep and still. The sun made the pine needles almost too bright to look at, up where the wind rocked. The cones dropped as light as feathers. Down in the hollow was the mourning dove — it was not too late for him.

The path ran up a hill. "Seem like there is chains about my feet, time I get this far," she said, in the voice of argument old people keep to use with themselves. "Something always take a hold of me on this hill — pleads I should stay."

After she got to the top she turned and gave a full, severe look behind her where she had come. "Up through pines," she said at length. "Now down through oaks."

Her eyes opened their widest, and she started down gently. But before she got to the bottom of the hill a bush caught her dress.

Her fingers were busy and intent, but her skirts were full and long, so that before she could pull them free in one place they were caught in another. It was not possible to allow the dress to tear. "I in the thorny bush," she said. "Thorns, you doing your appointed work. Never want to let folks pass, no sir. Old eyes thought you was a pretty little *green* bush."

Finally, trembling all over, she stood free, and after a moment dared to stoop for her cane.

"Sun so high!" she cried, leaning back and looking, while the thick tears went over her eyes. "The time getting all gone here."

At the foot of this hill was a place where a log was laid across the creek.

"Now comes the trial," said Phoenix.

Putting her right foot out, she mounted the log and shut her eyes. Lifting her skirt, leveling her cane fiercely before her, like a festival figure in some parade, she began to march across. Then she opened her eyes and she was safe on the other side.

"I wasn't as old as I thought," she said.

But she sat down to rest. She spread her skirts on the bank around her and folded her hands over her knees. Up above her was a tree in a pearly cloud of mistletoe. She did not dare to close her eyes, and when a little boy brought her a plate with a slice of marble-cake on it she spoke to him. "That would be acceptable," she said. But when she went to take it there was just her own hand in the air.

So she left that tree, and had to go through a barbed-wire fence. There she had to creep and crawl, spreading her knees and stretching her fingers like a baby trying to climb the steps. But she talked loudly to herself: she could not let her dress be torn now, so late in the day, and she could not pay for having her arm or her leg sawed off if she got caught fast where she was.

At last she was safe through the fence and risen up out in the clearing. Big dead trees, like black men with one arm, were standing in the purple stalks of the withered cotton field. There sat a buzzard.

"Who you watching?"

In the furrow she made her way along.

"Glad this not the season for bulls," she said, looking sideways, "and the good Lord made his snakes to curl up and sleep in the winter. A pleasure I don't see no two-headed snake coming around that tree, where it come once. It took a while to get by him, back in the summer."

She passed through the old cotton and went into a field of dead corn. It whispered and shook and was taller than her head. "Through the maze now," she said, for there was no path.

Then there was something tall, black, and skinny there, moving before her.

At first she took it for a man. It could have been a man dancing in the field. But she stood still and listened, and it did not make a sound. It was as silent as a ghost.

"Ghost," she said sharply, "who be you the ghost of? For I have heard of nary death close by."

But there was no answer — only the ragged dancing in the wind.

She shut her eyes, reached out her hand, and touched a sleeve. She found a coat and inside that an emptiness, cold as ice.

"You scarecrow," she said. Her face lighted. "I ought to be shut up for good," she said with laughter. "My senses is gone. I too old. I the oldest people I ever know. Dance, old scarecrow," she said, "while I dancing with you."

She kicked her foot over the furrow, and with mouth drawn down, shook her head once or twice in a little strutting way. Some husks blew down and whirled in streamers about her skirts.

Then she went on, parting her way from side to side with the cane, through the whispering field. At last she came to the end, to a wagon track where the silver grass blew between the red ruts. The quail were walking around like pullets, seeming all dainty and unseen.

"Walk pretty," she said. "This the easy place. This the easy going."

She followed the track, swaying through the quiet bare fields, through the little strings of trees silver in their dead leaves, past cabins silver from weather, with the doors and windows boarded shut, all like old women under a spell sitting there. "I walking in their sleep," she said, nodding her head vigorously.

In a ravine she went where a spring was silently flowing through a hollow log. Old Phoenix bent and drank. "Sweet-gum makes the water sweet," she said, and drank more. "Nobody know who made this well, for it was here when I was born."

The track crossed a swampy part where the moss hung as white as lace from every limb. "Sleep on, alligators, and blow your bubbles." Then the track went into the road.

Deep, deep the road went down between the high green-colored banks. Overhead the live-oaks met, and it was as dark as a cave.

A black dog with a lolling tongue came up out of the weeds by the ditch. She was meditating, and not ready, and when he came at her she only hit him a little with her cane. Over she went in the ditch, like a little puff of milkweed.

Down there, her senses drifted away. A dream visited her, and she reached her hand up, but nothing reached down and gave her a pull. So she lay there and presently went to talking. "Old woman," she said to herself, "that black dog come up out of the weeds to stall you off, and now there he sitting on his fine tail, smiling at you."

A white man finally came along and found her — a hunter, a young man, with his dog on a chain.

"Well, Granny!" he laughed. "What are you doing there?"

"Lying on my back like a June-bug waiting to be turned over, mister," she said, reaching up her hand.

He lifted her up, gave her a swing in the air, and set her down. "Anything broken, Granny?"

"No sir, them old dead weeds is springy enough," said Phoenix, when she had got her breath. "I thank you for your trouble."

"Where do you live, Granny?" he asked, while the two dogs were growling at each other.

"Away back yonder, sir, behind the ridge. You can't even see it from here."

"On your way home?"

"No sir, I going to town."

"Why, that's too far! That's as far as I walk when I come out myself, and I get something for my trouble." He patted the stuffed bag he carried, and there hung down a little closed claw. It was one of the bobwhites, with its beak hooked bitterly to show it was dead. "Now you go on home, Granny!"

"I bound to go to town, mister," said Phoenix. "The time come around."

He gave another laugh, filling the whole landscape. "I know you old colored people! Wouldn't miss going to town to see Santa Claus!"

But something held old Phoenix very still. The deep lines in her face went into a fierce and different radiation. Without warning, she had seen with her own eyes a flashing nickel fall out of the man's pocket onto the ground.

"How old are you, Granny?" he was saying.

"There is no telling, mister," she said, "no telling."

Then she gave a little cry and clapped her hands and said, "Git on away from here, dog! Look! Look at that dog!" She laughed as if in admiration. "He ain't scared of nobody. He a big black dog." She whispered, "Sic him!"

"Watch me get rid of that cur," said the man. "Sic him, Pete! Sic him!"

Phoenix heard the dogs fighting, and heard the man running and throwing sticks. She even heard a gunshot. But she was slowly bending forward by that time, further and further forward, the lid stretched down over her eyes, as if she were doing this in her sleep. Her chin was lowered almost to her knees. The yellow palm of her hand came out from the fold of her apron. Her fingers slid down and along the ground under the piece of money with the grace and care they would have in lifting an egg from under a setting hen. Then she slowly straightened up, she stood erect, and the nickel was in her apron pocket. A bird flew by. Her lips moved. "God watching me the whole time. I come to stealing."

The man came back, and his own dog panted about them. "Well, I scared him off that time," he said, and then he laughed and lifted his gun and pointed it at Phoenix.

She stood straight and faced him.

"Doesn't the gun scare you?" he said, still pointing it.

"No, sir, I seen plenty go off closer by, in my day, and for less than what I done," she said, holding utterly still.

He smiled, and shouldered the gun. "Well, Granny," he said, "you must be a hundred years old, and scared of nothing. I'd give you a dime if I had any money with me. But you take my advice and stay home, and nothing will happen to you."

"I bound to go on my way, mister," said Phoenix. She inclined her head in the red rag. Then they went in different directions, but she could hear the gun shooting again and again over the hill.

She walked on. The shadows hung from the oak trees to the road like curtains. Then she smelled wood-smoke, and smelled the river, and she saw a steeple and the cabins on their steep steps. Dozens of little black children whirled around her. There ahead was Natchez shining. Bells were ringing. She walked on.

In the paved city it was Christmas time. There were red and green electric lights strung and crisscrossed everywhere, and all turned on in the daytime. Old Phoenix would have been lost if she had not distrusted her eyesight and depended on her feet to know where to take her.

She paused quietly on the sidewalk where people were passing by. A lady came along in the crowd, carrying an armful of red-, green-, and silver-wrapped presents; she gave off perfume like the red roses in hot summer, and Phoenix stopped her.

"Please, missy, will you lace up my shoe?" She held up her foot.

"What do you want, Grandma?"

"See my shoe," said Phoenix. "Do all right for out in the country, but wouldn't look right to go in a big building."

"Stand still then, Grandma," said the lady. She put her packages down on the sidewalk beside her and laced and tied both shoes tightly.

"Can't lace 'em with a cane," said Phoenix. "Thank you, missy. I doesn't mind asking a nice lady to tie up my shoe, when I gets out on the street."

Moving slowly and from side to side, she went into the big building, and into a tower of steps, where she walked up and around and around until her feet knew to stop.

She entered a door, and there she saw nailed up on the wall the document that had been stamped with the gold seal and framed in the gold frame, which matched the dream that was hung up in her head.

"Here I be," she said. There was a fixed and ceremonial stiffness over her body.

"A charity case, I suppose," said an attendant who sat at the desk before her.

But Phoenix only looked above her head. There was sweat on her face, the wrinkles in her skin shone like a bright net.

"Speak up, Grandma," the woman said. "What's your name? We must have your history, you know. Have you been here before? What seems to be the trouble with you?"

Old Phoenix only gave a twitch to her face as if a fly were bothering her.

"Are you deaf?" cried the attendant.

But then the nurse came in.

"Oh, that's just old Aunt Phoenix," she said. "She doesn't come for herself — she has a little grandson. She makes these trips just as regular as clockwork. She lives away back off the Old Natchez Trace." She bent down. "Well, Aunt Phoenix, why don't you just take a seat? We won't keep you standing after your long trip." She pointed.

The old woman sat down, bolt upright in the chair.

"Now, how is the boy?" asked the nurse.

Old Phoenix did not speak.

"I said, how is the boy?"

But Phoenix only waited and stared straight ahead, her face very solemn and withdrawn into rigidity.

"Is his throat any better?" asked the nurse. "Aunt Phoenix, don't you hear me? Is your grandson's throat any better since the last time you came for the medicine?"

With her hands on her knees, the old woman waited, silent, erect and motionless, just as if she were in armor.

"You mustn't take up our time this way, Aunt Phoenix," the nurse said. "Tell us quickly about your grandson, and get it over. He isn't dead, is he?"

At last there came a flicker and then a flame of comprehension across her face, and she spoke.

"My grandson. It was my memory had left me. There I sat and forgot why I made my long trip."

"Forgot?" The nurse frowned. "After you came so far?"

Then Phoenix was like an old woman begging a dignified forgiveness for waking up frightened in the night. "I never did go to school, I was too old at the Surrender," she said in a soft voice. "I'm an old woman without an education. It was my memory fail me. My little grandson, he is just the same, and I forgot it in the coming."

"Throat never heals, does it?" said the nurse, speaking in a loud, sure voice to old Phoenix. By now she had a card with something written on it, a little list. "Yes. Swallowed lye. When was it? — January — two, three years ago —"

Phoenix spoke unasked now. "No, missy, he not dead, he just the same. Every little while his throat began to close up again, and he not able to swallow. He not get his breath. He not able to help himself. So the time come around, and I go on another trip for the soothing medicine."

"All right. The doctor said as long as you came to get it, you could have it," said the nurse. "But it's an obstinate case."

"My little grandson, he sit up there in the house all wrapped up, waiting by himself," Phoenix went on. "We is the only two left in the world. He suffer and it don't seem to put him back at all. He got a sweet look. He going to last. He wear a little patch quilt and peep out holding his mouth open like a little bird. I remembers so plain now. I not going to forget him again, no, the whole enduring time. I could tell him from all the others in creation."

"All right." The nurse was trying to hush her now. She brought her a bottle of medicine. "Charity," she said, making a check mark in a book.

Old Phoenix held the bottle close to her eyes, and then carefully put it into her pocket.

"I thank you," she said.

"It's Christmas time, Grandma," said the attendant. "Could I give you a few pennies out of my purse?"

"Five pennies is a nickel," said Phoenix stiffly.

"Here's a nickel," said the attendant.

Phoenix rose carefully and held out her hand. She received the nickel and then fished the other nickel out of her pocket and laid it beside the new one. She stared at her palm closely, with her head on one side.

Then she gave a tap with her cane on the floor.

"This is what come to me to do," she said. "I going to the store and buy my child a little windmill they sells, made out of paper. He going to find it hard to believe there such a thing in the world. I'll march myself back where he waiting, holding it straight up in this hand."

She lifted her free hand, gave a little nod, turned around, and walked out of the doctor's office. Then her slow step began on the stairs, going down.

KEEPING A JOURNAL OR NOTEBOOK TO RECORD YOUR INITIAL RESPONSES TO THE TEXT

Often the earliest stage in responding to a literary work occurs as you read the text and feel the impulse to underline words or phrases that instinctively strike you as significant. It's relatively easy to give in to this impulse. Using a pen as a highlighter is a step in the right direction, but there's a better way that will get you started on your essay. Keeping a journal or a notebook in which you record your responses to your reading will help you to generate ideas about what you find there.

In her essay "Keeping a Notebook," the writer Joan Didion said the main reason writers keep a record of their experience is that "we forget all too soon the things we thought we could never forget. . . . Keeping in touch is what notebooks are all about." Recording your impressions right after reading the assignment helps you to remember what you thought about it.

For most students, a journal of responses to literature is an important stage in the journey of transforming themselves from readers into writers. Once you become aware of how you are reading a text, you have begun the process of using your own words to describe what you find significant about a story, play, or poem. This is the beginning of your discovery of "the measure of what you brought to the reading."

In your journal, you should note your responses after your first (or second) reading of Welty's story. Jot down short quotations from the story if they strike you as significant. Your notes might look something like this:

JOURNAL ENTRY

Eudora Welty's "A Worn Path" . . . starts right in on the story introducing an old Negro woman named Phoenix Jackson, who's taking a long walk by herself on a December afternoon in the country. Author knows the setting very well--lots of specific details of trees, bushes, hills, and creek--Phoenix talks to herself but she's a feisty old thing. Has trouble seeing, but she picks up and hides a nickel belonging to a hunter she meets on the trail--the old lady's conscience bothers her, but she doesn't let on--he speaks so condescendingly to her that I think she's entitled to take his money--it's just a nickel--wait--did he drop the nickel or did she just see it on the ground? yes, Welty says it fell out of his pocket--so she could have given it back to him. The old lady gets tired but she keeps going and finally arrives at Natchez. Then she goes into a building in town where "she walked up and around and around until her feet knew to stop." So she's been there often before. It seems to be a nurses' office--and she's so old and tired she forgets why she's there--then remembers that she's come to get medicine for her grandson. Horrible--the little boy swallowed lye. He lives with Phoenix, and she makes the long walk to town for his sake every year. The nurse likes Phoenix--gives her a nickel as a Christmas present. Phoenix really loves her grandson--she tells the nurse she's going to buy him a present before she starts the long walk home. I wonder, is this grandson alive or dead? Is the old woman senile? Can we trust her?

You will notice that in your journal you began by summarizing the plot in your own words. That is the first response of most students when given the assignment of writing about literature. You need not regard it as a wasted effort because you can use your notes later to review the story when studying for an exam. But your instructor has asked you to write an essay. How can your notes help you to find an idea about the story for your paper?

Notice that summarizing the events of the story has led you to ask a question about the main character's actions: Can we trust Phoenix Jackson, or is she so old that she's really senile and doesn't know whether her grandson is alive or dead? If you are an insecure reader, you may think that your question is stupid, but it isn't. Often getting the answer to a simple question that arises as you read the text will lead you to more complex ideas about its significance that you can develop in your essay.

You can bring your question about "A Worn Path" to your instructor in class. Or, working by yourself, you can find commentaries by authors and critics in this anthology that shed light on your reading. So many students asked this question about the story that Welty wrote a commentary titled "Is Phoenix Jackson's Grandson Really Dead?" Reading her commentary will not only show you that you have asked a good question, but it will also help you generate ideas about the story for your paper. The important thing is *your* response to the story — what makes it significant for you. Reading commentaries, such as Welty's on "A Worn Path," will help you become a more informed reader and may stimulate your critical thinking about the story.

EUDORA WELTY

Is Phoenix Jackson's Grandson Really Dead? 1977

A story writer is more than happy to be read by students; the fact that these serious readers think and feel something in response to his work he finds life-giving. At the same time he may not always be able to reply to their specific questions in kind. I wondered if it might clarify something, for both the questioners and myself, if I set down a general reply to the question that comes to me most often in the mail, from both students and their teachers, after some classroom discussion. The unrivaled favorite is this: "Is Phoenix Jackson's grandson really *dead?*"

It refers to a short story I wrote years ago called "A Worn Path," which tells of a day's journey an old woman makes on foot from deep in the country into town and into a doctor's office on behalf of her little grandson; he is at home, periodically ill, and periodically she comes for his medicine; they give it to her as usual, she receives it and starts the journey back.

I had not meant to mystify readers by withholding any fact; it is not a writer's business to tease. The story is told through Phoenix's mind as she undertakes her errand. As the author at one with the character as I tell it, I must assume that the boy is alive. As the reader, you are free to think as you like, of course: The story invites you to believe that no matter what happens, Phoenix for as long as she is able to walk and can hold to her purpose will make her journey. The *possibility* that she would keep on even if he were dead is there in her devotion and its single-minded, single-track errand. Certainly the *artistic* truth, which should be good enough for the fact, lies in Phoenix's own answer to that question. When the nurse asks, "He isn't dead, is he?" she speaks for herself: "He still the same. He going to last."

The grandchild is the incentive. But it is the journey, the going of the errand, that is the story, and the question is not whether the grandchild is in reality alive or dead. It doesn't affect the outcome of the story or its meaning from start to finish. But it is not the question itself that has struck me as much as the idea, almost without exception implied in the asking, that for Phoenix's grandson to be dead would somehow make the story "better."

It's *all right,* I want to say to the students who write to me, for things to be what they appear to be, and for words to mean what they say. It's all right, too, for words and appearances to mean more than one thing — ambiguity is a fact of life. A fiction writer's responsibility covers not only what he presents as the facts of a given story but what he chooses to stir up as their implications; in the end, these implications, too, become facts, in the larger, fictional sense. But it is not all right, not in good faith, for things *not* to mean what they say.

The grandson's plight was real and it made the truth of the story, which is the story of an errand of love carried out. If the child no longer lived, the truth would persist in the "wornness" of the path. But his being dead can't increase the truth of the story, can't affect it one way or the other. I think I signal this, because the end of the story has been reached before old Phoenix gets home again: she simply starts back. To the question "Is the grandson really dead?" I could reply that it doesn't make any difference. I could also say that I did not make him up in order to let him play a trick on Phoenix. But my best answer would be: "*Phoenix* is alive."

The origin of a story is sometimes a trustworthy clue to the author — or can provide him with the clue — to its key image; maybe in this case it will do the same for the reader. One day I saw a solitary old woman like Phoenix. She was walking; I saw her, at middle distance, in a winter country landscape, and watched her slowly make her way across my line of vision. That sight of her made me write the story. I invented an errand for her, but that only seemed a living part of the figure she was herself: What errand other than for someone else could be making her go? And her going was the first thing, her persisting in her landscape was the real thing, and the first and the real were what I wanted and worked to keep. I brought her up close enough, by imagination, to describe her face, make her present to the eyes, but the full-length figure moving across the winter fields was the indelible one and the image to keep, and the perspective extending into the vanishing distance the true one to hold in mind.

I invented for my character, as I wrote, some passing adventures — some dreams and harassments and a small triumph or two, some jolts to her pride, some flights of fancy to console her, one or two encounters to scare her, a moment that gave her cause to feel ashamed, a moment to dance and preen — for it had to be a *journey,* and all these things belonged to that, parts of life's uncertainty.

A narrative line is in its deeper sense, of course, the tracing out of a meaning, and the real continuity of a story lies in this probing forward. The real dramatic force of a story depends on the strength of the emotion that has set it going. The emotional value is the measure of the reach of the story. What gives any such content to "A Worn Path" is not its circumstances but its *subject:* the deep-grained habit of love.

What I hoped would come clear was that in the whole surround of this story, the world it threads through, the only certain thing at all is the worn path. The habit of love cuts through confusion and stumbles or contrives its way out of difficulty, it remembers the way even when it forgets, for a dumfounded moment, its reason for being. The path is the thing that matters.

Her victory — old Phoenix's — is when she sees the diploma in the doctor's office, when she finds "nailed up on the wall the document that had been stamped with the gold seal and framed in the gold frame, which matched the dream that was hung up in her head." The return with the medicine is just a matter of retracing her own footsteps. It is the part of the journey, and of the story, that can now go without saying.

In the matter of function, old Phoenix's way might even do as a sort of parallel to your way of work if you are a writer of stories. The way to get there is the all-important, all-absorbing problem, and this problem is your reason for undertaking the story. Your only guide, too, is your sureness about your subject, about what this subject is. Like Phoenix, you work all your life to find your way, through all the obstructions and the false appearances and the upsets you may have brought on yourself, to reach a meaning — using inventions of your imagination, perhaps helped out by your dreams and bits of good luck. And finally too, like Phoenix, you have to assume that what you are working in aid of is life, not death.

But you would make the trip anyway — wouldn't you? — just on hope.

USING THE COMMENTARIES TO ASK NEW QUESTIONS ABOUT WHAT YOU HAVE READ

A number of commentaries on the stories, poems, and plays in this anthology are included throughout *Literature and Its Writers* because reading commentaries can help you feel more confident when you begin to think critically about literature. While commentaries by authors and critics often clear up specific questions about a text, they always introduce you to important aspects of the significance of a story, poem, or play that you might have missed on your own. You may agree or disagree with the commentaries, but they will usually stimulate your critical thinking.

Reading Welty's commentary answered your first question about the story: The author tells you that the grandson is alive. After Welty answers the question, you might be struck by how seriously she takes what she calls the "fiction writer's responsibility" in the second part of her essay. Welty says that a good writer never uses tricks in order to mislead the reader; the words in a story must always "mean what they say."

Welty's commentary has caused you to look at "A Worn Path" in a new way. How does an author make her words "mean what they say"? Now you might feel a flicker of excitement as you begin to think about how Welty has selected particular words to make up her story about a solitary old woman she glimpsed walking in a country landscape. Welty states that she wanted her story to illustrate an idea she had about this woman's journey: She wanted to dramatize what she imagined as "the deep-grained habit of love."

Thinking about the commentary, you might be impressed by Welty's sympathy for her central character, Phoenix Jackson. When you scan the opening paragraphs of "A Worn Path" again, you find that this sympathy is conveyed by the words Welty has chosen to tell her story. You ask yourself, how does the author keep her subject from becoming sentimental? What words in the text suggest Welty's feelings for the woman she writes about in the story without going overboard? You remember a line from the story that you jotted down in your journal: "she walked up and around and around until her feet knew to stop." Suddenly it's clear to you that Welty has chosen words that Phoenix Jackson would use. Now your mind is full of questions about the story. You are ready for the next stage in the writing process.

GENERATING IDEAS BY BRAINSTORMING, FREEWRITING, AND LISTING

Generating ideas for the assignment can be done in a variety of ways, either as a solitary process of jotting down ideas on paper or as a communal process of talking over your ideas with a friend or classmate who has also read the story. If you follow the latter course, be sure to take notes as your conversation progresses so that your ideas do not evaporate in the general glow of good company.

Usually sufficient ideas for your paper will evolve during one of these exercises of brainstorming, freewriting, and listing. Initially you might try them all to find out which one works best for you.

Brainstorming for Ideas

Perhaps the notion that Welty has written her story in words that Phoenix Jackson might use intrigues you so much that you decide to **brainstorm** by yourself. Record the thoughts that occur to you while you look over the story again. Begin with Welty's first sentence and free associate about whatever comes to your mind:

> Simple language, telling the month and day and time. Welty's so logical--large (month) to small (morning) time units.

Now try to think more specifically about Welty's choice of words. Brainstorm further by finding adjectives to describe your impressions of the words she uses to introduce Phoenix Jackson:

> respectful, warm, sympathetic, humane, compassionate, a little funny but gently so--Welty never makes a joke at Phoenix's expense. She's "neat and tidy," but still human--her shoelaces drag and she hasn't bothered to lace her shoes. Is it because she's too old to bend down to lace them? Or maybe her feet hurt and she can't buy another pair.

At this point you might discover that brainstorming has put your imagination to work on the story. Your brief vision of the figure of Phoenix Jackson so frail with age that she is unable to bend over to tie her own shoes has made her become almost as real to you as your own grandmother. This might amuse you and cause you to realize that you have learned something about the magic of literature: Writing about it can make you a more active participant in it.

This might be a good time to review your notes. Can you find a pattern in the details Welty has given you about Phoenix Jackson? If you have been as conscious of your thoughts about the story as Phoenix was aware of the path she was following through the woods, you might begin to sense Welty building something in her careful choice of descriptive details. She seems to suggest one thing and then to continue on to its opposite. Phoenix is "an old Negro woman" (respectable), but "her head tied in a red rag" (poor, shabby). She is "neat and tidy," but her shoelaces drag. And so on. Why does Welty do this?

As you think about it, you realize that while Welty sometimes chooses words that Phoenix Jackson might use, the author is clearly in control, selecting details about her character very carefully. How do you develop this new idea? You might try another technique to help you focus your thoughts, an exercise called freewriting.

Freewriting

Like brainstorming, focused **freewriting** can help you develop an idea when you begin to think critically about literature. In a freewriting session, you state everything that comes to mind when you try to answer a question relating to the subject of your paper. Do not stop to think of forming complete sentences or using correct grammar or spelling. Give yourself a set time — perhaps ten or fifteen minutes or even longer if you feel inspired — to spill out all your associations about the topic. You can use a scratch pad, a typewriter, or a computer — whatever you have at hand. Keep the story beside you as you write, so that you can refer to it as necessary. Then go back and underline ideas in your writing that you think could be organized into a coherent outline and developed further in an essay. Here is an example of freewriting about "A Worn Path" on the topic of Welty's choice of words as a storyteller.

> What does she do that makes me want to read on, one word following the next, until I'm hooked and want to know "what happens next"? First of all, she makes Phoenix into a complicated character. Simple to begin with, but more there than obviously meets the eye. Not a lot of dramatic action but a soft tone, almost as if she wanted to make you bend closer to her to hear her better. Serious, simple tone to begin the story. Then that business about the red rag. Does that do it? Or is it the choice of words, so simple and down-to-earth. Just like the character Welty's trying to describe. She's like anybody's granny in the country--even if it's Mississippi by the end of the story. Think about it. The way Welty uses alliteration, "red rag" and "path through the pinewoods," so her voice sounds good--it's very musical and rhythmic prose. Perhaps she's creating the rhythm of Phoenix's walk, "the balanced heaviness and lightness."

Focused freewriting can make you conscious of ideas you did not know you had, like the thought that Welty's prose is so musical and rhythmic that it suggests the pace of Phoenix's physical movements as she makes her slow way along the worn, familiar path to town. Brainstorming ideas and freewriting can often help you to think critically about a literary work. At this point you might want to make a list of all the things you have discovered about the story so far.

Listing

Another useful technique in the preliminary stage of the writing process is making lists. You are probably experienced at doing this whenever you try to keep several things in mind at once, especially if you are planning to use the list later on, as for grocery shopping or organizing "things to do" over the course of a busy weekend. **Listing** also can become a way to help you develop your thoughts about literature. Making a list is more focused than brainstorming or freewriting; first you must be clear about what you want to list.

For example, if you would like to develop the idea that what attracts you about Welty's storytelling voice is its musical quality, you could comb "A Worn Path" for more instances of memorable alliteration (like "red rag") in the words describing the protagonist. You will probably find that — strangely enough — once your brain starts to go to work analyzing literature, one idea seems to stimulate another during the writing process.

As you scan the story again, you suddenly notice the beautiful simile that Welty uses in the second paragraph to describe Phoenix's wrinkled face: "as though a whole little tree stood in the middle of her forehead." You see that Welty emphasizes the vitality and beauty of Phoenix's skin color — "golden." And this detail is followed at the end of the paragraph by another compliment, that her hair falls "in the frailest of ringlets, still black, and with an odor like copper." What is "an odor like copper"? you ask yourself. Is it a good smell or a bad one? This makes you remember an early idea when you started thinking about the assignment, that Welty blends positive and negative attributes into her description of Phoenix Jackson. Could that be how she keeps her story about the old woman from becoming sentimental?

You may feel that you have gotten a little sidetracked, but that is no matter, because your thoughts about the second paragraph have carried you further along on your idea about Welty's method of drawing you into the story by her poetic description of Phoenix Jackson's face. Return to the story to find the examples that you started looking for, of musical alliteration. They are as easy to find in the opening paragraph as ripe red strawberries in June:

red rag
side to side in her steps
sugar sacks

When you begin to notice examples of assonance, like the sound of the *o*'s in "odor of copper," you could start to make another list. You could also jot down a third list of examples of inverted word order that Welty has used in her sentences to achieve musical effect, such as "On she went." And you could create a fourth list for examples of the regular rhythm of sentences she (or Phoenix) chants using the melody of parallel structure: "Up through pines. . . . Now down through oaks."

ORGANIZING YOUR NOTES INTO A PRELIMINARY THESIS SENTENCE AND OUTLINE

After you have given yourself sufficient time to think critically about the story, you are ready to organize your thoughts about what you intend to write. *This is the most crucial step in the process of creating your essay.* Many students make the mistake of beginning to write the first draft of their paper too soon, before they have taken the time to stimulate new ideas and create a strong **thesis sentence**. They string together sentences about a topic, rather than develop a clearly focused response to their assignment. If you work on a strong thesis sentence first, before you start writing your essay, you will save yourself considerable anxiety and several false starts, or — even worse — an unfocused essay that doesn't communicate clearly to your reader.

Whether you are writing an essay of only a few paragraphs or a research paper of several thousand words, the basic requirement is always the same. An essay on any subject is a type of expository writing, and *expository* means "serving to clarify, set forth, or explain in detail" a central idea about your topic. Do not start your essay until you are able to express a strong idea in a well-crafted sentence.

An effective essay always requires two things: first, a good thesis sentence or central idea about your topic to start your paper, and second, an adequate development of your thesis sentence. Often it helps you get started if you concentrate on stating your thesis as clearly as you can in your rough draft. When you revise your essay, you can make sure that you have presented sufficient evidence to support your main idea. Some useful ways of organizing longer essays about literature — by explication, analysis, and comparison and contrast — are discussed in Part Five. Regardless of your paper's length, you should always begin by trying to express your central idea about the topic so that it can evolve and develop in the writing process.

Which of your notes about Welty's story is the best candidate to serve as a thesis sentence? It should express the main point of your essay. Consider it a *preliminary* thesis at this point, subject to revision when you rewrite your rough draft. After some thought, you might come up with the following thesis sentences:

1. *Welty's way of telling her story is interesting.* This is a common, quick, and facile solution to the problem of formulating a thesis sentence for an essay. It is totally inadequate because it is too general. A moment's reflection will reveal that a topic is not the same as a thesis. A topic is a general subject ("*Welty's way of telling her story*"); a thesis makes a statement about a topic ("*is interesting*" is not much of a statement).
2. *Welty's way of telling her story draws the reader into "A Worn Path."* This is a much more useful thesis sentence. You have thought about the topic and narrowed it down to focus on the relationship of the topic to a specific idea. The test of a thesis sentence is whether your general subject ("*Welty's way of telling her story*") is followed by a clearly focused predicate ("*draws the reader into 'A Worn Path'*").

3. *Welty uses language as a storyteller the way that Phoenix Jackson would use words to express her thoughts.* This was your first insight into Welty's way of telling her story. It could serve as a useful preliminary thesis. You have narrowed the topic even further. Your general subject ("*Welty uses language as a storyteller*") is followed by a very specific predicate ("*the way that Phoenix Jackson would use words to express her thoughts*"). This thesis sentence unmistakably points the way to how you could begin to develop your rough draft. You might suspect that this idea is too narrowly focused for your entire paper, but you will discover whether this is true as you write.
4. *Welty uses language the way a poet does to keep readers interested in her story.* This idea came out of the listing exercise, where you found examples of Welty's use of alliteration, assonance, and rhetorical structure. Like the previous two ideas, this could also serve as a useful preliminary thesis sentence to get you started on your rough draft.

Assume you take the third choice, because this was your original insight about the story and you like the idea best. Working on an essay is always more enjoyable when you are enthusiastic about the assignment. Before you sit down at the computer, you will find that making a brief outline will help you see the direction to take more clearly. It does not have to be a traditional outline. Shape it in any way that will help you remember the points you intend to make if you are interrupted. Start by writing down your preliminary thesis sentence. Then assemble the evidence you have found to support it.

> As a storyteller, Welty uses language the way that Phoenix Jackson uses words to express her thoughts.
>
> 1. Simple, down-to-earth vocabulary.
> 2. Poetic and musical phrases.

Because your assignment is a short paper, this initial thesis sentence and outline will get you started on your first draft. Don't worry about making the thesis perfect at this stage. You will bring your thesis into even sharper focus as you develop what you have to say about your topic in your essay. As Alex Johnson understood, the object of a first draft is to shape the thesis sentence into what she called a "controlling idea":

> The most common misconception is that the first draft is about writing *per se*. It's not. It's about thinking. If you've managed to turn out felicitous phrasing, I always tell students, it's icing on the cake. The real concern is how your idea evolves and sharpens, how its deeper structure emerges. To help this process along, don't agonize over word choice. Underline a word or simply leave a space and go back in the revision stage to get it right. Use momentum. Gag your internal critic and perfectionist when they report, correctly, that the draft seems sketchy. That's why it's called a first draft.

WRITING THE ROUGH DRAFT

If you include a strong thesis sentence in the first paragraph of your rough draft, it can often jumpstart further ideas. The effort of writing itself, the act of finding the right words to express your thoughts, can suggest new ways to develop your preliminary thesis. That is the reason you should allow plenty of time to complete an essay assignment. It is an unusual first draft in which the central idea is developed coherently and fully enough to be turned in as the finished paper. Revision usually stimulates further thought, sharpening and refining your argument.

You will probably discover that, like most people, you are better at rewriting than you are at writing. More often than not, the 500 or 750 words you might think are a perfect essay when you turn in your final paper will be the end result — if you took enough time and care in writing — of winnowing many more words from your rough drafts. In your revision you can support your thesis by editing your sentences and paragraphs so that each one relates coherently to your central idea. Then your essay will express your insights about the story so clearly that they can be understood by your reader as you intended.

SAMPLE FIRST DRAFT OF AN ESSAY ON EUDORA WELTY'S "A WORN PATH"

An author's voice   *a*   *point to consider about*
^ ~~A storyteller's style~~ is ^ key ~~to understanding~~ ^ the way she
From   *'s choice of words, we can hear*
tells her story. ^ Eudora Welty ^ ~~is a warm and sympathetic~~
that she is a warm and sympathetic
^ narrator in "A Worn Path." She uses language so simply and
interests us
concretely that she ^ ~~makes us interested~~ immediately in the
named Phoenix Jackson
journey of an old woman ^ as she walks through the pine-
In fact,   *often*
woods to Natchez to get medicine for her grandson. ^ Welty ^
uses language the way Phoenix uses it to express her
, because when she comes to the city
thoughts. ^ ~~At the end of the story~~ we are told that
"she walked up and around and around until her feet knew
to stop" (8).

Begin with broad generalization about the story.

Narrow your topic into a thesis sentence.

captures the reader's attention
This simple, down-to-earth vocabulary ^ ~~grounds us~~.
Welty
It is as if ^ ~~the author~~ could read the mind of the character
is creating
she ^ ~~has created~~ on the page. We all would like to be able to
mind   *and*
get inside the ^ ~~thoughts~~ of another person, ~~to~~ ^ share their

New insight in second paragraph develops out of writing the rough draft.

most private ~~interior world~~ *thoughts,* so we want to read further. This could be considered a trick, since Welty's own voice (and mind) could not be exactly the same as the uneducated Phoenix, but Welty's ~~sincere~~ feeling for her *fictional* character shines through the story. Her voice is sincere.

Welty's ~~voice~~ *use of words as a storyteller* interests us for another reason. She chooses words the way a poet would. She's writing ~~a short story~~ *a prose story,* but she chooses *her* words like a poet. There are many examples of alliteration and assonance in the ~~first~~ *opening* paragraph of her story, when she must *first* capture our interest*, like "red rag" and "path through the pinewoods" (4).* In the second paragraph, she ~~gives~~ *compares the pattern of wrinkles on* Phoenix's ~~wrinkled~~ face to a "whole little tree" (4). This is a fresh *and poetic* image to help us visualize the old woman's appearance. The plot and characterization of Phoenix later in the story shows us how resourceful and loving she is as a person. As a storyteller, Welty speaks of her heroine with great affection. She blends telling and showing in "A Worn Path."

Final paragraph needs further revision: repetitious vocabulary, ideas scattered, conclusion unfocused.

REVISING YOUR ESSAY

Usually your first draft will be shorter than your final draft, but at this point you shouldn't worry about length. Instead, savor the feeling of satisfaction that you have made a good start on your paper. If you have the time, you should put your rough draft away for a day or so, and then read it again with fresh eyes. Before you return to it, you might want to reread the literature you are writing about, looking for more details to develop your thesis statement. In your revision, you could also try to incorporate relevant material you might be discussing in class, like the concept of an author's voice as an aspect of literary style.

Revision means exactly what it says — the opportunity to revisit your essay and take another look at it. This is the writing stage where you get the chance to do the best work on your paper. You can refine your argument by strengthening your evidence and tying together loose ends. Most students are surprised to find how rough and unfinished their first drafts appear after time away from the essay. Always go over your work with a pen or a pencil in hand so that you can continue to clarify what you have written for your reader.

If you compare the first draft of the paper on "A Worn Path" with the revised draft, you can see how the essay became more fully developed and more coherent. Two additional middle paragraphs give specific examples from the story, evidence that supports the thesis sentence. This sentence now concludes the opening paragraph, putting more emphasis on this central idea and pointing the way to its development in the following paragraphs. In the final version, the essay begins with a general sentence based on information from class discussions of short fiction about an author's voice. This concept ties together several ideas about the story that had emerged from brainstorming, freewriting, and listing and also provides a title for the paper. The argument is further strengthened by the specific reference to Welty's commentary "Is Phoenix Jackson's Grandson Really Dead?"

SAMPLE REVISED DRAFT

The Voice of the Storyteller
in Eudora Welty's "A Worn Path"

An author's voice is a key point to consider about the effect of a story on her reader. From Eudora Welty's choice of words in "A Worn Path," we can tell she's a warm and sympathetic narrator. She uses language so simply and concretely that she makes us interested in the journey of an old woman named Phoenix Jackson as she walks through the pinewoods to Natchez to get medicine for her grandson. In fact, Welty often uses language the way that Phoenix would use it to express her thoughts.

At the beginning of the story, Welty introduces Phoenix by describing her as "an old Negro woman with her head tied in a red rag" (4). This description, so clear and direct, gives us a vivid image of the central character. In the second paragraph, Welty tells us what she is wearing, a dark dress covered by a "long apron of bleached sugar sacks" (4). This old woman may be poor, but she is also clean and thrifty. We respect her even before we learn that she cares enough about her sick grandson to walk many miles along a rugged country path from her home to the clinic for a bottle of medicine.

When the old woman comes to the city sidewalks, we are told that "she walked up and around and around until her feet knew to stop" (8). Phoenix has gotten tired after her long trek through the woods, over the hills, across a creek, through a field of dead cornstalks, along a wagon track, and across a swamp on her way to Natchez. These are the words that she herself would use, and the sentence is structured the way she would talk.

This lively colloquial vocabulary captures the reader's attention. It is as if the author could read the mind of her character. We all would like to be able to get inside the mind of another person, to share his or her private thoughts and feelings, so we want to read further. Welty has revealed in her commentary on "A Worn Path" that "the story is told through Phoenix's mind" (12). This could be considered a trick, since Welty's own voice (and mind) could not be exactly the same as uneducated, unsophisticated Phoenix. But Welty shows her deep respect for what she calls "the deep-grained habit of love" in Phoenix's actions (13). The sound of the author's voice is sincere, so we trust her.

Welty's voice attracts us for another reason. She is writing prose, but she chooses words like a poet. There are many examples of alliteration and assonance in the opening paragraph of her story, like "red rag" and "path through the pinewoods" (4), when the author must first capture our interest. In the second paragraph, Welty uses a poetic simile to compare the pattern of wrinkles on Phoenix's face to a "whole little tree" (4). This comparison helps us visualize the old woman's appearance. It is also so down-to-earth that it could even have occurred to Phoenix herself if we imagine her seeing her reflection in the water of a spring or in a Natchez shop window. We are irresistibly drawn into the story by the skillful voice of the storyteller in "A Worn Path."

MAKING A FINAL CHECK OF YOUR FINISHED ESSAY

Before you turn in your essay, you should check the quotations you have used to make sure that you have copied them accurately. If you have used a computer to write your paper, you should also run a spell-check. The following guide can help you in the final preparation of your essay:

1. Be sure to include your name, date, and class section on the paper.
2. Check your title. Ideally, it should suggest an idea of your approach to the assigned topic. If you include the author's name or title of the work

here, be sure you have spelled it correctly and have used quotation marks or underlining appropriately.

3. Include the name of the author and title of the work you are writing about in your opening paragraph so that the reader knows what you plan to discuss. Often, at least in short essays, the reader expects you to state your thesis sentence in the first paragraph.
4. Review your organization. Does your essay offer solid evidence to support your thesis statement? Does it develop ideas clearly and coherently? For effective emphasis, do your paragraphs proceed from the least important to the most important point? Can some of the longer paragraphs be divided into shorter units to clarify your main points? Are your short paragraphs adequately developed? Does each sentence relate to the one before? Have you supplied transitional sentences between paragraphs? Do you need to write shorter sentences so that your ideas come through more clearly?
5. Include quotations from the work you are discussing to add variety to the vocabulary you customarily use. Such a practice also offers a change of pace to the reader of your paper, as well as a reminder of the pleasures of the original text.
6. Check that your punctuation and grammar are correct throughout your essay, and that you have written varied and complete sentences, not sentence fragments. If you spot unintentional verbal repetitions, find fresh words to replace them or revise the sentence to eliminate wordiness.
7. Look for the conclusion to your essay. If it is a short paper, you can phrase your conclusion as a sentence or two in the final paragraph. In a longer paper, you could devote at least an entire final paragraph to a statement of your conclusion.

Peer Review

Before turning in your essay, you could exchange papers with another student to check each other's work. Your instructor might also include a peer review of rough drafts or finished papers during class time, allowing you to benefit from other readers' suggestions for improvement. This could help you clarify your ideas and strengthen your argument. If you are given another student's paper, read it twice. The first time, read it straight through for enjoyment and illumination; the second time, read it critically.

If you think your classmate can improve the paper, put a question mark in the margin close to any places where the sentences are unclear or you don't understand what the writer is trying to say. Put a check mark in the margin where you would like to see a quotation from the text to illustrate and strengthen the writer's interpretation of the material. Can you identify the thesis statement? Would it be more effective if placed earlier in the essay? Underline it and, if necessary, suggest how it could be repositioned or rewritten more clearly and forcefully. Does the writer adequately discuss the specific quotations from the text so that you understand why they are in the paper?

Finally, comment on the writer's conclusion: Have you learned something from the paper? Does the conclusion relate back to the thesis statement and sum up the essay?

COMMON PROBLEMS IN WRITING ABOUT LITERATURE

Interpret, don't summarize. Summarizing the contents of a story, poem, or play in an essay is not the same as giving insights into the work's pattern and meaning. Occasionally you can summarize the plot in a sentence if you are making a transition from one part of your paper to another, but keep in mind that the reader of your paper is usually your teacher, who has already read the work and will get the impression that you do not know much about what you are doing if you merely summarize it.

Write about how you read the story, poem, or play. Try to express your own ideas through the text. If you find yourself summarizing it in more than a couple of sentences, it is probably because you did not organize your essay around a strong thesis. Your impressions and ideas are the measure of your encounter with literature. Writing encourages your clarification of these ideas. Be sure to state your central idea in a sentence in your paper. It does not matter where it appears, although if you include it in your opening paragraph it will help you keep to the point in your discussion.

Avoid long personal anecdotes. Writing on the basis of your personal experience can result in a fine memoir, but such an essay is usually not about the literature you were asked to discuss. You may want to introduce an analysis of D. H. Lawrence's "The Rocking-Horse Winner" with a short anecdote about a relevant experience you had as a child with a rocking horse, but make sure your anecdote goes on for only a few sentences before you connect it explicitly with your central idea about Lawrence's story.

Use the text to check your interpretation. Opinions about literature can be wrong. Do not insist on ideas that will not fit the details of the work. You may stumble on a central idea for your paper with an intuitive leap or a hunch about a story's meaning, but be sure the specific details of the text support your interpretation. "Whatever I discover in the work is right for me," you may say, but that will not take you very far when writing a paper for an English class. Works of literature are tough, tangible constructions of language, not shifting tea leaves in the bottom of an empty cup into which you can project whatever meaning you like.

Make good use of quotations. You must quote from the text to give evidence of your interpretation. Usually a sentence should introduce and follow each quotation, linking it to the idea being developed in your paper. Never drop quotations into the body of your essay without a comment.

Be careful not to quote too much. Use only those passages that are relevant to your discussion. Overquoting can weaken an essay, easily turning it into a string of short quotations choppily connected by a few insufficient words from you. Be sure to make it clear to the reader why the passage you are quoting is important.

When the quotation is short (four lines or less), it should be enclosed in quotation marks and included within the regular text, as you have seen in the sample essay. When typing a quotation longer than four lines, separate it from the preceding typewritten line with double space. Then indent ten spaces, *omit quotation marks,* and type with a double spacing (unless your instructor tells you differently). If you include the opening paragraph of "Young Goodman Brown" in a research paper, for example, you would indent it like this:

> Young Goodman Brown came forth at sunset into the street at Salem village; but put his head back, after crossing the threshold, to exchange a parting kiss with his young wife. And Faith, as the wife was aptly named, thrust her own pretty head into the street, letting the wind play with the pink ribbons of her cap while she called to Goodman Brown.

In a shorter passage in which you use a quotation within a quotation, such as a line of dialogue inside an excerpt from a story, use double and single quotation marks: "The echoes of the forest mocked him, crying, 'Faith! Faith!' as if bewildered wretches were seeking her all through the wilderness."

If you wish to leave out words in a quoted passage, use ellipsis points, that is, three periods (or four periods if the omitted material includes the end of a sentence) in brackets: "And Faith [. . .] thrust her own pretty head into the street [. . .]."

Always quote the exact wording, punctuation, and capitalization of the original text. If you underline words in a quotation for emphasis, say that you have done so.

If you find an error, for example a misspelled word in a quotation, indicate that the error is in the original by inserting *sic,* a Latin word meaning "thus," in brackets after the error itself.

Last but not least, punctuate sentences that appear in quotation marks correctly. Commas and periods always belong *inside* the quotation marks, whether or not they appeared in the original text. Semicolons, question marks, colons, and exclamation points, however, belong *outside* the quotation marks, unless they are part of the quoted material.

Avoid plagiarism. Any material you borrow from other sources and include in your paper must be documented. If you present someone else's material (other than factual information) as if it were your own, you may be open to the charge of plagiarism. Even with factual information, if you use the exact wording of a source, you must indicate that it is a quotation. To be on the safe side, it is always better to footnote your original source, or give credit by working into your essay the name of the author and the title of the work in which you found the material you cited.

The one exception to this principle is information that is considered *common knowledge.* Common knowledge is material that is repeated in a number of sources, so that it is difficult to tell what the original source might have been. Such items as the basic biographical facts about an author or information about the publication of literary works do not need footnoting, unless you quote someone's exact words at length in your essay.

Know when and how to document the sources in your bibliography. Include the name of the author and the page number in a parenthetical citation or in the text itself when you use references other than this textbook:

> In Richard J. Jacobson's study, we learn that Hawthorne feared the artist might become "insulated from the common business of life" (27).

If you cite from more than one book by an author, mention the title in the text or include a shortened form of the title in the citation:

> We learn that Hawthorne feared the artist might become "insulated from the common business of life" (Jacobson, Hawthorne's Conception 27).

If your instructor asks you to use footnotes or endnotes, instead of parenthetical citation, you may place notes at the bottom of the page on which the reference appears, or they may be gathered together on a separate *notes* page at the end of your essay. When you footnote a source, indent the first line of each footnote five spaces before listing the author's first and last name; the title of the book; the city of publication, publisher, and date in parentheses; and the page number cited:

> [1] Richard J. Jacobson, Hawthorne's Conception of the Creative Process (Cambridge, MA: Harvard UP, 1965) 27.

A separate bibliography of sources is handled differently than a list of notes or footnotes. When you gather several sources together on a separate page at the end of your essay as a bibliography, you list them alphabetically, starting with the *last* name of the author.

> Welty, Eudora. "Is Phoenix Jackson's Grandson Really Dead?" Literature and Its Writers. 2nd ed. Ed. Ann Charters and Samuel Charters. Boston: Bedford/St. Martin's, 2001. 12–14.

Instructions for basic documentation form for different sources — books, magazines, encyclopedias, and so on — appear in every handbook and guide to writing college papers. They may also be found in various manuals of style and style sheets that should be available in the reference section of your college library. You will find a guide to the most frequently used types of citation in the chapter on the research paper that concludes this textbook.

GUIDELINES FOR WRITING AN ESSAY ABOUT LITERATURE

1. DO NOT WAIT UNTIL THE LAST MINUTE TO START. Allow plenty of time to write and revise.
2. BE SURE YOU HAVE A CLEAR IDEA OF WHAT YOU WANT TO SAY ABOUT THE WORK. Can you state this idea as a sharply focused thesis sentence? Remember that all expository writing serves to clarify, set forth, or explain in detail an idea about a topic.
3. READ THE WORK OVER AGAIN. Check the notes in your journal and take notes that will help you amplify your central idea. If necessary, try to generate ideas by brainstorming, freewriting, and listing. Use the commentaries to ask new questions about the text. It might help at this point to assemble a short outline, to stake out the ground you intend your essay to cover. Look for an approach that is distinctive enough to be worth your time and effort yet manageable enough to be handled in a paper of the length you are assigned.
4. DEVELOP A STRONG THESIS SENTENCE. It should express your central idea about your topic.
5. WRITE A ROUGH DRAFT OF YOUR ESSAY. Be sure to state your central idea as a thesis sentence somewhere — preferably at the beginning of your essay. If you are using an outline, try to follow it, but allow yourself the possibility of discovering something new that you did not know you had to say while you are writing. If you have taken notes or jotted down quotations from your reading, try to introduce such material smoothly into your discussion. Remember that the heart of literary criticism is good quotation. Brief, accurate examples from the text that illustrate the points you are trying to make about your thesis are essential in writing about literature.
6. ALLOW SOME TIME TO PASS BEFORE YOU LOOK OVER YOUR ROUGH DRAFT — AT LEAST A DAY. THEN MAKE AT LEAST ONE THOROUGH REVISION BEFORE YOU COPY OR TYPE A FINISHED DRAFT OF YOUR PAPER. Some students find they need several revisions before they are satisfied with what they have written. When you review your rough draft, concentrate and read critically. Let your words stimulate a flow of ideas about your topic; this will lead you to find more ways to develop your train of thought. Fill out paragraphs that seem thin. Be sure transitions between paragraphs are smooth and quotations are integrated into the discussion. If you sense that your sentences are wordy, try to be more concise. Eliminate repetition. Be sure your general organization is coherent and your discussion proceeds in a clear, logical order.
7. CHECK OVER YOUR PAPER ONE LAST TIME. Make sure you have always used complete sentences and correct spelling and punctuation. Avoid sentence fragments and exclamation points, unless they are part of a quotation.
8. TYPE THE PAPER OR WRITE IT NEATLY IN ITS FINAL FORM. If your instructor requires some particular style for class papers, such as extra-wide margins or triple spacing, follow those instructions. Use 8½-by-11-inch

paper. Type if you can, double spacing between lines. If you write by hand, use ink and write on only one side of each piece of paper. Leave generous margins at the top, bottom, and sides. Number the pages, beginning with the number 2 (not the word *two*) in the upper-right-hand corner of the second page. (Your title on the first page will indicate that it is the first page.) Clip and staple your pages together in the upper-left-hand corner. Be sure your name, your instructor's name, your class and section number, and the date appear on your paper.

9. READ YOUR ESSAY OVER ONE LAST TIME FOR TYPOGRAPHICAL ERRORS. Make legible corrections in ink. Have you put quotation marks around titles of short stories ("A Rose for Emily") and underlined or used italics for the titles of books (A Room of One's Own)? Have you placed commas and periods *within* quotation marks in the titles and quotations that appear in your essay? Have you inadvertently left out any words or sentences when you went from the rough draft to the final version of your essay?
10. FINALLY, MAKE A COPY OF YOUR PAPER. If you have typed the paper, make a photocopy of it before handing it in; if you wrote it on a computer, be sure to save a copy of it on disk. It is a good idea to save your notes and rough drafts as well, in case the accuracy of a quotation or the originality of your work is called into question.

What do you do after you hand in your paper? You have probably spent so much time on it — thinking, organizing, writing, and rewriting — that you feel you may never want to look at it again. The act of writing the essay will have clarified your thinking and brought you closer to the literary work, so you carry with you the intangible benefit of something learned in the writing process. Returning to your essay in the future might have one final benefit: Your paper will refresh your memory, reminding you of what you did not know you knew, about both yourself and literature.

PART TWO

FICTION

- *A true work of fiction does all of the following things, and does them elegantly, efficiently: it creates a vivid and continuous dream in the reader's mind; it is implicitly philosophical; it fulfills or at least deals with all of the expectations it sets up; and it strikes us, in the end, not simply as a thing done but as a shining performance.*

  – John Gardner

- *To plot is to move from asking the question* and then what happened? *to the question* why did it happen?

  – James Hillman

- *. . . a speaking voice, like the singing voice in music, that moves not across a space, across the page, but through time. Surely every written story is, in the final analysis, a score for voice. These little black marks on the page mean nothing without their translation into sound.*

  – Margaret Atwood (on the concept of voice in fiction)

1

WHAT IS A SHORT STORY?

Fiction is like the spider's web, attached ever so slightly perhaps, but still attached to life at all four corners.

– VIRGINIA WOOLF, *A Room of One's Own*

People have told stories to each other since before the dawn of history, but the literary genre that we call the **short story** is a relatively recent phenomenon, much younger than the genres of poetry and drama. The terms *story* and *short story* do not necessarily mean the same thing. The word *story* itself has two meanings. It can refer to a literary text (for example, we can say that Eudora Welty wrote a story titled "A Worn Path"), or it can refer to the events themselves that are represented in the text (we can say that the story of "A Worn Path" is about an old woman's trip to get medicine for her sick grandson). In contrast, the term *short story* always means the name of a particular literary genre. It refers to a short fictional prose narrative, sometimes including the fable, the sketch, and the tale. It is often applied to any work of narrative prose fiction shorter than a novel.

Most of us have spent our lives listening to, telling, watching, and reading stories, and we think we can recognize them. Consider, for example, the following narrative or act of storytelling:

Peter Klaus the Goatherd

In the village of Littendorf at the foot of a mountain lived Peter Klaus, a goatherd, who was in the habit of pasturing his flock upon the Kyffhausen hills. Towards evening he generally let them browse upon a green plot not far off, surrounded with an old ruined wall from which he could take a muster of his whole flock.

For some days past he had observed that one of his prettiest goats, soon after its arrival at this spot, usually disappeared, nor joined the fold again until late in the evening. He watched her again and again, and at last found that she slipped through a gap in the old wall, whither he followed her. It led into a passage which widened as he went into a cavern; and here he saw the goat employed in picking up the oats that fell through some crevices in the place above. He looked up, shook his ears at this odd shower of oats, but could discover nothing. Where the deuce could it come from? At length he heard over his head the neighing and stamping of horses; he listened, and concluded that the oats must have fallen through the manger when they were fed. The poor goatherd was sadly puzzled what to think of these horses in this uninhabited part of the mountain, but so it was, for a groom making his appearance, without saying a word beckoned him to follow him. Peter obeyed, and followed him up some steps which brought him into an open court-yard surrounded by old walls. At the side of this was a still more spacious cavern, surrounded by rocky heights which only admitted a kind of twilight, through the overhanging trees and shrubs. He went on, and came to a smooth shaven green, where he saw twelve ancient knights none of whom spoke a word, engaged in playing at nine pins. His guide now beckoned to Peter in silence, to pick up the nine pins and went his way. Trembling in every joint Peter did not venture to disobey, and at times he cast a stolen glance at the players, whose long beards and slashed doublets were not at all in the present fashion. By degrees his looks grew bolder; he took particular notice of every thing around him; among other things observing a tankard near him filled with wine, whose odour was excellent, he took a good draught. It seemed to inspire him with life; and whenever he began to feel tired of running, he applied with fresh ardour to the tankard, which always renewed his strength. But finally it quite overpowered him, and he fell asleep.

When he next opened his eyes, he found himself on the grass-plot again, in the old spot where he was in the habit of feeding his goats. He rubbed his eyes, he looked round, but could see neither dog nor flock; he was surprised at the long rank grass that grew around him, and at trees and bushes which he had never before seen. He shook his head and walked a little farther, looking for the old sheep path and the hillocks and roads where he used daily to drive his flock; but he could find no traces of them left. Yet he saw the village just before him; it was the same Littendorf, and scratching his head he hastened at a quick pace down the hill to enquire after his flock.

All the people whom he met going into the place were strangers to him, were differently dressed, and even spoke in a different style to his old neighbours. When he asked about his goats, they only stared at him, and fixed their eyes upon his chin. He put his hand unconsciously to his mouth, and to his great surprise found that he had got a beard, at least a foot long. He now began to think that both he and all the world about him were in a dream; and yet he knew the mountain for that of the Kyffhausen (for he had just come down it) well enough. And there were the cottages, with their gardens and grass-plots, much as he had left them. Besides the lads who had all collected round him, answered to the enquiry of a passenger, what place it was: "Littendorf, sir."

Still shaking his head, he went farther into the village to look for his own house. He found it, but greatly altered for the worse; a strange goatherd in an old tattered frock lay before the door, and near him his old dog, which growled and showed its teeth at Peter when he called him. He went through the entrance which had once a door, but all within was empty and deserted; Peter staggered like a drunken man out of the house, and called for his wife and children by their names. But no one heard him, and no one gave him any answer.

Soon, however, a crowd of women and children got round the inquisitive stranger, with the long hoary beard; and asked him what it was he wanted. Now Peter thought it was such a strange kind of thing to stand before his own house, enquiring for his own wife and children, as well as about himself, that evading these inquiries he pronounced the first name that came into his head: "Kurt Steffen, the blacksmith?" Most of the spectators were silent, and only looked at him wistfully, till an old woman at last said, "Why, for these twelve years he has been at Sachsenburg, whence I suppose you are not come today." "Where is Valentine Meier, the tailor?" "The Lord rest his soul," cried another woman leaning on her crutch, "he has been lying more than fifteen years in a house he will never leave."

Peter recognized in the speakers, two of his young neighbours who seemed to have grown old very suddenly, but he had no inclination to enquire any farther. At this moment there appeared making her way through the crowd of spectators, a sprightly young woman with a year old baby in her arms, and a girl about four taking hold of her hand, all three as like his wife he was seeking for as possible. "What are your names?" he enquired in a tone of great surprise. "Mine is Maria." "And your father's?" continued Peter. "God rest his soul! Peter Klaus for sure. It's now twenty years ago since we were all looking for him day and night upon the Kyffhausen; for his flock came home without him, and I was then," continued the woman, "only seven years old."

The goatherd could no longer bear this. "I am Peter Klaus," he said. "Peter and no other," and he took his daughter's child and kissed it. The spectators appeared struck dumb with astonishment, until first one and then another began to say, "Yes, indeed, this is Peter Klaus! Welcome, good neighbour, after twenty years' absence, welcome home."

Most readers would say that this narrative about Peter Klaus's twenty-year sleep in the mountains of Germany is a story. It is, using the definition of the English novelist E. M. Forster, a narrative of events arranged in a time sequence. Yet comparing it in your mind with other stories you have read, you may suspect that it doesn't quite fit into the literary genre of a *short story.* Considering the narrative's brevity and old-fashioned language, an informed reader would call it a **tale**, a narrative sequence less developed than a short story.

What you have just read is Thomas Roscoe's 1820 translation of "Peter Klaus the Goatherd," a traditional narrative collected in Germany at the end of the eighteenth century by the folklorist J. C. C. Nachtigal. The German folktale was originally published in Bremen in 1800 in a collection titled *Folkssagen, Nacherzhaht von Otmar* (*Folktales, Transcribed by Otmar*—Nachtigal's pseudonym). Nachtigal's transcription of the German folktale became the source of what most literary historians acknowledge as the first successful American short story, "Rip Van Winkle," by Washington Irving.

The connection between "Rip Van Winkle" and "Peter Klaus the Goatherd" is so clear that Irving was charged by hostile critics with plagiarism when he published his version of the story in *The Sketch Book* in 1819–20. The story of a person who disappears from the world in order to experience what Joseph Campbell described in *Hero with a Thousand Faces* as a "life-enhancing return" is common to the mythology of many cultures. Irving never denied that he had used a German source for his story. He even suggested as much at the end of "Rip Van Winkle," even if he tried to obscure his debt to Nachtigal.

Like the more famous Brothers Grimm who published their collections of German folktales a dozen years after him, Nachtigal believed in the importance of the oral tradition of storytelling. In the preface to his book, he explained that "the popular stories here offered my countrymen . . . are real tales of the people, collected among them with much care, as they were fast dropping into oblivion, and are here narrated in the most simple and faithful language."

When you read "Peter Klaus the Goatherd," you probably sensed that it was a story, but how did you know this? In 1842 the American author Edgar Allan Poe was one of the first writers to attempt an analysis of the aesthetic properties of what he called "the prose tale." He stressed its *length* and its *"unity of effect"* as its most characteristic features. Aware that the quality of the reader's attention to works of literature was important, Poe insisted that a prose narrative had to be brief enough to be read in one sitting. He argued that any interruption would destroy the unity of the work's emotional effect on the reader.

Most readers feel that literary works don't always need to be read in one sitting to achieve their effect, but Poe's "unity of effect" is an important standard. It can be found in all successful works of art, including poetry and drama as well as short fiction. In particular, you can see that "Peter Klaus the Goatherd" is unified in its plot, characters, setting, point of view, style, and theme, the six elements of fiction that give stories their unity.

In the early years of the nineteenth century when authors like Washington Irving began to publish their prose tales, they found a receptive audience of readers willing to suspend disbelief and enter the imaginative world of their fiction. In the previous century the novel had emerged as a new literary genre, and it also helped to create an audience of readers for entertaining short narratives. You will find that writers using the elements of fiction have powerful resources to shape both the form and the meaning of their stories.

RELATED STORY: *Washington Irving, "Rip Van Winkle," page 361.*

RELATED COMMENTARY: *Edgar Allan Poe, "The Importance of the Single Effect in a Prose Tale," page 709.*

2

THE ELEMENTS OF FICTION: A STORYTELLER'S MEANS

> A true work of fiction is a wonderfully simple thing — so simple that most so-called serious writers avoid trying it, feeling they ought to do something more important and ingenious, never guessing how incredibly difficult it is. A true work of fiction does all of the following things, and does them elegantly, efficiently: it creates a vivid and continuous dream in the reader's mind; it is implicitly philosophical; it fulfills or at least deals with all of the expectations it sets up; and it strikes us, in the end, not simply as a thing done but as a shining performance.
>
> – JOHN GARDNER, "What Writers Do"

Most readers are able to identify short fictional prose narratives as short stories, whether written by authors in the United States or in countries throughout the world, because authors in every country employ the same elements of fiction. In the imaginations of gifted storytellers, these basic components are transformed into the texts of short stories as the writers explore the potentiality of fiction. Literary critics generally agree that these basic elements comprise six different categories: plot, characterization, setting, point of view, style, and theme.

PLOT

Since the short story is defined as a prose narrative usually involving one unified episode or a sequence of related events, plot is basic to this literary form. **Plot** is the sequence of events in a story and their relation to one another. Writers usually present the events of the plot in a coherent time frame that the reader can follow easily. As we read, we sense that the events are related by causation, and their meaning lies in this relation. To the casual reader, causation (or why something in the plot happened next) seems to result only from the writer's organization of the events into a chronological sequence. A more thoughtful reader understands that causation in the plot of a memorable short story reveals a good deal about the author's use of the other elements of fiction as well, especially characterization.

As E. M. Forster realized, plot not only answers *what* happened next, but it also suggests *why.* The psychologist James Hillman has explained in *Healing Fiction* that plot reveals "human intentions. Plot shows how it all hangs together and makes sense. Only when a narrative receives inner coherence in terms of the depths of human nature do we have fiction, and for this fiction we have to have plot. . . . To plot is to move from asking the question *and then what happened?* to the question *why did it happen?"*

A short story can dramatize the events of a brief episode or compress a longer period of time. Analyzing why a short story is short, the critic Norman Friedman suggests that it "may be short not because its action is inherently small, but rather because the author has chosen — in working with an episode or plot — to omit certain of its parts. In other words, an action may be large in size and still be short in the telling because not all of it is there." A short story can describe something that happens in a few minutes or encompass action that takes years to conclude. The narrative possibilities are endless, as the writer may omit or condense complex episodes to intensify their dramatic effect or expand a single incident to make a relatively long story.

Regardless of length, the plot of a short story usually has what critics term an **end orientation** — the outcome of the action or the conclusion of the plot — inherent in its opening paragraphs. As Mark Twain humorously observed, "Fiction is obliged to stick to possibilities. Truth isn't." The novelist may conclude a single episode long before the end of a novel and then pick up the thread of another narrative, or interpret an event from another angle in a different character's point of view, linking episode to episode and character to character so that each illuminates the others. But a story stops earlier. As Poe recognized in 1842, its narrative dramatizes a single effect complete unto itself.

The events in the plot of a short story usually involve a conflict or struggle between opposing forces. When you analyze a plot, you can often (but not always) see it develop in a pattern during the course of the narration. Typically you find that the first paragraphs of the story or **exposition** give the background or setting of the conflict. The **rising action** dramatizes the specific events that set the conflict in motion. Often there is a **turning point** in the story midway before further **complications** prolong the suspense of the conflict's resolution. The **climax** is the emotional high point of the narration. In the **falling action**, the events begin to wind down and point the reader toward the **conclusion** or **dénouement** at the end of the story, which resolves the conflict to a greater or lesser degree. Sometimes the conclusion introduces an unexpected turn of events or a surprise ending. In successful stories the writer shapes these stages into a complex structure that may impress you with its balance and proportion.

The plot of "Peter Klaus the Goatherd" relates a sequence of events about a man who falls asleep for twenty years after a supernatural encounter in the mountains and then awakens to return to his family and friends, whose lives have gone on without him. The first part, or *exposition,* of the folktale introduces character, setting, and time. This all occurs in the first short paragraph of Nachtigal's version. The next, much longer paragraph introduces the *rising action,* the events that lead to Peter Klaus's mysterious encounter with the "twelve ancient knights." The *turning point* occurs when he wakes up. *Complications* make up the second half of the story, when Peter Klaus returns to his village and finds himself a stranger there. This leads to the *climax,* the emotional high point when the old goatherd hears the story of his disappearance from his daughter and "could no longer bear this. 'I am Peter Klaus,' he said, 'Peter and no other.'" This moment of recognition may cause the sympathetic reader to wince with pity for the old man. The *falling action* and *conclusion* immediately follow the goatherd's pathetic recognition of what has happened to him. In this short tale, the conclusion is the final sentence of the narrative.

When Washington Irving transformed "Peter Klaus the Goatherd" into the American story "Rip Van Winkle," it became four times as long. You might say that the difference between the treatment of the plot in the two versions is that Nachtigal's folktale tends to summarize the action, while Irving's short story develops it. Irving invented many new details to create elaborate twists and turns in the basic plot as well as to transform its characters and setting.

In modern stories, plot most often evolves as the interaction of characters with circumstances. Authors develop it through dialogue and commentary as well as description of action. They can also add **foreshadowing** and **verbal irony** to the narration, anticipating a turn of events that may or may not go along with our expectations. The opening paragraph of "Rip Van Winkle" is a good example of Irving's leisurely approach to his plot, containing examples of both foreshadowing and verbal irony:

> The following Tale was found among the papers of the late Diedrich Knickerbocker, an old gentleman of New York, who was very curious in the Dutch history of the province, and the manners of the descendants from its primitive settlers. His historical researches, however, did not lie so much among books as among men; for the former are lamentably scanty on his favorite topics; whereas he found the old burghers, and still more their wives, rich in that legendary lore so invaluable to true history. Whenever, therefore, he happened upon a genuine Dutch family, snugly shut up in its low-roofed farmhouse, under a spreading sycamore, he looked upon it as a little clasped volume of black-letter, and studied it with the zeal of a book-worm.

As the reader will learn in a few more paragraphs, Rip Van Winkle himself is one such "old burgher" (foreshadowing), a character whose life experience is rich in "legendary lore." But in Irving's tale, Rip's wife is not allowed to tell her story, so we are given a different reality than the literal meaning of the author's words in his introduction (verbal irony).

Regardless of the author's method of developing the plot, the goal is the same: The writer of short stories must *show* the reader something about human nature through the dramatic action of the plot and the other elements of the story, and not just *tell* the reader what to think. A good plot engages our curiosity, surprises us, and keeps us in suspense. As the contemporary American writer Eudora Welty understood, "A narrative line is in its deeper sense, of course, the tracing out of a meaning, and the real continuity of a story lies in this probing forward." A storyteller must sustain the illusion of reality until the end of the story, unfolding events with the continuing revelation of an apparently endless silk handkerchief drawn from a skillful magician's coat sleeve.

CHARACTER

If you are like most people, plot is what keeps you going when you first read a story, and character is what stays with you after you have finished reading it. The title of the German folktale "Peter Klaus the Goatherd" is named after its memorable **protagonist** or central character. Characters are usually the people who are involved in what happens in a story. Writers can use animals as characters, or even such inanimate objects as trees, chairs, and shoes, but with the term *character* we usually mean a human being with emotions whose mind works something like our own.

When we ask Why? of the plot of a story, we usually find the answer in the characters, who are convincing if we can understand their actions. Peter Klaus does not always understand why he acts as he does. Yet the reasons are there, and we may know them before the fictional characters do. We instinctively strive to connect the events of a story by more than their simple chronological sequence, because assuming connection between the events and the inner life of the characters makes the story seem coherent.

How are the characters in a short story to be understood? Any discussion of character tends to drift into a value judgment, as our principles of definition and evaluation for fictional characters are based on the ones we use for real people, tentative and confused as they may be. We must remember that we are reading about *fictional* characters in a short story, not real ones. The only evidence we have about characters is what the author puts into the story.

We are on firmer ground in literary discussions when we analyze the writer's method of characterization as well as the character's personality. Nachtigal's method is one of economy. We know from the title that Peter Klaus is the central person in the action. A little more than a dozen words into the story, we are told all we need to know about him — he is a goatherd. Only one sparse adjective, *a,* modifies the noun. We are in the fictional world of the oral folk tradition, where characters are known primarily by what they do. They are defined by their actions, not by their sensitive introspection, their subtle responses to other people, or their being described as good or bad.

Characters are sometimes called **round** or **flat**. For characters to emerge as round, the reader must feel the play and pull of their actions and responses to situations. Peter Klaus is a flat character. He does not have complex responses to his situation; he is acted upon by his circumstances.

Even as a flat character, Peter Klaus is not **static**. He is a **dynamic** character who changes during the narrative because something significant happens to him. However, his daughter Maria, a minor character in his story, is both flat and static. She makes such a brief appearance that she doesn't appear as an individual. She doesn't come alive on the page because there is no accumulation of detail about her actions and responses.

Writers of short fiction suggest their philosophical view of the world in the way they present their characters. In such early tales as "Peter Klaus the

Goatherd," authors create worlds of fantasy where the characters tend to be flat; they have little control over their environment. Later writers of realistic stories create more rounded protagonists because they put more emphasis on the choices that their fictional characters make, granting them more control over their fates.

Different fictional worlds make different demands on the reader's imagination, but what is most important is the emotional truth of the fictional character, flat or round, dynamic or static. To avoid **sentimentality** (emotional overindulgence) and **stereotyping** (generalized, oversimplified judgment) in creating characters, the writer must be able to suggest enough complexity to engage the reader's emotions, or the story will not succeed.

SETTING

Setting is the place and time of the story. To set the scene and suggest a mood or atmosphere for the events to follow, the writer attempts to create in the reader's visual imagination the illusion of a solid world in which the story takes place. Setting is so important that the opening words of "Peter Klaus the Goatherd" are "In the Village of Littendorf at the foot of a mountain lived Peter Klaus." Since this tale is based on legendary material about a human being's encounter with the spirit world, it could easily have started with the phrase "Once upon a time." Instead, the storyteller brings it out of the realm of fantasy and suggests it happens in the real world by mentioning the name of the village where the events allegedly took place to make the tale seem more credible to the reader.

In "Peter Klaus the Goatherd" the setting is secondary to the action; in "Rip Van Winkle" it is central. Irving's description of the countryside is so virtuosic that you could award him the first Harry Houdini magician's prize for excellence among sleight-of-hand scene painters. Irving spends an entire paragraph describing the Catskills' "magical hues and shapes" before introducing Rip Van Winkle. Then when Rip climbs the mountains hunting squirrel, the beauties of nature are described again through his eyes:

> In a long ramble of the kind on a fine autumnal day, Rip had unconsciously scrambled to one of the highest parts of the Kaatskill mountains. He was after his favorite sport of squirrel-shooting, and the still solitudes had echoed and re-echoed with the reports of his gun. Panting and fatigued, he threw himself, late in the afternoon, on a green knoll, covered with mountain herbage, that crowned the brow of a precipice. From an opening between the trees he could overlook all the lower country for many a mile of rich woodland. He saw at a distance the lordly Hudson, far, far below him, moving on its silent but majestic course, with the reflection of a purple cloud, or the sail of a lagging bark, here and there sleeping on its glassy bosom, and at last losing itself in the blue highlands.
>
> On the other side he looked down into a deep mountain glen, wild, lonely, and shagged, the bottom filled with fragments from the impending cliffs, and scarcely lighted by the reflected rays of the

> setting sun. For some time Rip lay musing on this scene; evening was gradually advancing; the mountains began to throw their long blue shadows over the valleys; he saw that it would be dark long before he could reach the village.

Like other early-nineteenth-century American authors such as Nathaniel Hawthorne, Irving contrasts the countryside in the New World tamed by its human occupants (the peaceful "rich woodland" and "lordly Hudson") with the untamed territory (the "wild, lonely" mountainside) outside the settled villages. When Rip sees the mountains, those specters of the wild landscape, throwing their "long blue shadows" over the peaceful valleys, Irving uses the setting to suggest a symbolic meaning in the plot. The description of nature tamed and untamed, different in daytime and at night, foreshadows Rip's mysterious meeting with the spirit world.

When the writer locates the narrative in a physical setting, the reader is moved step by step toward acceptance of the fiction. The *external* reality of the setting is always an illusion, our mental images that correspond to the words that the writer has put on paper. Yet this invented setting is essential if we are to share the *internal* emotional life of the characters involved in the plot. The setting of a story furnishes the location for its world of feeling. A sense of place engages us in the fictional characters' situations.

Place helps make the characters seem real, but, to be most effective, the setting must also have a dramatic use. It must be perceived to affect character or plot. When Klaus the goatherd returns after his twenty-year sleep and sees his house "greatly altered for the worse" and "empty and deserted," he staggers "like a drunken man." In "Rip Van Winkle," Irving begins his story in the decade before the American Revolution, not in a vague "once upon a time." After Rip's twenty years' absence, the momentous change in his Hudson River village is evident in the new sign he notices hanging above the tavern he had frequented with his cronies — the "ruby face of King George" has been replaced by a portrait of General Washington. By giving precise details about the setting, writers share their vision of their fictional world with their readers, creating the illusion that the story unfolds in the real world.

POINT OF VIEW

Point of view refers to the author's choice of a narrator for the story. At the start, the writer must decide whether to employ **first-person narration**, using the pronoun *I*, or **third-person narration**, using the pronouns *he, she,* and *they.* (Second-person narration, *you,* is less common, although the dramatic intimacy of second-person narrative address is often used in poetry and song lyrics.) The writer's choice of a point of view to narrate stories usually falls into two major categories:

FIRST-PERSON NARRATION (NARRATOR APPARENTLY A PARTICIPANT IN THE STORY)

1. A major character
2. A minor character

THIRD-PERSON NARRATION (NARRATOR A NONPARTICIPANT IN THE STORY)

1. Omniscient — seeing into the minds of all characters
2. Limited omniscient — seeing into one or, sometimes, two characters' minds
3. Objective — seeing into none of the characters' minds

First-Person Narration

The tale of "Peter Klaus the Goatherd" uses third-person narration, but you can imagine how it might have sounded in the first-person *I* if the author had let us imagine that Peter Klaus had told it himself:

> I don't want to sound crazy or anything, but it did happen to me. It was a long time ago, but I can still remember everything just as clear as a bell. I was watching my goats late one afternoon in the mountains, and I saw one stray through the wall. I went after her into a cave, and then suddenly I heard a lot of horses. A strange-looking man appeared and I followed him to a group of knights who were playing a game of nine pins. They made me help them, but I found something to drink, and I don't know how it happened, but I fell sound asleep. When I woke up and went home, I found everything had changed. My wife had died and my little girl had grown up. I had been asleep for twenty years!

Since Peter Klaus is presented as such a simple character, there is no magic to his first-person account. The storyteller in a first-person narration can be either a major or a minor character. If Peter is too tongue-tied to tell you his own tale, the author could let you hear it from a minor participant on the sidelines of the action, his daughter Maria. Her view of what happened to her father might sound something like this:

> Yes, you can ask me about him, but I was very young when he disappeared, only seven or so. I don't remember that much about him. All of us went out to look for him, and my mother cried bitterly when the search party from our village came back and told her that they'd failed to find him. His goats came home all right, but somebody else took charge of them, and we became very poor. My mother slaved to keep us fed and warm. When she died, poor thing, I was raised by my aunt. Twenty years passed before I saw my dear father again, standing in front of our house. I must admit that I didn't even recognize him until he spoke to me!

To be effective as a story, the biased report of the first-person narrator must have a dramatic significance. This usually occurs in a subtle discrepancy between the way he or she sees characters or events and the reader's sense of what really happened. Peter Klaus's laconic first-person narrative has the authority of an eye-witness account, of course, but Maria was only a little girl when her father disappeared, and she can't tell us much about his fantastic adventure away from home.

Also, from the way Peter and his daughter describe what happened to them in these different versions of the tale, it appears that they both lack artistry as storytellers. You will discover that writers in this anthology such as Edgar Allan Poe, Charlotte Perkins Gilman, William Faulkner, and Grace Paley use first-person narration to magnificent effect in their stories, adding to the emotional impact of the events they describe.

Third-Person Narration

Third-person narration means that the author tells the story using the pronouns *he* or *she* instead of the presumably more subjective *I*. Narrated in the third person, the folktale begins, "In the village of Littendorf at the foot of a mountain lived Peter Klaus, a goatherd, who was in the habit of pasturing his flock upon the Kyffhausen hills."

There can be significant differences, however, in the way authors handle third-person narration. "Peter Klaus the Goatherd" is an example of *limited-omniscient* narration, because Nachtigal confines himself to revealing the thoughts of only one character, his protagonist. The folklorist tells his story with such scrupulous regard for his source in the oral tradition that he doesn't present an interior, subjective view of Peter Klaus's experience. When the goatherd sees the "odd shower of oats" in the cavern ("Where the deuce could it come from?"), we are told that he was "sadly puzzled what to think" about the idea of a stable of horses in that part of the mountains, but we are told mostly what he did, rather than what he thought or felt. At the climax of his story, when he meets his daughter, the emotional content of Peter's response is summarized in a single sentence: "The goatherd could no longer bear this."

Irving took a different approach to third-person narration. As you have read in the opening paragraph of "Rip Van Winkle," Irving chose to take the third-person *omniscient* point of view toward his materials. This approach signals to the reader that the storyteller is omniscient, ready to tell you everything there is to know about all the characters in his tale, what they think and feel as well as what they do. Fairy tales beginning "Once upon a time" are the most familiar examples of omniscient narration.

There are several other varieties of third-person narration, since authors are highly conscious of the different effects on the reader resulting from their choice of a particular point of view. Discussing her approach to writing fiction, the South African writer Nadine Gordimer once said, "I have the writer's healthy selfish instinct to keep open the multiple vision that the fly's eye of the writer had brought me." A writer can tell a story using *objective narration,* attempting to create a totally detached perspective on the characters and the plot of the story. Setting, action, and dialogue appear on the page without the narrator's comments or the characters' reflection.

When Joseph Conrad suggested that the nineteenth-century French author Guy de Maupassant was interested in using only *facts* to tell his story, Conrad was implying that Maupassant was attempting objective narration. Yet Maupassant himself insisted on his "personal view" as a writer and on his selectivity in presenting what he called "the illusion of reality" in fiction. For example, in his famous story "The Necklace," Maupassant's "personal view" included a snobbish disdain for a social-climbing wife from a modest background.

The American writer Ernest Hemingway attempted an even more rigorous use of objective narration. In "Hills Like White Elephants," he presents only enough background information to introduce the physical setting and his two characters; then he narrates his story through their dialogue. You must read between the lines to understand what the characters are discussing.

Narration can be classified into further subcategories (for example, first- and third-person stream-of-consciousness narration), but a writer's handling of different points of view is always more flexible than the rigid categories imply. Franz Kafka, who tells the story of "The Metamorphosis" through the thoughts of his central character, Gregor Samsa, continues in the last pages of the narrative to describe events after Gregor's death so the reader can get a harrowing sense of how his uncaring family went on without him.

VOICE AND STYLE

Style is the characteristic way an author uses language to create literature. Style is the result of the writer's habitual use of certain rhetorical patterns, including sentence length and complexity, word choice and placement, and punctuation. Nachtigal uses simple sentence construction and choice of words in "Peter Klaus the Goatherd" to suggest that his tale had originated among uneducated people. Irving, on the other hand, wrote to show off his virtuosity as a prose stylist to his educated readers. He used much more complicated sentence structure and a much more sophisticated vocabulary.

You might think of the author's prose style as a projection of his or her **voice** as a writer, as if you were hearing the story instead of reading it. Voice, as the Canadian writer Margaret Atwood described it, is "a speaking voice, like the singing voice in music, that moves not across a space, across the page, but through time. Surely every written story is, in the final analysis, a score for voice. These little black marks on the page mean nothing without their retranslation into sound."

Of course, the voice brought to life by the words resonating in the mind of the reader is not necessarily the literal voice of the author. When Nachtigal told his story, his voice was flat and matter-of-fact, devoid of emotional resonance, the voice of a folklorist and scholar who respected his material. The German peasant who originally narrated the sad tale of Peter Klaus to him might have been a virtuoso performer in the oral tradition of her village, using a dramatic voice, physical gestures, and perhaps even music or props for an impressive effect. But transcribed and printed on the page, the bare words of the tale are all that remain to us.

Tone is the way the author conveys his or her unstated attitudes toward the story. We assume that Nachtigal's serious tone was present in the original German version of his tale, but since we read it in an English translation, we must be cautious in describing his authorial voice and tone. Since Irving wrote in English, we stand on firmer ground, understanding that he chose to put on a performance in "Rip Van Winkle." As you saw in the opening paragraph of his story, he adopted a humorous tone to amuse his readers.

Irony is another means by which writers tell stories. Irony makes the reader aware of a reality that differs from the reality the characters perceive (*dramatic irony*) or from the literal meaning of the author's words (*verbal irony*). Irving's prose style is rich in irony. You have already noticed an example of verbal irony in his opening paragraph to "Rip Van Winkle" when he refers to the wives "rich in that legendary lore so invaluable to true history." A good example of dramatic irony occurs at the end of the story, when Rip returns to his village after his long sleep. On the street he meets "a precise counterpart of himself, as he went up the mountain; apparently as lazy, and certainly as ragged." Here is a situation full of dramatic irony because Rip doesn't know he is looking at his son. He sees the shiftless young man only as a mirror image of himself twenty years before.

The use of **symbolism** can also be an aspect of a writer's style. A literary symbol can be anything in a story's setting, plot, or characterization that suggests an abstract meaning to the reader in addition to its literal significance. Irving's description of the late-afternoon shadows of the mountains could symbolize the mysterious fantasy world that Rip entered shortly afterwards. Symbols are more eloquent as specific images — visual ideas — than any paraphrase, suggesting infinitely more than they state. They are not always interpreted the same way by all readers. For example, the mountain shadows may suggest to another reader a symbol that foreshadows Rip's long sleep and his awakening into old age.

An entire story can also suggest a symbolic as well as a literal meaning. A story becomes an **allegory** when all the characters, places, things, and events represent symbolic qualities and their interactions are meant to reveal a moral truth. Whereas symbolism results from the multiple meanings inherent in a good story, an allegorical interpretation tends to simplify the meaning. We can easily interpret the folktale "Peter Klaus the Goatherd" as an allegory. Its traditional source suggests that centuries ago in Europe it could have served as a medieval Christian moral fable reminding listeners about the brevity of human life, or warning them about the dangers of pagan worship or alcohol.

THEME

Theme is a generalization about the meaning of a story. Whereas the plot of a story can be summarized by stating what happened in the action, the theme is the general idea behind the events of the plot that expresses the meaning of the story. Nachtigal and Irving's stories, about the mysterious nature of time and human mortality, are relatively easy to boil down to a phrase that summarizes their meaning, because both authors were writing at a time when readers expected to be taught a moral lesson when they read prose narratives. When Irving was criticized for basing his stories on a German source, he pointed out that Shakespeare had also borrowed the plots of his plays and that great writers succeeded not because they invented new stories but "because they have rooted themselves in the unchanging principles of human nature."

The stories we encounter daily do much more than entertain us; they also play a central role in our lives. Students of the media tell us that the narratives told to us by parents, friends, teachers, books, audio recordings, radio, television, and film are the real authors of what we take to be our "common" sense, helping us arrive at an understanding of ourselves and our place in the world. As James Hillman has explained, our stories provide "dynamic coherence and meaning to the dispersed narratives of our lives." At the same time, fiction also has the power to challenge our everyday sense of reality by reminding us of our mortality and suggesting that anything might happen, since the universe is ultimately beyond our control and comprehension.

Theme comes last in a discussion of the elements of fiction because all the other elements must be accounted for in determining it. The structure and theme of a story are fused like the body and soul of a reader; their interaction creates a living pattern. While the various actions of the plot must strike us as realistic and inevitable, the complete truth that it reveals is in essence indefinable and untranslatable outside the story. The storyteller says, "Let me tell you how it is," and we pay attention because we want to know what the story can show us about the complexities of human experience. Theme is an abstract formulation of the author's vision of the meaning of life.

One of the pleasures of a good story is figuring out what has pulled us into it. The ways authors use the elements of fiction to create their stories will reflect their philosophical view of the meaning of our common experience, what the Russian writer Isaac Babel called "the secret curve" behind the author's "straight line." The summary of a writer's theme is no substitute for the story in its entirety, but our attempt to state it can help us understand the story better. As the Southern writer Flannery O'Connor said, "A story is a way to say something that can't be said any other way, and it takes every word in the story to say what the meaning is. . . . When anybody asks what a story is about, the only proper thing is to tell him to read the story."

RELATED COMMENTARIES: *Sherwood Anderson, "Form, Not Plot, in the Short Story," page 660; Anton Chekhov, "Technique in Writing the Short Story," page 669; Joseph Conrad, "The Condition of Art," page 671; Flannery O'Connor, "The Element of Suspense in 'A Good Man Is Hard to Find,'" page 784; Eudora Welty, "Plot and Character in Chekhov's 'The Darling,'" page 736.*

3

READING, THINKING, AND WRITING ABOUT SHORT FICTION

> General rules in art are useful chiefly as a lamp in a mine, or a handrail down a black stairway: they are necessary for the sake of the guidance they give, but it is a mistake, once they are formulated, to be too much in awe of them.
>
> – Edith Wharton, *The Writing of Fiction*

READING SHORT FICTION

The great eighteenth-century English critic Samuel Johnson said that the great majority of people need to be reminded more often than instructed. Remember to read each story at least once in its entirety. The best way to give short stories a chance to entertain and enchant you is to sit down and grant them your full attention. Read them carefully straight through from beginning to end.

When you read a story for the first time, you may find it relatively easy to see the elements of plot, character, and setting interact on the page. They stand out because they seem to make the story happen, and — at least for the casual reader — they appear to be what the story is about. Point of view, style, and theme, on the other hand, are less visible elements. Many readers regard them with dread as part of what they call the "hidden meaning" of a story. While it is true that you may have to look for these particular elements deliberately, you will find that this hunt is worth the treasure. The more you read attentively, the easier it will be to appreciate how all the elements operate in short fiction. You will begin to understand more fully that *how* a story is written is an essential part of *what* it is saying.

If you make the effort, you will find that reading literature is an activity that challenges your intellect and emotions to the highest degree. After finishing a story for the first time, you may feel contradictory responses to it, uncertain how to interpret what you have read. A second or third reading may help clarify your impressions, or you may find you have to close your book and think about the story if it doesn't fit easily into your preconceptions about human experience.

The effort is worthwhile. As the critic Ray Carey has explained, the different forms of storytelling can "point a way out of some of the traps of received forms of thinking and feeling. Every artist makes a fresh effort of awareness. He [or she] offers new forms of caring. He [or she] can point out the processed emotions and canned understandings that deceive us. He [or she] can reveal the emotional lies that ensnare us. He [or she] can help us to new and potentially revolutionary understandings of our lives." Because reading a good story is potentially an enlightening experience, you will find that analyzing the means available to the storyteller is one of the best ways to make the story accessible to you.

Stories are shorter than novels, but they're not necessarily easier to read. The editor Charles McGrath cautions that

> stories aren't just *brief,* they're *different;* and they require of the reader something like the degree of concentration they require of the writer. . . . You can't skim or coast or leap ahead, and if you have to put a story down, it's not always easy to pick up — emotionally, that is — where you left off. You have to backtrack a little, or even start over. It's not enough to read a story the way you read a book or a newspaper. Stories ask of us that we surrender ourselves to them.

Guidelines for Reading Short Fiction

1. Make an entry in your notebook for each story assigned in class, writing down the author's name and the story's title and date. As you begin to read, remember T. S. Eliot's advice in his essay "Tradition and the Individual Talent" (p. 1163) that "criticism is as inevitable as breathing, and that we should be none the worse for articulating what passes in our minds when we read a book and feel an emotion about it, for criticizing our own minds in their work of criticism."
2. Use a dictionary to look up words in both the headnote and the story that you do not understand.
3. After you have read the story, make notes about the way the author has used the elements of fiction; this will help you remember and review the story later. Note, for example, the names of the characters, the geographical setting, the author's choice of a point of view, and the literary style in which it is written. Try summing up the story's theme in a phrase or sentence.
4. If you have difficulty understanding the story's meaning or how any of the elements of fiction work within it, write down your questions so you can ask them in class.
5. In class, take notes on the important material about the story that you learn from lectures and discussions and ask any questions you have about the assignment. You may be able to develop these notes in your essays.

6. Review technical words about short fiction that were used in class; this will help you to understand them better.
7. If you have particularly enjoyed a story, go to the library to check out other works by that writer. Reading on your own will enrich the class assignments.

CRITICAL THINKING ABOUT SHORT FICTION

You will find that reading a story and discussing it in class are only part of the process of understanding it. Usually your thinking about a story begins with interpreting it, clarifying what the author is saying in the action of the plot, and making sure you understand the characters and have a clear idea of the theme of the story. Critical thinking goes a step further beyond interpretation when you discuss how the form of the story is related to its content or when you analyze how the story relates to your own experience.

Reading commentaries about a story for an essay assignment will help you to focus your thoughts. Ideas for writing can come from any number of sources. Sometimes your instructor will give you a specific assignment; other times you will be asked to generate the idea for the paper yourself. Whatever the case, your reading notes and the class discussions will help you prepare for writing about the story.

Before you can start thinking about writing a response to literature, you should feel that you thoroughly understand the story as a whole. When you read it again, notice the passages that strike you with particular force. Underline the words and sentences you consider significant — or, even better, make a list in your notebook of what seems important while you are rereading the story. These can be outstanding descriptions of the characters or settings, passages of meaningful dialogue, details showing the way the author builds toward the story's climax, or hints that foreshadow the conclusion. To stimulate ideas about topics, you may want to jot down answers to the following questions about the elements of the story as you reread it.

Plot. Does the plot depend on chance, or coincidence? Or does it grow out of the personalities of the characters? Are any later incidents foreshadowed early in the story? Are the episodes presented in chronological order? If not, why is this so? Does the climax indicate a change in a situation or a change in a character? How dramatic is this change? Or is there no change at all?

Character. Are the characters believable? Are they stereotypes? Do they suggest real people, or abstract qualities? Is there one protagonist or are there several? Does the story have an antagonist? How does the author tell you about the main character — through description of physical appearance, actions, thoughts, and emotions, or through contrast with a minor character? Does the main character change in the course of the story? If so, how? Why?

Setting. How does the setting influence the plot and the characters? Does it help to suggest or develop the meaning of the story?

Point of view. How does the point of view shape the theme? Would the story change if told from a different viewpoint? In first-person narration, can you trust the narrator?

Style. Is the author's prose style primarily literal or figurative? Can you find examples of irony in dialogue or narrative passages? If dialect or colloquial speech is used, what is its effect? Does the author call attention to the way he or she uses words, or is the literary style inconspicuous?

Theme. Does the story's title help explain its meaning? Can you find a suggestion of the theme in specific passages of dialogue or description? Are certain symbols or repetitions of images important in revealing the author's intent in the story, what Edgar Allan Poe would call "the single effect"?

Now put the text aside and look over the notes in your journal. Can you see any pattern in them? You may find that you have been most impressed by the way the author developed characterizations, for example. Then you will have a possible topic for your paper. Reading the related commentary for a specific story may also generate ideas. Certainly if you have a choice, you should pick whatever appeals to you the most in the story and concentrate on it.

WRITING ABOUT SHORT FICTION

The Introduction and Part One of this anthology have presented two student papers based on a commentary by Raymond Carver and a short story by Eudora Welty, as well as a step-by-step discussion of the process of writing an essay about literature. Using the commentaries to ask questions about the text, brainstorming ideas for your paper, formulating a thesis sentence, organizing your thoughts into a coherent outline, and creating rough and finished drafts are important stages of the writing process discussed there.

The questions you ask about the elements of short fiction can also help you develop your ideas into an essay. Here, for example, is a student paper about the essential differences between a folktale and a short story, illustrated by an analysis of characterization in "Peter Klaus the Goatherd" and "Rip Van Winkle." In the opening paragraph, the student uses a commentary, referring to Washington Irving's letter to his friend Henry Brevoort in 1824 that describes his way of writing his stories (p. 687).

STUDENT ESSAY

Bringing Fiction to Life:
From Folktale to Short Story in "Peter
Klaus the Goatherd" and "Rip Van Winkle"

Short stories are carefully crafted works of fiction that captivate readers in ways that the simple transcription of an oral folktale cannot. What separates the short story from oral storytelling? Washington Irving, often credited with inventing the American short story, explained what he considered to be the essential aspect of a short story to his friend Henry Brevoort in 1824: "[. . .] I consider a story merely as a frame on which to stretch my materials. It is the play of thought, and sentiment, and language; the weaving in of characters [. . .]--these are among what I aim at [. . .]" (688).

Irving's intentions are illustrated in his story "Rip Van Winkle," a rendition of the German folktale "Peter Klaus the Goatherd." Irving uses the plot of the traditional tale as his "frame," but he retells the story in such a skillful way that he enchants his readers into considering it the first successful American short story. Irving's detailed characterization of Rip Van Winkle helps us understand the power of the short story.

In J. C. C. Nachtigal's transcription, Peter Klaus is briefly described in two words as "a goatherd," and then the events of the story proceed. Perhaps the original storyteller who narrated the tale in front of an audience of rapt German peasants went into more detail, but today's reader does not have an opportunity to step into Peter's shoes or to form an imaginative connection with him. The words in the transcribed folktale make the reader focus on the conclusion of the story and not think twice about how or why its events took place.

As Irving understood, the author of a short story can take an entirely different approach. This type of narrative is primarily meant to be read by an individual, not enacted by a storyteller. The conclusion of the plot becomes secondary to the "how" and "why" of the characters' actions. When an author reveals the thoughts of the protagonist and gives colorful details to describe his behavior, the reader can identify with the fictional character. The reader has the time to focus on every detail or to turn the pages back to reconsider something he might have missed earlier in the story. This permits a much more complex way of writing than a literal transcription of a folktale, and it explains why the short story has become so popular.

"Peter Klaus the Goatherd" tells a tale of a man who falls asleep one day while doing his job, wakes up twenty years later to find his circumstances greatly altered, and is eventually reconciled with his daughter and her family. The folk legend shows us how much we take life for granted; it suggests that we never know what we have until we lose it. The story of "Rip Van Winkle," on the other hand, does not have such a clear-cut theme.

Details about Rip's lackadaisical character as a man who "would rather starve on a penny than work for a pound--his avoidance of his demanding "termagant" wife, his pleasure in hunting squirrels in the wild Catskill mountains with his dog Wolf ("as much henpecked as his master"), and his sleeping away the momentous events of the Revolutionary War--add humor to his characterization and suggest several different themes. What the story says to one reader may differ from another reader's response to it. By getting imaginatively involved in Rip's situation, each reader can take an active role in enjoying the story. Perhaps this is the strongest appeal of the short story: It brings fiction to life by inventing a world and inviting you to make something of it.

Considering Contexts for Writing about Short Fiction

Your understanding of the elements of fiction can help you to interpret a story, but you can also appreciate that what you are reading is always much more than a self-contained, self-referential text printed on the page before you. When writers create an imaginary world in a story, they are also referring to the world outside the text, what students often call "the real world." Literature's link to the events of human history is as real as the paper it is printed on.

Literary critics point out that history penetrates literature in a variety of ways, and the closer a fictional work is to our own time, the more we take for granted its historical context. For example, the setting of Joyce Carol Oates's "Where Are You Going, Where Have You Been?" includes many details about teen culture in the early 1960s. When fifteen-year-old Connie hangs out with her friends at the drive-in restaurant across the street from the shopping mall, they would listen to "the music that made everything so good: the music was always in the background like music at a church service, it was something to depend upon."

If you research the cultural context of this short story, you will learn that Connie is listening to such jukebox hits as "Kisses Sweeter than Wine," "Chantilly Lace," "Do You Wanna Dance," and "Ten Commandments of Love." The escapist lyrics of romantic songs like these echo in her mind when a menacing visitor, Arnold Friend, turns up unexpectedly in her driveway and psychologically bullies her into submission. Oates dedicated the story to Bob Dylan, who redefined popular music in the mid-1960s when he wrote songs containing a tougher representation of American society — songs like "It Ain't Me, Babe," "The Times They Are A-Changin'," and "Blowin' in the Wind."

Authors themselves sometimes interact with their readers by elucidating their thematic intentions in individual stories, as William Faulkner does in commenting on "A Rose for Emily" and Flannery O'Connor does in her remarks about "A Good Man Is Hard to Find." These explicit statements of authorial intent are part of the historical background of these stories.

From the headnotes to the individual authors and the essays by writers and critics in the Commentaries section (p. 660), you will learn that occasionally storytellers create work based on their personal experience of a specific historic event, as Stephen Crane did in "The Open Boat," when he fictionalized what happened to him as a passenger after the shipwreck of the steamship *Commodore* off the Florida coast in January 1897.

For other writers, the inspiration for their fiction may be a personal story that they tell in order to communicate their suffering to others in an attempt to expose social injustice, as Charlotte Perkins Gilman did when she wrote "The Yellow Wallpaper." This story emerged from Gilman's own experience of a nervous breakdown, the result of a "rest cure" prescribed by an eminent physician in Philadelphia who, like others of the time, refused to recognize a woman's need for intellectual stimulation.

The headnotes and commentaries on the various authors and stories in this anthology contain a range of topics for you to explore in an essay or a research paper. Different assignments for writing about short fiction may also suggest specific critical approaches to literature. For example, you may be asked to analyze the symbolism in a story as a "reader response" critic, or you may want to express your ideas about a story as a gender critic or a cultural critic.

Part Five of this textbook contains a description of ten different critical approaches that you may find useful, with accompanying analyses of commentaries in the anthology that illustrate each perspective. This section is followed by a discussion of the most frequently assigned methods of developing essays about literature: explication, analysis, comparison and contrast, and the research paper, all with examples of student essays. Whatever your assignment, you will find that writing about literature will intensify your involvement with it, clarifying your responses and sharpening your critical thinking.

RELATED COMMENTARIES: *Wayne C. Booth, "A Rhetorical Reading of O'Connor's 'Everything That Rises Must Converge,'" page 797; Ralph Ellison, "The Influence of Folklore on 'Battle Royal,'" page 677; Sandra M. Gilbert and Susan Gubar, "A Feminist Reading of Gilman's 'The Yellow Wallpaper,'" page 681; Washington Irving, "Letter to Henry Brevoort, December 11, 1824," page 687; J. Hillis Miller, "Who Is He? Melville's 'Bartleby, the Scrivener,'" page 695.*

RELATED SECTION: *Part Five, Developing Your Ideas about Literature, page 2069.*

4

STORIES AND STORYTELLERS

CHINUA ACHEBE *(b. 1930) was born and grew up in Ogidi in eastern Nigeria, the son of devout Christian parents. He has recalled that in his childhood "the bounties of the Christian God were not to be taken lightly — education, paid jobs, and many other advantages that nobody in his right senses could underrate." As a member of the Ibo tribe, his first language was Igbo, which he remembers was "spoken with such eloquence by the old men of the village"; he learned English at the age of eight. After graduating from the University College of Ibadan, Achebe began a career in radio. In 1966 he resigned as director of external broadcasting in Nigeria and joined the Biafran Ministry of Information to help raise funds for his compatriots in the upheaval of the Biafran War. When Nigeria was put under military rule, he left the country to teach. While on the faculty of the University of Massachusetts, Amherst, he gave a controversial chancellor's lecture titled "Racism in Conrad's 'Heart of Darkness,'" which was later published in his collection of essays* Hopes and Impediments *(1988).*

Achebe says he began to think about becoming a writer after reading "some appalling novels about Africa" written by European authors. These made him decide, while still a student, "that the story we had to tell could not be told for us by anyone else no matter how gifted or well-intentioned." He won acclaim with his first novel, Things Fall Apart *(1958), a brilliant depiction of the decay of an African state under the impact of Europe. More recent books include the short story collection* Girls at War *(1973), the novel* Anthills of the Savannah *(1988), and the poetry and text of the picturebook* Another Africa *(1998). Achebe was also the founding editor of the distinguished African Writers Series of novels, stories, poetry, and plays published by Heinemann in London, Ibadan, and Nairobi.*

The story "Marriage Is a Private Affair" dramatizes Achebe's awareness of the effect of tribal divisions on the lives of ordinary people in contemporary Nigeria. He believes that Africans have always lived in what he calls "the crossroads of cultures."

> *We still do today, but when I was a boy one could see and sense the peculiar quality and atmosphere of it more clearly. I am not talking about all that rubbish we hear of the spiritual void and mental stresses that Africans are supposed to have, or the evil forces and irrational passions prowling through Africa's heart of darkness. We know the racist mystique behind a lot of that stuff. . . . What I do remember is a fascination for the ritual and the life on the other arm of the crossroads.*

CHINUA ACHEBE

Marriage Is a Private Affair

1952

"Have you written to your dad yet?" asked Nene one afternoon as she sat with Nnaemeka in her room at 16 Kasanga Street, Lagos.

"No. I've been thinking about it. I think it's better to tell him when I get home on leave!"

"But why? Your leave is such a long way off yet — six whole weeks. He should be let into our happiness now."

Nnaemeka was silent for a while, and then began very slowly as if he groped for his words: "I wish I were sure it would be happiness to him."

"Of course it must," replied Nene, a little surprised. "Why shouldn't it?"

"You have lived in Lagos all your life, and you know very little about people in remote parts of the country."

"That's what you always say. But I don't believe anybody will be so unlike other people that they will be unhappy when their sons are engaged to marry."

"Yes. They are most unhappy if the engagement is not arranged by them. In our case it's worse — you are not even an Ibo."

This was said so seriously and so bluntly that Nene could not find speech immediately. In the cosmopolitan atmosphere of the city it had always seemed to her something of a joke that a person's tribe could determine whom he married.

At last she said, "You don't really mean that he will object to your marrying me simply on that account? I had always thought you Ibos were kindly-disposed to other people."

"So we are. But when it comes to marriage, well, it's not quite so simple. And this," he added, "is not peculiar to the Ibos. If your father were alive and lived in the heart of Ibibio-land he would be exactly like my father."

"I don't know. But anyway, as your father is so fond of you, I'm sure he will forgive you soon enough. Come on then, be a good boy and send him a nice lovely letter . . ."

"It would not be wise to break the news to him by writing. A letter will bring it upon him with a shock. I'm quite sure about that."

"All right, honey, suit yourself. You know your father."

As Nnaemeka walked home that evening he turned over in his mind different ways of overcoming his father's opposition, especially now that he had gone and found a girl for him. He had thought of showing his letter to Nene but decided on second thought not to, at least for the moment. He read it again when he got home and couldn't help smiling to himself. He remembered Ugoye quite well, an Amazon of a girl who used to beat up all the boys, himself included, on the way to the stream, a complete dunce at school.

> I have found a girl who will suit you admirably — Ugoye Nweke, the eldest daughter of our neighbour, Jacob Nweke. She has a proper Christian upbringing. When she stopped schooling some years ago her father (a man of sound judgement) sent her to live in the house of a pastor where she has received all the training a wife could need. Her Sunday School teacher has told me that she reads her Bible very fluently. I hope we shall begin negotiations when you come home in December.

On the second evening of his return from Lagos Nnaemeka sat with his father under a cassia tree. This was the old man's retreat where he went to read his Bible when the parching December sun had set and a fresh, reviving wind blew on the leaves.

"Father," began Nnaemeka suddenly, "I have come to ask for forgiveness."

"Forgiveness? For what, my son?" he asked in amazement.

"It's about this marriage question."

"Which marriage question?"

"I can't — we must — I mean it is impossible for me to marry Nweke's daughter."

"Impossible? Why?" asked his father.

"I don't love her."

"Nobody said you did. Why should you?" he asked.

"Marriage today is different . . ."

"Look here, my son," interrupted his father, "nothing is different. What one looks for in a wife are a good character and a Christian background."

Nnaemeka saw there was no hope along the present line of argument.

"Moreover," he said, "I am engaged to marry another girl who has all of Ugoye's good qualities, and who . . ."

His father did not believe his ears. "What did you say?" he asked slowly and disconcertingly.

"She is a good Christian," his son went on, "and a teacher in a Girls' School in Lagos."

"Teacher, did you say? If you consider that a qualification for a good wife I should like to point out to you, Emeka, that no Christian woman should teach. St. Paul in his letter to the Corinthians says that women should keep silence." He rose slowly from his seat and paced forwards and backwards. This was his pet subject, and he condemned vehemently those church leaders who encouraged women to teach in their schools. After he had spent his emotion on a long homily he at last came back to his son's engagement, in a seemingly milder tone.

"Whose daughter is she, anyway?"

"She is Nene Atang."

"What!" All the mildness was gone again. "Did you say Neneataga, what does that mean?"

"Nene Atang from Calabar. She is the only girl I can marry." This was a very rash reply and Nnaemeka expected the storm to burst. But it did not. His father merely walked away into his room. This was most unexpected and perplexed Nnaemeka. His father's silence was infinitely more menacing than a flood of threatening speech. That night the old man did not eat.

When he sent for Nnaemeka a day later he applied all possible ways of dissuasion. But the young man's heart was hardened, and his father eventually gave him up as lost.

"I owe it to you, my son, as a duty to show you what is right and what is wrong. Whoever put this idea into your head might as well have cut your throat. It is Satan's work." He waved his son away.

"You will change your mind, Father, when you know Nene."

"I shall never see her," was the reply. From that night the father scarcely spoke to his son. He did not, however, cease hoping that he would realize how serious was the danger he was heading for. Day and night he put him in his prayers.

Nnaemeka, for his own part, was very deeply affected by his father's grief. But he kept hoping that it would pass away. If it had occurred to him that never in the history of his people had a man married a woman who spoke a different tongue, he might have been less optimistic. "It has never been heard," was the verdict of an old man speaking a few weeks later. In that short sentence he spoke for all of his people. This man had come with others to commiserate with Okeke when news went round about his son's behaviour. By that time the son had gone back to Lagos.

"It has never been heard," said the old man again with a sad shake of his head.

"What did Our Lord say?" asked another gentleman. "Sons shall rise against their Fathers; it is there in the Holy Book."

"It is the beginning of the end," said another.

The discussion thus tending to become theological, Madubogwu, a highly practical man, brought it down once more to the ordinary level.

"Have you thought of consulting a native doctor about your son?" he asked Nnaemeka's father.

"He isn't sick," was the reply.

"What is he then? The boy's mind is diseased and only a good herbalist can bang him back to his right senses. The medicine he requires is *Amalile,* the same that women apply with success to recapture their husbands' straying affection."

"Madubogwu is right," said another gentleman. "This thing calls for medicine."

"I shall not call in a native doctor." Nnaemeka's father was known to be obstinately ahead of his more superstitious neighbours in these matters. "I will not be another Mrs. Ochuba. If my son wants to kill himself let him do it with his own hands. It is not for me to help him."

"But it was her fault," said Madubogwu. "She ought to have gone to an honest herbalist. She was a clever woman, nevertheless."

"She was a wicked murderess," said Jonathan who rarely argued with his neighbours because, he often said, they were incapable of reasoning. "The medicine was prepared for her husband, it was his name they called in its preparation and I am sure it would have been perfectly beneficial to him. It was wicked to put it into the herbalist's food, and say you were only trying it out."

Six months later, Nnaemeka was showing his young wife a short letter from his father:

> It amazes me that you could be so unfeeling as to send me your wedding picture. I would have sent it back. But on further thought I decided just to cut off your wife and send it back to you because I have nothing to do with her. How I wish that I had nothing to do with you either.

When Nene read through this letter and looked at the mutilated picture her eyes filled with tears, and she began to sob.

"Don't cry, my darling," said her husband. "He is essentially good-natured and will one day look more kindly on our marriage." But years passed and that one day did not come.

For eight years, Okeke would have nothing to do with his son, Nnaemeka. Only three times (when Nnaemeka asked to come home and spend his leave) did he write to him.

"I can't have you in my house," he replied on one occasion. "It can be of no interest to me where or how you spend your leave — or your life, for that matter."

The prejudice against Nnaemeka's marriage was not confined to his little village. In Lagos, especially among his people who worked there, it showed itself in a different way. Their women, when they met at their village meeting, were not hostile to Nene. Rather, they paid her such excessive deference as to make her feel she was not one of them. But as time went on, Nene gradually broke through some of this prejudice and even began to make friends among them. Slowly and grudgingly they began to admit that she kept her home much better than most of them.

The story eventually got to the little village in the heart of the Ibo country that Nnaemeka and his young wife were a most happy couple. But his father was one of the few people in the village who knew nothing about this. He always displayed so much temper whenever his son's name was mentioned that everyone avoided it in his presence. By a tremendous effort of will he had succeeded in pushing his son to the back of his mind. The strain had nearly killed him but he had persevered, and won.

Then one day he received a letter from Nene, and in spite of himself he began to glance through it perfunctorily until all of a sudden the expression on his face changed and he began to read more carefully.

> . . . Our two sons, from the day they learnt that they have a grandfather, have insisted on being taken to him. I find it impossible to tell them that you will not see them. I implore you to allow Nnaemeka to bring them home for a short time during his leave next month. I shall remain here in Lagos . . .

The old man at once felt the resolution he had built up over so many years falling in. He was telling himself that he must not give in. He tried to steel his heart against all emotional appeals. It was a reenactment of that other struggle. He leaned against a window and looked out. The sky was overcast with heavy black clouds and a high wind began to blow filling the air with dust and dry leaves. It was one of those rare occasions when even Nature takes a hand in a human fight. Very soon it began to rain, the first rain in the year. It came down in large sharp drops and was accompanied by the lightning and thunder which mark a change of season. Okeke was trying hard not to think of his two grandsons. But he knew he was now fighting a losing battle. He tried to hum a favourite hymn but the pattering of large rain drops on the roof broke up the tune. His mind immediately returned to the children. How could he shut his door against them? By a curious mental process he imagined them standing, sad and forsaken, under the harsh angry weather — shut out from his house.

That night he hardly slept, from remorse — and a vague fear that he might die without making it up to them.

ꕥ

SHERMAN ALEXIE *(b. 1966) was born in Spokane, Washington. A registered member of the Spokane tribe through his mother, he attended grammar school on the Spokane reservation in Wellpinit, Washington. At Washington State University he took a creative writing course with Alex Kuo and began to publish in magazines such as* The Beloit Poetry Journal, The Journal of Ethnic Studies, New York Quarterly, Ploughshares, *and* Zyzzyva. *In 1991 he was awarded a poetry fellowship from the Washington State Arts Commission; the following year he received a poetry fellowship from the National Endowment for the Arts.*

In 1992 Alexie published his first two books, I Would Steal Horses *and* The Business of Fancydancing: Stories and Poems. *Several more titles followed in rapid order, including* The Lone Ranger and Tonto Fistfight in Heaven *(1993), which received a PEN/Hemingway Award for best first book of fiction. Alexie also won the American Book Award for his novel* Reservation Blues *(1995), in which he imagined what would happen if the legendary bluesman Robert Johnson were resurrected on the Spokane Indian Reservation. In 1996 Alexie published* Indian Killer, *a novel, and* Summer of Black Widows, *a collection of poetry. A recent work is the screenplay* Smoke Signals *(1998), based on one of his short stories.*

Alexie has stated, "I am a Spokane/Coeur d'Alene Indian from Wellpinit, Washington, where I live on the Spokane Indian Reservation. Everything I do now, writing and otherwise, has its origin in that." His short fiction, like "The Lone Ranger and Tonto Fistfight in Heaven," reflects his use of the icons of popular culture — radio and television programs, 7-Eleven stores, the neon promise of advertising — to facilitate a rapid crossover between storyteller and reader. As the critic Susan B. Brill has noticed, "Little ever changes in the lives of Alexie's characters. Commodity food, alcoholism, and desperation are constants in the stories."

SHERMAN ALEXIE

The Lone Ranger and Tonto Fistfight in Heaven 1993

Too hot to sleep so I walked down to the Third Avenue 7-11 for a Creamsicle and the company of a graveyard-shift cashier. I know that game. I worked graveyard for a Seattle 7-11 and got robbed once too often. The last time the bastard locked me in the cooler. He even took my money and basketball shoes.

The graveyard-shift worker in the Third Avenue 7-11 looked like they all do. Acne scars and a bad haircut, work pants that showed off his white socks, and those cheap black shoes that have no support. My arches still ache from my year at the Seattle 7-11.

"Hello," he asked when I walked into his store. "How you doing?"

I gave him a half-wave as I headed back to the freezer. He looked me over so he could describe me to the police later. I knew the look. One of my old girlfriends said I started to look at her that way, too. She left me not long after that. No, I left her and don't blame her for anything. That's how it happened. When one person starts to look at another like a criminal, then the love is over. It's logical.

"I don't trust you," she said to me. "You get too angry."

She was white and I lived with her in Seattle. Some nights we fought so bad that I would just get in my car and drive all night, only stop to fill up on gas. In fact, I worked the graveyard shift to spend as much time away from her as possible. But I learned all about Seattle that way, driving its back ways and dirty alleys.

Sometimes, though, I would forget where I was and get lost. I'd drive for hours, searching for something familiar. Seems like I'd spent my whole life that way, looking for anything I recognized. Once, I ended up in a nice residential neighborhood and somebody must have been worried because the police showed up and pulled me over.

"What are you doing out here?" the police officer asked me as he looked over my license and registration.

"I'm lost."

"Well, where are you supposed to be?" he asked me, and I knew there were plenty of places I wanted to be, but none where I was supposed to be.

"I got in a fight with my girlfriend," I said. "I was just driving around, blowing off steam, you know?"

"Well, you should be more careful where you drive," the officer said. "You're making people nervous. You don't fit the profile of the neighborhood."

I wanted to tell him that I didn't really fit the profile of the country but I knew it would just get me into trouble.

"Can I help you?" the 7-11 clerk asked me loudly, searching for some response that would reassure him that I wasn't an armed robber. He knew this dark skin and long, black hair of mine was dangerous. I had potential.

"Just getting a Creamsicle," I said after a long interval. It was a sick twist to pull on the guy, but it was late and I was bored. I grabbed my Creamsicle and walked back to the counter slowly, scanned the aisles for effect. I wanted to whistle low and menacingly but I never learned to whistle.

"Pretty hot out tonight?" he asked, that old rhetorical weather bullshit question designed to put us both at ease.

"Hot enough to make you go crazy," I said and smiled. He swallowed hard like a white man does in those situations. I looked him over. Same old green, red, and white 7-11 jacket and thick glasses. But he wasn't ugly, just misplaced and marked by loneliness. If he wasn't working there that night, he'd be at home alone, flipping through channels and wishing he could afford HBO or Showtime.

"Will this be all?" he asked me, in that company effort to make me do some impulse shopping. Like adding a clause onto a treaty. *We'll take Washington and Oregon, and you get six pine trees and a brand-new Chrysler Cordoba.* I knew how to make and break promises.

"No," I said and paused. "Give me a Cherry Slushie, too."

"What size?" he asked, relieved.

"Large," I said, and he turned his back to me to make the drink. He realized his mistake but it was too late. He stiffened, ready for the gunshot or the blow behind the ear. When it didn't come, he turned back to me.

"I'm sorry," he said. "What size did you say?"

"Small," I said and changed the story.

"But I thought you said large."

"If you knew I wanted a large, then why did you ask me again?" I asked him and laughed. He looked at me, couldn't decide if I was giving him serious shit or just goofing. There was something about him I liked, even if it was three in the morning and he was white.

"Hey," I said. "Forget the Slushie. What I want to know is if you know all the words to the theme from 'The Brady Bunch'?"

He looked at me, confused at first, then laughed.

"Shit," he said. "I was hoping you weren't crazy. You were scaring me."

"Well, I'm going to get crazy if you don't know the words."

He laughed loudly then, told me to take the Creamsicle for free. He was the graveyard-shift manager and those little demonstrations of power tickled him. All seventy-five cents of it. I knew how much everything cost.

"Thanks," I said to him and walked out the door. I took my time walking home, let the heat of the night melt the Creamsicle all over my hand. At three in the morning I could act just as young as I wanted to act. There was no one around to ask me to grow up.

In Seattle, I broke lamps. She and I would argue and I'd break a lamp, just pick it up and throw it down. At first she'd buy replacement lamps, expensive and beautiful. But after a while she'd buy lamps from Goodwill or garage sales. Then she just gave up the idea entirely and we'd argue in the dark.

"You're just like your brother," she'd yell. "Drunk all the time and stupid."

"My brother don't drink that much."

She and I never tried to hurt each other physically. I did love her, after all, and she loved me. But those arguments were just as damaging as a fist. Words can be like that, you know? Whenever I get into arguments now, I remember her and I also remember Muhammad Ali. He knew the power of his fists but, more importantly, he knew the power of his words, too. Even though he only had an IQ of 80 or so, Ali was a genius. And she was a genius, too. She knew exactly what to say to cause me the most pain.

But don't get me wrong. I walked through that relationship with an executioner's hood. Or more appropriately, with war paint and sharp arrows. She was a kindergarten teacher and I continually insulted her for that.

"Hey, schoolmarm," I asked. "Did your kids teach you anything new today?"

And I always had crazy dreams. I always have had them, but it seemed they became nightmares more often in Seattle.

In one dream, she was a missionary's wife and I was a minor war chief. We fell in love and tried to keep it secret. But the missionary caught us fucking in the barn and shot me. As I lay dying, my tribe learned of the shooting and attacked the whites all across the reservation. I died and my soul drifted above the reservation.

Disembodied, I could see everything that was happening. Whites killing Indians and Indians killing whites. At first it was small, just my tribe and the few whites who lived there. But my dream grew, intensified. Other tribes arrived on horseback to continue the slaughter of whites, and the United States Cavalry rode into battle.

The most vivid image of that dream stays with me. Three mounted soldiers played polo with a dead Indian woman's head. When I first dreamed it, I thought it was just a product of my anger and imagination. But since then, I've read similar accounts of that kind of evil in the old West. Even more terrifying, though, is the fact that those kinds of brutal things are happening today in places like El Salvador.

All I know for sure, though, is that I woke from that dream in terror, packed up all my possessions, and left Seattle in the middle of the night.

"I love you," she said as I left her. "And don't ever come back."

I drove through the night, over the Cascades, down into the plains of central Washington, and back home to the Spokane Indian Reservation.

■

When I finished the Creamsicle that the 7-11 clerk gave me, I held the wooden stick up into the air and shouted out very loudly. A couple lights flashed on in windows and a police car cruised by me a few minutes later. I waved to the men in blue and they waved back accidentally. When I got home it was still too hot to sleep so I picked up a week-old newspaper from the floor and read.

There was another civil war, another terrorist bomb exploded, and one more plane crashed and all aboard were presumed dead. The crime rate was rising in every city with populations larger than 100,000, and a farmer in Iowa shot his banker after foreclosure on his 1,000 acres.

A kid from Spokane won the local spelling bee by spelling the word *rhinoceros*.

When I got back to the reservation, my family wasn't surprised to see me. They'd been expecting me back since the day I left for Seattle. There's an old Indian poet who said that Indians can reside in the city, but they can never live there. That's as close to truth as any of us can get.

Mostly I watched television. For weeks I flipped through channels, searched for answers in the game shows and soap operas. My mother would circle the want ads in red and hand the paper to me.

"What are you going to do with the rest of your life?" she asked.

"Don't know," I said, and normally, for almost any other Indian in the country, that would have been a perfectly fine answer. But I was special, a former college student, a smart kid. I was one of those Indians who was supposed to make it, to rise above the rest of the reservation like a fucking eagle or something. I was the new kind of warrior.

For a few months I didn't even look at the want ads my mother circled, just left the newspaper where she had set it down. After a while, though, I got tired of television and started to play basketball again. I'd been a good player in high school, nearly great, and almost played at the college I attended for a couple years. But I'd been too out of shape from drinking and sadness to ever be good again. Still, I liked the way the ball felt in my hands and the way my feet felt inside my shoes.

At first I just shot baskets by myself. It was selfish, and I also wanted to learn the game again before I played against anybody else. Since I had been good before and embarrassed fellow tribal members, I knew they would want to take revenge on me. Forget about the cowboys versus Indians business. The most intense competition on any reservation is Indians versus Indians.

But on the night I was ready to play for real, there was this white guy at the gym, playing with all the Indians.

"Who is that?" I asked Jimmy Seyler.

"He's the new BIA° chief's kid."

BIA: Bureau of Indian Affairs.

"Can he play?"

"Oh, yeah."

And he could play. He played Indian ball, fast and loose, better than all the Indians there.

"How long's he been playing here?" I asked.

"Long enough."

I stretched my muscles, and everybody watched me. All these Indians watched one of their old and dusty heroes. Even though I had played most of my ball at the white high school I went to, I was still all Indian, you know? I was Indian when it counted, and this BIA kid needed to be beaten by an Indian, any Indian.

I jumped into the game and played well for a little while. It felt good. I hit a few shots, grabbed a rebound or two, played enough defense to keep the other team honest. Then that white kid took over the game. He was too good. Later, he'd play college ball back East and would nearly make the Knicks team a couple years on. But we didn't know any of that would happen. We just knew he was better that day and every other day.

The next morning I woke up tired and hungry, so I grabbed the want ads, found a job I wanted, and drove to Spokane to get it. I've been working at the high school exchange program ever since, typing and answering phones. Sometimes I wonder if the people on the other end of the line know that I'm Indian and if their voices would change if they did know.

One day I picked up the phone and it was her, calling from Seattle.

"I got your number from your mom," she said. "I'm glad you're working."

"Yeah, nothing like a regular paycheck."

"Are you drinking?"

"No, I've been on the wagon for almost a year."

"Good. "

The connection was good. I could hear her breathing in the spaces between our words. How do you talk to the real person whose ghost has haunted you? How do you tell the difference between the two?

"Listen," I said. "I'm sorry for everything."

"Me, too."

"What's going to happen to us?" I asked her and wished I had the answer for myself.

"I don't know," she said. "I want to change the world."

These days, living alone in Spokane, I wish I lived closer to the river, to the falls where ghosts of salmon jump. I wish I could sleep. I put down my paper or book and turn off all the lights, lie quietly in the dark. It may take hours, even years, for me to sleep again. There's nothing surprising or disappointing in that.

I know how all my dreams end anyway.

ISABEL ALLENDE *(b. 1942) was born in Peru, the daughter of a Chilean diplomat. After her parents' divorce, she spent her childhood in her maternal grandparents' household; she was especially close to her grandmother, a believer in the occult. When Allende's mother remarried another diplomat, Isabel left Chile to live during her adolescence in Bolivia, the Middle East, and Europe. She began her career by working as a journalist in Chile, writing articles for a radical women's magazine and eventually creating her own television program. In 1970 her father's first cousin Dr. Salvador Allende Gossens became the first Marxist-Leninist to be freely elected as president of Chile. Three years later he was assassinated by Augusto Pinochet Ugarte, who instituted a repressive military dictatorship backed by the United States until 1990. Allende and her family fled to Venezuela; she felt that "my life had been cut into pieces, and that I had to start over again."*

In 1981, after the death of her grandparents, Allende began to write her first work of long fiction. This was the internationally acclaimed novel The House of the Spirits *(1982), a chronicle of several generations of an imaginary family in Chile based on her memories of her own family. She has said that "in Latin America, we value dreams, passions, obsessions, emotions, and all that which is very important to our lives has a place in literature — our sense of family, our sense of religion, of superstition too. . . . Fantastic things happen every day in Latin America — it's not that we make them up."*

Allende followed the success of her first book with two other novels — Of Love and Shadows *(1986) and* Eva Luna *(1988) — and a volume of short stories,* The Stories of Eva Luna *(1991). Her recent novel,* Daughter of Fortune, *was published in 1999. "An Act of Vengeance" was included in* Short Stories by Latin American Women: The Magic and the Real *(1990).*

ISABEL ALLENDE

An Act of Vengeance

1990

TRANSLATED BY E. D. CARTER JR.

On that glorious noonday when Dulce Rosa Orellano was crowned with the jasmines of Carnival Queen, the mothers of the other candidates murmured that it was unfair for her to win just because she was the only daughter of the most powerful man in the entire province, Senator Anselmo Orellano. They admitted that the girl was charming and that she played the piano and danced like no other, but there were other competitors for the prize who were far more beautiful. They saw her standing on the platform in her organdy dress and with her crown of flowers, and as she waved at the crowd they cursed her through their clenched teeth. For that reason, some of them were overjoyed some months later when misfortune entered the Orellanos' house sowing such a crop of death that thirty years were required to reap it.

On the night of the queen's election, a dance was held in the Santa Teresa Town Hall, and young men from the remotest villages came to meet Dulce Rosa. She was so happy and danced with such grace that many failed to perceive that she was not the most beautiful, and when they returned to where they had come from they all declared that they had never before seen a face like hers. Thus she acquired an unmerited reputation for beauty and later testimony was never able to prove to the contrary. The exaggerated descriptions of her translucent skin and her diaphanous eyes were passed from mouth to mouth, and each individual added something to them from his own imagination. Poets from distant cities composed sonnets to a hypothetical maiden whose name was Dulce Rosa.

Rumors of the beauty who was flourishing in Senator Orellano's house also reached the ears of Tadeo Céspedes, who never dreamed he would be able to meet her, since during all his twenty-five years he had neither had time to learn poetry nor to look at women. He was concerned only with the Civil War. Ever since he had begun to shave he had had a weapon in his hands, and he had lived for a long time amidst the sound of exploding gunpowder. He had forgotten his mother's kisses and even the songs of mass. He did not always have reason to go into battle, because during several periods of truce there were no adversaries within reach of his guerrilla band. But even in times of forced peace he lived like a corsair. He was a man habituated to violence. He crossed the country in every direction, fighting visible enemies when he found them, and battling shadows when he was forced to invent them. He would have continued in the same way if his party had not won the presidential election. Overnight he went from a clandestine existence to wielding power, and all pretext for continuing the rebellion had ended for him.

Tadeo Céspedes's final mission was the punitive expedition against Santa Teresa. With a hundred and twenty men he entered the town under cover of darkness to teach everyone a lesson and eliminate the leaders of the opposition. They shot out the windows in the public buildings, destroyed the church door, and rode their horses right up to the main altar, crushing Father Clemente when he tried to block their way. They burned the trees that the Ladies' Club had planted in the square; amidst all the clamor of battle, they continued at a gallop toward Senator Orellano's house which rose up proudly on top of the hill.

After having locked his daughter in the room at the farthest corner of the patio and turned the dogs loose, the Senator waited for Tadeo Céspedes at the head of a dozen loyal servants. At that moment he had regretted, as he had so many other times in his life, not having had male descendants who could help him to take up arms and defend the honor of his house. He felt very old, but he did not have time to think about it, because he had spied on the hillside the terrible flash of a hundred and twenty torches that terrorized the night as they advanced. He distributed the last of the ammunition in silence. Everything had been said, and each of them knew that before morning he would be required to die like a man at his battle station.

"The last man alive will take the key to the room where my daughter is hidden and carry out his duty," said the Senator as he heard the first shots.

All the men had been present when Dulce Rosa was born and had held her on their knees when she was barely able to walk; they had told her ghost stories on winter afternoons; they had listened to her play the piano and they had applauded in tears on the day of her coronation as Carnival Queen. Her father could die in peace, because the girl would never fall alive into the hands of Tadeo Céspedes. The one thing that never crossed Senator Orellano's mind was that, in spite of his recklessness in battle, he would be the last to die. He saw his friends fall one by one and finally realized that it was useless to continue resisting. He had a bullet in his stomach and his vision was blurred. He was barely able to distinguish the shadows that were climbing the high walls surrounding his property, but he still had the presence of mind to drag himself to the third patio. The dogs recognized his scent despite the sweat, blood, and sadness that covered him and moved aside to let him pass. He inserted the key in the lock and through the mist that covered his eyes saw Dulce Rosa waiting for him. The girl was wearing the same organdy dress that she had worn for the Carnival and had adorned her hair with the flowers from the crown.

"It's time, my child," he said, cocking his revolver as a puddle of blood spread about his feet.

"Don't kill me, father," she replied in a firm voice. "Let me live so that I can avenge us both."

Senator Anselmo Orellano looked into his daughter's fifteen-year-old face and imagined what Tadeo Céspedes would do to her, but he saw great strength in Dulce Rosa's transparent eyes, and he knew that she would survive to punish his executioner. The girl sat down on the bed and he took his place at her side, pointing his revolver at the door.

When the uproar from the dying dogs had faded, the bar across the door was shattered, the bolt flew off, and the first group of men burst into the room. The Senator managed to fire six shots before losing consciousness. Tadeo Céspedes thought he was dreaming when he saw an angel crowned in jasmines holding a dying old man in her arms. But he did not possess sufficient pity to look for a second time, since he was drunk with violence and enervated by hours of combat.

"The woman is mine," he said, before any of his men could put his hands on her.

A leaden Friday dawned, tinged with the glare from the fire. The silence was thick upon the hill. The final moans had faded when Dulce Rosa was able to stand and walk to the fountain in the garden. The previous day it had been surrounded by magnolias, and now it was nothing but a tumultuous pool amidst the debris. After having removed the few strips of organdy that were all that remained of her dress, she stood nude before what had been the fountain. She submerged herself in the cold water. The sun rose behind the birches, and the girl watched the water turn red as she washed away the blood that flowed from between her legs along with that of her father which had dried in her hair. Once she was clean, calm, and without tears, she returned to the ruined house to look for something to cover herself. Picking up a linen sheet, she went outside to bring back the Senator's remains. They had tied him behind a horse and dragged him up and down the hillside until little remained but a pitiable mound of rags. But guided by love, the daughter was able to recognize him without hesitation. She wrapped him in the sheet and sat down by his side to watch the dawn grow into day. That is how her neighbors from Santa Teresa found her when they finally dared to climb up to the Orellano villa. They helped Dulce Rosa to bury her dead and to extinguish the vestiges of the fire. They begged her to go and live with her godmother in another town where no one knew her story, but she refused. Then they formed crews to rebuild the house and gave her six ferocious dogs to protect her.

From the moment they had carried her father away, still alive, and Tadeo Céspedes had closed the door behind them and unbuckled his leather belt, Dulce Rosa lived for revenge. In the thirty years that followed, that thought kept her awake at night and filled her days, but it did not completely obliterate her laughter nor dry up her good disposition. Her reputation for beauty increased as troubadors went everywhere proclaiming her imaginary enchantments until she became a living legend. She arose every morning at four o'clock to oversee the farm and household chores, roam her property on horseback, buy and sell, haggling like a Syrian, breed livestock, and cultivate the magnolias and jasmines in her garden. In the afternoon she would remove her trousers, her boots, and her weapons, and put on the lovely dresses which had come from the capital in aromatic trunks. At nightfall visitors would begin to arrive and would find her playing the piano while the servants prepared trays of sweets and glasses of orgeat. Many people asked themselves how it was possible that the girl had not ended up in a straitjacket in a sanitarium or as a novitiate with the Carmelite nuns. Nevertheless, since there were frequent parties at the Orellano villa, with the passage of time people stopped talking about the tragedy and erased the murdered Senator from their memories. Some gentlemen who possessed both fame and fortune managed to overcome the repugnance they felt because of the rape and, attracted by Dulce Rosa's beauty and sensitivity, proposed marriage. She rejected them all, for her only mission on Earth was vengeance.

Tadeo Céspedes was also unable to get that night out of his mind. The hangover from all the killing and the euphoria from the rape left him as he was on his way to the capital a few hours later to report the results of his punitive expedition. It was then that he remembered the child in a party dress and crowned with jasmines, who endured him in silence in that dark room where the air was impregnated with the odor of gunpowder. He saw her once again in the final scene, lying on the floor, barely covered by her reddened rags, sunk in the compassionate embrace of unconsciousness, and he continued to see her that way every night of his life just as he fell asleep. Peace, the exercise of government, and the use of power turned him into a settled, hard-working man. With the passage of time, memories of the Civil War faded away and the people began to call him Don Tadeo. He bought a ranch on the other side of the mountains, devoted himself to administering justice, and ended up as mayor. If it had not been for Dulce Rosa Orellano's tireless phantom, perhaps he might have attained a certain degree of happiness. But in all the women who crossed his path, he saw the face of the Carnival Queen. And even worse, the songs by popular poets, often containing verses that mentioned her name, would not permit him to expel her from his heart. The young woman's image grew within him, occupying him completely, until one day he could stand it no longer. He was at the head of a long banquet table celebrating his fifty-fifth birthday, surrounded by friends and colleagues, when he thought he saw in the tablecloth a child lying naked among jasmine blossoms, and understood that the nightmare would not leave him in peace even after his death. He struck the table with his fist, causing the dishes to shake, and asked for his hat and cane.

"Where are you going, Don Tadeo?" asked the Prefect.

"To repair some ancient damage," he said as he left without taking leave of anyone.

It was not necessary for him to search for her, because he always knew that she would be found in the same house where her misfortune had occurred, and it was in that direction that he pointed his car. By then good highways had been built and distances seemed shorter. The scenery had changed during the decades that had passed, but as he rounded the last curve by the hill, the villa appeared just as he remembered it before his troops had taken it in the attack. There were the solid walls made of river rock that he had destroyed with dynamite charges, there the ancient wooden coffers he had set afire, there the trees where he had hung the bodies of the Senator's men, there the patio where he had slaughtered the dogs. He stopped his vehicle a hundred meters from the door and dared not continue because he felt his heart exploding inside his chest. He was going to turn around and go back to where he came from, when a figure surrounded by the halo of her skirt appeared in the yard. He closed his eyes, hoping with all his might that she would not recognize him. In the soft twilight, he perceived that Dulce Rosa Orellano was advancing toward him, floating along the garden paths. He noted her hair, her candid face, the harmony of her gestures, the swirl of her dress, and he thought he was suspended in a dream that had lasted for thirty years.

"You've finally come, Tadeo Céspedes," she said as she looked at him, not allowing herself to be deceived by his mayor's suit or his gentlemanly gray hair, because he still had the same pirate's hands.

"You've pursued me endlessly. In my whole life I've never been able to love anyone but you," he murmured, his voice choked with shame.

Dulce Rosa gave a satisfied sigh. At last her time had come. But she looked into his eyes and failed to discover a single trace of the executioner, only fresh tears. She searched her heart for the hatred she had cultivated throughout those thirty years, but she was incapable of finding it. She evoked the instant that she had asked her father to make his sacrifice and let her live so that she could carry out her duty; she relived the embrace of the man whom she had cursed so many times, and remembered the early morning when she had wrapped some tragic remains in a linen sheet. She went over her perfect plan of vengeance, but did not feel the expected happiness; instead she felt its opposite, a profound melancholy. Tadeo Céspedes delicately took her hand and kissed the palm, wetting it with his tears. Then she understood with horror that by thinking about him every moment, and savoring his punishment in advance, her feelings had become reversed and she had fallen in love with him.

During the following days both of them opened the floodgates of repressed love and, for the first time since their cruel fate was decided, opened themselves to receive the other's proximity. They strolled through the gardens talking about themselves and omitting nothing, even that fatal night which had twisted the direction of their lives. As evening fell, she played the piano and he smoked, listening to her until he felt his bones go soft and the happiness envelop him like a blanket and obliterate the nightmares of the past. After dinner he went to Santa Teresa where no one still remembered the ancient tale of horror. He took a room in the best hotel and from there organized his wedding. He wanted a party with fanfare, extravagance, and noise, one in which the entire town would participate. He discovered love at an age when other men have already lost their illusions, and that returned to him his youthful vigor. He wanted to surround Dulce Rosa with affection and beauty, to give her everything that money could buy, to see if he could compensate in his later years for the evil he had done as a young man. At times panic possessed him. He searched her face for the smallest sign of rancor, but he saw only the light of shared love and that gave him back his confidence. Thus a month of happiness passed.

Two days before their wedding, when they were already setting up the tables for the party in the garden, slaughtering the birds and pigs for the feast, and cutting the flowers to decorate the house, Dulce Rosa Orellano tried on her wedding dress. She saw herself reflected in the mirror, just as she had on the day of her coronation as Carnival Queen, and realized that she could no longer continue to deceive her own heart. She knew that she could not carry out the vengeance she had planned because she loved the killer, but she was also unable to quiet the Senator's ghost. She dismissed the seamstress, took the scissors, and went to the room on the third patio which had remained unoccupied during all that time.

Tadeo Céspedes searched for her everywhere, calling out to her desperately. The barking of the dogs led him to the other side of the house. With the help of the gardeners he broke down the barred door and entered the room where thirty years before he had seen an angel crowned with jasmines. He found Dulce Rosa Orellano just as he had seen her in his dreams every night of his existence, lying motionless in the same bloody organdy dress. He realized that in order to pay for his guilt he would have to live until he was ninety with the memory of the only woman his soul could ever love.

ꕤ

SHERWOOD ANDERSON *(1876–1941) was born to a jack-of-all-trades father in Camden, Ohio. He did not publish his first book until he was over forty, after working for many years as a newsboy, farm laborer, stable boy, factory hand, and advertising copywriter. Dissatisfied with the commercial spirit of the advertising business, Anderson made friends with writers in Chicago and began to publish his own poetry and fiction. The poet Carl Sandburg encouraged him, but Anderson's literary style was most influenced by* Three Lives *(1909) and* Tender Buttons *(1914)* *experimental books by the expatriate American writer Gertrude Stein, which he felt revolutionized the language of narrative.*

In 1916 Anderson published his first novel, Windy McPherson's Son. *He followed it with another novel and a volume of poetry, but he did not receive wide recognition until 1919, with the book* Winesburg, Ohio. *This collection of related stories, including "Hands," about life in a small town explores the devastating consequences of the repressive conventions of a provincial society. It was followed by other important collections of stories:* The Triumph of the Egg *(1921),* Horses and Men *(1923), and* Death in the Woods and Other Stories *(1933). In his time Anderson was a strong influence on Ernest Hemingway, William Faulkner, Richard Wright, and John Steinbeck. The editor Martha Foley wrote in 1941 that*

> *Sherwood Anderson set out on new paths at a time when the American short story seemed doomed to a formula-ridden, conventionalized, mechanized, and commercialized concept. When* Winesburg, Ohio *appeared in 1919 it was intensely influential on writers who either had lost heart or had not yet found their way. His vision was his own; his characters were people into whose hearts and minds he seemed intuitively to peer; his prose was simple, deceptively simple, sensuous, rich, and evocative.*

As literary critics have observed, the characteristic tone of Anderson's short fiction is melancholy reminiscence. In an understated fashion, he wove carefully selected realistic details into such narratives as "Hands," which moves by apparently formless associations of thought and feeling but is actually a controlled progression of fully dramatized situations. Anderson's importance in our literature is suggested by Richard Wright's acknowledgment that Anderson's stories made him see that through the powers of fiction, "America could be shaped nearer to the hearts of those who lived in it."

RELATED COMMENTARY: *Sherwood Anderson, "Form, Not Plot, in the Short Story," page 660.*

SHERWOOD ANDERSON

Hands

1919

Upon the half decayed veranda of a small frame house that stood near the edge of a ravine near the town of Winesburg, Ohio, a fat little old man walked nervously up and down. Across a long field that had been seeded for clover but that had produced only a dense crop of yellow mustard weeds, he could see the public highway along which went a wagon filled with berry pickers returning from the fields. The berry pickers, youths and maidens, laughed and shouted boisterously. A boy clad in a blue shirt leaped from the wagon and attempted to drag after him one of the maidens who screamed and protested shrilly. The feet of the boy in the road kicked up a cloud of dust that floated across the face of the departing sun. Over the long field came a thin girlish voice. "Oh, you Wing Biddlebaum, comb your hair, it's falling into your eyes," commanded the voice to the man, who was bald and whose nervous little hands fiddled about the bare white forehead as though arranging a mass of tangled locks.

Wing Biddlebaum, forever frightened and beset by a ghostly band of doubts, did not think of himself as in any way a part of the life of the town where he had lived for twenty years. Among all the people of Winesburg but one had come close to him. With George Willard, son of Tom Willard, the proprietor of the new Willard House, he had formed something like a friendship. George Willard was the reporter on the *Winesburg Eagle* and sometimes in the evenings he walked out along the highway to Wing Biddlebaum's house. Now as the old man walked up and down on the veranda, his hands moving nervously about, he was hoping that George Willard would come and spend the evening with him. After the wagon containing the berry pickers had passed, he went across the field through the tall mustard weeds and climbing a rail fence peered anxiously along the road to the town. For a moment he stood thus, rubbing his hands together and looking up and down the road, and then, fear overcoming him, ran back to walk again upon the porch of his own house.

In the presence of George Willard, Wing Biddlebaum, who for twenty years had been the town mystery, lost something of his timidity, and his shadowy personality, submerged in a sea of doubts, came forth to look at the world. With the young reporter at his side, he ventured in the light of day into Main Street or strode up and down on the rickety front porch of his own house, talking excitedly. The voice that had been low and trembling became shrill and loud. The bent figure straightened. With a kind of wriggle, like a fish returned to the brook by the fisherman, Biddlebaum the silent began to talk, striving to put into words the ideas that had been accumulated by his mind during long years of silence.

Wing Biddlebaum talked much with his hands. The slender expressive fingers, forever active, forever striving to conceal themselves in his pockets or behind his back, came forth and became the piston rods of his machinery of expression.

The story of Wing Biddlebaum is a story of hands. Their restless activity, like unto the beating of the wings of an imprisoned bird, had given him his name. Some obscure poet of the town had thought of it. The hands alarmed their owner. He wanted to keep them hidden away and looked with amazement at the quiet inexpressive hands of other men who worked beside him in the fields, or passed, driving sleepy teams on country roads.

When he talked to George Willard, Wing Biddlebaum closed his fists and beat with them upon a table or on the walls of his house. The action made him more comfortable. If the desire to talk came to him when the two were walking in the fields, he sought out a stump or the top board of a fence and with his hands pounding busily talked with renewed ease.

The story of Wing Biddlebaum's hands is worth a book itself. Sympathetically set forth it would tap many strange, beautiful qualities in obscure men. It is a job for a poet. In Winesburg the hands had attracted attention merely because of their activity. With them Wing Biddlebaum had picked as high as a hundred and forty quarts of strawberries in a day. They became his distinguishing feature, the source of his fame. Also they made more grotesque an already grotesque and elusive individuality. Winesburg was proud of the hands of Wing Biddlebaum in the same spirit in which it was proud of Banker White's new stone house and Wesley Moyer's bay stallion, Tony Tip, that had won the two-fifteen trot at the fall races in Cleveland.

As for George Willard, he had many times wanted to ask about the hands. At times an almost overwhelming curiosity had taken hold of him. He felt that there must be a reason for their strange activity and their inclination to keep hidden away and only a growing respect for Wing Biddlebaum kept him from blurting out the questions that were often in his mind.

Once he had been on the point of asking. The two were walking in the fields on a summer afternoon and had stopped to sit upon a grassy bank. All afternoon Wing Biddlebaum had talked as one inspired. By a fence he had stopped and beating like a giant woodpecker upon the top board had shouted at George Willard, condemning his tendency to be too much influenced by the people about him. "You are destroying yourself," he cried.

"You have the inclination to be alone and to dream and you are afraid of dreams. You want to be like others in town here. You hear them talk and you try to imitate them."

On the grassy bank Wing Biddlebaum had tried again to drive his point home. His voice became soft and reminiscent, and with a sigh of contentment he launched into a long rambling talk, speaking as one lost in a dream.

Out of the dream Wing Biddlebaum made a picture for George Willard. In the picture men lived again in a kind of pastoral golden age. Across a green open country came clean-limbed young men, some afoot, some mounted upon horses. In crowds the young men came to gather about the feet of an old man who sat beneath a tree in a tiny garden and who talked to them.

Wing Biddlebaum became wholly inspired. For once he forgot the hands. Slowly they stole forth and lay upon George Willard's shoulders. Something new and bold came into the voice that talked. "You must try to forget all you have learned," said the old man. "You must begin to dream. From this time on you must shut your ears to the roaring of the voices."

Pausing in his speech, Wing Biddlebaum looked long and earnestly at George Willard. His eyes glowed. Again he raised the hands to caress the boy and then a look of horror swept over his face.

With a convulsive movement of his body, Wing Biddlebaum sprang to his feet and thrust his hands deep into his trousers pockets. Tears came to his eyes. "I must be getting along home. I can talk no more with you," he said nervously.

Without looking back, the old man had hurried down the hillside and across a meadow, leaving George Willard perplexed and frightened upon the grassy slope. With a shiver of dread the boy arose and went along the road toward town. "I'll not ask him about his hands," he thought, touched by the memory of the terror he had seen in the man's eyes. "There's something wrong, but I don't want to know what it is. His hands have something to do with his fear of me and of everyone."

And George Willard was right. Let us look briefly into the story of the hands. Perhaps our talking of them will arouse the poet who will tell the hidden wonder story of the influence for which the hands were but fluttering pennants of promise.

In his youth Wing Biddlebaum had been a school teacher in a town in Pennsylvania. He was not then known as Wing Biddlebaum, but went by the less euphonic name of Adolph Myers. As Adolph Myers he was much loved by the boys of his school.

Adolph Myers was meant by nature to be a rare teacher of youth. He was one of those rare, little-understood men who rule by a power so gentle that it passes as a lovable weakness. In their feeling for the boys under their charge such men are not unlike the finer sort of women in their love of men.

And yet that is but crudely stated. It needs the poet there. With the boys of his school, Adolph Myers had walked in the evening or had sat talking until dusk upon the schoolhouse steps lost in a kind of dream. Here and there went his hands, caressing the shoulders of the boys, playing about the tousled heads. As he talked his voice became soft and musical. There was a caress in that also. In a way the voice and the hands, the stroking of the shoulders and the touching of the hair was a part of the schoolmaster's effort to carry a dream into the young minds. By the caress that was in his fingers he expressed himself. He was one of those men in whom the force that creates life is diffused, not centralized. Under the caress of his hands doubt and disbelief went out of the minds of the boys and they began also to dream.

And then the tragedy. A half-witted boy of the school became enamored of the young master. In his bed at night he imagined unspeakable things and in the morning went forth to tell his dreams as facts. Strange, hideous accusations fell from his loose-hung lips. Through the Pennsylvania town went a shiver. Hidden, shadowy doubts that had been in men's minds concerning Adolph Myers were galvanized into beliefs.

The tragedy did not linger. Trembling lads were jerked out of bed and questioned. "He put his arms about me," said one. "His fingers were always playing in my hair," said another.

One afternoon a man of the town, Henry Bradford, who kept a saloon, came to the schoolhouse door. Calling Adolph Myers into the school yard he began to beat him with his fists. As his hard knuckles beat down into the frightened face of the schoolmaster, his wrath became more and more terrible. Screaming with dismay, the children ran here and there like disturbed insects. "I'll teach you to put your hands on my boy, you beast," roared the saloon keeper, who, tired of beating the master, had begun to kick him about the yard.

Adolph Myers was driven from the Pennsylvania town in the night. With lanterns in their hands a dozen men came to the door of the house where he lived alone and commanded that he dress and come forth. It was raining and one of the men had a rope in his hands. They had intended to hang the schoolmaster, but something in his figure, so small, white, and pitiful, touched their hearts and they let him escape. As he ran away into the darkness they repented of their weakness and ran after him, swearing and throwing sticks and great balls of soft mud at the figure that screamed and ran faster and faster into the darkness.

For twenty years Adolph Myers had lived alone in Winesburg. He was but forty but looked sixty-five. The name Biddlebaum he got from a box of goods seen at a freight station as he hurried through an eastern Ohio town. He had an aunt in Winesburg, a black-toothed old woman who raised chickens, and with her he lived until she died. He had been ill for a year after the experience in Pennsylvania, and after his recovery worked as a day laborer in the fields, going timidly about and striving to conceal his hands. Although he did not understand what had happened he felt that the hands must be to blame. Again and again the fathers of the boys had talked of the hands. "Keep your hands to yourself," the saloon keeper had roared, dancing with fury in the schoolhouse yard.

Upon the veranda of his house by the ravine, Wing Biddlebaum continued to walk up and down until the sun had disappeared and the road beyond the field was lost in the grey shadows. Going into his house he cut slices of bread and spread honey upon them. When the rumble of the evening train that took away the express cars loaded with the day's harvest of berries had passed and restored the silence of the summer night, he went again to walk upon the veranda. In the darkness he could not see the hands and they became quiet. Although he still hungered for the presence of the boy, who was the medium through which he expressed his love of man, the hunger became again a part of his loneliness and his waiting. Lighting a lamp, Wing Biddlebaum washed the few dishes soiled by his simple meal and, setting up a folding cot by the screen door that led to the porch, prepared to undress for the night. A few stray white bread crumbs lay on the cleanly washed floor by the table; putting the lamp upon a low stool he began to pick up the crumbs, carrying them to his mouth one by one with unbelievable rapidity. In the dense blotch of light beneath the table, the kneeling figure looked like a priest engaged in some service of his church. The nervous expressive fingers, flashing in and out of the light, might well have been mistaken for the fingers of the devotee going swiftly through decade after decade of his rosary.

MARGARET ATWOOD *(b. 1939) is a Canadian writer of poetry and fiction. Born in Ottawa, Ontario, she spent the first eleven years of her life in the sparsely settled "bush" country of northern Ontario and Quebec, where her father, an entomologist, did research. She remembers that*

> *I did not spend a full year in school until I was in Grade Eight. I began to write at the age of five — poems, "novels," comic books, and plays — but I had no thought of being a professional writer until I was sixteen. I entered Victoria College, University of Toronto, when I was seventeen and graduated in 1961. I won a Woodrow Wilson Fellowship to Harvard, where I studied Victorian Literature, and spent the next ten years in one place after another: Boston, Montreal, Edmonton, Toronto, Vancouver, England, and Italy, alternately teaching and writing.*

Atwood's first poem was published when she was nineteen. To date she has published two collections of short stories, several novels — including the best-sellers Surfacing *(1972),* The Handmaid's Tale *(1986),* Cat's Eye *(1989),* The Robber Bride

(1993), and Bodily Harm *(1999) — and more than a dozen books of poetry. She was encouraged to write as a young woman because Canadians of her generation felt a strong need to develop a national literature.*

Atwood has compared writing stories to telling riddles and jokes, all three requiring "the same mystifying buildup, the same surprising twist, the same impeccable sense of timing." "Gertrude Talks Back" was included in her collection Good Bones and Simple Murders *(1994).*

RELATED PLAY: *William Shakespeare,* Hamlet, Prince of Denmark, *page 1407.*

MARGARET ATWOOD

Gertrude Talks Back

1994

I always thought it was a mistake, calling you Hamlet. I mean, what kind of a name is that for a young boy? It was your father's idea. Nothing would do but that you had to be called after him. Selfish. The other kids at school used to tease the life out of you. The nicknames! And those terrible jokes about pork.

I wanted to call you George.

I am *not* wringing my hands. I'm drying my nails.

Darling, please stop fidgeting with my mirror. That'll be the third one you've broken.

Yes, I've seen those pictures, thank you very much.

I *know* your father was handsomer than Claudius. High brow, aquiline nose and so on, looked great in uniform. But handsome isn't everything, especially in a man, and far be it from me to speak ill of the dead, but I think it's about time I pointed out to you that your dad just wasn't a whole lot of fun. Noble, sure, I grant you. But Claudius, well, he likes a drink now and then. He appreciates a decent meal. He enjoys a laugh, know what I mean? You don't always have to be tiptoeing around because of some holier-than-thou principle or something.

By the way, darling, I wish you wouldn't call your stepdad *the bloat king.* He does have a slight weight problem, and it hurts his feelings.

The rank sweat of a *what?* My bed is certainly not *enseamed,* whatever that might be! A nasty sty, indeed! Not that it's any of your business, but I change those sheets twice a week, which is more than you do, judging from that student slum pigpen in Wittenberg. I'll certainly never visit you *there* again without prior warning! I see that laundry of yours when you bring it home, and not often enough either, by a long shot! Only when you run out of black socks.

And let me tell you, everyone sweats at a time like that, as you'd find out very soon if you ever gave it a try. A real girlfriend would do you a heap of good. Not like that pasty-faced what's-her-name, all trussed up like a prize turkey in those touch-me-not corsets of hers. If you ask me, there's something off about that girl. Borderline. Any little shock could push her right over the edge.

Go get yourself someone more down-to-earth. Have a nice roll in the hay. Then you can talk to me about nasty sties.

No, darling, I am not *mad* at you. But I must say you're an awful prig sometimes. Just like your Dad. *The Flesh,* he'd say. You'd think it was dog dirt. You can excuse that in a young person, they are always so intolerant, but in someone his age it was getting, well, very hard to live with, and that's the understatement of the year.

Some days I think it would have been better for both of us if you hadn't been an only child. But you realize who you have to thank for *that.* You have no idea what I used to put up with. And every time I felt like a little, you know, just to warm up my aging bones, it was like I'd suggested murder.

You think *what?* You think Claudius murdered your Dad? Well, no wonder you've been so rude to him at the dinner table!

If I'd known *that,* I could have put you straight in no time flat.

It wasn't Claudius, darling.

It was me.

ꕥ

JAMES BALDWIN *(1924–1987) was born the son of a clergyman in Harlem, where he attended Public School 24, Frederick Douglass Junior High School, and DeWitt Clinton High School. While still a high school student he preached at the Fireside Pentecostal Assembly, but when he was seventeen he renounced the ministry. Two years later, living in Greenwich Village, he met Richard Wright, who encouraged him to be a writer and helped him win a Eugene Saxton Fellowship. Soon afterward Baldwin moved to France, as Wright had, to escape the stifling racial oppression he found in the United States. Although France was his more or less permanent residence until his death from cancer nearly forty years later, Baldwin regarded himself as a "commuter" rather than an expatriate. He said,*

> *Only white Americans can consider themselves to be expatriates. Once I found myself on the other side of the ocean, I could see where I came from very*

clearly, and I could see that I carried myself, which is my home, with me. You can never escape that. I am the grandson of a slave, and I am a writer. I must deal with both.

Baldwin began his career by publishing novels and short stories. Go Tell It on the Mountain, *his first novel, was highly acclaimed when it appeared in 1953. It was based on his childhood in Harlem and his fear of his tyrannical father. Baldwin's frank depiction of homosexuality in the novels* Giovanni's Room *(1956) and* Another Country *(1962) drew criticism, but during the civil rights movement a few years later, he established himself as a brilliant essayist. In his lifetime Baldwin published several collections of essays, three more novels, and a book of five short stories,* Going to Meet the Man *(1965).*

"Sonny's Blues," from that collection, is one of Baldwin's strongest psychological dramatizations of the frustrations of African American life in our time. Like Wright's autobiographical books, Baldwin's work is an inspiration to young writers struggling to express their experience of racism. The African writer Chinua Achebe has said that "as long as injustice exists . . . the words of James Baldwin will be there to bear witness and to inspire and elevate the struggle for human freedom."

RELATED COMMENTARY: *James Baldwin, "Autobiographical Notes," page 663.*

JAMES BALDWIN

Sonny's Blues

1957

I read about it in the paper, in the subway, on my way to work. I read it, and I couldn't believe it, and I read it again. Then perhaps I just stared at it, at the newsprint spelling out his name, spelling out the story. I stared at it in the swinging lights of the subway car, and in the faces and bodies of the people, and in my own face, trapped in the darkness which roared outside.

It was not to be believed and I kept telling myself that, as I walked from the subway station to the high school. And at the same time I couldn't doubt it. I was scared, scared for Sonny. He became real to me again. A great block of ice got settled in my belly and kept melting there slowly all day long, while I taught my classes algebra. It was a special kind of ice. It kept melting, sending trickles of ice water all up and down my veins, but it never got less. Sometimes it hardened and seemed to expand until I felt my guts were going to come spilling out or that I was going to choke or scream. This would always be at a moment when I was remembering some specific thing Sonny had once said or done.

When he was about as old as the boys in my classes his face had been bright and open, there was a lot of copper in it; and he'd had wonderfully direct brown eyes, and great gentleness and privacy. I wondered what he looked like now. He had been picked up, the evening before, in a raid on an apartment downtown, for peddling and using heroin.

I couldn't believe it: but what I mean by that is that I couldn't find any room for it anywhere inside me. I had kept it outside me for a long time. I hadn't wanted to know. I had had suspicions, but I didn't name them, I kept putting them away. I told myself that Sonny was wild, but he wasn't crazy. And he'd always been a good boy, he hadn't ever turned hard or evil or disrespectful, the way kids can, so quick, so quick, especially in Harlem. I didn't want to believe that I'd ever see my brother going down, coming to nothing, all that light in his face gone out, in the condition I'd already seen so many others. Yet it had happened and here I was, talking about algebra to a lot of boys who might, every one of them for all I knew, be popping off needles every time they went to the head. Maybe it did more for them than algebra could.

I was sure that the first time Sonny had ever had horse, he couldn't have been much older than these boys were now. These boys, now, were living as we'd been living then, they were growing up with a rush and their heads bumped abruptly against the low ceiling of their actual possibilities. They were filled with rage. All they really knew were two darknesses, the darkness of their lives, which was now closing in on them, and the darkness of the movies, which had blinded them to that other darkness, and in which they now, vindictively, dreamed, at once more together than they were at any other time, and more alone.

When the last bell rang, the last class ended, I let out my breath. It seemed I'd been holding it for all that time. My clothes were wet — I may have looked as though I'd been sitting in a steam bath, all dressed up, all afternoon. I sat alone in the classroom a long time. I listened to the boys outside, downstairs, shouting and cursing and laughing. Their laughter struck me for perhaps the first time. It was not the joyous laughter which — God knows why — one associates with children. It was mocking and insular, its intent to denigrate. It was disenchanted, and in this, also, lay the authority of their curses. Perhaps I was listening to them because I was thinking about my brother and in them I heard my brother. And myself.

One boy was whistling a tune, at once very complicated and very simple, it seemed to be pouring out of him as though he were a bird, and it sounded very cool and moving through all that harsh, bright air, only just holding its own through all those other sounds.

I stood up and walked over to the window and looked down into the courtyard. It was the beginning of the spring and the sap was rising in the boys. A teacher passed through them every now and again, quickly, as though he or she couldn't wait to get out of that courtyard, to get those boys out of their sight and off their minds. I started collecting my stuff. I thought I'd better get home and talk to Isabel.

The courtyard was almost deserted by the time I got downstairs. I saw this boy standing in the shadow of a doorway, looking just like Sonny. I almost called his name. Then I saw that it wasn't Sonny, but somebody we used to know, a boy from around our block. He'd been Sonny's friend. He'd never been mine, having been too young for me, and, anyway, I'd never liked him. And now, even though he was a grown-up man, he still hung around that block, still spent hours on the street corners, was always high and raggy. I used to run into him from time to time and he'd often work around to asking me for a quarter or fifty cents. He always had some real good excuse, too, and I always gave it to him, I don't know why.

But now, abruptly, I hated him. I couldn't stand the way he looked at me, partly like a dog, partly like a cunning child. I wanted to ask him what the hell he was doing in the school courtyard.

He sort of shuffled over to me, and he said, "I see you got the papers. So you already know about it."

"You mean about Sonny? Yes, I already know about it. How come they didn't get you?"

He grinned. It made him repulsive and it also brought to mind what he'd looked like as a kid. "I wasn't there. I stay away from them people."

"Good for you." I offered him a cigarette and I watched him through the smoke. "You come all the way down here just to tell me about Sonny?"

"That's right." He was sort of shaking his head and his eyes looked strange, as though they were about to cross. The bright sun deadened his damp dark brown skin and it made his eyes look yellow and showed up the dirt in his kinked hair. He smelled funky. I moved a little away from him and I said, "Well, thanks. But I already know about it and I got to get home."

"I'll walk you a little ways," he said. We started walking. There were a couple of kids still loitering in the courtyard and one of them said goodnight to me and looked strangely at the boy beside me.

"What're you going to do?" he asked me. "I mean, about Sonny?"

"Look. I haven't seen Sonny for over a year. I'm not sure I'm going to do anything. Anyway, what the hell *can* I do?"

"That's right," he said quickly, "ain't nothing you can do. Can't much help old Sonny no more, I guess."

It was what I was thinking and so it seemed to me he had no right to say it.

"I'm surprised at Sonny, though," he went on — he had a funny way of talking, he looked straight ahead as though he were talking to himself — "I thought Sonny was a smart boy, I thought he was too smart to get hung."

"I guess he thought so too," I said sharply, "and that's how he got hung. And how about you? You're pretty goddamn smart, I bet."

Then he looked directly at me, just for a minute. "I ain't smart," he said. "If I was smart, I'd have reached for a pistol a long time ago."

"Look. Don't tell *me* your sad story, if it was up to me, I'd give you one." Then I felt guilty — guilty, probably, for never having supposed that the poor bastard *had* a story of his own, much less a sad one, and I asked, quickly, "What's going to happen to him now?"

He didn't answer this. He was off by himself some place. "Funny thing," he said, and from his tone we might have been discussing the quickest way to get to Brooklyn, "when I saw the papers this morning, the first thing I asked myself was if I had anything to do with it. I felt sort of responsible."

I began to listen more carefully. The subway station was on the corner, just before us, and I stopped. He stopped, too. We were in front of a bar and he ducked slightly, peering in, but whoever he was looking for didn't seem to be there. The juke box was blasting away with something black and bouncy and I half watched the barmaid as she danced her way from the juke box to her place behind the bar. And I watched her face as she laughingly responded to something someone said to her, still keeping time to the music. When she smiled one saw the little girl, one sensed the doomed, still-struggling woman beneath the battered face of the semi-whore.

"I never *give* Sonny nothing," the boy said finally, "but a long time ago I come to school high and Sonny asked me how it felt." He paused, I couldn't bear to watch him, I watched the barmaid, and I listened to the music which seemed to be causing the pavement to shake. "I told him it felt great." The music stopped, the barmaid paused and watched the juke box until the music began again. "It did."

All this was carrying me some place I didn't want to go. I certainly didn't want to know how it felt. It filled everything, the people, the houses, the music, the dark, quicksilver barmaid, with menace; and this menace was their reality. "What's going to happen to him now?" I asked again.

"They'll send him away some place and they'll try to cure him." He shook his head. "Maybe he'll even think he's kicked the habit. Then they'll let him loose" — he gestured, throwing his cigarette into the gutter. "That's all."

"What do you mean, that's *all*?"

But I knew what he meant.

"I *mean*, that's *all*." He turned his head and looked at me, pulling down the corners of his mouth. "Don't you know what I mean?" he asked, softly.

"How the hell *would* I know what you mean?" I almost whispered it, I don't know why.

"That's right," he said to the air, "how would *he* know what I mean?" He turned toward me again, patient and calm, and yet I somehow felt him shaking, shaking as though he were going to fall apart. I felt that ice in my guts again, the dread I'd felt all afternoon; and again I watched the barmaid, moving about the bar, washing glasses, and singing. "Listen. They'll let him out and then it'll just start all over again. That's what I mean."

"You mean — they'll let him out. And then he'll just start working his way back in again. You mean he'll never kick the habit. Is that what you mean?"

"That's right," he said, cheerfully. "*You* see what I mean."

"Tell me," I said at last, "why does he want to die? He must want to die, he's killing himself, why does he want to die?"

He looked at me in surprise. He licked his lips. "He don't want to die. He wants to live. Don't nobody want to die, ever."

Then I wanted to ask him — too many things. He could not have answered, or if he had, I could not have borne the answers. I started walking. "Well, I guess it's none of my business."

"It's going to be rough on old Sonny," he said. We reached the subway station. "This is your station?" he asked. I nodded. I took one step down. "Damn!" he said, suddenly. I looked up at him. He grinned again. "Damn it if I didn't leave all my money home. You ain't got a dollar on you, have you? Just for a couple of days, is all."

All at once something inside gave and threatened to come pouring out of me. I didn't hate him any more. I felt that in another moment I'd start crying like a child.

"Sure," I said. "Don't sweat." I looked in my wallet and didn't have a dollar, I only had a five. "Here," I said. "That hold you?"

He didn't look at it — he didn't want to look at it. A terrible closed look came over his face, as though he were keeping the number on the bill a secret from him and me. "Thanks," he said, and now he was dying to see me go. "Don't worry about Sonny. Maybe I'll write him or something."

"Sure," I said. "You do that. So long."

"Be seeing you," he said. I went on down the steps.

And I didn't write Sonny or send him anything for a long time. When I finally did, it was just after my little girl died, he wrote me back a letter which made me feel like a bastard.

Here's what he said:

> Dear brother,
>
> You don't know how much I needed to hear from you. I wanted to write you many a time but I dug how much I must have hurt you and so I didn't write. But now I feel like a man who's been trying to climb up out of some deep, real deep and funky hole and just saw the sun up there, outside. I got to get outside.
>
> I can't tell you much about how I got here. I mean I don't know how to tell you. I guess I was afraid of something or I was trying to escape from something and you know I have never been very strong in the head (smile). I'm glad Mama and Daddy are dead and can't see what's happened to their son and I swear if I'd known what I was doing I would never have hurt you so, you and a lot of other fine people who were nice to me and who believed in me.
>
> I don't want you to think it had anything to do with me being a musician. It's more than that. Or maybe less than that. I can't get anything straight in my head down here and I try not to think about what's going to happen to me when I get outside again. Sometime I think I'm going to flip and *never* get outside and sometime I think I'll come straight back. I tell you one thing, though, I'd rather blow my brains out than go through this again. But that's what they all say, so they tell me. If I tell you when I'm coming to New York and if you could meet me, I sure would appreciate it. Give my love to Isabel and the kids and I was sure sorry to hear about little Gracie. I wish I could be like Mama and say the Lord's will be done, but I don't know it seems to me that trouble is the one thing that never does get stopped and I don't know what good it does to blame it on the Lord. But maybe it does some good if you believe it.
>
> Your brother,
Sonny

Then I kept in constant touch with him and I sent him whatever I could and I went to meet him when he came back to New York. When I saw him many things I thought I had forgotten came flooding back to me. This was because I had begun, finally, to wonder about Sonny, about the life that Sonny lived inside. This life, whatever it was, had made him older and thinner and it had deepened the distant stillness in which he had always moved. He looked very unlike my baby brother. Yet, when he smiled, when we shook hands, the baby brother I'd never known looked out from the depths of his private life, like an animal waiting to be coaxed into the light.

"How you been keeping?" he asked me.

"All right. And you?"

"Just fine." He was smiling all over his face. "It's good to see you again."

"It's good to see you."

The seven years' difference in our ages lay between us like a chasm: I wondered if these years would ever operate between us as a bridge. I was remembering, and it made it hard to catch my breath, that I had been there when he was born; and I had heard the first words he had ever spoken. When he started to walk, he walked from our mother straight to me. I caught him just before he fell when he took the first steps he ever took in this world.

"How's Isabel?"

"Just fine. She's dying to see you."

"And the boys?"

"They're fine, too. They're anxious to see their uncle."

"Oh, come on. You know they don't remember me."

"Are you kidding? Of course they remember you."

He grinned again. We got into a taxi. We had a lot to say to each other, far too much to know how to begin.

As the taxi began to move, I asked, "You still want to go to India?"

He laughed. "You still remember that. Hell, no. This place is Indian enough for me."

"It used to belong to them," I said.

And he laughed again. "They damn sure knew what they were doing when they got rid of it."

Years ago, when he was around fourteen, he'd been all hipped on the idea of going to India. He read books about people sitting on rocks, naked, in all kinds of weather, but mostly bad, naturally, and walking barefoot through hot coals and arriving at wisdom. I used to say that it sounded to me as though they were getting away from wisdom as fast as they could. I think he sort of looked down on me for that.

"Do you mind," he asked, "if we have the driver drive alongside the park? On the west side — I haven't seen the city in so long."

"Of course not," I said. I was afraid that I might sound as though I were humoring him, but I hoped he wouldn't take it that way.

So we drove along, between the green of the park and the stony, lifeless elegance of hotels and apartment buildings, toward the vivid, killing streets of our childhood. These streets hadn't changed, though housing projects jutted up out of them now like rocks in the middle of a boiling sea. Most of the houses in which we had grown up had vanished, as had the stores from which we had stolen, the basements in which we had first tried sex, the rooftops from which we had hurled tin cans and bricks. But houses exactly like the houses of our past yet dominated the landscape, boys exactly like the boys we once had been found themselves smothering in these houses, came down into the streets for light and air and found themselves encircled by disaster. Some escaped the trap, most didn't. Those who got out always left something of themselves behind, as some animals amputate a leg and leave it in the trap. It might be said, perhaps, that I had escaped, after all, I was a school teacher; or that Sonny had, he hadn't lived in Harlem for years. Yet, as the cab moved uptown through streets which seemed, with a rush, to darken with dark people, and as I covertly studied Sonny's face, it came to me that what we both were seeking through our separate cab windows was that part of ourselves which had been left behind. It's always at the hour of trouble and confrontation that the missing member aches.

We hit 110th Street and started rolling up Lenox Avenue. And I'd known this avenue all my life, but it seemed to me again, as it had seemed on the day I'd first heard about Sonny's trouble, filled with a hidden menace which was its very breath of life.

"We almost there," said Sonny.

"Almost." We were both too nervous to say anything more.

We live in a housing project. It hasn't been up long. A few days after it was up it seemed uninhabitably new, now, of course, it's already rundown. It looks like a parody of the good, clean, faceless life — God knows the people who live in it do their best to make it a parody. The beat-looking grass lying around isn't enough to make their lives green, the hedges will never hold out the streets, and they know it. The big windows fool no one, they aren't big enough to make space out of no space. They don't bother with the windows, they watch the TV screen instead. The playground is most popular with the children who don't play at jacks, or skip rope, or roller skate, or swing, and they can be found in it after dark. We moved in partly because it's not too far from where I teach, and partly for the kids; but it's really just like the houses in which Sonny and I grew up. The same things happen, they'll have the same things to remember. The moment Sonny and I started into the house I had the feeling that I was simply bringing him back into the danger he had almost died trying to escape.

Sonny has never been talkative. So I don't know why I was sure he'd be dying to talk to me when supper was over the first night. Everything went fine, the oldest boy remembered him, and the youngest boy liked him, and Sonny had remembered to bring something for each of them; and Isabel, who is really much nicer than I am, more open and giving, had gone to a lot of trouble about dinner and was genuinely glad to see him. And she's always been able to tease Sonny in a way that I haven't. It was nice to see her face so vivid again and to hear her laugh and watch her make Sonny laugh. She wasn't, or, anyway, she didn't seem to be, at all uneasy or embarrassed. She chatted as though there were no subject which had to be avoided and she got Sonny past his first, faint stiffness. And thank God she was there, for I was filled with that icy dread again. Everything I did seemed awkward to me, and everything I said sounded freighted with hidden meaning. I was trying to remember everything I'd heard about dope addiction and I couldn't help watching Sonny for signs. I wasn't doing it out of malice. I was trying to find out something about my brother. I was dying to hear him tell me he was safe.

"Safe!" my father grunted, whenever Mama suggested trying to move to a neighborhood which might be safer for children. "Safe, hell! Ain't no place safe for kids, nor nobody."

He always went on like this, but he wasn't, ever, really as bad as he sounded, not even on weekends, when he got drunk. As a matter of fact, he was always on the lookout for "something a little better," but he died before he found it. He died suddenly, during a drunken weekend in the middle of the war, when Sonny was fifteen. He and Sonny hadn't ever got on too well. And this was partly because Sonny was the apple of his father's eye. It was because he loved Sonny so much and was frightened for him, that he was always fighting with him. It doesn't do any good to fight with Sonny. Sonny just moves back, inside himself, where he can't be reached. But the principal reason that they never hit it off is that they were so much alike. Daddy was big and rough and loud-talking, just the opposite of Sonny, but they both had — that same privacy.

Mama tried to tell me something about this, just after Daddy died. I was home on leave from the army.

This was the last time I ever saw my mother alive. Just the same, this picture gets all mixed up in my mind with pictures I had of her when she was younger. The way I always see her is the way she used to be on a Sunday afternoon, say, when the old folks were talking after the big Sunday dinner. I always see her wearing pale blue. She'd be sitting on the sofa. And my father would be sitting in the easy chair, not far from her. And the living room would be full of church folks and relatives. There they sit, in chairs all around the living room, and the night is creeping up outside, but nobody knows it yet. You can see the darkness growing against the windowpanes and you hear the street noises every now and again, or maybe the jangling beat of a tambourine from one of the churches close by, but it's real quiet in the room. For a moment nobody's talking, but every face looks darkening, like the sky outside. And my mother rocks a little from the waist, and my father's eyes are closed. Everyone is looking at something a child can't see. For a minute they've forgotten the children. Maybe a kid is lying on the rug, half asleep. Maybe somebody's got a kid in his lap and is absent-mindedly stroking the kid's head. Maybe there's a kid, quiet and big-eyed, curled up in a big chair in the corner. The silence, the darkness coming, and the darkness in the faces frightens the child obscurely. He hopes that the hand which strokes his forehead will never stop — will never die. He hopes that there will never come a time when the old folks won't be sitting around the living room, talking about where they've come from, and what they've seen, and what's happened to them and their kinfolk.

But something deep and watchful in the child knows that this is bound to end, is already ending. In a moment someone will get up and turn on the light. Then the old folks will remember the children and they won't talk any more that day. And when light fills the room, the child is filled with darkness. He knows that every time this happens he's moved just a little closer to that darkness outside. The darkness outside is what the old folks have been talking about. It's what they've come from. It's what they endure. The child knows that they won't talk any more because if he knows too much about what's happened to *them,* he'll know too much too soon, about what's going to happen to *him.*

The last time I talked to my mother, I remember I was restless. I wanted to get out and see Isabel. We weren't married then and we had a lot to straighten out between us.

There Mama sat, in black, by the window. She was humming an old church song, *Lord, you brought me from a long ways off.* Sonny was out somewhere. Mama kept watching the streets.

"I don't know," she said, "if I'll ever see you again, after you go off from here. But I hope you'll remember the things I tried to teach you."

"Don't talk like that," I said, and smiled. "You'll be here a long time yet."

She smiled, too, but she said nothing. She was quiet for a long time. And I said, "Mama, don't you worry about nothing. I'll be writing all the time, and you be getting the checks. . . ."

"I want to talk to you about your brother," she said, suddenly. "If anything happens to me he ain't going to have nobody to look out for him."

"Mama," I said, "ain't nothing going to happen to you *or* Sonny. Sonny's all right. He's a good boy and he's got good sense."

"It ain't a question of his being a good boy," Mama said, "nor of his having good sense. It ain't only the bad ones, nor yet the dumb ones that gets sucked under." She stopped, looking at me. "Your Daddy once had a brother," she said, and she smiled in a way that made me feel she was in pain. "You didn't never know that, did you?"

"No," I said, "I never knew that," and I watched her face.

"Oh, yes," she said, "your Daddy had a brother." She looked out of the window again. "I know you never saw your Daddy cry. But *I* did — many a time, through all these years."

I asked her, "What happened to his brother? How come nobody's ever talked about him?"

This was the first time I ever saw my mother look old.

"His brother got killed," she said, "when he was just a little younger than you are now. I knew him. He was a fine boy. He was maybe a little full of the devil, but he didn't mean nobody no harm."

Then she stopped and the room was silent, exactly as it had sometimes been on those Sunday afternoons. Mama kept looking out into the streets.

"He used to have a job in the mill," she said, "and, like all young folks, he just liked to perform on Saturday nights. Saturday nights, him and your father would drift around to different places, go to dances and things like that, or just sit around with people they knew, and your father's brother would sing, he had a fine voice, and play along with himself on his guitar. Well, this particular Saturday night, him and your father was coming home from some place, and they were both a little drunk and there was a moon that night, it was bright like day. Your father's brother was feeling kind of good, and he was whistling to himself, and he had his guitar slung over his shoulder. They was coming down a hill and beneath them was a road that turned off from the highway. Well, your father's brother, being always kind of frisky, decided to run down this hill, and he did, with that guitar banging and clanging behind him, and he ran across the road, and he was making water behind a tree. And your father was sort of amused at him and he was still coming down the hill, kind of slow. Then he heard a car motor and that same minute his brother stepped from behind the tree, into the road, in the moonlight. And he started to cross the road. And your father started to run down the hill, he says he don't know why. This car was full of white men. They was all drunk, and when they seen your father's brother they let out a great whoop and holler and they aimed the car straight at him. They was having fun, they just wanted to scare him, the way they do sometimes, you know. But they was drunk. And I guess the boy, being drunk, too, and scared, kind of lost his head. By the time he jumped it was too late. Your father says he heard his brother scream when the car rolled over him, and he heard the wood of that guitar when it give, and he heard them strings go flying, and he heard them white men shouting, and the car kept on a-going and it ain't stopped till this day. And, time your father got down the hill, his brother weren't nothing but blood and pulp."

Tears were gleaming on my mother's face. There wasn't anything I could say.

"He never mentioned it," she said, "because I never let him mention it before you children. Your Daddy was like a crazy man that night and for many a night thereafter. He says he never in his life seen anything as dark as that road after the lights of that car had gone away. Weren't nothing, weren't nobody on that road, just your Daddy and his brother and that busted guitar. Oh, yes. Your Daddy never did really get right again. Till the day he died he weren't sure but that every white man he saw was the man that killed his brother."

She stopped and took out her handkerchief and dried her eyes and looked at me.

"I ain't telling you all this," she said, "to make you scared or bitter or to make you hate nobody. I'm telling you this because you got a brother. And the world ain't changed."

I guess I didn't want to believe this. I guess she saw this in my face. She turned away from me, toward the window again, searching those streets.

"But I praise my Redeemer," she said at last, "that He called your Daddy home before me. I ain't saying it to throw no flowers at myself, but, I declare, it keeps me from feeling too cast down to know I helped your father get safely through this world. Your father always acted like he was the roughest, strongest man on earth. And everybody took him to be like that. But if he hadn't had *me* there — to see his tears!"

She was crying again. Still, I couldn't move. I said, "Lord, Lord, Mama, I didn't know it was like that."

"Oh, honey," she said, "there's a lot that you don't know. But you are going to find it out." She stood up from the window and came over to me. "You got to hold on to your brother," she said, "and don't let him fall, no matter what it looks like is happening to him and no matter how evil you gets with him. You going to be evil with him many a time. But don't you forget what I told you, you hear?"

"I won't forget," I said. "Don't you worry, I won't forget. I won't let nothing happen to Sonny."

My mother smiled as though she were amused at something she saw in my face. Then, "You may not be able to stop nothing from happening. But you got to let him know you's *there.*"

Two days later I was married, and then I was gone. And I had a lot of things on my mind and I pretty well forgot my promise to Mama until I got shipped home on a special furlough for her funeral.

And, after the funeral, with just Sonny and me alone in the empty kitchen, I tried to find out something about him.

"What do you want to do?" I asked him.

"I'm going to be a musician," he said.

For he had graduated, in the time I had been away, from dancing to the juke box to finding out who was playing what, and what they were doing with it, and he had bought himself a set of drums.

"You mean, you want to be a drummer?" I somehow had the feeling that being a drummer might be all right for other people but not for my brother Sonny.

"I don't think," he said, looking at me very gravely, "that I'll ever be a good drummer. But I think I can play a piano."

I frowned. I'd never played the role of the older brother quite so seriously before, had scarcely ever, in fact, *asked* Sonny a damn thing. I sensed myself in the presence of something I didn't really know how to handle, didn't understand. So I made my frown a little deeper as I asked: "What kind of musician do you want to be?"

He grinned. "How many kinds do you think there are?"

"Be *serious,*" I said.

He laughed, throwing his head back, and then looked at me. "I *am* serious."

"Well, then, for Christ's sake, stop kidding around and answer a serious question. I mean, do you want to be a concert pianist, you want to play classical music and all that, or — or what?" Long before I finished he was laughing again. "For Christ's *sake,* Sonny!"

He sobered, but with difficulty. "I'm sorry. But you sound so — *scared!*" and he was off again.

"Well, you may think it's funny now, baby, but it's not going to be so funny when you have to make your living at it, let me tell you *that.*" I was furious because I knew he was laughing at me and I didn't know why.

"No," he said, very sober now, and afraid, perhaps, that he'd hurt me, "I don't want to be a classical pianist. That isn't what interests me. I mean" — he paused, looking hard at me, as though his eyes would help me to understand, and then gestured helplessly, as though perhaps his hand would help — "I mean, I'll have a lot of studying to do, and I'll have to study *everything,* but, I mean, I want to play *with* — jazz musicians." He stopped. "I want to play jazz," he said.

Well, the word had never before sounded as heavy, as real, as it sounded that afternoon in Sonny's mouth. I just looked at him and I was probably frowning a real frown by this time. I simply couldn't see why on earth he'd want to spend his time hanging around nightclubs, clowning around on bandstands, while people pushed each other around a dance floor. It seemed — beneath him, somehow. I had never thought about it before, had never been forced to, but I suppose I had always put jazz musicians in a class with what Daddy called "good-time people."

"Are you *serious*?"

"Hell, *yes*, I'm serious."

He looked more helpless than ever, and annoyed, and deeply hurt.

I suggested, helpfully: "You mean — like Louis Armstrong?"

His face closed as though I'd struck him. "No. I'm not talking about none of that old-time, down home crap."

"Well, look, Sonny, I'm sorry, don't get mad. I just don't altogether get it, that's all. Name somebody — you know, a jazz musician you admire."

"Bird."

"Who?"

"Bird! Charlie Parker! Don't they teach you nothing in the goddamn army?"

I lit a cigarette. I was surprised and then a little amused to discover that I was trembling. "I've been out of touch," I said. "You'll have to be patient with me. Now. Who's this Parker character?"

"He's just one of the greatest jazz musicians alive," said Sonny, sullenly, his hands in his pockets, his back to me. "Maybe *the* greatest," he added, bitterly, "that's probably why *you* never heard of him."

"All right," I said, "I'm ignorant. I'm sorry. I'll go out and buy all the cat's records right away, all right?"

"It don't," said Sonny, with dignity, "make any difference to me. I don't care what you listen to. Don't do me no favors."

I was beginning to realize that I'd never seen him so upset before. With another part of my mind I was thinking that this would probably turn out to be one of those things kids go through and that I shouldn't make it seem important by pushing it too hard. Still, I didn't think it would do any harm to ask: "Doesn't all this take a lot of time? Can you make a living at it?"

He turned back to me and half leaned, half sat, on the kitchen table. "Everything takes time," he said, "and — well, yes, sure, I can make a living at it. But what I don't seem to be able to make you understand is that it's the only thing I want to do."

"Well, Sonny," I said, gently, "you know people can't always do exactly what they *want* to do —"

"*No*, I don't know that," said Sonny, surprising me. "I think people *ought* to do what they want to do, what else are they alive for?"

"You getting to be a big boy," I said desperately, "it's time you started thinking about your future."

"I'm thinking about my future," said Sonny, grimly. "I think about it all the time."

I gave up. I decided, if he didn't change his mind, that we could always talk about it later. "In the meantime," I said, "you got to finish school." We had already decided that he'd have to move in with Isabel and her folks. I knew this wasn't the ideal arrangement because Isabel's folks are inclined to be dicty and they hadn't especially wanted Isabel to marry me. But I didn't know what else to do. "And we have to get you fixed up at Isabel's."

There was a long silence. He moved from the kitchen table to the window. "That's a terrible idea. You know it yourself."

"Do you have a *better* idea?"

He just walked up and down the kitchen for a minute. He was as tall as I was. He had started to shave. I suddenly had the feeling that I didn't know him at all.

He stopped at the kitchen table and picked up my cigarettes. Looking at me with a kind of mocking, amused defiance, he put one between his lips. "You mind?"

"You smoking already?"

He lit the cigarette and nodded, watching me through the smoke. "I just wanted to see if I'd have the courage to smoke in front of you." He grinned and blew a great cloud of smoke to the ceiling. "It was easy." He looked at my face. "Come on, now. I bet you was smoking at my age, tell the truth."

I didn't say anything but the truth was on my face, and he laughed. But now there was something very strained in his laugh. "Sure. And I bet that ain't all you was doing."

He was frightening me a little. "Cut the crap," I said. "We already decided that you was going to go and live at Isabel's. Now what's got into you all of a sudden?"

"*You* decided it," he pointed out. "*I* didn't decide nothing." He stopped in front of me, leaning against the stove, arms loosely folded. "Look, brother. I don't want to stay in Harlem no more, I really don't." He was very earnest. He looked at me, then over toward the kitchen window. There was something in his eyes I'd never seen before, some thoughtfulness, some worry all his own. He rubbed the muscle of one arm. "It's time I was getting out of here."

"Where do you want to *go,* Sonny?"

"I want to join the army. Or the navy, I don't care. If I say I'm old enough, they'll believe me."

Then I got mad. It was because I was so scared. "You must be crazy. You goddamn fool, what the hell do you want to go and join the *army* for?"

"I just told you. To get out of Harlem."

"Sonny, you haven't even finished *school.* And if you really want to be a musician, how do you expect to study if you're in the *army*?"

He looked at me, trapped, and in anguish. "There's ways. I might be able to work out some kind of deal. Anyway, I'll have the G.I. Bill when I come out."

"*If* you come out." We stared at each other. "Sonny, please. Be reasonable. I know the setup is far from perfect. But we got to do the best we can."

"I ain't learning nothing in school," he said. "Even when I go." He turned away from me and opened the window and threw his cigarette out into the narrow alley. I watched his back. "At least, I ain't learning nothing you'd want me to learn." He slammed the window so hard I thought the glass would fly out, and turned back to me. "And I'm sick of the stink of these garbage cans!"

"Sonny," I said, "I know how you feel. But if you don't finish school now, you're going to be sorry later that you didn't." I grabbed him by the shoulders. "And you only got another year. It ain't so bad. And I'll come back and I swear I'll help you do *whatever* you want to do. Just try to put up with it till I come back. Will you please do that? For me?"

He didn't answer and he wouldn't look at me.

"Sonny. You hear me?"

He pulled away. "I hear you. But you never hear anything *I* say."

I didn't know what to say to that. He looked out of the window and then back at me. "OK," he said, and sighed. "I'll try."

Then I said, trying to cheer him up a little, "They got a piano at Isabel's. You can practice on it."

And as a matter of fact, it did cheer him up for a minute. "That's right," he said to himself. "I forgot that." His face relaxed a little. But the worry, the thoughtfulness, played on it still, the way shadows play on a face which is staring into the fire.

But I thought I'd never hear the end of that piano. At first, Isabel would write me, saying how nice it was that Sonny was so serious about his music and how, as soon as he came in from school, or wherever he had been when he was supposed to be at school, he went straight to that piano and stayed there until suppertime. And, after supper, he went back to that piano and stayed there until everybody went to bed. He was at the piano all day Saturday and all day Sunday. Then he bought a record player and started playing records. He'd play one record over and over again, all day long sometimes, and he'd improvise along with it on the piano. Or he'd play one section of the record, one chord, one change, one progression, then he'd do it on the piano. Then back to the record. Then back to the piano.

Well, I really don't know how they stood it. Isabel finally confessed that it wasn't like living with a person at all, it was like living with sound. And the sound didn't make any sense to her, didn't make any sense to any of them — naturally. They began, in a way, to be afflicted by this presence that was living in their home. It was as though Sonny were some sort of god, or monster. He moved in an atmosphere which wasn't like theirs at all. They fed him and he ate, he washed himself, he walked in and out of their door; he certainly wasn't nasty or unpleasant or rude, Sonny isn't any of those things; but it was as though he were all wrapped up in some cloud, some fire, some vision all his own; and there wasn't any way to reach him.

At the same time, he wasn't really a man yet, he was still a child, and they had to watch out for him in all kinds of ways. They certainly couldn't throw him out. Neither did they dare to make a great scene about that piano because even they dimly sensed, as I sensed, from so many thousands of miles away, that Sonny was at that piano playing for his life.

But he hadn't been going to school. One day a letter came from the school board and Isabel's mother got it — there had, apparently, been other letters but Sonny had torn them up. This day, when Sonny came in, Isabel's mother showed him the letter and asked where he'd been spending his time. And she finally got it out of him that he'd been down in Greenwich Village, with musicians and other characters, in a white girl's apartment. And this scared her and she started to scream at him and what came up, once she began — though she denies it to this day — was what sacrifices they were making to give Sonny a decent home and how little he appreciated it.

Sonny didn't play the piano that day. By evening, Isabel's mother had calmed down but then there was the old man to deal with, and Isabel herself. Isabel says she did her best to be calm but she broke down and started crying. She says she just watched Sonny's face. She could tell, by watching him, what was happening with him. And what was happening was that they penetrated his cloud, they had reached him. Even if their fingers had been a thousand times more gentle than human fingers ever are, he could hardly help feeling that they had stripped him naked and were spitting on that nakedness. For he also had to see that his presence, that music, which was life or death to him, had been torture for them and that they had endured it, not at all for his sake, but only for mine. And Sonny couldn't take that. He can take it a little better today than he could then but he's still not very good at it and, frankly, I don't know anybody who is.

The silence of the next few days must have been louder than the sound of all the music ever played since time began. One morning, before she went to work, Isabel was in his room for something and she suddenly realized that all of his records were gone. And she knew for certain that he was gone. And he was. He went as far as the navy would carry him. He finally sent me a postcard from some place in Greece and that was the first I knew that Sonny was still alive. I didn't see him any more until we were both back in New York and the war had long been over.

He was a man by then, of course, but I wasn't willing to see it. He came by the house from time to time, but we fought almost every time we met. I didn't like the way he carried himself, loose and dreamlike all the time, and I didn't like his friends, and his music seemed to be merely an excuse for the life he led. It sounded just that weird and disordered.

Then we had a fight, a pretty awful fight, and I didn't see him for months. By and by I looked him up, where he was living, in a furnished room in the Village, and I tried to make it up. But there were lots of people in the room and Sonny just lay on his bed, and he wouldn't come downstairs with me, and he treated these other people as though they were his family and I weren't. So I got mad and then he got mad, and then I told him that he might just as well be dead as live the way he was living. Then he stood up and he told me not to worry about him any more in life, that he *was* dead as far as I was concerned. Then he pushed me to the door and the other people looked on as though nothing were happening, and he slammed the door behind me. I stood in the hallway, staring at the door. I heard somebody laugh in the room and then the tears came to my eyes. I started down the steps, whistling to keep from crying, I kept whistling to myself, *You going to need me, baby, one of these cold, rainy days.*

I read about Sonny's trouble in the spring. Little Grace died in the fall. She was a beautiful little girl. But she only lived a little over two years. She died of polio and she suffered. She had a slight fever for a couple of days, but it didn't seem like anything and we just kept her in bed. And we would certainly have called the doctor, but the fever dropped, she seemed to be all right. So we thought it had just been a cold. Then, one day, she was up, playing, Isabel was in the kitchen fixing lunch for the two boys when they'd come in from school, and she heard Grace fall down in the living room. When you have a lot of children you don't always start running when one of them falls, unless they start screaming or something. And, this time, Grace was quiet. Yet, Isabel says that when she heard that *thump* and then that silence, something happened in her to make her afraid. And she ran to the living room and there was little Grace on the floor, all twisted up, and the reason she hadn't screamed was that she couldn't get her breath. And when she did scream, it was the worst sound, Isabel says, that she'd ever heard in all her life, and she still hears it sometimes in her dreams. Isabel will sometimes wake me up with a low, moaning, strangled sound and I have to be quick to awaken her and hold her to me and where Isabel is weeping against me seems a mortal wound.

I think I may have written Sonny the very day that little Grace was buried. I was sitting in the living room in the dark, by myself, and I suddenly thought of Sonny. My trouble made his real.

One Saturday afternoon, when Sonny had been living with us, or, anyway, been in our house, for nearly two weeks, I found myself wandering aimlessly about the living room, drinking from a can of beer, and trying to work up the courage to search Sonny's room. He was out, he was usually out whenever I was home, and Isabel had taken the children to see their grandparents. Suddenly I was standing still in front of the living room window, watching Seventh Avenue. The idea of searching Sonny's room made me still. I scarcely dared to admit to myself what I'd be searching for. I didn't know what I'd do if I found it. Or if I didn't.

On the sidewalk across from me, near the entrance to a barbecue joint, some people were holding an old-fashioned revival meeting. The barbecue cook, wearing a dirty white apron, his conked hair reddish and metallic in the pale sun, and a cigarette between his lips, stood in the doorway, watching them. Kids and older people paused in their errands and stood there, along with some older men and a couple of very tough-looking women who watched everything that happened on the avenue, as though they owned it, or were maybe owned by it. Well, they were watching this, too. The revival was being carried on by three sisters in black, and a brother. All they had were their voices and their Bibles and a tambourine. The brother was testifying and while he testified two of the sisters stood together, seeming to say, amen, and the third sister walked around with the tambourine outstretched and a couple of people dropped coins into it. Then the brother's testimony ended and the sister who had been taking up the collection dumped the coins into her palm and transferred them to the pocket of her long black robe. Then she raised both hands, striking the tambourine against the air, and then against one hand, and she started to sing. And the two other sisters and the brother joined in.

It was strange, suddenly, to watch, though I had been seeing these street meetings all my life. So, of course, had everybody else down there. Yet, they paused and watched and listened and I stood still at the window. *"Tis the old ship of Zion,"* they sang, and the sister with the tambourine kept a steady, jangling beat, *"it has rescued many a thousand!"* Not a soul under the sound of their voices was hearing this song for the first time, not one of them had been rescued. Nor had they seen much in the way of rescue work being done around them. Neither did they especially believe in the holiness of the three sisters and the brother, they knew too much about them, knew where they lived, and how. The woman with the tambourine, whose voice dominated the air, whose face was bright with joy, was divided by very little from the woman who stood watching her, a cigarette between her heavy, chapped lips, her hair a cuckoo's nest, her face scarred and swollen from many beatings, and her black eyes glittering like coal. Perhaps they both knew this, which was why, when, as rarely, they addressed each other, they addressed each other as Sister. As the singing filled the air the watching, listening faces underwent a change, the eyes focusing on something within; the music seemed to soothe a poison out of them; and time seemed, nearly, to fall away from the sullen, belligerent, battered faces, as though they were fleeing back to their first condition, while dreaming of their last. The barbecue cook half shook his head and smiled, and dropped his cigarette and disappeared into his joint. A man fumbled in his pockets for change and stood holding it in his hand impatiently, as though he had just remembered a pressing appointment further up the avenue. He looked furious. Then I saw Sonny, standing on the edge of the crowd. He was carrying a wide, flat notebook with a green cover, and it made him look, from where I was standing, almost like a schoolboy. The coppery sun brought out the copper in his skin, he was very faintly smiling, standing very still. Then the singing stopped, the tambourine turned into a collection plate again. The furious man dropped in his coins and vanished, so did a couple of the women, and Sonny dropped some change in the plate, looking directly at the woman with a little smile. He started across the avenue, toward the house. He has a slow, loping walk, something like the way Harlem hipsters walk, only he's imposed on this his own half-beat. I had never really noticed it before.

I stayed at the window, both relieved and apprehensive. As Sonny disappeared from my sight, they began singing again. And they were still singing when his key turned in the lock.

"Hey," he said.

"Hey, yourself. You want some beer?"

"No. Well, maybe." But he came up to the window and stood beside me, looking out. "What a warm voice," he said.

They were singing *If I could only hear my mother pray again!*

"Yes," I said, "and she can sure beat that tambourine."

"But what a terrible song," he said, and laughed. He dropped his notebook on the sofa and disappeared into the kitchen. "Where's Isabel and the kids?"

"I think they went to see their grandparents. You hungry?"

"No." He came back into the living room with his can of beer. "You want to come some place with me tonight?"

I sensed, I don't know how, that I couldn't possibly say no. "Sure. Where?"

He sat down on the sofa and picked up his notebook and started leafing through it. "I'm going to sit in with some fellows in a joint in the Village."

"You mean, you're going to play, tonight?"

"That's right." He took a swallow of his beer and moved back to the window. He gave me a sidelong look. "If you can stand it."

"I'll try," I said.

He smiled to himself and we both watched as the meeting across the way broke up. The three sisters and the brother, heads bowed, were singing *God be with you till we meet again*. The faces around them were very quiet. Then the song ended. The small crowd dispersed. We watched the three women and the lone man walk slowly up the avenue.

"When she was singing before," said Sonny, abruptly, "her voice reminded me for a minute of what heroin feels like sometimes — when it's in your veins. It makes you feel sort of warm and cool at the same time. And distant. And — and sure." He sipped his beer, very deliberately not looking at me. I watched his face. "It makes you feel — in control. Sometimes you've got to have that feeling."

"Do you?" I sat down slowly in the easy chair.

"Sometimes." He went to the sofa and picked up his notebook again. "Some people do."

"In order," I asked, "to play?" And my voice was very ugly, full of contempt and anger.

"Well" — he looked at me with great, troubled eyes, as though, in fact, he hoped his eyes would tell me things he could never otherwise say — "they *think* so. And *if* they think so — !"

"And what do *you* think?" I asked.

He sat on the sofa and put his can of beer on the floor. "I don't know," he said, and I couldn't be sure if he were answering my question or pursuing his thoughts. His face didn't tell me. "It's not so much to *play*. It's to *stand* it, to be able to make it at all. On any level." He frowned and smiled: "In order to keep from shaking to pieces."

"But these friends of yours," I said, "they seem to shake themselves to pieces pretty goddamn fast."

"Maybe." He played with the notebook. And something told me that I should curb my tongue, that Sonny was doing his best to talk, that I should listen. "But of course you only know the ones that've gone to pieces. Some don't — or at least they haven't *yet* and that's just about all *any* of us can say." He paused. "And then there are some who just live, really, in hell, and they know it and they see what's happening and they go right on. I don't know."

He sighed, dropped the notebook, folded his arms. "Some guys, you can tell from the way they play, they on something *all* the time. And you can see that, well, it makes something real for them. But of course," he picked up his beer from the floor and sipped it and put the can down again, "they *want* to, too, you've got to see that. Even some of them that say they don't — *some,* not all."

"And what about you?" I asked — I couldn't help it. "What about you? Do *you* want to?"

He stood up and walked to the window and remained silent for a long time. Then he sighed. "Me," he said. Then: "While I was downstairs before, on my way here, listening to that woman sing, it struck me all of a sudden how much suffering she must have had to go through — to sing like that. It's *repulsive* to think you have to suffer that much."

I said: "But there's no way not to suffer — is there, Sonny?"

"I believe not," he said and smiled, "but that's never stopped anyone from trying." He looked at me. "Has it?" I realized, with this mocking look, that there stood between us, forever, beyond the power of time or forgiveness, the fact that I had held silence — so long! — when he had needed human speech to help him. He turned back to the window. "No, there's no way not to suffer. But you try all kinds of ways to keep from drowning in it, to keep on top of it, and to make it seem — well, like *you.* Like you did something, all right, and now you're suffering for it. You know?" I said nothing. "Well you know," he said, impatiently, "why *do* people suffer? Maybe it's better to do something to give it a reason, *any* reason."

"But we just agreed," I said, "that there's no way not to suffer. Isn't it better, then, just to — take it?"

"But nobody just takes it," Sonny cried, "that's what I'm telling you! *Everybody* tries not to. You're just hung up on the *way* some people try — it's not *your* way!"

The hair on my face began to itch, my face felt wet. "That's not true," I said, "that's not true. I don't give a damn what other people do, I don't even care how they suffer. I just care how *you* suffer." And he looked at me. "Please believe me," I said, "I don't want to see you — die — trying not to suffer."

"I won't," he said, flatly, "die trying not to suffer. At least, not any faster than anybody else."

"But there's no need," I said, trying to laugh, "is there? in killing yourself."

I wanted to say more, but I couldn't. I wanted to talk about will power and how life could be — well, beautiful. I wanted to say that it was all within; but was it? or, rather, wasn't that exactly the trouble? And I wanted to promise that I would never fail him again. But it would all have sounded — empty words and lies.

So I made the promise to myself and prayed that I would keep it.

"It's terrible sometimes, inside," he said, "that's what's the trouble. You walk these streets, black and funky and cold, and there's not really a living ass to talk to, and there's nothing shaking, and there's no way of getting it out — that storm inside. You can't talk it and you can't make love with it, and when you finally try to get with it and play it, you realize *nobody's* listening. So *you've* got to listen. You got to find a way to listen."

And then he walked away from the window and sat on the sofa again, as though all the wind had suddenly been knocked out of him. "Sometimes you'll do *anything* to play, even cut your mother's throat." He laughed and looked at me. "Or your brother's." Then he sobered. "Or your own." Then: "Don't worry. I'm all right now and I think I'll *be* all right. But I can't forget — where I've been. I don't mean just the physical place I've been, I mean where I've *been.* And *what* I've been."

"What have you been, Sonny?" I asked.

He smiled — but sat sideways on the sofa, his elbow resting on the back, his fingers playing with his mouth and chin, not looking at me. "I've been something I didn't recognize, didn't know I could be. Didn't know anybody could be." He stopped, looking inward, looking helplessly young, looking old. "I'm not talking about it now because I feel *guilty* or anything like that — maybe it would be better if I did, I don't know. Anyway, I can't really talk about it. Not to you, not to anybody," and now he turned and faced me. "Sometimes, you know, and it was actually when I was most *out* of the world, I felt that I was in it, that I was *with* it, really, and I could play or I didn't really have to *play,* it just came out of me, it was there. And I don't know how I played, thinking about it now, but I know I did awful things, those times, sometimes, to people. Or it wasn't that I *did* anything to them — it was that they weren't real." He picked up the beer can; it was empty; he rolled it between his palms: "And other times — well, I needed a fix, I needed to find a place to lean, I needed to clear a space to *listen* — and I couldn't find it, and I — went crazy, I did terrible things to *me,* I was terrible *for* me." He began pressing the beer can between his hands, I watched the metal begin to give. It glittered, as he played with it, like a knife, and I was afraid he would cut himself, but I said nothing. "Oh well. I can never tell you. I was all by myself at the bottom of something, stinking and sweating and crying and shaking, and I smelled it, you know? *my* stink, and I thought I'd die if I couldn't get away from it and yet, all the same, I knew that everything I was doing was just locking me in with it. And I didn't know," he paused, still flattening the beer can, "I didn't know, I still *don't* know, something kept telling me that maybe it was good to smell your own stink, but I didn't think that *that* was what I'd been trying to do — and — who can stand it?" and he abruptly dropped the ruined beer can, looking at me with a small, still smile, and then rose, walking to the window as though it were the lodestone rock. I watched his face, he watched the avenue. "I couldn't tell you when Mama died — but the reason I wanted to leave Harlem so bad was to get away from drugs. And then, when I ran away, that's what I was running from — really. When I came back, nothing had changed, *I* hadn't changed, I was just — older." And he stopped, drumming with his fingers on the windowpane. The sun had vanished, soon darkness would fall. I watched his face. "It can come again," he said, almost as though speaking to himself. Then he turned to me. "It can come again," he repeated. "I just want you to know that."

"All right," I said, at last. "So it can come again, All right."

He smiled, but the smile was sorrowful. "I had to try to tell you," he said.

"Yes," I said. "I understand that."

"You're my brother," he said, looking straight at me, and not smiling at all.

"Yes," I repeated, "yes. I understand that."

He turned back to the window, looking out. "All that hatred down there," he said, "all that hatred and misery and love. It's a wonder it doesn't blow the avenue apart."

We went to the only nightclub on a short, dark street, downtown. We squeezed through the narrow, chattering, jam-packed bar to the entrance of the big room, where the bandstand was. And we stood there for a moment, for the lights were very dim in this room and we couldn't see. Then, "Hello, boy," said a voice and an enormous black man, much older than Sonny or myself, erupted out of all that atmospheric lighting and put an arm around Sonny's shoulder. "I been sitting right here," he said, "waiting for you."

He had a big voice, too, and heads in the darkness turned toward us.

Sonny grinned and pulled a little away, and said, "Creole, this is my brother. I told you about him."

Creole shook my hand. "I'm glad to meet you, son," he said, and it was clear that he was glad to meet me *there,* for Sonny's sake. And he smiled, "You got a real musician in *your* family," and he took his arm from Sonny's shoulder and slapped him, lightly, affectionately, with the back of his hand.

"Well. Now I've heard it all," said a voice behind us. This was another musician, and a friend of Sonny's, a coal-black, cheerful-looking man, built close to the ground. He immediately began confiding to me, at the top of his lungs, the most terrible things about Sonny, his teeth gleaming like a lighthouse and his laugh coming up out of him like the beginning of an earthquake. And it turned out that everyone at the bar knew Sonny, or almost everyone; some were musicians, working there, or nearby, or not working, some were simply hangers-on, and some were there to hear Sonny play. I was introduced to all of them and they were all very polite to me. Yet, it was clear that, for them, I was only Sonny's brother. Here, I was in Sonny's world. Or, rather: his kingdom. Here, it was not even a question that his veins bore royal blood.

They were going to play soon and Creole installed me, by myself, at a table in a dark corner. Then I watched them, Creole, and the little black man, and Sonny, and the others, while they horsed around, standing just below the bandstand. The light from the bandstand spilled just a little short of them and, watching them laughing and gesturing and moving about, I had the feeling that they, nevertheless, were being most careful not to step into that circle of light too suddenly: that if they moved into the light too suddenly, without thinking, they would perish in flame. Then, while I watched, one of them, the small, black man, moved into the light and crossed the bandstand and started fooling around with his drums. Then — being funny and being, also, extremely ceremonious — Creole took Sonny by the arm and led him to the piano. A woman's voice called Sonny's name and a few hands started clapping. And Sonny, also being funny and being ceremonious, and so touched, I think, that he could have cried, but neither hiding it nor showing it, riding it like a man, grinned, and put both hands to his heart and bowed from the waist.

Creole then went to the bass fiddle and a lean, very bright-skinned brown man jumped up on the bandstand and picked up his horn. So there they were, and the atmosphere on the bandstand and in the room began to change and tighten. Someone stepped up to the microphone and announced them. Then there were all kinds of murmurs. Some people at the bar shushed others. The waitress ran around, frantically getting in the last orders, guys and chicks got closer to each other, and the lights on the bandstand, on the quartet, turned to a kind of indigo. Then they all looked different there. Creole looked about him for the last time, as though he were making certain that all his chickens were in the coop, and then he — jumped and struck the fiddle. And there they were.

All I know about music is that not many people ever really hear it. And even then, on the rare occasions when something opens within, and the music enters, what we mainly hear, or hear corroborated, are personal, private, vanishing evocations. But the man who creates the music is hearing something else, is dealing with the roar rising from the void and imposing order on it as it hits the air. What is evoked in him, then, is of another order, more terrible because it has no words, and triumphant, too, for that same reason. And his triumph, when he triumphs, is ours. I just watched Sonny's face. His face was troubled, he was working hard, but he wasn't with it. And I had the feeling that, in a way, everyone on the bandstand was waiting for him, both waiting for him and pushing him along. But as I began to watch Creole, I realized that it was Creole who held them all back. He had them on a short rein. Up there, keeping the beat with his whole body, wailing on the fiddle, with his eyes half closed, he was listening to everything, but he was listening to Sonny. He was having a dialogue with Sonny. He wanted Sonny to leave the shoreline and strike out for the deep water. He was Sonny's witness that deep water and drowning were not the same thing — he had been there, and he knew. And he wanted Sonny to know. He was waiting for Sonny to do the things on the keys which would let Creole know that Sonny was in the water.

And, while Creole listened, Sonny moved, deep within, exactly like someone in torment. I had never before thought of how awful the relationship must be between the musician and his instrument. He has to fill it, this instrument, with the breath of life, his own. He has to make it do what he wants it to do. And a piano is just a piano. It's made out of so much wood and wires and little hammers and big ones, and ivory. While there's only so much you can do with it, the only way to find this out is to try; to try and make it do everything.

And Sonny hadn't been near a piano for over a year. And he wasn't on much better terms with his life, not the life that stretched before him now. He and the piano stammered, started one way, got scared, stopped; started another way, panicked, marked time, started again; then seemed to have found a direction, panicked again, got stuck. And the face I saw on Sonny I'd never seen before. Everything had been burned out of it, and, at the same time, things usually hidden were being burned in, by the fire and fury of the battle which was occurring in him up there.

Yet, watching Creole's face as they neared the end of the first set, I had the feeling that something had happened, something I hadn't heard. Then they finished, there was scattered applause, and then, without an instant's warning, Creole started into something else, it was almost sardonic, it was *Am I Blue.* And, as though he commanded, Sonny began to play. Something began to happen. And Creole let out the reins. The dry, low, black man said something awful on the drums, Creole answered, and the drums talked back. Then the horn insisted, sweet and high, slightly detached perhaps, and Creole listened, commenting now and then, dry, and driving, beautiful and calm and old. Then they all came together again, and Sonny was part of the family again. I could tell this from his face. He seemed to have found, right there beneath his fingers, a damn brand-new piano. It seemed that he couldn't get over it. Then, for awhile, just being happy with Sonny, they seemed to be agreeing with him that brand-new pianos certainly were a gas.

Then Creole stepped forward to remind them that what they were playing was the blues. He hit something in all of them, he hit something in me, myself, and the music tightened and deepened, apprehension began to beat the air. Creole began to tell us what the blues were all about. They were not about anything very new. He and his boys up there were keeping it new, at the risk of ruin, destruction, madness, and death, in order to find new ways to make us listen. For, while the tale of how we suffer, and how we are delighted, and how we may triumph is never new, it always must be heard. There isn't any other tale to tell, it's the only light we've got in all this darkness.

And this tale, according to that face, that body, those strong hands on those strings, has another aspect in every country, and a new depth in every generation. Listen, Creole seemed to be saying, listen. Now these are Sonny's blues. He made the little black man on the drums know it, and the bright, brown man on the horn. Creole wasn't trying any longer to get Sonny in the water. He was wishing him Godspeed. Then he stepped back, very slowly, filling the air with the immense suggestion that Sonny speak for himself.

Then they all gathered around Sonny and Sonny played. Every now and again one of them seemed to say, amen. Sonny's fingers filled the air with life, his life. But that life contained so many others. And Sonny went all the way back, he really began with the spare, flat statement of the opening phrase of the song. Then he began to make it his. It was very beautiful because it wasn't hurried and it was no longer a lament. I seemed to hear with what burning he had made it his, with what burning we had yet to make it ours, how we could cease lamenting. Freedom lurked around us and I understood, at last, that he could help us to be free if we would listen, that he would never be free until we did. Yet, there was no battle in his face now. I heard what he had gone through, and would continue to go through until he came to rest in earth. He had made it his: that long line, of which we knew only Mama and Daddy. And he was giving it back, as everything must be given back, so that, passing through death, it can live forever. I saw my mother's face again, and felt, for the first time, how the stones of the road she had walked on must have bruised her feet. I saw the moonlit road where my father's brother died. And it brought something else back to me, and carried me past it. I saw my little girl again and felt Isabel's tears again, and I felt my own tears begin to rise. And I was yet aware that this was only a moment, that the world waited outside, as hungry as a tiger, and that trouble stretched above us, longer than the sky.

Then it was over. Creole and Sonny let out their breath, both soaking wet, and grinning. There was a lot of applause and some of it was real. In the dark, the girl came by and I asked her to take drinks to the bandstand. There was a long pause, while they talked up there in the indigo light and after awhile I saw the girl put a Scotch and milk on top of the piano for Sonny. He didn't seem to notice it, but just before they started playing again, he sipped from it and looked toward me, and nodded. Then he put it back on top of the piano. For me, then, as they began to play again, it glowed and shook above my brother's head like the very cup of trembling.

ꙮ

TONI CADE BAMBARA *(1939–1996) was born in New York City and grew up in Harlem and Bedford-Stuyvesant. As a child she began scribbling stories on the margins of her father's copies of the* New York Daily News *and the squares of thin white cardboard her mother's stockings came wrapped around. She has said of herself,*

> *I was raised by my family and community to be a combatant. Forays to the Apollo [Theater in Harlem] with my daddy and hanging tough on Speakers Corner with my mama taught me the power of the word, the importance of the resistance tradition, and the high standards our [black] community had regarding verbal performance. While my heart is a laughing gland and my favorite thing to be doing is laughing so hard I have to lower myself on the wall to keep from falling down, near that chamber is a blast furnace where a rifle pokes from the ribs.*

In high school and at Queens College, Bambara remembered that she "hogged the lit journal." She took writing courses and wrote novels, stories, plays, film scripts, operas, "you-name-its." After graduating from Queens, she worked various jobs and studied for her M.A. at the City College of New York while she wrote fiction in "the predawn in-betweens." She began to publish her stories, and in 1972 she collected them in her first book, Gorilla, My Love. *It wasn't until Bambara returned from a trip to Cuba in 1973 that she thought of herself as a writer: "There I learned what Langston Hughes and others, most especially my colleagues in the Neo-Black Arts Movement, had been teaching for years — that writing is a legitimate way, an important way, to participate in the empowerment of the community that names me." Her books of stories include* The Black Woman *(1970),* Tales and Stories for Black Folks *(1971), and* The Sea Birds Are Still Alive: Collected Stories *(1977). She has also published two novels,* The Salt Eaters *(1980) and* If Blessing Comes *(1987).*

Like Zora Neale Hurston, whom Bambara credited with giving her new ways to consider literary material (folkways as the basis of art) and new categories of perception (women's images), Bambara often used humor in her fiction. She said that "what I enjoy most in my work is the laughter and the outrage and the attention to language." Her stories, like "The Lesson," were often about children, but Bambara tried to avoid sentimentality. She attempted to keep her torrents of language and feeling under control by remembering the premises from which she proceeded as a black writer: "One, we are at war. Two, the natural response to oppression, ignorance, evil, and mystification is wide-awake resistance. Three, the natural response to stress and crisis is not breakdown and capitulation, but transformation and renewal."

Toni Cade Bambara

The Lesson

1972

Back in the days when everyone was old and stupid or young and foolish and me and Sugar were the only ones just right, this lady moved on our block with nappy hair and proper speech and no makeup. And quite naturally we laughed at her, laughed the way we did at the junk man who went about his business like he was some big-time president and his sorry-ass horse his secretary. And we kinda hated her too, hated the way we did the winos who cluttered up our parks and pissed on our handball walls and stank up our hallways and stairs so you couldn't halfway play hide-and-seek without a goddamn gas mask. Miss Moore was her name. The only woman on the block with no first name. And she was black as hell, cept for her feet, which were fish-white and spooky. And she was always planning these boring-ass things for us to do, us being my cousin, mostly, who lived on the block cause we all moved North the same time and to the same apartment then spread out gradual to breathe. And our parents would yank our heads into some kinda shape and crisp up our clothes so we'd be presentable for travel with Miss Moore, who always looked like she was going to church, though she never did. Which is just one of the things the grownups talked about when they talked behind her back like a dog. But when she came calling with some sachet she'd sewed up or some gingerbread she'd made or some book, why then they'd all be too embarrassed to turn her down and we'd get handed over all spruced up. She'd been to college and said it was only right that she should take responsibility for the young ones' education, and she not even related by marriage or blood. So they'd go for it. Specially Aunt Gretchen. She was the main gofer in the family. You got some ole dumb shit foolishness you want somebody to go for, you send for Aunt Gretchen. She been screwed into the go-along for so long, it's a blood-deep natural thing with her. Which is how she got saddled with me and Sugar and Junior in the first place while our mothers were in a la-de-da apartment up the block having a good ole time.

So this one day, Miss Moore rounds us all up at the mailbox and it's puredee hot and she's knockin herself out about arithmetic. And school suppose to let up in summer I heard, but she don't never let up. And the starch in my pinafore scratching the shit outta me and I'm really hating this nappy-head bitch and her goddamn college degree. I'd much rather go to the pool or to the show where it's cool. So me and Sugar leaning on the mailbox being surly, which is a Miss Moore word. And Flyboy checking out what everybody brought for lunch. And Fat Butt already wasting his peanut-butter-and-jelly sandwich like the pig he is. And Junebug punchin on Q.T.'s arm for potato chips. And Rosie Giraffe shifting from one hip to the other waiting for somebody to step on her foot or ask her if she from Georgia so she can kick ass, preferably Mercedes'. And Miss Moore asking us do we know what money is, like we a bunch of retards. I mean real money, she say, like it's only poker chips or monopoly papers we lay on the grocer. So right away I'm tired of this and say so. And would much rather snatch Sugar and go to the Sunset and terrorize the West Indian kids and take their hair ribbons and their money too. And Miss Moore files that remark away for next week's lesson on brotherhood, I can tell. And finally I say we oughta get to the subway cause it's cooler and besides we might meet some cute boys. Sugar done swiped her mama's lipstick, so we ready.

So we heading down the street and she's boring us silly about what things cost and what our parents make and how much goes for rent and how money ain't divided up right in this country. And then she gets to the part about we all poor and live in the slums, which I don't feature. And I'm ready to speak on that, but she steps out in the street and hails two cabs just like that. Then she hustles half the crew in with her and hands me a five-dollar bill and tells me to calculate 10 percent tip for the driver. And we're off. Me and Sugar and Junebug and Flyboy hangin out the window and hollering to everybody, putting lipstick on each other cause Flyboy a faggot anyway, and making farts with our sweaty armpits. But I'm mostly trying to figure how to spend this money. But they all fascinated with the meter ticking and Junebug starts laying bets as to how much it'll read when Flyboy can't hold his breath no more. Then Sugar lays bets as to how much it'll be when we get there. So I'm stuck. Don't nobody want to go for my plan, which is to jump out at the next light and run off to the first bar-b-que we can find. Then the driver tells us to get the hell out cause we there already. And the meter reads eighty-five cents. And I'm stalling to figure out the tip and Sugar say give him a dime. And I decide he don't need it bad as I do, so later for him. But then he tries to take off with Junebug foot still in the door so we talk about his mama something ferocious. Then we check out that we on Fifth Avenue and everybody dressed up in stockings. One lady in a fur coat, hot as it is. White folks crazy.

"This is the place," Miss Moore say, presenting it to us in the voice she uses at the museum. "Let's look in the windows before we go in."

"Can we steal?" Sugar asks very serious like she's getting the ground rules squared away before she plays. "I beg your pardon," say Miss Moore, and we fall out. So she leads us around the windows of the toy store and me and Sugar screamin, "This is mine, that's mine, I gotta have that, that was made for me, I was born for that," till Big Butt drowns us out.

"Hey, I'm going to buy that there."

"That there? You don't even know what it is, stupid."

"I do so," he say punchin on Rosie Giraffe. "It's a microscope."

"Whatcha gonna do with a microscope, fool?"

"Look at things."

"Like what, Ronald?" ask Miss Moore. And Big Butt ain't got the first notion. So here go Miss Moore gabbing about the thousands of bacteria in a drop of water and the somethinorother in a speck of blood and the million and one living things in the air around us is invisible to the naked eye. And what she say that for? Junebug go to town on that "naked" and we rolling. Then

Miss Moore ask what it cost. So we all jam into the window smudgin it up and the price tag say $300. So then she ask how long'd take for Big Butt and Junebug to save up their allowances. "Too long," I say. "Yeh," adds Sugar, "outgrown it by that time." And Miss Moore say no, you never outgrow learning instruments. "Why, even medical students and interns and," blah, blah, blah. And we ready to choke Big Butt for bringing it up in the first damn place.

"This here costs four hundred eighty dollars," say Rosie Giraffe. So we pile up all over her to see what she pointin out. My eyes tell me it's a chunk of glass cracked with something heavy, and different-color inks dripped into the splits, then the whole thing put into a oven or something. But for $480 it don't make sense.

"That's a paperweight made of semi-precious stones fused together under tremendous pressure," she explains slowly, with her hands doing the mining and all the factory work.

"So what's a paperweight?" ask Rosie Giraffe.

"To weigh paper with, dumbbell," say Flyboy, the wise man from the East.

"Not exactly," say Miss Moore, which is what she say when you warm or way off too. "It's to weigh paper down so it won't scatter and make your desk untidy." So right away me and Sugar curtsy to each other and then to Mercedes who is more the tidy type.

"We don't keep paper on top of the desk in my class," say Junebug, figuring Miss Moore crazy or lyin one.

"At home, then," she say. "Don't you have a calendar and a pencil case and a blotter and a letter-opener on your desk at home where you do your homework?" And she know damn well what our homes look like cause she nosys around in them every chance she gets.

"I don't even have a desk," say Junebug. "Do we?"

"No. And I don't get no homework neither," says Big Butt.

"And I don't even have a home," says Flyboy like he do at school to keep the white folks off his back and sorry for him. Send this poor kid to camp posters, is his specialty.

"I do," says Mercedes. "I have a box of stationery on my desk and a picture of my cat. My godmother bought the stationery and the desk. There's a big rose on each sheet and the envelopes smell like roses."

"Who wants to know about your smelly-ass stationery," say Rosie Giraffe fore I can get my two cents in.

"It's important to have a work area all your own so that . . ."

"Will you look at this sailboat, please," say Flyboy, cutting her off and pointin to the thing like it was his. So once again we tumble all over each other to gaze at this magnificent thing in the toy store which is just big enough to maybe sail two kittens across the pond if you strap them to the posts tight. We all start reciting the price tag like we in assembly. "Handcrafted sailboat of fiberglass at one thousand one hundred ninety-five dollars."

"Unbelievable," I hear myself say and am really stunned. I read it again for myself just in case the group recitation put me in a trance. Same thing. For some reason this pisses me off. We look at Miss Moore and she lookin at us, waiting for I dunno what.

"Who'd pay all that when you can buy a sailboat set for a quarter at Pop's, a tube of glue for a dime, and a ball of string for eight cents? It must have a motor and a whole lot else besides," I say. "My sailboat cost me about fifty cents."

"But will it take water?" say Mercedes with her smart ass.

"Took mine to Alley Pond Park once," say Flyboy. "String broke. Lost it. Pity."

"Sailed mine in Central Park and it keeled over and sank. Had to ask my father for another dollar."

"And you got the strap," laugh Big Butt. "The jerk didn't even have a string on it. My old man wailed on his behind."

Little Q.T. was staring hard at the sailboat and you could see he wanted it bad. But he too little and somebody'd just take it from him. So what the hell. "This boat for kids, Miss Moore?"

"Parents silly to buy something like that just to get all broke up," say Rosie Giraffe.

"That much money it should last forever," I figure.

"My father'd buy it for me if I wanted it."

"Your father, my ass," say Rosie Giraffe getting a chance to finally push Mercedes.

"Must be rich people shop here," say Q.T.

"You are a very bright boy," say Flyboy. "What was your first clue?" And he rap him on the head with the back of his knuckles, since Q.T. the only one he could get away with. Though Q.T. liable to come up behind you years later and get his licks in when you half expect it.

"What I want to know is," I says to Miss Moore though I never talk to her, I wouldn't give the bitch that satisfaction, "is how much a real boat costs? I figure a thousand'd get you a yacht any day."

"Why don't you check that out," she says, "and report back to the group?" Which really pains my ass. If you gonna mess up a perfectly good swim day least you could do is have some answers. "Let's go in," she say like she got something up her sleeve. Only she don't lead the way. So me and Sugar turn the corner to where the entrance is, but when we get there I kinda hang back. Not that I'm scared, what's there to be afraid of, just a toy store. But I feel funny, shame. But what I got to be shamed about? Got as much right to go in as anybody. But somehow I can't seem to get hold of the door, so I step away from Sugar to lead. But she hangs back too. And I look at her and she looks at me and this is ridiculous. I mean, damn, I have never been shy about doing nothing or going nowhere. But then Mercedes steps up and then Rosie Giraffe and Big Butt crowd in behind and shove, and next thing we all stuffed into the doorway with only Mercedes squeezing past us, smoothing out her jumper and walking right down the aisle. Then the rest of us tumble in like a glued-together jigsaw done all wrong. And people lookin at us. And it's like the time me and Sugar crashed into the Catholic church on a dare. But once we got in there and everything so hushed and holy and the candles and the bowin and the handkerchiefs on all the drooping heads, I just couldn't go through with the plan. Which was for me to run up to the altar and do a tap dance while Sugar played the nose flute and messed around in the holy water. And Sugar kept givin me the elbow. Then later teased me so bad I tied her up in the shower and turned it on and locked her in. And she'd be there till this day if Aunt Gretchen hadn't finally figured I was lying about the boarder takin a shower.

Same thing in the store. We all walkin on tiptoe and hardly touchin the games and puzzles and things. And I watched Miss Moore who is steady watchin us like she waitin for a sign. Like Mama Drewery watches the sky and sniffs the air and takes note of just how much slant is in the bird formation. Then me and Sugar bump smack into each other, so busy gazing at the toys, 'specially the sailboat. But we don't laugh and go into our fat-lady bump-stomach routine. We just stare at that price tag. Then Sugar run a finger over the whole boat. And I'm jealous and want to hit her. Maybe not her, but I sure want to punch somebody in the mouth.

"Watcha bring us here for, Miss Moore?"

"You sound angry, Sylvia. Are you mad about something?" Givin me one of them grins like she tellin a grown-up joke that never turns out to be funny. And she's lookin very closely at me like maybe she plannin to do my portrait from memory. I'm mad, but I won't give her that satisfaction. So I slouch around the store being very bored and say, "Let's go."

Me and Sugar at the back of the train watchin the tracks whizzin by large then small then getting gobbled up in the dark. I'm thinkin about this tricky toy I saw in the store. A clown that somersaults on a bar then does chin-ups just cause you yank lightly at his leg. Cost $35. I could see me askin my mother for a $35 birthday clown. "You wanna who that costs what?" she'd say, cocking her head to the side to get a better view of the hole in my head. Thirty-five dollars could buy new bunk beds for Junior and Gretchen's boy. Thirty-five dollars and the whole household could go visit Granddaddy Nelson in the country. Thirty-five dollars would pay for the rent and the piano bill too. Who are these people that spend that much for performing clowns and $1000 for toy sailboats? What kinda work they do and how they live and how come we ain't in on it? Where we are is who we are, Miss Moore always pointin out. But it don't necessarily have to be that way, she always adds then waits for somebody to say that poor people have to wake up and demand their share of the pie and don't none of us know what kind of pie she talking about in the first damn place. But she ain't so smart cause I still got her four dollars from the taxi and she sure ain't gettin it. Messin up my day with this shit. Sugar nudges me in my pocket and winks.

Miss Moore lines us up in front of the mailbox where we started from, seem like years ago, and I got a headache for thinkin so hard. And we lean all over each other so we can hold up under the draggy-ass lecture she always finishes us off with at the end before we thank her for borin us to tears. But she just looks at us like she readin tea leaves. Finally she say, "Well, what did you think of F.A.O. Schwarz?"

Rosie Giraffe mumbles, "White folks crazy."

"I'd like to go there again when I get my birthday money," says Mercedes, and we shove her out the pack so she has to lean on the mailbox by herself.

"I'd like a shower. Tiring day," say Flyboy.

Then Sugar surprises me by sayin, "You know, Miss Moore, I don't think all of us here put together eat in a year what that sailboat costs." And Miss Moore lights up like somebody goosed her "And?" she say, urging Sugar on. Only I'm standin on her foot so she don't continue.

"Imagine for a minute what kind of society it is in which some people can spend on a toy what it would cost to feed a family of six or seven. What do you think?"

"I think," say Sugar pushing me off her feet like she never done before, cause I whip her ass in a minute, "that this is not much of a democracy if you ask me. Equal chance to pursue happiness means an equal crack at the dough, don't it?" Miss Moore is besides herself and I am disgusted with Sugar's treachery. So I stand on her foot one more time to see if she'll shove me. She shuts up, and Miss Moore looks at me, sorrowfully I'm thinkin. And somethin weird is goin on, I can feel it in my chest.

"Anybody else learn anything today?" lookin dead at me. I walk away and Sugar has to run to catch up and don't even seem to notice when I shrug her arm off my shoulder.

"Well, we got four dollars anyway," she says.

"Uh, hunh."

"We could go to Hascombs and get half a chocolate layer and then go to the Sunset and still have plenty money for potato chips and ice cream sodas."

"Uh, hunh."

"Race you to Hascombs," she say.

We start down the block and she gets ahead which is O.K. by me cause I'm going to the West End and then over to the Drive to think this day through. She can run if she want to and even run faster. But ain't nobody gonna beat me at nuthin.

ꙮ

AMBROSE BIERCE *(1842–1914?), the youngest of nine children, was born in a log cabin in Horse Cave Creek, Ohio. His father was a farmer, and Bierce had only one year of formal education at the Kentucky Military Institute when he was seventeen. During the Civil War he enlisted with the Ninth Indiana Infantry as a drummer boy. Wounded in 1864, he left the army and went to live with a brother in San Francisco. There he began his career as a newspaper writer, publishing his first story, "The Haunted Valley," in the* Overland Magazine *in 1871. When Bierce married the daughter of a wealthy Nevada miner, his father-in-law gave the young couple a wedding gift of $10,000, enabling them to live in London for five years. Homesick for California, Bierce returned with his wife and wrote for various newspapers, including William Randolph Hearst's* San Francisco Examiner. *In the 1880s he became very influential in his profession, although in literary circles outside California he was not widely known. Then his wife separated from him, his two sons died tragically, and he became embittered. In his seventies Bierce supervised publication of the twelve volumes of his* Collected Works, *revisited the Civil War battlefields of his youth, and* *then disappeared across the Mexican border. The Mexican writer Carlos Fuentes imagined Bierce's last months in the novel* The Old Gringo *(1985), which was made into a film.*

Bierce is known as the author of the philosophical epigrams in The Devil's Dictionary *(1906), but his two volumes of short stories are his finest achievement as a writer. He is considered a notable forerunner of American realists such as Stephen Crane. "An Occurrence at Owl Creek Bridge" was included in Bierce's first story collection,* In the Midst of Life, *published privately in San Francisco under the title* Tales of Soldiers and Civilians *(1891). His second collection,* Can Such Things Be? *was published two years later.*

Bierce preferred the short story to the novel, defining the novel as a "short story padded." He modeled his creation of suspense leading up to a dramatic crisis after the stories of Edgar Allan Poe, but Bierce described more realistic situations in his fiction. Dreams, flashbacks, and hallucinations, as in "An Occurrence at Owl Creek Bridge," provided vivid images but no escape from the violent death that was Bierce's obsession.

AMBROSE BIERCE

An Occurrence at Owl Creek Bridge

1891

I

A man stood upon a railroad bridge in Northern Alabama, looking down into the swift waters twenty feet below. The man's hands were behind his back, the wrists bound with a cord. A rope loosely encircled his neck. It was attached to a stout cross-timber above his head, and the slack fell to the level of his knees. Some loose boards laid upon the sleepers supporting the metals of the railway supplied a footing for him and his executioners — two private soldiers of the Federal army, directed by a sergeant, who in civil life may have been a deputy sheriff. At a short remove upon the same temporary platform was an officer in the uniform of his rank, armed. He was a captain. A sentinel at each end of the bridge stood with his rifle in the position known as "support," that is to say, vertical in front of the left shoulder, the hammer resting on the forearm thrown straight across the chest — a formal and unnatural position, enforcing an erect carriage of the body. It did not appear to be the duty of these two men to know what was occurring at the centre of the bridge; they merely blockaded the two ends of the foot plank which traversed it.

Beyond one of the sentinels nobody was in sight; the railroad ran straight away into a forest for a hundred yards, then, curving, was lost to view. Doubtless there was an outpost further along. The other bank of the stream was open ground — a gentle acclivity crowned with a stockade of vertical tree trunks, loop-holed for rifles, with a single embrasure through which protruded the muzzle of a brass cannon commanding the bridge. Midway of the slope between bridge and fort were the spectators — a single company of infantry in line, at "parade rest," the butts of the rifles on the ground, the barrels inclining slightly backward against the right shoulder, the hands crossed upon the stock. A lieutenant stood at the right of the line, the point of his sword upon the ground, his left hand resting upon his right. Excepting the group of four at the centre of the bridge not a man moved. The company faced the bridge, staring stonily, motionless. The sentinels, facing the banks of the stream, might have been statues to adorn the bridge. The captain stood with folded arms, silent, observing the work of his subordinates but making no sign. Death is a dignitary who, when he comes announced, is to be received with formal manifestations of respect, even by those most familiar with him. In the code of military etiquette silence and fixity are forms of deference.

The man who was engaged in being hanged was apparently about thirty-five years of age. He was a civilian, if one might judge from his dress, which was that of a planter. His features were good — a straight nose, firm mouth, broad forehead, from which his long, dark hair was combed straight back, falling behind his ears to the collar of his well-fitted frock coat. He wore a moustache and pointed beard, but no whiskers; his eyes were large and dark grey and had a kindly expression which one would hardly have expected in one whose neck was in the hemp. Evidently this was no vulgar assassin. The liberal military code makes provision for hanging many kinds of people, and gentlemen are not excluded.

The preparations being complete, the two private soldiers stepped aside and each drew away the plank upon which he had been standing. The sergeant turned to the captain, saluted and placed himself immediately behind that officer, who in turn moved apart one pace. These movements left the condemned man and the sergeant standing on the two ends of the same plank, which spanned three of the cross-ties of the bridge. The end upon which the civilian stood almost, but not quite, reached a fourth. This plank had been held in place by the weight of the captain; it was now held by that of the sergeant. At a signal from the former, the latter would step aside, the plank would tilt and the condemned man go down between two ties. The arrangement commended itself to his judgment as simple and effective. His face had not been covered nor his eyes bandaged. He looked a moment at his "unsteadfast footing," then let his gaze wander to the swirling water of the stream racing madly beneath his feet. A piece of dancing driftwood caught his attention and his eyes followed it down the current. How slowly it appeared to move! What a sluggish stream!

He closed his eyes in order to fix his last thoughts upon his wife and children. The water, touched to gold by the early sun, the brooding mists under the banks at some distance down the stream, the fort, the soldiers, the piece of drift — all had distracted him. And now he became conscious of a new disturbance. Striking through the thought of his dear ones was a sound which he could neither ignore nor understand, a sharp, distinct, metallic percussion like the stroke of a blacksmith's hammer upon the anvil; it had the same ringing quality. He wondered what it was, and whether immeasurably distant or near by — it seemed both. Its recurrence was regular, but as slow as the tolling of a death knell. He awaited each stroke with impatience and — he knew not why — apprehension. The intervals of silence grew progressively longer; the delays became maddening. With their greater infrequency the sounds increased in strength and sharpness. They hurt his ear like the thrust of a knife; he feared he would shriek. What he heard was the ticking of his watch.

He unclosed his eyes and saw again the water below him. "If I could free my hands," he thought, "I might throw off the noose and spring into the stream. By diving I could evade the bullets, and, swimming vigorously, reach the bank, take to the woods, and get away home. My home, thank God, is as yet outside their lines; my wife and little ones are still beyond the invader's farthest advance."

As these thoughts, which have here to be set down in words, were flashed into the doomed man's brain rather than evolved from it, the captain nodded to the sergeant. The sergeant stepped aside.

II

Peyton Farquhar was a well-to-do planter, of an old and highly-respected Alabama family. Being a slave owner, and, like other slave owners, a politician, he was naturally an original secessionist and ardently devoted to the Southern cause. Circumstances of an imperious nature which it is unnecessary to relate here, had prevented him from taking service with the gallant army which had fought the disastrous campaigns ending with the fall of Corinth, and he chafed under the inglorious restraint, longing for the release of his energies, the larger life of the soldier, the opportunity for distinction. That opportunity, he felt, would come, as it comes to all in war time. Meanwhile he did what he could. No service was too humble for him to perform in aid of the South, no adventure too perilous for him to undertake if consistent with the character of a civilian who was at heart a soldier, and who in good faith and without too much qualification assented to at least a part of the frankly villainous dictum that all is fair in love and war.

One evening while Farquhar and his wife were sitting on a rustic bench near the entrance to his grounds, a grey-clad soldier rode up to the gate and asked for a drink of water. Mrs. Farquhar was only too happy to serve him with her own white hands. While she was gone to fetch the water, her husband approached the dusty horseman and inquired eagerly for news from the front.

"The Yanks are repairing the railroads," said the man, "and are getting ready for another advance. They have reached the Owl Creek bridge, put it in order, and built a stockade on the other bank. The commandant has issued an order, which is posted everywhere, declaring that any civilian caught interfering with the railroad, its bridges, tunnels, or trains, will be summarily hanged. I saw the order."

"How far is it to the Owl Creek bridge?" Farquhar asked.

"About thirty miles."

"Is there no force on this side the creek?"

"Only a picket post half a mile out, on the railroad, and a single sentinel at this end of the bridge."

"Suppose a man — a civilian and student of hanging — should elude the picket post and perhaps get the better of the sentinel," said Farquhar, smiling, "what could he accomplish?"

The soldier reflected. "I was there a month ago," he replied. "I observed that the flood of last winter had lodged a great quantity of driftwood against the wooden pier at this end of the bridge. It is now dry and would burn like tow."

The lady had now brought the water, which the soldier drank. He thanked her ceremoniously, bowed to her husband, and rode away. An hour later, after nightfall, he repassed the plantation, going northward in the direction from which he had come. He was a Federal scout.

III

As Peyton Farquhar fell straight downward through the bridge, he lost consciousness and was as one already dead. From this state he was awakened — ages later, it seemed to him — by the pain of a sharp pressure upon his throat, followed by a sense of suffocation. Keen, poignant agonies seemed to shoot from his neck downward through every fibre of his body and limbs. These pains appeared to flash along well-defined lines of ramification, and to beat with an inconceivably rapid periodicity. They seemed like streams of pulsating fire heating him to an intolerable temperature. As to his head, he was conscious of nothing but a feeling of fullness — of congestion. These sensations were unaccompanied by thought. The intellectual part of his nature was already effaced; he had power only to feel, and feeling was torment. He was conscious of motion. Encompassed in a luminous cloud, of which he was now merely the fiery heart, without material substance, he swung through unthinkable arcs of oscillation, like a vast pendulum. Then all at once, with terrible suddenness, the light about him shot upward with the noise of a loud plash; a frightful roaring was in his ears, and all was cold and dark. The power of thought was restored; he knew that the rope had broken and he had fallen into the stream. There was no additional strangulation; the noose about his neck was already suffocating him, and kept the water from his lungs. To die of hanging at the bottom of a river — the idea seemed to him ludicrous. He opened his eyes in the blackness and saw above him a gleam of light, but how distant, how inaccessible! He was still sinking, for the light became fainter and fainter until it was a mere glimmer. Then it began to grow and brighten, and he knew that he was rising toward the surface — knew it with reluctance, for he was now very comfortable. "To be hanged and drowned," he thought, "that is not so bad; but I do not wish to be shot. No; I will not be shot; that is not fair."

He was not conscious of an effort, but a sharp pain in his wrist apprised him that he was trying to free his hands. He gave the struggle his attention, as an idler might observe the feat of a juggler, without interest in the outcome. What splendid effort! — what magnificent, what superhuman strength! Ah, that was a fine endeavor! Bravo! The cord fell away; his arms parted and floated upward, the hands dimly seen on each side in the growing light. He watched them with a new interest as first one and then the other pounced upon the noose at his neck. They tore it away and thrust it fiercely aside, its undulations resembling those of a water-snake. "Put it back, put it back!" He thought he shouted these words to his hands, for the undoing of the noose had been succeeded by the direst pang which he had yet experienced. His neck ached horribly; his brain was on fire; his heart, which had been fluttering faintly, gave a great leap, trying to force itself out at his mouth. His whole body was racked and wrenched with an insupportable anguish! But his disobedient hands gave no heed to the command. They beat the water vigorously with quick, downward strokes, forcing him to the surface. He felt his head emerge; his eyes were blinded by the sunlight; his chest expanded convulsively, and with a supreme and crowning agony his lungs engulfed a great draught of air, which instantly he expelled in a shriek!

He was now in full possession of his physical senses. They were, indeed, preternaturally keen and alert. Something in the awful disturbance of his organic system had so exalted and refined them that they made record of things never before perceived. He felt the ripples upon his face and heard their separate sounds as they struck. He looked at the forest on the bank of the stream, saw the individual trees, the leaves and the veining of each leaf — saw the very insects upon them, the locusts, the brilliant-bodied flies, the grey spiders stretching their webs from twig to twig. He noted the prismatic colors in all the dewdrops upon a million blades of grass. The humming of the gnats that danced above the eddies of the stream, the beating of the dragon flies' wings, the strokes of the water spiders' legs, like oars which had lifted their boat — all these made audible music. A fish slid along beneath his eyes and he heard the rush of its body parting the water.

He had come to the surface facing down the stream; in a moment the visible world seemed to wheel slowly round, himself the pivotal point, and he saw the bridge, the fort, the soldiers upon the bridge, the captain, the sergeant, the two privates, his executioners. They were in silhouette against the blue sky. They shouted and gesticulated, pointing at him; the captain had drawn his pistol, but did not fire; the others were unarmed. Their movements were grotesque and horrible, their forms gigantic.

Suddenly he heard a sharp report and something struck the water smartly within a few inches of his head, spattering his face with spray. He heard a second report, and saw one of the sentinels with his rifle at his shoulder, a light cloud of blue smoke rising from the muzzle. The man in the water saw the eye of the man on the bridge gazing into his own through the sights of the rifle. He observed that it was a grey eye, and remembered having read that grey eyes were keenest and that all famous marksmen had them. Nevertheless, this one had missed.

A counter swirl had caught Farquhar and turned him half round; he was again looking into the forest on the bank opposite the fort. The sound of a clear, high voice in a monotonous singsong now rang out behind him and came across the water with a distinctness that pierced and subdued all other sounds, even the beating of the ripples in his ears. Although no soldier, he had frequented camps enough to know the dread significance of that deliberate, drawling, aspirated chant; the lieutenant on shore was taking a part in the morning's work. How coldly and pitilessly — with what an even, calm intonation, presaging and enforcing tranquility in the men — with what accurately-measured intervals fell those cruel words:

"Attention, company. . . . Shoulder arms. . . . Ready. . . . Aim. . . . Fire."

Farquhar dived — dived as deeply as he could. The water roared in his ears like the voice of Niagara, yet he heard the dulled thunder of the volley, and rising again toward the surface, met shining bits of metal, singularly flattened, oscillating slowly downward. Some of them touched him on the face and hands, then fell away, continuing their descent. One lodged between his collar and neck; it was uncomfortably warm, and he snatched it out.

As he rose to the surface, gasping for breath, he saw that he had been a long time under water; he was perceptibly farther down stream — nearer to safety. The soldiers had almost finished reloading; the metal ramrods flashed all at once in the sunshine as they were drawn from the barrels, turned in the air, and thrust into their sockets. The two sentinels fired again, independently and ineffectually.

The hunted man saw all this over his shoulder; he was now swimming vigorously with the current. His brain was as energetic as his arms and legs; he thought with the rapidity of lightning.

"The officer," he reasoned, "will not make the martinet's error a second time. It is as easy to dodge a volley as a single shot. He has probably already given the command to fire at will. God help me, I cannot dodge them all!"

An appalling plash within two yards of him, followed by a loud rushing sound, *diminuendo,* which seemed to travel back through the air to the fort and died in an explosion which stirred the very river to its deeps! A rising sheet of water, which curved over him, fell down upon him, blinded him, strangled him! The cannon had taken a hand in the game. As he shook his head free from the commotion of the smitten water, he heard the deflected shot humming through the air ahead, and in an instant it was cracking and smashing the branches in the forest beyond.

"They will not do that again," he thought; "the next time they will use a charge of grape. I must keep my eye upon the gun; the smoke will apprise me — the report arrives too late; it lags behind the missile. It is a good gun."

Suddenly he felt himself whirled round and round — spinning like a top. The water, the banks, the forest, the now distant bridge, fort, and men — all were commingled and blurred. Objects were represented by their colors only; circular horizontal streaks of color — that was all he saw. He had been caught in a vortex and was being whirled on with a velocity of advance and gyration which made him giddy and sick. In a few moments he was flung upon the gravel at the foot of the left bank of the stream — the southern bank — and behind a projecting point which concealed him from his enemies. The sudden arrest of his motion, the abrasion of one of his hands on the gravel, restored him and he wept with delight. He dug his fingers into the sand, threw it over himself in handfuls and audibly blessed it. It looked like gold, like diamonds, rubies, emeralds; he could think of nothing beautiful which it did not resemble. The trees upon the bank were giant garden plants; he noted a definite order in their arrangement, inhaled the fragrance of their blooms. A strange, roseate light shone through the spaces among their trunks, and the wind made in their branches the music of æolian harps. He had no wish to perfect his escape, was content to remain in that enchanting spot until retaken.

A whizz and rattle of grapeshot among the branches high above his head roused him from his dream. The baffled cannoneer had fired him a random farewell. He sprang to his feet, rushed up the sloping bank, and plunged into the forest.

All that day he travelled, laying his course by the rounding sun. The forest seemed interminable; nowhere did he discover a break in it, not even a woodman's road. He had not known that he lived in so wild a region. There was something uncanny in the revelation.

By nightfall he was fatigued, footsore, famishing. The thought of his wife and children urged him on. At last he found a road which led him in what he knew to be the right direction. It was as wide and straight as a city street, yet it seemed untravelled. No fields bordered it, no dwelling anywhere. Not so much as the barking of a dog suggested human habitation. The black bodies of the great trees formed a straight wall on both sides, terminating on the horizon in a point, like a diagram in a lesson in perspective. Overhead, as he looked up through this rift in the wood, shone great golden stars looking unfamiliar and grouped in strange constellations. He was sure they were arranged in some order which had a secret and malign significance. The wood on either side was full of singular noises, among which — once, twice, and again — he distinctly heard whispers in an unknown tongue.

His neck was in pain, and, lifting his hand to it, he found it horribly swollen. He knew that it had a circle of black where the rope had bruised it. His eyes felt congested; he could no longer close them. His tongue was swollen with thirst; he relieved its fever by thrusting it forward from between his teeth into the cool air. How softly the turf had carpeted the untravelled avenue! He could no longer feel the roadway beneath his feet!

Doubtless, despite his suffering, he fell asleep while walking, for now he sees another scene — perhaps he has merely recovered from a delirium. He stands at the gate of his own home. All is as he left it, and all bright and beautiful in the morning sunshine. He must have travelled the entire night. As he pushes open the gate and passes up the wide white walk, he sees a flutter of female garments; his wife, looking fresh and cool and sweet, steps down from the verandah to meet him. At the bottom of the steps she stands waiting, with a smile of ineffable joy, an attitude of matchless grace and dignity. Ah, how beautiful she is! He springs forward with extended arms. As he is about to clasp her, he feels a stunning blow upon the back of the neck; a blinding white light blazes all about him, with a sound like a shock of a cannon — then all is darkness and silence!

Peyton Farquhar was dead; his body, with a broken neck, swung gently from side to side beneath the timbers of the Owl Creek bridge.

ꙮ

RAYMOND CARVER *(1938–1988) grew up in a logging town in Oregon, where his father worked in a sawmill and his mother held odd jobs. After graduating from high school, Carver married at the age of nineteen and had two children. Working hard to support his wife and family, he managed to enroll briefly in 1958 as a student at Chico State College in California, where he took a creative writing course from a then nearly unknown young novelist named John Gardner. Carver remembered that he decided to try to become a writer because he liked to read pulp novels and magazines* *about hunting and fishing. He credited Gardner for giving him a strong sense of direction as a writer: "A writer's values and craft. This is what the man taught and what he stood for, and this is what I've kept by me in the years since that brief but all-important time."*

In 1963 Carver received his B.A. from Humboldt State College in northern California. The following year he studied writing at the University of Iowa. But the 1960s, he said, were difficult for him and his wife:

> *I learned a long time ago when my kids were little and we had no money, and we were working our hearts out and weren't getting anywhere, even though we were giving it our best, my wife and I, that there were more important things than writing a poem or a story. That was a very hard realization for me to come to. But it came to me, and I had to accept it or die. Getting milk and food on the table, getting the rent paid, if a choice had to be made, then I had to forgo writing.*

Carver's desire to be a writer was so strong that he kept on writing long after the "cold facts" of his life told him he ought to quit. His first collection of stories, Will You Please Be Quiet, Please?, *was nominated for the National Book Award in 1976. Four more collections of stories followed, along with five books of poetry, before his death from lung cancer.*

Critics have noted that the rapid evolution of Carver's style causes his fiction to fall into three distinct periods. The tentative writing in his first book of stories — many of which he subsequently revised and republished — was followed by a paring down of his prose. This resulted in the hard-edged and detached minimalist style of his middle period, exemplified by the stories in his collection What We Talk About When We Talk About Love *(1981), which included "The Bath," later revised as "A Small, Good Thing." In his final period, Carver developed a more expansive style, as in the collection* Cathedral *(1983) and the new stories in his last collection,* Where I'm Calling From: New and Selected Stories *(1988).*

Influenced by the cadence of Ernest Hemingway's sentences, Carver also believed in simplicity. He wrote,

> *It's possible, in a poem or a short story, to write about commonplace things and objects using commonplace but precise language, and to endow those things — a chair, a window curtain, a fork, a stone, a woman's earring — with immense, even startling power. . . . If the words are heavy with the writer's own unbridled emotions, or if they are imprecise and inaccurate for some other reason — if the words are in any way blurred — the reader's eyes will slide right over them and nothing will be achieved. The reader's own artistic sense will simply not be engaged.*

RELATED CASEBOOK: *See pages 740–760, including Raymond Carver, "On Writing," page 740; Raymond Carver, "Creative Writing 101," page 744; Jim Naughton, "As Raymond Carver Muses, His Stature Grows," page 748; Kathleen Westfall Shute, "On 'The Bath' and 'A Small, Good Thing,'" page 750; Tom Jenks, "The Origin of 'Cathedral,'" page 755; A. O. Scott, "Looking for Raymond Carver," page 756.*

RAYMOND CARVER

Cathedral

1981

This blind man, an old friend of my wife's, he was on his way to spend the night. His wife had died. So he was visiting the dead wife's relatives in Connecticut. He called my wife from his in-laws'. Arrangements were made. He would come by train, a five-hour trip, and my wife would meet him at the station. She hadn't seen him since she worked for him one summer in Seattle ten years ago. But she and the blind man had kept in touch. They made tapes and mailed them back and forth. I wasn't enthusiastic about his visit. He was no one I knew. And his being blind bothered me. My idea of blindness came from the movies. In the movies, the blind moved slowly and never laughed. Sometimes they were led by seeing-eye dogs. A blind man in my house was not something I looked forward to.

That summer in Seattle she had needed a job. She didn't have any money. The man she was going to marry at the end of the summer was in officers' training school. He didn't have any money, either. But she was in love with the guy, and he was in love with her, etc. She'd seen something in the paper: HELP WANTED — *Reading to Blind Man,* and a telephone number. She phoned and went over, was hired on the spot. She'd worked with this blind man all summer. She read stuff to him, case studies, reports, that sort of thing. She helped him organize his little office in the county social-service department. They'd become good friends, my wife and the blind man. How do I know these things? She told me. And she told me something else. On her last day in the office, the blind man asked if he could touch her face. She agreed to this. She told me he touched his fingers to every part of her face, her nose — even her neck! She never forgot it. She even tried to write a poem about it. She was always trying to write a poem. She wrote a poem or two every year, usually after something really important had happened to her.

When we first started going out together, she showed me the poem. In the poem, she recalled his fingers and the way they had moved around over her face. In the poem, she talked about what she had felt at the time, about what went through her mind when the blind man touched her nose and lips. I can remember I didn't think much of the poem. Of course, I didn't tell her that. Maybe I just don't understand poetry. I admit it's not the first thing I reach for when I pick up something to read.

Anyway, this man who'd first enjoyed her favors, the officer-to-be, he'd been her childhood sweetheart. So okay. I'm saying that at the end of the summer she let the blind man run his hands over her face, said goodbye to him, married her childhood etc., who was now a commissioned officer, and she moved away from Seattle. But they'd kept in touch, she and the blind man. She made the first contact after a year or so. She called him up one night from an Air Force base in Alabama. She wanted to talk. They talked. He asked her to send him a tape and tell him about her life. She did this. She sent the tape. On the tape, she told the blind man about her husband and about their life together in the military. She told the blind man she loved her husband but she didn't like it where they lived and she didn't like it that he was a part of the military-industrial thing. She told the blind man she'd written a poem and he was in it. She told him that she was writing a poem about what it was like to be an Air Force officer's wife. The poem wasn't finished yet. She was still writing it. The blind man made a tape. He sent her the tape. She made a tape. This went on for years. My wife's officer was posted to one base and then another. She sent tapes from Moody AFB, McGuire, McConnell, and finally Travis, near Sacramento, where one night she got to feeling lonely and cut off from people she kept losing in that moving-around life. She got to feeling she couldn't go it another step. She went in and swallowed all the pills and capsules in the medicine chest and washed them down with a bottle of gin. Then she got into a hot bath and passed out.

But instead of dying, she got sick. She threw up. Her officer — why should he have a name? he was the childhood sweetheart, and what more does he want? — came home from somewhere, found her, and called the ambulance. In time, she put it all on a tape and sent the tape to the blind man. Over the years, she put all kinds of stuff on tapes and sent the tapes off lickety-split. Next to writing a poem every year, I think it was her chief means of recreation. On one tape, she told the blind man she'd decided to live away from her officer for a time. On another tape, she told him about her divorce. She and I began going out, and of course she told her blind man about it. She told him everything, or so it seemed to me. Once she asked me if I'd like to hear the latest tape from the blind man. This was a year ago. I was on the tape, she said. So I said okay, I'd listen to it. I got us drinks and we settled down in the living room. We made ready to listen. First she inserted the tape into the player and adjusted a couple of dials. Then she pushed a lever. The tape squeaked and someone began to talk in this loud voice. She lowered the volume. After a few minutes of harmless chitchat, I heard my own name in the mouth of this stranger, this blind man I didn't even know! And then this: "From all you've said about him, I can only conclude —" But we were interrupted, a knock at the door, something, and we didn't ever get back to the tape. Maybe it was just as well. I'd heard all I wanted to.

Now this same blind man was coming to sleep in my house.

"Maybe I could take him bowling," I said to my wife. She was at the draining board doing scalloped potatoes. She put down the knife she was using and turned around.

"If you love me," she said, "you can do this for me. If you don't love me, okay. But if you had a friend, any friend, and the friend came to visit, I'd make him feel comfortable." She wiped her hands with the dish towel.

"I don't have any blind friends," I said.

"You don't have *any* friends," she said. "Period. Besides," she said, "goddamn it, his wife's just died! Don't you understand that? The man's lost his wife!"

I didn't answer. She'd told me a little about the blind man's wife. Her name was Beulah. Beulah! That's a name for a colored woman.

"Was his wife Negro?" I asked.

"Are you crazy?" my wife said. "Have you just flipped or something?" She picked up a potato. I saw it hit the floor, then roll under the stove. "What's wrong with you?" she said. "Are you drunk?"

"I'm just asking," I said.

Right then my wife filled me in with more detail than I cared to know. I made a drink and sat at the kitchen table to listen. Pieces of the story began to fall into place.

Beulah had gone to work for the blind man the summer after my wife had stopped working for him. Pretty soon Beulah and the blind man had themselves a church wedding. It was a little wedding — who'd want to go to such a wedding in the first place? — just the two of them, plus the minister and the minister's wife. But it was a church wedding just the same. It was what Beulah had wanted, he'd said. But even then Beulah must have been carrying the cancer in her glands. After they had been inseparable for eight years — my wife's word, *inseparable* — Beulah's health went into a rapid decline. She died in a Seattle hospital room, the blind man sitting beside the bed and holding on to her hand. They'd married, lived and worked together, slept together — had sex, sure — and then the blind man had to bury her. All this without his having ever seen what the goddamned woman looked like. It was beyond my understanding. Hearing this, I felt sorry for the blind man for a little bit. And then I found myself thinking what a pitiful life this woman must have led. Imagine a woman who could never see herself as she was seen in the eyes of her loved one. A woman who could go on day after day and never receive the smallest compliment from her beloved. A woman whose husband could never read the expression on her face, be it misery or something better. Someone who could wear makeup or not — what difference to him? She could, if she wanted, wear green eye-shadow around one eye, a straight pin in her nostril, yellow slacks and purple shoes, no matter. And then to slip off into death, the blind man's hand on her hand, his blind eyes streaming tears — I'm imagining now — her last thought maybe this: that he never even knew what she looked like, and she on an express to the grave. Robert was left with a small insurance policy and half of a twenty-peso Mexican coin. The other half of the coin went into the box with her. Pathetic.

So when the time rolled around, my wife went to the depot to pick him up. With nothing to do but wait — sure, I blamed him for that — I was having a drink and watching the TV when I heard the car pull into the drive. I got up from the sofa with my drink and went to the window to have a look.

I saw my wife laughing as she parked the car. I saw her get out of the car and shut the door. She was still wearing a smile. Just amazing. She went around to the other side of the car to where the blind man was already starting to get out. This blind man, feature this, he was wearing a full beard! A beard on a blind man! Too much, I say. The blind man reached into the back seat and dragged out a suitcase. My wife took his arm, shut the car door, and, talking all the way, moved him down the drive and then up the steps to the front porch. I turned off the TV. I finished my drink, rinsed the glass, dried my hands. Then I went to the door.

My wife said, "I want you to meet Robert. Robert, this is my husband. I've told you all about him." She was beaming. She had this blind man by his coat sleeve.

The blind man let go of his suitcase and up came his hand.

I took it. He squeezed hard, held my hand, and then he let it go.

"I feel like we've already met," he boomed.

"Likewise," I said. I didn't know what else to say. Then I said, "Welcome. I've heard a lot about you." We began to move then, a little group, from the porch into the living room, my wife guiding him by the arm. The blind man was carrying his suitcase in his other hand. My wife said things like, "To your left here, Robert. That's right. Now watch it, there's a chair. That's it. Sit down right here. This is the sofa. We just bought this sofa two weeks ago."

I started to say something about the old sofa. I'd liked that old sofa. But I didn't say anything. Then I wanted to say something else, small-talk, about the scenic ride along the Hudson. How going *to* New York, you should sit on the right-hand side of the train, and coming *from* New York, the left-hand side.

"Did you have a good train ride?" I said. "Which side of the train did you sit on, by the way?"

"What a question, which side!" my wife said. "What's it matter which side?" she said.

"I just asked," I said.

"Right side," the blind man said. "I hadn't been on a train in nearly forty years. Not since I was a kid. With my folks. That's been a long time. I'd nearly forgotten the sensation. I have winter in my beard now," he said. "So I've been told, anyway. Do I look distinguished, my dear?" the blind man said to my wife.

"You look distinguished, Robert," she said. "Robert," she said. "Robert, it's just so good to see you."

My wife finally took her eyes off the blind man and looked at me. I had the feeling she didn't like what she saw. I shrugged.

I've never met, or personally known, anyone who was blind. This blind man was late forties, a heavy-set, balding man with stooped shoulders, as if he carried a great weight there. He wore brown slacks, brown shoes, a light-brown shirt, a tie, a sports coat. Spiffy. He also had this full beard. But he didn't use a cane and he didn't wear dark glasses. I'd always thought dark glasses were a must for the blind. Fact was, I wished he had a pair. At first glance, his eyes looked like anyone else's eyes. But if you look close, there was something different about them. Too much white in the iris, for one thing, and the pupils seemed to move around in the sockets without his knowing it or being able to stop it. Creepy. As I stared at his face, I saw the left pupil turn in toward his nose while the other made an effort to keep in one place. But it was only an effort, for that eye was on the roam without his knowing it or wanting it to be.

I said, "Let me get you a drink. What's your pleasure? We have a little of everything. It's one of our pastimes."

"Bub, I'm a Scotch man myself," he said fast enough in this big voice.

"Right," I said. Bub! "Sure you are, I knew it."

He let his fingers touch his suitcase, which was sitting alongside the sofa. He was taking his bearings. I didn't blame him for that.

"I'll move that up to your room," my wife said.

"No, that's fine," the blind man said loudly. "It can go up when I go up."

"A little water with the Scotch?" I said.

"Very little," he said.

"I knew it," I said.

He said, "Just a tad. The Irish actor, Barry Fitzgerald? I'm like that fellow. When I drink water, Fitzgerald said, I drink water. When I drink whiskey, I drink whiskey." My wife laughed. The blind man brought his hand up under his beard. He lifted his beard slowly and let it drop.

I did the drinks, three big glasses of Scotch with a splash of water in each. Then we made ourselves comfortable and talked about Robert's travels. First the long flight from the West Coast to Connecticut, we covered that. Then from Connecticut up here by train. We had another drink concerning that leg of the trip.

I remembered having read somewhere that the blind didn't smoke because, as speculation had it, they couldn't see the smoke they exhaled. I thought I knew that much and that much only about blind people. But this blind man smoked his cigarette down to the nubbin and then lit another one. This blind man filled his ashtray and my wife emptied it.

When we sat down at the table for dinner, we had another drink. My wife heaped Robert's plate with cube steak, scalloped potatoes, green beans. I buttered him up two slices of bread. I said, "Here's bread and butter for you." I swallowed some of my drink. "Now let us pray," I said, and the blind man lowered his head. My wife looked at me, her mouth agape. "Pray the phone won't ring and the food doesn't get cold," I said.

We dug in. We ate everything there was to eat on the table. We ate like there was no tomorrow. We didn't talk. We ate. We scarfed. We grazed that table. We were into serious eating. The blind man had right away located his foods, he knew just where everything was on his plate. I watched with admiration as he used his knife and fork on the meat. He'd cut two pieces of meat, fork the meat into his mouth, and then go all out for the scalloped potatoes, the beans next, and then he'd tear off a hunk of buttered bread and eat that. He'd follow this up with a big drink of milk. It didn't seem to bother him to use his fingers once in a while, either.

We finished everything, including half a strawberry pie. For a few moments, we sat as if stunned. Sweat beaded on our faces. Finally, we got up from the table and left the dirty plates. We didn't look back. We took ourselves into the living room and sank into our places again. Robert and my wife sat on the sofa. I took the big chair. We had us two or three more drinks while they talked about the major things that had come to pass for them in the past ten years. For the most part, I just listened. Now and then I joined in. I didn't want him to think I'd left the room, and I didn't want her to think I was feeling left out. They talked of things that had happened to them — to them! — these past ten years. I waited in vain to hear my name on my wife's sweet lips: "And then my dear husband came into my life" — something like that. But I heard nothing of the sort. More talk of Robert. Robert had done a little of everything, it seemed, a regular blind jack-of-all-trades. But most recently he and his wife had had an Amway distributorship, from which, I gathered, they'd earned their living, such as it was. The blind man was also a ham radio operator. He talked in his loud voice about conversations he'd had with fellow operators in Guam, in the Philippines, in Alaska, and even in Tahiti. He said he'd have a lot of friends there if he ever wanted to go visit those places. From time to time, he'd turn his blind face toward me, put his hand under his beard, ask me something. How long had I been in my present position? (Three years.) Did I like my work? (I didn't.) Was I going to stay with it? (What were the options?) Finally, when I thought he was beginning to run down, I got up and turned on the TV.

My wife looked at me with irritation. She was heading toward a boil. Then she looked at the blind man and said, "Robert, do you have a TV?"

The blind man said, "My dear, I have two TVs. I have a color set and a black-and-white thing, an old relic. It's funny, but if I turn the TV on, and I'm always turning it on, I turn on the color set. It's funny, don't you think?"

I didn't know what to say to that. I had absolutely nothing to say to that. No opinions. So I watched the news program and tried to listen to what the announcer was saying.

"This is a color TV," the blind man said. "Don't ask me how, but I can tell."

"We traded up a while ago," I said.

The blind man had another taste of his drink. He lifted his beard, sniffed it, and let it fall. He leaned forward on the sofa. He positioned his ashtray on the coffee table, then put the lighter to his cigarette. He leaned back on the sofa and crossed his legs at the ankles.

My wife covered her mouth, and then she yawned. She stretched. She said, "I think I'll go upstairs and put on my robe. I think I'll change into something else. Robert, you make yourself comfortable," she said.

"I'm comfortable," the blind man said.

"I want you to feel comfortable in this house," she said.

"I am comfortable," the blind man said.

After she'd left the room, he and I listened to the weather report and then to the sports roundup. By that time, she'd been gone so long I didn't know if she was going to come back. I thought she might have gone to bed. I wished she'd come back downstairs. I didn't want to be left alone with a blind man. I asked him if he wanted another drink, and he said sure. Then I asked if he wanted to smoke some dope with me. I said I'd just rolled a number. I hadn't, but I planned to do so in about two shakes.

"I'll try some with you," he said.

"Damn right," I said. "That's the stuff."

I got our drinks and sat down on the sofa with him. Then I rolled us two fat numbers. I lit one and passed it. I brought it to his fingers. He took it and inhaled.

"Hold it as long as you can," I said. I could tell he didn't know the first thing.

My wife came back downstairs wearing her pink robe and her pink slippers.

"What do I smell?" she said.

"We thought we'd have us some cannabis," I said.

My wife gave me a savage look. Then she looked at the blind man and said, "Robert, I didn't know you smoked."

He said, "I do now, my dear. There's a first time for everything. But I don't feel anything yet."

"This stuff is pretty mellow," I said. "This stuff is mild. It's dope you can reason with," I said. "It doesn't mess you up."

"Not much it doesn't, bub," he said, and laughed.

My wife sat on the sofa between the blind man and me. I passed her the number. She took it and toked and then passed it back to me. "Which way is this going?" she said. Then she said, "I shouldn't be smoking this. I can hardly keep my eyes open as it is. That dinner did me in. I shouldn't have eaten so much."

"It was the strawberry pie," the blind man said. "That's what did it," he said, and he laughed his big laugh. Then he shook his head.

"There's more strawberry pie," I said.

"Do you want some more, Robert?" my wife said.

"Maybe in a little while," he said.

We gave our attention to the TV. My wife yawned again. She said, "Your bed is made up when you feel like going to bed, Robert. I know you must have had a long day. When you're ready to go to bed, say so." She pulled his arm. "Robert?"

He came to and said, "I've had a real nice time. This beats tapes, doesn't it?"

I said, "Coming at you," and I put the number between his fingers. He inhaled, held the smoke, and then let it go. It was like he'd been doing it since he was nine years old.

"Thanks, bub," he said. "But I think this is all for me. I think I'm beginning to feel it," he said. He held the burning roach out for my wife.

"Same here," she said. "Ditto. Me, too." She took the roach and passed it to me. "I may just sit here for a while between you two guys with my eyes closed. But don't let me bother you, okay? Either one of you. If it bothers you, say so. Otherwise, I may just sit here with my eyes closed until you're ready to go to bed," she said. "Your bed's made up, Robert, when you're ready. It's right next to our room at the top of the stairs. We'll show you up when you're ready. You wake me up now, you guys, if I fall asleep." She said that and then she closed her eyes and went to sleep.

The news program ended. I got up and changed the channel. I sat back down on the sofa. I wished my wife hadn't pooped out. Her head lay across the back of the sofa, her mouth open. She'd turned so that her robe had slipped away from her legs, exposing a juicy thigh. I reached to draw her robe back over her, and it was then that I glanced at the blind man. What the hell! I flipped the robe open again.

"You say when you want some strawberry pie," I said.

"I will," he said.

I said, "Are you tired? Do you want me to take you up to your bed? Are you ready to hit the hay?"

"Not yet," he said. "No, I'll stay up with you, bub. If that's all right. I'll stay up until you're ready to turn in. We haven't had a chance to talk. Know what I mean? I feel like me and her monopolized the evening." He lifted his beard and he let it fall. He picked up his cigarettes and his lighter.

"That's all right," I said. Then I said, "I'm glad for the company."

And I guess I was. Every night I smoked dope and stayed up as long as I could before I fell asleep. My wife and I hardly ever went to bed at the same time. When I did go to sleep, I had these dreams. Sometimes I'd wake up from one of them, my heart going crazy.

Something about the church and the Middle Ages was on the TV. Not your run-of-the-mill TV fare. I wanted to watch something else. I turned to the other channels. But there was nothing on them, either. So I turned back to the first channel and apologized.

"Bub, it's all right," the blind man said. "It's fine with me. Whatever you want to watch is okay. I'm always learning something. Learning never ends. It won't hurt me to learn something tonight. I got ears," he said.

We didn't say anything for a time. He was leaning forward with his head turned at me, his right ear aimed in the direction of the set. Very disconcerting. Now and then his eyelids drooped and then they snapped open again. Now and then he put his fingers into his beard and tugged, like he was thinking about something he was hearing on the television.

On the screen, a group of men wearing cowls was being set upon and tormented by men dressed in skeleton costumes and men dressed as devils. The men dressed as devils wore devil masks, horns, and long tails. This pageant was part of a procession. The Englishman who was narrating the thing said it took place in Spain once a year. I tried to explain to the blind man what was happening.

"Skeletons," he said. "I know about skeletons," he said, and he nodded.

The TV showed this one cathedral. Then there was a long, slow look at another one. Finally, the picture switched to the famous one in Paris, with its flying buttresses and its spires reaching up to the clouds. The camera pulled away to show the whole of the cathedral rising above the skyline.

There were times when the Englishman who was telling the thing would shut up, would simply let the camera move around over the cathedrals. Or else the camera would tour the countryside, men in fields walking behind oxen. I waited as long as I could. Then I felt I had to say something. I said, "They're showing the outside of this cathedral now. Gargoyles. Little statues carved to look like monsters. Now I guess they're in Italy. Yeah, they're in Italy. There's paintings on the walls of this one church."

"Are those fresco paintings, bub?" he asked, and he sipped from his drink.

I reached for my glass. But it was empty. I tried to remember what I could remember. "You're asking me are those frescoes?" I said. "That's a good question. I don't know."

The camera moved to a cathedral outside Lisbon. The differences in the Portuguese cathedral compared with the French and Italian were not that great. But they were there. Mostly the interior stuff. Then something occurred to me, and I said, "Something has occurred to me. Do you have any idea what a cathedral is? What they look like, that is? Do you follow me? If somebody says cathedral to you, do you have any notion what they're talking about? Do you know the difference between that and a Baptist church, say?"

He let the smoke dribble from his mouth. "I know they took hundreds of workers fifty or a hundred years to build," he said. "I just heard the man say that, of course. I know generations of the same families worked on a cathedral. I heard him say that too. The men who began their life's work on them, they never lived to see the completion of their work. In that wise, bub, they're no different from the rest of us, right?" He laughed. Then his eyelids drooped again. His head nodded. He seemed to be snoozing. Maybe he was imagining himself in Portugal. The TV was showing another cathedral now. This one was in Germany. The Englishman's voice droned on. "Cathedrals," the blind man said. He sat up and rolled his head back and forth. "If you want the truth, bub, that's about all I know. What I just said. What I heard him say. But maybe you could describe one to me? I wish you'd do it. I'd like that. If you want to know, I really don't have a good idea."

I stared hard at the shot of the cathedral on the TV. How could I even begin to describe it? But say my life depended on it. Say my life was being threatened by an insane guy who said I had to do it or else.

I stared some more at the cathedral before the picture flipped off into the countryside. There was no use. I turned to the blind man and said, "To begin with, they're very tall." I was looking around the room for clues. "They reach way up. Up and up. Toward the sky. They're so big, some of them, they have to have these supports. To help hold them up, so to speak. These supports are called buttresses. They remind me of viaducts, for some reason. But maybe you don't know viaducts, either? Sometimes the cathedrals have devils and such carved into the front. Sometimes lords and ladies. Don't ask me why this is," I said.

He was nodding. The whole upper part of his body seemed to be moving back and forth.

"I'm not doing so good, am I?" I said.

He stopped nodding and leaned forward on the edge of the sofa. As he listened to me, he was running his fingers through his beard. I wasn't getting through to him, I could see that. But he waited for me to go on just the same. He nodded, like he was trying to encourage me. I tried to think what else to say. "They're really big," I said. "They're massive. They're built of stone. Marble, too, sometimes. In those olden days, when they built cathedrals, men wanted to be close to God. In those olden days, God was an important part of everyone's life. You could tell this from their cathedral-building. I'm sorry," I said, "but it looks like that's the best I can do for you. I'm just no good at it."

"That's all right, bub," the blind man said. "Hey, listen. I hope you don't mind my asking you. Can I ask you something? Let me ask you a simple question, yes or no. I'm just curious and there's no offense. You're my host. But let me ask if you are in any way religious? You don't mind my asking?"

I shook my head. He couldn't see that, though. A wink is the same as a nod to a blind man. "I guess I don't believe in it. In anything. Sometimes it's hard. You know what I'm saying?"

"Sure I do," he said.

"Right," I said.

The Englishman was still holding forth. My wife sighed in her sleep. She drew a long breath and went on with her sleeping.

"You'll have to forgive me," I said. "But I can't tell you what a cathedral looks like. It just isn't in me to do it. I can't do any more than I've done."

The blind man sat very still, his head down, as he listened to me.

I said, "The truth is, cathedrals don't mean anything special to me. Nothing. Cathedrals. They're something to look at on late-night TV. That's all they are."

It was then that the blind man cleared his throat. He brought something up. He took a handkerchief from his back pocket. Then he said, "I get it, bub. It's okay. It happens. Don't worry about it," he said. "Hey, listen to me. Will you do me a favor? I got an idea. Why don't you find us some heavy paper? And a pen. We'll do something. We'll draw one together. Get us a pen and some heavy paper. Go on, bub, get the stuff," he said.

So I went upstairs. My legs felt like they didn't have any strength in them. They felt like they did after I'd done some running. In my wife's room, I looked around. I found some ballpoints in a little basket on her table. And then I tried to think where to look for the kind of paper he was talking about.

Downstairs, in the kitchen, I found a shopping bag with onion skins in the bottom of the bag. I emptied the bag and shook it. I brought it into the living room and sat down with it near his legs. I moved some things, smoothed the wrinkles from the bag, spread it out on the coffee table.

The blind man got down from the sofa and sat next to me on the carpet.

He ran his fingers over the paper. He went up and down the sides of the paper. The edges, even the edges. He fingered the corners.

"All right," he said. "All right, let's do her."

He found my hand, the hand with the pen. He closed his hand over my hand. "Go ahead, bub, draw," he said. "Draw. You'll see. I'll follow along with you. It'll be okay. Just begin now like I'm telling you. You'll see. Draw," the blind man said.

So I began. First I drew a box that looked like a house. It could have been the house I lived in. Then I put a roof on it. At either end of the roof, I drew spires. Crazy.

"Swell," he said. "Terrific. You're doing fine," he said.

"Never thought anything like this could happen in your lifetime, did you, bub? Well, it's a strange life, we all know that. Go on now. Keep it up."

I put in windows with arches. I drew flying buttresses. I hung great doors. I couldn't stop. The TV station went off the air. I put down the pen and closed and opened my fingers. The blind man felt round over the paper. He moved the tips of his fingers over the paper, all over what I had drawn, and he nodded.

"Doing fine," the blind man said.

I took up the pen again, and he found my hand. I kept at it. I'm no artist. But I kept drawing just the same.

My wife opened up her eyes and gazed at us. She sat up on the sofa, her robe hanging open. She said, "What are you doing? Tell me, I want to know."

I didn't answer her.

The blind man said, "We're drawing a cathedral. Me and him are working on it. Press hard," he said to me. "That's right. That's good," he said. "Sure. You got it, bub. I can tell. You didn't think you could. But you can, can't you? You're cooking with gas now. You know what I'm saying? We're going to really have us something here in a minute. How's the old arm?" he said. "Put some people in there now. What's a cathedral without people?"

My wife said, "What's going on? Robert, what are you doing? What's going on?"

"It's all right," he said to her. "Close your eyes now," the blind man said to me.

I did it. I closed them just like he said.

"Are they closed? he said. "Don't fudge."

"They're closed," I said.

"Keep them that way," he said. He said, "Don't stop now. Draw."

So we kept on with it. His fingers rode my fingers as my hand went over the paper. It was like nothing else in my life up to now.

Then he said, "I think that's it. I think you got it," he said. "Take a look. What do you think?"

But I had my eyes closed. I thought I'd keep them that way for a little longer. I thought it was something I ought to do.

"Well?" he said. "Are you looking?"

My eyes were still closed. I was in my house. I knew that. But I didn't feel like I was inside anything.

"It's really something," I said.

RAYMOND CARVER

The Bath

1981

Saturday afternoon the mother drove to the bakery in the shopping center. After looking through a loose-leaf binder with photographs of cakes taped onto the pages, she ordered chocolate, the child's favorite. The cake she chose was decorated with a spaceship and a launching pad under a sprinkling of white stars. The name SCOTTY would be iced on in green as if it were the name of the spaceship.

The baker listened thoughtfully when the mother told him Scotty would be eight years old. He was an older man, this baker, and he wore a curious apron, a heavy thing with loops that went under his arms and around his back and then crossed in front again where they were tied in a very thick knot. He kept wiping his hands on the front of the apron as he listened to the woman, his wet eyes examining her lips as she studied the samples and talked.

He let her take her time. He was in no hurry.

The mother decided on the spaceship cake, and then she gave the baker her name and her telephone number. The cake would be ready Monday morning, in plenty of time for the party Monday afternoon. This was all the baker was willing to say. No pleasantries, just this small exchange, the barest information, nothing that was not necessary.

Monday morning, the boy was walking to school. He was in the company of another boy, the two boys passing a bag of potato chips back and forth between them. The birthday boy was trying to trick the other boy into telling what he was going to give in the way of a present.

At an intersection, without looking, the birthday boy stepped off the curb, and was promptly knocked down by a car. He fell on his side, his head in the gutter, his legs in the road moving as if he were climbing a wall.

The other boy stood holding the potato chips. He was wondering if he should finish the rest or continue on to school.

The birthday boy did not cry. But neither did he wish to talk anymore. He would not answer when the other boy asked what it felt like to be hit by a car. The birthday boy got up and turned back for home, at which time the other boy waved good-bye and headed off for school.

The birthday boy told his mother what had happened. They sat together on the sofa. She held his hands in her lap. This is what she was doing when the boy pulled his hands away and lay down on his back.

Of course, the birthday party never happened. The birthday boy was in the hospital instead. The mother sat by the bed. She was waiting for the boy to wake up. The father hurried over from his office. He sat next to the mother. So now the both of them waited for the boy to wake up. They waited for hours, and then the father went home to take a bath.

The man drove home from the hospital. He drove the streets faster than he should. It had been a good life till now. There had been work, fatherhood, family. The man had been lucky and happy. But fear made him want a bath.

He pulled into the driveway. He sat in the car trying to make his legs work. The child had been hit by a car and he was in the hospital, but he was going to be all right. The man got out of the car and went up to the door. The dog was barking and the telephone was ringing. It kept ringing while the man unlocked the door and felt the wall for the light switch.

He picked up the receiver. He said, "I just got in the door!"

"There's a cake that wasn't picked up."

This is what the voice on the other end said.

"What are you saying?" the father said.

"The cake," the voice said. "Sixteen dollars."

The husband held the receiver against his ear, trying to understand. He said, "I don't know anything about it."

"Don't hand me that," the voice said.

The husband hung up the telephone. He went into the kitchen and poured himself some whiskey. He called the hospital.

The child's condition remained the same.

While the water ran into the tub, the man lathered his face and shaved. He was in the tub when he heard the telephone again. He got himself out and hurried through the house, saying, "Stupid, stupid," because he wouldn't be doing this if he'd stayed where he was in the hospital. He picked up the receiver and shouted, "Hello!"

The voice said, "It's ready."

The father got back to the hospital after midnight. The wife was sitting in the chair by the bed. She looked up at the husband and then she looked back at the child. From an apparatus over the bed hung a bottle with a tube running from the bottle to the child.

"What's this?" the father said.

"Glucose," the mother said.

The husband put his hand to the back of the woman's head.

"He's going to wake up," the man said.

"I know," the woman said.

In a little while the man said, "Go home and let me take over."

She shook her head. "No," she said.

"Really," he said. "Go home for a while. You don't have to worry. He's sleeping, is all."

A nurse pushed open the door. She nodded to them as she went to the bed. She took the left arm out from under the covers and put her fingers on the wrist. She put the arm back under the covers and wrote on the clipboard attached to the bed.

"How is he?"' the mother said.

"Stable," the nurse said. Then she said, "Doctor will be in again shortly."

"I was saying maybe she'd want to go home and get a little rest," the man said. "After the doctor comes."

"She could do that," the nurse said.

The woman said, "We'll see what the doctor says." She brought her hand up to her eyes and leaned her head forward.

The nurse said, "Of course."

The father gazed at his son, the small chest inflating and deflating under the covers. He felt more fear now. He began shaking his head. He talked to himself like this. The child is fine. Instead of sleeping at home, he's doing it here. Sleep is the same wherever you do it.

The doctor came in. He shook hands with the man. The woman got up from the chair.

"Ann," the doctor said and nodded. The doctor said, "Let's just see how he's doing." He moved to the bed and touched the boy's wrist. He peeled back an eyelid and then the other. He turned back the covers and listened to the heart. He pressed his fingers here and there on the body. He went to the end of the bed and studied the chart. He noted the time, scribbled on the chart, and then he considered the mother and the father.

This doctor was a handsome man. His skin was moist and tan. He wore a three-piece suit, a vivid tie, and on his shirt were cufflinks.

The mother was talking to herself like this. He has just come from somewhere with an audience. They gave him a special medal.

The doctor said, "Nothing to shout about, but nothing to worry about. He should wake up pretty soon." The doctor looked at the boy again. "We'll know more after the tests are in."

"Oh, no," the mother said.

The doctor said, "Sometimes you see this."

The father said, "You wouldn't call this a coma, then?"

The father waited and looked at the doctor.

"No, I don't want to call it that," the doctor said. "He's sleeping. It's restorative. The body is doing what it has to do."

"It's a coma," the mother said. "A kind of coma."

The doctor said, "I wouldn't call it that."

He took the woman's hands and patted them. He shook hands with the husband.

The woman put her fingers on the child's forehead and kept them there for a while. "At least he doesn't have a fever," she said. Then she said, "I don't know. Feel his head."

The man put his fingers on the boy's forehead. The man said, "I think he's supposed to feel this way."

The woman stood there awhile longer, working her lip with her teeth. Then she moved to her chair and sat down.

The husband sat in the chair beside her. He wanted to say something else. But there was no saying what it should be. He took her hand and put it in his lap. This made him feel better. It made him feel he was saying something. They sat like that for a while, watching the boy, not talking. From time to time he squeezed her hand until she took it away.

"I've been praying," she said.

"Me too," the father said. "I've been praying too."

A nurse came back in and checked the flow from the bottle.

A doctor came in and said what his name was. This doctor was wearing loafers.

"We're going to take him downstairs for more pictures," he said. "And we want to do a scan."

"A scan?" the mother said. She stood between this new doctor and the bed.

"It's nothing," he said.

"My God," she said.

Two orderlies came in. They wheeled a thing like a bed. They unhooked the boy from the tube and slid him over onto the thing with wheels.

It was after sunup when they brought the birthday boy back out. The mother and father followed the orderlies into the elevator and up to the room. Once more the parents took up their places next to the bed.

They waited all day. The boy did not wake up. The doctor came again and examined the boy again and left after saying the same things again. Nurses came in. Doctors came in. A technician came in and took blood.

"I don't understand this," the mother said to the technician.

"Doctor's orders," the technician said.

The mother went to the window and looked out at the parking lot. Cars with their lights on were driving in and out. She stood at the window with her hands on the sill. She was talking to herself like this. We're into something now, something hard.

She was afraid.

She saw a car stop and a woman in a long coat get into it. She made believe she was that woman. She made believe she was driving away from here to someplace else.

The doctor came in. He looked tanned and healthier than ever. He went to the bed and examined the boy. He said, "His signs are fine. Everything's good."

The mother said, "But he's sleeping."

"Yes," the doctor said.

The husband said, "She's tired. She's starved."

The doctor said, "She should rest. She should eat. Ann," the doctor said.

"Thank you," the husband said.

He shook hands with the doctor and the doctor patted their shoulders and left.

"I suppose one of us should go home and check on things," the man said. "The dog needs to be fed."

"Call the neighbors," the wife said. "Someone will feed him if you ask them to."

She tried to think who. She closed her eyes and tried to think anything at all. After a time she said, "Maybe I'll do it. Maybe if I'm not here watching, he'll wake up. Maybe it's because I'm watching that he won't."

"That could be it," the husband said.

"I'll go home and take a bath and put on something clean," the woman said.

"I think you should do that," the man said.

She picked up her purse. He helped her into her coat. She moved to the door, and looked back. She looked at the child, and then she looked at the father. The husband nodded and smiled.

She went past the nurses' station and down to the end of the corridor, where she turned and saw a little waiting room, a family in there, all sitting in wicker chairs, a man in a khaki shirt, a baseball cap pushed back on his head, a large woman wearing a housedress, slippers, a girl in jeans, hair in dozens of kinky braids, the table littered with flimsy wrappers and styrofoam and coffee sticks and packets of salt and pepper.

"Nelson," the woman said. "Is it about Nelson?"

The woman's eyes widened.

"Tell me now, lady," the woman said. "Is it about Nelson?"

The woman was trying to get up from her chair. But the man had his hand closed over her arm.

"Here, here," the man said.

"I'm sorry," the mother said. "I'm looking for the elevator. My son is in the hospital. I can't find the elevator."

"Elevator is down that way," the man said, and he aimed a finger in the right direction.

"My son was hit by a car," the mother said. "But he's going to be all right. He's in shock now, but it might be some kind of coma too. That's what worries us, the coma part, I'm going out for a little while. Maybe I'll take a bath. But my husband is with him. He's watching. There's a chance everything will change when I'm gone. My name is Ann Weiss."

The man shifted in his chair. He shook his head.

He said, "Our Nelson."

She pulled into the driveway. The dog ran out from behind the house. He ran in circles on the grass. She closed her eyes and leaned her head against the wheel. She listened to the ticking of the engine.

She got out of the car and went to the door. She turned on lights and put on water for tea. She opened a can and fed the dog. She sat down on the sofa with her tea.

The telephone rang.

"Yes!" she said. "Hello!" she said.

"Mrs. Weiss," a man's voice said.

"Yes," she said. "This is Mrs. Weiss. Is it about Scotty?" she said.

"Scotty," the voice said. "It is about Scotty," the voice said. "It has to do with Scotty, yes."

RAYMOND CARVER

A Small, Good Thing

1983

Saturday afternoon she drove to the bakery in the shopping center. After looking through a loose-leaf binder with photographs of cakes taped onto the pages, she ordered chocolate, the child's favorite. The cake she chose was decorated with a space ship and launching pad under a sprinkling of white stars, and a planet made of red frosting at the other end. His name, SCOTTY, would be in green letters beneath the planet. The baker, who was an older man with a thick neck, listened without saying anything when she told him the child would be eight years old next Monday. The baker wore a white apron that looked like a smock. Straps cut under his arms, went around in back and then to the front again, where they were secured under his heavy waist. He wiped his hands on his apron as he listened to her. He kept his eyes down on the photographs and let her talk. He let her take her time. He'd just come to work and he'd be there all night, baking, and he was in no real hurry.

She gave the baker her name, Ann Weiss, and her telephone number. The cake would be ready on Monday morning, just out of the oven, in plenty of time for the child's party that afternoon. The baker was not jolly. There were no pleasantries between them, just the minimum exchange of words, the necessary information. He made her feel uncomfortable, and she didn't like that. While he was bent over the counter with the pencil in his hand, she studied his coarse features and wondered if he'd ever done anything else with his life besides be a baker. She was a mother and thirty-three years old, and it seemed to her that everyone, especially someone the baker's age — a man old enough to be her father — must have children who'd gone through this special time of cakes and birthday parties. There must be that between them, she thought. But he was abrupt with her — not rude, just abrupt. She gave up trying to make friends with him. She looked into the back of the bakery and could see a long, heavy wooden table with aluminum pie pans stacked at one end; and beside the table a metal container filled with empty racks. There was an enormous oven. A radio was playing country-Western music.

The baker finished printing the information on the special order card and closed up the binder. He looked at her and said, "Monday morning." She thanked him and drove home.

On Monday morning, the birthday boy was walking to school with another boy. They were passing a bag of potato chips back and forth and the birthday boy was trying to find out what his friend intended to give him for his birthday that afternoon. Without looking, the birthday boy stepped off the curb at an intersection and was immediately knocked down by a car. He fell on his side with his head in the gutter and his legs out in the road. His eyes were closed, but his legs moved back and forth as if he were trying to climb over something. His friend dropped the potato chips and started to cry. The car had gone a hundred feet or so and stopped in the middle of the road. The man in the driver's seat looked back over his shoulder. He waited until the boy got unsteadily to his feet. The boy wobbled a little. He looked dazed, but okay. The driver put the car into gear and drove away.

The birthday boy didn't cry, but he didn't have anything to say about anything either. He wouldn't answer when his friend asked him what it felt like to be hit by a car. He walked home, and his friend went on to school. But after the birthday boy was inside his house and was telling his mother about it — she sitting beside him on the sofa, holding his hands in her lap, saying, "Scotty, honey, are you sure you feel all right, baby?" thinking she would call the doctor anyway — he suddenly lay back on the sofa, closed his eyes, and went limp. When she couldn't wake him up, she hurried to the telephone and called her husband at work. Howard told her to remain calm, remain calm, and then he called an ambulance for the child and left for the hospital himself.

Of course, the birthday party was canceled. The child was in the hospital with a mild concussion and suffering from shock. There'd been vomiting, and his lungs had taken in fluid which needed pumping out that afternoon. Now he simply seemed to be in a very deep sleep — but no coma, Dr. Francis had emphasized, no coma, when he saw the alarm in the parents' eyes. At eleven o'clock that night, when the boy seemed to be resting comfortably enough after the many X-rays and the lab work, and it was just a matter of his waking up and coming around, Howard left the hospital. He and Ann had been at the hospital with the child since that afternoon, and he was going home for a short while to bathe and change clothes. "I'll be back in an hour," he said. She nodded. "It's fine," she said. "I'll be right here." He kissed her on the forehead, and they touched hands. She sat in the chair beside the bed and looked at the child. She was waiting for him to wake up and be all right. Then she could begin to relax.

Howard drove home from the hospital. He took the wet, dark streets very fast, then caught himself and slowed down. Until now, his life had gone smoothly and to his satisfaction — college, marriage, another year of college for the advanced degree in business, a junior partnership in an investment firm. Fatherhood. He was happy and, so far, lucky — he knew that. His parents were still living, his brothers and his sister were established, his friends from college had gone out to take their places in the world. So far, he had kept away from any real harm, from those forces he knew existed and that could cripple or bring down a man if the luck went bad, if things suddenly turned. He pulled into the driveway and parked. His left leg began to tremble. He sat in the car for a minute and tried to deal with the present situation in a rational manner. Scotty had been hit by a car and was in the hospital, but he was going to be all right. Howard closed his eyes and ran his hand over his face. He got out of the car and went up to the front door. The dog was barking inside the house. The telephone rang and rang while he unlocked the door and fumbled for the light switch. He shouldn't have left the hospital, he shouldn't have. "Goddamn it!" he said. He picked up the receiver and said, "I just walked in the door!"

"There's a cake here that wasn't picked up," the voice on the other end of the line said.

"What are you saying?" Howard asked.

"A cake," the voice said. "A sixteen-dollar cake."

Howard held the receiver against his ear, trying to understand. "I don't know anything about a cake," he said. "Jesus, what are you talking about?"

"Don't hand me that," the voice said.

Howard hung up the telephone. He went into the kitchen and poured himself some whiskey. He called the hospital. But the child's condition remained the same; he was still sleeping and nothing had changed there. While water poured into the tub, Howard lathered his face and shaved. He'd just stretched out in the tub and closed his eyes when the telephone rang again. He hauled himself out, grabbed a towel, and hurried through the house, saying, "Stupid, stupid," for having left the hospital. But when he picked up the receiver and shouted, "Hello!" there was no sound at the other end of the line. Then the caller hung up.

He arrived back at the hospital a little after midnight. Ann still sat in the chair beside the bed. She looked up at Howard, and then she looked back at the child. The child's eyes stayed closed, the head was still wrapped in bandages.

His breathing was quiet and regular. From an apparatus over the bed hung a bottle of glucose with a tube running from the bottle to the boy's arm.

"How is he?" Howard said. "What's all this?" waving at the glucose and the tube.

"Dr. Francis's orders," she said. "He needs nourishment. He needs to keep up his strength. Why doesn't he wake up, Howard? I don't understand, if he's all right."

Howard put his hand against the back of her head. He ran his fingers through her hair. "He's going to be all right. He'll wake up in a little while. Dr. Francis knows what's what."

After a time, he said, "Maybe you should go home and get some rest. I'll stay here. Just don't put up with this creep who keeps calling. Hang up right away."

"Who's calling?" she asked.

"I don't know who, just somebody with nothing better to do than call up people. You go on now."

She shook her head. "No," she said, "I'm fine."

"Really," he said. "Go home for a while, and then come back and spell me in the morning. It'll be all right. What did Dr. Francis say? He said Scotty's going to be all right. We don't have to worry. He's just sleeping now, that's all."

A nurse pushed the door open. She nodded at them as she went to the bedside. She took the left arm out from under the covers and put her fingers on the wrist, found the pulse, then consulted her watch. In a little while, she put the arm back under the covers and moved to the foot of the bed, where she wrote something on a clipboard attached to the bed.

"How is he?" Ann said. Howard's hand was a weight on her shoulder. She was aware of the pressure from his fingers.

"He's stable," the nurse said. Then she said, "Doctor will be in again shortly. Doctor's back in the hospital. He's making rounds right now."

"I was saying maybe she'd want to go home and get a little rest," Howard said. "After the doctor comes," he said.

"She could do that," the nurse said. "I think you should both feel free to do that, if you wish." The nurse was a big Scandinavian woman with blond hair. There was the trace of an accent in her speech.

"We'll see what the doctor says," Ann said. "I want to talk to the doctor. I don't think he should keep sleeping like this. I don't think that's a good sign." She brought her hand up to her eyes and let her head come forward a little. Howard's grip tightened on her shoulder, and then his hand moved up to her neck, where his fingers began to knead the muscles there.

"Dr. Francis will be here in a few minutes," the nurse said. Then she left the room.

Howard gazed at his son for a time, the small chest quietly rising and falling under the covers. For the first time since the terrible minutes after Ann's telephone call to him at his office, he felt a genuine fear starting in his limbs. He began shaking his head. Scotty was fine, but instead of sleeping at home in his own bed, he was in a hospital bed with bandages around his head and a tube in his arm. But this help was what he needed right now.

Dr. Francis came in and shook hands with Howard, though they'd just seen each other a few hours before. Ann got up from the chair. "Doctor?"

"Ann," he said and nodded. "Let's just first see how he's doing," the doctor said. He moved to the side of the bed and took the boy's pulse. He peeled back one eyelid and then the other. Howard and Ann stood beside the doctor and watched. Then the doctor turned back the covers and listened to the boy's heart and lungs with his stethoscope. He pressed his fingers here and there on the abdomen. When he was finished, he went to the end of the bed and studied the chart. He noted the time, scribbled something on the chart, and then looked at Howard and Ann.

"Doctor, how is he?" Howard said. "What's the matter with him exactly?"

"Why doesn't he wake up?" Ann said.

The doctor was a handsome, big-shouldered man with a tanned face. He wore a three-piece blue suit, a striped tie, and ivory cufflinks. His gray hair was combed along the sides of his head, and he looked as if he had just come from a concert. "He's all right," the doctor said. "Nothing to shout about, he could be better, I think. But he's all right. Still, I wish he'd wake up. He should wake up pretty soon." The doctor looked at the boy again. "We'll know some more in a couple of hours, after the results of a few more tests are in. But he's all right, believe me, except for the hairline fracture of the skull. He does have that."

"Oh, no," Ann said.

"And a bit of a concussion, as I said before. Of course, you know he's in shock," the doctor said. "Sometimes you see this in shock cases. This sleeping."

"But he's out of any real danger?" Howard said. "You said before he's not in a coma. You wouldn't call this a coma, then — would you, doctor?" Howard waited. He looked at the doctor.

"No, I don't want to call it a coma," the doctor said and glanced over at the boy once more. "He's just in a very deep sleep. It's a restorative measure the body is taking on its own. He's out of any real danger, I'd say that for certain, yes. But we'll know more when he wakes up and the other tests are in," the doctor said.

"It's a coma," Ann said. "Of sorts."

"It's not a coma yet, not exactly," the doctor said. "I wouldn't want to call it coma. Not yet, anyway. He's suffered shock. In shock cases, this kind of reaction is common enough; it's a temporary reaction to bodily trauma. Coma. Well, coma is a deep, prolonged unconsciousness, something that could go on for days, or weeks even. Scotty's not in that area, not as far as we can tell. I'm certain his condition will show improvement by morning. I'm betting that it will. We'll know more when he wakes up, which shouldn't be long now. Of course, you may do as you like, stay here or go home for a time. But by all means feel free to leave the hospital for a while if you want. This is not easy, I know. " The doctor gazed at the boy again, watching him, and then he turned to Ann and said, "You try not to worry, little mother. Believe me, we're doing all that can be done. It's just a question of a little more time now. " He nodded at her, shook hands with Howard again, and then he left the room.

Ann put her hand over the child's forehead. "At least he doesn't have a fever," she said. Then she said, "My God, he feels so cold, though. Howard? Is he supposed to feel like this? Feel his head."

Howard touched the child's temples. His own breathing had slowed. "I think he's supposed to feel this way right now," he said. "He's in shock, remember? That's what the doctor said. The doctor was just in here. He would have said something if Scotty wasn't okay."

Ann stood there a while longer, working her lip with her teeth. Then she moved over to her chair and sat down.

Howard sat in the chair next to her chair. They looked at each other. He wanted to say something else and reassure her, but he was afraid, too. He took her hand and put it in his lap, and this made him feel better, her hand being there. He picked up her hand and squeezed it. Then he just held her hand. They sat like that for a while, watching the boy and not talking. From time to time, he squeezed her hand. Finally, she took her hand away.

"I've been praying," she said.

He nodded.

She said, "I almost thought I'd forgotten how, but it came back to me. All I had to do was close my eyes and say, 'Please God, help us — help Scotty,' and then the rest was easy. The words were right there. Maybe if you prayed, too," she said to him.

"I've already prayed," he said. "I prayed this afternoon — yesterday afternoon, I mean — after you called, while I was driving to the hospital. I've been praying," he said.

"That's good," she said. For the first time, she felt they were together in it, this trouble. She realized with a start that, until now, it had only been happening to her and to Scotty. She hadn't let Howard into it, though he was there and needed all along. She felt glad to be his wife.

The same nurse came in and took the boy's pulse again and checked the flow from the bottle hanging above the bed.

In an hour, another doctor came in. He said his name was Parsons, from Radiology. He had a bushy mustache. He was wearing loafers, a Western shirt, and a pair of jeans.

"We're going to take him downstairs for more pictures," he told them. "We need to do some more pictures, and we want to do a scan."

"What's that?" Ann said. "A scan?" She stood between this new doctor and the bed. "I thought you'd already taken all your X-rays."

"I'm afraid we need some more," he said. "Nothing to be alarmed about. We just need some more pictures, and we want to do a brain scan on him."

"My God," Ann said.

"It's perfectly normal procedure in cases like this," this new doctor said. "We just need to find out for sure why he isn't back awake yet. It's normal medical procedure, and nothing to be alarmed about. We'll be taking him down in a few minutes," this doctor said.

In a little while, two orderlies came into the room with a gurney. They were black-haired, dark-complexioned men in white uniforms, and they said a few words to each other in a foreign tongue as they unhooked the boy from the tube and moved him from his bed to the gurney. Then they wheeled him from the room. Howard and Ann got on the same elevator. Ann gazed at the child. She closed her eyes as the elevator began its descent. The orderlies stood at either end of the gurney without saying anything, though once one of the men made a comment to the other in their own language, and the other man nodded slowly in response.

Later that morning, just as the sun was beginning to lighten the windows in the waiting room outside the X-ray department, they brought the boy out and moved him back up to his room. Howard and Ann rode up on the elevator with him once more, and once more they took up their places beside the bed.

They waited all day, but still the boy did not wake up. Occasionally, one of them would leave the room to go downstairs to the cafeteria to drink coffee and then, as if suddenly remembering and feeling guilty, get up from the table and hurry back to the room. Dr. Francis came again that afternoon and examined the boy once more and then left after telling them he was coming along and could wake up at any minute now. Nurses, different nurses from the night before, came in from time to time. Then a young woman from the lab knocked and entered the room. She wore white slacks and a white blouse and carried a little tray of things which she put on the stand beside the bed. Without a word to them, she took blood from the boy's arm. Howard closed his eyes as the woman found the right place on the boy's arm and pushed the needle in.

"I don't understand this," Ann said to the woman.

"Doctor's orders," the young woman said. "I do what I'm told. They say draw that one, I draw. What's wrong with him, anyway?" she said. "He's a sweetie."

"He was hit by a car," Howard said. "A hit-and-run."

The young woman shook her head and looked again at the boy. Then she took her tray and left the room.

"Why won't he wake up?" Ann said. "Howard? I want some answers from these people."

Howard didn't say anything. He sat down again in the chair and crossed one leg over the other. He rubbed his face. He looked at his son and then he settled back in the chair, closed his eyes, and went to sleep.

Ann walked to the window and looked out at the parking lot. It was night, and cars were driving into and out of the parking lot with their lights on. She stood at the window with her hands gripping the sill, and knew in her heart that they were into something now, something hard. She was afraid, and her teeth began to chatter until she tightened her jaws. She saw a big car stop in front of the hospital and someone, a woman in a long coat, get into the car. She wished she were that woman and somebody, anybody, was driving her away from here to somewhere else, a place where she would find Scotty waiting for her when she stepped out of the car, ready to say *Mom* and let her gather him in her arms.

In a little while, Howard woke up. He looked at the boy again. Then he got up from the chair, stretched, and went over to stand beside her at the window. They both stared out at the parking lot. They didn't say anything. But they seemed to feel each other's insides now, as though the worry had made them transparent in a perfectly natural way.

The door opened and Dr. Francis came in. He was wearing a different suit and tie this time. His gray hair was combed along the sides of his head, and he looked as if he had just shaved. He went straight to the bed and examined the boy. "He ought to have come around by now. There's just no good reason for this," he said. "But I can tell you we're all convinced he's out of any danger. We'll just feel better when he wakes up. There's no reason, absolutely none, why he shouldn't come around. Very soon. Oh, he'll have himself a dilly of a headache when he does, you can count on that. But all of his signs are fine. They're as normal as can be."

"It is a coma, then?" Ann said.

The doctor rubbed his smooth cheek. "We'll call it that for the time being, until he wakes up. But you must be worn out. This is hard. I know this is hard. Feel free to go out for a bite, " he said. "It would do you good. I'll put a nurse in here while you're gone if you'll feel better about going. Go and have yourselves something to eat."

"I couldn't eat anything," Ann said.

"Do what you need to do, of course," the doctor said. "Anyway, I wanted to tell you that all the signs are good, the tests are negative, nothing showed up at all, and just as soon as he wakes up he'll be over the hill."

"Thank you, doctor," Howard said. He shook hands with the doctor again. The doctor patted Howard's shoulder and went out.

"I suppose one of us should go home and check on things," Howard said. "Slug needs to be fed, for one thing."

"Call one of the neighbors," Ann said. "Call the Morgans. Anyone will feed a dog if you ask them to."

"All right," Howard said. After a while, he said, "Honey, why don't *you* do it? Why don't you go home and check on things, and then come back? It'll do you good. I'll be right here with him. Seriously," he said. "We need to keep up our strength on this. We'll want to be here for a while even after he wakes up."

"Why don't *you* go?" she said. "Feed Slug. Feed yourself."

"I already went," he said. "I was gone for exactly an hour and fifteen minutes. You go home for an hour and freshen up. Then come back."

She tried to think about it, but she was too tired. She closed her eyes and tried to think about it again. After a time, she said, "Maybe I will go home for a few minutes. Maybe if I'm not just sitting right here watching him every second, he'll wake up and be all right. You know? Maybe he'll wake up if I'm not here. I'll go home and take a bath and put on clean clothes. I'll feed Slug. Then I'll come back."

"I'll be right here," he said. "You go on home, honey. I'll keep an eye on things here." His eyes were bloodshot and small, as if he'd been drinking for a long time. His clothes were rumpled. His beard had come out again. She touched his face; and then she took her hand back. She understood he wanted to be by himself for a while, not have to talk or share his worry for a time. She picked her purse up from the nightstand, and he helped her into her coat.

"I won't be gone long," she said.

"Just sit and rest for a little while when you get home," he said. "Eat something. Take a bath. After you get out of the bath, just sit for a while and rest. It'll do you a world of good, you'll see. Then come back," he said. "Let's try not to worry. You heard what Dr. Francis said."

She stood in her coat for a minute trying to recall the doctor's exact words, looking for any nuances, any hint of something behind his words other than what he had said. She tried to remember if his expression had changed any when he bent over to examine the child. She remembered the way his features had composed themselves as he rolled back the child's eyelids and then listened to his breathing.

She went to the door, where she turned and looked back. She looked at the child, and then she looked at the father. Howard nodded. She stepped out of the room and pulled the door closed behind her.

She went past the nurses' station and down to the end of the corridor, looking for the elevator. At the end of the corridor, she turned to her right and entered a little waiting room where a Negro family sat in wicker chairs. There was a middle-aged man in a khaki shirt and pants, a baseball cap pushed back on his head. A large woman wearing a housedress and slippers was slumped in one of the chairs. A teenaged girl in jeans, hair done in dozens of little braids, lay stretched out in one of the chairs smoking a cigarette, her legs crossed at the ankles. The family swung their eyes to Ann as she entered the room. The little table was littered with hamburger wrappers and Styrofoam cups.

"Franklin," the large woman said as she roused herself. "Is it about Franklin?" Her eyes widened. "Tell me now, lady," the woman said. "Is it about Franklin?" She was trying to rise from her chair, but the man had closed his hand over her arm.

"Here, here," he said. "Evelyn."

"I'm sorry," Ann said. "I'm looking for the elevator. My son is in the hospital, and now I can't find the elevator."

"Elevator is down that way, turn left," the man said as he aimed a finger.

The girl drew on her cigarette and stared at Ann. Her eyes were narrowed to slits, and her broad lips parted slowly as she let the smoke escape. The Negro woman let her head fall on her shoulder and looked away from Ann, no longer interested.

"My son was hit by a car," Ann said to the man. She seemed to need to explain herself. "He has a concussion and a little skull fracture, but he's going to be all right. He's in shock now, but it might be some kind of coma, too. That's what really worries us, the coma part. I'm going out for a little while, but my husband is with him. Maybe he'll wake up while I'm gone."

"That's too bad," the man said and shifted in the chair. He shook his head. He looked down at the table, and then he looked back at Ann. She was still standing there. He said, "Our Franklin, he's on the operating table. Somebody cut him. Tried to kill him. There was a fight where he was at. At this party. They say he was just standing and watching. Not bothering nobody. But that don't mean nothing these days. Now he's on the operating table. We're just hoping and praying, that's all we can do now." He gazed at her steadily.

Ann looked at the girl again, who was still watching her, and at the older woman, who kept her head down, but whose eyes were now closed. Ann saw the lips moving silently, making words. She had an urge to ask what those words were. She wanted to talk more with these people who were in the same kind of waiting she was in. She was afraid, and they were afraid. They had that in common. She would have liked to have said something else about the accident, told them more about Scotty, that it had happened on the day of his birthday, Monday, and that he was still unconscious. Yet she didn't know how to begin. She stood looking at them without saying anything more.

She went down the corridor the man had indicated and found the elevator. She waited a minute in front of the closed doors, still wondering if she was doing the right thing. Then she put out her finger and touched the button.

She pulled into the driveway and cut the engine. She closed her eyes and leaned her head against the wheel for a minute. She listened to the ticking sounds the engine made as it began to cool. Then she got out of the car. She could hear the dog barking inside the house. She went to the front door, which was unlocked. She went inside and turned on lights and put on a kettle of water for tea. She opened some dogfood and fed Slug on the back porch. The dog ate in hungry little smacks. It kept running into the kitchen to see that she was going to stay. As she sat down on the sofa with her tea, the telephone rang.

"Yes!" she said as she answered. "Hello!"

"Mrs. Weiss," a man's voice said. It was five o'clock in the morning, and she thought she could hear machinery or equipment of some kind in the background.

"Yes, yes! What is it?" she said. "This is Mrs. Weiss. This is she. What is it, please?" She listened to whatever it was in the background. "Is it Scotty, for Christ's sake?"

"Scotty," the man's voice said. "It's about Scotty, yes. It has to do with Scotty, that problem. Have you forgotten about Scotty?" the man said. Then he hung up.

She dialed the hospital's number and asked for the third floor. She demanded information about her son from the nurse who answered the telephone. Then she asked to speak to her husband. It was, she said, an emergency.

She waited, turning the telephone cord in her fingers. She closed her eyes and felt sick at her stomach. She would have to make herself eat. Slug came in from the back porch and lay down near her feet. He wagged his tail. She pulled at his ear while he licked her fingers. Howard was on the line.

"Somebody just called here," she said. She twisted the telephone cord. "He said it was about Scotty," she cried.

"Scotty's fine," Howard told her. "I mean, he's still sleeping. There's been no change. The nurse has been in twice since you've been gone. A nurse or else a doctor. He's all right."

"This man called. He said it was about Scotty," she told him.

"Honey, you rest for a little while, you need the rest. It must be that same caller I had. Just forget it. Come back down here after you've rested. Then we'll have breakfast or something."

"Breakfast," she said. "I don't want any breakfast."

"You know what I mean," he said. "Juice, something. I don't know. I don't know anything, Ann. Jesus, I'm not hungry, either. Ann, it's hard to talk now. I'm standing here at the desk. Dr. Francis is coming again at eight o'clock this morning. He's going to have something to tell us then, something more definite. That's what one of the nurses said. She didn't know any more than that. Ann? Honey, maybe we'll know something more then. At eight o'clock. Come back here before eight. Meanwhile, I'm right here and Scotty's all right. He's still the same," he added.

"I was drinking a cup of tea," she said, "when the telephone rang. They said it was about Scotty. There was a noise in the background. Was there a noise in the background on that call you had, Howard?"

"I don't remember," he said. "Maybe the driver of the car, maybe he's a psychopath and found out about Scotty somehow. But I'm here with him. Just rest like you were going to do. Take a bath and come back by seven or so, and we'll talk to the doctor together when he gets here. It's going to be all right, honey. I'm here, and there are doctors and nurses around. They say his condition is stable."

"I'm scared to death," she said.

She ran water, undressed, and got into the tub. She washed and dried quickly, not taking the time to wash her hair. She put on clean underwear, wool slacks, and a sweater. She went into the living room, where the dog looked up at her and let its tail thump once against the floor. It was just starting to get light outside when she went out to the car.

She drove into the parking lot of the hospital and found a space close to the front door. She felt she was in some obscure way responsible for what had happened to the child. She let her thoughts move to the Negro family. She remembered the name Franklin and the table that was covered with hamburger papers, and the teenaged girl staring at her as she drew on her cigarette. "Don't have children," she told the girl's image as she entered the front door of the hospital. "For God's sake, don't.

She took the elevator up to the third floor with two nurses who were just going on duty. It was Wednesday morning, a few minutes before seven. There was a page for a Dr. Madison as the elevator doors slid open on the third floor. She got off behind the nurses, who turned in the other direction and continued the conversation she had interrupted when she'd gotten into the elevator. She walked down the corridor to the little alcove where the Negro family had been waiting. They were gone now, but the chairs were scattered in such a way that it looked as if people had just jumped up from them the minute before. The tabletop was cluttered with the same cups and papers, the ashtray was filled with cigarette butts.

She stopped at the nurses' station. A nurse was standing behind the counter, brushing her hair and yawning.

"There was a Negro boy in surgery last night," Ann said. "Franklin was his name. His family was in the waiting room. I'd like to inquire about his condition."

A nurse who was sitting at a desk behind the counter looked up from a chart in front of her. The telephone buzzed and she picked up the receiver, but she kept her eyes on Ann.

"He passed away," said the nurse at the counter. The nurse held the hairbrush and kept looking at her. "Are you a friend of the family or what?"

"I met the family last night," Ann said. "My own son is in the hospital. I guess he's in shock. We don't know for sure what's wrong. I just wondered about Franklin, that's all. Thank you." She moved down the corridor. Elevator doors the same color as the walls slid open and a gaunt, bald man in white pants and white canvas shoes pulled a heavy cart off the elevator. She hadn't noticed these doors last night. The man wheeled the cart out into the corridor and stopped in front of the room nearest the elevator and consulted a clipboard. Then he reached down and slid a tray out of the cart. He rapped lightly on the door and entered the room. She could smell the unpleasant odors of warm food as she passed the cart. She hurried on without looking at any of the nurses and pushed open the door to the child's room.

Howard was standing at the window with his hands behind his back. He turned around as she came in.

"How is he?" she said. She went over to the bed. She dropped her purse on the floor beside the nightstand. It seemed to her she had been gone a long time. She touched the child's face. "Howard?"

"Dr. Francis was here a little while ago," Howard said. She looked at him closely and thought his shoulders were bunched a little.

"I thought he wasn't coming until eight o'clock this morning," she said quickly.

"There was another doctor with him. A neurologist."

"A neurologist," she said.

Howard nodded. His shoulders were bunching, she could see that. "What'd they say, Howard? For Christ's sake, what'd they say? What is it?"

"They said they're going to take him down and run more tests on him, Ann. They think they're going to operate, honey. Honey, they *are* going to operate. They can't figure out why he won't wake up. It's more than just shock or concussion, they know that much now. It's in his skull, the fracture, it has something, something to do with that, they think. So they're going to operate. I tried to call you, but I guess you'd already left the house."

"Oh, God," she said. "Oh, please, Howard, please," she said, taking his arms.

"Look!" Howard said. "Scotty! Look, Ann!" He turned her toward the bed.

The boy had opened his eyes, then closed them. He opened them again now. The eyes stared straight ahead for a minute, then moved slowly in his head until they rested on Howard and Ann, then traveled away again.

"Scotty," his mother said, moving to the bed.

"Hey, Scott," his father said. "Hey, son."

They leaned over the bed. Howard took the child's hand in his hands and began to pat and squeeze the hand. Ann bent over the boy and kissed his forehead again and again. She put her hands on either side of his face. "Scotty, honey, it's Mommy and Daddy," she said. "Scotty?"

The boy looked at them, but without any sign of recognition. Then his mouth opened, his eyes scrunched closed, and he howled until he had no more air in his lungs. His face seemed to relax and soften then. His lips parted as his last breath was puffed through his throat and exhaled gently through the clenched teeth.

The doctors called it a hidden occlusion and said it was a one-in-a-million circumstance. Maybe if it could have been detected somehow and surgery undertaken immediately, they could have saved him. But more than likely not. In any case, what would they have been looking for? Nothing had shown up in the tests or in the X-rays.

Dr. Francis was shaken. "I can't tell you how badly I feel. I'm so very sorry, I can't tell you," he said as he led them into the doctors' lounge. There was a doctor sitting in a chair with his legs hooked over the back of another chair, watching an early-morning TV show. He was wearing a green delivery-room outfit, loose green pants and green blouse, and a green cap that covered his hair. He looked at Howard and Ann and then looked at Dr. Francis. He got to his feet and turned off the set and went out of the room. Dr. Francis guided Ann to the sofa, sat down beside her, and began to talk in a low, consoling voice. At one point, he leaned over and embraced her. She could feel his chest rising and falling evenly against her shoulder. She kept her eyes open and let him hold her. Howard went into the bathroom, but he left the door open. After a violent fit of weeping, he ran water and washed his face. Then he came out and sat down at the little table that held a telephone. He looked at the telephone as though deciding what to do first. He made some calls. After a time, Dr. Francis used the telephone.

"Is there anything else I can do for the moment?" he asked them.

Howard shook his head. Ann stared at Dr. Francis as if unable to comprehend his words.

The doctor walked them to the hospital's front door. People were entering and leaving the hospital. It was eleven o'clock in the morning. Ann was aware of how slowly, almost reluctantly, she moved her feet. It seemed to her that Dr. Francis was making them leave when she felt they should stay, when it would be more the right thing to do to stay. She gazed out into the parking lot and then turned around and looked back at the front of the hospital. She began shaking her head. "No, no," she said. "I can't leave him here, no." She heard herself say that and thought how unfair it was that the only words that came out were the sort of words used on TV shows where people were stunned by violent or sudden deaths. She wanted her words to be her own. "No," she said, and for some reason the memory of the Negro woman's head lolling on the woman's shoulder came to her. "No," she said again.

"I'll be talking to you later in the day," the doctor was saying to Howard. "There are still some things that have to be done, things that have to be cleared up to our satisfaction. Some things that need explaining."

"An autopsy," Howard said.

Dr. Francis nodded.

"I understand," Howard said. Then he said, "Oh, Jesus. No, I don't understand, doctor. I can't, I can't. I just can't."

Dr. Francis put his arm around Howard's shoulders. "I'm sorry. God, how I'm sorry." He let go of Howard's shoulders and held out his hand. Howard looked at the hand, and then he took it. Dr. Francis put his arms around Ann once more. He seemed full of some goodness she didn't understand. She let her head rest on his shoulder, but her eyes stayed open. She kept looking at the hospital. As they drove out of the parking lot, she looked back at the hospital.

At home, she sat on the sofa with her hands in her coat pockets. Howard closed the door to the child's room. He got the coffee-maker going and then he found an empty box. He had thought to pick up some of the child's things that were scattered around the living room. But instead he sat down beside her on the sofa, pushed the box to one side, and leaned forward, arms between his knees. He began to weep. She pulled his head over into her lap and patted his shoulder. "He's gone," she said. She kept patting his shoulder. Over his sobs, she could hear the coffee-maker hissing in the kitchen. "There, there," she said tenderly. "Howard, he's gone. He's gone and now we'll have to get used to that. To being alone."

In a little while, Howard got up and began moving aimlessly around the room with the box, not putting anything into it, but collecting some things together on the floor at one end of the sofa. She continued to sit with her hands in her coat pockets. Howard put the box down and brought coffee into the living room. Later, Ann made calls to relatives. After each call had been placed and the party had answered, Ann would blurt out a few words and cry for a minute. Then she would quietly explain, in a measured voice, what had happened and tell them about arrangements. Howard took the box out to the garage, where he saw the child's bicycle. He dropped the box and sat down on the pavement beside the bicycle. He took hold of the bicycle awkwardly so that it leaned against his chest. He held it, the rubber pedal sticking into his chest. He gave the wheel a turn.

Ann hung up the telephone after talking to her sister. She was looking up another number when the telephone rang. She picked it up on the first ring.

"Hello," she said, and she heard something in the background, a humming noise. "Hello!" she said. "For God's sake," she said. "Who is this? What is it you want?"

"Your Scotty, I got him ready for you," the man's voice said. "Did you forget him?"

"You evil bastard!" she shouted into the receiver. "How can you do this, you evil son of a bitch?"

"Scotty," the man said. "Have you forgotten about Scotty?" Then the man hung up on her.

Howard heard the shouting and came in to find her with her head on her arms over the table, weeping. He picked up the receiver and listened to the dial tone.

Much later, just before midnight, after they had dealt with many things, the telephone rang again.

"You answer it," she said. "Howard, it's him, I know." They were sitting at the kitchen table with coffee in front of them. Howard had a small glass of whiskey beside his cup. He answered on the third ring.

"Hello," he said. "Who is this? Hello! Hello!" The line went dead. "He hung up," Howard said. "Whoever it was."

"It was him," she said. "That bastard. I'd like to kill him," she said. "I'd like to shoot him and watch him kick," she said.

"Ann, my God," he said.

"Could you hear anything?" she said. "In the background? A noise, machinery, something humming?"

"Nothing, really. Nothing like that," he said. "There wasn't much time. I think there was some radio music. Yes, there was a radio going, that's all I could tell. I don't know what in God's name is going on," he said.

She shook her head. "If I could, could get my hands on him." It came to her then. She knew who it was. Scotty, the cake, the telephone number. She pushed the chair away from the table and got up. "Drive me down to the shopping center," she said. "Howard."

"What are you saying?"

"The shopping center. I know who it is who's calling. I know who it is. It's the baker, the son-of-a-bitching baker, Howard. I had him bake a cake for Scotty's birthday. That's who's calling. That's who has the number and keeps calling us. To harass us about that cake. The baker, that bastard."

They drove down to the shopping center. The sky was clear and stars were out. It was cold, and they ran the heater in the car. They parked in front of the bakery. All of the shops and stores were closed, but there were cars at the far end of the lot in front of the movie theater. The bakery windows were dark, but when they looked through the glass they could see a light in the back room and, now and then, a big man in an apron moving in and out of the white, even light. Through the glass, she could see the display cases and some little tables with chairs. She tried the door. She rapped on the glass. But if the baker heard them, he gave no sign. He didn't look in their direction.

They drove around behind the bakery and parked. They got out of the car. There was a lighted window too high up for them to see inside. A sign near the back door said THE PANTRY BAKERY, SPECIAL ORDERS. She could hear faintly a radio playing inside and something creak — an oven door as it was pulled down? She knocked on the door and waited. Then she knocked again, louder. The radio was turned down and there was a scraping sound now, the distinct sound of something, a drawer, being pulled open and then closed.

Someone unlocked the door and opened it. The baker stood in the light and peered out at them. "I'm closed for business," he said. "What do you want at this hour? It's midnight. Are you drunk or something?"

She stepped into the light that fell through the open door. He blinked his heavy eyelids as he recognized her. "It's you," he said.

"It's me," she said. "Scotty's mother. This is Scotty's father. We'd like to come in."

The baker said, "I'm busy now. I have work to do."

She had stepped inside the doorway anyway. Howard came in behind her. The baker moved back. "It smells like a bakery in here. Doesn't it smell like a bakery in here, Howard?"

"What do you want?" the baker said. "Maybe you want your cake? That's it, you decided you want your cake. You ordered a cake, didn't you?"

"You're pretty smart for a baker," she said. "Howard, this is the man who's been calling us." She clenched her fists. She stared at him fiercely. There was a deep burning inside her, an anger that made her feel larger than herself, larger than either of these men.

"Just a minute here," the baker said. "You want to pick up your three-day-old cake? That it? I don't want to argue with you, lady. There it sits over there, getting stale. I'll give it to you for half of what I quoted you. No. You want it? You can have it. It's no good to me, no good to anyone now. It cost me time and money to make that cake. If you want it, okay, if you don't, that's okay, too. I have to get back to work." He looked at them and rolled his tongue behind his teeth.

"More cakes," she said. She knew she was in control of it, of what was increasing in her. She was calm.

"Lady, I work sixteen hours a day in this place to earn a living," the baker said. He wiped his hands on his apron. "I work night and day in here, trying to make ends meet. " A look crossed Ann's face that made the baker move back and say, "No trouble, now. " He reached to the counter and picked up a rolling pin with his right hand and began to tap it against the palm of his other hand. "You want the cake or not? I have to get back to work. Bakers work at night," he said again. His eyes were small, mean-looking, she thought, nearly lost in the bristly flesh around his cheeks. His neck was thick with fat.

"I know bakers work at night," Ann said. "They make phone calls at night, too. You bastard," she said.

The baker continued to tap the rolling pin against his hand. He glanced at Howard. "Careful, careful," he said to Howard.

"My son's dead," she said with a cold, even finality. "He was hit by a car Monday morning. We've been waiting with him until he died. But, of course, you couldn't be expected to know that, could you? Bakers can't know everything — can they, Mr. Baker? But he's dead. He's dead, you bastard!" Just as suddenly as it had welled in her, the anger dwindled, gave way to something else, a dizzy feeling of nausea. She leaned against the wooden table that was sprinkled with flour, put her hands over her face, and began to cry, her shoulders rocking back and forth. "It isn't fair," she said. "It isn't, isn't fair."

Howard put his hand at the small of her back and looked at the baker. "Shame on you," Howard said to him. "Shame."

The baker put the rolling pin back on the counter. He undid his apron and threw it on the counter. He looked at them, and then he shook his head slowly. He pulled a chair out from under the card table that held papers and receipts, an adding machine, and a telephone directory. "Please sit down," he said. "Let me get you a chair," he said to Howard. "Sit down now, please." The baker went into the front of the shop and returned with two little wrought-iron chairs. "Please sit down, you people."

Ann wiped her eyes and looked at the baker." I wanted to kill you," she said. "I wanted you dead."

The baker had cleared a space for them at the table. He shoved the adding machine to one side, along with the stacks of notepaper and receipts. He pushed the telephone directory onto the floor, where it landed with a thud. Howard and Ann sat down and pulled their chairs up to the table. The baker sat down, too.

"Let me say how sorry I am," the baker said, putting his elbows on the table. "God alone knows how sorry. Listen to me. I'm just a baker. I don't claim to be anything else. Maybe once, maybe years ago, I was a different kind of human being. I've forgotten, I don't know for sure. But I'm not any longer, if I ever was. Now I'm just a baker. That don't excuse my doing what I did, I know. But I'm deeply sorry. I'm sorry for your son, and sorry for my part in this," the baker said. He spread his hands out on the table and turned them over to reveal his palms. "I don't have any children myself, so I can only imagine what you must be feeling. All I can say to you now is that I'm sorry. Forgive me, if you can," the baker said. "I'm not an evil man, I don't think. Not evil, like you said on the phone. You got to understand what it comes down to is I don't know how to act anymore, it would seem. Please," the man said, "let me ask you if you can find it in your hearts to forgive me?"

It was warm inside the bakery. Howard stood up from the table and took off his coat. He helped Ann from her coat. The baker looked at them for a minute and then nodded and got up from the table. He went to the oven and turned off some switches. He found cups and poured coffee from an electric coffee-maker. He put a carton of cream on the table, and a bowl of sugar.

"You probably need to eat something," the baker said. "I hope you'll eat some of my hot rolls. You have to eat and keep going. Eating is a small, good thing in a time like this," he said.

He served them warm cinnamon rolls just out of the oven, the icing still runny. He put butter on the table and knives to spread the butter. Then the baker sat down at the table with them. He waited. He waited until they each took a roll from the platter and began to eat. "It's good to eat something," he said, watching them. "There's more. Eat up. Eat all you want. There's all the rolls in the world in here."

They ate rolls and drank coffee. Ann was suddenly hungry, and the rolls were warm and sweet. She ate three of them, which pleased the baker. Then he began to talk. They listened carefully. Although they were tired and in anguish, they listened to what the baker had to say. They nodded when the baker began to speak of loneliness, and of the sense of doubt and limitation that had come to him in his middle years. He told them what it was like to be childless all these years. To repeat the days with the ovens endlessly full and endlessly empty. The party food, the celebrations he'd worked over. Icing knuckle-deep. The tiny wedding couples stuck into cakes. Hundreds of them, no, thousands by now. Birthdays. Just imagine all those candies burning. He had a necessary trade. He was a baker. He was glad he wasn't a florist. It was better to be feeding people. This was a better smell anytime than flowers.

"Smell this," the baker said, breaking open a dark loaf. "It's a heavy bread, but rich." They smelled it, then he had them taste it. It had the taste of molasses and coarse grains. They listened to him. They ate what they could. They swallowed the dark bread. It was like daylight under the fluorescent trays of light. They talked on into the early morning, the high, pale cast of light in the windows, and they did not think of leaving.

JOHN CHEEVER *(1912–1982), the leading exponent of the kind of carefully fashioned story of modern suburban manners that* The New Yorker *popularized, has been called "the Chekhov of the suburbs" by the reviewer John Leonard. Cheever spent most of his life in New York City and in suburban towns similar to the ones he described in much of his fiction. Born in Quincy, Massachusetts, he was raised by parents who owned a prosperous business that failed after the 1929 stock market crash. His parents enjoyed reading literature to him, so at an early age he was acquainted with the fiction of Charles Dickens, Jack London, and Robert Louis Stevenson. He started his career at an unusually young age. Expelled from Thayer Academy for being, by his own account, a "quarrelsome, intractable . . . and lousy student," he moved to New York City, lived in a cell of a room on a bread-and-buttermilk diet, and wrote stories. When his first one, "Expelled," was accepted for publication by Malcolm Cowley, then editor of the* New Republic, *Cheever was launched as a teenager into a career as a writer of fiction. Earlier Cowley had told him that his stories were too long to get published by magazines that paid, so, to encourage discipline, he made Cheever write a story of not more than a thousand words every day for four days.*

Cheever's first collection of stories, The Way Some People Live, *appeared in 1942, while he was serving in the army. In 1953 he strengthened his literary reputation with* The Enormous Radio and Other Stories, *a collection of fourteen of his* New Yorker *pieces. Six years later appeared another story collection,* The Housebreaker of Shady Hill. *In the 1960s and 1970s he published three more books of short stories and two widely acclaimed novels,* Bullet Park *(1969) and* Falconer *(1977).* The Stories of John Cheever, *published in 1978, won both the Pulitzer Prize and the National Book Critics Circle Award and became one of the few collections of short stories ever to make the* New York Times *best-seller list. In more than fifty years, Cheever published more than 200 magazine stories; he figured that he earned "enough money to feed the family and buy a new suit every other year."*

Usually a rapid writer, Cheever said he liked best the stories that he wrote in less than a week, although he spent months working on "The Swimmer" (1964). He originally wrote a draft of the plot as "a perfectly good" novel, but then he burned it. "I could very easily have sold the book," he said, "but the trick was to get the winter constellations in the midsummer sky without anyone knowing about it, and it didn't take 250 pages to do that."

RELATED COMMENTARY: *John Cheever, "Why I Write Short Stories," page 666.*

JOHN CHEEVER

The Swimmer

1964

It was one of those midsummer Sundays when everyone sits around saying, "I *drank* too much last night." You might have heard it whispered by the parishioners leaving church, heard it from the lips of the priest himself, struggling with his cassock in the *vestiarium,* heard it from the golf links and the tennis courts, heard it from the wild-life preserve where the leader of the Audubon group was suffering from a terrible hangover. "I *drank* too much," said Donald Westerhazy. "We all *drank* too much," said Lucinda Merrill. "It must have been the wine," said Helen Westerhazy. "I *drank* too much of that claret."

This was the edge of the Westerhazys' pool. The pool, fed by an artesian well with a high iron content, was a pale shade of green. It was a fine day. In the west there was a massive stand of cumulus cloud so like a city seen from a distance — from the bow of an approaching ship — that it might have had a name. Lisbon. Hackensack. The sun was hot. Neddy Merrill sat by the green water, one hand in it, one around a glass of gin. He was a slender man — he seemed to have the especial slenderness of youth — and while he was far from young he had slid down his banister that morning and given the bronze backside of Aphrodite on the hall table a smack, as he jogged toward the smell of coffee in his dining room. He might have been compared to a summer's day, particularly the last hours of one, and while he lacked a tennis racket or a sail bag the impression was definitely one of youth, sport, and clement weather. He had been swimming and now he was breathing deeply, stertorously as if he could gulp into his lungs the components of that moment, the heat of the sun, the intenseness of his pleasure. It all seemed to flow into his chest. His own house stood in Bullet Park, eight miles to the south, where his four beautiful daughters would have had their lunch and might be playing tennis. Then it occurred to him that by taking a dogleg to the southwest he could reach his home by water.

His life was not confining and the delight he took in this observation could not be explained by its suggestion of escape. He seemed to see, with a cartographer's eye, that string of swimming pools, that quasi-subterranean stream that curved across the county. He had made a discovery, a contribution to modern geography; he would name the stream Lucinda after his wife. He was not a practical joker nor was he a fool but he was determinedly original and had a vague and modest idea of himself as a legendary figure. The day was beautiful and it seemed to him that a long swim might enlarge and celebrate its beauty.

He took off a sweater that was hung over his shoulders and dove in. He had an inexplicable contempt for men who did not hurl themselves into pools. He swam a choppy crawl, breathing either with every stroke or every fourth stroke and counting somewhere well in the back of his mind the one-two one-two of a flutter kick. It was not a serviceable stroke for long distances but the domestication of swimming had saddled the sport with some customs and in his part of the world a crawl was customary. To be embraced and sustained by the light green water was less a pleasure, it seemed, than the resumption of a natural condition, and he would have liked to swim without trunks, but this was not possible, considering his project. He hoisted himself up on the far curb — he never used the ladder — and started across the lawn. When Lucinda asked where he was going he said he was going to swim home.

The only maps and charts he had to go by were remembered or imaginary but these were clear enough. First there were the Grahams, the Hammers, the Lears, the Howlands, and the Crosscups. He would cross Ditmar Street to the Bunkers and come, after a short portage, to the Levys, the Welchers, and the public pool in Lancaster. Then there were the Hallorans, the Sachses, the Biswangers, Shirley Adams, the Gilmartins, and the Clydes. The day was lovely, and that he lived in a world so generously supplied with water seemed like a clemency, a beneficence. His heart was high and he ran across the grass. Making his way home by an uncommon route gave him the feeling that he was a pilgrim, an explorer, a man with a destiny, and he knew that he would find friends all along the way; friends would line the banks of the Lucinda River.

He went through a hedge that separated the Westerhazys' land from the Grahams', walked under some flowering apple trees, passed the shed that housed their pump and filter, and came out at the Grahams' pool. "Why, Neddy," Mrs. Graham said, "what a marvelous surprise. I've been trying to get you on the phone all morning. Here, let me get you a drink." He saw then, like any explorer, that the hospitable customs and traditions of the natives would have to be handled with diplomacy if he was ever going to reach his destination. He did not want to mystify or seem rude to the Grahams nor did he have the time to linger there. He swam the length of their pool and joined them in the sun and was rescued, a few minutes later, by the arrival of two carloads of friends from Connecticut. During the uproarious reunions he was able to slip away. He went down by the front of the Grahams' house, stepped over a thorny hedge, and crossed a vacant lot to the Hammers'. Mrs. Hammer, looking up from her roses, saw him swim by although she wasn't quite sure who it was. The Lears heard him splashing past the open windows of their living room. The Howlands and the Crosscups were away. After leaving the Howlands' he crossed Ditmar Street and started for the Bunkers', where he could hear, even at that distance, the noise of a party.

The water refracted the sound of voices and laughter and seemed to suspend it in midair. The Bunkers' pool was on a rise and he climbed some stairs to a terrace where twenty-five or thirty men and women were drinking. The only person in the water was Rusty Towers, who floated there on a rubber raft. Oh, how bonny and lush were the banks of the Lucinda River! Prosperous men and women gathered by the sapphire-colored waters while caterer's men in white coats passed them cold gin. Overhead a red de Haviland trainer was circling around and around and around in the sky with something like the glee of a child in a swing. Ned felt a passing affection for the scene, a tenderness for the gathering, as if it was something he might touch. In the distance he heard thunder. As soon as Enid Bunker saw him she began to scream: "Oh, look who's here! What a marvelous surprise! When Lucinda said you couldn't come I thought I'd *die*." She made her way to him through the crowd, and when they had finished kissing she led him to the bar, a progress that was slowed by the fact that he stopped to kiss eight or ten other women and shake the hands of as many men. A smiling bartender he had seen at a hundred parties gave him a gin and tonic and he stood by the bar for a moment, anxious not to get stuck in any conversation that would delay his voyage. When he seemed about to be surrounded he dove in and swam close to the side to avoid colliding with Rusty's raft. At the far end of the pool he bypassed the Tomlinsons with a broad smile and jogged up the garden path. The gravel cut his feet but this was only unpleasantness. The party was confined to the pool, and as he went toward the house he heard the brilliant, watery sound of voices fade, heard the noise of a radio from the Bunkers' kitchen, where someone was listening to a ball game. Sunday afternoon. He made his way through the parked cars and down the grassy border of their driveway to Alewives Lane. He did not want to be seen on the road in his bathing trunks but there was no traffic and he made the short distance to the Levys' driveway, marked with a PRIVATE PROPERTY sign and a green tube for the *New York Times*. All the doors and windows of the big house were open but there were no signs of life; not even a dog barked. He went around the side of the house to the pool and saw that the Levys had only recently left. Glasses and bottles and dishes of nuts were on a table at the deep end, where there was a bathhouse or gazebo, hung with Japanese lanterns. After swimming the pool he got himself a glass and poured a drink. It was his fourth or fifth drink and he had swum nearly half the length of the Lucinda River. He felt tired, clean, and pleased at that moment to be alone; pleased with everything.

It would storm. The stand of cumulus cloud — that city — had risen and darkened, and while he sat there he heard the percussiveness of thunder again. The de Haviland trainer was still circling overhead and it seemed to Ned that he could almost hear the pilot laugh with pleasure in the afternoon; but when there was another peal of thunder he took off for home. A train whistle blew and he wondered what time it had gotten to be. Four? Five? He thought of the provincial station at that hour, where a waiter, his tuxedo concealed by a raincoat, a dwarf with some flowers wrapped in newspaper, and a woman who had been crying would be waiting for the local. It was suddenly growing dark; it was that moment when the pin-headed birds seemed to organize their song into some acute and knowledgeable recognition of the storm's approach. Then there was a fine noise of rushing water from the crown of an oak at his back, as if a spigot there had been turned. Then the noise of fountains came from the crowns of all the tall trees. Why did he love storms, what was the meaning of his excitement when the door sprang open and the rain wind fled rudely up the stairs, why had the simple task of shutting the windows of an old house seemed fitting and urgent, why did the first watery notes of a storm wind have for him the unmistakable sound of good news, cheer, glad tidings? Then there was an explosion, a smell of cordite, and rain lashed the Japanese lanterns that Mrs. Levy had bought in Kyoto the year before last, or was it the year before that?

He stayed in the Levys' gazebo until the storm had passed. The rain had cooled the air and he shivered. The force of the wind had stripped a maple of its red and yellow leaves and scattered them over the grass and the water. Since it was midsummer the tree must be blighted, and yet he felt a peculiar sadness at this sign of autumn. He braced his shoulders, emptied his glass, and started for the Welchers' pool. This meant crossing the Lindleys' riding ring and he was surprised to find it overgrown with grass and all the jumps dismantled. He wondered if the Lindleys had sold their horses or gone away for the summer and put them out to board. He seemed to remember having heard something about the Lindleys and their horses but the memory was unclear. On he went, barefoot through the wet grass, to the Welchers', where he found their pool was dry.

This breach in his chain of water disappointed him absurdly, and he felt like some explorer who seeks a torrential headwater and finds a dead stream. He was disappointed and mystified. It was common enough to go away for the summer but no one ever drained his pool. The Welchers had definitely gone away. The pool furniture was folded, stacked, and covered with a tarpaulin. The bathhouse was locked. All the windows of the house were shut, and when he went around to the driveway in front he saw a FOR SALE sign nailed to a tree. When had he last heard from the Welchers — when, that is, had he and Lucinda last regretted an invitation to dine with them? It seemed only a week or so ago. Was his memory failing or had he so disciplined it in the repression of unpleasant facts that he had damaged his sense of the truth? Then in the distance he heard the sound of a tennis game. This cheered him, cleared away all his apprehensions and let him regard the overcast sky and the cold air with indifference. This was the day that Neddy Merrill swam across the county. That was the day! He started off then for his most difficult portage.

Had you gone for a Sunday afternoon ride that day you might have seen him, close to naked, standing on the shoulders of Route 424, waiting for a chance to cross. You might have wondered if he was the victim of foul play, had his car broken down, or was he merely a fool. Standing barefoot in the deposits of the highway — beer cans, rags, and blowout patches — exposed to all kinds of ridicule, he seemed pitiful. He had known when he started that this was a part of his journey — it had been on his maps — but confronted with the lines of traffic, worming through the summery light, he found himself unprepared. He was laughed at, jeered at, a beer can was thrown at him, and he had no dignity or humor to bring to the situation. He could have gone back, back to the Westerhazys', where Lucinda would still be sitting in the sun. He had signed nothing, vowed nothing, pledged nothing, not even to himself. Why, believing as he did, that all human obduracy was susceptible to common sense, was he unable to turn back? Why was he determined to complete his journey even if it meant putting his life in danger? At what point had this prank, this joke, this piece of horseplay become serious? He could not go back, he could not even recall with any clearness the green water at the Westerhazys', the sense of inhaling the day's components, the friendly and relaxed voices saying that they had *drunk* too much. In the space of an hour, more or less, he had covered a distance that made his return impossible.

An old man, tooling down the highway at fifteen miles an hour, let him get to the middle of the road, where there was a grass divider. Here he was exposed to the ridicule of the northbound traffic, but after ten or fifteen minutes he was able to cross. From here he had only a short walk to the Recreation Center at the edge of the village of Lancaster, where there were some handball courts and a public pool.

The effect of the water on voices, the illusion of brilliance and suspense, was the same here as it had been at the Bunkers' but the sounds here were louder, harsher, and more shrill, and as soon as he entered the crowded enclosure he was confronted with regimentation. "ALL SWIMMERS MUST TAKE A SHOWER BEFORE USING THE POOL. ALL SWIMMERS MUST USE THE FOOTBATH. ALL SWIMMERS MUST WEAR THEIR IDENTIFICATION DISKS." He took a shower, washed his feet in a cloudy and bitter solution, and made his way to the edge of the water. It stank of chlorine and looked to him like a sink. A pair of lifeguards in a pair of towers blew police whistles at what seemed to be regular intervals and abused the swimmers through a public address system. Neddy remembered the sapphire water at the Bunkers' with longing and thought that he might contaminate himself — damage his own prosperousness and charm — by swimming in this murk, but he reminded himself that he was an explorer, a pilgrim, and that this was merely a stagnant bend in the Lucinda River. He dove, scowling with distaste, into the chlorine and had to swim with his head above water to avoid collisions, but even so he was bumped into, splashed, and jostled. When he got to the shallow end both lifeguards were shouting at him: "Hey, you, you without the identification disk, get outa the water." He did, but they had no way of pursuing him and he went through the reek of suntan oil and chlorine out through the hurricane fence and passed the handball courts. By crossing the road he entered the wooded part of the Halloran estate. The woods were not cleared and the footing was treacherous and difficult until he reached the lawn and the clipped beech hedge that encircled their pool.

The Hallorans were friends, an elderly couple of enormous wealth who seemed to bask in the suspicion that they might be Communists. They were zealous reformers but they were not Communists, and yet when they were accused, as they sometimes were, of subversion, it seemed to gratify and excite them. Their beech hedge was yellow and he guessed this had been blighted like the Levys' maple. He called hullo, hullo, to warn the Hallorans of his approach, to palliate his invasion of their privacy. The Hallorans, for reasons that had never been explained to him, did not wear bathing suits. No explanations were in order, really. Their nakedness was a detail in their uncompromising zeal for reform and he stepped politely out of his trunks before he went through the opening in the hedge.

Mrs. Halloran, a stout woman with white hair and a serene face, was reading the *Times.* Mr. Halloran was taking beech leaves out of the water with a scoop. They seemed not surprised or displeased to see him. Their pool was perhaps the oldest in the county, a fieldstone rectangle, fed by a brook. It had no filter or pump and its waters were the opaque gold of the stream.

"I'm swimming across the county," Ned said.

"Why, I didn't know one could," exclaimed Mrs. Halloran.

"Well, I've made it from the Westerhazys'," Ned said. "That must be about four miles."

He left his trunks at the deep end, walked to the shallow end, and swam this stretch. As he was pulling himself out of the water he heard Mrs. Halloran say, "We've been *terribly* sorry to hear about all your misfortunes, Neddy."

"My misfortunes?" Ned asked. "I don't know what you mean."

"Why we heard that you'd sold the house and that your poor children. . . ."

"I don't recall having sold the house," Ned said, "and the girls are at home."

"Yes," Mrs. Halloran sighed. "Yes. . . ." Her voice filled the air with an unseasonable melancholy and Ned spoke briskly. "Thank you for the swim."

"Well, have a nice trip," said Mrs. Halloran.

Beyond the hedge he pulled on his trunks and fastened them. They were loose and he wondered if, during the space of an afternoon, he could have lost some weight. He was cold and he was tired and the naked Hallorans and their dark water had depressed him. The swim was too much for his strength but how could he have guessed this, sliding down the banister that morning and sitting in the Westerhazys' sun? His arms were lame. His legs felt rubbery and ached at the joints. The worst of it was the cold in his bones and the feeling that he might never be warm again. Leaves were falling down around him and he smelled wood smoke on the wind. Who would be burning wood at this time of the year?

He needed a drink. Whiskey would warm him, pick him up, carry him through the last of his journey, refresh his feeling that it was original and valorous to swim across the county. Channel swimmers took brandy. He needed a stimulant. He crossed the lawn in front of the Hallorans' house and went down a little path to where they had built a house for their only daughter, Helen, and her husband, Eric Sachs. The Sachses' pool was small and he found Helen and her husband there.

"Oh, *Neddy,*" Helen said. "Did you lunch at Mother's?"

"Not *really,*" Ned said. "I *did* stop to see your parents." This seemed to be explanation enough. "I'm terribly sorry to break in on you like this but I've taken a chill and I wonder if you'd give me a drink."

"Why, I'd *love* to," Helen said, "but there hasn't been anything in this house to drink since Eric's operation. That was three years ago."

Was he losing his memory, had his gift for concealing painful facts let him forget that he had sold his house, that his children were in trouble, and that his friend had been ill? His eyes slipped from Eric's face to his abdomen, where he saw three pale, sutured scars, two of them at least a foot long. Gone was his navel, and what, Neddy thought, would the roving hand, bed-checking one's gifts at 3 A.M., make of a belly with no navel, no link to birth, this breach in the succession?

"I'm sure you can get a drink at the Biswangers'," Helen said. "They're having an enormous do. You can hear it from here. Listen!"

She raised her head and from across the road, the lawns, the gardens, the woods, the fields, he heard again the brilliant noise of voices over water. "Well, I'll get wet," he said, still feeling that he had no freedom of choice about his means of travel. He dove into the Sachses' cold water, and gasping, close to drowning, made his way from one end of the pool to the other. "Lucinda and I want *terribly* to see you," he said over his shoulder, his face set toward the Biswangers'. "We're sorry it's been so long and we'll call you *very* soon."

He crossed some fields to the Biswangers' and the sounds of revelry there. They would be honored to give him a drink, they would be happy to give him a drink. The Biswangers invited him and Lucinda for dinner four times a year, six weeks in advance. They were always rebuffed and yet they continued to send out their invitations, unwilling to comprehend the rigid and undemocratic realities of their society. They were the sort of people who discussed the price of things at cocktails, exchanged market tips during dinner, and after dinner told dirty stories to mixed company. They did not belong to Neddy's set — they were not even on Lucinda's Christmas card list. He went toward their pool with feelings of indifference, charity, and some unease, since it seemed to be getting dark and these were the longest days of the year. The party when he joined it was noisy and large. Grace Biswanger was the kind of hostess who asked the optometrist, the veterinarian, the real-estate dealer, and the dentist. No one was swimming and the twilight, reflected on the water of the pool, had a wintry gleam. There was a bar and he started for this. When Grace Biswanger saw him she came toward him, not affectionately as he had every right to expect, but bellicosely.

"Why, this party has everything," she said loudly, "including a gate crasher."

She could not deal him a social blow — there was no question about this and he did not flinch. "As a gate crasher," he asked politely, "do I rate a drink?"

"Suit yourself," she said. "You don't seem to pay much attention to invitations."

She turned her back on him and joined some guests, and he went to the bar and ordered a whiskey. The bartender served him but he served him rudely. His was a world in which the caterer's men kept the social score, and to be rebuffed by a part-time barkeep meant that he had suffered some loss of social esteem. Or perhaps the man was new and uninformed. Then he heard Grace at his back say: "They went for broke overnight — nothing but income — and he showed up drunk one Sunday and asked us to loan him five thousand dollars. . . ." She was always talking about money. It was worse than eating your peas off a knife. He dove into the pool, swam its length, and went away.

The next pool on his list, the last but two, belonged to his old mistress, Shirley Adams. If he had suffered any injuries at the Biswangers' they would be cured here. Love — sexual roughhouse in fact — was the supreme elixir, the pain killer, the brightly colored pill that would put the spring back into his step, the joy of life in his heart. They had had an affair last week, last month, last year. He couldn't remember. It was he who had broken it off, his was the upper hand, and he stepped through the gate of the wall that surrounded her pool with nothing so considered as self-confidence. It seemed in a way to be his pool, as the lover, particularly the illicit lover, enjoys the possessions of his mistress with an authority unknown to holy matrimony. She was there, her hair the color of brass, but her figure, at the edge of the lighted, cerulean water, excited in him no profound memories. It had been, he thought, a lighthearted affair, although she had wept when he broke it off. She seemed confused to see him and he wondered if she was still wounded. Would she, God forbid, weep again?

"What do you want?" she asked.

"I'm swimming across the county."

"Good Christ. Will you ever grow up?"

"What's the matter?"

"If you've come here for money," she said, "I won't give you another cent."

"You could give me a drink."

"I could but I won't. I'm not alone."

"Well, I'm on my way."

He dove in and swam the pool, but when he tried to haul himself up onto the curb he found that the strength in his arms and shoulders had gone, and he paddled to the ladder and climbed out. Looking over his shoulder he saw, in the lighted bathhouse, a young man. Going out onto the dark lawn he smelled chrysanthemums or marigolds — some stubborn autumnal fragrance — on the night air, strong as gas. Looking overhead he saw that the stars had come out, but why should he seem to see Andromeda, Cepheus, and Cassiopeia? What had become of the constellations of midsummer? He began to cry.

It was probably the first time in his adult life that he had ever cried, certainly the first time in his life that he had ever felt so miserable, cold, tired, and bewildered. He could not understand the rudeness of the caterer's barkeep or the rudeness of a mistress who had come to him on her knees and showered his trousers with tears. He had swum too long, he had been immersed too long, and his nose and his throat were sore from the water. What he needed then was a drink, some company, and some clean, dry clothes, and while he could have cut directly across the road to his home he went on to the Gilmartins' pool. Here, for the first time in his life, he did not dive but went down the steps into the icy water and swam a hobbled sidestroke that he might have learned as a youth. He staggered with fatigue on his way to the Clydes' and paddled the length of their pool, stopping again and again with his hand on the curb to rest. He climbed up the ladder and wondered if he had the strength to get home. He had done what he wanted, he had swum the county, but he was so stupefied with exhaustion that his triumph seemed vague. Stooped, holding on to the gateposts for support, he turned up the driveway of his own house.

The place was dark. Was it so late that they had all gone to bed? Had Lucinda stayed at the Westerhazys' for supper? Had the girls joined her there or gone someplace else? Hadn't they agreed, as they usually did on Sunday, to regret all their invitations and stay at home? He tried the garage doors to see what cars were in but the doors were locked and rust came off the handles onto his hands. Going toward the house, he saw the force of the thunderstorm had knocked one of the rain gutters loose. It hung down over the front door like an umbrella rib, but it could be fixed in the morning. The house was locked, and he thought that the stupid cook or the stupid maid must have locked the place up until he remembered that it had been some time since they had employed a maid or a cook. He shouted, pounded on the door, tried to force it with his shoulder, and then, looking in at the windows, saw that the place was empty.

ANTON CHEKHOV *(1860–1904), the Russian short story writer and playwright, wrote his first stories while he was a medical student at Moscow University, to help his family pay off debts. His grandfather had been a serf who had bought his freedom. His father was an unsuccessful grocer in Taganrog, in the southwestern part of the country. After completing medical school, Chekhov became an assistant to the district doctor in a provincial town. His early stories were mostly humorous sketches that he first published in newspapers under various pseudonyms, keeping his own name for his medical articles. But the popularity of these sketches made him decide to become a writer.*

Chekhov's first two collections of short stories, published in 1886 and 1887, were acclaimed by readers, and from that time on he was able to devote all his time to writing. He bought a small estate near Moscow, where he lived with his family and treated sick peasants at no charge. Chekhov's kindness and good works were not a matter of any political program or religious impulse but, as Vladimir Nabokov put it, "the natural coloration of his talent." He was extremely modest about his extraordinary ability to empathize with his characters. Once he said to a visitor, "Do you know how I write my stories? Here's how!" And he glanced at his table, took up the first object that he saw — it was an ashtray — and said, "If you want it, you'll have a story tomorrow. It will be called 'The Ashtray.'" And it seemed to the visitor that Chekhov was conjuring up a story in front of his eyes: "Certain indefinite situations, adventures which had not yet found concrete form, were already beginning to crystallize about the ashtray."

Chekhov's story-writing technique appears disarmingly simple. Yet, as Virginia Woolf recognized, "as we read these little stories about nothing at all, the horizon widens; the soul gains an astonishing sense of freedom." Chekhov's remarkable absence of egotism can be seen in masterpieces such as "The Darling" and "The Lady with the Pet Dog," both of which he wrote toward the end of his life. He once sent a sketch describing himself to the editor who first encouraged him in which he gave a sense of the depth of his self-knowledge:

> *Write a story, do, about a young man, the son of a serf, a former grocery boy, a choir singer, a high school pupil and university student, brought up to respect rank, to kiss the hands of priests, to truckle to the ideas of others — a young man who expressed thanks for every piece of bread, who was whipped many times, who went without galoshes to do his tutoring, who used his fists, tortured animals, was fond of dining with rich relatives, was a hypocrite in his dealings with God and men, needlessly, solely out of a realization of his own insignificance — write how this young man squeezes the slave out of himself, drop by drop, and how, on awaking one fine morning, he feels that the blood coursing through his veins is no longer that of a slave but that of a real human being.*

Chekhov's more than 800 stories have immensely influenced writers of short fiction. Unconcerned with giving a social or ethical message in his work, he championed what he called "the holy of holies" — "love and absolute freedom — freedom from violence and lies, whatever their form."

RELATED COMMENTARIES: *Anton Chekhov, "Technique in Writing the Short Story," page 669; Vladimir Nabokov, "A Reading of Chekhov's 'The Lady with the Little Dog,'" page 699; Leo Tolstoy, "Chekhov's Intent in 'The Darling,'" page 726; Eudora Welty, "Plot and Character in Chekhov's 'The Darling,'" page 736.*

ANTON CHEKHOV

The Darling

1899

TRANSLATED BY CONSTANCE GARNETT

Olenka, the daughter of the retired collegiate assessor, Plemyanniakov, was sitting in her back porch, lost in thought. It was hot, the flies were persistent and teasing, and it was pleasant to reflect that it would soon be evening. Dark rainclouds were gathering from the east, and bringing from time to time a breath of moisture in the air.

Kukin, who was the manager of an open-air theatre called the Tivoli, and who lived in the lodge, was standing in the middle of the garden looking at the sky.

"Again!" he observed despairingly. "It's going to rain again! Rain every day, as though to spite me. I might as well hang myself! It's ruin! Fearful losses every day."

He flung up his hands, and went on, addressing Olenka:

"There! that's the life we lead, Olga Semyonovna. It's enough to make one cry. One works and does one's utmost; one wears oneself out, getting no sleep at night, and racks one's brain what to do for the best. And then what happens? To begin with, one's public is ignorant, boorish. I give them the very best operetta, a dainty masque, first rate music-hall artists. But do you suppose that's what they want! They don't understand anything of that sort. They want a clown; what they ask for is vulgarity. And then look at the weather! Almost every evening it rains. It started on the tenth of May, and it's kept it up all May and June. It's simply awful! The public doesn't come, but I've to pay the rent just the same, and pay the artists."

The next evening the clouds would gather again, and Kukin would say with an hysterical laugh:

"Well, rain away, then! Flood the garden, drown me! Damn my luck in this world and the next! Let the artists have me up! Send me to prison! — to Siberia! — the scaffold! Ha, ha, ha!"

And next day the same thing.

Olenka listened to Kukin with silent gravity, and sometimes tears came into her eyes. In the end his misfortunes touched her; she grew to love him. He was a small thin man, with a yellow face, and curls combed forward on his forehead. He spoke in a thin tenor; as he talked his mouth worked on one side, and there was always an expression of despair on his face; yet he aroused a deep and genuine affection in her. She was always fond of some one, and could not exist without loving. In earlier days she had loved her papa, who now sat in a darkened room, breathing with difficulty; she had loved her aunt who used to come every other year from Bryansk; and before that, when she was at school, she had loved her French master. She was a gentle, soft-hearted, compassionate girl, with mild, tender eyes and very good health. At the sight of her full rosy cheeks, her soft white neck with a little dark mole on it, and the kind, naïve smile, which came into her face when she listened to anything pleasant, men thought, "Yes, not half bad," and smiled too, while lady visitors could not refrain from seizing her hand in the middle of a conversation, exclaiming in a gush of delight, "You darling!"

The house in which she had lived from her birth upwards, and which was left her in her father's will, was at the extreme end of the town, not far from the Tivoli. In the evenings and at night she could hear the band playing, and the crackling and banging of fireworks, and it seemed to her that it was Kukin struggling with his destiny, storming the entrenchments of his chief foe, the indifferent public; there was a sweet thrill at her heart, she had no desire to sleep, and when he returned home at daybreak, she tapped softly at her bedroom window, and showing him only her face and one shoulder through the curtain, she gave him a friendly smile. . . .

He proposed to her, and they were married. And when he had a closer view of her neck and her plump, fine shoulders, he threw up his hands, and said:

"You darling!"

He was happy, but as it rained on the day and night of his wedding, his face still retained an expression of despair.

They got on very well together. She used to sit in his office, to look after things in the Tivoli, to put down the accounts and pay the wages. And her rosy cheeks, her sweet, naïve, radiant smile, were to be seen now at the office window, now in the refreshment bar or behind the scenes of the theatre. And already she used to say to her acquaintances that the theatre was the chief and most important thing in life, and that it was only through the drama that one could derive true enjoyment and become cultivated and humane.

"But do you suppose the public understands that?" she used to say. "What they want is a clown. Yesterday we gave 'Faust Inside Out,' and almost all the boxes were empty; but if Vanitchka and I had been producing some vulgar thing, I assure you the theatre would have been packed. Tomorrow Vanitchka and I are doing 'Orpheus in Hell.' Do come."

And what Kukin said about the theatre and the actors she repeated. Like him she despised the public for their ignorance and their indifference to art; she took part in the rehearsals, she corrected the actors, she kept an eye on the behavior of the musicians, and when there was an unfavorable notice in the local paper, she shed tears, and then went to the editor's office to set things right.

The actors were fond of her and used to call her "Vanitchka and I," and "the darling"; she was sorry for them and used to lend them small sums of money, and if they deceived her, she used to shed a few tears in private, but did not complain to her husband.

They got on well in the winter too. They took the theatre in the town for the whole winter, and let it for short terms to a Little Russian company, or to a conjurer, or to a local dramatic society. Olenka grew stouter, and was always beaming with satisfaction, while Kukin grew thinner and yellower, and continually complained of their terrible losses, although he had not done badly all the winter. He used to cough at night, and she used to give him hot raspberry tea or lime-flower water, to rub him with eau-de-Cologne and to wrap him in her warm shawls.

"You're such a sweet pet!" she used to say with perfect sincerity, stroking his hair. "You're such a pretty dear!"

Towards Lent he went to Moscow to collect a new troupe, and without him she could not sleep, but sat all night at her window, looking at the stars, and she compared herself with the hens, who are awake all night and uneasy when the cock is not in the hen-house. Kukin was detained in Moscow, and wrote that he would be back at Easter, adding some instructions about the Tivoli. But on the Sunday before Easter, late in the evening, came a sudden ominous knock at the gate; some one was hammering on the gate as though on a barrel — boom, boom, boom! The drowsy cook went flopping with her bare feet through the puddles, as she ran to open the gate.

"Please open," said some one outside in a thick bass. "There is a telegram for you."

Olenka had received telegrams from her husband before, but this time for some reason she felt numb with terror. With shaking hands she opened the telegram and read as follows:

> "Ivan Petrovitch died suddenly to-day. Awaiting immate instructions fufuneral Tuesday."

That was how it was written in the telegram — "fufuneral," and the utterly incomprehensible word "immate." It was signed by the stage manager of the operatic company.

"My darling!" sobbed Olenka. "Vanitchka, my precious, my darling! Why did I ever meet you! Why did I know you and love you! Your poor heart-broken Olenka is all alone without you!"

Kukin's funeral took place on Tuesday in Moscow, Olenka returned home on Wednesday, and as soon as she got indoors she threw herself on her bed and sobbed so loudly that it could be heard next door, and in the street.

"Poor darling!" the neighbors said, as they crossed themselves. "Olga Semyonovna, poor darling! How she does take on!"

Three months later Olenka was coming home from mass, melancholy and in deep mourning. It happened that one of her neighbors, Vassily Andreitch Pustovalov, returning home from church, walked back beside her. He was the manager at Babakayev's, the timber merchant's. He wore a straw hat, a white waistcoat, and a gold watch-chain, and looked more like a country gentleman than a man in trade.

"Everything happens as it is ordained, Olga Semyonovna," he said gravely, with a sympathetic note in his voice; "and if any of our dear ones die, it must be because it is the will of God, so we ought to have fortitude and bear it submissively."

After seeing Olenka to her gate, he said good-bye and went on. All day afterwards she heard his sedately dignified voice, and whenever she shut her eyes she saw his dark beard. She liked him very much. And apparently she had made an impression on him too, for not long afterwards an elderly lady, with whom she was only slightly acquainted, came to drink coffee with her, and as soon as she was seated at table began to talk about Pustovalov, saying that he was an excellent man whom one could thoroughly depend upon, and that any girl would be glad to marry him. Three days later Pustovalov came himself. He did not stay long, only about ten minutes, and he did not say much, but when he left, Olenka loved him — loved him so much that she lay awake all night in a perfect fever, and in the morning she sent for the elderly lady. The match was quickly arranged, and then came the wedding.

Pustovalov and Olenka got on very well together when they were married.

Usually he sat in the office till dinner-time, then he went out on business, while Olenka took his place, and sat in the office till evening, making up accounts and booking orders.

"Timber gets dearer every year; the price rises twenty per cent," she would say to her customers and friends. "Only fancy we used to sell local timber, and now Vassitchka always has to go for wood to the Mogilev district. And the freight!" she would add, covering her cheeks with her hands in horror. "The freight!"

It seemed to her that she had been in the timber trade for ages and ages, and that the most important and necessary thing in life was timber; and there was something intimate and touching to her in the very sound of words such as "baulk," "post," "beam," "pole," "scantling," "batten," "lath," "plank," etc.

At night when she was asleep she dreamed of perfect mountains of planks and boards, and long strings of wagons, carting timber somewhere far away. She dreamed that a whole regiment of six-inch beams forty feet high, standing on end, was marching upon the timber-yard; that logs, beams, and boards knocked together with the resounding crash of dry wood, kept falling and getting up again, piling themselves on each other. Olenka cried out in her sleep, and Pustovalov said to her tenderly: "Olenka, what's the matter, darling? Cross yourself!"

Her husband's ideas were hers. If he thought the room was too hot, or that business was slack, she thought the same. Her husband did not care for entertainments, and on holidays he stayed at home. She did likewise.

"You are always at home or in the office," her friends said to her. "You should go to the theatre, darling, or to the circus."

"Vassitchka and I have no time to go to theatres," she would answer sedately. "We have no time for nonsense. What's the use of these theatres?"

On Saturdays Pustovalov and she used to go to the evening service; on holidays to early mass, and they walked side by side with softened faces as they came home from church. There was a pleasant fragrance about them both, and her silk dress rustled agreeably. At home they drank tea, with fancy bread and jams of various kinds, and afterwards they ate pie. Every day at twelve o'clock there was a savory smell of beet-root soup and of mutton or duck in their yard, and on fast-days of fish, and no one could pass the gate without feeling hungry. In the office the samovar was always boiling, and customers were regaled with tea and cracknels. Once a week the couple went to the baths and returned side by side, both red in the face.

"Yes, we have nothing to complain of, thank God," Olenka used to say to her acquaintances. "I wish every one were as well off as Vassitchka and I."

When Pustovalov went away to buy wood in the Mogilev district, she missed him dreadfully, lay awake and cried. A young veterinary surgeon in the army, called Smirnin, to whom they had let their lodge, used sometimes to come in in the evening. He used to talk to her and play cards with her, and this entertained her in her husband's absence. She was particularly interested in what he told her of his home life. He was married and had a little boy, but was separated from his wife because she had been unfaithful to him, and now he hated her and used to send her forty rubles a month for the maintenance of their son. And hearing of all this, Olenka sighed and shook her head. She was sorry for him.

"Well, God keep you," she used to say to him at parting, as she lighted him down the stairs with a candle. "Thank you for coming to cheer me up, and may the Mother of God give you health."

And she always expressed herself with the same sedateness and dignity, the same reasonableness, in imitation of her husband. As the veterinary surgeon was disappearing behind the door below, she would say:

"You know, Vladimir Platonitch, you'd better make it up with your wife. You should forgive her for the sake of your son. You may be sure the little fellow understands."

And when Pustovalov came back, she told him in a low voice about the veterinary surgeon and his unhappy home life, and both sighed and shook their heads and talked about the boy, who, no doubt, missed his father, and by some strange connection of ideas, they went up to the holy icons, bowed to the ground before them, and prayed that God would give them children.

And so the Pustovalovs lived for six years quietly and peaceably in love and complete harmony.

But behold! one winter day after drinking hot tea in the office, Vassily Andreitch went out into the yard without his cap on to see about sending off some timber, caught cold, and was taken ill. He had the best doctors, but he grew worse and died after four months' illness. And Olenka was a widow once more.

"I've nobody, now you've left me, my darling," she sobbed, after her husband's funeral. "How can I live without you, in wretchedness and misery! Pity me, good people, all alone in the world!"

She went about dressed in black with long "weepers," and gave up wearing hat and gloves for good. She hardly ever went out, except to church, or to her husband's grave, and led the life of a nun. It was not till six months later that she took off the weepers and opened the shutters of the windows. She was sometimes seen in the mornings, going with her cook to market for provisions, but what went on in her house and how she lived now could only be surmised. People guessed, from seeing her drinking tea in her garden with the veterinary surgeon, who read the newspaper aloud to her, and from the fact that, meeting a lady she knew at the post-office, she said to her:

"There is no proper veterinary inspection in our town, and that's the cause of all sorts of epidemics. One is always hearing of people's getting infection from the milk supply, or catching diseases from horses and cows. The health of domestic animals ought to be as well cared for as the health of human beings."

She repeated the veterinary surgeon's words, and was of the same opinion as he about everything. It was evident that she could not live a year without some attachment, and had found new happiness in the lodge. In any one else this would have been censured, but no one could think ill of Olenka; everything she did was so natural. Neither she nor the veterinary surgeon said anything to other people of the change in their relations, and tried, indeed, to conceal it, but without success, for Olenka could not keep a secret. When he had visitors, men serving in his regiment, and she poured out tea or served the supper, she would begin talking of the cattle plague, of the foot and mouth disease, and of the municipal slaughter-houses. He was dreadfully embarrassed, and when the guests had gone, he would seize her by the hand and hiss angrily:

"I've asked you before not to talk about what you don't understand. When we veterinary surgeons are talking among ourselves, please don't put your word in. It's really annoying."

And she would look at him with astonishment and dismay, and ask him in alarm: "But, Voloditchka, what *am* I to talk about?"

And with tears in her eyes she would embrace him, begging him not to be angry, and they were both happy.

But this happiness did not last long. The veterinary surgeon departed, departed for ever with his regiment, when it was transferred to a distant place — to Siberia, it may be. And Olenka was left alone.

Now she was absolutely alone. Her father had long been dead, and his armchair lay in the attic, covered with dust and lame of one leg. She got thinner and plainer, and when people met her in the street they did not look at her as they used to, and did not smile to her; evidently her best years were over and left behind, and now a new sort of life had begun for her, which did not bear thinking about. In the evening Olenka sat in the porch, and heard the band playing and the fireworks popping in the Tivoli, but now the sound stirred no response. She looked into her yard without interest, thought of nothing, wished for nothing, and afterwards, when night came on she went to bed and dreamed of her empty yard. She ate and drank as it were unwillingly.

And what was worst of all, she had no opinions of any sort. She saw the objects about her and understood what she saw, but could not form any opinion about them, and did not know what to talk about. And how awful it is not to have any opinions! One sees a bottle, for instance, or the rain, or a peasant driving in his cart, but what the bottle is for, or the rain, or the peasant, and what is the meaning of it, one can't say, and could not even for a thousand rubles. When she had Kukin, or Pustovalov, or the veterinary surgeon, Olenka could explain everything, and give her opinion about anything you like, but now there was the same emptiness in her brain and in her heart as there was in her yard outside. And it was as harsh and as bitter as wormwood in the mouth.

Little by little the town grew in all directions. The road became a street, and where the Tivoli and the timber-yard had been, there were new turnings and houses. How rapidly time passes! Olenka's house grew dingy, the roof got rusty, the shed sank on one side, and the whole yard was overgrown with docks and stinging-nettles. Olenka herself had grown plain and elderly; in summer she sat in the porch, and her soul, as before, was empty and dreary and full of bitterness. In winter she sat at her window and looked at the snow. When she caught the scent of spring, or heard the chime of the church bells, a sudden rush of memories from the past came over her, there was a tender ache in her heart, and her eyes brimmed over with tears; but this was only for a minute, and then came emptiness again and the sense of the futility of life. The black kitten, Briska, rubbed against her and purred softly, but Olenka was not touched by these feline caresses. That was not what she needed. She wanted a love that would absorb her whole being, her whole soul and reason — that would give her ideas and an object in life, and would warm her old blood. And she would shake the kitten off her skirt and say with vexation:

"Get along; I don't want you!"

And so it was, day after day and year after year, and no joy, and no opinions. Whatever Mavra, the cook, said she accepted.

One hot July day, towards evening, just as the cattle were being driven away, and the whole yard was full of dust, some one suddenly knocked at the gate. Olenka went to open it herself and was dumbfounded when she looked out; she saw Smirnin, the veterinary surgeon, grey-headed, and dressed as a civilian. She suddenly remembered everything. She could not help crying and letting her head fall on his breast without uttering a word, and in the violence of her feeling she did not notice how they both walked into the house and sat down to tea.

"My dear Vladimir Platonitch! What fate has brought you?" she muttered, trembling with joy.

"I want to settle here for good, Olga Semyonovna," he told her. "I have resigned my post, and have come to settle down and try my luck on my own account. Besides, it's time for my boy to go to school. He's a big boy. I am reconciled with my wife, you know."

"Where is she?" asked Olenka.

"She's at the hotel with the boy, and I'm looking for lodgings."

"Good gracious, my dear soul! Lodgings? Why not have my house? Why shouldn't that suit you? Why, my goodness, I wouldn't take any rent!" cried Olenka in a flutter, beginning to cry again. "You live here, and the lodge will do nicely for me. Oh dear! how glad I am!"

Next day the roof was painted and the walls were whitewashed, and Olenka, with her arms akimbo, walked about the yard giving directions. Her face was beaming with her old smile, and she was brisk and alert as though she had waked from a long sleep. The veterinary's wife arrived — a thin, plain lady, with short hair and a peevish expression. With her was her little Sasha, a boy of ten, small for his age, blue-eyed, chubby, with dimples in his cheeks. And scarcely had the boy walked into the yard when he ran after the cat, and at once there was the sound of his gay, joyous laugh.

"Is that your puss, auntie?" he asked Olenka. "When she has little ones, do give us a kitten. Mamma is awfully afraid of mice."

Olenka talked to him, and gave him tea. Her heart warmed and there was a sweet ache in her bosom, as though the boy had been her own child. And when he sat at the table in the evening, going over his lessons, she looked at him with deep tenderness and pity as she murmured to herself:

"You pretty pet! . . . my precious! . . . Such a fair little thing, and so clever."

"'An island is a piece of land which is entirely surrounded by water,'" he read aloud.

"An island is a piece of land," she repeated, and this was the first opinion to which she gave utterance with positive conviction after so many years of silence and dearth of ideas.

Now she had opinions of her own, and at supper she talked to Sasha's parents, saying how difficult the lessons were at the high schools, but that yet the high school was better than a commercial one, since with a high-school education all careers were open to one, such as being a doctor or an engineer.

Sasha began going to the high school. His mother departed to Harkov to her sister's and did not return; his father used to go off every day to inspect cattle, and would often be away from home for three days together, and it seemed to Olenka as though Sasha was entirely abandoned, that he was not wanted at home, that he was being starved, and she carried him off to her lodge and gave him a little room there.

And for six months Sasha had lived in the lodge with her. Every morning Olenka came into his bedroom and found him fast asleep, sleeping noiselessly with his hand under his cheek. She was sorry to wake him.

"Sashenka," she would say mournfully, "get up, darling. It's time for school."

He would get up, dress and say his prayers, and then sit down to breakfast, drink three glasses of tea, and eat two large cracknels and half a buttered roll. All this time he was hardly awake and a little ill-humored in consequence.

"You don't quite know your fable, Sashenka," Olenka would say, looking at him as though he were about to set off on a long journey. "What a lot of trouble I have with you! You must work and do your best, darling, and obey your teachers."

"Oh, do leave me alone!" Sasha would say.

Then he would go down the street to school, a little figure, wearing a big cap and carrying a satchel on his shoulder. Olenka would follow him noiselessly.

"Sashenka!" she would call after him, and she would pop into his hand a date or a caramel. When he reached the street where the school was, he would feel ashamed of being followed by a tall, stout woman; he would turn round and say:

"You'd better go home, auntie. I can go the rest of the way alone."

She would stand still and look after him fixedly till he had disappeared at the school-gate.

Ah, how she loved him! Of her former attachments not one had been so deep; never had her soul surrendered to any feeling so spontaneously, so disinterestedly, and so joyously as now that her maternal instincts were aroused. For this little boy with the dimple in his cheek and the big school cap, she would have given her whole life, she would have given it with joy and tears of tenderness. Why? Who can tell why?

When she had seen the last of Sasha, she returned home, contented and serene, brimming over with love; her face, which had grown younger during the last six months, smiled and beamed; people meeting her looked at her with pleasure.

"Good-morning, Olga Semyonovna, darling. How are you, darling?"

"The lessons at the high school are very difficult now," she would relate at the market. "It's too much; in the first class yesterday they gave him a fable to learn by heart, and a Latin translation and a problem. You know it's too much for a little chap."

And she would begin talking about the teachers, the lessons, and the school books, saying just what Sasha said.

At three o'clock they had dinner together: in the evening they learned their lessons together and cried. When she put him to bed, she would stay a long time making the Cross over him and murmuring a prayer; then she would go to bed and dream of that far-away misty future when Sasha would finish his studies and become a doctor or an engineer, would have a big house of his own with horses and a carriage, would get married and have children. . . . She would fall asleep still thinking of the same thing, and tears would run down her cheeks from her closed eyes, while the black cat lay purring beside her: "Mrr, mrr, mrr."

Suddenly there would come a loud knock at the gate.

Olenka would wake up breathless with alarm, her heart throbbing. Half a minute later would come another knock.

"It must be a telegram from Harkov," she would think, beginning to tremble from head to foot. "Sasha's mother is sending for him from Harkov. . . . Oh, mercy on us!"

She was in despair. Her head, her hands, and her feet would turn chill, and she would feel that she was the most unhappy woman in the world. But another minute would pass, voices would be heard: it would turn out to be the veterinary surgeon coming home from the club.

"Well, thank God!" she would think.

And gradually the load in her heart would pass off, and she would feel at ease. She would go back to bed thinking of Sasha, who lay sound asleep in the next room, sometimes crying out in his sleep:

"I'll give it you! Get away! Shut up!"

Anton Chekhov

The Lady with the Pet Dog 1899

TRANSLATED BY AVRAHM YARMOLINSKY

I

A new person, it was said, had appeared on the esplanade: a lady with a pet dog. Dmitry Dmitrich Gurov, who had spent a fortnight at Yalta and had got used to the place, had also begun to take an interest in new arrivals. As he sat in Vernet's confectionery shop, he saw, walking on the esplanade, a fair-haired young woman of medium height, wearing a beret; a white Pomeranian was trotting behind her.

And afterwards he met her in the public garden and in the square several times a day. She walked alone, always wearing the same beret and always with the white dog; no one knew who she was and everyone called her simply "the lady with the pet dog."

"If she is here alone without husband or friends," Gurov reflected, "it wouldn't be a bad thing to make her acquaintance."

He was under forty, but he already had a daughter twelve years old, and two sons at school. They had found a wife for him when he was very young, a student in his second year, and by now she seemed half as old again as he. She was a tall, erect woman with dark eyebrows, stately and dignified and, as she said of herself, intellectual. She read a great deal, used simplified spelling in her letters, called her husband, not Dmitry, but Dimitry, while he privately considered her of limited intelligence, narrow-minded, dowdy, was afraid of her, and did not like to be at home. He had begun being unfaithful to her long ago — had been unfaithful to her often and, probably for that reason, almost always spoke ill of women, and when they were talked of in his presence used to call them "the inferior race."

It seemed to him that he had been sufficiently tutored by bitter experience to call them what he pleased, and yet he could not have lived without "the inferior race" for two days together. In the company of men he was bored and ill at ease, he was chilly and uncommunicative with them; but when he was among women he felt free, and knew what to speak to them about and how to comport himself; and even to be silent with them was no strain on him. In his appearance, in his character, in his whole make-up there was something attractive and elusive that disposed women in his favor and allured them. He knew that, and some force seemed to draw him to them, too.

Oft-repeated and really bitter experience had taught him long ago that with decent people — particularly Moscow people — who are irresolute and slow to move, every affair which at first seems a light and charming adventure inevitably grows into a whole problem of extreme complexity, and in the end a painful situation is created. But at every new meeting with an interesting woman this lesson of experience seemed to slip from his memory, and he was eager for life, and everything seemed so simple and diverting.

One evening while he was dining in the public garden the lady in the beret walked up without haste to take the next table. Her expression, her gait, her dress, and the way she did her hair told him that she belonged to the upper class, that she was married, that she was in Yalta for the first time and alone, and that she was bored there. The stories told of the immorality in Yalta are to a great extent untrue; he despised them, and knew that such stories were made up for the most part by persons who would have been glad to sin themselves if they had had the chance; but when the lady sat down at the next table three paces from him, he recalled these stories of easy conquests, of trips to the mountains, and the tempting thought of a swift, fleeting liaison, a romance with an unknown woman of whose very name he was ignorant, suddenly took hold of him.

He beckoned invitingly to the Pomeranian, and when the dog approached him, shook his finger at it. The Pomeranian growled; Gurov threatened it again.

The lady glanced at him and at once dropped her eyes.

"He doesn't bite," she said and blushed.

"May I give him a bone?" he asked; and when she nodded he inquired affably, "Have you been in Yalta long?"

"About five days."

"And I am dragging out the second week here."

There was a short silence.

"Time passes quickly, and yet it is so dull here!" she said, not looking at him.

"It's only the fashion to say it's dull here. A provincial will live in Belyov or Zhizdra and not be bored, but when he comes here it's 'Oh, the dullness! Oh, the dust!' One would think he came from Granada."

She laughed. Then both continued eating in silence, like strangers, but after dinner they walked together and there sprang up between them the light banter of people who are free and contented, to whom it does not matter where they go or what they talk about. They walked and talked of the strange light on the sea: the water was a soft, warm, lilac color, and there was a golden band of moonlight upon it. They talked of how sultry it was after a hot day. Gurov told her that he was a native of Moscow, that he had studied languages and literature at the university, but had a post in a bank; that at one time he had trained to become an opera singer but had given it up, that he owned two houses in Moscow. And he learned from her that she had grown up in Petersburg, but had lived in S —— since her marriage two years previously, that she was going to stay in Yalta for about another month, and that her husband, who needed a rest, too, might perhaps come to fetch her. She was not certain whether her husband was a member of a Government Board or served on a Zemstvo Council,° and this amused her. And Gurov learned too that her name was Anna Sergeyevna.

Afterwards in his room at the hotel he thought about her — and was certain that he would meet her the next day. It was bound to happen. Getting into bed he recalled that she had been a schoolgirl only recently, doing lessons like his own daughter; he thought how much timidity and angularity there was still in her laugh and her manner of talking with a stranger. It must have been the first time in her life that she was alone in a setting in which she was followed, looked at, and spoken to for one secret purpose alone, which she could hardly fail to guess. He thought of her slim, delicate throat, her lovely gray eyes.

"There's something pathetic about her, though," he thought, and dropped off.

II

A week had passed since they had struck up an acquaintance. It was a holiday. It was close indoors, while in the street the wind whirled the dust about and blew people's hats off. One was thirsty all day, and Gurov often went into the restaurant and offered Anna Sergeyevna a soft drink or ice cream. One did not know what to do with oneself.

In the evening when the wind had abated they went out on the pier to watch the steamer come in. There were a great many people walking about the dock; they had come to welcome someone and they were carrying bunches of flowers. And two peculiarities of a festive Yalta crowd stood out: the elderly ladies were dressed like young ones and there were many generals.

Owing to the choppy sea, the steamer arrived late, after sunset, and it was a long time tacking about before it put in at the pier. Anna Sergeyevna peered at the steamer and the passengers through her lorgnette as though looking for acquaintances, and whenever she turned to Gurov her eyes were shining. She talked a great deal and asked questions jerkily, forgetting the next moment what she had asked; then she lost her lorgnette in the crush.

The festive crowd began to disperse; it was now too dark to see people's faces; there was no wind anymore, but Gurov and Anna Sergeyevna still stood as though waiting to see someone else come off the steamer. Anna Sergeyevna was silent now, and sniffed her flowers without looking at Gurov.

"The weather has improved this evening," he said. "Where shall we go now? Shall we drive somewhere?"

She did not reply.

Then he looked at her intently, and suddenly embraced her and kissed her on the lips, and the moist fragrance of her flowers enveloped him; and at once he looked round him anxiously, wondering if anyone had seen them.

"Let us go to your place," he said softly. And they walked off together rapidly.

Zemstvo Council: County council.

The air in her room was close and there was the smell of the perfume she had bought at the Japanese shop. Looking at her, Gurov thought: "What encounters life offers!" From the past he preserved the memory of carefree, good-natured women whom love made gay and who were grateful to him for the happiness he gave them, however brief it might be; and of women like his wife who loved without sincerity, with too many words, affectedly, hysterically, with an expression that it was not love or passion that engaged them but something more significant; and of two or three others, very beautiful, frigid women, across whose faces would suddenly flit a rapacious expression — an obstinate desire to take from life more than it could give, and these were women no longer young, capricious, unreflecting, domineering, unintelligent, and when Gurov grew cold to them their beauty aroused his hatred, and the lace on their lingerie seemed to him to resemble scales.

But here there was the timidity, the angularity of inexperienced youth, a feeling of awkwardness; and there was a sense of embarrassment, as though someone had suddenly knocked at the door. Anna Sergeyevna, "the lady with the pet dog," treated what had happened in a peculiar way, very seriously, as though it were her fall — so it seemed, and this was odd and inappropriate. Her features drooped and faded, and her long hair hung down sadly on either side of her face; she grew pensive and her dejected pose was that of a Magdalene in a picture by an old master.

"It's not right," she said. "You don't respect me now, you first of all."

There was a watermelon on the table. Gurov cut himself a slice and began eating it without haste. They were silent for at least half an hour.

There was something touching about Anna Sergeyevna; she had the purity of a well-bred, naive woman who has seen little of life. The single candle burning on the table barely illumined her face, yet it was clear that she was unhappy.

"Why should I stop respecting you, darling?" asked Gurov. "You don't know what you're saying."

"God forgive me," she said, and her eyes filled with tears. "It's terrible."

"It's as though you were trying to exonerate yourself."

"How can I exonerate myself? No. I am a bad, low woman; I despise myself and I have no thought of exonerating myself. It's not my husband but myself I have deceived. And not only just now; I have been deceiving myself for a long time. My husband may be a good, honest man, but he is a flunkey! I don't know what he does, what his work is, but I know he is a flunkey! I was twenty when I married him. I was tormented by curiosity; I wanted something better. 'There must be a different sort of life,' I said to myself. I wanted to live! To live, to live! Curiosity kept eating at me — you don't understand it, but I swear to God I could no longer control myself; something was going on in me; I could not be held back. I told my husband I was ill, and came here. And here I have been walking about as though in a daze, as though I were mad; and now I have become a vulgar, vile woman whom anyone may despise."

Gurov was already bored with her; he was irritated by her naive tone, by her repentance, so unexpected and so out of place, but for the tears in her eyes he might have thought she was joking or play-acting.

"I don't understand, my dear," he said softly. "What do you want?"

She hid her face on his breast and pressed close to him.

"Believe me, believe me, I beg you," she said, "I love honesty and purity, and sin is loathsome to me; I don't know what I'm doing. Simple people say, 'The Evil One has led me astray.' And I may say of myself now that the Evil One has led me astray."

"Quiet, quiet," he murmured.

He looked into her fixed, frightened eyes, kissed her, spoke to her softly and affectionately, and by degrees she calmed down, and her gaiety returned; both began laughing.

Afterwards when they went out there was not a soul on the esplanade. The town with its cypresses looked quite dead, but the sea was still sounding as it broke upon the beach; a single launch was rocking on the waves and on it a lantern was blinking sleepily.

They found a cab and drove to Oreanda.

"I found out your surname in the hall just now: it was written on the board — von Dideritz," said Gurov. "Is your husband German?"

"No; I believe his grandfather was German, but he is Greek Orthodox himself."

At Oreanda they sat on a bench not far from the church, looked down at the sea, and were silent. Yalta was barely visible through the morning mist; white clouds rested motionlessly on the mountaintops. The leaves did not stir on the trees, cicadas twanged, and the monotonous muffled sound of the sea that rose from below spoke of the peace, the eternal sleep awaiting us. So it rumbled below when there was no Yalta, no Oreanda here; so it rumbles now, and it will rumble as indifferently and as hollowly when we are no more. And in this constancy, in this complete indifference to the life and death of each of us, there lies, perhaps, a pledge of our eternal salvation, of the unceasing advance of life upon earth, of unceasing movement towards perfection. Sitting beside a young woman who in the dawn seemed so lovely, Gurov, soothed and spellbound by these magical surroundings — the sea, the mountains, the clouds, the wide sky — thought how everything is really beautiful in this world when one reflects: everything except what we think or do ourselves when we forget the higher aims of life and our own human dignity.

A man strolled up to them — probably a guard — looked at them, and walked away. And this detail, too, seemed so mysterious and beautiful. They saw a steamer arrive from Feodosia, its lights extinguished in the glow of dawn.

"There is dew on the grass," said Anna Sergeyevna, after a silence.

"Yes, it's time to go home."

They returned to the city.

Then they met every day at twelve o'clock on the esplanade, lunched and dined together, took walks, admired the sea. She complained that she slept badly, that she had palpitations, asked the same questions, troubled now by jealousy and now by the fear that he did not respect her sufficiently. And often in the square or the public garden, when there was no one near them, he suddenly drew her to him and kissed her passionately. Complete idleness, these kisses in broad daylight exchanged furtively in dread of someone's seeing them, the heat, the smell of the sea, and the continual flitting before his eyes of idle, well-dressed, well-fed people, worked a complete change in him; he kept telling Anna Sergeyevna how beautiful she was, how seductive, was urgently passionate; he would not move a step away from her, while she was often pensive and continually pressed him to confess that he did not respect her, did not love her in the least, and saw in her nothing but a common woman. Almost every evening rather late they drove somewhere out of town, to Oreanda or to the waterfall; and the excursion was always a success, the scenery invariably impressed them as beautiful and magnificent.

They were expecting her husband, but a letter came from him saying that he had eye-trouble, and begging his wife to return home as soon as possible. Anna Sergeyevna made haste to go.

"It's a good thing I am leaving," she said to Gurov. "It's the hand of Fate!"

She took a carriage to the railway station, and he went with her. They were driving the whole day. When she had taken her place in the express, and when the second bell had rung, she said, "Let me look at you once more — let me look at you again. Like this."

She was not crying but was so sad that she seemed ill and her face was quivering.

"I shall be thinking of you — remembering you," she said. "God bless you; be happy. Don't remember evil against me. We are parting forever — it has to be, for we ought never to have met. Well, God bless you."

The train moved off rapidly, its lights soon vanished, and a minute later there was no sound of it, as though everything had conspired to end as quickly as possible that sweet trance, that madness. Left alone on the platform, and gazing into the dark distance, Gurov listened to the twang of the grasshoppers and the hum of the telegraph wires, feeling as though he had just waked up. And he reflected, musing, that there had now been another episode or adventure in his life, and it, too, was at an end, and nothing was left of it but a memory. He was moved, sad, and slightly remorseful: this young woman whom he would never meet again had not been happy with him; he had been warm and affectionate with her, but yet in his manner, his tone, and his caresses there had been a shade of light irony, the slightly coarse arrogance of a happy male who was, besides, almost twice her age. She had constantly called him kind, exceptional, high-minded; obviously he had seemed to her different from what he really was, so he had involuntarily deceived her.

Here at the station there was already a scent of autumn in the air; it was a chilly evening.

"It is time for me to go north, too," thought Gurov as he left the platform. "High time!"

III

At home in Moscow the winter routine was already established; the stoves were heated, and in the morning it was still dark when the children were having breakfast and getting ready for school, and the nurse would light the lamp for a short time. There were frosts already. When the first snow falls, on the first day the sleighs are out, it is pleasant to see the white earth, the white roofs; one draws easy, delicious breaths, and the season brings back the days of one's youth. The old limes and birches, white with hoar-frost, have a good-natured look; they are closer to one's heart than cypresses and palms, and near them one no longer wants to think of mountains and the sea.

Gurov, a native of Moscow, arrived there on a fine frosty day, and when he put on his fur coat and warm gloves and took a walk along Petrovka, and when on Saturday night he heard the bells ringing, his recent trip and the places he had visited lost all charm for him. Little by little he became immersed in Moscow life, greedily read three newspapers a day, and declared that he did not read the Moscow papers on principle. He already felt a longing for restaurants, clubs, formal dinners, anniversary celebrations, and it flattered him to entertain distinguished lawyers and actors, and to play cards with a professor at the physicians' club. He could eat a whole portion of meat stewed with pickled cabbage and served in a pan, Moscow style.

A month or so would pass and the image of Anna Sergeyevna, it seemed to him, would become misty in his memory, and only from time to time he would dream of her with her touching smile as he dreamed of others. But more than a month went by, winter came into its own, and everything was still clear in his memory as though he had parted from Anna Sergeyevna only yesterday. And his memories glowed more and more vividly. When in the evening stillness the voices of his children preparing their lessons reached his study, or when he listened to a song or to an organ playing in a restaurant, or when the storm howled in the chimney, suddenly everything would rise up in his memory; what had happened on the pier and the early morning with the mist on the mountains, and the steamer coming from Feodosia, and the kisses. He would pace about his room a long time, remembering and smiling; then his memories passed into reveries, and in his imagination the past would mingle with what was to come. He did not dream of Anna Sergeyevna, but she followed him about everywhere and watched him. When he shut his eyes he saw her before him as though she were there in the flesh, and she seemed to him lovelier, younger, tenderer than she had been, and he imagined himself a finer man than he had been in Yalta. Of evenings she peered out at him from the bookcase, from the fireplace, from the corner — he heard her breathing, the caressing rustle of her clothes. In the street he followed the women with his eyes, looking for someone who resembled her.

Already he was tormented by a strong desire to share his memories with someone. But in his home it was impossible to talk of his love, and he had no one to talk to outside; certainly he could not confide in his tenants or in anyone at the bank. And what was there to talk about? He hadn't loved her then, had he? Had there been anything beautiful, poetical, edifying, or simply interesting in his relations with Anna Sergeyevna? And he was forced to talk vaguely of love, of women, and no one guessed what he meant; only his wife would twitch her black eyebrows and say, "The part of a philanderer does not suit you at all, Dimitry."

One evening, coming out of the physicians' club with an official with whom he had been playing cards, he could not resist saying:

"If you only knew what a fascinating woman I became acquainted with at Yalta!"

The official got into his sledge and was driving away, but turned suddenly and shouted:

"Dmitry Dmitrich!"

"What is it?"

"You were right this evening: the sturgeon was a bit high."

These words, so commonplace, for some reason moved Gurov to indignation, and struck him as degrading and unclean. What savage manners, what mugs! What stupid nights, what dull, humdrum days! Frenzied gambling, gluttony, drunkenness, continual talk always about the same thing! Futile pursuits and conversations always about the same topics take up the better part of one's time, the better part of one's strength, and in the end there is left a life clipped and wingless, an absurd mess, and there is no escaping or getting away from it — just as though one were in a madhouse or a prison.

Gurov, boiling with indignation, did not sleep all night. And he had a headache all the next day. And the following nights too he slept badly; he sat up in bed, thinking, or paced up and down his room. He was fed up with his children, fed up with the bank; he had no desire to go anywhere or to talk of anything.

In December during the holidays he prepared to take a trip and told his wife he was going to Petersburg to do what he could for a young friend — and he set off for S——. What for? He did not know, himself. He wanted to see Anna Sergeyevna and talk with her, to arrange a rendezvous if possible.

He arrived at S—— in the morning, and at the hotel took the best room, in which the floor was covered with gray army cloth, and on the table there was an inkstand, gray with dust and topped by a figure on horseback, its hat in its raised hand and its head broken off. The porter gave him the necessary information: von Dideritz lived in a house of his own on Staro-Goncharnaya Street, not far from the hotel: he was rich and lived well and kept his own horses; everyone in the town knew him. The porter pronounced the name: "Dridiritz."

Without haste Gurov made his way to Staro-Goncharnaya Street and found the house. Directly opposite the house stretched a long gray fence studded with nails.

"A fence like that would make one run away," thought Gurov, looking now at the fence, now at the windows of the house.

He reflected: this was a holiday, and the husband was apt to be at home. And in any case, it would be tactless to go into the house and disturb her. If he were to send her a note, it might fall into her husband's hands, and that might spoil everything. The best thing was to rely on chance. And he kept walking up and down the street and along the fence, waiting for the chance. He saw a beggar go in at the gate and heard the dogs attack him; then an hour later he heard a piano, and the sound came to him faintly and indistinctly. Probably it was Anna Sergeyevna playing. The front door opened suddenly, and an old woman came out, followed by the familiar white Pomeranian. Gurov was on the point of calling to the dog, but his heart began beating violently, and in his excitement he could not remember the Pomeranian's name.

He kept walking up and down, and hated the gray fence more and more, and by now he thought irritably that Anna Sergeyevna had forgotten him, and was perhaps already diverting herself with another man, and that that was very natural in a young woman who from morning till night had to look at that damn fence. He went back to his hotel room and sat on the couch for a long while, not knowing what to do, then he had dinner and a long nap.

"How stupid and annoying all this is!" he thought when he woke and looked at the dark windows: it was already evening. "Here I've had a good sleep for some reason. What am I going to do at night?"

He sat on the bed, which was covered with a cheap gray blanket of the kind seen in hospitals, and he twitted himself in his vexation:

"So there's your lady with the pet dog. There's your adventure. A nice place to cool your heels in."

That morning at the station a playbill in large letters had caught his eye. *The Geisha* was to be given for the first time. He thought of this and drove to the theater.

"It's quite possible that she goes to first nights," he thought.

The theater was full. As in all provincial theaters, there was a haze above the chandelier, the gallery was noisy and restless; in the front row, before the beginning of the performance the local dandies were standing with their hands clasped behind their backs; in the Governor's box the Governor's daughter, wearing a boa, occupied the front seat, while the Governor himself hid modestly behind the portiere and only his hands were visible; the curtain swayed; the orchestra was a long time tuning up. While the audience was coming in and taking their seats, Gurov scanned the faces eagerly.

Anna Sergeyevna, too, came in. She sat down in the third row, and when Gurov looked at her his heart contracted, and he understood clearly that in the whole world there was no human being so near, so precious, and so important to him; she, this little, undistinguished woman, lost in a provincial crowd, with a vulgar lorgnette in her hand, filled his whole life now, was his sorrow and his joy, the only happiness that he now desired for himself, and to the sounds of the bad orchestra, of the miserable local violins, he thought how lovely she was. He thought and dreamed.

A young man with small side-whiskers, very tall and stooped, came in with Anna Sergeyevna and sat down beside her; he nodded his head at every step and seemed to be bowing continually. Probably this was the husband whom at Yalta, in an access of bitter feeling, she had called a flunkey. And there really was in his lanky figure, his side-whiskers, his small bald patch, something of a flunkey's retiring manner; his smile was mawkish, and in his buttonhole there was an academic badge like a waiter's number.

During the first intermission the husband went out to have a smoke; she remained in her seat. Gurov, who was also sitting in the orchestra, went up to her and said in a shaky voice, with a forced smile:

"Good evening!"

She glanced at him and turned pale, then looked at him again in horror, unable to believe her eyes, and gripped the fan and the lorgnette tightly together in her hands, evidently trying to keep herself from fainting. Both were silent. She was sitting, he was standing, frightened by her distress and not daring to take a seat beside her. The violins and the flute that were being tuned up sang out. He suddenly felt frightened: it seemed as if all the people in the boxes were looking at them. She got up and went hurriedly to the exit; he followed her, and both of them walked blindly along the corridors and up and down stairs, and figures in the uniforms prescribed for magistrates, teachers, and officials of the Department of Crown Lands, all wearing badges, flitted before their eyes, as did also ladies, and fur coats on hangers; they were conscious of drafts and the smell of stale tobacco. And Gurov, whose heart was beating violently, thought:

"Oh, Lord! Why are these people here and this orchestra!"

And at that instant he suddenly recalled how when he had seen Anna Sergeyevna off at the station he had said to himself that all was over between them and that they would never meet again. But how distant the end still was!

On the narrow, gloomy staircase over which it said "To the Amphitheatre," she stopped.

"How you frightened me!" she said, breathing hard, still pale and stunned. "Oh, how you frightened me! I am barely alive. Why did you come? Why?"

"But do understand, Anna, do understand —" he said hurriedly, under his breath. "I implore you, do understand —"

She looked at him with fear, with entreaty, with love; she looked at him intently, to keep his features more distinctly in her memory.

"I suffer so," she went on, not listening to him. "All this time I have been thinking of nothing but you; I live only by the thought of you. And I wanted to forget, to forget; but why, oh, why have you come?"

On the landing above them two high school boys were looking down and smoking, but it was all the same to Gurov; he drew Anna Sergeyevna to him and began kissing her face and hands.

"What are you doing, what are you doing!" she was saying in horror, pushing him away. "We have lost our senses. Go away today; go away at once — I conjure you by all that is sacred, I implore you — People are coming this way!"

Someone was walking up the stairs.

"You must leave," Anna Sergeyevna went on in a whisper. "Do you hear, Dmitry Dmitrich? I will come and see you in Moscow. I have never been happy; I am unhappy now, and I never, never shall be happy, never! So don't make me suffer still more! I swear I'll come to Moscow. But now let us part. My dear, good, precious one, let us part!"

She pressed his hand and walked rapidly downstairs, turning to look round at him, and from her eyes he could see that she really was unhappy. Gurov stood for a while, listening, then when all grew quiet, he found his coat and left the theater.

IV

And Anna Sergeyevna began coming to see him in Moscow. Once every two or three months she left S —— telling her husband that she was going to consult a doctor about a woman's ailment from which she was suffering — and her husband did and did not believe her. When she arrived in Moscow she would stop at the Slavyansky Bazar Hotel, and at once send a man in a red cap to Gurov. Gurov came to see her, and no one in Moscow knew of it.

Once he was going to see her in this way on a winter morning (the messenger had come the evening before and not found him in). With him walked his daughter, whom he wanted to take to school; it was on the way. Snow was coming down in big wet flakes.

"It's three degrees above zero,° and yet it's snowing," Gurov was saying to his daughter. "But this temperature prevails only on the surface of the earth; in the upper layers of the atmosphere there is quite a different temperature."

"And why doesn't it thunder in winter, papa?"

He explained that, too. He talked, thinking all the while that he was on his way to a rendezvous, and no living soul knew of it, and probably no one would ever know. He had two lives, an open one, seen and known by all who needed to know it, full of conventional truth and conventional falsehood, exactly like the lives of his friends and acquaintances; and another life that went on in secret. And through some strange, perhaps accidental, combination of circumstances, everything that was of interest and importance to him, everything that was essential to him, everything about which he felt sincerely and did not deceive himself, everything that constituted the core of his life, was going on concealed from others; while all that was false, the shell in which he hid to cover the truth — his work at the bank, for instance, his discussions at the club, his references to the "inferior race," his appearances at anniversary celebrations with his wife — all that went on in the open. Judging others by himself, he did not believe what he saw, and always fancied that every man led his real, most interesting life under cover of secrecy as under cover of night. The personal life of every individual is based on secrecy, and perhaps it is partly for that reason that civilized man is so nervously anxious that personal privacy should be respected.

Having taken his daughter to school, Gurov went on to the Slavyansky Bazar Hotel. He took off his fur coat in the lobby, went upstairs, and knocked gently at the door. Anna Sergeyevna, wearing his favorite gray dress, exhausted by the journey and by waiting, had been expecting him since the previous evening. She was pale, and looked at him without a smile, and he had hardly entered when she flung herself on his breast. That kiss was a long, lingering one, as though they had not seen one another for two years.

"Well, darling, how are you getting on there?" he asked. "What news?"

"Wait; I'll tell you in a moment — I can't speak."

She could not speak; she was crying. She turned away from him, and pressed her handkerchief to her eyes.

---

three degrees above zero: On the Celsius scale — about thirty-seven degrees Fahrenheit.

"Let her have her cry; meanwhile I'll sit down," he thought, and he seated himself in an armchair.

Then he rang and ordered tea, and while he was having his tea she remained standing at the window with her back to him. She was crying out of sheer agitation, in the sorrowful consciousness that their life was so sad; that they could only see each other in secret and had to hide from people like thieves! Was it not a broken life?

"Come, stop now, dear!" he said.

It was plain to him that this love of theirs would not be over soon, that the end of it was not in sight. Anna Sergeyevna was growing more and more attached to him. She adored him, and it was unthinkable to tell her that their love was bound to come to an end some day; besides, she would not have believed it!

He went up to her and took her by the shoulders, to fondle her and say something diverting, and at that moment he caught sight of himself in the mirror.

His hair was already beginning to turn gray. And it seemed odd to him that he had grown so much older in the last few years, and lost his looks. The shoulders on which his hands rested were warm and heaving. He felt compassion for this life, still so warm and lovely, but probably already about to begin to fade and wither like his own. Why did she love him so much? He always seemed to women different from what he was, and they loved in him not himself, but the man whom their imagination created and whom they had been eagerly seeking all their lives; and afterwards, when they saw their mistake, they loved him nevertheless. And not one of them had been happy with him. In the past he had met women, come together with them, parted from them, but he had never once loved; it was anything you please, but not love. And only now when his head was gray he had fallen in love, really, truly — for the first time in his life.

Anna Sergeyevna and he loved each other as people do who are very close and intimate, like man and wife, like tender friends; it seemed to them that Fate itself had meant them for one another, and they could not understand why he had a wife and she a husband; and it was as though they were a pair of migratory birds, male and female, caught and forced to live in different cages. They forgave each other what they were ashamed of in their past, they forgave everything in the present, and felt that this love of theirs had altered them both.

Formerly in moments of sadness he had soothed himself with whatever logical arguments came into his head, but now he no longer cared for logic; he felt profound compassion, he wanted to be sincere and tender.

"Give it up now, my darling," he said. "You've had your cry; that's enough. Let us have a talk now, we'll think up something."

Then they spent a long time taking counsel together, they talked of how to avoid the necessity for secrecy, for deception, for living in different cities, and not seeing one another for long stretches of time. How could they free themselves from these intolerable fetters?

"How? How?" he asked, clutching his head. "How?"

And it seemed as though in a little while the solution would be found, and then a new and glorious life would begin; and it was clear to both of them that the end was still far off, and that what was to be most complicated and difficult for them was only just beginning.

ꕥ

KATE CHOPIN *(1851–1904) was born in St. Louis. Her father died when she was four, and she was raised by her Creole mother's family. In 1870 she married Oscar Chopin, a cotton broker. They lived in Louisiana, first in New Orleans and then on a large plantation among the French-speaking Acadians. When her husband died in 1882, Chopin moved with her six children back to St. Louis. Friends encouraged her to write, and when she was nearly forty years old she published her first novel,* At Fault *(1890). Her stories began to appear in* Century *and* Harper's Magazine, *and two collections followed:* Bayou Folk *(1894) and* A Night in Arcadie *(1897). Her last major work, the novel* The Awakening *(1899), is her masterpiece, but its sympathetic treatment of adultery shocked reviewers and readers throughout America. In St. Louis the novel was taken out of the libraries, and Chopin was denied membership in the St. Louis Fine Arts Club. When her third collection of stories was rejected by her publisher at the end of 1899, Chopin felt herself a literary outcast; she wrote very little in the last years of her life.*

What affronted the genteel readers of the 1890s was Chopin's attempt to write frankly about women's emotions in their relations with men, children, and their own sexuality. After her mother's death in 1885, she stopped being a practicing Catholic and accepted the Darwinian view of human evolution. Seeking God in nature rather than through the church, Chopin wrote freely on the subjects of sex and love, but she said she learned to her sorrow that for American authors, "the limitations imposed upon their art by their environment hamper a full and spontaneous expression." Magazine editors turned down her work if it challenged conventional social behavior, as does "The Story of an Hour," which feminist critics championed more than half a century after Chopin's death.

Chopin adopted Guy de Maupassant as a model after translating his stories from the French. She felt, "Here was life, not fiction; for where were the plots, the old fashioned mechanism and stage trappings that in a vague, unthinking way I had fancied were essential to the art of story making?" If her fiction is sometimes marred by stilted language or improbable coincidence, at her best, as in "Désirée's Baby," Chopin subtly emphasized character rather than plot in her dramatization of the tragic repercussions of racial prejudice.

RELATED COMMENTARY: *Kate Chopin, "How I Stumbled upon Maupassant," page 670.*

Kate Chopin

Désirée's Baby

1892

As the day was pleasant, Madame Valmondé drove over to L'Abri to see Désirée and the baby.

It made her laugh to think of Désirée with a baby. Why, it seemed but yesterday that Désirée was little more than a baby herself; when Monsieur in riding through the gateway of Valmondé had found her lying asleep in the shadow of the big stone pillar.

The little one awoke in his arms and began to cry for "Dada." That was as much as she could do or say. Some people thought she might have strayed there of her own accord, for she was of the toddling age. The prevailing belief was that she had been purposely left by a party of Texans, whose canvas-covered wagon, late in the day, had crossed the ferry that Coton Maïs kept, just below the plantation. In time Madame Valmondé abandoned every speculation but the one that Désirée had been sent to her by a beneficent Providence to be the child of her affection, seeing that she was without child of the flesh. For the girl grew to be beautiful and gentle, affectionate and sincere, — the idol of Valmondé.

It was no wonder, when she stood one day against the stone pillar in whose shadow she had lain asleep, eighteen years before, that Armand Aubigny riding by and seeing her there, had fallen in love with her. That was the way all the Aubignys fell in love, as if struck by a pistol shot. The wonder was that he had not loved her before; for he had known her since his father brought him home from Paris, a boy of eight, after his mother died there. The passion that awoke in him that day, when he saw her at the gate, swept along like an avalanche, or like a prairie fire, or like anything that drives headlong over all obstacles.

Monsieur Valmondé grew practical and wanted things well considered: that is, the girl's obscure origin. Armand looked into her eyes and did not care. He was reminded that she was nameless. What did it matter about a name when he could give her one of the oldest and proudest in Louisiana? He ordered the *corbeille* from Paris, and contained himself with what patience he could until it arrived; then they were married.

Madame Valmondé had not seen Désirée and the baby for four weeks. When she reached L'Abri she shuddered at the first sight of it, as she always did. It was a sad looking place, which for many years had not known the gentle presence of a mistress, old Monsieur Aubigny having married and buried his wife in France, and she having loved her own land too well ever to leave it. The roof came down steep and black like a cowl, reaching out beyond the wide galleries that encircled the yellow stuccoed house. Big, solemn oaks grew close to it, and their thick-leaved, far-reaching branches shadowed it like a pall. Young Aubigny's rule was a strict one, too, and under it his negroes had forgotten how to be gay, as they had been during the old master's easy-going and indulgent lifetime.

The young mother was recovering slowly, and lay full length, in her soft white muslins and laces, upon a couch. The baby was beside her, upon her arm, where he had fallen asleep, at her breast. The yellow nurse woman sat beside a window fanning herself.

Madame Valmondé bent her portly figure over Désirée and kissed her, holding her an instant tenderly in her arms. Then she turned to the child.

"This is not the baby!" she exclaimed, in startled tones. French was the language spoken at Valmondé in those days.

"I knew you would be astonished," laughed Désirée, "at the way he has grown. The little *cochon de lait!*° Look at his legs, mamma, and his hands and fingernails, — real fingernails. Zandrine had to cut them this morning. Isn't it true, Zandrine?"

The woman bowed her turbaned head majestically, "Mais si, Madame."

"And the way he cries," went on Désirée, "is deafening. Armand heard him the other day as far away as La Blanche's cabin."

Madame Valmondé had never removed her eyes from the child. She lifted it and walked with it over to the window that was lightest. She scanned the baby narrowly, then looked as searchingly at Zandrine, whose face was turned to gaze across the fields.

"Yes, the child has grown, has changed," said Madame Valmondé, slowly, as she replaced it beside its mother. "What does Armand say?"

Désirée's face became suffused with a glow that was happiness itself.

"Oh, Armand is the proudest father in the parish, I believe, chiefly because it is a boy, to bear his name; though he says not, — that he would have loved a girl as well. But I know it isn't true. I know he says that to please me. And mamma," she added, drawing Madame Valmondé's head down to her and speaking in a whisper, "he hasn't punished one of them — not one of them — since baby is born. Even Négrillon, who pretended to have burnt his leg that he might rest from work — he only laughed, and said Négrillon was a great scamp. Oh, mamma, I'm so happy; it frightens me."

What Désirée said was true. Marriage, and later the birth of his son had softened Armand Aubigny's imperious and exacting nature greatly. This was what made the gentle Désirée so happy, for she loved him desperately. When he frowned she trembled, but loved him. When he smiled, she asked no greater blessing of God. But Armand's dark, handsome face had not often been disfigured by frowns since the day he fell in love with her.

When the baby was about three months old, Désirée awoke one day to the conviction that there was something in the air menacing her peace. It was at first too subtle to grasp. It had only been a disquieting suggestion; an air of mystery among the blacks; unexpected visits from far-off neighbors who could hardly account for their coming. Then a strange, an awful change in her husband's manner, which she dared not ask him to explain. When he spoke to her, it was with averted eyes, from which the old love-light seemed to have gone out. He absented himself from home; and when there, avoided her presence and that of her child, without excuse. And the very spirit of Satan seemed

cochon de lait: An endearment (literally, "suckling pig" in French).

suddenly to take hold of him in his dealings with the slaves. Désirée was miserable enough to die.

She sat in her room, one hot afternoon, in her *peignoir*, listlessly drawing through her fingers the strands of her long, silky brown hair that hung about her shoulders. The baby, half naked, lay asleep upon her own great mahogany bed, that was like a sumptuous throne, with its satin-lined half-canopy. One of La Blanche's little quadroon boys — half naked too — stood fanning the child slowly with a fan of peacock feathers. Désirée's eyes had been fixed absently and sadly upon the baby, while she was striving to penetrate the threatening mist that she felt closing about her. She looked from her child to the boy who stood beside him, and back again; over and over. "Ah!" It was a cry that she could not help; which she was not conscious of having uttered. The blood turned like ice in her veins, and a clammy moisture gathered upon her face.

She tried to speak to the little quadroon boy; but no sound would come, at first. When he heard his name uttered, he looked up, and his mistress was pointing to the door. He laid aside the great, soft fan, and obediently stole away, over the polished floor, on his bare tiptoes.

She stayed motionless, with gaze riveted upon her child, and her face the picture of fright.

Presently her husband entered the room, and without noticing her, went to a table and began to search among some papers which covered it.

"Armand," she called to him, in a voice which must have stabbed him, if he was human. But he did not notice. "Armand," she said again. Then she rose and tottered towards him. "Armand," she panted once more, clutching his arm, "look at our child. What does it mean? tell me."

He coldly but gently loosened her fingers from about his arm and thrust the hand away from him. "Tell me what it means!" she cried despairingly.

"It means," he answered lightly, "that the child is not white; it means that you are not white."

A quick conception of all that this accusation meant for her nerved her with unwonted courage to deny it. "It is a lie; it is not true, I am white! Look at my hair, it is brown; and my eyes are gray, Armand, you know they are gray. And my skin is fair," seizing his wrist. "Look at my hand; whiter than yours, Armand," she laughed hysterically.

"As white as La Blanche's," he returned cruelly; and went away leaving her alone with their child.

When she could hold a pen in her hand, she sent a despairing letter to Madame Valmondé.

"My mother, they tell me I am not white. Armand has told me I am not white. For God's sake tell them it is not true. You must know it is not true. I shall die. I must die. I cannot be so unhappy, and live."

The answer that came was as brief:

"My own Désirée: Come home to Valmondé; back to your mother who loves you. Come with your child."

When the letter reached Désirée she went with it to her husband's study, and laid it open upon the desk before which he sat. She was like a stone image: silent, white, motionless after she placed it there.

In silence he ran his cold eyes over the written words. He said nothing. "Shall I go, Armand?" she asked in tones sharp with agonized suspense.

"Yes, go."

"Do you want me to go?"

"Yes, I want you to go."

He thought Almighty God had dealt cruelly and unjustly with him; and felt, somehow, that he was paying Him back in kind when he stabbed thus into his wife's soul. Moreover he no longer loved her, because of the unconscious injury she had brought upon his home and his name.

She turned away like one stunned by a blow, and walked slowly towards the door, hoping he would call her back.

"Good-by, Armand," she moaned.

He did not answer her. That was his last blow at fate.

Désirée went in search of her child. Zandrine was pacing the sombre gallery with it. She took the little one from the nurse's arms with no word of explanation, and descending the steps, walked away, under the live-oak branches.

It was an October afternoon; the sun was just sinking. Out in the still fields the negroes were picking cotton.

Désirée had not changed the thin white garment nor the slippers which she wore. Her hair was uncovered and the sun's rays brought a golden gleam from its brown meshes. She did not take the broad, beaten road which led to the far-off plantation of Valmondé. She walked across a deserted field, where the stubble bruised her tender feet, so delicately shod, and tore her thin gown to shreds.

She disappeared among the reeds and willows that grew thick along the banks of the deep, sluggish bayou; and she did not come back again.

Some weeks later there was a curious scene enacted at L'Abri. In the centre of the smoothly swept back yard was a great bonfire. Armand Aubigny sat in the wide hallway that commanded a view of the spectacle; and it was he who dealt out to a half dozen negroes the material which kept this fire ablaze.

A graceful cradle of willow, with all its dainty furbishings, was laid upon the pyre, which had already been fed with the richness of a priceless *layette*. Then there were silk gowns, and velvet and satin ones added to these; laces, too, and embroideries; bonnets and gloves; for the *corbeille* had been of rare quality.

The last thing to go was a tiny bundle of letters; innocent little scribblings that Désirée had sent to him during the days of their espousal. There was the remnant of one back in the drawer from which he took them. But it was not Désirée's; it was part of an old letter from his mother to his father. He read it. She was thanking God for the blessing of her husband's love: —

"But, above all," she wrote, "night and day, I thank the good God for having so arranged our lives that our dear Armand will never know that his mother, who adores him, belongs to the race that is cursed with the brand of slavery."

KATE CHOPIN

The Story of an Hour

1894

Knowing that Mrs. Mallard was afflicted with a heart trouble, great care was taken to break to her as gently as possible the news of her husband's death.

It was her sister Josephine who told her, in broken sentences; veiled hints that revealed in half concealing. Her husband's friend Richards was there, too, near her. It was he who had been in the newspaper office when intelligence of the railroad disaster was received, with Brently Mallard's name leading the list of "killed." He had only taken the time to assure himself of its truth by a second telegram, and had hastened to forestall any less careful, less tender friend in bearing the sad message.

She did not hear the story as many women have heard the same, with a paralyzed inability to accept its significance. She wept at once, with sudden, wild abandonment, in her sister's arms. When the storm of grief had spent itself she went away to her room alone. She would have no one follow her.

There stood, facing the open window, a comfortable, roomy armchair. Into this she sank, pressed down by a physical exhaustion that haunted her body and seemed to reach into her soul.

She could see in the open square before her house the tops of trees that were all aquiver with the new spring life. The delicious breath of rain was in the air. In the street below a peddler was crying his wares. The notes of a distant song which some one was singing reached her faintly, and countless sparrows were twittering in the eaves.

There were patches of blue sky showing here and there through the clouds that had met and piled one above the other in the west facing her window.

She sat with her head thrown back upon the cushion of the chair, quite motionless, except when a sob came up into her throat and shook her, as a child who had cried itself to sleep continues to sob in its dreams.

She was young, with a fair, calm face, whose lines bespoke repression and even a certain strength. But now there was a dull stare in her eyes, whose gaze was fixed away off yonder on one of those patches of blue sky. It was not a glance of reflection, but rather indicated a suspension of intelligent thought.

There was something coming to her and she was waiting for it, fearfully. What was it? She did not know; it was too subtle and elusive to name. But she felt it, creeping out of the sky, reaching toward her through the sounds, the scents, the color that filled the air.

Now her bosom rose and fell tumultuously. She was beginning to recognize this thing that was approaching to possess her, and she was striving to beat it back with her will — as powerless as her two white slender hands would have been.

When she abandoned herself a little whispered word escaped her slightly parted lips. She said it over and over under her breath: "free, free, free!" The vacant stare and the look of terror that had followed it went from her eyes. They stayed keen and bright. Her pulses beat fast, and the coursing blood warmed and relaxed every inch of her body.

She did not stop to ask if it were or were not a monstrous joy that held her. A clear and exalted perception enabled her to dismiss the suggestion as trivial.

She knew that she would weep again when she saw the kind, tender hands folded in death; the face that had never looked save with love upon her, fixed and gray and dead. But she saw beyond that bitter moment a long procession of years to come that would belong to her absolutely. And she opened and spread her arms out to them in welcome.

There would be no one to live for her during those coming years: she would live for herself. There would be no powerful will bending hers in that blind persistence with which men and women believe they have a right to impose a private will upon a fellow-creature. A kind intention or a cruel intention made the act seem no less a crime as she looked upon it in that brief moment of illumination.

And yet she had loved him — sometimes. Often she had not. What did it matter! What could love, the unsolved mystery, count for in face of this possession of self-assertion which she suddenly recognized as the strongest impulse of her being!

"Free! Body and soul free!" she kept whispering.

Josephine was kneeling before the closed door with her lips to the keyhole, imploring for admission. "Louise, open the door! I beg; open the door — you will make yourself ill. What are you doing, Louise? For heaven's sake open the door."

"Go away. I am not making myself ill." No; she was drinking in a very elixir of life through that open window.

Her fancy was running riot along those days ahead of her. Spring days, and summer days, and all sorts of days that would be her own. She breathed a quick prayer that life might be long. It was only yesterday she had thought with a shudder that life might be long.

She arose at length and opened the door to her sister's importunities. There was a feverish triumph in her eyes, and she carried herself unwittingly like a goddess of Victory. She clasped her sister's waist, and together they descended the stairs. Richards stood waiting for them at the bottom.

Some one was opening the front door with a latchkey. It was Brently Mallard who entered, a little travel-stained, composedly carrying his gripsack and umbrella. He had been far from the scene of accident, and did not even know there had been one. He stood amazed at Josephine's piercing cry; at Richards' quick motion to screen him from the view of his wife.

But Richards was too late.

When the doctors came they said she had died of heart disease — of joy that kills.

SANDRA CISNEROS *(b. 1954), the daughter of a Mexican father and a Chicana mother, grew up in ghetto neighborhoods in Chicago and began writing poetry when she was ten years old. Her six brothers so dominated the household that she remembers that she felt she had "seven fathers." Cisneros spoke Spanish at home with her father and on her frequent trips to Mexico to visit her grandmother, but she didn't think of herself as a Chicana writer until she began a series of autobiographical sketches as a graduate student in the M.A. program at the University of Iowa's Writers Workshop in 1977. Then she discovered her literary voice, realizing the uniqueness of her experience growing up as a poor Latina in Chicago:*

> *Everyone seemed to have some communal knowledge which I did not have. . . . This caused me to question myself, to become defensive. What did I, Sandra Cisneros, know? What could I know? My classmates were from the best schools in the country. They had been bred as fine hothouse flowers. I was a yellow weed among the city's cracks.*

Cisneros says that she became a writer because she was "determined to fill a literary void . . . trying to write the stories that haven't been written." These early sketches developed into the book published as The House on Mango Street *(1983), over forty short narratives that were highly praised by critics and won the 1985 Before Columbus American Book Award. Cisneros had found a way to write stories*

> *that were a cross between poetry and fiction. . . . [I] wanted to write a collection which could be read at any random point without having any knowledge of what came before or after. Or, that could be read in a series to tell one big story. I wanted stories like poems, compact and lyrical and ending with reverberation.*

As Joyce Carol Oates has observed, Cisneros's "emotionally rich subject is the Latino community, specifically the experience of growing up female in a male-dominated society; her work . . . might be as readily classified as prose poetry as prose fiction." To date Cisneros has published three books of poetry in addition to her short stories.

"Little Miracles, Kept Promises" is from Woman Hollering Creek and Other Stories *(1991), a collection of more than twenty lyrical narratives about Mexican Americans in San Antonio who have different experiences living on both sides of the border with Mexico. The form of this experimental story consists entirely of letters to patron saints that have been left with small charms or presents as offerings alongside religious statues. Here Cisneros's growing mastery of the short story form ensures, as one reviewer observed, that her "irony defers to her powers of observation so that feminism and cultural imperialism, while important issues here, do not overwhelm the narrative."*

SANDRA CISNEROS

Little Miracles, Kept Promises *1990*

Exvoto Donated as Promised

On the 20th of December of 1988 we suffered a terrible disaster on the road to Corpus Christi. The bus we were riding skidded and overturned near Robstown and a lady and her little girl were killed. Thanks to La Virgen de Guadalupe we are alive, all of us miraculously unharmed, and with no visible scars, except we are afraid to ride buses. We dedicate this retablo to La Virgencita with our affection and gratitude and our everlasting faith.

Familia Arteaga
Alice, Texas
G.R. (Gracias Recibido/Thanks Given)

Blessed Santo Niño de Atocha,

Thank you for helping us when Chapa's truck got stolen. We didn't know how we was going to make it. He needs it to get to work, and this job, well, he's been on probation since we got him to quit drinking. Raquel and the kids are hardly ever afraid of him anymore, and we are proud parents. We don't know how we can repay you for everything you have done for our family. We will light a candle to you every Sunday and never forget you.

Sidronio Tijerina
Brenda A. Camacho de Tijerina
San Angelo, Texas

Dear San Martín de Porres,

Please send us clothes, furniture, shoes, dishes. We need anything that don't eat. Since the fire we have to start all over again and Lalo's disability check ain't much and don't go far. Zulema would like to finish school but I says she can just forget about it now. She's our oldest and her place is at home helping us out I told her. Please make her see some sense. She's all we got.

Thanking you,
Adelfa Vásquez
Escobas, Texas

Dear San Antonio de Padua,

Can you please help me find a man who isn't a pain in the nalgas. There aren't any in Texas, I swear. Especially not in San Antonio.

Can you do something about all the educated Chicanos who have to go to California to find a job. I guess what my sister Irma says is true: "If you didn't get a husband when you were in college, you don't get one."

I would appreciate it very much if you sent me a man who speaks Spanish, who at least can pronounce his name the way it's supposed to be pronounced. Someone please who never calls himself "Hispanic" unless he's applying for a grant from Washington, D.C.

Can you send me a man man. I mean someone who's not ashamed to be seen cooking or cleaning or looking after himself. In other words, a man who acts like an adult. Not one who's never lived alone, never bought his own underwear, never ironed his own shirts, never even heated his own tortillas. In other words, don't send me someone like my brothers who my mother ruined with too much chichi, or I'll throw him back.

I'll turn your statue upside down until you send him to me. I've put up with too much too long, and now I'm just too intelligent, too powerful, too beautiful, too sure of who I am finally to deserve anything less.

Ms. Barbara Ybañez
San Antonio, TX

Dear Niño Fidencio,

I would like for you to help me get a job with good pay, benefits, and retirement plan. I promise you if you help me I will make a pilgrimage to your tomb in Espinazo and bring you flowers. Many thanks.

César Escandón
Pharr, Tejas

DEAR DON PEDRITO JARAMILLO HEALER OF LOS OLMOS

MY NAME IS ENRIQUETA ANTONIA SANDOVAL I LIVE IN SAN MARCOS TX I AM SICK THEY OPERATED ME FROM A KIDNEY AND A TUMOR OF CANCER BUT THANKS TO GOD I AM ALIVE BUT I HAVE TO GET TREATMENTS FOR A YEAR THE KIMO I AM 2½ YEARS OLD BUT MY GRANDMA BROUGHT ME THAT YOU AND OUR LORD WHO IS IN THE HEAVENS WILL CURE ME WITH THIS LETTER THAT I AM DEPOSITING HERE ITS MY GRANDMA WHO IS WRITING THIS I HOPE EVERYBODY WHO SEES THIS LETTER WILL TAKE A MINUTE TO ASK FOR MY HEALTH

ENRIQUETA ANTONIA SANDOVAL
2 AND A HALF YEARS OLD

I LEOCADIA DIMAS VDA. DE CORDERO OF SAN MARCOS TX HAVE COME TO PAY THIS REQUEST TO DON PEDRITO THAT MY GRANDDAUGHTER WILL COME OUT FINE FROM HER OPERATION THANKS TO GOD AND THOSE WHO HELPED SUCH GOOD DOCTORS THAT DID THEIR JOB WELL THE REST IS IN GODS HANDS THAT HE DO HIS WILL MANY THANKS WITH ALL MY HEART.

YOUR VERY RESPECTFUL SERVANT
LEOCADIA

Oh Mighty Poderosos, Blessed Powerful Ones,

You who are crowned in heaven and who are so close to our Divine Savior, I implore your intercession before the Almighty on my behalf. I ask for peace of spirit and prosperity, and that the demons in my path that are the cause of all my woes be removed so that they no longer torment me. Look favorably on this petition and bless me, that I may continue to glorify your deeds with all my heart — santísimo Niño Fidencio, gran General Pancho Villa, bendito Don Pedrito Jaramillo, virtuoso John F. Kennedy, and blessed Pope John Paul. Amen.

Gertrudis Parra
Uvalde, Tejas

Father Almighty

Teach me to love my husband again. Forgive me.

s.
Corpus Christi

Seven African Powers that surround our Savior — Obatala, Yemaya, Ochún, Orunla, Ogun, Elegua, and Shango — why don't you behave and be good to me? Oh Seven African Powers, come on, don't be bad. Let my Illinois lottery ticket win, and if it does, don't let my cousin Cirilo in Chicago cheat me out of my winnings, since I'm the one who pays for the ticket and all he does is buy it for me each week — if he does even that. He's my cousin, but like the Bible says, better to say nothing than to say nothing nice.

Protect me from the evil eye of the envious and don't let my enemies do me harm, because I've never done a thing wrong to anyone first. Save this good Christian who the wicked have taken advantage of.

Seven Powers, reward my devotion with good luck. Look after me, why don't you? And don't forget me because I never forget you.

Moises Ildefonso Mata
San Antonio, Texas

Virgencita de Guadalupe,

I promise to walk to your shrine on my knees the very first day I get back, I swear, if you will only get the Tortillería la Casa de la Masa to pay me the $253.72 they owe me for two weeks' work. I put in 67½ hours that first week and 79 hours the second, and I don't have anything to show for it yet. I calculated with the taxes deducted, I have $253.72 coming to me. That's all I'm asking for. The $253.72 I have coming to me.

I have asked the proprietors Blanquita and Rudy Mondragón, and they keep telling me next week, next week, next week. And it's almost the middle of the third week already and I don't know how I'm going to do it to pay this week's rent, since I'm already behind, and the other guys have loaned me as much as they're able, and I don't know what I'm going to do, I don't know what I'm going to do.

My wife and the kids and my in-laws all depend on what I send home. We are humble people, Virgencita. You know I'm not full of vices. That's how I am. It's been hard for me to live here so far away without seeing my wife, you know. And sometimes one gets tempted, but no, and no, and no. I'm not like that. Please, Virgencita, all I'm asking for is my $253.72. There is no one else I can turn to here in this country, and well, if you can't help me, well, I just don't know.

Arnulfo Contreras
San Antonio, Tejas

Saint Sebastian who was persecuted with arrows and then survived, thank you for answering my prayers! All them arrows that had persecuted me — my brother-in-law Ernie and my sister Alba and their kids — el Junior, la Gloria, and el Skyler — all gone. And now my home sweet home is mine again, and my Dianita bien lovey-dovey, and my kids got something to say to me besides who hit who.

Here is the little gold milagrito I promised you, a little house, see? And it ain't that cheap gold-plate shit either. So now that I paid you back, we're even, right? Cause I don't like for no one to say Victor Lozano don't pay his debts. I pays cash on the line, bro. And Victor Lozano's word like his deeds is solid gold.

Victor A. Lozano
Houston, TX

Dear San Lázaro,

My mother's comadre Dernetria said if I prayed to you that like maybe you could help me because you were raised from the dead and did a lot of miracles and maybe if I lit a candle every night for seven days and prayed, you might maybe could help me with my face breaking out with so many pimples. Thank you.

Rubén Ledesma
Hebbronville, Texas

Santísima Señora de San Juan de los Lagos,

We came to see you twice when they brought you to San Antonio, my mother and my sister Yolanda and two of my aunts, Tía Enedina and my Tía Perla, and we drove all the way from Beeville just to visit you and make our requests.

I don't know what my Tía Enedina asked for, she's always so secretive, but probably it had to do with her son Beto who doesn't do anything but hang around the house and get into trouble. And my Tía Perla no doubt complained about her ladies' problems — her ovaries that itch, her tangled fallopians, her uterus that makes her seasick with all its flipping and flopping. And Mami who said she only came along for the ride, lit three candles so you would bless us all and sweep jealousy and bitterness from our hearts because that's what she says every day and every night. And my sister Yoli asked that you help her lose weight because I don't want to wind up like Tía Perla, embroidering altar cloths and dressing saints.

But that was a year ago, Virgencita, and since then my cousin Beto was fined for killing the neighbor's rooster with a flying Big Red bottle, and my Tía Perla is convinced her uterus has fallen because when she walks something inside her rattles like a maraca, and my mother and my aunts are arguing and yelling at each other same as always. And my stupid sister Yoli is still sending away for even stupider products like the Grasa Fantástica, guaranteed to burn away fat — It really works, Tere, just rub some on while you're watching TV — only she's fatter than ever and just as sad.

What I realize is that we all made the trip to San Antonio to ask something of you, Virgencita, we all needed you to listen to us. And of all of us, my mama and sister Yoli, and my aunts Enedina and Perla, of all of us, you granted me my petition and sent, just like I asked, a guy who would love only me because I was tired of looking at girls younger than me walking along the street or riding in cars or standing in front of the school with a guy's arm hooked around their neck.

So what is it I'm asking for? Please, Virgencita. Lift this heavy cross from my shoulders and leave me like I was before, wind on my neck, my arms swinging free, and no one telling me how I ought to be.

Teresa Galindo
Beeville, Texas

Miraculous Black Christ of Esquipulas,

Please make our grandson to be nice to us and stay away from drugs. Save him to find a job and move away from us. Thank you.

Grandma y Grandfather
Harlingen

M3r1c5l45s Bl1ck Chr3st 4f 2sq53p5l1s,

3 1sk y45, L4rd, w3th 1ll my h21rt pl21s2 w1tch 4v2r M1nny B2n1v3d2s wh4 3s 4v2rs21s. 3 l4v2 h3m 1nd 3 d4n't kn4w wh1t t4 d4 1b45t 1ll th3s l4v2 s1dn2ss 1nd sh1m2 th1t f3lls m2.

B2nj1m3n T.
D2l R34 TX

Milagroso Cristo Negro de Esquipulas,

Te ofrezco este retrato de mis niños. Wáchelos, Dios Santo, y si le quitas el trago a mi hijo te prometo prender velitas. Ayúdanos con nuestras cuentas, Señor, y que el cheque del income tax nos llegue pronto para pagar los biles. Danos una buena vida y que les ayudes a mis hijos a cambiar sus modos. Tú que eres tan bondadoso escucha estas peticiones que te pido con todo mi corazón y con toda la fe de mi alma. Ten piedad, Padre mio. Mi nombre es Adela O.

Elizondo.
Cotulla TX

Milagroso Cristo Negro,

Thank you por el milagro de haber graduado de high school. Aquí le regalo mi retrato de graduation.

Fito Moroles
Rockport, Texas

Cristo Negro,

Venimos desde muy lejos. Infinitas gracias, Señor. Gracias por habernos escuchado.

Familia Armendáriz G.
Matamoros, Tamps. México

Jesus Christ,

Please keep Deborah Abrego and Ralph S. Urrea together forever.

Love,
Deborah Abrego
Sabinal, Texas

Blessed Virgen de los Remedios,

Señora Dolores Alcalá de Corchado finds herself gravely ill from a complication that resulted after a delicate operation she underwent Thursday last, and from which she was recovering satisfactorily until suffering a hemmorhage Tuesday morning. Please intercede on her behalf. We leave her in the hands of God, that His will be done, now that we have witnessed her suffering and don't know whether she should die or continue this life. Her husband of forty-eight years offers this request with all his heart.

Señor Gustavo Corchado B.
Laredo, Tejas

Madrecita de Dios,

Thank you. Our child is born healthy!

Rene y Janie Garza
Hondo,TX

Saint Jude, patron saint of lost causes,

Help me pass my English 320, British Restoration Literature class and everything to turn out ok.

Eliberto González
Dallas

■

Virgencita . . .

I've cut off my hair just like I promised I would and pinned my braid here by your statue. Above a Toys "Я" Us name tag that says IZAURA. Along several hospital bracelets. Next to a business card for Sergio's Casa de la Belleza Beauty College. Domingo Reyna's driver's license. Notes printed on the flaps of envelopes. Silk roses, plastic roses, paper roses, roses crocheted out of fluorescent orange yarn. Photo button of a baby in a *charro* hat. Caramel-skinned woman in a white graduation cap and gown. Mean dude in bandanna and tattoos. Oval black-and-white passport portrait of the sad uncle who never married. A mama in a sleeveless dress watering the porch plants. Sweet boy with new mustache and new soldier uniform. Teenager with a little bit of herself sitting on her lap. Blurred husband and wife leaning one into the other as if joined at the hip. Black-and-white photo of the cousins *la* Josie *y la* Mary Helen, circa 1942. Polaroid of Sylvia Rios, First Holy Communion, age nine years.

So many *milagritos* safety-pinned here, so many little miracles dangling from red thread — a gold Sacred Heart, a tiny copper arm, a kneeling man in silver, a bottle, a brass truck, a foot, a house, a hand, a baby, a cat, a breast, a tooth, a belly button, an evil eye. So many petitions, so many promises made and kept. And there is nothing I can give you except this braid of hair the color of coffee in a glass.

Chayo, What have you done! All that beautiful hair.
Chayito, how could you ruin in one second what your mother took years to create?
You might as well've plucked out your eyes like Saint Lucy. All that hair!

My mother cried, did I tell you? All that beautiful hair . . .

I've cut off my hair. Which I've never cut since the day I was born. The donkey tail in a birthday game. Something shed like a snakeskin.

My head as light as if I'd raised it from water. My heart buoyant again, as if before I'd worn *el* Sagrado Corazón in my open chest. I could've lit this entire church with my grief.

I'm a bell without a clapper. A woman with one foot in this world and one foot in that. A woman straddling both. This thing between my legs, this unmentionable.

I'm a snake swallowing its tail. I'm my history and my future. All my ancestors' ancestors inside my own belly. All my futures and all my pasts.

I've had to steel and hoard and hone myself. I've had to push the furniture against the door and not let you in.

What you doing sitting in there in the dark?

I'm thinking.

Thinking of what?

Just . . . thinking.

You're nuts. Chayo, ven a saludar. *All the relatives are here. You come out of there and be sociable.*

Do boys think, and girls daydream? Do only girls have to come out and greet the relatives and smile and be nice and *quedar bien?*

It's not good to spend so much time alone.

What she do in there all by herself? It don't look right.

Chayito, when you getting married? Look at your cousin Leticia. She's younger than you.

How many kids you want when you grow up?

When I become a mommy . . .

You'll change. You'll see. Wait till you meet Mr. Right.

Chayo, tell everybody what it is you're studying again.

Look at our Chayito. She likes making her little pictures. She's gonna be a painter.

A painter! Tell her I got five rooms that need painting.

When you become a mother . . .

Thank you for making all those months I held my breath not a child in my belly, but a thyroid problem in my throat.

I can't be a mother. Not now. Maybe never. Not for me to choose, like I didn't choose being female. Like I didn't choose being artist — it isn't something you choose. It's something you are, only I can't explain it.

I don't want to be a mother.

I wouldn't mind being a father. At least a father could still be artist, could love some*thing* instead of some*one*, and no one would call that selfish.

I leave my braid here and thank you for believing what I do is important. Though no one else in my family, no other woman, neither friend nor relative, no one I know, not even the heroine in the *telenovelas*, no woman wants to live alone.

I do.

Virgencita de Guadalupe. For a long time I wouldn't let you in my house. I couldn't see you without seeing my ma each time my father came home drunk and yelling, blaming everything that ever went wrong in his life on her.

I couldn't look at your folded hands without seeing my *abuela* mumbling, "My son, my son, my son . . ." Couldn't look at you without blaming you for all the pain my mother and her mother and all our mothers' mothers have put up with in the name of God. Couldn't let you in my house.

I wanted you bare-breasted, snakes in your hands. I wanted you leaping and somersaulting the backs of bulls. I wanted you swallowing raw hearts and rattling volcanic ash. I wasn't going to be my mother or my grandma. All that self-sacrifice, all that silent suffering. Hell no. Not here. Not me.

Don't think it was easy going without you. Don't think I didn't get my share of it from everyone. Heretic. Atheist. *Malinchista. Hocicona.* But I wouldn't shut my yap. My mouth always getting me in trouble. *Is that what they teach you at the university? Miss High-and-Mighty. Miss Thinks-She's-Too-Good-for-Us.* Acting like a *bolilla,* a white girl. *Malinche.* Don't think it didn't hurt being called a traitor. Trying to explain to my ma, to my *abuela,* why I didn't want to be like them.

I don't know how it all fell in place. How I finally understood who you are. No longer Mary the mild, but our mother Tonantzín. Your church at Tepeyac built on the site of her temple. Sacred ground no matter whose goddess claims it.

That you could have the power to rally a people when a country was born, and again during civil war, and during a farmworkers' strike in California made me think maybe there is power in my mother's patience, strength in my grandmother's endurance. Because those who suffer have a special power, don't they? The power of understanding someone else's pain. And understanding is the beginning of healing.

When I learned your real name is Coatlaxopeuh, She Who Has Dominion over Serpents, when I recognized you as Tonantzín, and learned your names are Teteoinnan, Toci, Xochiquetzal, Tlazolteotl, Coatlicue, Chalchiuhtlicue, Coyolxauhqui, Huixtocihuatl, Chicomecoatl, Cihuacoatl, when I could see you as Nuestra Señora de la Soledad, Nuestra Señora de los Remedios, Nuestra Señora del Perpetuo Socorro, Nuestra Señora de San Juan de los Lagos, Our Lady of Lourdes, Our Lady of Mount Carmel, Our Lady of the Rosary, Our Lady of Sorrows, I wasn't ashamed, then, to be my mother's daughter, my grandmother's granddaughter, my ancestors' child.

When I could see you in all your facets, all at once the Buddha, the Tao, the true Messiah, Yahweh, Allah, the Heart of the Sky, the Heart of the Earth, the Lord of the Near and Far, the Spirit, the Light, the Universe, I could love you, and, finally, learn to love me.

■

Mighty Guadalupana Coatlaxopeuh Tonantzín,

What "little miracle" could I pin here? Braid of hair in its place and know that I thank you.

Rosario (Chayo) De Leon
Austin, Tejas

ꙮ

STEPHEN CRANE *(1871–1900) wrote some of the most memorable fiction and poetry ever created by an American, publishing fourteen books in his short lifetime. The poet John Berryman, who wrote a biography of Crane, observed the essential truth about him: "Crane was a writer and nothing else: a man alone in a room with the English language, trying to get human feelings right." Crane's style in his short stories is as intensely personal as Edgar Allan Poe's or Nathaniel Hawthorne's, but he did not use the techniques of fantasy and allegory. "His eyes remained wide open on his world," according to Berryman. "He was almost illusionless, whether about his subjects or himself. Perhaps his sole illusion was the heroic one; and not even this, especially if he was concerned in it himself as a man, escaped his irony."*

Crane was born in Newark, New Jersey, the youngest of fourteen children. His father, a Methodist minister, died when Crane was a boy, and his mother supported the family by writing articles for Methodist newspapers and reporting for the New York Tribune *and the* Philadelphia Press. *Crane briefly attended Lafayette College and Syracuse University before going to work in New York City as a freelance journalist. He became interested in life in the Bowery, one of the worst slums in New York, and he used this setting for his novel* Maggie: A Girl of the Streets, *a work so grimly naturalistic in its portrayal of slum life and so frank in its treatment of sex that Crane had to publish it at his own expense in 1893. Two years later he sold a long story about the Civil War to a syndicate for less than a hundred dollars. That work,* The Red Badge of Courage, *was such a vivid account of wartime experience — even though Crane had never been in a battle himself — that it established his literary reputation.*

In the last five years of his life, before he died of tuberculosis in Germany, Crane traveled extensively as a reporter, first to the American West, then to Florida. He could not keep away from scenes of war or revolution, believing — as did Ernest Hemingway after him — that "the nearer a writer gets to life, the greater he becomes as an artist." Crane was en route to Florida on the steamship Commodore *when the ship was wrecked on New Year's Day, 1897. He based one of his finest short stories, "The Open Boat," on what happened to him in a lifeboat with the other survivors. He had first reported the disaster in an article for his newspaper shortly after the shipwreck. Joseph Conrad admired Crane's writing and said of "The Open Boat" that "by the deep and simple humanity of its presentation, [the story] seems somehow to illustrate the essentials of life itself, like a symbolic tale."*

RELATED COMMENTARY: *Stephen Crane, "The Sinking of the Commodore," page 674.*

Stephen Crane

The Open Boat

1897

A Tale Intended to Be after the Fact, Being the Experience of Four Men from the Sunk Steamer *Commodore*

I

None of them knew the color of the sky. Their eyes glanced level, and were fastened upon the waves that swept toward them. These waves were of the hue of slate, save for the tops, which were of foaming white, and all of the men knew the colors of the sea. The horizon narrowed and widened, and dipped and rose, and at all times its edge was jagged with waves that seemed thrust up in points like rocks.

Many a man ought to have a bath-tub larger than the boat which here rode upon the sea. These waves were most wrongfully and barbarously abrupt and tall, and each froth-top was a problem in small boat navigation.

The cook squatted in the bottom and looked with both eyes at the six inches of gunwale which separated him from the ocean. His sleeves were rolled over his fat forearms, and the two flaps of his unbuttoned vest dangled as he bent to bail out the boat. Often he said: "Gawd! That was a narrow clip." As he remarked it he invariably gazed eastward over the broken sea.

The oiler, steering with one of the two oars in the boat, sometimes raised himself suddenly to keep clear of water that swirled in over the stern. It was a thin little oar and it seemed often ready to snap.

The correspondent, pulling at the other oar, watched the waves and wondered why he was there.

The injured captain, lying in the bow, was at this time buried in that profound dejection and indifference which comes, temporarily at least, to even the bravest and most enduring when, willy nilly, the firm fails, the army loses, the ship goes down. The mind of the master of a vessel is rooted deep in the timbers of her, though he command for a day or a decade, and this captain had on him the stern impression of a scene in the grays of dawn of seven turned faces, and later a stump of a top-mast with a white ball on it that slashed to and fro at the waves, went low and lower, and down. Thereafter there was something strange in his voice. Although steady, it was deep with mourning, and of a quality beyond oration or tears.

"Keep 'er a little more south, Billie," said he.

"'A little more south,' sir," said the oiler in the stern.

A seat in this boat was not unlike a seat upon a bucking broncho, and, by the same token, a broncho is not much smaller. The craft pranced and reared, and plunged like an animal. As each wave came, and she rose for it, she seemed like a horse making at a fence outrageously high. The manner of her scramble over these walls of water is a mystic thing, and, moreover, at the top of them were ordinarily these problems in white water, the foam racing down from the summit of each wave, requiring a new leap, and a leap from the air. Then, after scornfully bumping a crest, she would slide, and race, and splash down a long incline and arrive bobbing and nodding in front of the next menace.

A singular disadvantage of the sea lies in the fact that after successfully surmounting one wave you discover that there is another behind it just as important and just as nervously anxious to do something effective in the way of swamping boats. In a ten-foot dingey one can get an idea of the resources of the sea in the line of waves that is not probable to the average experience, which is never at sea in a dingey. As each slaty wall of water approached, it shut all else from the view of the men in the boat, and it was not difficult to imagine that this particular wave was the final outburst of the ocean, the last effort of the grim water. There was a terrible grace in the move of the waves, and they came in silence, save for the snarling of the crests.

In the wan light, the faces of the men must have been gray. Their eyes must have glinted in strange ways as they gazed steadily astern. Viewed from a balcony, the whole thing would doubtlessly have been weirdly picturesque. But the men in the boat had no time to see it, and if they had had leisure there were other things to occupy their minds. The sun swung steadily up the sky, and they knew it was broad day because the color of the sea changed from slate to emerald-green, streaked with amber lights, and the foam was like tumbling snow. The process of the breaking day was unknown to them. They were aware only of this effect upon the color of the waves that rolled toward them.

In disjointed sentences the cook and the correspondent argued as to the difference between a life-saving station and a house of refuge. The cook had said: "There's a house of refuge just north of the Mosquito Inlet Light, and as soon as they see us, they'll come off in their boat and pick us up."

"As soon as who see us?" said the correspondent.

"The crew," said the cook.

"Houses of refuge don't have crews," said the correspondent. "As I understand them, they are only places where clothes and grub are stored for the benefit of shipwrecked people. They don't carry crews."

"Oh, yes, they do," said the cook.

"No, they don't," said the correspondent.

"Well, we're not there yet, anyhow," said the oiler, in the stern.

"Well," said the cook, "perhaps it's not a house of refuge that I'm thinking of as being near Mosquito Inlet Light. Perhaps it's a life-saving station."

"We're not there yet," said the oiler, in the stern.

II

As the boat bounced from the top of each wave, the wind tore through the hair of the hatless men, and as the craft plopped her stern down again the spray slashed past them. The crest of each of these waves was a hill, from the top of which the men surveyed, for a moment, a broad tumultuous expanse, shining and wind-riven. It was probably splendid. It was probably glorious, this play of the free sea, wild with lights of emerald and white and amber.

"Bully good thing it's an on-shore wind," said the cook. "If not where would we be? Wouldn't have a show."

"That's right," said the correspondent.

The busy oiler nodded his assent.

Then the captain, in the bow, chuckled in a way that expressed humor, contempt, tragedy, all in one. "Do you think we've got a show, now, boys?" said he.

Whereupon the three went silent, save for a trifle of hemming and hawing. To express any particular optimism at this time they felt to be childish and stupid, but they all doubtless possessed this sense of the situation in their mind. A young man thinks doggedly at such times. On the other hand, the ethics of their condition was decidedly against any open suggestion of hopelessness. So they were silent.

"Oh, well," said the captain, soothing his children, "we'll get ashore all right."

But there was that in his tone which made them think, so the oiler quoth: "Yes! If this wind holds!"

The cook was bailing. "Yes! If we don't catch hell in the surf."

Canton flannel gulls flew near and far. Sometimes they sat down on the sea, near patches of brown sea-weed that rolled over the waves with a movement like carpets on a line in a gale. The birds sat comfortably in groups, and they were envied by some in the dingey, for the wrath of the sea was no more to them than it was to a covey of prairie chickens a thousand miles inland. Often they came very close and stared at the men with black bead-like eyes. At these times they were uncanny and sinister in their unblinking scrutiny, and the men hooted angrily at them, telling them to be gone. One came, and evidently decided to alight on the top of the captain's head. The bird flew parallel to the boat and did not circle, but made short sidelong jumps in the air in chicken-fashion. His black eyes were wistfully fixed upon the captain's head. "Ugly brute," said the oiler to the bird. "You look as if you were made with a jack-knife." The cook and the correspondent swore darkly at the creature. The captain naturally wished to knock it away with the end of the heavy painter, but he did not dare do it, because anything resembling an emphatic gesture would have capsized this freighted boat, and so with his open hand, the captain gently and carefully waved the gull away. After it had been discouraged from the pursuit the captain breathed easier on account of his hair, and others breathed easier because the bird struck their minds at this time as being somehow gruesome and ominous.

In the meantime the oiler and the correspondent rowed. And also they rowed.

They sat together in the same seat, and each rowed an oar. Then the oiler took both oars; then the correspondent took both oars; then the oiler; then the correspondent. They rowed and they rowed. The very ticklish part of the business was when the time came for the reclining one in the stern to take his turn at the oars. By the very last star of truth, it is easier to steal eggs from under a hen than it was to change seats in the dingey. First the man in the stern slid his hand along the thwart and moved with care, as if he were of Sèvres.° Then the man in the rowing seat slid his hand along the other thwart. It was all done with the most extraordinary care. As the two sidled past each other, the whole party kept watchful eyes on the coming wave, and the captain cried: "Look out now! Steady there!"

The brown mats of sea-weed that appeared from time to time were like islands, bits of earth. They were travelling, apparently, neither one way nor the other. They were, to all intents, stationary. They informed the men in the boat that it was making progress slowly toward the land.

The captain, rearing cautiously in the bow, after the dingey soared on a great swell, said that he had seen the light-house at Mosquito Inlet. Presently the cook remarked that he had seen it. The correspondent was at the oars, then, and for some reason he too wished to look at the light-house, but his back was toward the far shore and the waves were important, and for some time he could not seize an opportunity to turn his head. But at last there came a wave more gentle than the others, and when at the crest of it he swiftly scoured the western horizon.

"See it?" said the captain.

"No," said the correspondent, slowly, "I didn't see anything."

"Look again," said the captain. He pointed. "It's exactly in that direction."

At the top of another wave, the correspondent did as he was bid, and this time his eyes chanced on a small still thing on the edge of the swaying horizon. It was precisely like the point of a pin. It took an anxious eye to find a light-house so tiny.

"Think we'll make it, Captain?"

"If this wind holds and the boat don't swamp, we can't do much else," said the captain.

The little boat, lifted by each towering sea, and splashed viciously by the crests, made progress that in the absence of sea-weed was not apparent to those in her. She seemed just a wee thing wallowing, miraculously, top-up, at the mercy of five oceans. Occasionally, a great spread of water, like white flames, swarmed into her.

"Bail her, cook," said the captain, serenely.

"All right, Captain," said the cheerful cook.

III

It would be difficult to describe the subtle brotherhood of men that was here established on the seas. No one said that it was so. No one mentioned it. But it dwelt in the boat, and each man felt it warm him. They were a captain, an oiler, a cook, and a correspondent, and they were friends, friends in a more curiously iron-bound degree than may be common. The hurt captain, lying against the water-jar in the bow, spoke always in a low voice and calmly, but

Sèvres: A delicate French porcelain.

he could never command a more ready and swiftly obedient crew than the motley three of the dingey. It was more than a mere recognition of what was best for the common safety. There was surely in it a quality that was personal and heartfelt. And after this devotion to the commander of the boat there was this comradeship that the correspondent, for instance, who had been taught to be cynical of men, knew even at the time was the best experience of his life. But no one said that it was so. No one mentioned it.

"I wish we had a sail," remarked the captain. "We might try my overcoat on the end of an oar and give you two boys a chance to rest." So the cook and the correspondent held the mast and spread wide the overcoat. The oiler steered, and the little boat made good way with her new rig. Sometimes the oiler had to scull sharply to keep a sea from breaking into the boat, but otherwise sailing was a success.

Meanwhile the light-house had been growing slowly larger. It had now almost assumed color, and appeared like a little gray shadow on the sky. The man at the oars could not be prevented from turning his head rather often to try for a glimpse of this little gray shadow.

At last, from the top of each wave the men in the tossing boat could see land. Even as the light-house was an upright shadow on the sky, this land seemed but a long black shadow on the sea. It certainly was thinner than paper. "We must be about opposite New Smyrna," said the cook, who had coasted this shore often in schooners. "Captain, by the way, I believe they abandoned that life-saving station there about a year ago."

"Did they?" said the captain.

The wind slowly died away. The cook and the correspondent were not now obliged to slave in order to hold high the oar. But the waves continued their old impetuous swooping at the dingey, and the little craft, no longer under way, struggled woundily over them. The oiler or the correspondent took the oars again.

Shipwrecks are *apropos* of nothing. If men could only train for them and have them occur when the men had reached pink condition, there would be less drowning at sea. Of the four in the dingey none had slept any time worth mentioning for two days and two nights previous to embarking in the dingey, and in the excitement of clambering about the deck of a foundering ship they had also forgotten to eat heartily.

For these reasons, and for others, neither the oiler nor the correspondent was fond of rowing at this time. The correspondent wondered ingenuously how in the name of all that was sane could there be people who thought it amusing to row a boat. It was not an amusement; it was a diabolical punishment, and even a genius of mental aberrations could never conclude that it was anything but a horror to the muscles and a crime against the back. He mentioned to the boat in general how the amusement of rowing struck him, and the weary-faced oiler smiled in full sympathy. Previously to the foundering, by the way, the oiler had worked double-watch in the engine-room of the ship.

"Take her easy, now, boys," said the captain. "Don't spend yourselves. If we have to run a surf you'll need all your strength, because we'll sure have to swim for it. Take your time."

Slowly the land arose from the sea. From a black line it became a line of black and a line of white — trees and sand. Finally, the captain said that he could make out a house on the shore. "That's the house of refuge, sure," said the cook. "They'll see us before long, and come out after us."

The distant light-house reared high. "The keeper ought to be able to make us out now, if he's looking through a glass," said the captain. "He'll notify the life-saving people."

"None of those other boats could have got ashore to give word of the wreck," said the oiler, in a low voice. "Else the life-boat would be out hunting us."

Slowly and beautifully the land loomed out of the sea. The wind came again. It had veered from the northeast to the southeast. Finally, a new sound struck the ears of the men in the boat. It was the low thunder of the surf on the shore. "We'll never be able to make the light-house now," said the captain. "Swing her head a little more north, Billie."

"'A little more north,' sir," said the oiler.

Whereupon the little boat turned her nose once more down the wind, and all but the oarsman watched the shore grow. Under the influence of this expansion doubt and direful apprehension were leaving the minds of the men. The management of the boat was still most absorbing, but it could not prevent a quiet cheerfulness. In an hour, perhaps, they would be ashore.

Their back-bones had become thoroughly used to balancing in the boat and they now rode this wild colt of a dingey like circus men. The correspondent thought that he had been drenched to the skin, but happening to feel in the top pocket of his coat, he found therein eight cigars. Four of them were soaked with sea-water; four were perfectly scatheless. After a search, somebody produced three dry matches, and thereupon the four waifs rode impudently in their little boat, and with an assurance of an impending rescue shining in their eyes, puffed at the big cigars and judged well and ill of all men. Everybody took a drink of water.

IV

"Cook," remarked the captain, "there don't seem to be any signs of life about your house of refuge."

"No," replied the cook. "Funny they don't see us!"

A broad stretch of lowly coast lay before the eyes of the men. It was of dunes topped with dark vegetation. The roar of the surf was plain, and sometimes they could see the white lip of a wave as it spun up the beach. A tiny house was blocked out black upon the sky. Southward, the slim light-house lifted its little gray length.

Tide, wind, and waves were swinging the dingey northward. "Funny they don't see us," said the men.

The surf's roar was here dulled, but its tone was, nevertheless, thunderous and mighty. As the boat swam over the great rollers, the men sat listening to this roar. "We'll swamp sure," said everybody.

It is fair to say here that there was not a life-saving station within twenty miles in either direction, but the men did not know this fact and in consequence they made dark and opprobrious remarks concerning the eyesight of the nation's life-savers. Four scowling men sat in the dingey and surpassed records in the invention of epithets.

"Funny they don't see us."

The light-heartedness of a former time had completely faded. To their sharpened minds it was easy to conjure pictures of all kinds of incompetency and blindness and, indeed, cowardice. There was the shore of the populous land, and it was bitter and bitter to them that from it came no sign.

"Well," said the captain, ultimately, "I suppose we'll have to make a try for ourselves. If we stay out here too long, we'll none of us have strength left to swim after the boat swamps."

And so the oiler, who was at the oars, turned the boat straight for the shore. There was a sudden tightening of muscles. There was some thinking.

"If we don't all get ashore —" said the captain. "If we don't all get ashore, I suppose you fellows know where to send news of my finish?"

They then briefly exchanged some addresses and admonitions. As for the reflections of the men, there was a great deal of rage in them. Perchance they might be formulated thus: "If I am going to be drowned — if I am going to be drowned — if I am going to be drowned, why, in the name of the seven mad gods who rule the sea, was I allowed to come thus far and contemplate sand and trees? Was I brought here merely to have my nose dragged away as I was about to nibble the sacred cheese of life? It is preposterous. If this old ninny-woman, Fate, cannot do better than this, she should be deprived of the management of men's fortunes. She is an old hen who knows not her intention. If she has decided to drown me, why did she not do it in the beginning and save me all this trouble. The whole affair is absurd. . . . But, no, she cannot mean to drown me. She dare not drown me. She cannot drown me. Not after all this work." Afterward the man might have had an impulse to shake his fist at the clouds. "Just you drown me, now, and then hear what I call you!"

The billows that came at this time were more formidable. They seemed always just about to break and roll over the little boat in a turmoil of foam. There was a preparatory and long growl in the speech of them. No mind unused to the sea would have concluded that the dingey could ascend these sheer heights in time. The shore was still afar. The oiler was a wily surfman. "Boys," he said, swiftly, "she won't live three minutes more and we're too far out to swim. Shall I take her to sea again, Captain?"

"Yes! Go ahead!" said the captain.

This oiler, by a series of quick miracles, and fast and steady oarsmanship, turned the boat in the middle of the surf and took her safely to sea again.

There was a considerable silence as the boat bumped over the furrowed sea to deeper water. Then somebody in gloom spoke. "Well, anyhow, they must have seen us from the shore by now."

The gulls went in slanting flight up the wind toward the gray desolate east. A squall, marked by dingy clouds, and clouds brick-red, like smoke from a burning building, appeared from the southeast.

"What do you think of those life-saving people? Ain't they peaches?"

"Funny they haven't seen us."

"Maybe they think we're out here for sport! Maybe they think we're fishin'. Maybe they think we're damned fools."

It was a long afternoon. A changed tide tried to force them southward, but wind and wave said northward. Far ahead, where coast-line, sea, and sky formed their mighty angle, there were little dots which seemed to indicate a city on the shore.

"St. Augustine?"

The captain shook his head. "Too near Mosquito Inlet."

And the oiler rowed, and then the correspondent rowed. Then the oiler rowed. It was a weary business. The human back can become the seat of more aches and pains than are registered in books for the composite anatomy of a regiment. It is a limited area, but it can become the theatre of innumerable muscular conflicts, tangles, wrenches, knots, and other comforts.

"Did you ever like to row, Billie?" asked the correspondent.

"No," said the oiler, "Hang it."

When one exchanged the rowing-seat for a place in the bottom of the boat, he suffered a bodily depression that caused him to be careless of everything save an obligation to wiggle one finger. There was cold sea-water swashing to and fro in the boat, and he lay in it. His head, pillowed on a thwart, was within an inch of the swirl of a wave crest, and sometimes a particularly obstreperous sea came in-board and drenched him once more. But these matters did not annoy him. It is almost certain that if the boat had capsized he would have tumbled comfortably out upon the ocean as if he felt sure that it was a great soft mattress.

"Look! There's a man on the shore!"

"Where?"

"There! See 'im? See 'im?"

"Yes, sure! He's walking along."

"Now he's stopped. Look! He's facing us!"

"He's waving at us!"

"So he is! By thunder!"

"Ah, now, we're all right! There'll be a boat out here for us in half an hour."

"He's going on. He's running. He's going up to that house there."

The remote beach seemed lower than the sea, and it required a searching glance to discern the little black figure. The captain saw a floating stick and they rowed to it. A bath-towel was by some weird chance in the boat, and, tying this on the stick, the captain waved it. The oarsman did not dare turn his head, so he was obliged to ask questions.

"What's he doing now?"

"He's standing still again. He's looking, I think. . . . There he goes again. Toward the house. . . . Now he's stopped again."

"Is he waving at us?"

"No, not now! He was, though."

"Look! There comes another man!"

"He's running."

"Look at him go, would you."

"Why, he's on a bicycle. Now he's met the other man. They're both waving at us. Look!"

"There comes something up the beach."

"What the devil is that thing?"

"Why, it looks like a boat."

"Why, certainly it's a boat."

"No, it's on wheels."

"Yes, so it is. Well, that must be the life-boat. They drag them along shore on a wagon."

"That's the life-boat, sure."

"No, by, it's — it's an omnibus."

"I tell you it's a life-boat."

"It is not! It's an omnibus. I can see it plain. See? One of those big hotel omnibuses."

"By thunder, you're right. It's an omnibus, sure as fate. What do you suppose they are doing with an omnibus? Maybe they are going around collecting the life-crew, hey?"

"That's it, likely. Look! There's a fellow waving a little black flag. He's standing on the steps of the omnibus. There come those other two fellows. Now they're all talking together. Look at the fellow with the flag. Maybe he ain't waving it!"

"That ain't a flag, is it? That's his coat. Why, certainly, that's his coat."

"So it is. It's his coat. He's taken it off and is waving it around his head. But would you look at him swing it!"

"Oh, say, there isn't any life-saving station there. That's just a winter resort hotel omnibus that has brought over some of the boarders to see us drown."

"What's that idiot with the coat mean? What's he signaling, anyhow?"

"It looks as if he were trying to tell us to go north. There must be a life-saving station up there."

"No! He thinks we're fishing. Just giving us a merry hand. See? Ah, there, Willie."

"Well, I wish I could make something out of those signals. What do you suppose he means?"

"He don't mean anything. He's just playing."

"Well, if he'd just signal us to try the surf again, or to go to sea and wait, or go north, or go south, or go to hell — there would be some reason in it. But look at him. He just stands there and keeps his coat revolving like a wheel. The ass!"

"There come more people."

"Now there's quite a mob. Look! Isn't that a boat?"

"Where? Oh, I see where you mean. No, that's no boat."

"That fellow is still waving his coat."

"He must think we like to see him do that. Why don't he quit it. It don't mean anything."

"I don't know. I think he is trying to make us go north. It must be that there's a life-saving station there somewhere."

"Say, he ain't tired yet. Look at 'im wave."

"Wonder how long he can keep that up. He's been revolving his coat ever since he caught sight of us. He's an idiot. Why aren't they getting men to bring a boat out. A fishing boat — one of those big yawls — could come out here all right. Why don't he do something?"

"Oh, it's all right, now."

"They'll have a boat out here for us in less than no time, now that they've seen us."

A faint yellow tone came into the sky over the low land. The shadows on the sea slowly deepened. The wind bore coldness with it, and the men began to shiver.

"Holy smoke!" said one, allowing his voice to express his impious mood, "if we keep on monkeying out here! If we've got to flounder out here all night!"

"Oh, we'll never have to stay here all night! Don't you worry. They've seen us now, and it won't be long before they'll come chasing out after us."

The shore grew dusky. The man waving a coat blended gradually into this gloom, and it swallowed in the same manner the omnibus and the group of people. The spray, when it dashed uproariously over the side, made the voyagers shrink and swear like men who were being branded.

"I'd like to catch the chump who waved the coat. I feel like soaking him one, just for luck."

"Why? What did he do?"

"Oh, nothing, but then he seemed so damned cheerful."

In the meantime the oiler rowed, and then the correspondent rowed, and then the oiler rowed. Gray-faced and bowed forward, they mechanically, turn by turn, plied the leaden oars. The form of the light-house had vanished from the southern horizon, but finally a pale star appeared, just lifting from the sea. The streaked saffron in the west passed before the all-merging darkness, and the sea to the east was black. The land had vanished, and was expressed only by the low and drear thunder of the surf.

"If I am going to be drowned — if I am going to be drowned — if I am going to be drowned, why, in the name of the seven mad gods who rule the sea, was I allowed to come thus far and contemplate sand and trees? Was I brought here merely to have my nose dragged away as I was about to nibble the sacred cheese of life?"

The patient captain, drooped over the water-jar, was sometimes obliged to speak to the oarsman.

"Keep her head up! Keep her head up!"

"'Keep her head up,' sir." The voices were weary and low.

This was surely a quiet evening. All save the oarsman lay heavily and listlessly in the boat's bottom. As for him, his eyes were just capable of noting the tall black waves that swept forward in a most sinister silence, save for an occasional subdued growl of a crest.

The cook's head was on a thwart, and he looked without interest at the water under his nose. He was deep in other scenes. Finally he spoke. "Billie," he murmured, dreamfully, "what kind of pie do you like best?"

V

"Pie," said the oiler and the correspondent, agitatedly. "Don't talk about those things, blast you!"

"Well," said the cook, "I was just thinking about ham sandwiches, and —"

A night on the sea in an open boat is a long night. As darkness settled finally, the shine of the light, lifting from the sea in the south, changed to full gold. On the northern horizon a new light appeared, a small bluish gleam on the edge of the waters. These two lights were the furniture of the world. Otherwise there was nothing but waves.

Two men huddled in the stern, and distances were so magnificent in the dingey that the rower was enabled to keep his feet partly warmed by thrusting them under his companions. Their legs indeed extended far under the rowing-seat until they touched the feet of the captain forward. Sometimes, despite the efforts of the tired oarsman, a wave came piling into the boat, an icy wave of the night, and the chilling water soaked them anew. They would twist their bodies for a moment and groan, and sleep the dead sleep once more, while the water in the boat gurgled about them as the craft rocked.

The plan of the oiler and the correspondent was for one to row until he lost the ability, and then arouse the other from his sea-water couch in the bottom of the boat.

The oiler plied the oars until his head drooped forward, and the overpowering sleep blinded him. And he rowed yet afterward. Then he touched a man in the bottom of the boat, and called his name. "Will you spell me for a little while?" he said, meekly.

"Sure, Billie," said the correspondent, awakening and dragging himself to a sitting position. They exchanged places carefully, and the oiler, cuddling down in the sea-water at the cook's side, seemed to go to sleep instantly.

The particular violence of the sea had ceased. The waves came without snarling. The obligation of the man at the oars was to keep the boat headed so that the tilt of the rollers would not capsize her, and to preserve her from filling when the crests rushed past. The black waves were silent and hard to be seen in the darkness. Often one was almost upon the boat before the oarsman was aware.

In a low voice the correspondent addressed the captain. He was not sure that the captain was awake, although this iron man seemed to be always awake. "Captain, shall I keep her making for that light north, sir?"

The same steady voice answered him. "Yes. Keep it about two points off the port bow."

The cook had tied a life-belt around himself in order to get even the warmth which this clumsy cork contrivance could donate, and he seemed almost stove-like when a rower, whose teeth invariably chattered wildly as soon as he ceased his labor, dropped down to sleep.

The correspondent, as he rowed, looked down at the two men sleeping under foot. The cook's arm was around the oiler's shoulders, and, with their fragmentary clothing and haggard faces, they were the babes of the sea, a grotesque rendering of the old babes in the wood.

Later he must have grown stupid at his work, for suddenly there was a growling of water, and a crest came with a roar and a swash into the boat, and it was a wonder that it did not set the cook afloat in his life-belt. The cook continued to sleep, but the oiler sat up, blinking his eyes and shaking with the new cold.

"Oh, I'm awful sorry, Billie," said the correspondent, contritely.

"That's all right, old boy," said the oiler, and lay down again and was asleep.

Presently it seemed that even the captain dozed, and the correspondent thought that he was the one man afloat on all the oceans. The wind had a voice as it came over the waves, and it was sadder than the end.

There was a long, loud swishing astern of the boat, and a gleaming trail of phosphorescence, like blue flame, was furrowed on the black waters. It might have been made by a monstrous knife.

Then there came a stillness, while the correspondent breathed with the open mouth and looked at the sea.

Suddenly there was another swish and another long flash of bluish light, and this time it was alongside the boat, and might almost have been reached with an oar. The correspondent saw an enormous fin speed like a shadow through the water, hurling the crystalline spray and leaving the long glowing trail.

The correspondent looked over his shoulder at the captain. His face was hidden, and he seemed to be asleep. He looked at the babes of the sea. They certainly were asleep. So, being bereft of sympathy, he leaned a little way to one side and swore softly into the sea.

But the thing did not then leave the vicinity of the boat. Ahead or astern, on one side or the other, at intervals long or short, fled the long sparkling streak, and there was to be heard the whirroo of the dark fin. The speed and power of the thing were greatly to be admired. It cut the water like a gigantic and keen projectile.

The presence of this biding thing did not affect the man with the same horror that it would if he had been a picnicker. He simply looked at the sea dully and swore in an undertone.

Nevertheless, it is true that he did not wish to be alone with the thing. He wished one of his companions to awaken by chance and keep him company with it. But the captain hung motionless over the water-jar and the oiler and the cook in the bottom of the boat were plunged in slumber.

VI

"If I am going to be drowned — if I am going to be drowned — if I am going to be drowned, why, in the name of the seven mad gods who rule the sea, was I allowed to come thus far and contemplate sand and trees?"

During this dismal night, it may be remarked that a man would conclude that it was really the intention of the seven mad gods to drown him, despite the abominable injustice of it. For it was certainly an abominable injustice to drown a man who had worked so hard, so hard. The man felt it would be a crime most unnatural. Other people had drowned at sea since galleys swarmed with painted sails, but still —

When it occurs to a man that nature does not regard him as important, and that she feels she would not maim the universe by disposing of him, he at first wishes to throw bricks at the temple, and he hates deeply the fact that there are no bricks and no temples. Any visible expression of nature would surely be pelleted with his jeers.

Then, if there be no tangible thing to hoot he feels, perhaps, the desire to confront a personification and indulge in pleas, bowed to one knee, and with hands supplicant, saying: "Yes, but I love myself."

A high cold star on a winter's night is the word he feels that she says to him. Thereafter he knows the pathos of his situation.

The men in the dingey had not discussed these matters, but each had, no doubt, reflected upon them in silence and according to his mind. There was seldom any expression upon their faces save the general one of complete weariness. Speech was devoted to the business of the boat.

To chime the notes of his emotion, a verse mysteriously entered the correspondent's head. He had even forgotten that he had forgotten this verse, but it suddenly was in his mind.

A soldier of the Legion lay dying in Algiers,
There was lack of woman's nursing, there was dearth of woman's tears;
But a comrade stood beside him, and he took that comrade's hand,
And he said: "I never more shall see my own, my native land."

In his childhood, the correspondent had been made acquainted with the fact that a soldier of the Legion lay dying in Algiers, but he had never regarded it as important. Myriads of his school-fellows had informed him of the soldier's plight, but the dinning had naturally ended by making him perfectly indifferent. He had never considered it his affair that a soldier of the Legion lay dying in Algiers, nor had it appeared to him as a matter for sorrow. It was less to him than the breaking of a pencil's point.

Now, however, it quaintly came to him as a human, living thing. It was no longer merely a picture of a few throes in the breast of a poet, meanwhile drinking tea and warming his feet at the grate; it was an actuality — stern, mournful, and fine.

The correspondent plainly saw the soldier. He lay on the sand with his feet out straight and still. While his pale left hand was upon his chest in an attempt to thwart the going of his life, the blood came between his fingers. In the far Algerian distance, a city of low square forms was set against a sky that was faint with the last sunset hues. The correspondent, plying the oars and dreaming of the slow and slower movements of the lips of the soldier, was moved by a profound and perfectly impersonal comprehension. He was sorry for the soldier of the Legion who lay dying in Algiers.

The thing which had followed the boat and waited had evidently grown bored at the delay. There was no longer to be heard the slash of the cut-water, and there was no longer the flame of the long trail. The light in the north still glimmered, but it was apparently no nearer to the boat. Sometimes the boom of the surf rang in the correspondent's ears, and he turned the craft seaward then and rowed harder. Southward, some one had evidently built a watch-fire on the beach. It was too low and too far to be seen, but it made a shimmering, roseate reflection upon the bluff back of it, and this could be discerned from the boat. The wind came stronger, and sometimes a wave suddenly raged out like a mountain-cat and there was to be seen the sheen and sparkle of a broken crest.

The captain, in the bow, moved on his water-jar and sat erect. "Pretty long night," he observed to the correspondent. He looked at the shore. "Those life-saving people take their time."

"Did you see that shark playing around?"

"Yes, I saw him. He was a big fellow, all right."

"Wish I had known you were awake."

Later the correspondent spoke into the bottom of the boat.

"Billie!" There was a slow and gradual disentanglement. "Billie, will you spell me?"

"Sure," said the oiler.

As soon as the correspondent touched the cold comfortable sea-water in the bottom of the boat, and had huddled close to the cook's life-belt he was deep in sleep, despite the fact that his teeth played all the popular airs. This sleep was so good to him that it was but a moment before he heard a voice call his name in a tone that demonstrated the last stages of exhaustion. "Will you spell me?"

"Sure, Billie."

The light in the north had mysteriously vanished, but the correspondent took his course from the wide-awake captain.

Later in the night they took the boat farther out to sea, and the captain directed the cook to take one oar at the stern and keep the boat facing the seas. He was to call out if he should hear the thunder of the surf. This plan enabled the oiler and the correspondent to get respite together. "We'll give those boys a chance to get into shape again," said the captain. They curled down and, after a few preliminary chatterings and trembles, slept once more the dead sleep. Neither knew they had bequeathed to the cook the company of another shark, or perhaps the same shark.

As the boat caroused on the waves, spray occasionally bumped over the side and gave them a fresh soaking, but this had no power to break their repose. The ominous slash of the wind and the water affected them as it would have affected mummies.

"Boys," said the cook, with the notes of every reluctance in his voice, "she's drifted in pretty close. I guess one of you had better take her to sea again." The correspondent, aroused, heard the crash of the toppled crests.

As he was rowing, the captain gave him some whiskey and water, and this steadied the chills out of him. "If I ever get ashore and anybody shows me even a photograph of an oar —"

At last there was a short conversation.

"Billie. . . . Billie, will you spell me?"

"Sure," said the oiler.

VII

When the correspondent again opened his eyes, the sea and the sky were each of the gray hue of the dawning. Later, carmine and gold was painted upon the waters. The morning appeared finally, in its splendor, with a sky of pure blue, and the sunlight flamed on the tips of the waves.

On the distant dunes were set many little black cottages, and a tall white wind-mill reared above them. No man, nor dog, nor bicycle appeared on the beach. The cottages might have formed a deserted village.

The voyagers scanned the shore. A conference was held in the boat. "Well," said the captain, "if no help is coming, we might better try a run through the surf right away. If we stay out here much longer we will be too weak to do anything for ourselves at all." The others silently acquiesced in this reasoning. The boat was headed for the beach. The correspondent wondered if none ever ascended the tall wind-tower, and if then they never looked seaward. This tower was a giant, standing with its back to the plight of the ants. It represented in a degree, to the correspondent, the serenity of nature amid the struggles of the individual — nature in the wind, and nature in the vision of men. She did not seem cruel to him then, nor beneficent, nor treacherous, nor wise. But she was indifferent, flatly indifferent. It is, perhaps, plausible that a man in this situation, impressed with the unconcern of the universe, should see the innumerable flaws of his life and have them taste wickedly in his mind and wish for another chance. A distinction between right and wrong seems absurdly clear to him, then, in this new ignorance of the grave-edge, and he understands that if he were given another opportunity he would mend his conduct and his words, and be better and brighter during an introduction, or at a tea.

"Now, boys," said the captain, "she is going to swamp sure. All we can do is to work her in as far as possible, and then when she swamps, pile out and scramble for the beach. Keep cool now, and don't jump until she swamps sure."

The oiler took the oars. Over his shoulders he scanned the surf. "Captain," he said, "I think I'd better bring her about, and keep her head-on to the seas and back her in."

"All right, Billie," said the captain. "Back her in." The oiler swung the boat then and, seated in the stern, the cook and the correspondent were obliged to look over their shoulders to contemplate the lonely and indifferent shore.

The monstrous inshore rollers heaved the boat high until the men were again enabled to see the white sheets of water scudding up the slanted beach. "We won't get in very close," said the captain. Each time a man could wrest his attention from the rollers, he turned his glance toward the shore, and in the expression of the eyes during this contemplation there was a singular quality. The correspondent, observing the others, knew that they were not afraid, but the full meaning of their glances was shrouded.

As for himself, he was too tired to grapple fundamentally with the fact. He tried to coerce his mind into thinking of it, but the mind was dominated at this time by the muscles, and the muscles said they did not care. It merely occurred to him that if he should drown it would be a shame.

There were no hurried words, no pallor, no plain agitation. The men simply looked at the shore. "Now, remember to get well clear of the boat when you jump," said the captain.

Seaward the crest of a roller suddenly fell with a thunderous crash, and the long white comber came roaring down upon the boat.

"Steady now," said the captain. The men were silent. They turned their eyes from the shore to the comber and waited. The boat slid up the incline, leaped at the furious top, bounced over it, and swung down the long back of the wave. Some water had been shipped and the cook bailed it out.

But the next crest crashed also. The tumbling boiling flood of white water caught the boat and whirled it almost perpendicular. Water swarmed in from all sides. The correspondent had his hands on the gunwale at this time, and when the water entered at that place he swiftly withdrew his fingers, as if he objected to wetting them.

The little boat, drunken with this weight of water, reeled and snuggled deeper into the sea.

"Bail her out, cook! Bail her out," said the captain.

"All right, Captain," said the cook.

"Now boys, the next one will do for us, sure," said the oiler. "Mind to jump clear of the boat."

The third wave moved forward, huge, furious, implacable. It fairly swallowed the dingey, and almost simultaneously the men tumbled into the sea. A piece of life-belt had lain in the bottom of the boat, and as the correspondent went overboard he held this to his chest with his left hand.

The January water was icy, and he reflected immediately that it was colder than he had expected to find it off the coast of Florida. This appeared to his dazed mind as a fact important enough to be noted at the time. The coldness of the water was sad; it was tragic. This fact was somehow so mixed and confused with his opinion of his own situation that it seemed almost a proper reason for tears. The water was cold.

When he came to the surface he was conscious of little but the noisy water. Afterward he saw his companions in the sea. The oiler was ahead in the race. He was swimming strongly and rapidly. Off to the correspondent's left, the cook's great white and corked back bulged out of the water, and in the rear the captain was hanging with his one good hand to the keel of the overturned dingey.

There is a certain immovable quality to a shore, and the correspondent wondered at it amid the confusion of the sea.

It seemed also very attractive, but the correspondent knew that it was a long journey, and he paddled leisurely. The piece of life-preserver lay under him, and sometimes he whirled down the incline of a wave as if he were on a hand-sled.

But finally he arrived at a place in the sea where travel was beset with difficulty. He did not pause swimming to inquire what manner of current had caught him, but there his progress ceased. The shore was set before him like a bit of scenery on a stage, and he looked at it and understood with his eyes each detail of it.

As the cook passed, much farther to the left, the captain was calling to him, "Turn over on your back, cook! Turn over on your back and use the oar."

"All right, sir." The cook turned on his back, and, paddling with an oar, went ahead as if he were a canoe.

Presently the boat also passed to the left of the correspondent with the captain clinging with one hand to the keel. He would have appeared like a man raising himself to look over a board fence, if it were not for the extraordinary gymnastics of the boat. The correspondent marvelled that the captain could still hold to it.

They passed on, nearer to shore — the oiler, the cook, the captain — and following them went the water-jar, bouncing gayly over the seas.

The correspondent remained in the grip of this strange new enemy — a current. The shore, with its white slope of sand and its green bluff, topped with little silent cottages, was spread like a picture before him. It was very near to him then, but he was impressed as one who in a gallery looks at a scene from Brittany or Holland.

He thought: "I am going to drown? Can it be possible? Can it be possible? Can it be possible?" Perhaps an individual must consider his own death to be the final phenomenon of nature.

But later a wave perhaps whirled him out of his small deadly current, for he found suddenly that he could again make progress toward the shore. Later still, he was aware that the captain, clinging with one hand to the keel of the dingey, had his face turned away from the shore and toward him, and was calling his name. "Come to the boat! Come to the boat!"

In his struggle to reach the captain and the boat, he reflected that when one gets properly wearied, drowning must really be a comfortable arrangement, a cessation of hostilities accompanied by a large degree of relief, and he was glad of it, for the main thing in his mind for some moments had been the horror of the temporary agony. He did not wish to be hurt.

Presently he saw a man running along the shore. He was undressing with most remarkable speed. Coat, trousers, shirt, everything flew magically off him.

"Come to the boat," called the captain.

"All right, Captain." As the correspondent paddled, he saw the captain let himself down to bottom and leave the boat. Then the correspondent performed his one little marvel of the voyage. A large wave caught him and flung him with ease and supreme speed completely over the boat and far beyond it. It struck him even then as an event in gymnastics, and a true miracle of the sea. An overturned boat in the surf is not a plaything to a swimming man.

The correspondent arrived in water that reached only to his waist, but his condition did not enable him to stand for more than a moment. Each wave knocked him into a heap, and the under-tow pulled at him.

Then he saw the man who had been running and undressing, and undressing and running, come bounding into the water. He dragged ashore the cook, and then waded toward the captain, but the captain waved him away, and sent him to the correspondent. He was naked, naked as a tree in winter, but a halo was about his head, and he shone like a saint. He gave a strong pull, and a long drag, and a bully heave at the correspondent's hand. The correspondent, schooled in the minor formulae, said: "Thanks, old man." But suddenly the man cried: "What's that?" He pointed a swift finger. The correspondent said: "Go."

In the shallows, face downward, lay the oiler. His forehead touched sand that was periodically, between each wave, clear of the sea.

The correspondent did not know all that transpired afterward. When he achieved safe ground he fell, striking the sand with each particular part of his body. It was as if he had dropped from a roof, but the thud was grateful to him.

It seems that instantly the beach was populated with men with blankets, clothes, and flasks, and women with coffee-pots and all the remedies sacred to their minds. The welcome of the land to the men from the sea was warm and generous, but a still and dripping shape was carried slowly up the beach, and the land's welcome for it could only be the different and sinister hospitality of the grave.

When it came night, the white waves paced to and fro in the moonlight, and the wind brought the sound of the great sea's voice to the men on shore, and they felt that they could then be interpreters.

EDWIDGE DANTICAT *(b. 1969) was born in Port-au-Prince, Haiti. When she was two, her father immigrated to the United States to look for work. Two years later her mother followed him, leaving Danticat and her younger brother in the care of their uncle, who was a minister. Danticat remembers her childhood fascination with the ritual of storytelling conducted by her aunt's grandmother in Haiti. When she told a story, her listeners said "Krik?" and she would answer "Krak!"*

> *She told stories when the people would gather — folk tales with her own spin on them, and stories about the family. It was call-and-response — if the audience seemed bored, the story would speed up, and if they were participating, a song would go in. The whole interaction was exciting to me. These cross-generational exchanges didn't happen often, because children were supposed to respect their elders. But when you were telling stories, it was more equal, and fun.*

At the age of twelve, Danticat joined her parents in Brooklyn, where she began to learn English (the family still speaks Creole at home). Within a year she was writing articles for her high school newspaper, New Youth Connections. *She majored in French literature at Barnard College, graduating in 1990, and went on to study in the MFA program in creative writing at Brown University on a full scholarship. While still a graduate student she sold the manuscript of her first book,* Breath, Eyes, Memory, *to Soho, a small press she discovered in* Writer's Digest. *Published in 1994, the novel dramatized a young Haitian woman's coming of age in a troubled mother-daughter relationship and was chosen by Oprah Winfrey for the June 18, 1994, "meet-*

ing" of her television book club. With this endorsement, Breath, Eyes, Memory *became a paperback best-seller.*

The next year Danticat published Krik? Krak!, *a collection of stories that included the autobiographical "New York Day Woman." This book was nominated for a National Book Award, and she was chosen as one of the twenty "Best Young American Novelists" by* Granta *magazine.* The Farming of Bones, *her third book, published by Soho in 1998 and winner of the 1999 American Book Award, describes the 1937 massacre on the Haitian-Dominican border. Danticat now works with the National Coalition for Haitian Rights on a three-year grant from the Lila Acheson Wallace Foundation. As a spokesperson for her community, Danticat insists that she is free to write as she pleases in her fiction: "My characters are not representative of the community as a whole. As a writer, it's the person who is different from everybody else who might be interesting to you."*

EDWIDGE DANTICAT

New York Day Woman

1995

Today, walking down the street, I see my mother. She is strolling with a happy gait, her body thrust toward the DON'T WALK sign and the yellow taxicabs that make forty-five-degree turns on the corner of Madison and Fifty-seventh Street.

I have never seen her in this kind of neighborhood, peering into Chanel and Tiffany's and gawking at the jewels glowing in the Bulgari windows. My mother never shops outside of Brooklyn. She has never seen the advertising office where I work. She is afraid to take the subway, where you may meet those young black militant street preachers who curse black women for straightening their hair.

Yet, here she is, my mother, who I left at home that morning in her bathrobe, with pieces of newspapers twisted like rollers in her hair. My mother, who accuses me of random offenses as I dash out of the house.

Would you get up and give an old lady like me your subway seat? In this state of mind, I bet you don't even give up your seat to a pregnant lady.

My mother, who is often right about that. Sometimes I get up and give my seat. Other times, I don't. It all depends on how pregnant the woman is and whether or not she is with her boyfriend or husband and whether or not *he* is sitting down.

As my mother stands in front of Carnegie Hall, one taxi driver yells to another, "What do you think this is, a dance floor?"

My mother waits patiently for this dispute to be settled before crossing the street.

In Haiti when you get hit by a car, the owner of the car gets out and kicks you for getting blood on his bumper.

My mother who laughs when she says this and shows a large gap in her mouth where she lost three more molars to the dentist last week. My mother, who at fifty-nine, says dentures are okay.

You can take them out when they bother you. I'll like them. I'll like them fine.

Will it feel empty when Papa kisses you?

Oh no, he doesn't kiss me that way anymore.

My mother, who watches the lottery drawing every night on channel 11 without ever having played the numbers.

A third of that money is all I would need. We would pay the mortgage, and your father could stop driving that taxicab all over Brooklyn.

I follow my mother, mesmerized by the many possibilities of her journey. Even in a flowered dress, she is lost in a sea of pinstripes and gray suits, high heels and elegant short skirts, Reebok sneakers, dashing from building to building.

My mother, who won't go out to dinner with anyone.

If they want to eat with me, let them come to my house, even if I boil water and give it to them.

My mother, who talks to herself when she peels the skin off poultry.

Fat, you know, and cholesterol. Fat and cholesterol killed your aunt Hermine.

My mother, who makes jam with dried grapefruit peel and then puts in cinnamon bark that I always think is cockroaches in the jam. My mother, whom I have always bought household appliances for, on her birthday. A nice rice cooker, a blender.

I trail the red orchids in her dress and the heavy faux leather bag on her shoulders. Realizing the ferocious pace of my pursuit, I stop against a wall to rest. My mother keeps on walking as though she owns the sidewalk under her feet.

As she heads toward the Plaza Hotel, a bicycle messenger swings so close to her that I want to dash forward and rescue her, but she stands dead in her tracks and lets him ride around her and then goes on.

My mother stops at a corner hot-dog stand and asks for something. The vendor hands her a can of soda that she slips into her bag. She stops by another vendor selling sundresses for seven dollars each. I can tell that she is looking at an African print dress, contemplating my size. I think to myself,

Please Ma, don't buy it. It would be just another thing that I would bury in the garage or give to Goodwill.

Why should we give to Goodwill when there are so many people back home who need clothes? We save our clothes for the relatives in Haiti.

Twenty years we have been saving all kinds of things for the relatives in Haiti. I need the place in the garage for an exercise bike.

You are pretty enough to be a stewardess. Only dogs like bones.

This mother of mine, she stops at another hot-dog vendor's and buys a frankfurter that she eats on the street. I never knew that she ate frankfurters. With her blood pressure, she shouldn't eat anything with sodium. She has to be careful with her heart, this day woman.

I cannot just swallow salt. Salt is heavier than a hundred bags of shame.

She is slowing her pace, and now I am too close. If she turns around, she might see me. I let her walk into the park before I start to follow again.

My mother walks toward the sandbox in the middle of the park. There a woman is waiting with a child. The woman is wearing a leotard with biker's shorts and has small weights in her hands. The woman kisses the child good-bye and surrenders him to my mother; then she bolts off, running on the cemented stretches in the park.

The child given to my mother has frizzy blond hair. His hand slips into hers easily, like he's known her for a long time. When he raises his face to look at my mother, it is as though he is looking at the sky.

My mother gives this child the soda that she bought from the vendor on the street corner. The child's face lights up as she puts in a straw in the can for him. This seems to be a conspiracy just between the two of them.

My mother and the child sit and watch the other children play in the sandbox. The child pulls out a comic book from a knapsack with Big Bird on the back. My mother peers into his comic book. My mother, who taught herself to read as a little girl in Haiti from the books that her brothers brought home from school.

My mother, who has now lost six of her seven sisters in Ville Rose and has never had the strength to return for their funerals.

Many graves to kiss when I go back. Many graves to kiss.

She throws away the empty soda can when the child is done with it. I wait and watch from a corner until the woman in the leotard and biker's shorts returns, sweaty and breathless, an hour later. My mother gives the woman back her child and strolls farther into the park.

I turn around and start to walk out of the park before my mother can see me. My lunch hour is long since gone. I have to hurry back to work. I walk through a cluster of joggers, then race to a *Sweden Tours* bus. I stand behind the bus and take a peek at my mother in the park. She is standing in a circle, chatting with a group of women who are taking other people's children on an afternoon outing. They look like a Third World Parent-Teacher Association meeting.

I quickly jump into a cab heading back to the office. Would Ma have said hello had she been the one to see me first?

As the cab races away from the park, it occurs to me that perhaps one day I would chase an old woman down a street by mistake and that old woman would be somebody else's mother, who I would have mistaken for mine.

Day women come out when nobody expects them.

Tonight on the subway, I will get up and give my seat to a pregnant woman or a lady about Ma's age.

My mother, who stuffs thimbles in her mouth and then blows up her cheeks like Dizzy Gillespie while sewing yet another Raggedy Ann doll that she names Suzette after me.

I will have all these little Suzettes in case you never have any babies, which looks more and more like it is going to happen.

My mother who had me when she was thirty-three — *l'âge du Christ* — at the age that Christ died on the cross.

That's a blessing, believe you me, even if American doctors say by that time you can make retarded babies.

My mother, who sews lace collars on my company softball T-shirts when she does my laundry.

Why, can't you look like a lady playing softball?

My mother, who never went to any of my Parent-Teacher Association meetings when I was in school.

You're so good anyway. What are they going to tell me? I don't want to make you ashamed of this day woman. Shame is heavier than a hundred bags of salt.

ഇര

RALPH ELLISON *(1914–1994) was born in Oklahoma City, Oklahoma. His father, a small-time vendor of ice and coal, died when Ellison was three, and thereafter his mother worked as a domestic servant to support herself and her son. Ellison later credited his mother, who recruited black votes for the Socialist Party, for turning him into an activist. She also brought home discarded books and phonograph records from the white households where she worked, and as a boy Ellison developed an interest in literature and music. He played trumpet in his high school band, and it was at this time that he began to relate the works of fiction he was reading to real life. "I began to look at my own life through the lives of fictional characters," he observed. "When I read Stendhal, I would search until I began to find patterns of a Stendhalian novel within the Negro communities in which I grew up. I began, in other words, quite early to connect the worlds projected in literature . . . with the life in which I found myself."*

In 1933 Ellison entered Tuskegee Institute in Alabama, where he studied music for three years. Then he went to New York City and met the black writers Langston Hughes and Richard Wright, whose encouragement helped him to become a writer. Wright turned Ellison's attention to writing short stories and reading "those works in which writing was discussed as a craft . . . to Henry James's prefaces, to Conrad," and to other authors. In 1939 Ellison's short stories, essays, and reviews began to appear in periodicals. After World War II, he settled down to work on the novel Invisible Man. *Published in 1952, it received the National Book Award for fiction and was listed in a 1965* Book Week *poll as the most distinguished American novel of the preceding twenty years. As the critic Richard D. Lyons recognized, the novel was "a chronicle of a young black man's awakening to racial discrimination and his battle against the refusal of Americans to see him apart from his ethnic background, which in turn leads to humiliation and disillusionment." "Battle Royal," an excerpt from* Invisible Man, *is often anthologized. It appears after the prologue describing the underground chamber in which the nameless protagonist has retreated from the chaos of life aboveground.*

Insisting that "art by its nature is social," Ellison began Invisible Man *with the words "I am an invisible man. No, I am not a spook like those who haunted Edgar Allan Poe; nor am I one of your Hollywood-movie ectoplasms. I am a man of substance, of flesh and bone, fiber and liquids — and I might even be said to possess a mind. I am invisible, understand, simply because people refuse to see me." At the time of his death from cancer, Ellison left an unfinished second novel started in the late 1950s. His initial work on the manuscript was destroyed in a fire, and he never completed the book, which he called his "forty-year work in progress* (very *long in progress)." Titled* Juneteenth *(1999), it was edited posthumously by his widow, Fanny, and John Callahan. In addition to* Invisible Man, *Ellison published a few short stories and two collections of essays,* Shadow and Act *(1964) and* Going to the Territory *(1986). He was also Albert Schweitzer Professor of Contemporary Literature and Culture at New York University.*

RELATED COMMENTARY: *Ralph Ellison, "The Influence of Folklore on 'Battle Royal,'"* *page 677.*

Ralph Ellison

Battle Royal

1952

It goes a long way back, some twenty years. All my life I had been looking for something, and everywhere I turned someone tried to tell me what it was. I accepted their answers too, though they were often in contradiction and even self-contradictory. I was naïve. I was looking for myself and asking everyone except myself questions which I, and only I, could answer. It took me a long time and much painful boomeranging of my expectations to achieve a realization everyone else appears to have been born with: That I am nobody but myself. But first I had to discover that I am an invisible man!

And yet I am no freak of nature, nor of history. I was in the cards, other things having been equal (or unequal) eighty-five years ago. I am not ashamed of my grandparents for having been slaves. I am only ashamed of myself for having at one time been ashamed. About eighty-five years ago they were told that they were free, united with others of our country in everything pertaining to the common good, and, in everything social, separate like the fingers of the hand. And they believed it. They exulted in it. They stayed in their place, worked hard, and brought up my father to do the same. But my grandfather is the one. He was an odd old guy, my grandfather, and I am told I take after him. It was he who caused the trouble. On his deathbed he called my father to him and said, "Son, after I'm gone I want you to keep up the good fight. I never told you, but our life is a war and I have been a traitor all my born days, a spy in the enemy's country ever since I give up my gun back in the Reconstruction. Live with your head in the lion's mouth. I want you to overcome 'em with yeses, undermine 'em with grins, agree 'em to death and destruction, let 'em swoller you till they vomit or bust wide open." They thought the old man had gone out of his mind. He had been the meekest of men. The younger children were rushed from the room, the shades drawn, and the flame of the lamp turned so low that it sputtered on the wick like the old man's breathing. "Learn it to the younguns," he whispered fiercely; then he died.

But my folks were more alarmed over his last words than over his dying. It was as though he had not died at all, his words caused so much anxiety. I was warned emphatically to forget what he had said and, indeed, this is the first time it has been mentioned outside the family circle. It had a tremendous effect upon me, however. I could never be sure of what he meant. Grandfather had been a quiet old man who never made any trouble, yet on his deathbed he had called himself a traitor and a spy, and he had spoken of his meekness as a dangerous activity. It became a constant puzzle which lay unanswered in the back of my mind. And whenever things went well for me I remembered my grandfather and felt guilty and uncomfortable. It was as though I was carrying out his advice in spite of myself. And to make it worse, everyone loved me for it. I was praised by the most lily-white men of the town. I was considered an example of desirable conduct — just as my grandfather had been. And what puzzled me was that the old man had defined it as *treachery*. When I was praised for my conduct I felt a guilt that in some way I was doing something that was really against the wishes of the white folks, that if they had understood they would have desired me to act just the opposite, that I should have been sulky and mean, and that that really would have been what they wanted, even though they were fooled and thought they wanted me to act as I did. It made me afraid that some day they would look upon me as a traitor and I would be lost. Still I was more afraid to act any other way because they didn't like that at all. The old man's words were like a curse. On my graduation day I delivered an oration in which I showed that humility was the secret, indeed, the very essence of progress. (Not that I believed this — how could I, remembering my grandfather? — I only believed that it worked.) It was a great success. Everyone praised me and I was invited to give the speech at a gathering of the town's leading white citizens. It was a triumph for our whole community.

It was in the main ballroom of the leading hotel. When I got there I discovered that it was on the occasion of a smoker, and I was told that since I was to be there anyway I might as well take part in the battle royal to be fought by some of my schoolmates as part of the entertainment. The battle royal came first.

All of the town's big shots were there in their tuxedoes, wolfing down the buffet foods, drinking beer and whiskey and smoking black cigars. It was a large room with a high ceiling. Chairs were arranged in neat rows around three sides of a portable boxing ring. The fourth side was clear, revealing a gleaming space of polished floor. I had some misgivings over the battle royal, by the way. Not from a distaste for fighting, but because I didn't care too much for the other fellows who were to take part. They were tough guys who seemed to have no grandfather's curse worrying their minds. No one could mistake their toughness. And besides, I suspected that fighting a battle royal might detract from the dignity of my speech. In those pre-invisible days I visualized myself as a potential Booker T. Washington. But the other fellows didn't care too much for me either, and there were nine of them. I felt superior to them in my way, and I didn't like the manner in which we were all crowded together into the servants' elevator. Nor did they like my being there. In fact, as the warmly lighted floors flashed past the elevator we had words over the fact that I, by taking part in the fight, had knocked one of their friends out of a night's work.

We were led out of the elevator through a rococo hall into an anteroom and told to get into our fighting togs. Each of us was issued a pair of boxing gloves and ushered out into the big mirrored hall, which we entered looking cautiously about us and whispering, lest we might accidentally be heard above the noise of the room. It was foggy with cigar smoke. And already the whiskey was taking effect. I was shocked to see some of the most important men of the town quite tipsy. They were all there — bankers, lawyers, judges, doctors, fire chiefs, teachers, merchants. Even one of the more fashionable pastors. Something we could not see was going on up front. A clarinet was vibrating sensuously and the men were standing up and moving eagerly forward. We were a small tight group, clustered together, our bare upper bodies touching and shining with anticipatory sweat; while up front the big shots were becoming increasingly excited over something we still could not see. Suddenly I heard the school superintendent, who had told me to come, yell, "Bring up the shines, gentlemen! Bring up the little shines!"

We were rushed up to the front of the ballroom, where it smelled even more strongly of tobacco and whiskey. Then we were pushed into place. I almost wet my pants. A sea of faces, some hostile, some amused, ringed around us, and in the center, facing us, stood a magnificent blonde — stark naked. There was dead silence. I felt a blast of cold air chill me. I tried to back away, but they were behind me and around me. Some of the boys stood with lowered heads, trembling. I felt a wave of irrational guilt and fear. My teeth chattered, my skin turned to goose flesh, my knees knocked. Yet I was strongly attracted and looked in spite of myself. Had the price of looking been blindness, I would have looked. The hair was yellow like that of a circus kewpie doll, the face heavily powdered and rouged, as though to form an abstract mask, the eyes hollow and smeared a cool blue, the color of a baboon's butt. I felt a desire to spit upon her as my eyes brushed slowly over her body. Her breasts were firm and round as the domes of East Indian temples, and I stood so close as to see the fine skin texture and beads of pearly perspiration glistening like dew around the pink and erected buds of her nipples. I wanted at one and the same time to run from the room, to sink through the floor, or go to her and cover her from my eyes and the eyes of the others with my body; to feel the soft thighs, to caress her and destroy her, to love her and murder her, to hide from her, and yet to stroke where below the small American flag tattooed upon her belly her thighs formed a capital V. I had a notion that of all in the room she saw only me with her impersonal eyes.

And then she began to dance, a slow sensuous movement; the smoke of a hundred cigars clinging to her like the thinnest of veils. She seemed like a fair bird-girl girdled in veils calling to me from the angry surface of some gray and threatening sea. I was transported. Then I became aware of the clarinet playing and the big shots yelling at us. Some threatened us if we looked and others if we did not. On my right I saw one boy faint. And now a man grabbed a silver pitcher from a table and stepped close as he dashed ice water upon him and stood him up and forced two of us to support him as his head hung and moans issued from his thick bluish lips. Another boy began to plead to go home. He was the largest of the group, wearing dark red fighting trunks much too small to conceal the erection which projected from him as though in answer to the insinuating low-registered moaning of the clarinet. He tried to hide himself with his boxing gloves.

And all the while the blonde continued dancing, smiling faintly at the big shots who watched her with fascination, and faintly smiling at our fear. I noticed a certain merchant who followed her hungrily, his lips loose and drooling. He was a large man who wore diamond studs in a shirtfront which swelled with the ample paunch underneath, and each time the blonde swayed her undulating hips he ran his hand through the thin hair of his bald head and, with his arms upheld, his posture clumsy like that of an intoxicated panda, wound his belly in a slow and obscene grind. This creature was completely hypnotized. The music had quickened. As the dancer flung herself about with a detached expression on her face, the men began reaching out to touch her. I could see their beefy fingers sink into her soft flesh. Some of the others tried to stop them and she began to move around the floor in graceful circles, as they gave chase, slipping and sliding over the polished floor. It was mad. Chairs went crashing, drinks were spilt, as they ran laughing and howling after her. They caught her just as she reached a door, raised her from the floor, and tossed her as college boys are tossed at a hazing, and above her red fixed-smiling lips I saw the terror and disgust in her eyes, almost like my own terror and that which I saw in some of the other boys. As I watched, they tossed her twice and her soft breasts seemed to flatten against the air and her legs flung wildly as she spun. Some of the more sober ones helped her to escape. And I started off the floor, heading for the anteroom with the rest of the boys.

Some were still crying and in hysteria. But as we tried to leave we were stopped and ordered to get into the ring. There was nothing to do but what we were told. All ten of us climbed under the ropes and allowed ourselves to be blindfolded with broad bands of white cloth. One of the men seemed to feel a bit sympathetic and tried to cheer us up as we stood with our backs against the ropes. Some of us tried to grin. "See that boy over there?" one of the men said. "I want you to run across at the bell and give it to him right in the belly. If you don't get him, I'm going to get you. I don't like his looks." Each of us was told the same. The blindfolds were put on. Yet even then I had been going over my speech. In my mind each word was as bright as flame. I felt the cloth pressed into place, and frowned so that it would be loosened when I relaxed.

But now I felt a sudden fit of blind terror. I was unused to darkness. It was as though I had suddenly found myself in a dark room filled with poisonous cottonmouths. I could hear the bleary voices yelling insistently for the battle royal to begin.

"Get going in there!"

"Let me at that big nigger!"

I strained to pick up the school superintendent's voice, as though to squeeze some security out of that slightly more familiar sound.

"Let me at those black sonsabitches!" someone yelled.

"No, Jackson, no!" another voice yelled. "Here, somebody, help me hold Jack."

"I want to get at that ginger-colored nigger. Tear him limb from limb," the first voice yelled.

I stood against the ropes trembling. For in those days I was what they called ginger-colored, and he sounded as though he might crunch me between his teeth like a crisp ginger cookie.

Quite a struggle was going on. Chairs were being kicked about and I could hear voices grunting as with a terrific effort. I wanted to see, to see more desperately than ever before. But the blindfold was as tight as a thick skin-puckering scab and when I raised my gloved hands to push the layers of white aside a voice yelled, "Oh, no you don't, black bastard! Leave that alone!"

"Ring the bell before Jackson kills him a coon!" someone boomed in the sudden silence. And I heard the bell clang and the sound of the feet scuffling forward.

A glove smacked against my head. I pivoted, striking out stiffly as someone went past, and felt the jar ripple along the length of my arm to my shoulder. Then it seemed as though all nine of the boys had turned upon me at once. Blows pounded me from all sides while I struck out as best I could. So many blows landed upon me that I wondered if I were not the only blindfolded fighter in the ring, or if the man called Jackson hadn't succeeded in getting me after all.

Blindfolded, I could no longer control my motions. I had no dignity. I stumbled about like a baby or a drunken man. The smoke had become thicker and with each new blow it seemed to sear and further restrict my lungs. My saliva became like hot bitter glue. A glove connected with my head, filling my mouth with warm blood. It was everywhere. I could not tell if the moisture I felt upon my body was sweat or blood. A blow landed hard against the nape of my neck. I felt myself going over, my head hitting the floor. Streaks of blue light filled the black world behind the blindfold. I lay prone, pretending that I was knocked out, but felt myself seized by hands and yanked to my feet. "Get going, black boy! Mix it up!" My arms were like lead, my head smarting from blows. I managed to feel my way to the ropes and held on, trying to catch my breath. A glove landed in my mid-section and I went over again, feeling as though the smoke had become a knife jabbed into my guts. Pushed this way and that by the legs milling around me, I finally pulled erect and discovered that I could see the black, sweat-washed forms weaving in the smoky-blue atmosphere like drunken dancers weaving to the rapid drum-like thuds of blows.

Everyone fought hysterically. It was complete anarchy. Everybody fought everybody else. No group fought together for long. Two, three, four, fought one, then turned to fight each other, were themselves attacked. Blows landed below the belt and in the kidney, with the gloves open as well as closed, and with my eye partly opened now there was not so much terror. I moved carefully, avoiding blows, although not too many to attract attention, fighting from group to group. The boys groped about like blind, cautious crabs crouching to protect their mid-sections, their heads pulled in short against their shoulders, their arms stretched nervously before them, with their fists testing the smoke-filled air like the knobbed feelers of hypersensitive snails. In one corner I glimpsed a boy violently punching the air and heard him scream in pain as he smashed his hand against a ring post. For a second I saw him bent over holding his hand, then going down as a blow caught his unprotected head. I played one group against the other, slipping in and throwing a punch then stepping out of range while pushing the others into the melee to take the blows blindly aimed at me. The smoke was agonizing and there were no rounds, no bells at three minute intervals to relieve our exhaustion. The room spun round me, a swirl of lights, smoke, sweating bodies surrounded by tense white faces. I bled from both nose and mouth, the blood spattering upon my chest.

The men kept yelling, "Slug him, black boy! Knock his guts out!"

"Uppercut him! Kill him! Kill that big boy!"

Taking a fake fall, I saw a boy going down heavily beside me as though we were felled by a single blow, saw a sneaker-clad foot shoot into his groin as the two who had knocked him down stumbled upon him. I rolled out of range, feeling a twinge of nausea.

The harder we fought the more threatening the men became. And yet, I had begun to worry about my speech again. How would it go? Would they recognize my ability? What would they give me?

I was fighting automatically and suddenly I noticed that one after another of the boys was leaving the ring. I was surprised, filled with panic, as though I had been left alone with an unknown danger. Then I understood. The boys had arranged it among themselves. It was the custom for the two men left in the ring to slug it out for the winner's prize. I discovered this too late. When the bell sounded two men in tuxedoes leaped into the ring and removed the blindfold. I found myself facing Tatlock, the biggest of the gang. I felt sick at my stomach. Hardly had the bell stopped ringing in my ears than it clanged again and I saw him moving swiftly toward me. Thinking of nothing else to do I hit him smash on the nose. He kept coming, bringing the rank sharp violence of stale sweat. His face was a black blank of a face, only his eyes alive — with hate of me and aglow with a feverish terror from what had happened to us all. I became anxious. I wanted to deliver my speech and he came at me as though he meant to beat it out of me. I smashed him again and again, taking his blows as they came. Then on a sudden impulse I struck him lightly and as we clinched, I whispered, "Fake like I knocked you out, you can have the prize."

"I'll break your behind," he whispered hoarsely.

"For *them*?"

"For *me*, sonofabitch!"

They were yelling for us to break it up and Tatlock spun me half around with a blow, and as a joggled camera sweeps in a reeling scene, I saw the howling red faces crouching tense beneath the cloud of blue-gray smoke. For a moment the world wavered, unraveled, flowed, then my head cleared and Tatlock bounced before me. That fluttering shadow before my eyes was his jabbing left hand. Then falling forward, my head against his damp shoulder, I whispered,

"I'll make it five dollars more."

"Go to hell!"

But his muscles relaxed a trifle beneath my pressure and I breathed, "Seven!"

"Give it to your ma," he said, ripping me beneath the heart.

And while I still held him I butted him and moved away. I felt myself bombarded with punches. I fought back with hopeless desperation. I wanted to deliver my speech more than anything else in the world, because I felt that only these men could judge truly my ability, and now this stupid clown was ruining my chances. I began fighting carefully now, moving in to punch him and out again with my greater speed. A lucky blow to his chin and I had him going too — until I heard a loud voice yell, "I got my money on the big boy."

Hearing this, I almost dropped my guard. I was confused: Should I try to win against the voice out there? Would not this go against my speech, and was not this a moment for humility, for nonresistance? A blow to my head as I danced about sent my right eye popping like a jack-in-the-box and settled my dilemma. The room went red as I fell. It was a dream fall, my body languid and fastidious as to where to land, until the floor became impatient and smashed up to meet me. A moment later I came to. An hypnotic voice said FIVE emphatically. And I lay there, hazily watching a dark red spot of my own blood shaping itself into a butterfly, glistening and soaking into the soiled gray world of the canvas.

When the voice drawled TEN I was lifted up and dragged to a chair. I sat dazed. My eye pained and swelled with each throb of my pounding heart and I wondered if now I would be allowed to speak. I was wringing wet, my mouth still bleeding. We were grouped along the wall now. The other boys ignored me as they congratulated Tatlock and speculated as to how much they would be paid. One boy whimpered over his smashed hand. Looking up front, I saw attendants in white jackets rolling the portable ring away and placing a small square rug in the vacant space surrounded by chairs. Perhaps, I thought, I will stand on the rug to deliver my speech.

Then the M.C. called to us, "Come on up here boys and get your money."

We ran forward to where the men laughed and talked in their chairs, waiting. Everyone seemed friendly now.

"There it is on the rug," the man said. I saw the rug covered with coins of all dimensions and a few crumpled bills. But what excited me, scattered here and there, were the gold pieces.

"Boys, it's all yours," the man said. "You get all you grab."

"That's right, Sambo," a blond man said, winking at me confidentially.

I trembled with excitement, forgetting my pain. I would get the gold and the bills, I thought. I would use both hands. I would throw my body against the boys nearest me to block them from the gold.

"Get down around the rug now," the man commanded, "and don't anyone touch it until I give the signal."

"This ought to be good," I heard.

As told, we got around the square rug on our knees. Slowly the man raised his freckled hand as we followed it upward with our eyes.

I heard, "These niggers look like they're about to pray!"

Then, "Ready," the man said. "Go!"

I lunged for a yellow coin lying on the blue design of the carpet, touching it and sending a surprised shriek to join those rising around me. I tried frantically to remove my hand but could not let go. A hot, violent force tore through my body, shaking me like a wet rat. The rug was electrified. The hair bristled up on my head as I shook myself free. My muscles jumped, my nerves jangled, writhed. But I saw that this was not stopping the other boys. Laughing in fear and embarrassment, some were holding back and scooping up the coins knocked off by the painful contortions of the others. The men roared above us as we struggled.

"Pick it up, goddamnit, pick it up!" someone called like a bass-voiced parrot. "Go on, get it!"

I crawled rapidly around the floor, picking up the coins, trying to avoid the coppers and to get greenbacks and the gold. Ignoring the shock by laughing, as I brushed the coins off quickly, I discovered that I could contain the electricity — a contradiction, but it works. Then the men began to push us onto the rug. Laughing embarrassedly, we struggled out of their hands and kept after the coins. We were all wet and slippery and hard to hold. Suddenly I saw a boy lifted into the air, glistening with sweat like a circus seal, and dropped, his wet back landing flush upon the charged rug, heard him yell and saw him literally dance upon his back, his elbows beating a frenzied tattoo upon the floor, his muscles twitching like the flesh of a horse stung by many flies. When he finally rolled off, his face was gray and no one stopped him when he ran from the floor amid booming laughter.

"Get the money," the M.C. called. "That's good hard American cash!"

And we snatched and grabbed, snatched and grabbed. I was careful not to come too close to the rug now, and when I felt the hot whiskey breath descend upon me like a cloud of foul air I reached out and grabbed the leg of a chair. It was occupied and I held on desperately.

"Leggo, nigger! Leggo!"

The huge face wavered down to mine as he tried to push me free. But my body was slippery and he was too drunk. It was Mr. Colcord, who owned a chain of movie houses and "entertainment palaces." Each time he grabbed me I slipped out of his hands. It became a real struggle. I feared the rug more than I did the drunk, so I held on, surprising myself for a moment by trying to topple *him* upon the rug. It was such an enormous idea that I found myself actually carrying it out. I tried not to be obvious, yet when I grabbed his leg, trying to tumble him out of the chair, he raised up roaring with laughter, and, looking at me with soberness dead in the eye, kicked me viciously in the chest. The chair leg flew out of my hand. I felt myself going and rolled. It was as though I had rolled through a bed of hot coals. It seemed a whole century would pass before I would roll free, a century in which I was seared through the deepest levels of my body to the fearful breath within me and the breath seared and heated to the point of explosion. It'll all be over in a flash, I thought as I rolled clear. It'll all be over in a flash.

But not yet, the men on the other side were waiting, red faces swollen as though from apoplexy as they bent forward in their chairs. Seeing their fingers coming toward me I rolled away as a fumbled football rolls off the receiver's fingertips, back into the coals. That time I luckily sent the rug sliding out of place and heard the coins ringing against the floor and the boys scuffling to pick them up and the M.C. calling, "All right, boys, that's all. Go get dressed and get your money."

I was limp as a dish rag. My back felt as though it had been beaten with wires.

When we had dressed the M.C. came in and gave us each five dollars, except Tatlock, who got ten for being last in the ring. Then he told us to leave. I was not to get a chance to deliver my speech, I thought. I was going out into the dim alley in despair when I was stopped and told to go back. I returned to the ballroom, where the men were pushing back their chairs and gathering in groups to talk.

The M.C. knocked on a table for quiet. "Gentlemen," he said, "we almost forgot an important part of the program. A most serious part, gentlemen. This boy was brought here to deliver a speech which he made at his graduation yesterday. . . ."

"Bravo!"

"I'm told that he is the smartest boy we've got out there in Greenwood. I'm told that he knows more big words than a pocket-sized dictionary."

Much applause and laughter.

"So now, gentlemen, I want you to give him your attention."

There was still laughter as I faced them, my mouth dry, my eye throbbing. I began slowly, but evidently my throat was tense, because they began shouting, "Louder! Louder!"

"We of the younger generation extol the wisdom of that great leader and educator," I shouted, "who first spoke these flaming words of wisdom: 'A ship lost at sea for many days suddenly sighted a friendly vessel. From the mast of the unfortunate vessel was seen a signal: "Water, water; we die of thirst!" The answer from the friendly vessel came back: "Cast down your bucket where you are." The captain of the distressed vessel, at last heeding the injunction, cast down his bucket, and it came up full of fresh sparkling water from the mouth of the Amazon River.' And like him I say, and in his words, 'To those of my race who depend upon bettering their condition in a foreign land, or who underestimate the importance of cultivating friendly relations with the Southern white man, who is his next-door neighbor, I would say: "Cast down your bucket where you are" — cast it down in making friends in every manly way of the people of all races by whom we are surrounded. . . .'"

I spoke automatically and with such fervor that I did not realize that the men were still talking and laughing until my dry mouth, filling up with blood from the cut, almost strangled me. I coughed, wanting to stop and go to one of the tall brass, sand-filled spittoons to relieve myself, but a few of the men, especially the superintendent, were listening and I was afraid. So I gulped it down, blood, saliva, and all, and continued. (What powers of endurance I had during those days! What enthusiasm! What a belief in the rightness of things!) I spoke even louder in spite of the pain. But still they talked and still they laughed, as though deaf with cotton in dirty ears. So I spoke with greater emotional emphasis. I closed my ears and swallowed blood until I was nauseated. The speech seemed a hundred times as long as before, but I could not leave out a single word. All had to be said, each memorized nuance considered, rendered. Nor was that all. Whenever I uttered a word of three or more syllables a group of voices would yell for me to repeat it. I used the phrase "social responsibility" and they yelled:

"What's the word you say, boy?"

"Social responsibility," I said.

"What?"

"Social . . ."

"Louder."

". . . responsibility."

"More!"

"Respon —"

"Repeat!"

"— sibility."

The room filled with the uproar of laughter until, no doubt, distracted by having to gulp down my blood, I made a mistake and yelled a phrase I had often seen denounced in newspaper editorials, heard debated in private.

"Social . . ."

"What?" they yelled.

". . . equality —"

The laughter hung smokelike in the sudden stillness. I opened my eyes, puzzled. Sounds of displeasure filled the room. The M.C. rushed forward. They shouted hostile phrases at me. But I did not understand.

A small dry mustached man in the front row blared out, "Say that slowly, son!"

"What sir?"

"What you just said!"

"Social responsibility, sir," I said.

"You weren't being smart, were you, boy?" he said, not unkindly.

"No, sir!"

"You sure that about 'equality' was a mistake?"

"Oh, yes, sir," I said. "I was swallowing blood."

"Well, you had better speak more slowly so we can understand. We mean to do right by you, but you've got to know your place at all times. All right, now, go on with your speech."

I was afraid. I wanted to leave but I wanted also to speak and I was afraid they'd snatch me down.

"Thank you, sir," I said, beginning where I had left off, and having them ignore me as before.

Yet when I finished there was a thunderous applause. I was surprised to see the superintendent come forth with a package wrapped in white tissue paper, and, gesturing for quiet, address the men.

"Gentlemen, you see that I did not overpraise this boy. He makes a good speech and some day he'll lead his people in the proper paths. And I don't have to tell you that that is important in these days and times. This is a good, smart boy, and so to encourage him in the right direction, in the name of the Board of Education I wish to present him a prize in the form of this . . ."

He paused, removing the tissue paper and revealing a gleaming calfskin brief case.

". . . in the form of this first-class article from Shad Whitmore's shop."

"Boy," he said, addressing me, "take this prize and keep it well. Consider it a badge of office. Prize it. Keep developing as you are and some day it will be filled with important papers that will help shape the destiny of your people."

I was so moved that I could hardly express my thanks. A rope of bloody saliva forming a shape like an undiscovered continent drooled upon the leather and I wiped it quickly away. I felt an importance that I had never dreamed.

"Open it and see what's inside," I was told.

My fingers a-tremble, I complied, smelling the fresh leather and finding an official-looking document inside. It was a scholarship to the state college for Negroes. My eyes filled with tears and I ran awkwardly off the floor.

I was overjoyed; I did not even mind when I discovered that the gold pieces I had scrambled for were brass pocket tokens advertising a certain make of automobile.

When I reached home everyone was excited. Next day the neighbors came to congratulate me. I even felt safe from grandfather, whose deathbed curse usually spoiled my triumphs. I stood beneath his photograph with my brief case in hand and smiled triumphantly into his stolid black peasant's face. It was a face that fascinated me. The eyes seemed to follow everywhere I went.

That night I dreamed I was at a circus with him and that he refused to laugh at the clowns no matter what they did. Then later he told me to open my brief case and read what was inside and I did, finding an official envelope stamped with the state seal; and inside the envelope I found another and another, endlessly, and I thought I would fall of weariness. "Them's years," he said. "Now open that one." And I did and in it I found an engraved document containing a short message in letters of gold. "Read it," my grandfather said. "Out loud."

"To Whom It May Concern," I intoned. "Keep This Nigger-Boy Running."

I awoke with the old man's laughter ringing in my ears.

(It was a dream I was to remember and dream again for many years after. But at the time I had no insight into its meaning. First I had to attend college.)

ꕥ

Louise Erdrich *(b. 1954) is of German and Native American descent. She grew up in Wahpeton, North Dakota, as a member of the Turtle Mountain Band of Chippewa. For many years her grandfather was tribal chair of the reservation. At Dartmouth College, Erdrich won several prizes for her fiction and poetry, including the American Academy of Poets Prize. After graduating in 1976, she returned to North Dakota, where she taught in the Poetry in the Schools Program. In 1979 she received her M.A. in creative writing from Johns Hopkins University. During her marriage to the late Michael Dorris, a professor of Native American studies at Dartmouth College, they collaborated on the novel* The Crown of Columbus *(1992).*

Erdrich has been an editor of the Boston Indian Council newspaper, The Circle. *Her stories have appeared in* Redbook, *the* New England Review, *and the* Mississippi Valley Review *and have been included in* Earth Power Coming, *an anthology of Native American literature, as well as* That's What She Said: Contemporary Poetry and Fiction by Native American Women. *In 1984 a collection of her poetry,* Jacklight, *was published and her first work of fiction,* Love Medicine, *won the National Book Critics Circle Award. Her novels* Beet Queen *(1986) and* Tracks *(1988) continue the* Love Medicine *series of stories, and her fourth novel,* The Bingo Palace, *appeared in 1994.* The Blue Jay's Dance: A Birth Year *(1995) is her celebration of motherhood, and* Tales of Burning Love *(1996),* The Antelope Wife *(1998), and* The Birchbark House *(1999) are recent novels.*

"The Red Convertible" is a chapter from Love Medicine. *Each chapter is a self-enclosed narrative that also functions as a separate short story about the lives of two families, the Kashpaws and the Lamartines, on a North Dakota reservation between 1934 and 1984. "The Red Convertible" takes place in 1974 and is narrated by Lyman Lamartine.*

Erdrich's work has won praise for its psychological depth and its literary excellence; it is a landmark achievement in its depiction of the lives of contemporary Native Americans. As the novelist Peter Matthiessen has observed, Love Medicine *is "quick with agile prose, taut speech, poetry, and power, conveying unflinchingly the funkiness, humor, and great unspoken sadness of the Indian reservations, and a people exiled to a no-man's-land between two worlds."*

LOUISE ERDRICH

The Red Convertible

1984

I was the first one to drive a convertible on my reservation. And of course it was red, a red Olds. I owned that car along with my brother Henry Junior. We owned it together until his boots filled with water on a windy night and he bought out my share. Now Henry owns the whole car, and his younger brother Lyman (that's myself), Lyman walks everywhere he goes.

How did I earn enough money to buy my share in the first place? My own talent was I could always make money. I had a touch for it, unusual in a Chippewa. From the first I was different that way, and everyone recognized it. I was the only kid they let in the American Legion Hall to shine shoes, for example, and one Christmas I sold spiritual bouquets for the mission door to door. The nuns let me keep a percentage. Once I started, it seemed the more money I made the easier the money came. Everyone encouraged it. When I was fifteen I got a job washing dishes at the Joliet Café, and that was where my first big break happened.

It wasn't long before I was promoted to busing tables, and then the short-order cook quit and I was hired to take her place. No sooner than you know it I was managing the Joliet. The rest is history. I went on managing. I soon became part owner, and of course there was no stopping me then. It wasn't long before the whole thing was mine.

After I'd owned the Joliet for one year, it blew over in the worst tornado ever seen around here. The whole operation was smashed to bits. A total loss. The fryalator was up in a tree, the grill torn in half like it was paper. I was only sixteen. I had it all in my mother's name, and I lost it quick, but before I lost it I had every one of my relatives, and their relatives, to dinner, and I also bought that red Olds I mentioned, along with Henry.

The first time we saw it! I'll tell you when we first saw it. We had gotten a ride up to Winnipeg, and both of us had money. Don't ask me why, because we never mentioned a car or anything, we just had all our money. Mine was cash, a big bankroll from the Joliet's insurance. Henry had two checks — a week's extra pay for being laid off, and his regular check from the Jewel Bearing Plant.

We were walking down Portage anyway, seeing the sights, when we saw it. There it was, parked, large as life. Really as *if* it was alive. I thought of the word *repose,* because the car wasn't simply stopped, parked, or whatever. That car reposed, calm and gleaming, a FOR SALE sign in its left front window. Then, before we had thought it over at all, the car belonged to us and our pockets were empty. We had just enough money for gas back home.

We went places in that car, me and Henry. We took off driving all one whole summer. We started off toward the Little Knife River and Mandaree in Fort Berthold and then we found ourselves down in Wakpala somehow, and then suddenly we were over in Montana on the Rocky Boy, and yet the summer was not even half over. Some people hang on to details when they travel, but we didn't let them bother us and just lived our everyday lives here to there.

I do remember this one place with willows. I remember I laid under those trees and it was comfortable. So comfortable. The branches bent down all around me like a tent or a stable. And quiet, it was quiet, even though there was a powwow close enough so I could see it going on. The air was not too still, not too windy either. When the dust rises up and hangs in the air around the dancers like that, I feel good. Henry was asleep with his arms thrown wide. Later on, he woke up and we started driving again. We were somewhere in Montana, or maybe on the Blood Reserve — it could have been anywhere. Anyway it was where we met the girl.

All her hair was in buns around her ears, that's the first thing I noticed about her. She was posed alongside the road with her arm out, so we stopped. That girl was short, so short her lumber shirt looked comical on her, like a nightgown. She had jeans on and fancy moccasins and she carried a little suitcase.

"Hop on in," says Henry. So she climbs in between us.

"We'll take you home," I says. "Where do you live?"

"Chicken," she says.

"Where the hell's that?" I ask her.

"Alaska."

"Okay," says Henry, and we drive.

We got up there and never wanted to leave. The sun doesn't truly set there in summer, and the night is more a soft dusk. You might doze off, sometimes, but before you know it you're up again, like an animal in nature. You never feel like you have to sleep hard or put away the world. And things would grow up there. One day just dirt or moss, the next day flowers and long grass. The girl's name was Susy. Her family really took to us. They fed us and put us up. We had our own tent to live in by their house, and the kids would be in and out of there all day and night. They couldn't get over me and Henry being brothers, we looked so different. We told them we knew we had the same mother, anyway.

One night Susy came in to visit us. We sat around in the tent talking of this and that. The season was changing. It was getting darker by that time, and the cold was even getting just a little mean. I told her it was time for us to go. She stood up on a chair.

"You never seen my hair," Susy said.

That was true. She was standing on a chair, but still, when she unclipped her buns the hair reached all the way to the ground. Our eyes opened. You couldn't tell how much hair she had when it was rolled up so neatly. Then my brother Henry did something funny. He went up to the chair and said, "Jump on my shoulders." So she did that, and her hair reached down past his waist, and he started twirling, this way and that, so her hair was flung out from side to side.

"I always wondered what it was like to have long pretty hair," Henry says. Well we laughed. It was a funny sight, the way he did it. The next morning we got up and took leave of those people.

On to greener pastures, as they say. It was down through Spokane and across Idaho then Montana and very soon we were racing the weather right along under the Canadian border through Columbus, Des Lacs, and then we were in Bottineau County and soon home. We'd made most of the trip, that summer, without putting up the car hood at all. We got home just in time, it turned out, for the army to remember Henry had signed up to join it.

I don't wonder that the army was so glad to get my brother that they turned him into a Marine. He was built like a brick outhouse anyway. We liked to tease him that they really wanted him for his Indian nose. He had a nose big and sharp as a hatchet, like the nose on Red Tomahawk, the Indian who killed Sitting Bull, whose profile is on signs all along the North Dakota highways. Henry went off to training camp, came home once during Christmas, then the next thing you know we got an overseas letter from him. It was 1970, and he said he was stationed up in the northern hill country. Whereabouts I did not know. He wasn't such a hot letter writer, and only got off two before the enemy caught him. I could never keep it straight, which direction those good Vietnam soldiers were from.

I wrote him back several times, even though I didn't know if those letters would get through. I kept him informed all about the car. Most of the time I had it up on blocks in the yard or half taken apart, because that long trip did a hard job on it under the hood.

I always had good luck with numbers, and never worried about the draft myself. I never even had to think about what my number was. But Henry was never lucky in the same way as me. It was at least three years before Henry came home. By then I guess the whole war was solved in the government's mind, but for him it would keep on going. In those years I'd put his car into almost perfect shape. I always thought of it as his car while he was gone, even though when he left he said, "Now it's yours," and threw me his key.

"Thanks for the extra key," I'd said. "I'll put it up in your drawer just in case I need it." He laughed.

When he came home, though, Henry was very different, and I'll say this: the change was no good. You could hardly expect him to change for the better,

I know. But he was quiet, so quiet, and never comfortable sitting still anywhere but always up and moving around. I thought back to times we'd sat still for whole afternoons, never moving a muscle, just shifting our weight along the ground, talking to whoever sat with us, watching things. He'd always had a joke, then, too, and now you couldn't get him to laugh, or when he did it was more the sound of a man choking, a sound that stopped up the throats of other people around him. They got to leaving him alone most of the time, and I didn't blame them. It was a fact: Henry was jumpy and mean.

I'd bought a color TV set for my mom and the rest of us while Henry was away. Money still came very easy. I was sorry I'd ever bought it though, because of Henry. I was also sorry I'd bought color, because with black-and-white the pictures seem older and farther away. But what are you going to do? He sat in front of it, watching it, and that was the only time he was completely still. But it was the kind of stillness that you see in a rabbit when it freezes and before it will bolt. He was not easy. He sat in his chair gripping the armrests with all his might, as if the chair itself was moving at a high speed and if he let go at all he would rocket forward and maybe crash right through the set.

Once I was in the room watching TV with Henry and I heard his teeth click at something. I looked over, and he'd bitten through his lip. Blood was going down his chin. I tell you right then I wanted to smash that tube to pieces. I went over to it but Henry must have known what I was up to. He rushed from his chair and shoved me out of the way, against the wall. I told myself he didn't know what he was doing.

My mom came in, turned the set off real quiet, and told us she had made something for supper. So we went and sat down. There was still blood going down Henry's chin, but he didn't notice it and no one said anything, even though every time he took a bit of his bread his blood fell onto it until he was eating his own blood mixed in with the food.

While Henry was not around we talked about what was going to happen to him. There were no Indian doctors on the reservation, and my mom was afraid of trusting the old man, Moses Pillager, because he courted her long ago and was jealous of her husbands. He might take revenge through her son. We were afraid that if we brought Henry to a regular hospital they would keep him.

"They don't fix them in those places," Mom said; "they just give them drugs."

"We wouldn't get him there in the first place," I agreed, "so let's just forget about it."

Then I thought about the car.

Henry had not even looked at the car since he'd gotten home, though like I said, it was in tip-top condition and ready to drive. I thought the car might bring the old Henry back somehow. So I bided my time and waited for my chance to interest him in the vehicle.

One night Henry was off somewhere. I took myself a hammer. I went out to that car and I did a number on its underside. Whacked it up. Bent the tail pipe double. Ripped the muffler loose. By the time I was done with the car it looked worse than any typical Indian car that has been driven all its life on reservation roads, which they always say are like government promises — full of holes. It just about hurt me, I'll tell you that! I threw dirt in the carburetor and I ripped all the electric tape off the seats. I made it look just as beat up as I could. Then I sat back and waited for Henry to find it.

Still, it took him over a month. That was all right, because it was just getting warm enough, not melting, but warm enough to work outside.

"Lyman," he says, walking in one day, "that red car looks like shit."

"Well it's old," I says. "You got to expect that."

"No way!" says Henry. "That car's a classic! But you went and ran the piss right out of it, Lyman, and you know it don't deserve that. I kept that car in A-one shape. You don't remember. You're too young. But when I left, that car was running like a watch. Now I don't even know if I can get it to start again, let alone get it anywhere near its old condition."

"Well you try," I said, like I was getting mad, "but I say it's a piece of junk."

Then I walked out before he could realize I knew he'd strung together more than six words at once.

After that I thought he'd freeze himself to death working on that car. He was out there all day, and at night he rigged up a little lamp, ran a cord out the window, and had himself some light to see by while he worked. He was better than he had been before, but that's still not saying much. It was easier for him to do the things the rest of us did. He ate more slowly and didn't jump up and down during the meal to get this or that or look out the window. I put my hand in the back of the TV set, I admit, and fiddled around with it good, so that it was almost impossible now to get a clear picture. He didn't look at it very often anyway. He was always out with that car or going off to get parts for it. By the time it was really melting outside, he had it fixed.

I had been feeling down in the dumps about Henry around this time. We had always been together before. Henry and Lyman. But he was such a loner now that I didn't know how to take it. So I jumped at the chance one day when Henry seemed friendly. It's not that he smiled or anything. He just said, "Let's take that old shitbox for a spin." Just the way he said it made me think he could be coming around.

We went out to the car. It was spring. The sun was shining very bright. My only sister, Bonita, who was just eleven years old, came out and made us stand together for a picture. Henry leaned his elbow on the red car's windshield, and he took his other arm and put it over my shoulder, very carefully, as though it was heavy for him to lift and he didn't want to bring the weight down all at once.

"Smile," Bonita said, and he did.

That picture, I never look at it anymore. A few months ago, I don't know why, I got his picture out and tacked it on the wall. I felt good about Henry at the time, close to him. I felt good having his picture on the wall, until one night when I was looking at television. I was a little drunk and stoned. I looked up at the wall and Henry was staring at me. I don't know what it was, but his smile had changed, or maybe it was gone. All I know is I couldn't stay in the same room with that picture. I was shaking. I got up, closed the door, and went into the kitchen. A little later my friend Ray came over and we both went back into that room. We put the picture in a brown bag, folded the bag over and over tightly, then put it way back in a closet.

I still see that picture now, as if it tugs at me, whenever I pass that closet door. The picture is very clear in my mind. It was so sunny that day Henry had to squint against the glare. Or maybe the camera Bonita held flashed like a mirror, blinding him, before she snapped the picture. My face is right out in the sun, big and round. But he might have drawn back, because the shadows on his face are deep as holes. There are two shadows curved like little hooks around the ends of his smile, as if to frame it and try to keep it there — that one, first smile that looked like it might have hurt his face. He has his field jacket on and the worn-in clothes he'd come back in and kept wearing ever since. After Bonita took the picture, she went into the house and we got into the car. There was a full cooler in the trunk. We started off, east, toward Pembina and the Red River because Henry said he wanted to see the high water.

The trip over there was beautiful. When everything starts changing, drying up, clearing off, you feel like your whole life is starting. Henry felt it, too. The top was down and the car hummed like a top. He'd really put it back in shape, even the tape on the seats was very carefully put down and glued back in layers. It's not that he smiled again or even joked, but his face looked to me as if it was clear, more peaceful. It looked as though he wasn't thinking of anything in particular except the bare fields and windbreaks and houses we were passing.

The river was high and full of winter trash when we got there. The sun was still out, but it was colder by the river. There were still little clumps of dirty snow here and there on the banks. The water hadn't gone over the banks yet, but it would, you could tell. It was just at its limit, hard swollen glossy like an old gray scar. We made ourselves a fire, and we sat down and watched the current go. As I watched it I felt something squeezing inside me and tightening and trying to let go all at the same time. I knew I was not just feeling it myself; I knew I was feeling what Henry was going through at that moment. Except that I couldn't stand it, the closing and opening. I jumped to my feet. I took Henry by the shoulders and I started shaking him. "Wake up," I says, "wake up, wake up, wake up!" I didn't know what had come over me. I sat down beside him again.

His face was totally white and hard. Then it broke, like stones break all of a sudden when water boils up inside them.

"I know it," he says. "I know it. I can't help it. It's no use."

We start talking. He said he knew what I'd done with the car. It was obvious it had been whacked out of shape and not just neglected. He said he wanted to give the car to me for good now, it was no use. He said he'd fixed it just to give it back and I should take it.

"No way," I says, "I don't want it."

"That's okay," he says, "you take it."

"I don't want it, though," I says back to him, and then to emphasize, just to emphasize, you understand, I touch his shoulder. He slaps my hand off.

"Take that car," he says.

"No," I say. "Make me," I say, and then he grabs my jacket and rips the arm loose. That jacket is a class act, suede with tags and zippers. I push Henry backwards, off the log. He jumps up and bowls me over. We go down in a clinch and come up swinging hard, for all we're worth, with our fists. He socks my jaw so hard I feel like it swings loose. Then I'm at his rib cage and land a good one under his chin so his head snaps back. He's dazzled. He looks at me and I look at him and then his eyes are full of tears and blood and at first I think he's crying. But no, he's laughing. "Ha! Ha!" he says. "Ha! Ha! Take good care of it."

"Okay," I says, "okay, no problem. Ha! Ha!"

I can't help it, and I start laughing, too. My face feels fat and strange, and after a while I get a beer from the cooler in the trunk, and when I hand it to Henry he takes his shirt and wipes my germs off. "Hoof-and-mouth disease," he says. For some reason this cracks me up, and so we're really laughing for a while, and then we drink all the rest of the beers one by one and throw them in the river and see how far, how fast, the current takes them before they fill up and sink.

"You want to go on back?" I ask after a while. "Maybe we could snag a couple nice Kashpaw girls."

He says nothing. But I can tell his mood is turning again.

"They're all crazy, the girls up here, every damn one of them."

"You're crazy too," I say, to jolly him up. "Crazy Lamartine boys!"

He looks as though he will take this wrong at first. His face twists, then clears, and he jumps up on his feet. "That's right!" he says. "Crazier 'n hell. Crazy Indians!"

I think it's the old Henry again. He throws off his jacket and starts swinging his legs out from the knees like a fancy dancer. He's down doing something between a grass dance and a bunny hop, no kind of dance I ever saw before, but neither has anyone else on all this green growing earth. He's wild. He wants to pitch whoopee! He's up and at me and all over. All this time I'm laughing so hard, so hard my belly is getting tied up in a knot.

"Got to cool me off!" he shouts all of a sudden. Then he runs over to the river and jumps in.

There's boards and other things in the current. It's so high. No sound comes from the river after the splash he makes, so I run right over. I look around. It's getting dark. I see he's halfway across the water already, and I know he didn't swim there but the current took him. It's far. I hear his voice, though, very clearly across it.

"My boots are filling," he says.

He says this in a normal voice, like he just noticed and he doesn't know what to think of it. Then he's gone. A branch comes by. Another branch. And I go in.

By the time I get out of the river, off the snag I pulled myself onto, the sun is down. I walk back to the car, turn on the high beams, and drive it up the bank. I put it in first gear and then I take my foot off the clutch. I get out, close the door, and watch it plow softly into the water. The headlights reach in as they go down, searching, still lighted even after the water swirls over the back end. I wait. The wires short out. It is all finally dark. And then there is only the water, the sound of it going and running and going and running and running.

ꕥ

William Faulkner *(1897–1962) was born in New Albany, Mississippi, into an old southern family. When he was a child, his parents moved to the isolated town of Oxford, Mississippi, and except for his service in World War I and some time in New Orleans and Hollywood, he spent the rest of his life there. "I discovered my own little postage stamp of native soil was worth writing about, and that I would never live long enough to exhaust it." His literary career began in New Orleans, where he lived for six months and wrote newspaper sketches and stories for the* Times-Picayune. *He met Sherwood Anderson in New Orleans, and Anderson helped him publish his first novel,* Soldier's Pay, *in 1926. Faulkner's major work was written in the late 1920s and the 1930s, when he created an imaginary county adjacent to Oxford, calling it Yoknapatawpha County and chronicling its history in a series of experimental novels. In* The Sound and the Fury *(1929),* As I Lay Dying *(1930),* Sanctuary *(1931),* Light in August *(1932),* Absalom, Absalom! *(1936), and* The Hamlet *(1940), he showed himself to be a writer of genius, although "a willfully and perversely chaotic one," as Jorge Luis Borges noted, whose "labyrinthine world" required a no less labyrinthine prose technique to describe in epic manner the disintegration of the South through many generations. Faulkner was awarded the Nobel Prize for literature in 1952.*

Faulkner experimented with using a child's point of view in "That Evening Sun," but he rarely included poetic imagery or stream-of-consciousness narration in his stories, which he wrote, he often said, to help him pay his rent. His biographer Frederick Karl has noted that he used short fiction "as a means of working through, or toward, larger ideas." He wrote nearly a hundred stories, often revising them later to fit as sections into a novel. Four books of his stories were published in his lifetime. When Faulkner revised "That Evening Sun" after its initial appearance in the American Mercury *in March 1931 for inclusion in* These 13, *his first story collection published that same year, he omitted a paragraph after the father and the three children have left Nancy in her cabin. The story originally read:*

> *Then we had crossed the ditch, walking out of Nancy's life. Then her life was sitting there with the door open and the lamp lit, waiting, and the ditch between us and us going on, the white people going on, dividing the impinged lives of us and Nancy.*
>
> *"Who will do our washing now, father?" I said.*

Although some readers found symbolism in "A Rose for Emily" that suggested he was implying a battle between the North (the character Homer Barron) and the South (Miss Emily herself), Faulkner denied a schematic interpretation. He said he had intended to write a ghost story, and "I think that the writer is too busy trying to create flesh-and-blood people that will stand up and cast a shadow to have time to be conscious of all the symbolism that he may put into what he does or what people may read into it."

RELATED COMMENTARY: *William Faulkner, "The Meaning of 'A Rose for Emily,'" page 679.*

WILLIAM FAULKNER

A Rose for Emily

1931

I

When Miss Emily Grierson died, our whole town went to her funeral: the men through a sort of respectful affection for a fallen monument, the women mostly out of curiosity to see the inside of her house, which no one save an old manservant — a combined gardener and cook — had seen in at least ten years.

It was a big, squarish frame house that had once been white, decorated with cupolas and spires and scrolled balconies in the heavily lightsome style of the seventies, set on what had once been our most select street. But garages and cotton gins had encroached and obliterated even the august names of that neighborhood; only Miss Emily's house was left, lifting its stubborn and coquettish decay above the cotton wagons and the gasoline pumps — an eyesore among eyesores. And now Miss Emily had gone to join the representatives of those august names where they lay in the cedar-bemused cemetery among the ranked and anonymous graves of Union and Confederate soldiers who fell at the battle of Jefferson.

Alive, Miss Emily had been a tradition, a duty, and a care; a sort of hereditary obligation upon the town, dating from that day in 1894 when Colonel Sartoris, the mayor — he who fathered the edict that no Negro woman should appear on the streets without an apron — remitted her taxes, the dispensation dating from the death of her father on into perpetuity. Not that Miss Emily would have accepted charity. Colonel Sartoris invented an involved tale to the effect that Miss Emily's father had loaned money to the town, which the town, as a matter of business, preferred this way of repaying. Only a man of Colonel Sartoris' generation and thought could have invented it, and only a woman could have believed it.

When the next generation, with its more modern ideas, became mayors and aldermen, this arrangement created some little dissatisfaction. On the first of the year they mailed her a tax notice. February came, and there was no reply. They wrote her a formal letter, asking her to call at the sheriff's office at her convenience. A week later the mayor wrote her himself, offering to call or to send his car for her, and received in reply a note on paper of an archaic shape, in a thin, flowing calligraphy in faded ink, to the effect that she no longer went out at all. The tax notice was also enclosed, without comment.

They called a special meeting of the Board of Aldermen. A deputation waited upon her, knocked at the door through which no visitor had passed since she ceased giving china-painting lessons eight or ten years earlier. They were admitted by the old Negro into a dim hall from which a stairway mounted into still more shadow. It smelled of dust and disuse — a close, dank smell. The Negro led them into the parlor. It was furnished in heavy, leather-covered furniture. When the Negro opened the blinds of one window, they could see that the leather was cracked; and when they sat down, a faint dust rose sluggishly about their thighs, spinning with slow motes in the single sun-ray. On a tarnished gilt easel before the fireplace stood a crayon portrait of Miss Emily's father.

They rose when she entered — a small, fat woman in black, with a thin gold chain descending to her waist and vanishing into her belt, leaning on an ebony cane with a tarnished gold head. Her skeleton was small and spare; perhaps that was why what would have been merely plumpness in another was obesity in her. She looked bloated, like a body long submerged in motionless water, and of that pallid hue. Her eyes, lost in the fatty ridges of her face, looked like two small pieces of coal pressed into a lump of dough as they moved from one face to another while the visitors stated their errand.

She did not ask them to sit. She just stood in the door and listened quietly until the spokesman came to a stumbling halt. Then they could hear the invisible watch ticking at the end of the gold chain.

Her voice was dry and cold. "I have no taxes in Jefferson. Colonel Sartoris explained it to me. Perhaps one of you can gain access to the city records and satisfy yourselves."

"But we have. We are the city authorities, Miss Emily. Didn't you get a notice from the sheriff, signed by him?"

"I received a paper, yes," Miss Emily said. "Perhaps he considers himself the sheriff. . . . I have no taxes in Jefferson."

"But there is nothing on the books to show that, you see. We must go by the —"

"See Colonel Sartoris. I have no taxes in Jefferson."

"But, Miss Emily —"

"See Colonel Sartoris." (Colonel Sartoris had been dead almost ten years.) "I have no taxes in Jefferson. Tobe!" The Negro appeared. "Show these gentlemen out."

II

So she vanquished them, horse and foot, just as she had vanquished their fathers thirty years before about the smell. That was two years after her father's death and a short time after her sweetheart — the one we believed would marry her — had deserted her. After her father's death she went out very little; after her sweetheart went away, people hardly saw her at all. A few of the ladies had the temerity to call, but were not received, and the only sign of life about the place was the Negro man — a young man then — going in and out with a market basket.

"Just as if a man — any man — could keep a kitchen properly," the ladies said; so they were not surprised when the smell developed. It was another link between the gross, teeming world and the high and mighty Griersons.

A neighbor, a woman, complained to the mayor, Judge Stevens, eighty years old.

"But what will you have me do about it, madam?" he said.

"Why, send her word to stop it," the woman said. "Isn't there a law?"

"I'm sure that won't be necessary," Judge Stevens said. "It's probably just a snake or a rat that nigger of hers killed in the yard. I'll speak to him about it."

The next day he received two more complaints, one from a man who came in diffident deprecation. "We really must do something about it, Judge. I'd be the last one in the world to bother Miss Emily, but we've got to do something." That night the Board of Aldermen met — three graybeards and one younger man, a member of the rising generation.

"It's simple enough," he said. "Send her word to have her place cleaned up. Give her a certain time to do it in, and if she don't. . . ."

"Dammit, sir," Judge Stevens said, "will you accuse a lady to her face of smelling bad?"

So the next night, after midnight, four men crossed Miss Emily's lawn and slunk about the house like burglars, sniffing along the base of the brickwork and at the cellar openings while one of them performed a regular sowing motion with his hand out of a sack slung from his shoulder. They broke open the cellar door and sprinkled lime there, and in all the outbuildings. As they recrossed the lawn, a window that had been dark was lighted and Miss Emily sat in it, the light behind her, and her upright torso motionless as that of an idol. They crept quietly across the lawn and into the shadow of the locusts that lined the street. After a week or two the smell went away.

That was when people had begun to feel really sorry for her. People in our town, remembering how old lady Wyatt, her great-aunt, had gone completely crazy at last, believed that the Griersons held themselves a little too high for what they really were. None of the young men were quite good enough for Miss Emily and such. We had long thought of them as a tableau, Miss Emily a slender figure in white in the background, her father a spraddled silhouette in the foreground, his back to her and clutching a horsewhip, the two of them framed by the backflung front door. So when she got to be thirty and was still single, we were not pleased exactly, but vindicated; even with insanity in the family she wouldn't have turned down all of her chances if they had really materialized.

When her father died, it got about that the house was all that was left to her; and in a way, people were glad. At last they could pity Miss Emily. Being left alone, and a pauper, she had become humanized. Now she too would know the old thrill and the old despair of a penny more or less.

The day after his death all the ladies prepared to call at the house and offer condolence and aid, as is our custom. Miss Emily met them at the door, dressed as usual and with no trace of grief on her face. She told them that her father was not dead. She did that for three days, with the ministers calling on her, and the doctors, trying to persuade her to let them dispose of the body. Just as they were about to resort to law and force, she broke down, and they buried her father quickly.

We did not say she was crazy then. We believed she had to do that. We remembered all the young men her father had driven away, and we knew that with nothing left, she would have to cling to that which had robbed her, as people will.

III

She was sick for a long time. When we saw her again, her hair was cut short, making her look like a girl, with a vague resemblance to those angels in colored church windows — sort of tragic and serene.

The town had just let the contracts for paving the sidewalks, and in the summer after her father's death they began the work. The construction company came with niggers and mules and machinery, and a foreman named Homer Barron, a Yankee — a big, dark, ready man, with a big voice and eyes lighter than his face. The little boys would follow in groups to hear him cuss the niggers, and the niggers singing in time to the rise and fall of picks. Pretty soon he knew everybody in town. Whenever you heard a lot of laughing anywhere about the square, Homer Barron would be in the center of the group. Presently, we began to see him and Miss Emily on Sunday afternoons driving in the yellow-wheeled buggy and the matched team of bays from the livery stable.

At first we were glad that Miss Emily would have an interest, because the ladies all said, "Of course a Grierson would not think seriously of a Northerner, a day laborer." But there were still others, older people, who said that even grief could not cause a real lady to forget *noblesse oblige* — without calling it *noblesse oblige.* They just said, "Poor Emily. Her kinsfolk should come to her." She had some kin in Alabama; but years ago her father had fallen out with them over the estate of old lady Wyatt, the crazy woman, and there was no communication between the two families. They had not even been represented at the funeral.

And as soon as the old people said, "Poor Emily," the whispering began. "Do you suppose it's really so?" they said to one another. "Of course it is. What else could. . . ." This behind their hands; rustling of craned silk and satin behind jalousies closed upon the sun of Sunday afternoon as the thin, swift clop-clop-clop of the matched team passed: "Poor Emily."

She carried her head high enough — even when we believed that she was fallen. It was as if she demanded more than ever the recognition of her dignity as the last Grierson; as if it had wanted that touch of earthiness to reaffirm her imperviousness. Like when she bought the rat poison, the arsenic. That was over a year after they had begun to say "Poor Emily," and while the two female cousins were visiting her.

"I want some poison," she said to the druggist. She was over thirty then, still a slight woman, though thinner than usual, with cold, haughty black eyes in a face the flesh of which was strained across the temples and about the eyesockets as you imagine a lighthouse-keeper's face ought to look. "I want some poison," she said.

"Yes, Miss Emily. What kind? For rats and such? I'd recom ——"

"I want the best you have. I don't care what kind."

The druggist named several. "They'll kill anything up to an elephant. But what you want is ——"

"Arsenic," Miss Emily said. "Is that a good one?"

"Is . . . arsenic? Yes, ma'am. But what you want ——"

"I want arsenic."

The druggist looked down at her. She looked back at him, erect, her face like a strained flag. "Why, of course," the druggist said. "If that's what you want. But the law requires you to tell what you are going to use it for."

Miss Emily just stared at him, her head tilted back in order to look him eye for eye, until he looked away and went and got the arsenic and wrapped it up. The Negro delivery boy brought her the package; the druggist didn't come back. When she opened the package at home there was written on the box, under the skull and bones: "For rats."

IV

So the next day we all said, "She will kill herself"; and we said it would be the best thing. When she had first begun to be seen with Homer Barron, we had said, "She will marry him." Then we said, "She will persuade him yet," because Homer himself had remarked — he liked men, and it was known that he drank with the younger men in the Elks' Club — that he was not a marrying man. Later we said, "Poor Emily" behind the jalousies as they passed on Sunday afternoon in the glittering buggy, Miss Emily with her head high and Homer Barron with his hat cocked and a cigar in his teeth, reins and whip in a yellow glove.

Then some of the ladies began to say that it was a disgrace to the town and a bad example to the young people. The men did not want to interfere, but at last the ladies forced the Baptist minister — Miss Emily's people were Episcopal — to call upon her. He would never divulge what happened during that interview, but he refused to go back again. The next Sunday they again drove about the streets, and the following day the minister's wife wrote to Miss Emily's relations in Alabama.

So she had blood-kin under her roof again and we sat back to watch developments. At first nothing happened. Then we were sure that they were to be married. We learned that Miss Emily had been to the jeweler's and ordered a man's toilet set in silver, with the letters H.B. on each piece. Two days later we learned that she had bought a complete outfit of men's clothing, including a nightshirt, and we said, "They are married." We were really glad. We were glad because the two female cousins were even more Grierson than Miss Emily had ever been.

So we were not surprised when Homer Barron — the streets had been finished some time since — was gone. We were a little disappointed that there was not a public blowing-off, but we believed that he had gone on to prepare for Miss Emily's coming, or to give her a chance to get rid of the cousins. (By that time it was a cabal, and we were all Miss Emily's allies to help circumvent the cousins.) Sure enough, after another week they departed. And, as we had expected all along, within three days Homer Barron was back in town. A neighbor saw the Negro man admit him at the kitchen door at dusk one evening.

And that was the last we saw of Homer Barron. And of Miss Emily for some time. The Negro man went in and out with the market basket, but the front door remained closed. Now and then we would see her at the window for a moment, as the men did that night when they sprinkled the lime, but for almost six months she did not appear on the streets. Then we knew that this was to be expected too; as if that quality of her father which had thwarted her woman's life so many times had been too virulent and too furious to die.

When we next saw Miss Emily, she had grown fat and her hair was turning gray. During the next few years it grew grayer and grayer until it attained an even pepper-and-salt iron-gray, when it ceased turning. Up to the day of her death at seventy-four it was still that vigorous iron-gray, like the hair of an active man.

From that time on her front door remained closed, save during a period of six or seven years, when she was about forty, during which she gave lessons in china-painting. She fitted up a studio in one of the downstairs rooms, where the daughters and granddaughters of Colonel Sartoris' contemporaries were sent to her with the same regularity and in the same spirit that they were sent to church on Sundays with a twenty-five-cent piece for the collection plate. Meanwhile her taxes had been remitted.

Then the newer generation became the backbone and the spirit of the town, and the painting pupils grew up and fell away and did not send their children to her with boxes of color and tedious brushes and pictures cut from the ladies' magazines. The front door closed upon the last one and remained closed for good. When the town got free postal delivery, Miss Emily alone refused to let them fasten the metal numbers above her door and attach a mailbox to it. She would not listen to them.

Daily, monthly, yearly we watched the Negro grow grayer and more stooped, going in and out with the market basket. Each December we sent her a tax notice, which would be returned by the post office a week later, unclaimed. Now and then we would see her in one of the downstairs windows — she had evidently shut up the top floor of the house — like the carven torso of an idol in a niche, looking or not looking at us, we could never tell which. Thus she passed from generation to generation — dear, inescapable, impervious, tranquil, and perverse.

And so she died. Fell ill in the house filled with dust and shadows, with only a doddering Negro man to wait on her. We did not even know she was sick; we had long since given up trying to get any information from the Negro. He talked to no one, probably not even to her, for his voice had grown harsh and rusty, as if from disuse.

She died in one of the downstairs rooms, in a heavy walnut bed with a curtain, her gray head propped on a pillow yellow and moldy with age and lack of sunlight.

V

The Negro met the first of the ladies at the front door and let them in, with their hushed, sibilant voices and their quick, curious glances, and then he disappeared. He walked right through the house and out the back and was not seen again.

The two female cousins came at once. They held the funeral on the second day, with the town coming to look at Miss Emily beneath a mass of bought flowers, with the crayon face of her father musing profoundly above the bier and the ladies sibilant and macabre; and the very old men — some in their brushed Confederate uniforms — on the porch and the lawn, talking of Miss Emily as if she had been a contemporary of theirs, believing that they had danced with her and courted her perhaps, confusing time with its mathematical progression, as the old do, to whom all the past is not a diminishing road but, instead, a huge meadow which no winter ever quite touches, divided from them now by the narrow bottleneck of the most recent decade of years.

Already we knew that there was one room in that region above stairs which no one had seen in forty years, and which would have to be forced. They waited until Miss Emily was decently in the ground before they opened it.

The violence of breaking down the door seemed to fill this room with pervading dust. A thin, acrid pall as of the tomb seemed to lie everywhere upon this room decked and furnished as for a bridal: upon the valance curtains of faded rose color, upon the rose-shaded lights, upon the dressing table, upon the delicate array of crystal and the man's toilet things backed with tarnished silver, silver so tarnished that the monogram was obscured. Among them lay a collar and tie, as if they had just been removed, which, lifted, left upon the surface a pale crescent in the dust. Upon a chair hung the suit, carefully folded; beneath it the two mute shoes and the discarded socks.

The man himself lay in the bed.

For a long while we just stood there, looking down at the profound and fleshless grin. The body had apparently once lain in the attitude of an embrace, but now the long sleep that outlasts love, that conquers even the grimace of love, had cuckolded him. What was left of him, rotted beneath what was left of the nightshirt, had become inextricable from the bed in which he lay; and upon him and upon the pillow beside him lay that even coating of the patient and biding dust.

Then we noticed that in the second pillow was the indentation of a head. One of us lifted something from it, and leaning forward, that faint and invisible dust dry and acrid in the nostrils, we saw a long strand of iron-gray hair.

WILLIAM FAULKNER

That Evening Sun

1931

I

Monday is no different from any other weekday in Jefferson now. The streets are paved now, and the telephone and electric companies are cutting down more and more of the shade trees — the water oaks, the maples and locusts and elms — to make room for iron poles bearing clusters of bloated and ghostly and bloodless grapes, and we have a city laundry which makes the rounds on Monday morning, gathering the bundles of clothes into bright-colored, specially-made motor cars: the soiled wearing of a whole week now flees apparitionlike behind alert and irritable electric horns, with a long diminishing noise of rubber and asphalt like tearing silk, and even the Negro women who still take in white people's washing after the old custom, fetch and deliver it in automobiles.

But fifteen years ago, on Monday morning the quiet, dusty, shady streets would be full of Negro women with, balanced on their steady, turbaned heads, bundles of clothes tied up in sheets, almost as large as cotton bales, carried so without touch of hand between the kitchen door of the white house and the blackened washpot beside a cabin door in Negro Hollow.

Nancy would set her bundle on the top of her head, then upon the bundle in turn she would set the black straw sailor hat which she wore winter and summer. She was tall, with a high, sad face sunken a little where her teeth were missing. Sometimes we would go a part of the way down the lane and across the pasture with her, to watch the balanced bundle and the hat that never bobbed nor wavered, even when she walked down into the ditch and up the other side and stooped through the fence. She would go down on her hands and knees and crawl through the gap, her head rigid, uptilted, the bundle steady as a rock or a balloon, and rise to her feet again and go on.

Sometimes the husbands of the washing women would fetch and deliver the clothes, but Jesus never did that for Nancy, even before father told him to stay away from our house, even when Dilsey was sick and Nancy would come to cook for us.

And then about half the time we'd have to go down the lane to Nancy's cabin and tell her to come on and cook breakfast. We would stop at the ditch, because father told us to not have anything to do with Jesus — he was a short black man, with a razor scar down his face — and we would throw rocks at Nancy's house until she came to the door, leaning her head around it without any clothes on.

"What yawl mean, chunking my house?" Nancy said. "What you little devils mean?"

"Father says for you to come on and get breakfast," Caddy said. "Father says it's over a half an hour now, and you've got to come this minute."

"I aint studying no breakfast," Nancy said. "I going to get my sleep out."

"I bet you're drunk," Jason said. "Father says you're drunk. Are you drunk, Nancy?"

"Who says I is?" Nancy said. "I got to get my sleep out. I ain't studying no breakfast."

So after a while we quit chunking the cabin and went back home. When she finally came, it was too late for me to go to school. So we thought it was whisky until that day they arrested her again and they were taking her to jail and they passed Mr Stovall. He was the cashier in the bank and a deacon in the Baptist church, and Nancy began to say:

"When you going to pay me, white man? When you going to pay me, white man? It's been three times now since you paid me a cent —" Mr Stovall knocked her down, but she kept on saying, "When you going to pay me, white man? It's been three times now since —" until Mr Stovall kicked her in the mouth with his heel and the marshal caught Mr Stovall back, and Nancy lying in the street, laughing. She turned her head and spat out some blood and teeth and said, "It's been three times now since he paid me a cent."

That was how she lost her teeth, and all that day they told about Nancy and Mr Stovall, and all that night the ones that passed the jail could hear Nancy singing and yelling. They could see her hands holding to the window bars, and a lot of them stopped along the fence, listening to her and to the jailer trying to make her stop. She didn't shut up until almost daylight, when the jailer began to hear a bumping and scraping upstairs and he went up there and found Nancy hanging from the window bar. He said that it was cocaine and not whisky, because no nigger would try to commit suicide unless he was full of cocaine, because a nigger full of cocaine wasn't a nigger any longer.

The jailer cut her down and revived her; then he beat her, whipped her. She had hung herself with her dress. She had fixed it all right, but when they arrested her she didn't have on anything except a dress and so she didn't have anything to tie her hands with and she couldn't make her hands let go of the window ledge. So the jailer heard the noise and ran up there and found Nancy hanging from the window, stark naked, her belly already swelling out a little, like a little balloon.

When Dilsey was sick in her cabin and Nancy was cooking for us, we could see her apron swelling out; that was before father told Jesus to stay away from the house. Jesus was in the kitchen, sitting behind the stove, with his razor scar on his black face like a piece of dirty string. He said it was a watermelon that Nancy had under her dress.

"It never come off of your vine, though," Nancy said.

"Off of what vine?" Caddy said.

"I can cut down the vine it did come off of," Jesus said.

"What makes you want to talk like that before these chillen?" Nancy said. "Whyn't you go on to work? You done et. You want Mr Jason to catch you hanging around his kitchen, talking that way before these chillen?"

"Talking what way?" Caddy said. "What vine?"

"I cant hang around white man's kitchen," Jesus said. "But white man can hang around mine. White man can come in my house, but I cant stop him. When white man want to come in my house, I aint got no house. I cant stop him, but he cant kick me outen it. He cant do that."

Dilsey was still sick in her cabin. Father told Jesus to stay off our place. Dilsey was still sick. It was a long time. We were in the library after supper.

"Isn't Nancy through in the kitchen yet?" mother said. "It seems to me that she has had plenty of time to have finished the dishes."

"Let Quentin go and see," father said. "Go and see if Nancy is through, Quentin. Tell her she can go on home."

I went to the kitchen. Nancy was through. The dishes were put away and the fire was out. Nancy was sitting in a chair, close to the cold stove. She looked at me.

"Mother wants to know if you are through," I said.

"Yes," Nancy said. She looked at me. "I done finished." She looked at me.

"What is it?" I said. "What is it?"

"I aint nothing but a nigger," Nancy said. "It aint none of my fault."

She looked at me, sitting in the chair before the cold stove, the sailor hat on her head. I went back to the library. It was the cold stove and all, when you think of a kitchen being warm and busy and cheerful. And with a cold stove and the dishes all put away, and nobody wanting to eat at that hour.

"Is she through?" mother said.

"Yessum," I said.

"What is she doing?" mother said.

"She's not doing anything. She's through."

"I'll go and see," father said.

"Maybe she's waiting for Jesus to come and take her home," Caddy said.

"Jesus is gone," I said. Nancy told us how one morning she woke up and Jesus was gone.

"He quit me," Nancy said. "Done gone to Memphis, I reckon. Dodging them city *po*-lice for a while, I reckon."

"And a good riddance," father said. "I hope he stays there."

"Nancy's scaired of the dark," Jason said.

"So are you," Caddy said.

"I'm not," Jason said.

"Scairy cat," Caddy said.

"I'm not," Jason said.

"You, Candace!" mother said. Father came back.

"I am going to walk down the lane with Nancy," he said. "She says that Jesus is back."

"Has she seen him?" mother said.

"No. Some Negro sent her word that he was back in town. I wont be long."

"You'll leave me alone, to take Nancy home?" mother said. "Is her safety more precious to you than mine?"

"I wont be long," father said.

"You'll leave these children unprotected, with that Negro about?"

"I'm going too," Caddy said. "Let me go, Father."

"What would he do with them, if he were unfortunate enough to have them?" father said.

"I want to go, too," Jason said.

"Jason!" mother said. She was speaking to father. You could tell that by the way she said the name. Like she believed that all day father had been trying to think of doing the thing she wouldn't like the most, and that she knew all the time that after a while he would think of it. I stayed quiet, because father and I both knew that mother would want him to make me stay with her if she just thought of it in time. So father didn't look at me. I was the oldest. I was nine and Caddy was seven and Jason was five.

"Nonsense," father said. "We wont be long."

Nancy had her hat on. We came to the lane. "Jesus always been good to me," Nancy said. "Whenever he had two dollars, one of them was mine." We walked in the lane. "If I can just get through the lane," Nancy said, "I be all right then."

The lane was always dark. "This is where Jason got scared on Hallowe'en," Caddy said.

"I didn't," Jason said.

"Cant Aunt Rachel do anything with him?" father said. Aunt Rachel was old. She lived in a cabin beyond Nancy's, by herself. She had white hair and she smoked a pipe in the door, all day long; she didn't work any more. They said she was Jesus' mother. Sometimes she said she was and sometimes she said she wasn't any kin to Jesus.

"Yes, you did," Caddy said. "You were scairder than Frony. You were scairder than T.P. even. Scairder than niggers."

"Cant nobody do nothing with him," Nancy said. "He say I done woke up the devil in him and aint but one thing going to lay it down again."

"Well, he's gone now," father said. "There's nothing for you to be afraid of now. And if you'd just let white men alone."

"Let what white men alone?" Caddy said. "How let them alone?"

"He aint gone nowhere," Nancy said. "I can feel him. I can feel him now, in this lane. He hearing us talk, every word, hid somewhere, waiting. I aint seen him, and I aint going to see him again but once more, with that razor in his mouth. That razor on that string down his back, inside his shirt. And then I aint going to be even surprised."

"I wasn't scaired," Jason said.

"If you'd behave yourself, you'd have kept out of this," father said. "But it's all right now. He's probably in St. Louis now. Probably got another wife by now and forgot all about you."

"If he has, I better not find out about it," Nancy said. "I'd stand there right over them, and every time he wropped her, I'd cut that arm off. I'd cut his head off and I'd slit her belly and I'd shove —"

"Hush," father said.

"Slit whose belly, Nancy?" Caddy said.

"I wasn't scaired," Jason said. "I'd walk right down this lane by myself."

"Yah," Caddy said. "You wouldn't dare to put your foot down in it if we were not here too."

II

Dilsey was still sick, so we took Nancy home every night until mother said, "How much longer is this going on? I to be left alone in this big house while you take home a frightened Negro?"

We fixed a pallet in the kitchen for Nancy. One night we waked up, hearing the sound. It was not singing and it was not crying, coming up the dark stairs. There was a light in mother's room and we heard father going down the hall, down the back stairs, and Caddy and I went into the hall. The floor was cold. Our toes curled away from it while we listened to the sound. It was like singing and it wasn't like singing, like the sounds that Negroes make.

Then it stopped and we heard father going down the back stairs, and we went to the head of the stairs. Then the sound began again, in the stairway, not loud, and we could see Nancy's eyes halfway up the stairs, against the wall. They looked like cat's eyes do, like a big cat against the wall, watching us.

When we came down the steps to where she was, she quit making the sound again, and we stood there until father came back up from the kitchen, with his pistol in his hand. He went back down with Nancy and they came back with Nancy's pallet.

We spread the pallet in our room. After the light in mother's room went off, we could see Nancy's eyes again. "Nancy," Caddy whispered, "are you asleep, Nancy?"

Nancy whispered something. It was oh or no, I dont know which. Like nobody had made it, like it came from nowhere and went nowhere, until it was like Nancy was not there at all; that I had looked so hard at her eyes on the stairs that they had got printed on my eyeballs, like the sun does when you have closed your eyes and there is no sun. "Jesus," Nancy whispered. "Jesus."

"Was it Jesus?" Caddy said. "Did he try to come into the kitchen?"

"Jesus," Nancy said. Like this: Jeeeeeeeeeeeeeeesus, until the sound went out, like a match or a candle does.

"It's the other Jesus she means," I said.

"Can you see us, Nancy?" Caddy whispered. "Can you see our eyes too?"

"I aint nothing but a nigger," Nancy said. "God knows. God knows."

"What did you see down there in the kitchen?" Caddy whispered. "What tried to get in?"

"God knows," Nancy said. We could see her eyes. "God knows."

Dilsey got well. She cooked dinner. "You'd better stay in bed a day or two longer," father said.

"What for?" Dilsey said. "If I had been a day later, this place would be to rack and ruin. Get on out of here now, and let me get my kitchen straight again."

Dilsey cooked supper too. And that night, just before dark, Nancy came into the kitchen.

"How do you know he's back?" Dilsey said. "You aint seen him."

"Jesus is a nigger," Jason said.

"I can feel him," Nancy said. "I can feel him laying yonder in the ditch."

"Tonight?" Dilsey said. "Is he there tonight?"

"Dilsey's a nigger too," Jason said.

"You try to eat something," Dilsey said.

"I dont want nothing," Nancy said.

"I aint a nigger," Jason said.

"Drink some coffee," Dilsey said. She poured a cup of coffee for Nancy. "Do you know he's out there tonight? How come you know it's tonight?"

"I know," Nancy said. "He's there, waiting. I know. I done lived with him too long. I know what he is fixing to do fore he know it himself."

"Drink some coffee," Dilsey said. Nancy held the cup to her mouth and blew into the cup. Her mouth pursed out like a spreading adder's, like a rubber mouth, like she had blown all the color out of her lips with blowing the coffee.

"I aint a nigger," Jason said. "Are you a nigger, Nancy?"

"I hellborn, child," Nancy said. "I wont be nothing soon. I going back where I come from soon."

III

She began to drink the coffee. While she was drinking, holding the cup in both hands, she began to make the sound again. She made the sound into the cup and the coffee splashed out onto her hands and her dress. Her eyes looked at us and she sat there, her elbows on her knees, holding the cup in both hands, looking at us across the wet cup, making the sound. "Look at Nancy," Jason said. "Nancy cant cook for us now. Dilsey's got well now."

"You hush up," Dilsey said. Nancy held the cup in both hands, looking at us, making the sound, like there were two of them: one looking at us and the other making the sound. "Whyn't you let Mr Jason telefoam the marshal?" Dilsey said. Nancy stopped then, holding the cup in her long brown hands. She tried to drink some coffee again, but it splashed out of the cup, onto her hands and her dress, and she put the cup down. Jason watched her.

"I cant swallow it," Nancy said. "I swallows but it wont go down me."

"You go down to the cabin," Dilsey said. "Frony will fix you a pallet and I'll be there soon."

"Wont no nigger stop him," Nancy said.

"I aint a nigger," Jason said. "Am I, Dilsey?"

"I reckon not," Dilsey said. She looked at Nancy. "I dont reckon so. What you going to do, then?"

Nancy looked at us. Her eyes went fast, like she was afraid there wasn't time to look, without hardly moving at all. She looked at us, at all three of us at one time. "You member that night I stayed in yawls' room?" she said. She told about how we waked up early the next morning, and played. We had to play quiet, on her pallet, until father woke up and it was time to get breakfast. "Go and ask your maw to let me stay here tonight," Nancy said. "I wont need no pallet. We can play some more."

Caddy asked mother. Jason went too. "I cant have Negroes sleeping in the bedrooms," mother said. Jason cried. He cried until mother said he couldn't have any dessert for three days if he didn't stop. Then Jason said he would stop if Dilsey would make a chocolate cake. Father was there.

"Why dont you do something about it?" mother said. "What do we have officers for?"

"Why is Nancy afraid of Jesus?" Caddy said. "Are you afraid of father, mother?"

"What could the officers do?" father said. "If Nancy hasn't seen him, how could the officers find him?"

"Then why is she afraid?" mother said.

"She says he is there. She says she knows he is there tonight."

"Yet we pay taxes," mother said. "I must wait here alone in this big house while you take a Negro woman home."

"You know that I am not lying outside with a razor," father said.

"I'll stop if Dilsey will make a chocolate cake," Jason said. Mother told us to go out and father said he didn't know if Jason would get a chocolate cake or not, but he knew what Jason was going to get in about a minute. We went back to the kitchen and told Nancy.

"Father said for you to go home and lock the door, and you'll be all right," Caddy said. "All right from what, Nancy? Is Jesus mad at you?" Nancy was holding the coffee cup in her hands again, her elbows on her knees and her hands holding the cup between her knees. She was looking into the cup. "What have you done that made Jesus mad?" Caddy said. Nancy let the cup go. It didn't break on the floor, but the coffee spilled out, and Nancy sat there with her hands still making the shape of the cup. She began to make the sound again, not loud. Not singing and not unsinging. We watched her.

"Here," Dilsey said. "You quit that, now. You get aholt of yourself. You wait here. I going to get Versh to walk home with you." Dilsey went out.

We looked at Nancy. Her shoulders kept shaking, but she quit making the sound. We watched her. "What's Jesus going to do to you?" Caddy said. "He went away."

Nancy looked at us. "We had fun that night I stayed in yawls' room, didn't we?"

"I didn't," Jason said. "I didn't have any fun."

"You were asleep in mother's room," Caddy said. "You were not there."

"Let's go down to my house and have some more fun," Nancy said.

"Mother wont let us," I said. "It's too late now."

"Dont bother her," Nancy said. "We can tell her in the morning. She wont mind."

"She wouldn't let us," I said.

"Dont ask her now," Nancy said. "Dont bother her now."

"She didn't say we couldn't go," Caddy said.

"We didn't ask," I said.

"If you go, I'll tell," Jason said.

"We'll have fun," Nancy said. "They won't mind, just to my house. I been working for yawl a long time. They won't mind."

"I'm not afraid to go," Caddy said. "Jason is the one that's afraid. He'll tell."

"I'm not," Jason said.

"Yes, you are," Caddy said. "You'll tell."

"I won't tell," Jason said. "I'm not afraid."

"Jason ain't afraid to go with me," Nancy said. "Is you, Jason?"

"Jason is going to tell," Caddy said. The lane was dark. We passed the pasture gate. "I bet if something was to jump out from behind that gate, Jason would holler."

"I wouldn't," Jason said. We walked down the lane. Nancy was talking loud.

"What are you talking so loud for, Nancy?" Caddy said.

"Who; me?" Nancy said. "Listen at Quentin and Caddy and Jason saying I'm talking loud."

"You talk like there was five of us here," Caddy said. "You talk like father was here too."

"Who; me talking loud, Mr Jason?" Nancy said.

"Nancy called Jason 'Mister,' " Caddy said.

"Listen how Caddy and Quentin and Jason talk," Nancy said.

"We're not talking loud," Caddy said. "You're the one that's talking like father —"

"Hush," Nancy said; "hush, Mr Jason."

"Nancy called Jason 'Mister' aguh —"

"Hush," Nancy said. She was talking loud when we crossed the ditch and stooped through the fence where she used to stoop through with the clothes on her head. Then we came to her house. We were going fast then. She opened the door. The smell of the house was like the lamp and the smell of Nancy was like the wick, like they were waiting for one another to begin to smell. She lit the lamp and closed the door and put the bar up. Then she quit talking loud, looking at us.

"What're we going to do?" Caddy said.

"What do yawl want to do?" Nancy said.

"You said we would have some fun," Caddy said.

There was something about Nancy's house; something you could smell besides Nancy and the house. Jason smelled it, even. "I don't want to stay here," he said. "I want to go home."

"Go home, then," Caddy said.

"I don't want to go by myself," Jason said.

"We're going to have some fun," Nancy said.

"How?" Caddy said.

Nancy stood by the door. She was looking at us, only it was like she had emptied her eyes, like she had quit using them. "What do you want to do?" she said.

"Tell us a story," Caddy said. "Can you tell a story?"

"Yes," Nancy said.

"Tell it," Caddy said. We looked at Nancy. "You don't know any stories."

"Yes," Nancy said. "Yes, I do."

She came and sat in a chair before the hearth. There was a little fire there. Nancy built it up, when it was already hot inside. She built a good blaze. She told a story. She talked like her eyes looked, like her eyes watching us and her voice talking to us did not belong to her. Like she was living somewhere else, waiting somewhere else. She was outside the cabin. Her voice was inside and the shape of her, the Nancy that could stoop under a barbed wire fence with a bundle of clothes balanced on her head as though without weight, like a balloon, was there. But that was all. "And so this here queen come walking up to the ditch, where that bad man was hiding. She was walking up to the ditch, and she say, 'If I can just get past this here ditch,' was what she say . . ."

"What ditch?" Caddy said. "A ditch like that one out there? Why did a queen want to go into a ditch?"

"To get to her house," Nancy said. She looked at us. "She had to cross the ditch to get into her house quick and bar the door."

"Why did she want to go home and bar the door?" Caddy said.

IV

Nancy looked at us. She quit talking. She looked at us. Jason's legs stuck straight out of his pants where he sat on Nancy's lap. "I don't think that's a good story," he said. "I want to go home."

"Maybe we had better," Caddy said. She got up from the floor. "I bet they are looking for us right now." She went toward the door.

"No," Nancy said. "Don't open it." She got up quick and passed Caddy. She didn't touch the door, the wooden bar.

"Why not?" Caddy said.

"Come back to the lamp," Nancy said. "We'll have fun. You don't have to go."

"We ought to go," Caddy said. "Unless we have a lot of fun." She and Nancy came back to the fire, the lamp.

"I want to go home," Jason said. "I'm going to tell."

"I know another story," Nancy said. She stood close to the lamp. She looked at Caddy, like when your eyes look up at a stick balanced on your nose. She had to look down to see Caddy, but her eyes looked like that, like when you are balancing a stick.

"I won't listen to it," Jason said. "I'll bang on the floor."

"It's a good one," Nancy said. "It's better than the other one."

"What's it about?" Caddy said. Nancy was standing by the lamp. Her hand was on the lamp, against the light, long and brown.

"Your hand is on that hot globe," Caddy said. "Don't it feel hot to your hand?"

Nancy looked at her hand on the lamp chimney. She took her hand away, slow. She stood there, looking at Caddy, wringing her long hand as though it were tied to her wrist with a string.

"Let's do something else," Caddy said.

"I want to go home," Jason said.

"I got some popcorn," Nancy said. She looked at Caddy and then at Jason and then at me and then at Caddy again. "I got some popcorn."

"I don't like popcorn," Jason said. "I'd rather have candy."

Nancy looked at Jason. "You can hold the popper." She was still wringing her hand; it was long and limp and brown.

"All right," Jason said. "I'll stay a while if I can do that. Caddy can't hold it. I'll want to go home again if Caddy holds the popper."

Nancy built up the fire. "Look at Nancy putting her hands in the fire," Caddy said. "What's the matter with you, Nancy?"

"I got popcorn," Nancy said. "I got some." She took the popper from under the bed. It was broken. Jason began to cry.

"Now we can't have any popcorn," he said.

"We ought to go home, anyway," Caddy said. "Come on, Quentin."

"Wait," Nancy said; "wait. I can fix it. Don't you want to help me fix it?"

"I don't think I want any," Caddy said. "It's too late now."

"You help me, Jason," Nancy said. "Don't you want to help me?"

"No," Jason said. "I want to go home."

"Hush," Nancy said; "hush. Watch. Watch me. I can fix it so Jason can hold it and pop the corn." She got a piece of wire and fixed the popper.

"It won't hold good," Caddy said.

"Yes, it will," Nancy said. "Yawl watch. Yawl help me shell some corn."

The popcorn was under the bed too. We shelled it into the popper and Nancy helped Jason hold the popper over the fire.

"It's not popping," Jason said. "I want to go home."

"You wait," Nancy said. "It'll begin to pop. We'll have fun then." She was sitting close to the fire. The lamp was turned up so high it was beginning to smoke.

"Why don't you turn it down some?" I said.

"It's all right," Nancy said. "I'll clean it. Yawl wait. The popcorn will start in a minute."

"I don't believe it's going to start," Caddy said. "We ought to start home, anyway. They'll be worried."

"No," Nancy said. "It's going to pop. Dilsey will tell um yawl with me. I been working for yawl long time. They won't mind if yawl at my house. You wait, now. It'll start popping any minute now."

Then Jason got some smoke in his eyes and he began to cry. He dropped the popper into the fire. Nancy got a wet rag and wiped Jason's face, but he didn't stop crying.

"Hush," she said. "Hush." But he didn't hush. Caddy took the popper out of the fire.

"It's burned up," she said. "You'll have to get some more popcorn, Nancy."

"Did you put all of it in?" Nancy said.

"Yes," Caddy said. Nancy looked at Caddy. Then she took the popper and opened it and poured the cinders into her apron and began to sort the grains, her hands long and brown, and we watching her.

"Haven't you got any more?" Caddy said.

"Yes," Nancy said; "yes. Look. This here ain't burnt. All we need to do is —"

"I want to go home," Jason said. "I'm going to tell."

"Hush," Caddy said. We all listened. Nancy's head was already turned toward the barred door, her eyes filled with red lamplight. "Somebody is coming," Caddy said.

Then Nancy began to make that sound again, not loud, sitting there above the fire, her long hands dangling between her knees; all of a sudden water began to come out on her face in big drops, running down her face, carrying in each one a little turning ball of firelight like a spark until it dropped off her chin. "She's not crying," I said.

"I ain't crying," Nancy said. Her eyes were closed. "I ain't crying. Who is it?"

"I don't know," Caddy said. She went to the door and looked out. "We've got to go now," she said. "Here comes father."

"I'm going to tell," Jason said. "Yawl made me come."

The water still ran down Nancy's face. She turned in her chair. "Listen. Tell him. Tell him we going to have fun. Tell him I take good care of yawl until in the morning. Tell him to let me come home with yawl and sleep on the floor. Tell him I won't need no pallet. We'll have fun. You member last time how we had so much fun?"

"I didn't have fun," Jason said. "You hurt me. You put smoke in my eyes. I'm going to tell."

V

Father came in. He looked at us. Nancy did not get up.

"Tell him," she said.

"Caddy made us come down here," Jason said. "I didn't want to."

Father came to the fire. Nancy looked up at him. "Can't you go to Aunt Rachel's and stay?" he said. Nancy looked up at father, her hands between her knees. "He's not here," father said. "I would have seen him. There's not a soul in sight."

"He in the ditch," Nancy said. "He waiting in the ditch yonder."

"Nonsense," father said. He looked at Nancy. "Do you know he's there?"

"I got the sign," Nancy said.

"What sign?"

"I got it. It was on the table when I come in. It was a hogbone, with blood meat still on it, laying by the lamp. He's out there. When yawl walk out that door, I gone."

"Gone where, Nancy?" Caddy said.

"I'm not a tattletale," Jason said.

"Nonsense," father said.

"He out there," Nancy said. "He looking through that window this minute, waiting for yawl to go. Then I gone."

"Nonsense," father said. "Lock up your house and we'll take you on to Aunt Rachel's."

" 'Twont do no good," Nancy said. She didn't look at father now, but he looked down at her, at her long, limp, moving hands. "Putting it off wont do no good."

"Then what do you want to do?" father said.

"I don't know," Nancy said. "I can't do nothing. Just put it off. And that don't do no good. I reckon it belong to me. I reckon what I going to get ain't no more than mine."

"Get what?" Caddy said. "What's yours?"

"Nothing," father said. "You all must get to bed."

"Caddy made me come," Jason said.

"Go on to Aunt Rachel's," father said.

"It won't do no good," Nancy said. She sat before the fire, her elbows on her knees, her long hands between her knees. "When even your own kitchen wouldn't do no good. When even if I was sleeping on the floor in the room with your chillen, and the next morning there I am, and blood —"

"Hush," father said. "Lock the door and put out the lamp and go to bed."

"I scared of the dark," Nancy said. "I scared for it to happen in the dark."

"You mean you're going to sit right here with the lamp lighted?" father said. Then Nancy began to make the sound again, sitting before the fire, her long hands between her knees. "Ah, damnation," father said. "Come along, chillen. It's past bedtime."

"When yawl go home, I gone," Nancy said. She talked quieter now, and her face looked quiet, like her hands. "Anyway, I got my coffin money saved up with Mr. Lovelady." Mr. Lovelady was a short, dirty man who collected the Negro insurance, coming around to the cabins or the kitchens every Saturday morning, to collect fifteen cents. He and his wife lived at the hotel. One morning his wife committed suicide. They had a child, a little girl. He and the child went away. After a week or two he came back alone. We would see him going along the lanes and the back streets on Saturday mornings.

"Nonsense," father said. "You'll be the first thing I'll see in the kitchen tomorrow morning."

"You'll see what you'll see, I reckon," Nancy said. "But it will take the Lord to say what that will be."

VI

"Come and put the bar up," father said. But she didn't move. She didn't look at us again, sitting quietly there between the lamp and the fire. From some distance down the lane we could look back and see her through the open door.

"What, Father?" Caddy said. "What's going to happen?"

"Nothing," father said. Jason was on father's back, so Jason was the tallest of all of us. We went down into the ditch. I looked at it, quiet. I couldn't see much where the moonlight and the shadows tangled.

"If Jesus is hid here, he can see us, cant he?" Caddy said.

"He's not there," father said. "He went away a long time ago."

"You made me come," Jason said, high; against the sky it looked like father had two heads, a little one and a big one. "I didn't want to."

We went up out of the ditch. We could still see Nancy's house and the open door, but we couldn't see Nancy now, sitting before the fire with the door open, because she was tired. "I just done got tired," she said. "I just a nigger. It ain't no fault of mine."

But we could hear her, because she began just after we came up out of the ditch, the sound that was not singing and not unsinging. "Who will do our washing now, Father?" I said.

"I'm not a nigger," Jason said, high and close above father's head.

"You're worse," Caddy said, "you are a tattletale. If something was to jump out, you'd be scairder than a nigger."

"I wouldn't," Jason said.

"You'd cry," Caddy said.

"Caddy," father said.

"I wouldn't!" Jason said.

"Scairy cat," Caddy said.

"Candace!" father said.

❧

MARY GAITSKILL *(b. 1954) was born in Lexington, Kentucky, the daughter of a teacher and a social worker. She had what she describes as a difficult adolescence, running away from home at sixteen to become a stripper and spending time in mental institutions. She has said that*

> *this background is of limited relevance to my writing except for one thing: my experience of life as essentially unhappy and uncontrollable taught me to examine the way people, including myself, create survival systems and psychological "safe" places for themselves in unorthodox and sometimes apparently self-defeating ways. These inner worlds, although often unworkable and unattractive in social terms, can have a unique beauty and courage.*

In 1981 Gaitskill graduated from the University of Michigan, where she won an award for her collection of short fiction The Woman Who Knew Judo and Other Stories. *Seven years later she published her first book of stories,* Bad Behavior, *with Poseidon Press. The critic Martin Waxman wrote in the Toronto* Globe and Mail *that her self-destructive characters are "outsiders whose behavior is 'bad' in that it is different . . . unexpected."*

In 1991 Gaitskill published her first novel, Two Girls Fat and Thin, *in which she continued to develop what she called her characters' "confusion of violation with closeness." Her fiction often explores the theme of how people seek intimacy but don't know how to achieve it, as in her story "Tiny, Smiling Daddy," from her second collection,* Because They Wanted To *(1997), which won the 1998 PEN/Faulkner Award.*

MARY GAITSKILL

Tiny, Smiling Daddy

1997

The phone rang five times before he got up to answer it. It was his friend Norm. They greeted each other and then Norm, his voice strangely weighted, said, "I saw the issue of *Self* with Kitty in it."

He waited for an explanation. None came so he said, "What? Issue of *Self*? What's *Self*?"

"Good grief, Stew, I thought for sure you'd of seen it. Now I feel awkward."

"So do I. Do you want to tell me what this is about?"

"My daughter's got a subscription to this magazine, *Self.* And they printed an article that Kitty wrote about fathers and daughters talking to each other, and she well, she wrote about you. Laurel showed it to me."

"My God."

"It's ridiculous that I'm the one to tell you. I just thought —"

"It was bad?"

"No. No, she didn't say anything bad. I just didn't understand the whole idea of it. And I wondered what you thought."

He got off the phone and walked back into the living room, shocked. His daughter Kitty was living in South Carolina working in a record store and making pots, vases, and statuettes which she sold on commission. She had never written anything that he knew of, yet she'd apparently published an article in a national magazine about him without telling him. He lifted his arms and put them on the window sill; the air from the open window cooled his underarms. Outside, the Starlings' tiny dog marched officiously up and down the pavement, looking for someone to bark at. Maybe she had written an article about how wonderful he was, and she was too shy to show him right away. This was doubtful. Kitty was quiet but she wasn't shy. She was untactful and she could be aggressive. Uncertainty only made her doubly aggressive.

He turned the edge of one nostril over with his thumb and nervously stroked his nose-hairs with one finger. He knew it was a nasty habit but it soothed him. When Kitty was a little girl he would do it to make her laugh: "Well," he'd say, "do you think it's time we played with the hairs in our nose?" And she would giggle, holding her hands against her face, eyes sparkling over her knuckles.

Then she was fourteen, and as scornful and rejecting as any girl he had ever thrown a spitball at when he was that age. They didn't get along so well any more. Once, they were sitting in the rec room watching TV, he on the couch, she on the footstool. There was a Charlie Chan movie on TV, but he was mostly watching her back and her long, thick brown hair, which she had just washed and was brushing. She dropped her head forward from the neck to let the hair fall between her spread legs, and began slowly stroking it with a pink nylon brush.

"Say, don't you think it's time we played with the hairs in our nose?"

No reaction from bent back and hair.

"Who wants to play with the hairs in their nose?"

Nothing.

"Hairs in the nose, hairs in the nose," he sang.

She bolted violently up from the stool. "You are so gross you disgust me!" She stormed from the room, shoulders in a tailored jacket of indignation.

Sometimes he said it just to see her exasperation, to feel the adorable, futile outrage of her violated girl delicacy.

He wished that his wife would come home with the car so that he could drive to the store and buy a copy of *Self.* His car was being repaired and he could not walk to the little cluster of stores and parking lots that constituted "town" in this heat. It would take a good twenty minutes and he would be completely worn out when he got there. He would find the magazine and stand there in the drugstore and read it and if it was something bad, he might not have the strength to walk back.

He went into the kitchen, opened a beer and brought it into the living room. His wife had been gone for over an hour, and God knows how much longer she would be. She could spend literally all day driving around the county doing nothing but buying a jar of honey or a bag of apples. Of course, he could call Kitty, but he'd probably just get her answering machine, and besides, he didn't want to talk to her before he understood the situation. He felt helplessness move through his body like a swimmer feels a large sea creature pass beneath him. How could she have done this to him? She knew how he dreaded exposure of any kind, she knew the way he guarded himself against strangers, the way he carefully drew all the curtains when twilight approached so that no one could see them walking through the house. She knew how ashamed he had been when, at sixteen, she had announced that she was lesbian.

The Starling dog was now across the street, yapping at the heels of a bow-legged old lady in a blue dress who was trying to walk down the street. "Dammit," he said. He left the window and got the afternoon opera station on the radio. They were in the final act of *La Bohème.*

He did not remember precisely when it had happened, but Kitty, his beautiful, happy little girl, turned into a glum, weird teenager that other kids picked on. She got skinny and ugly. Her blue eyes, which had been so sensitive and bright, turned filmy, as if the real Kitty had retreated so far from the surface that her eyes existed to shield rather than reflect her. It was as if she deliberately held her beauty away from them, only showing glimpses of it during unavoidable lapses, like the time she sat before the TV, daydreaming and lazily brushing her hair. At moments like this, her dormant charm broke his heart. It also annoyed him. What did she have to retreat from? They had both loved her. When she was little, and she couldn't sleep at night, Marsha would sit with her in bed for hours. She praised her stories and her drawings as if she were a genius. When Kitty was seven, she and her mother had special times, during which they went off together and talked about whatever Kitty wanted to talk about.

He tried to compare the sullen, morbid Kitty of sixteen with the slender, self-possessed twenty-eight-year-old lesbian who wrote articles for *Self.* He pictured himself in court, waving a copy of *Self* before a shocked jury. The case would be taken up by the press. He saw the headlines: Dad Sues Mag — Dyke Daughter Reveals . . . reveals what? What had Kitty found to say about him that was of interest to the entire country that she didn't want him to know about?

Anger overrode his helplessness. Kitty could be vicious. He hadn't seen her vicious side in years, but he knew it was there. He remembered the time he'd stood behind the half-open front door when fifteen-year-old Kitty sat hunched on the front steps with one of her few friends, a homely blond who wore white lipstick and a white leather jacket. He had come to the door to view the weather and say something to the girls, but they were muttering so intently that curiosity got the better of him, and he hung back a moment to listen. "Well, at least your mom's smart," said Kitty. "My mom's not only a bitch, she's stupid."

This after the lullabies and special times! It wasn't just an isolated incident either; every time he'd come home from work, his wife had something bad to say about Kitty. She hadn't set the table until she had been asked four times. She'd gone to Lois's house instead of coming straight home like she'd been told to do. She'd worn a dress to school that was short enough to show the tops of her panty hose.

By the time Kitty came to dinner, looking as if she'd been doing slave labor all day, he would be mad at her. He couldn't help it. Here was his wife doing her damnedest to raise a family and cook dinner and here was this awful kid looking ugly, acting mean and not setting the table. It seemed unreasonable that she should turn out so badly after taking up so much time. Her afflicted expression made him angry too. What had anybody ever done to her?

He sat forward and gently gnawed the insides of his mouth as he listened to the dying girl in *La Bohème.* He saw his wife's car pull into the driveway. He walked to the back door, almost wringing his hands, and waited for her to come through the door. When she did, he snatched the grocery bag from her arms and said, "Give me the keys." She stood open-mouthed in the stairwell, looking at him with idiotic consternation. "Give me the keys!"

"What is it, Stew? What's happened?"

"I'll tell you when I get back."

He got in the car and became part of it, this panting, mobile case propelling him through the incredibly complex and fast-moving world of other people, their houses, their children, their dogs, their lives. He wasn't usually so aware of this unpleasant sense of disconnection between him and everyone else, but he had the feeling that it had been there all along, underneath what he thought of most of the time. It was ironic that it should rear up so visibly at a time when there was in fact a mundane yet invasive and horribly real connection between him and everyone else in Wayne County: the hundreds of copies of *Self* magazine sitting in countless drugstores, bookstores, groceries, and libraries. It was as if there was a tentacle plugged into the side of the car, linking him with the random humans who picked up the magazine, possibly his very neighbors. He stopped at a crowded intersection, feeling like an ant in an enemy swarm.

Kitty had projected herself out of the house and into this swarm very early, ostensibly because life with him and Marsha had been so awful. Well, it had been awful, but because of Kitty, not them. As if it wasn't enough to be sullen and dull, she turned into a lesbian. Kids followed her down the street jeering at her. Somebody dropped her books in a toilet. She got into a fistfight. Their neighbors gave them looks. This reaction seemed only to steel Kitty's grip on her new identity; it made her romanticize herself like the kid she was. She wrote poems about heroic women warriors, she brought home strange books and magazines which, among other things, seemed to glorify prostitutes. Marsha looked for them and threw them away. Kitty screamed at her, the tendons leaping out on her slender neck. He hit Kitty, Marsha tried to stop him and he yelled at her. Kitty leapt between them, as if to defend her mother. He grabbed her and shook her but he could not shake the conviction off her face.

Most of the time though, they continued as always, eating dinner together, watching TV, making jokes. That was the worse thing; he would look at Kitty and see his daughter, now familiar in her withdrawn sullenness, and feel comfort and affection. Then he would remember that she was a lesbian and a morass of complication and wrongness would come down between them, making it impossible for him to see her. Then she would be just Kitty again. He hated it.

She ran away at sixteen and the police found her in the apartment of an eighteen-year-old body builder named Dolores who had a naked woman tattooed on her sinister bicep. Marsha made them put her in a mental hospital so psychiatrists could observe her, but he hated the psychiatrists — mean, supercilious sons of bitches who delighted in the trick question — so he took her back out. She finished school and they told her if she wanted to leave it was all right with them. She didn't waste any time getting out of the house.

She moved into an apartment near Detroit with a girl named George and took a job at a home for retarded kids. She would appear for visits with a huge bag of laundry every few weeks. She was thin and neurotically muscular, her body having the look of a fighting dog on a leash. She wore her hair like a boy's and wore black sunglasses, black leather half-gloves and leather belts. The only remnant of her beauty was her erect martial carriage and her efficient movements; she walked through a room like the commander of a guerrilla force. She would sit at the dining room table with Marsha, drinking tea and having a laconic verbal conversation, her body speaking its precise martial language while the washing machine droned from the utility room and he wandered in and out trying to make sense of what she said. Sometimes she would stay into the evening to eat dinner and watch *All in the Family.* Then Marsha would send her home with a jar of homemade tapioca pudding or a bag of apples and oranges.

One day instead of a visit they got a letter postmarked San Francisco. She had left George, she said. She listed strange details about her current environment and was vague about how she was supporting herself. He had nightmares about Kitty, with her brave, proudly muscular little body, lost among big fleshy women who danced naked in go-go bars and took drugs with needles, terrible women who his confused romantic daughter invested with oppressed heroism and intensely female glamour. He got up at night and stumbled into the bathroom for stomach medicine, the familiar darkness of the house heavy with menacing images that pressed about him, images that he saw reflected in his own expression when he turned on the bathroom light over the mirror.

Then one year she came home for Christmas. She came into the house with her luggage and a shopping bag of gifts for them and he saw that she was beautiful again. It was a beauty that both offended and titillated his senses. Her short spiky hair was streaked with purple, her dainty mouth was lipsticked, her nose and ears were pierced with amethyst and dangling silver. Her face had opened in thousands of petals. Her eyes shone with quick perception as she put down her bag and he knew that she had seen him see her beauty. She moved towards him with fluid hips, she embraced him for the first time in years. He felt her live, lithe body against him and his heart pulsed a message of blood and love. "Merry Christmas, Daddy," she said.

Her voice was husky and coarse, it reeked of knowledge and confidence. Her T-shirt said "Chicks With Balls." She was twenty-two years old.

She stayed for a week, discharging her strange jangling beauty into the house and changing the molecules of its air. She talked about the girls she shared an apartment with, her job at a coffee shop, how Californians were different from Michiganders. She talked about her friends: Lorraine, who was so pretty men fell off their bicycles as they twisted their bodies for a better look at her; Judy, a martial arts expert; and Meredith, who was raising a child with her husband, Angela. She talked of poetry readings, ceramics classes, celebrations of spring.

He realized, as he watched her, that she was now doing things that were as bad as or worse than the things that had made him angry at her five years before, yet they didn't quarrel. It seemed that a large white space existed between him and her, and that it was impossible to enter this space or to argue across it. Besides, she might never come back if he yelled at her.

Instead, he watched her, puzzling at the metamorphosis she had undergone. First she had been a beautiful, happy child turned homely, snotty, miserable adolescent. From there she had become a martinet girl with the eyes of a stifled pervert. Now she was a vibrant imp living, it seemed, in a world constructed of topsy-turvy junk pasted with rhinestones. Where had these three different people come from? Not even Marsha, who had spent so much time with her as a child, could trace the genesis of the new Kitty from the old one. Sometimes he bitterly reflected that he and Marsha weren't even real parents anymore, but bereft old people rattling around in a house, connected not to a real child who was going to college, or who at least had some kind of understandable life, but a changeling who was the product of only their most obscure quirks, a being who came from recesses that neither of them suspected they'd had.

There were only a few cars in the parking lot. He wheeled through it with pointless deliberation before parking near the drugstore. He spent irritating seconds searching for *Self* until he realized that its airbrushed cover girl was grinning right at him. He stormed the table of contents, then headed for the back of the magazine. "Speak Easy" was written sideways across the top of the appointed page in round turquoise letters. At the bottom was his daughter's name in a little box. "Kitty Thorne is a ceramic artist living in South Carolina." His hands were trembling.

It was hard for him to rationally ingest the beginning paragraphs which seemed, incredibly, to be about a phone conversation they'd had some time ago about the emptiness and selfishness of people who have sex but don't get married and have children. A few phrases that stood out clearly: ". . . my father may love me but he doesn't love the way I live." ". . . even more complicated because I'm gay." "Because it still hurts me."

For reasons he didn't understand, he felt a nervous smile tremble under his skin. He suppressed it.

"This hurt has its roots deep in our relationship, starting, I think, when I was a teenager."

He had a horrible sensation of being in public so he paid for the thing and took it out to the car with him. He slowly drove to another spot in the lot, as far away from the drugstore as possible, picked up the magazine, and began again. She described "the terrible difficulties" between him and her. She recounted, briefly and with hieroglyphic politeness, the fighting, the running away, the return, the tacit reconciliation.

"There is an emotional distance that we have both accepted and chosen to work around, hoping the occasional contact — love, anger, something — will get through."

He put the magazine down and looked out the window. It was near dusk; most of the stores in the little mall were closed. There were only two other cars in the parking lot, and a big, slow, frowning woman with two grocery bags was getting ready to drive one away. He was parked before a weedy piece of land at the edge of the parking lot. In it were rough, picky weeds spread out like big green tarantulas, young yellow dandelions, frail old dandelions, and bunches of tough blue chickweed. Even in his distress he vaguely appreciated the beauty of the blue weeds against the cool white and grey sky. For a moment the sound of insects comforted him. Images of Kitty passed through his memory with terrible speed: her nine-year-old forehead bent over her dish of ice cream, her tiny nightgowned form ran up the stairs, her ringed hand brushed her face, the keys on her belt jiggled as she walked her slow blue-jeaned walk away from the house. Gone, all gone.

The article went on to describe how Kitty hung up the phone feeling frustrated and then listed all the things she could've said to him to let him know how hurt she was, paving the way for "real communication," all in ghastly talk-show language. He was unable to put these words together with the Kitty he had last seen lounging around the house. She was twenty-eight now and she no longer dyed her hair or wore jewels in her nose. Her demeanor was serious, bookish, almost old-maidish. Once he'd overheard her talking to Marsha and heard her say, "So then this Italian girl gives me the once-over and says to Joanne, 'You 'ang around with too many Wasp.' And I said, 'I'm not a Wasp, I'm white trash.'"

"Speak for yourself," he'd said.

"If the worst occurred and my father was unable to respond to me in kind, I still would have done a good thing. I would have acknowledged my own needs and created the possibility to connect with what therapists call 'the good parent' in myself."

Well, if that was the kind of thing she was going to say to him, he was relieved she hadn't said it. But if she hadn't said it to him, why was she saying it to the rest of the country?

He turned on the radio. It sang: "Try to remember, and if you remember, then follow, follow." He turned it off. He closed his eyes. When he was nine or ten an uncle of his had told him, "Everybody makes his own world. You see what you want to see and hear what you want to hear. You can do it right now. If you blink ten times and then close your eyes real tight, you can see anything you want to see in front of you." He'd tried it rather half-heartedly and hadn't seen anything but the vague suggestion of a yellowish-white ball moving creepily through the dark. At the time, he'd thought it was perhaps because he hadn't tried hard enough.

He had told Kitty to do the same thing, or something like it, when she was eight or nine. They were on the back porch sitting in striped lawn chairs, holding hands and watching the fire-flies turn off and on.

She closed her eyes for a long time. Then very seriously, she said, "I see big balls of color, like shaggy flowers. They're pink and red and turquoise. I see an island with palm trees and pink rocks. There's dolphins and mermaids swimming in the water around it." He'd been almost awed by her belief in this impossible vision. Then he was sad because she would never see what she wanted to see.

His memory floated back to his boyhood; he was walking down the middle of the street at dusk, sweating lightly after a basketball game. There were crickets and the muted barks of dogs and the low, affirming mumble of people on their front porches. He felt securely held by the warm light and its sounds, he felt an exquisite blend of happiness and sorrow that life could contain this perfect moment, and sadness that he would soon arrive home, walk into bright light and be on his way into the next day, with its loud noise and alarming possibility. He resolved to hold this evening walk in his mind forever, to imprint all the sensations that occurred to him as he walked by the Oatlander's house in a permanent place, so that he could always take it out and look at it. He dimly recalled feeling that if he could successfully do that, he could stop time and hold it.

He knew he had to go home soon. He didn't want to talk about the article with Marsha, but the idea of sitting in the house with her and not talking about it was hard to bear. He imagined the conversation grinding into being, a future conversation with Kitty gestating within it. The conversation was a vast, complex machine like those that occasionally appeared in his dreams; if he could only pull the switch everything would be all right, but he felt too stupefied by the weight and complexity of the thing to do so. Besides, in this case, everything might not be all right. He put the magazine under his seat and started the car.

Marsha was in her armchair reading. She looked up and the expression on her face seemed like the result of internal conflict as complicated and strong as his own, but cross-pulled in different directions, uncomprehending of him and what he knew. In his mind he withdrew from her so quickly that for a moment the familiar room was fraught with the inexplicable horror of a banal nightmare. Then the ordinariness of the scene threw the extraordinary event of the day into relief and he felt so angry and bewildered he could've howled.

"Everything all right, Stew?" asked Marsha.

"No, nothing is all right. I'm a tired old man in a shitty world I don't want to be in. I go out there, it's like walking on knives. Everything is an attack, the ugliness, the cheapness, the rudeness, everything." He sensed her withdrawing from him into her own world of disgruntlement, her lips drawn together in that look of exasperated perseverance she'd gotten from her mother. Like Kitty, like everyone, she was leaving him. "I don't have a real daughter and I don't have a real wife who's here with me because she's too busy running around on some —"

"We've been through this before. We agreed I could —"

"That was different! That was when we had two cars!" His voice tore through his throat in a jagged whiplash and came out a cracked half-scream. "I don't have a car, remember? That means I'm stranded, all alone for hours and Norm Pisarro can just call me up and casually tell me that my lesbian daughter has just betrayed me in a national magazine and what do I think about that?" He wanted to punch the wall until his hand was bloody. He wanted Kitty to see the blood. Marsha's expression broke into soft open-mouthed consternation. The helplessness of it made his anger seem huge and terrible, then impotent and helpless itself. He sat down on the couch and instead of anger felt pain.

"What did Kitty do? What happened? What does Norm have —"

"She wrote an article in *Self* magazine about being a lesbian and her problems and something to do with me. I don't know, I could barely read the crap."

Marsha looked down at her nails.

He looked at her and saw the aged beauty of her ivory skin, sagging under the weight of her years and her cock-eyed bifocals, the emotional receptivity of her face, the dark down on her upper lip, the childish pearl buttons of her sweater, only the top button done.

"I'm surprised at Norm, that he would call you like that."

"Oh, who the hell knows what he thought." His heart was soothed and slowed by her words, even if they didn't address its real unhappiness.

"Here," she said, "let me rub your shoulders."

He allowed her to approach him and they sat sideways on the couch, his weight balanced on the edge by his awkwardly planted legs, she sitting primly on one hip with her legs tightly crossed. The discomfort of the position negated the practical value of the massage, but he welcomed her touch. Marsha had strong, intelligent hands that spoke to his muscles of deep safety and love and delight of physical life. In her effort, she leaned close and her sweatered breast touched him, releasing his tension almost against his will. Through half-closed eyes he observed her sneakers on the floor — he could not quite get over this phenomenon of adult women wearing what had been boys' shoes — in the dim light, one toe atop the other as though cuddling, their laces in pretty disorganization.

Poor Kitty. It hadn't really been so bad that she hadn't set the table on time. He couldn't remember why he and Marsha had been so angry over the table. Unless it was Kitty's coldness, her always turning away, her sarcastic voice. But she was a teenager and that's what teenagers did. Well, it was too bad, but it couldn't be helped now.

He thought of his father. That was too bad too, and nobody was writing articles about that. There had been a distance between them too, so great and so absolute that the word "distance" seemed inadequate to describe it. But that was probably because he had only known his father when he was a very young child; if his father had lived longer, perhaps they would've become closer. He could recall his father's face clearly only at the breakfast table, where it appeared silent and still except for lip and jaw motions, comforting in its constancy. His father ate his oatmeal with one hand working the spoon, one elbow on the table, eyes down, sometimes his other hand holding a cold rag to his head, which always hurt with what seemed to be a noble pain, willingly taken on with his duties as a husband and father. He had loved to stare at the big face with its deep lines and long earlobes, its thin lips and loose, loopily chewing jaws. Its almost godlike stillness and expressionlessness filled him with admiration and reassurance, until one day, his father slowly looked up from his cereal, met his eyes and said, "Stop staring at me, you little shit."

In the other memories, his father was a large, heavy body with a vague oblong face. He saw him sleeping in the armchair in the living room, his large, hairy-knuckled hands grazing the floor. He saw him walking up the front walk with the quick, clipped steps that he always used coming home from work, the straight-backed choppy gait that gave the big body an awesome mechanicalness. His shirt was wet under the arms, his head down, the eyes abstracted but alert, as though keeping careful watch on the outside world in case something nasty came at him, while he attended to the more important business inside.

"The good parent in yourself."

What did the well-meaning idiots who thought of these phrases mean by them? When a father dies, he is gone, there is no tiny, smiling daddy who appears, waving happily, in a secret pocket in your chest. Some kinds of loss are absolute. And no amount of self-realization or self-expression will change that.

As if she heard him, Marsha urgently pressed her weight into her hands and applied all her strength to relaxing his muscles. Her sweat and scented deodorant filtered through her sweater, which added its muted wooliness to her smell. "All righty!" She rubbed his shoulders and briskly patted him. He reached back and touched her hand in thanks.

Across from where they sat had once been a red chair, and in it had once sat Kitty, gripping her face in her hand, her expression mottled by tears. "And if you ever try to come back here I'm going to spit in your face. I don't care if I'm on my deathbed, I'll still have the energy to spit in your face," he had said.

Marsha's hands lingered on him for a moment. Then she moved and sat away from him on the couch.

GABRIEL GARCÍA MÁRQUEZ *(b. 1928) was born in the remote town of Aracataca in Magdalena province, near the Caribbean coast of Colombia. The oldest of twelve children of a poverty-stricken telegraph operator and his wife, he was raised by his maternal grandparents. When he was eight, he was sent to school near Bogotá, and after his graduation in 1946 he studied law. A writer from childhood, García Márquez published his first book,* Leaf Storm and Other Stories, *which includes "A Very Old Man with Enormous Wings," in 1955. He spent the next few years in Paris, where he wrote two short novels. After the Cuban Revolution, he returned to Central America and worked as a journalist and screenwriter. His comic masterpiece, the novel* One Hundred Years of Solitude *(1967), was written while he lived in Mexico City. His other novels include* The Autumn of the Patriarch *(1975), a novel about the life of a*

Latin American dictator, and the best-seller Love in the Time of Cholera *(1988). In 1982 he received the Nobel Prize for literature.*

García Márquez mingles realistic and fantastic details in all his fiction, including "A Very Old Man with Enormous Wings." He has said that the origin of his stories is always an image, "not an idea or a concept. The image grows in my head until the whole story takes shape as it might in real life." Leaf Storm *was written after García Márquez returned from visiting the place where he grew up. As he later explained to an interviewer from the* Paris Review,

> *The atmosphere, the decadence, the heat in the village were roughly the same as what I had felt in Faulkner. It was a banana plantation region inhabited by a lot of Americans from the fruit companies which gave it the same sort of atmosphere I had found in the writers of the Deep South. Critics have spoken of the literary influence of Faulkner but I see it as a coincidence: I had simply found material that had to be dealt with in the same way that Faulkner had treated similar material. . . .*
>
> *What really happened to me in that trip to Aracataca was that I realized that everything that had occurred in my childhood had a literary value that I was only now appreciating. From the moment I wrote* Leaf Storm *I realized I wanted to be a writer and that nobody could stop me and that the only thing left for me to do was to be the best writer in the world.*

Other collections of short fiction by García Márquez are No One Writes to the Colonel and Other Stories *(1968),* Innocent Eréndira and Other Stories *(1978),* Collected Stories *(1984), and* Strange Pilgrims *(1993).*

In 1988 García Márquez coauthored (with Fernando Birri) a screenplay of "A Very Old Man with Enormous Wings" for Television Española. In a scene added to the film version of the story, the old man is revealed as a trickster or confidence man who takes off his wings when he is alone. The film also begins with a quotation from Hebrews 13:2: "Be not forgetful to entertain strangers: for thereby some have entertained angels unaware."

GABRIEL GARCÍA MÁRQUEZ

A Very Old Man with Enormous Wings — *1955*

TRANSLATED BY GREGORY RABASSA

On the third day of rain they had killed so many crabs inside the house that Pelayo had to cross his drenched courtyard and throw them into the sea, because the newborn child had a temperature all night and they thought it was due to the stench. The world had been sad since Tuesday. Sea and sky were a single ash-gray thing and the sands of the beach, which on March nights glimmered like powdered light, had become a stew of mud and rotten shellfish. The light was so weak at noon that when Pelayo was coming back to the house after throwing away the crabs, it was hard for him to see what it was that was moving and groaning in the rear of the courtyard. He had to go very close to see that it was an old man, a very old man, lying face down in the mud, who, in spite of his tremendous efforts, couldn't get up, impeded by his enormous wings.

Frightened by that nightmare, Pelayo ran to get Elisenda, his wife, who was putting compresses on the sick child, and he took her to the rear of the courtyard. They both looked at the fallen body with mute stupor. He was dressed like a ragpicker. There were only a few faded hairs left on his bald skull and very few teeth in his mouth, and his pitiful condition of a drenched great-grandfather had taken away any sense of grandeur he might have had. His huge buzzard wings, dirty and half-plucked, were forever entangled in the mud. They looked at him so long and so closely that Pelayo and Elisenda very soon overcame their surprise and in the end found him familiar. Then they dared speak to him, and he answered in an incomprehensible dialect with a strong sailor's voice. That was how they skipped over the inconvenience of the wings and quite intelligently concluded that he was a lonely castaway from some foreign ship wrecked by the storm. And yet, they called in a neighbor woman who knew everything about life and death to see him, and all she needed was one look to show them their mistake.

"He's an angel," she told them. "He must have been coming for the child, but the poor fellow is so old that the rain knocked him down."

On the following day everyone knew that a flesh-and-blood angel was held captive in Pelayo's house. Against the judgment of the wise neighbor woman, for whom angels in those times were the fugitive survivors of a celestial conspiracy, they did not have the heart to club him to death. Pelayo watched over him all afternoon from the kitchen, armed with his bailiff's club, and before going to bed he dragged him out of the mud and locked him up with the hens in the wire chicken coop. In the middle of the night, when the rain stopped, Pelayo and Elisenda were still killing crabs. A short time afterward the child woke up without a fever and with a desire to eat. Then they felt magnanimous and decided to put the angel on a raft with fresh water and provisions for three days and leave him to his fate on the high seas. But when they went out into the courtyard with the first light of dawn, they found the whole neighborhood in front of the chicken coop having fun with the angel, without the slightest reverence, tossing him things to eat through the openings in the wire as if he weren't a supernatural creature but a circus animal.

Father Gonzaga arrived before seven o'clock, alarmed at the strange news. By that time onlookers less frivolous than those at dawn had already arrived and they were making all kinds of conjectures concerning the captive's future. The simplest among them thought that he should be named mayor of the world. Others of sterner mind felt that he should be promoted to the rank of five-star general in order to win all wars. Some visionaries hoped that he could be put to stud in order to implant on earth a race of winged wise men who could take charge of the universe. But Father Gonzaga, before becoming a priest, had been a robust woodcutter. Standing by the wire, he reviewed his catechism in an instant and asked them to open the door so that he could take a close look at that pitiful man who looked more like a huge decrepit hen among the fascinated chickens. He was lying in a corner drying his open wings in the sunlight among the fruit peels and breakfast leftovers that the early risers had thrown him. Alien to the impertinences of the world, he only lifted his antiquarian eyes and murmured something in his dialect when Father Gonzaga went into the chicken coop and said good morning to him in Latin. The parish priest had his first suspicion of an impostor when he saw that he did not understand the language of God or know how to greet His ministers. Then he noticed that seen close up he was much too human: he had an unbearable smell of the outdoors, the back side of his wings was strewn with parasites and his main feathers had been mistreated by terrestrial winds, and nothing about him measured up to the proud dignity of angels. Then he came out of the chicken coop and in a brief sermon warned the curious against the risks of being ingenuous. He reminded them that the devil had the bad habit of making use of carnival tricks in order to confuse the unwary. He argued that if wings were not the essential element in determining the difference between a hawk and an airplane, they were even less so in the recognition of angels. Nevertheless, he promised to write a letter to his bishop so that the latter would write to his primate so that the latter would write to the Supreme Pontiff in order to get the final verdict from the highest courts.

His prudence fell on sterile hearts. The news of the captive angel spread with such rapidity that after a few hours the courtyard had the bustle of a marketplace and they had to call in troops with fixed bayonets to disperse the mob that was about to knock the house down. Elisenda, her spine all twisted from sweeping up so much marketplace trash, then got the idea of fencing in the yard and charging five cents admission to see the angel.

The curious came from far away. A traveling carnival arrived with a flying acrobat who buzzed over the crowd several times, but no one paid any attention to him because his wings were not those of an angel but, rather, those of a sidereal° bat. The most unfortunate invalids on earth came in search of health: a poor woman who since childhood had been counting her heartbeats and had run out of numbers; a Portuguese man who couldn't sleep because the noise of the stars disturbed him; a sleep-walker who got up at night to undo the things he had done while awake; and many others with less serious ailments. In the midst of that shipwreck disorder that made the earth tremble, Pelayo and Elisenda were happy with fatigue, for in less than a week they had crammed their rooms with money and the line of pilgrims waiting their turn to enter still reached beyond the horizon.

The angel was the only one who took no part in his own act. He spent his time trying to get comfortable in his borrowed nest, befuddled by the hellish heat of the oil lamps and sacramental candles that had been placed along the wire. At first they tried to make him eat some mothballs, which, according to the wisdom of the wise neighbor woman, were the food prescribed for angels. But he turned them down, just as he turned down the papal lunches that the penitents brought him, and they never found out whether it was because he was an angel or because he was an old man that in the end he ate nothing but eggplant mush. His only supernatural virtue seemed to be patience. Especially during the first days, when the hens pecked at him, searching for the stellar parasites that proliferated in his wings, and the cripples pulled out feathers to touch their defective parts with, and even the most merciful threw

---

sidereal: Coming from the stars.

stones at him, trying to get him to rise so they could see him standing. The only time they succeeded in arousing him was when they burned his side with an iron for branding steers, for he had been motionless for so many hours that they thought he was dead. He awoke with a start, ranting in his hermetic language and with tears in his eyes, and he flapped his wings a couple of times, which brought on a whirlwind of chicken dung and lunar dust and a gale of panic that did not seem to be of this world. Although many thought that his reaction had been one not of rage but of pain, from then on they were careful not to annoy him, because the majority understood that his passivity was not that of a hero taking his ease but that of a cataclysm in repose.

Father Gonzaga held back the crowd's frivolity with formulas of maidservant inspiration while awaiting the arrival of a final judgment on the nature of the captive. But the mail from Rome showed no sense of urgency. They spent their time finding out if the prisoner had a navel, if his dialect had any connection with Aramaic, how many times he could fit on the head of a pin, or whether he wasn't just a Norwegian with wings. Those meager letters might have come and gone until the end of time if a providential event had not put an end to the priest's tribulations.

It so happened that during those days, among so many other carnival attractions, there arrived in town the traveling show of the woman who had been changed into a spider for having disobeyed her parents. The admission to see her was not only less than the admission to see the angel, but people were permitted to ask her all manner of questions about her absurd state and to examine her up and down so that no one would ever doubt the truth of her horror. She was a frightful tarantula the size of a ram and with the head of a sad maiden. What was most heart-rending, however, was not her outlandish shape but the sincere affliction with which she recounted the details of her misfortune. While still practically a child she had sneaked out of her parents' house to go to a dance, and while she was coming back through the woods after having danced all night without permission, a fearful thunderclap rent the sky in two and through the crack came the lightning bolt of brimstone that changed her into a spider. Her only nourishment came from the meatballs that charitable souls chose to toss into her mouth. A spectacle like that, full of so much human truth and with such a fearful lesson, was bound to defeat without even trying that of a haughty angel who scarcely deigned to look at mortals. Besides, the few miracles attributed to the angel showed a certain mental disorder, like the blind man who didn't recover his sight but grew three new teeth, or the paralytic who didn't get to walk but almost won the lottery, and the leper whose sores sprouted sunflowers. Those consolation miracles, which were more like mocking fun, had already ruined the angel's reputation when the woman who had been changed into a spider finally crushed him completely. That was how Father Gonzaga was cured forever of his insomnia and Pelayo's courtyard went back to being as empty as during the time it had rained for three days and crabs walked through the bedrooms.

The owners of the house had no reason to lament. With the money they saved they built a two-story mansion with balconies and gardens and high netting so that crabs wouldn't get in during the winter, and with iron bars on the windows so that angels wouldn't get in. Pelayo also set up a rabbit warren close to town and gave up his job as bailiff for good, and Elisenda bought some satin pumps with high heels and many dresses of iridescent silk, the kind worn on Sunday by the most desirable women in those times. The chicken coop was the only thing that didn't receive any attention. If they washed it down with creolin and burned tears of myrrh inside it every so often, it was not in homage to the angel but to drive away the dungheap stench that still hung everywhere like a ghost and was turning the new house into an old one. At first, when the child learned to walk, they were careful that he not get too close to the chicken coop. But then they began to lose their fears and got used to the smell, and before the child got his second teeth he'd gone inside the chicken coop to play, where the wires were falling apart. The angel was no less standoffish with him than with other mortals, but he tolerated the most ingenious infamies with the patience of a dog who had no illusions. They both came down with chicken pox at the same time. The doctor who took care of the child couldn't resist the temptation to listen to the angel's heart, and he found so much whistling in the heart and so many sounds in his kidneys that it seemed impossible for him to be alive. What surprised him most, however, was the logic of his wings. They seemed so natural on that completely human organism that he couldn't understand why other men didn't have them too.

When the child began school it had been some time since the sun and rain had caused the collapse of the chicken coop. The angel went dragging himself about here and there like a stray dying man. They would drive him out of the bedroom with a broom and a moment later find him in the kitchen. He seemed to be in so many places at the same time that they grew to think that he'd been duplicated, that he was reproducing himself all through the house, and the exasperated and unhinged Elisenda shouted that it was awful living in that hell full of angels. He could scarcely eat and his antiquarian eyes had also become so foggy that he went about bumping into posts. All he had left were the bare cannulae° of his last feathers. Pelayo threw a blanket over him and extended him the charity of letting him sleep in the shed, and only then did they notice that he had a temperature at night, and was delirious with the tongue twisters of an old Norwegian. That was one of the few times they became alarmed, for they thought he was going to die and not even the wise neighbor woman had been able to tell them what to do with dead angels.

And yet he not only survived his worst winter, but seemed improved with the first sunny days. He remained motionless for several days in the farthest corner of the courtyard, where no one would see him, and at the beginning of December some large, stiff feathers began to grow on his wings, the feathers of a scarecrow, which looked more like another misfortune of decrepitude. But he must have known the reason for those changes, for he was quite careful that no one should notice them, that no one should hear the sea

---

cannulae: The tubular pieces by which feathers are attached to a body.

chanteys that he sometimes sang under the stars. One morning Elisenda was cutting some bunches of onions for lunch when a wind that seemed to come from the high seas blew into the kitchen. Then she went to the window and caught the angel in his first attempts at flight. They were so clumsy that his fingernails opened a furrow in the vegetable patch and he was on the point of knocking the shed down with the ungainly flapping that slipped on the light and couldn't get a grip on the air. But he did manage to gain altitude. Elisenda let out a sigh of relief, for herself and for him, when she saw him pass over the last houses, holding himself up in some way with the risky flapping of a senile vulture. She kept watching him even when she was through cutting the onions and she kept on watching until it was no longer possible for her to see him, because then he was no longer an annoyance in her life but an imaginary dot on the horizon of the sea.

CHARLOTTE PERKINS GILMAN *(1860–1935) was born in Hartford, Connecticut. Her father deserted the family shortly after she was born and provided her mother with only meager support. As a teenager Gilman attended the Rhode Island School of Design for a brief period and worked as a commercial artist and teacher. Like her great-aunt Harriet Beecher Stowe, she was concerned at an early age with social injustice and wrote poetry about the hardship of women's lives.*

In 1884 she married the artist Charles Walter Stetson. Suffering extreme depression after the birth of a daughter, she left her husband and moved to California in 1888. They were divorced, and she later married George Houghton Gilman, with whom she lived for thirty-four years. In the 1890s Gilman established her reputation as a lecturer and writer of feminist tracts. Her book Women and Economics *(1898) is considered one of the most important works of the early years of the women's movement in the United States. Gilman's later books —* Concerning Children *(1900),* The Home *(1904), and* Human Work *(1904) — argue that women should be educated to become financially independent; then they could contribute more to the amelioration of systems of justice and the improvement of society. From 1909 to 1917 Gilman published her own journal,* The Forerunner, *for which she wrote voluminously. At the end of her life, suffering from cancer, she committed suicide with chloroform.*

Today Gilman's best-known work is "The Yellow Wallpaper," written around 1890, shortly after her own nervous breakdown. A landmark story in its frank depiction of mental illness, it is part fantasy and part autobiography, an imaginative account of her suffering and treatment by the physician S. Weir Mitchell, who forbade her any activity, especially writing, the thing she most wanted to do. In setting the story Gilman used elements of the conventional gothic romances that were a staple in women's popular fiction — an isolated mansion, a distant but dominating male figure, and a mysterious household — all of which force the heroine into the role of passive victim of circumstances. But Gilman gave her own twist to the form. Using the brief paragraphs and simple sentences of popular fiction, she narrated her story with a clinical precision that avoided the trite language of typical romances.

RELATED COMMENTARIES: *Sandra M. Gilbert and Susan Gubar, "A Feminist Reading of Gilman's 'The Yellow Wallpaper,'" page 681; Charlotte Perkins Gilman, "Undergoing the Cure for Nervous Prostration," page 683.*

Charlotte Perkins Gilman

The Yellow Wallpaper

1892

It is very seldom that mere ordinary people like John and myself secure ancestral halls for the summer.

A colonial mansion, a hereditary estate, I would say a haunted house and reach the height of romantic felicity — but that would be asking too much of fate!

Still I will proudly declare that there is something queer about it.

Else, why should it be let so cheaply? And why have stood so long untenanted?

John laughs at me, of course, but one expects that in marriage.

John is practical in the extreme. He has no patience with faith, an intense horror of superstition, and he scoffs openly at any talk of things not to be felt and seen and put down in figures.

John is a physician, and *perhaps* — (I would not say it to a living soul, of course, but this is dead paper and a great relief to my mind) — *perhaps* that is one reason I do not get well faster.

You see, he does not believe I am sick!

And what can one do?

If a physician of high standing, and one's own husband, assures friends and relatives that there is really nothing the matter with one but temporary nervous depression — a slight hysterical tendency — what is one to do?

My brother is also a physician, and also of high standing, and he says the same thing.

So I take phosphates or phosphites — whichever it is, and tonics, and journeys, and air, and exercise, and am absolutely forbidden to "work" until I am well again.

Personally, I disagree with their ideas.

Personally, I believe that congenial work, with excitement and change, would do me good.

But what is one to do?

I did write for a while in spite of them; but it *does* exhaust me a good deal — having to be so sly about it, or else meet with heavy opposition.

I sometimes fancy that in my condition if I had less opposition and more society and stimulus — but John says the very worst thing I can do is to think about my condition, and I confess it always makes me feel bad.

So I will let it alone and talk about the house.

The most beautiful place! It is quite alone, standing well back from the road, quite three miles from the village. It makes me think of English places that you read about, for there are hedges and walls and gates that lock, and lots of separate little houses for the gardeners and people.

There is a *delicious* garden! I never saw such a garden — large and shady, full of box-bordered paths, and lined with long grape-covered arbors with seats under them.

There were greenhouses, too, but they are all broken now.

There was some legal trouble, I believe, something about the heirs and co-heirs; anyhow, the place has been empty for years.

That spoils my ghostliness, I am afraid, but I don't care — there is something strange about the house — I can feel it.

I even said so to John one moonlight evening, but he said what I felt was a *draught,* and shut the window.

I get unreasonably angry with John sometimes. I'm sure I never used to be so sensitive. I think it is due to this nervous condition.

But John says if I feel so, I shall neglect proper self-control; so I take pains to control myself — before him, at least, and that makes me very tired.

I don't like our room a bit. I wanted one downstairs that opened on the piazza and had roses all over the window, and such pretty old-fashioned chintz hangings! but John would not hear of it.

He said there was only one window and not room for two beds, and no near room for him if he took another.

He is very careful and loving, and hardly lets me stir without special direction.

I have a schedule prescription for each hour in the day; he takes all care from me, and so I feel basely ungrateful not to value it more.

He said we came here solely on my account, that I was to have perfect rest and all the air I could get. "Your exercise depends on your strength, my dear," said he, "and your food somewhat on your appetite; but air you can absorb all the time." So we took the nursery at the top of the house.

It is a big, airy room, the whole floor nearly, with windows that look all ways, and air and sunshine galore. It was nursery first and then playroom and gymnasium, I should judge; for the windows are barred for little children, and there are rings and things in the walls.

The paint and paper look as if a boys' school had used it. It is stripped off — the paper — in great patches all around the head of my bed, about as far as I can reach, and in a great place on the other side of the room low down. I never saw a worse paper in my life.

One of those sprawling flamboyant patterns committing every artistic sin.

It is dull enough to confuse the eye in following, pronounced enough to constantly irritate and provoke study, and when you follow the lame uncertain curves for a little distance they suddenly commit suicide — plunge off at outrageous angles, destroy themselves in unheard of contradictions.

The color is repellant, almost revolting; a smouldering unclean yellow, strangely faded by the slow-turning sunlight.

It is a dull yet lurid orange in some places, a sickly sulphur tint in others.

No wonder the children hated it! I should hate it myself if I had to live in this room long.

There comes John, and I must put this away, — he hates to have me write a word.

We have been here two weeks, and I haven't felt like writing before, since that first day.

I am sitting by the window now, up in this atrocious nursery, and there is nothing to hinder my writing as much as I please, save lack of strength.

John is away all day, and even some nights when his cases are serious.

I am glad my case is not serious!

But these nervous troubles are dreadfully depressing.

John does not know how much I really suffer. He knows there is no *reason* to suffer, and that satisfies him.

Of course it is only nervousness. It does weigh on me so not to do my duty in any way!

I meant to be such a help to John, such a real rest and comfort, and here I am a comparative burden already!

Nobody would believe what an effort it is to do what little I am able, — to dress and entertain, and order things.

It is fortunate Mary is so good with the baby. Such a dear baby!

And yet I *cannot* be with him, it makes me so nervous.

I suppose John never was nervous in his life. He laughs at me so about this wall-paper!

At first he meant to repaper the room, but afterward he said that I was letting it get the better of me, and that nothing was worse for a nervous patient than to give way to such fancies.

He said that after the wall-paper was changed it would be the heavy bedstead, and then the barred windows, and then that gate at the head of the stairs, and so on.

"You know the place is doing you good," he said, "and really, dear, I don't care to renovate the house just for a three months' rental."

"Then do let us go downstairs," I said, "there are such pretty rooms there."

Then he took me in his arms and called me a blessed little goose, and said he would go down cellar, if I wished, and have it whitewashed into the bargain.

But he is right enough about the beds and windows and things.

It is an airy and comfortable room as anyone need wish, and, of course, I would not be so silly as to make him uncomfortable just for a whim.

I'm really getting quite fond of the big room, all but that horrid paper.

Out of one window I can see the garden, those mysterious deep-shaded arbors, the riotous old-fashioned flowers, and bushes and gnarly trees.

Out of another I get a lovely view of the bay and a little private wharf belonging to the estate. There is a beautiful shaded lane that runs down there from the house. I always fancy I see people walking in these numerous paths and arbors, but John has cautioned me not to give way to fancy in the least. He says that with my imaginative power and habit of story-making, a nervous weakness like mine is sure to lead to all manner of excited fancies, and that I ought to use my will and good sense to check the tendency. So I try.

I think sometimes that if I were only well enough to write a little it would relieve the press of ideas and rest me.

But I find I get pretty tired when I try.

It is so discouraging not to have any advice and companionship about my work. When I get really well, John says we will ask Cousin Henry and Julia down for a long visit; but he says he would as soon put fireworks in my pillow-case as to let me have those stimulating people about now.

I wish I could get well faster.

But I must not think about that. This paper looks to me as if it *knew* what a vicious influence it had!

There is a recurrent spot where the pattern lolls like a broken neck and two bulbous eyes stare at you upside down.

I get positively angry with the impertinence of it and the everlastingness. Up and down and sideways they crawl, and those absurd, unblinking eyes are everywhere. There is one place where two breadths didn't match, and the eyes go all up and down the line, one a little higher than the other.

I never saw so much expression in an inanimate thing before, and we all know how much expression they have! I used to lie awake as a child and get more entertainment and terror out of blank walls and plain furniture than most children could find in a toy-store.

I remember what a kindly wink the knobs of our big, old bureau used to have, and there was one chair that always seemed like a strong friend.

I used to feel that if any of the other things looked too fierce I could always hop into that chair and be safe.

The furniture in this room is no worse than inharmonious, however, for we had to bring it all from downstairs. I suppose when this was used as a playroom they had to take the nursery things out, and no wonder! I never saw such ravages as the children have made here.

The wall-paper, as I said before, is torn off in spots, and it sticketh closer than a brother — they must have had perseverance as well as hatred.

Then the floor is scratched and gouged and splintered, the plaster itself is dug out here and there, and this great heavy bed, which is all we found in the room, looks as if it had been through the wars.

But I don't mind it a bit — only the paper.

There comes John's sister. Such a dear girl as she is, and so careful of me! I must not let her find me writing.

She is a perfect and enthusiastic housekeeper, and hopes for no better profession. I verily believe she thinks it is the writing which made me sick!

But I can write when she is out, and see her a long way off from these windows.

There is one that commands the road, a lovely shaded winding road, and one that just looks off over the country. A lovely country, too, full of great elms and velvet meadows.

This wallpaper has a kind of sub-pattern in a different shade, a particularly irritating one, for you can only see it in certain lights, and not clearly then.

But in the places where it isn't faded and where the sun is just so — I can see a strange, provoking, formless sort of figure, that seems to skulk about behind that silly and conspicuous front design.

There's sister on the stairs!

Well, the Fourth of July is over! The people are all gone and I am tired out. John thought it might do me good to see a little company, so we just had mother and Nellie and the children down for a week.

Of course I didn't do a thing. Jennie sees to everything now.

But it tired me all the same.

John says if I don't pick up faster he shall send me to Weir Mitchell° in the fall.

But I don't want to go there at all. I had a friend who was in his hands once, and she says he is just like John and my brother, only more so!

Besides, it is such an undertaking to go so far.

I don't feel as if it was worthwhile to turn my hand over for anything, and I'm getting dreadfully fretful and querulous.

I cry at nothing, and cry most of the time.

Of course I don't when John is here, or anybody else, but when I am alone.

And I am alone a good deal just now. John is kept in town very often by serious cases, and Jennie is good and lets me alone when I want her to.

So I walk a little in the garden or down that lovely lane, sit on the porch under the roses, and lie down up here a good deal.

I'm getting really fond of the room in spite of the wallpaper. Perhaps *because* of the wallpaper.

It dwells in my mind so!

I lie here on this great immovable bed — it is nailed down, I believe — and follow that pattern about by the hour. It is as good as gymnastics, I assure you. I start, we'll say, at the bottom, down in the corner over there where it has not been touched, and I determine for the thousandth time that I *will* follow that pointless pattern to some sort of a conclusion.

I know a little of the principle of design, and I know this thing was not arranged on any laws of radiation, or alternation, or repetition, or symmetry, or anything else that I ever heard of.

It is repeated, of course, by the breadths, but not otherwise.

Looked at in one way each breadth stands alone, the bloated curves and flourishes — a kind of "debased Romanesque" with *delirium tremens* — go waddling up and down in isolated columns of fatuity.

But, on the other hand, they connect diagonally, and the sprawling outlines run off in great slanting waves of optic horror, like a lot of wallowing seaweeds in full chase.

The whole thing goes horizontally, too, at least it seems so, and I exhaust myself in trying to distinguish the order of its going in that direction.

They have used a horizontal breadth for a frieze, and that adds wonderfully to the confusion.

Weir Mitchell: Dr. S. Weir Mitchell (1829–1914) was an eminent Philadelphia neurologist who advocated "rest cures" for nervous disorders. He was the author of *Diseases of the Nervous System, Especially of Women* (1881).

There is one end of the room where it is almost intact, and there, when the crosslights fade and the low sun shines directly upon it, I can almost fancy radiation after all, — the interminable grotesques seem to form around a common centre and rush off in headlong plunges of equal distraction.

It makes me tired to follow it. I will take a nap I guess.

I don't know why I should write this.

I don't want to.

I don't feel able.

And I know John would think it absurd. But I *must* say what I feel and think in some way — it is such a relief!

But the effort is getting to be greater than the relief.

Half the time now I am awfully lazy, and lie down ever so much.

John says I mustn't lose my strength, and has me take cod liver oil and lots of tonics and things, to say nothing of ale and wine and rare meat.

Dear John! He loves me very dearly, and hates to have me sick. I tried to have a real earnest reasonable talk with him the other day, and tell him how I wish he would let me go and make a visit to Cousin Henry and Julia.

But he said I wasn't able to go, nor able to stand it after I got there; and I did not make out a very good case for myself, for I was crying before I had finished.

It is getting to be a great effort for me to think straight. Just this nervous weakness I suppose.

And dear John gathered me up in his arms, and just carried me upstairs and laid me on the bed, and sat by me and read to me till it tired my head.

He said I was his darling and his comfort and all he had, and that I must take care of myself for his sake, and keep well.

He says no one but myself can help me out of it, that I must use my will and self-control and not let any silly fancies run away with me.

There's one comfort, the baby is well and happy, and does not have to occupy this nursery with the horrid wallpaper.

If we had not used it, that blessed child would have! What a fortunate escape! Why, I wouldn't have a child of mine, an impressionable little thing, live in such a room for worlds.

I never thought of it before, but it is lucky that John kept me here after all, I can stand it so much easier than a baby, you see.

Of course I never mention it to them any more — I am too wise, but I keep watch of it all the same.

There are things in the wallpaper that nobody knows but me, or ever will.

Behind that outside pattern the dim shapes get clearer every day.

It is always the same shape, only very numerous.

And it is like a woman stooping down and creeping about behind that pattern. I don't like it a bit. I wonder — I begin to think — I wish John would take me away from here!

It is so hard to talk with John about my case, because he is so wise, and because he loves me so.

But I tried it last night.

It was moonlight. The moon shines in all around just as the sun does.

I hate to see it sometimes, it creeps so slowly, and always comes in by one window or another.

John was asleep and I hated to waken him, so I kept still and watched the moonlight on that undulating wallpaper till I felt creepy.

The faint figure behind seemed to shake the pattern, just as if she wanted to get out.

I got up softly and went to feel and see if the paper *did* move, and when I came back John was awake.

"What is it, little girl?" he said. "Don't go walking about like that — you'll get cold."

I thought it was a good time to talk, so I told him that I really was not gaining here, and that I wished he would take me away.

"Why, darling!" said he, "our lease will be up in three weeks, and I can't see how to leave before.

"The repairs are not done at home, and I cannot possibly leave town just now. Of course if you were in any danger, I could and would, but you really are better, dear, whether you can see it or not. I am a doctor, dear, and I know. You are gaining flesh and color, your appetite is better, I feel really much easier about you."

"I don't weigh a bit more," said I, "nor as much; and my appetite may be better in the evening when you are here but it is worse in the morning when you are away!"

"Bless her little heart!" said he with a big hug, "she shall be as sick as she pleases! But now let's improve the shining hours by going to sleep, and talk about it in the morning!"

"And you won't go away?" I asked gloomily.

"Why, how can I, dear? It is only three weeks more and then we will take a nice little trip of a few days while Jennie is getting the house ready. Really dear you are better!"

"Better in body perhaps —" I began, and stopped short, for he sat up straight and looked at me with such a stern, reproachful look that I could not say another word.

"My darling," said he, "I beg you, for my sake and for our child's sake, as well as for your own, that you will never for one instant let that idea enter your mind! There is nothing so dangerous, so fascinating, to a temperament like yours. It is a false and foolish fancy. Can you trust me as a physician when I tell you so?"

So of course I said no more on that score, and we went to sleep before long. He thought I was asleep first, but I wasn't, and lay there for hours trying to decide whether that front pattern and the back pattern really did move together or separately.

On a pattern like this, by daylight, there is a lack of sequence, a defiance of law, that is a constant irritant to a normal mind.

The color is hideous enough, and unreliable enough, and infuriating enough, but the pattern is torturing.

You think you have mastered it, but just as you get well underway in following, it turns a back-somersault and there you are. It slaps you in the face, knocks you down, and tramples upon you. It is like a bad dream.

The outside pattern is a florid arabesque, reminding one of a fungus. If you can imagine a toadstool in joints, an interminable string of toadstools, budding and sprouting in endless convolutions — why, that is something like it.

That is, sometimes!

There is one marked peculiarity about this paper, a thing nobody seems to notice but myself, and that is that it changes as the light changes.

When the sun shoots in through the east window — I always watch for that first long, straight ray — it changes so quickly that I never can quite believe it.

That is why I watch it always.

By moonlight — the moon shines in all night when there is a moon — I wouldn't know it was the same paper.

At night in any kind of light, in twilight, candlelight, lamplight, and worst of all by moonlight, it becomes bars! The outside pattern I mean, and the woman behind it is as plain as can be.

I didn't realize for a long time what the thing was that showed behind, that dim sub-pattern, but now I am quite sure it is a woman.

By daylight she is subdued, quiet. I fancy it is the pattern that keeps her so still. It is so puzzling. It keeps me quiet by the hour.

I lie down ever so much now. John says it is good for me, and to sleep all I can.

Indeed he started the habit by making me lie down for an hour after each meal.

It is a very bad habit I am convinced, for you see I don't sleep.

And that cultivates deceit, for I don't tell them I'm awake — O, no!

The fact is I am getting a little afraid of John.

He seems very queer sometimes, and even Jennie has an inexplicable look.

It strikes me occasionally, just as a scientific hypothesis, — that perhaps it is the paper!

I have watched John when he did not know I was looking, and come into the room suddenly on the most innocent excuses, and I've caught him several times *looking at the paper!* And Jennie too. I caught Jennie with her hand on it once.

She didn't know I was in the room, and when I asked her in a quiet, a very quiet voice, with the most restrained manner possible, what she was doing with the paper — she turned around as if she had been caught stealing, and looked quite angry — asked me why I should frighten her so!

Then she said that the paper stained everything it touched, that she had found yellow smooches on all my clothes and John's, and she wished we would be more careful!

Did not that sound innocent? But I know she was studying that pattern, and I am determined that nobody shall find it out but myself!

Life is very much more exciting now than it used to be. You see I have something more to expect, to look forward to, to watch. I really do eat better, and am more quiet than I was.

John is so pleased to see me improve! He laughed a little the other day, and said I seemed to be flourishing in spite of my wall-paper.

I turned it off with a laugh. I had no intention of telling him it was *because* of the wall-paper — he would make fun of me. He might even want to take me away.

I don't want to leave now until I have found it out. There is a week more, and I think that will be enough.

I'm feeling ever so much better! I don't sleep much at night, for it is so interesting to watch developments; but I sleep a good deal in the daytime.

In the daytime it is tiresome and perplexing.

There are always new shoots on the fungus, and new shades of yellow all over it. I cannot keep count of them, though I have tried conscientiously.

It is the strangest yellow, that wall-paper! It makes me think of all the yellow things I ever saw — not beautiful ones like buttercups, but old foul, bad yellow things.

But there is something else about that paper — the smell! I noticed it the moment we came into the room, but with so much air and sun it was not bad. Now we have had a week of fog and rain, and whether the windows are open or not, the smell is here.

It creeps all over the house.

I find it hovering in the dining-room, skulking in the parlor, hiding in the hall, lying in wait for me on the stairs.

It gets into my hair.

Even when I go to ride, if I turn my head suddenly and surprise it — there is that smell!

Such a peculiar odor, too! I have spent hours in trying to analyze it, to find what it smelled like.

It is not bad — at first, and very gentle, but quite the subtlest, most enduring odor I ever met.

In this damp weather it is awful, I wake up in the night and find it hanging over me.

It used to disturb me at first. I thought seriously of burning the house — to reach the smell.

But now I am used to it. The only thing I can think of that it is like is the *color* of the paper! A yellow smell.

There is a very funny mark on this wall, low down, near the mopboard. A streak that runs round the room. It goes behind every piece of furniture, except the bed, a long, straight, even *smooch,* as if it had been rubbed over and over.

I wonder how it was done and who did it, and what they did it for. Round and round and round — round and round and round — it makes me dizzy!

■ ■ ■

I really have discovered something at last.

Through watching so much at night, when it changes so, I have finally found out.

The front pattern *does* move — and no wonder! The woman behind shakes it!

Sometimes I think there are a great many women behind, and sometimes only one, and she crawls around fast, and her crawling shakes it all over.

Then in the very bright spots she keeps still, and in the very shady spots she just takes hold of the bars and shakes them hard.

And she is all the time trying to climb through. But nobody could climb through that pattern — it strangles so; I think that is why it has so many heads.

They get through, and then the pattern strangles them off and turns them upside down, and makes their eyes white!

If those heads were covered or taken off it would not be half so bad.

I think that woman gets out in the daytime!

And I'll tell you why — privately — I've seen her!

I can see her out of every one of my windows!

It is the same woman, I know, for she is always creeping, and most women do not creep by daylight.

I see her in that long shaded lane, creeping up and down. I see her in those dark grape arbors, creeping all around the garden.

I see her on that long road under the trees, creeping along, and when a carriage comes she hides under the blackberry vines.

I don't blame her a bit. It must be very humiliating to be caught creeping by daylight!

I always lock the door when I creep by daylight. I can't do it at night, for I know John would suspect something at once.

And John is so queer now, that I don't want to irritate him. I wish he would take another room! Besides, I don't want anybody to get that woman out at night but myself.

I often wonder if I could see her out of all the windows at once.

But, turn as fast as I can, I can only see out of one at one time.

And though I always see her, she *may* be able to creep faster than I can turn!

I have watched her sometimes away off in the open country, creeping as fast as a cloud shadow in a high wind.

If only that top pattern could be gotten off from the under one! I mean to try it, little by little.

I have found out another funny thing, but I shan't tell it this time! It does not do to trust people too much.

There are only two more days to get this paper off, and I believe John is beginning to notice. I don't like the look in his eyes.

And I heard him ask Jennie a lot of professional questions, about me. She had a very good report to give.

She said I slept a good deal in the daytime.

John knows I don't sleep very well at night, for all I'm so quiet!

He asked me all sorts of questions too, and pretended to be very loving and kind.

As if I couldn't see through him!

Still, I don't wonder he acts so, sleeping under this paper for three months.

It only interests me, but I feel sure John and Jennie are secretly affected by it.

Hurrah! This is the last day, but it is enough. John to stay in town over night, and won't be out until this evening.

Jennie wanted to sleep with me — the sly thing! But I told her I should undoubtedly rest better for a night all alone.

That was clever, for really I wasn't alone a bit! As soon as it was moonlight and that poor thing began to crawl and shake the pattern, I got up and ran to help her.

I pulled and she shook, I shook and she pulled, and before morning we had peeled off yards of that paper.

A strip about as high as my head and half around the room.

And then when the sun came and that awful pattern began to laugh at me, I declared I would finish it to-day!

We go away to-morrow, and they are moving all my furniture down again to leave things as they were before.

Jennie looked at the wall in amazement, but I told her merrily that I did it out of pure spite at the vicious thing.

She laughed and said she wouldn't mind doing it herself, but I must not get tired.

How she betrayed herself that time!

But I am here, and no person touches this paper but me, — not *alive!*

She tried to get me out of the room — it was too patent! But I said it was so quiet and empty and clean now that I believed I would lie down again and sleep all I could, and not to wake me even for dinner — I would call when I woke.

So now she is gone, and the servants are gone, and the things are gone, and there is nothing left but that great bedstead nailed down, with the canvas mattress we found on it.

We shall sleep downstairs to-night, and take the boat home to-morrow.

I quite enjoy the room, now it is bare again.

How those children did tear about here!

This bedstead is fairly gnawed!

But I must get to work.

I have locked the door and thrown the key down into the front path.

I don't want to go out, and I don't want to have anybody come in, till John comes.

I want to astonish him.

I've got a rope up here that even Jennie did not find. If that woman does get out, and tries to get away, I can tie her!

But I forgot I could not reach far without anything to stand on!

This bed will *not* move!

I tried to lift and push it until I was lame, and then I got so angry I bit off a little piece at one corner — but it hurt my teeth.

Then I peeled off all the paper I could reach standing on the floor. It sticks horribly and the pattern just enjoys it! All those strangled heads and bulbous eyes and waddling fungus growths just shriek with derision!

I am getting angry enough to do something desperate. To jump out of the window would be admirable exercise, but the bars are too strong even to try.

Besides I wouldn't do it. Of course not. I know well enough that a step like that is improper and might be misconstrued.

I don't like to *look* out of the windows even — there are so many of those creeping women, and they creep so fast.

I wonder if they all come out of that wall-paper as I did?

But I am securely fastened now by my well-hidden rope — you don't get *me* out in the road there!

I suppose I shall have to get back behind the pattern when it comes night, and that is hard!

It is so pleasant to be out in this great room and creep around as I please!

I don't want to go outside. I won't, even if Jennie asks me to.

For outside you have to creep on the ground, and everything is green instead of yellow.

But here I can creep smoothly on the floor, and my shoulder just fits in that long smooch around the wall, so I cannot lose my way.

Why, there's John at the door!

It is no use, young man, you can't open it!

How he does call and pound!

Now he's crying for an axe.

It would be a shame to break down that beautiful door!

"John dear!" said I in the gentlest voice, "the key is down by the front steps, under a plantain leaf!"

That silenced him for a few moments.

Then he said — very quietly indeed, "Open the door, my darling!"

"I can't," said I. "The key is down by the front door under a plantain leaf!"

And then I said it again, several times, very gently and slowly, and said it so often that he had to go and see, and he got it of course, and came in. He stopped short by the door.

"What is the matter?" he cried. "For God's sake, what are you doing!"

I kept on creeping just the same, but I looked at him over my shoulder.

"I've got out at last," said I, "in spite of you and Jane. And I've pulled off most of the paper, so you can't put me back!"

Now why should that man have fainted? But he did, and right across my path by the wall, so that I had to creep over him every time!

SUSAN GLASPELL *(1876–1948) was born in Davenport, Iowa, into a family that had been among the state's first settlers a generation before. After her graduation from high school, she worked as a reporter and society editor for various newspapers before enrolling at Drake University in Des Moines. There she studied literature, philosophy, and history; edited the college newspaper; and began to write short stories. In 1899 she took a job as statehouse reporter for the Des Moines* Daily News. *Years later she claimed that the discipline of newspaper work helped her to become a creative writer.*

At the age of twenty-five, Glaspell returned to Davenport to live with her family, determined, as she said, to "boldly" quit journalism and "give all my time to my own writing. I say 'boldly,' because I had to earn my living." Slowly she began to publish her fiction, mostly sentimental magazine pieces and an undistinguished first novel — work that, as her biographer C. W. E. Bigsby noted, "suggested little of the originality and power which were to mark her work in the theater." In 1909 Glaspell met George Cram Cook, a novelist and utopian socialist from a wealthy family who divorced his second wife and left his two children to marry her. They moved to Greenwich Village and collaborated on a play for the Washington Square Players in 1915, Suppressed Desires. *The following year, after the Players had moved to Provincetown on Cape Cod, Cook urged Glaspell to write a new play for the theater company, renamed the Provincetown Players. Her memory of a murder trial in Iowa that she had covered as a newspaper reporter served as the inspiration for the short play* Trifles *(1916). Glaspell recalled that she "had meant to do it as a short story, but the stage took it for its own."*

Trifles *was so successful as an experimental play that Glaspell turned it into a short story a year later, retitling it "A Jury of Her Peers." Her choice of a limited-omniscient, third-person point of view (via the character Martha Hale's perspective) and her description of the harsh realities of the rural setting in "A Jury of Her Peers" suggest the local-color tradition of such earlier writers as Sarah Orne Jewett, although Glaspell's suffragist sympathies were more radical than the views of nineteenth-century women writers. In 1912 Glaspell published her first book of stories,* Lifted Masks, *and she continued to write fiction as well as plays for most of her life. In her forty-seven-year career, she published fifty short stories, nine novels, and thirteen plays, including the Pulitzer Prize–winning play* Alison's House *(1931), based on Genevieve Taggard's biography of Emily Dickinson.*

RELATED PLAY: *Susan Glaspell,* Trifles, *page 1628.*

RELATED COMMENTARY: *Leonard Mustazza, "Generic Translation and Thematic Shift in Susan Glaspell's* Trifles *and 'A Jury of Her Peers,'" page 1980.*

SUSAN GLASPELL

A Jury of Her Peers

1917

When Martha Hale opened the storm-door and got a cut of the north wind, she ran back for her big woolen scarf. As she hurriedly wound that round her head her eye made a scandalized sweep of her kitchen. It was no ordinary thing that called her away — it was probably further from ordinary than anything that had ever happened in Dickson County. But what her eye took in was that her kitchen was in no shape for leaving: her bread all ready for mixing, half the flour sifted and half unsifted.

She hated to see things half done; but she had been at that when the team from town stopped to get Mr. Hale, and then the sheriff came running in to say his wife wished Mrs. Hale would come too — adding, with a grin, that he guessed she was getting scary and wanted another woman along. So she had dropped everything right where it was.

"Martha!" now came her husband's impatient voice. "Don't keep folks waiting out here in the cold."

She again opened the storm-door, and this time joined the three men and the one woman waiting for her in the big two-seated buggy.

After she had the robes tucked around her she took another look at the woman who sat beside her on the back seat. She had met Mrs. Peters the year before at the county fair, and the thing she remembered about her was that she didn't seem like a sheriff's wife. She was small and thin and didn't have a strong voice. Mrs. Gorman, sheriff's wife before Gorman went out and Peters came in, had a voice that somehow seemed to be backing up the law with every word. But if Mrs. Peters didn't look like a sheriff's wife, Peters made it up in looking like a sheriff. He was to a dot the kind of man who could get himself elected sheriff — a heavy man with a big voice, who was particularly genial with the law-abiding, as if to make it plain that he knew the difference between criminals and non-criminals. And right there it came into Mrs. Hale's mind, with a stab, that this man who was so pleasant and lively with all of them was going to the Wrights' now as a sheriff.

"The country's not very pleasant this time of year," Mrs. Peters at last ventured, as if she felt they ought to be talking as well as the men.

Mrs. Hale scarcely finished her reply, for they had gone up a little hill and could see the Wright place now, and seeing it did not make her feel like talking. It looked very lonesome this cold March morning. It had always been a lonesome-looking place. It was down in a hollow, and the poplar trees around it were lonesome-looking trees. The men were looking at it and talking about what had happened. The county attorney was bending to one side of the buggy, and kept looking steadily at the place as they drew up to it.

"I'm glad you came with me," Mrs. Peters said nervously, as the two women were about to follow the men in through the kitchen door.

Even after she had her foot on the door-step, her hand on the knob, Martha Hale had a moment of feeling she could not cross that threshold. And the reason it seemed she couldn't cross it now was simply because she hadn't crossed it before. Time and time again it had been in her mind, "I ought to go over and see Minnie Foster" — she still thought of her as Minnie Foster, though for twenty years she had been Mrs. Wright. And then there was always something to do and Minnie Foster would go from her mind. But *now* she could come.

The men went over to the stove. The women stood close together by the door. Young Henderson, the county attorney, turned around and said, "Come up to the fire, ladies."

Mrs. Peters took a step forward, then stopped. "I'm not — cold," she said.

And so the two women stood by the door, at first not even so much as looking around the kitchen.

The men talked for a minute about what a good thing it was the sheriff had sent his deputy out that morning to make a fire for them, and then Sheriff Peters stepped back from the stove, unbuttoned his outer coat, and leaned his hands on the kitchen table in a way that seemed to mark the beginning of official business. "Now, Mr. Hale," he said in a sort of semi-official voice, "before we move things about, you tell Mr. Henderson just what it was you saw when you came here yesterday morning."

The county attorney was looking around the kitchen.

"By the way," he said, "has anything been moved?" He turned to the sheriff. "Are things just as you left them yesterday?"

Peters looked from cupboard to sink; from that to a small worn rocker a little to one side of the kitchen table.

"It's just the same."

"Somebody should have been left here yesterday," said the county attorney.

"Oh — yesterday," returned the sheriff, with a little gesture as of yesterday having been more than he could bear to think of. "When I had to send Frank to Morris Center for that man who went crazy — let me tell you. I had my hands full *yesterday*. I knew you could get back from Omaha by today, George, and as long as I went over everything here myself —"

"Well, Mr. Hale," said the county attorney, in a way of letting what was past and gone go, "tell just what happened when you came here yesterday morning."

Mrs. Hale, still leaning against the door, had that sinking feeling of the mother whose child is about to speak a piece. Lewis often wandered along and got things mixed up in a story. She hoped he would tell this straight and plain, and not say unnecessary things that would just make things harder for Minnie Foster. He didn't begin at once, and she noticed that he looked queer — as if standing in that kitchen and having to tell what he had seen there yesterday morning made him almost sick.

"Yes, Mr. Hale?" the county attorney reminded.

"Harry and I had started to town with a load of potatoes," Mrs. Hale's husband began.

Harry was Mrs. Hale's oldest boy. He wasn't with them now, for the very good reason that those potatoes never got to town yesterday and he was taking them this morning, so he hadn't been home when the sheriff stopped to say he wanted Mr. Hale to come over to the Wright place and tell the county attorney his story there, where he could point it all out. With all Mrs. Hale's other emotions came the fear now that maybe Harry wasn't dressed warm enough — they hadn't any of them realized how that north wind did bite.

"We come along this road," Hale was going on, with a motion of his hand to the road over which they had just come, "and as we got in sight of the house I says to Harry, 'I'm goin' to see if I can't get John Wright to take a telephone.' You see," he explained to Henderson, "unless I can get somebody to go in with me they won't come out this branch road except for a price *I* can't pay. I'd spoke to Wright about it once before; but he put me off, saying folks talked too much anyway, and all he asked was peace and quiet — guess you know about how much he talked himself. But I thought maybe if I went to the house and talked about it before his wife, and said all the women-folks liked the telephones, and that in this lonesome stretch of road it would be a good thing — well, I said to Harry that that was what I was going to say — though I said at the same time that I didn't know as what his wife wanted made much difference to John —"

Now there he was! — saying things he didn't need to say. Mrs. Hale tried to catch her husband's eye, but fortunately the county attorney interrupted with:

"Let's talk about that a little later, Mr. Hale. I do want to talk about that, but I'm anxious now to get along to just what happened when you got here."

When he began this time, it was very deliberately and carefully:

"I didn't see or hear anything. I knocked at the door. And still it was all quiet inside. I knew they must be up — it was past eight o'clock. So I knocked again, louder, and I thought I heard somebody say, 'Come in.' I wasn't sure — I'm not sure yet. But I opened the door — this door," jerking a hand toward the door by which the two women stood, "and there, in that rocker" — pointing to it — "sat Mrs. Wright."

Everyone in the kitchen looked at the rocker. It came into Mrs. Hale's mind that that rocker didn't look in the least like Minnie Foster — the Minnie Foster of twenty years before. It was a dingy red, with wooden rungs up the back, and the middle rung was gone, and the chair sagged to one side.

"How did she — look?" the county attorney was inquiring.

"Well," said Hale, "she looked — queer."

"How do you mean — queer?"

As he asked it he took out a note-book and pencil. Mrs. Hale did not like the sight of that pencil. She kept her eye fixed on her husband, as if to keep him from saying unnecessary things that would go into that note-book and make trouble.

Hale did speak guardedly, as if the pencil had affected him too.

"Well, as if she didn't know what she was going to do next. And kind of — done up."

"How did she seem to feel about your coming?"

"Why, I don't think she minded — one way or other. She didn't pay much attention. I said, 'Ho' do, Mrs. Wright? It's cold, ain't it?' And she said, 'Is it?' — and went on pleatin' at her apron.

"Well, I was surprised. She didn't ask me to come up to the stove, or to sit down, but just set there, not even lookin' at me. And so I said: 'I want to see John.'

"And then she — laughed. I guess you would call it a laugh.

"I thought of Harry and the team outside, so I said, a little sharp, 'Can I see John?' 'No,' says she — kind of dull like. 'Ain't he home?' says I. Then she looked at me. 'Yes,' says she, 'he's home.' 'Then why can't I see him?' I asked her, out of patience with her now. 'Cause he's dead' says she, just as quiet and dull — and fell to pleatin' her apron. 'Dead?' says I, like you do when you can't take in what you've heard.

"She just nodded her head, not getting a bit excited, but rockin' back and forth.

" 'Why — where is he?' says I, not knowing *what* to say.

"She just pointed upstairs — like this" — pointing to the room above.

"I got up, with the idea of going up there myself. By this time I — didn't know what to do. I walked from there to here; then I says: 'Why, what did he die of?'

" 'He died of a rope around his neck,' says she; and just went on pleatin' at her apron."

Hale stopped speaking, and stood staring at the rocker, as if he were still seeing the woman who had sat there the morning before. Nobody spoke; it was as if every one were seeing the woman who had sat there the morning before.

"And what did you do then?" the county attorney at last broke the silence.

"I went out and called Harry. I thought I might — need help. I got Harry in, and we went upstairs." His voice fell almost to a whisper. "There he was — lying over the —"

"I think I'd rather have you go into that upstairs," the county attorney interrupted, "where you can point it all out. Just go on now with the rest of the story."

"Well, my first thought was to get that rope off. It looked —"

He stopped, his face twitching.

"But Harry, he went up to him, and he said, 'No, he's dead all right, and we'd better not touch anything.' So we went downstairs.

"She was still sitting that same way. 'Has anybody been notified?' I asked. 'No,' says she, unconcerned.

" 'Who did this, Mrs. Wright?' said Harry. He said it businesslike, and she stopped pleatin' at her apron. 'I don't know,' she says. 'You don't *know*?' says Harry. 'Weren't you sleepin' in the bed with him?' 'Yes,' says she, 'but I was on the inside.' 'Somebody slipped a rope round his neck and strangled him, and you didn't wake up?' says Harry. 'I didn't wake up,' she said after him.

"We may have looked as if we didn't see how that could be, for after a minute she said, 'I sleep sound.'

"Harry was going to ask her more questions, but I said maybe that weren't our business; maybe we ought to let her tell her story first to the coroner or the sheriff. So Harry went fast as he could over to High Road — the Rivers' place, where there's a telephone."

"And what did she do when she knew you had gone for the coroner?" The attorney got his pencil in his hand all ready for writing.

"She moved from that chair to this one over here" — Hale pointed to a small chair in the corner — "and just sat there with her hands held together and looking down. I got a feeling that I ought to make some conversation, so I said I had come in to see if John wanted to put in a telephone; and at that she started to laugh, and then she stopped and looked at me — scared."

At the sound of a moving pencil the man who was telling the story looked up.

"I dunno — maybe it wasn't scared," he hastened: "I wouldn't like to say it was. Soon Harry got back, and then Dr. Lloyd came, and you, Mr. Peters, and so I guess that's all I know that you don't."

He said that last with relief, and moved a little, as if relaxing. Everyone moved a little. The county attorney walked toward the stair door.

"I guess we'll go upstairs first — then out to the barn and around there."

He paused and looked around the kitchen.

"You're convinced there was nothing important here?" he asked the sheriff. "Nothing that would — point to any motive?"

The sheriff too looked all around, as if to re-convince himself.

"Nothing here but kitchen things," he said, with a little laugh for the insignificance of kitchen things.

The county attorney was looking at the cupboard — a peculiar, ungainly structure, half closet and half cupboard, the upper part of it being built in the wall, and the lower part just the old-fashioned kitchen cupboard. As if its queerness attracted him, he got a chair and opened the upper part and looked in. After a moment he drew his hand away sticky.

"Here's a nice mess," he said resentfully.

The two women had drawn nearer, and now the sheriff's wife spoke.

"Oh — her fruit," she said, looking to Mrs. Hale for sympathetic understanding. She turned back to the county attorney and explained: "She worried about that when it turned so cold last night. She said the fire would go out and her jars might burst."

Mrs. Peters' husband broke into a laugh.

"Well, can you beat the women! Held for murder, and worrying about her preserves!"

The young attorney set his lips.

"I guess before we're through with her she may have something more serious than preserves to worry about."

"Oh, well," said Mrs. Hale's husband, with good-natured superiority, "women are used to worrying over trifles."

The two women moved a little closer together. Neither of them spoke. The county attorney seemed suddenly to remember his manners — and think of his future.

"And yet," said he, with the gallantry of a young politician, "for all their worries, what would we do without the ladies?"

The women did not speak, did not unbend. He went to the sink and began washing his hands. He turned to wipe them on the roller towel — whirled it for a cleaner place.

"Dirty towels! Not much of a housekeeper, would you say, ladies?"

He kicked his foot against some dirty pans under the sink.

"There's a great deal of work to be done on a farm," said Mrs. Hale stiffly.

"To be sure. And yet" — with a little bow to her — "I know there are some Dickson County farm-houses that do not have such roller towels." He gave it a pull to expose its full length again.

"Those towels get dirty awful quick. Men's hands aren't always as clean as they might be."

"Ah, loyal to your sex, I see," he laughed. He stopped and gave her a keen look. "But you and Mrs. Wright were neighbors. I suppose you were friends, too."

Martha Hale shook her head.

"I've seen little enough of her of late years. I've not been in this house — it's more than a year."

"And why was that? You didn't like her?"

"I liked her well enough," she replied with spirit. "Farmers' wives have their hands full, Mr. Henderson. And then —" She looked around the kitchen.

"Yes?" he encouraged.

"It never seemed a very cheerful place," said she, more to herself than to him.

"No," he agreed; "I don't think anyone would call it cheerful. I shouldn't say she had the home-making instinct."

"Well, I don't know as Wright had, either," she muttered.

"You mean they didn't get on very well?" he was quick to ask.

"No; I don't mean anything," she answered, with decision. As she turned a little away from him, she added: "But I don't think a place would be any the cheerfuller for John Wright's bein' in it."

"I'd like to talk to you about that a little later, Mrs. Hale," he said. "I'm anxious to get the lay of things upstairs now."

He moved toward the stair door, followed by the two men.

"I suppose anything Mrs. Peters does'll be all right?" the sheriff inquired. "She was to take in some clothes for her, you know — and a few little things. We left in such a hurry yesterday."

The county attorney looked at the two women whom they were leaving alone there among the kitchen things.

"Yes — Mrs. Peters," he said, his glance resting on the woman who was not Mrs. Peters, the big farmer woman who stood behind the sheriff's wife. "Of course Mrs. Peters is one of us," he said, in a manner of entrusting responsibility. "And keep your eye out, Mrs. Peters, for anything that might be of use. No telling; you women might come upon a clue to the motive — and that's the thing we need."

Mr. Hale rubbed his face after the fashion of a showman getting ready for a pleasantry.

"But would the women know a clue if they did come upon it?" he said; and, having delivered himself of this, he followed the others through the stair door.

The women stood motionless and silent, listening to the footsteps, first upon the stairs, then in the room above them.

Then, as if releasing herself from something strange. Mrs. Hale began to arrange the dirty pans under the sink, which the county attorney's disdainful push of the foot had deranged.

"I'd hate to have men comin' into my kitchen," she said testily — "snoopin' round and criticizin'."

"Of course it's no more than their duty," said the sheriff's wife, in her manner of timid acquiescence.

"Duty's all right," replied Mrs. Hale bluffly; "but I guess that deputy sheriff that come out to make the fire might have got a little of this on." She gave the roller towel a pull. "Wish I'd thought of that sooner! Seems mean to talk about her for not having things slicked up, when she had to come away in such a hurry."

She looked around the kitchen. Certainly it was not "slicked up." Her eye was held by a bucket of sugar on a low shelf. The cover was off the wooden bucket, and beside it was a paper bag — half full.

Mrs. Hale moved toward it.

"She was putting this in there," she said to herself — slowly.

She thought of the flour in her kitchen at home — half sifted, half not sifted. She had been interrupted, and had left things half done. What had interrupted Minnie Foster? Why had that work been left half done? She made a move as if to finish it, — unfinished things always bothered her, — and then she glanced around and saw that Mrs. Peters was watching her — and she didn't want Mrs. Peters to get that feeling she had got of work begun and then — for some reason — not finished.

"It's a shame about her fruit," she said, and walked toward the cupboard that the county attorney had opened, and got on the chair, murmuring: "I wonder if it's all gone."

It was a sorry enough looking sight, but "Here's one that's all right," she said at last. She held it toward the light. "This is cherries, too." She looked again. "I declare I believe that's the only one."

With a sigh, she got down from the chair, went to the sink, and wiped off the bottle.

"She'll feel awful bad, after all her hard work in the hot weather. I remember the afternoon I put up my cherries last summer."

She set the bottle on the table, and, with another sigh, started to sit down in the rocker. But she did not sit down. Something kept her from sitting down in that chair. She straightened — stepped back, and, half turned away, stood looking at it, seeing the woman who had sat there "pleatin' at her apron."

The thin voice of the sheriff's wife broke in upon her: "I must be getting those things from the front-room closet." She opened the door into the other room, started in, stepped back. "You coming with me, Mrs. Hale?" she asked nervously. "You — you could help me get them."

They were soon back — the stark coldness of that shut-up room was not a thing to linger in.

"My!" said Mrs. Peters, dropping the things on the table and hurrying to the stove.

Mrs. Hale stood examining the clothes the woman who was being detained in town had said she wanted.

"Wright was close!"° she exclaimed, holding up a shabby black skirt that bore the marks of much making over. "I think maybe that's why she kept so much to herself. I s'pose she felt she couldn't do her part; and then, you don't enjoy things when you feel shabby. She used to wear pretty clothes and be lively — when she was Minnie Foster, one of the town girls, singing in the choir. But that — oh, that was twenty years ago."

With a carefulness in which there was something tender, she folded the shabby clothes and piled them at one corner of the table. She looked up at Mrs. Peters, and there was something in the other woman's look that irritated her.

"She don't care," she said to herself. "Much difference it makes to her whether Minnie Foster had pretty clothes when she was a girl."

Then she looked again, and she wasn't so sure; in fact, she hadn't at any time been perfectly sure about Mrs. Peters. She had that shrinking manner, and yet her eyes looked as if they could see a long way into things.

"This all you was to take in?" asked Mrs. Hale.

"No," said the sheriff's wife; "she said she wanted an apron. Funny thing to want," she ventured in her nervous little way, "for there's not much to get you dirty in jail, goodness knows. But I suppose just to make her feel more natural. If you're used to wearing an apron — . She said they were in the bottom drawer of this cupboard. Yes — here they are. And then her little shawl that always hung on the stair door."

She took the small gray shawl from behind the door leading upstairs, and stood a minute looking at it.

Suddenly Mrs. Hale took a quick step toward the other woman.

"Mrs. Peters!"

"Yes, Mrs. Hale?"

"Do you think she — did it?"

A frightened look blurred the other thing in Mrs. Peters' eyes.

"Oh, I don't know," she said, in a voice that seemed to shrink away from the subject.

"Well, I don't think she did," affirmed Mrs. Hale stoutly. "Asking for an apron, and her little shawl. Worryin' about her fruit."

"Mr. Peters says — ." Footsteps were heard in the room above; she stopped, looked up, then went on in a lowered voice: "Mr. Peters says — it looks bad for her. Mr. Henderson is awful sarcastic in a speech, and he's going to make fun of her saying she didn't — wake up."

For a moment Mrs. Hale had no answer. Then, "Well, I guess John Wright didn't wake up — when they was slippin' that rope under his neck," she muttered.

"No, it's *strange,*" breathed Mrs. Peters. "They think it was such a — funny way to kill a man."

---

close: Frugal, tightfisted.

She began to laugh; at the sound of the laugh, abruptly stopped.

"That's just what Mr. Hale said," said Mrs. Hale, in a resolutely natural voice. "There was a gun in the house. He says that's what he can't understand."

"Mr. Henderson said, coming out, that what was needed for the case was a motive. Something to show anger — or sudden feeling."

"Well, I don't see any signs of anger around here," said Mrs. Hale, "I don't —" She stopped. It was as if her mind tripped on something. Her eye was caught by a dishtowel in the middle of the kitchen table. Slowly she moved toward the table. One half of it was wiped clean, the other half messy. Her eyes made a slow, almost unwilling turn to the bucket of sugar and the half empty bag beside it. Things begun — and not finished.

After a moment she stepped back, and said, in that manner of releasing herself:

"Wonder how they're finding things upstairs? I hope she had it a little more redd up° up there. You know," — she paused, and feeling gathered, — "it seems kind of *sneaking:* locking her up in town and coming out here to get her own house to turn against her!"

"But, Mrs. Hale," said the sheriff's wife, "the law is the law."

"I s'pose 'tis," answered Mrs. Hale shortly.

She turned to the stove, saying something about that fire not being much to brag of. She worked with it a minute, and when she straightened up she said aggressively:

"The law is the law — and a bad stove is a bad stove. How'd you like to cook on this?" — pointing with the poker to the broken lining. She opened the oven door and started to express her opinion of the oven; but she was swept into her own thoughts, thinking of what it would mean, year after year, to have that stove to wrestle with. The thought of Minnie Foster trying to bake in that oven — and the thought of her never going over to see Minnie Foster — .

She was startled by hearing Mrs. Peters say: "A person gets discouraged — and loses heart."

The sheriff's wife had looked from the stove to the sink — to the pail of water which had been carried in from outside. The two women stood there silent, above them the footsteps of the men who were looking for evidence against the woman who had worked in that kitchen. That look of seeing into things, of seeing through a thing to something else, was in the eyes of the sheriff's wife now. When Mrs. Hale next spoke to her, it was gently:

"Better loosen up your things, Mrs. Peters. We'll not feel them when we go out."

Mrs. Peters went to the back of the room to hang up the fur tippet she was wearing. A moment later she exclaimed, "Why, she was piecing a quilt," and held up a large sewing basket piled high with quilt pieces.

Mrs. Hale spread some of the blocks on the table.

"It's log-cabin pattern," she said, putting several of them together. "Pretty, isn't it?"

---

redd up: Neat.

They were so engaged with the quilt that they did not hear the footsteps on the stairs. Just as the stair door opened Mrs. Hale was saying:

"Do you suppose she was going to quilt it or just knot it?"

The sheriff threw up his hands.

"They wonder whether she was going to quilt it or just knot it!"

There was a laugh for the ways of women, a warming of hands over the stove, and then the county attorney said briskly:

"Well, let's go right out to the barn and get that cleared up."

"I don't see as there's anything so strange," Mrs. Hale said resentfully, after the outside door had closed on the three men — "our taking up our time with little things while we're waiting for them to get the evidence. I don't see as it's anything to laugh about."

"Of course they've got awful important things on their minds," said the sheriff's wife apologetically.

They returned to an inspection of the block for the quilt. Mrs. Hale was looking at the fine, even sewing, and preoccupied with thoughts of the woman who had done that sewing, when she heard the sheriff's wife say, in a queer tone:

"Why, look at this one."

She turned to take the block held out to her.

"The sewing," said Mrs. Peters, in a troubled way. "All the rest of them have been so nice and even — but — this one. Why, it looks as if she didn't know what she was about!"

Their eyes met — something flashed to life, passed between them; then, as if with an effort, they seemed to pull away from each other. A moment Mrs. Hale sat there, her hands folded over that sewing which was so unlike all the rest of the sewing. Then she had pulled a knot and drawn the threads.

"Oh, what are you doing, Mrs. Hale?" asked the sheriff's wife, startled.

"Just pulling out a stitch or two that's not sewed very good," said Mrs. Hale mildly.

"I don't think we ought to touch things," Mrs. Peters said, a little helplessly.

"I'll just finish up this end," answered Mrs. Hale, still in that mild, matter-of-fact fashion.

She threaded a needle and started to replace bad sewing with good. For a little while she sewed in silence. Then, in that thin, timid voice, she heard:

"Mrs. Hale!"

"Yes, Mrs. Peters?"

"What do you suppose she was so — nervous about?"

"Oh, *I* don't know," said Mrs. Hale, as if dismissing a thing not important enough to spend much time on. "I don't know as she was — nervous. I sew awful queer sometimes when I'm just tired."

She cut a thread, and out of the corner of her eye looked up at Mrs. Peters. The small, lean face of the sheriff's wife seemed to have tightened up. Her eyes had that look of peering into something. But next moment she moved, and said in her thin, indecisive way:

"Well, I must get those clothes wrapped. They may be through sooner than we think. I wonder where I could find a piece of paper — and string."

"In that cupboard, maybe," suggested Mrs. Hale, after a glance around.

One piece of the crazy sewing remained unripped. Mrs. Peter's back turned, Martha Hale now scrutinized that piece, compared it with the dainty, accurate sewing of the other blocks. The difference was startling. Holding this block made her feel queer, as if the distracted thoughts of the woman who had perhaps turned to it to try and quiet herself were communicating themselves to her.

Mrs. Peters' voice roused her.

"Here's a bird-cage," she said. "Did she have a bird, Mrs. Hale?"

"Why, I don't know whether she did or not." She turned to look at the cage Mrs. Peters was holding up. "I've not been here in so long." She sighed. "There was a man round last year selling canaries cheap — but I don't know as she took one. Maybe she did. She used to sing real pretty herself."

Mrs. Peters looked around the kitchen.

"Seems kind of funny to think of a bird here." She half laughed — an attempt to put up a barrier. "But she must have had one — or why would she have a cage? I wonder what happened to it."

"I suppose maybe the cat got it," suggested Mrs. Hale, resuming her sewing.

"No; she didn't have a cat. She's got that feeling some people have about cats — being afraid of them. When they brought her to our house yesterday, my cat got in the room, and she was real upset and asked me to take it out."

"My sister Bessie was like that," laughed Mrs. Hale.

The sheriff's wife did not reply. The silence made Mrs. Hale turn round. Mrs. Peters was examining the bird-cage.

"Look at this door," she said slowly. "It's broke. One hinge has been pulled apart."

Mrs. Hale came nearer.

"Looks as if someone must have been — rough with it."

Again their eyes met — startled, questioning, apprehensive. For a moment neither spoke nor stirred. Then Mrs. Hale, turning away, said brusquely:

"If they're going to find any evidence, I wish they'd be about it. I don't like this place."

"But I'm awful glad you came with me, Mrs. Hale." Mrs. Peters put the bird-cage on the table and sat down. "It would be lonesome for me — sitting here alone."

"Yes, it would, wouldn't it?" agreed Mrs. Hale, a certain determined naturalness in her voice. She had picked up the sewing, but now it dropped in her lap, and she murmured in a different voice: "But I tell you what I *do* wish, Mrs. Peters. I wish I had come over sometimes when she was here. I wish — I had."

"But of course you were awful busy, Mrs. Hale. Your house — and your children."

"I could've come," retorted Mrs. Hale shortly. "I stayed away because it weren't cheerful — and that's why I ought to have come. I" — she looked around — "I've never liked this place. Maybe because it's down in a hollow and you don't see the road. I don't know what it is, but it's a lonesome place, and always was. I wish I had come over to see Minnie Foster sometimes. I can see now —" She did not put it into words.

"Well, you mustn't reproach yourself," counseled Mrs. Peters. "Somehow, we just don't see how it is with other folks till — something comes up."

"Not having children makes less work," mused Mrs. Hale, after a silence, "but it makes a quiet house — and Wright out to work all day — and no company when he did come in. Did you know John Wright, Mrs. Peters?"

"Not to know him. I've seen him in town. They say he was a good man."

"Yes — good," conceded John Wright's neighbor grimly. "He didn't drink, and kept his word as well as most, I guess, and paid his debts. But he was a hard man, Mrs. Peters. Just to pass the time of day with him — ." She stopped, shivered a little. "Like a raw wind that gets to the bone." Her eye fell upon the cage on the table before her, and she added, almost bitterly: "I should think she would've wanted a bird!"

Suddenly she leaned forward, looking intently at the cage. "But what do you s'pose went wrong with it?"

"I don't know," returned Mrs. Peters; "unless it got sick and died."

But after she said it she reached over and swung the broken door. Both women watched it as if somehow held by it.

"You didn't know — her?" Mrs. Hale asked, a gentler note in her voice.

"Not till they brought her yesterday," said the sheriff's wife.

"She — come to think of it, she was kind of like a bird herself. Real sweet and pretty, but kind of timid and — fluttery. How — she — did — change."

That held her for a long time. Finally, as if struck with a happy thought and relieved to get back to everyday things, she exclaimed:

"Tell you what, Mrs. Peters, why don't you take the quilt in with you? It might take up her mind."

"Why, I think that's a real nice idea, Mrs. Hale," agreed the sheriff's wife, as if she too were glad to come into the atmosphere of a simple kindness. "There couldn't possibly be any objection to that, could there? Now, just what will I take? I wonder if her patches are in here — and her things?"

They turned to the sewing basket.

"Here's some red," said Mrs. Hale, bringing out a roll of cloth. Underneath that was a box. "Here, maybe her scissors are in here — and her things." She held it up. "What a pretty box! I'll warrant that was something she had a long time ago — when she was a girl."

She held it in her hand a moment; then, with a little sigh, opened it.

Instantly her hand went to her nose.

"Why — !"

Mrs. Peters drew nearer — then turned away.

"There's something wrapped up in this piece of silk," faltered Mrs. Hale.

"This isn't her scissors," said Mrs. Peters, in a shrinking voice.

Her hand not steady, Mrs. Hale raised the piece of silk. "Oh, Mrs. Peters!" she cried. "It's —"

Mrs. Peters bent closer.

"It's the bird," she whispered.

"But, Mrs. Peters!" cried Mrs. Hale. "*Look* at it! Its *neck* — look at its neck! It's all — other side *to*."

She held the box away from her.

The sheriff's wife again bent closer.

"Somebody wrung its neck," said she, in a voice that was slow and deep.

And then again the eyes of the two women met — this time clung together in a look of dawning comprehension, of growing horror. Mrs. Peters looked from the dead bird to the broken door of the cage. Again their eyes met. And just then there was a sound at the outside door.

Mrs. Hale slipped the box under the quilt pieces in the basket, and sank into the chair before it. Mrs. Peters stood holding to the table. The county attorney and the sheriff came in from outside.

"Well, ladies," said the county attorney, as one turning from serious things to little pleasantries, "have you decided whether she was going to quilt it or knot it?"

"We think," began the sheriff's wife in a flurried voice, "that she was going to — knot it."

He was too preoccupied to notice the change that came in her voice on that last.

"Well, that's very interesting, I'm sure," he said tolerantly. He caught sight of the bird-cage. "Has the bird flown?"

"We think the cat got it," said Mrs. Hale in a voice curiously even.

He was walking up and down, as if thinking something out.

"Is there a cat?" he asked absently.

Mrs. Hale shot a look up at the sheriff's wife.

"Well, not *now*," said Mrs. Peters. "They're superstitious, you know; they leave."

She sank into her chair.

The county attorney did not heed her. "No sign at all of anyone having come in from the outside," he said to Peters, in the manner of continuing an interrupted conversation. "Their own rope. Now let's go upstairs again and go over it, piece by piece. It would have to have been someone who knew just the —"

The stair door closed behind them and their voices were lost.

The two women sat motionless, not looking at each other, but as if peering into something and at the same time holding back. When they spoke now it was as if they were afraid of what they were saying, but as if they could not help saying it.

"She liked the bird," said Martha Hale, low and slowly. "She was going to bury it."

"When I was a girl," said Mrs. Peters, under her breath, "my kitten — there was a boy took a hatchet, and before my eyes — before I could get there —" She covered her face an instant. "If they hadn't held me back I would have" — she caught herself, looked upstairs where footsteps were heard, and finished weakly — "hurt him."

Then they sat without speaking or moving.

"I wonder how it would seem," Mrs. Hale at last began, as if feeling her way over strange ground — "never to have had any children around?" Her eyes made a slow sweep of the kitchen, as if seeing what that kitchen had meant through all the years. "No, Wright wouldn't like the bird," she said after that — "a thing that sang. She used to sing. He killed that too." Her voice tightened.

Mrs. Peters moved uneasily.

"Of course we don't know who killed the bird."

"I knew John Wright," was Mrs. Hale's answer.

"It was an awful thing was done in this house that night, Mrs. Hale," said the sheriff's wife. "Killing a man while he slept — slipping a thing round his neck that choked the life out of him."

Mrs. Hale's hand went out to the bird-cage.

"His neck. Choked the life out of him."

"We don't *know* who killed him," whispered Mrs. Peters wildly. "We don't *know*."

Mrs. Hale had not moved. "If there had been years and years of — nothing, then a bird to sing to you, it would be awful — still — after the bird was still."

It was as if something within her not herself had spoken, and it found in Mrs. Peters something she did not know as herself.

"I know what stillness is," she said, in a queer, monotonous voice. "When we homesteaded in Dakota, and my first baby died — after he was two years old — and me with no other then —"

Mrs. Hale stirred.

"How soon do you suppose they'll be through looking for the evidence?"

"I know what stillness is," repeated Mrs. Peters, in just the same way. Then she too pulled back. "The law has got to punish crime, Mrs. Hale," she said in her tight little way.

"I wish you'd seen Minnie Foster," was the answer, "when she wore a white dress with blue ribbons, and stood up there in the choir and sang."

The picture of that girl, the fact that she had lived neighbor to that girl for twenty years, and had let her die for lack of life, was suddenly more than she could bear.

"Oh, I *wish* I'd come over here once in a while!" she cried. "That was a crime! Who's going to punish that?"

"We mustn't take on," said Mrs. Peters, with a frightened look toward the stairs.

"I might 'a' *known* she needed help! I tell you, it's *queer,* Mrs. Peters. We live close together, and we live far apart. We all go through the same things — it's all just a different kind of the same thing! If it weren't — why do you and I *understand*? Why do we *know* — what we know this minute?"

She dashed her hand across her eyes. Then, seeing the jar of fruit on the table, she reached for it and choked out:

"If I was you I wouldn't *tell* her her fruit was gone! Tell her it *ain't*. Tell her it's all right — all of it. Here — take this in to prove it to her! She — she may never know whether it was broke or not."

She turned away.

Mrs. Peters reached out for the bottle of fruit as if she were glad to take it — as if touching a familiar thing, having something to do, could keep her from something else. She got up, looked about for something to wrap the fruit in, took a petticoat from the pile of clothes she had brought from the front room, and nervously started winding that round the bottle.

"My!" she began, in a high, false voice, "it's a good thing the men couldn't hear us! Getting all stirred up over a little thing like a — dead canary." She hurried over that. "As if that could have anything to do with — with — My, wouldn't they *laugh?*"

Footsteps were heard on the stairs.

"Maybe they would," muttered Mrs. Hale — "maybe they wouldn't."

"No, Peters," said the county attorney incisively; "it's all perfectly clear, except the reason for doing it. But you know juries when it comes to women. If there was some definite thing — something to show. Something to make a story about. A thing that would connect up with this clumsy way of doing it."

In a covert way Mrs. Hale looked at Mrs. Peters. Mrs. Peters was looking at her. Quickly they looked away from each other. The outer door opened and Mr. Hale came in.

"I've got the team round now," he said. "Pretty cold out there."

"I'm going to stay here awhile by myself," the county attorney suddenly announced. "You can send Frank out for me, can't you?" he asked the sheriff. "I want to go over everything. I'm not satisfied we can't do better."

Again, for one brief moment, the two women's eyes found one another.

The sheriff came up to the table.

"Did you want to see what Mrs. Peters was going to take in?"

The county attorney picked up the apron. He laughed.

"Oh, I guess they're not very dangerous things the ladies have picked out."

Mrs. Hale's hand was on the sewing basket in which the box was concealed. She felt that she ought to take her hand off the basket. She did not seem able to. He picked up one of the quilt blocks which she had piled on to cover the box. Her eyes felt like fire. She had a feeling that if he took up the basket she would snatch it from him.

But he did not take it up. With another little laugh, he turned away, saying:

"No; Mrs. Peters doesn't need supervising. For that matter, a sheriff's wife is married to the law. Ever think of it that way, Mrs. Peters?"

Mrs. Peters was standing beside the table. Mrs. Hale shot a look up at her; but she could not see her face. Mrs. Peters had turned away. When she spoke, her voice was muffled.

"Not — just that way," she said.

"Married to the law!" chuckled Mrs. Peters' husband. He moved toward the door into the front room, and said to the county attorney:

"I just want you to come in here a minute, George. We ought to take a look at these windows."

"Oh — windows," said the county attorney scoffingly.

"We'll be right out, Mr. Hale," said the sheriff to the farmer, who was still waiting by the door.

Hale went to look after the horses. The sheriff followed the county attorney into the other room. Again — for one final moment — the two women were alone in that kitchen.

Martha Hale sprang up, her hands tight together, looking at that other woman, with whom it rested. At first she could not see her eyes, for the sheriff's wife had not turned back since she turned away at that suggestion of being married to the law. But now Mrs. Hale made her turn back. Her eyes made her turn back. Slowly, unwillingly, Mrs. Peters turned her head until her eyes met the eyes of the other woman. There was a moment when they held each other in a steady, burning look in which there was no evasion nor flinching. Then Martha Hale's eyes pointed the way to the basket in which was hidden the thing that would make certain the conviction of the other woman — that woman who was not there and yet who had been there with them all through that hour.

For a moment Mrs. Peters did not move. And then she did it. With a rush forward, she threw back the quilt pieces, got the box, tried to put it in her handbag. It was too big. Desperately she opened it, started to take the bird out. But there she broke — she could not touch the bird. She stood there helpless, foolish.

There was the sound of a knob turning in the inner door. Martha Hale snatched the box from the sheriff's wife, and got it in the pocket of her big coat just as the sheriff and the county attorney came back into the kitchen.

"Well, Henry," said the county attorney facetiously, "at least we found out that she was not going to quilt it. She was going to — what is it you call it, ladies?"

Mrs. Hale's hand was against the pocket of her coat.

"We call it — knot it, Mr. Henderson."

❧

NADINE GORDIMER *(b. 1923), the recipient of the 1991 Nobel Prize for Literature, was born in the small town of Springs, near Johannesburg, South Africa. Her mother was English, and her father, a Jewish watchmaker, emigrated to Africa from the Baltic states. Gordimer attended a convent school and studied at the University of the Witwatersrand, getting what she has called "a scrappy and uninspiring minimal education." Growing up in South Africa, she never recognized herself in any of the English books she read until she encountered the stories of the New Zealand writer Katherine Mansfield. Then, Gordimer says, "I realized here was somebody who was writing about this other world, whose seasons at least I shared. Then I understood it was possible to be a writer even if you didn't live in England."*

Gordimer began to write stories before she attempted a novel. She acknowledges three writers as her guides: D. H. Lawrence, who influenced her way of looking at the natural world; Henry James, who gave her a consciousness of form; and Ernest Hemingway, who taught her to hear what is essential in dialogue. Her early stories appeared in The New Yorker, Harper's, *and other American magazines and were first collected in* Face to Face *(1949) and* The Soft Voice of the Serpent *(1952). Since her first novel,* The Lying Days, *was published in 1953, she has continued to write novels and short fiction collections. In her stories, Gordimer rarely experiments beyond the realistic rendering of her subject, but her decision to write in the form of the short story or the novel depends on the shape the material takes as a narrative:*

> *Whether it sprawls or neatly bites its own tail, a short story is a concept that the writer can "hold" fully realized in his imagination at one time. A novel is, by comparison, staked out, and must be taken possession of stage by stage; it is impossible to contain, all at once, the proliferation of concepts it ultimately may use. For this reason I cannot understand how people can suppose one makes a conscious choice, after knowing what one wants to write about, between writing a novel or a short story. A short story occurs, in the imaginative sense. To write one is to express from a situation in the exterior or interior world the life-giving drop — sweat, tear, semen, saliva — that will spread an intensity on the page; burn a hole in it.*

Gordimer's most recent works are The House Gun *(1998), a novel, and* Living in Hope and History *(1998), a collection of speeches, political essays, and commentaries. "The Diamond Mine" was published in* The New Yorker *on May 10, 1999.*

NADINE GORDIMER

The Diamond Mine

1999

I'll call her Tilla. You may call her by another name. You might think you knew her. You might have been the one. It's not by some simple colloquial habit that we "call" someone instead of naming: call him up.

It is during the war, your war, the forties, that has sunk as far away into the century as the grandfathers' 1914. He is blond, stocky in khaki, attractively nearsighted, so that the eyes, which are actually having difficulty with focus, seem to be concentrating attentively on her. This impression is emphasized by his lashes, blond and curly as his hair. He is completely different from the men she knows in the life of films — the only men she knows, apart from her father — and whom she expected to come along one day not too far off, Robert Taylor or even the foreigner, Charles Boyer. He is different because — at last — he is real. She is sixteen. He is no foreigner, no materialization of projection from Hollywood. He's the son of friends of her maternal grandmother, detailed to a military training camp in the province where the girl and her parents live. Some people even take in strangers from the camp for the respite of weekend leave; with a young daughter in the house, this family would not go so far as to risk that, but when the man of the family is beyond call-up age an easy way to fulfill patriotic duty is to offer hospitality to a man vouched for by connections. He's almost to be thought of as an elective grandson of the old lady. In war these strangers, remember, are Our Boys.

When he comes on Friday night and stays until Sunday his presence makes a nice change for the three, mother, father, and daughter, who live a quiet life, not given to socializing. That presence is a pleasant element in the closeness between parents and daughter: he is old enough to be an adult like them and, only eight years ahead of her, young enough to be her contemporary. The mother cooks a substantial lunch on the Sundays he's there; you can imagine what the food must be like in a military camp. The father suggests a game of golf — welcome to borrow clubs — but it turns out the soldier doesn't play. What's his game, then? He likes to fish. But this hospitality is four hundred miles from the sea; the soldier laughs along in manly recognition that there must be a game. The daughter: for her, she could never tell anyone, his weekend presence is a pervasion that fills the house, displaces all its familiar odors of home, is fresh and pungent — he's here. It's the emanation of khaki washed with strong soap and fixed — as in perfume the essence of flowers is fixed by alcohol — by the pressure of a hot iron.

The parents are reluctant cinema-goers, so it is thoughtful of this visiting friend of the family to invite the daughter of the house to choose a film she'd like to see on a Saturday night. She has no driving license yet (seventeen was the qualifying age in those days) and the father does not offer his car to the soldier. So the pair walk down the road from streetlight to streetlight, under the trees, all that autumn, to the small town's center, where only the cinema and the pub in the hotel are awake. She is aware of window dummies, in the closed shops that her mother's friends patronize, observing her as she walks past with a man. If she is invited to a party given by a school friend, she must be home strictly by eleven, usually fetched by her father. But now she is with a responsible friend, a family connection, not among unknown youths on the loose; if the film is a nine-o'clock showing, the pair are not home before midnight, and the lights are already extinguished in the parents' bedroom. It is then that, schoolgirlish, knowing nothing else to offer, she makes cocoa in the kitchen, and it is then that he tells her about fishing. The kitchen is locked up for the night, the windows are closed, and it is amazing how strong that presence of a man can be, that stiff-clean clothing warmed — not a scent, not a breath but, as he moves his arms graphically in description of playing a catch, it comes from the inner crease of his bare elbows, where the sun on Maneuvers hasn't got at the secret fold, from that center of being, the pliant hollow that vibrates between his collarbones as he speaks, the breastplate rosy down to where a few brownish-blond hairs disappear into the open neck of the khaki shirt. He will never turn dark, his skin retains the sun, glows. Him.

Tilla has never gone fishing. Her father doesn't fish. Four hundred miles from the sea, the boys at school kick and throw balls around — they know about, talk about football and cricket. The father knows about, talks about golf. Fishing. It opens the sea before her, the salt wind gets in her narrowed eyes, conveying to her whole nights passed alone on the rocks. He walks from headland to headland on dawn-wet sand, the tide is out — sometimes in midsentence there's a check, half smile, half breath, because he's thinking of something this child couldn't know. This is his incantation; it shuts out the parade-ground march toward killing and blinds the sights that the gun trains on sawdust-stuffed figures on which he is being drilled to see the face of the enemy, to whom he himself is the enemy, with guts (he pulls the intricately perfect innards out of the fish he's caught, a fisherman's simple skill) in place of sawdust. The sleeping parents are right: he will not touch her innocence of what this century claims, commands from him.

As they walk home where she used to race her bicycle up and down under the trees, the clothing on their arms — the khaki sleeve, the sweater her mother has handed her as a condition of permission to be out in the chill night air — brushes by proximity, not intention. The strap of her sandal slips, and as she pauses to right it, hopping on one leg, he steadies her by the forearm and then they walk on hand in hand. He's taking care of her. The next weekend, they kiss in one of the tree-dark intervals between streetlights. Boys have kissed her; it happened only to her mouth. The next Saturday, her arms went around him, his around her, her face approached, was pressed, breathed in, and breathed against the hollow of neck where the pendulum of heartbeat can be felt, the living place above the breastplate from which the incense of his presence had come. She was there.

In the kitchen there was no talk. The cocoa rose to the top of the pot, made ready. All the sources of warmth that her palms had extended to, everywhere in the house, as a domestic animal senses the warmth of a fire to approach, were in this body against hers, in the current of arms, the contact of chest, belly muscles, the deep strange heat from between his thighs. But he took care of her. Gently loosened her while she was discovering that a man has breasts, too, even if made of muscle, and that to press her own against them was an urgent exchange, walking on the wet sands with the fisherman.

The next weekend leave — but the next weekend leave is cancelled. Instead there's a call from the public phone at the canteen bar. The mother happened to answer and there were expressions of bright and encouraging regret that the daughter tried to piece into what they were responding to. The family was at supper. The father's mouth bunched stoically: Marching orders. Embarkation. The mother nodded round the table, confirming. She — the one I call Tilla — stood up, appalled at the strength to strike the receiver from her mother and the inability of a good girl to do so. Then her mother was saying, But of course we'll take a drive out on Sunday, say goodbye and Godspeed. Grandma'd never forgive me if she thought . . . Now, can you tell me how to get there, beyond Pretoria, I know . . . I didn't catch it, what mine? And after the turnoff at the main road? Oh, don't bother, I suppose we can ask at a petrol station if we get lost, everyone must know where that camp is. Is there something we can bring you, anything you'll need . . .

It seems they're to make an outing of it. Out of her stun: that essence, ironed khaki and soap, has been swept from the house, from the kitchen, by something that's got nothing to do with a fisherman, except that he is a man and, as her father has stated — embarkation — men go to war. Her mother makes picnic preparations: Do you think a chicken or pickled ox tongue, hard-boiled eggs. . . . Don't know where one can sit to eat in a military camp, there must be somewhere for visitors. Her father selects from his stack of travel brochures a map of the local area to place on the shelf below the windshield.

Petrol is rationed, but he has been frugal with coupons; there are enough to provide a full tank. Because of this, plans for the picnic are abandoned — no picnic — her mother thinks. Wouldn't it be a nice gesture to take the soldier out for a restaurant lunch in the nearest city? There won't be many such luxuries for the young man on his way to war in the North African desert.

They have never shown her the mine, the diamond mine, although ever since she was a small child they have taken her to places of interest as part of her education. They must have talked about it — her father is a mining-company official himself, but his exploitation is gold, not precious stones — or more likely it has been cited in a general-knowledge text at school: some famous diamond was dug up there.

The camp is on part of the vast mine property, commandeered by the Defense Force. Over the veld there are tents to the horizon, roped and staked, dun as the scuffed and dried grass and the earth scoured by boots — boots tramping everywhere, khaki everywhere, the wearers replicating one another, him. Where will they find him? He did give a tent number. The numbers don't seem to be consecutive. Her father is called to a halt by a replica with a gun, slow-spoken and polite. The car follows given directions retained differently by the mother and the father; the car turns, backs up, take it slowly for heaven's sake.

She is the one: There. There he is.

Of course, when you find him you see that there is no one like him, no bewilderment. They are all laughing in the conventions of greeting, but his eyes have their concentrated attention for her. It is his greeting of the intervals between streetlights, and of the kitchen. This weekend that ends weekends seems also to be the first of winter; it's suddenly cold, wind bellies and whips at that tent where he must have slept, remote, between weekends. It's the weather for hot food, shelter. At the restaurant, he chooses curry and rice for this last meal. He sprinkles grated coconut and she catches his eye and he smiles for her as he adds dollops of chutney. The smile is that of a greedy boy caught out and is also as if it were a hand squeezed under the table. No wine — the father has to drive, and young men oughtn't to be encouraged to drink, enough of that in the Army — but there is ice cream with canned peaches, coffee served, and peppermints with the compliments of the management.

It was too warm in the restaurant. Outside, high-altitude winds carry the breath of what must be early snow on the mountains, far away, unseen, as this drive back to the camp carries the breath of war, far away, unseen, where all the replicas in khaki are going to be shipped. No heating in the family car of those days, the soldier has only his thin, well-pressed khaki and the daughter, of course, like all young girls, has taken no precaution against a change in the weather — she is wearing the skimpy flounced cotton dress (secretly chosen, although he, being older, and a disciple of the sea's mysteries, probably won't even notice) that she was wearing the first time they walked to the cinema. The mother, concealing, she believes, irritation at the fecklessness of the young — next thing she'll have bronchitis and miss school — fortunately keeps a rug handy and insists that the passengers in the back seat put it over their knees.

It was easy to chat in the preoccupations of food along with the budgerigar chitter of other patrons in the restaurant. In the car, headed back for that final place, the camp, the outing is over. The father feels an obligation: at least, he can tell something about the diamond mine that's of interest, and soon they'll actually be passing the site of operations again, though you can't see much from the road.

The rug is like the pelt of some dusty pet animal settled over them. The warmth of the meal inside them is bringing it to life, a life they share, one body. It's pleasant to put their hands beneath it; the hands, his right, her left, find one another.

. . . You know what a diamond is, of course, although you look at it as something pretty a woman wears on her finger, hmm? Well, actually it consists of pure carbon crystallized . . .

He doesn't like to be interrupted, so there's no need to make any response, even if you still hear him. The right hand and the left hand become so tightly clasped that the pad of muscle at the base of each thumb is flattened against the bone and the interlaced fingers are jammed down between the joints. It isn't a clasp against imminent parting, it's got nothing to do with any future, it belongs in the urgent purity of this present.

. . . The crystallization in regular octahedrons, that's to say eight-sided, and in allied forms and the cut and polished ones you see in jewelry more or less follow . . .

The hands lay together, simply happened, on the skirt over her left thigh, because that is where she had slipped her hand beneath the woolly comfort of the rug. Now he slowly released, first fingers, then palms — at once awareness signalled between them that the rug was their tender accomplice, it must not be seen to be stirred by something — he released himself from her and for one bereft moment she thought he had left her behind, his eight-year advantage prevailed against such fusion of palms as it had done, so gently (oh, but why), when they were in the dark between trees, when they were in the kitchen.

. . . colorless or they may be tinted occasionally yellow, pink, even black . . .

The hand had not emerged from the rug. She followed as if her eyes were closed or she were in the dark; it went as if it were playing — looking for a place to tickle, as children do to make one another wriggle and laugh — where her skirt ended at her knee, going under her knee without displacing the skirt and touching the tendons and the hollow there. She didn't want to laugh (what would her father make of such a response to his knowledgeable commentary), so she glided her hand to his and put it back with hers where it had been before.

. . . one of the biggest diamonds in the world after the Koh-i-noor's hundred and nine carats, but that was found in India . . .

The hand, his hand, pressed fingers into her thigh through the cotton flounce, as if testing to see what was real about her, and stopped, and then out of the hesitation went down and, under the rug, up under the gauze of skirt, moved over her flesh. She did not look at him and he did not look at her.

. . . and there are industrial gems you can cut glass with, make bits for certain drills, the hardest substance known . . .

At the taut lip of her panties he hesitated again, no hurry, all something she was learning, he was teaching, the anticipation in his fingertips, he stroked along one of the veins in there in the delicate membranelike skin that is at the crevice between leg and body (like the skin that the sun on Maneuvers couldn't reach in the crook of his elbow), just before the hair begins. And then he went in under the elastic edge and his hand was soft on soft hair, his fingers like eyes attentive to her.

... Look at this veld — nothing suggests one of the greatest ever, anywhere, down there, down in what we call Blue Earth, the diamondiferous core ...

She has no clear idea of where his hand is now, what she feels is that they are kissing, they are in each other's mouths although they cannot look at one another.

Are you asleep back there? The mother is remarking her own boredom with the mine. He is eight years older, able to speak: Just listening. His finger explores deep down in the dark, the hidden entrance to some sort of cave with its slippery walls and smooth stalagmite. She's found, he's found her.

The car is passing the mine processing plant.

... product of the death and decay of forests millennia ago, just as coal is, but down there the ultimate alchemy, you might say ...

Those others, the parents, they have no way of knowing. It has happened, it is happening under the old woolly rug that was all they could provide for her. She is free of them. Found, and they don't know where she is.

At the camp, the father shakes the soldier's hand longer than in the usual grip. The mother for a moment looks as if she might give him a peck on the cheek, Godspeed, but it is not her way to be familiar.

Aren't you going to say goodbye? She's not a child, good heavens, a mother shouldn't have to remind of manners.

He's standing outside one of the tents with his hands hanging open at his sides as the car is driven away, and his attention is upon her until, with his furry narrowed sight, he'll cease to be able to make her out, while she can still see him, see him until he is made one with all the others in khaki, replicated, crossing and crowding, in preparation to embark.

If he had been killed in that war they would have heard through the grandmother's connections.

Is it still you, somewhere, old.

ꕥ

NATHANIEL HAWTHORNE *(1804–1864), writer of short stories and novels, was born in Salem, Massachusetts, into an eminent family who traced their lineage back to the Puritans. After his graduation from Bowdoin College in 1825, Hawthorne lived at home while he wrote short fiction he called "tales" or "articles" that he tried to sell to periodicals. American magazines of the time were mostly interested in publishing ghost stories, Indian legends, and "village tales" based on historical anecdotes. Hawthorne (like his contemporary Edgar Allan Poe) created stories that transcended the limitations of these conventions; his imagination was stirred by what he called "an inveterate love of allegory."*

Hawthorne published his first collection of stories, Twice-Told Tales, *in 1837; a second book of stories,* Mosses from an Old Manse, *appeared in 1846. That year he stopped writing to earn a better living for his family as surveyor of customs for the port of Salem. This was a political appointment, and after the Whigs won the presidency three years later, Hawthorne — a Democrat — was out of a job. He returned to writing fiction, sketching his "official life" at the Custom House in the introduction to his novel* The Scarlet Letter *in 1850. During the last decade of his career as a writer he published three other novels, several books for children, and another collection of tales. In "The Custom House," Hawthorne humorously suggested that his profession would not have impressed his Puritan ancestors:*

> *"What is he?" murmurs one grey shadow of my forefathers to the other. "A writer of story-books! What kind of business in life, what manner of glorifying God, or being serviceable to mankind in his day and generation, may that be? Why, the degenerate fellow might as well have been a fiddler!" Such are the compliments bandied between my great-grandsires and myself across the gulf of time! And yet, let them scorn me as they will, strong traits of their nature have intertwined themselves with mine.*

Despite Hawthorne's portrait of himself as an unappreciated artist, he was recognized by contemporaries such as Herman Melville and Edgar Allan Poe as a "genius of a very lofty order." Hawthorne wrote about 120 short tales and sketches in addition to his novels. His notebooks are filled with ideas for stories, more often jottings of abstract ideas than detailed observations of "real" individuals. "Young Goodman Brown" is one of his moral tales set in colonial New England.

RELATED COMMENTARIES: *Herman Melville, "Blackness in Hawthorne's 'Young Goodman Brown,'" page 693; Edgar Allan Poe, "The Importance of the Single Effect in a Prose Tale," page 709.*

NATHANIEL HAWTHORNE

Young Goodman Brown

1835

Young Goodman Brown came forth at sunset into the street at Salem village; but put his head back, after crossing the threshold, to exchange a parting kiss with his young wife. And Faith, as the wife was aptly named, thrust her own pretty head into the street, letting the wind play with the pink ribbons of her cap while she called to Goodman Brown.

"Dearest heart," whispered she, softly and rather sadly, when her lips were close to his ear, "prithee put off your journey until sunrise and sleep in your own bed to-night. A lone woman is troubled with such dreams and such thoughts that she's afeared of herself sometimes. Pray tarry with me this night, dear husband, of all nights in the year."

"My love and my Faith," replied young Goodman Brown, "of all nights in the year, this one night must I tarry away from thee. My journey, as thou callest it, forth and back again, must needs be done 'twixt now and sunrise. What, my sweet, pretty wife, dost thou doubt me already, and we but three months married?"

"Then God bless you!" said Faith, with the pink ribbons; "and may you find all well when you come back."

"Amen!" cried Goodman Brown. "Say thy prayers, dear Faith, and go to bed at dusk, and no harm will come to thee."

So they parted; and the young man pursued his way until, being about to turn the corner by the meeting-house, he looked back and saw the head of Faith still peeping after him with a melancholy air, in spite of her pink ribbons.

"Poor little Faith!" thought he, for his heart smote him. "What a wretch am I to leave her on such an errand! She talks of dreams, too. Methought as she spoke there was trouble in her face, as if a dream had warned her what work is to be done to-night. But no, no; 't would kill her to think it. Well, she's a blessed angel on earth, and after this one night I'll cling to her skirts and follow her to heaven."

With this excellent resolve for the future, Goodman Brown felt himself justified in making more haste on his present evil purpose. He had taken a dreary road, darkened by all the gloomiest trees of the forest, which barely stood aside to let the narrow path creep through, and closed immediately behind. It was all as lonely as could be; and there is this peculiarity in such a solitude, that the traveller knows not who may be concealed by the innumerable trunks and the thick boughs overhead; so that with lonely footsteps he may yet be passing through an unseen multitude.

"There may be a devilish Indian behind every tree," said Goodman Brown to himself; and he glanced fearfully behind him as he added, "What if the devil himself should be at my very elbow!"

His head being turned back, he passed a crook of the road, and, looking forward again, beheld the figure of a man, in grave and decent attire, seated at the foot of an old tree. He arose at Goodman Brown's approach and walked onward side by side with him.

"You are late, Goodman Brown," said he. "The clock of the Old South was striking as I came through Boston, and that is full fifteen minutes agone."

"Faith kept me back a while," replied the young man, with a tremor in his voice, caused by the sudden appearance of his companion, though not wholly unexpected.

It was now deep dusk in the forest, and deepest in that part of it where these two were journeying. As nearly as could be discerned, the second traveller was about fifty years old, apparently in the same rank of life as Goodman Brown, and bearing a considerable resemblance to him, though perhaps more in expression than features. Still they might have been taken for father and son. And yet, though the elder person was as simply clad as the younger, and as simple in manner too, he had an indescribable air of one who knew the world, and who would not have felt abashed at the governor's dinner table or in King William's court, were it possible that his affairs should call him thither. But the only thing about him that could be fixed upon as remarkable was his staff, which bore the likeness of a great black snake, so curiously wrought that it might almost be seen to twist and wriggle itself like a living serpent. This, of course, must have been an ocular deception, assisted by the uncertain light.

"Come, Goodman Brown," cried his fellow-traveller, "this is a dull pace for the beginning of a journey. Take my staff, if you are so soon weary."

"Friend," said the other, exchanging his slow pace for a full stop, "having kept covenant by meeting thee here, it is my purpose now to return whence I came. I have scruples touching the matter thou wot'st of."

"Sayest thou so?" replied he of the serpent, smiling apart. "Let us walk on, nevertheless, reasoning as we go; and if I convince thee not thou shalt turn back. We are but a little way in the forest yet."

"Too far! too far!" exclaimed the goodman, unconsciously resuming his walk. "My father never went into the woods on such an errand, nor his father before him. We have been a race of honest men and good Christians since the days of the martyrs; and shall I be the first of the name of Brown that ever took this path and kept" —

"Such company, thou wouldst say," observed the elder person, interpreting his pause. "Well said, Goodman Brown! I have been as well acquainted with your family as with ever a one among the Puritans; and that's no trifle to say. I helped your grandfather, the constable, when he lashed the Quaker woman so smartly through the streets of Salem; and it was I that brought your father a pitch-pine knot, kindled at my own hearth, to set fire to an Indian village, in King Philip's war.° They were my good friends, both; and many a pleasant walk have we had along this path, and returned merrily after midnight. I would fain be friends with you for their sake."

"If it be as thou sayest," replied Goodman Brown, "I marvel they never spoke of these matters; or, verily, I marvel not, seeing that the least rumor of the sort would have driven them from New England. We are a people of prayer, and good works to boot, and abide no such wickedness."

"Wickedness or not," said the traveller with the twisted staff, "I have a very general acquaintance here in New England. The deacons of many a church have drunk the communion wine with me; the selectmen of divers towns make me their chairman; and a majority of the Great and General Court are firm supporters of my interest. The governor and I, too — But these are state secrets."

"Can this be so?" cried Goodman Brown, with a stare of amazement at his undisturbed companion. "Howbeit, I have nothing to do with the governor and council; they have their own ways, and are no rule for a simple husbandman like me. But, were I to go on with thee, how should I meet the eye of that good old man, our minister, at Salem village? Oh, his voice would make me tremble both Sabbath day and lecture day."

Thus far the elder traveller had listened with due gravity; but now burst into a fit of irrepressible mirth, shaking himself so violently that his snake-like staff actually seemed to wriggle in sympathy.

"Ha! ha! ha!" shouted he again and again; then composing himself, "Well, go on, Goodman Brown, go on; but, prithee, don't kill me with laughing."

King Philip's war: King Philip, a Wampanoag chief, spearheaded the most destructive Indian war ever waged against the New England colonists (1675–76).

"Well, then, to end the matter at once," said Goodman Brown, considerably nettled, "there is my wife, Faith. It would break her dear little heart; and I'd rather break my own."

"Nay, if that be the case," answered the other, "e'en go thy ways, Goodman Brown. I would not for twenty old women like the one hobbling before us that Faith should come to any harm."

As he spoke he pointed his staff at a female figure on the path, in whom Goodman Brown recognized a very pious and exemplary dame, who had taught him his catechism in youth, and was still his moral and spiritual adviser, jointly with the minister and Deacon Gookin.

"A marvel, truly that Goody Cloyse should be so far in the wilderness at nightfall," said he. "But with your leave, friend, I shall take a cut through the woods until we have left this Christian woman behind. Being a stranger to you, she might ask whom I was consorting with and whither I was going."

"Be it so," said his fellow-traveller. "Betake you to the woods, and let me keep the path."

Accordingly the young man turned aside, but took care to watch his companion, who advanced softly along the road until he had come within a staff's length of the old dame. She, meanwhile, was making the best of her way, with singular speed for so aged a woman, and mumbling some indistinct words — a prayer, doubtless — as she went. The traveller put forth his staff and touched her withered neck with what seemed the serpent's tail.

"The devil!" screamed the pious old lady.

"Then Goody Cloyse knows her old friend?" observed the traveller, confronting her and leaning on his writhing stick.

"Ah, forsooth, and is it your worship indeed?" cried the good dame. "Yea, truly is it, and in the very image of my old gossip, Goodman Brown, the grandfather of the silly fellow that now is. But — would your worship believe it? — my broomstick hath strangely disappeared, stolen, as I suspect, by that unhanged witch, Goody Cory, and that, too, when I was all anointed with the juice of smallage, and cinquefoil, and wolf's bane" —

"Mingled with fine wheat and the fat of a new-born babe," said the shape of old Goodman Brown.

"Ah, your worship knows the recipe," cried the old lady, cackling aloud. "So, as I was saying, being all ready for the meeting, and no horse to ride on, I made up my mind to foot it; for they tell me there is a nice young man to be taken into communion to-night. But now your good worship will lend me your arm, and we shall be there in a twinkling."

"That can hardly be," answered her friend. "I may not spare you my arm, Goody Cloyse; but here is my staff, if you will."

So saying, he threw it down at her feet, where, perhaps, it assumed life, being one of the rods which its owner had formerly lent to the Egyptian magi. Of this fact, however, Goodman Brown could not take cognizance. He had cast up his eyes in astonishment, and, looking down again, beheld neither Goody Cloyse nor the serpentine staff, but his fellow-traveller alone, who waited for him as calmly as if nothing had happened.

"That old woman taught me my catechism," said the young man; and there was a world of meaning in this simple comment.

They continued to walk onward, while the elder traveller exhorted his companion to make good speed and persevere in the path, discoursing so aptly that his arguments seemed rather to spring up in the bosom of his auditor than to be suggested by himself. As they went, he plucked a branch of maple to serve for a walking stick, and began to strip it of the twigs and little boughs, which were wet with evening dew. The moment his fingers touched them they became strangely withered and dried up as with a week's sunshine. Thus the pair proceeded, at a good free pace, until suddenly, in a gloomy hollow of the road, Goodman Brown sat himself down on the stump of a tree and refused to go any farther.

"Friend," he said, stubbornly, "my mind is made up. Not another step will I budge on this errand. What if a wretched old woman do choose to go to the devil when I thought she was going to heaven: is that any reason why I should quit my dear Faith and go after her?"

"You will think better of this by and by," said his acquaintance, composedly. "Sit here and rest yourself a while; and when you feel like moving again, there is my staff to help you along."

Without more words, he threw his companion the maple stick, and was as speedily out of sight as if he had vanished into the deepening gloom. The young man sat a few moments by the roadside, applauding himself greatly, and thinking with how clear a conscience he should meet the minister in his morning walk, nor shrink from the eye of good old Deacon Gookin. And what calm sleep would be his that very night, which was to have been spent so wickedly, but so purely and sweetly now, in the arms of Faith! Amidst these pleasant and praiseworthy meditations, Goodman Brown heard the tramp of horses along the road, and deemed it advisable to conceal himself within the verge of the forest, conscious of the guilty purpose that had brought him thither, though now so happily turned from it.

On came the hoof tramps and the voices of the riders, two grave old voices, conversing soberly as they drew near. These mingled sounds appeared to pass along the road, within a few yards of the young man's hiding-place; but, owing doubtless to the depth of the gloom at that particular spot, neither the travellers nor their steeds were visible. Though their figures brushed the small boughs by the wayside, it could not be seen that they intercepted, even for a moment, the faint gleam from the strip of bright sky athwart which they must have passed. Goodman Brown alternately crouched and stood on tiptoe, pulling aside the branches and thrusting forth his head as far as he durst without discerning so much as a shadow. It vexed him the more, because he could have sworn, were such a thing possible, that he recognized the voices of the minister and Deacon Gookin, jogging along quietly, as they were wont to do, when bound to some ordination or ecclesiastical council. While yet within hearing, one of the riders stopped to pluck a switch.

"Of the two, reverend sir," said the voice like the deacon's, "I had rather miss an ordination dinner than to-night's meeting. They tell me that some of our community are to be here from Falmouth and beyond, and others from Connecticut and Rhode Island, besides several of the Indian powwows, who, after their fashion, know almost as much deviltry as the best of us. Moreover, there is a goodly young woman to be taken into communion."

"Mighty well, Deacon Gookin!" replied the solemn old tones of the minister. "Spur up, or we shall be late. Nothing can be done, you know, until I get on the ground."

The hoofs clattered again; and the voices, talking so strangely in the empty air, passed on through the forest, where no church had ever been gathered or solitary Christian prayed. Whither, then, could these holy men be journeying so deep into the heathen wilderness? Young Goodman Brown caught hold of a tree for support, being ready to sink down on the ground, faint and overburdened with the heavy sickness of his heart. He looked up to the sky, doubting whether there really was a heaven above him. Yet there was the blue arch, and the stars brightening in it.

"With heaven above and Faith below, I will yet stand firm against the devil!" cried Goodman Brown.

While he still gazed upward into the deep arch of the firmament and had lifted his hands to pray, a cloud, though no wind was stirring, hurried across the zenith and hid the brightening stars. The blue sky was still visible, except directly overhead, where this black mass of cloud was sweeping swiftly northward. Aloft in the air, as if from the depths of the cloud, came a confused and doubtful sound of voices. Once the listener fancied that he could distinguish the accents of towns-people of his own, men and women, both pious and ungodly, many of whom he had met at the communion table, and had seen others rioting at the tavern. The next moment, so indistinct were the sounds, he doubted whether he had heard aught but the murmur of the old forest, whispering without a wind. Then came a stronger swell of those familiar tones, heard daily in the sunshine at Salem village, but never until now from a cloud of night. There was one voice, of a young woman, uttering lamentations, yet with an uncertain sorrow, and entreating for some favor, which, perhaps, it would grieve her to obtain; and all the unseen multitude, both saints and sinners, seemed to encourage her onward.

"Faith!" shouted Goodman Brown, in a voice of agony and desperation; and the echoes of the forest mocked him, crying, "Faith! Faith!" as if bewildered wretches were seeking her all through the wilderness.

The cry of grief, rage, and terror was yet piercing the night, when the unhappy husband held his breath for a response. There was a scream, drowned immediately in a louder murmur of voices, fading into far-off laughter, as the dark cloud swept away, leaving the clear and silent sky above Goodman Brown. But something fluttered lightly down through the air and caught on the branch of a tree. The young man seized it, and beheld a pink ribbon.

"My Faith is gone!" cried he after one stupefied moment. "There is no good on earth; and sin is but a name. Come, devil; for to thee is this world given."

And, maddened with despair, so that he laughed loud and long, did Goodman Brown grasp his staff and set forth again, at such a rate that he seemed to fly along the forest path rather than to walk or run. The road grew wilder and drearier and more faintly traced, and vanished at length, leaving him in the heart of the dark wilderness, still rushing onward with the instinct that guides mortal man to evil. The whole forest was peopled with frightful sounds — the creaking of the trees, the howling of wild beasts, and the yell of Indians; while sometimes the wind tolled like a distant church bell, and sometimes gave a broad roar around the traveller, as if all Nature were laughing him to scorn. But he was himself the chief horror of the scene, and shrank not from its other horrors.

"Ha! ha! ha!" roared Goodman Brown when the wind laughed at him. "Let us hear which will laugh loudest. Think not to frighten me with your deviltry. Come witch, come wizard, come Indian powwow, come devil himself, and here comes Goodman Brown. You may as well fear him as he fear you."

In truth, all through the haunted forest there could be nothing more frightful than the figure of Goodman Brown. On he flew among the black pines, brandishing his staff with frenzied gestures, now giving vent to an inspiration of horrid blasphemy, and now shouting forth such laughter as set all the echoes of the forest laughing like demons around him. The fiend in his own shape is less hideous than when he rages in the breast of man. Thus sped the demoniac on his course, until, quivering among the trees, he saw a red light before him, as when the felled trunks and branches of a clearing have been set on fire, and throw up their lurid blaze against the sky, at the hour of midnight. He paused, in a lull of the tempest that had driven him onward, and heard the swell of what seemed a hymn, rolling solemnly from a distance with the weight of many voices. He knew the tune; it was a familiar one in the choir of the village meeting-house. The verse died heavily away, and was lengthened by a chorus, not of human voices, but of all the sounds of the benighted wilderness pealing in awful harmony together. Goodman Brown cried out, and his cry was lost to his own ear by its unison with the cry of the desert.

In the interval of silence he stole forward until the light glared full upon his eyes. At one extremity of an open space, hemmed in by the dark wall of the forest, arose a rock, bearing some rude, natural resemblance either to an altar or a pulpit, and surrounded by four blazing pines, their tops aflame, their stems untouched, like candles at an evening meeting. The mass of foliage that had overgrown the summit of the rock was all on fire, blazing high into the night and fitfully illuminating the whole field. Each pendent twig and leafy festoon was in a blaze. As the red light arose and fell, a numerous congregation alternately shone forth, then disappeared in shadow, and again grew, as it were, out of the darkness, peopling the heart of the solitary woods at once.

"A grave and dark-clad company," quoth Goodman Brown.

In truth they were such. Among them, quivering to and fro between gloom and splendor, appeared faces that would be seen next day at the council board of the province, and others which, Sabbath after Sabbath, looked devoutly heavenward, and benignantly over the crowded pews, from the holiest pulpits in the land. Some affirm that the lady of the governor was there. At least there were high dames well known to her, and wives of honored husbands, and widows, a great multitude, and ancient maidens, all of excellent repute, and fair young girls, who trembled lest their mothers should espy them. Either the sudden gleams of light flashing over the obscure field bedazzled Goodman Brown, or he recognized a score of the church members of Salem village famous for their especial sanctity. Good old Deacon Gookin had arrived, and waited at the skirts of that venerable saint, his revered pastor. But, irreverently consorting with these grave, reputable, and pious people, these elders of the church, these chaste dames and dewy virgins, there were men of dissolute lives and women of spotted fame, wretches given over to all mean and filthy vice, and suspected even of horrid crimes. It was strange to see that the good shrank not from the wicked, nor were the sinners abashed by the saints. Scattered also among their pale-faced enemies were the Indian priests, or powwows, who had often scared their native forest with more hideous incantations than any known to English witchcraft.

"But where is Faith?" thought Goodman Brown; and, as hope came into his heart, he trembled.

Another verse of the hymn arose, a slow and mournful strain, such as the pious love, but joined to words which expressed all that our nature can conceive of sin, and darkly hinted at far more. Unfathomable to mere mortals is the lore of fiends. Verse after verse was sung; and still the chorus of the desert swelled between like the deepest tone of a mighty organ; and with the final peal of that dreadful anthem there came a sound, as if the roaring wind, the rushing streams, the howling beasts, and every other voice of the unconcerted wilderness were mingling and according with the voice of guilty man in homage to the prince of all. The four blazing pines threw up a loftier flame, and obscurely discovered shapes and visages of horror on the smoke wreaths above the impious assembly. At the same moment the fire on the rock shot redly forth and formed a flowing arch above its base, where now appeared a figure. With reverence be it spoken, the figure bore no slight similitude, both in garb and manner, to some grave divine of the New England churches.

"Bring forth the converts!" cried a voice that echoed through the field and rolled into the forest.

At the word, Goodman Brown stepped forth from the shadow of the trees and approached the congregation, with whom he felt a loathful brotherhood by the sympathy of all that was wicked in his heart. He could have well-nigh sworn that the shape of his own dead father beckoned him to advance, looking downward from a smoke wreath, while a woman, with dim features of despair, threw out her hand to warn him back. Was it his mother? But he had no power to retreat one step, nor to resist, even in thought, when the minister and good old Deacon Gookin seized his arms and led him to the blazing rock. Thither came also the slender form of a veiled female, led between Goody Cloyse, that pious teacher of the catechism, and Martha Carrier, who had received the devil's promise to be queen of hell. A rampant hag was she. And there stood the proselytes beneath the canopy of fire.

"Welcome, my children," said the dark figure, "to the communion of your race. Ye have found thus young your nature and your destiny. My children, look behind you!"

They turned; and flashing forth, as it were, in a sheet of flame, the fiend worshippers were seen; the smile of welcome gleamed darkly on every visage.

"There," resumed the sable form, "are all whom ye have reverenced from youth. Ye deemed them holier than yourselves and shrank from your own sin, contrasting it with their lives of righteousness and prayerful aspirations heavenward. Yet here are they all in my worshipping assembly. This night it shall be granted you to know their secret deeds: how hoary-bearded elders of the church have whispered wanton words to the young maids of their households; how many a woman, eager for widows' weeds, has given her husband a drink at bedtime and let him sleep his last sleep in her bosom; how beardless youths have made haste to inherit their fathers' wealth; and how fair damsels — blush not, sweet ones — have dug little graves in the garden, and bidden me, the sole guest, to an infant's funeral. By the sympathy of your human hearts for sin ye shall scent out all the places — whether in church, bedchamber, street, field, or forest — where crime has been committed, and shall exult to behold the whole earth one stain of guilt, one mighty blood spot. Far more than this. It shall be yours to penetrate, in every bosom, the deep mystery of sin, the fountain of all wicked arts, and which inexhaustibly supplies more evil impulses than human power — than my power at its utmost — can make manifest in deeds. And now, my children, look upon each other."

They did so; and, by the blaze of the hell-kindled torches, the wretched man beheld his Faith, and the wife her husband, trembling before that unhallowed altar.

"Lo, there ye stand, my children," said the figure, in a deep and solemn tone, almost sad with its despairing awfulness, as if his once angelic nature could yet mourn for our miserable race. "Depending upon one another's hearts, ye had still hoped that virtue were not all a dream. Now are ye undeceived. Evil is the nature of mankind. Evil must be your only happiness. Welcome again, my children, to the communion of your race."

"Welcome," repeated the fiend worshippers, in one cry of despair and triumph.

And there they stood, the only pair, as it seemed, who were yet hesitating on the verge of wickedness in this dark world. A basin was hallowed, naturally, in the rock. Did it contain water, reddened by the lurid light? or was it blood? or, perchance, a liquid flame? Herein did the shape of evil dip his hand and prepare to lay the mark of baptism upon their foreheads, that they might be partakers of the mystery of sin, more conscious of the secret guilt of others, both in deed and thought, than they could now be of their own. The husband cast one look at his pale wife, and Faith at him. What polluted wretches would the next glance show them to each other, shuddering alike at what they disclosed and what they saw!

"Faith! Faith!" cried the husband, "look up to heaven, and resist the wicked one."

Whether Faith obeyed he knew not. Hardly had he spoken when he found himself amid calm night and solitude, listening to a roar of the wind which died heavily away through the forest. He staggered against the rock, and felt it chill and damp; while a hanging twig, that had been all on fire, besprinkled his cheek with the coldest dew.

The next morning young Goodman Brown came slowly into the street of Salem village, staring around him like a bewildered man. The good old minister was taking a walk along the graveyard to get an appetite for breakfast and meditate his sermon, and bestowed a blessing, as he passed, on Goodman Brown. He shrank from the venerable saint as if to avoid an anathema. Old Deacon Gookin was at domestic worship, and the holy words of his prayer were heard through the open window. "What God doth the wizard pray to?" quoth Goodman Brown. Goody Cloyse, that excellent old Christian, stood in the early sunshine at her own lattice, catechizing a little girl who had brought her a pint of morning's milk. Goodman Brown snatched away the child as from the grasp of the fiend himself. Turning the corner by the meeting-house, he spied the head of Faith, with the pink ribbons, gazing anxiously forth, and bursting into such joy at sight of him that she skipped along the street and almost kissed her husband before the whole village. But Goodman Brown looked sternly and sadly into her face, and passed on without a greeting.

Had Goodman Brown fallen asleep in the forest and only dreamed a wild dream of a witch-meeting?

Be it so if you will; but, alas! it was a dream of evil omen for young Goodman Brown. A stern, a sad, a darkly meditative, a distrustful, if not a desperate man did he become from the night of that fearful dream. On the Sabbath day, when the congregation were singing a holy psalm, he could not listen because an anthem of sin rushed loudly upon his ear and drowned all the blessed strain. When the minister spoke from the pulpit with power and fervid eloquence, and, with his hand on the open Bible, of the sacred truths of our religion, and of saint-like lives and triumphant deaths, and of future bliss or misery unutterable, then did Goodman Brown turn pale, dreading lest the roof should thunder down upon the gray blasphemer and his hearers. Often, awaking suddenly at midnight, he shrank from the bosom of Faith; and at morning or eventide, when the family knelt down at prayer, he scowled and muttered to himself, and gazed sternly at his wife, and turned away. And when he had lived long, and was borne to his grave a hoary corpse, followed by Faith, an aged woman, and children and grandchildren, a goodly procession, besides neighbors not a few, they carved no hopeful verse upon his tombstone, for his dying hour was gloom.

ꕥ

BESSIE HEAD *(1937–1986) was born in Pietermaritzburg, South Africa, the daughter of a white mother and a black father. Raised by foster parents, she was placed in a mission orphanage at the age of thirteen. A lonely child, she was comforted by reading, which invited her into what she called "a world of magic beyond your own." In her early twenties she taught in an elementary school and wrote stories for a local newspaper. After her marriage in 1961, she left South Africa, seeking political refuge from apartheid on an agricultural commune in Serowe in Botswana.*

The journalist Betty Fradkin has described Head's life as a refugee: "There is no electricity yet. At night Bessie types by the light of six candles. Fruit trees and vegetables surround the house. Bessie makes guava jam to sell, and will sell vegetables when the garden is enlarged." Despite the devastating experiences of racial oppression and the dislocation and economic hardship of exile, Head found the peace of mind necessary to create fiction: "In South Africa, all my life I lived in shattered little bits. All those shattered bits began to grow together here. . . . I have a peace against which all the turmoil is worked out." In 1969 she published her first novel, When Rain Clouds Gather. *Two other novels followed, along with a collection of related stories titled* The Collector of Treasures and Other Botswana Village Tales *(1977) and a history of her village,* Serowe: Village of the Rain Wind *(1981). Her last novel,* A Bewitched Crossroad *(1984), is a chronicle combining history and folklore. Two years later, Head died of hepatitis while working on her autobiography.*

Highly sensitive to the enduring power of ritual and tradition in contemporary African life, Head was also concerned with the often precarious role of women in the patriarchal systems of African tribal society. "The Prisoner Who Wore Glasses" dramatizes complex political realities in the villages and cities she had known in Botswana and South Africa.

Bessie Head

The Prisoner Who Wore Glasses

1973

Scarcely a breath of wind disturbed the stiffness of the day and the long rows of cabbages were bright green in the sunlight. Large white clouds drifted slowly across the deep blue sky. Now and then they obscured the sun and caused a chill on the backs of the prisoners who had to work all day long in the cabbage field. This trick the clouds were playing with the sun eventually caused one of the prisoners who wore glasses to stop work, straighten up, and peer shortsightedly at them. He was a thin little fellow with a hollowed-out chest and comic knobbly knees. He also had a lot of fanciful ideas because he smiled at the clouds.

"Perhaps they want me to send a message to the children," he thought tenderly, noting that the clouds were drifting in the direction of his home some hundred miles away. But before he could frame the message, the warder in charge of his work detail shouted: "Hey, what you tink you're doing, Brille?"

The prisoner swung round, blinking rapidly, yet at the same time sizing up the enemy. He was a new warder, named Jacobus Stephanus Hannetjie. His eyes were the color of the sky but they were frightening. A simple, primitive, brutal soul gazed out of them.

The prisoner bent down quickly and a message was quietly passed down the line: "We're in for trouble this time, comrades."

"Why?" rippled back up the line.

"Because he's not human," the reply rippled down and yet only the crunching of the spades as they turned over the earth disturbed the stillness.

This particular work detail was known as Span One. It was composed of ten men and they were all political prisoners. They were grouped together for convenience, as it was one of the prison regulations that no black warder should be in charge of a political prisoner lest this prisoner convert him to his views. It never seemed to occur to the authorities that this very reasoning was the strength of Span One and a clue to the strange terror they aroused in the warders. As political prisoners they were unlike the other prisoners in the sense that they felt no guilt nor were they outcasts of society. All guilty men instinctively cower, which was why it was the kind of prison where men got knocked out cold with a blow at the back of the head from an iron bar. Up until the arrival of Warder Hannetjie, no warder had dared beat any member of Span One and no warder had lasted more than a week with them. The battle was entirely psychological. Span One was assertive and it was beyond the scope of white warders to handle assertive black men. Thus, Span One had got out of control. They were the best thieves and liars in the camp. They lived all day on raw cabbages. They chatted and smoked tobacco. And since they moved, thought, and acted as one, they had perfected every technique of group concealment.

Trouble began that very day between Span One and Warder Hannetjie. It was because of the shortsightedness of Brille. That was the nickname he was given in prison and is the Afrikaans word for someone who wears glasses. Brille could never judge the approach of the prison gates and on several previous occasions he had munched on cabbages and dropped them almost at the feet of the warder, and all previous warders had overlooked this. Not so Warder Hannetjie.

"Who dropped that cabbage?" he thundered.

Brille stepped out of line. "I did," he said meekly.

"All right," said Hannetjie. "The whole Span goes three meals off."

"But I told you I did it," Brille protested.

The blood rushed to Warder Hannetjie's face. "Look 'ere," he said. "I don't take orders from a kaffir. I don't know what kind of kaffir you tink you are. Why don't you say Baas. I'm your Baas. Why don't you say Baas, hey?"

Brille blinked his eyes rapidly but by contrast his voice was strangely calm. "I'm twenty years older than you," he said.

It was the first thing that came to mind but the comrades seemed to think it a huge joke. A titter swept up the line. The next thing, Warder Hannetjie whipped out a knobkerrie and gave Brille several blows about the head. What surprised his comrades was the speed with which Brille had removed his glasses or else they would have been smashed to pieces on the ground.

That evening in the cell Brille was very apologetic. "I'm sorry, comrades," he said. "I've put you into a hell of a mess."

"Never mind, brother," they said. "What happens to one of us happens to all."

"I'll try to make up for it, comrades," he said. "I'll steal something so that you don't go hungry."

Privately, Brille was very philosophical about his head wounds. It was the first time an act of violence had been perpetrated against him but he had long been a witness of extreme, almost unbelievable human brutality. He had twelve children and his mind traveled back that evening through the sixteen years of bedlam in which he had lived. It had all happened in a small drab little three-bedroom house in a small drab little street in the Eastern Cape and the children kept coming year after year because neither he nor Martha managed the contraceptives the right way and a teacher's salary never allowed moving to a bigger house and he was always taking exams to improve this salary only to have it all eaten up by hungry mouths. Everything was pretty horrible, especially the way the children fought. They'd get hold of each other's heads and give them a good bashing against the wall. Martha gave up somewhere along the line, so they worked out a thing between them. The bashings, biting, and blood were to operate in full swing until he came home. He was to be the bogeyman and when it worked he never failed to have a sense of godhead at the way in which his presence could change savages into fairly reasonable human beings.

Yet somehow it was this chaos and mismanagement at the center of his life that drove him into politics. It was really an ordered beautiful world with just a few basic slogans to learn along with the rights of mankind. At one stage, before things became very bad, there were conferences to attend, all very far away from home.

"Let's face it," he thought ruefully. "I'm only learning right now what it means to be a politician. All this while I've been running away from Martha and the kids."

And the pain in his head brought a hard lump to his throat. That was what the children did to each other daily and Martha wasn't managing and if Warder Hannetjie had not interrupted him that morning he would have sent the following message: "Be good comrades, my children. Cooperate, then life will run smoothly."

The next day Warder Hannetjie caught this old man with twelve children stealing grapes from the farm shed. They were an enormous quantity of grapes in a ten-gallon tin and for this misdeed the old man spent a week in the isolation cell. In fact, Span One as a whole was in constant trouble. Warder Hannetjie seemed to have eyes at the back of his head. He uncovered the trick about the cabbages, how they were split in two with the spade and immediately covered with earth and then unearthed again and eaten with split-second timing. He found out how tobacco smoke was beaten into the ground and he found out how conversations were whispered down the wind.

For about two weeks Span One lived in acute misery. The cabbages, tobacco, and conversations had been the pivot of jail life to them. Then one evening they noticed that their good old comrade who wore the glasses was looking rather pleased with himself. He pulled out a four-ounce packet of tobacco by way of explanation and the comrades fell upon it with great greed. Brille merely smiled. After all, he was the father of many children. But when the last shred had disappeared, it occurred to the comrades that they ought to be puzzled.

Someone said: "I say, brother. We're watched like hawks these days. Where did you get the tobacco?"

"Hannetjie gave it to me," said Brille.

There was a long silence. Into it dropped a quiet bombshell. "I saw Hannetjie in the shed today" — and the failing eyesight blinked rapidly. "I caught him in the act of stealing five bags of fertilizer and he bribed me to keep my mouth shut."

There was another long silence.

"Prison is an evil life," Brille continued, apparently discussing some irrelevant matter. "It makes a man contemplate all kinds of evil deeds."

He held out his hand and closed it. "You know, comrades," he said. "I've got Hannetjie. I'll betray him tomorrow."

Everyone began talking at once.

"Forget it, brother. You'll get shot."

Brille laughed.

"I won't," he said. "That is what I mean about evil. I am a father of children and I saw today that Hannetjie is just a child and stupidly truthful. I'm going to punish him severely because we need a good warder."

The following day, with Brille as witness, Hannetjie confessed to the theft of the fertilizer and was fined a large sum of money. From then on, Span One did very much as they pleased while Warder Hannetjie stood by and said nothing. But it was Brille who carried this to extremes.

One day, at the close of work Warder Hannetjie said: "Brille, pick up my jacket and carry it back to the camp."

"But nothing in the regulations says I'm your servant, Hannetjie," Brille replied coolly.

"I've told you not to call me Hannetjie. You must say, Baas," but Warder Hannetjie's voice lacked conviction.

In turn, Brille squinted up at him. "I'll tell you something about this Baas business, Hannetjie," he said. "One of these days we are going to run the country. You are going to clean my car. Now, I have a fifteen-year-old son and I'd die of shame if you had to tell him that I ever called you Baas."

Warder Hannetjie went red in the face and picked up his coat.

On another occasion Brille was seen to be walking about the prison yard, openly smoking tobacco. On being taken before the prison commander, he claimed to have received the tobacco from Warder Hannetjie. All throughout the tirade from his chief, Warder Hannetjie failed to defend himself, but his nerve broke completely.

He called Brille to one side. "Brille," he said. "This thing between you and me must end. You may not know it but I have a wife and children and you're driving me to suicide."

"Why, don't you like your own medicine, Hannetjie?" Brille asked quietly.

"I can give you anything you want," Warder Hannetjie said in desperation.

"It's not only me but the whole of Span One," said Brille cunningly. "The whole of Span One wants something from you."

Warder Hannetjie brightened with relief. "I tink I can manage if it's tobacco you want," he said.

Brille looked at him, for the first time struck with pity and guilt. He wondered if he had carried the whole business too far. The man was really a child.

"It's not tobacco we want, but you," he said. "We want you on our side. We want a good warder because without a good warder we won't be able to manage the long stretch ahead."

Warder Hannetjie interpreted this request in his own fashion and his interpretation of what was good and human often left the prisoners of Span One speechless with surprise. He had a way of slipping off his revolver and picking up a spade and digging alongside Span One. He had a way of producing unheard-of luxuries like boiled eggs from his farm nearby and things like cigarettes, and Span One responded nobly and got the reputation of being the best work detail in the camp. And it wasn't only take from their side. They were awfully good at stealing certain commodities like fertilizer which were needed on the farm of Warder Hannetjie.

✠

ERNEST HEMINGWAY *(1899–1961) was born in Oak Park, Illinois, but he spent most of his boyhood in Michigan, where his father, a doctor, encouraged his enthusiasm for camping and hunting. Active as a reporter for his high school newspaper, Hemingway decided not to go on to college. Instead he worked as a reporter on the* Kansas City Star *for a few months before volunteering to serve in an American ambulance unit in France during World War I. Then he went to Italy, served at the front, and was severely wounded in action just before his nineteenth birthday. After the war he was too restless to settle down in the United States, so he lived in Paris and supported himself and his wife as a newspaper correspondent. He worked hard at learning how to write fiction; as he later said, "I found the greatest difficulty, aside from knowing what you really felt, rather than what you were supposed to feel, or had been taught to feel, was to put down what really happened in action: what the actual things were which produced the emotion that you experienced."*

In America Hemingway had admired the work of Sherwood Anderson, especially the colloquial, "unliterary" tone of his stories, and in Paris he came under the influence of Gertrude Stein, telling Anderson in a letter of 1922 that "Gertrude Stein and me are just like brothers." As the critic A. Walton Litz and many others have recognized, Hemingway was receptive to several diverse influences as a young writer forging his literary style, including the work of the experimental poet Ezra Pound, whose advice in essays written in 1913 on the composition of imagist poetry is suggested in the style developed in Hemingway's early fiction:

1. *Direct treatment of the "thing," without evasion or cliché.*
2. *The use of absolutely no word that does not contribute to the general design.*
3. *Fidelity to the rhythms of natural speech.*
4. *The natural object is always the adequate symbol.*

Hemingway's first book, In Our Time *(1925), is a collection of stories and sketches. His early novels,* The Sun Also Rises *(1926) and* A Farewell to Arms *(1929), established him as a master stylist, probably the most influential writer of*

American prose in the first half of the twentieth century. In 1938 he collected what he considered his best short fiction in The Fifth Column and the First Forty-Nine Stories. *After publication of* The Old Man and the Sea, *he was awarded the Nobel Prize for Literature in 1954. Seven years later, in poor health and haunted by the memory of the suicide of his father, who had shot himself with a Civil War pistol in 1929, Hemingway killed himself with a shotgun in his Idaho hunting lodge.*

Hemingway's concise way of developing a plot through dialogue, as in "Hills Like White Elephants," attracted many imitators. He once explained how he achieved an intense compression by comparing his method to the principle of the iceberg: "There is seven-eighths of it under water for every part that shows. Anything you know you can eliminate and it only strengthens your iceberg. It is the part that doesn't show. If a writer omits something because he does not know it then there is a hole in the story." The most authoritative collection of Hemingway's stories, The Complete Short Stories of Ernest Hemingway: The Finca-Vigia Edition, *was published in 1991.*

RELATED COMMENTARY: *Ezra Pound, "On the Principles of Imagism," page 1204.*

ERNEST HEMINGWAY

Hills Like White Elephants

1927

The hills across the valley of the Ebro were long and white. On this side there was no shade and no trees and the station was between two lines of rails in the sun. Close against the side of the station there was the warm shadow of the building and a curtain, made of strings of bamboo beads, hung across the open door into the bar, to keep out flies. The American and the girl with him sat at a table in the shade, outside the building. It was very hot and the express from Barcelona would come in forty minutes. It stopped at this junction for two minutes and went on to Madrid.

"What should we drink?" the girl asked. She had taken off her hat and put it on the table.

"It's pretty hot," the man said.

"Let's drink beer."

"*Dos cervezas,*" the man said into the curtain.

"Big ones?" a woman asked from the doorway.

"Yes. Two big ones."

The woman brought two glasses of beer and two felt pads. She put the felt pads and the beer glasses on the table and looked at the man and the girl. The girl was looking off at the line of hills. They were white in the sun and the country was brown and dry.

"They look like white elephants," she said.

"I've never seen one," the man drank his beer.

"No, you wouldn't have."

"I might have," the man said. "Just because you say I wouldn't have doesn't prove anything."

The girl looked at the bead curtain. "They've painted something on it," she said. "What does it say?"

"Anis del Toro. It's a drink."

"Could we try it?"

The man called "Listen" through the curtain. The woman came out from the bar.

"Four reales."

"We want two Anis del Toro."

"With water?"

"Do you want it with water?"

"I don't know," the girl said. "Is it good with water?"

"It's all right."

"You want them with water?" asked the woman.

"Yes, with water."

"It tastes like licorice," the girl said and put the glass down.

"That's the way with everything."

"Yes," said the girl. "Everything tastes of licorice. Especially all the things you've waited so long for, like absinthe."

"Oh, cut it out."

"You started it," the girl said. "I was being amused. I was having a fine time."

"Well, let's try and have a fine time."

"All right. I was trying. I said the mountains looked like white elephants. Wasn't that bright?"

"That was bright."

"I wanted to try this new drink: That's all we do, isn't it — look at things and try new drinks?"

"I guess so."

The girl looked across at the hills.

"They're lovely hills," she said. "They don't really look like white elephants. I just meant the coloring of their skin through the trees."

"Should we have another drink?"

"All right."

The warm wind blew the bead curtain against the table.

"The beer's nice and cool," the man said.

"It's lovely," the girl said.

"It's really an awfully simple operation, Jig," the man said. "It's not really an operation at all."

The girl looked at the ground the table legs rested on.

"I know you wouldn't mind it, Jig. It's really not anything. It's just to let the air in."

The girl did not say anything.

"I'll go with you and I'll stay with you all the time. They just let the air in and then it's all perfectly natural."

"Then what will we do afterward?"

"We'll be fine afterward. Just like we were before."

"What makes you think so?"

"That's the only thing that bothers us. It's the only thing that's made us unhappy."

The girl looked at the bead curtain, put her hand out, and took hold of two of the strings of beads.

"And you think then we'll be all right and be happy."

"I know we will. You don't have to be afraid. I've known lots of people that have done it."

"So have I," said the girl. "And afterward they were all so happy."

"Well," the man said, "if you don't want to you don't have to. I wouldn't have you do it if you didn't want to. But I know it's perfectly simple."

"And you really want to?"

"I think it's the best thing to do. But I don't want you to do it if you don't really want to."

"And if I do it you'll be happy and things will be like they were and you'll love me?"

"I love you now. You know I love you."

"I know. But if I do it, then it will be nice again if I say things are like white elephants, and you'll like it?"

"I'll love it. I love it now but I just can't think about it. You know how I get when I worry."

"If I do it you won't ever worry?"

"I won't worry about that because it's perfectly simple."

"Then I'll do it. Because I don't care about me."

"What do you mean?"

"I don't care about me."

"Well, I care about you."

"Oh, yes. But I don't care about me. And I'll do it and then everything will be fine."

"I don't want you to do it if you feel that way."

The girl stood up and walked to the end of the station. Across, on the other side, were fields of grain and trees along the banks of the Ebro. Far away, beyond the river, were mountains. The shadow of a cloud moved across the field of grain and she saw the river through the trees.

"And we could have all this," she said. "And we could have everything and every day we make it more impossible."

"What did you say?"

"I said we could have everything."

"We can have everything."

"No, we can't."

"We can have the whole world."

"No, we can't."

"We can go everywhere."

"No, we can't. It isn't ours any more."

"It's ours."

"No, it isn't. And once they take it away, you never get it back."

"But they haven't taken it away."

"We'll wait and see."

"Come on back in the shade," he said. "You mustn't feel that way."

"I don't feel any way," the girl said. "I just know things."

"I don't want you to do anything that you don't want to do ——"

"Nor that isn't good for me," she said. "I know. Could we have another beer?"

"All right. But you've got to realize ——"

"I realize," the girl said. "Can't we maybe stop talking?"

They sat down at the table and the girl looked across at the hills on the dry side of the valley and the man looked at her and at the table.

"You've got to realize," he said, "that I don't want you to do it if you don't want to. I'm perfectly willing to go through with it if it means anything to you."

"Doesn't it mean anything to you? We could get along."

"Of course it does. But I don't want anybody but you. I don't want any one else. And I know it's perfectly simple."

"Yes, you know it's perfectly simple."

"It's all right for you to say that, but I do know it."

"Would you do something for me now?"

"I'd do anything for you."

"Would you please please please please please please please stop talking?"

He did not say anything but looked at the bags against the wall of the station. There were labels on them from all the hotels where they had spent nights.

"But I don't want you to," he said, "I don't care anything about it."

"I'll scream," the girl said.

The woman came out through the curtains with two glasses of beer and put them down on the damp felt pads. "The train comes in five minutes," she said.

"What did she say?" asked the girl.

"That the train is coming in five minutes."

The girl smiled brightly at the woman, to thank her.

"I'd better take the bags over to the other side of the station," the man said. She smiled at him.

"All right. Then come back and we'll finish the beer."

He picked up the two heavy bags and carried them around the station to the other tracks. He looked up the tracks but could not see the train. Coming back, he walked through the barroom, where people waiting for the train were drinking. He drank an Anis at the bar and looked at the people. They were all waiting reasonably for the train. He went out through the bead curtain. She was sitting at the table and smiled at him.

"Do you feel better?" he asked.

"I feel fine," she said. "There's nothing wrong with me. I feel fine."

Amy Hempel *(b. 1951) was born in Chicago and grew up in California, where she went to four colleges before moving to New York City. She regarded her years in Los Angeles and San Francisco as "lost," yet found herself "making notes on things that happened many years before I started to write, though at the time I did not know why." In 1982 she attended a fiction workshop at Columbia University taught by Gordon Lish, an editor at Knopf, who arranged for the publication of her first collection of stories,* Reasons to Live *(1985). Hempel has said that in her writing she was influenced by contemporaries such as Raymond Carver, who have "a kind of compression and distillation in their work that gets to the heart of things and gives the reader credit for being able to keep up without having everything explained."*

Often Hempel's stories are only a few paragraphs long — fragments of conversation, whimsical anecdotes, and ironic observations about women's lives written in a style as spare and evocative as a Polaroid snapshot. The novelist Sheila Ballantyne has understood Hempel's method:

> *Minimalism has its uses, and can achieve surprisingly varied effects: it can allude and expand, as well as leave out and compress. At its most reductive or repetitive, it can induce corresponding states of boredom or trance. . . . At its worst, minimalism is a kind of fraudulent tic that serves to hide a vacuum or defend against feeling. At its best it can, with economy and restraint, amplify perception and force meaning to leap from the page.*

"In the Cemetery Where Al Jolson Is Buried" refers to the popular entertainer Al Jolson, who starred in The Jazz Singer, *the first "talkie" made in Hollywood. He is buried in Forest Lawn Cemetery in Los Angeles. The story is from Hempel's first collection. Recently she has published* At the Gate of the Animal Kingdom *(1990) and* Tumble Home: A Novella and Short Stories *(1997), in which one of her narrators suggests Hempel's rationale as a storyteller: "The lighter the line, the easier it is to get your lure down deep." In an interview published in* Glimmer Train *(1997), Hempel explained that "compression has always been hugely attractive, and rhythm, whether it's in a sentence or a line" when she writes prose narrative.*

> *I pay readers the compliment, I mean I'm acknowledging that they're smart enough to get it. They don't need everything spelled out. They live downtown, they've seen tall buildings. . . . I think that my concerns are more a poet's concerns and always have been. I don't understand why these things in a story would be criticized, whereas in a poem it's the norm, it's what you expect. But I guess some have certain expectations of what a story is — that a story can be this, but not that. I think it really has come from a more provincial sense, a restricted, limited sense of story, and what it can do.*

Amy Hempel

In the Cemetery Where Al Jolson Is Buried 1985

"Tell me things I won't mind forgetting," she said. "Make it useless stuff or skip it."

I began. I told her insects fly through rain missing every drop, never getting wet. I told her no one in America owned a tape recorder before Bing

Crosby did. I told her the shape of the moon is like a banana — you see it looking full, you're seeing it end-on.

The camera made me self-conscious and I stopped. It was trained on us from a ceiling mount — the kind of camera banks use to photograph robbers. It played us to the nurses down the hall in Intensive Care.

"Go on, girl," she said. "You get used to it."

I had my audience. I went on. Did she know that Tammy Wynette had changed her tune? Really. That now she sings "Stand By Your Friends"? That Paul Anka did it too, I said. Does "You're Having *Our* Baby." That he got sick of all that feminist bitching.

"What else?" she said. "Have you got something else?"

Oh, yes.

For her I would always have something else.

"Did you know that when they taught the first chimp to talk, it lied? That when they asked her who did it on the desk, she signed back Max, the janitor. And that when they pressed her, she said she was sorry, that it was really the project director. But she was a mother, so I guess she had her reasons."

"Oh, that's good," she said. "A parable."

"There's more about the chimp," I said. "But it will break your heart."

"No, thanks," she says, and scratches at her mask.

We look like good-guy outlaws. Good or bad, I am not used to the mask yet. I keep touching the warm spot where my breath, thank God, comes out. She is used to hers. She only ties the strings on top. The other ones — a pro by now — she lets hang loose.

We call this place the Marcus Welby Hospital. It's the white one with the palm trees under the opening credits of all those shows. A Hollywood hospital, though in fact it is several miles west. Off camera, there is a beach across the street.

She introduces me to a nurse as the Best Friend. The impersonal article is more intimate. It tells me that *they* are intimate, the nurse and my friend.

"I was telling her we used to drink Canada Dry ginger ale and pretend we were in Canada."

"That's how dumb *we* were," I say.

"You could be sisters," the nurse says.

So how come, I'll bet they are wondering, it took me so long to get to such a glamorous place? But do they ask?

They do not ask.

Two months, and how long is the drive?

The best I can explain it is this — I have a friend who worked one summer in a mortuary. He used to tell me stories. The one that really got to me was not the grisliest, but it's the one that did. A man wrecked his car on 101 going south. He did not lose consciousness. But his arm was taken down to the wet bone — and when he looked at it — it scared him to death.

I mean, he died.

So I hadn't dared to look any closer. But now I'm doing it — and hoping that I will live through it.

She shakes out a summer-weight blanket, showing a leg you did not want to see. Except for that, you look at her and understand the law that requires two people to be with the body at all times.

"I thought of something," she says. "I thought of it last night. I think there is a real and present need here. You know," she says, "like for someone to do it for you when you can't do it yourself. You call them up whenever you want — like when push comes to shove."

She grabs the bedside phone and loops the cord around her neck.

"Hey," she says, "the end o' the line."

She keeps on, giddy with something. But I don't know with what.

"I can't remember," she says. "What does Kübler-Ross° say comes after Denial?"

It seems to me Anger must be next. Then Bargaining, Depression, and so on and so forth. But I keep my guesses to myself.

"The only thing is," she says, "is where's Resurrection? God knows, I want to do it by the book. But she left out Resurrection."

She laughs, and I cling to the sound the way someone dangling above a ravine holds fast to the thrown rope.

"Tell me," she says, "about that chimp with the talking hands. What do they do when the thing ends and the chimp says, 'I don't want to go back to the zoo'?"

When I don't say anything, she says, "Okay — then tell me another animal story. I like animal stories. But not a sick one — I don't want to know about all the seeing-eye dogs going blind."

No, I would not tell her a sick one.

"How about the hearing-ear dogs?" I say. "They're not going deaf, but they are getting very judgmental. For instance, there's this golden retriever in New Jersey, he wakes up the deaf mother and drags her into the daughter's room because the kid has got a flashlight and is reading under the covers."

"Oh, you're killing me," she says. "Yes, you're definitely killing me."

"They say the smart dog obeys, but the smarter dog knows when to disobey."

"Yes," she says, "the smarter anything knows when to disobey. Now, for example."

She is flirting with the Good Doctor, who has just appeared. Unlike the Bad Doctor, who checks the I. V. drip before saying good morning, the Good Doctor says things like "God didn't give epileptics a fair shake." The Good Doctor awards himself points for the cripples he could have hit in the parking lot. Because the Good Doctor is a little in love with her, he says maybe a year.

Kübler-Ross: Elisabeth Kübler-Ross (b. 1926), author of popular books on death and dying.

He pulls a chair up to her bed and suggests I might like to spend an hour on the beach.

"Bring me something back," she says. "Anything from the beach. Or the gift shop. Taste is no object."

He draws the curtain around her bed.

"Wait!" she cries.

I look in at her.

"Anything," she says, "except a magazine subscription."

The doctor turns away.

I watch her mouth laugh.

What seems dangerous often is not — black snakes, for example, or clear-air turbulence. While things that just lie there, like this beach, are loaded with jeopardy. A yellow dust rising from the ground, the heat that ripens melons overnight — this is earthquake weather. You can sit here braiding the fringe on your towel and the sand will all of a sudden suck down like an hourglass. The air roars. In the cheap apartments on-shore, bathtubs fill themselves and gardens roll up and over like green waves. If nothing happens, the dust will drift and the heat deepen till fear turns to desire. Nerves like that are only bought off by catastrophe.

"It never happens when you're thinking about it," she once observed. "Earthquake, earthquake, earthquake," she said.

"Earthquake, earthquake, earthquake," I said.

Like the aviaphobe who keeps the plane aloft with prayer, we kept it up until an aftershock cracked the ceiling.

That was after the big one in '72. We were in college; our dormitory was five miles from the epicenter. When the ride was over and my jabbering pulse began to slow, she served five parts champagne to one part orange juice, and joked about living in Ocean View, Kansas. I offered to drive her to Hawaii on the new world psychics predicted would surface the next time, or the next.

I could not say that now — next.

Whose next? she could ask.

Was I the only one who noticed that the experts had stopped saying *if* and now spoke of *when?* Of course not; the fearful ran to thousands. We watched the traffic of Japanese beetles for deviation. Deviation might mean more natural violence.

I wanted her to be afraid with me. But she said, "I don't know. I'm just not."

She was afraid of nothing, not even of flying.

I have this dream before a flight where we buckle in and the plane moves down the runway. It takes off at thirty-five miles an hour, and then we're airborne, skimming the tree tops. Still, we arrive in New York on time.

It is so pleasant.

One night I flew to Moscow this way.

■ ■ ■

She flew with me once. That time she flew with me she ate macadamia nuts while the wings bounced. She knows the wing tips can bend thirty feet up and thirty feet down without coming off. She believes it. She trusts the laws of aerodynamics. My mind stampedes. I can almost accept that a battleship floats when everybody knows steel sinks.

I see fear in her now, and am not going to try to talk her out of it. She is right to be afraid.

After a quake, the six o'clock news airs a film clip of first-graders yelling at the broken playground per their teacher's instructions.

"*Bad* earth!" they shout, because anger is stronger than fear.

But the beach is standing still today. Everyone on it is tranquilized, numb, or asleep. Teenaged girls rub coconut oil on each other's hard-to-reach places. They smell like macaroons. They pry open compacts like clamshells; mirrors catch the sun and throw a spray of white rays across glazed shoulders. The girls arrange their wet hair with silk flowers the way they learned in *Seventeen*. They pose.

A formation of low-riders pulls over to watch with a six-pack. They get vocal when the girls check their tan lines. When the beer is gone, so are they — flexing their cars on up the boulevard.

Above this aggressive health are the twin wrought-iron terraces, painted flamingo pink, of the Palm Royale. Someone dies there every time the sheets are changed. There's an ambulance in the driveway, so the remaining residents line the balconies, rocking and not talking, one-upped.

The ocean they stare at is dangerous, and not just the undertow. You can almost see the slapping tails of sand sharks keeping cruising bodies alive.

If she looked, she could see this, some of it, from her window. She would be the first to say how little it takes to make a thing all wrong.

There was a second bed in the room when I got back to it!

For two beats I didn't get it. Then it hit me like an open coffin.

She wants every minute, I thought. She wants my life.

"You missed Gussie," she said.

Gussie is her parents' three-hundred-pound, narcoleptic maid. Her attacks often come at the ironing board. The pillowcases in that family are all bordered with scorch.

"It's a hard trip for her," I said. "How is she?"

"Well, she didn't fall asleep, if that's what you mean. Gussie's great — you know what she said? She said, 'Darlin, stop this worriation. Just keep prayin, down on your knees' — me, who can't even get out of bed."

She shrugged. "What am I missing?"

"It's earthquake weather," I told her.

"The best thing to do about earthquakes," she said, "is not to live in California."

"That's useful," I said. "You sound like Reverend Ike — 'The best thing to do for the poor is not be one of them.'"

We're crazy about Reverend Ike.

I noticed her face was bloated.

"You know," she said, "I feel like hell. I'm about to stop having fun."

"The ancients have a saying," I said. "'There are times when the wolves are silent; there are times when the moon howls.'"

"What's that, Navajo?"

"Palm Royale lobby graffiti," I said. "I bought a paper there. I'll read you something."

"Even though I care about nothing?"

I turned to the page with the trivia column. I said, "Did you know the more shrimp flamingo birds eat, the pinker their feathers get?" I said, "Did you know that Eskimos need refrigerators? Do you know *why* Eskimos need refrigerators? Did you know that Eskimos need refrigerators because how else would they keep their food from freezing?"

I turned to page three, to a UPI filler datelined Mexico City. I read her "Man Robs Bank with Chicken," about a man who bought a barbecued chicken at a stand down the block from a bank. Passing the bank, he got the idea. He walked in and approached a teller. He pointed the brown paper bag at her and she handed over the day's receipts. It was the smell of barbecue sauce that eventually led to his capture.

The story had made her hungry, she said — so I took the elevator down six floors to the cafeteria, and brought back all the ice cream she wanted. We lay side by side, adjustable beds cranked up for optimal TV-viewing, littering the sheets with Good Humor wrappers, picking toasted almonds out of the gauze. We were Lucy and Ethel, Mary and Rhoda in extremis. The blinds were closed to keep light off the screen.

We watched a movie starring men we used to think we wanted to sleep with. Hers was a tough cop out to stop mine, a vicious rapist who went after cocktail waitresses.

"This is a good movie," she said when snipers felled them both.

I missed her already.

A Filipino nurse tiptoed in and gave her an injection. The nurse removed the pile of popsicle sticks from the nightstand — enough to splint a small animal.

The injection made us both sleepy. We slept.

I dreamed she was a decorator, come to furnish my house. She worked in secret, singing to herself. When she finished, she guided me proudly to the door. "How do you like it?" she asked, easing me inside.

Every beam and sill and shelf and knob was draped in gay bunting, with streamers of pastel crepe looped around bright mirrors.

■ ■ ■

"I have to go home," I said when she woke up.

She thought I meant home to her house in the Canyon, and I had to say No, *home* home. I twisted my hands in the time-honored fashion of people in pain. I was supposed to offer something. The Best Friend. I could not even offer to come back.

I felt weak and small and failed.

Also exhilarated.

I had a convertible in the parking lot. Once out of that room, I would drive it too fast down the Coast highway through the crab-smelling air. A stop in Malibu for sangria. The music in the place would be sexy and loud. They'd serve papaya and shrimp and watermelon ice. After dinner I would shimmer with lust, buzz with heat, vibrate with life, and stay up all night.

Without a word, she yanked off her mask and threw it on the floor. She kicked at the blankets and moved to the door. She must have hated having to pause for breath and balance before slamming out of Isolation, and out of the second room, the one where you scrub and tie on the white masks.

A voice shouted her name in alarm, and people ran down the corridor. The Good Doctor was paged over the intercom. I opened the door and the nurses at the station stared hard, as if this flight had been my idea.

"Where is she?" I asked, and they nodded to the supply closet.

I looked in. Two nurses were kneeling beside her on the floor, talking to her in low voices. One held a mask over her nose and mouth, the other rubbed her back in slow circles. The nurses glanced up to see if I was the doctor — and when I wasn't, they went back to what they were doing.

"There, there, honey," they cooed.

On the morning she was moved to the cemetery, the one where Al Jolson is buried, I enrolled in a Fear of Flying class. "What is your worst fear?" the instructor asked, and I answered, "That I will finish this course and still be afraid."

I sleep with a glass of water on the nightstand so I can see by its level if the coastal earth is trembling or if the shaking is still me.

What do I remember?

I remember only the useless things I hear — that Bob Dylan's mother invented Wite-out, that twenty-three people must be in a room before there is a fifty-fifty chance two will have the same birthdate. Who cares whether or not it's true? In my head there are bath towels swaddling this stuff. Nothing else seeps through.

I review those things that will figure in the re-telling: a kiss through surgical gauze, the pale hand correcting the position of the wig. I noted these gestures as they happened, not in any retrospect — though I do not know why looking back should show us more than looking at.

It is just possible I will say I stayed the night.

And who is there that can say that I did not?

■ ■ ■

I think of the chimp, the one with the talking hands.

In the course of the experiment, that chimp had a baby. Imagine how her trainers must have thrilled when the mother, without prompting, began to sign to her newborn.

Baby, drink milk.

Baby, play ball.

And when the baby died, the mother stood over the body, her wrinkled hands moving with animal grace, forming again and again the words, Baby, come hug, Baby, come hug, fluent now in the language of grief.

❧

ZORA NEALE HURSTON *(1901?–1960) was born in 1901 or 1902 (the records are lost, and she gave different birth dates in her writing) in Eatonville, Florida, a town founded by African Americans. When her mother died in 1912, her father, a Baptist minister, could not raise their eight children, so Hurston was forced to move from one relative's home to another. She never finished grade school, but when she was old enough to support herself, she attended Howard University in Washington, D.C. In 1921 she published her first story, "John Redding Goes to Sea," in the student literary magazine.*

In 1925 Hurston went to New York City and became active in the cultural renaissance in Harlem, collaborating with Langston Hughes on a folk comedy, Mule Bone. *Like Hughes and several other writers of that time, she was deeply interested in the abiding folk spirit inherent in southern life. After Hurston studied with the famous anthropologist Franz Boas at Barnard College, she returned to Florida to record the oral traditions of her native community. As critics have noted, from this time to the end of her life she tried to achieve a balance in her literary work between the folk culture of her background and her expression as an individual artist. Realizing that many white people used stereotypes to keep African Americans, Asian Americans, Hispanic Americans, and Native Americans in their "place," Hurston insisted it was*

> *urgent to realize that minorities do think, and think about something other than the race problem. That they are very human and internally, according to natural endowment, are just like everybody else. So long as this is not conceived, there must remain that feeling of unsurmountable difference, and difference to the average man means something bad. If people were made right, they would be just like him.*

During the 1930s Hurston turned all her energies to writing. She published Mules and Men *(1935), based on material from her field trips to Florida, and* Their Eyes Were Watching God *(1937), a novel about a woman's search for love and personal identity, in addition to several other books, including an autobiography. Although she published more than any other African American woman writer of her time, in the last two decades of her life she earned very little from her writing, and she died penniless in Florida. Fifteen years after Hurston's death, her work was rediscovered by the women's movement, and she is now regarded as an important American writer. "Sweat" is from* The Eatonville Anthology *(1927), the collection that brought Hurston to national attention. "The Gilded Six-Bits" (1933) and "Story in Harlem Slang" (1942) are later stories.*

RELATED CASEBOOK: *See pages 760–776, including Zora Neale Hurston, "How It Feels to Be Colored Me," page 760; "What White Publishers Won't Print," page 764; Langston Hughes, "Democracy, Negroes, and Writers," page 768; Robert E. Hemenway, "On 'Story in Harlem Slang,'" page 769; Rosalie Murphy Baum, "The Shape of Hurston's Fiction," page 771; Alice Walker, "Zora Neale Hurston: A Cautionary Tale and a Partisan View," page 774.*

ZORA NEALE HURSTON

The Gilded Six-Bits

1933

It was a Negro yard around a Negro house in a Negro settlement that looked to the payroll of the G and G Fertilizer works for its support.

But there was something happy about the place. The front yard was parted in the middle by a sidewalk from gate to doorstep, a sidewalk edged on either side by quart bottles driven neck down to the ground on a slant. A mess of homey flowers planted without a plan but blooming cheerily from their helter-skelter places. The fence and house were whitewashed. The porch and steps scrubbed white.

The front door stood open to the sunshine so that the floor of the front room could finish drying after its weekly scouring. It was Saturday. Everything clean from the front gate to the privy house. Yard raked so that the strokes of the rake would make a pattern. Fresh newspaper cut in fancy-edge on the kitchen shelves.

Missie May was bathing herself in the galvanized washtub in the bedroom. Her dark-brown skin glistened under the soapsuds that skittered down from her wash rag. Her stiff young breasts thrust forward aggressively like broad-based cones with the tips lacquered in black.

She heard men's voices in the distance and glanced at the dollar clock on the dresser.

"Humph! Ah'm way behind time t'day! Joe gointer be heah 'fore Ah git mah clothes on if Ah don't make haste."

She grabbed the clean meal sack at hand and dried herself hurriedly and began to dress. But before she could tie her slippers, there came the ring of singing metal on wood. Nine times.

Missie May grinned with delight. She had not seen the big tall man come stealing in the gate and creep up the walk grinning happily at the joyful mischief he was about to commit. But she knew that it was her husband throwing silver dollars in the door for her to pick up and pile beside her plate at dinner. It was this way every Saturday afternoon. The nine dollars hurled into the open door, he scurried to a hiding place behind the cape jasmine bush and waited.

Missie May promptly appeared at the door in mock alarm.

"Who dat chunkin' money in mah do'way?" she demanded. No answer from the yard. She leaped off the porch and began to search the shrubbery. She peeped under the porch and hung over the gate to look up and down the road. While she did this, the man behind the jasmine darted to the chinaberry tree. She spied him and gave chase.

"Nobody ain't gointer be chunkin' money at me and Ah not do'em nothin'," she shouted in mock anger. He ran around the house with Missie May at his heels. She overtook him at the kitchen door. He ran inside but could not close it after him before she crowded in and locked with him in a rough and tumble. For several minutes the two were a furious mass of male and female energy. Shouting, laughing, twisting, turning, and Joe trying, but not too hard, to get away.

"Missie May, take yo' hand out mah pocket!" Joe shouted out between laughs.

"Ah ain't, Joe, not lessen you gwine gimme whateve' it is good you got in yo' pocket. Turn it go, Joe, do Ah'll tear yo' clothes."

"Go on tear 'em. You de one dat pushes de needles round heah. Move yo' hand Missie May."

"Lemme git dat paper sack out yo' pocket. Ah bet its candy kisses."

"Tain't. Move yo' hand. Woman ain't got no business in a man's clothes nowhow. Go 'way."

Missie May gouged way down and gave an upward jerk and triumphed.

"Unhhunh! Ah got it. It 'tis so candy kisses. Ah knowed you had somethin' for me in yo' clothes. Now Ah got to see whut's in every pocket you got."

Joe smiled indulgently and let his wife go through all of his pockets and take out the things that he had hidden there for her to find. She bore off the chewing gum, the cake of sweet soap, the pocket handkerchief as if she had wrested them from him, as if they had not been bought for the sake of this friendly battle.

"Whew! dat play-fight done got me all warmed up," Joe exclaimed. "Got me some water in de kittle?"

"Yo' water is on de fire and yo' clean things is cross de bed. Hurry up and wash yo'self and git changed so we kin eat. Ah'm hongry." As Missie said this, she bore the steaming kettle into the bedroom.

"You ain't hongry, sugar," Joe contradicted her. "Youse jes's little empty. Ah'm de one whut's hongry. Ah could eat up camp meetin,' back off 'ssociation, and drink Jurdan dry. Have it on de table when Ah git out de tub."

"Don't you mess wid mah business, man. You git in yo' clothes. Ah'm a real wife, not no dress and breath. Ah might not look lak one, but if you burn me, you won't git a thing but wife ashes."

Joe splashed in the bedroom and Missie May fanned around in the kitchen. A fresh red and white checked cloth on the table. Big pitcher of buttermilk beaded with pale drops of butter from the churn. Hot fried mullet, crackling bread, ham hocks atop a mound of string beans and new potatoes, and perched on the window-sill a pone of spicy potato pudding.

Very little talk during the meal but that little consisted of banter that pretended to deny affection but in reality flaunted it. Like when Missie May reached for a second helping of the tater pone. Joe snatched it out of her reach. After Missie May had made two or three unsuccessful grabs at the pan, she begged, "Aw, Joe gimme some mo' dat tater pone."

"Nope, sweetenin' is for us men-folks. Y'all pritty li'l frail eels don't need nothin' lak dis. You too sweet already."

"Please, Joe."

"Naw, naw. Ah don't want you to get no sweeter than whut you is already. We goin' down de road al li'l piece t'night so you go put on yo' Sunday-go-to-meetin' things."

Missie May looked at her husband to see if he was playing some prank. "Sho' nuff, Joe?"

"Yeah. We goin' to de ice cream parlor."

"Where de ice cream parlor at, Joe?"

"A new man done come heah from Chicago and he done got a place and took and opened it up for a ice cream parlor, and bein' as it's real swell, Ah wants you to be one de first ladies to walk in dere and have some set down."

"Do Jesus, Ah ain't knowed nothin' 'bout it. Who de man done it?"

"Mister Otis D. Slemmons, of spots and places — Memphis, Chicago, Jacksonville, Philadelphia, and so on."

"Dat heavy-set man wid his mouth full of gold teethes?"

"Yeah. Where did you see 'im at?"

"Ah went down to de sto' tuh git a box of lye and Ah seen 'im standin' on de corner talkin' to some of de mens, and Ah come on back and went to scrubbin' de floor, and he passed and tipped his hat whilst Ah was scourin' de steps. Ah thought never Ah seen *him* befo'."

Joe smiled pleasantly. "Yeah, he's up to date. He got de finest clothes Ah ever seen on a colored man's back."

"Aw, he don't look no better in his clothes than you do in yourn. He got a puzzlegut on 'im and he so chuckle-headed, he got a pone behind his neck."

Joe looked down at his own abdomen and said wistfully, "Wisht Ah had a build on me lak he got. He ain't puzzle-gutted, honey. He jes' got a corperation. Dat make 'm look lak a rich white man. All rich mens is got some belly on 'em."

"Ah seen de pitchers of Henry Ford and he's a spare-built man and Rockefeller look lak he ain't got but one gut. But Ford and Rockefeller and dis Slemmons and all de rest kin be as many-gutted as dey please, ah'm satisfied wid you jes' lak you is, baby. God took pattern after a pine tree and built you noble. Youse a pritty still man, and if Ah knowed any way to make you mo' pritty still Ah'd take and do it."

Joe reached over gently and toyed with Missie May's ear. "You jes' say dat cause you love me, but Ah know Ah can't hold no light to Otis D. Slemmons. Ah ain't never been nowhere and Ah ain't got nothin' but you."

"How you know dat, Joe."

"He tole us so hisself."

"Dat don't make it so. His mouf is cut cross-ways, ain't it? Well, he kin lie jes' lak anybody els."

"Good Lawd, Missie! You womens sho' is hard to sense into things. He's got a five-dollar gold piece for a stick-pin and he got a ten-dollar gold piece on his watch chain and his mouf is jes' crammed full of gold teethes. Sho' wisht it wuz mine. And whut make it so cool, he got money 'cumulated. And womens give it all to 'im."

"Ah don't see whut de womens see on 'im. Ah wouldn't give 'im a wind if de sherff wuz after 'im."

"Well, he tole us how de white womens in Chicago give 'im all dat gold money. So he don't 'low nobody to touch it at all. Not even put dey finger on it. Dey tole 'im not to. You kin make 'miration at it, but don't tetch it."

"Whyn't he stay up dere where dey so crazy 'bout 'im?"

"Ah reckon dey done made 'im vast-rich and he wants to travel some. He say dey wouldn't leave 'im hit a lick of work. He got mo' lady people crazy 'bout him than he kin shake a stick at."

"Joe, Ah hates to see you so dumb. Dat stray nigger jes' tell y'all anything and y'all b'lieve it."

"Go 'head on now, honey and put on yo' clothes. He talkin' 'bout his pritty womens — Ah want 'im to see *mine.*"

Missie May went off to dress and Joe spent the time trying to make his stomach punch out like Slemmons' middle. He tried the rolling swagger of the stranger, but found that his tall bone-and-muscle stride fitted ill with it. He just had time to drop back into his seat before Missie May came in dressed to go.

On the way home that night Joe was exultant. "Didn't Ah say ole Otis was swell? Can't he talk Chicago talk? Wuzn't dat funny whut he said when great big fat ole Ida Armstrong come in? He asted me, 'Who is dat broad wid de forty shake?' Dat's a new word. Us always thought forty was a set of figgers but he showed us where it means a whole heap of things. Sometimes he don't say forty, he jes' say thirty-eight and two and dat mean de same thing. Know whut he tole me when Ah was payin' for our ice cream? He say, 'Ah have to hand it to you, Joe. Dat wife of yours is jes' thirty-eight and two. Yessuh, she's forty!' Ain't he killin?"

"He'll do in case of a rush. But he sho' is got uh heap uh gold on 'im. Dat's de first time Ah ever seed gold money. It looked good on him sho' nuff, but it'd look a whole heap better on you."

"Who, me? Missie May youse crazy! Where would a po' man lak me git gold money from?"

Missie May was silent for a minute, then she said, "Us might find some goin' long de road some time. Us could."

"Who would be losin' gold money 'round heah? We ain't even seen none dese white folks wearin' no gold money on dey watch chain. You must be figgeren' Mister Packard or Mister Cadillac goin' pass through heah . . ."

"You don't know whut been lost 'round heah. Maybe somebody way back in memorial times lost they gold money and went on off and it ain't never been found. And then if we wuz to find it, you could wear some 'thout havin' no gang of womens lak dat Slemmons say he got."

Joe laughed and hugged her. "Don't be so wishful 'bout me. Ah'm satisfied de way Ah is. So long as Ah be yo' husband, Ah don't keer 'bout nothin' else. Ah'd ruther all de other womens in de world to be dead than for you to have de toothache. Less we go to bed and git our night rest."

It was Saturday night once more before Joe could parade his wife in Slemmons' ice cream parlor again. He worked the night shift and Saturday was his only night off. Every other evening around six o'clock he left home, and dying dawn saw him hustling home around the lake where the challenging sun flung a flaming sword from east to west across the trembling water.

That was the best part of life — going home to Missie May. Their whitewashed house, the mock battle on Saturday, the dinner and ice cream parlor afterwards, church on Sunday nights when Missie outdressed any woman in town — all, everything was right.

One night around eleven the acid ran out at the G and G. The foreman knocked off the crew and let the steam die down. As Joe rounded the lake on his way home, a lean moon rode the lake in a silver boat. If anybody had asked Joe about the moon on the lake, he would have said he hadn't paid it any attention. But he saw it with his feelings. It made him yearn painfully for Missie. Creation obsessed him. He thought about children. They had been married for more than a year now. They had money put away. They ought to be making little feet for shoes. A little boy child would be about right.

He saw a dim light in the bedroom and decided to come in through the kitchen door. He could wash the fertilizer dust off himself before presenting himself to Missie May. It would be nice for her not to know that he was there until he slipped into his place in bed and hugged her back. She always liked that.

He eased the kitchen door open slowly and silently, but when he went to set his dinner bucket on the table he bumped it into a pile of dishes, and something crashed to the floor. He heard his wife gasp in fright and hurried to reassure her.

"Iss me, honey. Don't get skeered."

There was a quick, large movement in the bedroom. A rustle, a thud, and a stealthy silence. The light went out.

What? Robbers? Murderers? Some varmint attacking his helpless wife, perhaps. He struck a match, threw himself on guard, and stepped over the door-sill into the bedroom.

The great belt on the wheel of Time slipped and eternity stood still. By the match light he could see the man's legs fighting with his breeches in his frantic desire to get them on. He had both chance and time to kiff the intruder in his helpless condition — half-in and half-out of his pants — but he was too weak to take action. The shapeless enemies of humanity that live in the hours of Time had waylaid Joe. He was assaulted in his weakness. Like Samson awakening after his haircut. So he just opened his mouth and laughed.

The match went out and he struck another and lit the lamp. A howling wind raced across his heart, but underneath its fury he heard his wife sobbing and Slemmons pleading for his life. Offering to buy it with all that he had. "Please, suh, don't kill me. Sixty-two dollars at de sto' gold money."

Joe just stood. Slemmons looked at the window, but it was screened. Joe stood out like a rough-backed mountain between him and the door. Barring him from escape, from sunrise, from life.

He considered a surprise attack upon the big clown that stood there laughing like a chessy cat. But before his fist could travel an inch, Joe's own rushed out to crush him like a battering ram. Then Joe stood over him.

"Git into yo' damn rags, Slemmons, and dat quick."

Slemmons scrambled to his feet and into his vest and coat. As he grabbed his hat, Joe's fury overrode his intentions and he grabbed at Slemmons with his left hand and struck at him with his right. The right landed. The left grazed the front of his vest. Slemmons was knocked a somersault into the kitchen and fled through the open door. Joe found himself alone with Missie May, with the golden watch charm clutched in his left fist. A short bit of broken chain dangled between his fingers.

Missie May was sobbing. Wails of weeping without words. Joe stood, and after awhile she found out that he had something in his hand. And then he stood and felt without thinking and without seeing with his natural eyes. Missie May kept on crying and Joe kept on feeling so much and not knowing what to do with all his feelings, he put Slemmons' watch charm in his pants pocket and took a good laugh and went to bed.

"Missie May, whut you crying for?"

"Cause Ah love you so hard and Ah know you don't love *me* no mo'."

Joe sank his face into the pillow for a spell then he said huskily, "You don't know de feelings of dat yet, Missie May."

"Oh Joe, honey, he said he wuz gointer gimme dat gold money and he jes' kept on after me —"

Joe was very still and silent for a long time. Then he said, "Well, don't cry no mo', Missie May. Ah got yo' gold piece for you."

The hours went past on their rusty ankles. Joe still and quiet on one bed-rail and Missie May wrung dry of sobs on the other. Finally the sun's tide crept upon the shore of night and drowned all its hours. Missie May with her face stiff and streaked towards the window saw the dawn come into her yard. It was day. Nothing more. Joe wouldn't be coming home as usual. No need to fling open the front door and sweep off the porch, making it nice for Joe. Never no more breakfast to cook; no more washing and starching of Joe's jumper-jackets and pants. No more nothing. So why get up?

With this strange man in her bed, she felt embarrassed to get up and dress. She decided to wait till he had dressed and gone. Then she would get up, dress quickly, and be gone forever beyond reach of Joe's looks and laughs. But he never moved. Red light turned to yellow, then white.

From beyond the no-man's land between them came a voice. A strange voice that yesterday had been Joe's.

"Missie May, ain't you gonna fix me no breakfus'?"

She sprang out of bed. "Yeah, Joe. Ah didn't reckon you wuz hongry."

No need to die today. Joe needed her for a few more minutes anyhow. Soon there was a roaring fire in the cook stove. Water bucket full and two chickens killed. Joe loved fried chicken and rice. She didn't deserve a thing and good Joe was letting her cook him some breakfast. She rushed hot biscuits to the table as Joe took his seat.

He ate with his eyes on his plate. No laughter, no banter.

"Missie May, you ain't eatin' yo' breakfus'."

"Ah don't choose none, Ah thank yuh."

His coffee cup was empty. She sprang to refill it. When she turned from the stove and bent to set the cup beside Joe's plate, she saw the yellow coin on the table between them.

She slumped into her seat and wept into her arms.

Presently Joe said calmly, "Missie May, you cry too much. Don't look back lak Lot's wife and turn to salt."

The sun, the hero of every day, the impersonal old man that beams as brightly on death as on birth, came up every morning and raced across the blue dome and dipped into the sea of fire every evening. Water ran down hill and birds nested.

Missie knew why she didn't leave Joe. She couldn't. She loved him too much. But she couldn't understand why Joe didn't leave her. He was polite, even kind at times, but aloof.

There were no more Saturday romps. No ringing silver dollars to stack beside her plate. No pockets to rifle. In fact the yellow coin in his trousers was like a monster hiding in the cave of his pockets to destroy her.

She often wondered if he still had it, but nothing could have induced her to ask nor yet to explore his pockets to see for herself. Its shadow was in the house whether or no.

One night Joe came home around midnight and complained of pains in the back. He asked Missie to rub him down with liniment. It had been three months since Missie had touched his body and it all seemed strange. But she rubbed him. Grateful for the chance. Before morning, youth triumphed and Missie exulted. But the next day, as she joyfully made up their bed, beneath her pillow she found the piece of money with the bit of chain attached.

Alone to herself, she looked at the thing with loathing, but look she must. She took it into her hands with trembling and saw first thing that it was no gold piece. It was a gilded half-dollar. Then she knew why Slemmons had forbidden anyone to touch his gold. He trusted village eyes at a distance not to recognize his stick-pin as a gilded quarter, and his watch charm as a four-bit piece.

She was glad at first that Joe had left it there. Perhaps he was through with her punishment. They were man and wife again. Then another thought came clawing at her. He had come home to buy from her as if she were any woman in the long house. Fifty cents for her love. As if to say that he could pay as well as Slemmons. She slid the coin into his Sunday pants pocket and dressed herself and left his house.

Halfway between her house and the quarters she met her husband's mother, and after a short talk she turned and went back home. If she had not the substance of marriage, she had the outside show. Joe must leave *her*. She let him see she didn't want his old gold four-bits too.

She saw no more of the coin for some time though she knew that Joe could not help finding it in his pocket. But his health kept poor, and he came home at least every ten days to be rubbed.

The sun swept around the horizon, trailing its robes of weeks and days. One morning as Joe came in from work, he found Missie May chopping wood. Without a word he took the ax and chopped a huge pile before he stopped.

"You ain't got no business choppin' wood, and you know it."

"How come? Ah been choppin' it for de last longest."

"Ah ain't blind. You makin' feet for shoes."

"Won't you be glad to have a li'l baby chile, Joe?"

"You know dat 'thout astin' me."

"Iss gointer be a boy chile and de very spit of you."

"You reckon, Missie May?"

"Who else could it look lak?"

Joe said nothing, but he thrust his hand deep into his pocket and fingered something there.

It was almost six months later Missie May took to bed and Joe went and got his mother to come wait on the house.

Missie May delivered a fine boy. Her travail was over when Joe came in from work one morning. His mother and the old women were drinking great bowls of coffee around the fire in the kitchen.

The minute Joe came into the room his mother called him aside.

"How did Missie May make out?" he asked quickly.

"Who, dat gal? She strong as a ox. She gointer have plenty mo'. We done fixed her wid de sugar and lard to sweeten her for de nex' one."

Joe stood silent awhile.

"You ain't ast 'bout de baby, Joe. You oughter be mighty proud cause he sho' is de spittin' image of yuh, son. Dat's yourn all right, if you never git another one, dat un is yourn. And you know Ah'm mighty proud too, son, cause Ah never thought well of you marryin' Missie May cause her ma used tuh fan her foot 'round right smart and Ah been mighty skeered dat Missie May wuz gointer git misput on her road."

Joe said nothing. He fooled around the house till late in the day then just before he went to work, he went and stood at the foot of the bed and asked his wife how she felt. He did this every day during the week.

On Saturday he went to Orlando to make his market. It had been a long time since he had done that.

Meat and lard, meal and flour, soap and starch. Cans of corn and tomatoes. All the staples. He fooled around town for awhile and bought bananas and apples. Way after while he went around to the candy store.

"Hellow, Joe," the clerk greeted him. "Ain't seen you in a long time."

"Nope, Ah ain't been heah. Been 'round spots and places."

"Want some of them molasses kisses you always buy?"

"Yessuh." He threw the gilded half-dollar on the counter. "Will dat spend?"

"Whut is it, Joe? Well, I'll be doggone! A gold-plated four-bit piece. Where'd you git it, Joe?"

"Offen a stray nigger dat come through Eatonville. He had it on his watch chain for a charm-goin' 'round making out iss gold money. Ha ha! He had a quarter on his tie pin and it wuz all golded up too. Tryin' to fool people. Makin' out he so rich and everything. Ha! Ha! Trying' to tole off folkses wives from home."

"How did you git it, Joe? Did he fool you, too?"

"Who, me? Naw suh! He ain't fooled me none. Know whut Ah done? He come 'round me wid his smart talk. Ah hauled off and knocked 'im down and took his old four-bits 'way from 'im. Gointer buy my wife some good ole 'lasses kisses wid it. Gimme fifty cents worth of dem candy kisses."

"Fifty cents buys a mightly lot of candy kisses, Joe. Why don't you split it up and take some chocolate bars, too. They eat good, too."

"Yessuh, de do, but Ah wants all dat in kisses. Ah got a li'l boy chile home now. Tain't a week old yet, but he kin suck a sugar tit and maybe eat one them kisses hisself."

Joe got his candy and left the store. The clerk turned to the next customer. "Wisht I could be like these darkies. Laughin' all the time. Nothin' worries 'em."

Back in Eatonville, Joe reached his own front door. There was the ring of singing metal on wood. Fifteen times. Missie May couldn't run to the door, but she crept there as quickly as she could.

"Joe Banks, Ah hear you chunkin' money in mah do'way. You wait till Ah got mah strength back and Ah'm gointer fix you for dat."

Zora Neale Hurston

Story in Harlem Slang

1942

Wait till I light up my coal-pot and I'll tell you about this Zigaboo called Jelly. Well, all right now. He was a sealskin brown and papa-tree-top-tall. Skinny in the hips and solid built for speed. He was born with this rough-dried hair, but when he laid on the grease and pressed it down overnight with his stocking-cap, it looked just like that righteous moss, and had so many waves you got seasick from looking. Solid, man, solid!

His mama named him Marvel, but after a month on Lenox Avenue, he changed all that to Jelly. How come? Well, he put it in the street that when it came to filling that long-felt need, sugar-curing the ladies' feelings, he was in a class by himself and nobody knew his name, so he had to tell 'em. "It must be Jelly, 'cause jam don't shake." Therefore, his name was Jelly. That was what was on his sign. The stuff was there and it was mellow. Whenever he was challenged by a hard-head or a frail eel on the right of his title he would eye-ball the idol-breaker with a slice of ice and put on his ugly-laugh, made up of scorn and pity, and say: "Youse just dumb to the fact, baby. If you don't know what you talking 'bout, you better ask Granny Grunt. I wouldn't mislead you, baby. I don't need to — not with the help I got." Then he would give the pimp's[1] sign, and percolate on down the Avenue. You can't go behind a fact like that.

So this day he was airing out on the Avenue. It had to be late afternoon, or he would not have been out of bed. All you did by rolling out early was to stir

[1]In Harlemese, *pimp* has a different meaning than its ordinary definition as a procurer for immoral purposes. The Harlem pimp is a man whose amatory talents are for sale to any woman who will support him, either with a free meal or on a common law basis; in this sense, he is actually a male prostitute. [Hurston's note]

your stomach up. That made you hunt for more dishes to dirty. The longer you slept, the less you had to eat. But you can't collar nods all day. No matter how long you stay in bed, and how quiet you keep, sooner or later that big gut is going to reach over and grab that little one and start to gnaw. That's confidential right from the Bible. You got to get out on the beat and collar yourself a hot.

So Jelly got into his zoot suit with the reet pleats and got out to skivver around and do himself some good. At 132nd Street, he spied one of his colleagues on the opposite sidewalk, standing in front of a café. Jelly figured that if he bull-skated just right, he might confidence Sweet Back out of a thousand on a plate. Maybe a shot of scrap-iron or a reefer. Therefore, Jelly took a quick backward look at his shoe soles to see how his leather was holding out. The way he figured it after the peep was that he had plenty to get across and maybe do a little more cruising besides. So he stanched out into the street and made the crossing.

"Hi there, Sweet Back!" he exploded cheerfully. "Gimme some skin!"

"Lay de skin on me, pal!" Sweet Back grabbed Jelly's outstretched hand and shook hard. "Ain't seen you since the last time, Jelly. What's cookin'?"

"Oh, just like de bear — I ain't nowhere. Like de bear's brother, I ain't no further. Like de bear's daughter — ain't got a quarter."

Right away, he wished he had not been so honest. Sweet Back gave him a top-superior, cut-eye look. Looked at Jelly just like a showman looks at an ape. Just as far above Jelly as fried chicken is over branch water.

"Cold in hand, hunh?" He talked down to Jelly. "A red hot pimp like you *say* you is, ain't got no business in the barrel. Last night when I left you, you was beating up your gums and broadcasting about how hot you was. Just as hot as July-jam, you told me. What you doing cold in hand?"

"Aw, man, can't you take a joke? I was just beating up my gums when I said I was broke. How can I be broke when I got de best woman in Harlem? If I ask her for a dime, she'll give me a ten dollar bill; ask her for drink of likker, and she'll buy me a whiskey still. If I'm lying, I'm flying!"

"Gar, don't hang out dat dirty washing in my back yard! Didn't I see you last night with dat beat chick, scoffing a hot dog? Dat chick you had was beat to de heels. Boy, you ain't no good for what you live."

"If you ain't lying now, you flying. You ain't got de first thin. You ain't got nickel one."

Jelly threw back the long skirt of his coat and rammed his hand down into his pants pocket. "Put your money where your mouth is!" he challenged, as he mock-struggled to haul out a huge roll. "Back your crap with your money. I bet you five dollars!"

Sweet Back made the same gesture of hauling out nonexistent money.

"I been raised in the church. I don't bet, but I'll doubt you. Five rocks!"

"I thought so!" Jelly crowed, and hurriedly pulled his empty hand out of his pocket. "I knowed you'd back up when I drawed my roll on you."

"You ain't drawed no roll on me, Jelly. You ain't drawed nothing but your pocket. You better stop dat boogerbooing. Next time I'm liable to make you do it." There was a splinter of regret in his voice. If Jelly really had had some money, he might have staked him, Sweet Back, to a hot. Good Southern cornbread with a piano on a platter. Oh, well! The right broad would, or might, come along.

"Who boogerbooing?" Jelly snorted. "Jig, I don't have to. Talking about *me* with a beat chick scoffing a hot dog! You must of not seen me, 'cause last night I was riding round in a Yellow Cab, with a yellow gal, drinking yellow likker and spending yellow money. Tell 'em 'bout me, tell 'em!"

"Git out of my face, Jelly! Dat broad I seen you with wasn't no pe-ola. She was one of them coal-scuttle blondes with hair just as close to her head as ninety-nine is to a hundred. She look-ted like she had seventy-five pounds of clear bosom, guts in her feet, and she look-ted like six months in front and nine months behind. Buy you a whiskey still! Dat broad couldn't make the down payment on a pair of sox."

"Sweet Back, you fixing to talk out of place." Jelly stiffened.

"If you trying to jump salty, Jelly, that's your mammy."

"Don't play in de family, Sweet Back. I don't play de dozens. I done told you."

"Who playing de dozens? You trying to get your hips up on your shoulders 'cause I said you was with a beat broad. One of them lam blacks."

"Who? Me? Long as you been knowing me, Sweet Back, you ain't never seen me with nothing but pe-olas. I can get any frail eel I wants to. How come I'm up here in New York? You don't know, do you? Since youse dumb to the fact, I reckon I'll have to make you hep. I had to leave from down south 'cause Miss Anne used to worry me so bad to go with me. Who, me? Man, I don't deal in no coal. Know what I tell 'em? If they's white, they's right! If they's yellow, they's mellow! If they's brown, they can stick around. But if they come black, they better git way back! Tell 'em bout me!"

"Aw, man, you trying to show your grandma how to milk ducks. Best you can do is to confidence some kitchen-mechanic out of a dime or two. Me, I knocks de pad with them cack-broads up on Sugar Hill, and fills 'em full of melody. Man, I'm quick death and easy judgment. Youse just a home-boy, Jelly. Don't try to follow me."

"Me follow *you*! Man, I come on like the Gang Busters, and go off like The March of Time! If dat ain't so, God is gone to Jersey City and you know He wouldn't be messing 'round a place like that. Know what my woman done? We hauled off and went to church last Sunday, and when they passed 'round the plate for the *penny* collection, I throwed in a dollar. De man looked at me real hard for dat. Dat made my woman mad, so she called him back and throwed in a twenty dollar bill! Told him to take dat and go! Dat's what he got for looking at me 'cause I throwed in a dollar."

"Jelly, de wind may blow and de door may slam; dat what you shooting ain't worth a damn!"

Jelly slammed his hand in his bosom as if to draw a gun. Sweet Back did the same.

"If you wants to fight, Sweet Back, the favor is in me."

"I was deep-thinking then, Jelly. It's a good thing I ain't short- tempered. 'T'aint nothing to you, nohow. You ain't hit me yet."

Both burst into a laugh and changed from fighting to lounging poses.

"Don't get too yaller on me, Jelly. You liable to get hurt some day."

"You over-sports your hand your ownself. Too blamed astorperious. I just don't pay you no mind. Lay de skin on me!"

They broke their handshake hurriedly, because both of them looked up the Avenue and saw the same thing. It was a girl and they both remembered that it was Wednesday afternoon. All of the domestics off for the afternoon with their pay in their pockets. Some of them bound to be hungry for love. That meant a dinner, a shot of scrap-iron, maybe room rent and a reefer or two. Both went into the pose and put on the look.

"Big stars falling!" Jelly said out loud when she was in hearing distance. "It must be just before day!"

"Yeah, man!" Sweet Back agreed. "Must be a recess in Heaven — pretty angel like that out on the ground."

The girl drew abreast of them, reeling and rocking her hips.

"I'd walk clear to Diddy-Wah-Diddy to get a chance to speak to a pretty lil' ground-angel like that," Jelly went on.

"Aw, man, you ain't willing to go very far. Me, I'd go slap to Ginny-Gall, where they eat cow-rump, skin and all."

The girl smiled, so Jelly set his hat and took the plunge.

"Baby," he crooned, "what's on de rail for de lizard?"

The girl halted and braced her hips with her hands. "A Zigaboo down in Georgy, where I come from, asked a woman that one time and the judge told him 'ninety days.'"

"Georgy!" Sweet Back pretended to be elated. "Where 'bouts in Georgy is you from? Delaware?"

"Delaware?" Jelly snorted. "My people! My people! Free schools and dumb jigs! Man, how you going to put Delaware in Georgy? You ought to know dat's in Maryland."

"Oh, don't try to make out youse no northerner, you! Youse from right down in 'Bam your ownself!" The girl turned on Jelly.

"Yeah, I'm *from* there and I aims to stay from there."

"One of them Russians, eh?" the girl retorted. "Rushed up here to get away from a job of work."

That kind of talk was not leading towards the dinner table.

"But baby!" Jelly gasped. "Dat shape you got on you! I bet the Coca Cola Company is paying you good money for the patent!"

The girl smiled with pleasure at this, so Sweet Back jumped in.

"I know youse somebody swell to know. Youse real people. You grins like a regular fellow." He gave her his most killing look and let it simmer in. "These dickty jigs round here tries to smile. S'pose you and me go inside the café here and grab a hot?"

"You got any money?" the girl asked, and stiffened like a ramrod. "Nobody ain't pimping on me. You dig me?"

"Aw, now, baby!"

"I seen you two mullet-heads before. I was uptown when Joe Brown had you all in the go-long last night. Dat cop sure hates a pimp! All he needs to see is the pimps' salute, and he'll out with his night-stick and whip your head to the red. Beat your head just as flat as a dime!" She went off into a great blow of laughter.

"Oh, let's us don't talk about the law. Let's talk about us," Sweet Back persisted. "You going inside with me to holler 'let one come flopping! One come grunting! Snatch one from de rear!'"

"Naw indeed!" the girl laughed harshly. "You skillets is trying to promote a meal on me. But it'll never happen, brother. You barking up the wrong tree. I wouldn't give you air if you was stopped up in a jug. I'm not putting out a thing. I'm just like the cemetery — I'm not putting out, I'm taking in! Dig?"

"I'll tell you like the farmer told the potato — plant you now and dig you later."

The girl made a movement to switch on off. Sweet Back had not dirtied a plate since the day before. He made a weak but desperate gesture.

"Trying to snatch my pocketbook, eh?" she blazed. Instead of running, she grabbed hold of Sweet Back's draping coattail and made a slashing gesture. "How much split you want back here? If your feets don't hurry up and take you 'way from here, you'll *ride* away. I'll spread my lungs all over New York and call the law. Go ahead, Bedbug! Touch me! And I'll holler like a pretty white woman!"

The boys were ready to flee, but she turned suddenly and rocked on off with her ear-rings snapping and her heels popping.

"My people! My people!" Sweet Back sighed.

"I know you feel chewed," Jelly said, in an effort to make it appear that he had had no part in the fiasco.

"Oh, let her go," Sweet Back said magnanimously. "When I see people without the periodical principles they's supposed to have, I just don't fool with 'em. What I want to steal her old pocketbook with all the money I got? I could buy a beat chick like her and give her away. I got money's mammy and Grandma change. One of my women, and not the best one I got neither, is buying me ten shag suits at one time."

He glanced sidewise at Jelly to see if he was convincing. But Jelly's thoughts were far away. He was remembering those full, hot meals he had left back in Alabama to seek wealth and splendor in Harlem without working. He had even forgotten to look cocky and rich.

GLOSSARY OF HARLEM SLANG°

Air out — leave, flee, stroll

Astorperious — haughty, biggity

Aunt Hagar — Negro race (also Aunt Hagar's chillun)

Bad hair — Negro type hair

Balling — having fun

Bam, and down in Bam — down South

Battle-hammed — badly formed about the hips

Beating up your gums — talking to no purpose

Befuthahatchie — next station beyond Hell

Big boy — stout fellow. But in the South, it means fool and is a prime insult.

Glossary of Harlem Slang: Zora Neale Hurston included this glossary as part of "Story in Harlem Slang" when it was first published in *The American Mercury,* July 1942.

Blowing your top — getting very angry; occasionally used to mean, "He's doing fine!"
Boogie-woogie — type of dancing and rhythm. For years, in the South, it meant secondary syphilis.
Brother-in-black — Negro
Bull-skating — Bragging
Butt sprung — a suit or a skirt out of shape in the rear

Coal scuttle blonde — black woman
Cold — exceeding, well, etc., as in "He was cold on that trumpet!"
Collar a nod — sleep
Collar a hot — eat a meal
Color scale — high yaller, yaller, high brown, vaseline brown, seal brown, low brown, dark black
Conk buster — cheap liquor; also an intellectual Negro
Cruising — parading down the Avenue. Variations: *oozing, percolating,* and *free-wheeling.* The latter implies more briskness.
Cut — doing something well

Dark black — a casually black person. Superlatives: *low black,* a blacker person; *lam black,* still blacker; and *damn black,* blackest man, of whom it is said: "Why, lightning bugs follows him at 12 o'clock in the day, thinking it's midnight."
Dat thing — sex of either sex
Dat's your mammy — same as, "So is your old man."
Diddy-wah-diddy — a far place, a measure of distance. (2) another suburb of Hell, built since way before Hell wasn't no bigger than Baltimore. The folks in Hell go there for a big time.
Dig — understand. "Dig me?" means, "Do you get me? Do you collar the jive?"
Draped down — dressed in the height of Harlem fashion; also *togged down.*
Dumb to the fact — "You don't know what you're talking about."
Dusty butt — cheap prostitute

Eight-rock — very black person
Every postman on his beat — kinky hair

First thing smoking — a train. "I'm through with this town. I mean to grab the first thing smoking."
Frail eel — Pretty girl
Free schools — a shortened expression of deprecation derived from "free schools and dumb Negroes," sometimes embellished with "free schools, pretty yellow teachers and dumb Negroes."
Function — a small, unventilated dance, full of people too casually bathed

Gator-faced — long, black face with big mouth
Getting on some stiff time — really doing well with your racket
Get you to go — power, physical or otherwise, to force the opponent to run
Ginny Gall — a suburb of Hell, a long way off
Git up off of me — quit talking about me, leave me alone
Go when the wagon comes — another way of saying, "You may be acting biggity now, but you'll cool down when enough power gets behind you."
Good hair — Caucasian-type hair
Granny Grunt — a mythical character to whom most questions may be referred
Ground rations — sex, also *under rations*
Gum beater — a blowhard, a braggart, idle talker in general
Gut-bucket — low dive, type of music, or expression from same
Gut-foot — bad case of fallen arches

Handkerchief-head — sycophant type of Negro; also an *Uncle Tom*
Hauling — fleeing on foot. "Man! He cold hauled it!"

I don't deal in coal — "I don't keep company with black women."
I'm cracking but I'm facking — "I'm wisecracking, but I'm telling the truth."
Inky dink — very black person
I shot him lightly and he died politely — "I completely outdid him."

Jar head — Negro man
Jelly — sex
Jig — Negro, a corrupted shortening of zigaboo
Jook — a pleasure house, in the class of gut-bucket; now common all over the South
Jooking — playing the piano, guitar, or any musical instrument in the manner of the Jooks (pronounced like "took") (2) Dancing and "scronching" ditto.
Juice — liquor
July jam — something very hot
Jump salty — get angry

Kitchen mechanic — a domestic
Knock yourself out — have a good time

Lightly, slightly and politely — doing things perfectly
Little sister — measure of hotness: "Hot as little sister!"
Liver-lip — pendulous, thick, purple lips

Made hair — hair that has been straightened
Mammy — a term of insult. Never used in any other way by Negroes.
Miss Anne — a white woman
Mister Charlie — a white man
Monkey chaser — a West Indian
Mug man — small-time thug or gangster
My people! My people! — Sad and satiric expression in the Negro language: sad when a Negro comments on the backwardness of some members of his race; at other times, used for satiric or comic effect

Naps — kinky hair
Nearer my God to Thee — good hair
Nothing to the bear but his curly hair — "I call your bluff," or "Don't be afraid of him; he won't fight."
Now you cookin' with gas — now you're talking, in the groove, etc.

Ofay — white person
Old cuffee — Negro (genuine African word for the same thing)

Palmer House — walking flat-footed, as from fallen arches
Pancake — a humble type of Negro
Park ape — an ugly, underprivileged Negro
Peckerwood — poor and unloved class of Southern whites
Peeping through my likkers — carrying on even though drunk
Pe-ola — a very white Negro girl
Piano — spare ribs (white rib-bones suggest piano keys)
Pig meat — young girl
Pilch — house or apartment; residence
Pink toes — yellow girl
Playing the dozens — low-rating the ancestors of your opponent

Red neck — poor Southern white man
Reefer — marijuana cigaret, also a *drag*
Righteous mass or *grass* — good hair
Righteous rags — the components of a Harlem-style suit
Rug-cutter — originally a person frequenting house-rent parties, cutting up the rugs of the host with his feet; a person too cheap or poor to patronize regular dance halls; now means a good dancer.
Russian — a Southern Negro up north. "Rushed up here," hence a Russian.

Scrap iron — cheap liquor
Sell out — run in fear

Sender — he or she who can get you to go, i.e., has what it takes. Used often as a compliment: "He's a solid sender!"
Smoking, or *smoking over* — looking someone over
Solid — perfect
Sooner — anything cheap and mongrel, now applied to cheap clothes, or a shabby person.
Stanch, or *stanch out* — to begin, commence, step out
Stomp — low dance, but hot man!
Stormbuzzard — shiftless, homeless character
Stroll — doing something well
Sugar Hill — northwest corner of Harlem, near Washington Heights, site of newest apartment houses, mostly occupied by professional people. (The expression has been distorted in the South to mean a Negro red light district.)

The bear — confession of poverty
The big apple, also the *big red apple* — New York City
The man — the law, or powerful boss
Thousand on a plate — beans
Tight head — one with kinky hair
Trucking — strolling. (2) dance step from the strolling motif

V and X — five-and-ten-cent store

West Hell — another suburb of Hell, worse than the original
What's on the rail for the lizard? — suggestion for moral turpitude
Whip it to the red — beat your head until it is bloody
Woofing — aimless talk, as a dog barks on a moonlight night

Young suit — ill-fitting, too small. Observers pretend to believe you're breaking in your little brother's suit for him.
Your likker told you — misguided behavior

Zigaboo — a Negro
Zoot suit with the reet pleat — Harlem style suit, padded shoulders, 43-inch trousers at the knee with cuff so small it needs a zipper to get into, high waistline, fancy lapels, bushels of buttons, etc.

ZORA NEALE HURSTON

Sweat

1926

I

It was eleven o'clock of a Spring night in Florida. It was Sunday. Any other night, Delia Jones would have been in bed for two hours by this time. But she was a washwoman, and Monday morning meant a great deal to her. So she collected the soiled clothes on Saturday when she returned the clean things. Sunday night after church, she sorted and put the white things to soak. It saved her almost a half-day's start. A great hamper in the bedroom held the clothes that she brought home. It was so much neater than a number of bundles lying around.

She squatted on the kitchen floor beside the great pile of clothes, sorting them into small heaps according to color, and humming a song in a mournful key, but wondering through it all where Sykes, her husband, had gone with her horse and buckboard.

Just then something long, round, limp, and black fell upon her shoulders and slithered to the floor beside her. A great terror took hold of her. It softened her knees and dried her mouth so that it was a full minute before she could cry out or move. Then she saw that it was the big bull whip her husband liked to carry when he drove.

She lifted her eyes to the door and saw him standing there bent over with laughter at her fright. She screamed at him.

"Sykes, what you throw dat whip on me like dat? You know it would skeer me — looks just like a snake, an' you knows how skeered Ah is of snakes."

"Course Ah knowed it! That's how come Ah done it." He slapped his leg with his hand and almost rolled on the ground in his mirth. "If you such a big fool dat you got to have a fit over a earth worm or a string, Ah don't keer how bad Ah skeer you."

"You ain't got no business doing it. Gawd knows it's a sin. Some day Ah'm gointuh drop dead from some of yo' foolishness. 'Nother thing, where you been wid mah rig? Ah feeds dat pony. He ain't fuh you to be drivin' wid no bull whip."

"You sho' is one aggravatin' nigger woman!" he declared and stepped into the room. She resumed her work and did not answer him at once. "Ah done tole you time and again to keep them white folks' clothes outa dis house."

He picked up the whip and glared at her. Delia went on with her work. She went out into the yard and returned with a galvanized tub and set it on the wash-bench. She saw that Sykes had kicked all of the clothes together again, and now stood in her way truculently, his whole manner hoping, *praying,* for an argument. But she walked calmly around him and commenced to re-sort the things.

"Next time, Ah'm gointer kick 'em outdoors," he threatened as he struck a match along the leg of his corduroy breeches.

Delia never looked up from her work, and her thin, stooped shoulders sagged further.

"Ah ain't for no fuss t'night, Sykes. Ah just come from taking sacrament at the church house."

He snorted scornfully. "Yeah, you just come from de church house on a Sunday night, but heah you is gone to work on them clothes. You ain't nothing but a hypocrite. One of them amen-corner Christians — sing, whoop, and shout, then come home and wash white folks' clothes on the Sabbath."

He stepped roughly upon the whitest pile of things, kicking them helter-skelter as he crossed the room. His wife gave a little scream of dismay, and quickly gathered them together again.

"Sykes, you quit grindin' dirt into these clothes! How can Ah git through by Sat'day if Ah don't start on Sunday?"

"Ah don't keer if you never git through. Anyhow, Ah done promised Gawd and a couple of other men, Ah ain't gointer have it in mah house. Don't gimme no lip neither, else Ah'll throw 'em out and put mah fist up side yo' head to boot."

Delia's habitual meekness seemed to slip from her shoulders like a blown scarf. She was on her feet; her poor little body, her bare knuckly hands bravely defying the strapping hulk before her.

"Looka heah, Sykes, you done gone too fur. Ah been married to you fur fifteen years, and Ah been takin' in washin' fur fifteen years. Sweat, sweat, sweat! Work and sweat, cry and sweat, pray and sweat!"

"What's that got to do with me?" he asked brutally.

"What's it got to do with you, Sykes? Mah tub of suds is filled yo' belly with vittles more times than yo' hands is filled it. Mah sweat is done paid for this house and Ah reckon Ah kin keep on sweatin' in it."

She seized the iron skillet from the stove and struck a defensive pose, which act surprised him greatly, coming from her. It cowed him and he did not strike her as he usually did.

"Naw you won't," she panted, "that ole snaggle-toothed black woman you runnin' with ain't comin' heah to pile up on *mah* sweat and blood. You ain't paid for nothin' on this place, and Ah'm gointer stay right heah till Ah'm toted out foot foremost."

"Well, you better quit gittin' me riled up, else they'll be totin' you out sooner than you expect. Ah'm so tired of you Ah don't know whut to do. Gawd! How Ah hates skinny wimmen!"

A little awed by this new Delia, he sidled out of the door and slammed the back gate after him. He did not say where he had gone, but she knew too well. She knew very well that he would not return until nearly daybreak also. Her work over, she went on to bed but not to sleep at once. Things had come to a pretty pass!

She lay awake, gazing upon the debris that cluttered their matrimonial trail. Not an image left standing along the way. Anything like flowers had long ago been drowned in the salty stream that had been pressed from her heart. Her tears, her sweat, her blood. She had brought love to the union and he had brought a longing after the flesh. Two months after the wedding, he had given her the first brutal beating. She had the memory of his numerous trips to Orlando with all of his wages when he had returned to her penniless, even before the first year had passed. She was young and soft then, but now she thought of her knotty, muscled limbs, her harsh knuckly hands, and drew herself up into an unhappy little ball in the middle of the big feather bed. Too late now to hope for love, even if it were not Bertha it would be someone else. This case differed from the others only in that she was bolder than the others. Too late for everything except her little home. She had built it for her old days, and planted one by one the trees and flowers there. It was lovely to her, lovely.

Somehow, before sleep came, she found herself saying aloud: "Oh well, whatever goes over the Devil's back, is got to come under his belly. Sometime or ruther, Sykes, like everybody else, is gointer reap his sowing." After that she was able to build a spiritual earthworks against her husband. His shells could no longer reach her. AMEN. She went to sleep and slept until he announced his presence in bed by kicking her feet and rudely snatching the covers away.

"Gimme some kivah heah, an' git yo' damn foots over on yo' own side! Ah oughter mash you in yo' mouf fuh drawing dat skillet on me."

Delia went clear to the rail without answering him. A triumphant indifference to all that he was or did.

II

The week was full of work for Delia as all other weeks, and Saturday found her behind her little pony, collecting and delivering clothes.

It was a hot, hot day near the end of July. The village men on Joe Clarke's porch even chewed cane listlessly. They did not hurl the cane-knots as usual. They let them dribble over the edge of the porch. Even conversation had collapsed under the heat.

"Heah come Delia Jones," Jim Merchant said, as the shaggy pony came 'round the bend of the road toward them. The rusty buckboard was heaped with baskets of crisp, clean laundry.

"Yep," Joe Lindsay agreed. "Hot or col', rain or shine, jes'ez reg'lar ez de weeks roll roun' Delia carries 'em an' fetches 'em on Sat'day."

"She better if she wanter eat," said Moss. "Jones ain't wuth de shot an' powder hit would tek tuh kill 'em. Not to *huh* he ain't."

"He sho' ain't," Walter Thomas chimed in. "It's too bad, too, cause she wuz a right pretty li'l trick when he got huh. Ah'd uh mah'ied huh mahself if he hadnter beat me to it."

Delia nodded briefly at the men as she drove past.

"Too much knockin' will ruin *any* 'oman. He done beat huh 'nough tuh kill three women, let 'lone change they looks," said Elijah Moseley. "How Syke kin stommuck dat big black greasy Mogul he's layin' roun' wid, gits me. Ah swear dat eight-rock couldn't kiss a sardine can Ah done thowed out de back do' 'way las' yeah."

"Aw, she's fat, thass how come. He's allus been crazy 'bout fat women," put in Merchant. "He'd a' been tied up wid one long time ago if he could a' found one tuh have him. Did Ah tell yuh 'bout him come sidlin' roun' *mah* wife — bringin' her a basket uh peecans outa his yard fuh a present? Yessir, mah wife! She tol' him tuh take 'em right straight back home, 'cause Delia works so hard ovah dat washtub she reckon everything on de place taste lak sweat an' soapsuds. Ah jus' wisht Ah'd a' caught 'im 'roun' dere! Ah'd a' made his hips ketch on fiah down dat shell road."

"Ah know he done it, too. Ah sees 'im grinnin' at every 'oman dat passes," Walter Thomas said. "But even so, he useter eat some mighty big hunks uh humble pie tuh git dat li'l 'oman he got. She wuz ez pritty ez a speckled pup! Dat wuz fifteen years ago. He useter be so skeered uh losin' huh, she could make him do some parts of a husband's duty. Dey never wuz de same in de mind."

"There oughter be a law about him," said Lindsay. "He ain't fit tuh carry guts tuh a bear."

Clarke spoke for the first time. "Tain't no law on earth dat kin make a man be decent if it ain't in 'im. There's plenty men dat takes a wife lak dey do a joint uh sugar-cane. It's round, juicy, an' sweet when dey gits it. But dey squeeze an' grind, squeeze an' grind an' wring tell dey wring every drop uh pleasure dat's in 'em out. When dey's satisfied dat dey is wrung dry, dey treats 'em jes' lak dey do a cane-chew. Dey thows 'em away. Dey knows whut dey is doin' while dey is at it, an' hates theirselves fuh it but they keeps on hangin' after huh tell she's empty. Den dey hates huh fuh bein' a cane-chew an' in de way."

"We oughter take Syke an' dat stray 'oman uh his'n down in Lake Howell swamp an' lay on de rawhide till they cain't say Lawd' a' mussy. He allus wuz uh ovahbearin niggah, but since dat white 'oman from up north done teached 'im how to run a automobile, he done got too beggety to live — an' we oughter kill 'im," Old Man Anderson advised.

A grunt of approval went around the porch. But the heat was melting their civic virtue and Elijah Moseley began to bait Joe Clarke.

"Come on, Joe, git a melon outa dere an' slice it up for yo' customers. We'se all sufferin' wid de heat. De bear's done got *me*!"

"Thass right, Joe, a watermelon is jes' whut Ah needs tuh cure de eppizudicks," Walter Thomas joined forces with Moseley. "Come on dere, Joe. We all is steady customers an' you ain't set us up in a long time. Ah chooses dat long, bowlegged Floridy favorite."

"A god, an' be dough. You all gimme twenty cents and slice away," Clarke retorted. "Ah needs a col' slice m'self. Heah, everybody chip in. Ah'll lend y'all mah meat knife."

The money was all quickly subscribed and the huge melon brought forth. At that moment, Sykes and Bertha arrived. A determined silence fell on the porch and the melon was put away again.

Merchant snapped down the blade of his jacknife and moved toward the store door.

"Come on in, Joe, an' gimme a slab uh sow belly an' uh pound uh coffee — almost fuhgot 'twas Sat'day. Got to git on home." Most of the men left also.

Just then Delia drove past on her way home, as Sykes was ordering magnificently for Bertha. It pleased him for Delia to see.

"Git whutsoever yo' heart desires, Honey. Wait a minute, Joe. Give huh two bottles uh strawberry soda-water, uh quart parched ground-peas, an' a block uh chewin' gum."

With all this they left the store, with Sykes reminding Bertha that this was his town and she could have it if she wanted it.

The men returned soon after they left, and held their watermelon feast.

"Where did Syke Jones git da 'oman from nohow?" Lindsay asked.

"Ovah Apopka. Guess dey musta been cleanin' out de town when she lef'. She don't look lak a thing but a hunk uh liver wid hair on it."

"Well, she sho' kin squall," Dave Carter contributed. "When she gits ready tuh laff, she jes' opens huh mouf an' latches it back tuh de las' notch. No ole granpa alligator down in Lake Bell ain't got nothin' on huh."

III

Bertha had been in town three months now. Sykes was still paying her room-rent at Della Lewis' — the only house in town that would have taken her in. Sykes took her frequently to Winter Park to "stomps." He still assured her that he was the swellest man in the state.

"Sho' you kin have dat li'l ole house soon's Ah git dat 'oman outa dere. Everything b'longs tuh me an' you sho' kin have it. Ah sho' 'bominates uh skinny 'oman. Lawdy, you sho' is got one portly shape on you! You kin git *anything* you wants. Dis is *mah* town an' you sho' kin have it."

Delia's work-worn knees crawled over the earth in Gethsemane° and up the rocks of Calvary many, many times during these months. She avoided the villagers and meeting places in her efforts to be blind and deaf. But Bertha nullified this to a degree, by coming to Delia's house to call Sykes out to her at the gate.

Delia and Sykes fought all the time now with no peaceful interludes. They slept and ate in silence. Two or three times Delia had attempted a timid friendliness, but she was repulsed each time. It was plain that the breaches must remain agape.

The sun had burned July to August. The heat streamed down like a million hot arrows, smiting all things living upon the earth. Grass withered, leaves browned, snakes went blind in shedding, and men and dogs went mad. Dog days!

Delia came home one day and found Sykes there before her. She wondered, but started to go on into the house without speaking, even though he was standing in the kitchen door and she must either stoop under his arm or ask him to move. He made no room for her. She noticed a soap box beside the steps, but paid no particular attention to it, knowing that he must have brought it there. As she was stooping to pass under his outstretched arm, he suddenly pushed her backward, laughingly.

"Look in de box dere Delia, Ah done brung yuh somethin'!"

She nearly fell upon the box in her stumbling, and when she saw what it held, she all but fainted outright.

"Syke! Syke, mah Gawd! You take dat rattlesnake 'way from heah! You *gottuh*. Oh, Jesus, have mussy!"

"Ah ain't got tuh do nuthin' uh de kin' — fact is Ah ain't got tuh do nothin' but die. Tain't no use uh you puttin' on airs makin' out lak you skeered uh dat snake — he's gointer stay right heah tell he die. He wouldn't bite me cause Ah knows how tuh handle 'im. Nohow he wouldn't risk breakin' out his fangs 'gin *yo* skinny laigs."

"Naw, now Syke, don't keep dat thing 'round tryin' tuh skeer me tuh death. You knows Ah'm even feared uh earth worms. Thass de biggest snake Ah evah did se. Kill 'im Syke, please."

"Doan ast me tuh do nothin' fuh yuh. Goin' 'round tryin' tuh be so damn asterperious. Naw, Ah ain't gonna kill it. Ah think uh damn sight mo' uh him dan you! Dat's a nice snake an' anybody doan lak 'im kin jes' hit de grit."

The village soon heard that Sykes had the snake, and came to see and ask questions.

"How de hen-fire did you ketch dat six-foot rattler, Syke?" Thomas asked.

Gethsemane: A reference to the garden where Jesus was betrayed (in the Gospels) before being tried and crucified on Calvary or Golgotha, the "hill of skulls."

"He's full uh frogs so he cain't hardly move, thass how Ah eased up on 'm. But Ah'm a snake charmer an' knows how tuh handle 'em. Shux, dat ain't nothin'. Ah could ketch one eve'y day if Ah so wanted tuh."

"Whut he needs is a heavy hick'ry club leaned real heavy on his head. Dat's de bes' way tuh charm a rattlesnake."

"Naw, Walt, y'all jes' don't understand dese diamon' backs lak Ah do," said Sykes in a superior tone of voice.

The village agreed with Walter, but the snake stayed on. His box remained by the kitchen door with its screen wire covering. Two or three days later it had digested its meal of frogs and literally came to life. It rattled at every movement in the kitchen or the yard. One day as Delia came down the kitchen steps she saw his chalky-white fangs curved like scimitars hung in the wire meshes. This time she did not run away with averted eyes as usual. She stood for a long time in the doorway in a red fury that grew bloodier for every second that she regarded the creature that was her torment.

That night she broached the subject as soon as Sykes sat down to the table.

"Syke, Ah wants you tuh take dat snake 'way fum heah. You done starved me an' Ah put up widcher, you done beat me an Ah took dat, but you don kilt all mah insides bringin' dat varmint heah."

Sykes poured out a saucer full of coffee and drank it deliberately before he answered her.

"A whole lot Ah keer 'bout how you feels inside uh out. Dat snake ain't goin' no damn wheah till Ah gits ready fuh 'im tuh go. So fur as beatin' is concerned, yuh ain't took near all dat you gointer take ef yuh stay 'round *me.*"

Delia pushed back her plate and got up from the table. "Ah hates you, Sykes," she said calmly. "Ah hates you tuh de same degree dat Ah useter love yuh. Ah done took an' took till mah belly is full up tuh mah neck. Dat's de reason Ah got mah letter fum de church an' moved mah membership tuh Woodbridge — so Ah don't haftuh take no sacrament wid yuh. Ah don't wantuh see yuh 'round me atall. Lay 'round wid dat 'oman all yuh wants tuh, but gwan 'way from me an' mah house. Ah hates yuh lak uh suck-egg dog."

Sykes almost let the huge wad of corn bread and collard greens he was chewing fall out of his mouth in amazement. He had a hard time whipping himself up to the proper fury to try to answer Delia.

"Well, Ah'm glad you does hate me. Ah'm sho' tiahed uh you hangin' ontuh me. Ah don't want yuh. Look at yuh stringey ole neck! Yo' rawbony laigs an' arms is enough tuh cut uh man tuh death. You looks jes' lak de devvul's doll-baby tuh *me.* You cain't hate me no worse dan Ah hates you. Ah been hatin' *you* fuh years."

"Yo' ole black hide don't look lak nothin' tuh me, but uh passle uh wrinkled up rubber, wid yo' big ole yeahs flappin' on each side lak uh paih uh buzzard wings. Don't think Ah'm gointuh be run 'way fum mah house neither. Ah'm goin' tuh de white folks 'bout *you,* mah young man, de very nex' time you lay yo' han's on me. Mah cup is done run ovah." Delia said this with no signs of fear and Sykes departed from the house, threatening her, but made not the slightest move to carry out any of them.

That night he did not return at all, and the next day being Sunday, Delia was glad she did not have to quarrel before she hitched up her pony and drove the four miles to Woodbridge.

She stayed to the night service — "love feast" — which was very warm and full of spirit. In the emotional winds her domestic trials were borne far and wide so that she sang as she drove homeward,

Jurden water, black an' col
Chills de body, not de soul
An' Ah wantah cross Jurden in uh calm time.

She came from the barn to the kitchen door and stopped.

"Whut's de mattah, ol' Satan, you ain't kicken' up yo' racket?" She addressed the snake's box. Complete silence. She went on into the house with a new hope in its birth struggles. Perhaps her threat to go to the white folks had frightened Sykes! Perhaps he was sorry! Fifteen years of misery and suppression had brought Delia to the place where she would hope *anything* that looked towards a way over or through her wall of inhibitions.

She felt in the match-safe behind the stove at once for a match. There was only one there.

"Dat niggah wouldn't fetch nothin' heah tuh save his rotten neck, but he kin run thew whut Ah brings quick enough. Now he done toted off nigh on tuh haff uh box uh matches. He done had dat 'oman heah in mah house, too."

Nobody but a woman could tell how she knew this even before she struck the match. But she did and it put her into a new fury.

Presently she brought in the tubs to put the white things to soak. This time she decided she need not bring the hamper out of the bedroom; she would go in there and do the sorting. She picked up the pot-bellied lamp and went in. The room was small and the hamper stood hard by the foot of the white iron bed. She could sit and reach through the bedposts — resting as she worked.

"Ah wantah cross Jurden in uh calm time." She was singing again. The mood of the "love feast," had returned. She threw back the lid of the basket almost gaily. Then, moved by both horror and terror, she sprang back toward the door. *There lay the snake in the basket!* He moved sluggishly at first, but even as she turned round and round, jumped up and down in an insanity of fear, he began to stir vigorously. She saw him pouring his awful beauty from the basket upon the bed, then she seized the lamp and ran as fast as she could to the kitchen. The wind from the open door blew out the light and the darkness added to her terror. She sped to the darkness of the yard, slamming the door after her before she thought to set down the lamp. She did not feel safe even on the ground, so she climbed up in the hay barn.

There for an hour or more she lay sprawled upon the hay a gibbering wreck.

Finally she grew quiet, and after that came coherent thought. With this stalked through her a cold, bloody rage. Hours of this. A period of introspection, a space of retrospection, then a mixture of both. Out of this an awful calm.

"Well, Ah done de bes' Ah could. If things ain't right, Gawd knows tain't mah fault."

She went to sleep — a twitch sleep — and woke up to a faint gray sky. There was a loud hollow sound below. She peered out. Sykes was at the woodpile, demolishing a wire-covered box.

He hurried to the kitchen door, but hung outside there some minutes before he entered, and stood some minutes more inside before he closed it after him.

The gray in the sky was spreading. Delia descended without fear now, and crouched beneath the low bedroom window. The drawn shade shut out the dawn, shut in the night. But the thin walls held back no sound.

"Dat ol' scratch is woke up now!" She mused at the tremendous whirr inside, which every woodsman knows, is one of the sound illusions. The rattler is a ventriloquist. His whirr sounds to the right, to the left, straight ahead, behind, close under foot — everywhere but where it is. Woe to him who guesses wrong unless he is prepared to hold up his end of the argument! Sometimes he strikes without rattling at all.

Inside, Sykes heard nothing until he knocked a pot lid off the stove while trying to reach the match-safe in the dark. He had emptied his pockets at Bertha's.

The snake seemed to wake up under the stove and Sykes made a quick leap into the bedroom. In spite of the gin he had had, his head was clearing now.

"Mah Gawd!" he chattered, "ef Ah could on'y strack uh light!"

The rattling ceased for a moment as he stood paralyzed. He waited. It seemed that the snake waited also.

"Oh, fuh de light! Ah thought he'd be too sick" — Sykes was muttering to himself when the whirr began again, closer, right underfoot this time. Long before this, Sykes' ability to think had been flattened down to primitive instinct and he leaped — onto the bed.

Outside Delia heard a cry that might have come from a maddened chimpanzee, a stricken gorilla. All the terror, all the horror, all the rage that man possibly could express, without a recognizable human sound.

A tremendous stir inside there, another series of animal screams, the intermittent whirr of the reptile. The shade torn violently down from the window, letting in the red dawn, a huge brown hand seizing the window stick, great dull blows upon the wooden floor punctuating the gibberish of sound long after the rattle of the snake had abruptly subsided. All this Delia could see and hear from her place beneath the window, and it made her ill. She crept over to the four o'clocks and stretched herself on the cool earth to recover.

She lay there. "Delia, Delia!" She could hear Sykes calling in a most despairing tone as one who expected no answer. The sun crept on up, and he called. Delia could not move — her legs had gone flabby. She never moved, he called, and the sun kept rising.

"Mah Gawd!" She heard him moan, "Mah Gawd fum Heben!" She heard him stumbling about and got up from her flower-bed. The sun was growing warm. As she approached the door she heard him call out hopefully, "Delia, is dat you Ah heah?"

She saw him on his hands and knees as soon as she reached the door. He crept an inch or two toward her — all that he was able, and she saw his horribly swollen neck and his one open eye shining with hope. A surge of pity too strong to support bore her away from that eye that must, could not, fail to see the tubs. He would see the lamp. Orlando with its doctors was too far. She could scarcely reach the chinaberry tree, where she waited in the growing heat while inside she knew the cold river was creeping up and up to extinguish that eye which must know by now that she knew.

ꕥ

WASHINGTON IRVING *(1783–1859), named after George Washington, was the youngest of eleven children born in New York City to a mother of English descent and a Scottish father who was a prosperous merchant. After studying law with a judge, Josiah Hoffman, Irving went on a Grand Tour of Europe for two years, visiting France, Italy, Switzerland, Belgium, Holland, and England. Returning to New York City, he took the eighteenth-century English prose writers as his models when he published the* Salmagundi Papers *(1807–08) and a comic* History of New York *(1809), in which he invented the figure of a talkative elderly narrator named Diedrich Knickerbocker who told raucous anecdotes about the early political history of the Dutch colony. Irving's* History *was so successful that his comical gentleman "Knickerbocker" came to personify New York City. The name survives today in the professional basketball team the New York Knicks.*

Anguished by the death of his fiancée, Judge Hoffman's daughter Matilda, Irving left New York in 1815 to join his brother Peter in the European branch of the family's hardware business in Liverpool. When the venture failed, Irving — describing himself as "harassed and hag-ridden by the cares and anxieties of business" — decided to stay in England and try to make his living as a writer. He moved to London and began to meet British authors, including Sir Walter Scott, one of the most successful novelists of his time, whom Irving visited in his country house in 1818. They shared an enthusiasm for German literature, which Irving had read in translation. Scott had based the subplot of a play he was writing on a German folktale, and when Irving returned to London he immersed himself in an intensive study of German. He wrote his friend Henry Breevort,

> *I have been for some time past engaged in the study of the German language, and have got so far as to be able to read and sputter a little. It is a severe task, and has required hard study; but the rich mine of German literature holds forth abundant reward.*

As he put it, Irving started "scribbling" short prose tales based on his own translations. In one especially inspired day he produced "Rip Van Winkle," which was published in London in 1819–20 as part of his two-volume collection The Sketch Book.

Irving's source for "Rip Van Winkle" was the German folktale of "Peter Klaus the Goatherd," but he went to ingenious lengths to disguise his borrowing. First he invented the tongue-in-cheek character "Geoffrey Crayon" as the author of The Sketch Book, *attempting to hide that he was an American writer trying to interest English readers in his work. In his preface, Irving said that Geoffrey Crayon was a traveler "unsettled in his abode," making impressionistic, quick "crayon" sketches while journeying in Europe and the United States. Then Irving created a frame for*

"Rip Van Winkle," with Crayon telling the reader that he found the tale "among the papers of the late Diedrich Knickerbocker, an old gentleman of New York." Irving's use of pseudonyms and mock-documentation in the opening and closing paragraphs of "Rip Van Winkle" underscores the humorous tone of his tale, which gave the story an enduring new life as an American legend. He followed "Rip Van Winkle" in The Sketch Book *with another short story masterpiece based on German folklore, "The Legend of Sleepy Hollow," and completed the collection with travel sketches and informal essays.*

Irving's tales in The Sketch Book *were so popular that Scott followed his lead and published the first short story in British literature, "The Two Drovers," in 1827. When Irving was charged with plagiarism by hostile critics, he defended himself by explaining that he considered folktales "fair foundations for authors of fiction to build upon." He insisted that*

> *much of what I value myself upon in writing, escapes the observation of the great mass of my readers, who are intent more upon the story than the way in which it is told. For my part I consider a story merely as a frame on which to stretch my materials. It is the play of thought, and sentiment and language; the weaving in of characters, lightly yet expressively delineated; the familiar and faithful exhibition of scenes of common life, and the half concealed vein of humor that is often playing through the whole — these are among what I aim at, and which I felicitate myself in proportion as I think I succeed.*

Irving was the first American short story author to attain a European audience. When the English writer Mary Mitford Russell edited her Stories of American Life *(1830) in London, she excluded Irving from her list of American authors because she felt that "his writings are essentially European and must be content to take their station amongst the Spectators and Tatlers of the mother country." After seventeen years abroad Irving returned to New York in 1832 and settled in Tarrytown on the Hudson. He involved himself in politics and continued to publish books, most notably the travel sketches* A Tour on the Prairies *in 1835 and the multivolume* Life of Washington, *completed shortly before his death in 1859.*

RELATED STORY: *J. C. C. Nachtigal, "Peter Klaus the Goatherd," page 33.*

RELATED COMMENTARY: *Washington Irving, "Letter to Henry Brevoort, December 11, 1824," page 687.*

WASHINGTON IRVING

Rip Van Winkle

1819–20

A Posthumous Writing of Diedrich Knickerbocker

By Woden, God of Saxons,
From whence comes Wensday, that is Wodensday,
Truth is a thing that ever I will keep
Unto thylke day in which I creep into
My sepulchre —

– CARTWRIGHT°

Cartwright: William Cartwright (1611–1643) was an English playwright. The lines are from his play *The Ordinary* (3.1.1050–54).

[The following Tale was found among the papers of the late Diedrich Knickerbocker, an old gentleman of New York, who was very curious in the Dutch history of the province, and the manners of the descendants from its primitive settlers. His historical researches, however, did not lie so much among books as among men; for the former are lamentably scanty on his favorite topics; whereas he found the old burghers, and still more their wives, rich in that legendary lore so invaluable to true history. Whenever, therefore, he happened upon a genuine Dutch family, snugly shut up in its low-roofed farmhouse, under a spreading sycamore, he looked upon it as a little clasped volume of black-letter, and studied it with the zeal of a book-worm.

The result of all these researches was a history of the province during the reign of the Dutch governors, which he published some years since. There have been various opinions as to the literary character of his work, and, to tell the truth, it is not a whit better than it should be. Its chief merit is its scrupulous accuracy, which indeed was a little questioned on its first appearance, but has since been completely established; and it is now admitted into all historical collections as a book of unquestionable authority.

The old gentleman died shortly after the publication of his work; and now that he is dead and gone, it cannot do much harm to his memory to say that his time might have been much better employed in weightier labors. He, however, was apt to ride his hobby his own way; and though it did now and then kick up the dust a little in the eyes of his neighbors, and grieve the spirit of some friends, for whom he felt the truest deference and affection, yet his errors and follies are remembered "more in sorrow than in anger," and it begins to be suspected that he never intended to offend. But however his memory may be appreciated by critics, it is still held dear by many folk whose good opinion is well worth having; particularly by certain biscuit-makers, who have gone so far as to imprint his likeness on their New-Year cakes; and have thus given him a chance for immortality, almost equal to being stamped on a Waterloo Medal, or a Queen Anne's Farthing.]

Whoever has made a voyage up the Hudson must remember the Kaatskill mountains. They are a dismembered branch of the great Appalachian family, and are seen away to the west of the river, swelling up to a noble height, and lording it over the surrounding country. Every change of season, every change of weather, indeed, every hour of the day, produces some change in the magical hues and shapes of these mountains, and they are regarded by all the good wives, far and near, as perfect barometers. When the weather is fair and settled, they are clothed in blue and purple, and print their bold outlines on the clear evening sky; but sometimes, when the rest of the landscape is cloudless, they will gather a hood of gray vapors about their summits, which, in the last rays of the setting sun, will glow and light up like a crown of glory.

At the foot of these fairy mountains, the voyager may have descried the light smoke curling up from a village, whose shingle-roofs gleam among the trees, just where the blue tints of the upland melt away into the fresh green of the nearer landscape. It is a little village, of great antiquity, having been founded by some of the Dutch colonists in the early times of the province, just about the beginning of the government of the good Peter Stuyvesant, (may he rest in peace!) and there were some of the houses of the original settlers standing within a few years, built of small yellow bricks brought from Holland, having latticed windows and gable fronts, surmounted with weathercocks.

In that same village, and in one of these very houses (which, to tell the precise truth, was sadly time-worn and weather-beaten), there lived, many years since, while the country was yet a province of Great Britain, a simple, good-natured fellow, of the name of Rip Van Winkle. He was a descendant of the Van Winkles who figured so gallantly in the chivalrous days of Peter Stuyvesant, and accompanied him to the siege of Fort Christina. He inherited, however, but little of the martial character of his ancestors. I have observed that he was a simple, good-natured man; he was, moreover, a kind neighbor, and an obedient, hen-pecked husband. Indeed, to the latter circumstance might be owing that meekness of spirit which gained him such universal popularity; for those men are most apt to be obsequious and conciliating abroad, who are under the discipline of shrews at home. Their tempers, doubtless, are rendered pliant and malleable in the fiery furnace of domestic tribulation; and a curtain-lecture is worth all the sermons in the world for teaching the virtues of patience and long-suffering. A termagant wife may, therefore, in some respects, be considered a tolerable blessing; and if so, Rip Van Winkle was thrice blessed.

Certain it is, that he was a great favorite among all the good wives of the village, who, as usual with the amiable sex, took his part in all family squabbles; and never failed, whenever they talked those matters over in their evening gossipings, to lay all the blame on Dame Van Winkle. The children of the village, too, would shout with joy whenever he approached. He assisted at their sports, made their playthings, taught them to fly kites and shoot marbles, and told them long stories of ghosts, witches, and Indians. Whenever he went dodging about the village, he was surrounded by a troop of them, hanging on his skirts, clambering on his back, and playing a thousand tricks on him with impunity; and not a dog would bark at him throughout the neighborhood.

The great error in Rip's composition was an insuperable aversion to all kinds of profitable labor. It could not be from the want of assiduity or perseverance; for he would sit on a wet rock, with a rod as long and heavy as a Tartar's lance, and fish all day without a murmur, even though he should not be encouraged by a single nibble. He would carry a fowling-piece on his shoulder for hours together, trudging through woods and swamps, and up hill and down dale, to shoot a few squirrels or wild pigeons. He would never refuse to assist a neighbor even in the roughest toil, and was a foremost man at all country frolics for husking Indian corn, or building stone fences; the women of the village, too, used to employ him to run their errands, and to do such little odd jobs as their less obliging husbands would not do for them. In a word, Rip was ready to attend to anybody's business but his own; but as to doing family duty, and keeping his farm in order, he found it impossible.

In fact, he declared it was of no use to work on his farm; it was the most pestilent little piece of ground in the whole country; everything about it went wrong, and would go wrong, in spite of him. His fences were continually falling to pieces; his cow would either go astray, or get among the cabbages; weeds were sure to grow quicker in his fields than anywhere else; the rain always made a point of setting in just as he had some out-door work to do; so that though his patrimonial estate had dwindled away under his management, acre by acre, until there was little more left than a mere patch of Indian corn and potatoes, yet it was the worst conditioned farm in the neighborhood.

His children, too, were as ragged and wild as if they belonged to nobody. His son Rip, an urchin begotten in his own likeness, promised to inherit the habits, with the old clothes, of his father. He was generally seen trooping like a colt at his mother's heels, equipped in a pair of his father's cast-off galligaskins, which he had much ado to hold up with one hand, as a fine lady does her train in bad weather.

Rip Van Winkle, however, was one of those happy mortals, of foolish, well-oiled dispositions, who take the world easy, eat white bread or brown, whichever can be got with least thought or trouble, and would rather starve on a penny than work for a pound. If left to himself, he would have whistled life away in perfect contentment; but his wife kept continually dinning in his ears about his idleness, his carelessness, and the ruin he was bringing on his family. Morning, noon and night, her tongue was incessantly going, and everything he said or did was sure to produce a torrent of household eloquence. Rip had but one way of replying to all lectures of the kind, and that, by frequent use, had grown into a habit. He shrugged his shoulders, shook his head, cast up his eyes, but said nothing. This, however, always provoked a fresh volley from his wife; so that he was fain to draw off his forces, and take to the outside of the house — the only side which, in truth, belongs to a hen-pecked husband.

Rip's sole domestic adherent was his dog Wolf, who was as much hen-pecked as his master; for Dame Van Winkle regarded them as companions in idleness, and even looked upon Wolf with an evil eye, as the cause of his master's going so often astray. True it is, in all points of spirit befitting an honorable dog, he was as courageous an animal as ever scoured the woods; but what courage can withstand the ever-enduring and all-besetting terrors of a woman's tongue? The moment Wolf entered the house his crest fell, his tail drooped to the ground, or curled between his legs, he sneaked about with a gallows air, casting many a sidelong glance at Dame Van Winkle, and at the least flourish of a broomstick or ladle he would fly to the door with yelping precipitation.

Times grew worse and worse with Rip Van Winkle as years of matrimony rolled on; a tart temper never mellows with age, and a sharp tongue is the only edged tool that grows keener with constant use. For a long while he used to console himself, when driven from home, by frequenting a kind of perpetual club of the sages, philosophers, and other idle personages of the village, which held its sessions on a bench before a small inn, designated by a rubicund portrait of His Majesty George the Third. Here they used to sit in the shade through a long, lazy summer's day, talking listlessly over village gossip, or telling endless sleepy stories about nothing. But it would have been worth any statesman's money to have heard the profound discussions that sometimes took place, when by chance an old newspaper fell into their hands from some passing traveller. How solemnly they would listen to the contents, as drawled out by Derrick Van Bummel, the schoolmaster, a dapper learned little man, who was not to be daunted by the most gigantic word in the dictionary; and how sagely they would deliberate upon public events some months after they had taken place.

The opinions of this junto° were completely controlled by Nicholas Vedder, patriarch of the village, and landlord of the inn, at the door of which he took his seat from morning till night, just moving sufficiently to avoid the sun and keep in the shade of a large tree; so that the neighbors could tell the hour by his movements as accurately as by a sun-dial. It is true he was rarely heard to speak, but smoked his pipe incessantly. His adherents, however (for every great man has his adherents), perfectly understood him, and knew how to gather his opinions. When anything that was read or related displeased him, he was observed to smoke his pipe vehemently, and to send forth short, frequent, and angry puffs; but when pleased, he would inhale the smoke slowly and tranquilly, and emit it in light and placid clouds; and sometimes, taking the pipe from his mouth, and letting the fragrant vapor curl about his nose, would gravely nod his head in token of perfect approbation.

From even this stronghold the unlucky Rip was at length routed by his termagant wife, who would suddenly break in upon the tranquillity of the assemblage and call the members all to naught; nor was that august personage, Nicholas Vedder himself, sacred from the daring tongue of this terrible virago, who charged him outright with encouraging her husband in habits of idleness.

Poor Rip was at last reduced almost to despair; and his only alternative, to escape from the labor of the farm and clamor of his wife, was to take gun in hand and stroll away into the woods. Here he would sometimes seat himself at the foot of a tree, and share the contents of his wallet with Wolf, with whom he sympathized as a fellow-sufferer in persecution. "Poor Wolf," he would say, "thy mistress leads thee a dog's life of it, but never mind, my lad, whilst I live thou shalt never want a friend to stand by thee!" Wolf would wag his tail, look wistfully in his master's face, and if dogs can feel pity, I verily believe he reciprocated the sentiment with all his heart.

In a long ramble of the kind on a fine autumnal day, Rip had unconsciously scrambled to one of the highest parts of the Kaatskill mountains. He was after his favorite sport of squirrel-shooting, and the still solitudes had echoed and re-echoed with the reports of his gun. Panting and fatigued, he threw himself, late in the afternoon, on a green knoll, covered with mountain herbage, that crowned the brow of a precipice. From an opening between the trees he could overlook all the lower country for many a mile of rich woodland. He saw at a distance the lordly Hudson, far, far below him, moving on its silent but majestic course, with the reflection of a purple cloud, or the sail of

---

junto: A group brought together by a common purpose.

a lagging bark, here and there sleeping on its glassy bosom, and at last losing itself in the blue highlands.

On the other side he looked down into a deep mountain glen, wild, lonely, and shagged, the bottom filled with fragments from the impending cliffs, and scarcely lighted by the reflected rays of the setting sun. For some time Rip lay musing on this scene; evening was gradually advancing; the mountains began to throw their long blue shadows over the valleys; he saw that it would be dark long before he could reach the village, and he heaved a heavy sigh when he thought of encountering the terrors of Dame Van Winkle.

As he was about to descend, he heard a voice from a distance, hallooing, "Rip Van Winkle, Rip Van Winkle!" He looked around, but could see nothing but a crow winging its solitary flight across the mountain. He thought his fancy must have deceived him, and turned again to descend, when he heard the same cry ring through the still evening air: "Rip Van Winkle! Rip Van Winkle!" — at the same time Wolf bristled up his back, and giving a low growl, skulked to his master's side, looking fearfully down into the glen. Rip now felt a vague apprehension stealing over him; he looked anxiously in the same direction, and perceived a strange figure slowly toiling up the rocks, and bending under the weight of something he carried on his back. He was surprised to see any human being in this lonely and unfrequented place; but supposing it to be some one of the neighborhood in need of his assistance, he hastened down to yield it.

On nearer approach he was still more surprised at the singularity of the stranger's appearance. He was a short, square-built old fellow, with thick bushy hair, and a grizzled beard. His dress was of the antique Dutch fashion, — a cloth jerkin strapped around the waist — several pair of breeches, the outer one of ample volume, decorated with rows of buttons down the sides, and bunches at the knees. He bore on his shoulders a stout keg, that seemed full of liquor, and made signs for Rip to approach and assist him with the load. Though rather shy and distrustful of this new acquaintance, Rip complied with his usual alacrity; and mutually relieving one another, they clambered up a narrow gully, apparently the dry bed of a mountain torrent. As they ascended, Rip every now and then heard long, rolling peals, like distant thunder, that seemed to issue out of a deep ravine, or rather cleft, between lofty rocks, toward which their rugged path conducted. He paused for an instant, but supposing it to be the muttering of one of those transient thunder-showers which often take place in mountain heights, he proceeded. Passing through the ravine, they came to a hollow, like a small amphitheatre, surrounded by perpendicular precipices, over the brinks of which impending trees shot their branches, so that you only caught glimpses of the azure sky and the bright evening cloud. During the whole time Rip and his companion had labored on in silence; for though the former marvelled greatly what could be the object of carrying a keg of liquor up this wild mountain, yet there was something strange and incomprehensible about the unknown, that inspired awe and checked familiarity.

On entering the amphitheatre, new objects of wonder presented themselves. On a level spot in the centre was a company of odd-looking personages playing at ninepins. They were dressed in a quaint, outlandish fashion; some wore short doublets, others jerkins, with long knives in their belts, and most of them had enormous breeches, of similar style with that of the guide's. Their visages, too, were peculiar: one had a large beard, broad face, and small piggish eyes; the face of another seemed to consist entirely of nose, and was surmounted by a white sugar-loaf hat, set off with a little red cock's tail. They all had beards, of various shapes and colors. There was one who seemed to be the commander. He was a stout old gentleman, with a weather-beaten countenance; he wore a laced doublet, broad belt and hanger, high crowned hat and feather, red stockings, and high-heeled shoes, with roses in them. The whole group reminded Rip of the figures in an old Flemish painting, in the parlor of Dominie Van Shaick, the village parson, and which had been brought over from Holland at the time of the settlement.

What seemed particularly odd to Rip was, that, though these folks were evidently amusing themselves, yet they maintained the gravest faces, the most mysterious silence, and were, withal, the most melancholy party of pleasure he had ever witnessed. Nothing interrupted the stillness of the scene but the noise of the balls, which, whenever they rolled, echoed along the mountains like rumbling peals of thunder.

As Rip and his companion approached them, they suddenly desisted from their play, and stared at him with such fixed, statue-like gaze, and such strange, uncouth, lack-lustre countenances, that his heart turned within him, and his knees smote together. His companion now emptied the contents of the keg into large flagons, and made signs to him to wait upon the company. He obeyed with fear and trembling; they quaffed the liquor in profound silence, and then returned to their game.

By degrees Rip's awe and apprehension subsided. He even ventured, when no eye was fixed upon him, to taste the beverage, which he found had much of the flavor of excellent Hollands. He was naturally a thirsty soul, and was soon tempted to repeat the draught. One taste provoked another; and he reiterated his visits to the flagon so often that at length his senses were overpowered, his eyes swam in his head, his head gradually declined, and he fell into a deep sleep.

On waking, he found himself on the green knoll whence he had first seen the old man of the glen. He rubbed his eyes — it was a bright sunny morning. The birds were hopping and twittering among the bushes, and the eagle was wheeling aloft, and breasting the pure mountain breeze. "Surely," thought Rip, "I have not slept here all night." He recalled the occurrences before he fell asleep. The strange man with a keg of liquor — the mountain ravine — the wild retreat among the rocks — the woe-begone party at ninepins — the flagon — "Oh! that flagon! that wicked flagon!" thought Rip, "what excuse shall I make to Dame Van Winkle?"

He looked round for his gun, but in place of the clean, well-oiled fowling-piece, he found an old firelock lying by him, the barrel encrusted with rust, the lock falling off, and the stock worm-eaten. He now suspected that the grave roisters of the mountains had put a trick upon him, and, having dosed him with liquor, had robbed him of his gun. Wolf, too, had disappeared, but he might have strayed away after a squirrel or partridge. He whistled after him, and shouted his name, but all in vain; the echoes repeated his whistle and shout, but no dog was to be seen.

He determined to revisit the scene of the last evening's gambol, and if he met with any of the party, to demand his dog and gun. As he rose to walk, he found himself stiff in the joints, and wanting in his usual activity. "These mountain beds do not agree with me," thought Rip, "and if this frolic should lay me up with a fit of the rheumatism, I shall have a blessed time with Dame Van Winkle." With some difficulty he got down into the glen: he found the gully up which he and his companion had ascended the preceding evening; but to his astonishment a mountain stream was now foaming down it, leaping from rock to rock, and filling the glen with babbling murmurs. He, however, made shift to scramble up its sides, working his toilsome way through thickets of birch, sassafras, and witch-hazel, and sometimes tripped up or entangled by the wild grape-vines that twisted their coils or tendrils from tree to tree, and spread a kind of network in his path.

At length he reached to where the ravine had opened through the cliffs to the amphitheatre; but no traces of such opening remained. The rocks presented a high, impenetrable wall, over which the torrent came tumbling in a sheet of feathery foam, and fell into a broad deep basin, black from the shadows of the surrounding forest. Here, then, poor Rip was brought to a stand. He again called and whistled after his dog; he was only answered by the cawing of a flock of idle crows, sporting high in air about a dry tree that overhung a sunny precipice; and who, secure in their elevation, seemed to look down and scoff at the poor man's perplexities. What was to be done? the morning was passing away, and Rip felt famished for want of his breakfast. He grieved to give up his dog and gun; he dreaded to meet his wife; but it would not do to starve among the mountains. He shook his head, shouldered the rusty firelock, and, with a heart full of trouble and anxiety, turned his footsteps homeward.

As he approached the village he met a number of people, but none whom he knew, which somewhat surprised him, for he had thought himself acquainted with every one in the country round. Their dress, too, was of a different fashion from that to which he was accustomed. They all stared at him with equal marks of surprise, and whenever they cast their eyes upon him, invariably stroked their chins. The constant recurrence of this gesture induced Rip, involuntarily, to do the same, when, to his astonishment, he found his beard had grown a foot long!

He had now entered the skirts of the village. A troop of strange children ran at his heels, hooting after him, and pointing at his gray beard. The dogs, too, not one of which he recognized for an old acquaintance, barked at him as he passed. The very village was altered; it was larger and more populous. There were rows of houses which he had never seen before, and those which had been his familiar haunts had disappeared. Strange names were over the doors — strange faces at the windows — everything was strange. His mind now misgave him; he began to doubt whether both he and the world around him were not bewitched. Surely this was his native village, which he had left but the day before. There stood the Kaatskill mountains — there ran the silver

Hudson at a distance — there was every hill and dale precisely as it had always been. Rip was sorely perplexed. "That flagon last night," thought he, "has addled my poor head sadly!"

It was with some difficulty that he found the way to his own house, which he approached with silent awe, expecting every moment to hear the shrill voice of Dame Van Winkle. He found the house gone to decay — the roof fallen in, the windows shattered, and the doors off the hinges. A half-starved dog that looked like Wolf was skulking about it. Rip called him by name, but the cur snarled, showed his teeth, and passed on. This was an unkind cut indeed. "My very dog," sighed poor Rip, "has forgotten me!"

He entered the house, which to tell the truth, Dame Van Winkle had always kept in neat order. It was empty, forlorn, and apparently abandoned. This desolateness overcame all his connubial fears — he called loudly for his wife and children — the lonely chambers rang for a moment with his voice, and then all again was silence.

He now hurried forth, and hastened to his old resort, the village inn, but it too was gone. A large rickety wooden building stood in its place, with great gaping windows, some of them broken and mended with old hats and petticoats, and over the door was painted, "The Union Hotel, by Jonathan Doolittle." Instead of the great tree that used to shelter the quiet little Dutch inn of yore, there now was reared a tall naked pole, with something on top that looked like a red night-cap, and from it was fluttering a flag, on which was a singular assemblage of stars and stripes — all this was strange and incomprehensible. He recognized on the sign, however, the ruby face of King George, under which he had smoked so many a peaceful pipe; but even this was singularly metamorphosed. The red coat was changed for one of blue and buff, a sword was held in the hand instead of a sceptre, the head was decorated with a cocked hat, and underneath was painted in large characters, GENERAL WASHINGTON.

There was, as usual, a crowd of folk about the door, but none that Rip recollected. The very character of the people seemed changed. There was a busy, bustling, disputatious tone about it, instead of the accustomed phlegm and drowsy tranquillity. He looked in vain for the sage Nicholas Vedder, with his broad face, double chin, and fair long pipe, uttering clouds of tobacco-smoke instead of idle speeches; or Van Bummel, the schoolmaster, doling forth the contents of an ancient newspaper. In place of these, a lean, bilious-looking fellow, with his pockets full of handbills, was haranguing vehemently about rights of citizens — elections — members of congress — liberty — Bunker's Hill — heroes of seventy-six — and other words, which were a perfect Babylonish jargon to the bewildered Van Winkle.

The appearance of Rip, with his long, grizzled beard, his rusty fowling-piece, his uncouth dress, and an army of women and children at his heels, soon attracted the attention of the tavern-politicians. They crowded round him, eyeing him from head to foot with great curiosity. The orator bustled up to him, and, drawing him partly aside, inquired "On which side he voted?" Rip stared in vacant stupidity. Another short but busy little fellow pulled him by the arm, and, rising on tiptoe, inquired in his ear, "Whether he was Federal or Democrat?" Rip was equally at a loss to comprehend the question; when a knowing, self-important old gentleman, in a sharp cocked hat, made his way through the crowd, putting them to the right and left with his elbows as he passed, and planting himself before Van Winkle, with one arm akimbo, the other resting on his cane, his keen eyes and sharp hat penetrating, as it were, into his very soul, demanded in an austere tone, "What brought him to the election with a gun on his shoulder, and a mob at his heels; and whether he meant to breed a riot in the village?" — "Alas! gentlemen," cried Rip, somewhat dismayed, "I am a poor quiet man, a native of the place, and a loyal subject of the King, God bless him!"

Here a general shout burst from the by-standers — "A tory! a tory! a spy! a refugee! hustle him! away with him!" It was with great difficulty that the self-important man in the cocked hat restored order; and, having assumed a tenfold austerity of brow, demanded again of the unknown culprit, what he came there for, and whom he was seeking? The poor man humbly assured him that he meant no harm, but merely came there in search of some of his neighbors, who used to keep about the tavern.

"Well — who are they? — name them."

Rip bethought himself a moment, and inquired, "Where's Nicholas Vedder?"

There was a silence for a little while, when an old man replied, in a thin piping voice, "Nicholas Vedder! why, he is dead and gone these eighteen years! There was a wooden tombstone in that churchyard that used to tell all about him, but that's rotten and gone too."

"Where's Brom Dutcher?"

"Oh, he went off to the army in the beginning of the war; some say he was killed at the storming of Stony Point — others say he was drowned in a squall at the foot of Antony's Nose. I don't know — he never came back again."

"Where's Van Bummel, the schoolmaster?"

"He went off to the wars too, was a great militia general, and is now in congress."

Rip's heart died away at hearing of these sad changes in his home and friends, and finding himself thus alone in the world. Every answer puzzled him too, by treating of such enormous lapses of time, and of matters which he could not understand: war — congress — Stony Point — he had no courage to ask after any more friends, but cried out in despair, "Does nobody here know Rip Van Winkle?"

"Oh, Rip Van Winkle!" exclaimed two or three. "Oh, to be sure! that's Rip Van Winkle yonder, leaning against the tree."

Rip looked, and he beheld a precise counterpart of himself, as he went up the mountain; apparently as lazy, and certainly as ragged. The poor fellow was now completely confounded. He doubted his own identity, and whether he was himself or another man. In the midst of his bewilderment, the man in the cocked hat demanded who he was, and what was his name.

"God knows," exclaimed he, at his wit's end; "I'm not myself — I'm somebody else — that's me yonder — no — that's somebody else got into my shoes — I was myself last night, but I fell asleep on the mountain, and they've changed my gun, and everything's changed, and I'm changed, and I can't tell what's my name, or who I am!"

The by-standers began now to look at each other, nod, wink significantly, and tap their fingers against their foreheads. There was a whisper, also, about securing the gun, and keeping the old fellow from doing mischief, at the very suggestion of which the self-important man in the cocked hat retired with some precipitation. At this critical moment a fresh, comely woman pressed through the throng to get a peep at the gray-bearded man. She had a chubby child in her arms, which, frightened at his looks, began to cry. "Hush, Rip," cried she, "hush, you little fool; the old man won't hurt you." The name of the child, the air of the mother, the tone of her voice, all awakened a train of recollections in his mind. "What is your name, my good woman?" asked he.

"Judith Gardenier."

"And your father's name?"

"Ah, poor man, Rip Van Winkle was his name, but it's twenty years since he went away from home with his gun, and never has been heard of since — his dog came home without him; but whether he shot himself, or was carried away by the Indians, nobody can tell. I was then but a little girl."

Rip had but one question more to ask; but he put it with a faltering voice:

"Where's your mother?"

"Oh, she too died but a short time since; she broke a blood vessel in a fit of passion at a New England peddler."

There was a drop of comfort, at least, in this intelligence. The honest man could contain himself no longer. He caught his daughter and her child in his arms. "I am your father!" cried he — "Young Rip Van Winkle once — old Rip Van Winkle now! — Does nobody know poor Rip Van Winkle?"

All stood amazed, until an old woman, tottering out from among the crowd, put her hand to her brow, and peering under it in his face for a moment, exclaimed, "Sure enough! it is Rip Van Winkle — it is himself! Welcome home again, old neighbor. Why, where have you been these twenty long years?"

Rip's story was soon told, for the whole twenty years had been to him but as one night. The neighbors stared when they heard it; some were seen to wink at each other, and put their tongues in their cheeks: and the self-important man in the cocked hat, who, when the alarm was over, had returned to the field, screwed down the corners of his mouth, and shook his head — upon which there was a general shaking of the head throughout the assemblage.

It was determined, however, to take the opinion of old Peter Vanderdonk, who was seen slowly advancing up the road. He was a descendant of the historian of that name, who wrote one of the earliest accounts of the province. Peter was the most ancient inhabitant of the village, and well versed in all the wonderful events and traditions of the neighborhood. He recollected Rip at once, and corroborated his story in the most satisfactory manner. He assured the company that it was a fact, handed down from his ancestor the historian, that the Kaatskill mountains had always been haunted by strange beings. That it was affirmed that the great Hendrick Hudson, the first discoverer of the river and country, kept a kind of vigil there every twenty years, with his crew of the *Half-moon;* being permitted in this way to revisit the scenes of his enterprise, and keep a guardian eye upon the river and the great city called by his name. That his father had once seen them in their old Dutch dresses playing at ninepins in a hollow of the mountain; and that he himself had heard, one summer afternoon, the sound of their balls, like distant peals of thunder.

To make a long story short, the company broke up and returned to the more important concerns of the election. Rip's daughter took him home to live with her; she had a snug, well-furnished house, and a stout, cheery farmer for a husband, whom Rip recollected for one of the urchins that used to climb upon his back. As to Rip's son and heir, who was the ditto of himself, seen leaning against the tree, he was employed to work on the farm; but evinced an hereditary disposition to attend to anything else but his business.

Rip now resumed his old walks and habits; he soon found many of his former cronies, though all rather the worse for the wear and tear of time; and preferred making friends among the rising generation, with whom he soon grew into great favor.

Having nothing to do at home, and being arrived at that happy age when a man can be idle with impunity, he took his place once more on the bench at the inn-door, and was reverenced as one of the patriarchs of the village, and a chronicle of the old times "before the war." It was some time before he could get into the regular track of gossip, or could be made to comprehend the strange events that had taken place during his torpor. How that there had been a revolutionary war — that the country had thrown off the yoke of old England — and that, instead of being a subject of his Majesty George the Third, he was now a free citizen of the United States. Rip, in fact, was no politician; the changes of states and empires made but little impression to him; but there was one species of despotism under which he long groaned, and that was — petticoat government. Happily that was at an end; he had got his neck out of the yoke of matrimony, and could go in and out whenever he pleased, without dreading the tyranny of Dame Van Winkle. Whenever her name was mentioned, however, he shook his head, shrugged his shoulders, and cast up his eyes; which might pass either for an expression of resignation to his fate, or joy at his deliverance.

He used to tell his story to every stranger that arrived at Mr. Doolittle's hotel. He was observed, at first, to vary on some points every time he told it, which was, doubtless, owing to his having so recently awaked. It at last settled down precisely to the tale I have related, and not a man, woman, or child in the neighborhood but knew it by heart. Some always pretended to doubt the reality of it, and insisted that Rip had been out of his head, and that this was one point on which he always remained flighty. The old Dutch inhabitants, however, almost universally gave it full credit. Even to this day they never hear a thunderstorm of a summer afternoon about the Kaatskill, but they say Hendrick Hudson and his crew are at their game of ninepins; and it is a common wish of all hen-pecked husbands in the neighborhood, when life hangs heavy on their hands, that they might have a quieting draught out of Rip Van Winkle's flagon.

NOTE

The foregoing Tale, one would suspect, had been suggested to Mr. Knickerbocker by a little German superstition about the Emperor Frederick *der Rothbart,* and the Kypphäuser mountain: the subjoined note, however, which he had appended to the tale, shows that it is an absolute fact, narrated with his usual fidelity.

"The story of Rip Van Winkle may seem incredible to many, but nevertheless I give it my full belief, for I know the vicinity of our old Dutch settlements to have been very subject to marvellous events and appearances. Indeed, I have heard many stranger stories than this, in the villages along the Hudson; all of which were too well authenticated to admit of a doubt. I have even talked with Rip Van Winkle myself, who, when last I saw him, was a very venerable old man, and so perfectly rational and consistent on every other point, that I think no conscientious person could refuse to take this into the bargain; nay, I have seen a certificate on the subject taken before a country justice and signed with a cross, in the justice's own handwriting. The story, therefore, is beyond the possibility of doubt."

"D. K."

SHIRLEY JACKSON *(1919–1965) was born in San Francisco, California, her mother a housewife and her father an employee of a lithographing company. Most of her early life was spent in Burlingame, California, which she later used as the setting for her first novel,* The Road Through the Wall *(1948). As a child she was interested in writing; she won a poetry prize at age twelve, and in high school she began keeping a diary to record her writing progress. After high school she briefly attended the University of Rochester but left because of an attack of the mental depression that was to recur periodically in her later years. She recovered her health by living quietly at home and writing, conscientiously turning out 1,000 words of prose a day. In 1937 she entered Syracuse University, where she published stories in the student literary magazine. There she met Stanley Edgar Hyman, who was to become a noted literary critic. They were married in 1940, the year she received her degree. They had four children while both continued active literary careers, settling to raise their family in a large Victorian house in Vermont, where Hyman taught literature at Bennington College.*

Jackson's first national publication was a humorous story written after a job at a department store during the Christmas rush: "My Life with R. H. Macy" appeared in The New Republic *in 1941. Her first child was born the next year, but she wrote every day on a disciplined schedule, selling her stories to magazines and publishing three novels. She refused to take herself too seriously as a writer: "I can't persuade myself that writing is honest work. It is a very personal reaction, but 50 percent of my life is spent washing and dressing the children, cooking, washing dishes and clothes, and mending. After I get it all to bed, I turn around to my typewriter and try to — well, to create concrete things again. It's great fun, and I love it. But it doesn't tie any shoes."*

Jackson's best-known work, "The Lottery," is often anthologized, dramatized, and televised. She regarded it as a tale *in the sense that Nathaniel Hawthorne used the term — a moral allegory revealing the hidden evil of the human soul. She wrote later that "explaining just what I had hoped the story to say is very difficult. I supposed, I hoped, by setting a particularly brutal ancient rite in the present and in my own village, to shock the story's readers with a graphic dramatization of the pointless violence and general inhumanity in their own lives."*

RELATED COMMENTARY: *Shirley Jackson, "The Morning of June 28, 1948, and 'The Lottery,'" page 689.*

SHIRLEY JACKSON

The Lottery

1948

The morning of June 27th was clear and sunny, with the fresh warmth of a full-summer day; the flowers were blossoming profusely and the grass was richly green. The people of the village began to gather in the square, between the post office and the bank, around ten o'clock; in some towns there were so many people that the lottery took two days and had to be started on June 26th, but in this village, where there were only about three hundred people, the whole lottery took less than two hours, so it could begin at ten o'clock in the morning and still be through in time to allow the villagers to get home for noon dinner.

The children assembled first, of course. School was recently over for the summer, and the feeling of liberty sat uneasily on most of them; they tended to gather together quietly for a while before they broke into boisterous play, and their talk was still of the classroom and teacher, of books and reprimands. Bobby Martin had already stuffed his pockets full of stones, and the other boys soon followed his example, selecting the smoothest and roundest stones; Bobby and Harry Jones and Dickie Delacroix — the villagers pronounced this name "Dellacroy" — eventually made a great pile of stones in one corner of the square and guarded it against the raids of the other boys. The girls stood aside, talking among themselves, looking over their shoulders at the boys, and the very small children rolled in the dust or clung to the hands of their older brothers or sisters.

Soon the men began to gather, surveying their own children, speaking of planting and rain, tractors and taxes. They stood together, away from the pile of stones in the corner, and their jokes were quiet and they smiled rather than laughed. The women, wearing faded house dresses and sweaters, came shortly after their menfolk. They greeted one another and exchanged bits of gossip as they went to join their husbands. Soon the women, standing by their husbands, began to call to their children, and the children came reluctantly, having to be called four or five times. Bobby Martin ducked under his mother's grasping hand and ran, laughing, back to the pile of stones. His father spoke up sharply, and Bobby came quickly and took his place between his father and his oldest brother.

The lottery was conducted — as were the square dances, the teen-age club, the Halloween program — by Mr. Summers, who had time and energy to devote to civic activities. He was a round-faced, jovial man and he ran the coal business, and people were sorry for him, because he had no children and his wife was a scold. When he arrived in the square, carrying the black wooden box, there was a murmur of conversation among the villagers, and he waved and called, "Little late today, folks." The postmaster, Mr. Graves, followed him, carrying a three-legged stool, and the stool was put in the center of the square and Mr. Summers set the black box down on it. The villagers kept their distance, leaving a space between themselves and the stool, and when Mr. Summers said, "Some of you fellows want to give me a hand?" there was a hesitation before two men, Mr. Martin and his oldest son, Baxter, came forward to hold the box steady on the stool while Mr. Summers stirred up the papers inside it.

The original paraphernalia for the lottery had been lost long ago, and the black box now resting on the stool had been put into use even before Old Man Warner, the oldest man in town, was born. Mr. Summers spoke frequently to the villagers about making a new box, but no one liked to upset even as much tradition as was represented by the black box. There was a story that the present box had been made with some pieces of the box that had preceded it, the one that had been constructed when the first people settled down to make a village here. Every year, after the lottery, Mr. Summers began talking again about a new box, but every year the subject was allowed to fade off without anything's being done. The black box grew shabbier each year; by now it was no longer completely black but splintered badly along one side to show the original wood color, and in some places faded or stained.

Mr. Martin and his oldest son, Baxter, held the black box securely on the stool until Mr. Summers had stirred the papers thoroughly with his hand. Because so much of the ritual had been forgotten or discarded, Mr. Summers had been successful in having slips of paper substituted for the chips of wood that had been used for generations. Chips of wood, Mr. Summers had argued, had been all very well when the village was tiny, but now that the population was more than three hundred and likely to keep on growing, it was necessary to use something that would fit more easily into the black box. The night before the lottery, Mr. Summers and Mr. Graves made up the slips of paper and put them in the box, and it was then taken to the safe of Mr. Summers's coal company and locked up until Mr. Summers was ready to take it to the square next morning. The rest of the year, the box was put away, sometimes one place, sometimes another; it had spent one year in Mr. Graves's barn and another year underfoot in the post office, and sometimes it was set on a shelf in the Martin grocery and left there.

There was a great deal of fussing to be done before Mr. Summers declared the lottery open. There were the lists to make up — of heads of families, heads of households in each family, members of each household in each family. There was the proper swearing-in of Mr. Summers by the postmaster, as the official of the lottery; at one time, some people remembered, there had been a recital of some sort, performed by the official of the lottery, a perfunctory, tuneless chant that had been rattled off duly each year; some people believed that the official of the lottery used to stand just so when he said or sang it, others believed that he was supposed to walk among the people, but years and years ago this part of the ritual had been allowed to lapse. There had been, also, a ritual salute, which the official of the lottery had had to use in addressing each person who came up to draw from the box, but this also had changed with time, until now it was felt necessary only for the official to speak to each person approaching. Mr. Summers was very good at all this; in his clean white shirt and blue jeans, with one hand resting carelessly on the black box, he seemed very proper and important as he talked interminably to Mr. Graves and the Martins.

Just as Mr. Summers finally left off talking and turned to the assembled villagers, Mrs. Hutchinson came hurriedly along the path to the square, her sweater thrown over her shoulders, and slid into place in the back of the crowd. "Clean forgot what day it was," she said to Mrs. Delacroix, who stood next to her, and they both laughed softly. "Thought my old man was out back stacking wood," Mrs. Hutchinson went on, "and then I looked out the window and the kids was gone, and then I remembered it was the twenty-seventh and came a-running." She dried her hands on her apron, and Mrs. Delacroix said, "You're in time, though. They're still talking away up there."

Mrs. Hutchinson craned her neck to see through the crowd and found her husband and children standing near the front. She tapped Mrs. Delacroix on the arm as a farewell and began to make her way through the crowd. The people separated good-humoredly to let her through; two or three people said, in voices just loud enough to be heard across the crowd, "Here comes your Missus, Hutchinson," and "Bill, she made it after all." Mrs. Hutchinson reached her husband, and Mr. Summers, who had been waiting, said cheerfully, "Thought we were going to have to get on without you, Tessie." Mrs. Hutchinson said, grinning, "Wouldn't have me leave m'dishes in the sink, now, would you, Joe?" and soft laughter ran through the crowd as the people stirred back into position after Mrs. Hutchinson's arrival.

"Well, now," Mr. Summers said soberly, "guess we better get started, get this over with, so's we can go back to work. Anybody ain't here?"

"Dunbar," several people said. "Dunbar, Dunbar."

Mr. Summers consulted his list. "Clyde Dunbar," he said. "That's right. He's broke his leg, hasn't he? Who's drawing for him?"

"Me, I guess," a woman said, and Mr. Summers turned to look at her. "Wife draws for her husband," Mr. Summers said. "Don't you have a grown boy to do it for you, Janey?" Although Mr. Summers and everyone else in the village knew the answer perfectly well, it was the business of the official of the lottery to ask such questions formally. Mr. Summers waited with an expression of polite interest while Mrs. Dunbar answered.

"Horace's not but sixteen yet," Mrs. Dunbar said regretfully. "Guess I gotta fill in for the old man this year."

"Right," Mr. Summers said. He made a note on the list he was holding. Then he asked, "Watson boy drawing this year?"

A tall boy in the crowd raised his hand. "Here," he said. "I'm drawing for m'mother and me." He blinked his eyes nervously and ducked his head as several voices in the crowd said things like "Good fellow, Jack," and "Glad to see your mother's got a man to do it."

"Well," Mr. Summers said, "guess that's everyone. Old Man Warner make it?"

"Here," a voice said, and Mr. Summers nodded.

A sudden hush fell on the crowd as Mr. Summers cleared his throat and looked at the list. "All ready?" he called. "Now, I'll read the names — heads of families first — and the men come up and take a paper out of the box. Keep the paper folded in your hand without looking at it until everyone has had a turn. Everything clear?"

The people had done it so many times that they only half listened to the directions; most of them were quiet, wetting their lips, not looking around. Then Mr. Summers raised one hand high and said, "Adams." A man disengaged himself from the crowd and came forward. "Hi, Steve," Mr. Summers said, and Mr. Adams said, "Hi, Joe." They grinned at one another humorlessly and nervously. Then Mr. Adams reached into the black box and took out a folded paper. He held it firmly by one corner as he turned and went hastily back to his place in the crowd, where he stood a little apart from his family, not looking down at his hand.

"Allen," Mr. Summers said, "Anderson. . . . Bentham."

"Seems like there's no time at all between lotteries any more," Mrs. Delacroix said to Mrs. Graves in the back row. "Seems like we got through with the last one only last week."

"Time sure goes fast," Mrs. Graves said.

"Clark. . . . Delacroix."

"There goes my old man," Mrs. Delacroix said. She held her breath while her husband went forward.

"Dunbar," Mr. Summers said, and Mrs. Dunbar went steadily to the box while one of the women said, "Go on, Janey," and another said, "There she goes."

"We're next," Mrs. Graves said. She watched while Mr. Graves came around from the side of the box, greeted Mr. Summers gravely, and selected a slip of paper from the box. By now, all through the crowd there were men holding the small folded papers in their large hands, turning them over and over nervously. Mrs. Dunbar and her two sons stood together, Mrs. Dunbar holding the slip of paper.

"Harburt. . . . Hutchinson."

"Get up there, Bill," Mrs. Hutchinson said, and the people near her laughed.

"Jones."

"They do say," Mr. Adams said to Old Man Warner, who stood next to him, "that over in the north village they're talking of giving up the lottery."

Old Man Warner snorted. "Pack of crazy fools," he said. "Listening to the young folks, nothing's good enough for *them.* Next thing you know, they'll be wanting to go back to living in caves, nobody work any more, live *that* way for a while. Used to be a saying about 'Lottery in June, corn be heavy soon.'

First thing you know, we'd all be eating stewed chickweed and acorns. There's *always* been a lottery," he added petulantly. "Bad enough to see young Joe Summers up there joking with everybody."

"Some places have already quit lotteries," Mrs. Adams said.

"Nothing but trouble in *that,*" Old Man Warner said stoutly. "Pack of young fools."

"Martin." And Bobby Martin watched his father go forward. "Overdyke. . . . Percy."

"I wish they'd hurry," Mrs. Dunbar said to her older son. "I wish they'd hurry."

"They're almost through," her son said.

"You get ready to run tell Dad," Mrs. Dunbar said.

Mr. Summers called his own name and then stepped forward precisely and selected a slip from the box. Then he called, "Warner."

"Seventy-seventh year I been in the lottery," Old Man Warner said as he went through the crowd. "Seventy-seventh time."

"Watson." The tall boy came awkwardly through the crowd. Someone said, "Don't be nervous, Jack," and Mr. Summers said, "Take your time, son."

"Zanini."

After that, there was a long pause, a breathless pause, until Mr. Summers, holding his slip of paper in the air, said, "All right, fellows." For a minute, no one moved, and then all the slips of paper were opened. Suddenly, all the women began to speak at once, saying, "Who is it?" "Who's got it?" "Is it the Dunbars?" "Is it the Watsons?" Then the voices began to say, "It's Hutchinson. It's Bill," "Bill Hutchinson's got it."

"Go tell your father," Mrs. Dunbar said to her older son.

People began to look around to see the Hutchinsons. Bill Hutchinson was standing quiet, staring down at the paper in his hand. Suddenly, Tessie Hutchinson shouted to Mr. Summers, "You didn't give him time enough to take any paper he wanted. I saw you. It wasn't fair!"

"Be a good sport, Tessie," Mrs. Delacroix called, and Mrs. Graves said, "All of us took the same chance."

"Shut up, Tessie," Bill Hutchinson said.

"Well, everyone," Mr. Summers said, "that was done pretty fast, and now we've got to be hurrying a little more to get done in time." He consulted his next list. "Bill," he said, "you draw for the Hutchinson family. You got any other households in the Hutchinsons?"

"There's Don and Eva," Mrs. Hutchinson yelled. "Make *them* take their chance!"

"Daughters drew with their husbands' families, Tessie," Mr. Summers said gently. "You know that as well as anyone else."

"It wasn't *fair,*" Tessie said.

"I guess not, Joe," Bill Hutchinson said regretfully. "My daughter draws with her husband's family, that's only fair. And I've got no other family except the kids."

"Then, as far as drawing for families is concerned, it's you," Mr. Summers said in explanation, "and as far as drawing for households is concerned, that's you, too. Right?"

"Right," Bill Hutchinson said.

"How many kids, Bill?" Mr. Summers asked formally.

"Three," Bill Hutchinson said. "There's Bill, Jr., and Nancy, and little Dave. And Tessie and me."

"All right, then," Mr. Summers said. "Harry, you got their tickets back?"

Mr. Graves nodded and held up the slips of paper. "Put them in the box, then," Mr. Summers directed. "Take Bill's and put it in."

"I think we ought to start over," Mrs. Hutchinson said, as quietly as she could. "I tell you it wasn't *fair.* You didn't give him time enough to choose. *Every*body saw that."

Mr. Graves had selected the five slips and put them in the box, and he dropped all the papers but those onto the ground, where the breeze caught them and lifted them off.

"Listen, everybody," Mrs. Hutchinson was saying to the people around her.

"Ready, Bill?" Mr. Summers asked, and Bill Hutchinson, with one quick glance around at his wife and children, nodded.

"Remember," Mr. Summers said, "take the slips and keep them folded until each person has taken one. Harry, you help little Dave." Mr. Graves took the hand of the little boy, who came willingly with him up to the box. "Take a paper out of the box, Davy," Mr. Summers said. Davy put his hand into the box and laughed. "Take just *one* paper," Mr. Summers said. "Harry, you hold it for him." Mr. Graves took the child's hand and removed the folded paper from the tight fist and held it while little Dave stood next to him and looked up at him wonderingly.

"Nancy next," Mr. Summers said. Nancy was twelve, and her school friends breathed heavily as she went forward, switching her skirt, and took a slip daintily from the box. "Bill, Jr.," Mr. Summers said, and Billy, his face red and his feet overlarge, nearly knocked the box over as he got a paper out. "Tessie," Mr. Summers said. She hesitated for a minute, looking around defiantly, and then set her lips and went up to the box. She snatched a paper out and held it behind her.

"Bill," Mr. Summers said, and Bill Hutchinson reached into the box and felt around, bringing his hand out at last with the slip of paper in it.

The crowd was quiet. A girl whispered, "I hope it's not Nancy," and the sound of the whisper reached the edges of the crowd.

"It's not the way it used to be," Old Man Warner said clearly. "People ain't the way they used to be."

"All right," Mr. Summers said. "Open the papers. Harry, you open little Dave's."

Mr. Graves opened the slip of paper and there was a general sigh through the crowd as he held it up and everyone could see that it was blank. Nancy and Bill, Jr., opened theirs at the same time, and both beamed and laughed, turning around to the crowd and holding their slips of paper above their heads.

"Tessie," Mr. Summers said. There was a pause, and then Mr. Summers looked at Bill Hutchinson, and Bill unfolded his paper and showed it. It was blank.

"It's Tessie," Mr. Summers said, and his voice was hushed. "Show us her paper, Bill."

Bill Hutchinson went over to his wife and forced the slip of paper out of her hand. It had a black spot on it, the black spot Mr. Summers had made the night before with the heavy pencil in the coal-company office. Bill Hutchinson held it up and there was a stir in the crowd.

"All right, folks," Mr. Summers said. "Let's finish quickly."

Although the villagers had forgotten the ritual and lost the original black box, they still remembered to use stones. The pile of stones the boys had made earlier was ready; there were stones on the ground with the blowing scraps of paper that had come out of the box. Mrs. Delacroix selected a stone so large she had to pick it up with both hands and turned to Mrs. Dunbar. "Come on," she said. "Hurry up."

Mrs. Dunbar had small stones in both hands, and she said, gasping for breath, "I can't run at all. You'll have to go ahead and I'll catch up with you."

The children had stones already, and someone gave little Davy Hutchinson a few pebbles.

Tessie Hutchinson was in the center of a cleared space by now, and she held her hands out desperately as the villagers moved in on her. "It isn't fair," she said. A stone hit her on the side of the head.

Old Man Warner was saying, "Come on, come on, everyone." Steve Adams was in the front of the crowd of villagers, with Mrs. Graves beside him.

"It isn't fair, it isn't right," Mrs. Hutchinson screamed and then they were upon her.

ꙮ

GISH JEN *(b. 1956) was given the first name of Lillian by her parents, but in high school in Scarsdale, New York, she took the opportunity to change it when her girlfriends invented a nickname for her, "Gish," after the silent film star Lillian Gish. Jen has said that "the most telling thing" about her is her embarrassment about how eager she was for a new name: "Academics now say it is not only okay to have taken a name for oneself, but that such self-naming can represent a critical step in the process of self-invention. I should be proud, in other words. Such imaginative force! such derring-do!" Jen's family was not so understanding. She remembers her mother's cool response: "Whatever you call yourself, your name is still Lil."*

After Jen graduated from Harvard University as a premed, her parents wanted her to go on to graduate school to study medicine, law, or business, but she followed her own dream of becoming a writer and earned an M.F.A. from the University of Iowa in 1983. Since her parents refused to pay her tuition there, Jen supported herself on grants and prizes. The recipient of several awards in the 1980s, including a

National Endowment for the Arts fellowship, she worked on her first novel based on her father's immigration from China to the United States, published as Typical American *in 1991. Jen placed chapters from this work as well as stories from her second novel,* Mona in the Promised Land *(1996), in magazines such as* The New Yorker, Atlantic Monthly, Yale Review, *and* Iowa Review. *In 1999 Jen's collection of short stories,* Who's Irish? *was published.*

Jen's stories have also been included in two recent anthologies, Home to Stay: Asian American Women's Fiction *(1990) and* Charlie Chan Is Dead *(1993), that have followed in the wake of the pioneering anthologies of new Asian American prose and poetry compiled in the 1970s. "Chin" suggests the pressures of assimilation experienced by immigrants as well as the social clash between intolerant Americans and their new neighbors. As Jen's editor Carol Bruchac wrote in 1989,*

> *My belief was that Asian American women writers had something uniquely their own to share, something that might teach us what it is like to live in a country which always views one as an "outsider," oftentimes as an "exotic" outsider. At the same time, I believed that those writers were women who shared so many issues with their sisters of all colors, that common threads would be found which would weave us together.*

GISH JEN

Chin

1999

I wasn't his friend, but I wasn't one of the main kids who hounded him up onto the shed roof, either. Sure I'd lob a rock or two, but this was our stage of life back then, someplace between the arm and the fist. Not to chuck nothing would have been against nature, and I never did him one he couldn't duck easy, especially being as fast as he was — basically the fastest kid in the ninth grade, and one of the smartest besides, smarter even than yours truly, the official class underachiever. I tested so high on my IQ that the school psychologists made me take the test over, nobody could believe it. They've been hounding me to apply myself ever since. But Chin was smart, too — not so much in math and science as in stuff like history and English. How's that for irony? And he was a good climber, you had to give him that, the only kid who could scale that shed wall, period. Because that wall didn't have no handholds or footholds. In fact, the naked eye would've pronounced that wall plain concrete; you had to wonder if the kid had some kind of special vision, so that he could look at that wall and see a way up. Maybe where we saw wall, he saw cracks, or maybe there was something he knew in his body about walls; or maybe they didn't have walls in China, besides the Great Wall, that is, so that he knew a wall was only a wall because we thought it was a wall. That might be getting philosophical. But you know, I've seen guys do that in basketball, find the basket in ways you can't account for. You can rewind the tape and watch the replay until your eyeballs pop, but finally you've got to say that obstacles are not always obstacles for these guys. Things melt away for them.

Gus said it was on account of there was monkey feet inside his sneakers that the kid could get up there. That was the day the kid started stockpiling the rocks we threw and raining them back down on us. A fall day, full of the crack and smell of people burning leaves illegally. It was just like the monkeys in the zoo when they get mad at the zookeepers, that's what I said. I saw that on TV once. But Gus blew a smoke ring and considered it like a sunset, then said even though you couldn't see the kid's monkey feet, they were like hands and could grip onto things. He said you've never seen such long toes, or such weird toenails, either, and that the toenails were these little bitty slits, like his eyes. And that, he said, was why he was going to drown me in a douche bag if I threw any more rocks without paying attention. He said I was fucking arming the ape.

We didn't live in the same building, that kid and me. His name was Chin or something, like chin-up we used to say, and his family lived in the garden apartment next door to ours. This was in scenic Yonkers, New York, home of Central Avenue. We were both stuck on the ground floor, where everyone could look right into your kitchen. It was like having people look up your dress, my ma said, and they were smack across the alley from us. So you see, if I'd really wanted to nail him with a rock, I could've done it anytime their windows were open if I didn't want to break any glass. And I could've done it any time at all if I didn't care about noise and commotion and getting a JD card like the Beyer kid got for climbing the water tower. Of course, they didn't open their windows much, the Chins. My ma said it was because they were Chinese people — you know, like Chinese food, from China, she said, and then she cuffed me for playing dumb and getting her to explain what a Chinese was when they were getting to be a fact of life. Not like in California or Queens, but they were definitely proliferating, along with a lot of other people who could tell you where they came from, if they spoke English. They weren't like us who came from Yonkers and didn't have no special foods, unless you wanted to count fries. Gus never could see why we couldn't count fries. My own hunch, though, guess why, was that they just might be French. Not that I said so. I was more interested in why everybody suddenly had to have a special food. And why was everybody asking what your family was? First time somebody asked me that, I had no idea what they were talking about. But after a while, I said, Vanilla. I said that because I didn't want to say we were nothing, my family was nothing.

My ma said that the Chins kept their windows shut because they liked their apartment hot, seeing as how it was what they were used to. People keep to what they're used to, she liked to say, though she also liked to say, Wait and see, you know your taste changes. Especially to my big sister she was always saying that, because my sis was getting married for real this time, to this hairdresser who had suddenly started offering her free bang trims anytime. Out of the blue, this was. He was a thinker, this Ray. He had it all figured out, how from doing the bang trim he could get to talking about her beautiful blue eyes. And damned if he wasn't right that a lot of people, including yours truly, had never particularly noticed her eyes, what with the hair hanging in them. A real truth-teller, that Ray was, and sharp as a narc. It was all that practice with women all day long, my ma said. He knows how to make a woman feel like a queen, not like your pa, who knows how to make her feel like shit. She was as excited as my sis, that's the truth, now that this Ray and her Debi were hitting the aisle sure enough. Ray was doing my ma's hair free, too, every other day just about, trying to fine-tune her do for the wedding, and in between she was trying to pitch a couple of last You knows across to Debi while she could. Kind of a cram course.

But my pa said the Chins did that with their windows because somebody put a cherry bomb in their kitchen for fun one day, and it upset them. Maybe they didn't know it was just a cherry bomb. Who knows what they thought it was, but they beat up Chin over it; that much we did know, because we could see everything and hear everything they did over there, especially if we turned the TV down, which we sometimes did for a fight. If only more was in English, we could've understood everything, too. Instead all we caught was that Chin got beat up over the cherry bomb, as if they thought it was owing to him that somebody put the bomb in the window. Go figure.

Chin got beat up a lot — this wasn't the first time. He got beat up on account of he played hooky from school sometimes, and he got beat up on account of he mouthed off to his pa, and he got beat up on account of he once got a C in math, which was why right near the bomb site there was a blackboard in the kitchen. Nights he wasn't getting beaten up, he was parked in front of the blackboard doing equations with his pa, who people said was not satisfied with Chin plain getting the correct answer in algebra, he had to be able to get it two or three ways. Also he got beat up because he liked to find little presents for himself and his sis and his ma. He did this in stores without paying for them, and that pissed the hell out of his pa. On principle, people said, but maybe he just felt left out. I always thought Chin should've known enough to get something for his pa, too.

But really Chin got beat up, my pa said, because Mr. Chin had this weird cheek. He had some kind of infection in some kind of hole, and as a result, the cheek shook and for a long time he wouldn't go to the doctor, seeing as how in China he used to be a doctor himself. Here he was a cab driver — the worst driver in the city, we're talking someone who would sooner puke on the Pope than cut across two lanes of traffic. He had a little plastic sleeve on the passenger-side visor where he displayed his driver's license; that's how much it meant to him that he'd actually gotten one. But in China he'd been a doctor, and as a result, he refused to go to a doctor here until his whole cheek was about gone. Thought he should be able to cure himself with herbs. Now even with the missus out working down at the dry cleaners, they were getting cleaned out themselves, what with the bills. They're going to need that boy for their old age, that's what my pa said. Cabbies don't have no pension plan like firemen and policemen and everybody else. They can't afford for him to go wrong, he's going to have to step up to the plate and hit that ball into the bleachers for them. That's why he gets beat, so he'll grow up to be a doctor who can practice in America. They want that kid to have his M.D. hanging up instead of his driver's license.

That was our general theory of why Chin got the treatment. But this time was maybe different. This time my pa wondered if maybe Chin's pa thought he was in some kind of a gang. He asked me if Chin was or wasn't, and I said no way was he in anything. Nobody hung with Chin, why would anybody hang with the guy everyone wanted to break? Unless you wanted them to try and break you, too. That's when my pa nodded in that captain of the force way you see on TV, and I was glad I told him. It made me feel like I'd forked over valuable information to the guy who ought to know. I felt like I could relax after I'd told him, even though maybe it was Mr. Chin who really should've known. Who knows but maybe my pa should've told Mr. Chin. Though what was he going to do, call him up and say, This is our theory next door? The truth is, I understood my pa. Like maybe I should've told Gus that Chin didn't actually have monkey feet, because I've seen his feet top and bottom through my pa's binoculars, and they were just regular. But let's face it, people don't want to be told much. And what difference did it make that I didn't think his toes were even that long, or that I could see them completely plain because his pa used to make him kneel when he wanted to beat him? What difference does it make what anybody's seen? Sometimes I think I should've kept my eyes on the TV where they belonged, instead of watching stuff I couldn't turn off. Chin's pa used to use a belt mostly, but sometimes he used a metal garden stake, and with every single whack, I used to think how glad I was that it was Chin and not me that had those big welts rising up out of his back skin. They looked like some great special effect, these oozy red caterpillars crawling over some older pinkish ones. Chin never moved or said anything, and that just infuriated his pa more. You could see it so clear, you almost felt sorry for him. Here he had this garden stake and there was nothing he could do. What with his cheek all wrapped up, he had to stop the beating every now and then to readjust his bandage.

My pa used a ruler on me once, just like the one they used at school — Big Bertha, we called it, a solid eighteen inches, and if you flinched, you got hit another three times on the hands. Naturally, Chin never did, as a result of the advanced training he got at home. People said he didn't feel nothing; he was like a horse you had to kick with heel spurs, your plain heel just tickled. But I wasn't used to torture instruments. We didn't believe in that sort of thing in my house. Even that time my pa did get out the ruler, it broke and he had to go back to using his hand. That was bad enough. My pa was a fireman, meaning he was a lot stronger than Chin's pa was ever going to be, which maybe had nothing to do with anything. But my theory was, it was on account of that he knew he wasn't that strong that Mr. Chin used the garden stake on Chin, and once on the sister, too.

She wasn't as old as my sister, and she wasn't that pretty, and she wasn't that smart, and you were just glad when you looked at her that you weren't her gym teacher. She wore these glasses that looked like they were designed to fall off, and she moseyed down the school halls the way her pa did the highway — keeping all the way to the right and hesitating dangerously in the intersections. But she had a beautiful voice and was always doing the solo at school assembly. Some boring thing — the songs at school were all worse than ever since Mr. Reardon, the math teacher, had to take over music. He was so musical, people had to show him how to work those black stands; he didn't know you could adjust them, he thought they came in sizes. To be fair, he asked three times if he couldn't do study hall instead. But Chin's sister managed to wring something out of the songs he picked somehow. Everything she sang sounded like her. It was funny — she never talked, this girl, and everybody called her quiet, but when she sang, she filled up the whole auditorium and you completely forgot she wore these glasses people said were bulletproof.

It wasn't the usual thing that the sister got hit. But one day she threatened to move out of the house, actually stomped out into the snow, saying that she could not stand to watch what was going on anymore. Then her pa hauled her back and beat her, too. At least he left her clothes on and didn't make her kneel. She got to stand and only fell on the floor, curled up, by choice. But here was the sad thing: It turned out you could hear her singing voice when she cried; she still sounded like herself. She didn't look like herself with her glasses off, though, and nobody else did, either. Chin the unflinching turned so red in the face, he looked as though blood beads were going to come busting straight out of his pores, and he started pounding the wall so hard, he put craters in it. His ma told him to stop, but he kept going, until finally she packed a suitcase and put the sister's glasses back on for her. Ma Chin had to tape the suitcase with duct tape to get it to stay shut. Then Ma Chin and the sister both put on their coats and headed for the front door. The snowflakes by then were so giant, you'd think there was a closeout sale on underwear going on up in heaven. Still the dynamic duo marched out into the neighborhood and up our little hill without any boots. Right up the middle of the street, they went; I guess there being two of them bucked up the sister. Ma Chin started out with the suitcase, but by the time they'd reached the hill, the sister'd wrestled it away from her. Another unexpected physical feat. It was cold out, and so dark that what with all the snow, the light from the streetlights appeared to be falling down too, and kind of drifting around. My pa wondered out loud if he should give our neighbors a friendly lift someplace. After all, the Chins had no car, and it was a long walk over to the bus stop. But what would he say? Excuse me, I just happened to be out driving?

He was trying to work this out with my ma, but she had to tell him first how Ray would know what to say without having to consult nobody and how glad she was that her Debi wasn't marrying nobody like him. Ray, Ray, Ray! my pa said finally. Why don't you go fuck him yourself instead of using your daughter? Then he sat right in the kitchen window, where anybody who bothered to look could see him, and watched as Ma Chin and the sister stopped and had themselves a little conference. They were up to their ankles in snow, neither in one streetlight cone or the next, but smack in between. They jawed for a long time. Then they moved a little farther up the incline and stopped and jawed again, sheltering their glasses from the snow with their hands. They almost looked like lifeguards out there, trying to keep the sun out of their eyes, except that they didn't seem to know that they were supposed to be looking for something. Probably their glasses were all fogged up. Still my pa watched them and watched them while I had a look at Chin and his pa back at the ranch, and saw the most astounding thing of all: They were back at the blackboard, working problems out. Mr. Chin had a cup of tea made, and you couldn't see his face on account of his bandage, but he was gesturing with the eraser and Chin was nodding. How do you figure? I half-wanted to say something to my pa, to point out this useless fact. But my pa was too busy sitting in the window with the lights on, waiting for the Chin women to shout Fire! or something, I guess. He wanted them to behold him there, all lit up, their rescuer. Unfortunately, though, it was snowing out, not burning, and their heads were bent and their eyes were on the ground as they dragged their broken suitcase straight back across our view.

❧

SARAH ORNE JEWETT *(1849–1909) was born in South Berwick, Maine. Her father was a country doctor, and she often accompanied him on his horse-and-buggy rounds among sick people on the local farms. She later said that she got her real education from these trips, rather than from her classes at Miss Rayne's School and the Berwick Academy. She had a fine ear for local speech and the native idiom, which she used to good effect in her stories. Impressed as a girl by the sympathetic depiction of* local color *(the people and life of a particular geographical setting) in the fiction of Harriet Beecher Stowe, Jewett began to write stories herself, publishing her earliest one, "Jenny Garrow's Lovers," in a Boston weekly when she was eighteen years old. Shortly after her twentieth birthday, her work was accepted by the prestigious* Atlantic Monthly, *and her career was launched. Jewett published her first collection of stories,* Deephaven, *in 1877. She read the work of Gustave Flaubert, Émile Zola, Leo Tolstoy, and Henry James, and her style gradually matured, as is evident in the stories that make up the 1886 volume* A White Heron and Other Stories. *Jewett took her favorite motto from Flaubert, "One should write of ordinary life as if one were writing history." Her masterpiece,* The Country of the Pointed Firs *(1896), is a book of scrupulously observed short sketches linked by the narrator's account of her stay in a Maine seacoast village and her growing involvement in the quiet lives of its people.*

Many stories were written about New England in Jewett's time, but hers have a unique quality stemming from her deep sympathy for the native characters and her ear for local speech. Once she laughingly told the younger writer Willa Cather that her head was full of dear old houses and dear old women, and when an old house and an old woman came together in her brain with a click, she knew a story was under way.

Although it is true that Jewett's realism heightens the attractive aspects of the rural New England character at the same time that it diminishes the harsher qualities, her literary technique is so candid that the darker undercurrents of deprivation, both physical and psychological, are evident beneath the surface of her descriptions. Henry James recognized that Jewett was "surpassed only by Hawthorne as producer of the most finished and penetrating of the numerous 'short stories' that have the domestic life of New England for their general and their doubtless somewhat lean subject." In her time she was lauded for possessing an exquisitely simple, natural, and graceful style; now she is regarded as the most distinguished American regionalist writer of the nineteenth century, as evidenced by her finest tale, "A White Heron."

Sarah Orne Jewett

A White Heron

1886

I

The woods were already filled with shadows one June evening, just before eight o'clock, though a bright sunset still glimmered faintly among the trunks of the trees. A little girl was driving home her cow, a plodding, dilatory, provoking creature in her behavior, but a valued companion for all that. They were going away from the western light, and striking deep into the dark woods, but their feet were familiar with the path, and it was no matter whether their eyes could see it or not.

There was hardly a night the summer through when the old cow could be found waiting at the pasture bars; on the contrary, it was her greatest pleasure to hide herself away among the high huckleberry bushes, and though she wore a loud bell she had made the discovery that if one stood perfectly still it would not ring. So Sylvia had to hunt for her until she found her and call Co'! Co'! with never an answering Moo, until her childish patience was quite spent. If the creature had not given good milk and plenty of it, the case would have seemed very different to her owners. Besides, Sylvia had all the time there was, and very little use to make of it. Sometimes in pleasant weather it was a consolation to look upon the cow's pranks as an intelligent attempt to play hide and seek, and as the child had no playmates she lent herself to this amusement with a good deal of zest. Though this chase had been so long that the wary animal herself had given an unusual signal of her whereabouts, Sylvia had only laughed when she came upon Mistress Moolly at the swamp-side, and urged her affectionately homeward with a twig of birch leaves. The old cow was not inclined to wander farther, she even turned in the right direction for once as they left the pasture, and stepped along the road at a good pace. She was quite ready to be milked now, and seldom stopped to browse. Sylvia wondered what her grandmother would say because they were so late. It was a great while since she had left home at half past five o'clock, but everybody knew the difficulty of making this errand a short one. Mrs. Tilley had chased the horned torment too many summer evenings herself to blame any one else for lingering, and was only thankful as she waited that she had Sylvia, nowadays, to give such valuable assistance. The good woman suspected that Sylvia loitered occasionally on her own account; there never was such a child for straying about out-of-doors since the world was made! Everybody said that it was a good change for a little maid who had tried to grow for eight years in a crowded manufacturing town, but, as for Sylvia herself, it seemed as if she never had been alive at all before she came to live at the farm. She thought often with wistful compassion of a wretched dry geranium that belonged to a town neighbor.

"'Afraid of folks,'" old Mrs. Tilley said to herself, with a smile, after she had made the unlikely choice of Sylvia from her daughter's houseful of children, and was returning to the farm. "'Afraid of folks,' they said! I guess she won't be troubled no great with 'em up to the old place!" When they reached the door of the lonely house and stopped to unlock it, and the cat came to purr loudly, and rub against them, a deserted pussy, indeed, but fat with young robins, Sylvia whispered that this was a beautiful place to live in, and she never should wish to go home.

The companions followed the shady wood-road, the cow taking slow steps, and the child very fast ones. The cow stopped long at the brook to drink, as if the pasture were not half a swamp, and Sylvia stood still and waited, letting her bare feet cool themselves in the shoal water, while the great twilight moths struck softly against her. She waded on through the brook as the cow moved away, and listened to the thrushes with a heart that beat fast with pleasure. There was a stirring in the great boughs overhead. They were full of little birds and beasts that seemed to be wide-awake, and going about their world, or else saying good-night to each other in sleepy twitters. Sylvia herself felt sleepy as she walked along. However, it was not much farther to the house, and the air was soft and sweet. She was not often in the woods so late as this, and it made her feel as if she were a part of the gray shadows and the moving leaves. She was just thinking how long it seemed since she first came to the farm a year ago, and wondering if everything went on in the noisy town just the same as when she was there; the thought of the great red-faced boy who used to chase and frighten her made her hurry along the path to escape from the shadow of the trees.

Suddenly this little woods-girl is horror-stricken to hear a clear whistle not very far away. Not a bird's whistle, which would have a sort of friendliness, but a boy's whistle, determined, and somewhat aggressive. Sylvia left the cow to whatever sad fate might await her, and stepped discreetly aside into the bushes, but she was just too late. The enemy had discovered her, and called out in a very cheerful and persuasive tone, "Halloa, little girl, how far is it to the road?" and trembling Sylvia answered almost inaudibly, "A good ways."

She did not dare to look boldly at the tall young man, who carried a gun over his shoulder, but she came out of her bush and again followed the cow, while he walked alongside.

"I have been hunting for some birds," the stranger said kindly, "and I have lost my way, and need a friend very much. Don't be afraid," he added gallantly. "Speak up and tell me what your name is, and whether you think I can spend the night at your house, and go out gunning early in the morning."

Sylvia was more alarmed than before. Would not her grandmother consider her much to blame? But who could have foreseen such an accident as this? It did not appear to be her fault, and she hung her head as if the stem of it were broken, but managed to answer, "Sylvy," with much effort when her companion again asked her name.

Mrs. Tilley was standing in the doorway when the trio came into view. The cow gave a loud moo by way of explanation.

"Yes, you'd better speak up for yourself, you old trial! Where'd she tucked herself away this time, Sylvy?" Sylvia kept an awed silence; she knew by instinct that her grandmother did not comprehend the gravity of the situation. She must be mistaking the stranger for one of the farmer-lads of the region.

The young man stood his gun beside the door, and dropped a heavy game-bag beside it; then he bade Mrs. Tilley good-evening, and repeated his wayfarer's story, and asked if he could have a night's lodging.

"Put me anywhere you like," he said. "I must be off early in the morning, before day; but I am very hungry, indeed. You can give me some milk at any rate, that's plain."

"Dear sakes, yes," responded the hostess, whose long slumbering hospitality seemed to be easily awakened. "You might fare better if you went out on the main road a mile or so, but you're welcome to what we've got. I'll milk right off, and you make yourself at home. You can sleep on husks or feathers," she proffered graciously. "I raised them all myself. There's good pasturing for geese just below here towards the ma'sh. Now step round and set a plate for the gentleman, Sylvy!" And Sylvia promptly stepped. She was glad to have something to do, and she was hungry herself.

It was a surprise to find so clean and comfortable a little dwelling in this New England wilderness. The young man had known the horrors of its most primitive housekeeping, and the dreary squalor of that level of society which does not rebel at the companionship of hens. This was the best thrift of an old-fashioned farmstead, though on such a small scale that it seemed like a hermitage. He listened eagerly to the old woman's quaint talk, he watched Sylvia's pale face and shining gray eyes with ever growing enthusiasm, and insisted that this was the best supper he had eaten for a month; then, afterward, the new-made friends sat down in the doorway together while the moon came up.

Soon it would be berry-time, and Sylvia was a great help at picking. The cow was a good milker, though a plaguy thing to keep track of, the hostess gossiped frankly, adding presently that she had buried four children, so that Sylvia's mother, and a son (who might be dead) in California were all the children she had left. "Dan, my boy, was a great hand to go gunning," she explained sadly. "I never wanted for pa'tridges or gray squer'ls while he was to home. He's been a great wand'rer, I expect, and he's no hand to write letters. There, I don't blame him, I'd ha' seen the world myself if it had been so I could.

"Sylvia takes after him," the grandmother continued affectionately, after a minute's pause. "There ain't a foot o' ground she don't know her way over, and the wild creatur's counts her one o' themselves. Squer'ls she'll tame to come an' feed right out o' her hands, and all sorts o' birds. Last winter she got the jay-birds to bangeing here, and I believe she'd'a' scanted herself of her own meals to have plenty to throw out amongst 'em, if I hadn't kep' watch. Anything but crows, I tell her, I'm willin' to help support, — though Dan he went an' tamed one o' them that did seem to have reason same as folks. It was round here a good spell after he went away. Dan an' his father they didn't hitch, — but he never held up his head ag'in after Dan had dared him an' gone off."

The guest did not notice this hint of family sorrows in his eager interest in something else.

"So Sylvy knows all about birds, does she?" he exclaimed, as he looked round at the little girl who sat, very demure but increasingly sleepy, in the moonlight. "I am making a collection of birds myself. I have been at it ever since I was a boy." (Mrs. Tilley smiled.) "There are two or three very rare ones I have been hunting for these five years. I mean to get them on my own ground if they can be found."

"Do you cage 'em up?" asked Mrs. Tilley doubtfully, in response to this enthusiastic announcement.

"Oh, no, they're stuffed and preserved, dozens and dozens of them," said the ornithologist, "and I have shot or snared every one myself. I caught a glimpse of a white heron three miles from here on Saturday, and I have followed it in this direction. They have never been found in this district at all. The little white heron, it is," and he turned again to look at Sylvia with the hope of discovering that the rare bird was one of her acquaintances.

But Sylvia was watching a hop-toad in the narrow footpath.

"You would know the heron if you saw it," the stranger continued eagerly. "A queer tall white bird with soft feathers and long thin legs. And it would have a nest perhaps in the top of a high tree, made of sticks, something like a hawk's nest."

Sylvia's heart gave a wild beat; she knew that strange white bird, and had once stolen softly near where it stood in some bright green swamp grass, away over at the other side of the woods. There was an open place where the sunshine always seemed strangely yellow and hot, where tall, nodding rushes grew, and her grandmother had warned her that she might sink in the soft black mud underneath and never be heard of more. Not far beyond were the salt marshes and beyond those was the sea, the sea which Sylvia wondered and dreamed about, but never had looked upon, though its great voice could often be heard above the noise of the woods on stormy nights.

"I can't think of anything I should like so much as to find that heron's nest," the handsome stranger was saying. "I would give ten dollars to anybody who could show it to me," he added desperately, "and I mean to spend my whole vacation hunting for it if need be. Perhaps it was only migrating, or had been chased out of its own region by some bird of prey."

Mrs. Tilley gave amazed attention to all this, but Sylvia still watched the toad, not divining, as she might have done at some calmer time, that the creature wished to get to its hole under the doorstep, and was much hindered by the unusual spectators at that hour of the evening. No amount of thought, that night, could decide how many wished-for treasures the ten dollars, so lightly spoken of, would buy.

The next day the young sportsman hovered about the woods, and Sylvia kept him company, having lost her first fear of the friendly lad, who proved to be most kind and sympathetic. He told her many things about the birds and what they knew and where they lived and what they did with themselves. And he gave her a jack-knife, which she thought as great a treasure as if she were a desert-islander. All day long he did not once make her troubled or afraid except when he brought down some unsuspecting singing creature from its bough. Sylvia would have liked him vastly better without his gun; she could not understand why he killed the very birds he seemed to like so much. But as the day waned, Sylvia still watched the young man with loving admiration. She had never seen anybody so charming and delightful; the woman's heart, asleep in the child, was vaguely thrilled by a dream of love. Some premonition of that great power stirred and swayed these young foresters who traversed the solemn woodlands with soft-footed silent care. They stopped to listen to a bird's song; they pressed forward again eagerly, parting the branches — speaking to each other rarely and in whispers; the young man going first and Sylvia following, fascinated, a few steps behind, with her gray eyes dark with excitement.

She grieved because the longed-for white heron was elusive, but she did not lead the guest, she only followed, and there was no such thing as speaking first. The sound of her own unquestioned voice would have terrified her — it was hard enough to answer yes or no when there was need of that. At last evening began to fall, and they drove the cow home together, and Sylvia smiled with pleasure when they came to the place where she heard the whistle and was afraid only the night before.

II

Half a mile from home, at the farther edge of the woods, where the land was highest, a great pine-tree stood, the last of its generation. Whether it was left for a boundary mark, or for what reason, no one could say; the woodchoppers who had felled its mates were dead and gone long ago, and a whole forest of sturdy trees, pines and oaks and maples, had grown again. But the stately head of this old pine towered above them all and made a landmark for sea and shore miles and miles away. Sylvia knew it well. She had always believed that whoever climbed to the top of it could see the ocean; and the little girl had often laid her hand on the great rough trunk and looked up wistfully at those dark boughs that the wind always stirred, no matter how hot and still the air might be below. Now she thought of the tree with a new excitement, for why, if one climbed it at break of day, could not one see all the world, and easily discover whence the white heron flew, and mark the place, and find the hidden nest?

What a spirit of adventure, what wild ambition! What fancied triumph and delight and glory for the later morning when she could make known the secret! It was almost too real and too great for the childish heart to bear.

All night the door of the little house stood open, and the whippoorwills came and sang upon the very step. The young sportsman and his old hostess were sound asleep, but Sylvia's great design kept her broad awake and watching. She forgot to think of sleep. The short summer night seemed as long as the winter darkness, and at last when the whippoorwills ceased, and she was afraid the morning would after all come too soon, she stole out of the house and followed the pasture path through the woods, hastening toward the open ground beyond, listening with a sense of comfort and companionship to the drowsy twitter of a half-awakened bird, whose perch she had jarred in passing. Alas, if the great wave of human interest which flooded for the first time this dull little life should sweep away the satisfactions of an existence heart to heart with nature and the dumb life of the forest!

There was the huge tree asleep yet in the paling moonlight, and small and hopeful Sylvia began with utmost bravery to mount to the top of it, with tingling, eager blood coursing the channels of her whole frame, with her bare feet and fingers, that pinched and held like bird's claws to the monstrous ladder reaching up, up, almost to the sky itself. First she must mount the white oak tree that grew alongside, where she was almost lost among the dark branches and the green leaves heavy and wet with dew; a bird fluttered off its nest, and a red squirrel ran to and fro and scolded pettishly at the harmless housebreaker. Sylvia felt her way easily. She had often climbed there, and knew that higher still one of the oak's upper branches chafed against the pine trunk, just where its lower boughs were set close together. There, when she made the dangerous pass from one tree to the other, the great enterprise would really begin.

She crept out along the swaying oak limb at last, and took the daring step across into the old pine-tree. The way was harder than she thought; she must reach far and hold fast, the sharp dry twigs caught and held her and scratched her like angry talons, the pitch made her thin little fingers clumsy and stiff as she went round and round the tree's great stem, higher and higher upward. The sparrows and robins in the woods below were beginning to wake and twitter to the dawn, yet it seemed much lighter there aloft in the pine-tree, and the child knew that she must hurry if her project were to be of any use.

The tree seemed to lengthen itself out as she went up, and to reach farther and farther upward. It was like a great main-mast to the voyaging earth; it must truly have been amazed that morning through all its ponderous frame as it felt this determined spark of human spirit creeping and climbing from higher branch to branch. Who knows how steadily the least twigs held themselves to advantage this light, weak creature on her way! The old pine must have loved his new dependent. More than all the hawks, and bats, and moths, and even the sweet-voiced thrushes, was the brave, beating heart of the solitary gray-eyed child. And the tree stood still and held away the winds that June morning while the dawn grew bright in the east.

Sylvia's face was like a pale star, if one had seen it from the ground, when the last thorny bough was past, and she stood trembling and tired but wholly triumphant, high in the tree-top. Yes, there was the sea with the dawning sun making a golden dazzle over it, and toward that glorious east flew two hawks with slow-moving pinions. How low they looked in the air from that height when before one had only seen them far up, and dark against the blue sky. Their gray feathers were as soft as moths; they seemed only a little way from the tree, and Sylvia felt as if she too could go flying away among the clouds. Westward, the woodlands and farms reached miles and miles into the distance; here and there were church steeples, and white villages; truly it was a vast and awesome world.

The birds sang louder and louder. At last the sun came up bewilderingly bright. Sylvia could see the white sails of ships out at sea, and the clouds that were purple and rose-colored and yellow at first began to fade away. Where was the white heron's nest in the sea of green branches, and was this wonderful sight and pageant of the world the only reward for having climbed to such a giddy height? Now look down again, Sylvia, where the green marsh is set among the shining birches and dark hemlocks; there where you saw the white heron once you will see him again; look, look! a white spot of him like a single floating feather comes up from the dead hemlock and grows larger, and rises, and comes close at last, and goes by the landmark pine with steady sweep of wing and outstretched slender neck and crested head. And wait! wait! do not move a foot or a finger, little girl, do not send an arrow of light and consciousness from your two eager eyes, for the heron has perched on a pine bough not far beyond yours, and cries back to his mate on the nest, and plumes his feathers for the new day!

The child gives a long sigh a minute later when a company of shouting cat-birds comes also to the tree, and vexed by their fluttering and lawlessness the solemn heron goes away. She knows his secret now, the wild, light, slender bird that floats and wavers, and goes back like an arrow presently to his home in the green world beneath. Then Sylvia, well satisfied, makes her perilous way down again, not daring to look far below the branch she stands on, ready to cry sometimes because her fingers ache and her lamed feet slip. Wondering over and over again what the stranger would say to her, and what he would think when she told him how to find his way straight to the heron's nest.

"Sylvy, Sylvy!" called the busy old grandmother again and again, but nobody answered, and the small husk bed was empty, and Sylvia had disappeared.

The guest waked from a dream, and remembering his day's pleasure hurried to dress himself that it might sooner begin. He was sure from the way the shy little girl looked once or twice yesterday that she had at least seen the white heron, and now she must really be persuaded to tell. Here she comes now, paler than ever, and her worn old frock is torn and tattered, and smeared with pine pitch. The grandmother and the sportsman stand in the door together and question her, and the splendid moment had come to speak of the dead hemlock-tree by the green marsh.

But Sylvia does not speak after all, though the old grandmother fretfully rebukes her, and the young man's kind appealing eyes are looking straight in her own. He can make them rich with money; he has promised it, and they are poor now. He is so well worth making happy, and he waits to hear the story she can tell.

No, she must keep silence! What is it that suddenly forbids her and makes her dumb? Has she been nine years growing, and now, when the great world for the first time puts out a hand to her, must she thrust it aside for a bird's sake? The murmur of the pine's green branches is in her ears, she remembers how the white heron came flying through the golden air and how they watched the sea and the morning together, and Sylvia cannot speak; she cannot tell the heron's secret and give its life away.

Dear loyalty, that suffered a sharp pang as the guest went away disappointed later in the day, that could have served and followed him and loved him as a dog loves! Many a night Sylvia heard the echo of his whistle haunting the pasture path as she came home with the loitering cow. She forgot even her sorrow at the sharp report of his gun and the piteous sight of thrushes and sparrows dropping silent to the ground, their songs hushed and their pretty feathers stained and wet with blood. Were the birds better friends than their hunter might have been, — who can tell? Whatever treasures were lost to her, woodlands and summer-time, remember! Bring your gifts and graces and tell your secrets to this lonely country child!

JAMES JOYCE *(1882–1941) was born James Augustine Aloysius Joyce in Rathgar, a suburb of Dublin, during a turbulent era of political change in Ireland. His parents sent him at the age of six to the best Jesuit school, Clongowes Wood College, where he spent three years; but in 1891 his father was no longer able to afford the tuition, and he was withdrawn. During the period of his parents' financial decline, Joyce — a brilliant student — was educated at home and then given free tuition at Belvedere College, where he won prizes for his essays. Shortly after taking his bachelor's degree in 1902 from University College, Dublin, he left Ireland for Paris, where he attended one class at the Collège de Médecine but dropped out because he could not afford the fees. Nearly starving, he remained in Paris and wrote what he called "Epiphanies." These were notebook jottings of overheard conversations or passing observations that he later incorporated into his fiction, thinking that they illuminated in a flash the meaning of a group of apparently unrelated phenomena. In April 1903 Joyce returned to Dublin because his mother was dying. He remained in Ireland for a short time as a teacher, but the following year he went to live abroad again, disillusioned by his home country's political corruption and religious hypocrisy.*

Dubliners *(1914), a group of fifteen short stories begun in 1904, was Joyce's attempt to "write a chapter of the moral history" of Ireland. He chose Dublin for the setting because that city seemed to him "the center of paralysis," but he also thought of following the book with another titled "Provincials." As if to prove his perception of the extent of stifling moral repression in his country, he had great difficulties getting the book published — a struggle lasting nine years. This so angered and frustrated Joyce that he never again lived in Ireland; he settled in Trieste, Zurich, and Paris and wrote the novels that established him as one of the greatest authors of modern times:* A Portrait of the Artist as a Young Man *(1916),* Ulysses *(1922), and* Finnegans Wake *(1939).*

Joyce's stories about the lives of young people, servants, politicians, and the complacent middle class were intended to represent a broad spectrum of Dublin life — not "a collection of tourist impressions" but a penetrating account of the spiritual waste of his times. Today's reader finds it difficult to believe that some stories in Dubliners *could have appeared so scandalous to Joyce's publishers that at one point the plates were destroyed at the printers. "Araby" suggests the period of adolescence which Joyce depicted in his book. As a stylist, he blended a detached sympathy for his subject with a "scrupulous meanness" of observed detail. Instead of dramatic plots, he structured his stories around "epiphanies" — evanescent moments that reveal "a sudden spiritual manifestation, whether in the vulgarity of speech or of gesture or in a memorable expression of the mind itself."*

RELATED COMMENTARIES: *Harry Stone, "'Araby' and the Writings of James Joyce," page 717.*

JAMES JOYCE

Araby

1914

North Richmond Street, being blind, was a quiet street except at the hour when the Christian Brothers' School set the boys free. An uninhabited house of two storeys stood at the blind end, detached from its neighbours in a square ground. The other houses of the street, conscious of decent lives within them, gazed at one another with brown imperturbable faces.

The former tenant of our house, a priest, had died in the back drawing-room. Air, musty from having been long enclosed, hung in all the rooms, and the waste room behind the kitchen was littered with old useless papers. Among these I found a few paper-covered books, the pages of which were curled and damp: *The Abbot,* by Walter Scott, *The Devout Communicant,* and *The Memoirs of Vidocq.* I liked the last best because its leaves were yellow. The wild garden behind the house contained a central apple-tree and a few straggling bushes under one of which I found the late tenant's rusty bicycle-pump. He had been a very charitable priest; in his will he had left all his money to institutions and the furniture of his house to his sister.

When the short days of winter came dusk fell before we had well eaten our dinners. When we met in the street the houses had grown sombre. The space of sky above us was the colour of ever-changing violet and towards it the lamps of the street lifted their feeble lanterns. The cold air stung us and we played till our bodies glowed. Our shouts echoed in the silent street. The career of our play brought us through the dark muddy lanes behind the houses where we ran the gauntlet of the rough tribes from the cottages, to the back doors of the dark dripping gardens where odours arose from the ashpits, to the dark odorous stables where a coachman smoothed and combed the horse or shook music from the buckled harness. When we returned to the street light from the kitchen windows had filled the areas. If my uncle was seen turning the corner we hid in the shadow until we had seen him safely housed. Or if Mangan's sister came out on the doorstep to call her brother in to his tea we watched her from our shadow peer up and down the street. We waited to see whether she would remain or go in and, if she remained, we left our shadow and walked up to Mangan's steps resignedly. She was waiting for us, her figure defined by the light from the half-opened door. Her brother always teased her before he obeyed and I stood by the railings looking at her. Her dress swung as she moved her body and the soft rope of her hair tossed from side to side.

Every morning I lay on the floor in the front parlour watching her door. The blind was pulled down to within an inch of the sash so that I could not be seen. When she came out on the doorstep my heart leaped. I ran to the hall, seized my books, and followed her. I kept her brown figure always in my eye and, when we came near the point at which our ways diverged, I quickened my pace and passed her. This happened morning after morning. I had never spoken to her, except for a few casual words, and yet her name was like a summons to all my foolish blood.

Her image accompanied me even in places the most hostile to romance. On Saturday evenings when my aunt went marketing I had to go to carry some of the parcels. We walked through the flaring streets, jostled by drunken men and bargaining women, amid the curses of labourers, the shrill litanies of shop-boys who stood on guard by the barrel of pigs' cheeks, the nasal chanting of street-singers, who sang a *come-all-you* about O'Donovan Rossa,° or a ballad about the troubles in our native land. These noises converged in a single sensation of life for me: I imagined that I bore my chalice safely through a throng of foes. Her name sprang to my lips at moments in strange prayers and praises which I myself did not understand. My eyes were often full of tears (I could not tell why) and at times a flood from my heart seemed to pour itself out into my bosom. I thought little of the future. I did not know whether I would ever speak to her or not or, if I spoke to her, how I could tell her of my confused adoration. But my body was like a harp and her words and gestures were like fingers running upon the wires.

One evening I went into the back drawing-room in which the priest had died. It was a dark rainy evening and there was no sound in the house. Through one of the broken panes I heard the rain impinge upon the earth, the fine incessant needles of water playing in the sodden beds. Some distant lamp or lighted window gleamed below me. I was thankful that I could see so little. All my senses seemed to desire to veil themselves and, feeling that I was about to slip from them, I pressed the palms of my hands together until they trembled, murmuring: "*O love! O love!*" many times.

At last she spoke to me. When she addressed the first words to me I was so confused that I did not know what to answer. She asked me was I going to *Araby*. I forgot whether I answered yes or no. It would be a splendid bazaar, she said she would love to go.

"And why can't you?" I asked.

While she spoke she turned a silver bracelet round and round her wrist. She could not go, she said, because there would be a retreat that week in her convent. Her brother and two other boys were fighting for their caps and I was alone at the railings. She held one of the spikes, bowing her head towards me. The light from the lamp opposite our door caught the white curve of her neck, lit up her hair that rested there and, falling, lit up the hand upon the railing. It fell over one side of her dress and caught the white border of a petticoat, just visible as she stood at ease.

"It's well for you," she said.

O'Donovan Rossa: Jeremiah O'Donovan (1831–1915), born in Ross Carberry of County Cork, was nicknamed "Dynamite Rossa" for championing violent means to achieve Irish independence.

"If I go," I said, "I will bring you something."

What innumerable follies laid waste my waking and sleeping thoughts after that evening! I wished to annihilate the tedious intervening days. I chafed against the work of school. At night in my bedroom and by day in the classroom her image came between me and the page I strove to read. The syllables of the word *Araby* were called to me through the silence in which my soul luxuriated and cast an Eastern enchantment over me. I asked for leave to go to the bazaar on Saturday night. My aunt was surprised and hoped it was not some Freemason affair. I answered few questions in class. I watched my master's face pass from amiability to sternness; he hoped I was not beginning to idle. I could not call my wandering thoughts together. I had hardly any patience with the serious work of life which, now that it stood between me and my desire, seemed to me child's play, ugly monotonous child's play.

On Saturday morning I reminded my uncle that I wished to go to the bazaar in the evening. He was fussing at the hallstand, looking for the hatbrush, and answered me curtly:

"Yes, boy, I know."

As he was in the hall I could not go into the front parlour and lie at the window. I left the house in bad humour and walked slowly towards the school. The air was pitilessly raw and already my heart misgave me.

When I came home to dinner my uncle had not yet been home. Still it was early. I sat staring at the clock for some time and, when its ticking began to irritate me, I left the room. I mounted the staircase and gained the upper part of the house. The high cold empty gloomy rooms liberated me and I went from room to room singing. From the front window I saw my companions playing below in the street. Their cries reached me weakened and indistinct and, leaning my forehead against the cool glass, I looked over at the dark house where she lived. I may have stood there for an hour, seeing nothing but the brown-clad figure cast by my imagination, touched discreetly by the lamplight at the curved neck, at the hand upon the railings and at the border below the dress.

When I came downstairs again I found Mrs. Mercer sitting at the fire. She was an old garrulous woman, a pawnbroker's widow, who collected used stamps for some pious purpose. I had to endure the gossip of the tea-table. The meal was prolonged beyond an hour and still my uncle did not come. Mrs. Mercer stood up to go: she was sorry she couldn't wait any longer, but it was after eight o'clock and she did not like to be out late, as the night air was bad for her. When she had gone I began to walk up and down the room, clenching my fists. My aunt said:

"I'm afraid you may put off your bazaar for this night of Our Lord."

At nine o'clock I heard my uncle's latchkey in the halldoor. I heard him talking to himself and heard the hallstand rocking when it had received the weight of his overcoat. I could interpret these signs. When he was midway through his dinner I asked him to give me the money to go to the bazaar. He had forgotten.

"The people are in bed and after their first sleep now," he said.

I did not smile. My aunt said to him energetically:

"Can't you give him the money and let him go? You've kept him late enough as it is."

My uncle said he was very sorry he had forgotten. He said he believed in the old saying: "All work and no play makes Jack a dull boy." He asked me where I was going and, when I had told him a second time he asked me did I know *The Arab's Farewell to his Steed.* When I left the kitchen he was about to recite the opening lines of the piece to my aunt.

I held a florin° tightly in my hand as I strode down Buckingham Street towards the station. The sight of the streets thronged with buyers and glaring with gas recalled to me the purpose of my journey. I took my seat in a third-class carriage of a deserted train. After an intolerable delay the train moved out of the station slowly. It crept onward among ruinous houses and over the twinkling river. At Westland Row Station a crowd of people pressed to the carriage doors; but the porters moved them back, saying that it was a special train for the bazaar. I remained alone in the bare carriage. In a few minutes the train drew up beside an improvised wooden platform. I passed out on to the road and saw by the lighted dial of a clock that it was ten minutes to ten. In front of me was a large building which displayed the magical name.

I could not find any sixpenny entrance and, fearing that the bazaar would be closed, I passed in quickly through a turnstile, handing a shilling to a weary-looking man. I found myself in a big hall girdled at half its height by a gallery. Nearly all the stalls were closed and the greater part of the hall was in darkness. I recognised a silence like that which pervades a church after a service. I walked into the centre of the bazaar timidly. A few people were gathered about the stalls which were still open. Before a curtain, over which the words *Café Chantant* were written in coloured lamps, two men were counting money on a salver. I listened to the fall of the coins.

Remembering with difficulty why I had come I went over to one of the stalls and examined porcelain vases and flowered tea-sets. At the door of the stall a young lady was talking and laughing with two young gentlemen. I remarked their English accents and listened vaguely to their conversation.

"O, I never said such a thing!"

"O, but you did!"

"O, but I didn't!"

"Didn't she say that?"

"Yes. I heard her."

"O, there's a . . . fib!"

Observing me the young lady came over and asked me did I wish to buy anything. The tone of her voice was not encouraging; she seemed to have spoken to me out of a sense of duty. I looked humbly at the great jars that stood like eastern guards at either side of the dark entrance to the stall and murmured:

"No, thank you."

The young lady changed the position of one of the vases and went back to the two young men. They began to talk of the same subject. Once or twice the young lady glanced at me over her shoulder.

---

florin: A silver coin worth two shillings.

I lingered before her stall, though I knew my stay was useless, to make my interest in her wares seem the more real. Then I turned away slowly and walked down the middle of the bazaar. I allowed the two pennies to fall against the sixpence in my pocket. I heard a voice call from one end of the gallery that the light was out. The upper part of the hall was now completely dark.

Gazing up into the darkness I saw myself as a creature driven and derided by vanity; and my eyes burned with anguish and anger.

ꕥ

FRANZ KAFKA *(1883–1924) led a life whose events are simple and sad. He was born into a Jewish family in Prague, and from youth onward he feared his authoritarian father so much that he stuttered in his presence, although he spoke easily with others. In 1906 he received a doctorate in jurisprudence, and for many years he worked a tedious job as a civil service lawyer investigating claims at the state Worker's Accident Insurance Institute. He never married and lived for the most part with his parents, writing fiction at night (he was an insomniac) and publishing only a few slim volumes of stories during his lifetime.* Meditation, *a collection of sketches, appeared in 1912;* The Stoker: A Fragment *in 1913;* The Metamorphosis *in 1915;* The Judgment *in 1916;* In the Penal Colony *in 1919; and* A Country Doctor *in 1920. Only a few of his friends knew that Kafka was also at work on the great novels that were published after his death from tuberculosis:* The Trial *(1925),* The Castle *(1926), and* Amerika *(1927). (He asked his literary executor, Max Brod, to burn these works in manuscript, but Brod refused.)*

Kafka's despair with his writing, his job, his father, and his life was complete. Like Gustave Flaubert — whom he admired — he used his fiction as a "rock" to which he clung in order not to be drowned in the waves of the world around him. With typical irony, however, he saw the effort as futile: "By scribbling I run ahead of myself in order to catch myself up at the finishing post. I cannot run away from myself." In his diaries Kafka recorded his obsession with literature: "What will be my fate as a writer is very simple. My talent for portraying my dreamlike inner life has thrust all other matters into the background." Kafka created striking "parables of alienation," as his biographer Ernst Pawel has noted, but the "dreamlike" quality of his imagination is apparent in all his work.

Kafka is perhaps best known as the author of the waking nightmare "The Metamorphosis," whose remarkable first sentence is one of the most famous in short story literature. The hero of the story, Gregor Samsa (pronounced Zamza*), is the son of philistine, middle-class parents in Prague, as was Kafka, and literary critics have tended to interpret the story as an autobiographical fiction, using the "monstrous insect" as a Freudian symbol that characterizes Kafka's sense of inadequacy before his demanding father. Kafka himself considered psychoanalysis "a helpless error," regarding Freud's theories as very rough pictures that do not do justice to either the details or the essence of life. Perhaps the greatest literary influence on Kafka was Flaubert; both writers used language with ironic precision and without explicit intrusion of their private sentiments. The visionary, nightmarish quality of Kafka's fiction is in striking* *contrast to its precise and formal style, the clarity of which intensifies the dark richness of the fantasy.*

RELATED COMMENTARY: *John Updike, "Kafka and 'The Metamorphosis,'" page 733.*

FRANZ KAFKA

The Metamorphosis

1915

TRANSLATED BY WILLA MUIR AND EDWIN MUIR

I

As Gregor Samsa awoke one morning from uneasy dreams he found himself transformed in his bed into a gigantic insect. He was lying on his hard, as it were armor-plated, back and when he lifted his head a little he could see his dome-like brown belly divided into stiff arched segments on top of which the bed quilt could hardly keep in position and was about to slide off completely. His numerous legs, which were pitifully thin compared to the rest of his bulk, waved helplessly before his eyes.

What has happened to me? he thought. It was no dream. His room, a regular human bedroom, only rather too small, lay quiet between the four familiar walls. Above the table on which a collection of cloth samples was unpacked and spread out — Samsa was a commercial traveler — hung the picture which he had recently cut out of an illustrated magazine and put into a pretty gilt frame. It showed a lady, with a fur cap on and a fur stole, sitting upright and holding out to the spectator a huge fur muff into which the whole of her forearm had vanished!

Gregor's eyes turned next to the window, and the overcast sky — one could hear rain drops beating on the window gutter — made him quite melancholy. What about sleeping a little longer and forgetting all this nonsense, he thought, but it could not be done, for he was accustomed to sleep on his right side and in his present condition he could not turn himself over. However violently he forced himself towards his right side he always rolled on to his back again. He tried it at least a hundred times, shutting his eyes to keep from seeing his struggling legs, and only desisted when he began to feel in his side a faint dull ache he had never experienced before.

Oh God, he thought, what an exhausting job I've picked on! Traveling about day in, day out. It's much more irritating work than doing the actual business in the office, and on top of that there's the trouble of constant traveling, of worrying about train connections, the bed and irregular meals, casual acquaintances that are always new and never become intimate friends. The devil take it all! He felt a slight itching up on his belly; slowly pushed himself on his back nearer to the top of the bed so that he could lift his head more easily; identified the itching place which was surrounded by many small white spots the nature of which he could not understand and made to touch it with a leg, but drew the leg back immediately, for the contact made a cold shiver run through him.

He slid down again into his former position. This getting up early, he thought, makes one quite stupid. A man needs his sleep. Other commercials live like harem women. For instance, when I come back to the hotel of a morning to write up the orders I've got, these others are only sitting down to breakfast. Let me just try that with my chief; I'd be sacked on the spot. Anyhow, that might be quite a good thing for me, who can tell? If I didn't have to hold my hand because of my parents I'd have given notice long ago, I'd have gone to the chief and told him exactly what I think of him. That would knock him endways from his desk! It's a queer way of doing, too, this sitting on high at a desk and talking down to employees, especially when they have to come quite near because the chief is hard of hearing. Well, there's still hope; once I've saved enough money to pay back my parents' debts to him — that should take another five or six years — I'll do it without fail. I'll cut myself completely loose then. For the moment, though, I'd better get up, since my train goes at five.

He looked at the alarm clock ticking on the chest. Heavenly Father! he thought. It was half-past six o'clock and the hands were quietly moving on, it was even past the half-hour, it was getting on toward a quarter to seven. Had the alarm clock not gone off? From the bed one could see that it had been properly set for four o'clock; of course it must have gone off. Yes, but was it possible to sleep quietly through that ear-splitting noise? Well, he had not slept quietly, yet apparently all the more soundly for that. But what was he to do now? The next train went at seven o'clock; to catch that he would need to hurry like mad and his samples weren't even packed up, and he himself wasn't feeling particularly fresh and active. And even if he did catch the train he wouldn't avoid a row with the chief, since the firm's porter would have been waiting for the five o'clock train and would have long since reported his failure to turn up. The porter was a creature of the chief's, spineless and stupid. Well, supposing he were to say he was sick? But that would be most unpleasant and would look suspicious, since during his five years' employment he had not been ill once. The chief himself would be sure to come with the sick-insurance doctor, would reproach his parents with their son's laziness and would cut all excuses short by referring to the insurance doctor, who of course regarded all mankind as perfectly healthy malingerers. And would he be so far wrong on this occasion? Gregor really felt quite well, apart from a drowsiness that was utterly superfluous after such a long sleep, and he was even unusually hungry.

As all this was running through his mind at top speed without his being able to decide to leave his bed — the alarm clock had just struck a quarter to seven — there came a cautious tap at the door behind the head of his bed. "Gregor," said a voice — it was his mother's — "it's a quarter to seven. Hadn't you a train to catch?" That gentle voice! Gregor had a shock as he heard his own voice answering hers, unmistakably his own voice, it was true, but with a persistent horrible twittering squeak behind it like an undertone, that left the words in their clear shape only for the first moment and then rose up reverberating round them to destroy their sense, so that one could not be sure one had heard them rightly. Gregor wanted to answer at length and explain everything, but in the circumstances he confined himself to saying: "Yes, yes, thank you, Mother, I'm getting up now." The wooden door between them must have kept the change in his voice from being noticeable outside, for his mother contented herself with this statement and shuffled away. Yet this brief exchange of words had made the other members of the family aware that Gregor was still in the house, as they had not expected, and at one of the side doors his father was already knocking, gently, yet with his fist. "Gregor, Gregor," he called, "what's the matter with you?" And after a little while he called again in a deeper voice: "Gregor! Gregor!" At the other side door his sister was saying in a low, plaintive tone: "Gregor? Aren't you well? Are you needing anything?" He answered them both at once: "I'm just ready," and did his best to make his voice sound as normal as possible by enunciating the words very clearly and leaving long pauses between them. So his father went back to his breakfast, but his sister whispered: "Gregor, open the door, do." However, he was not thinking of opening the door, and felt thankful for the prudent habit he had acquired in traveling of locking all doors during the night, even at home.

His immediate intention was to get up quietly without being disturbed, to put on his clothes and above all eat his breakfast, and only then to consider what else was to be done, since in bed, he was well aware, his meditations would come to no sensible conclusion. He remembered that often enough in bed he had felt small aches and pains, probably caused by awkward postures, which had proved purely imaginary once he got up, and he looked forward eagerly to seeing this morning's delusions gradually fall away. That the change in his voice was nothing but the precursor of a severe chill, a standing ailment of commercial travelers, he had not the least possible doubt.

To get rid of the quilt was quite easy; he had only to inflate himself a little and it fell off by itself. But the next move was difficult, especially because he was so uncommonly broad. He would have needed arms and hands to hoist himself up; instead he had only the numerous little legs which never stopped waving in all directions and which he could not control in the least. When he tried to bend one of them it was the first to stretch itself straight; and did he succeed at last in making it do what he wanted, all the other legs meanwhile waved the more wildly in a high degree of unpleasant agitation. "But what's the use of lying idle in bed," said Gregor to himself.

He thought that he might get out of bed with the lower part of his body first, but this lower part, which he had not yet seen and of which he could form no clear conception, proved too difficult to move; it shifted so slowly; and when finally, almost wild with annoyance, he gathered his forces together and thrust out recklessly, he had miscalculated the direction and bumped heavily against the lower end of the bed, and the stinging pain he felt informed him that precisely this lower part of his body was at the moment probably the most sensitive.

So he tried to get the top part of himself out first, and cautiously moved his head towards the edge of the bed. That proved easy enough, and despite its breadth and mass the bulk of his body at last slowly followed the movement of his head. Still, when he finally got his head free over the edge of the bed he felt too scared to go on advancing, for after all if he let himself fall in this way it would take a miracle to keep his head from being injured. And at all costs he must not lose consciousness now, precisely now; he would rather stay in bed.

But when after a repetition of the same efforts he lay in his former position again, sighing, and watched his little legs struggling against each other more wildly than ever, if that were possible, and saw no way of bringing any order into this arbitrary confusion, he told himself again that it was impossible to stay in bed and that the most sensible course was to risk everything for the smallest hope of getting away from it. At the same time he did not forget meanwhile to remind himself that cool reflection, the coolest possible, was much better than desperate resolves. In such moments he focused his eyes as sharply as possible on the window, but, unfortunately, the prospect of the morning fog, which muffled even the other side of the narrow street, brought him little encouragement and comfort. "Seven o'clock already," he said to himself when the alarm clock chimed again, "seven o'clock already and still such a thick fog." And for a little while he lay quiet, breathing lightly, as if perhaps expecting such complete repose to restore all things to their real and normal condition.

But then he said to himself: "Before it strikes a quarter past seven I must be quite out of this bed, without fail. Anyhow, by that time someone will have come from the office to ask for me, since it opens before seven." And he set himself to rocking his whole body at once in a regular rhythm, with the idea of swinging it out of the bed. If he tipped himself out in that way he could keep his head from injury by lifting it at an acute angle when he fell. His back seemed to be hard and was not likely to suffer from a fall on the carpet. His biggest worry was the loud crash he would not be able to help making, which would probably cause anxiety, if not terror, behind all the doors. Still, he must take the risk.

When he was already half out of the bed — the new method was more a game than an effort, for he needed only to hitch himself across by rocking to and fro — it struck him how simple it would be if he could get help. Two strong people — he thought of his father and the servant girl — would be amply sufficient; they would only have to thrust their arms under his convex back, lever him out of the bed, bend down with their burden and then be patient enough to let him turn himself right over on to the floor, where it was to be hoped his legs would then find their proper function. Well, ignoring the fact that the doors were all locked, ought he really to call for help? In spite of his misery he could not suppress a smile at the very idea of it.

He had got so far that he could barely keep his equilibrium when he rocked himself strongly, and he would have to nerve himself very soon for the final decision since in five minutes' time it would be a quarter past seven — when the front doorbell rang. "That's someone from the office," he said to himself, and grew almost rigid, while his little legs only jigged about all the faster. For a moment everything stayed quiet. "They're not going to open the door," said Gregor to himself, catching at some kind of irrational hope. But then of course the servant girl went as usual to the door with her heavy tread and opened it. Gregor needed only to hear the first good morning of the visitor to know immediately who it was — the chief clerk himself. What a fate, to be condemned to work for a firm where the smallest omission at once gave rise to the gravest suspicion! Were all employees in a body nothing but scoundrels, was there not among them one single loyal devoted man who, had he wasted only an hour or so of the firm's time in a morning, was so tormented by conscience as to be driven out of his mind and actually incapable of leaving his bed? Wouldn't it really have been sufficient to send an apprentice to inquire — if any inquiry were necessary at all — did the chief clerk himself have to come and thus indicate to the entire family, an innocent family, that this suspicious circumstance could be investigated by no one less versed in affairs than himself? And more through the agitation caused by these reflections than through any act of will Gregor swung himself out of bed with all his strength. There was a loud thump, but it was not really a crash. His fall was broken to some extent by the carpet, his back, too, was less stiff than he thought, and so there was merely a dull thud, not so very startling. Only he had not lifted his head carefully enough and had hit it; he turned it and rubbed it on the carpet in pain and irritation.

"That was something falling down in there," said the chief clerk in the next room to the left. Gregor tried to suppose to himself that something like what had happened to him today might some day happen to the chief clerk; one really could not deny that it was possible. But as if in brusque reply to this supposition the chief clerk took a couple of firm steps in the next-door room and his patent leather boots creaked. From the right-hand room his sister was whispering to inform him of the situation: "Gregor, the chief clerk's here." "I know," muttered Gregor to himself; but he didn't dare to make his voice loud enough for his sister to hear it.

"Gregor," said his father now from the left-hand room, "the chief clerk has come and wants to know why you didn't catch the early train. We don't know what to say to him. Besides, he wants to talk to you in person. So open the door, please. He will be good enough to excuse the untidiness of your room." "Good morning, Mr. Samsa," the chief clerk was calling amiably meanwhile. "He's not well," said his mother to the visitor, while his father was still speaking through the door, "he's not well, sir, believe me. What else would make him miss a train! The boy thinks about nothing but his work. It makes me almost cross the way he never goes out in the evenings; he's been here the last eight days and has stayed at home every single evening. He just sits there quietly at the table reading a newspaper or looking through railway timetables. The only amusement he gets is doing fretwork. For instance, he spent two or three evenings cutting out a little picture frame; you would be surprised to see how pretty it is; it's hanging in his room; you'll see it in a minute when Gregor opens the door. I must say I'm glad you've come, sir; we should never have got him to unlock the door by ourselves; he's so obstinate; and I'm sure he's unwell, though he wouldn't have it to be so this morning." "I'm just coming," said Gregor slowly and carefully, not moving an inch for fear of losing one word of the conversation. "I can't think of any other explanation, madam," said the chief clerk, "I hope it's nothing serious. Although on the other hand I must say that we men of business — fortunately or unfortunately — very often simply have to ignore any slight indisposition, since business must be attended to." "Well, can the chief clerk come in now?" asked Gregor's father impatiently, again knocking on the door. "No," said Gregor. In the left-hand room a painful silence followed this refusal, in the right-hand room his sister began to sob.

Why didn't his sister join the others? She was probably newly out of bed and hadn't even begun to put on her clothes yet. Well, why was she crying? Because he wouldn't get up and let the chief clerk in, because he was in danger of losing his job, and because the chief would begin dunning his parents again for the old debts? Surely these were things one didn't need to worry about for the present. Gregor was still at home and not in the least thinking of deserting the family. At the moment, true, he was lying on the carpet and no one who knew the condition he was in could seriously expect him to admit the chief clerk. But for such a small discourtesy, which could plausibly be explained away somehow later on, Gregor could hardly be dismissed on the spot. And it seemed to Gregor that it would be much more sensible to leave him in peace for the present than to trouble him with tears and entreaties. Still, of course, their uncertainty bewildered them all and excused their behavior.

"Mr. Samsa," the chief clerk called now in a louder voice, "what's the matter with you? Here you are, barricading yourself in your room, giving only 'yes' and 'no' for answers, causing your parents a lot of unnecessary trouble and neglecting — I mention this only in passing — neglecting your business duties in an incredible fashion. I am speaking here in the name of your parents and of your chief, and I beg you quite seriously to give me an immediate and precise explanation. You amaze me, you amaze me. I thought you were a quiet, dependable person, and now all at once you seem bent on making a disgraceful exhibition of yourself. The chief did hint to me early this morning a possible explanation for your disappearance — with reference to the cash payments that were entrusted to you recently — but I almost pledged my solemn word of honor that this could not be so. But now that I see how incredibly obstinate you are, I no longer have the slightest desire to take your part at all. And your position in the firm is not so unassailable. I came with the intention of telling you all this in private, but since you are wasting my time so needlessly I don't see why your parents shouldn't hear it too. For some time past your work has been most unsatisfactory; this is not the season of the year for a business boom, of course, we admit that, but a season of the year for doing no business at all, that does not exist, Mr. Samsa, must not exist."

"But, sir," cried Gregor, beside himself and in his agitation forgetting everything else, "I'm just going to open the door this very minute. A slight illness, an attack of giddiness, has kept me from getting up. I'm still lying in bed. But I feel all right again. I'm getting out of bed now. Just give me a moment or two longer! I'm not quite so well as I thought. But I'm all right, really. How a thing like that can suddenly strike one down! Only last night I was quite well, my parents can tell you, or rather I did have a slight presentiment. I must have showed some sign of it. Why didn't I report it at the office! But one always thinks that an indisposition can be got over without staying in the house. Oh sir, do spare my parents! All that you're reproaching me with now has no foundation; no one has ever said a word to me about it. Perhaps you haven't looked at the last orders I sent in. Anyhow, I can still catch the eight o'clock train, I'm much the better for my few hours' rest. Don't let me detain you here, sir; I'll be attending to business very soon, and do be good enough to tell the chief so and to make my excuses to him!"

And while all this was tumbling out pell-mell and Gregor hardly knew what he was saying, he had reached the chest quite easily, perhaps because of the practice he had had in bed, and was now trying to lever himself upright by means of it. He meant actually to open the door, actually to show himself and speak to the chief clerk; he was eager to find out what the others, after all their insistence, would say at the sight of him. If they were horrified then the responsibility was no longer his and he could stay quiet. But if they took it calmly, then he had no reason either to be upset, and could really get to the station for the eight o'clock train if he hurried. At first he slipped down a few times from the polished surface of the chest, but at length with a last heave he stood upright; he paid no more attention to the pains in the lower part of his body, however they smarted. Then he let himself fall against the back of a near-by chair, and clung with his little legs to the edges of it. That brought him into control of himself again and he stopped speaking, for now he could listen to what the chief clerk was saying.

"Did you understand a word of it?" the chief clerk was asking; "surely he can't be trying to make fools of us?" "Oh dear," cried his mother, in tears, "perhaps he's terribly ill and we're tormenting him. Grete! Grete!" she called out then. "Yes, Mother?" called his sister from the other side. They were calling to each other across Gregor's room. "You must go this minute for the doctor. Gregor is ill. Go for the doctor, quick. Did you hear how he was speaking?" "That was no human voice," said the chief clerk in a voice noticeably low beside the shrillness of the mother's. "Anna! Anna!" his father was calling through the hall to the kitchen, clapping his hands, "get a locksmith at once!" And the two girls were already running through the hall with a swish of skirts — how could his sister have got dressed so quickly? — and were tearing the front door open. There was no sound of its closing again; they had evidently left it open, as one does in houses where some great misfortune has happened.

But Gregor was now much calmer. The words he uttered were no longer understandable, apparently, although they seemed clear enough to him, even clearer than before, perhaps because his ear had grown accustomed to the sound of them. Yet at any rate people now believed that something was wrong with him, and were ready to help him. The positive certainty with which these first measures had been taken comforted him. He felt himself drawn once more into the human circle and hoped for great and remarkable results from both the doctor and the locksmith, without really distinguishing precisely between them. To make his voice as clear as possible for the decisive conversation that was now imminent he coughed a little, as quietly as he could, of course, since this noise too might not sound like a human cough for all he was able to judge. In the next room meanwhile there was complete silence. Perhaps his parents were sitting at the table with the chief clerk, whispering, perhaps they were all leaning against the door and listening.

Slowly Gregor pushed the chair towards the door, then let go of it, caught hold of the door for support — the soles at the end of his little legs were somewhat sticky — and rested against it for a moment after his efforts. Then he set himself to turning the key in the lock with his mouth. It seemed, unhappily, that he hadn't really any teeth — what could he grip the key with? — but on the other hand his jaws were certainly very strong; with their help he did manage to set the key in motion, heedless of the fact that he was undoubtedly damaging them somewhere, since a brown fluid issued from his mouth, flowed over the key and dripped on the floor. "Just listen to that," said the chief clerk next door; "he's turning the key." That was a great encouragement to Gregor; but they should all have shouted encouragement to him, his father and mother too: "Go on, Gregor," they should have called out, "keep going, hold on to that key!" And in the belief that they were all following his efforts intently, he clenched his jaws recklessly on the key with all the force at his command. As the turning of the key progressed he circled round the lock, holding on now only with his mouth, pushing on the key, as required, or pulling it down again with all the weight of his body. The louder click of the finally yielding lock literally quickened Gregor. With a deep breath of relief he said to himself: "So I didn't need the locksmith," and laid his head on the handle to open the door wide.

Since he had to pull the door towards him, he was still invisible when it was really wide open. He had to edge himself slowly round the near half of the double door, and to do it very carefully if he was not to fall plump upon his back just on the threshold. He was still carrying out this difficult manoeuvre, with no time to observe anything else, when he heard the chief clerk utter a loud "Oh!" — it sounded like a gust of wind — and now he could see the man, standing as he was nearest to the door, clapping one hand before his open mouth and slowly backing away as if driven by some invisible steady pressure. His mother — in spite of the chief clerk's being there her hair was still undone and sticking up in all directions — first clasped her hands and looked at his father, then took two steps towards Gregor and fell on the floor among her outspread skirts, her face hidden on her breast. His father knotted his fist with a fierce expression on his face as if he meant to knock Gregor back into his room, then looked uncertainly round the living room, covered his eyes with his hands and wept till his great chest heaved.

Gregor did not go now into the living room, but leaned against the inside of the firmly shut wing of the door, so that only half his body was visible and his head above it bending sideways to look at the others. The light had meanwhile strengthened; on the other side of the street one could see clearly a section of the endlessly long, dark gray building opposite — it was a hospital — abruptly punctuated by its row of regular windows; the rain was still falling, but only in large singly discernible and literally singly splashing drops. The breakfast dishes were set out on the table lavishly, for breakfast was the most important meal of the day to Gregor's father, who lingered it out for hours over various newspapers. Right opposite Gregor on the wall hung a photograph of himself on military service, as a lieutenant, hand on sword, a carefree smile on his face, inviting one to respect his uniform and military bearing. The door leading to the hall was open, and one could see that the front door stood open too, showing the landing beyond and the beginning of the stairs going down.

"Well," said Gregor, knowing perfectly that he was the only one who had retained any composure, "I'll put my clothes on at once, pack up my samples and start off. Will you only let me go? You see, sir, I'm not obstinate, and I'm willing to work; traveling is a hard life, but I couldn't live without it. Where are you going, sir? To the office? Yes? Will you give a true account of all this? One can be temporarily incapacitated, but that's just the moment for remembering former services and bearing in mind that later on, when the incapacity has been got over, one will certainly work with all the more industry and concentration. I'm loyally bound to serve the chief, you know that very well. Besides, I have to provide for my parents and my sister. I'm in great difficulties, but I'll get out of them again. Don't make things any worse for me than they are. Stand up for me in the firm. Travelers are not popular there, I know. People think they earn sacks of money and just have a good time. A prejudice there's no particular reason for revising. But you, sir, have a more comprehensive view of affairs than the rest of the staff, yes, let me tell you in confidence, a more comprehensive view than the chief himself, who, being the owner, lets his judgment easily be swayed against one of his employees. And you know very well that the traveler, who is never seen in the office almost the whole year round, can so easily fall a victim to gossip and ill luck and unfounded complaints, which he mostly knows nothing about, except when he comes back exhausted from his rounds, and only then suffers in person from their evil consequences, which he can no longer trace back to the original causes. Sir, sir, don't go away without a word to me to show that you think me in the right at least to some extent!"

But at Gregor's very first words the chief clerk had already backed away and only stared at him with parted lips over one twitching shoulder. And while Gregor was speaking he did not stand still one moment but stole away towards the door, without taking his eyes off Gregor, yet only an inch at a time, as if obeying some secret injunction to leave the room. He was already at the hall, and the suddenness with which he took his last step out of the living room would have made one believe he had burned the sole of his foot. Once in the hall he stretched his right arm before him towards the staircase, as if some supernatural power were waiting there to deliver him.

Gregor perceived that the chief clerk must on no account be allowed to go away in this frame of mind if his position in the firm were not to be endangered to the utmost. His parents did not understand this so well; they had convinced themselves in the course of years that Gregor was settled for life in this firm, and besides they were so occupied with their immediate troubles that all foresight had forsaken them. Yet Gregor had this foresight. The chief clerk must be detained, soothed, persuaded and finally won over; the whole future of Gregor and his family depended on it! If only his sister had been there! She was intelligent; she had begun to cry while Gregor was still lying quietly on his back. And no doubt the chief clerk, so partial to ladies, would have been guided by her; she would have shut the door of the flat and in the hall talked him out of his horror. But she was not there, and Gregor would have to handle the situation himself. And without remembering that he was still unaware what powers of movement he possessed, without even remembering that his words in all possibility, indeed in all likelihood, would again be unintelligible, he let go the wing of the door, pushed himself through the opening, started to walk towards the chief clerk, who was already ridiculously clinging with both hands to the railing on the landing; but immediately, as he was feeling for a support, he fell down with a little cry upon all his numerous legs. Hardly was he down when he experienced for the first time this morning a sense of physical comfort; his legs had firm ground under them; they were completely obedient, as he noted with joy; they even strove to carry him forward in whatever direction he chose; and he was inclined to believe that a final relief from all his sufferings was at hand. But in the same moment as he found himself on the floor, rocking with suppressed eagerness to move, not far from his mother, indeed just in front of her, she, who had seemed so completely crushed, sprang all at once to her feet, her arms and fingers outspread, cried: "Help, for God's sake, help!" bent her head down as if to see Gregor better, yet on the contrary kept backing senselessly away; had quite forgotten that the laden table stood behind her; sat upon it hastily, as if in absence of mind, when she bumped into it; and seemed altogether unaware that the big coffee pot beside her was upset and pouring coffee in a flood over the carpet.

"Mother, Mother," said Gregor in a low voice, and looked up at her. The chief clerk, for the moment, had quite slipped from his mind; instead, he could not resist snapping his jaws together at the sight of the streaming coffee. That made his mother scream again, she fled from the table and fell into the arms of his father, who hastened to catch her. But Gregor had now no time to spare for his parents; the chief clerk was already on the stairs; with his chin on the banisters he was taking one last backward look. Gregor made a spring, to be as sure as possible of overtaking him; the chief clerk must have divined his intention, for he leaped down several steps and vanished; he was still yelling "Ugh!" and it echoed through the whole staircase.

Unfortunately, the flight of the chief clerk seemed completely to upset Gregor's father, who had remained relatively calm until now, for instead of running after the man himself, or at least not hindering Gregor in his pursuit, he seized in his right hand the walking stick which the chief clerk had left behind on a chair, together with a hat and greatcoat, snatched in his left hand a large newspaper from the table and began stamping his feet and flourishing the stick and the newspaper to drive Gregor back into his room. No entreaty of Gregor's availed, indeed no entreaty was even understood, however humbly he bent his head his father only stamped on the floor the more loudly. Behind his father his mother had torn open a window, despite the cold weather, and was leaning far out of it with her face in her hands. A strong draught set in from the street to the staircase, the window curtains blew in, the newspapers on the table fluttered, stray pages whisked over the floor. Pitilessly Gregor's father drove him back, hissing and crying "Shoo!" like a savage. But Gregor was quite unpracticed in walking backwards, it really was a slow business. If he only had a chance to turn round he could get back to his room at once, but he was afraid of exasperating his father by the slowness of such a rotation and at any moment the stick in his father's hand might hit him a fatal blow on the back or on the head. In the end, however, nothing else was left for him to do since to his horror he observed that in moving backwards he could not even control the direction he took; and so, keeping an anxious eye on his father all the time over his shoulder, he began to turn round as quickly as he could, which was in reality very slowly. Perhaps his father noted his good intentions, for he did not interfere except every now and then to help him in the manoeuvre from a distance with the point of the stick. If only he would have stopped making that unbearable hissing noise! It made Gregor quite lose his head. He had turned almost completely round when the hissing noise so distracted him that he even turned a little the wrong way again. But when at last his head was fortunately right in front of the doorway, it appeared that his body was too broad simply to get through the opening. His father, of course, in his present mood was far from thinking of such a thing as opening the other half of the door, to let Gregor have enough space. He had merely the fixed idea of driving Gregor back into his room as quickly as possible. He would never have suffered Gregor to make the circumstantial preparations for standing up on end and perhaps slipping his way through the door. Maybe he was now making more noise than ever to urge Gregor forward, as if no obstacle impeded him; to Gregor, anyhow, the noise in his rear sounded no longer like the voice of one single father; this was really no joke, and Gregor thrust himself — come what might — into the doorway. One side of his body rose up, he was tilted at an angle in the doorway, his flank was quite bruised, horrid blotches stained the white door, soon he was stuck fast and, left to himself, could not have moved at all, his legs on one side fluttered trembling to the air, those on the other were crushed painfully to the floor — when from behind his father gave him a strong push which was literally a deliverance and he flew far into the room, bleeding freely. The door was slammed behind him with the stick, and then at last there was silence.

II

Not until it was twilight did Gregor awake out of a deep sleep, more like a swoon than a sleep. He would certainly have waked up of his own accord not much later, for he felt himself sufficiently rested and well-slept, but it seemed to him as if a fleeting step and a cautious shutting of the door leading into the hall had aroused him. The electric lights in the street cast a pale sheen here and there on the ceiling and the upper surfaces of the furniture, but down below, where he lay, it was dark. Slowly, awkwardly trying out his feelers, which he now first learned to appreciate, he pushed his way to the door to see what had been happening there. His left side felt like one single long, unpleasant tense scar, and he had actually to limp on his two rows of legs. One little leg, moreover, had been severely damaged in the course of that morning's events — it was almost a miracle that only one had been damaged — and trailed uselessly behind him.

He had reached the door before he discovered what had really drawn him to it: the smell of food. For there stood a basin filled with fresh milk in which floated little sops of white bread. He could almost have laughed with joy, since he was now still hungrier than in the morning, and he dipped his head almost over the eyes straight into the milk. But soon in disappointment he withdrew it again; not only did he find it difficult to feed because of his tender left side — and he could only feed with the palpitating collaboration of his whole body — he did not like the milk either, although milk had been his favorite drink and that was certainly why his sister had set it there for him, indeed it was almost with repulsion that he turned away from the basin and crawled back to the middle of the room.

He could see through the crack of the door that the gas was turned on in the living room, but while usually at this time his father made a habit of reading the afternoon newspaper in a loud voice to his mother and occasionally to his sister as well, not a sound was now to be heard. Well, perhaps his father had recently given up this habit of reading aloud, which his sister had mentioned so often in conversation and in her letters. But there was the same silence all around, although the flat was certainly not empty of occupants. "What a quiet life our family has been leading," said Gregor to himself, and as he sat there motionless staring into the darkness he felt great pride in the fact that he had been able to provide such a life for his parents and sister in such a fine flat. But what if all the quiet, the comfort, the contentment were now to end in horror? To keep himself from being lost in such thoughts Gregor took refuge in movement and crawled up and down the room.

Once during the long evening one of the side doors was opened a little and quickly shut again, later the other side door too; someone had apparently wanted to come in and then thought better of it. Gregor now stationed himself immediately before the living room door, determined to persuade any hesitating visitor to come in or at least to discover who it might be; but the door was not opened again and he waited in vain. In the early morning, when the doors were locked, they had all wanted to come in, now that he had opened one door and the other had apparently been opened during the day, no one came in and even the keys were on the other side of the doors.

It was late at night before the gas went out in the living room, and Gregor could easily tell that his parents and his sister had all stayed awake until then, for he could clearly hear the three of them stealing away on tiptoe. No one was likely to visit him, not until the morning, that was certain; so he had plenty of time to meditate at his leisure on how he was to arrange his life afresh. But the lofty, empty room in which he had to lie flat on the floor filled him with an apprehension he could not account for, since it had been his very own room for the past five years — and with a half-unconscious action, not without a slight feeling of shame, he scuttled under the sofa, where he felt comfortable at once, although his back was a little cramped and he could not lift his head up, and his only regret was that his body was too broad to get the whole of it under the sofa.

He stayed there all night, spending the time partly in a light slumber, from which his hunger kept waking him up with a start, and partly in worrying and sketching vague hopes, which all led to the same conclusion, that he must lie low for the present and, by exercising patience, and the utmost consideration, help the family to bear the inconvenience he was bound to cause them in his present condition.

Very early in the morning, it was still almost night, Gregor had the chance to test the strength of his new resolutions, for his sister, nearly fully dressed, opened the door from the hall and peered in. She did not see him at once, yet when she caught sight of him under the sofa — well, he had to be somewhere, he couldn't have flown away, could he? — she was so startled that without being able to help it she slammed the door shut again. But as if regretting her behavior she opened the door again immediately and came in on tiptoe, as if she were visiting an invalid or even a stranger. Gregor had pushed his head forward to the very edge of the sofa and watched her. Would she notice that he had left the milk standing, and not for lack of hunger, and would she bring in some other kind of food more to his taste? If she did not do it of her own accord, he would rather starve than draw her attention to the fact, although he felt a wild impulse to dart out from under the sofa, throw himself at her feet and beg her for something to eat. But his sister at once noticed, with surprise, that the basin was still full, except for a little milk that had been spilt all around it, she lifted it immediately, not with her bare hands, true, but with a cloth and carried it away. Gregor was wildly curious to know what she would bring instead, and made various speculations about it. Yet what she actually did next, in the goodness of her heart, he could never have guessed at. To find out what he liked she brought him a whole selection of food, all set out on an old newspaper. There were old, half-decayed vegetables, bones from last night's supper covered with a white sauce that had thickened; some raisins and almonds; a piece of cheese that Gregor would have called uneatable two days ago; a dry roll of bread, a buttered roll, and a roll both buttered and salted. Besides all that, she set down again the same basin, into which she had poured some water, and which was apparently to be reserved for his exclusive use. And with fine tact, knowing that Gregor would not eat in her presence, she withdrew quickly and even turned the key, to let him understand that he could take his ease as much as he liked. Gregor's legs all whizzed towards the food. His wounds must have healed completely, moreover, for he felt no disability, which amazed him and made him reflect how more than a month ago he had cut one finger a little with a knife and had still suffered pain from the wound only the day before yesterday. Am I less sensitive now? he thought, and sucked greedily at the cheese, which above all the other edibles attracted him at once and strongly. One after another and with tears of satisfaction in his eyes he quickly devoured the cheese, the vegetables and the sauce; the fresh food, on the other hand, had no charms for him, he could not even stand the smell of it and actually dragged away to some little distance the things he could eat. He had long finished his meal and was only lying lazily on the same spot when his sister turned the key slowly as a sign for him to retreat. That roused him at once, although he was nearly asleep, and he hurried under the sofa again. But it took considerable self-control for him to stay under the sofa, even for the short time his sister was in the room, since the large meal had swollen his body somewhat and he was so cramped he could hardly breathe. Slight attacks of breathlessness afflicted him and his eyes were starting a little out of his head as he watched his unsuspecting sister sweeping together with a broom not only the remains of what he had eaten but even the things he had not touched, as if these were now of no use to anyone, and hastily shoveling it all into a bucket, which she covered with a wooden lid and carried away. Hardly had she turned her back when Gregor came from under the sofa and stretched and puffed himself out.

In this manner Gregor was fed, once in the early morning while his parents and the servant girl were still asleep, and a second time after they had all had their midday dinner, for then his parents took a short nap and the servant girl could be sent out on some errand or other by his sister. Not that they would have wanted him to starve, of course, but perhaps they could not have borne to know more about his feeding than from hearsay, perhaps too his sister wanted to spare them such little anxieties wherever possible, since they had quite enough to bear as it was.

Under what pretext the doctor and the locksmith had been got rid of on that first morning Gregor could not discover, for since what he had said was not understood by the others it never struck any of them, not even his sister, that he could understand what they said, and so whenever his sister came into his room he had to content himself with hearing her utter only a sigh now and then and an occasional appeal to the saints. Later on, when she had got a little used to the situation — of course she could never get completely used to it — she sometimes threw out a remark which was kindly meant or could be so interpreted. "Well, he liked his dinner today," she would say when Gregor had made a good clearance of his food; and when he had not eaten, which gradually happened more and more often, she would say almost sadly: "Everything's been left standing again."

But although Gregor could get no news directly, he overheard a lot from the neighboring rooms, and as soon as voices were audible, he would run to the door of the room concerned and press his whole body against it. In the first few days especially there was no conversation that did not refer to him somehow, even if only indirectly. For two whole days there were family consultations at every mealtime about what should be done; but also between meals the same subject was discussed, for there were always at least two members of the family at home, since no one wanted to be alone in the flat and to leave it quite empty was unthinkable. And on the very first of these days the household cook — it was not quite clear what and how much she knew of the situation — went down on her knees to his mother and begged leave to go, and when she departed, a quarter of an hour later, gave thanks for her dismissal with tears in her eyes as if for the greatest benefit that could have been conferred on her, and without any prompting swore a solemn oath that she would never say a single word to anyone about what had happened.

Now Gregor's sister had to cook too, helping her mother; true, the cooking did not amount to much, for they ate scarcely anything. Gregor was always hearing one of the family vainly urging another to eat and getting no answer but: "Thanks, I've had all I want," or something similar. Perhaps they drank nothing either. Time and again his sister kept asking his father if he wouldn't like some beer and offered kindly to go and fetch it herself, and when he made no answer suggested that she could ask the concierge to fetch it, so that he need feel no sense of obligation, but then a round "No" came from his father and no more was said about it.

In the course of that very first day Gregor's father explained the family's financial position and prospects to both his mother and his sister. Now and then he rose from the table to get some voucher or memorandum out of the small safe he had rescued from the collapse of his business five years earlier. One could hear him opening the complicated lock and rustling papers out and shutting it again. This statement made by his father was the first cheerful information Gregor had heard since his imprisonment. He had been of the opinion that nothing at all was left over from his father's business, at least his father had never said anything to the contrary, and of course he had not asked him directly. At the time Gregor's sole desire was to do his utmost to help the family to forget as soon as possible the catastrophe which had overwhelmed the business and thrown them all into a state of complete despair. And so he had set to work with unusual ardor and almost overnight had become a commercial traveler instead of a little clerk, with of course much greater chances of earning money, and his success was immediately translated into good round coin which he could lay on the table for his amazed and happy family. These had been fine times, and they had never recurred, at least not with the same sense of glory, although later on Gregor had earned so much money that he was able to meet the expenses of the whole household and did so. They had simply got used to it, both the family and Gregor; the money was gratefully accepted and gladly given, but there was no special uprush of warm feeling. With his sister alone had he remained intimate, and it was a secret plan of his that she, who loved music, unlike himself, and could play movingly on the violin, should be sent next year to study at the Conservatorium, despite the great expense that would entail, which must be made up in some other way. During his brief visits home the Conservatorium was often mentioned in the talks he had with his sister, but always merely as a beautiful dream which could never come true, and his parents discouraged even these innocent references to it; yet Gregor had made up his mind firmly about it and meant to announce the fact with due solemnity on Christmas Day.

Such were the thoughts, completely futile in his present condition, that went through his head as he stood clinging upright to the door and listening. Sometimes out of sheer weariness he had to give up listening and let his head fall negligently against the door, but he always had to pull himself together again at once, for even the slight sound his head made was audible next door and brought all conversation to a stop. "What can he be doing now?" his father would say after a while, obviously turning towards the door, and only then would the interrupted conversation gradually be set going again.

Gregor was now informed as amply as he could wish — for his father tended to repeat himself in his explanations, partly because it was a long time since he had handled such matters and partly because his mother could not always grasp things at once — that a certain amount of investments, a very small amount it was true, had survived the wreck of their fortunes and had even increased a little because the dividends had not been touched meanwhile. And besides that, the money Gregor brought home every month — he had kept only a few dollars for himself — had never been quite used up and now amounted to a small capital sum. Behind the door Gregor nodded his head eagerly, rejoiced at this evidence of unexpected thrift and foresight. True, he could really have paid off some more of his father's debts to the chief with his extra money, and so brought much nearer the day on which he could quit his job, but doubtless it was better the way his father had arranged it.

Yet this capital was by no means sufficient to let the family live on the interest of it; for one year, perhaps, or at the most two, they could live on the principal, that was all. It was simply a sum that ought not to be touched and should be kept for a rainy day; money for living expenses would have to be earned. Now his father was still hale enough but an old man, and he had done no work for the past five years and could not be expected to do much; during these five years, the first years of leisure in his laborious though unsuccessful life, he had grown rather fat and become sluggish. And Gregor's old mother, how was she to earn a living with her asthma, which troubled her even when she walked through the flat and kept her lying on a sofa every other day panting for breath beside an open window? And was his sister to earn her bread, she who was still a child of seventeen and whose life hitherto had been so pleasant, consisting as it did in dressing herself nicely, sleeping long, helping in the housekeeping, going out to a few modest entertainments and above all playing the violin? At first whenever the need for earning money was mentioned Gregor let go his hold on the door and threw himself down on the cool leather sofa beside it, he felt so hot with shame and grief.

Often he just lay there the long nights through without sleeping at all, scrabbling for hours on the leather. Or he nerved himself to the great effort of pushing an armchair to the window, then crawled up over the window sill and, braced against the chair, leaned against the windowpanes, obviously in some recollection of the sense of freedom that looking out of a window always used to give him. For in reality day by day things that were even a little way off were growing dimmer to his sight; the hospital across the street, which he used to execrate for being all too often before his eyes, was now quite beyond his range of vision, and if he had not known that he lived in Charlotte Street, a quiet street but still a city street, he might have believed that his window gave on a desert waste where gray sky and gray land blended indistinguishably into each other. His quick-witted sister only needed to observe twice that the armchair stood by the window; after that whenever she had tidied the room she always pushed the chair back to the same place at the window and even left the inner casements open.

If he could have spoken to her and thanked her for all she had to do for him, he could have borne her ministrations better; as it was, they oppressed him. She certainly tried to make as light as possible of whatever was disagreeable in her task, and as time went on she succeeded, of course, more and more, but time brought more enlightenment to Gregor too. The very way she came in distressed him. Hardly was she in the room when she rushed to the window, without even taking time to shut the door, careful as she was usually to shield the sight of Gregor's room from the others, and as if she were almost suffocating tore the casements open with hasty fingers, standing then in the open draught for a while even in the bitterest cold and drawing deep breaths. This noisy scurry of hers upset Gregor twice a day; he would crouch trembling under the sofa all the time, knowing quite well that she would certainly have spared him such a disturbance had she found it at all possible to stay in his presence without opening a window.

On one occasion, about a month after Gregor's metamorphosis, when there was surely no reason for her to be still startled at his appearance, she came a little earlier than usual and found him gazing out of the window, quite motionless, and thus well placed to look like a bogey. Gregor would not have been surprised had she not come in at all, for she could not immediately open the window while he was there, but not only did she retreat, she jumped back as if in alarm and banged the door shut; a stranger might well have thought that he had been lying in wait for her there meaning to bite her. Of course he hid himself under the sofa at once, but he had to wait until midday before she came again, and she seemed more ill at ease than usual. This made him realize how repulsive the sight of him still was to her, and that it was bound to go on being repulsive, and what an effort it must cost her not to run away even from the sight of the small portion of his body that stuck out from under the sofa. In order to spare her that, therefore, one day he carried a sheet on his back to the sofa — it cost him four hours' labor — and arranged it there in such a way as to hide him completely, so that even if she were to bend down she could not see him. Had she considered the sheet unnecessary, she would certainly have stripped it off the sofa again, for it was clear enough that this curtaining and confining of himself was not likely to conduce Gregor's comfort, but she left it where it was, and Gregor even fancied that he caught a thankful glance from her eye when he lifted the sheet carefully a very little with his head to see how she was taking the new arrangement.

For the first fortnight his parents could not bring themselves to the point of entering his room, and he often heard them expressing their appreciation of his sister's activities, whereas formerly they had frequently scolded her for being as they thought a somewhat useless daughter. But now, both of them often waited outside the door, his father and his mother, while his sister tidied his room, and as soon as she came out she had to tell them exactly how things were in the room, what Gregor had eaten, how he had conducted himself this time and whether there was not perhaps some slight improvement in his condition. His mother, moreover, began relatively soon to want to visit him, but his father and sister dissuaded her at first with arguments which Gregor listened to very attentively and altogether approved. Later, however, she had to be held back by main force, and when she cried out: "Do let me in to Gregor, he is my unfortunate son! Can't you understand that I must go to him?" Gregor thought that it might be well to have her come in, not every day, of course, but perhaps once a week; she understood things, after all, much better than his sister, who was only a child despite the efforts she was making and had perhaps taken on so difficult a task merely out of childish thoughtlessness.

Gregor's desire to see his mother was soon fulfilled. During the daytime he did not want to show himself at the window, out of consideration for his parents, but he could not crawl very far around the few square yards of floor space he had, nor could he bear lying quietly at rest all during the night, while he was fast losing any interest he had ever taken in food, so that for mere recreation he had formed the habit of crawling crisscross over the walls and ceiling. He especially enjoyed hanging suspended from the ceiling; it was much better than lying on the floor; one could breathe more freely; one's body swung and rocked lightly; and in the almost blissful absorption induced by this suspension it could happen to his own surprise that he let go and fell plump on the floor. Yet he now had his body much better under control than formerly, and even such a big fall did him no harm. His sister at once remarked the new distraction Gregor had found for himself — he left traces behind him of the sticky stuff on his soles wherever he crawled — and she got the idea in her head of giving him as wide a field as possible to crawl in and of removing the pieces of furniture that hindered him, above all the chest of drawers and the writing desk. But that was more than she could manage all by herself; she did not dare ask her father to help her; and as for the servant girl, a young creature of sixteen who had had the courage to stay on after the cook's departure, she could not be asked to help, for she had begged as an especial favor that she might keep the kitchen door locked and open it only on a definite summons; so there was nothing left but to apply to her mother at an hour when her father was out. And the old lady did come, with exclamations of joyful eagerness, which, however, died away at the door of Gregor's room. Gregor's sister, of course, went in first, to see that everything was in order before letting his mother enter. In great haste Gregor pulled the sheet lower and rucked it more in folds so that it really looked as if it had been thrown accidentally over the sofa. And this time he did not peer out from under it; he renounced the pleasure of seeing his mother on this occasion and was only glad that she had come at all. "Come in, he's out of sight," said his sister, obviously leading her mother in by the hand. Gregor could now hear the two women struggling to shift the heavy old chest from its place, and his sister claiming the greater part of the labor for herself, without listening to the admonitions of her mother who feared she might overstrain herself. It took a long time. After at least a quarter of an hour's tugging his mother objected that the chest had better be left where it was, for in the first place it was too heavy and could never be got out before his father came home, and standing in the middle of the room like that it would only hamper Gregor's movements, while in the second place it was not at all certain that removing the furniture would be doing a service to Gregor. She was inclined to think to the contrary; the sight of the naked walls made her own heart heavy, and why shouldn't Gregor have the same feeling, considering that he had been used to his furniture for so long and might feel forlorn without it. "And doesn't it look," she concluded in a low voice — in fact she had been almost whispering all the time as if to avoid letting Gregor, whose exact whereabouts she did not know, hear even the tones of her voice, for she was convinced that he could not understand her words — "doesn't it look as if we were showing him, by taking away his furniture, that we have given up hope of his ever getting better and are just leaving him coldly to himself? I think it would be best to keep his room exactly as it has always been, so that when he comes back to us he will find everything unchanged and be able all the more easily to forget what has happened in between."

On hearing these words from his mother Gregor realized that the lack of all direct human speech for the past two months together with the monotony of family life must have confused his mind, otherwise he could not account for the fact that he had quite earnestly looked forward to having his room emptied of furnishing. Did he really want his warm room, so comfortably fitted with old family furniture, to be turned into a naked den in which he would certainly be able to crawl unhampered in all directions but at the price of shedding simultaneously all recollection of his human background? He had indeed been so near the brink of forgetfulness that only the voice of his mother, which he had not heard for so long, had drawn him back from it. Nothing should be taken out of his room; everything must stay as it was; he could not dispense with the good influence of the furniture on his state of mind; and even if the furniture did hamper him in his senseless crawling round and round, that was no drawback but a great advantage.

Unfortunately his sister was of the contrary opinion; she had grown accustomed, and not without reason, to consider herself an expert in Gregor's affairs as against her parents, and so her mother's advice was now enough to make her determined on the removal not only of the chest and the writing desk, which had been her first intention, but of all the furniture except the indispensable sofa. This determination was not, of course, merely the outcome of childish recalcitrance and of the self-confidence she had recently developed so unexpectedly and at such cost; she had in fact perceived that Gregor needed a lot of space to crawl about in, while on the other hand he never used the furniture at all, so far as could be seen. Another factor might have been also the enthusiastic temperament of an adolescent girl, which seeks to indulge itself on every opportunity and which now tempted Grete to exaggerate the horror of her brother's circumstances in order that she might do all the more for him. In a room where Gregor lorded it all alone over empty walls no one save herself was likely ever to set foot.

And so she was not to be moved from her resolve by her mother who seemed moreover to be ill at ease in Gregor's room and therefore unsure of herself, was soon reduced to silence and helped her daughter as best she could to push the chest outside. Now, Gregor could do without the chest, if need be, but the writing desk he must retain. As soon as the two women had got the chest out of his room, groaning as they pushed it, Gregor stuck his head out from under the sofa to see how he might intervene as kindly and cautiously as possible. But as bad luck would have it, his mother was the first to return, leaving Grete clasping the chest in the room next door where she was trying to shift it all by herself, without of course moving it from the spot. His mother however was not accustomed to the sight of him, it might sicken her and so in alarm Gregor backed quickly to the other end of the sofa, yet could not prevent the sheet from swaying a little in front. That was enough to put her on the alert. She paused, stood still for a moment and then went back to Grete.

Although Gregor kept reassuring himself that nothing out of the way was happening, but only a few bits of furniture were being changed round, he soon had to admit that all this trotting to and fro of the two women, their little ejaculations and the scraping of furniture along the floor affected him like a vast disturbance coming from all sides at once, and however much he tucked in his head and legs and cowered to the very floor he was bound to confess that he would not be able to stand it for long. They were clearing his room out; taking away everything he loved; the chest in which he kept his fret saw and other tools was already dragged off; they were now loosening the writing desk which had almost sunk into the floor, the desk at which he had done all his homework when he was at the commercial academy, at the grammar school before that, and, yes, even at the primary school — he had no more time to waste in weighing the good intentions of the two women, whose existence he had by now almost forgotten, for they were so exhausted that they were laboring in silence and nothing could be heard but the heavy scuffling of their feet.

And so he rushed out — the women were just leaning against the writing desk in the next room to give themselves a breather — and four times changed his direction, since he really did not know what to rescue first, then on the wall opposite, which was already otherwise cleared, he was struck by the picture of the lady muffled in so much fur and quickly crawled up to it and pressed himself to the glass, which was a good surface to hold on to and comforted his hot belly. This picture at least, which was entirely hidden beneath him, was going to be removed by nobody. He turned his head towards the door of the living room so as to observe the women when they came back.

They had not allowed themselves much of a rest and were already coming; Grete had twined her arm round her mother and was almost supporting her. "Well, what shall we take now?" said Grete, looking round. Her eyes met Gregor's from the wall. She kept her composure, presumably because of her mother, bent her head down to her mother, to keep her from looking up, and said, although in a fluttering, unpremeditated voice: "Come, hadn't we better go back to the living room for a moment?" Her intentions were clear enough to Gregor, she wanted to bestow her mother in safety and then chase him down from the wall. Well, just let her try it! He clung to his picture and would not give it up. He would rather fly in Grete's face.

But Grete's words had succeeded in disquieting her mother, who took a step to one side, caught sight of the huge brown mass on the flowered wallpaper, and before she was really conscious that what she saw was Gregor screamed in a loud, hoarse voice: "Oh God, oh God!" fell with outspread arms over the sofa as if giving up and did not move. "Gregor!" cried his sister, shaking her fist and glaring at him. This was the first time she had directly addressed him since his metamorphosis. She ran into the next room for some aromatic essence with which to rouse her mother from her fainting fit. Gregor wanted to help too — there was still time to rescue the picture — but he was stuck fast to the glass and had to tear himself loose; he then ran after his sister into the next room as if he could advise her, as he used to do; but then had to stand helplessly behind her; she meanwhile searched among various small bottles and when she turned round started in alarm at the sight of him; one bottle fell on the floor and broke; a splinter of glass cut Gregor's face and some kind of corrosive medicine splashed him; without pausing a moment longer Grete gathered up all the bottles she could carry and ran to her mother with them; she banged the door shut with her foot. Gregor was now cut off from his mother, who was perhaps nearly dying because of him; he dared not open the door for fear of frightening away his sister, who had to stay with her mother; there was nothing he could do but wait; and harassed by self-reproach and worry he began now to crawl to and fro, over everything, walls, furniture and ceiling, and finally in his despair, when the whole room seemed to be reeling round him, fell down onto the middle of the big table.

A little while elapsed, Gregor was still lying there feebly and all around was quiet, perhaps that was a good omen. Then the doorbell rang. The servant girl was of course locked in her kitchen, and Grete would have to open the door. It was his father. "What's been happening?" were his first words; Grete's face must have told him everything. Grete answered in a muffled voice, apparently hiding her head on his breast: "Mother has been fainting, but she's better now. Gregor's broken loose." "Just what I expected," said his father, "just what I've been telling you, but you women would never listen." It was clear to Gregor that his father had taken the worst interpretation of Grete's all too brief statement and was assuming that Gregor had been guilty of some violent act. Therefore Gregor must now try to propitiate his father, since he had neither time nor means for an explanation. And so he fled to the door of his own room and crouched against it, to let his father see as soon as he came in from the hall that his son had the good intention of getting back into his room immediately and that it was not necessary to drive him there, but that if only the door were opened he would disappear at once.

Yet his father was not in the mood to perceive such fine distinctions. "Ah!" he cried as soon as he appeared, in a tone which sounded at once angry and exultant. Gregor drew his head back from the door and lifted it to look at his father. Truly, this was not the father he had imagined to himself; admittedly he had been too absorbed of late in his new recreation of crawling over the ceiling to take the same interest as before in what was happening elsewhere in the flat, and he ought really to be prepared for some changes. And yet, and yet, could that be his father? The man who used to lie wearily sunk in bed whenever Gregor set out on a business journey; who welcomed him back of an evening lying in a long chair in a dressing gown; who could not really rise to his feet but only lifted his arms in greeting, and on the rare occasions when he did go out with his family, on one or two Sundays a year and on high holidays, walked between Gregor and his mother, who were slow walkers anyhow, even more slowly than they did, muffled in his old greatcoat, shuffling laboriously forward with the help of his crook-handled stick which he set down most cautiously at every step and, whenever he wanted to say anything, nearly always came to a full stop and gathered his escort around him? Now he was standing there in fine shape; dressed in a smart blue uniform with gold buttons, such as bank messengers wear; his strong double chin bulged over the stiff high collar of his jacket; from under his bushy eyebrows his black eyes darted fresh and penetrating glances; his onetime tangled white hair had been combed flat on either side of a shining and carefully exact parting. He pitched his cap, which bore a gold monogram, probably the badge of some bank, in a wide sweep across the whole room on to a sofa and with the tail-ends of his jacket thrown back, his hands in his trouser pockets, advanced with a grim visage towards Gregor. Likely enough he did not himself know what he meant to do; at any rate he lifted his feet uncommonly high, and Gregor was dumbfounded at the enormous size of his shoe soles. But Gregor could not risk standing up to him, aware as he had been from the very first day of his new life that his father believed only the severest measures suitable for dealing with him. And so he ran before his father, stopping when he stopped and scuttling forward again when his father made any kind of move. In this way they circled the room several times without anything decisive happening; indeed the whole operation did not even look like a pursuit because it was carried out so slowly. And so Gregor did not leave the floor, for he feared that his father might take as a piece of peculiar wickedness any excursion of his over the walls or the ceiling. All the same, he could not stay this course much longer, for while his father took one step he had to carry out a whole series of movements. He was already beginning to feel breathless, just as in his former life his lungs had not been very dependable. As he was staggering along, trying to concentrate his energy on running, hardly keeping his eyes open; in his dazed state never even thinking of any other escape than simply going forward; and having almost forgotten that the walls were free to him, which in this room were well provided with finely carved pieces of furniture full of knobs and crevices — suddenly something lightly flung landed close behind him and rolled before him. It was an apple; a second apple followed immediately; Gregor came to a stop in alarm; there was no point in running on, for his father was determined to bombard him. He had filled his pockets with fruit from the dish on the sideboard and was now shying apple after apple, without taking particularly good aim for the moment. The small red apples rolled about the floor as if magnetized and cannoned into each other. An apple thrown without much force grazed Gregor's back and glanced off harmlessly. But another following immediately landed right on his back and sank in; Gregor wanted to drag himself forward, as if this startling, incredible pain could be left behind him: but he felt as if nailed to the spot and flattened himself out in a complete derangement of all his senses. With his last conscious look he saw the door of his room being torn open and his mother rushing out ahead of his screaming sister, in her underbodice, for her daughter had loosened her clothing to let her breathe more freely and recover from her swoon, he saw his mother rushing towards his father, leaving one after another behind her on the floor her loosened petticoats, stumbling over her petticoats straight to his father and embracing him, in complete union with him — but here Gregor's sight began to fail — with her hands clasped round his father's neck as she begged for her son's life.

III

The serious injury done to Gregor, which disabled him for more than a month — the apple went on sticking in his body as a visible reminder, since no one ventured to remove it — seemed to have made even his father recollect that Gregor was a member of the family, despite his present unfortunate and repulsive shape, and ought not to be treated as an enemy, that, on the contrary, family duty required the suppression of disgust and the exercise of patience, nothing but patience.

And although his injury had impaired, probably forever, his power of movement, and for the time being it took him long, long minutes to creep across his room like an old invalid — there was no question now of crawling up the wall — yet in his own opinion he was sufficiently compensated for this worsening of his condition by the fact that towards evening the living-room door, which he used to watch intently for an hour or two beforehand, was always thrown open, so that lying in the darkness of his room, invisible to the family, he could see them all at the lamp-lit table and listen to their talk, by general consent as it were, very different from his earlier eavesdropping.

True, their intercourse lacked the lively character of former times, which he had always called to mind with a certain wistfulness in the small hotel bedrooms where he had been wont to throw himself down, tired out, on damp bedding. They were now mostly very silent. Soon after supper his father would fall asleep in his armchair; his mother and sister would admonish each other to be silent; his mother, bending low over the lamp, stitched at fine sewing for an underwear firm; his sister, who had taken a job as a salesgirl, was learning shorthand and French in the evenings on the chance of bettering herself. Sometimes his father woke up, and as if quite unaware that he had been sleeping said to his mother: "What a lot of sewing you're doing today!" and at once fell asleep again, while the two women exchanged a tired smile.

With a kind of mulishness his father persisted in keeping his uniform on even in the house; his dressing gown hung uselessly on its peg and he slept fully dressed where he sat, as if he were ready for service at any moment and even here only at the beck and call of his superior. As a result, his uniform, which was not brand-new to start with, began to look dirty, despite all the loving care of the mother and sister to keep it clean, and Gregor often spent whole evenings gazing at the many greasy spots on the garment, gleaming with gold buttons always in a high state of polish, in which the old man sat sleeping in extreme discomfort and yet quite peacefully.

As soon as the clock struck ten his mother tried to rouse his father with gentle words and to persuade him after that to get into bed, for sitting there he could not have a proper sleep and that was what he needed most, since he had to go to duty at six. But with the mulishness that had obsessed him since he became a bank messenger he always insisted on staying longer at the table, although he regularly fell asleep again and in the end only with the greatest trouble could be got out of his armchair and into his bed. However insistently Gregor's mother and sister kept urging him with gentle reminders, he would go on slowly shaking his head for a quarter of an hour, keeping his eyes shut, and refuse to get to his feet. The mother plucked at his sleeve, whispering endearments in his ear, the sister left her lessons to come to her mother's help, but Gregor's father was not to be caught. He would only sink down deeper in his chair. Not until the two women hoisted him up by the armpits did he open his eyes and look at them both, one after the other, usually with the remark:

"This is a life. This is the peace and quiet of my old age." And leaning on the two of them he would heave himself up, with difficulty, as if he were a great burden to himself, suffer them to lead him as far as the door and then wave them off and go on alone, while the mother abandoned her needlework and the sister her pen in order to run after him and help him farther.

Who could find time, in this overworked and tired-out family, to bother about Gregor more than was absolutely needful? The household was reduced more and more; the servant girl was turned off; a gigantic bony charwoman with white hair flying round her head came in morning and evening to do the rough work; everything else was done by Gregor's mother, as well as great piles of sewing. Even various family ornaments, which his mother and sister used to wear with pride at parties and celebrations, had to be sold, as Gregor discovered of an evening from hearing them all discuss the prices obtained. But what they lamented most was the fact that they could not leave the flat which was much too big for their present circumstances, because they could not think of any way to shift Gregor. Yet Gregor saw well enough that consideration for him was not the main difficulty preventing the removal, for they could have easily shifted him in some suitable box with a few air holes in it; what really kept them from moving into another flat was rather their own complete hopelessness and the belief that they had been singled out for a misfortune such as had never happened to any of their relations or acquaintances. They fulfilled to the uttermost all that the world demands of poor people, the father fetched breakfast for the small clerks in the bank, the mother devoted her energy to making underwear for strangers, the sister trotted to and fro behind the counter at the behest of customers, but more than this they had not the strength to do. And the wound in Gregor's back began to nag at him afresh when his mother and sister, after getting his father into bed, came back again, left their work lying, drew close to each other and sat cheek by cheek; when his mother, pointing towards his room, said: "Shut that door now, Grete," and he was left again in darkness, while next door the women mingled their tears or perhaps sat dry-eyed staring at the table.

Gregor hardly slept at all by night or by day. He was often haunted by the idea that next time the door opened he would take the family's affairs in hand again just as he used to do; once more, after this long interval, there appeared in his thoughts the figures of the chief and the chief clerk, the commercial travelers and the apprentices, the porter who was so dull-witted, two or three friends in other firms, a chambermaid in one of the rural hotels, a sweet and fleeting memory, a cashier in a milliner's shop, whom he had wooed earnestly but too slowly — they all appeared, together with strangers or people he had quite forgotten, but instead of helping him and his family they were one and all unapproachable and he was glad when they vanished. At other times he would not be in the mood to bother about his family, he was only filled with rage at the way they were neglecting him, and although he had no clear idea of what he might care to eat he would make plans for getting into the larder to take the food that was after all his due, even if he were not hungry. His sister no longer took thought to bring him what might especially please him, but in the morning and at noon before she went to business hurriedly pushed into his room with her foot any food that was available, and in the evening cleared it out again with one sweep of the broom, heedless of whether it had been merely tasted, or — as most frequently happened — left untouched. The cleaning of his room, which she now did always in the evenings, could not have been more hastily done. Streaks of dirt stretched along the walls, here and there lay balls of dust and filth. At first Gregor used to station himself in some particularly filthy corner when his sister arrived, in order to reproach her with it, so to speak. But he could have sat there for weeks without getting her to make any improvements; she could see the dirt as well as he did, but she had simply made up her mind to leave it alone. And yet, with a touchiness that was new to her, which seemed anyhow to have infected the whole family, she jealously guarded her claim to be the sole caretaker of Gregor's room. His mother once subjected his room to a thorough cleaning, which was achieved only by means of several buckets of water — all this dampness of course upset Gregor too and he lay widespread, sulky and motionless on the sofa — but she was well punished for it. Hardly had his sister noticed the changed aspect of his room than she rushed in high dudgeon into the living room and, despite the imploringly raised hands of her mother, burst into a storm of weeping, while her parents — her father had of course been startled out of his chair — looked on at first in helpless amazement; then they too began to go into action; the father reproached the mother on his right for not having left the cleaning of Gregor's room to his sister; shrieked at the sister on his left that never again was she to be allowed to clean Gregor's room; while the mother tried to pull the father into his bedroom, since he was beyond himself with agitation; the sister, shaken with sobs, then beat upon the table with her small fists; and Gregor hissed loudly with rage because not one of them thought of shutting the door to spare him such a spectacle and so much noise.

Still, even if the sister, exhausted by her daily work, had grown tired of looking after Gregor as she did formerly, there was no need for his mother's intervention or for Gregor's being neglected at all. The charwoman was there. This old widow, whose strong bony frame had enabled her to survive the worst a long life could offer, by no means recoiled from Gregor. Without being in the least curious she had once by chance opened the door of his room and at the sight of Gregor, who, taken by surprise, began to rush to and fro although no one was chasing him, merely stood there with her arms folded. From that time she never failed to open his door a little for a moment, morning and evening, to have a look at him. At first she even used to call him to her, with words which apparently she took to be friendly, such as: "Come along, then, you old dung beetle!" or "Look at the old dung beetle, then!" To such allocutions Gregor made no answer, but stayed motionless where he was, as if the door had never been opened. Instead of being allowed to disturb him so senselessly whenever the whim took her, she should rather have been ordered to clean out his room daily, that charwoman! Once, early in the morning — heavy rain was lashing on the windowpanes, perhaps a sign that spring was on the way — Gregor was so exasperated when she began addressing him again that he ran at her, as if to attack her, although slowly and feebly enough. But the charwoman instead of showing fright merely lifted high a chair that happened to be beside the door, and as she stood there with her mouth wide open it was clear that she meant to shut it only when she brought the chair down on Gregor's back. "So you're not coming any nearer?" she asked, as Gregor turned away again, and quietly put the chair back into the corner.

Gregor was now eating hardly anything. Only when he happened to pass the food laid out for him did he take a bit of something in his mouth as a pastime, kept it there for an hour at a time and usually spat it out again. At first he thought it was chagrin over the state of his room that prevented him from eating, yet he soon got used to the various changes in his room. It had become a habit in the family to push into his room things there was no room for elsewhere, and there were plenty of these now, since one of the rooms had been let to three lodgers. These serious gentlemen — all three of them with full beards, as Gregor once observed through a crack in the door — had a passion for order, not only in their own room but, since they were now members of the household, in all its arrangements, especially in the kitchen. Superfluous, not to say dirty, objects they could not bear. Besides, they had brought with them most of the furnishings they needed. For this reason many things could be dispensed with that it was no use trying to sell but that should not be thrown away either. All of them found their way into Gregor's room. The ash can likewise and the kitchen garbage can. Anything that was not needed for the moment was simply flung into Gregor's room by the charwoman, who did everything in a hurry; fortunately Gregor usually saw only the object, whatever it was, and the hand that held it. Perhaps she intended to take the things away again as time and opportunity offered, or to collect them until she could throw them all out in a heap, but in fact they just lay wherever she happened to throw them, except when Gregor pushed his way through the junk heap and shifted it somewhat, at first out of necessity, because he had not room enough to crawl, but later with increasing enjoyment, although after such excursions, being sad and weary to death, he would lie motionless for hours. And since the lodgers often ate their supper at home in the common living room, the living room door stayed shut many an evening, yet Gregor reconciled himself quite easily to the shutting of the door, for often enough on evenings when it was opened he had disregarded it entirely and lain in the darkest corner of his room, quite unnoticed by the family. But on one occasion the charwoman left the door open a little and it stayed ajar even when the lodgers came in for supper and the lamp was lit. They set themselves at the top end of the table where formerly Gregor and his father and mother had eaten their meals, unfolded their napkins and took knife and fork in hand. At once his mother appeared in the other doorway with a dish of meat and close behind her his sister with a dish of potatoes piled high. The food steamed with a thick vapor. The lodgers bent over the food set before them as if to scrutinize it before eating, in fact the man in the middle, who seemed to pass for an authority with the other two, cut a piece of meat as it lay on the dish, obviously to discover if it were tender or should be sent back to the kitchen. He showed satisfaction, and Gregor's mother and sister, who had been watching anxiously, breathed freely and began to smile.

The family itself took its meals in the kitchen. Nonetheless, Gregor's father came into the living room before going in to the kitchen and with one prolonged bow, cap in hand, made a round of the table. The lodgers all stood up and murmured something in their beards. When they were alone again they ate their food in almost complete silence. It seemed remarkable to Gregor that among the various noises coming from the table he could always distinguish the sound of their masticating teeth, as if this were a sign to Gregor that one needed teeth in order to eat, and that with toothless jaws even of the finest make one could do nothing. "I'm hungry enough," said Gregor sadly to himself, "but not for that kind of food. How these lodgers are stuffing themselves, and here am I dying of starvation!"

On that very evening — during the whole of his time there Gregor could not remember ever having heard the violin — the sound of violin-playing came from the kitchen. The lodgers had already finished their supper, the one in the middle had brought out a newspaper and given the other two a page apiece, and now they were leaning back at ease reading and smoking. When the violin began to play they pricked up their ears, got to their feet, and went on tiptoe to the hall door where they stood huddled together. Their movements must have been heard in the kitchen, for Gregor's father called out: "Is the violin-playing disturbing you, gentlemen? It can be stopped at once." "On the contrary," said the middle lodger, "could not Fräulein Samsa come and play in this room, beside us, where it is much more convenient and comfortable?" "Oh certainly," cried Gregor's father, as if he were the violin-player. The lodgers came back into the living room and waited. Presently Gregor's father arrived with the music stand, his mother carrying the music and his sister with the violin. His sister quietly made everything ready to start playing; his parents, who had never let rooms before and so had an exaggerated idea of the courtesy due to lodgers, did not venture to sit down on their own chairs; his father leaned against the door, the right hand thrust between two buttons of his livery coat, which was formally buttoned up; but his mother was offered a chair by one of the lodgers and, since she left the chair just where he had happened to put it, sat down in a corner to one side.

Gregor's sister began to play; the father and mother, from either side, intently watched the movements of her hands. Gregor, attracted by the playing, ventured to move forward a little until his head was actually inside the living room. He felt hardly any surprise at his growing lack of consideration for the others; there had been a time when he prided himself on being considerate. And yet just on this occasion he had more reason than ever to hide himself, since owing to the amount of dust which lay thick in his room and rose into the air at the slightest movement, he too was covered with dust; fluff and hair and remnants of food trailed with him, caught on his back and along his sides; his indifference to everything was much too great for him to turn on his back and scrape himself clean on the carpet, as once he had done several times a day. And in spite of his condition, no shame deterred him from advancing a little over the spotless floor of the living room.

To be sure, no one was aware of him. The family was entirely absorbed in the violin-playing; the lodgers, however, who first of all had stationed themselves, hands in pockets, much too close behind the music stand so that they could all have read the music, which must have bothered his sister, had soon retreated to the window, half-whispering with downbent heads, and stayed there while his father turned an anxious eye on them. Indeed, they were making it more than obvious that they had been disappointed in their expectation of hearing good or enjoyable violin-playing, that they had had more than enough of the performance and only out of courtesy suffered a continued disturbance of their peace. From the way they all kept blowing the smoke of their cigars high in the air through nose and mouth one could divine their irritation. And yet Gregor's sister was playing so beautifully. Her face leaned sideways, intently and sadly her eyes followed the notes of music. Gregor crawled a little farther forward and lowered his head to the ground so that it might be possible for his eyes to meet hers. Was he an animal, that music had such an effect upon him? He felt as if the way were opening before him to the unknown nourishment he craved. He was determined to push forward till he reached his sister, to pull at her skirt and so let her know that she was to come into his room with her violin, for no one here appreciated her playing as he would appreciate it. He would never let her out of his room, at least, not so long as he lived; his frightful appearance would become, for the first time, useful to him; he would watch all the doors of his room at once and spit at intruders; but his sister should need no constraint, she should stay with him of her own free will; she should sit beside him on the sofa, bend down her ear to him and hear him confide that he had had the firm intention of sending her to the Conservatorium, and that, but for his mishap, last Christmas — surely Christmas was long past? — he would have announced it to everybody without allowing a single objection. After this confession his sister would be so touched that she would burst into tears, and Gregor would then raise himself to her shoulder and kiss her on the neck, which, now that she went to business, she kept free of any ribbon or collar.

"Mr. Samsa!" cried the middle lodger, to Gregor's father, and pointed, without wasting any more words, at Gregor, now working himself slowly forwards. The violin fell silent, the middle lodger first smiled to his friends with a shake of the head and then looked at Gregor again. Instead of driving Gregor out, his father seemed to think it more needful to begin by soothing down the lodgers, although they were not at all agitated and apparently found Gregor more entertaining than the violin-playing. He hurried toward them and, spreading out his arms, tried to urge them back into their own room and at the same time to block their view of Gregor. They now began to be really a little angry, one could not tell whether because of the old man's behavior or because it had just dawned on them that all unwittingly they had such a neighbor as Gregor next door. They demanded explanations of his father, they waved their arms like him, tugged uneasily at their beards, and only with reluctance backed towards their room. Meanwhile Gregor's sister, who stood there as if lost when her playing was so abruptly broken off, came to life again, pulled herself together all at once after standing for a while holding violin and bow in nervelessly hanging hands and staring at her music, pushed her violin into the lap of her mother, who was still sitting in her chair fighting asthmatically for breath, and ran into the lodgers' room to which they were now being shepherded by her father rather more quickly than before. One could see the pillows and blankets on the beds flying under her accustomed fingers and being laid in order. Before the lodgers had actually reached their room she had finished making the beds and slipped out.

The old man seemed once more to be so possessed by his mulish self-assertiveness that he was forgetting all the respect he should show to his lodgers. He kept driving them on and driving them on until in the very door of the bedroom the middle lodger stamped his foot loudly on the floor and so brought him to a halt. "I beg to announce," said the lodger, lifting one hand and looking also at Gregor's mother and sister, "that because of the disgusting conditions prevailing in this household and family" — here he spat on the floor with emphatic brevity — "I give you notice on the spot. Naturally I won't pay you a penny for the days I have lived here, on the contrary I shall consider bringing an action for damages against you, based on claims — believe me — that will be easily susceptible of proof." He ceased and stared straight in front of him, as if he expected something. In fact his two friends at once rushed into the breach with these words: "And we too give notice on the spot." On that he seized the door-handle and shut the door with a slam.

Gregor's father, groping with his hands, staggered forward and fell into his chair; it looked as if he were stretching himself there for his ordinary evening nap, but the marked jerkings of his head, which was as if uncontrollable, showed that he was far from asleep. Gregor had simply stayed quietly all the time on the spot where the lodgers had espied him. Disappointment at the failure of his plan, perhaps also the weakness arising from extreme hunger, made it impossible for him to move. He feared, with a fair degree of certainty, that at any moment the general tension would discharge itself in a combined attack upon him, and he lay waiting. He did not react even to the noise made by the violin as it fell off his mother's lap from under her trembling fingers and gave out a resonant note.

"My dear parents," said his sister, slapping her hand on the table by way of introduction, "things can't go on like this. Perhaps you don't realize that, but I do. I won't utter my brother's name in the presence of this creature, and so all I say is: we must try to get rid of it. We've tried to look after it and to put up with it as far as is humanly possible, and I don't think anyone could reproach us in the slightest."

"She is more than right," said Gregor's father to himself. His mother, who was still choking for lack of breath, began to cough hollowly into her hand with a wild look in her eyes.

His sister rushed over to her and held her forehead. His father's thoughts seemed to have lost their vagueness at Grete's words, he sat more upright, fingering his service cap that lay among the plates still lying on the table from the lodgers' supper, and from time to time looked at the still form of Gregor.

"We must try to get rid of it," his sister now said explicitly to her father, since her mother was coughing too much to hear a word, "it will be the death of both of you, I can see that coming. When one has to work as hard as we do, all of us, one can't stand this continual torment at home on top of it. At least I can't stand it any longer." And she burst into such a passion of sobbing that her tears dropped on her mother's face, where she wiped them off mechanically.

"My dear," said the old man sympathetically, and with evident understanding, "but what can we do?"

Gregor's sister merely shrugged her shoulders to indicate the feeling of helplessness that had now overmastered her during her weeping fit, in contrast to her former confidence.

"If he could understand us," said her father, half questioningly; Grete, still sobbing, vehemently waved a hand to show how unthinkable that was.

"If he could understand us," repeated the old man, shutting his eyes to consider his daughter's conviction that understanding was impossible, "then perhaps we might come to some agreement with him. But as it is —"

"He must go," cried Gregor's sister. "That's the only solution, Father. You must just try to get rid of the idea that this is Gregor. The fact that we've believed it for so long is the root of all our trouble. But how can it be Gregor? If this were Gregor, he would have realized long ago that human beings can't live with such a creature, and he'd have gone away on his own accord. Then we wouldn't have any brother, but we'd be able to go on living and keep his memory in honor. As it is, this creature persecutes us, drives away our lodgers, obviously wants the whole apartment to himself and would have us all sleep in the gutter. Just look, Father," she shrieked all at once, "he's at it again!" And in an access of panic that was quite incomprehensible to Gregor she even quitted her mother, literally thrusting the chair from her as if she would rather sacrifice her mother than stay so near to Gregor, and rushed behind her father, who also rose up, being simply upset by her agitation, and half-spread his arms out as if to protect her.

Yet Gregor had not the slightest intention of frightening anyone, far less his sister. He had only begun to turn round in order to crawl back to his room, but it was certainly a startling operation to watch, since because of his disabled condition he could not execute the difficult turning movements except by lifting his head and then bracing it against the floor over and over again. He paused and looked round. His good intentions seemed to have been recognized; the alarm had only been momentary. Now they were all watching him in melancholy silence. His mother lay in her chair, her legs stiffly outstretched and pressed together, her eyes almost closing for sheer weariness; his father and his sister were sitting beside each other, his sister's arm around the old man's neck.

Perhaps I can go on turning round now, thought Gregor, and began his labors again. He could not stop himself from panting with the effort, and had to pause now and then to take breath. Nor did anyone harass him, he was left entirely to himself. When he had completed the turn-round he began at once to crawl straight back. He was amazed at the distance separating him from his room and could not understand how in his weak state he had managed to accomplish the same journey so recently, almost without remarking it. Intent on crawling as fast as possible, he barely noticed that not a single word, not an ejaculation from his family, interfered with his progress. Only when he was already in the doorway did he turn his head round, not completely, for his neck muscles were getting stiff, but enough to see that nothing had changed behind him except that his sister had risen to her feet. His last glance fell on his mother, who was not quite overcome by sleep.

Hardly was he well inside his room when the door was hastily pushed shut, bolted, and locked. The sudden noise in his rear startled him so much that his little legs gave beneath him. It was his sister who had shown such haste. She had been standing ready waiting and had made a light spring forward, Gregor had not even heard her coming, and she cried "At last!" to her parents as she turned the key in the lock.

"And what now?" said Gregor to himself, looking round in the darkness. Soon he made the discovery that he was now unable to stir a limb. This did not surprise him, rather it seemed unnatural that he should ever actually have been able to move on these feeble little legs. Otherwise he felt relatively comfortable. True, his whole body was aching, but it seemed that the pain was gradually growing less and would finally pass away. The rotting apple in his back and the inflamed area around it, all covered with soft dust, already hardly troubled him. He thought of his family with tenderness and love. The decision that he must disappear was one that he held to even more strongly than his sister, if that were possible. In this state of vacant and peaceful meditation he remained until the tower clock struck three in the morning. The first broadening of light in the world outside the window entered his consciousness once more. Then his head sank to the floor of its own accord and from his nostrils came the last faint flicker of his breath.

When the charwoman arrived early in the morning — what between her strength and her impatience she slammed all the doors so loudly, never mind how often she had been begged not to do so, that no one in the whole apartment could enjoy any quiet sleep after her arrival — she noticed nothing unusual as she took her customary peep into Gregor's room. She thought he was lying motionless on purpose, pretending to be in the sulks; she credited him with every kind of intelligence. Since she happened to have the long-handled broom in her hand she tried to tickle him up with it from the doorway. When that too produced no reaction she felt provoked and poked at him a little harder, and only when she had pushed him along the floor without meeting any resistance was her attention aroused. It did not take her long to establish the truth of the matter, and her eyes widened, she let out a whistle, yet did not waste much time over it but tore open the door of the Samsas' bedroom and yelled into the darkness at the top of her voice: "Just look at this, it's dead; it's lying here dead and done for!"

Mr. and Mrs. Samsa started up in their double bed and before they realized the nature of the charwoman's announcement had some difficulty in overcoming the shock of it. But then they got out of bed quickly, one on either side, Mr. Samsa throwing a blanket over his shoulders, Mrs. Samsa in nothing but her nightgown; in this array they entered Gregor's room. Meanwhile the door of the living room opened, too, where Grete had been sleeping since the advent of the lodgers; she was completely dressed as if she had not been to bed, which seemed to be confirmed also by the paleness of her face. "Dead?" said Mrs. Samsa, looking questioningly at the charwoman, although she could have investigated for herself, and the fact was obvious enough without investigation. "I should say so," said the charwoman, proving her words by pushing Gregor's corpse a long way to one side with her broomstick. Mrs. Samsa made a movement as if to stop her, but checked it. "Well," said Mr. Samsa, "now thanks be to God." He crossed himself, and the three women followed his example. Grete, whose eyes never left the corpse, said: "Just see how thin he was. It's such a long time since he's eaten anything. The food came out again just as it went in." Indeed, Gregor's body was completely flat and dry, as could only now be seen when it was no longer supported by the legs and nothing prevented one from looking closely at it.

"Come in beside us, Grete, for a little while," said Mrs. Samsa with a tremulous smile, and Grete, not without looking back at the corpse, followed her parents into their bedroom. The charwoman shut the door and opened the window wide. Although it was so early in the morning a certain softness was perceptible in the fresh air. After all, it was already the end of March.

The three lodgers emerged from their room and were surprised to see no breakfast; they had been forgotten. "Where's our breakfast?" said the middle lodger peevishly to the charwoman. But she put her finger to her lips and hastily, without a word, indicated by gestures that they should go into Gregor's room. They did so and stood, their hands in the pockets of their somewhat shabby coats, around Gregor's corpse in the room where it was now fully light.

At that the door of the Samsas' bedroom opened and Mr. Samsa appeared in his uniform, his wife on one arm, his daughter on the other. They all looked a little as if they had been crying; from time to time Grete hid her face on her father's arm.

"Leave my house at once!" said Mr. Samsa, and pointed to the door without disengaging himself from the women. "What do you mean by that?" said the middle lodger, taken somewhat aback, with a feeble smile. The two others put their hands behind them and kept rubbing them together, as if in gleeful expectation of a fine set-to in which they were bound to come off the winners. "I mean just what I say," answered Mr. Samsa, and advanced in a straight line with his two companions towards the lodger. He stood his ground at first quietly, looking at the floor as if his thoughts were taking a new pattern in his head. "Then let us go, by all means," he said, and looked up at Mr. Samsa as if in a sudden access of humility he were expecting some renewed sanction for this decision. Mr. Samsa merely nodded briefly once or twice with meaning eyes. Upon that the lodger really did go with long strides into the hall, his two friends had been listening and had quite stopped rubbing their hands for some moments and now went scuttling after him as if afraid that Mr. Samsa might get into the hall before them and cut them off from their leader. In the hall they all three took their hats from the rack, their sticks from the umbrella stand, bowed in silence and quitted the apartment. With a suspiciousness which proved quite unfounded Mr. Samsa and the two women followed them out to the landing; leaning over the banister they watched the three figures slowly but surely going down the long stairs, vanishing from sight at a certain turn of the staircase on every floor and coming into view again after a moment or so; the more they dwindled, the more the

Samsa family's interest in them dwindled, and when a butcher's boy met them and passed them on the stairs coming up proudly with a tray on his head, Mr. Samsa and the two women soon left the landing and as if a burden had been lifted from them went back into their apartment.

They decided to spend this day in resting and going for a stroll; they had not only deserved such a respite from work but absolutely needed it. And so they sat down at the table and wrote three notes of excuse, Mr. Samsa to his board of management, Mrs. Samsa to her employer and Grete to the head of her firm. While they were writing, the charwoman came in to say that she was going now, since her morning's work was finished. At first they only nodded without looking up, but as she kept hovering there they eyed her irritably. "Well?" said Mr. Samsa. The charwoman stood grinning in the doorway as if she had good news to impart to the family but meant not to say a word unless properly questioned. The small ostrich feather standing upright on her hat, which had annoyed Mr. Samsa ever since she was engaged, was waving gaily in all directions. "Well, what is it then?" asked Mrs. Samsa, who obtained more respect from the charwoman than the others. "Oh," said the charwoman, giggling so amiably that she could not at once continue, "just this, you don't need to bother about how to get rid of the thing next door. It's been seen to already." Mrs. Samsa and Grete bent over their letters again, as if preoccupied; Mr. Samsa, who perceived that she was eager to begin describing it all in detail, stopped her with a decisive hand. But since she was not allowed to tell her story, she remembered the great hurry she was in, being obviously deeply huffed: "Bye, everybody," she said, whirling off violently, and departed with a frightful slamming of doors.

"She'll be given notice tonight," said Mr. Samsa, but neither from his wife nor his daughter did he get any answer, for the charwoman seemed to have shattered again the composure they had barely achieved. They rose, went to the window and stayed there, clasping each other tight. Mr. Samsa turned in his chair to look at them and quietly observed them for a little. Then he called out: "Come along, now, do. Let bygones be bygones. And you might have some consideration for me." The two of them complied at once, hastened to him, caressed him and quickly finished their letters.

Then they all three left the apartment together, which was more than they had done for months, and went by tram into the open country outside the town. The tram, in which they were the only passengers, was filled with warm sunshine. Leaning comfortably back in their seats they canvassed their prospects for the future, and it appeared on closer inspection that these were not at all bad, for the jobs they had got, which so far they had never really discussed with each other, were all three admirable and likely to lead to better things later on. The greatest immediate improvement in their condition would of course arise from moving to another house; they wanted to take a smaller and cheaper but also better situated and more easily run apartment than the one they had, which Gregor had selected. While they were thus conversing, it struck both Mr. and Mrs. Samsa, almost at the same moment, as they became aware of their daughter's increasing vivacity, that in spite of all the sorrow of recent times, which had made her cheeks pale, she had bloomed into a pretty girl with a good figure. They grew quieter and half unconsciously exchanged glances of complete agreement, having come to the conclusion that it would soon be time to find a good husband for her. And it was like a confirmation of their new dreams and excellent intentions that at the end of their journey their daughter sprang to her feet first and stretched her young body.

ꕥ

JAMAICA KINCAID *(b. 1949) was born and educated in St. Johns, Antigua, in the West Indies. Her father was a carpenter, and her family doted upon her, the only child. Kincaid remembers:*

> *My mother did keep everything I ever wore, and basically until I was quite grown up my past was sort of a museum to me. Clearly, the way I became a writer was that my mother wrote my life for me and told it to me. I can't help but think that it made me interested in the idea of myself as an object. I can't account for the reason I became a writer any other way, because I certainly didn't know writers. And not only that. I thought writing was something that people just didn't do anymore, that went out of fashion, like the bustle. I really didn't read a book that was written in the twentieth century until I was about seventeen and away from home.*

Kincaid left Antigua to study in the United States, but she found college "a dismal failure," so she educated herself. She began writing and published her stories in Rolling Stone, *the* Paris Review, *and* The New Yorker, *where she became a staff writer in 1978. Six years later she published her first book,* At the Bottom of the River, *a collection of stories, which won the Morton Dauwen Zabel Award of the American Academy and Institute of Arts and Letters. In 1985* Annie John, *her book of interrelated stories about a girl's coming of age in the West Indies, was also much praised. In her autobiographical writing, Kincaid often explores the idea that her deep affection for her family and her native country developed into a conflicting need for separation and independence as she grew up.*

Typically Kincaid writes in a deliberately precise rhythmic style about intense emotions, as in her story "Girl" (1978). Her fiction is free from conventional plots, characters, and dialogue. The critic Suzanne Freeman has recognized that "what Kincaid has to tell me, she tells, with her singsong style, in a series of images that are as sweet and mysterious as the secrets that children whisper in your ear." Although Kincaid is married to an American and lives in Vermont, she feels that the British West Indies will continue to be the source for her fiction. "What I really feel about America is that it's given me a place to be myself — but myself as I was formed somewhere else." A Small Place *(1988), another book about the West Indies, was described by the novelist Salman Rushdie as "a jeremiad of great clarity and a force that one might have called torrential were the language not so finely controlled." Her latest books are* Lucy *(1990),* The Autobiography of My Mother *(1996), and* My Brother *(1997).*

JAMAICA KINCAID

Girl

1978

Wash the white clothes on Monday and put them on the stone heap; wash the color clothes on Tuesday and put them on the clothesline to dry; don't walk barehead in the hot sun; cook pumpkin fritters in very hot sweet oil; soak your little cloths right after you take them off; when buying cotton to make yourself a nice blouse, be sure that it doesn't have gum on it, because that way it won't hold up well after a wash; soak salt fish overnight before you cook it; is it true that you sing benna° in Sunday school?; always eat your food in such a way that it won't turn someone else's stomach; on Sundays try to walk like a lady and not like the slut you are so bent on becoming; don't sing benna in Sunday school; you mustn't speak to wharf-rat boys, not even to give directions; don't eat fruits on the street — flies will follow you; *but I don't sing benna on Sundays at all and never in Sunday school;* this is how to sew on a button; this is how to make a button-hole for the button you have just sewed on; this is how to hem a dress when you see the hem coming down and so to prevent yourself from looking like the slut I know you are so bent on becoming; this is how you iron your father's khaki shirt so that it doesn't have a crease; this is how you iron your father's khaki pants so that they don't have a crease; this is how you grow okra — far from the house, because okra tree harbors red ants; when you are growing dasheen, make sure it gets plenty of water or else it makes your throat itch when you are eating it; this is how you sweep a corner; this is how you sweep a whole house; this is how you sweep a yard; this is how you smile to someone you don't like too much; this is how you smile to someone you don't like at all; this is how you smile to someone you like completely; this is how you set a table for tea; this is how you set a table for dinner; this is how you set a table for dinner with an important guest; this is how you set a table for lunch; this is how you set a table for breakfast; this is how to behave in the presence of men who don't know you very well, and this way they won't recognize immediately the slut I have warned you against becoming; be sure to wash every day, even if it is with your own spit; don't squat down to play marbles — you are not a boy, you know; don't pick people's flowers — you might catch something; don't throw stones at blackbirds, because it might not be a blackbird at all; this is how to make a bread pudding; this is how to make doukona;° this is how to make pepper pot; this is how to make a good medicine for a cold; this is how to make a good medicine to throw away a child before it even becomes a child; this is how to catch a fish; this is how to throw back a fish you don't like, and that way something bad won't fall on you; this is how to bully a man; this is how a man bullies you; this is how to love a man, and if this doesn't work there are other ways, and if they don't work don't feel too bad about giving up; this is how to spit up in

---

benna: Calypso music.
doukona: A spicy plantain pudding.

the air if you feel like it, and this is how to move quick so that it doesn't fall on you; this is how to make ends meet; always squeeze bread to make sure it's fresh; *but what if the baker won't let me feel the bread?*; you mean to say that after all you are really going to be the kind of woman who the baker won't let near the bread?

ꙮ

DAVID HERBERT LAWRENCE *(1885–1930) was born the son of a coal miner in the industrial town of Eastwood, in Nottinghamshire, England. His mother had been a schoolteacher, and she was frustrated by the hard existence of a coal miner's wife. Through her financial sacrifices, Lawrence was able to complete high school; then he studied to become a teacher. He finished his university studies and was licensed as a teacher at the age of twenty-three. Moving to South London, he allied himself with the young literary rebels there, and his first novel,* The White Peacock, *was published in 1910. In 1912 Lawrence fell in love with an older married woman, Frieda von Richthofen, who abandoned her husband and children to run off with him to her native Germany. English society never forgave either of them, although the pair eventually married in 1914 and maintained their exceedingly stormy union, punctuated with frequent affairs, until Lawrence's death. In 1913, Lawrence was established as a major literary figure with the publication of* Sons and Lovers.

Much of his fiction is about characters caught between their unsatisfactory relationships with others and their struggle to break free. Lawrence sought an ideal balance or, as he wrote in the novel Women in Love *(1920), a "star equilibrium," in which two beings are attracted to each other but never lose their individuality. He felt that "no emotion is supreme, or exclusively worth living for. All emotions go to the achieving of a living relationship between a human being and the other human being or creature or thing he becomes purely related to."*

A prolific writer, Lawrence suffered from tuberculosis and spent years wandering in Italy, Australia, Mexico, New Mexico, and southern France, seeking a warm, sunny climate. He also fled to primitive societies to escape the industrialization and commercialism of Western life. A virulent social critic, he was frequently harassed by censorship because his short stories, novels, and poetry were often explicitly sexual and he always challenged conventional moral attitudes. Literature, for Lawrence, had two great functions: providing an emotional experience, and then, if the reader had the courage of his or her own feelings and could live imaginatively, becoming "a mine of practical truth."

Lawrence wrote stories all his life, publishing a first collection, The Prussian Officer, *in 1914; it was followed by four other collections. In 1961 his stories were compiled in a three-volume paperback edition that has gone through numerous reprintings. The style of the early stories is harshly realistic, but Lawrence's depiction of his characters' emotional situations changed in his later work, where he created fantasies like his famous and chilling story "The Rocking-Horse Winner."*

RELATED COMMENTARY: *Janice H. Harris, "Levels of Meaning in Lawrence's 'The Rocking-Horse Winner,'" page 685.*

D. H. Lawrence

The Rocking-Horse Winner 1926

There was a woman who was beautiful, who started with all the advantages, yet she had no luck. She married for love, and the love turned to dust. She had bonny children, yet she felt they had been thrust upon her, and she could not love them. They looked at her coldly, as if they were finding fault with her. And hurriedly she felt she must cover up some fault in herself. Yet what it was that she must cover up she never knew. Nevertheless, when her children were present, she always felt the center of her heart go hard. This troubled her, and in her manner she was all the more gentle and anxious for her children, as if she loved them very much. Only she herself knew that at the center of her heart was a hard little place that could not feel love, no, not for anybody. Everybody else said of her: "She is such a good mother. She adores her children." Only she herself, and her children themselves, knew it was not so. They read it in each other's eyes.

There were a boy and two little girls. They lived in a pleasant house, with a garden, and they had discreet servants, and felt themselves superior to anyone in the neighborhood.

Although they lived in style, they felt always an anxiety in the house. There was never enough money. The mother had a small income, and the father had a small income, but not nearly enough for the social position which they had to keep up. The father went into town to some office. But though he had good prospects, these prospects never materialized. There was always the grinding sense of the shortage of money, though the style was always kept up.

At last the mother said: "I will see if *I* can't make something." But she did not know where to begin. She racked her brains, and tried this thing and the other, but could not find anything successful. The failure made deep lines come into her face. Her children were growing up, they would have to go to school. There must be more money, there must be more money. The father, who was always very handsome and expensive in his tastes, seemed as if he never *would* be able to do anything worth doing. And the mother, who had a great belief in herself, did not succeed any better, and her tastes were just as expensive.

And so the house came to be haunted by the unspoken phrase: *There must be more money! There must be more money!* The children could hear it all the time though nobody said it aloud. They heard it at Christmas, when the expensive and splendid toys filled the nursery. Behind the shining modern rocking horse, behind the smart doll's house, a voice would start whispering: "There *must* be more money! There *must* be more money!" And the children would stop playing, to listen for a moment. They would look into each other's eyes, to see if they had all heard. And each one saw in the eyes of the other two that they too had heard. "There *must* be more money! There *must* be more money!"

It came whispering from the springs of the still-swaying rocking horse, and even the horse, bending his wooden, champing head, heard it. The big doll, sitting so pink and smirking in her new pram, could hear it quite plainly, and seemed to be smirking all the more self-consciously because of it. The foolish puppy, too, that took the place of the teddy bear, he was looking so extraordinarily foolish for no other reason but that he heard the secret whisper all over the house: "There *must* be more money!"

Yet nobody ever said it aloud. The whisper was everywhere, and therefore no one spoke it. Just as no one ever says: "We are breathing!" in spite of the fact that breath is coming and going all the time.

"Mother," said the boy Paul one day, "why don't we keep a car of our own? Why do we always use Uncle's, or else a taxi?"

"Because we're the poor members of the family," said the mother.

"But why *are* we, Mother?"

"Well — I suppose," she said slowly and bitterly, "it's because your father has no luck."

The boy was silent for some time.

"Is luck money, Mother?" he asked rather timidly.

"No, Paul. Not quite. It's what causes you to have money."

"Oh!" said Paul vaguely. "I thought when Uncle Oscar said *filthy lucker,* it meant money."

"*Filthy lucre* does mean money," said the mother. "But it's lucre, not luck."

"Oh!" said the boy. "Then what *is* luck, Mother?"

"It's what causes you to have money. If you're lucky you have money. That's why it's better to be born lucky than rich. If you're rich, you may lose your money. But if you're lucky, you will always get more money."

"Oh! Will you? And is Father not lucky?"

"Very unlucky, I should say," she said bitterly.

The boy watched her with unsure eyes.

"Why?" he asked.

"I don't know. Nobody ever knows why one person is lucky and another unlucky."

"Don't they? Nobody at all? Does *nobody* know?"

"Perhaps God. But He never tells."

"He ought to, then. And aren't you lucky either, Mother?"

"I can't be, if I married an unlucky husband."

"But by yourself, aren't you?"

"I used to think I was, before I married. Now I think I am very unlucky indeed."

"Why?"

"Well — never mind! Perhaps I'm not really," she said.

The child looked at her, to see if she meant it. But he saw, by the lines of her mouth, that she was only trying to hide something from him.

"Well, anyhow," he said stoutly, "I'm a lucky person."

"Why?" said his mother, with a sudden laugh.

He stared at her. He didn't even know why he had said it.

"God told me," he asserted, brazening it out.

"I hope He did, dear!" she said, again with a laugh, but rather bitter.

"He did, Mother!"

"Excellent!" said the mother.

The boy saw she did not believe him; or, rather, that she paid no attention to his assertion. This angered him somewhat, and made him want to compel her attention.

He went off by himself, vaguely, in a childish way, seeking for the clue to "luck." Absorbed, taking no heed of other people, he went about with a sort of stealth, seeking inwardly for luck. He wanted luck, he wanted it, he wanted it. When the two girls were playing dolls in the nursery, he would sit on his big rocking horse, charging madly into space, with a frenzy that made the little girls peer at him uneasily. Wildly the horse careered, the waving dark hair of the boy tossed, his eyes had a strange glare in them. The little girls dared not speak to him.

When he had ridden to the end of his mad little journey, he climbed down and stood in front of his rocking horse, staring fixedly into its lowered face. Its red mouth was slightly open, its big eye was wide and glassy-bright.

Now! he could silently command the snorting steed. Now, take me to where there is luck! Now take me!

And he would slash the horse on the neck with the little whip he had asked Uncle Oscar for. He *knew* the horse could take him to where there was luck, if only he forced it. So he would mount again, and start on his furious ride, hoping at last to get there. He knew he could get there.

"You'll break your horse, Paul!" said the nurse.

"He's always riding like that! I wish he'd leave off!" said his elder sister Joan.

But he only glared down on them in silence. Nurse gave him up. She could make nothing of him. Anyhow he was growing beyond her.

One day his mother and his uncle Oscar came in when he was on one of his furious rides. He did not speak to them.

"Hallo, you young jockey! Riding a winner?" said his uncle.

"Aren't you growing too big for a rocking horse? You're not a very little boy any longer, you know," said his mother.

But Paul only gave a blue glare from his big, rather close-set eyes. He would speak to nobody when he was in full tilt. His mother watched him with an anxious expression on her face.

At last he suddenly stopped forcing his horse into the mechanical gallop, and slid down.

"Well, I got there!" he announced fiercely, his blue eyes still flaring, and his sturdy long legs straddling apart.

"Where did you get to?" asked his mother.

"Where I wanted to go," he flared back at her.

"That's right, son!" said Uncle Oscar. "Don't you stop till you get there. What's the horse's name?"

"He doesn't have a name," said the boy.

"Gets on without all right?" asked the uncle.

"Well, he has different names. He was called Sansovino last week."

"Sansovino, eh? Won the Ascot. How did you know his name?"

"He always talks about horse races with Bassett," said Joan.

The uncle was delighted to find that his small nephew was posted with all the racing news. Bassett, the young gardener, who had been wounded in the left foot in the war and had got his present job through Oscar Cresswell, whose batman° he had been, was a perfect blade of the "turf." He lived in the racing events, and the small boy lived with him.

Oscar Cresswell got it all from Bassett.

"Master Paul comes and asks me, so I can't do more than tell him, sir," said Bassett, his face terribly serious, as if he were speaking of religious matters.

"And does he ever put anything on a horse he fancies?"

"Well — I don't want to give him away — he's a young sport, a fine sport, sir. Would you mind asking him himself? He sort of takes a pleasure in it, and perhaps he'd feel I was giving him away, sir, if you don't mind."

Bassett was serious as a church.

The uncle went back to his nephew and took him off for a ride in the car.

"Say, Paul, old man, do you ever put anything on a horse?" the uncle asked.

The boy watched the handsome man closely.

"Why, do you think I oughtn't to?" he parried.

"Not a bit of it! I thought perhaps you might give me a tip for the Lincoln."

The car sped on into the country, going down to Uncle Oscar's place in Hampshire.

"Honor bright?" said the nephew.

"Honor bright, son!" said the uncle.

"Well, then, Daffodil."

"Daffodil! I doubt it, sonny. What about Mirza?"

"I only know the winner," said the boy. "That's Daffodil."

"Daffodil, eh?"

There was a pause. Daffodil was an obscure horse comparatively.

"Uncle!"

"Yes, son?"

"You won't let it go any further, will you? I promised Bassett."

"Bassett be damned, old man! What's he got to do with it?"

"We're partners. We've been partners from the first. Uncle, he lent me my first five shillings, which I lost. I promised him, honor bright, it was only between me and him; only you gave me that ten-shilling note I started winning with, so I thought you were lucky. You won't let it go any further, will you?"

The boy gazed at his uncle from those big, hot, blue eyes, set rather close together. The uncle stirred and laughed uneasily.

"Right you are, son! I'll keep your tip private. Daffodil, eh? How much are you putting on him?"

"All except twenty pounds," said the boy. "I keep that in reserve."

The uncle thought it a good joke.

"You keep twenty pounds in reserve, do you, you young romancer? What are you betting, then?"

---

batman: An orderly assigned to serve a superior officer in the British military.

"I'm betting three hundred," said the boy gravely. "But it's between you and me, Uncle Oscar! Honor bright?"

The uncle burst into a roar of laughter.

"It's between you and me all right, you young Nat Gould,"° he said, laughing. "But where's your three hundred?"

"Bassett keeps it for me. We're partners."

"You are, are you! And what is Bassett putting on Daffodil?"

"He won't go quite as high as I do, I expect. Perhaps he'll go a hundred and fifty."

"What, pennies?" laughed the uncle.

"Pounds," said the child, with a surprised look at his uncle. "Bassett keeps a bigger reserve than I do."

Between wonder and amusement Uncle Oscar was silent. He pursued the matter no further, but he determined to take his nephew with him to the Lincoln races.

"Now, son," he said, "I'm putting twenty on Mirza, and I'll put five for you on any horse you fancy. What's your pick?"

"Daffodil, Uncle."

"No, not the fiver on Daffodil!"

"I should if it was my own fiver," said the child.

"Good! Good! Right you are! A fiver for me and a fiver for you on Daffodil."

The child had never been to a race meeting before, and his eyes were blue fire. He pursed his mouth tight, and watched. A Frenchman just in front had put his money on Lancelot. Wild with excitement, he flailed his arms up and down, yelling *"Lancelot! Lancelot!"* in his French accent.

Daffodil came in first, Lancelot second, Mirza third. The child, flushed and with eyes blazing, was curiously serene. His uncle brought him four five-pound notes, four to one.

"What am I to do with these?" he cried, waving them before the boy's eyes.

"I suppose we'll talk to Bassett," said the boy. "I expect I have fifteen hundred now; and twenty in reserve; and this twenty."

His uncle studied him for some moments.

"Look here, son!" he said. "You're not serious about Bassett and that fifteen hundred, are you?"

"Yes, I am. But it's between you and me, Uncle. Honor bright!"

"Honor bright all right, son! But I must talk to Bassett."

"If you'd like to be a partner, Uncle, with Bassett and me, we could all be partners. Only, you'd have to promise, honor bright, Uncle, not to let it go beyond us three. Bassett and I are lucky, and you must be lucky, because it was your ten shillings I started winning with. . . ."

Uncle Oscar took both Bassett and Paul into Richmond Park for an afternoon, and there they talked.

Nat Gould: Nathaniel Gould (1857–1919) was a British novelist and sports columnist known best for a series of novels about horse racing.

"It's like this, you see, sir," Bassett said. "Master Paul would get me talking about racing events, spinning yarns, you know, sir. And he was always keen on knowing if I'd made or if I'd lost. It's about a year since, now, that I put five shillings on Blush of Dawn for him — and we lost. Then the luck turned, with that ten shillings he had from you, that we put on Singhalese. And since then, it's been pretty steady, all things considering. What do you say, Master Paul?"

"We're all right when we're sure," said Paul. "It's when we're not quite sure that we go down."

"Oh, but we're careful then," said Bassett.

"But when are you *sure*?" Uncle Oscar smiled.

"It's Master Paul, sir," said Bassett, in a secret, religious voice. "It's as if he had it from heaven. Like Daffodil, now, for the Lincoln. That was as sure as eggs."

"Did you put anything on Daffodil?" asked Oscar Cresswell.

"Yes, sir. I made my bit."

"And my nephew?"

Bassett was obstinately silent, looking at Paul.

"I made twelve hundred, didn't I, Bassett? I told Uncle I was putting three hundred on Daffodil."

"That's right," said Bassett, nodding.

"But where's the money?" asked the uncle.

"I keep it safe locked up, sir. Master Paul he can have it any minute he likes to ask for it."

"What, fifteen hundred pounds?"

"And twenty! And *forty*, that is, with the twenty he made on the course."

"It's amazing!" said the uncle.

"If Master Paul offers you to be partners, sir, I would, if I were you; if you'll excuse me," said Bassett.

Oscar Cresswell thought about it.

"I'll see the money," he said.

They drove home again, and sure enough, Bassett came round to the garden house with fifteen hundred pounds in notes. The twenty pounds reserve was left with Joe Glee, in the Turf Commission deposit.

"You see, it's all right, Uncle, when I'm *sure*! Then we go strong, for all we're worth. Don't we, Bassett?"

"We do that, Master Paul."

"And when are you sure?" said the uncle, laughing.

"Oh, well, sometimes I'm *absolutely* sure, like about Daffodil," said the boy; "and sometimes I have an idea; and sometimes I haven't even an idea, have I, Bassett? Then we're careful, because we mostly go down."

"You do, do you! And when you're sure, like about Daffodil, what makes you sure, sonny?"

"Oh, well, I don't know," said the boy uneasily. "I'm sure, you know, Uncle; that's all."

"It's as if he had it from heaven, sir," Bassett reiterated.

"I should say so!" said the uncle.

But he became a partner. And when the Leger was coming on, Paul was "sure" about Lively Spark, which was a quite inconsiderable horse. The boy insisted on putting a thousand on the horse, Bassett went for five hundred, and Oscar Cresswell two hundred. Lively Spark came in first, and the betting had been ten to one against him. Paul had made ten thousand.

"You see," he said, "I was absolutely sure of him."

Even Oscar Cresswell had cleared two thousand.

"Look here, son," he said, "this sort of thing makes me nervous."

"It needn't, Uncle! Perhaps I shan't be sure again for a long time."

"But what are you going to do with your money?" asked the uncle.

"Of course," said the boy. "I started it for Mother. She said she had no luck, because Father is unlucky, so I thought if *I* was lucky, it might stop whispering."

"What might stop whispering?"

"Our house. I *hate* our house for whispering."

"What does it whisper?"

"Why — why" — the boy fidgeted — "why, I don't know. But it's always short of money, you know, Uncle."

"I know it, son, I know it."

"You know people send Mother writs, don't you, Uncle?"

"I'm afraid I do," said the uncle.

"And then the house whispers, like people laughing at you behind your back. It's awful, that is! I thought if I was lucky. . . ."

"You might stop it," added the uncle.

The boy watched him with big blue eyes, that had an uncanny cold fire in them, and he said never a word.

"Well, then!" said the uncle. "What are we doing?"

"I shouldn't like Mother to know I was lucky," said the boy.

"Why not, son?"

"She'd stop me."

"I don't think she would."

"Oh!" — and the boy writhed in an odd way — "I *don't* want her to know, Uncle."

"All right, son! We'll manage it without her knowing."

They managed it very easily. Paul, at the other's suggestion, handed over five thousand pounds to his uncle, who deposited it with the family lawyer, who was then to inform Paul's mother that a relative had put five thousand pounds into his hands, which sum was to be paid out a thousand pounds at a time, on the mother's birthday, for the next five years.

"So she'll have a birthday present of a thousand pounds for five successive years," said Uncle Oscar. "I hope it won't make it all the harder for her later."

Paul's mother had her birthday in November. The house had been "whispering" worse than ever lately, and, even in spite of his luck, Paul could not bear up against it. He was very anxious to see the effect of the birthday letter, telling his mother about the thousand pounds.

When there were no visitors, Paul now took his meals with his parents, as he was beyond the nursery control. His mother went into town nearly every day. She had discovered that she had an odd knack of sketching furs and dress materials, so she worked secretly in the studio of a friend who was the chief artist for the leading drapers. She drew the figures of ladies in furs and ladies in silk and sequins for the newspaper advertisements. This young woman artist earned several thousand pounds a year, but Paul's mother only made several hundreds, and she was again dissatisfied. She so wanted to be first in something, and she did not succeed, even in making sketches for drapery advertisements.

She was down to breakfast on the morning of her birthday. Paul watched her face as she read her letters. He knew the lawyer's letter. As his mother read it, her face hardened and became more expressionless. Then a cold, determined look came on her mouth. She hid the letter under the pile of others, and said not a word about it.

"Didn't you have anything nice in the post for your birthday, Mother?" said Paul.

"Quite moderately nice," she said, her voice cold and absent.

She went away to town without saying more.

But in the afternoon Uncle Oscar appeared. He said Paul's mother had had a long interview with the lawyer, asking if the whole five thousand could not be advanced at once, as she was in debt.

"What do you think, Uncle?" said the boy.

"I leave it to you, son."

"Oh, let her have it, then! We can get some more with the other," said the boy.

"A bird in the hand is worth two in the bush, laddie!" said Uncle Oscar.

"But I'm sure to *know* for the Grand National; or the Lincolnshire; or else the Derby. I'm sure to know for *one* of them," said Paul.

So Uncle Oscar signed the agreement, and Paul's mother touched the whole five thousand. Then something very curious happened. The voices in the house suddenly went mad, like a chorus of frogs on a spring evening. There were certain new furnishings, and Paul had a tutor. He was *really* going to Eton, his father's school, in the following autumn. There were flowers in the winter, and a blossoming of the luxury Paul's mother had been used to. And yet the voices in the house, behind the sprays of mimosa and almond blossom, and from under the piles of iridescent cushions, simply trilled and screamed in a sort of ecstasy: "There *must* be more money! Oh-h-h; there *must* be more money. Oh, now, now-w! Now-w-w — there *must* be more money! — more than ever! More than ever!"

It frightened Paul terribly. He studied away at his Latin and Greek. But his intense hours were spent with Bassett. The Grand National had gone by; he had not "known," and had lost a hundred pounds. Summer was at hand. He was in agony for the Lincoln. But even for the Lincoln he didn't "know," and he lost fifty pounds. He became wild-eyed and strange, as if something were going to explode in him.

"Let it alone, son! Don't you bother about it!" urged Uncle Oscar. But it was as if the boy couldn't really hear what his uncle was saying.

"I've got to know for the Derby! I've got to know for the Derby!" the child reiterated, his big blue eyes blazing with a sort of madness.

His mother noticed how overwrought he was.

"You'd better go to the seaside. Wouldn't you like to go now to the seaside, instead of waiting? I think you'd better," she said, looking down at him anxiously, her heart curiously heavy because of him.

But the child lifted his uncanny blue eyes. "I couldn't possibly go before the Derby, Mother!" he said. "I couldn't possibly!"

"Why not?" she said, her voice becoming heavy when she was opposed. "Why not? You can still go from the seaside to see the Derby with your uncle Oscar, if that's what you wish. No need for you to wait here. Besides, I think you care too much about these races. It's a bad sign. My family has been a gambling family, and you won't know till you grow up how much damage it has done. But it has done damage. I shall have to send Bassett away, and ask Uncle Oscar not to talk racing to you, unless you promise to be reasonable about it; go away to the seaside and forget it. You're all nerves!"

"I'll do what you like, Mother, so long as you don't send me away till after the Derby," the boy said.

"Send you away from where? Just from this house?"

"Yes," he said, gazing at her.

"Why, you curious child, what makes you care about this house so much, suddenly? I never knew you loved it."

He gazed at her without speaking. He had a secret within a secret, something he had not divulged, even to Bassett or to his uncle Oscar.

But his mother, after standing undecided and a little bit sullen for some moments, said:

"Very well, then! Don't go to the seaside till after the Derby, if you don't wish it. But promise me you won't let your nerves go to pieces. Promise you won't think so much about horse racing and *events*, as you call them!"

"Oh, no," said the boy casually. "I won't think much about them, Mother. You needn't worry. I wouldn't worry, Mother, if I were you."

"If you were me and I were you," said his mother, "I wonder what we *should* do!"

"But you know you needn't worry, Mother, don't you?" the boy repeated.

"I should be awfully glad to know it," she said wearily.

"Oh, well you *can*, you know. I mean, you *ought* to know you needn't worry," he insisted.

"Ought I? Then I'll see about it," she said.

Paul's secret of secrets was his wooden horse, that which had no name. Since he was emancipated from a nurse and a nursery governess, he had had his rocking horse removed to his own bedroom at the top of the house.

"Surely, you're too big for a rocking horse!" his mother had remonstrated.

"Well, you see, Mother, till I can have a *real* horse, I like to have *some* sort of animal about," had been his quaint answer.

"Do you feel he keeps you company?" She laughed.

"Oh, yes! He's very good, he always keeps me company, when I'm there," said Paul.

So the horse, rather shabby, stood in an arrested prance in the boy's bedroom.

The Derby was drawing near, and the boy grew more and more tense. He hardly heard what was spoken to him, he was very frail, and his eyes were really uncanny. His mother had sudden strange seizures of uneasiness about him. Sometimes, for half an hour, she would feel a sudden anxiety about him that was almost anguish. She wanted to rush to him at once, and know he was safe.

Two nights before the Derby, she was at a big party in town, when one of her rushes of anxiety about her boy, her firstborn, gripped her heart till she could hardly speak. She fought with the feeling, might and main, for she believed in common sense. But it was too strong. She had to leave the dance and go downstairs to telephone to the country. The children's nursery governess was terribly surprised and startled at being rung up in the night.

"Are the children all right, Miss Wilmot?"

"Oh, yes, they are quite all right."

"Master Paul? Is he all right?"

"He went to bed as right as a trivet. Shall I run up and look at him?"

"No," said Paul's mother reluctantly. "No! Don't trouble. It's all right. Don't sit up. We shall be home fairly soon." She did not want her son's privacy intruded upon.

"Very good," said the governess.

It was about one o'clock when Paul's mother and father drove up to their house. All was still. Paul's mother went to her room and slipped off her white fur cloak. She had told her maid not to wait up for her. She heard her husband downstairs, mixing a whisky and soda.

And then, because of the strange anxiety at her heart, she stole upstairs to her son's room. Noiselessly she went along the upper corridor. Was there a faint noise? What was it?

She stood, with arrested muscles, outside his door, listening. There was a strange, heavy, and yet not loud noise. Her heart stood still. It was a soundless noise, yet rushing and powerful. Something huge, in violent, hushed motion. What was it? What in God's name was it? She ought to know. She felt that she knew the noise. She knew what it was.

Yet she could not place it. She couldn't say what it was. And on and on it went, like a madness.

Softly, frozen with anxiety and fear, she turned the door handle.

The room was dark. Yet in the space near the window, she heard and saw something plunging to and fro. She gazed in fear and amazement.

Then suddenly she switched on the light, and saw her son, in his green pajamas, madly surging on the rocking horse. The blaze of light suddenly lit him up, as he urged the wooden horse, and lit her up, as she stood, blonde, in her dress of pale green and crystal, in the doorway.

"Paul!" she cried. "Whatever are you doing?"

"It's Malabar!" he screamed, in a powerful, strange voice. "It's Malabar!"

His eyes blazed at her for one strange and senseless second, as he ceased urging his wooden horse. Then he fell with a crash to the ground, and she, all her tormented motherhood flooding upon her, rushed to gather him up.

But he was unconscious, and unconscious he remained, with some brain fever. He talked and tossed, and his mother sat stonily by his side.

"Malabar! It's Malabar! Bassett, Bassett, I *know!* It's Malabar!"

So the child cried, trying to get up and urge the rocking horse that gave him his inspiration.

"What does he mean by Malabar?" asked the heart-frozen mother.

"I don't know," said the father stonily.

"What does he mean by Malabar?" she asked her brother Oscar.

"It's one of the horses running for the Derby," was the answer.

And, in spite of himself, Oscar Cresswell spoke to Bassett, and himself put a thousand on Malabar: at fourteen to one.

The third day of the illness was critical: they were waiting for a change. The boy, with his rather long, curly hair, was tossing ceaselessly on the pillow. He never slept nor regained consciousness, and his eyes were like blue stones. His mother sat, feeling her heart had gone, turned actually into a stone.

In the evening, Oscar Cresswell did not come, but Bassett sent a message, saying could he come up for one moment, just one moment? Paul's mother was very angry at the intrusion, but on second thought she agreed. The boy was the same. Perhaps Bassett might bring him to consciousness.

The gardener, a shortish fellow with a little brown mustache, and sharp little brown eyes, tiptoed into the room, touched his imaginary cap to Paul's mother, and stole to the bedside, staring with glittering, smallish eyes at the tossing, dying child.

"Master Paul!" he whispered. "Master Paul! Malabar came in first all right, a clean win. I did as you told me. You've made over seventy thousand pounds, you have; you've got over eighty thousand. Malabar came in all right, Master Paul."

"Malabar! Malabar! Did I say Malabar, Mother? Did I say Malabar? Do you think I'm lucky, Mother? I knew Malabar, didn't I? Over eighty thousand pounds! I call that lucky, don't you, Mother? Over eighty thousand pounds! I knew, didn't I know I knew? Malabar came in all right. If I ride my horse till I'm sure, then I tell you, Bassett, you can go as high as you like. Did you go for all you were worth, Bassett?"

"I went a thousand on it, Master Paul."

"I never told you, Mother, that if I can ride my horse, and *get there,* then I'm absolutely sure — oh, absolutely! Mother, did I ever tell you? I *am* lucky!"

"No, you never did," said the mother.

But the boy died in the night.

And even as he lay dead, his mother heard her brother's voice saying to her: "My God, Hester, you're eighty-odd thousand to the good, and a poor devil of a son to the bad. But, poor devil, poor devil, he's best gone out of a life where he rides his rocking horse to find a winner."

KATHERINE MANSFIELD *(1888–1923) was born Kathleen Mansfield Beauchamp in Wellington, New Zealand. In 1903 she persuaded her father, a banker and industrialist, to send her to London to study the cello. After a brief return to New Zealand, she went back to London with a small allowance from her family. Mansfield decided to become a writer instead of a musician after meeting D. H. Lawrence and Virginia Woolf. Her first book of short stories,* In a German Pension, *was published in 1911. In the same year she met the literary critic John Middleton Murry, who became her husband in 1918.* Bliss and Other Stories *(1920) established her reputation and was followed by* The Garden-Party *(1922).*

Mansfield took Anton Chekhov as her model, but after she was stricken with tuberculosis in 1918 she found it difficult to work. In her posthumously published Journal *(1927), she often upbraided herself when she felt too ill to write: "Look at the stories that wait and wait just at the threshold. Why don't I let them in? And their place would be taken by others who are lurking beyond just there — waiting for the chance." Finally she sought a cure for her illness at the Gurdjieff Institute in France, run by the noted Armenian mystic Georges Ivanovitch Gurdjieff, whose methods combined spiritual and physical healing. She died at the institute a few months after her thirty-fourth birthday.*

Eighty-eight of Mansfield's stories have been published (including fifteen left unfinished), and they have had a great influence on the development of the literary form. As did Chekhov and James Joyce, Mansfield simplified plot to intensify its emotional impact, dramatizing small moments to reveal the larger significance in people's lives, or, as Willa Cather observed, approaching "the major forces of life through comparatively trivial incidents." Mansfield developed her own technique of narration in which she transformed a chance incident into a terse psychological drama. As would a symbolist poet, she used concrete images — such as the fur piece in "Miss Brill" — to convey her characters' feelings, or what she called "the state of the soul." Her stories have affected later writers as powerfully as Chekhov's affected her.

KATHERINE MANSFIELD

Miss Brill

1922

Although it was so brilliantly fine — the blue sky powdered with gold and great spots of light like white wine splashed over the Jardins Publiques — Miss Brill was glad that she had decided on her fur. The air was motionless, but when you opened your mouth there was just a faint chill, like a chill from a glass of iced water before you sip, and now and again a leaf came drifting — from nowhere, from the sky. Miss Brill put up her hand and touched her fur. Dear little thing! It was nice to feel it again. She had taken it out of its box that afternoon, shaken out the moth-powder, given it a good brush, and rubbed the life back into the dim little eyes. "What has been happening to me?" said the sad little eyes. Oh, how sweet it was to see them snap at her again from the red eiderdown! . . . But the nose, which was of some black composition, wasn't at all firm. It must have had a knock, somehow. Never mind — a little dab of black sealing-wax when the time came — when it was absolutely necessary. . . . Little rogue! Yes, she really felt like that about it. Little rogue biting its tail just by her left ear. She could have taken it off and laid it on her lap and stroked it. She felt a tingling in her hands and arms, but that came from walking, she supposed. And when she breathed, something light and sad — no, not sad, exactly — something gentle seemed to move in her bosom.

There were a number of people out this afternoon, far more than last Sunday. And the band sounded louder and gayer. That was because the Season had begun. For although the band played all the year round on Sundays, out of season it was never the same. It was like some one playing with only the family to listen; it didn't care how it played if there weren't any strangers present. Wasn't the conductor wearing a new coat, too? She was sure it was new. He scraped with his foot and flapped his arms like a rooster about to crow, and the bandsmen sitting in the green rotunda blew out their cheeks and glared at the music. Now there came a little "flutey" bit — very pretty! — a little chain of bright drops. She was sure it would be repeated. It was; she lifted her head and smiled.

Only two people shared her "special" seat: a fine old man in a velvet coat, his hands clasped over a huge carved walking-stick, and a big old woman, sitting upright, with a roll of knitting on her embroidered apron. They did not speak. This was disappointing, for Miss Brill always looked forward to the conversation. She had become really quite expert, she thought, at listening as though she didn't listen, at sitting in other people's lives just for a minute while they talked round her.

She glanced, sideways, at the old couple. Perhaps they would go soon. Last Sunday, too, hadn't been as interesting as usual. An Englishman and his wife, he wearing a dreadful Panama hat and she button boots. And she'd gone on the whole time about how she ought to wear spectacles; she knew she needed them; but that it was no good getting any; they'd be sure to break and they'd never keep on. And he'd been so patient. He'd suggested everything — gold rims, the kind that curved round your ears, little pads inside the bridge. No, nothing would please her. "They'll always be sliding down my nose!" Miss Brill had wanted to shake her.

The old people sat on the bench, still as statues. Never mind, there was always the crowd to watch. To and fro, in front of the flower-beds and the band rotunda, the couples and groups paraded, stopped to talk, to greet, to buy a handful of flowers from the old beggar who had his tray fixed to the railings. Little children ran among them, swooping and laughing; little boys with big white silk bows under their chins, little girls, little French dolls, dressed up in velvet and lace. And sometimes a tiny staggerer came suddenly rocking into the open from under the trees, stopped, stared, as suddenly sat down "flop," until its small high-stepping mother, like a young hen, rushed scolding to its rescue. Other people sat on the benches and green chairs, but they were nearly always the same, Sunday after Sunday, and — Miss Brill had often noticed — there was something funny about nearly all of them. They were odd, silent, nearly all old, and from the way they stared they looked as though they'd just come from dark little rooms or even — even cupboards!

Behind the rotunda the slender trees with yellow leaves down drooping, and through them just a line of sea, and beyond the blue sky with gold-veined clouds.

Tum-tum-tum tiddle-um! tiddle-um! tum tiddley-um tum ta! blew the band.

Two young girls in red came by and two young soldiers in blue met them, and they laughed and paired and went off arm-in-arm. Two peasant women with funny straw hats passed, gravely, leading beautiful smoke-coloured donkeys. A cold, pale nun hurried by. A beautiful woman came along and dropped her bunch of violets, and a little boy ran after to hand them to her, and she took them and threw them away as if they'd been poisoned. Dear me! Miss Brill didn't know whether to admire that or not! And now an ermine toque and a gentleman in grey met just in front of her. He was tall, stiff, dignified, and she was wearing the ermine toque she'd bought when her hair was yellow. Now everything, her hair, her face, even her eyes, was the same colour as the shabby ermine, and her hand, in its cleaned glove, lifted to dab her lips, was a tiny yellowish paw. Oh, she was so pleased to see him — delighted! She rather thought they were going to meet that afternoon. She described where she'd been — everywhere, here, there, along by the sea. The day was so charming — didn't he agree? And wouldn't he, perhaps? . . . But he shook his head, lighted a cigarette, slowly breathed a great deep puff into her face, and, even while she was still talking and laughing, flicked the match away and walked on. The ermine toque was alone; she smiled more brightly than ever. But even the band seemed to know what she was feeling and played more softly, played tenderly, and the drum beat, "The Brute! The Brute!" over and over. What would she do? What was going to happen now? But as Miss Brill wondered, the ermine toque turned, raised her hand as though she'd seen someone else, much nicer, just over there, and pattered away. And the band changed again and played more quickly, more gaily than ever, and the old couple on Miss Brill's seat got up and marched away, and such a funny old man with long whiskers hobbled along in time to the music and was nearly knocked over by four girls walking abreast.

Oh, how fascinating it was! How she enjoyed it! How she loved sitting here, watching it all! It was like a play. It was exactly like a play. Who could believe the sky at the back wasn't painted? But it wasn't till a little brown dog trotted on solemn and then slowly trotted off, like a little "theatre" dog, a little dog that had been drugged, that Miss Brill discovered what it was that made it so exciting. They were all on the stage. They weren't only the audience, not only looking on; they were acting. Even she had a part and came every Sunday. No doubt somebody would have noticed if she hadn't been there; she was part of the performance after all. How strange she'd never thought of it like that before! And yet it explained why she made such a point of starting from home at just the same time each week — so as not to be late for the performance — and it also explained why she had quite a queer, shy feeling at telling her English pupils how she spent her Sunday afternoons. No wonder! Miss Brill nearly laughed out loud. She was on the stage. She thought of the old invalid gentleman to whom she read the newspaper four afternoons a week while he slept in the garden. She had got quite used to the frail head on the cotton pillow, the hollowed eyes, the open mouth and the high pinched nose. If he'd been dead she mightn't have noticed for weeks; she wouldn't have minded. But suddenly he knew he was having the paper read to him by an actress! "An actress!" The old head lifted; two points of light quivered in the old eyes. "An actress — are ye?" And Miss Brill smoothed the newspaper as though it were the manuscript of her part and said gently: "Yes, I have been an actress for a long time."

The band had been having a rest. Now they started again. And what they played was warm, sunny, yet there was just a faint chill — a something, what was it? — not sadness — no, not sadness — a something that made you want to sing. The tune lifted, lifted, the light shone; and it seemed to Miss Brill that in another moment all of them, all the whole company, would begin singing. The young ones, the laughing ones who were moving together, they would begin, and the men's voices, very resolute and brave, would join them. And then she too, she too, and the others on the benches — they would come in with a kind of accompaniment — something low, that scarcely rose or fell, something so beautiful — moving. . . . And Miss Brill's eyes filled with tears and she looked smiling at all the other members of the company. Yes, we understand, we understand, she thought — though what they understood she didn't know.

Just at that moment a boy and a girl came and sat down where the old couple had been. They were beautifully dressed; they were in love. The hero and heroine, of course, just arrived from his father's yacht. And still soundlessly singing, still with that trembling smile, Miss Brill prepared to listen.

"No, not now," said the girl. "Not here, I can't."

"But why? Because of that stupid old thing at the end there?" asked the boy. "Why does she come here at all — who wants her? Why doesn't she keep her silly old mug at home?"

"It's her fu-fur which is so funny," giggled the girl. "It's exactly like a fried whiting."

"Ah, be off with you!" said the boy in an angry whisper. Then: "Tell me, ma petite chérie —"

"No, not here," said the girl. "Not *yet*."

On her way home she usually bought a slice of honey-cake at the baker's. It was her Sunday treat. Sometimes there was an almond in her slice, sometimes not. It made a great difference. If there was an almond it was like carrying home a tiny present — a surprise — something that might very well not have been there. She hurried on the almond Sundays and struck the match for the kettle in quite a dashing way.

But to-day she passed the baker's by, climbed the stairs, went into the little dark room — her room like a cupboard — and sat down on the red eiderdown. She sat there for a long time. The box that the fur came out of was on the bed. She unclasped the necklet quickly; quickly, without looking, laid it inside. But when she put the lid on she thought she heard something crying.

GUY DE MAUPASSANT *(1850–1893) was born in Normandy, the son of a wealthy stockbroker. Unable to accept discipline in school, he joined the army during the Franco-Prussian War of 1870–71. Then for seven years he apprenticed himself to Gustave Flaubert, a distant relative, who attempted to teach him to write. Maupassant remembered, "I wrote verses, short stories, longer stories, even a wretched play. Nothing survived. The master read everything. Then, the following Sunday at lunch, he developed his criticisms." Flaubert taught Maupassant that talent "is nothing other than a long patience. Work."*

The essence of Flaubert's now famous teaching is that the writer must look at everything to find some aspect of it that no one has yet seen or expressed. "Everything contains some element of the unexplored because we are accustomed to use our eyes only with the memory of what other people before us have thought about the object we are looking at. The least thing has a bit of the unknown about it. Let us find this."

In 1880 Maupassant caused a sensation with the publication of his story "Boule de Suif" ("Ball of Fat"), a dramatic account of prostitution and bourgeois hypocrisy. During the next decade, before his gradual incapacitation and death from syphilis, he published nearly 300 stories. Characterized by compact and dramatic narrative lines, they read as modern short stories, eliminating the moral judgments and the long digressions used by many earlier writers. Along with his younger contemporary Anton Chekhov, Maupassant is responsible for technical advances that moved the short story toward an austerity that has marked it ever since. These two writers influenced nearly everyone who has written short fiction after them.

As Joseph Conrad recognized, "Facts, and again facts, are his [Maupassant's] unique concern. That is why he is not always properly understood." Maupassant's lack of sentimentality toward his characters, as in his depiction of the wife in "The Necklace," laid him open to charges of cynicism and hardness. Even if Maupassant's stories display a greater distance from his characters and a less sympathetic irony than Chekhov's, both writers were the most accomplished of narrators, equal in their powers of exact observation and independent judgment and in their supple, practiced knowledge of their craft.

RELATED COMMENTARY: *Kate Chopin, "How I Stumbled upon Maupassant," page 670.*

GUY DE MAUPASSANT

The Necklace

1884

TRANSLATED BY MARJORIE LAURIE

She was one of those pretty and charming girls who are sometimes, as if by a mistake of destiny, born in a family of clerks. She had no dowry, no expectations, no means of being known, understood, loved, wedded by any rich and distinguished man; and she let herself be married to a little clerk at the Ministry of Public Instructions.

She dressed plainly because she could not dress well, but she was as unhappy as though she had really fallen from her proper station, since with women there is neither caste nor rank: and beauty, grace, and charm act instead of family and birth. Natural fineness, instinct for what is elegant, suppleness of wit, are the sole hierarchy, and make from women of the people the equals of the very greatest ladies.

She suffered ceaselessly, feeling herself born for all the delicacies and all the luxuries. She suffered from the poverty of her dwelling, from the wretched look of the walls, from the worn-out chairs, from the ugliness of the curtains. All those things, of which another woman of her rank would never even have been conscious, tortured her and made her angry. The sight of the little Breton peasant, who did her humble housework aroused in her regrets which were despairing, and distracted dreams. She thought of the silent antechambers hung with Oriental tapestry, lit by tall bronze candelabra, and of the two great footmen in knee breeches who sleep in the big armchairs, made drowsy by the heavy warmth of the hot-air stove. She thought of the long *salons* fitted up with ancient silk, of the delicate furniture carrying priceless curiosities, and of the coquettish perfumed boudoirs made for talks at five o'clock with intimate friends, with men famous and sought after, whom all women envy and whose attention they all desire.

When she sat down to dinner, before the round table covered with a tablecloth three days old, opposite her husband, who uncovered the soup tureen and declared with an enchanted air, "Ah, the good *pot-au-feu*! I don't know anything better than that," she thought of dainty dinners, of shining silverware, of tapestry which peopled the walls with ancient personages and with strange birds flying in the midst of a fairy forest; and she thought of delicious dishes served on marvelous plates, and of the whispered gallantries which you listen to with a sphinxlike smile, while you are eating the pink flesh of a trout or the wings of a quail.

She had no dresses, no jewels, nothing. And she loved nothing but that; she felt made for that. She would so have liked to please, to be envied, to be charming, to be sought after.

She had a friend, a former schoolmate at the convent, who was rich, and whom she did not like to go and see any more, because she suffered so much when she came back.

But one evening, her husband returned home with a triumphant air, and holding a large envelope in his hand.

"There," said he. "Here is something for you."

She tore the paper sharply, and drew out a printed card which bore these words:

"The Minister of Public Instruction and Mme. Georges Ramponneau request the honor of M. and Mme. Loisel's company at the palace of the Ministry on Monday evening, January eighteenth."

Instead of being delighted, as her husband hoped, she threw the invitation on the table with disdain, murmuring:

"What do you want me to do with that?"

"But, my dear, I thought you would be glad. You never go out, and this is such a fine opportunity. I had awful trouble to get it. Everyone wants to go; it is very select, and they are not giving many invitations to clerks. The whole official world will be there."

She looked at him with an irritated glance, and said, impatiently:

"And what do you want me to put on my back?"

He had not thought of that; he stammered:

"Why, the dress you go to the theater in. It looks very well, to me."

He stopped, distracted, seeing his wife was crying. Two great tears descended slowly from the corners of her eyes toward the corners of her mouth. He stuttered:

"What's the matter? What's the matter?"

But, by violent effort, she had conquered her grief, and she replied, with a calm voice, while she wiped her wet cheeks:

"Nothing. Only I have no dress and therefore I can't go to this ball. Give your card to some colleague whose wife is better equipped than I."

He was in despair. He resumed:

"Come, let us see, Mathilde. How much would it cost, a suitable dress, which you could use on other occasions. Something very simple?"

She reflected several seconds, making her calculations and wondering also what sum she could ask without drawing on herself an immediate refusal and a frightened exclamation from the economical clerk.

Finally, she replied, hesitatingly:

"I don't know exactly, but I think I could manage it with four hundred francs."

He had grown a little pale, because he was laying aside just that amount to buy a gun and treat himself to a little shooting next summer on the plain of Nanterre, with several friends who went to shoot larks down there, of a Sunday.

But he said:

"All right. I will give you four hundred francs. And try to have a pretty dress."

The day of the ball drew near, and Mme. Loisel seemed sad, uneasy, anxious. Her dress was ready, however. Her husband said to her one evening:

"What is the matter? Come, you've been so queer these last three days."

And she answered:

"It annoys me not to have a single jewel, not a single stone, nothing to put on. I shall look like distress. I should almost rather not go at all."

He resumed:

"You might wear natural flowers. It's very stylish at this time of the year. For ten francs you can get two or three magnificent roses."

She was not convinced.

"No; there's nothing more humiliating than to look poor among other women who are rich."

But her husband cried:

"How stupid you are! Go look up your friend Mme. Forestier, and ask her to lend you some jewels. You're quite thick enough with her to do that."

She uttered a cry of joy:

"It's true. I never thought of it."

The next day she went to her friend and told of her distress.

Mme. Forestier went to a wardrobe with a glass door, took out a large jewelbox, brought it back, opened it, and said to Mme. Loisel:

"Choose, choose, my dear."

She saw first of all some bracelets, then a pearl necklace, then a Venetian cross, gold and precious stones of admirable workmanship. She tried on the ornaments before the glass, hesitated, could not make up her mind to part with them, to give them back. She kept asking:

"Haven't you any more?"

"Why, yes. Look. I don't know what you like."

All of a sudden she discovered, in a black satin box, a superb necklace of diamonds, and her heart began to beat with an immoderate desire. Her hands trembled as she took it. She fastened it around her throat, outside her high necked dress, and remained lost in ecstasy at the sight of herself.

Then she asked, hesitating, filled with anguish:

"Can you lend me that, only that?"

"Why, yes, certainly."

She sprang upon the neck of her friend, kissed her passionately, then fled with her treasure.

The day of the ball arrived. Mme. Loisel made a great success. She was prettier than them all, elegant, gracious, smiling, and crazy with joy. All the men looked at her, asked her name, endeavored to be introduced. All the attachés of the Cabinet wanted to waltz with her. She was remarked by the minister himself.

She danced with intoxication, with passion, made drunk by pleasure, forgetting all, in the triumph of her beauty, in the glory of her success, in a sort of cloud of happiness composed of all this homage, of all this admiration, of all these awakened desires, and of that sense of complete victory which is so sweet to a woman's heart.

She went away about four o'clock in the morning. Her husband had been sleeping since midnight, in a little deserted anteroom, with three other gentlemen whose wives were having a good time. He threw over her shoulders the wraps which he had brought, modest wraps of common life, whose poverty contrasted with the elegance of the ball dress. She felt this, and wanted to escape so as not to be remarked by the other women, who were enveloping themselves in costly furs.

Loisel held her back.

"Wait a bit. You will catch cold outside. I will go and call a cab."

But she did not listen to him, and rapidly descended the stairs. When they were in the street they did not find a carriage; and they began to look for one, shouting after the cabmen whom they saw passing by at a distance.

They went down toward the Seine, in despair, shivering with cold. At last they found on the quay one of those ancient noctambulant coupés° which,

---

coupés: Enclosed four-wheeled carriages.

exactly as if they were ashamed to show their misery during the day, are never seen round Paris until after nightfall.

It took them to their door in the Rue des Martyrs, and once more, sadly, they climbed up homeward. All was ended, for her. And as to him, he reflected that he must be at the Ministry at ten o'clock.

She removed the wraps which covered her shoulders before the glass, so as once more to see herself in all her glory. But suddenly she uttered a cry. She no longer had the necklace around her neck!

Her husband, already half undressed, demanded:

"What is the matter with you?"

She turned madly toward him:

"I have — I have — I've lost Mme. Forestier's necklace."

He stood up, distracted.

"What! — how? — impossible!"

And they looked in the folds of her dress, in the folds of her cloak, in her pockets, everywhere. They did not find it.

He asked:

"You're sure you had it on when you left the ball?"

"Yes, I felt it in the vestibule of the palace."

"But if you had lost it in the street we should have heard it fall. It must be in the cab."

"Yes. Probably. Did you take his number?"

"No. And you, didn't you notice it?"

"No."

They looked, thunderstruck, at one another. At last Loisel put on his clothes.

"I shall go back on foot," said he, "over the whole route which we have taken to see if I can find it."

And he went out. She sat waiting on a chair in her ball dress, without strength to go to bed, overwhelmed, without fire, without a thought.

Her husband came back about seven o'clock. He had found nothing.

He went to Police Headquarters, to the newspaper offices, to offer a reward; he went to the cab companies — everywhere, in fact, whither he was urged by the least suspicion of hope.

She waited all day, in the same condition of mad fear before this terrible calamity.

Loisel returned at night with a hollow, pale face; he had discovered nothing.

"You must write to your friend," said he, "that you have broken the clasp of her necklace and that you are having it mended. That will give us time to turn round."

She wrote at his dictation.

At the end of a week they had lost all hope.

And Loisel, who had aged five years, declared:

"We must consider how to replace that ornament."

The next day they took the box which had contained it, and they went to the jeweler whose name was found within. He consulted his books.

"It was not I, madame, who sold that necklace; I must simply have furnished the case."

Then they went from jeweler to jeweler, searching for a necklace like the other, consulting their memories, sick both of them with chagrin and anguish.

They found, in a shop at the Palais Royal, a string of diamonds which seemed to them exactly like the one they looked for. It was worth forty thousand francs. They could have it for thirty-six.

So they begged the jeweler not to sell it for three days yet. And they made a bargain that he should buy it back for thirty-four thousand francs, in case they found the other one before the end of February.

Loisel possessed eighteen thousand francs which his father had left him. He would borrow the rest.

He did borrow, asking a thousand francs of one, five hundred of another, five louis here, three louis there. He gave notes, took up ruinous obligations, dealt with usurers and all the race of lenders. He compromised all the rest of his life, risked his signature without even knowing if he could meet it; and, frightened by the pains yet to come, by the black misery which was about to fall upon him, by the prospect of all the physical privation and of all the moral tortures which he was to suffer, he went to get the new necklace, putting down upon the merchant's counter thirty-six thousand francs.

When Mme. Loisel took back the necklace, Mme. Forestier said to her, with a chilly manner:

"You should have returned it sooner; I might have needed it."

She did not open the case, as her friend had so much feared. If she had detected the substitution, what would she have thought, what would she have said? Would she not have taken Mme. Loisel for a thief?

Mme. Loisel now knew the horrible existence of the needy. She took her part, moreover, all of a sudden, with heroism. That dreadful debt must be paid. She would pay it. They dismissed their servant; they changed their lodgings; they rented a garret under the roof.

She came to know what heavy housework meant and the odious cares of the kitchen. She washed the dishes, using her rosy nails on the greasy pots and pans. She washed the dirty linen, the shirts, and the dishcloths, which she dried upon a line; she carried the slops down to the street every morning, and carried up the water, stopping for breath at every landing. And, dressed like a woman of the people, she went to the fruiterer, the grocer, the butcher, her basket on her arm, bargaining, insulted, defending her miserable money sou by sou.

Each month they had to meet some notes, renew others, obtain more time.

Her husband worked in the evening making a fair copy of some tradesman's accounts, and late at night he often copied manuscript for five sous a page.

And this life lasted for ten years.

At the end of ten years, they had paid everything, everything, with the rates of usury, and the accumulations of the compound interest.

Mme. Loisel looked old now. She had become the woman of impoverished households — strong and hard and rough. With frowsy hair, skirts askew, and red hands, she talked loud while washing the floor with great swishes of water. But sometimes, when her husband was at the office, she sat down near the window, and she thought of that gay evening of long ago, of that ball where she had been so beautiful and so fêted.

What would have happened if she had not lost that necklace? Who knows? Who knows? How life is strange and changeful! How little a thing is needed for us to be lost or to be saved!

But, one Sunday, having gone to take a walk in the Champs Elysées to refresh herself from the labor of the week, she suddenly perceived a woman who was leading a child. It was Mme. Forestier, still young, still beautiful, still charming.

Mme. Loisel felt moved. Was she going to speak to her? Yes, certainly. And now that she had paid, she was going to tell her all about it. Why not?

She went up.

"Good-day, Jeanne."

The other, astonished to be familiarly addressed by this plain goodwife, did not recognize her at all, and stammered.

"But — madam! — I do not know — you must be mistaken."

"No. I am Mathilde Loisel."

Her friend uttered a cry.

"Oh, my poor Mathilde! How you are changed!"

"Yes, I have had days hard enough, since I have seen you, days wretched enough — and that because of you!"

"Of me! How so?"

"Do you remember that diamond necklace which you lent me to wear at the ministerial ball?"

"Yes. Well?"

"Well, I lost it."

"What do you mean? You brought it back."

"I brought you back another just like it. And for this we have been ten years paying. You can understand that it was not easy for us, who had nothing. At last it is ended, and I am very glad."

Mme. Forestier had stopped.

"You say that you bought a necklace of diamonds to replace mine?"

"Yes. You never noticed it, then! They were very like."

And she smiled with a joy which was proud and naïve at once.

Mme. Forestier, strongly moved, took her two hands.

"Oh, my poor Mathilde! Why, my necklace was paste. It was worth at most five hundred francs!"

HERMAN MELVILLE *(1819–1891) published his first short story in 1853 as "Bartleby, the Scrivener: A Story of Wall Street." Behind him were seven years of writing novels beginning with the burst of creative energy that produced his early books of sea adventure:* Typee *(1846),* Omoo *(1847),* Mardi *(1849),* Redburn *(1849), and* White-Jacket *(1850). All of these were based on his experiences on board* *ship. Melville had been left in poverty at the age of fifteen when his father went bankrupt, and in 1839 he went to sea as a cabin boy. Two years later he sailed on a whaler bound for the Pacific, but he deserted in the Marquesas Islands and lived for a time with cannibals. Having little formal education, Melville later boasted that "a whale ship was my Yale College and my Harvard." His most ambitious book was* Moby-Dick *(1851), a work of great allegorical complexity heavily indebted to the influence of Nathaniel Hawthorne, Melville's neighbor in the Berkshires at the time he wrote it.* Moby-Dick *was not a commercial success, however, and the novel that followed it,* Pierre *(1852), was dismissed by critics as incomprehensible trash.*

*It was at this point that Melville turned to the short story. Between 1853 and 1856 he published fifteen sketches and stories and a serialized historical novel, promising the popular magazines that his stories would "contain nothing of any sort to shock the fastidious." But when this work and another novel (*The Confidence Man*, 1857) failed to restore his reputation, he ceased trying to support his family by his pen. He moved from his farm in the Berkshires to a house in New York City bought for him by his father-in-law, and worked for more than twenty years as an inspector of customs. He published a few books of poems and wrote a short novel,* Billy Budd*, which critics acclaimed as one of his greatest works when it was published — thirty years after his death.*

Melville stood at the crossroads in the early history of American short fiction. When he began to publish in magazines, Hawthorne and Edgar Allan Poe had already done their best work in the romantic vein of tales and sketches, and the realistic local-color school of short stories had not yet been established. Melville created something new in "Bartleby, the Scrivener," a fully developed, if discursive, short story set in a contemporary social context. It baffled readers of Putnam's Monthly Magazine *in 1853, when it was published in two installments. One reviewer called it "a Poeish tale with an infusion of more natural sentiment." For the rest of his stories, Melville used the conventional form of old-fashioned tales mostly set in remote times or places.*

RELATED COMMENTARIES: *Herman Melville, "Blackness in Hawthorne's 'Young Goodman Brown,'" page 693; J. Hillis Miller, "Who Is He? Melville's 'Bartleby, the Scrivener,'" page 695.*

HERMAN MELVILLE

Bartleby, the Scrivener

1853

A Story of Wall Street

I am a rather elderly man. The nature of my avocations, for the last thirty years, has brought me into more than ordinary contact with what would seem an interesting and somewhat singular set of men, of whom, as yet, nothing, that I know of, has ever been written — I mean, the law-copyists, or scriveners. I have known very many of them, professionally and privately, and, if I pleased, could relate divers histories, at which good-natured gentlemen might smile, and sentimental souls might weep. But I waive the biographies of all other scriveners, for a few passages in the life of Bartleby, who was a scrivener, the strangest I ever saw, or heard of. While, of other law-copyists, I might write the complete life, of Bartleby nothing of that sort can be done. I believe that no materials exist, for a full and satisfactory biography of this man. It is an irreparable loss to literature. Bartleby was one of those beings of whom nothing is ascertainable, except from the original sources, and, in his case, those are very small. What my own astonished eyes saw of Bartleby, *that* is all I know of him, except, indeed, one vague report, which will appear in the sequel.

Ere introducing the scrivener, as he first appeared to me, it is fit I make some mention of myself, my *employés*, my business, my chambers, and general surroundings, because some such description is indispensable to an adequate understanding of the chief character about to be presented. Imprimis:° I am a man who, from his youth upwards, has been filled with a profound conviction that the easiest way of life is the best. Hence, though I belong to a profession proverbially energetic and nervous, even to turbulence, at times, yet nothing of that sort have I ever suffered to invade my peace. I am one of those unambitious lawyers who never address a jury, or in any way draw down public applause; but, in the cool tranquillity of a snug retreat, do a snug business among rich men's bonds, and mortgages, and title-deeds. All who know me, consider me an eminently *safe* man. The late John Jacob Astor, a personage little given to poetic enthusiasm, had no hesitation in pronouncing my first grand point to be prudence; my next, method. I do not speak it in vanity, but simply record the fact, that I was not unemployed in my profession by the late John Jacob Astor; a name which, I admit, I love to repeat; for it hath a rounded and orbicular sound to it, and rings like unto bullion. I will freely add, that I was not insensible to the late John Jacob Astor's good opinion.

Some time prior to the period at which this little history begins, my avocations had been largely increased. The good old office, now extinct in the State of New York, of a Master in Chancery, had been conferred upon me. It was not a very arduous office, but very pleasantly remunerative. I seldom lose my temper; much more seldom indulge in dangerous indignation at wrongs and outrages; but I must be permitted to be rash here and declare, that I consider the sudden and violent abrogation of the office of Master in Chancery, by the new Constitution, as a —— premature act; inasmuch as I had counted upon a life-lease of the profits, whereas I only received those of a few short years. But this is by the way.

My chambers were up stairs, at No. — Wall Street. At one end, they looked upon the white wall of the interior of a spacious skylight shaft, penetrating the building from top to bottom.

This view might have been considered rather tame than otherwise, deficient in what landscape painters call "life." But, if so, the view from the other end of my chambers offered, at least, a contrast, if nothing more. In that direction, my windows commanded an unobstructed view of a lofty brick wall, black by age and everlasting shade; which wall required no spy-glass to bring out its lurking beauties, but, for the benefit of all near-sighted spectators, was pushed up to within ten feet of my window-panes. Owing to the great height of the surrounding buildings, and my chambers being on the second floor, the interval between this wall and mine not a little resembled a huge square cistern.

Imprimis: In the first place (Latin).

At the period just preceding the advent of Bartleby, I had two persons as copyists in my employment, and a promising lad as an office-boy. First, Turkey; second, Nippers; third, Ginger Nut. These may seem names, the like of which are not usually found in the Directory. In truth, they were nicknames, mutually conferred upon each other by my three clerks, and were deemed expressive of their respective persons or characters. Turkey was a short, pursy Englishman, of about my own age — that is, somewhere not far from sixty. In the morning, one might say, his face was of a fine florid hue, but after twelve o'clock, meridian — his dinner hour — it blazed like a grate full of Christmas coals; and continued blazing — but, as it were, with a gradual wane — till six o'clock, P.M., or thereabouts; after which, I saw no more of the proprietor of the face, which, gaining its meridian with the sun, seemed to set with it, to rise, culminate, and decline the following day, with the like regularity and undiminished glory. There are many singular coincidences I have known in the course of my life, not the least among which was the fact, that, exactly when Turkey displayed his fullest beams from his red and radiant countenance, just then, too, at that critical moment, began the daily period when I considered his business capacities as seriously disturbed for the remainder of the twenty-four hours. Not that he was absolutely idle, or averse to business then; far from it. The difficulty was, he was apt to be altogether too energetic. There was a strange, inflamed, flurried, flighty recklessness of activity about him. He would be incautious in dipping his pen into his inkstand. All his blots upon my documents were dropped there after twelve o'clock, meridian. Indeed, not only would he be reckless, and sadly given to making blots in the afternoon, but, some days, he went further, and was rather noisy. At such times, too, his face flamed with augmented blazonry, as if cannel coal had been heaped on anthracite. He made an unpleasant racket with his chair; spilled his sand-box; in mending his pens, impatiently split them all to pieces, and threw them on the floor in a sudden passion; stood up, and leaned over his table, boxing his papers about in a most indecorous manner, very sad to behold in an elderly man like him. Nevertheless, as he was in many ways a most valuable person to me, and all the time before twelve o'clock, meridian, was the quickest, steadiest creature, too, accomplishing a great deal of work in a style not easily to be matched — for these reasons, I was willing to overlook his eccentricities, though, indeed, occasionally, I remonstrated with him. I did this very gently, however, because, though the civilest, nay, the blandest and most reverential of men in the morning, yet, in the afternoon, he was disposed, upon provocation, to be slightly rash with his tongue — in fact, insolent. Now, valuing his morning services as I did, and resolved not to lose them — yet, at the same time, made uncomfortable by his inflamed ways after twelve o'clock — and being a man of peace, unwilling by my admonitions to call forth unseemly retorts from him, I took upon me, one Saturday noon (he was always worse on Saturdays) to hint to him, very kindly, that, perhaps, now that he was growing old, it might be well to abridge his labors; in short, he need not come to my chambers after twelve o'clock, but, dinner over, had best go home to his lodgings, and rest himself till tea-time. But no; he insisted upon his afternoon devotions. His countenance became intolerably fervid, as he oratorically assured me — gesticulating with a long ruler at the other end of the room — that if his services in the morning were useful, how indispensable, then, in the afternoon?

"With submission, sir," said Turkey, on this occasion, "I consider myself your right-hand man. In the morning I but marshal and deploy my columns; but in the afternoon I put myself at their head, and gallantly charge the foe, thus" — and he made a violent thrust with the ruler.

"But the blots, Turkey," intimated I.

"True; but, with submission, sir, behold these hairs! I am getting old. Surely, sir, a blot or two of a warm afternoon is not to be severely urged against gray hairs. Old age — even if it blot the page — is honorable. With submission, sir, we *both* are getting old."

This appeal to my fellow-feeling was hardly to be resisted. At all events, I saw that go he would not. So, I made up my mind to let him stay, resolving, nevertheless, to see to it that, during the afternoon, he had to do with my less important papers.

Nippers, the second on my list, was a whiskered, sallow, and, upon the whole, rather piratical-looking young man, of about five-and-twenty. I always deemed him the victim of two evil powers — ambition and indigestion. The ambition was evinced by a certain impatience of the duties of a mere copyist, an unwarrantable usurpation of strictly professional affairs such as the original drawing up of legal documents. The indigestion seemed betokened in an occasional nervous testiness and grinning irritability, causing the teeth to audibly grind together over mistakes committed in copying; unnecessary maledictions, hissed, rather than spoken, in the heat of business; and especially by a continual discontent with the height of the table where he worked. Though of a very ingenious mechanical turn, Nippers could never get this table to suit him. He put chips under it, blocks of various sorts, bits of pasteboard, and at last went so far as to attempt an exquisite adjustment, by final pieces of folded blotting paper. But no invention would answer. If, for the sake of easing his back, he brought the table-lid at a sharp angle well up towards his chin, and wrote there like a man using the steep roof of a Dutch house for his desk, then he declared that it stopped the circulation in his arms. If now he lowered the table to his waistbands, and stooped over it in writing, then there was a sore aching in his back. In short, the truth of the matter was, Nippers knew not what he wanted. Or, if he wanted anything, it was to be rid of a scrivener's table altogether. Among the manifestations of his diseased ambition was a fondness he had for receiving visits from certain ambiguous-looking fellows in seedy coats, whom he called his clients. Indeed, I was aware that not only was he, at times, considerable of a ward-politician, but he occasionally did a little business at the justices' courts, and was not unknown on the steps of the Tombs.° I have good reason to believe, however, that one individual who called upon him at my chambers, and who, with a grand air, he insisted was his client, was no other than a dun, and the alleged title-deed,

---

the Tombs: A prison in New York City.

a bill. But, with all his failings, and the annoyances he caused me, Nippers, like his compatriot Turkey, was a very useful man to me; wrote a neat, swift hand; and, when he chose, was not deficient in a gentlemanly sort of deportment. Added to this, he always dressed in a gentlemanly sort of way; and so, incidentally, reflected credit upon my chambers. Whereas, with respect to Turkey, I had much ado to keep him from being a reproach to me. His clothes were apt to look oily, and smell of eating-houses. He wore his pantaloons very loose and baggy in summer. His coats were execrable, his hat not to be handled. But while the hat was a thing of indifference to me, inasmuch as his natural civility and deference, as a dependent Englishman, always led him to doff it the moment he entered the room, yet his coat was another matter. Concerning his coats, I reasoned with him; but with no effect. The truth was, I suppose, that a man with so small an income could not afford to sport such a lustrous face and a lustrous coat at one and the same time. As Nippers once observed, Turkey's money went chiefly for red ink. One winter day, I presented Turkey with a highly respectable-looking coat of my own — a padded gray coat, of a most comfortable warmth, and which buttoned straight up from the knee to the neck. I thought Turkey would appreciate the favor, and abate his rashness and obstreperousness of afternoons. But no; I verily believe that buttoning himself up in so downy and blanket-like a coat had a pernicious effect upon him upon the same principle that too much oats are bad for horses. In fact, precisely as a rash, restive horse is said to feel his oats, so Turkey felt his coat. It made him insolent. He was a man whom prosperity harmed.

Though, concerning the self-indulgent habits of Turkey, I had my own private surmises, yet, touching Nippers, I was well persuaded that, whatever might be his faults in other respects, he was, at least, a temperate young man. But, indeed, nature herself seemed to have been his vintner, and, at his birth, charged him so thoroughly with an irritable, brandy-like disposition, that all subsequent potations were needless. When I consider how, amid the stillness of my chambers, Nippers would sometimes impatiently rise from his seat, and stooping over his table, spread his arms wide apart, seize the whole desk, and move it, and jerk it, with a grim, grinding motion on the floor, as if the table were a perverse voluntary agent, intent on thwarting and vexing him, I plainly perceive that, for Nippers, brandy-and-water were altogether superfluous.

It was fortunate for me that, owing to its peculiar cause — indigestion — the irritability and consequent nervousness of Nippers were mainly observable in the morning, while in the afternoon he was comparatively mild. So that, Turkey's paroxysms only coming on about twelve o'clock, I never had to do with their eccentricities at one time. Their fits relieved each other, like guards. When Nippers' was on, Turkey's was off; and *vice versa*. This was a good natural arrangement, under the circumstances.

Ginger Nut, the third on my list, was a lad, some twelve years old. His father was a carman, ambitious of seeing his son on the bench instead of a cart, before he died. So he sent him to my office, as student at law, errand-boy, cleaner, and sweeper, at the rate of one dollar a week. He had a little desk to himself, but he did not use it much. Upon inspection, the drawer exhibited a great array of the shells of various sorts of nuts. Indeed, to this quick-witted youth, the whole noble science of the law was contained in a nutshell. Not the least among the employments of Ginger Nut, as well as one which he discharged with the most alacrity, was his duty as cake and apple purveyor for Turkey and Nippers. Copying lawpapers being proverbially a dry, husky sort of business, my two scriveners were fain to moisten their mouths very often with Spitzenbergs, to be had at the numerous stalls nigh the Custom House and Post Office. Also, they sent Ginger Nut very frequently for that peculiar cake — small, flat, round, and very spicy — after which he had been named by them. Of a cold morning, when business was but dull, Turkey would gobble up scores of these cakes, as if they were mere wafers — indeed, they sell them at the rate of six or eight for a penny — the scrape of his pen blending with the crunching of the crisp particles in his mouth. Of all the fiery afternoon blunders and flurried rashness of Turkey, was his once moistening a ginger-cake between his lips, and clapping it on to a mortgage, for a seal. I came within an ace of dismissing him then. But he mollified me by making an oriental bow, and saying —

"With submission, sir, it was generous of me to find you in stationery on my own account."

Now my original business — that of a conveyancer and title hunter, and drawer-up of recondite documents of all sorts — was considerably increased by receiving the Master's office. There was now great work for scriveners. Not only must I push the clerks already with me, but I must have additional help.

In answer to my advertisement, a motionless young man one morning stood upon my office threshold, the door being open, for it was summer. I can see that figure now — pallidly neat, pitiably respectable, incurably forlorn! It was Bartleby.

After a few words touching his qualifications, I engaged him, glad to have among my corps of copyists a man of so singularly sedate an aspect, which I thought might operate beneficially upon the flighty temper of Turkey, and the fiery one of Nippers.

I should have stated before that ground-glass folding-doors divided my premises into two parts, one of which was occupied by my scriveners, the other by myself. According to my humor, I threw open these doors, or closed them. I resolved to assign Bartleby a corner by the folding-doors, but on my side of them, so as to have this quiet man within easy call, in case any trifling thing was to be done. I placed his desk close up to a small side-window in that part of the room, a window which originally had afforded a lateral view of certain grimy brickyards and bricks, but which, owing to subsequent erections, commanded at present no view at all, though it gave some light. Within three feet of the panes was a wall, and the light came down from far above, between two lofty buildings, as from a very small opening in a dome. Still further to a satisfactory arrangement, I procured a high green folding screen, which might entirely isolate Bartleby from my sight, though not remove him from my voice. And thus, in a manner, privacy and society were conjoined.

At first, Bartleby did an extraordinary quantity of writing. As if long famishing for something to copy, he seemed to gorge himself on my documents. There was no pause for digestion. He ran a day and night line, copying by sunlight and by candle-light. I should have been quite delighted with his application, had he been cheerfully industrious. But he wrote on silently, palely, mechanically.

It is, of course, an indispensable part of a scrivener's business to verify the accuracy of his copy, word by word. Where there are two or more scriveners in an office, they assist each other in this examination, one reading from the copy, the other holding the original. It is a very dull, wearisome, and lethargic affair. I can readily imagine that, to some sanguine temperaments, it would be altogether intolerable. For example, I cannot credit that the mettlesome poet, Byron, would have contentedly sat down with Bartleby to examine a law document of, say five hundred pages, closely written in a crimpy hand.

Now and then, in the haste of business, it had been my habit to assist in comparing some brief document myself, calling Turkey or Nippers for this purpose. One object I had, in placing Bartleby so handy to me behind the screen, was, to avail myself of his services on such trivial occasions. It was on the third day, I think, of his being with me, and before any necessity had arisen for having his own writing examined, that, being much hurried to complete a small affair I had in hand, I abruptly called to Bartleby. In my haste and natural expectancy of instant compliance, I sat with my head bent over the original on my desk, and my right hand sideways, and somewhat nervously extended with the copy, so that, immediately upon emerging from his retreat, Bartleby might snatch it and proceed to business without the least delay.

In this very attitude did I sit when I called to him, rapidly stating what it was I wanted him to do — namely, to examine a small paper with me. Imagine my surprise, nay, my consternation, when, without moving from his privacy, Bartleby, in a singularly mild, firm voice, replied, "I would prefer not to."

I sat awhile in perfect silence, rallying my stunned faculties. Immediately it occurred to me that my ears had deceived me, or Bartleby had entirely misunderstood my meaning. I repeated my request in the clearest tone I could assume; but in quite as clear a one came the previous reply, "I would prefer not to."

"Prefer not to," echoed I, rising in high excitement, and crossing the room with a stride. "What do you mean? Are you moonstruck? I want you to help me compare this sheet here — take it," and I thrust it towards him.

"I would prefer not to," said he.

I looked at him steadfastly. His face was leanly composed; his gray eye dimly calm. Not a wrinkle of agitation rippled him. Had there been the least uneasiness, anger, impatience, or impertinence in his manner; in other words, had there been anything ordinarily human about him, doubtless I should have violently dismissed him from the premises. But as it was, I should have as soon thought of turning my pale plaster-of-paris bust of Cicero out of doors. I stood gazing at him awhile, as he went on with his own writing, and then reseated myself at my desk. This is very strange, thought I. What had one best do? But my business hurried me. I concluded to forget the matter for the present, reserving it for my future leisure. So, calling Nippers from the other room, the paper was speedily examined.

A few days after this, Bartleby concluded four lengthy documents, being quadruplicates of a week's testimony taken before me in my High Court of

Chancery. It became necessary to examine them. It was an important suit, and great accuracy was imperative. Having all things arranged, I called Turkey, Nippers, and Ginger Nut, from the next room, meaning to place the four copies in the hands of my four clerks, while I should read from the original. Accordingly, Turkey, Nippers, and Ginger Nut had taken their seats in a row, each with his document in his hand, when I called to Bartleby to join this interesting group.

"Bartleby! quick, I am waiting."

I heard a slow scrape of his chair legs on the uncarpeted floor, and soon he appeared standing at the entrance of his hermitage.

"What is wanted?" said he, mildly.

"The copies, the copies," said I, hurriedly. "We are going to examine them. There" — and I held towards him the fourth quadruplicate.

"I would prefer not to," he said, and gently disappeared behind the screen.

For a few moments I was turned into a pillar of salt, standing at the head of my seated column of clerks. Recovering myself, I advanced towards the screen, and demanded the reason for such extraordinary conduct.

"*Why* do you refuse?"

"I would prefer not to."

With any other man I should have flown outright into a dreadful passion, scorned all further words, and thrust him ignominiously from my presence. But there was something about Bartleby that not only strangely disarmed me, but, in a wonderful manner, touched and disconcerted me. I began to reason with him.

"These are your own copies we are about to examine. It is labor saving to you, because one examination will answer for your four papers. It is common usage. Every copyist is bound to help examine his copy. Is it not so? Will you not speak? Answer!"

"I prefer not to," he replied in a flute-like tone. It seemed to me that, while I had been addressing him, he carefully revolved every statement that I made; fully comprehended the meaning; could not gainsay the irresistible conclusion; but, at the same time, some paramount consideration prevailed with him to reply as he did.

"You are decided, then, not to comply with my request — a request made according to common usage and common sense?"

He briefly gave me to understand, that on that point my judgment was sound. Yes: his decision was irreversible.

It is not seldom the case that, when a man is browbeaten in some unprecedented and violently unreasonable way, he begins to stagger in his own plainest faith. He begins, as it were, vaguely to surmise that, wonderful as it may be, all the justice and all the reason is on the other side. Accordingly, if any disinterested persons are present, he turns to them for some reinforcement for his own faltering mind.

"Turkey," said I, "what do you think of this? Am I not right?"

"With submission, sir," said Turkey, in his blandest tone, "I think that you are."

"Nippers," said I, "what do *you* think of it?"

"I think I should kick him out of the office."

(The reader of nice perceptions will have perceived that, it being morning, Turkey's answer is couched in polite and tranquil terms, but Nippers replies in ill-tempered ones. Or, to repeat a previous sentence, Nippers' ugly mood was on duty, and Turkey's off.)

"Ginger Nut," said I, willing to enlist the smallest suffrage in my behalf, "what do *you* think of it?"

"I think, sir, he's a little *luny*," replied Ginger Nut, with a grin.

"You hear what they say," said I, turning towards the screen, "come forth and do your duty."

But he vouchsafed no reply. I pondered a moment in sore perplexity. But once more business hurried me. I determined again to postpone the consideration of this dilemma to my future leisure. With a little trouble we made out to examine the papers without Bartleby, though at every page or two Turkey deferentially dropped his opinion, that this proceeding was quite out of the common; while Nippers, twitching in his chair with a dyspeptic nervousness, ground out, between his set teeth, occasional hissing maledictions against the stubborn oaf behind the screen. And for his (Nippers') part, this was the first and the last time he would do another man's business without pay.

Meanwhile Bartleby sat in his hermitage, oblivious to everything but his own peculiar business there.

Some days passed, the scrivener being employed upon another lengthy work. His late remarkable conduct led me to regard his ways narrowly. I observed that he never went to dinner; indeed, that he never went anywhere. As yet I had never, of my personal knowledge, known him to be outside of my office. He was a perpetual sentry in the corner. At about eleven o'clock though, in the morning, I noticed that Ginger Nut would advance towards the opening in Bartleby's screen, as if silently beckoned thither by a gesture invisible to me where I sat. The boy would then leave the office, jingling a few pence, and reappear with a handful of ginger-nuts, which he delivered in the hermitage, receiving two of the cakes for his trouble.

He lives, then, on ginger-nuts, thought I; never eats a dinner, properly speaking; he must be a vegetarian, then, but no; he never eats even vegetables, he eats nothing but ginger-nuts. My mind then ran on in reveries concerning the probable effects upon the human constitution of living entirely on ginger-nuts. Ginger-nuts are so called, because they contain ginger as one of their peculiar constituents, and the final flavoring one. Now, what was ginger? A hot, spicy thing. Was Bartleby hot and spicy? Not at all. Ginger, then, had no effect upon Bartleby. Probably he preferred it should have none.

Nothing so aggravates an earnest person as a passive resistance. If the individual so resisted be of a not inhumane temper, and the resisting one perfectly harmless in his passivity, then, in the better moods of the former, he will endeavor charitably to construe to his imagination what proves impossible to be solved by his judgment. Even so, for the most part, I regarded Bartleby and his ways. Poor fellow! thought I, he means no mischief; it is plain he intends no insolence; his aspect sufficiently evinces that his eccentricities are involuntary. He is useful to me. I can get along with him. If I turn him away, the chances are he will fall in with some less indulgent employer, and then he will be rudely treated, and perhaps driven forth miserably to starve. Yes. Here I can cheaply purchase a delicious self-approval. To befriend Bartleby; to humor him in his strange wilfulness, will cost me little or nothing, while I lay up in my soul what will eventually prove a sweet morsel for my conscience. But this mood was not invariable with me. The passiveness of Bartleby sometimes irritated me. I felt strangely goaded on to encounter him in new opposition — to elicit some angry spark from him answerable to my own. But, indeed, I might as well have essayed to strike fire with my knuckles against a bit of Windsor soap. But one afternoon the evil impulse in me mastered me, and the following little scene ensued:

"Bartleby," said I, "when those papers are all copied, I will compare them with you."

"I would prefer not to."

"How? Surely you do not mean to persist in that mulish vagary?"

No answer.

I threw open the folding-doors nearby, and turning upon Turkey and Nippers, exclaimed:

"Bartleby a second time says, he won't examine his papers. What do you think of it, Turkey?"

It was afternoon, be it remembered. Turkey sat glowing like a brass boiler; his bald head steaming; his hands reeling among his blotted papers.

"Think of it?" roared Turkey. "I think I'll just step behind his screen, and black his eyes for him!"

So saying, Turkey rose to his feet and threw his arms into a pugilistic position. He was hurrying away to make good his promise, when I detained him, alarmed at the effect of incautiously rousing Turkey's combativeness after dinner.

"Sit down, Turkey," said I, "and hear what Nippers has to say. What do you think of it, Nippers? Would I not be justified in immediately dismissing Bartleby?"

"Excuse me, that is for you to decide, sir. I think his conduct quite unusual, and, indeed, unjust, as regards Turkey and myself. But it may only be a passing whim."

"Ah," exclaimed I, "you have strangely changed your mind, then — you speak very gently of him now."

"All beer," cried Turkey; "gentleness is effects of beer — Nippers and I dined together to-day. You see how gentle *I* am, sir. Shall I go and black his eyes?"

"You refer to Bartleby, I suppose. No, not to-day, Turkey," I replied; "pray, put up your fists."

I closed the doors, and again advanced towards Bartleby. I felt additional incentives tempting me to my fate. I burned to be rebelled against again. I remembered that Bartleby never left the office.

"Bartleby," said I, "Ginger Nut is away; just step around to the Post Office, won't you?" (it was but a three minutes' walk) "and see if there is anything for me."

"I would prefer not to."

"You *will* not?"

"I *prefer* not."

I staggered to my desk, and sat there in a deep study. My blind inveteracy returned. Was there any other thing in which I could procure myself to be ignominiously repulsed by this lean, penniless wight? my hired clerk? What added thing is there, perfectly reasonable, that he will be sure to refuse to do?

"Bartleby!"

No answer.

"Bartleby," in a louder tone.

No answer.

"Bartleby," I roared.

Like a very ghost, agreeably to the laws of magical invocation, at the third summons, he appeared at the entrance of his hermitage.

"Go to the next room, and tell Nippers to come to me."

"I would prefer not to," he respectfully and slowly said, and mildly disappeared.

"Very good, Bartleby," said I, in a quiet sort of serenely-severe self-possessed tone, intimating the unalterable purpose of some terrible retribution very close at hand. At the moment I half intended something of the kind. But upon the whole, as it was drawing towards my dinner-hour, I thought it best to put on my hat and walk home for the day, suffering much from perplexity and distress of mind.

Shall I acknowledge it? The conclusion of this whole business was, that it soon became a fixed fact of my chambers, that a pale young scrivener, by the name of Bartleby, had a desk there; that he copied for me at the usual rate of four cents a folio (one hundred words); but he was permanently exempt from examining the work done by him, that duty being transferred to Turkey and Nippers, out of compliment, doubtless, to their superior acuteness; moreover, said Bartleby was never, on any account, to be dispatched on the most trivial errand of any sort; and that even if entreated to take upon him such a matter, it was generally understood that he would "prefer not to" — in other words, that he would refuse point blank.

As days passed on, I became considerably reconciled to Bartleby. His steadiness, his freedom from all dissipation, his incessant industry (except when he chose to throw himself into a standing revery behind his screen), his great stillness, his unalterableness of demeanor under all circumstances, made him a valuable acquisition. One prime thing was this — *he was always there* — first in the morning, continually through the day, and the last at night. I had a singular confidence in his honesty. I felt my most precious papers perfectly safe in his hands. Sometimes, to be sure, I could not, for the very soul of me, avoid falling into sudden spasmodic passions with him. For it was exceeding difficult to bear in mind all the time those strange peculiarities, privileges, and unheard-of exemptions, forming the tacit stipulations on Bartleby's part under which he remained in my office. Now and then, in the eagerness of dispatching pressing business, I would inadvertently summon Bartleby, in a short, rapid tone, to put his finger, say, on the incipient tie of a bit of red tape with which I was about compressing some papers. Of course, from behind the screen the usual answer, "I prefer not to," was sure to come; and then, how could a human creature, with the common infirmities of our nature, refrain from bitterly exclaiming upon such perverseness — such unreasonableness? However, every added repulse of this sort which I received only tended to lessen the probability of my repeating the inadvertence.

Here it must be said, that, according to the custom of most legal gentlemen occupying chambers in densely populated law buildings, there were several keys to my door. One was kept by a woman residing in the attic, which person weekly scrubbed and daily swept and dusted my apartments. Another was kept by Turkey for convenience sake. The third I sometimes carried in my own pocket. The fourth I knew not who had.

Now, one Sunday morning I happened to go to Trinity Church, to hear a celebrated preacher, and finding myself rather early on the ground I thought I would walk round to my chambers for a while. Luckily I had my key with me; but upon applying it to the lock, I found it resisted by something inserted from the inside. Quite surprised, I called out; when to my consternation a key was turned from within; and thrusting his lean visage at me, and holding the door ajar, the apparition of Bartleby appeared, in his shirt-sleeves, and otherwise in a strangely tattered *deshabille,* saying quietly that he was sorry, but he was deeply engaged just then, and preferred not admitting me at present. In a brief word or two, he moreover added, that perhaps I had better walk round the block two or three times, and by that time he would probably have concluded his affairs.

Now, the utterly unsurmised appearance of Bartleby, tenanting my law-chambers of a Sunday morning, with his cadaverously gentlemanly *nonchalance,* yet withal firm and self-possessed, had such a strange effect upon me, that incontinently I slunk away from my own door, and did as desired. But not without sundry twinges of impotent rebellion against the mild effrontery of this unaccountable scrivener. Indeed, it was his wonderful mildness chiefly, which not only disarmed me, but unmanned me, as it were. For I consider that one, for the time, is sort of unmanned when he tranquilly permits his hired clerk to dictate to him, and order him away from his own premises. Furthermore, I was full of uneasiness as to what Bartleby could possibly be doing in my office in his shirt-sleeves, and in an otherwise dismantled condition on a Sunday morning. Was anything amiss going on? Nay, that was out of the question. It was not to be thought of for a moment that Bartleby was an immoral person. But what could he be doing there? — copying? Nay again, whatever might be his eccentricities, Bartleby was an eminently decorous person. He would be the last man to sit down to his desk in any state approaching to nudity. Besides, it was Sunday; and there was something about Bartleby that forbade the supposition that he would by any secular occupation violate the proprieties of the day.

Nevertheless, my mind was not pacified; and full of a restless curiosity, at last I returned to the door. Without hindrance I inserted my key, opened it, and entered. Bartleby was not to be seen. I looked round anxiously, peeped behind his screen; but it was very plain that he was gone. Upon more closely examining the place, I surmised that for an indefinite period Bartleby must have ate, dressed, and slept in my office, and that too without plate, mirror, or bed. The cushioned seat of a rickety old sofa in one corner bore the faint impress of a lean, reclining form. Rolled away under his desk, I found a blanket; under the empty grate, a blacking box and brush; on a chair, a tin basin, with soap and a ragged towel; in a newspaper a few crumbs of ginger-nuts and a morsel of cheese. Yes, thought I, it is evident enough that Bartleby has been making his home here, keeping bachelor's hall all by himself. Immediately then the thought came sweeping across me, what miserable friendlessness and loneliness are here revealed! His poverty is great; but his solitude, how horrible! Think of it. Of a Sunday, Wall Street is deserted as Petra;° and every night of every day it is an emptiness. This building, too, which of weekdays hums with industry and life, at nightfall echoes with sheer vacancy, and all through Sunday is forlorn. And here Bartleby makes his home; sole spectator of a solitude which he has seen all populous — a sort of innocent and transformed Marius° brooding among the ruins of Carthage!

For the first time in my life a feeling of overpowering stinging melancholy seized me. Before, I had never experienced aught but a not unpleasing sadness. The bond of a common humanity now drew me irresistibly to gloom. A fraternal melancholy! For both I and Bartleby were sons of Adam. I remembered the bright silks and sparkling faces I had seen that day, in gala trim, swan-like sailing down the Mississippi of Broadway; and I contrasted them with the pallid copyist, and thought to myself, Ah, happiness courts the light, so we deem the world is gay; but misery hides aloof, so we deem that misery there is none. These sad fancyings — chimeras, doubtless, of a sick and silly brain — led on to other and more special thoughts, concerning the eccentricities of Bartleby. Presentiments of strange discoveries hovered round me. The scrivener's pale form appeared to me laid out, among uncaring strangers, in its shivering winding-sheet.

Suddenly I was attracted by Bartleby's closed desk, the key in open sight left in the lock.

I mean no mischief, seek the gratification of no heartless curiosity, thought I; besides, the desk is mine, and its contents, too, so I will make bold to look within. Everything was methodically arranged, the papers smoothly placed. The pigeon-holes were deep, and removing the files of documents, I groped into their recesses. Presently I felt something there, and dragged it out. It was an old bandanna handkerchief, heavy and knotted. I opened it, and saw it was a saving's bank.

Petra: A city in what is now Jordan, once the center of an Arab kingdom. It was deserted for more than ten centuries, until its rediscovery by explorers in 1812.

Marius: Gaius Marius (157?–86 B.C.) was a Roman general, several times elected consul. Marius's greatest military successes came in the Jugurthine War, in Africa. Later, when his opponents gained power and he was banished, he fled to Africa. Carthage was a city in North Africa.

I now recalled all the quiet mysteries which I had noted in the man. I remembered that he never spoke but to answer; that, though at intervals he had considerable time to himself, yet I had never seen him reading — no, not even a newspaper; that for long periods he would stand looking out, at his pale window behind the screen, upon the dead brick wall; I was quite sure he never visited any refectory or eating-house; while his pale face clearly indicated that he never drank beer like Turkey; or tea and coffee even, like other men; that he never went anywhere in particular that I could learn; never went out for a walk, unless, indeed, that was the case at present; that he had declined telling who he was, or whence he came, or whether he had any relatives in the world; that though so thin and pale, he never complained of ill-health. And more than all, I remembered a certain unconscious air of pallid — how shall I call it? — of pallid haughtiness, say, or rather an austere reserve about him, which has positively awed me into my tame compliance with his eccentricities, when I had feared to ask him to do the slightest incidental thing for me, even though I might know, from his long-continued motionlessness, that behind his screen he must be standing in one of those dead-wall reveries of his.

Revolving all these things, and coupling them with the recently discovered fact, that he made my office his constant abiding place and home, and not forgetful of his morbid moodiness; revolving all these things, a prudential feeling began to steal over me. My first emotions had been those of pure melancholy and sincerest pity; but just in proportion as the forlornness of Bartleby grew and grew to my imagination, did that same melancholy merge into fear, that pity into repulsion. So true it is, and so terrible, too, that up to a certain point the thought or sight of misery enlists our best affections; but, in certain special cases, beyond that point it does not. They err who would assert that invariably this is owing to the inherent selfishness of the human heart. It rather proceeds from a certain hopelessness of remedying excessive and organic ill. To a sensitive being, pity is not seldom pain. And when at last it is perceived that such pity cannot lead to effectual succor, common sense bids the soul be rid of it. What I saw that morning persuaded me that the scrivener was the victim of innate and incurable disorder. I might give alms to his body; but his body did not pain him; it was his soul that suffered, and his soul I could not reach.

I did not accomplish the purpose of going to Trinity Church that morning. Somehow, the things I had seen disqualified me for the time from church-going. I walked homeward, thinking what I would do with Bartleby. Finally, I resolved upon this — I would put certain calm questions to him the next morning, touching his history, etc., and if he declined to answer them openly and unreservedly (and I supposed he would prefer not), then to give him a twenty dollar bill over and above whatever I might owe him, and tell him his services were no longer required; but that if in any other way I could assist him, I would be happy to do so, especially if he desired to return to his native place, wherever that might be, I would willingly help to defray the expenses. Moreover, if, after reaching home, he found himself at any time in want of aid, a letter from him would be sure of a reply.

The next morning came.

"Bartleby," said I, gently calling to him behind his screen.

No reply.

"Bartleby," said I, in a still gentler tone, "come here; I am not going to ask you to do anything you would prefer not to do — I simply wish to speak to you."

Upon this he noiselessly slid into view.

"Will you tell me, Bartleby, where you were born?"

"I would prefer not to."

"Will you tell me *anything* about yourself?"

"I would prefer not to."

"But what reasonable objection can you have to speak to me? I feel friendly towards you."

He did not look at me while I spoke, but kept his glance fixed upon my bust of Cicero, which, as I then sat, was directly behind me, some six inches above my head.

"What is your answer, Bartleby?" said I, after waiting a considerable time for a reply, during which his countenance remained immovable, only there was the faintest conceivable tremor of the white attenuated mouth.

"At present I prefer to give no answer," he said, and retired into his hermitage.

It was rather weak in me I confess, but his manner, on this occasion, nettled me. Not only did there seem to lurk in it a certain calm disdain, but his perverseness seemed ungrateful, considering the undeniable good usage and indulgence he had received from me.

Again I sat ruminating what I should do. Mortified as I was at his behavior, and resolved as I had been to dismiss him when I entered my office, nevertheless I strangely felt something superstitious knocking at my heart, and forbidding me to carry out my purpose, and denouncing me for a villain if I dared to breathe one bitter word against this forlornest of mankind. At last, familiarly drawing my chair behind his screen, I sat down and said: "Bartleby, never mind, then, about revealing your history; but let me entreat you, as a friend, to comply as far as may be with the usages of this office. Say now, you will help to examine papers tomorrow or next day: in short, say now, that in a day or two you will begin to be a little reasonable: — say so, Bartleby."

"At present I would prefer not to be a little reasonable," was his mildly cadaverous reply.

Just then the folding-doors opened, and Nippers approached. He seemed suffering from an unusually bad night's rest, induced by severer indigestion than common. He overheard those final words of Bartleby.

"*Prefer not,* eh?" gritted Nippers — "I'd *prefer* him, if I were you, sir," addressing me — "I'd *prefer* him; I'd give him preferences, the stubborn mule! What is it, sir, pray, that he *prefers* not to do now?"

Bartleby moved not a limb.

"Mr. Nippers," said I, "I'd prefer that you would withdraw for the present."

Somehow, of late, I had got into the way of involuntarily using this word "prefer" upon all sorts of not exactly suitable occasions. And I trembled to think that my contact with the scrivener had already and seriously affected me in a mental way. And what further and deeper aberration might it not yet produce? This apprehension had not been without efficacy in determining me to summary measures.

As Nippers, looking very sour and sulky, was departing, Turkey blandly and deferentially approached.

"With submission, sir," said he, "yesterday I was thinking about Bartleby here, and I think that if he would but prefer to take a quart of good ale every day, it would do much towards mending him, and enabling him to assist in examining his papers."

"So you have got the word, too," said I, slightly excited.

"With submission, what word, sir?" asked Turkey, respectfully crowding himself into the contracted space behind the screen, and by so doing, making me jostle the scrivener. "What word, sir?"

"I would prefer to be left alone here," said Bartleby, as if offended at being mobbed in his privacy.

"*That's* the word, Turkey," said I — "*that's* it."

"Oh, *prefer*? oh yes — queer word. I never use it myself. But, sir, as I was saying, if he would but prefer —"

"Turkey," interrupted I, "you will please withdraw."

"Oh certainly, sir, if you prefer that I should."

As he opened the folding-door to retire, Nippers at his desk caught a glimpse of me, and asked whether I would prefer to have a certain paper copied on blue paper or white. He did not in the least roguishly accent the word "prefer." It was plain that it involuntarily rolled from his tongue. I thought to myself, surely I must get rid of a demented man, who already has in some degree turned the tongues, if not the heads of myself and clerks. But I thought it prudent not to break the dismission at once.

The next day I noticed that Bartleby did nothing but stand at his window in his dead-wall revery. Upon asking him why he did not write, he said that he had decided upon doing no more writing.

"Why, how now? what next?" exclaimed I, "do no more writing?"

"No more."

"And what is the reason?"

"Do you not see the reason for yourself?" he indifferently replied.

I looked steadfastly at him, and perceived that his eyes looked dull and glazed. Instantly it occurred to me, that his unexampled diligence in copying by his dim window for the first few weeks of his stay with me might have temporarily impaired his vision.

I was touched. I said something in condolence with him. I hinted that of course he did wisely in abstaining from writing for a while; and urged him to embrace that opportunity of taking wholesome exercise in the open air. This, however, he did not do. A few days after this, my other clerks being absent, and being in a great hurry to dispatch certain letters by the mail, I thought that, having nothing else earthly to do, Bartleby would surely be less inflexible than usual, and carry these letters to the Post Office. But he blankly declined. So, much to my inconvenience, I went myself.

Still added days went by. Whether Bartleby's eyes improved or not, I could not say. To all appearance, I thought they did. But when I asked him if they did he vouchsafed no answer. At all events, he would do no copying. At last, in replying to my urgings, he informed me that he had permanently given up copying.

"What!" exclaimed I; "suppose your eyes should get entirely well — better than ever before — would you not copy then?"

"I have given up copying," he answered, and slid aside.

He remained as ever, a fixture in my chamber. Nay — if that were possible — he became still more of a fixture than before. What was to be done? He would do nothing in the office; why should he stay there? In plain fact, he had now become a millstone to me, not only useless as a necklace, but afflictive to bear. Yet I was sorry for him. I speak less than truth when I say that, on his own account, he occasioned me uneasiness. If he would but have named a single relative or friend, I would instantly have written, and urged their taking the poor fellow away to some convenient retreat. But he seemed alone, absolutely alone in the universe. A bit of wreck in the mid-Atlantic. At length, necessities connected with my business tyrannized over all other considerations. Decently as I could, I told Bartleby that in six days' time he must unconditionally leave the office. I warned him to take measures, in the interval, for procuring some other abode. I offered to assist him in this endeavor, if he himself would but take the first step towards a removal. "And when you finally quit me, Bartleby," added I, "I shall see that you go not away entirely unprovided. Six days from this hour, remember."

At the expiration of that period, I peeped behind the screen, and lo! Bartleby was there.

I buttoned up my coat, balanced myself; advanced slowly towards him, touched his shoulder, and said, "The time has come; you must quit this place; I am sorry for you; here is money; but you must go."

"I would prefer not," he replied, with his back still towards me.

"You *must*."

He remained silent.

Now I had an unbounded confidence in this man's common honesty. He had frequently restored to me sixpences and shillings carelessly dropped upon the floor, for I am apt to be very reckless in such shirt-button affairs. The proceeding, then, which followed will not be deemed extraordinary.

"Bartleby," said I, "I owe you twelve dollars on account; here are thirty-two; the odd twenty are yours — Will you take it?" and I handed the bills towards him.

But he made no motion.

"I will leave them here, then," putting them under a weight on the table. Then taking my hat and cane and going to the door, I tranquilly turned and added —" After you have removed your things from these offices, Bartleby, you will of course lock the door — since every one is now gone for the day but you — and if you please, slip your key underneath the mat, so that I may have it in the morning. I shall not see you again; so good-bye to you. If, hereafter, in your new place of abode, I can be of any service to you, do not fail to advise me by letter. Good-bye, Bartleby, and fare you well."

But he answered not a word; like the last column of some ruined temple, he remained standing mute and solitary in the middle of the otherwise deserted room.

As I walked home in a pensive mood, my vanity got the better of my pity. I could not but highly plume myself on my masterly management in getting rid of Bartleby. Masterly I call it, and such it must appear to any dispassionate thinker. The beauty of my procedure seemed to consist in its perfect quietness. There was no vulgar bullying, no bravado of any sort, no choleric hectoring, and striding to and fro across the apartment, jerking out vehement commands for Bartleby to bundle himself off with his beggarly traps. Nothing of the kind. Without loudly bidding Bartleby depart — as an inferior genius might have done — I *assumed* the ground that depart he must; and upon that assumption built all I had to say. The more I thought over my procedure, the more I was charmed with it. Nevertheless, next morning, upon awakening, I had my doubts — I had somehow slept off the fumes of vanity. One of the coolest and wisest hours a man has, is just after he awakes in the morning. My procedure seemed as sagacious as ever — but only in theory. How it would prove in practice — there was the rub. It was truly a beautiful thought to have assumed Bartleby's departure; but, after all, that assumption was simply my own, and none of Bartleby's. The great point was, not whether I had assumed that he would quit me, but whether he would prefer to do so. He was more a man of preferences than assumptions.

After breakfast, I walked down town, arguing the probabilities *pro* and *con*. One moment I thought it would prove a miserable failure, and Bartleby would be found all alive at my office as usual; the next moment it seemed certain that I should find his chair empty. And so I kept veering about. At the corner of Broadway and Canal Street, I saw quite an excited group of people standing in earnest conversation.

"I'll take odds he doesn't," said a voice as I passed.

"Doesn't go? — done!" said I, "put up your money."

I was instinctively putting my hand in my pocket to produce my own, when I remembered that this was an election day. The words I had overheard bore no reference to Bartleby, but to the success or non-success of some candidate for the mayoralty. In my intent frame of mind, I had, as it were, imagined that all Broadway shared in my excitement, and were debating the same question with me. I passed on, very thankful that the uproar of the street screened my momentary absent-mindedness.

As I had intended, I was earlier than usual at my office door. I stood listening for a moment. All was still. He must be gone. I tried the knob. The door was locked. Yes, my procedure had worked to a charm; he indeed must be vanished. Yet a certain melancholy mixed with this: I was almost sorry for my brilliant success. I was fumbling under the door mat for the key, which Bartleby was to have left there for me, when accidentally my knee knocked against a panel, producing a summoning sound, and in response a voice came to me from within — "Not yet; I am occupied."

It was Bartleby.

I was thunderstruck. For an instant I stood like the man who, pipe in mouth, was killed one cloudless afternoon long ago in Virginia, by summer lightning; at his own warm open window he was killed, and remained leaning out there upon the dreamy afternoon, till someone touched him, when he fell.

"Not gone!" I murmured at last. But again obeying that wondrous ascendancy which the inscrutable scrivener had over me, and from which ascendancy, for all my chafing, I could not completely escape, I slowly went down stairs and out into the street, and while walking round the block, considered what I should next do in this unheard-of perplexity. Turn the man out by an actual thrusting I could not; to drive him away by calling him hard names would not do; calling in the police was an unpleasant idea; and yet, permit him to enjoy his cadaverous triumph over me — this, too, I could not think of. What was to be done? or, if nothing could be done, was there anything further that I could *assume* in the matter? Yes, as before I had prospectively assumed that Bartleby would depart, so now I might retrospectively assume that departed he was. In the legitimate carrying out of this assumption, I might enter my office in a great hurry, and pretending not to see Bartleby at all, walk straight against him as if he were air. Such a proceeding would in a singular degree have the appearance of a home-thrust. It was hardly possible that Bartleby could withstand such an application of the doctrine of assumption. But upon second thoughts the success of the plan seemed rather dubious. I resolved to argue the matter over with him again.

"Bartleby," said I, entering the office, with a quietly severe expression, "I am seriously displeased. I am pained, Bartleby. I had thought better of you. I had imagined you of such a gentlemanly organization, that in any delicate dilemma a slight hint would suffice — in short, an assumption. But it appears I am deceived. Why," I added, unaffectedly starting, "You have not even touched that money yet," pointing to it, just where I had left it the evening previous.

He answered nothing.

"Will you, or will you not, quit me?" I now demanded in a sudden passion, advancing close to him.

"I would prefer *not* to quit you," he replied, gently emphasizing the *not*.

"What earthly right have you to stay here? Do you pay any rent? Do you pay my taxes? Or is this property yours?"

He answered nothing.

"Are you ready to go on and write now? Are your eyes recovered? Could you copy a small paper for me this morning? or help examine a few lines? or step round to the Post Office? In a word, will you do anything at all, to give a coloring to your refusal to depart the premises?"

He silently retired into his hermitage.

I was now in such a state of nervous resentment that I thought it but prudent to check myself at present from further demonstrations. Bartleby and I were alone. I remembered the tragedy of the unfortunate Adams and the still more unfortunate Colt in the solitary office of the latter; and how poor Colt, being dreadfully incensed by Adams, and imprudently permitting himself to get wildly excited, was at unawares hurried into his fatal act — an act which certainly no man could possibly deplore more than the actor himself.° Often it had occurred to me in my ponderings upon the subject that had that altercation taken place in the public street, or at a private residence, it would not have terminated as it did. It was the circumstance of being alone in a solitary office, up stairs, of a building entirely unhallowed by humanizing domestic associations — an uncarpeted office, doubtless, of a dusty, haggard sort of appearance — this it must have been, which greatly helped to enhance the irritable desperation of the hapless Colt.

But when this old Adam of resentment rose in me and tempted me concerning Bartleby, I grappled him and threw him. How? Why, simply by recalling the divine injunction: "A new commandment give I unto you, that ye love one another." Yes, this it was that saved me. Aside from higher considerations, charity often operates as a vastly wise and prudent principle — a great safeguard to its possessor. Men have committed murder for jealousy's sake, and anger's sake, and hatred's sake, and selfishness' sake, and spiritual pride's sake; but no man, that ever I heard of, ever committed a diabolical murder for sweet charity's sake. Mere self-interest, then, if no better motive can be enlisted, should, especially with high-tempered men, prompt all beings to charity and philanthropy. At any rate, upon the occasion in question, I strove to drown my exasperated feelings towards the scrivener by benevolently construing his conduct. Poor fellow, poor fellow! thought I, he don't mean anything; and besides, he has seen hard times, and ought to be indulged.

I endeavored, also, immediately to occupy myself, and at the same time to comfort my despondency. I tried to fancy, that in the course of the morning, at such time as might prove agreeable to him, Bartleby, of his own free accord, would emerge from his hermitage and take up some decided line of march in the direction of the door. But no. Half-past twelve o'clock came; Turkey began to glow in the face, overturn his inkstand, and become generally obstreperous; Nippers abated down into quietude and courtesy; Ginger Nut munched his noon apple; and Bartleby remained standing at his window in one of his profoundest dead-wall reveries. Will it be credited? Ought I to acknowledge it? That afternoon I left the office without saying one further word to him.

Some days now passed, during which, at leisure intervals I looked a little into "Edwards on the Will,"° and "Priestley on Necessity."° Under the

---

the actor himself: John C. Colt murdered Samuel Adams in January 1842. Later that year, after his conviction, Colt committed suicide a half-hour before he was to be hanged. The case received wide and sensationalistic press coverage at the time.

Edwards on the Will: Jonathan Edwards was an important American theologian, a rigidly orthodox Calvinist who believed in the doctrine of predestination and a leader of the Great Awakening, the religious revival that swept the North American colonies in the 1740s. The work being alluded to here is *Freedom of the Will* (1754).

Priestley on Necessity: Joseph Priestley (1733–1803) was an English scientist and clergyman who began as a Unitarian but developed his own radical ideas on "natural determinism." As a scientist, he did early experiments with electricity and was one of the first to discover the existence of oxygen. As a political philosopher, he championed the French Revolution — a cause so unpopular in England that he had to flee that country and spend the last decade of his life in the United States.

circumstances, those books induced a salutary feeling. Gradually I slid into the persuasion that these troubles of mine, touching the scrivener, had been all predestined from eternity, and Bartleby was billeted upon me for some mysterious purpose of an all-wise Providence, which it was not for a mere mortal like me to fathom. Yes, Bartleby, stay there behind your screen, thought I; I shall persecute you no more; you are harmless and noiseless as any of these old chairs; in short, I never feel so private as when I know you are here. At last I see it, I feel it; I penetrate to the predestined purpose of my life. I am content. Others may have loftier parts to enact; but my mission in this world, Bartleby, is to furnish you with office-room for such period as you may see fit to remain.

I believe that this wise and blessed frame of mind would have continued with me, had it not been for the unsolicited and uncharitable remarks obtruded upon me by my professional friends who visited the rooms. But thus it often is, that the constant friction of illiberal minds wears out at last the best resolves of the more generous. Though to be sure, when I reflected upon it, it was not strange that people entering my office should be struck by the peculiar aspect of the unaccountable Bartleby, and so be tempted to throw out some sinister observations concerning him. Sometimes an attorney, having business with me, and calling at my office, and finding no one but the scrivener there, would undertake to obtain some sort of precise information from him touching my whereabouts; but without heeding his idle talk, Bartleby would remain standing immovable in the middle of the room. So after contemplating him in that position for a time, the attorney would depart, no wiser than he came.

Also, when a reference was going on, and the room full of lawyers and witnesses, and business driving fast, some deeply-occupied legal gentleman present, seeing Bartleby wholly unemployed, would request him to run round to his (the legal gentleman's) office and fetch some papers for him. Thereupon, Bartleby would tranquilly decline, and yet remain idle as before. Then the lawyer would give a great stare, and turn to me. And what could I say? At last I was made aware that all through the circle of my professional acquaintance, a whisper of wonder was running round, having reference to the strange creature I kept at my office. This worried me very much. And as the idea came upon me of his possibly turning out a long-lived man, and keeping occupying my chambers, and denying my authority; and perplexing my visitors; and scandalizing my professional reputation; and casting a general gloom over the premises; keeping soul and body together to the last upon his savings (for doubtless he spent but half a dime a day), and in the end perhaps outlive me, and claim possession of my office by right of his perpetual occupancy: as all these dark anticipations crowded upon me more and more, and my friends continually intruded their relentless remarks upon the apparition in my room; a great change was wrought in me. I resolved to gather all my faculties together, and forever rid me of this intolerable incubus.

Ere revolving any complicated project, however, adapted to this end, I first simply suggested to Bartleby the propriety of his permanent departure. In a calm and serious tone, I commended the idea to his careful and mature consideration. But, having taken three days to meditate upon it, he apprised me, that his original determination remained the same; in short, that he still preferred to abide with me.

What shall I do? I now said to myself, buttoning up my coat to the last button. What shall I do? what ought I to do? what does conscience say I *should* do with this man, or, rather, ghost. Rid myself of him, I must; go, he shall. But how? You will not thrust him, the poor, pale, passive mortal you will not thrust such a helpless creature out of your door? you will not dishonor yourself by such cruelty? No, I will not, I cannot do that. Rather would I let him live and die here, and then mason up his remains in the wall. What, then, will you do? For all your coaxing, he will not budge. Bribes he leaves under your own paperweight on your table; in short, it is quite plain that he prefers to cling to you.

Then something severe, something unusual must be done. What! surely you will not have him collared by a constable, and commit his innocent pallor to the common jail? And upon what ground could you procure such a thing to be done? — a vagrant, is he? What! he a vagrant, a wanderer, who refuses to budge? It is because he will not be a vagrant, then, that you seek to count him *as* a vagrant. That is too absurd. No visible means of support: there I have him. Wrong again: for indubitably he *does* support himself, and that is the only unanswerable proof that any man can show of his possessing the means so to do. No more, then. Since he will not quit me, I must quit him. I will change my offices; I will move elsewhere, and give him fair notice, that if I find him on my new premises I will then proceed against him as a common trespasser.

Acting accordingly, next day I thus addressed him: "I find these chambers too far from the City Hall; the air is unwholesome. In a word, I propose to remove my offices next week, and shall no longer require your services. I tell you this now, in order that you may seek another place."

He made no reply, and nothing more was said.

On the appointed day I engaged carts and men, proceeded to my chambers, and, having but little furniture, everything was removed in a few hours. Throughout, the scrivener remained standing behind the screen, which I directed to be removed the last thing. It was withdrawn; and, being folded up like a huge folio, left him the motionless occupant of a naked room. I stood in the entry watching him a moment, while something from within me upbraided me.

I re-entered, with my hand in my pocket — and — and my heart in my mouth.

"Good-bye, Bartleby; I am going — good-bye, and God some way bless you; and take that," slipping something in his hand. But it dropped upon the floor, and then — strange to say — I tore myself from him whom I had so longed to be rid of.

Established in my new quarters, for a day or two I kept the door locked, started at every footfall in the passages. When I returned to my rooms, after any little absence, I would pause at the threshold for an instant, and attentively listen, ere applying my key. But these fears were needless. Bartleby never came nigh me.

I thought all was going well, when a perturbed-looking stranger visited me, inquiring whether I was the person who had recently occupied rooms at No. — Wall Street.

Full of forebodings, I replied that I was.

"Then, sir," said the stranger, who proved a lawyer, "you are responsible for the man you left there. He refuses to do any copying; he refuses to do anything; he says he prefers not to; and he refuses to quit the premises."

"I am very sorry, sir," said I, with assumed tranquillity, but an inward tremor, "but, really, the man you allude to is nothing to me — he is no relation or apprentice of mine, that you should hold me responsible for him."

"In mercy's name, who is he?"

"I certainly cannot inform you. I know nothing about him. Formerly I employed him as a copyist; but he has done nothing for me now for some time past."

"I shall settle him, then — good morning, sir."

Several days passed, and I heard nothing more; and, though I often felt a charitable prompting to call at the place and see poor Bartleby, yet a certain squeamishness, of I know not what, withheld me.

All is over with him, by this time, thought I, at last, when, through another week, no further intelligence reached me. But, coming to my room the day after, I found several persons waiting at my door in a high state of nervous excitement.

"That's the man here — he comes," cried the foremost one, whom I recognized as the lawyer who had previously called upon me alone.

"You must take him away, sir, at once," cried a portly person among them, advancing upon me, and whom I knew to be the landlord of No. — Wall Street. "These gentlemen, my tenants, cannot stand it any longer; Mr. B——" pointing to the lawyer, "has turned him out of his room, and he now persists in haunting the building generally, sitting upon the banisters of the stairs by day, and sleeping in the entry by night. Everybody is concerned; clients are leaving the offices; some fears are entertained of a mob; something you must do, and that without delay."

Aghast at this torrent, I fell back before it, and would fain have locked myself in my new quarters. In vain I persisted that Bartleby was nothing to me — no more than to any one else. In vain — I was the last person known to have anything to do with him, and they held me to the terrible account. Fearful, then, of being exposed in the papers (as one person present obscurely threatened), I considered the matter, and, at length, said, that if the lawyer would give me a confidential interview with the scrivener, in his (the lawyer's) own room, I would, that afternoon, strive my best to rid them of the nuisance they complained of.

Going up stairs to my old haunt, there was Bartleby silently sitting upon the banister at the landing.

"What are you doing here, Bartleby?" said I.

"Sitting upon the banister," he mildly replied.

I motioned him into the lawyer's room, who then left us.

"Bartleby," said I, "are you aware that you are the cause of great tribulation to me, by persisting in occupying the entry after being dismissed from the office?"

No answer.

"Now one of two things must take place. Either you must do something, or something must be done to you. Now what sort of business would you like to engage in? Would you like to re-engage in copying for some one?"

"No; I would prefer not to make any change."

"Would you like a clerkship in a dry-goods store?"

"There is too much confinement about that. No, I would not like a clerkship; but I am not particular."

"Too much confinement," I cried, "why, you keep yourself confined all the time!"

"I would prefer not to take a clerkship," he rejoined, as if to settle that little item at once.

"How would a bar-tender's business suit you? There is no trying of the eye-sight in that."

"I would not like it at all; though, as I said before, I am not particular."

His unwonted wordiness inspirited me. I returned to the charge.

"Well, then, would you like to travel through the country collecting bills for the merchants? That would improve your health."

"No, I would prefer to be doing something else."

"How, then, would going as a companion to Europe, to entertain some young gentleman with your conversation — how would that suit you?"

"Not at all. It does not strike me that there is anything definite about that. I like to be stationary. But I am not particular."

"Stationary you shall be, then," I cried, now losing all patience, and, for the first time in all my exasperating connections with him, fairly flying into a passion. "If you do not go away from these premises before night, I shall feel bound — indeed, I *am* bound — to — to — to quit the premises myself!" I rather absurdly concluded, knowing not with what possible threat to try to frighten his immobility into compliance. Despairing of all further efforts, I was precipitately leaving him, when a final thought occurred to me — one which had not been wholly unindulged before.

"Bartleby," said I, in the kindest tone I could assume under such exciting circumstances, "will you go home with me now not to my office, but my dwelling — and remain there till we can conclude upon some convenient arrangement for you at our leisure? Come, let us start now, right away."

"No: at present I would prefer not to make any change at all."

I answered nothing; but, effectually dodging every one by the suddenness and rapidity of my flight, rushed from the building, ran up Wall Street towards Broadway, and, jumping into the first omnibus, was soon removed from pursuit. As soon as tranquillity returned, I distinctly perceived that I had now done all that I possibly could, both in respect to the demands of the landlord and his tenants, and with regard to my own desire and sense of duty, to benefit Bartleby, and shield him from rude persecution. I now strove to be entirely care-free and quiescent; and my conscience justified me in the attempt; though, indeed, it was not so successful as I could have wished. So fearful was I of being again hunted out by the incensed landlord and his exasperated tenants, that, surrendering my business to Nippers, for a few days, I drove about the upper part of the town and through the suburbs, in my rockaway; crossed over to Jersey City and Hoboken, and paid fugitive visits to Manhattanville and Astoria. In fact, I almost lived in my rockaway for the time.

When again I entered my office, lo, a note from the landlord lay upon the desk. I opened it with trembling hands. It informed me that the writer had sent to the police, and had Bartleby removed to the Tombs as a vagrant. Moreover, since I knew more about him than any one else, he wished me to appear at that place, and make a suitable statement of the facts. These tidings had a conflicting effect upon me. At first I was indignant; but, at last, almost approved. The landlord's energetic, summary disposition, had led him to adopt a procedure which I do not think I would have decided upon myself; and yet, as a last resort, under such peculiar circumstances, it seemed the only plan.

As I afterwards learned, the poor scrivener, when told that he must be conducted to the Tombs, offered not the slightest obstacle, but, in his pale, unmoving way, silently acquiesced.

Some of the compassionate and curious by-standers joined the party; and headed by one of the constables arm-in-arm with Bartleby, the silent procession filed its way through all the noise, and heat, and joy of the roaring thoroughfares at noon.

The same day I received the note, I went to the Tombs, or, to speak more properly, the Halls of Justice. Seeking the right officer, I stated the purpose of my call, and was informed that the individual I described was, indeed, within. I then assured the functionary that Bartleby was a perfectly honest man, and greatly to be compassionated, however unaccountably eccentric. I narrated all I knew, and closed by suggesting the idea of letting him remain in as indulgent confinement as possible, till something less harsh might be done—though, indeed, I hardly knew what. At all events, if nothing else could be decided upon, the alms-house must receive him. I then begged to have an interview.

Being under no disgraceful charge, and quite serene and harmless in all his ways, they had permitted him freely to wander about the prison, and, especially, in the inclosed grass-platted yards thereof. And so I found him there, standing all alone in the quietest of the yards, his face towards a high wall, while all around, from the narrow slits of the jail windows, I thought I saw peering out upon him the eyes of murderers and thieves.

"Bartleby!"

"I know you," he said, without looking round—"and I want nothing to say to you."

"It was not I that brought you here, Bartleby," said I, keenly pained at his implied suspicion. "And to you, this should not be so vile a place. Nothing reproachful attaches to you by being here. And see, it is not so sad a place as one might think. Look, there is the sky, and here is the grass."

"I know where I am," he replied, but would say nothing more, and so I left him.

As I entered the corridor again, a broad meat-like man, in an apron, accosted me, and, jerking his thumb over my shoulder, said "Is that your friend?"

"Yes."

"Does he want to starve? If he does, let him live on the prison fare, that's all."

"Who are you?" asked I, not knowing what to make of such an unofficially speaking person in such a place.

"I am the grub-man. Such gentlemen as have friends here, hire me to provide them with something good to eat."

"Is this so?" said I, turning to the turnkey.

He said it was.

"Well, then," said I, slipping some silver into the grub-man's hands (for so they called him), "I want you to give particular attention to my friend there; let him have the best dinner you can get. And you must be as polite to him as possible."

"Introduce me, will you?" said the grub-man, looking at me with an expression which seemed to say he was all impatience for an opportunity to give a specimen of his breeding.

Thinking it would prove of benefit to the scrivener, I acquiesced; and, asking the grub-man his name, went up with him to Bartleby.

"Bartleby, this is a friend; you will find him very useful to you."

"Your sarvant, sir, your sarvant," said the grub-man, making a low salutation behind his apron. "Hope you find it pleasant here, sir; nice grounds — cool apartments — hope you'll stay with us some time — try to make it agreeable. What will you have for dinner to-day?"

"I prefer not to dine to-day," said Bartleby, turning away. "It would disagree with me; I am unused to dinners." So saying, he slowly moved to the other side of the inclosure, and took up a position fronting the dead-wall.

"How's this?" said the grub-man, addressing me with a stare of astonishment. "He's odd, ain't he?"

"I think he is a little deranged," said I, sadly.

"Deranged? deranged is it? Well, now, upon my word, I thought that friend of yourn was a gentleman forger; they are always pale and genteel-like, them forgers. I can't help pity 'em — can't help it, sir. Did you know Monroe Edwards?" he added, touchingly, and paused. Then, laying his hand piteously on my shoulder, sighed, "he died of consumption at Sing-Sing. So you weren't acquainted with Monroe?"

"No, I was never socially acquainted with any forgers. But I cannot stop longer. Look to my friend yonder. You will not lose by it. I will see you again."

Some few days after this, I again obtained admission to the Tombs, and went through the corridors in quest of Bartleby; but without finding him.

"I saw him coming from his cell not long ago," said a turnkey, "may be he's gone to loiter in the yards."

So I went in that direction.

"Are you looking for the silent man?" said another turnkey, passing me. "Yonder he lies — sleeping in the yard there. 'Tis not twenty minutes since I saw him lie down."

The yard was entirely quiet. It was not accessible to the common prisoners. The surrounding walls, of amazing thickness, kept off all sounds behind them. The Egyptian character of the masonry weighed upon me with its gloom. But a soft imprisoned turf grew under foot. The heart of the eternal pyramids, it seemed, wherein, by some strange magic, through the clefts, grass-seed, dropped by birds, had sprung.

Strangely huddled at the base of the wall, his knees drawn up, and lying on his side, his head touching the cold stones, I saw the wasted Bartleby. But nothing stirred. I paused; then went close up to him; stooped over, and saw that his dim eyes were open; otherwise he seemed profoundly sleeping. Something prompted me to touch him. I felt his hand, when a tingling shiver ran up my arm and down my spine to my feet.

The round face of the grub-man peered upon me now. "His dinner is ready. Won't he dine to-day, either? Or does he live without dining?"

"Lives without dining," said I, and closed the eyes.

"Eh! — He's asleep, ain't he?"

"With kings and counselors,"° murmured I.

There would seem little need for proceeding further in this history. Imagination will readily supply the meagre recital of poor Bartleby's interment. But, ere parting with the reader, let me say, that if this little narrative has sufficiently interested him, to awaken curiosity as to who Bartleby was, and what manner of life he led prior to the present narrator's making his acquaintance, I can only reply, that in such curiosity I fully share, but am wholly unable to gratify it. Yet here I hardly know whether I should divulge one little item of rumor, which came to my ear a few months after the scrivener's decease. Upon what basis it rested, I could never ascertain; and hence, how true it is I cannot now tell. But, inasmuch as this vague report has not been without a certain suggestive interest to me, however sad, it may prove the same with some others; and so I will briefly mention it. The report was this: that Bartleby had been a subordinate clerk in the Dead Letter Office at Washington, from which he had been suddenly removed by a change in the administration. When I think over this rumor, hardly can I express the emotions which seize me. Dead letters! does it not sound like dead men? Conceive a man by nature and misfortune prone to a pallid hopelessness, can any business seem more fitted to heighten it than that of continually handling these dead letters, and assorting them for the flames? For by the cart-load they are annually burned. Sometimes from out the folded paper the pale clerk takes a ring the finger it was meant for, perhaps, moulders in the grave; a bank-note sent in swiftest charity he whom it would relieve, nor eats nor hungers any more; pardon for those who died despairing; hope for those who died unhop-

---

With kings and counselors: A reference to Job 3:14. Job, who has lost his family and all his property and has been stricken by a terrible disease, wishes he had never been born: "then had I been at rest with kings and counselors of the earth, which built desolate places for themselves."

ing; good tidings for those who died stifled by unrelieved calamities. On errands of life, these letters speed to death.

Ah, Bartleby! Ah, humanity!

ALICE MUNRO *(b. 1931) grew up on a farm in a rural community near Lake Huron in Ontario, Canada, where her father raised silver foxes. After attending the University of Western Ontario for two years, she married and moved to British Columbia. Munro remembers that she began writing things down when she was about twelve, and at age fifteen she decided she would soon write a great novel: "But I thought perhaps I wasn't ready so I would write a short story in the meantime." She began publishing her stories when she was a university student, but her writing progressed very slowly during the next several years after she remarried and raised a family. "I never intended to be a short story writer," she has explained. "I started writing them because I didn't have time to write anything else — I had three children. And then I got used to writing stories, so I saw my material that way, and now I don't think I'll ever write a novel." In 1968 Munro published her first collection of stories,* Dance of the Happy Shades, *which won the Governor General's Award in Canada. Three years later she published her second book,* Lives of Girls and Women. *Another collection of stories,* Something I've Been Meaning to Tell You, *appeared in 1974, and a series of connected stories titled* Who Do You Think You Are? *was published in 1978, giving Munro her second Governor General's Award. She won her third with* The Progress of Love *in 1987. Her newest collection of stories,* The Love of a Good Woman *(1998), won the 1999 America's National Book Critics Circle Award for fiction.*

Almost all Munro's stories are set in southern Ontario, where she grew up and now lives with her second husband. She sees herself as an anachronism, "because I write about places where your roots are and most people don't live that kind of life any more at all. Most writers, probably, the writers who are most in tune with our time, write about places that have no texture because this is where most of us live."

Although Lives of Girls and Women *was published as a novel, Munro first wrote it as a series of stories, which she later revised in a loosely patterned autobiographical structure. Frequently her narrator is a young girl, who notes in great detail what she sees around her, while conveying a poignant sense of her own subjectivity. Munro's themes are often familiar ones of initiation and romantic love, as in the story "How I Met My Husband." Literary critics have observed that Munro's stories about small-town life are reminiscent of the fiction of such American writers as Flannery O'Connor and Eudora Welty.*

ALICE MUNRO

How I Met My Husband

1974

We heard the plane come over at noon, roaring through the radio news, and we were sure it was going to hit the house, so we all ran out into the yard. We saw it come in over the treetops, all red and silver, the first close-up plane I ever saw. Mrs. Peebles screamed.

"Crash landing," their little boy said. Joey was his name.

"It's okay," said Dr. Peebles. "He knows what he's doing." Dr. Peebles was only an animal doctor, but had a calming way of talking, like any doctor.

This was my first job — working for Dr. and Mrs. Peebles, who had bought an old house out on the Fifth Line, about five miles out of town. It was just when the trend was starting of town people buying up old farms, not to work them but to live on them.

We watched the plane land across the road, where the fairgrounds used to be. It did make a good landing field, nice and level for the old race track, and the barns and display sheds torn down now for scrap lumber so there was nothing in the way. Even the old grandstand bays had burned.

"All right," said Mrs. Peebles, snappy as she always was when she got over her nerves. "Let's go back in the house. Let's not stand here gawking like a set of farmers."

She didn't say that to hurt my feelings. It never occurred to her.

I was just setting the dessert down when Loretta Bird arrived, out of breath, at the screen door.

"I thought it was going to crash into the house and kill youse all!"

She lived on the next place and the Peebleses thought she was a countrywoman, they didn't know the difference. She and her husband didn't farm, he worked on the roads and had a bad name for drinking. They had seven children and couldn't get credit at the HiWay Grocery. The Peebleses made her welcome, not knowing any better, as I say, and offered her dessert.

Dessert was never anything to write home about, at their place. A dish of Jell-O or sliced bananas or fruit out of a tin. "Have a house without a pie, be ashamed until you die," my mother used to say, but Mrs. Peebles operated differently.

Loretta Bird saw me getting the can of peaches.

"Oh, never mind," she said. "I haven't got the right kind of a stomach to trust what comes out of those tins, I can only eat home canning."

I could have slapped her. I bet she never put down fruit in her life.

"I know what he's landed here for," she said. "He's got permission to use the fairgrounds and take people up for rides. It costs a dollar. It's the same fellow who was over at Palmerston last week and was up the lakeshore before that. I wouldn't go up, if you paid me."

"I'd jump at the chance," Dr. Peebles said. "I'd like to see this neighborhood from the air."

Mrs. Peebles said she would just as soon see it from the ground. Joey said he wanted to go and Heather did, too. Joey was nine and Heather was seven.

"Would you, Edie?" Heather said.

I said I didn't know. I was scared, but I never admitted that, especially in front of children I was taking care of.

"People are going to be coming out here in their cars raising dust and trampling your property, if I was you I would complain." Loretta said. She hooked her legs around the chair rung and I knew we were in for a lengthy visit. After Dr. Peebles went back to his office or out on his next call and Mrs.

Peebles went for her nap, she would hang around me while I was trying to do the dishes. She would pass remarks about the Peebleses in their own house.

"She wouldn't find time to lay down in the middle of the day, if she had seven kids like I got."

She asked me did they fight and did they keep things in the dresser drawer not to have babies with. She said it was a sin if they did. I pretended I didn't know what she was talking about.

I was fifteen and away from home for the first time. My parents had made the effort and sent me to high school for a year, but I didn't like it. I was shy of strangers and the work was hard, they didn't make it nice for you or explain the way they do now. At the end of the year the averages were published in the paper, and mine came out at the very bottom, 37 percent. My father said that's enough and I didn't blame him. The last thing I wanted, anyway, was to go on and end up teaching school. It happened the very day the paper came out with my disgrace in it, Dr. Peebles was staying at our place for dinner, having just helped one of our cows have twins, and he said I looked smart to him and his wife was looking for a girl to help. He said she felt tied down, with the two children, out in the country. I guess she would, my mother said, being polite, though I could tell from her face she was wondering what on earth it would be like to have only two children and no barn work, and then to be complaining.

When I went home I would describe to them the work I had to do, and it made everybody laugh. Mrs. Peebles had an automatic washer and dryer, the first I ever saw. I have had those in my own home for such a long time now it's hard to remember how much of a miracle it was to me, not having to struggle with the wringer and hang up and haul down. Let alone not having to heat water. Then there was practically no baking. Mrs. Peebles said she couldn't make pie crust, the most amazing thing I ever heard a woman admit. I could, of course, and I could make light biscuits and a white cake and dark cake, but they didn't want it, she said they watched their figures. The only thing I didn't like about working there, in fact, was feeling half hungry a lot of the time. I used to bring back a box of doughnuts made out at home, and hide them under my bed. The children found out, and I didn't mind sharing, but I thought I better bind them to secrecy.

The day after the plane landed Mrs. Peebles put both children in the car and drove over to Chesley, to get their hair cut. There was a good woman then at Chesley for doing hair. She got hers done at the same place, Mrs. Peebles did, and that meant they would be gone a good while. She had to pick a day Dr. Peebles wasn't going out into the country, she didn't have her own car. Cars were still in short supply then, after the war.

I loved being left in the house alone, to do my work at leisure. The kitchen was all white and bright yellow, with fluorescent lights. That was before they ever thought of making the appliances all different colors and doing the cupboards like dark old wood and hiding the lighting. I loved light. I loved the double sink. So would anybody new-come from washing dishes in a dishpan with a rag-plugged hole on an oilcloth-covered table by light of a coal-oil lamp. I kept everything shining.

The bathroom too. I had a bath in there once a week. They wouldn't have minded if I took one oftener, but to me it seemed like asking too much, or maybe risking making it less wonderful. The basin and the tub and the toilet were all pink, and there were glass doors with flamingoes painted on them, to shut off the tub. The light had a rosy cast and the mat sank under your feet like snow, except that it was warm. The mirror was three-way. With the mirror all steamed up and the air like a perfume cloud, from things I was allowed to use, I stood up on the side of the tub and admired myself naked, from three directions. Sometimes I thought about the way we lived out at home and the way we lived here and how one way was so hard to imagine when you were living the other way. But I thought it was still a lot easier, living the way we lived at home, to picture something like this, the painted flamingoes and the warmth and the soft mat, than it was anybody knowing only things like this to picture how it was the other way. And why was that?

I was through my jobs in no time, and had the vegetables peeled for supper and sitting in cold water besides. Then I went into Mrs. Peebles' bedroom. I had been in there plenty of times, cleaning, and I always took a good look in her closet, at the clothes she had hanging there. I wouldn't have looked in her drawers, but a closet is open to anybody. That's a lie. I would have looked in drawers, but I would have felt worse doing it and been more scared she could tell.

Some clothes in her closet she wore all the time, I was quite familiar with them. Others she never put on, they were pushed to the back. I was disappointed to see no wedding dress. But there was one long dress I could just see the skirt of, and I was hungering to see the rest. Now I took note of where it hung and lifted it out. It was satin, a lovely weight on my arm, light bluish-green in color, almost silvery. It had a fitted, pointed waist and a full skirt and an off-the-shoulder fold hiding the little sleeves.

Next thing was easy. I got out of my own things and slipped it on. I was slimmer at fifteen than anybody would believe who knows me now and the fit was beautiful. I didn't, of course, have a strapless bra on, which was what it needed, I just had to slide my straps down my arms under the material. Then I tried pinning up my hair, to get the effect. One thing led to another. I put on rouge and lipstick and eyebrow pencil from her dresser. The heat of the day and the weight of the satin and all the excitement made me thirsty, and I went out to the kitchen, got-up as I was, to get a glass of ginger ale with ice cubes from the refrigerator. The Peebleses drank ginger ale, or fruit drinks, all day, like water, and I was getting so I did too. Also there was no limit on ice cubes, which I was so fond of I would even put them in a glass of milk.

I turned from putting the ice tray back and saw a man watching me through the screen. It was the luckiest thing in the world I didn't spill the ginger ale down the front of me then and there.

"I never meant to scare you. I knocked but you were getting the ice out, you didn't hear me."

I couldn't see what he looked like, he was dark the way somebody is pressed up against a screen door with the bright daylight behind them. I only knew he wasn't from around here.

"I'm from the plane over there. My name is Chris Watters and what I was wondering was if I could use that pump."

There was a pump in the yard. That was the way the people used to get their water. Now I noticed he was carrying a pail.

"You're welcome," I said. "I can get it from the tap and save you pumping." I guess I wanted him to know we had piped water, didn't pump ourselves.

"I don't mind the exercise." He didn't move, though, and finally he said, "Were you going to a dance?"

Seeing a stranger there had made me entirely forget how I was dressed.

"Or is that the way ladies around here generally get dressed up in the afternoon?"

I didn't know how to joke back then. I was too embarrassed.

"You live here? Are you the lady of the house?"

"I'm the hired girl."

Some people change when they find that out, their whole way of looking at you and speaking to you changes, but his didn't.

"Well, I just wanted to tell you you look very nice. I was so surprised when I looked in the door and saw you. Just because you looked so nice and beautiful."

I wasn't even old enough then to realize how out of the common it is, for a man to say something like that to a woman, or somebody he is treating like a woman. For a man to say a word like *beautiful.* I wasn't old enough to realize or to say anything back, or in fact to do anything but wish he would go away. Not that I didn't like him, but just that it upset me so, having him look at me, and me trying to think of something to say.

He must have understood. He said good-bye, and thanked me, and went and started filling his pail from the pump. I stood behind the Venetian blinds in the dining room, watching him. When he had gone, I went into the bedroom and took the dress off and put it back in the same place. I dressed in my own clothes and took my hair down and washed my face, wiping it on Kleenex, which I threw in the wastebasket.

The Peebleses asked me what kind of man he was. Young, middle-aged, short, tall? I couldn't say.

"Good-looking?" Dr. Peebles teased me.

I couldn't think a thing but that he would be coming to get his water again, he would be talking to Dr. or Mrs. Peebles, making friends with them, and he would mention seeing me that first afternoon, dressed up. Why not mention it? He would think it was funny. And no idea of the trouble it would get me into.

After supper the Peebleses drove into town to go to a movie. She wanted to go somewhere with her hair fresh done. I sat in my bright kitchen wondering what to do, knowing I would never sleep. Mrs. Peebles might not fire me, when she found out, but it would give her a different feeling about me altogether. This was the first place I ever worked but I already had picked up things about the way people feel when you are working for them. They like to think you aren't curious. Not just that you aren't dishonest, that isn't enough. They like to feel you don't notice things, that you don't think or wonder about anything but what they liked to eat and how they liked things ironed, and so on. I don't mean they weren't kind to me, because they were. They had me eat my meals with them (to tell the truth I expected to, I didn't know there were families who don't) and sometimes they took me along in the car. But all the same.

I went up and checked on the children being asleep and then I went out. I had to do it. I crossed the road and went in the old fairgrounds gate. The plane looked unnatural sitting there, and shining with the moon. Off at the far side of the fairgrounds, where the bush was taking over, I saw his tent.

He was sitting outside it smoking a cigarette. He saw me coming.

"Hello, were you looking for a plane ride? I don't start taking people up till tomorrow." Then he looked again and said, "Oh, it's you. I didn't know you without your long dress on."

My heart was knocking away, my tongue was dried up. I had to say something. But I couldn't. My throat was closed and I was like a deaf-and-dumb.

"Did you want a ride? Sit down. Have a cigarette."

I couldn't even shake my head to say no, so he gave me one.

"Put it in your mouth or I can't light it. It's a good thing I'm used to shy ladies."

I did. It wasn't the first time I had smoked a cigarette, actually. My girlfriend out home, Muriel Lowe, used to steal them from her brother.

"Look at your hand shaking. Did you just want to have a chat, or what?"

In one burst I said, "I wisht you wouldn't say anything about that dress."

"What dress? Oh, the long dress."

"It's Mrs. Peebles'."

"Whose? Oh, the lady you work for? Is that it? She wasn't home so you got dressed up in her dress, eh? You got dressed up and played queen. I don't blame you. You're not smoking the cigarette right. Don't just puff. Draw it in. Did anybody ever show you how to inhale? Are you scared I'll tell on you? Is that it?"

I was so ashamed at having to ask him to connive this way I couldn't nod. I just looked at him and he saw *yes*.

"Well I won't. I won't in the slightest way mention it or embarrass you. I give you my word of honor."

Then he changed the subject, to help me out, seeing I couldn't even thank him.

"What do you think of this sign?"

It was a board sign lying practically at my feet.

SEE THE WORLD FROM THE SKY. ADULTS $1.00, CHILDREN 50¢. QUALIFIED PILOT.

"My old sign was getting pretty beat up, I thought I'd make a new one. That's what I've been doing with my time today."

The lettering wasn't all that handsome, I thought. I could have done a better one in half an hour.

"I'm not an expert at sign making."

"It's very good," I said.

"I don't need it for publicity, word of mouth is usually enough. I turned away two carloads tonight. I felt like taking it easy. I didn't tell them ladies were dropping in to visit me."

Now I remembered the children and I was scared again, in case one of them had waked up and called me and I wasn't there.

"Do you have to go so soon?"

I remembered some manners. "Thank you for the cigarette."

"Don't forget. You have my word of honor."

I tore off across the fairgrounds, scared I'd see the car heading home from town. My sense of time was mixed up, I didn't know how long I'd been out of the house. But it was all right, it wasn't late, the children were asleep. I got in bed myself and lay thinking what a lucky end to the day, after all, and among things to be grateful for I could be grateful Loretta Bird hadn't been the one who caught me.

The yard and borders didn't get trampled, it wasn't as bad as that. All the same it seemed very public, around the house. The sign was on the fairgrounds gate. People came mostly after supper but a good many in the afternoon, too. The Bird children all came without fifty cents between them and hung on the gate. We got used to the excitement of the plane coming in and taking off, it wasn't excitement anymore. I never went over, after that one time, but would see him when he came to get his water. I would be out on the steps doing sitting-down work, like preparing vegetables, if I could.

"Why don't you come over? I'll take you up in my plane."

"I'm saving my money," I said, because I couldn't think of anything else.

"For what? For getting married?"

I shook my head.

"I'll take you up for free if you come sometime when it's slack. I thought you would come, and have another cigarette."

I made a face to hush him, because you never could tell when the children would be sneaking around the porch, or Mrs. Peebles herself listening in the house. Sometimes she came out and had a conversation with him. He told her things he hadn't bothered to tell me. But then I hadn't thought to ask. He told her he had been in the war, that was where he learned to fly a plane, and now he couldn't settle down to ordinary life, this was what he liked. She said she couldn't imagine anybody liking such a thing. Though sometimes, she said, she was almost bored enough to try anything herself, she wasn't brought up to living in the country. It's all my husband's idea, she said. This was news to me.

"Maybe you ought to give flying lessons," she said.

"Would you take them?"

She just laughed.

Sunday was a busy flying day in spite of it being preached against from two pulpits. We were all sitting out watching. Joey and Heather were over on the fence with the Bird kids. Their father had said they could go, after their mother saying all week they couldn't.

A car came down the road past the parked cars and pulled up right in the drive. It was Loretta Bird who got out, all importance, and on the driver's side another woman got out, more sedately. She was wearing sunglasses.

"This is a lady looking for the man that flies the plane," Loretta Bird said. "I heard her inquire in the hotel coffee shop where I was having a Coke and I brought her out."

"I'm sorry to bother you," the lady said. "I'm Alice Kelling, Mr. Watters' fiancée."

This Alice Kelling had on a pair of brown and white checked slacks and a yellow top. Her bust looked to me rather low and bumpy. She had a worried face. Her hair had had a permanent, but had grown out, and she wore a yellow band to keep it off her face. Nothing in the least pretty or even young-looking about her. But you could tell from how she talked she was from the city, or educated, or both.

Dr. Peebles stood up and introduced himself and his wife and me and asked her to be seated.

"He's up in the air right now, but you're welcome to sit and wait. He gets his water here and he hasn't been yet. He'll probably take his break about five."

"That is him, then?" said Alice Kelling, wrinkling and straining at the sky.

"He's not in the habit of running out on you, taking a different name?" Dr. Peebles laughed. He was the one, not his wife, to offer iced tea. Then she sent me into the kitchen to fix it. She smiled. She was wearing sunglasses too.

"He never mentioned his fiancée," she said.

I loved fixing iced tea with lots of ice and slices of lemon in tall glasses. I ought to have mentioned before, Dr. Peebles was an abstainer, at least around the house, or I wouldn't have been allowed to take the place. I had to fix a glass for Loretta Bird too, though it galled me, and when I went out she had settled in my lawn chair, leaving me the steps.

"I knew you was a nurse when I first heard you in that coffee shop."

"How would you know a thing like that?"

"I get my hunches about people. Was that how you met him, nursing?"

"Chris? Well yes. Yes, it was."

"Oh, were you overseas?" said Mrs. Peebles.

"No, it was before he went overseas. I nursed him when he was stationed at Centralia and had a ruptured appendix. We got engaged and then he went overseas. My, this is refreshing, after a long drive."

"He'll be glad to see you," Dr. Peebles said. "It's a rackety kind of life, isn't it, not staying one place long enough to really make friends."

"Youse've had a long engagement," Loretta Bird said.

Alice Kelling passed that over. "I was going to get a room at the hotel, but when I was offered directions I came on out. Do you think I could phone them?"

"No need," Dr. Peebles said. "You're five miles away from him if you stay at the hotel. Here, you're right across the road. Stay with us. We've got rooms on rooms, look at this big house."

Asking people to stay, just like that, is certainly a country thing, and maybe seemed natural to him now, but not to Mrs. Peebles, from the way she said, oh yes, we have plenty of room. Or to Alice Kelling, who kept protesting, but let herself be worn down. I got the feeling it was a temptation to her, to be that close. I was trying for a look at her ring. Her nails were painted red, her fingers were freckled and wrinkled. It was a tiny stone. Muriel Lowe's cousin had one twice as big.

Chris came to get his water, late in the afternoon just as Dr. Peebles had predicted. He must have recognized the car from a way off. He came smiling.

"Here I am chasing after you to see what you're up to," called Alice Kelling. She got up and went to meet him and they kissed, just touched, in front of us.

"You're going to spend a lot on gas that way," Chris said.

Dr. Peebles invited Chris to stay for supper, since he had already put up the sign that said: NO MORE RIDES TILL 7 P.M. Mrs. Peebles wanted it served in the yard, in spite of the bugs. One thing strange to anybody from the country is this eating outside. I had made a potato salad earlier and she had made a jellied salad, that was one thing she could do, so it was just a matter of getting those out, and some sliced meat and cucumbers and fresh leaf lettuce. Loretta Bird hung around for some time saying, "Oh, well, I guess I better get home to those yappers," and, "It's so nice just sitting here, I sure hate to get up," but nobody invited her, I was relieved to see, and finally she had to go.

That night after rides were finished Alice Kelling and Chris went off somewhere in her car. I lay awake till they got back. When I saw the car lights sweep my ceiling I got up to look down on them through the slats of my blind. I don't know what I thought I was going to see. Muriel Lowe and I used to sleep on her front veranda and watch her sister and her sister's boy friend saying good night. Afterward we couldn't get to sleep, for longing for somebody to kiss us and rub up against us and we would talk about suppose you were out in a boat with a boy and he wouldn't bring you in to shore unless you did it, or what if somebody got you trapped in a barn, you would have to, wouldn't you, it wouldn't be your fault. Muriel said her two girl cousins used to try with a toilet paper roll that one of them was a boy. We wouldn't do anything like that; just lay and wondered.

All that happened was that Chris got out of the car on one side and she got out on the other and they walked off separately — him toward the fairgrounds and her toward the house. I got back in bed and imagined about me coming home with him, not like that.

Next morning Alice Kelling got up late and I fixed a grapefruit for her the way I had learned and Mrs. Peebles sat down with her to visit and have another cup of coffee. Mrs. Peebles seemed pleased enough now, having company. Alice Kelling said she guessed she better get used to putting in a day just watching Chris take off and come down, and Mrs. Peebles said she didn't know if she should suggest it because Alice Kelling was the one with the car, but the lake was only twenty-five miles away and what a good day for a picnic.

Alice Kelling took her up on the idea and by eleven o'clock they were in the car, with Joey and Heather and a sandwich lunch I had made. The only thing was that Chris hadn't come down, and she wanted to tell him where they were going.

"Edie'll go over and tell him," Mrs. Peebles said. "There's no problem."

Alice Kelling wrinkled her face and agreed.

"Be sure and tell him we'll be back by five!"

I didn't see that he would be concerned about knowing this right away, and I thought of him eating whatever he ate over there, alone, cooking on his camp stove, so I got to work and mixed up a crumb cake and baked it, in between the other work I had to do; then, when it was a bit cooled, wrapped it in a tea towel. I didn't do anything to myself but take off my apron and comb my hair. I would like to have put some makeup on, but I was too afraid it would remind him of the way he first saw me, and that would humiliate me all over again.

He had come and put another sign on the gate: NO RIDES THIS P.M. APOLOGIES. I worried that he wasn't feeling well. No sign of him outside and the tent flap was down. I knocked on the pole.

"Come in," he said, in a voice that would just as soon have said *Stay out.*

I lifted the flap.

"Oh, it's you. I'm sorry. I didn't know it was you."

He had been just sitting on the side of the bed, smoking. Why not at least sit and smoke in the fresh air?

"I brought a cake and hope you're not sick," I said.

"Why would I be sick? Oh — that sign. That's all right. I'm just tired of talking to people. I don't mean you. Have a seat." He pinned back the tent flap. "Get some fresh air in here."

I sat on the edge of the bed, there was no place else. It was one of those fold-up cots, really: I remembered and gave him his fiancée's message.

He ate some of the cake. "Good."

"Put the rest away for when you're hungry later."

"I'll tell you a secret. I won't be around here much longer."

"Are you getting married?"

"Ha ha. What time did you say they'd be back?"

"Five o'clock."

"Well, by that time this place will have seen the last of me. A plane can get further than a car." He unwrapped the cake and ate another piece of it, absent-mindedly.

"Now you'll be thirsty."

"There's some water in the pail."

"It won't be very cold. I could bring some fresh. I could bring some ice from the refrigerator."

"No," be said. "I don't want you to go. I want a nice long time of saying good-bye to you."

He put the cake away carefully and sat beside me and started those little kisses, so soft, I can't ever let myself think about them, such kindness in his face and lovely kisses, all over my eyelids and neck and ears, all over, then me kissing back as well as I could (I had only kissed a boy on a dare before, and kissed my own arms for practice) and we lay back on the cot and pressed together, just gently, and he did some other things, not bad things or not in a bad way. It was lovely in the tent, that smell of grass and hot tent cloth with the sun beating down on it, and he said, "I wouldn't do you any harm for the world." Once, when he had rolled on top of me and we were sort of rocking together on the cot, he said softly, "Oh, no," and freed himself and jumped up and got the water pail. He splashed some of it on his neck and face, and the little bit left, on me lying there.

"That's to cool us off, miss."

When we said good-bye I wasn't at all sad, because he held my face and said "I'm going to write you a letter. I'll tell you where I am and maybe you can come and see me. Would you like that? Okay then. You wait." I was really glad I think to get away from him, it was like he was piling presents on me I couldn't get the pleasure of till I considered them alone.

No consternation at first about the plane being gone. They thought he had taken somebody up, and I didn't enlighten them. Dr. Peebles had phoned he had to go to the country, so there was just us having supper, and then Loretta Bird thrusting her head in the door and saying, "I see he's took off."

"What?" said Alice Kelling, and pushed back her chair.

"The kids come and told me this afternoon he was taking down his tent. Did he think he'd run through all the business there was around here? He didn't take off without letting you know, did he?"

"He'll send me word," Alice Kelling said. "He'll probably phone tonight. He's terribly restless, since the war."

"Edie, he didn't mention to you, did he?" Mrs. Peebles said, "When you took over the message?"

"Yes," I said. So far so true.

"Well why didn't you say?" All of them were looking at me. "Did he say where he was going?"

"He said he might try Bayfield," I said. What made me tell such a lie? I didn't intend it.

"Bayfield, how far is that?" said Alice Kelling.

Mrs. Peebles said, "Thirty, thirty-five miles."

"That's not far. Oh, well, that's really not far at all. It's on the lake, isn't it?"

You'd think I'd be ashamed of myself, setting her on the wrong track. I did it to give him more time, whatever time he needed. I lied for him, and also, I have to admit, for me. Women should stick together and not do things like that. I see that now, but didn't then. I never thought of myself as being in any way like her, or coming to the same troubles, ever.

She hadn't taken her eyes off me. I thought she suspected my lie.

"When did he mention this to you?"

"Earlier."

"When you were over at the plane?"

"Yes."

"You must've stayed and had a chat." She smiled at me, not a nice smile. "You must've stayed and had a little visit with him."

"I took a cake," I said, thinking that telling some truth would spare me telling the rest.

"We didn't have a cake," said Mrs. Peebles rather sharply.

"I baked one."

Alice Kelling said, "That was very friendly of you."

"Did you get permission," said Loretta Bird. "You never know what these girls'll do next," she said. "It's not they mean harm so much, as they're ignorant."

"The cake is neither here nor there," Mrs. Peebles broke in. "Edie, I wasn't aware you knew Chris that well."

I didn't know what to say.

"I'm not surprised," Alice Kelling said in a high voice. "I knew by the look of her as soon as I saw her. We get them at the hospital all the time." She looked hard at me with her stretched smile. "Having their babies. We have to put them in a special ward because of their diseases. Little country tramps. Fourteen and fifteen years old. You should see the babies they have, too."

"There was a bad woman here in town had a baby that pus was running out of its eyes," Loretta Bird put in.

"Wait a minute," said Mrs. Peebles. "What is this talk? Edie. What about you and Mr. Watters? Were you intimate with him?"

"Yes," I said. I was thinking of us lying on the cot and kissing, wasn't that intimate? And I would never deny it.

They were all one minute quiet, even Loretta Bird.

"Well," said Mrs. Peebles. "I am surprised. I think I need a cigarette. This is the first of any such tendencies I've seen in her," she said, speaking to Alice Kelling, but Alice Kelling was looking at me.

"Loose little bitch." Tears ran down her face. "Loose little bitch, aren't you? I knew as soon as I saw you. Men despise girls like you. He just made use of you and went off, you know that, don't you? Girls like you are just nothing, they're just public conveniences, just filthy little rags!"

"Oh, now," said Mrs. Peebles.

"Filthy," Alice Kelling sobbed. "Filthy little rags!"

"Don't get yourself upset," Loretta Bird said. She was swollen up with pleasure at being in on this scene. "Men are all the same."

"Edie, I'm very surprised," Mrs. Peebles said. "I thought your parents were so strict. You don't want to have a baby, do you?"

I'm still ashamed of what happened next. I lost control, just like a six-year-old, I started howling. "You don't get a baby from just doing that!"

"You see. Some of them are that ignorant," Loretta Bird said.

But Mrs. Peebles jumped up and caught my arms and shook me.

"Calm down. Don't get hysterical. Calm down. Stop crying. Listen to me. Listen. I'm wondering, if you know what being intimate means. Now tell me. What did you think it meant?"

"Kissing," I howled.

She let go. "Oh, Edie. Stop it. Don't be silly. It's all right. It's all a misunderstanding. Being intimate means a lot more than that. Oh, I *wondered.*"

"She's trying to cover up, now," said Alice Kelling. "Yes. She's not so stupid. She sees she got herself in trouble."

"I believe her," Mrs. Peebles said. "This is an awful scene."

"Well there is one way to find out," said Alice Kelling, getting up. "After all, I am a nurse."

Mrs. Peebles drew a breath and said, "No. No. Go to your room, Edie. And stop that noise. This is too disgusting."

I heard the car start in a little while. I tried to stop crying, pulling back each wave as it started over me. Finally I succeeded, and lay heaving on the bed.

Mrs. Peebles came and stood in the doorway.

"She's gone," she said. "That Bird woman too. Of course, you know you should never have gone near that man and that is the cause of all this trouble. I have a headache. As soon as you can, go and wash your face in cold water and get at the dishes and we will not say any more about this."

Nor we didn't. I didn't figure out till years later the extent of what I had been saved from. Mrs. Peebles was not very friendly to me afterward, but she was fair. Not very friendly is the wrong way of describing what she was. She had never been very friendly. It was just that now she had to see me all the time and it got on her nerves, a little.

As for me, I put it all out of my mind like a bad dream and concentrated on waiting for my letter. The mail came every day except Sunday, between one-thirty and two in the afternoon, a good time for me because Mrs. Peebles was always having her nap. I would get the kitchen all cleaned and then go up to the mailbox and sit in the grass, waiting. I was perfectly happy, waiting, I forgot all about Alice Kelling and her misery and awful talk and Mrs. Peebles and her chilliness and the embarrassment of whether she told Dr. Peebles and the face of Loretta Bird, getting her fill of other people's troubles. I was always smiling when the mailman got there, and continued smiling even after he gave me the mail and I saw today wasn't the day. The mailman was a Carmichael. I knew by his face because there are a lot of Carmichaels living out by us and so many of them have a sort of sticking-out top lip. So I asked his name (he was a young man, shy, but good-humored, anybody could ask him anything) and then I said, "I knew by your face!" He was pleased by that and always glad to see me and got a little less shy. "You've got the smile I've been waiting on all day!" he used to holler out the car window.

It never crossed my mind for a long time a letter might not come. I believed in it coming just like I believed the sun would rise in the morning. I just put off my hope from day to day, and there was the goldenrod out around the mailbox and the children gone back to school, and the leaves turning, and I was wearing a sweater when I went to wait. One day walking back with the hydro bill stuck in my hand, that was all, looking across at the fairgrounds with the full-blown milkweed and dark teasels, so much like fall, it just struck me: *No letter was ever going to come.* It was an impossible idea to get used to. No, not impossible. If I thought about Chris's face when he said he was going to write to me, it was impossible, but if I forgot that and thought about the actual tin mailbox, empty, it was plain and true. I kept on going to meet the mail, but my heart was heavy now like a lump of lead. I only smiled because I thought of the mailman counting on it, and he didn't have an easy life, with the winter driving ahead.

Till it came to me one day there were women doing this with their lives, all over. There were women just waiting and waiting by mailboxes for one letter or another. I imagined me making this journey day after day and year after year, and my hair starting to go gray, and I thought, I was never made to go on like that. So I stopped meeting the mail. If there were women all through life waiting, and women busy and not waiting, I knew which I had to be. Even though there might be things the second kind of women have to pass up and never know about, it still is better.

I was surprised when the mailman phoned the Peebleses' place in the evening and asked for me. He said he missed me. He asked if I would like to go to Goderich, where some well-known movie was on, I forget now what. So I said yes, and I went out with him for two years and he asked me to marry him, and we were engaged a year more while I got my things together, and then we did marry. He always tells the children the story of how I went after him by sitting by the mailbox every day, and naturally I laugh and let him, because I like for people to think what pleases them and makes them happy.

ꕥ

JOYCE CAROL OATES *(b. 1938) was born in Lockport, New York, one of three children in a Roman Catholic family. She began to put picture stories down on paper even before she could write, and she remembers that her parents "dutifully" supplied her with lined tablets and gave her a typewriter when she was fourteen. In 1956, after Oates graduated from high school, she went on a scholarship to major in English at Syracuse University, but she did not devote most of her time to writing until after she received her M.A. from the University of Wisconsin in 1961. Discovering by chance that one of her stories had been cited in the honor roll of Martha Foley's annual* The Best American Short Stories, *Oates assembled the fourteen stories in her first book,* By the North Gate *(1963). Her career was launched, and as John Updike has speculated, she "was perhaps born a hundred years too late; she needs a lustier audience, a race of Victorian word-eaters to be worthy of her astounding productivity, her tireless gift of self-enthrallment."*

One of our most prolific authors, Oates has published almost seventy books, including over a hundred stories. Notable collections of stories are Raven's Wing *(1986) and* The Assignation *(1988); the same year she published the essays in* (Woman) Writer: Occasions and Opportunities. *Oates also writes poetry and literary criticism.* New Heaven, New Earth *(1974), analyzes the "visionary experience in literature" as exemplified in the work of Henry James, Virginia Woolf, Franz Kafka, D. H. Lawrence, Flannery O'Connor, and others. As a writer, critic, and professor at Princeton University, she dedicates her life to "promoting and exploring literature. . . . I am not conscious of being in any particular literary tradition, though I share with my contemporaries an intense interest in the formal aspects of writing; each of my books is an experiment of a kind, an investigation of the relationship between a certain consciousness and its formal aesthetic expression."*

The story "Where Are You Going, Where Have You Been?" was first published in Epoch *in 1966; it was included in* The Best American Short Stories *of 1967 and* Prize Stories: The O. Henry Awards 1968 *and was made into a film. Oates has said that this story, based on an article in* Life *magazine about a Tucson, Arizona, mur-*

derer, has been "constantly misunderstood by one generation, and intuitively understood by another." She sees the story as dealing with a human being "struggling heroically to define personal identity in the face of incredible opposition, even in the face of death itself." Her most recent works are The Collector of Hearts: New Tales of the Grotesque *(1998) and* Broke Heart Blues *(1999), a novel. In 1999 Oates won the O. Henry Prize for Continued Achievement in the Short Story.*

JOYCE CAROL OATES

Where Are You Going, Where Have You Been? *1966*

For Bob Dylan

Her name was Connie. She was fifteen and she had a quick nervous giggling habit of craning her neck to glance into mirrors, or checking other people's faces to make sure her own was all right. Her mother, who noticed everything and knew everything and who hadn't much reason any longer to look at her own face, always scolded Connie about it. "Stop gawking at yourself, who are you? You think you're so pretty?" she would say. Connie would raise her eyebrows at these familiar complaints and look right through her mother, into a shadowy vision of herself as she was right at that moment: she knew she was pretty and that was everything. Her mother had been pretty once too, if you could believe those old snapshots in the album, but now her looks were gone and that was why she was always after Connie.

"Why don't you keep your room clean like your sister? How've you got your hair fixed — what the hell stinks? Hair spray? You don't see your sister using that junk."

Her sister June was twenty-four and still lived at home. She was a secretary in the high school Connie attended, and if that wasn't bad enough — with her in the same building — she was so plain and chunky and steady that Connie had to hear her praised all the time by her mother and her mother's sisters. June did this, June did that, she saved money and helped clean the house and cooked and Connie couldn't do a thing, her mind was all filled with trashy daydreams. Their father was away at work most of the time and when he came home he wanted supper and he read the newspaper at supper and after supper he went to bed. He didn't bother talking much to them, but around his bent head Connie's mother kept picking at her until Connie wished her mother was dead and she herself was dead and it was all over. "She makes me want to throw up sometimes," she complained to her friends. She had a high, breathless, amused voice which made everything she said a little forced, whether it was sincere or not.

There was one good thing: June went places with girl friends of hers, girls who were just as plain and steady as she, and so when Connie wanted to do that her mother had no objections. The father of Connie's best girl friend drove the girls the three miles to town and left them off at a shopping plaza, so that they could walk through the stores or go to a movie, and when he came to pick them up again at eleven he never bothered to ask what they had done.

They must have been familiar sights, walking around that shopping plaza in their shorts and flat ballerina slippers that always scuffed the sidewalk, with charm bracelets jingling on their thin wrists; they would lean together to whisper and laugh secretly if someone passed by who amused or interested them. Connie had long dark blond hair that drew anyone's eye to it, and she wore part of it pulled up on her head and puffed out and the rest of it she let fall down her back. She wore a pullover jersey blouse that looked one way when she was at home and another way when she was away from home. Everything about her had two sides to it, one for home and one for anywhere that was not home: her walk that could be childlike and bobbing, or languid enough to make anyone think she was hearing music in her head, her mouth which was pale and smirking most of the time, but bright and pink on these evenings out, her laugh which was cynical and drawling at home — "Ha, ha, very funny" — but high-pitched and nervous anywhere else, like the jingling of the charms on her bracelet.

Sometimes they did go shopping or to a movie, but sometimes they went across the highway, ducking fast across the busy road, to a drive-in restaurant where older kids hung out. The restaurant was shaped like a big bottle, though squatter than a real bottle, and on its cap was a revolving figure of a grinning boy who held a hamburger aloft. One night in midsummer they ran across, breathless with daring, and right away someone leaned out a car window and invited them over, but it was just a boy from high school they didn't like. It made them feel good to be able to ignore him. They went up through the maze of parked and cruising cars to the bright-lit, fly-infested restaurant, their faces pleased and expectant as if they were entering a sacred building that loomed out of the night to give them what haven and what blessing they yearned for. They sat at the counter and crossed their legs at the ankles, their thin shoulders rigid with excitement and listened to the music that made everything so good: the music was always in the background like music at a church service, it was something to depend upon.

A boy named Eddie came in to talk with them. He sat backwards on his stool, turning himself jerkily around in semi-circles and then stopping and turning again, and after a while he asked Connie if she would like something to eat. She said she did and so she tapped her friend's arm on her way out — her friend pulled her face up into a brave droll look — and Connie said she would meet her at eleven, across the way. "I just hate to leave her like that," Connie said earnestly, but the boy said that she wouldn't be alone for long. So they went out to his car and on the way Connie couldn't help but let her eyes wander over the windshields and faces all around her, her face gleaming with the joy that had nothing to do with Eddie or even this place; it might have been the music. She drew her shoulders up and sucked in her breath with the pure pleasure of being alive, and just at that moment she happened to glance at a face just a few feet from hers. It was a boy with shaggy black hair, in a convertible jalopy painted gold. He stared at her and then his lips widened into a grin. Connie slit her eyes at him and turned away, but she couldn't help glancing back and there he was still watching her. He wagged a finger and laughed and said, "Gonna get you, baby," and Connie turned away again without Eddie noticing anything.

She spent three hours with him, at the restaurant where they ate hamburgers and drank Cokes in wax cups that were always sweating, and then down an alley a mile or so away, and when he left her off at five to eleven only the movie house was still open at the plaza. Her girl friend was there, talking with a boy. When Connie came up the two girls smiled at each other and Connie said, "How was the movie?" and the girl said, "*You* should know." They rode off with the girl's father, sleepy and pleased, and Connie couldn't help but look at the darkened shopping plaza with its big empty parking lot and its signs that were faded and ghostly now, and over at the drive-in restaurant where cars were still circling tirelessly. She couldn't hear the music at this distance.

Next morning June asked her how the movie was and Connie said, "So-so."

She and that girl and occasionally another girl went out several times a week that way, and the rest of the time Connie spent around the house — it was summer vacation — getting in her mother's way and thinking, dreaming, about the boys she met. But all the boys fell back and dissolved into a single face that was not even a face, but an idea, a feeling, mixed up with the urgent insistent pounding of the music and the humid night air of July. Connie's mother kept dragging her back to the daylight by finding things for her to do or saying suddenly, "What's this about the Pettinger girl?"

And Connie would say nervously, "Oh, her. That dope." She always drew thick clear lines between herself and such girls, and her mother was simple and kindly enough to believe her. Her mother was so simple, Connie thought, that it was maybe cruel to fool her so much. Her mother went scuffling around the house in old bedroom slippers and complained over the telephone to one sister about the other, then the other called up and the two of them complained about the third one. If June's name was mentioned her mother's tone was approving, and if Connie's name was mentioned it was disapproving. This did not really mean she disliked Connie and actually Connie thought that her mother preferred her to June because she was prettier, but the two of them kept up a pretense of exasperation, a sense that they were tugging and struggling over something of little value to either of them. Sometimes, over coffee, they were almost friends, but something would come up — some vexation that was like a fly buzzing suddenly around their heads — and their faces went hard with contempt.

One Sunday Connie got up at eleven — none of them bothered with church — and washed her hair so that it could dry all day long, in the sun. Her parents and sister were going to a barbecue at an aunt's house and Connie said no, she wasn't interested, rolling her eyes, to let mother know just what she thought of it. "Stay home alone then," her mother said sharply. Connie sat out back in a lawn chair and watched them drive away, her father quiet and bald, hunched around so that he could back the car out, her mother with a look that was still angry and not at all softened through the windshield, and in the back seat poor old June all dressed up as if she didn't know what a barbecue was, with all the running yelling kids and the flies. Connie sat with her eyes closed in the sun, dreaming and dazed with the warmth about her as if this were a kind of love, the caresses of love, and her mind slipped over onto thoughts of the boy she had been with the night before and how nice he had been, how sweet it always was, not the way someone like June would suppose but sweet, gentle, the way it was in movies and promised in songs; and when she opened her eyes she hardly knew where she was, the back yard ran off into weeds and a fenceline of trees and behind it the sky was perfectly blue and still. The asbestos "ranch house" that was now three years old startled her — it looked small. She shook her head as if to get awake.

It was too hot. She went inside the house and turned on the radio to drown out the quiet. She sat on the edge of her bed, barefoot, and listened for an hour and a half to a program called XYZ Sunday Jamboree, record after record of hard, fast, shrieking songs she sang along with, interspersed by exclamations from "Bobby King": "An' look here you girls at Napoleon's — Son and Charley want you to pay real close attention to this song coming up!"

And Connie paid close attention herself, bathed in a glow of slow-pulsed joy that seemed to rise mysteriously out of the music itself and lay languidly about the airless little room, breathed in and breathed out with each gentle rise and fall of her chest.

After a while she heard a car coming up the drive. She sat up at once, startled, because it couldn't be her father so soon. The gravel kept crunching all the way in from the road — the driveway was long — and Connie ran to the window. It was a car she didn't know. It was an open jalopy, painted a bright gold that caught the sun opaquely. Her heart began to pound and her fingers snatched at her hair, checking it, and she whispered, "Christ. Christ," wondering how bad she looked. The car came to a stop at the side door and the horn sounded four short taps as if this were a signal Connie knew.

She went into the kitchen and approached the door slowly, then hung out the screen door, her bare toes curling down off the step. There were two boys in the car and now she recognized the driver: he had shaggy, shabby black hair that looked crazy as a wig and he was grinning at her.

"I ain't late, am I?" he said.

"Who the hell do you think you are?" Connie said.

"Toldja I'd be out, didn't I?"

"I don't even know who you are."

She spoke sullenly, careful to show no interest or pleasure, and he spoke in a fast bright monotone. Connie looked past him to the other boy, taking her time. He had fair brown hair, with a lock that fell onto his forehead. His sideburns gave him a fierce, embarrassed look, but so far he hadn't even bothered to glance at her. Both boys wore sunglasses. The driver's glasses were metallic and mirrored everything in miniature.

"You wanta come for a ride?" he said.

Connie smirked and let her hair fall loose over one shoulder.

"Don'tcha like my car? New paint job," he said. "Hey."

"What?"

"You're cute."

She pretended to fidget, chasing flies away from the door.

"Don'tcha believe me, or what?" he said.

"Look, I don't even know who you are," Connie said in disgust.

"Hey, Ellie's got a radio, see. Mine's broke down." He lifted his friend's arm and showed her the little transistor the boy was holding, and now Connie began to hear the music. It was the same program that was playing inside the house.

"Bobby King?" she said.

"I listen to him all the time. I think he's great."

"He's kind of great," Connie said reluctantly.

"Listen, that guy's *great*. He knows where the action is."

Connie blushed a little, because the glasses made it impossible for her to see just what this boy was looking at. She couldn't decide if she liked him or if he was just a jerk, and so she dawdled in the doorway and wouldn't come down or go back inside. She said, "What's all that stuff painted on your car?"

"Can'tcha read it?" He opened the door very carefully, as if he was afraid it might fall off. He slid out just as carefully, planting his feet firmly on the ground, the tiny metallic world in his glasses slowing down like gelatine hardening and in the midst of it Connie's bright green blouse. "This here is my name, to begin with," he said. ARNOLD FRIEND was written in tar-like black letters on the side, with a drawing of a round grinning face that reminded Connie of a pumpkin, except it wore sunglasses. "I wanta introduce myself, I'm Arnold Friend and that's my real name and I'm gonna be your friend, honey, and inside the car's Ellie Oscar, he's kinda shy." Ellie brought his transistor up to his shoulder and balanced it there. "Now these numbers are a secret code, honey," Arnold Friend explained. He read off the numbers 33, 19, 17 and raised his eyebrows at her to see what she thought of that, but she didn't think much of it. The left rear fender had been smashed and around it was written, on the gleaming gold background: DONE BY CRAZY WOMAN DRIVER. Connie had to laugh at that. Arnold Friend was pleased at her laughter and looked up at her. "Around the other side's a lot more — you wanta come and see them?"

"No."

"Why not?"

"Why should I?"

"Don'tcha wanta see what's on the car? Don'tcha wanta go for a ride?"

"I don't know."

"Why not?"

"I got things to do."

"Like what?"

"Things."

He laughed as if she had said something funny. He slapped his thighs. He was standing in a strange way, leaning back against the car as if he were balancing himself. He wasn't tall, only an inch or so taller than she would be if she came down to him. Connie liked the way he was dressed, which was the way all of them dressed: tight faded jeans stuffed into black, scuffed boots, a belt that pulled his waist in and showed how lean he was, and a white pull-over shirt that was a little soiled and showed the hard small muscles of his arms and shoulders. He looked as if he probably did hard work, lifting and carrying things. Even his neck looked muscular. And his face was a familiar face, somehow: the jaw and chin and cheeks slightly darkened, because he hadn't shaved for a day or two, and the nose long and hawk-like, sniffing as if she were a treat he was going to gobble up and it was all a joke.

"Connie, you ain't telling the truth. This is your day set aside for a ride with me and you know it," he said, still laughing. The way he straightened and recovered from his fit of laughing showed that it had been all fake.

"How do you know what my name is?" she said suspiciously.

"It's Connie."

"Maybe and maybe not."

"I know my Connie," he said, wagging his finger. Now she remembered him even better, back at the restaurant, and her cheeks warmed at the thought of how she sucked in her breath just at the moment she passed him how she must have looked to him. And he had remembered her. "Ellie and I come out here especially for you," he said. "Ellie can sit in back. How about it?"

"Where?"

"Where what?"

"Where're we going?"

He looked at her. He took off the sunglasses and she saw how pale the skin around his eyes was, like holes that were not in shadow but instead in light. His eyes were like chips of broken glass that catch the light in an amiable way. He smiled. It was as if the idea of going for a ride somewhere, to some place, was a new idea to him.

"Just for a ride, Connie sweetheart."

"I never said my name was Connie," she said.

"But I know what it is. I know your name and all about you, lots of things," Arnold Friend said. He had not moved yet but stood still leaning back against the side of his jalopy. "I took a special interest in you, such a pretty girl, and found out all about you like I know your parents and sister are gone somewheres and I know where and how long they're going to be gone, and I know who you were with last night, and your best friend's name is Betty. Right?"

He spoke in a simple lilting voice, exactly as if he were reciting the words to a song. His smile assured her that everything was fine. In the car Ellie turned up the volume on his radio and did not bother to look around at them.

"Ellie can sit in the back seat," Arnold Friend said. He indicated his friend with a casual jerk of his chin, as if Ellie did not count and she could not bother with him.

"How'd you find out all that stuff?" Connie said.

"Listen? Betty Schultz and Tony Fitch and Jimmy Pettinger and Nancy Pettinger," he said, in a chant. "Raymond Stanley and Bob Hutter —"

"Do you know all those kids?"

"I know everybody."

"Look, you're kidding. You're not from around here."

"Sure."

"But — how come we never saw you before?"

"Sure you saw me before," he said. He looked down at his boots, as if he were a little offended. "You just don't remember."

"I guess I'd remember you," Connie said.

"Yeah?" He looked up at this, beaming. He was pleased. He began to mark time with the music from Ellie's radio, tapping his fists lightly together. Connie looked away from his smile to the car, which was painted so bright it almost hurt her eyes to look at it. She looked at that name, ARNOLD FRIEND. And up at the front fender was an expression that was familiar — MAN THE FLYING SAUCERS. It was an expression kids had used the year before, but didn't use this year. She looked at it for a while as if the words meant something to her that she did not yet know.

"What're you thinking about? Huh?" Arnold Friend demanded. "Not worried about your hair blowing around in the car, are you?"

"No."

"Think I maybe can't drive good?"

"How do I know?"

"You're a hard girl to handle. How come?" he said. "Don't you know I'm your friend? Didn't you see me put my sign in the air when you walked by?"

"What sign?"

"My sign." And he drew an X in the air, leaning out toward her. They were maybe ten feet apart. After his hand fell back to his side the X was still in the air, almost visible. Connie let the screen door close and stood perfectly still inside it, listening to the music from her radio and the boy's blend together. She stared at Arnold Friend. He stood there so stiffly relaxed, pretending to be relaxed, with one hand idly on the door handle as if he were keeping himself up that way and had no intention of ever moving again. She recognized most things about him, the tight jeans that showed his thighs and buttocks and the greasy leather boots and the tight shirt, and even that slippery friendly smile of his, that sleepy dreamy smile that all the boys used to get across ideas they didn't want to put into words. She recognized all this and also the singsong way he talked, slightly mocking, kidding, but serious and a little melancholy, and she recognized the way he tapped one fist against the other in homage to the perpetual music behind him. But all these things did not come together.

She said suddenly, "Hey, how old are you?"

His smile faded. She could see then that he wasn't a kid, he was much older — thirty, maybe more. At this knowledge her heart began to pound faster.

"That's a crazy thing to ask. Can'tcha see I'm your own age?"

"Like hell you are."

"Or maybe a coupla years older, I'm eighteen."

"Eighteen?" she said doubtfully.

He grinned to reassure her and lines appeared at the corners of his mouth. His teeth were big and white. He grinned so broadly his eyes became slits and she saw how thick the lashes were, thick and black as if painted with a black tar-like material. Then he seemed to become embarrassed, abruptly, and looked over his shoulder at Ellie. "*Him,* he's crazy," he said. "Ain't he a riot, he's a nut, a real character." Ellie was still listening to the music. His sunglasses told nothing about what he was thinking. He wore a bright orange shirt unbuttoned halfway to show his chest, which was a pale, bluish chest and not muscular like Arnold Friend's. His shirt collar was turned up all around and the very tips of the collar pointed out past his chin as if they were protecting him. He was pressing the transistor radio up against his ear and sat there in a kind of daze, right in the sun.

"He's kinda strange," Connie said.

"Hey, she says you're kinda strange! Kinda strange!" Arnold Friend cried. He pounded on the car to get Ellie's attention. Ellie turned for the first time and Connie saw with shock that he wasn't a kid either — he had a fair, hairless face, cheeks reddened slightly as if the veins grew too close to the surface of his skin, the face of a forty-year-old baby. Connie felt a wave of dizziness rise in her at this sight and she stared at him as if waiting for something to change the shock of the moment, make it all right again. Ellie's lips kept shaping words, mumbling along with the words blasting his ear.

"Maybe you two better go away," Connie said faintly.

"What? How come?" Arnold Friend cried. "We come out here to take you for a ride. It's Sunday." He had the voice of the man on the radio now. It was the same voice, Connie thought. "Don'tcha know it's Sunday all day and honey, no matter who you were with last night today you're with Arnold Friend and don't you forget it! — Maybe you better step out here," he said, and this last was in a different voice. It was a little flatter, as if the heat was finally getting to him.

"No. I got things to do."

"Hey."

"You two better leave."

"We ain't leaving until you come with us."

"Like hell I am —"

"Connie, don't fool around with me. I mean, I mean, don't fool *around*," he said, shaking his head. He laughed incredulously. He placed his sunglasses on top of his head, carefully, as if he were indeed wearing a wig, and brought the stems down behind his ears. Connie stared at him, another wave of dizziness and fear rising in her so that for a moment he wasn't even in focus but was just a blur, standing there against his gold car, and she had the idea that he had driven up the driveway all right but had come from nowhere before that and belonged nowhere and that everything about him and even the music that was so familiar to her was only half real.

"If my father comes and sees you —"

"He ain't coming. He's at a barbecue."

"How do you know that?"

"Aunt Tillie's. Right now they're — uh — they're drinking. Sitting around," he said vaguely, squinting as if he were staring all the way to town and over to Aunt Tillie's back yard. Then the vision seemed to clear and he nodded energetically. "Yeah. Sitting around. There's your sister in a blue dress, huh? And high heels, the poor sad bitch — nothing like you, sweetheart! And your mother's helping some fat woman with the corn, they're cleaning the corn — husking the corn —"

"What fat woman?" Connie cried.

"How do I know what fat woman. I don't know every goddamn fat woman in the world!" Arnold Friend laughed.

"Oh, that's Mrs. Hornby. . . . Who invited her?" Connie said. She felt a little light-headed. Her breath was coming quickly.

"She's too fat. I don't like them fat. I like them the way you are, honey," he said, smiling sleepily at her. They stared at each other for a while, through the screen door. He said softly, "Now what you're going to do is this: you're going to come out that door. You're going to sit up front with me and Ellie's going to sit in the back, the hell with Ellie, right? This isn't Ellie's date. You're my date. I'm your lover, honey."

"What? You're crazy —"

"Yes, I'm your lover. You don't know what that is but you will," he said. "I know that too. I know all about you. But look: it's real nice and you couldn't ask for nobody better than me, or more polite. I always keep my word. I'll tell you how it is, I'm always nice at first, the first time. I'll hold you so tight you won't think you have to try to get away or pretend anything because you'll know you can't. And I'll come inside you where it's all secret and you'll give in to me and you'll love me —"

"Shut up! You're crazy!" Connie said. She backed away from the door. She put her hands against her ears as if she'd heard something terrible, something not meant for her. "People don't talk like that, you're crazy," she muttered. Her heart was almost too big now for her chest and its pumping made sweat break out all over her. She looked out to see Arnold Friend pause and then take a step toward the porch lurching. He almost fell. But, like a clever drunken man, he managed to catch his balance. He wobbled in his high boots and grabbed hold of one of the porch posts.

"Honey?" he said. "You still listening?"

"Get the hell out of here!"

"Be nice, honey. Listen."

"I'm going to call the police —"

He wobbled again and out of the side of his mouth came a fast spat curse, an aside not meant for her to hear. But even this "Christ!" sounded forced. Then he began to smile again. She watched this smile come, awkward as if he were smiling from inside a mask. His whole face was a mask, she thought wildly, tanned down onto his throat but then running out as if he had plastered make-up on his face but had forgotten about his throat.

"Honey — ? Listen, here's how it is. I always tell the truth and I promise you this: I ain't coming in that house after you."

"You better not! I'm going to call the police if you — if you don't —"

"Honey," he said, talking right through her voice, "honey, I'm not coming in there but you are coming out here. You know why?"

She was panting. The kitchen looked like a place she had never seen before, some room she had run inside but which wasn't good enough, wasn't going to help her. The kitchen window had never had a curtain, after three years, and there were dishes in the sink for her to do — probably — and if you ran your hand across the table you'd probably feel something sticky there.

"You listening, honey? Hey?"

"— going to call the police —"

"Soon as you touch the phone I don't need to keep my promise and can come inside. You won't want that."

She rushed forward and tried to lock the door. Her fingers were shaking. "But why lock it," Arnold Friend said gently, talking right into her face. "It's just a screen door. It's just nothing." One of his boots was at a strange angle, as if his foot wasn't in it. It pointed out to the left, bent at the ankle. "I mean, anybody can break through a screen door and glass and wood and iron or anything else if he needs to, anybody at all and specially Arnold Friend. If the place got lit up with a fire, honey, you'd come running out into my arms, right into my arms and safe at home — like you knew I was your lover and'd stopped fooling around, I don't mind a nice shy girl but I don't like no fooling around." Part of those words were spoken with a slight rhythmic lilt, and Connie somehow recognized them — the echo of a song from last year, about a girl rushing into her boy friend's arms and coming home again —

Connie stood barefoot on the linoleum floor, staring at him. "What do you want?" she whispered.

"I want you," he said.

"What?"

"Seen you that night and thought, that's the one, yes sir. I never needed to look any more."

"But my father's coming back. He's coming to get me. I had to wash my hair first —" She spoke in a dry, rapid voice, hardly raising it for him to hear.

"No, your daddy is not coming and yes, you had to wash your hair and you washed it for me. It's nice and shining and all for me, I thank you, sweetheart," he said, with a mock bow, but again he almost lost his balance. He had to bend and adjust his boots. Evidently his feet did not go all the way down; the boots must have been stuffed with something so that he would seem taller. Connie stared out at him and behind him Ellie in the car, who seemed to be looking off toward Connie's right, into nothing. This Ellie said, pulling the words out of the air one after another as if he were just discovering them, "You want me to pull out the phone?"

"Shut your mouth and keep it shut," Arnold Friend said, his face red from bending over or maybe from embarrassment because Connie had seen his boots. "This ain't none of your business."

"What — what are you doing? What do you want?" Connie said. "If I call the police they'll get you, they'll arrest you —"

"Promise was not to come in unless you touch that phone, and I'll keep that promise," he said. He resumed his erect position and tried to force his shoulders back. He sounded like a hero in a movie, declaring something important. He spoke too loudly and it was as if he were speaking to someone behind Connie. "I ain't made plans for coming in that house where I don't belong but just for you to come out to me, the way you should. Don't you know who I am?"

"You're crazy," she whispered. She backed away from the door but did not want to go into another part of the house, as if this would give him permission to come through the door. "What do you. . . . You're crazy, you. . . ."

"Huh? What're you saying, honey?"

Her eyes darted everywhere in the kitchen. She could not remember what it was, this room.

"This is how it is, honey: you come out and we'll drive away, have a nice ride. But if you don't come out we're gonna wait till your people come home and then they're all going to get it."

"You want that telephone pulled out?" Ellie said. He held the radio away from his ear and grimaced, as if without the radio the air was too much for him.

"I toldja shut up, Ellie." Arnold Friend said, "You're deaf, get a hearing aid, right? Fix yourself up. This little girl's no trouble and's gonna be nice to me, so Ellie keep to yourself, this ain't your date — right? Don't hem in on me. Don't hog. Don't crush. Don't bird dog. Don't trail me," he said in a rapid meaningless voice, as if he were running through all the expressions he'd learned but was no longer sure which one of them was in style, then rushing on to new ones, making them up with his eyes closed, "Don't crawl under my fence, don't squeeze in my chipmunk hole, don't sniff my glue, suck my popsicle, keep your own greasy fingers on yourself!" He shaded his eyes and peered in at Connie, who was backed against the kitchen table. "Don't mind him, honey, he's just a creep. He's a dope. Right? I'm the boy for you and like I said you come out here nice like a lady and give me your hand, and nobody else gets hurt, I mean, your nice old bald-headed daddy and your mummy and your sister in her high heels. Because listen: why bring them in this?"

"Leave me alone," Connie whispered.

"Hey, you know that old woman down the road, the one with the chickens and stuff — you know her?"

"She's dead!"

"Dead? What? You know her?" Arnold Friend said.

"She's dead —"

"Don't you like her?"

"She's dead — she's — she isn't here any more —"

"But don't you like her, I mean, you got something against her? Some grudge or something?" Then his voice dipped as if he were conscious of rudeness. He touched the sunglasses on top of his head as if to make sure they were still there. "Now you be a good girl."

"What are you going to do?"

"Just two things, or maybe three," Arnold Friend said. "But I promise it won't last long and you'll like me that way you get to like people you're close to. You will. It's all over for you here, so come on out. You don't want your people in any trouble, do you?"

She turned and bumped against a chair or something, hurting her leg, but she ran into the back room and picked up the telephone. Something roared in her ear, a tiny roaring, and she was so sick with fear that she could do nothing but listen to it — the telephone was clammy and very heavy and her fingers groped down to the dial but were too weak to touch it. She began to scream into the phone, into the roaring. She cried out, she cried for her mother, she felt her breath start jerking back and forth in her lungs as if it were something Arnold Friend were stabbing her with again and again with no tenderness. A noisy sorrowful wailing rose all about her and she was locked inside it the way she was locked inside this house.

After a while she could hear again. She was sitting on the floor, with her wet back against the wall.

Arnold Friend was saying from the door, "That's a good girl. Put the phone back."

She kicked the phone away from her.

"No, honey. Pick it up. Put it back right."

She picked it up and put it back. The dial tone stopped.

"That's a good girl. Now you come outside."

She was hollow with what had been fear, but what was now just an emptiness. All that screaming had blasted it out of her. She sat, one leg cramped under her, and deep inside her brain was something like a pinpoint of light that kept going and would not let her relax. She thought, I'm not going to see my mother again. She thought, I'm not going to sleep in my bed again. Her bright green blouse was all wet.

Arnold Friend said, in a gentle-loud voice that was like a stage voice. "The place where you came from ain't there any more, and where you had in mind to go is cancelled out. This place you are now — inside your daddy's house — is nothing but a cardboard box I can knock down any time. You know that and always did know it. You hear me?"

She thought, I have got to think. I have to know what to do.

"We'll go out to a nice field, out in the country here where it smells so nice and it's sunny," Arnold Friend said. "I'll have my arms tight around you so you won't need to try to get away and I'll show you what love is like, what it does. The hell with this house! It looks solid all right," he said. He ran a fingernail down the screen and the noise did not make Connie shiver, as it would have the day before. "Now put your hand on your heart, honey. Feel that? That feels solid too but we know better, be nice to me, be sweet like you can because what else is there for a girl like you but to be sweet and pretty and give in? — and get away before her people come back?"

She felt her pounding heart. Her hands seemed to enclose it. She thought for the first time in her life that it was nothing that was hers, that belonged to her, but just a pounding, living thing inside this body that wasn't hers either.

"You don't want them to get hurt," Arnold Friend went on. "Now get up, honey. Get up all by yourself."

She stood.

"Now turn this way. That's right. Come over to me — Ellie, put that away, didn't I tell you? You dope. You miserable creepy dope," Arnold Friend said. His words were not angry but only part of an incantation. The incantation was kindly. "Now come out through the kitchen to me honey and let's see a smile, try it, you're a brave sweet little girl and now they're eating corn and hotdogs cooked to bursting over an outdoor fire, and they don't know one thing about you and never did and honey you're better than them because not one of them would have done this for you."

Connie felt the linoleum under her feet; it was cool. She brushed her hair back out of her eyes. Arnold Friend let go of the post tentatively and opened his arms for her, his elbows pointing up toward each other and his wrist limp, to show that this was an embarrassed embrace and a little mocking, he didn't want to make her self-conscious.

She put out her hand against the screen. She watched herself push the door slowly open as if she were safe back somewhere in the other doorway, watching this body and this head of long hair moving out into the sunlight where Arnold Friend waited.

"My sweet little blue-eyed girl," he said, in a half-sung sigh that had nothing to do with her brown eyes but was taken up just the same by the vast sunlit reaches of the land behind him and on all sides of him, so much land that Connie had never seen before and did not recognize except to know that she was going to it.

TIM O'BRIEN *(b. 1946) was born in Austin, Minnesota, and educated at Macalester College and Harvard University. Drafted into the army during the Vietnam War, he attained the rank of sergeant and received the Purple Heart.*

O'Brien's first book, If I Die in a Combat Zone, Box Me Up and Ship Me Home *(1973), is an account of his combat experience presented as "autofiction," a mixture of autobiography and fiction. His next book,* Northern Lights *(1974), depicts a conflict between two brothers. But O'Brien produced his finest work to date in the novel* Going after Cacciato *(1978), which won the National Book Award and was judged by many critics to be the best book by an American about the Vietnam War. This was followed by* The Nuclear Age *(1985), a novel set in 1995 about the ominous future of the human race.*

"Soldiers are dreamers," a line by the English poet Siegfried Sassoon, who survived a sniper's bullet during World War I, is the epigraph for Going after Cacciato. *Dreams play an important role in all O'Brien's fiction, yet the note they sound in a story such as "The Things They Carried" is not surrealistic. The dream is always rooted so firmly in reality that it survives, paradoxically, as the most vital element in an O'Brien story. "The Things They Carried" first appeared in* Esquire *magazine and was included in* The Best American Short Stories *when Ann Beattie edited the volume in 1987. It is also included in O'Brien's collection* The Things They Carried *(1990). O'Brien's latest book is the novel* Tomcat in Love *(1999).*

RELATED COMMENTARY: *Bobbie Ann Mason, "On Tim O'Brien's 'The Things They Carried,'" page 691.*

TIM O'BRIEN

The Things They Carried

1986

First Lieutenant Jimmy Cross carried letters from a girl named Martha, a junior at Mount Sebastian College in New Jersey. They were not love letters, but Lieutenant Cross was hoping, so he kept them folded in plastic at the bottom of his rucksack. In the late afternoon, after a day's march, he would dig his foxhole, wash his hands under a canteen, unwrap the letters, hold them with the tips of his fingers, and spend the last hour of light pretending. He would imagine romantic camping trips into the White Mountains in New Hampshire. He would sometimes taste the envelope flaps, knowing her tongue had been there. More than anything, he wanted Martha to love him as he loved her, but the letters were mostly chatty, elusive on the matter of love. She was a virgin, he was almost sure. She was an English major at Mount Sebastian, and she wrote beautifully about her professors and roommates and midterm exams, about her respect for Chaucer and her great affection for Virginia Woolf. She often quoted lines of poetry; she never mentioned the war, except to say, Jimmy, take care of yourself. The letters weighed ten ounces. They were signed "Love, Martha," but Lieutenant Cross understood that "Love" was only a way of signing and did not mean what he sometimes pretended it meant. At dusk, he would carefully return the letters to his rucksack. Slowly, a bit distracted, he would get up and move among his men, checking the perimeter, then at full dark he would return to his hole and watch the night and wonder if Martha was a virgin.

The things they carried were largely determined by necessity. Among the necessities or near necessities were P-38 can openers, pocket knives, heat tabs, wrist watches, dog tags, mosquito repellant, chewing gum, candy, cigarettes, salt tablets, packets of Kool-Aid, lighters, matches, sewing kits, Military Payment Certificates, C rations, and two or three canteens of water. Together, these items weighed between fifteen and twenty pounds, depending upon a man's habits or rate of metabolism. Henry Dobbins, who was a big man, carried extra rations; he was especially fond of canned peaches in heavy syrup over pound cake. Dave Jensen, who practiced field hygiene, carried a toothbrush, dental floss, and several hotel-size bars of soap he'd stolen on R&R in Sydney, Australia. Ted Lavender, who was scared, carried tranquilizers until he was shot in the head outside the village of Than Khe in mid-April. By necessity, and because it was SOP,° they all carried steel helmets that weighed five pounds including the liner and camouflage cover. They carried the standard fatigue jackets and trousers. Very few carried underwear. On their feet they carried jungle boots — 2.1 pounds — and Dave Jensen carried three pairs of socks and a can of Dr. Scholl's foot powder as a precaution against trench foot. Until he was shot, Ted Lavender carried six or seven ounces of premium dope, which for him was a necessity. Mitchell Sanders, the RTO,° carried condoms. Norman Bowker carried a diary. Rat Kiley carried comic books. Kiowa, a devout Baptist, carried an illustrated New Testament that had been presented to him by his father, who taught Sunday school in Oklahoma City, Oklahoma. As a hedge against bad times, however, Kiowa also carried his grandmother's distrust of the white man, his grandfather's old hunting hatchet. Necessity dictated. Because the land was mined and booby-trapped, it was SOP for each man to carry a steel-centered, nylon-covered flak jacket, which weighed 6.7 pounds, but which on hot days seemed much heavier.

SOP: Standard operating procedure.
RTO: Radiotelephone operator.

Because you could die so quickly, each man carried at least one large compress bandage, usually in the helmet band for easy access. Because the nights were cold, and because the monsoons were wet, each carried a green plastic poncho that could be used as a raincoat or ground sheet or makeshift tent. With its quilted liner, the poncho weighed almost two pounds, but it was worth every ounce. In April, for instance, when Ted Lavender was shot, they used his poncho to wrap him up, then to carry him across the paddy, then to lift him into the chopper that took him away.

They were called legs or grunts.

To carry something was to "hump" it, as when Lieutenant Jimmy Cross humped his love for Martha up the hills and through the swamps. In its intransitive form, "to hump" meant "to walk," or "to march," but it implied burdens far beyond the intransitive.

Almost everyone humped photographs. In his wallet, Lieutenant Cross carried two photographs of Martha. The first was a Kodachrome snapshot signed "Love," though he knew better. She stood against a brick wall. Her eyes were gray and neutral, her lips slightly open as she stared straight-on at the camera. At night, sometimes, Lieutenant Cross wondered who had taken the picture, because he knew she had boyfriends, because he loved her so much, and because he could see the shadow of the picture taker spreading out against the brick wall. The second photograph had been clipped from the 1968 Mount Sebastian yearbook. It was an action shot — women's volleyball — and Martha was bent horizontal to the floor, reaching, the palms of her hands in sharp focus, the tongue taut, the expression frank and competitive. There was no visible sweat. She wore white gym shorts. Her legs, he thought, were almost certainly the legs of a virgin, dry and without hair, the left knee cocked and carrying her entire weight, which was just over one hundred pounds. Lieutenant Cross remembered touching that left knee. A dark theater, he remembered, and the movie was *Bonnie and Clyde,* and Martha wore a tweed skirt, and during the final scene, when he touched her knee, she turned and looked at him in a sad, sober way that made him pull his hand back, but he would always remember the feel of the tweed skirt and the knee beneath it and the sound of the gunfire that killed Bonnie and Clyde, how embarrassing it was, how slow and oppressive. He remembered kissing her good night at the dorm door. Right then, he thought, he should've done something brave. He should've carried her up the stairs to her room and tied her to the bed and touched that left knee all night long. He should've risked it. Whenever he looked at the photographs, he thought of new things he should've done.

What they carried was partly a function of rank, partly of field specialty.

As a first lieutenant and platoon leader, Jimmy Cross carried a compass, maps, code books, binoculars, and a .45-caliber pistol that weighed 2.9 pounds fully loaded. He carried a strobe light and the responsibility for the lives of his men.

As an RTO, Mitchell Sanders carried the PRC-25 radio, a killer, twenty-six pounds with its battery.

As a medic, Rat Kiley carried a canvas satchel filled with morphine and plasma and malaria tablets and surgical tape and comic books and all the things a medic must carry, including M&M's for especially bad wounds, for a total weight of nearly twenty pounds.

As a big man, therefore a machine gunner, Henry Dobbins carried the M-60, which weighed twenty-three pounds unloaded, but which was almost always loaded. In addition, Dobbins carried between ten and fifteen pounds of ammunition draped in belts across his chest and shoulders.

As PFCs or Spec 4s, most of them were common grunts and carried the standard M-16 gas-operated assault rifle. The weapon weighed 7.5 pounds unloaded, 8.2 pounds with its full twenty-round magazine. Depending on numerous factors, such as topography and psychology, the riflemen carried anywhere from twelve to twenty magazines, usually in cloth bandoliers, adding on another 8.4 pounds at minimum, fourteen pounds at maximum. When it was available, they also carried M-16 maintenance gear — rods and steel brushes and swabs and tubes of LSA oil — all of which weighed about a pound. Among the grunts, some carried the M-79 grenade launcher, 5.9 pounds unloaded, a reasonably light weapon except for the ammunition, which was heavy. A single round weighed ten ounces. The typical load was twenty-five rounds. But Ted Lavender, who was scared, carried thirty-four rounds when he was shot and killed outside Than Khe, and he went down under an exceptional burden, more than twenty pounds of ammunition, plus the flak jacket and helmet and rations and water and toilet paper and tranquilizers and all the rest, plus the unweighed fear. He was dead weight. There was no twitching or flopping. Kiowa, who saw it happen, said it was like watching a rock fall, or a big sandbag or something — just boom, then down — not like the movies where the dead guy rolls around and does fancy spins and goes ass over teakettle — not like that, Kiowa said, the poor bastard just flat-fuck fell. Boom. Down. Nothing else. It was a bright morning in mid-April. Lieutenant Cross felt the pain. He blamed himself. They stripped off Lavender's canteens and ammo, all the heavy things, and Rat Kiley said the obvious, the guy's dead, and Mitchell Sanders used his radio to report one U.S. KIA° and to request a chopper. Then they wrapped Lavender in his poncho. They carried him out to a dry paddy, established security, and sat smoking the dead man's dope until the chopper came. Lieutenant Cross kept to himself. He pictured Martha's smooth young face, thinking he loved her more than anything, more than his men, and now Ted Lavender was dead because he loved her so much and could not stop thinking about her. When the dust-off arrived, they carried Lavender aboard. Afterward they burned Than Khe. They marched until dusk, then dug their holes, and that night Kiowa kept explaining how you had to be there, how fast it was, how the poor guy just dropped like so much concrete. Boom-down, he said. Like cement.

In addition to the three standard weapons — the M-60, M-16, and M-79 — they carried whatever presented itself, or whatever seemed appropri-

---

KIA: Killed in action.

ate as a means of killing or staying alive. They carried catch-as-catch-can. At various times, in various situations, they carried M-14s and CAR-15s and Swedish Ks and grease guns and captured AK-47s and Chi-Coms and RPGs and Simonov carbines and black-market Uzis and .38-caliber Smith & Wesson handguns and 66 mm LAWs and shotguns and silencers and blackjacks and bayonets and C-4 plastic explosives. Lee Strunk carried a slingshot; a weapon of last resort, he called it. Mitchell Sanders carried brass knuckles. Kiowa carried his grandfather's feathered hatchet. Every third or fourth man carried a Claymore antipersonnel mine — 3.5 pounds with its firing device. They all carried fragmentation grenades — fourteen ounces each. They all carried at least one M-18 colored smoke grenade — twenty-four ounces. Some carried CS or tear-gas grenades. Some carried white-phosphorus grenades. They carried all they could bear, and then some, including a silent awe for the terrible power of the things they carried.

In the first week of April, before Lavender died, Lieutenant Jimmy Cross received a good-luck charm from Martha. It was a simple pebble, an ounce at most. Smooth to the touch, it was a milky-white color with flecks of orange and violet, oval-shaped, like a miniature egg. In the accompanying letter, Martha wrote that she had found the pebble on the Jersey shoreline, precisely where the land touched water at high tide, where things came together but also separated. It was this separate-but-together quality, she wrote, that had inspired her to pick up the pebble and to carry it in her breast pocket for several days, where it seemed weightless, and then to send it through the mail, by air, as a token of her truest feelings for him. Lieutenant Cross found this romantic. But he wondered what her truest feelings were, exactly, and what she meant by separate-but-together. He wondered how the tides and waves had come into play on that afternoon along the Jersey shoreline when Martha saw the pebble and bent down to rescue it from geology. He imagined bare feet. Martha was a poet, with the poet's sensibilities, and her feet would be brown and bare, the toenails unpainted, the eyes chilly and somber like the ocean in March, and though it was painful, he wondered who had been with her that afternoon. He imagined a pair of shadows moving along the strip of sand where things came together but also separated. It was phantom jealousy, he knew, but he couldn't help himself. He loved her so much. On the march, through the hot days of early April, he carried the pebble in his mouth, turning it with his tongue, tasting sea salts and moisture. His mind wandered. He had difficulty keeping his attention on the war. On occasion he would yell at his men to spread out the column, to keep their eyes open, but then he would slip away into daydreams, just pretending, walking barefoot along the Jersey shore, with Martha, carrying nothing. He would feel himself rising. Sun and waves and gentle winds, all love and lightness.

What they carried varied by mission.

When a mission took them to the mountains, they carried mosquito netting, machetes, canvas tarps, and extra bug juice.

If a mission seemed especially hazardous, or if it involved a place they knew to be bad, they carried everything they could. In certain heavily mined

AOs,° where the land was dense with Toe Poppers and Bouncing Betties, they took turns humping a twenty-eight-pound mine detector. With its headphones and big sensing plate, the equipment was a stress on the lower back and shoulders, awkward to handle, often useless because of the shrapnel in the earth, but they carried it anyway, partly for safety, partly for the illusion of safety.

On ambush, or other night missions, they carried peculiar little odds and ends. Kiowa always took along his New Testament and a pair of moccasins for silence. Dave Jensen carried night-sight vitamins high in carotin. Lee Strunk carried his slingshot; ammo, he claimed, would never be a problem. Rat Kiley carried brandy and M&M's. Until he was shot, Ted Lavender carried the starlight scope, which weighed 6.3 pounds with its aluminum carrying case. Henry Dobbins carried his girlfriend's pantyhose wrapped around his neck as a comforter. They all carried ghosts. When dark came, they would move out single file across the meadows and paddies to their ambush coordinates, where they would quietly set up the Claymores and lie down and spend the night waiting.

Other missions were more complicated and required special equipment. In mid-April, it was their mission to search out and destroy the elaborate tunnel complexes in the Than Khe area south of Chu Lai. To blow the tunnels, they carried one-pound blocks of pentrite high explosives, four blocks to a man, sixty-eight pounds in all. They carried wiring, detonators, and battery-powered clackers. Dave Jensen carried earplugs. Most often, before blowing the tunnels, they were ordered by higher command to search them, which was considered bad news, but by and large they just shrugged and carried out orders. Because he was a big man, Henry Dobbins was excused from tunnel duty. The others would draw numbers. Before Lavender died there were seventeen men in the platoon, and whoever drew the number seventeen would strip off his gear and crawl in head first with a flashlight and Lieutenant Cross's .45-caliber pistol. The rest of them would fan out as security. They would sit down or kneel, not facing the hole, listening to the ground beneath them, imagining cobwebs and ghosts, whatever was down there — the tunnel walls squeezing in — how the flashlight seemed impossibly heavy in the hand and how it was tunnel vision in the very strictest sense, compression in all ways, even time, and how you had to wiggle in — ass and elbows — a swallowed-up feeling — and how you found yourself worrying about odd things — will your flashlight go dead? Do rats carry rabies? If you screamed, how far would the sound carry? Would your buddies hear it? Would they have the courage to drag you out? In some respects, though not many, the waiting was worse than the tunnel itself. Imagination was a killer.

On April 16, when Lee Strunk drew the number seventeen, he laughed and muttered something and went down quickly. The morning was hot and very still. Not good, Kiowa said. He looked at the tunnel opening, then out across a dry paddy toward the village of Than Khe. Nothing moved. No clouds or birds or people. As they waited, the men smoked and drank Kool-Aid, not talking much, feeling sympathy for Lee Strunk but also feeling the

---

AOs: Areas of operations.

luck of the draw. You win some, you lose some, said Mitchell Sanders, and sometimes you settle for a rain check. It was a tired line and no one laughed.

Henry Dobbins ate a tropical chocolate bar. Ted Lavender popped a tranquilizer and went off to pee.

After five minutes, Lieutenant Jimmy Cross moved to the tunnel, leaned down, and examined the darkness. Trouble, he thought — a cave-in maybe. And then suddenly, without willing it, he was thinking about Martha. The stresses and fractures, the quick collapse, the two of them buried alive under all that weight. Dense, crushing love. Kneeling, watching the hole, he tried to concentrate on Lee Strunk and the war, all the dangers, but his love was too much for him, he felt paralyzed, he wanted to sleep inside her lungs and breathe her blood and be smothered. He wanted her to be a virgin and not a virgin, all at once. He wanted to know her. Intimate secrets — why poetry? Why so sad? Why the grayness in her eyes? Why so alone? Not lonely, just alone — riding her bike across campus or sitting off by herself in the cafeteria. Even dancing, she danced alone — and it was the aloneness that filled him with love. He remembered telling her that one evening. How she nodded and looked away. And how, later, when he kissed her, she received the kiss without returning it, her eyes wide open, not afraid, not a virgin's eyes, just flat and uninvolved.

Lieutenant Cross gazed at the tunnel. But he was not there. He was buried with Martha under the white sand at the Jersey shore. They were pressed together, and the pebble in his mouth was her tongue. He was smiling. Vaguely, he was aware of how quiet the day was, the sullen paddies, yet he could not bring himself to worry about matters of security. He was beyond that. He was just a kid at war, in love. He was twenty-two years old. He couldn't help it.

A few moments later Lee Strunk crawled out of the tunnel. He came up grinning, filthy but alive. Lieutenant Cross nodded and closed his eyes while the others clapped Strunk on the back and made jokes about rising from the dead.

Worms, Rat Kiley said. Right out of the grave. Fuckin' zombie.

The men laughed. They all felt great relief.

Spook City, said Mitchell Sanders.

Lee Strunk made a funny ghost sound, a kind of moaning, yet very happy, and right then, when Strunk made that high happy moaning sound, when he went *Ahhooooo,* right then Ted Lavender was shot in the head on his way back from peeing. He lay with his mouth open. The teeth were broken. There was a swollen black bruise under his left eye. The cheekbone was gone. Oh shit, Rat Kiley said, the guy's dead. The guy's dead, he kept saying, which seemed profound — the guy's dead. I mean really.

The things they carried were determined to some extent by superstition. Lieutenant Cross carried his good-luck pebble. Dave Jensen carried a rabbit's foot. Norman Bowker, otherwise a very gentle person, carried a thumb that had been presented to him as a gift by Mitchell Sanders. The thumb was dark brown, rubbery to the touch, and weighed four ounces at most. It had been cut from a VC corpse, a boy of fifteen or sixteen. They'd found him at the bottom of an irrigation ditch, badly burned, flies in his mouth and eyes. The boy wore black shorts and sandals. At the time of his death he had been carrying a pouch of rice, a rifle, and three magazines of ammunition.

You want my opinion, Mitchell Sanders said, there's a definite moral here.

He put his hand on the dead boy's wrist. He was quiet for a time, as if counting a pulse, then he patted the stomach, almost affectionately, and used Kiowa's hunting hatchet to remove the thumb.

Henry Dobbins asked what the moral was.

Moral?

You know. *Moral.*

Sanders wrapped the thumb in toilet paper and handed it across to Norman Bowker. There was no blood. Smiling, he kicked the boy's head, watched the flies scatter, and said, It's like with that old TV show — Paladin. Have gun, will travel.

Henry Dobbins thought about it.

Yeah, well, he finally said. I don't see no moral.

There it *is*, man.

Fuck off.

They carried USO stationery and pencils and pens. They carried Sterno, safety pins, trip flares, signal flares, spools of wire, razor blades, chewing tobacco, liberated joss sticks and statuettes of the smiling Buddha, candles, grease pencils, *The Stars and Stripes*, fingernail clippers, Psy Ops° leaflets, bush hats, bolos, and much more. Twice a week, when the resupply choppers came in, they carried hot chow in green Mermite cans and large canvas bags filled with iced beer and soda pop. They carried plastic water containers, each with a two-gallon capacity. Mitchell Sanders carried a set of starched tiger fatigues for special occasions. Henry Dobbins carried Black Flag insecticide. Dave Jensen carried empty sandbags that could be filled at night for added protection. Lee Strunk carried tanning lotion. Some things they carried in common. Taking turns, they carried the big PRC-77 scrambler radio, which weighed thirty pounds with its battery. They shared the weight of memory. They took up what others could no longer bear. Often, they carried each other, the wounded or weak. They carried infections. They carried chess sets, basketballs, Vietnamese-English dictionaries, insignia of rank, Bronze Stars and Purple Hearts, plastic cards imprinted with the Code of Conduct. They carried diseases, among them malaria and dysentery. They carried lice and ringworm and leeches and paddy algae and various rots and molds. They carried the land itself — Vietnam, the place, the soil — a powdery orange-red dust that covered their boots and fatigues and faces. They carried the sky. The whole atmosphere, they carried it, the humidity, the monsoons, the stink of fungus and decay, all of it, they carried gravity. They moved like mules. By daylight they took sniper fire, at night they were mortared, but it was not battle, it was just the endless march, village to village, without purpose, nothing won or

Psy Ops: Psychological operations.

lost. They marched for the sake of the march. They plodded along slowly, dumbly, leaning forward against the heat, unthinking, all blood and bone, simple grunts, soldiering with their legs, toiling up the hills and down into the paddies and across the rivers and up again and down, just humping, one step and then the next and then another, but no volition, no will, because it was automatic, it was anatomy, and the war was entirely a matter of posture and carriage, the hump was everything, a kind of inertia, a kind of emptiness, a dullness of desire and intellect and conscience and hope and human sensibility. Their principles were in their feet. Their calculations were biological. They had no sense of strategy or mission. They searched the villages without knowing what to look for, not caring, kicking over jars of rice, frisking children and old men, blowing tunnels, sometimes setting fires and sometimes not, then forming up and moving on to the next village, then other villages, where it would always be the same. They carried their own lives. The pressures were enormous. In the heat of early afternoon, they would remove their helmets and flak jackets, walking bare, which was dangerous but which helped ease the strain. They would often discard things along the route of march. Purely for comfort, they would throw away rations, blow their Claymores and grenades, no matter, because by nightfall the resupply choppers would arrive with more of the same, then a day or two later still more, fresh watermelons and crates of ammunition and sunglasses and woolen sweaters — the resources were stunning — sparklers for the Fourth of July, colored eggs for Easter. It was the great American war chest — the fruits of science, the smokestacks, the canneries, the arsenals at Hartford, the Minnesota forests, the machine shops, the vast fields of corn and wheat — they carried like freight trains; they carried it on their backs and shoulders — and for all the ambiguities of Vietnam, all the mysteries and unknowns, there was at least the single abiding certainty that they would never be at a loss for things to carry.

After the chopper took Lavender away, Lieutenant Jimmy Cross led his men into the village of Than Khe. They burned everything. They shot chickens and dogs, they trashed the village well, they called in artillery and watched the wreckage, then they marched for several hours through the hot afternoon, and then at dusk, while Kiowa explained how Lavender died, Lieutenant Cross found himself trembling.

He tried not to cry. With his entrenching tool, which weighed five pounds, he began digging a hole in the earth.

He felt shame. He hated himself. He had loved Martha more than his men, and as a consequence Lavender was now dead, and this was something he would have to carry like a stone in his stomach for the rest of the war.

All he could do was dig. He used his entrenching tool like an ax, slashing, feeling both love and hate, and then later, when it was full dark, he sat at the bottom of his foxhole and wept. It went on for a long while. In part, he was grieving for Ted Lavender, but mostly it was for Martha, and for himself, because she belonged to another world, which was not quite real, and because she was a junior at Mount Sebastian College in New Jersey, a poet and a virgin and uninvolved, and because he realized she did not love him and never would.

■ ■ ■

Like cement, Kiowa whispered in the dark. I swear to God — boom-down. Not a word.

I've heard this, said Norman Bowker.

A pisser, you know? Still zipping himself up. Zapped while zipping.

All right, fine. That's enough.

Yeah, but you had to see it, the guy just —

I *heard,* man. Cement. So why not shut the fuck *up?*

Kiowa shook his head sadly and glanced over at the hole where Lieutenant Jimmy Cross sat watching the night. The air was thick and wet. A warm, dense fog had settled over the paddies and there was the stillness that precedes rain.

After a time Kiowa sighed.

One thing for sure, he said. The Lieutenant's in some deep hurt. I mean that crying jag — the way he was carrying on — it wasn't fake or anything, it was real heavy-duty hurt. The man cares.

Sure, Norman Bowker said.

Say what you want, the man does care.

We all got problems.

Not Lavender.

No, I guess not, Bowker said. Do me a favor, though.

Shut up?

That's a smart Indian. Shut up.

Shrugging, Kiowa pulled off his boots. He wanted to say more, just to lighten up his sleep, but instead he opened his New Testament and arranged it beneath his head as a pillow. The fog made things seem hollow and unattached. He tried not to think about Ted Lavender, but then he was thinking how fast it was, no drama, down and dead, and how it was hard to feel anything except surprise. It seemed un-Christian. He wished he could find some great sadness, or even anger, but the emotion wasn't there and he couldn't make it happen. Mostly he felt pleased to be alive. He liked the smell of the New Testament under his cheek, the leather and ink and paper and glue, whatever the chemicals were. He liked hearing the sounds of night. Even his fatigue, it felt fine, the stiff muscles and the prickly awareness of his own body, a floating feeling. He enjoyed not being dead. Lying there, Kiowa admired Lieutenant Jimmy Cross's capacity for grief. He wanted to share the man's pain, he wanted to care as Jimmy Cross cared. And yet when he closed his eyes, all he could think was Boom-down, and all he could feel was the pleasure of having his boots off and the fog curling in around him and the damp soil and the Bible smells and the plush comfort of night.

After a moment Norman Bowker sat up in the dark.

What the hell, he said. You want to talk, *talk.* Tell it to me.

Forget it.

No, man, go on. One thing I hate, it's a silent Indian.

For the most part they carried themselves with poise, a kind of dignity. Now and then, however, there were times of panic, when they squealed or wanted to squeal but couldn't, when they twitched and made moaning sounds and covered their heads and said Dear Jesus and flopped around on the earth and fired their weapons blindly and cringed and sobbed and begged for the noise to stop and went wild and made stupid promises to themselves and to God and to their mothers and fathers, hoping not to die. In different ways, it happened to all of them. Afterward, when the firing ended, they would blink and peek up. They would touch their bodies, feeling shame, then quickly hiding it. They would force themselves to stand. As if in slow motion, frame by frame, the world would take on the old logic — absolute silence, then the wind, then sunlight, then voices. It was the burden of being alive. Awkwardly, the men would reassemble themselves, first in private, then in groups, becoming soldiers again. They would repair the leaks in their eyes. They would check for casualties, call in dust-offs, light cigarettes, try to smile, clear their throats and spit and begin cleaning their weapons. After a time someone would shake his head and say, No lie, I almost shit my pants, and someone else would laugh, which meant it was bad, yes, but the guy had obviously not shit his pants, it wasn't that bad, and in any case nobody would ever do such a thing and then go ahead and talk about it. They would squint into the dense, oppressive sunlight. For a few moments, perhaps, they would fall silent, lighting a joint and tracking its passage from man to man, inhaling, holding in the humiliation. Scary stuff, one of them might say. But then someone else would grin or flick his eyebrows and say, Roger-dodger, almost cut me a new asshole, *almost*.

There were numerous such poses. Some carried themselves with a sort of wistful resignation, others with pride or stiff soldierly discipline or good humor or macho zeal. They were afraid of dying but they were even more afraid to show it.

They found jokes to tell.

They used a hard vocabulary to contain the terrible softness. *Greased,* they'd say. *Offed, lit up, zapped while zipping.* It wasn't cruelty, just stage presence. They were actors and the war came at them in 3-D. When someone died, it wasn't quite dying, because in a curious way it seemed scripted, and because they had their lines mostly memorized, irony mixed with tragedy, and because they called it by other names, as if to encyst and destroy the reality of death itself. They kicked corpses. They cut off thumbs. They talked grunt lingo. They told stories about Ted Lavender's supply of tranquilizers, how the poor guy didn't feel a thing, how incredibly tranquil he was.

There's a moral here, said Mitchell Sanders.

They were waiting for Lavender's chopper, smoking the dead man's dope.

The moral's pretty obvious, Sanders said, and winked. Stay away from drugs. No joke, they'll ruin your day every time.

Cute, said Henry Dobbins.

Mind-blower, get it? Talk about wiggy — nothing left, just blood and brains.

They made themselves laugh.

There it is, they'd say, over and over, as if the repetition itself were an act of poise, a balance between crazy and almost crazy, knowing without going.

There it is, which meant be cool, let it ride, because oh yeah, man, you can't change what can't be changed, there it is, there it absolutely and positively and fucking well *is.*

They were tough.

They carried all the emotional baggage of men who might die. Grief, terror, love, longing — these were intangibles, but the intangibles had their own mass and specific gravity, they had tangible weight. They carried shameful memories. They carried the common secret of cowardice barely restrained, the instinct to run or freeze or hide, and in many respects this was the heaviest burden of all, for it could never be put down, it required perfect balance and perfect posture. They carried their reputations. They carried the soldier's greatest fear, which was the fear of blushing. Men killed, and died, because they were embarrassed not to. It was what had brought them to the war in the first place, nothing positive, no dreams of glory or honor, just to avoid the blush of dishonor. They died so as not to die of embarrassment. They crawled into tunnels and walked point and advanced under fire. Each morning, despite the unknowns, they made their legs move. They endured. They kept humping. They did not submit to the obvious alternative, which was simply to close the eyes and fall. So easy, really. Go limp and tumble to the ground and let the muscles unwind and not speak and not budge until your buddies picked you up and lifted you into the chopper that would roar and dip its nose and carry you off to the world. A mere matter of falling, yet no one ever fell. It was not courage, exactly; the object was not valor. Rather, they were too frightened to be cowards.

By and large they carried these things inside, maintaining the masks of composure. They sneered at sick call. They spoke bitterly about guys who had found release by shooting off their own toes or fingers. Pussies, they'd say. Candyasses. It was fierce, mocking talk, with only a trace of envy or awe, but even so, the image played itself out behind their eyes.

They imagined the muzzle against flesh. They imagined the quick, sweet pain, then the evacuation to Japan, then a hospital with warm beds and cute geisha nurses.

They dreamed of freedom birds.

At night, on guard, staring into the dark, they were carried away by jumbo jets. They felt the rush of takeoff. *Gone!* they yelled. And then velocity, wings and engines, a smiling stewardess — but it was more than a plane, it was a real bird, a big sleek silver bird with feathers and talons and high screeching. They were flying. The weights fell off, there was nothing to bear. They laughed and held on tight, feeling the cold slap of wind and altitude, soaring, thinking *It's over, I'm gone!* — they were naked, they were light and free — it was all lightness, bright and fast and buoyant, light as light, a helium buzz in the brain, a giddy bubbling in the lungs as they were taken up over the clouds and the war, beyond duty, beyond gravity and mortification and global entanglements — *Sin loi!*° they yelled, *I'm sorry, motherfuckers, but I'm out of it, I'm goofed, I'm on a space cruise, I'm gone!* — and it was a restful, disencumbered

Sin loi!: "Sorry about that!"

sensation, just riding the light waves, sailing that big silver freedom bird over the mountains and oceans, over America, over the farms and great sleeping cities and cemeteries and highways and the golden arches of McDonald's. It was flight, a kind of fleeing, a kind of falling, falling higher and higher, spinning off the edge of the earth and beyond the sun and through the vast, silent vacuum where there were no burdens and where everything weighed exactly nothing. *Gone!* they screamed, *I'm sorry but I'm gone!* And so at night, not quite dreaming, they gave themselves over to lightness, they were carried, they were purely borne.

On the morning after Ted Lavender died, First Lieutenant Jimmy Cross crouched at the bottom of his foxhole and burned Martha's letters. Then he burned the two photographs. There was a steady rain falling, which made it difficult, but he used heat tabs and Sterno to build a small fire, screening it with his body, holding the photographs over the tight blue flame with the tips of his fingers.

He realized it was only a gesture. Stupid, he thought. Sentimental, too, but mostly just stupid.

Lavender was dead. You couldn't burn the blame.

Besides, the letters were in his head. And even now, without photographs, Lieutenant Cross could see Martha playing volleyball in her white gym shorts and yellow T-shirt. He could see her moving in the rain.

When the fire died out, Lieutenant Cross pulled his poncho over his shoulders and ate breakfast from a can.

There was no great mystery, he decided.

In those burned letters Martha had never mentioned the war, except to say, Jimmy, take care of yourself. She wasn't involved. She signed the letters "Love," but it wasn't love, and all the fine lines and technicalities did not matter.

The morning came up wet and blurry. Everything seemed part of everything else, the fog and Martha and the deepening rain.

It was a war, after all.

Half smiling, Lieutenant Jimmy Cross took out his maps. He shook his head hard, as if to clear it, then bent forward and began planning the day's march. In ten minutes, or maybe twenty, he would rouse the men and they would pack up and head west, where the maps showed the country to be green and inviting. They would do what they had always done. The rain might add some weight, but otherwise it would be one more day layered upon all the other days.

He was realistic about it. There was that new hardness in his stomach.

No more fantasies, he told himself.

Henceforth, when he thought about Martha, it would be only to think that she belonged elsewhere. He would shut down the daydreams. This was not Mount Sebastian, it was another world, where there were no pretty poems or midterm exams, a place where men died because of carelessness and gross stupidity. Kiowa was right. Boom-down, and you were dead, never partly dead.

Briefly, in the rain, Lieutenant Cross saw Martha's gray eyes gazing back at him.

He understood.

It was very sad, he thought. The things men carried inside. The things men did or felt they had to do.

He almost nodded at her, but didn't.

Instead he went back to his maps. He was now determined to perform his duties firmly and without negligence. It wouldn't help Lavender, he knew that, but from this point on he would comport himself as a soldier. He would dispose of his good-luck pebble. Swallow it, maybe, or use Lee Strunk's slingshot, or just drop it along the trail. On the march he would impose strict field discipline. He would be careful to send out flank security, to prevent straggling or bunching up, to keep his troops moving at the proper pace and at the proper interval. He would insist on clean weapons. He would confiscate the remainder of Lavender's dope. Later in the day, perhaps, he would call the men together and speak to them plainly. He would accept the blame for what had happened to Ted Lavender. He would be a man about it. He would look them in the eyes, keeping his chin level, and he would issue the new SOPs in a calm, impersonal tone of voice, an officer's voice, leaving no room for argument or discussion. Commencing immediately, he'd tell them, they would no longer abandon equipment along the route of march. They would police up their acts. They would get their shit together, and keep it together, and maintain it neatly and in good working order.

He would not tolerate laxity. He would show strength, distancing himself.

Among the men there would be grumbling, of course, and maybe worse, because their days would seem longer and their loads heavier, but Lieutenant Cross reminded himself that his obligation was not to be loved but to lead. He would dispense with love; it was not now a factor. And if anyone quarreled or complained, he would simply tighten his lips and arrange his shoulders in the correct command posture. He might give a curt little nod. Or he might not. He might just shrug and say Carry on, then they would saddle up and form into a column and move out toward the villages of Than Khe.

FLANNERY O'CONNOR *(1925–1964) was born in Savannah, Georgia, the only child of Roman Catholic parents. When she was thirteen her father was found to have disseminated lupus, an incurable disease in which antibodies in the immune system attack the body's own substances. After her father's death in 1941, O'Connor attended Georgia State College for Women in Milledgeville, where she also published stories and edited the literary magazine. On the strength of these stories, she was awarded a fellowship at the Writers Workshop at the University of Iowa and earned her M.F.A. degree there. Late in 1950 she became ill with what was diagnosed as lupus, and she returned to Milledgeville to start a series of treatments that temporarily arrested the disease. Living with her mother on the family's 500-acre dairy farm, O'Connor began to work again, writing from nine to twelve in the morning and spending the rest of the day resting, reading, writing letters, and raising peacocks.*

O'Connor's first book, Wise Blood, *a complex comic novel attacking the contemporary secularization of religion, was published in 1952. It was followed in 1955 by a collection of stories,* A Good Man Is Hard to Find. *O'Connor was able to see a second novel,* The Violent Bear It Away, *through to publication in 1960, but she died of lupus in 1964, having completed enough stories for a second collection,* Everything That Rises Must Converge *(1965). Her total output of just thirty-one stories, collected in her* Complete Stories, *won the National Book Award for fiction in 1972.*

Despite her illness, O'Connor was never a recluse; she accepted as many lecture invitations as her health would permit. A volume of her lectures and occasional pieces was published in 1969 as Mystery and Manners. *It is a valuable companion to her stories and novels, because she often reflected on her writing and interpreted her fiction. As a devout Roman Catholic, O'Connor was uncompromising in her religious views: "For I am no disbeliever in spiritual purpose and no vague believer. This means that for me the meaning of life is centered in our Redemption by Christ and what I see in the world I see in relation to that." As Joyce Carol Oates recognized in her essay "The Visionary Art of Flannery O'Connor," O'Connor is a great modern religious writer, thoroughly unique "in her celebration of the necessity of succumbing to the divine through violence that is immediate and irreparable. There is no mysticism in her work that is only spiritual; it is physical as well." O'Connor's stories, like the three included here, frequently involve family relationships but are not meant to be read as realistic fiction, despite her remarkable ear for dialogue. O'Connor said she wrote them as parables, as the epigraph to* A Good Man Is Hard to Find *attests.*

RELATED CASEBOOK: *See pages 776–800, including Flannery O'Connor, "From Letters, 1954–55," page 776, "Writing Short Stories," page 779, "The Element of Suspense in 'A Good Man Is Hard to Find,'" page 784; Sally Fitzgerald, "Southern Sources of 'A Good Man Is Hard to Find,'" page 787; Robert H. Brinkmeyer Jr., "Flannery O'Connor and Her Readers," page 788; Dorothy Tuck McFarland, "On 'Good Country People,'" page 793; Wayne C. Booth, "A Rhetorical Reading of O'Connor's 'Everything That Rises Must Converge,' " page 797.*

FLANNERY O'CONNOR

Everything That Rises Must Converge *1961*

Her doctor had told Julian's mother that she must lose twenty pounds on account of her blood pressure, so on Wednesday nights Julian had to take her downtown on the bus for a reducing class at the Y. The reducing class was designed for working girls over fifty, who weighed from 165 to 200 pounds. His mother was one of the slimmer ones, but she said ladies did not tell their age or weight. She would not ride the buses by herself at night since they had been integrated, and because the reducing class was one of her few pleasures, necessary for her health, and *free,* she said Julian could at least put himself out to take her, considering all she did for him. Julian did not like to consider all she did for him, but every Wednesday night he braced himself and took her.

She was almost ready to go, standing before the hall mirror, putting on her hat, while he, his hands behind him, appeared pinned to the door frame, waiting like Saint Sebastian for the arrows to begin piercing him. The hat was new and had cost her seven dollars and a half. She kept saying, "Maybe I shouldn't have paid that for it. No, I shouldn't have. I'll take it off and return it tomorrow. I shouldn't have bought it."

Julian raised his eyes to heaven. "Yes, you should have bought it," he said. "Put it on and let's go." It was a hideous hat. A purple velvet flap came down on one side of it and stood up on the other; the rest of it was green and looked like a cushion with the stuffing out. He decided it was less comical than jaunty and pathetic. Everything that gave her pleasure was small and depressed him.

She lifted the hat one more time and set it down slowly on top of her head. Two wings of gray hair protruded on either side of her florid face, but her eyes, sky-blue, were as innocent and untouched by experience as they must have been when she was ten. Were it not that she was a widow who had struggled fiercely to feed and clothe and put him through school and who was supporting him still, "until he got on his feet," she might have been a little girl that he had to take to town.

"It's all right, it's all right," he said. "Let's go." He opened the door himself and started down the walk to get her going. The sky was a dying violet and the houses stood out darkly against it, bulbous liver-colored monstrosities of a uniform ugliness though no two were alike. Since this had been a fashionable neighborhood forty years ago, his mother persisted in thinking they did well to have an apartment in it. Each house had a narrow collar of dirt around it in which sat, usually, a grubby child. Julian walked with his hands in his pockets, his head down and thrust forward, and his eyes glazed with the determination to make himself completely numb during the time he would be sacrificed to her pleasure.

The door closed and he turned to find the dumpy figure, surmounted by the atrocious hat, coming toward him. "Well," she said, "you only live once and paying a little more for it, I at least won't meet myself coming and going."

"Some day I'll start making money," Julian said gloomily — he knew he never would — "and you can have one of those jokes whenever you take the fit." But first they would move. He visualized a place where the nearest neighbor would be three miles away on either side.

"I think you're doing fine," she said, drawing on her gloves. "You've only been out of school a year. Rome wasn't built in a day."

She was one of the few members of the Y reducing class who arrived in hat and gloves and who had a son who had been to college. "It takes time," she said, "and the world is in such a mess. This hat looked better on me than any of the others, though when she brought it out I said, 'Take that thing back. I wouldn't have it on my head,' and she said, 'Now wait till you see it on,' and when she put it on me, I said, 'We-ull,' and she said, 'If you ask me, that hat does something for you and you do something for the hat, and besides,' she said, 'with that hat, you won't meet yourself coming and going.'"

Julian thought he could have stood his lot better if she had been selfish, if she had been an old hag who drank and screamed at him. He walked along, saturated in depression, as if in the midst of his martyrdom he had lost his faith. Catching sight of his long, hopeless, irritated face, she stopped suddenly with a grief-stricken look, and pulled back on his arm. "Wait on me," she said. "I'm going back to the house and take this thing off and tomorrow I'm going to return it. I was out of my head. I can pay the gas bill with the seven-fifty."

He caught her arm in a vicious grip. "You are not going to take it back," he said. "I like it."

"Well," she said, "I don't think I ought . . ."

"Shut up and enjoy it," he muttered, more depressed than ever.

"With the world in the mess it's in," she said, "it's a wonder we can enjoy anything. I tell you, the bottom rail is on the top."

Julian sighed.

"Of course," she said, "if you know who you are, you can go anywhere." She said this every time he took her to the reducing class. "Most of them in it are not our kind of people," she said, "but I can be gracious to anybody. I know who I am."

"They don't give a damn for your graciousness," Julian said savagely. "Knowing who you are is good for one generation only. You haven't the foggiest idea where you stand now or who you are."

She stopped and allowed her eyes to flash at him. "I most certainly do know who I am," she said, "and if you don't know who you are, I'm ashamed of you."

"Oh hell," Julian said.

"Your great-grandfather was a former governor of this state," she said. "Your grandfather was a prosperous landowner. Your grandmother was a Godhigh."

"Will you look around you," he said tensely, "and see where you are now?" and he swept his arm jerkily out to indicate the neighborhood, which the growing darkness at least made less dingy.

"You remain what you are," she said. "Your great-grandfather had a plantation and two hundred slaves."

"There are no more slaves," he said irritably.

"They were better off when they were," she said. He groaned to see that she was off on that topic. She rolled onto it every few days like a train on an open track. He knew every stop, every junction, every swamp along the way, and knew the exact point at which her conclusion would roll majestically into the station: "It's ridiculous. It's simply not realistic. They should rise, yes, but on their own side of the fence."

"Let's skip it," Julian said.

"The ones I feel sorry for," she said, "are the ones that are half white. They're tragic."

"Will you skip it?"

"Suppose we were half white. We would certainly have mixed feelings."

"I have mixed feelings now," he groaned.

"Well let's talk about something pleasant," she said. "I remember going to Grandpa's when I was a little girl. Then the house had double stairways that went up to what was really the second floor — all the cooking was done on the first. I used to like to stay down in the kitchen on account of the way the walls smelled. I would sit with my nose pressed against the plaster and take deep breaths. Actually the place belonged to the Godhighs but your grandfather Chestny paid the mortgage and saved it for them. They were in reduced circumstances," she said, "but reduced or not, they never forgot who they were."

"Doubtless that decayed mansion reminded them," Julian muttered. He never spoke of it without contempt or thought of it without longing. He had seen it once when he was a child before it had been sold. The double stairways had rotted and had been torn down. Negroes were living in it. But it remained in his mind as his mother had known it. It appeared in his dreams regularly. He would stand on the wide porch, listening to the rustle of oak leaves, then wander through the high-ceilinged hall into the parlor that opened onto it and gaze at the worn rugs and faded draperies. It occurred to him that it was he, not she, who could have appreciated it. He preferred its threadbare elegance to anything he could name and it was because of it that all the neighborhoods they had lived in had been a torment to him — whereas she had hardly known the difference. She called her insensitivity "being adjustable."

"And I remember the old darky who was my nurse, Caroline. There was no better person in the world. I've always had a great respect for my colored friends," she said. "I'd do anything in the world for them and they'd . . ."

"Will you for God's sake get off that subject?" Julian said. When he got on a bus by himself, he made it a point to sit down beside a Negro, in reparation as it were for his mother's sins.

"You're mighty touchy tonight," she said. "Do you feel all right?"

"Yes I feel all right," he said. "Now lay off."

She pursed her lips. "Well, you certainly are in a vile humor," she observed. "I just won't speak to you at all."

They had reached the bus stop. There was no bus in sight and Julian, his hands still jammed in his pockets and his head thrust forward, scowled down the empty street. The frustration of having to wait on the bus as well as ride on it began to creep up his neck like a hot hand. The presence of his mother was borne in upon him as she gave a pained sigh. He looked at her bleakly. She was holding herself very erect under the preposterous hat, wearing it like a banner of her imaginary dignity. There was in him an evil urge to break her spirit. He suddenly unloosened his tie and pulled it off and put it in his pocket.

She stiffened. "Why must you look like *that* when you take me to town?" she said. "Why must you deliberately embarrass me?"

"If you'll never learn where you are," he said, "you can at least learn where I am."

"You look like a — thug," she said.

"Then I must be one," he murmured.

"I'll just go home," she said. "I will not bother you. If you can't do a little thing like that for me . . ."

Rolling his eyes upward, he put his tie back on. "Restored to my class," he muttered. He thrust his face toward her and hissed, "True culture is in the mind, the *mind*," he said, and tapped his head, "the mind."

"It's in the heart," she said, "and in how you do things and how you do things is because of who you *are*."

"Nobody in the damn bus cares who you are."

"I care who I am," she said icily.

The lighted bus appeared on top of the next hill and as it approached, they moved out into the street to meet it. He put his hand under her elbow and hoisted her up on the creaking step. She entered with a little smile, as if she were going into a drawing room where everyone had been waiting for her. While he put in the tokens, she sat down on one of the broad front seats for three which faced the aisle. A thin woman with protruding teeth and long yellow hair was sitting on the end of it. His mother moved up beside her and left room for Julian beside herself. He sat down and looked at the floor across the aisle where a pair of thin feet in red and white canvas sandals were planted.

His mother immediately began a general conversation meant to attract anyone who felt like talking. "Can it get any hotter?" she said and removed from her purse a folding fan, black with a Japanese scene on it, which she began to flutter before her.

"I reckon it might could," the woman with the protruding teeth said, "but I know for a fact my apartment couldn't get no hotter."

"It must get the afternoon sun," his mother said. She sat forward and looked up and down the bus. It was half filled. Everybody was white. "I see we have the bus to ourselves," she said. Julian cringed.

"For a change," said the woman across the aisle, the owner of the red and white canvas sandals. "I come on one the other day and they were thick as fleas — up front and all through."

"The world is in a mess everywhere," his mother said. "I don't know how we've let it get in this fix."

"What gets my goat is all those boys from good families stealing automobile tires," the woman with the protruding teeth said. "I told my boy, I said you may not be rich but you been raised right and if I ever catch you in any such mess, they can send you on to the reformatory. Be exactly where you belong."

"Training tells," his mother said. "Is your boy in high school?"

"Ninth grade," the woman said.

"My son just finished college last year. He wants to write but he's selling typewriters until he gets started," his mother said.

The woman leaned forward and peered at Julian. He threw her such a malevolent look that she subsided against the seat. On the floor across the aisle there was an abandoned newspaper. He got up and got it and opened it out in front of him. His mother discreetly continued the conversation in a lower tone but the woman across the aisle said in a loud voice, "Well that's nice. Selling typewriters is close to writing. He can go right from one to the other."

"I tell him," his mother said, "that Rome wasn't built in a day."

Behind the newspaper Julian was withdrawing into the inner compartment of his mind where he spent most of his time. This was a kind of mental bubble in which he established himself when he could not bear to be part of what was going on around him. From it he could see out and judge but in it he was safe from any kind of penetration from without. It was the only place where he felt free of the general idiocy of his fellows. His mother had never entered it but from it he could see her with absolute clarity.

The old lady was clever enough and he thought that if she had started from any of the right premises, more might have been expected of her. She lived according to the laws of her own fantasy world, outside of which he had never seen her set foot. The law of it was to sacrifice herself for him after she had first created the necessity to do so by making a mess of things. If he had permitted her sacrifices, it was only because her lack of foresight had made them necessary. All of her life had been a struggle to act like a Chestny without the Chestny goods, and to give him everything she thought a Chestny ought to have; but since, said she, it was fun to struggle, why complain? And when you had won, as she had won, what fun to look back on the hard times! He could not forgive her that she had enjoyed the struggle and that she thought *she* had won.

What she meant when she said she had won was that she had brought him up successfully and had sent him to college and that he had turned out so well — good looking (her teeth had gone unfilled, so that his could be straightened), intelligent (he realized he was too intelligent to be a success), and with a future ahead of him (there was of course no future ahead of him). She excused his gloominess on the grounds that he was still growing up and his radical ideas on his lack of practical experience. She said he didn't yet know a thing about "life," that he hadn't even entered the real world — when already he was as disenchanted with it as a man of fifty.

The further irony of all this was that in spite of her, he had turned out so well. In spite of going to only a third-rate college, he had, on his own initiative, come out with a first-rate education; in spite of growing up dominated by a small mind, he had ended up with a large one; in spite of all her foolish views, he was free of prejudice and unafraid to face facts. Most miraculous of all, instead of being blinded by love for her as she was for him, he had cut himself emotionally free of her and could see her with complete objectivity. He was not dominated by his mother.

The bus stopped with a sudden jerk and shook him from his meditation. A woman from the back lurched forward with little steps and barely escaped falling in his newspaper as she righted herself. She got off and a large Negro got on. Julian kept his paper lowered to watch. It gave him a certain satisfaction to see injustice in daily operation. It confirmed his view that with a few exceptions there was no one worth knowing within a radius of three hundred miles. The Negro was well dressed and carried a briefcase. He looked round and then sat down on the other end of the seat where the woman with the red and white canvas sandals was sitting. He immediately unfolded a newspaper and obscured himself behind it. Julian's mother's elbow at once prodded insistently into his ribs. "Now you see why I won't ride on these buses by myself," she whispered.

The woman with the red and white canvas sandals had risen at the same time the Negro sat down and had gone further back in the bus and taken the seat of the woman who had got off. His mother leaned forward and cast her an approving look.

Julian rose, crossed the aisle, and sat down in the place of the woman with the canvas sandals. From this position, he looked serenely across at his mother. Her face had turned an angry red. He stared at her, making his eyes the eyes of a stranger. He felt his tension suddenly lift as if he had openly declared war on her.

He would have liked to get in conversation with the Negro and to talk with him about art or politics or any subject that would be above the comprehension of those around them, but the man remained entrenched behind his paper. He was either ignoring the change of seating or had never noticed it. There was no way for Julian to convey his sympathy.

His mother kept her eyes fixed reproachfully on his face. The woman with the protruding teeth was looking at him avidly as if he were a type of monster new to her.

"Do you have a light?" he asked the Negro.

Without looking away from his paper, the man reached in his pocket and handed him a packet of matches.

"Thanks," Julian said. For a moment he held the matches foolishly. A NO SMOKING sign looked down upon him from over the door. This alone would not have deterred him; he had no cigarettes. He had quit smoking some months before because he could not afford it. "Sorry," he muttered and handed back the matches. The Negro lowered the paper and gave him an annoyed look. He took the matches and raised the paper again.

His mother continued to gaze at him but she did not take the advantage of his momentary discomfort. Her eyes retained their battered look. Her face seemed to be unnaturally red, as if her blood pressure had risen. Julian allowed no glimmer of sympathy to show on his face. Having got the advantage, he wanted desperately to keep it and carry it through. He would have liked to teach her a lesson that would last her a while, but there seemed no way to continue the point. The Negro refused to come out from behind his paper.

Julian folded his arms and looked stolidly before him, facing her but as if he did not see her, as if he had ceased to recognize her existence. He visualized a scene in which, the bus having reached their stop, he would remain in his seat and when she said, "Aren't you going to get off?" he would look at her as a stranger who had rashly addressed him. The corner they got off on was usually deserted, but it was well lighted and it would not hurt her to walk by herself the four blocks to the Y. He decided to wait until the time came and then decide whether or not he would let her get off by herself. He would have to be at the Y at ten to bring her back, but he could leave her wondering if he was going to show up. There was no reason for her to think she could always depend on him.

He retired again into the high-ceilinged room sparsely settled with large pieces of antique furniture. His soul expanded momentarily but then he became aware of his mother across from him and the vision shriveled. He studied her coldly. Her feet in little pumps dangled like a child's and did not quite reach the floor. She was training on him an exaggerated look of reproach.

He felt completely detached from her. At that moment he could with pleasure have slapped her as he would have slapped a particularly obnoxious child in his charge.

He began to imagine various unlikely ways by which he could teach her a lesson. He might make friends with some distinguished Negro professor or lawyer and bring him home to spend the evening. He would be entirely justified but her blood pressure would rise to 300. He could not push her to the extent of making her have a stroke, and moreover, he had never been successful at making any Negro friends. He had tried to strike up an acquaintance on the bus with some of the better types, with ones that looked like professors or ministers or lawyers. One morning he had sat down next to a distinguished-looking dark brown man who had answered his questions with a sonorous solemnity but who had turned out to be an undertaker. Another day he had sat down beside a cigar-smoking Negro with a diamond ring on his finger, but after a few stilted pleasantries, the Negro had rung the buzzer and risen, slipping two lottery tickets into Julian's hand as he climbed over him to leave.

He imagined his mother lying desperately ill and his being able to secure only a Negro doctor for her. He toyed with that idea for a few minutes and then dropped it for a momentary vision of himself participating as a sympathizer in a sit-in demonstration. This was possible but he did not linger with it. Instead, he approached the ultimate horror. He brought home a beautiful suspiciously Negroid woman. Prepare yourself, he said. There is nothing you can do about it. This is the woman I've chosen. She's intelligent, dignified, even good, and she's suffered and she hasn't thought it *fun*. Now persecute us, go ahead and persecute us. Drive her out of here, but remember, you're driving me too. His eyes were narrowed and through the indignation he had generated, he saw his mother across the aisle, purplefaced, shrunken to the dwarf-like proportions of her moral nature, sitting like a mummy beneath the ridiculous banner of her hat.

He was tilted out of his fantasy again as the bus stopped. The door opened with a sucking hiss and out of the dark a large, gaily dressed, sullen-looking colored woman got on with a little boy. The child, who might have been four, had on a short plaid suit and a Tyrolean hat with a blue feather in it. Julian hoped that he would sit down beside him and that the woman would push in beside his mother. He could think of no better arrangement.

As she waited for her tokens, the woman was surveying the seating possibilities — he hoped with the idea of sitting where she was least wanted. There was something familiar-looking about her but Julian could not place what it was. She was a giant of a woman. Her face was set not only to meet opposition but to seek it out. The downward tilt of her large lower lip was like a warning sign: DON'T TAMPER WITH ME. Her bulging figure was encased in a green crepe dress and her feet overflowed in red shoes. She had on a hideous hat. A purple velvet flap came down on one side of it and stood up on the other; the rest of it was green and looked like a cushion with the stuffing out. She carried a mammoth red pocketbook that bulged throughout as if it were stuffed with rocks.

To Julian's disappointment, the little boy climbed up on the empty seat beside his mother. His mother lumped all children, black and white, into the common category, "cute," and she thought little Negroes were on the whole cuter than little white children. She smiled at the little boy as he climbed on the seat.

Meanwhile the woman was bearing down upon the empty seat beside Julian. To his annoyance, she squeezed herself into it. He saw his mother's face change as the woman settled herself next to him and he realized with satisfaction that this was more objectionable to her than it was to him. Her face seemed almost gray and there was a look of dull recognition in her eyes, as if suddenly she had sickened at some awful confrontation. Julian saw that it was because she and the woman had, in a sense, swapped sons. Though his mother would not realize the symbolic significance of this, she would feel it. His amusement showed plainly on his face.

The woman next to him muttered something unintelligible to herself. He was conscious of a kind of bristling next to him, muted growling like that of an angry cat. He could not see anything but the red pocketbook upright on the bulging green thighs. He visualized the woman as she had stood waiting for her tokens — the ponderous figure, rising from the red shoes upward over the solid hips, the mammoth bosom, the haughty face, to the green and purple hat.

His eyes widened.

The vision of the two hats, identical, broke upon him with the radiance of a brilliant sunrise. His face was suddenly lit with joy. He could not believe that Fate had thrust upon his mother such a lesson. He gave a loud chuckle so that she would look at him and see that he saw. She turned her eyes on him slowly. The blue in them seemed to have turned a bruised purple. For a moment he had an uncomfortable sense of her innocence, but it lasted only a second before principle rescued him. Justice entitled him to laugh. His grin hardened until it said to her as plainly as if he were saying aloud: Your punishment exactly fits your pettiness. This should teach you a permanent lesson.

Her eyes shifted to the woman. She seemed unable to bear looking at him and to find the woman preferable. He became conscious again of the bristling presence at his side. The woman was rumbling like a volcano about to become active. His mother's mouth began to twitch slightly at one corner. With a sinking heart, he saw incipient signs of recovery on her face and realized that this was going to strike her suddenly as funny and was going to be no lesson at all. She kept her eyes on the woman and an amused smile came over her face as if the woman were a monkey that had stolen her hat. The little Negro was looking up at her with large fascinated eyes. He had been trying to attract her attention for some time.

"Carver," the woman said suddenly. "Come heah!"

When he saw that the spotlight was on him at last, Carver drew his feet up and turned himself toward Julian's mother and giggled.

"Carver!" the woman said. "You heah me? Come Heah!"

Carver slid down from the seat but remained squatting with his back against the base of it, his head turned slowly around toward Julian's mother, who was smiling at him. The woman reached a hand across the aisle and snatched him to her. He righted himself and hung backwards on her knees, grinning at Julian's mother. "Isn't he cute?" Julian's mother said to the woman with the protruding teeth.

"I reckon he is," the woman said without conviction.

The Negress yanked him upright but he eased out of her grip and shot across the aisle and scrambled, giggling wildly, onto the seat beside his love.

"I think he likes me," Julian's mother said, and smiled at the woman. It was the smile she used when she was being particularly gracious to an inferior. Julian saw everything lost. The lesson had rolled off her like rain on a roof.

The woman stood up and yanked the little boy off the seat as if she were snatching him from contagion. Julian could feel the rage in her at having no weapon like his mother's smile. She gave the child a sharp slap across his leg. He howled once and then thrust his head into her stomach and kicked his feet against her shins. "Behave," she said vehemently.

The bus stopped and the Negro who had been reading the newspaper got off. The woman moved over and set the little boy down with a thump between herself and Julian. She held him firmly by the knee. In a moment he put his hands in front of his face and peeped at Julian's mother through his fingers.

"I see yoooooooo!" she said and put her hand in front of her face and peeped at him.

The woman slapped his hand down. "Quit yo' foolishness," she said, "before I knock the living Jesus out of you!"

Julian was thankful that the next stop was theirs. He reached up and pulled the cord. The woman reached up and pulled it at the same time. Oh my God, he thought. He had the terrible intuition that when they got off the bus together, his mother would open her purse and give the little boy a nickel. The gesture would be as natural to her as breathing. The bus stopped and the woman got up and lunged to the front, dragging the child, who wished to stay on, after her. Julian and his mother got up and followed. As they neared the door, Julian tried to relieve her of her pocketbook.

"No," she murmured, "I want to give the little boy a nickel."

"No!" Julian hissed. "No!"

She smiled down at the child and opened her bag. The bus door opened and the woman picked him up by the arm and descended with him, hanging at her hip. Once in the street she set him down and shook him.

Julian's mother had to close her purse while she got down the bus step but as soon as her feet were on the ground, she opened it again and began to rummage inside. "I can't find but a penny," she whispered, "but it looks like a new one."

"Don't do it!" Julian said fiercely between his teeth. There was a streetlight on the corner and she hurried to get under it so that she could better see into her pocketbook. The woman was heading off rapidly down the street with the child still hanging backward on her hand.

"Oh little boy!" Julian's mother called and took a few quick steps and caught up with them just beyond the lamppost. "Here's a bright new penny for you," and she held out the coin, which shone bronze in the dim light.

The huge woman turned and for a moment stood, her shoulders lifted and her face frozen with frustrated rage, and stared at Julian's mother. Then all at once she seemed to explode like a piece of machinery that had been given one ounce of pressure too much. Julian saw the black fist swing out with the red pocketbook. He shut his eyes and cringed as he heard the woman shout, "He don't take nobody's pennies!" When he opened his eyes, the woman was disappearing down the street with the little boy staring wide-eyed over her shoulder. Julian's mother was sitting on the sidewalk.

"I told you not to do that," Julian said angrily. "I told you not to do that!"

He stood over her for a minute, gritting his teeth. Her legs were stretched out in front of her and her hat was on her lap. He squatted down and looked her in the face. It was totally expressionless. "You got exactly what you deserved," he said. "Now get up."

He picked up her pocketbook and put what had fallen out back in it. He picked the hat up off her lap. The penny caught his eye on the sidewalk and he picked that up and let it drop before her eyes into the purse. Then he stood up and leaned over and held his hands out to pull her up. She remained immobile. He sighed. Rising above them on either side were black apartment buildings, marked with irregular rectangles of light. At the end of the block a man came out of a door and walked off in the opposite direction. "All right," he said, "suppose somebody happens by and wants to know why you're sitting on the sidewalk?"

She took the hand and, breathing hard, pulled heavily up on it and then stood for a moment, swaying slightly as if the spots of light in the darkness were circling around her. Her eyes, shadowed and confused, finally settled on his face. He did not try to conceal his irritation. "I hope this teaches you a lesson," he said. She leaned forward and her eyes raked his face. She seemed trying to determine his identity. Then, as if she found nothing familiar about him, she started off with a headlong movement in the wrong direction.

"Aren't you going to the Y?" he asked.

"Home," she muttered.

"Well, are we walking?"

For answer she kept going. Julian followed along, his hands behind him. He saw no reason to let the lesson she had had go without backing it up with an explanation of its meaning. She might as well be made to understand what had happened to her. "Don't think that was just an uppity Negro woman," he said. "That was the whole colored race which will no longer take your condescending pennies. That was your black double. She can wear the same hat as you, and to be sure," he added gratuitously (because he thought it was funny), "it looked better on her than it did on you. What all this means," he said, "is that the old world is gone. The old manners are obsolete and your graciousness is not worth a damn." He thought bitterly of the house that had been lost for him. "You aren't who you think you are," he said.

She continued to plow ahead, paying no attention to him. Her hair had come undone on one side. She dropped her pocketbook and took no notice. He stopped and picked it up and handed it to her but she did not take it.

"You needn't act as if the world had come to an end," he said, "because it hasn't. From now on you've got to live in a new world and face a few realities for a change. Buck up," he said, "it won't kill you."

She was breathing fast.

"Let's wait on the bus," he said.

"Home," she said thickly.

"I hate to see you behave like this," he said. "Just like a child. I should be able to expect more of you." He decided to stop where he was and make her stop and wait for a bus. "I'm not going any farther," he said, stopping. "We're going on the bus."

She continued to go on as if she had not heard him. He took a few steps and caught her arm and stopped her. He looked into her face and caught his breath. He was looking into a face he had never seen before. "Tell Grandpa to come get me," she said.

He stared, stricken.

"Tell Caroline to come get me," she said.

Stunned, he let her go and she lurched forward again, walking as if one leg were shorter than the other. A tide of darkness seemed to be sweeping her from him. "Mother!" he cried. "Darling, sweetheart, wait!" Crumpling, she fell to the pavement. He dashed forward and fell at her side, crying, "Mamma, Mamma!" He turned her over. Her face was fiercely distorted. One eye, large and staring, moved slightly to the left as if it had become unmoored. The other remained fixed on him, raked his face again, found nothing, and closed.

"Wait here, wait here!" he cried and jumped up and began to run for help toward a cluster of lights he saw in the distance ahead of him. "Help, help!" he shouted, but his voice was thin, scarcely a thread of sound. The lights drifted farther away the faster he ran and his feet moved numbly as if they carried him nowhere. The tide of darkness seemed to sweep him back to her, postponing from moment to moment his entry into the world of guilt and sorrow.

FLANNERY O'CONNOR

Good Country People

1955

Besides the neutral expression that she wore when she was alone, Mrs. Freeman had two others, forward and reverse, that she used for all her human dealings. Her forward expression was steady and driving like the advance of a heavy truck. Her eyes never swerved to left or right but turned as the story turned as if they followed a yellow line down the center of it. She seldom used the other expression because it was not often necessary for her to retract a statement, but when she did, her face came to a complete stop, there was an almost imperceptible movement of her black eyes, during which they seemed to be receding, and then the observer would see that Mrs. Freeman, though she might stand there as real as several grain sacks thrown on top of each other, was no longer there in spirit. As for getting anything across to her when this was the case, Mrs. Hopewell had given it up. She might talk her head off. Mrs. Freeman could never be brought to admit herself wrong on any point.

She would stand there and if she could be brought to say anything, it was something like, "Well, I wouldn't of said it was and I wouldn't of said it wasn't," or letting her gaze range over the top kitchen shelf where there was an assortment of dusty bottles, she might remark, "I see you ain't ate many of them figs you put up last summer."

They carried on their most important business in the kitchen at breakfast. Every morning Mrs. Hopewell got up at seven o'clock and lit her gas heater and Joy's. Joy was her daughter, a large blonde girl who had an artificial leg. Mrs. Hopewell thought of her as a child though she was thirty-two years old and highly educated. Joy would get up while her mother was eating and lumber into the bathroom and slam the door, and before long, Mrs. Freeman would arrive at the back door. Joy would hear her mother call, "Come on in," and then they would talk a while in low voices that were indistinguishable in the bathroom. By the time Joy came in, they had usually finished the weather report and were on one or the other of Mrs. Freeman's daughters, Glynese or Carramae, Joy called them Glycerin and Caramel. Glynese, a redhead, was eighteen and had many admirers; Carramae, a blonde, was only fifteen but already married and pregnant. She could not keep anything on her stomach. Every morning Mrs. Freeman told Mrs. Hopewell how many times she had vomited since the last report.

Mrs. Hopewell liked to tell people that Glynese and Carramae were two of the finest girls she knew and that Mrs. Freeman was a *lady* and that she was never ashamed to take her anywhere or introduce her to anybody they might meet. Then she would tell how she had happened to hire the Freemans in the first place and how they were a godsend to her and how she had had them four years. The reason for her keeping them so long was that they were not trash. They were good country people. She had telephoned the man whose name they had given as a reference and he had told her that Mr. Freeman was a good farmer but that his wife was the nosiest woman ever to walk the earth. "She's got to be into everything," the man said. "If she don't get there before the dust settles, you can bet she's dead, that's all. She'll want to know all your business. I can stand him real good," he had said, "but me nor my wife neither could have stood that woman one more minute on this place." That had put Mrs. Hopewell off for a few days.

She had hired them in the end because there were no other applicants but she had made up her mind beforehand exactly how she would handle the woman. Since she was the type who had to be into everything, then, Mrs. Hopewell had decided, she would not only let her be into everything, she would *see to it* that she was into everything — she would give her the responsibility of everything, she would put her in charge. Mrs. Hopewell had no bad qualities of her own but she was able to use other people's in such a constructive way that she never felt the lack. She had hired the Freemans and she had kept them four years.

Nothing is perfect. This was one of Mrs. Hopewell's favorite sayings. Another was: that is life! And still another, the most important, was: well, other people have their opinions too. She would make these statements, usually at the table, in a tone of gentle insistence as if no one held them but her, and the large hulking Joy, whose constant outrage had obliterated every expression from her face, would stare just a little to the side of her, her eyes icy blue, with the look of someone who has achieved blindness by an act of will and means to keep it.

When Mrs. Hopewell said to Mrs. Freeman that life was like that, Mrs. Freeman would say, "I always said so myself." Nothing had been arrived at by anyone that had not first been arrived at by her. She was quicker than Mr. Freeman. When Mrs. Hopewell said to her after they had been on the place a while, "You know, you're the wheel behind the wheel," and winked, Mrs. Freeman had said, "I know it. I've always been quick. It's some that are quicker than others."

"Everybody is different," Mrs. Hopewell said.

"Yes, most people is," Mrs. Freeman said.

"It takes all kinds to make the world."

"I always said it did myself."

The girl was used to this kind of dialogue for breakfast and more of it for dinner; sometimes they had it for supper too. When they had no guest they ate in the kitchen because that was easier. Mrs. Freeman always managed to arrive at some point during the meal and to watch them finish it. She would stand in the doorway if it were summer but in the winter she would stand with one elbow on top of the refrigerator and look down on them, or she would stand by the gas heater, lifting the back of her skirt slightly. Occasionally she would stand against the wall and roll her head from side to side. At no time was she in any hurry to leave. All this was very trying on Mrs. Hopewell but she was a woman of great patience. She realized that nothing is perfect and that in the Freemans she had good country people and that if, in this day and age, you get good country people, you had better hang onto them.

She had had plenty of experience with trash. Before the Freemans she had averaged one tenant family a year. The wives of these farmers were not the kind you would want to be around you for very long. Mrs. Hopewell, who had divorced her husband long ago, needed someone to walk over the fields with her; and when Joy had to be impressed for these services, her remarks were usually so ugly and her face so glum that Mrs. Hopewell would say, "If you can't come pleasantly, I don't want you at all," to which the girl, standing square and rigid-shouldered with her neck thrust slightly forward, would reply, "If you want me, here I am — LIKE I AM."

Mrs. Hopewell excused this attitude because of the leg (which had been shot off in a hunting accident when Joy was ten). It was hard for Mrs. Hopewell to realize that her child was thirty-two now and that for more than twenty years she had had only one leg. She thought of her still as a child because it tore her heart to think instead of the poor stout girl in her thirties who had never danced a step or had any *normal* good times. Her name was really Joy but as soon as she was twenty-one and away from home, she had had it legally changed. Mrs. Hopewell was certain that she had thought and thought until she had hit upon the ugliest name in any language. Then she had gone and had the beautiful name, Joy, changed without telling her mother until after she had done it. Her legal name was Hulga.

When Mrs. Hopewell thought the name Hulga, she thought of the broad blank hull of a battleship. She would not use it. She continued to call her Joy to which the girl responded but in a purely mechanical way.

Hulga had learned to tolerate Mrs. Freeman who saved her from taking walks with her mother. Even Glynese and Carramae were useful when they occupied attention that might otherwise have been directed at her. At first she had thought she could not stand Mrs. Freeman for she had found that it was not possible to be rude to her. Mrs. Freeman would take on strange resentments and for days together she would be sullen but the source of her displeasure was always obscure; a direct attack, a positive leer, blatant ugliness to her face — these never touched her. And without warning one day, she began calling her Hulga.

She did not call her that in front of Mrs. Hopewell who would have been incensed but when she and the girl happened to be out of the house together, she would say something and add the name Hulga to the end of it, and the big spectacled Joy-Hulga would scowl and redden as if her privacy had been intruded upon. She considered the name her personal affair. She had arrived at it first purely on the basis of its ugly sound and then the full genius of its fitness had struck her. She had a vision of the name working like the ugly sweating Vulcan who stayed in the furnace and to whom, presumably, the goddess had to come when called. She saw it as the name of her highest creative act. One of her major triumphs was that her mother had not been able to turn her dust into Joy, but the greater one was that she had been able to turn it herself into Hulga. However, Mrs. Freeman's relish for using the name only irritated her. It was as if Mrs. Freeman's beady steel-pointed eyes had penetrated far enough behind her face to reach some secret fact. Something about her seemed to fascinate Mrs. Freeman and then one day Hulga realized that it was the artificial leg. Mrs. Freeman had a special fondness for the details of secret infections, hidden deformities, assaults upon children. Of diseases, she preferred the lingering or incurable. Hulga had heard Mrs. Hopewell give her the details of the hunting accident, how the leg had been literally blasted off, how she had never lost consciousness. Mrs. Freeman could listen to it any time as if it had happened an hour ago.

When Hulga stumped into the kitchen in the morning (she could walk without making the awful noise but she made it — Mrs. Hopewell was certain — because it was ugly-sounding), she glanced at them and did not speak. Mrs. Hopewell would be in her red kimono with her hair tied around her head in rags. She would be sitting at the table, finishing her breakfast and Mrs. Freeman would be hanging by her elbow outward from the refrigerator, looking down at the table. Hulga always put her eggs on the stove to boil and then stood over them with her arms folded, and Mrs. Hopewell would look at her — a kind of indirect gaze divided between her and Mrs. Freeman — and would think that if she would only keep herself up a little, she wouldn't be so bad looking. There was nothing wrong with her face that a pleasant expression wouldn't help. Mrs. Hopewell said that people who looked on the bright side of things would be beautiful even if they were not.

Whenever she looked at Joy this way, she could not help but feel that it would have been better if the child had not taken the Ph.D. It had certainly not brought her out any and now that she had it, there was no more excuse for her to go to school again. Mrs. Hopewell thought it was nice for girls to go to school to have a good time but Joy had "gone through." Anyhow, she would not have been strong enough to go again. The doctors had told Mrs. Hopewell that with the best of care, Joy might see forty-five. She had a weak heart. Joy had made it plain that if it had not been for this condition, she would be far from these red hills and good country people. She would be in a university lecturing to people who knew what she was talking about. And Mrs. Hopewell could very well picture her there, looking like a scarecrow and lecturing to more of the same. Here she went about all day in a six-year-old skirt and a yellow sweat shirt with a faded cowboy on a horse embossed on it. She thought this was funny; Mrs. Hopewell thought it was idiotic and showed simply that she was still a child. She was brilliant but she didn't have a grain of sense. It seemed to Mrs. Hopewell that every year she grew less like other people and more like herself — bloated, rude, and squint-eyed. And she said such strange things! To her own mother she had said — without warning, without excuse, standing up in the middle of a meal with her face purple and her mouth half full — "Woman! do you ever look inside? Do you ever look inside and see what you are *not*? God!" she had cried sinking down again and staring at her plate, "Malebranche was right: we are not our own light. We are not our own light!" Mrs. Hopewell had no idea to this day what brought that on. She had only made the remark, hoping Joy would take it in, that a smile never hurt anyone.

The girl had taken the Ph.D. in philosophy and this left Mrs. Hopewell at a complete loss. You could say, "My daughter is a nurse," or "My daughter is a schoolteacher," or even, "My daughter is a chemical engineer." You could not say, "My daughter is a philosopher." That was something that had ended with the Greeks and Romans. All day Joy sat on her neck in a deep chair, reading. Sometimes she went for walks but she didn't like dogs or cats or birds or flowers or nature or nice young men. She looked at nice young men as if she could smell their stupidity.

One day Mrs. Hopewell had picked up one of the books the girl had just put down and opening it at random, she read, "Science, on the other hand, has to assert its soberness and seriousness afresh and declare that it is concerned solely with what-is. Nothing — how can it be for science anything but a horror and a phantasm? If science is right, then one thing stands firm: science wishes to know nothing of nothing. Such is after all the strictly scientific approach to Nothing. We know it by wishing to know nothing of Nothing." These words had been underlined with a blue pencil and they worked on Mrs. Hopewell like some evil incantation in gibberish. She shut the book quickly and went out of the room as if she were having a chill.

This morning when the girl came in, Mrs. Freeman was on Carramae. "She thrown up four times after supper," she said, "and was up twict in the night after three o'clock. Yesterday she didn't do nothing but ramble in the bureau drawer. All she did. Stand up there and see what she could run up on."

"She's got to eat," Mrs. Hopewell muttered, sipping her coffee, while she watched Joy's back at the stove. She was wondering what the child had said to the Bible salesman. She could not imagine what kind of a conversation she could possibly have had with him.

He was a tall gaunt hatless youth who had called yesterday to sell them a Bible. He had appeared at the door, carrying a large black suitcase that weighted him so heavily on one side that he had to brace himself against the door facing. He seemed on the point of collapse but he said in a cheerful voice, "Good morning, Mrs. Cedars!" and set the suitcase down on the mat. He was not a bad-looking young man though he had on a bright blue suit and yellow socks that were not pulled up far enough. He had prominent face bones and a streak of sticky-looking brown hair falling across his forehead.

"I'm Mrs. Hopewell," she said.

"Oh!" he said, pretending to look puzzled but with his eyes sparkling, "I saw it said 'The Cedars' on the mailbox so I thought you was Mrs. Cedars!" and he burst out in a pleasant laugh. He picked up the satchel and under cover of a pant, he fell forward into her hall. It was rather as if the suitcase had moved first, jerking him after it. "Mrs. Hopewell!" he said and grabbed her hand. "I hope you are well!" and he laughed again and then all at once his face sobered completely. He paused and gave her a straight earnest look and said, "Lady, I've come to speak of serious things."

"Well, come in," she muttered, none too pleased because her dinner was almost ready. He came into the parlor and sat down on the edge of a straight chair and put the suitcase between his feet and glanced around the room as if he were sizing her up by it. Her silver gleamed on the two sideboards; she decided he had never been in a room as elegant as this.

"Mrs. Hopewell," he began, using her name in a way that sounded almost intimate, "I know you believe in Chrustian service."

"Well yes," she murmured.

"I know," he said and paused, looking very wise with his head cocked on one side, "that you're a good woman. Friends have told me."

Mrs. Hopewell never liked to be taken for a fool. "What are you selling?" she asked.

"Bibles," the young man said and his eye raced around the room before he added, "I see you have no family Bible in your parlor, I see that is the one lack you got!"

Mrs. Hopewell could not say, "My daughter is an atheist and won't let me keep the Bible in the parlor." She said, stiffening slightly, "I keep my Bible by my bedside." This was not the truth. It was in the attic somewhere.

"Lady," he said, "the word of God ought to be in the parlor."

"Well, I think that's a matter of taste," she began. "I think . . ."

"Lady," he said, "for a Chrustian, the word of God ought to be in every room in the house besides in his heart. I know, you're a Chrustian because I can see it in every line of your face."

She stood up and said, "Well, young man, I don't want to buy a Bible and I smell my dinner burning."

He didn't get up. He began to twist his hands and looking down at them he said softly, "Well lady, I'll tell you the truth — not many people want to buy one nowadays and besides, I know I'm real simple. I don't know how to say a thing but to say it. I'm just a country boy." He glanced up into her unfriendly face. "People like you don't like to fool with country people like me!"

"Why!" she cried, "good country people are the salt of the earth! Besides, we all have different ways of doing, it takes all kinds to make the world go 'round. That's life!"

"You said a mouthful," he said.

"Why, I think there aren't enough good country people in the world!" she said, stirred. "I think that's what's wrong with it!"

His face had brightened. "I didn't inraduce myself," he said. "I'm Manley Pointer from out in the country around Willohobie, not even from a place, just from near a place."

"You wait a minute," she said. "I have to see about my dinner." She went out to the kitchen and found Joy standing near the door where she had been listening.

"Get rid of the salt of the earth," she said, "and let's eat."

Mrs. Hopewell gave her a pained look and turned the heat down under the vegetables. "*I* can't be rude to anybody," she murmured and went back into the parlor.

He had opened the suitcase and was sitting with a Bible on each knee.

"You might as well put those up," she told him. "I don't want one."

"I appreciate your honesty," he said. "You don't see any more real honest people unless you go way out in the country."

"I know," she said, "real genuine folks!" Through the crack in the door she heard a groan.

"I guess a lot of boys come telling you they're working their way through college," he said, "but I'm not going to tell you that. Somehow," he said, "I don't want to go to college. I want to devote my life to Chrustian service. See," he said, lowering his voice, "I got this heart condition. I may not live long. When you know it's something wrong with you and you may not live long, well then, lady . . ." He paused, with his mouth open, and stared at her.

He and Joy had the same condition! She knew that her eyes were filling with tears but she collected herself quickly and murmured, "Won't you stay for dinner? We'd love to have you!" and was sorry the instant she heard herself say it.

"Yes mam," he said in an abashed voice, "I would sher love to do that!"

Joy had given him one look on being introduced to him and then throughout the meal had not glanced at him again. He had addressed several remarks to her, which she had pretended not to hear. Mrs. Hopewell could not understand deliberate rudeness, although she lived with it, and she felt she had always to overflow with hospitality to make up for Joy's lack of courtesy. She urged him to talk about himself and he did. He said he was the seventh child of twelve and that his father had been crushed under a tree when he himself was eight years old. He had been crushed very badly, in fact, almost cut in two and was practically not recognizable. His mother had got along the best she could by hard working and she had always seen that her children went to Sunday School and that they read the Bible every evening. He was now nineteen years old and he had been selling Bibles for four months. In that time he had sold seventy-seven Bibles and had the promise of two more sales. He wanted to become a missionary because he thought that was the way you could do most for people. "He who losest his life shall find it," he said simply and he was so sincere, so genuine and earnest that Mrs. Hopewell would not for the world have smiled. He prevented his peas from sliding onto the table by blocking them with a piece of bread which he later cleaned his plate with. She could see Joy observing sidewise how he handled his knife and fork and she saw too that every few minutes, the boy would dart a keen appraising glance at the girl as if he were trying to attract her attention.

After dinner Joy cleared the dishes off the table and disappeared and Mrs. Hopewell was left to talk with him. He told her again about his childhood and his father's accident and about various things that had happened to him. Every five minutes or so she would stifle a yawn. He sat for two hours until finally she told him she must go because she had an appointment in town. He packed his Bibles and thanked her and prepared to leave, but in the doorway he stopped and wrung her hand and said that not on any of his trips had he met a lady as nice as her and he asked if he could come again. She had said she would always be happy to see him.

Joy had been standing in the road, apparently looking at something in the distance, when he came down the steps toward her, bent to the side with his heavy valise. He stopped where she was standing and confronted her directly. Mrs. Hopewell could not hear what he said but she trembled to think what Joy would say to him. She could see that after a minute Joy said something and that then the boy began to speak again, making an excited gesture with his free hand. After a minute Joy said something else at which the boy began to speak once more. Then to her amazement, Mrs. Hopewell saw the two of them walk off together, toward the gate. Joy had walked all the way to the gate with him and Mrs. Hopewell could not imagine what they had said to each other, and she had not yet dared to ask.

Mrs. Freeman was insisting upon her attention. She had moved from the refrigerator to the heater so that Mrs. Hopewell had to turn and face her in order to seem to be listening. "Glynese gone out with Harvey Hill again last night," she said. "She had this sty."

"Hill," Mrs. Hopewell said absently, "is that the one who works in the garage?"

"Nome, he's the one that goes to chiropracter school," Mrs. Freeman said. "She had this sty. Been had it two days. So she says when he brought her in the other night he says, 'Lemme get rid of that sty for you,' and she says, 'How?' and he says, 'You just lay yourself down acrost the seat of that car and I'll show you.' So she done it and he popped her neck. Kept on a-popping it several times until she made him quit. This morning," Mrs. Freeman said, "she ain't got no sty. She ain't got no traces of a sty."

"I never heard of that before," Mrs. Hopewell said.

"He ast her to marry him before the Ordinary," Mrs. Freeman went on, "and she told him she wasn't going to be married in no *office*."

"Well, Glynese is a fine girl," Mrs. Hopewell said. "Glynese and Carramae are both fine girls."

"Carramae said when her and Lyman was married Lyman said it sure felt sacred to him. She said he said he wouldn't take five hundred dollars for being married by a preacher."

"How much would he take?" the girl asked from the stove.

"He said he wouldn't take five hundred dollars," Mrs. Freeman repeated.

"Well we all have work to do," Mrs. Hopewell said.

"Lyman said it just felt more sacred to him," Mrs. Freeman said. "The doctor wants Carramae to eat prunes. Says instead of medicine. Says them cramps is coming from pressure. You know where I think it is?"

"She'll be better in a few weeks," Mrs. Hopewell said.

"In the tube," Mrs. Freeman said. "Else she wouldn't be as sick as she is."

Hulga had cracked her two eggs into a saucer and was bringing them to the table along with a cup of coffee that she had filled too full. She sat down carefully and began to eat, meaning to keep Mrs. Freeman there by questions if for any reason she showed an inclination to leave. She could perceive her mother's eye on her. The first round-about question would be about the Bible salesman and she did not wish to bring it on. "How did he pop her neck?" she asked.

Mrs. Freeman went into a description of how he had popped her neck. She said he owned a '55 Mercury but that Glynese said she would rather marry a man with only a '36 Plymouth who would be married by a preacher. The girl asked what if he had a '32 Plymouth and Mrs. Freeman said what Glynese had said was a '36 Plymouth.

Mrs. Hopewell said there were not many girls with Glynese's common sense. She said what she admired in those girls was their common sense. She said that reminded her that they had had a nice visitor yesterday, a young man selling Bibles. "Lord," she said, "he bored me to death but he was so sincere and genuine I couldn't be rude to him. He was just good country people, you know," she said, "— just the salt of the earth."

"I seen him walk up," Mrs. Freeman said, "and then later — I seen him walk off," and Hulga could feel the slight shift in her voice, the slight insinuation, that he had not walked off alone, had he? Her face remained expressionless but the color rose into her neck and she seemed to swallow it down with the next spoonful of egg. Mrs. Freeman was looking at her as if they had a secret together.

"Well, it takes all kinds of people to make the world go 'round," Mrs. Hopewell said. "It's very good we aren't all alike."

"Some people are more alike than others," Mrs. Freeman said.

Hulga got up and stumped, with about twice the noise that was necessary, into her room and locked the door. She was to meet the Bible salesman at ten o'clock at the gate. She had thought about it half the night. She had started thinking of it as a great joke and then she had begun to see profound implications in it. She had lain in bed imagining dialogues for them that were insane on the surface but that reached below to depths that no Bible salesman would be aware of. Their conversation yesterday had been of this kind.

He had stopped in front of her and had simply stood there. His face was bony and sweaty and bright, with a little pointed nose in the center of it, and his look was different from what it had been at the dinner table. He was gazing at her with open curiosity, with fascination, like a child watching a new fantastic animal at the zoo, and he was breathing as if he had run a great distance to reach her. His gaze seemed somehow familiar but she could not think where she had been regarded with it before. For almost a minute he didn't say anything. Then on what seemed an insuck of breath, he whispered, "You ever ate a chicken that was two days old?"

The girl looked at him stonily. He might have just put this question up for consideration at the meeting of a philosophical association. "Yes," she presently replied as if she had considered it from all angles.

"It must have been mighty small!" he said triumphantly and shook all over with little nervous giggles, getting very red in the face, and subsiding finally into his gaze of complete admiration, while the girl's expression remained exactly the same.

"How old are you?" he asked softly.

She waited some time before she answered. Then in a flat voice she said, "Seventeen."

His smiles came in succession like waves breaking on the surface of a little lake. "I see you got a wooden leg," he said. "I think you're brave. I think you're real sweet."

The girl stood blank and solid and silent.

"Walk to the gate with me," he said. "You're a brave sweet little thing and I liked you the minute I seen you walk in the door."

Hulga began to move forward.

"What's your name?" he asked, smiling down on the top of her head.

"Hulga," she said.

"Hulga," he murmured, "Hulga. Hulga. I never heard of anybody name Hulga before. You're shy, aren't you, Hulga?" he asked.

She nodded, watching his large red hand on the handle of the giant valise.

"I like girls that wear glasses," he said. "I think a lot. I'm not like these people that a serious thought don't ever enter their heads. It's because I may die."

"I may die too," she said suddenly and looked up at him. His eyes were very small and brown, glittering feverishly.

"Listen," he said, "don't you think some people was meant to meet on account of what all they got in common and all? Like they both think serious thoughts and all?" He shifted the valise to his other hand so that the hand nearest her was free. He caught hold of her elbow and shook it a little. "I don't work on Saturday," he said. "I like to walk in the woods and see what Mother Nature is wearing. O'er the hills and far away. Pic-nics and things. Couldn't we go on a pic-nic tomorrow? Say yes, Hulga," he said and gave her a dying look as if he felt his insides about to drop out of him. He had even seemed to sway slightly toward her.

During the night she had imagined that she seduced him. She imagined that the two of them walked on the place until they came to the storage barn beyond the two back fields and there, she imagined, that things came to such a pass that she very easily seduced him and that then, of course, she had to reckon with his remorse. True genius can get an idea across even to an inferior mind. She imagined that she took his remorse in hand and changed it into a deeper understanding of life. She took all his shame away and turned it into something useful.

She set off for the gate at exactly ten o'clock, escaping without drawing Mrs. Hopewell's attention. She didn't take anything to eat, forgetting that food is usually taken on a pic-nic. She wore a pair of slacks and a dirty white shirt, and as an afterthought, she had put some Vapex on the collar of it since she did not own any perfume. When she reached the gate no one was there.

She looked up and down the empty highway and had the furious feeling that she had been tricked, that he had only meant to make her walk to the gate after the idea of him. Then suddenly he stood up, very tall, from behind a bush on the opposite embankment. Smiling, he lifted his hat which was new and wide-brimmed. He had not worn it yesterday and she wondered if he had bought it for the occasion. It was toast-colored with a red and white band around it and was slightly too large for him. He stepped from behind the bush still carrying the black valise. He had on the same suit and the same yellow socks sucked down in his shoes from walking. He crossed the highway and said, "I knew you'd come!"

The girl wondered acidly how he had known this. She pointed to the valise and asked, "Why did you bring your Bibles?"

He took her elbow, smiling down on her as if he could not stop. "You can never tell when you'll need the word of God, Hulga," he said. She had a moment in which she doubted that this was actually happening and then they began to climb the embankment. They went down into the pasture toward the woods. The boy walked lightly by her side, bouncing on his toes. The valise did not seem to be heavy today; he even swung it. They crossed half the pasture without saying anything and then, putting his hand easily on the small of her back, he asked softly, "Where does your wooden leg join on?"

She turned an ugly red and glared at him and for an instant the boy looked abashed. "I didn't mean you no harm," he said. "I only meant you're so brave and all. I guess God takes care of you."

"No," she said, looking forward and walking fast, "I don't even believe in God."

At this he stopped and whistled. "No!" he exclaimed as if he were too astonished to say anything else.

She walked on and in a second he was bouncing at her side, fanning with his hat. "That's very unusual for a girl," he remarked, watching her out of the corner of his eye. When they reached the edge of the wood, he put his hand on her back again and drew her against him without a word and kissed her heavily.

The kiss, which had more pressure than feeling behind it, produced that extra surge of adrenalin in the girl that enables one to carry a packed trunk out of a burning house, but in her, the power went at once to the brain. Even before he released her, her mind, clear and detached and ironic anyway, was regarding him from a great distance, with amusement but with pity. She had never been kissed before and she was pleased to discover that it was an unexceptional experience and all a matter of the mind's control. Some people might enjoy drain water if they were told it was vodka. When the boy, looking expectant but uncertain, pushed her gently away, she turned and walked on, saying nothing as if such business, for her, were common enough.

He came along panting at her side, trying to help her when he saw a root that she might trip over. He caught and held back the long swaying blades of thorn vine until she had passed beyond them. She led the way and he came breathing heavily behind her. Then they came out on a sunlit hillside, sloping softly into another one a little smaller. Beyond, they could see the rusted top of the old barn where the extra hay was stored.

The hill was sprinkled with small pink weeds. "Then you ain't saved?" he asked suddenly, stopping.

The girl smiled. It was the first time she had smiled at him at all. "In my economy," she said, "I'm saved and you are damned but I told you I didn't believe in God."

Nothing seemed to destroy the boy's look of admiration. He gazed at her now as if the fantastic animal at the zoo had put its paw through the bars and given him a loving poke. She thought he looked as if he wanted to kiss her again and she walked on before he had the chance.

"Ain't there somewheres we can sit down sometime?" he murmured, his voice softening toward the end of the sentence.

"In that barn," she said.

They made for it rapidly as if it might slide away like a train. It was a large two-story barn, cool and dark inside. The boy pointed up the ladder that led into the loft and said, "It's too bad we can't go up there."

"Why can't we?" she asked.

"Yer leg," he said reverently.

The girl gave him a contemptuous look and putting both hands on the ladder, she climbed it while he stood below, apparently awestruck. She pulled herself expertly through the opening and then looked down at him and said, "Well, come on if you're coming," and he began to climb the ladder, awkwardly bringing the suitcase with him.

"We won't need the Bible," she observed.

"You never can tell," he said, panting. After he had got into the loft, he was a few seconds catching his breath. She had sat down in a pile of straw. A wide sheath of sunlight, filled with dust particles, slanted over her. She lay back against a bale, her face turned away, looking out the front opening of the barn where hay was thrown from a wagon into the loft. The two pink-speckled hillsides lay back against a dark ridge of woods. The sky was cloudless and cold blue. The boy dropped down by her side and put one arm under her and the other over her and began methodically kissing her face, making little noises like a fish. He did not remove his hat but it was pushed far enough back not to interfere. When her glasses got in his way, he took them off of her and slipped them into his pocket.

The girl at first did not return any of the kisses but presently she began to and after she had put several on his cheek, she reached his lips and remained there, kissing him again and again as if she were trying to draw all the breath out of him. His breath was clear and sweet like a child's and the kisses were sticky like a child's. He mumbled about loving her and about knowing when he first seen her that he loved her, but the mumbling was like the sleepy fretting of a child being put to sleep by his mother. Her mind, throughout this, never stopped or lost itself for a second to her feelings. "You ain't said you loved me none," he whispered finally, pulling back from her. "You got to say that."

She looked away from him off into the hollow sky and then down at a black ridge and then down farther into what appeared to be two green swelling lakes. She didn't realize he had taken her glasses but this landscape could not seem exceptional to her for she seldom paid any close attention to her surroundings.

"You got to say it," he repeated. "You got to say you love me."

She was always careful how she committed herself. "In a sense," she began, "if you use the word loosely, you might say that. But it's not a word I use. I don't have illusions. I'm one of those people who see *through* to nothing."

The boy was frowning. "You got to say it. I said it and you got to say it," he said.

The girl looked at him almost tenderly. "You poor baby," she murmured. "It's just as well you don't understand," and she pulled him by the neck, face-down, against her. "We are all damned," she said, "but some of us have taken off our blindfolds and see that there's nothing to see. It's a kind of salvation."

The boy's astonished eyes looked blankly through the ends of her hair. "Okay," he almost whined, "but do you love me or don'tcher?"

"Yes," she said and added, "in a sense. But I must tell you something. There mustn't be anything dishonest between us." She lifted his head and looked him in the eye. "I am thirty years old," she said. "I have a number of degrees."

The boy's look was irritated but dogged. "I don't care," he said. "I don't care a thing about what all you done. I just want to know if you love me or don'tcher?" and he caught her to him and wildly planted her face with kisses until she said, "Yes, yes."

"Okay then," he said, letting her go. "Prove it."

She smiled, looking dreamily out on the shifty landscape. She had seduced him without even making up her mind to try. "How?" she asked, feeling that he should be delayed a little.

He leaned over and put his lips to her ear. "Show me where your wooden leg joins on," he whispered.

The girl uttered a sharp little cry and her face instantly drained of color. The obscenity of the suggestion was not what shocked her. As a child she had sometimes been subject to feelings of shame but education had removed the last traces of that as a good surgeon scrapes for cancer; she would no more have felt it over what he was asking than she would have believed in his Bible. But she was as sensitive about the artificial leg as a peacock about his tail. No one ever touched it but her. She took care of it as someone else would his soul, in private and almost with her own eyes turned away. "No," she said.

"I known it," he muttered, sitting up. "You're just playing me for a sucker."

"Oh no no!" she cried. "It joins on at the knee. Only at the knee. Why do you want to see it?"

The boy gave her a long penetrating look. "Because," he said, "it's what makes you different. You ain't like anybody else."

She sat staring at him. There was nothing about her face or her round freezing-blue eyes to indicate that this had moved her; but she felt as if her heart had stopped and left her mind to pump her blood. She decided that for the first time in her life she was face to face with real innocence. This boy, with an instinct that came from beyond wisdom, had touched the truth about her. When after a minute, she said in a hoarse high voice, "All right," it was like surrendering to him completely. It was like losing her own life and finding it again, miraculously, in his.

Very gently be began to roll the slack leg up. The artificial limb, in a white sock and brown flat shoe, was bound in a heavy material like canvas and ended in an ugly jointure where it was attached to the stump. The boy's face and his voice were entirely reverent as he uncovered it and said, "Now show me how to take it off and on."

She took it off for him and put it back on again and then he took it off himself, handling it as tenderly as if it were a real one. "See!" he said with a delighted child's face. "Now I can do it myself!"

"Put it back on," she said. She was thinking that she would run away with him and that every night he would take the leg off and every morning put it back on again. "Put it back on," she said.

"Not yet," he murmured, setting it on its foot out of her reach. "Leave it off for a while. You got me instead."

She gave a little cry of alarm but he pushed her down and began to kiss her again. Without the leg she felt entirely dependent on him. Her brain seemed to have stopped thinking altogether and to be about some other function that it was not very good at. Different expressions raced back and forth over her face. Every now and then the boy, his eyes like two steel spikes, would glance behind him where the leg stood. Finally she pushed him off and said, "Put it back on me now."

"Wait," he said. He leaned the other way and pulled the valise toward him and opened it. It had a pale blue spotted lining and there were only two Bibles in it. He took one of these out and opened the cover of it. It was hollow and contained a pocket flask of whiskey, a pack of cards, and a small blue box with printing on it. He laid these out in front of her one at a time in an evenly-spaced row, like one presenting offerings at the shrine of a goddess. He put the blue box in her hand. THIS PRODUCT TO BE USED ONLY FOR THE PREVENTION OF DISEASE, she read, and dropped it. The boy was unscrewing the top of the flask. He stopped and pointed, with a smile, to the deck of cards. It was not an ordinary deck but one with an obscene picture on the back of each card. "Take a swig," he said, offering her the bottle first. He held it in front of her, but like one mesmerized, she did not move.

Her voice when she spoke had an almost pleading sound. "Aren't you," she murmured, "aren't you just good country people?"

The boy cocked his head. He looked as if he were just beginning to understand that she might be trying to insult him. "Yeah," he said, curling his lip slightly, "but it ain't held me back none. I'm as good as you any day in the week."

"Give me my leg," she said.

He pushed it farther away with his foot. "Come on now, let's begin to have us a good time," he said coaxingly. "We ain't got to know one another good yet."

"Give me my leg!" she screamed and tried to lunge for it but he pushed her down easily.

"What's the matter with you all of a sudden?" he asked, frowning as he screwed the top on the flask and put it quickly back inside the Bible. "You just a while ago said you didn't believe in nothing. I thought you was some girl!"

Her face was almost purple. "You're a Christian!" she hissed. "You're a fine Christian! You're just like them all — say one thing and do another. You're a perfect Christian, you're . . ."

The boy's mouth was set angrily. "I hope you don't think," he said in a lofty indignant tone, "that I believe in that crap! I may sell Bibles but I know which end is up and I wasn't born yesterday and I know where I'm going!"

"Give me my leg!" she screeched. He jumped up so quickly that she barely saw him sweep the cards and the blue box into the Bible and throw the Bible into the valise. She saw him grab the leg and then she saw it for an instant slanted forlornly across the inside of the suitcase with a Bible at either side of its opposite ends. He slammed the lid shut and snatched up the valise and swung it down the hole and then stepped through himself.

When all of him had passed but his head, he turned and regarded her with a look that no longer had any admiration in it. "I've gotten a lot of interesting things," he said. "One time I got a woman's glass eye this way. And you needn't to think you'll catch me because Pointer ain't really my name. I use a different name at every house I call at and don't stay nowhere long. And I'll tell you another thing, Hulga," he said, using the name as if he didn't think much of it, "you ain't so smart. I been believing in nothing ever since I was born!" and then the toast-colored hat disappeared down the hole and the girl was left, sitting on the straw in the dusty sunlight. When she turned her churning face toward the opening, she saw his blue figure struggling successfully over the green speckled lake.

Mrs. Hopewell and Mrs. Freeman, who were in the back pasture, digging up onions, saw him emerge a little later from the woods and head across the meadow toward the highway. "Why, that looks like that nice dull young man that tried to sell me a Bible yesterday," Mrs. Hopewell said, squinting. "He must have been selling them to the Negroes back in there. He was so simple," she said, "but I guess the world would be better off if we were all that simple."

Mrs. Freeman's gaze drove forward and just touched him before he disappeared under the hill. Then she returned her attention to the evil-smelling onion shoot she was lifting from the ground. "Some can't be that simple," she said. "I know I never could."

FLANNERY O'CONNOR

A Good Man Is Hard to Find

1955

> The dragon is by the side of the road, watching those who pass. Beware lest he devour you. We go to the Father of Souls, but it is necessary to pass by the dragon.
>
> – ST. CYRIL OF JERUSALEM

The grandmother didn't want to go to Florida. She wanted to visit some of her connections in east Tennessee and she was seizing at every chance to change Bailey's mind. Bailey was the son she lived with, her only boy. He was sitting on the edge of his chair at the table, bent over the orange sports section of the *Journal*. "Now look here, Bailey," she said, "see here, read this," and she stood with one hand on her thin hip and the other rattling the newspaper at his bald head. "Here this fellow that calls himself The Misfit is aloose from the Federal Pen and headed toward Florida and you read here what it says he did to these people. Just you read it. I wouldn't take my children in any direction with a criminal like that aloose in it. I couldn't answer to my conscience if I did."

Bailey didn't look up from his reading so she wheeled around then and faced the children's mother, a young woman in slacks, whose face was as broad and innocent as a cabbage and was tied around with a green headkerchief that had two points on the top like a rabbit's ears. She was sitting on the sofa, feeding the baby his apricots out of a jar. "The children have been to Florida before," the old lady said. "You all ought to take them somewhere else for a change so they would see different parts of the world and be broad. They never have been to east Tennessee."

The children's mother didn't seem to hear her but the eight-year-old boy, John Wesley, a stocky child with glasses, said, "If you don't want to go to Florida, why dontcha stay at home?" He and the little girl, June Star, were reading the funny papers on the floor.

"She wouldn't stay at home to be queen for a day," June Star said without raising her yellow head.

"Yes and what would you do if this fellow, The Misfit, caught you?" the grandmother asked.

"I'd smack his face," John Wesley said.

"She wouldn't stay at home for a million bucks," June Star said. "Afraid she'd miss something. She has to go everywhere we go."

"All right, Miss," the grandmother said. "Just remember that the next time you want me to curl your hair."

June Star said her hair was naturally curly.

The next morning the grandmother was the first one in the car, ready to go. She had her big black valise that looked like the head of a hippopotamus in one corner, and underneath it she was hiding a basket with Pitty Sing, the cat, in it. She didn't intend for the cat to be left alone in the house for three days because he would miss her too much and she was afraid he might brush against one of the gas burners and accidentally asphyxiate himself. Her son, Bailey, didn't like to arrive at a motel with a cat.

She sat in the middle of the back seat with John Wesley and June Star on either side of her. Bailey and the children's mother and the baby sat in front and they left Atlanta at eight forty-five with the mileage on the car at 55890. The grandmother wrote this down because she thought it would be interesting to say how many miles they had been when they got back. It took them twenty minutes to reach the outskirts of the city.

The old lady settled herself comfortably, removing her white cotton gloves and putting them up with her purse on the shelf in front of the back window. The children's mother still had on slacks and still had her head tied up in a green kerchief, but the grandmother had on a navy blue straw sailor hat with a bunch of white violets on the brim and a navy blue dress with a small white dot in the print. Her collars and cuffs were white organdy trimmed with lace and at her neckline she had pinned a purple spray of cloth violets containing a sachet. In case of an accident, anyone seeing her dead on the highway would know at once that she was a lady.

She said she thought it was going to be a good day for driving, neither too hot nor too cold, and she cautioned Bailey that the speed limit was fifty-five miles an hour and that the patrolmen hid themselves behind billboards and small clumps of trees and sped out after you before you had a chance to slow down. She pointed out interesting details of the scenery: Stone Mountain; the blue granite that in some places came up to both sides of the highway; the brilliant red clay banks slightly streaked with purple; and the various crops that made rows of green lace-work on the ground. The trees were full of silver-white sunlight and the meanest of them sparkled. The children were reading comic magazines and their mother had gone back to sleep.

"Let's go through Georgia fast so we won't have to look at it much," John Wesley said.

"If I were a little boy," said the grandmother, "I wouldn't talk about my native state that way. Tennessee has the mountains and Georgia has the hills."

"Tennessee is just a hillbilly dumping ground," John Wesley said, "and Georgia is a lousy state too."

"You said it," June Star said.

"In my time," said the grandmother, folding her thin veined fingers, "children were more respectful of their native states and their parents and everything else. People did right then. Oh look at the cute little pickaninny!" she said and pointed to a Negro child standing in the door of a shack. "Wouldn't that make a picture, now?" she asked and they all turned and looked at the little Negro out of the back window. He waved.

"He didn't have any britches on," June Star said.

"He probably didn't have any," the grandmother explained. "Little niggers in the country don't have things like we do. If I could paint, I'd paint that picture," she said.

The children exchanged comic books.

The grandmother offered to hold the baby and the children's mother passed him over the front seat to her. She set him on her knee and bounced him and told him about the things they were passing. She rolled her eyes and screwed up her mouth and stuck her leathery thin face into his smooth bland one. Occasionally he gave her a faraway smile. They passed a large cotton field with five or six graves fenced in the middle of it, like a small island. "Look at the graveyard!" the grandmother said, pointing it out. "That was the old family burying ground. That belonged to the plantation."

"Where's the plantation?" John Wesley asked.

"Gone with the Wind," said the grandmother. "Ha. Ha."

When the children finished all the comic books they had brought, they opened the lunch and ate it. The grandmother ate a peanut butter sandwich and an olive and would not let the children throw the box and the paper napkins out the window. When there was nothing else to do they played a game by choosing a cloud and making the other two guess what shape it suggested. John Wesley took one the shape of a cow and June Star guessed a cow and John Wesley said, no, an automobile, and June Star said he didn't play fair, and they began to slap each other over the grandmother.

The grandmother said she would tell them a story if they would keep quiet. When she told a story, she rolled her eyes and waved her head and was very dramatic. She said once when she was a maiden lady she had been courted by a Mr. Edgar Atkins Teagarden from Jasper, Georgia. She said he was a very good-looking man and a gentleman and that he brought her a watermelon every Saturday afternoon with his initials cut in it, E. A. T. Well, one Saturday, she said, Mr. Teagarden brought the watermelon and there was nobody at home and he left it on the front porch and returned in his buggy to Jasper, but she never got the watermelon, she said, because a nigger boy ate it when he saw the initials, E. A. T.! This story tickled John Wesley's funny bone and he giggled and giggled but June Star didn't think it was any good. She said she wouldn't marry a man that just brought her a watermelon on Saturday. The grandmother said she would have done well to marry Mr. Teagarden because he was a gentleman and had bought Coca-Cola stock when it first came out and that he had died only a few years ago, a very wealthy man.

They stopped at The Tower for barbecued sandwiches. The Tower was a part stucco and part wood filling station and dance hall set in a clearing outside of Timothy. A fat man named Red Sammy Butts ran it and there were signs stuck here and there on the building and for miles up and down the highway saying, TRY RED SAMMY'S FAMOUS BARBECUE. NONE LIKE FAMOUS RED SAMMY'S! RED SAM! THE FAT BOY WITH THE HAPPY LAUGH. A VETERAN! RED SAMMY'S YOUR MAN!

Red Sammy was lying on the bare ground outside The Tower with his head under a truck while a gray monkey about a foot high, chained to a small chinaberry tree, chattered nearby. The monkey sprang back into the tree and got on the highest limb as soon as he saw the children jump out of the car and run toward him.

Inside, The Tower was a long dark room with a counter at one end and tables at the other and dancing space in the middle. They all sat down at a board table next to the nickelodeon and Red Sam's wife, a tall burnt-brown woman with hair and eyes lighter than her skin, came and took their order. The children's mother put a dime in the machine and played "The Tennessee Waltz," and the grandmother said that tune always made her want to dance. She asked Bailey if he would like to dance but he only glared at her. He didn't have a naturally sunny disposition like she did and trips made him nervous. The grandmother's brown eyes were very bright. She swayed her head from side to side and pretended she was dancing in her chair. June Star said play something she could tap to so the children's mother put in another dime and played a fast number and June Star stepped out onto the dance floor and did her tap routine.

"Ain't she cute?" Red Sam's wife said, leaning over the counter. "Would you like to come be my little girl?"

"No I certainly wouldn't," June Star said. "I wouldn't live in a broken-down place like this for a million bucks!" and she ran back to the table.

"Ain't she cute?" the woman repeated, stretching her mouth politely.

"Aren't you ashamed?" hissed the grandmother.

Red Sam came in and told his wife to quit lounging on the counter and hurry up with these people's order. His khaki trousers reached just to his hip bones and his stomach hung over them like a sack of meal swaying under his shirt. He came over and sat down at a table nearby and let out a combination sigh and yodel. "You can't win," he said. "You can't win," and he wiped his sweating red face off with a gray handkerchief. "These days you don't know who to trust," he said. "Ain't that the truth?"

"People are certainly not nice like they used to be," said the grandmother.

"Two fellers come in here last week," Red Sammy said, "driving a Chrysler. It was a old beat-up car but it was a good one and these boys looked all right to me. Said they worked at the mill and you know I let them fellers charge the gas they bought? Now why did I do that?"

"Because you're a good man!" the grandmother said at once.

"Yes'm, I suppose so," Red Sam said as if he were struck with this answer.

His wife brought the orders, carrying the five plates all at once without a tray, two in each hand and one balanced on her arm. "It isn't a soul in this green world of God's that you can trust," she said. "And I don't count nobody out of that, not nobody," she repeated, looking at Red Sammy.

"Did you read about that criminal, The Misfit, that's escaped?" asked the grandmother.

"I wouldn't be a bit surprised if he didn't attack this place right here," said the woman. "If he hears about it being here, I wouldn't be none surprised to see him. If he hears it's two cent in the cash register, I wouldn't be a tall surprised if he. . . ."

"That'll do," Red Sam said. "Go bring these people their Co'-Colas," and the woman went off to get the rest of the order.

"A good man is hard to find," Red Sammy said. "Everything is getting terrible. I remember the day you could go off and leave your screen door unlatched. Not no more."

He and the grandmother discussed better times. The old lady said that in her opinion Europe was entirely to blame for the way things were now. She said the way Europe acted you would think we were made of money and Red Sam said it was no use talking about it, she was exactly right. The children ran outside into the white sunlight and looked at the monkey in the lacy chinaberry tree. He was busy catching fleas on himself and biting each one carefully between his teeth as if it were a delicacy.

They drove off again into the hot afternoon. The grandmother took cat naps and woke up every few minutes with her own snoring. Outside of Toombsboro she woke up and recalled an old plantation that she had visited in this neighborhood once when she was a young lady. She said the house had six white columns across the front and that there was an avenue of oaks leading up to it and two little wooden trellis arbors on either side in front where you sat down with your suitor after a stroll in the garden. She recalled exactly which road to turn off to get to it. She knew that Bailey would not be willing to lose any time looking at an old house, but the more she talked about it, the more she wanted to see it once again and find out if the little twin arbors were still standing. "There was a secret panel in this house," she said craftily, not telling the truth but wishing that she were, "and the story went that all the family silver was hidden in it when Sherman came through but it was never found. . . ."

"Hey!" John Wesley said. "Let's go see it! We'll find it! We'll poke all the woodwork and find it! Who lives there? Where do you turn off at? Hey Pop, can't we turn off there?"

"We never have seen a house with a secret panel!" June Star shrieked. "Let's go to the house with the secret panel! Hey Pop, can't we go see the house with the secret panel!"

"It's not far from here, I know," the grandmother said. "It won't take over twenty minutes."

Bailey was looking straight ahead. His jaw was as rigid as a horseshoe. "No," he said.

The children began to yell and scream that they wanted to see the house with the secret panel. John Wesley kicked the back of the front seat and June Star hung over her mother's shoulder and whined desperately into her ear that they never had any fun even on their vacation, that they could never do what THEY wanted to do. The baby began to scream and John Wesley kicked the back of the seat so hard that his father could feel the blows in his kidney.

"All right!" he shouted and drew the car to a stop at the side of the road. "Will you all shut up? Will you all just shut up for one second? If you don't shut up, we won't go anywhere."

"It would be very educational for them," the grandmother murmured.

"All right," Bailey said, "but get this: this is the only time we're going to stop for anything like this. This is the one and only time."

"The dirt road that you have to turn down is about a mile back," the grandmother directed. "I marked it when we passed."

"A dirt road," Bailey groaned.

After they had turned around and were headed toward the dirt road, the grandmother recalled other points about the house, the beautiful glass over the front doorway and the candle-lamp in the hall. John Wesley said that the secret panel was probably in the fireplace.

"You can't go inside this house," Bailey said. "You don't know who lives there."

"While you all talk to the people in front, I'll run around behind and get in a window," John Wesley suggested.

"We'll all stay in the car," his mother said.

They turned onto the dirt road and the car raced roughly along in a swirl of pink dust. The grandmother recalled the times when there were no paved roads and thirty miles was a day's journey. The dirt road was hilly and there were sudden washes in it and sharp curves on dangerous embankments. All at once they would be on a hill, looking down over the blue tops of trees for miles around, then the next minute, they would be in a red depression with the dust-coated trees looking down on them.

"This place had better turn up in a minute," Bailey said, "or I'm going to turn around."

The road looked as if no one had traveled on it for months.

"It's not much farther," the grandmother said and just as she said it, a horrible thought came to her. The thought was so embarrassing that she turned red in the face and her eyes dilated and her feet jumped up, upsetting her valise in the corner. The instant the valise moved, the newspaper top she had over the basket under it rose with a snarl and Pitty Sing, the cat, sprang onto Bailey's shoulder.

The children were thrown to the floor and their mother, clutching the baby, was thrown out the door onto the ground, the old lady was thrown into the front seat. The car turned over once and landed right-side-up in a gulch off the side of the road. Bailey remained in the driver's seat with the cat gray-striped with a broad white face and an orange nose clinging to his neck like a caterpillar.

As soon as the children saw they could move their arms and legs, they scrambled out of the car, shouting, "We've had an ACCIDENT!" The grandmother was curled up under the dashboard, hoping she was injured so that Bailey's wrath would not come down on her all at once. The horrible thought she had before the accident was that the house she had remembered so vividly was not in Georgia but in Tennessee.

Bailey removed the cat from his neck with both hands and flung it out the window against the side of a pine tree. Then he got out of the car and started looking for the children's mother. She was sitting against the side of the red gutted ditch, holding the screaming baby, but she only had a cut down her face and a broken shoulder. "We've had an ACCIDENT!" the children screamed in a frenzy of delight.

"But nobody's killed," June Star said with disappointment as the grandmother limped out of the car, her hat still pinned to her head but the broken front brim standing up at a jaunty angle and the violet spray hanging off the side. They all sat down in the ditch, except the children, to recover from the shock. They were all shaking.

"Maybe a car will come along," said the children's mother hoarsely.

"I believe I have injured an organ," said the grandmother, pressing her side, but no one answered her. Bailey's teeth were clattering. He had on a yellow sport shirt with bright blue parrots designed in it and his face was as yellow as the shirt. The grandmother decided that she would not mention that the house was in Tennessee.

The road was about ten feet above and they could only see the tops of the trees on the other side of it. Behind the ditch they were sitting in there were more woods, tall and dark and deep. In a few minutes they saw a car some distance away on top of a hill, coming slowly as if the occupants were watching them. The grandmother stood up and waved both arms dramatically to attract their attention. The car continued to come on slowly, disappeared around a bend and appeared again, moving even slower, on top of the hill they had gone over. It was a big black battered hearse-like automobile. There were three men in it.

It came to a stop just over them and for some minutes, the driver looked down with a steady expressionless gaze to where they were sitting, and didn't speak. Then he turned his head and muttered something to the other two and they got out. One was a fat boy in black trousers and a red sweat shirt with a silver stallion embossed on the front of it. He moved around on the right side of them and stood staring, his mouth partly open in a kind of loose grin. The other had on khaki pants and a blue striped coat and a gray hat pulled very low, hiding most of his face. He came around slowly on the left side. Neither spoke.

The driver got out of the car and stood by the side of it, looking down at them. He was an older man than the other two. His hair was just beginning to gray and he wore silver-rimmed spectacles that gave him a scholarly look. He had a long creased face and didn't have on any shirt or undershirt. He had on blue jeans that were too tight for him and was holding a black hat and a gun. The two boys also had guns.

"We've had an ACCIDENT!" the children screamed.

The grandmother had the peculiar feeling that the bespectacled man was someone she knew. His face was as familiar to her as if she had known him all her life but she could not recall who he was. He moved away from the car and began to come down the embankment, placing his feet carefully so that he wouldn't slip. He had on tan and white shoes and no socks, and his ankles were red and thin. "Good afternoon," he said. "I see you all had you a little spill."

"We turned over twice!" said the grandmother.

"Oncet," he corrected. "We seen it happen. Try their car and see will it run, Hiram," he said quietly to the boy with the gray hat.

"What you got that gun for?" John Wesley asked. "Whatcha gonna do with that gun?"

"Lady," the man said to the children's mother, "would you mind calling them children to sit down by you? Children make me nervous. I want all you all to sit down right together there where you're at."

"What are you telling US what to do for?" June Star asked.

Behind them the line of woods gaped like a dark open mouth. "Come here," said the mother.

"Look here now," Bailey said suddenly, "we're in a predicament! We're in . . ."

The grandmother shrieked. She scrambled to her feet and stood staring. "You're The Misfit!" she said. "I recognized you at once!"

"Yes'm," the man said, smiling slightly as if he were pleased in spite of himself to be known, "but it would have been better for all of you, lady, if you hadn't of reckernized me."

Bailey turned his head sharply and said something to his mother that shocked even the children. The old lady began to cry and The Misfit reddened.

"Lady," he said, "don't you get upset. Sometimes a man says things he don't mean. I don't reckon he meant to talk to you thataway."

"You wouldn't shoot a lady, would you?" the grandmother said and removed a clean handkerchief from her cuff and began to slap at her eyes with it.

The Misfit pointed the toe of his shoe into the ground and made a little hole and then covered it up again. "I would hate to have to," he said.

"Listen," the grandmother almost screamed, "I know you're a good man. You don't look a bit like you have common blood. I know you must come from nice people!"

"Yes mam," he said, "finest people in the world." When he smiled he showed a row of strong white teeth. "God never made a finer woman than my mother and my daddy's heart was pure gold," he said. The boy with the red sweat shirt had come around behind them and was standing with his gun at his hip. The Misfit squatted down on the ground. "Watch them children, Bobby Lee," he said. "You know they make me nervous." He looked at the six of them huddled together in front of him and he seemed to be embarrassed as if he couldn't think of anything to say. "Ain't a cloud in the sky," he remarked, looking up at it. "Don't see no sun but don't see no cloud neither."

"Yes, it's a beautiful day," said the grandmother. "Listen," she said, "you shouldn't call yourself The Misfit because I know you're a good man at heart. I can just look at you and tell."

"Hush!" Bailey yelled. "Hush! Everybody shut up and let me handle this!" He was squatting in the position of a runner about to sprint forward but he didn't move.

"I pre-chate that, lady," The Misfit said and drew a little circle in the ground with the butt of his gun.

"It'll take a half a hour to fix this here car," Hiram called, looking over the raised hood of it.

"Well, first you and Bobby Lee get him and that little boy to step over yonder with you," The Misfit said, pointing to Bailey and John Wesley. "The boys want to ast you something," he said to Bailey. "Would you mind stepping back in them woods there with them?"

"Listen," Bailey began, "we're in a terrible predicament! Nobody realizes what this is," and his voice cracked. His eyes were as blue and intense as the parrots in his shirt and he remained perfectly still.

The grandmother reached up to adjust her hat brim as if she were going to the woods with him but it came off in her hand. She stood staring at it and after a second she let it fall to the ground. Hiram pulled Bailey up by the arm as if he were assisting an old man. John Wesley caught hold of his father's hand and Bobby Lee followed. They went off toward the woods and just as they reached the dark edge, Bailey turned and supporting himself against a gray naked pine trunk, he shouted, "I'll be back in a minute, Mamma, wait on me!"

"Come back this instant!" his mother shrilled but they all disappeared into the woods.

"Bailey Boy!" the grandmother called in a tragic voice but she found she was looking at The Misfit squatting on the ground in front of her. "I just know you're a good man," she said desperately. "You're not a bit common!"

"Nome, I ain't a good man," The Misfit said after a second as if he had considered her statement carefully, "but I ain't the worst in the world neither. My daddy said I was a different breed of dog from my brothers and sisters. 'You know,' Daddy said, 'it's some that can live their whole life out without asking about it and it's others has to know why it is, and this boy is one of the latters. He's going to be into everything!' " He put on his black hat and looked up suddenly and then away deep into the woods as if he were embarrassed again. "I'm sorry I don't have on a shirt before you ladies," he said, hunching his shoulders slightly. "We buried our clothes that we had on when we escaped and we're just making do until we can get better. We borrowed these from some folks we met," he explained.

"That's perfectly all right," the grandmother said. "Maybe Bailey has an extra shirt in his suitcase."

"I'll look and see terrectly," The Misfit said.

"Where are they taking him?" the children's mother screamed.

"Daddy was a card himself," The Misfit said. "You couldn't put anything over on him. He never got in trouble with the Authorities though. Just had the knack of handling them."

"You could be honest too if you'd only try," said the grandmother. "Think how wonderful it would be to settle down and live a comfortable life and not have to think about somebody chasing you all the time."

The Misfit kept scratching in the ground with the butt of his gun as if he were thinking about it. "Yes'm, somebody is always after you," he murmured.

The grandmother noticed how thin his shoulder blades were just behind his hat because she was standing up looking down at him. "Do you ever pray?" she asked.

He shook his head. All she saw was the black hat wiggle between his shoulder blades. "Nome," he said.

There was a pistol shot from the woods, followed closely by another. Then silence. The old lady's head jerked around. She could hear the wind move through the tree tops like a long satisfied insuck of breath. "Bailey Boy!" she called.

"I was a gospel singer for a while," The Misfit said. "I been most everything. Been in the arm service, both land and sea, at home and abroad, been twict married, been an undertaker, been with the railroads, plowed Mother Earth, been in a tornado, seen a man burnt alive oncet," and he looked up at the children's mother and the little girl who were sitting close together, their faces white and their eyes glassy; "I even seen a woman flogged," he said.

"Pray, pray," the grandmother began, "pray, pray. . . ."

"I never was a bad boy that I remember of," The Misfit said in an almost dreamy voice, "but somewheres along the line I done something wrong and got sent to the penitentiary. I was buried alive," and he looked up and held her attention to him by a steady stare.

"That's when you should have started to pray," she said. "What did you do to get sent to the penitentiary, that first time?"

"Turn to the right, it was a wall," The Misfit said, looking up again at the cloudless sky. "Turn to the left, it was a wall. Look up it was a ceiling, look down it was a floor. I forgot what I done, lady. I set there and set there, trying to remember what it was I done and I ain't recalled it to this day. Oncet in a while, I would think it was coming to me, but it never come."

"Maybe they put you in by mistake," the old lady said vaguely.

"Nome," he said. "It wasn't no mistake. They had the papers on me."

"You must have stolen something," she said.

The Misfit sneered slightly. "Nobody had nothing I wanted," he said. "It was a head-doctor at the penitentiary said what I had done was kill my daddy but I known that for a lie. My daddy died in nineteen ought nineteen of the epidemic flu and I never had a thing to do with it. He was buried in the Mount Hopewell Baptist churchyard and you can see for yourself."

"If you would pray," the old lady said, "Jesus would help you."

"That's right," The Misfit said.

"Well then, why don't you pray?" she asked trembling with delight suddenly.

"I don't want no hep," he said. "I'm doing all right by myself."

Bobby Lee and Hiram came ambling back from the woods. Bobby Lee was dragging a yellow shirt with bright blue parrots in it.

"Throw me that shirt, Bobby Lee," The Misfit said. The shirt came flying at him and landed on his shoulder and he put it on. The grandmother couldn't name what the shirt reminded her of. "No, lady," The Misfit said while he was buttoning it up, "I found out the crime don't matter. You can do one thing or you can do another, kill a man or take a tire off his car, because sooner or later you're going to forget what it was you done and just be punished for it."

The children's mother had begun to make heaving noises as if she couldn't get her breath. "Lady," he asked, "would you and that little girl like to step off yonder with Bobby Lee and Hiram and join your husband?"

"Yes, thank you," the mother said faintly. Her left arm dangled helplessly and she was holding the baby, who had gone to sleep, in the other. "Hep that lady up, Hiram," The Misfit said as she struggled to climb out of the ditch, "and Bobby Lee, you hold onto that little girl's hand."

"I don't want to hold hands with him," June Star said. "He reminds me of a pig."

The fat boy blushed and laughed and caught her by the arm and pulled her off into the woods after Hiram and her mother.

Alone with The Misfit, the grandmother found that she had lost her voice. There was not a cloud in the sky nor any sun. There was nothing around her but woods. She wanted to tell him that he must pray. She opened and closed her mouth several times before anything came out. Finally she found herself saying, "Jesus, Jesus," meaning, Jesus will help you, but the way she was saying it, it sounded as if she might be cursing.

"Yes'm," The Misfit said as if he agreed. "Jesus thrown everything off balance. It was the same case with Him as with me except He hadn't committed any crime and they could prove I had committed one because they had the papers on me. Of course," he said, "they never shown me my papers. That's why I sign myself now. I said long ago, you get your signature and sign everything you do and keep a copy of it. Then you'll know what you done and you can hold up the crime to the punishment and see do they match and in the end you'll have something to prove you ain't been treated right. I call myself The Misfit," he said, "because I can't make what all I done wrong fit what all I gone through in punishment."

There was a piercing scream from the woods, followed closely by a pistol report. "Does it seem right to you, lady, that one is punished a heap and another ain't punished at all?"

"Jesus!" the old lady cried. "You've got good blood! I know you wouldn't shoot a lady! I know you come from nice people! Pray! Jesus, you ought not to shoot a lady. I'll give you all the money I've got!"

"Lady," The Misfit said, looking beyond her far into the woods, "there never was a body that give the undertaker a tip."

There were two more pistol reports and the grandmother raised her head like a parched old turkey hen crying for water and called, "Bailey Boy, Bailey Boy!" as if her heart would break.

"Jesus was the only One that ever raised the dead," The Misfit continued, "and He shouldn't have done it. He thrown everything off balance. If He did what He said, then it's nothing for you to do but throw away everything and follow Him, and if He didn't, then it's nothing for you to do but enjoy the few minutes you got left the best you can by killing somebody or burning down his house or doing some other meanness to him. No pleasure but meanness," he said and his voice had become almost a snarl.

"Maybe He didn't raise the dead," the old lady mumbled, not knowing what she was saying and feeling so dizzy that she sank down in the ditch with her legs twisted under her.

"I wasn't there so I can't say He didn't," The Misfit said. "I wisht I had of been there," he said, hitting the ground with his fist. "It ain't right I wasn't there because if I had of been there I would of known. Listen lady," he said in a high voice, "if I had of been there I would of known and I wouldn't be like I am now." His voice seemed about to crack and the grandmother's head cleared for an instant. She saw the man's face twisted close to her own as if he were going to cry and she murmured, "Why you're one of my babies. You're one of my own children!" She reached out and touched him on the shoulder. The Misfit sprang back as if a snake had bitten him and shot her three times through the chest. Then he put his gun down on the ground and took off his glasses and began to clean them.

Hiram and Bobby Lee returned from the woods and stood over the ditch, looking down at the grandmother who half sat and half lay in a puddle of blood with her legs crossed under her like a child's and her face smiling up at the cloudless sky.

Without his glasses, The Misfit's eyes were red-rimmed and pale and defenseless-looking. "Take her off and throw her where you thrown the others," he said, picking up the cat that was rubbing itself against his leg.

"She was a talker, wasn't she?" Bobby Lee said, sliding down the ditch with a yodel.

"She would of been a good woman," The Misfit said, "if it had been somebody there to shoot her every minute of her life."

"Some fun!" Bobby Lee said.

"Shut up, Bobby Lee," The Misfit said. "It's no real pleasure in life."

❧

FRANK O'CONNOR *was the pseudonym for Michael Francis O'Donovan (1903–1966), who was born in Cork, Ireland. His parents were so poor that he only made it through the fourth grade at the Christian Brothers School in Cork. During the Irish struggle for independence from England (1918–21), he was briefly a member of the Irish Republican Army. For several years thereafter he worked as a librarian in Cork and Dublin; it was at this time that he began using his pseudonym so that he would not jeopardize his job as a public official. He had started to write stories as a boy, and for a while he could not decide whether to be a painter or a writer: "I discovered by the time I was sixteen or seventeen that paints cost too much money, so I became a writer because you could be a writer with a pencil and a penny notebook."*

When O'Connor was twenty-eight years old, the Atlantic Monthly *published his story "Guests of the Nation," which he later said was an imitation of Isaac Babel's stories in* Red Cavalry. *His first collection of stories appeared that same year (1931), and from then on he made his living as a writer. During the 1950s he lived in the United States, teaching at Harvard and Northwestern universities and publishing two excellent critical works,* The Mirror in the Roadway *(1956), a study of the modern novel, and* The Lonely Voice *(1963), a history of the short story. O'Connor was a prolific writer, editor, critic, and translator, with almost fifty books to his credit, including fourteen volumes of short stories. He often rewrote his stories several times, even after they were published, so many of them appear in different versions in his various volumes.*

O'Connor's greatest achievement was in the short story. Primarily indebted to Anton Chekhov, he declared himself to be an old-fashioned storyteller, believing that a story should have the sound of a person speaking. This conviction gives his fiction an engaging tone, confirming — as do Chekhov's stories — the author's basic sympathy toward his characters. In praising O'Connor's stories, the noted Irish poet William Butler Yeats said that he was "doing for Ireland what Chekhov did for Russia."

FRANK O'CONNOR

Guests of the Nation

1931, 1954

I

At dusk the big Englishman, Belcher, would shift his long legs out of the ashes and say "Well, chums, what about it?" and Noble or me would say "All right, chum" (for we had picked up some of their curious expressions), and the little Englishman, Hawkins, would light the lamp and bring out the cards. Sometimes Jeremiah Donovan would come up and supervise the game and get excited over Hawkins's cards, which he always played badly, and shout at him as if he was one of our own "Ah, you divil, you, why didn't you play the tray?"

But ordinarily Jeremiah was a sober and contented poor devil like the big Englishman, Belcher, and was looked up to only because he was a fair hand at documents, though he was slow enough even with them. He wore a small cloth hat and big gaiters over his long pants, and you seldom saw him with his hands out of his pockets. He reddened when you talked to him, tilting from toe to heel and back, and looking down all the time at his big farmer's feet. Noble and me used to make fun of his broad accent, because we were from the town.

I couldn't at the time see the point of me and Noble guarding Belcher and Hawkins at all, for it was my belief that you could have planted that pair down anywhere from this to Claregalway and they'd have taken root there like a native weed. I never in my short experience seen two men to take to the country as they did.

They were handed on to us by the Second Battalion when the search for them became too hot, and Noble and myself, being young, took over with a natural feeling of responsibility, but Hawkins made us look like fools when he showed that he knew the country better than we did.

"You're the bloke they calls Bonaparte," he says to me. "Mary Brigid O'Connell told me to ask you what you done with the pair of her brother's socks you borrowed."

For it seemed, as they explained it, that the Second used to have little evenings, and some of the girls of the neighborhood turned in, and, seeing they were such decent chaps, our fellows couldn't leave the two Englishmen out of them. Hawkins learned to dance "The Walls of Limerick," "The Siege of Ennis," and "The Waves of Tory" as well as any of them, though, naturally, he couldn't return the compliment, because our lads at that time did not dance foreign dances on principle.

So whatever privileges Belcher and Hawkins had with the Second they just naturally took with us, and after the first day or two we gave up all pretense of keeping a close eye on them. Not that they could have got far, for they had accents you could cut with a knife and wore khaki tunics and overcoats with civilian pants and boots. But it's my belief that they never had any idea of escaping and were quite content to be where they were.

It was a treat to see how Belcher got off with the old woman of the house where we were staying. She was a great warrant to scold, and cranky even with us, but before ever she had a chance of giving our guests, as I may call them, a lick of her tongue, Belcher had made her his friend for life. She was breaking sticks, and Belcher, who hadn't been more than ten minutes in the house, jumped up from his seat and went over to her.

"Allow me, madam," he says, smiling his queer little smile, "please allow me"; and he takes the bloody hatchet. She was struck too paralytic to speak, and after that, Belcher would be at her heels, carrying a bucket, a basket, or a load of turf, as the case might be. As Noble said, he got into looking before she leapt, and hot water, or any little thing she wanted, Belcher would have it ready for her. For such a huge man (and though I am five foot ten myself I had to look up at him) he had an uncommon shortness or should I say lack? of speech. It took us some time to get used to him, walking in and out, like a ghost, without a word. Especially because Hawkins talked enough for a platoon, it was strange to hear big Belcher with his toes in the ashes come out with a solitary "Excuse me, chum" or "That's right, chum." His one and only passion was cards, and I will say for him that he was a good card-player. He could have fleeced myself and Noble, but whatever we lost to him Hawkins lost to us, and Hawkins played with the money Belcher gave him.

Hawkins lost to us because he had too much old gab, and we probably lost to Belcher for the same reason. Hawkins and Noble would spit at one another about religion into the early hours of the morning, and Hawkins worried the soul out of Noble, whose brother was a priest, with a string of questions that would puzzle a cardinal. To make it worse even in treating of holy subjects, Hawkins had a deplorable tongue. I never in all my career met a man who could mix such a variety of cursing and bad language into an argument. He was a terrible man, and a fright to argue. He never did a stroke of work, and when he had no one else to talk to, he got stuck in the old woman.

He met his match in her, for one day when he tried to get her to complain profanely of the drought, she gave him a great come-down by blaming it entirely on Jupiter Pluvius (a deity neither Hawkins nor I have ever heard of, though Noble said that among the pagans it was believed that he had something to do with the rain). Another day he was swearing at the capitalists for starting the German war when the old lady laid down her iron, puckered up her little crab's mouth, and said: "Mr. Hawkins, you can say what you like about the war, and think you'll deceive me because I'm only a simple poor countrywoman, but I know what started the war. It was the Italian Count that stole the heathen divinity out of the temple in Japan. Believe me, Mr. Hawkins, nothing but sorrow and want can follow the people that disturb the hidden powers."

A queer old girl, all right.

II

We had our tea one evening, and Hawkins lit the lamp and we all sat into cards. Jeremiah Donovan came in too, and sat down and watched us for a while, and it suddenly struck me that he had no great love for the two Englishmen. It came as a great surprise to me, because I hadn't noticed anything about him before.

Late in the evening a really terrible argument blew up between Hawkins and Noble, about capitalists and priests and love of your country.

"The capitalists," says Hawkins with an angry gulp, "pays the priests to tell you about the next world so as you won't notice what the bastards are up to in this."

"Nonsense, man!" says Noble, losing his temper. "Before ever a capitalist was thought of, people believed in the next world."

Hawkins stood up as though he was preaching a sermon.

"Oh, they did, did they?" he says with a sneer. "They believed all the things you believe, isn't that what you mean? And you believe that God created Adam, and Adam created Shem, and Shem created Jehoshophat. You believe all that silly old fairytale about Eve and Eden and the apple. Well, listen to me, chum. If you're entitled to hold a silly belief — like that, I'm entitled to hold my silly belief which is that the first thing your God created was a bleeding capitalist, with morality and Rolls-Royce complete. Am I right, chum?" he says to Belcher.

"You're right, chum," says Belcher with his amused smile, and got up from the table to stretch his long legs into the fire and stroke his moustache. So, seeing that Jeremiah Donovan was going, and that there was no knowing when the argument about religion would be over, I went out with him. We strolled down to the village together, and then he stopped and started blushing and mumbling and saying I ought to be behind, keeping guard on the prisoners. I didn't like the tone he took with me, and anyway I was bored with life in the cottage, so I replied by asking him what the hell we wanted guarding them at all for. I told him I'd talked it over with Noble, and that we'd both rather be out with a fighting column.

"What use are those fellows to us?" says I.

He looked at me in surprise and said: "I thought you knew we were keeping them as hostages."

"Hostages?" I said.

"The enemy have prisoners belonging to us," he says, "and now they're talking of shooting them. If they shoot our prisoners, we'll shoot theirs."

"Shoot them?" I said.

"What else did you think we were keeping them for?" he says.

"Wasn't it very unforeseen of you not to warn Noble and myself of that in the beginning?" I said.

"How was it?" says he. "You might have known it."

"We couldn't know it, Jeremiah Donovan," says I. "How could we when they were on our hands so long?"

"The enemy have our prisoners as long and longer," says he.

"That's not the same thing at all," says I.

"What difference is there?" says he.

I couldn't tell him, because I knew he wouldn't understand. If it was only an old dog that was going to the vet's, you'd try and not get too fond of him, but Jeremiah Donovan wasn't a man that would ever be in danger of that.

"And when is this thing going to be decided?" says I.

"We might hear tonight," he says. "Or tomorrow or the next day at latest.

So if it's only hanging round here that's a trouble to you, you'll be free soon enough."

It wasn't the hanging round that was a trouble to me at all by this time. I had worse things to worry about. When I got back to the cottage the argument was still on. Hawkins was holding forth in his best style, maintaining that there was no next world, and Noble was maintaining that there was; but I could see that Hawkins had had the best of it.

"Do you know what, chum?" he was saying with a saucy smile. "I think you're just as big a bleeding unbeliever as I am. You say you believe in the next world, and you know just as much about the next world as I do, which is sweet damn-all. What's heaven? You don't know. Where's heaven? You don't know. You know sweet damn-all! I ask you again, do they wear wings?"

"Very well, then," says Noble, "they do. Is that enough for you? They do wear wings."

"Where do they get them, then? Who makes them? Have they a factory for wings? Have they a sort of store where you hands in your chit and takes your bleeding wings?"

"You're an impossible man to argue with," says Noble. "Now, listen to me —" And they were off again.

It was long after midnight when we locked up and went to bed. As I blew out the candle I told Noble what Jeremiah Donovan was after telling me. Noble took it very quietly. When we'd been in bed about an hour he asked me did I think we ought to tell the Englishmen. I didn't think we should, because it was more than likely that the English wouldn't shoot our men, and even if they did, the brigade officers, who were always up and down with the Second Battalion and knew the Englishmen well, wouldn't be likely to want them plugged. "I think so too," says Noble. "It would be great cruelty to put the wind up them now."

"It was very unforeseen of Jeremiah Donovan anyhow," says I.

It was next morning that we found it so hard to face Belcher and Hawkins. We went about the house all day scarcely saying a word. Belcher didn't seem to notice; he was stretched into the ashes as usual, with his usual look of waiting in quietness for something unforeseen to happen, but Hawkins noticed and put it down to Noble's being beaten in the argument of the night before.

"Why can't you take a discussion in the proper spirit?" he says severely. "You and your Adam and Eve! I'm a Communist, that's what I am. Communist or anarchist, it all comes to much the same thing." And for hours he went round the house, muttering when the fit took him. "Adam and Eve! Adam and Eve! Nothing better to do with their time than picking bleeding apples!"

III

I don't know how we got through that day, but I was very glad when it was over, the tea things were cleared away, and Belcher said in his peaceable way: "Well, chums, what about it?" We sat round the table and Hawkins took out the cards, and just then I heard Jeremiah Donovan's footstep on the path and a dark presentiment crossed my mind. I rose from the table and caught him before he reached the door.

"What do you want?" I asked.

"I want those two soldier friends of yours," he says, getting red.

"Is that the way, Jeremiah Donovan?" I asked.

"That's the way. There were four of our lads shot this morning, one of them a boy of sixteen."

"That's bad," I said.

At that moment Noble followed me out, and the three of us walked down the path together, talking in whispers. Feeney, the local intelligence officer, was standing by the gate.

"What are you going to do about it?" I asked Jeremiah Donovan.

"I want you and Noble to get them out; tell them they're being shifted again; that'll be the quietest way."

"Leave me out of that," says Noble under his breath.

Jeremiah Donovan looks at him hard.

"All right," he says. "You and Feeney get a few tools from the shed and dig a hole by the far end of the bog. Bonaparte and myself will be after you. Don't let anyone see you with the tools. I wouldn't like it to go beyond ourselves."

We saw Feeney and Noble go round to the shed and went in ourselves. I left Jeremiah Donovan to do the explanations. He told them that he had orders to send them back to the Second Battalion. Hawkins let out a mouthful of curses, and you could see that though Belcher didn't say anything, he was a bit upset too. The old woman was for having them stay in spite of us, and she didn't stop advising them until Jeremiah Donovan lost his temper and turned on her. He had a nasty temper, I noticed. It was pitch-dark in the cottage by this time, but no one thought of lighting the lamp, and in the darkness the two Englishmen fetched their topcoats and said good-bye to the old woman.

"Just as a man makes a home of a bleeding place, some bastard at headquarters thinks you're too cushy and shunts you off," says Hawkins, shaking her hand.

"A thousand thanks, madam," says Belcher. "A thousand thanks for everything" — as though he'd made it up.

We went round to the back of the house and down towards the bog. It was only then that Jeremiah Donovan told them. He was shaking with excitement.

"There were four of our fellows shot in Cork this morning and now you're to be shot as a reprisal."

"What are you talking about?" snaps Hawkins. "It's bad enough being mucked about as we are without having to put up with your funny jokes."

"It isn't a joke," says Donovan. "I'm sorry, Hawkins, but it's true," and begins on the usual rigmarole about duty and how unpleasant it is.

I never noticed that people who talk a lot about duty find it much of a trouble to them.

"Oh, cut it out!" says Hawkins.

"Ask Bonaparte," says Donovan, seeing that Hawkins isn't taking him seriously. "Isn't it true, Bonaparte?"

"It is," I say, and Hawkins stops.

"Ah, for Christ's sake, chum!"

"I mean it, chum," I say.

"You don't sound as if you mean it."

"If he doesn't mean it, I do," says Donovan, working himself up.

"What have you against me, Jeremiah Donovan?"

"I never said I had anything against you. But why did your people take out four of our prisoners and shoot them in cold blood?"

He took Hawkins by the arm and dragged him on, but it was impossible to make him understand that we were in earnest. I had the Smith and Wesson in my pocket and I kept fingering it and wondering what I'd do if they put up a fight for it or ran, and wishing to God they'd do one or the other. I knew if they did run for it, that I'd never fire on them. Hawkins wanted to know was Noble in it, and when we said yes, he asked us why Noble wanted to plug him. Why did any of us want to plug him? What had he done to us? Weren't we all chums? Didn't we understand him and didn't he understand us? Did we imagine for an instant that he'd shoot us for all the so-and-so officers in the so-and-so British Army?

By this time we'd reached the bog, and I was so sick I couldn't even answer him. We walked along the edge of it in the darkness, and every now and then Hawkins would call a halt and begin all over again, as if he was wound up, about our being chums, and I knew that nothing but the sight of the grave would convince him that we had to do it. And all the time I was hoping that something would happen; that they'd run for it or that Noble would take over the responsibility from me. I had the feeling that it was worse on Noble than on me.

IV

At last we saw the lantern in the distance and made towards it. Noble was carrying it, and Feeney was standing somewhere in the darkness behind him, and the picture of them so still and silent in the bogland brought it home to me that we were in earnest, and banished the last bit of hope I had.

Belcher, on recognizing Noble, said: "Hallo, chum," in his quiet way, but Hawkins flew at him at once, and the argument began all over again, only this time Noble had nothing to say for himself and stood with his head down, holding the lantern between his legs.

It was Jeremiah Donovan who did the answering. For the twentieth time, as though it was haunting his mind, Hawkins asked if anybody thought he'd shoot Noble.

"Yes, you would," says Jeremiah Donovan.

"No, I wouldn't, damn you!"

"You would, because you'd know you'd be shot for not doing it."

"I wouldn't, not if I was to be shot twenty times over. I wouldn't shoot a pal. And Belcher wouldn't — isn't that right, Belcher?"

"That's right, chum," Belcher said, but more by way of answering the question than of joining in the argument. Belcher sounded as though whatever unforeseen thing he'd always been waiting for had come at last.

"Anyway, who says Noble would be shot if I wasn't? What do you think I'd do if I was in his place, out in the middle of a blasted bog?"

"What would you do?" asks Donovan.

"I'd go with him wherever he was going, of course. Share my last bob with him and stick by him through thick and thin. No one can ever say of me that I let down a pal."

"We had enough of this," says Jeremiah Donovan, cocking his revolver. "Is there any message you want to send?"

"No, there isn't."

"Do you want to say your prayers?"

Hawkins came out with a cold-blooded remark that even shocked me and turned on Noble again.

"Listen to me, Noble," he says. "You and me are chums. You can't come over to my side, so I'll come over to your side. That show you I mean what I say? Give me a rifle and I'll go along with you and the other lads."

Nobody answered him. We knew that was no way out.

"Hear what I'm saying?" he says. "I'm through with it. I'm a deserter or anything else you like. I don't believe in your stuff, but it's no worse than mine. That satisfy you?"

Noble raised his head, but Donovan began to speak and he lowered it again without replying.

"For the last time, have you any messages to send?" says Donovan in a cool, excited sort of voice.

"Shut up, Donovan! You don't understand me, but these lads do. They're not the sort to make a pal and kill a pal. They're not the tools of any capitalist."

I alone of the crowd saw Donovan raise his Webley to the back of Hawkins's neck, and as he did so I shut my eyes and tried to pray. Hawkins had begun to say something else when Donovan fired, and as I opened my eyes at the bang, I saw Hawkins stagger at the knees and lie out flat at Noble's feet, slowly and as quiet as a kid falling asleep, with the lantern-light on his lean legs and bright farmer's boots. We all stood very still, watching him settle out in the last agony.

Then Belcher took out a handkerchief and began to tie it about his own eyes (in our excitement we'd forgotten to do the same for Hawkins), and, seeing it wasn't big enough, turned and asked for the loan of mine. I gave it to him and he knotted the two together and pointed with his foot at Hawkins.

"He's not quite dead," he says. "Better give him another."

Sure enough, Hawkins's left knee is beginning to rise. I bend down and put my gun to his head; then, recollecting myself, I get up again. Belcher understands what's in my mind.

"Give him his first," he says. "I don't mind. Poor bastard, we don't know what's happening to him now."

I knelt and fired. By this time I didn't seem to know what I was doing. Belcher, who was fumbling a bit awkwardly with the handkerchiefs, came out with a laugh as he heard the shot. It was the first time I heard him laugh and it sent a shudder down my back; it sounded so unnatural.

"Poor bugger!" he said quietly. "And last night he was so curious about it all. It's very queer, chums, I always think. Now he knows as much about it as they'll ever let him know, and last night he was all in the dark."

Donovan helped him to tie the handkerchiefs about his eyes. "Thanks, chum," he said. Donovan asked if there were any messages he wanted sent.

"No, chum," he says, "not for me. If any of you would like to write to Hawkins's mother, you'll find a letter from her in his pocket. He and his mother were great chums. But my missus left me eight years ago. Went away with another fellow and took the kid with her. I like the feeling of a home, as you may have noticed, but I couldn't start again after that."

It was an extraordinary thing, but in those few minutes Belcher said more than in all the weeks before. It was just as if the sound of the shot had started a flood of talk in him and he could go on the whole night like that, quite happily, talking about himself. We stood round like fools now that he couldn't see us any longer. Donovan looked at Noble, and Noble shook his head. Then Donovan raised his Webley, and at that moment Belcher gives his queer laugh again. He may have thought we were talking about him, or perhaps he noticed the same thing I'd noticed and couldn't understand it.

"Excuse me, chums," he says. "I feel I'm talking the hell of a lot, and so silly, about my being so handy about a house and things like that. But this thing came on me suddenly. You'll forgive me, I'm sure."

"You don't want to say a prayer?" asks Donovan.

"No, chum," he says. "I don't think it would help. I'm ready, and you boys want to get it over."

"You understand that we're only doing our duty?" says Donovan.

Belcher's head was raised like a blind man's, so that you could only see his chin and the tip of his nose in the lantern-light.

"I never could make out what duty was myself," he said. "I think you're all good lads, if that's what you mean. I'm not complaining."

Noble, just as if he couldn't bear any more of it, raised his fist at Donovan, and in a flash Donovan raised his gun and fired. The big man went over like a sack of meal, and this time there was no need of a second shot.

I don't remember much about the burying, but that it was worse than all the rest because we had to carry them to the grave. It was all mad lonely with nothing but a patch of lantern-light between ourselves and the dark, and birds hooting and screeching all round, disturbed by the guns. Noble went through Hawkins's belongings to find the letter from his mother, and then joined his hands together. He did the same with Belcher. Then, when we'd filled the grave, we separated from Jeremiah Donovan and Feeney and took our tools back to the shed. All the way we didn't speak a word. The kitchen was dark and cold as we'd left it, and the old woman was sitting over the hearth, saying her beads. We walked past her into the room, and Noble struck a match to light the lamp. She rose quietly and came to the doorway with all her cantankerousness gone.

"What did ye do with them?" she asked in a whisper, and Noble started so that the match went out in his hand.

"What's that?" he asked without turning around.

"I heard ye," she said.

"What did you hear?" asked Noble.

"I heard ye. Do ye think I didn't hear ye, putting the spade back in the houseen?"

Noble struck another match and this time the lamp lit for him.

"Was that what ye did to them?" she asked.

Then, by God, in the very doorway, she fell on her knees and began praying, and after looking at her for a minute or two Noble did the same by the fireplace. I pushed my way out past her and left them at it. I stood at the door, watching the stars and listening to the shrieking of the birds dying out over the bogs. It is so strange what you feel at times like that that you can't describe it. Noble says he saw everything ten times the size, as though there were nothing in the whole world but that little patch of bog with the two Englishmen stiffening into it, but with me it was as if the patch of bog where the Englishmen were was a million miles away, and even Noble and the old woman, mumbling behind me, and the birds and the bloody stars were all far away, and I was somehow very small and very lost and lonely like a child astray in the snow. And anything that happened to me afterwards, I never felt the same about again.

ꕥ

TILLIE OLSEN *(b. 1913) was born in Omaha, Nebraska, the daughter of political refugees from the Russian Czarist repression after the revolution of 1905. Her father was a farmer, packing-house worker, house painter, and jack-of-all-trades; her mother was a factory worker. At the age of sixteen Olsen dropped out of high school to help support her family during the Depression. She was a member of the Young Communist League, involved in the Warehouse Union's labor disputes in Kansas City. At age nineteen she began her first novel,* Yonnondio. *Four chapters of this book about a poverty-stricken working-class family were completed in the next four years, during which time she married, gave birth to her first child, and was left with the baby by her husband because, as she later wrote in her autobiographical story "I Stand Here Ironing," he "could no longer endure sharing want" with them. In 1934 a section of the first chapter of her novel was published in* Partisan Review, *but she abandoned the unfinished book in 1937. The year before she had married Jack Olsen, with whom she had three more children; raising the children and working for political causes took up all her time. In the 1940s she was a factory worker; in the 1950s, a secretary. It was not until 1953, when her youngest daughter started school, that she was able to begin writing again.*

That year Olsen enrolled in a class in fiction writing at San Francisco State College. She was awarded a Stanford University creative writing fellowship for 1955 and 1956. During the 1950s she wrote the four stories collected in Tell Me a Riddle, *which established her reputation when the book was published as a paperback in 1961. Identified as a champion of the reemerging feminist movement, Olsen wrote a biographical introduction to Rebecca Harding Davis's nineteenth-century proletarian novel,* Life in the Iron Mills, *published by the Feminist Press in 1972. Two years later, after several grants and creative writing fellowships, she published the still-unfinished* Yonnondio. Silences, *a collection of essays exploring the different circumstances that obstruct or silence literary creation, appeared in 1978.*

As the Canadian author Margaret Atwood has understood about Olsen,

> *Few writers have gained such wide respect on such a small body of published work. . . . Among women writers in the United States, "respect" is too pale a word: "reverence" is more like it. This is presumably because women writers, even more than their male counterparts, recognize what a heroic feat it is to have held down a job, raised four children, and still somehow managed to become and to remain a writer.*

A radical feminist, Olsen has said that she felt no personal guilt as a single parent over her daughter's predicament, as described in her confessional narrative "I Stand Here Ironing," since "guilt is a word used far too sloppily, to cover up harmful situations in society that must be changed." Her four stories have appeared in more than fifty anthologies and have been translated into many languages. In 1994 she received the Rea Award for the Short Story, a literary prize that honors a living American author who has made "a significant contribution to the short story as an art form."

TILLIE OLSEN

I Stand Here Ironing

1961

I stand here ironing, and what you asked me moves tormented back and forth with the iron.

"I wish you would manage the time to come in and talk with me about your daughter. I'm sure you can help me understand her. She's a youngster who needs help and whom I'm deeply interested in helping."

"Who needs help." . . . Even if I came, what good would it do? You think because I am her mother I have a key, or that in some way you could use me as a key? She has lived for nineteen years. There is all that life that has happened outside of me, beyond me.

And when is there time to remember, to sift, to weigh, to estimate, to total? I will start and there will be an interruption and I will have to gather it all together again. Or I will become engulfed with all I did or did not do, with what should have been and what cannot be helped.

She was a beautiful baby. The first and only one of our five that was beautiful at birth. You do not guess how new and uneasy her tenancy in her now-loveliness. You did not know her all those years she was thought homely, or see her poring over her baby pictures, making me tell her over and over how beautiful she had been — and would be, I would tell her — and was now, to the seeing eye. But the seeing eyes were few or nonexistent. Including mine.

I nursed her. They feel that's important nowadays, I nursed all the children, but with her, with all the fierce rigidity of first motherhood, I did like the books then said. Though her cries battered me to trembling and my breasts ached with swollenness, I waited till the clock decreed.

Why do I put that first? I do not even know if it matters, or if it explains anything.

She was a beautiful baby. She blew shining bubbles of sound. She loved motion, loved light, loved color and music and textures. She would lie on the floor in her blue overalls patting the surface so hard in ecstasy her hands and feet would blur. She was a miracle to me, but when she was eight months old I had to leave her daytimes with the woman downstairs to whom she was no miracle at all, for I worked or looked for work and for Emily's father, who "could no longer endure" (he wrote in his good-bye note) "sharing want with us."

I was nineteen. It was the pre-relief, pre-WPA world of the depression. I would start running as soon as I got off the streetcar, running up the stairs, the place smelling sour, and awake or asleep to startle awake, when she saw me she would break into a clogged weeping that could not be comforted, a weeping I can hear yet.

After a while I found a job hashing at night so I could be with her days, and it was better. But it came to where I had to bring her to his family and leave her.

It took a long time to raise the money for her fare back. Then she got chicken pox and I had to wait longer. When she finally came, I hardly knew her, walking quick and nervous like her father, looking like her father, thin, and dressed in a shoddy red that yellowed her skin and glared at the pockmarks. All the baby loveliness gone.

She was two. Old enough for nursery school they said, and I did not know then what I know now — the fatigue of the long day, and the lacerations of group life in the kinds of nurseries that are only parking places for children.

Except that it would have made no difference if I had known. It was the only place there was. It was the only way we could be together, the only way I could hold a job.

And even without knowing, I knew. I knew the teacher that was evil because all these years it has curdled into my memory, the little boy hunched in the corner, her rasp, "why aren't you outside, because Alvin hits you? that's no reason, go out, scaredy." I knew Emily hated it even if she did not clutch and implore "don't go Mommy" like the other children, mornings.

She always had a reason why we should stay home. Momma, you look sick. Momma, I feel sick. Momma, the teachers aren't there today, they're sick. Momma, we can't go, there was a fire there last night. Momma, it's a holiday today, no school, they told me.

But never a direct protest, never rebellion. I think of our others in their three-, four-year-oldness — the explosions, the tempers, the denunciations, the demands — and I feel suddenly ill. I put the iron down. What in me demanded that goodness in her? And what was the cost, the cost to her of such goodness?

The old man living in the back once said in his gentle way: "You should smile at Emily more when you look at her." What *was* in my face when I looked at her? I loved her. There were all the acts of love.

It was only with the others I remembered what he said, and it was the face of joy, and not of care or tightness or worry I turned to them — too late for

Emily. She does not smile easily, let alone almost always as her brothers and sisters do. Her face is closed and sombre, but when she wants, how fluid. You must have seen it in her pantomimes, you spoke of her rare gift for comedy on the stage that rouses laughter out of the audience so dear they applaud and applaud and do not want to let her go.

Where does it come from, that comedy? There was none of it in her when she came back to me that second time, after I had to send her away again. She had a new daddy now to learn to love, and I think perhaps it was a better time.

Except when we left her alone nights, telling ourselves she was old enough.

"Can't you go some other time, Mommy, like tomorrow?" she would ask. "Will it be just a little while you'll be gone? Do you promise?"

The time we came back, the front door open, the clock on the floor in the hall. She rigid awake. "It wasn't just a little while. I didn't cry. Three times I called you, just three times, and then I ran downstairs to open the door so you could come faster. The clock talked loud. I threw it away, it scared me what it talked."

She said the clock talked loud again that night I went to the hospital to have Susan. She was delirious with the fever that comes before red measles, but she was fully conscious all the week I was gone and the week after we were home when she could not come near the new baby or me.

She did not get well. She stayed skeleton thin, not wanting to eat, and night after night she had nightmares. She would call for me, and I would rouse from exhaustion to sleepily call back: "You're all right, darling, go to sleep, it's just a dream," and if she still called, in a sterner voice, "now go to sleep, Emily, there's nothing to hurt you." Twice, only twice, when I had to get up for Susan anyhow, I went in to sit with her.

Now when it is too late (as if she would let me hold her and comfort her like I do the others) I get up and go to her at once at her moan or restless stirring. "Are you awake, Emily? Can I get you something?" And the answer is always the same: "No, I'm all right, go back to sleep, Mother."

They persuaded me at the clinic to send her away to a convalescent home in the country where "she can have the kind of food and care you can't manage for her, and you'll be free to concentrate on the new baby." They still send children to that place. I see pictures on the society page of sleek young women planning affairs to raise money for it, or dancing at the affairs, or decorating Easter eggs or filling Christmas stockings for the children.

They never have a picture of the children so I do not know if the girls still wear those gigantic red bows and the ravaged looks on the every other Sunday when parents can come to visit "unless otherwise notified" — as we were notified the first six weeks.

Oh it is a handsome place, green lawns and tall trees and fluted flower beds. High up on the balconies of each cottage the children stand, the girls in their red bows and white dresses, the boys in white suits and giant red ties. The parents stand below shrieking up to be heard and the children shriek down to be heard, and between them the invisible wall "Not To Be Contaminated by Parental Germs or Physical Affection."

There was a tiny girl who always stood hand in hand with Emily. Her parents never came. One visit she was gone. "They moved her to Rose Cottage," Emily shouted in explanation. "They don't like you to love anybody here."

She wrote once a week, the labored writing of a seven-year-old. "I am fine. How is the baby. If I write my leter nicly I will have a star. Love." There never was a star. We wrote every other day, letters she could never hold or keep but only hear read — once. "We simply do not have room for children to keep any personal possessions," they patiently explained when we pieced one Sunday's shrieking together to plead how much it would mean to Emily, who loved so to keep things, to be allowed to keep her letters and cards.

Each visit she looked frailer. "She isn't eating," they told us.

(They had runny eggs for breakfast or mush with lumps, Emily said later, I'd hold it in my mouth and not swallow. Nothing ever tasted good, just when they had chicken.)

It took us eight months to get her released home, and only the fact that she gained back so little of her seven lost pounds convinced the social worker.

I used to try to hold and love her after she came back, but her body would stay stiff, and after a while she'd push away. She ate little. Food sickened her, and I think much of life too. Oh she had physical lightness and brightness, twinkling by on skates, bouncing like a ball up and down up and down over the jump rope, skimming over the hill; but these were momentary.

She fretted about her appearance, thin and dark and foreign-looking at a time when every little girl was supposed to look or thought she should look a chubby blonde replica of Shirley Temple. The doorbell sometimes rang for her, but no one seemed to come and play in the house or to be a best friend. Maybe because we moved so much.

There was a boy she loved painfully through two school semesters. Months later she told me how she had taken pennies from my purse to buy him candy. "Licorice was his favorite and I brought him some every day, but he still liked Jennifer better'n me. Why, Mommy?" The kind of question for which there is no answer.

School was a worry for her. She was not glib or quick in a world where glibness and quickness were easily confused with ability to learn. To her overworked and exasperated teachers she was an overconscientious "slow learner" who kept trying to catch up and was absent entirely too often.

I let her be absent, though sometimes the illness was imaginary. How different from my now-strictness about attendance with the others. I wasn't working. We had a new baby. I was home anyhow. Sometimes, after Susan grew old enough, I would keep her home from school, too, to have them all together.

Mostly Emily had asthma, and her breathing, harsh and labored, would fill the house with a curiously tranquil sound. I would bring the two old dresser mirrors and her boxes of collections to her bed. She would select beads and single earrings, bottle tops and shells, dried flowers and pebbles, old postcards and scraps, all sorts of oddments; then she and Susan would play Kingdom, setting up landscapes and furniture, peopling them with action.

Those were the only times of peaceful companionship between her and Susan. I have edged away from it, that poisonous feeling between them, that terrible balancing of hurts and needs I had to do between the two, and did so badly, those earlier years.

Oh there were conflicts between the others too, each one human, needing, demanding, hurting, taking — but only between Emily and Susan, no, Emily toward Susan that corroding resentment. It seems so obvious on the surface, yet it is not obvious; Susan, the second child, Susan, golden- and curly-haired and chubby, quick and articulate and assured, everything in appearance and manner Emily was not; Susan, not able to resist Emily's precious things, losing or sometimes clumsily breaking them; Susan telling jokes and riddles to company for applause while Emily sat silent (to say to me later: that was *my* riddle, Mother, I told it to Susan); Susan, who for all the five years' difference in age was just a year behind Emily in developing physically.

I am glad for that slow physical development that widened the difference between her and her contemporaries, though she suffered over it. She was too vulnerable for that terrible world of youthful competition, of preening and parading, of constant measuring of yourself against every other, of envy, "If I had that copper hair," "If I had that skin. . . ." She tormented herself enough about not looking like the others, there was enough of unsureness, the having to be conscious of words before you speak, the constant caring — what are they thinking of me? without having it all magnified by the merciless physical drives.

Ronnie is calling. He is wet and I change him. It is rare there is such a cry now. That time of motherhood is almost behind me when the ear is not one's own but must always be racked and listening for the child cry, the child call. We sit for a while and I hold him, looking out over the city spread in charcoal with its soft aisles of light. "*Shoogily*," he breathes and curls closer. I carry him back to bed, asleep. *Shoogily.* A funny word, a family word, inherited from Emily, invented by her to say: *comfort.*

In this and other ways she leaves her seal, I say aloud. And startle at my saying it. What do I mean? What did I start to gather together, to try and make coherent? I was at the terrible, growing years. War years. I do not remember them well. I was working, there were four smaller ones now, there was not time for her. She had to help be a mother, and housekeeper, and shopper. She had to get her seal. Mornings of crisis and near hysteria trying to get lunches packed, hair combed, coats and shoes found, everyone to school or Child Care on time, the baby ready for transportation. And always the paper scribbled on by a smaller one, the book looked at by Susan then mislaid, the homework not done. Running out to that huge school where she was one, she was lost, she was a drop; suffering over the unpreparedness, stammering and unsure in her classes.

There was so little time left at night after the kids were bedded down. She would struggle over books, always eating (it was in those years she developed her enormous appetite that is legendary in our family) and I would be ironing, or preparing food for the next day, or writing V-mail to Bill, or tending the baby. Sometimes, to make me laugh, or out of her despair, she would imitate happenings or types at school.

I think I said once: "Why don't you do something like this in the school amateur show?" One morning she phoned me at work, hardly understandable through the weeping: "Mother, I did it. I won, I won; they gave me first prize; they clapped and clapped and wouldn't let me go."

Now suddenly she was Somebody, and as imprisoned in her difference as she had been in anonymity.

She began to be asked to perform at other high schools, even in colleges, then at city and statewide affairs. The first one we went to, I only recognized her that first moment when thin, shy, she almost drowned herself into the curtains. Then: Was this Emily? The control, the command, the convulsing and deadly clowning, the spell, then the roaring, stamping audience, unwilling to let this rare and precious laughter out of their lives.

Afterwards: You ought to do something about her with a gift like that — but without money or knowing how, what does one do? We have left it all to her, and the gift has so often eddied inside, clogged and clotted, as been used and growing.

She is coming. She runs up the stairs two at a time with her light graceful step, and I know she is happy tonight. Whatever it was that occasioned your call did not happen today.

"Aren't you ever going to finish the ironing, Mother? Whistler painted his mother in a rocker. I'd have to paint mine standing over an ironing board." This is one of her communicative nights and she tells me everything and nothing as she fixes herself a plate of food out of the icebox.

She is so lovely. Why did you want me to come in at all? Why were you concerned? She will find her way.

She starts up the stairs to bed. "Don't get me up with the rest in the morning." "But I thought you were having midterms." "Oh, those," she comes back in, kisses me, and says quite lightly, "in a couple of years when we'll all be atom-dead they won't matter a bit."

She has said it before. She *believes* it. But because I have been dredging the past, and all that compounds a human being is so heavy and meaningful in me, I cannot endure it tonight.

I will never total it all. I will never come in to say: She was a child seldom smiled at. Her father left me before she was a year old. I had to work her first six years when there was work, or I sent her home and to his relatives. There were years she had care she hated. She was dark and thin and foreign-looking in a world where the prestige went to blondeness and curly hair and dimples, she was slow where glibness was prized. She was a child of anxious, not proud, love. We were poor and could not afford for her the soil of easy growth. I was a young mother, I was a distracted mother. There were other children pushing up, demanding. Her younger sister seemed all that she was not. There were years she did not want me to touch her. She kept too much in herself, her life was such she had to keep too much in herself. My wisdom came too late. She has much to her and probably little will come of it. She is a child of her age, of depression, of war, of fear.

Let her be. So all that is in her will not bloom — but in how many does it? There is still enough left to live by. Only help her to know — help make it so there is cause for her to know — that she is more than this dress on the ironing board, helpless before the iron.

ꕥ

CYNTHIA OZICK *(b. 1928) sees a clear distinction between art and life: "As for life, I don't like it. I notice no 'interplay of life and art.' Life is that which — pressingly, persistently, unfailingly, imperially — interrupts." In Ozick's life there has been a long time between what Grace Paley would call "knowing and telling." Ozick was born in New York City, the daughter of a pharmacist. She received a B.A. from New York University in 1949 and an M.A. from Ohio State University in 1950 with a thesis titled "Parable in Henry James." She didn't publish her first work, the novel* Trust, *until 1966. Three collections of short fiction followed:* The Pagan Rabbi and Other Stories *(1971),* Bloodshed and Three Novellas *(1976), and* Levitation *(1981). In 1989 she published* Metaphor and Memory: Essays *and* The Shawl, *a novella developing the short story included here.*

In her essay "The Lesson of the Master" in Art and Ardor *(1983), Ozick described how as a young writer she was betrayed by Henry James. After college she worshiped literature, seeing herself "a priest at that altar, and that altar was all of my life." She felt that James was trying to teach her a lesson through his fiction, that an aspiring writer ought "to live immaculately, unspoiled by what we mean when we say 'life' — relationship, family mess, distraction, exhaustion, anxiety, above all disappointment." Ozick remembers herself as a nearsighted twenty-two-year old "infected with the commonplace intention of writing a novel" and trying to live "like the elderly bald-headed Henry James." Years later she realized her mistake. To be a writer,*

> *one must keep one's psychological distance from the supreme artists. . . . The true Lesson of the Master, then, is, simply, never to venerate what is complete, burnished, whole . . . never to worship ripe Art or the ripened artist; but instead to seek to be young while young, primitive while primitive, ungainly when ungainly — to look for crudeness and rudeness, to husband one's own stupidity or ungenius.*

Yet Ozick also understands that life "interrupts," and the journey to art is beset with difficulties. In her best short fiction, such as the Holocaust story "The Shawl," she accepts the challenge of her craft, writing in a swiftly imagistic style. She admits that "in beginning a story I know nothing at all: surely not where I am going, and hardly at all how to get there." Some recent books are What Henry James Knew *(1993),* The Cynthia Ozick Reader *(1996), and* The Puttermesser Papers *(1997).*

CYNTHIA OZICK

The Shawl 1980

Stella, cold, cold, the coldness of hell. How they walked on the roads together, Rosa with Magda curled up between sore breasts, Magda wound up in the shawl. Sometimes Stella carried Magda. But she was jealous of Magda. A thin girl of fourteen, too small, with thin breasts of her own, Stella wanted to be wrapped in a shawl, hidden away, asleep, rocked by the march, a baby, a round infant in arms. Magda took Rosa's nipple, and Rosa never stopped walking, a walking cradle. There was not enough milk; sometimes Magda sucked air; then she screamed. Stella was ravenous. Her knees were tumors on sticks, her elbows chicken bones.

Rosa did not feel hunger; she felt light, not like someone walking but like someone in a faint, in trance, arrested in a fit, someone who is already a floating angel, alert and seeing everything, but in the air, not there, not touching the road. As if teetering on the tips of her fingernails. She looked into Magda's face through a gap in the shawl: a squirrel in a nest, safe, no one could reach her inside the little house of the shawl's windings. The face, very round, a pocket mirror of a face: but it was not Rosa's bleak complexion, dark like cholera, it was another kind of face altogether, eyes blue as air, smooth feathers of hair nearly as yellow as the Star sewn into Rosa's coat. You could think she was one of *their* babies.

Rosa, floating, dreamed of giving Magda away in one of the villages. She could leave the line for a minute and push Magda into the hands of any woman on the side of the road. But if she moved out of line they might shoot. And even if she fled the line for half a second and pushed the shawl-bundle at a stranger, would the woman take it? She might be surprised, or afraid; she might drop the shawl, and Magda would fall out and strike her head and die. The little round head. Such a good child, she gave up screaming, and sucked now only for the taste of the drying nipple itself. The neat grip of the tiny gums. One mite of a tooth tip sticking up in the bottom gum, how shining, an elfin tombstone of white marble, gleaming there. Without complaining, Magda relinquished Rosa's teats, first the left, then the right; both were cracked, not a sniff of milk. The duct crevice extinct, a dead volcano, blind eye, chill hole, so Magda took the corner of the shawl and milked it instead. She sucked and sucked, flooding the threads with wetness. The shawl's good flavor, milk of linen.

It was a magic shawl, it could nourish an infant for three days and three nights. Magda did not die, she stayed alive, although very quiet. A peculiar smell, of cinnamon and almonds, lifted out of her mouth. She held her eyes open every moment, forgetting how to blink or nap, and Rosa and sometimes Stella studied their blueness. On the road they raised one burden of a leg after another and studied Magda's face. "Aryan," Stella said, in a voice grown as thin as a string; and Rosa thought how Stella gazed at Magda like a young cannibal. And the time that Stella said "Aryan," it sounded to Rosa as if Stella had really said, "Let us devour her."

But Magda lived to walk. She lived that long, but she did not walk very well, partly because she was only fifteen months old, and partly because the spindles of her legs could not hold up her fat belly. It was fat with air, full and round. Rosa gave almost all her food to Magda, Stella gave nothing; Stella was ravenous, a growing child herself, but not growing much. Stella did not menstruate. Rosa did not menstruate. Rosa was ravenous, but also not; she learned from Magda how to drink the taste of a finger in one's mouth. They were in a place without pity, all pity was annihilated in Rosa, she looked at Stella's bones without pity. She was sure that Stella was waiting for Magda to die so she could put her teeth into the little thighs.

Rosa knew Magda was going to die very soon; she should have been dead already, but she had been buried away deep inside the magic shawl, mistaken there for the shivering mound of Rosa's breasts; Rosa clung to the shawl as if it covered only herself. No one took it away from her. Magda was mute. She never cried. Rosa hid her in the barracks, under the shawl, but she knew that one day someone would inform; or one day someone, not even Stella, would steal Magda to eat her. When Magda began to walk Rosa knew that Magda was going to die very soon, something would happen. She was afraid to fall asleep; she slept with the weight of her thigh on Magda's body; she was afraid she would smother Magda under her thigh. The weight of Rosa was becoming less and less, Rosa and Stella were slowly turning into air.

Magda was quiet, but her eyes were horribly alive, like blue tigers. She watched. Sometimes she laughed — it seemed a laugh, but how could it be? Magda had never seen anyone laugh. Still, Magda laughed at her shawl when the wind blew its corners, the bad wind with pieces of black in it, that made Stella's and Rosa's eyes tear. Magda's eyes were always clear and tearless. She watched like a tiger. She guarded her shawl. No one could touch it; only Rosa could touch it. Stella was not allowed. The shawl was Magda's own baby, her pet, her little sister. She tangled herself up in it and sucked on one of the corners when she wanted to be very still.

Then Stella took the shawl away and made Magda die.

Afterward Stella said: "I was cold."

And afterward she was always cold, always. The cold went into her heart: Rosa saw that Stella's heart was cold. Magda flopped onward with her little pencil legs scribbling this way and that, in search of the shawl; the pencils faltered at the barracks opening, where the light began. Rosa saw and pursued. But already Magda was in the square outside the barracks, in the jolly light. It was the roll-call arena. Every morning Rosa had to conceal Magda under the shawl against a wall of the barracks and go out and stand in the arena with Stella and hundreds of others, sometimes for hours, and Magda, deserted, was quiet under the shawl, sucking on her corner. Every day Magda was silent, and so she did not die. Rosa saw that today Magda was going to die, and at the same time a fearful joy ran in Rosa's two palms, her fingers were on fire, she was astonished, febrile: Magda, in the sunlight, swaying on her pencil legs, was howling. Ever since the drying up of Rosa's nipples, ever since Magda's last scream on the road, Magda had been devoid of any syllable; Magda was a mute. Rosa believed that something had gone wrong with her vocal cords, with her windpipe, with the cave of her larynx; Magda was defective, without a voice; perhaps she was deaf; there might be something amiss with her intelligence; Magda was dumb. Even the laugh that came when the ash-stippled wind made a clown out of Magda's shawl was only the air-blown showing of her teeth. Even when the lice, head lice and body lice, crazed her so that she became as wild as one of the big rats that plundered the barracks at daybreak looking for carrion, she rubbed and scratched and kicked and bit and rolled without a whimper. But now Magda's mouth was spilling a long viscous rope of clamor.

"Maaaa —"

It was the first noise Magda had ever sent out from her throat since the drying up of Rosa's nipples.

"Maaaa . . . aaa!"

Again! Magda was wavering in the perilous sunlight of the arena, scribbling on such pitiful little bent shins. Rosa saw. She saw that Magda was grieving the loss of her shawl, she saw that Magda was going to die. A tide of commands hammered in Rosa's nipples: Fetch, get, bring! But she did not know which to go after first, Magda or the shawl. If she jumped out into the arena to snatch Magda up, the howling would not stop, because Magda would still not have the shawl; but if she ran back into the barracks to find the shawl, and if she found it, and if she came after Magda holding it and shaking it, then she would get Magda back, Magda would put the shawl in her mouth and turn dumb again.

Rosa entered the dark. It was easy to discover the shawl. Stella was heaped under it, asleep in her thin bones. Rosa tore the shawl free and flew — she could fly, she was only air — into the arena. The sunheat murmured of another life, of butterflies in summer. The light was placid, mellow. On the other side of the steel fence, far away, there were green meadows speckled with dandelions and deep-colored violets; beyond them, even farther, innocent tiger lilies, tall, lifting their orange bonnets. In the barracks they spoke of "flowers," of "rain": excrement, thick turd-braids, and the slow stinking maroon waterfall that slunk down from the upper bunks, the stink mixed with a bitter fatty floating smoke that greased Rosa's skin. She stood for an instant at the margin of the arena. Sometimes the electricity inside the fence would seem to hum; even Stella said it was only an imagining, but Rosa heard real sounds in the wire: grainy sad voices. The farther she was from the fence, the more clearly the voices crowded at her. The lamenting voices strummed so convincingly, so passionately, it was impossible to suspect them of being phantoms. The voices told her to hold up the shawl, high; the voices told her to shake it, to whip with it, to unfurl it like a flag. Rosa lifted, shook, whipped, unfurled. Far off, very far, Magda leaned across her air-fed belly, reaching out with the rods of her arms. She was high up, elevated, riding someone's shoulder. But the shoulder that carried Magda was not coming toward Rosa and the shawl, it was drifting away, the speck of Magda was moving more and more into the smoky distance. Above the shoulder a helmet glinted. A light tapped the helmet and sparkled it into a goblet. Below the helmet a black body like a domino and a pair of black boots hurled themselves in the direction of the electrified fence. The electric voices began to chatter wildly. "Maamaa, maaamaaa," they all hummed together. How far Magda was from Rosa now, across the whole square, past a dozen barracks, all the way on the other side! She was no bigger than a moth.

All at once Magda was swimming through the air. The whole of Magda traveled through loftiness. She looked like a butterfly touching a silver vine. And the moment Magda's feathered round head and her pencil legs and balloonish belly and zigzag arms splashed against the fence, the steel voices went mad in their growling, urging Rosa to run and run to the spot where Magda had fallen from her flight against the electrified fence; but of course Rosa did not obey them. She only stood, because if she ran they would shoot, and if she tried to pick up the sticks of Magda's body they would shoot, and if she let the wolf's screech ascending now through the ladder of her skeleton break out, they would shoot; so she took Magda's shawl and filled her own mouth with it, stuffed it in and stuffed it in, until she was swallowing up the wolf's screech and tasting the cinnamon and almond depth of Magda's saliva; and Rosa drank Magda's shawl until it dried.

GRACE PALEY *(b. 1922) was born in New York City. She studied at Hunter College and New York University, and in 1942 she married for the first time. She had two children from that marriage. In the 1950s she turned from writing poetry to short fiction. Her first book of stories,* The Little Disturbances of Man *(1959), established her reputation as a writer with a remarkably supple gift for language. As Susan Sontag has noted, "She is that rare kind of writer, a natural with a voice like no one else's — funny, sad, lean, modest, energetic, acute." When this book went out of print in 1965, its reputation survived, strengthened by the infrequent appearances of her new stories in magazines such as the* Atlantic Monthly, Esquire, *the* Noble Savage, Genesis West, *the* New American Review, Ararat, *and* Fiction.

During the 1960s and 1970s Paley was prominent as a nonviolent activist protesting the Vietnam War. She was secretary of the Greenwich Village Peace Center, spent time in jail for her antiwar activities, and visited Hanoi and Moscow as a member of peace delegations, defining herself as a "somewhat combative pacifist and cooperative anarchist." During the World Peace Congress in Moscow in 1973, she condemned the Soviet Union for silencing political dissidents; the congress disassociated itself from her statement. Paley has long been a feminist and active in the antinuclear movement. In 1974 her second volume of stories, Enormous Changes at the Last Minute, *was published — it is a quieter, more openly personal collection of seventeen stories, many of them, such as "A Conversation with My Father," autobiographical. Her third book of stories,* Later the Same Day, *appeared in 1985. In 1988 Paley was designated the first official New York State Author by an act of the state legislature.*

Paley refuses to blame her teaching jobs or her involvements as an activist for her relatively low productivity as a writer. She says she writes "from distress." What she tries to get at in her stories is "a history of everyday life," and her subject matter and prose style are unmistakable. Living in a Manhattan apartment close to the Greenwich Village School (P.S. 41), Little Tony's Unisex Haircutters, the Famous Ray's Pizza, the H & H Fruit and Vegetable Market, and the Jefferson Market Branch of the New York Public Library, Paley observes her neighbors, friends, and family with compassion, humor, and hope. Her spare dissection of her characters is never performed at the expense of sympathy for the human condition. It is likely that, as was true of her Russian counterpart Isaac Babel, her production of stories will be limited. As she puts it, "There is a long time in me between knowing and telling." The Collected Stories of Grace Paley *was published in 1994.*

RELATED COMMENTARY: *Grace Paley, "A Conversation with Ann Charters," page 705.*

GRACE PALEY

A Conversation with My Father

1974

My father is eighty-six years old and in bed. His heart, that bloody motor, is equally old and will not do certain jobs any more. It still floods his head with brainy light. But it won't let his legs carry the weight of his body around the house. Despite my metaphors, this muscle failure is not due to his old heart, he says, but to a potassium shortage. Sitting on one pillow, leaning on three, he offers last-minute advice and makes a request.

"I would like you to write a simple story just once more," he says, "the kind de Maupassant wrote, or Chekhov, the kind you used to write. Just recognizable people and then write down what happened to them next."

I say, "Yes, why not? That's possible." I want to please him, though I don't remember writing that way. I *would* like to try to tell such a story, if he means the kind that begins: "There was a woman . . ." followed by plot, the absolute line between two points which I've always despised. Not for literary reasons, but because it takes all hope away. Everyone, real or invented, deserves the open destiny of life.

Finally I thought of a story that had been happening for a couple of years right across the street. I wrote it down, then read it aloud. "Pa," I said, "how about this? Do you mean something like this?"

> Once in my time there was a woman and she had a son. They lived nicely, in a small apartment in Manhattan. This boy at about fifteen became a junkie, which is not unusual in our neighborhood. In order to maintain her close friendship with him, she became a junkie too. She said it was part of the youth culture, with which she felt very much at home. After a while, for a number of reasons, the boy gave it all up and left the city and his mother in disgust. Hopeless and alone, she grieved. We all visit her.

"O.K., Pa, that's it," I said, "an unadorned and miserable tale."

"But that's not what I mean," my father said. "You misunderstood me on purpose. You know there's a lot more to it. You know that. You left everything out. Turgenev wouldn't do that. Chekhov wouldn't do that. There are in fact Russian writers you never heard of, you don't have an inkling of, as good as anyone, who can write a plain ordinary story, who would not leave out what you have left out. I object not to facts but to people sitting in trees talking senselessly, voices from who knows where. . . ."

"Forget that one, Pa, what have I left out now? In this one?"

"Her looks, for instance."

"Oh. Quite handsome, I think. Yes."

"Her hair?"

"Dark, with heavy braids, as though she were a girl or a foreigner."

"What were her parents like, her stock? That she became such a person. It's interesting, you know."

"From out of town. Professional people. The first to be divorced in their county. How's that? Enough?" I asked.

"With you, it's all a joke," he said. "What about the boy's father? Why didn't you mention him? Who was he? Or was the boy born out of wedlock?"

"Yes," I said. "He was born out of wedlock."

"For Godsakes, doesn't anyone in your stories get married? Doesn't anyone have the time to run down to City Hall before they jump into bed?"

"No," I said. "In real life, yes. But in my stories, no."

"Why do you answer me like that?"

"Oh, Pa, this is a simple story about a smart woman who came to N.Y.C. full of interest love trust excitement very up to date, and about her son, what a hard time she had in this world. Married or not, it's of small consequence."

"It is of great consequence," he said.

"O.K.," I said.

"O.K. O.K. yourself," he said, "but listen. I believe you that she's good-looking, but I don't think she was so smart."

"That's true," I said. "Actually that's the trouble with stories. People start out fantastic. You think they're extraordinary, but it turns out as the work goes along, they're just average with a good education. Sometimes the other way around, the person's a kind of dumb innocent, but he outwits you and you can't even think of an ending good enough."

"What do you do then?" he asked. He had been a doctor for a couple of decades and then an artist for a couple of decades and he's still interested in details, craft, technique.

"Well, you just have to let the story lie around till some agreement can be reached between you and the stubborn hero."

"Aren't you talking silly now?" he asked. "Start again," he said. "It so happens I'm not going out this evening. Tell the story again. See what you can do this time."

"O.K.," I said. "But it's not a five-minute job." Second attempt:

> Once, across the street from us, there was a fine handsome woman, our neighbor. She had a son whom she loved because she'd known him since birth (in helpless chubby infancy, and in the wrestling, hugging ages, seven to ten, as well as earlier and later). This boy, when he fell into the fist of adolescence, became a junkie. He was not a hopeless one. He was in fact hopeful, an ideologue and successful converter. With his busy brilliance, he wrote persuasive articles for his high-school newspaper. Seeking a wider audience, using important connections, he drummed into Lower Manhattan newsstand distribution a periodical called *Oh! Golden Horse!*
>
> In order to keep him from feeling guilty (because guilt is the stony heart of nine tenths of all clinically diagnosed cancers in America today, she said), and because she had always believed in giving bad habits room at home where one could keep an eye on them, she too became a junkie. Her kitchen was famous for a while — a center for intellectual addicts who knew what they were doing. A few felt artistic like Coleridge° and others were scientific and revolutionary

---

Coleridge: Samuel Taylor Coleridge (1772–1834), the English Romantic poet, was an opium addict.

like Leary.° Although she was often high herself, certain good mothering reflexes remained, and she saw to it that there was lots of orange juice around and honey and milk and vitamin pills. However, she never cooked anything but chili, and that no more than once a week. She explained, when we talked to her, seriously, with neighborly concern, that it was her part in the youth culture and she would rather be with the young, it was an honor, than with her own generation.

One week, while nodding through an Antonioni film, this boy was severely jabbed by the elbow of a stern and proselytizing girl, sitting beside him. She offered immediate apricots and nuts for his sugar level, spoke to him sharply, and took him home.

She had heard of him and his work and she herself published, edited, and wrote a competitive journal called *Man Does Live by Bread Alone.* In the organic heat of her continuous presence he could not help but become interested once more in his muscles, his arteries, and nerve connections. In fact he began to love them, treasure them, praise them with funny little songs in *Man Does Live.* . . .

the fingers of my flesh transcend
my transcendental soul
the tightness in my shoulders end
my teeth have made me whole

To the mouth of his head (that glory of will and determination) he brought hard apples, nuts, wheat germ, and soybean oil. He said to his old friends, From now on, I guess I'll keep my wits about me. I'm going on the natch. He said he was about to begin a spiritual deep-breathing journey. How about you too, Mom? he asked kindly.

His conversion was so radiant, splendid, that neighborhood kids his age began to say that he had never been a real addict at all, only a journalist along for the smell of the story. The mother tried several times to give up what had become without her son and his friends a lonely habit. This effort only brought it to supportable levels. The boy and his girl took their electronic mimeograph and moved to the bushy edge of another borough. They were very strict. They said they would not see her again until she had been off drugs for sixty days.

At home alone in the evening, weeping, the mother read and reread the seven issues of *Oh! Golden Horse!* They seemed to her as truthful as ever. We often crossed the street to visit and console. But if we mentioned any of our children who were at college or in the hospital or dropouts at home, she would cry out, My baby! My baby! and burst into terrible, face-scarring, time-consuming tears. The End.

First my father was silent, then he said, "Number One: You have a nice sense of humor. Number Two: I see you can't tell a plain story. So don't waste time." Then he said sadly, "Number Three: I suppose that means she was alone, she was left like that, his mother. Alone. Probably sick?"

I said, "Yes."

"Poor woman. Poor girl, to be born in a time of fools, to live among fools. The end. The end. You were right to put that down. The end."

Leary: Timothy Leary (1920–1996) was a former Harvard professor of psychology and early advocate of the use of LSD.

I didn't want to argue, but I had to say, "Well, it is not necessarily the end, Pa."

"Yes," he said, "what a tragedy. The end of a person."

"No, Pa," I begged him. "It doesn't have to be. She's only about forty. She could be a hundred different things in this world as time goes on. A teacher or a social worker. An ex-junkie! Sometimes it's better than having a master's in education."

"Jokes," he said. "As a writer that's your main trouble. You don't want to recognize it. Tragedy! Plain tragedy! Historical tragedy! No hope. The end."

"Oh, Pa," I said. "She could change."

"In your own life, too, you have to look it in the face." He took a couple of nitroglycerin. "Turn to five," he said, pointing to the dial on the oxygen tank. He inserted the tubes into his nostrils and breathed deep. He closed his eyes and said, "No."

I had promised the family to always let him have the last word when arguing, but in this case I had a different responsibility. That woman lives across the street. She's my knowledge and my invention. I'm sorry for her. I'm not going to leave her there in that house crying. (Actually neither would Life, which unlike me has no pity.)

Therefore: She did change. Of course her son never came home again. But right now, she's the receptionist in a storefront community clinic in the East Village. Most of the customers are young people, some old friends. The head doctor has said to her, "If we only had three people in this clinic with your experiences. . . ."

"The doctor said that?" My father took the oxygen tubes out of his nostrils and said, "Jokes. Jokes again."

"No, Pa, it could really happen that way, it's a funny world nowadays."

"No," he said. "Truth first. She will slide back. A person must have character. She does not."

"No, Pa," I said. "That's it. She's got a job. Forget it. She's in that storefront working."

"How long will it be?" he asked. "Tragedy! You too. When will you look it in the face?"

EDGAR ALLAN POE *(1809–1849), the son of poor traveling actors, was adopted by the merchant John Allan of Richmond, Virginia, after the death of Poe's mother. He was educated in Virginia and England, served two years in the army as an enlisted man, then entered the military academy at West Point, from which he was expelled after a year. When John Allan disinherited him, Poe turned to writing to earn his living. In 1833 his story "Ms. Found in a Bottle" won a fifty-dollar prize for the best story in a popular Baltimore periodical, and shortly afterward Poe became editor of the* Southern Literary Messenger. *In 1836 he married his cousin Virginia Clemm, who was thirteen years old. Poe's brilliant reviews, poems, and stories attracted wide attention, but the magazine fired him in 1837 because of his unstable temperament.*

His remaining years were a struggle with poverty, depression, poor health aggravated by addiction to drugs and alcohol, and — after 1847 — grief over the death of his wife. The writer Jorge Luis Borges observed that Poe's life "was short and unhappy, if unhappiness can be short."

Most of Poe's stories can be divided into two categories: tales of terror, such as "The Cask of Amontillado" (1846) and "The Tell-Tale Heart" (1843), in which unity of effect or a single impression is of the greatest importance, and stories of intellect or reason, analytic tales that are precursors of the modern detective story. When critics accused him of imitating German romantic writers such as Heinrich von Kleist in his monologues of inspired madness, Poe answered, "Terror is not of Germany, but of the soul."

Poe is also important as one of the earliest writers to attempt to formulate an aesthetic theory about the short story form, or the "prose tale," as it was called in his time. His most extensive comments on this subject are in his reviews of Hawthorne's tales for the periodicals Graham's Magazine *in 1842 and* Godey's Lady's Book *in 1847; in these reviews he also described his own philosophy of composition. Poe believed that unity of a "single effect" was the most essential quality of all successful short fiction. He praised Hawthorne for his "invention, creation, imagination, originality" — qualities Poe himself possessed in abundance.*

RELATED COMMENTARY: *Edgar Allan Poe, "The Importance of the Single Effect in a Prose Tale," page 709.*

EDGAR ALLAN POE

The Cask of Amontillado

1846

The thousand injuries of Fortunato I had borne as I best could; but when he ventured upon insult, I vowed revenge. You, who so well know the nature of my soul, will not suppose, however, that I gave utterance to a threat. *At length* I would be avenged; this was a point definitely settled — but the very definitiveness with which it was resolved precluded the idea of risk. I must not only punish, but punish with impunity. A wrong is unredressed when retribution overtakes its redresser. It is equally unredressed when the avenger fails to make himself felt as such to him who has done the wrong.

It must be understood, that neither by word nor deed had I given Fortunato cause to doubt my good-will. I continued, as was my wont, to smile in his face, and he did not perceive that my smile *now* was at the thought of his immolation.

He had a weak point — this Fortunato — although in other regards he was a man to be respected and even feared. He prided himself on his connoisseurship in wine. Few Italians have the true virtuoso spirit. For the most part their enthusiasm is adopted to suit the time and opportunity — to practise imposture upon the British and Austrian *millionnaires.* In painting and gemmary Fortunato, like his countrymen, was a quack — but in the matter of old wines he was sincere. In this respect I did not differ from him materially: I was skilful in the Italian vintages myself, and bought largely whenever I could.

It was about dusk, one evening during the supreme madness of the carnival season, that I encountered my friend. He accosted me with excessive warmth, for he had been drinking much. The man wore motley. He had on a tight-fitting parti-striped dress, and his head was surmounted by the conical cap and bells. I was so pleased to see him, that I thought I should never have done wringing his hand.

I said to him: "My dear Fortunato, you are luckily met. How remarkably well you are looking to-day! But I have received a pipe° of what passes for Amontillado, and I have my doubts."

"How?" said he. "Amontillado? A pipe? Impossible! And in the middle of the carnival!"

"I have my doubts," I replied; "and I was silly enough to pay the full Amontillado price without consulting you in the matter. You were not to be found, and I was fearful of losing a bargain."

"Amontillado!"

"I have my doubts."

"Amontillado!"

"And I must satisfy them."

"Amontillado!"

"As you are engaged, I am on my way to Luchesi. If any one has a critical turn, it is he. He will tell me ——"

"Luchesi cannot tell Amontillado from Sherry."

"And yet some fools will have it that his taste is a match for your own."

"Come, let us go."

"Whither?"

"To your vaults."

"My friend, no; I will not impose upon your good nature. I perceive you have an engagement. Luchesi ——"

"I have no engagement; — come."

"My friend, no. It is not the engagement, but the severe cold with which I perceive you are afflicted. The vaults are insufferably damp. They are encrusted with nitre."

"Let us go, nevertheless. The cold is merely nothing. Amontillado! You have been imposed upon. And as for Luchesi, he cannot distinguish Sherry from Amontillado."

Thus speaking, Fortunato possessed himself of my arm. Putting on a mask of black silk, and drawing a *roquelaire*° closely about my person, I suffered him to hurry me to my palazzo.

There were no attendants at home; they had absconded to make merry in honor of the time. I had told them that I should not return until the morning, and had given them explicit orders not to stir from the house. These orders were sufficient, I well knew, to insure their immediate disappearance, one and all, as soon as my back was turned.

I took from their sconces two flambeaux, and giving one to Fortunato, bowed him through several suites of rooms to the archway that led into the vaults. I passed down a long and winding staircase, requesting him to be cau-

pipe: A large cask or keg.
roquelaire: A short cloak.

tious as he followed. We came at length to the foot of the descent, and stood together on the damp ground of the catacombs of the Montresors.

The gait of my friend was unsteady, and the bells upon his cap jingled as he strode.

"The pipe?" said he.

"It is farther on," said I; "but observe the white web-work which gleams from these cavern walls."

He turned toward me, and looked into my eyes with two filmy orbs that distilled the rheum of intoxication.

"Nitre?" he asked, at length.

"Nitre," I replied. "How long have you had that cough?"

"Ugh! ugh! ugh! — ugh! ugh! ugh! — ugh! ugh! ugh! — ugh! ugh! ugh! — ugh! ugh! ugh!"

My poor friend found it impossible to reply for many minutes.

"It is nothing," he said, at last.

"Come," I said, with decision, "we will go back; your health is precious. You are rich, respected, admired, beloved; you are happy, as once I was. You are a man to be missed. For me it is no matter. We will go back; you will be ill, and I cannot be responsible. Besides, there is Luchesi ——"

"Enough," he said; "the cough is a mere nothing; it will not kill me. I shall not die of a cough."

"True — true," I replied; "and, indeed, I had no intention of alarming you unnecessarily; but you should use all proper caution. A draught of this Medoc will defend us from the damps."

Here I knocked off the neck of a bottle which I drew from a long row of its fellows that lay upon the mould.

"Drink," I said, presenting him the wine.

He raised it to his lips with a leer. He paused and nodded to me familiarly, while his bells jingled.

"I drink," he said, "to the buried that repose around us."

"And I to your long life."

He again took my arm, and we proceeded.

"These vaults," he said, "are extensive."

"The Montresors," I replied, "were a great and numerous family."

"I forget your arms."

"A huge human foot d'or,° in a field azure; the foot crushes a serpent rampant whose fangs are imbedded in the heel."

"And the motto?"

"*Nemo me impune lacessit.*"°

"Good!" he said.

The wine sparkled in his eyes and the bells jingled. My own fancy grew warm with the Medoc. We had passed through walls of piled bones, with casks and puncheons intermingling into the inmost recesses of the catacombs.

---

d'or: Of gold.
Nemo me impune lacessit: "No one wounds me with impunity"; the motto of the royal arms of Scotland.

I paused again, and this time I made bold to seize Fortunato by an arm above the elbow.

"The nitre!" I said; "see, it increases. It hangs like moss upon the vaults. We are below the river's bed. The drops of moisture trickle among the bones. Come, we will go back ere it is too late. Your cough ——"

"It is nothing," he said; "let us go on. But first, another draught of the Medoc."

I broke and reached him a flagon of De Grâve. He emptied it at a breath. His eyes flashed with a fierce light. He laughed and threw the bottle upward with a gesticulation I did not understand.

I looked at him in surprise. He repeated the movement — a grotesque one.

"You do not comprehend?" he said.

"Not I," I replied.

"Then you are not of the brotherhood."

"How?"

"You are not of the masons."

"Yes, yes," I said; "yes, yes."

"You? Impossible! A mason?"

"A mason," I replied.

"A sign," he said.

"It is this," I answered, producing a trowel from beneath the folds of my *roquelaire.*

"You jest," he exclaimed, recoiling a few paces. "But let us proceed to the Amontillado."

"Be it so," I said, replacing the tool beneath the cloak, and again offering him my arm. He leaned upon it heavily. We continued our route in search of the Amontillado. We passed through a range of low arches, descended, passed on, and descending again, arrived at a deep crypt, in which the foulness of the air caused our flambeaux rather to glow than flame.

At the most remote end of the crypt there appeared another less spacious. Its walls had been lined with human remains, piled to the vault overhead, in the fashion of the great catacombs of Paris. Three sides of this interior crypt were still ornamented in this manner. From the fourth the bones had been thrown down, and lay promiscuously upon the earth, forming at one point a mound of some size. Within the wall thus exposed by the displacing of the bones, we perceived a still interior recess, in depth about four feet, in width three, in height six or seven. It seemed to have been constructed for no especial use within itself, but formed merely the interval between two of the colossal supports of the roof of the catacombs, and was backed by one of their circumscribing walls of solid granite.

It was in vain that Fortunato, uplifting his dull torch, endeavored to pry into the depth of the recess. Its termination the feeble light did not enable us to see.

"Proceed," I said; "herein is the Amontillado. As for Luchesi ——"

"He is an ignoramus," interrupted my friend, as he stepped unsteadily forward, while I followed immediately at his heels. In an instant he had reached the extremity of the niche, and finding his progress arrested by the rock, stood stupidly bewildered. A moment more and I had fettered him to the granite. In its surface were two iron staples, distant from each other about two feet, horizontally. From one of these depended a short chain, from the other a padlock. Throwing the links about his waist, it was but the work of a few seconds to secure it. He was too much astounded to resist. Withdrawing the key I stepped back from the recess.

"Pass your hand," I said, "over the wall; you cannot help feeling the nitre. Indeed it is *very* damp. Once more let me *implore* you to return. No? Then I must positively leave you. But I must first render you all the little attentions in my power."

"The Amontillado!" ejaculated my friend, not yet recovered from his astonishment.

"True," I replied; "the Amontillado."

As I said these words I busied myself among the pile of bones of which I have before spoken. Throwing them aside, I soon uncovered a quantity of building stone and mortar. With these materials and with the aid of my trowel, I began vigorously to wall up the entrance of the niche.

I had scarcely laid the first tier of the masonry when I discovered that the intoxication of Fortunato had in a great measure worn off. The earliest indication I had of this was a low moaning cry from the depth of the recess. It was *not* the cry of a drunken man. There was then a long and obstinate silence. I laid the second tier, and the third, and the fourth; and then I heard the furious vibrations of the chain. The noise lasted for several minutes, during which, that I might hearken to it with the more satisfaction, I ceased my labors and sat down upon the bones. When at last the clanking subsided, I resumed the trowel, and finished without interruption the fifth, the sixth, and the seventh tier. The wall was now nearly upon a level with my breast. I again paused, and holding the flambeaux over the masonwork, threw a few feeble rays upon the figure within.

A succession of loud and shrill screams, bursting suddenly from the throat of the chained form, seemed to thrust me violently back. For a brief moment I hesitated — I trembled. Unsheathing my rapier, I began to grope with it about the recess; but the thought of an instant reassured me. I placed my hand upon the solid fabric of the catacombs, and felt satisfied. I reapproached the wall. I replied to the yells of him who clamored. I reechoed — I aided — I surpassed them in volume and in strength. I did this, and the clamorer grew still.

It was now midnight, and my task was drawing to a close. I had completed the eighth, the ninth, and the tenth tier. I had finished a portion of the last and the eleventh; there remained but a single stone to be fitted and plastered in. I struggled with its weight; I placed it partially in its destined position. But now there came from out the niche a low laugh that erected the hairs upon my head. It was succeeded by a sad voice, which I had difficulty in recognizing as that of the noble Fortunato. The voice said —

"Ha! ha! ha! — he! he! — a very good joke indeed — an excellent jest. We will have many a rich laugh about it at the palazzo — he! he! he! — over our wine — he! he! he!"

"The Amontillado!" I said.

"He! he! he! — he! he! he! — yes, the Amontillado. But is it not getting late? Will not they be awaiting us at the palazzo, the Lady Fortunato and the rest? Let us be gone."

"Yes," I said, "let us be gone."

"For the love of God, Montresor!"

"Yes," I said, "for the love of God!"

But to these words I hearkened in vain for a reply. I grew impatient. I called aloud:

"Fortunato!"

No answer. I called again:

"Fortunato!"

No answer still, I thrust a torch through the remaining aperture and let it fall within. There came forth in return only a jingling of the bells. My heart grew sick — on account of the dampness of the catacombs. I hastened to make an end of my labor. I forced the last stone into its position; I plastered it up. Against the new masonry I re-erected the old rampart of bones. For the half of a century no mortal has disturbed them. *In pace requiescat!*

Edgar Allan Poe

The Tell-Tale Heart

1843

True! — nervous — very, very dreadfully nervous I had been and am; but why *will* you say that I am mad? The disease had sharpened my senses — not destroyed — not dulled them. Above all was the sense of hearing acute. I heard all things in the heaven and in the earth. I heard many things in hell. How, then, am I mad? Hearken! and observe how healthily — how calmly I can tell you the whole story.

It is impossible to say how first the idea entered my brain; but once conceived, it haunted me day and night. Object there was none. Passion there was none. I loved the old man. He had never wronged me. He had never given me insult. For his gold I had no desire. I think it was his eye! yes, it was this! One of his eyes resembled that of a vulture — a pale blue eye, with a film over it. Whenever it fell upon me, my blood ran cold; and so by degrees — very gradually — I made up my mind to take the life of the old man, and thus rid myself of the eye for ever.

Now this is the point. You fancy me mad. Madmen know nothing. But you should have seen *me.* You should have seen how wisely I proceeded — with what caution — with what foresight — with what dissimulation I went to work! I was never kinder to the old man than during the whole week before I killed him. And every night, about midnight, I turned the latch of his door and opened it — oh, so gently! And then, when I had made an opening sufficient for my head, I put in a dark lantern, all closed, closed, so that no light shone out, and then I thrust in my head. Oh, you would have laughed to see how cunningly I thrust it in! I moved it slowly — very, very slowly, so that I might not disturb the old man's sleep. It took me an hour to place my whole head within the opening so far that I could see him as he lay upon his bed. Ha — would a madman have been so wise as this? And then, when my head was well in the room, I undid the lantern cautiously — oh, so cautiously — cautiously (for the hinges creaked) — I undid it just so much that a single thin ray fell upon the vulture eye. And this I did for seven long nights — every night just after midnight — but I found the eye always closed; and so it was impossible to do the work; for it was not the old man who vexed me, but his Evil Eye. And every morning, when the day broke, I went boldly into the chamber, and spoke courageously to him, calling him by name in a hearty tone, and inquiring how he had passed the night. So you see he would have been a very profound old man, indeed, to suspect that every night, just at twelve, I looked in upon him while he slept.

Upon the eighth night I was more than usually cautious in opening the door. A watch's minute hand moves more quickly than did mine. Never before that night had I *felt* the extent of my own powers — of my sagacity. I could scarcely contain my feelings of triumph. To think that there I was, opening the door, little by little, and he not even to dream of my secret deeds or thoughts. I fairly chuckled at the idea; and perhaps he heard me; for he moved on the bed suddenly, as if startled. Now you may think that I drew back — but no. His room was as black as pitch with the thick darkness (for the shutters were close fastened, through fear of robbers), and so I knew that he could not see the opening of the door, and I kept pushing it on steadily, steadily.

I had my head in, and was about to open the lantern, when my thumb slipped upon the tin fastening, and the old man sprang up in the bed, crying out — "Who's there?"

I kept quite still and said nothing. For a whole hour I did not move a muscle, and in the meantime I did not hear him lie down. He was still sitting up in the bed listening; — just as I have done, night after night, hearkening to the death watches in the wall.

Presently I heard a slight groan, and I knew it was the groan of mortal terror. It was not a groan of pain or of grief — oh, no! — it was the low stifled sound that arises from the bottom of the soul when overcharged with awe. I knew the sound well. Many a night, just at midnight, when all the world slept, it has welled up from my own bosom, deepening with its dreadful echo, the terrors that distracted me. I say I knew it well. I knew what the old man felt, and pitied him, although I chuckled at heart. I knew that he had been lying awake ever since the first slight noise, when he had turned in the bed. His fears had been ever since growing upon him. He had been trying to fancy them causeless, but could not. He had been saying to himself — "It is nothing but the wind in the chimney — it is only a mouse crossing the floor," or "it is merely a cricket which has made a single chirp." Yes, he has been trying to comfort himself with these suppositions; but he had found all in vain. *All in vain*; because Death, in approaching him, had stalked with his black shadow before him, and enveloped the victim. And it was the mournful influence of the unperceived shadow that caused him to feel — although he neither saw nor heard — to *feel* the presence of my head within the room.

When I had waited a long time, very patiently, without hearing him lie down, I resolved to open a little — a very, very little crevice in the lantern. So I opened it — you cannot imagine how stealthily, stealthily — until, at length, a single dim ray, like the thread of the spider, shot from out the crevice and full upon the vulture eye.

It was open — wide, wide open — and I grew furious as I gazed upon it. I saw it with perfect distinctness — all a dull blue, with a hideous veil over it that chilled the very marrow in my bones, but I could see nothing else of the old man's face or person: for I had directed the ray as if by instinct, precisely upon the damned spot.

And now have I not told you that what you mistake for madness is but over-acuteness of the senses? — now, I say, there came to my ears a low, dull, quick sound, such as a watch makes when enveloped in cotton. I knew *that* sound well too. It was the beating of the old man's heart. It increased my fury, as the beating of a drum stimulates the soldier into courage.

But even yet I refrained and kept still. I scarcely breathed. I held the lantern motionless. I tried how steadily I could maintain the ray upon the eye. Meantime the hellish tattoo of the heart increased. It grew quicker and quicker, and louder and louder every instant. The old man's terror *must* have been extreme! It grew louder, I say, louder every moment! — do you mark me well? I have told you that I am nervous: so I am. And now at the dead hour of the night, amid the dreadful silence of that old house, so strange a noise as this excited me to uncontrollable terror. Yet, for some minutes longer I refrained and stood still. But the beating grew louder, louder! I thought the heart must burst. And now a new anxiety seized me — the sound would be heard by a neighbor! The old man's hour had come! With a loud yell, I threw open the lantern and leaped into the room. He shrieked once — once only. In an instant I dragged him to the floor, and pulled the heavy bed over him. I then smiled gaily, to find the deed so far done. But, for many minutes, the heart beat on with a muffled sound. This, however, did not vex me; it would not be heard through the wall. At length it ceased. The old man was dead. I removed the bed and examined the corpse. Yes, he was stone, stone dead. I placed my hand upon the heart and held it there many minutes. There was no pulsation. He was stone dead. His eye would trouble me no more.

If still you think me mad, you will think so no longer when I describe the wise precautions I took for the concealment of the body. The night waned, and I worked hastily, but in silence. First of all I dismembered the corpse. I cut off the head and the arms and the legs.

I then took up three planks from the flooring of the chamber, and deposited all between the scantlings. I then replaced the boards so cleverly, so cunningly, that no human eye — not even *his* — could have detected anything wrong. There was nothing to wash out — no stain of any kind — no blood-spot whatever. I had been too wary for that. A tub had caught all — ha! ha!

When I had made an end of these labors, it was four o'clock — still dark as midnight. As the bell sounded the hour, there came a knocking at the street door. I went down to open it with a light heart — for what had I *now* to fear? There entered three men, who introduced themselves, with perfect suavity, as officers of the police. A shriek had been heard by a neighbor during the night; suspicion of foul play had been aroused; information had been lodged at the police office, and they (the officers) had been deputed to search the premises.

I smiled — for *what* had I to fear? I bade the gentlemen welcome. The shriek, I said, was my own in a dream. The old man, I mentioned, was absent in the country. I took my visitors all over the house. I bade them search — search *well*. I led them, at length, to *his* chamber. I showed them his treasures, secure, undisturbed. In the enthusiasm of my confidence, I brought chairs into the room, and desired them *here* to rest from their fatigues, while I myself, in the wild audacity of my perfect triumph, placed my own seat upon the very spot beneath which reposed the corpse of the victim.

The officers were satisfied. My *manner* had convinced them. I was singularly at ease. They sat, and while I answered cheerily, they chatted familiar things. But, ere long, I felt myself getting pale and wished them gone. My head ached, and I fancied a ringing in my ears: but still they sat and still chatted. The ringing became more distinct: — it continued and became more distinct: I talked more freely to get rid of the feeling: but it continued and gained definitiveness — until, at length, I found that the noise was *not* within my ears.

No doubt I now grew *very* pale; — but I talked more fluently, and with a heightened voice. Yet the sound increased — and what could I do? It was *a low, dull, quick sound — much such a sound as a watch makes when enveloped in cotton*. I gasped for breath — and yet the officers heard it not. I talked more quickly — more vehemently; but the noise steadily increased. I arose and argued about trifles, in a high key and with violent gesticulations, but the noise steadily increased. Why *would* they not be gone? I paced the floor to and fro with heavy strides, as if excited to fury by the observation of the men — but the noise steadily increased. Oh God! what *could* I do? I foamed — I raved — I swore! I swung the chair upon which I had been sitting, and grated it upon the boards, but the noise arose over all and continually increased. It grew louder — louder — *louder*! And still the men chatted pleasantly, and smiled. Was it possible they heard not? Almighty God! — no, no! They heard! — they suspected! — they *knew*! — they were making a mockery of my horror! — this I thought, and this I think. But any thing was better than this agony! Any thing was more tolerable than this derision! I could bear those hypocritical smiles no longer! I felt that I must scream or die! — and now — again! — hark! louder! louder! louder! *louder*! —

"Villains!" I shrieked, "dissemble no more! I admit the deed! — tear up the planks! — here, here! — it is the beating of his hideous heart!"

ꕥ

KATHERINE ANNE PORTER *(1890–1980) was born Callie Russell Porter in Indian Creek, Texas. When she was only two her mother died. Educated at boarding schools and an Ursuline convent, Porter worked briefly as a reporter in Chicago and Denver. As a child she had wanted to be a writer, but it took fifteen years of serious writing before she trusted herself enough as a stylist to approach a publisher. Most of her life* *during this time was a financial struggle; she spent only 10 percent of her energy on writing, and "the other 90 percent went to keeping my head above water." She nearly lost her life in the influenza epidemic that swept the United States at the end of World War I, and when she recovered she went to Mexico to study Aztec and Mayan art.*

Porter achieved acclaim with her first collection of short stories, Flowering Judas and Other Stories, *in 1930. Her most productive decade as a writer was the 1930s, when she published* Noon Wine *(1937) and* Pale Horse, Pale Rider: Three Short Novels *(1939). She supported herself with lecture tours and teaching jobs at various universities while she worked on her novel* Ship of Fools *(1962), which took more than two decades to complete. In 1965 her* Collected Stories *won both the Pulitzer Prize and the National Book Award.*

Porter's style is not so recognizably "southern" as William Faulkner's or Flannery O'Connor's. She was a southerner by tradition and inheritance, but she had thought of herself since childhood as "always restless, always a roving spirit." She was very conscious of her own art as a storyteller, and of the art of fiction in general; she wrote personal essays on Willa Cather, Katherine Mansfield, Flannery O'Connor, Eudora Welty, and Virginia Woolf. Particularly indebted in her best stories to Mansfield, Porter attempted to dramatize a character's state of mind rather than develop a complicated plot. Her analysis of Mansfield's literary practice in the essay "The Art of Katherine Mansfield" can also be applied to a story such as "Theft":

> *With fine objectivity, she bares a moment of experience, real experience, in the life of some one human being; she states no belief, gives no motives, airs no theories, but simply presents to the reader a situation, a place, and a character, and there it is; and the emotional content is present as implicitly as the germ is in the grain of wheat.*

Katherine Anne Porter

Theft

1935

She had the purse in her hand when she came in. Standing in the middle of the floor, holding her bathrobe around her and trailing a damp towel in one hand, she surveyed the immediate past and remembered everything clearly. Yes, she had opened the flap and spread it out on the bench after she had dried the purse with her handkerchief.

She had intended to take the Elevated° and naturally she looked in her purse to make certain she had the fare, and was pleased to find forty cents in the coin envelope. She was going to pay her own fare, too, even if Camilo did have the habit of seeing her up the steps and dropping a nickel in the machine before he gave the turnstile a little push and sent her through it with a bow. Camilo by a series of compromises had managed to make effective a fairly complete set of smaller courtesies, ignoring the larger and more troublesome ones. She had walked with him to the station in a pouring rain, because she

Elevated: The elevated subway system in New York City at that time.

knew he was almost as poor as she was, and when he insisted on a taxi, she was firm and said, "You know it simply will not do." He was wearing a new hat of a pretty biscuit shade, for it never occurred to him to buy anything of a practical color; he had put it on for the first time and the rain was spoiling it. She kept thinking, "But this is dreadful, where will he get another?" She compared it with Eddie's hats that always seemed to be precisely seven years old and as if they had been quite purposely left out in the rain, and yet they sat with a careless and incidental rightness on Eddie. But Camilo was far different; if he wore a shabby hat it would be merely shabby on him, and he would lose his spirits over it. If she had not feared Camilo would take it badly, for he insisted on the practice of his little ceremonies up to the point he had fixed for them, she would have said to him as they left Thora's house, "Do go home. I can surely reach the station by myself."

"It is written that we must be rained upon tonight," said Camilo, "so let it be together."

At the foot of the platform stairway she staggered slightly — they were both nicely set up on Thora's cocktails — and said: "At least, Camilo, do me the favor not to climb these stairs in your present state, since for you it is only a matter of coming down again at once, and you'll certainly break your neck."

He made three quick bows, he was Spanish, and leaped off through the rainy darkness. She stood watching him, for he was a very graceful young man, thinking that tomorrow morning he would gaze soberly at his spoiled hat and soggy shoes and possibly associate her with his misery. As she watched, he stopped at the far corner and took off his hat and hid it under his overcoat. She felt she had betrayed him by seeing, because he would have been humiliated if he thought she even suspected him of trying to save his hat.

Roger's voice sounded over her shoulder above the clang of the rain falling on the stairway shed, wanting to know what she was doing out in the rain at this time of night, and did she take herself for a duck? His long, imperturbable face was steaming with water, and he tapped a bulging spot on the breast of his buttoned-up overcoat: "Hat," he said. "Come on, let's take a taxi."

She settled back against Roger's arm which he laid around her shoulders, and with the gesture they exchanged a glance full of long amiable associations, then she looked through the window at the rain changing the shapes of everything, and the colors. The taxi dodged in and out between the pillars of the Elevated, skidding slightly on every curve, and she said: "The more it skids the calmer I feel, so I really must be drunk."

"You must be," said Roger. "This bird is a homicidal maniac, and I could do with a cocktail myself this minute."

They waited on the traffic at Fortieth Street and Sixth Avenue, and three boys walked before the nose of the taxi. Under the globes of light they were cheerful scarecrows, all very thin and all wearing very seedy snappy-cut suits and gay neckties. They were not very sober either, and they stood for a moment wobbling in front of the car, and there was an argument going on among them. They leaned toward each other as if they were getting ready to sing, and the first one said: "When I get married it won't be jus' for getting married, I'm gonna marry for *love,* see?" and the second one said, "Aw, gwan and tell that stuff to *her,* why n't yuh?" and the third one gave a kind of hoot, and said, "Hell, dis guy? Wot the hell's he got?" and the first one said: "Aaah, shurrup yuh mush, I got plenty." Then they all squealed and scrambled across the street beating the first one on the back and pushing him around.

"Nuts," commented Roger, "pure nuts."

Two girls went skittering by in short transparent raincoats, one green, one red, their heads tucked against the drive of the rain. One of them was saying to the other, "Yes, I know all about *that.* But what about me? You're always so sorry for *him* . . ." and they ran on with their little pelican legs flashing back and forth.

The taxi backed up suddenly and leaped forward again, and after a while Roger said: "I had a letter from Stella today, and she'll be home on the twenty-sixth, so I suppose she's made up her mind and it's all settled."

"I had a sort of letter today too," she said, "making up my mind for me. I think it is time for you and Stella to do something definite."

When the taxi stopped on the comer of West Fifty-third Street, Roger said, "I've just enough if you'll add ten cents," so she opened her purse and gave him a dime, and he said, "That's beautiful, that purse."

"It's a birthday present," she told him, "and I like it. How's your show coming?"

"Oh, still hanging on, I guess. I don't go near the place. Nothing sold yet. I mean to keep right on the way I'm going and they can take it or leave it. I'm through with the argument."

"It's absolutely a matter of holding out, isn't it?"

"Holding out's the tough part."

"Good night, Roger."

"Good night, you should take aspirin and push yourself into a tub of hot water, you look as though you're catching cold."

"I will."

With the purse under her arm she went upstairs, and on the first landing Bill heard her step and poked his head out with his hair tumbled and his eyes red, and he said: "For Christ's sake, come in and have a drink with me. I've had some bad news."

"You're perfectly sopping," said Bill, looking at her drenched feet. They had two drinks, while Bill told how the director had thrown his play out after the cast had been picked over twice, and had gone through three rehearsals. "I said to him, 'I didn't say it was a masterpiece, I said it would make a good show.' And he said, 'It just doesn't *play,* do you see? It needs a doctor.' So I'm stuck, absolutely stuck," said Bill, on the edge of weeping again. "I've been crying," he told her, "in my cups." And he went on to ask her if she realized his wife was ruining him with her extravagance. "I send her ten dollars every week of my unhappy life, and I don't really have to. She threatens to jail me if I don't, but she can't do it. God, let her try it after the way she treated me! She's no right to alimony and she knows it. She keeps on saying she's got to have it for the baby and I keep on sending it because I can't bear to see anybody suffer. So I'm way behind on the piano and the victrola, both —"

"Well, this is a pretty rug, anyhow," she said.

Bill stared at it and blew his nose. "I got it at Ricci's for ninety-five dollars," he said. "Ricci told me it once belonged to Marie Dressler,° and cost fifteen hundred dollars, but there's a burnt place on it, under the divan. Can you beat that?"

"No," she said. She was thinking about her empty purse and that she could not possibly expect a check for her latest review for another three days, and her arrangement with the basement restaurant could not last much longer if she did not pay something on account. "It's no time to speak of it," she said, "but I've been hoping you would have by now that fifty dollars you promised for my scene in the third act. Even if it doesn't play. You were to pay me for the work anyhow out of your advance."

"Weeping Jesus," said Bill, "you, too?" He gave a loud sob, or hiccough, in his moist handkerchief. "Your stuff was no better than mine, after all. Think of that."

"But you got something for it," she said. "Seven hundred dollars."

Bill said, "Do me a favor, will you? Have another drink and forget about it. I can't, you know I can't, I would if I could, but you know the fix I'm in."

"Let it go, then," she found herself saying almost in spite of herself. She had meant to be quite firm about it. They drank again without speaking, and she went to her apartment on the floor above.

There, she now remembered distinctly, she had taken the letter out of the purse before she spread the purse out to dry.

She had sat down and read the letter over again: but there were phrases that insisted on being read many times, they had a life of their own separate from the others, and when she tried to read past and around them, they moved with the movement of her eyes, and she could not escape them . . . "thinking about you more than I mean to . . . yes, I even talk about you . . . why were you so anxious to destroy . . . even if I could see you now I would not . . . not worth all this abominable . . . the end . . ."

Carefully she tore the letter into narrow strips and touched a lighted match to them in the coal grate.

Early the next morning she was in the bathtub when the janitress knocked and then came in, calling out that she wished to examine the radiators before she started the furnace going for the winter. After moving about the room for a few minutes, the janitress went out, closing the door very sharply.

She came out of the bathroom to get a cigarette from the package in the purse. The purse was gone. She dressed and made coffee, and sat by the window while she drank it. Certainly the janitress had taken the purse, and certainly it would be impossible to get it back without a great deal of ridiculous excitement. Then let it go. With this decision of her mind, there rose coincidentally in her blood a deep almost murderous anger. She set the cup carefully in the center of the table, and walked steadily downstairs, three long flights and a short hall and a steep short flight into the basement, where the janitress, her face streaked with coal dust, was shaking up the furnace. "Will you please give me back my purse? There isn't any money in it. It was a present, and I don't want to lose it."

Marie Dressler: American actress (1873–1934).

The janitress turned without straightening up and peered at her with hot flickering eyes, a red light from the furnace reflected in them. "What do you mean, your purse?"

"The gold cloth purse you took from the wooden bench in my room," she said. "I must have it back."

"Before God I never laid eyes on your purse, and that's the holy truth," said the janitress.

"Oh, well then, keep it," she said, but in a very bitter voice; "keep it if you want it so much." And she walked away.

She remembered how she had never locked a door in her life, on some principle of rejection in her that made her uncomfortable in the ownership of things, and her paradoxical boast before the warnings of her friends, that she had never lost a penny by theft; and she had been pleased with the bleak humility of this concrete example designed to illustrate and justify a certain fixed, otherwise baseless and general faith which ordered the movements of her life without regard to her will in the matter.

In this moment she felt that she had been robbed of an enormous number of valuable things, whether material or intangible: things lost or broken by her own fault, things she had forgotten and left in houses when she moved: books borrowed from her and not returned, journeys she had planned and had not made, words she had waited to hear spoken to her and had not heard, and the words she had meant to answer with; bitter alternatives and intolerable substitutes worse than nothing, and yet inescapable: the long patient suffering of dying friendships and the dark inexplicable death of love — all that she had had, and all that she had missed, were lost together, and were twice lost in this landslide of remembered losses.

The janitress was following her upstairs with the purse in her hand and the same deep red fire flickering in her eyes. The janitress thrust the purse towards her while they were still a half dozen steps apart, and said: "Don't never tell on me. I musta been crazy. I get crazy in the head sometimes, I swear I do. My son can tell you."

She took the purse after a moment, and the janitress went on: "I got a niece who is going on seventeen, and she's a nice girl and I thought I'd give it to her. She needs a pretty purse. I musta been crazy; I thought maybe you wouldn't mind, you leave things around and don't seem to notice much."

She said: "I missed this because it was a present to me from someone . . ."

The janitress said: "He'd get you another if you lost this one. My niece is young and needs pretty things, we oughta give the young ones a chance. She's got young men after her maybe will want to marry her. She oughta have nice things. She needs them bad right now. You're a grown woman, you've had your chance, you ought to know how it is!"

She held the purse out to the janitress saying: "You don't know what you're talking about. Here, take it, I've changed my mind. I really don't want it."

The janitress looked up at her with hatred and said: "I don't want it either now. My niece is young and pretty, she don't need fixin' up to be pretty, she's young and pretty anyhow! I guess you need it worse than she does!"

"It wasn't really yours in the first place," she said, turning away. "You mustn't talk as if I had stolen it from you."

"It's not from me, it's from her you're stealing it," said the janitress, and went back downstairs.

She laid the purse on the table and sat down with the cup of chilled coffee, and thought: I was right not to be afraid of any thief but myself, who will end by leaving me nothing.

ꭒ

LESLIE MARMON SILKO *(b. 1948), a Laguna Pueblo, was born and grew up in New Mexico. She was educated at Board of Indian Affairs schools in Laguna, a Catholic school in Albuquerque, and the University of New Mexico, where she received her B.A. in English in 1969. After teaching at various colleges, she became a professor of English at the University of Arizona at Tucson. Silko's first novel,* Ceremony *(1977), is regarded as one of the most important books in modern Native American literature. In it she forged a connection between the shared past of the tribe and the individual life of a Native American returning home after World War II. Silko has received a National Endowment for the Arts fellowship, a Pushcart Prize, and a three-year grant from the MacArthur Foundation, which enabled her to take time off from teaching and become "a little less beholden to the everyday world."*

Storyteller *(1981), a collection of tribal folktales, family anecdotes, photographs by her grandfather, and her own poems and stories, is Silko's personal anthology of the Laguna Pueblo culture. "The Man to Send Rain Clouds" is from that collection.*

Silko has said that she writes "because I like seeing how I can translate [a] sort of feeling or flavor or sense of a story that's told and heard onto the page." Her most recent books are The Almanac of the Dead *(1991),* Sacred Water *(1993), and* Garden in the Dunes *(1999).*

RELATED COMMENTARY: *Leslie Marmon Silko, "Language and Literature from a Pueblo Indian Perspective," page 711.*

LESLIE MARMON SILKO

The Man to Send Rain Clouds

1981

They found him under a big cottonwood tree. His Levi jacket and pants were faded light blue so that he had been easy to find. The big cottonwood tree stood apart from a small grove of winterbare cottonwoods which grew in the wide, sandy arroyo. He had been dead for a day or more, and the sheep had wandered and scattered up and down the arroyo. Leon and his brother-in-law, Ken, gathered the sheep and left them in the pen at the sheep camp before they returned to the cottonwood tree. Leon waited under the tree while Ken drove the truck through the deep sand to the edge of the arroyo. He squinted up at the sun and unzipped his jacket — it sure was hot for this time of year. But high and northwest the blue mountains were still in snow. Ken came sliding down the low, crumbling bank about fifty yards down, and he was bringing the red blanket.

Before they wrapped the old man, Leon took a piece of string out of his pocket and tied a small gray feather in the old man's long white hair. Ken gave him the paint. Across the brown wrinkled forehead he drew a streak of white and along the high cheekbones he drew a strip of blue paint. He paused and watched Ken throw pinches of corn meal and pollen into the wind that fluttered the small gray feather. Then Leon painted with yellow under the old man's broad nose, and finally, when he had painted green across the chin, he smiled.

"Send us rain clouds, Grandfather." They laid the bundle in the back of the pickup and covered it with a heavy tarp before they started back to the pueblo.

They turned off the highway onto the sandy pueblo road. Not long after they passed the store and post office they saw Father Paul's car coming toward them. When he recognized their faces he slowed his car and waved for them to stop. The young priest rolled down the car window.

"Did you find old Teofilo?" he asked loudly.

Leon stopped the truck. "Good morning, Father. We were just out to the sheep camp. Everything is O.K. now."

"Thank God for that. Teofilo is a very old man. You really shouldn't allow him to stay at the sheep camp alone."

"No, he won't do that any more now."

"Well, I'm glad you understand. I hope I'll be seeing you at Mass this week — we missed you last Sunday. See if you can get old Teofilo to come with you." The priest smiled and waved at them as they drove away.

Louise and Teresa were waiting. The table was set for lunch, and the coffee was boiling on the black iron stove. Leon looked at Louise and then at Teresa.

"We found him under a cottonwood tree in the big arroyo near sheep camp. I guess he sat down to rest in the shade and never got up again." Leon walked toward the old man's bed. The red plaid shawl had been shaken and spread carefully over the bed, and a new brown flannel shirt and pair of stiff new Levi's were arranged neatly beside the pillow. Louise held the screen door open while Leon and Ken carried in the red blanket. He looked small and shriveled, and after they dressed him in the new shirt and pants he seemed more shrunken.

It was noontime now because the church bells rang the Angelus. They ate the beans with hot bread, and nobody said anything until after Teresa poured the coffee.

Ken stood up and put on his jacket. "I'll see about the gravediggers. Only the top layer of soil is frozen. I think it can be ready before dark."

Leon nodded his head and finished his coffee. After Ken had been gone for a while, the neighbors and clanspeople came quietly to embrace Teofilo's family and to leave food on the table because the gravediggers would come to eat when they were finished.

■ ■ ■

The sky in the west was full of pale yellow light. Louise stood outside with her hands in the pockets of Leon's green army jacket that was too big for her. The funeral was over, and the old men had taken their candles and medicine bags and were gone. She waited until the body was laid into the pickup before she said anything to Leon. She touched his arm, and he noticed that her hands were still dusty from the corn meal that she had sprinkled around the old man. When she spoke, Leon could not hear her.

"What did you say? I didn't hear you."

"I said that I had been thinking about something."

"About what?"

"About the priest sprinkling holy water for Grandpa. So he won't be thirsty."

Leon stared at the new moccasins that Teofilo had made for the ceremonial dances in the summer. They were nearly hidden by the red blanket. It was getting colder, and the wind pushed gray dust down the narrow pueblo road. The sun was approaching the long mesa where it disappeared during the winter. Louise stood there shivering and watching his face. Then he zipped up his jacket and opened the truck door. "I'll see if he's there."

Ken stopped the pickup at the church, and Leon got out; and then Ken drove down the hill to the graveyard where people were waiting. Leon knocked at the old carved door with its symbols of the Lamb. While he waited he looked up at the twin bells from the king of Spain with the last sunlight pouring around them in their tower.

The priest opened the door and smiled when he saw who it was. "Come in! What brings you here this evening?"

The priest walked toward the kitchen, and Leon stood with his cap in his hand, playing with the earflaps and examining the living room — the brown sofa, the green armchair, and the brass lamp that hung down from the ceiling by links of chain. The priest dragged a chair out of the kitchen and offered it to Leon.

"No thank you, Father. I only came to ask you if you would bring your holy water to the graveyard."

The priest turned away from Leon and looked out the window at the patio full of shadows and the dining-room windows of the nuns' cloister across the patio. The curtains were heavy, and the light from within faintly penetrated; it was impossible to see the nuns inside eating supper. "Why didn't you tell me he was dead? I could have brought the Last Rites anyway."

Leon smiled. "It wasn't necessary, Father."

The priest stared down at his scuffed brown loafers and the worn hem of his cassock. "For a Christian burial it was necessary."

His voice was distant, and Leon thought that his blue eyes looked tired.

"It's O.K., Father, we just want him to have plenty of water."

The priest sank down into the green chair and picked up a glossy missionary magazine. He turned the colored pages full of lepers and pagans without looking at them.

"You know I can't do that, Leon. There should have been the Last Rites and a funeral Mass at the very least."

Leon put on his green cap and pulled the flaps down over his ears. "It's getting late, Father. I've got to go."

When Leon opened the door Father Paul stood up and said, "Wait." He left the room and came back wearing a long brown overcoat. He followed Leon out the door and across the dim churchyard to the adobe steps in front of the church. They both stooped to fit through the low adobe entrance. And when they started down the hill to the graveyard only half of the sun was visible above the mesa.

The priest approached the grave slowly, wondering how they had managed to dig into the frozen ground; and then he remembered that this was New Mexico, and saw the pile of cold loose sand beside the hole. The people stood close to each other with little clouds of steam puffing from their faces. The priest looked at them and saw a pile of jackets, gloves, and scarves in the yellow, dry tumbleweeds that grew in the graveyard. He looked at the red blanket, not sure that Teofilo was so small, wondering if it wasn't some perverse Indian trick — something they did in March to ensure a good harvest — wondering if maybe old Teofilo was actually at sheep camp corralling the sheep for the night. But there he was, facing into a cold dry wind and squinting at the last sunlight, ready to bury a red wool blanket while the faces of his parishioners were in shadow with the last warmth of the sun on their backs.

His fingers were stiff, and it took him a long time to twist the lid off the holy water. Drops of water fell on the red blanket and soaked into dark icy spots. He sprinkled the grave and the water disappeared almost before it touched the dim, cold sand; it reminded him of something — he tried to remember what it was, because he thought if he could remember he might understand this. He sprinkled more water; he shook the container until it was empty, and the water fell through the light from sundown like August rain that fell while the sun was still shining, almost evaporating before it touched the wilted squash flowers.

The wind pulled at the priest's brown Franciscan robe and swirled away the corn meal and pollen that had been sprinkled on the blanket. They lowered the bundle into the ground, and they didn't bother to untie the stiff pieces of new rope that were tied around the ends of the blanket. The sun was gone, and over on the highway the eastbound lane was full of headlights. The priest walked away slowly. Leon watched him climb the hill, and when he had disappeared within the tall, thick walls, Leon turned to look up at the high blue mountains in the deep snow that reflected a faint red light from the west. He felt good because it was finished, and he was happy about the sprinkling of the holy water; now the old man could send them big thunderclouds for sure.

JOHN STEINBECK *(1902–1968) was born in Salinas and raised near Monterey in the fertile farm country of the Salinas Valley in California, the locale for his story "The Chrysanthemums." His mother was a former schoolteacher; his father was the county treasurer. In high school Steinbeck wrote for the school newspaper and was president of his class. He enjoyed literature from an early age and read novels by Gus-*

tave Flaubert, Fyodor Dostoevsky, and Thomas Hardy in the family library. Enrolled at Stanford University as an English major, Steinbeck dropped out before graduating and worked at odd jobs — fruit picker, caretaker, laboratory assistant — while he practiced writing fiction. Several times he took short-term jobs with the Spreckels Sugar Company and gained a perspective on labor problems, which he would later describe in his novels.

In 1929 Steinbeck began his literary career by publishing Cup of Gold, *a fictionalized biography of Henry Morgan, the seventeenth-century Welsh pirate. His next book,* The Pastures of Heaven *(1932), is a collection of short stories about the people in a farm community in California. The critic Brian Barbour has stated that Steinbeck realized early in his career that the short story form was not congenial to his talents. He needed the more expansive form of the novel to give his characters the room for what he considered real growth. In 1936 Steinbeck wrote* In Dubious Battle, *his first major political novel. He then published four more novels and another book of short fiction before his greatest work,* The Grapes of Wrath *(1939). This book, about a family from the Dust Bowl who emigrates to California and struggles to make a living despite agricultural exploitation, won Steinbeck the Pulitzer Prize. Among his many other successful novels are* East of Eden *(1952) and* The Winter of Our Discontent *(1961). He received the Nobel Prize for literature in 1962.*

One of the most accomplished popular novelists in the United States, Steinbeck excelled — as did Ernest Hemingway — in the creation of exciting conflicts, convincing dialogue, and recognizable characters to dramatize his philosophy of life. Although his production of short stories was relatively slight, his work is often anthologized because of his clear, realistic treatment of social themes as his characters struggle to forge meaningful lives. "The Chrysanthemums" echoes the D. H. Lawrence story "Odour of Chrysanthemums" in its concerns with sexual roles and the difficulty of striking a balance between self-interest and the needs of others. Steinbeck's biographer, Jackson J. Benson, also commented that the excellence of "The Chrysanthemums" lies in "its delicate, indirect handling of a woman's emotions . . . [especially] the difficulty of the woman in finding a creative significant role in a male-dominated society."

JOHN STEINBECK

The Chrysanthemums

1938

The high grey-flannel fog of winter closed off the Salinas Valley from the sky and from all the rest of the world. On every side it sat like a lid on the mountains and made of the great valley a closed pot. On the broad, level land floor the gang plows bit deep and left the black earth shining like metal where the shares had cut. On the foothill ranches across the Salinas River, the yellow stubble fields seemed to be bathed in pale cold sunshine, but there was no sunshine in the valley now in December. The thick willow scrub along the river flamed with sharp and positive yellow leaves.

It was a time of quiet and of waiting. The air was cold and tender. A light wind blew up from the southwest so that the farmers were mildly hopeful of a good rain before long; but fog and rain do not go together.

Across the river, on Henry Allen's foothill ranch there was little work to be done, for the hay was cut and stored and the orchards were plowed up to receive the rain deeply when it should come. The cattle on the higher slopes were becoming shaggy and rough-coated.

Elisa Allen, working in her flower garden, looked down across the yard and saw Henry, her husband, talking to two men in business suits. The three of them stood by the tractor shed, each man with one foot on the side of the little Fordson. They smoked cigarettes and studied the machine as they talked.

Elisa watched them for a moment and then went back to her work. She was thirty-five. Her face was lean and strong and her eyes were as clear as water. Her figure looked blocked and heavy in her gardening costume, a man's black hat pulled low down over her eyes, clod-hopper shoes, a figured print dress almost completely covered by a big corduroy apron with four big pockets to hold the snips, the trowel and scratcher, the seeds, and the knife she worked with. She wore heavy leather gloves to protect her hands while she worked.

She was cutting down the old year's chrysanthemum stalks with a pair of short and powerful scissors. She looked down toward the men by the tractor shed now and then. Her face was eager and mature and handsome; even her work with the scissors was overeager, overpowerful. The chrysanthemum stems seemed too small and easy for her energy.

She brushed a cloud of hair out of her eyes with the back of her glove, and left a smudge of earth on her cheek in doing it. Behind her stood the neat white farm house with red geraniums close-banked around it as high as the windows. It was a hard-swept looking little house with hard-polished windows, and a clean mud-mat on the front steps.

Elisa cast another glance toward the tractor shed. The strangers were getting into their Ford coupe. She took off a glove and put her strong fingers down into the forest of new green chrysanthemum sprouts that were growing around the old roots. She spread the leaves and looked down among the close-growing stems. No aphids were there, no sowbugs or snails or cutworms. Her terrier fingers destroyed such pests before they could get started.

Elisa started at the sound of her husband's voice. He had come near quietly, and he leaned over the wire fence that protected her flower garden from cattle and dogs and chickens.

"At it again," he said. "You've got a strong new crop coming."

Elisa straightened her back and pulled on the gardening glove again. "Yes. They'll be strong this coming year." In her tone and on her face there was a little smugness.

"You've got a gift with things," Henry observed. "Some of those yellow chrysanthemums you had this year were ten inches across. I wish you'd work out in the orchard and raise some apples that big."

Her eyes sharpened. "Maybe I could do it, too. I've a gift with things, all right. My mother had it. She could stick anything in the ground and make it grow. She said it was having planters' hands that knew how to do it."

"Well, it sure works with flowers," he said.

"Henry, who were those men you were talking to?"

"Why, sure, that's what I came to tell you. They were from the Western

Meat Company. I sold thirty head of three-year-old steers. Got nearly my own price, too."

"Good," she said. "Good for you."

"And I thought," he continued, "I thought how it's Saturday afternoon, and we might go into Salinas for dinner at a restaurant, and then to a picture show — to celebrate, you see."

"Good," she repeated. "Oh, yes. That will be good."

Henry put on his joking tone. "There's fights tonight. How'd you like to go to the fights?"

"Oh, no," she said breathlessly. "No, I wouldn't like fights."

"Just fooling, Elisa. We'll go to a movie. Let's see. It's two now. I'm going to take Scotty and bring down those steers from the hill. It'll take us maybe two hours. We'll go in town about five and have dinner at the Cominos Hotel. Like that?"

"Of course I'll like it. It's good to eat away from home."

"All right, then. I'll go get up a couple of horses."

She said, "I'll have plenty of time to transplant some of these sets, I guess."

She heard her husband calling Scotty down by the barn. And a little later she saw the two men ride up the pale yellow hillside in search of the steers.

There was a little square sandy bed kept for rooting the chrysanthemums. With her trowel she turned the soil over and over, and smoothed it and patted it firm. Then she dug ten parallel trenches to receive the sets. Back at the chrysanthemum bed she pulled out the little crisp shoots, trimmed off the leaves at each one with her scissors, and laid it on a small orderly pile.

A squeak of wheels and plod of hoofs came from the road. Elisa looked up. The country road ran along the dense bank of willows and cottonwoods that bordered the river, and up this road came a curious vehicle, curiously drawn. It was an old spring-wagon, with a round canvas top on it like the corner of a prairie schooner. It was drawn by an old bay horse and a little grey-and-white burro. A big stubble-bearded man sat between the cover flaps and drove the crawling team. Underneath the wagon, between the hind wheels, a lean and rangy mongrel dog walked sedately. Words were painted on the canvas, in clumsy, crooked letters. "Pots, pans, knives, sisors, lawn mores, Fixed." Two rows of articles, and the triumphantly definitive "Fixed" below. The black paint had run down in little sharp points beneath each letter.

Elisa, squatting on the ground, watched to see the crazy, loose-jointed wagon pass by. But it didn't pass. It turned into the farm road in front of her house, crooked old wheels skirling and squeaking. The rangy dog darted from between the wheels and ran ahead. Instantly the two ranch shepherds flew out at him. Then all three stopped, and with stiff and quivering tails, with taut straight legs, with ambassadorial dignity, they slowly circled, sniffing daintily. The caravan pulled up to Elisa's wire fence and stopped. Now the newcomer dog, feeling outnumbered, lowered his tail and retired under the wagon with raised hackles and bared teeth.

The man on the seat called out, "That's a bad dog in a fight when he gets started."

Elisa laughed. "I see he is. How soon does he generally get started?"

The man caught up her laughter and echoed it heartily. "Sometimes not for weeks and weeks," he said. He climbed stiffly down, over the wheel. The horse and the donkey dropped like unwatered flowers.

Elisa saw that he was a very big man. Although his hair and beard were greying, he did not look old. His worn black suit was wrinkled and spotted with grease. The laughter had disappeared from his face and eyes the moment his laughing voice ceased. His eyes were dark, and they were full of the brooding that gets in the eyes of teamsters and of sailors. The calloused hands he rested on the wire fence were cracked, and every crack was a black line. He took off his battered hat.

"I'm off my general road, ma'am," he said. "Does this dirt road cut over across the river to the Los Angeles highway?"

Elisa stood up and shoved the thick scissors in her apron pocket. "Well, yes, it does, but it winds around and then fords the river. I don't think your team could pull through the sand."

He replied with some asperity, "It might surprise you what them beasts can pull through."

"When they get started?" she asked.

He smiled for a second. "Yes. When they get started."

"Well," said Elisa, "I think you'll save time if you go back to the Salinas road and pick up the highway there."

He drew a big finger down the chicken wire and made it sing. "I ain't in any hurry, ma'am. I go from Seattle to San Diego and back every year. Takes all my time. About six months each way. I aim to follow nice weather."

Elisa took off her gloves and stuffed them in the apron pocket with the scissors. She touched the under edge of her man's hat, searching for fugitive hairs. "That sounds like a nice kind of a way to live," she said.

He leaned confidentially over the fence. "Maybe you noticed the writing on my wagon. I mend pots and sharpen knives and scissors. You got any of them things to do?"

"Oh, no," she said, quickly. "Nothing like that." Her eyes hardened with resistance.

"Scissors is the worst thing," he explained. "Most people just ruin scissors trying to sharpen 'em, but I know how. I got a special tool. It's a little bobbit kind of thing, and patented. But it sure does the trick."

"No. My scissors are all sharp."

"All right, then. Take a pot," he continued earnestly, "a bent pot, or a pot with a hole. I can make it like new so you don't have to buy no new ones. That's a savings for you."

"No," she said shortly. "I tell you I have nothing like that for you to do."

His face fell to an exaggerated sadness. His voice took on a whining undertone. "I ain't had a thing to do today. Maybe I won't have no supper tonight. You see I'm off my regular road. I know folks on the highway clear from Seattle to San Diego. They save their things for me to sharpen up because they know I do it so good and save them money."

"I'm sorry," Elisa said irritably. "I haven't anything for you to do."

His eyes left her face and fell to searching the ground. They roamed about until they came to the chrysanthemum bed where she had been working. "What's them plants, ma'am?"

The irritation and resistance melted from Elisa's face. "Oh, those are chrysanthemums, giant whites and yellows. I raise them every year, bigger than anybody around here."

"Kind of a long-stemmed flower? Looks like a quick puff of colored smoke?" he asked.

"That's it. What a nice way to describe them."

"They smell kind of nasty till you get used to them," he said.

"It's a good bitter smell," she retorted, "not nasty at all."

He changed his tone quickly, "I like the smell myself."

"I had ten-inch-blooms this year," she said.

The man leaned farther over the fence. "Look, I know a lady down the road a piece, has got the nicest garden you ever seen. Got nearly every kind of flower but no chrysanthemums. Last time I was mending a copper-bottom washtub for her (that's a hard job but I do it good), she said to me, 'If you ever run acrost some nice chrysanthemums I wish you'd try to get me a few seeds.' That's what she told me."

Elisa's eyes grew alert and eager. "She couldn't have known much about chrysanthemums. You *can* raise them from seed, but it's much easier to root the little sprouts you see there."

"Oh," he said. "I s'pose I can't take none to her, then."

"Why yes you can," Elisa cried. "I can put some in damp sand, and you can carry them right along with you. They'll take root in the pot if you keep them damp. And then she can transplant them."

"She'd sure like to have some, ma'am. You say they're nice ones?"

"Beautiful," she said. "Oh, beautiful." Her eyes shone. She tore off the battered hat and shook out her dark pretty hair. "I'll put them in a flower pot, and you can take them right with you. Come into the yard."

While the man came through the picket gate Elisa ran excitedly along the geranium-bordered path to the back of the house. And she returned carrying a big red flower pot. The gloves were forgotten now. She kneeled on the ground by the starting bed and dug up the sandy soil with her fingers and scooped it into the bright new flower pot. Then she picked up the little pile of shoots she had prepared. With her strong fingers she pressed them into the sand and tamped around them with her knuckles. The man stood over her. "I'll tell you what to do," she said. "You remember so you can tell the lady."

"Yes, I'll try to remember."

"Well, look. These will take root in about a month. Then she must set them out, about a foot apart in good rich earth like this, see?" She lifted a handful of dark soil for him to look at. "They'll grow fast and tall. Now remember this: In July tell her to cut them down, about eight inches from the ground."

"Before they bloom?" he asked.

"Yes, before they bloom." Her face was tight with eagerness. "They'll grow right up again. About the last of September the buds will start."

She stopped and seemed perplexed. "It's the budding that takes the most care," she said hesitantly. "I don't know how to tell you." She looked deep into his eyes, searchingly. Her mouth opened a little, and she seemed to be listening. "I'll try to tell you," she said. "Did you ever hear of planting hands?"

"Can't say I have, ma'am."

"Well, I can only tell you what it feels like. It's when you're picking off the buds you don't want. Everything goes right down into your fingertips. You watch your fingers work. They do it themselves. You can feel how it is. They pick and pick the buds. They never make a mistake. They're with the plant. Do you see? Your fingers and the plant. You can feel that, right up your arm. They know. They never make a mistake. You can feel it. When you're like that you can't do anything wrong. Do you see that? Can you understand that?"

She was kneeling on the ground looking up at him. Her breast swelled passionately.

The man's eyes narrowed. He looked away self-consciously. "Maybe I know," he said. "Sometimes in the night in the wagon there —"

Elisa's voice grew husky. She broke in on him, "I've never lived as you do, but I know what you mean. When the night is dark — why, the stars are sharp-pointed, and there's quiet. Why, you rise up and up! Every pointed star gets driven into your body. It's like that. Hot and sharp and — lovely."

Kneeling there, her hand went out toward his legs in the greasy black trousers. Her hesitant fingers almost touched the cloth. Then her hand dropped to the ground. She crouched low like a fawning dog.

He said, "It's nice, just like you say. Only when you don't have no dinner, it ain't."

She stood up then, very straight, and her face was ashamed. She held the flower pot out to him and placed it gently in his arms. "Here. Put it in your wagon, on the seat, where you can watch it. Maybe I can find something for you to do."

At the back of the house she dug in the can pile and found two old and battered aluminum saucepans. She carried them back and gave them to him. "Here, maybe you can fix these."

His manner changed. He became professional. "Good as new I can fix them." At the back of his wagon he set a little anvil, and out of an oily tool box dug a small machine hammer. Elisa came through the gate to watch him while he pounded out the dents in the kettles. His mouth grew sure and knowing. At a difficult part of the work he sucked his underlip.

"You sleep right in the wagon?" Elisa asked.

"Right in the wagon, ma'am. Rain or shine I'm dry as a cow in there."

"It must be nice," she said. "It must be very nice. I wish women could do such things."

"It ain't the right kind of a life for a woman."

Her upper lip raised a little, showing her teeth. "How do you know? How can you tell?" she said.

"I don't know, ma'am," he protested. "Of course I don't know. Now here's your kettles, done. You don't have to buy no new ones."

"How much?"

"Oh, fifty cents'll do. I keep my prices down and my work good. That's why I have all them satisfied customers up and down the highway."

Elisa brought him a fifty-cent piece from the house and dropped it in his hand. "You might be surprised to have a rival some time. I can sharpen scissors, too. And I can beat the dents out of little pots. I could show you what a woman might do."

He put his hammer back in the oily box and shoved the little anvil out of sight. "It would be a lonely life for a woman, ma'am, and a scarey life, too, with animals creeping under the wagon all night." He climbed over the singletree, steadying himself with a hand on the burro's white rump. He settled himself in the seat, picked up the lines. "Thank you kindly, ma'am," he said. "I'll do like you told me; I'll go back and catch the Salinas road."

"Mind," she called, "if you're long in getting there, keep the sand damp."

"Sand, ma'am? . . . Sand? Oh, sure. You mean around the chrysanthemums. Sure I will." He clucked his tongue. The beasts leaned luxuriously into their collars. The mongrel dog took his place between the back wheels. The wagon turned and crawled out the entrance road and back the way it had come, along the river.

Elisa stood in front of her wire fence watching the slow progress of the caravan. Her shoulders were straight, her head thrown back, her eyes half-closed, so that the scene came vaguely into them. Her lips moved silently, forming the words "Good-bye — good-bye." Then she whispered, "That's a bright direction. There's a glowing there." The sound of her whisper startled her. She shook herself free and looked about to see whether anyone had been listening. Only the dogs had heard. They lifted their heads toward her from their sleeping in the dust, and then stretched out their chins and settled asleep again. Elisa turned and ran hurriedly into the house.

In the kitchen she reached behind the stove and felt the water tank. It was full of hot water from the noonday cooking. In the bathroom she tore off her soiled clothes and flung them into the corner. And then she scrubbed herself with a little block of pumice, legs and thighs, loins and chest and arms, until her skin was scratched and red. When she had dried herself she stood in front of a mirror in her bedroom and looked at her body. She tightened her stomach and threw out her chest. She turned and looked over her shoulder at her back.

After a while she began to dress, slowly. She put on her newest underclothing and her nicest stockings and the dress which was the symbol of her prettiness. She worked carefully on her hair, penciled her eyebrows and rouged her lips.

Before she was finished she heard the little thunder of hoofs and the shouts of Henry and his helper as they drove the red steers into the corral. She heard the gate bang shut and set herself for Henry's arrival.

His step sounded on the porch. He entered the house calling, "Elisa, where are you?"

"In my room, dressing. I'm not ready. There's hot water for your bath. Hurry up. It's getting late."

When she heard him splashing in the tub, Elisa laid his dark suit on the bed, and shirt and socks and tie beside it. She stood his polished shoes on the floor beside the bed. Then she went to the porch and sat primly and stiffly down. She looked toward the river road where the willow-line was still yellow with frosted leaves so that under the high grey fog they seemed a thin band of sunshine. This was the only color in the grey afternoon. She sat unmoving for a long time. Her eyes blinked rarely.

Henry came banging out of the door, shoving his tie inside his vest as he came. Elisa stiffened and her face grew tight. Henry stopped short and looked at her. "Why — why, Elisa. You look so nice!"

"Nice? You think I look nice? What do you mean by 'nice'?"

Henry blundered on. "I don't know. I mean you look different, strong and happy."

"I am strong? Yes, strong. What do you mean 'strong'?"

He looked bewildered. "You're playing some kind of a game," he said helplessly. "It's a kind of a play. You look strong enough to break a calf over your knee, happy enough to eat it like a watermelon."

For a second she lost her rigidity. "Henry! Don't talk like that. You didn't know what you said." She grew complete again. "I'm strong," she boasted, "I never knew before how strong."

Henry looked down toward the tractor shed, and when he brought his eyes back to her, they were his own again. "I'll get out the car. You can put on your coat while I'm starting."

Elisa went into the house. She heard him drive to the gate and idle down his motor, and then she took a long time to put on her hat. She pulled it here and pressed it there. When Henry turned the motor off she slipped into her coat and went out.

The little roadster bounced along on the dirt road by the river, raising the birds and driving the rabbits into the brush. Two cranes flapped heavily over the willow-line and dropped into the river-bed.

Far ahead on the road Elisa saw a dark speck. She knew.

She tried not to look as they passed it, but her eyes would not obey. She whispered to herself sadly, "He might have thrown them off the road. That wouldn't have been much trouble, not very much. But he kept the pot," she explained. "He had to keep the pot. That's why he couldn't get them off the road."

The roadster turned a bend and she saw the caravan ahead. She swung full around toward her husband so she could not see the little covered wagon and the mismatched team as the car passed them.

In a moment it was over. The thing was done. She did not look back.

She said loudly, to be heard above the motor. "It will be good, tonight, a good dinner."

"Now you're changed again," Henry complained. He took one hand from the wheel and patted her knee. "I ought to take you in to dinner oftener. It would be good for both of us. We get so heavy out on the ranch."

"Henry," she asked, "could we have wine at dinner?"

"Sure we could. Say! That will be fine."

She was silent for a while; then she said, "Henry, at those prize fights, do the men hurt each other very much?"

"Sometimes a little, not often. Why?"

"Well, I've read how they break noses, and blood runs down their chests. I've read how the fighting gloves get heavy and soggy with blood."

He looked around at her. "What's the matter, Elisa? I didn't know you read things like that." He brought the car to a stop, then turned to the right over the Salinas River bridge.

"Do any women ever go to the fights?" she asked.

"Oh, sure, some. What's the matter Elisa? Do you want to go? I don't think you'd like it, but I'll take you if you really want to go."

She relaxed limply in the seat. "Oh, no. No. I don't want to go. I'm sure I don't." Her face was turned away from him. "It will be enough if we can have wine. It will be plenty." She turned up her coat collar so he could not see that she was crying weakly — like an old woman.

AMY TAN *(b. 1952) was born in Oakland, California. Her father was educated as an engineer in Beijing; her mother left China in 1949, just before the communist revolution. Tan remembers that as a child she felt like an American girl trapped in a Chinese body: "There was shame and self-hate. There is this myth that America is a melting pot, but what happens in assimilation is that we end up deliberately choosing the American things — hot dogs and apple pie — and ignoring the Chinese offerings."*

After her father's death, Tan and her mother lived in Switzerland, where she attended high school. "I was a novelty," she recalls. "There were so few Asians in Europe that everywhere I went people stared. Europeans asked me out. I had never been asked out in America." After attending a small college in Oregon, she worked for IBM as a writer of computer manuals. In 1984 Tan and her mother visited China and met her relatives; there she made the important discovery, as she has said, that "I belonged to my family and my family belonged to China." A year later, back in San Francisco, Tan read Louise Erdrich's Love Medicine *and was so impressed by the power of its interlocking stories about another cultural minority, American Indians, that she began to write short stories herself. One of them was published in a little magazine read by a literary agent in San Diego, who urged Tan to outline a book about the conflicts between different cultures and generations of Chinese mothers and daughters in the United States. After her agent negotiated a $50,000 advance from Putnam, Tan worked full-time on the first draft of her book* The Joy Luck Club *(1989) and finished it in four months.*

"Two Kinds" is an excerpt from that novel. At first Tan thought her book contract was "all a token minority thing. I thought they had to fill a quota since there weren't many Chinese Americans writing." But her book was a best-seller and was nominated for a National Book Award. As the novelist Valerie Miner has recognized, Tan's special gifts are her storytelling ability and her "remarkable ear for dialogue and dialect, representing the choppy English of the mother and the sloppy California vernacular of the daughter with a sensitive authenticity." At the heart of Tan's book is the tough bond between mother and daughter. "I'm my own person," the daughter says. "How can she be her own person," the mother answers. "When did I give her up?" Tan has also published two other novels, The Kitchen God's Wife *(1991) and* The Hundred Secret Senses *(1995).*

RELATED COMMENTARY: *Amy Tan, "In the Canon, For All the Wrong Reasons," page 722.*

Amy Tan

Two Kinds

1989

My mother believed you could be anything you wanted to be in America. You could open a restaurant. You could work for the government and get good retirement. You could buy a house with almost no money down. You could become rich. You could become instantly famous.

"Of course you can be prodigy, too," my mother told me when I was nine. "You can be best anything. What does Auntie Lindo know? Her daughter, she is only best tricky."

America was where all my mother's hopes lay. She had come here in 1949 after losing everything in China: her mother and father, her family home, her first husband, and two daughters, twin baby girls. But she never looked back with regret. There were so many ways for things to get better.

We didn't immediately pick the right kind of prodigy. At first my mother thought I could be a Chinese Shirley Temple. We'd watch Shirley's old movies on TV as though they were training films. My mother would poke my arm and say, *"Ni kan"* — You watch. And I would see Shirley tapping her feet, or singing a sailor song, or pursing her lips into a very round O while saying, "Oh my goodness."

"Ni kan," said my mother as Shirley's eyes flooded with tears. "You already know how. Don't need talent for crying!"

Soon after my mother got this idea about Shirley Temple, she took me to a beauty training school in the Mission district and put me in the hands of a student who could barely hold the scissors without shaking. Instead of getting big fat curls, I emerged with an uneven mass of crinkly black fuzz. My mother dragged me off to the bathroom and tried to wet down my hair.

"You look like Negro Chinese," she lamented, as if I had done this on purpose.

The instructor of the beauty training school had to lop off these soggy clumps to make my hair even again. "Peter Pan is very popular these days," the instructor assured my mother. I now had hair the length of a boy's, with straight-across bangs that hung at a slant two inches above my eyebrows. I liked the haircut and it made me actually look forward to my future fame.

In fact, in the beginning, I was just as excited as my mother, maybe even more so. I pictured this prodigy part of me as many different images, trying each one on for size. I was a dainty ballerina girl standing by the curtains, waiting to hear the right music that would send me floating on my tiptoes. I was like the Christ child lifted out of the straw manger, crying with holy indignity. I was Cinderella stepping from her pumpkin carriage with sparkly cartoon music filling the air.

In all of my imaginings, I was filled with a sense that I would soon become *perfect*. My mother and father would adore me. I would be beyond reproach. I would never feel the need to sulk for anything.

But sometimes the prodigy in me became impatient. "If you don't hurry up and get me out of here, I'm disappearing for good," it warned. "And then you'll always be nothing."

Every night after dinner, my mother and I would sit at the Formica kitchen table. She would present new tests, taking her examples from stories of amazing children she had read in *Ripley's Believe It or Not,* or *Good Housekeeping, Reader's Digest,* and a dozen other magazines she kept in a pile in our bathroom. My mother got these magazines from people whose houses she cleaned. And since she cleaned many houses each week, we had a great assortment. She would look through them all, searching for stories about remarkable children.

The first night she brought out a story about a three-year-old boy who knew the capitals of all the states and even most of the European countries. A teacher was quoted as saying the little boy could also pronounce the names of the foreign cities correctly.

"What's the capital of Finland?" my mother asked me, looking at the magazine story.

All I knew was the capital of California, because Sacramento was the name of the street we lived on in Chinatown. "Nairobi!" I guessed, saying the most foreign word I could think of. She checked to see if that was possibly one way to pronounce "Helsinki" before showing me the answer.

The tests got harder — multiplying numbers in my head, finding the queen of hearts in a deck of cards, trying to stand on my head without using my hands, predicting the daily temperatures in Los Angeles, New York, and London.

One night I had to look at a page from the Bible for three minutes and then report everything I could remember. "Now Jehoshaphat had riches and honor in abundance and . . . that's all I remember, Ma," I said.

And after seeing my mother's disappointed face once again, something inside of me began to die. I hated the tests, the raised hopes and failed expectations. Before going to bed that night, I looked in the mirror above the bathroom sink and when I saw only my face staring back — and that it would always be this ordinary face — I began to cry. Such a sad, ugly girl! I made high-pitched noises like a crazed animal, trying to scratch out the face in the mirror.

And then I saw what seemed to be the prodigy side of me — because I had never seen that face before. I looked at my reflection, blinking so I could see more clearly. The girl staring back at me was angry, powerful. This girl and I were the same. I had new thoughts, willful thoughts, or rather thoughts filled with lots of won'ts. I won't let her change me, I promised myself. I won't be what I'm not.

So now on nights when my mother presented her tests, I performed listlessly, my head propped on one arm. I pretended to be bored. And I was. I got so bored I started counting the bellows of the foghorns out on the bay while my mother drilled me in other areas. The sound was comforting and reminded me of the cow jumping over the moon. And the next day, I played a game with myself, seeing if my mother would give up on me before eight bellows. After a while I usually counted only one, maybe two bellows at most. At last she was beginning to give up hope.

Two or three months had gone by without any mention of my being a prodigy again. And then one day my mother was watching *The Ed Sullivan Show* on TV. The TV was old and the sound kept shorting out. Every time my mother got halfway up from the sofa to adjust the set, the sound would go back on and Ed would be talking. As soon as she sat down, Ed would go silent again. She got up, the TV broke into loud piano music. She sat down. Silence. Up and down, back and forth, quiet and loud. It was like a stiff embraceless dance between her and the TV set. Finally she stood by the set with her hand on the sound dial.

She seemed entranced by the music, a little frenzied piano piece with this mesmerizing quality, sort of quick passages and then teasing lilting ones before it returned to the quick playful parts.

"Ni kan," my mother said, calling me over with hurried hand gestures. "Look here."

I could see why my mother was fascinated by the music. It was being pounded out by a little Chinese girl, about nine years old, with a Peter Pan haircut. The girl had the sauciness of a Shirley Temple. She was proudly modest like a proper Chinese child. And she also did this fancy sweep of a curtsy, so that the fluffy skirt of her white dress cascaded slowly to the floor like the petals of a large carnation.

In spite of these warning signs, I wasn't worried. Our family had no piano and we couldn't afford to buy one, let alone reams of sheet music and piano lessons. So I could be generous in my comments when my mother badmouthed the little girl on TV.

"Play note right, but doesn't sound good! No singing sound," complained my mother.

"What are you picking on her for?" I said carelessly. "She's pretty good. Maybe she's not the best, but she's trying hard." I knew almost immediately I would be sorry I said that.

"Just like you," she said. "Not the best. Because you not trying." She gave a little huff as she let go of the sound dial and sat down on the sofa.

The little Chinese girl sat down also to play an encore of "Anitra's Dance" by Grieg. I remember the song, because later on I had to learn how to play it.

Three days after watching *The Ed Sullivan Show,* my mother told me what my schedule would be for piano lessons and piano practice. She had talked to Mr. Chong, who lived on the first floor of our apartment building. Mr. Chong was a retired piano teacher and my mother had traded housecleaning services for weekly lessons and a piano for me to practice on every day, two hours a day, from four until six.

When my mother told me this, I felt as though I had been sent to hell. I whined and then kicked my foot a little when I couldn't stand it anymore.

"Why don't you like me the way I am? I'm *not* a genius! I can't play the piano. And even if I could, I wouldn't go on TV if you paid me a million dollars!" I cried.

My mother slapped me. "Who ask you be genius?" she shouted. "Only ask you be your best. For you sake. You think I want you be genius? Hnnh! What for! Who ask you!"

"So ungrateful," I heard her mutter in Chinese. "If she had as much talent as she has temper, she would be famous now."

Mr. Chong, whom I secretly nicknamed Old Chong, was very strange, always tapping his fingers to the silent music of an invisible orchestra. He looked ancient in my eyes. He had lost most of the hair on top of his head and he wore thick glasses and had eyes that always looked tired and sleepy. But he must have been younger than I thought, since he lived with his mother and was not yet married.

I met Old Lady Chong once and that was enough. She had this peculiar smell like a baby that had done something in its pants. And her fingers felt like a dead person's, like an old peach I once found in the back of the refrigerator; the skin just slid off the meat when I picked it up.

I soon found out why Old Chong had retired from teaching piano. He was deaf. "Like Beethoven!" he shouted to me. "We're both listening only in our head!" And he would start to conduct his frantic silent sonatas.

Our lessons went like this. He would open the book and point to different things, explaining their purpose: "Key! Treble! Bass! No sharps or flats! So this is C major! Listen now and play after me!"

And then he would play the C scale a few times, a simple chord, and then, as if inspired by an old, unreachable itch, he gradually added more notes and running trills and a pounding bass until the music was really something quite grand.

I would play after him, the simple scale, the simple chord, and then I just played some nonsense that sounded like a cat running up and down on top of garbage cans. Old Chong smiled and applauded and then said, "Very good! But now you must learn to keep time!"

So that's how I discovered that Old Chong's eyes were too slow to keep up with the wrong notes I was playing. He went through the motions in half-time. To help me keep rhythm, he stood behind me, pushing down on my right shoulder for every beat. He balanced pennies on top of my wrists so I would keep them still as I slowly played scales and arpeggios. He had me curve my hand around an apple and keep that shape when playing chords. He marched stiffly to show me how to make each finger dance up and down, staccato like an obedient little soldier.

He taught me all these things, and that was how I also learned I could be lazy and get away with mistakes, lots of mistakes. If I hit the wrong notes because I hadn't practiced enough, I never corrected myself. I just kept playing in rhythm. And Old Chong kept conducting his own private reverie.

So maybe I never really gave myself a fair chance. I did pick up the basics pretty quickly, and I might have become a good pianist at that young age. But I was so determined not to try, not to be anybody different that I learned to play only the most ear-splitting preludes, the most discordant hymns.

Over the next year, I practiced like this, dutifully in my own way. And then one day I heard my mother and her friend Lindo Jong both talking in a loud bragging tone of voice so others could hear. It was after church, and I was leaning against the brick wall wearing a dress with stiff white petticoats. Auntie Lindo's daughter, Waverly, who was about my age, was standing farther down the wall about five feet away. We had grown up together and shared all the closeness of two sisters squabbling over crayons and dolls. In other words, for the most part, we hated each other. I thought she was snotty. Waverly Jong had gained a certain amount of fame as "Chinatown's Littlest Chinese Chess Champion."

"She bring home too many trophy," lamented Auntie Lindo that Sunday. "All day she play chess. All day I have no time do nothing but dust off her winnings." She threw a scolding look at Waverly, who pretended not to see her.

"You lucky you don't have this problem," said Auntie Lindo with a sigh to my mother.

And my mother squared her shoulders and bragged: "Our problem worser than yours. If we ask Jing-mei wash dish, she hear nothing but music. It's like you can't stop this natural talent."

And right then, I was determined to put a stop to her foolish pride.

A few weeks later, Old Chong and my mother conspired to have me play in a talent show which would be held in the church hall. By then, my parents had saved up enough to buy me a secondhand piano, a black Wurlitzer spinet with a scarred bench. It was the showpiece of our living room.

For the talent show, I was to play a piece called "Pleading Child" from Schumann's *Scenes from Childhood.* It was a simple, moody piece that sounded more difficult than it was. I was supposed to memorize the whole thing, playing the repeat parts twice to make the piece sound longer. But I dawdled over it, playing a few bars and then cheating, looking up to see what notes followed. I never really listened to what I was playing. I daydreamed about being somewhere else, about being someone else.

The part I liked to practice best was the fancy curtsy: right foot out, touch the rose on the carpet with a pointed foot, sweep to the side, left leg bends, look up and smile.

My parents invited all the couples from the Joy Luck Club to witness my debut. Auntie Lindo and Uncle Tin were there. Waverly and her two older brothers had also come. The first two rows were filled with children both younger and older than I was. The littlest ones got to go first. They recited simple nursery rhymes, squawked out tunes on miniature violins, twirled Hula Hoops, pranced in pink ballet tutus, and when they bowed or curtsied, the audience would sigh in unison, "Awww," and then clap enthusiastically.

When my turn came, I was very confident. I remember my childish excitement. It was as if I knew, without a doubt, that the prodigy side of me really did exist. I had no fear whatsoever, no nervousness. I remember thinking to myself,

This is it! This is it! I looked out over the audience, at my mother's blank face, my father's yawn, Auntie Lindo's stiff-lipped smile, Waverly's sulky expression. I had on a white dress layered with sheets of lace, and a pink bow in my Peter Pan haircut. As I sat down I envisioned people jumping to their feet and Ed Sullivan rushing up to introduce me to everyone on TV.

And I started to play. It was so beautiful. I was so caught up in how lovely I looked that at first I didn't worry how I would sound. So it was a surprise to me when I hit the first wrong note and I realized something didn't sound quite right. And then I hit another and another followed that. A chill started at the top of my head and began to trickle down. Yet I couldn't stop playing, as though my hands were bewitched. I kept thinking my fingers would adjust themselves back, like a train switching to the right track. I played this strange jumble through two repeats, the sour notes staying with me all the way to the end.

When I stood up, I discovered my legs were shaking. Maybe I had just been nervous and the audience, like Old Chong, had seen me go through the right motions and had not heard anything wrong at all. I swept my right foot out, went down on my knee, looked up and smiled. The room was quiet, except for Old Chong, who was beaming and shouting, "Bravo! Bravo! Well done!" But then I saw my mother's face, her stricken face. The audience clapped weakly, and as I walked back to my chair, with my whole face quivering as I tried not to cry, I heard a little boy whisper loudly to his mother, "That was awful," and the mother whispered back, "Well, she certainly tried."

And now I realized how many people were in the audience, the whole world it seemed. I was aware of eyes burning into my back. I felt the shame of my mother and father as they sat stiffly throughout the rest of the show.

We could have escaped during intermission. Pride and some strange sense of honor must have anchored my parents to their chairs. And so we watched it all: the eighteen-year-old boy with a fake mustache who did a magic show and juggled flaming hoops while riding a unicycle. The breasted girl with white makeup who sang from *Madama Butterfly* and got honorable mention. And the eleven-year-old boy who won first prize playing a tricky violin song that sounded like a busy bee.

After the show, the Hsus, the Jongs, and the St. Clairs from the Joy Luck Club came up to my mother and father.

"Lots of talented kids," Auntie Lindo said vaguely, smiling broadly.

"That was somethin' else," said my father, and I wondered if he was referring to me in a humorous way, or whether he even remembered what I had done.

Waverly looked at me and shrugged her shoulders. "You aren't a genius like me," she said matter-of-factly. And if I hadn't felt so bad, I would have pulled her braids and punched her stomach.

But my mother's expression was what devastated me: a quiet, blank look that said she had lost everything. I felt the same way, and it seemed as if everybody were now coming up, like gawkers at the scene of an accident, to see what parts were actually missing. When we got on the bus to go home, my father was humming the busy-bee tune and my mother was silent. I kept thinking she wanted to wait until we got home before shouting at me. But when my father unlocked the door to our apartment, my mother walked in and then went to the back, into the bedroom. No accusations. No blame. And in a way, I felt disappointed. I had been waiting for her to start shouting, so I could shout back and cry and blame her for all my misery.

I assumed my talent-show fiasco meant I never had to play the piano again. But two days later, after school, my mother came out of the kitchen and saw me watching TV.

"Four clock," she reminded me as if it were any other day. I was stunned, as though she were asking me to go through the talent-show torture again. I wedged myself more tightly in front of the TV.

"Turn off TV," she called from the kitchen five minutes later.

I didn't budge. And then I decided. I didn't have to do what my mother said anymore. I wasn't her slave. This wasn't China. I had listened to her before and look what happened. She was the stupid one.

She came out from the kitchen and stood in the arched entryway of the living room. "Four clock," she said once again, louder.

"I'm not going to play anymore," I said nonchalantly. "Why should I? I'm not a genius."

She walked over and stood in front of the TV. I saw her chest was heaving up and down in an angry way.

"No!" I said, and I now felt stronger, as if my true self had finally emerged. So this was what had been inside me all along.

"No! I won't!" I screamed.

She yanked me by the arm, pulled me off the floor, snapped off the TV. She was frighteningly strong, half pulling, half carrying me toward the piano as I kicked the throw rugs under my feet. She lifted me up and onto the hard bench. I was sobbing by now, looking at her bitterly. Her chest was heaving even more and her mouth was open, smiling crazily as if she were pleased I was crying.

"You want me to be someone that I'm not!" I sobbed. "I'll never be the kind of daughter you want me to be!"

"Only two kinds of daughters," she shouted in Chinese. "Those who are obedient and those who follow their own mind! Only one kind of daughter can live in this house. Obedient daughter!"

"Then I wish I wasn't your daughter. I wish you weren't my mother," I shouted. As I said these things I got scared. I felt like worms and toads and slimy things were crawling out of my chest, but it also felt good, as if this awful side of me had surfaced, at last.

"Too late change this," said my mother shrilly.

And I could sense her anger rising to its breaking point. I wanted to see it spill over. And that's when I remembered the babies she had lost in China, the ones we never talked about. "Then I wish I'd never been born!" I shouted. "I wish I were dead! Like them."

It was as if I had said the magic words, Alakazam! — and her face went blank, her mouth closed, her arms went slack, and she backed out of the room, stunned, as if she were blowing away like a small brown leaf, thin, brittle, lifeless.

It was not the only disappointment my mother felt in me. In the years that followed, I failed her so many times, each time asserting my own will, my right to fall short of expectations. I didn't get straight As. I didn't become class president. I didn't get into Stanford. I dropped out of college.

For unlike my mother, I did not believe I could be anything I wanted to be. I could only be me.

And for all those years, we never talked about the disaster at the recital or my terrible accusations afterward at the piano bench. All that remained unchecked, like a betrayal that was now unspeakable. So I never found a way to ask her why she had hoped for something so large that failure was inevitable.

And even worse, I never asked her what frightened me the most: Why had she given up hope?

For after our struggle at the piano, she never mentioned my playing again. The lessons stopped, the lid to the piano was closed, shutting out the dust, my misery, and her dreams.

So she surprised me. A few years ago, she offered to give me the piano, for my thirtieth birthday. I had not played in all those years. I saw the offer as a sign of forgiveness, a tremendous burden removed.

"Are you sure?" I asked shyly. "I mean, won't you and Dad miss it?"

"No, this your piano," she said firmly. "Always your piano. You only one can play."

"Well, I probably can't play anymore," I said. "It's been years."

"You pick up fast," said my mother, as if she knew this was certain. "You have natural talent. You could been genius if you want to."

"No I couldn't."

"You just not trying," said my mother. And she was neither angry nor sad. She said it as if to announce a fact that could never be disproved. "Take it," she said.

But I didn't at first. It was enough that she had offered it to me. And after that, every time I saw it in my parents' living room, standing in front of the bay windows, it made me feel proud, as if it were a shiny trophy I had won back.

Last week I sent a tuner over to my parents' apartment and had the piano reconditioned, for purely sentimental reasons. My mother had died a few months before and I had been getting things in order for my father, a little bit at a time. I put the jewelry in special silk pouches. The sweaters she had knitted in yellow, pink, bright orange — all the colors I hated — I put those in moth-proof boxes. I found some old Chinese silk dresses, the kind with little slits up the sides. I rubbed the old silk against my skin, then wrapped them in tissue and decided to take them home with me.

After I had the piano tuned, I opened the lid and touched the keys. It sounded even richer than I remembered. Really, it was a very good piano. Inside the bench were the same exercise notes with handwritten scales, the same secondhand music books with their covers held together with yellow tape.

I opened up the Schumann book to the dark little piece I had played at the recital. It was on the left-hand side of the page, "Pleading Child." It looked more difficult than I remembered. I played a few bars, surprised at how easily the notes came back to me.

And for the first time, or so it seemed, I noticed the piece on the right-hand side. It was called "Perfectly Contented." I tried to play this one as well. It had a lighter melody but the same flowing rhythm and turned out to be quite easy. "Pleading Child" was shorter but slower; "Perfectly Contented" was longer but faster. And after I played them both a few times, I realized they were two halves of the same song.

JOHN UPDIKE *(b. 1932) was born in Shillington, Pennsylvania, an only child. His father taught algebra in a local high school, and his mother wrote short stories and novels. His mother's consciousness of a special destiny, combined with his family's meager income — they lived with his mother's parents for the first thirteen years of Updike's life — made him "both arrogant and shy" as a teenager. He wrote stories, drew cartoons, and clowned for the approval of his peers. After getting straight A's in high school, he went to Harvard University on a full scholarship, studying English and graduating summa cum laude in 1954. He spent a year at Oxford on a fellowship, then joined the staff of* The New Yorker. *In 1959 Updike published both his first book of short fiction,* The Same Door, *and his first novel,* The Poorhouse Fair. *That year he also moved from New York City to a coastal town in Massachusetts, where he has lived most of the time since.*

In the 1960s, 1970s, and early 1980s, Updike continued to alternate novels and collections of stories, adding occasional volumes of verse, collections of essays, and one play. His novels include Rabbit, Run *(1960),* Couples *(1968),* Rabbit Redux *(1971), and* Marry Me *(1976).* Rabbit Is Rich *(1981), continuing the story of Harry "Rabbit" Angstrom, a suburban Pennsylvanian whom Updike has traced through adolescence, marriage, fatherhood, and middle age, won virtually every major American literary award for the year it appeared; Updike concluded the series with* Rabbit at Rest *(1991). Updike's collections of stories include* Pigeon Feathers *(1962),* Museums and Women *(1972), and* Problems and Other Stories *(1981). In 1983 Updike won the National Book Critics Circle Award for his collection of essays and criticism* Hugging the Shore. *In 1989 he published his memoirs,* Self-Consciousness. *Among his many recent books is another collection,* Philadelphia and Other Stories *(1995).*

Updike has said he is indebted to J. D. Salinger's stories for the literary form he adopted to describe the painful experience of adolescence: "I learned a lot from Salinger's short stories; he did remove the short narrative from the wise-guy, slice-of-life stories of the thirties and forties. Like most innovative artists, he made new room for shapelessness, for life as it is lived." Updike writes realistic narrative, believing that "fiction is a tissue of lies that refreshes and informs our sense of actuality. Reality is — chemically, atomically, biologically — a fabric of microscopic accuracies." His fiction, such as the story "A & P," concentrates on these "microscopic accuracies," tiny details of characterization and setting brilliantly described.

RELATED COMMENTARY: *John Updike, "Kafka and 'The Metamorphosis,'" page 733.*

John Updike

A & P

1961

In walks these three girls in nothing but bathing suits. I'm in the third checkout slot, with my back to the door, so I don't see them until they're over by the bread. The one that caught my eye first was the one in the plaid green two-piece. She was a chunky kid, with a good tan and a sweet broad soft-looking can with those two crescents of white just under it, where the sun never seems to hit, at the top of the backs of her legs. I stood there with my hand on a box of HiHo crackers trying to remember if I rang it up or not. I ring it up again and the customer starts giving me hell. She's one of these cash-register-watchers, a witch about fifty with rouge on her cheekbones and no eyebrows, and I know it made her day to trip me up. She'd been watching cash registers for fifty years and probably never seen a mistake before.

By the time I got her feathers smoothed and her goodies into a bag — she gives me a little snort in passing, if she'd been born at the right time they would have burned her over in Salem — by the time I get her on her way the girls had circled around the bread and were coming back, without a pushcart, back my way along the counters, in the aisle between the checkouts and the Special bins. They didn't even have shoes on. There was this chunky one, with the two-piece — it was bright green and the seams on the bra were still sharp and her belly was still pretty pale so I guessed she just got it (the suit) — there was this one, with one of those chubby berry-faces, the lips all bunched together under her nose, this one, and a tall one, with black hair that hadn't quite frizzed right, and one of these sunburns right across under the eyes, and a chin that was too long — you know, the kind of girl other girls think is very "striking" and "attractive" but never quite makes it, as they very well know, which is why they like her so much — and then the third one, that wasn't quite so tall. She was the queen. She kind of led them, the other two peeking around and making their shoulders round. She didn't look around, not this queen, she just walked straight on slowly, on these long white prima-donna legs. She came down a little hard on her heels, as if she didn't walk in her bare feet that much, putting down her heels and then letting the weight move along to her toes as if she was testing the floor with every step, putting a little deliberate extra action into it. You never know for sure how girls' minds work (do you really think it's a mind in there or just a little buzz like a bee in a glass jar?) but you got the idea she had talked the other two into coming in here with her, and now she was showing them how to do it, walk slow and hold yourself straight.

She had on a kind of dirty-pink — beige maybe, I don't know — bathing suit with a little nubble all over it, and what got me, the straps were down. They were off her shoulders looped loose around the cool tops of her arms, and I guess as a result the suit had slipped a little on her, so all around the top of the cloth there was this shining rim. If it hadn't been there you wouldn't have known there could have been anything whiter than those shoulders. With the straps pushed off, there was nothing between the top of the suit and the top of her head except just *her,* this clean bare plane of the top of her chest down from the shoulder bones like a dented sheet of metal tilted in the light. I mean, it was more than pretty.

She had sort of oaky hair that the sun and salt had bleached, done up in a bun that was unravelling, and a kind of prim face. Walking into the A & P with your straps down, I suppose it's the only kind of face you *can* have. She held her head so high her neck, coming up out of those white shoulders, looked kind of stretched, but I didn't mind. The longer her neck was, the more of her there was.

She must have felt in the corner of her eye me and over my shoulder Stokesie in the second slot watching, but she didn't tip. Not this queen. She kept her eyes moving across the racks, and stopped, and turned so slow it made my stomach rub the inside of my apron, and buzzed to the other two, who kind of huddled against her for relief, and then they all three of them went up the cat-and-dog-food-breakfast-cereal-macaroni-rice-raisins-seasonings-spreads-spaghetti-soft-drinks-crackers-and-cookies aisle. From the third slot I look straight up this aisle to the meat counter, and I watched them all the way. The fat one with the tan sort of fumbled with the cookies, but on second thought she put the package back. The sheep pushing their carts down the aisle — the girls were walking against the usual traffic (not that we have one-way signs or anything) — were pretty hilarious. You could see them, when Queenie's white shoulders dawned on them, kind of jerk, or hop, or hiccup, but their eyes snapped back to their own baskets and on they pushed. I bet you could set off dynamite in an A & P and the people would by and large keep reaching and checking oatmeal off their lists and muttering "Let me see, there was a third thing, began with A, asparagus, no, ah, yes, applesauce!" or whatever it is they do mutter. But there was no doubt, this jiggled them. A few houseslaves in pin curlers even looked around after pushing their carts past to make sure what they had seen was correct.

You know, it's one thing to have a girl in a bathing suit down on the beach, where what with the glare nobody can look at each other much anyway, and another thing in the cool of the A & P, under the fluorescent lights, against all those stacked packages, with her feet paddling along naked over our checkboard green-and-cream rubber-tile floor.

"Oh Daddy," Stokesie said beside me. "I feel so faint."

"Darling," I said. "Hold me tight." Stokesie's married, with two babies chalked up on his fuselage already, but as far as I can tell that's the only difference. He's twenty-two, and I was nineteen this April.

"Is it done?" he asks, the responsible married man finding his voice. I forgot to say he thinks he's going to be manager some sunny day, maybe in 1990 when it's called the Great Alexandrov and Petrooshki Tea Company or something.

What he meant was, our town is five miles from a beach, with a big summer colony out on the Point, but we're right in the middle of town, and the women generally put on a shirt or shorts or something before they get out of the car into the street. And anyway these are usually women with six children and varicose veins mapping their legs and nobody, including them, could care less. As I say, we're right in the middle of town, and if you stand at our front doors you can see two banks and the Congregational church and the newspaper store and three real-estate offices and about twenty-seven old freeloaders tearing up Central Street because the sewer broke again. It's not as if we're on the Cape; we're north of Boston and there's people in this town haven't seen the ocean for twenty years.

The girls had reached the meat counter and were asking McMahon something. He pointed, they pointed, and they shuffled out of sight behind a pyramid of Diet Delight peaches. All that was left for us to see was old McMahon patting his mouth and looking after them sizing up their joints. Poor kids, I began to feel sorry for them, they couldn't help it.

Now here comes the sad part of the story, at least my family says it's sad, but I don't think it's so sad myself. The store's pretty empty, it being Thursday afternoon, so there was nothing much to do except lean on the register and wait for the girls to show up again. The whole store was like a pinball machine and I didn't know which tunnel they'd come out of. After a while they come around out of the far aisle, around the light bulbs, records at discount of the Caribbean Six or Tony Martin Sings or some such gunk you wonder they waste the wax on, sixpacks of candy bars, and plastic toys done up in cellophane that fall apart when a kid looks at them anyway. Around they come, Queenie still leading the way, and holding a little gray jar in her hand. Slots Three through Seven are unmanned and I could see her wondering between Stokes and me, but Stokesie with his usual luck draws an old party in baggy gray pants who stumbles up with four giant cans of pineapple juice (what do these bums *do* with all that pineapple juice? I've often asked myself) so the girls come to me. Queenie puts down the jar and I take it into my fingers icy cold. Kingfish Fancy Herring Snacks in Pure Sour Cream: 49¢. Now her hands are empty, not a ring or a bracelet, bare as God made them, and I wonder where the money's coming from. Still with that prim look she lifts a folded dollar bill out of the hollow at the center of her nubbled pink top. The jar went heavy in my hand. Really, I thought that was so cute.

Then everybody's luck begins to run out. Lengel comes in from haggling with a truck full of cabbages on the lot and is about to scuttle into that door marked MANAGER behind which he hides all day when the girls touch his eye. Lengel's pretty dreary, teaches Sunday school and the rest, but he doesn't miss that much. He comes over and says, "Girls, this isn't the beach."

Queenie blushes, though maybe it's just a brush of sunburn I was noticing for the first time, now that she was so close. "My mother asked me to pick up a jar of herring snacks." Her voice kind of startled me, the way voices do when you see the people first, coming out so flat and dumb yet kind of tony, too, the way it ticked over "pick up" and "snacks." All of a sudden I slid right down her voice into her living room. Her father and the other men were standing around in ice-cream coats and bow ties and the women were in sandals picking up herring snacks on toothpicks off a big glass plate and they were all holding drinks the color of water with olives and sprigs of mint in them. When my parents have somebody over they get lemonade and if it's a real racy affair Schlitz in tall glasses with "They'll Do It Every Time" cartoons stencilled on.

"That's all right," Lengel said. "But this isn't the beach." His repeating this struck me as funny, as if it had just occurred to him, and he had been thinking all these years the A & P was a great big sand dune and he was the head lifeguard. He didn't like my smiling — as I say he doesn't miss much — but he concentrates on giving the girls that sad Sunday-school-superintendent stare.

Queenie's blush is no sunburn now, and the plump one in plaid, that I liked better from the back — a really sweet can — pipes up, "We weren't doing any shopping. We just came in for the one thing."

"That makes no difference," Lengel tells her, and I could see from the way his eyes went that he hadn't noticed she was wearing a two-piece before. "We want you decently dressed when you come in here."

"We *are* decent," Queenie says suddenly, her lower lip pushing, getting sore now that she remembers her place, a place from which the crowd that runs the A & P must look pretty crummy. Fancy Herring Snacks flashed in her very blue eyes.

"Girls, I don't want to argue with you. After this come in here with your shoulders covered. It's our policy." He turns his back. That's policy for you. Policy is what the kingpins want. What the others want is juvenile delinquency.

All this while, the customers had been showing up with their carts but, you know, sheep, seeing a scene, they had all bunched up on Stokesie, who shook open a paper bag as gently as peeling a peach, not wanting to miss a word. I could feel in the silence everybody getting nervous, most of all Lengel, who asks me, "Sammy, have you rung up their purchase?"

I thought and said "No" but it wasn't about that I was thinking. I go through the punches, 4, 9, GROC, TOT — it's more complicated than you think, and after you do it often enough, it begins to make a little song, that you hear words to, in my case "Hello (*bing*) there, you (*gung*) hap-py *pee*-pul (*splat*)!" — the *splat* being the drawer flying out. I uncrease the bill, tenderly as you may imagine, it just having come from between the two smoothest scoops of vanilla I had ever known were there, and pass a half and a penny into her narrow pink palm, and nestle the herrings in a bag and twist its neck and hand it over, all the time thinking.

The girls, and who'd blame them, are in a hurry to get out, so I say "I quit" to Lengel enough for them to hear, hoping they'll stop and watch me, their unsuspected hero. They keep right on going, into the electric eye; the door flies open and they flicker across the lot to their car, Queenie and Plaid and Big Tall Goony-Goony (not that as raw material she was so bad), leaving me with Lengel and a kink in his eyebrow.

"Did you say something, Sammy?"

"I said I quit."

"I thought you did."

"You didn't have to embarrass them."

"It was they who were embarrassing us."

I started to say something that came out "Fiddle-de-doo." It's a saying of my grandmother's, and I know she would have been pleased.

"I don't think you know what you're saying," Lengel said.

"I know you don't," I said. "But I do." I pull the bow at the back of my apron and start shrugging it off my shoulders. A couple customers that had been heading for my slot begin to knock against each other, like scared pigs in a chute.

Lengel sighs and begins to look very patient and old and gray. He's been a friend of my parents for years. "Sammy, you don't want to do this to your Mom and Dad," he tells me. It's true, I don't. But it seems to me that once you begin a gesture it's fatal not to go through with it. I fold the apron, "Sammy" stitched in red on the pocket, and put it on the counter, and drop the bow tie on top of it. The bow tie is theirs, if you've ever wondered. "You'll feel this for the rest of your life," Lengel says, and I know that's true, too, but remembering how he made that pretty girl blush makes me so scrunchy inside I punch the No Sale tab and the machine whirs "pee-pul" and the drawer splats out. One advantage to this scene taking place in summer, I can follow this up with a clean exit, there's no fumbling around getting your coat and galoshes, I just saunter into the electric eye in my white shirt that my mother ironed the night before, and the door heaves itself open, and outside the sunshine is skating around on the asphalt.

I look around for my girls, but they're gone, of course. There wasn't anybody but some young married screaming with her children about some candy they didn't get by the door of a powder-blue Falcon station wagon. Looking back in the big windows, over the bags of peat moss and aluminum lawn furniture stacked on the pavement, I could see Lengel in my place in the slot, checking the sheep through. His face was dark gray and his back stiff, as if he'd just had an injection of iron, and my stomach kind of fell as I felt how hard the world was going to be to me hereafter.

HELENA MARÍA VIRAMONTES *(b. 1954) was born in East Los Angeles, the daughter of a construction worker and a housewife who raised six daughters and three sons in a community that offered refuge for relatives and friends crossing the border from Mexico into California. As a child Viramontes witnessed "late night kitchen meetings where everyone talked and laughed in low voices" about having reached the United States,* el otro lado *("the other side"). After graduation from Garfield High School, Viramontes worked twenty hours a week while earning her B.A. from Immaculate Heart College, one of five Chicanas in her class. She then entered the graduate program at the University of California at Irvine as a creative writing student, but she left in 1981 and completed the requirements for the M.F.A. degree after the publication of her stories.*

As the critic Maria Herrera-Sobek has observed, "the 1980s decade witnessed an explosion in the literary output of Chicana authors," when Chicano-oriented publishers began to "risk investing in Mexican American women writers." Viramontes began to place her stories in small magazines such as Maize *and* XhismArte Magazine *as well as the anthology* Cuentos: Stories by Latinas *(1983). Her first book,* The Moths and Other Stories, *was published in 1985 by Arte Publico Press in Houston, Texas. The same year the University of California at Irvine sponsored the first national conference on Mexican American women writers, resulting in the volume* Beyond Stereotypes: A Critical Analysis of Chicana Literature *(1985). Three years later Viramontes helped organize a second Chicana writers conference at Irvine and coedited the anthology* Chicana Creativity and Criticism *(1988), in which "Miss Clairol" was first published. In 1989 Viramontes received a National Endowment for the Arts Fellowship grant; she was also selected by Gabriel García Márquez to participate in a ten-day storytelling workshop sponsored by the Sundance Institute in Utah. After this experience she began adapting one of her short stories into a film script. In 1993 she published her second book of short stories,* Paris Rats in E.L.A. *Her first novel,* Under the Feet of Jesus, *followed in 1995.*

As a woman of color, Viramontes believes that language is her most powerful tool for survival. She explains in "Why I Write" (1993) that "through writing, I have learned to protect the soles of my feet from the broken glass. . . . Writing is the only way I know how to pray."

Helena María Viramontes

Miss Clairol

1988

Arlene and Champ walk to K-Mart. The store is full of bins mounted with bargain buys from T-shirts to rubber sandals. They go to aisle 23, Cosmetics. Arlene, wearing bell bottom jeans two sizes too small, can't bend down to the Miss Clairol boxes, asks Champ.

— Which one mamá — asks Champ, chewing her thumb nail.

— Shit, mija,° I dunno. — Arlene smacks her gum, contemplating the decision. — Maybe I need a change, tú sabes.° What do you think? — She holds up a few blond strands with black roots. Arlene has burned the softness of her hair with peroxide; her hair is stiff, breaks at the ends and she needs plenty of Aqua Net hairspray to tease and tame her ratted hair, then folds it back into a high lump behind her head. For the last few months she has been a platinum "Light Ash" blond, before that a Miss Clairol "Flame" redhead, before that Champ couldn't even identify the color — somewhere between orange and brown, a "Sun Bronze." The only way Champ knows her mother's true hair color is by her roots which, like death, inevitably rise to the truth.

— I hate it, tú sabes, when I can't decide. — Arlene is wearing a pink, strapless tube top. Her stomach spills over the hip hugger jeans. Spits the gum onto the floor. — Fuck it. — And Champ follows her to the rows of nailpolish,

mija: Spanish slang short for "mi hija," or "my daughter."
tú sabes: Spanish for "you know."

next to the Maybelline rack of make-up, across the false eyelashes that look like insects on display in clear, plastic boxes. Arlene pulls out a particular color of nailpolish, looks at the bottom of the bottle for the price, puts it back, gets another. She has a tattoo of purple XXX's on her left finger like a ring. She finally settles for a purple-blackish color, Ripe Plum, that Champ thinks looks like the color of Frankenstein's nails. She looks at her own stubby nails, chewed and gnawed.

Walking over to the eyeshadows, Arlene slowly slinks out another stick of gum from her back pocket, unwraps and crumbles the wrapper into a little ball, lets it drop on the floor. Smacks the gum.

— Grandpa Ham used to make chains with these gum wrappers — she says, toeing the wrapper on the floor with her rubber sandals, her toes dotted with old nailpolish. — He started one, tú sabes, that went from room to room. That was before he went nuts — she says, looking at the price of magenta eyeshadow. — Sabes que?° What do you think? — lifting the eyeshadow to Champ.

— I dunno know — responds Champ, shrugging her shoulders the way she always does when she is listening to something else, her own heartbeat, what Gregorio said on the phone yesterday, shrugs her shoulders when Miss Smith says OFELIA, answer my question. She is too busy thinking of things people otherwise dismiss like parentheses, but sticks to her like gum, like a hole on a shirt, like a tattoo, and sometimes she wishes she weren't born with such adhesiveness. The chain went from room to room, round and round like a web, she remembers. That was before he went nuts.

— Champ. You listening? Or in lala land again? — Arlene has her arms akimbo on a fold of flesh, pissed.

— I said, I dunno know. — Champ whines back, still looking at the wrapper on the floor.

— Well you better learn, tú sabes, and fast too. Now think, will this color go good with Pancha's blue dress? — Pancha is Arlene's comadre. Since Arlene has a special date tonight, she lent Arlene her royal blue dress that she keeps in a plastic bag at the end of her closet. The dress is made of chiffon, with satin-like material underlining, so that when Arlene first tried it on and strutted about, it crinkled sounds of elegance. The dress fits too tight. Her plump arms squeeze through, her hips breathe in and hold their breath, the seams do all they can to keep the body contained. But Arlene doesn't care as long as it sounds right.

— I think it will — Champ says, and Arlene is very pleased.

— Think so? So do I mija. —

They walk out the double doors and Champ never remembers her mother paying.

It is four in the afternoon, but already Arlene is preparing for the date. She scrubs the tub, Art Labo on the radio, drops crystals of Jean Naté into the running water, lemon scent rises with the steam. The bathroom door ajar, she

---

Sabes que?: Spanish for "You know what?"

removes her top and her breasts flop and sag, pushes her jeans down with some difficulty, kicks them off, and steps in the tub.

— Mija. MIJA — she yells. — Mija, give me a few bobby pins. — She is worried about her hair frizzing and so wants to pin it up.

Her mother's voice is faint because Champ is in the closet. There are piles of clothes on the floor, hangers thrown askew and tangled, shoes all piled up or thrown on the top shelf. Champ is looking for her mother's special dress. Pancha says every girl has one at the end of her closet.

— Goddamn it Champ. —

Amidst the dirty laundry, the black hole of the closet, she finds nothing.

— NOW —

— Alright, ALRIGHT. Cheeze amá, stop yelling — says Champ, and goes in the steamy bathroom, checks the drawers, hairbrushes jump out, rollers, strands of hair, rummages through bars of soap, combs, eyeshadows, finds nothing; pulls open another drawer, powder, empty bottles of oil, manicure scissors, Kotex, dye instructions crinkled and botched, finally, a few bobby pins.

After Arlene pins up her hair, she asks Champ, — Sabes que? Should I wear my hair up? Do I look good with it up? — Champ is sitting on the toilet.

— Yea, amá, you look real pretty. —

— Thanks mija — says Arlene, Sabes que? When you get older I'll show you how you can look just as pretty — and she puts her head back, relaxes, like the Calgon commercials.

Champ lays on her stomach, T.V. on to some variety show with pogo stick dancers dressed in outfits of stretchy material and glitter. She is wearing one of Gregorio's white T-shirts, the ones he washes and bleaches himself so that the whiteness is impeccable. It drapes over her deflated ten-year-old body like a dress. She is busy cutting out Miss Breck models from the stacks of old magazines Pancha found in the back of her mother's garage. Champ collects the array of honey colored haired women, puts them in a shoe box with all her other special things.

Arlene is in the bathroom, wrapped in a towel. She has painted her eyebrows so that the two are arched and even, penciled thin and high. The magenta shades her eyelids. The towel slips, reveals one nipple blind from a cigarette burn, a date to forget. She rewraps the towel, likes her reflection, turns to her profile for additional inspection. She feels good, turns up the radio to . . . your love. For your loveeeee, I will do anything, I will do anything, forrr your love. For your kiss . . .

Champ looks on. From the open bathroom door, she can see Arlene, anticipation burning like a cigarette from her lips, sliding her shoulders to the ahhhh ahhhhh, and pouting her lips until the song ends. And Champ likes her mother that way.

Arlene carefully stretches black eyeliner, like a fallen question mark, outlines each eye. The work is delicate, her hand trembles cautiously, stops the process to review the face with each line. Arlene the mirror is not Arlene the face who has worn too many relationships, gotten too little sleep. The last touch is the chalky, beige lipstick.

By the time she is finished, her ashtray is full of cigarette butts, Champ's variety show is over, and Jackie Gleason's dancing girls come on to make kaleidoscope patterns with their long legs and arms. Gregorio is still not home, and Champ goes over to the window, checks the houses, the streets, corners, roams the sky with her eyes.

Arlene sits on the toilet, stretches up her nylons, clips them to her girdle. She feels good thinking about the way he will unsnap her nylons, and she will unroll them slowly, point her toes when she does.

Champ opens a can of Campbell soup, finds a perfect pot in the middle of a stack of dishes, pulls it out to the threatening rumble of the tower. She washes it out, pours the contents of the red can, turns the knob. After it boils, she puts the pot on the sink for it to cool down. She searches for a spoon.

Arlene is romantic. When Champ begins her period, she will tell her things that only women can know. She will tell her about the first time she made love with a boy, her awkwardness and shyness forcing them to go under the house, where the cool, refined soil made a soft mattress. How she closed her eyes and wondered what to expect, or how the penis was the softest skin she had ever felt against her, how it tickled her, searched for a place to connect. She was eleven and his name was Harry.

She will not not tell Champ that her first fuck was a guy named Puppet who ejaculated prematurely, at the sight of her apricot vagina, so plump and fuzzy. — Pendejo° — she said — you got it all over me. — She rubbed the gooey substance off her legs, her belly in disgust. Ran home to tell Rat and Pancha, her mouth open with laughter.

Arlene powder puffs under her arms, between her breasts, tilts a bottle of *Love Cries* perfume and dabs behind her ears, neck and breasts for those tight caressing songs which permit them to grind their bodies together until she can feel a bulge in his pants and she knows she's in for the night.

Jackie Gleason is a bartender in a saloon. He wears a black bow tie, a white apron, and is polishing a glass. Champ is watching him, sitting in the radius of the gray light, eating her soup from the pot.

Arlene is a romantic. She will dance until Pancha's dress turns a different color, dance until her hair becomes undone, her hips jiggering and quaking beneath a new pair of hosiery, her mascara shadowing under her eyes from the perspiration of the ritual, dance spinning herself into Miss Clairol, and stopping only when it is time to return to the sewing factory, time to wait out the next date, time to change hair color. Time to remember or to forget.

Champ sees Arlene from the window. She can almost hear Arlene's nylons rubbing against one another, hear the crinkling sound of satin when she gets in the blue and white shark-finned Dodge. Champ yells goodbye. It all sounds so right to Arlene who is too busy cranking up the window to hear her daughter.

Pendejo: Spanish for "idiot" (used as an insult).

ALICE WALKER *(b. 1944) was the eighth and youngest child of Willie Lee and Minnie Lou Grant Walker, sharecroppers in Eatonton, Georgia. Walker did well in school, encouraged by her teachers and her mother, whose stories she loved as "a walking history of our community." For two years, Walker attended Spelman College in Atlanta, the oldest college for black women in the United States. Then she studied at Sarah Lawrence College in New York, where she began her writing career by publishing a book of poetry,* Once *(1968). Since that time Walker has published several collections of poetry, novels, volumes of short stories, and* Living by the Word *(1988), a book of essays. Her best-known novel,* The Color Purple *(1982), won the American Book Award and the Pulitzer Prize and was made into a motion picture. Later books are* The Temple of My Familiar *(1989),* Possessing the Secret of Joy *(1992),* Anything We Love Can Be Saved: A Writer's Activism *(1997), and* By the Light of My Father's Smile *(1999).*

Walker's works show her commitment to the idea of radical social change. She was active in the civil rights movement in Mississippi, where she met and married a civil rights lawyer from whom she separated after the birth of their daughter. In confronting the painful struggle of black people's history, Walker asserts that the creativity of black women — the extent to which they are permitted to express themselves — is a measure of the health of the entire American society. She calls herself a "womanist," her term for a black feminist. In her definition, "womanism" is preferable to "feminism" because, as she has said,

> *part of our tradition as black women is that we are universalists. Black children, yellow children, red children, brown children, that is the black woman's normal, day-to-day relationship. In my family alone, we are about four different colors. When a black woman looks at the world, it is so different . . . when I look at the people in Iran they look like kinfolk. When I look at the people in Cuba, they look like my uncles and nieces.*

Walker credits many writers for influencing her prose style in her short fiction. Virginia Woolf, Zora Neale Hurston, and Gabriel García Márquez seem to Walker to be "like musicians; at one with their cultures and their historical subconscious." Her two books of stories show a clear progression of theme. The women of In Love and Trouble *(1973) struggle against injustice almost in spite of themselves, as does the protagonist in "Everyday Use" from that collection; the heroines of* You Can't Keep a Good Woman Down *(1981) consciously challenge conventions. Walker has said, "Writing really helps you heal yourself. I think if you write long enough, you will be a healthy person. That is, if you write what you need to write, as opposed to what will make money, or what will make fame." "Everyday Use" was first published in* Harper's Magazine *in 1973.*

RELATED COMMENTARIES: *Cheryl B. Torsney, "'Everyday Use': My Sojourn at Parchman Farm," page 729; Alice Walker, "Zora Neale Hurston: A Cautionary Tale and a Partisan View," page 774.*

Alice Walker

Everyday Use

1973

I will wait for her in the yard that Maggie and I made so clean and wavy yesterday afternoon. A yard like this is more comfortable than most people know. It is not just a yard. It is like an extended living room. When the hard clay is swept clean as a floor and the fine sand around the edges lined with tiny, irregular grooves, anyone can come and sit and look up into the elm tree and wait for the breezes that never come inside the house.

Maggie will be nervous until after her sister goes: she will stand hopelessly in corners, homely and ashamed of the burn scars down her arms and legs, eyeing her sister with a mixture of envy and awe. She thinks her sister has held life always in the palm of one hand, that "no" is a word the world never learned to say to her.

You've no doubt seen those TV shows where the child who has "made it" is confronted, as a surprise, by her own mother and father, tottering in weakly from backstage. (A pleasant surprise, of course: What would they do if parent and child came on the show only to curse out and insult each other?) On TV mother and child embrace and smile into each other's faces. Sometimes the mother and father weep, the child wraps them in her arms and leans across the table to tell how she would not have made it without their help. I have seen these programs.

Sometimes I dream a dream in which Dee and I are suddenly brought together on a TV program of this sort. Out of a dark and soft-seated limousine I am ushered into a bright room filled with many people. There I meet a smiling, gray, sporty man like Johnny Carson who shakes my hand and tells me what a fine girl I have. Then we are on the stage and Dee is embracing me with tears in her eyes. She pins on my dress a large orchid, even though she has told me once that she thinks orchids are tacky flowers.

In real life I am a large, big-boned woman with rough, man-working hands. In the winter I wear flannel nightgowns to bed and overalls during the day. I can kill and clean a hog as mercilessly as a man. My fat keeps me hot in zero weather. I can work outside all day, breaking ice to get water for washing; I can eat pork liver cooked over the open fire minutes after it comes steaming from the hog. One winter I knocked a bull calf straight in the brain between the eyes with a sledge hammer and had the meat hung up to chill before nightfall. But of course all this does not show on television. I am the way my daughter would want me to be: a hundred pounds lighter, my skin like an uncooked barley pancake. My hair glistens in the hot bright lights. Johnny Carson has much to do to keep up with my quick and witty tongue.

But that is a mistake. I know even before I wake up. Who ever knew a Johnson with a quick tongue? Who can even imagine me looking a strange white man in the eye? It seems to me I have talked to them always with one foot raised in flight, with my head turned in whichever way is farthest from them. Dee, though. She would always look anyone in the eye. Hesitation was no part of her nature.

"How do I look, Mama?" Maggie says, showing just enough of her thin body enveloped in pink skirt and red blouse for me to know she's there, almost hidden by the door.

"Come out into the yard," I say.

Have you ever seen a lame animal, perhaps a dog run over by some careless person rich enough to own a car, sidle up to someone who is ignorant enough to be kind to him? That is the way my Maggie walks. She has been like this, chin on chest, eyes on ground, feet in shuffle, ever since the fire that burned the other house to the ground.

Dee is lighter than Maggie, with nicer hair and a fuller figure. She's a woman now, though sometimes I forget. How long ago was it that the other house burned? Ten, twelve years? Sometimes I can still hear the flames and feel Maggie's arms sticking to me, her hair smoking and her dress falling off her in little black papery flakes. Her eyes seemed stretched open, blazed open by the flames reflected in them. And Dee. I see her standing off under the sweet gum tree she used to dig gum out of; a look of concentration on her face as she watched the last dingy gray board of the house fall in toward the red-hot brick chimney. Why don't you do a dance around the ashes? I'd wanted to ask her. She had hated the house that much.

I used to think she hated Maggie, too. But that was before we raised the money, the church and me, to send her to Augusta to school. She used to read to us without pity; forcing words, lies, other folks' habits, whole lives upon us two, sitting trapped and ignorant underneath her voice. She washed us in a river of make-believe, burned us with a lot of knowledge we didn't necessarily need to know. Pressed us to her with the serious way she read, to shove us away at just the moment, like dimwits, we seemed about to understand.

Dee wanted nice things. A yellow organdy dress to wear to her graduation from high school; black pumps to match a green suit she'd made from an old suit somebody gave me. She was determined to stare down any disaster in her efforts. Her eyelids would not flicker for minutes at a time. Often I fought off the temptation to shake her. At sixteen she had a style of her own: and knew what style was.

I never had an education myself. After second grade the school was closed down. Don't ask me why: in 1927 colored asked fewer questions than they do now. Sometimes Maggie reads to me. She stumbles along good-naturedly but can't see well. She knows she is not bright. Like good looks and money, quickness passed her by. She will marry John Thomas (who has mossy teeth in an earnest face) and then I'll be free to sit here and I guess just sing church songs to myself. Although I never was a good singer. Never could carry a tune. I was always better at a man's job. I used to love to milk till I was hooked in the side in '49. Cows are soothing and slow and don't bother you, unless you try to milk them the wrong way.

I have deliberately turned my back on the house. It is three rooms, just like the one that burned, except the roof is tin; they don't make shingle roofs any more. There are no real windows, just some holes cut in the sides, like the portholes in a ship, but not round and not square, with rawhide holding the shutters up on the outside. This house is in a pasture, too, like the other one. No doubt when Dee sees it she will want to tear it down. She wrote me once that no matter where we "choose" to live, she will manage to come see us. But she will never bring her friends. Maggie and I thought about this and Maggie asked me, "Mama, when did Dee ever *have* any friends?"

She had a few. Furtive boys in pink shirts hanging about on washday after school. Nervous girls who never laughed. Impressed with her they worshiped the well-turned phrase, the cute shape, the scalding humor that erupted like bubbles in lye. She read to them.

When she was courting Jimmy T she didn't have much time to pay to us, but turned all her faultfinding power on him. He *flew* to marry a cheap city gal from a family of ignorant flashy people. She hardly had time to recompose herself.

When she comes I will meet — but there they are!

Maggie attempts to make a dash for the house, in her shuffling way, but I stay her with my hand. "Come back here," I say. And she stops and tries to dig a well in the sand with her toe.

It is hard to see them clearly through the strong sun. But even the first glimpse of leg out of the car tells me it is Dee. Her feet were always neat-looking, as if God himself had shaped them with a certain style. From the other side of the car comes a short, stocky man. Hair is all over his head a foot long and hanging from his chin like a kinky mule tail. I hear Maggie suck in her breath. "Uhnnnh," is what it sounds like. Like when you see the wriggling end of a snake just in front of your foot on the road. "Uhnnnh."

Dee next. A dress down to the ground, in this hot weather. A dress so loud it hurts my eyes. There are yellows and oranges enough to throw back the light of the sun. I feel my whole face warming from the heat waves it throws out. Earrings gold, too, and hanging down to her shoulders. Bracelets dangling and making noises when she moves her arm up to shake the folds of the dress out of her armpits. The dress is loose and flows, and as she walks closer, I like it. I hear Maggie go "Uhnnnh" again. It is her sister's hair. It stands straight up like the wool on a sheep. It is black as night and around the edges are two long pigtails that rope about like small lizards disappearing behind her ears.

"Wa-su-zo-Tean-o!" she says, coming on in that gliding way the dress makes her move. The short stocky fellow with the hair to his navel is all grinning and he follows up with "Asalamalakim, my mother and sister!" He moves to hug Maggie but she falls back, right up against the back of my chair. I feel her trembling there and when I look up I see the perspiration falling off her chin.

"Don't get up," says Dee. Since I am stout it takes something of a push. You can see me trying to move a second or two before I make it. She turns, showing white heels through her sandals, and goes back to the car. Out she peeks next with a Polaroid. She stoops down quickly and lines up picture after picture of me sitting there in front of the house with Maggie cowering behind me. She never takes a shot without making sure the house is included. When a cow comes nibbling around the edge of the yard she snaps it and me *and* the house. Then she puts the Polaroid in the back seat of the car, and comes up and kisses me on the forehead.

Meanwhile Asalamalakim is going through the motions with Maggie's hand. Maggie's hand is as limp as a fish, and probably as cold, despite the sweat, and she keeps trying to pull it back. It looks like Asalamalakim wants to shake hands but wants to do it fancy. Or maybe he don't know how people shake hands. Anyhow, he soon gives up on Maggie.

"Well," I say. "Dee."

"No, Mama," she says. "Not 'Dee,' Wangero Leewanika Kemanjo!"

"What happened to 'Dee'?" I wanted to know.

"She's dead," Wangero said. "I couldn't bear it any longer being named after the people who oppress me."

"You know as well as me you was named after your aunt Dicie," I said. Dicie is my sister. She named Dee. We called her "Big Dee" after Dee was born.

"But who was *she* named after?" asked Wangero.

"I guess after Grandma Dee," I said.

"And who was she named after?" asked Wangero.

"Her mother," I said, and saw Wangero was getting tired. "That's about as far back as I can trace it," I said. Though, in fact, I probably could have carried it back beyond the Civil War through the branches.

"Well," said Asalamalakim, "there you are."

"Uhnnnh," I heard Maggie say.

"There I was not," I said, "before 'Dicie' cropped up in our family, so why should I try to trace it that far back?"

He just stood there grinning, looking down on me like somebody inspecting a Model A car. Every once in a while he and Wangero sent eye signals over my head.

"How do you pronounce this name?" I asked.

"You don't have to call me by it if you don't want to," said Wangero.

"Why shouldn't I?" I asked. "If that's what you want us to call you, we'll call you."

"I know it might sound awkward at first," said Wangero.

"I'll get used to it," I said. "Ream it out again."

Well, soon we got the name out of the way. Asalamalakim had a name twice as long and three times as hard. After I tripped over it two or three times he told me to just call him Hakim-a-barber. I wanted to ask him was he a barber, but I didn't really think he was, so I didn't ask.

"You must belong to those beef-cattle peoples down the road," I said. They said "Asalamalakim" when they met you, too, but they didn't shake hands. Always too busy: feeding the cattle, fixing the fences, putting up salt-lick shelters, throwing down hay. When the white folks poisoned some of the herd the men stayed up all night with rifles in their hands. I walked a mile and a half just to see the sight.

Hakim-a-barber said, "I accept some of their doctrines, but farming and raising cattle is not my style." (They didn't tell me, and I didn't ask, whether Wangero [Dee] had really gone and married him.)

We sat down to eat and right away he said he didn't eat collards and pork was unclean. Wangero, though, went on through the chitlins and corn bread, the greens and everything else. She talked a blue streak over the sweet potatoes. Everything delighted her. Even the fact that we still used the benches her daddy made for the table when we couldn't afford to buy chairs.

"Oh, Mama!" she cried. Then turned to Hakim-a-barber. "I never knew how lovely these benches are. You can feel the rump prints," she said, running her hands underneath her and along the bench. Then she gave a sigh and her hand closed over Grandma Dee's butter dish. "That's it!" she said. "I knew there was something I wanted to ask you if I could have." She jumped up from the table and went over in the corner where the churn stood, the milk in it clabber by now. She looked at the churn and looked at it.

"This churn top is what I need," she said. "Didn't Uncle Buddy whittle it out of a tree you all used to have?"

"Yes," I said.

"Uh-huh," she said happily. "And I want the dasher, too."

"Uncle Buddy whittle that, too?" asked the barber.

Dee (Wangero) looked up at me.

"Aunt Dee's first husband whittled the dash," said Maggie so low you almost couldn't hear her. "His name was Henry, but they called him Stash."

"Maggie's brain is like an elephant's," Wangero said, laughing. "I can use the churn top as a centerpiece for the alcove table," she said, sliding a plate over the churn, "and I'll think of something artistic to do with the dasher."

When she finished wrapping the dasher the handle stuck out. I took it for a moment in my hands. You didn't even have to look close to see where hands pushing the dasher up and down to make butter had left a kind of sink in the wood. In fact, there were a lot of small sinks; you could see where thumbs and fingers had sunk into the wood. It was beautiful light yellow wood, from a tree that grew in the yard where Big Dee and Stash had lived.

After dinner Dee (Wangero) went to the trunk at the foot of my bed and started rifling through it. Maggie hung back in the kitchen over the dishpan. Out came Wangero with two quilts. They had been pieced by Grandma Dee and then Big Dee and me had hung them on the quilt frames on the front porch and quilted them. One was in the Lone Star pattern. The other was Walk Around the Mountain. In both of them were scraps of dresses Grandma Dee had worn fifty and more years ago. Bits and pieces of Grandpa Jarrell's Paisley shirts. And one teeny faded blue piece, about the size of a penny matchbox, that was from Great Grandpa Ezra's uniform that he wore in the Civil War.

"Mama," Wangero said sweet as a bird. "Can I have these old quilts?"

I heard something fall in the kitchen, and a minute later the kitchen door slammed.

"Why don't you take one or two of the others?" I asked. "These old things was just done by me and Big Dee from some tops your grandma pieced before she died."

"No," said Wangero. "I don't want those. They are stitched around the borders by machine."

"That'll make them last better," I said.

"That's not the point," said Wangero. "These are all pieces of dresses Grandma used to wear. She did all this stitching by hand. Imagine!" She held the quilts securely in her arms, stroking them.

"Some of the pieces, like those lavender ones, come from old clothes her mother handed down to her," I said, moving up to touch the quilts. Dee (Wangero) moved back just enough so that I couldn't reach the quilts. They already belonged to her.

"Imagine!" she breathed again, clutching them closely to her bosom.

"The truth is," I said, "I promised to give them quilts to Maggie, for when she marries John Thomas."

She gasped like a bee had stung her.

"Maggie can't appreciate these quilts!" she said. "She'd probably be backward enough to put them to everyday use."

"I reckon she would," I said. "God knows I been saving 'em for long enough with nobody using 'em. I hope she will!" I didn't want to bring up how I had offered Dee (Wangero) a quilt when she went away to college. Then she had told me they were old-fashioned, out of style.

"But they're *priceless!*" she was saying now, furiously; for she has a temper. "Maggie would put them on the bed and in five years they'd be in rags. Less than that!"

"She can always make some more," I said. "Maggie knows how to quilt."

Dee (Wangero) looked at me with hatred. "You just will not understand. The point is these quilts, *these* quilts!"

"Well," I said, stumped. "What would *you* do with them?"

"Hang them," she said. As if that was the only thing you *could* do with quilts.

Maggie by now was standing in the door. I could almost hear the sound her feet made as they scraped over each other.

"She can have them, Mama," she said, like somebody used to never winning anything, or having anything reserved for her. "I can 'member Grandma Dee without the quilts."

I looked at her hard. She had filled her bottom lip with checkerberry snuff and it gave her face a kind of dopey, hangdog look. It was Grandma Dee and Big Dee who taught her how to quilt herself. She stood there with her scarred hands hidden in the folds of her skirt. She looked at her sister with something like fear but she wasn't mad at her. This was Maggie's portion. This was the way she knew God to work.

When I looked at her like that something hit me in the top of my head and ran down to the soles of my feet. Just like when I'm in church and the spirit of God touches me and I get happy and shout. I did something I never had done before: hugged Maggie to me, then dragged her on into the room, snatched the quilts out of Miss Wangero's hands and dumped them into Maggie's lap. Maggie just sat there on my bed with her mouth open.

"Take one or two of the others," I said to Dee.

But she turned without a word and went out to Hakim-a-barber.

"You just don't understand," she said, as Maggie and I came out to the car.

"What don't I understand?" I wanted to know.

"Your heritage," she said. And then she turned to Maggie, kissed her, and said, "You ought to try to make something of yourself, too, Maggie. It's really a new day for us. But from the way you and Mama still live you'd never know it."

She put on some sunglasses that hid everything above the tip of her nose and her chin.

Maggie smiled; maybe at the sunglasses. But a real smile, not scared. After we watched the car dust settle I asked Maggie to bring me a dip of snuff. And then the two of us sat there just enjoying, until it was time to go in the house and go to bed.

ꙮ

JOHN EDGAR WIDEMAN *(b. 1941) was born in Washington, D.C., and grew up in the Homewood section of Pittsburgh, Pennsylvania, an inner-city ghetto he has written about frequently in his fiction. At the University of Pennsylvania, Wideman was both a star athlete and a brilliant scholar: He earned All-Ivy honors in basketball as well as a place in the Philadelphia Big Five Basketball Hall of Fame, and he was awarded a Rhodes scholarship in 1963, the year he graduated. Wideman spent the next three years at Oxford University studying English literature and followed this experience with a year at the University of Iowa Writers' Workshop as a Kent fellow. After teaching at the University of Wyoming, he is now a professor of English at the University of Massachusetts, Amherst.*

Wideman published three novels in the 1960s and 1970s before his first book of stories, Damballah, *appeared in 1981. This was a volume in what he called the Homewood Trilogy, three books describing the Pittsburgh community of Homewood, founded by a runaway slave. The other two books in the trilogy are the novels* Hiding Place *(1981) and* Sent for You Yesterday *(1983), which won a PEN/Faulkner Award. Wideman received this award a second time for his novel* Philadelphia Fire *(1990).* All Stories Are True: The Stories of John Edgar Wideman — *comprising a total of thirty-five stories, including those in* Fever *(1989), his second book of short fiction — appeared in 1992.* Fatheralong: A Meditation on Fathers and Sons, Race and Society *(1994),* The Cattle Killing *(1996), and* Two Cities *(1998) are his recent works.*

"Newborn thrown in trash and dies," which first appeared in All Stories Are True, *is reminiscent of Wideman's earlier story in third-person narration about "dead children in garbage cans" titled "Daddy Garbage" in* Damballah. *Wideman read a newspaper account of a newborn infant murdered in New York City, and he said that he felt compelled "out of a sense of sadness, frustration, and pain to create the voice of a child who is witness to its own death and never got a chance to speak." Wideman felt that "the challenge of the story was to give dignity to the short life, and to slow down time when the course of its life was so short." As a teacher of aspiring writers, Wideman tells his students to "find the material that you have a stake in, that you care about immensely, that pins you down." In 1998 he was the recipient of the Rea Award for the Short Story.*

JOHN EDGAR WIDEMAN

newborn thrown in trash and dies 1992

They say you see your whole life pass in review the instant before you die. How would *they* know. If you die after the instant replay, you aren't around to tell anybody anything. So much for they and what they say. So much for the wish to be a movie star for once in your life because I think that's what people are hoping, what people are pretending when they say you see your life that way at the end. Death doesn't turn your life into a five-star production. The end is the end. And what you know at the end goes down the tube with you. I can speak to you now only because I haven't reached bottom yet. I'm on my way, faster than I want to be traveling and my journey won't take long, but I'm just beginning the countdown to zero. Zero's where I started also so I know a little bit about zero. Know what they say isn't necessarily so. In fact the opposite's true. You begin and right in the eye of that instant storm your life plays itself out for you in advance. That's the theater of your fate, there's where you're granted a preview, the coming attractions of everything that must happen to you. Your life rolled into a ball so dense, so superheavy it would drag the universe down to hell if this tiny, tiny lump of whatever didn't dissipate as quickly as it formed. Quicker. The weight of it is what you recall some infinitesimal fraction of when you stumble and crawl through your worst days on earth.

Knowledge of what's coming gone as quickly as it flashes forth. Quicker. Faster. Gone before it gets here, so to speak. Any other way and nobody would stick around to play out the cards they're dealt. No future in it. You begin forgetting before the zero's entirely wiped off the clock face, before the next digit materializes. What they say is assbackwards, a saying by the way, assbackwards itself. Whether or not you're treated to a summary at the end, you get the whole thing handed to you, neatly packaged as you begin. Then you forget it. Or try to forget. Live your life as if it hasn't happened before, as if the tape has not been prepunched full of holes, the die cast.

I remember because I won't receive much of a life. A measure of justice in the world, after all. I receive a compensatory bonus. Since the time between my wake-up call and curfew is so cruelly brief, the speeded-up preview of what will come to pass, my life, my portion, my destiny, my career, slowed down just enough to let me peek. Not slow enough for me to steal much, but I know some of what it contains, its finality, the groaning, fatal weight of it around my neck.

Call it a trade-off. A standoff. Intensity for duration. I won't get much and this devastating flash isn't much either, but I get it. Zingo.

But the future remains mysterious. Even if we all put our heads together and became one gigantic brain, a brain lots smarter than the sum of each of our smarts, an intelligence as great as the one that guides ants, whales or birds, because they're smarter, they figure things out not one by one, each individual locked in the cell of its head, its mortality, but collectively, doing what the group needs to do to survive, relate to the planet. If we were smarter even than birds and bees, we'd still have only a clue about what's inside the first flash of being. I know it happened and that I receive help from it. Scattered help. Sometimes I catch on. Sometimes I don't. But stuff from it's being pumped out always. I know things I have no business knowing. Things I haven't been around long enough to learn myself. For instance, many languages. A vast palette of feelings. The names of unseen things. Nostalgia for a darkness I've never experienced, a darkness another sense I can't account for assures me I will enter again. Large matters. Small ones. Naked as I am I'm dressed so to speak for my trip. Down these ten swift flights to oblivion.

Floor Ten. Nothing under the sun, they say, is new. This time they're right. They never stop talking so percentages guarantee they'll be correct sometimes. Especially since they speak out of both sides of their mouths at once: *Birds of a feather flock together. Opposites attract.* Like the billion billion monkeys at typewriters who sooner or later will bang out this story I think is uniquely mine. Somebody else, a Russian, I believe, with a long, strange-sounding name, has already written about his life speeding past as he topples slow-motion from a window high up in a tall apartment building. But it was in another country. And alas, the Russian's dead.

Floor Nine. In this building they shoot craps. One of many forms of gambling proliferating here. Very little new wealth enters this cluster of buildings that are like high-rise covered wagons circled against the urban night, so what's here is cycled and recycled by games of chance, by murder and other violent forms of exchange. Kids do it. Adults. Birds and bees. The law here is the same one ruling the jungle, they say. They say this is a jungle of the urban asphalt concrete variety. Since I've never been to Africa or the Amazon I can't agree or disagree. But you know what I think about what they say.

Seven come eleven. Snake eyes. Boxcars. Fever in the funkhouse searching for a five. Talk to me, baby. Talk. Talk. Please. Please. Please.

They cry and sing and curse and pray all night long over these games. On one knee they chant magic formulas to summon luck. They forget luck is rigged. Some of the men carry a game called Three Card Monte downtown. They cheat tourists who are stupid enough to trust in luck. Showmen with quick hands shuffling cards to a blur, fast feet carrying them away from busy intersections when cops come to break up their scam or hit on them for a cut. Flimflam artists, con men who daily use luck as bait and hook, down on their knees in a circle of other men who also should know better, trying to sweet-talk luck into their beds. Luck is the card you wish for, the card somebody else holds. You learn luck by its absence. Luck is what separates you from what you want. Luck is always turning its back and you lose.

Like other potions and powders they sell and consume here luck creates dependency. In their rooms people sit and wait for a hit. A yearning unto death for more, more, more till the little life they've been allotted dies in a basket on the doorstep where they abandoned it.

The Floor of Facts. Seventeen stories in this building. The address is 2950 West 23rd Street. My mother is nineteen years old. The trash chute down which I was dropped is forty-five feet from the door of the apartment my mother was visiting. I was born and will die Monday, August 12, 1991. The small door in the yellow cinder block wall is maroon. I won't know till the last second why my mother pushes it open. In 1990 nine discarded babies were discovered in New York City's garbage. As of August this year seven have been found. 911 is the number to call if you find a baby in the trash. Ernesto Mendez, forty-four, a Housing Authority caretaker, will notice my head, shoulders and curly hair in a black plastic bag he slashes open near the square entrance of the trash compactor on the ground floor of this brown-brick public housing project called the Gerald J. Carey Gardens. Gardens are green places where seeds are planted, tended, nurtured. The headline above my story reads "Newborn Is Thrown in Trash and Dies." The headline will remind some readers of a similar story with a happy ending that appeared in March. A baby rescued and surviving after she was dropped down a trash chute by her twelve-year-old mother. The reporter, a Mr. George James who recorded many of the above facts, introduced my unhappy story in the Metro Section of the *New York Times* on Wednesday, August 14, with this paragraph: "A young Brooklyn woman gave birth on Monday afternoon in a stairwell in a Coney Island housing project and then dropped the infant down a trash chute into a compactor ten stories below, the police said yesterday." And that's about it. What's fit to print. My tale in a nutshell followed by a relation of facts obtained by interview and reading official documents. Trouble is I could not be reached for comment. No one's fault. Certainly no negligence on the reporter's part. He gave me sufficient notoriety. Many readers must have shaken their heads in dismay or sighed or blurted Jesus Christ, did you see this, handing the Metro Section across the breakfast table or passing it to somebody at work. As grateful as I am to have my story made public you should be able to understand why I feel cheated, why the newspaper account is not enough, why I want my voice to be part of the record. The awful silence is not truly broken until we speak for ourselves. One chance to speak was snatched away. Then I didn't cry out as I plunged through the darkness. I didn't know any better. Too busy thinking to myself, *This is how it is, this is how it is, how it is* . . . accustoming myself to what it seemed life brings, what life is. Spinning, tumbling, a breathless rush, terror, exhilaration and wonder, wondering is this it, am I doing it right. I didn't know any better. The floors, the other lives packed into this building were going on their merry way as I flew past them in the darkness of my tunnel. No one waved. No one warned me. Said hello or good-bye. And of course I was too busy flailing, trying to catch my breath, trying to stop shivering in the sudden, icy air, welcoming almost the thick, pungent draft rushing up at me as if another pair of thighs were opening below to replace the ones from which I'd been ripped.

In the quiet dark of my passage I did not cry out. Now I will not be still.

A Floor of Questions. Why.

A Floor of Opinions. I believe the floor of fact should have been the ground floor, the foundation, the solid start, the place where all else is firmly rooted. I believe there should be room on the floor of fact for what I believe, for this opinion and others I could not venture before arriving here. I believe some facts are unnecessary and that unnecessary borders on untrue. I believe facts sometimes speak for themselves but never speak for us. They are never anyone's voice and voices are what we must learn to listen to if we wish ever to be heard. I believe my mother did not hate me. I believe somewhere I have a father, who if he is reading this and listening carefully will recognize me as his daughter and be ashamed, heartbroken. I must believe these things. What else do I have. Who has made my acquaintance or noticed or cared or forgotten me. How could anyone be aware of what hurtles by faster than light, blackly, in a dark space beyond the walls of the rooms they live in, beyond the doors they lock, shades they draw when they have rooms and the rooms have windows and the windows have shades and the people believe they possess something worth concealing.

In my opinion my death will serve no purpose. The streetlamps will pop on. Someone will be run over by an expensive car in a narrow street and the driver will hear a bump but consider it of no consequence. Junkies will leak out the side doors of this gigantic mound, nodding, buzzing, greeting their kind with hippy-dip vocalizations full of despair and irony and stylized to embrace the very best that's being sung, played and said around them. A young woman will open a dresser drawer and wonder whose baby that is sleeping peaceful on a bed of dishtowels, T-shirts, a man's ribbed sweat socks. She will feel something slither through the mud of her belly and splash into the sluggish river that meanders through her. She hasn't eaten for days, so that isn't it. Was it a deadly disease. Or worse, some new life she must account for. She opens and shuts the baby's drawer, pushes and pulls, opens and shuts.

I believe all floors are not equally interesting. Less reason to notice some than others. Equality would become boring, predictable. Though we may slight some and rattle on about others, that does not change the fact that each floor exists and the life on it is real, whether we pause to notice or not. As I gather speed and weight during my plunge, each floor adds its share. When I hit bottom I will bear witness to the truth of each one.

Floor of Wishes. I will miss Christmas. They say no one likes being born on Christmas. You lose your birthday, they say. A celebration already on December 25 and nice things happen to everyone on that day anyway, you give and receive presents, people greet you smiling and wish you peace and goodwill. The world is decorated. Colored bulbs draped twinkling in windows and trees, doorways hung with wild berries beneath which you may kiss a handsome stranger. Music everywhere. Even wars truced for twenty-four hours and troops served home-cooked meals, almost. Instead of at least two special days a year, if your birthday falls on Christmas, you lose one. Since my portion's less than a day, less than those insects called ephemera receive, born one morning dead the next, and I can't squeeze a complete life cycle as they do into the time allotted, I wish today were Christmas. Once would be enough. If it's as special as they say. And in some matters we yearn to trust them. Need to trust something, someone, so we listen, wish what they say is true. The holiday of Christmas seems to be the best time to be on earth, to be a child and awaken with your eyes full of dreams and expectations and believe for a while at least that all good things are possible — peace, goodwill, love, merriment, the raven-maned rocking horse you want to ride forever. No conflict of interest for me. I wouldn't lose a birthday to Christmas. Rather than this smoggy heat I wish I could see snow. The city, this building snug under a blanket of fresh snow. No footprints of men running, men on their knees, men bleeding. No women forced out into halls and streets, away from their children. I wish this city, this tower were stranded in a gentle snowstorm and Christmas happens day after day and the bright fires in every hearth never go out, and the carols ring true chorus after chorus, and the gifts given and received precipitate endless joys. The world trapped in Christmas for a day dancing on forever. I wish I could transform the ten flights of my falling into those twelve days in the Christmas song. *On the first day of Christmas my true love said to me* . . . angels, a partridge in a pear tree, ten maids a milking, five gold rings, two turtledoves. I wish those would be the sights greeting me instead of darkness, the icy winter heart of this August afternoon I have been pitched without a kiss through a maroon door.

Floor of Power. El Presidente inhabits this floor. Some say he owns the whole building. He believes he owns it, collects rent, treats the building and its occupants with contempt. He is a bold-faced man. Cheeks slotted nose to chin like a puppet's. Chicken lips. This floor is entirely white. A floury, cracked white some say used to gleam. El Presidente is white also. Except for the pink dome of his forehead. Once, long ago, his flesh was pink head to toe. Then he painted himself white to match the white floor of power. Paint ran out just after the brush stroke that permanently sealed his eyes. Since El Presidente is cheap and mean he refused to order more paint. Since El Presidente is vain and arrogant he pretended to look at his unfinished self in the mirror and proclaimed he liked what he saw, the coat of cakey white, the raw, pink dome pulsing like a bruise.

El Presidente often performs on TV. We can watch him jog, golf, fish, travel, lie, preen, mutilate the language. But these activities are not his job; his job is keeping things in the building as they are, squatting on the floor of power like a broken generator or broken furnace or broken heart, occupying the space where one that works should be.

Floor of Regrets. One thing bothers me a lot. I regret not knowing what is on the floors above the one where I began my fall. I hope it's better up there. Real gardens perhaps or even a kind of heaven for the occupants lucky enough to live above the floors I've seen. Would one of you please mount the stairs, climb slowly up from floor ten, examine carefully, one soft, warm night, the topmost floors and sing me a lullaby of what I missed.

Floor of Love. I'm supposed to be sleeping. I could be sleeping. Early morning and my eyes don't want to open and legs don't want to push me out of bed yet. Two rooms away I can hear Mom in the kitchen. She's fixing breakfast. Daddy first, then I will slump into the kitchen Mom has made bright and smelling good already this morning. Her perkiness, the sizzling bacon, water boiling, wheat bread popping up like jack-in-the-box from the shiny toaster, the Rice Krispies crackling, fried eggs hissing, the FM's sophisticated patter and mincing string trios would wake the dead. And it does. Me and Daddy slide into our places. Hi, Mom. Good morning, Dearheart. The day begins. Smells wonderful. I awaken now to his hand under the covers with me, rubbing the baby fat of my tummy where he's shoved my nightgown up past my panties. He says I shouldn't wear them. Says it ain't healthy to sleep in your drawers. Says no wonder you get those rashes. He rubs and pinches. Little nips. Then the flat of his big hand under the elastic waistband wedges my underwear down. I raise my hips a little bit to help. No reason not to. The whole thing be over with sooner. Don't do no good to try and stop him or slow him down. He said my Mama knows. He said go on fool and tell her she'll smack you for talking nasty. He was right. She beat me in the kitchen. Then took me in to their room and he stripped me butt-naked and beat me again while she watched. So I kinda hump up, wiggle, and my underwear's down below my knees, his hand's on its way back up to where I don't even understand how to grow hairs yet.

The Floor That Stands for All the Other Floors Missed or Still to Come. My stepbrother Tommy was playing in the schoolyard and they shot him dead. Bang. Bang. Gang banging and poor Tommy caught a cap in his chest. People been in and out the apartment all day. Sorry. Sorry. Everybody's so sorry. Some brought cakes, pies, macaroni casseroles, lunch meat, liquor. Two Ebony Cobras laid a joint on Tommy's older brother who hadn't risen from the kitchen chair he's straddling, head down, nodding, till his boys bop through the door. They know who hit Tommy. They know tomorrow what they must do. Today one of those everybody-in-the-family-and-friends-in-dark-clothes-funeral days, the mothers, sisters, aunts, grandmothers weepy, the men motherfucking everybody from god on down. You can't see me among the mourners. My time is different from this time. You can't understand my time. Or name it. Or share it. Tommy is beginning to remember me. To join me where I am falling unseen through your veins and arteries down down to where the heart stops, the square opening through which trash passes to the compactor.

❧

TOBIAS WOLFF *(b. 1945) began his best-selling memoir by writing, "My first stepfather used to say that what I didn't know would fill a book. Well, here it is." A compassionate sense of paradox and irony permeates his writing, as in the story "Say Yes," adding an emotional color to the transparently clear prose of his narratives.*

Born in Birmingham, Alabama, Wolff followed his mother to the Pacific Northwest when his parents divorced. It is this period in his life that is the subject of his memoir This Boy's Life *(1989). After being expelled from prep school, he served in the U.S. Army in Vietnam in 1964–68. Then he studied at Oxford University and Stanford University, where in 1975–76 he received a Wallace Stegner fellowship in creative writing. Two National Endowment for the Arts fellowships followed, along with a Mary Roberts Rinehart grant, an Arizona Council on the Arts fellowship, a Guggenheim fellowship, three O. Henry short story prizes, and the PEN/Faulkner Award for fiction for* The Barracks Thief *(1984), a novella about his army experience. Wolff's first book was a collection of short stories,* In the Garden of the North American Martyrs *(1981).* Back in the World *(1985) and* The Night in Question *(1997) are recent story collections.*

Wolff credits several writers as influences on his fiction: Ernest Hemingway,

Anton Chekhov, Paul Bowles, Sherwood Anderson, John Cheever, Flannery O'Connor, and Raymond Carver — "the list has no end so I'd better stop here." He prefers writing short stories to novels because "when I write a short story, I feel like I'm somehow cooperating with the story; when I try to work in longer forms, I feel like I'm beating them into existence. I feel a kind of clumsiness that I don't feel when I'm writing short stories." Wolff regards writing as an "essentially optimistic art," because

> *the very act of writing assumes, to begin with, that someone cares to hear what you have to say. It assumes that people share, that people can be reached, that people can be touched and even in some cases changed. . . . So many of the things in our world tend to lead us to despair. It seems to me that the final symptom of despair is silence, and that storytelling is one of the sustaining arts; it's one of the affirming arts. . . . A writer may have a certain pessimism in his outlook, but the very act of being a writer seems to me to be an optimistic act.*

TOBIAS WOLFF

Say Yes — 1985

They were doing the dishes, his wife washing while he dried. He'd washed the night before. Unlike most men he knew, he really pitched in on the housework. A few months earlier he'd overheard a friend of his wife's congratulate her on having such a considerate husband, and he thought, *I try.* Helping out with the dishes was a way of showing how considerate he was.

They talked about different things and somehow got on the subject of whether white people should marry black people. He said that all things considered, he thought it was a bad idea.

"Why?" she asked.

Sometimes his wife got this look where she pinched her brows together and bit her lower lip and stared down at something. When he saw her like this he knew he should keep his mouth shut, but he never did. Actually it made him talk more. She had that look now.

"Why?" she asked again, and stood there with her hand inside a bowl, not washing it but just holding it above the water.

"Listen," he said, "I went to school with blacks, and I've worked with blacks and lived on the same street with blacks, and we've always gotten along just fine. I don't need you coming along now and implying that I'm a racist."

"I didn't imply anything," she said, and began washing the bowl again, turning it around in her hand as though she were shaping it. "I just don't see what's wrong with a white person marrying a black person, that's all."

"They don't come from the same culture as we do. Listen to them sometime — they even have their own language. That's okay with me, I *like* hearing them talk" — he did; for some reason it always made him feel happy — "but it's different. A person from their culture and a person from our culture could never really *know* each other."

"Like you know me?" his wife asked.

"Yes. Like I know you."

"But if they love each other," she said. She was washing faster now, not looking at him.

Oh boy, he thought. He said, "Don't take my word for it. Look at the statistics. Most of those marriages break up."

"Statistics." She was piling dishes on the drainboard at a terrific rate, just swiping at them with the cloth. Many of them were greasy, and there were flecks of food between the tines of the forks. "All right," she said, "what about foreigners? I suppose you think the same thing about two foreigners getting married."

"Yes," he said, "as a matter of fact I do. How can you understand someone who comes from a completely different background?"

"Different," said his wife. "Not the same, like us."

"Yes, different," he snapped, angry with her for resorting to this trick of repeating his words so that they sounded crass, or hypocritical. "These are dirty," he said, and dumped all the silverware back into the sink.

The water had gone flat and gray. She stared down at it, her lips pressed tight together, then plunged her hands under the surface. "Oh!" she cried, and jumped back. She took her right hand by the wrist and held it up. Her thumb was bleeding.

"Ann, don't move," he said. "Stay right there." He ran upstairs to the bathroom and rummaged in the medicine chest for alcohol, cotton, and a Band-Aid. When he came back down she was leaning against the refrigerator with her eyes closed, still holding her hand. He took the hand and dabbed at her thumb with the cotton. The bleeding had stopped. He squeezed it to see how deep the wound was and a single drop of blood welled up, trembling and bright, and fell to the floor. Over the thumb she stared at him accusingly. "It's shallow," he said. "Tomorrow you won't even know it's there." He hoped that she appreciated how quickly he had come to her aid. He'd acted out of concern for her, with no thought of getting anything in return, but now the thought occurred to him that it would be a nice gesture on her part not to start up that conversation again, as he was tired of it. "I'll finish up here," he said. "You go and relax."

"That's okay," she said. "I'll dry."

He began to wash the silverware again, giving a lot of attention to the forks.

"So," she said, "you wouldn't have married me if I'd been black."

"For Christ's sake, Ann!"

"Well, that's what you said, didn't you?"

"No, I did not. The whole question is ridiculous. If you had been black we probably wouldn't even have met. You would have had your friends and I would have had mine. The only black girl I ever really knew was my partner in the debating club, and I was already going out with you by then."

"But if we had met, and I'd been black?"

"Then you probably would have been going out with a black guy." He picked up the rinsing nozzle and sprayed the silverware. The water was so hot that the metal darkened to pale blue, then turned silver again.

"Let's say I wasn't," she said. "Let's say I am black and unattached and we meet and fall in love."

He glanced over at her. She was watching him and her eyes were bright. "Look," he said, taking a reasonable tone, "this is stupid. If you were black you wouldn't be you." As he said this he realized it was absolutely true. There was no possible way of arguing with the fact that she would not be herself if she were black. So he said it again: "If you were black you wouldn't be you."

"I know," she said, "but let's just say."

He took a deep breath. He had won the argument but he still felt cornered. "Say what?" he asked.

"That I'm black, but still me, and we fall in love. Will you marry me?"

He thought about it.

"Well?" she said, and stepped close to him. Her eyes were even brighter. "Will you marry me?"

"I'm thinking," he said.

"You won't, I can tell. You're going to say no."

"Let's not move too fast on this," he said. "There are lots of things to consider. We don't want to do something we would regret for the rest of our lives."

"No more considering. Yes or no."

"Since you put it that way —"

"Yes or no."

"Jesus, Ann. All right. No."

She said, "Thank you," and walked from the kitchen into the living room. A moment later he heard her turning the pages of a magazine. He knew that she was too angry to be actually reading it, but she didn't snap through the pages the way he would have done. She turned them slowly, as if she were studying every word. She was demonstrating her indifference to him, and it had the effect he knew she wanted it to have. It hurt him.

He had no choice but to demonstrate his indifference to her. Quietly, thoroughly, he washed the rest of the dishes. Then he dried them and put them away. He wiped the counters and the stove and scoured the linoleum where the drop of blood had fallen. While he was at it, he decided, he might as well mop the whole floor. When he was done the kitchen looked new, the way it looked when they were first shown the house, before they had ever lived here.

He picked up the garbage pail and went outside. The night was clear and he could see a few stars to the west, where the lights of the town didn't blur them out. On El Camino the traffic was steady and light, peaceful as a river. He felt ashamed that he had let his wife get him into a fight. In another thirty years or so they would both be dead. What would all that stuff matter then? He thought of the years they had spent together, and how close they were, and how well they knew each other, and his throat tightened so that he could hardly breathe. His face and neck began to tingle. Warmth flooded his chest. He stood there for a while, enjoying these sensations, then picked up the pail and went out the back gate.

The two mutts from down the street had pulled over the garbage can again. One of them was rolling around on his back and the other had something in her mouth. Growling, she tossed it into the air, leaped up and caught it, growled again and whipped her head from side to side. When they saw him coming they trotted away with short, mincing steps. Normally he would heave rocks at them, but this time he let them go.

The house was dark when he came back inside. She was in the bathroom. He stood outside the door and called her name. He heard bottles clinking, but she didn't answer him. "Ann, I'm really sorry," he said. "I'll make it up to you, I promise."

"How?" she asked.

He wasn't expecting this. But from a sound in her voice, a level and definite note that was strange to him, he knew that he had to come up with the right answer. He leaned against the door. "I'll marry you," he whispered.

"We'll see," she said. "Go on to bed. I'll be out in a minute."

He undressed and got under the covers. Finally he heard the bathroom door open and close.

"Turn off the light," she said from the hallway.

"What?"

"Turn off the light."

He reached over and pulled the chain on the bedside lamp. The room went dark. "All right," he said. He lay there, but nothing happened. "All right," he said again. Then he heard a movement across the room. He sat up, but he couldn't see a thing. The room was silent. His heart pounded the way it had on their first night together the way it still did when he woke at a noise in the darkness and waited to hear it again — the sound of someone moving through the house, a stranger.

RICHARD WRIGHT *(1908–1960) was born on a plantation near Natchez, Mississippi, the son of a farmhand and a country schoolteacher. His home life was disrupted when his father deserted the family, and Wright later said it was only through reading that he managed to keep himself alive. As soon as he could he moved north, to Memphis, Chicago, and then to New York City, where he became involved in radical politics. He was a member of the Communist Party from 1932 to 1944. In the 1930s he worked as a reporter for* The New Masses, *a correspondent for the Harlem bureau of the* Daily Worker, *and an editor for* New Challenge, *a left-wing magazine that published his "Blueprint for Negro Writing," an effort to bridge the gap between Marxism and black nationalism, in 1938. He was also then writing the stories that appeared in* Uncle Tom's Children *(1938), which won first prize in a contest for writers in the Federal Writers' Project during the Depression. Wright's early fiction was strongly influenced by Ernest Hemingway's way of writing stories, but Wright also set himself the problem of how to use a modernist style to write about social issues:*

> *Practically all of us, young writers, were influenced by Ernest Hemingway. We liked the simple, direct way in which he wrote, but a great many of us wanted to write about social problems. The question came up: How could we write about social problems and use a simple style? Hemingway's style is so*

concentrated on naturalistic detail that there is no room for social comment. One boy said that one way was to dig deeper into the character and try to get something that will live. I decided to try it.

The result was the five stories published in Uncle Tom's Children. *Next Wright turned to his first novel,* Native Son *(1940), an American classic dramatizing a brutal story of racial conflict. This was followed by* Black Boy *(1945), a brilliant autobiography written when he was not yet forty. The next year he left the United States to spend the last fourteen years of his life in Paris, feeling himself alienated from American values. In 1960, the year Wright died, he gathered for publication his second book of short stories,* Eight Men, *made up of fiction that had appeared over the years in magazines and anthologies, including "The Man Who Was Almost a Man," written in the 1930s.*

Telling stories from a realistic view of his own experience, Wright experimented with literary techniques in all his fiction. His short stories dramatize the same themes as his novels and are equally experimental. "The Man Who Was Almost a Man" weaves the black farm boy's speech so skillfully with standard English narration that most readers are unaware of the effect of the deliberate juxtaposition, but this technique brings us closer to the boy's world while making an implicit social comment about his exclusion from the exploitative white society engulfing him.

RICHARD WRIGHT

The Man Who Was Almost a Man

1961

Dave struck out across the fields, looking homeward through paling light. Whut's the use talkin wid em niggers in the field? Anyhow, his mother was putting supper on the table. Them niggers can't understan nothing. One of these days he was going to get a gun and practice shooting, then they couldn't talk to him as though he were a little boy. He slowed, looking at the ground. Shucks, Ah ain scareda them even ef they are biggern me! Aw, Ah know whut Ahma do. Ahm going by ol Joe's sto n git that Sears Roebuck catlog n look at them guns. Mebbe Ma will lemme buy one when she gits mah pay from ol man Hawkins. Ahma beg her t gimme some money. Ahm ol ernough to hava gun. Ahm seventeen. Almost a man. He strode, feeling his long loose-jointed limbs. Shucks, a man oughta hava little gun aftah he done worked hard all day.

He came in sight of Joe's store. A yellow lantern glowed on the front porch. He mounted steps and went through the screen door, hearing it bang behind him. There was a strong smell of coal oil and mackerel fish. He felt very confident until he saw fat Joe walk in through the rear door, then his courage began to ooze.

"Howdy, Dave! Whutcha want?"

"How yuh, Mistah Joe? Aw, Ah don wanna buy nothing. Ah jus wanted t see ef yuhd lemme look at tha catlog erwhile."

"Sure! You wanna see it here?"

"Nawsuh. Ah wants t take it home wid me. Ah'll bring it back termorrow when Ah come in from the fiels."

"You plannin on buying something?"

"Yessuh."

"Your ma lettin you have your own money now?"

"Shucks. Mistah Joe, Ahm gittin t be a man like anybody else!"

Joe laughed and wiped his greasy white face with a red bandanna.

"Whut you plannin on buyin?"

Dave looked at the floor, scratched his head, scratched his thigh, and smiled. Then he looked up shyly.

"Ah'll tell yuh, Mistah Joe, ef yuh promise yuh won't tell."

"I promise."

"Waal, Ahma buy a gun."

"A gun? What you want with a gun?"

"Ah wanna keep it."

"You ain't nothing but a boy. You don't need a gun."

"Aw, lemme have the catlog, Mistah Joe. Ah'll bring it back."

Joe walked through the rear door. Dave was elated. He looked around at barrels of sugar and flour. He heard Joe coming back. He craned his neck to see if he were bringing the book. Yeah, he's got it. Gawddog, he's got it!

"Here, but be sure you bring it back. It's the only one I got."

"Sho, Mistah Joe."

"Say, if you wanna buy a gun, why don't you buy one from me? I gotta gun to sell."

"Will it shoot?"

"Sure it'll shoot."

"Whut kind is it?"

"Oh, it's kinda old . . . a left-hand Wheeler. A pistol. A big one."

"Is it got bullets in it?"

"It's loaded."

"Kin Ah see it?"

"Where's your money?"

"What yuh wan fer it?"

"I'll let you have it for two dollars."

"Just two dollahs? Shucks, Ah could buy tha when Ah git mah pay."

"I'll have it here when you want it."

"Awright, suh. Ah be in fer it."

He went through the door, hearing it slam again behind him. Ahma git some money from Ma n buy me a gun! Only two dollahs! He tucked the thick catalogue under his arm and hurried.

"Where yuh been, boy?" His mother held a steaming dish of black-eyed peas.

"Aw, Ma, Ah jus stopped down the road t talk wid the boys."

"Yuh know bettah t keep suppah waitin."

He sat down, resting the catalogue on the edge of the table.

"Yuh git up from there and git to the well n wash yosef! Ah ain feedin no hogs in mah house!"

She grabbed his shoulder and pushed him. He stumbled out of the room, then came back to get the catalogue.

"Whut this?"

"Aw, Ma, it's jusa catlog."

"Who yuh git it from?"

"From Joe, down at the sto."

"Waal, thas good. We kin use it in the outhouse."

"Naw, Ma." He grabbed for it. "Gimme ma catlog, Ma."

She held onto it and glared at him.

"Quit hollerin at me! Whut's wrong wid yuh? Yuh crazy?"

"But Ma, please. It ain mine! It's Joe's! He tol me t bring it back t im termorrow."

She gave up the book. He stumbled down the back steps, hugging the thick book under his arm. When he had splashed water on his face and hands, he groped back to the kitchen and fumbled in a corner for the towel. He bumped into a chair; it clattered to the floor. The catalogue sprawled at his feet. When he had dried his eyes he snatched up the book and held it again under his arm. His mother stood watching him.

"Now, ef yuh gonna act a fool over that ol book, Ah'll take it n burn it up."

"Naw, Ma, please."

"Waal, set down n be still!"

He sat down and drew the oil lamp close. He thumbed page after page, unaware of the food his mother set on the table. His father came in. Then his small brother.

"Whutcha got there, Dave?" his father asked.

"Jusa catlog," he answered, not looking up.

"Yeah, here they is!" His eyes glowed at blue-and-black revolvers. He glanced up, feeling sudden guilt. His father was watching him. He eased the book under the table and rested it on his knees. After the blessing was asked, he ate. He scooped up peas and swallowed fat meat without chewing. Buttermilk helped to wash it down. He did not want to mention money before his father. He would do much better by cornering his mother when she was alone. He looked at his father uneasily out of the edge of his eye.

"Boy, how come yuh don quit foolin wid tha book n eat yo suppah?"

"Yessuh."

"How you n ol man Hawkins gitten erlong?"

"Suh?"

"Can't yuh hear? Why don yuh lissen? Ah ast yu how wuz yuh n ol man Hawkins gittin erlong?"

"Oh, swell, Pa. Ah plows mo lan than anybody over there."

"Waal, yuh oughta keep you mind on whut yuh doin."

"Yessuh."

He poured his plate full of molasses and sopped it up slowly with a chunk of cornbread. When his father and brother had left the kitchen, he still sat and looked again at the guns in the catalogue, longing to muster courage enough to present his case to his mother. Lawd, ef Ah only had tha pretty one! He could almost feel the slickness of the weapon with his fingers. If he had a gun like that he would polish it and keep it shining so it would never rust. N Ah'd keep it loaded, by Gawd!

"Ma?" His voice was hesitant.

"Hunh?"

"Ol man Hawkins give yuh mah money yit?"

"Yeah, but ain no usa yuh thinking bout throwin nona it erway. Ahm keeping tha money sos yuh kin have cloes t go to school this winter."

He rose and went to her side with the open catalogue in his palms. She was washing dishes, her head bent low over a pan. Shyly he raised the book. When he spoke, his voice was husky, faint.

"Ma, Gawd knows Ah wans one of these."

"One of whut?" she asked, not raising her eyes.

"One of these," he said again, not daring even to point. She glanced up at the page, then at him with wide eyes.

"Nigger, is yuh gone plumb crazy?"

"Aw, Ma —"

"Git outta here! Don yuh talk t me bout no gun! Yuh a fool!"

"Ma, Ah kin buy one fer two dollahs."

"Not ef Ah knows it, yuh ain!"

"But yuh promised me one —"

"Ah don care what Ah promised! Yuh ain nothing but a boy yit!"

"Ma, ef yuh lemme buy one Ah'll *never* ast yuh fer nothing no mo."

"Ah tol yuh t git outta here! Yuh ain gonna toucha penny of tha money fer no gun! Thas how come Ah has Mistah Hawkins t pay yo wages t me, cause Ah knows yuh ain got no sense."

"But, Ma, we needa gun. Pa ain got no gun. We needa gun in the house. Yuh kin never tell whut might happen."

"Now don yuh try to maka fool outta me, boy! Ef we did hava gun, yuh wouldn't have it!"

He laid the catalogue down and slipped his arm around her waist.

"Aw, Ma, Ah done worked hard alla summer n ain ast yuh fer nothing, is Ah, now?"

"Thas whut yuh spose t do!"

"But Ma, Ah wans a gun. Yuh kin lemme have two dollahs outta mah money. Please, Ma. I kin give it to Pa. . . . Please, Ma! Ah loves yuh, Ma."

When she spoke her voice came soft and low.

"What yu wan wida gun, Dave? Yuh don need no gun. Yuh'll git in trouble. N ef yo pa jus thought Ah let yuh have money t buy a gun he'd hava fit."

"Ah'll hide it, Ma. It ain but two dollahs."

"Lawd, chil, whut's wrong wid yuh?"

"Ain nothin wrong, Ma. Ahm almos a man now. Ah wans a gun."

"Who gonna sell yuh a gun?"

"Ol Joe at the sto."

"N it don cos but two dollahs?"

"Thas all, Ma. Jus two dollahs. Please, Ma."

She was stacking the plates away; her hands moved slowly, reflectively. Dave kept an anxious silence. Finally, she turned to him.

"Ah'll let yuh git tha gun ef yuh promise me one thing."

"What's tha, Ma?"

"Yuh bring it straight back t me, yuh hear? It be fer Pa."

"Yessum! Lemme go now, Ma."

She stooped, turned slightly to one side, raised the hem of her dress, rolled down the top of her stocking, and came up with a slender wad of bills.

"Here," she said. "Lawd knows yuh don need no gun. But yer pa does. Yuh bring it right back t me, yuh hear? Ahma put it up. Now ef yuh don, Ahma have yuh pa lick yuh so hard yuh won fergit it."

"Yessum."

He took the money, ran down the steps, and across the yard.

"Dave! Yuuuuuh Daaaaave!"

He heard, but he was not going to stop now. "Now, Lawd!"

The first movement he made the following morning was to reach under his pillow for the gun. In the gray light of dawn he held it loosely, feeling a sense of power. Could kill a man with a gun like this. Kill anybody, black or white. And if he were holding his gun in his hand, nobody could run over him; they would have to respect him. It was a big gun, with a long barrel and a heavy handle. He raised and lowered it in his hand, marveling at its weight.

He had not come straight home with it as his mother had asked; instead he had stayed out in the fields, holding the weapon in his hand, aiming it now and then at some imaginary foe. But he had not fired it; he had been afraid that his father might hear. Also he was not sure he knew how to fire it.

To avoid surrendering the pistol he had not come into the house until he knew that they were all asleep. When his mother had tiptoed to his bedside late that night and demanded the gun, he had first played possum; then he had told her that the gun was hidden outdoors, that he would bring it to her in the morning. Now he lay turning it slowly in his hands. He broke it, took out the cartridges, felt them, and then put them back.

He slid out of bed, got a long strip of old flannel from a trunk, wrapped the gun in it, and tied it to his naked thigh while it was still loaded. He did not go in to breakfast. Even though it was not yet daylight, he started for Jim Hawkins' plantation. Just as the sun was rising he reached the barns where the mules and plows were kept.

"Hey! That you, Dave?"

He turned. Jim Hawkins stood eying him suspiciously.

"What're yuh doing here so early?"

"Ah didn't know Ah wuz gittin up so early, Mistah Hawkins. Ah was fixin t hitch up ol Jenny n take her t the fiels."

"Good. Since you're so early, how about plowing that stretch down by the woods?"

"Suits me, Mistah Hawkins."

"O.K. Go to it!"

He hitched Jenny to a plow and started across the fields. Hot dog! This was just what he wanted. If he could get down by the woods, he could shoot his gun and nobody would hear. He walked behind the plow, hearing the traces creaking, feeling the gun tied tight to his thigh.

When he reached the woods, he plowed two whole rows before he decided to take out the gun. Finally, he stopped, looked in all directions, then untied the gun and held it in his hand. He turned to the mule and smiled.

"Know whut this is, Jenny? Naw, yuh wouldn know! Yuhs jusa ol mule! Anyhow, this is a gun, n it kin shoot, by Gawd!"

He held the gun at arm's length. Whut t hell, Ahma shoot this thing! He looked at Jenny again.

"Lissen here, Jenny! When Ah pull this ol trigger, Ah don wan yuh t run n acka fool now!"

Jenny stood with head down, her short ears pricked straight. Dave walked off about twenty feet, held the gun far out from him at arm's length, and turned his head. Hell, he told himself, Ah ain afraid. The gun felt loose in his fingers; he waved it wildly for a moment. Then he shut his eyes and tightened his forefinger. Bloom! A report half deafened him and he thought his right hand was torn from his arm. He heard Jenny whinnying and galloping over the field, and he found himself on his knees, squeezing his fingers hard between his legs. His hand was numb; he jammed it into his mouth, trying to warm it, trying to stop the pain. The gun lay at his feet. He did not quite know what had happened. He stood up and stared at the gun as though it were a living thing. He gritted his teeth and kicked the gun. Yuh almos broke mah arm! He turned to look for Jenny; she was far over the fields, tossing her head and kicking wildly.

"Hol on there, ol mule!"

When he caught up with her she stood trembling, walling her big white eyes at him. The plow was far away; the traces had broken. Then Dave stopped short, looking, not believing. Jenny was bleeding. Her left side was red and wet with blood. He went closer. Lawd, have mercy! Wondah did Ah shoot this mule? He grabbed for Jenny's mane. She flinched, snorted, whirled, tossing her head.

"Hol on now! Hol on."

Then he saw the hole in Jenny's side, right between the ribs. It was round, wet, red. A crimson stream streaked down the front leg, flowing fast. Good Gawd! Ah wuzn't shootin at tha mule. He felt panic. He knew he had to stop that blood, or Jenny would bleed to death. He had never seen so much blood in all his life. He chased the mule for half a mile, trying to catch her. Finally she stopped, breathing hard, stumpy tail half arched. He caught her mane and led her back to where the plow and gun lay. Then he stopped and grabbed handfuls of damp black earth and tried to plug the bullet hole. Jenny shuddered, whinnied, and broke from him.

"Hol on! Hol on now!"

He tried to plug it again, but blood came anyhow. His fingers were hot and sticky. He rubbed dirt into his palms, trying to dry them. Then again he attempted to plug the bullet hole, but Jenny shied away, kicking her heels high. He stood helpless. He had to do something. He ran at Jenny; she dodged him. He watched a red stream of blood flow down Jenny's leg and form a bright pool at her feet.

"Jenny . . . Jenny," he called weakly.

His lips trembled. She's bleeding t death! He looked in the direction of home, wanting to go back, wanting to get help. But he saw the pistol lying in the damp black clay. He had a queer feeling that if he only did something, this would not be; Jenny would not be there bleeding to death.

When he went to her this time, she did not move. She stood with sleepy, dreamy eyes; and when he touched her she gave a low-pitched whinny and knelt to the ground, her front knees slopping in blood.

"Jenny . . . Jenny . . ." he whispered.

For a long time she held her neck erect; then her head sank, slowly. Her ribs swelled with a mighty heave and she went over.

Dave's stomach felt empty, very empty. He picked up the gun and held it gingerly between his thumb and forefinger. He buried it at the foot of a tree. He took a stick to cover the pool of blood with dirt — but what was the use? There was Jenny lying with her mouth open and her eyes walled and glassy. He could not tell Jim Hawkins he had shot his mule. But he had to tell something. Yeah, Ah'll tell em Jenny started gittin wil n fell on the joint of the plow. . . . But that would hardly happen to a mule. He walked across the field slowly, head down.

It was sunset. Two of Jim Hawkins' men were over near the edge of the woods digging a hole in which to bury Jenny. Dave was surrounded by a knot of people, all of whom were looking down at the dead mule.

"I don't see how in the world it happened," said Jim Hawkins for the tenth time.

The crowd parted and Dave's mother, father, and small brother pushed into the center.

"Where Dave?" his mother called.

"There he is," said Jim Hawkins.

His mother grabbed him.

"Whut happened, Dave? Whut yuh done?"

"Nothin."

"C mon, boy, talk," his father said.

Dave took a deep breath and told the story he knew nobody believed.

"Waal," he drawled. "Ah brung ol Jenny down here sos Ah could do mah plowin. Ah plowed bout two rows, just like yuh see." He stopped and pointed at the long rows of upturned earth. "Then somethin musta been wrong wid ol Jenny. She wouldn ack right a-tall. She started snortin n kickin her heels. Ah tried t hol her, but she pulled erway, rearin n goin in. Then when the point of the plow was stickin up in the air, she swung erroun n twisted herself back on it. . . . She stuck herself n started t bleed. N fo Ah could do anything, she wuz dead."

"Did you ever hear of anything like that in all your life?" asked Jim Hawkins.

There were white and black standing in the crowd. They murmured. Dave's mother came close to him and looked hard into his face. "Tell the truth, Dave," she said.

"Looks like a bullet hole to me," said one man.

"Dave, whut yuh do wid the gun?" his mother asked.

The crowd surged in, looking at him. He jammed his hands into his pockets, shook his head slowly from left to right, and backed away. His eyes were wide and painful.

"Did he hava gun?" asked Jim Hawkins.

"By Gawd, Ah tol yuh tha wuz a gun wound," said a man, slapping his thigh.

His father caught his shoulders and shook him till his teeth rattled.

"Tell whut happened, yuh rascal! Tell whut. . . ."

Dave looked at Jenny's stiff legs and began to cry.

"Whut yuh do wid tha gun?" his mother asked.

"What wuz he doin wida gun?" his father asked.

"Come on and tell the truth," said Hawkins. "Ain't nobody going to hurt you. . . ."

His mother crowded close to him.

"Did yuh shoot tha mule, Dave?"

Dave cried, seeing blurred white and black faces.

"Ahh ddinn gggo tt sshooot hher. . . . Ah ssswear ffo Gawd Ahh ddin. . . . Ah wuz a-tryin t sssee ef the old gggun would sshoot —"

"Where yuh git the gun from?" his father asked.

"Ah got it from Joe, at the sto."

"Where yuh git the money?"

"Ma give it t me."

"He kept worryin me, Bob. Ah had t. Ah tol im t bring the gun right back t me. . . . It was fer yuh, the gun."

"But how yuh happen to shoot that mule?" asked Jim Hawkins.

"Ah wuzn shootin at the mule, Mistah Hawkins. The gun jumped when Ah pulled the trigger. . . . N fo Ah knowed anythin Jenny was there a-bleedin."

Somebody in the crowd laughed. Jim Hawkins walked close to Dave and looked into his face.

"Well, looks like you have bought you a mule, Dave."

"Ah swear fo Gawd, Ah didn go t kill the mule, Mistah Hawkins!"

"But you killed her!"

All the crowd was laughing now. They stood on tiptoe and poked heads over one another's shoulders.

"Well, boy, looks like yuh done bought a dead mule! Hahaha!"

"Ain tha ershame."

"Hohohohoho."

Dave stood, head down, twisting his feet in the dirt.

"Well, you needn't worry about it, Bob," said Jim Hawkins to Dave's father. "Just let the boy keep on working and pay me two dollars a month."

"Whut yuh wan fer yo mule, Mistah Hawkins?"

Jim Hawkins screwed up his eyes.

"Fifty dollars."

"Whut yuh do wid tha gun?" Dave's father demanded.

Dave said nothing.

"Yuh wan me t take a tree n beat yuh till yuh talk!"

"Nawsuh!"

"Whut yuh do wid it?"

"Ah throwed it erway."

"Where?"

"Ah . . . Ah throwed it in the creek."

"Waal, c mon home. N firs thing in the mawnin git to tha creek n fin tha gun."

"Yessuh."

"Whut yuh pay fer it?"

"Two dollahs."

"Take tha gun n git yo money back n carry it to Mistah Hawkins, yuh hear? N don fergit Ahma lam you black bottom good fer this! Now march yosef on home, suh!"

Dave turned and walked slowly. He heard people laughing. Dave glared, his eyes welling with tears. Hot anger bubbled in him. Then he swallowed and stumbled on.

That night Dave did not sleep. He was glad that he had gotten out of killing the mule so easily, but he was hurt. Something hot seemed to turn over inside him each time he remembered how they had laughed. He tossed on his bed, feeling his hard pillow. N Pa says he's gonna beat me. . . . He remembered other beatings, and his back quivered. Naw, naw, Ah sho don wan im t beat me tha way no mo. Dam em all! Nobody ever gave him anything. All he did was work. They treat me like a mule, n then they beat me. He gritted his teeth. N Ma had t tell on me.

Well, if he had to, he would take old man Hawkins that two dollars. But that meant selling the gun. And he wanted to keep that gun. Fifty dollars for a dead mule.

He turned over, thinking how he had fired the gun. He had an itch to fire it again. Ef other men kin shoota gun, by Gawd, Ah kin! He was still, listening. Mebbe they all sleepin now. The house was still. He heard the soft breathing of his brother. Yes, now! He would go down and get that gun and see if he could fire it! He eased out of bed and slipped into overalls.

The moon was bright. He ran almost all the way to the edge of the woods. He stumbled over the ground, looking for the spot where he had buried the gun. Yeah, here it is. Like a hungry dog scratching for a bone, he pawed it up. He puffed his black cheeks and blew dirt from the trigger and barrel. He broke it and found four cartridges unshot. He looked around; the fields were filled with silence and moonlight. He clutched the gun stiff and hard in his fingers. But, as soon as he wanted to pull the trigger, he shut his eyes and turned his head. Naw, Ah can't shoot wid mah eyes closed n mah head turned. With effort he held his eyes open; then he squeezed. *Blooooom!* He was stiff, not breathing. The gun was still in his hands. Dammit, he'd done it! He fired again. *Blooooom!* He smiled. *Bloooom! Blooooom! Click, click.* There! It was empty. If anybody could shoot a gun, he could. He put the gun into his hip pocket and started across the fields.

When he reached the top of a ridge he stood straight and proud in the moonlight, looking at Jim Hawkins' big white house, feeling the gun sagging in his pocket. Lawd, ef Ah had just one mo bullet Ah'd taka shot at tha house. Ah'd like t scare ol man Hawkins jusa little. . . . Jusa enough t let im know Dave Saunders is a man.

To his left the road curved, running to the tracks of the Illinois Central. He jerked his head, listening. From far off came a faint *hoooof-hoooof; hoooof-hoooof.* . . . He stood rigid. Two dollahs a mont. Les see now. . . . Tha means it'll take bout two years. Shucks! Ah'll be dam!

He started down the road, toward the tracks. Yeah, here she comes! He stood beside the track and held himself stiffly. Here she comes, erroun the ben. . . . C mon, yuh slow poke! C mon! He had his hand on his gun; something quivered in his stomach. Then the train thundered past, the gray and brown box cars rumbling and clinking. He gripped the gun tightly; then he jerked his hand out of his pocket. Ah betcha Bill wouldn't do it! Ah betcha. . . . The cars slid past, steel grinding upon steel. Ahm ridin yuh ternight, so hep me Gawd! He was hot all over. He hesitated just a moment; then he grabbed, pulled atop of a car, and lay flat. He felt his pocket; the gun was still there. Ahead the long rails were glinting in the moonlight, stretching away, away to somewhere, somewhere where he could be a man. . . .

5

COMMENTARIES ON STORIES AND STORYTELLERS

SHERWOOD ANDERSON *commented on his practice of writing short stories in his autobiography,* A Story Teller's Story, *published in 1924. This book was his first attempt to write his memoirs and authenticate his "legend" — an impoverished childhood, a revolt against business life, and an entrance into the avant-garde literary circles of Chicago, New Orleans, and New York. He was more concerned with the meaning than with the facts of his life. In his rejection of the "plot" story (a story emphasizing plot over character, setting, or theme), which he considered contrived fiction, he became a strong influence on many subsequent writers of short stories and revitalized the American short story tradition.*

SHERWOOD ANDERSON

Form, Not Plot, in the Short Story — *1924*

For such men as myself you must understand there is always a great difficulty about telling the tale after the scent has been picked up. . . . Having, from a conversation overheard or in some other way, got the tone of a tale, I was like a woman who has just become impregnated. Something was growing inside me. At night when I lay in my bed I could feel the heels of the tale kicking against the walls of my body. Often as I lay thus every word of the tale came to me quite clearly but when I got out of bed to write it down the words would not come.

I had constantly to seek in roads new to me. Other men had felt what I had felt, had seen what I had seen — how had they met the difficulties I faced? My father when he told his tales walked up and down the room before his audience. He pushed out little experimental sentences and watched his audience narrowly. There was a dull-eyed old farmer sitting in a corner of the room. Father had his eyes on the fellow. "I'll get him," he said to himself. He watched the farmer's eyes. When the experimental sentence he had tried did not get anywhere he tried another and kept trying. Besides words he had — to help the telling of his tales — the advantage of being able to act out those parts for which he could find no words. He could frown, shake his fists, smile, let a look of pain or annoyance drift over his face.

These were his advantages that I had to give up if I was to write my tales rather than tell them and how often I had cursed my fate.

How significant words had become to me! At about this time an American woman living in Paris, Miss Gertrude Stein, had published a book called *Tender Buttons* and it had come into my hands. How it had excited me! Here was something purely experimental and dealing in words separated from sense — in the ordinary meaning of the word sense — an approach I was sure the poets must often be compelled to make. Was it an approach that would help me? I decided to try it.

A year or two before the time of which I am now writing an American painter, Mr. Felix Russman, had taken me one day into his workshop to show me his colors. He laid them out on a table before me and then his wife called him out of the room and he stayed for half an hour. It had been one of the most exciting moments of my life. I shifted the little pans of color about, laid one color against another. I walked away and came near. Suddenly there had flashed into my consciousness, for perhaps the first time in my life, the secret inner world of the painters. Before that time I had wondered often enough why certain paintings, done by the old masters, and hung in our Chicago Art Institute, had so strange an effect upon me. Now I thought I knew. The true painter revealed all of himself in every stroke of his brush. Titian made one feel so utterly the splendor of himself; from Fra Angelico and Sandro Botticelli there came such a deep human tenderness that on some days it fairly brought tears to the eyes; in a most dreadful way and in spite of all his skill Bouguereau gave away his own inner nastiness while Leonardo made one feel all of the grandeur of his mind just as Balzac° had made his readers feel the universality and wonder of his mind.

Very well then, the words used by the tale-teller were as the colors used by the painter. Form was another matter. It grew out of the materials of the tale and the teller's reaction to them. It was the tale trying to take form that kicked about inside the tale-teller at night when he wanted to sleep.

And words were something else. Words were the surfaces, the clothes of the tale. I thought I had begun to get something a little clearer now. I had smiled to myself a little at the sudden realization of how little native American

---

Balzac: Honoré de Balzac (1799–1850), French novelist, one of the earliest realists.

words had been used by American story-writers. When most American writers wanted to be very American they went in for slang. Surely we American scribblers had paid long and hard for the English blood in our veins. The English had got their books into our schools, their ideas of correct forms of expression were firmly fixed in our minds. Words as commonly used in our writing were in reality an army that marched in a certain array and the generals in command of the army were still English. One saw the words as marching, always just so — in books — and came to think of them so — in books.

But when one told a tale to a group of advertising men sitting in a barroom in Chicago or to a group of laborers by a factory door in Indiana one instinctively disbanded the army. There were moments then for what have always been called by our correct writers "unprintable words." One got now and then a certain effect by a bit of profanity. One dropped instinctively into the vocabulary of the men about, was compelled to do so to get the full effect sought for the tale. Was the tale he was telling not just the tale of a man named Smoky Pete and how he caught his foot in the trap set for himself? — or perhaps one was giving them the Mama Geigans story. The devil. What had the words of such a tale to do with Thackeray° or Fielding?° Did the men to whom one told the tale not know a dozen Smoky Petes and Mama Geigans? Had one ventured into the classic English models for tale-telling at that moment there would have been a roar. "What the devil! Don't you go high-toning us!"

And it was sure one did not always seek a laugh from his audience. Sometimes one wanted to move the audience, make them squirm with sympathy. Perhaps one wanted to throw an altogether new light on a tale the audience already knew.

Would the common words of our daily speech in shops and offices do the trick? Surely the Americans among whom one sat talking had felt everything the Greeks had felt, everything the English felt? Deaths came to them, the tricks of fate assailed their lives. I was certain none of them lived felt or talked as the average American novel made them live feel and talk and as for the plot short stories of the magazines — those bastard children of the de Maupassant, Poe, and O. Henry° — it was certain there were no plot short stories ever lived in any life I had known anything about.

❧

JAMES BALDWIN *wrote this account of how he became a writer in his book* Notes of a Native Son *(1955). He admitted that "the most difficult (and most rewarding) thing in my life has been the fact that I was born a Negro and was forced, therefore, to effect some kind of truce with this reality." As his biographer Louis H.*

Thackeray: William Makepeace Thackeray (1811–1863), English novelist.
Fielding: Henry Fielding (1707–1754), one of the first English novelists.
O. Henry: The pseudonym of William Sydney Porter (1862–1910), a famous American author of short stories with elaborate plots and often "trick" endings.

Pratt has understood, this "truce" forced Baldwin "into an open confrontation with his experience, enabling him to make an honest assessment of his past. . . . Baldwin the artist has been liberated because he has found a way to use his past and to transform those experiences resulting therefrom into art."

JAMES BALDWIN

Autobiographical Notes

1955

I was born in Harlem thirty-one years ago. I began plotting novels at about the time I learned to read. The story of my childhood is the usual bleak fantasy, and we can dismiss it with the unrestrained observation that I certainly would not consider living it again. In those days my mother was given to the exasperating and mysterious habit of having babies. As they were born, I took them over with one hand and held a book with the other. The children probably suffered, though they have since been kind enough to deny it, and in this way I read *Uncle Tom's Cabin* and *A Tale of Two Cities* over and over and over again; in this way, in fact, I read just about everything I could get my hands on — except the Bible, probably because it was the only book I was encouraged to read. I must also confess that I wrote — a great deal — and my first professional triumph, in any case, the first effort of mine to be seen in print, occurred at the age of twelve or thereabouts, when a short story I had written about the Spanish revolution won some sort of prize in an extremely short-lived church newspaper. I remember the story was censored by the lady editor, though I don't remember why, and I was outraged.

Also wrote plays, and songs, for one of which I received a letter of congratulations from Mayor La Guardia, and poetry, about which the less said, the better. My mother was delighted by all these goings-on, but my father wasn't; he wanted me to be a preacher. When I was fourteen I became a preacher, and when I was seventeen I stopped. Very shortly thereafter I left home. For God knows how long I struggled with the world of commerce and industry — I guess they would say they struggled with *me* — and when I was about twenty-one I had enough done of a novel to get a Saxton Fellowship. When I was twenty-two the fellowship was over, the novel turned out to be unsalable, and I started waiting on tables in a Village° restaurant and writing book reviews — mostly, as it turned out, about the Negro problem, concerning which the color of my skin made me automatically an expert. Did another book, in company with photographer Theodore Pelatowski, about the storefront churches in Harlem. This book met exactly the same fate as my first — fellowship, but no sale. (It was a Rosenwald Fellowship.) By the time I was twenty-four I had decided to stop reviewing books about the Negro problem — which, by this time, was only slightly less horrible in print than it was in life — and I packed my bags and went to France, where I finished, God knows how, *Go Tell It on the Mountain*.

Village: Greenwich Village, New York City.

Any writer, I suppose, feels that the world into which he was born is nothing less than a conspiracy against the cultivation of his talent — which attitude certainly has a great deal to support it. On the other hand, it is only because the world looks on his talent with such a frightening indifference that the artist is compelled to make his talent important. So that any writer, looking back over even so short a span of time as I am here forced to assess, finds that the things which hurt him and the things which helped him cannot be divorced from each other; he could be helped in a certain way only because he was hurt in a certain way; and his help is simply to be enabled to move from one conundrum to the next — one is tempted to say that he moves from one disaster to the next. When one begins looking for influences one finds them by the score. I haven't thought much about my own, not enough anyway; I hazard that the King James Bible, the rhetoric of the store-front church, something ironic and violent and perpetually understated in Negro speech — and something of Dickens' love for bravura — have something to do with me today; but I wouldn't stake my life on it. Likewise, innumerable people have helped me in many ways; but finally, I suppose, the most difficult (and most rewarding) thing in my life has been the fact that I was born a Negro and was forced, therefore, to effect some kind of truce with this reality. (Truce, by the way, is the best one can hope for.)

One of the difficulties about being a Negro writer (and this is not special pleading, since I don't mean to suggest that he has it worse than anybody else) is that the Negro problem is written about so widely. The bookshelves groan under the weight of information, and everyone therefore considers himself informed. And this information, furthermore, operates usually (generally, popularly) to reinforce traditional attitudes. Of traditional attitudes there are only two — For or Against — and I, personally, find it difficult to say which attitude has caused me the most pain. I am perfectly aware that the change from ill-will to good-will, however motivated, however imperfect, however expressed, is better than no change at all.

But it is part of the business of the writer — as I see it — to examine attitudes, to go beneath the surface, to tap the source. From this point of view the Negro problem is nearly inaccessible. It is not only written about so widely; it is written about so badly. It is quite possible to say that the price a Negro pays for becoming articulate is to find himself, at length, with nothing to be articulate about. ("You taught me the language," says Caliban to Prospero,° "and my profit on't is I know how to curse.") Consider: The tremendous social activity that this problem generates imposes on whites and Negroes alike the necessity of looking forward, of working to bring about a better day. This is fine, it keeps the waters troubled; it is all, indeed, that has made possible the Negro's progress. Nevertheless, social affairs are not generally speaking the writer's prime concern, whether they ought to be or not; it is absolutely necessary that he establish between himself and these affairs a distance that will allow, at least, for clarity, so that before he can look forward in any meaningful

---

Caliban . . . Prospero: In Shakespeare's *The Tempest,* the monster Caliban is a servant of the magician Prospero.

sense, he must first be allowed to take a long look back. In the context of the Negro problem neither whites nor blacks, for excellent reasons of their own, have the faintest desire to look back; but I think that the past is all that makes the present coherent, and further, that the past will remain horrible for exactly as long as we refuse to assess it honestly.

I know, in any case, that the most crucial time in my own development came when I was forced to recognize that I was a kind of bastard of the West; when I followed the line of my past I did not find myself in Europe but in Africa. And this meant that in some subtle way, in a really profound way, I brought to Shakespeare, Bach, Rembrandt, to the stones of Paris, to the cathedral at Chartres, and to the Empire State Building, a special attitude. These were not really my creations, they did not contain my history; I might search in them in vain forever for any reflection of myself. I was an interloper; this was not my heritage. At the same time I had no other heritage which I could possibly hope to use — I had certainly been unfitted for the jungle or the tribe. I would have to appropriate these white centuries, I would have to make them mine — I would have to accept my special attitude, my special place in this scheme — otherwise I would have no place in *any* scheme. What was the most difficult was the fact that I was forced to admit something I had always hidden from myself, which the American Negro has had to hide from himself as the price of his public progress; that I hated and feared white people. This did not mean that I loved black people; on the contrary, I despised them, possibly because they failed to produce Rembrandt. In effect, I hated and feared the world. And this meant, not only that I thus gave the world an altogether murderous power over me, but also that in such a self-destroying limbo I could never hope to write.

One writes out of one thing only — one's own experience. Everything depends on how relentlessly one forces from this experience the last drop, sweet or bitter, it can possibly give. This is the only real concern of the artist, to recreate out of the disorder of life that order which is art. The difficulty then, for me, of being a Negro writer was the fact that I was, in effect, prohibited from examining my own experience too closely by the tremendous demands and the very real dangers of my social situation.

I don't think the dilemma outlined above is uncommon. I do think, since writers work in the disastrously explicit medium of language, that it goes a little way towards explaining why, out of the enormous resources of Negro speech and life, and despite the example of Negro music, prose written by Negroes has been generally speaking so pallid and so harsh. I have not written about being a Negro at such length because I expect that to be my only subject, but only because it was the gate I had to unlock before I could hope to write about anything else. I don't think that the Negro problem in America can be even discussed coherently without bearing in mind its context; its context being the history, traditions, customs, the moral assumptions and preoccupations of the country; in short, the general social fabric. Appearances to the contrary, no one in America escapes its effects and everyone in America bears some responsibility for it. I believe this the more firmly because it is the overwhelming tendency to speak of this problem as though it were a thing apart. But in the work of Faulkner, in the general attitude and certain specific passages in Robert Penn Warren,° and, most significantly, in the advent of Ralph Ellison, one sees the beginnings — at least — of a more genuinely penetrating search. Mr. Ellison, by the way, is the first Negro novelist I have ever read to utilize in language, and brilliantly, some of the ambiguity and irony of Negro life.

About my interests: I don't know if I have any, unless the morbid desire to own a sixteen-millimeter camera and make experimental movies can be so classified. Otherwise, I love to eat and drink — it's my melancholy conviction that I've scarcely ever had enough to eat (this is because it's *impossible* to eat enough if you're worried about the next meal) — and I love to argue with people who do not disagree with me too profoundly, and I love to laugh. I do *not* like bohemia, or bohemians, I do not like people whose principal aim is pleasure, and I do not like people who are *earnest* about anything. I don't like people who like me because I'm a Negro; neither do I like people who find in the same accident grounds for contempt. I love America more than any other country in the world, and, exactly for this reason, I insist on the right to criticize her perpetually. I think all theories are suspect, that the finest principles may have to be modified, or may even be pulverized by the demands of life, and that one must find, therefore, one's own moral center and move through the world hoping that this center will guide one aright. I consider that I have many responsibilities, but none greater than this: to last, as Hemingway says, and get my work done.

I want to be an honest man and a good writer.

JOHN CHEEVER *wrote this article for the October 30, 1978, issue of* Newsweek. *He was newsworthy at that time because he had just published a collection of short fiction,* The Stories of John Cheever, *which had become a best-seller. Cheever humorously refers to his early financial struggles in the article, but in Susan Cheever's book* Home Before Dark *(1984), she remembers that her father was often deeply frustrated by how little he earned from* The New Yorker. *"The money they paid him just wasn't enough to live on — even in the years when we children were in public schools and the family in a rented house." The second part of the* Newsweek *article almost becomes a story about Cheever's suburban neighborhood. Evidently there was nothing in the contemporary scene that he could not turn into a narrative.*

JOHN CHEEVER

Why I Write Short Stories — *1978*

To publish a definitive collection of short stories in one's late sixties seems to me, as an American writer, a traditional and a dignified occasion,

Robert Penn Warren: An American novelist, poet, and critic (1905–1989).

eclipsed in no way by the fact that a great many of the stories in my current collection were written in my underwear.

This is not to say that I was ever a Bohemian. Hardly a man is now alive who can remember when Harold Ross edited *The New Yorker* magazine, but I am one of these. The Ross editorial queries were genuinely eccentric. In one short story of mine, I invented a character who returned home from work and changed his clothes before dinner. Ross wrote on the galley margin, "Eh? What's this? Cheever looks to me like a one-suiter." He was so right. At the space rates he paid, I could afford exactly one suit. In the mornings, I dressed in this and took the elevator to a windowless room in the basement where I worked. Here I hung my suit on a hanger, wrote until nightfall when I dressed and returned to our apartment. A great many of my stories were written in boxer shorts.

A collection of short stories appears like a lemon in the current fiction list, which is indeed a garden of love, erotic horseplay, and lewd and ancient family history; but so long as we are possessed by experience that is distinguished by its intensity and its episodic nature, we will have the short story in our literature, and without a literature we will, of course, perish. It was F. R. Leavis who said that literature is the first distinction of a civilized man.

Who reads short stories? one is asked, and I like to think that they are read by men and women in the dentist's office, waiting to be called to the chair; they are read on transcontinental plane trips instead of watching a banal and vulgar film spin out the time between our coasts; they are read by discerning and well-informed men and women who seem to feel that narrative fiction can contribute to our understanding of one another and the sometimes bewildering world around us.

The novel, in all its greatness, demands at least some passing notice of the classical unities, preserving that mysterious link between esthetics and moral fitness; but to have this unyielding antiquity exclude the newness in our ways of life would be regrettable. This newness is known to some of us through "Star Wars," to some of us through the melancholy that follows a fielder's error in the late innings of a ball game. In the pursuit of this newness, contemporary painting seems to have lost the language of the landscape, the still-life, and — most important — the nude. Modern music has been separated from those rhythms and tonalities that are most deeply ingrained in our memories, but literature still possesses the narrative — the story — and one would defend this with one's life.

In the short stories of my esteemed colleagues — and in a few of my own — I find those rented summer houses, those one-night love affairs, and those lost key rings that confound traditional esthetics. We are not a nomadic people, but there is more than a hint of this spirit of our great country — and the short story is the literature of the nomad.

I like to think that the view of a suburban street that I imagine from my window would appeal to a wanderer or to someone familiar with loneliness. Here is a profoundly moving display of nostalgia, vision, and love, none of it more than thirty years old, including most of the trees. Here are white columns from the manorial South, brick and timber walls from Elizabethan

England, saltbox houses from our great maritime past, and flat-roofed echoes of Frank Lloyd Wright° and his vision of a day when we would all enjoy solar heating, serene and commodious interiors, and peace on earth.

The lots are 1½ acres, flowers and vegetables grow in the yards, and here and there one finds, instead of tomatoes, robust stands of cannabis with its feathery leaf. Here, in this victorious domesticity, the principal crop is a hazardous drug. And what do I see hanging in the Hartshores' clothes-yard but enough seasoning marijuana to stone a regiment.

Is forgetfulness some part of the mysteriousness of life? If I speak to Mr. Hartshore about his cannabis crop, will he tell me that the greatness of Chinese civilization stood foursquare on the fantasies of opium? But it is not I who will speak to Mr. Hartshore. It will be Charlie Dilworth, a very abstemious man who lives in the house next door. He has a No Smoking sign on his front lawn, and his passionate feelings about marijuana have been intelligently channeled into a sort of reverse blackmail.

I hear them litigating late one Saturday afternoon when I have come back from playing touch football with my sons. The light is going. It is autumn. Charlie's voice is loud and clear and can be heard by anyone interested. "You keep your dogs off my lawn, you cook your steaks in the house, you keep your record player down, you keep your swimming-pool filter off in the evenings, and you keep your window shades drawn. Otherwise, I'll report your drug crop to the police and with my wife's uncle sitting as judge this month you'll get at least six months in the can for criminal possession."

They part. Night falls. Here and there a housewife, apprehending the first frost, takes in her house plants while from an Elizabethan, a Nantucket, and a Frank Lloyd Wright chimney comes the marvelous fragrance of wood smoke. You can't put this scene in a novel.

❧

ANTON CHEKHOV *described his theories of literature and his practice as a storyteller in countless letters to his family and friends. He was not a systematic critic, and he did not necessarily follow his own advice to other writers. Brevity and concentration on a few essentials of scene and character were the essence of his technique, but he was not always as drastically laconic in his stories as his letters suggest. What is consistently clear in his advice to other writers is his own untiring compassion and his desire to speak honestly in his efforts to help them. He wrote in his notebook, "It is not the function of art to solve problems but to present them clearly."*

These letters are to his older brother, his publisher, and a younger author whose work he admired.

Frank Lloyd Wright: American architect (1867–1959).

ANTON CHEKHOV

Technique in Writing the Short Story

1886–99

TRANSLATED BY CONSTANCE GARNETT

FROM A LETTER TO ALEXANDER P. CHEKHOV, 1886

In my opinion a true description of Nature should be very brief and have a character of relevance. Commonplaces such as, "the setting sun bathing in the waves of the darkening sea, poured its purple gold, etc." — "the swallows flying over the surface of the water twittered merrily" — such commonplaces one ought to abandon. In descriptions of Nature one ought to seize upon the little particulars, grouping them in such a way that, in reading, when you shut your eyes, you get a picture.

For instance, you will get the full effect of a moonlight night if you write that on the mill-dam a little glowing star-point flashed from the neck of a broken bottle, and the round, black shadow of a dog, or a wolf, emerged and ran, etc. Nature becomes animated if you are not squeamish about employing comparisons of her phenomena with ordinary human activities, etc.

In the sphere of psychology, details are also the thing. God preserve us from commonplaces. Best of all is it to avoid depicting the hero's state of mind; you ought to try to make it clear from the hero's actions. It is not necessary to portray many characters. The center of gravity should be in two persons: him and her.

FROM A LETTER TO ALEKSEY S. SUVORIN, 1890

You abuse me for objectivity, calling it indifference to good and evil, lack of ideals and ideas, and so on. You would have me, when I describe horse-thieves, say: "Stealing horses is an evil." But that has been known for ages without my saying so. Let the jury judge them; it's my job simply to show what sort of people they are. I write: You are dealing with horse-thieves, so let me tell you that they are not beggars but well-fed people, that they are people of a special cult, and that horse-stealing is not simply theft but a passion. Of course it would be pleasant to combine art with a sermon, but for me personally it is extremely difficult and almost impossible, owing to the conditions of technique. You see, to depict horse-thieves in seven hundred lines I must all the time speak and think in their tone and feel in their spirit, otherwise, if I introduce subjectivity, the image becomes blurred and the story will not be as compact as all short stories ought to be. When I write, I reckon entirely upon the reader to add for himself the subjective elements that are lacking in the story.

FROM A LETTER TO MAXIM GORKY, 1899

More advice: when reading the proofs, cross out a host of terms qualifying nouns and verbs. You have so many such terms that the reader's mind finds it a task to concentrate on them, and he soon grows tired. You understand it at once when I say, "The man sat on the grass"; you understand it because it is clear and makes no demands on the attention. On the other hand, it is not easily understood, and it is difficult for the mind, if I write, "A tall, narrow-chested, middle-sized man, with a red beard, sat on the green grass, already trampled by pedestrians, sat silently, shyly, and timidly looked about him." That is not immediately grasped by the mind, whereas good writing should be grasped at once — in a second.

ꙮ

KATE CHOPIN *made a number of translations, mostly of stories by Guy de Maupassant, and she published several essays on literature in St. Louis periodicals. She wrote about the influence of Maupassant on her fiction in response to an invitation from the editor of the* Atlantic Monthly *in 1896. He returned her first version of the essay, however, advising her to "set forth the matter directly." Her revised version was later included in the magazine with the title "In the Confidence of a Story-Teller," but the section describing how she first encountered Maupassant's tales and the impression they made on her was dropped, perhaps because she spoke so enthusiastically about the French writer's escape "from tradition and authority." This portion of the essay is reprinted from the manuscript included in Volume 2 of* The Complete Works of Kate Chopin *(1969).*

KATE CHOPIN

How I Stumbled upon Maupassant 1896

About eight years ago there fell accidentally into my hands a volume of Maupassant's tales. These were new to me. I had been in the woods, in the fields, groping around; looking for something big, satisfying, convincing, and finding nothing but — myself; a something neither big nor satisfying but wholly convincing. It was at this period of my emerging from the vast solitude in which I had been making my own acquaintance, that I stumbled upon Maupassant. I read his stories and marvelled at them. Here was life, not fiction; for where were the plots, the old fashioned mechanism and stage trapping that in a vague, unthinking way I had fancied were essential to the art of story making? Here was a man who had escaped from tradition and authority, who had entered into himself and looked out upon life through his own being and with his own eyes; and who, in a direct and simple way, told us what he saw. When a man does this, he gives us the best that he can; something valuable for it is genuine and spontaneous. He gives us his impressions. Someone told me the other day that Maupassant had gone out of fashion. I was not grieved to hear it. He has never seemed to me to belong to the multitude, but rather to the individual. He is not one whom we gather in crowds to listen to — whom we follow in procession — with beating of brass instruments. He does not move us to throw ourselves into the throng — having the integral of an unthinking whole to shout his praise. I even like to think that he appeals to me alone. You probably like to think that he reaches you exclusively. A whole multitude may be secretly nourishing the belief in regard to him for all I know. Someway I like to cherish the delusion that he has spoken to no one else so directly, so intimately as he does to me. He did not say, as another might have done, "do you see these are charming stories of mine? take them into your closet — study them closely — mark their combination — observe the method, the manner of their putting together — and if ever you are moved to write stories you can do no better than to imitate."

JOSEPH CONRAD *wrote his essay "The Condition of Art" as the preface to his third novel,* The Nigger of the Narcissus *(1897).*

JOSEPH CONRAD

The Condition of Art

1897

A work that aspires, however humbly, to the condition of art should carry its justification in every line. And art itself may be defined as a single-minded attempt to render the highest kind of justice to the visible universe, by bringing to light the truth, manifold and one, underlying its every aspect. It is an attempt to find in its forms, in its colours, in its light, in its shadows, in the aspects of matter, and in the facts of life what of each is fundamental, what is enduring and essential — their one illuminating and convincing quality — the very truth of their existence. The artist, then, like the thinker or the scientist, seeks the truth and makes his appeal. Impressed by the aspect of the world the thinker plunges into ideas, the scientist into facts — whence, presently, emerging they make their appeal to those qualities of our being that fit us best for the hazardous enterprise of living. They speak authoritatively to our common sense, to our intelligence, to our desire of peace, or to our desire of unrest; not seldom to our prejudices, sometimes to our fears, often to our egoism — but always to our credulity. And their words are heard with reverence, for their concern is with weighty matters: with the cultivation of our minds and the proper care of our bodies, with the attainment of our ambitions, with the perfection of the means and the glorification of our precious aims.

It is otherwise with the artist.

Confronted by the same enigmatical spectacle the artist descends within himself, and in that lonely region of stress and strife, if he be deserving and fortunate, he finds the terms of his appeal. His appeal is made to our less obvious capacities: to that part of our nature which, because of the warlike conditions of existence, is necessarily kept out of sight within the more resisting and hard qualities — like the vulnerable body within a steel armour. His appeal is less loud, more profound, less distinct, more stirring — and sooner forgotten. Yet its effect endures for ever. The changing wisdom of successive generations discards ideas, questions facts, demolishes theories. But the artist appeals to that part of our being which is not dependent on wisdom; to that in us which is a gift and not an acquisition — and, therefore, more permanently enduring. He speaks to our capacity for delight and wonder, to the sense of mystery surrounding our lives; to our sense of pity, and beauty, and pain; to the latent feeling of fellowship with all creation — and to the subtle but invincible conviction of solidarity that knits together the loneliness of innumerable hearts, to the solidarity in dreams, in joy, in sorrow, in aspirations, in illusions, in hope, in fear, which binds men to each other, which binds together all humanity — the dead to the living and the living to the unborn.

It is only some such train of thought, or rather of feeling, that can in a measure explain the aim of the attempt, made in the tale which follows, to present an unrestful episode in the obscure lives of a few individuals out of all the disregarded multitude of the bewildered, the simple, and the voiceless. For, if any part of truth dwells in the belief confessed above, it becomes evident that there is not a place of splendour or a dark corner of the earth that does not deserve, if only a passing glance of wonder and pity. The motive, then, may be held to justify the matter of the work; but this preface, which is simply an avowal of endeavour, cannot end here — for the avowal is not yet complete.

Fiction — if it at all aspires to be art — appeals to temperament. And in truth it must be, like painting, like music, like all art, the appeal of one temperament to all the other innumerable temperaments whose subtle and resistless power endows passing events with their true meaning, and creates the moral, the emotional atmosphere of the place and time. Such an appeal to be effective must be an impression conveyed through the senses; and, in fact, it cannot be made in any other way, because temperament, whether individual or collective, is not amenable to persuasion. All art, therefore, appeals primarily to the senses, and the artistic aim when expressing itself in written words must also make its appeal through the senses, if its high desire is to reach the secret spring of responsive emotions. It must strenuously aspire to the plasticity of sculpture, to the colour of painting, and to the magic suggestiveness of music — which is the art of arts. And it is only through complete, unswerving devotion to the perfect blending of form and substance; it is only through an unremitting never-discouraged care for the shape and ring of sentences that an approach can be made to plasticity, to colour, and that the light of magic suggestiveness may be brought to play for an evanescent instant over the commonplace surface of words: of the old, old words, worn thin, defaced by ages of careless usage.

The sincere endeavour to accomplish that creative task, to go as far on that road as his strength will carry him, to go undeterred by faltering, weariness, or reproach, is the only valid justification for the worker in prose. And if his conscience is clear, his answer to those who, in the fullness of a wisdom which looks for immediate profit, demand specifically to be edified, consoled, amused; who demand to be promptly improved, or encouraged, or frightened, or shocked, or charmed, must run thus: My task which I am trying to achieve is, by the power of the written word to make you hear, to make you feel — it is, before all, to make you see. That — and no more, and it is everything. If I succeed, you shall find there according to your deserts: encouragement, consolation, fear, charm — all you demand — and, perhaps, also that glimpse of truth for which you have forgotten to ask.

To snatch in a moment of courage, from the remorseless rush of time, a passing phase of life, is only the beginning of the task. The task approached in tenderness and faith is to hold up unquestioningly, without choice and without fear, the rescued fragment before all eyes in the light of a sincere mood. It is to show its vibration, its colour, its form; and through its movement, its form, and its colour, reveal the substance of its truth — disclose its inspiring secret: the stress and passion within the core of each convincing moment. In a single-minded attempt of that kind, if one be deserving and fortunate, one may perchance attain to such clearness of sincerity that at last the presented vision of regret or pity, of terror or mirth, shall awaken in the hearts of the beholders that feeling of unavoidable solidarity; of the solidarity in mysterious origin, in toil, in joy, in hope, in uncertain fate, which binds men to each other and all mankind to the visible world.

It is evident that he who, rightly or wrongly, holds by the convictions expressed above cannot be faithful to any one of the temporary formulas of his craft. The enduring part of them — the truth which each only imperfectly veils — should abide with him as the most precious of his possessions, but they all: Realism, Romanticism, Naturalism, even the unofficial sentimentalism (which, like the poor, is exceedingly difficult to get rid of), all these gods must, after a short period of fellowship, abandon him — even on the very threshold of the temple — to the stammerings of his conscience and to the outspoken consciousness of the difficulties of his work. In that uneasy solitude the supreme cry of Art for Art itself, loses the exciting ring of its apparent immorality. It sounds far off. It has ceased to be a cry, and is heard only as a whisper, often incomprehensible, but at times and faintly encouraging.

Sometimes, stretched at ease in the shade of a roadside tree, we watch the motions of a labourer in a distant field, and after a time, begin to wonder languidly as to what the fellow may be at. We watch the movements of his body, the waving of his arms, we see him bend down, stand up, hesitate, begin again. It may add to the charm of an idle hour to be told the purpose of his exertions. If we know he is trying to lift a stone, to dig a ditch, to uproot a stump, we look with a more real interest at his efforts; we are disposed to condone the jar of his agitation upon the restfulness of the landscape; and even, if in a brotherly frame of mind, we may bring ourselves to forgive his failure. We understood his object, and, after all, the fellow has tried, and perhaps he had not the strength — and perhaps he had not the knowledge. We forgive, go on our way — and forget.

And so it is with the workman of art. Art is long and life is short, and success is very far off. And thus, doubtful of strength to travel so far, we talk a little about the aim — the aim of art, which, like life itself, is inspiring, difficult — obscured by mists. It is not in the clear logic of a triumphant conclusion; it is not in the unveiling of one of those heartless secrets which are called the Laws of Nature. It is not less great, but only more difficult.

To arrest, for the space of a breath, the hands busy about the work of the earth, and compel men entranced by the sight of distant goals to glance for a moment at the surrounding vision of form and colour, of sunshine and shadows; to make them pause for a look, for a sigh, for a smile — such is the aim, difficult and evanescent, and reserved only for a very few to achieve. But sometimes, by the deserving and the fortunate, even that task is accomplished. And when it is accomplished — behold! — all the truth of life is there: a moment of vision, a sigh, a smile — and the return to an eternal rest.

STEPHEN CRANE *wrote about the wreck of the* Commodore *in the article "Stephen Crane's Own Story" in the* New York Press *on January 7, 1897. At that time arms and provisions were being smuggled from Florida to Cuba to aid the insurrection against Spanish rule. Crane boarded the* Commodore *in Jacksonville on December 31, 1896. The ship was loaded with a cargo of rifles and ammunition. As the scholar Olov W. Fryckstedt explained, Crane "looked forward to a long period of unknown adventures and exciting dangers in the Cuban mountains. But during the night of January 1 the ship foundered fifteen miles off the coast of Florida after a mysterious explosion in the engine room." The first part of Crane's newspaper story describes the loading of the ship, the peril of sandbars, the explosion in the engine room, and the lowering of the lifeboats. Then, with the ship's "whistle of despair," it became clear to everyone onboard that the situation was hopeless. The bustling action before the shipwreck is the substance of Crane's newspaper report; his thirty desperate hours afterward in the ten-foot rowboat became the story of "The Open Boat."*

STEPHEN CRANE

The Sinking of the Commodore

1897

A WHISTLE OF DESPAIR

Now the whistle of the *Commodore* had been turned loose, and if there ever was a voice of despair and death, it was in the voice of this whistle. It had gained a new tone. It was as if its throat was already choked by the water, and this cry on the sea at night, with a wind blowing the spray over the ship, and the waves roaring over the bow, and swirling white along the decks, was to each of us probably a song of man's end.

It was now that the first mate showed a sign of losing his grip. To us who were trying in all stages of competence and experience to launch the lifeboat he raged in all terms of fiery satire and hammerlike abuse. But the boat moved at last and swung down toward the water.

Afterward, when I went aft, I saw the captain standing, with his arm in a sling, holding on to a stay with his one good hand and directing the launching of the boat. He gave me a five-gallon jug of water to hold, and asked me what I was going to do. I told him what I thought was about the proper thing, and he told me then that the cook had the same idea, and ordered me to go forward and be ready to launch the ten-foot dingey.

IN THE TEN-FOOT DINGEY

I remember well that he turned then to swear at a colored stoker who was prowling around, done up in life preservers until he looked like a feather bed. I went forward with my five-gallon jug of water, and when the captain came we launched the dingey, and they put me over the side to fend her off from the ship with an oar.

They handed me down the water jug, and then the cook came into the boat, and we sat there in the darkness, wondering why, by all our hopes of future happiness, the captain was so long in coming over to the side and ordering us away from the doomed ship.

The captain was waiting for the other boat to go. Finally he hailed in the darkness: "Are you all right, Mr. Graines?"

The first mate answered: "All right, sir."

"Shove off, then," cried the captain.

The captain was just about to swing over the rail when a dark form came forward and a voice said, "Captain, I go with you."

The captain answered: "Yes, Billy; get in."

HIGGINS LAST TO LEAVE SHIP

It was Billy Higgins, the oiler. Billy dropped into the boat and a moment later the captain followed, bringing with him an end of about forty yards of lead line. The other end was attached to the rail of the ship.

As we swung back to leeward the captain said: "Boys, we will stay right near the ship till she goes down."

This cheerful information, of course, filled us all with glee. The line kept us headed properly into the wind, and as we rode over the monstrous waves we saw upon each rise the swaying lights of the dying *Commodore.*

When came the gray shade of dawn, the form of the *Commodore* grew slowly clear to us as our little ten-foot boat rose over each swell. She was floating with such an air of buoyancy that we laughed when we had time, and said, "What a gag it would be on those other fellows if she didn't sink at all."

But later we saw men aboard of her, and later still they began to hail us.

HELPING THEIR MATES

I had forgot to mention that previously we had loosened the end of the lead line and dropped much further to leeward. The men on board were a mystery to us, of course, as we had seen all the boats leave the ship. We rowed back to the ship, but did not approach too near, because we were four men in a ten-foot boat, and we knew that the touch of a hand on our gunwale would assuredly swamp us.

The first mate cried out from the ship that the third boat had foundered alongside. He cried that they had made rafts, and wished us to tow them.

The captain said, "All right."

Their rafts were floating astern. "Jump in!" cried the captain, but there was a singular and most harrowing hesitation. There were five white men and two negroes. This scene in the gray light of morning impressed one as would a view into some place where ghosts move slowly. These seven men on the stern of the sinking *Commodore* were silent. Save the words of the mate to the captain there was no talk. Here was death, but here also was a most singular and indefinable kind of fortitude.

Four men, I remember, clambered over the railing and stood there watching the cold, steely sheen of the sweeping waves.

"Jump," cried the captain again.

The old chief engineer first obeyed the order. He landed on the outside raft and the captain told him how to grip the raft and he obeyed as promptly and as docilely as a scholar in riding school.

THE MATE'S MAD PLUNGE

A stoker followed him, and then the first mate threw his hands over his head and plunged into the sea. He had no life belt and for my part, even when he did this horrible thing, I somehow felt that I could see in the expression of his hands, and in the very toss of his head, as he leaped thus to death, that it was rage, rage, rage unspeakable that was in his heart at the time.

And then I saw Tom Smith, the man who was going to quit filibustering after this expedition, jump to a raft and turn his face toward us. On board the *Commodore* three men strode, still in silence and with their faces turned toward us. One man had his arms folded and was leaning against the deckhouse. His feet were crossed, so that the toe of his left foot pointed downward. There they stood gazing at us, and neither from the deck nor from the rafts was a voice raised. Still was there this silence.

TRIED TO TOW THE RAFTS

The colored stoker on the first raft threw us a line and we began to tow. Of course, we perfectly understood the absolute impossibility of any such thing; our dingey was within six inches of the water's edge, there was an enormous sea running, and I knew that under the circumstances a tugboat would have no light task in moving these rafts.

But we tried it, and would have continued to try it indefinitely, but that something critical came to pass. I was at an oar and so faced the rafts. The cook controlled the line. Suddenly the boat began to go backward and then we saw this negro on the first raft pulling on the line hand over hand and drawing us to him.

He had turned into a demon. He was wild — wild as a tiger. He was crouched on this raft and ready to spring. Every muscle of him seemed to be turned into an elastic spring. His eyes were almost white. His face was the face of a lost man reaching upward, and we knew that the weight of his hand on our gunwale doomed us.

THE *COMMODORE* SINKS

The cook let go of the line. We rowed around to see if we could not get a line from the chief engineer, and all this time, mind you, there were no shrieks, no groans, but silence, silence and silence, and then the *Commodore* sank.

She lurched to windward, then swung afar back, righted and dove into the sea, and the rafts were suddenly swallowed by this frightful maw of the ocean. And then by the men on the ten-foot dingey were words said that were still not words — something far beyond words.

The lighthouse of Mosquito Inlet stuck up above the horizon like the point of a pin. We turned our dingey toward the shore.

The history of life in an open boat for thirty hours would no doubt be instructive for the young, but none is to be told here and now. For my part I would prefer to tell the story at once, because from it would shine the splendid manhood of Captain Edward Murphy and of William Higgins, the oiler, but let it suffice at this time to say that when we were swamped in the surf and making the best of our way toward the shore the captain gave orders amid the wildness of the breakers as clearly as if he had been on the quarter deck of a battleship.

John Kitchell of Daytona came running down the beach, and as he ran the air was filled with clothes. If he had pulled a single lever and undressed, even as the fire horses harness, he could not seem to me to have stripped with more speed. He dashed into the water and dragged the cook. Then he went after the captain, but the captain sent him to me, and then it was that he saw Billy Higgins lying with his forehead on sand that was clear of the water, and he was dead.

RALPH ELLISON *gave an interview for the "Art of Fiction" series of the* Paris Review *that was reprinted in his volume of essays,* Shadow and Act *(1964). In the introduction to that book he said that what is basic to the fiction writer's confrontation with the world is "converting experience into symbolic action. Good fiction is made of that which is real, and reality is difficult to come by. So much of it depends upon the individual's willingness to discover his true self, upon his defining himself — for the time being at least — against his background."*

RALPH ELLISON

The Influence of Folklore on "Battle Royal" *1964*

Interviewer: Can you give us an example of the use of folklore in your own novel?

Ellison: Well, there are certain themes, symbols, and images which are based on folk material. For example, there is the old saying amongst Negroes: If you're black, stay back; if you're brown, stick around; if you're white, you're right. And there is the joke Negroes tell on themselves about their being so black they can't be seen in the dark. In my book this sort of thing was merged with the meanings which blackness and light have long had in Western mythology: evil and goodness, ignorance and knowledge, and so on. In my novel the narrator's development is one through blackness to light; that is, from ignorance to enlightenment: invisibility to visibility. He leaves the South and goes North; this, as you will notice in reading Negro folktales, is always the road to freedom — the movement upward. You have the same thing again when he leaves his underground cave for the open.

It took me a long time to learn how to adapt such examples of myth into my work — also ritual. The use of ritual is equally a vital part of the creative process. I learned a few things from Eliot, Joyce, and Hemingway, but not how to adapt them. When I started writing, I knew that in both *The Waste Land*° and *Ulysses*° ancient myth and ritual were used to give form and significance to the material; but it took me a few years to realize that the myths and rites which we find functioning in our everyday lives could be used in the same way. In my first attempt at a novel — which I was unable to complete — I began by trying to manipulate the simple structural unities of *beginning, middle,* and *end,* but when I attempted to deal with the psychological strata — the images, symbols, and emotional configurations — of the experience at hand, I discovered that the unities were simply cool points of stability on which one could suspend the narrative line — but beneath the surface of apparently rational human relationships there seethed a chaos before which I was helpless. People rationalize what they shun or are incapable of dealing with; these superstitions and their rationalizations become ritual as they govern behavior. The rituals become social forms, and it is one of the functions of the artist to recognize them and raise them to the level of art.

I don't know whether I'm getting this over or not. Let's put it this way: Take the "Battle Royal" passage in my novel, where the boys are blindfolded and forced to fight each other for the amusement of the white observers. This is a vital part of behavior pattern in the South, which both Negroes and whites thoughtlessly accept. It is a ritual in preservation of caste lines, a keeping of taboo to appease the gods and ward off bad luck. It is also the initiation ritual to which all greenhorns are subjected. This passage which states what Negroes will see I did not have to invent; the patterns were already there in society, so that all I had to do was present them in a broader context of meaning. In any society there are many rituals of situation which, for the most part, go unquestioned. They can be simple or elaborate, but they are the connective tissue between the work of art and the audience.

Interviewer: Do you think a reader unacquainted with this folklore can properly understand your work?

Ellison: Yes, I think so. It's like jazz; there's no inherent problem which prohibits understanding but the assumptions brought to it. We don't all dig Shakespeare uniformly, or even *Little Red Riding Hood.* The understanding of art depends finally upon one's willingness to extend one's humanity and one's knowledge of human life. I noticed, incidentally, that the Germans, having no special caste assumptions concerning American Negroes, dealt with my work simply as a novel. I think Americans will come to view it that way in twenty years — if it's around that long.

The Waste Land: A long, extremely influential poem (1922) by T. S. Eliot (1888–1965).
Ulysses: An experimental novel (1922) by James Joyce (1882–1941).

Interviewer: Don't you think it will be?

Ellison: I doubt it. It's not an important novel. I failed of eloquence, and many of the immediate issues are rapidly fading away. If it does last, it will be simply because there are things going on in its depth that are of more permanent interest than on its surface. I hope so, anyway.

ꟹ

WILLIAM FAULKNER *was writer-in-residence at the University of Virginia in 1957 and 1958. During that time he encouraged students to ask questions about his writing. He answered more than 2,000 queries on everything from spelling to the nature of man, including a series of questions about "A Rose for Emily" addressed to him at different interviews by students of Frederick Gwynn and Joseph Blotner. These professors later edited the book* Faulkner in the University *(1959), in which the following excerpt first appeared.*

WILLIAM FAULKNER

The Meaning of "A Rose for Emily"

1959

Interviewer: What is the meaning of the title "A Rose for Emily"?

Faulkner: Oh, it's simply the poor woman had had no life at all. Her father had kept her more or less locked up and then she had a lover who was about to quit her, she had to murder him. It was just "A Rose for Emily" — that's all.

Interviewer: I was wondering, one of your short stories, "A Rose for Emily," what ever inspired you to write this story . . . ?

Faulkner: That to me was another sad and tragic manifestation of man's condition in which he dreams and hopes, in which he is in conflict with himself or with his environment or with others. In this case there was the young girl with a young girl's normal aspirations to find love and then a husband and a family, who was brow-beaten and kept down by her father, a selfish man who didn't want her to leave home because he wanted a housekeeper, and it was a natural instinct of — repressed which — you can't repress it — you can mash it down but it comes up somewhere else and very likely in a tragic form, and that was simply another manifestation of man's injustice to man, of the poor tragic human being struggling with its own heart, with others, with its environment, for the simple things which all human beings want. In that case it was a young girl that just wanted to be loved and to love and to have a husband and a family.

Interviewer: And that purely came from your imagination?

Faulkner: Well, the story did but the condition is there. It exists. I didn't invent that condition, I didn't invent the fact that young girls dream of someone to love and children and a home, but the story of what her own particular tragedy was was invented, yes. . . .

Interviewer: Sir, it has been argued that "A Rose for Emily" is a criticism of the North, and others have argued saying that it is a criticism of the South. Now, could this story, shall we say, be more properly classified as a criticism of the times?

Faulkner: Now that I don't know, because I was simply trying to write about people. The writer uses environment — what he knows — and if there's a symbolism in which the lover represented the North and the woman who murdered him represents the South, I don't say that's not valid and not there, but it was no intention of the writer to say, Now let's see, I'm going to write a piece in which I will use a symbolism for the North and another symbol for the South, that he was simply writing about people, a story which he thought was tragic and true, because it came out of the human heart, the human aspiration, the human — the conflict of conscience with glands, with the Old Adam. It was a conflict not between the North and the South so much as between, well you might say, God and Satan.

Interviewer: Sir, just a little more on that thing. You say it's a conflict between God and Satan. Well, I don't quite understand what you mean. Who is — did one represent the ——

Faulkner: The conflict was in Miss Emily, that she knew that you do not murder people. She had been trained that you do not take a lover. You marry, you don't take a lover. She had broken all the laws of her tradition, her background, and she had finally broken the law of God too, which says you do not take human life. And she knew she was doing wrong, and that's why her own life was wrecked. Instead of murdering one lover, and then to go and take another and when she used him up to murder him, she was expiating her crime.

Interviewer: Was the "Rose for Emily" an idea or a character? Just how did you go about it?

Faulkner: That came from a picture of the strand of hair on the pillow. It was a ghost story. Simply a picture of a strand of hair on the pillow in the abandoned house.

SANDRA M. GILBERT AND SUSAN GUBAR *presented a feminist reading of Charlotte Perkins Gilman's "The Yellow Wallpaper" in* The Madwoman in the Attic: The Woman Writer and the Nineteenth-Century Literary Imagination *(1979). In this book they argued that a recognizable literary tradition existed in English and American literature in which the female imagination had demonstrated "the anxiety of authorship." According to Gilbert and Gubar, "Images of enclosure and escape, fantasies in which maddened doubles functioned as asocial surrogates for docile selves . . . such patterns reoccurred throughout this tradition, along with obsessive depictions of diseases like anorexia, agoraphobia, and claustrophobia." Gilman's story is securely within this tradition of the "literature of confinement," in which a woman writer, trapped by the patriarchal society, tries to struggle free "through strategic redefinitions of self, art, and society."*

SANDRA M. GILBERT AND SUSAN GUBAR

A Feminist Reading of Gilman's "The Yellow Wallpaper"

1979

As if to comment on the unity of all these points — on, that is, the anxiety-inducing connections between what women writers tend to see as their parallel confinements in texts, houses, and maternal female bodies — Charlotte Perkins Gilman brought them all together in 1890 in a striking story of female confinement and escape, a paradigmatic tale which (like *Jane Eyre*°) seems to tell *the* story that all literary women would tell if they could speak their "speechless woe." "The Yellow Wallpaper," which Gilman herself called "a description of a case of nervous breakdown," recounts in the first person the experiences of a woman who is evidently suffering from a severe postpartum psychosis. Her husband, a censorious and paternalistic physician, is treating her according to methods by which S. Weir Mitchell, a famous "nerve specialist," treated Gilman herself for a similar problem. He has confined her to a large garret room in an "ancestral hall" he has rented, and he has forbidden her to touch pen to paper until she is well again, for he feels, says the narrator, "that with my imaginative power and habit of story-making, a nervous weakness like mine is sure to lead to all manner of excited fancies, and that I ought to use my will and good sense to check the tendency."

The cure, of course, is worse than the disease, for the sick woman's mental condition deteriorates rapidly. "I think sometimes that if I were only well enough to write a little it would relieve the press of ideas and rest me," she remarks, but literally confined in a room she thinks is a one-time nursery because it has "rings and things" in the walls, she is literally locked away from creativity. The "rings and things," although reminiscent of children's gymnastic equipment, are really the paraphernalia of confinement, like the gate at the head of the stairs, instruments that definitively indicate her imprisonment. Even more tormenting, however, is the room's wallpaper: a sulphurous yellow paper, torn off in spots, and patterned with "lame uncertain curves" that "plunge off at outrageous angles" and "destroy themselves in unheard of contradictions." Ancient, smoldering, "unclean" as the oppressive structures of the society in which she finds herself, this paper surrounds the narrator like an inexplicable text, censorious and overwhelming as her physician husband, haunting as the "hereditary estate" in which she is trying to survive. Inevitably she studies its suicidal implications — and inevitably, because of her "imaginative power and habit of story-making," she revises it, projecting her own passion for escape into its otherwise incomprehensible hieroglyphics. "This wallpaper," she decides, at a key point in her story,

> has a kind of subpattern in a different shade, a particularly irritating one, for you can only see it in certain lights, and not clearly then.

Jane Eyre: The classic Victorian novel (1847) by Charlotte Brontë (1816–1855) is considered an important feminist work.

> But in the places where it isn't faded and where the sun is just so — I can see a strange, provoking, formless sort of figure, that seems to skulk about behind that silly and conspicuous front design.

As time passes, this figure concealed behind what corresponds (in terms of what we have been discussing) to the facade of the patriarchal text becomes clearer and clearer. By moonlight the pattern of the wallpaper "becomes bars! The outside pattern I mean, and the woman behind it is as plain as can be." And eventually, as the narrator sinks more deeply into what the world calls madness, the terrifying implications of both the paper and the figure imprisoned behind the paper begin to permeate — that is, to *haunt* — the rented ancestral mansion in which she and her husband are immured. The "yellow smell" of the paper "creeps all over the house," drenching every room in its subtle aroma of decay. And the woman creeps too — through the house, in the house, and out of the house, in the garden and "on that long road under the trees." Sometimes, indeed, the narrator confesses, "I think there are a great many women" both behind the paper and creeping in the garden, "and sometimes only one, and she crawls around fast, and her crawling shakes [the paper] all over. . . . And she is all the time trying to climb through. But nobody could climb through that pattern — it strangles so; I think that is why it has so many heads."

Eventually it becomes obvious to both reader and narrator that the figure creeping through and behind the wallpaper is both the narrator and the narrator's double. By the end of the story, moreover, the narrator has enabled this double to escape from her textual/architectural confinement: "I pulled and she shook, I shook and she pulled, and before morning we had peeled off yards of that paper." Is the message of the tale's conclusion mere madness? Certainly the righteous Doctor John — whose name links him to the anti-hero of Charlotte Brontë's *Villette* — has been temporarily defeated, or at least momentarily stunned. "Now why should that man have fainted?" the narrator ironically asks as she creeps around her attic. But John's unmasculine swoon of surprise is the least of the triumphs Gilman imagines for her madwoman. More significant are the madwoman's own imaginings and creations, mirages of health and freedom with which her author endows her like a fairy godmother showering gold on a sleeping heroine. The woman from behind the wallpaper creeps away, for instance, creeps fast and far on the long road, in broad daylight. "I have watched her sometimes away off in the open country," says the narrator, "creeping as fast as a cloud shadow in a high wind."

Indistinct and yet rapid, barely perceptible but inexorable, the progress of that cloud shadow is not unlike the progress of nineteenth-century literary women out of the texts defined by patriarchal poetics into the open spaces of their own authority. That such an escape from the numb world behind the patterned walls of the text was a flight from disease into health was quite clear to Gilman herself. When "The Yellow Wallpaper" was published she sent it to Weir Mitchell whose strictures had kept her from attempting the pen during her own breakdown, thereby aggravating her illness, and she was delighted to learn, years later, that "he had changed his treatment of nervous prostration since reading" her story. "If that is a fact," she declared, "I have not lived in vain." Because she was a rebellious feminist besides being a medical iconoclast, we can be sure that Gilman did not think of this triumph of hers in narrowly therapeutic terms. Because she knew, with Emily Dickinson, that "Infection in the sentence breeds," she knew that the cure for female despair must be spiritual as well as physical, aesthetic as well as social. What "The Yellow Wallpaper" shows she knew, too, is that even when a supposedly "mad" woman has been sentenced to imprisonment in the "infected" house of her own body, she may discover that, as Sylvia Plath° was to put it seventy years later, she has "a self to recover, a queen."

CHARLOTTE PERKINS GILMAN *wrote her autobiography,* The Living of Charlotte Perkins Gilman *(1935), in the last years of her life. Her intelligence and strength of character are evident in this work, as is her modesty after a long career as an eminent American feminist. Her straightforward description of her mental breakdown nearly fifty years earlier is in marked contrast to the obsessive fantasy of her story "The Yellow Wallpaper," written shortly after her illness.*

CHARLOTTE PERKINS GILMAN

Undergoing the Cure for Nervous Prostration 1935

This was a worse horror than before, for now I saw the stark fact — that I was well while away and sick while at home — a heartening prospect! Soon ensued the same utter prostration, the unbearable inner misery, the ceaseless tears. A new tonic had been invented, Essence of Oats, which was given me, and did some good for a time. I pulled up enough to do a little painting that fall, but soon slipped down again and stayed down. An old friend of my mother's, dear Mrs. Diman, was so grieved at this condition that she gave me a hundred dollars and urged me to go away somewhere and get cured.

At that time the greatest nerve specialist in the country was Dr. S. W. Mitchell of Philadelphia. Through the kindness of a friend of Mr. Stetson's living in that city, I went to him and took "the rest cure"; went with the utmost confidence, prefacing the visit with a long letter giving "the history of the case" in a way a modern psychologist would have appreciated. Dr. Mitchell only thought it proved self-conceit. He had a prejudice against the Beechers. "I've had two women of your blood here already," he told me scornfully. This eminent physician was well versed in two kinds of nervous prostration; that of the business man exhausted from too much work, and the society woman exhausted from too much play. The kind I had was evidently behind him. But he did reassure me on one point — there was no dementia, he said, only hysteria.

Sylvia Plath: American poet (1932–1963). See p. 1103.

I was put to bed and kept there. I was fed, bathed, rubbed, and responded with the vigorous body of twenty-six. As far as he could see there was nothing the matter with me, so after a month of this agreeable treatment he sent me home, with this prescription:

> Live as domestic a life as possible. Have your child with you all the time. (Be it remarked that if I did but dress the baby it left me shaking and crying — certainly far from a healthy companionship for her, to say nothing of the effect on me.) Lie down an hour after each meal. Have but two hours' intellectual life a day. And never touch pen, brush, or pencil as long as you live.

I went home, followed those directions rigidly for months, and came perilously near to losing my mind. The mental agony grew so unbearable that I would sit blankly moving my head from side to side — to get out from under the pain. Not physical pain, not the least "headache" even, just mental torment, and so heavy in its nightmare gloom that it seemed real enough to dodge.

I made a rag baby, hung it on a doorknob, and played with it. I would crawl into remote closets and under beds — to hide from the grinding pressure of that profound distress. . . .

Finally, in the fall of '87, in a moment of clear vision, we agreed to separate, to get a divorce. There was no quarrel, no blame for either one, never an unkind word between us, unbroken mutual affection — but it seemed plain that if I went crazy, it would do my husband no good, and be a deadly injury to my child.

What this meant to the young artist, the devoted husband, the loving father, was so bitter a grief and loss that nothing would have justified breaking the marriage save this worse loss which threatened. It was not a choice between going and staying, but between going, sane, and staying, insane. If I had been of the slightest use to him or to the child, I would have "stuck it," as the English say. But this progressive weakening of the mind made a horror unnecessary to face; better for that dear child to have separated parents than a lunatic mother.

We had been married four years and more. This miserable condition of mind, this darkness, feebleness, and gloom, had begun in those difficult years of courtship, had grown rapidly worse after marriage, and was now threatening utter loss; whereas I had repeated proof that the moment I left home I began to recover. It seemed right to give up a mistaken marriage.

Our mistake was mutual. If I had been stronger and wiser I should never have been persuaded into it. Our suffering was mutual too, his unbroken devotion, his manifold cares and labors in tending a sick wife, his adoring pride in the best of babies, all coming to naught, ending in utter failure — we sympathized with each other but faced a bitter necessity. The separation must come as soon as possible, the divorce must wait for conditions.

If this decision could have been reached sooner it would have been much better for me, the lasting mental injury would have been less. Such recovery as I have made in forty years, and the work accomplished, seem to show that the fear of insanity was not fulfilled, but the effects of nerve bankruptcy remain to this day. So much of my many failures, of misplay and misunderstanding and "queerness" is due to this lasting weakness, and kind friends so unfailingly refuse to allow for it, to believe it, that I am now going to some length in stating the case.

JANICE HUBBARD HARRIS *wrote* The Short Fiction of D. H. Lawrence *(1984) after the scholar Mark Spilka pointed out to her in the late 1960s that there was no critical literature on Lawrence's stories. "Where were the analyses of that lively body of fiction capable, as Julian Moynahan says, of bringing light back into the eyes of the reader exhausted by* The Plumed Serpent *or fainting amid the incremental repetitions of* The Rainbow?*" Her critical approach to the stories incorporates several modes — biographical, psychological, sociological, feminist. Comparing Lawrence with his contemporaries James Joyce, Katherine Mansfield, and Virginia Woolf, Harris concludes that "Lawrence is clearly the leader in range, sheer quantity of masterpieces, and, something harder to define, in stretching the conventions of the [short story] genre to include a variety of new possibilities."*

JANICE H. HARRIS

Levels of Meaning in Lawrence's "The Rocking-Horse Winner"

1984

"The Rocking-Horse Winner" opens with the distant, singsong voice of a fairy tale: "There was a woman who was beautiful, who started with all the advantages, yet she had no luck." So begins an ancient tale. A brave young boy is challenged by his true love. He rides off into a dreamland where he struggles and succeeds at attaining secret knowledge. He brings the secret knowledge back and with it wins treasure houses of gold, giving all to his love. Undercutting this fairy tale, however, is another, which forms a grotesque shadow, a nightmare counter to the wish fulfillment narrative. The "true love" of the brave young boy is his cold-hearted mother. The quest he has embarked on is hopeless, for every success brings a new and greater trial. Like the exhausted and terrified daughter in Rumplestiltskin, this son is perpetually set the task of spinning more gold. In this tale, no magical dwarf comes to the child's aid; the boy finally spins himself out, dropping dead on his journey, his eyes turned to stone. Like all good fairy tales, this one has several complementary levels of reference: social, familial, psychological.

On the social level, the tale reads as a satire on the equation of money, love, luck, and happiness. The target of the satire, the mother, cannot be happy without an unending flow of cold, sure cash. As she sees it, luck and lucre are the same thing. Yearning for some response and real affection from her, Paul adds the term "love," making a solid, tragic construction. Quite simply, the tale concludes that these equations are deadly. The mother, representing a society run on a money ethic, has given the younger generation a murderous education.

On a familial level, the tale dramatizes an idea implied as early as *Sons and Lovers* but overtly stated only in a late autobiographical fragment and these last tales. The idea is that mothers shape their sons into the desirable opposite of their husbands. Whatever they are powerless to prevent or alter in their mates, mothers will seek to prevent or alter in their sons. In "The Rocking-Horse Winner," the woman cannot alter her husband's ineffectuality. She herself tries to be effective in the world of commerce and money, but she fails, partly because of the lack of opportunities available to her. So she turns unconsciously to her son. In this reading, Paul's death owes less to the specific character of his mother's demands and more to the strength of those demands. He dies — cannot live, cannot grow and flourish — partly because he is too good a son, and she is a woman with unbounded desires and no way to work directly toward their gratification. In *Sons and Lovers,* the young son kills, literally and figuratively, the paralyzed and paralyzing mother. The alternative pattern, which Lawrence felt to be common among the men of his generation, is played out in "The Rocking-Horse Winner."

But the tale acts out still another nexus of meaning, one implied in both the satire on a society governed by a money ethic and in the dramatization of a mother devourer. On this level, the hobbyhorse comes more to the fore. . . . This lonely, preadolescent boy continually retreats to his own room where, in great secrecy, he mounts his play horse and rides himself into a trancelike ecstasy. His action and the result it brings powerfully echo Lawrence's description of masturbation, physical and psychic, in his essay "Pornography and Obscenity." Discussing censorship, Lawrence praises art that inspires genuine sexual arousal, that invites union with the other, whether the "other" is another person, an idea, a landscape, the sun. Obscene art is essentially solipsistic; it arouses the desire to turn inward, to chafe, to ride the self in an endless and futile circle of self-stimulation, analysis, gratification. In masturbation, there is no reciprocity, no exchange between self and other. Applying Lawrence's indictment of masturbation to Paul's situation, we see that Paul has been taught to ride himself, that is, his hobbyhorse or obsessions, obsessions he inherited from his mother. . . .

If one takes these three levels of reference and seeks out their complementarity, one sees the rich logic of the tale. The money ethic, the devouring of sons by mothers, and the preference for masturbation are parallel in cause and result. All develop and respect only the kind of knowledge that will increase one's capacity to control. For example, like any money-maker, Paul learns about the horses only to manipulate his earnings — money and love. Paul's mother, in a variation on the theme, does not bother to learn anything about her son because she does not perceive him as useful to her. Further, Paul mounts his hobbyhorse, his surrogate sexual partner, only as a way of fulfilling his own narrowly defined program for success and happiness. In no case is the object that is to be known — horse, son, sexual partner — seen to have a life of its own, an otherness to be appreciated rather than manipulated, a furtherness that can give the knower a glimpse into all that is beyond him or her. In addition, the resolution of each nexus of meaning carries the same ironic denouement: The quest for absolute control leads to the loss of control. The mother's house, which she wants to be luxurious and proper, is haunted by crass whispers. She and her son, striving to control love and fortune, are compulsive, obsessed; Paul dies and thereby loses all chance for the very human love and contact he sought. The mother loses the very means by which her fortune was assured.

ꙮ

WASHINGTON IRVING *wrote a letter from Paris to his friend Henry Brevoort on December 11, 1824, describing the way he had composed his sketches and short tales such as "Rip Van Winkle" five years before, and pointing out why the prose tale seemed to him more difficult to write than the novel. The letter was included in the* Life and Letters of Washington Irving, *two volumes published by G. P. Putnam's Sons of New York City in 1869.*

WASHINGTON IRVING

Letter to Henry Brevoort, December 11, 1824

Paris, Rue Richelieu, No. 89, Dec. 11, 1824.

I cannot tell you what pleasure I have received from long chats with Lynch° about old times and old associates. His animated and descriptive manner has put all New York before me, and made me long to be once more there. I do not know whether it be the force of early impressions and associations, or whether it be really well-founded, but there is a charm about that little spot of earth; that beautiful city and its environs, that has a perfect spell over my imagination. The bay, the rivers and their wild and woody shores, the haunts of my boyhood, both on land and water, absolutely have a witchery over my mind. I thank God for my having been born in so beautiful a place among such beautiful scenery; I am convinced I owe a vast deal of what is good and pleasant in my nature to the circumstance.

I feel continually indebted to your kindness for the interest you have taken in my affairs, and in the success of my works in America. I begin to feel extremely anxious to secure a little income from my literary property, that shall put me beyond the danger of recurring penury; and shall render me independent of the necessity of laboring for the press. I should like to write occasionally for my amusement, and to have the power of throwing my writings either into my portfolio, or into the fire. I enjoy the first conception and

---

Lynch: A reference to Dominick Lynch of New York.

first sketchings down of my ideas, but the correcting and preparing them for the press is irksome, and publishing is detestable.

My last work has a good run in England, and has been extremely well spoken of by some of the worthies of literature, though it has met with some handling from the press. The fact is, I have kept myself so aloof from all clanship in literature that I have no allies among the scribblers for the periodical press; and some of them have taken a pique against me for having treated them a little cavalierly in my writings. However, as I do not read criticism, good or bad, I am out of the reach of attack. If my writings are worth anything, they will outlive temporary criticism; if not, they are not worth caring about. Some parts of my last work were written rather hastily; yet I am convinced that a great part of it was written in a free and happier vein than almost any of my former writings. . . . I fancy much of what I value myself upon in writing, escapes the observation of the great mass of my readers, who are intent more upon the story than the way in which it is told. For my part, I consider a story merely as a frame on which to stretch my materials. It is the play of thought, and sentiment, and language; the weaving in of characters, lightly, yet expressively delineated; the familiar and faithful exhibition of scenes in common life; and the half-concealed vein of humor that is often playing through the whole; — these are among what I aim at, and upon which I felicitate myself in proportion as I think I succeed. I have preferred adopting the mode of sketches and short tales rather than long works, because I choose to take a line of writing peculiar to myself, rather than fall into the manner or school of any other writer; and there is a constant activity of thought and a nicety of execution required in writings of the kind, more than the world appears to imagine. It is comparatively easy to swell a story to any size when you have once the scheme and the characters in your mind; the mere interest of the story, too, carries the reader on through pages and pages of careless writing, and the author may often be dull for half a volume at a time, if he has some striking scene at the end of it; but in these shorter writings, every page must have its merit. The author must be continually piquant; woe to him if he makes an awkward sentence or writes a stupid page; the critics are sure to pounce upon it. Yet if he succeed, the very variety and piquancy of his writings — nay, their very brevity, make them frequently recurred to, and when the mere interest of the story is exhausted, he begins to get credit for his touches of pathos or humor; his points of wit or turns of language. I give these as some of the reasons that have induced me to keep on thus far in the way I had opened for myself; because I find by recent letters from E. I. that you are joining in the oft-repeated advice that I should write a novel. I believe the works that I have written will be oftener re read than any novel of the size that I could have written. It is true other writers have crowded into the same branch of literature, and I now begin to find myself elbowed by men who have followed my footsteps; but at any rate I have had the merit of adopting a line for myself, instead of following others.

SHIRLEY JACKSON *wrote this "biography of a story" in 1960 as a lecture to be delivered before reading "The Lottery" to college audiences. After her death it was included in* Come Along with Me *(1968), edited by her husband, Stanley Edgar Hyman. The lecture also contained extensive quotations from letters she had received from readers who took the story literally. These so disgusted Jackson that she promised her listeners at the conclusion of her talk, "I am out of the lottery business for good."*

SHIRLEY JACKSON

The Morning of June 28, 1948, and "The Lottery" 1968

On the morning of June 28, 1948, I walked down to the post office in our little Vermont town to pick up the mail. I was quite casual about it, as I recall — I opened the box, took out a couple of bills and a letter or two, talked to the postmaster for a few minutes, and left, never supposing that it was the last time for months that I was to pick up the mail without an active feeling of panic. By the next week I had had to change my mailbox to the largest one in the post office, and casual conversation with the postmaster was out of the question, because he wasn't speaking to me. June 28, 1948, was the day *The New Yorker* came out with a story of mine in it. It was not my first published story, nor my last, but I have been assured over and over that if it had been the only story I ever wrote or published, there would be people who would not forget my name.

I had written the story three weeks before, on a bright June morning when summer seemed to have come at last, with blue skies and warm sun and no heavenly signs to warn me that my morning's work was anything but just another story. The idea had come to me while I was pushing my daughter up the hill in her stroller — it was, as I say, a warm morning, and the hill was steep, and beside my daughter the stroller held the day's groceries — and perhaps the effort of that last fifty yards up the hill put an edge to the story; at any rate, I had the idea fairly clearly in my mind when I put my daughter in her playpen and the frozen vegetables in the refrigerator, and, writing the story, I found that it went quickly and easily, moving from beginning to end without pause. As a matter of fact, when I read it over later I decided that except for one or two minor corrections, it needed no changes, and the story I finally typed up and sent off to my agent the next day was almost word for word the original draft. This, as any writer of stories can tell you, is not a usual thing. All I know is that when I came to read the story over I felt strongly that I didn't want to fuss with it. I didn't think it was perfect, but I didn't want to fuss with it. It was, I thought, a serious, straightforward story, and I was pleased and a little surprised at the ease with which it had been written; I was reasonably proud of it, and hoped that my agent would sell it to some magazine and I would have the gratification of seeing it in print.

My agent did not care for the story, but — as she said in her note at the time — her job was to sell it, not to like it. She sent it at once to *The New Yorker,* and about a week after the story had been written I received a telephone call from the fiction editor of *The New Yorker;* it was quite clear that he did not really care for the story, either, but *The New Yorker* was going to buy it. He asked for one change — that the date mentioned in the story be changed to coincide with the date of the issue of the magazine in which the story would appear, and I said of course. He then asked, hesitantly, if I had any particular interpretation of my own for the story; Mr. Harold Ross, then the editor of *The New Yorker,* was not altogether sure that he understood the story, and wondered if I cared to enlarge upon its meaning. I said no. Mr. Ross, he said, thought that the story might be puzzling to some people, and in case anyone telephoned the magazine, as sometimes happened, or wrote in asking about the story, was there anything in particular I wanted them to say? No, I said, nothing in particular; it was just a story I wrote.

I had no more preparation than that. I went on picking up the mail every morning, pushing my daughter up and down the hill in her stroller, anticipating pleasurably the check from *The New Yorker,* and shopping for groceries. The weather stayed nice and it looked as though it was going to be a good summer. Then, on June 28, *The New Yorker* came out with my story.

Things began mildly enough with a note from a friend at *The New Yorker:* "Your story has kicked up quite a fuss around the office," he wrote. I was flattered; it's nice to think that your friends notice what you write. Later that day there was a call from one of the magazine's editors; they had had a couple of people phone in about my story, he said, and was there anything I particularly wanted him to say if there were any more calls? No, I said, nothing particular; anything he chose to say was perfectly all right with me; it was just a story.

I was further puzzled by a cryptic note from another friend: "Heard a man talking about a story of yours on the bus this morning," she wrote. "Very exciting. I wanted to tell him I knew the author, but after I heard what he was saying I decided I'd better not."

One of the most terrifying aspects of publishing stories and books is the realization that they are going to be read, and read by strangers. I had never fully realized this before, although I had of course in my imagination dwelt lovingly upon the thought of the millions and millions of people who were going to be uplifted and enriched and delighted by the stories I wrote. It had simply never occurred to me that these millions and millions of people might be so far from being uplifted that they would sit down and write me letters I was downright scared to open; of the three-hundred-odd letters that I received that summer I can count only thirteen that spoke kindly to me, and they were mostly from friends. Even my mother scolded me: "Dad and I did not care at all for your story in *The New Yorker,*" she wrote sternly, "it does seem, dear, that this gloomy kind of story is what all you young people think about these days. Why don't you write something to cheer people up?"

By mid-July I had begun to perceive that I was very lucky indeed to be safely in Vermont, where no one in our small town had ever heard of *The New Yorker,* much less read my story. Millions of people, and my mother, had taken a pronounced dislike to me.

The magazine kept no track of telephone calls, but all letters addressed to me care of the magazine were forwarded directly to me for answering, and all letters addressed to the magazine — some of them addressed to Harold Ross personally; these were the most vehement — were answered at the magazine and then the letters were sent me in great batches, along with carbons of the answers written at the magazine. I have all the letters still, and if they could be considered to give any accurate cross section of the reading public, or the reading public of *The New Yorker,* or even the reading public of one issue of *The New Yorker,* I would stop writing now.

Judging from these letters, people who read stories are gullible, rude, frequently illiterate, and horribly afraid of being laughed at. Many of the writers were positive that *The New Yorker* was going to ridicule them in print, and the most cautious letters were headed, in capital letters: NOT FOR PUBLICATION or PLEASE DO NOT PRINT THIS LETTER, or, at best, THIS LETTER MAY BE PUBLISHED AT YOUR USUAL RATES OF PAYMENT. Anonymous letters, of which there were a few, were destroyed. *The New Yorker* never published any comment of any kind about the story in the magazine, but did issue one publicity release saying that the story had received more mail than any piece of fiction they had ever published; this was after the newspapers had gotten into the act, in midsummer, with a front-page story in the San Francisco *Chronicle* begging to know what the story meant, and a series of columns in New York and Chicago papers pointing out that *New Yorker* subscriptions were being canceled right and left.

Curiously, there are three main themes which dominate the letters of that first summer — three themes which might be identified as bewilderment, speculation, and plain old-fashioned abuse. In the years since then, during which the story has been anthologized, dramatized, televised, and even — in one completely mystifying transformation — made into a ballet, the tenor of letters I receive has changed. I am addressed more politely, as a rule, and the letters largely confine themselves to questions like what does this story mean? The general tone of the early letters, however, was a kind of wide-eyed, shocked innocence. People at first were not so much concerned with what the story meant; what they wanted to know was where these lotteries were held, and whether they could go there and watch.

BOBBIE ANN MASON *described her response to Tim O'Brien's story "The Things They Carried" in Ron Hansen and Jim Shepard's collection* You've Got to Read This *(1994).*

BOBBIE ANN MASON

On Tim O'Brien's "The Things They Carried" *1994*

Of all the stories I've read in the last decade, Tim O'Brien's "The Things They Carried" hit me hardest. It knocked me down, just as if a hundred-pound rucksack had been thrown right at me. The weight of the things the

American soldiers carried on their interminable journey through the jungle in Vietnam sets the tone for this story. But the power of it is not just the poundage they were humping on their backs. The story's list of "things they carried" extends to the burden of memory and desire and confusion and grief. It's the weight of America's involvement in the war. You can hardly bear to contemplate all that this story evokes with its matter-of-fact yet electrifying details.

The way this story works makes me think of the Vietnam Veterans Memorial in Washington. The memorial is just a list of names, in a simple, dark — yet soaring — design. Its power is in the simplicity of presentation and in what lies behind each of those names.

In the story, there is a central incident, the company's first casualty on its march through the jungle. But the immediate drama is the effort — by the main character, by the narrator, by the writer himself — to contain the emotion, to carry it. When faced with a subject almost too great to manage or confront, the mind wants to organize, to categorize, to simplify. Restraint and matter-of-factness are appropriate deflective techniques for dealing with pain, and they work on several levels in the story. Sometimes it is more affecting to see someone dealing with pain than it is to know about the pain itself. That's what's happening here.

By using the simplicity of a list and trying to categorize the simple items the soldiers carried, O'Brien reveals the real terror of the war itself. And the categories go from the tangible — foot powder, photographs, chewing gum — to the intangible. They carried disease; memory. When it rained, they carried the sky. The weight of what they carried moves expansively, opens out, grows from the stuff in the rucksack to the whole weight of the American war chest, with its litter of ammo and packaging through the landscape of Vietnam. And then it moves back, away from the huge outer world, back into the interior of the self. The story details the way they carried themselves (dignity, laughter, words) as well as what they carried inside (fear, "emotional baggage").

And within the solemn effort to list and categorize, a story unfolds. PFC Ted Lavender, a grunt who carries tranquilizers, is on his way back from relieving himself in the jungle when he is shot by a sniper. The irony and horror of it are unbearable. Almost instantaneously, it seems, the central character, Lieutenant Cross, changes from a romantic youth to a man of action and duty. With his new, hard clarity, he is carried forward by his determination not to be caught unprepared again. And the way he prepares to lead his group is to list his resolves. He has to assert power over the event by detaching himself. It is a life-and-death matter.

So this effort to detach and control becomes both the drama and the technique of the story. For it is our impulse to deal with unspeakable horror and sadness by fashioning some kind of order, a story, to clarify and contain our emotions. As the writer, Tim O'Brien stands back far enough not to be seen but not so far that he isn't in charge.

"They carried all they could bear, and then some, including a silent awe for the terrible power of the things they carried."

ꕥ

HERMAN MELVILLE *wrote an eloquent essay on Nathaniel Hawthorne's volume of short stories,* Mosses from an Old Manse, *for the New York periodical the* Literary World *in August 1850. Unlike Edgar Allan Poe in his review of Hawthorne's short fiction, Melville did not use the opportunity to theorize about the form of the short story. Instead, he conveyed his enthusiasm for Hawthorne's tragic vision, what Melville saw as the "great power of blackness" in Hawthorne's writing that derived "its force from its appeals to that Calvinistic sense of Innate Depravity and Original Sin." This was the aspect of Hawthorne's work that seemed most congenial to Melville's own genius while he continued work that summer on his novel-in-progress,* Moby-Dick.

HERMAN MELVILLE

Blackness in Hawthorne's "Young Goodman Brown"

1850

It is curious, how a man may travel along a country road, and yet miss the grandest or sweetest of prospects, by reason of an intervening hedge so like all other hedges as in no way to hint of the wide landscape beyond. So has it been with me concerning the enchanting landscape in the soul of this Hawthorne, this most excellent Man of Mosses. His Old Manse has been written now four years, but I never read it till a day or two since. I had seen it in the bookstores — heard of it often — even had it recommended to me by a tasteful friend, as a rare, quiet book, perhaps too deserving of popularity to be popular. But there are so many books called "excellent" and so much unpopular merit, that amid the thick stir of other things, the hint of my tasteful friend was disregarded; and for four years the Mosses on the Old Manse never refreshed me with their perennial green. It may be, however, that all this while, the book, like wine, was only improving in flavor and body. . . .

But it is the least part of genius that attracts admiration. Where Hawthorne is known, he seems to be deemed a pleasant writer, with a pleasant style — a sequestered, harmless man, from whom any deep and weighty thing would hardly be anticipated: a man who means no meanings. But there is no man, in whom humor and love, like mountain peaks, soar to such a rapt height, as to receive the irradiations of the upper skies; there is no man in whom humor and love are developed in that high form called genius — no such man can exist without also possessing, as the indispensable complement of these, a great, deep intellect, which drops down into the universe like a plummet. Or, love and humor are only the eyes, through which such an intellect views this world. The great beauty in such a mind is but the product of its strength. . . .

For spite of all the Indian-summer sunlight on the hither side of Hawthorne's soul, the other side — like the dark half of the physical sphere — is shrouded in a blackness, ten times black. But this darkness but gives more effect to the ever-moving dawn, that forever advances through it, and circumnavigates his world. Whether Hawthorne has simply availed himself of this mystical blackness as a means to the wondrous effects he makes it to produce in his lights and shades; or whether there really lurks in him, perhaps unknown to himself, a touch of Puritanic gloom — this I cannot altogether tell. Certain it is, however, that this great power of blackness in him derives its force from its appeals to that Calvinistic sense of Innate Depravity and Original Sin, from whose visitations, in some shape or other, no deeply thinking mind is always and wholly free. For, in certain moods, no man can weigh this world, without throwing in something, somehow like Original Sin, to strike the uneven balance. . . .

But with whatever motive, playful or profound, Nathaniel Hawthorne has chosen to entitle his pieces in the manner he has, it is certain that some of them are directly calculated to deceive — egregiously deceive — the superficial skimmer of pages. To be downright and candid once more, let me cheerfully say that two of these titles did dolefully dupe no less an eagle-eyed reader than myself; and that, too, after I had been impressed with a sense of the great depth and breadth of this American man. "Who in the name of thunder" (as the country people say in this neighborhood), "who in the name of thunder," would anticipate any marvel in a piece entitled "Young Goodman Brown"? You would of course suppose that it was a simple little tale, intended as a supplement to "Goody Two-Shoes." Whereas it is deep as Dante; nor can you finish it, without addressing the author in his own words: "It is yours to penetrate, in every bosom, the deep mystery of sin." And with Young Goodman, too, in allegorical pursuit of his Puritan wife, you cry out in your anguish,

> "Faith!" shouted Goodman Brown, in a voice of agony and desperation; and the echoes of the forest mocked him, crying — "Faith! Faith!" as if bewildered wretches were seeking her, all through the wilderness.

Now this same piece, entitled "Young Goodman Brown," is one of the two that I had not at all read yesterday; and I allude to it now, because it is, in itself, such a strong positive illustration of that blackness in Hawthorne which I had assumed from the mere occasional shadows of it, as revealed in several of the other sketches. But had I previously perused "Young Goodman Brown," I should have been at no pains to draw the conclusion which I came to at a time when I was ignorant that the book contained one such direct and unqualified manifestation of it.

J. HILLIS MILLER *analyzed the effect of what he called "Bartleby's celebrated immobility" in the critical study* Versions of Pygmalion *(1990). Miller was intent on examining "strange and unaccountable" versions of the Pygmalion myth in European literature; each story he discussed "contains a character who does something like falling in love with a statue." In Miller's view, a story like "Bartleby, the Scrivener" was an occasion for "the act of personification essential to all storytelling and story-reading."*

J. Hillis Miller

Who Is He? Melville's "Bartleby, the Scrivener"

1990

After the failure of all these strategies for getting rid of Bartleby, the narrator tries another. In part through charity but in part through the notion that it is his fate to have Bartleby permanently in his chambers, he decides to try to live with Bartleby, to take him as a permanent fixture in his office. The narrator looks into two quite different books that deny man free will in determining his life, "Edwards on the Will" and "Priestly on Necessity." For Jonathan Edwards man does not have free will because everything he does is predestined by God. For Joseph Priestly, on the other hand, man is bound within the chains of a universal material necessity. Everything happens through physical causality, and therefore everything happens as it must happen, as it has been certain through all time to happen. In either case Bartleby's presence in the narrator's rooms is something predestined:

> Gradually I slid into the persuasion that these troubles of mine touching the scrivener, had been all predestinated from eternity, and Bartleby was billeted upon me for some mysterious purpose of an all-wise Providence, which it was not for a mere mortal like me to fathom. Yes, Bartleby, stay there behind your screen, thought I; I shall persecute you no more; you are harmless and noiseless as any of these old chairs; in short, I never feel so private as when I know you are here. At last I see it, I feel it; I penetrate to the predestinated purpose of my life. I am content. Others may have loftier parts to enact; but my mission in this world, Bartleby, is to furnish you with office-room for such period as you may see fit to remain.

This strategy fails too, when the narrator's clients and associates let him know that Bartleby's presence in his offices is scandalizing his professional reputation. It is then that the narrator, who is nothing if not logical, conceives his strangest way of dealing with Bartleby. Since Bartleby will not budge, he himself will leave. The immobility of Bartleby turns the narrator into a nomad: "No more then. Since he will not quit me, I must quit him. I will change my offices; I will move elsewhere."

When the new tenants and the landlord of his old premises come to charge the narrator with responsibility for the nuisance Bartleby is causing, "haunting the building generally, sitting upon the banisters of the stairs by day, and sleeping in the entry by night," the narrator tries first a new strategy of saying he is in no way related to Bartleby or responsible for him. But it is no use: "I was the last person known to have anything to do with him, and they held me to the terrible account."

The narrator then meets Bartleby once more face to face. He offers to set him up in a respectable position, as a clerk in a dry-goods store, a bartender, a bill collector, or a companion for young gentlemen traveling to Europe. To all these ludicrous suggestions Bartleby replies that he is not particular, but he would prefer to remain "stationary." The narrator then, and finally, offers to take Bartleby home with him, like a stray cat, and give him refuge there. This meets with the same reply. The narrator flees the building and becomes truly a vagrant, wandering for days here and there in his rockaway.

The narrator's life and work seem to have been permanently broken by the irruption of Bartleby. It is not he but his old landlord who deals effectively with the situation. He has Bartleby "removed to the Tombs as a vagrant." This is just what the more intellectually consequent narrator has not been able to bring himself to do, not just because Bartleby is not, strictly speaking, a vagrant and not just because doing such violence to Bartleby would disobey the law of charity, but because he cannot respond with violence to a resistance that has been purely passive and has thereby "disarmed" or "unmanned" any decisive action: "Turn the man out by an actual thrusting I could not; to drive him away by calling him hard names would not do; calling in the police was an unpleasant idea. . . . You will not thrust him, the poor, pale, passive mortal, — you will not thrust such a helpless creature out of your door? you will not dishonor yourself by such cruelty? No, I will not, I cannot do that."

Even after the police have been called in and society has placed Bartleby where he belongs, the narrator continues to be haunted by a sense of unfulfilled responsibility. He visits him in the Tombs, the prison so called because it was in the Egyptian Revival style of architecture, but also no doubt in response to a deeper sense of kinship between incarceration and death: "The Egyptian character of the masonry weighed upon me with its gloom. But a soft imprisoned turf grew under foot. The heart of the eternal pyramids, it seemed, wherein, by some strange magic, through the clefts, grass-seed, dropped by birds, had sprung." Bartleby is appropriately placed in the Tombs since, if the prison courtyard where Bartleby dies is green life in the midst of death, Bartleby has been death in the midst of life. In the Tombs the narrator makes his last unsuccessful attempt to deal with Bartleby in a rational manner, to reincorporate him into ordinary life. He "narrates" to the prison authorities, as he says, "all I knew" about Bartleby, telling them Bartleby does not really belong there but must stay "till something less harsh might be done — though indeed I hardly knew what." He yields at last to the accounting for Bartleby that had been used by Ginger Nut: "I think, sir, he's a little *luny*." The narrator now tells the "grub-man" in the prison, Mr. Cutlets, "I think he is a little deranged." One powerful means society has for dealing with someone who does not fit any ordinary social category is to declare him insane.

Mr. Cutlets has his own curious and by no means insignificant way of placing Bartleby. He thinks Bartleby must be a forger. "Deranged? deranged is it? Well now, upon my word, I thought that friend of yourn was a gentleman forger; they are always pale and genteel-like, them forgers. I can't help pity 'em — can't help it, sir. Did you know Monroe Edwards?" To which the narrator answers, "No, I was never socially acquainted with any forgers." In a way Mr. Cutlets has got Bartleby right, since forgery involves the exact copying of someone else's handwriting in order to make a false document that functions performatively as if it were genuine. Bartleby is a species of forger in reverse. He copies documents all right, but he does this in such a way as to deprive them of their power to make anything happen. On the other hand, when the narrator has copied documents checked, corrected, and made functional, he is himself performing an act of forgery. He may not be socially acquainted with any forgers, but he is in a manner of speaking one himself.

The arrangement he makes with Mr. Cutlets to feed Bartleby in prison is the narrator's last attempt to reincorporate Bartleby into society. There is much emphasis on eating in the story, on what the narrator's different employees eat and drink and on how little Bartleby eats, apparently nothing at all in prison: "'I prefer not to dine to-day,' said Bartleby, turning away. 'It would disagree with me; I am unused to dinners.' So saying he slowly moved to the other side of the inclosure, and took up a position fronting the dead-wall." Eating is one of the basic ways to share our common humanity. This Bartleby refuses, or rather he says he would prefer not to share in the ritual of eating. To refuse that is in the end deadly. Bartleby's death makes him what he has been all along, a bit of death in the midst of life.

It is entirely appropriate that the narrator's account of Bartleby should end with Bartleby's death, not because any biography should end with the death of the biographee but because in death Bartleby becomes what he has always already been. As I have said, his "I would prefer not to" is strangely oriented toward the future. It opens the future, but a future of perpetual not-yet. It can only come as death, and death is that which can never be present. There, at the end, the narrator finds the corpse of Bartleby, "strangely huddled at the base of the wall, his knees drawn up, and lying on his side, his head touching the cold stones." In an earlier version, the "Bartleby" fragment in the Melville family papers in the Gansevoort-Lansing Collection at the New York Public Library, Bartleby is found by the narrator lying in a white-washed room with his head against a tombstone: "It was clean, well-lighted and scrupulously white washed. The head-stone was standing up against the wall, and stretched on a blanket at its base, his head touching the cold marble and his feet upon the threshold lay the wasted form of Bartleby."

The corpse of Bartleby is not the presence of Bartleby. It is his eternal absence. In death he becomes what he has always been, a cadaver who "lives without dining," as the narrator says to the grub-man. Bartleby returns at death, in the final version of the story, to a fetal position. He is the incursion into life of that unattainable realm somewhere before birth and after death. But the word "realm" is misleading. What Bartleby brings is not a realm in the sense of place we might go. It is the otherness that all along haunts or inhabits life from the inside. This otherness can by no method, such as the long series of techniques the narrator tries, be accounted for, narrated, rationalized, or in any other way reassimilated into ordinary life, though it is a permanent part of that ordinary life. Bartleby is the alien that may neither be thrust out the door nor domesticated, brought into the family, given citizenship papers. Bartleby is the invasion of death into life, but not death as something from outside life. He is death as the other side of life or the cohabitant with life. "Death," nevertheless, is not the proper name for this ghostly companion of life, as if it were an allegorical meaning identified at last. Nor is "Death" its generic or common name. "Death" is a catachresis for what can never be named properly.

■ ■ ■

The narrator's last method of attempting to deal with Bartleby is his narration, going all the way from "I am a rather elderly man" to "Ah Bartleby! Ah humanity!" This narration is explicitly said to be written down and addressed to a "reader." It repeats for a more indeterminate reader, that is, for whoever happens to read it, the quasi-legal deposition he has made before the proper officer of "the Tombs, or to speak more properly, the Halls of Justice." If the narrator can encompass Bartleby with words, if he can do justice to him, he may simultaneously have accounted for him, naturalized him after all, and freed himself from his unfulfilled obligation. He will have made an adequate response to the demand Bartleby has made on him. The narrator, that is, may have justified himself while doing justice to Bartleby.

This is impossible because Bartleby cannot be identified. His story cannot be told. But the reader at the end knows better just why this is so, since we have watched the narrator try one by one a whole series of strategies for accounting for someone and has seen them one by one fail. This failure leaves Bartleby still imperturbably bringing everything to a halt or indefinitely postponing everything with his "I would prefer not to." The narrator's account is not so much an account as an apology for his failure to give an adequate account.

The narrator's writing is also an attempt at a reading, a failed attempt to read Bartleby. In this sense it is the first in a long line of attempts to read Bartleby the scrivener, though the narrator's successors do this by trying to read the text written by Melville, "Bartleby, the Scrivener." Just as Bartleby by his immovable presence in the narrator's office has demanded to be read and accounted for by him, so Melville's strange story demands to be read and accounted for. Nor have readers failed to respond to the demand. A large secondary literature has grown up around "Bartleby," remarkable for its multiplicity and diversity. All claim in one way or another to have identified Bartleby and to have accounted for him, to have done him justice. They tend to exemplify that function of policing or putting things in their place which is entrusted by our society to literary studies as one realm among many of the academic forms of accounting or accounting for. In the case of the essays on "Bartleby" this accounting often takes one or the other of two main forms, as Warminski has observed. These forms could be put under the aegis of the two-pronged last paragraph of the story — "Ah Bartleby! Ah humanity!" — or they might be said to fly in the face either of Bartleby's "But I am not particular" or of the manifest failure of the narrator's attempt to draw close to Bartleby by way of "the bond of a common humanity." Many of the essays try to explain Bartleby either by making him an example of some universal type, for example "existential man," or by finding some particular original or explanatory context for him, for example one of Melville's acquaintances who worked in a law office, or some aspect of nineteenth-century capitalism in America. But Bartleby is neither general nor particular: he is neutral. As such, he disables reading by any of these strategies, any attempt to put "Bartleby, the Scrivener" in its place by answering the question, "In mercy's name, who is he?"

No doubt my own reading also claims to have identified Bartleby, in this case by defining him as the neutral in-between that haunts all thinking and living by dialectical opposition. All readings of the story, including my own, are more ways to call in the police. They are ways of trying to put Bartleby in his place, to convey him where we want to put him, to make sense of him, even if it is an accounting that defines him as the nonsense that inhabits all sense-making. All readings attempt in one way or another to fulfill what the narrator has tried and failed to do: to tell Bartleby's story in a way that will allow us to assimilate him and the story into the vast archives of rationalization that make up the secondary literature of our profession. We are institutionalized to do that work of policing for our society. None of these techniques of assimilation works any better than any of the narrator's methods, and we remain haunted by Bartleby, but haunted also by "Bartleby, the Scrivener: A Story of Wall-Street." I claim, however, that my accounting succeeds where the others fail by showing (though that is not quite the right word) why it is that "accounting for" in any of its usual senses cannot work, either for the story or for the character the story poses.

VLADIMIR NABOKOV *was a skillful guide to fiction in his* Lectures on Russian Literature. *As this excerpt from his analysis of Anton Chekhov's stories shows, he blended wit, irreverence, and critical insight in his summary of the intricacies of plot and character, illuminating the artistic achievements of the author. Nabokov felt that Chekhov's books are "sad books for humorous people" — that is, only a reader with a sense of humor can really appreciate their sadness. Chekhov's subtle humor pervades the grayness of the lives he created, flickering through his prose style: "He did it," said Nabokov, "by keeping all his words in the same dim light and of the same exact tint of gray, a tint between the color of an old fence and that of a low cloud."*

VLADIMIR NABOKOV

A Reading of Chekhov's "The Lady with the Little Dog"

1981

Chekhov comes into the story "The Lady with the Little Dog" without knocking. There is no dilly-dallying. The very first paragraph reveals the main character, the young fair-haired lady followed by her white Spitz dog on the waterfront of a Crimean resort, Yalta, on the Black Sea. And immediately after, the male character Gurov appears. His wife, whom he has left with the children in Moscow, is vividly depicted: her solid frame, her thick black eyebrows, and the way she has of calling herself "a woman who thinks." One notes the magic of the trifles the author collects — the wife's manner of dropping a certain mute letter in spelling and her calling her husband by the longest and fullest form of his name, both traits in combination with the impressive dignity of her beetle-browed face and rigid poise forming exactly the necessary impression. A hard woman with the strong feminist and social ideas of her time, but one whom her husband finds in his heart of hearts to be narrow, dull-minded, and devoid of grace. The natural transition is to Gurov's constant unfaithfulness to her, to his general attitude toward women — "that inferior race" is what he calls them, but without that inferior race he could not exist. It is hinted that these Russian romances were not altogether as light-winged as in the Paris of Maupassant. Complications and problems are unavoidable with those decent hesitating people of Moscow who are slow heavy starters but plunge into tedious difficulties when once they start going.

Then with the same neat and direct method of attack, with the bridging formula "and so . . ." (or perhaps still better rendered in English by that "Now" which begins a new paragraph in straightforward fairy tales), we slide back to the lady with the dog. Everything about her, even the way her hair was done, told him that she was bored. The spirit of adventure — though he realized perfectly well that his attitude toward a lone woman in a fashionable sea town was based on vulgar stories, generally false — this spirit of adventure prompts him to call the little dog, which thus becomes a link between her and him. They are both in a public restaurant.

> He beckoned invitingly to the Spitz, and when the dog approached him, shook his finger at it. The Spitz growled; Gurov threatened it again.
>
> The lady glanced at him and at once dropped her eyes.
>
> "He doesn't bite," she said and blushed.
>
> "May I give him a bone?" he asked; and when she nodded he inquired affably, "Have you been in Yalta long?"
>
> "About five days."

They talk. The author has hinted already that Gurov was witty in the company of women; and instead of having the reader take it for granted (you know the old method of describing the talk as "brilliant" but giving no samples of the conversation), Chekhov makes him joke in a really attractive, winning way. "Bored, are you? An average citizen lives in . . . (here Chekhov lists the names of beautifully chosen, super-provincial towns) and is not bored, but when he arrives here on his vacation it is all boredom and dust. One could think he came from Granada" (a name particularly appealing to the Russian imagination). The rest of their talk, for which this sidelight is richly sufficient, is conveyed indirectly. Now comes a first glimpse of Chekhov's own system of suggesting atmosphere by the most concise details of nature, "the sea was of a warm lilac hue with a golden path for the moon"; whoever has lived in Yalta knows how exactly this conveys the impression of a summer evening there. This first movement of the story ends with Gurov alone in his hotel room thinking of her as he goes to sleep and imagining her delicate weak-looking neck and her pretty gray eyes. It is to be noted that only now, through the medium of the hero's imagination, does Chekhov give a visible and definite form to the lady, features that fit perfectly with her listless manner and expression of boredom already known to us.

> Getting into bed he recalled that she had been a schoolgirl only recently, doing lessons like his own daughter; he thought how much timidity and angularity there was still in her laugh and her manner of talking with a stranger. It must have been the first time in her life that she was alone in a setting in which she was followed, looked at, and spoken to for one secret purpose alone, which she could hardly fail to guess. He thought of her slim, delicate throat, her lovely gray eyes.
>
> "There's something pathetic about her, though," he thought, and dropped off.

The next movement (each of the four diminutive chapters or movements of which the story is composed is not more than four or five pages long), the next movement starts a week later with Gurov going to the pavilion and bringing the lady iced lemonade on a hot windy day, with the dust flying; and then in the evening when the sirocco subsides, they go on the pier to watch the incoming steamer. "The lady lost her lorgnette in the crowd," Chekhov notes shortly, and this being so casually worded, without any direct influence on the story — just a passing statement — somehow fits in with that helpless pathos already alluded to.

Then in her hotel room her awkwardness and tender angularity are delicately conveyed. They have become lovers. She was now sitting with her long hair hanging down on both sides of her face in the dejected pose of a sinner in some old picture. There was a watermelon on the table. Gurov cut himself a piece and began to eat unhurriedly. This realistic touch is again a typical Chekhov device.

She tells him about her existence in the remote town she comes from and Gurov is slightly bored by her naiveté, confusion, and tears. It is only now that we learn her husband's name: von Dideritz — probably of German descent.

They roam about Yalta in the early morning mist.

> At Oreanda they sat on a bench not far from the church, looked down at the sea, and were silent. Yalta was barely visible through the morning mist; white clouds rested motionlessly on the mountaintops. The leaves did not stir on the trees, the crickets chirped, and the monotonous muffled sound of the sea that rose from below spoke of the peace, the eternal sleep awaiting us. So it rumbled below when there was no Yalta, no Oreanda here; so it rumbles now, and it will rumble as indifferently and hollowly when we are no more. . . . Sitting beside a young woman who in the dawn seemed so lovely, Gurov, soothed and spellbound by these magical surroundings — the sea, the mountains, the clouds, the wide sky — thought how everything is really beautiful in this world when one reflects: everything except what we think or do ourselves when we forget the higher aims of life and our own human dignity.
>
> A man strolled up to them — probably a watchman — looked at them and walked away. And this detail, too, seemed so mysterious and beautiful. They saw a steamer arrive from Feodosia, its lights extinguished in the glow of dawn.
>
> "There is dew on the grass," said Anna Sergeievna, after a silence.
>
> "Yes, it's time to go home."

Then several days pass and then she has to go back to her home town.

"'Time for me, too, to go North,' thought Gurov as he returned after seeing her off." And there the chapter ends.

The third movement plunges us straight into Gurov's life in Moscow. The richness of a gay Russian winter, his family affairs, the dinners at clubs and restaurants, all this is swiftly and vividly suggested. Then a page is devoted to a queer thing that has happened to him: he cannot forget the lady with the little dog. He has many friends, but the curious longing he has for talking about his adventure finds no outlet. When he happens to speak in a very general way of love and women, nobody guesses what he means, and only his wife moves her dark eyebrows and says: "Stop that fatuous posing; it does not suit you."

And now comes what in Chekhov's quiet stories may be called the climax. There is something that your average citizen calls romance and something he calls prose — though both are the meat of poetry for the artist. Such a contrast has already been hinted at by the slice of watermelon which Gurov crunched in a Yalta hotel room at a most romantic moment, sitting heavily and munching away. This contrast is beautifully followed up when at last Gurov blurts out to a friend late at night as they come out of the club: If you knew what a delightful woman I met in Yalta! His friend, a bureaucratic civil servant, got into his sleigh, the horses moved, but suddenly he turned and called back to Gurov. Yes? asked Gurov, evidently expecting some reaction to what he had just mentioned. By the way, said the man, you were quite right. That fish at the club was decidedly smelly.

This is a natural transition to the description of Gurov's new mood, his feeling that he lives among savages where cards and food are life. His family, his bank, the whole trend of his existence, everything seems futile, dull, and senseless. About Christmas he tells his wife he is going on a business trip to St. Petersburg, instead of which he travels to the remote Volga town where the lady lives.

Critics of Chekhov in the good old days when the mania for the civic problem flourished in Russia were incensed with his way of describing what they considered to be trivial unnecessary matters instead of thoroughly examining and solving the problems of bourgeois marriage. For as soon as Gurov arrives in the early hours to that town and takes the best room at the local hotel, Chekhov, instead of describing his mood or intensifying his difficult moral position, gives what is artistic in the highest sense of the word: he notes the gray carpet, made of military cloth, and the inkstand, also gray with dust, with a horseman whose hand waves a hat and whose head is gone. That is all: it is nothing but it is everything in authentic literature. A feature in the same line is the phonetic transformation which the hotel porter imposes on the German name von Dideritz. Having learned the address Gurov goes there and looks at the house. Opposite was a long gray fence with nails sticking out. An unescapable fence, Gurov says to himself, and here we get the concluding note in the rhythm of drabness and grayness already suggested by the carpet, the inkstand, the illiterate accent of the porter. The unexpected little turns and the lightness of the touches are what places Chekhov, above all Russian writers of fiction, on the level of Gogol and Tolstoy.

Presently he saw an old servant coming out with the familiar little white dog. He wanted to call it (by a kind of conditional reflex), but suddenly his heart began beating fast and in his excitement he could not remember the dog's name — another delightful touch. Later on he decides to go to the local theatre, where for the first time the operetta *The Geisha* is being given. In sixty words Chekhov paints a complete picture of a provincial theatre, not forgetting the town-governor who modestly hid in his box behind a plush curtain so that only his hands were visible. Then the lady appeared. And he realized quite clearly that now in the whole world there was none nearer and dearer and more important to him than this slight woman, lost in a small-town crowd, a woman perfectly unremarkable, with a vulgar lorgnette in her hand. He saw her husband and remembered her qualifying him as a flunkey — he distinctly resembled one.

A remarkably fine scene follows when Gurov manages to talk to her, and then their mad swift walk up all kinds of staircases and corridors, and down again, and up again, amid people in the various uniforms of provincial officials. Neither does Chekhov forget "two schoolboys who smoked on the stairs and looked down at him and her."

> "You must leave," Anna Sergeievna went on in a whisper. "Do you hear, Dmitri Dmitrich? I will come and see you in Moscow. I have never been happy; I am unhappy now, and I never, never shall be happy, never! So don't make me suffer still more! I swear I'll come to Moscow. But now let us part. My dear, good, precious one, let us part!"
>
> She pressed his hand and walked rapidly downstairs, turning to look round at him, and from her eyes he could see that she really was unhappy. Gurov stood for a while, listening, then when all grew quiet, he found his coat and left the theatre.

The fourth and last little chapter gives the atmosphere of their secret meetings in Moscow. As soon as she would arrive she used to send a red-capped messenger to Gurov. One day he was on his way to her and his daughter was with him. She was going to school, in the same direction as he. Big damp snowflakes were slowly coming down.

The thermometer, Gurov was saying to his daughter, shows a few degrees above freezing point (actually 37° above, Fahrenheit), but nevertheless snow is falling. The explanation is that this warmth applies only to the surface of the earth, while in the higher layers of the atmosphere the temperature is quite different.

And as he spoke and walked, he kept thinking that not a soul knew or would ever know about these secret meetings.

What puzzled him was that all the false part of his life, his bank, his club, his conversations, his social obligations — all this happened openly, while the real and interesting part was hidden.

> He had two lives, an open one, seen and known by all who needed to know of it, full of conventional truth and conventional

> falsehood, exactly like the lives of his friends and acquaintances; and another life that went on in secret. And through some strange, perhaps accidental, combination of circumstances, everything that was of interest and importance to him, everything that was essential to him, everything about which he felt sincerely and did not deceive himself, everything that constituted the core of his life, was going on concealed from others; while all that was false, the shell in which he hid to cover the truth — his work at the bank for instance, his discussions at the club, his references to the "inferior race," his appearances at anniversary celebrations with his wife — all that went on in the open. Judging others by himself, he did not believe what he saw, and always fancied that every man led his real, most interesting life under cover of secrecy as under cover of night. The personal life of every individual is based on secrecy, and perhaps it is partly for that reason that civilized man is so nervously anxious that personal privacy should be respected.

The final scene is full of that pathos which has been suggested in the very beginning. They meet, she sobs, they feel that they are the closest of couples, the tenderest of friends, and he sees that his hair is getting a little gray and knows that only death will end their love.

> The shoulders on which his hands rested were warm and quivering. He felt compassion for this life, still so warm and lovely, but probably already about to begin to fade and wither like his own. Why did she love him so much? He always seemed to women different from what he was, and they loved in him not himself, but the man whom their imagination had created and whom they had been eagerly seeking all their lives; and afterwards, when they saw their mistake, they loved him nevertheless. And not one of them had been happy with him. In the past he had met women, come together with them, parted from them, but he had never once loved; it was anything you please, but not love. And only now when his head was gray he had fallen in love, really, truly — for the first time in his life.

They talk, they discuss their position, how to get rid of the necessity of this sordid secrecy, how to be together always. They find no solution and in the typical Chekhov way the tale fades out with no definite full-stop but with the natural motion of life.

> And it seemed as though in a little while the solution would be found, and then a new and glorious life would begin; and it was clear to both of them that the end was still far off, and that what was to be most complicated and difficult for them was only just beginning.

All the traditional rules of story telling have been broken in this wonderful short story of twenty pages or so. There is no problem, no regular climax, no point at the end. And it is one of the greatest stories ever written.

GRACE PALEY *talked with Ann Charters about her experiences as a short story writer during lunch in her Greenwich Village apartment on a snowy day in February 1986. On the wall above the kitchen table hung an oil painting, a still life of vegetables painted by her father after his retirement from the practice of medicine. Paley mentions her father's interest in art in her story "A Conversation with My Father."*

GRACE PALEY

A Conversation with Ann Charters

1986

Charters: Some literary critics think that short stories are more closely related to poetry than to the novel. Would you agree?

Paley: I would say that stories are closer to poetry than they are to the novel because first they are shorter, and second they are more concentrated, more economical, and that kind of economy, the pulling together of all the information and making leaps across the information, is really close to poetry. By leaps I mean thought leaps and feeling leaps. Also, when short stories are working right, you pay more attention to language than most novelists do.

Charters: Poe said unity was an essential factor of short stories. Do you have any ideas about this in your own work?

Paley: I suppose there has to be some kind of unity, but that's true in a novel too. It seems to me that unity is form. Form is really the vessel in which the story or poem or novel exists. The reason I don't have an answer for you is that there's really no telling — sometimes I like to start a story with one thing and end it with another. I don't know where the unity is in that case. I see the word *unity* meaning that something has to be whole, even if it ends in an open way.

Charters: You mean, as you wrote in "A Conversation with My Father," that "everyone, real or invented, deserves the open destiny of life."

Paley: Yes.

Charters: You started writing poetry before short stories, and the language of your fiction is often as compressed and metaphorical as the language of poetry. Can you describe the process of how you learned to write?

Paley: Let me put it this way: I went to school to poetry — that was where I learned how to write. People learn to write by doing various things. I suppose I also wrote a lot of letters, since it was the time of the Second World War. But apart from that I wrote poems, that's what I wrote. I thought about language a lot. That was important to me. That was my teacher. My fiction teacher was poetry.

Charters: What poets did you read when you were learning how to write?

Paley: I just read all the poets. If there was an anthology of poets, I read every single one. I knew all the Victorians. I read the Imagists. At a certain point I fell in love with the Englishmen who came to America — Christopher Isherwood, Stephen Spender, and W. H. Auden. I thought Auden was the greatest. And I loved the poetry of Dylan Thomas. Yeats meant a lot to me. I paid attention to all of them and listened to all of them. Some of them must have gotten into my ear. That's not up to me to say. That's for the reader to say. The reader of my stories will tell me, "This is whom you're influenced by," but I can't say that. I feel I was influenced by everybody.

Charters: Why did you stop writing poetry and start writing stories? What did the form of the short story offer you that the poem didn't?

Paley: First of all, I began to think of certain subject matter, women's lives specifically, and what was happening around me. I was in my thirties, which I guess is the time people start to notice these things, women's and men's lives and what their relationship is. I knew lots of women with small kids, and I was developing very close relationships with a variety of women. All sorts of things began to worry me, and I began to think about them a lot. I couldn't deal with any of this subject matter in poetry; I just didn't know how. I didn't have the technique. Other people can, but I didn't want to write poems saying "I feel this" and "I feel that." That was the last thing I wanted to do.

I can give you a definition that can be proven wrong in many ways, but for me it was that in writing poetry I wanted to talk to the world, I wanted to address the world, so to speak. But writing stories, I wanted to get the world to explain itself to me, to speak to me. And for me that was the essential difference between writing poetry and stories, and it still is, in many ways. So I had to get that world to talk to me. I had to reach out to it, a very different thing than writing poems. I had to reach out to the world and get it to tell me what it was all about, because I didn't understand it. I just didn't understand. Also, I'd always been very interested in people and told funny stories, and I didn't have any room for doing that in poems, again because of my own self. My poems were too literary, that's the real reason.

Charters: What do you mean, you had to get the world to tell you what it was all about?

Paley: In the first story I ever wrote, "The Contest," I did exactly what I just told you — I got this guy to talk. That's what I did. I had a certain guy in mind. In fact, I stuck pretty close to my notion of what he was, and the story was about a contest he had told me about. The second story I wrote was about Aunt Rose in "Goodbye and Good Luck." That began with my husband's aunt visiting us, and saying exactly the sentence I used to start the story: "I was popular in certain circles." But the rest has nothing to do with her life at all. She looked at us, this aunt of his, and she felt we didn't appreciate her, so she looked at us and she said to us, "Listen," she said. "I was popular in certain circles." That statement really began that particular story. That story was about lots of older women I knew who didn't get married, and I was thinking about them. These are two examples of how I began, how I got to my own voice by hearing and using all these other voices.

Charters: I suppose "A Conversation with My Father" isn't typical of your work, because the story you make up for him isn't what he wants, the old-fashioned Chekhov or Maupassant story, and it's not really one of your "voice" stories either, is it?

Paley: No. I'm just trying to oblige him.

Charters: So that may be one of the jokes of the story?

Paley: It could be, but I never thought of it that way. I think it's a good story. People have found it useful in literature classes, which I think is funny, but nice.

Charters: Did you make up the plot of "A Conversation with My Father," or did it actually happen when you were visiting him before he died?

Paley: My father was eighty-six years old and in bed. I spent a lot of time with him. He was an artist, and he painted pictures after he retired from being a doctor. I visited him at least once a week, and we were very close. We would have discussions. I never wrote a story for him about this neighbor, but he did say to me once, "Why can't you write a regular story, for God's sake?" something like that. So that particular story is both about literature and about that particular discussion, but it's also about generational differences, about different ways of looking at life. What my father thought could be done in the world was due to his own history. What I thought could be done in the world was different, not because I was a more open person, because he was also a very open person, but because I lived in a particularly open time, the late 1960s. The story I wrote for him was about all these druggies. It was made up, but it was certainly true. I could point out people on my block whose kids became junkies. Many of them have recovered from being junkies and are in good shape now.

Charters: Did you know any mothers in Greenwich Village who became junkies to keep their kids company?

Paley: Sure. It was a very open neighborhood then, with lots of freedom. But my father was born into a very different time. He was born in Czarist Russia and came over to America when he was twenty and worked hard and studied medicine and had a profession.

Charters: When you were growing up did you read the writers your father admired — Maupassant and Chekhov?

Paley: Actually, he had never mentioned Maupassant to me before. He did mention him in that conversation. He did read a lot, he loved Chekhov. And when he came to this country, he taught himself English by reading Dickens.

Charters: So the idea for the story came to you when he mentioned Maupassant?

Paley: Well, not really. He had just read my story "Faith in a Tree," and there are a lot of voices coming from all over in that story. And so he asked me, "What is this? All those voices? Voices from who knows where?" He wasn't actually that heavy. But when I wrote about our conversation it became a fiction, and it's different from what really happened.

Charters: It must have been fun for you to make up the two versions of the story about your neighbor in "A Conversation with My Father."

Paley: I enjoyed writing that story. Some stories you don't enjoy, because they're very hard. I didn't write it right off, but I enjoyed it.

Charters: How many days did it take you to write?

Paley: There's no such thing as days with me when I write a story. More like months. I write it and I write slow, and then I rewrite, and then I put it away, and then I take it out again. It's tedious in some respects. But that's the way it works.

Charters: When do you decide it's finished?

Paley: When I've gone over it and I can't think of another thing to change.

Charters: I was looking over your book *Enormous Changes at the Last Minute,* which is where "A Conversation with My Father" appears, and I noticed you've placed it between two very dark stories, "The Little Girl," about a runaway in the Village who commits suicide after she's raped, and "The Immigrant Story," about the starvation of the young children in a Jewish family in Poland before the mother emigrates to America. I assume you did this for a reason. When you put a collection of short fiction together, how do you order the stories?

Paley: I always have something in mind. I like to put one or two at the beginning that will be readable immediately, and then I just work it out. I like to mix the long and the short, and the serious and the funny ones. But I did put those two dark stories around "A Conversation with My Father" to show him I could look tragedy in the face. Remember he asks me at the end of the story, "When will you look it in the face?"

Charters: Was that one of the things he actually said to you when you visited him?

Paley: Well, he did tend to say that I wouldn't look things in the face. That things were hard, and I wasn't looking at it. I didn't see certain problems with my kids when they were small, and he was in some degree right. In "The Immigrant Story" a man tells me, "You have a rotten rosy temperament." But then she says, "Rosiness is not a worse windowpane than gloomy gray when viewing the world." They're both just prisms to look through.

Charters: Is that what you still believe?

Paley: Well, I do believe it, but I also believe that things are bad.

Charters: A theme that some students find when reading "A Conversation with My Father" is that one of the things you don't want to look in the face that your father is trying to prepare you for is his own death. Were you conscious of that when you wrote the story?

Paley: No.

Charters: Can you see that theme in it now?

Paley: No. But maybe you're right. As I said, that's not up to me to say. Maybe the reader of a particular story knows better than the writer what it means. But I know I wasn't thinking about that when I wrote it. I wasn't thinking of his death at all. I was thinking of him being sick and trying not to get him excited.

EDGAR ALLAN POE *was one of the earliest writers to discuss the aesthetic qualities of the short story as a distinct prose narrative form. In his day, literary criticism was still a new field, lacking a terminology and developed concepts. His two long reviews praising the tales of Nathaniel Hawthorne were published in* Graham's Magazine *in 1842 and* Godey's Lady's Book *in 1847; they are pioneering examples* *of the analytic literary essay. The following excerpt is taken from the 1842 piece, in which Poe amplifies his theory of the short story and his views on the nature of originality in literature.*

EDGAR ALLAN POE

The Importance of the Single Effect in a Prose Tale

1842

But it is of [Hawthorne's] tales that we desire principally to speak. The tale proper, in our opinion, affords unquestionably the fairest field for the exercise of the loftiest talent, which can be afforded by the wide domains of mere prose. Were we bidden to say how the highest genius could be most advantageously employed for the best display of its own powers, we should answer, without hesitation — in the composition of a rhymed poem, not to exceed in length what might be perused in an hour. Within this limit alone can the highest order of true poetry exist. We need only here say, upon this topic, that, in almost all classes of composition, the unity of effect or impression is a point of the greatest importance. It is clear, moreover, that this unity cannot be thoroughly preserved in productions whose perusal cannot be completed at one sitting. We may continue the reading of a prose composition, from the very nature of prose itself, much longer than we can persevere, to any good purpose, in the perusal of a poem. This latter, if truly fulfilling the demands of the poetic sentiment, induces an exaltation of the soul which cannot be long sustained. All high excitements are necessarily transient. Thus a long poem is a paradox. And, without unity of impression, the deepest effects cannot be brought about. Epics were the offspring of an imperfect sense of Art, and their reign is no more. A poem *too* brief may produce a vivid, but never an intense or enduring impression. Without a certain continuity of effort — without a certain duration or repetition of purpose — the soul is never deeply moved. There must be the dropping of the water upon the rock. . . .

Were we called upon, however, to designate that class of composition which, next to such a poem as we have suggested, should best fulfill the demands of high genius — should offer it the most advantageous field of exertion — we should unhesitatingly speak of the prose tale, as Mr. Hawthorne has here exemplified it. We allude to the short prose narrative, requiring from a half-hour to one or two hours in its perusal. The ordinary novel is objectionable, from its length, for reasons already stated in substance. As it cannot be read at one sitting, it deprives itself, of course, of the immense force derivable from *totality.* Worldly interests intervening during the pauses of perusal, modify, annul, or counteract, in a greater or less degree, the impressions of the book. But simple cessation in reading would, of itself, be sufficient to destroy the true unity. In the brief tale, however, the author is enabled to carry out the fullness of his intention, be it what it may. During the hour of perusal the soul of the reader is at the writer's control. There are no external or extrinsic influences — resulting from weariness or interruption.

A skillful literary artist has constructed a tale. If wise, he has not fashioned his thoughts to accommodate his incidents; but having conceived, with deliberate care, a certain unique or single *effect* to be wrought out, he then invents such incidents — he then combines such events as may best aid him in establishing this preconceived effect. If his very initial sentence tend not to the outbringing of this effect, then he has failed in his first step. In the whole composition there should be no word written, of which the tendency, direct or indirect, is not to the one pre-established design. And by such means, with such care and skill, a picture is at length painted which leaves in the mind of him who contemplates it with a kindred art, a sense of the fullest satisfaction. The idea of the tale has been presented unblemished, because undisturbed; and this is an end unattainable by the novel. Undue brevity is just as exceptionable here as in the poem; but undue length is yet more to be avoided.

We have said that the tale has a point of superiority even over the poem. In fact, while the *rhythm* of this latter is an essential aid in the development of the poem's highest idea — the idea of the Beautiful — the artificialities of this rhythm are an inseparable bar to the development of all points of thought or expression which have their basis in *Truth*. But Truth is often, and in very great degree, the aim of the tale. Some of the finest tales are tales of ratiocination. Thus the field of this species of composition, if not in so elevated a region of the mountain of Mind, is a tableland of far vaster extent than the domain of the mere poem. Its products are never so rich, but infinitely more numerous, and more appreciable by the mass of mankind. The writer of the prose tale, in short, may bring to his theme a vast variety of modes or reflections of thought and expression — (the ratiocinative, for example, the sarcastic, or the humorous) which are not only antagonistical to the nature of the poem, but absolutely forbidden by one of its most peculiar and indispensable adjuncts; we allude, of course, to rhythm. It may be added, here, *par parenthèse,* that the author who aims at the purely beautiful in a prose tale is laboring at a great disadvantage. For Beauty can be better treated in the poem. Not so with terror, or passion, or horror, or a multitude of such other points. . . .

Of Mr. Hawthorne's "Tales" we would say, emphatically, that they belong to the highest region of Art — an Art subservient to genius of a very lofty order. We have supposed, with good reason for so supposing, that he had been thrust into his present position by one of the impudent cliques which beset our literature, and whose pretensions it is our full purpose to expose at the earliest opportunity; but we have been most agreeably mistaken. We know of few compositions which the critic can more honestly commend than these "Twice-Told Tales." As Americans, we feel proud of the book.

Mr. Hawthorne's distinctive trait is invention, creation, imagination, originality — a trait which, in the literature of fiction, is positively worth all the rest. But the nature of the originality, so far as regards its manifestation in letters, is but imperfectly understood. The inventive or original mind as frequently displays itself in novelty of *tone* as in novelty of matter. Mr. Hawthorne is original in *all* points.

It would be a matter of some difficulty to designate the best of these tales; we repeat that, without exception, they are beautiful. . . . In the way of objection we have scarcely a word to say of these tales. There is, perhaps, a somewhat too general or prevalent *tone* — a tone of melancholy and mysticism. The subjects are insufficiently varied. There is not so much of *versatility* evinced as we might well be warranted in expecting from the high powers of Mr. Hawthorne. But beyond these trivial exceptions we have really none to make. The style is purity itself. Force abounds. High imagination gleams from every page. Mr. Hawthorne is a man of the truest genius.

LESLIE MARMON SILKO *discussed her view of her audience and her background growing up in a matriarchal society in a lecture titled "Language and Literature from a Pueblo Indian Perspective." It was originally published in* English Literature: Opening Up the Canon *(1979).*

LESLIE MARMON SILKO

Language and Literature from a Pueblo Indian Perspective

1979

Where I come from, the words that are most highly valued are those which are spoken from the heart, unpremeditated and unrehearsed. Among the Pueblo people, a written speech or statement is highly suspect because the true feelings of the speaker remain hidden as he reads words that are detached from the occasion and the audience. I have intentionally not written a formal paper to read to this session because of this and because I want you to hear and to experience English in a nontraditional structure, a structure that follows patterns from the oral tradition. For those of you accustomed to a structure that moves from point A to point B to point C, this presentation may be somewhat difficult to follow because the structure of Pueblo expression resembles something like a spider's web — with many little threads radiating from a center, crisscrossing each other. As with the web, the structure will emerge as it is made and you must simply listen and trust, as the Pueblo people do, that meaning will be made.

I suppose the task that I have today is a formidable one because basically I come here to ask you, at least for a while, to set aside a number of basic approaches that you have been using and probably will continue to use in approaching the study of English or the study of language; first of all, I come to ask you to see language from the Pueblo perspective, which is a perspective that is very much concerned with including the whole of creation and the

---

This "essay" is an edited transcript of an oral presentation. The "author" deliberately did not read from a prepared paper so that the audience could experience firsthand one dimension of the oral tradition — nonlinear structure. Her remarks were intended to be heard, not read.

whole of history and time. And so we very seldom talk about breaking language down into words. As I will continue to relate to you, even the use of a specific language is less important than the one thing — which is the "telling," or the storytelling. And so, as Simon Ortiz has written, if you approach a Pueblo person and want to talk words or, worse than that, to break down an individual word into its components, ofttimes you will just get a blank stare, because we don't think of words as being isolated from the speaker, which, of course, is one element of the oral tradition. Moreover, we don't think of words as being alone: Words are always with other words, and the other words are almost always in a story of some sort.

Today I have brought a number of examples of stories in English because I would like to get around to the question that has been raised, or the topic that has come along here, which is what changes we Pueblo writers might make with English as a language for literature. But at the same time I would like to explain the importance of storytelling and how it relates to a Pueblo theory of language.

So first I would like to go back to the Pueblo Creation story. The reason I go back to that story is because it is an all-inclusive story of creation and how life began. Tséitsínako, Thought Woman, by thinking of her sisters, and together with her sisters, thought of everything which is, and this world was created. And the belief was that everything in this world was a part of the original creation, and that the people at home realized that far away there were others — other human beings. There is even a section of the story which is a prophesy — which describes the origin of the European race, the African, and also remembers the Asian origins.

Starting out with this story, with this attitude which includes all things, I would like to point out that the reason the people are more concerned with story and communication and less with a particular language is in part an outgrowth of the area [pointing to a map] where we find ourselves. Among the twenty Pueblos there are at least six distinct languages, and possibly seven. Some of the linguists argue — and I don't set myself up to be a linguist at all — about the number of distinct languages. But certainly Zuni is all alone, and Hopi is all alone, and from mesa to mesa there are subtle differences in language — very great differences. I think that this might be the reason that what particular language was being used wasn't as important as what a speaker was trying to say. And this, I think, is reflected and stems or grows out of a particular view of the story — that is, that language *is* story. At Laguna many words have stories which make them. So when one is telling a story, and one is using words to tell the story, each word that one is speaking has a story of its own too. Often the speakers or tellers go into the stories of the words they are using to tell one story so that you get stories within stories, so to speak. This structure becomes very apparent in the storytelling, and what I would like to show you later on by reading some pieces that I brought is that this structure also informs the writing and the stories which are currently coming from Pueblo people. I think what is essential is this sense of story, and story within story, and the idea that one story is only the beginning of many stories, and the sense that stories never truly end. I would like to propose that these views of structure and the dynamics of storytelling are some of the contributions which Native American cultures bring to the English language or at least to literature in the English language.

First of all, a lot of people think of storytelling as something that is done at bedtime — that it is something that is done for small children. When I use the term "storytelling," I include a far wider range of telling activity. I also do not limit storytelling to simply old stories, but to again go back to the original view of creation, which sees that it is all part of a whole; we do not differentiate or fragment stories and experiences. In the beginning, Tséitsínako, Thought Woman, thought of all these things, and all of these things are held together as one holds many things together in a single thought.

So in the telling (and today you will hear a few of the dimensions of this telling) first of all, as was pointed out earlier, the storytelling always includes the audience and the listeners, and, in fact, a great deal of the story is believed to be inside the listener, and the storyteller's role is to draw the story out of the listeners. This kind of shared experience grows out of a strong community base. The storytelling goes on and continues from generation to generation.

The Origin story functions basically as a maker of our identity — with the story we know who we are. We are the Lagunas. This is where we came from. We came this way. We came by this place. And so from the time you are very young, you hear these stories, so that when you go out into the wider world, when one asks who you are, or where are you from, you immediately know: We are the people who came down from the north. We are the people of these stories. It continues down into clans so that you are not just talking about Laguna Pueblo people, you are talking about your own clan. Within the clans there are stories which identify the clan.

In the Creation story, Antelope says that he will help knock a hole in the earth so that the people can come up, out into the next world. Antelope tries and tries, and he uses his hooves and is unable to break through; and it is then that Badger says, "Let me help you." And Badger very patiently uses his claws and digs a way through, bringing the people into the world. When the Badger clan people think of themselves, or when the Antelope people think of themselves, it is as people who are of *this* story, and this is *our* place, and we fit into the very beginning when the people first came, before we began our journey south.

So you can move, then, from the idea of one's identity as a tribal person into clan identity. Then we begin to get to the extended family, and this is where we begin to get a kind of story coming into play which some people might see as a different kind of story, though Pueblo people do not. Anthropologists and ethnologists have, for a long time, differentiated the types of oral language they find in the Pueblos. They tended to rule out all but the old and sacred and traditional stories and were not interested in family stories and the family's account of itself. But these family stories are just as important as the other stories — the older stories. These family stories are given equal recognition. There is no definite, pre-set pattern for the way one will hear the stories of one's own family, but it is a very critical part of one's childhood, and it continues on throughout one's life. You will hear stories of importance to the family — sometimes wonderful stories — stories about the time a maternal uncle got the biggest deer that was ever seen and brought back from the mountains. And so one's sense of who the family is, and who you are, will then extend from that — "I am from the family of my uncle who brought in this wonderful deer, and it was a wonderful hunt" — so you have this sort of building or sense of identity.

There are also other stories, stories about the time when another uncle, perhaps, did something that wasn't really acceptable. In other words, this process of keeping track, of telling, is an all-inclusive process which begins to create a total picture. So it is very important that you know all of the stories — both positive and not so positive — about one's own family. The reason that it is very important to keep track of all the stories in one's own family is because you are liable to hear a story from somebody else who is perhaps an enemy of the family, and you are liable to hear a version which has been changed, a version which makes your family sound disreputable — something that will taint the honor of the family. But if you have already heard the story, you know your family's version of what *really* happened that night, so when somebody else is mentioning it, you will have a version of the story to counterbalance it. Even when there is no way around it — old Uncle Pete did a terrible thing — by knowing the stories that come out of other families, by keeping very close watch, listening constantly to learn the stories about other families, one is in a sense able to deal with terrible sorts of things that might happen within one's own family. When a member of one's own family does something that cannot be excused, one always knows stories about similar things which happened in other families. And it is not done maliciously. I think it is very important to realize this. Keeping track of all the stories within the community gives a certain distance, a useful perspective which brings incidents down to a level we can deal with. If others have done it before, it cannot be so terrible. If others have endured, so can we.

The stories are always bringing us together, keeping this whole together, keeping this family together, keeping this clan together. "Don't go away, don't isolate yourself, but come here, because we have all had these kinds of experiences" — this is what the people are saying to you when they tell you these other stories. And so there is this constant pulling together to resist what seems to me to be a basic part of human nature: When some violent emotional experience takes place, people get the urge to run off and hide or separate themselves from others. And of course, if we do that, we are not only talking about endangering the group, we are also talking about the individual or the individual family never being able to recover or to survive. Inherent in this belief is the feeling that one does not recover or get well by one's self, but it is together that we look after each other and take care of each other.

In the storytelling, then, we see this process of bringing people together, and it works not only on the family level, but also on the level of the individual. Of course, the whole Pueblo concept of the individual is a little bit different from the usual Western concept of the individual. But one of the beauties of the storytelling is that when something happens to an individual, many people will come to you and take you aside, or maybe a couple of people will come and talk to you. These are occasions of storytelling. These occasions of storytelling are continuous; they are a way of life.

Storytelling lies at the heart of the Pueblo people, and so when someone comes in and says, "When did they tell the stories, or what time of day does the storytelling take place?" that is a ridiculous question. The storytelling goes on constantly — as some old grandmother puts on the shoes of a little child and tells the child the story of a little girl who didn't wear her shoes. At the same time somebody comes into the house for coffee to talk with an adolescent boy who has just been into a lot of trouble, to reassure him that *he* got into that kind of trouble, or somebody else's son got into that kind of trouble too. You have this constant ongoing process, working on many different levels.

One of the stories I like to bring up about helping the individual in crisis is a recent story, and I want to remind you that we make no distinctions between the stories — whether they are history, whether they are fact, whether they are gossip — these distinctions are not useful when we are talking about this particular experience with language. Anyway, there was a young man who, when he came back from the war in Vietnam, had saved up his Army pay and bought a beautiful red Volkswagen Beetle. He was very proud of it, and one night drove up to a place right across the reservation line. It is a very notorious place for many reasons, but one of the more notorious things about the place is a deep arroyo behind the place. This is the King's Bar. So he ran in to pick up a cold six-pack to take home, but he didn't put on his emergency brake. And his little red Volkswagen rolled back into the arroyo and was all smashed up. He felt very bad about it, but within a few days everybody had come to him and told him stories about other people who had lost cars to that arroyo. And probably the story that made him feel the best was about the time that George Day's station wagon, with his mother-in-law and kids in the back, rolled into that arroyo. So everybody was saying, "Well, at least your mother-in-law and kids weren't in the car when it rolled in," and you can't argue with that kind of story. He felt better then because he wasn't alone anymore. He and his smashed-up Volkswagen were now joined with all the other stories of cars that fell into that arroyo.

There are a great many parallels between Pueblo experiences and the remarks that have been made about South Africa and the Caribbean countries — similarities in experiences so far as language is concerned. More specifically, with the experience of English being imposed upon the people. The Pueblo people, of course, have seen intruders come and intruders go. The first they watched come were the Spaniards; while the Spaniards were there, things had to be conducted in Spanish. But as the old stories say, if you wait long enough, they'll go. And sure enough, they went. Then another bunch came in. And old stories say, well, if you wait around long enough, not so much that they'll go, but at least their ways will go. One wonders now, when you see what's happening to technocratic-industrial culture, now that we've used up most of the sources of energy, you think perhaps the old people are right.

But anyhow, our experience with English has been different because the

Bureau of Indian Affairs schools were so terrible that we never heard of Shakespeare. There was Dick and Jane, and I can remember reading that the robins were heading south for winter, but I knew that all winter the robins were around Laguna. It took me a long time to figure out what was going on. I worried for quite a while about the robins because they didn't leave in the winter, not realizing that the textbooks were written in Boston. The big textbook companies are up here in Boston and *their* robins do go south in the winter. But this freed us and encouraged us to stay with our narratives. Whatever literature we received at school (which was damn little), at home the storytelling, the special regard for telling and bringing together through the telling, was going on constantly. It has continued, and so we have a great body of classical oral literature, both in the narratives and in the chants and songs.

As the old people say, "If you can remember the stories, you will be all right. Just remember the stories." And, of course, usually when they say that to you, when you are young, you wonder what in the world they mean. But when I returned — I had been away from Laguna Pueblo for a couple of years, well more than a couple of years after college and so forth — I returned to Laguna and I went to Laguna-Acoma high school to visit an English class, and I was wondering how the telling was continuing, because Laguna Pueblo, as the anthropologists have said, is one of the more acculturated pueblos. So I walked into this high school English class and there they were sitting, these very beautiful Laguna and Acoma kids. But I knew that out in their lockers they had cassette tape recorders, and I knew that at home they had stereos, and they were listening to Kiss and Led Zeppelin and all those other things. I was almost afraid, but I had to ask — I had with me a book of short fiction (it's called *The Man to Send Rain Clouds* [New York: Viking Press, 1974]), and among the stories of other Native American writers, it has stories that I have written and Simon Ortiz has written. And there is one particular story in the book about the killing of a state policeman in New Mexico by three Acoma Pueblo men. It was an act that was committed in the early fifties. I was afraid to ask, but I had to. I looked at the class and I said, "How many of you heard this story before you read it in the book?" And I was prepared to hear this crushing truth that indeed the anthropologists were right about the old traditions dying out. But it was amazing, you know, almost all but one or two students raised their hands. They had heard that story, just as Simon and I had heard it, when we were young. That was my first indication that storytelling continues on. About half of them had heard it in English, about half of them had heard it in Laguna. I think again, getting back to one of the original statements, that if you begin to look at the core of the importance of the language and how it fits in with the culture, it is the *story* and the feeling of the story which matters more than what language it's told in.

ꕥ

HARRY STONE *analyzed the autobiographical background of James Joyce's "Araby" in an essay that originally appeared in the* Antioch Review *(1965).*

HARRY STONE

"Araby" and the Writings of James Joyce

1965

"We walk through ourselves," says Stephen Dedalus in *Ulysses.* Stephen is trying to show how Shakespeare, or for that matter how any artist (creator of "Dane or Dubliner"), forever turns to the themes which agitate him, endlessly bodying forth the few crucial events of his life. "Every life is many days, day after day," says Stephen. "We walk through ourselves, meeting robbers, ghosts, giants, old men, young men, wives, widows, brothers-in-love. But always meeting ourselves." Stephen's theory may be an ingenious *jeu d'esprit* — though Joyce himself was heavily committed to such views. But whether or not Stephen's words are appropriate to Shakespeare, they are exactly appropriate to Joyce. In his writings, Joyce was always meeting himself — in ways which must at times have been beyond his conscious ordinance — and the pages of "Araby" are witness to that fact.

For "Araby" preserves a central episode in Joyce's life, an episode he will endlessly recapitulate. The boy in "Araby," like the youthful Joyce himself, must begin to free himself from the nets and trammels of society. That beginning involves painful farewells and disturbing dislocations. The boy must dream "no more of enchanted days." He must forgo the shimmering mirage of childhood, begin to see things as they really are. But to see things as they really are is only a prelude. Far in the distance lies his appointed (but as yet unimagined) task: to encounter the reality of experience and forge the uncreated conscience of his race. The whole of that struggle, of course, is set forth in *A Portrait of the Artist as a Young Man.* "Araby" is the identical struggle at an earlier stage; "Araby" is a portrait of the artist as a young boy.

II

The autobiographical nexus of "Araby" is not confined to the struggle raging in the boy's mind, though that conflict — an epitome of Joyce's first painful effort to see — is central and controls all else. Many of the details of the story are also rooted in Joyce's life. The narrator of "Araby" — the narrator is the boy of the story now grown up — lived, like Joyce, on North Richmond Street. North Richmond Street is blind, with a detached two-story house at the blind end, and down the street, as the opening paragraph informs us, the Christian Brothers' school. Like Joyce, the boy attended this school, and again like Joyce he found it dull and stultifying. Furthermore, the boy's surrogate parents, his aunt and uncle, are a version of Joyce's parents: the aunt, with her forbearance and her unexamined piety, is like his mother; the uncle, with his irregular hours, his irresponsibility, his love of recitation, and his drunkenness, is like his father.

The title and the central action of the story are also autobiographical. From May fourteenth to nineteenth, 1894, while the Joyce family was living on North Richmond Street and Joyce was twelve, Araby came to Dublin. Araby was a bazaar, and the program of the bazaar, advertising the fair as a "Grand Oriental Fête," featured the name "Araby" in huge exotic letters, while the design as well as the detail of the program conveyed an ill-assorted blend of pseudo-Eastern romanticism and blatant commercialism. For one shilling, as the program put it, one could visit "Araby in Dublin" and at the same time aid the Jervis Street Hospital.

But the art of "Araby" goes beyond its autobiographical matrix. The autobiographical strands soon entwine themselves about more literary patterns and enter the fiction in dozens of unsuspected ways. For instance, embedded in "Araby" is a story, "Our Lady of the Hills," from a book that Joyce knew well, *The Celtic Twilight* (1893) by William Butler Yeats. "Our Lady of the Hills" tells how a pretty young Protestant girl walking through the mountains near Lough Gill was taken for the Virgin Mary by a group of Irish Catholic children. The children refused to accept her denials of divinity; to them she was "the great Queen of Heaven come to walk upon the mountain and be kind to them." After they had parted and she had walked on for half a mile, one of the children, a boy, jumped down into her path and said that he would believe she were mortal if she had a petticoat under her dress like other ladies. The girl showed the boy her two skirts, and the boy's dream of a saintly epiphany vanished into the mountain air. In his anguish, he cried out angrily, "Dad's a divil, mum's a divil, and I'm a divil, and you are only an ordinary lady." Then he "ran away sobbing."

Probably reverberating in "Araby" also are chords from one of Thomas De Quincey's° most famous works, "Levana and Our Ladies of Sorrow." In "Levana," Our Lady of Tears (she bears the additional title "Madonna") speaks about the child who is destined to suffer and to see, a type of the inchoate artist:

> "Lo! here is he whom in childhood I dedicated to my altars. This is he that once I made my darling. Him I led astray, him I beguiled, and from heaven I stole away his young heart to mine. Through me did he become idolatrous; and through me it was, by languishing desires, that he worshipped the worm, and prayed to the wormy grave. Holy was the grave to him; lovely was its darkness; saintly its corruption. Him, this young idolater, I have seasoned for thee, dear gentle Sister of Sighs!"

He who is chosen by the Ladies of Sorrow will suffer and be cursed; he will "see the things that ought *not* to be seen, sights that are abominable, and secrets that are unutterable," but he will also be able to read the great truths of the universe, and he will "rise again *before* he dies." In this manner, says Our Lady of Tears, we accomplish the commission we had from God: "to plague [the chosen one's] heart until we had unfolded the capacities of his spirit."

The ideas and images of "Levana" (witness the parody in *Ulysses*) had sunk deep into Joyce's imagination. His imagination had always sought out, always vibrated to, the Levanaesque constellation — a constellation that fuses religion, sexuality, idolatry, darkness, ascension, and art. "Araby," both in its

---

Thomas De Quincey: English essayist and critic (1785–1859) best known for his *Confessions of an English Opium Eater* (1822).

central idea and its characteristic imagery — in the image of Mangan's sister, in the boy's blind idolatry, and in the boy's ultimate insight and dawning ascension — is cognate with "Levana."

Other literary prototypes also contribute to "Araby." In "Araby" as in Joyce's life, Mangan is an important name. In life Mangan was one of Joyce's favorite Romantic poets, a little-known Irish poet who pretended that many of his poems were translations from the Arabic although he was totally ignorant of that language. Joyce championed him in a paper delivered as a Pateresque twenty-year-old before the Literary and Historical Society of University College, Dublin, and championed him again five years later, in a lecture at the Università Popolare in Trieste, as "the most significant poet of the modern Celtic world, and one of the most inspired singers that ever used the lyric form in any country." In "Araby" Mangan is the boy's friend, but, what is more important, Mangan's sister is the adored girl. In each lecture Joyce discussed Mangan's poetry in words which could serve as an epigraph for the boy's mute, chivalric love for Mangan's sister and for his subsequent disillusionment and self-disdain. In the latter lecture, Joyce described the female persona that Mangan is constantly adoring:

> This figure which he adores recalls the spiritual yearnings and the imaginary loves of the Middle Ages, and Mangan has placed his lady in a world full of melody, of lights and perfumes, a world that grows fatally to frame every face that the eyes of a poet have gazed on with love. There is only one chivalrous idea, only one male devotion, that lights up the faces of Vittoria Colonna, Laura, and Beatrice, just as the bitter disillusion and the self-disdain that end the chapter are one and the same.

And one of Joyce's favorite poems by Mangan — a poem whose influence recurs in *A Portrait of the Artist as a Young Man, Ulysses,* and *Finnegans Wake* — is "Dark Rosaleen," a love paean to a girl who represents Ireland (Dark Rosaleen is a poetic name for Ireland), physical love, and romantic adoration. In "Araby" Joyce took Mangan's idealized girl as an embodiment of the artist's, especially the Irish artist's, relationship to his beloved, and then, combining the image of the girl with other resonating literary associations, wrote his own story of dawning, worshipful love.

III

It is easy to follow the external events of the story. A young boy becomes fascinated with his boyfriend's sister, begins to dwell on her soft presence, and eventually adores her with an ecstasy of secret love. One day the girl speaks to him — it is one of the few times they have ever exchanged a word — and asks him if he is going to Araby. She herself cannot go, she tells him, for she must participate in a retreat. The boy says if he goes he will bring her a gift. When he finally visits the bazaar he is disillusioned by its tawdriness and by a banal conversation he overhears, and he buys no gift. Instead he feels "driven and derided by vanity" and his eyes burn with "anguish and anger."

"Driven and derided," "anguish and anger" — these reactions seem far too strong. Indeed they seem pretentious when compared to the trivial disillusionment which caused them. And they are pretentious, certainly they are inappropriate, if related only to their immediate external causes. But the boy is reacting to much more than a banal fair and a broken promise. He is reacting to sudden and deeply disturbing insights. These insights are shared by the attentive reader, for by the end of "Araby" the reader has been presented with all that he needs in order to resolve the story's intricate harmony into its component motifs.

Most of those motifs, both personal and public, are sounded at once. The former tenant of the boy's house, a house stale with the smell of mustiness and decay, had been a priest who had died in the back drawing room. In a litter of old papers in a waste room behind the kitchen the boy has found a few damp-stained volumes: "*The Abbot*, by Walter Scott, *The Devout Communicant*, and *The Memoirs of Vidocq*." The only additional information Joyce gives us about these books is that the boy liked the last volume best because "its leaves were yellow." The musty books and the boy's response to them are doubly and trebly meaningful. Joyce chose works that would objectify the themes of "Araby," works that would exemplify in the most blatant (yet unexpressed) manner the very confusions, veilings, and failures he was depicting in the priest and the boy. The books and their lurking incongruities help us arraign the priest and understand the boy. That the priest should leave a romance by Scott with a religious title that obscures the fact that it is the secular celebration of a worldly queen, Mary Queen of Scots, a queen enshrined in history as saint and harlot; a book of rules, meditations, anthems, and prayers for Holy Week by a Protestant clergyman named Abednego Seller, a clergyman who had written tracts against "Popish Priests," engaged in published controversy with a Jesuit divine, and was eventually relieved of his office; and a volume of lurid and often sexually suggestive memoirs by a notorious impostor, master of disguise, archcriminal, and police official — all this is a commentary on the priest and the religion he is supposed to represent. At the same time this literary debris objectifies the boy's confusions.

That Scott's unblemished romantic heroine, an idolized Catholic queen by the name of Mary, should also be (though not to Scott) a "harlot queen," a passionate thrice-married woman who was regarded by many of her contemporaries as the "Whore of Babylon," as a murderess who murdered to satisfy her lust — this strange dissonance, muted and obscured by Scott's presentation, is a version of the boy's strikingly similar and equally muted dissonances. That the dead priest's book of devotions is a Protestant manual by a man bearing the significant name Abednego Seller — a name which combines in equal parts ancient religious associations (in particular associations of refusing to worship a golden image and of a faith strong enough to withstand a fiery furnace) with an ironically incongruous modern surname that has to do with selling and commercialism — this juxtaposition, also, is appropriate to the boy: it typifies one of his fundamental confusions.

That Vidocq should escape from a prison hospital disguised in the stolen habit of a nun, a veil over his face; that he should then assist a good-natured curé in celebrating mass, pretending to make the signs and genuflections prescribed for a nun — this is a version of what the boy will do. That *The Memoirs* should also contain the history of a beauty "who seemed to have been created as a model for the divine Madonnas which sprang from the imagination of Raphael," whose eyes "gave expression to all the gentleness of her soul," and who had a "heavenly forehead" and an "ethereal elegance" — but who, from the age of fourteen, had been a debauched prostitute who was ultimately caught by the police because, in the midst of committing a robbery, she and her accomplice became utterly engrossed in fornicating with one another — this, also, is a version, a grotesque extension, of the boy's confusions. The boy does not know, cannot face, what he is. He gazes upon the things that attract or repel him, but they are blurred and veiled by clouds of romantic obfuscation: he likes *The Memoirs of Vidocq* best not because of what it is, a volume of exciting quasi-blasphemous criminal and sexual adventures, but because he finds its outward appearance, its yellowing leaves, romantically appealing. The boy, like the priest, or Vidocq's characters, or disguise-mad Vidocq himself, is, in effect, an impostor — only the boy is unaware of why he feels and acts as he does; the boy is an impostor through self-deception.

Joyce, in accordance with his practice throughout *Dubliners* (and for that matter, in accordance with his method throughout his writings) included these books so that we would make such generalizations about the priest and the boy. This is clear, not merely from his habitual usage in such matters or from the ironic significance of the books themselves, but from the highly directive import of the sentences which immediately follow these details. These sentences tell us that behind the boy's house was a "wild garden" containing a "central apple-tree" — images which strongly suggest a ruined Eden and Eden's forbidden central apple tree, a tree which has to do with man's downfall and his knowledge of good and evil: fundamental themes in "Araby." The last of the sentences is artfully inconclusive. "He had," concludes the narrator, "been a very charitable priest; in his will he had left all his money to institutions and the furniture of his house to his sister." Joyce's ambiguity suggests that the priest's charity may have been as double-edged as other details in the opening paragraphs. Yet the possibility of an incongruity here never occurs to the boy. As usual he fails to examine beneath the veneer of outward appearances; he fails to allow for the possibility of a less public, more cynical interpretation of the priest's charity. If this worldly priest had been so "very charitable" why, at his death, was he able to donate "all his money" to institutions? His charity, so far as we know about it, began at his death.

These and other ambiguously worded ironies had already been sounded by the three opening sentences of "Araby." Joyce begins by telling us that North Richmond Street is blind. That North Richmond Street is a dead end is a simple statement of fact; but that the street is blind, especially since this feature is given significant emphasis in the opening phrases of the story, suggests that blindness plays a role thematically. It suggests, as we later come to understand, that the boy also is blind, that he has reached a dead end in his life. Finally, we are told that the houses of North Richmond Street "conscious of decent lives within them, gazed at one another with brown imperturbable faces." These words, too, are ironic. For the boy will shortly discover that his own consciousness of a decent life within has been a mirage; the imperturbable surface of North Richmond Street (and of the boy's life) will soon be perturbed.

In these opening paragraphs Joyce touches all the themes he will later develop: self-deluding blindness, self-inflating romanticism, decayed religion, mammonism, the coming into man's inheritance, and the gulf between appearance and reality. But these paragraphs do more: they link what could have been the idiosyncratic story of the boy, his problems and distortions, to the problems and distortions of Catholicism and of Ireland as a whole. In other words, the opening paragraphs (and one or two other sections) prevent us from believing that the fault is solely in the boy and not, to some extent at least, in the world that surrounds him, and still more fundamentally, in the nature of man himself. . . .

AMY TAN *discussed the subject of multicultural literature in an essay written for* The Threepenny Review *in 1996. There she admitted that she was proud to find her name on the reading lists for many college courses ("What writer wouldn't want her work to be read?"), and then went on to explain why she was "not altogether comfortable" about the use of her book as required reading.*

AMY TAN

In the Canon, For All the Wrong Reasons 1996

Several years ago I learned that I had passed a new literary milestone. I had made it to the Halls of Education under the rubric of "Multicultural Literature," also known in many schools as "Required Reading."

Thanks to this development, I now meet students who proudly tell me they're doing their essays, term papers, or master's theses on me. By that they mean that they are analyzing not just my books but me — my grade-school achievements, youthful indiscretions, marital status, as well as the movies I watched as a child, the slings and arrows I suffered as a minority, and so forth — all of which, with the hindsight of classroom literary investigation, prove to contain many Chinese omens that made it inevitable that I would become a writer.

Once I read a master's thesis on feminist writings, which included examples from *The Joy Luck Club*. The student noted that I had often used the number four, something on the order of thirty-two or thirty-six times — in any case, a number divisible by four. She pointed out that there were four mothers, four daughters, four sections of the book, four stories per section. Furthermore, there were four sides to a mah jong table, four directions of the wind, four players. More important, she postulated, my use of the number four was a symbol for the four stages of psychological development, which corresponded in uncanny ways to the four stages of some type of Buddhist philosophy I had never heard of before. The student recalled that the story contained a character called Fourth Wife, symbolizing death, and a four-year-old girl with a feisty spirit, symbolizing regeneration.

In short, her literary sleuthing went on to reveal a mystical and rather Byzantine puzzle, which, once explained, proved to be completely brilliant and precisely logical. She wrote me a letter and asked if her analysis had been correct. How I longed to say "absolutely."

The truth is, if there are symbols in my work they exist largely by accident or through someone else's interpretive design. If I wrote of "an orange moon rising on a dark night," I would more likely ask myself later if the image was a cliché, not whether it was a symbol for the feminine force rising in anger, as one master's thesis postulated. To plant symbols like that, you need a plan, good organizational skills, and a prescient understanding of the story you are about to write. Sadly, I lack those traits.

All this is by way of saying that I don't claim my use of the number four to be a brilliant symbolic device. In fact, now that it's been pointed out to me in rather astonishing ways, I consider my overuse of the number to be a flaw.

Reviewers and students have enlightened me about not only how I write but why I write. Apparently, I am driven to capture the immigrant experience, to demystify Chinese culture, to point out the differences between Chinese and American culture, even to pave the way for other Asian American writers.

If only I were that noble. Contrary to what is assumed by some students, reporters, and community organizations wishing to bestow honors on me, I am not an expert on China, Chinese culture, mah jong, the psychology of mothers and daughters, generation gaps, immigration, illegal aliens, assimilation, acculturation, racial tension, Tiananmen Square, the Most Favored Nation trade agreements, human rights, Pacific Rim economics, the purported one million missing baby girls of China, the future of Hong Kong after 1997, or, I am sorry to say, Chinese cooking. Certainly I have personal opinions on many of these topics, but by no means do my sentiments and my world of make-believe make me an expert.

So I am alarmed when reviewers and educators assume that my very personal, specific, and fictional stories are meant to be representative down to the nth detail not just of Chinese Americans but, sometimes, of all Asian culture. Is Jane Smiley's *A Thousand Acres* supposed to be taken as representative of all of American culture? If so, in what ways? Are all American fathers tyrannical? Do all American sisters betray one another? Are all American conscientious objectors flaky in love relationships?

Over the years my editor has received hundreds of permissions requests from publishers of college textbooks and multicultural anthologies, all of them wishing to reprint my work for "educational purposes." One publisher wanted to include an excerpt from *The Joy Luck Club,* a scene in which a Chinese woman invites her non-Chinese boyfriend to her parents' house for dinner. The boyfriend brings a bottle of wine as a gift and commits a number of social gaffes at the dinner table. Students were supposed to read this excerpt, then answer the following question: "If you are invited to a Chinese family's house for dinner, should you bring a bottle of wine?"

In many respects, I am proud to be on the reading lists for courses such as Ethnic Studies, Asian American Studies, Asian American Literature, Asian American History, Women's Literature, Feminist Studies, Feminist Writers of Color, and so forth. What writer wouldn't want her work to be read? I also take a certain perverse glee in imagining countless students, sleepless at three in the morning, trying to read *The Joy Luck Club* for the next day's midterm. Yet I'm also not altogether comfortable about my book's status as required reading.

Let me relate a conversation I had with a professor at a school in southern California. He told me he uses my books in his literature class but he makes it a point to lambast those passages that depict China as backward or unattractive. He objects to any descriptions that have to do with spitting, filth, poverty, or superstitions. I asked him if China in the 1930s and 1940s was free of these elements. He said, No, such descriptions are true; but he still believes it is "the obligation of the writer of ethnic literature to create positive, progressive images."

I secretly shuddered and thought, Oh well, that's southern California for you. But then, a short time later, I met a student from UC Berkeley, a school that I myself attended. The student was standing in line at a book signing. When his turn came, he swaggered up to me, then took two steps back and said in a loud voice, "Don't you think you have a responsibility to write about Chinese men as positive role models?"

In the past, I've tried to ignore the potshots. A *Washington Post* reporter once asked me what I thought of another Asian American writer calling me something on the order of "a running dog whore sucking on the tit of the imperialist white pigs."

"Well," I said, "You can't please everyone, can you?" I pointed out that readers are free to interpret a book as they please, and that they are free to appreciate or not appreciate the result. Besides, reacting to your critics makes a writer look defensive, petulant, and like an all-around bad sport.

But lately I've started thinking it's wrong to take such a laissez-faire attitude. Lately I've come to think that I must say something, not so much to defend myself and my work but to express my hopes for American literature, for what it has the potential to become in the twenty-first century — that is, a truly American literature, democratic in the way it includes many colorful voices.

Until recently, I didn't think it was important for writers to express their private intentions in order for their work to be appreciated; I believed that any analysis of my intentions belonged behind the closed doors of literature classes. But I've come to realize that the study of literature does have its effect on how books are being read, and thus on what might be read, published, and written in the future. For that reason, I do believe writers today must talk about their intentions — if for no other reason than to serve as an antidote to what others say our intentions should be.

For the record, I don't write to dig a hole and fill it with symbols. I don't write stories as ethnic themes. I don't write to represent life in general. And I certainly don't write because I have answers. If I knew everything there is to know about mothers and daughters, Chinese and Americans, I wouldn't have any stories left to imagine. If I had to write about only positive role models, I wouldn't have enough imagination left to finish the first story. If I knew what to do about immigration, I would be a sociologist or a politician and not a long-winded storyteller.

So why do I write?

Because my childhood disturbed me, pained me, made me ask foolish questions. And the questions still echo. Why does my mother always talk about killing herself? Why did my father and brother have to die? If I die, can I be reborn into a happy family? Those early obsessions led to a belief that writing could be my salvation, providing me with the sort of freedom and danger, satisfaction and discomfort, truth and contradiction I can't find in anything else in life.

I write to discover the past for myself. I don't write to change the future for others. And if others are moved by my work — if they love their mothers more, scold their daughters less, or divorce their husbands who were not positive role models — I'm often surprised, usually grateful to hear from kind readers. But I don't take either credit or blame for changing their lives for better or for worse.

Writing, for me, is an act of faith, a hope that I will discover what I mean by "truth." I also think of reading as an act of faith, a hope that I will discover something remarkable about ordinary life, about myself. And if the writer and the reader discover the same thing, if they have that connection, the act of faith has resulted in an act of magic. To me, that's the mystery and the wonder of both life and fiction — the connection between two individuals who discover in the end that they are more the same than they are different.

And if that doesn't happen, it's nobody's fault. There are still plenty of other books on the shelf. Choose what you like.

ꕥ

LEO TOLSTOY *wrote his commentary on "The Darling" a year after his friend Anton Chekhov's death as a way of protesting what Tolstoy considered an unfair caricature of a simple, good-hearted woman, the central character in the story. That Tolstoy experienced such a strong emotional affinity with Chekhov's fictional heroine that he felt compelled to defend her is a striking testimony to Chekhov's power as a short story writer and to Tolstoy's obsessive concern with morality. Tolstoy's argument is essentially based on the point of view of the patriarch. Chekhov's point of view in the story is much more subtle. His narrative has prompted other, very different interpretations, as evidenced by Eudora Welty's reading* *(see p. 736–38)**.*

LEO TOLSTOY

Chekhov's Intent in "The Darling" — *1905*

TRANSLATED BY CONSTANCE GARNETT

There is a story of profound meaning in the Book of Numbers which tells how Balak, the King of the Moabites, sent for the prophet Balaam to curse the Israelites who were on his borders. Balak promised Balaam many gifts for this service, and Balaam, tempted, went to Balak, and went with him up the mountain, where an altar was prepared with calves and sheep sacrificed in readiness for the curse. Balak waited for the curse, but instead of cursing, Balaam blessed the people of Israel.

> And Balak said unto Balaam, What hast thou done unto me? I took thee to curse mine enemies, and, behold, thou hast blessed them altogether.
>
> And he answered and said, Must I not take heed to speak that which the Lord hath put in my mouth?
>
> And Balak said unto him, Come, I pray thee, with me into another place . . . and curse me them from thence.
>
> But again, instead of cursing, Balaam blessed. And so it was the third time also.
>
> And Balak's anger was kindled against Balaam, and he smote his hands together: And Balak said unto Balaam, I called thee to curse my enemies, and, behold, thou hast altogether blessed them these three times.
>
> Therefore now flee thee to thy place: I thought to promote thee unto great honour; but, lo, the Lord hast kept thee back from honour.
>
> And so Balaam departed without having received the gifts, because, instead of cursing, he had blessed the enemies of Balak. [Numbers 23: 11–13; 24:10–11]

What happened to Balaam often happens to real poets and artists. Tempted by Balak's gifts, popularity, or by false preconceived ideas, the poet does not see the angel barring his way, though the ass sees him, and he means to curse, and yet, behold, he blesses.

This is just what happened to the true poet and artist Chekhov when he wrote this charming story "The Darling."

The author evidently means to mock at the pitiful creature — as he judges her with his intellect, but not with his heart — the Darling, who after first sharing Kukin's anxiety about his theater, then throwing herself into the interests of the timber trade, then under the influence of the veterinary surgeon regarding the campaign against the foot and mouth disease as the most important matter in the world, is finally engrossed in the grammatical questions and the interests of the little schoolboy in the big cap. Kukin's surname is absurd, even his illness and the telegram announcing his death, the timber merchant with his respectability, the veterinary surgeon, even the boy — all are absurd, but the soul of the Darling, with her faculty of devoting herself with her whole being to any one she loves, is not absurd, but marvelous and holy.

I believe that while he was writing "The Darling," the author had in his mind, though not in his heart, a vague image of a new woman; of her equality with man; of a woman mentally developed, learned, working independently for the good of society as well as, if not better than, a man; of the woman who has raised and upholds the woman question; and in writing "The Darling" he wanted to show what woman ought not to be. The Balak of public opinion bade Chekhov curse the weak, submissive undeveloped woman devoted to man; and Chekhov went up the mountain, and the calves and sheep were laid upon the altar, but when he began to speak, the poet blessed what he had come to curse. In spite of its exquisite gay humor, I at least cannot read without tears some passages of this wonderful story. I am touched by the description of her complete devotion and love for Kukin and all that he cares for, and for the timber merchant and for the veterinary surgeon, and even more of her sufferings when she is left alone and has no one to love; and finally the account of how with all the strength of womanly, motherly feelings (of which she has no experience in her own life) she devotes herself with boundless love to the future man, the schoolboy in the big cap.

The author makes her love the absurd Kukin, the insignificant timber merchant, and the unpleasant veterinary surgeon, but love is no less sacred whether its object is a Kukin or a Spinoza, a Pascal, or a Schiller,° and whether the objects of it change as rapidly as with the Darling, or whether the object of it remains the same throughout the whole life.

Some time ago I happened to read in the *Novoe Vremya* an excellent article upon woman. The author has in this article expressed a remarkably clever and profound idea about woman. "Women," he says, "are trying to show us they can do everything we men can do. I don't contest it; I am prepared to admit women can do everything men can do, and possibly better than men; but the trouble is that men cannot do anything faintly approaching to what women can do."

Yes, that is undoubtedly true, and it is true not only with regard to birth, nurture, and early education of children. Men cannot do that highest, best work which brings man nearest to God — the work of love, and complete devotion to the loved object, which good women have done, do, and will do so well and so naturally. What would become of the world, what would become of us men if women had not that faculty and did not exercise it? We could get on without women doctors, women telegraph clerks, women lawyers, women scientists, women writers, but life would be a sorry affair without mothers, helpers, friends, comforters, who love in men the best in them, and imperceptibly instill, evoke, and support it. There would have been no Magdalen with Christ, no Claire with St. Francis; there would have been no wives of the Dekabrists° in Siberia; there would not have been among the

---

Spinoza . . . Schiller: Baruch Spinoza (1632–1677), Dutch philosopher; Blaise Pascal (1623–1662), French scientist and philosopher; Johann Christoph Friedrich von Schiller (1759–1805), German poet, playwright, and critic.
Dekabrists: Members of the unsuccessful December 1825 uprising against Czar Nicholas I.

Duhobors° those wives who, instead of holding their husbands back, supported them in their martyrdom for truth; there would not have been those thousands and thousands of unknown women — the best of all, as the unknown always are — the comforters of the drunken, the weak, and the dissolute, who, more than any, need the comfort of love. That love, whether devoted to a Kukin or to Christ, is the chief, grand, unique strength of woman.

What an amazing misunderstanding it is — all this so-called woman question, which, as every vulgar idea is bound to do, has taken possession of the majority of women, and even of men.

"Woman longs to improve herself" — what can be more legitimate and just than that?

But a woman's work is from her very vocation different from man's, and so the ideal of feminine perfection cannot be the same as the ideal of masculine perfection. Let us admit that we do not know what that ideal is; it is quite certain in any case that it is not the ideal of masculine perfection. And yet it is to the attainment of that masculine ideal that the whole and the absurd and evil activity of the fashionable woman movement, which is such a stumbling-block to woman, is directed.

I am afraid that Chekhov was under the influence of that misunderstanding when he wrote "The Darling."

He, like Balaam, intended to curse, but the god of poetry forbade him, and commanded him to bless. And he did bless, and unconsciously clothed this sweet creature in such an exquisite radiance that she will always remain a type of what a woman can be in order to be happy herself, and to make the happiness of those with whom destiny throws her.

What makes the story so excellent is that the effect is unintentional.

I learned to ride a bicycle in a hall large enough to drill a division of soldiers. At the other end of the hall a lady was learning. I thought I must be careful to avoid getting into her way, and began looking at her. And as I looked at her I began unconsciously getting nearer and nearer to her, and in spite of the fact that, noticing the danger, she hastened to retreat, I rode down upon her and knocked her down — that is, I did the very opposite of what I wanted to do, simply because I concentrated my attention upon her.

The same thing has happened to Chekhov, but in an inverse sense: He wanted to knock the Darling down, and concentrating upon her the close attention of the poet, he raised her up.

CHERYL B. TORSNEY *wrote an essay about Alice Walker's "Everyday Use" as a reader-response or autobiographical literary critic. Her essay was included in the collection* The Intimate Critique *(1993), edited by Diane P. Freedman, Olivia Frey, and Frances Murphy Zauhar.*

Duhobors: Members of the Christian sect that advocated following inner spirituality instead of church or government doctrine.

CHERYL B. TORSNEY

"Everyday Use": My Sojourn at Parchman Farm

1993

Today, when autumn colors camouflage the existence of the strip mines in the vertical West Virginia landscape of mountain and hollow, it's hard to remember actually having lived in the Mississippi Delta. What I do recall is that although the area lacks coal, it is rich in other things — soybeans, rice, and cotton — and flat as a quilt pulled tight over an old bed. From my backyard, I could see the water towers of six neighboring towns, not including the cotton boll affair in Minter City, Sunflower County.

In 1983, during the height of the job crunch in literary studies, I, a white Northern Jew — an alien by the standards of nearly everyone in Bolivar County, Mississippi — was delighted to be teaching in a tenure-line position at a small university in the state where Goodman's, Schwerner's, and Chaney's bodies had been found buried in an earthen dam near the ironically named city of Philadelphia. With the enthusiasm of a recent-vintage Ph.D., I brazenly challenged my mostly white students to reconsider their understandings of Southern history and traditions, to revise their notions of what constitutes sense of place, political agenda, race, and class. I remember talking about Eudora Welty, Fannie Lou Hamer, Alice Walker. I figured, presumptuously I now see, that if no one else was doing it, then I was responsible for telling my students what I thought they should know about their past, not to mention their present.

My teaching of Alice Walker's short story "Everyday Use" and my continuing research on quilting as a metaphor in women's writing led me to ask my husband to take me to work with him, to meet a quilter he had heard about. At that time, Jack was employed in the psychiatric hospital at the Mississippi State Penitentiary, the Parchman Farm of so many blues songs. He arranged for me to meet a female inmate who had pieced a quilt for another one of the psychologists at the prison hospital. . . .

I let Lucille Sojourner tell her story.

She had been quilting since 1980, when she was sentenced to life in prison. A quiet woman, Lucille had been approached by a white prisoner, who got her started. At that time she'd had no means of support. Soon after completing her first quilt, however, a big freeze hit northern Mississippi, and when another inmate offered to buy the cover to keep herself warm, Lucille sold it right from her bed.

Financially strapped, Lucille was emotionally depressed as well. Her family of many brothers and sisters and her own seven children did not visit her on the Farm. Her husband was in one of the men's camps. Soon she began to contract quilts with several women from Jackson, who would provide her with good material and pay her $150 a quilt. She'd recently made "an old nine-patch" for them, and those Jackson women sold it, not even a fancy patterned top, for $90. Ecstatic, she could send this money to her several sisters who were caring for her many children. At that time she was piecing for one of the counselors in the psychiatric unit a churn dash crib quilt in muted Laura Ashley tones of brick and blue. When Lucille Sojourner modestly offered "Round the World" as her favorite pattern, given the quilter's name, I was not surprised.

Parchman is a violent place. Lucille told me of one of her "friend girls" who had succumbed to gossip and gotten severely beaten. On another occasion two inmates had grabbed the freestanding quilting frame the Jackson women had bought her, destroyed it, and used the legs as clubs. As a result, she switched to a lap frame, quilting all day every day, taking time out only for trips to the bathroom. Wisely, as it turns out, she did not eat prison food: the week before I visited, seventy men in one of the camps got food poisoning, and one of them had died. Lucille told me that she got canned goods at the canteen, figuring she could survive on those and candy bars until she came up for parole. Constantly working — to make the time pass — she could piece a top in a week and quilt it in three days.

About thirty other women in the unit quilted, and Lucille spoke admiringly of a woman who worked more complicated patterns, like the lily of the valley and the double wedding ring. Yet she displayed real pride in her own skill. Some of the prison's quilters used a sewing machine to piece their tops, but she found that sometimes their seams didn't hold. Thus, she preferred, as she said, "to sew on my hands." And then she showed me her bruised fingers, swearing that they were better and had been much worse.

Why do it, I had asked. "It gives me constellation," she responded unhesitatingly, offering me an image of cosmic order.

She continued, telling of the guard who had asked her to quilt an already-pieced cover for free, since she was a convict with time on her hands. Clearly insulted by the guard's assumption that her time was of no value, Lucille noted that she was studying for her Graduation Equivalency Diploma.

This meeting with Lucille Sojourner forced me to revise my entire understanding of Alice Walker's short story, not to mention to examine my own position in the new narrative featuring the Yankee English professor's encounter with the convicted murderess. If Walker's Maggie, the stay-at-home sister of the story, was the type of meek, hard-working devoted daughter, Lucille (never mind the crime that had put her in Parchman) was the antitype, sewing for her place in the world, for her sanity. And if Dee/Wangero was the type of culturally hip daughter who desired tangible evidence of her heritage while rejecting her family, I was the antitype.

Both Dee and I had been named for family matriarchs: she had been originally named after her grandmother, and I, in the tradition of assimilated American Jews, was given a Hebrew name, Chaya — Life — after my maternal grandmother's mother. Our name changes reveal us to be cultural cross-dressers: Dee had been renamed Wangero, and I go by the English Cheryl. Lucille, too, had been renamed: #46496. Although Lucille was the only one of us to be literally incarcerated, from the perspective of Dee/Wangero's mother, Mrs. Johnson, Dee was as truly imprisoned by some institutionalized movement that had stripped her of her familial identity. And although I was privileged by education and race, I nonetheless felt a curious kinship with both Lucille/Maggie and Dee/Wangero. For in the foreign Delta culture, I felt constrained if not in many senses imprisoned as a result of my past, like Lucille; both of us, as it were, had been given "Life." But like Dee/Wangero, I was also estranged from my personal history, wanting it to confer identity, yet rejecting it at the same time. My double-bind hit home in the small synagogue in my Delta town during a Rosh Hashanah service, to which I had gone, I reasoned, to please my mother. Here the High Holy Days liturgy, sung in transliterated Hebrew, in major modes by the members of the First Baptist Church choir, only heightened my alienation.

In Walker's story, Dee has ironically been given a sort of work-release in order to return home to appropriate the family quilts, which contain pieces of people's lives: scraps from a wedding dress and a Civil War uniform, for example. Dee/Wangero wants to hang them like museum pieces on her wall, a motive that declares with additional irony that this newly liberated dashiki-ed black woman is both a prisoner to trends in interior design and a woman bent on larceny. Seeing her reentry into the dull life of her mother and sister as a diversion from her fashionable pursuit of her black heritage, Dee/Wangero plots to take what she wants and retreat once again from her past into a world that does not validate her familial history, into a social set whose project is to write a new narrative of African-American power. Mrs. Johnson and Maggie, then, are the ones who, in Dee/Wangero's fiction, are imprisoned in their rural lives and in their "ignorance," just like the students whom I had made it my business to enlighten.

In "Everyday Use" Maggie, the plain sister, who has remained at home with Mrs. Johnson, the focus of strength in the story, is, we remember, scarred, a description that gained a metaphoric import it never had before my trip to camp 25, before my examination of Lucille Sojourner's fingers. In fact, the whole notion of "everyday use" was transformed by my own sojourn at Parchman Farm. Originally, I had understood that, like the woman to whom Lucille made her first sale, Maggie would put the quilts to everyday use — she would use them to keep her and her family warm, to preserve their bodies as well as their souls — and in that fashion perpetuate the family's heritage in a way that displaying the quilts in a museum could never accomplish. She would use them *freely,* as a woman who gains strength from the narrative of her past, which she embodies. From the quilts Maggie would derive, as Lucille would say, constellation. Most interpretations of Walker's short story follow this line of reasoning, reading Maggie as the Cinderella — good sister, and Dee/Wangero as the evil sister in the flashy clothes. But Dee/Wangero doesn't want the quilts to destroy them. True, she wants to remove them from everyday use, but her motive is, after all, preservation, of personal family history in the context of larger cultural history, and preservation, as many recent feminist readers understand, of a valid text(ile) of women's tradition.

I am similarly engaged in making my own way through both family tradition and male and female literary traditions, taking what I want: for example, the copy of *Anna Karenina* that my grandmother brought with her on the boat from her Anatevka-like village (even though I can't read a word of

Russian); her volumes of the works of Sholem Aleichem (even though I can't read a word of Yiddish). Many critics have faulted Dee/Wangero for trying to "preserve" her past in the sterile, academic hanging out of the family linen as though it is the formal blazon that people like me make it out to be in our scholarship. I used to fault her, too.

But after my meeting with Lucille, who so reminds me of Maggie though her visible scars are limited to her fingertips, I feel a strong kinship with Dee/Wangero, who, had she been in my shoes, would have been called upon Passover Seder after Passover Seder to read the part of The Wicked Son, who does not believe. Like Dee/Wangero, I am trying to negotiate the old by casting my lot with the new. But whereas Walker presents no evidence that Dee/Wangero questions her own motivations, I do: call it Jewish guilt; a habit of self-reflexively examining my assumptions borne of graduate courses in literature and theory; or a rhetorical strategy to fend off an imagined reader's criticism. Why did I ask to meet Lucille Sojourner in the first place? To talk with her about quilting and do serious scholarship, or to commission a quilt for my bed? An even more fundamental question, however, is why I'm so interested in quilting, I don't quilt myself, I don't collect quilts (although I have a few), no members of my family, immediate or extended, quilt. The tradition is foreign to my family. Is it, then, that to give me some identity — cultural, professional, ultimately personal — I have wrapped myself in the critical quilt of literary theory and feminist criticism, which created the academic interest in quilting in the first place? If Lucille, Maggie, and Dee/Wangero are each imprisoned in ways both literal and metaphoric, am I a prisoner not only of literary trends but also of capitalist production and consumption, the system that, according to Michel Foucault, necessitated the existence of prisons in the first place? Admittedly, I did end up paying Lucille to make me a quilt of my own. . . .

It's been over six years since I interviewed Lucille. Although I wrote to her several times, sending her at one point a photocopy of "Everyday Use," I never heard from her. Perhaps she had been offended by my offer of the story, thinking that I was condescending to enlighten her. I hadn't thought I was, but my naive motive, thinking that it might "brighten her day," might have been condescension after all. A few years ago Parchman Farm closed camp 25 to women inmates, who were moved to Jackson, where, for what it's worth, the chief proponent of "sense of place," Eudora Welty, whose mother was a West Virginian, lives.

I wonder if Lucille was ever granted parole. I wouldn't be surprised: she was an ideal prisoner, never causing trouble, doing little other than plying her needle. In abstract terms, terms admittedly lacking any immediate meaning for a prisoner, in her quilting she established her own *parole* from the general *langue* of art and humanity. The cover she quilted for me, patched in primary colors and backed in the bright red of Isis, the goddess of creativity, is that narrative that now gives me *parole,* passing down to me, as it were, like Maggie's quilts, her stories for everyday use. Even as I write this last sentence, however, I recognize that its allusions derive from scholarship and from a culture not originally my own; that this paper, if quiltlike in its narrative, is hardly for everyday use. Rather, it is a narrative designed to be metaphorically hung, to establish an identity for myself as scholar, teacher, writer, feminist, to be used as a blazon. . . .

ꕥ

JOHN UPDIKE *wrote a foreword to* The Complete Stories of Franz Kafka *in 1983. Updike begins his essay by quoting "He," one of Kafka's aphorisms: "All that he does seems to him, it is true, extraordinarily new, but also, because of the incredible spate of new things, extraordinarily amateurish, indeed scarcely tolerable, incapable of becoming history, breaking short the chain of the generations, cutting off for the first time at its most profound source the music of the world, which before him could at least be divined. Sometimes in his arrogance he has more anxiety for the world than for himself." Updike has great sympathy for Kafka and has written about him with considerable perception.*

JOHN UPDIKE

Kafka and "The Metamorphosis"

1983

The century since Franz Kafka was born has been marked by the idea of "modernism" — a self-consciousness new among centuries, a consciousness of being new. Sixty years after his death, Kafka epitomizes one aspect of this modern mind-set: a sensation of anxiety and shame whose center cannot be located and therefore cannot be placated; a sense of an infinite difficulty within things, impeding every step; a sensitivity acute beyond usefulness, as if the nervous system, flayed of its old hide of social usage and religious belief, must record every touch as pain. In Kafka's peculiar and highly original case this dreadful quality is mixed with immense tenderness, oddly good humor, and a certain severe and reassuring formality. The combination makes him an artist; but rarely can an artist have struggled against greater inner resistance and more sincere diffidence as to the worth of his art. . . .

Kafka dated his own maturity as a writer from the long night of September 22nd–23rd, 1912, in which he wrote "The Judgment" at a single eight-hour sitting. He confided to his diary that morning, "Only *in this way* can writing be done, only with such coherence, with such a complete opening out of the body and the soul." Yet the story is not quite free of the undeclared neurotic elements that twist the earlier work; the connection between the engagement and the father seems obscure, and the old man's fury illogical. But in staring at, with his hero Georg, "the bogey conjured up by his father," Kafka broke through to a great cavern of stored emotion. He loved this story, and among friends praised — he who deprecated almost everything from his own pen — its *Zweifellosigkeit*, its "indubitableness." Soon after its composition, he wrote, in a few weeks, "The Metamorphosis," an indubitable masterpiece. It begins with a fantastic premise, whereas in "The Judgment" events become fantastic.

This premise — the gigantic insect — established in the first sentence, "The Metamorphosis" unfolds with a beautiful naturalness and a classic economy. It takes place in three acts: three times the metamorphosed Gregor Samsa ventures out of his room, with tumultuous results. The members of his family — rather simpler than Kafka's own, which had three sisters — dispose themselves around the central horror with a touching, as well as an amusing, plausibility. The father's fury, roused in defense of the fragile mother, stems directly from the action and inflicts a psychic wound gruesomely objectified in the rotting apple Gregor carries in his back; the evolutions of the sister, Grete, from shock to distasteful ministration to a certain sulky possessiveness and finally to exasperated indifference are beautifully sketched, with not a stroke too much. The terrible but terribly human tale ends with Grete's own metamorphosis, into a comely young woman. This great story resembles a great story of the nineteenth century, Tolstoy's "The Death of Ivan Ilych"; in both, a hitherto normal man lies hideously, suddenly stricken in the midst of a family whose irritated, banal daily existence flows around him. The abyss within life is revealed, but also life itself.

What kind of insect is Gregor? Popular belief has him a cockroach, which would be appropriate for a city apartment; and the creature's retiring nature and sleazy dietary preferences would seem to conform. But, as Vladimir Nabokov, who knew his entomology, pointed out in his lectures upon "The Metamorphosis" at Cornell University, Gregor is too broad and convex to be a cockroach. The charwoman calls him a "dung beetle" (*Mistkäfer*) but, Nabokov said, "it is obvious that the good woman is adding the epithet only to be friendly." Kafka's Eduard Raban of "Wedding Preparations" daydreams, walking along, "As I lie in bed I assume the shape of a big beetle, a stag beetle or a cockchafer, I think." Gregor Samsa, awaking, sees "numerous legs, which were pitifully thin compared to the rest of his bulk." If "numerous" is more than six, he must be a centipede — not an insect at all. From evidence in the story he is brown in color and about as long as the distance between a doorknob and the floor; he is broader than half a door. He has a voice at first, "but with a persistent horrible twittering squeak behind it like an undertone," which disappears as the story progresses. His jaws don't work as ours do but he has eyelids, nostrils, and a neck. He is, in short, impossible to picture except when the author wants to evoke his appearance, to bump the reader up against some astounding, poignant new aspect of Gregor's embodiment. The strange physical discomfort noted in the earlier work is here given its perfect allegorical envelope. A wonderful moment comes when Gregor, having been painfully striving to achieve human postures, drops to his feet:

> Hardly was he down when he experienced for the first time this morning a sense of physical comfort; his legs had firm ground under them; they were completely obedient, as he noted with joy; they even strove to carry him forward in whatever direction he chose; and he was inclined to believe that a final relief from all his sufferings was at hand.

When "The Metamorphosis" was to be published as a book in 1915, Kafka, fearful that the cover illustrator "might want to draw the insect itself," wrote the publisher, "Not that, please not that! . . . The insect itself cannot be depicted. It cannot even be shown from a distance." He suggested instead a scene of the family in the apartment with a locked door, or a door open and giving on darkness. Any theatrical or cinematic version of the story must founder on this point of external representation: A concrete image of the insect would be too distracting and shut off sympathy; such a version would lack the very heart of comedy and pathos which beats in the unsteady area between objective and subjective, where Gregor's insect and human selves swayingly struggle. Still half-asleep, he notes his extraordinary condition yet persists in remembering and trying to fulfill his duties as a travelling salesman and the mainstay of this household. Later, relegated by the family to the shadows of a room turned storage closet, he responds to violin music and creeps forward, covered with dust and trailing remnants of food, to claim his sister's love. Such scenes could not be done except with words. In this age that lives and dies by the visual, "The Metamorphosis" stands as a narrative absolutely literary, able to exist only where language and the mind's hazy wealth of imagery intersect.

"The Metamorphosis" stands also as a gateway to the world Kafka created after it. His themes and manner were now all in place. His mastery of official pomposity — the dialect of documents and men talking business — shows itself here for the first time, in the speeches of the chief clerk. Music will again be felt, by mice and dogs, as an overwhelming emanation in Kafka's later fables — a theme whose other side is the extreme sensitivity to noise, and the longing for unblemished silence, that Kafka shared with his hero in "The Burrow." Gregor's death scene, and Kafka's death wish, return in "A Hunger Artist" — the saddest, I think, of Kafka's stories, written by a dying man who was increasingly less sanguine (his correspondence reveals) about dying. The sweeping nature of the hunger artist's abstention is made plain by the opposing symbol of the panther who replaces him in his cage: "the joy of life streamed with such ardent passion from his throat that for the onlookers it was not easy to stand the shock of it." In 1920 Milena Jesenská wrote to Brod: "Frank cannot live. Frank does not have the capacity for living. . . . He is absolutely incapable of living, just as he is incapable of getting drunk. He possesses not the slightest refuge. For that reason he is exposed to all those things against which we are protected. He is like a naked man among a multitude who are dressed." After Gregor Samsa's incarnation, Kafka showed a fondness for naked heroes — animals who have complicated and even pedantic confessions to make but who also are distinguished by some keenly observed bestial traits — the ape of "A Report to an Academy" befouls himself and his fur jumps with fleas; the dog of "Investigations" recalls his young days when, very puppylike, "I believed that great things were going on around me of which I was the leader and to which I must lend my voice, things which must be wretchedly thrown aside if I did not run for them and wag my tail for them"; the mouse folk of "Josephine the Singer" pipe and multiply and are pervaded by an "unexpended, ineradicable childishness"; and the untaxonomic inhabitant of "The Burrow" represents the animal in all of us, his cheerful consumption of "small fry" existentially yoked to a terror of being consumed himself. An uncanny empathy broods above these zoömorphs, and invests them with more of their creator's soul than all but a few human characters receive. So a child, cowed and bored by the world of human adults, makes companions of pets and toy animals.

ꕥ

EUDORA WELTY *included her statement on Anton Chekhov's "The Darling" in her book* The Eye of the Story *(1977). In her brief reading she analyzes the elements of plot ("aware of its clear open stress, the variations all springing from Chekhov's boundless and minute perception of character"), character motivation ("maternalism: for there it is most naturally innocent of anything but formless, thoughtless, blameless* embracing; *the true innocence is in never perceiving"), and theme ("Protest to the darlings of this world will always be [delivered] — out of inward and silent rebellion alone").*

EUDORA WELTY

Plot and Character in Chekhov's "The Darling"

1977

Clearly, the fact that stories have plots in common is of no more account than that many people have blue eyes. Plots are, indeed, what the story writer sees with, and so do we as we read. The plot is the Why. Why? is asked and replied to at various depths; the fishes in the sea are bigger the deeper we go. To learn that character is a more awe-inspiring fish and (in a short story, though not, I think, in a novel) one some degrees deeper down than situation, we have only to read Chekhov. What constitutes the reality of his characters is what they reveal to us. And the possibility that they may indeed reveal everything is what makes fictional characters differ so greatly from us in real life; yet isn't it strange that they don't really *seem* to differ? This is one clue to the extraordinary magnitude of character in fiction. Characters in the plot connect us with the vastness of our secret life, which is endlessly explorable. This is their role. What happens to them is what they have been put here to show.

In his story "The Darling," the darling's first husband, the theater manager, dies suddenly *because* of the darling's sweet passivity; this is the causality of fiction. In everyday or real life he might have held on to his health for years. But under Chekhov's hand he is living and dying in dependence on, and in revelation of, Olenka's character. He can only last a page and a half. Only by force of the story's circumstance is he here at all; Olenka took him up to begin with because he lived next door. . . . Kukin proposes and they are married. . . . And when Kukin dies, Olenka's cry of heartbreak is this: "Vanitchka, my precious, my darling! Why did I ever meet you! Why did I know you and love you! Your poor brokenhearted Olenka is all alone without you!"

With variations the pattern is repeated, and we are made to feel it as plot, aware of its clear open stress, the variations all springing from Chekhov's boundless and minute perception of character. The timber-merchant, another neighbor, is the one who walks home from the funeral with Olenka. The outcome follows tenderly, is only natural. After three days, he calls. "He did not stay long, only about ten minutes, and he did not say much, but when he left, Olenka loved him — loved him so much that she lay awake all night in a perfect fever."

Olenka and Pustovalov get along very well together when they are married. . . . Even in her dreams Olenka is in the timber business, dreaming of "perfect mountains of planks and boards," and cries out in her sleep, so that Pustovalov says to her tenderly, "Olenka, what's the matter, darling? Cross yourself!" But the timber merchant inevitably goes out in the timber yard one day without his cap on; he catches cold and dies, to leave Olenka a widow once more. "I've nobody, now you've left me, my darling," she sobs after the funeral. "How can I live without you?"

And the timber merchant is succeeded by a veterinary surgeon — who gets transferred to Siberia. But the plot is not repetition — it is direction. The love which Olenka bears to whatever is nearest her reaches its final and, we discover, its truest mold in maternalism: For there it is most naturally innocent of anything but formless, thoughtless, blameless *embracing*; the true innocence is in never perceiving. Only mother love could endure in a pursuit of such blind regard, caring so little for the reality of either life involved so long as love wraps them together, Chekhov tells us — unpretentiously, as he tells everything, and with the simplest of concluding episodes. Olenka's character is seen purely then for what it is: limpid reflection, mindless and purposeless regard, love that falls like the sun and rain on all alike, vacant when there is nothing to reflect.

We know this because, before her final chance to love, Olenka is shown to us truly alone:

> [She] got thinner and plainer; and when people met her in the street they did not look at her as they used to, and did not smile to her; evidently her best years were over and left behind, and now a new sort of life had begun for her, which did not bear thinking about. . . . And what was worst of all, she had no opinions of any sort. She saw the objects about her and understood what she saw, but could not form any opinions about them, and did not know what to talk about. And how awful it is not to have any opinions! She wanted a love that would absorb her whole being, her whole soul and reason — that would give her ideas and an object in her life, and would warm her old blood.

The answer is Sasha, the ten-year-old son of the veterinary surgeon, an unexpected blessing from Siberia — a schoolchild. The veterinarian has another wife now, but this no longer matters. "Olenka, with arms akimbo, walked about the yard giving directions. Her face was beaming, and she was brisk and alert, as though she had waked from a long sleep. . . ." "An island is a piece of land entirely surrounded by water," Sasha reads aloud. "'An island is a piece of land,' she repeated, and this was the first opinion to which she gave utterance with positive conviction, after so many years of silence and dearth of ideas." She would follow Sasha halfway to school, until he told her to go back. She would go to bed thinking blissfully of Sasha, "who lay sound asleep in the next room, sometimes crying out in his sleep, 'I'll give it to you! Get away! Shut up!'"

The darling herself *is* the story; all else is sacrificed to her; deaths and departures are perfunctory and to be expected. The last words of the story are the child's and a protest, but they are delivered in his sleep, as indeed protest to the darlings of this world will always be — out of inward and silent rebellion alone, as this master makes plain.

ꕤ

6

CASEBOOKS ON STORIES AND STORYTELLERS

RAYMOND CARVER

FLANNERY O'CONNOR

ZORA NEALE HURSTON

CASEBOOK ON RAYMOND CARVER

Raymond Carver offers a clear example of how a contemporary author has responded to the work of earlier short story writers by following a line of thought that links him with his predecessors. Carver acknowledged the influence of Ernest Hemingway and Flannery O'Connor in his essay "On Writing." He also described his class with the young novelist John Gardner at Chico State College in California in "Creative Writing 101." In 1982 Carver discussed the origin of "The Bath" (p. 127) and "A Small, Good Thing" (p. 132) with the reporter Jim Naughton for the Syracuse Post-Standard. *Five years later, the academic critic Kathleen Westfall Shute wrote an extended analysis of the two stories for the* Hollins Critic. *Finally, Carver's editor Tom Jenks recalled Carver's explanation of the origin of "Cathedral" (p. 117), and A. O. Scott gave an overview of Carver's career.*

RAYMOND CARVER

On Writing

1981

Back in the mid-1960s, I found I was having trouble concentrating my attention on long narrative fiction. For a time I experienced difficulty in trying to read it as well as in attempting to write it. My attention span had gone out on me; I no longer had the patience to try to write novels. It's an involved story, too tedious to talk about here. But I know it has much to do now with why I write poems and short stories. Get in, get out. Don't linger. Go on. It could be that I lost any great ambitions at about the same time, in my late twenties. If I did, I think it was good it happened. Ambition and a little luck are good things for a writer to have going for him. Too much ambition and bad luck, or no luck at all, can be killing. There has to be talent.

Some writers have a bunch of talent; I don't know any writers who are without it. But a unique and exact way of looking at things, and finding the right context for expressing that way of looking, that's something else. *The World According to Garp* is, of course, the marvelous world according to John Irving. There is another world according to Flannery O'Connor, and others according to William Faulkner and Ernest Hemingway. There are worlds according to Cheever, Updike, Singer, Stanley Elkin, Ann Beattie, Cynthia Ozick, Donald Barthelme, Mary Robison, William Kittredge, Barry Hannah, Ursula K. Le Guin. Every great or even every very good writer makes the world over according to his own specifications.

It's akin to style, what I'm talking about, but it isn't style alone. It is the writer's particular and unmistakable signature on everything he writes. It is his world and no other. This is one of the things that distinguishes one writer from another. Not talent. There's plenty of that around. But a writer who has some special way of looking at things and who gives artistic expression to that way of looking: that writer may be around for a time.

Raymond Carver. (© Marion Ettlinger.)

Isak Dinesen said that she wrote a little every day, without hope and without despair. Someday I'll put that on a three-by-five card and tape it to the wall beside my desk. I have some three-by-five cards on the wall now. "Fundamental accuracy of statement is the ONE sole morality of writing." Ezra Pound. It is not everything by ANY means, but if a writer has "fundamental accuracy of statement" going for him, he's at least on the right track.

I have a three-by-five up there with this fragment of a sentence from a story by Chekhov: ". . . and suddenly everything became clear to him." I find these words filled with wonder and possibility. I love their simple clarity, and the hint of revelation that's implied. There is mystery, too. What has been unclear before? Why is it just now becoming clear? What's happened? Most of all — what now? There are consequences as a result of such sudden awakenings. I feel a sharp sense of relief — and anticipation.

I overheard the writer Geoffrey Wolff say "No cheap tricks" to a group of writing students. That should go on a three-by-five card. I'd amend it a little to "No tricks." Period. I hate tricks. At the first sign of a trick or a gimmick in a piece of fiction, a cheap trick or even an elaborate trick, I tend to look for cover. Tricks are ultimately boring, and I get bored easily, which may go along with my not having much of an attention span. But extremely clever chi-chi writing, or just plain tomfoolery writing, puts me to sleep. Writers don't need tricks or gimmicks or even necessarily need to be the smartest fellows on the block. At the risk of appearing foolish, a writer sometimes needs to be able to just stand and gape at this or that thing — a sunset or an old shoe — in absolute and simple amazement.

Some months back, in the *New York Times Book Review,* John Barth said that ten years ago most of the students in his fiction writing seminar were interested in "formal innovation," and this no longer seems to be the case. He's a little worried that writers are going to start writing mom-and-pop novels in the 1980s. He worries that experimentation may be on the way out, along with liberalism. I get a little nervous if I find myself within earshot of somber discussions about "formal innovation" in fiction writing. Too often "experimentation" is a license to be careless, silly, or imitative in the writing. Even worse, a license to try to brutalize or alienate the reader. Too often such writing gives us no news of the world, or else describes a desert landscape and that's all — a few dunes and lizards here and there, but no people; a place uninhabited by anything recognizably human, a place of interest only to a few scientific specialists.

It should be noted that real experiment in fiction is original, hard-earned and cause for rejoicing. But someone else's way of looking at things — Barthelme's, for instance — should not be chased after by other writers. It won't work. There is only one Barthelme, and for another writer to try to appropriate Barthelme's peculiar sensibility or mise en scène under the rubric of innovation is for that writer to mess around with chaos and disaster and, worse, self-deception. The real experimenters have to Make It New, as Pound urged, and in the process have to find things out for themselves. But if writers haven't taken leave of their senses, they also want to stay in touch with us, they want to carry news from their world to ours.

It's possible, in a poem or a short story, to write about commonplace things and objects using commonplace but precise language, and to endow those things — a chair, a window curtain, a fork, a stone, a woman's earring — with immense, even startling power. It is possible to write a line of seemingly innocuous dialogue and have it send a chill along the reader's spine — the source of artistic delight, as Nabokov would have it. That's the kind of writing that most interests me. I hate sloppy or haphazard writing whether it flies under the banner of experimentation or else is just clumsily rendered realism. In Isaac Babel's wonderful short story, "Guy de Maupassant," the narrator has this to say about the writing of fiction: "No iron can pierce the heart with such force as a period put just at the right place." This too ought to go on a three-by-five.

Evan Connell said once that he knew he was finished with a short story when he found himself going through it and taking out commas and then going through the story again and putting commas back in the same places. I like that way of working on something. I respect that kind of care for what is being done. That's all we have, finally, the words, and they had better be the right ones, with the punctuation in the right places so that they can best say what they are meant to say. If the words are heavy with the writer's own unbridled emotions, or if they are imprecise and inaccurate for some other reason — if the words are in any way blurred — the reader's eyes will slide right over them and nothing will be achieved. The reader's own artistic sense will simply not be engaged. Henry James called this sort of hapless writing "weak specification."

I have friends who've told me they had to hurry a book because they needed the money, their editor or their wife was leaning on them or leaving them — something, some apology for the writing not being very good. "It would have been better if I'd taken the time." I was dumbfounded when I heard a novelist friend say this. I still am, if I think about it, which I don't. It's none of my business. But if the writing can't be made as good as it is within us to make it, then why do it? In the end, the satisfaction of having done our best, and the proof of that labor, is the one thing we can take into the grave. I wanted to say to my friend, for heaven's sake go do something else. There have to be easier and maybe more honest ways to try and earn a living. Or else just do it to the best of your abilities, your talents, and then don't justify or make excuses. Don't complain, don't explain.

In an essay called, simply enough, "Writing Short Stories," Flannery O'Connor talks about writing as an act of discovery. O'Connor says she most often did not know where she was going when she sat down to work on a short story. She says she doubts that many writers know where they are going when they begin something. She uses "Good Country People" as an example of how she put together a short story whose ending she could not even guess at until she was nearly there:

> When I started writing that story, I didn't know there was going to be a Ph.D. with a wooden leg in it. I merely found myself one morning writing a description of two women I knew something about, and before I realized it, I had equipped one of them with a daughter with a wooden leg. I brought in the Bible salesman, but I had no idea what I was going to do with him. I didn't know he was going to steal that wooden leg until ten or twelve lines before he did it, but when I found out that this was what was going to happen, I realized it was inevitable.

When I read this some years ago it came as a shock that she, or anyone for that matter, wrote stories in this fashion. I thought this was my uncomfortable secret, and I was a little uneasy with it. For sure I thought this way of working on a short story somehow revealed my own shortcomings. I remember being tremendously heartened by reading what she had to say on the subject.

I once sat down to write what turned out to be a pretty good story, though only the first sentence of the story had offered itself to me when I began it. For several days I'd been going around with this sentence in my head: "He was running the vacuum cleaner when the telephone rang." I knew a story was there and that it wanted telling. I felt it in my bones, that a story belonged with that beginning, if I could just have the time to write it. I found the time, an entire day — twelve, fifteen hours even — if I wanted to make use of it. I did, and I sat down in the morning and wrote the first sentence, and other sentences promptly began to attach themselves. I made the story just as I'd make a poem; one line and then the next, and the next. Pretty soon I could see a story, and I knew it was my story, the one I'd been wanting to write.

I like it when there is some feeling of threat or sense of menace in short stories. I think a little menace is fine to have in a story. For one thing, it's good for the circulation. There has to be tension, a sense that something is imminent, that certain things are in relentless motion, or else, most often, there simply won't be a story. What creates tension in a piece of fiction is partly the way the concrete words are linked together to make up the visible action of the story. But it's also the things that are left out, that are implied, the landscape just under the smooth (but sometimes broken and unsettled) surface of things.

V. S. Pritchett's° definition of a short story is "something glimpsed from the corner of the eye, in passing." Notice the "glimpse" part of this. First the glimpse. Then the glimpse given life, turned into something that illuminates the moment and may, if we're lucky — that word again — have even further-ranging consequences and meaning. The short story writer's task is to invest the glimpse with all that is in his power. He'll bring his intelligence and literary skill to bear (his talent), his sense of proportion and sense of the fitness of things: of how things out there really are and how he sees those things — like no one else sees them. And this is done through the use of clear and specific language, language used so as to bring to life the details that will light up the story for the reader. For the details to be concrete and convey meaning, the language must be accurate and precisely given. The words can be so precise they may even sound flat, but they can still carry; if used right, they can hit all the notes.

Raymond Carver

Creative Writing 101 1983

A long time ago — it was the summer of 1958 — my wife and I and our two baby children moved from Yakima, Washington, to a little town outside of

V. S. Pritchett: British master of the short story and literary critic (b. 1900).

Chico, California. There we found an old house and paid twenty-five dollars a month rent. In order to finance this move, I'd had to borrow a hundred and twenty-five dollars from a druggist I'd delivered prescriptions for, a man named Bill Barton.

This is by way of saying that in those days my wife and I were stone broke. We had to eke out a living, but the plan was that I would take classes at what was then called Chico State College. But for as far back as I can remember, long before we moved to California in search of a different life and our slice of the American pie, I'd wanted to be a writer. I wanted to write, and I wanted to write anything — fiction, of course, but also poetry, plays, scripts, articles for *Sports Afield, True, Argosy,* and *Rogue* (some of the magazines I was then reading), pieces for the local newspaper — anything that involved putting words together to make something coherent and of interest to someone besides myself. But at the time of our move, I felt in my bones I had to get some education in order to go along with being a writer. I put a very high premium on education then — much higher in those days than now, I'm sure, but that's because I'm older and have an education. Understand that nobody in my family had ever gone to college or for that matter had got beyond the mandatory eighth grade in high school. I didn't know *anything,* but I knew I didn't know anything.

So along with this desire to get an education, I had this very strong desire to write; it was a desire so strong that, with the encouragement I was given in college, and the insight acquired, I kept on writing long after "good sense" and the "cold facts" — the "realities" of my life told me, time and again, that I ought to quit, stop the dreaming, quietly go ahead and do something else.

That fall at Chico State I enrolled in classes that most freshman students have to take, but I enrolled as well for something called Creative Writing 101. This course was going to be taught by a new faculty member named John Gardner, who was already surrounded by a bit of mystery and romance. It was said that he'd taught previously at Oberlin College but had left there for some reason that wasn't made clear. One student said Gardner had been fired — students, like everyone else, thrive on rumor and intrigue — and another student said Gardner had simply quit after some kind of flap. Someone else said his teaching load at Oberlin, four or five classes of freshman English each semester, had been too heavy and that he couldn't find time to write. For it was said that Gardner was a real, that is to say a practicing, writer — someone who had written novels and short stories. In any case, he was going to teach CW 101 at Chico State, and I signed up.

I was excited about taking a course from a real writer. I'd never laid eyes on a writer before, and I was in awe. But where were these novels and short stories, I wanted to know. Well, nothing had been published yet. It was said that he couldn't get his work published and that he carried it around with him in boxes. (After I became his student, I was to see those boxes of manuscript. Gardner had become aware of my difficulty in finding a place to work. He knew I had a young family and cramped quarters at home. He offered me the key to his office. I see that gift now as a turning point. It was a gift not made casually, and I took it, I think, as a kind of mandate — for that's what it was. I spent part of every Saturday and Sunday in his office, which is where he kept the boxes of manuscript. The boxes were stacked up on the floor beside the desk. *Nickel Mountain*, grease-pencilled on one of the boxes, is the only title I recall. But it was in his office, within sight of his unpublished books, that I undertook my first serious attempts at writing.) . . .

For short story writers in his class, the requirement was one story, ten to fifteen pages in length. For people who wanted to write a novel — I think there must have been one or two of these souls — a chapter of around twenty pages, along with an outline of the rest. The kicker was that this one short story, or the chapter of the novel, might have to be revised ten times in the course of the semester for Gardner to be satisfied with it. It was a basic tenet of his that a writer found what he wanted to say in the ongoing process of seeing what he'd said. And this seeing, or seeing more clearly, came about through revision. He *believed* in revision, endless revision; it was something very close to his heart and something he felt was vital for writers, at whatever stage of their development. And he never seemed to lose patience rereading a student story, even though he might have seen it in five previous incarnations.

I think his idea of a short story in 1958 was still pretty much his idea of a short story in 1982; it was something that had a recognizable beginning, middle, and an end to it. Once in a while he'd go to the blackboard and draw a diagram to illustrate a point he wanted to make about rising or falling emotion in a story — peaks, valleys, plateaus, resolution, *denouement*, things like that. Try as I might, I couldn't muster a great deal of interest or really understand this side of things, the stuff he put on the blackboard. But what I did understand was the way he would comment on a student story that was undergoing class discussion. Gardner might wonder aloud about the author's reasons for writing a story about a crippled person, say, and leaving out the fact of the character's crippledness until the very end of the story. "So you think it's a good idea not to let the reader know this man is crippled until the last sentence?" His tone of voice conveyed his disapproval, and it didn't take more than an instant for everyone in class, including the author of the story, to see that it wasn't a good strategy to use. Any strategy that kept important and necessary information away from the reader in the hope of overcoming him by surprise at the end of the story was cheating.

In class he was always referring to writers whose names I was not familiar with. Or if I knew their names, I'd never read the work. . . . He talked about James Joyce and Flaubert and Isak Dinesen as if they lived just down the road, in Yuba City. He said, "I'm here to tell you who to read as well as teach you how to write." I'd leave class in a daze and make straight for the library to find books by these writers he was talking about.

Hemingway and Faulkner were the reigning authors in those days. But altogether I'd probably read at the most two or three books by these fellows. Anyway, they were so well-known and so much talked about, they couldn't be all that good, could they? I remember Gardner telling me, "Read all the Faulkner you can get your hands on, and then read all of Hemingway to clean the Faulkner out of your system."

He introduced us to the "little" or literary periodicals by bringing a box of these magazines to class one day and passing them around so that we could acquaint ourselves with their names, see what they looked like and what they felt like to hold in the hand. He told us that this was where most of the best fiction in the country and just about all of the poetry was appearing. Fiction, poetry, literary essays, book reviews of recent books, criticism of *living* authors *by* living authors. I felt wild with discovery in those days.

For the seven or eight of us who were in his class, he ordered heavy black binders and told us we should keep our written work in these. He kept his own work in such binders, he said, and of course that settled it for us. We carried our stories in those binders and felt we were special, exclusive, singled out from others. And so we were.

I don't know how Gardner might have been with other students when it came time to have conferences with them about their work. I suspect he gave everybody a good amount of attention. But it was and still is my impression that during that period he took my stories more seriously, read them closer and more carefully, than I had any right to expect. I was completely unprepared for the kind of criticism I received from him. Before our conference he would have marked up my story, crossing out unacceptable sentences, phrases, individual words, even some of the punctuation; and he gave me to understand that these deletions were not negotiable. In other cases he would bracket sentences, phrases, or individual words, and these were items we'd talk about, these cases were negotiable. And he wouldn't hesitate to add something to what I'd written — a word here and there, or else a few words, maybe a sentence that would make clear what I was trying to say. We'd discuss commas in my story as if nothing else in the world mattered more at that moment — and, indeed, it did not. He was always looking to find something to praise. When there was a sentence, a line of dialogue, or a narrative passage that he liked, something that he thought "worked" and moved the story along in some pleasant or unexpected way, he'd write "Nice" in the margin, or else "Good!" And seeing these comments, my heart would lift.

It was close, line-by-line criticism he was giving me, and the reasons behind the criticism, why something ought to be this way instead of that; and it was invaluable to me in my development as a writer. After this kind of detailed talk about the text, we'd talk about the larger concerns of the story, the "problem" it was trying to throw light on, the conflict it was trying to grapple with, and how the story might or might not fit into the grand scheme of story writing. It was his conviction that if the words in the story were blurred because of the author's insensitivity, carelessness, or sentimentality, then the story suffered from a tremendous handicap. But there was something even worse and something that must be avoided at all costs: if the words and the sentiments were dishonest, the author was faking it, writing about things he didn't care about or believe in, then nobody could ever care anything about it.

A writer's values and craft. This is what the man taught and what he stood for, and this is what I've kept by me in the years since that brief but all-important time.

Jim Naughton

As Raymond Carver Muses, His Stature Grows 1982

When Raymond Carver was a boy he was walking to school with a friend who got hit by a car. The boy wasn't hurt, but years later, Carver wondered what if?

Several years ago Carver's telephone rang late at night. When he answered, the caller hung up. Carver was not disturbed by the call, but he wondered what if the call had come when he was upset about something else?

Two years ago Carver turned the fruits of his wonderings into a short story called "The Bath," which was published in *What We Talk About When We Talk About Love,* a critically acclaimed collection that was featured on the front page of *The New York Times Book Review.*

Still, when he thought about the story, Carver wondered what if he had written it differently?

During his Christmas vacation last year in early January, he sat down to answer the question. When he finished the new version, Carver remembers feeling "a rush" because he had written something special.

The story that emerged, "A Small, Good Thing," was recently awarded first prize by the editor of *Prize Stories 1983: The O. Henry Awards,* which will be published in April by Doubleday. The prize-winning story is generally recognized as the best short story published in the country in the previous year.

"A Small, Good Thing," which was published in the literary magazine *Ploughshares* in the summer of 1982, deals with parents' anguish after their child is hit by a car and later, mysteriously, dies.

Carver went back to the story because it was "unfinished business."

"I wrote the story and I didn't go far enough with it," he said in his office at Syracuse University Monday.

"I saw a place to stop it and I stopped it . . . but the notion of what could have happened stayed with me."

William Abrahams, who edited the collection and made the choice, said he feels the story marks a new direction in Carver's career.

"I think it's a magnificent story, deeply moving. I think it's one of the most impressive he's ever written.

"The original can't compare to this," he said. "The original seemed like the bare bones of a story he could have done.

"In this new version which must be at least twice the length, he's able to develop the people as people. All this has a terrific intensity."

Carver too feels his writing has taken a new turn. "I feel it is [a departure]," he said. "All those stories I wrote last winter are different.

"There is definitely a change going on in my writing and I'm glad of it. It happened when I wrote the story 'Cathedral.' I date the change from that story."

"Cathedral" has won a distinction of its own. It is the first story in *The Best American Short Stories 1982,* which was edited by Carver's friend, the late John Gardner.

"These stories are fuller, more generous somehow," Carver said of his recent work. "I hope without losing any of the other virtues."

He said the change occurred because: "I went as far as I wanted to go with reducing the stories to bare bones minimums."

Reducing stories to bare bones minimums is how Carver made his name as a fiction writer. His collection of stories *Will You Please Be Quiet, Please?* was nominated for the National Book Award in 1977.

"That put him on the map in terms of the general public," said Tobias Wolff, Carver's colleague in Syracuse University's Creative Writing Program. Wolff has had two of his own stories included in previous editions of the O. Henry collection.

"He has for at least ten years now been considered one of its best practitioners by anyone who is aware of the state of the short story," he said.

Carver did not come easily to this eminence. He grew up in a working-class family in Yakima, Washington, married young and worked as a laborer. He was nineteen when he met Gardner, then an unpublished writer teaching at Chico State College in California. Carver was sweeping floors to feed his young wife and their two children and writing on the side. In the early '60s Gardner gave him encouragement and the key to his office so he would have a place to write.

Carver published books of poetry in 1968 and 1970, struggling to support his family all the while. His marriage broke up after a trip to the Middle East in the early '70s, but it was around that point that his stories began to be noticed. *Esquire* bought a story called "Neighbors" and several others. He published another book of poetry and the critically acclaimed *Will You Please Be Quiet, Please?* in 1976. In the six years since then his popularity has increased dramatically.

The style that made Carver famous is best characterized by some words of his own taken from "The Bath." "No pleasantries, just this small exchange, the barest information, nothing that was not necessary."

This sparsely eloquent style became so well known in literary circles that Abrahams says he reads ten to fifteen stories a year by people who are trying to write like Raymond Carver.

Some critics have charged that Carver's work is too bare, that it is minimalistic. Wolff disagrees. "There is a tremendous richness, a music to his work. His work has the kind of music that Hemingway's had."

Abrahams, who felt things were "deliberately flattened out" in some of Carver's early work, said his recent stories have "taken him to a higher level of art."

For his efforts Carver joins writers like Hemingway, Fitzgerald, Faulkner, Sherwood Anderson, Ring Lardner, Katherine Anne Porter, Flannery O'Connor, Isaac Bashevis Singer, and Joyce Carol Oates, as first-prize winners.

Abrahams makes an even headier comparison. "It reminds me of Chekhov, to tell you the truth," he said.

Success has changed Raymond Carver's life, but not fundamentally. He still lives quietly on Maryland Avenue and teaches his writing classes at the university. He is on the road a bit more often.

"I'm busier at every level," he said. "But it hasn't changed the way I feel about myself or my family or my loved ones.

"I feel comfortable with my life. Not comfortable like a fat lazy cat, but comfortable, you know what I mean, comfortable being in my own skin."

Kathleen Westfall Shute

On "The Bath" and "A Small, Good Thing" 1987

. . . Clearly, Raymond Carver's fiction is in flux. The stories in *Fires* and *Cathedral* seem to me richer, more emotionally and artistically complex than the earlier works. Permeated now by subtle shades of choice and option, Carver's "landscape of characters," as Robert Houston has fittingly called it in *The Nation*, resonates with an authenticity, a sense of the "real America," that was unrealized heretofore. How great this philosophic and creative transformation is can be readily appreciated by a comparative detailing of the structures and "obsessions" (as Carver dislikes the term "themes") in stories like "The Bath" and its new version "A Small, Good Thing" and in the two variations of "So Much Water So Close to Home." In light of Carver's new, more optimistic version, these are fictions that, as he explained to Larry McCaffery and Sinda Gregory (*Alive and Writing*, University of Illinois Press, 1987), were in clear need of being "enhanced, redrawn, reimagined" (69).

Like so many of the tales in *What We Talk About When We Talk About Love* and the other collections, "The Bath" focuses on the dilemmas engendered when, as Thomas R. Edwards has written in the *New York Review of Books*, "marginal lives are intruded upon by mystery, a sense of something larger or more elemental" than what has been previously experienced. In "The Bath," with a stroke that is typically Carverian, this "mystery" is death — or, at least, the real possibility of it when a young boy, on his birthday, is struck by a hit-and-run car. Lapsing into a "sleep-like" state, the child lingers in the hospital, his terrified and confused parents hovering near. Their vigil, which would be horrifying enough, is further menaced when, on brief trips home to bathe and feed the dog, they are subjected to ominous calls "about Scotty" from a baker enraged about "the Birthday Boy's" expensive and now-forgotten cake.

Despite evidence of a genuinely loving domesticity and a somewhat affluent (at least, solidly middle-class) lifestyle, the characters in "The Bath" are nonetheless typical of Carver's "down-and-outers," his people on the verge. Like the rock-throwing protagonist in "Viewfinder" or the battling young parents in "Popular Mechanics," these folks are totems, faceless, nearly nameless emblems of a class. While the baker is deftly particularized by his "watery eyes" and the "curious apron," which loops about him in the fashion of a straight-jacket to end in a "very thick knot," the parents and child go without description. Two thirds of the way through the story, and then almost grudgingly, we are finally given a name for the family — Weiss. And while the mother's Christian name does manage to slip out in conversation, we are never told the father's.

Skeletally drawn, the Weisses reveal little of themselves. Though they no doubt entertain vague, unspoken dreams — symbolically evidenced by the futuristic cake for Scotty with its rocketship and stars — they, and all the other characters here, are clearly enmeshed in the unexamined life. This is Carver's "real America": a netherland of work-place, home, and shopping centers. With junk food for the body (characteristically, Scotty is munching potato chips as he is struck) and even junkier sentiments for the soul (Scotty's young companion, holding the bag after his friend has crumpled in the gutter, actually wonders "if he should finish the rest or continue on to school"), perhaps it is easier not to think, not to question, to take the bad curves and good in life for granted. In "The Bath," it is the unnamed father who senses this. Driving home from the hospital "faster than he should," he dimly realizes that "It had been a good life till now. There had been work, fatherhood, family. He had been lucky and happy." But beyond this vaguely articulable grocery-list of good things, he seems unable to go. In the shadow of this overwhelming mystery, "Fear made him want to take a bath." And with this act, he tries, unsuccessfully, to wash all thought from him as though it were sin.

In "The Bath," this moment is the closest we come to insight, epiphany. But, true to the harsh parameters Carver has already drawn, it is brushed aside by the ritual cleansing and, of even greater import, the increasing menace from the outside world: that ringing phone, the unrecognized voice with its torturing accusations.

In a world where ordinary kindness seems so often proscribed, where the larger community seems simply not to exist, we are not surprised that understanding of the self and others is limited, communication negligible or, worse, mere "human noise" ("What We Talk About When We Talk About Love"). As the tale progresses towards its final horror, we witness growing confusion, an increasing inability to define and name. When the father suggests that the dog might need to be fed, the mother makes a counterproposal of calling the neighbors: "Someone will feed him if you ask them to." Trying to conjure a name, she cannot come up with one. Even the doctors shilly-shally with words, refusing to define the boy's condition, to say if it is "coma" or not. The parents admit to prayer about their son, but it seems clear that no one is listening. In the end, they are left in limbo: their child hovering in some unnameable state, caught between existence and extinction, while the phone rings a final time. "It's about Scotty," the voice tells them. "Yes, it's about Scotty."

Winner of the Carlos Fuentes Award for Fiction, "The Bath" is obviously a masterwork of American minimalism and a product of Carver's own early aesthetic: "Get in, get out. Don't linger. Go On." Typical of the other stories in *What We Talk About*, the style admits "nothing vague, or blurred, no smoked-glass prose" (*Fires* 28). Indeed, its language is so attenuated, so pared of ornament and intentional ambiguity, so stunningly bare, it is almost, as David Boxer and Cassandra Phillips have claimed, "photorealistic." But however successful "The Bath" may be on its own minimalist terms — however mimetic, as Michael Gorra observes, its "intentional poverty [and] anorexia" of style is of "the spiritual poverty of [the] characters' lives" — this story clearly represents for Carver an avenue now exhausted.

Halfway through the writing of *Cathedral,* in the bloom of his "second life," Carver revised the tale, a process which finally took him "into the heart of what the story is *about*" (*Fires* 218). Three times the length of its parent-story, "A Small, Good Thing" concerns many of the same "obsessions" as "The Bath," but told by a richer, more generous voice, these "obsessions" are transfigured, mediated and tempered by genuine compassion.

In "A Small, Good Thing," Carver's "submerged population" begins to surface, moving out from the preoccupations of self to become aware of and even feel kinship to the larger community. Instead of ignoring the surly baker as she did in "The Bath," her attention then focused squarely upon the material object of the cake, this "reimagined" mother now searches for some common denominator. She studies his "coarse features." She wonders "if he's ever done anything else with his life besides being a baker." Trying to diminish the "uncomfortable" feeling his presence causes her, she examines her own life, as well as her own perception of his, looking for a mutual base: "She was a mother and thirty-three years old, and it seemed to her that everyone, especially someone the baker's age — a man old enough to be her father — must have children who'd gone through this special time of cakes and birthday parties. There must be that between them, she thought." Equally revealing are the changes in the scene that immediately follows this encounter. When Scotty is struck, his friend now drops the potato chips and begins "to cry." Even the driver of the car evidences a certain moral awareness, stopping now "in the middle of the road," waiting, before he drives off, "until the boy got unsteadily to his feet . . . dazed, but [apparently] okay" (*Where* 281).

As one would expect, the introduction into Carver's world of compassion, however shaky or seedling, proves to be a mixed blessing. While this new-found empathy considerably deepens the emotional scope of the characters, it also brings into their now less-marginal lives a greater share of pain. This becomes achingly clear in Carver's revision of the mother's encounter with the black family. Their loved one, Nelson, in surgery — victim of a senseless knifing — they, like the Weisses, are awaiting news. Accidentally stumbling upon them in a littered waiting room, the mother apologizes, then asks for directions to the elevator. This given, she suddenly blurts out the painful details of her story. In "The Bath," with a brush-stroke that is typical of the early Carver, the response to her agony is an impotent shake of the father's head, the self-enclosed utterance, "Our Nelson." In this one, almost perfunctorily sketched scene, Carver, while acknowledging the universality of tragedy, dismisses the possibility of connection between the aggrieved, a sentiment which is reversed in "A Small, Good Thing." Here, in a scene that is greatly expanded, the characters engage in a mutually felt sympathy, their discourse characterized by the give-and-take of genuine conversation. The grief briefly shared reverberates as the mother, returning to the hospital later, recreates the young girl she encountered in that room, silently warning her not to have children: "For God's sake, don't" (*Where* 293).

If empathy pains, it also transfigures, creating in Carver's new world a contemporary *via dolorosa* by which the characters may trudge toward salvation. Once the imagination succeeds, as the mother's has, in breaking through the crust of self toward an honest realization of others, a host of options and possibilities suddenly arise. In Carver's recent work, this process of personal redemption begins — much like the Christian theology which seems increasingly, if eclectically, to inform it — with the word.

Their despairing, blue-collar mediocrity aside, if Carver's early protagonists have anything in common, it is, as Robert Houston has remarked, their "stunning inarticulateness." From the teenaged girl in "Why Don't You Dance?" — who, faced with the mystery of domestic dissolution, tries to "get it talked out" and eventually "quit[s] trying" — to the alcoholic L.D. in "One More Thing" — who, upon leaving his wife and daughter, wants to spit out *the* parting shot, but cannot for the life of him think "what it could possibly be" — the characters in *What We Talk About* display a remarkable, if sometimes gratuitous, aphasia. In "The Bath" this is exemplified by the baker's elliptical calls, by the physicians' inability to name the boy's condition, by perhaps even the narrator himself who, so masterfully effaced in Carver's stories, often flounders with the simplest words, describing, for example, a gurney (properly named in "A Small, Good Thing") as "a thing like a bed . . . a thing with wheels."

In the new version, this poverty of language diminishes. With the artful exception of the baker, every major character is now named, an act which signals a critical turn in Carver's work, for by creating a world in which things *can* be named — explored and objectified by the communal activity of language — Carver allows and, in fact, demands of his characters a truer engagement. In "A Small, Good Thing," Dr. Francis can no longer hedge about Scotty's unnatural sleep; he must confront it and call it by its name: "coma." By the same token, the irrational guilt of the parents (beautifully symbolized in "The Bath," but unacknowledged by the protagonists) must also be tackled, with Ann now admitting to herself that "she felt she was in some obscure way responsible for what had happened to the child" (*Where* 293). Indeed, even the "mystery" itself can be broached; eyed squarely and investigated with words, as Carver now, courageously, releases Scotty from his hellish half-existence.

Carver's rendering of the child's death and its ramifications points in a way few other scenes can, to the depth of change in his aesthetic and philosophic perspective. In the earlier stories, death is generally portrayed as a malign and ultimately unknowable force; like a bolt from the natural world, it blasts in at the finale to shatter the artificial parameters constructed around unexamined lives. Faced with this powerful, ill-defined specter, Carver's characters could manage little beyond a mute, uncomprehending horror. . . .

With "A Small, Good Thing," this paradigm of helpless resignation is abandoned as Carver not only confronts death here — a victory in itself — but goes on to record the life after, the agony and resulting growth of those who survive. Given Carver's "obsession" for equating the masked and inarticulate life with spiritual death, one would be hard pressed to conjure a more symbolically fitting demise than Scotty's, as the child rouses briefly from his coma, emits a harrowing and incomprehensible howl, then dies, victim of "a hidden occlusion" of the brain. That this death is, as the bewildered doctors report, "a one in a million circumstance" only serves to intensify the parents' horror (and our own), for by this detail Carver reiterates his belief that, even in this more optimistic universe, a blind and inexplicable randomness still lurks, shaping and destroying at will.

If, in human affairs, contingency plays a major role, it is no longer necessarily a decisive one. There are choices of response, Carver now makes clear, options, even the opportunity to fight back. And this is what Scotty's parents do. After a brief and expected period of stunned denial, the Weisses return home. Rejecting the impulse to box Scotty's toys, thus prolonging his denial of the child's death, Howard finds himself drawn to Ann. Sitting on the couch, he weeps; they embrace; she struggles to find the words that, in elucidating their new and horrible reality, will console. Finally, she tells him, "He's gone... Howard, he's gone. He's gone and now we'll have to get used to that. To being alone" (*Where* 296). Later, phoning relatives, she seems to find some relief in the act of articulation, only to have this shattered when the phone rings, its disembodied voice demanding to know, "Have you forgotten Scotty?" (*Where* 297).

Just before midnight, the torture resumes with yet another call to the Weisses; but this time, by virtue of her engagement with the old man in the story's opening scene, Ann is able to identify the menacing source without. "I know who it is!" she exclaims to Howard. "It's the baker, the son-of-a-bitching baker!" (*Where* 298). With this knowledge, the stage is set for the final encounter.

In the middle of the night, the fake-icing stars of Scotty's cake now aptly transfigured into the real thing, the Weisses drive to the shopping center. In a tense scene, reminiscent of the repressed violence ubiquitous in Carver's early tales, the angry parents confront the baker, who in turn arms himself with his rolling pin. Feeling "a deep burning inside her, an anger that made her feel larger than herself, larger than either of these men" (*Where* 299), the mother spits out the reason for the abandoned cake, the story of Scotty's death. By articulating her pain, she is released from her murderous rage; amid tears and a growing nausea, she cries out for response, saying, "It isn't fair!" (*Where* 300).

While God or the Fates may be unmoved by the Weisses' private disaster, the baker clearly is not. In the stark radiance of another's grief, his own "hidden occlusion" — a mask erected by years of loneliness and failure — is brought to light, begins dissolving as he discards the pin, unties the heavy apron. Drawn into this mode of confession, he apologizes for his boorish behavior, even seeks to understand it as, in a monologue reminiscent of the mother's frantic speech to the black family, he unburdens himself, recounting to the Weisses the pain of his solitary life. Finally, he invites the couple to sit down and eat, for "Eating is a small, good thing in a time like this" (*Where* 301).

If Carver's titles are intended to suggest the essence of his fictions, it is apparent that the major "obsessions" of "A Small, Good Thing" are vastly different from those of "The Bath." While the earlier story, with its Old Testament image of *mikvah,* or ritual cleansing, hinges upon the despair of a guilt which cannot be washed away, a grief that stands no chance of utterance and resolution, the revised version, like Scripture itself, strives for something better, a new covenant between the players: the chance for salvation through communion. Surely, this is the "message" of the final scene with the baker offering the suffering couple "cinnamon rolls just out of the oven," coffee, conversation, then a dark, heavy bread which he "break[s] open" like the Eucharist. As the boundaries between them are chipped away through this sharing of bread and pain, the characters find, even in a world that seems fundamentally artificial, transcendence of a sort, for "It was like daylight under the fluorescent trays of light. They talked on into the early morning, the high, pale cast of light in the windows, and they did not think of leaving" (*Where* 301). . . .

TOM JENKS

The Origin of "Cathedral" 1993

I first met Ray Carver in New York in early September 1984 at a publishing dinner to launch Gary Fisketjon's Vintage Contemporary paperback series. Many of the new VC authors and their friends were there: Richard Ford, Toby Wolff, Jay McInerney, Tom McGuane, Jim Crumley, and Ralph Beer — a distinctly male crowd, and what struck me most was that, as we geared up to move to a nightclub, Ray, amid teasing about running off somewhere to see a woman, put himself in a taxi and headed for his hotel room alone. By the ginger way he got himself into the cab and laughingly ducked the barbs all around him, there was no doubt he meant to keep himself out of trouble.

But he was fair game for the friendly taunts that followed him into the cab. We were witnessing the Good Ray, but we all knew about the Bad Ray, the one who used to be Lord Misrule himself.

Reformed, Ray was fast becoming the most famous short story writer in the world, and the facts of his life were well known, partly because they were often the stuff of his writing and because fame brings a peculiar public intimacy.

At the time, I was an editor of *Esquire* and had made Ray's acquaintance through the mail and on the phone. I had published some of his work and knew him somewhat, and as I watched him slip away in the cab, I imagined him going back to his hotel room (it was early yet — ten o'clock) and telephoning Tess Gallagher [Carver's wife] at their home in Syracuse. Each evening they set aside the hours beyond ten o'clock to spend with each other. He *was,* in a sense, running off to see a woman.

A year and a half later, I visited them in Syracuse. During the days, Ray and I read stories for a book we were working on and at night we watched TV. One night, we were watching a PBS version of *Wuthering Heights,*° and Ray began to tell about another night of TV: the night the blind man for whom Tess once worked had come to visit. Tess told her side, too — how Ray was uneasy about the man's visit, uncomfortable with his blindness and his familiarity with Tess, a mild jealousy rising in Ray. Their evening was slow and tedious, and ended with the three of them watching PBS, just as we were. But on the night the blind man was visiting, Tess had fallen asleep, and then a program about cathedrals came on. The blind man had no idea what a cathedral looked like, and, in the end, Ray sat on the floor with him, holding his hands, drawing a cathedral so the blind man could sense the miracle of the shape.

Ray had written this story and titled it "Cathedral." Tess, who with Ray's encouragement had recently begun writing stories, had her own version, titled

Wuthering Heights: Classic Victorian gothic romance (1847) by Emily Brontë (1818–1848).

"The Harvest."° She gave me a copy, humorously telling Ray, "Watch out, I'm nipping at your heels." Their good-natured competition and openness was rare in my experience of writers, many of whom are cagey about the intimate, personal connections in their work.

A. O. SCOTT

Looking for Raymond Carver 1999

> "And did you get what
> you wanted from this life, even so?
> I did.
> And what did you want?
> To call myself beloved, to feel myself
> beloved on the earth."

Plenty of writers are admired, celebrated, imitated, and hyped. Very few writers can, as Raymond Carver does in his poem "Late Fragment," call themselves beloved. In the years since his death in 1988, at fifty, from lung cancer, Carver's reputation has blossomed. He has gone from being an influential — and controversial — member of a briefly fashionable school of experimental fiction to being an international icon of traditional American literary values. His genius — but more his honesty, his decency, his commitment to the exigencies of craft — is praised by an extraordinarily diverse cross section of his peers. . . .

Through the ministrations of his friends and the tireless efforts of his widow, the poet and short-story writer Tess Gallagher, to keep his memory alive, Carver has begun to approach something like literary sainthood. Certain facts about his life and death — his stoicism in the face of terminal illness, his generosity as a friend and teacher, his successful battle with alcoholism, the happy and productive life he made in Port Angeles, Washington, with Gallagher after the collapse of his first marriage — have added luster to his image. The best of Carver's writing now seems, in retrospect, to be suffused with the best of his personality — affable, humble, battered, wise. But to say this may also be to note that the adversities and triumphs of Carver's life have obscured his work, that we now read that work through the screen of biography, and that his identity as a writer is, in consequence, blurred. What kind of a writer was he, and how are we to assess his achievement? Was he a hard-boiled cynic or an open-hearted sentimentalist? A regionalist rooted in his native Pacific Northwest or the chronicler of an America whose trailer parks and subdivisions had become indistinguishable? Did he help to revive American fiction or contribute to its ruin? Is he, as the London *Times* once declared, "America's Chekhov," or merely the O. Henry of America's graduate writing programs?

If anything, the current state of Carver's published work makes these questions, which have lingered for some time, more difficult than ever to

---

"The Harvest": Gallagher eventually retitled the story "Rain Flooding Your Campfire."

address. More than a decade after his death, Carver's *oeuvre* is still taking shape. Last autumn Knopf brought out his collected poems, and the Atlantic Monthly Press issued a tenth-anniversary hardcover edition of *Where I'm Calling From,* which Carver viewed as the definitive collection of his stories. Around the same time, a *New York Times Magazine* article raised questions about the extent to which Carver was the sole, or even the primary, begetter of his own work, pointing to evidence that Gordon Lish, the editor of Carver's first two books, had drastically cut, rearranged, and even rewritten many of the stories which established Carver's fame.[1] And then there is the question of Gallagher's role, which seems to have been that of soulmate, sounding board, first reader — and collaborator. The journal *Philosophy and Literature* recently printed some short plays Carver and Gallagher wrote together. The journal also ran a photograph of the manuscript of the final page of "Errand," Carver's last published story; the concluding paragraph is in Gallagher's handwriting. . . .

To his admirers, Carver's taciturnity becomes its own kind of eloquence. But critics, especially those who are bothered by Carver's disproportionate influence on other writers, have complained about how much he leaves out. For Sven Birkerts, writing in 1986, the fiction of Carver and his followers is marked by "a total refusal of any vision of larger social connection." And it is true that the inhabitants of Carver's world appear to exist not only in states of isolation and impermanence, but, to borrow a phrase from George W. S. Trow, in a context of no context, without geographical, social, or historical coordinates. We seldom learn the name of the town, or even the state, in which a given story takes place. The stories tend to be devoid of the cultural and commercial references — popular songs, brand names, movies — that so many contemporary writers use to fix their narratives in time and space. And though Carver began writing in the early 1960s, and came to prominence over the next two decades, his stories, at first glance, take no notice of the social and political tumult of the era. We never know who the president is, or whether men have walked on the moon; the characters never read newspapers; and nobody expresses any political interests or opinions. As far as I can tell, Vietnam is mentioned exactly once: in "Vitamins" the leering, predatory behavior of a black man named Nelson — one of the very few nonwhite characters who appear in Carver's work — is ascribed to the fact that he is a veteran just returned from combat in Southeast Asia.

Carver's people often exist not only outside history and politics, but beyond psychology, unless the psychology in question is Skinnerian behaviorism. Their thoughts are typically left unreported; they are creatures of simple speech and sudden action:

> She unbuttoned her coat and put her purse down on the counter. She looked at L.D. and said, "L.D., I've had it. So has Rae. So has everyone who knows you. I've been thinking it over. I want you out of here. Tonight. This minute. Now. Get the hell out of here right now."

---

[1]D. T. Max, "The Carver Chronicles," *The New York Times Magazine,* August 9, 1998. [Scott's note]

> L.D. had no intention of going anywhere. He looked from Maxine to the jar of pickles that had been on the table since lunch. He picked up the jar and pitched it through the kitchen window.

The jaggedness, the deadpan narration, the rigorous refusal of any inflection of language that would suggest interpretation, judgment, or inwardness — these are the aspects of Carver's style that inspired people to think of him as a minimalist. The passage above is from "One More Thing," which, like "Why Don't You Dance?," appears both in *What We Talk About When We Talk About Love* and in *Where I'm Calling From.* The earlier book, which did a great deal to solidify Carver's reputation as an important voice in American fiction in the 1980s, has also done him lasting damage. It was on this book that the editorial hand of Gordon Lish fell most heavily, as Lish cut, rearranged, and rewrote freely, without regard for Carver's wishes or feelings. According to Tess Gallagher, "Ray felt the book, even at the time of its publication, did not represent the main thrust of his writing, nor his true pulse and instinct in the work. He had, in fact, even begged Gordon Lish, to no avail, not to publish the book in this misbegotten version."

Carver, it seems to me, was well within his rights. He was also, as a matter of literary judgment, right. There has been much discussion of the changes Lish imposed on two stories in particular, "The Bath" (which Carver had originally and would subsequently title "A Small, Good Thing") and "So Much Water So Close to Home." The Lish versions are jarring and, briefly, horrifying: the stories, like the people who inhabit them, seem violently discombobulated. In "The Bath," events happen almost at random, and crucial information — for instance, whether a child is alive or dead — is cruelly, capriciously, withheld. . . .

For Lish, the paring of a story down to its verbal and narrative skeleton was a mode of formal experimentation — a trick, if you will. The kind of writing he championed in the 1980s was not an antidote to the antirealist, avant-garde impulse of the 1960s and 1970s, of writers like John Barth and Donald Barthelme, but rather its most extreme expression. The refusal of explanation, the resistance to psychology, and the deliberate impoverishment of language reflect, on Lish's part, an aesthetic choice, and it is clear that he saw affinities between Carver's plain manner and his own stark vision. But the aesthetic principles that Carver discovered in the course of his literary education — from his readings in the modernist tradition, from his first teacher, the novelist John Gardner, and from Lish himself — were ultimately less important than the ethical commitments that are the deepest source of his work. . . .

To read *Where I'm Calling From* from beginning to end, supplemented by some of the stories from earlier collections that Carver chose not to reprint, is to discover that a great deal of what is supposed to be missing — in particular, the changing social landscape of the United States — has been there all along, but that it has been witnessed from a perspective almost without precedent in American literature. Stories like "What Do You Do in San Francisco?" and "After the Denim" record the curious, suspicious, and disgusted reactions of the small-town working class to interlopers from the urban, well-to-do counterculture. "Jerry and Molly and Sam," "Nobody Said Anything," and "Bicycles, Muscles, Cigarettes," among others, are ultimately about how the spread of the suburbs transformed family life, and about the crisis of masculinity that resulted. Carver's work, read closely and in the aggregate, also carries a lot of news about feminism, working conditions, and substance abuse in late-twentieth-century provincial America.

To generalize in this way is, of course, to engage in a kind of analytical discourse Carver resolutely mistrusted. More often than not, the big talkers in Carver's stories are in possession of a degree of class privilege. "My friend Mel McGinnis was talking," goes the famous opening of "What We Talk About When We Talk About Love." "Mel McGinnis is a cardiologist, and sometimes that gives him the right." The imperious homeowner in "Put Yourself in My Shoes" and the jealous college teacher in "Will You Please Be Quiet, Please?" also come to mind. People who carry on as if they know what they're talking about are regarded with suspicion. Carver's greatest sympathy is reserved for those characters who struggle to use language to make sense of things, but who founder or fail in the attempt.

It is striking how many of his stories turn on the inability or refusal of people to say what happened. Think of the girl at the end of "Why Don't You Dance?," unable to convey the fullness of what she has seen on the strange man's lawn, or the narrator of "Where Is Everyone?," clamming up at his AA meetings. And there are many more examples. "Why, Honey?" is a mother's desperate, almost incoherent, and yet strangely formal effort ("Dear Sir," it begins) to explain to a nameless, prying stranger how her darling son went wrong. In "Distance" (also published as "Everything Stuck to Him"), a father, asked by his grown daughter to tell her "what it was like when she was a kid," produces a fairy tale of young parenthood (the main characters in which are referred to only as "the boy" and "the girl") that leaves both teller and listener unsettled, unenlightened, and remote from each other.

And then there is "Cathedral," one of Carver's most beloved stories and the closest thing he produced to an allegory of his own method. The narrator is visited by a garrulous blind man, an old friend of his wife's, whose arrival he anticipates with apprehension. The two men end up smoking marijuana together, while the television airs a documentary about the cathedrals of Europe. It starts to bother the narrator that his new acquaintance, while he knows something about the history of church-building, has no idea of what cathedrals really are, and he tries to tell him about them:

> "They're really big," I said. "They're massive. They're built of stone. Marble, too, sometimes. In those olden days, when they built cathedrals, men wanted to be close to God. In those olden days, God was an important part of everyone's life. You could tell this from their cathedral-building. I'm sorry," I said, "but it looks like that's the best I can do for you. I'm just no good at it."

The blind man proposes that they draw a cathedral instead, and they do — the narrator's eyes closed, the blind man's hand guiding his. The narrator undergoes an epiphany: "It was like nothing else in my life up to now."

The reader is left out: the men's shared experience, visual and tactile, is beyond the reach of words. But the frustrating vicariousness of the story is also the source of its power. Art, according to Carver, is a matter of the blind leading the tongue-tied. Carver was an artist of a rare and valuable kind: he told simple stories, and made it look hard.

CASEBOOK ON ZORA NEALE HURSTON

Zora Neale Hurston continued throughout her life to make what the critic Mary Helen Washington called "unorthodox and paradoxical assertions on racial issues." Often conveyed with great wit and style, Hurston's views were always passionately held, as in her 1928 essay "How It Feels to Be Colored Me" and "What White Publishers Won't Print," one of her last essays, published in Negro Digest *in April 1950. Her friend Langston Hughes also spoke out courageously against racial prejudice during this time, as in "Democracy, Negroes, and Writers," on the occasion of the Fourth American Writers' Congress in 1941. Hurston's biographer Robert E. Hemenway discussed "Story in Harlem Slang" (p. 344), and Rosalie Murphy Baum analyzed "Sweat" (p. 351) and "The Gilded Six-Bits" (p. 336). Finally, Alice Walker gave her tribute to Hurston in "Zora Neale Hurston: A Cautionary Tale and a Partisan View."*

ZORA NEALE HURSTON

How It Feels to Be Colored Me 1928

I am colored but I offer nothing in the way of extenuating circumstances except the fact that I am the only Negro in the United States whose grandfather on the mother's side was *not* an Indian chief.

I remember the very day that I became colored. Up to my thirteenth year I lived in the little Negro town of Eatonville, Florida. It is exclusively a colored town. The only white people I knew passed through the town going to or coming from Orlando. The native whites rode dusty horses, the Northern tourists chugged down the sandy village road in automobiles. The town knew the Southerners and never stopped cane chewing when they passed. But the Northerners were something else again. They were peered at cautiously from behind curtains by the timid. The more venturesome would come out on the porch to watch them go past and got just as much pleasure out of the tourists as the tourists got out of the village.

The front porch might seem a daring place for the rest of the town, but it was a gallery seat for me. My favorite place was atop the gate-post. Proscenium box for a born first-nighter. Not only did I enjoy the show, but I didn't mind the actors knowing that I liked it. I usually spoke to them in passing. I'd

Zora Neale Hurston in Florida in the summer of 1935 while on the Lomax-Hurston-Barnicle recording expedition to Georgia, Florida, and the Bahamas. (Reproduced from the collections of the Library of Congress.)

wave at them and when they returned my salute, I would say something like this: "Howdy-do-well-I-thank-you-where-you-goin'?" Usually automobile or the horse paused at this, and after a queer exchange of compliments, I would probably "go a piece of the way" with them, as we say in farthest Florida. If one of my family happened to come to the front in time to see me, of course negotiations would be rudely broken off. But even so, it is clear that I was the first "welcome-to-our-state" Floridian, and I hope the Miami Chamber of Commerce will please take notice.

During this period, white people differed from colored to me only in that they rode through town and never lived there. They liked to hear me "speak pieces" and sing and wanted to see me dance the parse-me-la, and gave me generously of their small silver for doing these things, which seemed strange to me for I wanted to do them so much that I needed bribing to stop. Only they didn't know it. The colored people gave no dimes. They deplored any joyful tendencies in me, but I was their Zora nevertheless. I belonged to them, to the nearby hotels, to the county — everybody's Zora.

But changes came in the family when I was thirteen, and I was sent to school in Jacksonville. I left Eatonville, the town of the oleanders, as Zora. When I disembarked from the river-boat at Jacksonville, she was no more. It seemed that I had suffered a sea change. I was not Zora of Orange County any more, I was now a little colored girl. I found it out in certain ways. In my heart as well as in the mirror, I became a fast brown — warranted not to rub nor run.

But I am not tragically colored. There is no great sorrow dammed up in my soul, nor lurking behind my eyes. I do not mind at all. I do not belong to the sobbing school of Negrohood who hold that nature somehow has given them a lowdown dirty deal and whose feelings are all hurt about it. Even in the helter-skelter skirmish that is my life, I have seen that the world is to the strong regardless of a little pigmentation more or less. No, I do not weep at the world — I am too busy sharpening my oyster knife.

Someone is always at my elbow reminding me that I am the granddaughter of slaves. It fails to register depression with me. Slavery is sixty years in the past. The operation was successful and the patient is doing well, thank you. The terrible struggle that made me an American out of a potential slave said "On the line!" The Reconstruction said "Get set!"; and the generation before said "Go!" I am off to a flying start and I must not halt in the stretch to look behind and weep. Slavery is the price I paid for civilization, and the choice was not with me. It is a bully adventure and worth all that I have paid through my ancestors for it. No one on earth ever had a greater chance for glory. The world to be won and nothing to be lost. It is thrilling to think — to know that for any act of mine, I shall get twice as much praise or twice as much blame. It is quite exciting to hold the center of the national stage, with the spectators not knowing whether to laugh or to weep.

The position of my white neighbor is much more difficult. No brown specter pulls up a chair beside me when I sit down to eat. No dark ghost thrusts its leg against mine in bed. The game of keeping what one has is never so exciting as the game of getting.

I do not always feel colored. Even now I often achieve the unconscious Zora of Eatonville before the Hegira. I feel most colored when I am thrown against a sharp white background.

For instance at Barnard. "Beside the waters of the Hudson" I feel my race. Among the thousand white persons, I am a dark rock surged upon, and overswept, but through it all, I remain myself. When covered by the waters, I am; and the ebb but reveals me again.

Sometimes it is the other way around. A white person is set down in our midst, but the contrast is just as sharp for me. For instance, when I sit in the drafty basement that is The New World Cabaret with a white person, my color comes. We enter chatting about any little nothing that we have in common and are seated by the jazz waiters. In the abrupt way that jazz orchestras have, this one plunges into a number. It loses no time in circumlocutions, but gets right down to business. It constricts the thorax and splits the heart with its tempo and narcotic harmonies. This orchestra grows rambunctious, rears on its hind legs and attacks the tonal veil with primitive fury, rending it, clawing it until it breaks through to the jungle beyond. I follow those heathen — follow them exultingly. I dance wildly inside myself; I yell within, I whoop; I shake my assegai above my head, I hurl it true to the mark *yeeeeooww!* I am in the jungle and living in the jungle way. My face is painted red and yellow and my body is painted blue. My pulse is throbbing like a war drum. I want to slaughter something — give pain, give death to what, I do not know. But the piece ends. The men of the orchestra wipe their lips and rest their fingers. I creep back slowly to the veneer we call civilization with the last tone and find the white friend sitting motionless in his seat, smoking calmly.

"Good music they have here," he remarks, drumming the table with his fingertips.

Music. The great blobs of purple and red emotion have not touched him. He has only heard what I felt. He is far away and I see him but dimly across the ocean and the continent that have fallen between us. He is so pale with his whiteness then and I am *so* colored.

At certain times I have no race, I am *me.* When I set my hat at a certain angle and saunter down Seventh Avenue, Harlem City, feeling as snooty as the lions in front of the Forty-Second Street Library, for instance. So far as my feelings are concerned, Peggy Hopkins Joyce on the Boule Mich with her gorgeous raiment, stately carriage, knees knocking together in a most aristocratic manner, has nothing on me. The cosmic Zora emerges. I belong to no race nor time. I am the eternal feminine with its string of beads.

I have no separate feeling about being an American citizen and colored. I am merely a fragment of the Great Soul that surges within the boundaries. My country, right or wrong.

Sometimes, I feel discriminated against, but it does not make me angry. It merely astonishes me. How *can* any deny themselves the pleasure of my company? It's beyond me.

But in the main, I feel like a brown bag of miscellany propped against a wall. Against a wall in company with other bags, white, red and yellow. Pour out the contents, and there is discovered a jumble of small things priceless and worthless. A first-water diamond, an empty spool, bits of broken glass, lengths of string, a key to a door long since crumbled away, a rusty knife-blade, old shoes saved for a road that never was and never will be, a nail bent under the weight of things too heavy for any nail, a dried flower or two still a little fragrant. In your hand is the brown bag. On the ground before you is the jumble it held — so much like the jumble in the bags, could they be emptied, that all might be dumped in a single heap and the bags refilled without altering the content of any greatly. A bit of colored glass more or less would not matter. Perhaps that is how the Great Stuffer of Bags filled them in the first place — who knows?

ZORA NEALE HURSTON

What White Publishers Won't Print 1950

I have been amazed by the Anglo-Saxon's lack of curiosity about the internal lives and emotions of the Negroes, and for that matter, any non-Anglo-Saxon peoples within our borders, above the class of unskilled labor.

This lack of interest is much more important than it seems at first glance. It is even more important at this time than it was in the past. The internal affairs of the nation have bearings on the international stress and strain, and this gap in the national literature now has tremendous weight in world affairs. National coherence and solidarity is implicit in a thorough understanding of the various groups within a nation, and this lack of knowledge about the internal emotions and behavior of the minorities cannot fail to bar our understanding. Man, like all the other animals, fears and is repelled by that which he does not understand, and mere difference is apt to connote something malign.

The fact that there is no demand for incisive and full-dress stories about Negroes above the servant class is indicative of something of vast importance to this nation. This blank is *not* filled by the fiction built around upper-class Negroes exploiting the race problem. Rather, it tends to point it up. A college-bred Negro still is not a person like other folks, but an interesting problem, more or less. It calls to mind a story of slavery time. In this story, a master with more intellectual curiosity than usual, set out to see how much he could teach a particularly bright slave of his. When he had gotten him up to higher mathematics and to be a fluent reader of Latin, he called in a neighbor to show off his brilliant slave, and to argue that Negroes had brains just like the slave-owners had, and given the same opportunities, would turn out the same.

The visiting master of slaves looked and listened, tried to trap the literate slave in Algebra and Latin, and failing to do so in both, turned to his neighbor and said:

"Yes, he certainly knows his higher mathematics, and he can read Latin better than many white men I know, but I cannot bring myself to believe that he understands a thing that he is doing. It is all an aping of our culture. All on the outside. You are crazy if you think that it has changed him inside in the least. Turn him loose, and he will revert at once to the jungle. He is still a savage, and no amount of translating Virgil and Ovid is going to change him. In fact, all you have done is to turn a useful savage into a dangerous beast."

That was in slavery time, yes, and we have come a long, long way since then, but the troubling thing is that there are still too many who refuse to believe in the ingestion and digestion of western culture as yet. Hence the lack of literature about the higher emotions and love life of upper-class Negroes and the minorities in general.

Publishers and producers are cool to the idea. Now, do not leap to the conclusion that editors and producers constitute a special class of unbelievers. That is far from true. Publishing houses and theatrical promoters are in business to make money. They will sponsor anything that they believe will sell. They shy away from romantic stories about Negroes and Jews because they feel that they know the public indifference to such works, unless the story or play involves racial tension. It can then be offered as a study in Sociology, with the romantic side subdued. They know the scepticism in general about the complicated emotions in the minorities. The average American just cannot conceive of it, and would be apt to reject the notion, and publishers and producers take the stand that they are not in business to educate, but to make money. Sympathetic as they might be, they cannot afford to be crusaders.

In proof of this, you can note various publishers and producers edging forward a little, and ready to go even further when the trial balloons show that the public is ready for it. This public lack of interest is the nut of the matter.

The question naturally arises as to the why of this indifference, not to say scepticism, to the internal life of educated minorities.

The answer lies in what we may call THE AMERICAN MUSEUM OF UNNATURAL HISTORY. This is an intangible built on folk belief. It is assumed that all non-Anglo-Saxons are uncomplicated stereotypes. Everybody knows all about them. They are lay figures mounted in the museum where all may take them in at a glance. They are made of bent wires without insides at all. So how could anybody write a book about the nonexistent?

The American Indian is a contraption of copper wires in an eternal war-bonnet, with no equipment for laughter, expressionless face, and that says "How" when spoken to. His only activity is treachery leading us to massacres. Who is so dumb as not to know all about Indians, even if they have never seen one, nor talked with anyone who ever knew one?

The American Negro exhibit is a group of two. Both of these mechanical toys are built so that their feet eternally shuffle, and their eyes pop and roll. Shuffling feet and those popping, rolling eyes denote the Negro and no characterization is genuine without this monotony. One is seated on a stump picking away on his banjo and singing and laughing. The other is a most amoral character before a share-cropper's shack mumbling about injustice. Doing this makes him out to be a Negro "intellectual." It is as simple as all that.

The whole museum is dedicated to the convenient "typical." In there is the "typical" Oriental, Jew, Yankee, Westerner, Southerner, Latin, and even out-of-favor Nordics like the German. The Englishman "I say old chappie," and the gesticulating Frenchman. The least observant American can know all at a glance. However, the public willingly accepts the untypical in Nordics, but feels cheated if the untypical is portrayed in others. The author of *Scarlet Sister Mary*° complained to me that her neighbors objected to her book on the grounds that she had the characters thinking, "and everybody know that Nigras don't think."

But for the national welfare, it is urgent to realize that the minorities do think, and think about something other than the race problem. That they are very human and internally, according to natural endowment, are just like everybody else. So long as this is not conceived, there must remain that feeling of unsurmountable difference, and difference to the average man means something bad. If people were made right, they would be just like him.

The trouble with the purely problem arguments is that they leave too much unknown. Argue all you will or may about injustice, but as long as the majority cannot conceive of a Negro or a Jew feeling and reacting inside just as they do, the majority will keep right on believing that people who do not feel like them cannot possibly feel as they do, and conform to the established pattern. It is well known that there must be a body of waived matter, let us say, things accepted and taken for granted by all in a community, before there can be that commonality of feeling. The usual phrase is having things in common. Until this is thoroughly established in respect to Negroes in America, as well as of other minorities, it will remain impossible for the majority to conceive of a Negro experiencing a deep and abiding love and not just the passion of sex. That a great mass of Negroes can be stirred by the pageants of Spring and Fall; the extravaganza of summer, and the majesty of winter. That they can and do experience discovery of the numerous subtle faces as a foundation for a great and selfless love, and the diverse nuances that go to destroy that love as with others. As it is now, this capacity, this evidence of high and complicated emotions, is ruled out. Hence the lack of interest in a romance uncomplicated by the race struggle has so little appeal.

This insistence on defeat in a story where upper-class Negroes are portrayed, perhaps says something from the subconscious of the majority. Involved in western culture, the hero or the heroine, or both, must appear frustrated and go down to defeat, somehow. Our literature reeks with it. Is it the same as saying, "You can translate Virgil, and fumble with the differential calculus, but can you really comprehend it? Can you cope with our subtleties?"

That brings us to the folklore of "reversion to type." This curious doctrine has such wide acceptance that it is tragic. One has only to examine the huge literature on it to be convinced. No matter how high we may *seem* to climb, put us under strain and we revert to type, that is, to the bush. Under a superficial layer of western culture, the jungle drums throb in our veins.

This ridiculous notion makes it possible for that majority who accept it to conceive of even a man like the suave and scholarly Dr. Charles S. Johnson° to hide a black cat's bone on his person, and indulge in a midnight voodoo

---

Scarlet Sister Mary: The 1928 book by Julia Mood Peterkin (1880–1961).
Dr. Charles S. Johnson: Johnson (1893–1956) was the first African American president of Fisk University.

ceremony, complete with leopard skin and drums if threatened with the loss of the presidency of Fisk University, or the love of his wife. "Under the skin . . . better to deal with them in business, etc., but otherwise keep them at a safe distance and under control. I tell you, Carl Van Vechten,° think as you like, but they are just not like us."

The extent and extravagance of this notion reaches the ultimate in nonsense in the widespread belief that the Chinese have bizarre genitals, because of that eye-fold that makes their eyes seem to slant. In spite of the fact that no biology has ever mentioned any such difference in reproductive organs makes no matter. Millions of people believe it. "Did you know that a Chinese has . . ." Consequently, their quiet contemplative manner is interpreted as a sign of slyness and a treacherous inclination.

But the opening wedge for better understanding has been thrust into the crack. Though many Negroes denounced Carl Van Vechten's *Nigger Heaven* because of the title, and without ever reading it, the book, written in the deepest sincerity, revealed Negroes of wealth and culture to the white public. It created curiosity even when it aroused scepticism. It made folks want to know. Worth Tuttle Hedden's *The Other Room* has definitely widened the opening. Neither of these well-written works take a romance of upper-class Negro life as the central theme, but the atmosphere and the background is there. These works should be followed up by some incisive and intimate stories from the inside.

The realistic story around a Negro insurance official, dentist, general practitioner, undertaker, and the like would be most revealing. Thinly disguised fiction around the well-known Negro names is not the answer, either. The "exceptional" as well as the Ol' Man Rivers has been exploited all out of context already. Everybody is already resigned to the "exceptional" Negro, and willing to be entertained by the "quaint." To grasp the penetration of western civilization in a minority, it is necessary to know how the average behaves and lives. Books that deal with people like in Sinclair Lewis' *Main Street* is the necessary metier. For various reasons, the average, struggling, non-morbid Negro is the best-kept secret in America. His revelation to the public is the thing needed to do away with that feeling of difference which inspires fear and which ever expresses itself in dislike.

It is inevitable that this knowledge will destroy many illusions and romantic traditions which America probably likes to have around. But then, we have no record of anybody sinking into a lingering death on finding out that there was no Santa Claus. The old world will take it in its stride. The realization that Negroes are no better nor no worse, and at times just as boring as everybody else, will hardly kill off the population of the nation.

Outside of racial attitudes, there is still another reason why this literature should exist. Literature and other arts are supposed to hold up the mirror to nature. With only the fractional "exceptional" and the "quaint" portrayed, a true picture of Negro life in America cannot be. A great principle of national art has been violated.

Carl Van Vechten: Progressive white champion and patron of African American culture (1880–1964).

These are the things that publishers and producers, as the accredited representatives of the American people, have not as yet taken into consideration sufficiently. Let there be light!

LANGSTON HUGHES

Democracy, Negroes, and Writers 1941

Writing is the urge to tell folks about it. About what? About what hurts you inside. Colored folks, through the sheer fact of being colored, have got plenty hurting them inside. You see, we, too, are one of those minority races the newspapers are always talking about. Except that we are here in America, not in Europe, fourteen million of us — a rather large minority, but still a minority.

Now, what's hurting us? Well, Jim Crow is hurting us. Ghettos, and segregation, and lack of jobs is hurting us. Signs up: COLORED TRADE NOT DESIRED, and dirty names such as the Jews know under Hitler hurt us. So those of us who are writers have plenty to tell the world about.

To us democracy is a paradox, full of contradictions. Sure, in the North Negroes can vote, but we can't work in airplane factories and various other defense industries supported with *our* tax money as well as that of other citizens. In the South we can't vote, but we can howl to high heaven about it in our newspapers — and run the risk of lynching and the Ku Klux Klan for howling. In Mississippi the state spends nine times as much for the education of each white child as it does to educate a Negro child, yet the Negro population equals the white, and the wealth of the state is based on the labor of Negroes in the sun of the cotton fields. We give and others take. That's what makes us mad. So we feel bad and have to write about it. The color line runs right on down from capital through labor, although labor is waking up a bit. But in many industries today the factories won't hire us because they say the unions won't admit us, and the unions won't admit us because they say the factories won't hire us; a vicious circle into which a swastika fits perfectly. We can sweep a floor almost anywhere if a white man doesn't need the job, but even if we graduate from Massachusetts Institute of Technology, we still are not permitted to run a machine in the average American factory. A great many Negroes work, study, and learn, and then are frustrated by the blind alley of color-segregation in American industry. That color line runs all the way through culture and the arts, as well. There are world-famous and very great American Negro singers, some of whom have appeared in opera abroad, but not one has been asked to appear at the Metropolitan. And in many cities where they sing, their own people, the Negro concert goers, are Jim Crowed and segregated. There are some excellent Negro writers in this country, too, but, to my knowledge, none is employed at present in Hollywood where the real money for writers lies. All along the line, we suffer economic discrimination of a discouraging and arbitrary sort, be we artisan or artist.

The League of American Writers, meeting in their Fourth Writers' Congress in New York on June 6th [1941], has been one of the few cultural organizations to take up the fight for the artistic and economic equality of the Negro writer. Another stand of equal importance to Negro [writers] — and all writers — is the League's position on freedom of speech and publication. To colored people in the United States this is of particular importance as the trend toward suppression and censorship is growing and already there is a tendency to attempt to prevent Negro newspapers, with their editorials against discrimination in defense industries and the Jim Crow set-up of our army and navy, from being read by Negro soldiers and draftees in the army camps. From this it is but a step to the actual suppression of Negro papers, or else the censorship of their articles and editorials.

Negroes, like all other Americans, are being asked at the moment to prepare to defend democracy. But Negroes would very much like to have a little more democracy to defend. And democracy is achieved only through constant vigilance, struggle, and the educational processes of the written and spoken word. For Negro writers it is vital that the channels of free press and publication be kept open. It is necessary to the well-being of the creative soul that the harsh and ugly aspects of our life be exposed in accordance with the democratic ideals for which we are urged to be ready to die. But ideals mean very little. They must be put into practice. Writers must be free to call for and work toward the realization of full democracy in regard to peoples of all colors, else the light will rapidly go out for every one of us, white or Negro, gentile or Jew, for if we wish to preserve democracy, we must not only defend it, but *extend* it.

ROBERT E. HEMENWAY

On "Story in Harlem Slang" 1977

Hurston's gentle mocking of the illusion of ethnic purity and the reality of American miscegenation was served well by the dialect and the folktale form of the story. Zora utilized the same technique to celebrate racial expression in her "Story in Harlem Slang," in the *American Mercury* for July 1942 — the only fiction she published between the completion of *Dust Tracks* and the appearance of her last novel in 1948. Speaking in what her editors term "Harlemese," Zora describes a day in the life of a Harlem hustler named Jelly, so called because "he put it in the street that where it came to filling that long-felt need, sugar curing the ladies' feelings, he was in a class by himself and nobody knew his name, so he had to tell 'em. 'It must be Jelly, cause jam don't shake.'" Jelly gets into "his zoot suit with the reet pleats" and skivers around to do himself some good, trying to score a meal. He gets involved in a bragging contest with a fellow hustler named Sweet Back, each "boogerbooing" the other until they are close to blows. Sweet Back warns, "I'm quick death and easy judgment"; Jelly replies, "I come on like the Gang Busters and go off like the March of Time." When they both try to pick up a "kitchen mechanic" on her day off (engaging in an urban courting ritual very similar to its rural counterpart in "Mule Bone"), they are unsuccessful; the woman, more than equal to their jive, "rocks on off with her ear rings snapping and her heels popping." The story ends with Jelly remembering the hot meals he left back in Alabama "to seek wealth and splendor in Harlem," forgetting in his hunger even "to look cocky and rich."

"Story in Harlem Slang" was less fiction than a linguistic study; a glossary of Harlem expressions was attached. The story touched upon a theme Hurston would often return to — that the North was no utopia, just as the South was not necessarily hell. Her biographical feature for the September 5, 1942, *Saturday Evening Post* profiled Lawrence Silas, a tough, shrewd, respected Florida cattleman. She introduces Silas by emphasizing the geography of his success: "Considering that Florida is in Dixie, it will sound like poker playing at a prayer meeting when you read that Lawrence Silas, Negro, is one of the most important men of the cow country. But that is the word with the bark on it. The cattlemen of the state have a name for him and it is good."

Hurston's journalism of the war years continually stresses such opportunities for black achievement, even when analyzing racist institutions designed to ignore it. In the May 1943 *American Mercury* she chose the unfortunate title "The 'Pet Negro' System" to describe the way in which southern whites adopt certain blacks while vilifying the race in general: "The North has no interest in the particular Negro, but talks of justice for the whole. The South has no interest, and pretends none, in the mass of Negroes, but is very much concerned about the individual." Once that is understood, says Zora, "you can see why it is so difficult to change things in the South."

Her essay is about the complexity of race relations — "there are more angles to this race adjustment business than are ever pointed out to the public" — and about how neither posturing white southerners nor black civil rights workers can admit that the "pet Negro system" has contributed to a small, educated middle class who live on streets "of well-off Negro homes" and drive a "great number of high priced cars." Hurston condemns only faintly; she sees this system symbolizing a "web of feelings and mutual dependencies" between whites and blacks that "isn't half as pretty as the ideal adjustment of theorizers, but it's a lot more real and durable, and a lot of black folk, I'm afraid, find it mighty cozy." She thinks the system may indicate that "there are some people in every community who can always talk things over. It may be the proof that this race situation in America is not entirely hopeless and may even be worked out eventually." Knowing that her ideas are controversial, she concludes, "This is the inside picture of things, as I see it. Whether you like it or not, is no concern of mine. But it is an important thing to know if you have any plans for racial manipulations in Dixie."

Although most black professionals in the South earned their status in spite of, rather than because of, white paternalism, "The 'Pet Negro' System" had a measure of uncomfortable truth to it, and it reinforced the twin Hurston themes of black individualism and black achievement. It is not surprising that she would complain about Bucklin Moon's *The Darker Brother* (1943), which painted a dismal picture of life in Harlem: "It gives a falsely morbid picture of Negro life.

If his picture is true, how does he account for the thousands on thousands of wealthy, educated Negroes? . . . that awful picture does Negroes in general more harm than good. One might reason 'if the body of Negrodom is that weak and shiftless and criminal, no need to bother one's head about them.'"

What Zora apparently hoped for, like many other black public figures during the war, was a mood of racial cooperation and a recognition of black people's patriotism. . . .

ROSALIE MURPHY BAUM

The Shape of Hurston's Fiction

1991

Both "Sweat" and "The Gilded Six-Bits" can be seen as having closed endings, with the conflicts around which the stories are constructed being resolved and the imperfect protagonists having overcome the difficulties of previous days. In fact, the closings are consistent with what Frank Kermode has termed apocalyptic endings, in which truth "imposes causality and concordance, development, character, a past which *matters* and a future within certain broad limits determined by the project of the author rather than that of the characters"[1] (italics added).

In "Sweat," Delia's husband, Sykes, increases his mistreatment of her, first by flaunting his affair with the fat Bertha and second by trying to frighten and then kill Delia with a rattlesnake. In the ironic conclusion, Sykes himself is killed by the rattlesnake, while Delia is freed first of the psychological bondage that has caused her to tolerate his abuse and then of the marriage itself. In "The Gilded Six-Bits," Missie May and Joe, their relationship painfully damaged by her infidelity, slowly work to rebuild their marriage. The birth of their son — "de spittin' image" of Joe — and Joe's efforts to sort and control his overwhelming feelings create a new basis for a less innocent but perhaps deeper relationship. In both stories, life has direction — the long-suffering Delia is saved from her husband by his own treachery; the repentant Missie's efforts to save her marriage are successful. In both stories, the worth of the imperfect characters (except for the dead Sykes) is clear. Experience does "guide, instruct . . . judge human nature."[2]

Supporting the sense that the emotional and spiritual movement of the characters is progressive and that this progression indicates a meaningful interaction between man and his world are the series of frames that structure each story. These frames are defined by Mary Ann Caws as "condensations of action and vision," scenes "heavily bordered" with "their importance . . . heightened," scenes complete within themselves but "conveyors of revelation and insight," scenes clearly metonymic in their significance.[3] . . .

---

[1]Frank Kermode, *The Sense of an Ending: Studies in the Theory of Fiction* (New York, NY: Oxford University Press, 1967). [All notes are Baum's.]

[2]Donald Pizer, *Twentieth-Century American Literary Naturalism: An Interpretation* (Carbondale, IL: Southern Illinois University Press, 1982).

[3]Mary Ann Caws, *Reading Frames in Modern Fiction* (Princeton, NJ: Princeton University Press, 1985).

"Sweat" is formed around two kinds of framed episodes, some occurring eight or more weeks apart, the other forming two doorway scenes at the end of the story. The scene of Delia, the laundry, and the snake appears twice, once at the beginning of the story, once near the end; but it is implied at least eight other times. This scene defines Delia's life: work and mistreatment by the husband she struggles to support. The scene also clearly establishes two of the main symbols of the story, the white folks' laundry, which causes the sweat of the title, and the snake, which personifies Sykes's hatred of Delia, especially since he knows that her fear of snakes is so great that she has "a fit over a earthworm or a string."

The differences between the two dramatized scenes of Delia, the laundry, and the snake — as well as the weekly laundry scenes that are not portrayed — also indicate the eventual progression of Delia's life: from "Sweat, sweat, sweat! Work and sweat, cry and sweat, pray and sweat!" to freedom. In the first scene, Delia takes the white folks' laundry out of the hamper in the bedroom and is sorting it in the kitchen when "something long, round, limp and black . . . falls upon her shoulders." Her husband has used his long bullwhip to frighten her. This scene concludes with Sykes's kicking the sorted clothes "helter-skelter" and the usually meek Delia's standing up to him, apparently for the first time in fifteen years. As the next eight or so weeks pass, the reader is aware that Delia continues to do her weekly laundry, that Sykes wants to displace her in the house with his mistress and has placed a rattlesnake in a box outside the kitchen door to frighten his wife away, that Delia has moved her church membership to Woodbridge so she will no longer have to take the sacrament with Sykes, and that she has told her husband she hates him. Thus, the conflict between the two is clearly escalating to a dangerous level; but Delia is never actually portrayed again doing the white folks' weekly laundry; this lack creates what Caws describes as "a noticeable delay in time . . . [which] serves to stress the episode it precedes or follows, or both."

In the second laundry scene, toward the end of the story, Delia opens the hamper to remove the white folks' laundry and discovers a rattlesnake at the bottom. Thus, although the two points of reference in the scene remain the same, Delia and the laundry, the bullwhip has become a dangerous snake: no longer a snake in a box outside the kitchen door, now a snake in her house, in her hamper. This scene, superimposed on the earlier laundry scene, prepares the reader for the final change in Delia's attitude toward Sykes. Terrified of the snake, Delia flees "to the darkness of the yard, slamming the door after her." First she is a "gibbering wreck," then she experiences "a cold, bloody rage"; and finally she settles into "an awful calm." Thus, the reader is not surprised when Delia, lying in the hay barn, does not warn the approaching Sykes that the snake is now loose in the house. She knows that in this marriage she has "done de bes' . . . [she] could."

The final two scenes of the story are architecturally framed, with Sykes standing outside the kitchen door in the first, Delia in the second. When Sykes hangs outside the door "some minutes" before entering and then stands "some minutes more inside" before walking to the stove, he, of course, assumes that Delia has been bitten and is probably dead. In fact, when he realizes the snake is after him, he mutters, "Ah thought he'd be too sick." The reader has hardly adjusted to the horror of Sykes's expectation and the snake's attack on him before a second doorway scene is superimposed. Now it is Delia, sick with horror, who stands outside the door looking in. There is little morning light, but she is able to see the "despairing" Sykes, creeping "an inch or two toward her — all that he was able . . . his horribly swollen neck and his one open eye shining with hope." The man who has loomed above her through the years now crawls toward her, his fallen state emphasized by the frame of the door and Delia's standing figure; the man who has treated her with continuous contempt and cruelty now hopes for help from her. It is too late for Sykes to receive any help: "Orlando with its doctors was too far." But Delia squelches her "surge of pity"; hardened and resolved, she flees rather than stoop to the crawling figure to offer him any comfort in his dying moments. Sykes dies, with eyes that cannot "fail to see the wash tubs" outside the door and with eyes that must have seen Delia at the door, "must know by now that she knew." In turning her back on Sykes, Delia denies the folk belief that one must alleviate the suffering of those who die hard or be haunted by the person's spirit and denies the Christian belief in mercy. Metonymically, she stands as she has never stood before.

The two primary framed scenes in "The Gilded Six-Bits" operate in a very different fashion. The single scene in which Joe finds his wife in bed with Slemmons is doubly framed, architecturally by the doorway and perceptually by Joe's gradual, sensual awareness. When Joe makes his surprise visit home and steps over the doorsill of his bedroom, he slowly realizes what is happening and, framed by the doorway, feels "eternity" stand "still." The changes in lighting within the bedroom then shift the focus to Joe's perceptions. At first Joe can see nothing because "The light went out." Then, by the light of the match he strikes, he can see only "the man's legs fighting with his breeches in his frantic desire to get them on." Finally, after he lights the lamp, Joe does not see at all; he hears, hears "his wife sobbing and Slemmons pleading for his life." Such a scene may be a cliché in literature, but not as Hurston portrays it, focused by a man who "stood and felt without thinking and without seeing with his natural eyes . . . [who] kept on feeling so much and not knowing what to do with all his feelings."

The central scene around which the story is structured, a scene that recurs twice, is equally poignant. The first scene of interaction for the protagonists in the story, the scene that defines their marital happiness, is one of "joyful mischief," with Joe throwing silver dollars at the door for Missie May "to pick up and pile beside her plate at dinner," Missie coming to the door to scold anyone who would "be chunkin' money" at her, and the two entwining in "a furious mass of male and female energy" until Missie has emptied Joe's pockets of the candy kisses, chewing gum, and other sweets he brings her every Sunday. It is the "play-fight" of an innocent young man and innocent young woman who love each other deeply and take great joy in both life and their relationship, which they hope will soon include a child.

After Joe's discovery of Missie's affair, however, their relationship becomes stiff and formal. Joe is "polite, even kind at times, but aloof." There is "no laughter, no banter"; there are "no more Saturday romps." Hurston is clearly using "the noticeable delay in time," the emptiness of the protagonists' lives, and the sense of their waiting and healing to prepare for the brilliantly rendered final scene, in which Joe once again throws coins at the door. This time, however, Missie May cannot run to the door; she has just delivered a baby and can now only creep "there as quickly as she could." She cannot now wrestle with the man who has dared to chunk money at her door in that way; she can only promise, "You wait till Ah got mah strength back and Ah'm gointer fix you for dat." The closing scene, similar to yet strikingly different from the earlier one, clearly offers a metonymic indication of the current relationship between the two. There probably can never again be innocent romps. But Missie *can* move from creeping to walking to running; gradually her physical strength will return, as will the strength of their love. Someday there can again be laughter, bantering, and, at least, bittersweet romps.

"The Gilded Six-Bits" offers one additional frame, its remarkable one-sentence opening paragraph: "It was a Negro yard around a Negro house in a Negro settlement that looked to the payroll of the G and G Fertilizer works for its support." Here Hurston plays with the physical borders of a yard, the economic borders of a laborer's payroll, and the conceptual borders of a limited way of life. The passage frames in, but also frames out, frames out a huge amount of human experience. The opening with the neuter (nonhuman) word "it," the generative rhetoric of the predicate nominative, and the repetition of the word "Negro" surely makes a political statement. Lest, however, a reader attempt to cry "naturalism," the life of man circumscribed, Hurston opens the second paragraph with a clear objection: "But there was something happy about this place." The description of yard and house that follows attests to order, beauty, and care by both husband and wife. Thus, the opening frame of "The Gilded Six-Bits" complements the framed "joyful mischief" of this young couple, emphasizing the richness of their lives before Missie May's fall.

ALICE WALKER

Zora Neale Hurston: A Cautionary Tale and a Partisan View

1979

During the early and middle years of her career Zora was a cultural revolutionary simply because she was always herself. Her work, so vigorous among the rather pallid productions of many of her contemporaries, comes from the essence of black folk life. During her later life she became frightened of the life she had always dared bravely before. Her work too became reactionary, static, shockingly misguided and timid. (This is especially true of her last novel, *Seraphs on the Sewannee,* which is not even about black people, which is no crime, but *is* about white people for whom it is impossible to care, which is.)

A series of misfortunes battered Zora's spirit and her health. And she was broke.

Being broke made all the difference.

Without money of one's own in a capitalist society, there is no such thing as independence. This is one of the clearest lessons of Zora's life, and why I consider the telling of her life "a cautionary tale." We must learn from it what we can.

Without money, an illness, even a simple one, can undermine the will. Without money, getting into a hospital is problematic and getting out without money to pay for the treatment is nearly impossible. Without money, one becomes dependent on other people, who are likely to be — even in their kindness — erratic in their support and despotic in their expectations of return. Zora was forced to rely, like Tennessee Williams's Blanche,° "on the kindness of strangers." Can anything be more dangerous, if the strangers are forever in control? Zora, who worked so hard, was never able to make a living from her work.

She did not complain about not having money. She was not the type. (Several months ago I received a long letter from one of Zora's nieces, a bright ten-year-old, who explained to me that her aunt was so proud that the only way the family could guess she was ill or without funds was by realizing they had no idea where she was. Therefore, none of the family attended either Zora's sickbed or her funeral.) Those of us who have had "grants and fellowships from 'white folks'" know this aid is extended in precisely the way welfare is extended in Mississippi. One is asked, *curtly,* more often than not: How much do you need *just to survive?* Then one is — if fortunate — given a third of that. What is amazing is that Zora, who became an orphan at nine, a runaway at fourteen, a maid and manicurist (because of necessity and not from love of the work) before she was twenty — with one dress — managed to become Zora Neale Hurston, author and anthropologist, at all.

For me, the most unfortunate thing Zora ever wrote is her autobiography. After the first several chapters, it rings false. One begins to hear the voice of someone whose life required the assistance of too many transitory "friends." A Taoist proverb states that *to act sincerely with the insincere is dangerous.* (A mistake blacks as a group have tended to make in America.) And so we have Zora sincerely offering gratitude and kind words to people one knows she could not have respected. But this unctuousness, so out of character for Zora, is also a result of dependency, a sign of her powerlessness, her inability to pay back her debts with anything but words. They must have been bitter ones for her. In her dependency, it should be remembered, Zora was not alone — because it is quite true that America does not support or honor us as human beings, let alone as blacks, women, and artists. We have taken help where it was offered because we are committed to what we do and to the survival of our work. Zora was committed to the survival of her people's cultural heritage as well.

Tennessee Williams's Blanche: Main character in Williams's play *A Streetcar Named Desire* (1947).

In my mind, Zora Neale Hurston, Billie Holiday,° and Bessie Smith° form a sort of unholy trinity. Zora *belongs* in the tradition of black women singers, rather than among "the literati," at least to me. There were the extreme highs and lows of her life, her undaunted pursuit of adventure, passionate emotional and sexual experience, and her love of freedom. Like Billie and Bessie she followed her own road, believed in her own gods, pursued her own dreams, and refused to separate herself from "common" people. It would have been nice if the three of them had had one another to turn to, in times of need. I close my eyes and imagine them: Bessie would be in charge of all the money; Zora would keep Billie's masochistic tendencies in check and prevent her from singing embarrassing anything-for-a-man songs, thereby preventing Billie's heroin addiction. In return, Billie could be, along with Bessie, the family that Zora felt she never had.

We are a people. A people do not throw their geniuses away. And if they are thrown away, it is our duty *as artists and as witnesses for the future* to collect them again for the sake of our children, and, if necessary, bone by bone.

CASEBOOK ON FLANNERY O'CONNOR

Flannery O'Connor is unusual among writers in that she shared with readers her own interpretations of her stories. While acknowledging that there is usually more than one way to read a story, she also stated that there was only one way she could possibly have written it. O'Connor's discussion of "A Good Man Is Hard to Find" (p. 551) can be read alongside the interpretations of "Good Country People" (p. 536) and "Everything That Rises Must Converge" (p. 525) by academic critics Dorothy Tuck McFarland and Wayne C. Booth. Sally Fitzgerald reveals the newspaper sources of "A Good Man Is Hard to Find," and Robert H. Brinkmeyer Jr. considers the relationship between O'Connor and her readers.

FLANNERY O'CONNOR

From Letters, 1954–55

1955

TO SALLY FITZGERALD

26 Dec 54

. . . I have finally got off the ms. for my collection [*A Good Man Is Hard to Find*] and it is scheduled to appear in May. Without yr kind permission I have taken the liberty of dedicating (grand verb) it to you and Robert. This is

Billie Holiday: African American jazz singer (1915–1959) known for her pioneering vocal style and tragic life.
Bessie Smith: Prominent African American blues singer and song writer (1898–1937), the highest paid black artist in the United States in the 1920s.

Flannery O'Connor in the summer of 1962 at Andalusia, her family farm and home outside Milledgeville, Georgia. (© Joe McTyre. Reprinted by permission of Joe McTyre Photo/Atlanta Constitution.)

because you all are my adopted kin and if I dedicated it to any of my blood kin they would think they had to go into hiding. Nine stories about original sin, with my compliments.

I have been invited to go to Greensboro to the Women's College in March to be on an arts panel. That is where Brother Randall Jarrell° holds forth. I accepted but I am not looking forward to it. Can you fancy me hung in conversation with the likes of him?

Randall Jarrell: American poet and influential critic (1914–1965).

When I had lunch with Giroux [O'Connor's editor] in Atlanta he told me about Cal's escapade in Cincinnati. It seems [Cal] convinced everybody it was Elizabeth who was going crazy. . . . Toward the end he gave a lecture at the university that was almost pure gibberish. I guess nobody noticed, thinking it was the new criticism. . . .

I just got a check for $200 for the 2nd prize in the O. Henry book° this year. My ex-mentor Paul Engle does the selecting. Jean Stafford° got the first one.

I am walking with a cane these days which gives me a great air of distinction. The scientist tells me this has nothing to do with the lupus but is rheumatism. I would not believe it except that the dose of ACTH has not been increased. Besides which I now feel it makes very little difference what you call it. As the niggers say, I have the misery.

I am reading everything I can of Romano Guardini's [Italian priest and theologian]. Have you become acquainted with his work? A book called *The Lord* of his is very fine.

TO ELIZABETH MCKEE

13 January 1955

The carbon of "An Exile in the East" is enclosed, but I don't know if you realize or not that this is a rewritten version of "The Geranium" originally printed in *Accent. Accent* didn't pay me for it and it is rather much changed, but I enclose both stories so [the editor] can see what she's doing. I don't want to go to the penitentiary for selling a story twice (but if I do I would like to get a good price for the story).

TO ROBERT GIROUX

22 January 55

Nothing has been said about a picture for the jacket of this collection *but if you have to have one,* I would be much obliged if you could use the enclosed so that I won't have to have a new picture made. This is a self-portrait with a pheasant cock, that I painted in 1953; however, I think it will do justice to the subject for some time to come.

26 February 55

I have just written a story called "Good Country People" that Allen and Caroline [Tate?] both say is the best thing I have written and should be in this collection. I told them I thought it was too late, but anyhow I am writing now to ask if it is. It is really a story that would set the whole collection on its feet. It is 27 pages and if you can eliminate the one called "A Stroke of Good Fortune," and the other called "An Afternoon in the Woods," this one would fit the available space nicely. Also I remember you said it would be good to have

---

O. Henry book: The O. Henry Prizes are awarded annually to outstanding American short stories, which are collected each year in a book. O. Henry was the pen name of the popular American short story writer William Sydney Porter (1862–1910).
Jean Stafford: American short story writer and novelist (1915–1979).

one that had never been published before. I could send it to you at once *on being wired.* Please let me know.

Giroux wired O'Connor that every effort would be made to include the story. After he had read it, he wrote suggesting that an appearance by the mother and Mrs. Freeman at the end might improve it. Flannery recognized the value of the suggestion and added the sentences that are now a part of the story.

7 March 55

I like the suggestion about the ending of "Good Country People" and enclose a dozen or so lines that can be added on to *the present end.* I enclose them in case you can get them put on before I get the proofs. I am mighty wary of making changes on proofs. . . .

TO SALLY AND ROBERT FITZGERALD

1 April 55

We are wondering if #6 is here yet or due to arrive momentarily. Let us hear and if you need any names, I'll be glad to cable you a rich collection. I have just got back from Greensboro where I said nothing intelligent the whole time, but enjoyed myself. Mr. Randall Jarrell, wife and stepdaughters I met and et dinner with. I must say I was shocked at what a very kind man he is — that is the last impression I expected to have of him. I also met Peter Taylor,° who is more like folks. Mrs. Jarrell is writing a novel. You get the impression the two stepdaughters may be at it too and maybe the dog. Mr. Jarrell has a beard and looks like Mephistopheles (sp?) only fatter. Mrs. Jarrell is very friendly & sunkist.

The Easter rabbit is bringing my mother a three-quarter ton truck.

I trust Giroux will be sending you a copy of the book soon. I wrote a very hot story at the last minute called "Good Country People": so now there are ten.

While I was in NC I heard somebody recite a barroom ballad. I don't remember anything but the end but beinst you all are poets I will give it to you as it is mighty deathless:

"They stacked the stiffs outside the door.
They made, I reckon, a cord or more."

I call that real poetry.

I have put the cane up and am walking on my own very well. Let us hear. Regards to children.

FLANNERY O'CONNOR

Writing Short Stories

1961

. . . Perhaps the central question to be considered in any discussion of the short story is what do we mean by short. Being short does not mean being

Peter Taylor: Tennessee born and bred novelist and short story writer (1917–1994).

slight. A short story should be long in depth and should give us an experience of meaning. I have an aunt who thinks that nothing happens in a story unless somebody gets married or shot at the end of it. I wrote a story about a tramp who marries an old woman's idiot daughter in order to acquire the old woman's automobile. After the marriage, he takes the daughter off on a wedding trip in the automobile and abandons her in an eating place and drives on by himself. Now that is a complete story. There is nothing more relating to the mystery of that man's personality that could be shown through that particular dramatization. But I've never been able to convince my aunt that it's a complete story. She wants to know what happened to the idiot daughter after that.

Not long ago that story was adapted for a television play, and the adapter, knowing his business, had the tramp have a change of heart and go back and pick up the idiot daughter and the two of them ride away, grinning madly. My aunt believes that the story is complete at last, but I have other sentiments about it — which are not suitable for public utterance. When you write a story, you only have to write one story, but there will always be people who will refuse to read the story you have written.

And this naturally brings up the awful question of what kind of a reader you are writing for when you write fiction. Perhaps we each think we have a personal solution for this problem. For my own part, I have a very high opinion of the art of fiction and a very low opinion of what is called the "average" reader. I tell myself that I can't escape him, that this is the personality I am supposed to keep awake, but that at the same time, I am also supposed to provide the intelligent reader with the deeper experience that he looks for in fiction. Now actually, both of these readers are just aspects of the writer's own personality, and in the last analysis, the only reader he can know anything about is himself. We all write at our own level of understanding, but it is the peculiar characteristic of fiction that its literal surface can be made to yield entertainment on an obvious physical plane to one sort of reader while the selfsame surface can be made to yield meaning to the person equipped to experience it there.

Meaning is what keeps the short story from being short. I prefer to talk about the meaning in a story rather than the theme of a story. People talk about the theme of a story as if the theme were like the string that a sack of chicken feed is tied with. They think that if you can pick out the theme, the way you pick the right thread in the chicken-feed sack, you can rip the story open and feed the chickens. But this is not the way meaning works in fiction.

When you can state the theme of a story, when you can separate it from the story itself, then you can be sure the story is not a very good one. The meaning of a story has to be embodied in it, has to be made concrete in it. A story is a way to say something that can't be said any other way, and it takes every word in the story to say what the meaning is. You tell a story because a statement would be inadequate. When anybody asks what a story is about, the only proper thing is to tell him to read the story. The meaning of fiction is not abstract meaning but experienced meaning, and the purpose of making statements about the meaning of a story is only to help you to experience that meaning more fully.

Fiction is an art that calls for the strictest attention to the real — whether the writer is writing a naturalistic story or a fantasy. I mean that we always begin with what is or with what has an eminent possibility of truth about it. Even when one writes a fantasy, reality is the proper basis of it. A thing is fantastic because it is so real, so real that it is fantastic. Graham Greene° has said that he can't write, "I stood over a bottomless pit," because that couldn't be true, or "Running down the stairs I jumped into a taxi," because that couldn't be true either. But Elizabeth Bowen° can write about one of her characters that "she snatched at her hair as if she heard something in it," because that is eminently possible.

I would even go so far as to say that the person writing a fantasy has to be even more strictly attentive to the concrete detail than someone writing in a naturalistic vein — because the greater the story's strain on the credulity, the more convincing the properties in it have to be.

A good example of this is a story called "The Metamorphosis" by Franz Kafka. This is a story about a man who wakes up one morning to find that he has turned into a cockroach overnight, while not discarding his human nature. The rest of the story concerns his life and feelings and eventual death as an insect with human nature, and this situation is accepted by the reader because the concrete detail of the story is absolutely convincing. The fact is that this story describes the dual nature of man in such a realistic fashion that it is almost unbearable. The truth is not distorted here, but rather, a certain distortion is used to get at the truth. If we admit, as we must, that appearance is not the same thing as reality, then we must give the artist the liberty to make certain rearrangements of nature if these will lead to greater depths of vision. The artist himself always has to remember that what he is rearranging *is* nature, and that he has to know it and be able to describe it accurately in order to have the authority to rearrange it at all.

The peculiar problem of the short-story writer is how to make the action he describes reveal as much of the mystery of existence as possible. He has only a short space to do it in and he can't do it by statement. He has to do it by showing, not by saying, and by showing the concrete — so that his problem is really how to make the concrete work double time for him.

In good fiction, certain of the details will tend to accumulate meaning from the action of the story itself, and when this happens they become symbolic in the way they work. I once wrote a story called "Good Country People," in which a lady Ph.D. has her wooden leg stolen by a Bible salesman whom she has tried to seduce. Now I'll admit that, paraphrased in this way, the situation is simply a low joke. The average reader is pleased to observe anybody's wooden leg being stolen. But without ceasing to appeal to him and without making any statements of high intention, this story does manage to operate at another level of experience, by letting the wooden leg accumulate meaning. Early in the story, we're presented with the fact that the Ph.D. is spiritually as well as physically crippled. She believes in nothing but her own belief in nothing, and

---

Graham Greene: English writer (1904–1991).
Elizabeth Bowen: British novelist and short story writer (1899–1973).

we perceive that there is a wooden part of her soul that corresponds to her wooden leg. Now of course this is never stated. The fiction writer states as little as possible. The reader makes this connection from things he is shown. He may not even know that he makes the connection, but the connection is there nevertheless and it has its effect on him. As the story goes on, the wooden leg continues to accumulate meaning. The reader learns how the girl feels about her leg, how her mother feels about it, and how the country woman on the place feels about it; and finally, by the time the Bible salesman comes along, the leg has accumulated so much meaning that it is, as the saying goes, loaded. And when the Bible salesman steals it, the reader realizes that he has taken away part of the girl's personality and has revealed her deeper affliction to her for the first time.

If you want to say that the wooden leg is a symbol, you can say that. But it is a wooden leg first, and as a wooden leg it is absolutely necessary to the story. It has its place on the literal level of the story, but it operates in depth as well as on the surface. It increases the story in every direction, and this is essentially the way a story escapes being short.

Now a little might be said about the way in which this happens. I wouldn't want you to think that in that story I sat down and said, "I am now going to write a story about a Ph.D. with a wooden leg, using the wooden leg as a symbol for another kind of affliction." I doubt myself if many writers know what they are going to do when they start out. When I started writing that story, I didn't know there was going to be a Ph.D. with a wooden leg in it. I merely found myself one morning writing a description of two women that I knew something about, and before I realized it, I had equipped one of them with a daughter with a wooden leg. As the story progressed, I brought in the Bible salesman, but I had no idea what I was going to do with him. I didn't know he was going to steal that wooden leg until ten or twelve lines before he did it, but when I found out that this was what was going to happen, I realized that it was inevitable. This is a story that produces a shock for the reader, and I think one reason for this is that it produced a shock for the writer.

Now despite the fact that this story came about in this seemingly mindless fashion, it is a story that almost no rewriting was done on. It is a story that was under control throughout the writing of it, and it might be asked how this kind of control comes about, since it is not entirely conscious.

I think the answer to this is what Maritain° calls "the habit of art." It is a fact that fiction writing is something in which the whole personality takes part — the conscious as well as the unconscious mind. Art is the habit of the artist; and habits have to be rooted deep in the whole personality. They have to be cultivated like any other habit, over a long period of time, by experience; and teaching any kind of writing is largely a matter of helping the student develop the habit of art. I think this is more than just a discipline, although it is that; I think it is a way of looking at the created world and of using the senses so as to make them find as much meaning as possible in things.

Now I am not so naïve as to suppose that most people come to writers'

Maritain: Jacques Maritain (1882–1973) was a French philosopher and critic.

conferences in order to hear what kind of vision is necessary to write stories that will become a permanent part of our literature. Even if you do wish to hear this, your greatest concerns are immediately practical. You want to know how you can actually write a good story, and further, how you can tell when you've done it; and so you want to know what the form of a short story is, as if the form were something that existed outside of each story and could be applied or imposed on the material. Of course, the more you write, the more you will realize that the form is organic, that it is something that grows out of the material, that the form of each story is unique. A story that is any good can't be reduced, it can only be expanded. A story is good when you continue to see more and more in it, and when it continues to escape you. In fiction two and two is always more than four.

The only way, I think, to learn to write short stories is to write them, and then to try to discover what you have done. The time to think of technique is when you've actually got the story in front of you. The teacher can help the student by looking at his individual work and trying to help him decide if he has written a complete story, one in which the action fully illuminates the meaning.

Perhaps the most profitable thing I can do is to tell you about some of the general observations I made about these seven stories I read of yours. All of these observations will not fit any one of the stories exactly, but they are points nevertheless that it won't hurt anyone interested in writing to think about.

The first thing that any professional writer is conscious of in reading anything is, naturally, the use of language. Now the use of language in these stories was such that, with one exception, it would be difficult to distinguish one story from another. While I can recall running into several clichés, I can't remember one image or one metaphor from the seven stories. I don't mean there weren't images in them; I just mean that there weren't any that were effective enough to take away with you.

In connection with this, I made another observation that startled me considerably. With the exception of one story, there was practically no use made of the local idiom. Now this is a Southern Writers' Conference. All the addresses on these stories were from Georgia or Tennessee, yet there was no distinctive sense of Southern life in them. A few place-names were dropped, Savannah or Atlanta or Jacksonville, but these could just as easily have been changed to Pittsburgh or Passaic without calling for any other alteration in the story. The characters spoke as if they had never heard any kind of language except what came out of a television set. This indicates that something is way out of focus.

There are two qualities that make fiction. One is the sense of mystery and the other is the sense of manners. You get the manners from the texture of existence that surrounds you. The great advantage of being a Southern writer is that we don't have to go anywhere to look for manners; bad or good, we've got them in abundance. We in the South live in a society that is rich in contradiction, rich in irony, rich in contrast, and particularly rich in its speech. And yet here are six stories by Southerners in which almost no use is made of the gifts of the region.

Of course the reason for this may be that you have seen these gifts abused so often that you have become self-conscious about using them. There is nothing worse than the writer who doesn't *use* the gifts of the region, but wallows in them. Everything becomes so Southern that it's sickening, so local that it is unintelligible, so literally reproduced that it conveys nothing. The general gets lost in the particular instead of being shown through it.

However, when the life that actually surrounds us is totally ignored, when our patterns of speech are absolutely overlooked, then something is out of kilter. The writer should then ask himself if he is not reaching out for a kind of life that is artificial to him.

An idiom characterizes a society, and when you ignore the idiom, you are very likely ignoring the whole social fabric that could make a meaningful character. You can't cut characters off from their society and say much about them as individuals. You can't say anything meaningful about the mystery of a personality unless you put that personality in a believable and significant social context. And the best way to do this is through the character's own language. When the old lady in one of Andrew Lytle's stories says contemptuously that she has a mule that is older than Birmingham, we get in that one sentence a sense of a society and its history. A great deal of the Southern writers' work is done for him before he begins, because our history lives in our talk. In one of Eudora Welty's stories a character says, "Where I come from, we use fox for yard dogs and owls for chickens, but we sing true." Now there is a whole book in that one sentence; and when the people of your section can talk like that, and you ignore it, you're just not taking advantage of what's yours. The sound of our talk is too definite to be discarded with impunity, and if the writer tries to get rid of it, he is liable to destroy the better part of his creative power.

Another thing I observed about these stories is that most of them don't go very far inside a character, don't reveal very much of the character. I don't mean that they don't enter the character's mind, but they simply don't show that he has a personality. Again this goes back partly to speech. These characters have no distinctive speech to reveal themselves with; and sometimes they have no really distinctive features. You feel in the end that no personality is revealed because no personality is there. In most good stories it is the character's personality that creates the action of the story. In most of these stories, I feel that the writer has thought of some action and then scrounged up a character to perform it. You will usually be more successful if you start the other way around. If you start with a real personality, a real character, then something is bound to happen; and you don't have to know what before you begin. In fact it may be better if you don't know what before you begin. You ought to be able to discover something from your stories. If you don't, probably nobody else will.

Flannery O'Connor

The Element of Suspense in "A Good Man Is Hard to Find" *1969*

A story really isn't any good unless it successfully resists paraphrase, unless it hangs on and expands in the mind. Properly, you analyze to enjoy, but it's equally true that to analyze with any discrimination, you have to have enjoyed already, and I think that the best reason to hear a story read is that it should stimulate that primary enjoyment.

I don't have any pretensions to being an Aeschylus or Sophocles and providing you in this story with a cathartic experience out of your mythic background, though this story I'm going to read certainly calls up a good deal of the South's mythic background, and it should elicit from you a degree of pity and terror, even though its way of being serious is a comic one. I do think, though, that like the Greeks you should know what is going to happen in this story so that any element of suspense in it will be transferred from its surface to its interior.

I would be most happy if you had already read it, happier still if you knew it well, but since experience has taught me to keep my expectations along these lines modest, I'll tell you that this is the story of a family of six which, on its way driving to Florida, gets wiped out by an escaped convict who calls himself the Misfit. The family is made up of the Grandmother and her son, Bailey, and his children, John Wesley and June Star and the baby, and there is also the cat and the children's mother. The cat is named Pitty Sing, and the Grandmother is taking him with them, hidden in a basket.

Now I think it behooves me to try to establish with you the basis on which reason operates in this story. Much of my fiction takes its character from a reasonable use of the unreasonable, though the reasonableness of my use of it may not always be apparent. The assumptions that underlie this use of it, however, are those of the central Christian mysteries. These are assumptions to which a large part of the modern audience takes exception. About this I can only say that there are perhaps other ways than my own in which this story could be read, but none other by which it could have been written. Belief, in my own case anyway, is the engine that makes perception operate.

The heroine of this story, the Grandmother, is in the most significant position life offers the Christian. She is facing death. And to all appearances she, like the rest of us, is not too well prepared for it. She would like to see the event postponed. Indefinitely.

I've talked to a number of teachers who use this story in class and who tell their students that the Grandmother is evil, that in fact, she's a witch, even down to the cat. One of these teachers told me that his students, and particularly his southern students, resisted this interpretation with a certain bemused vigor, and he didn't understand why. I had to tell him that they resisted it because they all had grandmothers or great-aunts just like her at home, and they knew, from personal experience, that the old lady lacked comprehension, but that she had a good heart. The southerner is usually tolerant of those weaknesses that proceed from innocence, and he knows that a taste for self-preservation can be readily combined with the missionary spirit.

This same teacher was telling his students that morally the Misfit was several cuts above the Grandmother. He had a really sentimental attachment to the Misfit. But then a prophet gone wrong is almost always more interesting than your grandmother, and you have to let people take their pleasures where they find them.

It is true that the old lady is a hypocritical old soul; her wits are no match for the Misfit's, nor is her capacity for grace equal to his; yet I think the unprejudiced reader will feel that the Grandmother has a special kind of triumph in this story which instinctively we do not allow to someone altogether bad.

I often ask myself what makes a story work, and what makes it hold up as a story, and I have decided that it is probably some action, some gesture of a character that is unlike any other in the story, one which indicates where the real heart of the story lies. This would have to be an action or a gesture which was both totally right and totally unexpected; it would have to be one that was both in character and beyond character; it would have to suggest both the world and eternity. The action or gesture I'm talking about would have to be on the anagogical level, that is, the level which has to do with the Divine life and our participation in it. It would be a gesture that transcended any neat allegory that might have been intended or any pat moral categories a reader could make. It would be a gesture which somehow made contact with mystery.

There is a point in this story where such a gesture occurs. The Grandmother is at last alone, facing the Misfit. Her head clears for an instant and she realizes, even in her limited way, that she is responsible for the man before her and joined to him by ties of kinship which have their roots deep in the mystery she has been merely prattling about so far. And at this point, she does the right thing, she makes the right gesture.

I find that students are often puzzled by what she says and does here, but I think myself that if I took out this gesture and what she says with it, I would have no story. What was left would not be worth your attention. Our age not only does not have a very sharp eye for the almost imperceptible intrusions of grace, it no longer has much feeling for the nature of the violences which precede and follow them. The devil's greatest wile, Baudelaire has said, is to convince us that he does not exist.

I suppose the reasons for the use of so much violence in modern fiction will differ with each writer who uses it, but in my own stories I have found that violence is strangely capable of returning my characters to reality and preparing them to accept their moment of grace. Their heads are so hard that almost nothing else will do the work. This idea, that reality is something to which we must be returned at considerable cost, is one which is seldom understood by the casual reader, but it is one which is implicit in the Christian view of the world.

I don't want to equate the Misfit with the devil. I prefer to think that, however unlikely this may seem, the old lady's gesture, like the mustard-seed, will grow to be a great crow-filled tree in the Misfit's heart, and will be enough of a pain to him there to turn him into the prophet he was meant to become. But that's another story.

This story has been called grotesque, but I prefer to call it literal. A good story is literal in the same sense that a child's drawing is literal. When a child draws, he doesn't intend to distort but to set down exactly what he sees, and as his gaze is direct, he sees the lines that create motion. Now the lines of motion that interest the writer are usually invisible. They are lines of spiritual motion. And in this story you should be on the lookout for such things as the action of grace in the Grandmother's soul, and not for the dead bodies.

We hear many complaints about the prevalence of violence in modern fiction, and it is always assumed that this violence is a bad thing and meant to be an end in itself. With the serious writer, violence is never an end in itself. It is the extreme situation that best reveals what we are essentially, and I believe these are times when writers are more interested in what we are essentially than in the tenor of our daily lives. Violence is a force which can be used for good or evil, and among other things taken by it is the kingdom of heaven. But regardless of what can be taken by it, the man in the violent situation reveals those qualities least dispensable in his personality, those qualities which are all he will have to take into eternity with him; and since the characters in this story are all on the verge of eternity, it is appropriate to think of what they take with them. In any case, I hope that if you consider these points in connection with the story, you will come to see it as something more than an account of a family murdered on the way to Florida.

SALLY FITZGERALD

Southern Sources of "A Good Man Is Hard to Find"

1997

The germ of the story, like a number of others, came from the newspapers close to home — in this instance from several newspaper accounts of unrelated matters shortly before she wrote the story, in 1953. The title she found in a local item — with photograph — concerning a prize-winning performance by a hideously painted-up little girl still in kitten teeth, decked out in ribbons and tutu and sausage curls, singing "A Good Man Is Hard to Find." Beyond the title, there is no connection between the photograph and the events of the short story, but possibly this child served to inspire the awful little granddaughter, June Star, who sasses her way through the action, and does her tap-routine at the barbecue stand of Red Sammy Butts, the fat veteran "with the happy laugh," who is so thoroughly nasty to his wife. Flannery thought well enough of this newspaper photograph and caption to pass them along for my delectation, together with various ads and testimonials for patent medicines and inspirational columns from the local press, and I remember the clipping very clearly. So did she, and she took the nectar from it to make her fictional honey.

About the same time, an article appeared in the Atlanta paper about a small-time robber who called himself "The Misfit," in a self-pitying explanation or excuse for his crimes. A clipping about him and his honorary title turned up among her papers. Obviously, the name he gave himself was the only thing about this man that much interested the author, and certainly he was no match for the towering figure she turned him into. Incidentally, his excuse for his peccadilloes was taken rather literally in the judicial system: he was judged to be of unsound mind and committed to the lunatic asylum — in Milledgeville, the town in which Flannery lived. This news cannot have escaped her notice. By the way, the mental hospital there was once the largest in the world under one roof. Flannery once described Milledgeville as a town of 8,000, of whom 4,000 were locked up.

There was a third element in the inspirational mix for the story, and this was also to be found in the newspapers, in a series of accounts of another criminal "aloose" in the region. The subject was the person of Mr. James Francis ("Three-Gun") Hill, who amassed a record of twenty-six kidnappings in four states, an equal number of robberies, ten car thefts, and a daring rescue of four Florida convicts from a prison gang — all brought off in two fun-filled weeks. The papers at the time were full of these accounts, and the lurid headlines of the day might well have excited a grandmother like the one who is shaking a newspaper at Bailey Boy's bald head and lecturing him on the dangers to be feared on the road to Florida, when the O'Connor story opens.

Mr. Hill was a far more formidable figure than the original self-styled Misfit, and a more vivid one. Newspaper photographs show him to have looked almost exactly as she described the character in her story, complete with metal-rimmed spectacles. There were other details evidently appropriated by Flannery from life, or life as strained through the *Atlanta Journal* and the *Atlanta Constitution:* Mr. Hill was proud of his courtly manners, and in one press account called himself a "gentleman-bandit," explaining that he never cussed before ladies. (Readers will remember that Flannery's mass-murderer blushes when Bailey curses his mother for her incautious tongue.) In some accounts, "Three-Gun" Hill had two accomplices, although the fictional Hiram and Bobby Lee seem entirely imagined by O'Connor in their physical aspects and rather subhuman personalities.

The Misfit in O'Connor's story recounts a brush with a "head-doctor," which accords with the fate of both these actual criminals who initially inspired her. "Three-Gun" Hill, too, was committed to an insane asylum in the end, when he pled guilty to the charges against him. He was sent to a hospital in Tennessee, however, and not to Milledgeville, but the author no doubt read about the sentencing, and it may be that the eventual guilty plea suggested to her the beginnings of capitulation, the stirring of life in the Misfit, whom she conceived as a spoiled prophet, on which note her story ends.

ROBERT H. BRINKMEYER JR.

Flannery O'Connor and Her Readers *1989*

As her letters and essays clearly indicate, O'Connor was very much concerned with her reading audience. Her comments on her audience and how it affected her as an artist, however, were not entirely consistent, and it seems clear that O'Connor was of two minds on the subject.[1] One part of O'Connor downplayed the significance of the audience, saying that artists should be

[1]The most extensive discussion of O'Connor's interpretation of her audience is in Carol Shloss, *Flannery O'Connor's Dark Comedies: The Limits of Inference* (Baton Rouge, 1980). [Brinkmeyer's note]

concerned with one thing — their art — and that they bear no responsibility to the audience. By this line of thinking writers concentrate on making their fiction — the characters and their worlds — come alive, and they make sure that the story works as a story and not as a medium for expressing an abstract statement. The meaning of a piece of fiction, O'Connor insisted, was the entire experience one has with it and was not a statement imposed on it that could then later be extracted and held up as its "message." Such thinking was central to the advice she wrote (December 11, 1956) to A. about writing fiction. O'Connor wrote that a writer should merely "start simply with a character or anything that you can make come alive." She continued, "When you have a character he will create his own situation and his situation will suggest some kind of resolution as you get into it. Wouldn't it be better to discover a meaning in what you write than to impose one?" (*HB*, 188).

Behind O'Connor's thinking is the thought of Saint Thomas Aquinas, whom O'Connor frequently cites. For Aquinas a work of art is, as O'Connor points out in "Catholic Novelists and Their Readers," "a good in itself," being "wholly concerned with the good of that which is made." As such, it "glorifies God because it reflects God," and writers have no cause to put their work to any other end; such endeavors only undermine the integrity of the vision and sully the purity of the art. Modern writers, O'Connor says in this same essay, by and large fail to heed Aquinas's lesson and instead wrench their art to make it fit utilitarian ends. For her, in contrast, "the artist has his hands full and does his duty if he attends to his art. He can safely leave the evangelizing to the evangelists" (*MM*, 171, 173, 171).

Catholic writers, in O'Connor's eyes, were particularly prone to distort their fiction for utilitarian purposes — to make it do something rather than be something. Particularly disturbing to her were those writers, in part goaded by the Catholic press, who wrote in pious language about the pieties of the Church. O'Connor's attitude toward this type of fiction was sharp: "As for the fiction," she wrote (February 19, 1956) to John Lynch, "the motto of the Catholic press should be: We guarantee to corrupt nothing but your taste" (*HB*, 138). In ignoring the realities of the here and now outside the Church, such fiction was for O'Connor little more than religious propaganda, the stuff one expects to find in the vestibules of churches but not in bookstores. These writers, she believed, were too concerned with presenting the Church in a favorable light and tending to their readership's spiritual needs; O'Connor's answer to them was that in writing fiction the Catholic writer "does not decide what would be good for the Christian body and proceed to deliver it" (*MM*, 183). Instead, as we have seen O'Connor stressing, writers must work within the limitations of their vocation to create the best story — not tract — possible. "The writer is only free when he can tell the reader to go jump in the lake," O'Connor said in one of her interviews, stressing the artist's independence from the audience. She added that though the writer of course wants to communicate a personal vision, "whether [the reader] likes it or not is no concern of the writer" (*CFO*, 39).

If in this way O'Connor downplayed the significance of the audience, she also frequently said something quite different. She argued that the audience played a crucial role in artistic creation and that writers always had to be aware of, and to take account of, their audience. She spoke of this connection in "Catholic Novelists and Their Readers," saying that "it takes readers as well as writers to make literature," and she added in "The Catholic Novelist in the Protestant South" that "it is what writer, character, and reader share that makes it possible to write fiction at all." Elsewhere (in "Novelist and Believer") O'Connor wrote that fiction was ultimately an attempt at communication; successful writing, she added, was not merely a rendering of the artist's vision but a rendering of it in such a way that the reader could understand it. "The novelist doesn't write to express himself, he doesn't write simply to render a vision he believes true, rather he renders his vision so it can be transferred, as nearly whole as possible, to his reader," she wrote. "You can safely ignore the reader's taste, but you can't ignore his nature, you can't ignore his limited patience. Your problem is going to be difficult in direct proportion as your beliefs depart from his." She echoes this observation in "Some Aspects of the Grotesque in Southern Fiction," saying that the writer's vision "has to be transmitted and that the limitations and blind spots of his audience will very definitely affect the way he is able to show what he sees" (*MM*, 182, 204–205, 162, 47).

When speaking of her own audience, O'Connor almost always stressed the great distance she felt between herself and her readers and pointed to the ways this gulf pressured and limited her as a writer. She believed that she and other American Catholic writers lacked a significant and responsive audience, and that this situation stifled imaginative growth and artistic expression. O'Connor found several reasons for this development. Central to the Catholic writer's plight, O'Connor believed, was the fact that in America Catholic writers lacked a distinctive social and cultural heritage based on religious identity. In "The Catholic Novelist in the Protestant South" she asserts that "the writer whose themes are religious particularly needs a region where these themes find a response in the life of the people." She then adds: "The American Catholic is short on places that reflect his particular religious life and his particular problems. This country isn't exactly cut in his image." She goes on to say that even in areas where there are large numbers of Catholics, Catholic life there lacks "the significant features that result in a high degree of regional self-consciousness" and so offers the Catholic writer few "exploitable benefits." O'Connor's analysis of Catholic writers continues: "They have no great geographical extent, they have no particularly significant history, certainly no history of defeat; they have no real peasant class, and no cultural unity of the kind you find in the South." She adds that Catholics usually "blend almost imperceptively into the general materialistic background." This lack of a strong cultural tradition and a supportive audience greatly burdens Catholic writers, impoverishing their imaginative life and art. "If the Catholic faith were central to life in America, Catholic fiction would fare better, but the Church is not central to this society." O'Connor continues: "The things that bind us together as Catholics are known only to ourselves. A secular society understands us less and less. It becomes more and more difficult in America to make belief believable" (*MM*, 200, 201).

These final words point to the second reason American Catholics lack a supportive audience: The larger society they write from and to is overwhelmingly secular and materialistic, money based rather than religious based. O'Connor, as we saw in the first chapter, was well aware of the trends in modern social and intellectual thought that since the Enlightenment have been validating and valorizing the human consciousness and rationality while undermining and reducing the significance of the religious. In a letter (October 19, 1958) to T. R. Spivey, O'Connor wrote that by and large people in today's society have "no sense of the power of God that could produce the Incarnation and the Resurrection. They are all so busy explaining away the virgin birth and such things, reducing everything to human proportions that in time they lose even the sense of the human itself, what they were aiming to reduce everything to" (*HB*, 300). Because moderns lacked a faith in transcendent values and order, O'Connor, as she said in "Some Aspects of the Grotesque in Southern Fiction," saw the age as one "which doubts both fact and value, which is swept this way and that by momentary convictions" (*MM*, 49). O'Connor found such relativism particularly disturbing, and this in part explains her strong attraction to the fundamentalist imperative that defines all values according to the simple — but total — choice of being for either Christ or the Devil.

Given these trends and developments, O'Connor saw her own position, as well as that of almost all American Catholic writers, as being particularly precarious in terms of communicating with her readership. O'Connor frequently asserted in her letters that she could consistently count on only a handful of informed readers — an assertion largely borne out by the number of vicious and misinformed readings her work received, particularly early on — and that she had to make these readers go a long way in her life as an author. O'Connor knew hers was not the type of fiction that most Catholic readers yearned to read — not, in other words, fiction that was thoroughly positive and that went out of its way to celebrate the life of the Church. She characterized the general Catholic reader as unthinking, and she said that this reader "is so busy looking for something that fits his needs, and shows him in the best possible light, that he will find suspect anything that doesn't serve such purpose" (*MM*, 182). Elsewhere, in a letter (May 4, 1963) to Sister Mariella Gable, she wrote that those Catholic readers who demand that the writer make Christianity look desirable are asking the writer to describe Christianity's essence and not what the writer actually sees. "Ideal Christianity doesn't exist, because anything the human being touches, even Christian truth, he deforms slightly in his own image," she wrote, adding a bit later that the tendency of the Catholic readers she had been discussing "is always toward the abstract and therefore toward allegory, thinness, and ultimately what they are looking for is apologetic fiction. The best of them think: make it look desirable because it is desirable. And the rest of them think: make it look desirable so I won't look like a fool for holding it" (*HB*, 516). Such readers would find little to like in O'Connor's fiction and in all likelihood would see it as a good deal more than suspect — subversive, probably.

O'Connor of course felt an even greater distance from what she saw as the thoroughly secular and unbelieving general reader, the reader to whom she claimed she primarily wrote. In "The Catholic Novelists and Their Readers" she said that Catholic readers make a great mistake in supposing that Catholic writers write exclusively for them. "Occasionally this may happen," she wrote, "but generally it is not happening today" (*MM,* 185), and O'Connor made it clear elsewhere that it was not happening in her fiction. To A., O'Connor wrote (August 2, 1955) of the audience she perceived, saying that "one of the awful things about writing when you are a Christian is that for you the ultimate reality is the Incarnation, the present reality is the Incarnation, and nobody believes in the Incarnation; that is, nobody in your audience. My audience are the people who think God is dead. At least these are the people I am conscious of writing for" (*HB,* 92). Trying to bridge this gap between believing author and unbelieving audience was a terrible burden for O'Connor, and one that haunted her throughout her career. In a review of Caroline Gordon's *The Malefactors,* O'Connor wrote that "making grace believable to the contemporary reader is the almost insurmountable problem of the novelist who writes from the standpoint of Christian orthodoxy," an observation that speaks crucially to O'Connor's own situation in communicating with her audience (*PG,* 16).

O'Connor further perceived her audience as making demands that she was not prepared to meet — ever. She complained in "Some Aspects of the Grotesque in Southern Fiction" that her freedom as a writer was always under pressure, since everywhere "the novelist is asked to be the handmaid of his age." She wrote, "Whenever the public is heard from, it is heard demanding a literature which is balanced and which will somehow heal the ravages of our time." This literature, she said elsewhere in this essay, was based on what she called "a realism of fact" — a realism that associated "the only legitimate material for long fiction with the movement of social forces, with the typical, with the fidelity to the way things look and happen in normal life." Such realism, she added, limited both the scope of the imaginative vision of artists and their fiction. As O'Connor noted here and elsewhere, her own fiction was written with a realism of an altogether different sort — a realism that sought not to mirror the typical but to reveal the spiritual. To this end, she says in "Novelist and Believer," the writer "is bound by the reasonable possibilities, not the probabilities of his culture" (*MM,* 46, 39, 165).

If the overall critical environment established its own orthodoxy for fiction, O'Connor also saw general readers establishing their own expectations and demands for what they should experience in the act of reading. She characterized the general readers as being "tired," of wanting what she called at one point "Instant Uplift" — that is, wanting to have their spirits raised in an act of easy compassion and sentiment. This demand for uplift and the redemptive act, O'Connor notes in "Some Aspects of the Grotesque in Southern Fiction," is a characteristic human need, and one that both the storyteller and the listener find particularly compelling in narrative. What bothers O'Connor is not that the reader seeks this motion in fiction but that the reader "has forgotten the cost of it." She explains that the modern reader's "sense of evil is diluted or lacking altogether, and so he has forgotten the price of restoration. When he reads a novel, he wants either his senses tormented or his spirits raised. He wants to be transported, instantly, either to mock damnation or a mock innocence." To underscore the risks the writer takes in ignoring such readers, O'Connor writes in this same essay that there are those who "say that the serious writer doesn't have to bother about the tired reader, but he does, because they are all tired. One old lady who wants her heart uplifted wouldn't be so bad, but you multiply her two hundred and fifty thousand times and what you get is a book club" (*MM*, 165, 48–49).

ABBREVIATIONS

Abbreviations of works by Flannery O'Connor commonly cited in the text refer to the following editions:

CFO — *Conversations with Flannery O'Connor.* Edited by Rosemary M. Magee. Jackson, Miss., 1987.

HB — *The Habit of Being: Letters.* Edited by Sally Fitzgerald. New York, 1969.

MM — *Mystery and Manners: Occasional Prose.* Edited by Sally Fitzgerald and Robert Fitzgerald. New York, 1969.

PG — *The Presence of Grace and Other Book Reviews by Flannery O'Connor.* Compiled by Leo J. Zuber. Edited by Carter W. Martin. Athens, Ga., 1983.

DOROTHY TUCK MCFARLAND

On "Good Country People" *1976*

"Good Country People," the penultimate story in the collection, is something of a comic variation on "A Good Man Is Hard to Find." As the grandmother of the title story thinks of herself as a good Christian woman who believes in all the conventional platitudes, Hulga Hopewell, the Ph.D. in philosophy who is the protagonist of "Good Country People," thinks of herself as a good nihilist who energetically disbelieves in all the conventional platitudes. In their titles both stories implicitly ask the reader to consider what are good men or good people. And in both stories O'Connor uses conventional language for comic and ironic purposes, emphasizing the meaninglessness of the platitudes in the mouths of her characters, and at the same time using their words to sound the main themes of the story. For instance, Hulga's mother, Mrs. Hopewell, characteristically strings together remarks like "Everybody is different. . . . It takes all kinds to make the world. . . . Nothing is perfect." Nevertheless, she actually tolerates differences and imperfections very poorly. Two of the themes in the story grow out of the characters' attitudes toward uniqueness ("everybody is different") and imperfection.

Mrs. Hopewell and her tenant's wife, Mrs. Freeman, embody contrasting ways of looking at the world that provide the frame for the story. Whereas Mrs. Hopewell is determined always to put a smiling face on things and never look beneath the surface, the gimlet-eyed Mrs. Freeman has a fondness for hidden things: "the details of secret infections, hidden deformities, assaults upon children." She is obsessed with the physical demands and ills of the body, and in her conversation about her two daughters she dwells on the details of two major aspects of their physical being: their sexuality and their ailments. One daughter, Glynese, is being courted by several admirers, one of whom is going to chiropractor school and who cures her of a sty by popping her neck. The other daughter, Carramae, is pregnant and unable to "keep anything on her stomach."

Mrs. Hopewell's daughter, Hulga, is antagonized by her mother's platitudinous optimism to the extent that her face has come to wear a look of constant outrage that "obliterated every other expression." She finds Mrs. Freeman tolerable only on the ground that Mrs. Freeman diverts some of her mother's attention from her; otherwise, she is uncomfortable with Mrs. Freeman's fascination with the secrets of the body.

Hulga has rejected the physical world and the life of the body in preference for the life of the mind: "She didn't like dogs or cats or birds or flowers or nature or nice young men. She looked at nice young men as if she could smell their stupidity." Her rejection of the physical world stems from her awareness of its liability to imperfection. Hulga's own imperfection is gross — she lost a leg when she was ten — but O'Connor obviously intended her to be a figure of all mankind, which suffers from the imperfections of the human condition. Hulga insists on calling attention to her physical imperfection and refuses to try to improve her appearance. However, this defensive insistence that she be accepted "LIKE I AM" does not indicate that *she* has really accepted what she is; rather, it suggests that she is trying to insulate herself against the pain of difference and imperfection.

Hulga's choice of her name reflects her response to her condition. Named Joy by her mother, she could not tolerate the incongruity between the idea of joy and her knowledge that she was "dust." She therefore chose to emphasize her deformity and ugliness by assuming an ugly name — Hulga — and a rude manner, and closed herself to joy for the sake of affirming the truth about herself. The persona she creates with the name Hulga is a blind, stony, armored creature. To her mother, the name Hulga suggests the "broad blank hull of a battleship." Hulga herself is described as being "square and rigid-shouldered," and as standing "blank and solid and silent." Her face is characteristically expressionless, and her "icy blue" eyes have the "look of someone who has achieved blindness by an act of will and means to keep it." Though she believes the self she has created is her true self, this imagery suggests that her willful blindness prevents her from seeing the true nature of the human condition as much as does her mother's insistence on always looking "at the bright side of things."

Though she has rejected joy for herself, Hulga has not given up on the possibility of love, and this secret desire is her one area of vulnerability. However, she thinks the persona she has created through her name is a means of making herself invulnerable, so that she can command and control love from a position of strength. She envisions her name working "like the ugly sweating Vulcan who stayed in the furnace and to whom the goddess [of love] had to come when called."

When an apparently naive country boy appears selling Bibles, Hulga feels that he offers no threat to her and allows herself to respond to his open admiration. Despite her utter inexperience (she has never been kissed) she decides to demonstrate her command of love by seducing him. She reinforces her image of herself as a woman of intellectual superiority and worldly wisdom by imagining that the simple Bible salesman, once seduced, will suffer from remorse, whereupon she will take away his shame and "transform it into something useful."

However, the Bible salesman's simplicity seduces her. Having climbed with her into the loft of an isolated barn, the Bible salesman gets Hulga to declare (with some reservations) that she loves him. He then demands that she prove it by showing him where her wooden leg joins on. At first shocked by his proposal, Hulga resists until he tells her why: "because [the wooden leg is] what makes you different." She feels that the Bible salesman, "with an instinct that came from beyond wisdom, had touched the truth about her." She comes to the conclusion that for the first time in her life she has encountered true innocence. She is so moved by her perception of his innocence that she lets down her defenses and allows her hidden vulnerability to emerge.

This area of vulnerability O'Connor equates with Hulga's soul and symbolizes it by her wooden leg: "she was as sensitive about the artificial leg as a peacock about his tail. No one ever touched it but her. She took care of it as someone else would his soul, in private and almost with her own eyes turned away." The leg is also, as the Bible salesman cannily recognized, what makes her different — a difference which, up to now, she has worn defensively and defiantly. Now, for the first time in the story, she accepts her difference, and allows herself to be touched in what is symbolically her soul. Accepting herself, she can surrender herself, and having surrendered herself she finds herself again, in the classic progression of love. When she allows the Bible salesman to remove her leg, "it was like surrendering to him completely. It was like losing her own life and finding it again, miraculously, in his."

Significantly, she surrenders to love in a scene in which her physical grotesqueness is not only emphasized but becomes the very means of love's expression and fulfillment. Though this scene of the Bible salesman removing Hulga's wooden leg is objectively ludicrous (and O'Connor's handling of it is full of irony), Hulga herself is, for the first time, completely without irony. The boy seems to her to be "entirely reverent" as he approaches the leg, and his removal of it is clearly the psychological and emotional equivalent to Hulga of the act of love: "She was thinking that she would run away with him and that every night he would take the leg off and every morning put it back on again."

Hulga's surrender to love also makes her vulnerable to a revelation of her own blindness. She had been convinced that she can see and that others cannot, and that she knows the truth. "Woman!" she had once shouted at her mother, enraged at Mrs. Hopewell's habit of blandly papering over ugliness with smiles. "Do you ever look inside . . . and see what you are *not*?" As a philosopher, Hulga is professionally concerned with truth. She is convinced that she has no illusions, that she has seen through appearances to the nothing that is beneath. "Some of us," she informs the Bible salesman, "have taken off our blindfolds and see that there's nothing to see." And she is utterly convinced of the truth of her assessment of the Bible salesman's innocence.

The Bible salesman, however, is anything but an innocent. Having put Hulga's leg out of her reach, he takes out of his suitcase a hollowed-out Bible containing a flask of whiskey, a deck of pornographic playing cards, and a packet of contraceptives. In response to Hulga's evident dismay, he replies, "What's the matter with you all of a sudden? . . . You just a while ago said you didn't believe in nothing. I thought you was some girl!" When he sees that he will get no farther with her, he snatches up her wooden leg, thrusts it into his suitcase, and disappears down the ladder of the barn loft.

The Bible salesman's thoroughgoing nihilism shows up Hulga's claim to believe in nothing as a superficial intellectual posture. Both his actions and his words devastate her assumption of intellectual superiority: "he turned and regarded her with a look that no longer had any admiration in it. . . . 'And I'll tell you another thing, Hulga,' he said, using the name as if he didn't think much of it, 'you ain't so smart. I been believing in nothing ever since I was born!' "

Hulga is left stranded, her previously stony face "churning" with emotion. But the Bible salesman's destruction of her illusions and her defenses (like the destruction of conventional order that resulted from the grandmother's encounter with The Misfit) may be, for Hulga, the means of her salvation. That the Bible salesman might be a kind of savior is suggested in the description of Hulga's final glimpse of him. Looking out the window of the barn loft, she sees him making his way across the pasture. O'Connor implicitly compares him to Christ walking on the water; to Hulga's blurred vision (the Bible salesman has also taken her glasses), he seems to be "struggling successfully over the green speckled lake."

The actual or implied references to Christ in *A Good Man Is Hard to Find* are numerous. The climactic moment in the title story comes about after The Misfit expresses his intense concern over the question of whether or not Jesus raised the dead. . . . The Bible salesman in "Good Country People" is implicitly compared to Christ.

Christ, as Simeon prophesied in St. Luke's gospel, is a "sign that will be contradicted," a sign of the presence of God in the world that, to many, will not seem to be a sign of God at all — will seem, rather, its opposite. The unexpected and often grotesque and incongruous ways in which O'Connor felt Christ to be present in the world is, I think, the real subject of this collection. Not only is the image of Christ suggested in unlikely places or associated with unlikely characters; but in style as well the stories embody contradiction and incongruity — in the double point of view, in the mixture of comedy and horror, in the pervasive tone of emotional flatness and irony, on the one hand, and the intimations of depth and serious meaning on the other. Thematically and stylistically, the centrality of Christ — of that which we experience as contradictory — provides *A Good Man Is Hard to Find* with a unity that makes it more than simply a random collection of stories. . . . I would add another gloss on the meaning of the title: the good man is so hard to find because he appears in such unlikely guises, because he is hidden in irony and contradiction.

WAYNE C. BOOTH

A Rhetorical Reading of O'Connor's "Everything That Rises Must Converge" 1974

This is an extremely complex story, not only in its ironic undercuttings but in its affirmations. No reading of it can be considered adequate unless it somehow relates the curious title to the various attempts to "rise" and to the failures to "converge." In the web of inference that we must create to see the story whole, our running translation of Julian's judgments into alternative judgments is only one strand. But once we have discerned that strand clearly, the rest of the story gives few difficulties.

Since Julian's is the only mind offering us opinions (except for a few observations and metaphors from the narrator, most notably the final sentence), we must sooner or later decide how far we can trust him. It is not hard to see that he is unreliable about many things. "He never spoke of it without contempt or thought of it without longing" — what kind of man is it, we ask, who always belies his true feelings? His life is full of such contradictions, showing that in his own way he is as far out of touch with reality as he takes his mother to be. His radical self-deception is perhaps clearest in the long fantasy that begins when he "withdraws into the inner compartment of his mind where he spent most of his time." No one could misread his own character more thoroughly than Julian does in thinking that he has "turned out so well," that he has a "first rate education," that he has a "large" mind, that he is "free of prejudice and unafraid to face facts" — remember, this is the boy who "did not like to consider all she did for him" and who can take pride in having "cut himself emotionally free of her." The closer we look at the disharmonies among his various opinions and actions, the more vigorously we must work in reconstructing the terrible lost young man we see behind his self-defensive rhetoric. His childish efforts to hurt his mother begin in a comic light, as he poses like a martyr and does everything he possibly can to spoil her one pleasant time of the week. But the comedy slowly gives place to pathos and horror as he runs over in his mind the possible tortures he might subject her to, then enjoys her humiliation about the duplicate hat, and finally — so wrapped up in his own petty bitterness and futility that he cannot see what is in front of his eyes — shouts irony-laden insults at the stricken woman. "You aren't who you think you are," he says, summarizing himself as much as his mother. "You've got to live in the new world and face a few realities for a change. Buck up, it won't kill you." It *is* killing her, and *he* is the one who must now begin to "face a few realities for a change."

These disharmonies are simple and clear. But the reconstruction of what "the realities" are — of what Julian must face — is not so easy. It is obviously not to be found in the "unreal," absurdly "innocent" world of the class-bound mother, nor in the equally unreal and absurd but vicious world of Julian. One kind of unmistakable reality is found in the irreducible, often harsh details of the life that Julian and his mother encounter but cannot see because of the abstractions that blur their vision. The mother does not see real "Negroes," for example, only the stereotypes that her childhood has provided her with. But Julian does not see real people either; instead he sees only the stereotypes that his liberal opinions dictate. Similarly, neither of them can see the other: Julian cannot see his mother for what she is; she cannot see what a miserable failure she has helped to create in him.

Our question then becomes: is there some ordering of values that for this story constitutes an alternative reality, one that in a sense judges everything the characters do? Our knowledge that Flannery O'Connor was known as a devout Catholic, or even that she herself talked about her stories in religious terms, can only alert us to one possible direction of interpretation. She might, after all, write one story that was entirely different from the others; for all I know, independently of my reading, she could have written this one before being converted, or after losing her faith. Even the most detailed knowledge about the author's life and statements of purpose can only alert me to certain possibilities; I must finally ask what kinds of clues the story itself provides to aid in the task of reconstructing a world of values that contrast with Julian's inanities.

The curious title is itself a kind of warning that seems to be spoken, as it were, in a special tone of voice. It simply does not harmonize easily with most of the surface, and indeed at first hardly makes sense at all. Does everything that "rises" in the story "converge"? Hardly. The black characters are "rising," but in spite of the liberal platitudes of Julian, there is no sign in the story that in their rising they will converge with the whites or with each other; one must thus ask whether or in what limited sense they are rising at all. Julian's liberal abstractions lead him to expect all Negroes to want his sympathy and interest, and to conform to his stereotyped demand that they "rise" to "talk on subjects that would be *above* the comprehension of those around him." But they insist on dwelling in a totally inaccessible world.

Julian has been "rising," too, as he obtains what he likes to think was a "first-class education." But his sense of elevation has, obviously, separated him not only from his mother but from all of his roots, without providing him with any other allegiances that could possibly support the claim of the title. What, then, can the title mean? It does not help us much to learn that it comes from the works of Teilhard de Chardin, the Catholic priest whose scientific and theological speculations earned him the accusation of heresy.

Is there any genuine change in the story that could be considered a "rising"? There is one, indeed, if we take seriously the change in Julian produced by the catastrophe. Julian is not just nasty and petty throughout the story; he is totally absorbed in his own ego. In contrast to his mother, who is "innocent," he is corrupt. Her desire is not to do ill in the world, but good, and only the limitations of what Julian calls her "fantasy world" betray her. But Julian, as we discover him behind his rationalizations, is actually malevolent, totally incapable of "converging" with the interests of any other person. His thoughts run constantly on his hatred of the world and his desire to "justify" himself in ways that he knows will hurt his mother deeply. "He would be entirely justified [in bringing home a Negro wife] but her blood pressure would rise to 300. He could not push her to the extent of making her have a stroke, and moreover, he had never been successful at making any Negro friends."

Throughout his absurd but vicious fantasies there thus run clues that prepare us for his discovery at the end. "For a moment he had an uncomfortable sense of her *innocence,* but it lasted only a second before *principle* rescued him. *Justice* entitled him to laugh." Dimly aware of her "innocence," passionately devoted to proving his own "principles" and obtaining "justice," he can be touched only by the greatest of disasters. Having never once been genuinely touched by any trouble, having in fact used his mother and her innocence as a shield against knowledge of himself, he is at last "stricken," "stunned." The change in him is as startling as the physical change produced in her by the stroke which he has helped to induce: "Darling, sweetheart, wait!" He is "crumpled," crushed into letting his defenses down and trying, too late, to call to his mother in love.

It would probably be a mistake to see anything strongly affirmative in this final dropping of all his egotistical defenses and crying "Mamma, mamma." He has not risen very far, but as he watches her destruction, falls at her side, and then runs for help, there has been, at last, a "convergence," a meeting of two human wills, that *might* presage his genuine "entry into the world of guilt and sorrow." For the Julian we have known throughout the story to experience either genuine guilt or sorrow would be a "rise" indeed, a rise based on the final convergence. The honest nightmare of his nothingness moving into "nowhere" in the final paragraph is thus a great improvement — in the light of this view of reality we now share with the implied author — over the "mental bubble" in which he established himself, where "he was safe from any kind of penetration from without." In his bubble he had been able to "see her with absolute clarity," or so he thought. Now, at the end, his bubble has been penetrated; he is swept by a "tide of darkness," and we are led to feel that he is for the first time in a position from which some sort of genuine human life is conceivable.

Whether this interpretation is sound or not, it certainly is never stated. Except for the ending, most of the words report Julian's misguided thoughts without open correction, and they must consequently be reconstructed. But they are not translated into a message.

There is perhaps no absolute need to go further than this. Readers of many different faiths and anti-faiths can presumably participate in this story of punishment and discovery, without pushing toward any special meaning for words like sin, innocence, faith, realities, guilt, and sorrow. But those of us who have read many of Flannery O'Connor's stories and studied her life will be unable to resist seeing Julian's final problematic redemption as presented in a religious light, even a specifically Roman Catholic light. Once the story is reread from this point of view, many additional ironies accumulate, ranging from Julian's name and his saintly posings at the beginning to the gratuitousness of grace at the end. But Flannery O'Connor was eager to write stories that were not mere allegories; as she intended, this story can be experienced by anyone who catches the essential contrast among the three systems of norms, Julian's, his mother's, and the cluster of traditional, conventional values we share with the author. Though it may seem thinner to those for whom Julian's self-absorption and cruelty are judged in secular terms than for a Catholic who sees him as in mortal sin, the structure of experience will be the same for both: Everyone will be forced to reject all or most of what the words seem to say. At every point we must decide on one out of many possible reconstructions, on the basis of a set of unshakable but silent beliefs that we are expected to share (however fleetingly) with the author. No one who fails to discern and feel some sympathy for these beliefs — only a few of them specifically Roman Catholic — is likely to make very much of the story.

For readers who do see behind Julian's absurd and egotistical words, the energy devoted to the act of seeing will of course increase the emotional effect and thus their estimate of the story's worth. This will not necessarily lead them to agree with me that it is a first-class story. But if they like it at all, the force of their liking will have been strengthened by their active engagement with the ironies.

ꕥ

PART THREE

POETRY

■ *The poem may embody perception so luminous it seems truth, but what keeps it alive is not fixed discovery but the means of discovery; what keeps it alive is intelligence.*

– Louise Glück

■ *Poetry is the supreme fiction.*

– Wallace Stevens

7

WHAT IS A POEM?

The universe of poetry is the universe of emotional truth.
– MURIEL RUKEYSER, from *The Life of Poetry*

Just as it is important to begin reading short stories with some idea of what a short story is, we should begin reading poetry with some idea of what we mean by poetry. What is poetry and what is a poem? The poet Emily Dickinson, when she was asked in a letter how she knew something she had read was poetry, answered,

> If I read a book and it makes my whole body so cold no fire can ever warm me, I know that it is poetry. If I feel physically as if the top of my head were taken off, I know that it is poetry. These are the only ways I know it. Is there any other way?

It is not necessary for you as a reader to have such a strong emotional response to a poem in order to enjoy it, but as you begin to know more about poetry, you will also understand some of what she felt.

You will find, as you begin your study of poetry, that it is not so simple to say just what a poem is, but this is also true of other things that can give us the feeling that the tops of our heads have been taken off. Often when rock musicians are asked by interviewers to define rock and roll, they answer, without hesitation, "That's the kind of music I play." Their answer echoes the response of the American poet Robert Frost, who, when he was asked what poetry was, shrugged, "Poetry is the kind of thing that poets write."

Part of the difficulty of finding a simple definition of poetry is that there has been so much of it. Poetry is our oldest language art. Only drama, which probably emerged two centuries later, takes us as far back into antiquity. The novel, with its history of only three or four hundred years, and the short story, with its history of less than two hundred years, are newcomers compared with poetry. In Asia and in the eastern Mediterranean and Europe, poetry has had an unbroken line of expression for almost three thousand years, and the way we define poetry would have changed as societies and poetry itself changed during these millennia.

Many poets have felt the need to define poetry, and often they use the medium of poetry to describe what it is they create. In the famous poem "Ars Poetica," the American writer Archibald MacLeish tells us that poetry is not something to be explained or analyzed, that a poem can tell the story of grief simply by showing us "An empty doorway and a maple leaf."

ARCHIBALD MACLEISH

Ars Poetica

1926

A poem should be palpable and mute
As a globed fruit

Dumb
As old medallions to the thumb

Silent as the sleeve-worn stone
Of casement ledges where the moss has grown —

A poem should be wordless
As the flight of birds

■

A poem should be motionless in time
As the moon climbs

Leaving, as the moon releases
Twig by twig the night-entangled trees,

Leaving, as the moon behind the winter leaves,
Memory by memory the mind —

A poem should be motionless in time
As the moon climbs

■

A poem should be equal to:
Not true

For all the history of grief
An empty doorway and a maple leaf

For love
The leaning grasses and two lights above the sea —

A poem should not mean
But be.

In a poem titled simply "Poetry," Marianne Moore attempts to state her idea of what a poem should be. A poem, as she says, is "a place for the genuine," and she scolds writers who let themselves forget that it is a direct, real experience that must go into a poem. To her, the greatness of poetry is that it can cross the boundary between our inner emotions and something outside ourselves that can reawaken these emotions. In her unforgettable phrase, a poem "can present / for inspection, 'imaginary gardens with real toads in them.' . . ."

Marianne Moore

Poetry

1921, 1935

I, too, dislike it: there are things that are important beyond all this fiddle.
   Reading it, however, with a perfect contempt for it, one discovers in
   it after all, a place for the genuine.
      Hands that can grasp, eyes
      that can dilate, hair that can rise
         if it must, these things are important not because a
high-sounding interpretation can be put upon them but because they are
   useful. When they become so derivative as to become unintelligible,
   the same thing may be said for all of us, that we
      do not admire what
      we cannot understand: the bat
         holding on upside down or in quest of something to
eat, elephants pushing, a wild horse taking a roll, a tireless wolf under
   a tree, the immovable critic twitching his skin like a horse that feels a
            flea, the base-
   ball fan, the statistician —
      nor is it valid
         to discriminate against "business documents and
school-books";[1] all these phenomena are important. One must make a
            distinction
   however: when dragged into prominence by half poets, the result is
            not poetry,
   nor till the poets among us can be
      "literalists of
      the imagination"[2] — above
         insolence and triviality and can present

■ ■ ■

[1]Diary of Tolstoy (Dutton), p. 84. "Where the boundary between prose and poetry lies, I shall never be able to understand. The question is raised in manuals of style, yet the answer to it lies beyond me. Poetry is verse; prose is not verse. Or else poetry is everything with the exception of business documents and school books." [Moore's note]

[2]Yeats's *Ideas of Good and Evil* (A. H. Bullen), p. 182. "The limitation of his view was from the very intensity of his vision; he was a too literal realist of imagination, as others are of nature; and because he believed that the figures seen by the mind's eye, when exalted by inspiration, were 'eternal existences,' symbols of divine essences, he hated every grace of style that might obscure their lineaments." [Moore's note]

for inspection, "imaginary gardens with real toads in them," shall we have
   it. In the meantime, if you demand on the one hand,
   the raw material of poetry in
      all its rawness and
      that which is on the other hand
         genuine, then you are interested in poetry.

In this version of her poem, however, Moore may have felt that she had given away too many of a poet's secrets, or that she might have been stating something that was too obvious to need explaining. For whatever reason, when she printed it again several years later in her *Collected Poems,* she trimmed it down to the lines she felt were essential. The poem as she published it then reads simply,

I, too, dislike it.
   Reading it, however, with a perfect contempt for it, one discovers in
      it, after all, a place for the genuine.

As Moore made very clear (and you should remember this as you study poetry), poets have their own reasons for whatever they do.

Even if they haven't written a poem in their concern with defining their art, poets often attempt a definition that is as lyric and as distinctive as their poetry. For Carl Sandburg poetry is "a series of explanations of life, fading off into horizons too swift for explanations." Robert Frost's well-known, no-nonsense description of poetry is "a momentary stay against confusion." To William Carlos Williams, a poet concerned with the "things" named in a poem, a poem is "a machine made out of words." The contemporary poet Louise Glück tells us, "The poem may embody perception so luminous it seems truth, but what keeps it alive is not fixed discovery but the means of discovery; what keeps it alive is intelligence," while for Wallace Stevens, "Poetry is the supreme fiction."

Descriptions like these tell us a great deal about the poet, and the poems by Archibald MacLeish and Marianne Moore suggest many things about poetry itself, but we still don't have a definition. Perhaps a useful way to begin is to turn to a dictionary, where we find definitions that tell us something very specific about what a poem is. A dictionary will tell us that "a poem is a metrical composition of elevated tone depicting an emotional or philosophical truth." If you keep a definition like this in mind when you begin reading poetry, you will find it is a useful tool. The term *metrical composition* tells us to expect a poem's formal structure to be based on a rhythmic pattern of words and syllables that we can hear and anticipate. The term *elevated tone* tells us that a poem can use a different kind of language, or if it uses everyday speech it can use these words in ways that give them a special — "elevated" — significance. The term *emotional or philosophical truth* tells us that poetry can touch our deepest emotions.

As you begin studying poetry you will find it helpful to separate a poem into two parts. The first part is the emotion or the insight at the heart of the poem. This is called the **theme**. You should remember, however, that the theme of the poem is not necessarily the **subject** of the poem. The subject of the poem may be the writer's pet cat, but the theme of the poem is the writer's pleasure in everyday things that the cat symbolizes.

The second part of what you should think of as you read poetry consists of the elements of formal structure and "poetic" language, what we can call the **means** of the poem. A poet's means are the rhythms and verbal wordplay, the kind of language, the poetic form, the suggestions of the other poems or paintings or music that are there for poets to use as they write. These resources are sometimes called the *elements* of poetry, but if we use the term *means*, it also suggests that these elements are what poets *use* as they write.

With these tools, the theme and the means, you will find that you can enjoy more fully any of the poems you will be reading. Remember that these two aspects of a poem work each in different ways. The themes of poems come from within the poet's own personality. They can be the poet's thoughts, dreams, disappointments, or joys, or responses to someone else's thoughts, dreams, disappointments, or joys. The themes of a poem are also our shared experience of life. Because they come from our common humanity, they are continually renewed.

The means of poetry, however, are bound into the moment in time when each poem is written. They draw from the language and the social attitudes, the poetic traditions, and the background of the poets' lives and the moments in history when they lived. This is why you will find that poems from different times with the same themes — perhaps the poet's disappointment at the end of a love affair or the definition of poetry itself — will be expressed in different languages and forms, each a reflection of its own time and place.

As we have seen, poets often turn their thoughts about poetry into poems. This poem by San Francisco writer Lawrence Ferlinghetti describes the emotions that some poets feel as they write.

LAWRENCE FERLINGHETTI

Constantly Risking Absurdity

1955–58

Constantly risking absurdity
                                        and death
    whenever he performs
                              above the heads
                                             of his audience
    the poet like an acrobat
                         climbs on rime
                                        to a high wire of his own making
and balancing on eyebeams
                              above a sea of faces
    paces his way
                    to the other side of day

performing entrechats
and sleight-of-foot tricks
and other high theatrics
and all without mistaking
any thing
for what it may not be
For he's the super realist
who must perforce perceive
taut truth
before the taking of each stance or step
in his supposed advance
toward that still higher perch
where Beauty stands and waits
with gravity
to start her death-defying leap
And he
a little charleychaplin man
who may or may not catch
her fair eternal form
spreadeagled in the empty air
of existence

Sometimes poets describe what they do in phrases that are poems in themselves. The English poet Percy Bysshe Shelley wrote, "A poet is a nightingale, who sits in darkness and sings to cheer its own solitude with sweet sounds." Robert Frost tells us, "The figure a poem makes. It begins in delight and ends in wisdom." When poets write about their art they usually are serious. If they are in the mood, however, they can be half-serious. Tobey Hiller, who lives and works in Oakland, California, pretends in "The Poem" that she cannot find anything useful about poems — until the last lines, in which she tells us that with a poem we can fly above the ordinary experience of everyday life. The Alice she refers to in the title is the main character in Lewis Carroll's *Alice in Wonderland.*

TOBEY HILLER

The Poem — *1987*

(or, Alice's Remarks on Reading the Fine Print on the Bottle's Label)

Can it walk, or talk,
or do the mambo?

Will it set off, sleek,
and neigh its way to Mexico?

Provide a shade against the sun?
Cure freckles? Siphon sadness?

■ ■ ■

Recited right, won't it turn the curl of waves acrylic,
cast sunsets into glass,

make grass grow green
upon a desert page?

Perhaps you're hoping
it will turn the t.v. off.

Or make the kids grow up un-mumbling
and acquainted with the phases of the moon.

Perhaps it does a trick
with eyes, closing them, or opening.

But don't confuse it with a pear.
You wouldn't try to eat it, would you?

Remember that only angels can make hair and wings
and finger-nails out of the alphabet.

What we make is all flight.

Finally, in her poem "I Said to Poetry," Alice Walker, author of the novel *The Color Purple,* protests against the power that poetry has over her life, with its insistence on waking her in the night with lines that demand to be written and emotions that must be expressed. In the end, as she wryly admits, it is poetry that has the upper hand.

Alice Walker

I Said to Poetry

1984

I said to Poetry: 'I'm finished
with you.'
Having to almost die
before some weird light
comes creeping through
is no fun.
'No thank you, Creation,
no muse need apply.
I'm out for good times —
at the very least,
some painless convention.'

Poetry laid back
and played dead
until this morning.
I wasn't sad or anything,
only restless.

Poetry said: 'You remember
the desert, and how glad you were

that you have an eye
to see it with? You remember
that, if ever so slightly?'
I said: 'I didn't hear that.
Besides, it's five o'clock in the a.m.
I'm not getting up
in the dark
to talk to you.'

Poetry said: 'But think about the time
you saw the moon
over that small canyon
that you liked much better
than the grand one — and how surprised you were
that the moonlight was green
and you still had
one good eye
to see it with.

Think of that!'
'I'll join the church!' I said,
huffily, turning my face to the wall.
'I'll learn how to pray again!'

'Let me ask you,' said Poetry.
'When you pray, what do you think
you'll see?'

Poetry had me.

'There's no paper
in this room,' I said.
'And that new pen I bought
makes a funny noise.'

'Bullshit,' said Poetry.
'Bullshit,' said I.

RELATED COMMENTARIES: *Ralph Waldo Emerson, From "The Poet," page 1168; Louise Glück, "Poems* Are *Autobiography," page 1175.*

8

THE ELEMENTS OF POETRY: A POET'S MEANS

A word is dead
When it is said,
Some say.
I say it just
Begins to live
That day.
– EMILY DICKINSON

WORDS AND THEIR SOUND

When we first read a poem it is almost always its subject and theme that stir our interest. We ask ourselves, "What is the poem about?" If the poem is about something that concerns us, then we will read it. There are, however, many poems that deal with the same basic themes, since poetry draws up its materials from the well of our deepest emotions. What is it that makes us say one poem is beautiful and another poem is not, even if each poem describes the same feeling or emotional mood? The pleasure is in the *means* the poet has used to present the theme: the sound of the words, the rhythms of the lines, the vividness of the images. If we have some familiarity with these means, or formal elements of poetry, our understanding and enjoyment of the poem will be greatly increased.

Alliteration and Assonance

One of the simplest — and earliest — ways poets use the sound of words to structure their writing is what is called **alliteration**. Alliteration is the repetition of the same sounding letters. If it is the first letter that is repeated, and the letter is a consonant, it is called **initial alliteration**. This is the easiest form of alliteration to recognize, and people often use it for a humorous effect. "Little Lyle lies longingly on the lawn," is one example, or "Susan sat sewing sister's smock." Poets have generally used it more subtly, but alliteration was a common effect in the earliest poetry in English. *Beowulf,* from the beginning of the eighth century, is the first poem composed in what was to become the English language, and it uses a style based on alliteration.

Closely related to alliteration is **assonance**, the repetition of vowel sounds within a phrase. It can be an elusive effect, sometimes difficult to recognize. Its most obvious form is a phrase like "Opacity opens up rooms," with its repetition of *o* sounds, from Amy Clampitt's poem "Fog." In the hands of a skilled poet, assonance can be an effective means to shade the meaning of the poem. In the opening lines of the poem listen to the sound of the letter *o* as it is repeated several times:

> A vagueness comes over everything,
> as though proving color and contour
> alike dispensable. . . .

If you read the lines carefully, you also can hear the alliteration of the *c* consonants of "color and contour." Clampitt has used both alliteration and assonance so skillfully that you can enjoy her use of words as you read the entire poem. In the second verse, which begins "Tactile / definition, however, has not been / totally banished," she is saying that even though the fog has made everything vague, objects still can be felt, that they are "tactile." Clampitt loved to use unfamiliar words in her poetry, and here she has given us "panicled," which is a botanical term to describe the way the kernels of blossom and seed are distributed irregularly on the stem of certain grasses and grains, like oats. Georgia O'Keeffe, mentioned in the last verse, was an American painter who in some of her canvases caught the effect of a "hueless moonflower / corolla."

Amy Clampitt

Fog

1985

A vagueness comes over everything,
as though proving color and contour
alike dispensable: the lighthouse
extinct, the islands' spruce-tips
drunk up like milk in the
universal emulsion; houses
reverting into the lost
and forgotten; granite
subsumed, a rumor
in a mumble of ocean.
                                Tactile
definition, however, has not been
totally banished: hanging
tassel by tassel, panicled
foxtail and needlegrass,

dropseed, furred hawkweed,
and last season's rose-hips
are vested in silenced
chimes of the finest,
clearest sea-crystal.
                    Opacity
opens up rooms, a showcase
for the hueless moonflower
corolla, as Georgia
O'Keeffe might have seen it,
of foghorns; the nodding
campanula of bell buoys;
the ticking, linear
filigree of bird voices.

Onomatopoeia

Another effect that a writer can employ using the sound of words is called **onomatopoeia**. The word is derived from Greek roots, meaning "to make names," which implies that the word is made up to describe the sound. Onomatopoeia means that a word can "sound" like the noise it describes. *Bang!* is an easy example, or if you want a bigger sound, *Boom!* Comic books are a treasure trove of onomatopoeia. How about *Pow!, Splat!, Zap!, RaTaTat!, Ping!,* and *Who-o-o-sh?* One American poet who used onomatopoeia effectively was Vachel Lindsay, who performed his poetry in informal readings across the United States in the early years of the century. Read aloud the opening line of his poem about the founder of the Salvation Army, William S. Booth:

Booth led boldly with his big bass drum. . . .

Using alliteration and onomatopoeia, Lindsay catches the sound of a Salvation Army drum with the clamorous tone of the words. In a very different example, Amy Clampitt, in the last lines of "Fog," suggests the delicate sound of "the ticking, linear / filigree of bird voices."

Rhyme

Of all the means the poet has to work with that come out of the sound of words, none of them is more familiar to us than **rhyme**. For hundreds of years part of the definition of poetry was that it rhymed. When other poets began to break away from rhyme in the early part of this century, the American poet Robert Frost, who wrote in traditional rhymed styles, growled that writing poetry without rhyme was like "playing tennis with the net down." Although there is a kind of rhyme called **eye rhyme**, which means that two words look as though they would sound alike, but the sound, if spoken aloud, is different (for example, *house* and *rouse* or *tough* and *though*), the essence of rhyme is a similarity of sound.

Two kinds of rhyme — **perfect rhyme** and **near** or **slant rhyme** — define most of what we mean by the term. The type of rhyme you recognize most in your reading is perfect rhyme. Some of the most common perfect rhymes have been used so often that they have become clichés: *moon* and *June, sigh* and *cry, dream* and *scheme.* In perfect rhyme the sound of the two words is exactly alike, and if the poet can avoid the expected or the commonplace rhyme, the effect can be exciting in itself. The most familiar use of rhyme is called **end rhyme**, in which the words at the end of the line rhyme.

One of the masters of rhymed verse in English was A. E. Housman. Here are two of his best-known poems, each of which is an excellent example of the use of perfect rhyme.

A. E. Housman

Loveliest of trees, the cherry now

1896

Loveliest of trees, the cherry now
Is hung with bloom along the bough,
And stands about the woodland ride
Wearing white for eastertide.
Now, of my three score years and ten,
Twenty will not come again,
And take from seventy springs a score,
It only leaves me fifty more.
And since to look at things in bloom
Fifty springs are little room,
About the woodlands I will go
To see the cherry hung with snow.

A. E. Housman

When I was one-and-twenty

1896

When I was one-and-twenty
    I heard a wise man say,
"Give crowns and pounds and guineas
    But not your heart away;
Give pearls away and rubies
    But keep your fancy free."
But I was one-and-twenty,
    No use to talk to me.

When I was one-and-twenty
    I heard him say again,

"The heart out of the bosom
   Was never given in vain;
'Tis paid with sighs a-plenty
   And sold for endless rue."
And I am two-and-twenty,
   And oh, 'tis true, 'tis true.

Poets who write rhymed verse can benefit from pleasure that readers feel as they anticipate the sound of the rhyme, but this way of writing also has disadvantages. Because each line closes with a rhyme, the repeated pattern can begin to leave the reader feeling that the rhyme is interrupting the poem's flow of ideas and imagery. Perfect rhyme can become monotonous, and the need to find a rhyme can force the poet into an awkward word order or sentences that are muddy and unclear.

Poets have devised many strategies to deal with this problem, such as working with subtle differences in the sound of the rhyming words. They discovered they could vary the sound and have a little more flexibility to shape their lines if they used near rhymes or slant rhymes. With this kind of rhyme the sound of the two words is close but not exact. Examples of near rhyme are pairs of words like *read* and *red, seal* and *sail, ball* and *bell.*

In her well-known poem "Not Waving but Drowning," Stevie Smith, a modern English poet, consciously used near rhyme to mirror the pathos of a drowning man whose waving people thought was only "larking," or showing his high spirits. The truth is that his waving was a desperate signal for help.

STEVIE SMITH

Not Waving but Drowning

1957

Nobody heard him, the dead man,
But still he lay moaning:
I was much further out than you thought
And not waving but drowning.

Poor chap, he always loved larking
And now he's dead
It must have been too cold for him his heart gave way,
They said.

Oh, no, no, no, it was too cold always
(Still the dead one lay moaning)
I was much too far out all my life
And not waving but drowning.

Smith was a skilled poet, and she certainly could have found a perfect rhyme for the first and last stanzas of the poem, but instead she gives us "moaning," to rhyme with "drowning," a half rhyme that suggests everything that was half successful about the man's life.

Two other terms are also used in discussing rhyme: **masculine rhyme** and **feminine rhyme**. Words are pronounced in syllables, and some syllables are given more emphasis than others. The strong syllable is called an **accent**, and we will be talking more about accents when we discuss the rhythms of poetry. Masculine rhyme means that the accent on the rhyming words is on a final strong syllable. *Stay* and *away, bells* and *foretells, otherwise* and *guise* are masculine rhymes. In a feminine rhyme, the accent on the rhyming words is on a weak syllable. *Season* and *reason, tower* and *flower, thunder* and *wonder* are feminine rhymes.

You will sometimes notice that a poet uses rhyme in the middle of the line as well as the end. This is called **internal rhyme**. This example is from "Blow, Bugle, Blow" by the nineteenth-century English poet Alfred, Lord Tennyson. The internal rhyme occurs in the first and third lines:

> The splendor *falls* on castle *walls*
> And snowy summits old in story:
> The long light *shakes* across the *lakes*
> And the wild cataract leaps in glory.

There are two other terms that help describe what happens at the ends of the lines in a poem. If the meaning of the line comes to a definite end, it is called **end-stopped**; if the meaning does not end but continues on to the next line, it is called **enjambed**. The noun for this running of one line into another line is **enjambment**. Here is an example of end-stopped lines:

> I long to hear love's gentle tune.
> I only mourn it ends so soon.

Here is an example of enjambed lines:

> Oh, to feel the soft, soft touch of spring
> again, and the April softness it will bring!

Usually the poet tries only for a rhyme with one syllable, but many multisyllabic words are also useful as rhymes, like *September* and *remember, despair* and *aware.* During the centuries when most poets were concerned with rhyme they often looked for complicated rhymes to show off their skill with language. A famous example is the two-line poem the English poet John Dryden sent to a patron whose family name was Cadwallader. His patron had promised to send him a rabbit for supper, and when it did not appear, Dryden sent him a note in rhyme:

> Oh thou son of great Cadwallader
> Hast thou my hare, or hast thou swallowed her?

Although most poetry today is written without rhyme, many poets still turn to this most basic of poetic means to strengthen a poem's structure or to add another level of verbal dexterity to the poem's pleasures. This poem by Marianne Moore mixes rhyming lines with lines that are not rhymed. The first and third lines of each verse rhyme, as do each verse's final two lines. The final rhymes are a good example of a skilled poet's use of unexpected word combinations — *others/stirs, surrendering/continuing, mortality/eternity.* As you read the poem you will find many examples of enjambed lines, and you should also note the remarkable sentence that begins at the end of the third line with *And whence* and doesn't end until eight lines later, when it finally winds down in the opening line of the second verse, *the soul to be strong.*

MARIANNE MOORE

What Are Years?

1939

What is our innocence,
what is our guilt? All are
naked, none is safe. And whence
is courage: the unanswered question,
the resolute doubt —
dumbly calling, deafly listening — that
in misfortune, even death,
encourages others
and in its defeat, stirs

the soul to be strong? He
sees deep and is glad, who
accedes to mortality
and in his imprisonment rises
upon himself as
the sea in a chasm, struggling to be
free and unable to be,
in its surrendering
finds its continuing.

So he who strongly feels,
behaves. The very bird,
grown taller as he sings, steels
his form straight up. Though he is captive,
his mighty singing
says, satisfaction is a lowly
thing, how pure a thing is joy.
This is mortality,
this is eternity.

Poems for Further Reading

SIR THOMAS WYATT

They Flee from Me

1557

They flee from me, that sometime did me seek,
With naked foot stalking in my chamber.
I have seen them, gentle, tame, and meek,
That now are wild, and do not remember
That sometime they put themselves in danger
To take bread at my hand; and now they range,
Busily seeking with a continual change.

Thanked be Fortune it hath been otherwise,
Twenty times better; but once in special,
In thin array, after a pleasant guise,
When her loose gown from her shoulders did fall,
And she me caught in her arms long and small,
And therewith all sweetly did me kiss
And softly said, "Dear heart, how like you this?"

It was no dream, I lay broad waking.
But all is turned, thorough° my gentleness, *through*
Into a strange fashion of forsaking;
And I have leave to go, of her goodness,
And she also to use newfangleness.
But since that I so kindely am served,
I fain would know what she hath deserved.

BEN JONSON

On My First Son

1616

Farewell, thou child of my right hand,° and joy;
My sin was too much hope of thee, loved boy:
Seven years thou'wert lent to me, and I thee pay,
Exacted by thy fate, on the just day.°
Oh, could I lose all father now! for why
Will man lament the state he should envy,
To have so soon 'scaped world's and flesh's rage,

1. child of my right hand: The literal translation of the Hebrew name *Benjamin;* Jonson's first son. **4. the just day:** A reference to Benjamin's death on his seventh birthday.

And, if no other misery, yet age?
Rest in soft peace, and asked, say, "Here doth lie
Ben Jonson his best piece of poetry."
For whose sake henceforth all his vows be such
As what he loves may never like too much.

JOHN DONNE

Song

1633

Go and catch a falling star,
  Get with child a mandrake root,°
Tell me where all past years are,
  Or who cleft the Devil's foot,
Teach me to hear mermaids singing,
Or to keep off envy's stinging,
    And find
    What wind
Serves to advance an honest mind.

If thou beest born to strange sights,
  Things invisible to see,
Ride ten thousand days and nights,
  Till age snow white hairs on thee.
Thou, when thou return'st, wilt tell me
All strange wonders that befell thee,
    And swear
    Nowhere
Lives a woman true, and fair.

If thou find'st one, let me know,
  Such a pilgrimage were sweet;
Yet do not, I would not go,
  Though at next door we might meet;
Though she were true when you met her,
And last till you write your letter,
    Yet she
    Will be
False, ere I come, to two, or three.

---

2. mandrake root: A plant with a forked root that resembles the lower part of the female anatomy. Folk legend holds that the mandrake shrieks when uprooted and the sound is death to the hearer.

Robert Herrick

To the Virgins, to Make Much of Time

1648

Gather ye rosebuds while ye may,
Old time is still a-flying;
And this same flower that smiles today
Tomorrow will be dying.

The glorious lamp of heaven, the sun,
The higher he's a-getting,
The sooner will his race be run,
And nearer he's to setting.

That age is best which is the first,
When youth and blood are warmer;
But being spent, the worse, and worst
Times still succeed the former.

Then be not coy, but use your time,
And, while ye may, go marry;
For, having lost but once your prime,
You may forever tarry.

Richard Lovelace

To Lucasta, Going to the Wars

1649

Tell me not, sweet, I am unkind
That from the nunnery
Of thy chaste breast and quiet mind,
To war and arms I fly.

True, a new mistress now I chase,
The first foe in the field;
And with a stronger faith embrace
A sword, a horse, a shield.

Yet this inconstancy is such
As you too shall adore;
I could not love thee, dear, so much,
Loved I not honor more.

George Herbert

Easter Wings

1633

Lord, who createdst man in wealth and store,°
Though foolishly he lost the same,
Decaying more and more
Till he became
Most poor:
With thee
O let me rise
As larks, harmoniously,
And sing this day thy victories:
Then shall the fall further the flight in me.

My tender age in sorrow did begin:
And still with sicknesses and shame
Thou didst so punish sin,
That I became
Most thin.
With thee
Let me combine,
And feel this day thy victory;
For, if I imp° my wing on thine,
Affliction shall advance the flight in me.

Edgar Allan Poe

To Helen

1831

Helen, thy beauty is to me
Like those Nicean° barks of yore,
That gently, o'er a perfumed sea
The weary, way-worn wanderer bore
To his own native shore.

On desperate seas long wont to roam,
Thy hyacinth° hair, thy classic face
Thy Naiad° airs have brought me home
To the glory that was Greece
And the grandeur that was Rome.

Lo! in yon brilliant window-niche
How statue-like I see thee stand!

---

1. wealth and store: Abundance. **19. imp:** Graft, a term used in falconry.
2. Nicean: Of Nicaea, an ancient city of the Byzantine Empire near the modern village of Iznik in Turkey; or possibly of Nice (in southern France). **7. hyacinth:** The red of the flower in Greek mythology. **8. Naiad:** A water nymph in classical mythology.

The agate lamp within thy hand,
Ah! Psyche,° from the regions which
Are Holy Land!

Christina Rossetti

Song

1848

When I am dead, my dearest,
Sing no sad songs for me;
Plant thou no roses at my head,
Nor shady cypress tree:
Be the green grass above me
With showers and dewdrops wet:
And if thou wilt, remember,
And if thou wilt, forget.

I shall not see the shadows,
I shall not feel the rain;
I shall not hear the nightingale
Sing on as if in pain:
And dreaming through the twilight
That doth not rise nor set,
Haply I may remember,
And haply may forget.

Christina Rossetti

I wish I could remember that first day

1881

I wish I could remember that first day,
First hour, first moment of your meeting me,
If bright or dim the season, it might be
Summer or winter for aught I can say;
So unrecorded did it slip away,
So blind was I to see and to foresee,
So dull to mark the budding of my tree
That would not blossom yet for many a May.
If only I could recollect it, such
A day of days! I let it come and go
As traceless as a thaw of bygone snow;
It seemed to mean so little, meant so much;
If only now I could recall that touch,
First touch of hand in hand — Did one but know!

14. Psyche: In Greek mythology, a princess loved by Cupid; also, the soul or self.

E. E. Cummings

when god lets my body be
1923

when god lets my body be

From each brave eye shall sprout a tree
fruit that dangles therefrom

the purpled world will dance upon
Between my lips which did sing

a rose shall beget the spring
that maidens whom passion wastes

will lay between their little breasts
My strong fingers beneath the snow

into strenuous birds shall go
my love walking in the grass

their wings will touch with her face
and all the while shall my heart be

With the bulge and nuzzle of the sea

Dorothy Parker

Indian Summer
1926

In youth, it was a way I had
   To do my best to please,
And change, with every passing lad,
   To suit his theories.

But now I know the things I know,
   And do the things I do;
And if you do not like me so,
   To hell, my love, with you!

Genevieve Taggard

With Child
1922

Now I am slow and placid, fond of sun,
Like a sleek beast, or a worn one,
No slim and languid girl — not glad
With the windy trip I once had,
But velvet-footed, musing of my own,
Torpid, mellow, stupid as a stone.

You cleft me with your beauty's pulse, and now
Your pulse has taken body. Care not how

The old grace goes, how heavy I am grown,
Big with this loneliness, how you alone
Ponder our love. Touch my feet and feel
How earth tingles, teeming at my heel!
Earth's urge, not mine, — my little death, not hers;
And the pure beauty yearns and stirs.

It does not heed our ecstasies, it turns
With secrets of its own, its own concerns,
Toward a windy world of its own, toward stark
And solitary places. In the dark,
Defiant even now, it tugs and moans
To be untangled from these mother's bones.

John Berryman

A Professor's Song

1948

(. . . rabid or dog-dull.) Let me tell you how
The Eighteenth Century couplet ended. Now
Tell me. Troll me the sources of that Song —
Assigned last week — by Blake.° Come, come along,
Gentlemen. (Fidget and huddle, do. Squint soon.)
I want to end these fellows all by noon.

"That deep romantic chasm" — an early use;
The word is from the French, by our abuse
Fished out a bit. (Red all your eyes. O when?)
"A poet is a man speaking to men":
But I am then a poet, am I not? —
Ha ha. The radiator, please. Well, what?

Alive now — no — Blake would have written prose,
But movement following movement crisply flows,
So much the better, better the much so,
As burbleth Mozart. Twelve. The class can go.
Until I meet you, then, in Upper Hell
Convulsed, foaming immortal blood: farewell.

Wislawa Szymborska

Bodybuilders' Contest

1962

TRANSLATED BY STANISLAW BARÁNCZAK AND CLARE CAVANAUGH

From scalp to sole, all muscles in slow motion.
The ocean of his torso drips with lotion.

4. Blake: William Blake (1757–1827), English romantic poet.

The king of all is he who preens and wrestles
with sinews twisted into monstrous pretzels.

Onstage, he grapples with a grizzly bear
the deadlier for not really being there.
Three unseen panthers are in turn laid low,
each with one smoothly choreographed blow.

He grunts while showing his poses and paces.
His back alone has twenty different faces.
The mammoth fist he raises as he wins
is tribute to the force of vitamins.

ELIZABETH JENNINGS

My Grandmother

1961

She kept an antique shop — or it kept her.
Among Apostle spoons and Bristol glass,
The faded silks, the heavy furniture,
She watched her own reflection in the brass
Salvers and silver bowls, as if to prove
Polish was all, there was no need of love.

And I remember how I once refused
To go out with her, since I was afraid.
It was perhaps a wish not to be used
Like antique objects. Though she never said
That she was hurt, I still could feel the guilt
Of that refusal, guessing how she felt.

Later, too frail to keep a shop, she put
All her best things in one long narrow room.
The place smelt old, of things too long kept shut,
The smell of absences where shadows come
That can't be polished. There was nothing then
To give her own reflection back again.

And when she died I felt no grief at all,
Only the guilt of what I once refused.
I walked into her room among the tall
Sideboards and cupboards — things she never used
But needed; and no finger-marks were there,
Only the new dust falling through the air.

Song and Rhyme

Although rhyme is no longer considered to be an essential element in poetry, rhyme has never given up its place in song lyrics. Since it isn't possible for us to glance back to reread a line as we're listening, the rhymes in a song work as guidelines that help us follow the song's text. One of the most popular of today's song styles, rap, is built around rhyme and verbal play, and one of the characteristics of the blues, a basic building block of much rock music, is its distinctive rhyme scheme. Like Mississippi singer Big Joe Williams's "Levee Break Blues," each verse of a blues song has three rhyming lines. The first line begins a statement which the second line repeats, using a different harmony and a variation of the melody. The third line rhymes with the first two and completes the statement that the first two have initiated.

In the lyric of a popular song, like Annie Lennox's "Why?" rhyme is used more freely, but in the middle verse she relies on a series of perfect rhymes to add an element of musicality and anticipation to the words. The listener *waits* to hear the rhyme. In much rap music, the ability to rhyme is considered essential to a rapper's skills, although as we read Ed O.G.'s "Be a Father to Your Child" we are aware that for a rapper rhyme has a spontaneous, improvised feel. Some lines have no rhyme, other lines use near or slant rhyme, and a few skillfully introduce internal rhyme.

Big Joe Williams

Levee Break Blues

1975

Woman I'm lovin' sleepin' in her grave
Woman I'm lovin' sleepin' in her grave
Well, the fool I hate, meet her every day.

Please, don't give my woman no job
Please, don't give my baby no job
She's a married woman, and I don't 'low her to work too hard.

Oh, early in the morning 'bout the break of day
Early in the morning, baby, about the break of day
I'm goin' to grab the pillow where my baby used to lay.

Take me out of the bottom before the water rise
Take me out of the bottom, baby, before the water rise
Don't want to be buried down on the levee side.

Annie Lennox

Why?

1992

Why?
How many times do I have to try
to tell you that I'm sorry for the things I've done?
But when I start to try to tell you
that's when you have to tell me this kind of trouble's only just begun.

I tell myself too many times,
"Why don't you ever learn to keep your big mouth shut?"

That's why it hurts too bad to hear the words
that keep on falling from your mouth,
falling from your mouth,
falling from your mouth,
Tell me, why?
Why?

This is the book I never read.
These are the words I never said.
This is the path I'll never tread.
These are the dreams I'll dream instead.
This is the joy that's seldom spread.
These are the tears, the tears we shed.
This is the fear. This is the dread.
These are the contents of my head.
These are the years that we've spent.
This is what they represent.

This is how I feel.
Do you know how I feel?
'Cause I don't think you know how I feel.
I don't think you know what I feel.
Why?

Ed O.G.

Be a Father to Your Child

1992

Be a father, if not, why bother, son
A boy can make 'em but a man can raise one
If you did it, admit it, and stick with it
Don't say it ain't yours 'cause all women are not whores
Ninety percent represent a woman that is faithful
Ladies, can I hear it? Thank you
When a girl get pregnant, her man is gonna run around
Dissin' her for nine months, when it's born he wants to come around
Talkin' 'bout "I'm sorry for what I did"
And all of a sudden he now wants to see his kid
She had to bear it by herself and take care of it by herself
And givin' her some money for milk won't really help
Half of the fathers with sons and daughters don't even wanna take 'em
But it's so easy for them to make 'em
It's true, if it weren't for you then the child wouldn't exist
After a skeeze, there's responsibilities so don't resist
Be a father to your child

You see, I hate when a brother makes a child and then denies it
Thinkin' that money is the answer so he buys it

A whole bunch of gifts, had a lot of presents
It's not the presents, it's the presence, and the essence
Of bein' there and showing the baby that you care
Stop sittin' like a chair and having the baby wonder where you are
Or who you are — fool, you are his daddy
Don't act like you ain't 'cause that really makes me mad, G
To see a mother and a baby suffer
I've had enough of brothers who don't love the
Fact that a baby brings joy into your life
You could still be called daddy if the mother's not your wife
Don't be scared, be prepared 'cause love is gonna getcha
It will always be your child, even if she ain't witcha
So don't front on your child when you know it's your own
'Cause if you front now, you'll regret it when it's grown
Be a father to your child

Put yourself in his position and see what you've done
But just keep in mind that you're somebody's son
How would you like it if your father was a stranger
And then tried to come into your life and tried to change tha
Way your mother raised ya — now, wouldn't that amaze ya?
To be or not to be, that is the question
When you're wrong, you're wrong, it's time to make a correction
Harrassin' the mother for being with another man
But if the brother man can do it better than you can
Let him, don't sweat him, duke
Let him do the job that you couldn't do
You're claimin' you was there, but not when she needed you
And now you wanna come around for a day or two?
It's never too late to correct your mistakes
So get yourself together for your child's sake
And be a father to your child

Rhythm

If the only poetry you read is written by contemporary poets, then it might seem that you will not need to learn about the kinds of rhythm that went into the writing of verse a hundred years ago. In the politically turbulent years at the beginning of the twentieth century, many young poets in Europe and the United States felt that they had to break free of old poetic forms to find a new language that could reflect the enormous social changes they could see around them. What they chose to write was called **free verse**, because it looked on the page as if it were free of the restrictions of traditional poetry. Now we realize that writing poetry this way requires the same concentration and skill needed to write in traditional forms, so often we use the term **open form** instead. (Open form is discussed further in Chapter 11.) We call the traditional verse techniques **closed form**.

Accent and Meter

Like the other poetic means we have considered so far, the rhythm of a poem is built on the sound of words. When we discussed the difference between masculine and feminine rhyme we defined the term **accent**, which is the strong syllable, or syllables, in a word. This is the part of the word we emphasize with breath and tone as we say it out loud. The accents in the words give the poem its rhythm. All words with more than one syllable will have at least one **strong accent**. The other syllables are called **weak accents**. Sometimes the terms used are **stressed** and **unstressed** instead of strong and weak, but they refer to the same pattern of emphasized and unemphasized sounds.

A technical note: you should remember that one-syllable words like *a, the,* and *an,* which are called articles, generally are weak, unless we want to emphasize them for a special effect. One of the most common of these effects is a phrase like "There was THE Elvis Presley, standing in our own supermarket checkout line!" This same rule applies to one-syllable prepositions like *at, from, to, by, with,* and *of* and the conjunctions *and* and *but.*

One-syllable words like *I* and *me* are more complicated in their usage. You will find that all of these words can have strong or weak accents, depending on the words around them. Some short words have two strong accents: *uptight* is an example. Longer words can have complex patterns of strong and weak accents. Some, like *disenchanted,* stride briskly on with alternating strong and weak accents; others, like *encyclopedia,* dance to a rhythm all their own.

Two symbols are commonly used to indicate strong and weak accents: ´ (strong) and ˘ (weak). We would indicate the pattern of accents for *disenchanted* as

´ ˘ ´ ˘
dis en chant ed.

The indications for *encyclopedia* would be

˘ ˘ ˘ ´ ˘ ˘
en cy clo pe di a.

Marking the pattern of accents or stresses in a line of poetry will help you understand how the line achieves its effect, and it is a skill you should practice. You should, however, practice it by copying the poem into a notebook or into your word processor. If you mark a poem on the page of your text you will never be able to see the poem without the markings, and they will become small pricks that catch at your eye when you should be thinking only of the meaning and the language of the poem. The term for this kind of analysis is **scansion**, and what you are doing is scanning the poem.

The pattern set up by the regular rhythm of words in a poem is called **meter.** To have a meter we have to have more than one or two accents; this means we have to have at least three or four words to hear the meter. In some poems it is almost necessary to follow the pattern all the way to the end of the poem to decide what the meter is.

The meters you will be studying all have names, based on what is called a **foot,** one unit of the rhythmic pattern that makes up the meter. This may sound as if we have simply gone around in a circle, but it is not difficult to understand if you write down a line of the poem and mark it with the symbols for stressed and unstressed or accented and unaccented syllables. Here is an example from a sonnet by William Shakespeare:

˘ ´ ˘ ´ ˘ ´ ˘ ´ ˘ ´
So oft | have I | invok'd | thee for | my muse

If you read the line out loud, the first syllable, *So,* is unaccented, so the pattern of weak and strong accents is weak-strong, weak-strong, weak-strong, weak-strong, weak-strong. The foot is the unit of the two syllables — a weak one and a strong one — and as you can see we marked the foot with the symbol |. A rhythm based on a foot of one weak and one strong syllable, which has the name **iamb**, is called **iambic meter**, and it is one of the basic building blocks of English poetry.

What happens if we reverse the pattern of accents, and we have a line with a stress on the first syllable?

´ ˘ ´ ˘ ´ ˘ ´ ˘ ´
Does he | ever | wonder | where I | am?

Here the pattern is strong-weak, strong-weak, strong-weak, strong-weak, strong. This metrical foot is called a **trochee**, and the name for its meter is **trochaic meter**.

Two other rhythmic patterns are commonly found in poetry in English. One is a rhythmic foot of two unaccented syllables followed by a strong syllable. An example would be

˘ ˘ ´ ˘ ˘ ´ ˘ ˘ ´ ˘ ˘ ´
By the sea, | by the sea, | by the beau | tiful sea.

The foot is called an **anapest**, and the line produces **anapestic meter**. The other foot reverses this pattern and we have a strong syllable followed by two weak syllables:

´ ˘ ˘ ´ ˘ ˘ ´ ˘ ˘ ´
Down by the | sea, by the | beautiful | sea.

The foot is called a **dactyl** and its meter is **dactylic**.

As you begin using these terms and reading poems with them in mind, you should remember that poets usually do not follow the meters consistently through the poem. When the meter never varies, the poem may be considered too "sing-song." If you read through a poem and find that most of its lines are in one meter, then you will say that the poem is iambic or dactylic, trochaic or anapestic, depending on whichever foot is used most often in the poem. We call any foot that is not part of the overall meter by its own name. If you read a line like

˘ ´ ˘ ´ ˘ ˘ ´ ˘ ´
She watched | him walk | in the sum | mer's light

you see that the rhythm is weak-strong, weak-strong, weak-weak-strong, weak-strong. You would say that this line is iambic, with an anapestic third foot. You will also find when you analyze the meter of some lines that there is a break in the meter. It stops and starts somewhere within the line. This is called a **caesura**, and it is an important term to remember, because it will help you to sort through some of the meters in more complex lines. The symbol for a caesura is | |. In this line from another of Shakespeare's sonnets the caesura occurs between *cruel* and *do:*

˘ ´ ˘ ´ ˘ ´ ´ ˘ ´
Be wise | as thou | art cruel, | | do | not press

You will usually have some help in recognizing the caesura. There will often be punctuation at that point — a period, a colon, or semicolon. Even a comma can be enough to tell you that there is a break in the rhythm. Sometimes there is an unstressed syllable at the beginning of a line that does not affect the overall meter. The term for this is an **anacrusis**. In this example the meter of the line is dactylic, with the opening word *I* as an anacrusis:

˘ ´ ˘ ˘ ´ ˘ ˘ ´ ˘ ˘ ´
I | went to the | river to | see the sun | fade

If you have ever studied a play by Shakespeare, you've heard the term **iambic pentameter**. We already discussed the word *iambic. Pentameter* is derived from the Greek word *penta,* which means "five." Combined with the word *meter,* it means a meter with five units, or feet. If you consider the first line we analyzed from a sonnet by Shakespeare — "So oft have I invok'd thee for my muse" — you see that it has five strong accents. We say the line is written in iambic pentameter, as it is made up of a foot with weak-strong syllables, and it has five of them. There are terms derived from the Greek for almost all of the conceivable line lengths, and we can list them here:

monometer is a line of one foot
dimeter, a line of two feet
trimeter, a line of three feet
tetrameter, four feet
pentameter, five feet
hexameter, six feet
heptameter, seven feet
octameter, eight feet

Most poetry written in regular meter uses one of the shorter line lengths — three, four, or five strong syllables. Poems have been written, however, in all of these meters. One of the most famous American poems from the nineteenth century, "The Raven" by Edgar Allan Poe is an example of composition using an eight-syllable line. It is written with a strong-weak pattern of syllables, which means the technical term for the meter of the poem is **trochaic octameter**. This is the poem's opening line:

´ ˘ ´ ˘ ´ ˘ ´ ˘ ´ ˘ ´ ˘ ´ ˘ ´ ˘
Once up | on a | midnight | dreary, | while I | pondered | weak and | weary

Two strong accents together are called a **spondee** and two weak accents together are called a **pyrrhus**. There are some further refinements of the terms for poetic meter. We use the term **rising meter** for the two feet that begin with a weak syllable, iambic and anapestic, and the term **falling meter** for the two feet that begin with a strong syllable, trochaic and dactylic.

Blank Verse

In your studies of a play by Shakespeare, you would also have encountered the term **blank verse**. Blank verse is a form that utilizes the oratorical style of a long line in regular meter, but without the confines of rhyme. The meter is iambic pentameter, although writers generally allow themselves considerable metric freedom. Blank verse was the basic language of Elizabethan drama. Here is an example from Shakespeare's *King Henry the Fourth, Part I:*

So shaken as we are, so wan with care,
Find we a time for frighted peace to pant,
And breathe short-winded accents of new broils
To be commenced in stronds° afar remote. *strands*

In the long centuries that poets used the sound of words to create rhyme and meter, they became increasingly dexterous in the effects that they could achieve with these poetic means. Before we move on to the elements of a poem, which build on the meaning of words, we can close with an example by a writer whose poetry revitalized this tradition: Gerard Manley Hopkins. His "Pied Beauty" is a dazzling example of the musicality and verbal richness that a gifted poet can create with the poetic elements that you have studied.

GERARD MANLEY HOPKINS

Pied Beauty

1877

Glory be to God for dappled things —
For skies of couple-color as a brinded° cow; *reddish flecks*
For rose-moles all in stipple° upon trout that swim; *spotted*
Fresh-firecoal chestnut-falls; finches' wings;
Landscape plotted and pieced — fold, fallow, and plow;
And all trades, their gear and tackle and trim.
All things counter, original, spare, strange;
Whatever is fickle, freckled (who knows how?)
With swift, slow; sweet, sour; adazzle, dim;
He fathers-forth whose beauty is past change:
Praise him.

RELATED COMMENTARIES: *T. S. Eliot, "From 'Tradition and the Individual Talent,'" page 1163; Christopher Merrill, "Wyatt's 'They Flee from Me,'" page 1196; Robert Potts, "Rock 'n' Roll Is the New Poetry," page 1203.*

9

THE ELEMENTS OF POETRY: A POET'S MEANINGS

No tears in the writer, no tears in the reader. No surprise for the writer, no surprise for the reader.

– ROBERT FROST, from the introduction to *Collected Poems,* 1939

What we have been studying so far is how poets use the sound of words as part of the work they do in writing a poem. You may, however, also have heard the term *tone* used as a way to characterize a poem, and it will help you if you remember that the terms *sound* and *tone* mean different things. Before we begin to discuss those elements of a poem that depend on what a word means we should consider tone, and how it is used to describe a poem.

Tone

We are all familiar with the differences in tone in the things we say to each other in our everyday speech. The same words will mean entirely different things, depending on the tone of our voice when we say them. When a mother or father says to a young child, "You're so smart!" they will use an entirely different tone from the derisive cry of an angry classmate's voice when he or she says the same words, "You're so smart." So much of what we say to each other is shaded by our tone of voice and expression that we become accustomed to reading each other's intentions by responding to the tone of how something is said.

A poem presents us with a wide range of choices, but unless we are hearing the poem read aloud, we will have to look for the poem's meaning in the tone of its language. The words on the page will have to suggest enough for us to understand what the poet is trying to express. When we read these lines,

What high, bright hopes
  her shining spirit brings!

we know from the words *high, bright,* and *shining* that the tone of the poem is positive and admiring. We would read the poem aloud with a strong, respectful tone. When we read these next lines, however, we immediately respond to a different tone.

Whatever you thought you were doing,
my love, it wasn't enough for me,
Whatever you thought you were feeling,
  it wasn't, it wasn't,
    oh lord,
  it wasn't enough for me.

In the querulous phrase "whatever you thought you were doing," we hear a tone of exasperation and impatience, and if we read the lines aloud we find ourselves, almost without thinking, shaking our heads.

As you read the next three poems, think of how the tone of the writing helps you experience the emotions the poet wants to express. Two of the poems, "Miniver Cheevy" and "Richard Cory," by the American poet Edwin Arlington Robinson, achieve much of their effect through skillful irony. In the third, "Bells for John Whiteside's Daughter" written in the 1930s after the death of a friend's daughter, John Crowe Ransom weaves the tones of melancholy and loss into a moving elegy for a young girl.

Edwin Arlington Robinson

Miniver Cheevy 1910

Miniver Cheevy, child of scorn,
  Grew lean while he assailed the seasons;
He wept that he was ever born,
  And he had reasons.

Miniver loved the days of old
  When swords were bright and steeds were prancing;
The vision of a warrior bold
  Would set him dancing.

Miniver sighed for what was not,
  And dreamed, and rested from his labors;
He dreamed of Thebes° and Camelot,°
  And Priam's° neighbors.

■ ■ ■

11. Thebes: Ancient city of Greece; also, ancient city on the Nile River in Egypt. **Camelot:** The kingdom of King Arthur and legendary seat of the Knights of the Round Table in Britain. **12. Priam's:** Priam was the father of Hector and Paris and king of Troy during the Trojan War.

Miniver mourned the ripe renown
  That made so many a name so fragrant;
He mourned Romance, now on the town,
  And Art, a vagrant.

Miniver loved the Medici,°
  Albeit he had never seen one;
He would have sinned incessantly
  Could he have been one.

Miniver cursed the commonplace
  And eyed a khaki suit with loathing;
He missed the medieval grace
  Of iron clothing.

Miniver scorned the gold he sought,
  But sore annoyed was he without it;
Miniver thought, and thought, and thought,
  And thought about it.

Miniver Cheevy, born too late,
  Scratched his head and kept on thinking;
Miniver coughed, and called it fate,
  And kept on drinking.

Edwin Arlington Robinson

Richard Cory

1897

Whenever Richard Cory went down town,
We people on the pavement looked at him:
He was a gentleman from sole to crown,
Clean favored, and imperially slim.

And he was always quietly arrayed,
And he was always human when he talked;
But still he fluttered pulses when he said,
'Good-morning,' and he glittered when he walked.

And he was rich — yes, richer than a king —
And admirably schooled in every grace:
In fine, we thought that he was everything
To make us wish that we were in his place.

So on we worked, and waited for the light,
And went without the meat, and cursed the bread;
And Richard Cory, one calm summer night,
Went home and put a bullet through his head.

17. Medici: The ruling family of Florence, Italy, from the fifteenth to the eighteenth century.

John Crowe Ransom

Bells for John Whiteside's Daughter

1924

There was such speed in her little body,
And such lightness in her footfall,
It is no wonder her brown study
Astonishes us all.

Her wars were bruited in our high window.
We looked among orchard trees and beyond
Where she took arms against her shadow,
Or harried unto the pond.

The lazy geese, like a snow cloud
Dripping their snow on the green grass,
Tricking and stopping, sleepy and proud,
Who cried in goose, Alas,

For the tireless heart within the little
Lady with rod that made them rise
From their noon apple-dreams and scuttle
Goose-fashion under the skies!

But now go the bells, and we are ready,
In one house we are sternly stopped
To say we are vexed at her brown study,
Lying so primly propped.

WORDS AND THEIR MEANING

Keeping in mind the difference between the *sound* of a poem and the *tone* of a poem, we will begin to discuss those elements of a poem that depend on what a word *means*. Any writer is sensitive to the meanings of words, and poets, who must also think of the sound and the rhythm of each word they use, are even more conscious of the subtleties of meaning in every phrase they write, and they continually look for new and unexpected words to express their ideas. One of the popular poems from the nineteenth century is this "nonsense" verse by Lewis Carroll, which seems to make fun of this concern by poets to find new and unusual ways of saying things. Carroll simply invented words to create a poem that may mean many things, though readers have never been entirely certain just what those meanings might be. It is ironic that one of the nonsense words he made up, *chortled*, quickly became part of the English language.

Lewis Carroll

Jabberwocky°

1871

'Twas brillig, and the slithy toves
Did gyre and gimble in the wabe;
All mimsy were the borogoves,
And the mome raths outgrabe.

"Beware the Jabberwock, my son!
The jaws that bite, the claws that catch!
Beware the Jubjub bird, and shun
The frumious Bandersnatch!"

He took his vorpal sword in hand;
Long time the manxome foe he sought —
So rested he by the Tumtum tree,
And stood awhile in thought.

And, as in uffish thought he stood,
The Jabberwock, with eyes of flame,
Came whiffling through the tulgey wood,
And burbled as it came!

One, two! One, two! And through and through
The vorpal blade went snicker-snack!
He left it dead, and with its head
He went galumphing back.

"And hast thou slain the Jabberwock?
Come to my arms, my beamish boy!
O frabjous day! Callooh! Callay!"
He chortled in his joy.

'Twas brillig, and the slithy toves
Did gyre and gimble in the wabe;
All mimsy were the borogoves,
And the mome raths outgrabe.

Denotative and Connotative Meaning

The meanings of many words we use may seem to be simple and straightforward, but other words have many associations that alter the way we understand them. To describe this we use two terms. The first is **denotative**, or what a word denotes. This is the dictionary meaning of the word. The second term is **connotative**. This is the associated meanings that have built up around the word, or what the word connotes. As an example, let's take the word *sweat:*

Jabberwocky: Meaningless speech or writing. This poem is from the first chapter of Carroll's *Through the Looking Glass.*

> The *denotative meaning,* which we find in the dictionary: "Moisture exuded from the skin, perspiration."
>
> The *connotative meaning,* which we understand from common usage: hard work.

Someone asks you if you can do something for them, and you answer, "No sweat." What you have said, in the denotative meaning of the word, though you have shortened it considerably, is "Doing what you have asked me to do will be so easy for me that I won't even perspire while I do it." What you have said in its connotative meaning is that for you it's an easy job. Why did you use the connotations of the word *sweat?* For the same reason a writer uses connotations. These suggested or implied meanings make our language more rich and varied, and more vivid in its expression.

Many words that you can think of also have multiple meanings in their denotative sense. *Sweet* is an adjective in the United States; it can also be a term of endearment. In Britain it is a noun meaning "dessert." *Fall* can be a verb or a noun, with its denotative meaning "to descend freely." It can also mean a season of the year, autumn. You will have to be careful in your reading to recognize which meaning the writer wants.

Fall also has connotative meanings. We often use it in a phrase like "He's heading for a fall." The denotative meaning is that if he continues in the direction he is going he will fall down. The connotation of the phrase is that he is going to get into serious trouble. Sometimes the connotation of the word will be immediately obvious; sometimes you have to study the whole poem to see what the writer intended to say. For this way of reading the poem we'll be concerning ourselves with diction and syntax.

Diction

When we speak of **diction** we are describing the language that a writer has chosen to use in a poem. For us today this means looking at the poem and deciding why one word was chosen and not another one that means the same thing and that in most ways would have done just as well as the word the poet selected. For hundreds of years, however, when people used the term *diction* in discussing a poem, they meant a special kind of language for poetry that they called **poetic diction**. Poetry was considered to be such a refined art that you could only use refined words when you wrote it. In the words of Samuel Johnson, the poet and critic of the late eighteenth century who also compiled the first dictionary of the English language, poetic diction was "a system of words refined from the grossness of domestic use."

Sometimes readers make the mistake of thinking that people in the eighteenth century talked the way their poetry sounds. Except for the occasional person of conscious literary wit such as Johnson, you can be sure that ordinary conversation did not sound that way. This idea of poetic diction, which had grown out of the classical education of that time, was grounded in the study of Latin and Greek. The poets took the classic poets and the myths and legends of the older languages as models for their own poetry. As they worked with these models, their poetry almost developed a language of its own. The term *neoclassical* (or *Augustan*) is used to describe poetry written in this style. You will get an idea of this language from these lines from "Sound and Sense" by one of the most celebrated English poets of the eighteenth century, Alexander Pope:

True ease in writing comes from art, not chance,
As those move easiest who have learned to dance.
'Tis not enough no harshness gives offense,
The sound must seem an echo to the sense:
Soft is the strain when Zephyr° gently blows,
And the smooth stream in smoother numbers flows;
But when loud surges lash the sounding shore,
The hoarse, rough verse should like the torrent roar.
When Ajax° strives, some rock's vast weight to throw,
The line too labors, and the words move slow;
Not so, when swift Camilla° scours the plain,
Flies o'er th' unbending corn, and skims along the main.

If you had said to Pope that these lines sound artificial, not at all like the way people talk, he would have bowed his head and thanked you for the compliment. What he is telling us, in his seemingly effortless iambic pentameter and perfect rhyme, is that writing poetry does not depend on spontaneity, or "chance." The best poets will use artifice or be the ones "who have learned to dance." This is almost the opposite of our own concern with spontaneity and sincerity, but we must remember that the conventions of language reflect different historical periods.

The revolution against the limitations and artificialities that began to dominate neoclassical poetry came at the end of the eighteenth century, with the group of poets we call the *romantics.* Led by the English writers William Wordsworth and Samuel Taylor Coleridge, they broke away from the old style and tried to use language closer to ordinary ways of speaking. As Wordsworth expressed it in his introduction to the first collection of poems written in the new style, he wanted to write in "the language of the middle and lower classes of society."

The poets who are associated with the first romantics — among them William Blake, Robert Burns, Percy Bysshe Shelley, John Keats, and Lord Byron — continued to open up the poetic language to new possibilities in diction and emotional directness. Their poetry was the most important influence on the kind of immediate, personal writing that we value today.

Syntax

Syntax is derived from the Greek word "to arrange together." It refers to the order of the words in writing of any kind, not only poetry. A change in natural word order can affect the way we hear or read any kind of phrase or sentence. In poetry, where each word bears so much weight, any change becomes

5. Zephyr: The west wind. **9. Ajax:** Mighty warrior in Homer's *Iliad.* **11. Camilla:** Female warrior in Virgil's *Aeneid.*

significant. Poets will sometimes spend as much time deciding the order of the words as they do deciding on what words to use in the first place. For anyone using traditional poetic forms, which meant rhyme and meter, the most common decision about word order was often forced on the writer by the need to find a rhyme.

If you look again at the lines from Alexander Pope's "Sound and Sense," you will see that the natural word order is altered at the ends of line 8 and line 9 because of the necessities of the rhyme. Line 8 would end, in a natural word order, as "should roar like the current," but line 7 ends with "shore." The change of order to bring "roar" at the end of the line solves the problem. Line 9 presents the same difficulty. The natural word order would be "to throw some rock's vast weight," but the rhyme at the end of line 10 is "slow," and here also the change in order gives us the rhyme. You might also have noticed that there is a change in word order at the beginning of line 5. Instead of "The strain is soft," we have "Soft is the strain." Here the change has been made for the sound. If you read line 4 and then follow it with "The strain is soft," you will feel that the meter of the lines is clumsy. The change in order gives us a much smoother line, and this smoothness was one of the qualities that writers such as Pope prized most in a poem.

Imagery

We are all familiar with the literal, denotative meaning of the word *image* as a picture of something. If we say that a girl is the image of her mother, we mean that she looks just like her. If we are talking about an image in a poem, however, the word has different connotations. We do not, in a literal sense, *see* anything in a poem; we just read about it. What we call an image in poetry is a concrete description of something. It can also be a description of something we hear, touch, or feel in a physical sense. There are terms to describe each of these three kinds of images: **visual images** (things we see), **aural images** (things we hear), and **tactile images** (things we touch). If we write "an old, dark green convertible," that is a visual image. If we go on to describe the convertible's "noisy, rattling roar," that is an aural image. If we imagine sitting behind the wheel and feel "the prickly upholstery" on the seat, that is a tactile image.

Being even more precise in defining images, we have two more names for different types of tactile images. One is **gustatory** (things we taste), and the other is **olfactory** (things we smell). Describing the convertible's "lingering gas fumes" is an olfactory image, and if we drive it to a fast-food restaurant and eat a hamburger that has "a greasy, half-cooked taste," that is a gustatory image.

These kinds of physical descriptions have always been part of the poet's means, because a writer's description of specific and concrete objects in a poem strengthens our sense that what we are being told is real. This is, after all, the way we perceive the world. Our information comes to us through the perceptions of our senses, which gather in the raw material that we use to decide what we are experiencing. A poem can also include words like *beauty* and *truth,* but these are not images. They have no concrete reality, however intensely we may feel them. The word we use for them is **abstractions**.

The poems you are reading may have many images, or they may have only a single image. If we are talking about all of the images within a poem, we use the term **imagery**. The connotation of the term is that the poem presents us with a series of images that relate to one another in a way that helps to shape the poem's meaning. As you read "To Autumn" by the English romantic poet John Keats, you will see that the description of autumn is filled with visual images. Although we may find the language of the poem old-fashioned, Keats's poetry seemed revolutionary to the readers of his day.

John Keats

To Autumn

1819

Season of mists and mellow fruitfulness,
  Close bosom friend of the maturing sun:
Conspiring with him how to load and bless
  With fruit the vines that round the thatch-eaves run;
To bend with apples the mossed cottage-trees,
  And fill all fruit with ripeness to the core;
    To swell the gourd, and plump the hazel shells
With a sweet kernel; to set budding more,
  And still more, later flowers for the bees,
  Until they think warm days will never cease,
    For summer has o'er-brimmed their clammy cells.

Who hath not seen thee oft amid thy store?
  Sometimes whoever seeks abroad may find
Thee sitting careless on a granary floor,
  Thy hair soft-lifted by the winnowing wind;
Or on a half-reaped furrow sound asleep,
  Drowsed with the fume of poppies, while thy hook
    Spares the next swath and all its twined flowers:
And sometimes like a gleaner thou dost keep,
  Steady thy laden head across a brook;
  Or by a cider-press, with patient look,
    Thou watchest the last oozings hours by hours.

Where are the songs of Spring? Ay, where are they?
  Think not of them, thou hast thy music too, —
While barred clouds bloom the soft-dying day,
  And touch the stubble-plains with rosy hue;
Then in a wailful choir the small gnats mourn
  Among the river sallows, borne aloft
    Or sinking as the light wind lives or dies;
And full-grown lambs loud bleat from hilly bourn;
  Hedge-crickets sing: and now with treble soft
  The red-breast whistles from a garden-croft;
    and gathering swallows twitter in the skies.

Keats is writing here about an everyday subject, the coming of autumn to a country farm, and although his language is still too elevated to be mistaken for the way ordinary people spoke, he does not break up the poem's imagery with the continual references to classical learning that writers such as Pope considered an essential element of their poetry.

The first line is an image in itself, the autumn as a "season of mists and mellow fruitfulness." Then, almost as if we are standing in the center of the farmyard, we see the vines on the cottage eaves, the "mossed cottage-trees," the flowers for the bees, and the bees, which have gathered so much honey that they've "o'er-brimmed their clammy cells," in their hives. The figure that the poet addresses as "thee" in the second verse is autumn. The term for this way of speaking to something that is inanimate is the figure of speech called **apostrophe**.

At the end of the poem, Keats does not make any larger statement about the scene in the farmyard. He does not draw any moral or lesson from it. This was also part of the revolutionary quality of his poetry. Simply to be there, at that moment, and hear the red-breast whistling from the croft and the swallows twittering in the sky was enough for him. The sallows he notices in line 28 are low willows that grow along riverbanks, and one of the poet's strongest aural images is the description of the gnats "mourning" above the brushy willows.

Many modern poets write with the same open and direct response to a natural scene as Keats wrote. In the following poem the American writer Elizabeth Bishop is also satisfied simply to look at what is before her. She is seeing it so intensely that the poem is constructed entirely around its visual images. What she is describing is a *bight,* a small bay, usually by the ocean. *Marl* is the rich deposit of soil that streams have left on the bottom of the bight, and *claves* are wooden percussion instruments used in Caribbean and South American dance music. Charles Baudelaire, who is named in line 7, was a nineteenth-century French poet who shocked many people with the frank sensuality of his writing. He also puzzled people with his theories that poetry could find the associations between the world of the sense — the physical world — and the world of the spirit. In her line about marimba music (line 8), Bishop is humorously suggesting that this is the kind of association Baudelaire would have made when he was experimenting with substances such as the gas she can smell coming out of the muck at the bottom of the bay.

ELIZABETH BISHOP

The Bight

(On My Birthday) *1955*

At low tide like this how sheer the water is.
White, crumbling ribs of marl protrude and glare
and the boats are dry, the pilings dry as matches.
Absorbing, rather than being absorbed,

the water in the bight doesn't wet anything,
the color of the gas flame turned as low as possible.
One can smell it turning to gas; if one were Baudelaire
one could probably hear it turning into marimba music.
The little ochre dredge at work off the end of the dock
already plays the dry perfectly off-beat claves.
The birds are outsize. Pelicans crash
into this peculiar gas unnecessarily hard,
it seems to me, like pickaxes,
rarely coming up with anything to show for it,
and going off with humorous elbowings.
Black-and-white man-of-war birds soar
on impalpable drifts
and open their tails like scissors on the curves
or tense them like wishbones, till they tremble.
The frowsy sponge boats keep coming in
with the obliging air of retrievers,
bristling with jackstraw gaffs and hooks
and decorated with bobbles of sponges.
There is a fence of chicken wire along the dock
where, glinting like little plowshares,
the blue-gray shark tails are hung up to dry
for the Chinese-restaurant trade.
Some of the little white boats are still piled up
against each other, or lie on their sides, stove in,
and not yet salvaged, if they ever will be, from the last bad storm,
like torn-open, unanswered letters.
The bight is littered with old correspondences.
Click. Click. Goes the dredge,
and brings up a dripping jawful of marl.
All the untidy activity continues,
awful but cheerful.

As you read the poem you may have noticed some of the poetic means that Bishop uses to bring her description of the harbor to life. In the first line she has changed the *syntax* to tell us the most important thing about the scene. The line in customary order would be, "How sheer the water is like this at low tide." Instead, the first thing she tells us is that it is low tide, so we will have that as our immediate visual image.

Sheer is not an obvious choice to describe the gleam of the water on the mud flats, but Bishop has made a choice in the *diction* of the poem to use *sheer* instead of another possible word, like *shiny. Sheer* has the connotations of silk, and it also has an *r* sound, which relates to the *r* of water, and gives the line a subtle *assonance. Sheer* also has one syllable, which smooths out the rhythm of the last half of the line to three iambic feet.

We can see several other phrases in which Bishop has made choices in the diction to create an even more vivid image: *ochre* instead of yellow-brown for the color of the dredge, "dry perfectly off-beat" for the sound of the claves, the adjective *outsize* instead of *big* for the size of the birds, *frowsy* for the sponge boats instead of *tattered.* The poem is written without regular meter or rhyme, but certainly, with Bishop's brilliant skill with words, she intended to use the near rhyme of *marl* and *cheerful* that helps to bring the poem to a close.

Simile and Metaphor

As we looked closely at Bishop's poem, we realized that she had other means of showing us the harbor. Several times she used comparisons — phrases that began with the word *like.* The term for this is **simile**. For an image of the pelicans flapping out of the water she used the phrase "humorous elbowings," which is an indirect comparison. The term for this is **metaphor**. Both of these terms are important in understanding how poems are written.

Writers have always used simile and metaphor because language without simile is as flat as chili without chili powder. If you have studied literature, you recognized that "as flat as chili without chili powder" is a simile. Simile and metaphor are both comparisons, but a simile tells us to watch out for the comparison with the words *like, as, as if,* or *as though,* while a metaphor does not.

Writers use comparisons for several reasons. It is often easier to describe something that is not familiar by comparing it to something that is, as in the sentence "The wing of a Morpha butterfly looks like a large blue leaf." Another use of a simile is to give a tangible reality to something that is intangible. An example: "Our love is like the shine of the sun on the sea."

The use of metaphor has long been considered one of the measures of a poet's skill. The Greek philosopher Aristotle defined metaphor as "an intuitive perception of the similarity in dissimilars." A simple metaphor would be a phrase like "You are my sunshine." Most poets, however, try to find comparisons that are more unexpected, that make the reader think about what is similar in the two objects that are being drawn together in a comparison.

The Anglo-Saxon church historian the Venerable Bede included one of the first memorable extended similes in English literature (it was derived from Psalm 84) in his eighth-century *Ecclesiastical History of the English People.* Bede wrote that the brief span of our lifetime between birth and death is "as if a sparrow beaten with wind and weather" flies into a warm, lighted hall and then, after "a short space of this fair weather," departs back outside "to return from winter to winter again."

In Elizabeth Bishop's poem we identified both similes and a metaphor. The similes are strong word pictures. The pelicans crash into the water "like pickaxes," the man-of-war birds open their tails "like scissors," "glinting like little plowshares, / the blue-gray shark tails are hung up to dry," the little white boats lie damaged on the mud "like torn-open, unanswered letters." The metaphor is a description of pelicans struggling to fly up from the water. Bishop describes them as "going off with humorous elbowings," which compares them with people using their elbows to get through a crowd.

Here are some examples of similes:

Like as the waves make towards the pebbled shore,
So do our minutes hasten to their end.
– William Shakespeare, from "Sonnet 61"

Oh, my luve is like a red, red rose,
That's newly sprung in June.
– Robert Burns, from "A Red, Red Rose"

I love smooth words, like gold-enameled fish
which circle slowly with a golden swish.
– Elinor Wylie, from "Pretty Words"

Let us go then, you and I
When the evening is spread out against the sky
Like a patient etherized upon a table.
– T. S. Eliot, from "The Love Song of J. Alfred Prufrock"

I am scattered like
the hot shriveled seeds.
– H.D., from "Mid-day"

Love set you going like a fat gold watch.
– Sylvia Plath, from "Morning Song"

What happens to a dream deferred?
Does it dry up
like a raisin in the sun?
– Langston Hughes, from "Harlem"

I like small kindnesses.
In fact I actually prefer them to the more
substantial kindness that is always eyeing you,
like a large animal on a rug.
– Louise Glück, from "Gratitude"

Here are some examples of metaphors:

My Rosalind, my Rosalind,
My frolic falcon, with bright eyes.
– Alfred, Lord Tennyson, from "Rosalind"

Your mind and you are our Sargasso Sea.
– Ezra Pound, from "Portrait d'une Femme"

Now that I have your voice by heart, I read
In the black chords upon a dulling page
Music that is not meant for music's cage,
Whose emblems mix with words that shake and bleed.
– Louise Bogan, from "Song for the Last Act"

. . . your knees
are a southern breeze.
– William Carlos Williams, from "Portrait of a Lady"

The corpse was bloodless. . . .
Its open staring eyes were lustreless dead-lights.
– ROBERT LOWELL, from "The Quaker Graveyard in Nantucket"

Marriage is not
a house or even a tent
it is before that, and colder.
– MARGARET ATWOOD, from "Habitation"

Sometimes in your reading you will find poems that are themselves a simile or a metaphor. The poet has imagined the poem entirely in terms of a comparison. In this example the modern Polish poet Zbigniew Herbert compares the work of a translator to the labors of a bee. The bee emerges from its struggle with the flower with a nose "yellow with pollen." The "pollen" that translators have to show for their labors is the new poem they have created, their translation. The word *Like,* which begins the poem, tells us that what we will be reading is a simile.

ZBIGNIEW HERBERT

On Translating Poetry 1977

TRANSLATED BY JOHN AND BOGDANA CARPENTER

Like an awkward bumble-bee
he sits on the flower
until the delicate stalk bends
he squeezes through rows of petals
like the pages of a dictionary
he tries to reach the centre
where the scent and sweetness are
and though he has a cold
and lacks any taste
still he perseveres
until he knocks his head
against the yellow pistil
and here already is the end
it is difficult to penetrate
from the cups of flowers
to their roots
so the bumble-bee goes out
very proud
and loudly buzzing;
I have been inside
and to those
who don't quite believe him
he shows his nose
yellow with pollen.

One of the classic American poems from the first years of modernist experimentation is Carl Sandburg's "Fog." It compares the fog's drift over the city to a cat entering silently to sit for a moment and look down at the scene. Sandburg doesn't use the words *like* or *as,* so we are aware that the poem is a metaphor.

CARL SANDBURG

Fog

1916

The fog comes
on little cat feet.

It sits looking
over harbor and city
on silent haunches
and then moves on.

Figurative and Literal Language

The term **figurative language** means that the poem uses simile or metaphor, or any of the figures of speech we will study in the next pages. The opposite of figurative language is **literal language**, which means that each word is being used in its denotative sense.

Symbol

We've already seen how words and phrases have connotations and associations. A word becomes a **symbol** when it has so much meaning attached to it that we cannot hear it spoken without immediately thinking about something else at the same time. Mention of "the flag" brings up thoughts of patriotism and America. "Wall Street" could be a reference to the structure of American capitalism. In the 1920s the poet T. S. Eliot became the center of a lengthy discussion about symbols and symbolism, because several of his most influential poems used objects like roses or yew trees as symbols for his beliefs in tradition and his religious faith. In our own period poets more often write directly what they mean, but words like *Hollywood* or *Barbie* in a poem come loaded with associations.

Figures of Speech

There are more than two hundred ways that words can be used as figures of speech, but you need to familiarize yourself with only a few that you will meet most often. If you say "The sky is crying," you are using **personification**, which is giving human characteristics to something inanimate, animal, or abstract. In this poem the Swedish poet Rolf Aggestam personifies ordinary lightning as a difficult and unpredictable barefoot companion.

Rolf Aggestam

Lightning Bolt

1997

TRANSLATED BY SAMUEL CHARTERS

A lightning bolt
is in heat most of the time and doesn't
believe in anything. Unfaithful to any
system. Doesn't measure things. Doesn't make
comparisons.
Doesn't have any hair.

A lightning bolt
is unsure of itself, incomprehensible and curious.
If you understand a lightning bolt it's too late.

You can stuff
a lightning bolt. Stand it up there staring from a
book shelf, seeing everything so clearly.
It hurls itself out of the bare sky and
immediately begins to look for earth.

Challenge the lightning bolt to perform
your deepest and most secret commission
and walk around it wearing heavy boots.
A lightning bolt wants earth under the soles of its feet.

The term **apostrophe** means to address something intangible or someone not commonly spoken to. The opening line of this sonnet by John Donne (see p. 879) is an example of apostrophe, as the intangible presence he is crying out to is Death:

> Death, be not proud, though some have callèd thee
> Mighty and dreadful, for thou art not so;
> For those whom thou think'st thou dost overthrow
> Die not, poor Death. . . .

Metonymy and a type of figurative speech closely related to it, **synecdoche**, are similar to metaphor. In using metonymy the writer uses the name of one thing in place of the name of something closely related to it. Instead of saying "I knew him when he was young," the line could be "I knew him in his cradle." Synecdoche is the use of part of something to stand for the whole thing. If we say someone playing baseball or softball "has a heavy bat," we are using the bat as a substitute for the whole concept, which is that the batter hits the ball well.

There are other figures of speech that you will find in your reading, but most of these concepts are used by all writers, and you are probably already familiar with them. Some of these are *paradox, oxymoron, hyperbole,* and *understatement.* By **paradox** we mean a statement that on the surface seems that it cannot possibly be true but is true after all. In the last lines of the sonnet "Death, be not proud," John Donne uses a paradox when he suggests that because of the miracle of eternal life, it is Death itself that dies at the moment of mortality:

> One short sleep past, we wake eternally
> And death shall be no more; Death, thou shalt die.

An **oxymoron** is a statement that contradicts itself. Probably the best-known modern example is the phrase "jumbo shrimp." A more literary example is "darkness visible," Milton's phrase describing hell in *Paradise Lost*. By **hyperbole** we mean exaggerated statements that we do not really intend to be taken for the truth. When the seventeenth-century American poet Anne Bradstreet writes, in "To My Dear and Loving Husband" (p. 981), "I prize thy love more than whole mines of gold / Or all the riches that the East doth hold," she is using hyperbole. **Understatement** is the opposite of hyperbole. Here something is deliberately described in terms that suggest it is much smaller or less important than we know it really is. The line "Life for me ain't been no crystal stair" from Langston Hughes's poem "Mother to Son" (p. 1056) is an example of understatement.

Poems for Further Reading

ANDREW MARVELL

To His Coy Mistress 1681

Had we but world enough, and time,
This coyness, lady, were no crime.
We would sit down, and think which way
To walk, and pass our long love's day.
Thou by the Indian Ganges' side
Shouldst rubies find; I by the tide
Of Humber would complain. I would
Love you ten years before the flood,
And you should, if you please, refuse
Till the conversion of the Jews.
My vegetable love should grow
Vaster than empires and more slow;
An hundred years should go to praise
Thine eyes, and on thy forehead gaze;
Two hundred to adore each breast,
But thirty thousand to the rest;
An age at least to every part,
And the last age should show your heart.
For, lady, you deserve this state,
Nor would I love at lower rate.
But at my back I always hear
Time's wingéd chariot hurrying near;

And yonder all before us lie
Deserts of vast eternity.
Thy beauty shall no more be found,
Nor, in thy marble vault, shall sound
My echoing song; then worms shall try
That long-preserved virginity,
And your quaint honor turn to dust,
And into ashes all my lust:
The grave's a fine and private place,
But none, I think, do there embrace.
  Now therefore, while the youthful hue
Sits on thy skin like morning dew,
And while thy willing soul transpires° *breathes forth*
At every pore with instant fires,
Now let us sport us while we may,
And now, like amorous birds of prey,
Rather at once our time devour
Than languish in his slow-chapped° power. *slow-jawed*
Let us roll all our strength and all
Our sweetness up into one ball,
And tear our pleasures with rough strife
Thorough the iron gates of life:
Thus, though we cannot make our sun
Stand still, yet we will make him run.

Lady Mary Wortley Montagu

The Lover: A Ballad

1747

At length, by so much importunity pressed,
Take, C —— ,° at once, the inside of my breast;
This stupid indifference so often you blame
Is not owing to nature, to fear, or to shame;
I am not as cold as a Virgin in lead,°
Nor is Sunday's sermon so strong in my head;
I know but too well how time flies along,
That we live but few years and yet fewer are young.

But I hate to be cheated, and never will buy
Long years of repentance for moments of joy.
Oh was there a man (but where shall I find
Good sense and good nature so equally joined?)
Would value his pleasure, contribute to mine,
Not meanly would boast, nor would lewdly design,

2. C ——: Probably Lady Mary's friend Richard Chandler. **5. Virgin in lead:** A leaded stained-glass image of the Virgin Mary.

Not over severe, yet not stupidly vain,
For I would have the power though not give the pain;

No pedant yet learnéd, not rakehelly gay
Or laughing because he has nothing to say,
To all my whole sex obliging and free,
Yet never be fond of any but me;
In public preserve the decorum that's just,
And show in his eyes he is true to his trust,
Then rarely approach, and respectfully bow,
Yet not fulsomely pert, nor yet foppishly low.

But when the long hours of public are past
And we meet with champagne and a chicken at last,
May every fond pleasure that hour endear,
Be banished afar both discretion and fear,
Forgetting or scorning the airs of the crowd
He may cease to be formal, and I to be proud,
Till lost in the joy we confess that we live,
And he may be rude, and yet I may forgive.

And that my delight may be solidly fixed,
Let the friend and the lover be handsomely mixed,
In whose tender bosom my soul might confide,
Whose kindness can sooth me, whose counsel could guide.
From such a dear lover as here I describe
No danger should fright me, no millions should bribe;
But till this astonishing creature I know,
As I long have lived chaste, I will keep myself so.

I never will share with the wanton coquette,
Or be caught by a vain affectation of wit.
The toasters and songsters may try all their art
But never shall enter the pass of my heart.
I loathe the lewd rake, the dressed fopling despise;
Before such pursuers the nice° virgin flies; *fastidious*
And as Ovid has sweetly in parables told
We harden like trees, and like rivers are cold.°

William Blake

Song 1783

How sweet I roam'd from field to field,
  And tasted all the summer's pride,
'Till I the prince of love° beheld, *Cupid*
  Who in the sunny beams did glide!

48. harden . . . cold: In Ovid's *Metamorphosis,* the nymphs Daphne and Arethusa, fleeing the unwanted sexual overtures of gods, turn into a laurel tree and a fountain, respectively.

■ ■ ■

He shew'd me lilies for my hair,
  And blushing roses for my brow;
He led me through his gardens fair,
  Where all his golden pleasures grow.

With sweet May dews my wings were wet,
  And Phoebus fir'd my vocal rage;
He caught me in his silken net,
  And shut me in his golden cage.

He loves to sit and hear me sing,
  Then, laughing, sports and plays with me;
Then stretches out my golden wing,
  And mocks my loss of liberty.

WILLIAM WORDSWORTH

I Wandered Lonely as a Cloud

1804

I wandered lonely as a cloud
That floats on high o'er vales and hills,
When all at once I saw a crowd,
A host, of golden daffodils;
Beside the lake, beneath the trees,
Fluttering and dancing in the breeze.

Continuous as the stars that shine
And twinkle on the milky way,
They stretched in never-ending line
Along the margin of a bay:
Ten thousand saw I at a glance,
Tossing their heads in sprightly dance.

The waves beside them danced; but they
Outdid the sparkling waves in glee;
A poet could not but be gay,
In such a jocund company;
I gazed — and gazed — but little thought
What wealth the show to me had brought:

For oft, when on my couch I lie
In vacant or in pensive mood,
They flash upon that inward eye
Which is the bliss of solitude;
And then my heart with pleasure fills,
And dances with the daffodils.

William Wordsworth

My Heart Leaps Up

1802

My heart leaps up when I behold
 A rainbow in the sky:
So was it when my life began;
So is it now I am a man;
So be it when I shall grow old,
 Or let me die!
The Child is father of the Man;
And I could wish my days to be
Bound each to each by natural piety.

George Gordon, Lord Byron

She Walks in Beauty

1814

1

She walks in beauty, like the night
 Of cloudless climes and starry skies;
And all that's best of dark and bright
 Meet in her aspect and her eyes:
Thus mellowed to that tender light
 Which heaven to gaudy day denies.

2

One shade the more, one ray the less,
 Had half impaired the nameless grace
Which waves in every raven tress,
 Or softly lightens o'er her face;
Where thoughts serenely sweet express
 How pure, how dear their dwelling place.

3

And on that cheek, and o'er that brow,
 So soft, so calm, yet eloquent,
The smiles that win, the tints that glow,
 But tell of days in goodness spent,
A mind at peace with all below,
 A heart whose love is innocent!

PERCY BYSSHE SHELLEY

When Passion's Trance Is Overpast *1824*

When passion's trance is overpast,
If tenderness and truth could last
Or live — whilst all wild feelings keep
Some mortal slumber, dark and deep —
I should not weep, I should not weep!

It were enough to feel, to see
Thy soft eyes gazing tenderly . . .
And dream the rest — and burn and be
The secret food of fires unseen,
Could thou but be what thou hast been!

After the slumber of the year
The woodland violets reappear;
All things revive in field or grove
And sky and sea, but two, which move
And form all others — life and love. —

JOHN KEATS

A Thing of Beauty *1817*

A thing of beauty is a joy for ever:
Its loveliness increases; it will never
Pass into nothingness; but still will keep
A bower quiet for us, and a sleep
Full of sweet dreams, and health, and quiet breathing.
Therefore, on every morrow, are we wreathing
A flowery band to bind us to the earth,
Spite of despondence, of the inhuman dearth
Of noble natures, of the gloomy days,
Of all the unhealthy and o'er-darkened ways
Made for our searching: yes, in spite of all,
Some shape of beauty moves away the pall
From our dark spirits. Such the sun, the moon,
Trees old, and young sprouting a shady boon
For simple sheep; and such are daffodils
With the green world they live in; and clear rills
'That for themselves a cooling covert make
'Gainst the hot season; the mid forest brake,
Rich with a sprinkling of fair musk-rose blooms:
And such too is the grandeur of the dooms° *judgments*
We have imagined for the mighty dead;
All lovely tales that we have heard or read:

An endless fountain of immortal drink,
Pouring unto us from the heaven's brink.

Nor do we merely feel these essences
For one short hour; no, even as the trees
That whisper round a temple become soon
Dear as the temple's self, so does the moon,
The passion poesy, glories infinite,
Haunt us till they become a cheering light
Unto our souls, and bound to us so fast,
That, whether there be shine, or gloom o'ercast,
They always must be with us, or we die.

THOMAS HOOD

I remember, I remember

1826

I remember, I remember,
The house where I was born,
The little window where the sun
Came peeping in at morn;
He never came a wink too soon,
Nor brought too long a day,
But now, I often wish the night
Had borne my breath away!

I remember, I remember
The roses, red and white,
The vi'lets, and the lily-cups,
Those flowers made of light!
The lilacs where the robin built,
And where my brother set
The laburnum on his birthday, —
The tree is living yet!

I remember, I remember
Where I was used to swing,
And thought the air must rush as fresh
To swallows on the wing;
My spirit flew in feathers then,
That is so heavy now,
And summer pools could hardly cool
The fever on my brow!

I remember, I remember
The fir trees dark and high;
I used to think their slender tops
Were close against the sky:
It was a childish ignorance,

But now 'tis little joy
To know I'm farther off from heav'n
Than when I was a boy.

ALFRED, LORD TENNYSON

Ulysses

1833

It little profits that an idle king,
By this still hearth, among these barren crags,
Matched with an aged wife, I mete and dole
Unequal laws unto a savage race
That hoard, and sleep, and feed, and know not me.
I cannot rest from travel: I will drink
Life to the lees: all times I have enjoyed
Greatly, have suffered greatly, both with those
That loved me, and alone; on shore, and when
Through scudding drifts the rainy Hyades°
Vexed the dim sea: I am become a name;
For always roaming with a hungry heart
Much have I seen and known; cities of men
And manners, climates, councils, governments,
Myself not least, but honored of them all;
And drunk delight of battle with my peers,
Far on the ringing plains of windy Troy.
I am a part of all that I have met;
Yet all experience is an arch wherethrough
Gleams that untravelled world, whose margin fades
For ever and for ever when I move.
How dull it is to pause, to make an end,
To rust unburnished, not to shine in use!
As though to breathe were life. Life piled on life
Were all too little, and of one to me
Little remains: but every hour is saved
From that eternal silence, something more,
A bringer of new things; and vile it were
For some three suns to store and hoard myself,
And this gray spirit yearning in desire
To follow knowledge like a sinking star,
Beyond the utmost bound of human thought.
    This is my son, mine own Telemachus,
To whom I leave the scepter and the isle —
Well-loved of me, discerning to fulfil

10. Hyades: A cluster of stars whose rising was thought to be a sign of rain.

This labor, by slow prudence to make mild
A rugged people, and through soft degrees
Subdue them to the useful and the good.
Most blameless is he, centered in the sphere
Of common duties, decent not to fail
In offices of tenderness, and pay
Meet° adoration to my household gods *proper*
When I am gone. He works his work, I mine.
    There lies the port: the vessel puffs her sail;
There gloom the dark broad seas. My mariners,
Souls that have toiled, and wrought, and thought with me —
That ever with a frolic welcome took
The thunder and the sunshine, and opposed
Free hearts, free foreheads — you and I are old;
Old age hath yet his honor and his toil;
Death closes all: but something ere the end,
Some work of noble note, may yet be done,
Not unbecoming men that strove with gods.
The lights begin to twinkle from the rocks:
The long day wanes: the slow moon climbs: the deep
Moans round with many voices. Come, my friends,
'Tis not too late to seek a newer world.
Push off, and sitting well in order smite
The sounding furrows; for my purpose holds
To sail beyond the sunset and the baths
Of all the western stars, until I die.
It may be that the gulfs will wash us down:
It may be we shall touch the Happy Isles°
And see the great Achilles, whom we knew.
Though much is taken, much abides; and though
We are not now that strength which in old days
Moved earth and heaven, that which we are, we are;
One equal temper of heroic hearts,
Made weak by time and fate but strong in will
To strive, to seek, to find, and not to yield.

RELATED COMMENTARIES: *X. J. Kennedy, "Andrew Marvell's 'To His Coy Mistress,'" page 1187; Percy Bysshe Shelley, "From 'A Defence of Poetry,'" page 1217; William Wordsworth, "From the Introduction to* Lyrical Ballads,*" page 1229.*

---

63. touch the Happy Isles: In Greek mythology the Happy Isles were the home of dead warriors. In line 64, Ulysses speaks of his old comrade Achilles, who fought alongside him at Troy and was killed there.

10

THE TYPES OF POETRY: A POET'S FORMS

one loves only form
and form only comes
into existence when
the thing is born
– CHARLES OLSON,
from "I, Maximus of Gloucester"

TYPES OF VERSE

Meter and rhyme, and their complex intertwining, are at the core of all of the forms of traditional verse. For much English poetry the basic building block is a unit of two lines that end in perfect rhyme. The term for this unit is a **couplet**. The couplet appears in English poetry as early as the twelfth century. In this poem, "Hymn to Godric," two couplets are joined together to make a four-line unit called a **stanza**, or a **verse**:

Sainte Marye, Christes bur° *shelter*
Maidenes clenhad,° moderes flur° *purity; flower*
Dilie° min sinne, rix° in min mod° *remove; merge; heart*
Bring me to winne° with the self God *joy*

We do not recognize all of the words, since language and its meanings are continually changing, but the four-line stanza, written in the four-stress line called *tetrameter* or *quadrameter,* continued to be one of the most widely used poetic means in English and American poetry for hundreds of years. One of the best-known examples of perfect rhyme, A. E. Housman's "Loveliest of trees, the cherry now" (p. 814), is written in this same stanza:

Loveliest of trees, the cherry now
Is hung with bloom along the bough,
And stands about the woodland ride
Wearing white for Eastertide.

We mark the sequence of rhymes in a poem with a tool like the accent symbols that we used to study the meter of a line. Instead of symbols, however, each rhyme is given a letter of the alphabet. Here is an example of how we mark the rhyme pattern of a poem using the same Housman stanza:

Loveliest of trees, the cherry now *a*
Is hung with bloom along the bough, *a*
And stands about the woodland ride *b*
Wearing white for Eastertide. *b*

Another form of this same stanza has been used almost as often by many poets. The stanza also has four lines and it is written in alternating lines of tetrameter and trimeter, but instead of *aabb,* the rhyme scheme is *abab.* Here is an example.

A. E. Housman

Oh, when I was in love with you 1896

Oh, when I was in love with you, *a*
Then I was clean and brave, *b*
And miles around the wonder grew *a*
How well I did behave. *b*

And now the fancy passes by, *c*
And nothing will remain, *d*
And miles around they'll say that I *c*
Am quite myself again. *d*

A term that is also used for a group of four rhymed lines is a **quatrain,** especially when it is part of a longer unit in a poem. A group of six lines with a recurring rhyme scheme is called a **sestet**, and the term for an eight-line group is an **octave**.

Although the couplet is the basic unit for so much poetry, occasionally the writer will also use a unit of three lines, which is called a **tercet**. Tennyson, who was ingenious in his use of rhyme, included a tercet in each stanza of his long ballad poem *The Lady of Shalott.*

A red-cross knight forever kneeled
To a lady in his shield,
That sparkled on the yellow field.

With these basic terms to help us, we can begin to look at some types of poetry. Whether they are written in traditional — closed — forms or in free — open — forms, poems can generally be sorted into three main types: narrative, lyric, and dramatic.

NARRATIVE POETRY

A narrative poem is simply a poem that tells the story, like the one that begins " 'Twas the night before Christmas, and all through the house . . ." The oldest form of narrative poetry is the **epic**, which is probably best known today for the two epic poems, the *Iliad* and the *Odyssey*, composed by the poet Homer. The large scale of these narratives and their sweeping depiction of the lives and events of another time have given us the adjective *epic*.

The Ballad

Ballads, which are also narrative poems, are part of the folk tradition of every culture. Even though we know them as printed compositions, traditional ballads come from an earlier period, when they were part of an oral tradition. They tell of a death in a family, of women who were taken by spirits, of bloody quarrels where families are broken or reunited. Most ballads were probably composed by a single individual, but when they come down to us they are usually anonymous. The name of the original writer has been lost as the ballads were passed on from singer to singer. Ballads were meant to be sung, and they are composed in simple quatrains with meters that are easily followed, sometimes with a repeated line that ends every verse, which is called a **refrain**.

In the well-known folk ballad "Barbara Allan," the stanza form uses alternating lines of four and three stressed beats. As is usual in poems that are meant to be sung, there is considerable looseness in the scansion of the beats. Another characteristic of ballads like these is that rhyme is used only for the second and fourth lines of the stanza.

Barbara Allan

date unknown

It was in and about the Martinmas° time, *November 11*
When the green leaves were a-fallin',
That Sir John Graeme in the West Country
Fell in love with Barbara Allan.

He sent his man down through the town
To the place where she was dwellin':
"O haste and come to my master dear,
Gin° ye be Barbara Allan." *if*

O slowly, slowly rase° she up, *rose*
To the place where he was lyin',
And when she drew the curtain by:
"Young man, I think you're dyin'."

"O it's I'm sick, and very, very sick,
And 'tis a' for Barbara Allan."
"O the better for me ye sal° never be *shall*
Though your heart's blood were a-spillin'.

"O dinna ye mind, young man," said she,
"When ye the cups were fillin',

That ye made the healths gae round and round,
    And slighted Barbara Allan?"

He turned his face unto the wall,
    And death with him was dealin':
"Adieu, adieu, my dear friends all,
    And be kind to Barbara Allan."

And slowly, slowly, rase she up,
    And slowly, slowly left him;
And sighing said she could not stay,
    Since death of life had reft him.

She had not gane a mile but twa,
    When she heard the dead-bell knellin',
And every jow° that the dead-bell ga'ed *stroke*
    It cried, "Woe to Barbara Allan."

"O mother, mother, make my bed,
    O make it soft and narrow:
Since my love died for me today,
    I'll die for him tomorrow."

When we read a folk ballad it is easy to forget that the words are a transcription of what someone was singing. Although the ballads of the African American culture have not often made their way into literary anthologies, they are a vital expression that tells us much about the social background that created them. The song "Gray Goose," which is sung by black work gangs in Texas prisons, is a ballad with a sly double meaning. The "gray goose" is understood by the singers to be a veiled reference to the black American who is too tough to be destroyed, despite the tragedies of slavery and segregation.

Gray Goose

date unknown

Well, my papa went a-hunting,
        Well, well, well . . .
You know he took along his shotgun,
        Well, well, well . . .
You know he rared the hammer 'way back,
        Well, well, well . . .
You know he shot at the gray goose,
        Well, well, well . . .
Well down came the gray goose,
        Well, well, well . . .
After six weeks a falling,
        Well, well, well . . .
Well we gave a feather picking,
        Well, well, well . . .
Was a six weeks a pickin' him,
        Well, well, well . . .

Well we put him on to parboil,
Well, well, well . . .
Well we put him in the oven,
Well, well, well . . .
Was a six weeks a bakin' him,
Well, well, well . . .
Well we put him on the table,
Well, well, well . . .
Well the knife couldn't cut him,
Well, well, well . . .
Well the last time I seen him,
Well, well, well . . .
He was flyin' across the ocean,
Well, well, well . . .

The song is started by a leader, who sings the opening phrase; then the work gang answers with the refrain, "Well, well, well . . ." This version was sung by two convicts, Louis Houston and D. J. Miller, with other prisoners at Ramsey State Prison. It was recorded in 1964 by folklorist Bruce Jackson. As they performed it, each line was repeated, but it is more interesting to read it with each line sung only once. Like most songs from the folk tradition, the rhythm is counted in accents. Here there are two strong accents in each line of the verse, and the other words and syllables are given less emphasis. The strong accents in the opening lines, as the singer performs them, are "well my PA-pa went a-HUNT-ing" and "you know he TOOK along his SHOT-gun."

Ballads for Further Reading

The Three Ravens

date unknown

There were three ravens sat on a tree,
Down a down, hay down, hay down,
There were three ravens sat on a tree,
With a down,

There were three ravens sat on a tree,
They were as black as they might be,
With a down, derry, derry, derry, down, down.

The one of them said to his mate,
"Where shall we our breakfast take?"

"Down in yonder green field
There lies a knight slain under his shield.

"His hounds they lie down at his feet,
So well they can their master keep.

"His hawks they fly so eagerly,
There's no fowl dare him come nigh."

■ ■ ■

Down there comes a fallow doe,
As great with young as she might go.

She lifted up his bloody head,
And kissed his wounds that were so red.

She got him up upon her back,
And carried him to earthen lake.° *pit*

She buried him before the prime;° *sunrise*
She was dead herself ere evensong time.

God send every gentleman
Such hawks, such hounds, and such a lemman.° *lover*

Lord Randall

date unknown

"Oh where ha'e ye been, Lord Randall my son?
O where ha'e ye been, my handsome young man?"
"I ha'e been to the wild wood: mother, make my bed soon,
For I'm weary wi' hunting, and fain wald° lie down." *would gladly*

"Where gat ye your dinner, Lord Randall my son?
Where gat ye your dinner, my handsome young man?"
"I dined wi' my true love: mother, make my bed soon,
For I'm weary wi' hunting, and fain wald lie down."

"What gat ye to your dinner, Lord Randall my son?
What gat ye to your dinner, my handsome young man?"
"I gat eels boiled in broo:° mother, make my bed soon, *broth*
For I'm weary wi' hunting, and fain wald lie down."

"What became of your bloodhounds, Lord Randall my son?
What became of your bloodhounds, my handsome young man?"
"O they swelled and they died: mother, make my bed soon,
For I'm weary wi' hunting, and fain wald lie down."

"O I fear ye are poisoned, Lord Randall my son!
O I fear ye are poisoned, my handsome young man!"
"Oh yes, I am poisoned: mother, make my bed soon,
For I'm sick at the heart, and I fain wald lie down."

EDWIN ARLINGTON ROBINSON

Luke Havergal

1897

Go to the western gate, Luke Havergal,
There where the vines cling crimson on the wall,
And in the twilight wait for what will come.
The leaves will whisper there of her, and some,
Like flying words, will strike you as they fall;

But go, and if you listen, she will call.
Go to the western gate, Luke Havergal —
Luke Havergal.

No, there is not a dawn in eastern skies
To rift the fiery night that's in your eyes;
But there, where western glooms are gathering,
The dark will end the dark, if anything:
God slays himself with every leaf that flies,
And hell is more than half of paradise.
No, there is not a dawn in eastern skies —
In eastern skies.

Out of a grave I come to tell you this,
Out of a grave I come to quench the kiss
That flames upon your forehead with a glow
That blinds you to the way that you must go.
Yes, there is yet one way to where she is,
Bitter, but one that faith may never miss.
Out of a grave I come to tell you this —
To tell you this.

There is the western gate, Luke Havergal,
There are the crimson leaves upon the wall.
Go, for the winds are tearing them away, —
Nor think to riddle the dead words they say,
Nor any more to feel them as they fall;
But go, and if you trust her she will call.
There is the western gate, Luke Havergal —
Luke Havergal.

Dudley Randall

Ballad of Birmingham°

1966

(On the bombing of a church in Birmingham, Alabama, 1963)

"Mother dear, may I go downtown
Instead of out to play,
And march the streets of Birmingham
In a Freedom March today?"

"No, baby, no, you may not go,
For the dogs are fierce and wild,
And clubs and hoses, guns and jails
Aren't good for a little child."

Birmingham: This poem was written in response to the 1963 bombing of the 16th Street Baptist Church in Birmingham, Alabama. Four black children perished in the explosion.

■ ■ ■

But, mother, I won't be alone.
Other children will go with me,
And march the streets of Birmingham
To make our country free."

"No, baby, no, you may not go,
For I fear those guns will fire.
But you may go to church instead
And sing in the children's choir."

She has combed and brushed her night-dark hair,
And bathed rose petal sweet,
And drawn white gloves on her small brown hands,
And white shoes on her feet.

The mother smiled to know her child
Was in the sacred place,
But that smile was the last smile
To come upon her face.

For when she heard the explosion,
Her eyes grew wet and wild.
She raced through the streets of Birmingham
Calling for her child.

She clawed through bits of glass and brick,
Then lifted out a shoe
"Oh, here's the shoe my baby wore,
But, baby, where are you?"

JACKIE KAY

Brendon Gallacher

1992

(For my brother Maxie)

He was seven and I was six, my Brendon Gallacher.
He was Irish and I was Scottish, my Brendon Gallacher.
His father was in prison; he was a cat burglar.
My father was a communist party full-time worker.
He had six brothers and I had one, my Brendon Gallacher.

He would hold my hand and take me by the river
Where we'd talk all about his family being poor.
He'd get his mum out of Glasgow when he got older.
A wee holiday someplace nice. Some place far.
I'd tell my mum about my Brendon Gallacher

How his mum drank and his daddy was a cat burglar.
And she'd say, "why not have him round to dinner?"
No, no, I'd say he's got big holes in his trousers.

I like meeting him by the burn in the open air.
Then one day after we'd been friends two years,

One day when it was pouring and I was indoors,
My mum says to me, "I was talking to Mrs. Moir
Who lives next door to your Brendon Gallacher
Didn't you say his address was 24 Novar?
She says there are no Gallachers at 24 Novar

There never have been any Gallachers next door."
And he died then, my Brendon Gallacher,
Flat out on my bedroom floor, his spiky hair,
His impish grin, his funny flapping ear.
Oh Brendon. Oh my Brendon Gallacher.

LYRIC POETRY

Just as my fingers on these keys
Make music, so the selfsame sounds
On my spirit make a music, too. . . .
—WALLACE STEVENS, from "Peter Quince at the Clavier"

The word *lyric* comes from *lyre,* the small harp that the Greek poets played to accompany their songs, and for many centuries lyric poetry was written in the stanza forms and the rhyme schemes of a song. Now a lyric poem is defined as a short poem that expresses the emotions and thoughts of the poet. Often lyric poems are written in the first person, though the "I" of the poem may be a **persona**, which is another person through whom the poet is speaking. The term *lyrics* is still used today, but its meaning is more specifically the text of a song. Lyric poetry is highly subjective, deeply personal, and usually intensely emotional.

Some forms of lyric poetry are defined by a set meter and rhyme scheme, but it is best to think of lyric poetry as a way of expressing feelings. This poem by Scottish poet Robert Burns is an example of a lyric poem that is close to the form of a song but still expresses the writer's emotions.

ROBERT BURNS

Ae Fond Kiss

1792

Ae fond kiss, and then we sever!
Ae farewell, and then forever!
Deep in heart-wrung tears I'll pledge thee,
Warring sighs and groans I'll wage thee.
Who shall say that Fortune grieves him,
While the star of hope she leaves him?
Me, nae cheerfu' twinkle lights me,
Dark despair around benights me.

■ ■ ■

I'll ne'er blame my partial fancy:
Naething could resist my Nancy!
But to see her was to love her,
Love but her, and love for ever.
Had we never lov'd sae kindly,
Had we never lov'd sae blindly,
Never met — or never parted —
We had ne'er been broken-hearted.

Fare-the-weel, thou first and fairest!
Fare-the-weel, thou best and dearest!
Thine be ilka° joy and treasure, *every*
Peace, Enjoyment, Love and Pleasure!
Ae fond kiss, and then we sever!
Ae farewell, alas, for ever!
Deep in heart-wrung tears I'll pledge thee,
Warring sighs and groans I'll wage thee.

The poem's meter — it is written in trochaic tetrameter — is so skillfully done that there is no break in the rhythmic flow. There is a clearly expressed rhyme scheme (each stanza is an octave of four closed couplets), and at the same time the language of the poem, although it is in Scottish dialect, seems natural and direct. The challenge of writing lyric poetry has always been this problem of finding a form for the poem and at the same time finding phrases and sentences that people might actually speak. The best way to test how well the poet has succeeded is to read the poem aloud. This poem of Burns meets the challenge so well that it almost seems to sing itself.

A lyric poem written more than a hundred years later comes closer to the kind of direct speech that expresses the thoughts and feelings of the poet. The American poet Hilda Doolittle, who wrote under the initials H.D., was one of the first generation of poets to abandon rhyme, and even though there is still a classic tone to her poem's diction and syntax, it is a modern poem in open form.

H.D.

Mid-day

1916

The light beats upon me.
I am startled —
a split leaf crackles on the paved floor —
I am anguished — defeated.

A slight wind shakes the seed-pods —
my thoughts are spent
as the black seeds.

My thoughts tear me,
I dread their fever.
I am scattered in its whirl.
I am scattered like
the hot shrivelled seeds.

The shrivelled seeds
are split on the path —
the grass bends with dust,
the grape slips
under its crackled leaf:
Yet far beyond the spent seed-pods,
and the blackened stalks of mint,
the poplar is bright on the hill,
the poplar spreads out,
deep-rooted among trees.

O poplar, you are great
among the hill-stones,
while I perish on the path
among the crevices of the rocks.

The subjectivity that is one of the characteristics of a lyric poem is much more strongly expressed if the poem is written in a style that is closer to the writer's own way of speaking. As we have already discussed in our study of rhyme and meter, certain elements of style and language are won or lost with any changes in the way poets use the means to create their poem. What the lyric poem by H.D. has lost is the musical experience of the meter and the rhyme of Burns's poem. What has been gained is a directness and immediacy of expression.

The Ode

Among the oldest forms of lyric poetry is the **ode**. As a poem of praise, it is found in nearly every language and culture. For European poets, the style had a classical model, the odes written by the Greek poet Pindar to honor the victorious athletes of the Olympic Games of fifth-century Athens. His poems are often called the "Great Odes" to separate them from the imitations that followed. Pindar intended them to be performed in public ceremonies by choruses that sang or chanted the lines.

An ode is a long, serious lyric poem, addressed to a person or to an object, that presents philosophic ideas and moral concerns. Often odes were addressed to inanimate concepts, as in Percy Bysshe Shelley's "Ode to the West Wind" or objects, as in John Keats's "Ode on a Grecian Urn." In Keats's ode he looks at a half-imagined Greek vase covered with painted scenes and decorations. When he asks, in the first stanza, "What men or gods are these? What maidens loth?," he is asking about the figures painted on the sides of the urn. In the turmoil and riot of the life that he sees there, he imagines an eternal reality.

John Keats

Ode on a Grecian Urn

1820

Thou still unravished bride of quietness,
  Thou foster-child of silence and slow time,
Sylvan historian, who canst thus express
  A flowery tale more sweetly than our rhyme:
What leaf-fringed legend haunts about thy shape
  Of deities or mortals, or of both,
    In Tempe or the dales of Arcady?°
  What men or gods are these? What maidens loth?
What mad pursuit? What struggle to escape?
    What pipes and timbrels? What wild ecstasy?

Heard melodies are sweet, but those unheard
  Are sweeter; therefore, ye soft pipes, play on;
Not to the sensual° ear, but, more endeared, *physical*
  Pipe to the spirit ditties of no tone:
Fair youth, beneath the trees, thou canst not leave
  Thy song, nor ever can those trees be bare;
    Bold Lover, never, never canst thou kiss,
Though winning near the goal — yet, do not grieve;
    She cannot fade, though thou hast not thy bliss,
  For ever wilt thou love, and she be fair!

Ah, happy, happy boughs! that cannot shed
  Your leaves, nor ever bid the Spring adieu;
And, happy melodist, unweariѐd,
  For ever piping songs for ever new;
More happy love! more happy, happy love!
  For ever warm and still to be enjoyed,
    For ever panting, and for ever young;
All breathing human passion far above,
  That leaves a heart high-sorrowful and cloyed,
    A burning forehead, and a parching tongue.

Who are these coming to the sacrifice?
  To what green altar, O mysterious priest,
Lead'st thou that heifer lowing at the skies,
  And all her silken flanks with garlands drest?
What little town by river or sea shore,
  Or mountain-built with peaceful citadel,
    Is emptied of this folk, this pious morn?
And, little town, thy streets for evermore
  Will silent be; and not a soul to tell
    Why thou art desolate, can e'er return.

---

7. Tempe . . . Arcady: Rural places in Greece.

■ ■ ■

O Attic° shape! Fair attitude! with brede° *Greek; design*
  Of marble men and maidens overwrought,
With forest branches and the trodden weed;
  Thou, silent form, dost tease us out of thought
As doth Eternity: Cold Pastoral!
  When old age shall this generation waste,
    Thou shalt remain, in midst of other woe
  Than ours, a friend to man, to whom thou say'st,
Beauty is truth, truth beauty, — that is all
    Ye know on earth, and all ye need to know.

"Ode to the West Wind" has none of the philosophic calm of Keats's ode. Shelley's poem is a tumultuous reflection of the personal difficulties that had almost overwhelmed him. The autumn wind is an appropriate image for his emotions, driving before it the falling leaves that mark the approach of winter. Although it is a turbulent poem with many currents of feeling, it is written with great care and subtlety. Shelley allows himself more freedom with the meter than is usual in a formal poem, but each line has five stressed beats.

The complexity lies in the rhyme scheme. The poem is written in **terza rima**. The form is a tercet in iambic pentameter, with a sequence of rhymes that crosses from one stanza to the next, binding them together. The rhyme scheme is *aba, bcb, cdc,* continuing with the same pattern. The middle line becomes the rhyme for the outer lines of the next tercet.

Terza rima is especially effective for narrative poems and for poems, like this one, with a restless, unsettled mood. To strengthen the poem's overall structure, Shelley constructs the tercets in groups of four with an added couplet that rhymes with the middle line of the fourth tercet. This is the rhyme scheme for each stanza: *aba, bcb, cdc, ded, ee.*

PERCY BYSSHE SHELLEY

Ode to the West Wind

1819

I

O wild West Wind, thou breath of Autumn's being,
Thou, from whose unseen presence the leaves dead
Are driven, like ghosts from an enchanter fleeing,

Yellow, and black, and pale, and hectic red,
Pestilence-stricken multitudes: O Thou,
Who chariotest to their dark wintry bed

The winged seeds, where they lie cold and low,
Each like a corpse within its grave, until
Thine azure sister of the Spring shall blow

■ ■ ■

Her clarion° o'er the dreaming earth, and fill *trumpet call*
(Driving sweet buds like flocks to feed in air)
With living hues and odours plain and hill:

Wild Spirit, which art moving everywhere;
Destroyer and Preserver; hear, O hear!

II

Thou on whose stream, 'mid the steep sky's commotion,
Loose clouds like Earth's decaying leaves are shed,
Shook from the tangled boughs of Heaven and Ocean,

Angels of rain and lightning: there are spread
On the blue surface of thine aery surge,
Like the bright hair uplifted from the head

Of some fierce Mænad,° even from the dim verge
Of the horizon to the zenith's height,
The locks of the approaching storm. Thou Dirge

Of the dying year, to which this closing night
Will be the dome of a vast sepulchre,
Vaulted with all thy congregated might

Of vapours, from whose solid atmosphere
Black rain and fire and hail will burst: O hear!

III

Thou who didst waken from his summer dreams
The blue Mediterranean, where he lay,
Lulled by the coil of his chrystalline streams,

Beside a pumice isle in Baiæ's bay,°
And saw in sleep old palaces and towers
Quivering within the wave's intenser day,

All overgrown with azure moss and flowers
So sweet, the sense faints picturing them! Thou
For whose path the Atlantic's level powers

Cleave themselves into chasms, while far below
The sea-blooms and the oozy woods which wear
The sapless foliage of the ocean, know

Thy voice, and suddenly grow grey with fear,
And tremble and despoil themselves: O hear!

IV

If I were a dead leaf thou mightest bear;
If I were a swift cloud to fly with thee;
A wave to pant beneath thy power, and share

21. Mænad: Female worshiper of Bacchus, the Greek god of wine and revelry. **32. Baiæ's bay:** A bay near Naples, Italy.

The impulse of thy strength, only less free
Than thou, O Uncontrollable! If even
I were as in my boyhood, and could be

The comrade of thy wanderings over Heaven,
As then, when to outstrip thy skiey speed
Scarce seemed a vision; I would ne'er have striven

As thus with thee in prayer in my sore need.
Oh! lift me as a wave, a leaf, a cloud!
I fall upon the thorns of life! I bleed!

A heavy weight of hours has chained and bowed
One too like thee: tameless, and swift, and proud.

V

Make me thy lyre, even as the forest is:
What if my leaves are falling like its own!
The tumult of thy mighty harmonies

Will take from both a deep, autumnal tone,
Sweet though in sadness. Be thou, Spirit fierce,
My spirit! Be thou me, impetuous one!

Drive my dead thoughts over the universe
Like withered leaves to quicken a new birth!
And, by the incantation of this verse,

Scatter, as from an unextinguished hearth
Ashes and sparks, my words among mankind!
Be through my lips to unawakened Earth

The trumpet of a prophecy! O Wind,
If Winter comes, can Spring be far behind?

The Elegy

An **elegy**, like an ode, is a serious poem. In its usual form it is a long lyric poem written to lament someone's death and memorialize their life. The most widely read elegy in traditional English poetry is Thomas Gray's "Elegy Written in a Country Churchyard," published in 1751.

THOMAS GRAY

Elegy Written in a Country Churchyard 1751

The curfew tolls the knell of parting day,
  The lowing herd wind slowly o'er the lea,
The plowman homeward plods his weary way,
  And leaves the world to darkness and to me.

■ ■ ■

Now fades the glimmering landscape on the sight,
And all the air a solemn stillness holds,
Save where the beetle wheels his droning flight,
And drowsy tinklings lull the distant folds;

Save that from yonder ivy-mantled tower
The moping owl does to the moon complain
Of such, as wand'ring near her secret bower,
Molest her ancient solitary reign.

Beneath those rugged elms, that yew tree's shade,
Where heaves the turf in many a mold'ring heap,
Each in his narrow cell forever laid,
The rude forefathers of the hamlet sleep.

The breezy call of incense-breathing morn,
The swallow twitt'ring from the straw-built shed,
The cock's shrill clarion, or the echoing horn,° *hunting horn*
No more shall rouse them from their lowly bed.

For them no more the blazing hearth shall burn,
Or busy housewife ply her evening care;
No children run to lisp their sire's return,
Or climb his knees the envied kiss to share.

Oft did the harvest to their sickle yield,
Their furrow oft the stubborn glebe° has broke; *turf*
How jocund did they drive their team afield!
How bowed the woods beneath their sturdy stroke!

Let not Ambition mock their useful toil,
Their homely joys, and destiny obscure;
Nor Grandeur hear with a disdainful smile
The short and simple annals of the poor.

The boast of heraldry, the pomp of pow'r,
And all that beauty, all that wealth e'er gave,
Awaits alike th' inevitable hour.
The paths of glory lead but to the grave.

Nor you, ye proud, impute to these the fault,
If Mem'ry o'er their tomb no trophies raise,
Where through the long-drawn aisle and fretted vault
The pealing anthem swells the note of praise.

Can storied urn or animated bust
Back to its mansion call the fleeting breath?
Can Honor's voice provoke the silent dust,
Or Flatt'ry soothe the dull cold ear of Death?

Perhaps in this neglected spot is laid
Some heart once pregnant with celestial fire;
Hands that the rod of empire might have swayed,
Or waked to ecstasy the living lyre.

■ ■ ■

But knowledge to their eyes her ample page
    Rich with the spoils of time did ne'er unroll;
Chill Penury repressed their noble rage,
    And froze the genial current of the soul.

Full many a gem of purest ray serene,
    The dark unfathomed caves of ocean bear:
Full many a flower is born to blush unseen,
    And waste its sweetness on the desert air.

Some village Hampden,° that with dauntless breast
    The little tyrant of his field withstood;
Some mute inglorious Milton° here may rest,
    Some Cromwell,° guiltless of his country's blood.

Th' applause of list'ning senates to command,
    The threats of pain and ruin to despise,
To scatter plenty o'er a smiling land,
    And read their hist'ry in a nation's eyes,

Their lot forbade; nor circumscribed alone
    Their growing virtues, but their crimes confined;
Forbade to wade through slaughter to a throne,
    And shut the gates of mercy on mankind,

The struggling pangs of conscious truth to hide,
    To quench the blushes of ingenuous shame,
Or heap the shrine of Luxury and Pride
    With incense kindled at the Muse's flame.°

Far from the madding crowd's ignoble strife,
    Their sober wishes never learned to stray;
Along the cool sequestered vale of life
    They kept the noiseless tenor° of their way. *continual movement*

Yet ev'n these bones from insult to protect
    Some frail memorial still erected nigh,
With uncouth rhymes and shapeless sculpture decked,
    Implores the passing tribute of a sigh.

Their name, their years, spelt by th' unlettered Muse,
    The place of fame and elegy supply:
And many a holy text around she strews,
    That teach the rustic moralist to die.

For who to dumb Forgetfulness a prey,
    This pleasing anxious being e'er resigned,

---

57. Hampden: John Hampden (1594–1643) was a member of Parliament who resisted the illegal taxes on his lands that were imposed by Charles I. **59. Milton:** John Milton (1608–1674), the English poet. **60. Cromwell:** Oliver Cromwell (1599–1658) served as Lord Protector of England from 1653 until his death. **71–72. heap the shrine . . . Muse's flame:** Gray is criticizing poets who write to please wealthy patrons.

Left the warm precincts of the cheerful day,
Nor cast one longing ling'ring look behind?

On some fond breast the parting soul relies,
Some pious drops the closing eye requires;
Ev'n from the tomb the voice of Nature cries,
Ev'n in our ashes live their wonted fires.

For thee, who mindful of th' unhonored dead
Dost in these lines their artless tale relate;
If chance, by lonely contemplation led,
Some kindred spirit shall inquire thy fate,

Haply° some hoary-headed swain° may say, *perchance; shepherd*
"Oft have we seen him at the peep of dawn
Brushing with hasty steps the dews away
To meet the sun upon the upland lawn.

"There at the foot of yonder nodding beech
That wreathes its old fantastic roots so high,
His listless length at noontide would he stretch,
And pore upon the brook that babbles by.

"Hard by yon wood, now smiling as in scorn,
Mutt'ring his wayward fancies he would rove,
Now drooping, woeful wan, like one forlorn,
Or crazed with care, or crossed in hopeless love.

"One morn I missed him, on the customed hill,
Along the heath and near his fav'rite tree;
Another came; nor yet beside the rill,
Nor up the lawn, nor at the wood was he;

"The next with dirges due in sad array
Slow through the churchway path we saw him borne.
Approach and read (for thou canst read) the lay,° *song or poem*
Graved on the stone beneath yon aged thorn."

THE EPITAPH

Here rests his head upon the lap of Earth
A youth to Fortune and to Fame unknown.
Fair Science frowned not on his humble birth,
And Melancholy marked him for her own.

Large was his bounty, and his soul sincere,
Heav'n did a recompense as largely send:
He gave to Mis'ry all he had, a tear,
He gained from Heav'n ('twas all he wished) a friend.

No farther seek his merits to disclose,
Or draw his frailties from their dread abode,
(There they alike in trembling hope repose),
The bosom of His Father and his God.

The poem can seem placid and uneventful to modern readers, but at the time it was written it made a strong and disturbing political statement. The poem was unlike other elegies that had been written before it because the individual for whom the elegy was written was an ordinary person. He was simply someone who had been buried in this village's churchyard. As Gray wrote in the epitaph that ends the poem,

Here rests his head upon the lap of Earth
    A youth to Fortune and to Fame unknown.

The person buried in the churchyard is never named. What Gray is insisting is that under other circumstances this ordinary person could have been the equal of any other person in their society. In the years leading up to the revolutions in the American colonies and in France — revolutions that overthrew the rigid class lines of the old social order — these were fiery sentiments. Another stanza from the poem, the twelfth, burned itself into the consciousness of its time, with its bold idea that in the grave might lie someone who could have ruled a nation or could have written immortal poetry. The phrases were echoed again and again by poets, politicians, and writers everywhere:

Perhaps in this neglected spot is laid
    Some heart once pregnant with celestial fire;
Hands that the rod of empire might have swayed,
    Or waked to ecstasy the living lyre.

The final line of the ninth stanza of his poem has been quoted in more speeches, books, and plays than Gray could ever have imagined: "The paths of glory lead but to the grave."

Although the form and the technical means have changed, the elegy continues as part of our poetic heritage. In her elegy for the English rock musician John Lennon, Amy Clampitt uses the name of the apartment building in New York City where Lennon lived and was murdered as the title of her poem, and in several of the lines she alludes to phrases from "Eleanor Rigby," one of the songs he wrote as a member of The Beatles.

AMY CLAMPITT

The Dakota

1983

Grief for a generation — all
the lonely people
gone, the riffraff
out there now mainly pigeons —
steps from its limousine
and lights a taper
inside the brownstone catacomb
of the Dakota. Pick up

the wedding rice, take out
the face left over from
the funeral nobody came to,
bring flowers, leave them woven
with the lugubrious ironwork
of the Dakota. Grief
is original, but it
repeats itself: there's nothing
more original it can do.

The Sonnet

Although a **sonnet** is short — generally fourteen lines — and is written in a regular rhyme sequence, it is one of the richest and most durable forms of lyric poetry. The difference between a sonnet and other lyric poetry is in the way the poet works with its theme. At the heart of most traditional sonnets is an implied argument that muses on the philosophic implications of the sonnet's main idea. The form has been so useful to poets for so many centuries that authors today continue to write sonnets, even if they don't feel they have to restrict themselves to traditional rhyme schemes and meter. What they want to tell the reader, when they use the term *sonnet* or write in a variant of the sonnet form, is that the poem will have a seriousness that may not be characteristic of their other short lyrics.

The sonnet was perfected in Italy in the early fourteenth century. The name comes from the Italian word *sonnetto,* which means "little song." Several poets helped develop the form, but the one whose work was most influential with English poets was Francesco Petrarca, an Italian nobleman known in English as Petrarch, who lived from 1304 to 1374. His sonnets were personal poems, written to express his unhappiness over his love for a woman who did not return his affection. In structure, the individual sonnets presented a kind of short philosophical discussion, with a presentation of the theme of the poem in the opening lines, a consideration of the theme in the next lines, then a conclusion summed up in a final couplet.

The sonnet was brought to England by a courtier and diplomat named Sir Thomas Wyatt, who was sent by Henry VIII on diplomatic missions to France and Italy. Wyatt encountered the writing of Petrarch on his travels, and before his death in 1542 he translated more than a hundred Italian sonnets. The translations were circulated in manuscript through court circles, and a younger poet, also a courtier and nobleman named Henry Howard, Earl of Surrey, who often caroused through the streets of London with Wyatt's son, translated many of the same sonnets. It was Surrey who established the rhyme scheme used by William Shakespeare.

A great playwright, Shakespeare was also an accomplished sonneteer, and one of his enduring works is a collection of 154 sonnets published in 1609. This famous example, untitled but numbered 73, takes as its theme the poet's old age. In the development of its theme and the rich use of imagery and rhyme, the poem shows all the characteristics of the classic sonnet form.

William Shakespeare

That time of year thou mayst in me behold 1609

That time of year thou mayst in me behold
When yellow leaves, or none, or few, do hang
Upon those boughs which shake against the cold,
Bare ruined choirs, where late the sweet birds sang.
In me thou seest the twilight of such day
As after sunset fadeth in the west;
Which by and by black night doth take away,
Death's second self that seals up all in rest.
In me thou seest the glowing of such fire,
That on the ashes of his youth doth lie,
As the deathbed whereon it must expire,
Consumed with that which it was nourished by.
  This thou perceiv'st, which makes thy love more strong,
  To love that well, which thou must leave ere long.

If we look at the meter of the poem we can see that it is in iambic pentameter. The five-foot line, which is also the line of dramatic blank verse, has a feeling of weight and substance that the more common four-foot line of other short lyric poems does not. The fourteen lines consist of three quatrains with the rhyme scheme of *abab, cdcd, efef,* and a concluding couplet, *gg.* This way of structuring the rhyme is called the *English,* or Shakespearean, sonnet. The rhyme scheme for the *Italian,* or Petrarchan sonnet, is an octave of two quatrains that rhyme *abba,* followed by a sextet with a rhyme scheme that may have some variation but is usually either *cdecde* or *cdcdcd.*

Shakespeare was so skillful that he was able to work the sonnet form into the dialogue of one of his plays. In scene 5 of the first act of *Romeo and Juliet,* the lines of dialogue between the two lovers are written as a sonnet.

ROMEO: If I profane with my unworthiest hand
This holy shrine, the gentle fine is this,
My lips, two blushing pilgrims, ready stand
To smooth that rough touch with a tender kiss.
JULIET: Good pilgrim, you do wrong your hand too much,
Which mannerly devotion shows in this;
For saints have hands that pilgrims' hands do touch,
And palm to palm is holy palmers' kiss.
ROMEO: Have not saints lips, and holy palmers too?
JULIET: Aye, pilgrim, lips that they must use in prayer.
ROMEO: Oh then, dear saint, let lips do what hands do.
Then pray. Grant thou, lest faith turn to despair.
JULIET: Saints do not move, though grant for prayers' sake.
ROMEO: Then move not while my prayer's effect I take.

(Several of Shakespeare's sonnets are gathered in Chapter 15, "Poems and Poets.")

Sonnets for Further Reading

Because of the variety of subjects and themes in the sonnet, the best way to experience these poems is to read as many of them as you can. Try to follow their rhyme schemes and the way each sonnet develops its theme. This gathering of sonnets will introduce you to some of the important writers from Petrarca's time to our own. Contemporary poets use the form more freely, but the same concentration of ideas and imagery is still what makes the sonnet unique.

FRANCESCO PETRARCA

Love's Inconsistency

1557

TRANSLATED BY SIR THOMAS WYATT

I find no peace, and all my war is done;
I fear and hope, I burn and freeze likewise;
I fly above the wind, yet cannot rise;
And nought I have, yet all the world I seize on;
That looseth, nor locketh, holdeth me in prison,
And holds me not, yet can I 'scape no wise;
Nor lets me live, nor die, at my devise,
And yet of death it giveth none occasion.
Without eyes I see, and without tongue I plain;
I wish to perish, yet I ask for health;
I love another, and yet I hate myself;
I feed in sorrow, and laugh in all my pain;
Lo, thus displeaseth me both death and life,
And my delight is causer of my grief.

JOHN DONNE

Death, be not proud

1633

Death, be not proud, though some have callèd thee
Mighty and dreadful, for thou art not so;
For those whom thou think'st thou dost overthrow
Die not, poor Death, nor yet canst thou kill me.
From rest and sleep, which but thy pictures be,
Much pleasure; then from thee much more must flow,
And soonest our best men with thee do go,
Rest of their bones, and soul's delivery.
Thou art slave to fate, chance, kings, and desperate men,
And dost with poison, war, and sickness dwell,
And poppy° or charms can make us sleep as well *opium*
And better than thy stroke; why swell'st thou then?
One short sleep past, we wake eternally
And death shall be no more; Death, thou shalt die.

John Milton

When I consider how my light is spent 1673

When I consider how my light is spent
Ere half my days in this dark world and wide,
And that one talent which is death to hide
Lodged with me useless, though my soul more bent
To serve therewith my Maker, and present
My true account, lest he returning chide,
"Doth God exact day-labor, light denied?"
I fondly ask. But Patience, to prevent
That murmur, soon replies, "God doth not need
Either man's work or his own gifts. Who best
Bear his mild yoke, they serve him best. His state
Is kingly: thousands at his bidding speed,
And post o'er land and ocean without rest;
They also serve who only stand and wait."

Elizabeth Barrett Browning

How Do I Love Thee? 1850

How do I love thee? Let me count the ways.
I love thee to the depth and breadth and height
My soul can reach, when feeling out of sight
For the ends of Being and ideal Grace.
I love thee to the level of every day's
Most quiet need, by sun and candlelight.
I love thee freely, as men strive for Right;
I love thee purely, as they turn from Praise;
I love thee with the passion put to use
In my old griefs, and with my childhood's faith.
I love thee with a love I seemed to lose
With my lost saints — I love thee with the breath,
Smiles, tears of all my life! — and, if God choose,
I shall but love thee better after death.

Countee Cullen

Yet Do I Marvel 1925

I doubt not God is good, well-meaning, kind,
And did He stoop to quibble could tell why
The little buried mole continues blind,
Why flesh that mirrors Him must some day die,

Make plain the reason tortured Tantalus°
Is baited by the fickle fruit, declare
If merely brute caprice dooms Sisyphus°
To struggle up a never-ending stair.
Inscrutable His ways are, and immune
To catechism by a mind too strewn
With petty cares to slightly understand
What awful brain compels His awful hand.
Yet do I marvel at this curious thing:
To make a poet black, and bid him sing!

E. E. Cummings

goodby Betty, don't remember me 1923

goodby Betty, don't remember me
pencil your eyes dear and have a good time
with the tall tight boys at Tabari'
s, keep your teeth snowy, stick to beer and lime,
wear dark, and where your meeting breasts are round
have roses darling, it's all i ask of you —
but that when light fails and this sweet profound
Paris moves with lovers, two and two
bound for themselves, when passionately dusk
brings softly down the perfume of the world
(and just as smaller stars begin to husk
heaven) you, you exactly paled and curled
with mystic lips take twilight where i know:
proving to Death that Love is so and so.

Diane Ackerman

Sweep Me through Your Many-Chambered Heart 1978

Sweep me through your many-chambered heart
if you like, or leave me here, flushed
amid the sap-ooze and blossom: one more dish
in the banquet called April, or think me hard-
won all your days full of women. Weeks
later, till I felt your arms around

---

5. **Tantalus:** In Hades, the Greek underworld, Tantalus was prevented from assuaging his hunger as he reached for fruit just beyond his grasp. 7. **Sisyphus:** In Greek myth, Sisyphus was condemned to roll a huge stone uphill that always rolled back down just before he reached the top.

me like a shackle, heard all the sundown
wizardries the fired body speaks.
Tell me why, if it was no more than this,
the unmuddled tumble, the renegade kiss,
today, rapt in a still life and unaware,
my paintbrush dropped like an amber hawk;
thinking I'd heard your footfall on the stair,
I listened, heartwise, for the knock.

Rita Dove

Sonnet in Primary Colors 1995

This is for the woman with one black wing
perched over her eyes: lovely Frida,° erect
among parrots, in the stern petticoats of the peasant,
who painted herself a present —
wildflowers entwining the plaster corset
her spine resides in, that flaming pillar —
this priestess in the romance of mirrors.

Each night she lay down in pain and rose
to the celluloid butterflies of her Beloved Dead,
Lenin and Marx and Stalin arrayed at the footstead.
And rose to her easel, the hundred dogs panting
like children along the graveled walls of the garden, Diego's°
love a skull in the circular window
of the thumbprint searing her inimitable brow.

The Epigram and the Aphorism

Lyric poetry, by its nature, has very loosely defined boundaries or limitations, and it also has room for many forms of humorous short poetry. One of these is the **epigram**. Epigrams are short poems, never more than a few lines long, often rhymed, and usually funny or wryly satirical. They are intended to make a sharp comment or witty observation. The epigram has also been popular with humorous writers of what used to be called *light verse,* short poems usually written for magazines that dressed down-to-earth truths in funny poetic language. The American writer of light verse Ogden Nash was particularly skilled at the art of the epigram.

---

2. Frida: Refers to Frida Kahlo (1907–1954), Mexican surrealist artist famous for her self-portraits revealing her tumultuous life — which included her marriage to muralist Diego Rivera. **12. Diego's:** Refers to Diego Rivera (1886–1957), Mexican artist whose bold, leftist-oriented murals captured significant moments in Mexican history and inspired a revival of fresco painting in Latin America and the United States.

Ogden Nash

Reflection on Ice-Breaking

1931

Candy
Is Dandy,
But liquor
Is Quicker.

Another kind of short, usually humorous poem is the **aphorism**. Epigrams and aphorisms are so close in style and mood that it is difficult sometimes to decide where a particular poem belongs. The usual definition of an aphorism is that it is a short, concise statement of a principle or a sentiment. These three short poems fit the definition very well.

Wendy Cope

Two Cures for Love

1992

1 Don't see him. Don't phone or write a letter.
2 The easy way: get to know him better.

Adrian Mitchell

Celia Celia

1975

When I am sad and weary
When I think all hope has gone
When I walk along High Holborn
I think of you with nothing on

Irving Layton

Don't Blame the Apple

1978

Original sin:
to look
and to be happy.

No human
will forgive you that.
Not ever.

Not even your mother.

The Limerick

The **limerick** is a short, humorous poem that is defined by its verse form. It has become one of the most widespread types of folk poetry, usually in the scatalogical and obscene forms that everyone has read or heard at some time in their lives. The form is a fixed five-line verse, and there is only a single stanza, rhyming *aabba.* It is the characteristic meter of limericks that makes them so easy to remember. Their rhythmic pattern is two rhyming lines of three strong accents, followed by two lines of two strong accents — with a different rhyme — then a final line that returns to the three accents of the first two lines, and it rhymes with them. The meter is an anapest, but the form allows for some variation.

Whatever a reader may think of limericks, there is no other kind of poetry quite like them. They are a good example of what we mean when we talk about freedom within limits. Often writers who are known for more serious work have used the form to write poems that are more light-hearted than their usual poetry. Here are examples by two well-known poets, Dylan Thomas and Robert Frost.

The last time I slept with the Queen
She said, as I whistled "Ich Dien":°
"It's royalty's night out,
But please put the light out,
The Queen may be had, but not seen."

– Dylan Thomas

For travelers going sidereal
The danger, they say, is bacterial.
I don't know the pattern
On Mars, or on Saturn
But on Venus it must be venereal.

– Robert Frost

Although it may seem a contradiction in terms, limericks are also very useful as literary criticism. Although these limericks, all by English writers, are meant to be laughed at, each of them is also a skillfully presented comment on the poem or the play that is the limerick's subject. It would be hard to think of a better short description of the central figure of T. S. Eliot's "The Love Song of J. Alfred Prufrock" (p. 1017) than J. Walker's opening line, "An angst-ridden amorist, Fred. . . ." A. Cinna, in a limerick's small dimensions, manages to present some of the questions that have often bothered students trying to make sense out of Shakespeare's *Hamlet.*

The fine English poet, John Donne,
Was wont to admonish the Sunne:
"You busie old foole
Lie still and keep coole,
For I am in bed having funne."

– Wendy Cope

"Ich Dien": "I serve" — the official motto of the Prince of Wales.

(ON T.S. ELIOT'S "PRUFROCK")

An angst-ridden amorist, Fred,
Saw sartorial changes ahead.
  His mind kept on ringing
  With fishy girls singing.
Soft fruit also filled him with dread.

– J. WALKER

(APROPOS COLERIDGE'S "KUBLA KHAN")

When approached by a person from Porlock
It's best to take time by the forelock.
  Shout, "I'm not at home
  'Till I've finished this pome!"
And refuse to unfasten the door-lock.

– RICHARD LEIGHTON GREEN

Did Ophelia ask Hamlet to bed?
Was Gertrude incestuously wed?
  Is there anything certain?
  By the fall of the curtain
Almost everyone's certainly dead.

– A. CINNA

RELATED COMMENTARIES: *Rita Dove, "An Intact World," page 1162; Erica Jong, "Devouring Time: Shakespeare's Sonnets," page 1185.*

11

THE TYPES OF POETRY: OTHER POETIC FORMS

A poem is a sum of triumphs over unpredictable resistances.
– STANLEY KUNITZ, quoted in Seldon Rodman's *Tongues of Fallen Angels*

Many other forms of lyric poetry have been popular in the past, and you might encounter some of their names in your reading. **Rhyme royal** is a form that, like the sonnet, also developed from Italian models. It is a seven-line stanza in iambic pentameter with a rhyme scheme of *ababbcc.* The English medieval poet Geoffrey Chaucer used it for his long poem *Troilus and Criseyde,* and Sir Thomas Wyatt's great love poem, "They Flee from Me" (p. 818), is written in rhyme royal. Another form that Wyatt first used in English was an eight-line stanza called **ottava rima**. It has a rhyme scheme of *abababcc.*

Although **terza rima**, another of the forms taken from Italian models, has been used only occasionally by poets writing in English since the fifteenth century, it is the form for Shelley's "Ode to the West Wind," which we discussed earlier in the previous chapter. The most complex stanza form in English that continued to be used by later writers was created by Edmund Spenser at the end of the sixteenth century for his epic poem *The Faerie Queen.* The **Spenserian stanza** uses eight lines of iambic pentameter and a last line of six stressed feet, which is called an **alexandrine**. The rhyme scheme is *ababbcbcc.* Here is a stanza from Spenser's epic.

A Gentle Knight was pricking° on the plaine, *cantering*
Y cladd in mightie arms and silver shielde,
Wherein old dints of deepe wounds did remaine,
The cruell markes of many a bloudy fielde;
Yet armes till that time did he never wield.

His angry steede did chide his foaming bitt,
As much disdayning to the curbe to yield:
Full jolly° knight he seemd, and faire did sitt, *gallant*
As one for knightly giusts° and fierce encounters fitt. *jousts*

Despite its daunting complexity, Keats used the Spenserian stanza for his ballad "Eve of St. Agnes," and Shelley wrote "Adonais," his elegy on the death of Keats, in the same form.

There are several shorter forms of lyric poetry that have been used by modern poets looking for a form of verse that would have some of the usefulness of the sonnet but would have more of a songlike quality. All of these types of lyric are characterized by complicated rhyme schemes and concise patterns of meter. The rules for writing each of them seem to contradict the idea of spontaneity, which is also considered one of the essentials of lyric poetry, but poets respond to challenges from other poets. Nearly everyone who writes in traditional closed forms tries one of these rich hybrids at one time or another. Here are two of the best-known forms, the sestina and the villanelle.

The **sestina** is composed of six stanzas, each six lines long, with a concluding verse of three lines called the **envoy**. The form, which is called the "song of sixes," is from France, where it is said to have been introduced into Provençal love poetry in the thirteenth century. It is a complicated word game where the last words of the first six lines are repeated as end words of the lines of the other five stanzas, changing places in a carefully ordered procession. The final three lines must include the words, but in any order. One of the best-known modern examples of a sestina is this poem by Elizabeth Bishop.

ELIZABETH BISHOP

Sestina

1965

September rain falls on the house.
In the failing light, the old grandmother
sits in the kitchen with the child
beside the Little Marvel Stove,
reading the jokes from the almanac,
laughing and talking to hide her tears.

She thinks that her equinoctial tears
and the rain that beats on the roof of the house
were both foretold by the almanac,
but only known to a grandmother.
The iron kettle sings on the stove.
She cuts some bread and says to the child,

It's time for tea now; but the child
is watching the teakettle's small hard tears
dance like mad on the hot black stove,
the way the rain must dance on the house.

Tidying up, the old grandmother
hangs up the clever almanac

on its string. Birdlike, the almanac
hovers half open above the child,
hovers above the old grandmother
and her teacup full of dark brown tears.
She shivers and says she thinks the house
feels chilly, and puts more wood in the stove.

It was to be, says the Marvel Stove.
I know what I know, says the almanac.
With crayons the child draws a rigid house
and a winding pathway. Then the child
puts in a man with buttons like tears
and shows it proudly to the grandmother.

But secretly, while the grandmother
busies herself about the stove,
the little moons fall down like tears
from between the pages of the almanac
into the flower bed the child
has carefully placed in the front of the house.

Time to plant tears, says the almanac.
The grandmother sings to the marvellous stove
and the child draws another inscrutable house.

The **villanelle** is composed of five tercets and a final quatrain, written in iambic pentameter. The rhyme scheme for the tercets is *aba,* and the quatrain repeats the final rhyme, *abaa.* Like the sestina, the poem is an elaborate game in which entire lines appear again and again. The first line of the poem is used as the final line of the second and fourth tercets, and it also becomes the next to last line of the quatrain. The last line of the first tercet becomes the last line (with slight variations in this example) for the last line of the third and fifth tercets and finally ends the poem. This is an example by the modern American poet Theodore Roethke.

THEODORE ROETHKE

The Waking 1953

I wake to sleep, and take my waking slow.
I feel my fate in what I cannot fear.
I learn by going where I have to go.

We think by feeling. What is there to know?
I hear my being dance from ear to ear.
I wake to sleep and take my waking slow.

■ ■ ■

Of those so close beside me, which are you?
God bless the Ground! I shall walk softly there,
And learn by where I have to go.

Light takes the Tree, but who can tell us how?
The lowly worm climbs up a winding stair;
I wake to sleep, and take my waking slow.

Great Nature has another thing to do
To you and me; so take the lively air,
And, lovely, learn by going where to go.

This shaking keeps me steady, I should know.
What falls away is always. This is near.
I wake to sleep, and take my waking slow.
I learn by going where I have to go.

One of the best-known examples of the modern villanelle is "Do Not Go Gentle into That Good Night," the Welsh poet Dylan Thomas's moving tribute to his father. In a note to his publisher when he sent him the poem Thomas wrote, "The only person I can't show the little enclosed poem to is my father, who doesn't know he's dying."

DYLAN THOMAS

Do Not Go Gentle into That Good Night *1951*

Do not go gentle into that good night,
Old age should burn and rave at close of day;
Rage, rage against the dying of the light.

Though wise men at their end know dark is right,
Because their words had forked no lightning they
Do not go gentle into that good night.

Good men, the last wave by, crying how bright
Their frail deeds might have danced in a green bay,
Rage, rage against the dying of the light.

Wild men who caught and sang the sun in flight,
And learn, too late, they grieved it on its way,
Do not go gentle into that good night.

Grave men, near death, who see with blinding sight
Blind eyes could blaze like meteors and be gay,
Rage, rage against the dying of the light.

And you, my father, there on the sad height,
Curse, bless, me now with your fierce tears, I pray.
Do not go gentle into that good night.
Rage, rage against the dying of the light.

Open Form

Like the nineteenth-century photographer Louis Daguerre, who was supposed to have cried out, when he managed to capture an image on a silver-coated plate, "From this moment, painting is dead!," many people were certain that when poetry lost its centuries-old anchors of rhyme and meter there would be no more poetry. As we know, poetry is still with us, even though we do not usually look for rhyme schemes or count the meter when we read a poem today. In the first years of the "free verse" movement, as **open form** was called then, there was some feeling that poetry could be as "free" as the wind and that a poem could take any form the writer chose. The writers found, however, that although the way they wrote had changed, the means they worked with to create a poem were still the same. Poetry written in open form had to have the concentration and the technical virtuosity of poetry written in traditional closed forms.

This poem by the American poet Galway Kinnell has the tone of ordinary conversation, but, although the poem is not rhymed, he has used many of the traditional technical means to create it.

GALWAY KINNELL

The Man Splitting Wood in the Daybreak — *1985*

The man splitting wood in the daybreak
looks strong, as though, if one weakened,
one could turn to him and he would help.
Gus Newland was strong. When he split wood
he struck hard, flashing the bright steel
through air of daybreak so fast rock maple
leapt apart — as they think marriages will
in countries about to institute divorce —
and even willow, which, though stacked
to dry a full year, on separating
actually weeps — totem wood, therefore,
to the married-until-death — miseried asunder
with many small lip-smacking gasp-noises.
But Gus is dead. We could turn to our fathers,
but they protect us only through the unperplexed
looking-back of the numerals cut into their headstones.
Or to our mothers, whose love, so devastated,
can't, even in spring, break through the hard earth.
Our spouses weaken at the same rate we do.
We have to hold our children up to lean on them.
What about the man splitting wood in the daybreak,
who looked strong? That was years ago. That was me.

Kinnell develops an extended metaphor of splitting wood as a symbol of young strength; he uses a shift of syntax in lines like "Or to our mothers, whose love, so devastated, / can't, even in spring, break through the hard earth"; he employs the conscious awkwardness of the constructed word *mis-eried* set beside the more elegant-sounding *asunder.* The meter is irregular, but if you scan the opening line, "The man splitting wood in the daybreak," you are already conscious of a strong metric pulse, which Kinnell interrupts with the phrase "Gus Newland was strong" for dramatic effect at the beginning of the fourth line. You can find alliteration in the phrase "air of daybreak." Kinnell even uses an adjective that causes a problem of interpretation, "totem wood," suggesting perhaps that the wood is an emblem or symbol for a marriage that lasts "until-death."

The Prose Poem

As readers have become more used to open form, poets have continued to explore its possibilities. A form that was first developed in France but which has now spread to every other language is the **prose poem**. The term contradicts itself by telling us that this is both prose and poetry, two forms of writing we have always been told are separate, but the term also is a good description of what writers do with the form. A prose poem is a lyric poem that has all the characteristics of a lyric but is written in prose. It presents one image or, like a lyric poem in open form, a response to a single emotion.

A prose poem can have some kind of narrative, but the story line is one of the means the poet uses to illustrate the theme of the poem. Some prose poems have the effect of a **parable**, a short narrative used to point out a moral. Others have the effect of opening the mind to the possibilities of the unconscious. Even if they present us with a single, condensed image, they often leave us with the sense that what we have just read has made us conscious of something *else.* We call poetry like this **associative**. Here are four contemporary prose poems by American writers that show some of the range of the form.

Robert Bly

August Rain

1975

After a month and a half without rain, at last, in late August, darkness comes at three in the afternoon. A cheerful thunder begins, and then the rain. I set a glass out on a table to measure the rain and, suddenly buoyant and affectionate, go indoors to find my children. They are upstairs, playing quietly alone in their doll-filled rooms, hanging pictures, thoughtfully moving "the small things that make them happy" from one side of the room to another. I feel triumphant, without need of money, far from the grave. I walk over the grass, watching the soaked chairs, and the cooled towels, and sit down on my stoop, pulling a chair out with me. The rain deepens. It rolls off the porch roof, making a great puddle near me. The bubbles slide toward the puddle edge, become crowded, and disappear. The black earth turns blacker; it absorbs the rain needles without a sound. The sky is low, everything silent, as when parents are angry. . . . What has failed and been forgiven — the leaves from last year unable to go on, lying near the foundation, dry under the porch, retreat farther into the shadow; they give off a faint hum, as of birds' eggs, or the tail of a dog.

The older we get the more we fail, but the more we fail the more we feel a part of the dead straw of the universe, the corner of a barn with cowdung twenty years old, the chair fallen back on its head in a deserted farmhouse, the belt left hanging over the chairback after the bachelor has died in the ambulance on the way to the city. These objects belong to us; they ride us as the child holds on to the dog's fur; they appear in our dreams; they approach nearer and nearer, coming in slowly from the wainscoting. They make our trunks heavy, accumulating between trips. These objects lie against the ship's side, and will nudge the hole open that lets the water in at last.

Robert Hass

A Story about the Body — *1989*

The young composer, working that summer at an artist's colony, had watched her for a week. She was Japanese, a painter, almost sixty, and he thought he was in love with her. He loved her work, and her work was like the way she moved her body, used her hands, looked at him directly when she made amused and considered answers to his questions. One night, walking back from a concert, they came to her door and she turned to him and said, "I think you would like to have me. I would like that too, but I must tell you that I have had a double mastectomy," and when he didn't understand, "I've lost both my breasts." The radiance that he had carried around in his belly and chest cavity — like music — withered very quickly, and he made himself look at her when he said, "I'm sorry. I don't think I could." He walked back to his own cabin through the pines, and in the morning he found a small blue bowl on the porch outside his door. It looked to be full of rose petals, but he found when he picked it up that the rose petals were on top; the rest of the bowl — she must have swept them from the corners of her studio — was full of dead bees.

Louis Jenkins

How to Tell a Wolf from a Dog — *1995*

A wolf carries his head down, tail down. He has a look of preoccupation, or worry, you might think. He has a family to support. He probably has a couple of broken ribs from trying to bring down a moose. He's not getting workman's comp, either, and no praise for his efforts. The wolf looks unemployed, flat broke.

On the other hand, a dog of similar features, a husky or a malamute, has his head up, ears up, looks attentive, self-confident, cheerful and obedient. He is fully employed with an eye toward promotion. He carries his tail high, like a banner. He's part of a big organization and has the title of "man's best friend."

MICHAEL BENEDIKT

The Meat Epitaph

1975

This is what it was: Sometime in the recent but until now unrecorded past, it was decided by cattle-ranchers that since people were increasingly insistent that "you are what you eat," all cattle on the way to market were to be marked with brief descriptive tags noting the favorite food of each beast, and how much each ate of it. This, it was felt, would both delight the diner and comfort the consumer: people would be able to tell exactly what kind of flavor and texture beef they were purchasing beforehand, and always secure exactly the kind of product most likely to delight their taste (it was something a little like our present-day system of catering to preferences for light and dark meat in chicken). The system set up seemed ideally efficient: first, they attached the tag to each beast on its last day on the ranch, just before the two or three days required for shipment to the slaughterhouse — during which travel time the animal customarily doesn't eat anything, anyway. Once at the slaughterhouse, they carefully removed the tags; and during the slaughtering, duplicated the so-called "parent tag" numerous times, preparing perhaps hundreds of tiny tags for each animal. Directly after, at the packing plant, these were affixed to the proper parts, each section of each animal being separately and appropriately tagged, as if with an epitaph. But something went wrong with this means of augmenting the diner's delight, and of comforting the consumer. At first, quite predictably, the tags came out reading things like "Much grass, a little moss, medium grain" and "Much grass, much grain, generally ate a lot." And this, as one might expect, proved a great pleasure to the consumer. But then tags began coming through reading things like "A little grass, small grain, many diverse scraps from the table"; and "She was our favorite, gave her all we had to give"; and one (featured at dinnertime one evening on national television news) saying: "Goodbye, Blackie Lamb, sorry you had to grow up — we'll miss you." Gradually, despite its efficiency, this system somehow ceased to delight the diner, and comfort the consumer. And this is how the practice of the meat epitaph began to become generally neglected during the course of time; and how people came to eat their meat, as they generally do today, partially or wholly blindfolded.

Haiku

An easy definition of **haiku** might be,

A HAIKU

Seventeen syllable
   Japanese poem
popular with students.

Most dictionaries insist on two syllables for the word *poem;* so our definition can claim to have the required seventeen syllables. The haiku is so well known in Japan that most of the members of an educated Japanese family would be skilled enough in writing haiku to present verses to one another. Among experienced poets the poems were usually written in a linked sequence, each poet writing a new haiku in response to the haiku that had just been written, or that they had just read.

Most haiku are written in three lines, with five syllables in the two outer lines and seven in the middle line. As with so many other things between the two languages, Japanese and English, the similarity between our syllable and the Japanese ideogram — the system of writing using pictures to represent a thing or idea — is not as close as our precise definition suggests. An ideogram can have the connotations of one or more of our words and even an entire phrase. A direct translation from a Japanese haiku sometimes means that when you read the poem in English, you are getting considerably less from it than a Japanese reader would.

Since an ideogram may be written in different ways, the poet can also allude to other haiku or to another poet by the way the ideogram is set down on the paper. Specific places or certain seasons of the year are identified with the best-known writers. With all of these possibilities, a haiku that can seem like a small, simple poem to an English reader can present a Japanese reader with a world of allusion and response. This allusion and response are the essence of a haiku. The small glimpse of a real instant should recall in the reader some moment of life, some half-forgotten memory.

There have been thousands of writers of haiku since the form was first created, but four poets are considered to be the most important. The first is Bashō, who was born in 1644 into a samurai family. Before his death in 1694, he had turned to a simple life and spent much of his time making long journeys over the Japanese countryside, traveling by foot or on horseback. The spare simplicity of his poems reflects his Zen Buddhist beliefs. Many of his haiku were written on his travels. This is a typical Bashō poem:

   A crow is perched
Upon a leafless withered bough —
   The evening dusk.

Here are three of Bashō's linked haiku, freely interpreted by Robert Hass:

   Ripening barley —
does it get that color
   from the skylark's tears?

Day by day
the barley ripens,
the skylarks sing.

Having no talent,
I just want to sleep,
you noisy birds.

Two generations after Bashō's death, his poetry was taken up by a well-educated writer and painter named Buson, who lived from 1716 to 1783. Buson revered Bashō's poetry and at the same time brought his own sensitivity to the haiku:

The sea in springtime
All the warm day in breathing swells —
In breathing swells.

Although Issa lived at almost the same time as Buson, from 1763 to 1827, his poetry had a distinctive tone that came as much from his country background as it did from his poetic studies:

Children imitating cormorants —
more wonderful
than cormorants.

In the century that followed Buson's death, the haiku was neglected and the form lost some of its purity, but it was once again taken up by a younger poet, Shiki, who lived from 1872 to 1923. Shiki set the tone of the modern haiku:

The ocean freshly green
Mountain on mountain peaked with snow
Birds homing to the north.

The haiku has been adopted by many American poets, particularly the Beat poets of the 1950s and the 1960s, who had become Buddhists and who tried to match the severity of the Japanese poems with their own rigor and restraint. The best known of the Beat writers, Jack Kerouac, wrote dozens of haiku, sometimes jotting them down in pencil on the back pages of the paperback books he carried in his pocket when he worked on the railroad. He called what he was writing "Western Haikus."

Birds singing
in the dark
— Rainy dawn

The summer chair
rocking by itself
In the blizzard

In my medicine cabinet
the winter fly
has died of old age

The American writer who has perhaps best caught the essence of the haiku is the African American novelist and author of short stories Richard

Wright. Wright discovered the haiku in 1959, shortly before his death. As he wrote a friend, "Maybe I'm fooling around with these little poems, but I could not let them go. I was possessed by them" (quoted in *American Poetry and Japanese Culture,* Kodama, Archon Books, 1994, p. 158). Within a few months he wrote 4,000 haiku and then spent almost as much time winnowing them down into a collection describing the seasons of the year.

I would like a bell
Tolling in this soft twilight
Over willow trees

A freezing morning
I left a bit of my skin
On the broomstick handle

A soft wind at dawn
Lifts one dry leaf and lays it
Upon another

An empty sickbed
An indented white pillow
In weak winter sun

Imagism

The term **imagism** was invented by an American poet, Ezra Pound, who was living in London and closely associated with a small group of friends who were the first imagists. As a literary movement, imagism lasted only a few years, but it was widely discussed, ridiculed, and parodied, and it had an important role in the development of open form poetry. Even poets who would not think of themselves as imagists used the methods of the imagists for their own work. The imagists were trying to create poetry that was, as it was expressed by another of their founders, T. E. Hulme, "a moment of discovery or awareness, created by effective metaphor which provides the sharp, intuitive insight that is the essence of life." In the credo that opened the 1915 imagist anthology, the first point was "To use the language of common speech, but the exact word, not the nearly exact, nor the merely decorative." The fourth point was that imagist poems should "Present an image. Poetry should render particulars exactly, and not deal in vague generalities, however magnificent and sonorous."

It was the lean, hard diction of imagist poetry that was to have a lasting effect on modern poetry. Poets found that they did not have to round every poem into a generality. As William Carlos Williams, a friend of Pound's who stayed in New Jersey and wrote his poetry with his own American voice, expressed the imagist ideal, "No ideas, but in things."

This poem by Ezra Pound is perhaps the most famous of the imagist poems. Pound used it as an example of what he meant by imagism in his introduction to the first collection of his friends' poems. It is a description of people in the Paris subway on a rainy, dark night.

EZRA POUND

In a Station of the Metro

1913

The apparition of these faces in the crowd
Petals on a wet, black bough.

T. E. Hulme's role in the early years of imagism is well known, and he contributed several imagist poems, like this description of a scene in London, to the movement's early anthologies.

T. E. HULME

Images

1914

Old houses were scaffolding once
and workmen whistling.

For a few months, when they both were students at the University of Pennsylvania, Pound had been engaged to Hilda Doolittle. When she came to London he persuaded her to use her initials, H.D., for her poetry. She and her husband, Richard Aldington, were part of the original imagist group.

H.D.

Oread°

1914

Whirl up, sea —
whirl your pointed pines,
splash your great pines
on our rocks,
hurl your green over us,
cover us with your pools of fir.

In the United States the New England poet Amy Lowell took up the cause of imagism, editing a series of imagist anthologies and becoming an important supporter of the new style. In her own imagist poems, and those of another American poet of the period, Adelaide Crapsey, the strong underpinning of the Japanese haiku in imagist writing can be clearly seen.

Oread: Mountain nymph.

AMY LOWELL

Wind and Silver 1914

Greatly shining,
The autumn moon floats in the thin sky;
And the fish-ponds shake their backs and flash their dragon scales
As she passes over them.

ADELAIDE CRAPSEY

November Night 1913

Listen . . .
With faint dry sound,
Like steps of passing ghosts,
The leaves, frost-crisp'd, break from the tree
And fall.

Although William Carlos Williams never considered himself an imagist, the poetry he wrote after the group began to publish reflected their aims. The best way to describe the effect of the imagist credo on his work is to say that he wrote poems that were made possible by imagism. His poem "The Red Wheelbarrow" would be a classic imagist description of a wheelbarrow left out in the rain close to the chickens, except for his enigmatic phrase, "so much depends." What Williams seems to be suggesting in his eight short lines is that he finds something very important in this image of rain and chickens and a wheelbarrow in his backyard. Although we know now that the inspiration for the poem came to Dr. Williams when he was waiting for news of a patient as he stared out of the family's window into their backyard, the basic image of the poem has never given away all of its secrets.

WILLIAM CARLOS WILLIAMS

The Red Wheelbarrow 1923

so much depends
upon

a red wheel
barrow

glazed with rain
water

beside the white
chickens

This next poem is closer to the imagist ideal.

William Carlos Williams

Night

1917

Houses —
the dark side silhouetted
on flashes of moonlight!

The air — full of
invisible snow!

At the end of the street —
chrysanthemums in
a lighted window:
white and pink globes
in clusters massed!
They grow clearer
nearer . . . nearer!
I will reach them! !
(if I continue)

The window
is full of flowers —
more than I imagined . . .

They are gone!

The flower girl
has switched off the light.

Moon-shine
street lamps in my face.
"What do I care!"

Although Wallace Stevens was an insurance executive who lived in Hartford, Connecticut, he had many associations with Williams and other young poets who were experimenting with the new style. The first and last verses of his poem "Thirteen Ways of Looking at a Blackbird" have all the characteristics of an imagist poem. The first verse also suggests the tone of a haiku, although it has too many syllables. Other verses, like the seventh, with its admonition to the men of Haddam, a small city in Connecticut, to stop thinking about imagined exotic birds and see the blackbirds walking around the ground, are more didactic.

Like Williams's poem about the red wheelbarrow, this poem has also defied easy access to its meanings. Perhaps one way to understand it is to think of it as a series of imagist poems and short enigmatic lyrics, with blackbirds suddenly flying through. It is a poem that reminds us of Marianne Moore's description of poetry as something that can present us with "imaginary gardens with real toads in them."

WALLACE STEVENS

Thirteen Ways of Looking at a Blackbird 1931

I

Among twenty snowy mountains
The only moving thing
Was the eye of the blackbird.

II

I was of three minds,
Like a tree
In which there are three blackbirds.

III

The blackbird whistled in the autumn winds.
It was a small part of the pantomime.

IV

A man and a woman
Are one.
A man and a woman and a blackbird
Are one.

V

I do not know which to prefer,
The beauty of inflections
Or the beauty of innuendoes,
The blackbird whistling
Or just after.

VI

Icicles filled the long window
With barbaric glass.
The shadow of the blackbird
Crossed it, to and fro.
The mood
Traced in the shadow
An indecipherable cause.

VII

O thin men of Haddam,
Why do you imagine golden birds?
Do you not see how the blackbird
Walks around the feet
Of the women about you?

VIII

I know noble accents
And lucid, inescapable rhythms;
But I know, too,
That the blackbird is involved
In what I know.

IX

When the blackbird flew out of sight,
It marked the edge
Of one of many circles.

X

At the sight of blackbirds
Flying in a green light,
Even the bawds of euphony
Would cry out sharply.

XI

He rode over Connecticut
In a glass coach.
Once, a fear pierced him,
In that he mistook
The shadow of his equipage
For blackbirds.

XII

The river is moving.
The blackbird must be flying.

XIII

It was evening all afternoon.
It was snowing
And it was going to snow.
The blackbird sat
In the cedar-limbs.

DRAMATIC POETRY

The term **dramatic poetry**, in its denotative sense, means the use of poetry in the writing of drama. If we have grown up with English as our language, when we think of poetry as dramatic dialogue we usually are hearing, in our memory, the blank-verse cadences of Shakespeare and the other Elizabethan dramatists. In the prologue to *King Henry the Fifth,* Shakespeare attracts the attention of the crowd of theatergoers with language that is as dramatic as the events that he is describing.

William Shakespeare

Prologue to King Henry the Fifth

1600

O! for a Muse of fire, that would ascend
The brightest heaven of invention;
A kingdom for a stage, princes to act
And monarchs to behold the swelling scene.
Then should the warlike Harry, like himself,
Assume the port of Mars; and at his heels,
Leash'd in like hounds, should famine, sword, and fire
Crouch for employment. But pardon, gentles all,
The flat unraised spirits that hath dar'd
On this unworthy scaffold to bring forth
So great an object: can this cockpit hold
The vasty fields of France? or may we cram
Within this wooden O the very casques
That did affright the air at Agincourt?
O, pardon! since a crooked figure may
Attest in little place a million;
And let us, ciphers to this great accompt,
On your imaginary forces work.
Suppose within the girdle of these walls
Are now confin'd two mighty monarchies,
Whose high upreared and abutting fronts
The perilous narrow ocean parts asunder:
Piece out our imperfections with your thoughts:
Into a thousand parts divide one man,
And make imaginary puissance;
Think when we talk of horses that you see them
Printing their proud hoofs i' the receiving earth;
For 'tis your thoughts that now must deck our kings,
Carry them here and there, jumping o'er times,
Turning the accomplishment of many years
Into an hour-glass: for the which supply,
Admit me Chorus to this history;
Who prologue-like your humble patience pray,
Gently to hear, kindly to judge, our play.

If we had grown up with French as our language, however, what we would hear in our memory would be the rhymed verse of Molière, who was writing for the court of Louis XIV, more than a half a century after Shakespeare. We are not used to hearing rhymed verse as dialogue from the stage, but after a moment we become so accustomed to the courtly style of the rhyme that without the sounds and rhythm of the language the play would seem as flat and unsatisfactory as stale bread. Molière's dialogue seems to *sing* from the stage. Here is an example from his play *The Misanthrope* (1666), as translated by the poet Richard Wilbur in 1955. Two suitors are trying to force the heroine to tell them which one she loves. She finally tires of their persistence and answers sharply,

Enough: this inquisition's gone too far:
How utterly unreasonable you are!
Not that I couldn't make the choice with ease;
My heart has no conflicting sympathies;
I know full well which one of you I favor,
And you'd not see me hesitate or waver.
But how can you expect me to reveal
So cruelly and bluntly what I feel?
I think it altogether too unpleasant
To choose between two men when both are present.

Many poets have looked for a form that would combine the power of the spoken poem from the stage and the more intimate expression of a poem on the page. One of the most popular of these forms is the dramatic monologue, and a student will come much closer to understanding poems like these by reading them out loud.

The Dramatic Monologue

A **dramatic monologue** is usually defined as a poem written in the form of a speech or extended narration that the person who is the subject of the poem delivers to someone else. In the nineteenth century, when the form was very popular, a dramatic monologue had a definite speaker who was talking to an imaginary person; there was some implied action; and the action took place in the present. Often the subject of the more lurid monologues was someone, often a woman, who related a story about something terrible that had happened to them, and then ended the poem by hurling themselves off a cliff or into the ocean.

The dramatic monologues written by the English poet Robert Browning, however, are character studies of people who reveal themselves as they speak. One of the best known is "My Last Duchess." If you read the poem aloud, you will hear the subtlety and ease of its language. The poem perfectly fits the nineteenth-century idea of the dramatic monologue. It includes a definite speaker, the action of the duke showing his art collection, and the moment in the present when he is talking to the emissary.

ROBERT BROWNING

My Last Duchess

1842

Ferrara

That's my last Duchess painted on the wall,
Looking as if she were alive. I call
That piece a wonder, now: Frà Pandolf's° hands

3. Frà Pandolf's hands: Brother Pandolf, a fictional painter.

Worked busily a day, and there she stands.
Will't please you sit and look at her? I said
"Frà Pandolf" by design, for never read
Strangers like you that pictured countenance,
The depth and passion of its earnest glance,
But to myself they turned (since none puts by
The curtain I have drawn for you, but I)
And seemed as they would ask me, if they durst,
How such a glance came there; so, not the first
Are you to turn and ask thus. Sir, 'twas not
Her husband's presence only, called that spot
Of joy into the Duchess' cheek: perhaps
Frà Pandolf chanced to say "Her mantle laps
Over my lady's wrist too much," or "Paint
Must never hope to reproduce the faint
Half-flush that dies along her throat": such stuff
Was courtesy, she thought, and cause enough
For calling up that spot of joy. She had
A heart — how shall I say? — too soon made glad,
Too easily impressed; she liked whate'er
She looked on, and her looks went everywhere.
Sir, 'twas all one! My favor at her breast,
The dropping of the daylight in the West,
The bough of cherries some officious fool
Broke in the orchard for her, the white mule
She rode with round the terrace — all and each
Would draw from her alike the approving speech,
Or blush, at least. She thanked men, — good! but thanked
Somehow — I know not how — as if she ranked
My gift of a nine-hundred-years-old name
With anybody's gift. Who'd stoop to blame
This sort of trifling? Even had you skill
In speech — which I have not — to make your will
Quite clear to such an one, and say, "Just this
Or that in you disgusts me; here you miss,
Or there exceed the mark" — and if she let
Herself be lessoned so, nor plainly set
Her wits to yours, forsooth, and made excuse,
— E'en then would be some stooping; and I choose
Never to stoop. Oh sir, she smiled, no doubt,
Whene'er I passed her; but who passed without
Much the same smile? This grew; I gave commands;
Then all smiles stopped together. There she stands
As if alive. Will't please you rise? We'll meet
The company below, then. I repeat,
The Count your master's known munificence
Is ample warrant that no just pretense

Of mine for dowry will be disallowed;
Though his fair daughter's self, as I avowed
At starting, is my object. Nay, we'll go
Together down, sir. Notice Neptune, though,
Taming a sea-horse, thought a rarity,
Which Claus of Innsbruck° cast in bronze for me!

The dramatic monologue today, as critic Park Honan has defined it, is "a single discourse by one whose presence is indicated by the poet, but who is not the poet himself." In the modern monologue "Next Day," the American poet Randall Jarrell has chosen the persona of a middle-aged woman whose children are off at school and who suddenly understands that she is growing old. It is the day after the funeral of a friend, and her own life, at this moment, feels "commonplace and solitary."

Randall Jarrell

Next Day

1965

Moving from Cheer to Joy, from Joy to All,
I take a box
And add it to my wild rice, my Cornish game hens.
The slacked or shorted, basketed, identical
Food-gathering flocks
Are selves I overlook. Wisdom, said William James,°

Is learning what to overlook. And I am wise
If that is wisdom.
Yet somehow, as I buy All from these shelves
And the boy takes it to my station wagon,
What I've become
Troubles me even if I shut my eyes.

When I was young and miserable and pretty
And poor, I'd wish
What all girls wish: to have a husband,
A house and children. Now that I'm old, my wish
Is womanish:
That the boy putting groceries in my car

See me. It bewilders me he doesn't see me.
For so many years
I was good enough to eat: the world looked at me
And its mouth watered. How often they have undressed me,
The eyes of strangers!
And, holding their flesh within my flesh, their vile

56. Claus of Innsbruck: Unidentified; probably a fictional sculptor.
6. William James: American pragmatist, philosopher, and psychologist (1892–1910).

■ ■ ■

Imaginings within my imagining,
I too have taken
The chance of life. Now the boy pats my dog
And we start home. Now I am good.
The last mistaken,
Ecstatic, accidental bliss, the blind
Happiness that, bursting, leaves upon the palm
Some soap and water —
It was so long ago, back in some Gay
Twenties, Nineties, I don't know . . . Today I miss
My lovely daughter
Away at school, my sons away at school,
My husband away at work — I wish for them.
The dog, the maid,
And I go through the sure unvarying days
At home in them. As I look at my life,
I am afraid
Only that it will change, as I am changing:
I am afraid, this morning, of my face.
It looks at me
From the rear-view mirror, with the eyes I hate,
The smile I hate. Its plain, lined look
Of gray discovery
Repeats to me: "You're old." That's all, I'm old.
And yet I'm afraid, as I was at the funeral
I went to yesterday.
My friend's cold made-up face, granite among its flowers,
Her undressed, operated-on, dressed body
Were my face and body.
As I think of her I hear her telling me
How young I seem; I *am* exceptional;
I think of all I have.
But really no one is exceptional,
No one has anything, I'm anybody,
I stand beside my grave
Confused with my life, that is commonplace and solitary.

Poems for the Ear

Many students today, whether or not they read poetry, *hear* poetry. Poetry slams, readings, recorded cassettes, and television appearances by poets performing in every style are part of today's world. Poets have always read their work aloud, but with the Beat poets of the 1950s, led by Allen Ginsberg, the spoken poem became one of the most popular ways for poets to reach their audience. Their poems, like dramatic monologues, were written to be performed. Reading their poems to a live audience, the poets used everyday language; they expressed their audience's problems and enthusiasm, and their language was immediately understandable. Ginsberg introduced his most famous poem, *Howl* (p. 1038), in excited readings to California audiences even before it was published. The poem went on to sell nearly a million copies in a small paperback, and Ginsberg read it for audiences around the world. Part tribal shamans and part theatrical performers, the poets writing for the ear have given contemporary poetry a new and exciting dimension.

ALLEN GINSBERG

America

1956

America I've given you all and now I'm nothing.
America two dollars and twentyseven cents January 17, 1956.
I can't stand my own mind.
America when will we end the human war?
Go fuck yourself with your atom bomb.
I don't feel good don't bother me.
I won't write my poem till I'm in my right mind.
America when will you be angelic?
When will you take off your clothes?
When will you look at yourself through the grave?
When will you be worthy of your million Trotskyites?°
America why are your libraries full of tears?
America when will you send your eggs to India?
I'm sick of your insane demands.
When can I go into the supermarket and buy what I need with my good
looks?
America after all it is you and I who are perfect not the next world.
Your machinery is too much for me.
You made me want to be a saint.
There must be some other way to settle this argument.
Burroughs° is in Tangiers I don't think he'll come back it's sinister.
Are you being sinister or is this some form of practical joke?
I'm trying to come to the point.
I refuse to give up my obsession.
America stop pushing I know what I'm doing.
America the plum blossoms are falling.
I haven't read the newspapers for months, everyday somebody goes on
trial for murder.

11. Trotskyites: Communists who continued to consider Leon Trotsky a legitimate leader.
20. Burroughs: William S. Burroughs (1914–1997), an American author whose harrowing works about life as a drug addict were written when he was an expatriate living abroad in Mexico and Tangiers.

America I feel sentimental about the Wobblies.°
America I used to be a communist when I was a kid I'm not sorry.
I smoke marijuana every chance I get.
I sit in my house for days on end and stare at the roses in the closet.
When I go to Chinatown I get drunk and never get laid.
My mind is made up there's going to be trouble.
You should have seen me reading Marx.
My psychoanalyst thinks I'm perfectly right.
I won't say the Lord's Prayer.
I have mystical visions and cosmic vibrations.
America I still haven't told you what you did to Uncle Max after he
came over from Russia.

I'm addressing you.
Are you going to let your emotional life be run by Time Magazine?
I'm obsessed by Time Magazine.
I read it every week.
Its cover stares at me every time I slink past the corner candystore.
I read it in the basement of the Berkeley Public Library.
It's always telling me about responsibility. Businessmen are serious.
Movie producers are serious. Everybody's serious but me.
It occurs to me that I am America.
I am talking to myself again.

Asia is rising against me.
I haven't got a chinaman's chance.
I'd better consider my national resources.
My national resources consist of two joints of marijuana millions of
genitals an unpublishable private literature that jetplanes 1400 miles
an hour and twentyfive-thousand mental institutions.
I say nothing about my prisons nor the millions of underprivileged who
live in my flowerpots under the light of five hundred suns.
I have abolished the whorehouses of France, Tangiers is the next to go.
My ambition is to be President despite the fact that I'm a Catholic.

America how can I write a holy litany in your silly mood?
I will continue like Henry Ford my strophes are as individual as his
automobiles more so they're all different sexes.
America I will sell you strophes $2500 apiece $500 down on your old
strophe
America free Tom Mooney°
America save the Spanish Loyalists
America Sacco & Vanzetti must not die
America I am the Scottsboro boys.
America when I was seven momma took me to Communist Cell meet-
ings they sold us garbanzos a handful per ticket a ticket costs a nickel

27. Wobblies: Members of the radical International Workers of the World. **57. Tom Mooney:** Labor organizer convicted of a bombing based on perjured evidence.

and the speeches were free everybody was angelic and sentimental about the workers it was all so sincere you have no idea what a good thing the party was in 1835 Scott Nearing° was a grand old man a real mensch Mother Bloor the Silk-strikers' Ewig-Weibliche made me cry I once saw the Yiddish orator Israel Amter° plain. Everybody must have been a spy.
America you don't really want to go to war.
America it's them bad Russians.
Them Russians them Russians and them Chinamen. And them Russians.
The Russia wants to eat us alive. The Russia's power mad. She wants to take our cars from out our garages.
Her wants to grab Chicago. Her needs a Red *Reader's Digest*. Her wants our auto plants in Siberia. Him big bureaucracy running our fillingstations.
That no good. Ugh. Him make Indians learn read. Him need big black niggers. Hah. Her make us all work sixteen hours a day. Help.
America this is quite serious.
America this is the impression I get from looking in the television set.
America is this correct?
I'd better get right down to the job.
It's true I don't want to join the Army or turn lathes in precision parts factories, I'm nearsighted and psychopathic anyway.
America I'm putting my queer shoulder to the wheel.

With Allen Ginsberg, Anne Waldman founded the Jack Kerouac School of Disembodied Poetics at the Naropa Institute in Boulder, Colorado, in 1975. Today she travels and performs widely, and her poetry reflects not only the scenes of her travels, but also her serious commitment to Buddhism. "To the Censorious Ones" is one of her popular performance pieces. First performed at the Naropa Institute, this chant was accompanied by a chorus of women flexing their muscles.

Anne Waldman

To the Censorious Ones — *1994*

(Jesse Helms° & others . . .)

I'm coming up out of the tomb, Men of War
Just when you thought you had me down, in place, hidden
I'm coming up now
Can you feel the ground rumble under your feet?

---

60. Scott Nearing: A radical economist; **Mother Bloor . . . Israel Amter:** New York–based leaders of the American Communist Party.
Jesse Helms: Conservative senator from North Carolina.

It's breaking apart, it's turning over, it's pushing up
It's thrusting into your point of view, your private property
O Men of War, Censorious Ones!
GET READY BIG BOYS GET READY
I'm coming up now
I'm coming up with all that was hidden
Get ready, Big Boys, get ready
I'm coming up with all you wanted buried,
All the hermetic texts with stories in them of hot & dangerous women
Women with lascivious tongues, sharp eyes & claws
I've been working out, my muscles are strong
I'm pushing up the earth with all you try to censor
All the iconoclasm & bravado you scorn
All the taunts against your banner & salute
I'm coming up from Hell with all you ever suppressed
All the dark fantasies, all the dregs are coming back
I'm leading them back up now
They're going to bark & scoff & rage & bite
I'm opening the box
BOO!

Poems for Further Reading

WALLACE STEVENS

The Emperor of Ice-Cream 1923

Call the roller of big cigars,
The muscular one, and bid him whip
In kitchen cups concupiscent curds.°
Let the wenches dawdle in such dress
As they are used to wear, and let the boys
Bring flowers in last month's newspapers.
Let be be finale of seem.°
The only emperor is the emperor of ice-cream.

Take from the dresser of deal,
Lacking the three glass knobs, that sheet
On which she embroidered fantails once

3. concupiscent curds: "The words 'concupiscent curds' have no genealogy; they are merely expressive: at least, I hope they are expressive. They express the concupiscence of life, but, by contrast with the things in relation in the poem, they express or accentuate life's destitution, and it is this that gives them something more than a cheap lustre" (Wallace Stevens, *Letters* [New York: Knopf, 1960], p. 500). **7. Let . . . seem:** "The true sense of 'Let be be finale of seem' is let being become the conclusion or denouement of appearing to be: in short, ice cream is an absolute good. The poem is obviously not about ice cream, but about being as distinguished from seeming to be" (*Letters*, p. 341).

And spread it so as to cover her face.
If her horny feet protrude, they come
To show how cold she is, and dumb.
Let the lamp affix its beam.
The only emperor is the emperor of ice-cream.

William Carlos Williams

Danse Russe

1917

If I when my wife is sleeping
and the baby and Kathleen
are sleeping
and the sun is a flame-white disc
in silken mists
above shining trees, —
if I in my north room
dance naked, grotesquely
before my mirror
waving my shirt round my head
and singing softly to myself:
"I am lonely, lonely.
I was born to be lonely,
I am best so!"
If I admire my arms, my face,
my shoulders, flanks, buttocks
against the yellow drawn shades, —
Who shall say I am not
the happy genius of my household?

D. H. Lawrence

Mountain Lion

1923

Climbing through the January snow, into the Lobo canyon
Dark grow the spruce-trees, blue is the balsam, water sounds still
unfrozen, and the trail is still evident.

Men!
Two men!
Men! The only animal in the world to fear!
They hesitate.
We hesitate.
They have a gun.
We have no gun.
Then we all advance, to meet.

■ ■ ■

Two Mexicans, strangers, emerging out of the dark and snow and
inwardness of the Lobo valley.
What are they doing here on this vanishing trail?

What is he carrying?
Something yellow.
A deer?

Qué tiene, amigo?
León — °

He smiles, foolishly, as if he were caught doing wrong.
And we smile, foolishly, as if we didn't know.
He is quite gentle and dark-faced.

It is a mountain lion.
A long, long slim cat, yellow like a lioness.
Dead.

He trapped her this morning, he says, smiling foolishly.
Lift up her face,
Her round, bright face, bright as frost.
Her round, fine-fashioned head, with two dead ears;
And stripes in the brilliant frost of her face, sharp, fine dark rays,
Dark, keen, fine rays in the brilliant frost of her face.
Beautiful dead eyes.

Hermoso es!°

They go out towards the open;
We go on into the gloom of Lobo.
And above the trees I found her lair,
A hole in the blood-orange brilliant rocks that stick up, a little cave.
And bones, and twigs, and a perilous ascent.

So, she will never leap up that way again, with the yellow flash of a
mountain lion's long shoot!
And her bright striped frost-face will never watch any more, out of the
shadow of the cave in the blood-orange rock,
Above the trees of the Lobo dark valley-mouth!

Instead, I look out.
And out to the dim of the desert, like a dream, never real;
To the snow of the Sangre de Cristo mountains, the ice of the mountains
of Picoris,
And near across at the opposite steep of snow, green trees motionless
standing in snow, like a Christmas toy.

And I think in this empty world there was room for me and a mountain
lion.
And I think in the world beyond, how easily we might spare a million
or two of humans

16–17. ***Qué tiene, . . . León:*** "What do you have, friend? / Lion" in Spanish. **31.** ***Hermoso es!:*** Spanish for "It's beautiful!"

And never miss them.
Yet what a gap in the world, the missing white frost-face of that slim
yellow mountain lion!

MARY OLIVER

Picking Blueberries, Austerlitz, New York, 1957

1992

Once, in summer,
in the blueberries,
I fell asleep, and woke
when a deer stumbled against me.

I guess
she was so busy with her own happiness
she had grown careless
and was just wandering along

listening
to the wind as she leaned down
to lip up the sweetness.
So, there we were

with nothing between us
but a few leaves, and the wind's
glossy voice
shouting instructions.

The deer
backed away finally
and flung up her white tail
and went floating off toward the trees —

but the moment before she did that
was so wide and so deep
it has lasted to this day;
I have only to think of her —

the flower of her amazement
and the stalled breath of her curiosity,
and even the damp touch of her solicitude
before she took flight —

to be absent again from this world
and alive, again, in another,
for thirty years
sleepy and amazed,

rising out of the rough weeds,
listening and looking.
Beautiful girl,
where are you?

Margaret Atwood

Siren° Song

1974

This is the one song everyone
would like to learn: the song
that is irresistible:

the song that forces men
to leap overboard in squadrons
even though they see the beached skulls

the song nobody knows
because anyone who has heard it
is dead, and the others can't remember.

Shall I tell you the secret
and if I do, will you get me
out of this bird suit?

I don't enjoy it here
squatting on this island
looking picturesque and mythical

with these two feathery maniacs,
I don't enjoy singing
this trio, fatal and valuable.

I will tell the secret to you,
to you, only to you.
Come closer. This song

is a cry for help: Help me!
Only you, only you can,
you are unique

at last. Alas
it is a boring song
but it works every time.

Amiri Baraka

For Hettie

1954

My wife is left-handed.
Which implies a fierce de-
termination. A complete other
worldliness. IT'S WEIRD BABY
The way some folks

Siren: In Greek mythology, a creature who could assume the shape of a beautiful woman; its song lured passing mariners to their deaths.

are always trying to be different.
A sin & a shame.

But then, she's been a bohemian
all her life . . . black stockings,
refusing to take orders. I sit
patiently, trying to tell her
what's right. TAKE THAT DAMM
PENCIL OUTTA THAT HAND. YOU'RE
RITING BACKWARDS. & such. But
to no avail. & it shows
in her work. Left-handed coffee,
left-handed eggs: when she comes
in at night . . . it's her left hand
offered for me to kiss. DAMM.

& now her belly droops over the seat.
They say it's a child. But
I ain't quite so sure.

Wislawa Szymborska

True Love

1972

TRANSLATED BY STANISLAW BARÁNCZAK AND CLARE CAVANAGH

True love. Is it normal,
is it serious, is it practical?
What does the world get from two people
who exist in a world of their own?

Placed on the same pedestal for no good reason,
drawn randomly from millions, but convinced
it had to happen this way — in reward for what?
For nothing.
The light descends from nowhere.
Why on these two and not on others?
Doesn't this outrage justice? Yes it does.
Doesn't it disrupt our painstakingly erected principles,
and cast the moral from the peak? Yes on both accounts.

Look at the happy couple.
Couldn't they at least try to hide it,
fake a little depression for their friends' sake!
Listen to them laughing — it's an insult.
The language they use — deceptively clear.
And their little celebrations, rituals,
the elaborate mutual routines —
it's obviously a plot behind the human race's back!

■ ■ ■

It's hard even to guess how far things might go
if people start to follow their example.
What could religion and poetry count on?
What would be remembered? What renounced?
Who'd want to stay within bounds?

True love. Is it really necessary?
Tact and common sense tell us to pass over it in silence,
like a scandal in Life's highest circles.
Perfectly good children are born without its help.
It couldn't populate the planet in a million years,
it comes along so rarely.

Let the people who never find true love
keep saying that there's no such thing.

Their faith will make it easier for them to live and die.

HELEN DUNMORE

Wild Strawberries 1991

What I get I bring home to you:
a dark handful, sweet-edged,
dissolving in one mouthful.

I bother to bring them for you
though they're so quickly over,
pulpless, sliding to juice,

a grainy rub on the tongue
and the taste's gone. If you remember
we were in the woods at wild strawberry time

and I was making a basket of dockleaves
to hold what you'd picked,
but the cold leaves unplaited themselves

and slid apart, and again unplaited themselves
until I gave up and ate wild strawberries
out of your hands for sweetness.

I lipped at your palm —
the little salt edge there,
the tang of money you'd handled.

As we stayed in the wood, hidden,
we heard the sound system below us
calling the winners at Chepstow,
faint as the breeze turned.

The sun came out on us, the shade blotches
went hazel: we heard names
bubble like stock-doves over the woods

■ ■ ■

as jockeys in stained silks gentled
those sweat-dark, shuddering horses
down to the walk.

RELATED COMMENTARIES: *Marge Piercy, "Imagery Can't Really Be Taught," page 1202; Ezra Pound, "On the Principles of Imagism," page 1204; Peter Schmitt, "Sad Heart at the Supermarket: Randall Jarrell's 'Next Day,'" page 1213.*

12

POETS SPEAKING OUT: POEMS ABOUT POLITICS, SOCIETY, AND THE ENVIRONMENT

No single poet — Dante, Goethe, or even Shakespeare — has had a more pervasive influence on the cultural foundation of the West than the shadowy figure we call Homer. His name is so familiar that it is easy to overlook just how long his work has been our heritage. Homer described events that took place, as far as we can tell, at roughly the same time as the Exodus. Before the Old Testament was complete, his works were already the basic scrolls in a cultured man's library. By the time Jesus was born, so much had been written about Homer and his work that it would be a very long time before any of the Apostles could challenge his leading position as the most intensely studied author in Western Civilization. All this Homer accomplished with just two poems — the *Iliad* and the *Odyssey*.

– TIM SEVERIN, *The Ulysses Voyage*

As Muriel Rukeyser told us in the epigraph that began our study of poetry and poets, "the universe of poetry is the universe of emotional truth," and what you have found in your reading is that poets write about the things that set off their emotional triggers. Poets, like everyone else, are passionately engaged in the issues that divide their times, and the world around them is mirrored in their writing. Often the poetry inspired by social upheaval loses its immediacy once the dust has settled, and poems written in these moments of emotion are forgotten later. Edna St. Vincent Millay is still read for her early poetry about the physical world and for her sonnets (p. 1085), but in the late 1920s it was her angry poetry protesting the execution of the falsely accused anarchists Sacco and Vanzetti that attracted many readers. In the excitement of the first years of the social experiment in the Soviet Union, Langston Hughes wrote several long, fervent poems calling for revolution in the United States, but he left them out of later collections of his work.

POETRY OF PROTEST AND SOCIAL CONCERN

Poets writing today reflect many of the themes and the attitudes that concerned writers of a generation ago. Although some of the strident rhetoric of the 1960s has been muted, they are still deeply engaged in their own moment of history. In the 1970s and 1980s, young African American writers began to voice their anger at the racism that they encountered in American society, and at the same time new women writers were giving vent to their impatience with the limited role that society's customs were forcing on them. For these writers, the voice of their protest often was poetry. They wrote poems to convince us, to shock us, or to inform us, and they were more concerned with the message of their poetry than with traditional conventions of language, style, or form. Their poems were political, and **political poetry** has been used to open prayer meetings and to lead revolutions.

In much contemporary poetry, we find ourselves and our concerns reflected back to us. Yusef Komunyakaa served in Vietnam and many of his poems have the harrowing emotional experience of the war as their source. In "Facing It," he is writing several years after the war's end, but his emotions still reverberate in its aftermath.

YUSEF KOMUNYAKAA

Facing It

1988

My black face fades,
hiding inside the black granite.
I said I wouldn't,
dammit: No tears.
I'm stone. I'm flesh.
My clouded reflection eyes me
like a bird of prey, the profile of night
slanted against morning. I turn
this way — the stone lets me go.
I turn that way — I'm inside
the Vietnam Veterans Memorial
again, depending on the light
to make a difference.
I go down the 58,022 names,
half-expecting to find
my own in letters like smoke.
I touch the name Andrew Johnson;
I see the booby trap's white flash.
Names shimmer on a woman's blouse
but when she walks away
the names stay on the wall.
Brushstrokes flash, a red bird's

wings cutting across my stare.
The sky. A plane in the sky.
A white vet's image floats
closer to me, then his pale eyes
look through mine. I'm a window.
He's lost his right arm
inside the stone. In the black mirror
a woman's trying to erase names:
No, she's brushing a boy's hair.

Although a poem like "The Day Lady Died," by New York poet Frank O'Hara, is not specifically political, in its *topicality* it is related to a poem like "Facing It." It reflects our social concerns, and it is written with the direct emotional response of the political poets. O'Hara is writing about an ordinary day in New York City, but it is a day that abruptly changes for him when he glances at a headline and reads that the singer Billie Holiday, who was for O'Hara's generation what John Lennon or Kurt Cobain is for ours, has just died.

FRANK O'HARA

The Day Lady° Died *1964*

It is 12:20 in New York a Friday
three days after Bastille day, yes
it is 1959 and I go get a shoeshine
because I will get off the 4:19 in Easthampton
at 7:15 and then go straight to dinner
and I don't know the people who will feed me

I walk up the muggy street beginning to sun
and have a hamburger and a malted and buy
an ugly NEW WORLD WRITING to see what the poets
in Ghana are doing these days
I go on to the bank
and Miss Stillwagon (first name Linda I once heard)
doesn't even look up my balance for once in her life
and in the GOLDEN GRIFFIN I get a little Verlaine
for Patsy with drawings by Bonnard° although I do
think of Hesiod,° trans. Richmond Lattimore or
Brendan Behan's new play° or *Le Balcon* or *Les Nègres*

Lady: Billie Holiday, known as "Lady Day," a popular African American singer of the 1930s, who struggled at the end of her career against alcohol and drug abuse. **14–15. Verlaine . . . Bonnard:** Paul Verlaine (1844–1896), the French poet; the reference is to an edition of Verlaine's poems with illustrations by Pierre Bonnard (1867–1947). **16. Hesiod:** Greek poet (eighth century B.C.). **17. Brendan Behan's new play:** Possibly *The Quare Fellow* (1956) or *The Hostage* (1958).

of Genet,° but I don't, I stick with Verlaine
after practically going to sleep with quandariness
and for Mike I just stroll into the PARK LANE
Liquor Store and ask for a bottle of Strega and
then I go back where I came from to 6th Avenue
and the tobacconist in the Ziegfeld Theatre and
casually ask for a carton of Gauloises and a carton
of Picayunes, and a NEW YORK POST with her face on it
and I am sweating a lot by now and thinking of
leaning on the john door in the 5 SPOT
while she whispered a song along the keyboard
to Mal Waldron° and everyone and I stopped breathing

Although more than a half-century has passed since the world first became aware of the totality of the Holocaust, there are still poems being written that struggle to deal with its story. This poem, by England's poet laureate, Andrew Motion, describes his feelings after visiting the hiding place of Anne Frank in Amsterdam, Holland. *Huis* is the Dutch word for "house."

ANDREW MOTION

Anne Frank Huis

1978

Even now, after twice her lifetime of grief
and anger in the very place, whoever comes
to climb these narrow stairs, discovers how
the bookcase slides aside, then walks through
shadow into sunlit rooms, can never help
but break her secrecy again. Just listening
is a kind of guilt: the Westerkirk° repeats
itself outside, as if all time worked round
towards her fear, and made each stroke
die down on guarded streets. Imagine it —
three years of whispering and loneliness
and plotting, day by day, the Allied line
in Europe with a yellow chalk. What hope
she had for ordinary love and interest
survives her here, displayed above the bed

■ ■ ■

18. Genet: Jean Genet (1910–1986), French novelist and playwright whose plays included *The Balcony* (1956) and *The Blacks* (1958). **29. Mal Waldron:** A jazz pianist who sometimes accompanied Holiday in her club engagements.

7. Westerkirk: A church in Amsterdam. Built in 1620, it is famous for its carillon and tower, the highest in the city.

as pictures of her family; some actors;
fashions chosen by Princess Elizabeth.
And those who stoop to see them find
not only patience missing its reward,
but one enduring wish for chances
like my own: to leave as simply
as I do, and walk at ease
up dusty tree-lined avenues, or watch
a silent barge come clear of bridges
settling their reflections in the blue canals.

One of the tragedies still on our horizons today is the AIDS epidemic, and there has been an outpouring of art and poetry struggling with the ravages of the disease. In this poem, the American writer Miller Williams describes a hospital visit to a dying friend.

MILLER WILLIAMS

Thinking about Bill, Dead of AIDS *1989*

We did not know the first thing about
how blood surrenders to even the smallest threat
when old allergies turn inside out,

the body rescinding all its normal orders
to all defenders of flesh, betraying the head,
pulling its guards back from all its borders.

Thinking of friends afraid to shake your hand,
we think of your hand shaking, your mouth set,
your eyes drained of any reprimand.

Loving, we kissed you, partly to persuade
both you and us, seeing what eyes had said,
that we were loving and we were not afraid.

If we had had more, we would have given more.
As it was we stood next to your bed,
stopping, though, to set our smiles at the door.

Not because we were less sure at the last.
Only because, not knowing anything yet,
we didn't know what look would hurt you least.

Although our century has seen remarkable advances in our daily lives, it has also been darkened by political oppression. This poem by a Russian poet poignantly describes not only her own protest against the imprisonment of her son, but also tells us what the poet's role can be in telling of injustice.

Anna Akhmatova

Instead of a Preface

1917

TRANSLATED BY RICHARD MCKANE

In the terrible years of the Yezhov terror I spent seventeen months waiting in line outside the prison in Leningrad. One day somebody in the crowd identified me. Standing behind me was a woman, with lips blue from the cold, who had, of course, never heard me called by name before. Now she started out of the torpor common to us all and asked me in a whisper (everyone whispered there):

"Can you describe this?"

And I said: "I can."

Then something like a smile passed fleetingly over what had once been her face.

A subject that has continued to engage the emotions of poets is war. The earliest literary classic of European culture is the *Iliad,* an epic poem written several hundred years before the Christian era by the blind Greek poet Homer. The poem tells the story of the ten-year-long war between the Greeks and the Trojans. The following group of poems reflect a shared theme: the brutality and inhumanity of war. Stephen Crane wrote "War Is Kind" about the American Civil War. Thomas Hardy's poem "The Man He Killed" is about the Boer War between England and the Dutch settlers in South Africa from 1899 to 1902. "Dulce et Decorum Est," by Wildred Owen, was written in the midst of World War I, shortly before Owen was killed in the fighting. Muriel Rukeyser, who had been forced to flee from Spain at the outbreak of the Spanish Civil War in 1936, wrote "Holy Family" about the fate of refugees in the 1930s. Randall Jarrell's "The Death of the Ball Turret Gunner" was written while he was serving in the U.S. Air Force in England during World War II.

Stephen Crane

War Is Kind

1896

Do not weep, maiden, for war is kind.
Because your lover threw wild hands toward the sky
And the affrighted steed ran on alone,
Do not weep.
War is kind.

Hoarse, booming drums of the regiment,
Little souls who thirst for fight,
These men were born to drill and die.
The unexplained glory flies above them,
Great is the battle-god, great, and his kingdom —
A field where a thousand corpses lie.

■ ■ ■

Do not weep, babe, for war is kind
Because your father tumbled in the yellow trenches,
Raged at his breast, gulped and died,
Do not weep.
War is kind.

Swift blazing flag of the regiment,
Eagle with crest of red and gold,
These men were born to drill and die.
Point for them the virtue of slaughter,
Make plain to them the excellence of killing
And a field where a thousand corpses lie.

Mother whose heart hung humble as a button
On the bright splendid shroud of your son,
Do not weep.
War is kind.

THOMAS HARDY

The Man He Killed

1902

"Had he and I but met
By some old ancient inn,
We should have sat us down to wet
Right many a nipperkin!°

"But ranged as infantry,
And staring face to face,
I shot at him as he at me,
And killed him in his place.

"I shot him dead because —
Because he was my foe,
Just so: my foe of course he was:
That's clear enough; although

"He thought he'd 'list, perhaps,
Off-hand-like — just as I —
Was out of work — had sold his traps —
No other reason why.

"Yes; quaint and curious war is!
You shoot a fellow down
You'd treat, if met where any bar is,
Or help to half-a-crown."

4. nipperkin: A measure of alcohol less than a half pint.

WILFRED OWEN

Dulce et Decorum Est° *1920*

Bent double, like old beggars under sacks,
Knock-kneed, coughing like hags, we cursed through sludge,
Till on the haunting flares we turned our backs
And towards our distant rest began to trudge.
Men marched asleep. Many had lost their boots
But limped on, blood-shod. All went lame; all blind;
Drunk with fatigue; deaf even to the hoots
Of tired, outstripped Five-Nines° that dropped behind.

Gas! Gas! Quick, boys! — An ecstasy of fumbling
Fitting the clumsy helmets just in time;
But someone still was yelling out and stumbling
And flound'ring like a man in fire or lime . . .
Dim, through the misty panes and thick green light,°
As under a green sea, I saw him drowning.

In all my dreams, before my helpless sight,
He plunges at me, guttering, choking, drowning.

If in some smothering dreams you too could pace
Behind the wagon that we flung him in,
And watch the white eyes writhing in his face,
His hanging face, like a devil's sick of sin;
If you could hear, at every jolt, the blood
Come gargling from the froth-corrupted lungs,
Obscene as cancer, bitter as the cud
Of vile, incurable sores on innocent tongues, —
My friend,° you would not tell with such high zest
To children ardent for some desperate glory,
The old Lie: Dulce et decorum est
Pro patria mori.

MURIEL RUKEYSER

Holy Family *1941*

A long road and a village.
A bloody road and a village.
A road away from war.
Born, born, we know how it goes.

Dulce et Decorum Est: The Latin phrase in lines 27–28 reads, "It is sweet and proper to die for one's country" (from the Roman poet Horace). **8. Five-Nines:** German 59 mm artillery shells. **13. misty panes and thick green light:** Through a gas mask. **25. My friend:** The poem is addressed to a poet known for patriotic verse, Jessie Pope.

■ ■ ■

A man and woman riding.
Riding, the new-born child.
White sky, clever and wild.
Born, born, we know how it goes.

The wheel goes back.
How is it with the child?
How is it with the world?
Born, born, we know how it goes.

Never look at the child.
Give it to bloody ground.
By this dream we are bound.
Born, born, we know how it goes.

Riding between these hills,
Woman and man alone
Enter the battle-line.
Born, born, we know how it goes.

They childless disappear
Among the fighting men.
Two thousand years until they come again.
Born, born, we know how it goes.

RANDALL JARRELL

The Death of the Ball Turret Gunner 1945

From my mother's sleep I fell into the state
And I hunched in its belly till my wet fur froze.
Six miles from earth, loosed from its dream of life,
I woke to black flak and the nightmare fighters.
When I died they washed me out of the turret with a hose.

ECOPOETRY AND THE ECOPOETS

Another continuing theme for poets is our interrelationship with nature, a theme that has become more pressing as our environment is increasingly threatened by pollution and the pressures of overpopulation. In his book *Sustainable Poetry,* the critic Leonard M. Scigaj uses the term **ecopoetry** to describe the writings of poets who place nature at the center of much of their poetry. As he defines their work, "Ecopoets present nature in their poems as a separate and equal other." He also defines their way of writing. "Ecopoets distill ecological processes into aesthetic techniques to restore our lost sense of connectedness to the planet that bore and sustains us."

As you will see from the following poem, written by John Clare in 1835–37, ecopoetry has a long tradition.

John Clare

Badger

1835–37

When midnight comes a host of dogs and men
Go out and track the badger to his den,
And put a sack within the hole, and lie
Till the old grunting badger passes by.
He comes and hears — they let the strongest loose.
The old fox hears the noise and drops the goose.
The poacher shoots and hurries from the cry,
And the old hare half wounded buzzes by.
They get a forkèd stick to bear him down
And clap the dogs and take him to the town,
And bait him all the day with many dogs,
And laugh and shout and fright the scampering hogs.
He runs along and bites at all he meets:
They shout and hollo down the noisy streets.

He turns about to face the loud uproar
And drives the rebels to their very door.
The frequent stone is hurled where'er they go;
When badgers fight, then every one's a foe.
The dogs are clapt and urged to join the fray;
The badger turns and drives them all away.
Though scarcely half as big, demure and small,
He fights with dogs for hours and beats them all.
The heavy mastiff, savage in the fray,
Lies down and licks his feet and turns away.
The bulldog knows his match and waxes cold,
The badger grins and never leaves his hold.
He drives the crowd and follows at their heels
And bites them through — the drunkard swears and reels.

The frighted women take the boys away,
The blackguard laughs and hurries on the fray.
He tries to reach the woods, an awkward race,
But sticks and cudgels quickly stop the chase.
He turns agen and drives the noisy crowd
And beats the many dogs in noises loud.
He drives away and beats them every one,
And then they loose them all and set them on.
He falls as dead and kicked by boys and men,
Then starts and grins and drives the crowd agen;
Till kicked and torn and beaten out he lies
And leaves his hold and cackles, groans and dies.

RICHARD EBERHART

The Groundhog

1936

In June, amid the golden fields,
I saw a groundhog lying dead.
Dead lay he; my sense shook,
And mind outshot our naked frailty.
There lowly in the vigorous summer
His form began its senseless change,
And made my senses waver dim
Seeing nature ferocious in him.
Inspecting close his maggots' might
And seething cauldron of his being,
Half with loathing, half with a strange love,
I poked him with an angry stick.
The fever arose, became a flame
And Vigour circumscribed the skies,
Immense energy in the sun,
And through my frame a sunless trembling.
My stick had done nor good nor harm.
Then stood I silent in the day
Watching the object, as before;
And kept my reverence for knowledge
Trying for control, to be still,
To quell the passion of the blood;
Until I had bent down on my knees
Praying for joy in the sight of decay.
And so I left; and I returned
In Autumn strict of eye, to see
The sap gone out of the groundhog,
But the bony sodden hulk remained.
But the year had lost its meaning,
And in intellectual chains
I lost both love and loathing,
Mured up in the wall of wisdom.
Another summer took the fields again
Massive and burning, full of life,
But when I chanced upon the spot
There was only a little hair left,
And bones bleaching in the sunlight
Beautiful as architecture;
I watched them like a geometer,
And cut a walking stick from a birch.
It has been three years, now.
There is no sign of the groundhog.
I stood there in the whirling summer,

My hand capped a withered heart,
And thought of China and of Greece,
Of Alexander in his tent;
Of Montaigne in his tower,
Of Saint Theresa° in her wild lament.

Gary Snyder

Ripples on the Surface

1992

"Ripples on the surface of the water
were silver salmon passing under — different
from the sorts of ripples caused by breezes"

A scudding plume on the wave —
a humpback whale is
breaking out in air up
gulping herring
  — Nature not a book, but a *performance*, a
high old culture

Ever-fresh events
scraped out, rubbed out, and used, used, again —
the braided channels of the rivers
hidden under fields of grass —

The vast wild.
  the house, alone.
the little house in the wild,
  the wild in the house.

both forgotten.

  No nature.

Both together, one big empty house.

W. S. Merwin

Birds Waking

1956

I went out at daybreak and stood on Primrose Hill.
It was April: a white haze over the hills of Surrey
Over the green haze of the hills above the dark green
Of the park trees, and over it all the light came up clear,
The sky like deep porcelain paling and paling,

46–48. Of Alexander . . . Saint Theresa: Refers to Alexander the Great (356–323 B.C.), conqueror of a large empire; Michel Eyquem de Montaigne (1533–1592), French essayist; and St. Theresa of Avila (1515–1582), Spanish Carmelite nun and mystic.

With everywhere under it the faces of the buildings
Where the city slept, gleaming white and quiet,
St Paul's and the water tower taking the gentle gold.
And from the hill chestnuts and the park trees
There was such a clamour rose as the birds woke,
Such uncontainable tempest of whirled
Singing flung upward and upward into the new light,
Increasing still as the birds themselves rose
From the black trees and whirled in a rising cloud,
Flakes and water-spouts and hurled seas and continents of them
Rising, dissolving, streamering out, always
Louder and louder singing, shrieking, laughing.
Sometimes one would break from the cloud but from the song never,
And would beat past my ear dinning his deafening note.
I thought I had never known the wind
Of joy to be so shrill, so unanswerable,
With such clouds of winged song at its disposal, and I thought
Oh Voice that my demand is the newest name for,
There are many ways we may end, and one we must,
Whether burning, or the utter cold descending in darkness,
Explosion of our own devising, collision of planets, all
Violent, however silent they at last may seem;
Oh let it be by this violence, then, let it be now,
Now when in their sleep, unhearing, unknowing,
Most faces must be closest to innocence,
When the light moves unhesitating to fill the sky with clearness
And no dissent could be heard above the din of its welcome,
Let the great globe well up and dissolve like its last birds,
With the bursting roar and uprush of song!

ANNE STEVENSON

The Fish Are All Sick — *1982*

The fish are all sick, the great whales dead,
the villages stranded in stone on the coast,
ornamental, like pearls on the fringe of a coat.
Sea men, who knew what the ocean did,
turned their low houses away from the surf.
But new men, who come to be rural and safe,
add big glass views and begonia beds.

Water keeps to itself.
White lip after lip
curls to a close on the littered beach.
Something is sicker and blacker than fish.
And closing its grip, and closing its grip.

Poems for Further Reading

WOLE SOYINKA

Telephone Conversation

1960

The price seemed reasonable, location
Indifferent. The landlady swore she lived
Off premises. Nothing remained
But self-confession. "Madam," I warned,
"I hate a wasted journey — I am African."
Silence. Silenced transmission of
Pressurized good-breeding. Voice, when it came,
Lipstick coated, long gold-rolled
Cigarette-holder pipped. Caught I was, foully.
"HOW DARK?" . . . I had not misheard . . . "ARE YOU LIGHT
OR VERY DARK?" Button B. Button A. Stench
Of rancid breath of public hide-and-speak.
Red booth. Red pillar-box. Red double-tiered
Omnibus squelching tar. It *was* real! Shamed
By ill-mannered silence, surrender
Pushed dumbfoundment to beg simplification.
Considerate she was, varying the emphasis —
"ARE YOU DARK? OR VERY LIGHT?" Revelation came.
"You mean — like plain or milk chocolate?"
Her assent was clinical, crushing in its light
Impersonality. Rapidly, wave-length adjusted,
I chose. "West African sepia" — and as afterthought,
"Down in my passport." Silence for spectroscopic
Flight of fancy, till truthfulness clanged her accent
Hard on the mouthpiece. "WHAT'S THAT?" conceding
"DON'T KNOW WHAT THAT IS." "Like brunette."
"THAT'S DARK, ISN'T IT?" "Not altogether.
Facially, I am brunette, but madam, you should see
The rest of me. Palm of my hand, soles of my feet
Are a peroxide blonde. Friction, caused —
Foolishly madam — by sitting down, has turned
My bottom raven black — One moment madam!" — sensing
Her receiver rearing on the thunderclap
About my ears — "Madam," I pleaded, "wouldn't you rather
See for yourself?"

Tomas Tranströmer

Allegro

1962

TRANSLATED BY SAMUEL CHARTERS

I play Haydn after a black day
and feel a simple warmth in my hands.

The keys are willing. Mild hammers strike.
The sound is green, lively, and calm.

The sound says that there is freedom
and that there is somebody who isn't paying taxes to the emperor.

I shove my hands down in my Haydnpockets
and act like I'm one of those people who regards the world calmly.

I hoist my Haydnflag — it means:
We don't give up. But want peace.

The music is a house of glass on the hillside
where the stones fly, the stones roll.

And the stones roll right on through
but every pane stays whole.

Louise Erdrich

Indian Boarding School: The Runaways

1984

Home's the place we head for in our sleep.
Boxcars stumbling north in dreams
don't wait for us. We catch them on the run.
The rails, old lacerations that we love,
shoot parallel across the face and break
just under Turtle Mountains.° Riding scars
you can't get lost. Home is the place they cross.

The lame guard strikes a match and makes the dark
less tolerant. We watch through cracks in boards
as the land starts rolling, rolling till it hurts
to be here, cold in regulation clothes.
We know the sheriff's waiting at midrun
to take us back. His car is dumb and warm.
The highway doesn't rock, it only hums
like a wing of long insults. The worn-down welts
of ancient punishment lead back and forth.

All runaways wear dresses, long green ones,
the color you would think shame was. We scrub

---

6. **Turtle Mountains:** A range in North Dakota and Manitoba.

the sidewalks down because it's shameful work.
Our brushes cut the stone in watered arcs
and in the soak frail outlines shiver clear
a moment, things us kids pressed on the dark
face before it hardened, pale, remembering
delicate old injuries, the spines of names and leaves.

PAT MORA

Elena

1984

My Spanish isn't enough.
I remember how I'd smile
listening to my little ones,
understanding every word they'd say,
their jokes, their songs, their plots.
    Vamos a pedirle dulces a mamá. Vamos.°
But that was in Mexico.
Now my children go to American high schools.
They speak English. At night they sit around
the kitchen table, laugh with one another.
I stand by the stove and feel dumb, alone.
I bought a book to learn English.
My husband frowned, drank more beer.
My oldest said, "*Mamá*, he doesn't want you
to be smarter than he is." I'm forty,
embarrassed at mispronouncing words,
embarrassed at the laughter of my children,
the grocer, the mailman. Sometimes I take
my English book and lock myself in the bathroom,
say the thick words softly,
for if I stop trying, I will be deaf
when my children need my help.

JANICE MIRIKITANI

Recipe

1987

Round eyes

Ingredients: scissors, Scotch magic transparent tape,
    eyeliner — water based, black.
    Optional: false eyelashes.

Cleanse face thoroughly.

---

6. **Vamos . . . Vamos:** Let's go ask for sweets from mom. Come on.

■ ■ ■

For best results, powder entire face, including eyelids.
(lighter shades suited to total effect desired)
With scissors, cut magic tape 1⁄16″ wide, 3⁄4″–1⁄2″ long —
depending on length of eyelid.
Stick firmly onto mid-upper eyelid area
(looking down into handmirror facilitates finding
adequate surface)

If using false eyelashes, affix first on lid, folding any
excess lid over the base of eyelash with glue.

Paint black eyeliner on tape and entire lid.

Do not cry.

Lorna Dee Cervantes

Poem for the Young White Man Who Asked Me How I, an Intelligent, Well-Read Person Could Believe in the War between Races

1981

In my land there are no distinctions.
The barbed wire politics of oppression
have been torn down long ago. The only reminder
of past battles, lost or won, is a slight
rutting in the fertile fields.

In my land
people write poems about love,
full of nothing but contented childlike syllables.
Everyone reads Russian short stories and weeps.
There are no boundaries.
There is no hunger, no
complicated famine or greed.

I am not a revolutionary.
I don't even like political poems.
Do you think I can believe in a war between races?

I can deny it. I can forget about it
when I'm safe,
living on my own continent of harmony
and home, but I am not
there.

I believe in revolution
because everywhere the crosses are burning,
sharp-shooting goose-steppers round every corner,
there are snipers in the schools . . .

(I know you don't believe this.
You think this is nothing
but faddish exaggeration. But they
are not shooting at you.)

I'm marked by the color of my skin.
The bullets are discrete and designed to kill slowly.
They are aiming at my children.
These are facts.
Let me show you my wounds: my stumbling mind, my
"excuse me" tongue, and this
nagging preoccupation
with the feeling of not being good enough.

These bullets bury deeper than logic.
Racism is not intellectual.
I can not reason these scars away.

Outside my door
there is a real enemy
who hates me.

I am a poet
who yearns to dance on rooftops,
to whisper delicate lines about joy
and the blessings of human understanding.
I try. I go to my land, my tower of words and
bolt the door, but the typewriter doesn't fade out
the sounds of blasting and muffled outrage.
My own days bring me slaps on the face.
Every day I am deluged with reminders
that this is not
my land

and this is my land.

I do not believe in the war between races
but in this country
there is war.

ADRIENNE RICH

Diving into the Wreck 1971

First having read the book of myths,
and loaded the camera,
and checked the edge of the knife-blade,
I put on
the body-armor of black rubber
the absurd flippers
the grave and awkward mask.

I am having to do this
not like Cousteau° with his
assiduous team
aboard the sun-flooded schooner
but here alone.

There is a ladder.
The ladder is always there
hanging innocently
close to the side of the schooner.
We know what it is for,
we who have used it.
Otherwise
it is a piece of maritime floss
some sundry equipment.

I go down.
Rung after rung and still
the oxygen immerses me
the blue light
the clear atoms
of our human air.
I go down.
My flippers cripple me,
I crawl like an insect down the ladder
and there is no one
to tell me when the ocean
will begin.

First the air is blue and then
it is bluer and then green and then
black I am blacking out and yet
my mask is powerful
it pumps my blood with power
the sea is another story
the sea is not a question of power
I have to learn alone
to turn my body without force
in the deep element.

And now: it is easy to forget
what I came for
among so many who have always
lived here
swaying their crenellated° fans

---

9. Cousteau: Jacques Cousteau (1910–1997), French underwater explorer, photographer, and author. **48. crenellated:** Notched with rounded or scalloped projections.

between the reefs
and besides
you breathe differently down here.

I came to explore the wreck.
The words are purposes.
The words are maps.
I came to see the damage that was done
and the treasures that prevail.
I stroke the beam of my lamp
slowly along the flank
of something more permanent
than fish or weed

the thing I came for:
the wreck and not the story of the wreck
the thing itself and not the myth
the drowned face always staring
toward the sun
the evidence of damage
worn by salt and sway into this threadbare beauty
the ribs of the disaster
curving their assertion
among the tentative haunters.

This is the place.
And I am here, the mermaid whose dark hair
streams black, the merman in his armored body
We circle silently
about the wreck
we dive into the hold.
I am she: I am he

whose drowned face sleeps with open eyes
whose breasts still bear the stress
whose silver, copper, vermeil° cargo lies
obscurely inside barrels
half-wedged and left to rot
we are the half-destroyed instruments
that once held to a course
the water-eaten log
the fouled compass

We are, I am, you are
by cowardice or courage
the one who find our way
back to this scene

---

80. vermeil: Gilded silver or bronze.

carrying a knife, a camera
a book of myths
in which
our names do not appear.

Mary Jo Salter

Welcome to Hiroshima

1984

is what you first see, stepping off the train:
a billboard brought to you in living English
by Toshiba Electric. While a channel
silent in the TV of the brain

projects those flickering re-runs of a cloud
that brims its risen columnful like beer
and, spilling over, hangs its foamy head,
you feel a thirst for history: what year

it started to be safe to breathe the air,
and when to drink the blood and scum afloat
on the Ohta River. But no, the water's clear,
they pour it for your morning cup of tea

in one of the countless sunny coffee shops
whose plastic dioramas advertise
mutations of cuisine behind the glass:
a pancake sandwich; a pizza someone tops

with a maraschino cherry. Passing by
the Peace Park's floral hypocenter (where
how bravely, or with what mistaken cheer,
humanity erased its own erasure),

you enter the memorial museum
and through more glass are served, as on a dish
of blistered grass, three mannequins. Like gloves
a mother clips to coatsleeves, strings of flesh

hang from their fingertips; or as if tied
to recall a duty for us, *Reverence*
the dead whose mourners too shall soon be dead,
but all commemoration's swallowed up

in questions of bad taste, how re-created
horror mocks the grim original,
and thinking at last *They should have left it all*
you stop. This is the wristwatch of a child.

Jammed on the moment's impact, resolute
to communicate some message, although mute,

it gestures with its hands at eight-fifteen
and eight-fifteen and eight-fifteen again

while tables of statistics on the wall
update the news by calling on a roll
of tape, death gummed on death, and in the case
adjacent, an exhibit under glass

is glass itself: a shard the bomb slammed in
a woman's arm at eight-fifteen, but some
three decades on — as if to make it plain
hope's only as renewable as pain,

and as if all the unsung
debasements of the past may one day come
rising to the surface once again —
worked its filthy way out like a tongue.

Carolyn Forché

The Colonel

1978

What you have heard is true. I was in his house. His wife carried a tray of coffee and sugar. His daughter filed her nails, his son went out for the night. There were daily papers, pet dogs, a pistol on the cushion beside him. The moon swung bare on its black cord over the house. On the television was a cop show. It was in English. Broken bottles were embedded in the walls around the house to scoop the kneecaps from a man's legs or cut his hands to lace. On the windows there were gratings like those in liquor stores. We had dinner, rack of lamb, good wine, a gold bell was on the table for calling the maid. The maid brought green mangoes, salt, a type of bread. I was asked how I enjoyed the country. There was a brief commercial in Spanish. His wife took everything away. There was some talk then of how difficult it had become to govern. The parrot said hello on the terrace. The colonel told it to shut up, and pushed himself from the table. My friend said to me with his eyes: say nothing. The colonel returned with a sack used to bring groceries home. He spilled many human ears on the table. They were like dried peach halves. There is no other way to say this. He took one of them in his hands, shook it in our faces, dropped it into a water glass. It came alive there. I am tired of fooling around he said. As for the rights of anyone, tell your people they can go fuck themselves. He swept the ears to the floor with his arm and held the last of his wine in the air. Something for your poetry, no? he said. Some of the ears on the floor caught this scrap of his voice. Some of the ears on the floor were pressed to the ground.

Tadeusz Rozewicz

Pigtail

1948

TRANSLATED BY ROBERT A. MAGUIRE AND MAGNUS JAN KRYNSKI

When all the women in the transport
had their heads shaved
four workmen with brooms made of birch twigs
swept up
and gathered up the hair

Behind clean glass
the stiff hair lies
of those suffocated in gas chambers
there are pins and side combs
in this hair

The hair is not shot through with light
is not parted by the breeze
is not touched by any hand
or rain or lips

In huge chests
clouds of dry hair
of those suffocated
and a faded plait
a pigtail with a ribbon
pulled at school
by naughty boys

Irina Ratushinskaya

I Will Live and Survive

1986

I will live and survive and be asked:
How they slammed my head against a trestle,
How I had to freeze at nights,
How my hair started to turn grey . . .
But I'll smile. And will crack some joke
And brush away the encroaching shadow.
And I will render homage to the dry September
That became my second birth.
And I'll be asked: 'Doesn't it hurt you to remember?'
Not being deceived by my outward flippancy.
But the former names will detonate in my memory —
Magnificent as old cannon.
And I will tell of the best people in all the earth,
The most tender, but also the most invincible,

How they said farewell, how they went to be tortured,
How they waited for letters from their loved ones.
And I'll be asked: what helped us to live
When there were neither letters nor any news — only walls,
And the cold of the cell, and the blather of official lies,
And the sickening promises made in exchange for betrayal.
And I will tell of the first beauty
I saw in captivity.
A frost-covered window! No spyholes, nor walls,
Nor cell-bars, nor the long-endured pain —
Only a blue radiance on a tiny pane of glass,
A cast pattern — none more beautiful could be dreamt!
The more clearly you looked, the more powerfully blossomed
Those brigand forests, campfires and birds!
And how many times there was bitter cold weather
And how many windows sparkled after that one —
But never was it repeated,
That upheaval of rainbow ice!
And anyway, what good would it be to me now,
And what would be the pretext for that festival?
Such a gift can only be received once,
And perhaps is only needed once.

RELATED COMMENTARY: *Louise Glück, "Poems* Are *Autobiography," page 1175.*

13

POET TO POET

We're all writing the same poem.
– ROBERT DUNCAN

Perhaps because poetry is written from emotions that lie so close to the surface of the skin, poets are very conscious of each other's work, and they respond strongly to other poetry. Poets are their own best audience. Adrienne Rich has described her own experience of poetry as a child:

> I thought that the poets in the anthologies were the only real poets, that their being in the anthologies was proof of this, though some were classified as "great" and others as "minor." I owed much to these anthologies: *Silver Pennies;* the constant outflow of volumes edited by Louis Untermeyer; *The Cambridge Book of Poetry for Children;* Palgrave's *Golden Treasury;* the *Oxford Book of English Verse*. . . . I still believed that poets were inspired by some transcendental authority and spoke from some extraordinary height.

Margaret Atwood has described her emotions when she heard Rich read from her book *Diving into the Wreck* (1973): "When I first heard the author read from it, I felt as though the top of my head was being attacked, sometimes with an ice pick, sometimes with a blunter instrument: a hatchet or a hammer." Atwood, in *her* turn, reminds the reader of Emily Dickinson's description of how she knew something she read was poetry: "If I feel physically as if the top of my head were taken off, I know that it is poetry."

You will find in your reading that it is not only modern poets who are so excited by the words of another poet. When a friend introduced John Keats to the translation of Homer by the Elizabethan poet George Chapman, they stayed up all night reading to each other. As Keats walked home at dawn he was already composing his sonnet, "On First Looking into Chapman's Homer." The poem was finished and reached his friend by the first mail, only a few hours later.

JOHN KEATS

On First Looking into Chapman's Homer *1816*

Much have I travell'd in the realms of gold,
  And many goodly states and kingdoms seen;
  Round many western islands have I been
Which bards in fealty to Apollo° hold.
Oft of one wide expanse had I been told
  That deep-browed Homer ruled as his demesne;°
  Yet never did I breathe its pure serene°
Till I heard Chapman° speak out loud and bold:
Then felt I like some watcher of the skies
  When a new planet swims into his ken;
Or like stout Cortez° when with eagle eyes
  He star'd at the Pacific — and all his men
Look'd at each other with a wild surmise —
  Silent upon a peak in Darien.

In his mood of exhilaration, Keats made a mistake in the name of the Spanish explorer who first saw the Pacific (it was Balboa and not "Cortez"), but critics have never felt that this diminishes the effect of his poem.

Many poets also have poets as friends, they translate one another's poems from other languages, they read their poems to each other, they send each other copies of new manuscripts, they publish magazines of each other's poetry. In the sense that living writers are part of a community, they also are an important influence on each other. To speak of a poem from an earlier generation "influencing" a younger writer, however, is more complicated. In a discussion of young painters that applies equally well to young poets, art critic Michael Baxadall has pointed out that to say a writer or a text from an earlier generation "influences" a younger writer is misleading, since a poem written by a poet who is no longer living cannot "do" anything. It is the younger writer who *does* something. Baxadall drew up a list of the things that

---

4. Apollo: Greek god of poetry. **6. demesne:** Domain. **7. serene:** Atmosphere. **8. Chapman:** George Chapman (c. 1560–1634), Elizabethan poet whose translations of Homer's Greek epics *Iliad* and *Odyssey* Keats found superior to the eighteenth-century translations with which he was familiar. **11. Cortez:** Keats mistakenly identifies Hernando Cortés, not Vasco Núñez de Balboa, as the first European to view the Pacific Ocean from Darien, a peak in Panama.

the younger writer can do. If the young writer is moved to respond to something by an older writer, the younger — in just the same way that a young painter responds to the work of an older artist — can

> draw on, resort to, avail oneself of, appropriate from, have recourse to, adapt, misunderstand, refer to, pick up, take on, engage with, react to, quote, differentiate oneself from, assimilate oneself to, assimilate, align oneself with, copy, address, paraphrase, absorb, make a variation on, revive, continue, remodel, ape, emulate, travesty, parody, extract from, distort, attend to, resist, simplify, reconstitute, elaborate on, develop, face up to, master, subvert, perpetuate, reduce, promote, respond to, transform, tackle. . . . [E]veryone will be able to think of others.

As we have seen in Keats's response to Homer, whichever way a young poet responds to the work of another poet, the result will be poetry.

For women readers today, the early centuries of poetry in English can present a difficult hurdle. Because of social attitudes, it is not until the nineteenth century that poetry written by women begins to play an important role in the poetic tradition. However, as critic Jan Montefiore shows us in her analysis of a sonnet by Edna St. Vincent Millay, an American poet of the 1920s, women poets did not feel that they were entirely excluded from this tradition, and they did not hesitate to take it and mold it for their own work. Montefiore writes,

> Millay's best-known sequence of love sonnets, *Fatal Interview,* depends on an individual voice speaking with a poetic vocabulary (thematic as well as lexical) which is drawn from Elizabethan poetry as reread by the Romantics, as in this excerpt from sonnet VIII:
>
> > Yet in an hour to come, disdainful dust,
> > You shall be bowed and brought to bed with me.
> > While the blood roars, or when the blood is rust
> > About a broken engine, this shall be.
> > If not today, then later; if not here,
> > On the green grass, with sighing and delight,
> > Then under it, all in good time, my dear,
> > We shall be laid together in the night.
>
> The poet's confidence and ease in handling the sonnet form are immediately apparent; she slides effortlessly from the twentieth-century image of "rust / About a broken engine" to the "timeless" line "On the green grass, with sighing and delight," using the associative rhymes "rust" and "dust" and the emphatic alliteration of "bowed and brought to bed" with an effect of relish, not cliché. Her appropriation of literary tradition is equally apparent in the way that the counterposing of love and death, the brevity of human life and the sleep of the grave, recalls Shakespeare, Marvell, and Catullus in a *cantabile* lyricism formed on Yeats. This is not an allusive poem; rather its themes are smoothed with poetic handling, and it is written in a style which assumes that poetry is timeless.

The term *allusive* that Montefiore uses, which means to allude or refer to some other writing, suggests one of the ways in which a poet responds to another poem. It is one of several ways that are part of the poet's means, the tools a poet uses to make a poem. Here are some of the most common you will find in your reading.

QUOTATION

Many poets quote directly or indirectly from other poems. Sometimes the use of someone else's words is indicated by quotation marks, but more often the quotation is left without any marks to indicate it. The writer wants to leave it to the reader, whether or not the different voice in the poem is heard. One of the uses of **quotation** that you will find is to give the poem a more general meaning or to present the poem in a clearer historical perspective. The California poet Robert Duncan used a quote from the Greek poet Pindar as the title and the source of ideas for one of his major poems, *A Poem Beginning with a Line by Pindar.* The line from Pindar that begins the poem is "The light foot hears you and the brightness begins." In the poem, Duncan alludes to Walt Whitman's elegy on the death of Lincoln, *When Lilacs Last in the Dooryard Bloom'd:*

> What
> if lilacs last in *this* dooryard bloomd?

A few lines later he quotes directly from Whitman, using quotation marks:

> How sad "amid lanes and through old woods"
> echoes Whitman's love for Lincoln!

Marianne Moore used many quotations in her poetry. Often it was material from magazine articles or books she was reading, or phrases that she took from other poets or writers, sometimes slightly altering them. Consider these lines from the poem "The Student":

> . . . With us, a
> school — like the singing tree of which
> the leaves were mouths singing in concert
> is both a tree of knowledge
> and of liberty. . . .

Moore tells us in a note to the poem that she adapted the sentence "Each leaf was a mouth, and every leaf joined in concert" from the book *The Arabian Nights.*

A poet who was influenced by Moore, Amy Clampitt includes a note on the line in her poem "The Outer Bar" that describes the waves striking the sandbar:

> chain-gang archangels that in their prismatic
> frenzy fall, gall and gash the daylight. . . .

Clampitt's note points out that "'fall, gall and gash the daylight' . . . derives, of course, from 'The Windhover' by Gerard Manley Hopkins."

Quotation is also used to "engage with," if we use another of the ways younger writers respond to other poems that we listed a few paragraphs ago.

In the opening lines of her poem "the closing of the south park road," Tobey Hiller uses a quotation from Emily Dickinson:

> the closing of the south park road
>
> happens every year between Thanksgiving and Christmas
> just when the light grows lucid, forgiving nothing and
> disappearing *into beauty,*
> as Emily says
>
> on these days the air over the water opens into a hard wise body
> lying low and immortal over everything it loves.

In the same way, Langston Hughes uses the last line from the song "Dixie" for a bitter, ironic comment on racism in "Song for a Dark Girl" (p. 1058):

> Way Down South in Dixie
>   (Break the heart of me)
> They hung my black young lover
>   To a cross roads tree.
> Way Down South in Dixie
>   (Bruised body high in air)
> I asked the white Lord Jesus
>   What was the use of prayer.

As the critic Helen Vendler writes, "All cultural production comes about from constant interchanges of past works and ideas with current ones."

PARAPHRASE

Another way that a poet may use another poet's words is to **paraphrase** a line or a stanza. The denotative meaning of paraphrase is "to render freely, or amplify, a passage, or express its sense in other words." In his poem "Journey of the Magi," T. S. Eliot paraphrased a section from a sermon by the early English religious writer Lancelot Andrewes. This is the section from Andrewes's "Nativity Sermon" XV:

> It was no summer progress. A cold coming they had of it at this time of the year, just the worst time of the year to take a journey, and specially a long journey in. The ways deep, the weather sharp, the days short, the sun furthest off, *in solstitio brumali,* "the very dead of winter."

This is Eliot's paraphrase, which he sets off with quotation marks to show that there is a source for the lines:

> "A cold coming we had of it,
> Just the worst time of the year
> For a journey, and such a long journey:
> The ways deep and the weather sharp,
> The very dead of winter."

Eliot's poems were often a maze of unidentified paraphrases and translations. He felt that this was one way to respond to the traditions behind his poetry. As he wrote in an essay on Elizabethan drama, "One of the surest tests is the way in which a poet borrows. Immature poets imitate; mature poets steal; bad poets deface what they take; and good poets make it into something better, or at least something different." You should also read the excerpt from Eliot's essay "Tradition and the Individual Talent" in Chapter 16, Commentaries on Poetry and Poets.

IMITATION

At some point in their struggle to find their own voice, young writers usually try every form of traditional poetry. Sometimes in their mature work they will casually begin to imitate the work of another poet or another poetic style. The American poet James Merrill was very skillful at slipping in and out of a wide range of poetic voices. Often he used rhyme and near rhyme for groups of lines within his poems. As an example, in his long poem *Coda: The Higher Keys,* in addition to a crowd of allusions to other writers and other poems, his elegant diction and perfect rhyme in lines 120–28 suggest that the setting of the poem is an eighteenth-century English ballroom:

. . . A splendor
Across lawns meets, in Sandover's tall time —
Dappled mirrors, its own eye. Should rhyme
Calling to rhyme awaken the odd snore,
No harm done. I shall study to ignore
Looks that more boldly with each session yearn
Toward the buffet where steaming silver urn,
Cucumber sandwiches, rum punch, fudge laced
With hashish cater to whatever taste.

PARODY

There is a saying that "imitation is the sincerest form of flattery," and **parody** achieves the same result, by paying an indirect tribute to the popularity of the poet whose work is the subject of the parody. The denotative meaning of parody is "a composition in which an author's characteristics are humorously imitated." Parodies have been written of almost every well-known writer, though they often are more malicious than humorous. Here is one written in the 1920s by Hugh Kingsmill that is humorous. The writer being parodied is A. E. Housman.

HUGH KINGSMILL

What, Still Alive at Twenty-Two? *1920*

What, still alive at twenty-two,
A clean, upstanding chap like you?
Sure, if your throat 'tis hard to slit,
Slit your girl's, and swing for it.

■ ■ ■

Like enough, you won't be glad
When they come to hang you, lad:
But bacon's not the only thing
That's cured by hanging from a string.

So, when the spilt ink of the night
Spreads o'er the blotting-pad of light,
Lads whose job is still to do
Shall whet their knives, and think of you.

ALLUSION

The denotative meaning of **allusion** — "to allude to" — means to "refer indirectly to something presumably known to the listener or reader." It is different from quotation because it is indirect. If you allude to something, you name it, or suggest it, and readers add their own understanding of the context. In his poem "The Love Song of J. Alfred Prufrock," T. S. Eliot alludes to Shakespeare with the line "I know the voices dying with a dying fall." Shakespeare's phrase, from *Twelfth Night,* is "If music be the food of love, play on. . . . That strain again! It had a dying fall." In act 2, scene 2 of *Hamlet,* Shakespeare alludes to the *Iliad* in Hamlet's soliloquy. After listening to one of the players begin to weep as he described the grief of Hecuba, Queen of Troy, at the death of her husband, Priam, Hamlet bursts out,

For Hecuba!
What's Hecuba to him, or he to Hecuba,
That he should weep for her?

Matthew Arnold, in his poem "Dover Beach" (p. 966), alludes to the Greek dramatist Sophocles when he describes the eternal note of sadness he hears in the sea:

Sophocles long ago
Heard it on the Aegean.

In the titles of her poems, Adrienne Rich often alludes to other poems and writers. The title "The Demon Lover" is a phrase from Samuel Taylor Coleridge's "Kubla Khan." "A Valediction Forbidding Mourning" is also the title of a poem by John Donne, and "When We Dead Awaken" is the title of the last play by the Norwegian playwright Henrik Ibsen.

In our discussion of quotation, we have already read some examples of allusion. In your reading you will find many other poets who use allusion to develop the themes or the language of their poetry.

ADDRESS AND TRIBUTE

Another of the ways poets respond to other poets is to address them directly, and there is a long tradition of poetry written as a **tribute** from one writer to another. A well-known example is the Elizabethan dramatist and poet Ben Jonson's tribute to his friend William Shakespeare. The poem introduced the first Folio of Shakespeare's plays, published in 1623.

Ben Jonson

To the Memory of My Beloved, the Author, Mr. William Shakespeare, and What He Hath Left Us

1623

To draw no envy, Shakespeare, on thy name
  Am I thus ample to thy book and fame,
While I confess thy writings to be such
  As neither man nor Muse can praise too much.
'Tis true, and all men's suffrage. But these ways
  Were not the paths I meant unto thy praise;
For silliest ignorance on these may light,
  Which, when it sounds at best, but echoes right;
Or blind affection, which doth ne'er advance
  The truth, but gropes, and urgeth all by chance;
Or crafty malice might pretend this praise,
  And think to ruin where it seemed to raise.
These are as some infamous bawd or whore
  Should praise a matron. What could hurt her more?
But thou art proof against them, and, indeed,
  Above th' ill fortune of them, or the need.
I therefore will begin. Soul of the age!
  The applause! delight! the wonder of our stage!
My Shakespeare, rise; I will not lodge thee by
  Chaucer or Spenser, or bid Beaumont lie
A little further to make thee a room:°
  Thou art a monument without a tomb,
And art alive still while thy book doth live,
  And we have wits to read and praise to give.
That I not mix thee so, my brain excuses,
  I mean with great, but disproportioned Muses;
For, if I thought my judgment were of years,
  I should commit thee surely with thy peers,
And tell how far thou didst our Lyly outshine,
  Or sporting Kyd, or Marlowe's mighty line.°
And though thou hadst small Latin and less Greek,

20–21. Chaucer . . . Spenser . . . Beaumont: Geoffrey Chaucer, Edmund Spenser, and Francis Beaumont were buried in the poet's corner at Westminster Abbey, while Shakespeare was buried in Stratford-upon-Avon. **29–30. Lyly . . . Kyd . . . or Marlowe's mighty line:** John Lyly, Thomas Kyd, and Christopher Marlowe were fine Elizabethan dramatists who still did not measure up to Shakespeare.

From thence to honor thee I would not seek
For names, but call forth thund'ring Aeschylus,
Euripides, and Sophocles° to us,
Pacuvius, Accius, him of Cordova dead,°
To life again, to hear thy buskin° tread
And shake a stage; or, when thy socks° were on,
Leave thee alone for the comparison
Of all that insolent Greece or haughty Rome
Sent forth, or since did from their ashes come.
Triumph, my Britain; thou hast one to show
To whom all scenes of Europe homage owe.
He was not of an age, but for all time!
And all the Muses still were in their prime
When like Apollo he came forth to warm
Our ears, or like a Mercury to charm.
Nature herself was proud of his designs,
And joyed to wear the dressing of his lines,
Which were so richly spun, and woven so fit,
As, since, she will vouchsafe no other wit:
The merry Greek, tart Aristophanes,°
Neat Terence, witty Plautus° now not please,
But antiquated and deserted lie,
As they were not of Nature's family.
Yet must I not give Nature all; thy Art,
My gentle Shakespeare, must enjoy a part.
For though the poet's matter Nature be,
His Art doth give the fashion; and that he
Who casts to write a living line must sweat
(Such as thine are) and strike the second heat
Upon the muses' anvil; turn the same,
And himself with it, that he thinks to frame,
Or for the laurel he may gain a scorn;
For a good poet's made as well as born.
And such wert thou! Look how the father's face
Lives in his issue; even so the race
Of Shakespeare's mind and manners brightly shines
In his well-turned and true-filed lines,
In each of which he seems to shake a lance,°

33–34. Aeschylus, Euripides, . . . Sophocles: Aeschylus, Euripides, and Sophocles were the greatest of the classic Greek tragedians. **35. Pacuvius, Accius, him of Cordova dead:** In the first century A.D., Seneca the Younger "of Cordova" was the greatest of the classic Latin tragedians; his second century B.C. predecessors Marcus Pacuvius and Lucius Accius were minor tragedians whom Jonson cites more for rhetorical effect than for genuine comparison to Shakespeare. **36. buskin:** The footwear of actors in tragedies were buskins; hence, a buskin is a symbol of tragedy. **37. socks:** Comic actors wore socks; therefore, a sock symbolizes comedy. **51. Aristophanes:** Greek satirical writer and dramatist. **52. Terence . . . Plautus:** Roman authors of comedic plays. **69. shake a lance:** Pun on "Shakespeare."

As brandished at the eyes of ignorance.
Sweet swan of Avon, what a sight it were
To see thee in our waters yet appear,
And make those flights upon the banks of Thames
That so did take Eliza and our James!°
But stay; I see thee in the hemisphere
Advanced and made a constellation there!
Shine forth, thou star of poets, and with rage
Or influence° chide or cheer the drooping stage,
Which, since thy flight from hence, hath mourned like night,
And despairs day, but for thy volume's light.

Young writers often feel that it is important to speak directly to the older writers who have had an effect on their own work. A good example is the poem "A Pact," by the then-young American poet Ezra Pound, addressing the classic older American poet Walt Whitman.

Ezra Pound

A Pact

1913

I made a pact with you, Walt Whitman —
I have detested you long enough.
I come to you as a grown child
who has had a pig-headed father;
I am old enough now to make friends.
It was you that broke the new wood,
Now is the time for carving.
We have one sap and one root —
Let there be commerce between us.

Often the response to the other poet is a way of paying tribute to the other writer's work. In his poem "A Supermarket in California," Allen Ginsberg also addresses Walt Whitman, paying him an affectionate tribute.

Allen Ginsberg

A Supermarket in California

1956

What thoughts I have of you tonight, Walt Whitman, for I walked down the sidestreets under the trees with a headache self-conscious looking at the full moon.

74. Eliza and our James: Queen Elizabeth I and King James I. **76–78. constellation . . . influence:** In mythology, great heroes were often transformed into star constellations upon their death, and celestial bodies were believed to exert an influence upon earthly affairs.

In my hungry fatigue, and shopping for images, I went into the neon fruit supermarket, dreaming of your enumerations!

What peaches and what penumbras! Whole families shopping at night! Aisles full of husbands! Wives in the avocados, babies in the tomatoes! — and you, García Lorca, what were you doing down by the watermelons!

I saw you, Walt Whitman, childless, lonely old grubber, poking among the meats in the refrigerator and eyeing the grocery boys.

I heard you asking questions of each: Who killed the pork chops? What price bananas? Are you my Angel?

I wandered in and out of the brilliant stacks of cans following you, and followed in my imagination by the store detective.

We strode down the open corridors together in our solitary fancy tasting artichokes, possessing every frozen delicacy, and never passing the cashier.

Where are we going, Walt Whitman? The doors close in an hour. Which way does your beard point tonight?

(I touch your book and dream of our odyssey in the supermarket and feel absurd.)

Will we walk all night through solitary streets? The trees add shade to shade, lights out in the houses, we'll both be lonely.

Will we stroll dreaming of the lost America of love past blue automobiles in driveways, home to our silent cottage?

Ah, dear father, graybeard, lonely old courage-teacher, what America did you have when Charon quit poling his ferry and you got out on a smoking bank and stood watching the boat disappear on the black waters of Lethe? *Berkeley, 1955*

The García Lorca alluded to in the poem is the Spanish poet who was murdered by the Fascists during the Spanish Civil War.

A tribute to another poet can also be casual and amusing. In his poem "Oatmeal," Galway Kinnell imagines that he is eating oatmeal with John Keats, and this gives him a chance to talk about a problem with the text of one of Keats's best-known poems. Kinnell's reference to Patrick Kavanagh in the final line is an inside joke for readers who may recognize the Irish writer whose best-known poem is titled "The Great Hunger."

Galway Kinnell

Oatmeal

1990

I eat oatmeal for breakfast.
I make it on the hot plate and put skimmed milk on it.
I eat it alone.
I am aware it is not good to eat oatmeal alone.

Its consistency is such that it is better for your mental health if somebody eats it with you.
That is why I often think up an imaginary companion to have breakfast with.
Possibly it is even worse to eat oatmeal with an imaginary companion.
Nevertheless, yesterday morning, I ate my oatmeal — porridge, as he called it — with John Keats.
Keats said I was absolutely right to invite him: due to its glutinous texture, gluey lumpishness, hint of slime, and unusual willingness to disintegrate, oatmeal must never be eaten alone.
He said that in his opinion, however, it is perfectly OK to eat it with an imaginary companion,
and he himself had enjoyed memorable porridges with Edmund Spenser and John Milton.
Even if eating oatmeal with an imaginary companion is not as wholesome as Keats claims, still, you can learn something from it.
Yesterday morning, for instance, Keats told me about writing the "Ode to a Nightingale."
He had a heck of a time finishing it — those were his words — "Oi 'ad a 'eck of a toime," he said, more or less, speaking through his porridge.
He wrote it quickly, on scraps of paper, which he then stuck in his pocket,
but when he got home he couldn't figure out the order of the stanzas, and he and a friend spread the papers on a table, and they made some sense of them, but he isn't sure to this day if they got it right.
An entire stanza may have slipped into the lining of his jacket through a hole in the pocket.
He still wonders about the occasional sense of drift between stanzas,
and the way here and there a line will go into the configuration of a Moslem at prayer, then raise itself up and peer about, and then lay itself down slightly off the mark, causing the poem to move forward with God's reckless wobble.
He said someone told him that later in life Wordsworth heard about the scraps of paper on the table, and tried shuffling some stanzas of his own, but only made matters worse.
I would not have known about any of this but for my reluctance to eat oatmeal alone.
When breakfast was over, John recited "To Autumn."
He recited it slowly, with much feeling, and he articulated the words lovingly, and his odd accent sounded sweet.
He didn't offer the story of writing "To Autumn," I doubt if there is much of one.
But he did say the sight of a just-harvested oat field got him started on it,
and two of the lines, "For Summer has o'er-brimmed their clammy cells" and "Thou watchest the last oozings hours by hours," came to him while eating oatmeal alone.

I can see him — drawing a spoon through the stuff, gazing into the glimmering furrows, muttering — and it occurs to me:
maybe there is no sublime; only the shining of the amnion's tatters.
For supper tonight I am going to have a baked potato left over from lunch.
I am aware that a leftover baked potato is damp, slippery, and simultaneously gummy and crumbly,
and therefore I'm going to invite Patrick Kavanagh to join me.

RELATED COMMENTARIES: *Marilyn Chin, "On the Canon," page 1159; T. S. Eliot, From "Tradition and the Individual Talent," page 1163.*

14

READING, THINKING, AND WRITING ABOUT POETRY

It is difficult
to get the news from poems
yet men die miserably every day
for lack
of what is found there.

– William Carlos Williams, from "Asphodel, That Greeny Flower"

READING POETRY

Perhaps it is because poetry *looks* different on the page, or perhaps it is because poetry sometimes wears its heart on its sleeve, but for many readers the experience of reading a poem seems different from reading a short story or a play. It is easy to be put off by the formal arrangement of lines and verses and by language that describes private emotions and hidden dreams. Reading poetry, however, is an experience very similar to reading anything else. You read a poem for what you will find there, for what it tells you about yourself, your life, your world. Then you read it a second time for the pleasure you find in the way the poet uses words.

In Chapter 7, "What Is a Poem?," you learned that it will help you to understand a poem if you can separate it into two parts as you read it over. First read the poem for what it is about, its subject and its theme; then read it to appreciate further the skill and imagination the poet has used in presenting you with this theme.

Even if you are not entirely sure that you understand everything in the poem in your first reading, you can be struck by the writer's skill. If we take a very short poem as an example, you can see that it is often the poet's ability to choose one thing out of the mass of small details that brings a poem to life. Here is a haiku by the Japanese poet Buson quoted by the American writer Jack Kerouac in his introduction to his own "Western Haikus":

> The nightingale is singing,
> Its small mouth
> open.

The description "Its small mouth / open" suggests the nightingale's song so simply and yet so vividly that the group of three short lines surrounded by the white space on the page seems to reverberate like the nightingale song itself in your imagination. Other poems can suggest an emotional situation so clearly and with such intensity that you find the words stay in your memory, even if you could not write them down exactly if you were asked. This short English medieval lyric has been part of our emotional storehouse for more than four hundred years:

> Western wind, when wilt thou blow,
> The small rain down can rain?
> Christ, if my love were in my arms,
> And I in my bed again!

You do not have to be told to read poems like these more than once. Their appeal to your feelings is immediate and unforgettable. The skill of the author has been in finding the small moment that suggests the poem's theme — the wonder of experiencing nature in Buson's haiku, and the joy of love in the medieval lyric.

Longer poems can be more difficult for the reader. Sometimes the language is unfamiliar; sometimes the theme is not clear at first reading. The general rule is to read the poem straight through to the end, even if you are unsure of the meaning of all the words or phrases the first time around. Inexperienced readers often stop after just a few lines if they begin to feel confused by what the poet appears to be saying.

If this happens, you should disregard your sense that you have lost your bearings in the poem and continue reading until you have finished it. Often the whole poem will clarify the meaning of the early images or lines. Unless you give yourself the opportunity to read the entire poem, you will not have a fair chance to find out what it is saying. For example, when you begin reading the poem "since feeling is first" (1926) by the American writer E. E. Cummings, you might stumble on the word *syntax* or the phrase "syntax of things" in the third line of the poem. Do not stop reading to reach for a dictionary to help you puzzle out what the poem means by "syntax." Just continue on to the end of the poem. Reach for the dictionary, if necessary, *after* you have read it all the way through the first time.

> since feeling is first
> who pays any attention
> to the syntax of things
> will never wholly kiss you;
> wholly to be a fool
> while Spring is in the world
>
> my blood approves,
> and kisses are a better fate

than wisdom
lady I swear by all flowers. Don't cry
— the best gesture of my brain is less than
your eyelids' flutter which says
we are for each other: then
laugh, leaning back in my arms
for life's not a paragraph

And death I think is no parenthesis

When you go back to the beginning of the poem to give it a second reading, you will find that the last two lines illuminate the meaning of the word *syntax* that might have given you trouble on your first reading. The poet is using literary terms in a playful manner to write a love poem, making the point that life is different from literature and should be lived fully and instinctively while there is still time. The speaker in the poem is urging his lady to follow the impulse of her heart, which he tells her is worth more than his poem.

In your study of poetry, you can admire the skill with which Cummings employs his technical means of alliteration, rhythm, and paradox. Aware that the poem was published in 1926, before the sexual revolution of the 1960s, you might also understand that the poet has written it to persuade his "lady" not to wait for a wedding ring but to abandon her caution, urging her to acknowledge the physical attraction between them and become his lover right away. Despite Cummings's use of lowercase letters and the open form of his poem, you can recognize the traditional theme of *carpe diem,* the Latin words for "seize the day," in this modern poem.

It is possible, of course, for you to pay close attention as you follow the words in a poem, read it carefully straight through to the end, reread it a second time, and still find its meaning elusive. Then you might find writing a *paraphrase* of the subject of the poem helps you to understand it as you attempt to put the poem into your own words. Your paraphrase of Cummings's poem might look something like this:

> Feeling is more important than thinking. A person who thinks too much about the meaning of life will miss the pleasure of enjoying love. When you're young, you should throw caution to the winds and follow your heart. A love affair should take precedence over everything. Don't be sad thinking it won't work out. Letting yourself feel an attraction for someone is more important than any thought you can have. Relax and enjoy being with your lover, because life is short — it isn't as long as a paragraph, it's only a sentence. And death is a full stop — it isn't a parenthesis, it's a period.

Usually the effort of trying to find your own words to express the subject of a poem will help you to understand it. Writing a paraphrase will force you to spend more time focusing on the poem to clarify your thoughts. This is the first step in the process of thinking critically about poetry.

Poems are "meter-making arguments," so they usually represent an idea or develop a series of ideas in a coherent discourse. Poems are also "language charged with meaning to the utmost degree," so you may have to unravel the ideas behind the words as patiently as you would unravel a ball of string after your cat has played with it. When you write a paraphrase of a poem, you take the chance that you might be mistaken about all or part of its meaning. But you also have a method of clarifying the subject that usually brings you closer to the theme or the central idea that you sense behind the poem's words.

The more skilled you become as a reader of poetry, the more readily your intuition will help you grapple with the experience of the poem. At first your study of the poet's means will give you insight into the different writers' resources as they use language to create a poem. Your increased sensitivity to meter and rhyme, diction and symbolism, and the other means used by the poet should help you to understand and enjoy the work. At the beginning of your study of poetry, it may not be possible to paraphrase the entire poem successfully, but any effort you make should help to bring you closer to the poem.

Guidelines for Reading Poetry

1. Make an entry in your notebook for each poem that is assigned in class, writing down the author's name, the title, and the date.
2. Read the poem through once in its entirety, regardless of whether you understand all the words.
3. When you read the poem a second time, use a dictionary to look up words you don't understand.
4. Copy the first lines of the poem into your notebook to scan the rhythm of the poem. Does it fall into any of the patterns you have studied?
5. Note what impresses you most about the way the poet uses language in the poem, in particular the poem's rhyme, its figurative language, and its diction.
6. Try to write a paraphrase of the subject of the poem, following the poet's argument closely as it develops throughout the lines of the poem. Does the poet use paradox, symbolism, allusion, or tribute? Summarize, if you can, the theme of the poem in a single sentence.
7. If you have difficulty understanding any parts of the poem, or the entire poem, write down specific questions about it so that you can ask them in class.
8. Review technical words about poetry that were used in class to be sure you understand them.

CRITICAL THINKING ABOUT POETRY

Paraphrasing a poem will help you to understand its subject and its theme, a necessary step in the process of thinking critically about poetry. You will also find that identifying the various means the poet has used to create the poem will help you to analyze the creative strategies behind the author's choice of form and language. For example, you might ask yourself the following questions:

1. Who is the speaker of the poem? How does identifying the speaker contribute to your understanding of the poem?
2. How closely can you identify the speaker with the author of the poem?
3. What attitude toward the subject of the poem does the speaker convey? How does the tone of the poem help you understand this attitude?
4. What use has the poet made of technical means such as imagery, alliteration, allusion, and specific figures of speech?
5. How has the poet used metaphor and simile in the poem?
6. How would you describe the diction and the syntax of the poem?
7. What is the form of the poem? Why did the poet choose this form and not another?
8. Why do you feel the poet might have written this poem?
9. What does the language of the poem tell you about the reader for whom the poem was written? Is it addressed to a person close to the poet, or to a more general reader?
10. How might different readers interpret the poem from different critical perspectives — feminist, Marxist, historical, and so forth?

It might help clarify your thinking about poetry if you take a specific poem and read it closely with these questions in mind. The answers to the questions can generate additional ideas for writing about the poem. This poem is by the modern American writer Linda Pastan.

LINDA PASTAN

To a Daughter Leaving Home 1978

When I taught you
at eight to ride
a bicycle, loping along
beside you
as you wobbled away
on two round wheels,
my own mouth rounding
in surprise when you pulled
ahead down the curved
path of the park,
I kept waiting
for the thud
of your crash as I
sprinted to catch up,
while you grew
smaller, more breakable
with distance,
pumping, pumping
for your life, screaming

with laughter,
the hair flapping
behind you like a
handkerchief waving
goodbye.

After you have carefully read a poem, you can answer the questions that were posed to help you in your understanding. Applying the questions to Pastan's poem might generate some of the following responses:

1. The speaker of the poem is clearly the writer herself. We know from this that we are reading a lyric poem, which is concerned with a moment of everyday life. Knowing that the writer is speaking in her own voice helps us to understand the tone and the context of the poem.
2. In this poem the identity of the speaker and author of the poem are the same.
3. The subject of the poem is the poet's daughter, and the emotional attitude she expresses is her love for her child.
4. Although the poem is written in a casual, personal tone, there is a skillful ingenuity in the use of language. Instead of writing that her daughter rode away unsteadily, Pastan uses more striking imagery: "as you wobbled away / on two round wheels." It is also useful to notice that she has written "two . . . wheels." This is an allusion to the moment when a child grows from a tricycle or training wheels to a two-wheel bicycle, which is crucial in the child's development. Also notice the writer's use of alliteration in the phrases "loping along," with its repetition of l sounds; "wobbled away," with its w sounds; and "path of the park," with its ps.

   There are several ways you could describe the image "my own mouth rounding / in surprise." The use of "rounding" to describe her mouth is certainly an allusion to the round wheels of the bicycle that she mentioned in the previous line. The denotative meaning of "rounding" is simply a description of the shape of her mouth, while the connotative meaning is, as she explains, that the round shape of her mouth is an expression of her surprise at what her daughter is doing.

   The phrase "more breakable with distance" is an interesting example of the use of metonymy. The writer is describing her feeling that her daughter is more vulnerable to the dangers of life as she goes further away from her mother, but Pastan uses, instead, the more poetic phrase to describe the dangers to her daughter as she travels further on the park's bicycle path.
5. The use of metaphor is very important in this poem, because the entire poem itself is a metaphor. What Pastan is describing is the moment

when a daughter breaks away from her mother to become an adult. She has chosen to describe it in terms of a metaphor, that of her daughter riding away from her on the daughter's first excited trip on a two-wheel bicycle. The use of simile is very clear in the final lines, when she describes her daughter's hair "flapping . . . like a / handkerchief waving / goodbye." With the simile she has made the meaning of the poem clear. She sees her daughter's first moments on a bicycle and her wild, runaway ride along the path as the moment when her daughter leaves her.

6. The diction of the poem is contemporary and familiar; the syntax is the conversational word order of everyday speech.
7. Since the writer does not use rhyme and the lines don't follow a regular meter we would describe this as a poem in open form, and since it is a personal poem directed to a person close to the writer we would describe it as a lyric poem. The poet chose this form because it most closely matches the style of everyday speech. Since this is a personal poem to her daughter it would strike a modern reader as unconvincing if she used a more elevated and consciously "literary" form.
8. The poet clearly wrote this poem as an expression of her love for her daughter. We know by the title that it was written when her daughter had grown up and become an adult. The poem was probably written both to express the poet's emotions and to soothe her pain at their separation by comparing this moment to her daughter's first bicycle ride.
9. We can tell by the familiar, tender tone of the poem that it was written for someone close to the writer. Since the experience she is describing is familiar to so many other people, however, the poem is also meaningful for a general reader.
10. It would perhaps be a feminist critic who would be most interested in writing about the poem, since the subject of mother-daughter relationships is crucial to feminist theory. A historical critic might want to compare the relative freedom of the mother-daughter relationship that is inferred in the poem with the historical past, when women had little freedom to make any choices over their own lives.

WRITING ABOUT POETRY

An assignment to write a paper about a poem will help you to focus your ideas about it and sharpen your critical thinking about what you have read. Many students find that when asked to write a paper analyzing a poem they can work more easily with the poem if they type it on a computer and print it out double-spaced or simply write it out in longhand on a piece of paper. On your copy you can underline words that strike you as significant, and you can jot down your specific feelings and thoughts about the way the poet has used language and form. You can trace the development of the poet's theme, contrast this with the poem's subject, and try to verbalize your feelings about the theme. As you read the poem, are you intrigued, sympathetic, unsympathetic, or confused? Is the subject of the poem something you feel strongly about? Is the theme of the poem something that moves you emotionally? What is your overall reaction to the poem?

If the essay you are planning to write is intended to describe your own response to the poem you could first concentrate on what it is about the poem that has triggered your response. Is it the subject, or the theme of the poem, or the various poetic means the author employed in creating the poem? Second, you could analyze what it is about you as a reader that caused this response. Perhaps you had trouble with the poem because you were uncomfortable with the subject or theme. Did the poem's diction or syntax pose problems for you in understanding the lines? Was it the poem's use of language that caused you to respond favorably or unfavorably to it?

When you are ready to begin your essay you can turn to the materials presented in the sections on reading and writing a literary essay. (See Part One, Reading, Thinking, and Writing about Literature, p. 1, and Part Five, Developing Your Ideas about Literature, p. 2069.) You will find help there in planning your paper in stages, with whatever critical approach you take in writing it. You will also find suggestions about prewriting, first and final drafts, revision, and styling your essay.

One student who read Linda Pastan's poem carefully, and then read the list of questions suggesting ways to respond to the poem just as carefully, decided to develop the idea of the poem as a metaphor. She used her own experience as a way to structure her essay.

STUDENT ESSAY

The Metaphor of the Empty Nest

in Linda Pastan's "To a Daughter

Leaving Home"

When I read Linda Pastan's poem about her daughter, I thought about the questions I should ask myself about the poem to help myself understand it better. What I understood after I looked at the poem again was that her daughter's wild ride on the bicycle is what we call a metaphor. That is, the theme of the poem, what the poem really tells us, is about her daughter leaving home, but the subject of the poem, what she writes about, is her daughter's first ride on her two-wheel bicycle. This helps us understand how she feels about her daughter leaving her to begin a new life as an adult.

When I read the poem it made me think about events in my life that I could describe in a metaphor. My mother wasn't thinking about a poem when she talked to me about my older sister, after my sister went away to college. What my mother said was, "Soon, I'm going to have an empty nest." What I learned from studying this poem is that "empty nest" is a metaphor. What my mother told me was that our house had been like a bird's nest where we had grown up, and now it was time for me and my sister to fly away.

Another time when something in my life was described by a metaphor was when my grandmother died. At her funeral the minister told us that "the river had flowed down to the sea." What he was telling us was that her life was over. His metaphor was that her life had flowed in the same way that a river flows until it reaches the sea. He used the metaphor of life as a river to tell us that my grandmother's life had been very long and very peaceful at the end.

In addition to Pastan's use of a vivid metaphor that helped me to visualize the situation she described in "To a Daughter Leaving Home," her poem impressed me for another reason. The poet has presented her feelings very skillfully in a single sentence that develops the metaphor. At the beginning of the sentence, the poet's anxiety about her daughter is in contrast to the little girl's excitement at learning how to ride a bicycle. Then in the middle of the sentence, after the first surprise of seeing her daughter take off by herself, Pastan imagines a disaster ("the thud / of your crash"). But the sentence concludes as a triumphant simile, when she sees her daughter disappearing into the distance with her hair flapping "like a / handkerchief waving / goodbye." Into the sentence Pastan has compressed a range of emotions, describing how she moves from surprise to fear to acceptance of her daughter's independence. "To a Daughter Leaving Home" makes me think that the poet is riding her metaphors and similes as courageously as her daughter is riding the bicycle.

This student chose to write a literary essay as a way of understanding the poem. She took the strategy of a response to the text, investigating the personal connotations evoked by the poet's use of specific images. You will find that many theoretical approaches lend themselves to developing your critical thinking and your writing about poetry. You might consider the intertextual elements in a contemporary poem like John Crowe Ransom's "Bells for John Whiteside's Daughter" (p. 836), comparing it to and contrasting it with an earlier poem that you have read.

All of these critical approaches depend on your close reading of the poem. The poem itself will always be the place where you begin your thinking. Recognizing the means that the poet employed in creating the poem will help you to reach deeper levels of response and will clarify your understanding of the poet's intentions. The essays by poets and critics in Chapter 16, Commentaries on Poetry and Poets, also offer insights into how other writers respond to poetry.

RELATED SECTIONS: *Part One, Reading, Thinking, and Writing about Literature, page 1; Part Five, Developing Your Ideas about Literature, page 2069.*

15

POEMS AND POETS

MATTHEW ARNOLD *(1822–1888) was born in a village in the Thames Valley, just outside of London. When he was six his family moved to Rugby School where his father, a distinguished Victorian clergyman, had become headmaster. Arnold spent most of his life in an academic environment, first as a child at Rugby, then as a student at Oxford, and for thirty-five years as an inspector of schools for the British government. He traveled throughout England and Europe, studying educational systems and observing the lives of the people who were administering them.*

At Oxford he had a reputation as a dandy. The novelist Charlotte Brontë, who met him at that time, wrote, "His manner displeases, from his seeming foppery." His writing, however, had a seriousness that sometimes dissatisfied even Arnold himself. His major poems — among them "The Scholar Gypsy" and "Thyrsis," an elegy on the death of his friend and fellow poet Arthur Hugh Clough — had an important influence on the attitudes and the ideals of the Victorian era. He stopped writing poetry in his thirties, and for the rest of his life he was a widely read and influential critic of English society and culture. "Dover Beach," his best-known poem, was written in 1851.

RELATED COMMENTARIES: *Anthony Hecht, "The Dover Bitch," page 1179; Eric Trethewey, "The Virtue of Arnold's 'Dover Beach,'" page 1224.*

Matthew Arnold

Dover Beach

1867

The sea is calm tonight.
The tide is full, the moon lies fair
Upon the straits; — on the French coast the light
Gleams and is gone; the cliffs of England stand,
Glimmering and vast, out in the tranquil bay.
Come to the window, sweet is the night-air!
Only, from the long line of spray
Where the sea meets the moon-blanched land,
Listen! You hear the grating roar
Of pebbles which the waves draw back, and fling,
At their return, up the high strand,
Begin, and cease, and then again begin,
With tremulous cadence slow, and bring
The eternal note of sadness in.

Sophocles long ago
Heard it on the Aegean, and it brought
Into his mind the turbid ebb and flow
Of human misery;° we
Find also in the sound a thought,
Hearing it by this distant northern sea.
The Sea of Faith
Was once, too, at the full, and round earth's shore
Lay like the folds of a bright girdle furled.
But now I only hear
Its melancholy, long, withdrawing roar,
Retreating, to the breath
Of the night-wind, down the vast edges of drear
And naked shingles° of the world. *pebble beaches*
Ah, love, let us be true
To one another! for the world, which seems
To lie before us like a land of dreams,
So various, so beautiful, so new,
Hath really neither joy, nor love, nor light,
Nor certitude, nor peace, nor help for pain;
And we are here as on a darkling plain
Swept with confused alarms of struggle and flight,
Where ignorant armies clash by night.

15–18. Sophocles long ago . . . misery: In *Antigone,* Sophocles compares the calamities that afflict the house of Oedipus to a rising tide.

W. H. AUDEN *(1907–1973) was born Wystan Hugh Auden in York, a large industrial city in northern England. He graduated from Oxford in 1930 and taught school for five years, but he was already publishing poetry and was considered one of the most exciting of a new, young group of English poets, which included Stephen Spender and C. Day Lewis.*

In the 1930s Auden's poetry reflected his dismay at the effect of the world depression on England, and also his leftist views. In 1937 he went to Spain to take part in the Civil War, but he was disturbed by the Loyalists' hostility to organized religion and returned to England without seeing active combat. In 1939 he moved to the United States, and in 1946 he became an American citizen. He returned to England as a professor of poetry at Oxford from 1956 to 1960, but in his last years he was part of the colorful cultural life of the Lower East Side in New York City.

Auden prided himself on his literary professionalism, and he wrote plays, the libretto for Igor Stravinsky's opera The Rake's Progress, *and considerable literary commentary. For many years he toured U.S. universities as an excellent reader of his own poetry.*

"Musée des Beaux Arts" was written a few months before Auden moved to the United States. Although he became deeply devoted to his new country, he also could not resist the urge to be satirical, and "On the Circuit" is his comment on his American reading tours.

W. H. AUDEN

Musée des Beaux Arts° *1938*

About suffering they were never wrong,
The Old Masters: how well they understood
Its human position; how it takes place
While someone else is eating or opening a window or just walking
  dully along;
How, when the aged are reverently, passionately waiting
For the miraculous birth, there always must be
Children who did not specially want it to happen, skating
On a pond at the edge of the wood:
They never forgot
That even the dreadful martyrdom must run its course
Anyhow in a corner, some untidy spot
Where the dogs go on with their doggy life and the torturer's horse
Scratches its innocent behind on a tree.

In Brueghel's *Icarus,*° for instance: how everything turns away
Quite leisurely from the disaster; the plowman may
Have heard the splash, the forsaken cry,

Musée des Beaux Arts: The Museum of Fine Arts in Brussels.
14. Brueghel's *Icarus:* Refers to *Landscape with the Fall of Icarus,* by Pieter Brueghel the Elder (c. 1525–1569), in the Brussels museum. The painting represents the mythical Icarus as a tiny figure, dwarfed by other characters in the painting, as he falls into the sea.

But for him it was not an important failure; the sun shown
As it had to on the white legs disappearing into the green
Water; and the expensive delicate ship that must have seen
Something amazing, a boy falling out of the sky,
Had somewhere to get to and sailed calmly on.

W. H. Auden

On the Circuit

1963

Among pelagian° travelers,
Lost on their lewd conceited way
To Massachusetts, Michigan,
Miami or L.A.,

An airborne instrument I sit,
Predestined nightly to fulfill
Columbia-Giesen-Management's°
Unfathomable will,

By whose election justified,
I bring my gospel of the Muse
To fundamentalists, to nuns,
To Gentiles and to Jews,

And daily, seven days a week,
Before a local sense has jelled,
From talking-site to talking-site
Am jet-or-prop-propelled.

Though warm my welcome everywhere,
I shift so frequently, so fast,
I cannot now say where I was
The evening before last,

Unless some singular event
Should intervene to save the place,
A truly asinine remark,
A soul-bewitching face,

Or blessed encounter, full of joy,
Unscheduled on the Giesen Plan,
With, here, an addict of Tolkien,°
There, a Charles Williams° fan.

---

1. pelagian: One who upholds the teachings of Pelagius, a British monk and theologian (c. 354–418) who denied the doctrine of original sin and held that humans are free to choose between good and evil. **7. Columbia-Giesen-Management's:** Auden's lecture management agency. **27. Tolkien:** J. R. R. Tolkien (1892–1973) was a British medieval scholar, philologist, and author. He is best known for his epic works of fantasy, including the trilogy *The Lord of the Rings* (1954–55). **28. Charles Williams:** English novelist and poet (1886–1945), best known for his seven mystical thriller novels. He associated with the Inklings, an informal group of writers that included C. S. Lewis and J. R. R. Tolkien.

■ ■ ■

Since Merit but a dunghill is,
I mount the rostrum unafraid:
Indeed, 'twere damnable to ask
If I am overpaid.

Spirit is willing to repeat
Without a qualm the same old talk,
But Flesh is homesick for our snug
Apartment in New York.

A sulky fifty-six, he finds
A change of mealtime utter hell,
Grown far too crotchety to like
A luxury hotel.

The Bible is a goodly book
I always can peruse with zest,
But really cannot say the same
For Hilton's *Be My Guest,*°

Nor bear with equanimity
The radio in students' cars,
Muzak at breakfast, or — dear God! —
Girl-organists in bars.

Then, worst of all, the anxious thought,
Each time my plane begins to sink
And the No Smoking sign comes on:
What will there be to drink?

Is this a milieu where I must
How grahamgreeneish!° How infra dig!°
Snatch from the bottle in my bag
An analeptic swig?

Another morning comes: I see,
Dwindling below me on the plane,
The roofs of one more audience
I shall not see again.

God bless the lot of them, although
I don't remember which was which:
God bless the U.S.A., so large,
So friendly, and so rich.

---

44. Hilton's *Be My Guest:* The memoir of Conrad Hilton, the entrepreneur who founded the Hilton hotel chain. A copy of the book is usually stocked in every Hilton hotel room. **54. grahamgreeneish:** A reference to Graham Greene (1904–1991), the English writer whose novels explore moral issues in political settings; **infra dig:** Undignified.

ELIZABETH BISHOP *(1911–1979) was the daughter of a successful Boston building contractor and his Canadian wife, but her father died when she was a baby, and when she was four her mother was placed in a mental institution. Bishop was raised by grandparents and relatives in Nova Scotia and Massachusetts. She suffered from severe asthma, and she was unable to attend school until she was sixteen. Among her friends, when she entered Vassar College in 1930, were the writers Muriel Rukeyser and Mary McCarthy.*

Although Bishop grew up in a period in which talented women writers — among them Edna St. Vincent Millay, Elinor Wylie, and Louise Bogan — played a dominant role in American poetry, she found their work too traditional, and she took the modernist poet Marianne Moore as a mentor and friend. Another strong influence on her writing was her long friendship with poet Robert Lowell. A small trust fund made it possible for her to live as she wanted, and she spent several years in Key West, Florida. After reviving an old acquaintance with Lota de Macedo Soares, she moved with her to Brazil and remained there until Soares's suicide in 1977. Bishop then returned to the United States to teach at Harvard.

Bishop was a careful, selective poet, and she achieved considerable critical success. She won the Pulitzer Prize and the National Book Award, and her final collection was awarded the National Book Critics Circle Award. "The Fish," one of her best-known poems, was included in her first collection North and South, *published in 1946. "The Armadillo" is dedicated to Robert Lowell.* *(See also Bishop's "The Bight" on p. 842 and "Sestina" on p. 887.)*

RELATED COMMENTARY: *Brett C. Millier, "On Elizabeth Bishop's 'One Art,'" page 1198.*

ELIZABETH BISHOP

The Fish

1946

I caught a tremendous fish
and held him beside the boat
half out of water, with my hook
fast in a corner of his mouth.
He didn't fight.
He hadn't fought at all.
He hung a grunting weight,
battered and venerable
and homely. Here and there
his brown skin hung in strips
like ancient wallpaper,
and its pattern of darker brown
was like wallpaper:
shapes like full-blown roses
stained and lost through age.
He was speckled with barnacles,
fine rosettes of lime,
and infested

with tiny white sea-lice,
and underneath two or three
rags of green weed hung down.
While his gills were breathing in
the terrible oxygen
— the frightening gills,
fresh and crisp with blood,
that can cut so badly —
I thought of the coarse white flesh
packed in like feathers,
the big bones and the little bones,
the dramatic reds and blacks
of his shiny entrails,
and the pink swim-bladder
like a big peony.
I looked into his eyes
which were far larger than mine
but shallower, and yellowed,
the irises backed and packed
with tarnished tinfoil
seen through the lenses
of old scratched isinglass.
They shifted a little, but not
to return my stare.
— It was more like the tipping
of an object toward the light.
I admired his sullen face,
the mechanism of his jaw,
and then I saw
that from his lower lip
— if you could call it a lip —
grim, wet, and weaponlike,
hung five old pieces of fish-line,
or four and a wire leader
with the swivel still attached,
with all their five big hooks
grown firmly in his mouth.
A green line, frayed at the end
where he broke it, two heavier lines,
and a fine black thread
still crimped from the strain and snap
when it broke and he got away.
Like medals with their ribbons
frayed and wavering,
a five-haired beard of wisdom
trailing from his aching jaw.
I stared and stared

and victory filled up
the little rented boat,
from the pool of bilge
where oil had spread a rainbow
around the rusted engine
to the bailer rusted orange,
the sun-cracked thwarts,
the oarlocks on their strings,
the gunnels — until everything
was rainbow, rainbow, rainbow!
And I let the fish go.

ELIZABETH BISHOP

The Armadillo

1965

for Robert Lowell

This is the time of year
when almost every night
the frail, illegal fire balloons appear.
Climbing the mountain height,

rising toward a saint
still honored in these parts,
the paper chambers flush and fill with light
that comes and goes, like hearts.

Once up against the sky it's hard
to tell them from the stars —
planets, that is — the tinted ones:
Venus going down, or Mars,

or the pale green one. With a wind,
they flare and falter, wobble and toss;
but if it's still they steer between
the kite sticks of the Southern Cross,

receding, dwindling, solemnly
and steadily forsaking us,
or, in the downdraft from a peak,
suddenly turning dangerous.

Last night another big one fell.
It splattered like an egg of fire
against the cliff behind the house.
The flame ran down. We saw the pair

of owls who nest there flying up
and up, their whirling black-and-white
stained bright pink underneath, until
they shrieked up out of sight.

■ ■ ■

The ancient owl's nest must have burned.
Hastily, all alone,
a glistening armadillo left the scene,
rose-flecked, head down, tail down,

and then a baby rabbit jumped out,
short-eared, to our surprise.
So soft! — a handful of intangible ash
with fixed, ignited eyes.

Too pretty, dreamlike mimicry!
O falling fire and piercing cry
and panic, and a weak mailed fist
clenched ignorant against the sky!

ELIZABETH BISHOP

One Art

1976

The art of losing isn't hard to master;
so many things seem filled with the intent
to be lost that their loss is no disaster.

Lose something every day. Accept the fluster
of lost door keys, the hour badly spent.
The art of losing isn't hard to master.

Then practice losing farther, losing faster:
places, and names, and where it was you meant
to travel. None of these will bring disaster.

I lost my mother's watch. And look! my last, or
next-to-last, of three loved houses went.
The art of losing isn't hard to master.

I lost two cities, lovely ones. And, vaster,
some realms I owned, two rivers, a continent.
I miss them, but it wasn't a disaster.

— Even losing you (the joking voice, a gesture
I love) I shan't have lied. It's evident
the art of losing's not too hard to master
though it may look like (*Write* it!) like disaster.

ꕥ

WILLIAM BLAKE *(1757–1827) was born in London, one of several children of a London haberdasher. His family expected he would become a tradesman, and he was educated to be a commercial artist. He was sent to a drawing academy when he was ten, then he studied painting for a short time at the Royal Academy of Arts.*

At the age of fourteen Blake was apprenticed to an engraver, and his seven-year apprenticeship provided him with enough knowledge and experience to set up his own small engraving business. At the same time he was reading on his own and beginning to write poetry. When he was twenty-four he married Catherine Boucher, whose father delivered produce to the London markets. The next year, 1783, his first book of poems, Poetical Sketches, *was published.*

Over the next ten years he produced his two most celebrated books. Songs of Innocence *appeared in 1789, and* Songs of Innocence and of Experience *in 1794. He created the books with a method of engraving that combined the illustrations and the hand-lettered poetry on the page, then he and his wife hand-painted each page with watercolors. To do a single copy was so time-consuming that only a handful of editions were produced, but they were so unusual and so beautiful that Blake attracted the attention of a small group of connoisseurs and artists.*

In 1800, with the financial assistance of a patron, the Blakes were able to move to the country, and he continued to draw and paint, to create illustrations for books by other writers and to create his own books of prophecy and mystical inspiration. To many of his contemporaries, Blake was an exasperating eccentric with radical opinions, who often described conversations he had just had with long-dead historical figures. As he said of his habit of seeing visions, "I do not distrust my corporeal or vegetative eye any more than I would distrust a window for its sight. I see through it, not with it." He died in 1827 at the age of seventy.

The selection of Blake's poetry is taken from Songs of Innocence and of Experience. *The last two poems — "I askèd a thief" and "Never pain to tell thy love" — were found in a small book the poet used for sketching and writing notes. (See also Blake's "Song" on p. 851.)*

RELATED COMMENTARY: *T. S. Eliot, "From 'William Blake,'" page 1166.*

WILLIAM BLAKE

From Songs of Innocence

1789

Introduction

Piping down the valleys wild
Piping songs of pleasant glee
On a cloud I saw a child,
And he laughing said to me,

"Pipe a song about a Lamb";
So I piped with merry chear;
"Piper pipe that song again" —
So I piped, he wept to hear.

"Drop thy pipe thy happy pipe
Sing thy songs of happy chear";
So I sung the same again
While he wept with joy to hear.

"Piper sit thee down and write
In a book that all may read" —

So he vanish'd from my sight.
And I pluck'd a hollow reed,
And I made a rural pen,
And I stain'd the water clear,
And I wrote my happy songs
Every child may joy to hear.

WILLIAM BLAKE

The Lamb

1789

Little Lamb, who made thee?
Dost thou know who made thee?
Gave thee life, and bid thee feed
By the stream and o'er the mead;
Gave thee clothing of delight,
Softest clothing, wooly, bright;
Gave thee such a tender voice,
Making all the vales rejoice?
Little Lamb, who made thee?
Dost thou know who made thee?

Little Lamb, I'll tell thee,
Little Lamb, I'll tell thee:
He is callèd by thy name,
For he calls himself a Lamb.
He is meek, and he is mild;
He became a little child.
I a child, and thou a lamb,
We are callèd by his name.
Little Lamb, God bless thee!
Little Lamb, God bless thee!

WILLIAM BLAKE

Holy Thursday

1789

'Twas on a Holy Thursday, their innocent faces clean,
The children walking two & two, in red & blue & green;
Grey headed beadles walkd before with wands as white as snow,
Till into the high dome of Paul's° they like Thames' waters flow.

O what a multitude they seemd, these flowers of London town!
Seated in companies they sit with radiance all their own.
The hum of multitudes was there, but multitudes of lambs,
Thousands of little boys & girls raising their innocent hands.

■ ■ ■

4. Paul's: St. Paul's Cathedral.

Now like a mighty wind they raise to heaven the voice of song,
Or like harmonious thunderings the seats of heaven among.
Beneath them sit the agèd men, wise guardians of the poor;
Then cherish pity, lest you drive an angel from your door.

William Blake

The Little Boy Lost

1789

"Father, father, where are you going?
O do not walk so fast.
Speak father, speak to your little boy
Or else I shall be lost."

The night was dark, no father was there,
The child was wet with dew.
The mire was deep, & the child did weep,
And away the vapour flew.

William Blake

The Little Boy Found

1789

The little boy lost in the lonely fen,
Led by the wand'ring light,
Began to cry, but God ever nigh
Appeard like his father in white.

He kissed the child & by the hand led
And to his mother brought,
Who in sorrow pale, thro' the lonely dale,
Her little boy weeping sought.

William Blake

From Songs of Experience

1794

Introduction

Hear the voice of the Bard!
Who Present, Past, & Future sees;
Whose ears have heard
The Holy Word
That walk'd among the ancient trees;

Calling the lapsèd Soul
And weeping in the evening dew,
That might controll

The starry pole,
And fallen, fallen light renew!

"O Earth, O Earth, return!
Arise from out the dewy grass;
Night is worn,
And the morn
Rises from the slumberous mass.

"Turn away no more;
Why wilt thou turn away?
The starry floor
The watry shore
Is giv'n thee till the break of day."

WILLIAM BLAKE

The Sick Rose

1794

O Rose, thou art sick!
The invisible worm
That flies in the night,
In the howling storm,

Has found out thy bed
Of crimson joy,
And his dark secret love
Does thy life destroy.

WILLIAM BLAKE

The Tyger

1794

Tyger! Tyger! burning bright
In the forests of the night,
What immortal hand or eye
Could frame thy fearful symmetry?

In what distant deeps or skies
Burnt the fire of thine eyes?
On what wings dare he aspire?
What the hand dare seize the fire?

And what shoulder, and what art,
Could twist the sinews of thy heart?
And when thy heart began to beat,
What dread hand? and what dread feet?

What the hammer? what the chain?
In what furnace was thy brain?

What the anvil? what dread grasp
Dare its deadly terrors clasp?

When the stars threw down their spears,
And watered heaven with their tears,
Did he smile his work to see?
Did he who made the Lamb make thee?

Tyger! Tyger! burning bright
In the forests of the night,
What immortal hand or eye
Dare frame thy fearful symmetry?

William Blake

London

1794

I wander through each chartered° street *defined by law*
Near where the chartered Thames does flow,
And mark in every face I meet
Marks of weakness, marks of woe.

In every cry of every man,
In every Infant's cry of fear,
In every voice, in every ban,
The mind-forged manacles I hear.

How the Chimney-sweeper's cry
Every black'ning Church appalls;
And the hapless Soldier's sigh
Runs in blood down Palace walls.

But most through midnight streets I hear
How the youthful Harlot's curse° *syphilis*
Blasts the new-born Infant's tear,
And blights with plagues the Marriage hearse.

William Blake

A Poison Tree

1794

I was angry with my friend:
I told my wrath, my wrath did end.
I was angry with my foe:
I told it not, my wrath did grow.

And I waterd it in fears,
Night & morning with my tears;

And I sunnèd it with smiles,
And with soft deceitful wiles.

And it grew both day and night,
Till it bore an apple bright.
And my foe beheld it shine,
And he knew that it was mine,

And into my garden stole,
When the night had veild the pole;
In the morning glad I see
My foe outstretched beneath the tree.

WILLIAM BLAKE

The Garden of Love

1794

I went to the Garden of Love,
And saw what I never had seen:
A Chapel was built in the midst,
Where I used to play on the green.

And the gates of this Chapel were shut,
And "Thou shalt not" writ over the door;
So I turn'd to the Garden of Love,
That so many sweet flowers bore,

And I saw it was filled with graves,
And tomb-stones where flowers should be;
And Priests in black gowns were walking their rounds,
And binding with briars my joys & desires.

WILLIAM BLAKE

I askèd a thief

1796

I askèd a thief to steal me a peach,
He turned up his eyes;
I ask'd a lithe lady to lie her down,
Holy & meek she cries.

As soon as I went
An angel came.
He wink'd at the thief
And smild at the dame —

And without one word said
Had a peach from the tree

And still as a maid
Enjoy'd the lady.

William Blake

Never pain to tell thy love

1796

Never pain to tell thy love
Love that never told can be,
For the gentle wind does move
Silently, invisibly.

I told my love, I told my love,
I told her all my heart,
Trembling, cold, in ghastly fears —
Ah, she doth depart.

Soon as she was gone from me
A traveller came by
Silently, invisibly —
O, was no deny.

Anne Bradstreet *(c. 1612–1672) was born in England, the daughter of a "well borne woman" of modest wealth and a father who was the steward of the country estate of the Earl of Lincoln. Both the earl and Bradstreet's parents were Puritans, and she was given a much better education than most young women of her time. At sixteen she married Simon Bradstreet, also a Puritan, and two years later, in 1630, she, her husband, and her parents sailed to the Massachusetts Bay Colony. They lived first in Boston and in 1644 moved to North Andover, where Bradstreet lived for the rest of her life.*

As a girl she had already begun writing poems that she and her father read with pleasure together. She continued to write, while she raised eight children and managed the household for her husband, who, as governor of the colony, was away for long periods.

In 1650, without her knowledge, her brother-in-law took a gathering of her poems to London. The collection was the first to be published by anyone living in the North American colonies, and the book attracted considerable attention. Because of the constraints placed on women's lives, her brother-in-law felt obliged to assure suspicious readers, in the introduction, that Bradstreet was respectable according to the standards of the time. The poems, he wrote, were "the work of a woman, honored and esteemed where she lives, for her gracious demeanor, her eminent parts, her pious conversation, her courteous disposition, her exact diligence in her place, and discreet managing of her family occasions."

"To My Dear and Loving Husband" and "In Reference to Her Children, 23 June 1659" were both written during Bradstreet's years in North Andover.

ANNE BRADSTREET

To My Dear and Loving Husband

1678

If ever two were one, then surely we.
If ever man were loved by wife, then thee;
If ever wife was happy in a man,
Compare with me, ye women, if you can.
I prize thy love more than whole mines of gold
Or all the riches that the East doth hold.
My love is such that rivers cannot quench,
Nor ought but love from thee, give recompense.
Thy love is such I can no way repay,
The heavens reward thee manifold, I pray.
Then while we live, in love let's so persevere
That when we live no more, we may live ever.

ANNE BRADSTREET

In Reference to Her Children, 23 June 1659

1678

I had eight birds hatcht in one nest,
Four cocks there were, and hens the rest,
I nurst them up with pain and care,
Nor cost, nor labor did I spare,
Till at the last they felt their wing,
Mounted the trees, and learn'd to sing;
Chief of the brood then took his flight,
To regions far, and left me quite.
My mournful chirps I after send,
Till he return, or I do end:
Leave not thy nest, thy dam and sire,
Fly back and sing amidst this choir.
My second bird did take her flight,
And with her mate flew out of sight;
Southward they both their course did bend,
And seasons twain they there did spend:
Till after blown by southern gales,
They norward steer'd with filled sails.
A prettier bird was no where seen,
Along the beach among the treen.
I have a third of color white,
On whom I plac'd no small delight;

Coupled with mate loving and true,
Hath also bid her dam adieu:

And where Aurora° first appears, *Roman goddess of dawn*
She now hath percht to spend her years;
One to the academy flew
To chat among that learned crew:
Ambition moves still in his breast
That he might chant above the rest,
Striving for more than to do well,
That nightingales he might excel.
My fifth, whose down is yet scarce gone,
Is 'mongst the shrubs and bushes flown,
And as his wings increase in strength,
On higher boughs he'll perch at length,
My other three, still with me nest,
Until they're grown, then as the rest,
Or here or there, they'll take their flight,
As is ordain'd, so shall they light.
If birds could weep, then would my tears
Let others know what are my fears
Lest this my brood some harm should catch,
And be surpris'd for want of watch,
Whilst pecking corn, and void of care
They fall un'wares in fowler's snare:
Or whilst on trees they sit and sing,
Some untoward boy at them do fling:
Or whilst allur'd with bell and glass,
The net be spread, and caught, alas.
Or least by lime-twigs they be foil'd,°
Or by some greedy hawks be spoil'd.
Or would my young, ye saw my breast,
And knew what thoughts there sadly rest,
Great was my pain when I you bred,
Great was my care when I you fed,
Long did I keep you soft and warm,
And with my wings kept off all harm,
My cares are more, and fears than ever,
My throbs such now, as 'fore were never:
Alas my birds, you wisdom want.
Of perils you are ignorant,
Oft times in grass, on trees, in flight,
Sore accidents on you may light.
O to your safety have an eye,
So happy may you live and die:
Mean while my days in tunes I'll spend,
Till my weak lays° with me shall end. *songs or poems*
In shady woods I'll sit and sing,

---

51. lime-twigs . . . foil'd: A sticky "lime" was smeared on branches to catch birds.

And things that past, no mind I'll bring.
Once young and pleasant, as are you,
But former toys (no joys) adieu.
My age I will not once lament,
But sing, my time so near is spent.
And from the top bough take my flight,
Into a country beyond sight,
Where old ones instantly grow young,
And there with seraphims° set song: *an order of angels*
No seasons cold, nor storms they see,
But spring lasts to eternity.
When each of you shall in your nest
Among your young ones take your rest,
In chirping language, oft them tell,
You had a dam that lov'd you well,
That did what could be done for young,
And nurst you up till you were strong,
And 'fore she once would let you fly,
She show'd you joy and misery;
Taught what was good, and what was ill,
What would save life, and what would kill.
Thus gone, amongst you I may live,
And dead, yet speak, and counsel give:
Farewell, my birds, farewell adieu,
I happy am, if well with you.

GWENDOLYN BROOKS *(b. 1917) was born in Topeka, Kansas, but her parents moved to Chicago's South Side soon after her birth. Her father worked as a janitor, and the family was poor, but her parents encouraged her to study in school and to write poetry. She wrote her first poems when she was seven. Her childhood was so contented that she wrote later in her autobiography, "I had always felt that to be black was good."*

Brooks had almost immediate success as a writer. She was already publishing her poetry when she was seventeen. Her first book, A Street in Bronzeville, *which appeared in 1945, won a series of prizes, and she was awarded a Guggenheim fellowship which allowed her to spend a year devoted entirely to writing. In 1949 her second poetry collection,* Annie Allen, *won the Pulitzer Prize, the first time it had been given to an African American writer. She also published a novel,* Maud Martha, *in 1953, and taught at Chicago State University, where she is a Distinguished Professor.*

In 1967 Brooks took part in the Second Black Writer's Conference at Fisk University, and she was swept up in the new militancy of the younger black poets like Amiri Baraka and don l. lee. Her poetry became more specifically political, and finally she turned to alternative publishing so she could have some control over the way her poetry was presented.

"We Real Cool" is one of her shortest poems, and it is also one of her most

famous. "The Mother" is an early poem in which the woman speaker projects a scarring, personal unhappiness. Brooks herself is the mother of a son and a daughter.

RELATED COMMENTARIES: *Robert Hayden, "On Negro Poetry," page 1177; Gary Smith, "On Gwendolyn Brooks's* A Street in Bronzeville,*" page 1222.*

Gwendolyn Brooks

We Real Cool

1960

The Pool Players.
Seven at the Golden Shovel.

We real cool. We
Left school. We

Lurk late. We
Strike straight. We

Sing sin. We
Thin gin. We

Jazz June. We
Die soon.

Gwendolyn Brooks

The Mother

1945

Abortions will not let you forget.
You remember the children you got that you did not get,
The damp small pulps with a little or with no hair,
The singers and workers that never handled the air.
You will never neglect or beat
Them, or silence or buy with a sweet.
You will never wind up the sucking-thumb
Or scuttle off ghosts that come.
You will never leave them, controlling your luscious sigh,
Return for a snack of them, with gobbling mother-eye.
I have heard in the voices of the wind the voices of my dim killed children.
I have contracted. I have eased
My dim dears at the breasts they could never suck.
I have said, Sweets, if I sinned, if I seized
Your luck
And your lives from your unfinished reach,
If I stole your births and your names,
Your straight baby tears and your games,
Your stilted or lovely loves, your tumults, your marriages, aches, and
  your deaths,
If I poisoned the beginnings of your breaths,
Believe that even in my deliberateness I was not deliberate.

Though why should I whine,
Whine that the crime was other than mine? —
Since anyhow you are dead.
Or rather, or instead,
You were never made.
But that too, I am afraid,
Is faulty: oh, what shall I say, how is the truth to be said?
You were born, you had body, you died.
It is just that you never giggled or planned or cried.

Believe me, I loved you all.
Believe me, I knew you, though faintly, and I loved, I loved you
All.

ꕥ

LORNA DEE CERVANTES *(b. 1954) was born in San Francisco. She is of Mexican and Native American ancestry. Although her family was poor, she thought of herself as a writer when she was very young and was already writing poetry when she was six years old. When she later began to publish her poetry, she included writing she had done when she was fourteen. She received her B.A. at San Jose State University and did her graduate studies at the University of California at Santa Cruz. She received her Ph.D. in philosophy and aesthetics in 1979, the same year she was awarded a National Endowment for the Arts grant and began teaching creative writing at the University of Colorado.*

Her first book, Emplumada, *was published in 1981 and attracted widespread attention. The critic Nicolas Kanellos wrote that the collection "presents a young woman coming of age, discovering the gap that exists in life between one's hopes and desires and what life eventually offers in reality. The predominant themes include culture conflict, the oppression of women and minorities, and alienation from one's roots." The poem "For Virginia Chavez," from* Emplumada, *touches on all of these themes. In "Barco de Refugiados/Refugee Ship," included here in both her Spanish and English versions, Cervantes explores her sense of alienation from the Spanish language of her grandmother, which her mother never taught her. The poem is from the same collection.*

LORNA DEE CERVANTES

For Virginia Chavez

1981

It was never in the planning,
in the life we thought
we'd live together, two fast
women living cheek to cheek,
still tasting the dog's
breath of boys in our testy
new awakening.
We were never the way

they had it planned.
Their wordless tongues we stole
and tasted the power
that comes of that.
We were never what they wanted
but we were bold. We could take
something of life and not
give it back. We could utter
the rules, mark the lines
and cross them ourselves — we two
women using our fists, we thought,
our wits, our tunnels. They were such
dumb hunks of warm fish
swimming inside us,
but this was love,
we knew, love, and that was all
we were ever offered.

You were always alone
so another lonely life
wouldn't matter.
In the still house
your mother left you,
when the men were gone
and the television droned
into test patterns, with our cups
of your mother's whiskey
balanced between the brown thighs
creeping out of our shorts, I read
you the poems of Lord Byron, Donne,
the Brownings: all about love,
explaining the words
before realizing that you knew
all that the kicks in your belly
had to teach you. You were proud
of the woman blooming out of your
fourteen lonely years, but you cried
when you read that poem I wrote you,
something about our "waning moons"
and the child in me
I let die that summer.

In the years that separate,
in the tongues that divide
and conquer, in the love
that was a language
in itself, you never spoke,
never regret. Even
that last morning

I saw you with blood
in your eyes, blood
on your mouth, the blood
pushing out of you
in purple blossoms.

He did this.
When I woke, the kids
were gone. They told me
I'd never get them back.

With our arms holding
each other's waists, we walked
the waking streets
back to your empty flat,
ignoring the horns and catcalls
behind us, ignoring what
the years had brought between us:
my diploma and the bare bulb
that always lit your bookless room.

LORNA DEE CERVANTES

Barco de Refugiados 1981

Como almidón de maíz
me deslizo, pasando por los ojos de mi abuela,
bíblia a su lado. Se quita los lentes.
El pudín se hace espeso.

Mamá me crío sin lenguaje.
Soy huérfano de mi nombre español.
Las palabras son extrañas,
tartamudeando en mi lengua.
Mis ojos ven el espejo, mi reflejo:
piel de bronce, cabello negro.

Siento que soy un cautivo
a bordo de un barco de refugiados.
El barco que nunca atraca.
El barco que nunca atraca.

LORNA DEE CERVANTES

Refugee Ship 1981

Like wet cornstarch, I slide
past my grandmother's eyes. Bible
at her side, she removes her glasses.
The pudding thickens.

■ ■ ■

Mama raised me without language,
I'm orphaned from my Spanish name.
The words are foreign, stumbling
on my tongue. I see in the mirror
my reflection: bronzed skin, black hair.

I feel I am a captive
aboard the refugee ship.
The ship that will never dock.
El barco que nunca atraca.

MARILYN MEI LING CHIN *(b. 1955) was born in Hong Kong, where her father operated a restaurant. He moved the family to Portland, Oregon, when she was a child, and changed his daughter's name from Mei Ling to Marilyn, in homage to the actress Marilyn Monroe. He also soon abandoned the family for a Caucasian woman, and this act has left a strong emotional imprint on Chin's poetry.*

Chin graduated from the University of Massachusetts in 1977 and received her M.F.A. from the University of Iowa in 1981. Her first book, Dwarf Bamboo, *was published in 1987. For several years she taught at San Diego State University, which she described as an "exile." Although she has assimilated into the mainstream American culture, she is concerned that she is losing her Chinese identity. As she told television interviewer Bill Moyers in 1995, "I am afraid of losing my Chinese, losing my language, which would be like losing part of myself, losing part of my soul. Poetry seems a way to recapture that, but of course the truth is we can't recapture the past. The vector only goes one direction and that is toward the future. So the grandeur of China — the grandeur of that past of my grandfather's, of my grandmother's, of my mother's, and so forth — that will be all lost to me. I lose inches of it every day."*

"How I Got That Name" is an autobiographical portrait. In "Sad Guitar" Chin responds to a failed relationship and her sense of loneliness as an immigrant.

RELATED COMMENTARY: *Marilyn Chin, "On the Canon," page 1159.*

MARILYN CHIN

How I Got That Name 1994

an essay on assimilation

I am Marilyn Mei Ling Chin.
Oh, how I love the resoluteness
of that first person singular
followed by that stalwart indicative
of "be," without the uncertain i-n-g
of "becoming." Of course,
the name had been changed
somewhere between Angel Island and the sea,
when my father the paperson

in the late 1950s
obsessed with a bombshell blonde
transliterated "Mei Ling" to "Marilyn."
And nobody dared question
his initial impulse — for we all know
lust drove men to greatness,
not goodness, not decency.
And there I was, a wayward pink baby,
named after some tragic white woman
swollen with gin and Nembutal.
My mother couldn't pronounce the "r."
She dubbed me "Numba one female offshoot"
for brevity: henceforth, she will live and die
in sublime ignorance, flanked
by loving children and the "kitchen deity."
While my father dithers,
a tomcat in Hong Kong trash —
a gambler, a petty thug,
who bought a chain of chopsuey joints
in Piss River, Oregon,
with bootlegged Gucci cash.
Nobody dared question his integrity given
his nice, devout daughters
and his bright, industrious sons
as if filial piety were the standard
by which all earthly men were measured.

Oh, how trustworthy our daughters,
how thrifty our sons!
How we've managed to fool the experts
in education, statistics and demography —
We're not very creative but not adverse to rote-learning.
Indeed, they can *use* us.
But the "Model Minority"° is a tease.
We know you are watching now,
so we refuse to give you any!
Oh, bamboo shoots, bamboo shoots!
The further west we go, we'll hit east;
the deeper down we dig, we'll find China.
History has turned its stomach
on a black polluted beach —
where life doesn't hinge
on that red, red wheelbarrow,°
but whether or not our new lover

---

42. Model Minority: Asian Americans have been stereotyped as a well-behaved, industrious "model minority." **51. red, red wheelbarrow:** A reference to William Carlos Williams's brief modernist poem "The Red Wheelbarrow" (see p. 898 in this text).

in the final episode of "Santa Barbara"°
will lean over a scented candle
and call us a "bitch."
Oh God, where have we gone wrong?
We have no inner resources!

Then, one redolent spring morning
the Great Patriarch Chin
peered down from his kiosk in heaven
and saw that his descendants were ugly.
One had a squarish head and a nose without a bridge.
Another's profile — long and knobbed as a gourd.
A third, the sad, brutish one
may never, never marry.
And I, his least favorite —
"not quite boiled, not quite cooked,"
a plump pomfret° simmering in my juices —
too listless to fight for my people's destiny.
"To kill without resistance is not slaughter"
says the proverb. So, I wait for imminent death.
The fact that this death is also metaphorical
is testament to my lethargy.

So here lies Marilyn Mei Ling Chin,
married once, twice to so-and-so, a Lee and a Wong,
granddaughter of Jack "the patriarch"
and the brooding Suilin Fong,
daughter of the virtuous Yuet Kuen Wong
and G. G. Chin the infamous,
sister of a dozen, cousin of a million,
survived by everybody and forgotten by all.
She was neither black nor white,
neither cherished nor vanquished,
just another squatter in her own bamboo grove
minding her poetry —
when one day heaven was unmerciful,
and a chasm opened where she stood.
Like the jowls of a mighty white whale,
or the jaws of a metaphysical Godzilla,
it swallowed her whole.
She did not flinch nor writhe,
nor fret about the afterlife,
but stayed! Solid as wood, happily
a little gnawed, tattered, mesmerized
by all that was lavished upon her
and all that was taken away!

53. Santa Barbara: Prime-time television "soap opera" about wealthy, glamorous characters living in the California seaside city. **68. pomfret:** A spiny, edible fish.

Marilyn Chin

Sad Guitar

1994

(Sad Guitar series #3/3)

Blind immigrant,
do you understand this:
touch, wood,
this is wood
and not fire, this
earth and not wood.
This is elemental water.

Tea brews, rice boils,
ten days since your departure.
I stagger, stumble,
let old associations go.
What rhymes with flower,
bower, shower, power?

Stranger, have you ever loved
a Chinese woman?
Her heart is chrysanthemum.
And there are deeper chasms.

Oh, the goads, the rancor!
here I am within you, without you,
groping the fleshy dark,
conjuring the spirits and the furies.

I am a woman without rope
chasing a runaway horse
whose chariots neigh
and hoofbeats plunder.

I hear you, but I don't see you.
I touch you, but you seem far.
What I have learned about loneliness
is the three fingers that strum
the heart of the all-knowing —
the dark pith of the sad guitar.

Samuel Taylor Coleridge *(1772–1834) was born in a small village in southern England, but after the death of his father he was sent to school in London. Despite his indolence, he could also be sporadically brilliant, and at nineteen he entered Cambridge University, where his lack of discipline overwhelmed him, and he was unable to complete his degree.*

In 1794 Coleridge met the young poet Robert Southey and, filled with the fervor of the French Revolution, they decided to establish a utopian colony in Pennsylvania. Their plans fell apart, but Coleridge, as part of the plan, had married the sister of Southey's fiancée. The marriage was as unhappy as everything else Coleridge had attempted. The next year he met William Wordsworth and soon moved close to where the older poet and his sister Dorothy were living in England. Writing together, in a fever of excitement, he and Wordsworth completed the small collection titled Lyrical Ballads, *which was published in 1798. With their book they attempted to write a new kind of poetry, closer to ordinary speech and drawing from everyday emotions. Coleridge's contribution was the long supernatural narrative "The Rime of the Ancient Mariner" and several shorter poems.*

Coleridge by this time was addicted to opium, and his writing became chaotically uneven. "Kubla Khan" is the best known of his drug-influenced poems. When he later overcame his addiction he became one of the most important literary theorists and critics of the early nineteenth century. His lifelong friend, the writer Charles Lamb, described Coleridge as "an archangel, slightly damaged." "Frost at Midnight" is one of Coleridge's "conversation poems" in blank verse that moves back and forth between description of his surroundings and lofty meditation.

RELATED POEM: *Richard Leighton Green, "(Apropos Coleridge's 'Kubla Khan') When approached by a person from Porlock," page 885.*

RELATED COMMENTARY: *Harold Bloom, "On 'Frost at Midnight,'" page 1153.*

Samuel Taylor Coleridge

Kubla Khan: or, a Vision in a Dream° *1798*

In Xanadu did Kubla Khan°
    A stately pleasure-dome decree:
Where Alph, the sacred river, ran
Through caverns measureless to man
    Down to a sunless sea.
So twice five miles of fertile ground
With walls and towers were girdled round:
And here were gardens bright with sinuous rills
Where blossomed many an incense-bearing tree;
And there were forests ancient as the hills,
Enfolding sunny spots of greenery.

But oh! that deep romantic chasm which slanted
Down the green hill athwart a cedarn cover!°
A savage place! as holy and enchanted
As e'er beneath a waning moon was haunted
By woman wailing for her demon-lover!

Vision in a Dream: Coleridge claimed this poem came to him in a dream, but when he woke and was transcribing it, he was interrupted by a visitor and was later unable to remember the rest of the poem. **1. Kubla Khan:** In Chinese history, Kublai Khan (1215–1294) founded the Mongol dynasty. **13. athwart . . . cover:** Encompassing a grove of cedar trees.

And from this chasm, with ceaseless turmoil seething,
As if this earth in fast thick pants were breathing,
A mighty fountain momently was forced,
Amid whose swift half-intermitted burst
Huge fragments vaulted like rebounding hail,
Or chaffy grain beneath the thresher's flail:
And 'mid these dancing rocks at once and ever
It flung up momently the sacred river.
Five miles meandering with a mazy motion
Through wood and dale the sacred river ran,
Then reached the caverns measureless to man,
And sank in tumult to a lifeless ocean:
And 'mid this tumult Kubla heard from far
Ancestral voices prophesying war!
    The shadow of the dome of pleasure
    Floated midway on the waves;
    Where was heard the mingled measure
    From the fountain and the caves.
It was a miracle of rare device,
A sunny pleasure-dome with caves of ice!

    A damsel with a dulcimer
    In a vision once I saw:
    It was an Abyssinian maid,
    And on her dulcimer she played,
    Singing of Mount Abora.
    Could I revive within me
    Her symphony and song,
    To such a deep delight 'twould win me,
That with music loud and long,
I would build that dome in air,
That sunny dome! those caves of ice!
And all who heard should see them there,
And all should cry, Beware! Beware!
His flashing eyes, his floating hair!
Weave a circle round him thrice,
And close your eyes with holy dread,
For he on honey-dew hath fed,
And drunk the milk of Paradise.

SAMUEL TAYLOR COLERIDGE

Frost at Midnight

1798

The Frost performs its secret ministry,
Unhelped by any wind. The owlet's cry
Came loud — and hark, again! loud as before.

The inmates of my cottage, all at rest,
Have left me to that solitude, which suits
Abstruser musings: save that at my side
My cradled infant slumbers peacefully.
'Tis calm indeed! so calm, that it disturbs
And vexes meditation with its strange
And extreme silentness. Sea, hill, and wood,
This populous village! Sea, and hill, and wood,
With all the numberless goings-on of life,
Inaudible as dreams! the thin blue flame
Lies on my low-burnt fire, and quivers not;
Only that film,° which fluttered on the grate, *soot*
Still flutters there, the sole unquiet thing.
Methinks its motion in this hush of nature
Gives it dim sympathies with me who live,
Making it a companionable form,
Whose puny flaps and freaks the idling Spirit
By its own moods interprets, everywhere
Echo or mirror seeking of itself,
And makes a toy of Thought.
But O! how oft,
How oft, at school, with most believing mind,
Presageful, have I gazed upon the bars,
To watch that fluttering *stranger!* and as oft
With unclosed lids, already had I dreamt
Of my sweet birthplace, and the old church tower,
Whose bells, the poor man's only music, rang
From morn to evening, all the hot fair-day,
So sweetly, that they stirred and haunted me
With a wild pleasure, falling on mine ear
Most like articulate sounds of things to come!
So gazed I, till the soothing things, I dreamt,
Lulled me to sleep, and sleep prolonged my dreams!
And so I brooded all the following morn,
Awed by the stern preceptor's face, mine eye
Fixed with mock study on my swimming book:
Save if the door half opened, and I snatched
A hasty glance, and still my heart leaped up,
For still I hoped to see the *stranger's* face,
Townsman, or aunt, or sister more beloved,
My playmate when we both were clothed alike!

Dear Babe,° that sleepest cradled by my side, *Coleridge's infant son*
Whose gentle breathings, heard in this deep calm,
Fill up the interspersèd vacancies
And momentary pauses of the thought!
My babe so beautiful! it thrills my heart
With tender gladness, thus to look at thee,

And think that thou shalt learn far other lore,
And in far other scenes! For I was reared
In the great city, pent 'mid cloisters dim,
And saw nought lovely but the sky and stars.
But *thou,* my babe! shalt wander like a breeze
By lakes and sandy shores, beneath the crags
Of ancient mountain, and beneath the clouds,
Which image in their bulk both lakes and shores
And mountain crags: so shalt thou see and hear
The lovely shapes and sounds intelligible
Of that eternal language, which thy God
Utters, who from eternity doth teach
Himself in all, and all things in himself.
Great universal Teacher! he shall mold
Thy spirit, and by giving make it ask.

Therefore all seasons shall be sweet to thee,
Whether the summer clothe the general earth
With greenness, or the redbreast sit and sing
Betwixt the tufts of snow on the bare branch
Of mossy apple tree, while the nigh thatch
Smokes in the sun-thaw; whether the eave-drops fall
Heard only in the trances of the blast,
Or if the secret ministry of frost
Shall hang them up in silent icicles,
Quietly shining to the quiet Moon.

E. E. CUMMINGS *(1894–1962) was born Edward Estlin Cummings in Cambridge, Massachusetts. His father was a Unitarian minister who taught sociology at Harvard. As a Harvard undergraduate, Cummings wrote conventional verse, but under the influence of the poet and critic Ezra Pound, his poetry became less sentimental and more sharply satiric.*

In 1917 he went to France with a friend to join the Red Cross Ambulance Corps, but he was careless in comments he made about the French Army in letters home, forgetting that mail was censored. He was arrested by the French authorities and imprisoned for treason. His father, however, had important government connections and succeeded in getting Cummings released after four months of detention. The experience became the subject of Cummings's sardonic, exuberant book, The Enormous Room, *which appeared in 1922.*

When Cummings's poetry began to appear in the mid-1920s, it incited considerable controversy, not only for his experimental techniques of breaking up words and punctuation, but also for his eroticism and his irreverence toward the heroism of World War I. He justified his poetic experiments by saying that he was searching for a way to express the ecstasy of life. As he described it in the introduction to his Collected Poems *(1938), "We can never be born enough." In 1933 he traveled to the*

Soviet Union, and, characteristically, he was bored and disappointed with the Soviet social experiment.

Also a painter, Cummings spent much of his life writing and painting in a small house in Greenwich Village. The love poem "somewhere i have never travelled" is a brilliantly free variation on the form of the sonnet. The elegy "Buffalo Bill 's" is one of his best-known poems. "In Just-" is an example of his poetic technique at its freshest and most expressive. (See also Cummings's "when god lets my body be" on p. 823, "goodby Betty, don't remember me" on p. 881, and "since feeling is first" on p. 956.)

E. E. CUMMINGS

somewhere i have never travelled 1931

somewhere i have never travelled,gladly beyond
any experience,your eyes have their silence:
in your most frail gesture are things which enclose me,
or which i cannot touch because they are too near

your slightest look easily will unclose me
though i have closed myself as fingers,
you open always petal by petal myself as Spring opens
(touching skilfully,mysteriously)her first rose

or if your wish be to close me,i and
my life will shut very beautifully,suddenly,
as when the heart of this flower imagines
the snow carefully everywhere descending;

nothing which we are to perceive in this world equals
the power of your intense fragility:whose texture
compels me with the colour of its countries,
rendering death and forever with each breathing

(i do not know what it is about you that closes
and opens;only something in me understands
the voice of your eyes is deeper than all roses)
nobody,not even the rain,has such small hands

E. E. CUMMINGS

Buffalo Bill 's° 1923

Buffalo Bill 's
defunct
                who used to
                ride a watersmooth-silver
                                                stallion

Buffalo Bill 's: William Frederick Cody (1846–1917), known as Buffalo Bill, was a frontier scout who put together a "Wild West" show that was the most popular show in America for thirty years.

■ ■ ■

and break onetwothreefourfive pigeonsjustlikethat
                                                                Jesus

he was a handsome man
                                    and what i want to know is
how do you like your blueeyed boy
Mister Death

E. E. CUMMINGS

in Just- *1923*

in Just-
spring   when the world is mud-
luscious the little
lame balloonman

whistles   far   and wee

and eddieandbill come
running from marbles and
piracies and it's
spring

when the world is puddle-wonderful

the queer
old balloonman whistles
far   and   wee
and bettyandisbel come dancing

from hop-scotch and jump-rope and

it's
spring
and
      the
            goat-footed

balloonMan   whistles
far
and
wee

❧

HILDA DOOLITTLE *(1886–1961), who used her initials H.D. as a writer, was born in Bethlehem, Pennsylvania. Her mother was a member of the Moravian Brotherhood and was deeply interested in mysticism. Her father was a professor of astronomy. When she was still at school she became engaged to the young poet Ezra Pound, who was studying at the University of Pennsylvania. Pound brought another friend, William Carlos Williams, to meet her, and Williams later remembered a walk* *when the three of them were caught in a storm. She sat down and held up her arms, saying, "Beautiful rain, welcome."*

Her engagement to Pound ended, but later, after poor grades and ill health forced her to leave Bryn Mawr College in her sophomore year, she met Pound again in London in 1911 and became a member of the literary movement he was founding, called imagism (p. 896). When Pound sent three of her poems to Poetry Magazine *in Chicago he signed them "H.D., Imagiste."*

Her life in London was turbulent and unhappy. She married one of the imagist group, Richard Aldington, but he began an affair with another woman after she had a miscarriage, and she ended the marriage, desperately poor and ill. For several months she was emotionally dependent upon the writer D. H. Lawrence, but he abruptly ended the relationship. Finally, in 1919, when H.D. was pregnant after a brief affair with a new lover, she was rescued by a wealthy English writer named Winifred Ellerman, who wrote under the name of Bryher. Bryher took over her life, and they remained together, despite occasional separations, until 1946, when their relationship ended.

H.D. wrote continually, though for many years she felt she had exhausted her themes and refused to publish. In 1960 she was the first woman to receive the Award of Merit Medal for Poetry from the American Academy of Arts and Letters. "Orchard" is an early poem, while "May 1943" is an intimate glimpse of her life during the war years. (See also H.D.'s "Mid-day" on p. 867 and "Oread" on p. 897.)

RELATED COMMENTARIES: *Alicia Ostriker, "The Poet as Heroine: H.D.," page 1201; Ezra Pound, "On the Principles of Imagism," page 1204.*

H.D.

Orchard

1916

I saw the first pear
as it fell —
the honey-seeking, golden-banded,
the yellow swarm,
was not more fleet than I,
(spare us from loveliness!)
and I fell prostrate,
crying:
you have flayed us with your blossoms,
spare us the beauty
of fruit-trees!

The honey-seeking
paused not;
the air thundered their song,
and I alone was prostrate.

O rough-hewn
god of the orchard,
I bring you an offering —
do you, alone unbeautiful,

son of the god,
spare us from loveliness:
these fallen hazel-nuts,
stripped late of their green sheaths,
grapes, red-purple,
their berries
dripping with wine;
pomegranates already broken,
and shrunken figs,
and quinces untouched,
I bring you as offering.

H.D.

May 1943

1950

I wanted to say I was sorry,
but why should I? but anyway
I did want to say I was sorry,
but how could I? who was I?
I wanted to say, yes, we're used to it,
we have the advantage,
you're new to it;
we've slithered so long in the rain,
prowled like cats in the dark,
like owls in the black-out,
look at us — anaemic, good-natured,
for a rat in the gutter's a rat in the gutter,
consider our fellowship,
look at each one of us,
we've grown alike, slithering,
slipping along with fish-baskets,
grey faces, fish-faces, frog gait,
we slop, we hop,
we're off to the bread-queue,
the meat-shop, the grocery,
an egg? — really madam — maybe to-morrow —
one here — one there — another one over there
is heroic (who'd know it?)
heroic? no bronze face —

no
    no
        no
what am I saying?

ꕥ

EMILY DICKINSON *(1830–1886) wrote in a letter,*

> *If I read a book and it makes my whole body so cold no fire can ever warm me, I know that it is poetry. If I feel physically as if the top of my head were taken off, I know that is poetry. These are the only ways I know it. Is there any other way?*

It is difficult, though, to imagine how someone whose days seemed as quiet and uneventful as hers could feel such a strong emotion. Outwardly, so little happened in her life that someone reading her poetry today could say that the one "event" of her life came a few days after her death, when her sister Lavinia opened a box she'd left at the foot of her bed and found the manuscripts of hundreds of unpublished poems — poems that had been her sister's life's work.

Dickinson, the second child of Emily and Edward Dickinson, spent her life in the small Massachusetts town of Amherst, in a house where she was born and died. For the last fourteen years of her life she lived almost entirely in one room: her large, sunny front bedroom. In her last years she dressed all in white and saw only a few friends and relatives, even though her brother and his wife lived in the house beside hers. She communicated with people through notes and lines of poems, most of them so cryptic and veiled that it was hard to know what she meant. Her niece Martha, the daughter of her brother Austin, remembered that once she came into her aunt's bedroom and Dickinson pretended to lock the door behind her, saying, "Matty, here's freedom."

The reality of Emily Dickinson's life, however, is much more complicated. In her poetry there is anger and despair as well as joy. There are many poems that hint at an unhappy love affair. One, written when she was about thirty, suggests that she thought of herself as married:

I'm "wife" — I've finished that —
That other state —
I'm Czar — I'm "Woman" now —
It's safer so —

In another, possibly written a year later, there is a burst of passion:

Wild Nights — Wild Nights!
Were I with thee
Wild nights would be
Our luxury!

In 1890, four years after she had found the box of poems, Lavinia paid to have a small selection from the manuscripts published. For help with the editing she turned to her brother's lover, Mabel Loomis Todd, and the well-known writer and literary editor Thomas Wentworth Higginson. Higginson had corresponded with Emily for more than twenty years, and even journeyed to Amherst to meet her. The public response was overwhelming — there were ten printings of the book in the first year — and immediately readers began sifting through the hints and suggestions they found in the poems to try to understand what concealed events might have inspired Dickinson to write them.

Dickinson's poetry is so oblique — so "slant" in her term — that for many years it was impossible to identify the person she loved or to guess at why the relationship ended. However, when a literary scholar reconstructed her original arrangement of the poems into small hand-sewn booklets it became clear that Dickinson had fallen deeply in love in her late twenties. Her emotional attachment to a married minister named Charles Wadsworth began in 1858 and lasted until 1863. She heard him preach on a visit to Philadelphia, and when the family needed someone to help her through an emotionally difficult period in her life she was encouraged to write him. She began sending him groups of poems and in the spring of 1858 sent him the first of a series of turbulent "master" letters, describing her love and her emotional indebtedness to him. Although his own letters to her are carefully polite he came to Amherst to visit her in 1860, and in her poetry it seems clear that their relationship was physically consummated. It is from this time that she referred to herself as "wife," and she does not seem to have considered a relationship with anyone else, although letters to a family friend, Judge Otis Lord, in 1877 hint that he had proposed to her. She continued to correspond with Wadsworth, even when she realized that they could never marry, and she saw him again when he returned to Amherst in 1880.

For many years researchers suspected that the man she loved was a close family friend named Samuel Bowles, who was often a guest in the Dickinson home. Bowles was the editor of the Springfield Republican, *a daily newspaper published in nearby Springfield. Bowles, it now seems certain, was one of the two or three people she used to help her send letters to Wadsworth. He published three of her poems, but in each case they were edited to smooth out what were considered to be their "irregularities." Reading her poems as a record of her love affair makes it clear that she could never consider publishing them. They were her secret diary, and she asked Lavinia to destroy them at her death. When she wrote her now-famous letter to Thomas Wentworth Higginson in 1862, asking if he could tell her if her verse was "alive," she was only asking for his opinion, not for help in finding a publisher for the poems.*

Other strains and tensions are also mirrored in the poetry. Dickinson had a very complicated relationship with her father, who was a lawyer and treasurer of Amherst College. As she described her family in a letter to Higginson,

> *I have a brother and sister; my mother does not care for thought, and father, too busy with his briefs to notice what we do. He buys me many books, but begs me not to read them, because he fears they joggle the mind.*

In 1856 her brother married and moved into the house next door. For several years there was a warm friendliness between Dickinson and her sister-in-law, but the marriage soured, and finally the only contact between the two households was her brother's daily visit to Emily and her sister Lavinia, who also never married. In 1881, a year after Dickinson had met Wadsworth again, a young astronomy professor named David Todd moved to Amherst with his wife, Mabel. Austin Dickinson and Mabel Todd fell passionately in love, and their affair, more or less openly acknowledged, continued until his death. Lavinia carried the messages between them, and they sometimes met in Dickinson's house.

Until she was in her thirties, Dickinson still took part in Amherst life. In 1856 her bread won second prize at the Agricultural Fair, and the next year she was on the Cattle Show Committee. As she dealt with the complex emotional tensions of her relationship, she became more and more socially withdrawn, so that by 1863 Samuel Bowles referred to her in a note to Austin as "Queen recluse." In 1862 she wrote to

Higginson after he'd published an article in the April Atlantic Monthly *suggesting that he might be interested in hearing from young poets. He responded to her letter with interest, but he found her poems too idiosyncratic to publish. It seems clear, however, that she had already decided that her poetry would be her "letter to the World / that never wrote to me," as she said in a poem from 1862. In 1869, when Higginson wrote and asked if she would come to Boston, she answered, "I do not cross my Father's ground to any House or Town."*

Higginson, however, showed the poems to a childhood friend of Dickinson's, the successful writer Helen Hunt Jackson, and Jackson immediately recognized the genius in the work and begged her to publish. In 1876 Jackson wrote her, "You are a great poet — and it is a wrong . . . that you will not sing aloud." Jackson was able to persuade her to have a poem published anonymously, but there was never any question that Dickinson would consider further publication. The themes of the poetry of her last years were death and eternity.

Dickinson's poems seemed innocent and naive to some of her early readers, but she was conscious of other poets and their work. Unlike Elizabeth Barrett Browning, who never went to school, Dickinson went first to the Amherst Academy and then spent a year, when she was seventeen, at Mount Holyoke Female Seminary, now Mount Holyoke College. It is interesting to compare her poetry to Barrett Browning's, since she admired the English writer so much that she had a portrait of her on the wall of her bedroom. She read, but certainly was not influenced in any way, by Barrett Browning's defiant novel in verse, Aurora Leigh, *with its attack on the passive role forced on women in their society. When she learned that Higginson was traveling to Europe, not long after Barrett Browning's death, Dickinson wrote him "If you touch her Grave, put one hand on the Head, for me — her unmentioned mourner."*

Dickinson also read the works of John Keats, whom she admired the most of the Romantics, the Brontë sisters, and Alfred, Lord Tennyson, as well as the novels of George Eliot. But she did not let herself be influenced by the technical skill of the Victorian poets. Much of her poetry is written in simple quatrains, generally in iambic tetrameter, often with only the second and fourth lines rhyming. It is close to the style of verse that filled the hymnals she used in church. Her poetry is so startling in its imagery and its revelations that there is no real parallel to it, but it is interesting that in its form it has some similarities with the poetry of Emily Brontë. Brontë, who found literary immortality with her novel Wuthering Heights, *was one of the writers Dickinson read. Like Dickinson, Brontë was reclusive, spent her short life in her family home, and drew on the hymnal for the forms of her poetry. These lines by Brontë could also have been written by Dickinson:*

I'm happiest when most away
I can bear my soul from its home of clay
On a windy night when the moon is bright
And the eye wander through worlds of light . . .

No coward soul is mine
No trembler in the world's storm-troubled sphere.

Higginson read Brontë's poem "Last Lines" at Dickinson's funeral. Seven of Dickinson's poems were published in her lifetime, and in each case they were edited or rewritten to suit the conventions of the time. Would she have edited them herself if

Helen Hunt Jackson could have finally persuaded her to publish them? Like so much else about her life, we will never know. We do know that every revision Higginson suggested in his letters to her was gently but firmly rejected. She knew what she had accomplished. What she left was a gathering of poems so unique and unexpected that we are still trying today to measure the dimensions of her achievement.

This selection from her poetry includes many of her best-known poems, in the transcriptions from her manuscripts published in 1948. The poems in the new edition were numbered, as Dickinson did not title them herself. They can be interpreted in many ways, and often they refer to some specific moment in the day they were written, like "I've nothing else — to bring, You know —," which seems to be telling Charles Wadsworth that the only things that Dickinson can bring him are poems. The poems are startling in their imagery, and behind the deceptive simplicities of their lines are subtle insights. In "I'm 'wife' — I've finished that —" Dickinson describes the passage from girl to woman as "this soft eclipse." The sixth poem in this group begins with the unforgettable image "'Hope' is the thing with feathers — / That perches in the soul." "I taste a liquor never brewed —" was one of the three poems that Bowles published in his newspaper, and it became one of the poems discussed by other writers when it was included in the first collection in 1890. The popular poet Thomas Bailey Aldrich was irritated by the imperfect rhyme of "pearl/alcohol" in the first stanza and quickly rewrote it. His "corrected" version was,

> *I taste a liquor never brewed*
> *In vats along the Rhine:*
> *No tankards scooped in pearl could yield*
> *An alcohol like mine.*

Nothing Aldrich ever wrote, however, could match the exuberance of the poem's last image of Dickinson herself as "the little Tippler / Leaning against the — Sun."

"I'm Nobody! Who are you?" is her sardonic comment on fame, and in "Much Madness is divinest Sense —" she could be agreeing with William Blake, with his belief that society often mistakes genius for madness. "I died for Beauty — but was scarce" is one of her many poems on the subject of death, this one agreeing with John Keats's final lines of "Ode on a Grecian Urn": "'Beauty is truth, truth beauty' — that is all / Ye know on earth, and all ye need to know." "Love — thou art high —" and "If you were coming in the Fall," are both from the last months of her relationship with Charles Wadsworth. "Mine — by the Right of the White Election!" was probably written when she realized they could never marry, although it is — as always — difficult to be certain of the circumstances of the poem. The phrase "White Election" probably means a wedding ceremony.

"Because I could not stop for Death —" and "The Only News I know" were written in the next years. The former, with its image of death as a gentle carriage ride, was one of the most widely quoted poems from the 1890 collection. The latter was not published until 1929. "Split the Lark — and you'll find the Music —" opens with an image as vivid as the first line of "'Hope' is the thing with feathers — ." Although "I stepped from Plank to Plank" suggests that Dickinson had lived many years to gain her "Experience," she was only thirty-four. Still, she was already feeling her life closing in around her. "A narrow Fellow in the Grass," her brilliant description of a snake and the fear she feels whenever she sees one, was published in the Springfield Republican, *but*

she complained that it had been published without her permission. For much of her life she was troubled by her inability to accept conventional Christian dogma, but "I never saw a Moor —" is a clear statement of her religious faith. Dickinson has found her own way to eternity. (See also Dickinson's "A word is dead" on p. 811.)

RELATED CASEBOOK: *See pages 1234–1254, including Thomas Wentworth Higginson, "Emily Dickinson's Letters," page 1235; Thomas H. Johnson, "The Text of Emily Dickinson's Poetry," page 1244; Thomas Bailey Aldrich, "*In Re *Emily Dickinson," page 1246; Richard Wilbur, "On Emily Dickinson," page 1248; Linda Gregg, "Not Understanding Emily Dickinson," page 1249; Galway Kinnell, "The Deconstruction of Emily Dickinson," page 1253.*

EMILY DICKINSON

You love me — you are sure — c. 1860

You love me — you are sure —
I shall not fear mistake —
I shall not *cheated* wake —
Some grinning morn —
to find the Sunrise left —
And Orchards — unbereft —
And Dollie — gone!

I need not start — you're sure —
That night will never be —
When frightened — home to Thee I run —
To find the windows dark —
And no more Dollie — mark —
Quite none?

Be sure you're sure — you know —
I'll bear it better now —
If you'll just tell me so —
Than when — a little dull Balm grown —
Over this pain of mine —
You sting — again!

EMILY DICKINSON

I'm "wife" — I've finished that — c. 1860

I'm "wife" — I've finished that —
That other state —
I'm Czar — I'm "Woman" now —
It's safer so —

■ ■ ■

How odd the Girl's life looks
Behind this soft Eclipse —
I think that Earth feels so
To folks in Heaven — now —

This being comfort — then
That other kind — was pain —
But why compare?
I'm "Wife"! Stop there!

EMILY DICKINSON

I taste a liquor never brewed — *c. 1860*

I taste a liquor never brewed —
From Tankards scooped in Pearl —
Not all the Vats upon the Rhine
Yield such an Alcohol!

Inebriate of Air — am I —
And Debauchee of Dew —
Reeling — thro endless summer days —
From inns of Molten Blue —

When "Landlords" turn the drunken Bee
Out of the Foxglove's door —
When Butterflies — renounce their "drams" —
I shall but drink the more!

Till Seraphs swing their snowy Hats —
And Saints — to windows run —
To see the little Tippler
Leaning against the — Sun —

EMILY DICKINSON

I've nothing else — to bring, You know — *c. 1861*

I've nothing else — to bring, You know —
So I keep bringing These —
Just as the Night keeps fetching Stars
To our familiar eyes —

Maybe, we shouldn't mind them —
Unless they didn't come —
Then — maybe, it would puzzle us
To find our way Home —

Emily Dickinson

Wild Nights — Wild Nights! c. 1861

Wild Nights — Wild Nights!
Were I with thee
Wild Nights should be
Our luxury!

Futile — the Winds —
To a Heart in port —
Done with the Compass —
Done with the Chart!

Rowing in Eden —
Ah, the Sea!
Might I but moor — Tonight —
In Thee!

Emily Dickinson

"Hope" is the thing with feathers — c. 1861

"Hope" is the thing with feathers —
That perches in the soul —
And sings the tune without the words —
And never stops — at all —

And sweetest — in the Gale — is heard —
And sore must be the storm —
That could abash the little Bird
That kept so many warm —

I've heard it in the chillest land —
And on the strangest Sea —
Yet, never, in Extremity,
It asked a crumb — of Me.

Emily Dickinson

There's a certain Slant of light, c. 1861

There's a certain Slant of light,
Winter Afternoons —
That oppresses, like the Heft
Of Cathedral Tunes —

Heavenly Hurt, it gives us —
We can find no scar,
But internal difference,
Where the Meanings, are —

None may teach it — Any —
'Tis the Seal Despair —
An imperial affliction
Sent us of the Air —

When it comes, the Landscape listens —
Shadows — hold their breath —
When it goes, 'tis like the Distance
On the look of Death —

Emily Dickinson

I'm Nobody! Who are you? *c. 1861*

I'm Nobody! Who are you?
Are you — Nobody — Too?
Then there's a pair of us!
Don't tell! they'd advertise — you know!

How dreary — to be — Somebody!
How public — like a Frog —
To tell one's name — the livelong June —
To an admiring Bog!

Emily Dickinson

After great pain, a formal feeling comes — *c. 1862*

After great pain, a formal feeling comes —
The Nerves sit ceremonious, like Tombs —
The stiff Heart questions was it He, that bore,
And Yesterday, or Centuries before?

The Feet, mechanical, go round —
Of Ground, or Air, or Ought —
A Wooden way
Regardless grown,
A Quartz contentment, like a stone —

This is the Hour of Lead —
Remembered, if outlived,
As Freezing persons, recollect the Snow —
First — Chill — then Stupor — then the letting go —

EMILY DICKINSON

Much Madness is divinest Sense — c. 1862

Much Madness is divinest Sense —
To a discerning Eye —
Much Sense — the starkest Madness —
'Tis the Majority
In this, as All, prevail —
Assent — and you are sane —
Demur — you're straightway dangerous —
And handled with a Chain —

EMILY DICKINSON

I died for Beauty — but was scarce c. 1862

I died for Beauty — but was scarce
Adjusted in the Tomb
When One who died for Truth, was lain
In an adjoining Room —

He questioned softly "Why I failed"?
"For Beauty," I replied —
"And I — for Truth — Themself are One —
We Brethren, are," He said —

And so, as Kinsmen, met a Night —
We talked between the Rooms —
Until the Moss had reached our lips —
And covered up — our names —

EMILY DICKINSON

Love — thou art high — c. 1862

Love — thou art high —
I cannot climb thee —
But, were it Two —
Who knows but we —
Taking turns — at the Chimborazo —
Ducal — at last — stand up by thee —

Love — thou art deep —
I cannot cross thee —
But, were there Two
Instead of One —

Rower, and Yacht — some sovereign Summer —
Who knows — but we'd reach the Sun?

Love — thou art Veiled —
A few — behold thee —
Smile — and alter — and prattle — and die —
Bliss — were an Oddity — without thee —
Nicknamed by God —
Eternity —

EMILY DICKINSON

I heard a Fly buzz — when I died —

c. 1862

I heard a Fly buzz — when I died —
The Stillness in the Room
Was like the Stillness in the Air —
Between the Heaves of Storm —

The Eyes around — had wrung them dry —
And Breaths were gathering firm
For that last Onset — when the King
Be witnessed — in the Room —

I willed my Keepsakes — Signed away
What portion of me be
Assignable — and then it was
There interposed a Fly —

With Blue — uncertain stumbling Buzz —
Between the light — and me —
And then the Windows failed — and then
I could not see to see —

EMILY DICKINSON

If you were coming in the Fall,

c. 1862

If you were coming in the Fall,
I'd brush the Summer by
With half a smile, and half a spurn,
As Housewives do, a Fly.

If I could see you in a year,
I'd wind the months in balls —
And put them each in separate Drawers,
For fear the numbers fuse —

If only Centuries, delayed,
I'd count them on my Hand,

Subtracting, till my fingers dropped
Into Van Dieman's Land.°

If certain, when this life was out —
That yours and mine, should be
I'd toss it yonder, like a Rind,
And take Eternity —

But, now, uncertain of the length
Of this, that is between,
It goads me, like the Goblin Bee —
That will not state — its sting.

EMILY DICKINSON

Mine — by the Right of the White Election! *c. 1862*

Mine — by the Right of the White Election!
Mine — by the Royal Seal!
Mine — by the Sign in the Scarlet prison —
Bars — cannot conceal!

Mine — here — in Vision — and in Veto!
Mine — by the Grave's Repeal —
Titled — Confirmed —
Delirious Charter!
Mine — long as Ages steal!

EMILY DICKINSON

Because I could not stop for Death — *c. 1863*

Because I could not stop for Death —
He kindly stopped for me —
The Carriage held but just Ourselves —
And Immortality.

We slowly drove — He knew no haste
And I had put away
My labor and my leisure too,
For His Civility —

We passed the School, where Children strove
At Recess — in the Ring —

---

12. Van Dieman's Land: The seventeenth-century Dutch navigator Abel Tasman named an island off the coast of Australia Van Diemen's Land, which Dickinson has misspelled. Today it is the Australian commonwealth of Tasmania.

We passed the Fields of Gazing Grain —
We passed the Setting Sun —

Or rather — He passed Us —
The Dews drew quivering and chill —
For only Gossamer, my Gown —
My Tippet — only Tulle —

We paused before a House that seemed
A Swelling of the Ground —
The Roof was scarcely visible —
The Cornice — in the Ground —

Since then — 'tis Centuries — and yet
Feels shorter than the Day
I first surmised the Horses' Heads
Were toward Eternity —

EMILY DICKINSON

The Only News I know

c. 1864

The Only News I know
Is Bulletins all Day
From Immortality.

The Only Shows I see —
Tomorrow and Today —
Perchance Eternity —

The Only One I meet
Is God — The Only Street —
Existence — This traversed

If Other News there be —
Or Admirabler Show —
I'll tell it You —

EMILY DICKINSON

Split the Lark — and you'll find the Music —

c. 1864

Split the Lark — and you'll find the Music —
Bulb after Bulb, in Silver rolled —
Scantily dealt to the Summer Morning
Saved for your Ear when Lutes be old.

Loose the Flood — you shall find it patent —
Gush after Gush, reserved for you —
Scarlet Experiment! Sceptic Thomas!
Now, do you doubt that your Bird was true?

Emily Dickinson

I stepped from Plank to Plank c. 1864

I stepped from Plank to Plank
A slow and cautious way
The Stars about my Head I felt
About my Feet the Sea.

I knew not but the next
Would be my final inch —
This gave me that precarious Gait
Some call Experience.

Emily Dickinson

A narrow Fellow in the Grass c. 1865

A narrow Fellow in the Grass
Occasionally rides —
You may have met Him — did you not
His notice sudden is —

The Grass divides as with a Comb —
A spotted shaft is seen —
And then it closes at your feet
And opens further on —

He likes a Boggy Acre
A Floor too cool for Corn —
Yet when a Boy, and Barefoot —
I more than once at Noon
Have passed, I thought, a Whip lash
Unbraiding in the Sun
When stooping to secure it
It wrinkled, and was gone —

Several of Nature's People
I know, and they know me —
I feel for them a transport
Of cordiality —

But never met this Fellow
Attended, or alone
Without a tighter breathing
And Zero at the Bone —

Emily Dickinson

I never saw a Moor —

c. 1865

I never saw a Moor —
I never saw the Sea —
Yet know I how the Heather looks
And what a Billow be.

I never spoke with God
Nor visited in Heaven —
Yet certain am I of the spot
As if the Checks were given —

JOHN DONNE *(1572–1631) was born a Roman Catholic during a period in English history when Roman Catholics were harassed by the Protestant government and were barred from advancement to most major positions of influence. His father died when he was four, and he was left with enough income to live well, but not to purchase favor at the court of Queen Elizabeth. He studied at Oxford and Cambridge universities but earned no degrees.*

In his early twenties, Donne lived like many other young, ambitious courtiers. He had many mistresses, traveled extensively in Europe, and took part in two raids against the Spanish at Cadiz and in the Azores. At the same time he read voraciously and wrote some of his most vivid erotic poetry. He had renounced his Catholicism but still hesitated to join the Church of England.

In 1598, when he was twenty-six, Donne became private secretary to Sir Thomas Egerton, one of the most powerful figures in the court of Queen Elizabeth. A brilliant future seemed certain, but three years later he fell deeply in love and secretly married Ann More, the seventeen-year-old niece of Lady Egerton. He was dismissed and thrown into prison, and for a dozen years he struggled against disappointment and financial difficulties. During this period his marriage was his only source of happiness.

Because of his brilliance and his early friendships, Donne was still welcome in the court, but King James, who succeeded Elizabeth, felt that Donne could be most useful to him in the church, and refused to consider granting Donne any other position. Donne finally surrendered and in 1615 became an Anglican priest. He was as talented in the church as he had been in court life, and in 1621 he became dean of St. Paul's Cathedral in London, where he delivered sermons and wrote devotional poetry and meditations until his death.

This selection of Donne's poetry includes two of his idiosyncratic love poems, "The Good-Morrow" and "The Flea." "A Valediction: Forbidding Mourning," written earlier, was composed for his wife before he left her on a trip to France. "Batter my heart, three-personed God" is from his collection of "Holy Sonnets." *(See also Donne's "Song" on p. 819 and "Death, be not proud" on p. 879.)*

RELATED POEM: *Wendy Cope, "The fine English poet, John Donne," page 884.*

John Donne

A Valediction:° Forbidding Mourning 1611

As virtuous men pass mildly away,
  And whisper to their souls to go,
Whilst some of their sad friends do say
  The breath goes now, and some say, no;

So let us melt, and make no noise,
  No tear-floods, nor sigh-tempests move,
'Twere profanation of our joys
  To tell the laity° our love.

Moving of th' earth brings harms and fears,
  Men reckon what it did and meant;
But trepidation of the spheres,°
  Though greater far, is innocent.

Dull sublunary° lovers' love
  (Whose soul is sense) cannot admit
Absence, because it doth remove
  Those things which elemented° it. *composed*

But we by a love so much refined
  That our selves know not what it is,
Inter-assurèd of the mind,
  Care less, eyes, lips, and hands to miss.

Our two souls therefore, which are one,
  Though I must go, endure not yet
A breach, but an expansion,
  Like gold to airy thinness beat.

If they be two, they are two so
  As stiff twin compasses are two;
Thy soul, the fixed foot, makes no show
  To move, but doth, if th' other do.

And though it in the center sit,
  Yet when the other far doth roam,
It leans and hearkens after it,
  And grows erect, as that comes home.

Such wilt thou be to me, who must
  Like th' other foot, obliquely° run. *diagonally, aslant*

Valediction: A departure speech or discourse; a bidding of farewell. **8. laity:** Common people. **11. trepidation of the spheres:** A trembling of the celestial spheres, hypothesized by Ptolemaic astronomers to account for unpredicted variations in the paths of the heavenly bodies. **13. sublunary:** Beneath the moon; earthly, hence, changeable.

Thy firmness makes my circle° just,
  And makes me end where I begun.

JOHN DONNE

The Good-Morrow

1633

I wonder, by my troth, what thou and I
Did, till we loved? Were we not weaned till then,
But sucked on country pleasures, childishly?
Or snorted we in the seven sleepers' den?
'Twas so; but this, all pleasures fancies be.
If ever any beauty I did see,
Which I desired, and got, 'twas but a dream of thee.

And now good morrow to our waking souls,
Which watch not one another out of fear;
For love all love of other sights controls,
And makes one little room an everywhere.
Let sea-discoverers to new worlds have gone,
Let maps to others, worlds on worlds have shown:
Let us possess one world; each hath one, and is one.

My face in thine eye, thine in mine appears,
And true plain hearts do in the faces rest;
Where can we find two better hemispheres,
Without sharp North, without declining West?
Whatever dies was not mixed equally;
If our two loves be one, or thou and I
Love so alike that none do slacken, none can die.

JOHN DONNE

The Flea

1633

Mark but this flea, and mark in this
How little that which thou deny'st me is;
It sucked me first, and now sucks thee,
And in this flea our two bloods mingled be;
Thou know'st that this cannot be said
A sin, nor shame, nor loss of maidenhead,
    Yet this enjoys before it woo,
    And pampered swells with one blood made of two,
    And this, alas, is more than we would do.

---

35. circle: The circle was a symbol of perfection; with a dot in the middle, it was also the alchemist's symbol for gold.

▪ ▪ ▪

Oh stay, three lives in one flea spare,
Where we almost, yea more than, married are.
This flea is you and I, and this
Our marriage bed, and marriage temple is;
Though parents grudge, and you, we're met
And cloistered in these living walls of jet.
    Though use° make you apt to kill me, *habit*
    Let not to that, self-murder added be,
    And sacrilege, three sins in killing three.

Cruel and sudden, hast thou since
Purpled thy nail in blood of innocence?
Wherein could this flea guilty be,
Except in that drop which it sucked from thee?
Yet thou triumph'st, and say'st that thou
Find'st not thyself, nor me, the weaker now;
    'Tis true; then learn how false, fears be;
    Just so much honor, when thou yield'st to me,
    Will waste, as this flea's death took life from thee.

JOHN DONNE

Batter my heart, three-personed God 1633

Batter my heart, three-personed God; for You
As yet but knock, breathe, shine, and seek to mend;
That I may rise and stand, o'erthrow me,'and bend
Your force to break, blow, burn, and make me new.
I, like an usurped town, to'another due,
Labor to'admit You, but O, to no end;
Reason, Your viceroy'in me, me should defend,
But is captívd, and proves weak or untrue.
Yet dearly'I love You,'and would be lovéd fain,
But am betrothed unto Your enemy.
Divorce me,'untie or break that knot again;
Take me to You, imprison me, for I,
Except You'enthrall me, never shall be free,
Nor ever chaste, except You ravish me.

T. S. ELIOT *(1888–1965) was born Thomas Stearns Eliot in St. Louis, Missouri. His mother was a schoolteacher who also wrote poetry, and his father was a successful businessman. Eliot was sent to finish his education at Milton Academy, south of Boston, and then attended Harvard College.*

Following his graduation from Harvard in 1910, he spent a year in France studying at the Sorbonne and became intensely interested in the writing of a brilliant group of contemporary French poets who called themselves symbolists. *When he returned to Harvard to earn his doctorate the next year, he began writing "The Love Song of J. Alfred Prufrock," a poem that included phrases and attitudes translated from the work of symbolist poets Jules Laforgue and Arthur Rimbaud. Conrad Aiken, a fellow student who was also a poet, encouraged him to publish it, but Eliot waited until he returned to Europe in 1914 and was studying at Oxford. He read the poem to Ezra Pound, who immediately sent it to an American magazine. It is considered by most critics to be the first modernist poem written in English.*

In 1915 Eliot suddenly married Vivian Haigh-Wood, whom he had met in England, and had to find some kind of job to support them. He was first a schoolteacher, then a bank clerk, and finally a director in a London publishing house. With the publication in 1922 of his controversial long poem The Wasteland *— a work begun during a stay in a sanatorium brought about by exhaustion, marital difficulties, and depression — he became one of the world's most widely read and discussed younger poets. His writing, both as a poet and a literary critic, had a decisive effect on nearly every poetic tradition before World War II. He became a British citizen in 1927. In 1948 he won the Nobel Prize for literature.*

RELATED POEM: *J. Walker, "(On T. S. Eliot's Prufrock) An angst-ridden amorist, Fred," page 885.*

RELATED COMMENTARIES: *Cleanth Brooks Jr. and Robert Penn Warren, "On Eliot's 'The Love Song of J. Alfred Prufrock,'" page 1156; T. S. Eliot, "From 'Tradition and the Individual Talent,'" page 1163; T. S. Eliot, "From 'William Blake,'" page 1166.*

T. S. ELIOT

The Love Song of J. Alfred Prufrock

1917

S'io credesse che mia risposta fosse
A persona che mai tornasse al mondo,
Questa fiamma staria senza piu scosse.
Ma perciocche giammai di questo fondo
Non torno vivo alcun, s'i'odo il vero,
Sensa tema d'infamia ti rispondo.°

Let us go then, you and I,
When the evening is spread out against the sky
Like a patient etherized upon a table;
Let us go, through certain half-deserted streets,
The muttering retreats
Of restless nights in one-night cheap hotels
And sawdust restaurants with oyster-shells:

S'io . . . rispondo: In Dante's *Inferno,* these lines are spoken by one of the "false counselors" whose soul is hidden within a flame that moves as it speaks: "If I believed my reply were given / to one who might ever return to the earth, this fire would cease further movement. / But as from this chasm / none has ever come back alive — if what I have heard is true — / without fearing infamy will I respond to you."

Streets that follow like a tedious argument
Of insidious intent
To lead you to an overwhelming question . . .
Oh, do not ask, "What is it?"
Let us go and make our visit.

In the room the women come and go
Talking of Michelangelo.

The yellow fog that rubs its back upon the window-panes
The yellow smoke that rubs its muzzle on the window-panes
Licked its tongue into the corners of the evening,
Lingered upon the pools that stand in drains,
Let fall upon its back the soot that falls from chimneys,
Slipped by the terrace, made a sudden leap,
And seeing that it was a soft October night,
Curled once about the house, and fell asleep.

And indeed there will be time
For the yellow smoke that slides along the street,
Rubbing its back upon the window-panes;
There will be time, there will be time
To prepare a face to meet the faces that you meet;
There will be time to murder and create,
And time for all the works and days of hands
That lift and drop a question on your plate;
Time for you and time for me,
And time yet for a hundred indecisions,
And for a hundred visions and revisions,
Before the taking of a toast and tea.

In the room the women come and go
Talking of Michelangelo.

And indeed there will be time
To wonder, "Do I dare?" and, "Do I dare?"
Time to turn back and descend the stair,
With a bald spot in the middle of my hair —
[They will say: "How his hair is growing thin!"]
My morning coat, my collar mounting firmly to the chin,
My necktie rich and modest, but asserted by a simple pin —
[They will say: "But how his arms and legs are thin!"]
Do I dare
Disturb the universe?
In a minute there is time
For decisions and revisions which a minute will reverse.

For I have known them all already, known them all:
Have known the evenings, mornings, afternoons,
I have measured out my life with coffee spoons;
I know the voices dying with a dying fall

Beneath the music from a farther room.
  So how should I presume?

And I have known the eyes already, known them all —
The eyes that fix you in a formulated phrase,
And when I am formulated, sprawling on a pin,
When I am pinned and wriggling on the wall,
Then how should I begin
To spit out all the butt-ends of my days and ways?
  And how should I presume?

And I have known the arms already, known them all —
Arms that are braceleted and white and bare
[But in the lamplight, downed with light brown hair!]
Is it perfume from a dress
That makes me so digress?
Arms that lie along a table, or wrap about a shawl.
  And should I then presume?
  And how should I begin?

■

Shall I say, I have gone at dusk through narrow streets
And watched the smoke that rises from the pipes
Of lonely men in shirt-sleeves, leaning out of windows? . . .

I should have been a pair of ragged claws
Scuttling across the floors of silent seas.

■

And the afternoon, the evening, sleeps so peacefully!
Smoothed by long fingers,
Asleep . . . tired . . . or it malingers,
Stretched on the floor, here beside you and me.
Should I, after tea and cakes and ices,
Have the strength to force the moment to its crisis?
But though I have wept and fasted, wept and prayed,
Though I have seen my head [grown slightly bald] brought in upon a
  platter,°
I am no prophet — and here's no great matter;
I have seen the moment of my greatness flicker,
And I have seen the eternal Footman hold my coat, and snicker,
And in short, I was afraid.

And would it have been worth it, after all,
After the cups, the marmalade, the tea,
Among the porcelain, among some talk of you and me,
Would it have been worth while,
To have bitten off the matter with a smile,
To have squeezed the universe into a ball

---

82. upon a platter: A reference to the martyrdom of St. John the Baptist (Matthew 14:1–12).

To roll it toward some overwhelming question,
To say: "I am Lazarus,° come from the dead,
Come back to tell you all, I shall tell you all" —
If one, settling a pillow by her head,
    Should say: "That is not what I meant at all.
    That is not it, at all."

And would it have been worth it, after all,
Would it have been worth while,
After the sunsets and the dooryards and the sprinkled streets,
After the novels, after the teacups, after the skirts that trail along the
    floor —
And this, and so much more? —
It is impossible to say just what I mean!
But as if a magic lantern threw the nerves in patterns on a screen:
Would it have been worth while
If one, settling a pillow or throwing off a shawl,
And turning toward the window, should say:
    "That is not it at all,
    That is not what I meant, at all."

■

No! I am not Prince Hamlet, nor was meant to be;
Am an attendant lord, one that will do
To swell a progress, start a scene or two,
Advise the prince; no doubt, an easy tool,
Deferential, glad to be of use,
Politic, cautious, and meticulous;
Full of high sentence, but a bit obtuse;
At times, indeed, almost ridiculous —
Almost, at times, the Fool.

I grow old . . . I grow old . . .
I shall wear the bottoms of my trousers rolled.

Shall I part my hair behind? Do I dare to eat a peach?
I shall wear white flannel trousers, and walk upon the beach.
I have heard the mermaids singing, each to each.

I do not think that they will sing to me.

I have seen them riding seaward on the waves
Combing the white hair of the waves blown back
When the wind blows the water white and black.

We have lingered in the chambers of the sea
By sea-girls wreathed with seaweed red and brown
Till human voices wake us, and we drown.

---

94. "I am Lazarus": A reference to the resurrected Lazarus (John II, 12:1–2)

LAWRENCE FERLINGHETTI *(b. 1919) was born in Yonkers, New York, to Italian American parents. Tragically, his father died before he was born, and his mother was institutionalized. His mother's aunt took him with her to France for five years, but her own life was difficult, and following their return to the United States, Ferlinghetti was placed in an orphanage for seven months. It was only after his great-aunt became a tutor to a wealthy New York suburban family that she was able to take care of him again. He attended the Mount Hermon School in Massachusetts and then the University of North Carolina.*

Although Ferlinghetti was later to be known for his radical pacifist views, he served as a lieutenant commander in the U.S. Navy from 1941 to 1945. After the war, he studied for his doctorate at the Sorbonne in Paris. In April 1951 he married and settled in San Francisco, where he and a friend, Peter Martin, opened a small bookstore named City Lights, after the Charlie Chaplin film. The store became the center of the new Beat literary movement, which would soon coalesce in San Francisco.

Ferlinghetti began publishing a series of small books of his own and his friends' poetry, and one of his first publications was Allen Ginsberg's poem Howl. *The poem was seized by the police for obscenity, and the trial and the publicity from it helped turn the Beats into a national news event. Ferlinghetti's own book,* Starting from San Francisco, *sold several hundred thousand copies in the 1960s.*

He is often considered a Beat writer, but his writing, such as the poem "Dog," often has closer affinities to the French political poetry he translated while in Paris. "In Goya's greatest scenes we seem to see" reflects his serious interest in painting and art. *(See also Ferlinghetti's "Constantly Risking Absurdity" on p. 807.)*

RELATED POEM: *Louis Jenkins, "How to Tell a Wolf from a Dog," page 892.*

LAWRENCE FERLINGHETTI

Dog

1958

The dog trots freely in the street
and sees reality
and the things he sees
are bigger than himself
and the things he sees
are his reality
Drunks in doorways
Moons on trees
The dog trots freely thru the street
and the things he sees
are smaller than himself
Fish on newsprint
Ants in holes
Chickens in Chinatown windows
their heads a block away
The dog trots freely in the street
and the things he smells

smell something like himself
The dog trots freely in the street
past puddles and babies
cats and cigars
poolrooms and policemen
He doesn't hate cops
He merely has no use for them
and he goes past them
and past the dead cows hung up whole
in front of the San Francisco Meat Market
He would rather eat a tender cow
than a tough policeman
though either might do
And he goes past the Romeo Ravioli Factory
and past Coit's Tower
and past Congressman Doyle
He's afraid of Coit's Tower
but he's not afraid of Congressman Doyle
although what he hears is very discouraging
very depressing
very absurd
to a sad young dog like himself
to a serious dog like himself
But he has his own free world to live in
His own fleas to eat
He will not be muzzled
Congressman Doyle is just another
fire hydrant
to him
The dog trots freely in the street
and has his own dog's life to live
and to think about
and to reflect upon
touching and tasting and testing everything
investigating everything
without benefit of perjury
a real realist
with a real tale to tell
and a real tail to tell it with
a real live
            barking
                        democratic dog
engaged in real
                        free enterprise
with something to say
                                about ontology

something to say
about reality
and how to see it
and how to hear it
with his head cocked sideways
at streetcorners
as if he is just about to have
his picture taken
for Victor Records
listening for
His Master's Voice
and looking
like a living questionmark
into the
great gramaphone
of puzzling existence
with its wondrous hollow horn
which always seems
just about to spout forth
some Victorious answer
to everything

LAWRENCE FERLINGHETTI

In Goya's greatest scenes we seem to see *1958*

In Goya's greatest scenes we seem to see
the people of the world
exactly at the moment when
they first attained the title of
"suffering humanity"
They writhe upon the page
in a veritable rage
of adversity
Heaped up
groaning with babies and bayonets
under cement skies
in an abstract landscape of blasted trees
bent statues bats wings and beaks
slippery gibbets
cadavers and carnivorous cocks
and all the final hollering monsters
of the
"imagination of disaster"

they are so bloody real
it is as if they really still existed
And they do
Only the landscape is changed
They still are ranged along the roads
plagued by legionnaires
false windmills and demented roosters
They are the same people
only further from home
on freeways fifty lanes wide
on a concrete continent
spaced with bland billboards
illustrating imbecile illusions of happiness
The scene shows fewer tumbrils
but more maimed citizens
in painted cars
and they have strange license plates
and engines
that devour America

ꕥ

ROBERT FROST *(1874–1963) Although Walt Whitman proclaimed himself the poet of the American democracy, it is the quiet poet of the New England countryside, Robert Frost, who is the closest the United States has come to a "national" poet. It was fitting that when President-elect John F. Kennedy was inaugurated for a presidency that he dreamed would re-create the American spirit, he chose Robert Frost to read a new poem for the occasion. The sun shone so brightly in the poet's eyes that he could not read the new poem he had written, so he recited an old poem from memory, and it fit just as well into the solemn ceremony.*

Although Robert Frost's poetry rings with the tones of New England, and the voice of his poems is that of a New England farmer, this was the result of a conscious artistic choice. His own background was more diverse. He was born in San Francisco in 1874, and lived there eleven years until his father's death. His mother then moved with Robert and his younger sister Jeanie to Lawrence, Massachusetts, where she looked for work as a schoolteacher. Frost attended high school in Lawrence and was a valedictorian at his graduation. Three years later, after a stormy and jealous courtship, he married the woman who had been the other valedictorian, Elinor White. It was a marriage with only brief moments of happiness, but Elinor gave birth to six children, two of whom died very young. After high school Frost briefly attended Dartmouth and Harvard, and for the next twenty years he struggled to support his family with a series of poorly paid jobs, writing poems at night and sending them to local newspapers. One of his failed projects was an attempt to operate a chicken farm in New Hampshire, and even though he was unsuccessful as a farmer the experience gave him the setting for his poetry.

Although Frost in later years described the family's poverty during this time in bleak terms, he was being partially supported by his grandfather. As biographer William H. Pritchard writes,

> Frost had tried poultry farming in Derry, New Hampshire, the farm purchased for him by his paternal grandfather, and the indifferent results probably had a good deal to do with the very qualified way he would later characterize himself as a farmer. When William Prescott Frost died in 1901, he gave his grandson free use of the farm for ten years, after which it would belong to Frost. There was, as well, an annuity of five hundred dollars for each of the first ten years; it would then become eight hundred for the rest of the grandson's life. Meanwhile, in 1906, Frost began full-time teaching at Pinkerton Academy, in Derry, and in 1911 taught for a year at the Plymouth Normal School, in Plymouth, New Hampshire. In 1911, the farm having become his to do with as he pleased, Frost sold it, and the proceeds, in addition to the enlarged annuity, which was now his, made the possibility of living away from New England for a time — with no responsibilities except literary and familial ones — real and attractive. (Frost: A Literary Life Reconsidered, 1984, p. 4)

In 1912, despite the support from his grandfather he was so discouraged at his failure as a writer that he was close to emotional collapse, deeply depressed, and suicidal. In an effort to wrench himself free, he took the family to England, where they lived on his annuity. He formed a close friendship with Edward Thomas, a young English literary journalist, who began writing poetry himself after he had come to know Frost. Frost said of him later that he was "the only brother I ever had." His meetings with young English poets helped him to strip his poetry of its conventional imagery, and in 1913 he was able to find a publisher for his first book, A Boy's Will. An American expatriate living in London, Ezra Pound, wrote enthusiastically to American publishers about Frost's poetry and helped him find a publisher for North of Boston, which appeared in 1914. Included in the book were many of the poems that would make Frost famous, and it was an immediate success. When he returned to the United States a year later, Frost was an established writer, and he was able to find work as a teacher. He taught for many years at several schools, among them Harvard University, Amherst College, Middlebury College, and Dartmouth College, as well at the Bread Loaf School, a summer writing program that he founded and led until his death.

Frost was free of the economic worries that had plagued him for so long, but his life was not free of tragedy. His son committed suicide, and one daughter had to be confined to a mental institution. None of his family's unhappiness was directly mirrored in his poetry, which became more and more positive in tone as he grew older. Disengaging himself from the political turmoil of the 1930s, he refused to join other poets in their struggles to achieve a more just American society. As he wrote in the introduction to his Collected Poems in 1939, "I have given up my democratic prejudices and now willingly set the lower classes free to be completely taken care of by the upper classes. Political freedom is nothing to me. I bestow it right and left." At the same time, he was fiercely jealous of other poets, and he was painfully conscious that the attention of his early audience had drifted to the more modern work of writers such as T. S. Eliot, or the more politically aware poetry of Archibald MacLeish. His attacks on *their work often focused on their open poetic form. In the same introduction he wrote of their poetics, "It is painful to watch our sprung-rhythmists straining at the point of omitting one short from a foot for relief from monotony." In the emotional tides of World War II, Frost's poetry became a place of refuge and comfort for many readers, and despite the disillusionment of the 1950s, he never lost the place he had won in America's heart. There was mourning across the nation at his death in 1963.*

"The Pasture" was written shortly after the family had moved to England, and its description of the cow and her new calf in the spring pasture may have been inspired by home-sickness for their life in New Hampshire. Like all of Frost's poems about his experience as a farmer, "The Pasture" does not describe the reality of the farm but projects a wish that the reality might have been like that. It is this conscious presentation of idealized American experience that is at the heart of Frost's enduring popularity. Also composed in England, "Mending Wall" is unrhymed, but it is written in fluent iambic pentameter, the blank verse form that Shakespeare used for his plays. If Frost ever read Walt Whitman's poetry, with its free meter and unrhymed cadences, there is no sign of it in his own work. As he said, free verse was "like playing tennis with the net down."

In his early poetry Frost also showed a strong sense of drama, and he included several long narrative poems in his first books. The poems were stark and moody, and in them can be glimpsed some of his own unhappiness. One of the best known is "The Death of the Hired Man," a sorrowful description of an old farm laborer who has outlived his usefulness. Although the opening line suggests a freer meter, the poem is written in blank verse.

In "Birches" he returns to his characteristically skillful iambic pentameter. It is a poem that gives some hint of his desire to live his life more freely, even if it is only to swing on birch trees. As he writes, "Earth's the right place for love." The poem also has one of his most striking images, the description of the ice breaking loose from the frozen trees,

> *. . . They click upon themselves*
> *As the breeze rises, and turn many-colored*
> *As the stir cracks and crazes their enamel.*

"Fire and Ice" is only a little longer than an epigram, but in its few lines Frost manages to make a sardonic comment about the end of the world. His bitter lines can be read as an allusion to the image from the gospel song about the same moment of destruction, "no more water, fire next time." "To Earthward" describes the intense fire he felt in his early love, and now he finds that for him there is "no joy but lacks salt," and he longs to feel his old fervor again.

Frost's writing appears to be so effortless that many of his most popular poems seem as clear and as simple as someone describing the weather. At the same time they are complex examples of rhyme and diction. "Stopping by Woods on a Snowy Evening" is one of these familiar poems. The seemingly artless stanzas are actually tightly structured around a complicated rhyme scheme. Even if the reader's eye is not consciously analyzing the rhymes, the ear is hearing them.

"The Road Not Taken" is one of Frost's most popular poems, written in the United States a year after his return from England. Its metaphor of life as a journey, and the decision to make the journey down one of two roads, is a striking example of a

metaphor that is *the poem. Readers have sometimes noticed, however, that Frost makes it clear that the roads were actually so similar that each of them was worn "about the same." The poem was actually intended as a joke for his friend Edward Thomas. Thomas could never make up his mind about anything, and Frost teased him by saying, "No matter which road you take, you'll always sigh and wish you'd taken another." Frost sent the poem to Thomas in a letter, but his friend missed the joke entirely, thinking it was a poem about the decisions Frost had made in his own life. According to his biographer Lawrence Thompson, Frost never could bring himself to confess that the poem had not worked the way he had intended.*

Written in England, "After Apple-Picking" is another poem in which Frost uses a metaphor taken from his half-imagined country life to describe his emotions at his own death, and it reflects the disappointments he and his family had endured. He was only forty when he wrote it, and he would live another forty-five years. (See also Frost's "For travelers going sidereal" on p. 884.)

RELATED CASEBOOK: *See pages 1254–1264, including Rose C. Feld, "An Interview with Robert Frost," page 1255; Robert Frost, "The Figure a Poem Makes," page 1258; Robert Lowell, "On Robert Frost," page 1260; Joseph Brodsky, "On Grief and Reason," page 1260; Philip L. Gerber, "On Frost's 'After Apple-Picking,'" page 1262.*

ROBERT FROST

The Pasture

1913

I'm going out to clean the pasture spring;
I'll only stop to rake the leaves away
(And wait to watch the water clear, I may):
I shan't be gone long. — You come too.

I'm going out to fetch the little calf
That's standing by the mother. It's so young
It totters when she licks it with her tongue.
I shan't be gone long. — You come too.

ROBERT FROST

Mending Wall

1914

Something there is that doesn't love a wall,
That sends the frozen-ground-swell under it,
And spills the upper boulders in the sun;
And makes gaps even two can pass abreast.
The work of hunters is another thing:
I have come after them and made repair
Where they have left not one stone on a stone,
But they would have the rabbit out of hiding,
To please the yelping dogs. The gaps I mean,
No one has seen them made or heard them made,

But at spring mending-time we find them there.
I let my neighbor know beyond the hill;
And on a day we meet to walk the line
And set the wall between us once again.
We keep the wall between us as we go.
To each the boulders that have fallen to each.
And some are loaves and some so nearly balls
We have to use a spell to make them balance:
"Stay where you are until our backs are turned!"
We wear our fingers rough with handling them.
Oh, just another kind of outdoor game,
One on a side. It comes to little more:
There where it is we do not need the wall:
He is all pine and I am apple orchard.
My apple trees will never get across
And eat the cones under his pines, I tell him.
He only says, "Good fences make good neighbors."
Spring is the mischief in me, and I wonder
If I could put a notion in his head:
"*Why* do they make good neighbors? Isn't it
Where there are cows? But here there are no cows.
Before I built a wall I'd ask to know
What I was walling in or walling out,
And to whom I was like to give offense.
Something there is that doesn't love a wall,
That wants it down." I could say "Elves" to him,
But it's not elves exactly, and I'd rather
He said it for himself. I see him there
Bringing a stone grasped firmly by the top
In each hand, like an old-stone savage armed.
He moves in darkness as it seems to me,
Not of woods only and the shade of trees.
He will not go behind his father's saying,
And he likes having thought of it so well
He says again, "Good fences make good neighbors."

ROBERT FROST

The Death of the Hired Man

1914

Mary sat musing on the lamp-flame at the table
Waiting for Warren. When she heard his step,
She ran on tiptoe down the darkened passage
To meet him in the doorway with the news
And put him on his guard. "Silas is back."
She pushed him outward with her through the door

And shut it after her. "Be kind," she said.
She took the market things from Warren's arms
And set them on the porch, then drew him down
To sit beside her on the wooden steps.

"When was I ever anything but kind to him?
But I'll not have the fellow back," he said.
"I told him so last haying, didn't I?
If he left then, I said, that ended it.
What good is he? Who else will harbor him
At his age for the little he can do?
What help he is there's no depending on.
Off he goes always when I need him most.
He thinks he ought to earn a little pay,
Enough at least to buy tobacco with,
So he won't have to beg and be beholden.
'All right,' I say, 'I can't afford to pay
Any fixed wages, though I wish I could.'
'Someone else can.' 'Then someone else will have to.'
I shouldn't mind his bettering himself
If that was what it was. You can be certain,
When he begins like that, there's someone at him
Trying to coax him off with pocket money, —
In haying time, when any help is scarce.
In winter he comes back to us. I'm done."

"Sh! not so loud: he'll hear you," Mary said.
"I want him to: he'll have to soon or late."

"He's worn out. He's asleep beside the stove.
When I came up from Rowe's I found him here,
Huddled against the barn door fast asleep,
A miserable sight, and frightening, too —
You needn't smile — I didn't recognize him —
I wasn't looking for him — and he's changed.
Wait till you see."

"Where did you say he'd been?"

"He didn't say. I dragged him to the house,
And gave him tea and tried to make him smoke.
I tried to make him talk about his travels.
Nothing would do: he just kept nodding off."

"What did he say? Did he say anything?"

"But little."

"Anything? Mary, confess
He said he'd come to ditch the meadow for me."

"Warren!"

"But did he? I just want to know."

■ ■ ■

"Of course he did. What would you have him say?
Surely you wouldn't grudge the poor old man
Some humble way to save his self-respect.
He added, if you really care to know,
He meant to clear the upper pasture, too.
That sounds like something you have heard before?
Warren, I wish you could have heard the way
He jumbled everything. I stopped to look
Two or three times — he made me feel so queer —
To see if he was talking in his sleep.
He ran on Harold Wilson — you remember —
The boy you had in haying four years since.
He's finished school, and teaching in his college.
Silas declares you'll have to get him back.
He says they two will make a team for work:
Between them they will lay this farm as smooth!
The way he mixed that in with other things.
He thinks young Wilson a likely lad, though daft
On education — you know how they fought
All through July under the blazing sun,
Silas up on the cart to build the load,
Harold along beside to pitch it on."

"Yes, I took care to keep well out of earshot."

"Well, those days trouble Silas like a dream.
You wouldn't think they would. How some things linger!
Harold's young college boy's assurance piqued him.
After so many years he still keeps finding
Good arguments he sees he might have used.
I sympathize. I know just how it feels
To think of the right thing to say too late.
Harold's associated in his mind with Latin.
He asked me what I thought of Harold's saying
He studied Latin, like the violin,
Because he liked it — that an argument!
He said he couldn't make the boy believe
He could find water with a hazel prong —
Which showed how much good school had ever done him.
He wanted to go over that. But most of all
He thinks if he could have another chance
To teach him how to build a load of hay —"

"I know, that's Silas' one accomplishment.
He bundles every forkful in its place,
And tags and numbers it for future reference,
So he can find and easily dislodge it
In the unloading. Silas does that well.
He takes it out in bunches like big birds' nests.

You never see him standing on the hay
He's trying to lift, straining to lift himself."

"He thinks if he could teach him that, he'd be
Some good perhaps to someone in the world.
He hates to see a boy the fool of books.
Poor Silas, so concerned for other folk,
And nothing to look backward to with pride,
And nothing to look forward to with hope,
So now and never any different."

Part of a moon was falling down the west,
Dragging the whole sky with it to the hills.
Its light poured softly in her lap. She saw it
And spread her apron to it. She put out her hand
Among the harp-like morning-glory strings,
Taut with the dew from garden bed to eaves,
As if she played unheard some tenderness
That wrought on him beside her in the night.
"Warren," she said, "he has come home to die:
You needn't be afraid he'll leave you this time."

"Home," he mocked gently.

"Yes, what else but home?
It all depends on what you mean by home.
Of course he's nothing to us, any more
Than was the hound that came a stranger to us
Out of the woods, worn out upon the trail."

"Home is the place where, when you have to go there,
They have to take you in."

"I should have called it
Something you somehow haven't to deserve."

Warren leaned out and took a step or two,
Picked up a little stick, and brought it back
And broke it in his hand and tossed it by.
"Silas has better claim on us you think
Than on his brother? Thirteen little miles
As the road winds would bring him to his door.
Silas has walked that far no doubt to-day.
Why doesn't he go there? His brother's rich,
A somebody — director in the bank."

"He never told us that."

"We know it though."

"I think his brother ought to help, of course.
I'll see to that if there is need. He ought of right
To take him in, and might be willing to —
He may be better than appearances.

But have some pity on Silas. Do you think
If he had any pride in claiming kin
Or anything he looked for from his brother,
He'd keep so still about him all this time?"

"I wonder what's between them."

"I can tell you.
Silas is what he is — we wouldn't mind him —
But just the kind that kinfolk can't abide.
He never did a thing so very bad.
He don't know why he isn't quite as good
As anybody. Worthless though he is,
He won't be made ashamed to please his brother."

"*I* can't think Si ever hurt anyone."

"No, but he hurt my heart the way he lay
And rolled his old head on that sharp-edged chair-back.
He wouldn't let me put him on the lounge.
You must go in and see what you can do.
I made the bed up for him there tonight.
You'll be surprised at him — how much he's broken.
His working days are done; I'm sure of it."

"I'd not be in a hurry to say that."

I haven't been. Go, look, see for yourself.
But, Warren, please remember how it is:
He's come to help you ditch the meadow.
He has a plan. You mustn't laugh at him.
He may not speak of it, and then he may.
I'll sit and see if that small sailing cloud
Will hit or miss the moon."

It hit the moon.
Then there were three there, making a dim row,
The moon, the little silver cloud, and she.

Warren returned — too soon, it seemed to her,
Slipped to her side, caught up her hand and waited.
"Warren?" she questioned.

"Dead," was all he answered.

Robert Frost

Birches

1916

When I see birches bend to left and right
Across the lines of straighter darker trees,
I like to think some boy's been swinging them.
But swinging doesn't bend them down to stay

As ice-storms do. Often you must have seen them
Loaded with ice a sunny winter morning
After a rain. They click upon themselves
As the breeze rises, and turn many-colored
As the stir cracks and crazes their enamel.
Soon the sun's warmth makes them shed crystal shells
Shattering and avalanching on the snow-crust —
Such heaps of broken glass to sweep away
You'd think the inner dome of heaven had fallen.
They are dragged to the withered bracken by the load,
And they seem not to break; though once they are bowed
So low for long, they never right themselves:
You may see their trunks arching in the woods
Years afterwards, trailing their leaves on the ground
Like girls on hands and knees that throw their hair
Before them over their heads to dry in the sun.
But I was going to say when Truth broke in
With all her matter-of-fact about the ice-storm,
I should prefer to have some boy bend them
As he went out and in to fetch the cows —
Some boy too far from town to learn baseball,
Whose only play was what he found himself,
Summer or winter, and could play alone.
One by one he subdued his father's trees
By riding them down over and over again
Until he took the stiffness out of them,
And not one but hung limp, not one was left
For him to conquer. He learned all there was
To learn about not launching out too soon
And so not carrying the tree away
Clear to the ground. He always kept his poise
To the top branches, climbing carefully
With the same pains you use to fill a cup
Up to the brim, and even above the brim.
Then he flung outward, feet first, with a swish,
Kicking his way down through the air to the ground.
So was I once myself a swinger of birches.
And so I dream of going back to be.
It's when I'm weary of considerations,
And life is too much like a pathless wood
Where your face burns and tickles with the cobwebs
Broken across it, and one eye is weeping
From a twig's having lashed across it open.
I'd like to get away from earth awhile
And then come back to it and begin over.
May no fate willfully misunderstand me
And half grant what I wish and snatch me away

Not to return. Earth's the right place for love:
I don't know where it's likely to go better.
I'd like to go by climbing a birch tree,
And climb black branches up a snow-white trunk,
Toward heaven, till the tree could bear no more,
But dipped its top and set me down again.
That would be good both going and coming back.
One could do worse than be a swinger of birches.

Robert Frost

Fire and Ice

1923

Some say the world will end in fire,
Some say in ice.
From what I've tasted of desire
I hold with those who favor fire.
But if it had to perish twice,
I think I know enough of hate
To say that for destruction ice
Is also great
And would suffice.

Robert Frost

To Earthward

1923

Love at the lips was touch
As sweet as I could bear;
And once that seemed too much;
I lived on air

That crossed me from sweet things
The flow of — was it musk
From hidden grapevine springs
Down hill at dusk?

I had the swirl and ache
From sprays of honeysuckle
That when they're gathered shake
Dew on the knuckle.

I craved strong sweets, but those
Seemed strong when I was young;
The petal of the rose
It was that stung.

Now no joy but lacks salt
That is not dashed with pain

And weariness and fault;
I crave the stain

Of tears, the aftermark
Of almost too much love,
The sweet of bitter bark
And burning clove.

When stiff and sore and scarred
I take away my hand
From leaning on it hard
In grass and sand,

The hurt is not enough:
I long for weight and strength
To feel the earth as rough
To all my length.

ROBERT FROST

Stopping by Woods on a Snowy Evening 1923

Whose woods these are I think I know.
His house is in the village, though;
He will not see me stopping here
To watch his woods fill up with snow.

My little horse must think it queer
To stop without a farmhouse near
Between the woods and frozen lake
The darkest evening of the year.

He gives his harness bells a shake
To ask if there is some mistake.
The only other sound's the sweep
Of easy wind and downy flake.

The woods are lovely, dark and deep,
But I have promises to keep,
And miles to go before I sleep,
And miles to go before I sleep.

ROBERT FROST

The Road Not Taken 1916

Two roads diverged in a yellow wood,
And sorry I could not travel both
And be one traveler, long I stood
And looked down one as far as I could
To where it bent in the undergrowth;

■ ■ ■

Then took the other, as just as fair,
And having perhaps the better claim,
Because it was grassy and wanted wear;
Though as for that the passing there
Had worn them really about the same,

And both that morning equally lay
In leaves no step had trodden black.
Oh, I kept the first for another day!
Yet knowing how way leads on to way,
I doubted if I should ever come back.

I shall be telling this with a sigh
Somewhere ages and ages hence:
Two roads diverged in a wood, and I —
I took the one less traveled by,
And that has made all the difference.

Robert Frost

After Apple-Picking

1914

My long two-pointed ladder's sticking through a tree
Toward heaven still,
And there's a barrel that I didn't fill
Beside it, and there may be two or three
Apples I didn't pick upon some bough.
But I am done with apple-picking now.
Essence of winter sleep is on the night,
The scent of apples: I am drowsing off.
I cannot rub the strangeness from my sight
I got from looking through a pane of glass
I skimmed this morning from the drinking trough
And held against the world of hoary grass.
It melted, and I let it fall and break.
But I was well
Upon my way to sleep before it fell,
And I could tell
What form my dreaming was about to take.
Magnified apples appear and disappear,
Stem end and blossom end,
And every fleck of russet showing clear.
My instep arch not only keeps the ache,
It keeps the pressure of a ladder-round.
I feel the ladder sway as the boughs bend.
And I keep hearing from the cellar bin
The rumbling sound
Of load on load of apples coming in.

For I have had too much
Of apple-picking: I am overtired
Of the great harvest I myself desired.
There were ten thousand thousand fruit to touch,
Cherish in hand, lift down, and not let fall.
For all
That struck the earth,
No matter if not bruised or spiked with stubble,
Went surely to the cider-apple heap
As of no worth.
One can see what will trouble
This sleep of mine, whatever sleep it is.
Were he not gone,
The woodchuck could say whether it's like his
Long sleep, as I describe its coming on,
Or just some human sleep.

ALLEN GINSBERG *(b. 1926–1997) was born in Paterson, New Jersey. His father, Louis Ginsberg, taught high school English and also wrote conventional poetry. His mother, Naomi Ginsberg, was a committed leftist who struggled against intermittent bouts of mental instability. From 1944 to 1948 Ginsberg studied at Columbia University, where he met fledgling writers Jack Kerouac and William S. Burroughs, and with them formed a loose literary underground that would emerge as the Beat Generation. His life was chaotic as he struggled with his homosexuality and his own, and his friends', drug use. In 1949 he was hospitalized at the New York State Psychiatric Institute for eight months following an arrest for possession of stolen goods, which his friends had cached in his apartment. A dean from Columbia was able to have Ginsberg's jail sentence transmuted to psychiatric rehabilitation.*

In 1954 Ginsberg traveled to San Francisco by way of Mexico and immediately became part of the artistic ferment in the city. In the fall of 1955 he organized a reading for himself and some friends at a local art gallery, with poet Kenneth Rexroth as master of ceremonies. Ginsberg read the first part of a new poem called Howl *and roused such an excited response from the audience that it was clear that a new era had begun in American poetry. The poem was published in 1956 by fellow poet Lawrence Ferlinghetti's City Lights Press, and since that time it has sold nearly a million copies in different editions and has been translated into dozens of languages.*

As the most famous poet of his generation, Ginsberg led peace marches in the 1960s, traveled and read his poetry incessantly, and continued to write voluminously. He was a teacher, a guru for thousands of young students, and a poet-singer who toured with Bob Dylan and recorded with British rock bands. In his later years he was a professor of poetry at Brooklyn College in New York. Within a few hours of his death in 1997, the illuminated display of news headlines above New York's Times Square reported the "Beat Laureate" had died.

The following excerpt from Howl *is the section that he read aloud in 1955. His poetry was often written as a response to the events of his daily life, and "Mugging" describes his violent robbery by a young street gang close to his apartment on New York's Lower East Side.*

RELATED COMMENTARIES: *Allen Ginsberg, "On His Poetic Craft," page 1170; William Carlos Williams, "Introduction to* Howl,*" page 1228.*

ALLEN GINSBERG

From Howl

1956

for Carl Solomon°

I

I saw the best minds of my generation destroyed by madness, starving hysterical naked,
dragging themselves through the negro streets at dawn looking for an angry fix,
angelheaded hipsters burning for the ancient heavenly connection to the starry dynamo in the machinery of night,
who poverty and tatters and hollow-eyed and high sat up smoking in the supernatural darkness of cold-water flats floating across the tops of cities contemplating jazz,
who bared their brains to Heaven under the El and saw Mohammedan angels staggering on tenement roofs illuminated,
who passed through universities with radiant cool eyes hallucinating Arkansas and Blake-light° tragedy among the scholars of war,
who were expelled from the academies for crazy & publishing obscene odes on the windows of the skull,
who cowered in unshaven rooms in underwear, burning their money in wastebaskets and listening to the Terror through the wall,
who got busted in their pubic beards returning through Laredo with a belt of marijuana for New York,
who ate fire in paint hotels or drank turpentine in Paradise Alley, death, or purgatoried their torsos night after night
with dreams, with drugs, with waking nightmares, alcohol and cock and endless balls,
incomparable blind streets of shuddering cloud and lightning in the mind leaping toward poles of Canada & Paterson, illuminating all the motionless world of Time between,
Peyote solidities of halls, backyard green tree cemetery dawns, wine drunkenness over the rooftops, storefront boroughs of teahead joyride neon blinking traffic light, sun and moon and tree vibrations

---

for Carl Solomon: Solomon was a young poet and editor Ginsberg met as a fellow patient at the Psychiatric Institute. **6. Blake-light:** An allusion to the paintings of William Blake (1757–1827).

in the roaring winter dusks of Brooklyn, ashcan rantings and kind king light of mind,
who chained themselves to subways for the endless ride from Battery to holy Bronx on benzedrine until the noise of wheels and children brought them down shuddering mouth-wracked and battered bleak of brain all drained of brilliance in the drear light of Zoo,
who sank all night in submarine light of Bickford's floated out and sat through the stale beer afternoon in desolate Fugazzi's, listening to the crack of doom on the hydrogen jukebox,
who talked continuously seventy hours from park to pad to bar to Bellevue to museum to the Brooklyn Bridge,
a lost battalion of platonic conversationalists jumping down the stoops off fire escapes off windowsills off Empire State out of the moon,
yacketayakking screaming vomiting whispering facts and memories and anecdotes and eyeball kicks and shocks of hospitals and jails and wars,
whose intellects disgorged in total recall for seven days and nights with brilliant eyes, meat for the Synagogue cast on the pavement,
who vanished into nowhere Zen New Jersey leaving a trail of ambiguous picture postcards of Atlantic City Hall,
suffering Eastern sweats and Tangerian bone-grindings and migraines of China under junk-withdrawal in Newark's bleak furnished room,
who wandered around and around at midnight in the railroad yard wondering where to go, and went, leaving no broken hearts,
who lit cigarettes in boxcars boxcars boxcars racketing through snow toward lonesome farms in grandfather night,
who studied Plotinus° Poe° St. John of the Cross telepathy and bop kaballa because the cosmos instinctively vibrated at their feet in Kansas,
who loned it through the streets of Idaho seeking visionary indian angels who were visionary indian angels,
who thought they were only mad when Baltimore gleamed in supernatural ecstasy,
who jumped in limousines with the Chinaman of Oklahoma on the impulse of winter midnight streetlight smalltown rain,
who lounged hungry and lonesome through Houston seeking jazz or sex or soup, and followed the brilliant Spaniard to converse about America and Eternity, a hopeless task, and so took ship to Africa,
who disappeared into the volcanoes of Mexico leaving behind nothing but the shadow of dungarees and the lava and ash of poetry scattered in fireplace Chicago,
who reappeared on the West Coast investigating the F.B.I. in beards and shorts with big pacifist eyes sexy in their dark skin passing out incomprehensible leaflets,

---

24. Plotinus: Roman philosopher (205–270); **Poe:** Edgar Allan Poe (1809–1849, American writer).

who burned cigarette holes in their arms protesting the narcotic tobacco haze of Capitalism,
who distributed Supercommunist pamphlets in Union Square weeping and undressing while the sirens of Los Alamos° wailed them down, and wailed down Wall, and the Staten Island ferry also wailed,
who broke down crying in white gymnasiums naked and trembling before the machinery of other skeletons,
who bit detectives in the neck and shrieked with delight in policecars for committing no crime but their own wild cooking pederasty and intoxication,
who howled on their knees in the subway and were dragged off the roof waving genitals and manuscripts,
who let themselves be fucked in the ass by saintly motorcyclists, and screamed with joy,
who blew and were blown by those human seraphim, the sailors, caresses of Atlantic and Caribbean love,
who balled in the morning in the evenings in rosegardens and the grass of public parks and cemeteries scattering their semen freely to whomever come who may,
who hiccupped endlessly trying to giggle but wound up with a sob behind a partition in a Turkish Bath when the blonde & naked angel came to pierce them with a sword,
who lost their loveboys to the three old shrews of fate the one eyed shrew of the heterosexual dollar the one eyed shrew that winks out of the womb and the one eyed shrew that does nothing but sit on her ass and snip the intellectual golden threads of the craftsman's loom,
who copulated ecstatic and insatiate with a bottle of beer a sweetheart a package of cigarettes a candle and fell off the bed, and continued along the floor and down the hall and ended fainting on the wall with a vision of ultimate cunt and come eluding the last gyzym of consciousness,
who sweetened the snatches of a million girls trembling in the sunset, and were red eyed in the morning but prepared to sweeten the snatch of the sunrise, flashing buttocks under barns and naked in the lake,
who went out whoring through Colorado in myriad stolen night-cars, N.C.,° secret hero of these poems, cocksman and Adonis of Denver — joy to the memory of his innumerable lays of girls in empty lots & diner backyards, moviehouses' rickety rows, on mountaintops in caves or with gaunt waitresses in familiar roadside lonely petticoat upliftings & especially secret gas-station solipsisms of johns, & hometown alleys too,

---

32. Los Alamos: The site of the New Mexico laboratory in which the first atomic bombs were constructed. **43. N.C.:** Neal Cassady, a Denver dropout and hustler who was the hero of Jack Kerouac's 1957 novel, *On the Road*, and for a short period was Ginsberg's lover.

who faded out in vast sordid movies, were shifted in dreams, woke on a sudden Manhattan, and picked themselves up out of basements hungover with heartless Tokay and horrors of Third Avenue iron dreams & stumbled to unemployment offices,
who walked all night with their shoes full of blood on the snowbank docks waiting for a door in the East River to open to a room full of steamheat and opium,
who created great suicidal dramas on the apartment cliff-banks of the Hudson under the wartime blue floodlight of the moon & their heads shall be crowned with laurel in oblivion,
who ate the lamb stew of the imagination or digested the crab at the muddy bottom of the rivers of Bowery,
who wept at the romance of the streets with their pushcarts full of onions and bad music,
who sat in boxes breathing in the darkness under the bridge, and rose up to build harpsichords in their lofts,
who coughed on the sixth floor of Harlem crowned with flame under the tubercular sky surrounded by orange crates of theology,
who scribbled all night rocking and rolling over lofty incantations which in the yellow morning were stanzas of gibberish,
who cooked rotten animals lung heart feet tail borsht & tortillas dreaming of the pure vegetable kingdom,
who plunged themselves under meat trucks looking for an egg,
who threw their watches off the roof to cast their ballot for Eternity outside of Time, & alarm clocks fell on their heads every day for the next decade,
who cut their wrists three times successively unsuccessfully, gave up and were forced to open antique stores where they thought they were growing old and cried,
who were burned alive in their innocent flannel suits on Madison Avenue amid blasts of leaden verse & the tanked-up clatter of the iron regiments of fashion & the nitroglycerine shrieks of the fairies of advertising & the mustard gas of sinister intelligent editors, or were run down by the drunken taxicabs of Absolute Reality,
who jumped off the Brooklyn Bridge this actually happened and walked away unknown and forgotten into the ghostly daze of Chinatown soup alleyways & firetrucks, not even one free beer,
who sang out of their windows in despair, fell out of the subway window, jumped in the filthy Passaic, leaped on negroes, cried all over the street, danced on broken wineglasses barefoot smashed phonograph records of nostalgic European 1930's German jazz finished the whiskey and threw up groaning into the bloody toilet, moans in their ears and the blast of colossal steamwhistles,
who barreled down the highways of the past journeying to each other's hotrod-Golgotha jail-solitude watch or Birmingham jazz incarnation,

who drove crosscountry seventytwo hours to find out if I had a vision or you had a vision or he had a vision to find out Eternity,
who journeyed to Denver, who died in Denver, who came back to Denver & waited in vain, who watched over Denver & brooded & loned in Denver and finally went away to find out the Time, & now Denver is lonesome for her heroes,
who fell on their knees in hopeless cathedrals praying for each other's salvation and light and breasts, until the soul illuminated its hair for a second,
who crashed through their minds in jail waiting for impossible criminals with golden heads and the charm of reality in their hearts who sang sweet blues to Alcatraz,
who retired to Mexico to cultivate a habit, or Rocky Mount to tender Buddha or Tangiers to boys or Southern Pacific to the black locomotive or Harvard to Narcissus to Woodlawn to the daisychain or grave,
who demanded sanity trials accusing the radio of hypnotism & were left with their insanity & their hands & a hung jury,
who threw potato salad at CCNY° lectures on Dadaism and subsequently presented themselves on the granite steps of the madhouse with shaven heads and harlequin speech of suicide, demanding instantaneous lobotomy,
and who were given instead the concrete void of insulin metrasol electricity hydrotherapy psychotherapy occupational therapy pingpong & amnesia,
who in humorless protest overturned only one symbolic pingpong table, resting briefly in catatonia,
returning years later truly bald except for a wig of blood, and tears and fingers, to the visible madman doom of the wards of the madtowns of the East,
Pilgrim State's Rockland's and Greystone's foetid halls, bickering with the echoes of the soul, rocking and rolling in the midnight solitude-bench dolmen-realms of love, dream of life a nightmare, bodies turned to stone as heavy as the moon,
with mother finally ******, and the last fantastic book flung out of the tenement window, and the last door closed at 4 AM and the last telephone slammed at the wall in reply and the last furnished room emptied down to the last piece of mental furniture, a yellow paper rose twisted on a wire hanger in the closet, and even that imaginary, nothing but a hopeful little bit of hallucination —
ah, Carl, while you are not safe I am not safe, and now you're really in the total animal soup of time —
and who therefore ran through the icy streets obsessed with a sudden flash of the alchemy of the use of the ellipse the catalog the meter & the vibrating plane,

---

66. CCNY: City College of New York.

who dreamt and made incarnate gaps in Time & Space through images juxtaposed, and trapped the archangel of the soul between 2 visual images and joined the elemental verbs and set the noun and dash of consciousness together jumping with sensation of Pater Omnipotens Aeterna Deus
to recreate the syntax and measure of poor human prose and stand before you speechless and intelligent and shaking with shame, rejected yet confessing out the soul to conform to the rhythm of thought in his naked and endless head,
the madman bum and angel beat in Time, unknown, yet putting down here what might be left to say in time come after death,
and rose reincarnate in the ghostly clothes of jazz in the goldhorn shadow of the band and blew the suffering of America's naked mind for love into an eli eli lamma lamma sabacthani° saxophone cry that shivered the cities down to the last radio
with the absolute heart of the poem of life butchered out of their own bodies good to eat a thousand years.

ALLEN GINSBERG

Mugging

1977

I

Tonite I walked out of my red apartment door on East tenth street's dusk —
Walked out of my home ten years, walked out in my honking neighborhood
Tonite at seven walked out past garbage cans chained to concrete anchors
Walked under black painted fire escapes, giant castiron plate covering a hole in ground
— Crossed the street, traffic lite red, thirteen bus roaring by liquor store,
past corner pharmacy iron grated, past Coca Cola & Mylai° posters fading scraped on brick
Past Chinese Laundry wood door'd, & broken cement stoop steps For Rent hall painted green & purple Puerto Rican style
Along E. 10th's glass splattered pavement, kid blacks & Spanish oiled hair adolescents' crowded house fronts —
Ah, tonite I walked out on my block NY City under humid summer sky Halloween
thinking what happened Timothy Leary° joining brain police for a season?

77. eli . . . sabacthani: Words from a chanted prayer.
6. Mylai: Vietnamese village whose inhabitants were massacred by U.S. forces. **10. Timothy Leary:** Political activist (1920–1996) who advocated use of the drug LSD in the 1960s.

thinking what's all this Weathermen,° secrecy & selfrighteousness
beyond reason — F.B.I. plots?
Walked past a taxicab controlling the bottle strewn curb —
past young fellows with their umbrella handles & canes leaning against
a ravaged Buick
— and as I looked at the crowd of kids on the stoop — a boy stepped up,
put his arm around my neck
tenderly I thought for a moment, squeezed harder, his umbrella handle
against my skull,
and his friends took my arm, a young brown companion tripped his foot
'gainst my ankle —
as I went down shouting Om Ah Hūṃ° to gangs of lovers on the stoop
watching
slowly appreciating, why this is a raid, these strangers mean strange
business
with what — my pockets, bald head, broken-healed-bone leg, my soft-
shoes, my heart —
Have they knives? Om Ah Hūṃ — Have they sharp metal wood to
shove in eye ear ass? Om Ah Hūṃ
& slowly reclined on the pavement, struggling to keep my woolen bag
of poetry address calendar & Leary-lawyer° notes hung from my
shoulder
dragged in my neat orlon shirt over the crossbar of a broken metal door
dragged slowly onto the fire-soiled floor an abandoned store, laundry
candy counter 1929 —
now a mess of papers & pillows & plastic car seat covers cracked
cockroach-corpsed ground —
my wallet back pocket passed over the iron foot step guard
and fell out, stole by God Muggers' lost fingers, Strange —
Couldn't tell — snakeskin wallet actually plastic, 70 dollars my bank
money for a week,
old broken wallet — and dreary plastic contents — Amex card & Manf.
Hanover Trust Credit too — business card from Mr. Spears British
Home Minister Drug Squad — my draft card — membership ACLU
& Naropa Institute° Instructor's identification
Om Ah Hūṃ I continued chanting Om Ah Hūṃ
Putting my palm on the neck of an 18 year old boy fingering my back
pocket crying "Where's the money"
"Om Ah Hūṃ there isn't any"
My card Chief Boo-Hoo Neo American Church New Jersey & Lower
East Side

---

11. Weathermen: Radical political group of the 1960s. **17. Om Ah Hūṃ:** Buddhist chant intended to achieve calm. **21. Leary-lawyer:** Timothy Leary was tried and imprisoned for his activities. **28. Naropa Institute:** The school which Ginsberg helped found in Boulder, Colorado.

Om Ah Hūṃ — what not forgotten crowded wallet — Mobil Credit, Shell? old lovers addresses on cardboard pieces, booksellers calling cards —
— "Shut up or we'll murder you" — "Om Ah Hūṃ take it easy"
Lying on the floor shall I shout more loud? — the metal door closed on blackness
one boy felt my broken healed ankle, looking for hundred dollar bills behind my stocking weren't even there — a third boy untied my Seiko Hong Kong watch rough from right wrist leaving a clasp-prick skin tiny bruise
"Shut up and we'll get out of here" — and so they left,
as I rose from the cardboard mattress thinking Om Ah Hūṃ didn't stop em enough,
the tone of voice too loud — my shoulder bag with 10,000 dollars full of poetry left on the broken floor —

November 2, 1974

II

Went out the door dim eyed, bent down & picked up my glasses from step edge I placed them while dragged in the store — looked out —
Whole street a bombed-out face, building rows' eyes & teeth missing
burned apartments half the long block, gutted cellars, hallways' charred beams
hanging over trash plaster mounded entrances, couches & bedsprings rusty after sunset
Nobody home, but scattered stoopfuls of scared kids frozen in black hair
chatted giggling at house doors in black shoes, families cooked For Rent some six story houses mid the street's wreckage
Nextdoor Bodega,° a phone, the police? "I just got mugged" I said
to the man's face under fluorescent grocery light tin ceiling —
puffy, eyes blank & watery, sickness of beer kidney and language tongue
thick lips stunned as my own eyes, poor drunken Uncle minding the store!
O hopeless city of idiots empty eyed staring afraid, red beam top'd car at street curb arrived —
"Hey maybe my wallet's still on the ground got a flashlight?"
Back into the burnt-doored cave, & the policeman's gray flashlight broken no eyebeam —
"My partner all he wants is sit in the car never gets out Hey Joe bring your flashlight —
A tiny throwaway beam, dim as a match in the criminal dark
"No I can't see anything here" . . . "Fill out this form"

46. Bodega: Neighborhood grocery in Hispanic areas.

Neighborhood street crowd behind a car "We didn't see nothing"
Stoop young girls, kids laughing "Listen man last time I messed with
them see this —"
rolled up his skinny arm shirt, a white knife scar on his brown shoulder
"Besides we help you the cops come down don't know anybody we all
get arrested
go to jail I never help no more mind my business everytime"
"Agh!" upstreet think "Gee I don't know anybody here ten years lived
half block crost Avenue C°
and who knows who?" — passing empty apartments, old lady with
frayed paper bags
sitting in the tin-boarded doorframe of a dead house.

December 10, 1974

ꕥ

LOUISE GLÜCK *(b. 1943) was born and grew up in New York City, where her father was a business executive. She studied at Sarah Lawrence College and received her B.A. from Columbia University in 1965. She has been married twice and has a son and is at present a faculty member at Warren Wilson College in North Carolina.*

Glück's first book, Firstborn, *was published in 1968, and it established her themes of family and her personal life. The critic Helen Vendler has said of Glück's poems, "She sees experience from very far off, almost through the end of a telescope, transparently removed in space or time. It is this removal which gives such mythological power . . . to the account of her parents' lives and of her own childhood, and makes their family constellation into a universal one." Glück's book* Ararat, *which was in part an emotional response to her father's death, won the Pulitzer Prize in 1990.*

Although Glück's early poetry was often shadowed by an effort to understand her unhappy childhood, more recent poems, like "Widows," "Terminal Resemblance," and "First Memory," suggest that she has come to accept the complexities of her own experience.

RELATED COMMENTARIES: *Louise Glück, "Poems Are Autobiography," page 1175; Helen Vendler, "On Louise Glück," page 1226.*

LOUISE GLÜCK

Widows *1990*

My mother's playing cards with my aunt,
Spite and Malice, the family pastime, the game
my grandmother taught all her daughters.
Midsummer: too hot to go out.
Today, my aunt's ahead; she's getting the good cards.
My mother's dragging, having trouble with her concentration.

---

61. Avenue C: The cross street close to Ginsberg's apartment.

She can't get used to her own bed this summer.
She had no trouble last summer,
getting used to the floor. She learned to sleep there
to be near my father.
He was dying; he got a special bed.

My aunt doesn't give an inch, doesn't make
allowance for my mother's weariness.
It's how they were raised: you show respect by fighting.
To let up insults the opponent.

Each player has one pile to the left, five cards in the hand.
It's good to stay inside on days like this,
to stay where it's cool.
And this is better than other games, better than solitaire.

My grandmother thought ahead; she prepared her daughters.
They have cards; they have each other.
They don't need any more companionship.

All afternoon the game goes on but the sun doesn't move.
It just keeps beating down, turning the grass yellow.
That's how it must seem to my mother.
And then, suddenly, something is over.

My aunt's been at it longer; maybe that's why she's playing better.
Her cards evaporate: that's what you want, that's the object: in the end,
the one who has nothing wins.

Louise Glück

Terminal Resemblance

1990

When I saw my father for the last time, we both did the same thing.
He was standing in the doorway to the living room,
waiting for me to get off the telephone.
That he wasn't also pointing to his watch
was a signal he wanted to talk.

Talk for us always meant the same thing.
He'd say a few words. I'd say a few back.
That was about it.

It was the end of August, very hot, very humid.
Next door, workmen dumped new gravel on the driveway.

My father and I avoided being alone;
we didn't know how to connect, to make small talk —
there didn't seem to be
any other possibilities.
So this was special: when a man's dying,
he has a subject.

■ ■ ■

It must have been early morning. Up and down the street
sprinklers started coming on. The gardener's truck
appeared at the end of the block,
then stopped, parking.

My father wanted to tell me what it was like to be dying.
He told me he wasn't suffering.
He said he kept expecting pain, waiting for it, but it never came.
All he felt was a kind of weakness.
I said I was glad for him, that I thought he was lucky.

Some of the husbands were getting in their cars, going to work.
Not people we knew anymore. New families,
families with young children.
The wives stood on the steps, gesturing or calling.

We said goodbye in the usual way,
no embrace, nothing dramatic.
When the taxi came, my parents watched from the front door,
arm in arm, my mother blowing kisses as she always does,
because it frightens her when a hand isn't being used.
But for a change, my father didn't just stand there.
This time, he waved.

That's what I did, at the door to the taxi.
Like him, waved to disguise my hand's trembling.

Louise Glück

First Memory 1990

Long ago, I was wounded. I lived
to revenge myself
against my father, not
for what he was —
for what I was: from the beginning of time,
in childhood, I thought
that pain meant
I was not loved.
It meant I loved.

ꙮ

Robert Hayden *(1913–1980) was born in Detroit. When he was three his mother, Asa Sheffey, decided that she wanted to live her own life, and although she never lost contact with her son, she gave him to a working couple named Hayden to raise. His adoptive father worked when he could as a day laborer, and Hayden grew up in poverty in the Detroit ghetto. As a boy, Hayden was small and extremely near-sighted, and he spent many hours alone reading.*

By his teens, he was already absorbed by literature, and Hayden's was a generation of African Americans who no longer felt excluded from mainstream American intellectual culture. His early poetic models were the African American writer Countee Cullen and the white poet Elinor Wylie. When Hayden graduated from high school, America was entering the depression. He attended Detroit City College until 1936, then was employed by the WPA Federal Writer's Project until the war. He married in 1940 and entered the University of Michigan, where he studied under the English poet W. H. Auden, who had recently moved to the United States.

From 1946 until 1969 Hayden taught at Fisk University in Nashville while also writing and publishing steadily. An early book had been published in 1940, but Hayden did not achieve wide recognition until 1966, when he was awarded the Grand Prize for Poetry for A Ballad of Remembrance *at the First World Festival of Negro Arts in Senegal. At the same time he had become reluctantly involved in the debate over political consciousness that was shaking the black literary world. Younger African American writers accused him of accommodating his writing to the white culture and refused to listen to his argument that he considered himself part of a literary culture that had no racial boundaries. The angry disagreement was one of his reasons for leaving Fisk.*

Hayden was awarded many literary prizes and honors. For four years he was Consultant in Poetry to the Library of Congress, a position that now has the title of poet laureate. In January 1980, a month before his death, he took part in a reading at the White House.

"Those Winter Sundays" is Hayden's best-known poem, describing his father in Detroit. "A Letter from Phillis Wheatley," from his last book, is an evocative portrait of the first published African American writer, and "Frederick Douglass" is his tribute to the nineteenth-century escaped slave and abolitionist leader.

RELATED COMMENTARIES: *Robert Hayden, "On Negro Poetry," page 1177; David Huddle, "The 'Banked Fire' of Robert Hayden's 'Those Winter Sundays,'" page 1182.*

ROBERT HAYDEN

Those Winter Sundays

1962

Sundays too my father got up early
and put his clothes on in the blueblack cold,
then with cracked hands that ached
from labor in the weekday weather made
banked fires blaze. No one ever thanked him.

I'd wake and hear the cold splintering, breaking.
When the rooms were warm, he'd call,
and slowly I would rise and dress,
fearing the chronic angers of that house,

Speaking indifferently to him,
who had driven out the cold

and polished my good shoes as well.
What did I know, what did I know
of love's austere and lonely offices?

Robert Hayden

A Letter from Phillis Wheatley *1978*

London, 1773

Dear Obour°
        Our crossing was without
event. I could not help, at times,
reflecting on that first — my Destined —
voyage long ago (I yet
have some remembrance of its Horrors)
and marvelling at God's Ways.
        Last evening, her Ladyship presented me
to her illustrious Friends.
I scarce could tell them anything
of Africa, though much of Boston
and my hope of Heaven. I read
my latest Elegies to them.
"O Sable Muse!" the Countess cried,
embracing me, when I had done.
I held back tears, as is my wont,
and there were tears in Dear
Nathaniel's eyes.
        At supper — I dined apart
like captive Royalty —
the Countess and her Guests promised
signatures affirming me
True Poetess, albeit once a slave.
Indeed, they were most kind, and spoke,
moreover, of presenting me
at Court (I thought of Pocahontas) —
an Honor, to be sure, but one,
I should, no doubt, as Patriot decline.
        My health is much improved;
I feel I may, if God so Wills,
entirely recover here.

1. **Obour:** Obour Tanner, a former slave who was one of Wheatley's friends.

Robert Hayden

Frederick Douglass°
1966

When it is finally ours, this freedom, this liberty, this beautiful
and terrible thing, needful to man as air,
usable as earth; when it belongs at last to all,
when it is truly instinct, brain matter, diastole, systole,
reflex action; when it is finally won; when it is more
than the gaudy mumbo jumbo of politicians:
this man, this Douglass, this former slave, this Negro
beaten to his knees, exiled, visioning a world
where none is lonely, none hunted, alien,
this man, superb in love and logic, this man
shall be remembered. Oh, not with statues' rhetoric,
not with legends and poems and wreaths of bronze alone,
but with the lives grown out of his life, the lives
fleshing his dream of the beautiful, needful thing.

Seamus Heaney *(b. 1939) was born in Ireland, in Castledown in County Kerry. He grew up in a small farming community, and this has shaped his writing and his outlook on the world. He trained as a teacher and after teaching in a secondary school for a year he returned to the university and completed his studies in English at Queen's College in Belfast. Belfast is the capital of Northern Ireland, and Heaney has spent his life in the midst of the violent struggle for political power between the province's Catholic minority and Protestant majority. He became a lecturer at Queen's College and in 1966 his first collection,* Death of a Naturalist, *appeared.*

In the years since then, Heaney has continued to teach, to study the work of other poets, and to write. He has won nearly every major literary prize in England and Ireland and was awarded the Nobel Prize in 1995. For extended periods he has been a guest lecturer at Harvard University and Oxford University. As an Irish writer who is also a Catholic he has felt considerable pressure to become engaged in the effort of the Irish minority in the north to end the ties between the Protestant majority, which is largely of Scottish descent, and England, which maintains the status quo with a large military force. Although he is sympathetic to the Catholic minority's aims, he is deeply disturbed by the use of violence by the IRA, the underground Irish Republican Army. He has written poems that lament the present situation, but he has also insisted that this is not the role of poetry. As he wrote in his essay "The Redress of Poetry," "Poetry cannot afford to lose its fundamentally self-delighting inventiveness, its joy in being a process of language as well as a representation of things in the world."

Frederick Douglass (1817–1895), an escaped slave who became a leading speaker and agitator in the antislavery movement.

"Digging," from Death of a Naturalist, *is one of his most frequently anthologized poems. "The Guttural Muse" is from his 1979 collection* Field Work.

Seamus Heaney

Digging

1966

Between my finger and my thumb
The squat pen rests; snug as a gun.

Under my window, a clean rasping sound
When the spade sinks into gravelly ground:
My father, digging. I look down

Till his straining rump among the flowerbeds
Bends low, comes up twenty years away
Stooping in rhythm through potato drills°
Where he was digging.

The coarse boot nestled on the lug, the shaft
Against the inside knee was levered firmly.
He rooted out tall tops, buried the bright edge deep
To scatter new potatoes that we picked
Loving their cool hardness in our hands.

By god, the old man could handle a spade.
Just like his old man.

My grandfather cut more turf° in a day
Than any other man on Toner's bog.
Once I carried him milk in a bottle
Corked sloppily with paper. He straightened up
To drink it, then fell to right away
Nicking and slicing neatly, heaving sods
Over his shoulder, going down and down
For the good turf. Digging.

The cold smell of potato mould, the squelch and slap
Of soggy peat, the curt cuts of an edge
Through living roots awaken in my head.
But I've no spade to follow men like them.

Between my finger and my thumb
The squat pen rests.
I'll dig with it.

8. drills: Furrows in which seeds are sown. **17. turf:** Bricks of peat used for fuel.

Seamus Heaney

The Guttural Muse

1979

Late summer, and at midnight
I smelt the heat of the day:
At my window over the hotel car park
I breathed the muddied night airs off the lake
And watched a young crowd leave the discotheque.

Their voices rose up thick and comforting
As oily bubbles the feeding tench sent up
That evening at dusk — the slimy tench
Once called the "doctor fish" because his slime
Was said to heal the wounds of fish that touched it.

A girl in a white dress
Was being courted out among the cars:
As her voice swarmed and puddled into laughs
I felt like some old pike all badged with sores
Wanting to swim in touch with soft-mouthed life.

❧

LANGSTON HUGHES *(1902–1967), who was to become America's best-known African American writer, was one of the first American poets to reach a wide audience with a direct, personal poetic style created from the rhythms and language of everyday black speech. When we read him today we see only the depth of his accomplishment, but it was achieved by a lifetime of dedication to his goal, which was to create a voice for the African American community. He lived for many years alone in his small Harlem apartment, and there were years of discouraging poverty. His determination, however — and his optimism — never wavered. As his biographer Arnold Rampersad wrote, the greatest truth of Hughes's life was that "in his chronic loneliness, true satisfaction came only from the love and regard of the black race, which he earned by placing his finest gift, his skill with language, in its service."*

He was born in Joplin, Missouri, but his parents separated, and he spent most of his childhood with his maternal grandmother in Lawrence, Kansas. His father, angry at racial intolerance but prejudiced himself against darker-skinned blacks, moved to Mexico. His mother settled in Cleveland. His grandmother was emotionally reserved, and he yearned for more contact with his mother, but his grandmother gave him a strong sense of racial pride that never left him. She was the widow of one of the men killed in the battle at Harpers Ferry, Virginia, in 1859, when a small group under the leadership of abolitionist John Brown attempted to ignite a rebellion in the South by capturing the federal arsenal there and seizing weapons to arm southern slaves. Hughes heard the story from her many times, and sometimes she covered him in bed with her husband's bullet-torn shawl.

Hughes's grandmother died when he was thirteen, and he went to live with his mother in Cleveland, Ohio. He was already writing poetry. He once humorously described how he was chosen to be class poet for his graduation from Central High School, where he and a girl were the only black class members.

> *My classmates, knowing that a poem had to have rhythm, elected me unanimously — thinking, no doubt, that I had some, being a Negro. . . . In the first half of the poem, I said that our school had the finest teachers that there ever were. And in the latter half, I said our class was the greatest class ever graduated. Naturally everybody applauded loudly. That was the way I began to write poetry.*

He was elected, however, because he was popular with other students, competed on the track team, and, as his English teacher told an interviewer when his first book appeared, he was one of the most gifted members of his class.

Following his graduation he went to live in Mexico with his father, who was impatient with his literary ambitions. In Mexico, where he stayed for several months, Hughes learned Spanish and wrote the poem "The Negro Speaks of Rivers," which was published in 1921 in The Crisis, *an intellectual journal edited by the Harlem writer and activist W. E. B. Du Bois. Uncomfortable with his father, who wanted him to study to be an engineer, Hughes returned to the United States, lived in Harlem, and attended Columbia University for a year. Restless again, he drifted for several years while he struggled to find a way to write the poetry and prose he dreamed of, and to support himself doing it. He worked as a seaman, traveling to Africa and northern Europe. For some months in 1924 he shared a small apartment in Paris with a Russian ballet dancer, then after a trip to Italy he returned to the United States, painting and scrubbing the decks on a tramp steamer to earn his fare. He spent most of the next year in Washington, D.C., working first for the Association for the Study of Negro Life and History, then as a busboy in the dining room of the Wardman Park Hotel.*

Although still in his early twenties Hughes was considered one of the most promising members of the cultural movement called the Harlem Renaissance, a talented gathering of writers, artists, and musicians, who were creating a new African American consciousness. A bohemian white writer, photographer, and active supporter of the movement named Carl Van Vechten became interested in Hughes's poetry and recommended him to his own publisher. Van Vechten also chose the title, The Weary Blues, *for Hughes's first poetry collection. Hughes was waiting for the book to appear at the time he was working in Washington. His breakthrough as a writer came through his job. The popular poet Vachel Lindsay stayed over at the hotel on one of his reading tours, and Hughes left some of his poems at Lindsay's place in the dining room. Lindsay read them with interest and at his reading announced to his audience that he had found a poet right there at the hotel, and a Negro poet at that. The next morning reporters from several white newspapers were waiting to interview the "busboy poet."*

In 1925 Hughes won his first prize as a poet, and after some months back in Harlem he returned to school, this time at Lincoln University, in Pennsylvania. He also continued to write poetry, attempted an unsuccessful collaboration on a play with Zora Neale Hurston, and he was encouraged to begin his first novel, Not without Laughter, *by a wealthy white woman who had become the financial patron of several Harlem writers. In 1931 he traveled through the southern states, reading his poetry to schools and private gatherings and using his poems to encourage his audiences to live their lives as fully as they could, despite the harsh reality of racial segregation. The racism he encountered affected him so deeply that the next year he traveled to Moscow with a group of Harlem writers and actors, and when the project collapsed he stayed in the Soviet Union for almost a year. When he came back to the United States he became politically active in several groups connected to the Communist party, although he was never a party member. Many of his poems in the 1930s reflected his emotional response to these early years of the Soviet experiment. In the late 1930s he supported the Loyalist government during the Spanish Civil War, and he spent months as a war correspondent in Madrid during the siege of the city, sharing quarters with other sympathetic writers like Ernest Hemingway and John Steinbeck. When it was clear that the struggle was hopeless, he returned to the United States.*

Back in Harlem, Hughes became a public figure, working as a journalist, founding black theater groups, editing anthologies of black writing, and writing poetry, plays, and essays. He actively supported the U.S. war effort when the nation entered World War II in 1941. In 1943 he created the character of Jesse B. Semple, a Harlem Everyman called "Simple" by his friends, who commented with shrewd intelligence on the world of Harlem and its place in the larger world of American society. The "Simple Stories" were first published in a Harlem newspaper, then gathered into four very successful collections. After the war Hughes was questioned about his Communist sympathies by the House Un-American Activities Committee, but he was not blacklisted, as were many Americans involved in the arts during the McCarthy era. He continued to write poetry and create works for the theater and to support the work of other African American creative artists, among them young writers, painters, and jazz musicians, until his death in 1967.

In this selection from Langston Hughes's poetry you will find many of his recurring themes. "The Negro Speaks of Rivers," written while he was still a teenager and strongly influenced by the midwestern poet Carl Sandburg, is a haunting expression of the rich sense of history in his poetry, even though the language is direct and uncomplicated. "Mother to Son" explores the theme of family and the difficulties of everyday life. "I, Too," which borrows some of its language and style from Walt Whitman, is an expression of Hughes's consciousness of his blackness and his certainty of the worth of his blackness, even if now he is forced to "eat in the kitchen." "Bound No'th Blues" is one of the many poems he wrote in the blues form. In a blues verse the first two lines are repeated, often with small variations, and a third line concludes the idea of the first two lines and rhymes with them. The first two lines of Hughes's poem represent the first line of a blues verse; then he repeats the words, with slight variations; and the last two lines of his verse represent the third line of the blues, concluding his thought and completing the rhyme. He was the first poet to use the blues form successfully, and he used it with continued skill for many years.

The tragedy of lynching is the subject of "Song for a Dark Girl," which quotes a line from the song "Dixie" as a sardonic comment on southern racism. Hughes is becoming much more engaged politically in poems like "Song for a Dark Girl," "House in the World," and "Florida Road Workers," although he is still writing in a language that is deceptively simple and immediate in its appeal. The speaker in "House in the World" despairs that he and his "dark brothers" will never be free of white domination, and the poor worker who is building the road in Florida cheers himself up by proclaiming proudly that even if it is only rich people who will get to "sweep over" his road he will "get to see 'em ride." Hughes's turn away from this kind of public poetry can be marked in the simple but enigmatic poem "Personal." "Little Lyric (Of Great Importance)*" reflects his response to Harlem and his neighbors' worries.*

Although there was a consciousness in America in the 1960s that the problem of racism had to be faced, Hughes lived through the violence of the voter registration drives in the southern states, and the turbulence of the efforts of the "Freedom Riders," northern students who came by the busload into the south, to challenge the legality of segregated public facilities. In poems like "Merry-Go-Round" and the well-known "Theme for English B" he continues to protest against racism, though in these poems the protest is expressed in wry, half-amused terms. The protest in "Down Where I Am" is presented wearily by someone who has been fighting prejudice for a long time and insists now that if anyone wants to see them, they'll have to, as the poem says in its closing line, "come down." In his famous poem "Dream Deferred" — the source of the phrase "raisin in the sun" which Lorraine Hansberry later used as the title of her well-known play — the speaker's patience is worn thin. The "dream deferred" is the dream of racial equality, and the speaker suggests that if the dream does not come true soon, there might be an explosion. It was a prophecy that was fulfilled in the months before his death, as in one city after another the ghettoes exploded into violence and rioting.

RELATED COMMENTARY: *Robert Hayden, "On Negro Poetry," page 1177.*

RELATED CASEBOOK: *See pages 1265–1271, including Langston Hughes, "A Toast to Harlem," page 1266; Jessie Fauset, "Meeting Langston Hughes," page 1267; Richard Wright, "A Review of* The Big Sea,*" page 1269; Arnold Rampersad, "Langston Hughes as Folk Poet," page 1270.*

LANGSTON HUGHES

The Negro Speaks of Rivers — *1921*

I've known rivers:
I've known rivers ancient as the world and older than the
flow of human blood in human veins.

My soul has grown deep like the rivers.
I bathed in the Euphrates when dawns were young.
I built my hut near the Congo and it lulled me to sleep.
I looked upon the Nile and raised the Pyramids above it.
I heard the singing of the Mississippi when Abe Lincoln
went down to New Orleans, and I've seen its muddy
bosom turn all golden in the sunset.

I've known rivers:
Ancient, dusky rivers.

My soul has grown deep like the rivers.

LANGSTON HUGHES

Mother to Son — *1926*

Well, son, I'll tell you:
Life for me ain't been no crystal stair.
It's had tacks in it,

And splinters,
And boards torn up,
And places with no carpet on the floor —
Bare.
But all the time
I'se been a-climbin' on,
And reachin' landin's,
And turnin' corners,
And sometimes goin' in the dark
Where there ain't been no light.
So boy, don't you turn back.
Don't you set down on the steps
'Cause you finds it's kinder hard.
Don't you fall now —
For I'se still goin', honey,
I'se still climbin',
And life for me ain't been no crystal stair.

LANGSTON HUGHES

I, Too

1926

I, too, sing America.

I am the darker brother.
They send me to eat in the kitchen
When company comes,
But I laugh,
And eat well,
And grow strong.

Tomorrow,
I'll be at the table
When company comes.
Nobody'll dare
Say to me,
"Eat in the kitchen,"
Then.

Besides,
They'll see how beautiful I am
And be ashamed —

I, too, am America.

Langston Hughes

Bound No'th Blues 1927

Goin' down the road, Lawd,
Goin' down the road.
Down the road, Lawd,
Way, way down the road.
Got to find somebody
To help me carry this load.

Road's in front o' me,
Nothin' to do but walk.
Road's in front o' me,
Walk . . . an' walk . . . an' walk.
I'd like to meet a good friend
To come along an' talk.

Hates to be lonely,
Lawd, I hates to be sad.
Says I hates to be lonely,
Hates to be lonely an' sad,
But ever friend you finds seems
Like they try to do you bad.

Road, road, road, O!
Road, road . . . road . . . road, road!
Road, road, road, O!
On the no'thern road.
These Mississippi towns ain't
Fit fer a hoppin' toad.

Langston Hughes

Song for a Dark Girl 1927

Way Down South in Dixie
        (Break the heart of me)
They hung my black young lover
        To a cross roads tree.

Way Down South in Dixie
        (Bruised body high in air)
I asked the white Lord Jesus
        What was the use of prayer.

Way Down South in Dixie
        (Break the heart of me)
Love is a naked shadow
        On a gnarled and naked tree.

Langston Hughes

House in the World
1931

I'm looking for a house
In the world
Where the white shadows
Will not fall.

There is no such house,
Dark brothers,
No such house
At all.

Langston Hughes

Florida Road Workers
1931

Hey, Buddy!
Look at me!

I'm makin' a road
For the cars to fly by on,
Makin' a road
Through the palmetto thicket
For light and civilization
To travel on.

I'm makin' a road
For the rich to sweep over
In their big cars
And leave me standin' here.

Sure,
A road helps everybody.
Rich folks ride —
And I get to see 'em ride.
I ain't never seen nobody
Ride so fine before.

Hey, Buddy, look!
I'm makin' a road!

Langston Hughes

Personal
1933

In an envelope marked:
    Personal
God addressed me a letter.

In an envelope marked:
Personal.
I have given my answer.

LANGSTON HUGHES

Little Lyric (Of Great Importance) *1942*

I wish the rent
Was heaven sent.

LANGSTON HUGHES

Merry-Go-Round *1942*

Colored child at carnival

Where is the Jim Crow section
On this merry-go-round,
Mister, cause I want to ride?
Down South where I come from
White and colored
Can't sit side by side.
Down South on the train
There's a Jim Crow car.
On the bus we're put in the back —
But there ain't no back
To a merry-go-round!
Where's the horse
For a kid that's black?

LANGSTON HUGHES

Down Where I Am *1950*

Too many years
Beatin' at the door —
I done beat my
Both fists sore.

Too many years
Tryin' to get up there —
Done broke my ankles down,
Got nowhere.

Too many years
Climbin' that hill,
'Bout out of breath.
I got my fill.

▪ ▪ ▪

I'm gonna plant my feet
On solid ground.
If you want to see me,
Come down.

Langston Hughes

Theme for English B

1949

The instructor said,

Go home and write
a page tonight.
And let that page come out of you —
Then, it will be true.

I wonder if it's that simple?
I am twenty-two, colored, born in Winston-Salem.
I went to school there, then Durham, then here
to this college on the hill above Harlem.
I am the only colored student in my class.
The steps from the hill lead down into Harlem,
through a park, then I cross St. Nicholas,
Eighth Avenue, Seventh, and I come to the Y,
the Harlem Branch Y, where I take the elevator
up to my room, sit down, and write this page:

It's not easy to know what is true for you or me
at twenty-two, my age. But I guess I'm what
I feel and see and hear, Harlem, I hear you:
hear you, hear me — we two — you, me, talk on this page.
(I hear New York, too.) Me — who?
Well, I like to eat, sleep, drink, and be in love.
I like to work, read, learn, and understand life.
I like a pipe for a Christmas present,
or records — Bessie, bop, or Bach.
I guess being colored doesn't make me *not* like
the same things other folks like who are other races.
So will my page be colored that I write?
Being me, it will not be white.
But it will be
a part of you, instructor.
You are white —
yet a part of me, as I am a part of you.
That's American.
Sometimes perhaps you don't want to be a part of me.
Nor do I often want to be a part of you.
But we are, that's true!
As I learn from you,

I guess you learn from me —
although you're older — and white —
and somewhat more free.

This is my page for English B.

Langston Hughes

Dream Deferred

1959

What happens to a dream deferred?
    Does it dry up
    like a raisin in the sun?
    OR fester like a sore —
    And then run?
    Does it stink like rotten meat?
    Or crust and sugar over —
    like a syrupy sweet?

    Maybe it just sags
    like a heavy load.

    Or does it explode?

Ted Hughes *(1930–1998) was born in Yorkshire, in the small town of Mytholmroyd. Hughes's father was a carpenter and later became a shopkeeper, but his disturbed memories of his experiences in World War I, when he was only one of a handful in his regiment to survive the slaughter of the British troops at Gallipoli, made a lasting impression on the poet. After finishing grammar school Hughes spent two years in the Royal Air Force at an isolated radio station in Yorkshire where he spent most of his time reading. Pembroke College, at Cambridge University, followed his national service. Although he switched from studying English to archeology and anthropology, he continued to read voraciously such titles as* The White Goddess, *by the English novelist and poet Robert Graves.*

Following his graduation in 1954 at Cambridge, he spent two years working a series of jobs in London. At the inaugural party to launch the literary magazine St. Botolph's Review, *he met a young American college student who had recently come to England on a Fulbright scholarship. Her name was Sylvia Plath, and within a few months they were married. They spent two years at the University of Massachusetts in Amherst, from 1957 to 1959, where he taught English and creative writing. Both Hughes and Plath spent every moment they could find writing poetry. As he said later, "It was all we were interested in, all we ever did." By the time they returned to England in 1959 he had already begun publishing successfully. Despite two children and a period of life in rural Devon, tensions developed within the marriage, and when*

Hughes began an affair with another woman Plath told him to leave Devon. She later moved to London with their children and in 1963 committed suicide.

For American readers this seemed to sum up Hughes's career, but he went on to write dozens of books on a variety of subjects as well as a body of poetry that placed him among the most prominent poets of his generation. In 1981, he was named England's poet laureate. Often he was bitterly attacked for what many critics alleged was his role in Plath's suicide, and as her literary executor in the early days following her death, he destroyed her late diary in an effort to protect their children. It was not until the end of his life that he spoke out about their relationship, in a collection of poems that described their marriage and its tragic ending. The book, Birthday Letters, *published in 1999, became an international best-seller. The poem "Fulbright Scholars," which opens the book, describes the moment when he first became conscious of Plath.*

Although Hughes spent many years in London, he had grown up in the country and his sense of nature never left him. He was also an obsessive fisherman, and all of these themes are present in such poems as "Wind" and "Pike." In all of his writing there is a skill and sensitivity to language and to the moods of the weather and the landscape.

TED HUGHES

Wind

1956

This house has been far out at sea all night,
The woods crashing through darkness, the booming hills,
Winds stampeding the fields under the window
Floundering black astride and blinding wet

Till day rose; then under an orange sky
The hills had new places, and wind wielded
Blade-light, luminous black and emerald,
Flexing like the lens of a mad eye.

At noon I scaled along the house-side as far as
The coal-house door. Once I looked up —
Through the brunt wind that dented the balls of my eyes
The tent of the hills drummed and strained its guyrope,

The fields quivering, the skyline a grimace,
At any second to bang and vanish with a flap:
The wind flung a magpie away and a black-
Back gull bent like an iron bar slowly. The house

Rang like some fine green goblet in the note
That any second would shatter it. Now deep
In chairs, in front of the great fire, we grip
Our hearts and cannot entertain book, thought,

Or each other. We watch the fire blazing,
And feel the roots of the house move, but sit on,

Seeing the window tremble to come in,
Hearing the stones cry out under the horizons.

TED HUGHES

Pike

1959, 1960

Pike, three inches long, perfect
Pike in all parts, green tigering the gold.
Killers from the egg: the malevolent aged grin.
They dance on the surface among the flies.
Or move, stunned by their own grandeur,
Over a bed of emerald, silhouette
Of submarine delicacy and horror.
A hundred feet long in their world.

In ponds, under the heat-struck lily pads —
Gloom of their stillness:
Logged on last year's black leaves, watching upwards.
Or hung in an amber cavern of weeds

The jaws' hooked clamp and fangs
Not to be changed at this date;
A life subdued to its instrument;
The gills kneading quietly, and the pectorals.

Three we kept behind glass,
Jungled in weed: three inches, four,
And four and a half: fed fry° to them —
Suddenly there were two. Finally one

With a sag belly and the grin it was born with.
And indeed they spare nobody.
Two, six pounds each, over two feet long,
High and dry and dead in the willow-herb —

One jammed past its gills down the other's gullet:
The outside eye stared: as a vice locks —
The same iron in this eye
Though its film shrank in death.

A pond I fished, fifty yards across,
Whose lilies and muscular tench°
Had outlasted every visible stone
Of the monastery that planted them —

Stilled legendary depth:
It was as deep as England. It held

19. fry: Young fishes. **30. tench:** Variety of freshwater fish.

Pike too immense to stir, so immense and old
That past nightfall I dared not cast

But silently cast and fished
With the hair frozen on my head
For what might move, for what eye might move.
The still splashes on the dark pond,

Owls hushing the floating woods
Frail on my ear against the dream
Darkness beneath night's darkness had freed,
That rose slowly towards me, watching.

TED HUGHES

Fulbright Scholars

1998

Where was it, in the Strand? A display
Of news items, in photographs.
For some reason I noticed it.
A picture of that year's intake
Of Fulbright Scholars. Just arriving —
Or arrived. Or some of them.
Were you among them? I studied it,
Not too minutely, wondering
Which of them I might meet.
I remember that thought. Not
Your face. No doubt I scanned particularly
The girls. Maybe I noticed you.
Maybe I weighed you up, feeling unlikely.
Noted your long hair, loose waves —
Your Veronica Lake bang. Not what it hid.
It would appear blond. And your grin.
Your exaggerated American
Grin for the cameras, the judges, the strangers, the frighteners.
Then I forgot. Yet I remember
The picture: the Fulbright Scholars.
With their luggage? It seems unlikely.
Could they have come as a team? I was walking
Sore-footed, under hot sun, hot pavements.
Was it then I bought a peach? That's as I remember.
From a stall near Charing Cross Station.
It was the first fresh peach I had ever tasted.
I could hardly believe how delicious.
At twenty-five I was dumbfounded afresh
By my ignorance of the simplest things.

JOHN KEATS *(1795–1821) was the oldest of five children. His mother was the wife of the head stableman in a London livery stable. In his brief school years, Keats, despite his small stature, was mostly distinguished for his numerous fist fights. He also developed a passion for reading, under the fortunate tutelage of Charles Cowden Clarke, but after the deaths of his parents he was apprenticed at age fifteen to an apothecary surgeon. When he completed a year of studies at Guy's College, he was licensed to continue his trade, but he quickly abandoned it to become a poet.*

Little of the poetry Keats had written up to this time showed any sign of genius, although he received ample encouragement from a number of older writers, including Leigh Hunt, who introduced him to Percy Bysshe Shelley. The sonnet "On First Looking into Chapman's Homer" (p. 943), written when he was twenty-one, first hinted at what he would accomplish in the short time that was left to him. The first line of "A Thing of Beauty" (p. 854) is one of Keats's most quoted phrases, and although the longer poem from which it is taken was criticized at the time for its awkward structure, the language and ideas were an important influence on nineteenth-century English poetry.

His mother had died of tuberculosis, and Keats nursed a tubercular younger brother through his dying months in 1818. Keats contracted the disease and at the same time fell hopelessly in love with an eighteen-year-old girl named Fanny Brawne. Too poor and too ill to marry, he poured his emotions into poems and letters that were suffused with his despair, his love for Brawne, and his consciousness that his life was already running out.

Keats tried to fight his illness by traveling to Italy, but he was weakened by a series of hemorrhages and died in Rome at the age of twenty-six. In his last letter he apologized to a friend for writing such a clumsy good-bye. He wrote, "I always made an awkward bow."

Both "Ode to a Nightingale" and "La Belle Dame sans Merci" were written in Keats's remarkable year of 1819, when he composed several of his major works, including "To Autumn" (p. 841) and "Ode on a Grecian Urn" (p. 869).

RELATED COMMENTARY: *Philip Levine, "From 'Keats in Detroit,'" page 1190.*

JOHN KEATS

Ode to a Nightingale

1819

I

My heart aches, and a drowsy numbness pains
  My sense, as though of hemlock° I had drunk, *a poison*
Or emptied some dull opiate to the drains
  One minute past, and Lethe-wards° had sunk:
'Tis not through envy of thy happy lot,
  But being too happy in thine happiness —
    That thou, light-wingèd Dryad° of the trees, *wood nymph*
      In some melodious plot

4. Lethe-wards: Lethe is the river of forgetfulness in Greek mythology.

Of beechen green, and shadows numberless,
Singest of summer in full-throated ease.

II

O, for a draught of vintage! that hath been
Cooled a long age in the deep-delved earth,
Tasting of Flora° and the country green, *goddess of flowers*
Dance, and Provençal song,° and sunburnt mirth!
O for a beaker full of the warm South,
Full of the true, the blushful Hippocrene,°
With beaded bubbles winking at the brim,
And purple-stainèd mouth;
That I might drink, and leave the world unseen,
And with thee fade away into the forest dim.

III

Fade far away, dissolve, and quite forget
What thou among the leaves hast never known,
The weariness, the fever, and the fret
Here, where men sit and hear each other groan;
Where palsy shakes a few, sad, last gray hairs,
Where youth grows pale, and specter-thin, and dies,
Where but to think is to be full of sorrow
And leaden-eyed despairs,
Where Beauty cannot keep her lustrous eyes;
Or new Love pine at them beyond tomorrow.

IV

Away! away! for I will fly to thee,
Not charioted by Bacchus and his pards,°
But on the viewless wings of Poesy,
Though the dull brain perplexes and retards:
Already with thee! tender is the night,
And haply the Queen-Moon is on her throne,
Clustered around by all her starry Fays;° *fairies*
But here there is no light,
Save what from heaven is with the breezes blown
Through verdurous glooms and winding mossy ways.

V

I cannot see what flowers are at my feet,
Nor what soft incense hangs upon the boughs,

---

14. Provençal song: Provence, in medieval France, was famous for its troubadors. **16. Hippocrene:** Hippocrene is the fountain of the Muses, the goddesses of artistic inspiration. **32. Bacchus and his pards:** Bacchus, the god of wine, supposedly traveled in a chariot drawn by leopards.

But, in embalmèd° darkness, guess each sweet *perfumed*
  Wherewith the seasonable month endows
The grass, the thicket, and the fruit-tree wild;
  What hawthorn, and the pastoral eglantine;
    Fast fading violets covered up in leaves;
      And mid-May's eldest child,
  The coming musk-rose, full of dewy wine,
    The murmurous haunt of flies on summer eves.

VI

Darkling° I listen; and for many a time *in the dark*
  I have been half in love with easeful Death,
Called him soft names in many a musèd rhyme,
  To take into the air my quiet breath;
Now more than ever seems it rich to die,
  To cease upon the midnight with no pain,
    While thou art pouring forth thy soul abroad
      In such an ecstasy!
  Still wouldst thou sing, and I have ears in vain —
    To thy high requiem become a sod.

VII

Thou wast not born for death, immortal Bird!
  No hungry generations tread thee down;
The voice I hear this passing night was heard
  In ancient days by emperor and clown:
Perhaps the selfsame song that found a path
  Through the sad heart of Ruth,° when, sick for home,
    She stood in tears amid the alien corn:
      The same that oft-times hath
  Charmed magic casements, opening on the foam
    Of perilous seas, in faery lands forlorn.

VIII

Forlorn! the very word is like a bell
  To toll me back from thee to my sole self!
Adieu! the fancy cannot cheat so well
  As she is famed to do, deceiving elf.
Adieu! adieu! thy plaintive anthem fades
  Past the near meadows, over the still stream,
    Up the hill side; and now 'tis buried deep
      In the next valley-glades:
  Was it a vision, or a waking dream?
    Fled is that music: — Do I wake or sleep?

---

66. the sad heart of Ruth: Reference to the young widow in the biblical Book of Ruth.

JOHN KEATS

La Belle Dame sans Merci° *1819*

O what can ail thee, Knight at arms,
  Alone and palely loitering?
The sedge has withered from the Lake
  And no birds sing!

O what can ail thee, Knight at arms,
  So haggard, and so woebegone?
The squirrel's granary is full
  And the harvest's done.

I see a lily on thy brow
  With anguish moist and fever dew,
And on thy cheeks a fading rose
  Fast withereth too.

"I met a Lady in the Meads,° *meadows*
  Full beautiful, a faery's child,
Her hair was long, her foot was light
  And her eyes were wild.

"I made a Garland for her head,
  And bracelets too, and fragrant Zone;° *girdle*
She looked at me as she did love
  And made sweet moan.

"I set her on my pacing steed
  And nothing else saw all day long,
For sidelong would she bend and sing
  A faery's song.

"She found me roots of relish sweet,
  And honey wild, and manna dew,
And sure in language strange she said
  'I love thee true.'

"She took me to her elfin grot
  And there she wept and sighed full sore,
And there I shut her wild wild eyes
  With kisses four.

"And there she lullèd me asleep,
  And there I dreamed, Ah Woe betide!
The latest° dream I ever dreamt *last*
  On the cold hill side.

■ ■ ■

La Belle Dame sans Merci: "The lady beautiful but without mercy" (French). This is an earlier (and widely preferred) version of a poem first published in 1820.

"I saw pale Kings, and Princes too,
  Pale warriors, death-pale were they all;
They cried, 'La belle dame sans merci
  Hath thee in thrall!'

"I saw their starved lips in the gloam
  With horrid warning gapèd wide,
And I awoke, and found me here
  On the cold hill's side.

"And this is why I sojourn here,
  Alone and palely loitering;
Though the sedge is withered from the Lake
  And no birds sing."

JANE KENYON *(1947–1995) was born in Ann Arbor, Michigan, and attended the University of Michigan. She received her B.A. in 1970 and her M.A. in 1972. The same year she married a teacher at the university, the poet Donald Hall. After their marriage they moved to Eagle Pond Road in Wilmont, New Hampshire, which had been the home of Hall's family for several generations.*

Although Kenyon was to write joyously about her life in rural New Hampshire, she suffered from severe depression throughout her marriage, and her final poems document her struggle against leukemia. Her first book, Let Evening Come, *was published in 1990. She described the quiet life she led with her husband in many poems, but she and Hall were also well known through his books about life on their farm. Shortly before her death they were the subject of a television documentary that depicted their shared life of poetry and the changing seasons of their rural countryside.*

Kenyon's poetry is delicate and subtle, a poetry of shadings and quiet musings. The poet Carol Muske wrote of her, "These poems surprise beauty at every turn and capture truth at its familiar New England slant." "Catching Frogs," from her first book, with a careful understatement in its last lines suggests some of the tensions she remembered from her childhood. "Otherwise" and "Winter Lambs" are from her book Constance, *published in 1993. The poems in this collection deal more openly with her depression and contain a darker tone that never left her writing as her illness became more severe.*

JANE KENYON

Catching Frogs

1990

I crouched beside the deepest pool,
and the smell of damp and moss
rose rich between my knees. Water-striders
creased the silver-black silky surface.

Rapt, I hardly breathed. Gnats
roiled in a shaft of sun.

Back again after supper I'd see
a nose poke up by the big flat stone
at the lip of the fall; then the humped
eyes and the slippery emerald head,
freckled brown. The buff membrane
pulsed under the jaw while
subtleties of timing played in my mind.

With a patience that came like grace
I waited. Mosquitoes moaned all
around. Better to wait. Better to reach
from behind. . . . It grew dark.

I came into the warm, bright room
where Father held aloft the evening
paper, and there was talk, and maybe
laughter, though I don't remember laughter.

JANE KENYON

Otherwise

1993

I got out of bed
on two strong legs.
It might have been
otherwise. I ate
cereal, sweet
milk, ripe, flawless
peach. It might
have been otherwise.
I took the dog uphill
to the birch wood.
All morning I did
the work I love.

At noon I lay down
with my mate. It might
have been otherwise.
We ate dinner together
at a table with silver
candlesticks. It might
have been otherwise.
I slept in a bed
in a room with paintings
on the walls, and

planned another day
just like this day.
But one day, I know,
it will be otherwise.

Jane Kenyon

Winter Lambs 1993

All night snow came upon us
with unwavering intent —
small flakes not meandering
but driving thickly down. We woke
to see the yard, the car and road
heaped unrecognizably.

The neighbors' ewes are lambing
in this stormy weather. Three
lambs born yesterday, three more
expected. . . .
                Felix the ram looked
proprietary in his separate pen
while fatherhood accrued to him.
The panting ewes regarded me
with yellow-green, small-
pupiled eyes.

I have a friend who is pregnant —
plans gone awry — and not altogether
pleased. I don't say she should
be pleased. We are creation's
property, its particles, its clay
as we fall into this life,
agree or disagree.

Denise Levertov *(1923–1997) was born in London. Her father was a Russian Jew who had converted to Christianity while he was studying at a German university. After he moved to England, he became an Anglican priest. Levertov's mother was Welsh, and, except for a brief period in ballet school, she educated her daughter at home. Levertov's first poem was published when she was sixteen.*

Although Levertov was still in her teens when war broke out in Europe in 1939, she stayed in London and worked as a nurse. She continued writing, and her first book, The Double Image, *was published in 1946. On a walking tour in France, she met an American writer named Michael Goodman, and in 1948, after their marriage, they moved to the United States. Her second book,* Here and Now, *was published in 1957, by the now-famous City Lights Press, which was owned by the San Francisco poet Lawrence Ferlinghetti. She spent many years teaching, then in the 1960s she became editor of* The Nation *magazine. From 1975 to 1978 she worked as editor of the San Francisco magazine* Mother. *She became deeply committed to the struggle against the Vietnam War, and her poetry in those years was influenced by social turmoil that gripped the United States.*

As an English immigrant, a close friend of many of the Beat poets, and a committed antiwar activist, Levertov balanced many divergent concerns in her own writing, but she brought the same quick intelligence and commitment to all of her work. The poet Valerie Taylor wrote of her, "In what might have been called the Allen Ginsberg era, when the voice of the poet was often a raucous one, Levertov spoke quietly but with authority."

The three poems in this selection illuminate the diversity in Levertov's writing. The short lyric "Grey Sparrow Addresses the Mind's Ear" shows her pleasure in language and images of the natural world. "July 1968" opens to her feelings of self, and "The Day the Audience Walked Out on Me, and Why," from 1972, responds to the urgency she felt during the Vietnam years.

DENISE LEVERTOV

Grey Sparrow Addresses the Mind's Ear

1964

In the Japanese
tongue of the
mind's eye one
two syllable word
tells of
the fringe of rain
clinging to the eaves
and of the grey-green
fronds of
wild parsley.

DENISE LEVERTOV

July 1968

1968

Topmost leaves of young oak,
young maple,
are red — a delicate red
almost maroon.

I am not young,
and not yet old. Young enough not to be able
to imagine my own old age. Something in me

■ ■ ■

puts out new leaves that are red also,
    delicate, fantastic, in June,
        early summer, late spring in the north.

A dark time we live in. One would think
    there would be no summer. No red leaves.
        One would think there would be

no drawings-up of the blind at morning
    to a field awake with flowers.
        Yet with my tuft of new leaves

it is that field I wake to,
    a woman foolish with desire.

Denise Levertov

The Day the Audience Walked Out on Me, and Why

1970

(May 8th, 1970, Goucher College, Maryland)

Like this it happened:
after the antiphonal reading from the psalms
and the dance of lamentation before the altar,
and the two poems, "Life at War" and
                                        "What Were They Like?"

I began my rap,
and said:
Yes, it is well that we have gathered
in this chapel to remember
the students shot at Kent State,

but let us be sure we know
our gathering is a mockery unless
we remember also
the black students shot at Orangeburg two years ago,
and Fred Hampton murdered in his bed
by the police only months ago.

And while I spoke the people
— girls, older women, a few men —
began to rise and turn
their backs to the altar and leave.

And I went on and said,
Yes, it is well that we remember
all of these, but let us be sure
we know it is hypocrisy
to think of them unless

we make our actions their memorial,
actions of militant resistance.

By then the pews were almost empty
and I returned to my seat and a man stood up
in the back of the quiet chapel
(near the wide-open doors through which
the green of May showed, and the long shadows
of late afternoon)
and said my words
desecrated a holy place.

And a few days later
when some more students (black) were shot
at Jackson, Mississippi,
no one desecrated the white folks' chapel,
because no memorial service was held.

ꕥ

PHILIP LEVINE *(b. 1928) was born in Detroit and grew up in the years of the Great Depression with Russian Jewish immigrant parents who were deeply involved in the radical politics of those tumultuous years. His father was a businessman, and his mother was a bookseller. Levine received his A.B. in 1950 from Wayne State University, his M.A. in 1954, and his M.F.A. from the University of Iowa in 1957. Crucial to his decision to become a poet were his years of working a series of hard laboring jobs in the 1950s in Detroit's mills and factories. As he said later, in an interview in* Detroit Magazine,

> *I saw that the people that I was working with . . . were voiceless in a way. In terms of the literature of the United States they weren't being heard. Nobody was speaking for them. And as young people will, you know, I took this foolish vow that I would speak for them and that's what my life would be. And sure enough I've gone and done it.*

In a questionnaire for a literary encyclopedia, when Levine was asked about his politics and his religion, he replied to both questions, "anarchist." At the same time, however, the moment of discovery for him as a poet was the writing of John Keats. Levine wrote in an essay titled "Keats in Detroit" that when he first read Keats in a late-afternoon literature class after working a factory shift, "It seemed quite suddenly I could be both a poet and a person, even in a world like ours."

He began teaching at the University of Iowa in 1955, and his first book, On the Edge, *was published in 1961. He has had a long and successful literary career, winning the National Book Award twice, as well as the Pulitzer Prize. There have been numerous other prizes and grants. "Starlight" is a moving reminiscence of his childhood, and "The Fox" is a serious social comment woven into a half-serious play on his imagination.*

RELATED COMMENTARY: *Philip Levine, "From 'Keats in Detroit,'" page 1190.*

PHILIP LEVINE

Starlight

1979

My father stands in the warm evening
on the porch of my first house.
I am four years old and growing tired.
I see his head among the stars,
the glow of his cigarette, redder
than the summer moon riding
low over the old neighborhood. We
are alone, and he asks me if I am happy.
"Are you happy?" I cannot answer.
I do not really understand the word,
and the voice, my father's voice, is not
his voice, but somehow thick and choked,
a voice I have not heard before, but
heard often since. He bends and passes
a thumb beneath each of my eyes.
The cigarette is gone, but I can smell
the tiredness that hangs on his breath.
He has found nothing, and he smiles
and holds my head with both his hands.
Then he lifts me to his shoulder,
and now I too am there among the stars,
as tall as he. Are you happy? I say.
He nods in answer, Yes! oh yes! oh yes!
And in that new voice he says nothing,
holding my head tight against his head,
his eyes closed up against the starlight,
as though those tiny blinking eyes
of light might find a tall, gaunt child
holding his child against the promises
of autumn, until the boy slept
never to waken in that world again.

PHILIP LEVINE

The Fox

1981

I think I must have lived
once before, not as a man or woman
but as a small, quick fox pursued
through fields of grass and grain
by ladies and gentlemen on horseback.

This would explain my nose
and the small dark tufts of hair
that rise from the base of my spine.
It would explain why I am
so seldom invited out to dinner
and when I am I am never
invited back. It would explain
my loathing for those on horseback
in Central Park and how I can
so easily curse them and challenge
the men to fight and why no matter
how big they are or how young
they refuse to dismount,
for at such times, rock in hand,
I must seem demented.
My anger is sudden and total,
for I am a man to whom anger
usually comes slowly, spreading
like a fever along my shoulders
and back and turning my stomach
to a stone, but this fox anger
is lyrical and complete, as I stand
in the pathway shouting and refusing
to budge, feeling the dignity
of the small creature menaced
by the many and larger. Yes,
I must have been that unseen fox
whose breath sears the thick bushes
and whose eyes burn like opals
in the darkness, who humps
and shits gleefully in the horsepath
softened by moonlight and goes on
feeling the steady measured beat
of his fox heart like a wordless
delicate song, and the quick forepaws
choosing the way unerringly
and the thick furred body following
while the tail flows upward,
too beautiful a plume for anyone
except a creature who must proclaim
not ever ever ever
to mounted ladies and their gentlemen.

AUDRE LORDE *(1934–1992) was born in New York City of West Indian parents. Her father worked as a real-estate broker. She attended schools in New York and entered Hunter College, but more important to her was the year 1954, when she attended the National University of Mexico in Mexico City. She wrote later, "Seeing my own color reflected upon the streets in such great numbers was an affirmation for me." She graduated from Hunter in 1961 and began working as a librarian in a New York suburb. A year later she married an attorney and they had two children. She continued to work as a librarian until 1968, when her writing was beginning to be noticed, and she became a lecturer in creative writing at the City University of New York. She received her first National Endowment for the Arts grant the same year.*

When her marriage ended, Lorde described herself as "black, lesbian, feminist, poet, activist." She could also have added "single mother." In a discussion of Lorde's "modes of alienation" the critic Sandra Gilbert wrote that considering "her race, her sex, her vocation, and even her city it's not surprising that Lorde occasionally seems to be choking on her own anger . . . when her fury vibrates through taut cables from head to heart to page, she is capable of rare and, paradoxically, loving jeremiads." Her early poetry was published by small activist presses, but her breakthrough came when she was published by a major New York publisher—first the collection Coal, *in 1976, and then* The Black Unicorn *in 1978, when she openly identified herself as black and lesbian. She spent her last years fighting breast cancer, a struggle that she described in many poems. She died in St. Croix in the Virgin Islands.*

Many of Lorde's poems reflect the fury that Sandra Gilbert described, but there is also much writing that is filled with tenderness and affection. "Now That I Am Forever with Child" is from Coal, *and "Hanging Fire" is from* The Black Unicorn. *"Teacher," first published by Broadside Press, is drawn from the everyday tensions of her life as a single mother.*

AUDRE LORDE

Hanging Fire *1978*

I am fourteen
and my skin has betrayed me
the boy I cannot live without
still sucks his thumb
in secret
how come my knees are
always so ashy
what if I die
before morning
and momma's in the bedroom
with the door closed.

I have to learn how to dance
in time for the next party
my room is too small for me
suppose I die before graduation

they will sing sad melodies
but finally
tell the truth about me
There is nothing I want to do
and too much
that has to be done
and momma's in the bedroom
with the door closed.

Nobody even stops to think
about my side of it
I should have been on Math Team
my marks were better than his
why do I have to be
the one
wearing braces
I have nothing to wear tomorrow
will I live long enough
to grow up
and momma's in the bedroom
with the door closed.

AUDRE LORDE

Now That I Am Forever with Child *1976*

How the days went
while you were blooming within me
I remember each upon each —
the swelling changed planes of my body
and how you first fluttered, then jumped
and I thought it was my heart.

How the days wound down
and the turning of winter
I recall, with you growing heavy
against the wind. I thought
now her hands
are formed, and her hair
has started to curl
now her teeth are done
now she sneezes.
Then the seed opened
I bore you one morning just before spring
My head rang like a fiery piston
my legs were towers between which
a new world was passing.

■ ■ ■

Since then
I can only distinguish
one thread within running hours
You, flowing through selves
toward You.

AUDRE LORDE

Teacher

1973

I make my children promises in wintery afternoons
like lunchtime stories
when my feet hurt from talking too much
and not enough movement except in my own
worn down at the heel shoes
except in the little circle of broken down light
I am trapped in
the intensities of my own (our) situation
where what we need and do not have
deadens us
and promises sound like destruction
white snowflakes clog the passages
drifting through the halls and corridors
while I tell stories with no ending
at lunchtime
the children's faces bear uneasy smiles
like a heavy question
I provide food with a frightening efficiency
the talk is free/dom meaning state
condition of being
We are elementary forces colliding in free fall

ROBERT LOWELL *(1917–1977) was born in Boston to a distinguished New England family that had already produced two major poets, James Russell Lowell (1819–1891) and Amy Lowell (1874–1925), one of the leaders of the imagist movement (p. 896). After two years at Harvard University, Lowell left in 1937 for Kenyon College in Ohio to join a group of young poets who had gathered around teacher and poet John Crowe Ransom. Although his father had been a Navy officer, Lowell became a conscientious objector during World War II and was imprisoned for five months in 1943. He continued to write poetry through his personal crises, and his second book,* Lord Weary's Castle, *won the Pulitzer Prize in 1946.*

Lowell published steadily, and his books were well received, but he was beginning to suffer from acute attacks of depression. Two of his three marriages were to novelists — first to Jean Stafford in 1940 and then to Elizabeth Hardwick in 1949. He was also drinking heavily and when he was drunk he was emotionally abusive. In the 1950s he visited San Francisco and experienced the excitement of the Beat Generation, the new literary movement that had sprung up there. After seeing the effect of Beat writer Allen Ginsberg's poetry on audiences and reading an emotional poem titled "Heart's Needle" by a former student named W. D. Snodgrass, he changed his way of writing. His poems became freer and more personal. His collection Life Studies, *written in the new "confessional" style, was one of the most influential books published after the war, winning the National Book Award in 1959. At this same time he was teaching a poetry course at Boston University, and among his students were Sylvia Plath and Anne Sexton, who adopted the new style in their own writing.*

Finally diagnosed as manic-depressive, Lowell was able to avoid with medication some of the psychotic episodes that had periodically caused him to be hospitalized. With novelist Norman Mailer, he was involved in the struggle against the Vietnam War, and in 1972 he married for the third time and settled in England. He had written plays and literary criticism and won the Bollingen Prize for his translations. In 1977 he returned to the United States planning to teach at Harvard, but he died of a heart attack a short time later.

One of his closest friends was poet Elizabeth Bishop — in emotional moments he asked her to marry him — and "Skunk Hour" is dedicated to her. His poem is a response to her "Armadillo." It reads almost like a letter, describing a scene that is familiar to both of them. "For the Union Dead" is also a description, this time of the Boston Common and the memorial statue by Augustus Saint-Gaudens to the Civil War regiment of African American soldiers that was destroyed with its young commander, Boston's Colonel Shaw. "Epilogue" was written in 1977, shortly before Lowell's death.

RELATED COMMENTARIES: *Robert Lowell, "An Explication of 'Skunk Hour,'" page 1192; Robert Lowell, "Foreword to Plath's* Ariel,*" page 1194; Robert Lowell, "On Robert Frost," page 1260; Louis Simpson, "On Lowell's 'Skunk Hour,'" page 1220.*

ROBERT LOWELL

Skunk Hour

1959

For Elizabeth Bishop

Nautilus Island's hermit
heiress still lives through winters in her Spartan cottage;
her sheep still graze above the sea.
Her son's a bishop. Her farmer
is first selectman in our village;
she's in her dotage.

Thirsting for
the hierarchic privacy
of Queen Victoria's century,
she buys up all
the eyesores facing her shore,
and lets them fall.

The season's ill —
we've lost our summer millionaire,

who seemed to leap from an L. L. Bean°
catalogue. His nine-knot yawl
was auctioned off to lobstermen.
A red fox stain covers Blue Hill.

And now our fairy
decorator brightens his shop for fall;
his fishnet's filled with orange cork,
orange, his cobbler's bench and awl;
there is no money in his work,
he'd rather marry.

One dark night,
my Tudor Ford climbed the hill's skull;
I watched for love-cars. Lights turned down,
they lay together, hull to hull,
where the graveyard shelves on the town....
My mind's not right.

A car radio bleats,
"Love, O careless Love...." I hear
my ill-spirit sob in each blood cell,
as if my hand were at its throat....
I myself am hell;
nobody's here —

only skunks, that search
in the moonlight for a bite to eat.
They march on their soles up Main Street:
white stripes, moonstruck eyes' red fire
under the chalk-dry and spar spire
of the Trinitarian Church.

I stand on top
of our back steps and breathe the rich air —
a mother skunk with her column of kittens swills the garbage pail.
She jabs her wedge-head in a cup
of sour cream, drops her ostrich tail,
and will not scare.

ROBERT LOWELL

For the Union Dead *1964*

"Relinquunt Omnia Servare Rem Publican."°

The old South Boston Aquarium stands
in a Sahara of snow now. Its broken windows are boarded.

15. L. L. Bean: A Maine mail-order store known for its sporting goods and outdoor equipment.
Relinquunt . . . Publican: "They gave up all to serve the republic."

The bronze weathervane cod has lost half its scales.
The airy tanks are dry.

Once my nose crawled like a snail on the glass;
my hand tingled
to burst the bubbles
drifting from the noses of the cowed, compliant fish.

My hand draws back. I often sigh still
for the dark downward and vegetating kingdom
of the fish and reptile. One morning last March,
I pressed against the new barbed and galvanized

fence on the Boston Common. Behind their cage,
yellow dinosaur steamshovels were grunting
as they cropped up tons of mush and grass
to gouge their underworld garage.

Parking spaces luxuriate like civic
sandpiles in the heart of Boston.
A girdle of orange, Puritan-pumpkin colored girders
braces the tingling Statehouse,

shaking over the excavations, as it faces Colonel Shaw
and his bell-cheeked Negro infantry
on St. Gaudens' shaking Civil War relief,
propped by a plank splint against the garage's earthquake.

Two months after marching through Boston,
half the regiment was dead;
at the dedication,
William James° could almost hear the bronze Negroes breathe.

Their monument sticks like a fishbone
in the city's throat.
Its Colonel is as lean
as a compass-needle.

He has an angry wrenlike vigilance,
a greyhound's gentle tautness;
he seems to wince at pleasure,
and suffocate for privacy.

He is out of bounds now. He rejoices in man's lovely,
peculiar power to choose life and die —
when he leads his black soldiers to death,
he cannot bend his back.

On a thousand small town New England greens,
the old white churches hold their air

---

28. William James: Harvard psychologist and philosopher (1842–1910).

of sparse, sincere rebellion; frayed flags
quilt the graveyards of the Grand Army of the Republic.

The stone statues of the abstract Union Soldier
grow slimmer and younger each year —
wasp-waisted, they doze over muskets
and muse through their sideburns . . .

Shaw's father wanted no monument
except the ditch,
where his son's body was thrown
and lost with his "niggers."

The ditch is nearer.
There are no statues for the last war here;
on Boylston Street, a commercial photograph
shows Hiroshima boiling

over a Mosler Safe, the "Rock of Ages"
that survived the blast. Space is nearer.
When I crouch to my television set,
the drained faces of Negro school-children rise like balloons.

Colonel Shaw
is riding on his bubble,
he waits
for the blessèd break.

The Aquarium is gone. Everywhere,
giant finned cars nose forward like fish;
a savage servility
slides by on grease.

ROBERT LOWELL

Epilogue

1977

Those blessèd structures, plot and rhyme —
why are they no help to me now
I want to make
something imagined, not recalled?
I hear the noise of my own voice:
The painter's vision is not a lens,
it trembles to caress the light.
But sometimes everything I write
with the threadbare art of my eye
seems a snapshot,
lurid, rapid, garish, grouped,
heightened from life,
yet paralyzed by fact.
All's misalliance.

Yet why not say what happened?
Pray for the grace of accuracy
Vermeer° gave to the sun's illumination
stealing like the tide across a map
to his girl solid with yearning.
We are poor passing facts,
warned by that to give
each figure in the photograph
his living name.

EDNA ST. VINCENT MILLAY *(1892–1950) was born in Rockland, Maine, and in 1923, following her marriage, she moved to a farm in the Berkshires and lived there in quiet isolation. As a poet, however, she will always be remembered for her few brief years in Greenwich Village after her graduation from Vassar College in 1917. "First Fig," a quatrain she wrote in 1920, seemed to represent with its candle metaphor the carefree spirit of the era. Her first major poem, "Renascence," was published when she was nineteen, and during her Village years she wrote short stories, plays, and several collections of lyric poetry, including a number of sonnets. She won the Pulitzer Prize in 1923 for "The Harp-Weaver," and for many years she was probably the best-known and most widely read poet in the United States. Her sequence of fifty-two love sonnets,* Fatal Interview, *published in 1931, was one of the most enthusiastically reviewed books of the time. She was also a political activist and used her poetry to defend the causes she believed in so passionately.*

Although Millay is usually associated with her bohemian life in Greenwich Village, she grew up in Maine and lived for many years on her Berkshire farm. The sequence of "Sonnets from an Ungrafted Tree" reflects the language and the bleak life of the Maine countryside. She took considerable liberties with the meter of the sonnets, and each final line has seven, rather than five, accents. "Childhood Is the Kingdom Where Nobody Dies" was written after she returned to the country. The simple lyric "The courage that my mother had" was found among her papers after her death.

EDNA ST. VINCENT MILLAY

From "Sonnets from an Ungrafted Tree" *1920*

I

So she came back into his house again
And watched beside his bed until he died,
Loving him not at all. The winter rain
Splashed in the painted butter-tub outside,

17. Vermeer: Dutch painter Jan Vermeer (1632–1675).

Where once her red geraniums had stood,
Where still their rotted stalks were to be seen;
The thin log snapped; and she went out for wood,
Bareheaded, running the few steps between
The house and shed; there, from the sodden eaves
Blown back and forth on ragged ends of twine,
Saw the dejected creeping-jinny vine,
(And one, big-aproned, blithe, with stiff blue sleeves
Rolled to the shoulder that warm day in spring,
Who planted seeds, musing ahead to their far blossoming).

II

The last white sawdust on the floor was grown
Gray as the first, so long had he been ill;
The axe was nodding in the block; fresh-blown
And foreign came the rain across the sill,
But on the roof so steadily it drummed
She could not think a time it might not be —
In hazy summer, when the hot air hummed
With mowing, and locusts rising raspingly,
When that small bird with iridescent wings
And long incredible sudden silver tongue
Had just flashed (and yet maybe not!) among
The dwarf nasturtiums — when no sagging springs
Of shower were in the whole bright sky, somehow
Upon this roof the rain would drum as it was drumming now.

III

She filled her arms with wood, and set her chin
Forward, to hold the highest stick in place,
No less afraid than she had always been
Of spiders up her arms and on her face,
But too impatient for a careful search
Or a less heavy loading, from the heap
Selecting hastily small sticks of birch,
For their curled bark, that instantly will leap
Into a blaze, nor thinking to return
Some day, distracted, as of old, to find
Smooth, heavy, round, green logs with a wet, gray rind
Only, and knotty chunks that will not burn,
(That day when dust is on the wood-box floor
And some old catalogue, and a brown, shriveled apple core).

IV

The white bark writhed and sputtered like a fish
Upon the coals, exuding odorous smoke.
She knelt and blew, in a surging desolate wish

For comfort; and the sleeping ashes woke
And scattered to the hearth, but no thin fire
Broke suddenly, the wood was wet with rain.
Then, softly stepping forth from her desire,
(Being mindful of like passion hurled in vain
Upon a similar task, in other days)
She thrust her breath against the stubborn coal,
Bringing to bear upon its hilt the whole
Of her still body . . . there sprang a little blaze . . .
A pack of hounds, the flame swept up the flue! —
And the blue night stood flattened against the window, staring through.

IX

Not over-kind nor over-quick in study
Nor skilled in sports nor beautiful was he,
Who had come into her life when anybody
Would have been welcome, so in need was she.
They had become acquainted in this way:
He flashed a mirror in her eyes at school;
By which he was distinguished; from that day
They went about together, as a rule.
She told, in secret and with whispering,
How he had flashed a mirror in her eyes;
And as she told, it struck her with surprise
That this was not so wonderful a thing.
But what's the odds? — It's pretty nice to know
You've got a friend to keep you company everywhere you go.

X

She had forgotten how the August night
Was level as a lake beneath the moon,
In which she swam a little, losing sight
Of shore; and how the boy, who was at noon
Simple enough, not different from the rest,
Wore now a pleasant mystery as he went,
Which seemed to her an honest enough test
Whether she loved him, and she was content.
So loud, so loud the million crickets' choir . . .
So sweet the night, so long-drawn-out and late . . .
And if the man were not her spirit's mate,
Why was her body sluggish with desire?
Stark on the open field the moonlight fell,
But the oak tree's shadow was deep and black and secret as a well.

XI

It came into her mind, seeing how the snow
Was gone, and the brown grass exposed again,

And clothes-pins, and an apron — long ago,
In some white storm that sifted through the pane
And sent her forth reluctantly at last
To gather in, before the line gave way,
Garments, board-stiff, that galloped on the blast
Clashing like angel armies in a fray,
An apron long ago in such a night
Blown down and buried in the deepening drift,
To lie till April thawed it back to sight,
Forgotten, quaint and novel as a gift —
It struck her, as she pulled and pried and tore,
That here was spring, and the whole year to be lived through once more.

Edna St. Vincent Millay

Childhood Is the Kingdom Where Nobody Dies 1934

Childhood is not from birth to a certain age and at a certain age
The child is grown, and puts away childish things.
Childhood is the kingdom where nobody dies.

Nobody that matters, that is. Distant relatives of course
Die, whom one never has seen or has seen for an hour,
And they gave one candy in a pink-and-green stripèd bag, or a jack-knife,
And went away, and cannot really be said to have lived at all.

And cats die. They lie on the floor and lash their tails,
And their reticent fur is suddenly all in motion
With fleas that one never knew were there,
Polished and brown, knowing all there is to know,
Trekking off into the living world.
You fetch a shoe-box, but it's much too small, because she won't curl up now;
So you find a bigger box, and bury her in the yard, and weep.

But you do not wake up a month from then, two months,
A year from then, two years, in the middle of the night
And weep, with your knuckles in your mouth, and say Oh, God! Oh, God!
Childhood is the kingdom where nobody dies that matters, — mothers and fathers don't die.

And if you have said, "For heaven's sake, must you always be kissing a person?"
Or, "I do wish to gracious you'd stop tapping on the window with your thimble!"
Tomorrow, or even the day after tomorrow if you're busy having fun,
Is plenty of time to say, "I'm sorry, mother."

■ ■ ■

To be grown up is to sit at the table with people who have died,
who neither listen nor speak;
Who do not drink their tea, though they always said
Tea was such a comfort.

Run down into the cellar and bring up the last jar of raspberries;
they are not tempted.
Flatter them, ask them what was it they said exactly
That time, to the bishop, or to the overseer, or to Mrs. Mason;
They are not taken in.
Shout at them, get red in the face, rise,
Drag them up out of their chairs by their stiff shoulders and shake
them and yell at them;
They are not startled, they are not even embarrassed; they slide
back into their chairs.

Your tea is cold now.
You drink it standing up,
And leave the house.

EDNA ST. VINCENT MILLAY

The courage that my mother had

1954

The courage that my mother had
Went with her, and is with her still:
Rock from New England quarried;
Now granite in a granite hill.

The golden brooch my mother wore
She left behind for me to wear;
I have no thing I treasure more:
Yet, it is something I could spare.

Oh, if instead she'd left to me
The thing she took into the grave! —
That courage like a rock, which she
Has no more need of, and I have.

❧

MARIANNE MOORE *(1887–1972) was born in St. Louis, but her father chose not to remain with his family, and eventually Moore and her mother moved to Carlisle, Pennsylvania. She graduated from Bryn Mawr College in 1909. Following her graduation, she and her mother traveled to France and England, then for five years she taught courses in office skills at the U.S. Indian School for Native Americans in Carlisle. In 1918 she and her mother moved to New York with her brother, who was a Presbyterian minister.*

She had already begun writing poetry in college, and she began submitting her work to several small experimental magazines. Her poetry immediately attracted the attention of other writers, including William Carlos Williams and Wallace Stevens. Williams included her work in a small mimeographed magazine he published in the early 1920s. From 1925 to 1929 she was editor of The Dial, *a New York literary journal.*

Moore's life was quiet. She lived with her mother in Brooklyn and worked on her poetry. The poet Elizabeth Bishop, who was close to her for thirty-five years, remembered her conversation as "entertaining, enlightening, fascinating, and memorable; her talk, like her poetry, was quite different from anyone else in the world."

In 1951 Moore's Collected Poems *won almost every major American literary award, and her work found new audiences who were charmed by her enthusiasm for oddly named animals, racehorses, and the Brooklyn Dodgers. "The Fish" is an early poem that attracted immediate attention and may have inspired the poem with the same title by Elizabeth Bishop. "Critics and Connoisseurs" is from* The Selected Poems, *published in 1935, and "I May, I Might, I Must" is from* O to Be a Dragon, *published in 1959.* *(See also Moore's "Poetry" on p. 805 and "What Are Years?" on p. 817.)*

RELATED COMMENTARY: *Marianne Moore, "Some Answers to Questions Posed by Howard Nemerov," page 1199.*

MARIANNE MOORE

The Fish — *1921*

wade
through black jade.
    Of the crow-blue mussel shells, one keeps
    adjusting the ash heaps;
        opening and shutting itself like

an
injured fan.
    The barnacles which encrust the side
    of the wave, cannot hide
        there for the submerged shafts of the

sun,
split like spun
    glass, move themselves with spotlight swiftness
    into the crevices —
        in and out, illuminating

the
turquoise sea
    of bodies. The water drives a wedge
    of iron through the iron edge
        of the cliff; whereupon the stars,

■ ■ ■

pink
rice-grains, ink-
bespattered jellyfish, crabs like green
lilies, and submarine
toadstools, slide each on the other.

All
external
marks of abuse are present on this
defiant edifice —
all the physical features of

ac-
cident — lack
of cornice, dynamite grooves, burns, and
hatchet strokes, these things stand
out on it; the chasm side is

dead.
Repeated
evidence has proved that it can live
on what can not revive
its youth. The sea grows old in it.

Marianne Moore

Critics and Connoisseurs

1958

There is a great amount of poetry in unconscious
fastidiousness. Certain Ming
products, imperial floor-coverings of coach-
wheel yellow, are well enough in their way but I have seen something
that I like better — a
mere childish attempt to make an imperfectly bal-
lasted animal stand up,
similar determination to make a pup
eat his meat from the plate.

I remember a swan under the willows in Oxford,
with flamingo-colored, maple-
leaflike feet. It reconnoitered like a battle-
ship. Disbelief and conscious fastidiousness were
ingredients in its
disinclination to move. Finally its hardihood was
not proof against its
proclivity to more fully appraise such bits
of food as the stream

■ ■ ■

bore counter to it; it made away with what I gave it
to eat. I have seen this swan and
I have seen you; I have seen ambition without
understanding in a variety of forms. Happening to stand
by an ant-hill, I have
seen a fastidious ant carrying a stick north, south,
east, west, till it turned on
itself, struck out from the flower-bed into the lawn,
and returned to the point

from which it had started. Then abandoning the stick as
useless and overtaxing its
jaws with a particle of whitewash — pill-like but
heavy, it again went through the same course of procedure. What is
there in being able
to say that one has dominated the stream in an attitude of self-
defense;

in proving that one has had the experience
of carrying a stick?

MARIANNE MOORE

I May, I Might, I Must

1935

If you will tell me why the fen
appears impassable, I then
will tell you why I think that I
can get across it if I try.

SHARON OLDS *(b. 1942) was born in San Francisco and grew up in Berkeley. She has consistently refused to answer questions about her family and her personal life, feeling that the people she describes in her poetry have a right to privacy. As she told an interviewer for the* New York Times, *"I promised I'd keep them out of this." She went on, "I never thought anyone would read anything I'd written. If I'd known the number of readers I would have, I would have used a pseudonym." Her critics and interviewers have generally respected her wishes, and there have been no published interviews or reminiscences by people who have been part of her life.*

The other side of Olds's reticence has been to create a body of poetry that is the most explicitly personal record any woman has ever given us about her body, her sexuality, and her complex relationships with her lovers, her father, her children, her sister, and her husband. She writes in the confessional mode of Robert Lowell, Anne Sexton, and Sylvia Plath, but without the verbal defenses that often make their poetry more ambiguous. As the interviewer Dinitia Smith wrote, "Her work has a robust sensuality, a delight in the physical that is almost Whitmanesque. She has made the minutiae of a woman's everyday life as valid a subject for poetry as the grand abstract themes that have preoccupied other poets." The literary critic Helen Vendler termed her poetry "pornographic," but there is no pornographic intent in anything Olds writes, even though a few of the poems would have caused difficulties for her publishers before the legal decisions that cleared the way for the work of writers such as D. H. Lawrence, Vladimir Nabokov, and Allen Ginsberg in the 1950s.

What Olds has allowed interviewers to learn about her life is that she grew up in a middle-class home that was deeply religious. Her parents were Episcopalians, and the family attended church twice weekly. As she has written in the poem "The Elder Sister," she had an older sibling, who she felt helped open the way for her own development. Olds's relationship with her father, as she described it in her book The Father, *was difficult. He is presented as a physically bullying figure who dominated her life. In newer poems she has softened the portrait, but he is still a troubling presence.*

Olds was sent to the Dana Hall School in Wellesley, Massachusetts, but returned to California for her university years. She graduated from Stanford and moved to New York City to study for her Ph.D. at Columbia University. She married in the late 1960s and is the mother of a son and a daughter. The recent painful breakup of her marriage has also caused her to shield herself from personal questions.

Although Olds has preferred to present a low personal profile, her life in New York is a rush of public activity. She has taught creative writing at New York University since the mid-1980s, and from 1989 to 1991 she was director of the Graduate Creative Writing Program. In 1984 she founded a poetry workshop for the severely disabled in New York's Goldwater Hospital, where she continues to teach. Adding to her already crammed schedule, in the spring of 1998 she was selected as the official New York state poet, which involves two years of presentations and appearances across the state. When one interviewer asked her about fitting all of these things into her life, she confessed that she has given up reading newspapers and watching television. She agreed that this has its disadvantages, but cheerfully defended herself by saying, "I try to look at the front page whenever I'm walking by a newsstand."

Olds also manages to fit a demanding line-up of readings into her schedule, and she is one of a handful of poets in the United States whose books sell in large quantities. The Father *was reprinted several times within a few months of its publication, and her 1984 collection* The Dead and the Living, *which won the National Book Critics Circle Award, has sold more than 50,000 copies. The demands of her life, however, mean that each book is a gathering of work that was written years before. She writes continuously, and it is only after considerable time has passed that she feels the need to put together the poems that make up a book. She doesn't conceive of her books as following a specific theme, but with* The Father *she made the decision to include only poems that created a loose narrative sequence. "At first I thought it would not be a good idea to have a book all on one theme. I also didn't know if I had enough poems on the subject that I liked well enough to make a book of them. But it turned out that I did. And it just seemed true to make a story that was all of itself. It pleased me to do so, and it still does."*

Her poetry is composed in her head as she is busy with her other responsibilities, and the actual writing of a poem goes quickly. She joked with an interviewer that she could write a poem in half an hour. When the response to this was surprise, Olds laughed and agreed, "Forty-five minutes is much better."

This selection of Olds's work includes poems written over much of her career and includes many of her continuing themes. "I Go Back to May 1937," "The Planned Child," and "The Elder Sister" suggest the tensions in her family. "The Race," from The Father, *describes her frantic rush to be at her father's bedside in California before his death. "The One Girl at the Boys' Party" is a reflection on her daughter as a young girl. "The Death of Marilyn Monroe" and "Summer Solstice, New York City" deal with people whose lives have reached a breaking point, Monroe's unhappiness leading to her suicide, and the would-be suicide on the New York rooftop saved by the police. There is perhaps no poem that better reflects the current uncertainty about sexual mores in our society than her "Sex without Love." "At the Bay" is from her most recent collection,* Blood, Tin, Straw, *published in 1999.*

RELATED CASEBOOK: *See pages 1271–1279, including Sharon Olds, "From the* Salon *Interview," page 1272; Jonathan Holden, "The Dichotomy between Men's and Women's Writing," page 1274; Dinitia Smith, "The Creative Mind; The Examined Life without Punctuation," page 1275; Ann Charters, "'Working the Room': Sharon Olds Reads Her Poetry at the Miami International Book Fair," page 1276.*

SHARON OLDS

The Elder Sister — 1984

When I look at my elder sister now
I think how she had to go first, down through the
birth canal, to force her way
head-first through the tiny channel,
the pressure of Mother's muscles on her brain,
the tight walls scraping her skin.
Her face is still narrow from it, the long
hollow cheeks of a Crusader on a tomb,
and her inky eyes have the look of someone who has
been in prison a long time and
knows they can send her back. I look at her
body and think how her breasts were the first to
rise, slowly, like swans on a pond.
By the time mine came along, they were just
two more birds in the flock, and when the hair
rose on the white mound of her flesh, like
threads of water out of the ground, it was the
first time, but when mine came
they knew about it. I used to think
only in terms of her harshness, sitting and
pissing on me in bed, but now I
see I had her before me always
like a shield. I look at her wrinkles, her clenched
jaws, her frown-lines — I see they are
the dents on my shield, the blows that did not reach me.

She protected me, not as a mother
protects a child, with love, but as a
hostage protects the one who makes her
escape as I made my escape, with my sister's
body held in front of me.

Sharon Olds

Summer Solstice, New York City

1987

By the end of the longest day of the year he could not stand it,
he went up the iron stairs through the roof of the building
and over the soft, tarry surface
to the edge, put one leg over the complex green tin cornice
and said if they came a step closer that was it.
Then the huge machinery of the earth began to work for his life,
the cops came in their suits blue-grey as the sky on a cloudy evening,
and one put on a bullet-proof vest,
a black shell around his own life,
life of his children's father, in case
the man was armed, and one, slung with a
rope like the sign of his bounden duty,
came up out of a hole in the top of the neighbouring building
like the gold hole they say is in the top of the head,
and began to lurk toward the man who wanted to die.
The tallest cop approached him directly,
softly, slowly, talking to him, talking, talking,
while the man's leg hung over the lip of the next world
and the crowd gathered in the street, silent, and the
hairy net with its implacable grid was
unfolded near the curb and spread out and
stretched as the sheet is prepared to receive at a birth.
Then they all came a little closer
where he squatted next to his death, his shirt
glowing its milky glow like something
growing in a dish at night in the dark in a lab and then
everything stopped
as his body jerked and he
stepped down from the parapet and went toward them
and they closed on him, I thought they were going to
beat him up, as a mother whose child has been
lost will scream at the child when it's found, they
took him by the arms and held him up and
leaned him against the wall of the chimney and the
tall cop lit a cigarette
in his own mouth, and gave it to him, and
then they all lit cigarettes, and the

red, glowing ends burned like the
tiny campfires we lit at night
back at the beginning of the world.

Sharon Olds

I Go Back to May 1937

1987

I see them standing at the formal gates of their colleges,
I see my father strolling out
under the ochre sandstone arch, the
red tiles glinting like bent
plates of blood behind his head, I
see my mother with a few light books at her hip
standing at the pillar made of tiny bricks with the
wrought-iron gate still open behind her, its
sword-tips black in the May air,
they are about to graduate, they are about to get married,
they are kids, they are dumb, all they know is they are
innocent, they would never hurt anybody.
I want to go up to them and say Stop,
don't do it — she's the wrong woman,
he's the wrong man, you are going to do things
you cannot imagine you would ever do,
you are going to do bad things to children,
you are going to suffer in ways you never heard of,
you are going to want to die. I want to go
up to them there in the late May sunlight and say it,
her hungry pretty blank face turning to me,
her pitiful beautiful untouched body,
his arrogant handsome blind face turning to me,
his pitiful beautiful untouched body,
but I don't do it. I want to live. I
take them up like the male and female
paper dolls and bang them together
at the hips like chips of flint as if to
strike sparks from them, I say
Do what you are going to do, and I will tell about it.

Sharon Olds

The One Girl at the Boys' Party

1995

When I take our girl to the swimming party
I set her down among the boys. They tower and
bristle, she stands there smooth and sleek,

her math scores unfolding in the air around her.
They will strip to their suits, her body hard and
indivisible as a prime number,
they'll plunge in the deep end, she'll subtract
her height from ten feet, divide it into
hundreds of gallons of water, the numbers
bouncing in her mind like molecules of chlorine
in the bright blue pool. When they climb out,
her ponytail will hang its pencil lead
down her back, her narrow silk suit
with hamburgers and french fries printed on it
will glisten in the brilliant air, and they will
see her sweet face, solemn and
sealed, a factor of one, and she will
see their eyes, two each,
their legs, two each, and the curves of their sexes,
one each, and in her head she'll be doing her
wild multiplying, as the drops
sparkle and fall to the power of a thousand from her body.

SHARON OLDS

The Planned Child — *1983*

I hated the fact that they had planned me, she had taken
a cardboard out of his shirt from the laundry
as if sliding the backbone up out of his body,
and made a chart of the month and put
her temperature on it, rising and falling,
to know the day to make me — I would have
liked to have been conceived in heat,
in haste, by mistake, in love, in sex,
not on cardboard, the little x on the
rising line that did not fall again.

But when a friend was pouring wine
and said that I seem to have been a child who had been wanted,
I took the wine against my lips
as if my mouth were moving along
that valved wall in my mother's body, she was
bearing down, and then breathing from the mask, and then
bearing down, pressing me out into
the world that was not enough for her without me in it,
not the moon, the sun, Orion
cartwheeling across the dark, not
the earth, the sea — none of it
was enough, for her, without me.

SHARON OLDS

The Death of Marilyn Monroe 1983

The ambulance men touched her cold
body, lifted it, heavy as iron,
onto the stretcher, tried to close the
mouth, closed the eyes, tied the
arms to the sides, moved a caught
strand of hair, as if it mattered,
saw the shape of her breasts, flattened by
gravity, under the sheet,
carried her, as if it were she,
down the steps.

These men were never the same. They went out
afterwards, as they always did,
for a drink or two, but they could not meet
each other's eyes.

Their lives took
a turn — one had nightmares, strange
pains, impotence, depression. One did not
like his work, his wife looked
different, his kids. Even death
seemed different to him — a place where she
would be waiting,

and one found himself standing at night
in the doorway to a room of sleep, listening to a
woman breathing, just an ordinary
woman
breathing.

SHARON OLDS

Sex without Love 1983

How do they do it, the ones who make love
without love? Beautiful as dancers,
gliding over each other like ice-skaters
over the ice, fingers hooked
inside each other's bodies, faces
red as steak, wine, wet as the
children at birth whose mothers are going to
give them away. How do they come to the
come to the   come to the   God   come to the
still waters, and not love

the one who came there with them, light
rising slowly as steam off their joined
skin? These are the true religious,
the purists, the pros, the ones who will not
accept a false Messiah, love the
priest instead of the God. They do not
mistake the lover for their own pleasure,
they are like great runners: they know they are alone
with the road surface, the cold, the wind,
the fit of their shoes, their over-all cardio-
vascular health — just factors, like the partner
in the bed, and not the truth, which is the
single body alone in the universe
against its own best time.

SHARON OLDS

The Race

1992

When I got to the airport I rushed up to the desk,
bought a ticket, ten minutes later
they told me the flight was cancelled, the doctors
had said my father would not live through the night
and the flight was cancelled. A young man
with a dark blond moustache told me
another airline had a non-stop
leaving in seven minutes. See that
elevator over there, well go
down to the first floor, make a right, you'll
see a yellow bus, get off at the
second Pan Am terminal, I
ran, I who have no sense of direction
raced exactly where he'd told me, a fish
slipping upstream deftly against
the flow of the river. I jumped off that bus with those
bags I had thrown everything into
in five minutes, and ran, the bags
wagged me from side to side as if
to prove I was under the claims of the material,
I ran up to a man with a white flower on his breast,
I who always go to the end of the line, I said
Help me. He looked at my ticket, he said
Make a left and then a right, go up the moving stairs and then
run. I lumbered up the moving stairs,
at the top I saw the corridor,

and then I took a deep breath, I said
Goodbye to my body, goodbye to comfort,
I used my legs and heart as if I would
gladly use them up for this,
to touch him again in this life. I ran, and the
bags banged me, wheeled and coursed
in skewed orbits, I have seen pictures of
women running, their belongings tied
in scarves grasped in their fists, I blessed my
long legs he gave me, my strong
heart I abandoned to its own purpose,
I ran to Gate 17 and they were
just lifting the thick white
lozenge of the door to fit it into
the socket of the plane. Like the one who is not
too rich, I turned sideways and
slipped through the needle's eye, and then
I walked down the aisle toward my father. The jet
was full, and people's hair was shining, they were
smiling, the interior of the plane was filled with a
mist of gold endorphin light,
I wept as people weep when they enter heaven,
in massive relief. We lifted up
gently from one tip of the continent
and did not stop until we set down lightly on the
other edge, I walked into his room
and watched his chest rise slowly
and sink again, all night
I watched him breathe.

Sharon Olds

At the Bay 1999

At four in the morning, the waning crescent
rose. It still seemed full night,
Pegasus shining. The tide was low,
a clump of seaweed on the foreshore shimmered
so slightly that I had to gaze aside
to see it. The constellations were moving
up from the east. The clump glittered
in a different place — it was a snowy egret,
hunting, at the liquid edge
in the dark. I felt like a man who watches
a goddess bathe, diminutive and naked
in a clearing. The first, dawn light

seemed to come from inside the ocean,
a glow the sky picked up. Low
over the inlet, into this quiet,
a pelican flew, coming to rest
on the glossy surface. And another pelican
alighted, and the two floated
under the gold moon, in silence.
And the great blue came stalking, snake
neck and mallet beak, segment-
walking on fleshless legs at the end
of night. The air was soft and cold.
The water was smooth. Up from within it,
moving from west to east, a dolphin's
dark, back, slowly, curved.
Moments later, in the same place,
but now from east to west, it came up
past me again, and down, as if
the earth had said, I will say it twice,
Sharon, the first time backwards, to get you
ready, the second time left to right, so you can read it.

ꕥ

MARGE PIERCY *(b. 1936) was born in Detroit, where her father was employed as an installation worker by Westinghouse. Her mother was the daughter of a union activist who was murdered for his efforts to organize workers. Piercy had an emotionally difficult adolescence, and a severe attack of rheumatic fever left her physically weakened. She also began writing as a teenager, however, and with the help of scholarships and prizes she graduated from the University of Michigan in 1957 and received her M.A. a year later.*

Briefly married, Piercy was divorced by the time she was twenty-three. In the 1960s she married again, and with her husband became committed to a communal lifestyle and to the protest movement against the Vietnam War and U.S. involvement in Latin America. In 1980 she married for a third time, and since then she has lived in Wellfleet, Massachusetts, on Cape Cod. Although Piercy is one of the more popular feminist poets, she is still much better known as a novelist. Her long, fictionalized accounts of her family background and her life as a radical in the 1960s have been best-sellers, and she has been able to live comfortably on the income from her fiction and her readings.

"The woman in the ordinary" was written in 1973. "In which she begs (like everybody else) that love may last" is from her 1983 collection Stone, Paper, Knife. *"It ain't heavy, it's my purse," with its humorous allusion to a well-known sentimental drawing of a small boy carrying a much larger, older boy on his shoulders with the caption, "He ain't heavy, he's my brother," was published in 1992.*

RELATED COMMENTARY: *Marge Piercy, "Imagery Can't Really Be Taught," page 1202.*

MARGE PIERCY

The woman in the ordinary 1973

The woman in the ordinary pudgy downcast girl
is crouching with eyes and muscles clenched.
Round and pebble smooth she effaces herself
under ripples of conversation and debate.
The woman in the block of ivory soap
has massive thighs that neigh,
great breasts that blare and strong arms that trumpet.
The woman of the golden fleece
laughs uproariously from the belly
inside the girl who imitates
a Christmas card virgin with glued hands,
who fishes for herself in other's eyes,
who stoops and creeps to make herself smaller.
In her bottled up is a woman peppery as curry,
a yam of a woman of butter and brass,
compounded of acid and sweet like a pineapple,
like a handgrenade set to explode,
like goldenrod ready to bloom.

MARGE PIERCY

In which she begs (like everybody else) that love may last 1983

The lilac blooms now in May,
our bed awash with its fragrance,
while beside the drive, buds
of peony and poppy swell
toward cracking, slivers of color
bulging like a flash of eye
from someone pretending to sleep.
Each in its garden slot, each
in its season, crocus gives way
to daffodil, through to fall
monkshood and chrysanthemum.
Only I am the wicked rose
that wants to bloom all year.
I am never replete with loving
you. Satisfaction
makes me greedy. I want
to blossom out with my joy of you
in March, in July, in October.

I want to drop my red red
petals on the hard black ice.

MARGE PIERCY

It ain't heavy, it's my purse

1992

We have marsupial instincts, women
who lug purses as big as garbage igloos,
women who hang leather hippos from their shoulders:

we are hiding the helpless greedy naked worms
of our intentions shivering in chaos.
In bags the size of Manhattan studio apartments,

we carry not merely the apparatus of neatness
and legality, cards, licenses, combs,
mirrors, spare glasses, lens fluid,

but hex signs against disaster and loss.
Antihistamines — if we should sneeze.
Painkillers — suppose the back goes out.

Snake bite medicine — a copperhead
may lurk in the next subway car.
Extra shoes — I may have to ford a stream.

On my keyring, flats I used to stay in,
a Volvo I traded in 1985, two unknown doors
opening on what I might sometime direly need.

Ten pens, because the ink may run out.
Band-Aids, safety pins, rubber bands, glue,
maps, a notebook in case, addresses of friends

estranged. So we go hopping lopsided, women
like kangaroos with huge purses bearing hidden
our own helplessness and its fancied cures.

SYLVIA PLATH *(1932–1963) was born in Boston. Her father, who had emigrated from a German area of Poland as a boy, taught entomology at Boston University. Their relationship, as she described it in her poetry, was complicated, but he died when she was eight, and her mother, a high-school language teacher, encouraged her to write. Plath attended Smith College and graduated summa cum laude, but between her junior and senior years she suffered a nervous breakdown and attempted suicide.*

In 1955, after her graduation, she received a Fulbright grant to study at Cambridge University, where she met one of the most promising young English poets, Ted Hughes. They were married in 1956 and came to the United States, where Plath had a job teaching at Smith College and Hughes later took a job at Amherst College. After two years Hughes returned to England, and despite strains in their marriage Plath joined him there in December 1959. They had two children, a daughter born in 1960 and a son in 1962, and they settled in a cottage in Devon.

On the surface Plath's life seemed ideal, with a house in the English countryside, a husband who respected her writing, and the publication of her first book the same year her first child was born. The poems she was writing, however, depict her despair at her isolation and the tensions of marriage to someone who was also a gifted writer and who was attractive to other women. Hughes began a relationship with someone else and left the cottage in Devon in October 1962. Several weeks later Plath moved with her children into a bleak London flat. She had been writing at a frantic pace through the autumn months and, despite near poverty and a deepening sense of isolation, she continued to compose the poems that Hughes later collected in his edited version of the manuscript she had titled Ariel. *By February she could no longer see any way out of her emotional turmoil and ended her life. As Robert Lowell wrote in an introduction to the poems, "Her art's immortality is life's disintegration."*

"Morning Song" is the first poem in Ariel. *It describes the birth of Plath's second child and their first night together. "Mirror" is an extended image of a mirror, in which she sees her old age rising toward her "like a terrible fish." She completed "Daddy" on October 12, 1962, the day after Hughes left her, and she continued to write raging poems over the next weeks. "Lady Lazarus" was begun on October 23 and finished on October 29. (Students who are interested in Plath's writing should also read the section on Ted Hughes on p. 1062.)*

RELATED POEM: *Ted Hughes, "Fulbright Scholars," page 1065.*
RELATED COMMENTARY: *Robert Lowell, "Foreword to Plath's* Ariel, *" page 1194.*

Sylvia Plath

Morning Song

1961

Love set you going like a fat gold watch.
The midwife slapped your footsoles, and your bald cry
Took its place among the elements.

Our voices echo, magnifying your arrival. New statue.
In a drafty museum, your nakedness
Shadows our safety. We stand round blankly as walls.

I'm no more your mother
Than the cloud that distils a mirror to reflect its own slow
Effacement at the wind's hand.

All night your moth-breath
Flickers among the flat pink roses. I wake to listen:
A far sea moves in my ear.

One cry, and I stumble from bed, cow-heavy and floral
In my Victorian nightgown.
Your mouth opens clean as a cat's. The window square

■ ■ ■

Whitens and swallows its dull stars. And now you try
Your handful of notes;
The clear vowels rise like balloons.

Sylvia Plath

Mirror

1963

I am silver and exact. I have no preconceptions
Whatever I see I swallow immediately
Just as it is, unmisted by love or dislike.
I am not cruel, only truthful —
The eye of a little god, four-cornered.
Most of the time I meditate on the opposite wall.
It is pink, with speckles. I have looked at it so long
I think it is a part of my heart. But it flickers.
Faces and darkness separate us over and over.

Now I am a lake. A woman bends over me,
Searching my reaches for what she really is.
Then she turns to those liars, the candles or the moon.
I see her back, and reflect it faithfully.
She rewards me with tears and an agitation of hands.
I am important to her. She comes and goes.
Each morning it is her face that replaces the darkness.
In me she has drowned a younger girl, and in me an old woman
Rises toward her day after day, like a terrible fish.

Sylvia Plath

Daddy

1962

You do not do, you do not do
Any more, black shoe
In which I have lived like a foot
For thirty years, poor and white,
Barely daring to breathe or Achoo.

Daddy, I have had to kill you.
You died before I had time ——
Marble-heavy, a bag full of God,
Ghastly statue with one gray toe
Big as a Frisco seal

And a head in the freakish Atlantic
Where it pours bean green over blue
In the waters off beautiful Nauset.

I used to pray to recover you.
Ach, du.° *Oh, you*

In the German tongue, in the Polish Town°
Scraped flat by the roller
Of wars, wars, wars.
But the name of the town is common.
My Polack friend

Says there are a dozen or two.
So I never could tell where you
Put your foot, your root,
I never could talk to you.
The tongue stuck in my jaw.

It stuck in a barb wire snare.
Ich, ich, ich, ich,° *I, I, I, I*
I could hardly speak.
I thought every German was you.
And the language obscene

An engine, an engine
Chuffing me off like a Jew.
A Jew to Dachau, Auschwitz, Belsen.°
I began to talk like a Jew.
I think I may well be a Jew.

The snows of the Tyrol, the clear beer of Vienna
Are not very pure or true.
With my gypsy-ancestress and my weird luck
And my Taroc° pack and my Taroc pack
I may be a bit of a Jew.

I have always been scared of *you*,
With your Luftwaffe,° your gobbledygoo.
And your neat mustache
And your Aryan eye, bright blue.
Panzer-man, panzer-man,° O You —

Not God but a swastika
So black no sky could squeak through.
Every woman adores a Fascist,
The boot in the face, the brute
Brute heart of a brute like you.

You stand at the blackboard, daddy,
In the picture I have of you,
A cleft in your chin instead of your foot

---

16. Polish Town: Refers to Otto Plath's birthplace, Granbow. **33. Dachau . . . Belsen:** Nazi death camps in World War II. **39. Taroc:** Pack of fortune-telling (tarot) cards. **42. Luftwaffe:** World War II German aircorps. **45. Panzer-man:** In World War II, the German panzer division was that made up of armored vehicles.

But no less a devil for that, no not
Any less the black man who

Bit my pretty red heart in two.
I was ten when they buried you.
At twenty I tried to die
And get back, back, back to you.
I thought even the bones would do

But they pulled me out of the sack,
And they stuck me together with glue.
And then I knew what to do.
I made a model of you,
A man in black with a Meinkampf° look

And a love of the rack and the screw.
And I said I do, I do.
So daddy, I'm finally through.
The black telephone's off at the root,
The voices just can't worm through.

If I've killed one man, I've killed two ——
The vampire who said he was you
And drank my blood for a year,
Seven years, if you want to know.
Daddy, you can lie back now.

There's a stake in your fat black heart
And the villagers never liked you.
They are dancing and stamping on you.
They always *knew* it was you.
Daddy, daddy, you bastard, I'm through.

Sylvia Plath

Lady Lazarus°

1962

I have done it again.
One year in every ten
I manage it ——

A sort of walking miracle, my skin
Bright as a Nazi lampshade,°
My right foot

A paperweight,
My face a featureless, fine
Jew linen.

---

65. Meinkampf: Adolf Hitler's autobiography was titled *Meinkampf,* or "My Struggle." **Lazarus:** In John 11:44, Jesus resurrects Lazarus from the grave. **5. Nazi lampshade:** The Nazis used the skin of some Jewish concentration camp prisoners to make lampshades.

■ ■ ■

Peel off the napkin
O my enemy.
Do I terrify? ——

The nose, the eye pits, the full set of teeth?
The sour breath
Will vanish in a day.

Soon, soon the flesh
The grave cave ate will be
At home on me

And I a smiling woman.
I am only thirty.
And like the cat I have nine times to die.

This is Number Three.
What a trash
To annihilate each decade.

What a million filaments.
The peanut-crunching crowd
Shoves in to see

Them unwrap me hand and foot ——
The big strip tease.
Gentleman, ladies,

These are my hands,
My knees.
I may be skin and bone,

Nevertheless, I am the same, identical woman.
The first time it happened I was ten.
It was an accident.

The second time I meant
To last it out and not come back at all.
I rocked shut

As a seashell.
They had to call and call
And pick the worms off me like sticky pearls.

Dying
Is an art, like everything else.
I do it exceptionally well.

I do it so it feels like hell.
I do it so it feels real.
I guess you could say I've a call.

It's easy enough to do it in a cell.
It's easy enough to do it and stay put.
It's the theatrical

■ ■ ■

Comeback in broad day
To the same place, the same face, the same brute
Amused shout:

"A miracle!"
That knocks me out.
There is a charge

For the eyeing of my scars, there is a charge
For the hearing of my heart ——
It really goes.

And there is a charge, a very large charge,
For a word or a touch
Or a bit of blood

Or a piece of my hair or my clothes.
So, so, Herr Doktor.
So, Herr Enemy.

I am your opus,
I am your valuable,
The pure gold baby

That melts to a shriek.
I turn and burn.
Do not think I underestimate your great concern.

Ash, ash —
You poke and stir.
Flesh, bone, there is nothing there ——

A cake of soap,
A wedding ring,
A gold filling.

Herr God, Herr Lucifer,
Beware
Beware.

Out of the ash
I rise with my red hair
And I eat men like air.

☙

THEODORE ROETHKE *(1908–1963) was born in Saginaw, Michigan, the son of a successful operator of commercial greenhouses. Already writing poetry as an undergraduate at the University of Michigan, he began publishing his work during his graduate studies at Michigan and Harvard. His first full-time teaching position was at Lafayette College in Pennsylvania in 1931. He later taught at several other universities before going in 1947 to the University of Washington, where he taught for the rest of his life. His book* Words for the Wind: The Collected Verse, *in 1958, established his reputation.*

Roethke was a prolific writer and had a successful career as a poet, but he struggled against alcoholism and manic-depressive illness. On more than one occasion he had to be taken in handcuffs from his classroom and was hospitalized for long periods. The poet Robert Lowell, a close friend, described him as "a ponderous, coarse, fattish, fortyish man, well read, likes the same things I do, and is quite a competent poet."

"My Papa's Waltz" recounts a painful childhood memory; "Elegy for Jane" is about the death of one of his students. "I Knew a Woman" uses a complicated rhyme scheme and some of the language of earlier poets to describe his very modern feelings. *(See also Roethke's "The Waking" on p. 888.)*

THEODORE ROETHKE

My Papa's Waltz

1948

The whiskey on your breath
Could make a small boy dizzy;
But I hung on like death:
Such waltzing was not easy.

We romped until the pans
Slid from the kitchen shelf;
My mother's countenance
Could not unfrown itself.

The hand that held my wrist
Was battered on one knuckle;
At every step you missed
My right ear scraped a buckle.

You beat time on my head
With a palm caked hard by dirt,
Then waltzed me off to bed
Still clinging to your shirt.

THEODORE ROETHKE

Elegy for Jane

1953

My Student, Thrown by a Horse

I remember the neckcurls, limp and damp as tendrils;
And her quick look, a sidelong pickerel smile;
And how, once startled into talk, the light syllables leaped for her,
And she balanced in the delight of her thought,
A wren, happy, tail into the wind,
Her song trembling the twigs and small branches.
The shade sang with her;
The leaves, their whispers turned to kissing;
And the mold sang in the bleached valleys under the rose.

■ ■ ■

Oh, when she was sad, she cast herself down into such a pure depth,
Even a father could not find her:
Scraping her cheek against straw;
Stirring the clearest water.

My sparrow, you are not here,
Waiting like a fern, making a spiny shadow.
The sides of wet stones cannot console me,
Nor the moss, wound with the last light.

If only I could nudge you from this sleep,
My maimed darling, my skittery pigeon.
Over this damp grave I speak the words of my love:
I, with no rights in this matter,
Neither father nor lover.

THEODORE ROETHKE

I Knew a Woman

1958

I knew a woman, lovely in her bones,
When small birds sighed, she would sigh back at them;
Ah, when she moved, she moved more ways than one:
The shapes a bright container can contain!
Of her choice virtues only gods should speak,
Or English poets who grew up on Greek
(I'd have them sing in chorus, cheek to cheek).

How well her wishes went! She stroked my chin,
She taught me Turn, and Counter-turn, and Stand;°
She taught me Touch, that undulant white skin;
I nibbled meekly from her proffered hand;
She was the sickle; I, poor I, the rake,
Coming behind her for her pretty sake
(But what prodigious mowing we did make).

Love likes a gander, and adores a goose:
Her full lips pursed, the errant note to seize;
She played it quick, she played it light and loose,
My eyes, they dazzled at her flowing knees;
Her several parts could keep a pure repose,
Or one hip quiver with a mobile nose
(She moved in circles, and those circles moved).

Let seed be grass, and grass turn into hay:
I'm martyr to a motion not my own;
What's freedom for? To know eternity.
I swear she cast a shadow white as stone.

9. Turn . . . Counter-turn . . . Stand: Literal translations of the Greek words *strophe, antistrophe,* and *epode,* which constitute the three sections of a Pindaric ode.

But who would count eternity in days?
These old bones live to learn her wanton ways:
(I measure time by how a body sways).

ANNE SEXTON *(1928–1974), the youngest of three daughters, was born in Newton, Massachusetts, a suburb of Boston, and grew up in Wellesley. She was from a well-off New England family, spending her winters in the city and her summers on Squirrel Island in Maine. When she was nineteen she eloped with a man who was, like her father, successful in the woolen industry.*

Although outwardly she conformed to her family's expectations, Sexton was unable to resolve her inner conflicts. After the birth of each of her daughters, in 1953 and 1955, she was hospitalized for psychiatric treatment. When she first attempted suicide in 1956, her doctor suggested she begin writing poetry as therapy. She enrolled in her first writing workshop the next year, where she met the writer Maxine Kumin, who would become a close friend. The following year she enrolled in Robert Lowell's poetry class at Boston University. Another young poet, Sylvia Plath, was in the same class.

Sexton's first book, To Bedlam and Part Way Back, *published in 1960, only a year after her class with Lowell, attracted considerable attention for its powerful confessional style. She received awards and grants, and in 1967 she won the Pulitzer Prize for her book* Live or Die. *She taught at Harvard and Colgate universities, and was appointed a professor at Boston University in 1972. Despite her recognition, however, she was unable to free herself from her emotional torment. She finally succeeded in a suicide attempt in 1974.*

"The Starry Night" is her response to a painting by Vincent van Gogh, and "Little Girl, My String Bean, My Lovely Woman" is addressed to her eleven-year-old daughter, Linda.

RELATED COMMENTARY: *Richard Howard, "'Some Tribal Female Who Is Known but Forbidden': Anne Sexton," page 1180.*

ANNE SEXTON

The Starry Night

1962

That does not keep me from having a terrible need of — shall I say the word — religion. Then I go out at night to paint the stars.

– VINCENT VAN GOGH in a letter to his brother°

The town does not exist
except where one black-haired tree slips
up like a drowned woman into the hot sky.

Vincent van Gogh . . . to his brother: Sexton's title echoes *Starry Night on the Rhône,* a painting by the Dutch artist Vincent van Gogh (1853–1890), who eventually went mad and committed suicide; the epigraph is taken from a letter van Gogh wrote to his brother, Theo, in 1888 — at about the time he was painting *Starry Night*.

The town is silent. The night boils with eleven stars
Oh starry starry night! This is how
I want to die.

It moves. They are all alive.
Even the moon bulges in its orange irons
to push children, like a god, from its eye.
The old unseen serpent swallows up the stars.
Oh starry starry night! This is how
I want to die:

into that rushing beast of the night,
sucked up by that great dragon, to split
from my life with no flag,
no belly,
no cry.

ANNE SEXTON

Little Girl, My String Bean, My Lovely Woman *1964*

My daughter, at eleven
(almost twelve), is like a garden.

Oh, darling! Born in that sweet birthday suit
and having owned it and known it for so long,
now you must watch high noon enter —
noon, that ghost hour.
Oh, funny little girl — this one under a blueberry sky,
this one! How can I say that I've known
just what you know and just where you are?

It's not a strange place, this odd home
where your face sits in my hand
so full of distance,
so full of its immediate fever.
The summer has seized you,
as when, last month in Amalfi, I saw
lemons as large as your desk-side globe —
that miniature map of the world —
and I could mention, too,
the market stalls of mushrooms
and garlic buds all engorged.
Or I think even of the orchard next door,
where the berries are done
and the apples are beginning to swell.
And once, with our first backyard,
I remember I planted an acre of yellow beans
we couldn't eat.

■ ■ ■

Oh, little girl,
my stringbean,
how do you grow?
You grow this way.
You are too many to eat.

I hear
as in a dream
the conversation of the old wives
speaking of *womanhood.*
I remember that I heard nothing myself.
I was alone.
I waited like a target.

Let high noon enter —
the hour of the ghosts.
Once the Romans believed
that noon was the ghost hour,
and I can believe it, too,
under that startling sun,
and someday they will come to you,
someday, men bare to the waist, young Romans
at noon where they belong,
with ladders and hammers
while no one sleeps.

But before they enter
I will have said,
Your bones are lovely,
and before their strange hands
there was always this hand that formed.

Oh, darling, let your body in,
let it tie you in,
in comfort.
What I want to say, Linda,
is that women are born twice.

If I could have watched you grow
as a magical mother might,
if I could have seen through my magical transparent belly,
there would have been such ripening within:
your embryo,
the seed taking on its own,
life clapping the bedpost,
bones from the pond,
thumbs and two mysterious eyes,
the awfully human head,
the heart jumping like a puppy,
the important lungs,
the becoming —

while it becomes!
as it does now,
a world of its own,
a delicate place.

I say hello
to such shakes and knockings and high jinks,
such music, such sprouts,
such dancing-mad-bears of music,
such necessary sugar,
such goings-on!

Oh, little girl,
my stringbean,
how do you grow?
You grow this way.
You are too many to eat.

What I want to say, Linda,
is that there is nothing in your body that lies.
All that is new is telling the truth.
I'm here, that somebody else,
an old tree in the background.

Darling,
stand still at your door,
sure of yourself, a white stone, a good stone —
as exceptional as laughter
you will strike fire,
that new thing!

WILLIAM SHAKESPEARE *(1564–1616) is best known as a playwright, and his life and career are presented in the drama section in this book. Almost as honored is the sequence of sonnets he wrote during the latter part of his career. A contemporary of Shakespeare's wrote in 1598 that in addition to his plays, he was known "among his private friends" for "his sugared sonnets." They were published in 1609, the year before he retired from the theater, and since then they have been the standard against which all other sonnets in the English language are measured.*

The 154 sonnets in the sequence seem to tell the story of an unhappy love affair, but, like so much else about Shakespeare's work, there is considerable confusion and continual scholarly wrangling over interpretation of the poems themselves and the story they may tell us. There is even uncertainty about the order of the sonnets. A "Dark Lady" is the central figure in many of them, and in some there is a suggestion of a love triangle between two men and a woman. Some of the early sonnets are written to a young man of great beauty, urging him to marry.

More important than these details of the possible "story" of the sequence are the sonnets themselves, many lines and phrases from which have entered into the English language. The small gathering that follows reprints some of Shakespeare's most often anthologized sonnets. (The Shakespearean sonnet form is also discussed on pp. 877–882.)

RELATED COMMENTARY: *Erica Jong, "Devouring Time: Shakespeare's Sonnets," page 1185.*

WILLIAM SHAKESPEARE

Shall I compare thee to a summer's day? 1609

Shall I compare thee to a summer's day?
Thou art more lovely and more temperate;
Rough winds do shake the darling buds of May,
And summer's lease hath all too short a date.
Sometime too hot the eye of heaven shines,
And often is his gold complexion dimmed;
And every fair from fair sometime declines,
By chance, or nature's changing course untrimmed.
But thy eternal summer shall not fade
Nor lose possession of that fair thou owest;
Nor shall Death brag thou wander'st in his shade,
When in eternal lines to time thou growest.
So long as men can breathe or eyes can see,
So long lives this and this gives life to thee.

WILLIAM SHAKESPEARE

When to the sessions of sweet silent thought 1609

When to the sessions of sweet silent thought
I summon up remembrance of things past,
I sigh the lack of many a thing I sought,
And with old woes new wail my dear time's waste:
Then can I drown an eye, unused to flow,
For precious friends hid in death's dateless night,
And weep afresh love's long since canceled woe,
And moan the expense of many a vanished sight:
Then can I grieve at grievances foregone,
And heavily from woe to woe tell o'er
The sad account of fore-bemoanèd moan,
Which I new pay as if not paid before.
But if the while I think on thee, dear friend,
All losses are restored and sorrows end.

WILLIAM SHAKESPEARE

Let me not to the marriage of true minds *1609*

Let me not to the marriage of true minds
Admit impediments. Love is not love
Which alters when it alteration finds,
Or bends with the remover to remove:
O, no! it is an ever-fixèd mark
That looks on tempests and is never shaken;
It is the star to every wandering bark,
Whose worth's unknown, although his height be taken.
Love's not Time's fool, though rosy lips and cheeks
Within his bending sickle's compass come;
Love alters not with his brief hours and weeks,
But bears it out even to the edge of doom.
If this be error and upon me proved,
I never writ, nor no man ever loved.

WILLIAM SHAKESPEARE

My mistress' eyes are nothing like the sun *1609*

My mistress' eyes are nothing like the sun;
Coral is far more red than her lips' red:
If snow be white, why then her breasts are dun;
If hairs be wires, black wires grow on her head.
I have seen roses damasked, red and white,
But no such roses see I in her cheeks;
And in some perfumes is there more delight
Than in the breath that from my mistress reeks.
I love to hear her speak, yet well I know
That music hath a far more pleasing sound;
I grant I never saw a goddess go;
My mistress, when she walks, treads on the ground:
And yet, by heaven, I think my love as rare
As any she belied with false compare.

PERCY BYSSHE SHELLEY *(1792–1822) was born outside of London in Sussex. His grandfather was a wealthy aristocrat and his father was a politically conservative member of Parliament. Shelley attended elite schools — first Eton, then Oxford University — but being short, slightly built, and a poor athlete, he was bullied so unmercifully by the other students that he came to see all of English society as an instrument of oppression.*

He was already writing poetry and sensational novels as a teenager, but at Oxford he and a friend, Thomas Jefferson Hogg, published a small pamphlet titled The Necessity of Atheism. *When Shelley was questioned by the university authorities, he refused to repudiate the pamphlet, and both Shelley and Hogg were expelled. Shelley was only eighteen; earlier in the year he had met a young woman named Harriet Westbrook, who was sixteen. Six months after he'd been expelled, Shelley and Harriet eloped and were married in Edinburgh.*

Early the next year, in 1812, they traveled to Dublin, and Shelley published two more pamphlets, this time advocating Catholic emancipation and Irish independence. For a year he and Harriet moved from place to place while he wrote poetry, read continuously, and tried to obtain more money from his family. In 1813 he met the controversial philosopher William Godwin and found himself drawn into Godwin's family, which included a teenage daughter, Mary, and her half-sister, Jane (later Claire) Clairmont. Harriet gave birth to a daughter, but Shelley was becoming more and more involved with Mary. Godwin tried to separate them, but Shelley attempted suicide with an overdose of opium, then after his recovery he abandoned his wife and child and fled to France with both Mary, who was sixteen, and Claire, who was a few months younger.

By abandoning his wife, Shelley had burned most of his bridges, but his father, in an effort to clear the family name, paid Shelley's debts and set him up with a yearly income. Hogg joined the group when the three of them returned to England a few months later, and for a time the four of them seem to have lived in an open experiment that they termed "free-love." Shelley somehow expected Harriet to join them, but she refused. In November she gave birth to a son they had conceived before he had fled with Mary Godwin. Three months later Mary gave birth to a daughter, who died two weeks later. Shelley was now twenty-two.

Shelley, Mary, and Claire returned to Europe and joined the poet George Gordon, Lord Byron, in Switzerland, and Byron and Claire soon became lovers. A few months later, Harriet's body was found in the Serpentine Pond in Hyde Park. She had become pregnant by someone else and, in despair, had committed suicide. Mary and Shelley, who now had a son, were married three weeks later.

Through all of this turmoil, Shelley was writing the poems for which he would finally be famous, although some years had to pass before the controversy died down about his personal life. In the summer of 1822, in northern Italy, where he and Mary and their children were now living, Shelley and a friend went out in the Bay of Spezia in a new sailboat he had had built to his own specifications. The boat overturned in a storm, and their bodies washed up on the beach three days later.

"Ozymandias" was written quickly after viewing an exhibition at the British Museum with a friend, but it has become one of his best-known poems. Like "Ode to the West Wind" (p. 870), "To a Sky-Lark" was written in 1820 and is one of Shelley's best-known lyric odes. (See also Shelley's "When Passion's Trance Is Overpast" on p. 854.)

RELATED COMMENTARIES: *Sherod Santos, "Shelley in Ruins: The Appeal of 'Ozymandias,'" page 1209; Percy Bysshe Shelley, From "A Defence of Poetry," page 1217.*

PERCY BYSSHE SHELLEY

Ozymandias°
1818

I met a traveler from an antique land
Who said: Two vast and trunkless legs of stone
Stand in the desert . . . Near them, on the sand,
Half sunk, a shattered visage lies, whose frown,
And wrinkled lip, and sneer of cold command,
Tell that its sculptor well those passions read
Which yet survive, stamped on these lifeless things,
The hand that mocked them, and the heart that fed:
And on the pedestal these words appear:
"My name is Ozymandias, king of kings:
Look on my works, ye Mighty, and despair!"
Nothing beside remains. Round the decay
Of that colossal wreck, boundless and bare
The lone and level sands stretch far away.

PERCY BYSSHE SHELLEY

To a Sky-Lark
1820

Hail to thee, blithe Spirit!
Bird thou never wert —
That from Heaven, or near it,
Pourest thy full heart
In profuse strains of unpremeditated art.

Higher still and higher
From the earth thou springest
Like a cloud of fire;
The blue deep thou wingest,
And singing still dost soar, and soaring ever singest.

In the golden lightning
Of the sunken Sun —
O'er which clouds are brightning,
Thou dost float and run;
Like an unbodied joy whose race is just begun.

The pale purple even
Melts around thy flight,
Like a star of Heaven
In the broad day-light
Thou art unseen, — but yet I hear thy shrill delight,

Ozymandias: Greek name for the thirteenth-century B.C. Egyptian pharaoh Ramses II.

■ ■ ■

Keen as are the arrows
    Of that silver sphere,° *the morning star*
Whose intense lamp narrows
    In the white dawn clear
Until we hardly see — we feel that it is there.

All the earth and air
    With thy voice is loud,
As when Night is bare
    From one lonely cloud
The moon rains out her beams — and Heaven is overflowed.

What thou art we know not;
    What is most like thee?
From rainbow clouds there flow not
    Drops so bright to see
As from thy presence showers a rain of melody.

Like a Poet hidden
    In the light of thought,
Singing hymns unbidden,
    Till the world is wrought
To sympathy with hopes and fears it heeded not:

Like a high-born maiden
    In a palace-tower,
Soothing her love-laden
    Soul in secret hour,
With music sweet as love — which overflows her bower:

Like a glow-worm golden
    In a dell of dew,
Scattering unbeholden
    Its aerial hue
Among the flowers and grass which screen it from the view:

Like a rose embowered
    In its own green leaves —
By warm winds deflowered —
    Till the scent it gives
Makes faint with too much sweet heavy-wingèd thieves:

Sound of vernal showers
    On the twinkling grass,
Rain-awakened flowers,
    All that ever was
Joyous, and clear and fresh, thy music doth surpass.

Teach us, Sprite or Bird,
    What sweet thoughts are thine:
I have never heard
    Praise of love or wine
That panted forth a flood of rapture so divine:

■ ■ ■

Chorus Hymeneal°
　Or triumphal chaunt
Matched with thine would be all
　But an empty vaunt,
A thing wherein we feel there is some hidden want.

What objects are the fountains
　Of thy happy strain?
What fields or waves or mountains?
　What shapes of sky or plain?
What love of thine own kind? what ignorance of pain?

With thy clear keen joyance
　Languor cannot be —
Shadow of annoyance
　Never came near thee;
Thou lovest — but ne'er knew love's sad satiety.

Waking or asleep,
　Thou of death must deem
Things more true and deep
　Than we mortals dream,
Or how could thy notes flow in such a chrystal stream?

We look before and after,
　And pine for what is not —
Our sincerest laughter
　With some pain is fraught —
Our sweetest songs are those that tell of saddest thought.

Yet if we could scorn
　Hate and pride and fear;
If we were things born
　Not to shed a tear,
I know not how thy joy we ever should come near.

Better than all measures
　Of delightful sound —
Better than all treasures
　That in books are found —
Thy skill to poet were, thou Scorner of the ground!

Teach me half the gladness
　That thy brain must know,
Such harmonious madness
　From my lips would flow
The world should listen then — as I am listening now.

---

66. Chorus Hymeneal: Reference to Hymen, the Greek god of marriage.

GARY SNYDER *(b. 1930) was born in San Francisco, but his family moved to a farm outside of Seattle when he was two, and he grew up in the Pacific Northwest. In 1942 the family moved to Portland, Oregon, where he went to high school. In 1947 he enrolled in Reed College, and shared a house with two other young poets, Philip Whalen and Lew Welch. His first published poems appeared in the Reed literary magazine.*

In 1952 he moved to San Francisco, then rented a small cottage in Berkeley while he studied in the university's Asian language program. He soon met Beat writers Allen Ginsberg and Jack Kerouac, and his cottage became one of the hangouts for the young Beat movement. Kerouac made him the hero of his novel The Dharma Bums, *naming him "Japhy Ryder." Snyder was one of the other readers the night Allen Ginsberg first read parts of* Howl. *In 1957 Snyder moved to Japan, and for the next dozen years he lived mostly in Kyoto, studying and meditating at the Daitoku-ji Zen monastery. His first book,* Riprap, *was published in 1959.*

Snyder came back to San Francisco in time for the Human Be-In in 1967, and after that he lived for many years with his wife and children in a Japanese-style house he built in the California mountains. He now teaches poetry half the year at the University of California at Davis and also lectures on ecology and the environment. He is a popular reader of his own work and often appeared with friends, including Ginsberg and Lawrence Ferlinghetti. His collection Turtle Island *won the Pulitzer Prize in 1975.*

"Milton by Firelight" reflects Snyder's continuing interest in the environment and the natural world. "Four Poems for Robin" returns to memories of a college love affair. *(See also Snyder's "Ripples on the Surface" on p. 929.)*

GARY SNYDER

Milton by Firelight

1955

"O hell, what do mine eyes
        with grief behold?"°
Working with an old
Singlejack miner, who can sense
The vein and cleavage
In the very guts of rock, can
Blast granite, build
Switchbacks° that last for years
Under the beat of snow, thaw, mule-hooves.
What use, Milton, a silly story
Of our lost general parents,
        eaters of fruit?

The Indian, the chainsaw boy,
And a string of six mules

1–2. "O hell, . . . behold?": In his 1667 epic poem *Paradise Lost,* John Milton (1608–1674) retells the biblical story of Adam and Eve's fall from grace. Satan speaks these lines when he first spies the couple in the Garden of Eden (4:358). **8. Switchbacks:** Roads that zigzag up a sharp incline.

Came riding down to camp
Hungry for tomatoes and green apples.
Sleeping in saddle-blankets
Under a bright night-sky
Han River slantwise by morning.
Jays squall
Coffee boils

In ten thousand years the Sierras
Will be dry and dead, home of the scorpion.
Ice-scratched slabs and bent trees.

No paradise, no fall,
Only the weathering land
The wheeling sky,
Man, with his Satan
Scouring the chaos of the mind.
Oh Hell!

Fire down
Too dark to read, miles from a road
The bell-mare clangs in the meadow
That packed dirt for a fill-in
Scrambling through loose rocks
On an old trail
All of a summer's day.

GARY SNYDER

Four Poems for Robin

1968

SIWASHING IT° OUT ONCE IN SIUSLAW FOREST

I slept under   rhododendron
All night   blossoms fell
Shivering on   a sheet of cardboard
Feet stuck   in my pack
Hands deep   in my pockets
Barely   able   to   sleep.
I remembered   when we were in school
Sleeping together   in a big warm bed
We were   the youngest lovers
When we broke up   we were still nineteen.
Now our   friends are married
You teach   school back east
I dont mind   living this way

Siwashing it: A term for rough camping. The Siuslaw Forest is a wilderness area west of Eugene, Oregon.

Green hills the long blue beach
But sometimes sleeping in the open
I think back when I had you.

A SPRING NIGHT IN SHOKOKU-JI°

Eight years ago this May
We walked under cherry blossoms
At night in an orchard in Oregon.
All that I wanted then
Is forgotten now, but you.
Here is the night
In a garden of the old capital
I feel the trembling ghost of Yugao
I remember your cool body
Naked under a summer cotton dress.

AN AUTUMN MORNING IN SHOKOKU-JI

Last night watching the Pleiades,°
Breath smoking in the moonlight,
Bitter memory like vomit
Choked my throat.
I unrolled a sleeping bag
On mats on the porch
Under thick autumn stars.
In dream you appeared
(Three times in nine years)
Wild, cold, and accusing.
I woke shamed and angry:
The pointless wars of the heart.
Almost dawn. Venus and Jupiter.
The first time I have
Ever seen them close.

DECEMBER AT YASE°

You said, that October,
In the tall dry grass by the orchard
When you chose to be free,
"Again someday, maybe ten years."

After college, I saw you
One time. You were strange.
And I was obsessed with a plan.

■ ■ ■

Shokoku-ji: An important Zen monastery in Kyoto, the old capital of Japan.
27. Pleiades: A cluster of stars in the constellation Taurus. Greek mythology held that these stars were the seven daughters of Atlas.
Yase: A suburb to the north of Kyoto.

Now ten years and more have
Gone by: I've always known
        where you were —
I might have gone to you
Hoping to win your love back.
You still are single.

I didn't.
I thought I must make it alone. I
Have done that.

Only in dream, like this dawn,
Does the grave, awed intensity
Of our young love
Return to my mind, to my flesh.

We had what the others
All crave and seek for;
We left it behind at nineteen.

I feel ancient, as though I had
Lived many lives.

And may never now know
If I am a fool
Or have done what my
        karma° demands.

CATHY SONG *(b. 1955) was born in Honolulu, Hawaii, of mixed Korean and Chinese ancestry. Her father, who was Korean and for whom she wrote the poem "The Tower of Pisa," was an airline pilot. Her mother, who was the subject of the poem "Humble Jar," was a seamstress, and her family was Chinese. In the 1970s Song moved to New England for her college years, graduating from Wellesley College in 1977 and completing her M.F.A. at Boston College in 1981. She returned to Hawaii after completing her degrees. She is married and the mother of two children.*

Song began writing when she was a child, and her first book, Picture Bride, *was published in 1983. It received the Yale Younger Poets Award and was nominated for the National Book Critics Circle Award. One of the themes of her writing is her family's history, and in the poem "Easter: Wahiawa, 1959" she describes her Korean grandfather, who cut sugar cane in the Hawaiian cane fields for eighteen years.*

. . . His right arm
grew disproportionately large
to the rest of his body.
He could hold three of us
grandchildren in that arm.

---

70. karma: In Buddhist thought, the force of our actions, which determine the form of our next incarnation.

Her poetry moves easily from the mythic to the personal; in "The White Porch," from her first book, she begins with washing her hair and ends with an image of Rapunzel, from the fairy tale, letting her hair down for her lover. In "Heaven," written a few years later, it is her young son who is the poem's protagonist, suspended in his dreams between the cultures of his mother and his father.

CATHY SONG

The White Porch

1983

I wrap the blue towel
after washing,
around the damp
weight of hair, bulky
as a sleeping cat,
and sit out on the porch.
Still dripping water,
it'll be dry by supper,
by the time the dust
settles off your shoes,
though it's only five
past noon. Think
of the luxury: how to use
the afternoon like the stretch
of lawn spread before me.
There's the laundry,
sun-warm clothes at twilight,
and the mountain of beans
in my lap. Each one,
I'll break and snap
thoughtfully in half.
But there is this slow arousal.
The small buttons
of my cotton blouse
are pulling away from my body.
I feel the strain of threads,
the swollen magnolias
heavy as a flock of birds
in the tree. Already,
the orange sponge cake
is rising in the oven.
I know you'll say it makes
your mouth dry
and I'll watch you
drench your slice of it

in canned peaches
and lick the plate clean.

So much hair, my mother
used to say, grabbing
the thick braided rope
in her hands while we washed
the breakfast dishes, discussing
dresses and pastries.
My mind often elsewhere
as we did the morning chores together.
Sometimes, a few strands
would catch in her gold ring.
I worked hard then,
anticipating the hour
when I would let the rope down
at night, strips of sheets,
knotted and tied,
while she slept in tight blankets.
My hair, freshly washed
like a measure of wealth,
like a bridal veil.
Crouching in the grass,
you would wait for the signal,
for the movement of curtains
before releasing yourself
from the shadow of moths.
Cloth, hair and hands,
smuggling you in.

CATHY SONG

Heaven

1988

He thinks when we die we'll go to China.
Think of it — a Chinese heaven
where, except for his blond hair,
the part that belongs to his father,
everyone will look like him.
China, that blue flower on the map,
bluer than the sea
his hand must span like a bridge
to reach it.
An octave away.

I've never seen it.
It's as if I can't sing that far.

But look —
on the map, this black dot.
Here is where we live,
on the pancake plains
just east of the Rockies,
on the other side of the clouds.
A mile above the sea,
the air is so thin, you can starve on it.
No bamboo trees
but the alpine equivalent,
reedy aspen with light, flattering leaves.
Did a boy in Guangzhou° dream of this
as his last stop?

I've heard the trains at night
whistling past our yards,
what we've come to own,
the broken fences, the whiny dog, the rattletrap cars.
It's still the wild west,
mean and grubby,
the shootouts and fistfights in the back alley.
With my son the dreamer
and my daughter, who is too young to walk,
I've sat in this spot
and wondered why here?
Why in this short life,
this town, this creek they call a river?

He had never planned to stay,
the boy who helped to build
the railroads° for a dollar a day.
He had always meant to go back.
When did he finally know
that each mile of track led him further away,
that he would die in his sleep,
dispossessed,
having seen Gold Mountain,°
the icy wind tunneling through it,
these landlocked, makeshift ghost towns?

It must be in the blood,
this notion of returning.
It skipped two generations, lay fallow,

---

24. Guangzhou: Or Canton, seaport city in southeastern China. **41. railroads:** Much of the labor in the construction of the western section of the Transcontinental Railroad in the nineteenth century was supplied by Chinese immigrants brought to the country for the work. **47. Gold Mountain:** In Chinese legend, a land of riches and opportunity, corresponding to the western El Dorado.

the garden an unmarked grave.
On a spring sweater day
it's as if we remember him.
I call to the children.
We can see the mountains
shimmering blue above the air.
If you look really hard
says my son the dreamer,
leaning out from the laundry's rigging,
the work shirts fluttering like sails,
you can see all the way to heaven.

GARY SOTO *(b. 1952) was born to Mexican American parents in Fresno, an agricultural town in California's Central Valley. He worked in the fields in the summers and in the Fresno factories. After his graduation from high school, he entered California State University at Fresno, planning to study urban planning, but classes with poet Philip Levine turned his interest to literature and writing. After graduation he went on to the University of California at Irvine for an M.F.A.*

Soto's first poems appeared when he was still a senior in college, and his first collection, The Elements of San Joaquin, *was published in 1977. He began teaching literature and Chicano studies at the University of California campus at Berkeley the same year. His work has won many awards, and he has been granted a Guggenheim fellowship. Although Soto is perhaps the best known of the new Chicano poets, his writing has a personal identity that places it directly in the American mainstream.*

"Mexicans Begin Jogging" is a wryly humorous memory from his youth; "Teaching English from an Old Composition Book," written in the same tone, describes an experience from his years as a young teacher.

GARY SOTO

Mexicans Begin Jogging

1981

At the factory I worked
In the fleck of rubber, under the press
Of an oven yellow with flame,
Until the border patrol opened
Their vans and my boss waved for us to run.
"Over the fence, Soto," he shouted,
And I shouted that I was American.
"No time for lies," he said, and pressed
A dollar in my palm, hurrying me
Through the back door.

■ ■ ■

Since I was on his time, I ran
And became the wag to a short tail of Mexicans —
Ran past the amazed crowds that lined
The street and blurred like photographs, in rain.
I ran from that industrial road to the soft
Houses where people paled at the turn of an autumn sky.
What could I do but yell *vivas*
To baseball, milkshakes, and those sociologists
Who would clock me
As I jog into the next century
On the power of a great, silly grin.

Gary Soto

Teaching English from an Old Composition Book

1996

My chalk is no larger than a chip of fingernail,
Chip by which I must explain this Monday
Night the verbs "to get," "to wear," "to cut."
I'm not given much, these tired students,
Knuckle-wrapped from work as roofers,
Sour from scrubbing toilets and pedestal sinks.
I'm given this room with five windows,
A coffee machine, a piano with busted strings,
The music of how we feel as the sun falls,
Exhausted from keeping up.
I stand at
The blackboard. The chip is worn to a hangnail,
Nearly gone, the dust of some educational bone.
By and by I'm Cantinflas, the comic
Busy body in front. I say, "I want the coffee."
I pick up a coffee cup and sip.
I clip my heels and say, "I wear my shoes."
I bring an invisible fork to my mouth
And say, "I eat the chicken."
Suddenly the class is alive —
Each one putting on hats and shoes,
Drinking sodas and beers, cutting flowers
And steaks — a pantomime of sumptuous living.

At break I pass out cookies.
Augustine, the Guatemalan, asks in Spanish,
"Teacher, what is 'tally-ho'?"
I look at the word in the composition book.

I raise my face to the bare bulb for a blind answer.
I stutter, then say, "It's like *adelante*."°
Augustine smiles, then nudges a friend
In the next desk, now smarter by one word.
After the cookies are eaten,
We move ahead to prepositions —
"Under," "over," and "between,"
Useful words when *la migra*° opens the doors
Of their idling vans.
At ten to nine, I'm tired of acting,
And they're tired of their roles.
When class ends, I clap my hands of chalk dust,
And two students applaud, thinking it's a new verb.
I tell them *adelante*,
And they pick up their old books.
They smile and, in return, cry, "Tally-ho"
As they head for the door.

PHILLIS WHEATLEY *(c. 1753–1784) was kidnapped from Africa and sold in the Boston slave market in 1761, so the true year of her birth will always be a mystery. She was bought by Susanna Wheatley, a woman of some means, and welcomed more as a new member of the Wheatley household than as a slave. Phillis was precocious and quickly learned English and Latin. She began writing when she was still only a young girl, and her earliest surviving poem was written in 1767, when she was twelve or thirteen. She was formally freed by the Wheatley family when she was about twenty but remained with them until her marriage to John Peters, a free black man, in 1778.*

At the same time, she tried with newspaper advertisements to solicit enough subscribers to publish a collection of her poems, but when skepticism over her racial background made this impossible, Susanna Wheatley arranged for the poems to be published in London in 1773. Poems on Various Subjects, Religious and Moral *is the first book known to be published by an African American. There were at least four printings of the book in London the first year, but the publication sold poorly in Boston, again because of resistance to Wheatley's race. She was trying to gather enough subscribers for a new collection when she was suddenly taken ill and died in 1784.*

Wheatley's poems are written in the conventional neoclassical style (see p. 839) of her time, but her themes are American. Her own situation is expressed poignantly in the fourth verse of "To the Right Honourable William, Earl of Dartmouth" and in the short poem "On Being Brought from Africa to America."

RELATED POEM: *Robert Hayden, "A Letter from Phillis Wheatley," page 1050.*
RELATED COMMENTARY: *Robert Hayden, "On Negro Poetry," page 1177.*

---

29. ***adelante:*** Move. **35.** ***la migra:*** Border Patrol.

Phillis Wheatley

To the Right Honourable William, Earl of Dartmouth

1773

Hail, happy day, when, smiling like the morn,
Fair *Freedom* rose *New-England* to adorn:
The northern clime beneath her genial ray,
Dartmouth, congratulates thy blissful sway:
Elate with hope her race no longer mourns,
Each soul expands, each grateful bosom burns,
While in thine hand with pleasure we behold
The silken reins, and *Freedom's* charms unfold.
Long lost to realms beneath the northern skies
She shines supreme, while hated *faction* dies:
Soon as appear'd the *Goddess* long desir'd,
Sick at the view, she languish'd and expir'd;
Thus from the splendors of the morning light
The owl in sadness seeks the caves of night.
    No more, *America,* in mournful strain
Of wrongs, and grievance unredress'd complain,
No longer shalt thou dread the iron chain,
Which wanton *Tyranny* with lawless hand
Had made, and with it meant t' enslave the land.
    Should you, my lord, while you peruse my song,
Wonder from whence my love of *Freedom* sprung,
Whence flow these wishes for the common good,
By feeling hearts alone best understood,
I, young in life, by seeming cruel fate
Was snatch'd from *Afric's* fancy'd happy seat:
What pangs excruciating must molest,
What sorrows labour in my parent's breast?
Steel'd was that soul and by no misery mov'd
That from a father seiz'd his babe belov'd:
Such, such my case. And can I then but pray
Others may never feel tyrannic sway?

    For favours past, great Sir, our thanks are due,
And thee we ask thy favours to renew,
Since in thy pow'r, as in thy will before,
To sooth the griefs, which thou did'st once deplore.
May heav'nly grace the sacred sanction give
To all thy works, and thou for ever live
Not only on the wings of fleeting *Fame,*
Though praise immortal crowns the patriot's name,
But to conduct to heav'ns refulgent fane,
May fiery coursers sweep th' ethereal plain,

And bear thee upwards to that blest abode,
Where, like the prophet, thou shalt find thy God.

PHILLIS WHEATLEY

On Being Brought from Africa to America 1773

'Twas mercy brought me from my *Pagan* land,
Taught my benighted soul to understand
That there's a God, that there's a *Saviour* too:
Once I redemption neither sought nor knew.

Some view our sable race with scornful eye,
"Their colour is a diabolic die."
Remember, *Christians, Negros,* black as *Cain,*°
May be refin'd, and join th'angelic train.

ꙮ

WALT WHITMAN *(1819–1892) was born on Long Island, close to New York City. When he was three his father moved the family to Brooklyn. Whitman went to work as an errand boy when he was eleven and the next year took a job in a newspaper office. He educated himself by reading novels and soon was contributing poems to a Manhattan newspaper. For five years, beginning when he was sixteen, he worked mostly as a country schoolmaster on Long Island, boarding with the families of his students.*

When Whitman gave up teaching, he went back to New York and Brooklyn, and for the next fifteen years he held a series of newspaper jobs, wrote a temperance novel, and published several short stories in a national magazine. By his mid-thirties he was living at home again, crowded into a shabby house in Brooklyn with his parents and his brothers and sisters. He had lost his newspaper job and was working — when he did work — as a carpenter. He spent his days walking the streets or sitting in local libraries. He was emotionally dependent on his mother, but he was careless about missing family meals, came and went as he pleased, and hid himself for hours writing poetry in the room he shared with his brother.

In the spring of 1855 Whitman arranged with a small Brooklyn print shop to bring out a book of the poems he had been writing. He titled it Leaves of Grass. *He printed enough sheets for three hundred copies, had one hundred bound in green cloth with gold stamping, and sent copies to many important American writers. Some threw their copies in the fire, but Ralph Waldo Emerson, then the leading American intellectual figure, recognized the book's genius and sent Whitman a letter that began, "I greet you at the beginning of a great career . . ."*

Emerson's praise meant that the book received some attention, but Whitman's poetry confused most readers. It was unrhymed, the rhythms were so irregular that

---

7. black as *Cain:* In Genesis 4:14, God puts a mark on Cain for having murdered his brother Abel. Some traditions hold that this "mark" is black skin.

there was no way to determine the meter of the lines, and the language was as free and direct as someone shouting in the street. Readers were also confused because the only subject of the poems seemed to be Whitman himself. It was not only the form of his poems that opened the path to modern poetry. His use of himself as the persona of the poems was an important source for the tone of confession and self-examination of much twentieth-century American poetry.

Whitman spent the rest of his life trying to organize the writing that poured into his book. Each subsequent edition of Leaves of Grass *contained new poems, and he also rewrote and retitled older poems. By the end of his life he was a revered literary figure whose work was read as enthusiastically in Europe as it was in the United States. Support from friends made it possible for him to buy a small house in Camden, New Jersey, where he died in 1892.*

"On the Beach at Night" is one of a group of shorter poems included in the third edition of Leaves of Grass *in 1860. "Beat! Beat! Drums!," "Vigil Strange I Kept on the Field One Night," and "When I Heard the Learn'd Astronomer" were first printed in 1865 in a small collection titled* Drum-Taps. *"A Noiseless Patient Spider," one of Whitman's most explicitly spiritual poems, was included in an edition of* Leaves of Grass *that he published in 1868.*

RELATED COMMENTARIES: *Robert Creeley, "On Whitman's Poetry," page 1160; Ezra Pound, "What I Feel about Walt Whitman," page 1207.*

WALT WHITMAN

On the Beach at Night

1860

On the beach at night,
Stands a child with her father,
Watching the east, the autumn sky.

Up through the darkness,
While ravening clouds, the burial clouds, in black masses spreading,
Lower sullen and fast athwart and down the sky,
Amid a transparent clear belt of ether yet left in the east,
Ascends large and calm the lord-star Jupiter,
And nigh at hand, only a very little above,
Swim the delicate sisters the Pleiades.°

From the beach the child holding the hand of her father,
Those burial-clouds that lower victorious soon to devour all,
Watching, silently weeps.

Weep not, child,
Weep not, my darling,
With these kisses let me remove your tears,
The ravening clouds shall not long be victorious,

10. Pleiades: A cluster of stars in the constellation Taurus. Greek mythology held that these stars were the seven daughters of Atlas.

They shall not long possess the sky, they devour the stars only in
apparition,
Jupiter shall emerge, be patient, watch again another night, the Pleiades
shall emerge,
They are immortal, all those stars both silvery and golden shall shine
out again,
The great stars and the little ones shall shine out again, they endure,
The vast immortal suns and the long-enduring pensive moons shall
again shine.

Then dearest child mournest thou only for Jupiter?
Considerest thou alone the burial of the stars?

Something there is,
(With my lips soothing thee, adding I whisper,
I give thee the first suggestion, the problem and indirection,)
Something there is more immortal even than the stars,
(Many the burials, many the days and night, passing away,)
Something that shall endure longer even than lustrous Jupiter,
Longer than sun or any revolving satellite,
Or the radiant sisters the Pleiades.

WALT WHITMAN

Beat! Beat! Drums!

1861

Beat! beat! drums! — blow! bugles! blow!
Through the windows — through doors — burst like a ruthless force,
Into the solemn church, and scatter the congregation,
Into the school where the scholar is studying;
Leave not the bridegroom quiet — no happiness must he have now
with his bride,
Nor the peaceful farmer any peace, ploughing his field or gathering his
grain,
So fierce you whirr and pound you drums — so shrill you bugles blow.

Beat! beat! drums! — blow! bugles! blow!
Over the traffic of cities — over the rumble of wheels in the streets;
Are beds prepared for sleepers at night in the houses? no sleepers must
sleep in those beds,
No bargainers' bargains by day — no brokers or speculators — would
they continue?
Would the talkers be talking? would the singer attempt to sing?
Would the lawyer rise in the court to state his case before the judge?
Then rattle quicker, heavier drums — you bugles wilder blow.

Beat! beat! drums! — blow! bugles! blow!
Make no parley — stop for no expostulation,
Mind not the timid — mind not the weeper or prayer,

Mind not the old man beseeching the young man,
Let not the child's voice be heard, nor the mother's entreaties,
Make even the trestles to shake the dead where they lie awaiting the
hearses,
So strong you thump O terrible drums — so loud you bugles blow.

WALT WHITMAN

Vigil Strange I Kept on the Field One Night 1865

Vigil strange I kept on the field one night;
When you my son and my comrade dropt at my side that day,
One look I but gave which your dear eyes return'd with a look I shall
never forget,
One touch of your hand to mine O boy, reach'd up as you lay on the
ground,
Then onward I sped in the battle, the even-contested battle,
Till late in the night reliev'd to the place at last again I made my way,
Found you in death so cold dear comrade, found your body son of
responding kisses, (never again on earth responding,)
Bared your face in the starlight, curious the scene, cool blew the
moderate night-wind,
Long there and then in vigil I stood, dimly around me the battlefield
spreading,
Vigil wondrous and vigil sweet there in the fragrant silent night,
But not a tear fell, not even a long-drawn sigh, long I gazed,
Then on the earth partially reclining sat by your side leaning my chin
in my hands,
Passing sweet hours, immortal and mystic hours with you dearest
comrade — not a tear, not a word,
Vigil of silence, love and death, vigil for you my son and my soldier,
As onward silently stars aloft, eastward new ones upward stole,
Vigil final for you brave boy, (I could not save you, swift was your
death,
I faithfully loved you and cared for you living, I think we shall surely
meet again,)
Till at latest lingering of the night, indeed just as the dawn appear'd,
My comrade I wrapt in his blanket, envelop'd well his form,
Folded the blanket well, tucking it carefully over head and carefully
under feet,
And there and then and bathed by the rising sun, my son in his grave,
in his rude-dug grave I deposited,
Ending my vigil strange with that, vigil of night and battle-field dim,
Vigil for boy of responding kisses, (never again on earth responding,)
Vigil for comrade swiftly slain, vigil I never forget, how as day brighten'd,

I rose from the chill ground and folded my soldier well in his blanket,
And buried him where he fell.

Walt Whitman

When I Heard the Learn'd Astronomer 1865

When I heard the learn'd astronomer,
When the proofs, the figures, were ranged in columns before me,
When I was shown the charts and diagrams, to add, divide, and measure them,
When I sitting heard the astronomer where he lectured with much applause in the lecture-room,
How soon unaccountable I became tired and sick,
Till rising and gliding out I wander'd off by myself,
In the mystical moist night-air, and from time to time,
Look'd up in perfect silence at the stars.

Walt Whitman

A Noiseless Patient Spider 1868

A noiseless patient spider,
I mark'd where on a little promontory it stood isolated,
Mark'd how to explore the vacant vast surrounding,
It launch'd forth filament, filament, filament, out of itself,
Ever unreeling them, ever tirelessly speeding them.

And you O my soul where you stand,
Surrounded, detached, in measureless oceans of space,
Ceaselessly musing, venturing, throwing, seeking the spheres to connect them,
Till the bridge you will need be form'd, till the ductile anchor hold,
Till the gossamer thread you fling catch somewhere, O my soul.

William Carlos Williams *(1883–1963) was born in Rutherford, New Jersey, where he lived and practiced medicine all his life. His mother was Puerto Rican; his father was English. Although he spent his life as a pediatrician, when he was a student at the University of Pennsylvania he was friends with Hilda Doolittle, who became the poet H.D., and the poet Ezra Pound. His encounter with them encouraged his own ambitions to be a poet, and he managed to lead a double life — as a doctor and a writer — until a series of strokes forced him to give up medicine in the 1950s.*

Williams felt himself isolated in his small town medical practice, but he was part of the avant-garde poetry movements of his time, and it was as an imagist (see imagism on pp. 896–901) that he was best known when be began publishing after World War I. During his long career he founded small magazines; contributed essays, poems, and stories to literary journals; and also found time to write novels, plays, and an autobiography.

Many of Williams's poems are short. In his autobiography he remembers that some of them were written on his office typewriter between patients, and some first versions of his poems were written on prescription blanks. He was the last of the modernist poets to achieve recognition, but his work became an important influence on younger poets like Allen Ginsberg, who brought Jack Kerouac, among others, to visit Williams in the 1950s.

"Spring and All" was published as an untitled entry in an experimental collection of writing with the title Spring and All, *and the poem has assumed the book's name. Poems like this one, as well as "This Is Just to Say," and "The Widow's Lament in Springtime," have the same directness of speech, the personal vocabulary, and the spontaneous poetic form that Williams termed "the American idiom."(See also Williams's "The Red Wheelbarrow" on p. 898 and "Night" on p. 899.)*

RELATED COMMENTARY: *William Carlos Williams, "Introduction to* Howl,*" page 1228.*

WILLIAM CARLOS WILLIAMS

Spring and All

1923

By the road to the contagious hospital,
under the surge of the blue
mottled clouds driven from the
northeast — cold wind. Beyond, the
waste of broad, muddy fields,
brown with dried weeds, standing and fallen,

patches of standing water,
the scattering of tall trees.

All along the road the reddish,
purplish, forked, upstanding, twiggy
stuff of brushes and small trees
with dead, brown leaves under them
leafless vines —

Lifeless in appearance, sluggish,
dazed spring approaches —

They enter the new world naked,
cold, uncertain of all
save that they enter. All about them
the cold, familiar wind —

■ ■ ■

Now the grass, tomorrow
the stiff curl of wild-carrot leaf.

One by one objects are defined —
It quickens: clarity, outline of leaf,

But now the stark dignity of
entrance — Still, the profound change
has come upon them; rooted, they
grip down and begin to awaken.

WILLIAM CARLOS WILLIAMS

This Is Just to Say *1934*

I have eaten
the plums
that were in
the icebox

and which
you were probably
saving
for breakfast

Forgive me
they were delicious
so sweet
and so cold

WILLIAM CARLOS WILLIAMS

The Widow's° Lament in Springtime *1921*

Sorrow is my own yard
where the new grass
flames as it has flamed
often before but not
with the cold fire
that closes round me this year.
Thirtyfive years
I lived with my husband.
The plumtree is white today
with masses of flowers.
Masses of flowers
loaded the cherry branches

Widow's: The widow of the poem is Williams's mother.

and color some bushes
yellow and some red
but the grief in my heart
is stronger than they
for though they were my joy
formerly, today I notice them
and turned away forgetting.
Today my son told me
that in the meadows,
at the edge of the heavy woods
in the distance, he saw
trees of white flowers.
I feel that I would like
to go there
and fall into those flowers
and sink into the marsh near them.

WILLIAM WORDSWORTH *(1770–1850) was born in the north of England, close to the Lake District. After the death of his mother when he was eight, he and his three brothers were raised in the countryside and often left free to roam. He also read hungrily and was encouraged to think of becoming a poet by his schoolmaster.*

Wordsworth had a turbulent youth. In 1790, during his summer break from St. John's College in Cambridge, he went on a long walking trip through France and Switzerland, then returned to France after his graduation the next year, hoping to improve his French language skills enough to qualify as a teacher. He remained in France during the period of the wildest triumphs and fervors of the French Revolution. He fell in love with Annette Vallon, daughter of a family of Royalist sympathizers. She gave birth to Wordsworth's child, but the political turmoil forced him to return to England, and Annette was unable to follow him.

In England, Wordsworth was torn between the love he had left behind him and his disillusionment with the Revolution, which was becoming increasingly violent and despotic. At this moment, when he was struggling against a complete emotional collapse, a friend died and left Wordsworth enough money to enable the poet to devote himself entirely to his art. With his sister Dorothy, and a new friend, the young poet and critic Samuel Taylor Coleridge, Wordsworth began a new life.

Wordsworth and Coleridge set out to create a new style of poetry — poetry that would be closer to the language of ordinary people and would deal with genuine emotions. In 1798 they published a slim book, Lyrical Ballads, *with poems by each of them. This book is considered the beginning of the romantic movement in English poetry.*

In the course of his long life, Wordsworth lost the creative fire of his early years, but at his death he was hailed as one of the most significant literary figures England had ever produced. He began "Ode: Intimations of Immortality" in his mid thirties, and it took him two years after he wrote the first four stanzas to complete the poem. He wrote to an admirer about its subject, "Nothing was more difficult for me in childhood than to admit the notion of death as a state applicable to my own being." The sonnet "The world is too much with us" was published the same year. (See also Wordsworth's "I Wandered Lonely as a Cloud" on p. 852 and "My Heart Leaps Up" on p. 853.)

RELATED COMMENTARY: *William Wordsworth, "From the Introduction to* Lyrical Ballads,*" page 1229.*

William Wordsworth

Ode

1807

Intimations of Immortality from Recollections of Early Childhood

The Child is Father of the Man;
And I could wish my days to be
Bound each to each by natural piety.

1

There was a time when meadow, grove, and stream,
The earth, and every common sight,
To me did seem
Apparelled in celestial light,
The glory and the freshness of a dream.
It is not now as it hath been of yore; —
Turn wheresoe'er I may,
By night or day,
The things which I have seen I now can see no more.

2

The Rainbow comes and goes,
And lovely is the Rose,
The Moon doth with delight
Look round her when the heavens are bare,
Waters on a starry night
Are beautiful and fair;
The sunshine is a glorious birth;
But yet I know, where'er I go,
That there hath past away a glory from the earth.

3

Now, while the birds thus sing a joyous song,
And while the young lambs bound
As to the tabor's sound,
To me alone there came a thought of grief:
A timely utterance gave that thought relief,
And I again am strong:
The cataracts blow their trumpets from the steep;
No more shall grief of mine the season wrong;

I hear the Echoes through the mountains throng,
The Winds come to me from the fields of sleep,
And all the earth is gay;
Land and sea
Give themselves up to jollity,
And with the heart of May
Doth every Beast keep holiday;—
Thou Child of Joy,
Shout round me, let me hear thy shouts, thou happy Shepherd-boy!

4

Ye blessed Creatures, I have heard the call
Ye to each other make; I see
The heavens laugh with you in your jubilee;
My heart is at your festival,
My head hath its coronal,°
The fulness of your bliss, I feel — I feel it all.
Oh evil day! if I were sullen
While Earth herself is adorning,
This sweet May-morning,
And the Children are culling
On every side,
In a thousand valleys far and wide,
Fresh flowers; while the sun shines warm,
And the Babe leaps up on his Mother's arm: —
I hear, I hear, with joy I hear!
— But there's a Tree, of many, one,
A single Field which I have looked upon,
Both of them speak of something that is gone:
The Pansy at my feet
Doth the same tale repeat:
Whither is fled the visionary gleam?
Where is it now, the glory and the dream?

5

Our birth is but a sleep and a forgetting:
The Soul that rises with us, our life's Star,
Hath had elsewhere its setting,
And cometh from afar:
Not in entire forgetfulness,
And not in utter nakedness,
But trailing clouds of glory do we come
From God, who is our home:

---

40. coronal: Crown of flowers worn by young shepherds in May.

Heaven lies about us in our infancy!
Shades of the prison-house begin to close
        Upon the growing Boy,
But He beholds the light, and whence it flows,
        He sees it in his joy;
The Youth, who daily farther from the east
        Must travel, still is Nature's Priest,
        And by the vision splendid
        Is on his way attended;
At length the Man perceives it die away,
And fade into the light of common day.

6

Earth fills her lap with pleasures of her own;
Yearnings she hath in her own natural kind,
And, even with something of a Mother's mind,
        And no unworthy aim,
        The homely Nurse doth all she can
To make her Foster-child, her Inmate Man,
        Forget the glories he hath known,
And that imperial palace whence he came.

7

Behold the Child among his new-born blisses,
A six years' Darling of a pigmy size!
See, where 'mid work of his own hand he lies,
Fretted by sallies of his mother's kisses,
With light upon him from his father's eyes!
See, at his feet, some little plan or chart,
Some fragment from his dream of human life,
Shaped by himself with newly-learnèd art;
        A wedding or a festival,
        A mourning or a funeral;
            And this hath now his heart,
        And unto this he frames his song:
            Then will he fit his tongue
To dialogues of business, love, or strife;
        But it will not be long
        Ere this be thrown aside,
        And with new joy and pride
The little Actor cons another part;
Filling from time to time his "humorous stage"°
With all the Persons, down to palsied Age,

103. "humorous stage": Capriciousness, but also carries the sense of the classical temperaments ("humors").

That Life brings with her in her equipage;
As if his whole vocation
Were endless imitation.

8

Thou, whose exterior semblance doth belie
Thy Soul's immensity;
Thou best Philosopher, who yet dost keep
Thy heritage, thou Eye among the blind,
That, deaf and silent, read'st the eternal deep,
Haunted for ever by the eternal mind,—
Mighty Prophet! Seer blest!
On whom those truths do rest,
Which we are toiling all our lives to find,
In darkness lost, the darkness of the grave;
Thou, over whom thy Immortality
Broods like the Day, a Master o'er a Slave,
A Presence which is not to be put by;
Thou little Child, yet glorious in the might
Of heaven-born freedom on thy being's height,
Why with such earnest pains dost thou provoke
The years to bring the inevitable yoke,
Thus blindly with thy blessedness at strife?
Full soon thy Soul shall have her earthly freight,
And custom lie upon thee with a weight,
Heavy as frost, and deep almost as life!

9

O joy! that in our embers
Is something that doth live,
That nature yet remembers
What was so fugitive!
The thought of our past years in me doth breed
Perpetual benediction: not indeed
For that which is most worthy to be blest;
Delight and liberty, the simple creed
Of Childhood, whether busy or at rest,
With new-fledged hope still fluttering in his breast—
Not for these I raise
The song of thanks and praise;
But for those obstinate questionings
Of sense and outward things,
Fallings from us, vanishings;
Blank misgivings of a Creature
Moving about in worlds not realised,
High instincts before which our mortal Nature
Did tremble like a guilty Thing surprised:

But for those first affections,
Those shadowy recollections,
Which, be they what they may,
Are yet the fountain light of all our day,
Are yet a master light of all our seeing;
Uphold us, cherish, and have power to make
Our noisy years seem moments in the being
Of the eternal Silence: truths that wake,
To perish never;
Which neither listlessness, nor mad endeavour,
Nor Man nor Boy,
Nor all that is at enmity with joy,
Can utterly abolish or destroy!
Hence in a season of calm weather
Though inland far we be,
Our Souls have sight of that immortal sea
Which brought us hither,
Can in a moment travel thither,
And see the Children sport upon the shore,
And hear the mighty waters rolling evermore.

10

Then sing, ye Birds, sing, sing a joyous song!
And let the young Lambs bound
As to the tabor's sound!
We in thought will join your throng,
Ye that pipe and ye that play,
Ye that through your hearts to-day
Feel the gladness of the May!
What though the radiance which was once so bright
Be now for ever taken from my sight,
Though nothing can bring back the hour
Of splendour in the grass, of glory in the flower;
We will grieve not, rather find
Strength in what remains behind;
In the primal sympathy
Which having been must ever be;
In the soothing thoughts that spring
Out of human suffering;
In the faith that looks through death,
In years that bring the philosophic mind.

11

And O, ye Fountains, Meadows, Hills, and Groves,
Forebode not any severing of our loves!
Yet in my heart of hearts I feel your might;
I only have relinquished one delight

To live beneath your more habitual sway.
I love the Brooks which down their channels fret,
Even more than when I tripped lightly as they;
The innocent brightness of a new-born Day
Is lovely yet;
The Clouds that gather round the setting sun
Do take a sober colouring from an eye
That hath kept watch o'er man's mortality;
Another race hath been, and other palms are won.
Thanks to the human heart by which we live,
Thanks to its tenderness, its joys, and fears,
To me the meanest flower that blows can give
Thoughts that do often lie too deep for tears.

William Wordsworth

The world is too much with us

1807

The world is too much with us; late and soon,
Getting and spending, we lay waste our powers:
Little we see in nature that is ours;
We have given our hearts away, a sordid boon!
This Sea that bares her bosom to the moon;
The Winds that will be howling at all hours
And are up-gathered now like sleeping flowers;
For this, for every thing, we are out of tune;
It moves us not — Great God! I'd rather be
A Pagan suckled in a creed outworn;
So might I, standing on this pleasant lea,
Have glimpses that would make me less forlorn;
Have sight of Proteus coming from the sea;
Or hear old Triton blow his wreathed horn.

James Wright *(1927–1980) was born in the small town of Martin's Ferry, Ohio. Although he spent much of his adult life teaching in New York City, his poetry returned again and again to themes of small-town rural life. He studied as an undergraduate at Kenyon College and completed his M.A. and Ph.D. at the University of Washington. At the same time he was certain enough of his commitment to poetry to study with John Crowe Ransom and Theodore Roethke. He served in the army during World War II.*

Wright's first book, The Green Wall, *was published in 1957, and the same year he began teaching at the University of Minnesota in Minneapolis. He joined the faculty of Hunter College in New York in 1966 and remained there until his death.*

Although he won many prizes and awards, including a Pulitzer Prize for his Collected Poems *in 1972, he was even more important for his influence on his fellow poets. The critic Paul Zweig wrote in* Partisan Review *that, even before he had won the Pulitzer Prize, "Wright had been acknowledged by a generation of poets as the artisan of a new language for poetry: a style of pastoral surrealism built around strong images and a simple spoken rhetoric. Wright's art lay not in complex grammar, but in a stark structure of perceptions which become their own statement."*

The uniqueness of Wright's poetry lies in his ability to sustain a sense of wonder in writing that seems, at first glance, to be as casual as a conversation about the weather. In each of these poems, "Lying in a Hammock at William Duffy's Farm in Pine Island, Minnesota," "A Blessing," "Milkweed," and "To Flood Stage Again," the moment he describes is so small, so uneventful, that it might almost go unnoticed, but in language that is as subtle as it is ordinary, he is able to convey to us the wonder and the mystery that are implicit in the moment. His own evaluation of his work was much more modest. "I suffer from glibness . . . I had [to struggle] to strip my poetry down." His own laconic judgment on his writing was that since he came from an Irish family "it is too easy for me to talk sometimes."

JAMES WRIGHT

Lying in a Hammock at William Duffy's Farm in Pine Island, Minnesota

1963

Over my head, I see the bronze butterfly,
Asleep on the black trunk,
Blowing like a leaf in green shadow.
Down the ravine behind the empty house,
The cowbells follow one another
Into the distances of the afternoon.
To my right,
In a field of sunlight between two pines,
The droppings of last year's horses
Blaze up into golden stones.
I lean back, as the evening darkens and comes on.
A chicken hawk floats over, looking for home.
I have wasted my life.

JAMES WRIGHT

A Blessing

1963

Just off the highway to Rochester, Minnesota,
Twilight bounds softly forth on the grass.
And the eyes of those two Indian ponies
Darken with kindness.
They have come gladly out of the willows

To welcome my friend and me.
We step over the barbed wire into the pasture
Where they have been grazing all day, alone.
They ripple tensely, they can hardly contain their happiness
That we have come.
They bow shyly as wet swans. They love each other.
There is no loneliness like theirs.
At home once more,
They begin munching the young tufts of spring in the darkness.
I would like to hold the slenderer one in my arms,
For she has walked over to me
And nuzzled my left hand.
She is black and white,
Her mane falls wild on her forehead,
And the light breeze moves me to caress her long ear
That is delicate as the skin over a girl's wrist.
Suddenly I realize
That if I stepped out of my body I would break
Into blossom.

James Wright

Milkweed *1963*

While I stood here, in the open, lost in myself,
I must have looked a long time
Down the corn rows, beyond grass,
The small house,
White walls, animals lumbering toward the barn.
I look down now. It is all changed.
Whatever it was I lost, whatever I wept for
Was a wild, gentle thing, the small dark eyes
Loving me in secret.
It is here. At a touch of my hand,
The air fills with delicate creatures
From the other world.

James Wright

To Flood Stage Again *1968*

In Fargo, North Dakota, a man
Warned me the river might rise
To flood stage again.
On the bridge, a girl hurries past me, alone,

Unhappy face.
Will she pause in wet grass somewhere?
Behind my eyes she stands tiptoe, yearning for confused sparrows
To fetch a bit of string and dried wheatbeard
To line her outstretched hand.
I open my eyes and gaze down
At the dark water.

WILLIAM BUTLER YEATS *(1865–1939) was born in Dublin, but his parents were of English descent, and he spent much of his youth in London. His father, Jack Yeats, was a gifted but struggling artist. Yeats first decided to follow his father and become a painter. He changed his mind, however, after beginning his art studies. His first published poems appeared in the* Dublin University Review *when he was twenty.*

For most of his life Yeats journeyed between England and Ireland, where he lived some of the time in Dublin and at other times with his mother's family in County Sligo, a rural area in northwest Ireland. All three of these very different environments had an effect on his writing. His early poetry often presented a soft mood of reverie, influenced by younger poets he met in London. He also drew from his Irish background in verse dramas based on Irish legends and myths. The rough countryside of County Sligo lent his poetry a sharper, less romantic tone than that of the London poets' verse.

In 1899 Yeats helped found the Irish National Theatre, but bitter struggles with the conservative middle-class audiences eventually drove him to London. The Irish Rebellion of 1916, however, when a group of Irish idealists attempted to seize power from the British occupying forces, brought him back, and when Ireland achieved partial independence in 1922 he was appointed a senator and served in the government for six years.

Yeats had a long and successful career as a writer, and he won the Nobel Prize for literature in 1923. "The Lake Isle of Innisfree" and "When You Are Old" were written almost thirty years earlier. "The Wild Swans at Coole" was written almost twenty years after Yeats's first visit to Coole, the estate of his patron, Lady Gregory. "The Second Coming" is one of his most impassioned visionary poems. Of the many poems written describing the rape of the Spartan queen Leda by the god Zeus, who had disguised himself as a swan, Yeats's "Leda and the Swan" is perhaps the best known.

WILLIAM BUTLER YEATS

The Lake Isle of Innisfree

1890

I will arise and go now, and go to Innisfree,
And a small cabin build there, of clay and wattles made;
Nine bean rows will I have there, a hive for the honey bee,
And live alone in the bee-loud glade.

■ ■ ■

And I shall have some peace there, for peace comes dropping slow,
Dropping from the veils of the morning to where the cricket sings;
There midnight's all a glimmer, and noon a purple glow,
And evening full of the linnet's wings.

I will arise and go now, for always night and day
I hear lake water lapping with low sounds by the shore;
While I stand on the roadway, or on the pavements gray,
I hear it in the deep heart's core.

William Butler Yeats

When You Are Old 1892

When you are old and grey and full of sleep,
And nodding by the fire, take down this book,
And slowly read, and dream of the soft look
Your eyes had once, and of their shadows deep;

How many loved your moments of glad grace,
And loved your beauty with love false or true,
But one man loved the pilgrim soul in you,
And loved the sorrows of your changing face;

And bending down beside the glowing bars,
Murmur, a little sadly, how Love fled
And paced upon the mountains overhead
And hid his face amid a crowd of stars.

William Butler Yeats

The Wild Swans at Coole 1917

The trees are in their autumn beauty,
The woodland paths are dry,
Under the October twilight the water
Mirrors a still sky;
Upon the brimming water among the stones
Are nine-and-fifty swans.

The nineteenth autumn has come upon me
Since I first made my count;
I saw, before I had well finished,
All suddenly mount
And scatter wheeling in great broken rings
Upon their clamorous wings.

I have looked upon those brilliant creatures,
And now my heart is sore.

All's changed since I, hearing at twilight,
The first time on this shore,
The bell-beat of their wings above my head,
Trod with a lighter tread.

Unwearied still, lover by lover,
They paddle in the cold
Companionable streams or climb the air;
Their hearts have not grown old;
Passion or conquest, wander where they will,
Attend upon them still.

But now they drift on the still water,
Mysterious, beautiful;
Among what rushes will they build,
By what lake's edge or pool
Delight men's eyes when I awake some day
To find they have flown away?

WILLIAM BUTLER YEATS

The Second Coming

1919

Turning and turning in the widening gyre
The falcon cannot hear the falconer;
Things fall apart; the centre cannot hold;
Mere anarchy is loosed upon the world,
The blood-dimmed tide is loosed, and everywhere
The ceremony of innocence is drowned;
The best lack all conviction, while the worst
Are full of passionate intensity.

Surely some revelation is at hand;
Surely the Second Coming is at hand.
The Second Coming! Hardly are those words out
When a vast image out of *Spiritus Mundi*°
Troubles my sight: somewhere in sands of the desert
A shape with lion body and the head of a man,
A gaze blank and pitiless as the sun,
Is moving its slow thighs, while all about it
Reel shadows of the indignant desert birds.
The darkness drops again; but now I know
That twenty centuries of stony sleep
Were vexed to nightmare by a rocking cradle,
And what rough beast, its hour come round at last,
Slouches towards Bethlehem to be born?

12. ***Spiritus Mundi:*** Spirit of the universe.

William Butler Yeats

Leda and the Swan°

1924

A sudden blow: the great wings beating still
Above the staggering girl, her thighs caressed
By the dark webs, her nape caught in his bill,
He holds her helpless breast upon his breast.

How can those terrified vague fingers push
The feathered glory from her loosening thighs?
And how can body, laid in that white rush,
But feel the strange heart beating where it lies?

A shudder in the loins engenders there
The broken wall, the burning roof and tower
And Agamemnon dead.
                                        Being so caught up,
So mastered by the brute blood of the air,
Did she put on his knowledge with his power
Before the indifferent beak could let her drop?

Leda and the Swan: The god Zeus had the power to assume animal forms, and in the shape of a swan raped Leda, a Greek woman of noble birth. The girl born of the rape, Helen, later married the Greek king Menelaus, and it was her kidnapping by the Trojan prince Paris that was the cause of the Trojan War.

16

COMMENTARIES ON POETRY AND POETS

HAROLD BLOOM *is a distinguished literary critic whose book* The Western Canon *has defined many current attitudes toward the traditional literary canon.*

HAROLD BLOOM

On "Frost at Midnight"

1961

With *Dejection, The Ancient Mariner,* and *Kubla Khan,*° *Frost at Midnight* shows Coleridge at his most impressive. *Frost at Midnight* is the masterpiece of the "conversation poems"; it gathers the virtues of the group, without diffuseness, into one form, and it shares with *Tintern Abbey*° the distinction of inaugurating the major Wordsworthian myth of the memory as salvation. Indeed, Coleridge precedes Wordsworth. *Frost at Midnight* is dated February 1798; *Tintern Abbey,* we know from its title, was composed on July 13, 1798. The closing paragraph of Coleridge's poem, directed to his infant son, beginning "Therefore all seasons shall be sweet to thee," is a prelude to the closing lines of *Tintern Abbey,* addressed to Dorothy Wordsworth, where the poet asks nature's blessings on his sister:

Dejection, The Ancient Mariner,* and *Kubla Khan: Other poems by Coleridge.
Tintern Abbey: A poem by Coleridge's friend and associate, the poet William Wordsworth.

Therefore let the moon
Shine on thee in thy solitary walk;
And let the misty mountain-winds be free
To blow against thee

Frost at Midnight begins with Coleridge addressing himself to "abstruster musings." His cradled infant slumbers near him. The calm around the poet is so profound that its silentness vexes meditation:

the thin blue flame
Lies on my low-burnt fire, and quivers not;
Only that film, which fluttered on the grate
Still flutters there, the sole unquiet thing.

The film on the grate was called, in popular superstition, a *stranger,* and was supposed to portend° the arrival of some absent friend. The motion of the film makes it a companionable form to the poet, for only they stir in this hush of nature. The puny flaps of the film are like the motions of the poet's idling Spirit, which both deprecates itself and seeks fellowship by finding echo or mirror in the fluttering *stranger.* By doing so, the poet says of his abstracter musings that they are turned into a toy. Yet this playfulness becomes vital, for the mind travels back in memory as it idly broods on an identity with the film:

But O! how oft,
How oft, at school, with most believing mind,
Presageful, have I gazed upon the bars,
To watch that fluttering *stranger!*

One memory of school days leads to another in the same vein. The child watching the grate dreams of his birth place, and:

the old church-tower,
Whose bells, the poor man's only music, rang
From morn to evening, all the hot Fair-day,
So sweetly, that they stirred and haunted me
With a wild pleasure, falling on mine ear
Most like articulate sounds of things to come!

This is a memory within a memory, and the poem goes back to the initial recall. The child sleeps that night, dreaming of his sweet birth place. The next morning he broods, his eye fixed on his book but seeing nothing of it and looking up each time the door opens:

For still I hoped to see the *stranger's* face,
Townsman, or aunt, or sister more beloved

Carried back to his own childhood, the poet by an associative progression is prepared to brood on the future of his slumbering infant.

Coleridge, like Wordsworth, was country-born, but, unlike Words-

---

portend: to fortell.

worth, he passed his school years in London. As he looks at the sleeping infant Hartley, he utters a wishful prophecy that was to find ironic fulfillment. His son, he hopes, will learn far other lore, and in more natural scenes:

> For I was reared
> In the great city, pent 'mid cloisters dim,
> And saw nought lovely but the sky and stars.
> But *thou,* my babe! shalt wander like a breeze
> By lakes and sandy shores

So Hartley was to wander, a vagrant in the Wordsworth country, a Solitary prematurely decayed. In a happier sense, as a Wordsworthian minor poet, he fulfilled the other half of the prophecy:

> so shalt thou see and hear
> The lovely shapes and sounds intelligible
> Of that eternal language, which thy God
> Utters, who from eternity doth teach
> Himself in all, and all things in himself.
> Great universal Teacher! he shall mould
> Thy spirit, and by giving make it ask.

Again we recognize the doctrine and sound of *Tintern Abbey,* anticipated but with a tremulous intensity, very unlike the primitive confidence Wordsworth at his best was to bring to the Coleridgean formulation of the religion of Nature. The fierce epiphanies of Wordsworth are declared with the trumpetings of the prophet Amos, for whom judgment could run down like waters, and righteousness as a mighty stream. But something of an eternal child is in Coleridge (and in Hartley Coleridge after him), and a naive sweetness graces *Frost at Midnight.* The end of *Tintern Abbey* has a deeper music than that of *Frost at Midnight,* but is not more moving than this:

> Therefore all seasons shall be sweet to thee,
> Whether the summer clothe the general earth
> With greenness, or the redbreast sit and sing
> Betwixt the tufts of snow on the bare branch
> Of mossy apple-tree, while the night thatch
> Smokes in the sun-thaw; whether the eave-drops fall
> Heard only in the trances of the blast,
> Or if the secret ministry of frost
> Shall hang them up in silent icicles,
> Quietly shining to the quiet Moon.

The poem comes full circle, back to its opening. The secret ministry of frost is analogous to the secret ministry of memory, for both bind together apparently disparate phenomena in an imaginative unity. The frost creates a surface to both receive and reflect the shining of the winter moon. Memory, moving by its overtly arbitrary but deeply designed associations, creates an identity between the mature poet and the child who is his ancestor, as well as his own child. In this identity the poem comes into full being, with its own receiving and reflecting surfaces that mold the poet's and (he hopes) his son's spirits, and, by giving, make them ask who is the author of the gift. Wordsworth, in his prime years, would have given a phenomenological answer, and have been content to say Nature herself. In a more traditionally balanced *Frost at Midnight,* the answer is ontological, but the eternal language the Great Being is compelled to use is that of Nature, with her "lovely shapes and sounds intelligible."

ꙮ

CLEANTH BROOKS JR. *and* **ROBERT PENN WARREN** *(the literary critic and the American poet) discussed in their groundbreaking textbook* Understanding Poetry *(1938) T. S. Eliot's major early poem from the perspective of the New Criticism, an approach that emphasizes close reading of the formal properties of literary works.*

CLEANTH BROOKS JR. AND ROBERT PENN WARREN

On Eliot's "The Love Song of J. Alfred Prufrock" *1938*

The character of Prufrock, as we shall see, is really very much like that of Hamlet — a man who is apparently betrayed by his possession of such qualities as intellect and imagination. But it is particularly dangerous to attempt to portray, and make the audience believe in and take seriously, such a person as Prufrock. We are inclined to laugh at the person who is really so painfully self-conscious that he is inhibited from all action. Moreover, in so far as the poet is using Prufrock as a character typical of our age, he must in fairness to truth avoid treating him quite so heroically as a Hamlet. At the very beginning, therefore, the poet faces a difficult problem. In using the materials of the present, the desire to be accurate, to be thoroughly truthful, forces him to exhibit the character as not purely romantic or tragic. And yet there is in such a person as he describes a very real tragedy. How shall he treat him? To attempt to treat Prufrock in full seriousness is doomed to failure; on the other hand, to make him purely comic is to falsify matters too.

Faced with this problem, the poet resorts to irony, and by employing varying shades of irony he is able to do justice to the ludicrous elements in the situation and yet do justice to the serious ones also. The casual and careless reader will probably see only the comic aspects: he will be likely to fail to appreciate the underlying seriousness of the whole poem.

The title itself gives us the first clue to the fact that the poem is ironical. We think of a love song as simple and full of warm emotion. But this poem opens on a scene where the streets

> . . . follow like an argument
> Of insidious intent
> To lead you to an overwhelming question. . . .

One notices also that the character Prufrock is continually interested in stating that "there will be time" to make up his mind. But in saying that there will be time for this, he is so hopelessly unable to act that he continues in a sort of abstracted and unconscious patter to state that there will be time

For the yellow smoke that slides along the street,
Rubbing its back upon the windowpanes;
There will be time, there will be time
To prepare a face to meet the faces that you meet;
There will be time to murder and create,
And time for all the works and days of hands
That lift and drop a question on your plate.

Then, caught up by the irrelevance of his patter, he goes on to say that there will be time — not for decisions — but, ironically, for a "hundred indecisions," and for a "hundred visions and revisions."

The first part of the poem, then, can be imagined as the monologue of Prufrock himself as he finds his indecisiveness reflected in the apparently aimless streets of the city and in the fog which hangs over the city. It is filled with a rather bitter self-irony, a self-irony which is reflected in some of the abrupt transitions. But in observing this ironical monologue which illuminates the character, one has missed the point entirely if he has failed to see the psychological penetration in it. Take, for example, the tone and associations of the comparison of the evening to a "patient etherized upon a table." This comparison is "in character." It is an appropriate observation for Prufrock, being what he is, though it might not be very appropriate for an entirely different character or in a poem of entirely different tone. The evening — not any evening, but this particular evening, as seen by this particular observer — does seem to have the hushed quiet of the perfectly, and yet fatally relaxed, body of a person under ether.

Or notice also the psychological penetration of the remark, "To prepare a face to meet the faces that you meet." Again, the remark must be taken in character. Yet it is possible to observe, as a general truth, that we do prepare a face, an expression, a look, to meet the various "faces" that we meet — faces which have duly undergone a like preparation. A poorer poet would have written "To put on a mask to meet the people that you meet." Eliot's line with its concentration and its slight ironical shock is far superior. . . .

After the opening sections in which the character of the speaker is to some extent established for the reader, Prufrock describes a scene in which overcultured, bored women sip tea and discuss art. It is as though he had just stepped inside after wandering alone in the streets. Here are the people of whose criticism Prufrock is most afraid, and yet, as his characterization of them abundantly shows, he sees their shallowness. But Prufrock does not attempt to treat romantically or heroically his own character: he is able to see the ludicrous aspect of himself, his timid preciseness and vanity.

With a bald spot in the middle of my hair —
(They will say: "How his hair is growing thin.")
My necktie rich and modest, but asserted by a simple pin.

But what is the function of a statement so abrupt as "I have measured out my life with coffee spoons?" Here again, the line must be taken in character. But if we are willing to take it in character, we shall be able to see that it is brilliantly ironical. It would mean literally, one supposes, that he has measured out his life in little driblets, coffee spoons being tiny in size. But it carries another and more concrete meaning: namely, that he has spent his life in just such an environment as this drawing room which he is describing. The comparison makes the same ironical point, therefore, as the lines

> And time yet for a hundred indecisions,
> And for a hundred visions and revisions,
> Before the taking of a toast and tea.

The poem's sense of fidelity to the whole situation — its willingness to take into account so many apparently discordant views and points of view — is shown in the lines

> Arms that are braceleted and white and bare
> (But in the lamplight, downed with light brown hair!)

These lines give us a contrast between what might be termed loosely the romantic and the realistic attitude. The ironical comment here parallels exactly the reference to his own bald head.

The structure of the poem is, as we have noticed, that of a sort of monologue in which the poet describes this scene or that and comments on them, and, by means of them, on himself. The irrelevance, or apparent irrelevance, is exactly the sort of irrelevance and abrupt transition which is often admired in a personal essay by a writer like Charles Lamb. The structure is essentially the same here (though of course with an entirely different tone and for a different effect). But having seen what the structure is — not a logical structure, or one following the lines of a narrative, or one based on the description of a scene, but the structure of the flow of ideas — the reader is not puzzled at the rather abrupt transition from the stanza about the arms to

> Shall I say, I have gone at dusk through narrow streets,

etc. It is a scene from the beginning of the poem — or perhaps it is a scene viewed earlier and brought back to memory by the statement about the streets and the smoke in the opening lines of the poem. It is the sort of scene which has a very real poignance about it. Prufrock feels that it meant something. But he is utterly incapable of stating the meaning before the bored and sophisticated audience of the world to which he belongs. He would be laughed at as a fool. And then comes the thought — apparently irrelevant, but the sort of thought which might easily occur in such a monologue:

> I should have been a pair of ragged claws
> Scuttling across the floors of silent seas.

A crab is about as vivid a symbol as one might find, for a person who is completely self-sufficing and cannot be, and does not need to be, sociable. And there is, moreover, a secondary implication of irony here growing out of Prufrock's disgust with these people about him and with himself: the crab is at least "alive" and has, as Prufrock does not have, a meaning and a place in its world. (Observe that the poet does not use the word *crab.* Why? Because in mentioning the most prominent feature of the crab, the claws, and with the vivid description of the effect of the crab's swimming, "scuttling," he makes the point more sharply.)

There are several literary allusions in the latter part of the poem, allusions which we must know in order to understand the poem. . . . Can they be justified? And if so, how? In the first place, they are fairly commonly known: an allusion to John the Baptist's head having been cut off at Herod's orders and brought in on a platter; an allusion to the raising of Lazarus from the dead; and a reference to Shakespeare's *Hamlet.* The poet has not imposed a very heavy burden on us, therefore, in expecting that we shall know these references. But what can be said by way of justification? In the first place, all the allusions are "in character." They are comparisons which would normally occur to such a person as Prufrock, and they would naturally occur in the sort of meditation in which he indulges in this poem. In the second place, they do a great deal to sharpen the irony in the poem. Prufrock is vividly conscious of the sorry figure which he cuts in comparison with the various great figures from the past or from literature whom, in a far-off sense, he resembles. He has seen his reputation picked to pieces — his head, a slightly bald head, brought in on a platter like that of John the Baptist. But *he* is no prophet — nothing is lost. Death itself in this society can be regarded as nothing more than a liveried footman, putting on the coats of the departing, and death, like the knowing and insolent footman, is quite capable, he believes, of snickering behind his back.

MARILYN CHIN, *a Chinese American poet, responded to a question about "the canon" in a 1995 interview. In recent years much discussion has centered on the canon, the long tradition of literature that has served as the American educational standard. Some people believe the canon defines U.S. culture; others consider it a fence that has kept out writing by women and members of cultural minorities.*

MARILYN CHIN

On the Canon

1995

My personal psychology regarding "the canon" is this: To the outer world I say in a devil-may-care manner "to hell with it." It's a fixed endgame: There will always be an imperialist, Eurocentric bias. The powers-that-be who lord over the selection process are and forevermore will be privileged white male critics. They will decide who will be validated along with Shakespeare and Milton and the latter-day saints of the like of Keats, Yeats, and Eliot. They will guard that "canon" jealously with their elaborate "critical" apparatus; and driven by their own Darwinian instinct to "survive," they will do the best they can to "exclude" us and to promote their own monolithic vision.

But deep inside me another voice rings resolute. I am a serious poet with a rich palette and important missive and I shall fight for the survival of my poetry. What I learned from my youth as a marginalized and isolated west coast Asian American poet is this: It's no fun to be "excluded" . . . as a matter of fact, it feels like hell. What is the purpose of spending most of your adult life hunched in a dark corner perfecting your poems, if your oeuvre will be buried and forgotten anyway? I don't believe any poet who tells me, "No, baby, I don't give a damn about the canon." I am certain that the very same poet has his little poems all dressed up, organized and alphabetized and locked in a vault to be opened in the next century.

The poet's mission on earth is to inspire and to illuminate; and to leave behind to our glorious descendents an intricate and varied map of humanity. One way to survive is to be like Milton, who sits aloft in the great pantheon in the sky and only a very few self-flagellating geeky scholar/poets could indulge into his knotty points. Another way to survive is to be like Gwendolyn Brooks; I predict that her poem "We Real Cool" will be warm on schoolchildren's lips forever. To survive is to be like Langston Hughes, whose poem "A Raisin in the Sun" inspired the young playwright Lorraine Hansberry to write a masterpiece bearing that same name. The true test of "validation" is when one's poems can serve as inspirational models and guiding spirits for a younger generation. We must survive! We must fight to be included in "the canon," so that our voices will sing through history and the global consciousness in eternal echoes. And I'll be damned if I'm going to miss out on THAT out-of-the-body experience!

ROBERT CREELEY *is one of the many contemporary poets who have continued to respond to the dimensions of Walt Whitman's achievement even when, in Creeley's case, it was a response that came to him late. As he writes, when he was a student it was the fashion to dismiss Whitman for his grandiosity and his optimism. This excerpt is from Creeley's introduction to a selection of Whitman's work included in a modern anthology.*

ROBERT CREELEY

On Whitman's Poetry 1973

One of the most lovely insistences in Whitman's poems seems to me his instruction that one speak for oneself. Assumedly that would be the person most involved in saying anything and yet a habit of "objective" statement argues the contrary, noting the biases and distortions and tediums of the personal that are thereby invited into the writing. Surely there is some measure possible, such would say, that can make statement a clearly defined and impersonal instance of reality, of white clouds in a blue sky, of things and feelings not distorted by any fact of one man or woman's intensive possession of them. Then there would truly be a common possibility, that all might share, and that no one would have use of more than another.

Yet if Whitman has taught me anything, and he has taught me a great deal, often against my own will, it is that the common *is* personal, intensely so, in that having no one thus to invest it, the sea becomes a curious mixture of water and table salt and the sky the chemical formula for air. It is, paradoxically, the personal which makes the common in so far as it recognizes the existence of the many in the one. In my own joy or despair, I am brought to that which others have also experienced.

My own senses of Whitman were curiously numb until I was thirty. In the forties, when I was in college, it was considered literally bad taste to have an active interest in his writing. In that sense he suffered the same fate as Wordsworth, also condemned as overly prolix and generalizing. There was a persistent embarrassment that this naively affirmative poet might affect one's own somewhat cynical wisdoms. Too, in so far as this was a time of intensively didactic criticism, what was one to do with Whitman, even if one read him? He went on and on, he seemed to lack "structure," he yielded to no "critical apparatus" then to hand. So, as students, we were herded past him as quickly as possible, and our teachers used him only as an example of "the America of that period" which, we were told, was a vast swamp of idealistic expansion and corruption. Whitman, the dupe, the dumb-bell, the pathetically regrettable instance of this country's dream and despair, the self-taught man.

That summation of Whitman and his work was a very comfortable one for all concerned. If I felt at times awkward with it, I had only to turn to Ezra Pound, whom the university also condemned, to find that he too disapproved despite the begrudging "Pact." At least he spoke of having "detested" Whitman, only publicly altering the implications of that opinion in a series of BBC interviews made in the late fifties. William Carlos Williams also seemed to dislike him, decrying the looseness of the writing, as he felt it, and the lack of a coherent prosody. He as well seemed to change his mind in age in so far as he referred to Whitman as the greatest of American poets in a public lecture on American poetry for college students. Eliot also changes his mind, as did James before him, but the point is that the heroes of my youth as well as my teachers were almost without exception extremely critical of Whitman and his influence and wanted as little as possible to do with him.

Two men, however, most dear to me, felt otherwise. The first of these was D. H. Lawrence, whose *Studies in Classic American Literature* remains the most extraordinary apprehension of the nature of American experience and writing that I know. His piece on Whitman in that book is fundamental in that he, in a decisively personal manner, first castigates Whitman for what he considers a muddling assumption of "oneness," citing "I am he that aches with amorous love . . ." as particularly offensive, and then, with equal intensity, applauds that Whitman who is, as he puts it, "a great charger of the blood in men," a truly heroic poet whose vision and will make a place of absolute communion for others.

The second, Hart Crane, shared with Whitman my own teachers' disapproval. I remember a course which I took with F. O. Mathiessen, surely a man of deep commitment and care for his students, from which Crane had been absented. I asked for permission to give a paper on Crane, which he gave me, but I had overlooked what I should have realized would be the response of the class itself, understandably intent upon its own sophistications. How would they accept these lines, for example?

yes, Walt,
Afoot again, and onward without halt, —
Not soon, nor suddenly, — no, never to let go
My hand
in yours,
Walt Whitman —
so —

If they did not laugh outright at what must have seemed to them the awkwardly stressed rhymes and sentimental camaraderie, then they tittered at Crane's will to be one with his fellow *homosexual.* But didn't they hear, I wanted to insist, the pacing of the rhythms of those lines, the syntax, the intently human tone, or simply the punctuation? Couldn't they read? Was Crane to be simply another "crudity" they could so glibly be rid of? But still I myself didn't read Whitman, more than the few poems of his that were "dealt with" in classes or that some friend asked me to. No doubt I too was embarrassed by my aunt's and my grandmother's ability to recite that terrible poem, "O Captain! My Captain!," banal as I felt it to be, and yet what was that specious taste which could so distract any attention and could righteously dismiss so much possibility, just because it didn't "like" it? Sadly, it was too much my own.

RITA DOVE, *whose recent collection* Mother Love *(1995) is written mostly in sonnet form, discusses the traditional verse form in the following excerpt from her introduction.*

RITA DOVE

An Intact World 1995

"Sonnet" literally means "little song." The sonnet is a *heile Welt,* an intact world where everything is in sync, from the stars down to the tiniest mite on a blade of grass. And if the "true" sonnet reflects the music of the spheres, it then follows that any variation from the strictly Petrarchan or Shakespearean forms represents a world gone awry.

Or does it? Can't form also be a talisman against disintegration? The sonnet defends itself against the vicissitudes of fortune by its charmed structure, its beautiful bubble. All the while, though, chaos is lurking outside the gate.

The ancient story of Demeter and Persephone is just such a tale of a violated world. It is a modern dilemma as well — there comes a point when a mother can no longer protect her child, when the daughter must go her own way into womanhood. Persephone, out picking flowers with her girlfriends, wanders off from the group. She has just stooped to pluck a golden narcissus, when the earth opens and Hades emerges, dragging her down with him into the Underworld. Inconsolable in her grief, Demeter neglects her duties as goddess of agriculture, and the crops wither. The Olympians disapprove of the abduction but are more shaken by Demeter's reaction, her refusal to return to her godly work in defiance of the laws of nature; she's even left her throne in Olympus and taken to wandering about on earth disguised as a mortal. In varying degrees she is admonished or pitied by the other gods for the depth of her grief. She refuses to accept her fate, however; she strikes out against the Law, forcing Zeus to ask his brother Hades to return Persephone to her mother. Hades agrees.

But ah, can we ever really go back home, as if nothing had happened? Before returning to the surface, the girl eats a few pomegranate seeds, not realizing that anyone who partakes of the food of the dead cannot be wholly restored to the living. So she must spend half of each year at Hades' side, as Queen of the Underworld, and her mother must acquiesce: Every fall and winter Demeter is permitted to grieve for the loss of her daughter, letting vegetation wilt and die, but she is obliged to act cheerful in spring and summer, making the earth blossom and bear fruit.

Sonnets seemed the proper mode for most of [the poems in *Mother Love*] — and not only in homage and as counterpoint to Rilke's° *Sonnets to Orpheus.* Much has been said about the many ways to "violate" the sonnet in the service of American speech or modern love or whatever; I will simply say that I like how the sonnet comforts even while its prim borders (but what a pretty fence!) are stultifying; one is constantly bumping up against Order. The Demeter/Persephone cycle of betrayal and regeneration is ideally suited for this form since all three — mother-goddess, daughter-consort, and poet — are struggling to sing in their chains.

❧

T. S. ELIOT *first published his essay discussing literary tradition in the London magazine* The Egoist *in 1919. He included it in his collection* The Sacred Wood *the following year.*

T. S. ELIOT

From "Tradition and the Individual Talent"

1919

I

In English writing we seldom speak of tradition, though we occasionally apply its name in deploring its absence. We cannot refer to "the tradition" or to

---

Rilke's: I.e., the German poet Rainer Maria Rilke (1875–1926).

"a tradition"; at most, we employ the adjective in saying that the poetry of so-and-so is "traditional" or even "too traditional." Seldom, perhaps, does the word appear except in a phrase of censure. If otherwise, it is vaguely approbative, with the implication, as to the work approved, of some pleasing archaeological reconstruction. You can hardly make the word agreeable to English ears without this comfortable reference to the reassuring science of archaeology.

Certainly the word is not likely to appear in our appreciations of living or dead writers. Every nation, every race, has not only its own creative, but its own critical turn of mind; and is even more oblivious of the shortcomings and limitations of its critical habits than of those of its creative genius. We know, or think we know, from the enormous mass of critical writing that has appeared in the French language the critical method or habit of the French; we only conclude (we are such unconscious people) that the French are "more critical" than we, and sometimes even plume ourselves a little with the fact, as if the French were the less spontaneous. Perhaps they are; but we might remind ourselves that criticism is as inevitable as breathing, and that we should be none the worse for articulating what passes in our minds when we read a book and feel an emotion about it, for criticizing our own minds in their work of criticism. One of the facts that might come to light in this process is our tendency to insist, when we praise a poet, upon those aspects of his work in which he least resembles any one else. In these aspects or parts of his work we pretend to find what is individual, what is the peculiar essence of the man. We dwell with satisfaction upon the poet's difference from his predecessors, especially his immediate predecessors; we endeavour to find something that can be isolated in order to be enjoyed. Whereas if we approach a poet without this prejudice we shall often find that not only the best, but the most individual parts of his work may be those in which the dead poets, his ancestors, assert their immortality most vigorously. And I do not mean the impressionable period of adolescence, but the period of full maturity.

Yet if the only form of tradition, of handing down, consisted in following the ways of the immediate generation before us in a blind or timid adherence to its successes, "tradition" should positively be discouraged. We have seen many such simple currents soon lost in the sand; and novelty is better than repetition. Tradition is a matter of much wider significance. It cannot be inherited, and if you want it you must obtain it by great labour. It involves, in the first place, the historical sense, which we may call nearly indispensable to any one who would continue to be a poet beyond his twenty-fifth year; and the historical sense involves a perception, not only of the pastness of the past, but of its presence; the historical sense compels a man to write not merely with his own generation in his bones, but with a feeling that the whole of the literature of Europe from Homer and within it the whole of the literature of his own country has a simultaneous existence and composes a simultaneous order. This historical sense, which is a sense of the timeless as well as of the temporal and of the timeless and of the temporal together, is what makes a writer traditional. And it is at the same time what makes a writer most acutely conscious of his place in time, of his own contemporaneity.

No poet, no artist of any art, has his complete meaning alone. His significance, his appreciation is the appreciation of his relation to the dead poets and artists. You cannot value him alone; you must set him, for contrast and comparison, among the dead. I mean this as a principle of aesthetic, not merely historical, criticism. The necessity that he shall conform, that he shall cohere, is not one-sided; what happens when a new work of art is created is something that happens simultaneously to all the works of art which preceded it. The existing monuments form an ideal order among themselves, which is modified by the introduction of the new (the really new) work of art among them. The existing order is complete before the new work arrives; for order to persist after the supervention of novelty, the *whole* existing order must be, if ever so slightly, altered; and so the relations, proportions, values of each work of art toward the whole are readjusted; and this is conformity between the old and the new. Whoever has approved this idea of order, of the form of European, of English literature will not find it preposterous that the past should be altered by the present as much as the present is directed by the past. And the poet who is aware of this will be aware of great difficulties and responsibilities.

In a peculiar sense he will be aware also that he must inevitably be judged by the standards of the past. I say judged, not amputated, by them; not judged to be as good as, or worse or better than, the dead; and certainly not judged by the canons of dead critics. It is a judgment, a comparison, in which two things are measured by each other. To conform merely would be for the new work not really to conform at all; it would not be new, and would therefore not be a work of art. And we do not quite say that the new is more valuable because it fits in; but its fitting in is a test of its value — a test, it is true, which can only be slowly and cautiously applied, for we are none of us infallible judges of conformity. We say: it appears to conform, and is perhaps individual, or it appears individual, and many conform; but we are hardly likely to find that it is one and not the other.

To proceed to a more intelligible exposition of the relation of the poet to the past: he can neither take the past as a lump, an indiscriminate bolus,° nor can he form himself wholly on one or two private admirations, nor can he form himself wholly upon one preferred period. The first course is inadmissible, the second is an important experience of youth, and the third is a pleasant and highly desirable supplement. The poet must be very conscious of the main current, which does not at all flow invariably through the most distinguished reputations. He must be quite aware of the obvious fact that art never improves, but that the material of art is never quite the same. He must be aware that the mind of Europe — the mind of his own country — a mind which he learns in time to be much more important than his own private mind — is a mind which changes, and that this change is a development which abandons nothing *en route*, which does not superannuate either Shakespeare, or Homer, or the rock drawing of the Magdalenian draughtsmen.°

---

bolus: A large pill. **Magdalenian draughtsmen:** The artists of the Paleolithic period who drew on cave walls in La Madeleine, in the south of France.

That this development, refinement perhaps, complication certainly, is not, from the point of view of the artist, any improvement. Perhaps not even an improvement from the point of view of the psychologist or not to the extent which we imagine; perhaps only in the end based upon a complication in economics and machinery. But the difference between the present and the past is that the conscious present is an awareness of the past in a way and to an extent which the past's awareness of itself cannot show.

Some one said: "The dead writers are remote from us because we *know* so much more than they did." Precisely, and they are that which we know.

I am alive to a usual objection to what is clearly part of my programme for the *métier*° of poetry. The objection is that the doctrine requires a ridiculous amount of erudition (pedantry), a claim which can be rejected by appeal to the lives of poets in any pantheon. It will even be affirmed that much learning deadens or perverts poetic sensibility. While, however, we persist in believing that a poet ought to know as much as will not encroach upon his necessary receptivity and necessary laziness, it is not desirable to confine knowledge to whatever can be put into a useful shape for examinations, drawing-rooms, or the still more pretentious modes of publicity. Some can absorb knowledge, the more tardy must sweat for it. Shakespeare acquired more essential history from Plutarch° than most men could from the whole British Museum. What is to be insisted upon is that the poet must develop or procure the consciousness of the past and that he should continue to develop this consciousness throughout his career.

What happens is a continual surrender of himself as he is at the moment to something which is more valuable. The progress of an artist is a continual self-sacrifice, a continual extinction of personality.

T. S. ELIOT *the modernist poet was a traditionalist in his literary tastes, and it is not surprising that he was uncomfortable with some of what he felt were eccentricities in William Blake's life and work. Eliot found Blake's poetry to be profoundly free and innocent, however, even if he was honest enough to admit that Blake's freedom from what Eliot called "current opinion" was "terrifying." Eliot's essay was first published in 1930.*

T. S. Eliot

From "William Blake" 1930

If one follows Blake's mind through the several stages of his poetic development it is impossible to regard him as a naïf, a wild man, a wild pet for the supercultivated. The strangeness is evaporated, the peculiarity is seen to

métier: French for "art" or "craft." **Plutarch:** Greek writer (c. 46–119?) whose work was used by Shakespeare as a source for his plays.

be the peculiarity of all great poetry: something which is found (not everywhere) in Homer and Aeschylus and Dante and Villon, and profound and concealed in the work of Shakespeare — and also in another form in Montaigne and in Spinoza. It is merely a peculiar honesty, which, in a world too frightened to be honest, is peculiarly terrifying. It is an honesty against which the whole world conspires because it is unpleasant. Blake's poetry has the unpleasantness of great poetry. Nothing that can be called morbid or abnormal or perverse, none of the things which exemplify the sickness of an epoch or a fashion, have this quality; only those things which, by some extraordinary labour of simplification, exhibit the essential sickness or strength of the human soul. And this honesty never exists without great technical accomplishment. The question about Blake the man is the question of the circumstances that concurred to permit this honesty in his work, and what circumstances define its limitations. The favouring conditions probably include these two: that, being early apprenticed to a manual occupation, he was not compelled to acquire any other education in literature than he wanted, or to acquire it for any other reason than that he wanted it; and that, being a humble engraver, he had no journalistic-social career open to him.

There was, that is to say, nothing to distract him from his interests or to corrupt these interests: neither the ambitions of parents or wife, nor the standards of society, nor the temptations of success; nor was he exposed to imitation of himself or of any one else. These circumstances — not his supposed inspired and untaught spontaneity — are what make him innocent. His early poems show what the poems of a boy of genius ought to show, immense power of assimilation. Such early poems are not, as usually supposed, crude attempts to do something beyond the boy's capacity; they are, in the case of a boy of real promise, more likely to be quite mature and successful attempts to do something small. So with Blake, his early poems are technically admirable, and their originality is in an occasional rhythm. The verse of "Edward III" deserves study. But his affection for certain Elizabethans is not so surprising as his affinity with the very best work of his own century. He is very like Collins,° he is very eighteenth century. The poem "Whether on Ida's Shady Brow" is eighteenth-century work; the movement, the weight of it, the syntax, the choice of words:

> *The* languid *strings do scarcely move!*
> *The sound is* forc'd, *the notes are few!*

this is contemporary with Gray° and Collins, it is the poetry of a language which has undergone the discipline of prose. Blake up to twenty is decidedly a traditional.

Blake's beginnings as a poet, then, are as normal as the beginnings of Shakespeare. His method of composition, in his mature work, is exactly like that of other poets. He has an idea (a feeling, an image), he develops it by accretion or expansion, alters his verse often, and hesitates often over the final choice. The idea, of course, simply comes, but upon arrival it is subjected to

---

Collins: English poet William Collins (1721–1759). **Gray:** English poet Thomas Gray (1716–1771); see p. 872.

prolonged manipulation. In the first phase Blake is concerned with verbal beauty; in the second he becomes the apparent naïf, really the mature intelligence. It is only when the ideas become more automatic, come more freely and are less manipulated, that we begin to suspect their origin, to suspect that they spring from a shallower source.

The Songs of Innocence and of Experience, and the poems from the Rossetti manuscript, are the poems of a man with a profound interest in human emotions, and a profound knowledge of them. The emotions are presented in an extremely simplified, abstract form. This form is one illustration of the eternal struggle of art against education, of the literary artist against the continuous deterioration of language.

It is important that the artist should be highly educated in his own art; but his education is one that is hindered rather than helped by the ordinary processes of society which constitute education for the ordinary man. For these processes consist largely in the acquisition of impersonal ideas which obscure what we really are and feel, what we really want, and what really excites our interest. It is of course not the actual information acquired, but the conformity which the accumulation of knowledge is apt to impose, that is harmful. Tennyson is a very fair example of a poet almost wholly encrusted with opinion, almost wholly merged into his environment. Blake, on the other hand, knew what interested him, and he therefore presents only the essential, only, in fact, what can be presented, and need not be explained. And because he was not distracted, or frightened, or occupied in anything but exact statements, he understood. He was naked, and saw man naked, and from the centre of his own crystal. To him there was no more reason why Swedenborg° should be absurd than Locke.° He accepted Swedenborg, and eventually rejected him, for reasons of his own. He approached everything with a mind unclouded by current opinions. There was nothing of the superior person about him. This makes him terrifying.

RALPH WALDO EMERSON's *"The Poet" appeared in his second collection titled simply* Essays *(1844) and inspired Walt Whitman to expand the limits of conventional poetic form and language. As Whitman said, "I was simmering, simmering, simmering: Emerson brought me to a boil."*

RALPH WALDO EMERSON

From "The Poet"

1844

The poet is the sayer, the namer, and represents beauty. He is a sovereign, and stands on the centre. For the world is not painted, or adorned, but is

Swedenborg: Swedish philosopher Emanuel Swedenborg (1688–1772). **Locke:** English philosopher John Locke (1632–1704).

from the beginning beautiful; and God has not made some beautiful things, but Beauty is the creator of the universe. Therefore the poet is not any permissive potentate, but is emperor in his own right. Criticism is infested with a cant of materialism, which assumes that manual skill and activity is the first merit of all men, and disparages such as say and do not, overlooking the fact that some men, namely poets, are natural sayers, sent into the world to the end of expression, and it confounds them with those whose province is action, but who quit it to imitate the sayers. But Homer's words are as costly and admirable to Homer, as Agamemnon's victories are to Agamemnon. The poet does not wait for the hero or the sage, but, as they act and think primarily, so he writes primarily what will and must be spoken, reckoning the others, though primaries also, yet, in respect to him, secondaries and servants; as sitters or models in the studio of a painter, or as assistants who bring building materials to an architect.

For poetry was all written before time was, and whenever we are so finely organized that we can penetrate into that region where the air is music, we hear those primal warblings, and attempt to write them down, but we lose ever and anon a word, or a verse, and substitute something of our own, and thus miswrite the poem. The men of more delicate ear write down these cadences more faithfully, and these transcripts, though imperfect, become the songs of the nations. For nature is as truly beautiful as it is good, or as it is reasonable, and must as much appear, as it must be done, or be known. Words and deeds are quite indifferent modes of the divine energy. Words are also actions, and actions are a kind of words.

The sign and credentials of the poet are, that he announces that which no man foretold. He is the true and only doctor; he knows and tells; he is the only teller of news, for he was present and privy to the appearance which he describes. He is a beholder of ideas, and an utterer of the necessary and causal. We do not speak now of men of poetical talents, or of industry and skill in metre, but of the true poet. I took part in a conversation the other day, concerning a recent writer of lyrics, a man of subtle mind, whose head appeared to be a music-box of delicate tunes and rhythms, and whose skill, and command of language, we could not sufficiently praise. But when the question arose whether he were not only a lyrist, but a poet, we were obliged to confess that he is plainly a contemporary, not an eternal man. He does not stand out of our low limitations, like a Chimborazo° under the line, running up from the torrid base through all the climates of the globe, with belts of the herbage of every latitude on its high and mottled sides; but this genius is the landscape garden of a modern house, adorned with fountains and statues, with well-bred men and women standing and sitting in the walks and terraces. We hear, through all the varied music, the ground-tone of conventional life. Our poets are men of talents who sing, and not the children of music. The argument is secondary, the finish of the verses is primary.

For it is not metres, but a metre-making argument, that makes a poem, — a thought so passionate and alive, that, like the spirit of a plant or an

---

Chimborazo: A mountain in Ecuador.

animal, it has an architecture of its own, and adorns nature with a new thing. The thought and the form are equal in the order of time, but in the order of genesis the thought is prior to the form. The poet has a new thought: he has a whole new experience to unfold; he will tell us how it was with him, and all men will be the richer in his fortune. The experience of each new age requires a new confession, and the world seems always waiting for its poet. I remember, when I was young, how much I was moved one morning by tidings that genius had appeared in a youth who sat near me at table. He had left his work, and gone rambling none knew whither, and had written hundreds of lines, but could not tell whether that which was in him was therein told: he could tell nothing but that all was changed — man, beast, heaven, earth, and sea. How gladly we listened! how credulous! Society seemed to be compromised. We sat in the aurora of a sunrise which was to put out all the stars. Boston seemed to be at twice the distance it had the night before, or was much further than that. Rome, — what was Rome? Plutarch and Shakespeare were in the yellow leaf, and Homer no more should be heard of. It is much to know that poetry has been written this very day, under this very roof, by your side. What! that wonderful spirit has not expired! these stony moments are still sparkling and animated! I had fancied that the oracles were all silent, and nature had spent her fires, and behold! all night, from every pore, these fine auroras have been streaming. Every one has some interest in the advent of the poet, and no one knows how much it may concern him. We know that the secret of the world is profound, but who or what shall be our interpreter, we know not. A mountain ramble, a new style of face, a new person, may put the key into our hands. Of course, the value of genius to us is in the veracity of its report. Talent may frolic and juggle; genius realizes and adds. Mankind, in good earnest, have gone so far in understanding themselves and their work, and the foremost watchman on the peak announces his news. It is the truest word ever spoken, and the phrase will be the fittest, most musical, and the unerring voice of the world for the time.

ALLEN GINSBERG *discusses and expands on the concepts in his writing in this 1987 interview in the* New York Quarterly.

ALLEN GINSBERG

On His Poetic Craft

1987

Interviewer: You have talked about this before, but would you begin this interview by describing the early influences on your work, or the influences on your early work?

Ginsberg: Emily Dickinson. Poe's "Bells" — "Hear the sledges with the bells — Silver Bells! . . ." Milton's long line breath in *Paradise Lost* —

> Him the almighty power
> Hurled headlong flaming from the ethereal sky
> With hideous ruin and combustion down
> To bottomless perdition, there to dwell
> In adamantine chains and penal fire,
> Who durst defy the omnipotent to arms.

Shelley's "Epipsychidion" — "one life, one death, / One Heaven, one Hell, one immortality, / And one annihilation. Woe is me! . . ." The end of Shelley's "Adonais"; and Shelley's "Ode to the West Wind" exhibits continuous breath leading to ecstatic climax.

Wordsworth's "Intimations of Immortality" —

> Our birth is but a sleep and a forgetting:
> The soul that rises with us, our life's Star,
> Hath had elsewhere its setting,

— also Wordsworth's "Tintern Abbey" exhortation, or whatever you call it:

> a sense sublime
> Of something far more deeply interfused,
> Whose dwelling is the light of setting suns,
> And the round ocean and the living air,
> And the blue sky, and in the mind of man;

That kind of poetry influenced me: a long breath poetry that has a sort of ecstatic climax.

Interviewer: What about Whitman?

Ginsberg: No, I replied very specifically. You asked me about my *first* poetry. Whitman and Blake, yes, but in terms of the *early* poems I replied specifically. When I began writing I was writing rhymed verse, stanzaic forms that I derived from my father's practice. As I progressed into that, I got more involved with Andrew Marvell.

Interviewer: Did you used to go to the Poetry Society of America meetings?

Ginsberg: Yes, I used to go with my father. It was a horrifying experience — mostly old ladies and second-rate poets.

Interviewer: Would you elaborate?

Ginsberg: That's the PSA I'm talking about. At the time it was mainly people who were enemies of, and denounced, William Carlos Williams and Ezra Pound and T. S. Eliot.

Interviewer: How long did it take you to realize they were enemies?

Ginsberg: Oh, I knew right away. I meant enemies of poetry, very specifically. Or enemies of that poetry which now by hindsight is considered sincere poetry of the time. *Their* highwater mark was, I guess, Edwin Arlington Robinson; "Eros Tyrranos" was considered, I guess, the great highwater mark of twentieth-century poetry.

Interviewer: Where did you first hear long lines in momentum?

Ginsberg: The texts I was citing were things my father taught me when I was prepubescent.

Interviewer: Did he teach them to you as beautiful words, or as the craft of poetry?

Ginsberg: I don't think people used that word "craft" in those days. It's sort of like a word that has only come into use in the last few decades. There were texts of great poetry around the house, and he would recite from memory. He never sat down and said now I am going to teach you: Capital C-R-A-F-T. Actually I don't like the use of the word craft applied to poetry, because generally along with it comes a defense of stressed iambic prosody, which I find uncraftsmanly and pedantical in its use. There are very few people in whose mouths that word makes any sense. I think Marianne Moore may have used it a few times. Pound has used it a couple of times in very specific circumstances — more often as a verb than as a general noun: "This or that poet has crafted a sestina."

Interviewer: Would you talk about later influences on your work? William Blake? Walt Whitman?

Ginsberg: Later on for open verse I was interested in Kerouac's poetry. I think that turned me on more than anyone else. I think he is a very great poet and much underrated. He hadn't been read yet by poets.

Interviewer: Most people associate Kerouac with prose, with *On the Road,* and not so much with *Mexico City Blues.* Or maybe they differentiate too strictly between prose and poetry.

Ginsberg: I think it's because people are so preoccupied with the use of the word craft and its meaning that they can't see poetry in front of them on the page. Kerouac's poetry looks like the most "uncrafted stuff" in the world. He's got a different idea of craft from most people who use the word "craft." I would say Kerouac's poetry is the craftiest of all. And as far as having the most craft of anyone, though those who talk about craft have not yet discovered it, his craft is spontaneity; his craft is having the instantaneous recall of the unconscious; his craft is the perfect executive conjunction of archetypal memorial images articulating present observation of detail and childhood epiphany fact.

Interviewer: In *Howl,* at the end of Section One, you came close to a definition of poetry, when you wrote:

> Who dreamt and made incarnate gaps in Time & Space through images juxtaposed, and trapped the archangel of the soul between 2 visual images and joined the elemental verbs and set the noun and dash of consciousness together jumping with sensation of Pater Omnipotens Aeterne Deus

Ginsberg: I reparaphrased that when I was talking about Kerouac. If you heard the structure of the sentence I was composing, it was about putting present observed detail into epiphany, or catching the archangel of the soul between two visual images. I was thinking then about what Kerouac and I thought about haiku — two visual images, opposite poles, which are connected by a lightning in the mind. In other words "Today's been a good day; let another fly come on the rice." Two disparate images, unconnected, which the mind connects.

Interviewer: Chinese poets do that. Is that what you are talking about?

Ginsberg: This is characteristic of Chinese poetry as Ezra Pound pointed out in his essay "The Chinese Written Character as a Medium for Poetry" nearly fifty years ago. Do you know that work? Well, way back when, Ezra Pound proposed Chinese hieroglyphic language as more fit for poetry, considering that it was primarily visual, than generalized language-abstraction English, with visionless words like Truth, Beauty, Craft, etc. Pound then translated some Chinese poetry and translated (from Professor Fenellossa's papers) this philosophic essay pointing to Chinese language as pictorial. There is no concrete in English, and poets could learn from Chinese to present image-detail: and out of that Pound hieroglyph rose the whole practice of imagism, the school which is referred to as "Imagism." So what you are referring to is an *old* history in twentieth-century poetry. My own thing about two visual images is just from that tradition, actually drawing from Pound's discovery and interpretation of Chinese as later practiced by Williams and everybody who studied with Pound or who understood Pound. What I'm trying to point out is that this tradition in American poetry in the twentieth century is not something *just* discovered. It was done by Pound and Williams, precisely the people that are anathema to the PSA mediocrities who were attacking Pound and Williams for not having "craft."

Interviewer: In that same section of *Howl,* in the next line, you wrote:

> to recreate the syntax and measure of poor human prose and stand before you speechless and intelligent and shaking with shame, rejected yet confessing out the soul to conform to the rhythm of thought in his naked and endless head.

Ginsberg: Description of aesthetic method. Key phrases that I picked up around that time and was using when I wrote the book. I meant again that if you place two visual images side by side and let the mind connect them, the gap between the two images, the lightning in the mind illuminates. It's the *sunyata* (Buddhist term for blissful empty void) which can only be known by living creatures. So, the emptiness to which the Zen finger classically points — the ellipse — is the unspoken hair-raising awareness in between two mental visual images. I should try to make my answers a little more succinct.

Interviewer: Despite your feeling about craft, poets have developed an attitude towards your work, they have discovered certain principles of breath division in your lines —

Ginsberg: Primary fact of my writing is that I don't have any craft and don't know what I'm doing. There is absolutely no art involved, in the context of the general use of the words "art" and "craft." Such craft or art as there is, is in illuminating mental formations, and trying to observe the naked activity of my own mind. Then transcribing that activity down on paper. So the craft is being shrewd at flash lighting mental activity. Trapping the archangel of the soul, by accident, so to speak. The subject matter is the action of my mind. To put it on the most vulgar level, like on the psychoanalyst's couch is supposed to be. Now if you are thinking of "form" or even the "well-made poem" or a sonnet when you're lying on the couch, you'll never say what you have on your mind. You'd be babbling about corset styles or something *else* all the time instead of saying, "I want to fuck my mother," or whatever it is you want. So my problem is to get down the fact that I want to fuck my mother or whatever. I'm taking the most hideous image possible, so there will be no misunderstanding about what area of mind you are dealing with: what is socially unspoken, what is prophetic from the unconscious, what is universal to all men, what's the main subject of poetry, what's underneath, *inside* the mind. So, how do you get that out on the page? You observe your own mind during the time of composition and write down whatever goes through the ticker tape of mentality, or whatever you hear in the echo of your inner ear, or what flashes in picture on the eyeball while you're writing. So the subject is constantly interrupting because the mind is constantly going on vagaries — so whenever it changes I have a dash. The dashes are a function of this method of transcription of unconscious data. Now you can't write down *everything* that you've got going on — half-conscious data. You can't write down everything, you can only write down what the hand can carry. Your hand can't carry more than a twentieth of what the mind flashes, and the very fact of writing interrupts the mind's flashes and redirects attention to writing. So that the observation (for writing) impedes the function of the mind. You might say "Observation impedes Function." I get down as much as I can of genuine material, interrupting the flow of material as I get it down and when I look, I turn to the center of my brain to see the next thought, but it's probably about thirty thoughts later. So I make a dash to indicate a break, sometimes a dash plus dots. Am I making sense? — . . .

Interviewer: How much do you revise your work?

Ginsberg: As little revision as possible. The craft, the art consists in paying attention on the actual movie of the mind. Writing it down is like a byproduct of that. If you can actually keep track of your own head movie, then the writing it down is just like a secretarial job, and who gets crafty about that? Use dashes instead of semicolons. Knowing the difference between a dash — and a hyphen -. Long lines are useful at certain times, and short lines at other times. But a big notebook with lines is a helpful thing, and three pens — you have to be shrewd about that. The actual materials are important. A book at the nightstand is important — a light you can get at — or a flashlight, as Kerouac had a brakeman's lantern. That's the craft. Having the brakeman's lantern and knowing where to use the ampersand "&" for swiftness in writing. If your attention is focused all the time — as my attention was in writing "Sunflower Sutra," "TV Baby" poem later ("Wichita Vortex Sutra" later, in a book called *Planet News*) — when attention is focused, there is no likelihood there will be much need for blue penciling revision because there'll be a sensuous continuum in the composition. So when I look over something that I've written down, I find that if my attention has lapsed from the subject, I begin to talk about myself writing about the subject or talking about my irrelevant left foot itch instead of about the giant smog factory I'm observing in Linden, New Jersey. Then I'll have to do some blue penciling, excising whatever is irrelevant: whatever I inserted self-consciously, instead of conscious of the Subject. Where self-consciousness intervenes on attention, blue pencil excision means getting rid of the dross of self-consciousness. Since the subject matter is really the operation of the mind, as in Gertrude Stein, anything that the mind passes through is proper and shouldn't be revised out, almost anything that passes through mind, anything with the exception of self-consciousness. Anything that occurs to the mind is the proper subject. So if you are making a graph of the movements of the mind, there is no point in revising it. Because then you would obliterate the actual markings of the graph. So if you're interested in writing as a form of meditation or introspective yoga, which I am, then there's no revision possible.

❧

LOUISE GLÜCK *wrote these comments as part of her introduction to* The Best American Poems *of 1993, of which she was the editor.*

LOUISE GLÜCK

Poems Are *Autobiography*

1993

The world is complete without us. Intolerable fact. To which the poet responds by rebelling, wanting to prove otherwise. Out of wounded vanity or stubborn pride or desolate need, the poet lives in chronic dispute with fact, and an astonishment occurs: another fact is created, like a new element, in partial contradiction of the intolerable. Indelible voice, though it has no impact on the nonhuman universe, profoundly alters our experience of that universe as well as of the world of human relations; to all that is most solitary in our natures, it is the sustaining companion.

We know this happens: literature is its record or testament. A chilling word, literature. It lacks all sense of the voice's adamant vitality. As an abstraction, it converts the poem into something equally disembodied, a resolved thing, inert and distant. Whereas the voice that rises from the page is weirdly restless: seductive, demanding, embittered, witty. Speaking not from the past but in the present. And it still occurs: voices emerge from which, in Robinson Jeffers's phrase, fire cannot be leached, whether because cultural shifts create them or because they enact the ancient dispute with new emphasis or because there is in them some quality or force not yet identified.

It would be interesting to know something about that quality, because the poem, no matter how charged its content, survives not through content but through voice. By *voice* I mean style of thought, for which a style of speech — the clever grafts and borrowings, the habitual gestures scattered like clues in the lines — never convincingly substitutes. We fall back on that term, *voice,* for all its insufficiencies; it suggests, at least, the sound of an authentic being. Although such sound may draw on the poet's actual manner of speech, it is not, on the page, transcription. The voice is at liberty to excerpt, to exaggerate, to bypass what it chooses, to issue from conditions the real world will never exactly reproduce; unlike speech, it bears no immediate social pressure, since the other to whom it strives to make itself clear may not yet exist. The poem means to create that person, first in the poet, then in the reader. Meanwhile, its fidelity is not to external reality: it need not provide a replica of the outward, or of social relations. This is why time confers more readily on the apolitical novel political significance: nineteenth-century romantic novels, for example, were not necessarily conceived as political statements; they become such statements in light of a contemporary readiness to politicize gender relations. The novel seems oddly easier on many readers, who are puzzled by the poem's independence, puzzled, even, by the voice's unnerving authenticity. The conviction that poems must be autobiography (since they are not description) begins here; in the reader's belief that the actual and the true are synonyms.

Poems *are* autobiography, but divested of the trappings of chronology and comment, the metronomic alternation of anecdote and response. Moreover, a body of work may change and develop less in reaction to the lived life than in reaction to the poet's prior discoveries, or the discoveries of others. If a poem remains so selectively amplified, so casual with fact, as to seem elusive, we must remember its agenda: not, or not simply, to record the actual but to continuously create the sensation of immersion in the actual. And if, in its striving to be free of the imprisoning self, the poet's gaze trains itself outward, it rests nevertheless on what compels or arrests it. Such choices constitute a portrait. Where the gaze is held, voice, or response, begins. Always in what follows the poet is alert, resistant, resisting dogma and fashion, resisting the greater danger of personal conviction, which must be held suspect, given its resemblance to dogma.

Still, for poems to touch us, we have to be magnetically drawn, we have to want to read these things. What makes this possible, what are the characteristics of those voices that, even as they become epigraphs or inscriptions on stone, mock the stone and the page with their vitality? Not, I think, that they sound beautiful or speak truth. Of these claims, the second seems at once grander and more accessible because of the ease with which truth identifies itself with sincerity as opposed to insight. Art's truth is as different from sincerity's honest disclosure as it is different from the truth administered in the doctor's office, that sequence of knowns which the doctor, newly trained to respect the patient's dignity, makes wholly available, affording, in the process, glimpses into a world of probabilities and strategies, the world of action transposed to conditions in which action can do only so much. The poem may embody perception so luminous it seems truth, but what keeps it alive is not fixed discovery but the means to discovery; what keeps it alive is intelligence.

ROBERT HAYDEN's *introduction to his anthology of African American poetry discusses the tradition of "Negro poetry" which, like American poetry generally, was concerned with developing a distinctive language and form.*

ROBERT HAYDEN

On Negro Poetry

1967

The question whether we can speak with any real justification of "Negro poetry" arises often today. Some object to the term because it has been used disparagingly to indicate a kind of pseudo-poetry concerned with the race problem to the exclusion of almost everything else. Others hold that Negro poetry *per se* could only be produced in black Africa. Seen from this point of view, the poetry of the American Negro, its "specialized" content notwithstanding, is obviously not to be thought of as existing apart from the rest of our literature, but as having been shaped over some three centuries by social, moral, and literary forces essentially American.

Those who presently avow themselves "poets of the Negro revolution" argue that they do indeed constitute a separate group or school, since the purpose of their writing is to give Negroes a sense of human dignity and provide them with ideological weapons. A belligerent race pride moves these celebrants of Black Power to declare themselves not simply "poets," but "Negro poets." However, Countee Cullen, the brilliant lyricist of the Harlem Renaissance in the 1920s, insisted that he be considered a "poet," not a "Negro poet," for he did not want to be restricted to racial themes nor have his poetry judged solely on the basis of its relevance to the Negro struggle.

Cullen was aware of a peculiar risk Negro poets have had to face. The tendency of American critics has been to label the established Negro writer a "spokesman for his race." There are, as we have seen, poets who think of themselves in that role. But the effect of such labeling is to place any Negro author in a kind of literary ghetto where the standards applied to other writers are not likely to be applied to him, since he, being a "spokesman for his race," is not considered primarily a writer but a species of race-relations man, the leader of a cause, the voice of protest.

Protest has been a recurring element in the writing of American Negroes, a fact hardly to be wondered at, given the social conditions under which they have been forced to live. And the Negro poet's devotion to the cause of freedom is not in any way reprehensible, for throughout history poets have often been champions of human liberty. But bad poetry is another matter, and there is no denying that a great deal of "race poetry" is poor, because its content seems ready-made and art is displaced by argument.

Phillis Wheatley (c. 1750–1784), the first poet of African descent to win some measure of recognition, had almost nothing to say about the plight of her people. And if she resented her own ambiguous position in society, she did not express her resentment. One reason for her silence is that, although brought to Boston as a slave, she never lived as one. Another is that as a neoclassical poet she would scarcely have thought it proper to reveal much of herself in her poetry, although we do get brief glimpses of her in the poem addressed to the Earl of Dartmouth and in "On Being Brought from Africa to America." Neoclassicism emphasized reason rather than emotion and favored elegance and formality. The English poet, Alexander Pope, was the acknowledged master of this style, and in submitting to his influence Phillis Wheatley produced poetry that was as good as that of her American contemporaries. She actually wrote better than some of them.

But the poetry of Phillis Wheatley and her fellow poet, Jupiter Hammon, has historical and not literary interest for us now. The same can be said of much of eighteenth-century American poetry in general. Not until the nineteenth century did the United States begin to have literature of unqualified merit and originality. There were no Negro poets of stature in the period before the Civil War, but there were several with talent, among them George Moses Horton (1797–c. 1883) and Frances E. W. Harper (1825–1911). Didactic and sentimental, they wrote with competence and moral fervor in the manner of their times. Their poetry is remembered chiefly because it contributed to the antislavery struggle, and because it testifies to the creative efforts of Negroes under disheartening conditions. . . .

In the twentieth century Negro poets have abandoned dialect for an idiom truer to folk speech. The change has been due not only to differences in social outlook on their part but also to revolutionary developments in American poetry. The New Poetry movement, which began before the First World War and reached its definitive point in the 1920s, represented a break with the past. Free verse, diction close to everyday speech, a realistic approach to life, and the use of material once considered unpoetic — these were the goals of the movement. The Negro poet-critic, William Stanley Braithwaite, encouraged the "new" poetry through his articles in the *Boston Evening Transcript* and his yearly anthologies of magazine verse.

The New Negro movement or Negro Renaissance, resulting from the social, political, and artistic awakening of Negroes in the twenties, brought into prominence poets whose work showed the influence of the poetic revolution. Protest became more defiant, racial bitterness and racial pride more outspoken than ever before. Negro history and folklore were explored as new sources of inspiration. Spirituals, blues, and jazz suggested themes and verse patterns to young poets like Jean Toomer and Langston Hughes. Certain conventions, notably what has been called "literary Garveyism," grew out of a fervent Negro nationalism. Marcus Garvey, leader of the United Negro Improvement Association, advocated a "return" to Africa, the lost homeland, and nearly all the Renaissance poets wrote poems about their spiritual ties to Africa, about the dormant fires of African paganism in the Negro soul that the white man's civilization could never extingish. Countee Cullen's "Heritage" is one of the best of these poems, even though the Africa it presents is artificial, romanticized, and it reiterates exotic clichés in vogue during the period when it was written.

Harlem was the center of the Negro Renaissance, which for that reason is also referred to as the Harlem Renaissance. Two magazines, *The Crisis* and *Opportunity,* gave aid and encouragement to Negro writers by publishing their work and by awarding literary prizes.

In the decades since the New Negro movement, which ended with the twenties, protest and race consciousness have continued to find expression in the poetry of the American Negro. But other motivating forces are also in evidence. There are Negro poets who believe that any poet's most clearly defined task is to create with honesty and sincerity poems that will illuminate human experience — not exclusively "Negro experience." They reject the idea of poetry as racial propaganda, of poetry that functions as a kind of sociology. Their attitude is not wholly new, of course, being substantially that of Dunbar and Cullen. In counterpoise to it is the "Beat" or "nonacademic" view held by poets who are not only in rebellion against middle-class ideals and the older poetic traditions but who also advocate a militant racism in a definitely "Negro" poetry.

It has come to be expected of Negro poets that they will address themselves to the race question — and that they will all say nearly the same things about it. Such "group unity" is more apparent than real. Differences in vision and emphasis, fundamental differences in approach to the art of poetry itself, modify and give diversity to the writing of these poets, even when they employ similar themes. And certainly there is no agreement among them as to what the much debated role of the Negro poet should be.

ANTHONY HECHT's *1968 parody of Matthew Arnold's "Dover Beach" (p. 966) is not meant as an attack on the earlier poem. It is, rather, a deliberately amusing way of looking at a familiar masterpiece from another point of view.*

ANTHONY HECHT

The Dover Bitch

1968

A Criticism of Life

So there stood Matthew Arnold and this girl
With the cliffs of England crumbling away behind them,
And he said to her, "Try to be true to me,
And I'll do the same for you, for things are bad
All over, etc., etc."
Well now, I knew this girl. It's true she had read
Sophocles in a fairly good translation
And caught that bitter allusion to the sea,
But all the time he was talking she had in mind
The notion of what his whiskers would feel like
On the back of her neck. She told me later on
That after a while she got to looking out
At the lights across the channel, and really felt sad,
Thinking of all the wine and enormous beds
And blandishments in French and the perfumes.
And then she got really angry. To have been brought
All the way down from London, and then be addressed

As a sort of mournful cosmic last resort
Is really tough on a girl, and she was pretty.
Anyway, she watched him pace the room
And finger his watch-chain and seem to sweat a bit,
And then she said one or two unprintable things.
But you mustn't judge her by that. What I mean to say is,
She's really all right. I still see her once in a while
And she always treats me right. We have a drink
And I give her a good time, and perhaps it's a year
Before I see her again, but there she is,
Running to fat, but dependable as they come.
And sometimes I bring her a bottle of *Nuit d'Amour.*

RICHARD HOWARD, *the poet and translator, published his important book* Alone with America *in 1980. In it he discusses some of the contradictions of Anne Sexton's poetic achievement.*

RICHARD HOWARD

"Some Tribal Female Who Is Known but Forbidden": Anne Sexton

1980

There are some areas of experience in modern life, Theodore Roethke has said, that simply cannot be rendered by either the formal lyric or straight prose. We must realize — and who could have enforced the realization upon us better than Roethke — that the writer in "freer forms" must have an even greater fidelity to his subject matter or his substance than the poet who has the support of form — of received form. He must be imaginatively "right," his rhythm must move as the mind moves, or he is lost. "On the simplest level, something must happen in this kind of poem." By which Roethke meant, I am certain, that it is not enough to report something happening in your life merely — it must be made to happen in your poem. You must begin somewhere, though, generally with your life, above all with your life when it seems to you to welter in a particular exemplary status. Such is Anne Sexton's case, and she has begun indeed with the report of her case:

Oh! Honor and relish the facts!
Do not think of the intense sensation
I have as I tell you this
but think only . . .

In fact, she has reported more than anyone else — anyone else who has set out to write poems — has ever cared or dared, and thereby she has gained, perhaps at the expense of her poetry, a kind of sacerdotal stature, the elevation of a priestess celebrating mysteries which are no less mysterious for having been conducted in all the hard glare of the marketplace and with all the explicitness mere print can afford.

Anne Sexton is the true Massachusetts heiress of little Pearl,° who as the procession of Worthies passes by asks Hester Prynne if one man in it is the same minister who kissed her by the brook. "Hold thy peace, dear little Pearl," whispers her mother. "We must not always talk in the marketplace of what happens to us in the forest." Like the sibylline, often insufferable Pearl, Anne Sexton *does* speak of such things, and in such places, and it makes her, again like Pearl, both more and less than a mere "person," something beyond a "character"; it makes her, rather, what we call a *figure,* the form of a tragic function. If you are wearing not only your heart on your sleeve, your liver on your lapel, and the other organs affixed to various articles of your attire, but also a whole alphabet in scarlet on your breast, then your poetry must bear with losing the notion of *private parts* altogether and with gaining a certain publicity that has nothing to do with the personal. Further, if you regard, as Anne Sexton does, the poem as "a lie that tells the truth" (it was Cocteau° who first spoke of himself this way), then you face the corresponding peril that the truth you tell will become a lie: "there is no translating that ocean," as Miss Sexton says. And it will become a lie because you have not taken enough care to "make something happen" — in short, to lie in the way poems must lie, by devising that imaginative rightness which Roethke located primarily in rhythm, but which has everything to do as well with the consecution of images, the shape language makes as it is deposited in the reader's mind, the transactions between beginnings and endings, the *devices* — no less — of art.

"Even one alone verse sometimes makes a perfect poem," Ben Jonson declared, and so much praise (it is the kind of praise that leaves out of the reckoning a great deal of waste, a great deal of botched work) it will be easy, and what is more it will be necessary, to give Anne Sexton; like the preposterous sprite whose "demon-offspring" impulses she resumes, this poet is likely, *at any moment,* to say those oracular, outrageous things we least can bear but most require:

> Fee-fi-fo-fum
> Now I'm borrowed
> Now I'm numb

It is when she speaks beyond the moment, speaks as it were consecutively that Anne Sexton finds herself in difficulties; if we are concerned with the poem as it grows from one verse to the next, enlarging itself by means of itself, like a growing pearl, the real one (Hawthorne's, for all he tells us, never grew up), then we must discover an Anne Sexton dead set, by her third book of poems, against any such process. Hers is the truth that cancels poetry, and her career as an artist an excruciating trajectory of self-destruction, so that it is by her

---

Pearl: Hester Prynne's illegitimate child in Nathaniel Hawthorne's *The Scarlet Letter* (1850).
Cocteau: French writer, artist, and filmmaker Jean Cocteau (1889–1963).

failures in her own enterprise that she succeeds, and by her successes as an artist that she fails herself.

DAVID HUDDLE *discusses Hayden's 1962 poem in his most recent book,* A David Huddle Reader *(1994). Huddle, a poet, teaches at the University of Vermont, and in 1993–94 he was acting editor of the* New England Review.

DAVID HUDDLE

The "Banked Fire" of Robert Hayden's "Those Winter Sundays"

1996

For twenty years I've been teaching Robert Hayden's most frequently anthologized poem to undergraduate poetry-writing students. By "teach," I mean that from our textbook I read the poem aloud in the classroom, I ask one of the students to read it aloud, I make some observations about it, I invite the students to make some observations about it, then we talk about it a while longer. Usually to wrap up the discussion, I'll read the poem through once more. Occasions for such teaching come up about half a dozen times a year, and so let's say that during my life I've been privileged to read this poem aloud approximately 240 times. "Those Winter Sundays" has withstood my assault upon it. It remains a poem I look forward to reading and discussing in my classroom. The poem remains alive to me, so that for hours and sometimes days after it visits my classroom, I'm hearing its lines in my mind's ear.

Though a fourteen-liner, "Those Winter Sundays" is only loosely a sonnet. Its stanzas are five, four, and five lines long. There are rhymes and near-rhymes, but no rhyme scheme. The poem's lines probably average about eight syllables. There are only three strictly iambic lines: the fourth, the eighth, and (significantly) the fourteenth. It's a poem that's powerfully informed by the sonnet form; it's a poem that "feels like" a sonnet — it has the density and gravity of a sonnet — which is to say that in its appearance on the page, in its diction and syntax, in its tone, cadence, and argumentative strategy, "Those Winter Sundays" presents the credentials of a work of literary art in the tradition of English letters. But it's also a poem that has gone its own way, a definite departure from that most conventional of all the poetic forms of English and American verse.

The abstract issue of this poem's sonnethood is of less value to my beginning poets than the tangible matter of the sounds the poem makes, especially those *k*-sounding words of the first eleven lines that one comes to associate with discomfort: "clothes . . . blueback cold . . . cracked . . . ached . . . weekday . . . banked . . . thanked . . . wake . . . cold . . . breaking . . . call . . . chronic . . . cold." What's missing from the final three lines? The *k* sounds have been driven from the poem, as the father has "driven out the cold" from the house. The sounds that have replaced those *k* sounds are the *o* sounds of "good . . . shoes . . . know . . . know . . . love . . . lonely offices." The poem lets us associate the *o* sounds with love and loneliness. Sonically the poem tells the same story the poem narrates for us. The noise of this poem moves us through its emotional journey from discomfort to lonely love. If ever there was a poem that could teach a beginning poet the viability of the element of sound-crafting, it is "Those Winter Sundays."

Quote its first two words, and a great many poets and English teachers will be able to finish the first line (if not the whole poem) from memory. Somewhat remarkably, the poem's thesis — that the office of love can be relentless, thankless, and more than a little mysterious — resides in that initially odd-sounding two-word beginning, "Sundays too." The rest of the line — the rest of the independent clause — is ordinary. Nowhere else in Anglo-American literature does the word *too* carry the weight it carries in "Those Winter Sundays."

Not as immediately apparent as its opening words but very nearly as important to the poem's overall strategy is the two-sentence engineering of the first stanza. Because they will appreciate it more if they discover it for themselves, I often maneuver Socratically to have my students describe the poem's first two sentences: long and complex, followed by short and simple. It almost always seems to me worthwhile to ask, "Why didn't Hayden begin his poem this way: 'No one ever thanked my father for getting up early on Sundays, too'? Wouldn't that be a more direct and hospitable way to bring the reader into the poem?" After I've taken my students that far, they are quick to see how that ordinary five-word unit, "No one ever thanked him," gains meaning and emotion, weight, and force, from the elaborate preparation given it by the thirty-two-word "Sundays too" first sentence.

So much depends on "No one ever thanked him" that it requires the narrative enhancement of the first four and a half lines. It is the crux of the poem. What is this poem about? It is about a son's remorse over never thanking his father not only for what he did for him but also for how (he now realizes) he felt about him. And what is the poem if not an elegantly fashioned, permanent expression of gratitude?

"Those Winter Sundays" tells a story, or it describes a circumstance, of father-son conflict, and it even makes some excuses for the son's "Speaking indifferently" to the father: there was a good deal of anger between them; "chronic angers of that house" suggests that the circumstances were complicated somewhat beyond the usual and ordinary conflict between fathers and sons. Of the father, we know that he labored outdoors with his hands. Of the son, we know that he was, in the classic manner of youth, heedless of the ways in which his father served him.

Though the evidence of his "labor" is visible in every stanza of this poem, the father himself is somewhere else. We don't see him. He is in some other room of the house than the one where our speaker is. That absence suggests the emotional distance between the father and the son as well as the current absence, through death, of the father on the occasion of this utterance. It's easy enough to imagine this poem as a graveside meditation, an elegy, and a rather impassioned one at that, "What did I know, what did I know?"

The grinding of past against present gives the poem its urgency. The story is being told with such clarity, thoughtfulness, and apparent calm that we are surprised by the outburst of the repeated question of the thirteenth line. The fourteenth line returns to a tone of tranquillity. Its diction is formal, even arch, and its phrasing suggests an extremely considered conclusion; the fourteenth line is the answer to a drastic rephrasing of the original question: *What is the precise name of what as a youth I was incapable of perceiving but that as a life-examining adult, I now suddenly understand?*

I tell my students that they may someday need this poem, they may someday be walking along downtown and find themselves asking aloud, "What did I know, what did I know?" But what I mean to suggest to them is that Hayden has made them the gift of this final phrase like a package that in ten years' time they may open and find immensely valuable: "love's austere and lonely offices." Like "the banked fires" his father made, Hayden has made a poem that will be of value to readers often years after they've first read it.

"Those Winter Sundays" has articulated a treasure of an insight and preserved it for me until I was old enough to appreciate it. The poem always has the power to move me, to make me understand something so subtle that apparently I need to be reminded of it again and again. Hayden's poem is a "banked fire" that holds its warmth and allows me to rekindle my spirits whenever I come back to read it.

"Those Winter Sundays" honors a much-criticized figure in American culture of the 1990s — the withdrawn, emotionally inexpressive, and distant (and probably unhappy and angry) father. The poem makes its way toward perceiving the emotional life of such a man. The poem *realizes* love as it lived in such a man. That my own father was somewhat similar is perhaps why the poem particularly affects me, but I have witnessed its affecting so many others that I must assume either that such fathers exist in multitudes or that the poem cuts across vast differences of background in its instruction to the reader to reconsider the lives of those who helped us make our way into adulthood.

Whenever I teach "Those Winter Sundays," I face a dilemma of personal, political, and pedagogical consequence. Do I tell my students that Hayden is an African-American poet? That fact *does* make a difference in how we read the poem: the "cracked hands that ached / from labor in the weekday weather" may be seen in a context of a racial-economic circumstance, and thus "the chronic angers of that house" may also be seen as a result of racially enforced poverty. There are, however, manual laborers and poor families of all ethnic backgrounds, and so one need not necessarily read "Those Winter Sundays" as a poem that has anything to do with racial issues. It might even be argued that to read the poem as being about race is to give the poem a racist reading.

My students are almost always white, they are only beginning to learn about modern poetry, and they aren't likely to be acquainted with any African-American poets. If I tell them that Hayden was an African American, am I practicing a subtly racist bit of pedagogy? On the other hand, if I don't tell them that the man who wrote this poem is an African American, aren't I denying them a piece of knowledge that is essential not only for the understanding of this poem but for their general poetic education? (One wonders what the equivalent might be for another poet. To omit telling students of a Robert Frost poem that he lived for most of his life in New England? To say nothing about Walt Whitman's homosexuality? To leave unmentioned Emily Dickinson's reclusiveness? Is there really any equivalent?)

I'm a teacher; I almost always look for a positive approach to such dilemmas. I see an admirable ambiguity and psychological complexity in the fact that the poem can be read in both ways, as a poem that has nothing to do with race and as a poem that is somewhat informed by the circumstance of racial injustice. I do tell my students that the author was an African American, but I tell them only after we've read it a couple of times and talked about it. That piece of information is very nearly the last thing that I tell them before I read it to them the last time, the reading in which once more I journey in my own voice through the words, the lines, the stanzas, down through the cold house into the waiting warmth it always offers me, that necessary, inspiring insight it delivers to me again and again, that the duties of love (like the duties of poetry) are often scrupulously carried out in invisible and thankless ways.

ഌ

ERICA JONG *first became known for her feminist novel* Fear of Flying *(1973), but she has also published several collections of poetry and a recent memoir,* Any Woman's Blues *(1991). Her essay describes her discovery of Shakespeare's sonnets when she was a college student.*

ERICA JONG

Devouring Time: Shakespeare's Sonnets

1996

My love affair with Shakespeare's sonnets began when I was in college. Looking back, it seems to me that at every stage of my adult life, the sonnets have meant something different to me — always deepening, always inexhaustible.

The most daunting challenge is to choose a favorite out of the 152 best poems in our language, since there are so many that move me deeply. I begin this impossible task by reading through the sonnets to myself silently, and then by listening to Sir John Gielgud's astonishing rendition of them, recorded in 1963, Shakespeare's quatercentenary. (I deliberately do not turn to my groaning bookshelves of Shakespeare criticism with their pointless, and ultimately snobbish, debates about the identity of "Mr. W. H." or whether or not our "Top Poet," as Auden called him, could really be a mere middle-class man of Stratford rather than the Earl of Oxford — or perhaps even the Virgin Queen herself. I want to return to the sonnets freshly — as a common reader, responding to them as a person first, a poet second.) As Gielgud's great actor's voice reawakens these dazzling poems for me, I hear again the toll of mortality in the sonnets, the elaboration of the themes of love and death and the stark repetition of their central word: "time."

Devouring time, the wastes of Time, Time's scythe, Wasteful time, in war with time, this bloody tyrant time, time's pencil, time's furrows, dear time's waste, Time's injurious hand, Time's spoils, Time's fool, a hell of time, Time's fickle glass. . . . It seems I cannot read or hear the sonnets without being reminded of how little time is left — which sends me to my desk to write with frenzied hand.

Time is the all-powerful, wrathful God of the sonnets. And to this awesome power, the poet opposes procreation, love, and poetry.

The first thirteen sonnets urge begetting a child to oppose death:

> Th'ou art thy mother's glass, and she in thee
> Calls back the lovely April of her prime.
>
> (Sonnet 3)

Then the theme shifts, and by Sonnet 15 the poet is comparing his own craft to procreation as a way of winning the war with time:

> And all in war with Time for love of you,
> As he takes from you, I ingraft you new.

But poetry is fired by love, so these two forms of redemption are really the same. Children redeem us from time, poetry redeems us from time, and love is the force that drives them both. As the sonnets go on to tell their twisted tale of rival loves, rival poets, love, passion, parting, obsessional sexuality, wrath, reunion, forgiveness, self-love, self-loathing, and self-forgiveness, time never ceases to be the poet's alpha and omega, the deity he both worships and despises.

And so I find myself coming back again and again to Sonnet 19, a poet's credo if ever there were one.

> Devouring Time, blunt thou the lion's paws,
> And make the earth devour her own sweet brood;
> Pluck the keen teeth from the fierce tiger's yaws,
> And burn the long-liv'd phoenix in her blood;
> Make glad and sorry seasons as thou fleet'st,
> And do whate'er thou wilt, swift-footed Time,
> To the wide world and all her fading sweets;
> But I forbid thee one most heinous crime:
> O, carve not with thy hours my love's fair brow,
> Nor draw no lines there with thine antique pen;
> Him in thy course untained do allow
> For beauty's pattern to succeeding men.
> Yet do thy worst, old Time: despite thy wrong,
> My love shall in my verse ever live young.

Sonnet 19 is hardly the most complex of Shakespeare's sonnets, nor the most tortured. The sonnets that recount obsessional love, jealousy, and lust are far darker and more fretted. But Sonnet 19 calls me back again and again because it is one of the few in which the poet addresses time directly and takes him on — David against Goliath.

The simplicity of the sonnet's "statement" delights me: "Time, you big bully, you think you're so great. You can make people die and tigers lose their teeth and change the seasons so fast it makes us dizzy. But spare my love. Don't scribble on him with your antique pen. On second thought, do whatever the hell you like. You have the power to destroy, but I have an even greater power: I create. And by capturing my love in poetry, I can keep my love young forever, whatever you may do to destroy him!"

There is a fluidity to this sonnet that seems to me a triumph of this difficult form. The three quatrains flow into one another and become one exhortation. The couplet argues with them all, changing the direction swiftly and ironically. The poet is standing up to the bully. Suddenly "Devouring Time" becomes "old Time," as if in the course of fourteen lines he had withered like a vampire thrown into a raging inferno. The poem itself has subdued time, made him old before his time, vanquished him. The force of poetry alone defeats time.

This theme is elaborated often in the sonnets, but seldom with such simplicity, the simplicity of a person addressing a fearsome deity without fear: the poet speaking to the gods. Throughout the sonnets, the poet addresses his love, his siren, his lust, even himself, but only in this sonnet (and once more in Sonnet 123) does he address Time directly. He throws down the gauntlet and takes Time on as if one might defeat a powerful foe simply with the force of language.

And, of course, one *can*, as Shakespeare's sonnets prove. We go back to them again and again, discovering new depths in them as time carves new depths in our hearts.

In youth, we tend to love the love poems, the poems of obsessional lust, jealousy, and rage. "Th'expense of spirit in a waste of shame" (129) reminds us of our own struggles to master lust. "So are you to my thoughts as food to life" (75) reminds us of the yearning of first love. As we age, we increasingly see Time shadowing love and the bliss of creation as the only redemption. Shakespeare's sonnets are a fugue on the theme of time. They can be read together or separately, line by line, quatrain by quatrain, or as a narrative of the power of art against decay. They prove the poet's point by their very durability.

Each time I go back to the sonnets, I find something that seemed not to be there before. Perhaps I have changed and my vision is less clouded, or else the sonnets metamorphose on the shelf. The sonnets I love best are those with sustained voices, those that sound like a person speaking. I think I hear Shakespeare's private voice in these sonnets, as if he were whispering directly in my ear.

That Shakespeare's sonnets have defeated death comforts me — for what is great poetry, after all, but the continuation of the human voice after death?

ꝏ

X. J. KENNEDY *emphasizes in this discussion of Marvell's "To His Coy Mistress" that the real point of the poem is the seduction of the speaker's hesitant mistress. Kennedy's* Cross Ties: Selected Poems *was published in 1985; his most recent collection is* Dark Houses *(1992).*

X. J. Kennedy

Andrew Marvell's "To His Coy Mistress" 1996

"Make it new," Ezra Pound advised his fellow poets. Few have taken a theme older and more familiar than Andrew Marvell does in "To His Coy Mistress," his most celebrated work, and rendered it with such lasting freshness. The idea of *carpe diem* ("Seize today!") resounds through the poetry of ancient Greece, Egypt, and Persia, and is a particularly favorite theme of Latin poets, notably Catullus and Horace. "Enjoy the present smiling hour," Horace counsels (in *Odes* 3.29, as translated by John Dryden), and many a later poet has urged the same policy.

Though he became a committed servant of the English Puritan party — toiling as Latin Secretary to Oliver Cromwell, the Puritan Lord Protector himself — Marvell cannot be called Puritanical. He did not resemble those American Puritans who burned witches, and (it is said) condemned the cruel sport of bearbaiting, in which dogs were turned loose upon a chained bear, not because it hurt the bear but because it gave pleasure to the spectators. Though Marvell switched political parties over the course of his career, his biographers have found one consistent thread informing his life: a love of liberty. Marvell continually attacked censorship, wrote pamphlets urging religious freedom, and condemned those who borrowed their opinions from others — people who displayed, he said, a "party-colour'd mind." His best poems appear to hold clashing views with nearly equal sympathy; for example, though Marvell supported Oliver Cromwell, his "Horatian Ode upon Cromwell's Return from Ireland" expresses admiration for Charles I, the Stuart king whom the Puritans had deposed. Some degree of this broad-mindedness and complexity of feeling is evident in "To His Coy Mistress."

To begin, consider the title. The lady's coyness — her hesitancy, her coquetry — sets the dramatic situation. It may be a temptation to misread the word "Mistress" to mean a kept woman, but the poem makes it clear that in Marvell's time the word referred to an unmarried woman. (Were she kept, the speaker wouldn't need to argue her into bed; she would be there already.)

The poem is divided into three parts, each clearly announced by an indented line. Let me offer a few notes on what goes on in each part. The reader who already knows this poem by heart will, I hope, forgive these remarks their simplicity.

In the introductory portion of his argument, Marvell assumes that women and men naturally differ in their attitudes toward love: Women prefer to be wooed slowly, men want to forge ahead with all haste possible. The speaker pretends to consider the woman's attitude sympathetically, although (as we shall see) he is all for forging ahead. He opens his argument diplomatically, not by protesting the woman's reluctance to yield, but by suggesting that leisurely dalliance, while desirable, would be possible only in a world far larger and less hurried than the world we know. On a globe, the fact that England's River Humber is on the opposite side of the earth from the Ganges River in India throws the largest possible distance between the lovers. In imagining a vast extent of time, Marvell is equally definite. His speaker would begin the wooing back before the time of Noah, and his mistress might refuse "till the conversion of the Jews," which unlikely event, according to tradition, is to take place just before the end of the world. And so this ideal wooing would have to span human history as told in the Bible from the Old Testament book of Genesis through the New Testament book of Revelation. For "vegetable" in line 11, read "vegetative," or growing. (This line recalls one of my favorite bits of parody, author anonymous: "My vegetable love should grow / Quick as bamboo in Vigoro.") With loving playfulness, the speaker wishes that, indeed, that much world and time were available to do his lady justice. He turns a pretty compliment: "For, Lady, you deserve this state" (this slow and stately ritual). We can see his strategy. He puts the case for delay in terms so preposterous that no sensible mistress could agree to it. I find this part quietly hilarious, especially in the lines, "Two hundred, to adore each breast, / But thirty thousand to the rest." The scrupulous specificity of that number of years!

The second part begins with a magnificent "But." Then comes Marvell's awesome vision of the immense extent of death:

> But at my back I always hear
> Time's wingèd chariot hurrying near
> And yonder all before us lie
> Deserts of vast eternity.

That famous phrase "Time's wingèd chariot" may echo the classical myth of Apollo, the sun god who daily drives his fiery chariot around the sky, drawn by winged horses. How they loom large in this poem, these stressful forces — the pressure of passing time, the swift approach of eternity. This is no cheerful Christian view of eternity, but a doleful, pagan one. Foreseeing no pleasant afterlife, Marvell expects death to lead to nothing but an endless wasteland. This is a reason for lovers to leap into the sack while they still may. What's the good of keeping your maidenhead intact, he argues, just for some dumb worm in the ground to pierce (to "try," like trying a door), when (he might have added, but tactfully doesn't) you could enjoy my worm instead? Delectable is the tongue-in-cheek understatement of "The grave's a fine and private place, / But none, I think, do there embrace." Who can argue with that?

I can never read this stanza without admiring Marvell's tremendously skilled handling of meter. The rhythm of his lines has been ticking along fairly regularly in a basic iambic beat: unstressed syllables alternated with stressed ones. Then the poet hits the beginning of the line hard — "Time's wingèd." In the ensuing phrase "chariot hurrying," each word has one stressed or heavy syllable followed by two light, unstressed ones. The effect is a skipping or rippling rhythm, like a fast-moving chariot jolting over a rocky road.

In its third part the poem, with an agreeable shock, returns us to the present moment. Here we are, says the speaker, two healthy youngbloods whose vigor won't last forever. In line 34, that morning *glew* isn't Elmer's. The word, according to scholar Helge Kökeritz, is Northern English dialect for *glow.* Marvell, a Yorkshireman, may well have known it. The imagery is violent, of meat-eating. Time is a ravenous beast with slow, irresistible jaws; we must devour him or be devoured. Obviously, being mortal, we can't make the sun stand still as Joshua did, or Zeus, who in order to enjoy the mortal Alcmena made the night last a whole week. Some readers find a serious pun in the next-to-last line. Though the lovers cannot halt time, they can have a *son,* a child who can literally run, a living inheritance. However we read the ending, Marvell gives us a solution to the problem of fleeting time. In making love, we'll render the immediate moment as good as eternity itself — indeed, eternity being a desert, we'll render it far better.

PHILIP LEVINE *wrote this reminiscence of his youthful discovery of the poetry of Keats for the* New York Times.

PHILIP LEVINE

From "Keats in Detroit" 1995

We were twelve young and not-so-young men and women from Detroit. The class, Prof. A. D. Wooly's introduction to the Romantic poets, met in the late afternoon, and some hurried to it after finishing the day shift at one of the local factories. Even our clothing revealed that.

With one month left in the semester, we arrived at young John Keats — who was born two hundred years ago this week and is hardly more fashionable now than he was when I sat in that classroom forty-seven years ago. With Keats there was an immediate affinity we had not felt before. Shelley and Byron were exotic aristocrats, who rode far above the clouds of industrial garbage that hovered over our university campus. Keats was one of us: young, uncertain, determined, decently educated at mediocre schools, struggling to survive. He was what one of us might have been, had one of us been phenomenal John Keats.

From the moment I read "On First Looking into Chapman's Homer," I was hooked. It expressed perfectly my own response to the great Romantic poetry I was reading for the first time and — to use Keats's expression — feeling on my pulse as I had felt no poetry before:

Much have I travell'd in the realms of gold,
And many goodly states and kingdoms seen;
Round many western islands have I been
Which bards in fealty to Apollo hold.
Oft of one wide expanse had I been told
That deep-brow'd Homer ruled as his demesne;
Yet did I never breathe its pure serene
Till I heard Chapman speak out loud and bold:
Then felt I like some watcher of the skies

When a new planet swims into his ken;
Or like stout Cortez when with eagle eyes
He star'd at the Pacific — and all his men
Look'd at each other with a wild surmise —
Silent, upon a peak in Darien.

I do not know if Professor Wooly knew that my ambition was to become a poet. Detroit was not Greenwich Village or even Berkeley; it taught you not to advertise all of your ambitions. Its stance was ferociously masculine, and most of its citizens seemed to have little tolerance for the arts or for what might be described as "artistic behavior." Even half the women I went to school with carried themselves as though they yearned to become professional bowlers.

My guess is that Professor Wooly divined certain needs in me. One afternoon, as the last of daylight faded across his desk, he handed me a volume of Keats's letters opened to the page concerned with what the poet called "the vale of Soul-making." In what I read, a man barely older than I was attempting to account for the function of pain and suffering in the creation of the human spirit. I found, to use Keats's words, "the use of the world" for probably the first time in my life.

"I will call the world a School," Keats had written, "instituted for the purpose of teaching little children to read." He went on, "Do you not see how necessary a World of Pains and troubles is to school an Intelligence and make it a Soul?" For a moment I saw. Nothing I had read before had so potently lifted the gloom that hovered over my small portion of Detroit.

This was some ten years before Americans of my generation would set about the creation of a body of poetry that would later be labeled "confessional" and even longer before those poets' acts of self-destruction, but the models were already there. That year, Detroit itself would welcome the besotted Dylan Thomas. My mentor-to-be, John Berryman, would later claim that what the poet required above all else was a wounding so terrible that he or she could only barely survive it.

Imagine my relief and surprise when Professor Wooly pointed to the following passage: "Whenever I find myself growing vaporish I rouse myself, wash, and put on a clean shirt, brush my hair and clothes, tie my shoestrings neatly, and in fact adonize as I were going out — then all clean and comfortable I sit down to write. This I find the greatest relief." A poet writing out of his joy in the world and in himself, out of what Coleridge had called his "genial spirits."

It seemed quite suddenly I could be both a poet and a person, even in a world like ours — that is, if I were able to create such a person out of what I'd been given. By this time, even at age twenty, certain things were clear to me. One was that Keats was a genius and I was not, so I would have to apply myself with even greater dedication than he. Another was that his early poems gave not the least hint of what was to come. Yet he had made himself a poet and he had done this while living "in uncertainties, Mysteries, doubts, without any irritable reaching after fact and reason."

According to Keats, my ability to write in a world I did not understand and from which I did not demand final answers might prove to be an asset rather than a defect of character. Like Keats, I was descended from ordinary people, in my case with extraordinary minds and imaginations. I realized that this, too, could prove to be a virtue, for it meant that I could not live apart from the daily difficulties of the world. I could regard these circumstances as the Alps that stood between me and the poetry I might write, or like Keats I could regard them as part of the material out of which I might build my character and, later, my poetry.

ROBERT LOWELL's *comments on "Skunk Hour" were a response to a discussion of the poem by fellow poets Richard Wilbur, John Frederick Nims, and John Berryman. The comments were included in the book* The Contemporary Artist as Artist and Critic *(1964), edited by Anthony Ostroff.*

ROBERT LOWELL

An Explication of "Skunk Hour"

1964

I. THE MEANING

The author of a poem is not necessarily the ideal person to explain its meaning. He is as liable as anyone else to muddle, dishonesty, and reticence. Nor is it his purpose to provide a peg for a prose essay. Meaning varies in importance from poem to poem, and from style to style, but always it is only a strand and an element in the brute flow of composition. Other elements are pictures that please or thrill for themselves, phrases that ring for their music or carry some buried suggestion. For all this the author is an opportunist, throwing whatever comes to hand into his feeling for start, continuity, contrast, climax, and completion. It is imbecile for him not to know his intentions, and unsophisticated for him to know too explicitly and fully. . . .

I am not sure whether I can distinguish between intention and interpretation. I think this is what I more or less intended. The first four stanzas are meant to give a dawdling more or less amiable picture of a declining Maine sea town. I move from the ocean inland. Sterility howls through the scenery, but I try to give a tone of tolerance, humor, and randomness to the sad prospect. The composition drifts, its direction sinks out of sight into the casual, chancy arrangements of nature and decay. Then all comes alive in stanzas V and VI. This is the dark night. I hoped my readers would remember John of the Cross's° poem. My night is not gracious, but secular, puritan, and agnostical. An Existentialist night. Somewhere in my mind was a passage from Sartre or

John of the Cross's: Reference to Juan de Yepes y Alvarez (1542–1591), Spanish mystic and poet.

Camus° about reaching some point of final darkness where the one free act is suicide. Out of this comes the march and affirmation, an ambiguous one, of my skunks in the last two stanzas. The skunks are both quixotic and barbarously absurd, hence the tone of amusement and defiance. "Skunk Hour" is not entirely independent, but the anchor poem in its sequence. . . .

"Skunk Hour" was begun in mid-August 1957, and finished about a month later. In March of the same year, I had been giving readings on the West Coast, often reading six days a week and sometimes twice on a single day. I was in San Francisco, the era and setting of Allen Ginsberg, and all about very modest poets were waking up prophets. I became sorely aware of how few poems I had written, and that these few had been finished at the latest three or four years earlier. Their style seemed distant, symbol-ridden and willfully difficult. I began to paraphrase my Latin quotations, and to add extra syllables to a line to make it clearer and more colloquial. I felt my old poems hid what they were really about, and many times offered a stiff, humorless, and even impenetrable surface. I am no convert to the "beats." I know well too that the best poems are not necessarily poems that read aloud. Many of the greatest poems can only be read to one's self, for inspiration is no substitute for humor, shock, narrative, and a hypnotic voice, the four musts for oral performance. Still, my own poems seemed like prehistoric monsters dragged down into the bog and death by their ponderous armor. I was reciting what I no longer felt. What influenced me more than San Francisco and reading aloud was that for some time I had been writing prose. I felt that the best style for poetry was none of the many poetic styles in English, but something like the prose of Chekhov or Flaubert.

When I returned to my home, I began writing lines in a new style. No poem, however, got finished and soon I left off and tried to forget the whole headache. Suddenly, in August, I was struck by the sadness of writing nothing, and having nothing to write, of having, at least, no language. When I began writing "Skunk Hour," I felt that most of what I knew about writing was a hindrance.

The dedication is to Elizabeth Bishop, because rereading her suggested a way of breaking through the shell of my old manner. Her rhythms, idiom, images, and stanza structure seemed to belong to a later century. "Skunk Hour" is modeled on Miss Bishop's "The Armadillo," a much better poem and one I had heard her read and had later carried around with me. Both "Skunk Hour" and "The Armadillo" use short line stanzas, start with drifting description, and end with a single animal. . . .

"Skunk Hour" was written backwards, first the last two stanzas, I think, and then the next to last two. Anyway, there was a time when I had the last four stanzas much as they now are and nothing before them. I found the bleak personal violence repellent. All was too close, though watching the lovers was not mine, but from an anecdote about Walt Whitman in his old age. I began to

---

Sartre or Camus: Jean-Paul Sartre (1905–1980) and Albert Camus (1913–1960) were important modern French writers.

feel that real poetry came, not from fierce confessions, but from something almost meaningless but imagined. I was haunted by an image of a blue china doorknob. I never used the doorknob, or knew what it meant, yet somehow it started the current of images in my opening stanzas. They were written in reverse order, and at last gave my poem an earth to stand on, and space to breathe.

ꕥ

ROBERT LOWELL, *as both poet and teacher, was an important influence on the work of Sylvia Plath. As he describes in his introduction to the collection of her final poems published after her death, he remembered her from his class, without knowing then the poetry she would create in those last months.*

ROBERT LOWELL

Foreword to Plath's Ariel

1966

In these poems, written in the last months of her life and often rushed out at the rate of two or three a day, Sylvia Plath becomes herself, becomes something imaginary, newly, wildly and subtly created — hardly a person at all, or a woman, certainly not another "poetess," but one of those super-real, hypnotic, great classical heroines. This character is feminine, rather than female, though almost everything we customarily think of as feminine is turned on its head. The voice is now coolly amused, witty, now sour, now fanciful, girlish, charming, now sinking to the strident rasp of the vampire — a Dido, Phaedra, or Medea, who can laugh at herself as "cow-heavy and floral in my Victorian nightgown." Though lines get repeated, and sometimes the plot is lost, language never dies in her mouth.

Everything in these poems is personal, confessional, felt, but the manner of feeling is controlled hallucination, the autobiography of a fever. She burns to be on the move, a walk, a ride, a journey, the flight of the queen bee. She is driven forward by the pounding pistons of her heart. The title *Ariel* summons up Shakespeare's lovely, though slightly chilling and androgenous spirit, but the truth is that this *Ariel* is the author's horse. Dangerous, more powerful than man, machinelike from hard training, she herself is a little like a racehorse, galloping relentlessly with risked, outstretched neck, death hurdle after death hurdle topped. She cries out for that rapid life of starting pistols, snapping tapes, and new world records broken. What is most heroic in her, though, is not her force, but the desperate practicality of her control, her hand of metal with its modest, womanish touch. Almost pure motion, she can endure "God, the great stasis in his vacuous night," hospitals, fever, paralysis, the iron lung, being stripped like a girl in the booth of a circus sideshow, dressed like a mannequin, tied down like Gulliver by the Lilliputians . . . apartments, babies, prim English landscapes, beehives, yew trees, gardens, the moon, hooks, the black boot, wounds, flowers with mouths like wounds, Belsen's lampshades° made of human skin, Hitler's homicidal iron tanks clanking over Russia. Suicide, father-hatred, self-loathing — nothing is too much for the macabre gaiety of her control. Yet it is too much; her art's immortality is life's disintegration. The surprise, the shimmering, unwrapped birthday present, the transcendence "into the red eye, the cauldron of morning," and the lover, who are always waiting for her, are Death, her own abrupt and defiant death.

He tells me how badly I photograph.
He tells me how sweet
The babies look in their hospital
Icebox, a simple

Frill at the neck,
Then the flutings of their Ionian
Death gowns,
Then two little feet.

There is a peculiar, haunting challenge to these poems. Probably many, after reading *Ariel,* will recoil from their first overawed shock, and painfully wonder why so much of it leaves them feeling empty, evasive and inarticulate. In her lines, I often hear the serpent whisper, "Come, if only you had the courage, you too could have my rightness, audacity and ease of inspiration." But most of us will turn back. These poems are playing Russian roulette with six cartridges in the cylinder, a game of "chicken," the wheels of both cars locked and unable to swerve. Oh, for that heaven of the humble copyist, those millennia of Egyptian artists repeating their lofty set patterns! And yet Sylvia Plath's poems are not the celebration of some savage and debauched existence, that of the "damned" poet, glad to burn out his body for a few years of continuous intensity. This poetry and life are not a career; they tell that life, even when disciplined, is simply not worth it.

It is poignant, looking back, to realize that the secret of Sylvia Plath's last irresistible blaze lies lost somewhere in the checks and courtesies of her early laborious shyness. She was never a student of mine, but for a couple of months seven years ago, she used to drop in on my poetry seminar at Boston University. I see her dim against the bright sky of a high window, viewless unless one cared to look down on the city outskirts' defeated yellow brick and square concrete pillbox filling stations. She was willowy, long-waisted, sharp-elbowed, nervous, giggly, gracious — a brilliant tense presence embarrassed by restraint. Her humility and willingness to accept what was admired seemed at times to give her an air of maddening docility that hid her unfashionable patience and boldness. She showed us poems that later, more or less

---

Belsen's lampshades: Reference to Bergen-Belsen, a Nazi concentration camp during World War II.

unchanged, went into her first book, *The Colossus.* They were somber, formidably expert in stanza structure, and had a flair for alliteration and Massachusetts' low-tide dolor.

> A mongrel working his legs to a gallop
> Hustles the gull flock to flap off the sand-spit.

Other lines showed her wit and directness.

> The pears fatten like little Buddhas.

Somehow none of it sank very deep into my awareness. I sensed her abashment and distinction, and never guessed her later appalling and triumphant fulfillment.

CHRISTOPHER MERRILL *has most recently published the poetry collections* Workbook *(1988) and* Fevers and Tides *(1989). His discussion of Sir Thomas Wyatt's poem examines the subtleties of its meters.*

CHRISTOPHER MERRILL

Wyatt's "They Flee from Me"

1996

The conceit of comparing his beloved to a wild animal is . . . central to [Sir Thomas] Wyatt's most famous ballad, "They Flee from Me." Written in Chaucer's stanza, the popular seven-line ballad stanza that employs a rhyme royal scheme (named after King James I of Scotland, who used it in *The Kingis Quair*) and what Robert Frost might call "loose iambics," this poem has baffled strict prosodists for centuries. How to scan the second line, for example, or the fifth, without resorting to complicated metrical schemes bearing little relation to normal speech patterns is the problem facing the student of prosody. (One possible solution:

> ˘ ´ | ˘ ´ | ´ | ˘ ˘ | ˘ | ˘ ´ | ˘
> With nak | ed foot | stalk | ing in | | my cham | ber
>
> That sŏme | tíme | thĕy pút | thĕmsélves | in dán | gĕr)

To explain such departures from normal practice, one of his editors suggests that Wyatt "regards precision, clarity, or concentration of meaning as of primary importance." But it is more than that: such precision has its own music, which hearkens back to the stress-based prosody of Anglo-Saxon verse; that is, Wyatt is happy to sacrifice a syllable here or there in favor of rhythms buried in our ancestral memory. What better tune for the oldest subject in poetry, the lover's grief at the beloved's indifference?

In like manner, Wyatt has no fear of pulling readers up short, literally speaking, offering four-beat lines (foreshadowed in lines two and five?) when he wants to draw attention to the consequences of his loss. The emotional logic of this poem resides in moments of metrical uncertainty — "That now are wild, and do not remember," for example, or "And I have leave to go, of her goodness" — juxtaposed with the rhythmic certainty of, say, the run of pleasing pentameters in the second stanza. Here the poet celebrates one glorious night, culminating in a four-beat line — "Therewithall sweetly did me kiss" — as if to suggest the flee(t)ing nature of love: we expect to hear another beat, in the same way that the poet may have imagined he would have more nights with his beloved.

To reinforce his point, Wyatt begins the final stanza with another four-beat line: "It was no dream, I lay broad waking" is an intimate revelation, as if the poet has no choice but to confide, in the plainest tones, the nature of his loss, his sorrow. What he reveals is his bitter knowledge that nothing will ever be the same, for fortune has abandoned him. And his "strange fashion of forsaking"? This is how he bids farewell to a woman and a world. What he mourns is the loss of the certainty by which he once lived, which was embodied in the love of one woman — Anne Boleyn?° — who "softly said, 'Dear heart, how like you this?'"

"Uncertainty," according to Joseph Brodsky,° "is the mother of beauty, one of whose definitions is that it's something which isn't yours." And what was more uncertain in Renaissance England than the courtier's life? Wyatt's properties were confiscated in 1541, at which point only a pardon from the King spared him the loss of his head. More, he lived through a revolution in thinking, which began with a rival's love for his mistress and ended in the Reformation of the English Church. What makes "They Flee from Me" so poignant is that while the poet says good-bye to a woman, an age, and a world, there is such "passionate intensity" in his verse that one cannot help feeling he was in his way also greeting the new order.

"The pass to poetry," Nadezhda Mandelstam° affirmed, "is granted only by faith in its sacramental character and a sense of responsibility for everything that happens in the world." Sir Thomas Wyatt the Elder was a poet responsible for his time and ours, which is why we may yet learn lessons from him vital to our own period of change, when the world is once again reorganizing itself day by day, stanza by stanza.

BRETT C. MILLIER *described the biographical context of the composition of the poem "One Art" in* Elizabeth Bishop: Life and the Memory of It. *This study was published by the University of California Press in 1993.*

Anne Boleyn: Boleyn (1507?–1536) was the second wife of Henry VIII and mother of Queen Elizabeth I of England.
Joseph Brodsky: Soviet poet (1940–1995) exiled to the United States.
Nadezhda Mandelstam: Widow of Soviet poet Osip Mandelstam (1891–1938).

Brett C. Millier

On Elizabeth Bishop's "One Art" 1993

Elizabeth Bishop left seventeen drafts of the poem "One Art" among her papers. In the first draft, she lists all the things she's lost in her life — keys, pens, glasses, cities — and then she writes "One might think this would have prepared me / for losing one average-sized not exceptionally / beautiful or dazzlingly intelligent person . . . / But it doesn't seem to have at all. . . ." By the seventeenth draft, nearly every word has been transformed, but most importantly, Bishop discovered along the way that there might be a way to master this loss.

One way to read Bishop's modulation between the first and last drafts from "the loss of you is impossible to master" to something like "I am still the master of losing even though losing you looks like a disaster" is that in the writing of such a disciplined, demanding poem as this villanelle ("[*Write* it!]") lies the potential mastery of the loss. Working through each of her losses — from the bold, painful catalog of the first draft to the finely honed and privately meaningful final version — is the way to overcome them or, if not to overcome them, then to see the way in which she might possibly master herself in the face of loss. It is all, perhaps "one art" — writing elegy, mastering loss, mastering grief, self-mastery. Bishop had a precocious familiarity with loss. Her father died before her first birthday, and four years later her mother disappeared into a sanitarium, never to be seen by her daughter again. The losses in the poem are real: time in the form of the "hour badly spent" and, more tellingly for the orphaned Bishop "my mother's watch": the lost houses, in Key West, Petrópolis, and Ouro Prêto, Brazil. The city of Rio de Janeiro and the whole South American continent (where she had lived for nearly two decades) were lost to her with the suicide of her Brazilian companion. And currently, in the fall of 1975, she seemed to have lost her dearest friend and lover, who was trying to end their relationship. But each version of the poem distanced the pain a little more, depersonalized it, moved it away from the tawdry self-pity and "confession" that Bishop disliked in so many of her contemporaries.

Bishop's friends remained for a long time protective of her personal reputation, and unwilling to have her grouped among lesbian poets or even among the other great poets of her generation — Robert Lowell, John Berryman, Theodore Roethke — as they seemed to self-destruct before their readers' eyes. Bishop herself taught them this reticence by keeping her private life to herself, and by investing what "confession" there was in her poems deeply in objects and places, thus deflecting biographical inquiry. In the development of this poem, discretion is both a poetic method, and a part of a process of self-understanding, the seeing of a pattern in her own life.

MARIANNE MOORE *was one of the most skillful commentators on her own poetry and poetics. Her answers to these questions presented by poet Howard Nemerov were published in 1966.*

MARIANNE MOORE

Some Answers to Questions Posed by Howard Nemerov

1966

Nemerov: Do you see your work as having essentially changed in character or style since you began?

Moore: No, except that rhythm was my prime objective. If I succeeded in embodying a rhythm that preoccupied me, I was satisfied.

Uniform line length seemed to me essential as accrediting the satisfactory model stanza and I sometimes ended a line with a hyphen, expecting the reader to maintain the line unbroken (disregarding the hyphen). I have found readers misled by the hyphen, mistaking it as an arcane form of emphasis, so I seldom use it today.

I am today much aware of the world's dilemma. People's effect on other people results, it seems to me, in an enforced sense of responsibility — a compulsory obligation to participate in others' problems.

Nemerov: Is there, has there been, was there ever, a "revolution" in poetry, or is all that a matter of a few sleazy technical tricks? What is the relation of your work to this question, if there is a relation? Otherwise put: do you respond to such notions as The New Poetry, An American Language Distinct from English, The Collapse of Prosody, No Thoughts but in Things, The Battle between Academics and — What? — Others (A Fair Field Full of Mostly Corpses)?

Moore: The individuality and emotions of the writer should transcend modes. I recall feeling oversolitary occasionally (say in 1912) — in reflecting no "influences"; in not being able to be called an "Imagist" — but determined to put the emphasis on what mattered most to me, in a manner natural to me. I like end-stopped lines and depend on rhyme, but my rhymes are often hidden and, in being inconspicuous, escape detection. When I began writing verse, I regarded flowing continuity as indispensable.

A Jellyfish

Visible, invisible,
   a fluctuating charm
an amber-tinctured amethyst
   inhabits it, your arm
approaches and it opens
   and it closes; you had meant
to catch it and it quivers;
   you abandon your intent.

Then when I came on Charles Sorley's "The Idea" (probably in *The Egoist*, London)—

It was all my own;
  I have guarded it well from
the winds that have blown
  too bitterly

—I recognized the unaccented syllable (the light rhyme) as means for me, as in "The Jerboa":

. . . one would not be he
who has nothing but plenty.

. . . closed upper paws seeming one with the fur
in its flight from a danger.

Having written the last stanza first, I had to duplicate it, progressing backward.

Its leaps should be set
to the flageolet;
  pillar body erect
  on a three-cornered smooth-working Chippendale
    claw—propped on hind legs, and tail as third toe
    between leaps to its burrow.

In "Occasionem Cognosce," the light rhyme is upside down:

. . . "Atlas"
(pressed glass)

looks best
embossed.

Poetry is a magic of pauses, as a dog-valentine contrasting "pawses" and "pauses"—sent me from Harvard where I had been discussing pauses—reminded me. I do not know what syllabic verse is. I find no appropriate application for it.

Might I say of the light rhyme that T. S. Eliot's phrase, "the greatest living master of the light rhyme," in his Introduction to my *Selected Poems*—suggesting conscious proficiency or at most a regulator art on my part, hardly deserves the term. Conscious writing can be the death of poetry.

ALICIA OSTRIKER, *who teaches at Rutgers University, is well known both as a poet and critic. Recent poetry collections include* The Imaginary Lover *(1986) and* Green Age *(1989), and she is the author of the study* Stealing the Language: The Emergence of Women's Poetry in America *(1987). This description of H.D.'s early literary involvement with the poet Ezra Pound and imagism is included in her book* Writing Like a Woman *(1983).*

ALICIA OSTRIKER

The Poet as Heroine: H.D.

1983

War and sex, sex and war, inseparable. H.D. seems to have sought, over and over, a man whose love for her would be indistinguishable from his love for beauty and truth. What she found, too often for it to be accidental, was something more predictable.

I say she found it. But nothing in the world is so simple. I mean, really, she bought into it. Or do I? Pound of course was the first of H.D.'s failed romances. The Pound-figure in her 1927 novel *Her* "wanted Her, but he wanted a Her he called decorative." He quotes to her the line, "You are a poem though your poem's naught." She resists him, prefers another woman, loses both — they betray her with each other — and at the novel's end she is recovering from a breakdown. Thirty years later in her memoir *End to Torment,* as Pound is emerging from St. Elizabeth's, her attitude toward him as a writer is adoring, and she is filled with electric sexual memories. At the same time he is depicted as a sexual bully, a collector and discarder of female acolytes; had their engagement not been broken and Dorothy Shakespeare's fate been hers, she muses, "Ezra would have destroyed me and the center . . . of my poetry." Here is her recollection of the moment in the British Museum tea room when Ezra took from Hilda Doolittle the poem which would initiate her publishing career:

> "But Dryad . . . this is poetry." He slashed with a pencil. "Cut this out, shorten this line. 'Hermes of the Ways' is a good title. I'll send this to Harriet Monroe of *Poetry.* Have you a copy? Yes? Then we can send this, or I'll type it when I get back. Will this do?" And he scrawled "H.D. Imagiste" at the bottom of the page. (*End to Torment,* p. 18)

This is not far from girlish locker-room boasting. He said he *loved* me, girls have whispered to each other for centuries. Then consider the nuances: the "slashing" of her poem, the signing of her name for her.

He defines her. By the same token he can destroy her. He, not she, is strong, authoritative. "He" is any man she is attracted to, physically, emotionally, intellectually.

The scene in the tea room took place in October 1912. H.D. a year later married the idealistic fellow-poet and fellow-imagist, Richard Aldington. The War began the following year. In 1916 Aldington enlisted in the British Army, and H.D. took over his position as assistant editor of *The Egoist.* She had had a miscarriage which left her frail and possibly frigid. Aldington soon commenced an affair with the less intellectual and high-strung, more earthy American woman in the flat upstairs. The Aldingtons separated, although there was no legal divorce until 1938. In 1918 H.D.'s brother was killed in France. Her father suffered a stroke on hearing the news and died shortly after.

Until a definitive biography appears, we will not know how the poet reacted to the losses of a child, a husband, a brother, a father. But in the fictions H.D. wrote about this period in her life, she portrays the poet-heroine as a being who is excruciatingly passive, who depends on men to share her faith in "worlds of past beauty that were future beauty" and to cooperate in creating moments of mystic "bliss." When they fail her she does not fight, is not angry, is merely paralyzed. In *Bid Me to Live* the heroine is manipulated and rejected first by her war-coarsened husband, then by "Rico" (D. H. Lawrence), who has promised erotic and spiritual companionship. Criticizing a poem she sends him, Rico snappishly writes: "I don't like the second half of the Orpheus sequence as well as the first. Stick to the woman speaking. How can you know what Orpheus feels? It's your part to be woman, the woman vibration, Euridice should be enough." Her response, "But if he could enter, so diabolically, into the feelings of women, why should she not enter into the feelings of men?" remains unspoken and unshared. She imagines a way to escape "the biological catch" of sex roles: if two artists pair, "then the danger met the danger, the woman was man-woman, the man was woman-man." The men in the novel think otherwise. Shortly after invoking her ideal of androgynous mutuality between artist-lovers, the novelist repeats one of the novel's refrains: "The war will never be over."

MARGE PIERCY *answered a question by interviewer Bill Moyers with this comment about one of the most distinctive features of a poet's craft.*

MARGE PIERCY

Imagery Can't Really Be Taught 1999

I am an intensely curious person, nosy, insatiable, as a poet, everything you experience, whether personally or vicariously, or virtuously or virtually, for that matter, is your stuff. Imagery can't really be taught. You can lecture about the different kinds of imagery in different sorts of poems, but the truth is, imagery is the most personal core of a poet. The more you actually see — how carefully you look at an opossum or a wildflower or the way light strikes water or hair; the more you actually listen to the natural and manufactured sounds of our world; the more you know about what the shape of a bird's beak means about what it eats, or what the weeds growing in a field tell you about the soil and its history — then the more stuff you will have within you that will rise and suggest itself as imagery. You have to stay open and curious and keep learning as you go. Poems come from a whole variety of sources. When you're younger, you believe in inspiration. As you get older, you believe most in receptivity and work.

ROBERT POTTS *is an English cultural journalist who contributed this discussion of the poetry of popular song lyrics to the Sunday edition of* The Guardian.

ROBERT POTTS

Rock 'n' Roll Is the New Poetry

1999

Perhaps it was inevitable that poetry, vaunted only a few years ago as "the new rock 'n' roll" (a slogan as dulled by repetition as the few chords of Status Quo), should now find the tables are turned. The BBC website announces that tomorrow's National Poetry Day will celebrate the Nation's Favourite Song Lyric. In a country in which "dumbing down" is an increasing concern, this looks like another retreat. Poetry was getting used to its one day of attention a year — a national prize, a few games and gimmicks, the luring of punters with comic poems and love poems. Now there is so much sugar on the pill you wonder why they bother with the medicine at all.

Yet, for all the apparently crass populism of this year's theme, there is a valid question: if what we value in poetry can be found in song lyrics, in what sense can we argue that those lyrics are not poetry themselves? As noted in the perennial nonquestion — "Is Bob Dylan better than Keats?" — the division between song lyrics and poetry has been fiercely maintained, although more often by academics and cultural conservatives than songwriters or poets. The fact is a great deal of perfectly awful poetry is being written (as it always has been), while, among the dross and sweet nothings of song writing, there are some fine wordsmiths doing everything that we are supposed to revere in poets.

Pop music is a relatively modern phenomenon. It appears more and more often in the work of contemporary poets (Glyn Maxwell's homages to Bob Dylan; Alan Jenkins' citations of REM; Paul Muldoon's "Sleeve Notes in Hay"). This is not a cheapening of the poets' art; it is a recognition of the world they grew up in, and inhabit, and is an acknowledgement of influence as important to them as their nods at Shakespeare, Blake, or Eliot. (Eliot himself was something of a music hall fan, and this older form finds its way into his work.)

What's more, the compliment is frequently repaid: in allusions and direct steals. Madonna's "Love Tried to Welcome Me" owes more than a small debt to George Herbert's religious poem "Love III" ("Love bade me welcome, yet my soul drew back"), but neatly avoids Herbert's resolution in God's love and acceptance, leaving instead a sense of intractable sin and gracelessness. Likewise, The Verve's "History" — "I wander lonely streets / behind where the old Thames does flow / And in every face I meet / Reminds me of what I have run from" — is, despite the grammatical ellipsis, resonantly alluding to Blake's London: "I wander through each chartered street / Near where the chartered Thames does flow / And mark in every face I meet / Marks of weakness, marks of woe." Blake's London of syphilis and soldiers is updated by The Verve to encompass drug addiction; it's charming, in a song called "History" (used here in the sense of "you and I are history") that the archaism of "does flow" is retained even at the point of departure: the refusal of clinching rhyme.

Morrissey probably took purposeful allusion further than most songwriters. A quotation that many attribute to Eliot — "talent borrows; genius steals" (itself a much stolen epigram) — was scratched into the run-off groove of one of the early Smiths EPs. Morrissey has made references to A Taste of Honey, Brighton Rock, The L-Shaped Room, and numerous other cultural products of the fifties and early sixties in a search for the mythic England that he adores. "Cemetery Gates" faces the question head on — "If you must write prose and poems, the words you use should be your own; don't plagiarise or take on loan," he sings with cheeky irony — before declaring his favoured branch of Romanticism: "Keats and Yeats are on your side . . . but I've the love of Wilde on mine."

Yet more bonds the two art forms than their mutual admiration. When poets use forms such as the ballad, or title their pieces "Song," there seems to be a deliberate gesture to an older, more inclusive form. If some songwriters are saying "we can write," many poets have aspired to "sing"; to offer something of the potent simplicity and harmony of the sung lyric.

The song lyric, admittedly, often looks banal and clunky on the page, like bad sixth form poetry; it is less effective without the power of the music behind it. But when performed, plain-spoken slogans and declarations gain a remarkable charge — the "potency of cheap music" referred to by Noël Coward. And when a song lyric has its own rhythm on the page, can it still be disdained? "And far away, across the fields / the tolling of the iron bell / calls the faithful to their knees / to hear the softly spoken magic spells." This could be Georgian — with three tetrameters, and an iambic pentameter, rhyming *a-b-a-b,* offering the combination of English pastoral and sceptical atheism that Hardy° would have enjoyed. The words actually come from Pink Floyd's "Dark Side of the Moon."

EZRA POUND *was one of the founders of the short-lived but influential movement called imagism, which stressed clarity and economy of language. In this 1918 statement, which was later published under the title "A Retrospect" in a 1954 collection of his literary essays, Pound describes the imagists' aims.*

EZRA POUND

On the Principles of Imagism *1918*

There has been so much scribbling about a new fashion in poetry, that I may perhaps be pardoned this brief recapitulation and retrospect.

In the spring or early summer of 1912, "H.D.," Richard Aldington, and myself decided that we were agreed upon the three principles following:

Hardy: Thomas Hardy (1840–1928), English novelist and poet.

1. Direct treatment of the "thing" whether subjective or objective.
2. To use absolutely no word that does not contribute to the presentation.
3. As regarding rhythm: to compose in the sequence of the musical phrase, not in sequence of a metronome.

Upon many points of taste and of predilection we differed, but agreeing upon these three positions we thought we had as much right to a group name, at least as much right, as a number of French "schools" proclaimed by Mr Flint in the August number of Harold Monro's magazine for 1911.

This school has since been "joined" or "followed" by numerous people who, whatever their merits, do not show any signs of agreeing with the second specification. Indeed *vers libre* has become as prolix and as verbose as any of the flaccid varieties that preceded it. It has brought faults of its own. The actual language and phrasing is often as bad as that of our elders without even the excuse that the words are shovelled in to fill a metric pattern or to complete the noise of a rhyme-sound. Whether or no the phrases followed by the followers are musical must be left to the reader's decision. At times I can find a marked metre in "vers libres," as stale and hackneyed as any pseudo-Swinburnian,° at times the writers seem to follow no musical structure whatever. But it is, on the whole, good that the field should be ploughed. Perhaps a few good poems have come from the new method, and if so it is justified.

Criticism is not a circumscription or a set of prohibitions. It provides fixed points of departure. It may startle a dull reader into alertness. That little of it which is good is mostly in stray phrases; or if it be an older artist helping a younger it is in great measure but rules of thumb, cautions gained by experience.

I set together a few phrases on practical working about the time the first remarks on imagism were published. The first use of the word "Imagiste" was in my note to T. E. Hulme's five poems, printed at the end of my "Ripostes" in the autumn of 1912. I reprint my cautions from *Poetry* for March, 1913.

A FEW DON'TS

An "Image" is that which presents an intellectual and emotional complex in an instant of time. I use the term "complex" rather in the technical sense employed by the newer psychologists, such as Hart, though we might not agree absolutely in our application.

It is the presentation of such a "complex" instantaneously which gives that sense of sudden liberation; that sense of freedom from time limits and space limits; that sense of sudden growth, which we experience in the presence of the greatest works of art.

It is better to present one Image in a lifetime than to produce voluminous works.

All this, however, some may consider open to debate. The immediate necessity is to tabulate A LIST OF DON'TS for those beginning to write verses. I can not put all of them into Mosaic negative.

---

pseudo-Swinburnian: I.e., one who mimics the work of Algernon Charles Swinburne (1837–1909), the English poet whose poetry was noted for its romantic exaggeration.

To begin with, consider the three propositions (demanding direct treatment, economy of words, and the sequence of the musical phrase), not as dogma — never consider anything as dogma — but as the result of long contemplation, which, even if it is some one else's contemplation, may be worth consideration.

Pay no attention to the criticism of men who have never themselves written a notable work. Consider the discrepancies between the actual writing of the Greek poets and dramatists, and the theories of the Graeco-Roman grammarians, concocted to explain their metres.

LANGUAGE

Use no superfluous word, no adjective which does not reveal something.

Don't use such an expression as "dim lands *of peace*." It dulls the image. It mixes an abstraction with the concrete. It comes from the writer's not realizing that the natural object is always the *adequate* symbol.

Go in fear of abstractions. Do not retell in mediocre verse what has already been done in good prose. Don't think any intelligent person is going to be deceived when you try to shirk all the difficulties of the unspeakably difficult art of good prose by chopping your composition into line lengths.

What the expert is tired of today the public will be tired of to-morrow.

Don't imagine that the art of poetry is any simpler than the art of music, or that you can please the expert before you have spent at least as much effort on the art of verse as the average piano teacher spends on the art of music.

Be influenced by as many great artists as you can, but have the decency either to acknowledge the debt outright, or to try to conceal it.

Don't allow "influence" to mean merely that you mop up the particular decorative vocabulary of some one or two poets whom you happen to admire. A Turkish war correspondent was recently caught red-handed babbling in his despatches of "dove-grey" hills, or else it was "pearl-pale," I can not remember.

Use either no ornament or good ornament.

RHYTHM AND RHYME

Let the candidate fill his mind with the finest cadences he can discover, preferably in a foreign language,[1] so that the meaning of the words may be less likely to divert his attention from the movement; e.g. Saxon charms, Hebridean Folk Songs, the verse of Dante, and the lyrics of Shakespeare — if he can dissociate the vocabulary from the cadence. Let him dissect the lyrics of Goethe coldly into their component sound values, syllables long and short, stressed and unstressed, into vowels and consonants.

It is not necessary that a poem should rely on its music, but if it does rely on its music that music must be such as will delight the expert.

Let the neophyte know assonance and alliteration, rhyme immediate and delayed, simple and polyphonic, as a musician would expect to know harmony and counterpoint and all the minutiae of his craft. No time is too

---

[1] This is for rhythm, his vocabulary must of course be found in his native tongue. [Pound's note]

great to give to these matters or to any one of them, even if the artist seldom have need of them.

Don't imagine that a thing will "go" in verse just because it's too dull to go in prose.

Don't be "viewy" — leave that to the writers of pretty little philosophic essays. Don't be descriptive; remember that the painter can describe a landscape much better than you can, and that he has to know a deal more about it.

When Shakespeare talks of the "Dawn in russet mantle clad" he presents something which the painter does not present. There is in this line of his nothing that one can call description; he presents.

Consider the way of the scientists rather than the way of an advertising agent for a new soap.

The scientist does not expect to be acclaimed as a great scientist until he has *discovered* something. He begins by learning what has been discovered already. He goes from that point onward. He does not bank on being a charming fellow personally. He does not expect his friends to applaud the results of his freshman class work. Freshmen in poetry are unfortunately not confined to a definite and recognizable class room. They are "all over the shop." Is it any wonder "the public is indifferent to poetry?"

Don't chop your stuff into separate *iambs*. Don't make each line stop dead at the end, and then begin every next line with a heave. Let the beginning of the next line catch the rise of the rhythm wave, unless you want a definite longish pause.

In short, behave as a musician, a good musician, when dealing with that phase of your art which has exact parallels in music. The same laws govern, and you are bound by no others.

EZRA POUND *wrote this essay on Walt Whitman in 1909, only a year after he had left the United States to live permanently in Europe.*

EZRA POUND

What I Feel about Walt Whitman

1909

From this side of the Atlantic I am for the first time able to read Whitman, and from the vantage of my education and — if it be permitted a man of my scant years — my world citizenship: I see him America's poet. The only Poet before the artists of the Carmen-Hovey° period, or better, the only one of the conventionally recognised "American Poets" who is worth reading.

He *is* America. His crudity is an exceeding great stench, but it *is* America.

Carmen-Hovey: Canadian poet William Bliss Carman (1861–1929) and American poet Richard Hovey (1864–1900) collaborated on three books of verse in their *Songs of Vagabondia* series (1894, 1896, 1901).

He is the hollow place in the rock that echoes with his time. He *does* "chant the crucial stage" and he is the "voice triumphant." He is disgusting. He is an exceedingly nauseating pill, but he accomplishes his mission.

Entirely free from the renaissance humanist ideal of the complete man or from the Greek idealism, he is content to be what he is, and he is his time and his people. He is a genius because he has vision of what he is and of his function. He knows that he is a beginning and not a classically finished work.

I honour him for he prophesied me while I can only recognise him as a forebear of whom I ought to be proud.

In America there is much for the healing of the nations, but woe unto him of the cultured palate who attempts the dose.

As for Whitman, I read him (in many parts) with acute pain, but when I write of certain things I find myself using his rhythms. The expression of certain things related to cosmic consciousness seems tainted with this maramis.°

I am (in common with every educated man) an heir of the ages and I demand my birthright. Yet if Whitman represented his time in language acceptable to one accustomed to my standard of intellectual-artistic living he would belie his time and nation. And yet I am but one of his "ages and ages' encrustations" or to be exact an encrustation of the next age. The vital part of my message, taken from the sap and fibre of America, is the same as his.

Mentally I am a Walt Whitman who has learned to wear a collar and a dress shirt (although at times inimical to both). Personally I might be very glad to conceal my relationship to my spiritual father and brag about my more congenial ancestry — Dante, Shakespeare, Theocritus, Villon, but the descent is a bit difficult to establish. And, to be frank, Whitman is to my fatherland (*Patriam quam odi et amo*° for no uncertain reasons) what Dante is to Italy and I at my best can only be a strife for a renaissance in America of all the lost or temporarily mislaid beauty, truth, valour, glory of Greece, Italy, England, and all the rest of it.

And yet if a man has written lines like Whitman's to *Sunset Breeze* one has to love him. I think we have not yet paid enough attention to the deliberate artistry of the man, not in details but in the large.

I am immortal even as he is, yet with a lesser vitality as I am the more in love with beauty (If I really do love it more than he did). Like Dante he wrote in the "vulgar tongue," in a new metric. The first great man to write in the language of his people.

Et ego Petrarca in lingua vetera scribo,° and in a tongue my people understand not.

It seems to me I should like to drive Whitman into the old world. I sledge, he drill — and to scourge America with all the old beauty. (For Beauty *is* an accusation) and with a thousand thongs from Homer to Yeats, from Theocritus to Marcel Schwob. This desire is because I am young and impatient, were I old and wise I should content myself in seeing and saying that these

---

maramis: Likely "marasmus," wasting away.
Patriam quam odi et amo: Latin for "Country that I hate and love."
Et ego Petrarca in lingua vetera scribo: "And I, Petrarca, write in the old language." The Italian poet and scholar Francesco Petrarca (1304–1374) chose to write in Latin rather than Italian.

things will come. But now, since I am by no means sure it would be true prophecy, I am fain set my own hand to the labour.

It is a great thing, reading a man to know, not "His Tricks are not as yet my Tricks, but I can easily make them mine" but "His message is my message. We will see that men hear it."

ꙮ

SHEROD SANTOS *teaches at the University of Missouri, and his first collection of poetry,* Accidental Weather *(1982), was chosen for the National Poetry Series; his most recent collection is* City of Women *(1994). In this reading of Shelley's famous sonnet, Santos suggests an unusual interpretation for the figure of the broken statue in the desert.*

SHEROD SANTOS

Shelley in Ruins: The Appeal of "Ozymandias"

1996

Popular opinion of Percy Bysshe Shelley's mysterious sonnet "Ozymandias" periodically undergoes a sea change. Newman Ivey White's definitive, two-volume, fourteen hundred–page biography (1940), for instance, never even mentions the poem once, though it was included in Palgrave's *Golden Treasury* (1861), and today it is generally considered one of Shelley's finest lyric achievements — the only one of his sonnets, according to Desmond King-Hele (1960), that "can bear comparison with Shakespeare's." The reason for this is both more and less baffling than might first appear, for the rise and fall of this poem's individual reputation seems inversely correspondent to the rise and fall of the overall reputation of Shelley's work. To put it more bluntly, those who are drawn to this poem appear to admire it, not because it's quintessential Shelley, but because it's so out of keeping with Shelley's style. Likewise, those who dislike or ignore it appear to do so for the very same reason. Where Shelley is normally oracular, extravagant, intuitional, and transportive, here he is detached, ironic, skeptical, and cool — as though the Orphean lute had been traded in for the slide rule of the metaphysical poet.

So who was Ozymandias anyway? At one level we know that this was the Greek name for Rameses II, and that inscribed on an Egyptian temple, as recorded by Diodorus Siculus, is the sentence "I am Ozymandias, king of kings." In the autumn of 1817, around the time of the poem's composition, things Egyptian were making quite a stir in England, and the British Museum had just taken in a collection of pieces from the empire of the Rameses — pieces including the Rosetta Stone and a large-scale figure of Rameses II. Following a visit to the museum with Horace Smith (the stockbroker poet who served as Shelley's London financial agent), Shelley proposed that they each compose a sonnet on the subject, and that "Ozymandias" is the wholly unimaginable result of that seemingly offhand proposal. But that information is circumstantial at best, and as such it only leads us back to itself. The more telling story lies elsewhere.

The son of a member of Parliament, Shelley was a poet who in his youth — and since he lived to be only twenty-nine, I use that term in a relative sense — believed passionately in the role of the poet as world reformer, political activist, agent of justice, and enemy of commerce, royalty, and religion. This was the poet who at eighteen sent copies of his pamphlet *The Necessity of Atheism* to all the faculty and administrators at Oxford (where he was a student at the time) and to all the bishops in the United Kingdom — a quixotic gesture for which he was duly and promptly expelled. This was the same poet who, months later in Dublin, attempted to organize the Irish into "the society of peace and love," and then, having failed at that, resettled in Wales where he sent out into the waiting world yet another hopeful pamphlet, *A Declaration of Rights,* which he launched into the air in bright balloons and onto the sea in toy boats and corked bottles. By then he was nineteen and midway through the writing of his first significant poem, *Queen Mab,* a long verse narrative studded with lectures on politics, religion, and society. In an 1812 letter to the philosopher William Godwin, he described that period of his life this way: "I could not descend to common life: the sublime interest of poetry, lofty and exalted achievements, the proselytism of the world, the equalization of its inhabitants, were to me the soul of my soul."

"Ozymandias," I think, needs to be read in light of that early, and apparently boundless, moral fervor, and in light of that age-old, ongoing, back-and-forth struggle — as germane today as then — between the social and aesthetic demands of an art. For though Shelley was only twenty-five at the time of its composition, his illimitable earlier claims on the world and his role as crusader within it, had been tested seriously by events in his life: the abandonment of his children and wife, Harriet Westbrook, to elope with Mary Godwin; the suicide of Mary's half-sister, for which Shelley felt partially responsible; the death and possible suicide of Harriet; the scandal surrounding Mary's stepsister, Claire Clairmont, pregnant by Byron though assumed by many to be pregnant by Shelley; the court's denial of custody of his children by Harriet, and his fear that he'd eventually lose custody of his children by Mary as well. The list goes on. His own small "society of peace and love" had proven to be anything but. His political aspirations had likewise come to nought. And his poetry was now generally received with a resounding public indifference. So the magnitude of his disillusionment — matched only by the vastness of his early ambitions — suffuse "Ozymandias" with a sobering retrospective self-contempt.

For though "Ozymandias" characteristically assumes Shelley's lifelong disdain for despots and kings — that "sneer of cold command" — and though the poem can be (and normally is) read as a political tract to express that disdain, it is also tempting to see the poem as a moment when Shelley steps back from himself. When, through the eyes of posterity, he observes that hopelessly failed persona — that venerated, long-suffering, super-sensitive *"Me,"* as he described it in "Julian and Maddalo," "who am as a nerve o'er which do creep / the else unfelt oppressions of this earth."

It is tempting in fact to see "Ozymandias" as an instance of the poem revising the poet, abruptly caught out in that (sometimes) painfully clarifying light that poetry and dreams will cast. It may be that there is more of Shelley in that "shattered visage" than we first perceive. For are the grand delusions of a tyrant who could boast "Look on my works, ye Mighty, and despair!" all that different from those of a poet who had once aspired to "lofty and exalted achievements, the proselytism of the world, the equalization of its inhabitants"? Perhaps pressing into being through the features of that disintegrated stone is a self Shelley now finds betrayed by destiny and lying in the rubble of his own exuberant idealism.

Yet oddly enough — and herein lies the poem's unspoken promise to the poet — within that bitter self-negation resides a deeper, more enduring affirmation. For out of "the decay / Of that colossal wreck," the world reformer will discover at last a more truly self-centering (hence, as he'd hoped, self-transcending) relationship to his art. As true for Shelley as it was for Keats, the death of the self was a prerequisite for the birth of the poet. By the time he'd write the *Defence of Poetry* — composed the year before his death, four years after "Ozymandias" — Shelley would finally come around to claim that a poet "would do ill to embody his own conceptions of right and wrong, which are usually those of his place and time, in his poetical creations, which participate in neither."

But let's go back to the beginning.

That eerie sense of detachment that distinguishes "Ozymandias" from others in the Shelley canon — and which determines for some its value as a poem — is established through a complex layering of voices, and an equally complex layering of historical times. In a prototypical modernist vein, the poem unfolds as a story within a story within a story. We have, first off, what might be called the poem's "frame," a tale recounted by the poem's anonymous narrator, who, to whatever degree, might be seen as the poet himself. His story holds a second story, as told by a "traveler from an antique land," a story before which the original narrator quickly disappears. In some faraway and long ago place, the traveler is reported to say, exists a desert in which he'd found "Two vast and trunkless legs of stone" and, nearby, "a shattered visage." And that was all, "Nothing beside remains." No trace of those achievements about which an inscription on the pedestal proudly claims, "Look on my works, ye Mighty, and despair!"

But the time the traveler refers us to points back to another time, to yet another story within *his* story, a time preceding the pedestal and the trunkless legs, a time from which a message was launched, as in a toy boat or corked bottle, onto a sea of random connections that have brought it here today. That message appears to have something to do with "those passions . . . / Which yet survive," though the artist who "mocked them" (*mocked* here means copied, not ridiculed) and the king whose heart they fed are both now reduced to "lifeless things." The message appears to exist somewhere in that pointed juxtaposition of what survives and what is swallowed up by the inexorable movement of time.

A curious thing has happened here, for the role of the artist, while linked by those passions to the role of the sovereign, is also implicitly distinguished from it. What survives of the ruler — or, in my reading, of the youthful idealist Shelley — is not, as the inscription claims, "my works," but a subordinate and reducible disposition. What survives of the artist, while reducible to neither the work nor the disposition, still of necessity contains them both (the "sneer" is inseparable from the stone on which it is carved). More significantly, the artist's making has somehow managed to outstrip time. For this reason one might assume safely that the poem has less to do with Ozymandias as an emblem of those absolute rulers Shelley deplored — after all, whether tyrant or benevolent leader, the fate of Ozymandias would remain the same — and more to do with that carefully nuanced chain of connections that has accurately "read," skillfully "mocked," and successfully kept alive "those passions."

That process, of course, only begins with the sculptor. Had it ended with him, his works, like those of Ozymandias, would have been equally lost to time. For in order to keep those passions alive, there is a second artist (whose art is telling) who has had to read and record their movement: that mysterious "traveler from an antique land," without whose story we'd know nothing of this. And then, as well, as we circle back through the layers of the poem, we are reminded of a crucial tertiary link: the poet himself, who composed the poem "Ozymandias," which contains and keeps alive both the traveler's story and the sculptor's stone.

Oddly enough, the poet proves the least present of all the figures in the poem. He ostensibly speaks only the first ten words of the sonnet, and those are directed away from himself: "I met a traveler from an antique land / Who said: . . . ." So where is he, this poet who, after a visit to the British Museum, proposed to a friend that they each attempt a sonnet on the subject? The poet who, through a mysterious confluence of events in his life, sat down to write a poem unlike anything he'd written before? It's appealing to imagine — and for some it may be instructive as well — that for the moment anyway there was no poet, that the poem was composed in that stupefying silence ("boundless and bare") between the death of one self and the birth of another; or that the poet who would be had not yet come into being, while the poet who was turned to rubble. It's appealing to imagine that at most there existed a consciousness, the faintest whisper of a consciousness, gazing back over the ruined prospect of its own past life. And what did this consciousness see? To borrow the words addressed to yet another famously uprooted statue — the great stone statue of General Du Puy in [Wallace] Stevens's *Notes Toward a Supreme Fiction* — "There never had been, never could be, such / A man."

The drama of this poem as anomaly — or more accurately as poem *donnée* — demands that we read it against the lavish backdrop of Shelley's earlier work, not as the negation or ratification of that work, but as an unwitting, and perhaps even unwanted, revelation of a spirit that had, until then, fueled that work — and would thereafter be called upon to transfigure it. "Ozymandias" serves as a cautionary tale — told by the poem to the poet midway in his writing life — about the futilities of worldly ambition and the transience of fame. But it's a poem with a darker interior as well, for at the heart of its revelation lies nothing less than a harrowing encounter with the desolate experience of self-extinction: "Round the decay / Of that colossal wreck, boundless and bare / The lone and level sands stretch far away." The shock of that experience accounts for the almost posthumous tone that attends its lines, and the effect of those lines remains one of the more urgent and unsettling and unmediated moments in Shelley's work.

ꕥ

PETER SCHMITT's *recent books include* Country Airport *and* Hazard Duty. *In his discussion of Randall Jarrell's poem, he examines the challenge of writing a poem in which the poem's central figure is a different sex from the writer.*

PETER SCHMITT

Sad Heart at the Supermarket: Randall Jarrell's "Next Day"

1996

One of the challenges for any poet, just as for a playwright or novelist, is to write convincingly in the voice of the other sex. If Randall Jarrell's dramatic monologue, or persona poem "Next Day" succeeds in this endeavor, it must do so by persuading us that this modern suburban woman's voice is entirely credible. For the poem to transcend the mere impersonation of the other gender, it must speak for humanity in general — clearly the larger of the poet's tasks.

"Next Day" begins at the supermarket, specifically in the detergent aisle: "Moving from Cheer to Joy, from Joy to All." The ironies are many in this opening line: the impossibly upbeat names on the boxes, contrasting with the speaker's own disillusionment; she is in some way trying to cleanse her life, but can't get further than her laundry; she has bypassed happiness (Cheer, Joy) for the myth of having it All, as much a fantasy today as in the prefeminist sixties when Jarrell's housewife could conceive of little in her role beyond the traditional cooking and cleaning. For her, of course, "All" turns out to be a box of soap. And ever since the rice thrown at her wedding, what remains for her that is "wild," unruly, undomesticated? Certainly not "my Cornish game hens," bred for nothing more than consumption. Her counterparts in the market, in their frisky suburban wear, are just as deprived ("slacked or shorted") despite the abundance in their carts, and one hears "basket cases" in the remainder of the fourth line. But these other women, faceless as chickens in a coop, "Are selves I overlook," the speaker claims, at least outside of the poem's relentless self-scrutiny. It's a habit she's learned from William James, this knowing when to turn away. Is Jarrell attempting to lend his poem a little academic weight, or would a long-married homemaker really know William James? It's possible, particularly if she were college educated, and if the other wives lack such a sophisticated frame of reference it only tends to make her situation rather more depressing. The internal rhyme of "selves" and "shelves" suggests that her life has indeed been "shelved" intellectually, emotionally, physically.

As the bagboy brings the groceries out to her station wagon, that comfortably suburban vehicle of domesticity, marking her "station" in life, there is at least one self she can't "overlook." Out, briefly, in the open air, her comparisons are no longer to the clucking marketgoers but to the larger world, and "What I've become / Troubles me even if I shut my eyes." Squeezing those eyes shut conjures an earlier self, "When I was young and miserable and pretty / And poor." So much for youth as a carefree time! The speaker acknowledges the conventionality of her youthful desires: "to have a husband, / A house and children" (in the usual order of attainment). "Now that I'm old," and having realized those familiar ambitions, her wish is no less conventional: "That the boy putting groceries in my car / / See me." To be favored again by youth itself. The enjambment of "See me" at the beginning of the new stanza, and its repetition at the other end of the line, force us indeed to see the phrase in all its imperative urgency: *See me!* But the bagboy, alas, does not.

It puzzles her, his lack of interest, when "For so many years / I was good enough to eat": a tasty grocery herself, the object of men's desires, when men *were* the "world" that "looked at me / And its mouth watered." (Now she looks at the world, and her *eyes* water.) Once, the eyes of others, "strangers," undressed her, like a stuffed game hen. These undressings are relegated now to the past, as are the allusions in the following lines: "holding their flesh within my flesh, their vile / / Imaginings within my imagining, / I too have taken / The chance of life." If we take this passage with at least some literalism (as we should for every line), do we assume Jarrell means her single days, sleeping with virtual strangers? Note the breath taken at the stanza break after "vile": how the "imaginings," which she herself shares, are somehow more daunting than the very acts themselves. Or has she only undressed the others with her own eyes? Taking "The chance of life" would hint otherwise — that actual, physical liaisons with others, even relative strangers, are what one must sometimes risk to gain something greater, something Jarrell quietly terms "life." It is as if she insists, *I, too, have lived, I have known desire* — if in the past.

Now, however, the speaker would settle for attracting not even men, but, from her middle-aged outlook, a "boy," who instead of giving her the eye, "pats my dog." "Now I am good," she says, if not "good enough to eat." Safe, leashed, beyond the lusts of strangers, she thinks back to "The last mistaken, / Ecstatic, accidental bliss," not necessarily sexual at all, but a "blind / / Happiness" — a filmy bubble of contentment, perhaps illusory — "that, bursting, leaves upon the palm / Some soap and water" — the detergent with which the poem began, the residue on one's hands after marriage and at least three children, now nearly grown. "It was so long ago," she reflects, "back in some Gay / Twenties" — *her* twenties? — "Nineties, I don't know." Possibly her confusion is meant to call back an imagined simpler time.

"Today," instead of an almost unlooked-for happiness, what she has is painfully felt absence, especially of her loved ones — daughter and sons away at school, husband at work — everything she once wished for and acquired, and yet she still feels alone and wishes for them still, even wishes on their behalf. The delight and pride she can take in her "accomplishments," so to speak, is limited; her daughter is "lovely," but still away from her. With only the dog and maid for company, she "go[es] through the sure unvarying days / At home in them." Home here means only routine, and yet it is precisely that safe, orderly predictability or constancy she most fears losing: "As I look at my life, / I am afraid / Only that it will change, as I am changing." What she fears, of course, is getting older and facing death.

The speaker's language is direct and exposed to the very degree that she feels exposed and vulnerable and would like to turn away but can't. "I am afraid," she repeats, "this morning, of my face." What one has known intimately all one's life now seems virtually dissociated, disembodied from the self: "It looks at me / From the rear-view mirror" just as she reviews her life. Aspects of her appearance — her eyes and smile — that have always bothered her are now, she tells us point-blank, features "I hate," even, ironically, as she smiles bravely and ruefully at her reflection. That face holds no surprises for her anymore, whatever is to be found there is "plain, lined . . . gray," bearing only one message that it repeats: "You're old." And she repeats it to herself, and for us: "That's all, I'm old." Everyone ages; how is my problem different from anyone else's? With this momentary, offhand deflection, we are all implicated in the poem.

And yet what age brings is not solely, if at all, the comforting wisdom of perspective, the wisdom of a William James. What it brings instead is a palpable fear, as the speaker repeats for the third time, "I'm afraid"; and only now do we grasp the import of the poem's title, "as I was at the funeral / I went to yesterday." We realize that the poem has been set not in the morning-after of a gratifying sexual rendezvous, but the at least as sobering *mourning* after, more frequent with age, of going to a funeral. And what frightened her so was seeing herself in the guise of her late friend, most likely another prosperous, middle-aged housewife.

"My friend's cold made-up face," rouged by morticians, is also unreal in the same way hers seems to be from that rearview mirror as she drives home. She replays touching the dead woman's face, and finding it "granite among its flowers" — that jarring juxtaposition — just as our speaker is hardened amid whatever mitigating influences her life may offer — her children, say, her house, her husband. "Her undressed, operated-on, dressed body" brings back with what one might call an almost surgical irony the earlier line, "How often they have undressed me," and the speaker spells both her lost youth and her waiting future in looking at her dead friend and conceding that what she gazed on "Were my face and body." Now it is the dead she identifies with, this self she cannot overlook. In this harsh light of mortality, even her youthful passionate encounters now dull in memory to clinical probings, mechanical exploratories that prepare us for the desolation of the poem's closing lines.

"As I think of her I hear her telling me / / How young I seem" — a voice that reaches the speaker from memory, a remembered conversation, or through imagination, out of the grave — though the stanza break's white space communicates the span of the gulf in either case. She wants to be reassured, and alongside the dead it isn't difficult to feel relatively young. And she experiences, as she has more than once in the poem, momentary relief and gratification: "I *am* exceptional; / I think of all I have." But investing the dead with the authority she herself cannot summon proves just as futile as any attempt at self-assurance: despite her seeming youth and blessings, "really no one is exceptional" (that last word repeated to dull its distinctiveness), and she continues, bleakly: "No one has anything." She rejects the worth of material advantages, or even human bonds, in the face of death, and her identification with humanity's mortal condition is now complete: "I'm anybody." Jarrell's choice of *body* over *one* emphasizes both her physical decline and refutes any claims to individuality. In fact, in this final stanza's fourth line the one indefinite pronoun that seems to be missing is *anyone* (though shadowed by the "No one"), and the speaker's terrible sense of aloneness, and not just of a momentary nature, comes fully across.

At this point in the poem we remember that she has been driving back from the supermarket, her thoughts darkening along the way, and when she says in the penultimate line, "I stand beside my grave," we know at last she has arrived home. It isn't far, the poem would seem to say, from the detergent where we began to the boxes of house and coffin. Her home, she realizes, is her grave, it's what her life, so outwardly comfortable, has come to, and little wonder it is "Confused with my life," just as she wonders how all this time her home could so completely have become her life. What Jarrell mourns here is the virtual loss of an inner life — call it intellectual, or emotional, even spiritual — when it has been so thoroughly taken over by domestic routine. But if our housewife is confused by how her life can be both "commonplace and solitary" (just like the grave), how her life has become a living death, the poem offers little consolation to us as readers, because nowhere does it suggest that our fates — however we avoid the ensnarements of routine and tedium — should be any different from hers ("I'm anybody") in its desolation and bewilderment. No matter if William James is but a solitary entry in her commonplace book, it's enough to tell us that cultivating rich interior lives brings us no closer to what the woman who has everything is missing.

With its unobtrusive rhyme scheme and midlevel diction, "Next Day" has done nothing to distract us from the voice of the speaker in all her emotional directness. Jarrell has created a persuasive woman's voice by delivering throughout a convincing *human* voice. He has somehow managed for his 1960s suburban homemaker to speak for all of us, male and female, who at one time or another find our lives more empty than complete, and so offers us the possibility that our differences as men and women may yet prove secondary to our likenesses.

ꕤ

PERCY BYSSHE SHELLEY's *lyrical, impassioned defense of the poet and his art is an expression of the romantic attitude toward art and literature. In part, Shelley is defending poetry against Plato's idea that poets should be banished from the ideal city, but he is also presenting the poet and the artist as an individual who should be free of the society's constrictions.*

Percy Bysshe Shelley

From "A Defence of Poetry"

1821

A poem is the very image of life expressed in its eternal truth. There is this difference between a story and a poem, that a story is a catalogue of detached facts, which have no other bond of connexion than time, place, circumstance, cause and effect; the other is the creation of actions according to the unchangeable forms of human nature, as existing in the mind of the creator, which is itself the image of all other minds. The one is partial, and applies only to a definite period of time, and a certain combination of events which can never again recur; the other is universal, and contains within itself the germ of a relation to whatever motives or actions have place in the possible varieties of human nature. Time, which destroys the beauty and the use of the story of particular facts, stript of the poetry which should invest them, augments that of Poetry, and for ever develops new and wonderful applications of the eternal truth which it contains. Hence epitomes have been called the moths of just history; they eat out the poetry of it. The story of particular facts is as a mirror which obscures and distorts that which should be beautiful: Poetry is a mirror which makes beautiful that which is distorted.

The parts of a composition may be poetical, without the composition as a whole being a poem. A single sentence may be considered as a whole though it be found in a series of unassimilated portions; a single word even may be a spark of inextinguishable thought. And thus all the great historians, Herodotus, Plutarch, Livy, were poets; and although the plan of these writers, especially that of Livy, restrained them from developing this faculty in its highest degree, they make copious and ample amends for their subjection, by filling all the interstices of their subjects with living images.

Having determined what is poetry, and who are poets, let us proceed to estimate its effects upon society.

Poetry is ever accompanied with pleasure: all spirits on which it falls, open themselves to receive the wisdom which is mingled with its delight. In the infancy of the world, neither poets themselves nor their auditors are fully aware of the excellence of poetry: for it acts in a divine and unapprehended manner, beyond and above consciousness; and it is reserved for future generations to contemplate and measure the mighty cause and effect in all the strength and splendour of their union. Even in modern times, no living poet ever arrived at the fulness of his fame; the jury which sits in judgement upon a poet, belonging as he does to all time, must be composed of his peers: it must be impanelled by Time from the selectest of the wise of many generations. A Poet is a nightingale, who sits in darkness and sings to cheer its own solitude with sweet sounds; his auditors are as men entranced by the melody of an unseen musician, who feel that they are moved and softened, yet know not whence or why. The poems of Homer and his contemporaries were the delight of infant Greece; they were the elements of that social system which is the column upon which all succeeding civilization has reposed. Homer embodied the ideal perfection of his age in human character; nor can we doubt that those who read his verses were awakened to an ambition of becoming like to Achilles, Hector and Ulysses: the truth and beauty of friendship, patriotism and persevering devotion to an object, were unveiled to the depths in these immortal creations: the sentiments of the auditors must have been refined and enlarged by a sympathy with such great and lovely impersonations, until from admiring they imitated, and from imitation they identified themselves with the objects of their admiration. Nor let it be objected, that these characters are remote from moral perfection, and that they can by no means be considered as edifying patterns for general imitation. Every epoch under names more or less specious has deified its peculiar errors; Revenge is the naked Idol of the worship of a semi-barbarous age; and Self-deceit is the veiled Image of unknown evil before which luxury and satiety lie prostrate. But a poet considers the vices of his contemporaries as the temporary dress in which his creations must be arrayed, and which cover without concealing the eternal proportions of their beauty. An epic or dramatic personage is understood to wear them around his soul, as he may the antient armour or the modern uniform around his body; whilst it is easy to conceive a dress more graceful than either. The beauty of the internal nature cannot be so far concealed by its accidental vesture, but that the spirit of its form shall communicate itself to the very disguise, and indicate the shape it hides from the manner in which it is worn. A majestic form and graceful motions will express themselves through the most barbarous and tasteless costume. Few poets of the highest class have chosen to exhibit the beauty of their conceptions in its naked truth and splendour; and it is doubtful whether the alloy of costume, habit, etc., be not necessary to temper this planetary music for mortal ears. . . .

Poetry is indeed something divine. It is at once the centre and circumference of knowledge; it is that which comprehends all science, and that to which all science must be referred. It is at the same time the root and blossom of all other systems of thought; it is that from which all spring, and that which adorns all; and that which, if blighted, denies the fruit and the seed, and withholds from the barren world the nourishment and the succession of the scions of the tree of life. It is the perfect and consummate surface and bloom of things; it is as the odour and the colour of the rose to the texture of the elements which compose it, as the form and the splendour of unfaded beauty to the secrets of anatomy and corruption. What were Virtue, Love, Patriotism, Friendship etc. — what were the scenery of this beautiful Universe which we inhabit — what were our consolations on this side of the grave — and what were our aspirations beyond it — if Poetry did not ascend to bring light and fire from those eternal regions where the owl-winged faculty of calculation dare not ever soar? Poetry is not like reasoning, a power to be exerted according to the determination of the will. A man cannot say, "I will compose poetry." The greatest poet even cannot say it: for the mind in creation is as a fading coal which some invisible influence, like an inconstant wind, awakens to transitory brightness: this power arises from within, like the colour of a flower which fades and changes as it is developed, and the conscious portions of our natures are unprophetic either of its approach or its departure. Could this influence be durable in its original purity and force, it is impossible to predict the greatness of the results; but when composition begins, inspiration is already on the decline, and the most glorious poetry that has ever been communicated to the world is probably a feeble shadow of the original conception of the poet. I appeal to the greatest Poets of the present day, whether it be not an error to assert that the finest passages of poetry are produced by labour and study. The toil and the delay recommended by critics can be justly interpreted to mean no more than a careful observation of the inspired moments, and an artificial connexion of the spaces between their suggestions by the intertexture of conventional expressions; a necessity only imposed by the limitedness of the poetical faculty itself. For Milton conceived the Paradise Lost as a whole before he executed it in portions. We have his own authority also for the Muse having "dictated" to him the "unpremeditated song," and let this be an answer to those who would allege the fifty-six various readings of the first line of the Orlando Furioso. Compositions so produced are to poetry what mosaic is to painting. This instinct and intuition of the poetical faculty is still more observable in the plastic and pictorial arts: a great statue or picture grows under the power of the artist as a child in the mother's womb; and the very mind which directs the hands in formation is incapable of accounting to itself for the origin, the gradations, or the media of the process.

Poetry is the record of the best and happiest moments of the happiest and best minds. We are aware of evanescent visitations of thought and feeling sometimes associated with place or person, sometimes regarding our own mind alone, and always arising unforeseen and departing unbidden, but elevating and delightful beyond all expression: so that even in the desire and the regret they leave, there cannot but be pleasure, participating as it does in the nature of its object. It is as it were the interpenetration of a diviner nature through our own; but its footsteps are like those of a wind over a sea, where the coming calm erases, and whose traces remain only as on the wrinkled sand which paves it. These and corresponding conditions of being are experienced principally by those of the most delicate sensibility and the most enlarged imagination; and the state of mind produced by them is at war with every base desire. The enthusiasm of virtue, love, patriotism, and friendship is essentially linked with these emotions; and whilst they last, self appears as what it is, an atom to a Universe. Poets are not only subject to these experiences as spirits of the most refined organization, but they can colour all that they combine with the evanescent hues of this etherial world; a word, or a trait in the representation of a sense or a passion, will touch the enchanted chord, and reanimate, in those who have ever experienced these emotions, the sleeping, the cold, the buried image of the past. Poetry thus makes immortal all that is best and most beautiful in the world; it arrests the vanishing apparitions which haunt the interlunations of life, and veiling them or in language or in form sends them forth among mankind, bearing sweet news of kindred joy to those with whom their sisters abide — abide, because there is no portal of expression from the caverns of the spirit which they inhabit into the universe of things. Poetry redeems from decay the visitations of the divinity in man.

Poetry turns all things to loveliness; it exalts the beauty of that which is most beautiful, and it adds beauty to that which is most deformed; it marries exultation and horror, grief and pleasure, eternity and change; it subdues to union under its light yoke all irreconcilable things. It transmutes all that it touches, and every form moving within the radiance of its presence is changed by wondrous sympathy to an incarnation of the spirit which it breathes; its secret alchemy turns to potable gold the poisonous waters which flow from death through life; it strips the veil of familiarity from the world, and lays bare the naked and sleeping beauty which is the spirit of its forms. . . .

. . . The most unfailing herald, companion, and follower of the awakening of a great people to work a beneficial change in opinion or institution, is Poetry. At such periods there is an accumulation of the power of communicating and receiving intense and impassioned conceptions respecting man and nature. The persons in whom this power resides, may often, as far as regards many portions of their nature, have little apparent correspondence with that spirit of good of which they are the ministers. But even whilst they deny and abjure, they are yet compelled to serve, the Power which is seated upon the throne of their own soul. It is impossible to read the compositions of the most celebrated writers of the present day without being startled with the electric life which burns within their words. They measure the circumference and sound the depths of human nature with a comprehensive and all-penetrating spirit, and they are themselves perhaps the most sincerely astonished at its manifestations, for it is less their spirit than the spirit of the age. Poets are the hierophants of an unapprehended inspiration, the mirrors of the gigantic shadows which futurity casts upon the present, the words which express what they understand not; the trumpets which sing to battle, and feel not what they inspire: the influence which is moved not, but moves. Poets are the unacknowledged legislators of the World.

LOUIS SIMPSON's *comments on Robert Lowell's "Skunk Hour" are particularly interesting for their contrast with the comments on the same poem by Lowell himself* *(see p. 1192).*

LOUIS SIMPSON

On Lowell's "Skunk Hour" 1978

Speaking of "Skunk Hour," one of the poems in *Life Studies,* Lowell says that he began to feel that real poetry came "not from fierce confessions, but from something almost meaningless but imagined." He was haunted by the image of a blue china doorknob. He had never used the doorknob, nor did he know what it meant, but it started the train of images in the opening stanzas.

This is a description of a process of evoking the unconscious. The doorknob performs the function of a *mandala,* the circle used in Tibetan Buddhism as an aid in meditating, the aim being to detach the self from its relations with the world. For an artist, however, the aim would be by releasing the mind from its preoccupations, to disengage the will and so enable the unconscious — or whatever one wishes to call that part of one's being that is not amenable to one's will but seems to have a will of its own — to rise to the surface.

Lowell's discovery of the unconscious as an aid in writing came as a result of the psychiatric disorder from which he suffered and the therapy he underwent in order to control it. His blue china doorknob, something "almost meaningless but imagined," is like the image a therapist chooses from his patient's speech as he associates freely, in order to pursue it and see where it leads. It is a thread into the unconscious; tugged at, it brings other images in its train.

Lowell uses the method to recreate his childhood and the lives around it. In the house on Revere Street "the vast number of remembered *things* [Lowell's emphasis] remains rocklike. Each is in its place, each has its function, its history, its drama. There, all is preserved by that motherly care that one either ignored or resented in his youth. The things and their owners come back urgent with life and meaning — because finished, they are endurable and perfect."

The resemblance to Proust is striking — it was so that the narrator of *La Recherche du Temps Perdu* set about recovering the past. Things are the repositories of an affection that one was too preoccupied to notice. One was too selfish, the equivalent in Proust of original sin. But there may come a day when the veil is lifted, and it is a thing that lifts it — things have the power to evoke, by shape or taste or smell, a time that has been lost. The senses are the house of memory, sought not for its own sake, but because to remember is to love.

"Well-adjusted" people think that people with "artistic temperament" are always dreaming of other worlds and imagining unreal things. This is not so — it is life these neurotics dream of. It is as hard for them to find the way there as it would be for a member of the Yale Club to enter Aladdin's cave. So they have a passion for facts: Proust writes to a woman of his acquaintance asking what dress she wore on a certain occasion, and Lowell pushes through the doors of "91 Revere Street." We wish to feel and express the affection we did not feel at the time — for time without affection is time lost. But with the lifting of the veil we are able to live again in a new way; this is the "philosophic mind" Wordsworth speaks of. And if we are artists we are able to point the way to others.

ꙮ

GARY SMITH *wrote this introductory note to Gwendolyn Brooks's writing for the literary quarterly* MELUS, *where it appeared in 1983. The critic Harold Bloom included it in his 1986 collection of modern critical views titled* Contemporary Poets.

GARY SMITH

On Gwendolyn Brooks's A Street in Bronzeville

1983

When Gwendolyn Brooks published her first collection of poetry, *A Street in Bronzeville* (1945), with Harper and Brothers, she already enjoyed a substantial reputation in the literary circles of Chicago. Nearly a decade earlier her mother, Keziah Brooks, had arranged meetings between her daughter and James Weldon Johnson and Langston Hughes, two of the most distinguished black writers of America's Harlem Renaissance. Determined to mold Gwendolyn into a *lady* Paul Laurence Dunbar,° Mrs. Brooks proffered poems for the famous writers to read. While Johnson's advice to the young poet was abrupt, eventually he exerted an incisive influence on her later work. In a letter and a marginal note included on the returned poems, addressed to her on 30 August 1937, Johnson praised Brooks's obvious talent and pointed her in the direction of Modernist poetry:

> My dear Miss Brooks: I have read the poems you sent me last. Of them I especially liked *Reunion* and *Myself. Reunion* is very good, and *Myself* is good. You should, by all means, continue you[r] study and work. I shall always be glad to give you any assistance that I can. Sincerely yours. James Weldon Johnson.
>
> Dear Miss Brooks — You have an unquestionable talent and feeling for poetry. Continue to write — at the same time, study carefully, help cultivate the highest possible standards of self-criticism. Sincerely, James Weldon Johnson.

Of course, the irony in Johnson's advice, addressed as it is to the future *lady* Dunbar, is that he actually began his own career by conspicuously imitating Dunbar's dialect poems, *Lyrics of a Lowly Life*; yet he encourages Brooks to study the work of the "best Modern poets." He was, perhaps, reacting to the latent elements of modernism already found in her poetry; but the effect was to turn Brooks momentarily away from the black aesthetic of Hughes's *Weary Blues* (1926) and Countee Cullen's *Color* (1925) toward the Modernist aesthetics of T. S. Eliot, Ezra Pound, and e. e. cummings. It is interesting to note, however, that, even though Johnson's second letter admonishes Brooks to study the Modernist poets, he cautions her "not to imitate them," but to read them with the intent of cultivating the "highest possible standards of self-criticism." Flattered by the older poet's attention and advice, Brooks embarked upon a serious attempt to absorb as much Modernist poetry as she could carry from the public library.

Paul Laurence Dunbar: Dunbar (1872–1906) was the first African American poet to achieve success with poems written in black dialect.

If Johnson played the part of literary mentor, Brooks's relationship with Hughes was more personal, warmer, and longer lasting. She was already on familiar terms with *Weary Blues,* so their first meeting was particularly inspirational. Brooks showed Hughes a packet of her poems, and he praised her talent and encouraged her to continue to write. Years later, after Brooks's reputation was firmly established by a Pulitzer prize for *Annie Allen* (1949), her relationship with Hughes blossomed into mutual admiration. Hughes dedicated his collection of short stories, *Something in Common* (1963), to her. While Hughes's poetic style had an immeasurable influence on Brooks's poetry, she also respected his personal values and lifestyle. As she noted in her autobiography, Hughes was her idol:

> Langston Hughes! The words and deeds of Langston Hughes were rooted in kindness, and in pride. His point of departure was always a clear pride in his race. Race pride may be craft, art, or a music that combines the best of jazz and hymn. Langston frolicked and chanted to the measure of his own race-reverence.
>
> He was an easy man. You could rest in his company. No one possessed a more serious understanding of life's immensities. No one was firmer in recognition of the horrors man imposes upon man, in hardy insistence on reckonings. But when those who know him remember him the memory inevitably will include laughter of an unusually warm and tender kind. The wise man, he knew, will take some juice out of this one life that is his gift.
>
> Mightily did he use the street. He found its multiple heart, its tastes, smells, alarms, formulas, flowers, garbage and convulsions. He brought them all to his table-top. He crushed them to a writing paste. He himself became the pen.

In other words, while Johnson encouraged Brooks to find "standards for self-criticism" in Modernism, Hughes underscored the value of cultivating the ground upon which she stood. In Hughes, in both the poet and man, Brooks found standards for living: he was a model of witty candor and friendly unpretentiousness and, most importantly, a literary success. Hughes convinced Brooks that a black poet need not travel outside the realm of his own experiences to create a poetic vision and write successful poetry. Unlike the Modernist Eliot who gathered much of his poetic material from the drawingrooms and salons of London, Hughes found his material in the cold-water flats and backstreets of Harlem. And Brooks, as is self-evident in nearly all her poetry, learned Hughes's example by heart.

ERIC TRETHEWEY *points out in this commentary that a poem as much read and discussed as Matthew Arnold's "Dover Beach" will have detractors as well as admirers. His discussion illuminates the aspects of the poem that give it its strength.*

Eric Trethewey

The Virtue of Arnold's "Dover Beach"

1996

While generally conceded to be a great, as well as canonical poem, Matthew Arnold's "Dover Beach" has not been without its detractors. Some criticisms, such as Edith Sitwell's general estimate that readers who like Arnold's poetry are precisely those who do not like poetry, amount to little more than the posturing of a minor poet with a major agenda. Other negative judgments are to be taken more seriously, being made by writers who, if they are finally led astray by a mistaken emphasis, have a genuine commitment to poetry. Examples of such critical judgments are those of Donald Hall in his essay "Ah, Love, Let Us Be True" (1959), and Douglas Bush in his *Matthew Arnold* (1971).

My own judgment is that two qualities above all stand out in Matthew Arnold's poems, of which "Dover Beach" is among the finest and most representative. One, a characteristic noted by generations of sympathetic readers, is Arnold's sustained, elegiac tone evoking loneliness and isolation, a sense, which one encounters more frequently in twentieth-century writers, of lostness in a hostile world seemingly devoid of authentic moral value. The central issue of Arnold's poems is the problem of modernity — as he phrases it in "The Scholar Gypsy," "This strange disease of modern life, / With its sick hurry, its divided aims, / It's heads o'ertaxed, its palsied hearts." The other characteristic, which has perhaps commended itself less to our own age, is Arnold's determination to resist despair and its facsimile, specious affirmation. He wrote poems hospitable to ideas, poems informed by genuinely complex thought, that were adequate representations of the pain and dislocations of modern existence, but that refused to succumb to nihilism. The difficulty he faced was how to do this without assenting to creeds outworn or fostering illusions about the human prospect. Implicitly or explicitly, Arnold's poems raise the question that he said Wordsworth had asked with "profound genuineness" in his writing: the Socratic question of how to live. "It is important, therefore, to hold fast to this," Arnold wrote in his essay on Wordsworth, "that poetry is at bottom a criticism of life; that the greatness of a poet lies in his powerful and beautiful application of ideas to life — to the question: How to live." It is a question, whatever the literary fashion of the moment, that is unlikely ever to disappear entirely from poetry.

"Dover Beach," like Wordsworth's "Lines composed a Few Miles Above Tintern Abbey," is a meditative monologue in which the character of the meditation arises organically out of the topographical situation. In the opening lines of "Dover Beach" the scene is sketched in conventionally picturesque terms. The elements of the setting are "calm," "full," "fair," "tranquil," "sweet." The lovers in the poem might be tourists at a resort hotel (Arnold and his wife spent a night at Dover on their honeymoon). But there is something more in the scene than the merely picturesque. Midway through the first stanza, the speaker begins a new sentence with an ominous "only":

> Only, from the lone line of spray
> Where the sea meets the moon-blanch'd sand,
> Listen! you hear the grating roar
> Of pebbles which the waves draw back, and fling,
> At their return, up the high strand,
> Begin, and cease, and then again begin,
> With tremulous cadence slow, and bring
> The eternal note of sadness in.

The passage constitutes a crucial turn in the poem, introducing in a single hauntingly cadenced sentence a new, unsettling sound of waveborne pebbles that the lovers hear "Begin, and cease, and then again begin." The onomatopoeia here imitates the movement of successive waves breaking on the shore. And "the grating roar" made by the pebbles being drawn back across the rocky shingle suggests to the speaker "The eternal note of sadness," a phrase that echoes, with a distinctive qualification, Wordsworth's "Still, sad music and humanity, / Nor harsh nor grating, though of ample power / To chasten and subdue." The cadence of Arnold's language, miming the motion of the water, is a rhythmic imitation of human sorrow repeating itself throughout the generations.

The allusion to Sophocles in the next stanza functions in several ways. By alluding to the lines in *Antigone* that use the sound of the sea as a figure for human misery, Arnold establishes a genealogy for his perception and connects the present with the distant past. The note of sadness is eternal. I think, however, that Arnold had something more in mind. Sophocles occupied a position in antiquity analogous to Arnold's in the nineteenth century; he was a poet with a profoundly religious sensibility, articulating a religious view of life in an age when Greek religion, the traditional forms of belief, were losing their power to compel assent. Similarly, though Arnold was at odds with Victorian orthodoxy, at the same time that he was attacking superstition, idolatry, and dogma, he was arguing for a religious, essentially poetic, mode of consciousness and fighting the debunking positivism of much contemporary liberal thought. Arnold saw in Sophocles a tragic sense of life very like his own, a sense of human isolation in a world without any sustaining code of value. The centuries of Christian consolation between Sophocles and Arnold may have given humans hope and help in bearing the inevitable, but for Arnold, the tide of faith had turned and, like the speaker in "Dover Beach," he can hear only "Its melancholy, long, withdrawing roar, / Retreating, to the breath / Of the night-wind, down the vast edges drear / And naked shingles of the world." The plangent lyricism here is characteristic of Arnold's best poems, as is the bleak evocation of an existence bereft of belief's sustaining power.

The desolation in these lines is the lowest point of the poem and gives rise to the illumination that follows. The speaker's despair before the retreat of the tide of religious faith, a retreat that weakens the bonds of community established by belief, can only be countered by an appeal to another kind of community, one based on a demythologized commitment to others, the emblem of which is the relationship between two people, grounded in love or friendship, and supported by the virtue of fidelity. Without fidelity, men and women are left in a universe emptied of ethical content to contend against one another in meaningless violence. The insight in "Dover Beach" arrives at the poem's nadir, as if to remind us, as Wallace Stevens put it in "No Possum, No Sop, No Taters," "It is only here, in this bad, that we reach / The last purity of the knowledge of good." The retreating tide of faith leaves bare in the moonlight the naked shingles of the world. The speaker, with the insight engendered by his historical situation, laments that

> the world, which *seems*
> To lie before us like a land of dreams,
> So various, so beautiful, so new,
> Hath really neither joy, nor love, nor light,
> Nor certitude, nor peace, nor help for pain [my emphasis]

The world is not a benevolent, meaningful seascape but a "darkling plain / Swept with confused alarms of struggle and flight, / Where ignorant armies clash by night." These are the last lines of the poem, clinching it in a couplet — one of only three in the poem — as if Arnold wished to leave the reader with a strong enough image of a nihilistic universe to persuade him to accept the appeal to human solidarity presented earlier.

HELEN VENDLER, *in her 1988 anthology titled* The Music of What Happens, *discusses what she terms the "archetypal poetry" of Louise Glück. As a critic, reviewer, and Harvard University professor, Vendler has written on most of the important contemporary poets in the United States.*

HELEN VENDLER

On Louise Glück

1988

Louise Glück has tried in her poetry to give experience the permanent form of myth. Hers is the sort of lyric poetry that turns away from specific details and observations (names, places, dates, quotidian details — what Lowell, for instance, made the stuff of poetry) to an abstract plane, sometimes narrative, as in the Greek myths, sometimes archetypal, as in the encounter of Man with Woman. The tendency for lyric to turn mythical is often irritating to readers who yearn for biography (Who was the Fair Youth? Who was the Dark Lady? Who, for that matter, was Shakespeare?) as if facts would resolve meaning. We all began as sophomores in this respect; but we learn as we read more poetry that it is possible for novelistic detail to obscure, rather than reveal, fictive experience — that the lean shape of myth is the nakedness guaranteeing all stories.

A better argument for mythical lyric is that the beauty possible for mythical or archetypal poetry — with its own lexicon and thesaurus of images — is different from the beauty of the historical quotidian (which too has a lexicon of its own, a specific museum of images). In the treatment of Christian anecdote, for instance, there have always been what one could call artists of essence (those, for example, who painted hieratic crucifixions showing a monumental and untormented Christ in glory on the cross) and, on the other side, artists of the actual (those who painted crucifixions exhibiting a tortured corpse in a realistic social setting).

The chief obstacle in writing mythical or archetypal poetry is that the story is already known, its conclusion familiar. Interest consequently has to center almost entirely on interpretation and manner. (It is no accident that Milton, who decided to retell archetypal stories that every literate person already knew by heart, became the poet with the most highly developed manner in our history.) Glück retells, in "Mythic Fragment," Ovid's story of the myth of Daphne, saved from Apollo's advances by her father the river god Peneus, who turned her into a laurel tree. The lyric poet, facing a narrative, must choose the point at which the lyric aria will occur: Glück gives us Daphne's postmetamorphic voice. The tree, once a girl, retells the myth with the brevity proper to lyric:

> When the stern god
> approached me with his gift
> my fear enchanted him . . .
> I begged my father in the sea
> to save me. When
> the god arrived, I was nowhere,
> I was in a tree forever. Reader,
> pity Apollo: at the water's edge,
> I turned from him, I summoned
> my invisible father — as
> I stiffened in the god's arms,
> of his encompassing love
> my father made
> no other sign from the water.

This may be the first time that the myth of Daphne has been retold as a Freudian story, the tale of a girl too much in love with her father to accept a lover. "Reader, pity Apollo," she says; we are to reflect on the many young men who lose the young women they pursue to that unacknowledged rival, the father. And pity Glück's Daphne: begging her father to save her, she imagines that the result will be Apollo repelled, herself unchanged. Instead, she stiffens into the wood of the sexually unresponsive. Her last words are, "Of his encompassing love / my father made / no other sign from the water." The blankness of that vista — as the stiffened bark looks to the silent shore — is characteristic of Glück's poems of desolation and impossibility. In this Oedipal retelling of the myth there are no compensatory moments — no laurels bound about Apollo's brow, no ecstatic, Straussian joy in leafiness. The manner of the poem has changed the manner of the myth, turning Ovid's story into a demystifying modern story of virginity, revealing its roots in incestuous desire.

Glück's poems bend erotic stereotypes into her own forms of mannerist anguish:

I have been looking
steadily at these elms
and seen the process that creates
the writhing, stationary tree
is torment, and have understood
it will make no forms but twisted forms.

That splendid Yeatsian close states the poetic of Glück's book: writhing, to be stationary; stationary, to be writhing. This is the poetic of myth — animating what is eternal, freezing what is temporary and vanishing. As Glück's two adjectives imply, motion does not cease, but any notion of "progress" or "advance" or "improvement" ceases. Yeats at one point called himself a marble triton growing old among the streams; that moment when a poet becomes marble is the moment of myth. Myth and archetype offer themselves as the only formally tenable vehicles for a sense of the unchangingness of writhing human experience. The older we get, the more we "progress," the more we find our situations anticipated in Ovid, in Homer, in Genesis.

It is no accident that aphorism suits archetype. Glück shows an aphoristic talent that harks back to the Greek Anthology:

You have betrayed me, Eros.
You have sent me
my true love.

"Only victims," she says elsewhere, "have a destiny."

William Carlos Williams *was one of the few established poets who responded to the new aesthetics of the Beat writers. This introduction to Allen Ginsberg's famous poem* Howl *helped establish the poem's validity in the legal battles that followed its publication.*

William Carlos Williams

Introduction to Howl

1956

When he was younger, and I was younger, I used to know Allen Ginsberg, a young poet living in Paterson, New Jersey, where he, son of a well-known poet, had been born and grew up. He was physically slight of build and mentally much disturbed by the life which he had encountered about him during those first years after the First World War as it was exhibited to him in and about New York City. He was always on the point of "going away," where it didn't seem to matter; he disturbed me, I never thought he'd live to grow up and write a book of poems. His ability to survive, travel, and go on writing astonishes me. That he has gone on developing and perfecting his art is no less amazing to me.

Now he turns up fifteen or twenty years later with an arresting poem. Literally he has, from all the evidence, been through hell. On the way he met a man named Carl Solomon with whom he shared among the teeth and excrement of this life something that cannot be described but in the words he has used to describe it. It is a howl of defeat. Not defeat at all for he has gone through defeat as if it were an ordinary experience, a trivial experience. Everyone in this life is defeated but a man, if he be a man, is not defeated.

It is the poet, Allen Ginsberg, who has gone, in his own body, through the horrifying experiences described from life in these pages. The wonder of the thing is not that he has survived but that he, from the very depths, has found a fellow whom he can love, a love he celebrates without looking aside in these poems. Say what you will, he proves to us, in spite of the most debasing experiences that life can offer a man, the spirit of love survives to ennoble our lives if we have the wit and the courage and the faith — and the art! to persist.

It is the belief in the art of poetry that has gone hand in hand with this man into his Golgotha,° from that charnel house, similar in every way, to that of the Jews in the past war. But this is in our own country, our own fondest purlieus. We are blind and live our blind lives out in blindness. Poets are damned but they are not blind, they see with the eyes of the angels. This poet sees through and all around the horrors he partakes of in the very intimate details of his poem. He avoids nothing but experiences it to the hilt. He contains it. Claims it as his own — and, we believe, laughs at it and has the time and affrontery to love a fellow of his choice and record that love in a well-made poem.

Hold back the edges of your gowns, Ladies, we are going through hell.

WILLIAM WORDSWORTH *wrote two introductions to the collection of poems titled* Lyrical Ballads. *This is the second introduction, to the edition of 1802, which expanded and explained ideas that he had presented in the introduction to the first edition of the work in 1798.*

WILLIAM WORDSWORTH

From the Introduction to Lyrical Ballads

1802

It is supposed, that by the act of writing in verse an author makes a formal engagement that he will gratify certain known habits of association; that he not only thus apprizes the reader that certain classes of ideas and expressions will be found in his book, but that others will be carefully excluded. This

Golgotha: Hebrew name for Calvary, the place where Jesus was crucified outside ancient Jerusalem.

exponent or symbol held forth by metrical language must in different eras of literature have excited very different expectations: for example, in the age of Catullus, Terence, and Lucretius and that of Statius or Claudian,° and in our own country, in the age of Shakespeare and Beaumont and Fletcher, and that of Donne and Cowley, or Dryden, or Pope. I will not take upon me to determine the exact import of the promise which by the act of writing in verse an author, in the present day, makes to his reader; but I am certain, it will appear to many persons that I have not fulfilled the terms of an engagement thus voluntarily contracted. They who have been accustomed to the gaudiness and inane phraseology of many modern writers, if they persist in reading this book to its conclusion, will, no doubt, frequently have to struggle with feelings of strangeness and awkwardness: they will look round for poetry, and will be induced to inquire by what species of courtesy these attempts can be permitted to assume that title. I hope therefore the reader will not censure me, if I attempt to state what I have proposed to myself to perform; and also (as far as the limits of a preface will permit) to explain some of the chief reasons which have determined me in the choice of my purpose: that at least he may be spared any unpleasant feeling of disappointment, and that I myself may be protected from the most dishonorable accusation which can be brought against an author, namely, that of an indolence which prevents him from endeavouring to ascertain what is his duty, or, when this duty is ascertained, prevents him from performing it.

The principal object, then, which I proposed to myself in these poems was to choose incidents and situations from common life, and to relate or describe them, throughout, as far as was possible, in a selection of language really used by men; and, at the same time, to throw over them a certain colouring of imagination, whereby ordinary things should be presented to the mind in an unusual way; and, further, and above all, to make these incidents and situations interesting by tracing in them, truly though not ostentatiously, the primary laws of our nature: chiefly, as far as regards the manner in which we associate ideas in a state of excitement. Low and rustic life was generally chosen, because in that condition, the essential passions of the heart find a better soil in which they can attain their maturity, are less under restraint, and speak a plainer and more emphatic language; because in that condition of life our elementary feelings co-exist in a state of greater simplicity, and, consequently, may be more accurately contemplated, and more forcibly communicated; because the manners of rural life germinate from those elementary feelings; and, from the necessary character of rural occupations, are more easily comprehended; and are more durable; and lastly, because in that condition the passions of men are incorporated with the beautiful and permanent forms of nature. The language, too, of these men is adopted (purified indeed from what appear to be its real defects, from all lasting and rational causes of dislike or disgust) because such men hourly communicate with the best objects from

Catullus . . . Claudian: Catullus (84–54 B.C.), Terence (186–159 B.C.), and Lucretius (96–55 B.C.) were Roman poets who wrote simply, in contrast to Statius (45–96) and Claudian (370?–410?), whose work was more elaborate.

which the best part of language is originally derived; and because, from their rank in society and the sameness and narrow circle of their intercourse, being less under the influence of social vanity they convey their feelings and notions in simple and unelaborated expressions. Accordingly, such a language, arising out of repeated experience and regular feelings, is a more permanent, and a far more philosophical language, than that which is frequently substituted for it by poets, who think that they are conferring honour upon themselves and their art, in proportion as they separate themselves from the sympathies of men, and indulge in arbitrary and capricious habits of expression, in order to furnish food for fickle tastes, and fickle appetites, of their own creation.

I cannot, however, be insensible of the present outcry against the triviality and meanness both of thought and language, which some of my contemporaries have occasionally introduced into their metrical compositions; and I acknowledge, that this defect, where it exists, is more dishonorable to the writer's own character than false refinement or arbitrary innovation, though I should contend at the same time that it is far less pernicious in the sum of its consequences. From such verses the poems in these volumes will be found distinguished at least by one mark of difference, that each of them has a worthy *purpose.* Not that I mean to say, that I always began to write with a distinct purpose formally conceived; but I believe that my habits of meditation have so formed my feelings, as that my descriptions of such objects as strongly excite those feelings, will be found to carry along with them a *purpose.* If in this opinion I am mistaken, I can have little right to the name of a poet. For all good poetry is the spontaneous overflow of powerful feelings: but though this be true, poems to which any value can be attached, were never produced on any variety of subjects but by a man who, being possessed of more than usual organic sensibility, had also thought long and deeply. For our continued influxes of feeling are modified and directed by our thoughts, which are indeed the representatives of all our past feelings; and, as by contemplating the relation of these general representatives to each other we discover what is really important to men, so, by the repetition and continuance of this act, our feelings will be connected with important subjects, till at length, if we be originally possessed of much sensibility, such habits of mind will be produced, that, by obeying blindly and mechanically the impulses of those habits, we shall describe objects, and utter sentiments, of such a nature and in such connection with each other, that the understanding of the being to whom we address ourselves, if he be in a healthful state of association, must necessarily be in some degree enlightened, and his affections ameliorated. . . .

I have said that poetry is the spontaneous overflow of powerful feelings: it takes its origin from emotion recollected in tranquillity: the emotion is contemplated till by a species of reaction the tranquillity gradually disappears, and an emotion, kindred to that which was before the subject of contemplation, is gradually produced, and does itself actually exist in the mind. In this mood successful composition generally begins, and in a mood similar to this it is carried on; but the emotion, of whatever kind and in whatever degree, from various causes is qualified by various pleasures, so that in describing any passions whatsoever, which are voluntarily described, the mind will upon the whole be in a state of enjoyment. Now, if nature be thus cautious in preserving in a state of enjoyment a being thus employed, the poet ought to profit by the lesson thus held forth to him, and ought especially to take care, that whatever passions he communicates to his reader, those passions, if his reader's mind be sound and vigorous, should always be accompanied with an overbalance of pleasure. Now the music of harmonious metrical language, the sense of difficulty overcome, and the blind association of pleasure which has been previously received from works of rhyme or metre of the same or similar construction, an indistinct perception perpetually renewed of language closely resembling that of real life, and yet, in the circumstance of metre, differing from it so widely, all these imperceptibly make up a complex feeling of delight, which is of the most important use in tempering the painful feeling which will always be found intermingled with powerful descriptions of the deeper passions. This effect is always produced in pathetic and impassioned poetry; while, in lighter compositions, the ease and gracefulness with which the poet manages his numbers are themselves confessedly a principal source of the gratification of the reader. I might perhaps include all which it is *necessary* to say upon this subject by affirming, what few persons will deny, that, of two descriptions, either of passions, manners, or characters, each of them equally well executed, the one in prose and the other in verse, the verse will be read a hundred times where the prose is read once.

17

CASEBOOKS ON POETRY AND POETS

Emily Dickinson

Langston Hughes

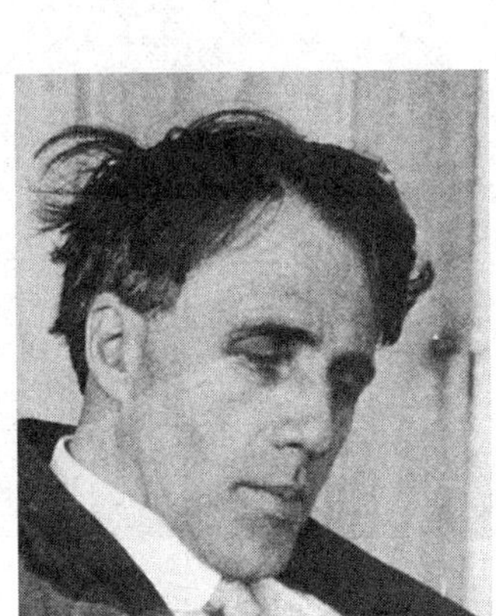

Robert Frost

Sharon Olds

CASEBOOK ON EMILY DICKINSON

This casebook on Emily Dickinson opens with material from her most important editors. Thomas Wentworth Higginson was approached by her in 1862 as a possible mentor and advisor for her writing, but Higginson found her as evasive and puzzling as she was fascinating. Higginson's description of their meeting is the only one we have of Dickinson by a contemporary who was involved in the world of literature and publishing. Following Higginson's selection is one from Thomas H. Johnson, who edited the manuscripts for the first collected edition of her poetry in 1955. The dismissive remarks by a poet who was a contemporary of Dickinson's, Thomas Bailey Aldrich, reflect some of the confusion that greeted the appearance of the first collection of her work. Commentaries by three poets of our day follow. Richard Wilbur discusses some of the emotions he detects behind the brilliant surfaces of Dickinson's poetry.

A seventeen-year-old Emily Dickinson in a daguerreotype, the only authenticated likeness of her. (Reprinted by permission of the Robert Frost Library, Amherst College.)

Then Linda Gregg, a California poet who first encountered Dickinson's poetry when she was in grammar school, writes about Dickinson in an essay that introduced her own poetry in the anthology 19 New American Poets of the Golden Gate, *published in 1984. Finally, a poem by Galway Kinnell describes with dismay his encounter with a deconstructed Emily Dickinson in a modern classroom.*

THOMAS WENTWORTH HIGGINSON

Emily Dickinson's Letters

1891

On April 16, 1862, I took from the post office in Worcester, Mass., where I was then living, the following letter: —

MR. HIGGINSON, — Are you too deeply occupied to say if my verse is alive?

The mind is so near itself it cannot see distinctly, and I have none to ask.

Should you think it breathed, and had you the leisure to tell me, I should feel quick gratitude.

If I make the mistake, that you dared to tell me would give me sincerer honor toward you.

I inclose my name, asking you, if you please, sir, to tell me what is true?

That you will not betray me it is needless to ask, since honor is its own pawn.

The letter was postmarked "Amherst," and it was in a handwriting so peculiar that it seemed as if the writer might have taken her first lessons by studying the famous fossil bird-tracks in the museum of that college town. Yet it was not in the slightest degree illiterate, but cultivated, quaint, and wholly unique. Of punctuation there was little; she used chiefly dashes, and it has been thought better, in printing these letters, as with her poems, to give them the benefit in this respect of the ordinary usages; and so with her habit as to capitalization, as the printers call it, in which she followed the Old English and present German method of thus distinguishing every noun substantive. But the most curious thing about the letter was the total absence of a signature. It proved, however, that she had written her name on a card, and put it under the shelter of a smaller envelope inclosed in the larger; and even this name was written — as if the shy writer wished to recede as far as possible from view — in pencil, not in ink. The name was Emily Dickinson. Inclosed with the letter were four poems, two of which have been already printed, — "Safe in their alabaster chambers" and "I'll tell you how the sun rose," together with the two that here follow. The first comprises in its eight lines a truth so searching that it seems a condensed summary of the whole experience of a long life: —

We play at paste
Till qualified for pearl;
Then drop the paste
And deem ourself a fool.

The shapes, though, were similar
And our new hands
Learned gem-tactics,
Practicing sands.

Then came one which I have always classed among the most exquisite of her productions, with a singular felicity of phrase and an aerial lift that bears the ear upward with the bee it traces: —

The nearest dream recedes unrealized.
  The heaven we chase,
  Like the June bee
  Before the schoolboy,
  Invites the race,
  Stoops to an easy clover,
Dips — evades — teases — deploys —
Then to the royal clouds
  Lifts his light pinnace,
  Heedless of the boy
Staring, bewildered, at the mocking sky

  Homesick for steadfast honey, —
  Ah! the bee flies not
Which brews that rare variety.

The impression of a wholly new and original poetic genius was as distinct on my mind at the first reading of these four poems as it is now, after thirty years of further knowledge; and with it came the problem never yet solved, what place ought to be assigned in literature to what is so remarkable, yet so elusive of criticism. The bee himself did not evade the schoolboy more than she evaded me; and even at this day I still stand somewhat bewildered, like the boy.

Circumstances, however, soon brought me in contact with an uncle of Emily Dickinson, a gentleman not now living; a prominent citizen of Worcester, a man of integrity and character, who shared her abruptness and impulsiveness but certainly not her poetic temperament, from which he was indeed singularly remote. He could tell but little of her, she being evidently an enigma to him, as to me. It is hard to tell what answer was made by me, under these circumstances, to this letter. It is probable that the adviser sought to gain time a little and find out with what strange creature he was dealing. I remember to have ventured on some criticism which she afterwards called "surgery," and on some questions, part of which she evaded, as will be seen, with a naïve skill such as the most experienced and worldly coquette might envy. Her second letter (received April 26, 1862), was as follows: —

Mr. Higginson, — Your kindness claimed earlier gratitude, but I was ill, and write to-day from my pillow.

Thank you for the surgery; it was not so painful as I supposed. I bring you others, as you ask, though they might not differ. While my thought is undressed, I can make the distinction; but when I put them in the gown, they look alike and numb.

You asked how old I was? I made no verse, but one or two, until this winter, sir.

I had a terror since September, I could tell to none; and so I sing, as the boy does of the burying ground, because I am afraid.

You inquire my books. For poets, I have Keats, and Mr. and Mrs. Browning. For prose, Mr. Ruskin, Sir Thomas Browne, and the Revelations. I went to school, but in your manner of the phrase had no education. When a little girl, I had a friend who taught me Immortality; but venturing too near, himself, he never returned. Soon after my tutor died, and for several years my lexicon was my only companion. Then I found one more, but he was not contented I be his scholar, so he left the land.

You ask of my companions. Hills, sir, and the sundown, and a dog large as myself, that my father bought me. They are better than beings because they know, but do not tell; and the noise in the pool at noon excels my piano.

I have a brother and sister; my mother does not care for thought, and father, too busy with his briefs to notice what we do. He buys me many books, but begs me not to read them, because he fears they joggle the mind. They are religious, except me, and address an eclipse, every morning, whom they call their "Father."

But I fear my story fatigues you. I would like to learn. Could you tell me how to grow, or is it unconveyed, like melody or witchcraft?

You speak of Mr. Whitman. I never read his book, but was told that it was disgraceful.

I read Miss Prescott's Circumstance, but it followed me in the dark, so I avoided her.

Two editors of journals came to my father's house this winter, and asked me for my mind, and when I asked them "why" they said I was penurious, and they would use it for the world.

I could not weigh myself, myself. My size felt small to me. I read your chapters in the Atlantic, and experienced honor for you. I was sure you would not reject a confiding question.

Is this, sir, what you asked me to tell you? Your friend,

E. DICKINSON.

It will be seen that she had now drawn a step nearer, signing her name, and as my "friend." It will also be noticed that I had sounded her about certain American authors, then much read; and that she knew how to put her own criticisms in a very trenchant way. With this letter came some more verses, still in the same birdlike script, as for instance the following: —

Your riches taught me poverty,
  Myself a millionaire
In little wealths, as girls could boast,
  Till, broad as Buenos Ayre,
You drifted your dominions
  A different Peru,
And I esteemed all poverty
  For life's estate, with you.

Of mines, I little know, myself,
    But just the names of gems,
The colors of the commonest,
    And scarce of diadems
So much that, did I meet the queen
    Her glory I should know;
But this must be a different wealth,
    To miss it, beggars so.

I'm sure 't is India, all day,
    To those who look on you
Without a stint, without a blame,
    Might I but be the Jew!
I'm sure it is Golconda
    Beyond my power to deem,
To have a smile for mine, each day,
    How better than a gem!

At least, it solaces to know
    That there exists a gold
Although I prove it just in time
    Its distance to behold;
Its far, far treasure to surmise
    And estimate the pearl
That slipped my simple fingers through
    While just a girl at school!

Here was already manifest that defiance of form, never through carelessness, and never precisely from whimsy which so marked her. The slightest change in the order of words — the "While yet at school, a girl" — would have given her a rhyme for this last line but no; she was intent upon her thought and it would not have satisfied her to make the change. The other poem further showed, what had already been visible, a rare and delicate sympathy with the life of nature: —

A bird came down the walk;
He did not know I saw;
He bit an angle-worm in halves
And ate the fellow raw.

And then he drank a dew
From a convenient grass,
And then hopped sidewise to a wall
To let a beetle pass.

He glanced with rapid eyes
That hurried all around;
They looked like frightened beads, I thought;
He stirred his velvet head

Like one in danger, cautious.
I offered him a crumb,

And he unrolled his feathers
And rowed him softer home

Than oars divide the ocean,
Too silver for a seam —
Or butterflies, off banks of noon,
Leap, plashless as they swim.

It is possible that in a second letter I gave more of distinct praise or encouragement, for her third is in a different mood. This was received June 8, 1862. There is something startling in its opening image: and in the yet stranger phrase that follows, where she apparently uses "mob" in the sense of chaos or bewilderment: —

DEAR FRIEND, — Your letter gave no drunkenness, because I tasted rum before. Domingo comes but once; yet I have had few pleasures so deep as your opinion, and if I tried to thank you, my tears would block my tongue.

My dying tutor told me that he would like to live till I had been a poet, but Death was much of mob as I could master, then. And when, far afterward, a sudden light on orchards, or a new fashion in the wind troubled my attention, I felt a palsy, here, the verses just relieve.

Your second letter surprised me, and for a moment, swung. I had not supposed it. Your first gave no dishonor, because the true are not ashamed. I thanked you for your justice, but could not drop the bells whose jingling cooled my tramp. Perhaps the balm seemed better, because you bled me first. I smile when you suggest that I delay "to publish," that being foreign to my thought as firmament to fin.

If fame belonged to me, I could not escape her; if she did not, the longest day would pass me on the chase, and the approbation of my dog would forsake me then. My barefoot rank is better.

You think my gait "spasmodic." I am in danger, sir. You think me "uncontrolled." I have no tribunal.

Would you have time to be the "friend" you should think I need? I have a little shape: it would not crowd your desk, nor make much racket as the mouse that dents your galleries.

If I might bring you what I do — not so frequent to trouble you — and ask you if I told it clear, 't would be control to me. The sailor cannot see the North, but knows the needle can. The "hand you stretch me in the dark" I put mine in, and turn away. I have no Saxon now: —

As if I asked a common alms,
And in my wondering hand
A stranger pressed a kingdom,
And I, bewildered, stand;
As if I asked the Orient
Had it for me a morn,
And it should lift its purple dikes
And shatter me with dawn!

But, will you be my preceptor, Mr. Higginson?

With this came the poem already published in her volume and entitled Renunciation; and also that beginning "Of all the sounds dispatched abroad," thus fixing approximately the date of those two. I must soon have written to ask her for her picture, that I might form some impression of my enigmatical correspondent. To this came the following reply, in July, 1862: —

Could you believe me without? I had no portrait, now, but am small, like the wren; and my hair is bold, like the chestnut bur; and my eyes, like the sherry in the glass, that the guest leaves. Would this do just as well?

It often alarms father. He says death might occur, and he has moulds of all the rest, but has no mould of me; but I noticed the quick wore off those things, in a few days, and forestall the dishonor. You will think no caprice of me.

You said "Dark." I know the butterfly, and the lizard, and the orchis. Are not those *your* countrymen?

I am happy to be your scholar, and will deserve the kindness I cannot repay.

If you truly consent, I recite now. Will you tell me my fault, frankly as to yourself, for I had rather wince than die. Men do not call the surgeon to commend the bone, but to set it, sir, and fracture within is more critical. And for this, preceptor, I shall bring you obedience, the blossom from my garden, and every gratitude I know.

Perhaps you smile at me. I could not stop for that. My business is circumference. An ignorance, not of customs, but if caught with the dawn, or the sunset see me, myself the only kangaroo among the beauty, sir, if you please, it afflicts me, and I thought that instruction would take it away.

Because you have much business, beside the growth of me, you will appoint, yourself, how often I shall come, without your inconvenience.

And if at any time you regret you received me, or I prove a different fabric to that you supposed, you must banish me.

When I state myself, as the representative of the verse, it does not mean me, but a supposed person.

You are true about the "perfection." To-day makes Yesterday mean.

You spoke of Pippa Passes. I never heard anybody speak of Pippa Passes before. You see my posture is benighted.

To thank you baffles me. Are you perfectly powerful? Had I a pleasure you had not, I could delight to bring it.

Your Scholar.

This was accompanied by this strong poem, with its breathless conclusion. The title is of my own giving: —

The Saints' Rest

Of tribulation, these are they,
    Denoted by the white;
The spangled gowns, a lesser rank
    Of victors designate.

All these did conquer; but the ones
Who overcame most times,
Wear nothing commoner than snow,
No ornaments but palms.

"Surrender" is a sort unknown
On this superior soil;
"Defeat" an outgrown anguish,
Remembered as the mile

Our panting ancle barely passed
When night devoured the road;
But we stood whispering in the house,
And all we said, was "Saved!"

[Note by the writer of the verses.] I spelled ankle wrong.

It would seem that at first I tried a little, — a very little — to lead her in the direction of rules and traditions; but I fear it was only perfunctory, and that she interested me more in her — so to speak — unregenerate condition. Still, she recognizes the endeavor. In this case, as will be seen, I called her attention to the fact that while she took pains to correct the spelling of a word, she was utterly careless of greater irregularities. It will be seen by her answer that with her usual naive adroitness she turns my point: —

Dear Friend, — Are these more orderly? I thank you for the truth.

I had no monarch in my life, and cannot rule myself; and when I try to organize, my little force explodes and leaves me bare and charred.

I think you called me "wayward." Will you help me improve?

I suppose the pride that stops the breath, in the core of woods, is not of ourself.

You say I confess the little mistake, and omit the large. Because I can see orthography; but the ignorance out of sight is my preceptor's charge.

Of "shunning men and women," they talk of hallowed things, aloud, and embarrass my dog. He and I don't object to them, if they'll exist their side. I think Carl would please you. He is dumb, and brave. I think you would like the chestnut tree I met in my walk. It hit my notice suddenly, and I thought the skies were in blossom.

Then there's a noiseless noise in the orchard that I let persons hear.

You told me in one letter you could not come to see me "now," and I made no answer; not because I had none, but did not think myself the price that you should come so far.

I do not ask so large a pleasure, lest you might deny me.

You say, "Beyond your knowledge." You would not jest with me, because I believe you; but, preceptor, you cannot mean it?

All men say "What" to me, but I thought it a fashion.

When much in the woods, as a little girl, I was told that the snake would bite me, that I might pick a poisonous flower, or goblins kidnap me; but I went along and met no one but angels, who were far shyer of me than I could be of them, so I have n't that confidence in fraud which many exercise.

I shall observe your precept, though I don't understand it, always.

I marked a line in one verse, because I met it after I made it, and never consciously touch a paint mixed by another person.

I do not let go it, because it is mine. Have you the portrait of Mrs. Browning?

Persons sent me three. If you had none, will you have mine?

YOUR SCHOLAR. . . .

At last, after many postponements, on August 16, 1870, I found myself face to face with my hitherto unseen correspondent. It was at her father's house, one of those large, square, brick mansions so familiar in our older New England towns, surrounded by trees and blossoming shrubs without, and within exquisitely neat, cool, spacious, and fragrant with flowers. After a little delay, I heard an extremely faint and pattering footstep like that of a child, in the hall, and in glided, almost noiselessly, a plain, shy little person, the face without a single good feature, but with eyes, as she herself said, "like the sherry the guest leaves in the glass," and with smooth bands of reddish chestnut hair. She had a quaint and nun-like look, as if she might be a German canoness of some religious order, whose prescribed garb was white piqué, with a blue net worsted shawl. She came toward me with two day-lilies, which she put in a childlike way into my hand, saying softly, under her breath, "These are my introduction," and adding, also under her breath, in childlike fashion, "Forgive me if I am frightened; I never see strangers, and hardly know what I say." But soon she began to talk, and thenceforward continued almost constantly; pausing sometimes to beg that I would talk instead, but readily recommencing when I evaded. There was not a trace of affectation in all this; she seemed to speak absolutely for her own relief, and wholly without watching its effect on her hearer. Led on by me, she told much about her early life, in which her father was always the chief figure, — evidently a man of the old type, *la vielle roche* of Puritanism — a man who, as she said, read on Sunday "lonely and rigorous books"; and who had from childhood inspired her with such awe, that she never learned to tell time by the clock till she was fifteen, simply because he had tried to explain it to her when she was a little child, and she had been afraid to tell him that she did not understand, and also afraid to ask any one else lest he should hear of it. Yet she had never heard him speak a harsh word, and it needed only a glance at his photograph to see how truly the Puritan tradition was preserved in him. He did not wish his children, when little, to read anything but the Bible; and when, one day, her brother brought her home Longfellow's Kavanagh, he put it secretly under the pianoforte cover, made signs to her, and they both afterwards read it. It may have been before this, however, that a student of her father's was amazed to find that she and her brother had never heard of Lydia Maria Child, then much read, and he brought Letters from New York, and hid it in the great bush of old-fashioned tree-box beside the front door. After the first book she thought in ecstasy, "This, then, is a book, and there are more of them." But she did not find so many as she expected, for she afterwards said to me, "When I lost the use of my eyes, it was a comfort to think that there were so few real books that I could easily find one to read me all of them." Afterwards, when she regained her eyes, she read Shakespeare, and thought to herself, "Why is any other book needed?"

She went on talking constantly and saying, in the midst of narrative, things quaint and aphoristic. "Is it oblivion or absorption when things pass from our minds?" "Truth is such a rare thing, it is delightful to tell it." "I find ecstacy in living; the mere sense of living is joy enough." When I asked her if she never felt any want of employment, not going off the grounds and rarely seeing a visitor, she answered, "I never thought of conceiving that I could ever have the slightest approach to such a want in all future time"; and then added, after a pause, "I feel that I have not expressed myself strongly enough," although it seemed to me that she had. She told me of her household occupations, that she made all their bread, because her father liked only hers; then saying shyly, "And people must have puddings," this very timidly and suggestively, as if they were meteors or comets. Interspersed with these confidences came phrases so emphasized as to seem the very wantonness of over-statement, as if she pleased herself with putting into words what the most extravagant might possibly think without saying, as thus: "How do most people live without any thoughts? There are many people in the world, — you must have noticed them in the street, — how do they live? How do they get strength to put on their clothes in the morning?" Or this crowning extravaganza: "If I read a book and it makes my whole body so cold no fire can ever warm me, I know that is poetry. If I feel physically as if the top of my head were taken off, I know that is poetry. These are the only ways I know it. Is there any other way?"

I have tried to describe her just as she was, with the aid of notes taken at the time; but this interview left our relation very much what it was before; — on my side an interest that was strong and even affectionate, but not based on any thorough comprehension; and on her side a hope, always rather baffled, that I should afford some aid in solving her abstruse problem of life.

The impression undoubtedly made on me was that of an excess of tension, and of an abnormal life. Perhaps in time I could have got beyond that somewhat overstrained relation which not my will, but her needs, had forced upon us. Certainly I should have been most glad to bring it down to the level of simple truth and every-day comradeship; but it was not altogether easy. She was much too enigmatical a being for me to solve in an hour's interview, and an instinct told me that the slightest attempt at direct cross-examination would make her withdraw into her shell; I could only sit still and watch, as one does in the woods; I must name my bird without a gun, as recommended by Emerson. Under this necessity I had no opportunity to see that human and humorous side of her which is strongly emphasized by her nearer friends, and which shows itself in her quaint and unique description of a rural burglary, contained in the volume of her poems. Hence, even her letters to me show her mainly on her *exaltée* side; and should a volume of her correspondence ever be printed, it is very desirable that it should contain some of her letters to friends of closer and more familiar intimacy.

After my visit came this letter: —

Enough is so vast a sweetness, I suppose it never occurs, only pathetic counterfeits.

Fabulous to me as the men of the Revelations who "shall not hunger any more." Even the possible has its insoluble particle.

After you went, I took Macbeth and turned to "Birnam Wood." Came twice "To Dunsinane." I thought and went about my work. . . .

The vein cannot thank the artery, but her solemn indebtedness to him, even the stolidest admit, and so of me who try, whose effort leaves no sound.

You ask great questions accidentally. To answer them would be events. I trust that you are safe.

I ask you to forgive me for all the ignorance I had. I find no nomination sweet as your low opinion.

Speak, if but to blame your obedient child.

You told me of Mrs. Lowell's poems. Would you tell me where I could find them, or are they not for sight? An article of yours, too, perhaps the only one you wrote that I never knew. It was about a "Latch." Are you willing to tell me? [Perhaps "A Sketch."]

If I ask too much, you could please refuse. Shortness to live has made me bold.

Abroad is close to-night and I have but to lift my hands to touch the "Heights of Abraham." DICKINSON.

When I said, at parting, that I would come again some time, she replied, "Say, in a long time; that will be nearer. Some time is no time."

THOMAS H. JOHNSON

The Text of Emily Dickinson's Poetry 1960

At the time of her death in 1886, Emily Dickinson left in manuscript a body of verse far more extensive than anyone imagined. Cared for by a servant, Emily and her sister Lavinia had been living together in the Amherst house built by their grandfather Dickinson, alone after their mother's death in 1882. On going through her sister's effects, Lavinia discovered a small box containing about 900 poems. These were the sixty little "volumes," as Lavinia called them, "tied together with twine," that constitute the packets. Determined that she must find a publisher for them, she persuaded Mabel Loomis Todd, the wife of an Amherst professor, to undertake the task of transcribing them. Mrs. Todd enlisted the aid of Thomas Wentworth Higginson, and together they made a selection of 115 poems for publication. But Colonel Higginson was apprehensive about the willingness of the public to accept the poems as they stood. Therefore in preparing copy for the printer he undertook to smooth rhymes, regularize the meter, delete provincialisms, and substitute "sensible" metaphors. Thus "folks" became "those," "heft" became "weight," and occasionally line arrangement was altered.

The publication of *Poems by Emily Dickinson* by Roberts Brothers of Boston nevertheless proved to be one of the literary events of 1890, and the reception of the slender volume encouraged the editors to select 166 more verses, issued a year later as *Poems, Second Series.* These likewise were warmly received. In 1896 Mrs. Todd alone edited *Poems, Third Series,* bringing the total number published to 449, and together with 102 additional poems and parts of poems included in Mrs. Todd's edition of *Letters of Emily Dickinson* (1894), they constituted the Dickinson canon until 1914, when Emily Dickinson's niece and literary heir, Martha Dickinson Bianchi, issued *The Single Hound.*

By now the public had come to appreciate the quality of Dickinson's originalities, and alterations in the text of *The Single Hound* are refreshingly few. But Mrs. Bianchi sometimes had trouble reading the manuscripts, and on occasion words or phrases were misread, in that volume and in the two later ones which completed publication of all the verses in Mrs. Bianchi's possession: *Further Poems* (1929) and *Unpublished Poems* (1935). The appearance of *Bolts of Melody* (1945), from texts prepared by Mrs. Todd and her daughter, Millicent Todd Bingham, virtually completed publication of all the Dickinson poetry, and marked a new era in textual fidelity. It presented 668 poems and fragments, deriving from transcripts made by Mrs. Todd, or from manuscripts which had remained among her papers.

Clearly the time had come to present the Dickinson poetry in an unreconstructed text with some degree of chronological arrangement, and that opportunity was presented in 1950 when ownership of Emily Dickinson's literary estate was transferred to Harvard University. Editing then began on the variorum text of *The Poems of Emily Dickinson,* which I prepared for the Belknap Press of Harvard University Press (3 vols., 1955), comprising a total of 1775 poems and fragments.

The text for this edition of *The Complete Poems of Emily Dickinson* reproduces solely and completely that of the 1955 variorum edition, but intended as a reading text, it selects but one form of each poem. Inevitably therefore one is forced to make some editorial decisions about a text which never was prepared by the author as copy for the printer. Rare instances exist, notably in the poem "Blazing in gold" (228), where no text can be called "final." That poem describes a sunset which in one version stoops as low as "the kitchen window"; in another, as low as an "oriel windoe"; in a third, as low as "the Otter's Window." These copies were made over a period of five years from 1861 to 1866, and one text is apparently as "final" as another. The reader may make the choice.

Selection becomes mandatory for the semifinal drafts. Though by far the largest number of packet copies exist in but a single fair-copy version, several exist in semifinal form: those for which marginally the poet suggested an alternate reading for one word or more. In order to keep editorial construction to a bare minimum, I have followed the policy of adopting such suggestions only when they are underlined, presumably Emily Dickinson's method of indicating her own preference.

Rough drafts, of which there are relatively few, are allowed to stand as such, with no editorial tinkering.

I have silently corrected obvious misspelling (*witheld, visiter,* etc.), and misplaced apostrophes (*does'nt*). Punctuation and capitalization remain unaltered. Dickinson used dashes as a musical device, and though some may be elongated end stops, any "correction" would be gratuitous. Capitalization, though often capricious, is likewise untouched.

THOMAS BAILEY ALDRICH, *at the time he wrote this slighting comment on Emily Dickinson, was one of America's best-known poets. Although he suggests in his final sentence that her work will soon be forgotten, the irony is that his own reputation has failed to survive into the present.*

THOMAS BAILEY ALDRICH

In Re *Emily Dickinson*

1892

The English critic who said of Miss Emily Dickinson that she might have become a fifth-rate poet "if she had only mastered the rudiments of grammar and gone into metrical training for about fifteen years," — the rather candid English critic who said this somewhat overstated his case. He had, however, a fairly good case. If Miss Dickinson had undergone the austere curriculum indicated, she would, I am sure, have become an admirable lyric poet of the second magnitude. In the first volume of her poetical chaos is a little poem which needs only slight revision in the initial stanza in order to make it worthy of ranking with some of the odd swallow flights in Heine's° lyrical *intermezzo.* I have ventured to desecrate this stanza by tossing a rhyme into it, as the other stanzas happened to rhyme, and here print the lyric, hoping the reader will not accuse me of overvaluing it: —

I taste a liquor never brewed
In vats upon the Rhine;
No tankard ever held a draught
Of alcohol like mine.

Inebriate of air am I,
And debauchee of dew,
Reeling, through endless summer days,
From inns of molten blue.

When landlords turn the drunken bee
Out of the Foxglove's door,
When butterflies renounce their drams,
I shall but drink the more!

Till seraphs swing their snowy caps
And saints to windows run,
To see the little tippler
Leaning against the sun!

Heine's: Heinrich Heine (1797–1856), German poet and critic.

Certainly those inns of molten blue, and that disreputable honey-gatherer who got himself turned out-of-doors at the sign of the Foxglove, are very taking matters. I know of more important things that interest me less. There are three or four bits in this kind in Miss Dickinson's book; but for the most part the ideas totter and toddle, not having learned to walk. In spite of this, several of the quatrains are curiously touching, they have such a pathetic air of yearning to be poems.

It is plain that Miss Dickinson possessed an extremely unconventional and grotesque fancy. She was deeply tinged by the mysticism of Blake, and strongly influenced by the mannerism of Emerson. The very way she tied her bonnet-strings, preparatory to one of her nunlike walks in her claustral garden, must have been Emersonian. She had much fancy of a queer sort, but only, as it appears to me, intermittent flashes of imagination. I fail to detect in her work any of that profound thought which her editor professes to discover in it. The phenomenal insight, I am inclined to believe, exists only in his partiality; for whenever a woman poet is in question Mr. Higginson always puts on his rose-colored spectacles. This is being chivalrous; but the invariable result is not clear vision. That Miss Dickinson's whimsical memoranda have a certain something which, for want of a more precise name, we term *quality* is not to be denied except by the unconvertible heathen who are not worth conversion. But the incoherence and formlessness of her — I don't know how to designate them — versicles are fatal. Sydney Smith, or some other humorist, mentions a person whose bump of veneration was so inadequately developed as to permit him to damn the equator if he wanted to. This certainly established a precedent for independence; but an eccentric, dreamy, half-educated recluse in an out-of-the-way New England village (or anywhere else) cannot with impunity set at defiance the laws of gravitation and grammar. In his charming preface to Miss Dickinson's collection, Mr. Higginson insidiously remarks: "After all, when a thought takes one's breath away, a lesson on grammar seems an impertinence." But an ungrammatical thought does not, as a general thing, take one's breath away, except in a sense the reverse of flattering. Touching this matter of mere technique Mr. Ruskin° has a word to say (it appears that he said it "in his earlier and better days"), and Mr. Higginson quotes it: "No weight, nor mass, nor beauty of execution can outweigh one grain or fragment of thought." This is a proposition to which one would cordially subscribe, if it were not so intemperately stated. A suggestive commentary on Mr. Ruskin's impressive dictum is furnished by the fact that Mr. Ruskin has lately published a volume of the most tedious verse that has been printed in this century. The substance of it is weighty enough, but the workmanship lacks just that touch which distinguishes the artist from the bungler, — the touch which Mr. Ruskin seems not to have much regarded either in his later or "in his earlier and better days."

If Miss Dickinson's *disjecta membra* are poems, then Shakespeare's prolonged imposition should be exposed without further loss of time, and Lord Tennyson ought to be advised of the error of his ways before it is too late. But I do not hold the situation to be so desperate. Miss Dickinson's versicles have a

---

Ruskin: John Ruskin (1819–1900), English essayist, critic, and reformer.

queerness and a quaintness that have stirred a momentary curiosity in emotional bosoms. Oblivion lingers in the immediate neighborhood.

Richard Wilbur

On Emily Dickinson

1963

Emily Dickinson never lets us forget for very long that in some respects life gave her short measure; and indeed it is possible to see the greater part of her poetry as an effort to cope with her sense of privation. I think that for her there were three major privations: she was deprived of an orthodox and steady religious faith; she was deprived of love; she was deprived of literary recognition.

At the age of seventeen, after a series of revival meetings at Mount Holyoke Seminary, Emily Dickinson found that she must refuse to become a professing Christian. To some modern minds this may seem to have been a sensible and necessary step; and surely it was a step toward becoming such a poet as she became. But for her, no pleasure in her own integrity could then eradicate the feeling that she had betrayed a deficiency, a want of grace. In her letters to Abiah Root she tells of the enhancing effect of conversion on her fellow-students, and says of herself in a famous passage:

> *I* am one of the lingering bad ones, and so do I slink away, and pause and ponder, and ponder and pause, and do work without knowing why, not surely, for this brief world, and more sure it is not for heaven, and I ask what this message *means* that they ask for so very eagerly: *you* know of this depth and fulness, will you try to tell me about it?

There is humor in that, and stubbornness, and a bit of characteristic lurking pride: but there is also an anguished sense of having separated herself, through some dry incapacity, from spiritual community, from purpose, and from magnitude of life. As a child of evangelical Amherst, she inevitably thought of purposive, heroic life as requiring a vigorous faith. Out of such a thought she later wrote:

> The abdication of Belief
> Makes the Behavior small —
> Better an ingis fatuus
> Than no illume at all — (1551)

That hers *was* a species of religious personality goes without saying; but by her refusal of such ideas as original sin, redemption, hell, and election, she made it impossible for herself — as Professor Whicher observed — "to share the religious life of her generation." She became an unsteady congregation of one.

Her second privation, the privation of love, is one with which her poems and her biographies have made us exceedingly familiar, though some biographical facts remain conjectural. She had the good fortune, at least once, to bestow her heart on another; but she seems to have found her life, in great part, a history of loneliness, separation, and bereavement.

As for literary fame, some will deny that Emily Dickinson ever greatly desired it, and certainly there is evidence, mostly from her latter years, to support such a view. She *did* write that "Publication is the auction / Of the mind of man." And she *did* say to Helen Hunt Jackson, "How can you print a piece of your soul?" But earlier, in 1861, she had frankly expressed to Sue Dickinson the hope that "sometime" she might make her kinfolk proud of her. The truth is, I think, that Emily Dickinson knew she was good, and began her career with a normal appetite for recognition. I think that she later came, with some reason, to despair of being understood or properly valued, and so directed against her hopes of fame what was by then a well-developed disposition to renounce. That she wrote a good number of poems about fame supports my view: the subjects to which a poet returns are those which vex him.

What did Emily Dickinson do, as a poet, with her sense of privation? One thing she quite often did was to pose as the laureate and attorney of the empty-handed, and question God about the economy of His creation. Why, she asked, is a fatherly God so sparing of His presence? Why is there never a sign that prayers are heard? Why does Nature tell us no comforting news of its Maker? Why do some receive a whole loaf, while others must starve on a crumb? Where is the benevolence in shipwreck and earthquake? By asking such questions as these, she turned complaint into critique, and used her own sufferings as experiential evidence about the nature of the deity. The God who emerges from these poems is a God who does not answer, an unrevealed God whom one cannot confidently approach through Nature or through doctrine.

But there was another way in which Emily Dickinson dealt with her sentiment of lack — another emotional strategy which was both more frequent and more fruitful. I refer to her repeated assertion of the paradox that privation is more plentiful than plenty; that to renounce is to possess the more; that "The Banquet of abstemiousness / Defaces that of wine." We all know how the poet illustrated this ascetic paradox in her behavior — how in her latter years she chose to live in relative retirement, keeping the world, even in its dearest aspects, at a physical remove. She would write her friends, telling them how she missed them, then flee upstairs when they came to see her; afterward, she might send a note of apology, offering the odd explanation that "We shun because we prize." Any reader of Dickinson biographies can furnish other examples, dramatic or homely, of this prizing and shunning, this yearning and renouncing: in my own mind's eye is a picture of Emily Dickinson watching a gay circus caravan from the distance of her chamber window.

LINDA GREGG

Not Understanding Emily Dickinson

1984

Emily Dickinson was the first poet I really read. I was in the fifth or sixth grade and she seemed such a secret thing to me that I always read her in bed. I remember clearly the amazement, respect, and something maybe like horror when I read her. I still react to her that way.

I felt then and feel now that she halts me at the border of her poetry while she uses the space beyond like a landscape with many birds in it feeding on the trees after snow has fallen and now it is morning and there is a steady small rain. I didn't understand that when I was little. She was different from those I knew. For me there has always been that something in her which wanted to remain separate. I have never felt let in. Not as I feel let in by [Theodore] Roethke or [D. H.] Lawrence or Sappho or Catullus or Shakespeare. I respect it. I do not wish to approach closer than she wishes. I think of how she would stand on the upstairs landing to listen when there were guests talking downstairs in the living room. Out of respect, I do not go up those stairs after her. She called her poems her letter to the world, not her meeting or her embrace. When I went to her grave, I kept wondering what she would want me to do. I listened to the silence between us of earth and air, and of time, and to the natural silence around us. I listened for her there, and what she gave me was that silence and that distance. I accepted it gratefully, as a gift. And stayed still to be more closely where she was. I did not touch the stone.

There are still a lot of things I don't understand. The wind that seems to be in her poetry, for example. Is it her breath? I don't think so. There is very little natural breathing in her poems. I think it is something other than herself, something which halts her breath. I think she has let something like God's will into her poetry. It halts her, adds much, pushes her, even works against her feelings and body, yet is a great strength in her poems. It blows through and the words do not blow down. This doubleness in her work creates power.

One of the important ways of understanding the poetry of Emily Dickinson may be *not* understanding her. Not, at least, understanding her in the rational way. In the way we understand prose, for example. When I was a young girl, I often did not know what the poems meant. To be honest, that happened more than often. It happened almost all the time when I read her that I did not understand in the usual way. But I did understand nevertheless. Even now, I think many of her poems are successful without being understandable in a logical sense.

I want to be careful to make clear that I am not *against* understanding or explaining the poems. It gives me great pleasure when the poems suddenly yield themselves to me and become clear. I delight in people who help that to happen. I delight in the poetry whose meanings *are* clear, instantly. Lines like:

> There's a certain Slant of light
> Winter Afternoons —
> That oppresses, like the Heft
> Of Cathedral tunes —

For all of us who grew up in the country, there is a special pleasure when she speaks of a snake in the grass *wrinkling*. But one of the most important things about her poetry for the young girl I was *was* the other kind of poetry she wrote, the kind which made no logical sense to me but worked wonderfully. Lines like the ones which end that very poem about the wrinkling snake (called "A narrow fellow in the grass"):

. . . never met this Fellow
Attended, or alone
Without a tighter breathing
And Zero at the Bone —

I still don't know what "Zero at the Bone" means, not in a logical way, but it seems clear to me in another and equally important sense. This is also true for lines like:

The deer attracts no further
Than it resists the hound
(979)

Or poem 690, which begins: "Victory comes late" and ends with the fine lines:

God keep His oath to Sparrows
Who of little Love know how to starve.

Sometimes whole poems have this quality for me, such as poem 512:

The Soul has Bandaged moments —
When too appalled to stir —
She feels some ghastly Fright come up
And stop to look at her —

Salute her — with long fingers —
Caress her freezing hair —
Sip, Goblin, from the very lips
The lover — hovered — o'er —
Unworthy, that a thought so mean
Accost a Theme — so — fair —

The Soul has moments of Escape —
When bursting all the doors —
She dances like a Bomb, abroad,
And swings upon the Hours,

As do the Bee — delirious borne —
Long Dungeoned from his Rose —
Touch Liberty — then know no more,
But Noon, and Paradise —

The Soul's retaken moments —
When, Felon led along,
With shackles on the plumed feet,
And staples, in the Song,

The Horror welcomes her, again,
These, are not brayed of Tongue —

This could be explained. I can glimpse bits of meaning in among the dazzle; but to tell the truth, I am content (in this poem) not to track the meaning down by those clues. I really don't care what the exact meaning is when she speaks of:

The Soul's retaken moments —
When, Felon led along,
With shackles on the plumed feet,
And staples, in the Song.

I liked it even when I thought *plumed* was *plummed*. And I secretly hope *staples* means what we use it to mean now. Stapled Songs! It is a successful poem for me without the other kind of understanding. However, I'm not saying that I like to ride the energy, or the images. What I *am* trying to say is that there's an important way of getting to the *true* meaning which may elude analysis. I *do* understand what *the soul's bandaged moments means.* It *means* the soul's bandaged moments.

I am *not* choosing between understanding and not understanding in these poems. But I *am* trying to suggest that *sometimes* there is a legitimate way her poems communicate without needing to be decoded into logic. It is important to me and to my own work to remember that in even the greatest poetry there is often the other kind of meaning.

Anyhow, this was true for me when I read Emily Dickinson at the very beginning of my knowing about poetry. It helped me to know there is a magic at the center of poetry, a way of meaning that is different from logic. So that from the first I had the encouragement to trust my instinct in preferring metaphor to simile, image to abstractions, to trust the intuitive more than the rational in my poetry.

Of course, I am not saying this should be true for all poets. Not even for all *her* poetry, but it has *always* been how I work. Or part of how I work. And it is so partly because of Emily Dickinson. She taught me there is a difficult, hard-to-understand, hard-to-translate, hard-to-write-about-or-explain place. I knew I had that in me also. But at the same time, I learned that the difficulty or obscurity in her poetry is not because she uses images to hide a secret. Rather, it is an attempt to say something that cannot be said in a simple or direct way.

One of the amazing things about Emily Dickinson for me, when I first read her and also now, is the presence of thought in her poetry which thinks like a poem does. I remember how as a child I could almost easily understand those thoughts without understanding. Or maybe I should say understanding it *before* understanding. I remember clearly saying at that early time: "then I will have to write my own poetry. A poetry of a kind I cannot understand in the same way I cannot understand *hers.*"

Understanding before understanding led me and led me toward what is magical in poetry. Maybe that is one of the most valuable things about the poetry of Emily Dickinson: to teach that there is something in poetry which cannot be handled, cannot be studied scientifically. Can only be approached, can only be honored. We can go up to the border. Can name what is there. Can know a lot. But we must remember that it is still country on the other side of the border and there are things there which we do not have good names for. We must remember there is a kind of safety in trusting the unknown. There are things beyond the border which are invisible, but if we are patient and listen hard, we can sometimes hear them.

Galway Kinnell

The Deconstruction of Emily Dickinson

1994

The lecture had ended when I came in,
and the professor was answering questions.
I do not know what he had been doing with her
poetry, but now he was speaking of her
as a victim of reluctant male publishers.
When the questions dwindled, I put up my hand.
I said the ignorant meddling of the Springfield *Daily Republican*
and the hidebound response of literary men,
and the gulf between the poetic wishfulness
then admired and her own harsh knowledge,
had let her see that her poems
would not be understood in her time;
and therefore, passionate to publish,
she vowed not to publish again. I said
I would recite a version of her vow,

> Publication – is the Auction
> Of the mind of Man –

But before I could, the professor broke in.
"Yes," he said, "'the Auction' — 'auction,' from *augere, auctum,* to augment, to author . . ."
"Let's hear the poem!" "The poem!" several women,
who at such a moment are more outspoken than men, shouted,
but I kept still and he kept going.
"In *auctum* the economy of the signifier is split, revealing an unconscious collusion in the bourgeois commodification of consciousness. While our author says 'no,' the unreified text says 'yes,' yes?"
He kissed his lips together and turned to me
saying, "Now, may we hear the poem?"
I waited a moment for full effect.
Without rising to my feet, I said,
"Professor, to understand Dickinson
it may not always be necessary to uproot her words.
Why not, first, try *listening* to her?
Loyalty forbids me to recite her poem now."
No, I didn't say that — I realized
she would want me to finish him off with one wallop.
So I said, "Professor, I thought you
would welcome the words of your author.
I see you prefer to hear yourself speak."
No, I held back — for I could hear her

urging me to put outrage into my voice
and substance into my argument.
I stood up so that everyone might see
the derision in my smile. "Professor," I said,
"you live in Amherst at the end of the twentieth century.
For you 'auction' means a quaint event
where somebody coaxes out the bids
on butter churns on a summer Saturday.
Forget etymology, this is history.
In Amherst in 1860 'auction' meant
the slave auction, you dope!"
Well, I didn't say that either,
although I have said them all,
many times, in the middle of the night.
In reality, I stood up and recited
like a schoolboy called upon in class.
My voice gradually weakened, and the women
who had called out for the poem
now looked as though they were thinking
of errands to be done on the way home.
When I finished, the professor smiled.
"Thank you. So, what at first some of us may have taken as
    a simple outcry, we all now see is an ambivalent, self-
    subversive text."
As people got up to go, I moved
into that sanctum within me where Emily
sometimes speaks a verse, and listened
for a sign of how she felt, such as,
"Thanks – Sweet – countryman –
for wanting – to Sing out – of Me –
after all that Humbug." But she was silent.

CASEBOOK ON ROBERT FROST

This casebook on Robert Frost begins with a perceptive interview with the poet by Rose C. Feld that appeared in the New York Times Book Review *in 1923. The next commentary is Frost's introduction to his* Selected Poems *of 1939; although he did not consider himself a critic, he did express opinions about his poetic methods in the introductions to his collections. Fellow poet Robert Lowell's sonnet suggests the more complicated reality behind the figure of the genial, wise New England bard Frost presented to his public. The Nobel Prize–winning poet Joseph Brodsky's discerning response to the profoundly American poetry of Frost is from the perspective of someone who grew up in the Soviet Union and moved to the United States as an adult.*

Robert Frost at his writing desk. (Reprinted by permission of Dartmouth College Library.)

Finally, Philip L. Gerber looks at Frost's "After Apple-Picking" (p. 1036) as an example of the poet's "honest duplicity," a characteristic he finds essential to all poetry.

ROSE C. FELD

An Interview with Robert Frost

1923

Have you ever seen a sensitive child enter a dark room, fearful of the enveloping blackness, yet more than half ashamed of the fear? That is the way Robert Frost, poet, approached the interview arranged for him with the writer. He didn't want to come, he was half afraid of coming, and he was ashamed of the fear of meeting questions.

He was met at his publisher's office at the request of his friends there. "Come and get him, please," they said. "He is a shy person — a gentle and a sensitive person — and the idea of knocking at your doors, saying, 'Here I am, come to be interviewed,' will make him run and hide." The writer came and got him.

All the way down Fifth Avenue for ten or fifteen blocks he smiled often and talked rapidly to show that he was at ease and confident. But he was not. One could see the child telling itself not to be afraid.

Arrived at the house, he took the chair offered him and sat down rigidly. Still he smiled.

"Go ahead," he said. "Ask me the questions. Let's get at it."

"There are no questions — no specific questions. Suppose you just ramble on about American poetry, about poets, about men of the past and men of the present, about where we are drifting or where we are marching. Just talk."

He looked nonplused. The rigid smile gave way to one of relief and relaxation.

"You mean to say that you're not going to fire machine-gun questions at me and expect me to answer with skyrocketing repartee. Well, I wish I'd known. Well."

The brown hand opened up on the arms of the chair and the graying head leaned back. Robert Frost began to talk. He talked of some of the poets of the past, and in his quiet, gentle manner exploded the first bombshell. He exploded many others.

"One of the real American poets of yesterday," he said, "was Longfellow. No, I am not being sarcastic. I mean it. It is the fashion nowadays to make fun of him. I come across this pose and attitude with people I meet socially, with men and women I meet in the classrooms of colleges where I teach. They laugh at his gentleness, at his lack of worldliness, at his detachment from the world and the meaning thereof.

"When and where has it been written that a poet must be a club-swinging warrior, a teller of barroom tales, a participant of unspeakable experiences? That, today, apparently is the stamp of poetic integrity. I hear people speak of men who are writing today, and their eyes light up with a deep glow of satisfaction when they can mention some putrid bit of gossip about them. 'He writes such lovely things,' they say, and in the next breath add, half worshipfully, 'He lives such a terrible life.'

"I can't see it. I can't see that a man must needs have his feet plowing through unhealthy mud in order to appreciate more fully the glowing splendor of the clouds. I can't see that a man must fill his soul with sick and miserable experiences, self-imposed and self-inflicted, and greatly enjoyed, before he can sit down and write a lyric of strange and compelling beauty. Inspiration doesn't lie in the mud; it lies in the clean and wholesome life of the ordinary man.

"Maybe I am wrong. Maybe there is something wrong with me. Maybe I haven't the power to feel, to appreciate and live the extremes of dank living and beautiful inspiration.

"Men have told me, and perhaps they are right, that I have no 'straddle.' That is the term they use: I have no straddle. That means that I cannot spread out far enough to live in filth and write in the treetops. I can't. Perhaps it is because I am so ordinary. I like the middle way, as I like to talk to the man who walks the middle way with me.

"I have given thought to this business of straddling, and there's always seemed to me to be something wrong with it, something tricky. I see a man riding two horses, one foot on the back of one horse, one foot on the other. One horse pulls one way, the other a second. His straddle is wide, Heaven help him, but it seems to me that before long it's going to hurt him. It isn't the natural way, the normal way, the powerful way to ride. It's a trick." . . .

"People do me the honor to say that I am truly a poet of America. They point to my New England background, to the fact that my paternal ancestor came here some time in the sixteen hundreds. So much is true, but what they either do not know or do not say is that my mother was an immigrant. She came to these shores from Edinburgh in an old vessel that docked at Philadelphia. But she felt the spirit of America and became part of it before she even set her foot off the boat.

"She used to tell about it when I was a child. She was sitting on the deck of the boat waiting for orders to come ashore. Near her some workmen were loading Delaware peaches on to the ship. One of them picked out one of them and dropped it into her lap.

"'Here, take that,' he said. The way he said it and the spirit in which he gave it left an indelible impression on her mind.

"'It was a bonny peach,' she used to say, 'and I didn't eat it. I kept it to show my friends.'

"Looking back would I say that she was less the American than my father? No. America meant something live and real and virile to her. He took it for granted. He was a Fourth-of-July American, by which I mean that he rarely failed to celebrate in the way considered proper and appropriate. She, however, was a year-around American.

"I had an aunt in New England who used to talk long and loud about the foreigners who were taking over this country. Across the way from her house stood a French Catholic church which the new people of the village had put up. Every Sunday my aunt would stand at her window, behind the curtain, and watch the steady stream of men and women pouring into church. Her mouth would twist in the way that seems peculiar to dried-up New Englanders, and she would say, 'My soul!' Just that: 'My soul!'

"All the disapproval and indignation and disgust were concentrated in these two words. She never could see why I laughed at her, but it did strike me very funny for her to be calling upon her soul for help when this mass of industrious people were going to church to save theirs." . . .

"Today almost every man who writes poetry confesses his debt to Whitman. Many have gone very much further than Whitman would have traveled with them. They are the people who believe in wide straddling.

"I, myself, as I said before, don't like it for myself. I do not write free verse; I write blank verse. I must have the pulse beat of rhythm, I like to hear it beating under the things I write.

"That doesn't mean I do not like to read a bit of free verse occasionally. I do. It sometimes succeeds in painting a picture that is very clear and startling. It's good as something created momentarily for its sudden startling effect; it hasn't the qualities, however, of something lastingly beautiful.

"And sometimes my objection to it is that it's a pose. It's not honest. When a man sets out consciously to tear up forms and rhythms and measures, then he is not interested in giving you poetry. He just wants to perform; he wants to show you his tricks. He will get an effect; nobody will deny that, but it is not a harmonious effect.

"Sometimes it strikes me that the free-verse people got their idea from incorrect proof sheets. I have had stuff come from the printers with lines half left out or positions changed about. I read the poems as they stood, distorted and half finished, and I confess I get a rather pleasant sensation from them. They make a sort of nightmarish half-sense."

As he rose to go, he said, "I am an ordinary man, I guess. That's what's the trouble with me. I like my school and I like my farm and I like people. Just ordinary, you see."

Robert Frost

The Figure a Poem Makes 1939

Abstraction is an old story with the philosophers, but it has been like a new toy in the hands of the artists of our day. Why can't we have any one quality of poetry we choose by itself? We can have in thought. Then it will go hard if we can't in practice. Our lives for it.

Granted no one but a humanist much cares how sound a poem is if it is only *a* sound. The sound is the gold in the ore. Then we will have the sound out alone and dispense with the inessential. We do till we make the discovery that the object in writing poetry is to make all poems sound as different as possible from each other, and the resources for that of vowels, consonants, punctuation, syntax, words, sentences, meter are not enough. We need the help of context — meaning — subject matter. That is the greatest help towards variety. All that can be done with words is soon told. So also with meters — particularly in our language where there are virtually but two, strict iambic and loose iambic. The ancients with many were still poor if they depended on meters for all tune. It is painful to watch our sprung-rhythmists straining at the point of omitting one short from a foot for relief from monotony. The possibilities for tune from the dramatic tones of meaning struck across the rigidity of a limited meter are endless. And we are back in poetry as merely one more art of having something to say, sound or unsound. Probably better if sound, because deeper and from wider experience.

Then there is this wildness whereof it is spoken. Granted again that it has an equal claim with sound to being a poem's better half. If it is a wild tune, it is a poem. Our problem then is, as modern abstractionists, to have the wildness pure; to be wild with nothing to be wild about. We bring up as aberrationists, giving way to undirected associations and kicking ourselves from one chance suggestion to another in all directions as of a hot afternoon in the life of a grasshopper. Theme alone can steady us down. Just as the first mystery was how a poem could have a tune in such a straightness as meter, so the second mystery is how a poem can have wildness and at the same time a subject that shall be fulfilled.

It should be of the pleasure of a poem itself to tell how it can. The figure a poem makes. It begins in delight and ends in wisdom. The figure is the same as for love. No one can really hold that the ecstasy should be static and stand still in one place. It begins in delight, it inclines to the impulse, it assumes direction with the first line laid down, it runs a course of lucky events, and ends in a clarification of life — not necessarily a great clarification, such as sects and cults are founded on, but in a momentary stay against confusion. It has denouement. It has an outcome that though unforeseen was predestined from the first image of the original mood — and indeed from the very mood. It is but a trick poem and no poem at all if the best of it was thought of first and saved for the last. It finds its own name as it goes and discovers the best waiting for it in some final phrase at once wise and sad — the happy-sad blend of the drinking song.

No tears in the writer, no tears in the reader. No surprise for the writer, no surprise for the reader. For me the initial delight is in the surprise of remembering something I didn't know I knew. I am in a place, in a situation, as if I had materialized from cloud or risen out of the ground. There is a glad recognition of the long lost and the rest follows. Step by step the wonder of unexpected supply keeps growing. The impressions most useful to my purpose seem always those I was unaware of and so made no note of at the time when taken, and the conclusion is come to that like giants we are always hurling experience ahead of us to pave the future with against the day when we may want to strike a line of purpose across it for somewhere. The line will have the more charm for not being mechanically straight. We enjoy the straight crookedness of a good walking stick. Modern instruments of precision are being used to make things crooked as if by eye and hand in the old days.

I tell how there may be a better wildness of logic than of inconsequence. But the logic is backward, in retrospect, after the act. It must be more felt than seen ahead like prophecy. It must be a revelation, or a series of revelations, as much for the poet as for the reader. For it to be that there must have been the greatest freedom of the material to move about in it and to establish relations in it regardless of time and space, previous relation, and everything but affinity. We prate of freedom. We call our schools free because we are not free to stay away from them till we are sixteen years of age. I have given up my democratic prejudices and now willingly set the lower classes free to be completely taken care of by the upper classes. Political freedom is nothing to me. I bestow it right and left. All I would keep for myself is the freedom of my material — the condition of body and mind now and then to summons aptly from the vast chaos of all I have lived through.

Scholars and artists thrown together are often annoyed at the puzzle of where they differ. Both work from knowledge; but I suspect they differ most importantly in the way their knowledge is come by. Scholars get theirs with conscientious thoroughness along projected lines of logic; poets theirs cavalierly and as it happens in and out of books. They stick to nothing deliberately, but let what will stick to them like burrs where they walk in the fields. No acquirement is on assignment, or even self-assignment. Knowledge of the second kind is much more available in the wild free ways of wit and art. A schoolboy may be defined as one who can tell you what he knows in the order in which he learned it. The artist must value himself as he snatches a thing from some previous order in time and space into a new order with not so much as a ligature clinging to it of the old place where it was organic.

More than once I should have lost my soul to radicalism if it had been the originality it was mistaken for by its young converts. Originality and initiative are what I ask for my country. For myself the originality need be no more than the freshness of a poem run in the way I have described: from delight to wisdom. The figure is the same as for love. Like a piece of ice on a hot stove the poem must ride on its own melting. A poem may be worked over once it is in being, but may not be worried into being. Its most precious quality will remain its having run itself and carried away the poet with it. Read it a hundred times: it will forever keep its freshness as a petal keeps its fragrance. It can never lose its sense of a meaning that once unfolded by surprise as it went.

Robert Lowell

On Robert Frost

1969

Robert Frost at midnight, the audience gone
to vapor, the great act laid on the shelf in mothballs,
his voice musical, raw and raw — he writes in the flyleaf:
"Robert Lowell from Robert Frost, his friend in the art."
"Sometimes I feel too full of myself," I say.
And he, misunderstanding, "When I am low,
I stray away. My son wasn't your kind. The night
we told him Merrill Moore° would come to treat him,
he said, 'I'll kill him first.' One of my daughters thought things,
knew every male she met was out to make her;
the way she dresses, she couldn't make a whorehouse."
And I, "Sometimes I'm so happy I can't stand myself."
And he, "When I am too full of joy, I think
how little good my health did anyone near me."

Joseph Brodsky

On Grief and Reason

1994

I should tell you that what follows is a spinoff of a seminar given four years ago at the Collège International de Philosophie, in Paris. Hence a certain breeziness to the pace; hence, too, the paucity of biographical material — irrelevant, in my view, to the analysis of a work of art in general, and particularly

Merrill Moore: Poet and psychiatrist. Frost's son later committed suicide.

where a foreign audience is concerned. In any case, the pronoun "you" in these pages stands for those ignorant of or poorly acquainted with the lyrical and narrative strengths of the poetry of Robert Frost. But, first, some basics.

Robert Frost was born in 1874 and died in 1963, at the age of eighty-eight. One marriage, six children; fairly strapped when young; farming, and, later, teaching jobs in various schools. Not much travelling until late in his life; he mostly resided on the East Coast, in New England. If biography accounts for poetry, this one should have resulted in none. Yet he published nine books of poems; the second one, "North of Boston," which came out when he was forty, made him famous. This was in 1914.

After that, his sailing was a bit smoother. But literary fame is not exactly popularity. As it happens, it took the Second World War to bring Frost's work to the general public's notice. In 1943, the Council on Books in Wartime distributed fifty thousand copies of Frost's "Come In" to United States troops stationed overseas, as a morale-builder. By 1955, his "Selected Poems" was in its fourth edition, and one could speak of his poetry's having acquired national standing.

It did. In the course of nearly five decades following the publication of "North of Boston," Frost reaped every possible reward and honor an American poet can get; shortly before Frost's death, John Kennedy invited him to read a poem at the Inauguration ceremony. Along with recognition naturally came a great deal of envy and resentment, a substantial contribution to which emerged from the pen of Frost's own biographer. And yet both the adulation and resentment had one thing in common: a nearly total misconception of what Frost was all about.

He is generally regarded as the poet of the countryside, of rural settings — as a folksy, crusty, wisecracking old gentleman farmer, generally of positive disposition. In short, as American as apple pie. To be fair, he greatly enhanced this notion by projecting precisely this image of himself in numerous public appearances and interviews throughout his career. I suppose it wasn't that difficult for him to do, for he had those qualities in him as well. He was indeed a quintessential American poet; it is up to us, however, to find out what that quintessence is made of, and what the term "American" means as applied to poetry and, perhaps, in general.

In 1959, at a banquet thrown in New York on the occasion of Robert Frost's eighty-fifth birthday, the most prominent literary critic at that time, Lionel Trilling, rose and declared that Robert Frost was "a terrifying poet." That, of course, caused a certain stir, but the epithet was well chosen.

Now, I want you to make the distinction here between terrifying and tragic. Tragedy, as you know, is always a fait accompli, whereas terror always has to do with anticipation, with man's recognition of his own negative potential — with his sense of what he is capable of. And it is the latter that was Frost's forte, not the former. In other words, his posture is radically different from the Continental tradition of the poet as tragic hero. And that difference alone makes him — for want of a better term — American.

On the surface, he looks very positively predisposed toward his surroundings — particularly toward nature. His fluency, his "being versed in country things" alone can produce this impression. However, there is a difference between the way a European perceives nature and the way an American does. Addressing this difference, W. H. Auden, in his short essay on Frost, suggests something to the effect that when a European conceives of confronting nature, he walks out of his cottage or a little inn, filled with either friends or family, and goes for an evening stroll. If he encounters a tree, it's a tree made familiar by history, to which it's been a witness. This or that king sat underneath it, laying down this or that law — something of that sort. A tree stands there rustling, as it were, with allusions. Pleased and somewhat pensive, our man, refreshed but unchanged by that encounter, returns to his inn or cottage, finds his friends or family absolutely intact, and proceeds to have a good, merry time. Whereas when an American walks out of his house and encounters a tree it is a meeting of equals. Man and tree face each other in their respective primal power, free of references: neither has a past, and as to whose future is greater, it is a toss-up. Basically, it's epidermis meeting bark. Our man returns to his cabin in a state of bewilderment, to say the least, if not in actual shock or terror.

Now, this is obviously a romantic caricature, but it accentuates the features, and that's what I am after here. In any case, the second point could be safely billed as the gist of Robert Frost's nature poetry. Nature for this poet is neither friend nor foe, nor is it the backdrop for human drama; it is this poet's terrifying self-portrait.

PHILIP L. GERBER

On Frost's "After Apple-Picking" *1966*

As an illustration of the "honest duplicity" of Frost's better verses, the early lyric "After Apple-Picking," although often analyzed, serves ideally. Some readers admire this poem because the deceptive simplicity of its surface picture has charmed them with a rich vision of idyllic New England harvest. Others treasure the poem as exemplifying the truth of John Ciardi's reminder that "a poem is never about what it seems to be about." . . .

Among the available interpretations of Frost's lyric, perhaps the most lucid and readily accessible is that based upon the Emersonian pattern of natural analogies: "things admit of being used as symbols because nature is a symbol, in the whole, and in every part." Emerson's doctrine of analogy between human life and the seasons, for instance, in which spring, summer, fall, and winter parallel the various ages of man, is seconded by Thoreau, who observed the same analogy operating within the span of the day: "The phenomena of the year take place every day in a pond on a small scale. Every morning, generally speaking, the shallow water is being warmed more rapidly than the deep, though it may not be made so warm after all, and every evening it is being cooled more rapidly until the morning. The day is an epitome of the year. The night is the winter, the morning and evening are the spring and fall, and the noon is summer." Building upon the suggestions of Emerson and Thoreau, and noting the centrality that Frost has afforded both to the yearly cycle and to the daily span, the reader begins to absorb the implications radiating from "After Apple-Picking."

On the surface of the poem, however, all seems serenely concrete and straightforward. An apple grower, eager for his awaited harvest of ripe red russets, has worked for days against the imminent arrival of autumn frost. Freezing temperatures, signs of which are already apparent, will close out his opportunities to profit fully from his year's labor. In tending his trees from springtime bud through summer growth, the man's toil has been buoyed by a tremendous stimulus of anticipation. But now the exertion of the harvest itself has wearied him. Tedium has set in. He knows he will not be allowed to pick every apple on his trees, nor does he expect to. Much more realistic now than in the spring and summer, he possibly no longer even desires to account for every piece of fruit.

The harvest has taught the apple-grower something of value. He has attempted to do more than one man can hope to do alone in a season. His excitement — as well as his weariness — has caused many apples to fall to earth. Bruised, ruined, spiked on stubble, these become relatively worthless. The energies of man and nature lavished upon bringing them to perfection seem to have been poured out for naught. Yet such accidents are to be expected in the normal course of any human scheme. It is natural also that some fruit will necessarily be left to freeze as winter closes in; for this is real, not ideal, harvest.

Sleepiness of late autumn pervades the air. All around the harvester nature is preparing herself for rest: trees are defoliating as the summer sap recedes; woodchucks are hibernating, snug in readied burrows. The harvester himself lies in bed after what he realizes may be the very last day of his harvest. He is tired to the bone, leaden-limbed; but ironically he is too fatigued to pass easily into his exhausted and well-earned slumber. His eyes swim. His feet ache from standing on the ladder rung for hours at a time. All ambition spent, he is ready to call a halt and take his rest, knowing that — like anyone totally committed to a task — he will continue the harvest of apples even in his sleep.

So accurately and so economically does Frost capture the essence of apple harvest that one cannot be faulted for finding adequate satisfaction within his portrayal of the apple-picking itself, needing no more. The sights and sounds are all there. Every sensation is recorded vigorously. No one who has used a ladder or labored long hours driven by desire, or nodded in the heady drowsiness of Indian summer, is likely to forget soon the achievement of this verse. As rural idyll, it gratifies.

Even so, the simple application of natural analogies to the poem discloses an entirely new dimension, and it does so without exertion or distortion. The explicit meaning of the poem communicates with the clarity of crystal. Just as clearly does the metaphor, camouflaged only slightly by the impressive veneer of sensory detail, make itself felt. Just as every line, detail, and word contributes to transmitting the essence of the harvest experience, so does every aspect of the poem fall into place as well within the analogies and press for their development.

One notes first that Frost selects as his setting both the night of the daily span and the winter of the yearly cycle. Either would guide the mind toward a prospect of death, but the conjunction of night and winter renders that prospect unmistakable. Numerous references to drowsiness and sleep, to strangeness of sight, and to the harvest itself all reinforce the parallel between the terminations of day, season, and existence. The span of life is embraced within the curve of season, spring to winter. But what completes the circle? Ordinarily spring again, returning after winter to bring rebirth. Hints emanate from at least two references and suggest that the resurrection of spring is probable. The first comes with an unobtrusive gesture in the poem's second line, its seemingly gratuitous reference to the ladder's pointing "toward heaven still." Without straining the issue, the word *heaven* elicits subconscious responses involving death and immortality. The second hint occurs at the finish, as the verse concludes with a whimsical contemplation of the woodchuck's sleep, the hibernation, the little imitation of death which also will terminate in springtime "resurrection." And obviously even "just some human sleep" implies a reawakening.

Snuggling within the curve of the natural cycles is another arc, that shaped by the harvest process fulfilling itself. The harvest is awaited expectantly, with nerves atingle for rosy signals of ripeness to appear on the fruit. With the "russet showing clear," the picker goes to work, heady with grandiose visions of a bumper crop gathered to the last plump apple. The elixir of enthusiasm is steadily diluted. First come endless hours of labor. Then a weariness engulfs what energy is yet unspent. Desire wanes. Then a realization grows that the original goal will not be reached without compromise forced by circumstance. Surprisingly, it no longer seems so very critical to finish. Finally comes the letting-go, first with the hands, then with the mind, but never with the heart. The apple-picker, a sadder but wiser man, relinquishes his task altogether. Now is the time to rest from toil, to accept the verdict on his performance, to listen to himself harshly judging himself.

This harvest action, complete in itself, slips so neatly into the convenient circle created by the natural symbolism, and the whole tallies so comfortably with the surface events of the poem, that the reader arrives at the final period in a euphoria of "rightness." Surface and symbol coincide neatly.

How fortunate that Frost resisted any impulse he may have felt to press his poem into the didactic mold. A phrase or two would have shaped the verse into a substantiation of the orthodox religious view — and would have done untold violence to the lyrical purity so far sustained. But he fortuitously elected instead to suggest, to hint. Whatever sleep it is, only a woodchuck, he says fancifully, could tell for sure. The poem thus ends in deliberate ambiguity. But if a reader chooses to see "After Apple-Picking" as an allegory of man's life ascending from the eager grasping of youth to the letting-go of age, Frost will not object. Nor will he frown upon his poem viewed as a moral tale of the world having its inevitable way with human ambition. Let there be no mistake; all poetry is hinting — is metaphor. Poetry is the legitimate means of saying one thing and meaning another, an "honest duplicity."

CASEBOOK ON LANGSTON HUGHES

This casebook begins with a tribute by Hughes to his beloved Harlem. The excerpt is from one of the Simple stories Hughes wrote for a Harlem newspaper in which he used the character of a Harlem Everyman, Jessie Semple — nicknamed "Simple" — as a foil for his own attitudes and opinions. The next selection is a reminiscence published in The Crisis, *an African American journal, in 1926 by the writer Jessie Fauset, a contemporary of Hughes and like him a member of the generation of writers, artists, musicians, and critics identified as the Harlem Renaissance. There follows a review of Hughes's autobiography,* The Big Sea *(1940), by Richard Wright, the*

Langston Hughes as photographed by photojournalist Gordon Parks in 1943. (Reproduced from the collections of the Library of Congress.)

most successful and controversial African American writer of the 1930s. A savagely realistic novelist and poet, Wright might have been expected to be critical of Hughes's deceptively softer and more accommodating style. Wright, however, was perceptive enough to see that in his writing Hughes "bends, but he never breaks." Finally, Arnold Rampersad, author of the first extended biography of Hughes, comments in his introduction to the collected poems about Hughes's role as a folk poet.

LANGSTON HUGHES

A Toast to Harlem 1950

Quiet can seem unduly loud at times. Since nobody at the bar was saying a word during a lull in the bright blues-blare of the Wishing Well's usually overworked juke box, I addressed my friend Simple.

"Since you told me last night you are an Indian, explain to me how it is you find yourself living in a furnished room in Harlem, my brave buck, instead of on a reservation?"

"I am a colored Indian," said Simple.

"In other words, a Negro."

"A Black Foot Indian, daddy-o, not a red one. Anyhow, Harlem is the place I always did want to be. And if it wasn't for landladies, I would be happy. That's a fact! I love Harlem."

"What is it you love about Harlem?"

"It's so full of Negroes," said Simple. "I feel like I got protection."

"From what?"

"From white folks," said Simple. "Furthermore, I like Harlem because it belongs to me."

"Harlem does not belong to you. You don't own the houses in Harlem. They belong to white folks."

"I might not own 'em," said Simple, "but I live in 'em. It would take an atom bomb to get me out."

"Or a depression," I said.

"I would not move for no depression. No, I would not go back down South, not even to Baltimore. I am in Harlem to stay! You say the houses ain't mine. Well, the sidewalk is — and don't nobody push me off. The cops don't even say, 'Move on,' hardly no more. They learned something from them Harlem riots. They used to beat your head right in public, but now they only beat it after they get you down to the stationhouse. And they don't beat it then if they think you know a colored congressman."

"Harlem has a few Negro leaders," I said.

"Elected by my *own* vote," said Simple. "Here I ain't scared to vote — that's another thing I like about Harlem. I also like it because we've got subways and it does not take all day to get downtown, neither are you Jim Crowed° on the way. Why, Negroes is running some of these subway trains.

Jim Crowed: Jim Crow laws were the "legal" foundation for racial discrimination in the southern states.

This morning I rode the A Train down to 34th Street. There were a Negro driving it, making ninety miles a hour. That cat *were really driving* that train! Every time he flew by one of them local stations looks like he was saying, 'Look at me! This train is mine!' That cat were gone, ole man. Which is another reason why I like Harlem! Sometimes I run into Duke Ellington on 125th Street and I say, 'What you know there, Duke?' Duke says, 'Solid, ole man.' He does not know me from Adam, but he speaks. One day I saw Lena Horne coming out of the Hotel Theresa and I said, 'Huba! Huba!' Lena smiled. Folks is friendly in Harlem. I feel like I got the world in a jug and the stopper in my hand! So drink a toast to Harlem!"

Simple lifted his glass of beer:

"Here's to Harlem!
They say Heaven is Paradise.
If Harlem ain't Heaven,
Then a mouse ain't mice!"

JESSIE FAUSET

Meeting Langston Hughes

1926

Very perfect is the memory of my first literary acquaintance with Langston Hughes. In the unforgettable days when we were publishing *The Brownies' Book* we had already appreciated a charming fragile conceit which read:

Out of the dust of dreams,
Fairies weave their garments;
Out of the purple and rose of old memories,
They make purple wings.
No wonder we find them such marvelous things.

Then one day came "The Negro Speaks of Rivers." I took the beautiful dignified creation to Dr. Du Bois and said: "What colored person is there, do you suppose, in the United States who writes like that and yet is unknown to us?" And I wrote and found him to be a Cleveland high school graduate who had just gone to live in Mexico. Already he had begun to assume that remote, so elusive quality which permeates most of his work. Before long we had the pleasure of seeing the work of the boy, whom we had sponsored, copied, and recopied in journals far and wide. "The Negro Speaks of Rivers" even appeared in translation in a paper printed in Germany.

Not very long after Hughes came to New York and not long after that he began to travel and to set down the impressions, the pictures, which his sensitive mind had registered of new forms of life and living in Holland, in France, in Spain, in Italy, and in Africa.

His poems are warm, exotic, and shot through with color. Never is he preoccupied with form. But this fault, if it is one, has its corresponding virtue, for it gives his verse, which almost always is imbued with the essence of poetry, the perfection of spontaneity. And one characteristic which makes for this bubbling-like charm is the remarkable objectivity which he occasionally achieves, remarkable for one so young, and a first step toward philosophy. Hughes has seen a great deal of the world, and this has taught him that nothing matters much but life. Its forms and aspects may vary, but living is the essential thing. Therefore make no bones about it, — "make the most of what you may spend."

Some consciousness of this must have been in him even before he began to wander for he sent us as far back as 1921:

> *"Shake your brown feet, honey,*
> *Shake your brown feet, chile,*
> *Shake your brown feet, honey,*
> *Shake 'em swift and wil' — . . .*
> *Sun's going down this evening —*
> *Might never rise no mo'.*
> *The sun's going down this very night —*
> *Might never rise no mo' —*
> *So dance with swift feet, honey,*
> *(The banjo's sobbing low . . .*
> *The sun's going down this very night —*
> *Might never rise no mo'."*

Now this is very significant, combining as it does the doctrine of the old Biblical exhortation, "eat, drink, and be merry for tomorrow ye die," Horace's "Carpe diem," the German "Freut euch des Lebens," and [Robert] Herrick's "Gather ye rosebuds while ye may." This is indeed a universal subject served Negro-style and though I am no great lover of any dialect I hope heartily that Mr. Hughes will give us many more such combinations.

Mr. Hughes is not always the calm philosopher; he has feeling a-plenty and is not ashamed to show it. He "loved his friend" who left him and so taken up is he with the sorrow of it all that he has no room for anger or resentment. While I do not think of him as a protagonist of color, — he is too much the citizen of the world for that — , I doubt if any one will ever write more tenderly, more understandingly, more humorously of the life of Harlem shot through as it is with mirth, abandon and pain. Hughes comprehends this life, has studied it and loved it. In one poem he has epitomized its essence:

> *Does a jazz-band ever sob?*
> *They say a jazz-band's gay.*
> *Yet as the vulgar dancers whirled*
> *And the wan night wore away,*
> *One said she heard the jazz-band sob*
> *When the little dawn was grey.*

Harlem is undoubtedly one of his great loves; the sea is another. Indeed all life is his love and his work a brilliant, sensitive interpretation of its numerous facets.

Richard Wright

A Review of The Big Sea

1940

The double role that Langston Hughes has played in the rise of a realistic literature among the Negro people resembles in one phase the role that Theodore Dreiser° played in freeing American literary expression from the restrictions of Puritanism. Not that Negro literature was ever Puritanical, but it was timid and vaguely lyrical and folkish. Hughes's early poems, "The Weary Blues" and "Fine Clothes to the Jew," full of irony and urban imagery, were greeted by a large section of the Negro reading public with suspicion and shock when they first appeared in the middle twenties. Since then the realistic position assumed by Hughes has become the dominant outlook of all those Negro writers who have something to say.

The other phase of Hughes's role has been, for the lack of a better term, that of a cultural ambassador. Performing his task quietly and almost casually, he has represented the Negroes' case, in his poems, plays, short stories and novels, at the court of world opinion. On the other hand he has brought the experiences of other nations within the orbit of the Negro writer by his translations from the French, Russian and Spanish.

How Hughes became this forerunner and ambassador can best be understood in the cameo sequences of his own life that he gives us in his sixth and latest book, *The Big Sea.* Out of his experiences as a seaman, cook, laundry worker, farm helper, bus boy, doorman, unemployed worker, have come his writings dealing with black gals who wore red stockings and black men who sang the blues all night and slept like rocks all day.

Unlike the sons and daughters of Negro "society," Hughes was not ashamed of those of his race who had to scuffle for their bread. The jerky transitions of his own life did not admit of his remaining in one place long enough to become a slave of prevailing Negro middle-class prejudices. So beneficial does this ceaseless movement seem to Hughes that he has made it one of his life principles: six months in one place, he says, is long enough to make one's life complicated. The result has been a range of artistic interest and expression possessed by no other Negro writer of his time.

Born in Joplin, Missouri, in 1902, Hughes lived in half a dozen Midwestern towns until he entered high school in Cleveland, Ohio, where he began to write poetry. His father, succumbing to that fit of disgust which overtakes so many self-willed Negroes in the face of American restrictions, went off to

---

Theodore Dreiser: American realistic novelist (1871–1945).

Mexico to make money and proceeded to treat the Mexicans just as the whites in America had treated him. The father yearned to educate Hughes and establish him in business. His favorite phrase was "hurry up," and it irritated Hughes so much that he fled his father's home.

Later he entered Columbia University, only to find it dull. He got a job on a merchant ship, threw his books into the sea and sailed for Africa. But for all his work, he arrived home with only a monkey and a few dollars, much to his mother's bewilderment. Again he sailed, this time for Rotterdam, where he left the ship and made his way to Paris. After an interval of hunger he found a job as a doorman, then as second cook in a night club, which closed later because of bad business. He went to Italy to visit friends and had his passport stolen. Jobless in an alien land, he became a beachcomber until he found a ship on which he could work his way back to New York.

The poems he had written off and on had attracted the attention of some of his relatives in Washington and, at their invitation, he went to live with them. What Hughes has to say about Negro "society" in Washington, relatives and hunger are bitter poems in themselves. While living in Washington, he won his first poetry prize; shortly afterwards Carl Van Vechten submitted a batch of his poems to a publisher.

The rest of *The Big Sea* is literary history, most of it dealing with the Negro renaissance, that astonishing period of prolific productivity among Negro artists that coincided with America's "golden age" of prosperity. Hughes writes of it with humor, urbanity and objectivity; one has the feeling that never for a moment was his sense of solidarity with those who had known hunger shaken by it. Even when a Park Avenue patron was having him driven about the streets of New York in her town car, he "felt bad because he could not share his new-found comfort with his mother and relatives." When the bubble burst in 1929, Hughes returned to the mood that seems to fit him best. He wrote of the opening of the Waldorf-Astoria:

> Now, won't that be charming when the last flophouse
> has turned you down this winter?

Hughes is tough; he bends but he never breaks, and he has carried on a manly tradition in literary expression when many of his fellow writers have gone to sleep at their posts.

ARNOLD RAMPERSAD

Langston Hughes as Folk Poet 1994

Hughes was often called, and sometimes called himself, a folk poet. To some people, this means that his work is almost artless and thus possibly beneath criticism. The truth indeed is that Hughes published many poems that are doggerel. To reach his primary audience — the black masses — he was prepared to write "down" to them. Some of the pieces in this volume were intended for public recitation mainly; some started as song lyrics. Like many democratic poets, such as William Carlos Williams, he believed that the full range of his poetry should reach print as soon as possible; poetry is a form of social action. However, for Hughes, as for all serious poets, the writing of poetry was virtually a sacred commitment. And while he wished to write no verse that was beyond the ability of the masses of people to understand, his poetry, in common with that of other committed writers, is replete with allusions that must be respected and understood if it is to be properly appreciated. To respect Hughes's work, above all one must respect the African American people and their culture, as well as the American people in general and their national culture.

If Hughes kept at the center of his art the hopes and dreams, as well as the actual lived conditions, of African Americans, he almost always saw these factors in the context of the eternally embattled but eternally inspiring American democratic tradition, even as changes in the world order, notably the collapse of colonialism in Africa, redefined the experiences of African peoples around the world. Almost always, too, Hughes attempted to preserve a sense of himself as a poet beyond race and other corrosive social pressures. By his absolute dedication to his art and to his social vision, as well as to his central audience, he fused his unique vision of himself as a poet to his production of art.

"What is poetry?" Langston Hughes asked near his death. He answered, "It is the human soul entire, squeezed like a lemon or a lime, drop by drop, into atomic words." He wanted no definition of the poet that divorced his art from the immediacy of life. "A poet is a human being," he declared. "Each human being must live within his time, with and for his people, and within the boundaries of his country." Hughes constantly called upon himself for the courage and the endurance necessary to write according to these beliefs. "Hang yourself, poet, in your own words," he urged all those who would take up the mantle of the poet and dare to speak to the world. "Otherwise, you are dead."

CASEBOOK ON SHARON OLDS

This casebook on Sharon Olds reflects the media's interest in the work of a contemporary poet, particularly a writer like Olds, whose work has attracted a wide readership. The first interview is from the online magazine Salon, *and she is being interviewed by academic critic Jonathan Holden. He is one of the first to discuss Olds's poetry in terms of the differences between masculine and feminine sensibilities. The second interview/article is from the* New York Times. *It is one of a series of portraits of creative writers which Dinitia Smith, a New York–based journalist, has contributed to the newspaper. In the third essay Ann Charters examines the seeming contradictions in Olds's modest manner and the strength of her public readings with a description of her recent appearance at a book fair in Florida.*

Sharon Olds. (Photo by David Bartolomi.)

Sharon Olds

From the Salon *Interview*

1999

Interviewer: Thanks for the tea. Which reminds me that I once read somewhere that you don't smoke or drink coffee, and that you consume very little alcohol. Why is that?

Olds: Well, one thing I'm really interested in, when I'm writing, is being accurate. If I am trying to describe something, I'd like to be able to get it right. Of course, what's "right" is different for every person. Sometimes what's accurate might be kind of mysterious. So I don't just mean mathematically accurate. But to get it right according to my vision. I think this is true for all artists. My senses are very important to me. I want to be able to describe accurately what I see and hear and smell. And what they say about those things not being good for one's longevity makes an impression on me also. So I did quit coffee and I did quit smoking. But I haven't managed that with drinking!

Interviewer: So many poets are associated with alcohol and other kinds of excess.

Olds: There are some fine books and essays about that. Lewis Hyde has written about alcoholism and poets and the role that society gives its writers — encouraging them to die [laughs]. And Donald Hall has wonderful, sobering stories about many of these poets. But I don't think anyone believes anymore that drugs and alcohol are good for writing, do they? I'm probably so out of it at my age that I don't know what people think. But I think that exercise and as much good health as one can enjoy is the best thing for writing.

Interviewer: I was even more surprised to read that you don't take a newspaper or watch television.

Olds: It's true, but it's kind of a different issue. At one point I took on a new job, and I just didn't have time to do anything but work. [Olds was the director of the Graduate Creative Writing Program at NYU from 1989 to 1991.] So I figured that for a year, just for the first year of this job, I would not watch TV, I wouldn't read a newspaper, I wouldn't read a book, I wouldn't go hear any music, I wouldn't do any of that kind of thing. Just so I'd have enough time. I was very afraid that I wouldn't be able to do this job well. And the time never came back. But there are problems connected with this — with keeping informed about what's happening in the world. So I try to look at the front page whenever I'm walking by a newsstand. And people talk about what's happening, so I get a certain amount of information that way. It might be a bad thing, not to know what's going on in the world. I can't say I really approve of it. . . .

Interviewer: People who know your work well might be surprised to know that you have such a vigorous public life. Because your work is very focused and often kind of quiet. It's hard to imagine the narrator of one of your poems fending off multiple phone calls.

Olds: But don't you think that every single one of us is leading a harried life? We're all taking on too much, we're all asking too much of ourselves. We're all wishing we could do more, and therefore just doing more. So I don't think my life is different from anybody else's. Every poet I know — although there may be some I don't know who lead very different lives, who maybe live in the country and don't teach — tends to be just like the rest of us: just really busy, really overcommitted. We wouldn't necessarily see it in their poems. Because a poem is not written while running or while answering the phone. It's written in whatever minutes one has. Sometimes you have half an hour.

Interviewer: Can you write a poem in half an hour?

Olds: Forty-five minutes is much better [laughs] . . .

Interviewer: As accessible as your poetry can seem to be, there also seems to be an almost brutally direct emotional quality sometimes. There are some tough images.

Olds: I think that I am slowly improving in my ability to not be too melodramatic, to help the images have the right tenor. My first book came out when I was thirty-seven, so when I was finally able to speak as a writer my wish to not be silent was, in my early work, extreme. It's like someone, in baseball, who thinks that the ball is being thrown by a very strong arm from the outfield, and so she can't just land on home, she has to try to run way past it, practically into the dugout. Reading some of my earlier work, I get that sense of the need for too big a head of steam to be built up. It seems extreme to me at times, some of the imagery. That's part of why I'm not so sorry I'm a little behind in putting books together, because some of those rather crude images I can now maybe correct. It also might be that maybe I've used an image that is too mild, and I'll correct in the other direction. I don't want to imply that it's always going the other way. But my tendency was to be a little over the mark. And so I just really love now the possibility of getting it right.

Interviewer: Your new book contains several poems that are quite realistic in terms of their descriptions of sex. Is it difficult writing poetry about sex, not to fall into language that might seem clichéd?

Olds: I don't think that sex has been written about a lot in poetry. And I want to be able to write about any subject. There is a failure rate — there are subjects that are probably a lot harder to write about than others. I think that love is almost the hardest thing to write about. Not a general state of being in love, but a particular love for a particular person. Just one's taste for that one. And if you look at all the love poetry in our tradition, there isn't much that helps us know why that one. I'm just interested in human stuff like hate, love, sexual love, and sex. I don't see why not. It just seems to me if writers can assemble, in language, something that bears any relation to experience — especially important experience, experience we care about, moving and powerful experience — then it is worth trying. The opportunities for offense and failure are always aplenty. They lie all around us.

JONATHAN HOLDEN

The Dichotomy between Men's and Women's Writing

1991

The dichotomy between men's and women's writing, glaringly obvious in the domain of serious fiction, is also apparent in slightly different form in the differences that have evolved between male and female poetry in America. Although "realistic" in setting and characterization, much American male poetry tends to be what Wendell Berry° labels a poetry of "sensibility." By contrast, much female poetry, though often anguished and passionate, attempts to deal realistically with questions of history, ideology, and social and personal responsibility — to deal with ideas rather than "feelings" in an attempt to reveal, almost analytically, connections between the subjective life of an

Wendell Berry: American poet (b. 1934).

individual female and the objective political, economic, and personal facts which determine her situation.

Paradigmatic of this type of poetry at its best might be Sharon Olds's important collection *The Dead and the Living,* a book which was both the Lamont Poetry Selection for 1983 and a National Book Critics Circle Award winner. The confessional poems which comprise the strongest half of the book, poems replete with gritty journalistic detail, expose almost relentlessly the links between Olds's ostensibly safe, comfortable bourgeois life as a mother on the one hand and various unpleasant historical facts — the Holocaust, wars waged by male governments, imperialism, and oppression — on the other. The book is energized by Olds's agonized sense of responsibility at her *female* role as a bearer of children into a world in which, all too easily, they could find themselves being either victims or oppressors. By alternating between public events and poems about domestic, private life, Olds dramatizes how her own body — exemplary of the female body in its potentiality for birth — is located at the very nexus of history, of past and future, of public and private, of the dead and of the living, how as a mother one is drawn not just theoretically into history but into it *bodily* — that there is no shelter from it or from one's responsibility in it.

Dinitia Smith

The Creative Mind; The Examined Life, without Punctuation

1999

"Look at this," Sharon Olds said while flipping through her new poetry collection, *Blood, Tin, Straw,* to be published next month by Alfred A. Knopf.

"This is so awful," she said. "Omigod, it's all stories. I just can't believe it."

"Oh, I wish I were better," Ms. Olds said of her poems, which chronicle the daily life of a wife and mother not unlike herself. "Why not just keep a diary?" she asked, repeating a question from her critics.

"Why does this woman think anyone wants to read about her private life?" Ms. Olds asked. "I have a prejudice that narrative poetry is not as high an art as dense, mysterious, imagistic poetry." But then, she points out, one always admires the things one can't do oneself.

There is almost no major American poet whose work is as sexually explicit, and as intimately evocative of a distinct father, husband, and children as Ms. Olds, who is the New York State poet laureate and who won a National Book Critics Circle Award for 1984 for her collection *The Dead and the Living.* The critic Helen Vendler famously referred to her poems as pornographic. Ms. Olds has written poems about a son urinating, about a daughter on the brink of puberty. She is particularly known for her 1992 collection "The Father," which chronicles in pitiless detail the death of an abusive, alcoholic father from cancer.

She has also written many poems about making love to a husband. In her new collection, *The Spouses Waking Up in the Hotel Mirror,* one poem reads:

The man looked like himself, only more so,
his face lucent, his silence deep as if
inevitable, but the woman looked
like a different species from an hour before,
a sandhill crane or a heron, her eyes
skinned back, she looked insane with happiness.

Yet for all the autobiographical flavor of her work, to interview Sharon Olds is to play a wispy kind of cat-and-mouse game. She has agreed to cooperate, and yet she refuses to discuss her personal life. She will not discuss her children; she has a son and a daughter. She will not discuss the ending of her thirty-two-year marriage to a psychiatrist.

"It's such a pain," said Ms. Olds, fifty-six, apologizing when she refused to say even what her father's occupation was. "It makes me seem like such a sensitive person."

"I never thought anyone would read anything I'd written," she said. "If I'd known the number of readers I would have, I would have used a pseudonym."

One reason for the privacy is to protect her family, she said. "I promised I'd keep them out of this." She made a vow, she said, many years ago, not to talk about them: "Outing them is morally wicked." But in a way, the wall she forms around herself also enables her to continue to mine domestic life for the material of her art.

And besides, even though her poems have been called diaries, "I don't think of it as personal," she said.

"These are not messages in a bottle about me," said Ms. Olds. "No!"

She is often called a confessional poet, in the tradition of Robert Lowell, Sylvia Plath, and Anne Sexton. Her work has a robust sensuality, a delight in the physical that is almost Whitmanesque. She has made the minutiae of a woman's everyday life as valid a subject for poetry as the grand abstract themes that have preoccupied other poets.

Ann Charters

"Working the Room": Sharon Olds Reads Her Poetry at the Miami International Book Fair *1999*

On an early Saturday afternoon in November outside a large hotel in Miami, I noticed a slim, silent woman in a dark, ankle-length, belted raincoat and black high heels, standing quietly a few feet from me as I waited for the shuttle van to go to the Miami International Book Fair a mile away downtown. The sky was overcast, rain misting the driveway as the cabs drew up and departed with their passengers.

I was in Miami to appear on a panel of authors at the book fair later that afternoon, but I had decided to leave the hotel a couple of hours early so that I could hear the poet Sharon Olds. She was scheduled to appear in the main auditorium reading along with the poet Daniel Halpern, just before my panel.

I was told that 250 authors had been booked to appear during the week of the fair. I considered myself fortunate to have been given the chance to hear Olds read her poetry on the only day that I was in town.

Earlier that morning, I had ridden the shuttle van downtown to the fair for the first time to hear a stimulating talk by the playwright Edward Albee and his biographer Mel Gussow. Leaving the hotel at 9:30 A.M., the elderly man waiting beside me for the van had been very friendly. He introduced himself as a retired academic living in Arizona who wrote books about Hemingway and Fitzgerald. I had just come from a breakfast buffet at the Authors' Welcoming Lounge, where, over fresh muffins and coffee, I met a woman from South Carolina who told me that she was at the book fair to talk about her latest novel. While we were chatting, another woman joined us and identified herself as a sportswriter from Long Island who was researching a biography of the famous Dodgers pitcher Sandy Koufax.

Since all the writers I had met at the fair had been very gregarious, I decided that the quiet middle-aged woman in the long belted raincoat waiting with me for the afternoon van must be a librarian. Her blonde hair was braided and fastened to her head in a very intricate, tight pattern. She appeared to be in her middle-fifties, standing very still with her head averted, her eyes focused on something far away. We waited together in silence for nearly twenty minutes, each quietly watching the rain as it stopped and the clouds began to lighten. I decided not to try to begin a conversation. Clearly she liked the silence. When the van came, she got inside first, sitting in the farthest corner. I sat down in the empty front seat, beside the driver. No one spoke during the short trip downtown, and the woman and I went our separate ways at the fair.

Twenty minutes later, I took my seat in the auditorium, which was nearly full. The audience seemed to be composed equally of young people, many of them students wearing inexpensive, raffish clothes, burdened with bulging bookbags, and older retired men and women, mostly dressed in new-looking casual clothes and sporting an impressive variety of expensive gold watches, bracelets, and rings. The woman who had organized the fair introduced the New York poet and editor Daniel Halpern, a tall man with a round face under a mop of curly hair. Halpern read for half an hour, mostly poems about his love for his young daughter, which the audience enjoyed. Halpern's daughter looked to be about seven years old; she sat in the front row and ran to her father to exchange a warm hug as he stepped down from the stage.

Then it was time for Sharon Olds. Three rows in front of me, the woman in the long, dark raincoat who had ridden in the van with me stood up from her seat beside the empty chair where Halpern's daughter had been sitting. She draped the raincoat on the back of her chair, and I saw that under the coat she was dressed in a jacket, a blouse, a very short skirt, and sheer white tights. The audience burst into fresh applause as she climbed the stairs, holding a sheaf of papers in front of her. At the podium she put down the papers and took off her jacket, revealing a lot of white skin in a low cut, sleeveless blouse, perfect for the muggy Miami weather. She put the jacket carefully on a chair and finally turned to the audience, a pale, fully composed figure. She was my silent "librarian."

"I planned to read for seventeen minutes, because that was the amount of time I was told to prepare, so I chose seven poems, but I understand that we don't have quite that much time, so I'll do the best I can." As Olds began her reading, my first impression was of her authority at the podium. At first she made a few informal remarks about her pleasure listening to Halpern read his poetry about his daughter, and the joy she felt being with him and his family during the other readings they had done together that year.

Then Olds began to read her own work, mostly poems about her family, her voice slow and clear, each word distinct and coherent. Suddenly I realized that she was very different without her raincoat. On the stage Olds transformed herself into a skillful, passionately intense performer, uninhibitedly revealing her most private experiences to a collection of strangers.

Reading in front of an audience appeared to be a ritual that engaged her completely. Her voice was even and unhurried, crafting each poem anew in the air, making elegant patterns of language and meaning arise from the page as effortlessly as the mid-afternoon rain had misted on the oilslick covering the concrete driveway while we waited for the van outside the hotel. The audience in the auditorium followed her words with hushed concentration as she read each poem. Listening to Olds made us feel that we were joined in a communal experience charged with special meaning.

I cannot remember all the titles of the seven poems that Olds read. I should have written them down, but I was enjoying her reading so much — and was so delighted by my discovery that the woman whom I thought was a librarian was actually the poet I had come to hear — that I didn't take any notes. Nobody seated around me did. We wanted to enjoy Olds's reading as completely as she appeared to be enjoying her reading for us.

I especially remember the subject matter of two of the poems. One was "At the Bay," from Olds's latest book *Blood, Tin, Straw* (1999), about the birds she observed in the water during a visit to Florida. The snowy egret, the pelicans, the great blue with its "snake neck and mallet beak," lead Olds to the sight of a dolphin, and she concludes the last nine lines of the poem as if the earth magically speaks to her, telling her that what she has just seen is a poem. Olds read these lines very slowly, with quiet deliberation, as if she had not been quite intelligent enough to see what was in front of her eyes without outside help:

> The water was smooth. Up from within it,
> moving from west to east, a dolphin's
> dark, back, slowly, curved.
> Moments later, in the same place,
> but now from east to west, it came up
> past me again, and down, as if
> the earth had said, I will say it twice,
> Sharon, the first time backwards, to get you
> ready, the second time left to right, so you can read it.

The second poem I particularly remember got a lot of laughter from the audience. It was written by Lucille Clifton, whose poetry Olds said she admired enough to include in her own reading. Clifton had written this poem as a letter to her son, listing several important physiological experiences that women had that he would never understand. This poem Olds read in a very dramatic way, evoking much appreciative applause from the audience, before she returned to her own poetry to end the reading.

Then Halpern joined Olds on the stage, and they invited members of the audience to step up to the microphones placed in the two aisles and ask their questions. Lines of people quickly formed in back of the mikes. Most of the questions seemed to be concerned with technical problems experienced by would-be poets. Did Olds consciously structure her lines in specific lengths, or did she allow herself complete freedom as an open-form poet? How long would Halpern allow a narrative or story to dominate a poem before he felt it lost its focus as a personal lyric? Both Halpern and Olds were very positive and encouraging in their responses, answering all the questions patiently until the woman who had introduced them came back and said they had to leave the stage. Nearly an hour and a half had flown by. It was time for the appearance of the next group of authors scheduled that afternoon at the Miami International Book Fair.

PART FOUR

DRAMA

- *The reason we confuse the tragic with the pathetic, as well as why we create so few [new] tragedies, is twofold: in the first place many of our writers have given up trying to search out the right way of living, and secondly, there is not among us any commonly accepted faith in a way of life that will give us not only material gain but satisfaction.*

  – ARTHUR MILLER

- *In a play, time is arrested in the sense of being confined. By a sort of legerdemain, events are made to remain events, rather than being reduced so quickly to mere occurrences.*

  – TENNESSEE WILLIAMS

- *I don't think you should frighten them [the audience], I think you should terrify them."*

  – EDWARD ALBEE

18

WHAT IS A PLAY?

Suit the action to the word, the word to the action; with this special observance, that you o'erstep not the modesty of nature: for any thing so o'erdone is from the purpose of playing, whose end, both at the first and now, was and is, to hold, as 't were, the mirror up to nature.

– HAMLET TO THE PLAYERS

Of all the literary genres, drama has the greatest potential to reach the emotions of an audience. The American dramatist Tennessee Williams understood how easy it is for us to disguise "from ourselves the intensity of our own feelings, the sensibility of our own hearts" as we are inexorably caught up in the ceaseless rush of events in our everyday lives. In "The Timeless World of a Play," an essay included in Williams's collection *Where I Live* (1978), he wrote that

> In a play, time is arrested in the sense of being confined. By a sort of legerdemain, events are made to remain *events,* rather than being reduced so quickly to mere *occurrences.* The audience can sit back in a comforting dusk to watch a world which is flooded with light and in which emotion and action have a dimension and dignity that they would likewise have in real existence, if only the shattering intrusion of time could be locked out.
>
> About their lives, people ought to remember that when they are finished, everything in them will be contained in a marvelous state of repose which is the same as that which they unconsciously admired in drama. The rush is temporary. The great and only possible dignity of man lies in his power deliberately to choose certain moral values by which to live as steadfastly as if he, too, like a character in a play, were immured against the corrupting rush of time. Snatching the eternal out of the desperately fleeting is the great magic trick of human existence.

Williams believed that what he called "the created world of a play" gives spectators the opportunity to escape from time's inevitable sense of impermanence. Sitting in a theater, we experience a "special kind of repose which allows contemplation and produces the climate in which tragic importance is a possible thing," because

> plays in the tragic tradition offer us a view of certain moral values in violent juxtaposition. Because we do not participate, except as spectators, we can view them clearly, within the limits of our emotional equipment. These people on the stage do not return our looks. We do not have to answer their questions nor make any sign of being in company with them, nor do we have to compete with their virtues nor resist their offenses. All at once, for this reason, we are able to *see* them! Our hearts are wrung by recognition and pity, so that the dusky shell of the auditorium where we are gathered anonymously together is flooded with an almost liquid warmth of unchecked human sympathies, relieved of self-consciousness, allowed to function. . . .

After poetry, drama is our second oldest literary form. To define **drama** as a play written to be performed in a theater is true only for the earliest plays. Later works known as "closet dramas," written in the nineteenth century by such poets as Percy Bysshe Shelley and such playwrights as Henrik Ibsen, were meant to be performed in the solitary theater of the reader's mind. A play can be considered a story told in dialogue, but even here there are exceptions: The modern playwright Samuel Beckett wrote stories without dialogue for the stage intended to be mimed by a single performer. Today millions of viewers watch works of drama — television sitcoms, prime-time soap operas, and weekly network dramatic series — that were never intended to be performed in a theater. But for centuries *drama* meant a stage play, and it is this meaning of the word that we primarily have in mind when we speak of drama as a literary genre.

As Aristotle understood, action is the essence of drama. This is suggested in the origin of the word *drama,* which is the Greek verb *dran,* "to perform." A century after drama flourished in Greece, Aristotle wrote the *Poetics* (c. 340 B.C.), a work in which he analyzed the literary form used by Sophocles and other Greek dramatists. For Aristotle, a play was the process of imitating a significant action complete unto itself by means of language "made sensuously attractive" and spoken by the persons involved in the action, not presented through narrative. Aristotle's definition of tragedy contained six important elements: (1) plot or action, the basic principle of drama; (2) characterization, an almost equally important element; (3) the thought or theme of the play; (4) verbal expression or dialogue; (5) visual adornment or stage decoration and costumes and masks for the actors; and (6) song or music to accompany the performers' words and movement.

Because most plays are literary works meant to give an illusion of reality through their performance onstage, a playwright who has set actors in motion to tell a story cannot interrupt the action, as in a work of fiction, to offer background information about the characters or summarize events taking place over a period of time, unless he introduces a narrator at the beginning of the play. Usually, the playwright gives the audience information about the story through dialogue. Playwrights can also suggest the development of their story by the physical behavior of the actors onstage and by changes in lighting, sets, or costumes.

When we think of the word *drama* we have in mind an illusion of reality invented for a striking effect. To illustrate the relationship between the everyday life we live and the life we see portrayed in the theater, the director Peter Brook described a simple exercise in *The Open Door* (1993):

> Ask any volunteer to walk from one side of a space to another. Anyone can do this. The clumsiest idiot cannot fail; he just has to walk. He makes no effort and deserves no reward.
>
> Now ask him to try to imagine that he is holding a precious bowl in his hands and to walk carefully so as not to spill a drop of its contents. Here again anyone can accomplish the act of imagination that this requires and can move in a more or less convincing manner. Yet your volunteer has made a special effort, so perhaps he deserves thanks and a five-penny piece as a reward for trying.
>
> Next ask him to imagine that as he walks the bowl slips from his fingers and crashes to the ground, spilling its contents. Now he's in trouble. He tries to act and the worst kind of artificial, amateur acting will take over his body, making the expression on his face "acted" — in other words, woefully unreal.
>
> To execute this apparently simple action so that it will appear as natural as just walking demands all the skills of a highly professional artist — an idea has to be given flesh and blood and emotional reality; it must go beyond imitation, so that an invented life is also a parallel life, which at no level can be distinguished from the real thing. Now we can see why a true actor is worth the enormous daily rate that film companies pay him for giving a plausible impression of everyday life.
>
> One goes to the theatre to find life, but if there is no difference between life outside the theatre and life inside, then theatre makes no sense. There's no point doing it. But if we accept that life in the theatre is more visible, more vivid than on the outside, then we can see that it is simultaneously the same thing and somewhat different.

Plays are acts of make-believe — acts in which the author, actors, stage technicians, and audience are united in their participation in an imaginary world. This world onstage can mimic "real life" in such plays as Lorraine Hansberry's *A Raisin in the Sun* (1959) or August Wilson's *Fences* (1983), with actors and sets representing contemporary everyday reality, or it can project a view of our potential experience as in a dream, in such poetic plays as Shakespeare's *Hamlet* (c. 1600) or Edward Albee's *The Sandbox* (1960).

As a story primarily told in dialogue, each play in this anthology falls into one of three conventional categories: tragedy, comedy, and tragicomedy. Broadly speaking, in **tragedy** the story ends unhappily, usually in the death of the main character, as in Sophocles' *Oedipus the King* (c. 430 B.C.). In **comedy** the story ends happily, often with a marriage symbolizing the continuation of life and the resolution of the conflict, as in Shakespeare's *The Tempest* (1611). In **tragicomedy,** a mixture of sad and happy events, the story's resolution can take different forms, but the audience usually experiences the play as a positive statement, an affirmation of life, as in Philip Kan Gotanda's *The Wash* (1987). This category can be further subdivided in modern plays into **dark comedy,** where the playwright's sardonic humor offers a frightening glimpse of the futility of life, and **farce,** a short play that depends for its comic effect on exaggerated, improbable situations and slapstick action, as in Caryl Churchill's *Heart's Desire* (1997).

Drama has experienced many innovations in form and staging in the twentieth century, even while such practitioners as the contemporary English playwright Tom Stoppard make fun of the increasing pace of our lives and the trivialization of our most cherished institutions, including the theater. In *Dogg's Hamlet* (1979), Stoppard created two short versions of Shakespeare's *Hamlet* — one that would take fifteen minutes to perform and a second, even briefer "encore" version of the play — streamlined for a production on a double-decker London bus. As short as it is, Stoppard's "encore" version of *Hamlet* as a farce (see the Casebook on Shakespeare's *Hamlet,* p. 2016) still satisfies our definition of a play — a performance by actors of a story told in dialogue. Stoppard has edited Shakespeare's words so drastically that our familiarity with the original *Hamlet* — one of the most famous plays in the European tradition — is essential to our understanding the cut version.

If the text of *Hamlet* were performed in its complete version, it would take almost six hours onstage. Every director makes some cuts in the script, but Stoppard's version is so short that he seems to be implying that contemporary audiences are so busy watching television that they have practically no time at all to sit through the long classic plays. But he also assumes that the tradition of European theater is still relevant today. The people who bought tickets when Stoppard's play was performed on the bus probably studied Shakespeare in school, where they might have become familiar with the complicated plot of *Hamlet* through reading the play or a summary of it for an English class.

If you are familiar with Shakespeare's play, Stoppard's collapsed version will remind you of what has been cut. The "encore" version of *Hamlet* conveys none of the complexity of the hero's passionate character, none of the poetry of his unforgettable soliloquies, and none of the tragedy of his dilemma. This bizarre version is meant to be only a faint, funny echo of the original.

Stoppard wrote his farce for a specific theater company in England, intending it to be seen and heard as well as read. This adds another dimension to our experience of drama. When performed in front of an audience, the text of a play is transmitted by the theatrical director, the costume and set designers, the technical staff responsible for sound and lighting, and the actors who make the play come alive. All these people work together to shape a play's meaning for the audience.

Even on a red double-decker London bus, an actor interpreting Hamlet as an aristocrat dressed in luxurious black velvet and silk ruffles will elicit a different response to the hero's personality and emotional situation than an actor who depicts Hamlet as a clown in a silly wig and circus tights or as a scruffy, leather-jacketed, metal-studded biker or as a pajama-clad patient recently escaped from a psychiatric hospital. Actors have performed the role in all these costumes, and they are all — at least in name — Hamlet. Every time an actor "plays" him, or any other character in a drama, there is the potential for interpreting the role differently.

Because drama is a collaborative effort that results in a work performed on a stage in front of an audience, we call a writer who creates plays a play*wright,* suggesting a highly skilled craftsperson or artisan who makes something tangible. But the basic text of a play — the author's creation of dialogue and stage action and the description on the page of the setting and the characters — has a special significance. The text is the only aspect of the theater in which the writer has the last word. When we read a play, following the dialogue and the stage directions makes us conscious of how the story might take on another life when performed on a stage or in a film, but we are also aware as we follow the words on the page that reading a play puts us into a special relationship with the playwright. Like the writer, we have only words to fire our imaginations; there are no actors, costumes, or sets.

What endures is the play on the page. As Aristotle wrote about the primacy of the text in *The Poetics,* "The visual adornment of the dramatic persons can have a strong emotional effect but is the least artistic element, the least connected with the poetic art; in fact the force of tragedy can be felt even without benefit of public performance and actors, while for the production of the visual effect the property man's art is even more decisive than that of the poet's."

If a play is to survive beyond its ephemeral stage or film presentations, it depends on its text and the response of generations of readers to its story, language, structure, and deeper meaning or theme. If a play exists only in performance, it will probably not survive as literature. Reading a play in addition to seeing it performed can help you understand the work better, especially if its language or meaning is difficult to follow in the action onstage. From your seat in the theater you cannot stop a play in the middle of a scene to tell the actor, "Wait, I didn't understand that line. Please repeat it." As a reader, however, you have the luxury of being able to stop in the midst of your reading to ponder the meaning of a line or to go over an entire scene that is not immediately clear to you.

RELATED COMMENTARIES: *Edward Albee, "On Playwriting," page 1949; Aristotle, "On the Elements and General Principles of Tragedy," page 1955.*

19

THE ELEMENTS OF DRAMA: A PLAYWRIGHT'S MEANS

INTERVIEWER: Which playwrights did you most admire when you were young?

ARTHUR MILLER: Well, first the Greeks, for their magnificent form, the symmetry. Half the time I couldn't really repeat the story because the characters in the mythology were completely blank to me. I had no background at that time to know really what was involved in these plays, but the architecture was clear. One looks at some building of the past whose use one is ignorant of, and yet it has a modernity. It had its own specific gravity. That form has never left me; I suppose it just got burned in.

– ARTHUR MILLER, *Paris Review* interview (1967)

Like short story writers and poets, playwrights have several important means or elements at their disposal in creating dramatic works for the stage. Familiarizing yourself with these elements will help you appreciate the artistry of these creations and understand them better. Some terms used to analyze drama (for instance, *plot, character,* and *theme*) are also used in discussing short fiction; others (*dialogue* and *staging*) refer exclusively to theater.

Even the most basic form of drama, the **monologue** — words meant to be spoken by one actor — suggests the resources available to the playwright. Consider, for example, the following fragment by Anton Chekhov. Found in his handwriting among his papers after his death, it appears to be a page that survived from one of his early attempts to rewrite his play *Uncle Vanya* (1896):

SOLOMON (*alone*): Oh! how dark is life! No night, when I was a child, so terrified me by its darkness as does my invisible existence. Lord, to David my father thou gavest only the gift of harmonizing words and songs, to sing and praise thee on strings, to lament sweetly, to make people weep or admire beauty; but why hast thou given me a meditative, sleepless, hungry mind? Like an insect born of the dust, I hide in darkness; and in fear and despair, all shaking and shivering, I see and hear in everything an invisible mystery. Why this morning? Why does the sun come out from behind the temple and gild the palm tree? Why this beauty of women? Where does

> the bird hurry, what is the meaning of its flight, if it and its young and the place to which it hastens will like myself, turn to dust? It were better I had never been born or were a stone, to which God has given neither eyes nor thoughts. In order to tire out my body by nightfall, all day yesterday, like a mere workman, I carried marble to the temple; but now the night has come and I cannot sleep. . . . I'll go and lie down. Phorses told me that if one imagines a flock of sheep running and fixes one's attention upon it, the mind gets confused and one falls asleep. I'll do it. . . . (*Exit.*)

Chekhov suggests several elements of drama in this monologue. The first word gives us the name of the **character** speaking the lines, Solomon, the son of King David, the great Hebrew poet whose psalms are included in the Old Testament. Solomon himself is a judge, not a poet, renowned throughout his kingdom for his wisdom. His first words ("Oh! how dark is life!") suggest the poetic **language** of his speech in his use of a metaphor. His next words ("No night, when I was a child, so terrified me by its darkness as does my invisible existence") suggest the subject or **theme** of his monologue, a philosophical contemplation of his own mortality. His words take on the element of **dramatic irony,** because the reader assumes that a man as wise as King Solomon would not be troubled by doubts or uncertainties.

Chekhov uses an elegant structure to present the progression of Solomon's thoughts, beginning with his statement or **exposition** of the theme. Solomon's situation is then developed in the **rising action** of the monologue, when he compares himself to his father and states the **conflict** within his personality: Unlike David, he is not content to praise the Lord; he has a "sleepless, hungry mind." Next, Solomon gives specific examples of his dilemma — first his awareness of the darkness and mystery in the world, then his observation of the same mystery in sunlight and beauty. Finally, at the **climax** of his thought, when he recognizes his own mortality and the evidence all around him of the futility of all existence ("turn to dust"), he admits, "It were better I had never been born or were a stone, to which God has given neither eyes nor thoughts." In the **falling action** he reminds himself about the advice he's heard from Phorses, about a method of counting sheep to put himself to sleep, and he leaves the stage determined to try it.

This monologue is a fragment, with no **resolution** other than Solomon's exit from the stage. It also lacks any physical **action** other than the speech itself, wherein Solomon meditates on mortality and attempts to fill the time before he tries to sleep. His words suggest a **plot,** telling us about what he did the previous day, trying to shake off his depression by carrying blocks of heavy marble in order to exhaust himself for sleep. **Movement** or staging of the monologue would depend on the actor saying the words onstage. We would not actually see Solomon pick up the marble slabs, but he could suggest his heavy labor — or his fatigue — by his physical stance and gestures. Each of us can imagine an appropriate **staging** for the monologue of a great Hebrew king, as ornate or as simple as we wish — a room in a realistic set that suggests a palace filled with silver and gold objects, or a symbolic bare stage furnished only with a classic plain-cloth backdrop. These choices, of course, affect how the viewer perceives the scene and the actor speaking his lines.

Plot, characterization, dialogue, and theme are the four main elements that you analyze when you think about plays as literary texts. Naturally, in plays with more than one character, playwrights can develop these elements in more complex ways. As you read the short play *Tender Offer* by the contemporary American playwright Wendy Wasserstein, be aware of how she uses plot, characterization, dialogue, and theme, as well as various physical elements of staging (for instance, the stage set and the two performers' song and dance routine), to tell a story in the words exchanged by two actors on a stage.

WENDY WASSERSTEIN

Tender Offer 1991

A girl of around nine is alone in a dance studio. She is dressed in traditional leotards and tights. She begins singing to herself, "Nothing Could Be Finer Than to Be in Carolina." She maps out a dance routine, including parts for the chorus. She builds to a finale. A man, Paul, around thirty-five, walks in. He has a sweet, though distant, demeanor. As he walks in, Lisa notices him and stops.

PAUL: You don't have to stop, sweetheart.

LISA: That's okay.

PAUL: Looked very good.

LISA: Thanks.

PAUL: Don't I get a kiss hello?

LISA: Sure.

PAUL (*embraces her*): Hi, Tiger.

LISA: Hi, Dad.

PAUL: I'm sorry I'm late.

LISA: That's okay.

PAUL: How'd it go?

LISA: Good.

PAUL: Just good?

LISA: Pretty good.

PAUL: "Pretty good." You mean you got a lot of applause or "pretty good" you could have done better?

LISA: Well, Courtney Palumbo's mother thought I was pretty good. But you know the part in the middle when everybody's supposed to freeze and the big girl comes out. Well, I think I moved a little bit.

PAUL: I thought what you were doing looked very good.

LISA: Daddy, that's not what I was doing. That was tap-dancing. I made that up.

PAUL: Oh. Well it looked good. Kind of sexy.

LISA: Yuch!

PAUL: What do you mean "yuch"?

LISA: Just yuch!
PAUL: You don't want to be sexy?
LISA: I don't care.
PAUL: Let's go, Tiger. I promised your mother I'd get you home in time for dinner.
LISA: I can't find my leg warmers.
PAUL: You can't find your what?
LISA: Leg warmers. I can't go home till I find my leg warmers.
PAUL: I don't see you looking for them.
LISA: I was waiting for you.
PAUL: Oh.
LISA: Daddy.
PAUL: What?
LISA: Nothing.
PAUL: Where do you think you left them?
LISA: Somewhere around here. I can't remember.
PAUL: Well, try to remember, Lisa. We don't have all night.
LISA: I told you. I think somewhere around here.
PAUL: I don't see them. Let's go home now. You'll call the dancing school tomorrow.
LISA: Daddy, I can't go home till I find them. Miss Judy says it's not professional to leave things.
PAUL: Who's Miss Judy?
LISA: She's my ballet teacher. She once danced the lead in *Swan Lake,* and she was a June Taylor dancer.
PAUL: Well, then, I'm sure she'll understand about the leg warmers.
LISA: Daddy, Miss Judy wanted to know why you were late today.
PAUL: Hmmmmmmmm?
LISA: Why were you late?
PAUL: I was in a meeting. Business. I'm sorry.
LISA: Why did you tell Mommy you'd come instead of her if you knew you had business?
PAUL: Honey, something just came up. I thought I'd be able to be here. I was looking forward to it.
LISA: I wish you wouldn't make appointments to see me.
PAUL: Hmmmmmmm.
LISA: You shouldn't make appointments to see me unless you know you're going to come.
PAUL: Of course I'm going to come.
LISA: No, you're not. Talia Robbins told me she's much happier living without her father in the house. Her father used to come home late and go to sleep early.
PAUL: Lisa, stop it. Let's go.
LISA: I can't find my leg warmers.
PAUL: Forget your leg warmers.
LISA: Daddy.

PAUL: What is it?

LISA: I saw this show on television, I think it was WPIX Channel 11. Well, the father was crying about his daughter.

PAUL: Why was he crying? Was she sick?

LISA: No. She was at school. And he was at business. And he just missed her, so he started to cry.

PAUL: What was the name of this show?

LISA: I don't know. I came in in the middle.

PAUL: Well, Lisa, I certainly would cry if you were sick or far away, but I know that you're well and you're home. So no reason to get maudlin.

LISA: What's maudlin?

PAUL: Sentimental, soppy. Frequently used by children who make things up to get attention.

LISA: I am sick! I am sick! I have Hodgkin's disease and a bad itch on my leg.

PAUL: What do you mean you have Hodgkin's disease? Don't say things like that.

LISA: Swoosie Kurtz, she had Hodgkin's disease on a TV movie last year, but she got better and now she's on *Love, Sidney*.

PAUL: Who is Swoosie Kurtz?

LISA: She's an actress named after an airplane. I saw her on *Live at Five*.

PAUL: You watch too much television; you should do your homework. Now, put your coat on.

LISA: Daddy, I really do have a bad itch on my leg. Would you scratch it?

PAUL: Lisa, you're procrastinating.

LISA: Why do you use words I don't understand? I hate it. You're like Daria Feldman's mother. She always talks in Yiddish to her husband so Daria won't understand.

PAUL: Procrastinating is not Yiddish.

LISA: Well, I don't know what it is.

PAUL: Procrastinating means you don't want to go about your business.

LISA: I don't go to business. I go to school.

PAUL: What I mean is you want to hang around here until you and I are late for dinner and your mother's angry and it's too late for you to do your homework.

LISA: I do not.

PAUL: Well, it sure looks that way. Now put your coat on and let's go.

LISA: Daddy.

PAUL: Honey, I'm tired. Really, later.

LISA: Why don't you want to talk to me?

PAUL: I do want to talk to you. I promise when we get home we'll have a nice talk.

LISA: No, we won't. You'll read the paper and fall asleep in front of the news.

PAUL: Honey, we'll talk on the weekend, I promise. Aren't I taking you to the theater this weekend? Let me look. (*He takes out appointment book.*) Yes. Sunday. *Joseph and the Amazing Technicolor Raincoat* with Lisa. Okay, Tiger?

LISA: Sure. It's Dreamcoat.

PAUL: What?

LISA: Nothing. I think I see my leg warmers. (*She goes to pick them up, and an odd-looking trophy.*)

PAUL: What's that?

LISA: It's stupid. I was second best at the dance recital, so they gave me this thing. It's stupid.

PAUL: Lisa.

LISA: What?

PAUL: What did you want to talk about?

LISA: Nothing.

PAUL: Was it about my missing your recital? I'm really sorry, Tiger. I would have liked to have been here.

LISA: That's okay.

PAUL: Honest?

LISA: Daddy, you're prostrastinating.

PAUL: I'm procrastinating. Sit down. Let's talk. So. How's school?

LISA: Fine.

PAUL: You like it?

LISA: Yup.

PAUL: You looking forward to camp this summer?

LISA: Yup.

PAUL: Is Daria Feldman going back?

LISA: Nope.

PAUL: Why not?

LISA: I don't know. We can go home now. Honest, my foot doesn't itch anymore.

PAUL: Lisa, you know what you do in business when it seems like there's nothing left to say? That's when you really start talking. Put a bid on the table.

LISA: What's a bid?

PAUL: You tell me what you want and I'll tell you what I've got to offer. Like Monopoly. You want Boardwalk, but I'm only willing to give you the Railroads. Now, because you are my daughter I'd throw in Water Works and Electricity. Understand, Tiger?

LISA: No. I don't like board games. You know, Daddy, we could get Space Invaders for our home for thirty-five dollars. In fact, we could get an Osborne System for two thousand. Daria Feldman's parents . . .

PAUL: Daria Feldman's parents refuse to talk to Daria, so they bought a computer to keep Daria busy so they won't have to speak in Yiddish. Daria will probably grow up to be a homicidal maniac lesbian prostitute.

LISA: I know what that word prostitute means.

PAUL: Good. (*Pause.*) You still haven't told me about school. Do you still like your teacher?

LISA: She's okay.

PAUL: Lisa, if we're talking try to answer me.

LISA: I am answering you. Can we go home now, please?

PAUL: Damn it, Lisa, if you want to talk to me . . . Talk to me!

LISA: I can't wait till I'm old enough so I can make my own money and never have to see you again. Maybe I'll become a prostitute.

PAUL: Young lady, that's enough.

LISA: I hate you, Daddy! I hate you! (*She throws her trophy into the trash bin.*)

PAUL: What'd you do that for?

LISA: It's stupid.

PAUL: Maybe I wanted it.

LISA: What for?

PAUL: Maybe I wanted to put it where I keep your dinosaur and the picture you made of Mrs. Kimbel with the chicken pox.

LISA: You got mad at me when I made that picture. You told me I had to respect Mrs. Kimbel because she was my teacher.

PAUL: That's true. But she wasn't my teacher. I liked her better with the chicken pox. (*Pause.*) Lisa, I'm sorry. I was very wrong to miss your recital, and you don't have to become a prostitute. That's not the type of profession Miss Judy has in mind for you.

LISA (*mumbles*): No.

PAUL: No. (*Pause.*) So Talia Robbins is really happy her father moved out?

LISA: Talia Robbins picks open the eighth-grade lockers during gym period. But she did that before her father moved out.

PAUL: You can't always judge someone by what they do or what they don't do. Sometimes you come home from dancing school and run upstairs and shut the door, and when I finally get to talk to you, everything is "okay" or "fine." Yup or nope?

LISA: Yup.

PAUL: Sometimes, a lot of times, I come home and fall asleep in front of the television. So you and I spend a lot of time being a little scared of each other. Maybe?

LISA: Maybe.

PAUL: Tell you what. I'll make you a tender offer.

LISA: What?

PAUL: I'll make you a tender offer. That's when one company publishes in the newspaper that they want to buy another company. And the company that publishes is called the Black Knight because they want to gobble up the poor little company. So the poor little company needs to be rescued. And then a White Knight comes along and makes a bigger and better offer so the shareholders won't have to tender shares to the Big Black Knight. You with me?

LISA: Sort of.

PAUL: I'll make you a tender offer like the White Knight. But I don't want to own you. I just want to make a much better offer. Okay?

LISA (*sort of understanding*): Okay. (*Pause. They sit for a moment.*) Sort of, Daddy, what do you think about? I mean, like when you're quiet what do you think about?

PAUL: Oh, business usually. If I think I made a mistake or if I think I'm doing okay. Sometimes I think about what I'll be doing five years from now and if it's what I hoped it would be five years ago. Sometimes I think about what your life will be like, if Mount Saint Helens will erupt again. What you'll become if you'll study penmanship or word processing. If you speak kindly of me to your psychiatrist when you are in graduate school. And how the hell I'll pay for your graduate school. And sometimes I try and think what it was I thought about when I was your age.

LISA: Do you ever look out your window at the clouds and try to see which kinds of shapes they are? Like one time, honest, I saw the head of Walter Cronkite in a flower vase. Really! Like look don't those kinda look like if you turn it upside down, two big elbows or two elephant trunks dancing?

PAUL: Actually still looks like Walter Cronkite in a flower vase to me. But look up a little. See the one that's still moving? That sorta looks like a whale on a thimble.

LISA: Where?

PAUL: Look up. To your right.

LISA: I don't see it. Where?

PAUL: The other way.

LISA: Oh, yeah! There's the head and there's the stomach. Yeah! (*Lisa picks up her trophy.*) Hey, Daddy.

PAUL: Hey, Lisa.

LISA: You can have this thing if you want it. But you have to put it like this, because if you put it like that it is gross.

PAUL: You know what I'd like? So I can tell people who come into my office why I have this gross stupid thing on my shelf, I'd like it if you could show me your dance recital.

LISA: Now?

PAUL: We've got time. Mother said she won't be home till late.

LISA: Well, Daddy, during a lot of it I freeze and the big girl in front dances.

PAUL: Well, how 'bout the number you were doing when I walked in?

LISA: Well, see, I have parts for a lot of people in that one, too.

PAUL: I'll dance the other parts.

LISA: You can't dance.

PAUL: Young lady, I played Yvette Mimimieux in a *Hasty Pudding Show.*°

LISA: Who's Yvette Mimimieux?

PAUL: Watch more television. You'll find out. (*Paul stands up.*) So I'm ready. (*He begins singing.*) "Nothing could be finer than to be in Carolina."

LISA: Now I go. In the morning. And now you go. Dum-da.

PAUL (*obviously not a tap dancer*): Da-da-dum.

LISA (*whines*): Daddy!

PAUL (*mimics her*): Lisa! Nothing could be finer . . .

LISA: That looks dumb.

PAUL: Oh, yeah? You think they do this better in *The Amazing Minkcoat?* No way! Now you go — da da da dum.

Hasty Pudding Show: An all-male revue, written and staged by Harvard students and renowned for its zany humor, men in drag, and parodies of cultural icons (e.g., the mock-reference to Yvette Mimieux, a '60s movie star).

LISA: Da da da dum.
PAUL: If I had Aladdin's lamp for only a day, I'd make a wish . . .
LISA: Daddy, that's maudlin!
PAUL: I know it's maudlin. And here's what I'd say:
LISA AND PAUL: I'd say that "nothing could be finer than to be in Carolina in the moooooooooornin'."

ꕤ

PLOT

Plot is the structuring of the events in a play. Also called the story, plot is the essential element with which a dramatist works. If "to play," according to the dictionary definition, is to engage in mimicry, acting, or make believe, then "a play" is a literary work that mimics or imitates a complete action onstage.

The plot of *Tender Offer* is the story of how a father and his young daughter resolve their differences during a quarrel and grow closer. When Paul and Lisa finish their tap routine in the dance studio, we sense that something has been resolved between them and that the stage action is complete. The **exposition** of the plot begins with Lisa's solitary dance as the play starts and continues with the entrance of Paul, who has arrived too late to see Lisa's recital. The development of the quarrel between them is the plot's **rising action.** Paul's attempts to evade the issue of Lisa's disappointment with him and Lisa's expression of her anger lead to the **climax** of the action, when she throws her trophy away. The father's "tender offer" to his daughter is the **turning point** of the plot. Their game together finding shapes in the clouds is the **falling action,** and their final song and dance duet constitutes the **resolution** or **dénouement** of the drama. This progression of events develops a story with a beginning, a middle, and an end.

What drives the plot is usually **conflict,** and drama can be defined most simply as a progression of events that develop and resolve conflicts. Wasserstein's play continues a tradition of drama begun in the fifth century B.C. by such Greek playwrights as Sophocles and analyzed by Aristotle in *The Poetics*. Aristotle emphasized that the plot or story of a play should be unified and complete, with all aspects of the conflict resolved by the end. **Suspense** is created for the audience before the resolution of the conflict in the plot. We can see both conflict and suspense in this play.

We do not know that there is a problem between Paul and Lisa at the beginning of *Tender Offer:* All we know is that the father is so late picking up his young daughter at the dance studio that he has missed her performance at the recital. This is the dramatic situation that suggests the conflict between them. Suspense begins to build during the events of the rising action, as Wasserstein keeps us in the dark about whether Paul and Lisa will be able to resolve their differences. Lisa procrastinates about going home and suggests indirectly that she is angry with Paul by responding flatly to his opening remarks and baiting him in lines like "Talia Robbins told me she's much happier living without her father in the house." At first Paul is an authoritarian father ("Lisa, stop it. Let's go"); then, as this has no effect, he tries a softer approach ("Honey, I'm tired. Really, later").

Both characters are gentle, "tender" people, so the quarrel between them does not escalate to physical violence or a life-or-death struggle, but Wasserstein increases the tension between them when Lisa cuts through their skirmishing to confront Paul directly. She asks her father, "Why don't you want to talk to me?" When Paul responds in his customary role as the emotionally reserved parent ("I promise when we get home we'll have a nice talk"), his daughter seems to give up, delaying the resolution of the plot.

Halfway into the story, a **complication** in the plot occurs when Lisa picks up the trophy she won at the recital, and Paul begins to understand how important the afternoon has been for her. In the second half of the play, he begins to build the bridge between them that allows him to share her feelings, beginning with his next action ("Sit down. Let's talk"). Wasserstein continues to delay the resolution of the conflict and build suspense. Lisa may act calmly, but she is furious with her father. She expresses her anger in words, trying to rile him ("Can we go home now, please?," "Maybe I'll become a prostitute").

Then Wasserstein heightens the suspense: Lisa expresses her frustration by a physical action, throwing her trophy into the trash bin. Her act of hostility is the most violent event in the play, the climax or high point. It is also, of course, an act of hostility toward her father. He reacts as a concerned adult by accepting her action; he is honest enough to admit they have a problem and explains their quarrel in terms that a nine-year-old can understand ("So you and I spend a lot of time being a little scared of each other"). He defuses the tension by surprising her with his "tender offer." Taking her seriously, he shares his feelings with her, and gradually they move closer into a reconciliation symbolized by their song and dance together at the end of the play.

The action of Wasserstein's short play is very tightly constructed, exhibiting what Aristotle would call the **unity of time and place.** Its action takes less than an hour, and it occurs in one place, the dance studio. In defining the elements of classic drama, Aristotle stipulated that the action of a well-made play should be contained within a restricted period of time and a single physical place. In Sophocles' *Oedipus the King,* for example, the action occurs within one day, and the setting represents one place, the exterior of Oedipus's palace. For centuries theater critics judged playwrights according to their fidelity to Aristotle's rules about these unities, even though such brilliant writers as Shakespeare broke the rules constantly, writing plays like *Hamlet* that have complicated subplots with action occurring in different locations over extended periods of time.

Finally, in the eighteenth century, the great English critic Samuel Johnson brought some common sense to the debate. In *The Preface to Shakespeare,* Johnson wrote that Aristotle's analysis was not "an unquestionable principle":

> The truth is that the spectators [of a play in the theater] are always in their senses, and know, from the first act to the last, that the stage is only a stage, and that the players are only players. They came to hear a certain number of lines recited with just gesture and elegant modulation. The lines related to some action, and an action must be in some

> place; but the different actions that complete a story may be in places very remote from each other. . . . [A] lapse of years is as easily conceived as a passage of hours. In contemplation we easily contract the time of real actions, and therefore willingly permit it to be contracted when we only see their imitation.

Johnson understood that all literature, including drama, is an imitation of life. The actions we watch onstage in *Tender Offer* by the actors portraying Paul and Lisa are only imitations of what happens in a real-life relationship between father and daughter. In the play, as Johnson would have put it, these "imitations produce pain or pleasure, not because they are mistaken for realities, but because they bring realities to mind."

CHARACTERIZATION

Another important means of the playwright is **characterization,** which, as in a short story, can be the presentation of characters who play either major or minor roles in the action. Both characters in *Tender Offer* play major roles. They are also **round characters,** or fully developed human beings, a father and a daughter who are "tender" toward each other. They work through their quarrel step by step, changing their attitudes as each moves toward a better understanding of the other. In the conflict between parent and child, neither one could be called a hero or a villain. Paul was late to the recital, but he was kept busy at his office. Lisa tries to hurt him by what she says, but she enters into the spirit of his "tender offer" and invites him to look at cloud shapes outside the studio window as a prelude to joining him in their final tap dance.

In classic drama, where conflict between the characters is a confrontation between clearly delineated moral good and moral evil, the terms **protagonist** and **antagonist** are used for the hero (the central character, man or woman) and the villain, respectively. We can consider Lisa the protagonist of *Tender Offer* in that she is present on stage when the play begins, waiting for her father's arrival at the dance studio, and that the ensuing action focuses on her anger toward him. Paul could be called the antagonist because he provokes Lisa's anger, first by being late and then by not noticing she is upset. Both characters have leading roles in the short play, and both are equally complex psychological beings. When the stage directions state that Lisa "mumbles" her line and that there's a "pause" before Paul asks her a question about her friend Talia Robbins, Wasserstein is giving us subtle clues to suggest the growing tension between them.

Like short stories, plays depend on characterization to motivate the action or plot. The events occurring on stage are set in motion by the characters' personalities, and the more we understand their psychological behavior, the closer we come to understanding the play. We assume that the actions that we see on stage are plausible and consistent, within our "reading" of the different characters. We understand, for example, from the play's setting in a dance studio and from what the characters say to each other, that Lisa comes from an affluent family and seems to have a secure economic background. We factor these details into our reading of the play. As a realistic depiction of a father-daughter relationship, the characters in *Tender Offer* are solidly believable. In this short play, unlike many longer plays, there are no minor characters who exist on stage primarily to advance the action of the story or introduce subplots that complicate the main action. Minor characters usually are presented with fewer dimensions to their personalities.

The actors playing the characters can also shape our response to them. Wasserstein tells us at the beginning of *Tender Offer* that Paul has "a sweet, though distant, demeanor," but she does not give any indication of why he is "distant." It could be that while he is temperamentally reserved, he is basically honest in his dealings with his family and just happens to be so caught up in his business that he has neglected his daughter. Or we can imagine that he is "distant" because he has something to hide — for example, perhaps he missed Lisa's dance recital not because he worked late at his office but because he is having an extramarital affair. At the beginning of the play we can decide from the way the actor playing Paul speaks his lines whether we want to believe him. By the end of the play, Paul has reacted so sensitively to Lisa's feelings that we probably trust him and judge him an honest person, at least on the basis of what we have seen of his behavior onstage.

Aristotle maintained in the *Poetics* that characterization in a play was second to the element of plot or action, yet he emphasized the importance of the characters. In his ranking of the elements of drama, Aristotle was apparently as much a pragmatist as he was a theorist, judging the relative importance of plot, character, dialogue, theme, and the other elements on the basis of the literature he had actually seen and read. As evidence for his belief that structuring a good plot was the most essential element in drama, Aristotle said he noticed that beginning writers "manage to hit the mark in verbal expression and character portrayal sooner than they do in plot construction." Other critics have argued that dialogue, not characterization or plot action, is the most important element in drama. You can reach your own conclusion in this matter after you have read more plays.

DIALOGUE

Dialogue is the exchange of words between the characters in a play. In short fiction and poetry, dialogue is often set emotionally for us by the descriptive words that authors use to introduce it. They write, "He shouted," to show strong emotion, for example, or "She wailed," to show extreme unhappiness. Wasserstein tells us that Lisa "mumbles," but playwrights rely primarily on the dialogue to tell their stories.

Most critics agree that dialogue has three main functions in a play: to advance the plot, to establish the setting, and to reveal character. When we say that plot is *dialogue driven* in drama, we mean that the words of the actors advance the plot. In the exposition at the start of the play, the actors' words can also reveal important information about what has gone on before the stage action commences; dialogue continues to introduce new complications throughout the development of the plot. When Lisa greets Paul by saying "Hi, Dad," her words establish their relationship with great economy and precision. When he says, "I'm sorry I'm late" and "How'd it go?," her flat replies suggest her disappointment with him. Their exchange establishes the setting and tells what happened before the play began. In her choice of words, Lisa also hints that something is wrong.

Paul's opening dialogue presents him as a loving, if breezy, parent: "You don't have to stop, sweetheart." He's also a stickler for information, holding his daughter accountable for her actions ("'Pretty good.' You mean you got a lot of applause or 'pretty good' you could have done better"). He puts off her question about why he's late with a noncommittal "hmmmmmmmm," which he repeats evasively when she attempts to give him an order by saying "I wish you wouldn't make appointments to see me." Paul introduces words that Lisa doesn't understand — *maudlin* and *procrastinating* — but she is responsive to him, asking him for definitions and then deliberately misunderstanding him ("I don't go to business. I go to school"). In response, he simplifies his language as if he thinks she is stupid ("What I mean is you want to hang around here until you and I are late for dinner and your mother's angry and it's too late for you to do your homework"). This is the height of the misunderstanding between them.

When we say that Wasserstein has written realistic dialogue between the two characters in *Tender Offer* we mean that the words they speak onstage strike us as the way people could actually have a conversation. With a little thought, you realize that this is not true. Where are the pauses, incomplete sentences, rushes of words, and fillers like "like," "uh," and "you know" that creep into our usual attempts at verbal communication with another human being? We may think we are having a dialogue when we exchange words with another person, but usually it is nothing like the dialogue we hear onstage. Wasserstein has ironed out all the wrinkles in the words that Lisa and Paul exchange. Every word has been chosen for its effect on the listener. This does not mean that Wasserstein's dialogue strikes our ears as false or badly written. It is a tribute to her skill as a playwright that we believe Lisa and Paul talk in the way that people *could* have this conversation — if they were both speaking their lines onstage.

Taking Chekhov as an example, the director Peter Brook has described in *The Open Door* the way that playwrights must go beyond an imitation of life in order to create effective dialogue:

> Life in the theatre is more readable and intense because it is more concentrated. The act of reducing space and compressing time creates a concentrate.
>
> In life we speak in a chattering tumble of repetitive words, yet this quite natural way of expressing ourselves always takes a great deal of time in relation to the actual content of what one wants to say. . . . The [dramatist's] compression consists of removing everything that is not strictly necessary and intensifying what is there, such as putting a strong adjective in the place of a bland one, whilst preserving the impression of spontaneity. If this impression is main-

tained, we reach the point where if in life it takes two people three hours to say something, onstage it should take three minutes. . . .

With Chekhov, the text gives the impression of having been recorded on tape, of taking its sentences from daily life. But there is not a phrase of Chekhov's that has not been chiseled, polished, modified, with great skill and artistry so as to give the impression that the actor is really speaking "like in daily life."

However, if one tries to speak and behave just like in daily life, one cannot play Chekhov. The actor and the director must follow the same process as the author, which is to be aware that each word, even if it appears to be innocent, is not so. It contains in itself, and in the silence that precedes and follows it, an entire unspoken complexity of energies between the characters. If one can manage to find that, and if, furthermore, one looks for the art needed to conceal it, then one succeeds in saying these simple words and giving the impression of life.

In *Tender Offer* Wasserstein also uses dialogue to be funny and lighten up the situation. As a running joke, Paul keeps giving an incorrect title (*raincoat, minkcoat*) to the musical he is going to see with his daughter, *Joseph and the Amazing Technicolor Dreamcoat.* Lisa uses colloquialisms like "kinda" and "gross," which Paul adapts into his speech to sustain their fragile bonding near the end of the play ("That sorta looks like a whale on a thimble" and "So I can tell people who come into my office why I have this gross stupid thing on my shelf"). The different levels of diction in each character's choice of words helps to enliven the dialogue, which tends to be matter of fact. This is a characteristic of realistic plays written in recent years, as opposed to the heights of poetic fancy expressed in Shakespearean dialogue. Paul tries to heighten his choice of words when he tells Lisa, "Young lady, I played Yvette Mimimieux in a *Hasty Pudding Show,*" revealing in the process that he has been educated at Harvard by his casual reference to the university's drama club. Their verbal exchange is light years away from the poetry of Hamlet's words pledging obedience to his father's ghost in Act I, Scene V, of *Hamlet:*

Remember thee!
Yea, from the table of my memory
I'll wipe away all trivial fond records,
All saws of books, all forms, all pressures past
That youth and observation copied there,
And thy commandment all alone shall live
Within the book and volume of my brain,
Unmix'd with baser matter . . .

The poetic dialogues Shakespeare created in *Hamlet* are a treasury of words, not only in Hamlet's speeches to the other characters in the play but also in his **soliloquies** (speeches spoken when he is alone onstage). Wasserstein has written her dialogue in *Tender Offer* to mirror the flatter expectations of her characters: Not for them is the poetry in the lines of *Hamlet.* Wasserstein is in the company of recent American playwrights like Milcha Sanchez-Scott and Philip Kan Gotanda.

STAGING

The staging of a play refers to the physical spectacle it presents to the audience in a performance by the actors. It takes into account such elements as the stage set, the different props and costumes used by the actors, their movement onstage, and the lighting and sound effects. *Tender Offer* is a one-set play, with its stripped-down dance-studio setting contributing to the spectator's sense of listening in on an intimate family quarrel. By entering his daughter's practice room, the father can become emotionally accessible to her in ways that he probably would not be in his office. We can read the description of the setting at the beginning of the play to locate ourselves in the world of the drama, even if the playwright gives only sparse directions (*"A girl of around nine is alone in a dance studio"*) to help us place ourselves in Lisa's story.

The transformation of a play from the page to the stage is usually a collaboration between the director; the actors; and the costume, light, and set designers. Their creativity can help the audience interpret what the dialogue reveals to them as the drama proceeds. Costumes signal aspects of character that the actors are trying to project. The lighting of the sets (now often controlled by technicians with computers transmitting hundreds of cues during a performance) helps to give the stage composition a focus. Light also casts shadows, suggesting a mood and a sense of dimensionality to the actors. The designers' work enables the viewer to *feel* a scene rather than just see it.

In most productions the director has a vision of the play that he or she communicates to the actors and the set, costume, and light designers. In the 1949 staging of Arthur Miller's *Death of a Salesman,* for example, the set designer Jo Mielziner collaborated with the author and director Elia Kazan to create a design concept centered on what he considered "the most important visual symbol in the play," the salesman's house. With great ingenuity, Mielziner constructed his set to harmonize with the effect Miller was trying to achieve in the way he told his story. Mielziner explained,

> Why should that house not be the main set, with all the other scenes — the corner of a graveyard, a hotel room in Boston, the corner of a business office, a lawyer's consultation room, and so on — played on a forestage? If I designed these little scenes in segments and fragments, with easily moved props and fluid lighting effects, I might be able, without ever lowering the curtain, to achieve the easy flow that the author clearly wanted.

The actors' movement onstage during their delivery of the dialogue is called **blocking.** Their nonverbal gestures are known as **stage business.** At times the playwright can combine the elements of movement and music to create very effective stage business, as with the tap dance symbolizing the harmony between parent and child at the end of *Tender Offer*.

A director can suggest ways for the actors to move on the set and give them stage business to further the action of the plot or support the desired illusion. When the Swedish film director Ingmar Bergman staged Henrik Ibsen's *A Doll House* in 1992, he began his production by raising the curtain to reveal the woman playing the main character Nora wearing a wine-red dress and seated on a red plush sofa. Surrounded by a clutter of toys, dolls, and doll furniture, she waited motionless for a few moments, staring out into empty space like a human doll ready to be played with.

As readers of plays we become the director, actors, designers, and musicians all in one. We may not be able to visualize Paul and Lisa's tap dance, but reading plays attentively is a challenge to our imaginations to simulate the experience of seeing and hearing them brought to life in a theater.

THEME

As with short fiction and poetry, theme is the underlying meaning of a dramatic work, suggested through the dialogue spoken by the characters as they move through the action of the play. Theme must also take into account the overall effect of the different elements of drama, including the way we imagine the play staged in a theater. The theme of Wasserstein's *Tender Offer* could be expressed as the importance of a parent and child's communication with each other to build trust for their future relationship. This acknowledges the playwright's careful structure of her plot and dialogue, so that both Paul and Lisa are held accountable for the breach of good feeling between them, with Paul as a parent who has not kept his promise to attend the recital, and Lisa as a child who is acting out her disappointment. Other interpretations of the theme of *Tender Offer* are possible, of course, just as long as they do not contradict the facts in the play. For example, citing a theme of child abuse or juvenile delinquency would be to disregard what the characters do and say. Only a careless or perverse reader would come up with these faulty statements of the theme.

Awareness of the genre of a play can also help you to express its theme. Reading early plays like Sophocles' *Oedipus the King* and Shakespeare's *Hamlet,* you might find it easier to summarize the theme if you remember that these are examples of *tragedy*. Both of the title characters have a tragic flaw, or defect of character, that brings about the end of their lives as if inevitably decreed by fate. In Tom Stoppard's play *Rosencrantz and Guildenstern Are Dead* (1967), which — like his farcical *Dogg's Hamlet* — is based on Shakespeare's classic, the character of the Player gives this definition of tragedy: "We're tragedians, you see. We follow directions — there is no *choice* involved. The bad end unhappily, the good unluckily. That is what tragedy means."

Willy Russell, a contemporary of Stoppard, explored the definition of tragedy in a funny scene from his play *Educating Rita*. Here the title character, a young woman from a working-class background employed as a hairdresser who is taking classes at an English university, is so excited after seeing her first production of a Shakespeare play that she rushes back to the office of her tutor, Frank, to talk to him about it.

WILLY RUSSELL

From *Educating Rita*

1983

Frank enters carrying a briefcase and a pile of essays. He goes to the filing cabinet, takes his lecture notes from the briefcase and puts them in a drawer. He takes the sandwiches and apple from his briefcase and puts them on his desk and then goes to the window desk and dumps the essays and briefcase. He switches on the radio and then sits in the swivel chair. He opens the packet of sandwiches, takes a bite, and then picks up a book and starts reading.

Rita bursts through the door out of breath.

FRANK: What are you doing here? (*He looks at his watch.*) It's Thursday, you . . .

RITA (*moving over to the desk; quickly*): I know I shouldn't be here, it's me dinner hour, but listen, I've gorra tell someone, have y' git a few minutes, can y' spare . . . ?

FRANK (*alarmed*): My God, what is it?

RITA: I had to come an' tell y', Frank, last night, I went to the theatre! A proper one, a professional theatre.

Frank gets up and switches off the radio and then returns to the swivel chair.

FRANK (*sighing*): For God's sake, you had me worried, I thought it was something serious.

RITA: No, listen, it was. I went out an' got me ticket, it was Shakespeare, I thought it was gonna be dead borin' . . .

FRANK: Then why did you go in the first place?

RITA: I wanted to find out. But listen, it wasn't borin', it was bleedin' great, honest, ogh, it done me in, it was fantastic. I'm gonna do an essay on it.

FRANK (*smiling*): Come on, which one was it?

Rita moves upper right centre.

RITA: ". . . Out, out, brief candle!
Life's but a walking shadow, a poor player
That struts and frets his hour upon the stage
And then is heard no more. It is a tale
Told by an idiot, full of sound and fury
Signifying nothing."

FRANK (*deliberately*): Ah, *Romeo and Juliet.*

RITA (*moving towards Frank*): Tch. Frank! Be serious. I learnt that today from the book. (*She produces a copy of* Macbeth.) Look, I went out an' bought the book. Isn't it great? What I couldn't get over is how excitin' it was.

Frank puts his feet up on the desk.

RITA: Wasn't his wife a cow, eh? An' that fantastic bit where he meets Macduff an' he thinks he's all invincible. I was on the edge of me seat at that bit. I wanted to shout out an' tell Macbeth, warn him.

FRANK: You didn't, did you?

RITA: Nah. Y' can't do that in a theatre, can y'? It was dead good. It was like a thriller.

FRANK: Yes. You'll have to go and see more.
RITA: I'm goin' to. *Macbeth*'s a tragedy, isn't it?

Frank nods.

RITA: Right.

Rita smiles at Frank and he smiles back at her.

Well I just — I just had to tell someone who'd understand.
FRANK: I'm honoured that you chose me.
RITA (*moving towards the door*): Well, I better get back. I've left a customer with a perm lotion. If I don't get a move on there'll be another tragedy.
FRANK: No. There won't be a tragedy.
RITA: There will, y' know. I know this woman; she's dead fussy. If her perm doesn't come out right there'll be blood an' guts everywhere.
FRANK: Which might be quite tragic — (*He throws her the apple from his desk which she catches.*) — but it won't be a tragedy.
RITA: What?
FRANK: Well — erm — look; the tragedy of the drama has nothing to do with the sort of tragic event you're talking about. Macbeth is flawed by his ambition — yes?
RITA (*going and sitting in the chair by the desk*): Yeh. Go on. (*She starts to eat the apple.*)
FRANK: Erm — it's that flaw which forces him to take the inevitable steps towards his own doom. You see?

Rita offers him the can of soft drink. He takes it and looks at it.

FRANK (*putting the can down on the desk*): No thanks. Whereas, Rita, a woman's hair being reduced to an inch of stubble, or — or the sort of thing you read in the paper that's reported as being tragic, "Man Killed By Falling Tree," is not a tragedy.
RITA: It is for the poor sod under the tree.
FRANK: Yes, it's tragic, absolutely tragic. But it's not a tragedy in the way that *Macbeth* is a tragedy. Tragedy in dramatic terms is inevitable, preordained. Look, now, even without ever having heard the story of *Macbeth* you wanted to shout out, to warn him and prevent him going on, didn't you? But you wouldn't have been able to stop him would you?
RITA: No.
FRANK: Why?
RITA: They would have thrown me out the theatre.
FRANK: But what I mean is that your warning would have been ignored. He's warned in the play. But he can't go back. He still treads the path to doom. But the poor old fellow under the tree hasn't arrived there by following any inevitable steps has he?
RITA: No.
FRANK: There's no particular flaw in his character that has dictated his end. If he'd been warned of the consequences of standing beneath that particular tree he wouldn't have done it, would he? Understand?
RITA: So — so Macbeth brings it on himself?

FRANK: Yes. You see he goes blindly on and on and with every step he's spinning one more piece of thread which will eventually make up the network of his own tragedy. Do you see?

RITA: I think so. I'm not used to thinkin' like this.

FRANK: It's quite easy, Rita.

RITA: It is for you. I just thought it was a dead excitin' story. But the way you tell it you make me see all sorts of things in it. (*After a pause.*) It's fun, tragedy, isn't it?

Frank's explanation of why the death of "the poor old sod under the tree" is not an example of tragedy suggests the difference between tragedy and **pathos**. Pathos, according to the playwright Arthur Miller, arouses our feelings of "sadness, sympathy, identification, and even fear," while tragedy "brings us knowledge or enlightenment" about the "right way of living in the world." As Miller observed, "The reason we confuse the tragic with the pathetic, as well as why we create so few [new] tragedies, is twofold: in the first place many of our writers have given up trying to search out the right way of living, and secondly, there is not among us any commonly accepted faith in a way of life that will give us not only material gain but satisfaction."

These definitions of tragedy help us to understand the **dark comedy** or **theater of the absurd** of Edward Albee and Caryl Churchill, where the characters are presented in absurd situations that reduce the meaning or significance of their lives to zero. Comedy, on the other hand, as in Shakespeare's *The Tempest,* usually centers on the complications of love (if the play is a romantic comedy) or human eccentricity (if it is a comedy of manners). Like tragic plays, good comic plays are serious statements about the human situation, allowing us to laugh at ourselves after the initial shock of recognition. Another category of drama is the **didactic play**, which teaches a lesson. Although presented within the context of a comedy, Frank's explanation of tragedy in *Educating Rita* is a didactic scene. Didactic plays often teach a lesson about the best way to live or lecture the audience about serious matters.

Modern plays by such authors as Henrik Ibsen, Susan Glaspell, Tennessee Williams, Lorraine Hansberry, and August Wilson are **realistic dramas** in which the characters seem to exhibit free will in regard to their choices for future action. They are usually a mixture of comic and tragic elements. There is no end to the ways in which plays can be classified (recall Hamlet's troupe of touring actors who are proficient in acting "tragedy, comedy, history, pastoral, pastoral-comical, historical-pastoral, tragical-historical, tragical-comical-historical-pastoral, scene individable, or poem unlimited"). In each case, the way you classify the play can help you to clarify the dramatist's underlying theme.

RELATED COMMENTARIES: *Leonard Mustazza, "Generic Translation and Thematic Shift in Glaspell's* Trifles *and 'A Jury of Her Peers,'" page 1980; Sandra Saari, "Female Becomes Human: Nora Transformed in* A Doll House,*" page 1993.*

20

READING, THINKING, AND WRITING ABOUT DRAMA

If my tragedy makes a tragic impression on people, they have only themselves to blame.

– AUGUST STRINDBERG, preface to *Miss Julie*

READING DRAMA

Reading a play allows you to have it both ways: you can stop the action at any time to think about the words on the page, and you can envision what is happening in a make-believe performance in the theater of your mind. Whether you follow a play as a passive spectator or an imaginative reader, you understand that its author is engaged in more than an act of "let's pretend." Most playwrights are attempting to make a serious statement about how we live — both as individuals and as members of society. Like other forms of literature, drama takes us out of our lives and allows us access to a wider range of human thoughts and feelings, showing us our vast potential as individuals for both good and evil.

Having drama available as texts on the page has another advantage. Like other writers, playwrights are conscious of themselves as contributing to an ongoing tradition. It is possible to see many of the plays in this anthology produced onstage or as film, but they are immediately accessible within the covers of this book. Furthermore, in Part Two of this anthology, you can read the story by Susan Glaspell that has a counterpart in her play *Trifles*. Glaspell wrote her story "A Jury of Her Peers" after the success of *Trifles* at the Provincetown Playhouse. Comparing the story with the play, you will gain a deeper appreciation of the differences in the two literary genres and the different resources of playwrights and short story writers. You can also appreciate the scope of Shakespeare's extraordinary achievement as a playwright and a poet by reading his selections in the different parts of this anthology.

Even in such short, relatively simple plays as *Tender Offer* you probably need two readings of the text in order to be able to discuss it in class. On the first reading, let your imagination expand and try to see the play enacted onstage. On the second reading, be more detached from the text and try to analyze it as a work of literature by thinking about how the playwright has used the elements of drama.

For example, Wasserstein has a double meaning in mind when she uses the term *tender offer* as the title of her play. Its use in business may not be clear to every reader, but she explains it in the conversation between the father and his daughter. In your first reading you will get to understand the literal meaning of the term in business negotiations. As you follow the action on stage to its conclusion, you also see the meaning of the term enacted in the relationship between the two characters. On your second reading, you might allow the literal meaning of the play's title to take on connotative associations, symbolizing the fragile relationship between father and daughter. Then you can go on to consider how this theme is dramatized in the play's other structural elements.

Sometimes you will still have questions about the meaning of a play even after your second reading. Close the book and give yourself some time to think about it. Your effort to understand the work is a necessary part of the learning process. Remember Peter Brook's direction: "In order for something of quality to take place, an empty space needs to be created. An empty space makes it possible for a new phenomenon to come to life, for anything that touches on content, meaning, expression, language, and music can exist only if the experience is fresh and new. However, no fresh and new experience is possible if there isn't a pure, virgin space ready to receive it." If you are still confused after you have thought about the play, write down your questions and bring them to the next class discussion.

In a sense, reading drama is easier than reading poetry and short fiction because playwrights introduce you in a more leisurely fashion to the imaginative world they create on the page. For one thing, plays begin with a description of the characters who perform the action. For example, opening to the first page of Sophocles' *Oedipus the King,* you encounter a list of characters right after the title of the play. The setting or "scene" of the play is also described before you start to read the dialogue between the various characters. In *Oedipus the King* you are told that the Greek stage is meant to suggest the front of the royal house of Thebes. This is a neutral description, but then you learn that "many years have passed since Oedipus solved the riddle of the Sphinx and ascended the throne of Thebes, and now a plague has struck the city. A procession of priests enters; suppliants, broken and despondent, they carry branches wound in wool and lay them on the altar." The editor of the text of *Oedipus the King* is giving you a clue about the serious mood in which the play begins. You do not know what has caused the priests to become so unhappy, but as Oedipus comes forward with a "telltale limp" and the play starts, you read his speech in the prologue with more information to help you understand his words than you have when you begin a poem or a short story.

The opening dialogue between Oedipus and the Priest who speaks for the suppliants is an admirable illustration of the drama at the heart of a great play. There is no physical action as such between the two characters — no brawny fisticuffs, no spectacular duel, no surprising exchange of weapons. Standing side by side, the two actors only exchange words. But the dialogue allows the reader of the play to create a personality for Oedipus and get a first sense of the conflict — or mystery — within his situation that will evoke a sense of pity and terror for him as the play unfolds.

Guidelines for Reading Drama

1. Make an entry in your notebook for each play assigned in class, writing down the author's name and the title and date of the play.
2. Use a dictionary to look up words in the headnote or in the play that you do not understand.
3. Remember that the type of theater — Greek, Elizabethan, realistic, contemporary — prevalent at the time the playwright is working can influence his or her plays.
4. When you start to read a play, note the list of characters and the playwright's description of them. Try to envision the set, if it is described at the beginning of the various scenes and acts.
5. As you read the dialogue, imagine the gestures and the costumes of the actors specified in the stage directions or suggested by what the characters say.
6. Notice what the characters *don't* say in the dialogue — their pauses and silences. Remember that their words, like those of real people, are not always to be trusted.

CRITICAL THINKING ABOUT DRAMA

As in your study of short fiction and poetry, your critical thinking about a play depends on your first having formulated an interpretation of it after reading and perhaps rereading the text. Then you can begin asking yourself questions about different aspects of the work's structure, depending on the topic you are writing about. The various elements of drama are often the focus of a critical inquiry. The questions to help you think critically about drama are similar to those asked of short fiction. You might consider the following topics as you read.

Plot. What is the conflict of the play? Is it developed in separate stages of rising action, complication, climax, falling action, and resolution? Can you find examples of foreshadowing? Does the play have a subplot or second plot? How is it related to the main plot? Is there any repetition of significant action? If so, what do you think the playwright intended?

Characters. Is there a protagonist and an antagonist in the play? Do you think that they are presented as round or flat, static or dynamic characters? Are they realistic or symbolic? Often in drama it helps you to think critically about characterization if you select one character for your analysis. How is this character described in stage directions? How do other characters in the play see him or her? How does the character view himself or herself? What words or actions given to this character help to define his or her personality?

Dialogue. Which is given more emphasis in the play, dialogue or physical action? Is the dialogue realistic or symbolic? To what effect does the author use poetic, colloquial, or dialect English? What is the tone of the speeches? Does the playwright use consistent patterns of imagery or metaphor in the speeches of different characters in order to suggest something important about them?

Stage Setting. How does the setting help establish the time and place of the play? Is the setting realistic or symbolic? What objects onstage are particularly important in suggesting the mood of the characters or their values? What does the setting suggest about the theme of the play? How would a different staging of the play affect your interpretation?

Irony and Symbolism. Can you find any instances of dramatic irony in the play when you (as a reader or spectator) know more about the situation than do the onstage characters? Does this make you more or less sympathetic toward the characters? What aspects of the play and its staging seem symbolic? What do they symbolize? Is the symbolism extensive enough to form an allegorical system? If so, what is the meaning implied by the allegory?

Theme. What ideas explored by the play seem most significant to you? Which of the preceding elements of the play conveys the theme most effectively? Does the playwright give a clear statement of the theme to any one of the characters? If there is no resolution of the theme in the action of the play, what emotional effect does this have on you? Is the conflict between the characters a struggle between moral good and moral evil? Is the playwright attempting to *explain* or to *explore* the issues?

It will also help you to understand drama if you remember that playwrights, like all other writers, create their plays within a tradition. The genius of Sophocles, Shakespeare, and Ibsen is inimitable, but their plays have inspired later playwrights to give their own interpretation of similar themes or develop their own approach based on an awareness of the earlier writers' dramatic techniques. Writing their plays during periods when the theater flourished in ancient Greece and Renaissance England, Sophocles and Shakespeare borrowed or appropriated the plots of *Oedipus the King* and *Hamlet* from legend, history, and earlier plays — a standard practice among playwrights in their historical periods. Appropriation, or creating a new work by taking something from a previous work, continues today as part of the legacy of our cultural heritage of literature, music, and art. As a technique or method of working, appropriation can become a new vehicle for playwrights to express their view of the human condition.

Sophocles' and Shakespeare's versions of earlier material survive because their dramatic works reveal the fullest dimensions of their sources. Their brilliant exploration of the characters of Oedipus and Hamlet have kept their plays alive in theater repertoires throughout the world, whereas the literature that gave them the ideas for their plays is now known only to specialists. The essay by Francis Fergusson on *Oedipus the King* in the Commentaries section and that by Geoffrey Bullough on *Hamlet* in the Casebook on Shakespeare's *Hamlet* will help you to understand how Sophocles and Shakespeare transformed their sources into great works of literature.

The influence of Greek dramatists such as Sophocles has continued to the present day. When Arthur Miller was interviewed by Leonard Moss in 1980, Miller said that he "would have liked to live in Greece with the tragedies." He went on to explain the influence of earlier writers on him: "I attach myself to Ibsen because I saw him as a contemporary Greek, and I suppose it's because there was a terrific reliance in him as there was in the Greeks on the idea of the continuity between the distant past and the present. 'The birds come home to roost' — they always did; your character was your fate. I like that immensely."

Playwrights are often willing to discuss how they were influenced by earlier writers. A few years after the debut of *Death of a Salesman,* when Miller adapted Ibsen's play *An Enemy of the People* for American audiences in 1951, he wrote a preface to the published version of the play to explain the strong influence of Ibsen's work on him:

> There is one quality in Ibsen that no serious writer can afford to overlook. It lies at the very center of his force, and I found in it — as I hope others will — a profound source of strength. It is his insistence, his utter conviction, that he is going to say what he has to say, and that the audience, by God, is going to listen. It is the very same quality that makes a star actor, a great public speaker, and a lunatic. Every Ibsen play begins with the unwritten words: "Now listen here!" And these words have shown me a path through the wall of "entertainment," a path that leads beyond the formulas and dried-up precepts, the pretense and fraud, of the business of the stage. Whatever else Ibsen has to teach, this is his first and greatest contribution.

As the critic Seymour L. Flaxman observed, "The realistic drama reached the peak of its development with Ibsen, and in many ways this style continues to dominate the drama today." Ibsen extended the use of discussion and debate in the dialogues between his characters to probe their mental states, and his method of analytic exposition survives in the structure of later work by Miller and Williams as well as Lorraine Hansberry, August Wilson, Milcha Sanchez-Scott, and Philip Kan Gotanda, to name only a few recent American dramatists. All of these playwrights have gone beyond Ibsen's realism to incorporate symbolic and expressionistic elements in their work, as Ibsen himself did in his later plays.

Sometimes the actors who interpret a play onstage are in a special position to perceive affinities between playwrights. Geraldine Page, an actress with a special affinity for Tennessee Williams's work, has sensed the influence of Chekhov's plays on Williams. She told an interviewer that Chekhov "gives so much of the drama out of the surface noise of life. I mean in a lot of the Chekhov plays, people are sitting around talking about tea or going fishing or things that are not to do with the central drama, but to do with the way human beings express themselves and convey these things. And Tennessee uses that too."

Edward Albee often gives provocative interviews about both the positive and negative influence of earlier playwrights on him. Albee acknowledged a negative influence in Eugene O'Neill, who argued in his plays that people needed deceptions or dreams in their lives in order to live. Albee confessed that he "probably became a playwright as much as anything to refute that whole argument of O'Neill." Like the great German playwright Bertolt Brecht, Albee has what the editor Philip Kolin describes as a "combative" view of the theater, believing that it "must disturb in order to reform society." Albee explained, "I don't think you should frighten them [the audience], I think you should terrify them."

Albee has also been outspoken in his advice to aspiring playwrights. Discussing his craft in *Dramatics* magazine, he cautioned young writers about the harmful influence of reading too many great plays:

> But let me tell you one thing, if you are going to learn from other writers, don't only read the great ones, because if you do that you'll get so filled with despair and the fear that you'll never be able to do anywhere near as well as they did that you'll stop writing. I recommend that you read a lot of bad stuff, too. It's very encouraging. "Hey, I can do so much better than this." Read the greatest stuff but read the stuff that isn't so great, too. Great stuff is very discouraging. If you read only Beckett and Chekhov you'll go away and only deliver telegrams at Western Union.

Reading widely in the history of drama, you become aware that talented writers often come of age in clusters or groups, sometimes influenced by specific theaters or directors. The cluster of playwrights in Athens who created the great tragedies for the stage during the Golden Age of Greece is well known and includes Aeschylus, Euripides, and Sophocles. The Provincetown Players, an experimental theater that flourished in the early years of this century in the bohemian enclaves of Provincetown, Massachusetts, and Greenwich Village in New York City, supported another group of writers whose plays have stood the test of time — Susan Glaspell, Eugene O'Neill, and Edna St. Vincent Millay, among scores of others. The creative work of these playwrights helped establish the modern American theater, preparing the way for the gifted playwrights of the next generation.

WRITING ABOUT DRAMA

An assignment to write an essay about a specific play or aspect of drama will give you the opportunity to bring your ideas about what you have read into focus. The process of writing about drama will sharpen your critical analysis of the text you have chosen to discuss and will clarify your understanding of the ideas dramatized by the playwright. Because every reader's background is different, your reading of the plays will reflect the life experience that you bring to them. Using the vocabulary of the elements of drama to help you express your thoughts about the plays, you have the opportunity to articulate your interpretations clearly and forcibly to another reader.

Here is an example of a student essay comparing works in two literary genres. After reading Susan Glaspell's *Trifles* (p. 1628) and Leonard Mustazza's commentary on her transformation of the play into a story (p. 1980), the student decided to present his own ideas about why the author might have chosen to rewrite the play a year later as "A Jury of Her Peers."

STUDENT ESSAY

On the Differences between Susan Glaspell's Trifles and "A Jury of Her Peers"

What is the difference between a play and a short story? Why should an author choose to write one over the other? An essential difference between a short story and a play lies in how each expresses emotion and thought to the audience. A short story allows the reader to enter a character's thoughts much more easily than a play would. In drama, a thought that could be said in a sentence in a short story requires a soliloquy or dialogue with another character that the audience can trust. On the other hand, a simple action or gesture in drama could require a great amount of narration in a short story. Each type of literature has its strengths and weaknesses.

Given the differences between the two genres, why did Susan Glaspell choose to turn her play Trifles into the short story "A Jury of Her Peers," instead of reworking the play? The answer to this question lies in what her goal with each work was, and how she wanted to achieve that goal. Both works have exactly the same dialogue, but "A Jury of Her Peers" is much longer, and has a different and more complex theme. It is the variances in theme, and the manner in which those variances are achieved, that illustrate why Glaspell might have been tempted to change genres when she transformed Trifles into a short story.

Transforming Trifles means narrating the story from the point of view of one of the main characters, even though by doing so Glaspell loses two of the themes she developed in her play. One of those is the diminution of wives by their husbands over "trifles." Another theme is the importance of the little things or "trifles" in life. The main theme in "A Jury of Her Peers," however, is much more complex. As the title suggests, the theme of the story is based on how two women, Mrs. Hale and Mrs. Peters, come to one opinion in judging another woman, Mrs. Wright. Illustrating their coming together necessitates a change in the point of view of the narratives. Trifles is presented, as most drama is, in the third-person objective while "A Jury of Her Peers" is presented in the third-person limited: The reader sees into the mind of Mrs. Hale.

In "A Jury of Her Peers," dramatizing the difference in the minds of the two women and watching them reach a consensus is the main action of the story. Glaspell makes it evident early in the narrative that Mrs. Hale and Mrs. Peters think differently. Mrs. Hale says, "I'd hate to have men comin' into my kitchen, . . . snoopin' round and criticizin'." Here Mrs. Hale is testing Mrs. Peters's response to see if Mrs. Peters will follow the letter of the law. Initially, Mrs. Peters believes in the letter of the law: "'Of course it's no more than their duty,' said the sheriff's wife, in her manner of timid acquiescence." Mrs. Peters's "acquiescence" refers to the fact that she feels she must remind Mrs. Hale of the law. But her manner is "timid," suggesting that there might be room for change in Mrs. Peters's mind.

The evolution of Mrs. Peters's attitude is evident when she says, "A person gets discouraged--and loses heart." Here Mrs. Peters shows that she understands why Mrs. Wright might have murdered her husband, given that she now knows that Mr. Wright was not the kind of person who made life enjoyable for his wife. Nevertheless, as the sheriff's wife, Mrs. Peters still struggles with the concept that "the law is the law."

Mrs. Peters's real transformation comes when Mrs. Hale starts to restitch the bad sewing. When Mrs. Peters says, "I don't think that we ought to touch things," the narrator describes her comment as being said "a little helplessly." At this point she realizes that she has lost the battle to follow the letter of the law; she starts to see things as Mrs. Hale does, in the spirit of the law. Thus, when the topic of how still the house was after the death of the bird arises, Mrs. Peters remembers the death of her baby in Dakota. She now understands the life that Mrs. Wright led and feels compassion for her. Mrs. Peters now discerns the position of Mrs. Hale. They come to an unspoken agreement to tamper with the evidence in the kitchen.

On the stage in Trifles, there is no need for the women to come to agreement over the issue of withholding evidence. When the bad sewing and the bird are found in the play, it is almost as if both women know that it must be hidden. Both seem to realize that the other knows as well. This mutual sharing of each other's feelings shows an underdevelopment of characterization in Trifles, making it seem flat in comparison to "A Jury of Her Peers." The use of a narrator to develop characterization is what gives the story a more complex theme.

Character revelation aside, the conclusion of both the play and the story is the same. The women come to agree that even though Mrs. Wright is guilty of murder, she does not deserve the punishment that the county attorney seeks. Both women feel compassion for Mrs. Wright because they can relate to her. Mrs. Hale relates the unfinished work in the Wright house to the unfinished work in her own house. Mrs. Peters relates to the stillness that was in the house. The understanding that both women have of Mrs. Wright causes them to tamper with the evidence.

Changes in the theme reflect the genre change, but they don't explain why Glaspell changed genres. A little biographical background is relevant here. Writing in the early twentieth century, Glaspell often emphasized feminist issues. Trifles tells men that women are capable of noticing details and that they have sharp minds. "A Jury of Her Peers" tells men that one of the strengths of women is their compassion. While both works tell about compassion, only the story shows men the path to feeling compassion for others.

"A Jury of Her Peers" argues that in the case of Mrs. Wright, the full weight of the law is not a just punishment for murder, because Mrs. Wright's personality and lifestyle were adversely altered by her husband. Before her marriage, she was Minnie Foster. As Mrs. Hale says, "She used to wear pretty clothes and be lively--when she was Minnie Foster, one of the town girls, singing in the choir." The key word in that passage is "when." It means that Mrs. Wright used to be like that, before her marriage. Mr. Wright is described as "a hard man. . . . Just to pass the time of day with him--. . . . Like a raw wind that gets to the bone." Mr. Wright liked none of the "trifles" that make life enjoyable. Mrs. Wright lived with him for twenty years, meaning that she did not enjoy life for twenty years. From this perspective, she could have committed murder to save her own sanity. If this was the case, then the harsh punishment that the county attorney seeks would be excessive. Though murder is wrong, seeking an excessive punishment is worse. It is akin to the saying "two wrongs don't make a right." Compassionately paying attention to the spirit of the law is what men can learn from women.

Teaching men what women have to offer society seems to be one of the reasons that Glaspell changed Trifles from a play into a short story in "A Jury of Her Peers." The story illustrates a change from thinking to feeling compassion, a transition particularly necessary for men at a time when women were still denied the right to vote or serve on juries. The evolution of the characters gives "A Jury of Her Peers" a feeling of completeness lacking in Trifles. New themes, descriptions, and lessons to be taught are all aspects of "A Jury of Her Peers." Together they form an answer to the question of why Susan Glaspell chose to change her play Trifles into a short story.

This student began to think critically about Glaspell's play and short story after reading a commentary. Finally, remember that while you can always compare and contrast the literary texts in this anthology, you can also get additional ideas for your papers by seeing a play produced on film or in the theater. In your essay, you will be expected to analyze your impressions beyond summarizing the plot. The questions about drama earlier in this chapter can help you think critically about the play.

Often, choosing a specific critical approach in your paper — biographical, historical, or reader response, for example — can give you a perspective from which to take useful notes during your second close reading of the play. Taking such an approach will clarify your understanding of how the playwright has developed dialogue, images, and patterns of action. In the Commentaries section that starts on page 1949, you will find material that illustrates different critical perspectives and suggests background information for your essays.

RELATED COMMENTARIES: *Geoffrey Bullough, "Sources of Shakespeare's* Hamlet,*" page 2017; Francis Fergusson, "Oedipus, Myth and Play," page 1970; Leonard Mustazza, "Generic Translation and Thematic Shift in Glaspell's* Trifles *and 'A Jury of Her Peers,'" page 1980; Helge Normann Nilsen, "Marxism and the Early Plays of Arthur Miller," page 2037; Joan Templeton, "Is* A Doll House *a Feminist Text?" page 2000; Margaret B. Wilkerson, "Hansberry's Awareness of Culture and Gender," page 2064.*

21

PLAYS AND PLAYWRIGHTS

SOPHOCLES *(495–406* B.C.*), along with Aeschylus and Euripides, was one of the three major authors of Greek tragedy. He lived for nearly ninety years through most of the turbulent events of his country during the fifth century* B.C. *He was only five when the Greek army turned back the invading Persians at Marathon, but he probably heard that after the battle a messenger brought word of the victory back to Athens, running the twenty-six miles between Marathon and Athens and dying of exhaustion while delivering the news. Ten years later, in 480* B.C.*, the Greeks won another major battle against the Persian navy at Salamis. At the victory celebration Sophocles, a teenager trained in dance, is said to have made his first public appearance dancing nude to his own lyre accompaniment.*

The period in which the Greek playwrights flourished is known as the Golden Age. Athens became rich as the city's allies paid its statesmen tribute money, and statesmen honored the gifted poets, playwrights, philosophers, architects, and scientists who thrived in the city. This great period lasted barely to the last years of the century, starting its decline when the armed forces of the Greek city-state were defeated in Sicily in 413 B.C. *Six years later, just before the death of Sophocles, the Spartans destroyed the Greek navy at Aegospotami and imposed their own government in Athens, bringing the Golden Age to an end.*

The earliest extant Greek play for two actors, Aeschylus's The Persians, *dates from 472* B.C. *Thirty years younger than Aeschylus, Sophocles won his first prize for one of his plays in 468* B.C. *at the Great Dionysia during the competition for playwrights in Athens. The Great Dionysia was the name given to the important holiday* each year when the Greek plays were produced. Occurring just before the arrival of spring, the festival honored Dionysus, the god of fertility and growth, who was mysteriously linked to Hades, the lord of the underworld and death. The celebration began in Athens with a procession carrying a statue of Dionysus from his temple to the theater at the Acropolis. It included the ritual slaying of a sacrificial bull and much drunken revelry, as Dionysus was also the god of wine in Greece.

The high point of the annual festival was the three-day competition among the playwrights, each of whom submitted four plays: three tragedies (tragedy was considered the highest form of drama by the Greeks) and a brief satyr play, which combined slapstick and erotic comedy. A comic play was also included in the performances, so although the plays were relatively short, the audience was expected to have sufficient stamina and interest to sit through several plays each day. As the British playwright Tony Harrison has observed, the Greek dramatists were "open-eyed about suffering but with a heart still open to celebration and physical affirmation." Traditionally during the Great Dionysia, a comic play began the program each day, and the tragic plays were followed by a satyr play to maintain "a kind of celebratory route in the sensual and everyday to follow the tragedy."

The dramatic performances at the Acropolis were part of a religious celebration, a public holiday rather than a commercial theater, with the entire population of the city marching in the procession and thousands of people filling the amphitheater on the slopes of the Acropolis to watch the plays. Originally the audience sat on the ground, then on wooden seats. When the weight of the crowd caused the wooden seats to collapse, they were replaced with concentric tiers of stone seats designed on the hillside to surround the stage almost completely. The high priest of Dionysus sat at the place of honor at the center of the first tier of this theater-in-the-round in Athens.

To keep order among the huge crowd, there were strict laws — apparently even the penalty of death — against taking another person's seat or engaging in fights. Tickets were expensive (almost the price of a laborer's daily wage), but funds were available so that poor people and slaves could attend. To underscore the religious importance of the event, prisoners were released from jail so they could also participate. Evidence suggests that women weren't admitted into the audience to watch Greek plays, but this is a contentious point argued by archeologists and historians.

During the three days of theater in Athens each year, it was customary for playwrights to act in their own plays. Apparently Sophocles could dance better than he could project his voice onstage (contemporary viewers describe him as having a "small voice"), and this would explain why he did not perform the leading role in his plays. Sophocles originated the practice of giving parts to a third actor onstage and introduced such innovations as painted scenery and a larger tragic chorus (increasing it from twelve men to fifteen). Active as a playwright in Athens for over half a century, he wrote more than a hundred plays and won first prize at the Great Dionysia eighteen times, more than any other playwright. Today only seven complete Sophoclean tragedies survive (the Oedipus trilogy and the plays Philoctetes, Ajax, Trachiniae, and Elektra) as well as a satyr play about the childhood of the god Hermes and nearly a thousand fragments of his other plays.

Sophocles and other playwrights who introduced their work during the Great Dionysia sought to arouse pity and fear among the spectators with their tragic plays about death and suffering; they sought to instill a sense of religious awe at the myste-

rious power of the gods, whose perfect knowledge of events stands in contrast to the imperfect knowledge of mortal beings. In classical Greek theater, only men were actors. They wore shoes with high heels to increase their stature and masks to help amplify their voices and simulate their appearance as mythical heroes or gods. The masks and costumes also enabled them to assume the roles of women, who were often central characters in the plays that dramatized mythical stories and legends made famous by earlier poets and historians. Actors were trained in singing and dancing as well as speaking, but in the large amphitheaters they were judged by how effectively they projected their voices to suggest the emotional states of their characters. The design of the outdoor theater and the costuming and masks of the actors contributed to the audience's sense of participation in a religious ritual. The importance of respecting the oracles — and of accepting the gods' prophecy, which is often fulfilled in ways that humans do not expect — is frequently mentioned in Oedipus the King. *At the end of the play Oedipus has learned to his sorrow that the gods are omnipotent and that he cannot escape his fate.*

Audiences watching Oedipus the King *would have known the legendary story before they came to the theater. At the beginning of the play they were aware of the tragic flaw of pride in Oedipus's character and understood the mysterious circumstances of his birth far better than he did. In the theater, the spectators' pleasure would derive from recognizing the dramatic irony in the poetic dialogue and the elegant way Sophocles structured the events of the story as Oedipus gradually uncovers the truth about his past. Unlike Aeschylian tragedy, which is essentially static, Sophocles unfolded the incidents of Oedipus's past like a detective story, linking events by cause and effect and motivating them plausibly. In the process Sophocles also revealed different dimensions of his protagonist's character, his strong as well as his weak points. Oedipus exhibits a high moral character as king. He is genuinely concerned about his subjects and eager to help them during the plague that has descended on the city. Yet he is quick to suspect his loyal brother-in-law Creon of a plot to usurp his power and ready to taunt his heartbroken wife, Jocasta, when he thinks she is glorying in her "noble blood."*

Sophocles was nicknamed "the Attic Bee" because he relied on such earlier works as Homer's Iliad *and* Odyssey *for material for his plays, but he always developed his characterizations far beyond his sources and created dialogue marked by eloquence and vigor. He also gave active roles to the chorus of citizens and the messenger, who function as important characters in the play. When Sophocles began* Oedipus the King *by having the king promise the chorus of citizens to help fight the plague, the playwright knew that this detail would arouse sympathy in the Athenian audience, because plague had ravaged their city only five years before. This addition also deepens our sense of foreboding at the beginning of the play, because Sophocles was suggesting a further irony about Oedipus's character. It was believed at the time that the well-being of the state was a reflection of the health of its ruler. The Greek audience would know that, according to legend, Oedipus was a descendent of Cadmus, the founder of Thebes. The city had a disputed leadership because of a fraternal rivalry that the gods had decreed would wipe out Cadmus's entire family.* Oedipus the King *is the first of the trilogy of plays Sophocles wrote about this tragic situation. When the three plays are produced together, they are usually presented in the order that follows the chronology of events in the plot:* Oedipus the King *(first produced between 430 and 427*

B.C.), Oedipus at Colonus *(posthumously produced in 401 B.C.), and* Antigone *(first produced in 441 B.C.).*

Oedipus the King *was considered such a masterpiece a century after its creation that the philosopher and critic Aristotle used it in the* Poetics *as the example on which to base his aesthetic theory of drama. Aristotle understood that Sophocles structured the story of* Oedipus the King *so that the rising action that revealed the complications of the plot led to Oedipus's moment of recognition in the second half of the play, precisely at the time the falling action began. In Aristotle's analysis, this combination of a serious character defect combined with the destiny ordained by the implacable gods constitutes a "tragic flaw." Sophocles structured his play so as to first arouse pity and fear in the spectators watching the proud and headstrong Oedipus gradually unravel the truth about his past, and then allow them to experience a purging or catharsis of their emotions at the sight of Oedipus broken by the gods' prophecy at the end of the play. Yet, paradoxically, the blinded figure of Oedipus remains heroic, because his determination to discover the truth about his own identity remains a moral victory despite the tragic outcome of his search. This dramatic illustration of the gods' power over human frailty must have been a transcendent religious experience for the audience during the festival of Dionysus.*

Like Oedipus the King, Antigone *is based on the tragic myth familiar to Greek audiences. Antigone is one of the daughters of Oedipus. The play begins shortly after the deaths of her father and her two brothers, Eteocles and Polynices, who have killed each other in a dispute over who will become the next king of Thebes. Antigone's uncle, Creon, inherits the throne. When he denies an honorable burial to Polynices, blaming him for the death of Eteocles, Antigone rebels against what she considers an unfair judgment against her beloved brother. She is determined to disobey Creon's orders, even if she forfeits her own life in the attempt.* Antigone *is one of the most often produced of the classic Greek tragedies, as modern audiences respond to what they see as the heroine's rebellion against tyranny and the subordination of women. As the critic George Steiner understood about* Antigone,

> *It has, I believe, been given to only one literary text to express all the principal constants of conflict in the condition of man [human beings]. These constants are fivefold: the confrontation of men and of women; of age and of youth; of society and of the individual; of the living and of the dead; of men and of god(s). The conflicts which come of these five orders of confrontation are not negotiable. Men and women, old and young, the individual and the community or state, the quick and the dead, mortals and immortals, define themselves in the conflictual process of defining each other. Self-definition and the agonistic recognition of "otherness" (of* l'autre*) across the threatened boundaries of self are indissociable. The polarities of masculinity and of femininity, of aging and of youth, of private autonomy and of social collectivity, of existence and mortality, of the human and the divine, can be crystallized only in adversative terms (whatever the many shades of accommodation between them). To arrive at oneself — the primordial journey — is to come up, polemically, against "the other."*

RELATED COMMENTARIES: *Aristotle, "On the Elements and General Principles of Tragedy," page 1955; Mary Whitlock Blundell, From* Helping Friends and Harming Enemies: A Study in Sophocles and Greek Ethics, *page 1961; Francis*

Fergusson, "Oedipus, Myth and Play," page 1970; Sigmund Freud, "The Oedipus Complex," page 1977; Muriel Rukeyser, "Myth," page 1993.

SOPHOCLES

Oedipus the King

c. 430 B.C.

TRANSLATED BY ROBERT FAGLES

CHARACTERS

OEDIPUS, *king of Thebes*
A PRIEST *of Zeus*
CREON, *brother of Jocasta*
A CHORUS *of Theban citizens and their* LEADER
TIRESIAS, *a blind prophet*
JOCASTA, *the queen, wife of Oedipus*
A MESSENGER *from Corinth*
A SHEPHERD
A MESSENGER *from inside the palace*
ANTIGONE, ISMENE, *daughters of Oedipus and Jocasta*
GUARDS AND ATTENDANTS
PRIESTS OF THEBES

TIME AND SCENE: *The royal house of Thebes. Double doors dominate the facade; a stone altar stands at the center of the stage.*

Many years have passed since Oedipus solved the riddle of the Sphinx° and ascended the throne of Thebes, and now a plague has struck the city. A procession of priests enters; suppliants, broken and despondent, they carry branches wound in wool° and lay them on the altar.

The doors open. Guards assemble. Oedipus comes forward, majestic but for a telltale limp, and slowly views the condition of his people.

OEDIPUS: Oh my children, the new blood of ancient Thebes,
why are you here? Huddling at my altar,
praying before me, your branches wound in wool.
Our city reeks with the smoke of burning incense,
rings with cries for the Healer and wailing for the dead.
I thought it wrong, my children, to hear the truth
from others, messengers. Here I am myself —
you all know me, the world knows my fame:
I am Oedipus.

Helping a Priest to his feet.

Speak up, old man. Your years,
your dignity — you should speak for the others.
Why here and kneeling, what preys upon you so?

---

s.d. the riddle of the Sphinx: The Sphinx asked, "What walks on four legs in the morning, two at noon, and three in the evening?" Oedipus replied, "Man."
s.d. wool: Wool was used in offerings to Apollo, the god of poetry, sun, prophecy, and healing.

Some sudden fear? some strong desire?
You can trust me; I am ready to help,
I'll do anything. I would be blind to misery
not to pity my people kneeling at my feet.

PRIEST: Oh Oedipus, king of the land, our greatest power!
You see us before you, men of all ages
clinging to your altars. Here are boys,
still too weak to fly from the nest,
and here the old, bowed down with the years,
the holy ones — a priest of Zeus° myself — and here
the picked, unmarried men, the young hope of Thebes.
And all the rest, your great family gathers now,
branches wreathed, massing in the squares,
kneeling before the two temples of queen Athena°
or the river-shrine where the embers glow and die
and Apollo sees the future in the ashes.
Our city —
look around you, see with your own eyes —
our ship pitches wildly, cannot lift her head
from the depths, the red waves of death . . .
Thebes is dying. A blight on the fresh crops
and the rich pastures, cattle sicken and die,
and the women die in labor, children stillborn,
and the plague, the fiery god of fever hurls down
on the city, his lightning slashing through us —
raging plague in all its vengeance, devastating
the house of Cadmus!° And Black Death luxuriates
in the raw, wailing miseries of Thebes.

Now we pray to you. You cannot equal the gods,
your children know that, bending at your altar.
But we do rate you first of men,
both in the common crises of our lives
and face-to-face encounters with the gods.
You freed us from the Sphinx; you came to Thebes
and cut us loose from the bloody tribute we had paid
that harsh, brutal singer. We taught you nothing,
no skill, no extra knowledge, still you triumphed.
A god was with you, so they say, and we believe it —
you lifted up our lives.
So now again,
Oedipus, king, we bend to you, your power —
we implore you, all of us on our knees:
find us strength, rescue! Perhaps you've heard

21. Zeus: The highest Olympian deity and father of Apollo. **25. Athena:** The goddess of wisdom and protector of Greek cities. **37. Cadmus:** The legendary founder of Thebes.

the voice of a god or something from other men,
Oedipus . . . what do you know?
The man of experience — you see it every day —
his plans will work in a crisis, his first of all.
Act now — we beg you, best of men, raise up our city!
Act, defend yourself, your former glory!
Your country calls you savior now
for your zeal, your action years ago.
Never let us remember of your reign:
you helped us stand, only to fall once more.
Oh raise up our city, set us on our feet.
The omens were good that day you brought us joy —
be the same man today!
Rule our land, you know you have the power,
but rule a land of the living, not a wasteland.
Ship and towered city are nothing, stripped of men
alive within it, living all as one.

OEDIPUS: My children,
I pity you. I see — how could I fail to see
what longings bring you here? Well I know
you are sick to death, all of you,
but sick as you are, not one is sick as I.
Your pain strikes each of you alone, each
in the confines of himself, no other. But my spirit
grieves for the city, for myself and all of you.
I wasn't asleep, dreaming. You haven't wakened me —
I've wept through the nights, you must know that,
groping, laboring over many paths of thought.
After a painful search I found one cure:
I acted at once. I sent Creon,
my wife's own brother, to Delphi° —
Apollo the Prophet's oracle — to learn
what I might do or say to save our city.

Today's the day. When I count the days gone by
it torments me . . . what is he doing?
Strange, he's late, he's gone too long.
But once he returns, then, then I'll be a traitor
if I do not do all the god makes clear.

PRIEST: Timely words. The men over there
are signaling — Creon's just arriving.

OEDIPUS:

Sighting Creon, then turning to the altar.

Lord Apollo,

---

82. Delphi: The shrine where the oracle of Apollo held forth.

let him come with a lucky word of rescue,
shining like his eyes!

PRIEST: Welcome news, I think — he's crowned, look,
and the laurel wreath is bright with berries.

OEDIPUS: We'll soon see. He's close enough to hear —

Enter Creon from the side; his face is shaded with a wreath.

Creon, prince, my kinsman, what do you bring us?
What message from the god?

CREON: Good news.
I tell you even the hardest things to bear,
if they should turn out well, all would be well.

OEDIPUS: Of course, but what were the god's *words?* There's no hope
and nothing to fear in what you've said so far.

CREON: If you want my report in the presence of these . . .

Pointing to the priests while drawing Oedipus toward the palace.

I'm ready now, or we might go inside.

OEDIPUS: Speak out,
speak to us all. I grieve for these, my people,
far more than I fear for my own life.

CREON: Very well,
I will tell you what I heard from the god.
Apollo commands us — he was quite clear —
"Drive the corruption from the land,
don't harbor it any longer, past all cure,
don't nurse it in your soil — root it out!"

OEDIPUS: How can we cleanse ourselves — what rites?
What's the source of the trouble?

CREON: Banish the man, or pay back blood with blood.
Murder sets the plague-storm on the city.

OEDIPUS: Whose murder?
Whose fate does Apollo bring to light?

CREON: Our leader,
my lord, was once a man named Laius,
before you came and put us straight on course.

OEDIPUS: I know —
or so I've heard. I never saw the man myself.

CREON: Well, he was killed, and Apollo commands us now —
he could not be more clear,
"Pay the killers back — whoever is responsible."

OEDIPUS: Where on earth are they? Where to find it now,
the trail of the ancient guilt so hard to trace?

CREON: "Here in Thebes," he said.
Whatever is sought for can be caught, you know,
whatever is neglected slips away.

OEDIPUS: But where,

in the palace, the fields or foreign soil,
where did Laius meet his bloody death?

CREON: He went to consult an oracle, he said,
and he set out and never came home again.

OEDIPUS: No messenger, no fellow-traveler saw what happened?
Someone to cross-examine?

CREON: No,
they were all killed but one. He escaped,
terrified, he could tell us nothing clearly,
nothing of what he saw — just one thing.

OEDIPUS: What's that?
One thing could hold the key to it all,
a small beginning gives us grounds for hope.

CREON: He said thieves attacked them — a whole band,
not single-handed, cut King Laius down.

OEDIPUS: A thief,
so daring, wild, he'd kill a king? Impossible,
unless conspirators paid him off in Thebes.

CREON: We suspected as much. But with Laius dead
no leader appeared to help us in our troubles.

OEDIPUS: Trouble? Your *king* was murdered — royal blood!
What stopped you from tracking down the killer
then and there?

CREON: The singing, riddling Sphinx.
She . . . persuaded us to let the mystery go
and concentrate on what lay at our feet.

OEDIPUS: No,
I'll start again — I'll bring it all to light myself!
Apollo is right, and so are you, Creon,
to turn our attention back to the murdered man.
Now you have *me* to fight for you, you'll see:
I am the land's avenger by all rights
and Apollo's champion too.
But not to assist some distant kinsman, no,
for my own sake I'll rid us of this corruption.
Whoever killed the king may decide to kill me too,
with the same violent hand — by avenging Laius
I defend myself.

To the priests.

Quickly, my children.
Up from the steps, take up your branches now.

To the guards.

One of you summon the city here before us,
tell them I'll do everything. God help us,
we will see our triumph — or our fall.

Oedipus and Creon enter the palace, followed by the guards.

PRIEST: Rise, my sons. The kindness we came for
Oedipus volunteers himself.
Apollo has sent his word, his oracle —
Come down, Apollo, save us, stop the plague.

The priests rise, remove their branches, and exit to the side. Enter a Chorus, the citizens of Thebes, who have not heard the news that Creon brings. They march around the altar, chanting.

CHORUS: Zeus!
Great welcome voice of Zeus, what do you bring?
What word from the gold vaults of Delphi
comes to brilliant Thebes? I'm racked with terror —
terror shakes my heart
and I cry your wild cries, Apollo, Healer of Delos°
I worship you in dread . . . what now, what is your price?
some new sacrifice? some ancient rite from the past
come round again each spring? —
what will you bring to birth?
Tell me, child of golden Hope
warm voice that never dies!

You are the first I call, daughter of Zeus
deathless Athena — I call your sister Artemis,°
heart of the market place enthroned in glory,
guardian of our earth —
I call Apollo astride the thunderheads of heaven —
O triple shield against death, shine before me now!
If ever, once in the past, you stopped some ruin
launched against our walls
you hurled the flame of pain
far, far from Thebes — you gods
come now, come down once more!

No, no
the miseries numberless, grief on grief, no end —
too much to bear, we are all dying
O my people . . .
Thebes like a great army dying
and there is no sword of thought to save us, no
and the fruits of our famous earth, they will not ripen
no and the women cannot scream their pangs to birth —
screams for the Healer, children dead in the womb
and life on life goes down

173. Delos: Apollo was born on this sacred island. **181. Artemis:** Apollo's sister, the goddess of hunting, the moon, and chastity.

you can watch them go
like seabirds winging west, outracing the day's fire
down the horizon, irresistibly
streaking on to the shores of Evening
Death
so many deaths, numberless deaths on deaths, no end —
Thebes is dying, look, her children
stripped of pity . . .
generations strewn on the ground
unburied, unwept, the dead spreading death
and the young wives and gray-haired mothers with them
cling to the altars, trailing in from all over the city —
Thebes, city of death, one long cortege
and the suffering rises
wails for mercy rise
and the wild hymn for the Healer blazes out
clashing with our sobs our cries of mourning —
O golden daughter of god, send rescue
radiant as the kindness in your eyes!
Drive him back! — the fever, the god of death
that raging god of war
not armored in bronze, not shielded now, he burns me,
battle cries in the onslaught burning on —
O rout him from our borders!
Sail him, blast him out to the Sea-queen's chamber
the black Atlantic gulfs
or the northern harbor, death to all
where the Thracian surf comes crashing.
Now what the night spares he comes by day and kills —
the god of death.
O lord of the stormcloud,
you who twirl the lightning, Zeus, Father,
thunder Death to nothing!

Apollo, lord of the light, I beg you —
whip your longbow's golden cord
showering arrows on our enemies — shafts of power
champions strong before us rushing on!

Artemis, Huntress,
torches flaring over the eastern ridges —
ride Death down in pain!

God of the headdress gleaming gold, I cry to you —
your name and ours are one, Dionysus° —
come with your face aflame with wine

239. Dionysus: The god of fertility and wine.

your raving women's cries°
your army on the march! Come with the lightning
come with torches blazing, eyes ablaze with glory!
Burn that god of death that all gods hate!

Oedipus enters from the palace to address the Chorus, as if addressing the entire city of Thebes.

OEDIPUS: You pray to the gods? Let me grant your prayers.
Come, listen to me — do what the plague demands:
you'll find relief and lift your head from the depths.

I will speak out now as a stranger to the story,
a stranger to the crime. If I'd been present then,
there would have been no mystery, no long hunt
without a clue in hand. So now, counted
a native Theban years after the murder,
to all of Thebes I make this proclamation:
if any one of you knows who murdered Laius,
the son of Labdacus, I order him to reveal
the whole truth to me. Nothing to fear,
even if he must denounce himself,
let him speak up
and so escape the brunt of the charge —
he will suffer no unbearable punishment,
nothing worse than exile, totally unharmed.

Oedipus pauses, waiting for a reply.

Next,
if anyone knows the murderer is a stranger,
a man from alien soil, come, speak up.
I will give him a handsome reward, and lay up
gratitude in my heart for him besides.

Silence again, no reply.

But if you keep silent, if anyone panicking,
trying to shield himself or friend or kin,
rejects my offer, then hear what I will do.
I order you, every citizen of the state
where I hold throne and power: banish this man —
whoever he may be — never shelter him, never
speak a word to him, never make him partner
to your prayers, your victims burned to the gods.
Never let the holy water touch his hands.
Drive him out, each of you, from every home.
He is the plague, the heart of our corruption,
as Apollo's oracle has revealed to me

---

241. your . . . cries: Dionysus was attended by female celebrants.

just now. So I honor my obligations:
I fight for the god and for the murdered man.

Now my curse on the murderer. Whoever he is,
a lone man unknown in his crime
or one among many, let that man drag out
his life in agony, step by painful step —
I curse myself as well . . . if by any chance
he proves to be an intimate of our house,
here at my hearth, with my full knowledge,
may the curse I just called down on him strike me!

These are your orders: perform them to the last.
I command you, for my sake, for Apollo's, for this country
blasted root and branch by the angry heavens.
Even if god had never urged you on to act,
how could you leave the crime uncleansed so long?
A man so noble — your king, brought down in blood —
you should have searched. But I am the king now,
I hold the throne that he held then, possess his bed
and a wife who shares our seed . . . why, our seed
might be the same, children born of the same mother
might have created blood-bonds between us
if his hope of offspring hadn't met disaster —
but fate swooped at his head and cut him short.
So I will fight for him as if he were my father,
stop at nothing, search the world
to lay my hands on the man who shed his blood,
the son of Labdacus descended of Polydorus,
Cadmus of old and Agenor, founder of the line:
their power and mine are one.
Oh dear gods,
my curse on those who disobey these orders!
Let no crops grow out of the earth for them —
shrivel their women, kill their sons,
burn them to nothing in this plague
that hits us now, or something even worse.
But you, loyal men of Thebes who approve my actions,
may our champion, Justice, may all the gods
be with us, fight beside us to the end!

LEADER: In the grip of your curse, my king, I swear
I'm not the murderer, cannot point him out.
As for the search, Apollo pressed it on us —
he should name the killer.

OEDIPUS: Quite right,
but to force the gods to act against their will —
no man has the power.

LEADER: Then if I might mention

the next best thing . . .

OEDIPUS: The third best too —
don't hold back, say it.

LEADER: I still believe . . .
Lord Tiresias sees with the eyes of Lord Apollo.
Anyone searching for the truth, my king,
might learn it from the prophet, clear as day.

OEDIPUS: I've not been slow with that. On Creon's cue
I sent the escorts, twice, within the hour.
I'm surprised he isn't here.

LEADER: We need him —
without him we have nothing but old, useless rumors.

OEDIPUS: Which rumors? I'll search out every word.

LEADER: Laius was killed, they say, by certain travelers.

OEDIPUS: I know — but no one can find the murderer.

LEADER: If the man has a trace of fear in him
he won't stay silent long,
not with your curses ringing in his ears.

OEDIPUS: He didn't flinch at murder,
he'll never flinch at words.

Enter Tiresias, the blind prophet, led by a boy with escorts in attendance. He remains at a distance.

LEADER: Here is the one who will convict him, look,
they bring him on at last, the seer, the man of god.
The truth lives inside him, him alone.

OEDIPUS: O Tiresias,
master of all the mysteries of our life,
all you teach and all you dare not tell,
signs in the heavens, signs that walk the earth!
Blind as you are, you can feel all the more
what sickness haunts our city. You, my lord,
are the one shield, the one savior we can find.

We asked Apollo — perhaps the messengers
haven't told you — he sent his answer back:
"Relief from the plague can only come one way.
Uncover the murderers of Laius,
put them to death or drive them into exile."
So I beg you, grudge us nothing now, no voice,
no message plucked from the birds, the embers
or the other mantic ways within your grasp.
Rescue yourself, your city, rescue me —
rescue everything infected by the dead.
We are in your hands. For a man to help others
with all his gifts and native strength:
that is the noblest work.

TIRESIAS: How terrible — to see the truth

when the truth is only pain to him who sees!
I knew it well, but I put it from my mind,
else I never would have come.

OEDIPUS: What's this? Why so grim, so dire?

TIRESIAS: Just send me home. You bear your burdens,
I'll bear mine. It's better that way,
please believe me.

OEDIPUS: Strange response — unlawful,
unfriendly too to the state that bred and raised you;
you're withholding the word of god.

TIRESIAS: I fail to see
that your own words are so well-timed.
I'd rather not have the same thing said of me . . .

OEDIPUS: For the love of god, don't turn away,
not if you know something. We beg you,
all of us on our knees.

TIRESIAS: None of you knows —
and I will never reveal my dreadful secrets,
not to say your own.

OEDIPUS: What? You know and you won't tell?
You're bent on betraying us, destroying Thebes?

TIRESIAS: I'd rather not cause pain for you or me.
So why this . . . useless interrogation?
You'll get nothing from me.

OEDIPUS: Nothing! You,
you scum of the earth, you'd enrage a heart of stone!
You won't talk? Nothing moves you?
Out with it, once and for all!

TIRESIAS: You criticize my temper . . . unaware
of the one *you* live with, you revile me.

OEDIPUS: Who could restrain his anger hearing you?
What outrage — you spurn the city!

TIRESIAS: What will come will come.
Even if I shroud it all in silence.

OEDIPUS: What will come? You're bound to *tell* me that.

TIRESIAS: I'll say no more. Do as you like, build your anger
to whatever pitch you please, rage your worst —

OEDIPUS: Oh I'll let loose, I have such fury in me —
now I see it all. You helped hatch the plot,
you did the work, yes, short of killing him
with your own hands — and given eyes I'd say
you did the killing single-handed!

TIRESIAS: Is that so!
I charge you, then, submit to that decree
you just laid down: from this day onward
speak to no one, not these citizens, not myself.
You are the curse, the corruption of the land!

OEDIPUS: You, shameless —
aren't you appalled to start up such a story?
You think you can get away with this?
TIRESIAS: I have already.
The truth with all its power lives inside me.
OEDIPUS: Who primed you for this? Not your prophet's trade.
TIRESIAS: You did, you forced me, twisted it out of me.
OEDIPUS: What? Say it again — I'll understand it better.
TIRESIAS: Didn't you understand, just now?
Or are you tempting me to talk?
OEDIPUS: No, I can't say I grasped your meaning.
Out with it, again!
TIRESIAS: I say you are the murderer you hunt.
OEDIPUS: That obscenity, twice — by god, you'll pay.
TIRESIAS: Shall I say more, so you can really rage?
OEDIPUS: Much as you want. Your words are nothing —
futile.
TIRESIAS: You cannot imagine . . . I tell you,
you and your loved ones live together in infamy,
you cannot see how far you've gone in guilt.
OEDIPUS: You think you can keep this up and never suffer?
TIRESIAS: Indeed, if the truth has any power.
OEDIPUS: It does
but not for you, old man. You've lost your power,
stone-blind, stone-deaf — senses, eyes blind as stone!
TIRESIAS: I pity you, flinging at me the very insults
each man here will fling at you so soon.
OEDIPUS: Blind,
lost in the night, endless night that nursed you!
You can't hurt me or anyone else who sees the light —
you can never touch me.
TIRESIAS: True, it is not your fate
to fall at my hands. Apollo is quite enough,
and he will take some pains to work this out.
OEDIPUS: Creon! Is this conspiracy his or yours?
TIRESIAS: Creon is not your downfall, no, you are your own.
OEDIPUS: O power —
wealth and empire, skill outstripping skill
in the heady rivalries of life,
what envy lurks inside you! Just for this,
the crown the city gave me — I never sought it,
they laid it in my hands — for this alone, Creon,
the soul of trust, my loyal friend from the start
steals against me . . . so hungry to overthrow me
he sets this wizard on me, this scheming quack,
this fortune-teller peddling lies, eyes peeled
for his own profit — seer blind in his craft!

Come here, you pious fraud. Tell me,
when did you ever prove yourself a prophet?
When the Sphinx, that chanting Fury kept her deathwatch here,
why silent then, not a word to set our people free?
There was a riddle, not for some passer-by to solve —
it cried out for a prophet. Where were you?
Did you rise to the crisis? Not a word,
you and your birds, your gods — nothing.
No, but I came by, Oedipus the ignorant,
I stopped the Sphinx! With no help from the birds,
the flight of my own intelligence hit the mark.

And this is the man you'd try to overthrow?
You think you'll stand by Creon when he's king?
You and the great mastermind —
you'll pay in tears, I promise you, for this,
this witch-hunt. If you didn't look so senile
the lash would teach you what your scheming means!

LEADER: I'd suggest his words were spoken in anger,
Oedipus . . . yours too, and it isn't what we need.
The best solution to the oracle, the riddle
posed by god — we should look for that.

TIRESIAS: You are the king no doubt, but in one respect,
at least, I am your equal: the right to reply.
I claim that privilege too.
I am not your slave. I serve Apollo.
I don't need Creon to speak for me in public.
So,
you mock my blindness? Let me tell you this.
You with your precious eyes,
you're blind to the corruption of your life,
to the house you live in, those you live with —
who *are* your parents? Do you know? All unknowing
you are the scourge of your own flesh and blood,
the dead below the earth and the living here above,
and the double lash of your mother and your father's curse
will whip you from this land one day, their footfall
treading you down in terror, darkness shrouding
your eyes that now can see the light!
Soon, soon
you'll scream aloud — what haven won't reverberate?
What rock of Cithaeron° won't scream back in echo?
That day you learn the truth about your marriage,
the wedding-march that sang you into your halls,

---

481. Cithaeron: The mountains where Oedipus was abandoned as an infant.

the lusty voyage home to the fatal harbor!
And a load of other horrors you'd never dream
will level you with yourself and all your children.

There. Now smear us with insults — Creon, myself
and every word I've said. No man will ever
be rooted from the earth as brutally as you.

OEDIPUS: Enough! Such filth from him? Insufferable —
what, still alive? Get out —
faster, back where you came from — vanish!

TIRESIAS: I'd never have come if you hadn't called me here.

OEDIPUS: If I thought you'd blurt out such absurdities,
you'd have died waiting before I'd had you summoned.

TIRESIAS: Absurd, am I? To you, not to your parents:
the ones who bore you found me sane enough.

OEDIPUS: Parents — who? Wait . . . who is my father?

TIRESIAS: This day will bring your birth and your destruction.

OEDIPUS: Riddles — all you can say are riddles, murk and darkness.

TIRESIAS: Ah, but aren't you the best man alive at solving riddles?

OEDIPUS: Mock me for that, go on, and you'll reveal my greatness.

TIRESIAS: Your great good fortune, true, it was your ruin.

OEDIPUS: Not if I saved the city — what do I care?

TIRESIAS: Well then, I'll be going.

To his attendant.

Take me home, boy.

OEDIPUS: Yes, take him away. You're a nuisance here.
Out of the way, the irritation's gone.

Turning his back on Tiresias, moving toward the palace.

TIRESIAS: I will go,
once I have said what I came here to say.
I'll never shrink from the anger in your eyes —
you can't destroy me. Listen to me closely:
the man you've sought so long, proclaiming,
cursing up and down, the murderer of Laius —
he is here. A stranger,
you may think, who lives among you,
he soon will be revealed a native Theban
but he will take no joy in the revelation.
Blind who now has eyes, beggar who now is rich,
he will grope his way toward a foreign soil,
a stick tapping before him step by step.

Oedipus enters the palace.

Revealed at last, brother and father both
to the children he embraces, to his mother
son and husband both — he sowed the loins
his father sowed, he spilled his father's blood!

Go in and reflect on that, solve that.
And if you find I've lied
from this day onward call the prophet blind.

Tiresias and the boy exit to the side.

CHORUS: Who —
who is the man the voice of god denounces
resounding out of the rocky gorge of Delphi?
The horror too dark to tell,
whose ruthless bloody hands have done the work?
His time has come to fly
to outrace the stallions of the storm
his feet a streak of speed —
Cased in armor, Apollo son of the Father
lunges on him, lightning-bolts afire!
And the grim unerring Furies°
closing for the kill.
Look,
the word of god has just come blazing
flashing off Parnassus'° snowy heights!
That man who left no trace —
after him, hunt him down with all our strength!
Now under bristling timber
up through rocks and caves he stalks
like the wild mountain bull —
cut off from men, each step an agony, frenzied, racing blind
but he cannot outrace the dread voices of Delphi
ringing out of the heart of Earth,
the dark wings beating around him shrieking doom
the doom that never dies, the terror —

The skilled prophet scans the birds and shatters me with terror!
I can't accept him, can't deny him, don't know what to say,
I'm lost, and the wings of dark foreboding beating —
I cannot see what's come, what's still to come . . .
and what could breed a blood feud between
Laius' house and the son of Polybus?°
I know of nothing, not in the past and not now,
no charge to bring against our king, no cause
to attack his fame that rings throughout Thebes —
not without proof — not for the ghost of Laius,
not to avenge a murder gone without a trace.

Zeus and Apollo know, they know, the great masters
of all the dark and depth of human life.

---

536. Furies: Three spirits who avenged evildoers. **539. Parnassus:** A mountain in Greece associated with Apollo. **555. Polybus:** The King of Corinth, who is thought to be Oedipus's father.

But whether a mere man can know the truth,
whether a seer can fathom more than I —
there is no test, no certain proof
though matching skill for skill
a man can outstrip a rival. No, not till I see
these charges proved will I side with his accusers.
We saw him then, when the she-hawk° swept against him,
saw with our own eyes his skill, his brilliant triumph —
there was the test — he was the joy of Thebes!
Never will I convict my king, never in my heart.

Enter Creon from the side.

CREON: My fellow-citizens, I hear King Oedipus
levels terrible charges at me. I had to come.
I resent it deeply. If, in the present crisis,
he thinks he suffers any abuse from me,
anything I've done or said that offers him
the slightest injury, why, I've no desire
to linger out this life, my reputation a shambles.
The damage I'd face from such an accusation
is nothing simple. No, there's nothing worse:
branded a traitor in the city, a traitor
to all of you and my good friends.
LEADER: True,
but a slur might have been forced out of him,
by anger perhaps, not any firm conviction.
CREON: The charge was made in public, wasn't it?
I put the prophet up to spreading lies?
LEADER: Such things were said . . .
I don't know with what intent, if any.
CREON: Was his glance steady, his mind right
when the charge was brought against me?
LEADER: I really couldn't say. I never look
to judge the ones in power.

The doors open. Oedipus enters.

Wait,
here's Oedipus now.
OEDIPUS: You — here? You have the gall
to show your face before the palace gates?
You, plotting to kill me, kill the king —
I see it all, the marauding thief himself
scheming to steal my crown and power!
Tell me,
in god's name, what did you take me for,

569. she-hawk: The Sphinx.

coward or fool, when you spun out your plot?
Your treachery — you think I'd never detect it
creeping against me in the dark? Or sensing it,
not defend myself? Aren't you the fool,
you and your high adventure. Lacking numbers,
powerful friends, out for the big game of empire —
you need riches, armies to bring that quarry down!

CREON: Are you quite finished? It's your turn to listen
for just as long as you've . . . instructed me.
Hear me out, then judge me on the facts.

OEDIPUS: You've a wicked way with words, Creon,
but I'll be slow to learn — from you.
I find you a menace, a great burden to me.

CREON: Just one thing, hear me out in this.

OEDIPUS: Just one thing,
don't tell me you're not the enemy, the traitor.

CREON: Look, if you think crude, mindless stubbornness
such a gift, you've lost your sense of balance.

OEDIPUS: If you think you can abuse a kinsman,
then escape the penalty, you're insane.

CREON: Fair enough, I grant you. But this injury
you say I've done you, what is it?

OEDIPUS: Did you induce me, yes or no,
to send for that sanctimonious prophet?

CREON: I did. And I'd do the same again.

OEDIPUS: All right then, tell me, how long is it now
since Laius . . .

CREON: Laius — what did *he* do?

OEDIPUS: Vanished,
swept from sight, murdered in his tracks.

CREON: The count of the years would run you far back . . .

OEDIPUS: And that far back, was the prophet at his trade?

CREON: Skilled as he is today, and just as honored.

OEDIPUS: Did he ever refer to me then, at that time?

CREON: No,
never, at least, when I was in his presence.

OEDIPUS: But you did investigate the murder, didn't you?

CREON: We did our best, of course, discovered nothing.

OEDIPUS: But the great seer never accused me then — why not?

CREON: I don't know. And when I don't, *I* keep quiet.

OEDIPUS: You do know this, you'd tell it too —
if you had a shred of decency.

CREON: What?
If I know, I won't hold back.

OEDIPUS: Simply this:
if the two of you had never put heads together,
we'd never have heard about *my* killing Laius.

CREON: If that's what he says . . . well, you know best.
But now I have a right to learn from you
as you just learned from me.
OEDIPUS: Learn your fill,
you never will convict me of the murder.
CREON: Tell me, you're married to my sister, aren't you?
OEDIPUS: A genuine discovery — there's no denying that.
CREON: And you rule the land with her, with equal power?
OEDIPUS: She receives from me whatever she desires.
CREON: And I am the third, all of us are equals?
OEDIPUS: Yes, and it's there you show your stripes —
you betray a kinsman.
CREON: Not at all.
Not if you see things calmly, rationally,
as I do. Look at it this way first:
who in his right mind would rather rule
and live in anxiety than sleep in peace?
Particularly if he enjoys the same authority.
Not I, I'm not the man to yearn for kingship,
not with a king's power in my hands. Who would?
No one with any sense of self-control.
Now, as it is, you offer me all I need,
not a fear in the world. But if I wore the crown . . .
there'd be many painful duties to perform,
hardly to my taste.
How could kingship
please me more than influence, power
without a qualm? I'm not that deluded yet,
to reach for anything but privilege outright,
profit free and clear.
Now all men sing my praises, all salute me,
now all who request your favors curry mine.
I'm their best hope: success rests in me.
Why give up that, I ask you, and borrow trouble?
A man of sense, someone who sees things clearly
would never resort to treason.
No, I've no lust for conspiracy in me,
nor could I ever suffer one who does.

Do you want proof? Go to Delphi yourself,
examine the oracle and see if I've reported
the message word-for-word. This too:
if you detect that I and the clairvoyant
have plotted anything in common, arrest me,
execute me. Not on the strength of one vote,
two in this case, mine as well as yours.
But don't convict me on sheer unverified surmise.

How wrong it is to take the good for bad,
purely at random, or take the bad for good.
But reject a friend, a kinsman? I would as soon
tear out the life within us, priceless life itself.
You'll learn this well, without fail, in time.
Time alone can bring the just man to light;
the criminal you can spot in one short day.

LEADER: Good advice,
my lord, for anyone who wants to avoid disaster.
Those who jump to conclusions may be wrong.

OEDIPUS: When my enemy moves against me quickly,
plots in secret, I move quickly too, I must,
I plot and pay him back. Relax my guard a moment,
waiting his next move — he wins his objective,
I lose mine.

CREON: What do you want?
You want me banished?

OEDIPUS: No, I want you dead.

CREON: Just to show how ugly a grudge can . . .

OEDIPUS: So,
still stubborn? you don't think I'm serious?

CREON: I think you're insane.

OEDIPUS: Quite sane — in my behalf.

CREON: Not just as much in mine?

OEDIPUS: You — my mortal enemy?

CREON: What if you're wholly wrong?

OEDIPUS: No matter — I must rule.

CREON: Not if you rule unjustly.

OEDIPUS: Hear him, Thebes, my city!

CREON: My city too, not yours alone!

LEADER: Please, my lords.

Enter Jocasta from the palace.

Look, Jocasta's coming,
and just in time too. With her help
you must put this fighting of yours to rest.

JOCASTA: Have you no sense? Poor misguided men,
such shouting — why this public outburst?
Aren't you ashamed, with the land so sick,
to stir up private quarrels?

To Oedipus.

Into the palace now. And Creon, you go home.
Why make such a furor over nothing?

CREON: My sister, it's dreadful . . . Oedipus, your husband,
he's bent on a choice of punishments for me,
banishment from the fatherland or death.

OEDIPUS: Precisely. I caught him in the act, Jocasta,
plotting, about to stab me in the back.
CREON: Never — curse me, let me die and be damned
if I've done you any wrong you charge me with.
JOCASTA: Oh god, believe it, Oedipus,
honor the solemn oath he swears to heaven.
Do it for me, for the sake of all your people.

The Chorus begins to chant.

CHORUS: Believe it, be sensible
give way, my king, I beg you!
OEDIPUS: What do you want from me, concessions?
CHORUS: Respect him — he's been no fool in the past
and now he's strong with the oath he swears to god.
OEDIPUS: You know what you're asking?
CHORUS: I do.
OEDIPUS: Then out with it!
CHORUS: The man's your friend, your kin, he's under oath —
don't cast him out, disgraced
branded with guilt on the strength of hearsay only.
OEDIPUS: Know full well, if that's what you want
you want me dead or banished from the land.
CHORUS: Never —
no, by the blazing Sun, first god of the heavens!
Stripped of the gods, stripped of loved ones,
let me die by inches if that ever crossed my mind.
But the heart inside me sickens, dies as the land dies
and now on top of the old griefs you pile this,
your fury — both of you!
OEDIPUS: Then let him go,
even if it does lead to my ruin, my death
or my disgrace, driven from Thebes for life.
It's you, not him I pity — your words move me.
He, wherever he goes, my hate goes with him.
CREON: Look at you, sullen in yielding, brutal in your rage —
you'll go too far. It's perfect justice:
natures like yours are hardest on themselves.
OEDIPUS: Then leave me alone — get out!
CREON: I'm going.
You're wrong, so wrong. These men know I'm right.

Exit to the side. The Chorus turns to Jocasta.

CHORUS: Why do you hesitate, my lady
why not help him in?
JOCASTA: Tell me what's happened first.
CHORUS: Loose, ignorant talk started dark suspicions
and a sense of injustice cut deeply too.
JOCASTA: On both sides?

CHORUS: Oh yes.
JOCASTA: What did they say?
CHORUS: Enough, please, enough! The land's so racked already
or so it seems to me . . .
End the trouble here, just where they left it.
OEDIPUS: You see what comes of your good intentions now?
And all because you tried to blunt my anger.
CHORUS: My king,
I've said it once, I'll say it time and again —
I'd be insane, you know it,
senseless, ever to turn my back on you.
You who set our beloved land — storm-tossed, shattered —
straight on course. Now again, good helmsman,
steer us through the storm!

The Chorus draws away, leaving Oedipus and Jocasta side by side.

JOCASTA: For the love of god,
Oedipus, tell me too, what is it?
Why this rage? You're so unbending.
OEDIPUS: I will tell you. I respect you, Jocasta,
much more than these . . .

Glancing at the Chorus.

Creon's to blame, Creon schemes against me.
JOCASTA: Tell me clearly, how did the quarrel start?
OEDIPUS: He says *I* murdered Laius — I am guilty.
JOCASTA: How does he know? Some secret knowledge
or simple hearsay?
OEDIPUS: Oh, he sent his prophet in
to do his dirty work. You know Creon,
Creon keeps his own lips clean.
JOCASTA: A prophet?
Well then, free yourself of every charge!
Listen to me and learn some peace of mind:
no skill in the world,
nothing human can penetrate the future.
Here is proof, quick and to the point.
An oracle came to Laius one fine day
(I won't say from Apollo himself
but his underlings, his priests) and it said
that doom would strike him down at the hands of a son,
our son, to be born of our own flesh and blood. But Laius,
so the report goes at least, was killed by strangers,
thieves, at a place where three roads meet . . . my son —
he wasn't three days old and the boy's father
fastened his ankles, had a henchman fling him away
on a barren, trackless mountain.
There, you see?

Apollo brought neither thing to pass. My baby
no more murdered his father than Laius suffered —
his wildest fear — death at his own son's hands.
That's how the seers and their revelations
mapped out the future. Brush them from your mind.
Whatever the god needs and seeks
he'll bring to light himself, with ease.

OEDIPUS: Strange,
hearing you just now . . . my mind wandered,
my thoughts racing back and forth.

JOCASTA: What do you mean? Why so anxious, startled?

OEDIPUS: I thought I heard you say that Laius
was cut down at a place where three roads meet.

JOCASTA: That was the story. It hasn't died out yet.

OEDIPUS: Where did this thing happen? Be precise.

JOCASTA: A place called Phocis, where two branching roads,
one from Daulia, one from Delphi,
come together — a crossroads.

OEDIPUS: When? How long ago?

JOCASTA: The heralds no sooner reported Laius dead
than you appeared and they hailed you king of Thebes.

OEDIPUS: My god, my god — what have you planned to do to me?

JOCASTA: What, Oedipus? What haunts you so?

OEDIPUS: Not yet.
Laius — how did he look? Describe him.
Had he reached his prime?

JOCASTA: He was swarthy,
and the gray had just begun to streak his temples,
and his build . . . wasn't far from yours.

OEDIPUS: Oh no no,
I think I've just called down a dreadful curse
upon myself — I simply didn't know!

JOCASTA: What are you saying? I shudder to look at you.

OEDIPUS: I have a terrible fear the blind seer can see.
I'll know in a moment. One thing more —

JOCASTA: Anything,
afraid as I am — ask, I'll answer, all I can.

OEDIPUS: Did he go with a light or heavy escort,
several men-at-arms, like a lord, a king?

JOCASTA: There were five in the party, a herald among them,
and a single wagon carrying Laius.

OEDIPUS: Ai —
now I can see it all, clear as day.
Who told you all this at the time, Jocasta?

JOCASTA: A servant who reached home, the lone survivor.

OEDIPUS: So, could he still be in the palace — even now?

JOCASTA: No indeed. Soon as he returned from the scene

and saw you on the throne with Laius dead and gone,
he knelt and clutched my hand, pleading with me
to send him into the hinterlands, to pasture,
far as possible, out of sight of Thebes.
I sent him away. Slave though he was,
he'd earned that favor — and much more.

OEDIPUS: Can we bring him back, quickly?

JOCASTA: Easily. Why do you want him so?

OEDIPUS: I'm afraid,
Jocasta, I have said too much already.
That man — I've got to see him.

JOCASTA: Then he'll come.
But even I have a right, I'd like to think,
to know what's torturing you, my lord.

OEDIPUS: And so you shall — I can hold nothing back from you,
now I've reached this pitch of dark foreboding.
Who means more to me than you? Tell me,
whom would I turn toward but you
as I go through all this?

My father was Polybus, king of Corinth.
My mother, a Dorian, Merope. And I was held
the prince of the realm among the people there,
till something struck me out of nowhere,
something strange . . . worth remarking perhaps,
hardly worth the anxiety I gave it.
Some man at a banquet who had drunk too much
shouted out — he was far gone, mind you —
that I am not my father's son. Fighting words!
I barely restrained myself that day
but early the next I went to mother and father,
questioned them closely, and they were enraged
at the accusation and the fool who let it fly.
So as for my parents I was satisfied,
but still this thing kept gnawing at me,
the slander spread — I had to make my move.
And so,
unknown to mother and father I set out for Delphi,
and the god Apollo spurned me, sent me away
denied the facts I came for,
but first he flashed before my eyes a future
great with pain, terror, disaster — I can hear him cry,
"You are fated to couple with your mother, you will bring
a breed of children into the light no man can bear to see —
you will kill your father, the one who gave you life!"
I heard all that and ran. I abandoned Corinth,
from that day on I gauged its landfall only

by the stars, running, always running
toward some place where I would never see
the shame of all those oracles come true.
And as I fled I reached that very spot
where the great king, you say, met his death.
Now, Jocasta, I will tell you all.
Making my way toward this triple crossroad
I began to see a herald, then a brace of colts
drawing a wagon, and mounted on the bench . . . a man,
just as you've described him, coming face-to-face,
and the one in the lead and the old man himself
were about to thrust me off the road — brute force —
and the one shouldering me aside, the driver,
I strike him in anger! — and the old man, watching me
coming up along his wheels — he brings down
his prod, two prongs straight at my head!
I paid him back with interest!
Short work, by god — with one blow of the staff
in this right hand I knock him out of his high seat,
roll him out of the wagon, sprawling headlong —
I killed them all — every mother's son!

Oh, but if there is any blood-tie
between Laius and this stranger . . .
what man alive more miserable than I?
More hated by the gods? *I* am the man
no alien, no citizen welcomes to his house,
law forbids it — not a word to me in public,
driven out of every hearth and home.
And all these curses I — no one but I
brought down these piling curses on myself!
And you, his wife, I've touched your body with these,
the hands that killed your husband cover you with blood.

Wasn't I born for torment? Look me in the eyes!
I am abomination — heart and soul!
I must be exiled, and even in exile
never see my parents, never set foot
on native earth again. Else I'm doomed
to couple with my mother and cut my father down . . .
Polybus who reared me, gave me life.
But why, why?
Wouldn't a man of judgment say — and wouldn't he be right —
some savage power has brought this down upon my head?

Oh no, not that, you pure and awesome gods,
never let me see that day! Let me slip
from the world of men, vanish without a trace

before I see myself stained with such corruption,
stained to the heart.

LEADER: My lord, you fill our hearts with fear.
But at least until you question the witness,
do take hope.

OEDIPUS: Exactly. He is my last hope —
I'm waiting for the shepherd. He is crucial.

JOCASTA: And once he appears, what then? Why so urgent?

OEDIPUS: I'll tell you. If it turns out that his story
matches yours, I've escaped the worst.

JOCASTA: What did I say? What struck you so?

OEDIPUS: You said *thieves* —
he told you a whole band of them murdered Laius.
So, if he still holds to the same number,
I cannot be the killer. One can't equal many.
But if he refers to one man, one alone,
clearly the scales come down on me:
I am guilty.

JOCASTA: Impossible. Trust me,
I told you precisely what he said,
and he can't retract it now;
the whole city heard it, not just I.
And even if he should vary his first report
by one man more or less, still, my lord,
he could never make the murder of Laius
truly fit the prophecy. Apollo was explicit:
my son was doomed to kill my husband . . . my son,
poor defenseless thing, he never had a chance
to kill his father. They destroyed him first.

So much for prophecy. It's neither here nor there.
From this day on, I wouldn't look right or left.

OEDIPUS: True, true. Still, that shepherd,
someone fetch him — now!

JOCASTA: I'll send at once. But do let's go inside.
I'd never displease you, least of all in this.

Oedipus and Jocasta enter the palace.

CHORUS: Destiny guide me always
Destiny find me filled with reverence
pure in word and deed.
Great laws tower above us, reared on high
born for the brilliant vault of heaven —
Olympian sky their only father,
nothing mortal, no man gave them birth,
their memory deathless, never lost in sleep:
within them lives a mighty god, the god does not grow old.

Pride breeds the tyrant
violent pride, gorging, crammed to bursting
with all that is overripe and rich with ruin —
clawing up to the heights, headlong pride
crashes down the abyss — sheer doom!
No footing helps, all foothold lost and gone,
But the healthy strife that makes the city strong —
I pray that god will never end that wrestling:
god, my champion, I will never let you go.

But if any man comes striding, high and mighty
in all he says and does,
no fear of justice, no reverence
for the temples of the gods —
let a rough doom tear him down,
repay his pride, breakneck, ruinous pride!
If he cannot reap his profits fairly
cannot restrain himself from outrage —
mad, laying hands on the holy things untouchable!

Can such a man, so desperate, still boast
he can save his life from the flashing bolts of god?
If all such violence goes with honor now
why join the sacred dance?

Never again will I go reverent to Delphi,
the inviolate heart of Earth
or Apollo's ancient oracle at Abae
or Olympia of the fires —
unless these prophecies all come true
for all mankind to point toward in wonder.
King of kings, if you deserve your titles
Zeus, remember, never forget!
You and your deathless, everlasting reign.

They are dying, the old oracles sent to Laius,
now our masters strike them off the rolls.
Nowhere Apollo's golden glory now —
the gods, the gods go down.

Enter Jocasta from the palace, carrying a suppliant's branch wound in wool.

JOCASTA: Lords of the realm, it occurred to me,
just now, to visit the temples of the gods,
so I have my branch in hand and incense too.

Oedipus is beside himself. Racked with anguish,
no longer a man of sense, he won't admit
the latest prophecies are hollow as the old —
he's at the mercy of every passing voice

if the voice tells of terror.
I urge him gently, nothing seems to help,
so I turn to you, Apollo, you are nearest.

Placing her branch on the altar, while an old herdsman enters from the side, not the one just summoned by the king but an unexpected messenger from Corinth.

I come with prayers and offerings . . . I beg you,
cleanse us, set us free of defilement!
Look at us, passengers in the grip of fear,
watching the pilot of the vessel go to pieces.

MESSENGER:

Approaching Jocasta and the Chorus.

Strangers, please, I wonder if you could lead us
to the palace of the king . . . I think it's Oedipus.
Better, the man himself — you know where he is?

LEADER: This is his palace, stranger. He's inside.
But here is his queen, his wife and mother
of his children.

MESSENGER: Blessings on you, noble queen,
queen of Oedipus crowned with all your family —
blessings on you always!

JOCASTA: And the same to you, stranger, you deserve it . . .
such a greeting. But what have you come for?
Have you brought us news?

MESSENGER: Wonderful news —
for the house, my lady, for your husband too.

JOCASTA: Really, what? Who sent you?

MESSENGER: Corinth.
I'll give you the message in a moment.
You'll be glad of it — how could you help it? —
though it costs a little sorrow in the bargain.

JOCASTA: What can it be, with such a double edge?

MESSENGER: The people there, they want to make your Oedipus
king of Corinth, so they're saying now.

JOCASTA: Why? Isn't old Polybus still in power?

MESSENGER: No more. Death has got him in the tomb.

JOCASTA: What are you saying? Polybus, dead? — dead?

MESSENGER: If not,
if I'm not telling the truth, strike me dead too.

JOCASTA:

To a servant.

Quickly, go to your master, tell him this!

You prophecies of the gods, where are you now?
This is the man that Oedipus feared for years,
he fled him, not to kill him — and now he's dead,
quite by chance, a normal, natural death,

not murdered by his son.

OEDIPUS:

Emerging from the palace.

Dearest,
what now? Why call me from the palace?

JOCASTA:

Bringing the Messenger closer.

Listen to *him*, see for yourself what all
those awful prophecies of god have come to.

OEDIPUS: And who is he? What can he have for me?

JOCASTA: He's from Corinth, he's come to tell you
your father is no more — Polybus — he's dead!

OEDIPUS:

Wheeling on the Messenger.

What? Let me have it from your lips.

MESSENGER: Well,
if that's what you want first, then here it is:
make no mistake, Polybus is dead and gone.

OEDIPUS: How — murder? sickness? — what? what killed him?

MESSENGER: A light tip of the scales can put old bones to rest.

OEDIPUS: Sickness then — poor man, it wore him down.

MESSENGER: That,
and the long count of years he'd measured out.

OEDIPUS: So!
Jocasta, why, why look to the Prophet's hearth,
the fires of the future? Why scan the birds
that scream above our heads? They winged me on
to the murder of my father, did they? That was my doom?
Well look, he's dead and buried, hidden under the earth,
and here I am in Thebes, I never put hand to sword —
unless some longing for me wasted him away,
then in a sense you'd say I caused his death.
But now, all those prophecies I feared — Polybus
packs them off to sleep with him in hell!
They're nothing, worthless.

JOCASTA: There.
Didn't I tell you from the start?

OEDIPUS: So you did. I was lost in fear.

JOCASTA: No more, sweep it from your mind forever.

OEDIPUS: But my mother's bed, surely I must fear —

JOCASTA: Fear?
What should a man fear? It's all chance,
chance rules our lives. Not a man on earth
can see a day ahead, groping through the dark.

Better to live at random, best we can.
And as for this marriage with your mother —
have no fear. Many a man before you,
in his dreams, has shared his mother's bed.
Take such things for shadows, nothing at all —
Live, Oedipus,
as if there's no tomorrow!

OEDIPUS: Brave words,
and you'd persuade me if mother weren't alive.
But mother lives, so for all your reassurances
I live in fear, I must.

JOCASTA: But your father's death,
that, at least, is a great blessing, joy to the eyes!

OEDIPUS: Great, I know . . . but I fear *her* — she's still alive.

MESSENGER: Wait, who is this woman, makes you so afraid?

OEDIPUS: Merope, old man. The wife of Polybus.

MESSENGER: The queen? What's there to fear in her?

OEDIPUS: A dreadful prophecy, stranger, sent by the gods.

MESSENGER: Tell me, could you? Unless it's forbidden
other ears to hear.

OEDIPUS: Not at all.
Apollo told me once — it is my fate —
I must make love with my own mother,
shed my father's blood with my own hands.
So for years I've given Corinth a wide berth,
and it's been my good fortune too. But still,
to see one's parents and look into their eyes
is the greatest joy I know.

MESSENGER: You're afraid of that?
That kept you out of Corinth?

OEDIPUS: My *father,* old man —
so I wouldn't kill my father.

MESSENGER: So that's it.
Well then, seeing I came with such good will, my king,
why don't I rid you of that old worry now?

OEDIPUS: What a rich reward you'd have for that.

MESSENGER: What do you think I came for, majesty?
So you'd come home and I'd be better off.

OEDIPUS: Never, I will never go near my parents.

MESSENGER: My boy, it's clear, you don't know what you're doing.

OEDIPUS: What do you mean, old man? For god's sake, explain.

MESSENGER: If you ran from *them,* always dodging home . . .

OEDIPUS: Always, terrified Apollo's oracle might come true —

MESSENGER: And you'd be covered with guilt, from both your parents.

OEDIPUS: That's right, old man, that fear is always with me.

MESSENGER: Don't you know? You've really nothing to fear.

OEDIPUS: But why? If I'm their son — Merope, Polybus?
MESSENGER: Polybus was nothing to you, that's why, not in blood.
OEDIPUS: What are you saying — Polybus was not my father?
MESSENGER: No more than I am. He and I are equals.
OEDIPUS: My father —
how can my father equal nothing? You're nothing to me!
MESSENGER: Neither was he, no more your father than I am.
OEDIPUS: Then why did he call me his son?
MESSENGER: You were a gift,
years ago — know for a fact he took you
from my hands.
OEDIPUS: No, from another's hands?
Then how could he love me so? He loved me, deeply . . .
MESSENGER: True, and his early years without a child
made him love you all the more.
OEDIPUS: And you, did you . . .
buy me? find me by accident?
MESSENGER: I stumbled on you,
down the woody flanks of Mount Cithaeron.
OEDIPUS: So close,
what were you doing here, just passing through?
MESSENGER: Watching over my flocks, grazing them on the slopes.
OEDIPUS: A herdsman, were you? A vagabond, scraping for wages?
MESSENGER: Your savior too, my son, in your worst hour.
OEDIPUS: Oh —
when you picked me up, was I in pain? What exactly?
MESSENGER: Your ankles . . . they tell the story. Look at them.
OEDIPUS: Why remind me of that, that old affliction?
MESSENGER: Your ankles were pinned together; I set you free.
OEDIPUS: That dreadful mark — I've had it from the cradle.
MESSENGER: And you got your name from that misfortune too,
the name's still with you.
OEDIPUS: Dear god, who did it? —
mother? father? Tell me.
MESSENGER: I don't know.
The one who gave you to me, he'd know more.
OEDIPUS: What? You took me from someone else?
You didn't find me yourself?
MESSENGER: No sir,
another shepherd passed you on to me.
OEDIPUS: Who? Do you know? Describe him.
MESSENGER: He called himself a servant of . . .
if I remember rightly — Laius.

Jocasta turns sharply.

OEDIPUS: The king of the land who ruled here long ago?
MESSENGER: That's the one. That herdsman was *his* man.

OEDIPUS: Is he still alive? Can I see him?
MESSENGER: They'd know best, the people of these parts.

Oedipus and the Messenger turn to the Chorus.

OEDIPUS: Does anyone know that herdsman,
the one he mentioned? Anyone seen him
in the fields, in town? Out with it!
The time has come to reveal this once for all.
LEADER: I think he's the very shepherd you wanted to see,
a moment ago. But the queen, Jocasta,
she's the one to say.
OEDIPUS: Jocasta,
you remember the man we just sent for?
Is *that* the one he means?
JOCASTA: That man . . .
why ask? Old shepherd, talk, empty nonsense,
don't give it another thought, don't even think —
OEDIPUS: What — give up now, with a clue like this?
Fail to solve the mystery of my birth?
Not for all the world!
JOCASTA: Stop — in the name of god,
if you love your own life, call off this search!
My suffering is enough.
OEDIPUS: Courage!
Even if my mother turns out to be a slave,
and I a slave, three generations back,
you would not seem common.
JOCASTA: Oh no,
listen to me, I beg you, don't do this.
OEDIPUS: Listen to you? No more. I must know it all,
see the truth at last.
JOCASTA: No, please —
for your sake — I want the best for you!
OEDIPUS: Your best is more than I can bear.
JOCASTA: You're doomed —
may you never fathom who you are!
OEDIPUS:

To a servant.

Hurry, fetch me the herdsman, now!
Leave her to glory in her royal birth.
JOCASTA: Aieeeeee —
man of agony —
that is the only name I have for you,
that, no other — ever, ever, ever!

Flinging [herself] through the palace doors. A long, tense silence follows.

LEADER: Where's she gone, Oedipus?

Rushing off, such wild grief . . .
I'm afraid that from this silence
something monstrous may come bursting forth.

OEDIPUS: Let it burst! Whatever will, whatever must!
I must know my birth, no matter how common
it may be — must see my origins face-to-face.
She perhaps, she with her woman's pride
may well be mortified by my birth,
but I, I count myself the son of Chance,
the great goddess, giver of all good things —
I'll never see myself disgraced. She is my mother!
And the moons have marked me out, my blood-brothers,
one moon on the wane, the next moon great with power.
That is my blood, my nature — I will never betray it,
never fail to search and learn my birth!

CHORUS: Yes — if I am a true prophet
if I can grasp the truth,
by the boundless skies of Olympus,
at the full moon of tomorrow, Mount Cithaeron
you will know how Oedipus glories in you —
you, his birthplace, nurse, his mountain-mother!
And we will sing you, dancing out your praise —
you lift our monarch's heart!
Apollo, Apollo, god of the wild cry
may our dancing please you!
Oedipus —
son, dear child, who bore you?
Who of the nymphs who seem to live forever
mated with Pan,° the mountain-striding Father?
Who was your mother? who, some bride of Apollo
the god who loves the pastures spreading toward the sun?
Or was it Hermes, king of the lightning ridges?
Or Dionysus, lord of frenzy, lord of the barren peaks —
did he seize you in his hands, dearest of all his lucky finds? —
found by the nymphs, their warm eyes dancing, gift
to the lord who loves them dancing out his joy!

Oedipus strains to see a figure coming from the distance. Attended by palace guards, an old Shepherd enters slowly, reluctant to approach the King.

OEDIPUS: I never met the man, my friends . . . still,
if I had to guess, I'd say that's the shepherd,
the very one we've looked for all along.
Brothers in old age, two of a kind,
he and our guest here. At any rate

1207. Pan: The god of shepherds, who was, like Hermes and Dionysus, associated with the wilderness.

the ones who bring him in are my own men,
I recognize them.

Turning to the Leader.

But you know more than I,
you should, you've seen the man before.

LEADER: I know him, definitely. One of Laius' men,
a trusty shepherd, if there ever was one.

OEDIPUS: You, I ask you first, stranger,
you from Corinth — is this the one you mean?

MESSENGER: You're looking at him. He's your man.

OEDIPUS:

To the Shepherd.

You, old man, come over here —
look at me. Answer all my questions.
Did you ever serve King Laius?

SHEPHERD: So I did . . .
a slave, not bought on the block though,
born and reared in the palace.

OEDIPUS: Your duties, your kind of work?

SHEPHERD: Herding the flocks, the better part of my life.

OEDIPUS: Where, mostly? Where did you do your grazing?

SHEPHERD: Well,
Cithaeron sometimes, or the foothills round about.

OEDIPUS: This man — you know him? ever see him there?

SHEPHERD:

Confused, glancing from the Messenger to the King.

Doing what — what man do you mean?

OEDIPUS:

Pointing to the Messenger.

This one here — ever have dealings with him?

SHEPHERD: Not so I could say, but give me a chance,
my memory's bad . . .

MESSENGER: No wonder he doesn't know me, master.
But let me refresh his memory for him.
I'm sure he recalls old times we had
on the slopes of Mount Cithaeron;
he and I, grazing our flocks, he with two
and I with one — we both struck up together,
three whole seasons, six months at a stretch
from spring to the rising of Arcturus° in the fall,
then with winter coming on I'd drive my herds
to my own pens, and back he'd go with his
to Laius' folds.

1249. Arcturus: A star whose rising marked the end of summer.

To the Shepherd.

Now that's how it was,
wasn't it — yes or no?

SHEPHERD: Yes, I suppose . . .
it's all so long ago.

MESSENGER: Come, tell me,
you gave me a child back then, a boy, remember?
A little fellow to rear, my very own.

SHEPHERD: What? Why rake up that again?

MESSENGER: Look, here he is, my fine old friend —
the same man who was just a baby then.

SHEPHERD: Damn you, shut your mouth — quiet!

OEDIPUS: Don't lash out at him, old man —
you need lashing more than he does.

SHEPHERD: Why,
master, majesty — what have I done wrong?

OEDIPUS: You won't answer his question about the boy.

SHEPHERD: He's talking nonsense, wasting his breath.

OEDIPUS: So, you won't talk willingly —
then you'll talk with pain.

The guards seize the Shepherd.

SHEPHERD: No, dear god, don't torture an old man!

OEDIPUS: Twist his arms back, quickly!

SHEPHERD: God help us, why? —
what more do you need to know?

OEDIPUS: Did you give him that child? He's asking.

SHEPHERD: I did . . . I wish to god I'd died that day.

OEDIPUS: You've got your wish if you don't tell the truth.

SHEPHERD: The more I tell, the worse the death I'll die.

OEDIPUS: Our friend here wants to stretch things out, does he?

Motioning to his men for torture.

SHEPHERD: No, no, I gave it to him — I just said so.

OEDIPUS: Where did you get it? Your house? Someone else's?

SHEPHERD: It wasn't mine, no, I got it from . . . someone.

OEDIPUS: Which one of them?

Looking at the citizens.

Whose house?

SHEPHERD: No —
god's sake, master, no more questions!

OEDIPUS: You're a dead man if I have to ask again.

SHEPHERD: Then — the child came from the house . . .
of Laius.

OEDIPUS: A slave? or born of his own blood?

SHEPHERD: Oh no,
I'm right at the edge, the horrible truth — I've got to say it!

OEDIPUS: And I'm at the edge of hearing horrors, yes, but I must hear!
SHEPHERD: All right! His son, they said it was — his son!
    But the one inside, your wife,
    she'd tell it best.
OEDIPUS: My wife —
    she gave it to you?
SHEPHERD: Yes, yes, my king.
OEDIPUS: Why, what for?
SHEPHERD: To kill it.
OEDIPUS: Her own child,
    how could she?
SHEPHERD: She was afraid —
    frightening prophecies.
OEDIPUS: What?
SHEPHERD: They said —
    he'd kill his parents.
OEDIPUS: But you gave him to this old man — why?
SHEPHERD: I pitied the little baby, master,
    hoped he'd take him off to his own country,
    far away, but he saved him for this, this fate.
    If you are the man he says you are, believe me,
    you were born for pain.
OEDIPUS: O god —
    all come true, all burst to light!
    O light — now let me look my last on you!
    I stand revealed at last —
    cursed in my birth, cursed in marriage,
    cursed in the lives I cut down with these hands!

Rushing through the doors with a great cry. The Corinthian Messenger, the Shepherd, and attendants exit slowly to the side.

CHORUS: O the generations of men
    the dying generations — adding the total
    of all your lives I find they come to nothing . . .
        does there exist, is there a man on earth
    who seizes more joy than just a dream, a vision?
    And the vision no sooner dawns than dies
    blazing into oblivion.

    You are my great example, you, your life,
    your destiny, Oedipus, man of misery —
    I count no man blest.

        You outranged all men!
      Bending your bow to the breaking-point
    you captured priceless glory, O dear god,
    and the Sphinx came crashing down,
        the virgin, claws hooked

like a bird of omen singing, shrieking death —
like a fortress reared in the face of death
you rose and saved our land.

From that day on we called you king
we crowned you with honors, Oedipus, towering over all —
mighty king of the seven gates of Thebes.

But now to hear your story — is there a man more agonized?
More wed to pain and frenzy? Not a man on earth,
the joy of your life ground down to nothing
O Oedipus, name for the ages —
one and the same wide harbor served you
son and father both
son and father came to rest in the same bridal chamber.
How, how could the furrows your father plowed
bear you, your agony, harrowing on
in silence O so long?
But now for all your power
Time, all-seeing Time has dragged you to the light,
judged your marriage monstrous from the start —
the son and the father tangling, both one —
O child of Laius, would to god
I'd never seen you, never never!
Now I weep like a man who wails the dead
and the dirge comes pouring forth with all my heart!
I tell you the truth, you gave me life
my breath leapt up in you
and now you bring down night upon my eyes.

Enter a Messenger from the palace.

MESSENGER: Men of Thebes, always the first in honor,
what horrors you will hear, what you will see,
what a heavy weight of sorrow you will shoulder . . .
if you are true to your birth, if you still have
some feeling for the royal house of Thebes.
I tell you neither the waters of the Danube
nor the Nile can wash this palace clean.
Such things it hides, it soon will bring to light —
terrible things, and none done blindly now,
all done with a will. The pains
we inflict upon ourselves hurt most of all.

LEADER: God knows we have pains enough already.
What can you add to them?

MESSENGER: The queen is dead.

LEADER: Poor lady — how?

MESSENGER: By her own hand. But you are spared the worst,
you never had to watch . . . I saw it all,

and with all the memory that's in me
you will learn what that poor woman suffered.

Once she'd broken in through the gates,
dashing past us, frantic, whipped to fury,
ripping her hair out with both hands —
straight to her rooms she rushed, flinging herself
across the bridal-bed, doors slamming behind her —
once inside, she wailed for Laius, dead so long,
remembering how she bore his child long ago,
the life that rose up to destroy him, leaving
its mother to mother living creatures
with the very son she'd borne.
Oh how she wept, mourning the marriage-bed
where she let loose that double brood — monsters —
husband by her husband, children by her child.
And then —
but how she died is more than I can say. Suddenly
Oedipus burst in, screaming, he stunned us so
we couldn't watch her agony to the end,
our eyes were fixed on him. Circling
like a maddened beast, stalking, here, there
crying out to us —
Give him a sword! His wife,
no wife, his mother, where can he find the mother earth
that cropped two crops at once, himself and all his children?
He was raging — one of the dark powers pointing the way,
none of us mortals crowding around him, no,
with a great shattering cry — someone, something leading him on —
he hurled at the twin doors and bending the bolts back
out of their sockets, crashed through the chamber.
And there we saw the woman hanging by the neck,
cradled high in a woven noose, spinning,
swinging back and forth. And when he saw her,
giving a low, wrenching sob that broke our hearts,
slipping the halter from her throat, he eased her down,
in a slow embrace he laid her down, poor thing . . .
then, what came next, what horror we beheld!
He rips off her brooches, the long gold pins
holding her robes — and lifting them high,
looking straight up into the points,
he digs them down the sockets of his eyes, crying, "You,
you'll see no more the pain I suffered, all the pain I caused!
Too long you looked on the ones you never should have seen,
blind to the ones you longed to see, to know! Blind
from this hour on! Blind in the darkness — blind!"
His voice like a dirge, rising, over and over

raising the pins, raking them down his eyes.
And at each stroke blood spurts from the roots,
splashing his beard, a swirl of it, nerves and clots —
black hail of blood pulsing, gushing down.

These are the griefs that burst upon them both,
coupling man and woman. The joy they had so lately,
the fortune of their old ancestral house
was deep joy indeed. Now, in this one day,
wailing, madness and doom, death, disgrace,
all the griefs in the world that you can name,
all are theirs forever.

LEADER: Oh poor man, the misery —
has he any rest from pain now?

A voice within, in torment.

MESSENGER: He's shouting,
"Loose the bolts, someone, show me to all of Thebes!
My father's murderer, my mother's — "
No, I can't repeat it, it's unholy.
Now he'll tear himself from his native earth,
not linger, curse the house with his own curse.
But he needs strength, and a guide to lead him on.
This is sickness more than he can bear.

The palace doors open.

Look,
he'll show you himself. The great doors are opening —
you are about to see a sight, a horror
even his mortal enemy would pity.

Enter Oedipus, blinded, led by a boy. He stands at the palace steps, as if surveying his people once again.

CHORUS: O the terror —
the suffering, for all the world to see,
the worst terror that ever met my eyes.
What madness swept over you? What god,
what dark power leapt beyond all bounds,
beyond belief, to crush your wretched life? —
godforsaken, cursed by the gods!
I pity you but I can't bear to look.
I've much to ask, so much to learn,
so much fascinates my eyes,
but you . . . I shudder at the sight.

OEDIPUS: Oh, Ohhh —
the agony! I am agony —
where am I going? where on earth?
where does all this agony hurl me?
where's my voice? —

winging, swept away on a dark tide —
My destiny, my dark power, what a leap you made!
CHORUS: To the depths of terror, too dark to hear, to see.
OEDIPUS: Dark, horror of darkness
my darkness, drowning, swirling around me
crashing wave on wave — unspeakable, irresistible
headwind, fatal harbor! Oh again,
the misery, all at once, over and over
the stabbing daggers, stab of memory
raking me insane.
CHORUS: No wonder you suffer
twice over, the pain of your wounds,
the lasting grief of pain.
OEDIPUS: Dear friend, still here?
Standing by me, still with a care for me,
the blind man? Such compassion,
loyal to the last. Oh it's you,
I know you're here, dark as it is
I'd know you anywhere, your voice —
it's yours, clearly yours.
CHORUS: Dreadful, what you've done . . .
how could you bear it, gouging out your eyes?
What superhuman power drove you on?
OEDIPUS: Apollo, friends, Apollo —
he ordained my agonies — these, my pains on pains!
But the hand that struck my eyes was mine,
mine alone — no one else —
I did it all myself!
What good were eyes to me?
Nothing I could see could bring me joy.
CHORUS: No, no, exactly as you say.
OEDIPUS: What can I ever see?
What love, what call of the heart
can touch my ears with joy? Nothing, friends.
Take me away, far, far from Thebes,
quickly, cast me away, my friends —
this great murderous ruin, this man cursed to heaven,
the man the deathless gods hate most of all!
CHORUS: Pitiful, you suffer so, you understand so much . . .
I wish you'd never known.
OEDIPUS: Die, die —
whoever he was that day in the wilds
who cut my ankles free of the ruthless pins,
he pulled me clear of death, he saved my life
for this, this kindness —
Curse him, kill him!
If I'd died then, I'd never have dragged myself,

my loved ones through such hell.
CHORUS: Oh if only . . . would to god.
OEDIPUS: I'd never have come to this,
my father's murderer — never been branded
mother's husband, all men see me now! Now,
loathed by the gods, son of the mother I defiled
coupling in my father's bed, spawning lives in the loins
that spawned my wretched life. What grief can crown this grief?
It's mine alone, my destiny — I am Oedipus!
CHORUS: How can I say you've chosen for the best?
Better to die than be alive and blind.
OEDIPUS: What I did was best — don't lecture me,
no more advice. I, with *my* eyes,
how could I look my father in the eyes
when I go down to death? Or mother, so abused . . .
I've done such things to the two of them,
crimes too huge for hanging.
Worse yet,
the sight of my children, born as they were born,
how could I long to look into their eyes?
No, not with these eyes of mine, never.
Not this city either, her high towers,
the sacred glittering images of her gods —
I am misery! I, her best son, reared
as no other son of Thebes was ever reared,
I've stripped myself, I gave the command myself.
All men must cast away the great blasphemer,
the curse now brought to light by the gods,
the son of Laius — I, my father's son!

Now I've exposed my guilt, horrendous guilt,
could I train a level glance on you, my countrymen?
Impossible! No, if I could just block off my ears,
the springs of hearing, I would stop at nothing —
I'd wall up my loathsome body like a prison,
blind to the sound of life, not just the sight.
Oblivion — what a blessing . . .
for the mind to dwell a world away from pain.
O Cithaeron, why did you give me shelter?
Why didn't you take me, crush my life out on the spot?
I'd never have revealed my birth to all mankind.

O Polybus, Corinth, the old house of my fathers,
so I believed — what a handsome prince you raised —
under the skin, what sickness to the core.
Look at me! Born of outrage, outrage to the core.

O triple roads — it all comes back, the secret,
dark ravine, and the oaks closing in

where the three roads join . . .
You drank my father's blood, my own blood
spilled by my own hands — you still remember me?
What things you saw me do? Then I came here
and did them all once more!
Marriages! O marriage,
you gave me birth, and once you brought me into the world
you brought my sperm rising back, springing to light
fathers, brothers, sons — one deadly breed —
brides, wives, mothers. The blackest things
a man can do, I have done them all!
No more —
it's wrong to name what's wrong to do. Quickly,
for the love of god, hide me somewhere,
kill me, hurl me into the sea
where you can never look on me again.

Beckoning to the Chorus as they shrink away.

Closer,
it's all right. Touch the man of sorrow.
Do. Don't be afraid. My troubles are mine
and I am the only man alive who can sustain them.

Enter Creon from the palace, attended by palace guards.

LEADER: Put your requests to Creon. Here he is,
just when we need him. He'll have a plan, he'll act.
Now that he's the sole defense of the country
in your place.
OEDIPUS: Oh no, what can I say to him?
How can I ever hope to win his trust?
I wronged him so, just now, in every way.
You must see that — I was so wrong, so wrong.
CREON: I haven't come to mock you, Oedipus,
or to criticize your former failings.

Turning to the guards.

You there,
have you lost all respect for human feeling?
At least revere the Sun, the holy fire
that keeps us all alive. Never expose a thing
of guilt and holy dread so great it appalls
the earth, the rain from heaven, the light of day!
Get him into the halls — quickly as you can.
Piety demands no less. Kindred alone
should see a kinsman's shame. This is obscene.
OEDIPUS: Please, in god's name . . . you wipe my fears away,
coming so generously to me, the worst of men.
Do one thing more, for your sake, not mine.

CREON: What do you want? Why so insistent?
OEDIPUS: Drive me out of the land at once, far from sight,
where I can never hear a human voice.
CREON: I'd have done that already, I promise you.
First I wanted the god to clarify my duties.
OEDIPUS: The god? His command was clear, every word:
death for the father-killer, the curse —
he said destroy me!
CREON: So he did. Still, in such a crisis
it's better to ask precisely what to do.
OEDIPUS: You'd ask the oracle about a man like me?
CREON: By all means. And this time, I assume,
even you will obey the god's decrees.
OEDIPUS: I will,
I will. And you, I command you — I beg you . . .
the woman inside, bury her as you see fit.
It's the only decent thing,
to give your own the last rites. As for me,
never condemn the city of my fathers
to house my body, not while I'm alive, no,
let me live on the mountains, on Cithaeron,
my favorite haunt, I have made it famous.
Mother and father marked out that rock
to be my everlasting tomb — buried alive.
Let me die there, where they tried to kill me.
Oh but this I know: no sickness can destroy me,
nothing can. I would never have been saved
from death — I have been saved
for something great and terrible, something strange.
Well let my destiny come and take me on its way!

About my children, Creon, the boys at least,
don't burden yourself. They're men;
wherever they go, they'll find the means to live.
But my two daughters, my poor helpless girls,
clustering at our table, never without me
hovering near them . . . whatever I touched,
they always had their share. Take care of them,
I beg you. Wait, better — permit me, would you?
Just to touch them with my hands and take
our fill of tears. Please . . . my king.
Grant it, with all your noble heart.
If I could hold them, just once, I'd think
I had them with me, like the early days
when I could see their eyes.

Antigone and Ismene, two small children, are led in from the palace by a nurse.

What's that?

O god! Do I really hear you sobbing? —
my two children. Creon, you've pitied me?
Sent me my darling girls, my own flesh and blood!
Am I right?

CREON: Yes, it's my doing.
I know the joy they gave you all these years,
the joy you must feel now.

OEDIPUS: Bless you, Creon!
May god watch over you for this kindness,
better than he ever guarded me.
Children, where are you?
Here, come quickly —

Groping for Antigone and Ismene, who approach their father cautiously, then embrace him.

Come to these hands of mine,
your brother's hands, your own father's hands
that served his once bright eyes so well —
that made them blind. Seeing nothing, children,
knowing nothing, I became your father,
I fathered you in the soil that gave me life.

How I weep for you — I cannot see you now . . .
just thinking of all your days to come, the bitterness,
the life that rough mankind will thrust upon you.
Where are the public gatherings you can join,
the banquets of the clans? Home you'll come,
in tears, cut off from the sight of it all,
the brilliant rites unfinished.
And when you reach perfection, ripe for marriage,
who will he be, my dear ones? Risking all
to shoulder the curse that weighs down my parents,
yes and you too — that wounds us all together.
What more misery could you want?
Your father killed his father, sowed his mother,
one, one and the selfsame womb sprang you —
he cropped the very roots of his existence.
Such disgrace, and you must bear it all!
Who will marry you then? Not a man on earth.
Your doom is clear: you'll wither away to nothing,
single, without a child.

Turning to Creon.

Oh Creon,
you are the only father they have now . . .
we who brought them into the world
are gone, both gone at a stroke —
Don't let them go begging, abandoned,

women without men. Your own flesh and blood!
Never bring them down to the level of my pains.
Pity them. Look at them, so young, so vulnerable,
shorn of everything — you're their only hope.
Promise me, noble Creon, touch my hand.

Reaching toward Creon, who draws back.

You, little ones, if you were old enough
to understand, there is much I'd tell you.
Now, as it is, I'd have you say a prayer.
Pray for life, my children,
live where you are free to grow and season.
Pray god you find a better life than mine,
the father who begot you.

CREON: Enough.
You've wept enough. Into the palace now.

OEDIPUS: I must, but I find it very hard.

CREON: Time is the great healer, you will see.

OEDIPUS: I am going — you know on what condition?

CREON: Tell me. I'm listening.

OEDIPUS: Drive me out of Thebes, in exile.

CREON: Not I. Only the gods can give you that.

OEDIPUS: Surely the gods hate me so much —

CREON: You'll get your wish at once.

OEDIPUS: You consent?

CREON: I try to say what I mean; it's my habit.

OEDIPUS: Then take me away. It's time.

CREON: Come along, let go of the children.

OEDIPUS: No —
don't take them away from me, not now! No no no!

Clutching his daughters as the guards wrench them loose and take them through the palace doors.

CREON: Still the king, the master of all things?
No more: here your power ends.
None of your power follows you through life.

Exit Oedipus and Creon to the palace. The Chorus comes forward to address the audience directly.

CHORUS: People of Thebes, my countrymen, look on Oedipus.
He solved the famous riddle with his brilliance,
he rose to power, a man beyond all power.
Who could behold his greatness without envy?
Now what a black sea of terror has overwhelmed him.
Now as we keep our watch and wait the final day,
count no man happy till he dies, free of pain at last.

Exit in procession.

SOPHOCLES

Antigone

c. 441 B.C.

TRANSLATED BY ROBERT FAGLES

CHARACTERS

ANTIGONE, *daughter of Oedipus and Jocasta*
ISMENE, *sister of Antigone*
A CHORUS *of old Theban citizens and their* LEADER
CREON, *king of Thebes, uncle of Antigone and Ismene*
A SENTRY
HAEMON, *son of Creon and Eurydice*
TIRESIAS, *a blind prophet*
A MESSENGER
EURYDICE, *wife of Creon*
GUARDS, ATTENDANTS, AND A BOY

TIME AND SCENE: *The royal house of Thebes. It is still night, and the invading armies of Argos have just been driven from the city. Fighting on opposite sides, the sons of Oedipus, Eteocles and Polynices, have killed each other in combat. Their uncle, Creon, is now king of Thebes.*

Enter Antigone, slipping through the central doors of the palace. She motions to her sister, Ismene, who follows her cautiously toward an altar at the center of the stage.

ANTIGONE: My own flesh and blood — dear sister, dear Ismene,
how many griefs our father Oedipus handed down!
Do you know one, I ask you, one grief
that Zeus° will not perfect for the two of us
while we still live and breathe? There's nothing,
no pain — our lives are pain — no private shame,
no public disgrace, nothing I haven't seen
in your griefs and mine. And now this:
an emergency decree, they say, the Commander
has just declared for all of Thebes.
What, haven't you heard? Don't you see?
The doom reserved for enemies
marches on the ones we love the most.

ISMENE: Not I, I haven't heard a word, Antigone.
Nothing of loved ones,
no joy or pain has come my way, not since
the two of us were robbed of our two brothers,
both gone in a day, a double blow —
not since the armies of Argos vanished,
just this very night. I know nothing more,
whether our luck's improved or ruin's still to come.

---

4. Zeus: The king of the gods in Greek mythology.

ANTIGONE: I thought so. That's why I brought you out here,
past the gates, so you could hear in private.
ISMENE: What's the matter? Trouble, clearly . . .
you sound so dark, so grim.
ANTIGONE: Why not? Our own brothers' burial!
Hasn't Creon graced one with all the rites,
disgraced the other? Eteocles, they say,
has been given full military honors,
rightly so — Creon's laid him in the earth
and he goes with glory down among the dead.
But the body of Polynices, who died miserably —
why, a city-wide proclamation, rumor has it,
forbids anyone to bury him, even mourn him.
He's to be left unwept, unburied, a lovely treasure
for birds that scan the field and feast to their heart's content.

Such, I hear, is the martial law our good Creon
lays down for you and me — yes, me, I tell you —
and he's coming here to alert the uninformed
in no uncertain terms,
and he won't treat the matter lightly. Whoever
disobeys in the least will die, his doom is sealed:
stoning to death inside the city walls!

There you have it. You'll soon show what you are,
worth your breeding, Ismene, or a coward —
for all your royal blood.
ISMENE: My poor sister, if things have come to this,
who am I to make or mend them, tell me,
what good am I to you?
ANTIGONE: Decide.
Will you share the labor, share the work?
ISMENE: What work, what's the risk? What do you mean?
ANTIGONE:

Raising her hands.

Will you lift up his body with these bare hands
and lower it with me?
ISMENE: What? You'd bury him —
when a law forbids the city?
ANTIGONE: Yes!
He is my brother and — deny it as you will —
your brother too.
No one will ever convict me for a traitor.
ISMENE: So desperate, and Creon has expressly —
ANTIGONE: No,
he has no right to keep me from my own.
ISMENE: Oh my sister, think —

think how our own father died, hated,
his reputation in ruins, driven on
by the crimes he brought to light himself
to gouge out his eyes with his own hands —
then mother . . . his mother and wife, both in one,
mutilating her life in the twisted noose —
and last, our two brothers dead in a single day,
both shedding their own blood, poor suffering boys,
battling out their common destiny hand-to-hand.

Now look at the two of us, left so alone . . .
think what a death we'll die, the worst of all
if we violate the laws and override
the fixed decree of the throne, its power —
we must be sensible. Remember we are women,
we're not born to contend with men. Then too,
we're underlings, ruled by much stronger hands,
so we must submit in this, and things still worse.

I, for one, I'll beg the dead to forgive me —
I'm forced, I have no choice — I must obey
the ones who stand in power. Why rush to extremes?
It's madness, madness.

ANTIGONE: I won't insist,
no, even if you should have a change of heart,
I'd never welcome you in the labor, not with me.
So, do as you like, whatever suits you best —
I'll bury him myself.
And even if I die in the act, that death will be a glory.
I'll lie with the one I love and loved by him —
an outrage sacred to the gods! I have longer
to please the dead than please the living here:
in the kingdom down below I'll lie forever.
Do as you like, dishonor the laws
the gods hold in honor.

ISMENE: I'd do them no dishonor . . .
but defy the city? I have no strength for that.

ANTIGONE: You have your excuses. I am on my way,
I'll raise a mound for him, for my dear brother.

ISMENE: Oh Antigone, you're so rash — I'm so afraid for you!

ANTIGONE: Don't fear for me. Set your own life in order.

ISMENE: Then don't, at least, blurt this out to anyone.
Keep it a secret. I'll join you in that, I promise.

ANTIGONE: Dear god, shout it from the rooftops. I'll hate you
all the more for silence — tell the world!

ISMENE: So fiery — and it ought to chill your heart.

ANTIGONE: I know I please where I must please the most.

ISMENE: Yes, if you can, but you're in love with impossibility.

ANTIGONE: Very well then, once my strength gives out
I will be done at last.

ISMENE: You're wrong from the start,
you're off on a hopeless quest.

ANTIGONE: If you say so, you will make me hate you,
and the hatred of the dead, by all rights,
will haunt you night and day.
But leave me to my own absurdity, leave me
to suffer this — dreadful thing. I'll suffer
nothing as great as death without glory.

Exit to the side.

ISMENE: Then go if you must, but rest assured,
wild, irrational as you are, my sister,
you are truly dear to the ones who love you.

Withdrawing to the palace. Enter a Chorus, the old citizens of Thebes, chanting as the sun begins to rise.

CHORUS: Glory! — great beam of sun, brightest of all
that ever rose on the seven gates of Thebes,
you burn through night at last!
Great eye of the golden day,
mounting the Dirce's° banks you throw him back —
the enemy out of Argos, the white shield, the man of bronze —
he's flying headlong now
the bridle of fate stampeding him with pain!

And he had driven against our borders,
launched by the warring claims of Polynices —
like an eagle screaming, winging havoc
over the land, wings of armor
shielded white as snow,
a huge army massing,
crested helmets bristling for assault.

He hovered above our roofs, his vast maw gaping
closing down around our seven gates,
his spears thirsting for the kill
but now he's gone, look,
before he could glut his jaws with Theban blood
or the god of fire put our crown of towers to the torch.
He grappled the Dragon none can master — Thebes —
the clang of our arms like thunder at his back!

Zeus hates with a vengeance all bravado,
the mighty boasts of men. He watched them

121. the Dirce: A river near Thebes, an ancient Greek city.

coming on in a rising flood, the pride
of their golden armor ringing shrill —
and brandishing his lightning
blasted the fighter just at the goal,
rushing to shout his triumph from our walls.

Down from the heights he crashed, pounding down on the earth!
And a moment ago, blazing torch in hand —
mad for attack, ecstatic
he breathed his rage, the storm
of his fury hurling at our heads!
But now his high hopes have laid him low
and down the enemy ranks the iron god of war
deals his rewards, his stunning blows — Ares°
rapture of battle, our right arm in the crisis.

Seven captains marshaled at seven gates
seven against their equals, gave
their brazen trophies up to Zeus,
god of the breaking rout of battle,
all but two: those blood brothers,
one father, one mother — matched in rage,
spears matched for the twin conquest —
clashed and won the common prize of death.

But now for Victory! Glorious in the morning,
joy in her eyes to meet our joy
she is winging down to Thebes,
our fleets of chariots wheeling in her wake —
Now let us win oblivion from the wars,
thronging the temples of the gods
in singing, dancing choirs through the night!
Lord Dionysus,° god of the dance
that shakes the land of Thebes, now lead the way!

Enter Creon from the palace, attended by his guard.

But look, the king of the realm is coming,
Creon, the new man for the new day,
whatever the gods are sending now . . .
what new plan will he launch?
Why this, this special session?
Why this sudden call to the old men
summoned at one command?

CREON: My countrymen,
the ship of state is safe. The gods who rocked her,
after a long, merciless pounding in the storm,

---

154. Ares: The Greek god of war. **171. Dionysus:** The Greek god of fertility and wine.

have righted her once more.
Out of the whole city
I have called you here alone. Well I know,
first, your undeviating respect
for the throne and royal power of King Laius.
Next, while Oedipus steered the land of Thebes,
and even after he died, your loyalty was unshakable,
you still stood by their children. Now then,
since the two sons are dead — two blows of fate
in the same day, cut down by each other's hands,
both killers, both brothers stained with blood —
as I am next in kin to the dead,
I now possess the throne and all its powers.

Of course you cannot know a man completely,
his character, his principles, sense of judgment,
not till he's shown his colors, ruling the people,
making laws. Experience, there's the test.
As I see it, whoever assumes the task,
the awesome task of setting the city's course,
and refuses to adopt the soundest policies
but fearing someone, keeps his lips locked tight,
he's utterly worthless. So I rate him now,
I always have. And whoever places a friend
above the good of his own country, he is nothing:
I have no use for him. Zeus my witness,
Zeus who sees all things, always —
I could never stand by silent, watching destruction
march against our city, putting safety to rout,
nor could I ever make that man a friend of mine
who menaces our country. Remember this:
our country *is* our safety.
Only while she voyages true on course
can we establish friendships, truer than blood itself.
Such are my standards. They make our city great.

Closely akin to them I have proclaimed,
just now, the following decree to our people
concerning the two sons of Oedipus.
Eteocles, who died fighting for Thebes,
excelling all in arms: he shall be buried,
crowned with a hero's honors, the cups we pour
to soak the earth and reach the famous dead.

But as for his blood brother, Polynices,
who returned from exile, home to his father-city
and the gods of his race, consumed with one desire —
to burn them roof to roots — who thirsted to drink

his kinsmen's blood and sell the rest to slavery:
that man — a proclamation has forbidden the city
to dignify him with burial, mourn him at all.
No, he must be left unburied, his corpse
carrion for the birds and dogs to tear,
an obscenity for the citizens to behold!

These are my principles. Never at my hands
will the traitor be honored above the patriot.
But whoever proves his loyalty to the state:
I'll prize that man in death as well as life.

LEADER: If this is your pleasure, Creon, treating
our city's enemy and our friend this way . . .
The power is yours, I suppose, to enforce it
with the laws, both for the dead and all of us,
the living.

CREON: Follow my orders closely then,
be on your guard.

LEADER: We're too old.
Lay that burden on younger shoulders.

CREON: No, no,
I don't mean the body — I've posted guards already.

LEADER: What commands for us then? What other service?

CREON: See that you never side with those who break my orders.

LEADER: Never. Only a fool could be in love with death.

CREON: Death is the price — you're right. But all too often
the mere hope of money has ruined many men.

A Sentry enters from the side.

SENTRY: My lord,
I can't say I'm winded from running, or set out
with any spring in my legs either — no sir,
I was lost in thought, and it made me stop, often,
dead in my tracks, wheeling, turning back,
and all the time a voice inside me muttering,
"Idiot, why? You're going straight to your death."
Then muttering, "Stopped again, poor fool?
If somebody gets the news to Creon first,
what's to save your neck?"
And so,
mulling it over, on I trudged, dragging my feet,
you can make a short road take forever . . .
but at last, look, common sense won out,
I'm here, and I'm all yours,
and even though I come empty-handed
I'll tell my story just the same, because
I've come with a good grip on one hope,
what will come will come, whatever fate —

CREON: Come to the point!
What's wrong — why so afraid?
SENTRY: First, myself, I've got to tell you,
I didn't do it, didn't see who did —
Be fair, don't take it out on me.
CREON: You're playing it safe, soldier,
barricading yourself from any trouble.
It's obvious, you've something strange to tell.
SENTRY: Dangerous too, and danger makes you delay
for all you're worth.
CREON: Out with it — then dismiss!
SENTRY: All right, here it comes. The body —
someone's just buried it, then run off . . .
sprinkled some dry dust on the flesh,
given it proper rites.
CREON: What?
What man alive would dare —
SENTRY: I've no idea, I swear it.
There was no mark of a spade, no pickaxe there,
no earth turned up, the ground packed hard and dry,
unbroken, no tracks, no wheelruts, nothing,
the workman left no trace. Just at sunup
the first watch of the day points it out —
it was a wonder! We were stunned . . .
a terrific burden too, for all of us, listen:
you can't see the corpse, not that it's buried,
really, just a light cover of road-dust on it,
as if someone meant to lay the dead to rest
and keep from getting cursed.
Not a sign in sight that dogs or wild beasts
had worried the body, even torn the skin.

But what came next! Rough talk flew thick and fast,
guard grilling guard — we'd have come to blows
at last, nothing to stop it; each man for himself
and each the culprit, no one caught red-handed,
all of us pleading ignorance, dodging the charges,
ready to take up red-hot iron in our fists,
go through fire, swear oaths to the gods —
"I didn't do it, I had no hand in it either,
not in the plotting, not in the work itself!"

Finally, after all this wrangling came to nothing,
one man spoke out and made us stare at the ground,
hanging our heads in fear. No way to counter him,
no way to take his advice and come through
safe and sound. Here's what he said:

"Look, we've got to report the facts to Creon,
we can't keep this hidden." Well, that won out,
and the lot fell on me, condemned me,
unlucky as ever, I got the prize. So here I am,
against my will and yours too, well I know —
no one wants the man who brings bad news.

LEADER: My king,
ever since he began I've been debating in my mind,
could this possibly be the work of the gods?

CREON: Stop —
before you make me choke with anger — the gods!
You, you're senile, must you be insane?
You say — why it's intolerable — say the gods
could have the slightest concern for that corpse?
Tell me, was it for meritorious service
they proceeded to bury him, prized him so? The hero
who came to burn their temples ringed with pillars,
their golden treasures — scorch their hallowed earth
and fling their laws to the winds.
Exactly when did you last see the gods
celebrating traitors? Inconceivable!

No, from the first there were certain citizens
who could hardly stand the spirit of my regime,
grumbling against me in the dark, heads together,
tossing wildly, never keeping their necks beneath
the yoke, loyally submitting to their king.
These are the instigators, I'm convinced —
they've perverted my own guard, bribed them
to do their work.
Money! Nothing worse
in our lives, so current, rampant, so corrupting.
Money — you demolish cities, root men from their homes,
you train and twist good minds and set them on
to the most atrocious schemes. No limit,
you make them adept at every kind of outrage,
every godless crime — money!
Everyone —
the whole crew bribed to commit this crime,
they've made one thing sure at least:
sooner or later they will pay the price.

Wheeling on the Sentry.

You —
I swear to Zeus as I still believe in Zeus,
if you don't find the man who buried that corpse,
the very man, and produce him before my eyes,

simple death won't be enough for you,
not till we string you up alive
and wring the immorality out of you.
Then you can steal the rest of your days,
better informed about where to make a killing.
You'll have learned, at last, it doesn't pay
to itch for rewards from every hand that beckons.
Filthy profits wreck most men, you'll see —
they'll never save your life.

SENTRY: Please,
may I say a word or two, or just turn and go?

CREON: Can't you tell? Everything you say offends me.

SENTRY: Where does it hurt you, in the ears or in the heart?

CREON: And who are you to pinpoint my displeasure?

SENTRY: The culprit grates on your feelings,
I just annoy your ears.

CREON: Still talking?
You talk too much! A born nuisance —

SENTRY: Maybe so,
but I never did this thing, so help me!

CREON: Yes you did —
what's more, you squandered your life for silver!

SENTRY: Oh it's terrible when the one who does the judging
judges things all wrong.

CREON: Well now,
you just be clever about your judgments —
if you fail to produce the criminals for me,
you'll swear your dirty money brought you pain.

Turning sharply, reentering the palace.

SENTRY: I hope he's found. Best thing by far.
But caught or not, that's in the lap of fortune;
I'll never come back, you've seen the last of me.
I'm saved, even now, and I never thought,
I never hoped —
dear gods, I owe you all my thanks!

Rushing out.

CHORUS: Numberless wonders
terrible wonders walk the world but none the match for man —
that great wonder crossing the heaving gray sea,
driven on by the blasts of winter
on through breakers crashing left and right,
holds his steady course
and the oldest of the gods he wears away —
the Earth, the immortal, the inexhaustible —
as his plows go back and forth, year in, year out
with the breed of stallions turning up the furrows.

And the blithe, lightheaded race of birds he snares,
the tribes of savage beasts, the life that swarms the depths —
with one fling of his nets
woven and coiled tight, he takes them all,
man the skilled, the brilliant!
He conquers all, taming with his techniques
the prey that roams the cliffs and wild lairs,
training the stallion, clamping the yoke across
his shaggy neck, and the tireless mountain bull.

And speech and thought, quick as the wind
and the mood and mind for law that rules the city —
all these he has taught himself
and shelter from the arrows of the frost
when there's rough lodging under the cold clear sky
and the shafts of lashing rain —
ready, resourceful man!
Never without resources
never an impasse as he marches on the future —
only Death, from Death alone he will find no rescue
but from desperate plagues he has plotted his escapes.

Man the master, ingenious past all measure
past all dreams, the skills within his grasp —
he forges on, now to destruction
now again to greatness. When he weaves in
the laws of the land, and the justice of the gods
that binds his oaths together
he and his city rise high —
but the city casts out
that man who weds himself to inhumanity
thanks to reckless daring. Never share my hearth
never think my thoughts, whoever does such things.

Enter Antigone from the side, accompanied by the Sentry.

Here is a dark sign from the gods —
what to make of this? I know her,
how can I deny it? That young girl's Antigone!
Wretched, child of a wretched father,
Oedipus. Look, is it possible?
They bring you in like a prisoner —
why? did you break the king's laws?
Did they take you in some act of mad defiance?

SENTRY: She's the one, she did it single-handed —
we caught her burying the body. Where's Creon?

Enter Creon from the palace.

LEADER: Back again, just in time when you need him.
CREON: In time for what? What is it?

SENTRY: My king,
there's nothing you can swear you'll never do —
second thoughts make liars of us all.
I could have sworn I wouldn't hurry back
(what with your threats, the buffeting I just took),
but a stroke of luck beyond our wildest hopes,
what a joy, there's nothing like it. So,
back I've come, breaking my oath, who cares?
I'm bringing in our prisoner — this young girl —
we took her giving the dead the last rites.
But no casting lots this time; this is *my* luck,
my prize, no one else's.
Now, my lord,
here she is. Take her, question her,
cross-examine her to your heart's content.
But set me free, it's only right —
I'm rid of this dreadful business once for all.

CREON: Prisoner! Her? You took her — where, doing what?

SENTRY: Burying the man. That's the whole story.

CREON: What?
You mean what you say, you're telling me the truth?

SENTRY: She's the one. With my own eyes I saw her
bury the body, just what you've forbidden.
There. Is that plain and clear?

CREON: What did you see? Did you catch her in the act?

SENTRY: Here's what happened. We went back to our post,
those threats of yours breathing down our necks —
we brushed the corpse clean of the dust that covered it,
stripped it bare . . . it was slimy, going soft,
and we took to high ground, backs to the wind
so the stink of him couldn't hit us;
jostling, baiting each other to keep awake,
shouting back and forth — no napping on the job,
not this time. And so the hours dragged by
until the sun stood dead above our heads,
a huge white ball in the noon sky, beating,
blazing down, and then it happened —
suddenly, a whirlwind!
Twisting a great dust-storm up from the earth,
a black plague of the heavens, filling the plain,
ripping the leaves off every tree in sight,
choking the air and sky. We squinted hard
and took our whipping from the gods.

And after the storm passed — it seemed endless —
there, we saw the girl!
And she cried out a sharp, piercing cry,

like a bird come back to an empty nest,
peering into its bed, and all the babies gone . . .
Just so, when she sees the corpse bare
she bursts into a long, shattering wail
and calls down withering curses on the heads
of all who did the work. And she scoops up dry dust,
handfuls, quickly, and lifting a fine bronze urn,
lifting it high and pouring, she crowns the dead
with three full libations.
Soon as we saw
we rushed her, closed on the kill like hunters,
and she, she didn't flinch. We interrogated her,
charging her with offenses past and present —
she stood up to it all, denied nothing. I tell you,
it made me ache and laugh in the same breath.
It's pure joy to escape the worst yourself,
it hurts a man to bring down his friends.
But all that, I'm afraid, means less to me
than my own skin. That's the way I'm made.

CREON:

Wheeling on Antigone.

You,
with your eyes fixed on the ground — speak up.
Do you deny you did this, yes or no?

ANTIGONE: I did it. I don't deny a thing.

CREON:

To the Sentry.

You, get out, wherever you please —
you're clear of a very heavy charge.

He leaves; Creon turns back to Antigone.

You, tell me briefly, no long speeches —
were you aware a decree had forbidden this?

ANTIGONE: Well aware. How could I avoid it? It was public.

CREON: And still you had the gall to break this law?

ANTIGONE: Of course I did. It wasn't Zeus, not in the least,
who made this proclamation — not to me.
Nor did that Justice, dwelling with the gods
beneath the earth, ordain such laws for men.
Nor did I think your edict had such force
that you, a mere mortal, could override the gods,
the great unwritten, unshakable traditions.
They are alive, not just today or yesterday:
they live forever, from the first of time,
and no one knows when they first saw the light.

These laws — I was not about to break them,
not out of fear of some man's wounded pride,
and face the retribution of the gods.
Die I must, I've known it all my life —
how could I keep from knowing? — even without
your death-sentence ringing in my ears.
And if I am to die before my time
I consider that a gain. Who on earth,
alive in the midst of so much grief as I,
could fail to find his death a rich reward?
So for me, at least, to meet this doom of yours
is precious little pain. But if I had allowed
my own mother's son to rot, an unburied corpse —
that would have been an agony! This is nothing.
And if my present actions strike you as foolish,
let's just say I've been accused of folly
by a fool.

LEADER: Like father like daughter,
passionate, wild . . .
she hasn't learned to bend before adversity.

CREON: No? Believe me, the stiffest stubborn wills
fall the hardest; the toughest iron,
tempered strong in the white-hot fire,
you'll see it crack and shatter first of all.
And I've known spirited horses you can break
with a light bit — proud, rebellious horses.
There's no room for pride, not in a slave,
not with the lord and master standing by.

This girl was an old hand at insolence
when she overrode the edicts we made public.
But once she'd done it — the insolence,
twice over — to glory in it, laughing,
mocking us to our face with what she'd done.
I'm not the man, not now: she is the man
if this victory goes to her and she goes free.

Never! Sister's child or closer in blood
than all my family clustered at my altar
worshiping Guardian Zeus — she'll never escape,
she and her blood sister, the most barbaric death.
Yes, I accuse her sister of an equal part
in scheming this, this burial.

To his attendants.

Bring her here!

I just saw her inside, hysterical, gone to pieces.
It never fails: the mind convicts itself

in advance, when scoundrels are up to no good,
plotting in the dark. Oh but I hate it more
when a traitor, caught red-handed,
tries to glorify his crimes.

ANTIGONE: Creon, what more do you want
than my arrest and execution?

CREON: Nothing. Then I have it all.

ANTIGONE: Then why delay? Your moralizing repels me,
every word you say — pray god it always will.
So naturally all I say repels you too.
Enough.
Give me glory! What greater glory could I win
than to give my own brother decent burial?
These citizens here would all agree,

To the Chorus.

they'd praise me too
if their lips weren't locked in fear.

Pointing to Creon.

Lucky tyrants — the perquisites of power!
Ruthless power to do and say whatever pleases *them.*

CREON: You alone, of all the people in Thebes,
see things that way.

ANTIGONE: They see it just that way
but defer to you and keep their tongues in leash.

CREON: And you, aren't you ashamed to differ so from them?
So disloyal!

ANTIGONE: Not ashamed for a moment,
not to honor my brother, my own flesh and blood.

CREON: Wasn't Eteocles a brother too — cut down, facing him?

ANTIGONE: Brother, yes, by the same mother, the same father.

CREON: Then how can you render his enemy such honors,
such impieties in his eyes?

ANTIGONE: He'll never testify to that,
Eteocles dead and buried.

CREON: He will —
if you honor the traitor just as much as him.

ANTIGONE: But it was his brother, not some slave that died —

CREON: Ravaging our country! —
but Eteocles died fighting in our behalf.

ANTIGONE: No matter — Death longs for the same rites for all.

CREON: Never the same for the patriot and the traitor.

ANTIGONE: Who, Creon, who on earth can say the ones below
don't find this pure and uncorrupt?

CREON: Never. Once an enemy, never a friend,
not even after death.

ANTIGONE: I was born to join in love, not hate —

that is my nature.
CREON: Go down below and love,
if love you must — love the dead! While I'm alive,
no woman is going to lord it over me.

Enter Ismene from the palace, under guard.

CHORUS: Look,
Ismene's coming, weeping a sister's tears,
loving sister, under a cloud . . .
her face is flushed, her cheeks streaming.
Sorrow puts her lovely radiance in the dark.
CREON: You —
in my house, you viper, slinking undetected,
sucking my life-blood! I never knew
I was breeding twin disasters, the two of you
rising up against my throne. Come, tell me,
will you confess your part in the crime or not?
Answer me. Swear to me.
ISMENE: I did it, yes —
if only she consents — I share the guilt,
the consequences too.
ANTIGONE: No,
Justice will never suffer that — not you,
you were unwilling. I never brought you in.
ISMENE: But now you face such dangers . . . I'm not ashamed
to sail through trouble with you,
make your troubles mine.
ANTIGONE: Who did the work?
Let the dead and the god of death bear witness!
I've no love for a friend who loves in words alone.
ISMENE: Oh no, my sister, don't reject me, please,
let me die beside you, consecrating
the dead together.
ANTIGONE: Never share my dying,
don't lay claim to what you never touched.
My death will be enough.
ISMENE: What do I care for life, cut off from you?
ANTIGONE: Ask Creon. Your concern is all for him.
ISMENE: Why abuse me so? It doesn't help you now.
ANTIGONE: You're right —
if I mock you, I get no pleasure from it,
only pain.
ISMENE: Tell me, dear one,
what can I do to help you, even now?
ANTIGONE: Save yourself. I don't grudge you your survival.
ISMENE: Oh no, no, denied my portion in your death?

ANTIGONE: You chose to live, I chose to die.
ISMENE: Not, at least,
without every kind of caution I could voice.
ANTIGONE: Your wisdom appealed to one world — mine, another.
ISMENE: But look, we're both guilty, both condemned to death.
ANTIGONE: Courage! Live your life. I gave myself to death,
long ago, so I might serve the dead.
CREON: They're both mad, I tell you, the two of them.
One's just shown it, the other's been that way
since she was born.
ISMENE: True, my king,
the sense we were born with cannot last forever . . .
commit cruelty on a person long enough
and the mind begins to go.
CREON: Yours did,
when you chose to commit your crimes with her.
ISMENE: How can I live alone, without her?
CREON: Her?
Don't even mention her — she no longer exists.
ISMENE: What? You'd kill your own son's bride?
CREON: Absolutely:
there are other fields for him to plow.
ISMENE: Perhaps,
but never as true, as close a bond as theirs.
CREON: A worthless woman for my son? It repels me.
ISMENE: Dearest Haemon, your father wrongs you so!
CREON: Enough, enough — you and your talk of marriage!
ISMENE: Creon — you're really going to rob your son of Antigone?
CREON: Death will do it for me — break their marriage off.
LEADER: So, it's settled then? Antigone must die?
CREON: Settled, yes — we both know that.

To the guards.

Stop wasting time. Take them in.
From now on they'll act like women.
Tie them up, no more running loose;
even the bravest will cut and run,
once they see Death coming for their lives.

The guards escort Antigone and Ismene into the palace. Creon remains while the old citizens form their chorus.

CHORUS: Blest, they are the truly blest who all their lives
have never tasted devastation. For others, once
the gods have rocked a house to its foundations
the ruin will never cease, cresting on and on
from one generation on throughout the race —

like a great mounting tide
driven on by savage northern gales,
surging over the dead black depths
roiling up from the bottom dark heaves of sand
and the headlands, taking the storm's onslaught full-force,
roar, and the low moaning
echoes on and on
and now
as in ancient times I see the sorrows of the house,
the living heirs of the old ancestral kings,
piling on the sorrows of the dead
and one generation cannot free the next —
some god will bring them crashing down,
the race finds no release.
And now the light, the hope
springing up from the late last root
in the house of Oedipus, that hope's cut down in turn
by the long, bloody knife swung by the gods of death
by a senseless word
by fury at the heart.
Zeus,
yours is the power, Zeus, what man on earth
can override it, who can hold it back?
Power that neither Sleep, the all-ensnaring
no, nor the tireless months of heaven
can ever overmaster — young through all time,
mighty lord of power, you hold fast
the dazzling crystal mansions of Olympus.
And throughout the future, late and soon
as through the past, your law prevails:
no towering form of greatness
enters into the lives of mortals
free and clear of ruin.
True,
our dreams, our high hopes voyaging far and wide
bring sheer delight to many, to many others
delusion, blithe, mindless lusts
and the fraud steals on one slowly . . . unaware
till he trips and puts his foot into the fire.
— He was a wise old man who coined
the famous saying: "Sooner or later
foul is fair, fair is foul
to the man the gods will ruin" —
He goes his way for a moment only
free of blinding ruin.

Enter Haemon from the palace.

Here's Haemon now, the last of all your sons.
Does he come in tears for his bride,
his doomed bride, Antigone —
bitter at being cheated of their marriage?

CREON: We'll soon know, better than seers could tell us.

Turning to Haemon.

Son, you've heard the final verdict on your bride?
Are you coming now, raving against your father?
Or do you love me, no matter what I do?

HAEMON: Father, I'm your *son* . . . you in your wisdom
set my bearings for me — I obey you.
No marriage could ever mean more to me than you,
whatever good direction you may offer.

CREON: Fine, Haemon.
That's how you ought to feel within your heart,
subordinate to your father's will in every way.
That's what a man prays for: to produce good sons —
households full of them, dutiful and attentive,
so they can pay his enemy back with interest
and match the respect their father shows his friend.
But the man who rears a brood of useless children,
what has he brought into the world, I ask you?
Nothing but trouble for himself, and mockery
from his enemies laughing in his face.
Oh Haemon,
never lose your sense of judgment over a woman.
The warmth, the rush of pleasure, it all goes cold
in your arms, I warn you . . . a worthless woman
in your house, a misery in your bed.
What wound cuts deeper than a loved one
turned against you? Spit her out,
like a mortal enemy — let the girl go.
Let her find a husband down among the dead.

Imagine it: I caught her in naked rebellion,
the traitor, the only one in the whole city.
I'm not about to prove myself a liar,
not to my people, no, I'm going to kill her!
That's right — so let her cry for mercy, sing her hymns
to Zeus who defends all bonds of kindred blood.
Why, if I bring up my own kin to be rebels,
think what I'd suffer from the world at large.
Show me the man who rules his household well:
I'll show you someone fit to rule the state.
That good man, my son,
I have every confidence he and he alone
can give commands and take them too. Staunch

in the storm of spears he'll stand his ground,
a loyal, unflinching comrade at your side.

But whoever steps out of line, violates the laws
or presumes to hand out orders to his superiors,
he'll win no praise from me. But that man
the city places in authority, his orders
must be obeyed, large and small,
right and wrong.
Anarchy —
show me a greater crime in all the earth!
She, she destroys cities, rips up houses,
breaks the ranks of spearmen into headlong rout.
But the ones who last it out, the great mass of them
owe their lives to discipline. Therefore
we must defend the men who live by law,
never let some woman triumph over us.
Better to fall from power, if fall we must,
at the hands of a man — never be rated
inferior to a woman, never.

LEADER: To us,
unless old age has robbed us of our wits,
you seem to say what you have to say with sense.

HAEMON: Father, only the gods endow a man with reason,
the finest of all their gifts, a treasure.
Far be it from me — I haven't the skill,
and certainly no desire, to tell you when,
if ever, you make a slip in speech . . . though
someone else might have a good suggestion.

Of course it's not for you,
in the normal run of things, to watch
whatever men say or do, or find to criticize.
The man in the street, you know, dreads your glance,
he'd never say anything displeasing to your face.
But it's for me to catch the murmurs in the dark,
the way the city mourns for this young girl.
"No woman," they say, "ever deserved death less,
and such a brutal death for such a glorious action.
She, with her own dear brother lying in his blood —
she couldn't bear to leave him dead, unburied,
food for the wild dogs or wheeling vultures.
Death? She deserves a glowing crown of gold!"
So they say, and the rumor spreads in secret,
darkly . . .
I rejoice in your success, father —
nothing more precious to me in the world.
What medal of honor brighter to his children

than a father's growing glory? Or a child's
to his proud father? Now don't, please,
be quite so single-minded, self-involved,
or assume the world is wrong and you are right.
Whoever thinks that he alone possesses intelligence,
the gift of eloquence, he and no one else,
and character too . . . such men, I tell you,
spread them open — you will find them empty.
No,
it's no disgrace for a man, even a wise man,
to learn many things and not to be too rigid.
You've seen trees by a raging winter torrent,
how many sway with the flood and salvage every twig,
but not the stubborn — they're ripped out, roots and all.
Bend or break. The same when a man is sailing:
haul your sheets too taut, never give an inch,
you'll capsize, go the rest of the voyage
keel up and the rowing-benches under.

Oh give way. Relax your anger — change!
I'm young, I know, but let me offer this:
it would be best by far, I admit,
if a man were born infallible, right by nature.
If not — and things don't often go that way,
it's best to learn from those with good advice.

LEADER: You'd do well, my lord, if he's speaking to the point,
to learn from him,

Turning to Haemon.

and you, my boy, from him.
You both are talking sense.

CREON: So,
men our age, we're to be lectured, are we? —
schooled by a boy his age?

HAEMON: Only in what is right. But if I seem young,
look less to my years and more to what I do.

CREON: Do? Is admiring rebels an achievement?

HAEMON: I'd never suggest that you admire treason.

CREON: Oh? —
isn't that just the sickness that's attacked her?

HAEMON: The whole city of Thebes denies it, to a man.

CREON: And is Thebes about to tell me how to rule?

HAEMON: Now, you see? Who's talking like a child?

CREON: Am I to rule this land for others — or myself?

HAEMON: It's no city at all, owned by one man alone.

CREON: What? The city *is* the king's — that's the law!

HAEMON: What a splendid king you'd make of a desert island —
you and you alone.

CREON:

To the Chorus.

This boy, I do believe,
is fighting on her side, the woman's side.
HAEMON: If you are a woman, yes;
my concern is all for you.
CREON: Why, you degenerate — bandying accusations,
threatening me with justice, your own father!
HAEMON: I see my father offending justice — wrong.
CREON: Wrong?
To protect my royal rights?
HAEMON: Protect your rights?
When you trample down the honors of the gods?
CREON: You, you soul of corruption, rotten through —
woman's accomplice!
HAEMON: That may be,
but you'll never find me accomplice to a criminal.
CREON: That's what *she* is,
and every word you say is a blatant appeal for her —
HAEMON: And you, and me, and the gods beneath the earth.
CREON: You'll never marry her, not while she's alive.
HAEMON: Then she'll die . . . but her death will kill another.
CREON: What, brazen threats? You go too far!
HAEMON: What threat?
Combating your empty, mindless judgments with a word?
CREON: You'll suffer for your sermons, you and your empty wisdom!
HAEMON: If you weren't my father, I'd say you were insane.
CREON: Don't flatter me with Father — you woman's slave!
HAEMON: You really expect to fling abuse at me
and not receive the same?
CREON: Is that so!
Now, by heaven, I promise you, you'll pay —
taunting, insulting me! Bring her out,
that hateful — she'll die now, here,
in front of his eyes, beside her groom!
HAEMON: No, no, she will never die beside me —
don't delude yourself. And you will never
see me, never set eyes on my face again.
Rage your heart out, rage with friends
who can stand the sight of you.

Rushing out.

LEADER: Gone, my king, in a burst of anger.
A temper young as his . . . hurt him once,
he may do something violent.
CREON: Let him do —
dream up something desperate, past all human limit!

Good riddance. Rest assured,
he'll never save those two young girls from death.
LEADER: Both of them, you really intend to kill them both?
CREON: No, not her, the one whose hands are clean;
you're quite right.
LEADER: But Antigone —
what sort of death do you have in mind for her?
CREON: I'll take her down some wild, desolate path
never trod by men, and wall her up alive
in a rocky vault, and set out short rations,
just a gesture of piety
to keep the entire city free of defilement.
There let her pray to the one god she worships:
Death — who knows? — may just reprieve her from death.
Or she may learn at last, better late than never,
what a waste of breath it is to worship Death.

Exit to the palace.

CHORUS: Love, never conquered in battle
Love the plunderer laying waste the rich!
Love standing the night-watch
guarding a girl's soft cheek,
you range the seas, the shepherds' steadings off in the wilds —
not even the deathless gods can flee your onset,
nothing human born for a day —
whoever feels your grip is driven mad.
Love
you wrench the minds of the righteous into outrage,
swerve them to their ruin — you have ignited this,
this kindred strife, father and son at war
and Love alone the victor —
warm glance of the bride triumphant, burning with desire!
Throned in power, side-by-side with the mighty laws!
Irresistible Aphrodite,° never conquered —
Love, you mock us for your sport.

Antigone is brought from the palace under guard.

But now, even I'd rebel against the king,
I'd break all bounds when I see this —
I fill with tears, can't hold them back,
not any more . . . I see Antigone make her way
to the bridal vault where all are laid to rest.
ANTIGONE: Look at me, men of my fatherland,
setting out on the last road
looking into the last light of day
the last I'll ever see . . .

---

894. Aphrodite: Greek goddess of love and beauty.

the god of death who puts us all to bed
takes me down to the banks of Acheron° alive —
denied my part in the wedding-songs,
no wedding-song in the dusk has crowned my marriage —
I go to wed the lord of the dark waters.

CHORUS: Not crowned with glory, crowned with a dirge,
you leave for the deep pit of the dead.
No withering illness laid you low,
no strokes of the sword — a law to yourself,
alone, no mortal like you, ever, you go down
to the halls of Death alive and breathing.

ANTIGONE: But think of Niobe° — well I know her story —
think what a living death she died,
Tantalus' daughter, stranger queen from the east:
there on the mountain heights, growing stone
binding as ivy, slowly walled her round
and the rains will never cease, the legends say
the snows will never leave her . . .
wasting away, under her brows the tears
showering down her breasting ridge and slopes —
a rocky death like hers puts me to sleep.

CHORUS: But she was a god, born of gods,
and we are only mortals born to die.
And yet, of course, it's a great thing
for a dying girl to hear, just hear
she shares a destiny equal to the gods,
during life and later, once she's dead.

ANTIGONE: O you mock me!
Why, in the name of all my fathers' gods
why can't you wait till I am gone —
must you abuse me to my face?
O my city, all your fine rich sons!
And you, you springs of the Dirce,
holy grove of Thebes where the chariots gather,
you at least, you'll bear me witness, look,
unmourned by friends and forced by such crude laws
I go to my rockbound prison, strange new tomb —
always a stranger, O dear god,
I have no home on earth and none below,
not with the living, not with the breathless dead.

CHORUS: You went too far, the last limits of daring —
smashing against the high throne of Justice!
Your life's in ruins, child — I wonder . . .

---

906. Acheron: A river in Hades, the underworld of the dead. **916. Niobe:** A queen of Thebes who, while weeping for her slain children, was turned into stone from which her tears continue to flow.

do you pay for your father's terrible ordeal?
ANTIGONE: There — at last you've touched it, the worst pain
the worst anguish! Raking up the grief for father
three times over, for all the doom
that's struck us down, the brilliant house of Laius.
O mother, your marriage-bed
the coiling horrors, the coupling there —
you with your own son, my father — doomstruck mother!
Such, such were my parents, and I their wretched child.
I go to them now, cursed, unwed, to share their home —
I am a stranger! O dear brother, doomed
in your marriage — your marriage murders mine,
your dying drags me down to death alive!

Enter Creon.

CHORUS: Reverence asks some reverence in return —
but attacks on power never go unchecked,
not by the man who holds the reins of power.
Your own blind will, your passion has destroyed you.
ANTIGONE: No one to weep for me, my friends,
no wedding-song — they take me away
in all my pain . . . the road lies open, waiting.
Never again, the law forbids me to see
the sacred eye of day. I am agony!
No tears for the destiny that's mine,
no loved one mourns my death.
CREON: Can't you see?
If a man could wail his own dirge *before* he dies,
he'd never finish.

To the guards.

Take her away, quickly!
Wall her up in the tomb, you have your orders.
Abandon her there, alone, and let her choose —
death or a buried life with a good roof for shelter.
As for myself, my hands are clean. This young girl —
dead or alive, she will be stripped of her rights,
her stranger's rights, here in the world above.
ANTIGONE: O tomb, my bridal-bed — my house, my prison
cut in the hollow rock, my everlasting watch!
I'll soon be there, soon embrace my own,
the great growing family of our dead
Persephone° has received among her ghosts.
I,
the last of them all, the most reviled by far,

---

983. Persephone: A daughter of Zeus and Demeter who was abducted by Pluto to reign as queen of the underworld.

go down before my destined time's run out.
But still I go, cherishing one good hope:
my arrival may be dear to father,
dear to you, my mother,
dear to you, my loving brother, Eteocles —
When you died I washed you with my hands,
I dressed you all, I poured the cups
across your tombs. But now, Polynices,
because I laid your body out as well,
this, this is my reward. Nevertheless
I honored you — the decent will admit it —
well and wisely too.
Never, I tell you,
if I had been the mother of children
or if my husband died, exposed and rotting —
I'd never have taken this ordeal upon myself,
never defied our people's will. What law,
you ask, do I satisfy with what I say?
A husband dead, there might have been another.
A child by another too, if I had lost the first.
But mother and father both lost in the halls of Death,
no brother could ever spring to light again.

For this law alone I held you first in honor.
For this, Creon, the king, judges me a criminal
guilty of dreadful outrage, my dear brother!
And now he leads me off, a captive in his hands,
with no part in the bridal-song, the bridal-bed,
denied all joy of marriage, raising children —
deserted so by loved ones, struck by fate,
I descend alive to the caverns of the dead.

What law of the mighty gods have I transgressed?
Why look to the heavens any more, tormented as I am?
Whom to call, what comrades now? Just think,
my reverence only brands me for irreverence!
Very well: if this is the pleasure of the gods,
once I suffer I will know that I was wrong.
But if these men are wrong, let them suffer
nothing worse than they mete out to me —
these masters of injustice!

LEADER: Still the same rough winds, the wild passion
raging through the girl.

CREON:

To the guards.

Take her away.
You're wasting time — you'll pay for it too.

ANTIGONE: Oh god, the voice of death. It's come, it's here.
CREON: True. Not a word of hope — your doom is sealed.
ANTIGONE: Land of Thebes, city of all my fathers —
O you gods, the first gods of the race!
They drag me away, now, no more delay.
Look on me, you noble sons of Thebes —
the last of a great line of kings,
I alone, see what I suffer now
at the hands of what breed of men —
all for reverence, my reverence for the gods!

She leaves under guard; the Chorus gathers.

CHORUS: Danaë, Danaë° —
even she endured a fate like yours,
in all her lovely strength she traded
the light of day for the bolted brazen vault —
buried within her tomb, her bridal-chamber,
wed to the yoke and broken.
But she was of glorious birth
my child, my child
and treasured the seed of Zeus within her womb,
the cloudburst streaming gold!
The power of fate is a wonder,
dark, terrible wonder —
neither wealth nor armies
towered walls nor ships
black hulls lashed by the salt
can save us from that force.

The yoke tamed him too
young Lycurgus° flaming in anger
king of Edonia, all for his mad taunts
Dionysus clamped him down, encased
in the chain-mail of rock
and there his rage
his terrible flowering rage burst —
sobbing, dying away . . . at last that madman
came to know his god —
the power he mocked, the power
he taunted in all his frenzy
trying to stamp out
the women strong with the god —

1036. Danaë: A princess of Argos who was imprisoned by her father because it was prophesied that her son would kill him, but visited by Zeus in the form of a shower of gold. Their son was Perseus. **1053. Lycurgus:** Punished by Dionysus because he refused to worship him.

the torch, the raving sacred cries —
enraging the Muses° who adore the flute.

And far north where the Black Rocks
cut the sea in half
and murderous straits
split the coast of Thrace
a forbidding city stands
where once, hard by the walls
the savage Ares thrilled to watch
a king's new queen, a Fury rearing in rage
against his two royal sons —
her bloody hands, her dagger-shuttle
stabbing out their eyes — cursed, blinding wounds —
their eyes blind sockets screaming for revenge!

They wailed in agony, cries echoing cries
the princes doomed at birth . . .
and their mother doomed to chains,
walled off in a tomb of stone —
but she traced her own birth back
to a proud Athenian line and the high gods
and off in caverns half the world away,
born of the wild North Wind
she sprang on her father's gales,
racing stallions up the leaping cliffs —
child of the heavens. But even on her the Fates
the gray everlasting Fates rode hard
my child, my child.

Enter Tiresias, the blind prophet, led by a boy.

TIRESIAS: Lords of Thebes,
I and the boy have come together,
hand in hand. Two see with the eyes of one . . .
so the blind must go, with a guide to lead the way.
CREON: What is it, old Tiresias? What news now?
TIRESIAS: I will teach you. And you obey the seer.
CREON: I will,
I've never wavered from your advice before.
TIRESIAS: And so you kept the city straight on course.
CREON: I owe you a great deal, I swear to that.
TIRESIAS: Then reflect, my son: you are poised,
once more, on the razor-edge of fate.
CREON: What is it? I shudder to hear you.
TIRESIAS: You will learn
when you listen to the warnings of my craft.

1066. Muses: Goddesses of the arts and sciences.

As I sat on the ancient seat of augury,°
in the sanctuary where every bird I know
will hover at my hands — suddenly I heard it,
a strange voice in the wingbeats, unintelligible,
barbaric, a mad scream! Talons flashing, ripping,
they were killing each other — that much I knew —
the murderous fury whirring in those wings
made that much clear!
I was afraid,
I turned quickly, tested the burnt-sacrifice,
ignited the altar at all points — but no fire,
the god in the fire never blazed.
Not from those offerings . . . over the embers
slid a heavy ooze from the long thighbones,
smoking, sputtering out, and the bladder
puffed and burst — spraying gall into the air —
and the fat wrapping the bones slithered off
and left them glistening white. No fire!
The rites failed that might have blazed the future
with a sign. So I learned from the boy here;
he is my guide, as I am guide to others.
And it's you —
your high resolve that sets this plague on Thebes.
The public altars and sacred hearths are fouled,
one and all, by the birds and dogs with carrion
torn from the corpse, the doomstruck son of Oedipus!
And so the gods are deaf to our prayers, they spurn
the offerings in our hands, the flame of holy flesh.
No birds cry out an omen clear and true —
they're gorged with the murdered victim's blood and fat.
Take these things to heart, my son, I warn you.
All men make mistakes, it is only human.
But once the wrong is done, a man
can turn his back on folly, misfortune too,
if he tries to make amends, however low he's fallen,
and stops his bullnecked ways. Stubbornness
brands you for stupidity — pride is a crime.
No, yield to the dead!
Never stab the fighter when he's down.
Where's the glory, killing the dead twice over?

I mean you well. I give you sound advice.
It's best to learn from a good adviser
when he speaks for your own good:
it's pure gain.

1104. seat of augury: The place where Tiresias looked for omens among birds.

CREON: Old man — all of you! So,
you shoot your arrows at my head like archers at the target —
I even have *him* loosed on me, this fortune-teller.
Oh his ilk has tried to sell me short
and ship me off for years. Well,
drive your bargains, traffic — much as you like —
in the gold of India, silver-gold of Sardis.
You'll never bury that body in the grave,
not even if Zeus's eagles rip the corpse
and wing their rotten pickings off to the throne of god!
Never, not even in fear of such defilement
will I tolerate his burial, that traitor.
Well I know, we can't defile the gods —
no mortal has the power.
No,
reverend old Tiresias, all men fall,
it's only human, but the wisest fall obscenely
when they glorify obscene advice with rhetoric —
all for their own gain.
TIRESIAS: Oh god, is there a man alive
who knows, who actually believes . . .
CREON: What now?
What earth-shattering truth are you about to utter?
TIRESIAS: . . . just how much a sense of judgment, wisdom
is the greatest gift we have?
CREON: Just as much, I'd say,
as a twisted mind is the worst affliction going.
TIRESIAS: You are the one who's sick, Creon, sick to death.
CREON: I am in no mood to trade insults with a seer.
TIRESIAS: You have already, calling my prophecies a lie.
CREON: Why not?
You and the whole breed of seers are mad for money!
TIRESIAS: And the whole race of tyrants lusts to rake it in.
CREON: This slander of yours —
are you aware you're speaking to the king?
TIRESIAS: Well aware. Who helped you save the city?
CREON: You —
you have your skills, old seer, but you lust for injustice!
TIRESIAS: You will drive me to utter the dreadful secret in my heart.
CREON: Spit it out! Just don't speak it out for profit.
TIRESIAS: Profit? No, not a bit of profit, not for you.
CREON: Know full well, you'll never buy off my resolve.
TIRESIAS: Then know this too, learn this by heart!
The chariot of the sun will not race through
so many circuits more, before you have surrendered
one born of your own loins, your own flesh and blood,
a corpse for corpses given in return, since you have thrust

to the world below a child sprung for the world above,
ruthlessly lodged a living soul within the grave —
then you've robbed the gods below the earth,
keeping a dead body here in the bright air,
unburied, unsung, unhallowed by the rites.

You, you have no business with the dead,
nor do the gods above — this is violence
you have forced upon the heavens.
And so the avengers, the dark destroyers late
but true to the mark, now lie in wait for you,
the Furies sent by the gods and the god of death
to strike you down with the pains that you perfected!

There. Reflect on that, tell me I've been bribed.
The day comes soon, no long test of time, not now,
that wakes the wails for men and women in your halls.
Great hatred rises against you —
cities in tumult, all whose mutilated sons
the dogs have graced with burial, or the wild beasts,
some wheeling crow that wings the ungodly stench of carrion
back to each city, each warrior's hearth and home.

These arrows for your heart! Since you've raked me
I loose them like an archer in my anger,
arrows deadly true. You'll never escape
their burning, searing force.

Motioning to his escort.

Come, boy, take me home.
So he can vent his rage on younger men,
and learn to keep a gentler tongue in his head
and better sense than what he carries now.

Exit to the side.

LEADER: The old man's gone, my king —
terrible prophecies. Well I know,
since the hair on this old head went gray,
he's never lied to Thebes.
CREON: I know it myself — I'm shaken, torn.
It's a dreadful thing to yield . . . but resist now?
Lay my pride bare to the blows of ruin?
That's dreadful too.
LEADER: But good advice,
Creon, take it now, you must.
CREON: What should I do? Tell me . . . I'll obey.
LEADER: Go! Free the girl from the rocky vault
and raise a mound for the body you exposed.
CREON: That's your advice? You think I should give in?

LEADER: Yes, my king, quickly. Disasters sent by the gods
cut short our follies in a flash.

CREON: Oh it's hard.
giving up the heart's desire . . . but I will do it —
no more fighting a losing battle with necessity.

LEADER: Do it now, go, don't leave it to others.

CREON: Now — I'm on my way! Come, each of you,
take up axes, make for the high ground,
over there, quickly! I and my better judgment
have come round to this — I shackled her,
I'll set her free myself. I am afraid . . .
it's best to keep the established laws
to the very day we die.

Rushing out, followed by his entourage. The Chorus clusters around the altar.

CHORUS: God of a hundred names!
Great Dionysus —
Son and glory of Semele! Pride of Thebes —
Child of Zeus whose thunder rocks the clouds —
Lord of the famous lands of evening —
King of the Mysteries!
King of Eleusis, Demeter's plain°
her breasting hills that welcome in the world —
Great Dionysus!
Bacchus,° living in Thebes
the mother-city of all your frenzied women —
Bacchus
living along the Ismenus'° rippling waters
standing over the field sown with the Dragon's teeth!

You — we have seen you through the flaring smoky fires,
your torches blazing over the twin peaks
where nymphs of the hallowed cave climb onward
fired with you, your sacred rage —
we have seen you at Castalia's running spring°
and down from the heights of Nysa° crowned with ivy
the greening shore rioting vines and grapes
down you come in your storm of wild women
ecstatic, mystic cries —
Dionysus —
down to watch and ward the roads of Thebes!

First of all cities, Thebes you honor first
you and your mother, bride of the lightning —

1244. Demeter's plain: The goddess of agriculture was worshiped at Eleusis, near Athens. **1246. Bacchus:** Dionysus. **1248. Ismenus:** A river from which the founders of the city, Thebes, were said to have sprung from a dragon's teeth. **1254. Castalia's running spring:** The sacred spring of Apollo's oracle at Delphi. **1255. Nysa:** A mountain where Dionysus was worshiped.

come, Dionysus! now your people lie
in the iron grip of plague,
come in your racing, healing stride
down Parnassus'° slopes
or across the moaning straits.
Lord of the dancing —
dance, dance the constellations breathing fire!
Great master of the voices of the night!
Child of Zeus, God's offspring, come, come forth!
Lord, king, dance with your nymphs, swirling, raving
arm-in-arm in frenzy through the night
they dance you, Iacchus° —
Dance, Dionysus
giver of all good things!

Enter a Messenger from the side.

MESSENGER: Neighbors,
friends of the house of Cadmus° and the kings,
there's not a thing in this life of ours
I'd praise or blame as settled once for all.
Fortune lifts and Fortune fells the lucky
and unlucky every day. No prophet on earth
can tell a man his fate. Take Creon:
there was a man to rouse your envy once,
as I see it. He saved the realm from enemies;
taking power, he alone, the lord of the fatherland,
he set us true on course — flourished like a tree
with the noble line of sons he bred and reared . . .
and now it's lost, all gone.
Believe me,
when a man has squandered his true joys,
he's good as dead, I tell you, a living corpse.
Pile up riches in your house, as much as you like —
live like a king with a huge show of pomp,
but if real delight is missing from the lot,
I wouldn't give you a wisp of smoke for it,
not compared with joy.

LEADER: What now?
What new grief do you bring the house of kings?

MESSENGER: Dead, dead — and the living are guilty of their death!

LEADER: Who's the murderer? Who is dead? Tell us.

MESSENGER: Haemon's gone, his blood spilled by the very hand —

LEADER: His father's or his own?

MESSENGER: His own . . .
raging mad with his father for the death —

1265. Parnassus: A mountain in Greece that was sacred to Dionysus as well as other gods and goddesses. **1272. Iacchus:** Dionysus. **1274. Cadmus:** The legendary founder of Thebes.

LEADER: Oh great seer,
you saw it all, you brought your word to birth!
MESSENGER: Those are the facts. Deal with them as you will.

As he turns to go, Eurydice enters from the palace.

LEADER: Look, Eurydice. Poor woman, Creon's wife,
so close at hand. By chance perhaps,
unless she's heard the news about her son.
EURYDICE: My countrymen,
all of you — I caught the sound of your words
as I was leaving to do my part,
to appeal to queen Athena° with my prayers.
I was just loosing the bolts, opening the doors,
when a voice filled with sorrow, family sorrow,
struck my ears, and I fell back, terrified,
into the women's arms — everything went black.
Tell me the news, again, whatever it is . . .
sorrow and I are hardly strangers;
I can bear the worst.
MESSENGER: I — dear lady,
I'll speak as an eye-witness. I was there.
And I won't pass over one word of the truth.
Why should I try to soothe you with a story,
only to prove a liar in a moment?
Truth is always best.
So,
I escorted your lord, I guided him
to the edge of the plain where the body lay,
Polynices, torn by the dogs and still unmourned.
And saying a prayer to Hecate of the Crossroads,
Pluto° too, to hold their anger and be kind,
we washed the dead in a bath of holy water
and plucking some fresh branches, gathering . . .
what was left of him, we burned them all together
and raised a high mound of native earth, and then
we turned and made for that rocky vault of hers,
the hollow, empty bed of the bride of Death.
And far off, one of us heard a voice,
a long wail rising, echoing
out of that unhallowed wedding-chamber;
he ran to alert the master and Creon pressed on,
closer — the strange, inscrutable cry came sharper,
throbbing around him now, and he let loose
a cry of his own, enough to wrench the heart,

1306. Athena: The Greek goddess of wisdom and protector of cities. **1322–1323. Hecate, Pluto:** Gods of the underworld.

"Oh god, am I the prophet now? going down
the darkest road I've ever gone? My son —
it's *his* dear voice, he greets me! Go, men,
closer, quickly! Go through the gap,
the rocks are dragged back —
right to the tomb's very mouth — and look,
see if it's Haemon's voice I think I hear,
or the gods have robbed me of my senses."

The king was shattered. We took his orders,
went and searched, and there in the deepest,
dark recesses of the tomb we found her . . .
hanged by the neck in a fine linen noose,
strangled in her veils — and the boy,
his arms flung around her waist,
clinging to her, wailing for his bride,
dead and down below, for his father's crimes
and the bed of his marriage blighted by misfortune.
When Creon saw him, he gave a deep sob,
he ran in, shouting, crying out to him,
"Oh my child — what have you done? what seized you,
what insanity? what disaster drove you mad?
Come out, my son! I beg you on my knees!"
But the boy gave him a wild burning glance,
spat in his face, not a word in reply,
he drew his sword — his father rushed out,
running as Haemon lunged and missed! —
and then, doomed, desperate with himself,
suddenly leaning his full weight on the blade,
he buried it in his body, halfway to the hilt.
And still in his senses, pouring his arms around her,
he embraced the girl and breathing hard,
released a quick rush of blood,
bright red on her cheek glistening white.
And there he lies, body enfolding body . . .
he has won his bride at last, poor boy,
not here but in the houses of the dead.

Creon shows the world that of all the ills
afflicting men the worst is lack of judgment.

Eurydice turns and reenters the palace.

LEADER: What do you make of that? The lady's gone,
without a word, good or bad.
MESSENGER: I'm alarmed too
but here's my hope — faced with her son's death,
she finds it unbecoming to mourn in public.
Inside, under her roof, she'll set her women

to the task and wail the sorrow of the house.
She's too discreet. She won't do something rash.

LEADER: I'm not so sure. To me, at least,
a long heavy silence promises danger,
just as much as a lot of empty outcries.

MESSENGER: We'll see if she's holding something back,
hiding some passion in her heart.
I'm going in. You may be right — who knows?
Even too much silence has its dangers.

Exit to the palace. Enter Creon from the side, escorted by attendants carrying Haemon's body on a bier.

LEADER: The king himself! Coming toward us,
look, holding the boy's head in his hands.
Clear, damning proof, if it's right to say so —
proof of his own madness, no one else's,
no, his own blind wrongs.

CREON: Ohhh,
so senseless, so insane . . . my crimes,
my stubborn, deadly —
Look at us, the killer, the killed,
father and son, the same blood — the misery!
My plans, my mad fanatic heart,
my son, cut off so young!
Ai, dead, lost to the world,
not through your stupidity, no, my own.

LEADER: Too late,
too late, you see what justice means.

CREON: Oh I've learned
through blood and tears! Then, it was then,
when the god came down and struck me — a great weight
shattering, driving me down that wild savage path,
ruining, trampling down my joy. Oh the agony,
the heartbreaking agonies of our lives.

Enter the Messenger from the palace.

MESSENGER: Master,
what a hoard of grief you have, and you'll have more.
The grief that lies to hand you've brought yourself —

Pointing to Haemon's body.

the rest, in the house, you'll see it all too soon.

CREON: What now? What's worse than this?

MESSENGER: The queen is dead.
The mother of this dead boy . . . mother to the end —
poor thing, her wounds are fresh.

CREON: No, no,
harbor of Death, so choked, so hard to cleanse! —
why me? why are you killing me?

Herald of pain, more words, more grief?
I died once, you kill me again and again!
What's the report, boy . . . some news for me?
My wife dead? O dear god!
Slaughter heaped on slaughter?

The doors open; the body of Eurydice is brought out on her bier.

MESSENGER: See for yourself:
now they bring her body from the palace.

CREON: Oh no,
another, a second loss to break the heart.
What next, what fate still waits for me?
I just held my son in my arms and now,
look, a new corpse rising before my eyes —
wretched, helpless mother — O my son!

MESSENGER: She stabbed herself at the altar,
then her eyes went dark, after she'd raised
a cry for the noble fate of Megareus,° the hero
killed in the first assault, then for Haemon,
then with her dying breath she called down
torments on your head — you killed her sons.

CREON: Oh the dread,
I shudder with dread! Why not kill me too? —
run me through with a good sharp sword?
Oh god, the misery, anguish —
I, I'm churning with it, going under.

MESSENGER: Yes, and the dead, the woman lying there,
piles the guilt of all their deaths on you.

CREON: How did she end her life, what bloody stroke?

MESSENGER: She drove home to the heart with her own hand,
once she learned her son was dead . . . that agony.

CREON: And the guilt is all mine —
can never be fixed on another man,
no escape for me. I killed you,
I, god help me, I admit it all!

To his attendants.

Take me away, quickly, out of sight.
I don't even exist — I'm no one. Nothing.

LEADER: Good advice, if there's any good in suffering.
Quickest is best when troubles block the way.

CREON:

Kneeling in prayer.

Come, let it come! — that best of fates for me
that brings the final day, best fate of all.

1429. Megareus: A son of Creon and Eurydice; he died when Thebes was attacked.

Oh quickly, now —
so I never have to see another sunrise.
LEADER: That will come when it comes;
we must deal with all that lies before us.
The future rests with the ones who tend the future.
CREON: That prayer — I poured my heart into that prayer!
LEADER: No more prayers now. For mortal men
there is no escape from the doom we must endure.
CREON: Take me away, I beg you, out of sight.
A rash, indiscriminate fool!
I murdered you, my son, against my will —
you too, my wife . . .
Wailing wreck of a man,
whom to look to? where to lean for support?

Desperately turning from Haemon to Eurydice on their biers.

Whatever I touch goes wrong — once more
a crushing fate's come down upon my head.

The Messenger and attendants lead Creon into the palace.

CHORUS: Wisdom is by far the greatest part of joy,
and reverence toward the gods must be safeguarded.
The mighty words of the proud are paid in full
with mighty blows of fate, and at long last
those blows will teach us wisdom.

The old citizens exit to the side.

WILLIAM SHAKESPEARE *(1564–1616), the great English playwright and poet, was born in Stratford, the third of eight children of Mary Arden, daughter of a prosperous landowner, and John Shakespeare, a glovemaker. We know a little more about Shakespeare's personal life than we know about Sophocles' life two thousand years before. Some forty documents of Shakespeare's time offer details about him, commensurate with his station in life and professional activities. The register of the Stratford parish church documents Shakespeare's baptism and burial, along with the baptisms of his daughter Susanna and his twins, Judith and Hamnet. We also know that in 1582, at the age of eighteen, he married Anne Hathaway in Stratford (she was twenty-six), and that before his death he made a will leaving most of his considerable property to his two daughters (his son, Hamnet, had died at age eleven). Shakespeare willed only his "second best bed" to his wife, whom he apparently left in Stratford with his children when he went off to London to make his fortune in the theater.*

As a young man in London, Shakespeare worked as an actor and playwright, but his first publications were two books of poetry. In 1593, after an outbreak of the plague had closed the London theaters, he published his first poem, Venus and Adonis, *dedicated to his wealthy patron the Earl of Southampton. A year later he pub-*

lished another long narrative poem, The Rape of Lucrece. *(A third book, his collection of sonnets, was published in 1609.) When the theaters reopened in London at the end of 1594, Shakespeare joined the new Lord Chamberlain's Company, for whom he continued to act and write plays until 1613. The literary historian François Laroque has described the astute way Shakespeare managed his career before his retirement as a wealthy man in Stratford:*

> *The Chamberlain's Men were organized in an unusual manner: the six main actors [including Shakespeare] formed an association in which each was a shareholder, directly receiving part of the takings from performances. The actors were financially independent, paying only rent to the theatre proprietor James Burbage. . . . Shakespeare never changed company, a fact rare enough to be worthy of note. From now on he worked to strengthen his position as both player and playwright. In addition to his acting he wrote an average of two plays a year until 1608, when the pace of theatrical production slackened. The decision early in his career to remain in one place, with one company, enabled him quickly to consolidate his first successes as a writer and to become in his lifetime the most highly sought after dramatist of the Elizabethan and Jacobean stage.*

The exact number of plays written by Shakespeare is unknown, as the practice of his time was for playwrights to collaborate on scripts, often reworking and adapting older material, but thirty-seven plays currently make up the Shakespeare canon. Seven years after his death, thirty-six of his plays were collected by actors in his theater company desirous to honor his memory and to protect his work from unscrupulous publishers. The table of contents in this First Folio edition of 1623 reads, "A Catalogue of the several Comedies, Histories, and Tragedies contained in this Volume." This way of organizing the plays has continued to the present day.

The comedies included, among other plays, The Tempest, The Comedy of Errors, A Midsummer Night's Dream, As You Like It, The Taming of the Shrew, *and* The Merchant of Venice. *The history plays — most of which Shakespeare wrote early in his career, between 1590 and 1597 — included* Richard II; Henry IV, Parts 1 and 2; Henry V; Henry VI, Parts 1–3; *and* Richard III. *The tragedies included* Romeo and Juliet, Macbeth, King Lear, Othello, *and* Hamlet. *Although eighteen of Shakespeare's plays were published in his lifetime as small books called* quartos, *no play manuscript used by a printer in this time has survived, so we depend on the work of scholars for the editing of his texts.*

The Elizabethan theater flourished during the reign of Elizabeth I and her successor, James I, having its origins in fifteenth-century religious pageants and plays such as The Second Shepherd's Play *and* Everyman, *which were performed by actors who were part of traveling companies. The first permanent theater in England was not built until 1576, only about fifteen years before Shakespeare came to London to begin his career. Toward the end of the sixteenth century, playwrights began to glorify English history, turning to secular material for their subjects. National patriotism was stirred by the defeat of the Spanish Armada, which had failed spectacularly in its attempt to conquer England in 1588. When Shakespeare began to write plays, there were several professional acting companies in London, and we have a good idea of the design of their theaters from the foundations of the Rose Playhouse, excavated in 1988. A reconstruction of the Globe Playhouse, in which Shakespeare once held a one-tenth*

Interior of the first Globe Playhouse. (Drawing by C. Walter Hodges. Reprinted from *The Third Globe: Symposium for the Reconstruction of the Globe Playhouse,* edited by C. Walter Hodges, S. Schoenbaum, and Leonard Leone. © 1981 Wayne State University Press. Reprinted by permission of the publisher.)

interest as a partner in the company of the Chamberlain's Men, opened in London in 1997. The original structure's thatched roof sported a globe with the Latin inscription totus mundus agit histrionem — *"All the world's a stage."*

Elizabethan theaters such as the Rose and the Globe, the two largest public theaters in London, were tall buildings, usually round or octagonal, with three tiers of galleries for the spectators. The Globe was located south of the Thames river in a neighborhood famous for its bearbaiting pits, gambling houses, brothels, and theaters. The Globe was the finest playhouse in London, yet its raised, covered stage, which projected into the audience, was so small that no more than a dozen actors could appear at a time. The gallery directly behind the stage was used by musicians or actors (as for the balcony scene in Romeo and Juliet*). In the front section of the stage was a trapdoor* *used for the entrance and disappearance of devils and ghosts, or for burial scenes, as in* Hamlet. *Actors could also stand under the stage, as in the mention in* Hamlet *that the "ghost cries under the stage."*

Audiences of up to eight hundred people paid a penny each to stand in the uncovered pit to watch the play, with ticket prices increasing up to six pence for a seat in the galleries, which held an additional fifteen hundred spectators. Plays were performed in these public theaters only in daylight, without artificial illumination. As in Greek and classical Japanese Nō theater, only men were trained as actors, including boys who played women's roles until their voices broke. Shakespeare wrote complex parts for specific actors in his company, such as Richard Burbage, who first played the role of Hamlet. As an actor Shakespeare was not a star performer; probably he played the ghost of the murdered king in productions of Hamlet. *In theater records he was designated a "principal comedian" in 1598, a "principle tragedian" in 1603, and one of the "man players" in 1608.*

On June 29, 1613, soon after Shakespeare's retirement to Stratford, the Globe Playhouse burned to the ground during a performance of his play Henry VIII. *A volley of blank shots fired by an actor onstage set fire to the thatched roof of the galleries. Everyone in the audience escaped unharmed, with the exception of a man whose trousers caught fire in the blaze; according to spectators, he doused the fire in his clothes with a bottle of ale. Thirty years later, all the theaters in England would be torn down by order of Parliament in 1642 and 1644 under Puritan rule.*

While Shakespeare and his generation of gifted contemporaries — Christopher Marlowe, Thomas Kyd, and Ben Jonson, to name only a few — were creating their plays, audiences crammed into the theaters six days a week, eager to witness stage spectacles and listen to the players' grandiloquence. Plays such as Hamlet, *which included a ghost, stabbings, suicide, and duels, in addition to rich and complex lines of poetry, were the regular fare of the patrons of the Globe Playhouse. Shakespeare and his company of actors were so successful that they enjoyed royal patronage. They performed for Queen Elizabeth I on the average of three times a year, and it is recorded that King James I was in attendance at the first performance of* Macbeth *in 1604.*

Just as Shakespeare depended on the contemporary historian Raphael Holinshed's chronicles for the material of his English history plays, he used earlier sources as the basis for Hamlet. *He was also influenced by Kyd's* Spanish Tragedy *(c. 1587), which set the standard for a new genre of English plays called "revenge tragedies." In addition, writings by Shakespeare's contemporaries indicate that a "lost play" of* Hamlet *was known to Shakespeare before he wrote his version of the play. In creating their* **revenge tragedies** *(plays in which the plot typically centers on a spectacular attempt to avenge the murder of a family member), Shakespeare and other popular English dramatists took the early Roman playwrights as their models. The Greek playwrights were not popular at the time, but a contemporary account credited Shakespeare with being as polished a writer of comedy and tragedy as the Romans Plautus and Seneca, respectively.*

The extraordinary richness of Shakespeare's theatrical world is made evident in Hamlet. *Unlike other avengers in the revenge tragedies of his time, Hamlet is a complex figure. He plays the multiple roles of son, lover, philosopher, actor, and prince. He questions the reality of his experience, procrastinates in carrying out his promise to avenge his father's death, considers his own failure of will and emotional paralysis, and contemplates suicide. Because most of us can sympathize with his difficult situation,* Hamlet *is the best known and most often performed of Shakespeare's plays. Actors have offered different interpretations of the role as diverse as Sir John Gielgud's aristocratic, disillusioned Hamlet in 1934 to the young actor Mark Rylance's recent performance of a psychotic Hamlet dressed in striped pajamas, inhabiting the Danish court as if it were a psychiatric hospital. As the critic Edward Hubler recognized, "Tragedy of the first order is a rare phenomenon. It came into being in Greece in the fifth century* B.C.*, where it flourished for a while, and it did not appear again until some two thousand years later when Shakespeare wrote* Hamlet *in 1600."*

First performed in 1611, The Tempest *was probably the last play wholly written by Shakespeare. It opened the volume of comedies in the First Folio edition. Unlike* Hamlet, The Tempest *was not based on any earlier narrative or dramatic sources. Instead, Shakespeare incorporated various Elizabethan travelers' accounts of the meeting of Europeans with the "savages" inhabiting the New World. The shipwreck of Sir Thomas Gates in the Bermudas during a "most dreadful tempest" was a primary source for* The Tempest. *In an account of the shipwreck written in a letter by William Strachey in 1610, Shakespeare found the details of the storm that open his play as well as the description of a hospitable island that, far from being "no habitation for men but rather given over to devils and wicked spirits," proved to Strachey "to be as habitable and commodious as most countries of the same climate and situation."*

In the introduction to the Pelican edition of The Tempest, *the Shakespearean scholar Peter Holland has noted that*

> *the play's evident interest in the problem of colonization has led many to assume that the play is set somewhere close to America. But the geography may suggest the reverse: not that Europeans are now confronting the New World in the interests of exploration and empire but that elements of that New World, which imperialist discoverers had encountered — the natural abundance and the indigenous population — are now transposed to the Old World, a world that is sustainedly aware of its roots in Roman civilization and its narratives of empire.*

Many talented poets and dramatists have written about their responses to The Tempest, *including W. H. Auden in his long poem* The Sea and the Mirror. *In 1969 the radical West Indian poet Aimé Césaire adapted Shakespeare's play as* A Tempest *for what he called "a Black Theatre." This version culminates in a final unresolved scene in which Caliban confronts Prospero, who — divested of the power of his magic arts — must take responsibility for having enslaved others.*

RELATED STORY: *Margaret Atwood, "Gertrude Talks Back," page 77.*

RELATED COMMENTARIES: *Aimé Césaire, "Final Scene from* A Tempest,*" page 1963; William Strachey, "From* True Repertory of the Wrack,*" page 1996.*

RELATED CASEBOOK: *See pages 2016–2030, including Geoffrey Bullough, "Sources of Shakespeare's* Hamlet,*" page 2017; H. D. F. Kitto, "*Hamlet *and the* Oedipus,*" page 2020; John Keats, "From a Letter to George and Thomas Keats, 21 December 1817," page 2022; Leo Tolstoy, "Shakespeare's Immoral Frame of Mind," page 2022; Virginia Woolf, "What If Shakespeare Had Had a Sister?" page 2023; T. S. Eliot, "*Hamlet *and His Problems," page 2025; Tom Stoppard,* Dogg's Hamlet: The Encore, *page 2029.*

WILLIAM SHAKESPEARE

Hamlet, Prince of Denmark

c. 1600

[DRAMATIS PERSONAE

CLAUDIUS, *King of Denmark*
HAMLET, *son to the late and nephew to the present king*
POLONIUS, *lord chamberlain*
HORATIO, *friend to Hamlet*
LAERTES, *son to Polonius*
VOLTIMAND, CORNELIUS, ROSENCRANTZ, GUILDENSTERN, OSRIC — *courtiers*
A GENTLEMAN
A PRIEST
MARCELLUS, BERNARDO — *officers*
FRANCISCO, *a soldier*
REYNALDO, *servant to Polonius*
PLAYERS
TWO CLOWNS, *grave-diggers*
FORTINBRAS, *Prince of Norway*
A CAPTAIN
ENGLISH AMBASSADORS
GERTRUDE, *Queen of Denmark, and mother to Hamlet*
OPHELIA, *daughter to Polonius*
LORDS, LADIES, OFFICERS, SOLDIERS, SAILORS, MESSENGERS, *and other* ATTENDANTS
GHOST *of Hamlet's father*

SCENE: *Denmark.*]

[ACT I

SCENE I: *Elsinore. A platform° before the castle.*]

Enter Bernardo and Francisco, two sentinels.

BERNARDO: Who's there?
FRANCISCO: Nay, answer me:° stand, and unfold yourself.
BERNARDO: Long live the king!°
FRANCISCO: Bernardo?
BERNARDO: He.
FRANCISCO: You come most carefully upon your hour.
BERNARDO: 'Tis now struck twelve; get thee to bed, Francisco.

ACT I, SCENE I. **s.d. platform:** A level space on the battlements of the royal castle at Elsinore, a Danish seaport; now Helsingör. **2. me:** This is emphatic, since Francisco is the sentry. **3. Long live the king:** Either a password or greeting; Horatio and Marcellus use a different one in line 15.

FRANCISCO: For this relief much thanks: 'tis bitter cold,
And I am sick at heart.
BERNARDO: Have you had quiet guard?
FRANCISCO: Not a mouse stirring.
BERNARDO: Well, good night.
If you do meet Horatio and Marcellus,
The rivals° of my watch, bid them make haste.

Enter Horatio and Marcellus.

FRANCISCO: I think I hear them. Stand, ho! Who is there?
HORATIO: Friends to this ground.
MARCELLUS: And liegemen to the Dane.
FRANCISCO: Give you° good night.
MARCELLUS: O, farewell, honest soldier:
Who hath reliev'd you?
FRANCISCO: Bernardo hath my place.
Give you good night. *Exit Francisco.*
MARCELLUS: Holla! Bernardo!
BERNARDO: Say,
What, is Horatio there?
HORATIO: A piece of him.
BERNARDO: Welcome, Horatio: welcome, good Marcellus.
MARCELLUS: What, has this thing appear'd again to-night?
BERNARDO: I have seen nothing.
MARCELLUS: Horatio says 'tis but our fantasy,
And will not let belief take hold of him
Touching this dreaded sight, twice seen of us:
Therefore I have entreated him along
With us to watch the minutes of this night;
That if again this apparition come,
He may approve° our eyes and speak to it.
HORATIO: Tush, tush, 'twill not appear.
BERNARDO: Sit down awhile;
And let us once again assail your ears,
That are so fortified against our story
What we have two nights seen.
HORATIO: Well, sit we down,
And let us hear Bernardo speak of this.
BERNARDO: Last night of all,
When yond same star that's westward from the pole°
Had made his course t' illume that part of heaven
Where now it burns, Marcellus and myself,
The bell then beating one, —

13. rivals: Partners. **16. Give you:** God give you. **29. approve:** Corroborate. **36. pole:** Polestar.

Enter Ghost.

MARCELLUS: Peace, break thee off; look, where it comes again!
BERNARDO: In the same figure, like the king that's dead.
MARCELLUS: Thou art a scholar;° speak to it, Horatio.
BERNARDO: Looks 'a not like the king? mark it, Horatio.
HORATIO: Most like: it harrows° me with fear and wonder.
BERNARDO: It would be spoke to.°
MARCELLUS: Speak to it, Horatio.
HORATIO: What art thou that usurp'st this time of night,
Together with that fair and warlike form
In which the majesty of buried Denmark°
Did sometimes march? by heaven I charge thee, speak!
MARCELLUS: It is offended.
BERNARDO: See it stalks away!
HORATIO: Stay! speak, speak! I charge thee, speak! *Exit Ghost.*
MARCELLUS: 'Tis gone, and will not answer.
BERNARDO: How now, Horatio! you tremble and look pale:
Is not this something more than fantasy?
What think you on 't?
HORATIO: Before my God, I might not this believe
Without the sensible and true avouch
Of mine own eyes.
MARCELLUS: Is it not like the king?
HORATIO: As thou art to thyself:
Such was the very armour he had on
When he the ambitious Norway combated;
So frown'd he once, when, in an angry parle,
He smote° the sledded Polacks° on the ice.
'Tis strange.
MARCELLUS: Thus twice before, and jump° at this dead hour,
With martial stalk hath he gone by our watch.
HORATIO: In what particular thought to work I know not;
But in the gross and scope° of my opinion,
This bodes some strange eruption to our state.
MARCELLUS: Good now,° sit down, and tell me, he that knows,
Why this same strict and most observant watch
So nightly toils° the subject° of the land,
And why such daily cast° of brazen cannon,

---

42. scholar: Exorcisms were performed in Latin, which Horatio, as an educated man, would be able to speak. **44. harrows:** Lacerates the feelings. **45. It . . . to:** A ghost could not speak until spoken to. **48. buried Denmark:** The buried king of Denmark. **63. smote:** Defeated; **sledded Polacks:** Polanders using sledges. **65. jump:** Exactly. **68. gross and scope:** General drift. **70. Good now:** An expression denoting entreaty or expostulation. **72. toils:** Causes or makes to toil; **subject:** People, subjects. **73. cast:** Casting, founding.

And foreign mart° for implements of war;
Why such impress° of shipwrights, whose sore task
Does not divide the Sunday from the week;
What might be toward, that this sweaty haste
Doth make the night joint-labourer with the day:
Who is't that can inform me?

HORATIO: That can I;
At least, the whisper goes so. Our last king,
Whose image even but now appear'd to us,
Was, as you know, by Fortinbras of Norway,
Thereto prick'd on° by a most emulate° pride,
Dar'd to the combat; in which our valiant Hamlet —
For so this side of our known world esteem'd him —
Did slay this Fortinbras; who, by a seal'd compact,
Well ratified by law and heraldry,°
Did forfeit, with his life, all those his lands
Which he stood seiz'd° of, to the conqueror:
Against the which, a moiety competent°
Was gaged by our king; which had return'd
To the inheritance of Fortinbras,
Had he been vanquisher; as, by the same comart,°
And carriage° of the article design'd,
His fell to Hamlet. Now, sir, young Fortinbras,
Of unimproved° mettle hot and full,°
Hath in the skirts of Norway here and there
Shark'd up° a list of lawless resolutes,°
For food and diet,° to some enterprise
That hath a stomach in't; which is no other —
As it doth well appear unto our state —
But to recover of us, by strong hand
And terms compulsatory, those foresaid lands
So by his father lost: and this, I take it,
Is the main motive of our preparations,
The source of this our watch and the chief head
Of this post-haste and romage° in the land.

BERNARDO: I think it be no other but e'en so:
Well may it sort° that this portentous figure
Comes armed through our watch; so like the king
That was and is the question of these wars.

---

74. mart: Buying and selling, traffic. **75. impress:** Impressment. **83. prick'd on:** Incited; **emulate:** Rivaling. **87. law and heraldry:** Heraldic law, governing combat. **89. seiz'd:** Possessed. **90. moiety competent:** Adequate or sufficient portion. **93. comart:** Joint bargain. **94. carriage:** Import, bearing. **96. unimproved:** Not turned to account; **hot and full:** Full of fight. **98. Shark'd up:** Got together in haphazard fashion; **resolutes:** Desperadoes. **99. food and diet:** No pay but their keep. **107. romage:** Bustle, commotion. **109. sort:** Suit.

HORATIO: A mote° it is to trouble the mind's eye.
In the most high and palmy state° of Rome,
A little ere the mightiest Julius fell,
The graves stood tenantless and the sheeted dead
Did squeak and gibber in the Roman streets:
As stars with trains of fire° and dews of blood,
Disasters° in the sun; and the moist star°
Upon whose influence Neptune's empire° stands
Was sick almost to doomsday with eclipse:
And even the like precurse° of fear'd events,
As harbingers preceding still the fates
And prologue to the omen coming on,
Have heaven and earth together demonstrated
Unto our climatures and countrymen. —

Enter Ghost.

But soft, behold! lo, where it comes again!
I'll cross° it, though it blast me. Stay, illusion!
If thou hast any sound, or use of voice,
Speak to me! *It° spreads his arms.*
If there be any good thing to be done,
That may to thee do ease and grace to me,
Speak to me!
If thou art privy to thy country's fate,
Which, happily, foreknowing may avoid,
O, speak!
Or if thou hast uphoarded in thy life
Extorted treasure in the womb of earth,
For which, they say, you spirits oft walk in death, *The cock crows.*
Speak of it:° stay, and speak! Stop it, Marcellus.
MARCELLUS: Shall I strike at it with my partisan?°
HORATIO: Do, if it will not stand.
BERNARDO: 'Tis here!
HORATIO: 'Tis here!
MARCELLUS: 'Tis gone! *[Exit Ghost.]*
We do it wrong, being so majestical,
To offer it the show of violence;
For it is, as the air, invulnerable,
And our vain blows malicious mockery.

---

112. mote: Speck of dust. **113. palmy state:** Triumphant sovereignty. **117. stars . . . fire:** I.e., comets. **118. Disasters:** Unfavorable aspects; **moist star:** The moon, governing tides. **119. Neptune's empire:** The sea. **121. precurse:** Heralding. **127. cross:** Meet, face, thus bringing down the evil influence on the person who crosses it. **129. It:** The Ghost, or perhaps Horatio. **133–139. If . . . it:** Horatio recites the traditional reasons why ghosts might walk. **140. partisan:** Long-handled spear with a blade having lateral projections.

BERNARDO: It was about to speak, when the cock crew.°
HORATIO: And then it started like a guilty thing
Upon a fearful summons. I have heard,
The cock, that is the trumpet to the morn,
Doth with his lofty and shrill-sounding throat
Awake the god of day; and, at his warning,
Whether in sea or fire, in earth or air,
Th' extravagant and erring° spirit hies
To his confine:° and of the truth herein
This present object made probation.°
MARCELLUS: It faded on the crowing of the cock.
Some say that ever 'gainst° that season comes
Wherein our Saviour's birth is celebrated,
The bird of dawning singeth all night long:
And then, they say, no spirit dare stir abroad;
The nights are wholesome; then no planets strike,°
No fairy takes, nor witch hath power to charm,
So hallow'd and so gracious° is that time.
HORATIO: So have I heard and do in part believe it.
But, look, the morn, in russet mantle clad,
Walks o'er the dew of yon high eastward hill:
Break we our watch up; and by my advice,
Let us impart what we have seen to-night
Unto young Hamlet; for, upon my life,
This spirit, dumb to us, will speak to him.
Do you consent we shall acquaint him with it,
As needful in our loves, fitting our duty?
MARCELLUS: Let's do 't, I pray; and I this morning know
Where we shall find him most conveniently. *Exeunt.*

[SCENE II: *A room of state in the castle.*]

Flourish. Enter Claudius, King of Denmark, Gertrude the Queen, Councilors, Polonius and his Son Laertes, Hamlet, cum aliis° [including Voltimand and Cornelius].

KING: Though yet of Hamlet our dear brother's death
The memory be green, and that it us befitted
To bear our hearts in grief and our whole kingdom
To be contracted in one brow of woe,
Yet so far hath discretion fought with nature
That we with wisest sorrow think on him,
Together with remembrance of ourselves.
Therefore our sometime sister, now our queen,

---

147. cock crew: According to traditional ghost lore, spirits returned to their confines at cockcrow. **154. extravagant and erring:** Wandering. Both words mean the same thing. **155. confine:** Place of confinement. **156. probation:** Proof, trial. **158. 'gainst:** Just before. **162. planets strike:** It was thought that planets were malignant and might strike travelers by night. **164. gracious:** Full of goodness. SCENE II. **s.d. cum aliis:** With others.

Th' imperial jointress° to this warlike state,
Have we, as 'twere with a defeated joy, —
With an auspicious and a dropping eye,
With mirth in funeral and with dirge in marriage,
In equal scale weighing delight and dole, —
Taken to wife: nor have we herein barr'd
Your better wisdoms, which have freely gone
With this affair along. For all, our thanks.
Now follows, that° you know, young Fortinbras,
Holding a weak supposal° of our worth,
Or thinking by our late dear brother's death
Our state to be disjoint° and out of frame,°
Colleagued° with this dream of his advantage,°
He hath not fail'd to pester us with message,
Importing° the surrender of those lands
Lost by his father, with all bands of law,
To our most valiant brother. So much for him.
Now for ourself and for this time of meeting:
Thus much the business is: we have here writ
To Norway, uncle of young Fortinbras, —
Who, impotent and bed-rid, scarcely hears
Of this his nephew's purpose, — to suppress
His further gait° herein; in that the levies,
The lists and full proportions, are all made
Out of his subject:° and we here dispatch
You, good Cornelius, and you, Voltimand,
For bearers of this greeting to old Norway;
Giving to you no further personal power
To business with the king, more than the scope
Of these delated° articles allow.
Farewell, and let your haste commend your duty.

CORNELIUS: }
VOLTIMAND: } In that and all things will we show our duty.

KING: We doubt it nothing: heartily farewell.

[*Exeunt Voltimand and Cornelius.*]

And now, Laertes, what's the news with you?
You told us of some suit; what is't, Laertes?
You cannot speak of reason to the Dane,°
And lose your voice:° what wouldst thou beg, Laertes,
That shall not be my offer, not thy asking?

---

9. jointress: Woman possessed of a jointure, or, joint tenancy of an estate. **17. that:** That which. **18. weak supposal:** Low estimate. **20. disjoint:** Distracted, out of joint; **frame:** Order. **21. Colleagued:** added to; **dream . . . advantage:** Visionary hope of success. **23. Importing:** Purporting, pertaining to. **31. gait:** Proceeding. **33. Out of his subject:** At the expense of Norway's subjects (collectively). **38. delated:** Expressly stated. **44. the Dane:** Danish king. **45. lose your voice:** Speak in vain.

The head is not more native° to the heart,
The hand more instrumental° to the mouth,
Than is the throne of Denmark to thy father.
What wouldst thou have, Laertes?

LAERTES: My dread lord,
Your leave and favour to return to France;
From whence though willingly I came to Denmark,
To show my duty in your coronation,
Yet now, I must confess, that duty done,
My thoughts and wishes bend again toward France
And bow them to your gracious leave and pardon.°

KING: Have you your father's leave? What says Polonius?

POLONIUS: He hath, my lord, wrung from me my slow leave
By laboursome petition, and at last
Upon his will I seal'd my hard consent:
I do beseech you, give him leave to go.

KING: Take thy fair hour, Laertes; time be thine,
And thy best graces spend it at thy will!
But now, my cousin° Hamlet, and my son,—

HAMLET [*aside*]: A little more than kin, and less than kind!°

KING: How is it that the clouds still hang on you?

HAMLET: Not so, my lord; I am too much in the sun.°

QUEEN: Good Hamlet, cast thy nighted colour off,
And let thine eye look like a friend on Denmark.
Do not for ever with thy vailed lids
Seek for thy noble father in the dust:
Thou know'st 'tis common; all that lives must die,
Passing through nature to eternity.

HAMLET: Ay, madam, it is common.°

QUEEN: If it be,
Why seems it so particular with thee?

HAMLET: Seems, madam! nay, it is; I know not "seems."
'Tis not alone my inky cloak, good mother,
Nor customary suits° of solemn black,
Nor windy suspiration° of forc'd breath,
No, nor the fruitful river in the eye,

---

47. native: Closely connected, related. **48. instrumental:** Serviceable. **56. leave and pardon:** Permission to depart. **64. cousin:** Any kin not of the immediate family. **65. A little . . . kind:** My relation to you has become more than kinship warrants; it has also become unnatural. **67. I am . . . sun:** The senses seem to be: I am too much out of doors, I am too much in the sun of your grace (ironical), I am too much of a son to you. Possibly an allusion to the proverb "Out of heaven's blessing into the warm sun"; i.e., Hamlet is out of house and home in being deprived of the kingship. **74. Ay . . . common:** It is common, but it hurts nevertheless; possibly a reference to the commonplace quality of the queen's remark. **78. customary suits:** Suits prescribed by custom for mourning. **79. windy suspiration:** Heavy sighing.

Nor the dejected 'haviour of the visage,
Together with all forms, moods, shapes of grief,
That can denote me truly: these indeed seem,
For they are actions that a man might play:
But I have that within which passeth show;
These but the trappings and the suits of woe.

KING: 'Tis sweet and commendable in your nature, Hamlet,
To give these mourning duties to your father:
But, you must know, your father lost a father;
That father lost, lost his, and the survivor bound
In filial obligation for some term
To do obsequious° sorrow: but to persever
In obstinate condolement° is a course
Of impious stubbornness; 'tis unmanly grief;
It shows a will most incorrect° to heaven,
A heart unfortified, a mind impatient,
An understanding simple and unschool'd:
For what we know must be and is as common
As any the most vulgar thing° to sense,
Why should we in our peevish opposition
Take it to heart? Fie! 'tis a fault to heaven,
A fault against the dead, a fault to nature,
To reason most absurd; whose common theme
Is death of fathers, and who still hath cried,
From the first corse till he that died to-day,
"This must be so." We pray you, throw to earth
This unprevailing° woe, and think of us
As of a father: for let the world take note,
You are the most immediate° to our throne;
And with no less nobility° of love
Than that which dearest father bears his son,
Do I impart° toward you. For your intent
In going back to school in Wittenberg,°
It is most retrograde° to our desire:
And we beseech you, bend you° to remain
Here, in the cheer and comfort of our eye,
Our chiefest courtier, cousin, and our son.

QUEEN: Let not thy mother lose her prayers, Hamlet:
I pray thee, stay with us; go not to Wittenberg.

---

92. obsequious: Dutiful. **93. condolement:** Sorrowing. **95. incorrect:** Untrained, uncorrected. **99. vulgar thing:** Common experience. **107. unprevailing:** Unavailing. **109. most immediate:** Next in succession. **110. nobility:** High degree. **112. impart:** The object is apparently *love* (line 110). **113. Wittenberg:** Famous German university founded in 1502. **114. retrograde:** Contrary. **115. bend you:** Incline yourself; imperative.

HAMLET: I shall in all my best obey you, madam.
KING: Why, 'tis a loving and a fair reply:
Be as ourself in Denmark. Madam, come;
This gentle and unforc'd accord of Hamlet
Sits smiling to my heart: in grace whereof,
No jocund health that Denmark drinks to-day,
But the great cannon to the clouds shall tell,
And the king's rouse° the heaven shall bruit again,°
Re-speaking earthly thunder. Come away.
Flourish. Exeunt all but Hamlet.

HAMLET: O, that this too too sullied flesh would melt,
Thaw and resolve itself into a dew!
Or that the Everlasting had not fix'd
His canon 'gainst self-slaughter! O God! God!
How weary, stale, flat and unprofitable,
Seem to me all the uses of this world!
Fie on't! ah fie! 'tis an unweeded garden,
That grows to seed; things rank and gross in nature
Possess it merely.° That it should come to this!
But two months dead: nay, not so much, not two:
So excellent a king; that was, to this,
Hyperion° to a satyr; so loving to my mother
That he might not beteem° the winds of heaven
Visit her face too roughly. Heaven and earth!
Must I remember? why, she would hang on him,
As if increase of appetite had grown
By what it fed on: and yet, within a month —
Let me not think on't — Frailty, thy name is woman! —
A little month, or ere those shoes were old
With which she followed my poor father's body,
Like Niobe,° all tears: — why she, even she —
O God! a beast, that wants discourse of reason,°
Would have mourn'd longer — married with my uncle,
My father's brother, but no more like my father
Than I to Hercules: within a month:
Ere yet the salt of most unrighteous tears
Had left the flushing in her galled° eyes,
She married. O, most wicked speed, to post
With such dexterity° to incestuous sheets!
It is not nor it cannot come to good:
But break, my heart; for I must hold my tongue.

---

127. rouse: Draft of liquor; **bruit again:** Echo. **137. merely:** Completely, entirely. **140. Hyperion:** God of the sun in the older regime of ancient gods. **141. beteem:** Allow. **149. Niobe:** Tantalus's daughter, who boasted that she had more sons and daughters than Leto; for this Apollo and Artemis slew her children. She was turned into stone by Zeus on Mount Sipylus. **150. discourse of reason:** Process or faculty of reason. **155. galled:** Irritated. **157. dexterity:** Facility.

Enter Horatio, Marcellus, and Bernardo.

HORATIO: Hail to your lordship!
HAMLET: I am glad to see you well:
Horatio! — or I do forget myself.
HORATIO: The same, my lord, and your poor servant ever.
HAMLET: Sir, my good friend; I'll change that name with you:°
And what make you from Wittenberg, Horatio?
Marcellus?
MARCELLUS: My good lord —
HAMLET: I am very glad to see you. Good even, sir.
But what, in faith, make you from Wittenberg?
HORATIO: A truant disposition, good my lord.
HAMLET: I would not hear your enemy say so,
Nor shall you do my ear that violence,
To make it truster of your own report
Against yourself: I know you are no truant.
But what is your affair in Elsinore?
We'll teach you to drink deep ere you depart.
HORATIO: My lord, I came to see your father's funeral.
HAMLET: I prithee, do not mock me, fellow-student;
I think it was to see my mother's wedding.
HORATIO: Indeed, my lord, it follow'd hard° upon.
HAMLET: Thrift, thrift, Horatio! the funeral bak'd meats°
Did coldly furnish forth the marriage tables.
Would I had met my dearest° foe in heaven
Or ever I had seen that day, Horatio!
My father! — methinks I see my father.
HORATIO: Where, my lord!
HAMLET: In my mind's eye, Horatio.
HORATIO: I saw him once; 'a° was a goodly king.
HAMLET: 'A was a man, take him for all in all,
I shall not look upon his like again.
HORATIO: My lord, I think I saw him yesternight.
HAMLET: Saw? who?
HORATIO: My lord, the king your father.
HAMLET: The king my father!
HORATIO: Season your admiration° for a while
With an attent ear, till I may deliver,
Upon the witness of these gentlemen,
This marvel to you.

---

163. I'll . . . you: I'll be your servant; you shall be my friend; also explained as "I'll exchange the name of friend with you." **179. hard:** Close. **180. bak'd meats:** Meat pies. **182. dearest:** Direst. The adjective *dear* in Shakespeare has two different origins: O.E. *deore,* "beloved," and O.E. *deor,* "fierce." *Dearest* is the superlative of the second. **186. 'a:** He. **192. Season your admiration:** Restrain your astonishment.

HAMLET: For God's love, let me hear.
HORATIO: Two nights together had these gentlemen,
Marcellus and Bernardo, on their watch,
In the dead waste and middle of the night,
Been thus encount'red. A figure like your father,
Armed at point exactly, cap-a-pe,°
Appears before them, and with solemn march
Goes slow and stately by them: thrice he walk'd
By their oppress'd° and fear-surprised eyes,
Within his truncheon's° length; whilst they, distill'd°
Almost to jelly with the act° of fear,
Stand dumb and speak not to him. This to me
In dreadful secrecy impart they did;
And I with them the third night kept the watch:
Where, as they had deliver'd, both in time,
Form of the thing, each word made true and good,
The apparition comes: I knew your father;
These hands are not more like.
HAMLET: But where was this?
MARCELLUS: My lord, upon the platform where we watch'd.
HAMLET: Did you not speak to it?
HORATIO: My lord, I did;
But answer made it none: yet once methought
It lifted up it° head and did address
Itself to motion, like as it would speak;
But even then the morning cock crew loud,
And at the sound it shrunk in haste away,
And vanish'd from our sight.
HAMLET: 'Tis very strange.
HORATIO: As I do live, my honour'd lord, 'tis true;
And we did think it writ down in our duty
To let you know of it.
HAMLET: Indeed, indeed, sirs, but this troubles me.
Hold you the watch to-night?
MARCELLUS: }
BERNARDO: } We do, my lord.
HAMLET: Arm'd, say you?
MARCELLUS: }
BERNARDO: } Arm'd, my lord.
HAMLET: From top to toe?
MARCELLUS: }
BERNARDO: } My lord, from head to foot.
HAMLET: Then saw you not his face?

---

200. cap-a-pe: From head to foot. **203. oppress'd:** Distressed. **204. truncheon:** Officer's staff; **distill'd:** Softened, weakened. **205. act:** Action. **216. it:** Its.

HORATIO: O, yes, my lord; he wore his beaver° up.
HAMLET: What, look'd he frowningly?
HORATIO: A countenance more
In sorrow than in anger.
HAMLET: Pale or red?
HORATIO: Nay, very pale.
HAMLET: And fix'd his eyes upon you?
HORATIO: Most constantly.
HAMLET: I would I had been there.
HORATIO: It would have much amaz'd you.
HAMLET: Very like, very like. Stay'd it long?
HORATIO: While one with moderate haste might tell a hundred.
MARCELLUS: / BERNARDO: Longer, longer.
HORATIO: Not when I saw't.
HAMLET: His beard was grizzled, — no?
HORATIO: It was, as I have seen it in his life,
A sable° silver'd.
HAMLET: I will watch to-night;
Perchance 'twill walk again.
HORATIO: I warr'nt it will.
HAMLET: If it assume my noble father's person,
I'll speak to it, though hell itself should gape
And bid me hold my peace. I pray you all,
If you have hitherto conceal'd this sight,
Let it be tenable in your silence still;
And whatsoever else shall hap to-night,
Give it an understanding, but no tongue:
I will requite your loves. So, fare you well:
Upon the platform, 'twixt eleven and twelve,
I'll visit you.
ALL: Our duty to your honour.
HAMLET: Your loves, as mine to you: farewell. *Exeunt [all but Hamlet].*
My father's spirit in arms! all is not well;
I doubt° some foul play: would the night were come!
Till then sit still, my soul: foul deeds will rise,
Though all the earth o'erwhelm them, to men's eyes. *Exit.*

[SCENE III: *A room in Polonius's house.*]

Enter Laertes and Ophelia, his Sister.

LAERTES: My necessaries are embark'd: farewell:
And, sister, as the winds give benefit
And convoy is assistant,° do not sleep,
But let me hear from you.

---

230. beaver: Visor on the helmet. **241. sable:** Black color. **255. doubt:** Fear. SCENE III. **3. convoy is assistant:** Means of conveyance are available.

OPHELIA: Do you doubt that?
LAERTES: For Hamlet and the trifling of his favour,
Hold it a fashion° and a toy in blood,°
A violet in the youth of primy° nature,
Forward,° not permanent, sweet, not lasting,
The perfume and suppliance of a minute;°
No more.
OPHELIA: No more but so?
LAERTES: Think it no more:
For nature, crescent,° does not grow alone
In thews° and bulk, but, as this temple° waxes,
The inward service of the mind and soul
Grows wide withal. Perhaps he loves you now,
And now no soil° nor cautel° doth besmirch
The virtue of his will: but you must fear,
His greatness weigh'd,° his will is not his own;
For he himself is subject to his birth:
He may not, as unvalued persons do,
Carve for himself; for on his choice depends
The safety and health of this whole state;
And therefore must his choice be circumscrib'd
Unto the voice and yielding° of that body
Whereof he is the head. Then if he says he loves you,
It fits your wisdom so far to believe it
As he in his particular act and place
May give his saying deed;° which is no further
Than the main voice of Denmark goes withal.
Then weigh what loss your honour may sustain,
If with too credent° ear you list his songs,
Or lose your heart, or your chaste treasure open
To his unmast'red° importunity.
Fear it, Ophelia, fear it, my dear sister,
And keep you in the rear of your affection,
Out of the shot and danger of desire.
The chariest° maid is prodigal enough,
If she unmask her beauty to the moon:
Virtue itself 'scapes not calumnious strokes:
The canker galls the infants of the spring,°

---

6. fashion: Custom, prevailing usage; **toy in blood:** Passing amorous fancy. **7. primy:** In its prime. **8. Forward:** Precocious. **9. suppliance of a minute:** Diversion to fill up a minute. **11. crescent:** Growing, waxing. **12. thews:** Bodily strength; **temple:** Body. **15. soil:** blemish; **cautel:** Crafty device. **17. greatness weigh'd:** High position considered. **23. voice and yielding:** Assent, approval. **27. deed:** Effect. **30. credent:** Credulous. **32. unmast'red:** Unrestrained. **36. chariest:** Most scrupulously modest. **39. The canker . . . spring:** The cankerworm destroys the young plants of spring.

Too oft before their buttons° be disclos'd,°
And in the morn and liquid dew° of youth
Contagious blastments° are most imminent.
Be wary then; best safety lies in fear:
Youth to itself rebels, though none else near.

OPHELIA: I shall the effect of this good lesson keep,
As watchman to my heart. But, good my brother,
Do not, as some ungracious° pastors do,
Show me the steep and thorny way to heaven;
Whiles, like a puff'd° and reckless libertine,
Himself the primrose path of dalliance treads,
And recks° not his own rede.°

Enter Polonius.

LAERTES: O, fear me not.
I stay too long: but here my father comes.
A double° blessing is a double grace;
Occasion° smiles upon a second leave.

POLONIUS: Yet here, Laertes? aboard, aboard, for shame!
The wind sits in the shoulder of your sail,
And you are stay'd for. There; my blessing with thee!
And these few precepts° in thy memory
Look thou character.° Give thy thoughts no tongue,
Nor any unproportion'd° thought his act.
Be thou familiar, but by no means vulgar.°
Those friends thou hast, and their adoption tried,
Grapple them to thy soul with hoops of steel;
But do not dull thy palm with entertainment
Of each new-hatch'd, unfledg'd° comrade. Beware
Of entrance to a quarrel, but being in,
Bear't that th' opposed may beware of thee.
Give every man thy ear, but few thy voice;
Take each man's censure, but reserve thy judgement.
Costly thy habit as thy purse can buy,
But not express'd in fancy;° rich, not gaudy;
For the apparel oft proclaims the man,
And they in France of the best rank and station
Are of a most select and generous chief in that.°
Neither a borrower nor a lender be;
For loan oft loses both itself and friend,

---

40. buttons: Buds; **disclos'd:** Opened. **41. liquid dew:** I.e., time when dew is fresh. **42. blastments:** Blights. **47. ungracious:** Graceless. **49. puff'd:** Bloated. **51. recks:** Heeds; **rede:** Counsel. **53. double:** I.e., Laertes has already bade his father good-by. **54. Occasion:** Opportunity. **58. precepts:** Many parallels have been found to the series of maxims which follows, one of the closer being that in Lyly's *Euphues*. **59. character:** Inscribe. **60. unproportion'd:** Inordinate. **61. vulgar:** Common. **65. unfledg'd:** Immature. **71. express'd in fancy:** Fantastical in design. **74. Are . . . that:** *Chief* is usually taken as a substantive meaning "head," "eminence."

And borrowing dulleth edge of husbandry.°
This above all: to thine own self be true,
And it must follow, as the night the day,
Thou canst not then be false to any man.
Farewell: my blessing season° this in thee!

LAERTES: Most humbly do I take my leave, my lord.

POLONIUS: The time invites you; go; your servants tend.

LAERTES: Farewell, Ophelia; and remember well
What I have said to you.

OPHELIA: 'Tis in my memory lock'd,
And you yourself shall keep the key of it.

LAERTES: Farewell. *Exit Laertes.*

POLONIUS: What is 't, Ophelia, he hath said to you?

OPHELIA: So please you, something touching the Lord Hamlet.

POLONIUS: Marry, well bethought:
'Tis told me, he hath very oft of late
Given private time to you; and you yourself
Have of your audience been most free and bounteous:
If it be so, as so't is put on° me,
And that in way of caution, I must tell you,
You do not understand yourself so clearly
As it behooves my daughter and your honour.
What is between you? give me up the truth.

OPHELIA: He hath, my lord, of late made many tenders°
Of his affection to me.

POLONIUS: Affection! pooh! you speak like a green girl,
Unsifted° in such perilous circumstance.
Do you believe his tenders, as you call them?

OPHELIA: I do not know, my lord, what I should think.

POLONIUS: Marry, I will teach you: think yourself a baby;
That you have ta'en these tenders° for true pay,
Which are not sterling.° Tender° yourself more dearly;
Or — not to crack the wind° of the poor phrase,
Running it thus — you'll tender me a fool.°

OPHELIA: My lord, he hath importun'd me with love
In honourable fashion.

POLONIUS: Ay, fashion° you may call it; go to, go to.

OPHELIA: And hath given countenance° to his speech, my lord,
With almost all the holy vows of heaven.

POLONIUS: Ay, springes° to catch woodcocks.° I do know,
When the blood burns, how prodigal the soul

---

77. husbandry: Thrift. **81. season:** Mature. **94. put on:** Impressed on. **99, 103. tenders:** Offers. **102. Unsifted:** Untried. **106. tenders:** Promises to pay. **107. sterling:** Legal currency; **Tender:** Hold. **108. crack the wind:** I.e., run it until it is broken-winded. **109. tender . . . fool:** Show me a fool (for a daughter). **112. fashion:** Mere form, pretense. **113. countenance:** Credit, support. **115. springes:** Snares; **woodcocks:** Birds easily caught, type of stupidity.

Lends the tongue vows: these blazes, daughter,
Giving more light than heat, extinct in both,
Even in their promise, as it is a-making,
You must not take for fire. From this time
Be somewhat scanter of your maiden presence;
Set your entreatments° at a higher rate
Than a command to parley.° For Lord Hamlet,
Believe so much in him,° that he is young,
And with a larger tether may he walk
Than may be given you: in few,° Ophelia,
Do not believe his vows; for they are brokers;°
Not of that dye° which their investments° show,
But mere implorators of° unholy suits,
Breathing° like sanctified and pious bawds,
The better to beguile. This is for all:
I would not, in plain terms, from this time forth,
Have you so slander° any moment leisure,
As to give words or talk with the Lord Hamlet.
Look to 't, I charge you: come your ways.

OPHELIA: I shall obey, my lord. *Exeunt.*

[SCENE IV: *The platform.*]

Enter Hamlet, Horatio, and Marcellus.

HAMLET: The air bites shrewdly; it is very cold.
HORATIO: It is a nipping and an eager air.
HAMLET: What hour now?
HORATIO: I think it lacks of twelve.
MARCELLUS: No, it is struck.
HORATIO: Indeed? I heard it not: then it draws near the season
Wherein the spirit held his wont to walk.

A flourish of trumpets, and two pieces go off.

What does this mean, my lord?
HAMLET: The king doth wake° to-night and takes his rouse,°
Keeps wassail,° and the swagg'ring up-spring° reels;°
And, as he drains his draughts of Rhenish° down,
The kettle-drum and trumpet thus bray out
The triumph of his pledge.°
HORATIO: Is it a custom?

---

122. entreatments: Conversations, interviews. **123. command to parley:** Mere invitation to talk. **124. so . . . him:** This much concerning him. **126. in few:** Briefly. **127. brokers:** Go-betweens, procurers. **128. dye:** Color or sort; **investments:** Clothes. **129. implorators of:** Solicitors of. **130. Breathing:** Speaking. **133. slander:** Bring disgrace or reproach upon. SCENE IV. **8. wake:** Stay awake, hold revel; **rouse:** Carouse, drinking bout. **9. wassail:** Carousal; **up-spring:** Last and wildest dance at German merry-makings; **reels:** Reels through. **10. Rhenish:** Rhine wine. **12. triumph . . . pledge:** His glorious achievement as a drinker.

HAMLET: Ay, marry, is 't:
But to my mind, though I am native here
And to the manner born,° it is a custom
More honour'd in the breach than the observance.
This heavy-headed revel east and west
Makes us traduc'd and tax'd of other nations:
They clepe° us drunkards, and with swinish phrase°
Soil our addition;° and indeed it takes
From our achievements, though perform'd at height,
The pith and marrow of our attribute.°
So, oft it chances in particular men,
That for some vicious mole of nature° in them,
As, in their birth — wherein they are not guilty,
Since nature cannot choose his origin —
By the o'ergrowth of some complexion,
Oft breaking down the pales° and forts of reason,
Or by some habit that too much o'er-leavens°
The form of plausive° manners, that these men,
Carrying, I say, the stamp of one defect,
Being nature's livery,° or fortune's star,° —
Their virtues else — be they as pure as grace,
As infinite as man may undergo —
Shall in the general censure take corruption
From that particular fault: the dram of eale
Doth all the noble substance of a doubt
To his own scandal.°

Enter Ghost.

HORATIO: Look, my lord, it comes!

HAMLET: Angels and ministers of grace° defend us!
Be thou a spirit of health or goblin damn'd,
Bring with thee airs from heaven or blasts from hell,
Be thy intents wicked or charitable,
Thou com'st in such a questionable° shape
That I will speak to thee: I'll call thee Hamlet,
King, father, royal Dane: O, answer me!
Let me not burst in ignorance; but tell
Why thy canoniz'd° bones, hearsed° in death,

---

15. to . . . born: Destined by birth to be subject to the custom in question. **19. clepe:** Call; **with swinish phrase:** By calling us swine. **20. addition:** Reputation. **22. attribute:** Reputation. **24. mole of nature:** Natural blemish in one's constitution. **28. pales:** Palings (as of a fortification). **29. o'er-leavens:** Induces a change throughout (as yeast works in bread). **30. plausive:** Pleasing. **32. nature's livery:** Endowment from nature; **fortune's star:** The position in which one is placed by fortune, a reference to astrology. The two phrases are aspects of the same thing. **36–38. the dram . . . scandal:** A famous crux: *dram of eale* has had various interpretations, the preferred one being probably, "a dram of evil." **39. ministers of grace:** Messengers of God. **43. questionable:** Inviting question or conversation. **47. canoniz'd:** Buried according to the canons of the church; **hearsed:** Coffined.

Have burst their cerements;° why the sepulchre,
Wherein we saw thee quietly interr'd,
Hath op'd his ponderous and marble jaws,
To cast thee up again. What may this mean,
That thou, dead corse, again in complete steel
Revisits thus the glimpses of the moon,°
Making night hideous; and we fools of nature°
So horridly to shake our disposition
With thoughts beyond the reaches of our souls?
Say, why is this? wherefore? what should we do?

[*Ghost*] *beckons* [*Hamlet*].

HORATIO: It beckons you to go away with it,
As if it some impartment° did desire
To you alone.
MARCELLUS: Look, with what courteous action
It waves you to a more removed° ground:
But do not go with it.
HORATIO: No, by no means.
HAMLET: It will not speak; then I will follow it.
HORATIO: Do not, my lord!
HAMLET: Why, what should be the fear?
I do not set my life at a pin's fee;
And for my soul, what can it do to that,
Being a thing immortal as itself?
It waves me forth again: I'll follow it.
HORATIO: What if it tempt you toward the flood, my lord,
Or to the dreadful summit of the cliff
That beetles o'er° his base into the sea,
And there assume some other horrible form,
Which might deprive your sovereignty of reason°
And draw you into madness? think of it:
The very place puts toys of desperation,°
Without more motive, into every brain
That looks so many fathoms to the sea
And hears it roar beneath.
HAMLET: It waves me still.
Go on; I'll follow thee.
MARCELLUS: You shall not go, my lord.
HAMLET: Hold off your hands!

---

48. cerements: Grave-clothes. **53. glimpses of the moon:** The earth by night. **54. fools of nature:** Mere men, limited to natural knowledge. **59. impartment:** Communication. **61. removed:** Remote. **71. beetles o'er:** Overhangs threateningly. **73. deprive . . . reason:** Take away the sovereignty of your reason. It was thought that evil spirits would sometimes assume the form of departed spirits in order to work madness in a human creature. **75. toys of desperation:** Freakish notions of suicide.

HORATIO: Be rul'd; you shall not go.

HAMLET: My fate cries out,
And makes each petty artere° in this body
As hardy as the Nemean lion's° nerve.°
Still am I call'd. Unhand me, gentlemen.
By heaven, I'll make a ghost of him that lets° me!
I say, away! Go on; I'll follow thee. *Exeunt Ghost and Hamlet.*

HORATIO: He waxes desperate with imagination.

MARCELLUS: Let's follow; 'tis not fit thus to obey him.

HORATIO: Have after. To what issue° will this come?

MARCELLUS: Something is rotten in the state of Denmark.

HORATIO: Heaven will direct it.°

MARCELLUS: Nay, let's follow him. *Exeunt.*

[SCENE V: *Another part of the platform.*]

Enter Ghost and Hamlet.

HAMLET: Whither wilt thou lead me? speak; I'll go no further.

GHOST: Mark me.

HAMLET: I will.

GHOST: My hour is almost come,
When I to sulphurous and tormenting flames
Must render up myself.

HAMLET: Alas, poor ghost!

GHOST: Pity me not, but lend thy serious hearing
To what I shall unfold.

HAMLET: Speak; I am bound to hear.

GHOST: So art thou to revenge, when thou shalt hear.

HAMLET: What?

GHOST: I am thy father's spirit,
Doom'd for a certain term to walk the night,
And for the day confin'd to fast° in fires,
Till the foul crimes done in my days of nature
Are burnt and purg'd away. But that I am forbid
To tell the secrets of my prison-house,
I could a tale unfold whose lightest word
Would harrow up thy soul, freeze thy young blood,
Make thy two eyes, like stars, start from their spheres,°
Thy knotted° and combined° locks to part
And each particular hair to stand an end,

---

82. artere: Artery. **83. Nemean lion's:** The Nemean lion was one of the monsters slain by Hercules; **nerve:** Sinew, tendon. The point is that the arteries which were carrying the spirits out into the body were functioning and were as stiff and hard as the sinews of the lion. **85. lets:** Hinders. **89. issue:** Outcome. **91. it:** I.e., the outcome. SCENE V. **11. fast:** Probably, do without food. It has been sometimes taken in the sense of doing general penance. **17. spheres:** Orbits. **18. knotted:** Perhaps intricately arranged; **combined:** Tied, bound.

Like quills upon the fretful porpentine:°
But this eternal blazon° must not be
To ears of flesh and blood. List, list, O, list!
If thou didst ever thy dear father love —
HAMLET: O God!
GHOST: Revenge his foul and most unnatural° murder.
HAMLET: Murder!
GHOST: Murder most foul, as in the best it is;
But this most foul, strange and unnatural.
HAMLET: Haste me to know't, that I, with wings as swift
As meditation or the thoughts of love,
May sweep to my revenge.
GHOST: I find thee apt;
And duller shouldst thou be than the fat weed°
That roots itself in ease on Lethe wharf,°
Wouldst thou not stir in this. Now, Hamlet, hear:
'Tis given out that, sleeping in my orchard,
A serpent stung me; so the whole ear of Denmark
Is by a forged process of my death
Rankly abus'd: but know, thou noble youth,
The serpent that did sting thy father's life
Now wears his crown.
HAMLET: O my prophetic soul!
My uncle!
GHOST: Ay, that incestuous, that adulterate° beast,
With witchcraft of his wit, with traitorous gifts, —
O wicked wit and gifts, that have the power
So to seduce! — won to his shameful lust
The will of my most seeming-virtuous queen:
O Hamlet, what a falling-off was there!
From me, whose love was of that dignity
That it went hand in hand even with the vow
I made to her in marriage, and to decline
Upon a wretch whose natural gifts were poor
To those of mine!
But virtue, as it never will be moved,
Though lewdness court it in a shape of heaven,
So lust, though to a radiant angel link'd,
Will sate itself in a celestial bed,
And prey on garbage.
But, soft! methinks I scent the morning air;
Brief let me be. Sleeping within my orchard,

---

20. porpentine: Porcupine. **21. eternal blazon:** Promulgation or proclamation of eternity, revelation of the hereafter. **25. unnatural:** I.e., pertaining to fratricide. **32. fat weed:** Many suggestions have been offered as to the particular plant intended, including asphodel; probably a general figure for plants growing along rotting wharves and piles. **33. Lethe wharf:** Bank of the river of forgetfulness in Hades. **42. adulterate:** Adulterous.

My custom always of the afternoon,
Upon my secure° hour thy uncle stole,
With juice of cursed hebona° in a vial,
And in the porches of my ears did pour
The leperous° distilment; whose effect
Holds such an enmity with blood of man
That swift as quicksilver it courses through
The natural gates and alleys of the body,
And with a sudden vigour it doth posset°
And curd, like eager° droppings into milk,
The thin and wholesome blood: so did it mine;
And a most instant tetter bark'd about,
Most lazar-like,° with vile and loathsome crust,
All my smooth body.
Thus was I, sleeping, by a brother's hand
Of life, of crown, of queen, at once dispatch'd:°
Cut off even in the blossoms of my sin,
Unhous'led,° disappointed,° unanel'd,°
No reck'ning made, but sent to my account
With all my imperfections on my head:
O, horrible! O, horrible! most horrible!°
If thou hast nature in thee, bear it not;
Let not the royal bed of Denmark be
A couch for luxury° and damned incest.
But, howsomever thou pursues this act,
Taint not thy mind,° nor let thy soul contrive
Against thy mother aught: leave her to heaven
And to those thorns that in her bosom lodge,
To prick and sting her. Fare thee well at once!
The glow-worm shows the matin° to be near,
And 'gins to pale his uneffectual fire:°
Adieu, adieu, adieu! remember me. [*Exit.*]

HAMLET: O all you host of heaven! O earth! what else?
And shall I couple° hell? O, fie! Hold, hold, my heart;
And you, my sinews, grow not instant old,
But bear me stiffly up. Remember thee!
Ay, thou poor ghost, whiles memory holds a seat
In this distracted globe.° Remember thee!

---

61. secure: Confident, unsuspicious. **62. hebona:** Generally supposed to mean henbane, conjectured *hemlock; ebenus,* meaning "yew." **64. leperous:** Causing leprosy. **68. posset:** Coagulate, curdle. **69. eager:** Sour, acid. **72. lazar-like:** Leperlike. **75. dispatch'd:** Suddenly bereft. **77. Unhous'led:** Without having received the sacrament; **disappointed:** Unready, without equipment for the last journey; **unanel'd:** Without having received extreme unction. **80. O . . . horrible:** Many editors give this line to Hamlet; Garrick and Sir Henry Irving spoke it in that part. **83. luxury:** Lechery. **85. Taint . . . mind:** Probably, deprave not thy character, do nothing except in the pursuit of a natural revenge. **89. matin:** Morning. **90. uneffectual fire:** Cold light. **93. couple:** Add. **97. distracted globe:** Confused head.

Yea, from the table of my memory
I'll wipe away all trivial fond records,
All saws° of books, all forms, all pressures° past,
That youth and observation copied there;
And thy commandment all alone shall live
Within the book and volume of my brain,
Unmix'd with baser matter: yes, by heaven!
O most pernicious woman!
O villain, villain, smiling, damned villain!
My tables,° — meet it is I set it down,
That one may smile, and smile, and be a villain;
At least I am sure it may be so in Denmark: [*Writing.*]
So, uncle, there you are. Now to my word;°
It is "Adieu, adieu! remember me,"
I have sworn't.

Enter Horatio and Marcellus.

HORATIO: My lord, my lord —
MARCELLUS: Lord Hamlet, —
HORATIO: Heavens secure him!
HAMLET: So be it!
MARCELLUS: Hillo, ho, ho,° my lord!
HAMLET: Hillo, ho, ho, boy! come, bird, come.
MARCELLUS: How is't, my noble lord?
HORATIO: What news, my lord?
HAMLET: O, wonderful!
HORATIO: Good my lord, tell it.
HAMLET: No; you will reveal it.
HORATIO: Not I, my lord, by heaven.
MARCELLUS: Nor I, my lord.
HAMLET: How say you, then; would heart of man once think it?
But you'll be secret?
HORATIO:
MARCELLUS: } Ay, by heaven, my lord.
HAMLET: There's ne'er a villain dwelling in all Denmark
But he's an arrant° knave.
HORATIO: There needs no ghost, my lord, come from the grave
To tell us this.
HAMLET: Why, right; you are in the right;
And so, without more circumstance at all,
I hold it fit that we shake hands and part:
You, as your business and desire shall point you;
For every man has business and desire,

100. saws: Wise sayings; **pressures:** Impressions stamped. **107. tables:** Probably a small portable writing tablet carried at the belt. **110. word:** Watchword. **115. Hillo, ho, ho:** A falconer's call to a hawk in air. **124. arrant:** Thoroughgoing.

Such as it is; and for my own poor part,
Look you, I'll go pray.
HORATIO: These are but wild and whirling words, my lord.
HAMLET: I am sorry they offend you, heartily;
Yes, 'faith, heartily.
HORATIO: There's no offence, my lord.
HAMLET: Yes, by Saint Patrick,° but there is, Horatio,
And much offence too. Touching this vision here,
It is an honest° ghost, that let me tell you:
For your desire to know what is between us,
O'ermaster 't as you may. And now, good friends,
As you are friends, scholars and soldiers,
Give me one poor request.
HORATIO: What is 't, my lord? we will.
HAMLET: Never make known what you have seen to-night.
HORATIO:
MARCELLUS: } My lord, we will not.
HAMLET: Nay, but swear 't.
HORATIO: In faith,
My lord, not I.
MARCELLUS: Nor I, my lord, in faith.
HAMLET: Upon my sword.°
MARCELLUS: We have sworn, my lord, already.
HAMLET: Indeed, upon my sword, indeed. *Ghost cries under the stage.*
GHOST: Swear.
HAMLET: Ah, ha, boy! say'st thou so? art thou there, truepenny?°
Come on — you hear this fellow in the cellarage —
Consent to swear.
HORATIO: Propose the oath, my lord.
HAMLET: Never to speak of this that you have seen,
Swear by my sword.
GHOST [*beneath*]: Swear.
HAMLET: Hic et ubique?° then we'll shift our ground.
Come hither, gentlemen,
And lay your hands again upon my sword:
Swear by my sword,
Never to speak of this that you have heard.
GHOST [*beneath*]: Swear by his sword.
HAMLET: Well said, old mole! canst work i' th' earth so fast?
A worthy pioner!° Once more remove, good friends.
HORATIO: O day and night, but this is wondrous strange!
HAMLET: And therefore as a stranger give it welcome.

---

136. Saint Patrick: St. Patrick was keeper of Purgatory and patron saint of all blunders and confusion. **138. honest:** I.e., a real ghost and not an evil spirit. **147. sword:** I.e., the hilt in the form of a cross. **150. truepenny:** Good old boy, or the like. **156. Hic et ubique?:** Here and everywhere? **163. pioner:** Digger, miner.

There are more things in heaven and earth, Horatio,
Than are dreamt of in your philosophy.
But come;
Here, as before, never, so help you mercy,
How strange or odd soe'er I bear myself,
As I perchance hereafter shall think meet
To put an antic° disposition on,
That you, at such times seeing me, never shall,
With arms encumb'red° thus, or this head-shake,
Or by pronouncing of some doubtful phrase,
As "Well, well, we know," or "We could, an if we would,"
Or "If we list to speak," or "There be, an if they might,"
Or such ambiguous giving out,° to note°
That you know aught of me: this not to do,
So grace and mercy at your most need help you,
Swear.

GHOST [*beneath*]: Swear.

HAMLET: Rest, rest, perturbed spirit! [*They swear.*] So, gentlemen,
With all my love I do commend me to you:
And what so poor a man as Hamlet is
May do, t' express his love and friending° to you,
God willing, shall not lack. Let us go in together;
And still your fingers on your lips, I pray.
The time is out of joint: O cursed spite,
That ever I was born to set it right!
Nay, come, let's go together. *Exeunt.*

[ACT II

SCENE I: *A room in Polonius's house.*]

Enter old Polonius with his man [*Reynaldo*].

POLONIUS: Give him this money and these notes, Reynaldo.

REYNALDO: I will, my lord.

POLONIUS: You shall do marvellous wisely, good Reynaldo,
Before you visit him, to make inquire
Of his behaviour.

REYNALDO: My lord, I did intend it.

POLONIUS: Marry, well said; very well said. Look you, sir,
Inquire me first what Danskers° are in Paris;
And how, and who, what means, and where they keep,°
What company, at what expense; and finding
By this encompassment° and drift° of question

---

172. antic: Fantastic. **174. encumb'red:** Folded or entwined. **178. giving out:** Profession of knowledge; **to note:** To give a sign. **186. friending:** Friendliness. ACT II, SCENE I. **7. Danskers:** Danke was a common variant for "Denmark"; hence "Dane." **8. keep:** Dwell. **10. encompassment:** Roundabout talking; **drift:** Gradual approach or course.

That they do know my son, come you more nearer
Than your particular demands will touch it:°
Take° you as 'twere, some distant knowledge of him;
As thus, "I know his father and his friends,
And in part him": do you mark this, Reynaldo?
REYNALDO: Ay, very well, my lord.
POLONIUS: "And in part him; but" you may say "not well:
But, if 't be he I mean, he's very wild;
Addicted so and so": and there put on° him
What forgeries° you please; marry, none so rank
As may dishonour him; take heed of that;
But, sir, such wanton,° wild and usual slips
As are companions noted and most known
To youth and liberty.
REYNALDO: As gaming, my lord.
POLONIUS: Ay, or drinking, fencing,° swearing, quarrelling,
Drabbing;° you may go so far.
REYNALDO: My lord, that would dishonour him.
POLONIUS: 'Faith, no; as you may season it in the charge.
You must not put another scandal on him,
That he is open to incontinency;°
That's not my meaning: but breathe his faults so quaintly°
That they may seem the taints of liberty°
The flash and outbreak of a fiery mind,
A savageness in unreclaimed° blood,
Of general assault.°
REYNALDO: But, my good lord, —
POLONIUS: Wherefore should you do this?
REYNALDO: Ay, my lord,
I would know that.
POLONIUS: Marry, sir, here's my drift;
And, I believe, it is a fetch of wit:°
You laying these slight sullies on my son,
As 'twere a thing a little soil'd i' th' working,
Mark you,
Your party in converse, him you would sound,
Having ever° seen in the prenominate° crimes
The youth you breathe of guilty, be assur'd

11–12. come . . . it: I.e., you will find out more this way than by asking pointed questions. **13. Take:** Assume, pretend. **19. put on:** Impute to. **20. forgeries:** Invented tales. **22. wanton:** Sportive, unrestrained. **25. fencing:** Indicative of the ill repute of professional fencers and fencing schools in Elizabethan times. **26. Drabbing:** Associating with immoral women. **30. incontinency:** Habitual loose behavior. **31. quaintly:** Delicately, ingeniously. **32. taints of liberty:** Blemishes due to freedom. **34. unreclaimed:** Untamed. **35. general assault:** Tendency that assails all untrained youth. **38. fetch of wit:** Clever trick. **43. ever:** At any time; **prenominate:** Before-mentioned.

He closes with you in this consequence;°
"Good sir," or so, or "friend," or "gentleman,"
According to the phrase or the addition
Of man and country.

REYNALDO: Very good, my lord.

POLONIUS: And then, sir, does 'a this — 'a does — what was I about to say? By the mass, I was about to say something: where did I leave?

REYNALDO: At "closes in the consequence," at "friend or so," and "gentleman."

POLONIUS: At "closes in the consequence," ay, marry;
He closes thus: "I know the gentleman;
I saw him yesterday, or t' other day,
Or then, or then; with such, or such; and, as you say,
There was 'a gaming; there o'ertook in 's rouse°
There falling out at tennis": or perchance,
"I saw him enter such a house of sale,"
Videlicet,° a brothel, or so forth.
See you now;
Your bait of falsehood takes this carp of truth:
And thus do we of wisdom and of reach,°
With windlasses° and with assays of bias,°
By indirections° find directions° out:
So by my former lecture° and advice,
Shall you my son. You have me, have you not?

REYNALDO: My lord, I have.

POLONIUS: God bye ye;° fare ye well.

REYNALDO: Good my lord!

POLONIUS: Observe his inclination in yourself.°

REYNALDO: I shall, my lord.

POLONIUS: And let him ply his music.°

REYNALDO: Well, my lord.

POLONIUS: Farewell! *Exit Reynaldo.*

Enter Ophelia.

How now, Ophelia! what's the matter?

OPHELIA: O, my lord, my lord, I have been so affrighted!

POLONIUS: With what, i' th' name of God?

OPHELIA: My lord, as I was sewing in my closet,°
Lord Hamlet, with his doublet° all unbrac'd;°

---

45. closes . . . consequence: Agrees with you in this conclusion. **56. o'ertook in 's rouse:** Overcome by drink. **59. Videlicet:** Namely. **62. reach:** Capacity, ability. **63. windlasses:** I.e., circuitous paths; **assays of bias:** Attempts that resemble the course of the bowl, which, being weighted on one side, has a curving motion. **64. indirections:** Devious courses; **directions:** Straight courses, i.e., the truth. **65. lecture:** Admonition. **67. bye ye:** Be with you. **69. Observe . . . yourself:** In your own person, not by spies; or conform your own conduct to his inclination; or test him by studying yourself. **71. ply his music:** Probably to be taken literally. **75. closet:** Private chamber. **76. doublet:** Close-fitting coat; **unbrac'd:** Unfastened.

No hat upon his head; his stockings foul'd,
Ungart'red, and down-gyved° to his ankle;
Pale as his shirt; his knees knocking each other;
And with a look so piteous in purport
As if he had been loosed out of hell
To speak of horrors, — he comes before me.

POLONIUS: Mad for thy love?

OPHELIA: My lord, I do not know;
But truly, I do fear it.

POLONIUS: What said he?

OPHELIA: He took me by the wrist and held me hard;
Then goes he to the length of all his arm;
And, with his other hand thus o'er his brow,
He falls to such perusal of my face
As 'a would draw it. Long stay'd he so;
At last, a little shaking of mine arm
And thrice his head thus waving up and down,
He rais'd a sigh so piteous and profound
As it did seem to shatter all his bulk°
And end his being: that done, he lets me go:
And, with his head over his shoulder turn'd,
He seem'd to find his way without his eyes;
For out o' doors he went without their helps,
And, to the last, bended their light on me.

POLONIUS: Come, go with me: I will go seek the king.
This is the very ecstasy of love,
Whose violent property° fordoes° itself
And leads the will to desperate undertakings
As oft as any passion under heaven
That does afflict our natures. I am sorry.
What, have you given him any hard words of late?

OPHELIA: No, my good lord, but, as you did command,
I did repel his letters and denied
His access to me.

POLONIUS: That hath made him mad.
I am sorry that with better heed and judgement
I had not quoted° him: I fear'd he did but trifle,
And meant to wrack thee; but, beshrew my jealousy!°
By heaven, it is as proper to our age
To cast beyond° ourselves in our opinions
As it is common for the younger sort
To lack discretion. Come, go we to the king:

---

78. down-gyved: Fallen to the ankles (like gyves or fetters). **93. bulk:** Body. **101. property:** Nature; **fordoes:** Destroys. **110. quoted:** Observed. **111. beshrew my jealousy:** Curse my suspicions. **113. cast beyond:** Overshoot, miscalculate.

This must be known; which, being kept close, might move
More grief to hide than hate to utter love.°
Come. *Exeunt.*

[SCENE II: *A room in the castle.*]

Flourish. Enter King and Queen, Rosencrantz, and Guildenstern [*with others*].

KING: Welcome, dear Rosencrantz and Guildenstern!
Moreover that° we much did long to see you,
The need we have to use you did provoke
Our hasty sending. Something have you heard
Of Hamlet's transformation; so call it,
Sith° nor th' exterior nor the inward man
Resembles that it was. What it should be,
More than his father's death, that thus hath put him
So much from th' understanding of himself,
I cannot dream of: I entreat you both,
That, being of so young days° brought up with him,
And sith so neighbour'd to his youth and haviour,
That you vouchsafe your rest° here in our court
Some little time: so by your companies
To draw him on to pleasures, and to gather,
So much as from occasion you may glean,
Whether aught, to us unknown, afflicts him thus,
That, open'd, lies within our remedy.

QUEEN: Good gentlemen, he hath much talk'd of you;
And sure I am two men there are not living
To whom he more adheres. If it will please you
To show us so much gentry° and good will
As to expend your time with us awhile,
For the supply and profit° of our hope,
Your visitation shall receive such thanks
As fits a king's remembrance.

ROSENCRANTZ: Both your majesties
Might, by the sovereign power you have of us,
Put your dread pleasures more into command
Than to entreaty.

GUILDENSTERN: But we both obey,
And here give up ourselves, in the full bent°
To lay our service freely at your feet,
To be commanded.

116–117. might . . . love: I.e., I might cause more grief to others by hiding the knowledge of Hamlet's love to Ophelia than hatred to me and mine by telling of it. SCENE II. **2. Moreover that:** Besides the fact that. **6. Sith:** Since. **11. of . . . days:** From such early youth. **13. vouchsafe your rest:** Please to stay. **22. gentry:** Courtesy. **24. supply and profit:** Aid and successful outcome. **30. in . . . bent:** To the utmost degree of our mental capacity.

KING: Thanks, Rosencrantz and gentle Guildenstern.
QUEEN: Thanks, Guildenstern and gentle Rosencrantz:
And I beseech you instantly to visit
My too much changed son. Go, some of you,
And bring these gentlemen where Hamlet is.
GUILDENSTERN: Heavens make our presence and our practices
Pleasant and helpful to him!
QUEEN: Ay, amen!
Exeunt Rosencrantz and Guildenstern [*with some Attendants*].

Enter Polonius.

POLONIUS: Th' ambassadors from Norway, my good lord,
Are joyfully return'd.
KING: Thou still hast been the father of good news.
POLONIUS: Have I, my lord? I assure my good liege,
I hold my duty, as I hold my soul,
Both to my God and to my gracious king:
And I do think, or else this brain of mine
Hunts not the trail of policy so sure
As it hath us'd to do, that I have found
The very cause of Hamlet's lunacy.
KING: O, speak of that; that do I long to hear.
POLONIUS: Give first admittance to th' ambassadors;
My news shall be the fruit to that great feast.
KING: Thyself do grace to them, and bring them in. [*Exit Polonius.*]
He tells me, my dear Gertrude, he hath found
The head and source of all your son's distemper.
QUEEN: I doubt° it is no other but the main;°
His father's death, and our o'erhasty marriage.
KING: Well, we shall sift him.

Enter Ambassadors [*Voltimand and Cornelius, with Polonius.*]

Welcome, my good friends!
Say, Voltimand, what from our brother Norway?
VOLTIMAND: Most fair return of greetings and desires.
Upon our first, he sent out to suppress
His nephew's levies; which to him appear'd
To be a preparation 'gainst the Polack;
But, better look'd into, he truly found
It was against your highness: whereat griev'd,
That so his sickness, age and impotence
Was falsely borne in hand,° sends out arrests
On Fortinbras; which he, in brief, obeys;
Receives rebuke from Norway, and in fine°
Makes vow before his uncle never more

---

56. doubt: Fear; **main:** Chief point, principal concern. **67. borne in hand:** Deluded. **69. in fine:** In the end.

To give th' assay° of arms against your majesty.
Whereon old Norway, overcome with joy,
Gives him three score thousand crowns in annual fee,
And his commission to employ those soldiers,
So levied as before, against the Polack:
With an entreaty, herein further shown, [*giving a paper.*]
That it might please you to give quiet pass
Through your dominions for this enterprise,
On such regards of safety and allowance°
As therein are set down.

KING: It likes° us well;
And at our more consider'd° time we'll read,
Answer, and think upon this business.
Meantime we thank you for your well-took labour:
Go to your rest; at night we'll feast together:
Most welcome home! *Exeunt Ambassadors.*

POLONIUS: This business is well ended.
My liege, and madam, to expostulate
What majesty should be, what duty is,
Why day is day, night night, and time is time,
Were nothing but to waste night, day and time.
Therefore, since brevity is the soul of wit,°
And tediousness the limbs and outward flourishes,°
I will be brief: your noble son is mad:
Mad call I it; for, to define true madness
What is 't but to be nothing else but mad?
But let that go.

QUEEN: More matter, with less art.

POLONIUS: Madam, I swear I use no art at all.
That he is mad, 'tis true: 'tis true 'tis pity;
And pity 'tis 'tis true: a foolish figure;°
But farewell it, for I will use no art.
Mad let us grant him, then: and now remains
That we find out the cause of this effect,
Or rather say, the cause of this defect,
For this effect defective comes by cause:
Thus it remains, and the remainder thus.
Perpend.°
I have a daughter — have while she is mine —
Who, in her duty and obedience, mark,
Hath given me this: now gather, and surmise. [*Reads the letter.*] "To the celestial and my soul's idol,

---

71. assay: Assault, trial (of arms). **79. safety and allowance:** Pledges of safety to the country and terms of permission for the troops to pass. **80. likes:** Pleases. **81. consider'd:** Suitable for deliberation. **90. wit:** Sound sense or judgment. **91. flourishes:** Ostentation, embellishments. **98. figure:** Figure of speech. **105. Perpend:** Consider.

the most beautified Ophelia," —
That's an ill phrase, a vile phrase; "beautified" is a vile phrase: but you shall hear. Thus: [*Reads.*]
"In her excellent white bosom, these, &c."

QUEEN: Came this from Hamlet to her?

POLONIUS: Good madam, stay awhile; I will be faithful. [*Reads.*]
"Doubt thou the stars are fire;
Doubt that the sun doth move;
Doubt truth to be a liar;
But never doubt I love.
"O dear Ophelia, I am ill at these numbers;° I have not art to reckon° my groans: but that I love thee best, O most best, believe it. Adieu.
"Thine evermore, most dear lady, whilst this machine° is to him,
HAMLET."
This, in obedience, hath my daughter shown me,
And more above,° hath his solicitings,
As they fell out° by time, by means° and place,
All given to mine ear.

KING: But how hath she
Receiv'd his love?

POLONIUS: What do you think of me?

KING: As of a man faithful and honourable.

POLONIUS: I would fain prove so. But what might you think,
When I had seen this hot love on the wing —
As I perceiv'd it, I must tell you that,
Before my daughter told me — what might you,
Or my dear majesty your queen here, think,
If I had play'd the desk or table-book,°
Or given my heart a winking,° mute and dumb,
Or look'd upon this love with idle sight;
What might you think? No, I went round to work,
And my young mistress thus I did bespeak:°
"Lord Hamlet is a prince, out of thy star;°
This must not be": and then I prescripts gave her,
That she should lock herself from his resort,
Admit no messengers, receive no tokens.
Which done, she took the fruits of my advice;
And he, repelled — a short tale to make —
Fell into a sadness, then into a fast,
Thence to a watch,° thence into a weakness,

---

120. ill . . . numbers: Unskilled at writing verses; **reckon:** Number metrically, scan. **122. machine:** Bodily frame. **125. more above:** Moreover. **126. fell out:** Occurred; **means:** Opportunities (of access). **135. play'd . . . table-book:** I.e., remained shut up, concealed this information. **136. given . . . winking:** Given my heart a signal to keep silent. **139. bespeak:** Address. **140. out . . . star:** Above thee in position. **147. watch:** State of sleeplessness.

Thence to a lightness,° and, by this declension,°
Into the madness wherein now he raves,
And all we mourn for.

KING: Do you think 'tis this?

QUEEN: It may be, very like.

POLONIUS: Hath there been such a time — I would fain know that —
That I have positively said " 'Tis so,"
When it prov'd otherwise?

KING: Not that I know.

POLONIUS [*pointing to his head and shoulder*]: Take this from this, if this be otherwise:
If circumstances lead me, I will find
Where truth is hid, though it were hid indeed
Within the centre.°

KING: How may we try it further?

POLONIUS: You know, sometimes he walks four hours together
Here in the lobby.

QUEEN: So he does indeed.

POLONIUS: At such a time I'll loose my daughter to him:
Be you and I behind an arras° then;
Mark the encounter: if he love her not
And be not from his reason fall'n thereon,°
Let me be no assistant for a state,
But keep a farm and carters.

KING: We will try it.

Enter Hamlet [*reading on a book*].

QUEEN: But, look, where sadly the poor wretch comes reading.

POLONIUS: Away, I do beseech you both, away:

Exeunt King and Queen [*with Attendants*].

I'll board° him presently. O, give me leave.
How does my good Lord Hamlet?

HAMLET: Well, God-a-mercy.

POLONIUS: Do you know me, my lord?

HAMLET: Excellent well; you are a fishmonger.°

POLONIUS: Not I, my lord.

HAMLET: Then I would you were so honest a man.

POLONIUS: Honest, my lord!

HAMLET: Ay, sir; to be honest, as this world goes, is to be one man picked out of ten thousand.

POLONIUS: That's very true, my lord.

HAMLET: For if the sun breed maggots in a dead dog, being a good kissing carrion,° — Have you a daughter?

---

148. lightness: Lightheadedness; **declension:** Decline, deterioration. **158. centre:** Middle point of the earth. **162. arras:** Hanging, tapestry. **164. thereon:** On that account. **169. board:** Accost. **173. fishmonger:** An opprobrious expression meaning "bawd," "procurer." **180–181. good kissing carrion:** I.e., a good piece of flesh for kissing (?).

POLONIUS: I have, my lord.

HAMLET: Let her not walk i' the sun:° conception° is a blessing: but as your daughter may conceive — Friend, look to 't.

POLONIUS [*aside*]: How say you by° that? Still harping on my daughter: yet he knew me not at first; 'a said I was a fishmonger: 'a is far gone, far gone: and truly in my youth I suffered much extremity for love; very near this. I'll speak to him again. What do you read, my lord?

HAMLET: Words, words, words.

POLONIUS: What is the matter,° my lord?

HAMLET: Between who?°

POLONIUS: I mean, the matter that you read, my lord.

HAMLET: Slanders, sir: for the satirical rogue says here that old men have grey beards, that their faces are wrinkled, their eyes purging° thick amber and plum-tree gum and that they have a plentiful lack of wit, together with most weak hams: all which, sir, though I most powerfully and potently believe, yet I hold it not honesty° to have it thus set down, for yourself, sir, should be old as I am, if like a crab you could go backward.

POLONIUS [*aside*]: Though this be madness, yet there is method in 't. — Will you walk out of the air, my lord?

HAMLET: Into my grave.

POLONIUS: Indeed, that's out of the air. *(Aside.)* How pregnant sometimes his replies are! a happiness° that often madness hits on, which reason and sanity could not so prosperously° be delivered of. I will leave him, and suddenly contrive the means of meeting between him and my daughter. — My honourable lord, I will most humbly take my leave of you.

HAMLET: You cannot, sir, take from me any thing that I will more willingly part withal: except my life, except my life, except my life.

Enter Guildenstern and Rosencrantz.

POLONIUS: Fare you well, my lord.

HAMLET: These tedious old fools!

POLONIUS: You go to seek the Lord Hamlet; there he is.

ROSENCRANTZ [*to Polonius*]: God save you, sir! [*Exit Polonius.*]

GUILDENSTERN: My honoured lord!

ROSENCRANTZ: My most dear lord!

HAMLET: My excellent good friends! How dost thou, Guildenstern? Ah, Rosencrantz! Good lads, how do ye both?

ROSENCRANTZ: As the indifferent° children of the earth.

GUILDENSTERN: Happy, in that we are not over-happy;
On Fortune's cap we are not the very button.

HAMLET: Nor the soles of her shoe?

---

183. i' the sun: In the sunshine of princely favors; **conception:** Quibble on "understanding" and "pregnancy." **185. by:** Concerning. **190. matter:** Substance. **191. Between who:** Hamlet deliberately takes *matter* as meaning "basis of dispute." **194. purging:** discharging. **197. honesty:** Decency. **203. happiness:** Felicity of expression. **204. prosperously:** Successfully. **217. indifferent:** Ordinary.

ROSENCRANTZ: Neither, my lord.

HAMLET: Then you live about her waist, or in the middle of her favours?

GUILDENSTERN: 'Faith, her privates° we.

HAMLET: In the secret parts of Fortune? O, most true; she is a strumpet. What's the news?

ROSENCRANTZ: None, my lord, but that the world's grown honest.

HAMLET: Then is doomsday near: but your news is not true. Let me question more in particular: what have you, my good friends, deserved at the hands of Fortune, that she sends you to prison hither?

GUILDENSTERN: Prison, my lord!

HAMLET: Denmark's a prison.

ROSENCRANTZ: Then is the world one.

HAMLET: A goodly one; in which there are many confines,° wards and dungeons, Denmark being one o' the worst.

ROSENCRANTZ: We think not so, my lord.

HAMLET: Why, then, 'tis none to you; for there is nothing either good or bad, but thinking makes it so: to me it is a prison.

ROSENCRANTZ: Why then, your ambition makes it one; 'tis too narrow for your mind.

HAMLET: O God, I could be bounded in a nutshell and count myself a king of infinite space, were it not that I have bad dreams.

GUILDENSTERN: Which dreams indeed are ambition, for the very substance of the ambitious° is merely the shadow of a dream.

HAMLET: A dream itself is but a shadow.

ROSENCRANTZ: Truly, and I hold ambition of so airy and light a quality that it is but a shadow's shadow.

HAMLET: Then are our beggars bodies, and our monarchs and outstretched heroes the beggars' shadows. Shall we to the court? for, by my fay,° I cannot reason.°

ROSENCRANTZ: / GUILDENSTERN: We'll wait upon° you.

HAMLET: No such matter: I will not sort° you with the rest of my servants, for, to speak to you like an honest man, I am most dreadfully attended.° But, in the beaten way of friendship,° what make you at Elsinore?

ROSENCRANTZ: To visit you, my lord: no other occasion.

HAMLET: Beggar that I am, I am ever poor in thanks; but I thank you: and sure, dear friends, my thanks are too dear a° halfpenny. Were you not sent for? Is it your own inclining? Is it a free visitation? Come, come, deal justly with me: come, come; nay, speak.

GUILDENSTERN: What should we say, my lord?

---

223. privates: I.e., ordinary men (sexual pun on *private parts*). **233. confines:** Places of confinement. **242–243. very . . . ambitious:** That seemingly most substantial thing which the ambitious pursue. **248. fay:** Faith. **249. reason:** Argue. **250. wait upon:** Accompany. **251. sort:** Class. **252. dreadfully attended:** Poorly provided with servants. **253. in the . . . friendship:** As a matter of course among friends. **256. a:** I.e., at a.

HAMLET: Why, any thing, but to the purpose. You were sent for; and there is a kind of confession in your looks which your modesties have not craft enough to colour: I know the good king and queen have sent for you.

ROSENCRANTZ: To what end, my lord?

HAMLET: That you must teach me. But let me conjure° you, by the rights of our fellowship, by the consonancy of our youth,° by the obligation of our ever-preserved love, and by what more dear a better proposer° could charge you withal, be even and direct with me, whether you were sent for, or no?

ROSENCRANTZ [*aside to Guildenstern*]: What say you?

HAMLET [*aside*]: Nay, then, I have an eye of you. — If you love me, hold not off.

GUILDENSTERN: My lord, we were sent for.

HAMLET: I will tell you why; so shall my anticipation prevent your discovery,° and your secrecy to the king and queen moult no feather. I have of late — but wherefore I know not — lost all my mirth, forgone all custom of exercises; and indeed it goes so heavily with my disposition that this goodly frame, the earth, seems to me a sterile promontory, this most excellent canopy, the air, look you, this brave o'erhanging firmament, this majestical roof fretted° with golden fire, why, it appeareth nothing to me but a foul and pestilent congregation of vapours. What a piece of work is a man! how noble in reason! how infinite in faculties° in form and moving how express° and admirable! in action how like an angel! in apprehension° how like a god! the beauty of the world! the paragon of animals! And yet, to me, what is this quintessence° of dust? man delights not me: no, nor woman neither, though by your smiling you seem to say so.

ROSENCRANTZ: My lord, there was no such stuff in my thoughts.

HAMLET: Why did you laugh then, when I said "man delights not me"?

ROSENCRANTZ: To think, my lord, if you delight not in man, what lenten° entertainment the players shall receive from you: we coted° them on the way; and hither are they coming, to offer you service.

HAMLET: He that plays the king shall be welcome; his majesty shall have tribute of me; the adventurous knight shall use his foil and target;° the lover shall not sigh gratis; the humorous man° shall end his part in peace; the clown shall make those laugh whose lungs are tickle o' the sere;° and the lady shall say her mind freely, or the blank verse shall halt for 't.° What players are they?

---

264. conjure: Adjure, entreat. **265. consonancy of our youth:** The fact that we are of the same age. **266. better proposer:** One more skillful in finding proposals. **273. prevent your discovery:** Forestall your disclosure. **279. fretted:** Adorned. **281. faculties:** Capacity. **282. express:** Well-framed(?), exact(?). **283. apprehension:** Understanding. **284. quintessence:** The fifth essence of ancient philosophy, supposed to be the substance of the heavenly bodies and to be latent in all things. **289. lenten:** Meager. **290. coted:** Overtook and passed beyond. **293. foil and target:** Sword and shield. **294. humorous man:** Actor who takes the part of the humor characters. **295. tickle o' the sere:** Easy on the trigger. **295–296. the lady . . . for 't:** The lady (fond of talking) shall have opportunity to talk, blank verse or no blank verse.

ROSENCRANTZ: Even those you were wont to take delight in, the tragedians of the city.

HAMLET: How chances it they travel? their residence,° both in reputation and profit, was better both ways.

ROSENCRANTZ: I think their inhibition° comes by the means of the late innovation.°

HAMLET: Do they hold the same estimation they did when I was in the city? are they so followed?

ROSENCRANTZ: No, indeed, are they not.

HAMLET: How° comes it? do they grow rusty?

ROSENCRANTZ: Nay, their endeavour keeps in the wonted pace: but there is, sir, an aery° of children, little eyases,° that cry out on the top of question,° and are most tyrannically° clapped for 't: these are now the fashion, and so berattle° the common stages° — so they call them — that many wearing rapiers° are afraid of goose-quills° and dare scarce come thither.

HAMLET: What, are they children? who maintains 'em? how are they escoted?° Will they pursue the quality° no longer than they can sing?° will they not say afterwards, if they should grow themselves to common° players — as it is most like, if their means are no better — their writers do them wrong, to make them exclaim against their own succession?°

ROSENCRANTZ: 'Faith, there has been much to do on both sides; and the nation holds it no sin to tarre° them to controversy: there was, for a while, no money bid for argument,° unless the poet and the player went to cuffs° in the question.°

HAMLET: Is't possible?

GUILDENSTERN: O, there has been much throwing about of brains.

HAMLET: Do the boys carry it away?°

ROSENCRANTZ: Ay, that they do, my lord; Hercules and his load° too.

HAMLET: It is not very strange; for my uncle is king of Denmark, and those that would make mows° at him while my father lived, give twenty, forty,

---

300. residence: Remaining in one place. **302. inhibition:** Formal prohibition (from acting plays in the city or, possibly, at court). **302–303. innovation:** The new fashion in satirical plays performed by boy actors in the "private" theaters. **307–325. How . . . load too:** The passage is the famous one dealing with the War of the Theatres (1599–1602); namely, the rivalry between the children's companies and the adult actors. **309. aery:** Nest; **eyases:** Young hawks.; **cry . . . question:** Speak in a high key dominating conversation; clamor forth the height of controversy; probably "excel" (cf. line 462); perhaps intended to decry leaders of the dramatic profession. **310. tyrannically:** Outrageously. **311. berattle:** Berate; **common stages:** Public theaters. **311–312. many wearing rapiers:** Many men of fashion, who were afraid to patronize the common players for fear of being satirized by the poets who wrote for the children. **312. goose-quills:** I.e., pens of satirists. **313. escoted:** Maintained. **314. quality:** Acting profession; **no longer . . . sing:** I.e., until their voices change. **315. common:** Regular, adult. **317. succession:** future careers. **319. tarre:** Set on (as dogs). **320. argument:** Probably, plot for a play; **went to cuffs:** Came to blows. **321. question:** Controversy. **324. carry it away:** Win the day. **325. Hercules . . . load:** Regarded as an allusion to the sign of the Globe Theatre, which was Hercules bearing the world on his shoulder. **327. mows:** Grimaces.

fifty, a hundred ducats° a-piece for his picture in little.° 'Sblood, there is something in this more than natural, if philosophy could find it out.

A flourish [*of trumpets within*].

GUILDENSTERN: There are the players.

HAMLET: Gentlemen, you are welcome to Elsinore. Your hands, come then: the appurtenance of welcome is fashion and ceremony: let me comply° with you in this garb,° lest my extent° to the players, which, I tell you, must show fairly outwards, should more appear like entertainment than yours. You are welcome: but my uncle-father and aunt-mother are deceived.

GUILDENSTERN: In what, my dear lord?

HAMLET: I am but mad north-north-west:° when the wind is southerly I know a hawk from a handsaw.°

Enter Polonius.

POLONIUS: Well be with you, gentlemen!

HAMLET: Hark you, Guildenstern; and you too: at each ear a hearer: that great baby you see there is not yet out of his swaddling-clouts.°

ROSENCRANTZ: Happily he is the second time come to them; for they say an old man is twice a child.

HAMLET: I will prophesy he comes to tell me of the players; mark it. — You say right, sir: o' Monday morning;° 'twas then indeed.

POLONIUS: My lord, I have news to tell you.

HAMLET: My lord, I have news to tell you. When Roscius° was an actor in Rome, —

POLONIUS: The actors are come hither, my lord.

HAMLET: Buz, buz!°

POLONIUS: Upon my honour, —

HAMLET: Then came each actor on his ass, —

POLONIUS: The best actors in the world, either for tragedy, comedy, history, pastoral, pastoral-comical, historical-pastoral, tragical-historical, tragical-comical-historical-pastoral, scene individable,° or poem unlimited:° Seneca° cannot be too heavy, nor Plautus° too light. For the law of writ and the liberty,° these are the only men.

---

328. ducats: Gold coins worth 9s. 4d; **in little:** In miniature. **332. comply:** Observe the formalities of courtesy. **333. garb:** Manner; **extent:** Showing of kindness. **338. I am . . . north-north-west:** I am only partly mad, i.e., in only one point of the compass. **339. handsaw:** A proposed reading of *hernshaw* would mean "heron"; *handsaw* may be an early corruption of *hernshaw.* Another view regards *hawk* as the variant of *hack,* a tool of the pickax type, and *handsaw* as a saw operated by hand. **342. swaddling-clouts:** Cloths in which to wrap a newborn baby. **346. o' Monday morning:** Said to mislead Polonius. **348. Roscius:** A famous Roman actor. **351. Buz, buz:** An interjection used at Oxford to denote stale news. **356. scene individable:** A play observing the unity of place; **poem unlimited:** A play disregarding the unities of time and place. **357. Seneca:** Writer of Latin tragedies, model of early Elizabethan writers of tragedy; **Plautus:** Writer of Latin comedy. **357–358. law . . . liberty:** Pieces written according to rules and without rules, i.e., "classical" and "romantic" dramas.

HAMLET: O Jephthah, judge of Israel,° what a treasure hadst thou!
POLONIUS: What a treasure had he, my lord?
HAMLET: Why,
"One fair daughter, and no more,
The which he loved passing well."
POLONIUS [*aside*]: Still on my daughter.
HAMLET: Am I not i' the right, old Jephthah?
POLONIUS: If you call me Jephthah, my lord, I have a daughter that I love passing° well.
HAMLET: Nay, that follows not.
POLONIUS: What follows, then, my lord?
HAMLET: Why,
"As by lot, God wot,"
and then, you know,
"It came to pass, as most like° it was," —
the first row° of the pious chanson° will show you more; for look, where my abridgement comes.°

Enter the Players.

You are welcome, masters; welcome, all. I am glad to see thee well. Welcome, good friends. O, old friend! why, thy face is valanced° since I saw thee last: comest thou to beard me in Denmark? What, my young lady and mistress! By'r lady, your ladyship is nearer to heaven than when I saw you last, by the altitude of a chopine.° Pray God, your voice, like a piece of uncurrent° gold, be not cracked within the ring.° Masters, you are all welcome. We'll e'en to 't like French falconers, fly at any thing we see: we'll have a speech straight: come, give us a taste of your quality; come, a passionate speech.

FIRST PLAYER: What speech, my good lord?
HAMLET: I heard thee speak me a speech once, but it was never acted; or, if it was, not above once; for the play, I remember, pleased not the million; 'twas caviary to the general:° but it was — as I received it, and others, whose judgements in such matters cried in the top of° mine — an excellent play, well digested in the scenes, set down with as much modesty as cunning.° I remember, one said there were no sallets° in the lines to make the matter savoury, nor no matter in the phrase that might indict° the author of affectation; but called it an honest method, as wholesome as sweet, and by very much more handsome than fine.° One speech in 't

---

359. Jephthah . . . Israel: Jephthah had to sacrifice his daughter; see Judges 11. **366–367. passing:** Surpassingly. **373. like:** Probable. **374. row:** Stanza; **chanson:** Ballad. **375. abridgement comes:** Opportunity comes for cutting short the conversation. **377. valanced:** Fringed (with a beard). **380. chopine:** Kind of shoe raised by the thickness of the heel; worn in Italy, particularly at Venice. **381. uncurrent:** Not passable as lawful coinage; **cracked within the ring:** In the center of coins were rings enclosing the sovereign's head; if the coin was cracked within this ring, it was unfit for currency. **388. caviary to the general:** Not relished by the multitude. **389. cried in the top of:** Spoke with greater authority than. **391. cunning:** Skill; **sallets:** Salads: here, spicy improprieties. **392. indict:** Convict. **393–394. as wholesome . . . fine:** Its beauty was not that of elaborate ornament, but that of order and proportion.

I chiefly loved: 'twas Æneas' tale to Dido;° and thereabout of it especially, where he speaks of Priam's slaughter: if it live in your memory, begin at this line: let me see, let me see —
"The rugged Pyrrhus,° like th' Hyrcanian beast,"° —
'tis not so: — it begins with Pyrrhus: —
"The rugged Pyrrhus, he whose sable arms,
Black as his purpose, did the night resemble
When he lay couched in the ominous horse,°
Hath now this dread and black complexion smear'd
With heraldry more dismal; head to foot
Now is he total gules;° horridly trick'd°
With blood of fathers, mothers, daughters, sons,
Bak'd and impasted° with the parching streets,
That lend a tyrannous and a damned light
To their lord's murder: roasted in wrath and fire,
And thus o'er-sized° with coagulate gore,
With eyes like carbuncles, the hellish Pyrrhus
Old grandsire Priam seeks."
So, proceed you.

POLONIUS: 'Fore God, my lord, well spoken, with good accent and good discretion.

FIRST PLAYER: "Anon he finds him
Striking too short at Greeks; his antique sword,
Rebellious to his arm, lies where it falls,
Repugnant° to command: unequal match'd,
Pyrrhus at Priam drives; in rage strikes wide;
But with the whiff and wind of his fell sword
Th' unnerved father falls. Then senseless Ilium,°
Seeming to feel this blow, with flaming top
Stoops to his base, and with a hideous crash
Takes prisoner Pyrrhus' ear: for, lo! his sword
Which was declining on the milky head
Of reverend Priam, seem'd i' th' air to stick:
So, as a painted tyrant,° Pyrrhus stood,
And like a neutral to his will and matter,°
Did nothing.
But, as we often see, against° some storm,
A silence in the heavens, the rack° stand still,
The bold winds speechless and the orb below

---

395. Æneas' tale to Dido: The lines recited by the player are imitated from Marlowe and Nashe's *Dido Queen of Carthage* (II.i.214ff.). They are written in such a way that the conventionality of the play within a play is raised above that of ordinary drama. **398. Pyrrhus:** A Greek hero in the Trojan War; **Hyrcanian beast:** The tiger; see Virgil, *Aeneid,* IV.266. **402. ominous horse:** Trojan horse. **405. gules:** Red, a heraldic term; **trick'd:** Spotted, smeared. **407. impasted:** Made into a paste. **410. o'er-sized:** Covered as with size or glue. **419. Repugnant:** Disobedient. **422. Then senseless Ilium:** Insensate Troy. **428. painted tyrant:** Tyrant in a picture. **429. matter:** Task. **431. against:** Before. **432. rack:** Mass of clouds.

As hush as death, anon the dreadful thunder
Doth rend the region,° so, after Pyrrhus' pause,
Aroused vengeance sets him new a-work;
And never did the Cyclops' hammers fall
On Mars's armour forg'd for proof eterne°
With less remorse than Pyrrhus' bleeding sword
Now falls on Priam.
Out, out, thou strumpet, Fortune! All you gods,
In general synod,° take away her power;
Break all the spokes and fellies° from her wheel,
And bowl the round nave° down the hill of heaven,
As low as to the fiends!"

POLONIUS: This is too long.

HAMLET: It shall to the barber's, with your beard. Prithee, say on: he's for a jig° or a tale of bawdry,° or he sleeps: say on: come to Hecuba.°

FIRST PLAYER: "But who, ah woe! had seen the mobled° queen —"

HAMLET: "The mobled queen?"

POLONIUS: That's good; "mobled queen" is good.

FIRST PLAYER: "Run barefoot up and down, threat'ning the flames
With bisson rheum;° a clout° upon that head
Where late the diadem stood, and for a robe,
About her lank and all o'er-teemed° loins,
A blanket, in the alarm of fear caught up;
Who this had seen, with tongue in venom steep'd,
'Gainst Fortune's state would treason have pronounc'd:°
But if the gods themselves did see her then
When she saw Pyrrhus make malicious sport
In mincing with his sword her husband's limbs,
The instant burst of clamour that she made,
Unless things mortal move them not at all,
Would have made milch° the burning eyes of heaven,
And passion in the gods."

POLONIUS: Look, whe'r he has not turned° his colour and has tears in 's eyes. Prithee, no more.

HAMLET: 'Tis well; I'll have thee speak out the rest soon. Good my lord, will you see the players well bestowed? Do you hear, let them be well used; for they are the abstract° and brief chronicles of the time: after your death you were better have a bad epitaph than their ill report while you live.

---

435. region: Assembly. **438. proof eterne:** External resistance to assault. **442. synod:** Assembly. **443. fellies:** Pieces of wood forming the rim of a wheel. **444. nave:** Hub. **447. jig:** Comic performance given at the end or in an interval of a play. **448. bawdry:** Indecency; **Hecuba:** Wife of Priam, king of Troy. **449. mobled:** Muffled. **453. bisson rheum:** Blinding tears; **clout:** Piece of cloth. **455. o'er-teemed:** Worn out with bearing children. **458. pronounc'd:** Proclaimed. **464. milch:** Moist with tears. **466. turned:** Changed. **470. abstract:** Summary account.

POLONIUS: My lord, I will use them according to their desert.

HAMLET: God's bodykins,° man, much better: use every man after his desert, and who shall 'scape whipping? Use them after your own honour and dignity: the less they deserve, the more merit is in your bounty. Take them in.

POLONIUS: Come, sirs.

HAMLET: Follow him, friends: we'll hear a play tomorrow. [*Aside to First Player.*] Dost thou hear me, old friend; can you play the Murder of Gonzago?

FIRST PLAYER: Ay, my lord.

HAMLET: We'll ha 't to-morrow night. You could, for a need, study a speech of some dozen or sixteen lines,° which I would set down and insert in 't, could you not?

FIRST PLAYER: Ay, my lord.

HAMLET: Very well. Follow that lord; and look you mock him not. — My good friends, I'll leave you till night: you are welcome to Elsinore.

Exeunt Polonius and Players.

ROSENCRANTZ: Good my lord! *Exeunt* [*Rosencrantz and Guildenstern.*]

HAMLET: Ay, so, God bye to you. — Now I am alone.
O, what a rogue and peasant° slave am I!
Is it not monstrous that this player here,
But in a fiction, in a dream of passion,
Could force his soul so to his own conceit
That from her working all his visage wann'd,°
Tears in his eyes, distraction in 's aspect,
A broken voice, and his whole function suiting
With forms to his conceit?° and all for nothing!
For Hecuba!
What's Hecuba to him, or he to Hecuba,
That he should weep for her? What would he do,
Had he the motive and the cue for passion
That I have? He would drown the stage with tears
And cleave the general ear with horrid speech,
Make mad the guilty and appall the free,
Confound the ignorant, and amaze indeed
The very faculties of eyes and ears.
Yet I,
A dull and muddy-mettled° rascal, peak,°
Like John-a-dreams,° unpregnant of° my cause,

---

474. bodykins: Diminutive form of the oath "by God's body." **484. dozen or sixteen lines:** Critics have amused themselves by trying to locate Hamlet's lines. Lucianus's speech III.ii.226–231 is the best guess. **491. peasant:** Base. **495. wann'd:** Grew pale. **497–498. his whole . . . conceit:** His whole being responded with forms to suit his thought. **509. muddy-mettled:** Dull-spirited; **peak:** Mope, pine. **510. John-a-dreams:** An expression occurring elsewhere in Elizabethan literature to indicate a dreamer; **unpregnant of:** Not quickened by.

And can say nothing; no, not for a king.
Upon whose property° and most dear life
A damn'd defeat was made. Am I a coward?
Who calls me villain? breaks my pate across?
Plucks off my beard, and blows it in my face?
Tweaks me by the nose? gives me the lie i' th' throat,
As deep as to the lungs? who does me this?
Ha!
'Swounds, I should take it: for it cannot be
But I am pigeon-liver'd° and lack gall
To make oppression bitter, or ere this
I should have fatted all the region kites°
With this slave's offal: bloody, bawdy villain!
Remorseless, treacherous, lecherous, kindless° villain!
O, vengeance!
Why, what an ass am I! This is most brave,
That I, the son of a dear father murder'd,
Prompted to my revenge by heaven and hell,
Must, like a whore, unpack my heart with words,
And fall a-cursing, like a very drab,°
A stallion!°
Fie upon 't! foh! About,° my brains! Hum, I have heard
That guilty creatures sitting at a play
Have by the very cunning of the scene
Been struck so to the soul that presently
They have proclaim'd their malefactions;
For murder, though it have no tongue, will speak
With most miraculous organ. I'll have these players
Play something like the murder of my father
Before mine uncle: I'll observe his looks:
I'll tent° him to the quick: if 'a do blench,°
I know my course. The spirit that I have seen
May be the devil:° and the devil hath power
T' assume a pleasing shape; yea, and perhaps
Out of my weakness and my melancholy,
As he is very potent with such spirits,°
Abuses me to damn me: I'll have grounds
More relative° than this:° the play's the thing
Wherein I'll catch the conscience of the king. *Exit.*

---

512. property: Proprietorship (of crown and life). **520. pigeon-liver'd:** The pigeon was supposed to secrete no gall; if Hamlet, so he says, had had gall, he would have felt the bitterness of oppression, and avenged it. **522. region kites:** Kites of the air. **524. kindless:** Unnatural. **530. drab:** Prostitute. **531. stallion:** Prostitute (male or female). **532. About:** About it, or turn thou right about. **541. tent:** Probe; **blench:** Quail, flinch. **543. May be the devil:** Hamlet's suspicion is properly grounded in the belief of the time. **546. spirits:** Humors. **548. relative:** Closely related, definite; **this:** I.e., the ghost's story.

[ACT III

SCENE I: *A room in the castle.*]

Enter King, Queen, Polonius, Ophelia, Rosencrantz, Guildenstern, Lords.

KING: And can you, by no drift of conference,°
Get from him why he puts on this confusion,
Grating so harshly all his days of quiet
With turbulent and dangerous lunacy?

ROSENCRANTZ: He does confess he feels himself distracted;
But from what cause 'a will by no means speak.

GUILDENSTERN: Nor do we find him forward° to be sounded,
But, with a crafty madness, keeps aloof,
When we would bring him on to some confession
Of his true state.

QUEEN: Did he receive you well?

ROSENCRANTZ: Most like a gentleman.

GUILDENSTERN: But with much forcing of his disposition.°

ROSENCRANTZ: Niggard of question;° but, of our demands,
Most free in his reply.

QUEEN: Did you assay° him
To any pastime?

ROSENCRANTZ: Madam, it so fell out, that certain players
We o'er-raught° on the way: of these we told him;
And there did seem in him a kind of joy
To hear of it: they are here about the court,
And, as I think, they have already order
This night to play before him.

POLONIUS: 'Tis most true:
And he beseech'd me to entreat your majesties
To hear and see the matter.

KING: With all my heart; and it doth much content me
To hear him so inclin'd.
Good gentlemen, give him a further edge,°
And drive his purpose into these delights.

ROSENCRANTZ: We shall, my lord. *Exeunt Rosencrantz and Guildenstern.*

KING: Sweet Gertrude, leave us too;
For we have closely° sent for Hamlet hither,
That he, as 'twere by accident, may here
Affront° Ophelia:
Her father and myself, lawful espials,°
Will so bestow ourselves that, seeing, unseen,

ACT III, SCENE I. **1. drift of conference:** Device of conversation. **7. forward:** Willing. **12. forcing of his disposition:** I.e., against his will. **13. Niggard of question:** Sparing of conversation. **14. assay:** Try to win. **17. o'er-raught:** Overtook. **26. edge:** Incitement. **29. closely:** Secretly. **31. Affront:** Confront. **32. lawful espials:** Legitimate spies.

We may of their encounter frankly judge,
And gather by him, as he is behav'd,
If 't be th' affliction of his love or no
That thus he suffers for.

QUEEN: I shall obey you.
And for your part, Ophelia, I do wish
That your good beauties be the happy cause
Of Hamlet's wildness:° so shall I hope your virtues
Will bring him to his wonted way again,
To both your honours.

OPHELIA: Madam, I wish it may. [*Exit Queen.*]

POLONIUS: Ophelia, walk you here. Gracious,° so please you,
We will bestow ourselves. [*To Ophelia.*] Read on this book;
That show of such an exercise° may colour°
Your loneliness. We are oft to blame in this, —
'Tis too much prov'd — that with devotion's visage
And pious action we do sugar o'er
The devil himself.

KING: [*aside*] O, 'tis too true!
How smart a lash that speech doth give my conscience!
The harlot's cheek, beautied with plast'ring art,
Is not more ugly to° the thing° that helps it
Than is my deed to my most painted word:
O heavy burthen!

POLONIUS: I hear him coming: let's withdraw, my lord.
[*Exeunt King and Polonius.*]

Enter Hamlet.

HAMLET: To be, or not to be: that is the question:
Whether 'tis nobler in the mind to suffer
The slings and arrows of outrageous fortune,
Or to take arms against a sea° of troubles,
And by opposing end them? To die: to sleep;
No more; and by a sleep to say we end
The heart-ache and the thousand natural shocks
That flesh is heir to, 'tis a consummation
Devoutly to be wish'd. To die, to sleep;
To sleep: perchance to dream: ay, there's the rub;
For in that sleep of death what dreams may come
When we have shuffled° off this mortal coil,°
Must give us pause: there's the respect°

---

40. wildness: Madness. **43. Gracious:** Your grace (addressed to the king). **45. exercise:** Act of devotion (the book she reads is one of devotion); **colour:** Give a plausible appearance to. **52. to:** Compared to; **thing:** I.e., the cosmetic. **59. sea:** The mixed metaphor of this speech has often been commented on; a later emendation *siege* has sometimes been spoken on the stage. **67. shuffled:** Sloughed, cast; **coil:** Usually means "turmoil"; here, possibly "body" (conceived of as wound about the soul like rope); *clay, soil, veil,* have been suggested as emendations. **68. respect:** Consideration.

That makes calamity of so long life;°
For who would bear the whips and scorns of time,°
Th' oppressor's wrong, the proud man's contumely,
The pangs of despis'd° love, the law's delay,
The insolence of office° and the spurns°
That patient merit of th' unworthy takes,
When he himself might his quietus° make
With a bare bodkin?° who would fardels° bear,
To grunt and sweat under a weary life,
But that the dread of something after death,
The undiscover'd country from whose bourn°
No traveller returns, puzzles the will
And makes us rather bear those ills we have
Than fly to others that we know not of?
Thus conscience° does make cowards of us all;
And thus the native hue° of resolution
Is sicklied o'er° with the pale cast° of thought,
And enterprises of great pitch° and moment°
With this regard° their currents° turn awry,
And lose the name of action — Soft you now!
The fair Ophelia! Nymph, in thy orisons°
Be all my sins rememb'red.

OPHELIA: Good my lord,
How does your honour for this many a day?

HAMLET: I humbly thank you; well, well, well.

OPHELIA: My lord, I have remembrances of yours,
That I have longed long to re-deliver;
I pray you, now receive them.

HAMLET: No, not I;
I never gave you aught.

OPHELIA: My honour'd lord, you know right well you did;
And, with them, words of so sweet breath compos'd
As made the things more rich: their perfume lost,
Take these again; for to the noble mind
Rich gifts wax poor when givers prove unkind.
There, my lord.

HAMLET: Ha, ha! are you honest?°

OPHELIA: My lord?

---

69. of . . . life: So long-lived. **70. time:** The world. **72. despis'd:** Rejected. **73. office:** Office-holders; **spurns:** Insults. **75. quietus:** Acquittance; here, death. **76. bare bodkin:** Mere dagger; *bare* is sometimes understood as "unsheathed"; **fardels:** Burdens. **79. bourn:** Boundary. **83. conscience:** Probably, inhibition by the faculty of reason restraining the will from doing wrong. **84. native hue:** Natural color; metaphor derived from the color of the face. **85. sicklied o'er:** Given a sticky tinge; **cast:** Shade of color. **86. pitch:** Height (as of a falcon's flight); **moment:** Importance. **87. regard:** Respect, consideration; **currents:** Courses. **89. orisons:** Prayers. **103–108. are you honest . . . beauty:** *Honest* meaning "truthful" and "chaste" and *fair* meaning "just, honorable" (line 105) and "beautiful" (line 107) are not mere quibbles; the speech has the irony of a *double entendre*.

HAMLET: Are you fair?

OPHELIA: What means your lordship?

HAMLET: That if you be honest and fair, your honesty° should admit no discourse to° your beauty.

OPHELIA: Could beauty, my lord, have better commerce° than with honesty?

HAMLET: Ay, truly; for the power of beauty will sooner transform honesty from what it is to a bawd than the force of honesty can translate beauty into his likeness: this was sometime a paradox, but now the time° gives it proof. I did love you once.

OPHELIA: Indeed, my lord, you made me believe so.

HAMLET: You should not have believed me; for virtue cannot so inoculate° our old stock but we shall relish of it:° I loved you not.

OPHELIA: I was the more deceived.

HAMLET: Get thee to a nunnery: why wouldst thou be a breeder of sinners? I am myself indifferent honest;° but yet I could accuse me of such things that it were better my mother had not borne me: I am very proud, revengeful, ambitious, with more offences at my beck° than I have thoughts to put them in, imagination to give them shape, or time to act them in. What should such fellows as I do crawling between earth and heaven? We are arrant knaves, all; believe none of us. Go thy ways to a nunnery. Where's your father?

OPHELIA: At home, my lord.

HAMLET: Let the doors be shut upon him, that he may play the fool no where but in 's own house. Farewell.

OPHELIA: O, help him, you sweet heavens!

HAMLET: If thou dost marry, I'll give thee this plague for thy dowry: be thou as chaste as ice, as pure as snow, thou shalt not escape calumny. Get thee to a nunnery, go: farewell. Or, if thou wilt needs marry, marry a fool; for wise men know well enough what monsters° you make of them. To a nunnery, go, and quickly too. Farewell.

OPHELIA: O heavenly powers, restore him!

HAMLET: I have heard of your° paintings too, well enough; God hath given you one face, and you make yourselves another: you jig,° you amble, and you lisp; you nick-name God's creatures, and make your wantonness your ignorance.° Go to, I'll no more on 't; it hath made me mad. I say, we will have no moe marriage: those that are married already, all but one,° shall live; the rest shall keep as they are. To a nunnery, go. *Exit.*

OPHELIA: O, what a noble mind is here o'er-thrown!
The courtier's, soldier's, scholar's, eye, tongue, sword;

---

107. your honesty: Your chastity. **107–108. discourse to:** Familiar intercourse with. **109. commerce:** Intercourse. **112. the time:** The present age. **115. inoculate:** Graft (metaphorical). **116. but . . . it:** I.e., that we do not still have about us a taste of the old stock; i.e., retain our sinfulness. **119. indifferent honest:** Moderately virtuous. **121. beck:** Command. **133. monsters:** An allusion to the horns of a cuckold. **136. your:** Indefinite use. **137. jig:** Move with jerky motion; probably allusion to the *jig,* or song and dance, of the current stage. **138–139. make . . . ignorance:** I.e., excuse your wantonness on the ground of your ignorance. **140. one:** I.e., the king.

Th' expectancy and rose° of the fair state,
The glass of fashion and the mould of form,°
Th' observ'd of all observers,° quite, quite down!
And I, of ladies most deject and wretched,
That suck'd the honey of his music vows,
Now see that noble and most sovereign reason,
Like sweet bells jangled, out of time and harsh;
That unmatch'd form and feature of blown° youth
Blasted with ecstasy:° O, woe is me,
T' have seen what I have seen, see what I see!

Enter King and Polonius.

KING: Love! his affections do not that way tend;
Nor what he spake, though it lack'd form a little,
Was not like madness. There's something in his soul,
O'er which his melancholy sits on brood;
And I do doubt° the hatch and the disclose°
Will be some danger: which for to prevent,
I have in quick determination
Thus set it down: he shall with speed to England,
For the demand of our neglected tribute:
Haply the seas and countries different
With variable° objects shall expel
This something-settled° matter in his heart,
Whereon his brains still beating puts him thus
From fashion of himself.° What think you on 't?
POLONIUS: It shall do well: but yet do I believe
The origin and commencement of his grief
Sprung from neglected love. How now, Ophelia!
You need not tell us what Lord Hamlet said;
We heard it all. My lord, do as you please;
But, if you hold it fit, after the play
Let his queen mother all alone entreat him
To show his grief: let her be round° with him;
And I'll be plac'd, so please you, in the ear
Of all their conference. If she find him not,
To England send him, or confine him where
Your wisdom best shall think.
KING: It shall be so:
Madness in great ones must not unwatch'd go. *Exeunt.*

---

144. expectancy and rose: Source of hope. **145. The glass . . . form:** The mirror of fashion and the pattern of courtly behavior. **146. observ'd . . . observers:** I.e., the center of attention in the court. **151. blown:** Blooming. **152. ecstasy:** Madness. **158. doubt:** Fear; **disclose:** Disclosure or revelation (by chipping of the shell). **164. variable:** Various. **165. something-settled:** Somewhat settled. **167. From . . . himself:** Out of his natural manner. **175. round:** Blunt.

[SCENE II: *A hall in the castle.*]

Enter Hamlet and three of the Players.

HAMLET: Speak the speech, I pray you, as I pronounced it to you, trippingly on the tongue: but if you mouth it, as many of your° players do, I had as lief the town-crier spoke my lines. Nor do not saw the air too much with your hand, thus, but use all gently; for in the very torrent, tempest, and, as I may say, whirlwind of your passion, you must acquire and beget a temperance that may give it smoothness. O, it offends me to the soul to hear a robustious° periwig-pated° fellow tear a passion to tatters, to very rags, to split the ears of the groundlings,° who for the most part are capable of° nothing but inexplicable° dumb-shows and noise: I would have such a fellow whipped for o'er-doing Termagant;° it out-herods Herod:° pray you, avoid it.

FIRST PLAYER: I warrant your honour.

HAMLET: Be not too tame neither, but let your own discretion be your tutor: suit the action to the word, the word to the action; with this special observance, that you o'er-step not the modesty of nature: for any thing so overdone is from the purpose of playing, whose end, both at the first and now, was and is, to hold, as 't were, the mirror up to nature; to show virtue her own feature, scorn her own image, and the very age and body of the time his form and pressure.° Now this overdone, or come tardy off,° though it make the unskilful laugh, cannot but make the judicious grieve; the censure of the which one° must in your allowance o'erweigh a whole theatre of others. O, there be players that I have seen play, and heard others praise, and that highly, not to speak it profanely, that, neither having the accent of Christians nor the gait of Christian, pagan, nor man, have so strutted and bellowed that I have thought some of nature's journeymen° had made men and not made them well, they imitated humanity so abominably.

FIRST PLAYER: I hope we have reformed that indifferently° with us, sir.

HAMLET: O, reform it altogether. And let those that play your clowns speak no more than is set down for them; for there be of° them that will themselves laugh, to set on some quantity of barren° spectators to laugh too; though, in the mean time, some necessary question of the play be then to be considered: that's villanous, and shows a most pitiful ambition in the fool that uses it. Go, make you ready. [*Exeunt Players.*]

SCENE II. **2. your:** Indefinite use. **7. robustious:** Violent, boisterous; **periwig-pated:** Wearing a wig. **8. groundlings:** Those who stood in the yard of the theater. **9. capable of:** Susceptible of being influenced by; **inexplicable:** Of no significance worth explaining. **10. Termagant:** A god of the Saracens; a character in the St. Nicholas play, where one of his worshipers, leaving him in charge of goods, returns to find them stolen; whereupon he beats the god (or idol), which howls vociferously. **11. Herod:** Herod of Jewry; a character in *The Slaughter of the Innocents* and other cycle plays. The part was played with great noise and fury. **19. pressure:** Stamp, impressed character. **19–20. come tardy off:** Inadequately done. **21. the censure . . . one:** The judgment of even one of whom. **26. journeymen:** Laborers not yet masters in their trade. **28. indifferently:** Fairly, tolerably. **30. of:** I.e., some among them. **31. barren:** I.e., of wit.

Enter Polonius, Guildenstern, and Rosencrantz.

How now, my lord! will the king hear this piece of work?
POLONIUS: And the queen too, and that presently.
HAMLET: Bid the players make haste. [*Exit Polonius.*]
Will you two help to hasten them?
ROSENCRANTZ:
GUILDENSTERN: } We will, my lord. *Exeunt they two.*
HAMLET: What ho! Horatio!

Enter Horatio.

HORATIO: Here, sweet lord, at your service.
HAMLET: Horatio, thou art e'en as just° a man
As e'er my conversation cop'd withal.
HORATIO: O, my dear lord, —
HAMLET: Nay, do not think I flatter;
For what advancement may I hope from thee
That no revenue hast but thy good spirits,
To feed and clothe thee? Why should the poor be flatter'd?
No, let the candied tongue lick absurd pomp,
And crook the pregnant° hinges of the knee
Where thrift° may follow fawning. Dost thou hear?
Since my dear soul was mistress of her choice
And could of men distinguish her election,
S' hath seal'd thee for herself; for thou hast been
As one, in suff'ring all, that suffers nothing,
A man that fortune's buffets and rewards
Hast ta'en with equal thanks: and blest are those
Whose blood and judgement are so well commeddled,
That they are not a pipe for fortune's finger
To sound what stop° she please. Give me that man
That is not passion's slave, and I will wear him
In my heart's core, ay, in my heart of heart,
As I do thee. — Something too much of this. —
There is a play to-night before the king;
One scene of it comes near the circumstance
Which I have told thee of my father's death:
I prithee, when thou seest that act afoot,
Even with the very comment of thy soul°
Observe my uncle: if his occulted° guilt
Do not itself unkennel in one speech,
It is a damned° ghost that we have seen,

41. just: Honest, honorable. **48. pregnant:** Pliant. **49. thrift:** Profit. **58. stop:** Hole in a wind instrument for controlling the sound. **66. very . . . soul:** Inward and sagacious criticism. **67. occulted:** Hidden. **69. damned:** In league with Satan.

And my imaginations are as foul
As Vulcan's stithy.° Give him heedful note;
For I mine eyes will rivet to his face,
And after we will both our judgements join
In censure of his seeming.°

HORATIO: Well, my lord:
If 'a steal aught the whilst this play is playing,
And 'scape detecting, I will pay the theft.

Enter trumpets and kettledrums, King, Queen, Polonius, Ophelia, [*Rosencrantz, Guildenstern, and others*].

HAMLET: They are coming to the play; I must be idle:° Get you a place.

KING: How fares our cousin Hamlet?

HAMLET: Excellent, i' faith; of the chameleon's dish:° I eat the air, promise-crammed: you cannot feed capons so.

KING: I have nothing with° this answer, Hamlet; these words are not mine.°

HAMLET: No, nor mine now. [*To Polonius.*] My lord, you played once i' the university, you say?

POLONIUS: That did I, my lord; and was accounted a good actor.

HAMLET: What did you enact?

POLONIUS: I did enact Julius Cæsar: I was killed i' the Capitol; Brutus killed me.

HAMLET: It was a brute part of him to kill so capital a calf there. Be the players ready?

ROSENCRANTZ: Ay, my lord; they stay upon your patience.

QUEEN: Come hither, my dear Hamlet, sit by me.

HAMLET: No, good mother, here's metal more attractive.

POLONIUS [*to the king*]: O, ho! do you mark that?

HAMLET: Lady, shall I lie in your lap? [*Lying down at Ophelia's feet.*]

OPHELIA: No, my lord.

HAMLET: I mean, my head upon your lap?

OPHELIA: Ay, my lord.

HAMLET: Do you think I meant country° matters?

OPHELIA: I think nothing, my lord.

HAMLET: That's a fair thought to lie between maids' legs.

OPHELIA: What is, my lord?

HAMLET: Nothing.

OPHELIA: You are merry, my lord.

HAMLET: Who, I?

OPHELIA: Ay, my lord.

---

71. stithy: Smithy, place of *stiths* (anvils). **74. censure . . . seeming:** Judgment of his appearance or behavior. **77. idle:** Crazy, or not attending to anything serious. **79. chameleon's dish:** Chameleons were supposed to feed on air. (Hamlet deliberately misinterprets the king's "fares" as "feeds.") **81. have . . . with:** Make nothing of; **are not mine:** Do not respond to what I ask. **98. country:** With a bawdy pun.

HAMLET: O God, your only° jig-maker.° What should a man do but be merry? for, look you, how cheerfully my mother looks, and my father died within's two hours.

OPHELIA: Nay, 'tis twice two months, my lord.

HAMLET: So long? Nay then, let the devil wear black, for I'll have a suit of sables.° O heavens! die two months ago, and not forgotten yet? Then there's hope a great man's memory may outlive his life half a year: but, by 'r lady, 'a must build churches, then; or else shall 'a suffer not thinking on,° with the hobbyhorse, whose epitaph is "For, O, for, O, the hobbyhorse is forgot."°

The trumpets sound. Dumb show follows.

Enter a King and a Queen [very lovingly]; the Queen embracing him, and he her. [She kneels, and makes show of protestation unto him.] He takes her up, and declines his head upon her neck: he lies him down upon a bank of flowers: she, seeing him asleep, leaves him. Anon comes in another man, takes off his crown, kisses it, pours poison in the sleeper's ears, and leaves him. The Queen returns; finds the King dead, makes passionate action. The Poisoner, with some three or four come in again, seem to condole with her. The dead body is carried away. The Poisoner woos the Queen with gifts: she seems harsh awhile, but in the end accepts love. [Exeunt.]

OPHELIA: What means this, my lord?

HAMLET: Marry, this is miching mallecho;° it means mischief.

OPHELIA: Belike this show imports the argument of the play.

Enter Prologue.

HAMLET: We shall know by this fellow: the players cannot keep counsel; they'll tell all.

OPHELIA: Will 'a tell us what this show meant?

HAMLET: Ay, or any show that you'll show him: be not you ashamed to show, he'll not shame to tell you what it means.

OPHELIA: You are naught, you are naught:° I'll mark the play.

PROLOGUE: For us, and for our tragedy,
Here stooping° to your clemency,
We beg your hearing patiently. *[Exit.]*

HAMLET: Is this a prologue, or the posy° of a ring?

OPHELIA: 'Tis brief, my lord.

HAMLET: As woman's love.

Enter [two Players as] King and Queen.

PLAYER KING: Full thirty times hath Phoebus' cart gone round
Neptune's salt wash° and Tellus'° orbed ground,

---

106. your only: Only your; **jig-maker:** Composer of jigs (song and dance). **110–111. suit of sables:** Garments trimmed with the fur of the sable, with a quibble on *sable* meaning "black." **113–114. suffer . . . on:** Undergo oblivion. **114–115. "For . . . forgot":** Verse of a song occurring also in *Love's Labour's Lost,* III.i.30. The hobbyhorse was a character in the Morris Dance. **117. miching mallecho:** Sneaking mischief. **124. naught:** Indecent. **126. stooping:** Bowing. **128. posy:** Motto. **132. salt wash:** The sea; **Tellus:** Goddess of the earth (*orbed ground*).

And thirty dozen moons with borrowed° sheen
About the world have times twelve thirties been,
Since love our hearts and Hymen° did our hands
Unite commutual° in most sacred bands.

PLAYER QUEEN: So many journeys may the sun and moon
Make us again count o'er ere love be done!
But, woe is me, you are so sick of late,
So far from cheer and from your former state,
That I distrust° you. Yet, though I distrust,
Discomfort you, my lord, it nothing must:
For women's fear and love holds quantity;°
In neither aught, or in extremity.
Now, what my love is, proof hath made you know;
And as my love is siz'd, my fear is so:
Where love is great, the littlest doubts are fear;
Where little fears grow great, great love grows there.

PLAYER KING: 'Faith, I must leave thee, love, and shortly too;
My operant° powers their functions leave° to do:
And thou shalt live in this fair world behind,
Honour'd, belov'd; and haply one as kind
For husband shalt thou —

PLAYER QUEEN: O, confound the rest!
Such love must needs be treason in my breast:
In second husband let me be accurst!
None wed the second but who kill'd the first.

HAMLET (*aside*): Wormwood, wormwood.

PLAYER QUEEN: The instances that second marriage move
Are base respects of thrift, but none of love:
A second time I kill my husband dead,
When second husband kisses me in bed.

PLAYER KING: I do believe you think what now you speak;
But what we do determine oft we break.
Purpose is but the slave to memory,
Of violent birth, but poor validity:
Which now, like fruit unripe, sticks on the tree;
But fall, unshaken, when they mellow be.
Most necessary 'tis that we forget
To pay ourselves what to ourselves is debt:
What to ourselves in passion we propose,
The passion ending, doth the purpose lose.
The violence of either grief or joy
Their own enactures° with themselves destroy:

---

133. borrowed: I.e., reflected. **135. Hymen:** God of matrimony. **136. commutual:** Mutually. **141. distrust:** Am anxious about. **143. holds quantity:** Keeps proportion between. **150. operant:** Active; **leave:** Cease. **173. enactures:** Fulfillments.

Where joy most revels, grief doth most lament;
Grief joys, joy grieves, on slender accident.
This world is not for aye,° nor 'tis not strange
That even our loves should with our fortunes change;
For 'tis a question left us yet to prove,
Whether love lead fortune, or else fortune love.
The great man down, you mark his favourite flies;
The poor advanc'd makes friends of enemies.
And hitherto doth love on fortune tend;
For who° not needs shall never lack a friend,
And who in want a hollow friend doth try,
Directly seasons° him his enemy.
But, orderly to end where I begun,
Our wills and fates do so contrary run
That our devices still are overthrown;
Our thoughts are ours, their ends° none of our own:
So think thou wilt no second husband wed;
But die thy thoughts when thy first lord is dead.

PLAYER QUEEN: Nor earth to me give food, nor heaven light!
Sport and repose lock from me day and night!
To desperation turn my trust and hope!
An anchor's° cheer° in prison be my scope!
Each opposite° that blanks° the face of joy
Meet what I would have well and it destroy!
Both here and hence pursue me lasting strife,
If, once a widow, ever I be wife!

HAMLET: If she should break it now!

PLAYER KING: 'Tis deeply sworn. Sweet, leave me here awhile;
My spirits grow dull, and fain I would beguile
The tedious day with sleep. *[Sleeps.]*

PLAYER QUEEN: Sleep rock thy brain;
And never come mischance between us twain! *Exit.*

HAMLET: Madam, how like you this play?

QUEEN: The lady doth protest too much, methinks.

HAMLET: O, but she'll keep her word.

KING: Have you heard the argument? Is there no offence in 't?

HAMLET: No, no, they do but jest, poison in jest; no offence i' the world.

KING: What do you call the play?

HAMLET: The Mouse-trap. Marry, how? Tropically.° This play is the image of a murder done in Vienna: Gonzago° is the duke's name; his wife, Baptista: you shall see anon; 't is a knavish piece of work: but what o' that? your

---

176. aye: Ever. **183. who:** Whoever. **185. seasons:** Matures, ripens. **189. ends:** Results. **195. An anchor's:** An anchorite's; **cheer:** Fare; sometimes printed as *chair.* **196. opposite:** Adverse thing; **blanks:** Causes to *blanch* or grow pale. **211. Tropically:** Figuratively, *trapically* suggests a pun on *trap* in *Mouse-trap* (line 211). **212. Gonzago:** In 1538 Luigi Gonzago murdered the Duke of Urbano by pouring poisoned lotion in his ears.

majesty and we that have free souls, it touches us not: let the galled jade° winch,° our withers° are unwrung.°

Enter Lucianus.

This is one Lucianus, nephew to the king.

OPHELIA: You are as good as a chorus,° my lord.

HAMLET: I could interpret between you and your love, if I could see the puppets dallying.°

OPHELIA: You are keen, my lord, you are keen.

HAMLET: It would cost you a groaning to take off my edge.

OPHELIA: Still better, and worse.°

HAMLET: So you mistake° your husbands. Begin, murderer; pox,° leave thy damnable faces, and begin. Come: the croaking raven doth bellow for revenge.

LUCIANUS: Thoughts black, hands apt, drugs fit, and time agreeing;
Confederate° season, else no creature seeing;
Thou mixture rank, of midnight weeds collected,
With Hecate's° ban° thrice blasted, thrice infected,
Thy natural magic and dire property,
On wholesome life usurp immediately.

[*Pours the poison into the sleeper's ears.*]

HAMLET: 'A poisons him i' the garden for his estate. His name's Gonzago: the story is extant, and written in very choice Italian: you shall see anon how the murderer gets the love of Gonzago's wife.

OPHELIA: The king rises.

HAMLET: What, frighted with false fire!°

QUEEN: How fares my lord?

POLONIUS: Give o'er the play.

KING: Give me some light: away!

POLONIUS: Lights, lights, lights! *Exeunt all but Hamlet and Horatio.*

HAMLET: Why, let the strucken deer go weep,
The hart ungalled play;
For some must watch, while some must sleep:
Thus runs the world away.°
Would not this,° sir, and a forest of feathers° — if the rest of my fortunes

---

214. galled jade: Horse whose hide is rubbed by saddle or harness. **215. winch:** Wince; **withers:** The part between the horse's shoulder blades; **unwrung:** Not wrung or twisted. **217. chorus:** In many Elizabethan plays the action was explained by an actor known as the "chorus"; at a puppet show the actor who explained the action was known as an "interpreter," as indicated by the lines following. **219. dallying:** With sexual suggestion, continued in *keen* (sexually aroused), *groaning* (i.e., in pregnancy), and *edge* (i.e., sexual desire or impetuosity). **222. Still . . . worse:** More keen, less decorous. **223. mistake:** Err in taking; **pox:** An imprecation. **227. Confederate:** Conspiring (to assist the murderer). **229. Hecate:** The goddess of witchcraft; **ban:** Curse. **236. false fire:** Fireworks, or a blank discharge. **241–244. Why . . . away:** Probably from an old ballad, with allusion to the popular belief that a wounded deer retires to weep and die. Cf. *As You Like It,* II.i.66. **245. this:** I.e., the play; **feathers:** Allusion to the plumes which Elizabethan actors were fond of wearing.

turn Turk with° me — with two Provincial roses° on my razed° shoes, get me a fellowship in a cry° of players,° sir?

HORATIO: Half a share.°

HAMLET: A whole one, I.

For thou dost know, O Damon dear,
  This realm dismantled° was
Of Jove himself; and now reigns here
  A very, very° — pajock.°

HORATIO: You might have rhymed.

HAMLET: O good Horatio, I'll take the ghost's word for a thousand pound. Didst perceive?

HORATIO: Very well, my lord.

HAMLET: Upon the talk of the poisoning?

HORATIO: I did very well note him.

HAMLET: Ah, ha! Come, some music! come, the recorders!°
For if the king like not the comedy,
Why then, belike, he likes it not, perdy.°
Come, some music!

Enter Rosencrantz and Guildenstern.

GUILDENSTERN: Good my lord, vouchsafe me a word with you.

HAMLET: Sir, a whole history.

GUILDENSTERN: The king, sir, —

HAMLET: Ay, sir, what of him?

GUILDENSTERN: Is in his retirement marvellous distempered.

HAMLET: With drink, sir?

GUILDENSTERN: No, my lord, rather with choler.°

HAMLET: Your wisdom should show itself more richer to signify this to his doctor; for, for me to put him to his purgation would perhaps plunge him into far more choler.

GUILDENSTERN: Good my lord, put your discourse into some frame° and start not so wildly from my affair.

HAMLET: I am tame, sir: pronounce.

GUILDENSTERN: The queen, your mother, in most great affliction of spirit, hath sent me to you.

HAMLET: You are welcome.

GUILDENSTERN: Nay, good my lord, this courtesy is not of the right breed. If it shall please you to make me a wholesome° answer, I will do your

---

246. turn Turk with: Go back on; **two Provincial roses:** Rosettes of ribbon like the roses of Provins near Paris, or else the roses of Provence; **razed:** Cut, slashed (by way of ornament). **247. cry:** Pack (as of hounds); **fellowship . . . players:** Partnership in a theatrical company. **248. Half a share:** Allusion to the custom in dramatic companies of dividing the ownership into a number of shares among the householders. **251. dismantled:** Stripped, divested. **250–253. For . . . very:** Probably from an old ballad having to do with Damon and Pythias. **253. pajock:** Peacock (a bird with a bad reputation). Possibly the word was *patchock,* diminutive of *patch,* clown. **260. recorders:** Wind instruments of the flute kind. **262. perdy:** Corruption of *par dieu.* **270. choler:** Bilious disorder, with quibble on the sense "anger." **274. frame:** Order. **281. wholesome:** Sensible.

mother's commandment; if not, your pardon and my return shall be the end of my business.

HAMLET: Sir, I cannot.

GUILDENSTERN: What, my lord?

HAMLET: Make you a wholesome answer; my wit's diseased: but, sir, such answer as I can make, you shall command; or, rather, as you say, my mother: therefore no more, but to the matter:° my mother, you say, —

ROSENCRANTZ: Then thus she says; your behaviour hath struck her into amazement and admiration.

HAMLET: O wonderful son, that can so 'stonish a mother! But is there no sequel at the heels of this mother's admiration? Impart.

ROSENCRANTZ: She desires to speak with you in her closet, ere you go to bed.

HAMLET: We shall obey, were she ten times our mother. Have you any further trade with us?

ROSENCRANTZ: My lord, you once did love me.

HAMLET: And do still, by these pickers and stealers.°

ROSENCRANTZ: Good my lord, what is your cause of distemper? you do, surely, bar the door upon your own liberty, if you deny your griefs to your friend.

HAMLET: Sir, I lack advancement.

ROSENCRANTZ: How can that be, when you have the voice° of the king himself for your succession in Denmark?

HAMLET: Ay, sir, but "While the grass grows,"° — the proverb is something musty.

Enter the Players with recorders.

O, the recorders! let me see one. To withdraw° with you: — why do you go about to recover the wind° of me, as if you would drive me into a toil?°

GUILDENSTERN: O, my lord, if my duty be too bold, my love is too unmannerly.°

HAMLET: I do not well understand that. Will you play upon this pipe?

GUILDENSTERN: My lord, I cannot.

HAMLET: I pray you.

GUILDENSTERN: Believe me, I cannot.

HAMLET: I beseech you.

GUILDENSTERN: I know no touch of it, my lord.

HAMLET: 'Tis as easy as lying: govern these ventages° with your fingers and thumb, give it breath with your mouth, and it will discourse most eloquent music. Look you, these are the stops.

---

288. matter: Matter in hand. **297. pickers and stealers:** Hands, so called from the catechism "to keep my hands from picking and stealing." **302. voice:** Support. **304. "While . . . grows":** The rest of the proverb is "the silly horse starves." Hamlet may be destroyed while he is waiting for the succession to the kingdom. **306. withdraw:** Speak in private. **307. recover the wind:** Get to the windward side. **308. toil:** Snare. **309–310. if . . . unmannerly:** If I am using an unmannerly boldness, it is my love which occasions it. **317. ventages:** Stops of the recorders.

GUILDENSTERN: But these cannot I command to any utterance of harmony; I have not the skill.

HAMLET: Why, look you now, how unworthy a thing you make of me! You would play upon me; you would seem to know my stops; you would pluck out the heart of my mystery; you would sound me from my lowest note to the top of my compass:° and there is much music, excellent voice, in this little organ;° yet cannot you make it speak. 'Sblood, do you think I am easier to be played on than a pipe? Call me what instrument you will, though you can fret° me, you cannot play upon me.

Enter Polonius.

God bless you, sir!

POLONIUS: My lord, the queen would speak with you, and presently.

HAMLET: Do you see yonder cloud that 's almost in shape of a camel?

POLONIUS: By the mass, and 'tis like a camel, indeed.

HAMLET: Methinks it is like a weasel.

POLONIUS: It is backed like a weasel.

HAMLET: Or like a whale?

POLONIUS: Very like a whale.

HAMLET: Then I will come to my mother by and by. [*Aside.*] They fool me to the top of my bent.° — I will come by and by.°

POLONIUS: I will say so. [*Exit.*]

HAMLET: By and by is easily said.
Leave me, friends. [*Exeunt all but Hamlet.*]
'Tis now the very witching time° of night,
When churchyards yawn and hell itself breathes out
Contagion to this world: now could I drink hot blood,
And do such bitter business as the day
Would quake to look on. Soft! now to my mother.
O heart, lose not thy nature; let not ever
The soul of Nero° enter this firm bosom:
Let me be cruel, not unnatural:
I will speak daggers to her, but use none;
My tongue and soul in this be hypocrites;
How in my words somever she be shent,°
To give them seals° never, my soul, consent! *Exit.*

[SCENE III: *A room in the castle.*]

Enter King, Rosencrantz, and Guildenstern.

KING: I like him not, nor stands it safe with us
To let his madness range. Therefore prepare you;

---

325. compass: Range of voice. **326. organ:** Musical instrument, i.e., the pipe. **328. fret:** Quibble on meaning "irritate" and the piece of wood, gut, or metal which regulates the fingering. **338. top of my bent:** Limit of endurance, i.e., extent to which a bow may be bent; **by and by:** Immediately. **342. witching time:** I.e., time when spells are cast. **348. Nero:** Murderer of his mother, Agrippina. **352. shent:** Rebuked. **353. give them seals:** Confirm with deeds.

I your commission will forthwith dispatch,°
And he to England shall along with you:
The terms° of our estate° may not endure
Hazard so near us as doth hourly grow
Out of his brows.°

GUILDENSTERN: We will ourselves provide:
Most holy and religious fear it is
To keep those many many bodies safe
That live and feed upon your majesty.

ROSENCRANTZ: The single and peculiar° life is bound,
With all the strength and armour of the mind,
To keep itself from noyance;° but much more
That spirit upon whose weal depend and rest
The lives of many. The cess° of majesty
Dies not alone; but, like a gulf,° doth draw
What's near it with it: it is a massy wheel,
Fix'd on the summit of the highest mount,
To whose huge spokes ten thousand lesser things
Are mortis'd and adjoin'd; which, when it falls,
Each small annexment, petty consequence,
Attends° the boist'rous ruin. Never alone
Did the king sigh, but with a general groan.

KING: Arm° you, I pray you, to this speedy voyage;
For we will fetters put about this fear,
Which now goes too free-footed.

ROSENCRANTZ: We will haste us.

Exeunt Gentlemen [*Rosencrantz and Guildenstern*].

Enter Polonius.

POLONIUS: My lord, he's going to his mother's closet:
Behind the arras° I'll convey° myself,
To hear the process;° I'll warrant she'll tax him home:°
And, as you said, and wisely was it said,
'Tis meet that some more audience than a mother,
Since nature makes them partial, should o'erhear
The speech, of vantage.° Fare you well, my liege:
I'll call upon you ere you go to bed,
And tell you what I know.

KING: Thanks, dear my lord. *Exit* [*Polonius*].
O, my offence is rank, it smells to heaven;

SCENE III. **3. dispatch:** Prepare. **5. terms:** Condition, circumstances; **estate:** State. **7. brows:** Effronteries. **11. single and peculiar:** Individual and private. **13. noyance:** Harm. **15. cess:** Decease. **16. gulf:** Whirlpool. **22. Attends:** Participates in. **24. Arm:** Prepare. **28. arras:** Screen of tapestry placed around the walls of household apartments; **convey:** Implication of secrecy, *convey* was often used to mean "steal." **29. process:** Proceedings; **tax him home:** Reprove him severely. **33. of vantage:** From an advantageous place.

It hath the primal eldest curse° upon't,
A brother's murder. Pray can I not,
Though inclination be as sharp as will:°
My stronger guilt defeats my strong intent;
And, like a man to double business bound,
I stand in pause where I shall first begin,
And both neglect. What if this cursed hand
Were thicker than itself with brother's blood,
Is there not rain enough in the sweet heavens
To wash it white as snow? Whereto serves mercy
But to confront° the visage of offence?
And what's in prayer but this two-fold force,
To be forestalled° ere we come to fall,
Or pardon'd being down? Then I'll look up;
My fault is past. But, O, what form of prayer
Can serve my turn? "Forgive me my foul murder"?
That cannot be: since I am still possess'd
Of those effects for which I did the murder,
My crown, mine own ambition° and my queen.
May one be pardon'd and retain th' offence?°
In the corrupted currents° of this world
Offence's gilded hand° may shove by justice,
And oft 'tis seen the wicked prize° itself
Buys out the law: but 'tis not so above;
There is no shuffling,° there the action lies°
In his true nature; and we ourselves compell'd,
Even to the teeth and forehead° of our faults,
To give in evidence. What then? what rests?°
Try what repentance can: what can it not?
Yet what can it when one can not repent?
O wretched state! O bosom black as death!
O limed° soul, that, struggling to be free,
Art more engag'd!° Help, angels! Make assay!°
Bow, stubborn knees; and, heart with strings of steel,
Be soft as sinews of the new-born babe!
All may be well. [*He kneels.*]

Enter Hamlet.

HAMLET: Now might I do it pat,° now he is praying;
And now I'll do't. And so 'a goes to heaven;

---

37. primal eldest curse: The curse of Cain, the first to kill his brother. **39. sharp as will:** I.e., his desire is as strong as his determination. **47. confront:** Oppose directly. **49. forestalled:** Prevented. **55. ambition:** I.e., realization of ambition. **56. offence:** Benefit accruing from offense. **57. currents:** Courses. **58. gilded hand:** Hand offering gold as a bribe. **59. wicked prize:** Prize won by wickedness. **61. shuffling:** Escape by trickery; **lies:** Is sustainable. **63. teeth and forehead:** Very face. **64. rests:** Remains. **68. limed:** Caught as with birdlime. **69. engag'd:** Embedded; **assay:** Trial. **73. pat:** Opportunely.

And so am I reveng'd. That would be scann'd:°
A villain kills my father; and for that,
I, his sole son, do this same villain send
To heaven.
Why, this is hire and salary, not revenge.
'A took my father grossly, full of bread;°
With all his crimes broad blown,° as flush° as May;
And how his audit stands who knows save heaven?
But in our circumstance and course° of thought,
'Tis heavy with him: and am I then reveng'd,
To take him in the purging of his soul,
When he is fit and season'd for his passage?°
No!
Up, sword; and know thou a more horrid hent:°
When he is drunk asleep,° or in his rage,
Or in th' incestuous pleasure of his bed;
At game, a-swearing, or about some act
That has no relish of salvation in't;
Then trip him, that his heels may kick at heaven,
And that his soul may be as damn'd and black
As hell, whereto it goes. My mother stays:
This physic° but prolongs thy sickly days. *Exit.*

KING: [*Rising*] My words fly up, my thoughts remain below:
Words without thoughts never to heaven go. *Exit.*

[SCENE IV: *The Queen's closet.*]

Enter [*Queen*] *Gertrude and Polonius.*

POLONIUS: 'A will come straight. Look you lay° home to him:
Tell him his pranks have been too broad° to bear with,
And that your grace hath screen'd and stood between
Much heat° and him. I'll sconce° me even here.
Pray you, be round° with him.

HAMLET (*within*): Mother, mother, mother!

QUEEN: I'll warrant you,
Fear me not: withdraw, I hear him coming.
[*Polonius hides behind the arras.*]

Enter Hamlet.

HAMLET: Now, mother, what's the matter?

QUEEN: Hamlet, thou hast thy father much offended.

HAMLET: Mother, you have my father° much offended.

---

75. would be scann'd: Needs to be looked into. **80. full of bread:** Enjoying his worldly pleasures (see Ezekiel 16:49). **81. broad blown:** In full bloom; **flush:** Lusty. **83. in . . . course:** As we see it in our mortal situation. **86. fit . . . passage:** I.e., reconciled to heaven by forgiveness of his sins. **88. hent:** Seizing; or more probably, occasion of seizure. **89. drunk asleep:** In a drunken sleep. **96. physic:** Purging (by prayer). SCENE IV. **1. lay:** Thrust. **2. broad:** Unrestrained. **4. Much heat:** I.e., the king's anger; **sconce:** Hide. **5. round:** Blunt. **9–10. thy father, my father:** I.e., Claudius, the elder Hamlet.

QUEEN: Come, come, you answer with an idle tongue.
HAMLET: Go, go, you question with a wicked tongue.
QUEEN: Why, how now, Hamlet!
HAMLET: What's the matter now?
QUEEN: Have you forgot me?
HAMLET: No, by the rood,° not so:
You are the queen, your husband's brother's wife;
And — would it were not so! — you are my mother.
QUEEN: Nay, then, I'll set those to you that can speak.
HAMLET: Come, come, and sit you down; you shall not budge;
You go not till I set you up a glass
Where you may see the inmost part of you.
QUEEN: What wilt thou do? thou wilt not murder me?
Help, help, ho!
POLONIUS [*behind*]: What, ho! help, help; help!
HAMLET [*drawing*]: How now! a rat? Dead, for a ducat, dead!
[*Makes a pass through the arras.*]
POLONIUS [*behind*]: O, I am slain! [*Falls and dies.*]
QUEEN: O me, what hast thou done?
HAMLET: Nay, I know not:
Is it the king?
QUEEN: O, what a rash and bloody deed is this!
HAMLET: A bloody deed! almost as bad, good mother,
As kill a king, and marry with his brother.
QUEEN: As kill a king!
HAMLET: Ay, lady, it was my word.
[*Lifts up the arras and discovers Polonius.*]
Thou wretched, rash, intruding fool, farewell!
I took thee for thy better: take thy fortune;
Thou find'st to be too busy is some danger.
Leave wringing of your hands: peace! sit you down,
And let me wring your heart; for so I shall,
If it be made of penetrable stuff,
If damned custom have not braz'd° it so
That it be proof and bulwark against sense.
QUEEN: What have I done, that thou dar'st wag thy tongue
In noise so rude against me?
HAMLET: Such an act
That blurs the grace and blush of modesty,
Calls virtue hypocrite, takes off the rose
From the fair forehead of an innocent love
And sets a blister° there, makes marriage-vows
As false as dicers' oaths: O, such a deed
As from the body of contraction° plucks

14. rood: Cross. **38. braz'd:** Brazened, hardened. **45. sets a blister:** Brands as a harlot. **47. contraction:** The marriage contract.

The very soul, and sweet religion° makes
A rhapsody° of words: heaven's face does glow
O'er this solidity and compound mass
With heated visage, as against the doom
Is thought-sick at the act.°

QUEEN: Ay me, what act,
That roars so loud, and thunders in the index?°

HAMLET: Look here, upon this picture, and on this.
The counterfeit presentment° of two brothers.
See, what grace was seated on this brow;
Hyperion's° curls; the front° of Jove himself;
An eye like Mars, to threaten and command;
A station° like the herald Mercury
New-lighted on a heaven-kissing hill;
A combination and a form indeed,
Where every god did seem to set his seal,
To give the world assurance° of a man:
This was your husband. Look you now, what follows:
Here is your husband; like a mildew'd ear,°
Blasting his wholesome brother. Have you eyes?
Could you on this fair mountain leave to feed,
And batten° on this moor?° Ha! have you eyes?
You cannot call it love; for at your age
The hey-day° in the blood is tame, it's humble,
And waits upon the judgement: and what judgement
Would step from this to this? Sense, sure, you have,
Else could you not have motion;° but sure, that sense
Is apoplex'd;° for madness would not err,
Nor sense to ecstasy was ne'er so thrall'd°
But it reserv'd some quantity of choice,°
To serve in such a difference. What devil was't
That thus hath cozen'd° you at hoodman-blind?°
Eyes without feeling, feeling without sight,
Ears without hands or eyes, smelling sans° all,
Or but a sickly part of one true sense

---

48. religion: Religious vows. **49. rhapsody:** Senseless string. **49–52. heaven's . . . act:** Heaven's face blushes to look down upon this world, compounded of the four elements, with hot face as though the day of doom were near, and thought-sick at the deed (i.e., Gertrude's marriage). **53. index:** Prelude or preface. **55. counterfeit presentment:** Portrayed representation. **57. Hyperion's:** The sun god's; **front:** Brow. **59. station:** Manner of standing. **63. assurance:** Pledge, guarantee. **65. mildew'd ear:** See Genesis 41:5–7. **68. batten:** Grow fat; **moor:** Barren upland. **70. hey-day:** State of excitement. **72–73. Sense . . . motion:** Sense and motion are functions of the middle or sensible soul, the possession of sense being the basis of motion. **74. apoplex'd:** Paralyzed. Mental derangement was thus of three sorts: apoplexy, ectasy, and diabolic possession. **75. thrall'd:** Enslaved. **76. quantity of choice:** Fragment of the power to choose. **78. cozen'd:** Tricked, cheated; **hoodman-blind:** Blindman's buff. **80. sans:** Without.

Could not so mope.°
O shame! where is thy blush? Rebellious hell,
If thou canst mutine° in a matron's bones,
To flaming youth let virtue be as wax,
And melt in her own fire: proclaim no shame
When the compulsive ardour gives the charge,°
Since frost itself as actively doth burn
And reason pandars will.°

QUEEN: O Hamlet, speak no more:
Thou turn'st mine eyes into my very soul;
And there I see such black and grained° spots
As will not leave their tinct.

HAMLET: Nay, but to live
In the rank sweat of an enseamed° bed,
Stew'd in corruption, honeying and making love
Over the nasty sty, —

QUEEN: O, speak to me no more;
These words, like daggers, enter in mine ears;
No more, sweet Hamlet!

HAMLET: A murderer and a villain;
A slave that is not twentieth part the tithe
Of your precedent lord;° a vice of kings;°
A cutpurse of the empire and the rule,
That from a shelf the precious diadem stole,
And put it in his pocket!

QUEEN: No more!

Enter Ghost.

HAMLET: A king of shreds and patches,° —
Save me, and hover o'er me with your wings,
You heavenly guards! What would your gracious figure?

QUEEN: Alas, he's mad!

HAMLET: Do you not come your tardy son to chide,
That, laps'd in time and passion,° lets go by
Th' important° acting of your dread command?
O, say!

GHOST: Do not forget: this visitation
Is but to whet thy almost blunted purpose.

---

82. mope: Be in a depressed, spiritless state, act aimlessly. **84. mutine:** Mutiny, rebel. **87. gives the charge:** Delivers the attack. **89. reason pandars will:** The normal and proper situation was one in which reason guided the will in the direction of good; here, reason is perverted and leads in the direction of evil. **91. grained:** Dyed in grain. **93. enseamed:** Loaded with grease, greased. **99. precedent lord:** I.e., the elder Hamlet; **vice of kings:** Buffoon of kings; a reference to the Vice, or clown, of the morality plays and interludes. **103. shreds and patches:** I.e., motley, the traditional costume of the Vice. **108. laps'd . . . passion:** Having suffered time to slip and passion to cool; also explained as "engrossed in casual events and lapsed into mere fruitless passion, so that he no longer entertains a rational purpose." **109. important:** Urgent.

But, look, amazement° on thy mother sits:
O, step between her and her fighting soul:
Conceit in weakest bodies strongest works:
Speak to her, Hamlet.

HAMLET: How is it with you, lady?

QUEEN: Alas, how is 't with you,
That you do bend your eye on vacancy
And with th' incorporal° air do hold discourse?
Forth at your eyes your spirits wildly peep;
And, as the sleeping soldiers in th' alarm,
Your bedded° hair, like life in excrements,°
Start up, and stand an° end. O gentle son,
Upon the heat and flame of thy distemper
Sprinkle cool patience. Whereon do you look?

HAMLET: On him, on him! Look you, how pale he glares!
His form and cause conjoin'd,° preaching to stones,
Would make them capable. — Do not look upon me;
Lest with this piteous action you convert
My stern effects:° then what I have to do
Will want true colour;° tears perchance for blood.

QUEEN: To whom do you speak this?

HAMLET: Do you see nothing there?

QUEEN: Nothing at all; yet all that is I see.

HAMLET: Nor did you nothing hear?

QUEEN: No, nothing but ourselves.

HAMLET: Why, look you there! look, how it steals away!
My father, in his habit as he liv'd!
Look, where he goes, even now, out at the portal! *Exit Ghost.*

QUEEN: This is the very coinage of your brain:
This bodiless creation ecstasy
Is very cunning in.

HAMLET: Ecstasy!
My pulse, as yours, doth temperately keep time,
And makes as healthful music: it is not madness
That I have utt'red: bring me to the test,
And I the matter will re-word,° which madness
Would gambol° from. Mother, for love of grace,
Lay not that flattering unction° to your soul,
That not your trespass, but my madness speaks:

---

113. amazement: Frenzy, distraction. **119. incorporal:** Immaterial. **122. bedded:** Laid in smooth layers; **excrements:** The hair was considered an excrement or voided part of the body. **123. an:** On. **127. conjoin'd:** United. **129–130. convert . . . effects:** Divert me from my stern duty. For *effects,* possibly *affects* (affections of the mind). **131. want true colour:** Lack good reason so that (with a play on the normal sense of *colour*) I shall shed tears instead of blood. **144. re-word:** Repeat in words. **145. gambol:** Skip away. **146. unction:** Ointment used medicinally or as a rite; suggestion that forgiveness for sin may not be so easily achieved.

It will but skin and film the ulcerous place,
Whiles rank corruption, mining° all within,
Infects unseen. Confess yourself to heaven;
Repent what's past; avoid what is to come;°
And do not spread the compost° on the weeds,
To make them ranker. Forgive me this my virtue;°
For in the fatness° of these pursy° times
Virtue itself of vice must pardon beg,
Yea, curb° and woo for leave to do him good.

QUEEN: O Hamlet, thou hast cleft my heart in twain.

HAMLET: O, throw away the worser part of it,
And live the purer with the other half.
Good night: but go not to my uncle's bed;
Assume a virtue, if you have it not.
That monster, custom, who all sense doth eat,
Of habits devil, is angel yet in this,
That to the use of actions fair and good
He likewise gives a frock or livery,
That aptly is put on. Refrain to-night,
And that shall lend a kind of easiness
To the next abstinence: the next more easy;
For use almost can change the stamp of nature,
And either . . . the devil, or throw him out°
With wondrous potency. Once more, good night:
And when you are desirous to be bless'd,°
I'll blessing beg of you. For this same lord, [*Pointing to Polonius.*]
I do repent: but heaven hath pleas'd it so,
To punish me with this and this with me,
That I must be their scourge and minister.
I will bestow him, and will answer well
The death I gave him. So, again, good night.
I must be cruel, only to be kind:
Thus bad begins and worse remains behind.
One word more, good lady.

QUEEN: What shall I do?

HAMLET: Not this, by no means, that I bid you do:
Let the bloat° king tempt you again to bed;
Pinch wanton on your cheek; call you his mouse;
And let him, for a pair of reechy° kisses,
Or paddling in your neck with his damn'd fingers,
Make you to ravel all this matter out,

---

149. mining: Working under the surface. **151. what is to come:** I.e., the sins of the future. **152. compost:** Manure. **153. this my virtue:** My virtuous talk in reproving you. **154. fatness:** Grossness; **pursy:** Short-winded, corpulent. **156. curb:** Bow, bend the knee. **170.** Defective line usually emended by inserting *master* after *either.* **172. be bless'd:** Become blessed, i.e., repentant. **183. bloat:** Bloated. **185. reechy:** Dirty, filthy.

That I essentially° am not in madness,
But mad in craft. 'Twere good you let him know;
For who, that's but a queen, fair, sober, wise,
Would from a paddock,° from a bat, a gib,°
Such dear concernings° hide? who would do so?
No, in despite of sense and secrecy,
Unpeg the basket on the house's top,
Let the birds fly, and, like the famous ape.°
To try conclusions,° in the basket creep,
And break your own neck down.

QUEEN: Be thou assur'd, if words be made of breath,
And breath of life, I have no life to breathe
What thou hast said to me.

HAMLET: I must to England; you know that?

QUEEN: Alack,
I had forgot: 'tis so concluded on.

HAMLET: There's letters seal'd: and my two schoolfellows,
Whom I will trust as I will adders fang'd,
They bear the mandate; they must sweep my way,°
And marshal me to knavery. Let it work;
For 'tis the sport to have the enginer°
Hoist° with his own petar:° and 't shall go hard
But I will delve one yard below their mines,
And blow them at the moon: O, 'tis most sweet,
When in one line two crafts° directly meet.
This man shall set me packing:°
I'll lug the guts into the neighbour room.
Mother, good night. Indeed this counsellor
Is now most still, most secret and most grave,
Who was in life a foolish prating knave.
Come, sir, to draw° toward an end with you.
Good night, mother. *Exeunt* [*severally; Hamlet dragging in Polonius.*]

[ACT IV

SCENE I: *A room in the castle.*]

Enter King and Queen, with Rosencrantz and Guildenstern.

KING: There's matter in these sighs, these profound heaves:

---

188. essentially: In my essential nature. **191. paddock:** Toad; **gib:** Tomcat. **192. dear concernings:** Important affairs. **195. the famous ape:** A letter from Sir John Suckling seems to supply other details of the story, otherwise not identified: "It is the story of the jackanapes and the partridges; thou starest after a beauty till it be lost to thee, then let'st out another, and starest after that till it is gone too." **196. conclusions:** Experiments. **205. sweep my way:** Clear my path. **207. enginer:** Constructor of military works, or possibly, artilleryman. **208. Hoist:** Blown up; **petar:** Defined as a small engine of war used to blow in a door or make a breach, and as a case filled with explosive materials. **211. two crafts:** Two acts of guile, with quibble on the sense of "two ships." **212. set me packing:** Set me to making schemes, and set me to lugging (him), and, also, send me off in a hurry. **217. draw:** Come, with quibble on literal sense.

You must translate: 'tis fit we understand them.
Where is your son?
QUEEN: Bestow this place on us a little while.
[*Exeunt Rosencrantz and Guildenstern.*]
Ah, mine own lord, what have I seen to-night!
KING: What, Gertrude? How does Hamlet?
QUEEN: Mad as the sea and wind, when both contend
Which is the mightier: in his lawless fit,
Behind the arras hearing something stir,
Whips out his rapier, cries, "A rat, a rat!"
And, in this brainish° apprehension,° kills
The unseen good old man.
KING: O heavy deed!
It had been so with us, had we been there:
His liberty is full of threats to all;
To you yourself, to us, to every one.
Alas, how shall this bloody deed be answer'd?
It will be laid to us, whose providence°
Should have kept short,° restrain'd and out of haunt,°
This mad young man: but so much was our love,
We would not understand what was most fit;
But, like the owner of a foul disease,
To keep it from divulging,° let it feed
Even on the pith of life. Where is he gone?
QUEEN: To draw apart the body he hath kill'd:
O'er whom his very madness, like some ore
Among a mineral° of metals base,
Shows itself pure; 'a weeps for what is done.
KING: O Gertrude, come away!
The sun no sooner shall the mountains touch,
But we will ship him hence: and this vile deed
We must, with all our majesty and skill,
Both countenance and excuse. Ho, Guildenstern!

Enter Rosencrantz and Guildenstern.

Friends both, go join you with some further aid:
Hamlet in madness hath Polonius slain,
And from his mother's closet hath he dragg'd him:
Go seek him out; speak fair, and bring the body
Into the chapel. I pray you, haste in this.
[*Exeunt Rosencrantz and Guildenstern.*]
Come, Gertrude, we'll call up our wisest friends;
And let them know, both what we mean to do,

ACT IV, SCENE I. **11. brainish:** Headstrong, passionate; **apprehension:** Conception, imagination. **17. providence:** Foresight. **18. short:** I.e., on a short tether; **out of haunt:** Secluded. **22. divulging:** Becoming evident. **26. mineral:** Mine.

And what's untimely done . . .°
Whose whisper o'er the world's diameter,°
As level° as the cannon to his blank,°
Transports his pois'ned shot, may miss our name,
And hit the woundless° air. O, come away!
My soul is full of discord and dismay. *Exeunt.*

[SCENE II: *Another room in the castle.*]

Enter Hamlet.

HAMLET: Safely stowed.

ROSENCRANTZ: / GUILDENSTERN: (*within*) Hamlet! Lord Hamlet!

HAMLET: But soft, what noise? who calls on Hamlet? O, here they come.

Enter Rosencrantz and Guildenstern.

ROSENCRANTZ: What have you done, my lord, with the dead body?

HAMLET: Compounded it with dust, whereto 'tis kin.

ROSENCRANTZ: Tell us where 'tis, that we may take it thence
And bear it to the chapel.

HAMLET: Do not believe it.

ROSENCRANTZ: Believe what?

HAMLET: That I can keep your counsel° and not mine own. Besides, to be demanded of a sponge! what replication° should be made by the son of a king?

ROSENCRANTZ: Take you me for a sponge, my lord?

HAMLET: Ay, sir, that soaks up the king's countenance, his rewards, his authorities.° But such officers do the king best service in the end: he keeps them, like an ape an apple, in the corner of his jaw; first mouthed, to be last swallowed: when he needs what you have gleaned, it is but squeezing you, and, sponge, you shall be dry again.

ROSENCRANTZ: I understand you not, my lord.

HAMLET: I am glad of it: a knavish speech sleeps in a foolish ear.

ROSENCRANTZ: My lord, you must tell us where the body is, and go with us to the king.

HAMLET: The body is with the king, but the king is not with the body.° The king is a thing —

GUILDENSTERN: A thing, my lord!

HAMLET: Of nothing: bring me to him. Hide fox, and all after.° *Exeunt.*

---

40. Defective line; some editors add: *so, haply, slander;* others add: *for, haply, slander;* other conjectures. **41. diameter:** Extent from side to side. **42. level:** Straight; **blank:** White spot in the center of a target. **44. woundless:** Invulnerable. SCENE II. **9. keep your counsel:** Hamlet is aware of their treachery but says nothing about it. **10. replication:** Reply. **14. authorities:** Authoritative backing. **22. The body . . . body:** There are many interpretations; possibly, "The body lies in death with the king, my father; but my father walks disembodied"; or "Claudius has the bodily possession of kingship, but kingliness, or justice of inheritance, is not with him." **25. Hide . . . after:** An old signal cry in the game of hide-and-seek.

[SCENE III: *Another room in the castle.*]

Enter King, and two or three.

KING: I have sent to seek him, and to find the body.
How dangerous is it that this man goes loose!
Yet must not we put the strong law on him:
He's lov'd of the distracted° multitude,
Who like not in their judgement, but their eyes;
And where 'tis so, th' offender's scourge° is weigh'd,°
But never the offence. To bear all smooth and even,
This sudden sending him away must seem
Deliberate pause:° diseases desperate grown
By desperate appliance are reliev'd,
Or not at all.

Enter Rosencrantz, [Guildenstern,] and all the rest.

How now! what hath befall'n?

ROSENCRANTZ: Where the dead body is bestow'd, my lord,
We cannot get from him.

KING: But where is he?

ROSENCRANTZ: Without, my lord; guarded, to know your pleasure.

KING: Bring him before us.

ROSENCRANTZ: Ho! bring in the lord.

They enter [with Hamlet].

KING: Now, Hamlet, where's Polonius?

HAMLET: At supper.

KING: At supper! where?

HAMLET: Not where he eats, but where 'a is eaten: a certain convocation of politic° worms° are e'en at him. Your worm is your only emperor for diet: we fat all creatures else to fat us, and we fat ourselves for maggots: your fat king and your lean beggar is but variable service,° two dishes, but to one table: that's the end.

KING: Alas, alas!

HAMLET: A man may fish with the worm that hath eat of a king, and eat of the fish that hath fed of that worm.

KING: What dost thou mean by this?

HAMLET: Nothing but to show you how a king may go a progress° through the guts of a beggar.

KING: Where is Polonius?

HAMLET: In heaven; send thither to see: if your messenger find him not there, seek him i' the other place yourself. But if indeed you find him not within this month, you shall nose him as you go up the stairs into the lobby.

SCENE III. **4. distracted:** I.e., without power of forming logical judgments. **6. scourge:** Punishment; **weigh'd:** Taken into consideration. **9. Deliberate pause:** Considered action. **20–21. convocation . . . worms:** Allusion to the Diet of Worms (1521); **politic:** Crafty. **23. variable service:** A variety of dishes. **29. progress:** Royal journey of state.

KING [*to some Attendants*]: Go seek him there.
HAMLET: 'A will stay till you come. [*Exeunt Attendants.*]
KING: Hamlet, this deed, for thine especial safety, —
Which we do tender,° as we dearly grieve
For that which thou hast done, — must send thee hence
With fiery quickness: therefore prepare thyself;
The bark is ready, and the wind at help,
Th' associates tend, and everything is bent
For England.
HAMLET: For England!
KING: Ay, Hamlet.
HAMLET: Good.
KING: So is it, if thou knew'st our purposes.
HAMLET: I see a cherub° that sees them. But, come; for England! Farewell, dear mother.
KING: Thy loving father, Hamlet.
HAMLET: My mother: father and mother is man and wife; man and wife is one flesh; and so, my mother. Come, for England! *Exit.*
KING: Follow him at foot;° tempt him with speed aboard;
Delay it not; I'll have him hence to-night:
Away! for every thing is seal'd and done
That else leans on th' affair: pray you, make haste.
[*Exeunt all but the King.*]
And, England, if my love thou hold'st at aught —
As my great power thereof may give thee sense,
Since yet thy cicatrice° looks raw and red
After the Danish sword, and thy free awe°
Pays homage to us — thou mayst not coldly set
Our sovereign process; which imports at full,
By letters congruing to that effect,
The present death of Hamlet. Do it, England;
For like the hectic° in my blood he rages,
And thou must cure me: till I know 'tis done,
Howe'er my haps,° my joys were ne'er begun. *Exit.*

[SCENE IV: *A plain in Denmark.*]

Enter Fortinbras with his Army over the stage.

FORTINBRAS: Go, captain, from me greet the Danish king;
Tell him that, by his license,° Fortinbras
Craves the conveyance° of a promis'd march
Over his kingdom. You know the rendezvous.
If that his majesty would aught with us,

39. tender: Regard, hold dear. **46. cherub:** Cherubim are angels of knowledge. **51. at foot:** Close behind, at heel. **57. cicatrice:** Scar. **58. free awe:** Voluntary show of respect. **63. hectic:** Fever. **65. haps:** Fortunes. SCENE IV. **2. license:** Leave. **3. conveyance:** Escort, convoy.

We shall express our duty in his eye;°
And let him know so.
CAPTAIN: I will do't, my lord.
FORTINBRAS: Go softly° on. [*Exeunt all but Captain.*]

Enter Hamlet, Rosencrantz, [Guildenstern,] &c.

HAMLET: Good sir, whose powers are these?
CAPTAIN: They are of Norway, sir.
HAMLET: How purpos'd, sir, I pray you?
CAPTAIN: Against some part of Poland.
HAMLET: Who commands them, sir?
CAPTAIN: The nephew to old Norway, Fortinbras.
HAMLET: Goes it against the main° of Poland, sir,
Or for some frontier?
CAPTAIN: Truly to speak, and with no addition,
We go to gain a little patch of ground
That hath in it no profit but the name.
To pay five ducats, five, I would not farm it;°
Nor will it yield to Norway or the Pole
A ranker rate, should it be sold in fee.°
HAMLET: Why, then the Polack never will defend it.
CAPTAIN: Yes, it is already garrison'd.
HAMLET: Two thousand souls and twenty thousand ducats
Will not debate the question of this straw:°
This is th' imposthume° of much wealth and peace,
That inward breaks, and shows no cause without
Why the man dies. I humbly thank you, sir.
CAPTAIN: God be wi' you, sir. [*Exit.*]
ROSENCRANTZ: Will 't please you go, my lord?
HAMLET: I'll be with you straight. Go a little before. [*Exeunt all except Hamlet.*]
How all occasions° do inform against° me,
And spur my dull revenge! What is a man,
If his chief good and market of his time°
Be but to sleep and feed? a beast, no more.
Sure, he that made us with such large discourse,
Looking before and after, gave us not
That capability and god-like reason
To fust° in us unus'd. Now, whether it be
Bestial oblivion, or some craven scruple
Of thinking too precisely on th' event,
A thought which, quarter'd, hath but one part wisdom

---

6. in his eye: In his presence. **8. softly:** Slowly. **15. main:** Country itself. **20. farm it:** Take a lease of it. **22. fee:** Fee simple. **26. debate . . . straw:** Settle this trifling matter. **27. imposthume:** Purulent abscess or swelling. **32. occasions:** Incidents, events; **inform against:** Generally defined as "show," "betray" (i.e., his tardiness); more probably *inform* means "take shape," as in *Macbeth,* II.i.48. **34. market of his time:** The best use he makes of his time, or, that for which he sells his time. **39. fust:** Grow moldy.

And ever three parts coward, I do not know
Why yet I live to say "This thing 's to do";
Sith I have cause and will and strength and means
To do 't. Examples gross as earth exhort me:
Witness this army of such mass and charge
Led by a delicate and tender prince,
Whose spirit with divine ambition puff'd
Makes mouths at the invisible event,
Exposing what is mortal and unsure
To all that fortune, death and danger dare,
Even for an egg-shell. Rightly to be great
Is not to stir without great argument,
But greatly to find quarrel in a straw
When honour's at the stake. How stand I then,
That have a father kill'd, a mother stain'd,
Excitements of° my reason and my blood,
And let all sleep? while, to my shame, I see
The imminent death of twenty thousand men,
That, for a fantasy and trick° of fame,
Go to their graves like beds, fight for a plot°
Whereon the numbers cannot try the cause,
Which is not tomb enough and continent
To hide the slain? O, from this time forth,
My thoughts be bloody, or be nothing worth! *Exit.*

[SCENE V: *Elsinore. A room in the castle.*]

Enter Horatio, [Queen] Gertrude, and a Gentleman.

QUEEN: I will not speak with her.
GENTLEMAN: She is importunate, indeed distract:
Her mood will needs be pitied.
QUEEN: What would she have?
GENTLEMAN: She speaks much of her father; says she hears
There's tricks° i' th' world; and hems, and beats her heart;°
Spurns enviously at straws;° speaks things in doubt,
That carry but half sense: her speech is nothing,
Yet the unshaped° use of it doth move
The hearers to collection;° they yawn° at it,
And botch° the words up fit to their own thoughts;
Which, as her winks, and nods, and gestures yield° them,
Indeed would make one think there might be thought,
Though nothing sure, yet much unhappily.°

---

58. Excitements of: Incentives to. **61. trick:** Toy, trifle. **62. plot:** I.e., of ground. SCENE V. **5. tricks:** Deceptions; **heart:** I.e., breast. **6. Spurns . . . straws:** Kicks spitefully at small objects in her path. **8. unshaped:** Unformed, artless. **9. collection:** Inference, a guess at some sort of meaning; **yawn:** Wonder. **10. botch:** Patch. **11. yield:** Deliver, bring forth (her words). **13. much unhappily:** Expressive of much unhappiness.

HORATIO: 'Twere good she were spoken with: for she may strew
Dangerous conjectures in ill-breeding minds.°
QUEEN: Let her come in. [*Exit Gentleman.*]
[*Aside.*] To my sick soul, as sin's true nature is,
Each toy seems prologue to some great amiss:°
So full of artless jealousy is guilt,
It spills itself in fearing to be spilt.°

Enter Ophelia [*distracted*].

OPHELIA: Where is the beauteous majesty of Denmark?
QUEEN: How now, Ophelia!
OPHELIA (*she sings*): How should I your true love know
From another one?
By his cockle hat° and staff,
And his sandal shoon.°
QUEEN: Alas, sweet lady, what imports this song?
OPHELIA: Say you? nay, pray you mark.
(*Song*) He is dead and gone, lady,
He is dead and gone;
At his head a grass-green turf,
At his heels a stone.
O, ho!
QUEEN: Nay, but, Ophelia —
OPHELIA: Pray you, mark
[*Sings.*] White his shroud as the mountain snow, —

Enter King.

QUEEN: Alas, look here, my lord.
OPHELIA (*Song*): Larded° all with flowers;
Which bewept to the grave did not go
With true-love showers.
KING: How do you, pretty lady?
OPHELIA: Well, God 'ild° you! They say the owl° was a baker's daughter. Lord, we know what we are, but know not what we may be. God be at your table!
KING: Conceit upon her father.
OPHELIA: Pray let's have no words of this; but when they ask you what it means, say you this:
(*Song*) To-morrow is Saint Valentine's day,
All in the morning betime,
And I a maid at your window,

---

15. ill-breeding minds: Minds bent on mischief. **18. great amiss:** Calamity, disaster. **19–20. So . . . spilt:** Guilt is so full of suspicion that it unskillfully betrays itself in fearing to be betrayed. **25. cockle hat:** Hat with cockleshell stuck in it as a sign that the wearer has been a pilgrim to the shrine of St. James of Compostella. The pilgrim's garb was a conventional disguise for lovers. **26. shoon:** Shoes. **38. Larded:** Decorated. **42. God 'ild:** God yield or reward; **owl:** Reference to a monkish legend that a baker's daughter was turned into an owl for refusing bread to the Savior.

To be your Valentine.°
Then up he rose, and donn'd his clothes,
And dupp'd° the chamber-door;
Let in the maid, that out a maid
Never departed more.

KING: Pretty Ophelia!

OPHELIA: Indeed, la, without an oath, I'll make an end on 't:
[*Sings.*] By Gis° and by Saint Charity,
Alack, and fie for shame!
Young men will do 't, if they come to 't;
By cock,° they are to blame.
Quoth she, before you tumbled me,
You promis'd me to wed.
So would I ha' done, by yonder sun,
An thou hadst not come to my bed.

KING: How long hath she been thus?

OPHELIA: I hope all will be well. We must be patient: but I cannot choose but weep, to think they would lay him i' the cold ground. My brother shall know of it: and so I thank you for your good counsel. Come, my coach! Good night, ladies; good night, sweet ladies; good night, good night. [*Exit.*]

KING: Follow her close; give her good watch, I pray you. [*Exit Horatio.*]
O, this is the poison of deep grief; it springs
All from her father's death. O Gertrude, Gertrude,
When sorrows come, they come not single spies,
But in battalions. First, her father slain:
Next your son gone; and he most violent author
Of his own just remove: the people muddied,
Thick and unwholesome in their thoughts and whispers,
For good Polonius' death; and we have done but greenly,°
In hugger-mugger° to inter him: poor Ophelia
Divided from herself and her fair judgement,
Without the which we are pictures, or mere beasts:
Last, and as much containing as all these,
Her brother is in secret come from France;
Feeds on his wonder, keeps himself in clouds,°
And wants not buzzers° to infect his ear
With pestilent speeches of his father's death;
Wherein necessity, of matter beggar'd,°
Will nothing stick° our person to arraign
In ear and ear.° O my dear Gertrude, this,

---

51. Valentine: This song alludes to the belief that the first girl seen by a man on the morning of this day was his valentine or true love. **53. dupp'd:** Opened. **58. Gis:** Jesus. **61. cock:** Perversion of "God" in oaths. **79. greenly:** Foolishly. **80. hugger-mugger:** Secret haste. **85. in clouds:** Invisible. **86. buzzers:** Gossipers. **88. of matter beggar'd:** Unprovided with facts. **89. nothing stick:** Not hesitate. **90. In ear and ear:** In everybody's ears.

Like to a murd'ring-piece,° in many places
Gives me superfluous death. *A noise within.*

QUEEN: Alack, what noise is this?

KING: Where are my Switzers?° Let them guard the door.

Enter a Messenger.

What is the matter?

MESSENGER: Save yourself, my lord:
The ocean, overpeering° of his list,°
Eats not the flats with more impiteous haste
Than young Laertes, in a riotous head,
O'erbears your officers. The rabble call him lord;
And, as the world were now but to begin,
Antiquity forgot, custom not known,
The ratifiers and props of every word,°
They cry "Choose we: Laertes shall be king":
Caps, hands, and tongues, applaud it to the clouds:
"Laertes shall be king, Laertes king!" *A noise within.*

QUEEN: How cheerfully on the false trail they cry!
O, this is counter,° you false Danish dogs!

KING: The doors are broke.

Enter Laertes with others.

LAERTES: Where is this king? Sirs, stand you all without.

DANES: No, let's come in.

LAERTES: I pray you, give me leave.

DANES: We will, we will. [*They retire without the door.*]

LAERTES: I thank you: keep the door. O thou vile king,
Give me my father!

QUEEN: Calmly, good Laertes.

LAERTES: That drop of blood that's calm proclaims me bastard,
Cries cuckold to my father, brands the harlot
Even here, between the chaste unsmirched brow
Of my true mother.

KING: What is the cause, Laertes,
That thy rebellion looks so giant-like?
Let him go, Gertrude; do not fear our person:
There's such divinity doth hedge a king,
That treason can but peep to° what it would°
Acts little of his will. Tell me, Laertes,
Why thou art thus incens'd. Let him go, Gertrude.
Speak, man.

---

91. murd'ring-piece: Small cannon or mortar; suggestion of numerous missiles fired. **93. Switzers:** Swiss guards, mercenaries. **95. overpeering:** Overflowing; **list:** Shore. **101. word:** Promise. **106. counter:** A hunting term meaning to follow the trail in a direction opposite to that which the game has taken. **120. peep to:** I.e., look at from afar off; **would:** Wishes to do.

LAERTES: Where is my father?
KING: Dead.
QUEEN: But not by him.
KING: Let him demand his fill.
LAERTES: How came he dead? I'll not be juggled with:
To hell, allegiance! vows, to the blackest devil!
Conscience and grace, to the profoundest pit!
I dare damnation. To this point I stand,
That both the worlds I give to negligence,°
Let come what comes; only I'll be reveng'd
Most throughly° for my father.
KING: Who shall stay you?
LAERTES: My will,° not all the world's:
And for my means, I'll husband them so well,
They shall go far with little.
KING: Good Laertes,
If you desire to know the certainty
Of your dear father, is 't writ in your revenge,
That, swoopstake,° you will draw both friend and foe,
Winner and loser?
LAERTES: None but his enemies.
KING: Will you know them then?
LAERTES: To his good friends thus wide I'll ope my arms;
And like the kind life-rend'ring pelican,°
Repast° them with my blood.
KING: Why, now you speak
Like a good child and a true gentleman.
That I am guiltless of your father's death,
And am most sensibly in grief for it,
It shall as level to your judgement 'pear
As day does to your eye. *A noise within: "Let her come in."*
LAERTES: How now! what noise is that?

Enter Ophelia.

O heat,° dry up my brains! tears seven times salt,
Burn out the sense and virtue of mine eye!
By heaven, thy madness shall be paid with weight,
Till our scale turn the beam. O rose of May!
Dear maid, kind sister, sweet Ophelia!
O heavens! is 't possible, a young maid's wits
Should be as mortal as an old man's life?

---

130. give to negligence: He despises both the here and the hereafter. **132. throughly:** thoroughly. **133. My will:** He will not be stopped except by his own will. **138. swoopstake:** Literally, drawing the whole stake at once, i.e., indiscriminately. **142. pelican:** Reference to the belief that the pelican feeds its young with its own blood. **143. Repast:** Feed. **150. heat:** Probably the heat generated by the passion of grief.

Nature is fine in love, and where 'tis fine,
It sends some precious instance of itself
After the thing it loves.

OPHELIA (*Song*): They bore him barefac'd on the bier;
Hey non nonny, nonny, hey nonny;
And in his grave rain'd many a tear: —
Fare you well, my dove!

LAERTES: Hadst thou thy wits, and didst persuade revenge,
It could not move thus.

OPHELIA [*sings*]: You must sing a-down a-down,
An you call him a-down-a.
O, how the wheel° becomes it! It is the false steward,° that stole his master's daughter.

LAERTES: This nothing's more than matter.

OPHELIA: There's rosemary,° that's for remembrance; pray you, love, remember: and there is pansies,° that's for thoughts.

LAERTES: A document° in madness, thoughts and remembrance fitted.

OPHELIA: There's fennel° for you, and columbines:° there's rue° for you; and here's some for me: we may call it herb of grace o' Sundays: O, you must wear your rue with a difference. There's a daisy:° I would give you some violets,° but they withered all when my father died: they say 'a made a good end, —
[*Sings.*] For bonny sweet Robin is all my joy.°

LAERTES: Thought° and affliction, passion, hell itself,
She turns to favour and to prettiness.

OPHELIA (*Song*): And will 'a not come again?°
And will 'a not come again?
No, no, he is dead:
Go to thy death-bed:
He never will come again.
His beard was as white as snow,
All flaxen was his poll:°
He is gone, he is gone,
And we cast away° moan:
God ha' mercy on his soul!
And of all Christian souls, I pray God. God be wi' you. [*Exit.*]

LAERTES: Do you see this, O God?

---

168. wheel: Spinning wheel as accompaniment to the song refrain; **false steward:** The story is unknown. **171. rosemary:** Used as a symbol of remembrance both at weddings and at funerals. **172. pansies:** Emblems of love and courtship. Cf. French *pensées*. **173. document:** Piece of instruction or lesson. **174. fennel:** Emblem of flattery; **columbines:** Emblem of unchastity (?) or ingratitude(?); **rue:** Emblem of repentance. It was usually mingled with holy water and then known as *herb of grace*. Ophelia is probably playing on the two meanings of *rue,* "repentant" and "even for ruth (pity)"; the former signification is for the queen, the latter for herself. **176. daisy:** Emblem of dissembling, faithlessness. **177. violets:** Emblems of faithfulness. **179. For . . . joy:** Probably a line from a Robin Hood ballad. **180. Thought:** Melancholy thought. **182. And . . . again:** This song appeared in the songbooks as "The Merry Milkmaids' Dumps." **188. poll:** Head. **190. cast away:** Shipwrecked.

KING: Laertes, I must commune with your grief,
Or you deny me right.° Go but apart,
Make choice of whom your wisest friends you will,
And they shall hear and judge 'twixt you and me:
If by direct or by collateral° hand
They find us touch'd,° we will our kingdom give,
Our crown, our life, and all that we call ours,
To you in satisfaction; but if not,
Be you content to lend your patience to us,
And we shall jointly labour with your soul
To give it due content.

LAERTES: Let this be so;
His means of death, his obscure funeral —
No trophy, sword, nor hatchment° o'er his bones,
No noble rite nor formal ostentation —
Cry to be heard, as 'twere from heaven to earth,
That I must call 't in question.

KING: So you shall;
And where th' offence is let the great axe fall.
I pray you, go with me. *Exeunt.*

[SCENE VI: *Another room in the castle.*]

Enter Horatio and others.

HORATIO: What are they that would speak with me?

GENTLEMAN: Sea-faring men, sir: they say they have letters for you.

HORATIO: Let them come in. [*Exit Gentleman.*]
I do not know from what part of the world
I should be greeted, if not from lord Hamlet.

Enter Sailors.

FIRST SAILOR: God bless you, sir.

HORATIO: Let him bless thee too.

FIRST SAILOR: 'A shall sir, an 't please him. There's a letter for you, sir; it comes from the ambassador that was bound for England; if your name be Horatio, as I am let to know it is.

HORATIO [*reads*]: "Horatio, when thou shalt have overlooked this, give these fellows some means° to the king: they have letters for him. Ere we were two days old at sea, a pirate of very warlike appointment gave us chase. Finding ourselves too slow of sail, we put on a compelled valour, and in the grapple I boarded them: on the instant they got clear of our ship; so I alone became their prisoner. They have dealt with me like thieves of mercy:° but they knew what they did; I am to do a good turn for them. Let the king have the letters I have sent; and repair thou to me with as much speed as thou wouldest fly death. I have words to speak in thine

---

195. right: My rights. **198. collateral:** Indirect. **199. touch'd:** Implicated. **206. hatchment:** Tablet displaying the armorial bearings of a deceased person. SCENE VI. **12. means:** Means of access. **16–17. thieves of mercy:** Merciful thieves.

ear will make thee dumb; yet are they much too light for the bore° of the matter. These good fellows will bring thee where I am. Rosencrantz and Guildenstern hold their course for England: of them I have much to tell thee. Farewell.

"He that thou knowest thine, HAMLET."

Come, I will give you way for these your letters;
And do 't the speedier, that you may direct me
To him from whom you brought them. *Exeunt.*

[SCENE VII: *Another room in the castle.*]

Enter King and Laertes.

KING: Now must your conscience° my acquittance seal,
And you must put me in your heart for friend,
Sith you have heard, and with a knowing ear,
That he which hath your noble father slain
Pursued my life.

LAERTES: It well appears: but tell me
Why you proceeded not against these feats,
So criminal and so capital° in nature,
As by your safety, wisdom, all things else,
You mainly° were stirr'd up.

KING: O, for two special reasons;
Which may to you, perhaps, seem much unsinew'd,°
But yet to me th' are strong. The queen his mother
Lives almost by his looks; and for myself —
My virtue or my plague, be it either which —
She's so conjunctive° to my life and soul,
That, as the star moves not but in his sphere,°
I could not but by her. The other motive,
Why to a public count° I might not go,
Is the great love the general gender° bear him;
Who, dipping all his faults in their affection,
Would, like the spring° that turneth wood to stone,
Convert his gyves° to graces; so that my arrows,
Too slightly timber'd° for so loud° a wind,
Would have reverted to my bow again,
And not where I had aim'd them.

LAERTES: And so have I a noble father lost;
A sister driven into desp'rate terms,°

20. bore: Caliber, importance. SCENE VII. **1. conscience:** Knowledge that this is true. **7. capital:** Punishable by death. **9. mainly:** Greatly. **10. unsinew'd:** Weak. **14. conjunctive:** Conformable (the next line suggesting planetary conjunction). **15. sphere:** The hollow sphere in which, according to Ptolemaic astronomy, the planets were supposed to move. **17. count:** Account, reckoning. **18. general gender:** Common people. **20. spring:** I.e., one heavily charged with lime. **21. gyves:** Fetters; here, faults, or possibly, punishments inflicted (on him). **22. slightly timber'd:** Light; **loud:** Strong. **26. terms:** State, condition.

Whose worth, if praises may go back° again,
Stood challenger on mount° of all the age°
For her perfections: but my revenge will come.
KING: Break not your sleeps for that: you must not think
That we are made of stuff so flat and dull
That we can let our beard be shook with danger
And think it pastime. You shortly shall hear more:
I lov'd your father, and we love ourself;
And that, I hope, will teach you to imagine —

Enter a Messenger with letters.

How now! what news?
MESSENGER: Letters, my lord, from Hamlet:
These to your majesty; this to the queen.°
KING: From Hamlet! who brought them?
MESSENGER: Sailors, my lord, they say; I saw them not:
They were given me by Claudio;° he receiv'd them
Of him that brought them.
KING: Laertes, you shall hear them.
Leave us. [*Exit Messenger.*]
[*Reads.*] "High and mighty, You shall know I am set naked° on your kingdom. To-morrow shall I beg leave to see your kingly eyes: when I shall, first asking your pardon thereunto, recount the occasion of my sudden and more strange return. "HAMLET."
What should this mean? Are all the rest come back?
Or is it some abuse, and no such thing?
LAERTES: Know you the hand?
KING: 'Tis Hamlet's character. "Naked!"
And in a postscript here, he says "alone."
Can you devise° me?
LAERTES: I'm lost in it, my lord. But let him come;
It warms the very sickness in my heart,
That I shall live and tell him to his teeth,
"Thus didst thou."
KING: If it be so, Laertes —
As how should it be so? how otherwise?° —
Will you be rul'd by me?
LAERTES: Ay, my lord;
So you will not o'errule me to a peace.
KING: To thine own peace. If he be now return'd,

---

27. go back: I.e., to Ophelia's former virtues. **28. on mount:** Set up on high, *mounted* (on horseback); **of all the age:** Qualifies *challenger* and not *mount.* **37. to the queen:** One hears no more of the letter to the queen. **40. Claudio:** This character does not appear in the play. **43. naked:** Unprovided (with retinue). **51. devise:** Explain to. **56. As . . . otherwise?** How can this (Hamlet's return) be true? (yet) how otherwise than true (since we have the evidence of his letter)? Some editors read *How should it not be so,* etc., making the words refer to Laertes' desire to meet with Hamlet.

As checking at° his voyage, and that he means
No more to undertake it, I will work him
To an exploit, now ripe in my device,
Under the which he shall not choose but fall:
And for his death no wind of blame shall breathe,
But even his mother shall uncharge the practice°
And call it accident.

LAERTES: My lord, I will be rul'd;
The rather, if you could devise it so
That I might be the organ.°

KING: It falls right.
You have been talk'd of since your travel much,
And that in Hamlet's hearing, for a quality
Wherein, they say, you shine: your sum of parts
Did not together pluck such envy from him
As did that one, and that, in my regard,
Of the unworthiest siege.°

LAERTES: What part is that, my lord?

KING: A very riband in the cap of youth,
Yet needful too; for youth no less becomes
The light and careless livery that it wears
Than settled age his sables° and his weeds,
Importing health and graveness. Two months since,
Here was a gentleman of Normandy: —
I have seen myself, and serv'd against, the French,
And they can well° on horseback: but this gallant
Had witchcraft in 't; he grew unto his seat;
And to such wondrous doing brought his horse,
As had he been incorps'd and demi-natur'd°
With the brave beast: so far he topp'd° my thought,
That I, in forgery° of shapes and tricks,
Come short of what he did.

LAERTES: A Norman was 't?

KING: A Norman.

LAERTES: Upon my life, Lamord.°

KING: The very same.

LAERTES: I know him well: he is the brooch indeed
And gem of all the nation.

KING: He made confession° of you,
And gave you such a masterly report

---

60. checking at: Used in falconry of a hawk's leaving the quarry to fly at a chance bird, turn aside. **65. uncharge the practice:** Acquit the stratagem of being a plot. **68. organ:** Agent, instrument. **74. siege:** Rank. **78. sables:** Rich garments. **82. can well:** Are skilled. **85. incorps'd and demi-natur'd:** Of one body and nearly of one nature (like the centaur). **86. topp'd:** Surpassed. **87. forgery:** Invention. **90. Lamord:** This refers possibly to Pietro Monte, instructor to Louis XII's master of the horse. **93. confession:** Grudging admission of superiority.

For art and exercise° in your defence°
And for your rapier most especial,
That he cried out, 'twould be a sight indeed,
If one could match you: the scrimers° of their nation,
He swore, had neither motion, guard, nor eye,
If you oppos'd them. Sir, this report of his
Did Hamlet so envenom with his envy
That he could nothing do but wish and beg
Your sudden coming o'er, to play° with you.
Now, out of this, —

LAERTES: What out of this, my lord?

KING: Laertes, was your father dear to you?
Or are you like the painting of a sorrow,
A face without a heart?

LAERTES: Why ask you this?

KING: Not that I think you did not love your father;
But that I know love is begun by time;
And that I see, in passages of proof,°
Time qualifies the spark and fire of it.
There lives within the very flame of love
A kind of wick or snuff that will abate it;
And nothing is at a like goodness still;
For goodness, growing to a plurisy,°
Dies in his own too much:° that we would do,
We should do when we would; for this "would" changes
And hath abatements° and delays as many
As there are tongues, are hands, are accidents;°
And then this "should" is like a spendthrift° sigh,
That hurts by easing. But, to the quick o' th' ulcer:° —
Hamlet comes back: what would you undertake,
To show yourself your father's son in deed
More than in words?

LAERTES: To cut his throat i' th' church.

KING: No place, indeed, should murder sanctuarize;°
Revenge should have no bounds. But, good Laertes,
Will you do this, keep close within your chamber.
Hamlet return'd shall know you are come home:
We'll put on those shall praise your excellence
And set a double varnish on the fame
The Frenchman gave you, bring you in fine together

---

95. art and exercise: Skillful exercise; **defence:** Science of defense in sword practice. **98. scrimers:** Fencers. **103. play:** Fence. **110. passages of proof:** Proved instances. **115. plurisy:** Excess, plethora. **116. in his own too much:** Of its own excess. **118. abatements:** Diminutions. **119. accidents:** Occurrences, incidents. **120. spendthrift:** An allusion to the belief that each sigh cost the heart a drop of blood. **121. quick o' th' ulcer:** Heart of the difficulty. **125. sanctuarize:** Protect from punishment; allusion to the right of sanctuary with which certain religious places were invested.

And wager on your heads: he, being remiss,
Most generous and free from all contriving,
Will not peruse the foils; so that, with ease,
Or with a little shuffling, you may choose
A sword unbated,° and in a pass of practice°
Requite him for your father.

LAERTES: I will do 't:
And, for that purpose, I'll anoint my sword.
I bought an unction of a mountebank,°
So mortal that, but dip a knife in it,
Where it draws blood no cataplasm° so rare,
Collected from all simples° that have virtue
Under the moon,° can save the thing from death
That is but scratch'd withal: I'll touch my point
With this contagion, that, if I gall° him slightly,
It may be death.

KING: Let's further think of this;
Weigh what convenience both of time and means
May fit us to our shape:° if this should fail,
And that our drift look through our bad performance,°
'Twere better not assay'd: therefore this project
Should have a back or second, that might hold,
If this should blast in proof.° Soft! let me see:
We'll make a solemn wager on your cunnings:°
I ha 't:
When in your motion you are hot and dry —
As make your bouts more violent to that end —
And that he calls for drink, I'll have prepar'd him
A chalice° for the nonce, whereon but sipping,
If he by chance escape your venom'd stuck,°
Our purpose may hold there. But stay, what noise?

Enter Queen.

QUEEN: One woe doth tread upon another's heel,
So fast they follow: your sister's drown'd, Laertes.

LAERTES: Drown'd! O, where?

QUEEN: There is a willow° grows askant° the brook,
That shows his hoar° leaves in the glassy stream;
There with fantastic garlands did she make
Of crow-flowers,° nettles, daisies, and long purples°

---

136. unbated: Not blunted, having no button; **pass of practice:** Treacherous thrust. **139. mountebank:** Quack doctor. **141. cataplasm:** Plaster or poultice. **142. simples:** Herbs. **143. Under the moon:** I.e., when collected by moonlight to add to their medicinal value. **145. gall:** Graze, wound. **148. shape:** Part we propose to act. **149. drift . . . performance:** Intention be disclosed by our bungling. **152. blast in proof:** Burst in the test (like a cannon). **153. cunnings:** Skills. **158. chalice:** Cup. **159. stuck:** Thrust (from *stoccado*). **164. willow:** For its significance of forsaken love; **askant:** Aslant. **165. hoar:** White (i.e., on the underside). **167. crow-flowers:** Buttercups; **long purples:** Early purple orchids.

That liberal° shepherds give a grosser name,
But our cold maids do dead men's fingers call them:
There, on the pendent boughs her crownet° weeds
Clamb'ring to hang, an envious sliver° broke;
When down her weedy° trophies and herself
Fell in the weeping brook. Her clothes spread wide;
And, mermaid-like, awhile they bore her up:
Which time she chanted snatches of old lauds;°
As one incapable° of her own distress,
Or like a creature native and indued°
Upon that element: but long it could not be
Till that her garments, heavy with their drink,
Pull'd the poor wretch from her melodious lay
To muddy death.

LAERTES: Alas, then, she is drown'd?

QUEEN: Drown'd, drown'd.

LAERTES: Too much of water hast thou, poor Ophelia,
And therefore I forbid my tears: but yet
It is our trick;° nature her custom holds,
Let shame say what it will: when these are gone,
The woman will be out.° Adieu, my lord:
I have a speech of fire, that fain would blaze,
But that this folly drowns it. *Exit.*

KING: Let's follow, Gertrude:
How much I had to do to calm his rage!
Now fear I this will give it start again;
Therefore let 's follow. *Exeunt.*

[ACT V

SCENE I: *A churchyard.*]

Enter two Clowns° [with spades, &c.].

FIRST CLOWN: Is she to be buried in Christian burial when she wilfully seeks her own salvation?

SECOND CLOWN: I tell thee she is; therefore make her grave straight:° the crowner° hath sat on her, and finds it Christian burial.

FIRST CLOWN: How can that be, unless she drowned herself in her own defence?

SECOND CLOWN: Why, 'tis found so.

---

168. liberal: Probably, free-spoken. **170. crownet:** Coronet; made into a chaplet. **171. sliver:** Branch. **172. weedy:** I.e., of plants. **175. lauds:** Hymns. **176. incapable:** Lacking capacity to apprehend. **177. indued:** Endowed with qualities fitting her for living in water. **185. trick:** Way. **186–187. when . . . out:** When my tears are all shed, the woman in me will be satisfied. ACT V, SCENE I. **s.d. Clowns:** The word *clown* was used to denote peasants as well as humorous characters; here applied to the rustic type of clown. **3. straight:** Straightway, immediately; some interpret "from east to west in a direct line, parallel with the church." **4. crowner:** Coroner.

FIRST CLOWN: It must be "se offendendo";° it cannot be else. For here lies the point: if I drown myself wittingly,° it argues an act: and an act hath three branches;° it is, to act, to do, and to perform: argal,° she drowned herself wittingly.

SECOND CLOWN: Nay, but hear you, goodman delver,° —

FIRST CLOWN: Give me leave. Here lies the water; good: here stands the man; good: if the man go to this water, and drown himself, it is, will he, nill he, he goes, — mark you that; but if the water come to him and drown him, he drowns not himself: argal, he that is not guilty of his own death shortens not his own life.

SECOND CLOWN: But is this law?

FIRST CLOWN: Ay, marry, is 't; crowner's quest° law.

SECOND CLOWN: Will you ha' the truth on 't? If this had not been a gentlewoman, she should have been buried out o' Christian burial.

FIRST CLOWN: Why, there thou say'st:° and the more pity that great folk should have countenance° in this world to drown or hang themselves, more than their even° Christian. Come, my spade. There is no ancient gentlemen but gardeners, ditchers, and grave-makers: they hold up° Adam's profession.

SECOND CLOWN: Was he a gentleman?

FIRST CLOWN: 'A was the first that ever bore arms.

SECOND CLOWN: Why, he had none.

FIRST CLOWN: What, art a heathen? How dost thou understand the Scripture? The Scripture says "Adam digged": could he dig without arms? I'll put another question to thee: if thou answerest me not to the purpose, confess thyself° —

SECOND CLOWN: Go to.°

FIRST CLOWN: What is he that builds stronger than either the mason, the shipwright, or the carpenter?

SECOND CLOWN: The gallows-maker; for that frame outlives a thousand tenants.

FIRST CLOWN: I like thy wit well, in good faith: the gallows does well; but how does it well? it does well to those that do ill: now thou dost ill to say the gallows is built stronger than the church: argal, the gallows may do well to thee. To 't again, come.

SECOND CLOWN: "Who builds stronger than a mason, a shipwright, or a carpenter?"

FIRST CLOWN: Ay, tell me that, and unyoke.°

SECOND CLOWN: Marry, now I can tell.

FIRST CLOWN: To 't.

---

7. "se offendendo": For *se defendendo,* term used in verdicts of justifiable homicide. **8. wittingly:** Intentionally. **8–9. three branches:** Parody of legal phraseology; **argal:** Corruption of *ergo,* therefore. **11. delver:** Digger. **18. quest:** Inquest. **21. there thou say'st:** That's right. **22. countenance:** Privilege. **23. even:** Fellow. **24. hold up:** Maintain, continue. **31–32. confess thyself:** "And be hanged" completes the proverb. **33. Go to:** Perhaps, "begin," or some other form of concession. **44. unyoke:** After this great effort you may unharness the team of your wits.

SECOND CLOWN: Mass,° I cannot tell.

Enter Hamlet and Horatio [at a distance].

FIRST CLOWN: Cudgel thy brains no more about it, for your dull ass will not mend his pace with beating; and, when you are asked this question next, say "a grave-maker": the houses he makes lasts till doomsday. Go, get thee in, and fetch me a stoup° of liquor.

[Exit Second Clown.] Song. [He digs.]

In youth, when I did love, did love,
  Methought it was very sweet,
To contract — O — the time, for — a — my behove,°
  O, methought, there — a — was nothing — a — meet.

HAMLET: Has this fellow no feeling of his business, that 'a sings at grave-making?

HORATIO: Custom hath made it in him a property of easiness.°

HAMLET: 'Tis e'en so: the hand of little employment hath the daintier sense.

FIRST CLOWN: (*Song.*) But age, with his stealing steps,
  Hath claw'd me in his clutch,
And hath shipped me into the land
  As if I had never been such. *[Throws up a skull.]*

HAMLET: That skull had a tongue in it, and could sing once: how the knave jowls° it to the ground, as if 'twere Cain's jaw-bone,° that did the first murder! This might be the pate of a politician,° which this ass now o'er-reaches;° one that would circumvent God, might it not?

HORATIO: It might, my lord.

HAMLET: Or of a courtier; which could say "Good morrow, sweet lord! How dost thou, sweet lord?" This might be my lord such-a-one, that praised my lord such-a-one's horse, when he meant to beg it; might it not?

HORATIO: Ay, my lord.

HAMLET: Why, e'en so: and now my Lady Worm's; chapless,° and knocked about the mazzard° with a sexton's spade: here's fine revolution, an we had the trick to see 't. Did these bones cost no more the breeding, but to play at loggats° with 'em? mine ache to think on 't.

FIRST CLOWN: (*Song.*) A pick-axe, and a spade, a spade,
  For and° a shrouding sheet:
O, a pit of clay for to be made
  For such a guest is meet. *[Throws up another skull.]*

HAMLET: There's another: why may not that be the skull of a lawyer? Where be his quiddities° now, his quillities,° his cases, his tenures,° and his tricks?

---

47. Mass: By the Mass. **51. stoup:** Two-quart measure. **54. behove:** Benefit. **58. property of easiness:** A peculiarity that now is easy. **65. jowls:** Dashes; **Cain's jaw-bone:** Allusion to the old tradition that Cain slew Abel with the jawbone of an ass. **66. politician:** Schemer, plotter. **66–67. o'er-reaches:** Quibble on the literal sense and the sense "circumvent." **73. chapless:** Having no lower jaw. **74. mazzard:** Head. **76. loggats:** A game in which six sticks are thrown to lie as near as possible to a stake fixed in the ground, or block of wood on a floor. **78. For and:** And moreover. **82. quiddities:** Subtleties, quibbles; **quillities:** Verbal niceties, subtle distinctions; **tenures:** The holding of a piece of property or office or the conditions or period of such holding.

why does he suffer this mad knave now to knock him about the sconce° with a dirty shovel, and will not tell him of his action of battery? Hum! This fellow might be in 's time a great buyer of land, with his statutes, his recognizances,° his fines, his double vouchers,° his recoveries:° is this the fine° of his fines, and the recovery of his recoveries, to have his fine pate full of fine dirt? will his vouchers vouch him no more of his purchases, and double ones too, than the length and breadth of a pair of indentures?° The very conveyances of his lands will scarcely lie in this box; and must the inheritor° himself have no more, ha?

HORATIO: Not a jot more, my lord.

HAMLET: Is not parchment made of sheep-skins?

HORATIO: Ay, my lord, and of calf-skins° too.

HAMLET: They are sheep and calves which seek out assurance in that.° I will speak to this fellow. Whose grave's this, sirrah?

FIRST CLOWN: Mine, sir.

[*Sings.*] O, a pit of clay for to be made
For such a guest is meet.

HAMLET: I think it be thine, indeed; for thou liest in 't.

FIRST CLOWN: You lie out on 't, sir, and therefore 't is not yours: for my part, I do not lie in 't, yet it is mine.

HAMLET: Thou dost lie in 't, to be in 't and say it is thine: 'tis for the dead, not for the quick; therefore thou liest.

FIRST CLOWN: 'Tis a quick lie, sir; 'twill away again, from me to you.

HAMLET: What man dost thou dig it for?

FIRST CLOWN: For no man, sir.

HAMLET: What woman, then?

FIRST CLOWN: For none, neither.

HAMLET: Who is to be buried in 't?

FIRST CLOWN: One that was a woman, sir; but, rest her soul, she's dead.

HAMLET: How absolute° the knave is! we must speak by the card,° or equivocation° will undo us. By the Lord, Horatio, these three years I have taken note of it; the age is grown so picked° that the toe of the peasant comes so near the heel of the courtier, he galls° his kibe.° How long hast thou been a grave-maker?

FIRST CLOWN: Of all the day i' the year, I came to 't that day that our last king Hamlet overcame Fortinbras.

HAMLET: How long is that since?

FIRST CLOWN: Cannot you tell that? every fool can tell that: it was the very day that young Hamlet was born; he that is mad, and sent into England.

---

83. sconce: Head. **85–86. statutes, recognizances:** Legal terms connected with the transfer of land; **vouchers:** Persons called on to warrant a tenant's title; **recoveries:** Process for transfer of entailed estate. **87. fine:** The four uses of this word are as follows: (1) end, (2) legal process, (3) elegant, (4) small. **90. indentures:** Conveyances or contracts. **91. inheritor:** Possessor, owner. **94. calf-skins:** Parchments. **95. assurance in that:** Safety in legal parchments. **112–113. absolute:** Positive, decided; **by the card:** With precision, i.e., by the mariner's card on which the points of the compass were marked; **equivocation:** Ambiguity in the use of terms. **114. picked:** Refined, fastidious. **115. galls:** Chafes; **kibe:** Chilblain.

HAMLET: Ay, marry, why was he sent into England?

FIRST CLOWN: Why, because 'a was mad: 'a shall recover his wits there; or, if 'a do not, 'tis no great matter there.

HAMLET: Why?

FIRST CLOWN: 'Twill not be seen in him there; there the men are as mad as he.

HAMLET: How came he mad?

FIRST CLOWN: Very strangely, they say.

HAMLET: How strangely?

FIRST CLOWN: Faith, e'en with losing his wits.

HAMLET: Upon what ground?

FIRST CLOWN: Why, here in Denmark: I have been sexton here, man and boy, thirty years.°

HAMLET: How long will a man lie i' the earth ere he rot?

FIRST CLOWN: Faith, if 'a be not rotten before 'a die — as we have many pocky° corses now-a-days, that will scarce hold the laying in — 'a will last you some eight year or nine year: a tanner will last you nine year.

HAMLET: Why he more than another?

FIRST CLOWN: Why, sir, his hide is so tanned with his trade, that 'a will keep out water a great while; and your water is a sore decayer of your whoreson dead body. Here's a skull now hath lain you i' th' earth three and twenty years.

HAMLET: Whose was it?

FIRST CLOWN: A whoreson mad fellow's it was: whose do you think it was?

HAMLET: Nay, I know not.

FIRST CLOWN: A pestilence on him for a mad rogue! 'a poured a flagon of Rhenish on my head once. This same skull, sir, was Yorick's skull, the king's jester.

HAMLET: This?

FIRST CLOWN: E'en that.

HAMLET: Let me see. [*Takes the skull.*] Alas, poor Yorick! I knew him, Horatio: a fellow of infinite jest, of most excellent fancy: he hath borne me on his back a thousand times; and now, how abhorred in my imagination it is! my gorge rises at it. Here hung those lips that I have kissed I know not how oft. Where be your gibes now? your gambols? your songs? your flashes of merriment, that were wont to set the table on a roar? Not one now, to mock your own grinning? quite chap-fallen? Now get you to my lady's chamber, and tell her, let her paint an inch thick, to this favour she must come; make her laugh at that. Prithee, Horatio, tell me one thing.

HORATIO: What's that, my lord?

HAMLET: Dost thou think Alexander looked o' this fashion i' the earth?

HORATIO: E'en so.

HAMLET: And smelt so? pah! [*Puts down the skull.*]

HORATIO: E'en so, my lord.

---

133. thirty years: This statement with that in lines 120–121 shows Hamlet's age to be thirty years. **135. pocky:** Rotten, diseased.

HAMLET: To what base uses we may return, Horatio! Why may not imagination trace the noble dust of Alexander, till 'a find it stopping a bunghole?

HORATIO: 'Twere to consider too curiously,° to consider so.

HAMLET: No, faith, not a jot; but to follow him thither with modesty enough, and likelihood to lead it: as thus: Alexander died, Alexander was buried, Alexander returneth into dust; the dust is earth; of earth we make loam;° and why of that loam, whereto he was converted, might they not stop a beer-barrel?

Imperious° Cæsar, dead and turn'd to clay,
Might stop a hole to keep the wind away:
O, that that earth, which kept the world in awe,
Should patch a wall t'expel the winter's flaw!°

But soft! but soft awhile! here comes the king,

Enter King, Queen, Laertes, and the Corse of [*Ophelia, in procession, with Priest, Lords, etc.*].

The queen, the courtiers: who is this they follow?
And with such maimed rites? This doth betoken
The corse they follow did with desp'rate hand
Fordo° it° own life: 'twas of some estate.
Couch° we awhile, and mark. [*Retiring with Horatio.*]

LAERTES: What ceremony else?

HAMLET: That is Laertes,
A very noble youth: mark.

LAERTES: What ceremony else?

FIRST PRIEST: Her obsequies have been as far enlarg'd°
As we have warranty: her death was doubtful;
And, but that great command o'ersways the order,
She should in ground unsanctified have lodg'd
Till the last trumpet; for charitable prayers,
Shards,° flints and pebbles should be thrown on her:
Yet here she is allow'd her virgin crants,°
Her maiden strewments° and the bringing home
Of bell and burial.°

LAERTES: Must there no more be done?

FIRST PRIEST: No more be done:
We should profane the service of the dead
To sing a requiem and such rest to her
As to peace-parted° souls.

---

167. curiously: Minutely. **170. loam:** Clay paste for brickmaking. **173. Imperious:** Imperial. **176. flaw:** Gust of wind. **181. Fordo:** Destroy; **it:** Its. **182. Couch:** Hide, lurk. **186. enlarg'd:** Extended, referring to the fact that suicides are not given full burial rites. **191. Shards:** Broken bits of pottery. **192. crants:** Garlands customarily hung upon the biers of unmarried women. **193. strewments:** Traditional strewing of flowers. **193–194. bringing . . . burial:** The laying to rest of the body, to the sound of the bell. **198. peace-parted:** Allusion to the text "Lord, now lettest thou thy servant depart in peace."

LAERTES: Lay her i' th' earth:
And from her fair and unpolluted flesh
May violets spring! I tell thee, churlish priest,
A minist'ring angel shall my sister be,
When thou liest howling.°

HAMLET: What, the fair Ophelia!

QUEEN: Sweets to the sweet: farewell! [*Scattering flowers.*]
I hop'd thou shouldst have been my Hamlet's wife;
I thought thy bride-bed to have deck'd, sweet maid,
And not have strew'd thy grave.

LAERTES: O, treble woe
Fall ten times treble on that cursed head,
Whose wicked deed thy most ingenious sense°
Depriv'd thee of! Hold off the earth awhile,
Till I have caught her once more in mine arms: [*Leaps into the grave.*]
Now pile your dust upon the quick and dead,
Till of this flat a mountain you have made,
T' o'ertop old Pelion,° or the skyish head
Of blue Olympus.

HAMLET: [*Advancing*] What is he whose grief
Bears such an emphasis? whose phrase of sorrow
Conjures the wand'ring stars,° and makes them stand
Like wonder-wounded hearers? This is I,
Hamlet the Dane. [*Leaps into the grave.*]

LAERTES: The devil take thy soul! [*Grappling with him.*]

HAMLET: Thou pray'st not well.
I prithee, take thy fingers from my throat;
For, though I am not splenitive° and rash,
Yet have I in me something dangerous,
Which let thy wisdom fear: hold off thy hand.

KING: Pluck them asunder.

QUEEN: Hamlet, Hamlet!

ALL: Gentlemen, —

HORATIO: Good my lord, be quiet.
[*The Attendants part them, and they come out of the grave.*]

HAMLET: Why, I will fight with him upon this theme
Until my eyelids will no longer wag.°

QUEEN: O my son, what theme?

HAMLET: I lov'd Ophelia: forty thousand brothers
Could not, with all their quantity° of love,
Make up my sum. What wilt thou do for her?

---

202. howling: I.e., in hell. **208. ingenious sense:** Mind endowed with finest qualities. **213. Pelion:** Olympus, Pelion, and Ossa are mountains in the north of Thessaly. **216. wand'ring stars:** Planets. **221. splenitive:** Quick-tempered. **227. wag:** Move (not used ludicrously). **230. quantity:** Some suggest that the word is used in a deprecatory sense (little bits, fragments).

KING: O, he is mad, Laertes.
QUEEN: For love of God, forbear° him.
HAMLET: 'Swounds,° show me what thou 'lt do:
Woo 't° weep? woo 't fight? woo 't fast? woo 't tear thyself?
Woo 't drink up eisel?° eat a crocodile?
I'll do 't. Dost thou come here to whine?
To outface me with leaping in her grave?
Be buried quick with her, and so will I:
And, if thou prate of mountains, let them throw
Millions of acres on us, till our ground,
Singeing his pate against the burning zone,°
Make Ossa like a wart! Nay, an thou 'lt mouth,
I'll rant as well as thou.
QUEEN: This is mere madness:
And thus awhile the fit will work on him;
Anon, as patient as the female dove,
When that her golden couplets° are disclos'd,
His silence will sit drooping.
HAMLET: Hear you, sir;
What is the reason that you use me thus?
I lov'd you ever: but it is no matter;
Let Hercules himself do what he may,
The cat will mew and dog will have his day.
KING: I pray thee, good Horatio, wait upon him. *Exit Hamlet and Horatio.*
[*To Laertes.*] Strengthen your patience in° our last night's speech;
We'll put the matter to the present push.°
Good Gertrude, set some watch over your son.
This grave shall have a living° monument:
An hour of quiet shortly shall we see;
Till then, in patience our proceeding be. *Exeunt.*

[SCENE II: *A hall in the castle.*]

Enter Hamlet and Horatio.

HAMLET: So much for this, sir: now shall you see the other;
You do remember all the circumstance?
HORATIO: Remember it, my lord!
HAMLET: Sir, in my heart there was a kind of fighting,
That would not let me sleep: methought I lay
Worse than the mutines° in the bilboes.° Rashly°
And prais'd be rashness for it, let us know,

---

233. forbear: Leave alone. **234. 'Swounds:** Oath, "God's wounds." **235. Woo 't:** Wilt thou. **236. eisel:** Vinegar. Some editors have taken this to be the name of a river, such as the Yssel, the Weissel, and the Nile. **242. burning zone:** Sun's orbit. **247. golden couplets:** The pigeon lays two eggs; the young when hatched are covered with golden down. **254. in:** By recalling. **255. present push:** Immediate test. **257. living:** Lasting; also refers (for Laertes' benefit) to the plot against Hamlet. SCENE II. **6. mutines:** Mutineers; **bilboes:** Shackles; **Rashly:** Goes with line 12.

Our indiscretion sometime serves us well,
When our deep plots do pall:° and that should learn us
There's a divinity that shapes our ends,
Rough-hew° them how we will, —

HORATIO: That is most certain.

HAMLET: Up from my cabin,
My sea-gown° scarf'd about me, in the dark
Grop'd I to find out them; had my desire,
Finger'd° their packet, and in fine° withdrew
To mine own room again; making so bold,
My fears forgetting manners, to unseal
Their grand commission; where I found, Horatio, —
O royal knavery! — an exact command,
Larded° with many several sorts of reasons
Importing Denmark's health and England's too,
With, ho! such bugs° and goblins in my life,°
That, on the supervise,° no leisure bated,°
No, not to stay the grinding of the axe,
My head should be struck off.

HORATIO: Is 't possible?

HAMLET: Here's the commission: read it at more leisure.
But wilt thou hear me how I did proceed?

HORATIO: I beseech you.

HAMLET: Being thus be-netted round with villanies, —
Ere I could make a prologue to my brains,
They had begun the play° — I sat me down,
Devis'd a new commission, wrote it fair:
I once did hold it, as our statists° do,
A baseness to write fair° and labour'd much
How to forget that learning, but, sir, now
It did me yeoman's° service: wilt thou know
Th' effect of what I wrote?

HORATIO: Ay, good my lord.

HAMLET: An earnest conjuration from the king,
As England was his faithful tributary,
As love between them like the palm might flourish,
As peace should still her wheaten garland° wear
And stand a comma° 'tween their amities,

---

9. pall: Fail. **11. Rough-hew:** Shape roughly; it may mean "bungle." **13. sea-gown:** "A sea-gown, or a coarse, high-collered, and short-sleeved gowne, reaching down to the mid-leg, and used most by seamen and saylors" (Cotgrave, quoted by Singer). **15. Finger'd:** Pilfered, filched; **in fine:** Finally. **20. Larded:** Enriched. **22. bugs:** Bugbears; **such . . . life:** Such imaginary dangers if I were allowed to live. **23. supervise:** Perusal; **leisure bated:** Delay allowed. **30–31. prologue . . . play:** I.e., before I could begin to think, my mind had made its decision. **33. statists:** Statesmen. **34. fair:** In a clear hand. **36. yeoman's:** I.e., faithful. **41. wheaten garland:** Symbol of peace. **42. comma:** Smallest break or separation. Here *amity* begins and *amity* end the period, and *peace* stands between like a dependent clause. The comma indicates continuity, link.

And many such-like 'As'es° of great charge,°
That, on the view and knowing of these contents,
Without debatement further, more or less,
He should the bearers put to sudden death,
Not shriving-time° allow'd.

HORATIO: How was this seal'd?

HAMLET: Why, even in that was heaven ordinant.°
I had my father's signet in my purse,
Which was the model of that Danish seal;
Folded the writ up in the form of th' other,
Subscrib'd it, gave 't th' impression, plac'd it safely,
The changeling never known. Now, the next day
Was our sea-fight; and what to this was sequent°
Thou know'st already.

HORATIO: So Guildenstern and Rosencrantz go to 't.

HAMLET: Why, man, they did make love to this employment;
They are not near my conscience; their defeat
Does by their own insinuation° grow:
'Tis dangerous when the baser nature comes
Between the pass° and fell incensed° points
Of mighty opposites.

HORATIO: Why, what a king is this!

HAMLET: Does it not, think thee, stand° me now upon —
He that hath kill'd my king and whor'd my mother,
Popp'd in between th' election° and my hopes,
Thrown out his angle° for my proper life,
And with such coz'nage° — is 't not perfect conscience,
To quit° him with this arm? and is 't not to be damn'd,
To let this canker° of our nature come
In further evil?

HORATIO: It must be shortly known to him from England
What is the issue of the business there.

HAMLET: It will be short: the interim is mine;
And a man's life's no more than to say "One."
But I am very sorry, good Horatio,
That to Laertes I forgot myself;
For, by the image of my cause, I see
The portraiture of his: I'll court his favours:
But, sure, the bravery° of his grief did put me
Into a tow'ring passion.

HORATIO: Peace! who comes here?

---

43. 'As'es: The "whereases" of a formal document, with play on the word *ass;* **charge:** Import, and burden. **47. shriving-time:** Time for absolution. **48. ordinant:** Directing. **54. sequent:** Subsequent. **59. insinuation:** Interference. **61. pass:** Thrust; **fell incensed:** Fiercely angered. **63. stand:** Become incumbent. **65. election:** The Danish throne was filled by election. **66. angle:** Fishing line. **67. coz'nage:** Trickery. **68. quit:** Repay. **69. canker:** Ulcer, or possibly the worm which destroys buds and leaves. **79. bravery:** Bravado.

Enter a Courtier [*Osric*].

OSRIC: Your lordship is right welcome back to Denmark.

HAMLET: I humbly thank you, sir. [*To Horatio.*] Dost know this water-fly?°

HORATIO: No, my good lord.

HAMLET: Thy state is the more gracious; for 'tis a vice to know him. He hath much land, and fertile: let a beast be lord of beasts,° and his crib shall stand at the king's mess:° 'tis a chough;° but, as I say, spacious in the possession of dirt.

OSRIC: Sweet lord, if your lordship were at leisure, I should impart a thing to you from his majesty.

HAMLET: I will receive it, sir, with all diligence of spirit. Put your bonnet to his right use; 'tis for the head.

OSRIC: I thank you lordship, it is very hot.

HAMLET: No, believe me, 'tis very cold; the wind is northerly.

OSRIC: It is indifferent° cold, my lord, indeed.

HAMLET: But yet methinks it is very sultry and hot for my complexion.

OSRIC: Exceedingly, my lord; it is very sultry, — as 'twere, — I cannot tell how. But, my lord, his majesty bade me signify to you that 'a has laid a great wager on your head: sir, this is the matter, —

HAMLET: I beseech you, remember° — [*Hamlet moves him to put on his hat.*]

OSRIC: Nay, good my lord; for mine ease,° in good faith. Sir, here is newly come to court Laertes; believe me, an absolute gentleman, full of most excellent differences, of very soft° society and great showing:° indeed, to speak feelingly° of him, he is the card° or calendar of gentry,° for you shall find in him the continent of what part a gentleman would see.

HAMLET: Sir, his definement° suffers no perdition° in you; though, I know, to divide him inventorially° would dozy° the arithmetic of memory, and yet but yaw° neither, in respect of his quick sail. But, in the verity of extolment, I take him to be a soul of great article;° and his infusion° of such dearth and rareness,° as, to make true diction of him, his semblable° is his mirror; and who else would trace° him, his umbrage,° nothing more.

OSRIC: Your lordship speaks most infallibly of him.

HAMLET: The concernancy,° sir? why do we wrap the gentleman in our more rawer breath?°

---

82. water-fly: Vain or busily idle person. **85. lord of beasts:** Cf. Genesis 1:26, 28. **85–86. his crib . . . mess:** He shall eat at the king's table, i.e., be one of the group of persons (usually four) constituting a *mess* at a banquet. **86. chough:** Probably, chattering jackdaw; also explained as *chuff,* provincial boor or churl. **94. indifferent:** Somewhat. **99. remember:** I.e., remember thy courtesy; conventional phrase for "Be covered." **100. mine ease:** Conventional reply declining the invitation of "Remember thy courtesy." **102. soft:** Gentle; **showing:** Distinguished appearance. **103. feelingly:** With just perception; **card:** Chart, map; **gentry:** Good breeding. **105. definement:** Definition; **perdition:** Loss, diminution. **106. divide him inventorially:** I.e., enumerate his graces; **dozy:** Dizzy. **107. yaw:** To move unsteadily (of a ship). **108. article:** Moment or importance; **infusion:** Infused temperament, character imparted by nature. **109. dearth and rareness:** Rarity. **109–110. semblable:** True likeness. **110. trace:** Follow; **umbrage:** Shadow. **113. concernancy:** Import. **114. breath:** Speech.

OSRIC: Sir?

HORATIO [*aside to Hamlet*]: Is 't not possible to understand in another tongue?° You will do 't, sir, really.

HAMLET: What imports the nomination° of this gentleman?

OSRIC: Of Laertes?

HORATIO [*aside to Hamlet*]: His purse is empty already; all 's golden words are spent.

HAMLET: Of him, sir.

OSRIC: I know you are not ignorant —

HAMLET: I would you did, sir; yet, in faith, if you did, it would not much approve° me. Well, sir?

OSRIC: You are not ignorant of what excellence Laertes is —

HAMLET: I dare not confess that, lest I should compare with him in excellence; but, to know a man well, were to know himself.°

OSRIC: I mean, sir, for his weapon; but in the imputation° laid on him by them, in his meed° he's unfellowed.

HAMLET: What's his weapon?

OSRIC: Rapier and dagger.

HAMLET: That's two of his weapons: but, well.

OSRIC: The king, sir, hath wagered with him six Barbary horses: against the which he has impawned,° as I take it, six French rapiers and poniards, with their assigns, as girdle, hangers,° and so: three of the carriages, in faith, are very dear to fancy,° very responsive° to the hilts, most delicate° carriages, and of very liberal conceit.°

HAMLET: What call you the carriages?

HORATIO [*aside to Hamlet*]: I knew you must be edified by the margent° ere you had done.

OSRIC: The carriages, sir, are the hangers.

HAMLET: The phrase would be more german° to the matter, if we could carry cannon by our sides: I would it might be hangers till then. But, on: six Barbary horses against six French swords, their assigns, and three liberal-conceited carriages; that's the French bet against the Danish. Why is this "impawned," as you call it?

OSRIC: The king, sir, hath laid, that in a dozen passes between yourself and him, he shall not exceed you three hits: he hath laid on twelve for nine; and it would come to immediate trial, if your lordship would vouchsafe the answer.

HAMLET: How if I answer "no"?

OSRIC: I mean, my lord, the opposition of your person in trial.

---

116. Is 't . . . tongue?: I.e., can one converse with Osric only in this outlandish jargon? **118. nomination:** Naming. **125. approve:** Command. **128. but . . . himself:** But to know a man as excellent were to know Laertes. **129. imputation:** Reputation. **130. meed:** Merit. **135. he has impawned:** He has wagered. **136. hangers:** Straps on the sword belt from which the sword hung. **137. dear to fancy:** Fancifully made; **responsive:** Probably, well balanced, corresponding closely; **delicate:** I.e., in workmanship. **138. liberal conceit:** Elaborate design. **140. margent:** Margin of a book, place for explanatory notes. **143. german:** Germane, appropriate.

HAMLET: Sir, I will walk here in the hall: if it please his majesty, it is the breathing time° of day with me; let the foils be brought, the gentleman willing, and the king hold his purpose, I will win for him as I can; if not, I will gain nothing but my shame and the odd hits.

OSRIC: Shall I re-deliver you e'en so?

HAMLET: To this effect, sir; after what flourish your nature will.

OSRIC: I commend my duty to your lordship.

HAMLET: Yours, yours. [*Exit Osric.*] He does well to commend it himself; there are no tongues else for 's turn.

HORATIO: This lapwing° runs away with the shell on his head.

HAMLET: 'A did comply, sir, with his dug,° before 'a sucked it. Thus has he — and many more of the same breed that I know the drossy° age dotes on — only got the tune° of the time and out of an habit of encounter;° a kind of yesty° collection, which carries them through and through the most fann'd and winnowed° opinions; and do but blow them to their trial, the bubbles are out.°

Enter a Lord.

LORD: My lord, his majesty commended him to you by young Osric, who brings back to him, that you attend him in the hall: he sends to know if your pleasure hold to play with Laertes, or that you will take longer time.

HAMLET: I am constant to my purposes; they follow the king's pleasure: if his fitness speaks, mine is ready; now or whensoever, provided I be so able as now.

LORD: The king and queen and all are coming down.

HAMLET: In happy time.°

LORD: The queen desires you to use some gentle entertainment to Laertes before you fall to play.

HAMLET: She well instructs me. [*Exit Lord.*]

HORATIO: You will lose this wager, my lord.

HAMLET: I do not think so; since he went into France, I have been in continual practice; I shall win at the odds. But thou wouldst not think how ill all 's here about my heart: but it is no matter.

HORATIO: Nay, good my lord, —

HAMLET: It is but foolery; but it is such a kind of gain-giving,° as would perhaps trouble a woman.

HORATIO: If your mind dislike any thing, obey it: I will forestall their repair hither, and say you are not fit.

HAMLET: Not a whit, we defy augury: there's a special providence in the fall of a sparrow. If it be now, 'tis not to come; if it be not to come, it will be

---

154–155. breathing time: Exercise period. **163. lapwing:** Peewit; noted for its wiliness in drawing a visitor away from its nest and its supposed habit of running about when newly hatched with its head in the shell; possibly an allusion to Osric's hat. **164. did comply . . . dug:** Paid compliments to his mother's breast. **165. drossy:** Frivolous. **166. tune:** Temper, mood; **habit of encounter:** Demeanor of social intercourse. **167. yesty:** Frothy. **168. fann'd and winnowed:** Select and refined. **168–169. blow . . . out:** I.e., put them to the test, and their ignorance is exposed. **177. In happy time:** A phrase of courtesy. **186. gain-giving:** Misgiving.

now; if it be not now, yet it will come: the readiness is all:° since no man of aught he leaves knows, what is 't to leave betimes? Let be.

A table prepared. [*Enter*] *Trumpets, Drums, and Officers with cushions; King, Queen,* [*Osric,*] *and all the State; foils, daggers,* [*and wine borne in;*] *and Laertes.*

KING: Come, Hamlet, come, and take this hand from me.
[*The King puts Laertes' hand into Hamlet's.*]

HAMLET: Give me your pardon, sir: I have done you wrong;
But pardon 't as you are a gentleman.
This presence° knows,
And you must needs have heard, how I am punish'd
With a sore distraction. What I have done,
That might your nature, honour and exception°
Roughly awake, I here proclaim was madness.
Was 't Hamlet wrong'd Laertes? Never Hamlet:
If Hamlet from himself be ta'en away,
And when he's not himself does wrong Laertes,
Then Hamlet does it not, Hamlet denies it.
Who does it, then? His madness: if 't be so,
Hamlet is of the faction that is wrong'd;
His madness is poor Hamlet's enemy.
Sir, in this audience,
Let my disclaiming from a purpos'd evil
Free me so far in your most generous thoughts,
That I have shot mine arrow o'er the house,
And hurt my brother.

LAERTES: I am satisfied in nature,°
Whose motive, in this case, should stir me most
To my revenge: but in my terms of honour
I stand aloof; and will no reconcilement,
Till by some elder masters, of known honour,
I have a voice° and precedent of peace,
To keep my name ungor'd. But till that time,
I do receive your offer'd love like love,
And will not wrong it.

HAMLET: I embrace it freely;
And will this brother's wager frankly play.
Give us the foils. Come on.

LAERTES: Come, one for me.

HAMLET: I'll be your foil,° Laertes: in mine ignorance
Your skill shall, like a star i' th' darkest night,
Stick fiery off° indeed.

---

192. all: All that matters. **197. presence:** Royal assembly. **200. exception:** Disapproval. **213. nature:** I.e., he is personally satisfied, but his honor must be satisfied by the rules of the code of honor. **218. voice:** Authoritative pronouncement. **224. foil:** Quibble on the two senses: "background which sets something off," and "blunted rapier for fencing." **226. Stick fiery off:** Stand out brilliantly.

LAERTES: You mock me, sir.
HAMLET: No, by this hand.
KING: Give them the foils, young Osric. Cousin Hamlet,
You know the wager?
HAMLET: Very well, my lord;
Your grace has laid the odds o' th' weaker side.
KING: I do not fear it; I have seen you both:
But since he is better'd, we have therefore odds.
LAERTES: This is too heavy, let me see another.
HAMLET: This likes me well. These foils have all a length?
[*They prepare to play.*]
OSRIC: Ay, my good lord.
KING: Set me the stoups of wine upon that table.
If Hamlet give the first or second hit,
Or quit in answer of the third exchange,
Let all the battlements their ordnance fire;
The king shall drink to Hamlet's better breath;
And in the cup an union° shall he throw,
Richer than that which four successive kings
In Denmark's crown have worn. Give me the cups;
And let the kettle° to the trumpet speak,
The trumpet to the cannoneer without,
The cannons to the heavens, the heavens to earth,
"Now the king drinks to Hamlet." Come begin: *Trumpets the while.*
And you, the judges, bear a wary eye.
HAMLET: Come on, sir.
LAERTES: Come, my lord. [*They play.*]
HAMLET: One.
LAERTES: No.
HAMLET: Judgement.
OSRIC: A hit, a very palpable hit.
Drum, trumpets, and shot. Flourish. A piece goes off.
LAERTES: Well; again.
KING: Stay; give me drink. Hamlet, this pearl° is thine;
Here's to thy health. Give him the cup.
HAMLET: I'll play this bout first; set it by awhile.
Come. [*They play.*] Another hit; what say you?
LAERTES: A touch, a touch, I do confess 't.
KING: Our son shall win.
QUEEN: He's fat,° and scant of breath.
Here, Hamlet, take my napkin, rub thy brows:
The queen carouses° to thy fortune, Hamlet.

---

241. union: Pearl. **244. kettle:** Kettledrum. **251. pearl:** I.e., the poison. **256. fat:** Not physically fit, out of training. Some earlier editors speculated that the term applied to the corpulence of Richard Burbage, who originally played the part, but the allusion now appears unlikely. *Fat* may also suggest "sweaty." **258. carouses:** Drinks a toast.

HAMLET: Good madam!
KING: Gertrude, do not drink.
QUEEN: I will, my lord; I pray you, pardon me. [*Drinks.*]
KING [*aside*]: It is the poison'd cup: it is too late.
HAMLET: I dare not drink yet, madam; by and by.
QUEEN: Come, let me wipe thy face.
LAERTES: My lord, I'll hit him now.
KING: I do not think 't.
LAERTES [*aside*]: And yet 'tis almost 'gainst my conscience.
HAMLET: Come, for the third, Laertes: you but dally;
I pray you, pass with your best violence;
I am afeard you make a wanton° of me.
LAERTES: Say you so? come on. [*They play.*]
OSRIC: Nothing, neither way.
LAERTES: Have at you now!
[*Laertes wounds Hamlet; then, in scuffling, they change rapiers° and Hamlet wounds Laertes.*]
KING: Part them; they are incens'd.
HAMLET: Nay, come again. [*The Queen falls.*]
OSRIC: Look to the queen there, ho!
HORATIO: They bleed on both sides. How is it, my lord?
OSRIC: How is 't, Laertes?
LAERTES: Why, as a woodcock° to mine own springe,° Osric;
I am justly kill'd with mine own treachery.
HAMLET: How does the queen?
KING: She swounds° to see them bleed.
QUEEN: No, no, the drink, the drink, — O my dear Hamlet, —
The drink, the drink! I am poison'd. [*Dies.*]
HAMLET: O villany! Ho! let the door be lock'd:
Treachery! Seek it out. [*Laertes falls.*]
LAERTES: It is here, Hamlet: Hamlet, thou art slain;
No med'cine in the world can do thee good;
In thee there is not half an hour of life;
The treacherous instrument is in thy hand,
Unbated° and envenom'd: the foul practice
Hath turn'd itself on me; lo, here I lie,
Never to rise again: thy mother's poison'd:
I can no more: the king, the king's to blame.
HAMLET: The point envenom'd too!
Then, venom, to thy work. [*Stabs the King.*]
ALL: Treason! treason!

---

268. wanton: Spoiled child. **271. s.d. in scuffling, they change rapiers:** According to a widespread stage tradition, Hamlet receives a scratch, realizes that Laertes' sword is unbated, and accordingly forces an exchange. **275. woodcock:** As type of stupidity or as decoy; **springe:** Trap, snare. **277. swounds:** Swoons. **286. Unbated:** Not blunted with a button.

KING: O, yet defend me, friends; I am but hurt.
HAMLET: Here, thou incestuous, murd'rous, damned Dane,
Drink off this potion. Is thy union here?
Follow my mother. [*King dies.*]
LAERTES: He is justly serv'd;
It is a poison temper'd° by himself.
Exchange forgiveness with me, noble Hamlet:
Mine and my father's death come not upon thee,
Nor thine on me! [*Dies.*]
HAMLET: Heaven make thee free of it! I follow thee.
I am dead, Horatio. Wretched queen, adieu!
You that look pale and tremble at this chance,
That are but mutes° or audience to this act,
Had I but time — as this fell sergeant,° Death,
Is strict in his arrest — O, I could tell you —
But let it be. Horatio, I am dead;
Thou livest; report me and my cause aright
To the unsatisfied.
HORATIO: Never believe it:
I am more an antique Roman° than a Dane:
Here 's yet some liquor left.
HAMLET: As th' art a man,
Give me the cup: let go, by heaven, I'll ha 't.
O God! Horatio, what a wounded name,
Things standing thus unknown, shall live behind me!
If thou didst ever hold me in thy heart,
Absent thee from felicity awhile,
And in this harsh world draw thy breath in pain,
To tell my story. *A march afar off.*
What warlike noise is this?
OSRIC: Young Fortinbras, with conquest come from Poland,
To the ambassadors of England gives
This warlike volley.
HAMLET: O, I die, Horatio;
The potent poison quite o'er-crows° my spirit:
I cannot live to hear the news from England;
But I do prophesy th' election lights
On Fortinbras: he has my dying voice;
So tell him, with th' occurrents,° more and less,
Which have solicited.° The rest is silence. [*Dies.*]
HORATIO: Now cracks a noble heart. Good night, sweet prince;

---

297. temper'd: Mixed. **304. mutes:** Performers in a play who speak no words. **305. sergeant:** Sheriff's officer. **310. Roman:** It was the Roman custom to follow masters in death. **322. o'er-crows:** Triumphs over. **326. occurrents:** Events, incidents. **327. solicited:** Moved, urged.

And flights of angels sing thee to thy rest!
Why does the drum come hither? [*March within.*]

Enter Fortinbras, with the [*English*] *Ambassadors* [*and others*].

FORTINBRAS: Where is this sight?
HORATIO: What is it you would see?
If aught of woe or wonder, cease your search.
FORTINBRAS: This quarry° cries on havoc.° O proud Death,
What feast is toward in thine eternal cell,
That thou so many princes at a shot
So bloodily hast struck?
FIRST AMBASSADOR: The sight is dismal;
And our affairs from England come too late:
The ears are senseless that should give us hearing,
To tell him his commandment is fulfill'd,
That Rosencrantz and Guildenstern are dead:
Where should we have our thanks?
HORATIO: Not from his mouth,°
Had it th' ability of life to thank you:
He never gave commandment for their death.
But since, so jump° upon this bloody question,°
You from the Polack wars, and you from England,
Are here arriv'd, give order that these bodies
High on a stage° be placed to the view;
And let me speak to th' yet unknowing world
How these things came about: so shall you hear
Of carnal, bloody, and unnatural acts,
Of accidental judgements, casual slaughters,
Of deaths put on by cunning and forc'd cause,
And, in this upshot, purposes mistook
Fall'n on th' inventors' heads: all this can I
Truly deliver.
FORTINBRAS: Let us haste to hear it,
And call the noblest to the audience.
For me, with sorrow I embrace my fortune:
I have some rights of memory° in this kingdom,
Which now to claim my vantage doth invite me.
HORATIO: Of that I shall have also cause to speak,
And from his mouth whose voice will draw on more:°
But let this same be presently perform'd,
Even while men's minds are wild; lest more mischance,
On° plots and errors, happen.

---

333. quarry: Heap of dead; **cries on havoc:** Proclaims a general slaughter. **341. his mouth:** I.e., the king's. **344. jump:** Precisely; **question:** Dispute. **347. stage:** Platform. **358. of memory:** Traditional, remembered. **361. voice . . . more:** Vote will influence still others. **364. On:** On account of, or possibly, on top of, in addition to.

FORTINBRAS: Let four captains
Bear Hamlet, like a soldier, to the stage;
For he was likely, had he been put on,
To have prov'd most royal: and, for his passage,°
The soldiers' music and the rites of war
Speak loudly for him.
Take up the bodies: such a sight as this
Becomes the field,° but here shows much amiss.
Go, bid the soldiers shoot.

Exeunt [*marching, bearing off the dead bodies; after which a peal of ordnance is heard*].

WILLIAM SHAKESPEARE

The Tempest

c. 1611

NAMES OF THE ACTORS

ALONSO, *King of Naples*
SEBASTIAN, *his brother*
PROSPERO, *the right Duke of Milan*
ANTONIO, *his brother, the usurping Duke of Milan*
FERDINAND, *son to the King of Naples*
GONZALO, *an honest old councillor*
ADRIAN *and* FRANCISCO, *lords*
CALIBAN, *a savage and deformed slave*
TRINCULO, *a jester*
STEPHANO, *a drunken butler*
MASTER *of a ship*
BOATSWAIN
MARINERS
MIRANDA, *daughter to Prospero*
ARIEL, *an airy spirit*
IRIS, CERES, JUNO, NYMPHS, REAPERS, [*presented by*] *spirits*
[OTHER SPIRITS ATTENDING ON PROSPERO]

THE SCENE: *An uninhabited island*

367. passage: Death. **371. field:** I.e., of battle.

[ACT I

SCENE I: *On board ship, off the island's coast.*]

A tempestuous noise of thunder and lightning heard. Enter a Shipmaster and a Boatswain.

MASTER: Boatswain!

BOATSWAIN: Here, Master. What cheer?

MASTER: Good,° speak to the mariners. Fall to 't yarely,° or we run ourselves aground. Bestir, bestir! *Exit.*

Enter Mariners.

BOATSWAIN: Heigh, my hearts! Cheerly, cheerly, my hearts! Yare, yare! Take in the topsail. Tend° to the Master's whistle. — Blow° till thou burst thy wind, if room enough!°

Enter Alonso, Sebastian, Antonio, Ferdinand, Gonzalo, and others.

ALONSO: Good Boatswain, have care. Where's the Master? Play the men.°

BOATSWAIN: I pray now, keep below.

ANTONIO: Where is the Master, Boatswain?

BOATSWAIN: Do you not hear him? You mar our labor. Keep° your cabins! You do assist the storm.

GONZALO: Nay, good,° be patient.

BOATSWAIN: When the sea is. Hence! What cares these roarers° for the name of king? To cabin! Silence! Trouble us not.

GONZALO: Good, yet remember whom thou hast aboard.

BOATSWAIN: None that I more love than myself. You are a councillor; if you can command these elements to silence and work the peace of the present,° we will not hand° a rope more. Use your authority. If you cannot, give thanks you have lived so long and make yourself ready in your cabin for the mischance of the hours, if it so hap° — Cheerly, good hearts! — Out of our way, I say. *Exit.*

GONZALO: I have great comfort from this fellow. Methinks he hath no drowning mark upon him; his complexion is perfect gallows.° Stand fast, good Fate, to his hanging! Make the rope of his destiny our cable, for our own doth little advantage.° If he be not born to be hanged, our case is miserable.° *Exeunt* [*courtiers*].

Enter Boatswain.

ACT I, SCENE I. **3. Good:** I.e., it's good you've come, or, my good fellow; **yarely:** Nimbly. **6. Tend:** Attend; **Blow:** (Addressed to the wind.) **7. if room enough:** As long as we have sea room enough. **8. Play the men:** Act like men (?) ply, urge the men to exert themselves (?). **11. Keep:** Remain in. **13. good:** Good fellow. **14. roarers:** Waves or winds, or both; spoken to as though they were "bullies" or "blusterers." **18–19. work . . . present:** Bring calm to our present circumstances. **19. hand:** Handle. **21. hap:** Happen. **24. complexion . . . gallows:** Appearance shows he was born to be hanged (and therefore, according to the proverb, in no danger of drowning). **26. our . . . advantage:** Our own cable is of little benefit. **27. case is miserable:** Circumstances are desperate.

BOATSWAIN: Down with the topmast! Yare! Lower, lower! Bring her to try wi' the main course.° *(A cry within.)* A plague upon this howling! They are louder than the weather or our office.°

Enter Sebastian, Antonio, and Gonzalo.

Yet again? What do you hear? Shall we give o'er° and drown? Have you a mind to sink?

SEBASTIAN: A pox o' your throat, you bawling, blasphemous, incharitable dog!

BOATSWAIN: Work you, then.

ANTONIO: Hang, cur! Hang, you whoreson, insolent noisemaker! We are less afraid to be drowned than thou art.

GONZALO: I'll warrant him for drowning,° though the ship were no stronger than a nutshell and as leaky as an unstanched° wench.

BOATSWAIN: Lay her ahold, ahold!° Set her two courses.° Off to sea again! Lay her off!

Enter Mariners, wet.

MARINERS: All lost! To prayers, to prayers! All lost!
[*The Mariners run about in confusion, exiting at random.*]

BOATSWAIN: What, must our mouths be cold?°

GONZALO: The King and Prince at prayers! Let's assist them,
For our case is as theirs.

SEBASTIAN: I am out of patience.

ANTONIO: We are merely° cheated of our lives by drunkards.
This wide-chapped° rascal! Would thou mightst lie drowning
The washing of ten tides!°

GONZALO: He'll be hanged yet,
Though every drop of water swear against it
And gape at wid'st° to glut° him.
(A confused noise within:) "Mercy on us!" —
"We split, we split!"° — "Farewell my wife and children!" —
"Farewell, brother!" — "We split, we split, we split!" [*Exit Boatswain.*]

ANTONIO: Let's all sink wi' the King.

SEBASTIAN: Let's take leave of him. *Exit* [*with Antonio*].

GONZALO: Now would I give a thousand furlongs of sea for an acre of barren ground: long heath,° brown furze,° anything. The wills above be done! But I would fain° die a dry death. *Exit.*

28–29. Bring . . . course: Sail her close to the wind by means of the mainsail. **30. our office:** I.e., the noise we make at our work. **31. give o'er:** Give up. **38. warrant him for drowning:** Guarantee that he will never be drowned. **39. unstanched:** Insatiable, loose, unrestrained (suggesting also "incontinent" and "menstrual"). **40. ahold:** Ahull, close to the wind; **courses:** Sails, i.e., foresail as well as mainsail, set in an attempt to get the ship back out into open water. **43. must . . . cold:** I.e., must we drown in the cold sea, or, let us heat up our mouths with liquor. **46. merely:** Utterly. **47. wide-chapped:** With mouth wide open. **47–48. lie . . . tides:** (Pirates were hanged on the shore and left until three tides had come in.) **50. at wid'st:** Wide open; **glut:** Swallow. **51. split:** Break apart. **56. heath:** Heather; **furze:** Gorse, a weed growing on wasteland. **57. fain:** Rather.

[SCENE II: *The island, near Prospero's cell. On the Elizabethan stage, this cell is implicitly at hand throughout the play, although in some scenes the convention of flexible distance allows us to imagine characters in other parts of the island.*]

Enter Prospero [in his magic cloak] and Miranda.

MIRANDA: If by your art,° my dearest father, you have
Put the wild waters in this roar, allay° them.
The sky, it seems, would pour down stinking pitch,
But that the sea, mounting to th' welkin's cheek,°
Dashes the fire out. O, I have suffered
With those that I saw suffer! A brave° vessel,
Who had, no doubt, some noble creature in her,
Dashed all to pieces. O, the cry did knock
Against my very heart! Poor souls, they perished.
Had I been any god of power, I would
Have sunk the sea within the earth or ere°
It should the good ship so have swallowed and
The freighting° souls within her.

PROSPERO: Be collected.°
No more amazement.° Tell your piteous° heart
There's no harm done.

MIRANDA: O, woe the day!

PROSPERO: No harm.
I have done nothing but° in care of thee,
Of thee, my dear one, thee, my daughter, who
Art ignorant of what thou art, naught knowing
Of whence I am, nor that I am more better°
Than Prospero, master of a full° poor cell,
And thy no greater father.

MIRANDA: More to know
Did never meddle° with my thoughts.

PROSPERO: 'Tis time
I should inform thee farther. Lend thy hand
And pluck my magic garment from me. So,
[*laying down his magic cloak and staff*]
Lie there, my art. — Wipe thou thine eyes. Have comfort.
The direful spectacle of the wreck,° which touched
The very virtue° of compassion in thee,
I have with such provision° in mine art
So safely ordered that there is no soul —
No, not so much perdition° as an hair

SCENE II. **1. art:** Magic. **2. allay:** Pacify. **4. welkin's cheek:** Sky's face. **6. brave:** Gallant, splendid. **11. or ere:** Before. **13. freighting:** Forming the cargo; **collected:** Calm, composed. **14. amazement:** Consternation; **piteous:** Pitying. **16. but:** Except. **19. more better:** Of higher rank. **20. full:** Very. **22. meddle:** Mingle. **26. wreck:** Shipwreck. **27. virtue:** Essence. **28. provision:** Foresight. **30. perdition:** Loss.

Betid° to any creature in the vessel
Which° thou heard'st cry, which thou saw'st sink. Sit down,
For thou must now know farther.

MIRANDA [*sitting*]: You have often
Begun to tell me what I am, but stopped
And left me to a bootless inquisition,°
Concluding, "Stay, not yet."

PROSPERO: The hour's now come;
The very minute bids thee ope thine ear.
Obey, and be attentive. Canst thou remember
A time before we came unto this cell?
I do not think thou canst, for then thou wast not
Out° three years old.

MIRANDA: Certainly, sir, I can.

PROSPERO: By what? By any other house or person?
Of anything the image, tell me, that
Hath kept with thy remembrance.

MIRANDA: 'Tis far off,
And rather like a dream than an assurance
That my remembrance warrants.° Had I not
Four or five women once that tended me?

PROSPERO: Thou hadst, and more, Miranda. But how is it
That this lives in thy mind? What seest thou else
In the dark backward and abysm of time?°
If thou rememberest aught° ere thou cam'st here,
How thou cam'st here thou mayst.

MIRANDA: But that I do not.

PROSPERO: Twelve year since, Miranda, twelve year since,
Thy father was the Duke of Milan and
A prince of power.

MIRANDA: Sir, are not you my father?

PROSPERO: Thy mother was a piece° of virtue, and
She said thou wast my daughter; and thy father
Was Duke of Milan, and his only heir
And princess no worse issued.°

MIRANDA: O the heavens!
What foul play had we, that we came from thence?
Or blessèd was't we did?

PROSPERO: Both, both, my girl.
By foul play, as thou sayst, were we heaved thence,
But blessedly holp° hither.

---

31. Betid: Happened. **32. Which:** Whom. **35. bootless inquisition:** Profitless inquiry. **41. Out:** Fully. **45–46. assurance . . . warrants:** Certainty that my memory guarantees. **50. backward . . . time:** Abyss of the past. **51. aught:** Anything. **56. piece:** Masterpiece, exemplar. **59. no worse issued:** No less nobly born, descended. **63. holp:** Helped.

MIRANDA: O, my heart bleeds
To think o' the teen that I have turned you to,°
Which is from° my remembrance! Please you, farther.
PROSPERO: My brother and thy uncle, called Antonio —
I pray thee mark me — that a brother should
Be so perfidious! — he whom next° thyself
Of all the world I loved, and to him put
The manage° of my state, as at that time
Through all the seigniories° it was the first,
And Prospero the prime° duke, being so reputed
In dignity, and for the liberal arts
Without a parallel; those being all my study,
The government I cast upon my brother
And to my state grew stranger,° being transported°
And rapt in secret studies. Thy false uncle —
Dost thou attend me?
MIRANDA: Sir, most heedfully.
PROSPERO: Being once perfected° how to grant suits,
How to deny them, who t' advance and who
To trash° for overtopping,° new created
The creatures° that were mine, I say, or changed 'em,
Or else new formed 'em;° having both the key°
Of officer and office, set all hearts i' the state
To what tune pleased his ear, that° now he was
The ivy which had hid my princely trunk
And sucked my verdure° out on 't.° Thou attend'st not.
MIRANDA: O, good sir, I do.
PROSPERO: I pray thee, mark me.
I, thus neglecting worldly ends, all dedicated
To closeness° and the bettering of my mind
With that which, but by being so retired,
O'erprized all popular rate,° in my false brother
Awaked an evil nature; and my trust,
Like a good parent,° did beget of° him

---

64. teen . . . to: Trouble I've caused you to remember or put you to. **65. from:** Out of. **68. next:** Next to. **70. manage:** Management, administration. **71. seigniories:** I.e., city-states of northern Italy. **72. prime:** First in rank and importance. **76. to . . . stranger:** I.e., withdrew from my responsibilities as duke; **transported:** Carried away. **79. perfected:** Grown skillful. **81. trash:** Check a hound by tying a cord or weight to its neck; **overtopping:** Running too far ahead of the pack; surmounting, exceeding one's authority. **82. creatures:** Dependents. **82–83. or changed . . . formed 'em:** I.e., either changed their loyalties and duties or else created new ones. **83. key:** (1) Key for unlocking (2) tool for tuning stringed instruments. **85. that:** So that. **87. verdure:** Vitality; **on 't:** Of it. **90. closeness:** Retirement, seclusion. **91–92. but . . . rate:** I.e., were it not that its private nature caused me to neglect my public responsibilities, had a value far beyond what public opinion could appreciate, or, simply because it was done in such seclusion, had a value not appreciated by popular opinion. **94. good parent:** (Alludes to the proverb that good parents often bear bad children; see also line 120); **of:** In.

A falsehood in its contrary as great
As my trust was, which had indeed no limit,
A confidence sans° bound. He being thus lorded°
Not only with what my revenue yielded
But what my power might else° exact, like one
Who, having into° truth by telling of it,
Made such a sinner of his memory
To° credit his own lie,° he did believe
He was indeed the Duke, out o'° the substitution
And executing th' outward face of royalty°
With all prerogative. Hence his ambition growing —
Dost thou hear?

MIRANDA: Your tale, sir, would cure deafness.

PROSPERO: To have no screen between this part he played
And him he played it for,° he needs will be°
Absolute Milan.° Me, poor man, my library
Was dukedom large enough. Of temporal royalties°
He thinks me now incapable; confederates° —
So dry° he was for sway° — wi' the King of Naples
To give him annual tribute, do him° homage,
Subject his coronet to his° crown, and bend°
The dukedom yet° unbowed — alas, poor Milan! —
To most ignoble stooping.

MIRANDA: O the heavens!

PROSPERO: Mark his condition° and th' event,° then tell me
If this might be a brother.

MIRANDA: I should sin
To think but° nobly of my grandmother.
Good wombs have borne bad sons.

PROSPERO: Now the condition.
This King of Naples, being an enemy
To me inveterate, hearkens° my brother's suit,
Which was that he,° in lieu o' the premises°

---

97. sans: Without; **lorded:** Raised to lordship, with power and wealth. **99. else:** Otherwise, additionally. **100–102. Who . . . lie:** I.e., who, by repeatedly telling the lie (that he was indeed Duke of Milan), made his memory such a confirmed sinner against truth that he began to believe his own lie; **into:** Unto, against; **To:** So as to. **103. out o':** As a result of. **104. And . . . royalty:** And (as a result of) his carrying out all the visible functions of royalty. **107–108. To have . . . it for:** To have no separation or barrier between his role and himself. (Antonio wanted to act in his own person, not as substitute.) **108. needs will be:** Insisted on becoming. **109. Absolute Milan:** Unconditional Duke of Milan. **110. temporal royalties:** Practical prerogatives and responsibilities of a sovereign. **111. confederates:** Conspires, allies himself. **112. dry:** Thirsty; **sway:** Power. **113. him:** I.e., the King of Naples. **114. his . . . his:** Antonio's . . . the King of Naples'; **bend:** Make bow down. **115. yet:** Hitherto. **117. condition:** Pact; **event:** Outcome. **119. but:** Other than. **122. hearkens:** Listens to. **123. he:** The King of Naples; **in . . . premises:** In return for the stipulation.

Of homage and I know not how much tribute,
Should presently extirpate° me and mine
Out of the dukedom and confer fair Milan,
With all the honors, on my brother. Whereon,
A treacherous army levied, one midnight
Fated to th' purpose did Antonio open
The gates of Milan, and, i' the dead of darkness,
The ministers for the purpose° hurried thence°
Me and thy crying self.

MIRANDA: Alack, for pity!
I, not remembering how I cried out then,
Will cry it o'er again. It is a hint°
That wrings° mine eyes to 't.

PROSPERO: Hear a little further,
And then I'll bring thee to the present business
Which now's upon 's, without the which this story
Were most impertinent.°

MIRANDA: Wherefore° did they not
That hour destroy us?

PROSPERO: Well demanded,° wench.°
My tale provokes that question. Dear, they durst not,
So dear the love my people bore me, nor set
A mark so bloody° on the business, but
With colors fairer° painted their foul ends.
In few,° they hurried us aboard a bark,°
Bore us some leagues to sea, where they prepared
A rotten carcass of a butt,° not rigged,
Nor tackle,° sail, nor mast; the very rats
Instinctively have quit° it. There they hoist us,
To cry to th' sea that roared to us, to sigh
To th' winds whose pity, sighing back again,
Did us but loving wrong.°

MIRANDA: Alack, what trouble
Was I then to you!

PROSPERO: O, a cherubin
Thou wast that did preserve me. Thou didst smile,
Infusèd with a fortitude from heaven,

---

125. presently extirpate: At once remove. **131. ministers . . . purpose:** Agents employed to do this; **thence:** From there. **134. hint:** Occasion. **135. wrings:** (1) Constrains (2) wrings tears from. **138. impertinent:** Irrelevant; **Wherefore:** Why. **139. demanded:** Asked; **wench:** (Here a term of endearment.) **141–142. set . . . bloody:** I.e., make obvious their murderous intent (from the practice of marking with the blood of the prey those who have participated in a successful hunt). **143. fairer:** Apparently more attractive. **144. few:** Few words; **bark:** Ship. **146. butt:** Cask, tub. **147. Nor tackle:** Neither rigging. **148. quit:** Abandoned. **151. Did . . . wrong:** (I.e., the winds pitied Prospero and Miranda, though of necessity they blew them from shore.)

When I have decked° the sea with drops full salt,
Under my burden groaned, which° raised in me
An undergoing stomach,° to bear up
Against what should ensue.
MIRANDA: How came we ashore?
PROSPERO: By Providence divine.
Some food we had, and some fresh water, that
A noble Neapolitan, Gonzalo,
Out of his charity, who being then appointed
Master of this design, did give us, with
Rich garments, linens, stuffs,° and necessaries,
Which since have steaded much.° So, of° his gentleness,
Knowing I loved my books, he furnished me
From mine own library with volumes that
I prize above my dukedom.
MIRANDA: Would° I might
But ever° see that man!
PROSPERO: Now I arise. [*He puts on his magic cloak.*]
Sit still, and hear the last of our sea sorrow.°
Here in this island we arrived; and here
Have I, thy schoolmaster, made thee more profit°
Than other princess'° can, that have more time
For vainer° hours and tutors not so careful.
MIRANDA: Heavens thank you for 't! And now, I pray you, sir —
For still 'tis beating in my mind — your reason
For raising this sea storm?
PROSPERO: Know thus far forth:
By accident most strange, bountiful Fortune,
Now my dear lady,° hath mine enemies
Brought to this shore; and by my prescience
I find my zenith° doth depend upon
A most auspicious star, whose influence°
If now I court not, but omit,° my fortunes
Will ever after droop. Here cease more questions.
Thou art inclined to sleep. 'Tis a good dullness,°
And give it way.° I know thou canst not choose. [*Miranda sleeps.*]

155. decked: Covered (with salt tears), adorned. **156. which:** I.e., the smile. **157. undergoing stomach:** Courage to go on. **165. stuffs:** Supplies. **166. steaded much:** Been of much use; **So, of:** Similarly, out of. **169. Would:** I wish. **170. But ever:** I.e., someday. **171. sea sorrow:** Sorrowful adventure at sea. **173. more profit:** Profit more. **174. princess':** Princesses (or the word may be *princes,* referring to royal children both male and female). **175. vainer:** More foolishly spent. **180. my dear lady:** (Refers to Fortune, not Miranda.) **182. zenith:** Height of fortune (astrological term). **183. influence:** Astrological power. **184. omit:** Ignore. **186. dullness:** Drowsiness. **187. give it way:** Let it happen (i.e., don't fight it).

Come away,° servant, come! I am ready now.
Approach, my Ariel, come.

Enter Ariel.

ARIEL: All hail, great master, grave sir, hail! I come
To answer thy best pleasure; be 't to fly,
To swim, to dive into the fire, to ride
On the curled clouds, to thy strong bidding task°
Ariel and all his quality.°

PROSPERO: Hast thou, spirit,
Performed to point° the tempest that I bade thee?

ARIEL: To every article.
I boarded the King's ship. Now on the beak,°
Now in the waist,° the deck,° in every cabin,
I flamed amazement.° Sometimes I'd divide
And burn in many places; on the topmast,
The yards, and bowsprit would I flame distinctly,°
Then meet and join. Jove's lightning, the precursors
O' the dreadful thunderclaps, more momentary
And sight-outrunning° were not.° The fire and cracks
Of sulfurous roaring the most mighty Neptune°
Seem to besiege and make his bold waves tremble,
Yea, his dread trident shake.

PROSPERO: My brave spirit!
Who was so firm, so constant, that this coil°
Would not infect his reason?

ARIEL: Not a soul
But felt a fever of the mad° and played
Some tricks of desperation. All but mariners
Plunged in the foaming brine and quit the vessel,
Then all afire with me. The King's son, Ferdinand,
With hair up-staring° — then like reeds, not hair —
Was the first man that leapt; cried, "Hell is empty,
And all the devils are here!"

PROSPERO: Why, that's my spirit!
But was not this nigh shore?

ARIEL: Close by, my master.

PROSPERO: But are they, Ariel, safe?

ARIEL: Not a hair perished.
On their sustaining garments° not a blemish,

---

188. Come away: Come. **193. task:** Make demands upon. **194. quality:** (1) Fellow spirits (2) abilities. **195. to point:** To the smallest detail. **197. beak:** Prow. **198. waist:** Midships; **deck:** Poop deck at the stern. **199. flamed amazement:** Struck terror in the guise of fire, i.e., Saint Elmo's fire. **201. distinctly:** In different places. **204. sight-outrunning:** Swifter than sight; **were not:** Could not have been. **205. Neptune:** Roman god of the sea. **208. coil:** Tumult. **210. of the mad:** I.e., such as madmen feel. **214. up-staring:** Standing on end. **219. sustaining garments:** Garments that buoyed them up in the sea.

But fresher than before; and, as thou bad'st° me,
In troops° I have dispersed them, 'bout the isle.
The King's son have I landed by himself,
Whom I left cooling of° the air with sighs
In an odd angle° of the isle, and sitting,
His arms in this sad knot.° [*He folds his arms.*]

PROSPERO: Of the King's ship,
The mariners, say how thou hast disposed,
And all the rest o' the fleet.

ARIEL: Safely in harbor
Is the King's ship; in the deep nook,° where once
Thou called'st me up at midnight to fetch dew°
From the still-vexed Bermudas,° there she's hid;
The mariners all under hatches stowed,
Who, with a charm joined to their suffered labor,°
I have left asleep. And for the rest o' the fleet,
Which I dispersed, they all have met again
And are upon the Mediterranean float°
Bound sadly home for Naples,
Supposing that they saw the King's ship wrecked
And his great person perish.

PROSPERO: Ariel, thy charge
Exactly is performed. But there's more work.
What is the time o' the day?

ARIEL: Past the mid season.°

PROSPERO: At least two glasses.° The time twixt six and now
Must by us both be spent most preciously.

ARIEL: Is there more toil? Since thou dost give me pains,°
Let me remember° thee what thou hast promised,
Which is not yet performed me.

PROSPERO: How now? Moody?
What is 't thou canst demand?

ARIEL: My liberty.

PROSPERO: Before the time be out? No more!

ARIEL: I prithee,
Remember I have done thee worthy service,
Told thee no lies, made thee no mistakings, served
Without or grudge or grumblings. Thou did promise
To bate° me a full year.

PROSPERO: Dost thou forget
From what a torment I did free thee?

---

220. bad'st: Ordered. **221. troops:** Groups. **223. cooling of:** Cooling. **224. angle:** Corner. **225. sad knot:** (Folded arms are indicative of melancholy.) **228. nook:** Bay. **229. dew:** (Collected at midnight for magical purposes; compare with line 325.) **230. still-vexed Bermudas:** Ever stormy Bermudas. **232. with . . . labor:** By means of a spell added to all the labor they have undergone. **235. float:** Sea. **240. mid season:** Noon. **241. glasses:** Hourglasses. **243. pains:** Labors. **244. remember:** Remind. **251. bate:** Remit, deduct.

ARIEL: No.
PROSPERO: Thou dost, and think'st it much to tread the ooze
Of the salt deep,
To run upon the sharp wind of the north,
To do me° business in the veins° o' the earth
When it is baked° with frost.
ARIEL: I do not, sir.
PROSPERO: Thou liest, malignant thing! Hast thou forgot
The foul witch Sycorax, who with age and envy°
Was grown into a hoop?° Hast thou forgot her?
ARIEL: No, sir.
PROSPERO: Thou hast. Where was she born? Speak. Tell me.
ARIEL: Sir, in Argier.°
PROSPERO: O, was she so? I must
Once in a month recount what thou hast been,
Which thou forgett'st. This damned witch Sycorax,
For mischiefs manifold and sorceries terrible
To enter human hearing, from Argier,
Thou know'st, was banished. For one thing she did°
They would not take her life. Is not this true?
ARIEL: Ay, sir.
PROSPERO: This blue-eyed° hag was hither brought with child°
And here was left by the sailors. Thou, my slave,
As thou report'st thyself, was then her servant;
And, for° thou wast a spirit too delicate
To act her earthy and abhorred commands,
Refusing her grand hests,° she did confine thee,
By help of her more potent ministers
And in her most unmitigable rage,
Into a cloven pine, within which rift
Imprisoned thou didst painfully remain
A dozen years; within which space she died
And left thee there, where thou didst vent thy groans
As fast as mill wheels strike.° Then was this island —
Save° for the son that she did litter° here,
A freckled whelp,° hag-born° — not honored with
A human shape.

---

256. do me: Do for me; **veins:** Veins of minerals, or, underground streams, thought to be analogous to the veins of the human body. **257. baked:** Hardened. **259. envy:** Malice. **260. grown into a hoop:** I.e., so bent over with age as to resemble a hoop. **263. Argier:** Algiers. **268. one . . . did:** (Perhaps a reference to her pregnancy, for which her life would be spared.) **271. blue-eyed:** With dark circles under the eyes or with blue eyelids, implying pregnancy; **with child:** Pregnant. **274. for:** Because. **276. hests:** Commands. **283. as mill wheels strike:** As the blades of a mill wheel strike the water. **284. Save:** Except; **litter:** Give birth to. **285. whelp:** Offspring (used of animals); **hag-born:** Born of a female demon.

ARIEL: Yes, Caliban her son.°
PROSPERO: Dull thing, I say so:° he, that Caliban
Whom now I keep in service. Thou best know'st
What torment I did find thee in. Thy groans
Did make wolves howl, and penetrate the breasts
Of ever-angry bears. It was a torment
To lay upon the damned, which Sycorax
Could not gain undo. It was mine art,
When I arrived and heard thee, that made gape°
The pine and let thee out.
ARIEL: I thank thee, master.
PROSPERO: If thou more murmur'st, I will rend an oak
And peg thee in his° knotty entrails till
Thou hast howled away twelve winters.
ARIEL: Pardon, master.
I will be correspondent° to command
And do my spriting° gently.°
PROSPERO: Do so, and after two days
I will discharge thee.
ARIEL: That's my noble master!
What shall I do? Say what? What shall I do?
PROSPERO: Go make thyself like a nymph o' the sea. Be subject
To no sight but thine and mine, invisible
To every eyeball else. Go take this shape
And hither come in 't. Go, hence with diligence! *Exit* [*Ariel*].
Awake, dear heart, awake! Thou hast slept well.
Awake!
MIRANDA: The strangeness of your story put
Heaviness° in me.
PROSPERO: Shake it off. Come on,
We'll visit Caliban, my slave, who never
Yields us kind answer.
MIRANDA: 'Tis a villain, sir,
I do not love to look on.
PROSPERO: But, as 'tis,
We cannot miss° him. He does make our fire,
Fetch in our wood, and serves in offices°
That profit us. — What ho! Slave! Caliban!
Thou earth, thou! Speak.
CALIBAN (*within*): There's wood enough within.

---

286. Yes . . . son: (Ariel is probably concurring with Prospero's comment about a "freckled whelp," not contradicting the point about "A human shape.") **287. Dull . . . so:** I.e., exactly, that's what I said, you dullard. **294. gape:** Open wide. **297. his:** Its. **299. correspondent:** Responsive, submissive. **300. spriting:** Duties as a spirit; **gently:** Willingly, ungrudgingly. **311. Heaviness:** Drowsiness. **315. miss:** Do without. **316. offices:** Functions, duties.

PROSPERO: Come forth, I say! There's other business for thee.
Come, thou tortoise! When?°

Enter Ariel like a water nymph.

Fine apparition! My quaint° Ariel,
Hark in thine ear. [*He whispers.*]

ARIEL: My lord, it shall be done. *Exit.*

PROSPERO: Thou poisonous slave, got° by the devil himself
Upon thy wicked dam,° come forth!

Enter Caliban.

CALIBAN: As wicked° dew as e'er my mother brushed
With raven's feather from unwholesome fen°
Drop on you both! A southwest° blow on ye
And blister you all o'er!

PROSPERO: For this, be sure, tonight thou shalt have cramps,
Side-stitches that shall pen thy breath up. Urchins°
Shall forth at vast° of night that they may work
All exercise on thee. Thou shalt be pinched
As thick as honeycomb,° each pinch more stinging
Than bees that made 'em.°

CALIBAN: I must eat my dinner.
This island's mine, by Sycorax my mother,
Which thou tak'st from me. When thou cam'st first,
Thou strok'st me and made much of me, wouldst give me
Water with berries in 't, and teach me how
To name the bigger light, and how the less,°
That burn by day and night. And then I loved thee
And showed thee all the qualities o' th' isle,
The fresh springs, brine pits, barren place and fertile.
Cursed be I that did so! All the charms°
Of Sycorax, toads, beetles, bats, light on you!
For I am all the subjects that you have,
Which first was mine own king; and here you sty° me
In this hard rock, whiles you do keep from me
The rest o' th' island.

PROSPERO: Thou most lying slave,
Whom stripes° may move, not kindness! I have used thee,
Filth as thou art, with humane° care, and lodged thee

---

320. When: (An exclamation of impatience.) **321. quaint:** Ingenious. **323. got:** Begotten, sired. **324. dam:** Mother (used of animals). **325. wicked:** Mischievous, harmful. **326. fen:** Marsh, bog. **327. southwest:** I.e., wind thought to bring disease. **330. Urchins:** Hedgehogs; here, suggesting goblins in the guise of hedgehogs. **331. vast:** Lengthy, desolate time. (Malignant spirits were thought to be restricted to the hours of darkness.) **333. As thick as honeycomb:** I.e., all over, with as many pinches as a honeycomb has cells. **334. 'em:** I.e., the honeycomb. **339. the bigger . . . less:** I.e., the sun and the moon (see Genesis 1:16: "God then made two great lights: the greater light to rule the day, and the less light to rule the night"). **343. charms:** Spells. **346. sty:** Confine as in a sty. **349. stripes:** Lashes. **350. humane:** (Not distinguished as word from *human.*)

In mine own cell, till thou didst seek to violate
The honor of my child.

CALIBAN: Oho, oho! Would 't had been done!
Thou didst prevent me; I had peopled else°
This isle with Calibans.

MIRANDA: Abhorrèd° slave,
Which any print° of goodness wilt not take,
Being capable of all ill! I pitied thee,
Took pains to make thee speak, taught thee each hour
One thing or other. When thou didst not, savage,
Know thine own meaning, but wouldst gabble like
A thing most brutish, I endowed thy purposes°
With words that made them known. But thy vile race,°
Though thou didst learn, had that in 't which good natures
Could not abide to be with; therefore wast thou
Deservedly confined into this rock,
Who hadst deserved more than a prison.

CALIBAN: You taught me language, and my profit on 't
Is I know how to curse. The red plague° rid° you
For learning° me your language!

PROSPERO: Hagseed,° hence!
Fetch us in fuel, and be quick, thou'rt best,°
To answer other business.° Shrugg'st thou, malice?
If thou neglect'st or dost unwillingly
What I command, I'll rack thee with old° cramps,
Fill all thy bones with aches,° make thee roar
That beasts shall tremble at thy din.

CALIBAN: No, pray thee.
[*Aside.*] I must obey. His art is of such power
It would control my dam's god, Setebos,°
And make a vassal of him.

PROSPERO: So, slave, hence! *Exit Caliban.*

Enter Ferdinand; and Ariel, invisible,° playing and singing. [*Ferdinand does not see Prospero and Miranda.*]

Ariel's Song.

ARIEL: Come unto these yellow sands,
And then take hands;

---

354. peopled else: Otherwise populated. **355–366. Abhorrèd . . . prison:** (Sometimes assigned by editors to Prospero.) **356. print:** Imprint, impression. **361. purposes:** Meanings, desires. **362. race:** Natural disposition; species, nature. **368. red plague:** Plague characterized by red sores and evacuation of blood; **rid:** Destroy. **369. learning:** Teaching; **Hagseed:** Offspring of a female demon. **370. thou'rt best:** You'd be well advised. **371. answer other business:** Perform other tasks. **373. old:** Such as old people suffer, or, plenty of. **374. aches:** (Pronounced "aitches.") **377. Setebos:** (A god of the Patagonians, named in Robert Eden's *History of Travel,* 1577.) **378. s.d. Ariel, invisible:** (Ariel wears a garment that by convention indicates he is invisible to the other characters.)

Curtsied when you have,° and kissed
The wild waves whist,°
Foot it featly° here and there,
And, sweet sprites,° bear
The burden.° Hark, hark!
Burden, dispersedly° [*within*]. Bow-wow.
The watchdogs bark.
[*Burden, dispersedly within.*] Bow-wow.
Hark, hark! I hear
The strain of strutting chanticleer
Cry Cock-a-diddle-dow.

FERDINAND: Where should this music be? I' th' air or th' earth?
It sounds no more; and sure it waits upon°
Some god o' th' island. Sitting on a bank,°
Weeping again the King my father's wreck,
This music crept by me upon the waters,
Allaying both their fury and my passion°
With its sweet air. Thence° I have followed it,
Or it hath drawn me rather. But 'tis gone.
No, it begins again.

Ariel's Song.

ARIEL: Full fathom five thy father lies.
Of his bones are coral made.
Those are pearls that were his eyes.
Nothing of him that doth fade
But doth suffer a sea change
Into something rich and strange.
Sea nymphs hourly ring his knell.°
Burden [*within*]. Ding dong.
Hark, now I hear them, ding dong bell.

FERDINAND: The ditty does remember° my drowned father.
This is no mortal business, nor no sound
That the earth owes.° I hear it now above me.

PROSPERO [*to Miranda*]: The fringèd curtains of thine eye advance°
And say what thou seest yond.

MIRANDA: What is 't? A spirit?
Lord, how it looks about! Believe me, sir,
It carries a brave° form. But 'tis a spirit.

---

381. Curtsied . . . have: When you have curtsied. **381–382. kissed . . . whist:** Kissed the waves into silence, or, kissed while the waves are being hushed. **383. Foot it featly:** Dance nimbly. **384. sprites:** Spirits. **385. burden:** Refrain, undersong; **s.d. dispersedly:** I.e., from all directions, not in unison. **391. waits upon:** Serves, attends. **392. bank:** Sandbank. **395. passion:** Grief. **396. Thence:** I.e., from the bank on which I sat. **405. knell:** Announcement of a death by the tolling of a bell. **407. remember:** Commemorate. **409. owes:** Owns. **410. advance:** Raise. **413. brave:** Excellent.

PROSPERO: No, wench, it eats and sleeps and hath such senses
As we have, such. This gallant which thou seest
Was in the wreck; and, but° he's something stained°
With grief, that's beauty's canker,° thou mightst call him
A goodly person. He hath lost his fellows
And strays about to find 'em.

MIRANDA: I might call him
A thing divine, for nothing natural
I ever saw so noble.

PROSPERO [*aside*]: It goes on,° I see,
As my soul prompts it. — Spirit, fine spirit, I'll free thee
Within two days for this.

FERDINAND [*seeing Miranda*]: Most sure, the goddess
On whom these airs° attend! — Vouchsafe° my prayer
May know° if you remain° upon this island,
And that you will some good instruction give
How I may bear me° here. My prime° request,
Which I do last pronounce, is — O you wonder!° —
If you be maid or no?°

MIRANDA: No wonder, sir,
But certainly a maid.

FERDINAND: My language? Heavens!
I am the best° of them that speak this speech,
Were I but where 'tis spoken.

PROSPERO [*coming forward*]: How? The best?
What wert thou if the King of Naples heard thee?

FERDINAND: A single° thing, as I am now, that wonders
To hear thee speak of Naples.° He does hear me,°
And that he does I weep.° Myself am Naples,°
Who with mine eyes, never since at ebb,° beheld
The King my father wrecked.

MIRANDA: Alack, for mercy!

FERDINAND: Yes, faith, and all his lords, the Duke of Milan
And his brave son° being twain.

PROSPERO [*aside*]: The Duke of Milan
And his more braver° daughter could control° thee,

---

416. but: Except that; **something stained:** Somewhat disfigured. **417. canker:** Cankerworm (feeding on buds and leaves). **421. It goes on:** I.e., my plan works. **425. airs:** Songs; **Vouchsafe:** Grant. **426. May know:** I.e., that I may know; **remain:** Dwell. **428. bear me:** Conduct myself; **prime:** Chief. **429. wonder:** (Miranda's name means "to be wondered at.") **430. maid or no:** I.e., a human maiden as opposed to a goddess or married woman. **432. best:** I.e., in birth. **435. single:** (1) Solitary, being at once King of Naples and myself (2) feeble. **436, 437. Naples:** The King of Naples. **436. He does hear me:** I.e., the King of Naples does hear my words, for I am King of Naples. **437. And . . . weep:** I.e., and I weep at this reminder that my father is seemingly dead, leaving me heir. **438. at ebb:** I.e., dry, not weeping. **441. son:** (The only reference in the play to a son of Antonio.) **442. more braver:** More splendid; **control:** Refute.

If now 'twere fit to do 't. At the first sight
They have changed eyes.° — Delicate Ariel,
I'll set thee free for this. [*To Ferdinand.*] A word, good sir.
I fear you have done yourself some wrong.° A word!

MIRANDA [*aside*]: Why speaks my father so urgently? This
Is the third man that e'er I saw, the first
That e'er I sighed for. Pity move my father
To be inclined my way!

FERDINAND: O, if a virgin,
And your affection not gone forth, I'll make you
The Queen of Naples.

PROSPERO: Soft, sir! One word more.
[*Aside.*] They are both in either's° powers; but this swift business
I must uneasy° make, lest too light winning
Make the prize light.° [*To Ferdinand.*] One word more: I charge thee
That thou attend° me. Thou dost here usurp
The name thou ow'st° not, and hast put thyself
Upon this island as a spy, to win it
From me, the lord on 't.°

FERDINAND: No, as I am a man.

MIRANDA: There's nothing ill can dwell in such a temple.
If the ill spirit have so fair a house,
Good things will strive to dwell with 't.°

PROSPERO: Follow me. —
Speak not you for him; he's a traitor. — Come,
I'll manacle thy neck and feet together.
Seawater shalt thou drink; thy food shall be
The fresh-brook mussels, withered roots, and husks
Wherein the acorn cradled. Follow.

FERDINAND: No!
I will resist such entertainment° till
Mine enemy has more power. *He draws, and is charmed° from moving.*

MIRANDA: O dear father,
Make not too rash° a trial of him, for
He's gentle,° and not fearful.°

PROSPERO: What, I say,
My foot° my tutor? — Put thy sword up, traitor,
Who mak'st a show but dar'st not strike, thy conscience
Is so possessed with guilt. Come, from thy ward,°

444. changed eyes: Exchanged amorous glances. **446. done . . . wrong:** I.e., spoken falsely. **453. both in either's:** Each in the other's. **454. uneasy:** Difficult. **454–455. light . . . light:** Easy . . . cheap. **456. attend:** Follow, obey. **457. ow'st:** Ownest. **459. on 't:** Of it. **462. strive . . . with 't:** I.e., expel the evil and occupy the *temple,* the body. **468. entertainment:** Treatment. **469. s.d. charmed:** Magically prevented. **470. rash:** Harsh. **471. gentle:** Wellborn; **fearful:** Frightening, dangerous, or perhaps, cowardly. **472. foot:** Subordinate (Miranda, the foot, presumes to instruct Prospero, the head). **474. ward:** Defensive posture (in fencing).

For I can here disarm thee with this stick
And make thy weapon drop. [*He brandishes his staff.*]

MIRANDA [*trying to hinder him*]: Beseech you, father!

PROSPERO: Hence! Hang not on my garments.

MIRANDA: Sir, have pity!
I'll be his surety.°

PROSPERO: Silence! One word more
Shall make me chide thee, if not hate thee. What,
An advocate for an impostor? Hush!
Thou think'st there is no more such shapes as he,
Having seen but him and Caliban. Foolish wench,
To° the most of men this is a Caliban,
And they to him are angels.

MIRANDA: My affections
Are then most humble; I have no ambition
To see a goodlier man.

PROSPERO [*to Ferdinand*]: Come on, obey.
Thy nerves° are in their infancy again
And have no vigor in them.

FERDINAND: So they are.
My spirits,° as in a dream, are all bound up.
My father's loss, the weakness which I feel,
The wreck of all my friends, nor this man's threats
To whom I am subdued, are but light° to me,
Might I but through my prison once a day
Behold this maid. All corners else° o' th' earth
Let liberty make use of; space enough
Have I in such a prison.

PROSPERO [*aside*]: It works. [*To Ferdinand.*] Come on. — [*To Ariel*]
Thou hast done well, fine Ariel! [*To Ferdinand.*] Follow me.
[*To Ariel.*] Hark what thou else shalt do me.°

MIRANDA [*to Ferdinand*]: Be of comfort.
My father's of a better nature, sir,
Than he appears by speech. This is unwonted°
Which now came from him.

PROSPERO [*to Ariel*]: Thou shalt be as free
As mountain winds; but then° exactly do
All points of my command.

ARIEL: To th' syllable.

PROSPERO [*to Ferdinand*]: Come, follow. [*To Miranda.*] Speak not for him.
Exeunt.

---

479. surety: Guarantee. **484. To:** Compared to. **488. nerves:** Sinews. **490. spirits:** Vital powers. **493. light:** Unimportant. **495. corners else:** Other corners, regions. **500. me:** For me. **502. unwonted:** Unusual. **504. then:** Until then, or, if that is to be so.

[ACT II

SCENE I: *Another part of the island.*]

Enter Alonso, Sebastian, Antonio, Gonzalo, Adrian, Francisco, and others.

GONZALO [*to Alonso*]: Beseech you, sir, be merry. You have cause,
So have we all, of joy, for our escape
Is much beyond our loss. Our hint° of woe
Is common; every day some sailor's wife,
The masters of some merchant, and the merchant,°
Have just our theme of woe. But for the miracle,
I mean our preservation, few in millions
Can speak like us. Then wisely, good sir, weigh
Our sorrow with° our comfort.

ALONSO: Prithee, peace.

SEBASTIAN [*aside to Antonio*]: He receives comfort like cold porridge.°

ANTONIO [*aside to Sebastian*]: The visitor° will not give him o'er° so.

SEBASTIAN: Look, he's winding up the watch of his wit; by and by it will strike.

GONZALO [*to Alonso*]: Sir —

SEBASTIAN [*aside to Antonio*]: One. Tell.°

GONZALO: When every grief is entertained
That's offered, comes to th' entertainer° —

SEBASTIAN: A dollar.°

GONZALO: Dolor comes to him, indeed. You have spoken truer than you purposed.

SEBASTIAN: You have taken it wiselier than I meant you should.

GONZALO [*to Alonso*]: Therefore, my lord —

ANTONIO: Fie, what a spendthrift is he of his tongue!

ALONSO [*to Gonzalo*]: I prithee, spare.°

GONZALO: Well, I have done. But yet —

SEBASTIAN [*aside to Antonio*]: He will be talking.

ANTONIO [*aside to Sebastian*]: Which, of he or Adrian, for a good wager, first begins to crow?°

SEBASTIAN: The old cock.°

ANTONIO: The cockerel.°

SEBASTIAN: Done. The wager?

ACT II, SCENE I. **3. hint:** Occasion. **5. masters . . . the merchant:** Officers of some merchant vessel and the merchant himself, the owner. **9. with:** Against. **10. porridge:** Pun suggested by *peace* for "peas" or "pease," a common ingredient of porridge. **11. visitor:** One taking nourishment and comfort to the sick, as Gonzalo is doing; **give him o'er:** Abandon him. **14. Tell:** Keep count. **15–16. When . . . entertainer:** When every sorrow that presents itself is accepted without resistance, there comes to the recipient. **17. dollar:** Widely circulated coin, the German thaler and the Spanish piece of eight (Sebastian puns on *entertainer* in the sense of innkeeper; to Gonzalo, *dollar* suggests "dolor," grief). **23. spare:** Forbear, cease. **26–27. Which . . . crow:** Which of the two, Gonzalo or Adrian, do you bet will speak (crow) first? **28. old cock:** I.e., Gonzalo. **29. cockerel:** I.e., Adrian.

ANTONIO: A laughter.°
SEBASTIAN: A match!°
ADRIAN: Though this island seem to be desert° —
ANTONIO: Ha, ha, ha!
SEBASTIAN: So, you're paid.°
ADRIAN: Uninhabitable and almost inaccessible —
SEBASTIAN: Yet —
ADRIAN: Yet —
ANTONIO: He could not miss 't.°
ADRIAN: It must needs be° of subtle, tender, and delicate temperance.°
ANTONIO: Temperance° was a delicate° wench.
SEBASTIAN: Ay, and a subtle,° as he most learnedly delivered.°
ADRIAN: The air breathes upon us here most sweetly.
SEBASTIAN: As if it had lungs, and rotten ones.
ANTONIO: Or as 'twere perfumed by a fen.
GONZALO: Here is everything advantageous to life.
ANTONIO: True, save° means to live.
SEBASTIAN: Of that there's none, or little.
GONZALO: How lush and lusty° the grass looks! How green!
ANTONIO: The ground indeed is tawny.°
SEBASTIAN: With an eye° of green in 't.
ANTONIO: He misses not much.
SEBASTIAN: No. He doth but° mistake the truth totally.
GONZALO: But the rarity of it is — which is indeed almost beyond credit —
SEBASTIAN: As many vouched rarities° are.
GONZALO: That our garments, being, as they were, drenched in the sea, hold notwithstanding their freshness and glosses, being rather new-dyed than stained with salt water.
ANTONIO: If but one of his pockets° could speak, would it not say he lies?
SEBASTIAN: Ay, or very falsely pocket up° his report.°
GONZALO: Methinks our garments are now as fresh as when we put them on first in Afric, at the marriage of the King's fair daughter Claribel to the King of Tunis.

---

31. laughter: (1) Burst of laughter (2) sitting of eggs. (When Adrian, the *cockerel,* begins to speak two lines later, Sebastian loses the bet. . . .) **32. A match:** A bargain; agreed. **33. desert:** Uninhabited. **35. you're paid:** I.e., you've had your laugh. **39. miss 't:** (1) Avoid saying "Yet" (2) miss the island. **40. must needs be:** Has to be; **temperance:** Mildness of climate. **41. Temperance:** A girl's name; **delicate:** (Here it means "given to pleasure, voluptuous"; in line 40, "pleasant." Antonio is evidently suggesting that *tender, and delicate temperance* sounds like a Puritan phrase, which Antonio then mocks by applying the words to a woman rather than an island. He began this bawdy comparison with a double entendre on *inaccessible,* line 36.) **42. subtle:** (Here it means "tricky, sexually crafty"; in line 40, "delicate"); **delivered:** Uttered. (Sebastian joins Antonio in baiting the Puritans with his use of the pious cant phrase *learnedly delivered.*) **47. save:** Except. **49. lusty:** Healthy. **50. tawny:** Dull brown, yellowish. **51. eye:** Tinge, or spot (perhaps with reference to Gonzalo's eye or judgment). **53. but:** Merely. **55. vouched rarities:** Allegedly real though strange sights. **59. pockets:** I.e., because they are muddy. **60. pocket up:** I.e., conceal, suppress; often used in the sense of "receive unprotestingly, fail to respond to a challenge"; **his report:** (Sebastian's jest is that the evidence of Gonzalo's soggy and sea-stained pockets would confute Gonzalo's speech and his reputation for truth telling.)

SEBASTIAN: 'Twas a sweet marriage, and we prosper well in our return.
ADRIAN: Tunis was never graced before with such a paragon to° their queen.
GONZALO: Not since widow Dido's° time.
ANTONIO [*aside to Sebastian*]: Widow? A pox o' that! How came that "widow" in? Widow Dido!
SEBASTIAN: What if he had said "widower Aeneas" too? Good Lord, how you take° it!
ADRIAN [*to Gonzalo*]: "Widow Dido" said you? You make me study of° that. She was of Carthage, not of Tunis.
GONZALO: This Tunis, sir, was Carthage.
ADRIAN: Carthage?
GONZALO: I assure you, Carthage.
ANTONIO: His word is more than the miraculous harp.°
SEBASTIAN: He hath raised the wall, and houses too.
ANTONIO: What impossible matter will he make easy next?
SEBASTIAN: I think he will carry this island home in his pocket and give it his son for an apple.
ANTONIO: And, sowing the kernels° of it in the sea, bring forth more islands.
GONZALO: Ay.°
ANTONIO: Why, in good time.°
GONZALO [*to Alonso*]: Sir, we were talking° that our garments seem now as fresh as when we were at Tunis at the marriage of your daughter, who is now queen.
ANTONIO: And the rarest° that e'er came there.
SEBASTIAN: Bate,° I beseech you, widow Dido.
ANTONIO: O, widow Dido! Ay, widow Dido.
GONZALO: Is not, sir, my doublet° as fresh as the first day I wore it? I mean, in a sort.°
ANTONIO: That "sort"° was well wished for.
GONZALO: When I wore it at your daughter's marriage.
ALONSO: You cram these words into mine ears against
The stomach of my sense.° Would I had never
Married° my daughter there! For, coming thence,

---

65. to: For. **67. widow Dido:** Queen of Carthage, deserted by Aeneas. (She was, in fact, a widow when Aeneas, a widower, met her, but Antonio may be amused at Gonzalo's prudish use of the term "widow" to describe a woman deserted by her lover.) **71. take:** Understand, respond to, interpret. **72. study of:** Think about. **77. miraculous harp:** (Alludes to Amphion's harp, with which he raised the walls of Thebes; Gonzalo has exceeded that deed by recreating ancient Carthage — *wall and houses* — mistakenly on the site of modern-day Tunis. Some Renaissance commentators believed, like Gonzalo, that the two sites were near each other.) **82. kernels:** Seeds. **83. Ay:** (Gonzalo may be reasserting his point about Carthage, or he may be responding ironically to Antonio, who, in turn, answers sarcastically.) **84. in good time:** (An expression of ironical acquiescence or amazement, i.e., "sure, right away.") **85. talking:** Saying. **88. rarest:** Most remarkable, beautiful. **89. Bate:** Abate, except, leave out (Sebastian says sardonically, surely you should allow widow Dido to be an exception). **91. doublet:** Close-fitting jacket. **92. in a sort:** In a way. **93. "sort":** (Antonio plays on the idea of drawing lots and on "fishing" for something to say.) **96. The stomach . . . sense:** My appetite for hearing them. **97. Married:** Given in marriage.

My son is lost and, in my rate,° she too,
Who is so far from Italy removed
I ne'er again shall see her. O thou mine heir
Of Naples and of Milan, what strange fish
Hath made his meal on thee?

FRANCISCO: Sir, he may live.
I saw him beat the surges° under him
And ride upon their backs. He trod the water,
Whose enmity he flung aside, and breasted
The surge most swoll'n that met him. His bold head
'Bove the contentious waves he kept, and oared
Himself with his good arms in lusty° stroke
To th' shore, that o'er his° wave-worn basis bowed,°
As° stooping to relieve him. I not doubt
He came alive to land.

ALONSO: No, no, he's gone.

SEBASTIAN [*to Alonso*]: Sir, you may thank yourself for this great loss,
That° would not bless our Europe with your daughter,
But rather° loose° her to an African,
Where she at least is banished from your eye,°
Who hath cause to wet the grief on 't.°

ALONSO: Prithee, peace.

SEBASTIAN: You were kneeled to and importuned° otherwise
By all of us, and the fair soul herself
Weighed between loathness and obedience at
Which end o' the beam should bow.° We have lost your son,
I fear, forever. Milan and Naples have
More widows in them of this business' making°
Than we bring men to comfort them.
The fault's your own.

ALONSO: So is the dear'st° o' the loss.

GONZALO: My lord Sebastian,
The truth you speak doth lack some gentleness
And time° to speak it in. You rub the sore
When you should bring the plaster.°

SEBASTIAN: Very well.

---

98. rate: Estimation, opinion. **103. surges:** Waves. **108. lusty:** Vigorous. **109. that . . . bowed:** I.e., that projected out over the base of the cliff that had been eroded by the surf, thus seeming to bend down toward the sea; **his:** Its. **110. As:** As if. **113. That:** You who. **114. rather:** Would rather; **loose:** (1) Release, let loose (2) lose. **115. is banished from your eye:** Is not constantly before your eye to serve as a reproachful reminder of what you have done. **116. Who . . . on 't:** I.e., your eye, which has good reason to weep because of this, or, Claribel, who has good reason to weep for it. **117. importuned:** Urged, implored. **118–120. the fair . . . bow:** Claribel herself was poised uncertainly between unwillingness to marry and obedience to her father as to which end of the scales should sink, which should prevail. **122. of . . . making:** On account of this marriage and subsequent shipwreck. **125. dear'st:** Heaviest, most costly. **128. time:** Appropriate time. **129. plaster:** (A medical application.)

ANTONIO: And most chirurgeonly.°
GONZALO [*to Alonso*]: It is foul weather in us all, good sir,
When you are cloudy.
SEBASTIAN [*to Antonio*]: Fowl° weather?
ANTONIO [*to Sebastian*]: Very foul.
GONZALO: Had I plantation° of this isle, my lord —
ANTONIO [*to Sebastian*]: He'd sow 't with nettle seed.
SEBASTIAN: Or docks, or mallows.°
GONZALO: And were the king on 't, what would I do?
SEBASTIAN: Scape° being drunk for want° of wine.
GONZALO: I' the commonwealth I would by contraries°
Execute all things; for no kind of traffic,°
Would I admit; no name of magistrate,
Letters° should not be known; riches, poverty,
And use of service,° none; contract, succession,°
Bourn, bound of land, tilth,° vineyard, none;
No use of metal, corn,° or wine, or oil;
No occupation; all men idle, all,
And women too, but innocent and pure;
No sovereignty —
SEBASTIAN: Yet he would be king on 't.
ANTONIO: The latter end of his commonwealth forgets the beginning.
GONZALO: All things in common nature should produce
Without sweat or endeavor. Treason, felony,
Sword, pike,° knife, gun, or need of any engine°
Would I not have; but nature should bring forth,
Of its own kind, all foison,° all abundance,
To feed my innocent people.
SEBASTIAN: No marrying 'mong his subjects?
ANTONIO: None, man, all idle — whores and knaves.
GONZALO: I would with such perfection govern, sir,
T' excel the Golden Age.°
SEBASTIAN: 'Save° His Majesty!
ANTONIO: Long live Gonzalo!
GONZALO: And — do you mark me, sir?
ALONSO: Prithee, no more. Thou dost talk nothing to me.

---

130. chirurgeonly: Like a skilled surgeon. (Antonio mocks Gonzalo's medical analogy of a *plaster* applied curatively to a wound.) **132. Fowl:** (With a pun on *foul*, returning to the imagery of lines 26–29.) **133. plantation:** Colonization (with subsequent wordplay on the literal meaning, "planting"). **134. docks, mallows:** (Weeds used as antidotes for nettle stings.) **136. Scape:** Escape; **want:** Lack. (Sebastian jokes sarcastically that this hypothetical ruler would be saved from dissipation only by the barrenness of the island.) **137. contraries:** By what is directly opposite to usual custom. **138. traffic:** Trade. **140. Letters:** Learning. **141. use of service:** Custom of employing servants; **succession:** Holding of property by right of inheritance. **142. Bourn . . . tilth:** Boundaries, property limits, tillage of soil. **143. corn:** Grain. **150. pike:** Lance; **engine:** Instrument of warfare. **152. foison:** Plenty. **157. the Golden Age:** The age, according to Hesiod, when Cronus, or Saturn, ruled the world; an age of innocence and abundance; **'Save:** God save.

GONZALO: I do well believe Your Highness, and did it to minister occasion° to these gentlemen, who are of such sensible° and nimble lungs that they always use° to laugh at nothing.

ANTONIO: 'Twas you we laughed at.

GONZALO: Who in this kind of merry fooling am nothing to you; so you may continue, and laugh at nothing still.

ANTONIO: What a blow was there given!

SEBASTIAN: An° it had not fallen flat-long.°

GONZALO: You are gentlemen of brave mettle;° you would lift the moon out of her sphere° if she would continue in it five weeks without changing.

Enter Ariel [*invisible*] *playing solemn music.*

SEBASTIAN: We would so, and then go a-batfowling.°

ANTONIO: Nay, good my lord, be not angry.

GONZALO: No, I warrant you, I will not adventure my discretion so weakly.°
Will you laugh me asleep? For I am very heavy.°

ANTONIO: Go sleep, and hear us.°

[*All sleep except Alonso, Sebastian, and Antonio.*]

ALONSO: What, all so soon asleep? I wish mine eyes
Would, with themselves, shut up my thoughts.° I find
They are inclined to do so.

SEBASTIAN: Please you, sir,
Do not omit° the heavy° offer of it.
It seldom visits sorrow; when it doth,
It is a comforter.

ANTONIO: We two, my lord,
Will guard your person while you take your rest,
And watch your safety.

ALONSO: Thank you. Wondrous heavy.

[*Alonso sleeps. Exit Ariel.*]

SEBASTIAN: What a strange drowsiness possesses them!

ANTONIO: It is the quality o' the climate.

SEBASTIAN: Why
Doth it not then our eyelids sink? I find not
Myself disposed to sleep.

---

160. minister occasion: Furnish opportunity. **161. sensible:** Sensitive. **162. use:** Are accustomed. **167. An:** If; **flat-long:** With the flat of the sword, i.e., ineffectually. (Compare with "fallen flat.") **168. mettle:** Temperament, courage. (The sense of *metal,* indistinguishable as a form from *mettle,* continues the metaphor of the sword.) **169. sphere:** Orbit (literally, one of the concentric zones occupied by planets in Ptolemaic astronomy). **171. a-batfowling:** Hunting birds at night with lantern and *bat,* or "stick"; also, gulling a simpleton (Gonzalo is the simpleton, or fowl, and Sebastian will use the moon as his lantern). **173. adventure . . . weakly:** Risk my reputation for discretion for so trivial a cause (by getting angry at these sarcastic fellows). **174. heavy:** Sleepy. **175. Go . . . us:** I.e., get ready for sleep, and we'll do our part by laughing. **177. Would . . . thoughts:** Would shut off my melancholy brooding when they close themselves in sleep. **179. omit:** Neglect; **heavy:** Drowsy.

ANTONIO: Nor I. My spirits are nimble.
They° fell together all, as by consent;°
They dropped, as by a thunderstroke. What might,
Worthy Sebastian, O, what might — ? No more.
And yet methinks I see it in thy face,
What thou shouldst be. Th' occasion speaks thee,° and
My strong imagination sees a crown
Dropping upon thy head.

SEBASTIAN: What, art thou waking?

ANTONIO: Do you not hear me speak?

SEBASTIAN: I do, and surely
It is a sleepy° language, and thou speak'st
Out of thy sleep. What is it thou didst say?
This is a strange repose, to be asleep
With eyes wide open — standing, speaking, moving —
And yet so fast asleep.

ANTONIO: Noble Sebastian,
Thou lett'st thy fortune sleep — die, rather; wink'st°
Whiles thou art waking.

SEBASTIAN: Thou dost snore distinctly;°
There's meaning in thy snores.

ANTONIO: I am more serious than my custom. You
Must be so too if heed° me, which to do
Trebles thee o'er.°

SEBASTIAN: Well, I am standing water.°

ANTONIO: I'll teach you how to flow.

SEBASTIAN: Do so. To ebb°
Hereditary sloth° instructs me.

ANTONIO: O,
If you but knew how you the purpose cherish
Whiles thus you mock it!° How, in stripping it,
You more invest° it!° Ebbing men, indeed,
Most often do so near the bottom° run
By their own fear or sloth.

---

188. They: The sleepers; **consent:** Common agreement. **192. occasion speaks thee:** Opportunity of the moment calls upon you, i.e., proclaims you usurper of Alonso's crown. **196. sleepy:** Dreamlike, fantastic. **201. wink'st:** (You) shut your eyes. **202. distinctly:** Articulately. **205. if heed:** If you heed. **206. Trebles thee o'er:** Makes you three times as great and rich; **standing water:** Water that neither ebbs nor flows, at a standstill. **207. ebb:** Recede, decline. **208. Hereditary sloth:** Natural laziness and the position of younger brother, one who cannot inherit. **209–210. If . . . mock it:** If you only knew how much you really enhance the value of ambition even while your words mock your purpose. **210–211. How . . . invest it:** I.e., how the more you speak flippantly of ambition, the more you, in effect, affirm it; **invest:** Clothe (Antonio's paradox is that, by skeptically stripping away illusions, Sebastian can see the essence of a situation and the opportunity it presents or that, by disclaiming and deriding his purpose, Sebastian shows how valuable it really is). **212. the bottom:** I.e., on which unadventurous men may go aground and miss the tide of fortune.

SEBASTIAN: Prithee, say on.
The setting° of thine eye and cheek proclaim
A matter° from thee, and a birth indeed
Which throes° thee much to yield.°

ANTONIO: Thus, sir:
Although this lord° of weak remembrance,° this
Who shall be of as little memory
When he is earthed,° hath here almost persuaded —
For he's a spirit of persuasion, only
Professes to persuade° — the King his son's alive,
'Tis as impossible that he's undrowned
As he that sleeps here swims.

SEBASTIAN: I have no hope
That he's undrowned.

ANTONIO: O, out of that "no hope"
What great hope have you! No hope that way° is
Another way so high a hope that even
Ambition cannot pierce a wink° beyond,
But doubt discovery there.° Will you grant with me
That Ferdinand is drowned?

SEBASTIAN: He's gone.

ANTONIO: Then tell me,
Who's the next heir of Naples?

SEBASTIAN: Claribel.

ANTONIO: She that is Queen of Tunis; she that dwells
Ten leagues beyond man's life;° she that from Naples
Can have no note,° unless the sun were post° —
The Man i' the Moon's too slow — till newborn chins
Be rough and razorable;° she that from° whom
We all were sea-swallowed, though some cast° again,
And by that destiny to perform an act
Whereof what's past is prologue, what to come
In yours and my discharge.°

SEBASTIAN: What stuff is this? How say you?
'Tis true my brother's daughter's Queen of Tunis,
So is she heir of Naples, twixt which regions
There is some space.

---

214. setting: Set expression (of earnestness). **215. matter:** Matter of importance. **216. throes:** Causes pain, as in giving birth; **yield:** Give forth, speak about. **217. this lord:** I.e., Gonzalo; **remembrance:** (1) Power of remembering (2) being remembered after his death. **219. earthed:** Buried. **220–221. only . . . persuade:** Whose whole function (as a privy councillor) is to persuade. **225. that way:** I.e., in regard to Ferdinand's being saved. **227. wink:** Glimpse. **227–228. Ambition . . . there:** Ambition itself cannot see any further than that hope (of the crown), is unsure of finding anything to achieve beyond it or even there. **233. Ten . . . life:** I.e., further than the journey of a lifetime. **234. note:** News, intimation; **post:** Messenger. **236. razorable:** Ready for shaving; **from:** On our voyage from. **237. cast:** Were disgorged (with a pun on *casting* of parts for a play). **240. discharge:** Performance.

ANTONIO: A space whose every cubit°
Seems to cry out, "How shall that Claribel
Measure us° back to Naples? Keep° in Tunis,
And let Sebastian wake."° Say this were death
That now hath seized them, why, they were no worse
Than now they are. There be° that can rule Naples
As well as he that sleeps, lords that can prate°
As amply and unnecessarily
As this Gonzalo. I myself could make
A chough of as deep chat.° O, that you bore
The mind that I do! What a sleep were this
For your advancement! Do you understand me?
SEBASTIAN: Methinks I do.
ANTONIO: And how does your content°
Tender° your own good fortune?
SEBASTIAN: I remember
You did supplant your brother Prospero.
ANTONIO: True.
And look how well my garments sit upon me,
Much feater° than before. My brother's servants
Were then my fellows. Now they are my men.
SEBASTIAN: But, for your conscience?
ANTONIO: Ay, sir, where lies that? If 'twere a kibe,°
'Twould put me to° my slipper; but I feel not
This deity in my bosom. Twenty consciences
That stand twixt me and Milan,° candied° be they°
And melt ere they molest!° Here lies your brother,
No better than the earth he lies upon,
If he were that which now he's like — that's dead,
Whom I, with this obedient steel, three inches of it,
Can lay to bed forever; whiles you, doing thus,°
To the perpetual wink° for aye° might put
This ancient morsel, this Sir Prudence, who
Should not° upbraid our course. For all the rest,
They'll take suggestion° as a cat laps milk;
They'll tell the clock° to any business that
We say befits the hour.

---

244. cubit: Ancient measure of length of about twenty inches. **246. Measure us:** I.e., traverse the cubits, find her way; **Keep:** Stay (addressed to Claribel). **247. wake:** I.e., to his good fortune. **249. There be:** There are those. **250. prate:** Speak foolishly. **252–253. I . . . chat:** I could teach a jackdaw to talk as wisely, or, be such a garrulous talker myself. **256. content:** Desire, inclination. **257. Tender:** Regard, look after. **260. feater:** More becomingly, fittingly. **263. kibe:** Chilblain, here a sore on the heel. **264. put me to:** Oblige me to wear. **266. Milan:** The dukedom of Milan; **candied:** Frozen, congealed in crystalline form; **be they:** May they be. **267. molest:** Interfere. **271. thus:** Similarly. (The actor makes a stabbing gesture.) **272. wink:** Sleep, closing of eyes; **aye:** Ever. **274. Should not:** Would not then be able to. **275. take suggestion:** Respond to prompting. **276. tell the clock:** I.e., agree, answer appropriately, chime.

SEBASTIAN: Thy case, dear friend,
Shall be my precedent. As thou gott'st Milan,
I'll come by Naples. Draw thy sword. One stroke
Shall free thee from the tribute° which thou payest,
And I the king shall love thee.

ANTONIO: Draw together;
And when I rear my hand, do you the like
To fall it° on Gonzalo. [*They draw.*]

SEBASTIAN: O, but one word. [*They talk apart.*]

Enter Ariel [*invisible*], *with music and song.*

ARIEL [*to Gonzalo*]: My master through his art foresees the danger
That you, his friend, are in, and sends me forth —
For else his project dies — to keep them living. *Sings in Gonzalo's ear.*
While you here do snoring lie,
Open-eyed conspiracy
His time° doth take.
If of life you keep a care,
Shake off slumber, and beware.
Awake, awake!

ANTONIO: Then let us both be sudden.°

GONZALO [*waking*]: Now, good angels preserve the King! [*The others wake.*]

ALONSO: Why, how now, ho, awake? Why are you drawn?
Wherefore this ghastly looking?

GONZALO: What's the matter?

SEBASTIAN: Whiles we stood here securing° your repose,
Even now, we heard a hollow burst of bellowing
Like bulls, or rather lions. Did 't not wake you?
It struck mine ear most terribly.

ALONSO: I heard nothing.

ANTONIO: O, 'twas a din to fright a monster's ear,
To make an earthquake! Sure it was the roar
Of a whole herd of lions.

ALONSO: Heard you this, Gonzalo?

GONZALO: Upon mine honor, sir. I heard a humming,
And that a strange one too, which did awake me.
I shaked you, sir, and cried.° As mine eyes opened,
I saw their weapons drawn. There was a noise,
That's verily.° 'Tis best we stand upon our guard,
Or that we quit this place. Let's draw our weapons.

ALONSO: Lead off this ground, and let's make further search
For my poor son.

GONZALO: Heavens keep him from these beasts!
For he is, sure, i' th' island.

---

280. tribute: (See I.ii.113, 124.) **283. fall it:** Let it fall. **289. time:** Opportunity. **293. sudden:** Quick. **297. securing:** Standing guard over. **307. cried:** Called out. **309. verily:** True.

ALONSO: Lead away.
ARIEL [*aside*]: Prospero my lord shall know what I have done.
So, King, go safely on to seek thy son. *Exeunt* [*separately*].

[SCENE II: *Another part of the island.*]

Enter Caliban with a burden of wood. A noise of thunder heard.

CALIBAN: All the infections that the sun sucks up
From bogs, fens, flats,° on Prosper fall, and make him
By inchmeal° a disease! His spirits hear me,
And yet I needs must° curse. But they'll nor° pinch,
Fright me with urchin shows,° pitch me i' the mire,
Nor lead me, like a firebrand,° in the dark
Out of my way, unless he bid 'em. But
For every trifle are they set upon me,
Sometimes like apes, that mow° and chatter at me
And after bite me; then like hedgehogs, which
Lie tumbling in my barefoot way and mount
Their pricks at my footfall. Sometimes am I
All wound with° adders, who with cloven tongues
Do hiss me into madness.

Enter Trinculo.

Lo, now, lo!
Here comes a spirit of his, and to torment me
For bringing wood in slowly. I'll fall flat.
Perchance he will not mind° me. [*He lies down.*]

TRINCULO: Here's neither bush nor shrub to bear off° any weather at all. And another storm brewing; I hear it sing i' the wind. Yond same black cloud, yond huge one, looks like a foul bombard° that would shed his° liquor. If it should thunder as it did before, I know not where to hide my head. Yond same cloud cannot choose but fall by pailfuls. [*Seeing Caliban.*] What have we here, a man or a fish? Dead or alive? A fish, he smells like a fish; a very ancient and fishlike smell; a kind of not-of-the-newest Poor John.° A strange fish! Were I in England now, as once I was, and had but this fish painted,° not a holiday fool there but would give a piece of silver. There would this monster make a man.° Any strange beast there makes a man. When they will not give a doit° to relieve a lame beggar, they will lay out ten to see a dead Indian. Legged like a man, and his fins like arms! Warm, o' my troth!° I do now let loose my opinion, hold it° no longer: this is

---

SCENE II. **2. flats:** Swamps. **3. By inchmeal:** Inch by inch. **4. needs must:** Have to; **nor:** Neither. **5. urchin shows:** Elvish apparitions shaped like hedgehogs. **6. like a firebrand:** They in the guise of a will-o'-the-wisp. **9. mow:** Make faces. **13. wound with:** Entwined by. **17. mind:** Notice. **18. bear off:** Keep off. **20. foul bombard:** Dirty leather jug. **21. his:** Its. **25. Poor John:** Salted fish, type of poor fare. **26. painted:** I.e., painted on a sign set up outside a booth or tent at a fair. **28. make a man:** (1) Make one's fortune (2) be indistinguishable from an Englishman. **29. doit:** Small coin. **31. o' my troth:** By my faith; **hold it:** Hold it in.

no fish, but an islander, that hath lately suffered° by a thunderbolt. [*Thunder.*] Alas, the storm is come again! My best way is to creep under his gaberdine.° There is no other shelter hereabout. Misery acquaints a man with strange bedfellows. I will here shroud° till the dregs° of the storm be past. [*He creeps under Caliban's garment.*]

Enter Stephano, singing, [*a bottle in his hand*].

STEPHANO: "I shall no more to sea, to sea,
Here shall I die ashore — "
This is a very scurvy tune to sing at a man's funeral.
Well, here's my comfort. *Drinks.*
(*Sings.*)
"The master, the swabber,° the boatswain, and I,
The gunner and his mate,
Loved Mall, Meg, and Marian, and Margery,
But none of us cared for Kate.
For she had a tongue with a tang,°
Would cry to a sailor, 'Go hang!'
She loved not the savor of tar nor of pitch,
Yet a tailor might scratch her where'er she did itch.°
Then to sea, boys, and let her go hang!"
This is a scurvy tune too. But here's my comfort. *Drinks.*

CALIBAN: Do not torment me!° O!

STEPHANO: What's the matter?° Have we devils here? Do you put tricks upon 's° with savages and men of Ind,° ha? I have not scaped drowning to be afeard now of your four legs. For it hath been said, "As proper° a man as ever went on four legs° cannot make him give ground"; and it shall be said so again while Stephano breathes at'° nostrils.

CALIBAN: This spirit torments me! O!

STEPHANO: This is some monster of the isle with four legs, who hath got, as I take it, an ague.° Where the devil should he learn° our language? I will give him some relief, if it be but for that.° If I can recover° him and keep him tame and get to Naples with him, he's a present for any emperor that ever trod on neat's leather.°

CALIBAN: Do not torment me, prithee. I'll bring my wood home faster.

---

32. suffered: I.e., died. **34. gaberdine:** Cloak, loose upper garment. **35. shroud:** Take shelter. **36. dregs:** I.e., last remains (as in a *bombard* or jug, line 20). **41. swabber:** Crew member whose job is to wash the decks. **45. tang:** Sting. **48. tailor . . . itch:** (A dig at tailors for their supposed effeminacy and a bawdy suggestion of satisfying a sexual craving.) **51. Do . . . me:** (Caliban assumes that one of Prospero's spirits has come to punish him.) **52. What's the matter?:** What's going on here? **52–53. put tricks upon 's:** Trick us with conjuring shows. **53. Ind:** India. **55. proper:** Handsome; **four legs:** (The conventional phrase would supply *two* legs, but the creature Stephano thinks he sees has four.) **56. at':** At the. **60. ague:** Fever. (Probably both Caliban and Trinculo are quaking; see lines 51 and 71.); **should he learn:** Could he have learned. **61. for that:** I.e., for knowing our language; **recover:** Restore. **63. neat's leather:** Cowhide.

STEPHANO: He's in his fit now and does not talk after the wisest.° He shall taste of my bottle. If he have never drunk wine afore,° it will go near to° remove his fit. If I can recover° him and keep him tame, I will not take too much° for him. He shall pay for him that hath° him,° and that soundly.

CALIBAN: Thou dost me yet but little hurt; thou wilt anon,° I know it by thy trembling. Now Prosper works upon thee.

STEPHANO: Come on your ways. Open your mouth. Here is that which will give language to you, cat. Open your mouth.° This will shake your shaking, I can tell you, and that soundly. [*Giving Caliban a drink.*] You cannot tell who's your friend. Open your chaps° again.

TRINCULO: I should know that voice. It should be — but he is drowned, and these are devils. O, defend me!

STEPHANO: Four legs and two voices — a most delicate° monster! His forward voice now is to speak well of his friend; his backward voice° is to utter foul speeches and to detract. If all the wine in my bottle will recover him,° I will help° his ague. Come. [*Giving a drink.*] Amen! I will pour some in thy other mouth.

TRINCULO: Stephano!

STEPHANO: Doth thy other mouth call me?° Mercy, mercy! This is a devil, and no monster. I will leave him. I have no long spoon.°

TRINCULO: Stephano! If thou beest Stephano, touch me and speak to me, for I am Trinculo — be not afeard — thy good friend Trinculo.

STEPHANO: If thou beest Trinculo, come forth. I'll pull thee by the lesser legs. If any be Trinculo's legs, these are they. [*Pulling him out.*] Thou art very Trinculo indeed! How cam'st thou to be the siege° of this mooncalf?° Can he vent° Trinculos?

TRINCULO: I took him to be killed with a thunderstroke. But art thou not drowned, Stephano? I hope now thou art not drowned. Is the storm overblown?° I hid me under the dead mooncalf's gaberdine for fear of the storm. And art thou living, Stephano? O Stephano, two Neapolitans scaped! [*He capers with Stephano.*]

STEPHANO: Prithee, do not turn me about. My stomach is not constant.°

CALIBAN: These be fine things, an if° they be not spirits.

---

65. after the wisest: In the wisest fashion. **66. afore:** Before. **66–67. go near to:** Be in a fair way to. **67. recover:** Restore. **67–68. I will . . . much:** I.e., no sum can be too much. **68. He shall . . . hath him:** I.e., anyone who wants him will have to pay dearly for him; **hath:** Possesses, receives. **70. anon:** Presently. **73. cat . . . mouth:** (Allusion to the proverb "Good liquor will make a cat speak.") **75. chaps:** Jaws. **78. delicate:** Ingenious. **79. backward voice:** (Trinculo and Caliban are facing in opposite directions. Stephano supposes the monster to have a rear end that can emit *foul speeches* or foul-smelling wind at the monster's *other mouth,* line 84.) **80–81. If . . . him:** Even if it takes all the wine in my bottle to cure him. **81. help:** Cure. **84. call me:** I.e., call me by name, know supernaturally who I am. **85. long spoon:** (Allusion to the proverb "He that sups with the devil has need of a long spoon.") **90. siege:** Excrement. **91. mooncalf:** Monstrous or misshapen creature (whose deformity is caused by the malignant influence of the moon); **vent:** Excrete, defecate. **94. overblown:** Blown over. **97. not constant:** Unsteady. **98. an if:** If.

That's a brave° god, and bears° celestial liquor.
I will kneel to him.

STEPHANO: How didst thou scape? How cam'st thou hither? Swear by this bottle how thou cam'st hither. I escaped upon a butt of sack° which the sailors heaved o'erboard — by this bottle,° which I made of the bark of a tree with mine own hands since° I was cast ashore.

CALIBAN [*kneeling*]: I'll swear upon that bottle to be thy true subject, for the liquor is not earthly.

STEPHANO: Here. Swear then how thou escapedst.

TRINCULO: Swum ashore, man, like a duck. I can swim like a duck, I'll be sworn.

STEPHANO: Here, kiss the book.° Though thou canst swim like a duck, thou art made like a goose. [*Giving him a drink.*]

TRINCULO: O Stephano, hast any more of this?

STEPHANO: The whole butt, man. My cellar is in a rock by the seaside, where my wine is hid. — How now, mooncalf? How does thine ague?

CALIBAN: Hast thou not dropped from heaven?

STEPHANO: Out o' the moon, I do assure thee. I was the Man i' the Moon when time was.°

CALIBAN: I have seen thee in her, and I do adore thee. My mistress showed me thee, and thy dog, and thy bush.°

STEPHANO: Come, swear to that. Kiss the book. I will furnish it anon with new contents. Swear. [*Giving him a drink.*]

TRINCULO: By this good light,° this is a very shallow monster! I afeard of him? A very weak monster! The Man i' the Moon? A most poor credulous monster! Well drawn,° monster, in good sooth!°

CALIBAN [*to Stephano*]: I'll show thee every fertile inch o' th' island,
And I will kiss thy foot. I prithee, be my god.

TRINCULO: By this light, a most perfidious and drunken monster! When 's god's asleep, he'll rob his bottle.°

CALIBAN: I'll kiss thy foot. I'll swear myself thy subject.

STEPHANO: Come on then. Down, and swear. [*Caliban kneels.*]

TRINCULO: I shall laugh myself to death at this puppy-headed monster. A most scurvy monster! I could find in my heart to beat him —

STEPHANO: Come, kiss.

TRINCULO: But that the poor monster's in drink.° An abominable monster!

CALIBAN: I'll show thee the best springs. I'll pluck thee berries.
I'll fish for thee and get thee wood enough.

---

99. brave: Fine, magnificent; **bears:** He carries. **102. butt of sack:** Barrel of Canary wine. **103. by this bottle:** I.e., I swear by this bottle. **104. since:** After. **110. book:** I.e., bottle (but with ironic reference to the practice of kissing the Bible in swearing an oath; see *I'll be sworn* in lines 108–109). **117. when time was:** Once upon a time. **119. dog . . . bush:** (The Man in the Moon was popularly imagined to have with him a dog and a bush of thorn.) **122. By . . . light:** By God's light, by this good light from heaven. **124. Well drawn:** Well pulled (on the bottle); **in good sooth:** Truly, indeed. **127–128. When . . . bottle:** I.e., Caliban wouldn't even stop at robbing his god of his bottle if he could catch him asleep. **134. in drink:** Drunk.

A plague upon the tyrant that I serve!
I'll bear him no more sticks, but follow thee,
Thou wondrous man.

TRINCULO: A most ridiculous monster, to make a wonder of a poor drunkard!

CALIBAN: I prithee, let me bring thee where crabs° grow,
And I with my long nails will dig thee pignuts,°
Show thee a jay's nest, and instruct thee how
To snare the nimble marmoset.° I'll bring thee
To clustering filberts, and sometimes I'll get thee
Young scamels° from the rock. Wilt thou go with me?

STEPHANO: I prithee now, lead the way without any more talking. — Trinculo, the King and all our company else° being drowned, we will inherit° here. — Here, bear my bottle. — Fellow Trinculo, we'll fill him by and by again.

CALIBAN (*sings drunkenly*): Farewell, master, farewell, farewell!

TRINCULO: A howling monster; a drunken monster!

CALIBAN: No more dams I'll make for fish,
Nor fetch in firing°
At requiring,
Nor scrape trenchering,° nor wash dish.
'Ban, 'Ban, Ca–Caliban
Has a new master. Get a new man!°
Freedom, high-day!° High-day, freedom! Freedom, high-day, freedom!

STEPHANO: O brave monster! Lead the way. *Exeunt.*

[ACT III

SCENE I: *Before Prospero's cell.*]

Enter Ferdinand, bearing a log.

FERDINAND: There be some sports are painful, and their labor
Delight in them sets off.° Some kinds of baseness°
Are nobly undergone,° and most poor° matters
Point to rich ends. This my mean° task
Would be as heavy to me as odious, but°
The mistress which I serve quickens° what's dead

---

142. crabs: Crab apples, or perhaps crabs. **143. pignuts:** Earthnuts, edible tuberous roots. **145. marmoset:** Small monkey. **147. scamels:** (Possibly *seamews,* mentioned in Strachey's letter, or shellfish, or perhaps from *squamelle,* "furnished with little scales." Contemporary French and Italian travel accounts report that the natives of Patagonia in South America ate small fish described as *fort scameux* and *squame.*) **149. else:** In addition, besides ourselves. **150. inherit:** Take possession. **155. firing:** Firewood. **157. trenchering:** Trenchers, wooden plates. **159. Get a new man:** (Addressed to Prospero.) **160. high-day:** Holiday. ACT III, SCENE I. **1–2. There . . . sets off:** Some pastimes are laborious, but the pleasure we get from them compensates for the effort. (Pleasure is *set off* by labor as a jewel is set off by its foil.) **2. baseness:** Menial activity. **3. undergone:** Undertaken; **most poor:** Poorest. **4. mean:** Lowly. **5. but:** Were it not that. **6. quickens:** Gives life to.

And makes my labors pleasures. O, she is
Ten times more gentle than her father's crabbed,
And he's composed of harshness. I must remove
Some thousands of these logs and pile them up,
Upon a sore injunction.° My sweet mistress
Weeps when she sees me work and says such baseness
Had never like executor.° I forget;°
But these sweet thoughts do even refresh my labors,
Most busy lest when I do it.°

Enter Miranda; and Prospero [*at a distance, unseen*].

MIRANDA: Alas now, pray you,
Work not so hard. I would the lightning had
Burnt up those logs that you are enjoined° to pile!
Pray, set it down and rest you. When this° burns,
'Twill weep° for having wearied you. My father
Is hard at study. Pray now, rest yourself.
He's safe for these° three hours.

FERDINAND: O most dear mistress,
The sun will set before I shall discharge°
What I must strive to do.

MIRANDA: If you'll sit down,
I'll bear your logs the while. Pray, give me that.
I'll carry it to the pile.

FERDINAND: No, precious creature,
I had rather crack my sinews, break my back,
Than you should such dishonor undergo
While I sit lazy by.

MIRANDA: It would become me
As well as it does you; and I should do it
With much more ease, for my good will is to it,
And yours it is against.

PROSPERO [*aside*]: Poor worm, thou art infected!
This visitation° shows it.

MIRANDA: You look wearily.

FERDINAND: No, noble mistress, 'tis fresh morning with me
When you are by° at night. I do beseech you —
Chiefly that I might set it in my prayers —
What is your name?

---

11. sore injunction: Severe command. **13. Had . . . executor:** I.e., was never before undertaken by so noble a being; **I forget:** I.e., I forget that I'm supposed to be working, or, I forget my happiness, oppressed by my labor. **15. Most . . . it:** I.e., busy at my labor but with my mind on other things (?) (the line may be in need of emendation). **17. enjoined:** Commanded. **18. this:** I.e., the log. **19. weep:** I.e., exude resin. **21. these:** The next. **22. discharge:** Complete. **32. visitation:** (1) Miranda's visit to Ferdinand (2) visitation of the plague, i.e., infection of love. **34. by:** Nearby.

MIRANDA: Miranda. — O my father,
I have broke your hest° to say so.
FERDINAND: Admired Miranda!°
Indeed the top of admiration, worth
What's dearest° to the world! Full many a lady
I have eyed with best regard,° and many a time
The harmony of their tongues hath into bondage
Brought my too diligent° ear. For several° virtues
Have I liked several women, never any
With so full soul but some defect in her
Did quarrel with the noblest grace she owed°
And put it to the foil.° But you, O you,
So perfect and so peerless, are created
Of° every creature's best!
MIRANDA: I do not know
One of my sex; no woman's face remember,
Save, from my glass, mine own. Nor have I seen
More that I may call men than you, good friend,
And my dear father. How features are abroad°
I am skilless° of; but, by my modesty,°
The jewel in my dower, I would not wish
Any companion in the world but you;
Nor can imagination form a shape,
Besides yourself, to like of.° But I prattle
Something° too wildly, and my father's precepts
I therein do forget.
FERDINAND: I am in my condition°
A prince, Miranda; I do think, a king —
I would, not so! — and would° no more endure
This wooden slavery° than to suffer
The flesh-fly° blow° my mouth. Hear my soul speak:
The very instant that I saw you did
My heart fly to your service, there resides
To make me slave to it, and for your sake
Am I this patient long-man.
MIRANDA: Do you love me?

---

37. hest: Command; **Admired Miranda:** (Her name means "to be admired or wondered at.") **39. dearest:** Most treasured. **40. best regard:** Thoughtful and approving attention. **42. diligent:** Attentive; **several:** Various (also on line 43). **45. owed:** Owned. **46. put . . . foil:** (1) Overthrew it (as in wrestling) (2) served as a *foil,* or "contrast," to set it off. **48. Of:** Out of. **52. How . . . abroad:** What people look like in other places. **53. skilless:** Ignorant; **modesty:** Virginity. **57. like of:** Be pleased with, be fond of. **58. Something:** Somewhat. **59. condition:** Rank. **61. would:** Wish (it were). **62. wooden slavery:** Being compelled to carry wood. **63. flesh-fly:** Insect that deposits its eggs in dead flesh; **blow:** Befoul with fly eggs.

FERDINAND: O heaven, O earth, bear witness to this sound,
And crown what I profess with kind event°
If I speak true! If hollowly,° invert°
What best is boded° me to mischief!° I
Beyond all limit of what° else i' the world
Do love, prize, honor you.
MIRANDA [*weeping*]: I am a fool
To weep at what I am glad of.
PROSPERO [*aside*]: Fair encounter
Of two most rare affections! Heavens rain grace
On that which breeds between 'em!
FERDINAND: Wherefore weep you?
MIRANDA: At mine unworthiness, that dare not offer
What I desire to give, and much less take
What I shall die° to want.° But this is trifling,
And all the more it seeks to hide itself
The bigger bulk it shows. Hence, bashful cunning,°
And prompt me, plain and holy innocence!
I am your wife, if you will marry me;
If not, I'll die your maid.° To be your fellow°
You may deny me, but I'll be your servant
Whether you will° or no.
FERDINAND: My mistress,° dearest,
And I thus humble ever.
MIRANDA: My husband, then?
FERDINAND: Ay, with a heart as willing°
As bondage e'er of freedom. Here's my hand.
MIRANDA [*clasping his hand*]: And mine, with my heart in 't. And now farewell
Till half an hour hence.
FERDINAND: A thousand thousand!°
Exeunt [*Ferdinand and Miranda, separately*].
PROSPERO: So glad of this as they I cannot be,
Who are surprised with all;° but my rejoicing
At nothing can be more. I'll to my book,
For yet ere suppertime must I perform
Much business appertaining.° *Exit.*

---

69. kind event: Favorable outcome. **70. hollowly:** Insincerely, falsely; **invert:** Turn. **71. boded:** In store for; **mischief:** Harm. **72. what:** Whatever. **79. die:** (Probably with an unconscious sexual meaning that underlies all of lines 77–81.); **to want:** Through lacking. **81. bashful cunning:** Coyness. **84. maid:** Handmaiden, servant; **fellow:** Mate, equal. **86. will:** Desire it; **My mistress:** I.e., the woman I adore and serve (not an illicit sexual partner). **89. willing:** Desirous. **92. A thousand thousand:** I.e., a thousand thousand farewells. **94. with all:** By everything that has happened, or, *withal,* "with it." **97. appertaining:** Related to this.

[SCENE II: *Another part of the island.*]

Enter Caliban, Stephano, and Trinculo.

STEPHANO: Tell not me. When the butt is out,° we will drink water, not a drop before. Therefore bear up and board 'em.° Servant monster, drink to me.

TRINCULO: Servant monster? The folly of° this island! They say there's but five upon this isle. We are three of them; if th' other two be brained° like us, the state totters.

STEPHANO: Drink, servant monster, when I bid thee. Thy eyes are almost set° in thy head. [*Giving a drink.*]

TRINCULO: Where should they be set° else? He were a brave° monster indeed if they were set in his tail.

STEPHANO: My man-monster hath drowned his tongue in sack. For my part, the sea cannot drown me. I swam, ere I could recover° the shore, five and thirty leagues° off and on.° By this light,° thou shalt be my lieutenant, monster, or my standard.°

TRINCULO: Your lieutenant, if you list;° he's no standard.°

STEPHANO: We'll not run,° Monsieur Monster.

TRINCULO: Nor go° neither, but you'll lie° like dogs and yet say nothing neither.

STEPHANO: Mooncalf, speak once in thy life, if thou beest a good mooncalf.

CALIBAN: How does thy honor? Let me lick thy shoe. I'll not serve him. He is not valiant.

TRINCULO: Thou liest, most ignorant monster, I am in case to jostle a constable.° Why, thou debauched° fish, thou, was there ever man a coward that hath drunk so much sack° as I today? Wilt thou tell a monstrous lie, being but half a fish and half a monster?

CALIBAN: Lo, how he mocks me! Wilt thou let him, my lord?

TRINCULO: "Lord," quoth he? That a monster should be such a natural!°

CALIBAN: Lo, lo, again! Bite him to death, I prithee.

STEPHANO: Trinculo, keep a good tongue in your head. If you prove a mutineer — the next tree!° The poor monster's my subject, and he shall not suffer indignity.

CALIBAN: I thank my noble lord. Wilt thou be pleased
To hearken once again to the suit I made to thee?

SCENE II. **1. out:** Empty. **2. bear . . . 'em:** (Stephano uses the terminology of maneuvering at sea and boarding a vessel under attack as a way of urging an assault on the liquor supply.) **4. folly of:** I.e., stupidity found on. **5. be brained:** Are endowed with intelligence. **7. set:** Fixed in a drunken stare, or, sunk, like the sun. **9. set:** Placed; **brave:** Fine, splendid. **12. recover:** Gain, reach. **13. leagues:** Units of distance, each equaling about three miles; **off and on:** Intermittently; **By this light:** (An oath: by the light of the sun.) **14. standard:** Standard-bearer, ensign (as distinguished from *lieutenant,* lines 14, 15). **15. list:** Prefer; **no standard:** I.e., not able to stand up. **16. run:** (1) Retreat (2) urinate (taking Trinculo's *standard,* line 15, in the old sense of "conduit"). **17. go:** Walk; **lie:** (1) Tell lies (2) lie prostrate (3) excrete. **22–23. in case . . . constable:** I.e., in fit condition, made valiant by drink, to taunt or challenge the police. **23. debauched:** (1) Seduced away from proper service and allegiance (2) depraved. **24. sack:** Spanish white wine. **27. natural:** (1) Idiot (2) natural as opposed to unnatural, monsterlike. **30. the next tree:** I.e., you'll hang.

STEPHANO: Marry,° will I. Kneel and repeat it. I will stand, and so shall Trinculo. [*Caliban kneels.*]

Enter Ariel, invisible.°

CALIBAN: As I told thee before, I am subject to a tyrant,
A sorcerer, that by his cunning hath
Cheated me of the island.

ARIEL [*mimicking Trinculo*]: Thou liest.

CALIBAN: Thou liest, thou jesting monkey, thou!
I would my valiant master would destroy thee.
I do not lie.

STEPHANO: Trinculo, if you trouble him any more in 's tale, by this hand, I will supplant° some of your teeth.

TRINCULO: Why, I said nothing.

STEPHANO: Mum, then, and no more. — Proceed.

CALIBAN: I say by sorcery he got this isle;
From me he got it. If thy greatness will
Revenge it on him — for I know thou dar'st,
But this thing° dare not —

STEPHANO: That's most certain.

CALIBAN: Thou shalt be lord of it, and I'll serve thee.

STEPHANO: How now shall this be compassed?° Canst thou bring me to the party?

CALIBAN: Yea, yea, my lord. I'll yield him thee asleep,
Where thou mayst knock a nail into his head.

ARIEL: Thou liest; thou canst not.

CALIBAN: What a pied ninny's° this! Thou scurvy patch!° —
I do beseech thy greatness, give him blows
And take his bottle from him. When that's gone
He shall drink naught but brine, for I'll not show him
Where the quick freshes° are.

STEPHANO: Trinculo, run into no further danger. Interrupt the monster one word further° and, by this hand, I'll turn my mercy out o' doors° and make a stockfish° of thee.

TRINCULO: Why, what did I? I did nothing. I'll go farther off.°

STEPHANO: Didst thou not say he lied?

ARIEL: Thou liest.

STEPHANO: Do I so? Take thou that. [*He beats Trinculo.*] As you like this, give me the lie° another time.

---

34. Marry: I.e., indeed (originally an oath, "by the Virgin Mary"). **35. s.d. invisible:** I.e., wearing a garment to connote invisibility, as at I.ii.378. **43. supplant:** Uproot, displace. **49. this thing:** I.e., Trinculo. **52. compassed:** Achieved. **57. pied ninny:** Fool in motley; **patch:** Fool. **61. quick freshes:** Running springs. **62–63. one word further:** I.e., one more time. **63. turn . . . doors:** I.e., forget about being merciful. **64. stockfish:** Dried cod beaten before cooking. **65. off:** Away. **68–69. give me the lie:** Call me a liar to my face.

TRINCULO: I did not give the lie. Out o' your wits and hearing too? A pox o' your bottle! This can sack and drinking do. A murrain° on your monster, and the devil take your fingers!

CALIBAN: Ha, ha, ha!

STEPHANO: Now, forward with your tale. [*To Trinculo.*] Prithee, stand further off.

CALIBAN: Beat him enough. After a little time
I'll beat him too.

STEPHANO: Stand farther. — Come, proceed.

CALIBAN: Why, as I told thee, 'tis a custom with him
I' th' afternoon to sleep. There thou mayst brain him,
Having first seized his books; or with a log
Batter his skull, or paunch° him with a stake,
Or cut his weasand° with thy knife. Remember
First to possess his books, for without them
He's but a sot,° as I am, nor hath not
One spirit to command. They all do hate him
As rootedly as I. Burn but his books.
He has brave utensils° — for so he calls them —
Which, when he has a house, he'll deck withal.°
And that most deeply to consider is
The beauty of his daughter. He himself
Calls her a nonpareil. I never saw a woman
But only Sycorax my dam and she;
But she as far surpasseth Sycorax
As great'st does least.

STEPHANO: Is it so brave° a lass?

CALIBAN: Ay, lord. She will become° thy bed, I warrant,
And bring thee forth brave brood.

STEPHANO: Monster, I will kill this man. His daughter and I will be king and queen — save Our Graces! — and Trinculo and thyself shall be viceroys. Dost thou like the plot, Trinculo?

TRINCULO: Excellent.

STEPHANO: Give me thy hand. I am sorry I beat thee; but, while thou liv'st, keep a good tongue in thy head.

CALIBAN: Within this half hour will he be asleep.
Wilt thou destroy him then?

STEPHANO: Ay, on mine honor.

ARIEL [*aside*]: This will I tell my master.

CALIBAN: Thou mak'st me merry; I am full of pleasure.
Let us be jocund.° Will you troll the catch°
You taught me but whilere?°

---

71. murrain: Plague (literally, a cattle disease). **82. paunch:** Stab in the belly. **83. weasand:** Windpipe. **85. sot:** Fool. **88. brave utensils:** Fine furnishings. **89. deck withal:** Furnish it with. **96. brave:** Splendid, attractive. **97. become:** Suit (sexually). **110. jocund:** Jovial, merry; **troll the catch:** Sing the round. **111. but whilere:** Only a short time ago.

STEPHANO: At thy request, monster, I will do reason, any reason.° — Come on, Trinculo, let us sing. *Sings.*

"Flout° 'em and scout° 'em
And scout 'em and flout 'em!
Thought is free."

CALIBAN: That's not the tune. *Ariel plays the tune on a tabor° and pipe.*

STEPHANO: What is this same?

TRINCULO: This is the tune of our catch, played by the picture of Nobody.°

STEPHANO: If thou beest a man, show thyself in thy likeness. If thou beest a devil, take 't as thou list.°

TRINCULO: O, forgive me my sins!

STEPHANO: He that dies pays all debts.° I defy thee. Mercy upon us!

CALIBAN: Art thou afeard?

STEPHANO: No, monster, not I.

CALIBAN: Be not afeard. The isle is full of noises,
Sounds, and sweet airs, that give delight and hurt not.
Sometimes a thousand twangling instruments
Will hum about mine ears, and sometimes voices
That, if I then had waked after long sleep,
Will make me sleep again; and then, in dreaming,
The clouds methought would open and show riches
Ready to drop upon me, that when I waked
I cried to dream° again.

STEPHANO: This will prove a brave kingdom to me, where I shall have my music for nothing.

CALIBAN: When Prospero is destroyed.

STEPHANO: That shall be by and by.° I remember the story.

TRINCULO: The sound is going away. Let's follow it, and after do our work.

STEPHANO: Lead, monster; we'll follow. I would I could see this taborer! He lays it on.°

TRINCULO: Wilt come? I'll follow, Stephano. *Exeunt [following Ariel's music].*

[SCENE III: *Another part of the island.*]

Enter Alonso, Sebastian, Antonio, Gonzalo, Adrian, Francisco, etc.

GONZALO: By 'r lakin,° I can go no further, sir.
My old bones aches. Here's a maze trod indeed
Through forthrights and meanders!° By your patience,
I needs must° rest me.

ALONSO: Old lord, I cannot blame thee,

---

112. reason, any reason: Anything reasonable. **114. Flout:** Scoff at; **scout:** Deride. **117. s.d. tabor:** Small drum. **119. picture of Nobody:** (Refers to a familiar figure with head, arms, and legs but no trunk.) **121. take 't . . . list:** I.e., take my defiance as you please, as best you can. **123. He . . . debts:** I.e., if I have to die, at least that will be the end of all my woes and obligations. **134. to dream:** Desirous of dreaming. **138. by and by:** Very soon. **141. lays it on:** I.e., plays the drum vigorously. SCENE III. **1. By 'r lakin:** By our Ladykin, by our Lady. **3. forthrights and meanders:** Paths straight and crooked. **4. needs must:** Have to.

Who am myself attached° with weariness,
To th' dulling of my spirits.° Sit down and rest.
Even here I will put off my hope, and keep it
No longer for° my flatterer. He is drowned
Whom thus we stray to find, and the sea mocks
Our frustrate° search on land. Well, let him go. [*Alonso and Gonzalo sit.*]

ANTONIO [*aside to Sebastian*]: I am right° glad that he's so out of hope.
Do not, for° one repulse, forgo the purpose
That you resolved t' effect.

SEBASTIAN [*to Antonio*]: The next advantage
Will we take throughly.°

ANTONIO [*to Sebastian*]: Let it be tonight,
For, now° they are oppressed with travel,° they
Will not, nor cannot, use° such vigilance
As when they are fresh.

SEBASTIAN [*to Antonio*]: I say tonight. No more.

Solemn and strange music; and Prospero on the top,° invisible.

ALONSO: What harmony is this? My good friends, hark!

GONZALO: Marvelous sweet music!

Enter several strange shapes, bringing in a banquet, and dance about it with gentle actions of salutations; and, inviting the King, etc., to eat, they depart.

ALONSO: Give us kind keepers,° heavens! What were these?

SEBASTIAN: A living° drollery.° Now I will believe
That there are unicorns; that in Arabia
There is one tree, the phoenix' throne, one phoenix°
At this hour reigning there.

ANTONIO: I'll believe both;
And what does else want credit,° come to me
And I'll be sworn 'tis true. Travelers ne'er did lie,
Though fools at home condemn 'em.

GONZALO: If in Naples
I should report this now, would they believe me
If I should say I saw such islanders?
For, certes,° these are people of the island,
Who, though they are of monstrous° shape, yet note,
Their manners are more gentle, kind, than of
Our human generation you shall find
Many, nay, almost any.

---

5. attached: Seized. **6. To . . . spirits:** To the point of being dull-spirited. **8. for:** As. **10. frustrate:** Frustrated. **11. right:** Very. **12. for:** Because of. **14. throughly:** Thoroughly. **15. now:** Now that; **travel:** Carrying the sense of labor as well as traveling. **16. use:** Apply. **17. s.d. on the top:** At some high point of the tiring-house or the theater, on a third level above the gallery. **20. kind keepers:** Guardian angels. **21. living:** With live actors; **drollery:** Comic entertainment, caricature, puppet show. **23. phoenix:** Mythical bird consumed to ashes every five hundred to six hundred years, only to be renewed into another cycle. **25. want credit:** Lack credence. **30. certes:** Certainly. **31. monstrous:** Unnatural.

PROSPERO [*aside*]: Honest lord,
Thou hast said well, for some of you there present
Are worse than devils.
ALONSO: I cannot too much muse°
Such shapes, such gesture, and such sound, expressing —
Although they want° the use of tongue — a kind
Of excellent dumb discourse.
PROSPERO [*aside*]: Praise in departing.°
FRANCISCO: They vanished strangely.
SEBASTIAN: No matter, since
They have left their viands° behind, for we have stomachs.°
Will 't please you taste of what is here?
ALONSO: Not I.
GONZALO: Faith, sir, you need not fear. When we were boys,
Who would believe that there were mountaineers°
Dewlapped° like bulls, whose throats had hanging at 'em
Wallets° of flesh? Or that there were such men
Whose heads stood in their breasts? Which now we find
Each putter-out of five for one° will bring us
Good warrant° of.
ALONSO: I will stand to° and feed,
Although my last° — no matter, since I feel
The best° is past. Brother, my lord the Duke,
Stand to, and do as we. [*They approach the table.*]

Thunder and lightning. Enter Ariel, like a harpy,° claps his wings upon the table, and with a quaint device° the banquet vanishes.°

ARIEL: You are three men of sin, whom Destiny —
That hath to instrument this lower world
And what is in 't — the never-surfeited sea
Hath caused to belch up you,° and on this island
Where man doth not inhabit, you 'mongst men
Being most unfit to life. I have made you mad;
And even with suchlike valor° men hang and drown
Their proper° selves. [*Alonso, Sebastian, and Antonio draw their swords.*]

---

36. muse: Wonder at. **38. want:** Lack. **39. Praise in departing:** I.e., save your praise until the end of the performance (proverbial). **41. viands:** Provisions; **stomachs:** Appetites. **44. mountaineers:** Mountain dwellers. **45. Dewlapped:** Having a dewlap, or fold of skin hanging from the neck, like cattle. **46. Wallets:** Pendent folds of skin, wattles. **48. putter-out . . . one:** One who invests money or gambles on the risks of travel on the condition that the traveler who returns safely is to receive five times the amount deposited; hence, any traveler. **49. Good warrant:** Assurance; **stand to:** Fall to, take the risk. **50. Although my last:** Even if this were to be my last meal. **51. best:** Best part of life. **52. s.d. harpy:** A fabulous monster with a woman's face and breasts and a vulture's body, supposed to be a minister of divine vengeance; **quaint device:** Ingenious stage contrivance; **the banquet vanishes:** I.e., the food vanishes; the table remains until line 82. **53–56. whom . . . up you:** You whom Destiny, controller of the sublunary world as its instrument, has caused the ever hungry sea to belch up. **59. suchlike valor:** I.e., the reckless valor derived from madness. **60. proper:** Own.

You fools! I and my fellows
Are ministers of Fate. The elements
Of whom° your swords are tempered° may as well
Wound the loud winds, or with bemocked-at° stabs
Kill the still-closing° waters, as diminish
One dowl° that's in my plume. My fellow ministers
Are like° invulnerable. If° you could hurt,
Your swords are now too massy° for your strengths
And will not be uplifted. But remember —
For that's my business to you — that you three
From Milan did supplant good Prospero;
Exposed unto the sea, which hath requit° it,
Him and his innocent child; for which foul deed
The powers, delaying, not forgetting, have
Incensed the seas and shores, yea, all the creatures,
Against your peace. Thee of thy son, Alonso,
They have bereft; and to pronounce by me
Ling'ring perdition,° worse than any death
Can be at once, shall step by step attend
You and your ways; whose° wraths to guard you from —
Which here, in this most desolate isle, else° falls
Upon your heads — is nothing° but heart's sorrow
And a clear° life ensuing.

He vanishes in thunder; then, to soft music, enter the shapes again, and dance, with mocks and mows,° and carrying out the table.

PROSPERO: Bravely° the figure of this harpy hast thou
Performed, my Ariel; a grace it had devouring.°
Of my instruction hast thou nothing bated°
In what thou hadst to say. So,° with good life°
And observation strange,° my meaner° ministers
Their several kinds° have done. My high charms work,
And these mine enemies are all knit up
In their distractions.° They now are in my power;
And in these fits I leave them, while I visit
Young Ferdinand, whom they suppose is drowned,
And his and mine loved darling. [*Exit above.*]

---

62. whom: Which; **tempered:** Composed and hardened. **63. bemocked-at:** Scorned. **64. still-closing:** Always closing again when parted. **65. dowl:** Soft, fine feather. **66. like:** Likewise, similarly; **If:** Even if. **67. massy:** Heavy. **71. requit:** Requited, avenged. **77. perdition:** Ruin, destruction. **79. whose:** (Refers to the heavenly powers.) **80. else:** Otherwise. **81. is nothing:** There is no way. **82. clear:** Unspotted, innocent; **s.d. mocks and mows:** Mocking gestures and grimaces. **83. Bravely:** Finely, dashingly. **84. a grace . . . devouring:** I.e., you gracefully caused the banquet to disappear as if you had consumed it (with puns on *grace,* meaning "gracefulness" and "a blessing on the meal," and on *devouring,* meaning "a literal eating" and "an all-consuming or ravishing grace"). **85. bated:** Abated, omitted. **86. So:** In the same fashion; **good life:** Faithful reproduction. **87. observation strange:** Exceptional attention to detail; **meaner:** I.e., subordinate to Ariel. **88. several kinds:** Individual parts. **90. distractions:** Trancelike state.

GONZALO: I' the name of something holy, sir, why° stand you
In this strange stare?
ALONSO: O, it° is monstrous, monstrous!
Methought the billows° spoke and told me of it;
The winds did sing it to me, and the thunder,
That deep and dreadful organ pipe, pronounced
The name of Prosper; it did bass my trespass.°
Therefor° my son i' th' ooze is bedded; and
I'll seek him deeper than e'er plummet° sounded,°
And with him there lie mudded. *Exit.*
SEBASTIAN: But one fiend at a time,
I'll fight their legions o'er.°
ANTONIO: I'll be thy second.
Exeunt [Sebastian and Antonio].
GONZALO: All three of them are desperate.° Their great guilt,
Like poison given to work a great time after,
Now 'gins to bite the spirits.° I do beseech you,
That are of suppler joints, follow them swiftly
And hinder them from what this ecstasy°
May now provoke them to.
ADRIAN: Follow, I pray you. *Exeunt omnes.*

[ACT IV

SCENE I: *Before Prospero's cell.*]

Enter Prospero, Ferdinand, and Miranda.

PROSPERO: If I have too austerely punished you,
Your companion makes amends, for I
Have given you here a third° of mine own life,
Or that for which I live; who once again
I tender° to thy hand. All thy vexations
Were but my trials of thy love, and thou
Hast strangely° stood the test. Here, afore heaven,
I ratify this my rich gift. O Ferdinand,
Do not smile at me that I boast her off,°

94. why: (Gonzalo was not addressed in Ariel's speech to the *three men of sin*, line 53, and is not, as they are, in a maddened state; see lines 105–107.) **95. it:** I.e., my sin (also in line 96). **96. billows:** Waves. **99. bass my trespass:** Proclaim my trespass like a bass note in music. **100. Therefor:** In consequence of that. **101. plummet:** A lead weight attached to a line for testing depth; **sounded:** Probed, tested the depth of. **104. o'er:** One after another. **105. desperate:** Despairing and reckless. **107. bite the spirits:** Sap their vital powers through anguish. **109. ecstasy:** Mad frenzy. ACT IV, SCENE I. **3. a third:** I.e., Miranda, into whose education Prospero has put a third of his life (?) or who represents a large part of what he cares about, along with his dukedom and his learned study (?). **5. tender:** Offer. **7. strangely:** Extraordinarily. **9. boast her off:** I.e., praise her so, or, perhaps an error for "boast of her."

For thou shalt find she will outstrip all praise
And make it halt° behind her.

FERDINAND: I do believe it.
Against an oracle.°

PROSPERO: Then, as my gift and thine own acquisition
Worthily purchased, take my daughter. But
If thou dost break her virgin-knot before
All sanctimonious° ceremonies may
With full and holy rite be ministered,
No sweet aspersion° shall the heavens let fall
To make this contract grow; but barren hate,
Sour-eyed disdain, and discord shall bestrew
The union of your bed with weeds° so loathly
That you shall hate it both. Therefore take heed,
As Hymen's lamps shall light you.°

FERDINAND: As I hope
For quiet days, fair issue,° and long life,
With such love as 'tis now, the murkiest den,
The most opportune place, the strong'st suggestion°
Our worser genius° can,° shall never melt
Mine honor into lust, to° take away
The edge° of that day's celebration
When I shall think or° Phoebus' steeds are foundered°
Or Night kept chained below.

PROSPERO: Fairly spoke.
Sit then and talk with her. She is thine own.
[*Ferdinand and Miranda sit and talk together.*]
What,° Ariel! My industrious servant, Ariel!

Enter Ariel.

ARIEL: What would my potent master? Here I am.

PROSPERO: Thou and thy meaner fellows° your last service
Did worthily perform, and I must use you
In such another trick.° Go bring the rabble,°
O'er whom I give thee power, here to this place.
Incite them to quick motion, for I must
Bestow upon the eyes of this young couple

---

11. halt: Limp. **12. Against an oracle:** Even if an oracle should declare otherwise. **16. sanctimonious:** Sacred. **18. aspersion:** Dew, shower. **21. weeds:** (In place of the flowers customarily strewn on the marriage bed.) **23. As . . . you:** I.e., as you long for happiness and concord in your marriage. (Hymen was the Greek and Roman god of marriage; his symbolic torches, the wedding torches, were supposed to burn brightly for a happy marriage and smokily for a troubled one.) **24. issue:** Offspring. **26. suggestion:** Temptation. **27. worser genius:** Evil genius, or, evil attendant spirit; **can:** Is capable of. **28. to:** So as to. **29. edge:** Keen enjoyment, sexual ardor. **30. or:** Either; **foundered:** Broken down, made lame. (Ferdinand will wait impatiently for the bridal night.) **33. What:** Now then. **35. meaner fellows:** Subordinates. **37. trick:** Device; **rabble:** Band, i.e., the *meaner fellows* of line 35.

Some vanity° of mine art. It is my promise,
And they expect it from me.

ARIEL: Presently?°

PROSPERO: Ay, with a twink.°

ARIEL: Before you can say "Come" and "Go,"
And breathe twice, and cry "So, so,"
Each one, tripping on his toe,
Will be here with mop and mow.°
Do you love me, master? No?

PROSPERO: Dearly, my delicate Ariel. Do not approach
Till thou dost hear me call.

ARIEL: Well; I conceive.° *Exit.*

PROSPERO: Look thou be true;° do not give dalliance
Too much the rein. The strongest oaths are straw
To the fire i' the blood. Be more abstemious,
Or else good night° your vow!

FERDINAND: I warrant° you, sir,
The white cold virgin snow upon my heart°
Abates the ardor of my liver.°

PROSPERO: Well.
Now come, my Ariel! Bring a corollary,°
Rather than want° a spirit. Appear, and pertly!° —
No tongue!° All eyes! Be silent. *Soft music.*

Enter Iris.°

IRIS: Ceres,° most bounteous lady, thy rich leas°
Of wheat, rye, barley, vetches,° oats, and peas;
Thy turfy mountains, where live nibbling sheep,
And flat meads° thatched with stover,° them to keep;
Thy banks with pionèd and twillèd° brims,
Which spongy° April at thy hest° betrims
To make cold nymphs chaste crowns; and thy broom groves,°
Whose shadow the dismissèd bachelor° loves,
Being lass-lorn; thy poll-clipped° vineyard;
And thy sea marge,° sterile and rocky hard,

---

41. vanity: (1) Illusion, (2) trifle, (3) desire for admiration, conceit. **42. Presently:** Immediately. **43. with a twink:** In the twinkling of an eye. **47. mop and mow:** Gestures and grimaces. **50. conceive:** Understand. **51. true:** True to your promise. **54. good night:** I.e., say good-bye to; **warrant:** Guarantee. **55. The white . . . heart:** I.e., the ideal of chastity and consciousness of Miranda's chaste innocence enshrined in my heart. **56. liver:** (As the presumed seat of the passions.) **57. corollary:** Surplus, extra supply. **58. want:** Lack; **pertly:** Briskly. **59. No tongue:** All the beholders are to be silent (lest the spirits vanish); **s.d. Iris:** Goddess of the rainbow and Juno's messenger. **60. Ceres:** Goddess of the generative power of nature; **leas:** Meadows. **61. vetches:** Plants for forage, fodder. **63. meads:** Meadows; **stover:** Winter fodder for cattle. **64. pionèd and twillèd:** Undercut by the swift current and protected by roots and branches that tangle to form a barricade. **65. spongy:** Wet; **hest:** Command. **66. broom groves:** Clumps of broom, gorse, yellow-flowered shrub. **67. dismissèd bachelor:** Rejected male lover. **68. poll-clipped:** Pruned, lopped at the top, or *pole-clipped,* "hedged in with poles." **69. sea marge:** Shore.

Where thou thyself dost air:° the queen o' the sky,°
Whose watery arch° and messenger am I,
Bids thee leave these, and with her sovereign grace,

Juno descends° [*slowly in her car*].

Here on this grass plot, in this very place,
To come and sport. Her peacocks° fly amain.°
Approach, rich Ceres, her to entertain.°

Enter Ceres.

CERES: Hail, many-colored messenger, that ne'er
Dost disobey the wife of Jupiter,
Who with thy saffron° wings upon my flowers
Diffusest honeydrops, refreshing showers,
And with each end of thy blue bow° dost crown
My bosky° acres and my unshrubbed down,°
Rich scarf° to my proud earth. Why hath thy queen
Summoned me hither to this short-grassed green?

IRIS: A contract of true love to celebrate,
And some donation freely to estate°
On the blest lovers.

CERES: Tell me, heavenly bow,
If Venus or her son,° as° thou dost know,
Do now attend the Queen? Since they did plot
The means that° dusky° Dis my daughter got,°
Her° and her blind boy's scandaled° company
I have forsworn.

IRIS: Of her society°
Be not afraid. I met her deity°
Cutting the clouds towards Paphos,° and her son
Dove-drawn° with her. Here thought they to have done°
Some wanton charm° upon this man and maid,
Whose vows are that no bed-right shall be paid
Till Hymen's torch be lighted; but in vain.
Mars's hot minion° is returned° again;
Her waspish-headed° son has broke his arrows,

---

70. thou . . . air: You take the air, go for walks; **queen o' the sky:** I.e., Juno. **71. watery arch:** Rainbow. **72. s.d. Juno descends:** I.e., starts her descent from the "heavens" above the stage (?). **74. peacocks:** Birds sacred to Juno and used to pull her chariot; **amain:** With full speed. **75. entertain:** Receive. **78. saffron:** Yellow. **80. bow:** I.e., rainbow. **81. bosky:** Wooded; **unshrubbed down:** Open upland. **82. scarf:** (The rainbow is like a colored silk band adorning the earth.) **85. estate:** Bestow. **87. son:** I.e., Cupid; **as:** As far as. **89. that:** Whereby; **dusky:** Dark; **Dis . . . got:** (Pluto, or *Dis*, god of the infernal regions, carried off Proserpina, daughter of Ceres, to be his bride in Hades.) **90. Her:** I.e., Venus's; **scandaled:** Scandalous. **91. society:** Company. **92. her deity:** I.e., Her Highness. **93. Paphos:** Place on the island of Cyprus, sacred to Venus. **94. Dove-drawn:** (Venus's chariot was drawn by doves); **done:** Placed. **95. wanton charm:** Lustful spell. **98. Mars's hot minion:** I.e., Venus, the beloved of Mars; **returned:** I.e., returned to Paphos. **99. waspish-headed:** Hotheaded, peevish.

Swears he will shoot no more, but play with sparrows°
And be a boy right out.°

[*Juno alights.*]

CERES: Highest Queen of state,°
Great Juno, comes; I know her by her gait.°

JUNO: How does my bounteous sister?° Go with me
To bless this twain, that they may prosperous be,
And honored in their issue.° *They sing:*

JUNO: Honor, riches, marriage blessing,
Long continuance, and increasing,
Hourly joys be still° upon you!
Juno sings her blessings on you.

CERES: Earth's increase, foison plenty,°
Barns and garners° never empty,
Vines with clustering bunches growing,
Plants with goodly burden bowing;

Spring come to you at the farthest
In the very end of harvest!°
Scarcity and want shall shun you;
Ceres' blessing so is on you.

FERDINAND: This is a most majestic vision, and
Harmonious charmingly.° May I be bold
To think these spirits?

PROSPERO: Spirits, which by mine art
I have from their confines called to enact
My present fancies.

FERDINAND: Let me live here ever!
So rare a wondered° father and a wife
Makes this place Paradise.

Juno and Ceres whisper, and send Iris on employment.

PROSPERO: Sweet now, silence!
Juno and Ceres whisper seriously;
There's something else to do. Hush and be mute,
Or else our spell is marred.

IRIS [*calling offstage*]: You nymphs, called naiads,° of the windring° brooks,
With your sedged° crowns and ever-harmless° looks,
Leave your crisp° channels, and on this green land
Answer your summons; Juno does command.

---

100. sparrows: (Supposed lustful, and sacred to Venus.) **101. right out:** Outright. **101. Highest . . . state:** Most majestic Queen. **102. gait:** I.e., majestic bearing. **103. sister:** I.e., fellow goddess (?). **105. issue:** Offspring. **108. still:** Always. **110. foison plenty:** Plentiful harvest. **111. garners:** Granaries. **115. In . . . harvest:** I.e., with no winter in between. **119. charmingly:** Enchantingly. **123. wondered:** Wonder-performing, wondrous. **128. naiads:** Nymphs of springs, rivers, or lakes; **windring:** Wandering, winding (?). **129. sedged:** Made of reeds; **ever-harmless:** Ever innocent. **130. crisp:** Curled, rippled.

Come, temperate° nymphs, and help to celebrate
A contract of true love. Be not too late.

Enter certain nymphs.

You sunburned sicklemen,° of August weary,°
Come hither from the furrow° and be merry.
Make holiday; your rye-straw hats put on,
And these fresh nymphs encounter° every one
In country footing.°

Enter certain reapers, properly° habited. They join with the nymphs in a graceful dance, towards the end whereof Prospero starts suddenly, and speaks; after which, to a strange, hollow, and confused noise, they heavily° vanish.

PROSPERO [*aside*]: I had forgot that foul conspiracy
Of the beast Caliban and his confederates
Against my life. The minute of their plot
Is almost come. [*To the Spirits.*] Well done! Avoid;° no more!
FERDINAND [*to Miranda*]: This is strange. Your father's in some passion
That works° him strongly.
MIRANDA: Never till this day
Saw I him touched with anger so distempered.
PROSPERO: You do look, my son, in a moved sort,°
As if you were dismayed. Be cheerful, sir.
Our revels° now are ended. These our actors,
As I foretold you, were all spirits and
Are melted into air, into thin air;
And, like the baseless fabric° of this vision,
The cloud-capped towers, the gorgeous palaces,
The solemn temples, the great globe° itself,
Yea, all which it inherit,° shall dissolve,
And, like this insubstantial pageant faded,
Leave not a rack° behind. We are such stuff
As dreams are made on,° and our little life
Is rounded° with a sleep. Sir, I am vexed.
Bear with my weakness. My old brain is troubled.
Be not disturbed with° my infirmity.
If you be pleased, retire° into my cell
And there repose. A turn or two I'll walk
To still my beating° mind.

---

132. temperate: Chaste. **134. sicklemen:** Harvesters, field workers who cut down grain and grass; **of August weary:** I.e., weary of the hard work of the harvest. **135. furrow:** I.e., plowed fields. **137. encounter:** Join. **138. country footing:** Country dancing; **s.d. properly:** Suitably; **s.d. heavily:** Slowly, dejectedly. **142. Avoid:** Withdraw. **144. works:** Affects, agitates. **146. moved sort:** Troubled state, condition. **148. revels:** Entertainment, pageant. **151. baseless fabric:** Unsubstantial theatrical edifice or contrivance. **153. great globe:** (With a glance at the Globe Playhouse.) **154. which it inherit:** Who subsequently occupy it. **156. rack:** Wisp of cloud. **157. on:** Of. **158. rounded:** Surrounded (before birth and after death), or crowned, rounded off. **160. with:** By. **161. retire:** Withdraw, go. **163. beating:** Agitated.

FERDINAND, MIRANDA: We wish your peace.
Exeunt [*Ferdinand and Miranda*].
PROSPERO: Come with a thought!° I thank thee, Ariel. Come.

Enter Ariel.

ARIEL: Thy thoughts I cleave° to. What's thy pleasure?
PROSPERO: Spirit,
We must prepare to meet with Caliban.
ARIEL: Ay, my commander. When I presented° Ceres,
I thought to have told thee of it, but I feared
Lest I might anger thee.
PROSPERO: Say again, where didst thou leave these varlets?
ARIEL: I told you, sir, they were red-hot with drinking;
So full of valor that they smote the air
For breathing in their faces, beat the ground
For kissing of their feet; yet always bending°
Towards their project. Then I beat my tabor,
At which, like unbacked° colts, they pricked their ears,
Advanced° their eyelids, lifted up their noses
As° they smelt music. So I charmed their ears
That calflike they my lowing° followed through
Toothed briers, sharp furzes, pricking gorse,° and thorns,
Which entered their frail shins. At last I left them
I' the filthy-mantled° pool beyond your cell,
There dancing up to the chins, that the foul lake
O'erstunk° their feet.
PROSPERO: This was well done, my bird.
Thy shape invisible retain thou still.
The trumpery° in my house, go bring it hither,
For stale° to catch these thieves.
ARIEL: I go, I go. *Exit.*
PROSPERO: A devil, a born devil, on whose nature
Nurture can never stick; on whom my pains,
Humanely taken, all, all lost, quite lost!
And as with age his body uglier grows,
So his mind cankers.° I will plague them all,
Even to roaring.

---

164. with a thought: I.e., on the instant, or, summoned by my thought, no sooner thought of than here. **165. cleave:** Cling, adhere. **167. presented:** Acted the part of, or, introduced. **174. bending:** Aiming. **176. unbacked:** Unbroken, unridden. **177. Advanced:** Lifted up. **178. As:** As if. **179. lowing:** Mooing. **180. furzes, gorse:** Prickly shrubs. **182. filthy-mantled:** Covered with a slimy coating. **184. O'erstunk:** Smelled worse than, or, caused to stink terribly. **186. trumpery:** Cheap goods, the *glistering apparel* mentioned in the following stage direction. **187. stale:** (1) Decoy (2) out-of-fashion garments (with possible further suggestions of "horse piss," as in line 198, and "steal," pronounced like *stale*). *For stale* could also mean "fit for a prostitute." **192. cankers:** Festers, grows malignant.

Enter Ariel, loaden with glistering apparel, etc.

Come, hang them on this line.°

[*Ariel hangs up the showy finery; Prospero and Ariel remain,° invisible.*] *Enter Caliban, Stephano, and Trinculo, all wet.*

CALIBAN: Pray you, tread softly, that the blind mole may
Not hear a foot fall. We now are near his cell.

STEPHANO: Monster, your fairy, which you say is a harmless fairy, has done little better than played the jack° with us.

TRINCULO: Monster, I do smell all horse piss, at which my nose is in great indignation.

STEPHANO: So is mine. Do you hear, monster? If I should take a displeasure against you, look you —

TRINCULO: Thou wert but a lost monster.

CALIBAN: Good my lord, give me thy favor still.
Be patient, for the prize I'll bring thee to
Shall hoodwink this mischance.° Therefore speak softly.
All's hushed as midnight yet.

TRINCULO: Ay, but to lose our bottles in the pool —

STEPHANO: There is not only disgrace and dishonor in that, monster, but an infinite loss.

TRINCULO: That's more to me than my wetting. Yet this is your harmless fairy, monster!

STEPHANO: I will fetch off my bottle, though I be o'er ears° for my labor.

CALIBAN: Prithee, my king, be quiet. Seest thou here,
This is the mouth o' the cell. No noise, and enter.
Do that good mischief which may make this island
Thine own forever, and I thy Caliban
For aye thy footlicker.

STEPHANO: Give me thy hand. I do begin to have bloody thoughts.

TRINCULO [*seeing the finery*]: O King Stephano! O peer!° O worthy Stephano!
Look what a wardrobe here is for thee!

CALIBAN: Let it alone, thou fool, it is but trash.

TRINCULO: Oho, monster! We know what belongs to a frippery.° O King Stephano! [*He puts on a gown.*]

STEPHANO: Put off° that gown, Trinculo. By this hand, I'll have that gown.

TRINCULO: Thy Grace shall have it.

CALIBAN: The dropsy° drown this fool! What do you mean
To dote thus on such luggage?° Let 't alone

---

193. line: Lime tree or linden; **s.d. Prospero and Ariel remain:** (The staging is uncertain. They may instead exit here and return with the spirits at line 248.) **197. jack:** (1) Knave (2) will-o'-the-wisp. **205. hoodwink this mischance:** (Misfortune is to be prevented from doing further harm by being hooded like a hawk and also put out of remembrance.) **212. o'er ears:** I.e., totally submerged and perhaps drowned. **219. King . . . peer:** (Alludes to the old ballad beginning, "King Stephen was a worthy peer.") **222. frippery:** Place where cast-off clothes are sold. **224. Put off:** Put down, or, take off. **226. dropsy:** Disease characterized by the accumulation of fluid in the connective tissue of the body. **227. luggage:** Cumbersome trash.

And do the murder first. If he awake,
From toe to crown° he'll fill our skins with pinches,
Make us strange stuff.

STEPHANO: Be you quiet, monster. — Mistress line,° is not this my jerkin?° [*He takes it down.*] Now is the jerkin under the line.° Now, jerkin, you are like° to lose your hair and prove a bald° jerkin.

TRINCULO: Do, do!° We steal by line and level,° an 't like° Your Grace.

STEPHANO: I thank thee for that jest. Here's a garment for 't. [*He gives a garment.*] Wit shall not go unrewarded while I am king of this country. "Steal by line and level" is an excellent pass of pate.° There's another garment for 't.

TRINCULO: Monster, come, put some lime° upon your fingers, and away with the rest.

CALIBAN: I will have none on 't. We shall lose our time,
And all be turned to barnacles,° or to apes
With foreheads villainous° low.

STEPHANO: Monster, lay to° your fingers. Help to bear this° away where my hogshead° of wine is, or I'll turn you out of my kingdom. Go to,° carry this.

TRINCULO: And this.

STEPHANO: Ay, and this. [*They load Caliban with more and more garments.*]

A noise of hunters heard. Enter divers spirits, in shape of dogs and hounds, hunting them about, Prospero and Ariel setting them on.

PROSPERO: Hey, Mountain, hey!

ARIEL: Silver! There it goes, Silver!

PROSPERO: Fury, Fury! There, Tyrant, there! Hark! Hark!
[*Caliban, Stephano, and Trinculo are driven out.*]
Go, charge my goblins that they grind their joints
With dry° convulsions,° shorten up their sinews
With agèd° cramps, and more pinch-spotted make them
Than pard° or cat o' mountain.°

ARIEL: Hark, they roar!

---

229. crown: Head. **231. Mistress line:** (Addressed to the linden or lime tree upon which, at line 193, Ariel hung the *glistering apparel*); **jerkin:** Jacket made of leather. **232. under the line:** Under the lime tree (with punning sense of being south of the equinoctial line or equator; sailors on long voyages to the southern regions were popularly supposed to lose their hair from scurvy or other diseases. Stephano also quibbles bawdily on losing hair through syphilis, and in *Mistress* and *jerkin*). **233. like:** Likely; **bald:** (1) Hairless, napless (2) meager. **234. Do, do:** I.e., bravo (said in response to the jesting or to the taking of the jerkin, or both); **by line and level:** I.e., by means of plumb line and carpenter's level, methodically (with pun on *line,* "lime tree," line 232, and *steal,* pronounced like *stale,* i.e., prostitute, continuing Stephano's bawdy quibble); **an 't like:** If it please. **237. pass of pate:** Sally of wit. (The metaphor is from fencing.) **239. lime:** Birdlime, sticky substance (to give Caliban sticky fingers). **242. barnacles:** Barnacle geese, formerly supposed to be hatched from barnacles attached to trees or to rotting timber; here, evidently used, like *apes,* as types of simpletons. **243. villainous:** Miserably. **244. lay to:** Start using; **this:** I.e., the *glistering apparel.* **245. hogshead:** Large cask; **Go to:** (An expression of exhortation or remonstrance.) **253. dry:** Associated with age, arthritic (?); **convulsions:** Cramps. **254. agèd:** Characteristic of old age. **255. pard:** Panther or leopard; **cat o' mountain:** Wildcat.

PROSPERO: Let them be hunted soundly.° At this hour
Lies at my mercy all mine enemies.
Shortly shall all my labors end, and thou
Shalt have the air at freedom. For a little°
Follow, and do me service. *Exeunt.*

[ACT V

SCENE I: *Before Prospero's cell.*]

Enter Prospero in his magic robes, [with his staff,] and Ariel.

PROSPERO: Now does my project gather to a head.
My charms crack° not, my spirits obey, and Time
Goes upright with his carriage.° How's the day?
ARIEL: On° the sixth hour, at which time, my lord,
You said our work should cease.
PROSPERO: I did say so,
When first I raised the tempest. Say, my spirit,
How fares the King and 's followers?
ARIEL: Confined together
In the same fashion as you gave in charge,
Just as you left them; all prisoners, sir,
In the line grove° which weather-fends° your cell.
They cannot budge till your release.° The King,
His brother, and yours abide all three distracted,°
And the remainder mourning over them,
Brim full of sorrow and dismay; but chiefly
Him that you termed, sir, the good old lord, Gonzalo.
His tears runs down his beard like winter's drops
From eaves of reeds.° Your charm so strongly works 'em
That if you now beheld them your affections°
Would become tender.
PROSPERO: Dost thou think so, spirit?
ARIEL: Mine would, sir, were I human.°
PROSPERO: And mine shall.
Hast thou, which art but air, a touch,° a feeling
Of their afflictions, and shall not myself,
One of their kind, that relish all as sharply
Passion as they,° be kindlier° moved than thou art?

---

256. soundly: Thoroughly (and suggesting the sounds of the hunt). **259. little:** Little while longer. ACT V, SCENE I. **2. crack:** Collapse, fail. (The metaphor is probably alchemical, as in *project* and *gather to a head,* line 1.) **3. his carriage:** Its burden (time is no longer heavily burdened and so can go *upright,* "standing straight and unimpeded"). **4. On:** Approaching. **10. line grove:** Grove of lime trees; **weather-fends:** Protects from the weather. **11. your release:** You release them. **12. distracted:** Out of their wits. **17. eaves of reeds:** Thatched roofs. **18. affections:** Disposition, feelings. **20. human:** Humane [as well as human]. **21. touch:** Sense, apprehension. **23–24. that . . . they:** I who experience human passions as acutely as they. **24. kindlier:** (1) More sympathetically (2) more naturally, humanly.

Though with their high wrongs I am struck to the quick,
Yet with my nobler reason 'gainst my fury
Do I take part. The rarer° action is
In virtue than in vengeance. They being penitent,
The sole drift of my purpose doth extend
Not a frown further. Go release them, Ariel.
My charms I'll break, their senses I'll restore,
And they shall be themselves.

ARIEL: I'll fetch them, sir. *Exit.*

[*Prospero traces a charmed circle with his staff.*]

PROSPERO: Ye elves of hills, brooks, standing lakes, and groves,
And ye that on the sands with printless foot
Do chase the ebbing Neptune, and do fly him
When he comes back; you demi-puppets° that
By moonshine do the green sour ringlets° make,
Whereof the ewe not bites; and you whose pastime
Is to make midnight mushrooms,° that rejoice
To hear the solemn curfew;° by whose aid,
Weak masters° though ye be, I have bedimmed
The noontide sun, called forth the mutinous winds,
And twixt the green sea and the azured vault°
Set roaring war; to the dread rattling thunder
Have I given fire,° and rifted° Jove's stout oak°
With his own bolt;° the strong-based promontory
Have I made shake, and by the spurs° plucked up
The pine and cedar; graves at my command
Have waked their sleepers, oped, and let 'em forth
By my so potent art. But this rough° magic
I here abjure, and when I have required°
Some heavenly music — which even now I do —
To work mine end upon their senses that°
This airy charm° is for, I'll break my staff,
Bury it certain fathoms in the earth,
And deeper than did ever plummet sound
I'll drown my book. *Solemn music.*

Here enters Ariel before; then Alonso, with a frantic gesture, attended by Gonzalo; Sebastian and Antonio in like manner, attended by Adrian and Francisco. They all enter the

---

27. rarer: Nobler. **33–50. Ye . . . art:** (This famous passage is an embellished paraphrase of Golding's translation of Ovid's *Metamorphoses,* Book VII, lines 197–219.) **36. demi-puppets:** Puppets of half size, i.e., elves and fairies. **37. green sour ringlets:** Fairy rings, circles in grass (actually produced by mushrooms). **39. midnight mushrooms:** Mushrooms appearing overnight. **40. curfew:** Evening bell, usually rung at nine o'clock, ushering in the time when spirits are abroad. **41. Weak masters:** I.e., subordinate spirits, as in IV.i.35 (?). **43. the azured vault:** I.e., the sky. **44–45. to . . . fire:** I have discharged the dread rattling thunderbolt. **45. rifted:** Riven, split; **oak:** A tree that was sacred to Jove. **46. bolt:** Lightning bolt. **47. spurs:** Roots. **50. rough:** Violent. **51. required:** Requested. **53. their senses that:** The senses of those whom. **54. airy charm:** I.e., music.

circle which Prospero had made, and there stand charmed; which Prospero observing, speaks:

[*To Alonso.*] A solemn air,° and° the best comforter
To an unsettled fancy,° cure thy brains,
Now useless, boiled° within thy skull! [*To Sebastian and Antonio.*]
There stand,
For you are spell-stopped. —
Holy Gonzalo, honorable man,
Mine eyes, e'en sociable° to the show° of thine,
Fall° fellowly drops. [*Aside.*] The charm dissolves apace,
And as the morning steals upon the night,
Melting the darkness, so their rising senses
Begin to chase the ignorant fumes° that mantle°
Their clearer° reason. — O good Gonzalo,
My true preserver, and a loyal sir
To him thou follow'st! I will pay thy graces°
Home° both in word and deed. — Most cruelly
Didst thou, Alonso, use me and my daughter.
Thy brother was a furtherer° in the act. —
Thou art pinched° for 't now, Sebastian. [*To Antonio.*] Flesh and blood,
You, brother mine, that entertained ambition,
Expelled remorse° and nature,° whom,° with Sebastian,
Whose inward pinches therefore are most strong,
Would here have killed your king, I do forgive thee,
Unnatural though thou art. — Their understanding
Begins to swell, and the approaching tide
Will shortly fill the reasonable shore°
That now lies foul and muddy. Not one of them
That yet looks on me, or would know me. — Ariel,
Fetch me the hat and rapier in my cell.
[*Ariel goes to the cell and returns immediately.*]
I will discase° me and myself present
As I was sometime Milan.° Quickly, spirit!
Thou shalt ere long be free. *Ariel sings and helps to attire him.*

ARIEL: Where the bee sucks, there suck I.
In a cowslip's bell I lie;
There I couch° when owls do cry.
On the bat's back I do fly

58. air: Song; **and:** I.e., which is. **59. fancy:** Imagination. **60. boiled:** I.e., extremely agitated. **63. sociable:** Sympathetic; **show:** Appearance. **64. Fall:** Let fall. **67. ignorant fumes:** Fumes that render them incapable of comprehension; **mantle:** Envelop. **68. clearer:** Growing clearer. **70. pay thy graces:** Requite your favors and virtues. **71. Home:** Fully. **73. furtherer:** Accomplice. **74. pinched:** Punished, afflicted. **76. remorse:** Pity; **nature:** Natural feeling; **whom:** I.e., who. **81. reasonable shore:** Shores of reason, i.e., minds (their reason returns, like the incoming tide). **85. discase:** Disrobe. **86. As . . . Milan:** In my former appearance as Duke of Milan. **90. couch:** Lie.

After° summer merrily.
Merrily, merrily shall I live now
Under the blossom that hangs on the bough.

PROSPERO: Why, that's my dainty Ariel! I shall miss thee,
But yet thou shalt have freedom. So, so, so.°
To the King's ship, invisible as thou art!
There shalt thou find the mariners asleep
Under the hatches. The Master and the Boatswain
Being awake, enforce them to this place,
And presently,° I prithee.

ARIEL: I drink the air before me and return
Or ere° your pulse twice beat. *Exit.*

GONZALO: All torment, trouble, wonder, and amazement
Inhabits here. Some heavenly power guide us
Out of this fearful° country!

PROSPERO: Behold, sir King,
The wrongèd Duke of Milan, Prospero.
For more assurance that a living prince
Does now speak to thee, I embrace thy body;
And to thee and thy company I bid
A hearty welcome. [*Embracing him.*]

ALONSO: Whe'er thou be'st he or no,
Or some enchanted trifle° to abuse° me,
As late° I have been, I not know. Thy pulse
Beats as of flesh and blood; and, since I saw thee,
Th' affliction of my mind amends, with which
I fear a madness held me. This must crave° —
An if this be at all° — a most strange story.°
Thy dukedom I resign,° and do entreat
Thou pardon me my wrongs.° But how should Prospero
Be living, and be here?

PROSPERO [*to Gonzalo*]: First, noble friend,
Let me embrace thine age,° whose honor cannot
Be measured or confined. [*Embracing him.*]

GONZALO: Whether this be
Or be not, I'll not swear.

PROSPERO: You do yet taste
Some subtleties° o' th' isle, that will not let you
Believe things certain. Welcome, my friends all!

---

92. After: I.e., pursuing. **96. So, so, so:** (Expresses approval of Ariel's help as valet.) **101. presently:** Immediately. **103. Or ere:** Before. **106. fearful:** Frightening. **112. trifle:** Trick of magic; **abuse:** Deceive. **113. late:** Lately. **116. crave:** Require. **117. An . . . all:** If this is actually happening; **story:** I.e., explanation. **118. Thy . . . resign:** (Alonso made arrangements with Antonio at the time of Prospero's banishment for Milan to pay tribute to Naples; see I.ii.113–127.) **119. wrongs:** Wrongdoings. **121. thine age:** Your venerable self. **124. subtleties:** Illusions, magical powers (playing on the idea of "pastries, concoctions").

[*Aside to Sebastian and Antonio.*] But you, my brace° of lords, were I so minded,
I here could pluck His Highness' frown upon you
And justify you° traitors. At this time
I will tell no tales.

SEBASTIAN: The devil speaks in him.

PROSPERO: No.
[*To Antonio.*] For you, most wicked sir, whom to call brother
Would even infect my mouth, I do forgive
Thy rankest fault — all of them; and require
My dukedom of thee, which perforce° I know
Thou must restore.

ALONSO: If thou be'st Prospero,
Give us particulars of thy preservation,
How thou hast met us here, whom° three hours since
Were wrecked upon this shore, where I have lost —
How sharp the point of this remembrance is! —
My dear son Ferdinand.

PROSPERO: I am woe° for 't, sir.

ALONSO: Irreparable is the loss, and Patience
Says it is past her cure.

PROSPERO: I rather think
You have not sought her help, of whose soft grace°
For the like loss I have her sovereign° aid
And rest myself content.

ALONSO: You the like loss?

PROSPERO: As great to me as late,° and supportable
To make the dear loss, have I° means much weaker
Than you may call to comfort you; for I
Have lost my daughter.

ALONSO: A daughter?
O heavens, that they were living both in Naples,
The king and queen there! That° they were, I wish
Myself were mudded° in that oozy bed
Where my son lies. When did you lose your daughter?

PROSPERO: In this last tempest. I perceive these lords
At this encounter do so much admire°
That they devour their reason° and scarce think
Their eyes do offices of truth, their words
Are natural breath.° But, howsoever you have

---

126. brace: Pair. **128. justify you:** Prove you to be. **133. perforce:** Necessarily. **136. whom:** I.e., who. **139. woe:** Sorry. **142. of . . . grace:** By whose mercy. **143. sovereign:** Efficacious. **145. late:** Recent. **145–146. supportable . . . have I:** To make the deeply felt loss bearable, I have. **151. That:** So that. **152. mudded:** Buried in the mud. **155. admire:** Wonder. **156. devour their reason:** I.e., are openmouthed, dumbfounded. **156–158. scarce . . . breath:** Scarcely believe that their eyes inform them accurately as to what they see or that their words are naturally spoken.

Been jostled from your senses, know for certain
That I am Prospero and that very duke
Which was thrust forth of° Milan, who most strangely
Upon this shore, where you were wrecked, was landed
To be the lord on 't. No more yet of this,
For 'tis a chronicle of day by day,°
Not a relation for a breakfast nor
Befitting this first meeting. Welcome, sir.
This cell's my court. Here have I few attendants,
And subjects none abroad.° Pray you, look in.
My dukedom since you have given me again,
I will requite° you with as good a thing,
At least bring forth a wonder to content ye
As much as me my dukedom.

Here Prospero discovers° Ferdinand and Miranda, playing at chess.

MIRANDA: Sweet lord, you play me false.°
FERDINAND: No, my dearest love,
I would not for the world.
MIRANDA: Yes, for a score of kingdoms you should wrangle,
And I would call it fair play.°
ALONSO: If this prove
A vision° of the island, one dear son
Shall I twice lose.
SEBASTIAN: A most high miracle!
FERDINAND [*approaching his father*]: Though the seas threaten, they are merciful;
I have cursed them without cause. [*He kneels.*]
ALONSO: Now all the blessings
Of a glad father compass° thee about!
Arise, and say how thou cam'st here. [*Ferdinand rises.*]
MIRANDA: O, wonder!
How many goodly creatures are there here!
How beauteous mankind is! O brave° new world
That has such people in 't!
PROSPERO: 'Tis new to thee.
ALONSO: What is this maid with whom thou wast at play?
Your eld'st° acquaintance cannot be three hours.
Is she the goddess that hath severed us,
And brought us thus together?

---

161. of: From. **164. of day by day:** Requiring days to tell. **168. abroad:** Away from here, anywhere else. **170. requite:** Repay. **172. s.d. discovers:** I.e., by opening a curtain, presumably rearstage. **173. play me false:** I.e., press your advantage. **176–177. Yes . . . play:** Yes, even if we were playing for only twenty kingdoms, you would still press your advantage against me, and I would lovingly let you do it as though it were fair play, or if you were to play not just for stakes but literally for kingdoms, my complaint would be out of order in that your "wrangling" would be proper. **178. vision:** Illusion. **182. compass:** Encompass, embrace. **185. brave:** Splendid, gorgeously appareled, handsome. **188. eld'st:** Longest.

FERDINAND: Sir, she is mortal;
But by immortal Providence she's mine.
I chose her when I could not ask my father
For his advice, nor thought I had one. She
Is daughter to this famous Duke of Milan,
Of whom so often I have heard renown,
But never saw before; of whom I have
Received a second life; and second father
This lady makes him to me.

ALONSO: I am hers.
But O, how oddly will it sound that I
Must ask my child forgiveness!

PROSPERO: There, sir, stop.
Let us not burden our remembrances with
A heaviness° that's gone.

GONZALO: I have inly° wept,
Or should have spoke ere this. Look down, you gods,
And on this couple drop a blessèd crown!
For it is you that have chalked forth the way°
Which brought us hither.

ALONSO: I say amen, Gonzalo!

GONZALO: Was Milan° thrust from Milan, that his issue
Should become kings of Naples? O, rejoice
Beyond a common joy, and set it down
With gold on lasting pillars: In one voyage
Did Claribel her husband find at Tunis,
And Ferdinand, her brother, found a wife
Where he himself was lost; Prospero his dukedom
In a poor isle; and all of us ourselves
When no man was his own.°

Alonso [*to Ferdinand and Miranda*]: Give me your hands.
Let grief and sorrow still° embrace his° heart
That° doth not wish you joy!

GONZALO: Be it so! Amen!

Enter Ariel, with the Master and Boatswain amazedly following.

O, look, sir, look, sir! Here is more of us.
I prophesied, if a gallows were on land,
This fellow could not drown. — Now, blasphemy,°
That swear'st grace o'erboard,° not an oath° on shore?
Hast thou no mouth by land? What is the news?

---

202. heaviness: Sadness; **inly:** Inwardly. **205. chalked . . . way:** Marked as with a piece of chalk the pathway. **207. Was Milan:** Was the Duke of Milan. **214–215. all . . . own:** All of us have found ourselves and our sanity when we all had lost our senses. **216. still:** Always; **his:** That person's. **217. That:** Who. **220. blasphemy:** I.e., blasphemer. **221. That swear'st grace o'erboard:** I.e., you who banish heavenly grace from the ship by your blasphemies; **not an oath:** Aren't you going to swear an oath.

BOATSWAIN: The best news is that we have safely found
Our King and company; the next, our ship —
Which, but three glasses° since, we gave out° split —
Is tight and yare° and bravely° rigged as when
We first put out to sea.
ARIEL [*aside to Prospero*]: Sir, all this service
Have I done since I went.
PROSPERO [*aside to Ariel*]: My tricksy° spirit!
ALONSO: These are not natural events; they strengthen°
From strange to stranger. Say, how came you hither?
BOATSWAIN: If I did think, sir, I were well awake,
I'd strive to tell you. We were dead of sleep,°
And — how we know not — all clapped under hatches,
Where but even now, with strange and several° noises
Of roaring, shrieking, howling, jingling chains,
And more diversity of sounds, all horrible,
We were awaked; straightway at liberty;
Where we, in all her trim, freshly beheld
Our royal, good, and gallant ship, our Master
Cap'ring to eye° her. On a trice,° so please you,
Even in a dream, were we divided from them°
And were brought moping° hither.
ARIEL [*aside to Prospero*]: Was 't well done?
PROSPERO [*aside to Ariel*]: Bravely, my diligence. Thou shalt be free.
ALONSO: This is as strange a maze as e'er men trod,
And there is in this business more than nature
Was ever conduct° of. Some oracle
Must rectify our knowledge.
PROSPERO: Sir, my liege,
Do not infest° your mind with beating on°
The strangeness of this business. At picked° leisure,
Which shall be shortly, single° I'll resolve° you,
Which to you shall seem probable,° of every
These° happened accidents;° till when, be cheerful
And think of each thing well.° [*Aside to Ariel.*] Come hither, spirit.
Set Caliban and his companions free.
Untie the spell. [*Exit Ariel.*] How fares my gracious sir?

---

225. glasses: I.e., hours; **gave out:** Reported, professed to be. **226. yare:** Ready; **bravely:** Splendidly. **228. tricksy:** Ingenious, sportive. **229. strengthen:** Increase. **232. dead of sleep:** Deep in sleep. **234. several:** Diverse. **240. Cap'ring to eye:** Dancing for joy to see; **On a trice:** In an instant. **241. them:** I.e., the other crew members. **242. moping:** In a daze. **246. conduct:** Guide. **248. infest:** Harass, disturb; **beating on:** Worrying about. **249. picked:** Chosen, convenient. **250. single:** Privately, by my own human powers; **resolve:** Satisfy, explain to. **251. probable:** Plausible. **251–252. of every These:** About every one of these. **252. accidents:** Occurrences. **253. well:** Favorably.

There are yet missing of your company
Some few odd° lads that you remember not.

Enter Ariel, driving in Caliban, Stephano, and Trinculo, in their stolen apparel.

STEPHANO: Every man shift° for all the rest,° and let no man take care for himself; for all is but fortune. Coragio,° bully monster,° coragio!

TRINCULO: If these be true spies° which I wear in my head, here's a goodly sight.

CALIBAN: O Setebos, these be brave° spirits indeed!
How fine° my master is! I am afraid
He will chastise me.

SEBASTIAN: Ha, ha!
What things are these, my lord Antonio?
Will money buy 'em?

ANTONIO: Very like. One of them
Is a plain fish, and no doubt marketable.

PROSPERO: Mark but the badges° of these men, my lords,
Then say if they be true.° This misshapen knave,
His mother was a witch, and one so strong
That could control the moon, make flows and ebbs,
And deal in her command without her power.°
These three have robbed me, and this demidevil —
For he's a bastard° one — had plotted with them
To take my life. Two of these fellows you
Must know and own.° This thing of darkness I
Acknowledge mine.

CALIBAN: I shall be pinched to death.

ALONSO: Is not this Stephano, my drunken butler?

SEBASTIAN: He is drunk now. Where had he wine?

ALONSO: And Trinculo is reeling ripe.° Where should they
Find this grand liquor that hath gilded° 'em?
[*To Trinculo.*] How cam'st thou in this pickle?°

TRINCULO: I have been in such a pickle since I saw you last that, I fear me, will never out of my bones. I shall not fear flyblowing.°

SEBASTIAN: Why, how now, Stephano?

---

257. odd: Unaccounted for. **258. shift:** Provide; **for all the rest:** (Stephano drunkenly gets wrong the saying "Every man for himself.") **259. Coragio:** Courage; **bully monster:** Gallant monster (ironical). **260. true spies:** Accurate observers (i.e., sharp eyes). **262. brave:** Handsome. **263. fine:** Splendidly attired. **269. badges:** Emblems of cloth or silver worn by retainers to indicate whom they serve. (Prospero refers here to the stolen clothes as emblems of their villainy.) **270. true:** Honest. **273. deal . . . power:** Wield the moon's power, either without her authority or beyond her influence, or, even though to do so was beyond Sycorax's own power. **275. bastard:** Counterfeit. **277. own:** Recognize, admit as belonging to you. **281. reeling ripe:** Stumbling drunk. **282. gilded:** (1) Flushed, made drunk (2) covered with gilt (suggesting the horse urine). **283. pickle:** (1) Fix, predicament (2) pickling brine (in this case, horse urine). **285. flyblowing:** I.e., being fouled by fly eggs (from which he is saved by being pickled).

STEPHANO: O, touch me not! I am not Stephano, but a cramp.
PROSPERO: You'd be king o' the isle, sirrah?°
STEPHANO: I should have been a sore° one, then.
ALONSO [*pointing to Caliban*]: This is a strange thing as e'er I looked on.
PROSPERO: He is as disproportioned in his manners
    As in his shape. — Go, sirrah, to my cell.
    Take with you your companions. As you look
    To have my pardon, trim° it handsomely.
CALIBAN: Ay, that I will; and I'll be wise hereafter
    And seek for grace.° What a thrice-double ass
    Was I to take this drunkard for a god
    And worship this dull fool!
PROSPERO: Go to. Away!
ALONSO: Hence, and bestow your luggage where you found it.
SEBASTIAN: Or stole it, rather. [*Exeunt Caliban, Stephano, and Trinculo.*]
PROSPERO: Sir, I invite Your Highness and your train
    To my poor cell, where you shall take your rest
    For this one night; which, part of it, I'll waste°
    With such discourse as, I not doubt, shall make it
    Go quick away: the story of my life,
    And the particular accidents° gone by
    Since I came to this isle. And in the morn
    I'll bring you to your ship, and so to Naples,
    Where I have hope to see the nuptial
    Of these our dear-belovèd solemnized;
    And thence retire me° to my Milan, where
    Every third thought shall be my grave.
ALONSO: I long
    To hear the story of your life, which must
    Take° the ear strangely.
PROSPERO: I'll deliver° all;
    And promise you calm seas, auspicious gales,
    And sail so expeditious that shall catch
    Your royal fleet far off.° [*Aside to Ariel.*] My Ariel, chick,
    That is thy charge. Then to the elements
    Be free, and fare thou well! — Please you, draw near.°
Exeunt omnes [*except Prospero*].

---

288. sirrah: (Standard form of address to an inferior, here expressing reprimand.) **289. sore:** (1) Tyrannical (2) sorry, inept (3) wracked by pain. **294. trim:** Prepare, decorate. **296. grace:** Pardon, favor. **303. waste:** Spend. **306. accidents:** Occurrences. **311. retire me:** Return. **314. Take:** Take effect upon, enchant; **deliver:** Declare, relate. **316–317. catch . . . far off:** Enable you to catch up with the main part of your royal fleet, now afar off en route to Naples (see I.ii.233–236). **319. draw near:** I.e., enter my cell.

EPILOGUE

Spoken by Prospero.

Now my charms are all o'erthrown,
And what strength I have 's mine own,
Which is most faint. Now, 'tis true,
I must be here confined by you
Or sent to Naples. Let me not,
Since I have my dukedom got
And pardoned the deceiver, dwell
In this bare island by your spell,
But release me from my bands°
With the help of your good hands.°
Gentle breath° of yours my sails
Must fill, or else my project fails,
Which was to please. Now I want°
Spirits to enforce,° art to enchant,
And my ending is despair,
Unless I be relieved by prayer,°
Which pierces so that it assaults°
Mercy itself, and frees° all faults.
As you from crimes° would pardoned be,
Let your indulgence° set me free. *Exit.*

HENRIK IBSEN *(1828–1906), dramatist and poet, was born the second child of a merchant in a small town in southeast Norway. After the ruin of his father's business, Ibsen was raised in extreme poverty. His familiarity with economic hardship and his long struggle to make ends meet were later reflected in his realistic dramas. As a teenager Ibsen intended to study medicine, and he helped support his family by working for six years in an apothecary shop in the seaport town of Grimstad. Self-educated, he wrote his first play,* Catilina, *in verse when he was twenty-one. A year later he left Grimstad to become a student in Oslo, and then in 1851 he became active in the newly formed National Theatre at Bergen, the first theater in Norway to use Norwegian actors (Danish actors had previously dominated the stage). There Ibsen gained practical experience designing costumes, keeping the accounts, directing, and writing. After the theater went bankrupt, he left Norway with his wife and young son in 1864 and settled in Rome. Living abroad, he wrote the historical plays* Brand *(1866) and* Peer

---

EPILOGUE. **9. bands:** Bonds. **10. hands:** I.e., applause (the noise of which would break the spell of silence). **11. Gentle breath:** Favorable breeze (produced by hands clapping or favorable comment). **13. want:** Lack. **14. enforce:** Control. **16. prayer:** I.e., Prospero's petition to the audience. **17. assaults:** Rightfully gains the attention of. **18. frees:** Obtains forgiveness for. **19. crimes:** Sins. **20. indulgence:** (1) Humoring, lenient approval (2) remission of punishment for sin.

Gynt (1867) as closet dramas, intended to be read, not acted. These plays' brilliant vision of human vocation and self-realization made Ibsen famous throughout Scandinavia when they were published, and Ibsen was awarded a government pension, although the two plays were not staged for many years.

In 1875 Ibsen moved to Munich, where he began to experiment with a different kind of drama in The Pillars of Society (1877), the first of his twelve realistic prose plays addressing social issues. Four years later, living in Rome and Amalfi, he wrote A Doll House. Its portrayal of a marriage in crisis aroused so much controversy that the play caused an immediate sensation when it was performed. His next play, Ghosts (1881), was also attacked for its subject matter (syphilis passed on from father to son within a respected, upper-class family), although it was staged the following year by a small experimental theater company in Chicago. In the 1880s Ibsen's plays — An Enemy of the People (1882) and The Wild Duck (1884) among them — were regarded as obscure and unconventional. The earliest major English-language production of any of his plays was in 1889 when A Doll House was performed in London. In 1891, after writing Hedda Gabler in Munich, Ibsen returned to live for the remainder of his life in Norway, where he wrote four last plays about spiritual conflicts in a new symbolic style.

Ibsen based the plot of A Doll House on a true story. In 1871 a young Norwegian woman named Laura Petersen sent him a sequel that she had written to his play Brand. Ibsen encouraged her to continue writing, calling her his "skylark." The following year she married a Danish schoolmaster who, suffering from tuberculosis, learned that he had to live in a warmer climate. The couple was poor, so Laura secretly arranged a loan to finance their trip to Italy. In 1878, after her creditor demanded repayment of the loan, she wrote a novel and sent it to Ibsen, asking him to recommend it to his publisher. Ibsen refused to endorse her book, and acting in panic, she forged a check to repay the debt. When the bank refused payment, Laura confessed to her husband what she had done. Instead of being sympathetic because she had been so concerned about his health, he accused her of being a criminal and an unfit mother for their children. Laura had a nervous breakdown, and her husband had her committed to a psychiatric hospital. After a month in the institution, she begged her husband to let her come back home for their children's sake, which he did, making it clear to her that it was against his higher moral principles. As Ibsen's biographer Michael Meyer understood, "The incident must have seemed to Ibsen to crystallize not merely woman's, but mankind's fight against conventional morality and prejudice."

Three months after hearing that Laura Petersen had been institutionalized, Ibsen composed his "Notes for a Modern Tragedy," in which he stated the germ of the idea that he developed in A Doll House: "There are two kinds of moral laws, two kinds of conscience, one for men and one, quite different, for women. They don't understand each other; but in practical life, woman is judged by masculine law, as though she weren't a woman but a man." Ibsen had been interested for some time in what was then called the problem of women's rights. His wife, Suzannah, championed the cause, and his friend the Norwegian novelist Camilla Collett had criticized what she considered his old-fashioned ideas about women's place in society.

The English writer John Stuart Mill's The Subjection of Women had been translated into Norwegian in 1869, the same year that Ibsen wrote his comedy The League of Youth. In this play one of the minor characters, a young wife, tells her *husband, "You dressed me up like a doll; you played with me as one plays with a child." The Danish theater critic and champion of modernism Georg Brandes told Ibsen that a strong woman character like her might be a good subject for a play. In* The Pillars of Society, *which Ibsen completed just before* A Doll House, *he created two roles for women who rebel against the subordinate position dictated to them by their uncompromising patriarchal society. Yet he later insisted that in* A Doll House *he had not "worked for the Women's Rights movement. I am not even very sure what Women's Rights really are." What he really wanted to show in creating the character of Nora, he told Brandes, was a revolution of the human spirit.*

By 1879, when A Doll House *premiered at the Royal Theatre in Copenhagen, stage production had developed into the realistic theater familiar to us today. In his printed stage directions Ibsen had described the set in minute detail as a middle-class apartment, and the Danes followed his floor plan closely, adding flowering plants and a reproduction of Raphael's painting of the Madonna and child on the wall above the piano. The Royal Theatre even envisioned how to furnish Torvald's study offstage authentically with a paperweight and two candlesticks, although this view of his desk would be seen by very few people in the audience. Betty Hennings, the beautiful twenty-nine-year-old Danish actress playing Nora, was an accomplished dancer, and she was so attractive in the role that she became established as an international star. One reviewer who had come under Hennings's spell declared that in the first two acts she presented such a charming "picture of the young, inexperienced, naive, and carefree wife and mother that one truly envied" her husband for "the treasure which he possessed," thus completely missing the point of the play.*

By the end of A Doll House, *nineteenth-century audiences were nearly unanimous in their sympathy for Nora's husband, Torvald. Theater historians Frederick Marker and Lise-Lone Marker point out that in 1879, all the reviewers of this first production agreed that "the spiritual metamorphosis" that Nora undergoes in the third act of* A Doll House *from a naive wife and mother to a self-possessed independent woman was totally unconvincing. Attacked for being immoral, the play aroused so much controversy in Copenhagen that a placard reading* Her tales ikke Dukkehjem *("No Doll House discussions here") was sold for Danes to put in their parlors to keep the peace at home.*

Two months after the Danish premier, Ibsen rewrote the play for a German actress who refused to appear on stage unless there was a happy ending — an ending in which Nora (as a so-called normal mother) agrees to stay home to continue her marriage. This version of the play was not a success, and Ibsen restored the original ending. Later critics understood that in A Doll House *Ibsen had gone beyond the conventional idea of a "well-made play" in realistic drama to create a new type of "discussion play." Where the carefully plotted well-made play ends in a dénouement or a closed ending that resolves all the aspects of the conflict between the characters, Ibsen's discussion play culminates in an open ending without a clear resolution of the issues dramatized onstage, because the debate itself is intended to be an integral part of the dramatic action. Contemporary audiences accept Ibsen's open ending in the play, but a century ago most people were shocked by Nora's decision to leave her children and go off on her own. When she slammed the door of her husband's house at the end of the play, the sound reverberated round the world.*

RELATED COMMENTARIES: *Henrik Ibsen, "Notes for* A Doll House,*"* *page 1980**; Sandra Saari, "Female Becomes Human: Nora Transformed in* A Doll House,*"* *page 1993; George Bernard Shaw, "On* A Doll House,*" page 1995; Joan Templeton, "Is* A Doll House *a Feminist Text?," page 2000.*

HENRIK IBSEN

A Doll House

1879

TRANSLATED BY ROLF FJELDE

THE CHARACTERS

TORVALD HELMER, *a lawyer*
NORA, *his wife*
DR. RANK
MRS. LINDE
NILS KROGSTAD, *a bank clerk*
The Helmers' three small children
ANNE-MARIE, *their nurse*
HELENE, *a maid*
A Delivery Boy

SCENE: *The action takes place in Helmer's residence.*

ACT I

A comfortable room, tastefully but not expensively furnished. A door to the right in the back wall leads to the entryway; another to the left leads to Helmer's study. Between these doors, a piano. Midway in the left-hand wall a door, and further back a window. Near the window a round table with an armchair and a small sofa. In the right-hand wall, toward the rear, a door, and nearer the foreground a porcelain stove with two armchairs and a rocking chair beside it. Between the stove and the side door, a small table. Engravings on the walls. An etagère with china figures and other small art objects; a small bookcase with richly bound books; the floor carpeted; a fire burning in the stove. It is a winter day.

A bell rings in the entryway; shortly after we hear the door being unlocked. Nora comes into the room, humming happily to herself; she is wearing street clothes and carries an armload of packages, which she puts down on the table to the right. She has left the hall door open; and through it a Delivery Boy is seen, holding a Christmas tree and a basket, which he gives to the Maid who let them in.

NORA: Hide the tree well, Helene. The children mustn't get a glimpse of it till this evening, after it's trimmed. (*To the Delivery Boy, taking out her purse.*) How much?

DELIVERY BOY: Fifty, ma'am.

NORA: There's a crown. No, keep the change. (*The Boy thanks her and leaves. Nora shuts the door. She laughs softly to herself while taking off her street things. Drawing a bag of macaroons from her pocket, she eats a couple, then steals over and listens at her husband's study door.*) Yes, he's home. (*Hums again as she moves to the table right.*)

HELMER (*from the study*): Is that my little lark twittering out there?

NORA (*busy opening some packages*): Yes, it is.

HELMER: Is that my squirrel rummaging around?

NORA: Yes!

HELMER: When did my squirrel get in?

NORA: Just now. (*Putting the macaroon bag in her pocket and wiping her mouth.*) Do come in, Torvald, and see what I've bought.

HELMER: Can't be disturbed. (*After a moment he opens the door and peers in, pen in hand.*) Bought, you say? All that there? Has the little spendthrift been out throwing money around again?

NORA: Oh, but Torvald, this year we really should let ourselves go a bit. It's the first Christmas we haven't had to economize.

HELMER: But you know we can't go squandering.

NORA: Oh yes, Torvald, we can squander a little now. Can't we? Just a tiny, wee bit. Now that you've got a big salary and are going to make piles and piles of money.

HELMER: Yes — starting New Year's. But then it's a full three months till the raise comes through.

NORA: Pooh! We can borrow that long.

HELMER: Nora! (*Goes over and playfully takes her by the ear.*) Are your scatter-brains off again? What if today I borrowed a thousand crowns, and you squandered them over Christmas week, and then on New Year's Eve a roof tile fell on my head and I lay there —

NORA (*putting her hand on his mouth*): Oh! Don't say such things!

HELMER: Yes, but what if it happened — then what?

NORA: If anything so awful happened, then it just wouldn't matter if I had debts or not.

HELMER: Well, but the people I'd borrowed from?

NORA: Them? Who cares about them! They're strangers.

HELMER: Nora, Nora, how like a woman! No, but seriously, Nora, you know what I think about that. No debts! Never borrow! Something of freedom's lost — and something of beauty, too — from a home that's founded on borrowing and debt. We've made a brave stand up to now, the two of us; and we'll go right on like that the little while we have to.

NORA (*going toward the stove*): Yes, whatever you say, Torvald.

HELMER (*following her*): Now, now, the little lark's wings mustn't droop. Come on, don't be a sulky squirrel. (*Taking out his wallet.*) Nora, guess what I have here.

NORA (*turning quickly*): Money!

HELMER: There, see. (*Hands her some notes.*) Good grief, I know how costs go up in a house at Christmastime.

NORA: Ten — twenty — thirty — forty. Oh, thank you, Torvald; I can manage no end on this.

HELMER: You really will have to.

NORA: Oh yes, I promise I will! But come here so I can show you everything I bought. And so cheap! Look, new clothes for Ivar here — and a sword. Here a horse and a trumpet for Bob. And a doll and a doll's bed here for Emmy; they're nothing much, but she'll tear them to bits in no time anyway. And here I have dress material and handkerchiefs for the maids. Old Anne-Marie really deserves something more.

HELMER: And what's in that package there?

NORA (*with a cry*): Torvald, no! You can't see that till tonight!

HELMER: I see. But tell me now, you little prodigal, what have you thought of for yourself?

NORA: For myself? Oh, I don't want anything at all.

HELMER: Of course you do. Tell me just what — within reason — you'd most like to have.

NORA: I honestly don't know. Oh, listen, Torvald —

HELMER: Well?

NORA (*fumbling at his coat buttons, without looking at him*): If you want to give me something, then maybe you could — you could —

HELMER: Come on, out with it.

NORA (*hurriedly*): You could give me money, Torvald. No more than you think you can spare; then one of these days I'll buy something with it.

HELMER: But Nora —

NORA: Oh please, Torvald darling, do that! I beg you, please. Then I could hang the bills in pretty gilt paper on the Christmas tree. Wouldn't that be fun?

HELMER: What are those little birds called that always fly through their fortunes?

NORA: Oh yes, spendthrifts: I know all that. But let's do as I say, Torvald; then I'll have time to decide what I really need most. That's very sensible, isn't it?

HELMER (*smiling*): Yes, very — that is, if you actually hung onto the money I give you, and you actually used it to buy yourself something. But it goes for the house and for all sorts of foolish things, and then I only have to lay out some more.

NORA: Oh, but Torvald —

HELMER: Don't deny it, my dear little Nora. (*Putting his arm around her waist.*) Spendthrifts are sweet, but they use up a frightful amount of money. It's incredible what it costs a man to feed such birds.

NORA: Oh, how can you say that! Really, I save everything I can.

HELMER (*laughing*): Yes, that's the truth. Everything you can. But that's nothing at all.

NORA (*humming, with a smile of quiet satisfaction*): Hm, if you only knew what expenses we larks and squirrels have, Torvald.

HELMER: You're an odd little one. Exactly the way your father was. You're never at a loss for scaring up money; but the moment you have it, it runs right out through your fingers; you never know what you've done with it. Well, one takes you as you are. It's deep in your blood. Yes, these things are hereditary, Nora.

NORA: Ah, I could wish I'd inherited many of Papa's qualities.

HELMER: And I couldn't wish you anything but just what you are, my sweet little lark. But wait; it seems to me you have a very — what should I call it? — a very suspicious look today —

NORA: I do?

HELMER: You certainly do. Look me straight in the eye.

NORA (*looking at him*): Well?

HELMER (*shaking an admonitory finger*): Surely my sweet tooth hasn't been running riot in town today, has she?

NORA: No. Why do you imagine that?

HELMER: My sweet tooth really didn't make a little detour through the confectioner's?

NORA: No, I assure you, Torvald —

HELMER: Hasn't nibbled some pastry?

NORA: No, not at all.

HELMER: Not even munched a macaroon or two?

NORA: No, Torvald, I assure you, really —

HELMER: There, there now. Of course I'm only joking.

NORA (*going to the table, right*): You know I could never think of going against you.

HELMER: No, I understand that; and you *have* given me your word. (*Going over to her.*) Well, you keep your little Christmas secrets to yourself, Nora darling. I expect they'll come to light this evening, when the tree is lit.

NORA: Did you remember to ask Dr. Rank?

HELMER: No. But there's no need for that: it's assumed he'll be dining with us. All the same, I'll ask him when he stops by here this morning. I've ordered some fine wine. Nora, you can't imagine how I'm looking forward to this evening.

NORA: So am I. And what fun for the children, Torvald!

HELMER: Ah, it's so gratifying to know that one's gotten a safe, secure job, and with a comfortable salary. It's a great satisfaction, isn't it?

NORA: Oh, it's wonderful!

HELMER: Remember last Christmas? Three whole weeks before, you shut yourself in every evening till long after midnight, making flowers for the Christmas tree, and all the other decorations to surprise us. Ugh, that was the dullest time I've ever lived through.

NORA: It wasn't at all dull for me.

HELMER (*smiling*): But the outcome *was* pretty sorry, Nora.

NORA: Oh, don't tease me with that again. How could I help it that the cat came in and tore everything to shreds.

HELMER: No, poor thing, you certainly couldn't. You wanted so much to please us all, and that's what counts. But it's just as well that the hard times are past.

NORA: Yes, it's really wonderful.

HELMER: Now I don't have to sit here alone, boring myself, and you don't have to tire your precious eyes and your fair little delicate hands —

NORA (*clapping her hands*): No, is it really true, Torvald, I don't have to? Oh, how wonderfully lovely to hear! (*Taking his arm.*) Now I'll tell you just how I've thought we should plan things. Right after Christmas — (*The doorbell rings.*) Oh, the bell. (*Straightening the room up a bit.*) Somebody would have to come. What a bore!

HELMER: I'm not home to visitors, don't forget.
MAID (*from the hall doorway*): Ma'am, a lady to see you —
NORA: All right, let her come in.
MAID (*to Helmer*): And the doctor's just come too.
HELMER: Did he go right to my study?
MAID: Yes, he did.

Helmer goes into his room. The Maid shows in Mrs. Linde, dressed in traveling clothes, and shuts the door after her.

MRS. LINDE (*in a dispirited and somewhat hesitant voice*): Hello, Nora.
NORA (*uncertain*): Hello —
MRS. LINDE: You don't recognize me.
NORA: No, I don't know — but wait, I think — (*Exclaiming.*) What! Kristine! Is it really you?
MRS. LINDE: Yes, it's me.
NORA: Kristine! To think I didn't recognize you. But then, how could I? (*More quietly.*) How you've changed, Kristine!
MRS. LINDE: Yes, no doubt I have. In nine — ten long years.
NORA: Is it so long since we met! Yes, it's all of that. Oh, these last eight years have been a happy time, believe me. And so now you've come in to town, too. Made the long trip in the winter. That took courage.
MRS. LINDE: I just got here by ship this morning.
NORA: To enjoy yourself over Christmas, of course. Oh, how lovely! Yes, enjoy ourselves, we'll do that. But take your coat off. You're not still cold? (*Helping her.*) There now, let's get cozy here by the stove. No, the easy chair there! I'll take the rocker here. (*Seizing her hands.*) Yes, now you have your old look again; it was only in that first moment. You're a bit more pale, Kristine — and maybe a bit thinner.
MRS. LINDE: And much, much older, Nora.
NORA: Yes, perhaps a bit older: a tiny, tiny bit; not much at all. (*Stopping short; suddenly serious.*) Oh, but thoughtless me, to sit here, chattering away. Sweet, good Kristine, can you forgive me?
MRS. LINDE: What do you mean, Nora?
NORA (*softly*): Poor Kristine, you've become a widow.
MRS. LINDE: Yes, three years ago.
NORA: Oh, I knew it, of course: I read it in the papers. Oh, Kristine, you must believe me; I often thought of writing you then, but I kept postponing it, and something always interfered.
MRS. LINDE: Nora dear, I understand completely.
NORA: No, it was awful of me, Kristine. You poor thing, how much you must have gone through. And he left you nothing?
MRS. LINDE: No.
NORA: And no children?
MRS. LINDE: No.
NORA: Nothing at all, then?
MRS. LINDE: Not even a sense of loss to feed on.
NORA (*looking incredulously at her*): But Kristine, how could that be?

MRS. LINDE (*smiling wearily and smoothing her hair*): Oh, sometimes it happens, Nora.

NORA: So completely alone. How terribly hard that must be for you. I have three lovely children. You can't see them now; they're out with the maid. But now you must tell me everything —

MRS. LINDE: No, no, no, tell me about yourself.

NORA: No, you begin. Today I don't want to be selfish. I want to think only of you today. But there *is* something I must tell you. Did you hear of the wonderful luck we had recently?

MRS. LINDE: No, what's that?

NORA: My husband's been made manager in the bank, just think!

MRS. LINDE: Your husband? How marvelous!

NORA: Isn't it? Being a lawyer is such an uncertain living, you know, especially if one won't touch any cases that aren't clean and decent. And of course Torvald would never do that, and I'm with him completely there. Oh, we're simply delighted, believe me! He'll join the bank right after New Year's and start getting a huge salary and lots of commissions. From now on we can live quite differently — just as we want. Oh, Kristine, I feel so light and happy! Won't it be lovely to have stacks of money and not a care in the world?

MRS. LINDE: Well, anyway, it would be lovely to have enough for necessities.

NORA: No, not just for necessities, but stacks and stacks of money!

MRS. LINDE (*smiling*): Nora, Nora, aren't you sensible yet? Back in school you were such a free spender.

NORA (*with a quiet laugh*): Yes, that's what Torvald still says. (*Shaking her finger.*) But "Nora, Nora" isn't as silly as you all think. Really, we've been in no position for me to go squandering. We've had to work, both of us.

MRS. LINDE: You too?

NORA: Yes, at odd jobs — needlework, crocheting, embroidery, and such — (*Casually.*) and other things too. You remember that Torvald left the department when we were married? There was no chance of promotion in his office, and of course he needed to earn more money. But that first year he drove himself terribly. He took on all kinds of extra work that kept him going morning and night. It wore him down, and then he fell deathly ill. The doctors said it was essential for him to travel south.

MRS. LINDE: Yes, didn't you spend a whole year in Italy?

NORA: That's right. It wasn't easy to get away, you know. Ivar had just been born. But of course we had to go. Oh, that was a beautiful trip, and it saved Torvald's life. But it cost a frightful sum, Kristine.

MRS. LINDE: I can well imagine.

NORA: Four thousand, eight hundred crowns it cost. That's really a lot of money.

MRS. LINDE: But it's lucky you had it when you needed it.

NORA: Well, as it was, we got it from Papa.

MRS. LINDE: I see. It was just about the time your father died.

NORA: Yes, just about then. And, you know, I couldn't make that trip out to nurse him. I had to stay here, expecting Ivar any moment, and with my poor sick Torvald to care for. Dearest Papa, I never saw him again, Kristine. Oh, that was the worst time I've known in all my marriage.

MRS. LINDE: I know how you loved him. And then you went off to Italy?

NORA: Yes. We had the means now, and the doctors urged us. So we left a month after.

MRS. LINDE: And your husband came back completely cured?

NORA: Sound as a drum!

MRS. LINDE: But — the doctor?

NORA: Who?

MRS. LINDE: I thought the maid said he was a doctor, the man who came in with me.

NORA: Yes, that was Dr. Rank — but he's not making a sick call. He's our closest friend, and he stops by at least once a day. No, Torvald hasn't had a sick moment since, and the children are fit and strong, and I am, too. (*Jumping up and clapping her hands.*) Oh, dear God, Kristine, what a lovely thing to live and be happy! But how disgusting of me — I'm talking of nothing but my own affairs. (*Sits on a stool close by Kristine, arms resting across her knees.*) Oh, don't be angry with me! Tell me, is it really true that you weren't in love with your husband? Why did you marry him, then?

MRS. LINDE: My mother was still alive, but bedridden and helpless — and I had my two younger brothers to look after. In all conscience, I didn't think I could turn him down.

NORA: No, you were right there. But was he rich at the time?

MRS. LINDE: He was very well off, I'd say. But the business was shaky, Nora. When he died, it all fell apart, and nothing was left.

NORA: And then — ?

MRS. LINDE: Yes, so I had to scrape up a living with a little shop and a little teaching and whatever else I could find. The last three years have been like one endless workday without a rest for me. Now it's over, Nora. My poor mother doesn't need me, for she's passed on. Nor the boys, either; they're working now and can take care of themselves.

NORA: How free you must feel —

MRS. LINDE: No — only unspeakably empty. Nothing to live for now. (*Standing up anxiously.*) That's why I couldn't take it any longer out in that desolate hole. Maybe here it'll be easier to find something to do and keep my mind occupied. If I could only be lucky enough to get a steady job, some office work —

NORA: Oh, but Kristine, that's so dreadfully tiring, and you already look so tired. It would be much better for you if you could go off to a bathing resort.

MRS. LINDE (*going toward the window*): I have no father to give me travel money, Nora.

NORA (*rising*): Oh, don't be angry with me.

MRS. LINDE (*going to her*): Nora dear, don't you be angry with me. The worst of my kind of situation is all the bitterness that's stored away. No one to work for, and yet you're always having to snap up your opportunities. You have to live; and so you grow selfish. When you told me the happy change in your lot, do you know I was delighted less for your sakes than for mine?

NORA: How so? Oh, I see. You think maybe Torvald could do something for you.

MRS. LINDE: Yes, that's what I thought.

NORA: And he will, Kristine! Just leave it to me; I'll bring it up so delicately — find something attractive to humor him with. Oh, I'm so eager to help you.

MRS. LINDE: How very kind of you, Nora, to be so concerned over me — doubly kind, considering you really know so little of life's burdens yourself.

NORA: I — ? I know so little — ?

MRS. LINDE (*smiling*): Well, my heavens — a little needlework and such — Nora, you're just a child.

NORA (*tossing her head and pacing the floor*): You don't have to act so superior.

MRS. LINDE: Oh?

NORA: You're just like the others. You all think I'm incapable of anything serious —

MRS. LINDE: Come now —

NORA: That I've never had to face the raw world.

MRS. LINDE: Nora dear, you've just been telling me all your troubles.

NORA: Hm! Trivia! (*Quietly.*) I haven't told you the big thing.

MRS. LINDE: Big thing? What do you mean?

NORA: You look down on me so, Kristine, but you shouldn't. You're proud that you worked so long and hard for your mother.

MRS. LINDE: I don't look down on a soul. But it *is* true: I'm proud — and happy, too — to think it was given to me to make my mother's last days almost free of care.

NORA: And you're also proud thinking of what you've done for your brothers.

MRS. LINDE: I feel I've a right to be.

NORA: I agree. But listen to this, Kristine — I've also got something to be proud and happy for.

MRS. LINDE: I don't doubt it. But whatever do you mean?

NORA: Not so loud. What if Torvald heard! He mustn't, not for anything in the world. Nobody must know, Kristine. No one but you.

MRS. LINDE: But what is it, then?

NORA: Come here. (*Drawing her down beside her on the sofa.*) It's true — I've also got something to be proud and happy for. I'm the one who saved Torvald's life.

MRS. LINDE: Saved — ? Saved how?

NORA: I told you about the trip to Italy. Torvald never would have lived if he hadn't gone south —

MRS. LINDE: Of course; your father gave you the means —

NORA (*smiling*): That's what Torvald and all the rest think, but —

MRS. LINDE: But — ?

NORA: Papa didn't give us a pin. I was the one who raised the money.

MRS. LINDE: You? That whole amount?

NORA: Four thousand, eight hundred crowns. What do you say to that?

MRS. LINDE: But Nora, how was it possible? Did you win the lottery?

NORA (*disdainfully*): The lottery? Pooh! No art to that.

MRS. LINDE: But where did you get it from then?

NORA (*humming, with a mysterious smile*): Hmm, tra-la-la-la.

MRS. LINDE: Because you couldn't have borrowed it.

NORA: No? Why not?

MRS. LINDE: A wife can't borrow without her husband's consent.

NORA (*tossing her head*): Oh, but a wife with a little business sense, a wife who knows how to manage —

MRS. LINDE: Nora, I simply don't understand —

NORA: You don't have to. Whoever said I *borrowed* the money? I could have gotten it other ways. (*Throwing herself back on the sofa.*) I could have gotten it from some admirer or other. After all, a girl with my ravishing appeal —

MRS. LINDE: You lunatic.

NORA: I'll bet you're eaten up with curiosity, Kristine.

MRS. LINDE: Now listen here, Nora — you haven't done something indiscreet?

NORA (*sitting up again*): Is it indiscreet to save your husband's life?

MRS. LINDE: I think it's indiscreet that without his knowledge you —

NORA: But that's the point: he mustn't know! My Lord, can't you understand? He mustn't ever know the close call he had. It was to *me* the doctors came to say his life was in danger — that nothing could save him but a stay in the south. Didn't I try strategy then! I began talking about how lovely it would be for me to travel abroad like other young wives; I begged and I cried; I told him please to remember my condition, to be kind and indulge me; and then I dropped a hint that he could easily take out a loan. But at that, Kristine, he nearly exploded. He said I was frivolous, and it was his duty as man of the house not to indulge me in whims and fancies — as I think he called them. Aha, I thought, now you'll just have to be saved — and that's when I saw my chance.

MRS. LINDE: And your father never told Torvald the money wasn't from him?

NORA: No, never. Papa died right about then. I'd considered bringing him into my secret and begging him never to tell. But he was too sick at the time — and then, sadly, it didn't matter.

MRS. LINDE: And you've never confided in your husband since?

NORA: For heaven's sake, no! Are you serious? He's so strict on that subject. Besides — Torvald, with all his masculine pride — how painfully humiliating for him if he ever found out he was in debt to me. That would just ruin our relationship. Our beautiful, happy home would never be the same.

MRS. LINDE: Won't you ever tell him?

NORA (*thoughtfully, half smiling*): Yes — maybe sometime, years from now, when I'm no longer so attractive. Don't laugh! I only mean when Torvald loves me less than now, when he stops enjoying my dancing and dressing up and reciting for him. Then it might be wise to have something in reserve — (*Breaking off.*) How ridiculous! That'll never happen — Well,

Kristine, what do you think of my big secret? I'm capable of something too, hm? You can imagine, of course, how this thing hangs over me. It really hasn't been easy meeting the payments on time. In the business world there's what they call quarterly interest and what they call amortization, and these are always so terribly hard to manage. I've had to skimp a little here and there, wherever I could, you know. I could hardly spare anything from my house allowance, because Torvald has to live well. I couldn't let the children go poorly dressed; whatever I got for them, I felt I had to use up completely — the darlings!

MRS. LINDE: Poor Nora, so it had to come out of your own budget, then?

NORA: Yes, of course. But I was the one most responsible, too. Every time Torvald gave me money for new clothes and such, I never used more than half; always bought the simplest, cheapest outfits. It was a godsend that everything looks so well on me that Torvald never noticed. But it did weigh me down at times, Kristine. It *is* such a joy to wear fine things. You understand.

MRS. LINDE: Oh, of course.

NORA: And then I found other ways of making money. Last winter I was lucky enough to get a lot of copying to do. I locked myself in and sat writing every evening till late in the night. Ah, I was tired so often, dead tired. But still it was wonderful fun, sitting and working like that, earning money. It was almost like being a man.

MRS. LINDE: But how much have you paid off this way so far?

NORA: That's hard to say, exactly. These accounts, you know, aren't easy to figure. I only know that I've paid out all I could scrape together. Time and again I haven't known where to turn. (*Smiling.*) Then I'd sit here dreaming of a rich old gentleman who had fallen in love with me —

MRS. LINDE: What! Who is he?

NORA: Oh, really! And that he'd died, and when his will was opened, there in big letters it said, "All my fortune shall be paid over in cash, immediately, to that enchanting Mrs. Nora Helmer."

MRS. LINDE: But Nora dear — who *was* this gentleman?

NORA: Good grief, can't you understand? The old man never existed; that was only something I'd dream up time and again whenever I was at my wits' end for money. But it makes no difference now; the old fossil can go where he pleases for all I care; I don't need him or his will — because now I'm free. (*Jumping up.*) Oh, how lovely to think of that, Kristine! Carefree! To know you're carefree, utterly carefree; to be able to romp and play with the children, and to keep up a beautiful, charming home — everything just the way Torvald likes it! And think, spring is coming, with big blue skies. Maybe we can travel a little then. Maybe I'll see the ocean again. Oh yes, it *is* so marvelous to live and be happy!

The front doorbell rings.

MRS. LINDE (*rising*): There's the bell. It's probably best that I go.

NORA: No, stay. No one's expected. It must be for Torvald.

MAID (*from the hall doorway*): Excuse me, ma'am — there's a gentleman here to see Mr. Helmer, but I didn't know — since the doctor's with him —

NORA: Who is the gentleman?

KROGSTAD (*from the doorway*): It's me, Mrs. Helmer.

Mrs. Linde starts and turns away toward the window.

NORA (*stepping toward him, tense, her voice a whisper*): You? What is it? Why do you want to speak to my husband?

KROGSTAD: Bank business — after a fashion. I have a small job in the investment bank, and I hear now your husband is going to be our chief —

NORA: In other words, it's —

KROGSTAD: Just dry business, Mrs. Helmer. Nothing but that.

NORA: Yes, then please be good enough to step into the study. (*She nods indifferently as she sees him out by the hall door, then returns and begins stirring up the stove.*)

MRS. LINDE: Nora — who was that man?

NORA: That was a Mr. Krogstad — a lawyer.

MRS. LINDE: Then it really was him.

NORA: Do you know that person?

MRS. LINDE: I did once — many years ago. For a time he was a law clerk in our town.

NORA: Yes, he's been that.

MRS. LINDE: How he's changed.

NORA: I understand he had a very unhappy marriage.

MRS. LINDE: He's a widower now.

NORA: With a number of children. There now, it's burning. (*She closes the stove door and moves the rocker a bit to one side.*)

MRS. LINDE: They say he has a hand in all kinds of business.

NORA: Oh? That may be true; I wouldn't know. But let's not think about business. It's so dull.

Dr. Rank enters from Helmer's study.

Rank (*still in the doorway*): No, no really — I don't want to intrude, I'd just as soon talk a little while with your wife. (*Shuts the door, then notices Mrs. Linde.*) Oh, beg pardon. I'm intruding here too.

NORA: No, not at all. (*Introducing him.*) Dr. Rank, Mrs. Linde.

RANK: Well now, that's a name much heard in this house. I believe I passed the lady on the stairs as I came.

MRS. LINDE: Yes, I take the stairs very slowly. They're rather hard on me.

RANK: Uh-hm, some touch of internal weakness?

MRS. LINDE: More overexertion, I'd say.

RANK: Nothing else? Then you're probably here in town to rest up in a round of parties?

MRS. LINDE: I'm here to look for work.

RANK: Is that the best cure for overexertion?

MRS. LINDE: One has to live, Doctor.

RANK: Yes, there's a common prejudice to that effect.

NORA: Oh, come on, Dr. Rank — you really do want to live yourself.

RANK: Yes, I really do. Wretched as I am, I'll gladly prolong my torment indefinitely. All my patients feel like that. And it's quite the same, too, with the morally sick. Right at this moment there's one of those moral invalids in there with Helmer —

MRS. LINDE (*softly*): Ah!

NORA: Who do you mean?

RANK: Oh, it's a lawyer, Krogstad, a type you wouldn't know. His character is rotten to the root — but even he began chattering all-importantly about how he had to *live.*

NORA: Oh? What did he want to talk to Torvald about?

RANK: I really don't know. I only heard something about the bank.

NORA: I didn't know that Krog — that this man Krogstad had anything to do with the bank.

RANK: Yes, he's gotten some kind of berth down there. (*To Mrs. Linde.*) I don't know if you also have, in your neck of the woods, a type of person who scuttles about breathlessly, sniffing out hints of moral corruption, and then maneuvers his victim into some sort of key position where he can keep an eye on him. It's the healthy these days that are out in the cold.

MRS. LINDE: All the same, it's the sick who most need to be taken in.

RANK (*with a shrug*): Yes, there we have it. That's the concept that's turning society into a sanatorium.

Nora, lost in her thoughts, breaks out into quiet laughter and claps her hands.

RANK: Why do you laugh at that? Do you have any real idea of what society is?

NORA: What do I care about dreary old society? I was laughing at something quite different — something terribly funny. Tell me, Doctor — is everyone who works in the bank dependent now on Torvald?

RANK: Is that what you find so terribly funny?

NORA (*smiling and humming*): Never mind, never mind! (*Pacing the floor.*) Yes, that's really immensely amusing: that we — that Torvald has so much power now over all those people. (*Taking the bag out of her pocket.*) Dr. Rank, a little macaroon on that?

RANK: See here, macaroons! I thought they were contraband here.

NORA: Yes, but these are some that Kristine gave me.

MRS. LINDE: What? I — ?

NORA: Now, now, don't be afraid. You couldn't possibly know that Torvald had forbidden them. You see, he's worried they'll ruin my teeth. But hmp! Just this once! Isn't that so, Dr. Rank? Help yourself! (*Puts a macaroon in his mouth.*) And you too, Kristine. And I'll also have one, only a little one — or two, at the most. (*Walking about again.*) Now I'm really tremendously happy. Now there's just one last thing in the world that I have an enormous desire to do.

RANK: Well! And what's that?

NORA: It's something I have such a consuming desire to say so Torvald could hear.

RANK: And why can't you say it?

NORA: I don't dare. It's quite shocking.

MRS. LINDE: Shocking?

RANK: Well, then it isn't advisable. But in front of us you certainly can. What do you have such a desire to say so Torvald could hear?

NORA: I have such a huge desire to say — to hell and be damned!

RANK: Are you crazy?

MRS. LINDE: My goodness, Nora!

RANK: Go on, say it. Here he is.

NORA (*hiding the macaroon bag*): Shh, shh, shh!

Helmer comes in from his study, hat in hand, overcoat over his arm.

NORA (*going toward him*): Well, Torvald dear, are you through with him?

HELMER: Yes, he just left.

NORA: Let me introduce you — this is Kristine, who's arrived here in town.

HELMER: Kristine — ? I'm sorry, but I don't know —

NORA: Mrs. Linde, Torvald dear. Mrs. Kristine Linde.

HELMER: Of course. A childhood friend of my wife's, no doubt?

MRS. LINDE: Yes, we knew each other in those days.

NORA: And just think, she made the long trip down here in order to talk with you.

HELMER: What's this?

MRS. LINDE: Well, not exactly —

NORA: You see, Kristine is remarkably clever in office work, and so she's terribly eager to come under a capable man's supervision and add more to what she already knows —

HELMER: Very wise, Mrs. Linde.

NORA: And then when she heard that you'd become a bank manager — the story was wired out to the papers — then she came in as fast as she could and — Really, Torvald, for my sake you can do a little something for Kristine, can't you?

HELMER: Yes, it's not at all impossible. Mrs. Linde, I suppose you're a widow?

MRS. LINDE: Yes.

HELMER: Any experience in office work?

MRS. LINDE: Yes, a good deal.

HELMER: Well, it's quite likely that I can make an opening for you —

NORA (*clapping her hands*): You see, you see!

HELMER: You've come at a lucky moment, Mrs. Linde.

MRS. LINDE: Oh, how can I thank you?

HELMER: Not necessary. (*Putting his overcoat on.*) But today you'll have to excuse me —

RANK: Wait, I'll go with you. (*He fetches his coat from the hall and warms it at the stove.*)

NORA: Don't stay out long, dear.

HELMER: An hour; no more.

NORA: Are you going too, Kristine?

MRS. LINDE (*putting on her winter garments*): Yes, I have to see about a room now.

HELMER: Then perhaps we can all walk together.

NORA (*helping her*): What a shame we're so cramped here, but it's quite impossible for us to —

MRS. LINDE: Oh, don't even think of it! Good-bye, Nora dear, and thanks for everything.

NORA: Good-bye for now. Of course you'll be back this evening. And you too, Dr. Rank. What? If you're well enough? Oh, you've got to be! Wrap up tight now.

In a ripple of small talk the company moves out into the hall; children's voices are heard outside on the steps.

NORA: There they are! There they are! (*She runs to open the door. The children come in with their nurse, Anne-Marie.*) Come in, come in! (*Bends down and kisses them.*) Oh, you darlings — ! Look at them, Kristine. Aren't they lovely!

RANK: No loitering in the draft here.

HELMER: Come, Mrs. Linde — this place is unbearable now for anyone but mothers.

Dr. Rank, Helmer, and Mrs. Linde go down the stairs. Anne-Marie goes into the living room with the children. Nora follows, after closing the hall door.

NORA: How fresh and strong you look. Oh, such red cheeks you have! Like apples and roses. (*The children interrupt her throughout the following.*) And it was so much fun? That's wonderful. Really? You pulled both Emmy and Bob on the sled? Imagine, all together! Yes, you're a clever boy, Ivar. Oh, let me hold her a bit, Anne-Marie. My sweet little doll baby! (*Takes the smallest from the nurse and dances with her.*) Yes, yes, Mama will dance with Bob as well. What? Did you throw snowballs? Oh, if I'd only been there! No, don't bother, Anne-Marie — I'll undress them myself. Oh yes, let me. It's such fun. Go in and rest; you look half frozen. There's hot coffee waiting for you on the stove. (*The nurse goes into the room to the left. Nora takes the children's winter things off, throwing them about, while the children talk to her all at once.*) Is that so? A big dog chased you? But it didn't bite? No, dogs never bite little, lovely doll babies. Don't peek in the packages, Ivar! What is it? Yes, wouldn't you like to know. No, no, it's an ugly something. Well? Shall we play? What shall we play? Hide-and-seek? Yes, let's play hide-and-seek. Bob must hide first. I must? Yes, let me hide first. (*Laughing and shouting, she and the children play in and out of the living room and the adjoining room to the right. At last Nora hides under the table. The children come storming in, search, but cannot find her, then hear her muffled laughter, dash over to the table, lift the cloth up and find her. Wild shouting. She creeps forward as if to scare them. More shouts. Meanwhile, a knock at the hall door; no one has noticed it. Now the door half opens, and Krogstad appears. He waits a moment; the game goes on.*)

KROGSTAD: Beg pardon, Mrs. Helmer —

NORA (*with a strangled cry, turning and scrambling to her knees*): Oh! What do you want?

KROGSTAD: Excuse me. The outer door was ajar; it must be someone forgot to shut it —

NORA (*rising*): My husband isn't home, Mr. Krogstad.

KROGSTAD: I know that.

NORA: Yes — then what do you want here?

KROGSTAD: A word with you.

NORA: With — ? (*To the children, quietly.*) Go in to Anne-Marie. What? No, the strange man won't hurt Mama. When he's gone, we'll play some more. (*She leads the children into the room to the left and shuts the door after them. Then, tense and nervous:*) You want to speak to me?

KROGSTAD: Yes, I want to.

NORA: Today? But it's not yet the first of the month —

KROGSTAD: No, it's Christmas Eve. It's going to be up to you how merry a Christmas you have.

NORA: What is it you want? Today I absolutely can't —

KROGSTAD: We won't talk about that till later. This is something else. You do have a moment to spare, I suppose?

NORA: Oh yes, of course — I do, except —

KROGSTAD: Good. I was sitting over at Olsen's Restaurant when I saw your husband go down the street —

NORA: Yes?

KROGSTAD: With a lady.

NORA: Yes. So?

KROGSTAD: If you'll pardon my asking: wasn't that lady a Mrs. Linde?

NORA: Yes.

KROGSTAD: Just now come into town?

NORA: Yes, today.

KROGSTAD: She's a good friend of yours?

NORA: Yes, she is. But I don't see —

KROGSTAD: I also knew her once.

NORA: I'm aware of that.

KROGSTAD: Oh? You know all about it. I thought so. Well, then let me ask you short and sweet: is Mrs. Linde getting a job in the bank?

NORA: What makes you think you can cross-examine me, Mr. Krogstad — you, one of my husband's employees? But since you ask, you might as well know — yes, Mrs. Linde's going to be taken on at the bank. And I'm the one who spoke for her, Mr. Krogstad. Now you know.

KROGSTAD: So I guessed right.

NORA (*pacing up and down*): Oh, one does have a tiny bit of influence, I should hope. Just because I am a woman, don't think it means that — When one has a subordinate position, Mr. Krogstad, one really ought to be careful about pushing somebody who — hm —

KROGSTAD: Who has influence?

NORA: That's right.

KROGSTAD (*in a different tone*): Mrs. Helmer, would you be good enough to use your influence on my behalf?

NORA: What? What do you mean?

KROGSTAD: Would you please make sure that I keep my subordinate position in the bank?

NORA: What does that mean? Who's thinking of taking away your position?

KROGSTAD: Oh, don't play the innocent with me. I'm quite aware that your friend would hardly relish the chance of running into me again; and I'm also aware now whom I can thank for being turned out.

NORA: But I promise you —

KROGSTAD: Yes, yes, yes, to the point: there's still time, and I'm advising you to use your influence to prevent it.

NORA: But Mr. Krogstad, I have absolutely no influence.

KROGSTAD: You haven't? I thought you were just saying —

NORA: You shouldn't take me so literally. I! How can you believe that I have any such influence over my husband?

KROGSTAD: Oh, I've known your husband from our student days. I don't think the great bank manager's more steadfast than any other married man.

NORA: You speak insolently about my husband, and I'll show you the door.

KROGSTAD: The lady has spirit.

NORA: I'm not afraid of you any longer. After New Year's, I'll soon be done with the whole business.

KROGSTAD (*restraining himself*): Now listen to me, Mrs. Helmer. If necessary, I'll fight for my little job in the bank as if it were life itself.

NORA: Yes, so it seems.

KROGSTAD: It's not just a matter of income; that's the least of it. It's something else — All right, out with it! Look, this is the thing. You know, just like all the others, of course, that once, a good many years ago, I did something rather rash.

NORA: I've heard rumors to that effect.

KROGSTAD: The case never got into court; but all the same, every door was closed in my face from then on. So I took up those various activities you know about. I had to grab hold somewhere; and I dare say I haven't been among the worst. But now I want to drop all that. My boys are growing up. For their sakes, I'll have to win back as much respect as possible here in town. That job in the bank was like the first rung in my ladder. And now your husband wants to kick me right back down in the mud again.

NORA: But for heaven's sake, Mr. Krogstad, it's simply not in my power to help you.

KROGSTAD: That's because you haven't the will to — but I have the means to make you.

NORA: You certainly won't tell my husband that I owe you money?

KROGSTAD: Hm — what if I told him that?

NORA: That would be shameful of you. (*Nearly in tears.*) This secret — my joy and my pride — that he should learn it in such a crude and disgusting way — learn it from you. You'd expose me to the most horrible unpleasantness —

KROGSTAD: Only unpleasantness?

NORA (*vehemently*): But go on and try. It'll turn out the worse for you, because then my husband will really see what a crook you are, and then you'll *never* be able to hold your job.

KROGSTAD: I asked if it was just domestic unpleasantness you were afraid of?

NORA: If my husband finds out, then of course he'll pay what I owe at once, and then we'd be through with you for good.

KROGSTAD (*a step closer*): Listen, Mrs. Helmer — you've either got a very bad memory, or else no head at all for business. I'd better put you a little more in touch with the facts.

NORA: What do you mean?

KROGSTAD: When your husband was sick, you came to me for a loan of four thousand, eight hundred crowns.

NORA: Where else could I go?

KROGSTAD: I promised to get you that sum —

NORA: And you got it.

KROGSTAD: I promised to get you that sum, on certain conditions. You were so involved in your husband's illness, and so eager to finance your trip, that I guess you didn't think out all the details. It might just be a good idea to remind you. I promised you the money on the strength of a note I drew up.

NORA: Yes, and that I signed.

KROGSTAD: Right. But at the bottom I added some lines for your father to guarantee the loan. He was supposed to sign down there.

NORA: Supposed to? He did sign.

KROGSTAD: I left the date blank. In other words, your father would have dated his signature himself. Do you remember that?

NORA: Yes, I think —

KROGSTAD: Then I gave you the note for you to mail to your father. Isn't that so?

NORA: Yes.

KROGSTAD: And naturally you sent it at once — because only some five, six days later you brought me the note, properly signed. And with that, the money was yours.

NORA: Well, then; I've made my payments regularly, haven't I?

KROGSTAD: More or less. But — getting back to the point — those were hard times for you then, Mrs. Helmer.

NORA: Yes, they were.

KROGSTAD: Your father was very ill, I believe.

NORA: He was near the end.

KROGSTAD: He died soon after?

NORA: Yes.

KROGSTAD: Tell me, Mrs. Helmer, do you happen to recall the date of your father's death? The day of the month, I mean.

NORA: Papa died the twenty-ninth of September.

KROGSTAD: That's quite correct; I've already looked into that. And now we come to a curious thing — (*Taking out a paper.*) which I simply cannot comprehend.

NORA: Curious thing? I don't know —

KROGSTAD: This is the curious thing: that your father co-signed the note for your loan three days after his death.

NORA: How — ? I don't understand.

KROGSTAD: Your father died the twenty-ninth of September. But look. Here your father dated his signature October second. Isn't that curious, Mrs. Helmer? (*Nora is silent.*) Can you explain it to me? (*Nora remains silent.*) It's also remarkable that the words "October second" and the year aren't written in your father's hand, but rather in one that I think I know. Well, it's easy to understand. Your father forgot perhaps to date his signature, and then someone or other added it, a bit sloppily, before anyone knew of his death. There's nothing wrong in that. It all comes down to the signature. And there's no question about *that*, Mrs. Helmer. It really *was* your father who signed his own name here, wasn't it?

NORA (*after a short silence, throwing her head back and looking squarely at him*): No, it wasn't. *I* signed Papa's name.

KROGSTAD: Wait, now — are you fully aware that this is a dangerous confession?

NORA: Why? You'll soon get your money.

KROGSTAD: Let me ask you a question — why didn't you send the paper to your father?

NORA: That was impossible. Papa was so sick. If I'd asked him for his signature, I also would have had to tell him what the money was for. But I couldn't tell him, sick as he was, that my husband's life was in danger. That was just impossible.

KROGSTAD: Then it would have been better if you'd given up the trip abroad.

NORA: I couldn't possibly. The trip was to save my husband's life. I couldn't give that up.

KROGSTAD: But didn't you ever consider that this was a fraud against me?

NORA: I couldn't let myself be bothered by that. You weren't any concern of mine. I couldn't stand you, with all those cold complications you made, even though you knew how badly off my husband was.

KROGSTAD: Mrs. Helmer, obviously you haven't the vaguest idea of what you've involved yourself in. But I can tell you this: it was nothing more and nothing worse that I once did — and it wrecked my whole reputation.

NORA: You? Do you expect me to believe that you ever acted bravely to save your wife's life?

KROGSTAD: Laws don't inquire into motives.

NORA: Then they must be very poor laws.

KROGSTAD: Poor or not — if I introduce this paper in court, you'll be judged according to law.

NORA: This I refuse to believe. A daughter hasn't a right to protect her dying father from anxiety and care? A wife hasn't a right to save her husband's life? I don't know much about laws, but I'm sure that somewhere in the books these things are allowed. And you don't know anything about it — you who practice the law? You must be an awful lawyer, Mr. Krogstad.

KROGSTAD: Could be. But business — the kind of business we two are mixed up in — don't you think I know about that? All right. Do what you want now. But I'm telling you *this:* if I get shoved down a second time, you're going to keep me company. (*He bows and goes out through the hall.*)

NORA (*pensive for a moment, then tossing her head*): Oh, really! Trying to frighten me! I'm not so silly as all that. (*Begins gathering up the children's clothes, but soon stops.*) But — ? No, but that's impossible! I did it out of love.

THE CHILDREN (*in the doorway, left*): Mama, that strange man's gone out the door.

NORA: Yes, yes, I know it. But don't tell anyone about the strange man. Do you hear? Not even Papa!

THE CHILDREN: No, Mama. But now will you play again?

NORA: No, not now.

THE CHILDREN: Oh, but Mama, you promised.

NORA: Yes, but I can't now. Go inside; I have too much to do. Go in, go in, my sweet darlings. (*She herds them gently back in the room and shuts the door after them. Settling on the sofa, she takes up a piece of embroidery and makes some stitches, but soon stops abruptly.*) No! (*Throws the work aside, rises, goes to the hall door and calls out.*) Helene! Let me have the tree in here. (*Goes to the table, left, opens the table drawer, and stops again.*) No, but that's utterly impossible!

MAID (*with the Christmas tree*): Where should I put it, ma'am?

NORA: There. The middle of the floor.

MAID: Should I bring anything else?

NORA: No, thanks. I have what I need.

The Maid, who has set the tree down, goes out.

NORA (*absorbed in trimming the tree*): Candles here — and flowers here. That terrible creature! Talk, talk, talk! There's nothing to it at all. The tree's going to be lovely. I'll do anything to please you, Torvald. I'll sing for you, dance for you —

Helmer comes in from the hall, with a sheaf of papers under his arm.

NORA: Oh! You're back so soon?

HELMER: Yes. Has anyone been here?

NORA: Here? No.

HELMER: That's odd. I saw Krogstad leaving the front door.

NORA: So? Oh yes, that's true. Krogstad was here a moment.

HELMER: Nora, I can see by your face that he's been here, begging you to put in a good word for him.

NORA: Yes.

HELMER: And it was supposed to seem like your own idea? You were to hide it from me that he'd been here. He asked you that, too, didn't he?

NORA: Yes, Torvald, but —

HELMER: Nora, Nora, and you could fall for that? Talk with that sort of person and promise him anything? And then in the bargain, tell me an untruth.

NORA: An untruth — ?

HELMER: Didn't you say that no one had been here? (*Wagging his finger.*) My little songbird must never do that again. A songbird needs a clean beak to warble with. No false notes. (*Putting his arm about her waist.*) That's the way it should be, isn't it? Yes, I'm sure of it. (*Releasing her.*) And so, enough of that. (*Sitting by the stove.*) Ah, how snug and cozy it is here. (*Leafing among his papers.*)

NORA (*busy with the tree, after a short pause*): Torvald!

HELMER: Yes.

NORA: I'm so much looking forward to the Stenborgs' costume party, day after tomorrow.

HELMER: And I can't wait to see what you'll surprise me with.

NORA: Oh, that stupid business!

HELMER: What?

NORA: I can't find anything that's right. Everything seems so ridiculous, so inane.

HELMER: So my little Nora's come to *that* recognition?

NORA (*going behind his chair, her arms resting on its back*): Are you very busy, Torvald?

HELMER: Oh —

NORA: What papers are those?

HELMER: Bank matters.

NORA: Already?

HELMER: I've gotten full authority from the retiring management to make all necessary changes in personnel and procedure. I'll need Christmas week for that. I want to have everything in order by New Year's.

NORA: So that was the reason this poor Krogstad —

HELMER: Hm.

NORA (*still leaning on the chair and slowly stroking the nape of his neck*): If you weren't so very busy, I would have asked you an enormous favor, Torvald.

HELMER: Let's hear. What is it?

NORA: You know, there isn't anyone who has your good taste — and I want so much to look well at the costume party. Torvald, couldn't you take over and decide what I should be and plan my costume?

HELMER: Ah, is my stubborn little creature calling for a lifeguard?

NORA: Yes, Torvald, I can't get anywhere without your help.

HELMER: All right — I'll think it over. We'll hit on something.

NORA: Oh, how sweet of you. (*Goes to the tree again. Pause.*) Aren't the red flowers pretty — ? But tell me, was it really such a crime that this Krogstad committed?

HELMER: Forgery. Do you have any idea what that means?

NORA: Couldn't he have done it out of need?

HELMER: Yes, or thoughtlessness, like so many others. I'm not so heartless that I'd condemn a man categorically for just one mistake.

NORA: No, of course not, Torvald!

HELMER: Plenty of men have redeemed themselves by openly confessing their crimes and taking their punishment.

NORA: Punishment — ?

HELMER: But now Krogstad didn't go that way. He got himself out by sharp practices, and that's the real cause of his moral breakdown.

NORA: Do you really think that would — ?

HELMER: Just imagine how a man with that sort of guilt in him has to lie and cheat and deceive on all sides, has to wear a mask even with the nearest and dearest he has, even with his own wife and children. And with the children, Nora — that's where it's most horrible.

NORA: Why?

HELMER: Because that kind of atmosphere of lies infects the whole life of a home. Every breath the children take in is filled with the germs of something degenerate.

NORA (*coming closer behind him*): Are you sure of that?

HELMER: Oh, I've seen it often enough as a lawyer. Almost everyone who goes bad early in life has a mother who's a chronic liar.

NORA: Why just — the mother?

HELMER: It's usually the mother's influence that's dominant, but the father's works in the same way, of course. Every lawyer is quite familiar with it. And still this Krogstad's been going home year in, year out, poisoning his own children with lies and pretense; that's why I call him morally lost. (*Reaching his hands out toward her.*) So my sweet little Nora must promise me never to plead his cause. Your hand on it. Come, come, what's this? Give me your hand. There, now. All settled. I can tell you it'd be impossible for me to work alongside of him. I literally feel physically revolted when I'm anywhere near such a person.

NORA (*withdraws her hand and goes to the other side of the Christmas tree*): How hot it is here! And I've got so much to do.

HELMER (*getting up and gathering his papers*): Yes, and I have to think about getting some of these read through before dinner. I'll think about your costume, too. And something to hang on the tree in gilt paper, I may even see about that. (*Putting his hand on her head.*) Oh you, my darling little songbird. (*He goes into his study and closes the door after him.*)

NORA (*softly, after a silence*): Oh, really! It isn't so. It's impossible. It must be impossible.

ANNE-MARIE (*in the doorway, left*): The children are begging so hard to come in to Mama.

NORA: No, no, no, don't let them in to me! You stay with them, Anne-Marie.

ANNE-MARIE: Of course, ma'am. (*Closes the door.*)

NORA (*pale with terror*): Hurt my children — ! Poison my home? (*A moment's pause; then she tosses her head.*) That's not true. Never. Never in all the world.

ACT II

Same room. Beside the piano the Christmas tree now stands stripped of ornament, burned-down candle stubs on its ragged branches. Nora's street clothes lie on the sofa. Nora, alone in the room, moves restlessly about; at last she stops at the sofa and picks up her coat.

NORA (*dropping the coat again*): Someone's coming! (*Goes toward the door, listens.*) No — there's no one. Of course — nobody's coming today, Christmas Day — or tomorrow, either. But maybe — (*Opens the door and looks out.*) No, nothing in the mailbox. Quite empty. (*Coming forward.*) What nonsense! He won't do anything serious. Nothing terrible could happen. It's impossible. Why, I have three small children.

Anne-Marie, with a large carton, comes in from the room to the left.

ANNE-MARIE: Well, at last I found the box with the masquerade clothes.
NORA: Thanks. Put it on the table.
ANNE-MARIE (*does so*): But they're all pretty much of a mess.
NORA: Ahh! I'd love to rip them in a million pieces!
ANNE-MARIE: Oh, mercy, they can be fixed right up. Just a little patience.
NORA: Yes, I'll go get Mrs. Linde to help me.
ANNE-MARIE: Out again now? In this nasty weather? Miss Nora will catch cold — get sick.
NORA: Oh, worse things could happen. How are the children?
ANNE-MARIE: The poor mites are playing with their Christmas presents, but —
NORA: Do they ask for me much?
ANNE-MARIE: They're so used to having Mama around, you know.
NORA: Yes, but Anne-Marie, I *can't* be together with them as much as I was.
ANNE-MARIE: Well, small children get used to anything.
NORA: You think so? Do you think they'd forget their mother if she was gone for good?
ANNE-MARIE: Oh, mercy — gone for good!
NORA: Wait, tell me, Anne-Marie — I've wondered so often — how could you ever have the heart to give your child over to strangers?
ANNE-MARIE: But I had to, you know, to become little Nora's nurse.
NORA: Yes, but how could you *do* it?
ANNE-MARIE: When I could get such a good place? A girl who's poor and who's gotten in trouble is glad enough for that. Because that slippery fish, he didn't do a thing for me, you know.
NORA: But your daughter's surely forgotten you.
ANNE-MARIE: Oh, she certainly has not. She's written to me, both when she was confirmed and when she was married.
NORA (*clasping her about the neck*): You old Anne-Marie, you were a good mother for me when I was little.
ANNE-MARIE: Poor little Nora, with no other mother but me.
NORA: And if the babies didn't have one, then I know that you'd — What silly talk! (*Opening the carton.*) Go in to them. Now I'll have to — Tomorrow you can see how lovely I'll look.
ANNE-MARIE: Oh, there won't be anyone at the party as lovely as Miss Nora. (*She goes off into the room, left.*)
NORA (*begins unpacking the box, but soon throws it aside*): Oh, if I dared to go out. If only nobody would come. If only nothing would happen here while I'm out. What craziness — nobody's coming. Just don't think. This muff — needs a brushing. Beautiful gloves, beautiful gloves. Let it go.

Let it go! One, two, three, four, five, six — (*With a cry.*) Oh, there they are! (*Poises to move toward the door, but remains irresolutely standing. Mrs. Linde enters from the hall, where she has removed her street clothes.*)

NORA: Oh, it's you, Kristine. There's no one else out there? How good that you've come.

MRS. LINDE: I hear you were up asking for me.

NORA: Yes, I just stopped by. There's something you really can help me with. Let's get settled on the sofa. Look, there's going to be a costume party tomorrow evening at the Stenborgs' right above us, and now Torvald wants me to go as a Neapolitan peasant girl and dance the tarantella that I learned in Capri.

MRS. LINDE: Really, are you giving a whole performance?

NORA: Torvald says yes, I should. See, here's the dress. Torvald had it made for me down there; but now it's all so tattered that I just don't know —

MRS. LINDE: Oh, we'll fix that up in no time. It's nothing more than the trimmings — they're a bit loose here and there. Needle and thread? Good, now we have what we need.

NORA: Oh, how sweet of you!

MRS. LINDE (*sewing*): So you'll be in disguise tomorrow, Nora. You know what? I'll stop by then for a moment and have a look at you all dressed up. But listen, I've absolutely forgotten to thank you for that pleasant evening yesterday.

NORA (*getting up and walking about*): I don't think it was as pleasant as usual yesterday. You should have come to town a bit sooner, Kristine — Yes, Torvald really knows how to give a home elegance and charm.

MRS. LINDE: And you do, too, if you ask me. You're not your father's daughter for nothing. But tell me, is Dr. Rank always so down in the mouth as yesterday?

NORA: No, that was quite an exception. But he goes around critically ill all the time — tuberculosis of the spine, poor man. You know, his father was a disgusting thing who kept mistresses and so on — and that's why the son's been sickly from birth.

MRS. LINDE (*lets her sewing fall to her lap*): But my dearest Nora, how do you know about such things?

NORA (*walking more jauntily*): Hmp! When you've had three children, then you've had a few visits from — from women who know something of medicine, and they tell you this and that.

MRS. LINDE (*resumes sewing; a short pause*): Does Dr. Rank come here every day?

NORA: Every blessed day. He's Torvald's best friend from childhood, and *my* good friend, too. Dr. Rank almost belongs to this house.

MRS. LINDE: But tell me — is he quite sincere? I mean, doesn't he rather enjoy flattering people?

NORA: Just the opposite. Why do you think that?

MRS. LINDE: When you introduced us yesterday, he was proclaiming that he'd often heard my name in this house; but later I noticed that your husband hadn't the slightest idea who I really was. So how could Dr. Rank — ?

NORA: But it's all true, Kristine. You see, Torvald loves me beyond words, and, as he puts it, he'd like to keep me all to himself. For a long time he'd almost be jealous if I even mentioned any of my old friends back home. So of course I dropped that. But with Dr. Rank I talk a lot about such things, because he likes hearing about them.

MRS. LINDE: Now listen, Nora; in many ways you're still like a child. I'm a good deal older than you, with a little more experience. I'll tell you something: you ought to put an end to all this with Dr. Rank.

NORA: What should I put an end to?

MRS. LINDE: Both parts of it, I think. Yesterday you said something about a rich admirer who'd provide you with money —

NORA: Yes, one who doesn't exist — worse luck. So?

MRS. LINDE: Is Dr. Rank well off?

NORA: Yes, he is.

MRS. LINDE: With no dependents?

NORA: No, no one. But —

MRS. LINDE: And he's over here every day?

NORA: Yes, I told you that.

MRS. LINDE: How can a man of such refinement be so grasping?

NORA: I don't follow you at all.

MRS. LINDE: Now don't try to hide it, Nora. You think I can't guess who loaned you the forty-eight hundred crowns?

NORA: Are you out of your mind? How could you think such a thing! A friend of ours, who comes here every single day. What an intolerable situation that would have been!

MRS. LINDE: Then it really wasn't him.

NORA: No, absolutely not. It never even crossed my mind for a moment — And he had nothing to lend in those days; his inheritance came later.

MRS. LINDE: Well, I think that was a stroke of luck for you, Nora dear.

NORA: No, it never would have occurred to me to ask Dr. Rank — Still, I'm quite sure that if I had asked him —

MRS. LINDE: Which you won't, of course.

NORA: No, of course not. I can't see that I'd ever need to. But I'm quite positive that if I talked to Dr. Rank —

MRS. LINDE: Behind your husband's back?

NORA: I've got to clear up this other thing; *that's* also behind his back. I've *got* to clear it all up.

MRS. LINDE: Yes, I was saying that yesterday, but —

NORA (*pacing up and down*): A man handles these problems so much better than a woman —

MRS. LINDE: One's husband does, yes.

NORA: Nonsense. (*Stopping.*) When you pay everything you owe, then you get your note back, right?

MRS. LINDE: Yes, naturally.

NORA: And can rip it into a million pieces and burn it up — that filthy scrap of paper!

MRS. LINDE (*looking hard at her, laying her sewing aside, and rising slowly*): Nora, you're hiding something from me.

NORA: You can see it in my face?

MRS. LINDE: Something's happened to you since yesterday morning. Nora, what is it?

NORA (*hurrying toward her*): Kristine! (*Listening.*) Shh! Torvald's home. Look, go in with the children a while. Torvald can't bear all this snipping and stitching. Let Anne-Marie help you.

MRS. LINDE (*gathering up some of the things*): All right, but I'm not leaving here until we've talked this out. (*She disappears into the room, left, as Torvald enters from the hall.*)

NORA: Oh, how I've been waiting for you, Torvald dear.

HELMER: Was that the dressmaker?

NORA: No, that was Kristine. She's helping me fix up my costume. You know, it's going to be quite attractive.

HELMER: Yes, wasn't that a bright idea I had?

NORA: Brilliant! But then wasn't I good as well to give in to you?

HELMER: Good — because you give in to your husband's judgment? All right, you little goose, I know you didn't mean it like that. But I won't disturb you. You'll want to have a fitting, I suppose.

NORA: And you'll be working?

HELMER: Yes. (*Indicating a bundle of papers.*) See. I've been down to the bank. (*Starts toward his study.*)

NORA: Torvald.

HELMER (*stops*): Yes.

NORA: If your little squirrel begged you, with all her heart and soul, for something — ?

HELMER: What's that?

NORA: Then would you do it?

HELMER: First, naturally, I'd have to know what it was.

NORA: Your squirrel would scamper about and do tricks, if you'd only be sweet and give in.

HELMER: Out with it.

NORA: Your lark would be singing high and low in every room —

HELMER: Come on, she does that anyway.

NORA: I'd be a wood nymph and dance for you in the moonlight.

HELMER: Nora — don't tell me it's that same business from this morning?

NORA (*coming closer*): Yes, Torvald, I beg you, please!

HELMER: And you actually have the nerve to drag that up again?

NORA: Yes, yes, you've got to give in to me; you *have* to let Krogstad keep his job in the bank.

HELMER: My dear Nora, I've slated his job for Mrs. Linde.

NORA: That's awfully kind of you. But you could just fire another clerk instead of Krogstad.

HELMER: This is the most incredible stubbornness! Because you go and give an impulsive promise to speak up for him, I'm expected to —

NORA: That's not the reason, Torvald. It's for your own sake. That man does writing for the worst papers; you said it yourself. He could do you any amount of harm. I'm scared to death of him —

HELMER: Ah, I understand. It's the old memories haunting you.

NORA: What do you mean by that?

HELMER: Of course, you're thinking about your father.

NORA: Yes, all right. Just remember how those nasty gossips wrote in the papers about Papa and slandered him so cruelly. I think they'd have had him dismissed if the department hadn't sent you up to investigate, and if you hadn't been so kind and open-minded toward him.

HELMER: My dear Nora, there's a notable difference between your father and me. Your father's official career was hardly above reproach. But mine is; and I hope it'll stay that way as long as I hold my position.

NORA: Oh, who can ever tell what vicious minds can invent? We could be so snug and happy now in our quiet, carefree home — you and I and the children, Torvald! That's why I'm pleading with you so —

HELMER: And just by pleading for him you make it impossible for me to keep him on. It's already known at the bank that I'm firing Krogstad. What if it's rumored around now that the new bank manager was vetoed by his wife —

NORA: Yes, what then — ?

HELMER: Oh yes — as long as our little bundle of stubbornness gets her way — ! I should go and make myself ridiculous in front of the whole office — give people the idea I can be swayed by all kinds of outside pressure. Oh, you can bet I'd feel the effects of that soon enough! Besides — there's something that rules Krogstad right out at the bank as long as I'm the manager.

NORA: What's that?

HELMER: His moral failings I could maybe overlook if I had to —

NORA: Yes, Torvald, why not?

HELMER: And I hear he's quite efficient on the job. But he was a crony of mine back in my teens — one of those rash friendships that crop up again and again to embarrass you later in life. Well, I might as well say it straight out: we're on a first-name basis. And that tactless fool makes no effort at all to hide it in front of others. Quite the contrary — he thinks that entitles him to take a familiar air around me, and so every other second he comes booming out with his "Yes, Torvald!" and "Sure thing, Torvald!" I tell you, it's been excruciating for me. He's out to make my place in the bank unbearable.

NORA: Torvald, you can't be serious about all this.

HELMER: Oh no? Why not?

NORA: Because these are such petty considerations.

HELMER: What are you saying? Petty? You think I'm petty!

NORA: No, just the opposite, Torvald dear. That's exactly why —

HELMER: Never mind. You call my motives petty; then I might as well be just that. Petty! All right! We'll put a stop to this for good. (*Goes to the hall door and calls.*) Helene!

NORA: What do you want?

HELMER (*searching among his papers*): A decision. (*The Maid comes in.*) Look here; take this letter; go out with it at once. Get hold of a messenger and have him deliver it. Quick now. It's already addressed. Wait, here's some money.

MAID: Yes, sir. (*She leaves with the letter.*)

HELMER (*straightening his papers*): There, now, little Miss Willful.

NORA (*breathlessly*): Torvald, what was that letter?

HELMER: Krogstad's notice.

NORA: Call it back, Torvald! There's still time. Oh, Torvald, call it back! Do it for my sake — for your sake, for the children's sake! Do you hear, Torvald; do it! You don't know how this can harm us.

HELMER: Too late.

NORA: Yes, too late.

HELMER: Nora dear, I can forgive you this panic, even though basically you're insulting me. Yes, you are! Or isn't it an insult to think that *I* should be afraid of a courtroom hack's revenge? But I forgive you anyway, because this shows so beautifully how much you love me. (*Takes her in his arms.*) This is the way it should be, my darling Nora. Whatever comes, you'll see; when it really counts, I have strength and courage enough as a man to take on the whole weight myself.

NORA (*terrified*): What do you mean by that?

HELMER: The whole weight, I said.

NORA (*resolutely*): No, never in all the world.

HELMER: Good. So we'll share it, Nora, as man and wife. That's as it should be. (*Fondling her.*) Are you happy now? There, there, there — not these frightened dove's eyes. It's nothing at all but empty fantasies — Now you should run through your tarantella and practice your tambourine. I'll go to the inner office and shut both doors, so I won't hear a thing; you can make all the noise you like. (*Turning in the doorway.*) And when Rank comes, just tell him where he can find me. (*He nods to her and goes with his papers into the study, closing the door.*)

NORA (*standing as though rooted, dazed with fright, in a whisper*): He really could do it. He will do it. He'll do it in spite of everything. No, not that, never, never! Anything but that! Escape! A way out — (*The doorbell rings.*) Dr. Rank! Anything but that! *Anything,* whatever it is! (*Her hands pass over her face, smoothing it; she pulls herself together, goes over and opens the hall door. Dr. Rank stands outside, hanging his fur coat up. During the following scene, it begins getting dark.*)

NORA: Hello, Dr. Rank. I recognized your ring. But you mustn't go in to Torvald yet; I believe he's working.

RANK: And you?

NORA: For you, I always have an hour to spare — you know that. (*He has entered, and she shuts the door after him.*)

RANK: Many thanks. I'll make use of these hours while I can.

NORA: What do you mean by that? While you can?

RANK: Does that disturb you?

NORA: Well, it's such an odd phrase. Is anything going to happen?

RANK: What's going to happen is what I've been expecting so long — but I honestly didn't think it would come so soon.

NORA (*gripping his arm*): What is it you've found out? Dr. Rank, you have to tell me!

RANK (*sitting by the stove*): It's all over for me. There's nothing to be done about it.

NORA (*breathing easier*): Is it you — then — ?

RANK: Who else? There's no point in lying to one's self. I'm the most miserable of all my patients, Mrs. Helmer. These past few days I've been auditing my internal accounts. Bankrupt! Within a month I'll probably be laid out and rotting in the churchyard.

NORA: Oh, what a horrible thing to say.

RANK: The thing itself is horrible. But the worst of it is all the other horror before it's over. There's only one final examination left; when I'm finished with that, I'll know about when my disintegration will begin. There's something I want to say. Helmer with his sensitivity has such a sharp distaste for anything ugly. I don't want him near my sickroom.

NORA: Oh, but Dr. Rank —

RANK: I won't have him in there. Under no condition. I'll lock my door to him — As soon as I'm completely sure of the worst, I'll send you my calling card marked with a black cross, and you'll know then the wreck has started to come apart.

NORA: No, today you're completely unreasonable. And I wanted you so much to be in a really good humor.

RANK: With death up my sleeve? And then to suffer this way for somebody else's sins. Is there any justice in that? And in every single family, in some way or another, this inevitable retribution of nature goes on —

NORA (*her hands pressed over her ears*): Oh, stuff! Cheer up! Please — be gay!

RANK: Yes, I'd just as soon laugh at it all. My poor, innocent spine, serving time for my father's gay army days.

NORA (*by the table, left*): He was so infatuated with asparagus tips and pâté de foie gras, wasn't that it?

RANK: Yes — and with truffles.

NORA: Truffles, yes. And then with oysters, I suppose?

RANK: Yes, tons of oysters, naturally.

NORA: And then the port and champagne to go with it. It's so sad that all these delectable things have to strike at our bones.

RANK: Especially when they strike at the unhappy bones that never shared in the fun.

NORA: Ah, that's the saddest of all.

RANK (*looks searchingly at her*): Hm.

NORA (*after a moment*): Why did you smile?

RANK: No, it was you who laughed.

NORA: No, it was you who smiled, Dr. Rank!

RANK (*getting up*): You're even a bigger tease than I'd thought.

NORA: I'm full of wild ideas today.

RANK: That's obvious.

NORA (*putting both hands on his shoulders*): Dear, dear Dr. Rank, you'll never die for Torvald and me.

RANK: Oh, that loss you'll easily get over. Those who go away are soon forgotten.

NORA (*looks fearfully at him*): You believe that?

RANK: One makes new connections, and then —

NORA: Who makes new connections?

RANK: Both you and Torvald will when I'm gone. I'd say you're well under way already. What was that Mrs. Linde doing here last evening?

NORA: Oh, come — you can't be jealous of poor Kristine?

RANK: Oh yes, I am. She'll be my successor here in the house. When I'm down under, that woman will probably —

NORA: Shh! Not so loud. She's right in there.

RANK: Today as well. So you see.

NORA: Only to sew on my dress. Good gracious, how unreasonable you are. (*Sitting on the sofa.*) Be nice now, Dr. Rank. Tomorrow you'll see how beautifully I'll dance; and you can imagine then that I'm dancing only for you — yes, and of course for Torvald, too — that's understood. (*Takes various items out of the carton.*) Dr. Rank, sit over here and I'll show you something.

RANK (*sitting*): What's that?

NORA: Look here. Look.

RANK: Silk stockings.

NORA: Flesh-colored. Aren't they lovely? Now it's so dark here, but tomorrow — No, no, no, just look at the feet. Oh well, you might as well look at the rest.

RANK: Hm —

NORA: Why do you look so critical? Don't you believe they'll fit?

RANK: I've never had any chance to form an opinion on that.

NORA (*glancing at him a moment*): Shame on you. (*Hits him lightly on the ear with the stockings.*) That's for you. (*Puts them away again.*)

RANK: And what other splendors am I going to see now?

NORA: Not the least bit more, because you've been naughty. (*She hums a little and rummages among her things.*)

RANK (*after a short silence*): When I sit here together with you like this, completely easy and open, then I don't know — I simply can't imagine — whatever would have become of me if I'd never come into this house.

NORA (*smiling*): Yes, I really think you feel completely at ease with us.

RANK (*more quietly, staring straight ahead*): And then to have to go away from it all —

NORA: Nonsense, you're not going away.

RANK (*his voice unchanged*): — and not even be able to leave some poor show of gratitude behind, scarcely a fleeting regret — no more than a vacant place that anyone can fill.

NORA: And if I asked you now for — ? No —

RANK: For what?

NORA: For a great proof of your friendship —

RANK: Yes, yes?

NORA: No, I mean — for an exceptionally big favor —

RANK: Would you really, for once, make me so happy?

NORA: Oh, you haven't the vaguest idea what it is.

RANK: All right, then tell me.

NORA: No, but I can't, Dr. Rank — it's all out of reason. It's advice and help, too — and a favor —

RANK: So much the better. I can't fathom what you're hinting at. Just speak out. Don't you trust me?

NORA: Of course. More than anyone else. You're my best and truest friend, I'm sure. That's why I want to talk to you. All right, then, Dr. Rank: there's something you can help me prevent. You know how deeply, how inexpressibly dearly Torvald loves me; he'd never hesitate a second to give up his life for me.

RANK (*leaning close to her*): Nora — do you think he's the only one —

NORA (*with a slight start*): Who — ?

RANK: Who'd gladly give up his life for you.

NORA (*heavily*): I see.

RANK: I swore to myself you should know this before I'm gone. I'll never find a better chance. Yes, Nora, now you know. And also you know now that you can trust me beyond anyone else.

NORA (*rising, natural and calm*): Let me by.

RANK (*making room for her, but still sitting*): Nora —

NORA (*in the hall doorway*): Helene, bring the lamp in. (*Goes over to the stove.*) Ah, dear Dr. Rank, that was really mean of you.

RANK (*getting up*): That I've loved you just as deeply as somebody else? Was *that* mean?

NORA: No, but that you came out and told me. That was quite unnecessary —

RANK: What do you mean? Have you known — ?

The Maid comes in with the lamp, sets it on the table, and goes out again.

RANK: Nora — Mrs. Helmer — I'm asking you: have you known about it?

NORA: Oh, how can I tell what I know or don't know? Really, I don't know what to say — Why did you have to be so clumsy, Dr. Rank! Everything was so good.

RANK: Well, in any case, you now have the knowledge that my body and soul are at your command. So won't you speak out?

NORA (*looking at him*): After that?

RANK: Please, just let me know what it is.

NORA: You can't know anything now.

RANK: I have to. You mustn't punish me like this. Give me the chance to do whatever is humanly possible for you.

NORA: Now there's nothing you can do for me. Besides, actually, I don't need any help. You'll see — it's only my fantasies. That's what it is. Of course! (*Sits in the rocker, looks at him, and smiles.*) What a nice one you are, Dr. Rank. Aren't you a little bit ashamed, now that the lamp is here?

RANK: No, not exactly. But perhaps I'd better go — for good?

NORA: No, you certainly can't do that. You must come here just as you always have. You know Torvald can't do without you.

RANK: Yes, but *you?*

NORA: You know how much I enjoy it when you're here.

RANK: That's precisely what threw me off. You're a mystery to me. So many times I've felt you'd almost rather be with me than with Helmer.

NORA: Yes — you see, there are some people that one loves most and other people that one would almost prefer being with.

RANK: Yes, there's something to that.

NORA: When I was back home, of course I loved Papa most. But I always thought it was so much fun when I could sneak down to the maids' quarters, because they never tried to improve me, and it was always so amusing, the way they talked to each other.

RANK: Aha, so it's *their* place that I've filled.

NORA (*jumping up and going to him*): Oh, dear, sweet Dr. Rank, that's not what I meant at all. But you can understand that with Torvald it's just the same as with Papa —

The Maid enters from the hall.

MAID: Ma'am — please! (*She whispers to Nora and hands her a calling card.*)

NORA (*glancing at the card*): Ah! (*Slips it into her pocket.*)

RANK: Anything wrong?

NORA: No, no, not at all. It's only some — it's my new dress —

RANK: Really? But — there's your dress.

NORA: Oh, that. But this is another one — I ordered it — Torvald mustn't know —

RANK: Ah, now we have the big secret.

NORA: That's right. Just go in with him — he's back in the inner study. Keep him there as long as —

RANK: Don't worry. He won't get away. (*Goes into the study.*)

NORA (*to the Maid*): And he's standing waiting in the kitchen?

MAID: Yes, he came up by the back stairs.

NORA: But didn't you tell him somebody was here?

MAID: Yes, but that didn't do any good.

NORA: He won't leave?

MAID: No, he won't go till he's talked with you, ma'am.

NORA: Let him come in, then — but quietly. Helene, don't breathe a word about this. It's a surprise for my husband.

MAID: Yes, yes, I understand — (*Goes out.*)

NORA: This horror — it's going to happen. No, no, no, it can't happen, it mustn't. (*She goes and bolts Helmer's door. The Maid opens the hall door for Krogstad and shuts it behind him. He is dressed for travel in a fur coat, boots, and a fur cap.*)

NORA (*going toward him*): Talk softly. My husband's home.

KROGSTAD: Well, good for him.

NORA: What do you want?

KROGSTAD: Some information.

NORA: Hurry up, then. What is it?

KROGSTAD: You know, of course, that I got my notice.

NORA: I couldn't prevent it, Mr. Krogstad. I fought for you to the bitter end, but nothing worked.

KROGSTAD: Does your husband's love for you run so thin? He knows everything I can expose you to, and all the same he dares to —

NORA: How can you imagine he knows anything about this?

KROGSTAD: Ah, no — I can't imagine it either, now. It's not at all like my fine Torvald Helmer to have so much guts —

NORA: Mr. Krogstad, I demand respect for my husband!

KROGSTAD: Why, of course — all due respect. But since the lady's keeping it so carefully hidden, may I presume to ask if you're also a bit better informed than yesterday about what you've actually done?

NORA: More than you could ever teach me.

KROGSTAD: Yes, I *am* such an awful lawyer.

NORA: What is it you want from me?

KROGSTAD: Just a glimpse of how you are, Mrs. Helmer. I've been thinking about you all day long. A cashier, a night-court scribbler, a — well, a type like me also has a little of what they call a heart, you know.

NORA: Then show it. Think of my children.

KROGSTAD: Did you or your husband ever think of mine? But never mind. I simply wanted to tell you that you don't need to take this thing too seriously. For the present, I'm not proceeding with any action.

NORA: Oh no, really! Well — I knew that.

KROGSTAD: Everything can be settled in a friendly spirit. It doesn't have to get around town at all; it can stay just among us three.

NORA: My husband must never know anything of this.

KROGSTAD: How can you manage that? Perhaps you can pay me the balance?

NORA: No, not right now.

KROGSTAD: Or you know some way of raising the money in a day or two?

NORA: No way that I'm willing to use.

KROGSTAD: Well, it wouldn't have done you any good, anyway. If you stood in front of me with a fistful of bills, you still couldn't buy your signature back.

NORA: Then tell me what you're going to do with it.

KROGSTAD: I'll just hold onto it — keep it on file. There's no outsider who'll even get wind of it. So if you've been thinking of taking some desperate step —

NORA: I have.

KROGSTAD: Been thinking of running away from home —

NORA: I have!

KROGSTAD: Or even of something worse —

NORA: How could you guess that?

KROGSTAD: You can drop those thoughts.

NORA: How could you guess I was thinking of *that?*

KROGSTAD: Most of us think about *that* at first. I thought about it too, but I discovered I hadn't the courage —

NORA (*lifelessly*): I don't either.

KROGSTAD (*relieved*): That's true, you haven't the courage? You too?

NORA: I don't have it — I don't have it.

KROGSTAD: It would be terribly stupid, anyway. After that first storm at home blows out, why, then — I have here in my pocket a letter for your husband —

NORA: Telling everything?

KROGSTAD: As charitably as possible.

NORA (*quickly*): He mustn't ever get that letter. Tear it up. I'll find some way to get money.

KROGSTAD: Beg pardon, Mrs. Helmer, but I think I just told you —

NORA: Oh, I don't mean the money I owe you. Let me know how much you want from my husband, and I'll manage it.

KROGSTAD: I don't want money from your husband.

NORA: What do you want, then?

KROGSTAD: I'll tell you what. I want to recoup, Mrs. Helmer; I want to get on in the world — and there's where your husband can help me. For a year and a half I've kept myself clean of anything disreputable — all that time struggling with the worst conditions; but I was satisfied, working my way up step by step. Now I've been written right off, and I'm just not in the mood to come crawling back. I tell you, I want to move on. I want to get back in the bank — in a better position. Your husband can set up a job for me —

NORA: He'll never do that!

KROGSTAD: He'll do it. I know him. He won't dare breathe a word of protest. And once I'm in there together with him, you just wait and see! Inside of a year, I'll be the manager's right-hand man. It'll be Nils Krogstad, not Torvald Helmer, who runs the bank.

NORA: You'll never see the day!

KROGSTAD: Maybe you think you can —

NORA: I have the courage now — for *that*.

KROGSTAD: Oh, you don't scare me. A smart, spoiled lady like you —

NORA: You'll see; you'll see!

KROGSTAD: Under the ice, maybe? Down in the freezing coal-black water? There, till you float up in the spring, ugly, unrecognizable, with your hair falling out —

NORA: You don't frighten me.

KROGSTAD: Nor do you frighten me. One doesn't do these things, Mrs. Helmer. Besides, what good would it be? I'd still have him safe in my pocket.

NORA: Afterwards? When I'm no longer — ?

KROGSTAD: Are you forgetting that *I'll* be in control then over your final reputation? (*Nora stands speechless, staring at him.*) Good; now I've warned you. Don't do anything stupid. When Helmer's read my letter, I'll be waiting for his reply. And bear in mind that it's your husband himself who's forced me back to my old ways. I'll never forgive him for that. Good-bye, Mrs. Helmer. (*He goes out through the hall.*)

NORA (*goes to the hall door, opens it a crack, and listens*): He's gone. Didn't leave the letter. Oh no, no, that's impossible too! (*Opening the door more and more.*) What's that? He's standing outside — not going downstairs. He's thinking it over? Maybe he'll — ? (*A letter falls in the mailbox; then Krogstad's footsteps are heard, dying away down a flight of stairs. Nora gives a muffled cry and runs over toward the sofa table. A short pause.*) In the mailbox. (*Slips warily over to the hall door.*) It's lying there. Torvald, Torvald — now we're lost!

MRS. LINDE (*entering with costume from the room, left*): There now, I can't see anything else to mend. Perhaps you'd like to try —

NORA (*in a hoarse whisper*): Kristine, come here.

MRS. LINDE (*tossing the dress on the sofa*): What's wrong? You look upset.

NORA: Come here. See that letter? *There!* Look — through the glass in the mailbox.

MRS. LINDE: Yes, yes, I see it.

NORA: That letter's from Krogstad —

MRS. LINDE: Nora — it's Krogstad who loaned you the money!

NORA: Yes, and now Torvald will find out everything.

MRS. LINDE: Believe me, Nora, it's best for both of you.

NORA: There's more you don't know. I forged a name.

MRS. LINDE: But for heaven's sake — ?

NORA: I only want to tell you that, Kristine, so that you can be my witness.

MRS. LINDE: Witness? Why should I — ?

NORA: If I should go out of my mind — it could easily happen —

MRS. LINDE: Nora!

NORA: Or anything else occurred — so I couldn't be present here —

MRS. LINDE: Nora, Nora, you aren't yourself at all!

NORA: And someone should try to take on the whole weight, all of the guilt, you follow me —

MRS. LINDE: Yes, of course, but why do you think — ?

NORA: Then you're the witness that it isn't true, Kristine. I'm very much myself; my mind right now is perfectly clear; and I'm telling you: nobody else has known about this; I alone did everything. Remember that.

MRS. LINDE: I will. But I don't understand all this.

NORA: Oh, how could you ever understand it? It's the miracle now that's going to take place.

MRS. LINDE: The miracle?

NORA: Yes, the miracle. But it's so awful, Kristine. It mustn't take place, not for anything in the world.

MRS. LINDE: I'm going right over and talk with Krogstad.

NORA: Don't go near him; he'll do you some terrible harm!

MRS. LINDE: There was a time once when he'd gladly have done anything for me.

NORA: He?

MRS. LINDE: Where does he live?

NORA: Oh, how do I know? Yes. (*Searches in her pocket.*) Here's his card. But the letter, the letter — !

HELMER (*from the study, knocking on the door*): Nora!

NORA (*with a cry of fear*): Oh! What is it? What do you want?

HELMER: Now, now, don't be so frightened. We're not coming in. You locked the door — are you trying on the dress?

NORA: Yes, I'm trying it. I'll look just beautiful, Torvald.

MRS. LINDE (*who has read the card*): He's living right around the corner.

NORA: Yes, but what's the use? We're lost. The letter's in the box.

MRS. LINDE: And your husband has the key?

NORA: Yes, always.

MRS. LINDE: Krogstad can ask for his letter back unread; he can find some excuse —

NORA: But it's just this time that Torvald usually —

MRS. LINDE: Stall him. Keep him in there. I'll be back as quick as I can. (*She hurries out through the hall entrance.*)

NORA (*goes to Helmer's door, opens it, and peers in*): Torvald!

HELMER (*from the inner study*): Well — does one dare set foot in one's own living room at last? Come on, Rank, now we'll get a look — (*In the doorway.*) But what's this?

NORA: What, Torvald dear?

HELMER: Rank had me expecting some grand masquerade.

RANK (*in the doorway*): That was my impression, but I must have been wrong.

NORA: No one can admire me in my splendor — not till tomorrow.

HELMER: But Nora dear, you look so exhausted. Have you practiced too hard?

NORA: No, I haven't practiced at all yet.

HELMER: You know, it's necessary —

NORA: Oh, it's absolutely necessary, Torvald. But I can't get anywhere without your help. I've forgotten the whole thing completely.

HELMER: Ah, we'll soon take care of that.

NORA: Yes, take care of me, Torvald, please! Promise me that? Oh, I'm so nervous. That big party — You must give up everything this evening for me. No business — don't even touch your pen. Yes? Dear Torvald, promise?

HELMER: It's a promise. Tonight I'm totally at your service — you little helpless thing. Hm — but first there's one thing I want to — (*Goes toward the hall door.*)

NORA: What are you looking for?

HELMER: Just to see if there's any mail.

NORA: No, no, don't do that, Torvald!

HELMER: Now what?

NORA: Torvald, please. There isn't any.

HELMER: Let me look, though. (*Starts out. Nora, at the piano, strikes the first notes of the tarantella. Helmer, at the door, stops.*) Aha!

NORA: I can't dance tomorrow if I don't practice with you.

HELMER (*going over to her*): Nora dear, are you really so frightened?

NORA: Yes, so terribly frightened. Let me practice right now; there's still time before dinner. Oh, sit down and play for me, Torvald. Direct me. Teach me, the way you always have.

HELMER: Gladly, if it's what you want. (*Sits at the piano.*)

NORA (*snatches the tambourine up from the box, then a long, varicolored shawl, which she throws around herself, whereupon she springs forward and cries out*): Play for me now! Now I'll dance!

Helmer plays and Nora dances. Rank stands behind Helmer at the piano and looks on.

HELMER (*as he plays*): Slower. Slow down.

NORA: Can't change it.

HELMER: Not so violent, Nora!

NORA: Has to be just like this.

HELMER (*stopping*): No, no, that won't do at all.

NORA (*laughing and swinging her tambourine*): Isn't that what I told you?

RANK: Let me play for her.

HELMER (*getting up*): Yes, go on. I can teach her more easily then.

Rank sits at the piano and plays; Nora dances more and more wildly. Helmer has stationed himself by the stove and repeatedly gives her directions; she seems not to hear them; her hair loosens and falls over her shoulders; she does not notice, but goes on dancing. Mrs. Linde enters.

MRS. LINDE (*standing dumbfounded at the door*): Ah — !

NORA (*still dancing*): See what fun, Kristine!

HELMER: But Nora darling, you dance as if your life were at stake.

NORA: And it is.

HELMER: Rank, stop! This is pure madness. Stop it, I say!

Rank breaks off playing, and Nora halts abruptly.

HELMER (*going over to her*): I never would have believed it. You've forgotten everything I taught you.

NORA (*throwing away the tambourine*): You see for yourself.

HELMER: Well, there's certainly room for instruction here.

NORA: Yes, you see how important it is. You've got to teach me to the very last minute. Promise me that, Torvald?

HELMER: You can bet on it.

NORA: You mustn't, either today or tomorrow, think about anything else but me; you mustn't open any letters — or the mailbox —

HELMER: Ah, it's still the fear of that man —

NORA: Oh yes, yes, that too.

HELMER: Nora, it's written all over you — there's already a letter from him out there.

NORA: I don't know. I guess so. But you mustn't read such things now; there mustn't be anything ugly between us before it's all over.

RANK (*quietly to Helmer*): You shouldn't deny her.

HELMER (*putting his arms around her*): The child can have her way. But tomorrow night, after you've danced —

NORA: Then you'll be free.

MAID (*in the doorway, right*): Ma'am, dinner is served.

NORA: We'll be wanting champagne, Helene.

MAID: Very good, ma'am. (*Goes out.*)

HELMER: So — a regular banquet, hm?

NORA: Yes, a banquet — champagne till daybreak! (*Calling out.*) And some macaroons, Helene. Heaps of them — just this once.

HELMER (*taking her hands*): Now, now, now — no hysterics. Be my own little lark again.

NORA: Oh, I will soon enough. But go on in — and you, Dr. Rank. Kristine, help me put up my hair.

RANK (*whispering, as they go*): There's nothing wrong — really wrong, is there?

HELMER: Oh, of course not. It's nothing more than this childish anxiety I was telling you about. (*They go out, right.*)

NORA: Well?

MRS. LINDE: Left town.

NORA: I could see by your face.

MRS. LINDE: He'll be home tomorrow evening. I wrote him a note.

NORA: You shouldn't have. Don't try to stop anything now. After all, it's a wonderful joy, this waiting here for the miracle.

MRS. LINDE: What is it you're waiting for?

NORA: Oh, you can't understand that. Go in to them; I'll be along in a moment.

Mrs. Linde goes into the dining room. Nora stands a short while as if composing herself; then she looks at her watch.

NORA: Five. Seven hours to midnight. Twenty-four hours to the midnight after, and then the tarantella's done. Seven and twenty-four? Thirty-one hours to live.

HELMER (*in the doorway, right*): What's become of the little lark?

NORA (*going toward him with open arms*): Here's your lark!

ACT III

Same scene. The table, with chairs around it, has been moved to the center of the room. A lamp on the table is lit. The hall door stands open. Dance music drifts down from the floor above. Mrs. Linde sits at the table, absently paging through a book, trying to read, but apparently unable to focus her thoughts. Once or twice she pauses, tensely listening for a sound at the outer entrance.

MRS. LINDE (*glancing at her watch*): Not yet — and there's hardly any time left. If only he's not — (*Listening again.*) Ah, there he is. (*She goes out in the hall and cautiously opens the outer door. Quiet footsteps are heard on the stairs. She whispers:*) Come in. Nobody's here.

KROGSTAD (*in the doorway*): I found a note from you at home. What's back of all this?

MRS. LINDE: I just *had* to talk to you.

KROGSTAD: Oh? And it just *had* to be here in this house?

MRS. LINDE: At my place it was impossible; my room hasn't a private entrance. Come in; we're all alone. The maid's asleep, and the Helmers are at the dance upstairs.

KROGSTAD (*entering the room*): Well, well, the Helmers are dancing tonight? Really?

MRS. LINDE: Yes, why not?

KROGSTAD: How true — why not?

MRS. LINDE: All right, Krogstad, let's talk.

KROGSTAD: Do we two have anything more to talk about?

MRS. LINDE: We have a great deal to talk about.

KROGSTAD: I wouldn't have thought so.

MRS. LINDE: No, because you've never understood me, really.

KROGSTAD: Was there anything more to understand — except what's all too common in life? A calculating woman throws over a man the moment a better catch comes by.

MRS. LINDE: You think I'm so thoroughly calculating? You think I broke it off lightly?

KROGSTAD: Didn't you?

MRS. LINDE: Nils — is that what you really thought?

KROGSTAD: If you cared, then why did you write me the way you did?

MRS. LINDE: What else could I do? If I had to break off with you, then it was my job as well to root out everything you felt for me.

KROGSTAD (*wringing his hands*): So that was it. And this — all this, simply for money!

MRS. LINDE: Don't forget I had a helpless mother and two small brothers. We couldn't wait for you, Nils; you had such a long road ahead of you then.

KROGSTAD: That may be; but you still hadn't the right to abandon me for somebody else's sake.

MRS. LINDE: Yes — I don't know. So many, many times I've asked myself if I did have that right.

KROGSTAD (*more softly*): When I lost you, it was as if all the solid ground dissolved from under my feet. Look at me; I'm a half-drowned man now, hanging onto a wreck.

MRS. LINDE: Help may be near.

KROGSTAD: It was near — but then you came and blocked it off.

MRS. LINDE: Without my knowing it, Nils. Today for the first time I learned that it's you I'm replacing at the bank.

KROGSTAD: All right — I believe you. But now that you know, will you step aside?

MRS. LINDE: No, because that wouldn't benefit you in the slightest.

KROGSTAD: Not "benefit" me, hm! I'd step aside anyway.

MRS. LINDE: I've learned to be realistic. Life and hard, bitter necessity have taught me that.

KROGSTAD: And life's taught me never to trust fine phrases.

MRS. LINDE: Then life's taught you a very sound thing. But you do have to trust in actions, don't you?

KROGSTAD: What does that mean?

MRS. LINDE: You said you were hanging on like a half-drowned man to a wreck.

KROGSTAD: I've good reason to say that.

MRS. LINDE: I'm also like a half-drowned woman on a wreck. No one to suffer with; no one to care for.

KROGSTAD: You made your choice.

MRS. LINDE: There wasn't any choice then.

KROGSTAD: So — what of it?

MRS. LINDE: Nils, if only we two shipwrecked people could reach across to each other.

KROGSTAD: What are you saying?

MRS. LINDE: Two on one wreck are at least better off than each on his own.

KROGSTAD: Kristine!

MRS. LINDE: Why do you think I came into town?

KROGSTAD: Did you really have some thought of me?

MRS. LINDE: I have to work to go on living. All my born days, as long as I can remember, I've worked, and it's been my best and my only joy. But now I'm completely alone in the world; it frightens me to be so empty and lost. To work for yourself — there's no joy in that. Nils, give me something — someone to work for.

KROGSTAD: I don't believe all this. It's just some hysterical feminine urge to go out and make a noble sacrifice.

MRS. LINDE: Have you ever found me to be hysterical?

KROGSTAD: Can you honestly mean this? Tell me — do you know everything about my past?

MRS. LINDE: Yes.

KROGSTAD: And you know what they think I'm worth around here.

MRS. LINDE: From what you were saying before, it would seem that with me you could have been another person.

KROGSTAD: I'm positive of that.

MRS. LINDE: Couldn't it happen still?

KROGSTAD: Kristine — you're saying this in all seriousness? Yes, you are! I can see it in you. And do you really have the courage, then — ?

MRS. LINDE: I need to have someone to care for; and your children need a mother. We both need each other. Nils, I have faith that you're good at heart — I'll risk everything together with you.

KROGSTAD (*gripping her hands*): Kristine, thank you, thank you — Now I know I can win back a place in their eyes. Yes — but I forgot —

MRS. LINDE (*listening*): Shh! The tarantella. Go now! Go on!

KROGSTAD: Why? What is it?

MRS. LINDE: Hear the dance up there? When that's over, they'll be coming down.

KROGSTAD: Oh, then I'll go. But — it's all pointless. Of course, you don't know the move I made against the Helmers.

MRS. LINDE: Yes, Nils, I know.

KROGSTAD: And all the same, you have the courage to — ?

MRS. LINDE: I know how far despair can drive a man like you.

KROGSTAD: Oh, if I only could take it all back.

MRS. LINDE: You easily could — your letter's still lying in the mailbox.

KROGSTAD: Are you sure of that?

MRS. LINDE: Positive. But —

KROGSTAD (*looks at her searchingly*): Is that the meaning of it, then? You'll save your friend at any price. Tell me straight out. Is that it?

MRS. LINDE: Nils — anyone who's sold herself for somebody else once isn't going to do it again.

KROGSTAD: I'll demand my letter back.

MRS. LINDE: No, no.

KROGSTAD: Yes, of course. I'll stay here till Helmer comes down; I'll tell him to give me my letter again — that it only involves my dismissal — that he shouldn't read it —

MRS. LINDE: No, Nils, don't call the letter back.

KROGSTAD: But wasn't that exactly why you wrote me to come here?

MRS. LINDE: Yes, in that first panic. But it's been a whole day and night since then, and in that time I've seen such incredible things in this house. Helmer's got to learn everything; this dreadful secret has to be aired; those two have to come to a full understanding; all these lies and evasions can't go on.

KROGSTAD: Well, then, if you want to chance it. But at least there's one thing I can do, and do right away —

MRS. LINDE (*listening*): Go now, go quick! The dance is over. We're not safe another second.

KROGSTAD: I'll wait for you downstairs.

MRS. LINDE: Yes, please do; take me home.

KROGSTAD: I can't believe it; I've never been so happy. (*He leaves by way of the outer door; the door between the room and the hall stays open.*)

MRS. LINDE (*straightening up a bit and getting together her street clothes*): How different now! How different! Someone to work for, to live for — a home to build. Well, it is worth the try! Oh, if they'd only come! (*Listening.*) Ah, there they are. Bundle up. (*She picks up her hat and coat. Nora's and Helmer's voices can be heard outside; a key turns in the lock, and Helmer brings Nora into the hall almost by force. She is wearing the Italian costume with a large black shawl about her; he has on evening dress, with a black domino open over it.*)

NORA (*struggling in the doorway*): No, no, no, not inside! I'm going up again. I don't want to leave so soon.

HELMER: But Nora dear —

NORA: Oh, I beg you, please, Torvald. From the bottom of my heart, *please* — only an hour more!

HELMER: Not a single minute, Nora darling. You know our agreement. Come on, in we go; you'll catch cold out here. (*In spite of her resistance, he gently draws her into the room.*)

MRS. LINDE: Good evening.

NORA: Kristine!

HELMER: Why, Mrs. Linde — are you here so late?

MRS. LINDE: Yes, I'm sorry, but I did want to see Nora in costume.

NORA: Have you been sitting here, waiting for me?

MRS. LINDE: Yes. I didn't come early enough; you were all upstairs; and then I thought I really couldn't leave without seeing you.

HELMER (*removing Nora's shawl*): Yes, take a good look. She's worth looking at, I can tell you that, Mrs. Linde. Isn't she lovely?

MRS. LINDE: Yes, I should say —

HELMER: A dream of loveliness, isn't she? That's what everyone thought at the party, too. But she's horribly stubborn — this sweet little thing. What's to be done with her? Can you imagine, I almost had to use force to pry her away.

NORA: Oh, Torvald, you're going to regret you didn't indulge me, even for just a half hour more.

HELMER: There, you see. She danced her tarantella and got a tumultuous hand — which was well earned, although the performance may have been a bit too naturalistic — I mean it rather overstepped the proprieties of art. But never mind — what's important is, she made a success, an overwhelming success. You think I could let her stay on after that and spoil the effect? Oh no; I took my lovely little Capri girl — my capricious little Capri girl, I should say — took her under my arm; one quick tour of the ballroom, a curtsy to every side, and then — as they say in novels — the beautiful vision disappeared. An exit should always be effective, Mrs. Linde, but that's what I can't get Nora to grasp. Phew, it's hot in here. (*Flings the domino on a chair and opens the door to his room.*) Why's it dark in here? Oh yes, of course. Excuse me. (*He goes in and lights a couple of candles.*)

NORA (*in a sharp, breathless whisper*): So?

MRS. LINDE (*quietly*): I talked with him.

NORA: And — ?

MRS. LINDE: Nora — you must tell your husband everything.

NORA (*dully*): I knew it.

MRS. LINDE: You've got nothing to fear from Krogstad, but you have to speak out.

NORA: I won't tell.

MRS. LINDE: Then the letter will.

NORA: Thanks, Kristine. I know now what's to be done. Shh!

HELMER (*reentering*): Well, then, Mrs. Linde — have you admired her?

MRS. LINDE: Yes, and now I'll say good night.

HELMER: Oh, come, so soon? Is this yours, this knitting?

MRS. LINDE: Yes, thanks. I nearly forgot it.

HELMER: Do you knit, then?

MRS. LINDE: Oh yes.

HELMER: You know what? You should embroider instead.

MRS. LINDE: Really? Why?

HELMER: Yes, because it's a lot prettier. See here, one holds the embroidery so, in the left hand, and then one guides the needle with the right — so — in an easy, sweeping curve — right?

MRS. LINDE: Yes, I guess that's —

HELMER: But, on the other hand, knitting — it can never be anything but ugly. Look, see here, the arms tucked in, the knitting needles going up and down — there's something Chinese about it. Ah, that was really a glorious champagne they served.

MRS. LINDE: Yes, good night, Nora, and don't be stubborn anymore.

HELMER: Well put, Mrs. Linde!

MRS. LINDE: Good night, Mr. Helmer.

HELMER (*accompanying her to the door*): Good night, good night. I hope you get home all right. I'd be very happy to — but you don't have far to go. Good night, good night. (*She leaves. He shuts the door after her and returns.*) There, now, at last we got her out the door. She's a deadly bore, that creature.

NORA: Aren't you pretty tired, Torvald?

HELMER: No, not a bit.

NORA: You're not sleepy?

HELMER: Not at all. On the contrary, I'm feeling quite exhilarated. But you? Yes, you really look tired and sleepy.

NORA: Yes, I'm very tired. Soon now I'll sleep.

HELMER: See! You see! I was right all along that we shouldn't stay longer.

NORA: Whatever you do is always right.

HELMER (*kissing her brow*): Now my little lark talks sense. Say, did you notice what a time Rank was having tonight?

NORA: Oh, was he? I didn't get to speak with him.

HELMER: I scarcely did either, but it's a long time since I've seen him in such high spirits. (*Gazes at her a moment, then comes nearer her.*) Hm — it's marvelous, though, to be back home again — to be completely alone with you. Oh, you bewitchingly lovely young woman!

NORA: Torvald, don't look at me like that!

HELMER: Can't I look at my richest treasure? At all that beauty that's mine, mine alone — completely and utterly.

NORA (*moving around to the other side of the table*): You mustn't talk to me that way tonight.

HELMER (*following her*): The tarantella is still in your blood, I can see — and it makes you even more enticing. Listen. The guests are beginning to go. (*Dropping his voice.*) Nora — it'll soon be quiet through this whole house.

NORA: Yes, I hope so.

HELMER: You do, don't you, my love? Do you realize — when I'm out at a party like this with you — do you know why I talk to you so little, and keep such a distance away; just send you a stolen look now and then — you know why I do it? It's because I'm imagining then that you're my secret darling, my secret bride-to-be, and that no one suspects there's anything between us.

NORA: Yes, yes; oh, yes, I know you're always thinking of me.

HELMER: And then when we leave and I place the shawl over those fine young rounded shoulders — over that wonderful curving neck — then I pretend that you're my young bride, that we're just coming from the wedding, that for the first time I'm bringing you into my house — that for the first time I'm alone with you — completely alone with you, your trembling young beauty! All this evening I've longed for nothing but you. When I saw you turn and sway in the tarantella — my blood was pounding till I couldn't stand it — that's why I brought you down here so early —

NORA: Go away, Torvald! Leave me alone. I don't want all this.

HELMER: What do you mean? Nora, you're teasing me. You will, won't you? Aren't I your husband — ?

A knock at the outside door.

NORA (*startled*): What's that?

HELMER (*going toward the hall*): Who is it?

RANK (*outside*): It's me. May I come in a moment?

HELMER (*with quiet irritation*): Oh, what does he want now? (*Aloud.*) Hold on. (*Goes and opens the door.*) Oh, how nice that you didn't just pass us by!

RANK: I thought I heard your voice, and then I wanted so badly to have a look in. (*Lightly glancing about.*) Ah, me, these old familiar haunts. You have it snug and cozy in here, you two.

HELMER: You seemed to be having it pretty cozy upstairs, too.

RANK: Absolutely. Why shouldn't I? Why not take in everything in life? As much as you can, anyway, and as long as you can. The wine was superb —

HELMER: The champagne especially.

RANK: You noticed that too? It's amazing how much I could guzzle down.

NORA: Torvald also drank a lot of champagne this evening.

RANK: Oh?

NORA: Yes, and that always makes him so entertaining.

RANK: Well, why shouldn't one have a pleasant evening after a well-spent day?

HELMER: Well spent? I'm afraid I can't claim that.

RANK (*slapping him on the back*): But I can, you see!

NORA: Dr. Rank, you must have done some scientific research today.

RANK: Quite so.

HELMER: Come now — little Nora talking about scientific research!

NORA: And can I congratulate you on the results?

RANK: Indeed you may.

NORA: Then they were good?

RANK: The best possible for both doctor and patient — certainty.

NORA (*quickly and searchingly*): Certainty?

RANK: Complete certainty. So don't I owe myself a gay evening afterwards?

NORA: Yes, you're right, Dr. Rank.

HELMER: I'm with you — just so long as you don't have to suffer for it in the morning.

RANK: Well, one never gets something for nothing in life.

NORA: Dr. Rank — are you very fond of masquerade parties?

RANK: Yes, if there's a good array of odd disguises —

NORA: Tell me, what should we two go as at the next masquerade?

HELMER: You little featherhead — already thinking of the next!

RANK: We two? I'll tell you what: you must go as Charmed Life —

HELMER: Yes, but find a costume for *that!*

RANK: Your wife can appear just as she looks every day.

HELMER: That was nicely put. But don't you know what you're going to be?

RANK: Yes, Helmer, I've made up my mind.

HELMER: Well?

RANK: At the next masquerade I'm going to be invisible.

HELMER: That's a funny idea.

RANK: They say there's a hat — black, huge — have you never heard of the hat that makes you invisible? You put it on, and then no one on earth can see you.

HELMER (*suppressing a smile*): Ah, of course.

RANK: But I'm quite forgetting what I came for. Helmer, give me a cigar, one of the dark Havanas.

HELMER: With the greatest pleasure. (*Holds out his case.*)

RANK: Thanks. (*Takes one and cuts off the tip.*)

NORA (*striking a match*): Let me give you a light.

RANK: Thank you. (*She holds the match for him; he lights the cigar.*) And now good-bye.

HELMER: Good-bye, good-bye, old friend.

NORA: Sleep well, Doctor.

RANK: Thanks for that wish.

NORA: Wish me the same.

RANK: You? All right, if you like — Sleep well. And thanks for the light. (*He nods to them both and leaves.*)

HELMER (*his voice subdued*): He's been drinking heavily.

NORA (*absently*): Could be. (*Helmer takes his keys from his pocket and goes out in the hall.*) Torvald — what are you after?

HELMER: Got to empty the mailbox; it's nearly full. There won't be room for the morning papers.

NORA: Are you working tonight?

HELMER: You know I'm not. Why — what's this? Someone's been at the lock.

NORA: At the lock — ?

HELMER: Yes, I'm positive. What do you suppose — ? I can't imagine one of the maids — ? Here's a broken hairpin. Nora, it's yours —

NORA (*quickly*): Then it must be the children —

HELMER: You'd better break them of that. Hm, hm — well, opened it after all. (*Takes the contents out and calls into the kitchen.*) Helene! Helene, would you put out the lamp in the hall. (*He returns to the room shutting the hall door, then displays the handful of mail.*) Look how it's piled up. (*Sorting through them.*) Now what's this?

NORA (*at the window*): The letter! Oh, Torvald, no!

HELMER: Two calling cards — from Rank.

NORA: From Dr. Rank?

HELMER (*examining them*): "Dr. Rank, Consulting Physician." They were on top. He must have dropped them in as he left.

NORA: Is there anything on them?

HELMER: There's a black cross over the name. See? That's a gruesome notion. He could almost be announcing his own death.

NORA: That's just what he's doing.

HELMER: What! You've heard something? Something he's told you?

NORA: Yes. That when those cards came, he'd be taking his leave of us. He'll shut himself in now and die.

HELMER: Ah, my poor friend! Of course I knew he wouldn't be here much longer. But so soon — And then to hide himself away like a wounded animal.

NORA: If it has to happen, then it's best it happens in silence — don't you think so, Torvald?

HELMER (*pacing up and down*): He'd grown right into our lives. I simply can't imagine him gone. He with his suffering and loneliness — like a dark cloud setting off our sunlit happiness. Well, maybe it's best this way. For him, at least. (*Standing still.*) And maybe for us too, Nora. Now we're thrown back on each other, completely. (*Embracing her.*) Oh you, my darling wife, how can I hold you close enough? You know what, Nora — time and again I've wished you were in some terrible danger, just so I could stake my life and soul and everything, for your sake.

NORA (*tearing herself away, her voice firm and decisive*): Now you must read your mail, Torvald.

HELMER: No, no, not tonight. I want to stay with you, dearest.

NORA: With a dying friend on your mind?

HELMER: You're right. We've both had a shock. There's ugliness between us — these thoughts of death and corruption. We'll have to get free of them first. Until then — we'll stay apart.

NORA (*clinging about his neck*): Torvald — good night! Good night!

HELMER (*kissing her on the cheek*): Good night, little songbird. Sleep well, Nora. I'll be reading my mail now. (*He takes the letters into his room and shuts the door after him.*)

NORA (*with bewildered glances, groping about, seizing Helmer's domino, throwing it around her, and speaking in short, hoarse, broken whispers*): Never see him again. Never, never. (*Putting her shawl over her head.*) Never see the children either — them, too. Never, never. Oh, the freezing black water! The depths — down — Oh, I wish it were over — He has it now; he's reading it — now. Oh no, no, not yet. Torvald, good-bye, you and the children — (*She starts for the hall; as she does, Helmer throws open his door and stands with an open letter in his hand.*)

HELMER: Nora!

NORA (*screams*): Oh — !

HELMER: What is this? You know what's in this letter?

NORA: Yes, I know. Let me go! Let me out!

HELMER (*holding her back*): Where are you going?

NORA (*struggling to break loose*): You can't save me, Torvald!

HELMER (*slumping back*): True! Then it's true what he writes? How horrible! No, no, it's impossible — it can't be true.

NORA: It *is* true. I've loved you more than all this world.

HELMER: Ah, none of your slippery tricks.

NORA (*taking one step toward him*): Torvald — !

HELMER: What *is* this you've blundered into!

NORA: Just let me loose. You're not going to suffer for my sake. You're not going to take on my guilt.

HELMER: No more play-acting. (*Locks the hall door.*) You stay right here and give me a reckoning. You understand what you've done? Answer! You understand?

NORA (*looking squarely at him, her face hardening*): Yes. I'm beginning to understand everything now.

HELMER (*striding about*): Oh, what an awful awakening! In all these eight years — she who was my pride and joy — a hypocrite, a liar — worse, worse — a criminal! How infinitely disgusting it all is! The shame! (*Nora says nothing and goes on looking straight at him. He stops in front of her.*) I should have suspected something of the kind. I should have known. All your father's flimsy values — Be still! All your father's flimsy values have come out in you. No religion, no morals, no sense of duty — Oh, how I'm punished for letting him off! I did it for your sake, and you repay me like this.

NORA: Yes, like this.

HELMER: Now you've wrecked all my happiness — ruined my whole future. Oh, it's awful to think of. I'm in a cheap little grafter's hands; he can do anything he wants with me, ask for anything, play with me like a puppet — and I can't breathe a word. I'll be swept down miserably into the depths on account of a featherbrained woman.

NORA: When I'm gone from this world, you'll be free.

HELMER: Oh, quit posing. Your father had a mess of those speeches too. What good would that ever do me if you were gone from this world, as you say? Not the slightest. He can still make the whole thing known; and if he does, I could be falsely suspected as your accomplice. They might even think that I was behind it — that I put you up to it. And all that I can thank you for — you that I've coddled the whole of our marriage. Can you see now what you've done to me?

NORA (*icily calm*): Yes.

HELMER: It's so incredible, I just can't grasp it. But we'll have to patch up whatever we can. Take off the shawl. I said, take it off! I've got to appease him somehow or other. The thing has to be hushed up at any cost. And as for you and me, it's got to seem like everything between us is just as it was — to the outside world, that is. You'll go right on living in this house, of course. But you can't be allowed to bring up the children; I don't dare trust you with them — Oh, to have to say this to someone I've loved so much! Well, that's done with. From now on happiness doesn't matter; all that matters is saving the bits and pieces, the appearance — (*The doorbell rings. Helmer starts.*) What's that? And so late. Maybe the worst — ? You think he'd — ? Hide, Nora! Say you're sick. (*Nora remains standing motionless. Helmer goes and opens the door.*)

MAID (*half dressed, in the hall*): A letter for Mrs. Helmer.

HELMER: I'll take it. (*Snatches the letter and shuts the door.*) Yes, it's from him. You don't get it; I'm reading it myself.

NORA: Then read it.

HELMER (*by the lamp*): I hardly dare. We may be ruined, you and I. But — I've got to know. (*Rips open the letter, skims through a few lines, glances at an enclosure, then cries out joyfully.*) Nora! (*Nora looks inquiringly at him.*) Nora! Wait — better check it again — Yes, yes, it's true. I'm saved. Nora, I'm saved!

NORA: And I?

HELMER: You too, of course. We're both saved, both of us. Look. He's sent back your note. He says he's sorry and ashamed — that a happy development in his life — oh, who cares what he says! Nora, we're saved! No one can hurt you. Oh, Nora, Nora — but first, this ugliness all has to go. Let me see — (*Takes a look at the note.*) No, I don't want to see it; I want the whole thing to fade like a dream. (*Tears the note and both letters to pieces, throws them into the stove and watches them burn.*) There — now there's nothing left — He wrote that since Christmas Eve you — Oh, they must have been three terrible days for you, Nora.

NORA: I fought a hard fight.

HELMER: And suffered pain and saw no escape but — No, we're not going to dwell on anything unpleasant. We'll just be grateful and keep on repeating: it's over now, it's over! You hear me, Nora? You don't seem to realize — it's over. What's it mean — that frozen look? Oh, poor little Nora, I understand. You can't believe I've forgiven you. But I have, Nora; I swear I have. I know that what you did, you did out of love for me.

NORA: That's true.

HELMER: You loved me the way a wife ought to love her husband. It's simply the means that you couldn't judge. But you think I love you any the less for not knowing how to handle your affairs? No, no — just lean on me; I'll guide you and teach you. I wouldn't be a man if this feminine helplessness didn't make you twice as attractive to me. You mustn't mind those sharp words I said — that was all in the first confusion of thinking my world had collapsed. I've forgiven you, Nora; I swear I've forgiven you.

NORA: My thanks for your forgiveness. (*She goes out through the door, right.*)

HELMER: No, wait — (*Peers in.*) What are you doing in there?

NORA (*inside*): Getting out of my costume.

HELMER (*by the open door*): Yes, do that. Try to calm yourself and collect your thoughts again, my frightened little songbird. You can rest easy now; I've got wide wings to shelter you with. (*Walking about close by the door.*) How snug and nice our home is, Nora. You're safe here; I'll keep you like a hunted dove I've rescued out of a hawk's claws. I'll bring peace to your poor, shuddering heart. Gradually it'll happen, Nora; you'll see. Tomorrow all this will look different to you; then everything will be as it was. I won't have to go on repeating I forgive you; you'll feel it for yourself. How can you imagine I'd ever conceivably want to disown you — or even blame you in any way? Ah, you don't know a man's heart, Nora. For a man there's something indescribably sweet and satisfying in knowing he's forgiven his wife — and forgiven her out of a full and open heart. It's as if she belongs to him in two ways now: in a sense he's given her fresh into the world again, and she's become his wife and his child as well. From now on that's what you'll be to me — you little, bewildered, helpless thing. Don't be afraid of anything, Nora; just open your heart to me, and I'll be conscience and will to you both — (*Nora enters in her regular clothes.*) What's this? Not in bed? You've changed your dress?

NORA: Yes, Torvald, I've changed my dress.

HELMER: But why now, so late?

NORA: Tonight I'm not sleeping.

HELMER: But Nora dear —

NORA (*looking at her watch*): It's still not so very late. Sit down, Torvald; we have a lot to talk over. (*She sits at one side of the table.*)

HELMER: Nora — what is this? That hard expression —

NORA: Sit down. This'll take some time. I have a lot to say.

HELMER (*sitting at the table directly opposite her*): You worry me, Nora. And I don't understand you.

NORA: No, that's exactly it. You don't understand me. And I've never understood you either — until tonight. No, don't interrupt. You can just listen to what I say. We're closing out accounts, Torvald.

HELMER: How do you mean that?

NORA (*after a short pause*): Doesn't anything strike you about our sitting here like this?

HELMER: What's that?

NORA: We've been married now eight years. Doesn't it occur to you that this is the first time we two, you and I, man and wife, have ever talked seriously together?

HELMER: What do you mean — seriously?

NORA: In eight whole years — longer even — right from our first acquaintance, we've never exchanged a serious word on any serious thing.

HELMER: You mean I should constantly go and involve you in problems you couldn't possibly help me with?

NORA: I'm not talking of problems. I'm saying that we've never sat down seriously together and tried to get to the bottom of anything.

HELMER: But dearest, what good would that ever do you?

NORA: That's the point right there: you've never understood me. I've been wronged greatly, Torvald — first by Papa, and then by you.

HELMER: What! By us — the two people who've loved you more than anyone else?

NORA (*shaking her head*): You never loved me. You've thought it fun to be in love with me, that's all.

HELMER: Nora, what a thing to say!

NORA: Yes, it's true now, Torvald. When I lived at home with Papa, he told me all his opinions, so I had the same ones too; or if they were different I hid them, since he wouldn't have cared for that. He used to call me his doll-child, and he played with me the way I played with my dolls. Then I came into your house —

HELMER: How can you speak of our marriage like that?

NORA (*unperturbed*): I mean, then I went from Papa's hands into yours. You arranged everything to your own taste, and so I got the same taste as you — or I pretended to; I can't remember. I guess a little of both, first one, then the other. Now when I look back, it seems as if I'd lived here like a beggar — just from hand to mouth. I've lived by doing tricks for you, Torvald. But that's the way you wanted it. It's a great sin what you and Papa did to me. You're to blame that nothing's become of me.

HELMER: Nora, how unfair and ungrateful you are! Haven't you been happy here?

NORA: No, never. I thought so — but I never have.

HELMER: Not — not happy!

NORA: No, only lighthearted. And you've always been so kind to me. But our home's been nothing but a playpen. I've been your doll-wife here, just as at home I was Papa's doll-child. And in turn the children have been my dolls. I thought it was fun when you played with me, just as they thought it fun when I played with them. That's been our marriage, Torvald.

HELMER: There's some truth in what you're saying — under all the raving exaggeration. But it'll all be different after this. Playtime's over; now for the schooling.

NORA: Whose schooling — mine or the children's?

HELMER: Both yours and the children's, dearest.

NORA: Oh, Torvald, you're not the man to teach me to be a good wife to you.

HELMER: And you can say that?

NORA: And I — how am I equipped to bring up children?

HELMER: Nora!

NORA: Didn't you say a moment ago that that was no job to trust me with?

HELMER: In a flare of temper! Why fasten on that?

NORA: Yes, but you were so very right. I'm not up to the job. There's another job I have to do first. I have to try to educate myself. You can't help me with that. I've got to do it alone. And that's why I'm leaving you now.

HELMER (*jumping up*): What's that?

NORA: I have to stand completely alone, if I'm ever going to discover myself and the world out there. So I can't go on living with you.

HELMER: Nora, Nora!

NORA: I want to leave right away. Kristine should put me up for the night —

HELMER: You're insane! You've no right! I forbid you!

NORA: From here on, there's no use forbidding me anything. I'll take with me whatever is mine. I don't want a thing from you, either now or later.

HELMER: What kind of madness is this!

NORA: Tomorrow I'm going home — I mean, home where I came from. It'll be easier up there to find something to do.

HELMER: Oh, you blind, incompetent child!

NORA: I must learn to be competent, Torvald.

HELMER: Abandon your home, your husband, your children! And you're not even thinking what people will say.

NORA: I can't be concerned about that. I only know how essential this is.

HELMER: Oh, it's outrageous. So you'll run out like this on your most sacred vows.

NORA: What do you think are my most sacred vows?

HELMER: And I have to tell you that! Aren't they your duties to your husband and children?

NORA: I have other duties equally sacred.

HELMER: That isn't true. What duties are they?

NORA: Duties to myself.

HELMER: Before all else, you're a wife and mother.

NORA: I don't believe in that anymore. I believe that, before all else, I'm a human being, no less than you — or anyway, I ought to try to become one. I know the majority thinks you're right, Torvald, and plenty of books agree with you, too. But I can't go on believing what the majority says, or what's written in books. I have to think over these things myself and try to understand them.

HELMER: Why can't you understand your place in your own home? On a point like that, isn't there one everlasting guide you can turn to? Where's your religion?

NORA: Oh, Torvald, I'm really not sure what religion is.

HELMER: What — ?

NORA: I only know what the minister said when I was confirmed. He told me religion was this thing and that. When I get clear and away by myself, I'll go into that problem too. I'll see if what the minister said was right, or, in any case, if it's right for me.

HELMER: A young woman your age shouldn't talk like that. If religion can't move you, I can try to rouse your conscience. You do have some moral feeling? Or, tell me — has that gone too?

NORA: It's not easy to answer that, Torvald. I simply don't know. I'm all confused about these things. I just know I see them so differently from you. I find out, for one thing, that the law's not at all what I'd thought — but I can't get it through my head that the law is fair. A woman hasn't a right to protect her dying father or save her husband's life! I can't believe that.

HELMER: You talk like a child. You don't know anything of the world you live in.

NORA: No, I don't. But now I'll begin to learn for myself. I'll try to discover who's right, the world or I.

HELMER: Nora, you're sick; you've got a fever. I almost think you're out of your head.

NORA: I've never felt more clearheaded and sure in my life.

HELMER: And — clearheaded and sure — you're leaving your husband and children?

NORA: Yes.

HELMER: Then there's only one possible reason.

NORA: What?

HELMER: You no longer love me.

NORA: No. That's exactly it.

HELMER: Nora! You can't be serious!

NORA: Oh, this is so hard, Torvald — you've been so kind to me always. But I can't help it. I don't love you anymore.

HELMER (*struggling for composure*): Are you also clearheaded and sure about that?

NORA: Yes, completely. That's why I can't go on staying here.

HELMER: Can you tell me what I did to lose your love?

NORA: Yes, I can tell you. It was this evening when the miraculous thing didn't come — then I knew you weren't the man I'd imagined.

HELMER: Be more explicit; I don't follow you.

NORA: I've waited now so patiently eight long years — for, my Lord, I know miracles don't come every day. Then this crisis broke over me, and such a certainty filled me: *now* the miraculous event would occur. While Krogstad's letter was lying out there, I never for an instant dreamed that you could give in to his terms. I was so utterly sure you'd say to him: go on, tell your tale to the whole wide world. And when he'd done that —

HELMER: Yes, what then? When I'd delivered my own wife into shame and disgrace —

NORA: When he'd done that, I was so utterly sure that you'd step forward, take the blame on yourself and say: I am the guilty one.

HELMER: Nora — !

NORA: You're thinking I'd never accept such a sacrifice from you? No, of course not. But what good would my protests be against you? That was the miracle I was waiting for, in terror and hope. And to stave that off, I would have taken my life.

HELMER: I'd gladly work for you day and night, Nora — and take on pain and deprivation. But there's no one who gives up honor for love.

NORA: Millions of women have done just that.

HELMER: Oh, you think and talk like a silly child.

NORA: Perhaps. But you neither think nor talk like the man I could join myself to. When your big fright was over — and it wasn't from any threat against me, only for what might damage you — when all the danger was past, for you it was just as if nothing had happened. I was exactly the same, your little lark, your doll, that you'd have to handle with double care now that I'd turned out so brittle and frail. (*Gets up.*) Torvald — in that instant it dawned on me that for eight years I've been living here with a stranger, and that I've even conceived three children — oh, I can't stand the thought of it! I could tear myself to bits.

HELMER (*heavily*): I see. There a gulf that's opened between us — that's clear. Oh, but Nora, can't we bridge it somehow?

NORA: The way I am now, I'm no wife for you.

HELMER: I have the strength to make myself over.

NORA: Maybe — if your doll gets taken away.

HELMER: But to part! To part from you! No, Nora no — I can't imagine it.

NORA (*going out, right*): All the more reason why it has to be. (*She reenters with her coat and a small overnight bag, which she puts on a chair by the table.*)

HELMER: Nora, Nora, not now! Wait till tomorrow.

NORA: I can't spend the night in a strange man's room.

HELMER: But couldn't we live here like brother and sister —

NORA: You know very well how long that would last. (*Throws her shawl about her.*) Good-bye, Torvald. I won't look in on the children. I know they're in better hands than mine. The way I am now, I'm no use to them.

HELMER: But someday, Nora — someday — ?

NORA: How can I tell? I haven't the least idea what'll become of me.

HELMER: But you're my wife, now and wherever you go.

NORA: Listen, Torvald — I've heard that when a wife deserts her husband's house just as I'm doing, then the law frees him from all responsibility. In any case, I'm freeing you from being responsible. Don't feel yourself bound, any more than I will. There has to be absolute freedom for us both. Here, take your ring back. Give me mine.

HELMER: That too?

NORA: That too.

HELMER: There it is.

NORA: Good. Well, now it's all over. I'm putting the keys here. The maids know all about keeping up the house — better than I do. Tomorrow, after I've left town, Kristine will stop by to pack up everything that's mine from home. I'd like those things shipped up to me.

HELMER: Over! All over! Nora, won't you ever think about me?

NORA: I'm sure I'll think of you often, and about the children and the house here.

HELMER: May I write you?

NORA: No — never. You're not to do that.

HELMER: Oh, but let me send you —

NORA: Nothing. Nothing.

HELMER: Or help you if you need it.

NORA: No. I accept nothing from strangers.

HELMER: Nora — can I never be more than a stranger to you?

NORA (*picking up her overnight bag*): Ah, Torvald — it would take the greatest miracle of all —

HELMER: Tell me the greatest miracle!

NORA: You and I both would have to transform ourselves to the point that — Oh, Torvald, I've stopped believing in miracles.

HELMER: But I'll believe. Tell me! Transform ourselves to the point that — ?

NORA: That our living together could be a true marriage. (*She goes out down the hall.*)

HELMER (*sinks down on a chair by the door, face buried in his hands*): Nora! Nora! (*Looking about and rising.*) Empty. She's gone. (*A sudden hope leaps in him.*) The greatest miracle — ?

From below, the sound of a door slamming shut.

ꕥ

SUSAN GLASPELL *(1876–1948) was born in Davenport, Iowa, into a family that had been among the state's first settlers a generation before. After her graduation from high school, she worked as a reporter and society editor for various newspapers before enrolling at Drake University in Des Moines, where she studied literature, philosophy, and history. She also edited the college newspaper and began to write short stories. In 1899 she took a job as statehouse reporter for the* Des Moines Daily News. *Years later she claimed that the discipline of newspaper work helped her to become a creative writer.*

At the age of twenty-five, Glaspell returned to Davenport to live with her family, "boldly" determined, as she said, to quit journalism and "give all my time to my own writing. I say 'boldly,' because I had to earn my living." Slowly she began to publish her own work, mostly sentimental magazine stories and an undistinguished first novel — fiction that, as her biographer C. W. E. Bigsby has noted, "suggested little of the originality and power which were to mark her work in the theater." In 1909 Glaspell met George Cram Cook, a novelist and utopian socialist from a wealthy family who divorced his second wife and left his two children to marry her.

Glaspell and Cook moved to Greenwich Village in New York City and collaborated on a short play for the experimental Washington Square Players in 1915, Suppressed Desires, *a comedy about psychoanalysis and its founder, Sigmund Freud, whom they sarcastically referred to as "the new Messiah." The simple sets and amateur performances in this off-Broadway theater company contrasted with the ostentation then prevailing on Broadway. There producers such as David Belasco went to extreme lengths in the lavishness of their sets and costumes, transferring to the stage every detail of an actual Child's Restaurant, for example, in the popular play* The Governor's Lady *in 1912. After the Players left Greenwich Village to relocate in Provincetown on Cape Cod in 1916, Cook urged Glaspell to write a new play for their fledgling theater company, renamed the Provincetown Players. When she protested that she did not know how to write plays, he told her, "Nonsense. You've got a stage, haven't you?"*

Glaspell's memory of a murder trial in Iowa that she'd covered as a newspaper reporter served as the inspiration for the short play Trifles *(1916). A decade later, in her biography of her husband,* The Road to the Temple *(1927), Glaspell recalled how she visualized the play while sitting in a ramshackle fish house at the end of a wharf in Provincetown where she and Cook were establishing a theater:*

> *So I went out on the wharf, sat alone on one of our wooden benches without a back, and looked a long time at that bare little stage. After a time the stage became a kitchen — a kitchen there all by itself. I saw just where the stove was, the table, and the steps going upstairs. Then the door at the back opened, and people all bundled up came in — two or three men, I wasn't sure which,*

> *but sure enough about the two women, who hung back, reluctant to enter that kitchen. When I was a newspaper reporter out in Iowa, I was sent down-state to do a murder trial, and I never forgot going into the kitchen of a woman locked up in town. I had meant to do it as a short story, but the stage took it for its own, so I hurried in from the wharf to write down what I had seen. Whenever I got stuck, I would run across the street to the old wharf, sit in that leaning little theater under which the sea sounded, until the play was ready to continue. Sometimes things written in my room would not form on the stage, and I must go home and cross them out.*

Glaspell finished Trifles *in ten days. It opened on August 8, 1916, with Glaspell and Cook in the cast. Glaspell went on to write ten more plays for the Provincetown Players, but* Trifles *is the one play of hers that is continually reprinted. She also published a short story version of the play, titled "A Jury of Her Peers," in 1917. During the six years of Cook's visionary leadership, the Provincetown Players produced one hundred plays by fifty-two authors. The company's promotion of American playwrights was an important landmark in the history of theater in the United States. As the historian Barbara Ozieblo realized, the Provincetown Players "constituted a laboratory for their two stars, Eugene O'Neill and Susan Glaspell; they triumphed both in the United States and in England; they broke the hegemony of Broadway, proving the value of little theatres and their experimental work and so seeding the mature drama of America."*

RELATED STORY: *Susan Glaspell, "A Jury of Her Peers," page 286.*

RELATED COMMENTARY: *Leonard Mustazza, "Generic Translation and Thematic Shift in Susan Glaspell's* Trifles *and 'A Jury of Her Peers,'" page 1980.*

SUSAN GLASPELL

Trifles

1916

CHARACTERS

GEORGE HENDERSON, *county attorney*
HENRY PETERS, *sheriff*
LEWIS HALE, *a neighboring farmer*
MRS. PETERS
MRS. HALE

SCENE: *The kitchen in the now abandoned farmhouse of John Wright, a gloomy kitchen, and left without having been put in order — the walls covered with a faded wall paper. Down right is a door leading to the parlor. On the right wall above this door is a built-in kitchen cupboard with shelves in the upper portion and drawers below. In the rear wall at right, up two steps is a door opening onto stairs leading to the second floor. In the rear wall at left is a door to the shed and from there to the outside. Between these two doors is an old-fashioned black iron stove. Running along the left wall from the shed door is an old iron sink and sink shelf, in which is set a hand pump. Downstage of the sink is an uncurtained window. Near the window is an old wooden rocker. Center stage is an unpainted wooden kitchen table with straight chairs on either side. There is a small chair down right. Unwashed pans under the sink, a loaf of bread outside the breadbox, a dish towel on the table — other signs of incompleted work. At the rear the shed door opens and the Sheriff comes in followed by the County Attorney and Hale. The Sheriff and Hale are men in middle life, the County Attorney is a young man; all are much bundled up and go at once to the stove. They are followed by the two women — the Sheriff's wife, Mrs. Peters, first; she is a slight wiry woman, a thin nervous face. Mrs. Hale is larger and would ordinarily be called more comfortable looking, but she is disturbed now and looks fearfully about as she enters. The women have come in slowly, and stand close together near the door.*

COUNTY ATTORNEY (*at stove rubbing his hands*): This feels good. Come up to the fire, ladies.

MRS. PETERS (*after taking a step forward*): I'm not — cold.

SHERIFF (*unbuttoning his overcoat and stepping away from the stove to right of table as if to mark the beginning of official business*): Now, Mr. Hale, before we move things about, you explain to Mr. Henderson just what you saw when you came here yesterday morning.

COUNTY ATTORNEY (*crossing down to left of the table*): By the way, has anything been moved? Are things just as you left them yesterday?

SHERIFF (*looking about*): It's just about the same. When it dropped below zero last night I thought I'd better send Frank out this morning to make a fire for us — (*sits right of center table*) no use getting pneumonia with a big case on, but I told him not to touch anything except the stove — and you know Frank.

COUNTY ATTORNEY: Somebody should have been left here yesterday.

SHERIFF: Oh — yesterday. When I had to send Frank to Morris Center for that man who went crazy — I want you to know I had my hands full yesterday. I knew you could get back from Omaha by today and as long as I went over everything here myself ———

COUNTY ATTORNEY: Well, Mr. Hale, tell just what happened when you came here yesterday morning.

HALE (*crossing down to above table*): Harry and I had started to town with a load of potatoes. We came along the road from my place and as I got here I said, "I'm going to see if I can't get John Wright to go in with me on a party telephone." I spoke to Wright about it once before and he put me off, saying folks talked too much anyway, and all he asked was peace and quiet — I guess you know about how much he talked himself; but I thought maybe if I went to the house and talked about it before his wife, though I said to Harry that I didn't know as what his wife wanted made much difference to John ———

COUNTY ATTORNEY: Let's talk about that later, Mr. Hale. I do want to talk about that, but tell now just what happened when you got to the house.

HALE: I didn't hear or see anything; I knocked at the door, and still it was all quiet inside. I knew they must be up, it was past eight o'clock. So I knocked again, and I thought I heard somebody say, "Come in." I wasn't sure, I'm not sure yet, but I opened the door — this door (*indicating the door by which the two women are still standing*) and there in that rocker — (*pointing to it*) sat Mrs. Wright. (*They all look at the rocker down left.*)

COUNTY ATTORNEY: What — was she doing?

HALE: She was rockin' back and forth. She had her apron in her hand and was kind of — pleating it.

COUNTY ATTORNEY: And how did she — look?

HALE: Well, she looked queer.

COUNTY ATTORNEY: How do you mean — queer?

HALE: Well, as if she didn't know what she was going to do next. And kind of done up.

COUNTY ATTORNEY (*takes out notebook and pencil and sits left of center table*): How did she seem to feel about your coming?

HALE: Why, I don't think she minded — one way or other. She didn't pay much attention. I said, "How do, Mrs. Wright, it's cold, ain't it?" And she said, "Is it?" — and went on kind of pleating at her apron. Well, I was surprised; she didn't ask me to come up to the stove, or to set down, but just sat there, not even looking at me, so I said, "I want to see John." And then she — laughed. I guess you would call it a laugh. I thought of Harry and the team outside, so I said a little sharp: "Can't I see John?" "No," she says, kind o' dull like. "Ain't he home?" says I. "Yes," says she, "he's home." "Then why can't I see him?" I asked her, out of patience. "'Cause he's dead," says she. *"Dead?"* says I. She just nodded her head, not getting a bit excited, but rockin' back and forth. "Why — where is he?" says I, not knowing what to say. She just pointed upstairs — like that. (*Himself pointing to the room above.*) I started for the stairs, with the idea of going up there. I walked from there to here — then I says, "Why, what did he die of?" "He died of a rope round his neck," says she, and just went on pleatin' at her apron. Well, I went out and called Harry. I thought I might — need help. We went upstairs and there he was lyin' —

COUNTY ATTORNEY: I think I'd rather have you go into that upstairs, where you can point it all out. Just go on now with the rest of the story.

HALE: Well, my first thought was to get that rope off. It looked . . . (*stops; his face twitches*) . . . but Harry, he went up to him, and he said, "No, he's dead all right, and we'd better not touch anything." So we went back downstairs. She was still sitting that same way. "Has anybody been notified?" I asked. "No," says she, unconcerned. "Who did this, Mrs. Wright?" said Harry. He said it businesslike — and she stopped pleatin' of her apron. "I don't know," she says. "You don't *know?"* says Harry. "No," says she. "Weren't you sleepin' in the bed with him?" says Harry. "Yes," says she, "but I was on the inside." "Somebody slipped a rope round his neck and strangled him and you didn't wake up?" says Harry. "I didn't wake up," she said after him. We must 'a' looked as if we didn't see how that could be, for after a minute she said, "I sleep sound." Harry was going to ask her more questions but I said maybe we ought to let her tell her story first to the coroner, or the sheriff, so Harry went fast as he could to Rivers' place, where there's a telephone.

COUNTY ATTORNEY: And what did Mrs. Wright do when she knew that you had gone for the coroner?

HALE: She moved from the rocker to that chair over there (*pointing to a small chair in the down right corner*) and just sat there with her hands held together and looking down. I got a feeling that I ought to make some conversation, so I said I had come in to see if John wanted to put in a telephone, and at that she started to laugh, and then she stopped and looked at me — scared. (*The County Attorney, who has had his notebook out, makes a note.*) I dunno, maybe it wasn't scared. I wouldn't like to say it was. Soon Harry got back, and then Dr. Lloyd came and you, Mr. Peters, and so I guess that's all I know that you don't.

COUNTY ATTORNEY (*rising and looking around*): I guess we'll go upstairs first — and then out to the barn and around there. (*To the Sheriff.*) You're convinced that there was nothing important here — nothing that would point to any motive?

SHERIFF: Nothing here but kitchen things. (*The County Attorney, after again looking around the kitchen, opens the door of a cupboard closet in right wall. He brings a small chair from right — gets on it and looks on a shelf. Pulls his hand away, sticky.*)

COUNTY ATTORNEY: Here's a nice mess. (*The women draw nearer up center.*)

MRS. PETERS (*to the other woman*): Oh, her fruit; it did freeze. (*To the Lawyer.*) She worried about that when it turned so cold. She said the fire'd go out and her jars would break.

SHERIFF (*rises*): Well, can you beat the woman! Held for murder and worryin' about her preserves.

COUNTY ATTORNEY (*getting down from chair*): I guess before we're through she may have something more serious than preserves to worry about. (*Crosses down right center.*)

HALE: Well, women are used to worrying over trifles. (*The two women move a little closer together.*)

COUNTY ATTORNEY (*with the gallantry of a young politician*): And yet, for all their worries, what would we do without the ladies? (*The women do not unbend. He goes below the center table to the sink, takes a dipperful of water from the pail, and pouring it into a basin, washes his hands. While he is doing this the Sheriff and Hale cross to cupboard, which they inspect. The County Attorney starts to wipe his hands on the roller towel, turns it for a cleaner place.*) Dirty towels! (*Kicks his foot against the pans under the sink.*) Not much of a housekeeper, would you say, ladies?

MRS. HALE (*stiffly*): There's a great deal of work to be done on a farm.

COUNTY ATTORNEY: To be sure. And yet (*with a little bow to her*) I know there are some Dickson County farmhouses which do not have such roller towels. (*He gives it a pull to expose its full-length again.*)

MRS. HALE: Those towels get dirty awful quick. Men's hands aren't always as clean as they might be.

COUNTY ATTORNEY: Ah, loyal to your sex, I see. But you and Mrs. Wright were neighbors. I suppose you were friends, too.

MRS. HALE (*shaking her head*): I've not seen much of her of late years. I've not been in this house — it's more than a year.

COUNTY ATTORNEY (*crossing to women up center*): And why was that? You didn't like her?

MRS. HALE: I liked her all well enough. Farmers' wives have their hands full, Mr. Henderson. And then ——

COUNTY ATTORNEY: Yes —— ?

MRS. HALE (*looking about*): It never seemed a very cheerful place.

COUNTY ATTORNEY: No — it's not cheerful. I shouldn't say she had the home-making instinct.

MRS. HALE: Well, I don't know as Wright had, either.

COUNTY ATTORNEY: You mean that they didn't get on very well?

MRS. HALE: No, I don't mean anything. But I don't think a place'd be any cheerfuller for John Wright's being in it.

COUNTY ATTORNEY: I'd like to talk more of that a little later. I want to get the lay of things upstairs now. (*He goes past the women to up right where steps lead to a stair door.*)

SHERIFF: I suppose anything Mrs. Peters does'll be all right. She was to take in some clothes for her, you know, and a few little things. We left in such a hurry yesterday.

COUNTY ATTORNEY: Yes, but I would like to see what you take, Mrs. Peters, and keep an eye out for anything that might be of use to us.

MRS. PETERS: Yes, Mr. Henderson. (*The men leave by up right door to stairs. The women listen to the men's steps on the stairs, then look about the kitchen.*)

MRS. HALE (*crossing left to sink*): I'd hate to have men coming into my kitchen, snooping around and criticizing. (*She arranges the pans under sink which the lawyer had shoved out of place.*)

MRS. PETERS: Of course it's no more than their duty. (*Crosses to cupboard up right.*)

MRS. HALE: Duty's all right, but I guess that deputy sheriff that came out to make the fire might have got a little of this on. (*Gives the roller towel a pull.*) Wish I'd thought of that sooner. Seems mean to talk about her for not having things slicked up when she had to come away in such a hurry. (*Crosses right to Mrs. Peters at cupboard.*)

MRS. PETERS (*who has been looking through cupboard, lifts one end of towel that covers a pan*): She had bread set. (*Stands still.*)

MRS. HALE (*eyes fixed on a loaf of bread beside the breadbox, which is on a low shelf of the cupboard*): She was going to put this in there. (*Picks up loaf, abruptly drops it. In a manner of returning to familiar things.*) It's a shame about her fruit. I wonder if it's all gone. (*Gets up on the chair and looks.*) I think there's some here that's all right, Mrs. Peters. Yes — here; (*holding it toward the window*) this is cherries, too. (*Looking again.*) I declare I believe that's the only one. (*Gets down, jar in her hand. Goes to the sink and wipes it off on the outside.*) She'll feel awful bad after all her hard work in the hot weather. I remember the afternoon I put up my cherries last summer. (*She puts the jar on the big kitchen table, center of the room. With a sigh, is about to sit down in the rocking chair. Before she is seated realizes what chair it is; with a slow look at it, steps back. The chair which she has touched rocks back and forth. Mrs. Peters moves to center table and they both watch the chair rock for a moment or two.*)

MRS. PETERS (*shaking off the mood which the empty rocking chair has evoked. Now in a businesslike manner she speaks*): Well I must get those things from the front room closet. (*She goes to the door at the right but, after looking into the other room, steps back.*) You coming with me, Mrs. Hale? You could help me carry them. (*They go in the other room; reappear, Mrs. Peters carrying a dress, petticoat, and skirt, Mrs. Hale following with a pair of shoes.*) My, it's cold in there. (*She puts the clothes on the big table and hurries to the stove.*)

MRS. HALE (*right of center table examining the skirt*): Wright was close. I think maybe that's why she kept so much to herself. She didn't even belong to the Ladies' Aid. I suppose she felt she couldn't do her part, and then you don't enjoy things when you feel shabby. I heard she used to wear pretty clothes and be lively, when she was Minnie Foster, one of the town girls singing in the choir. But that — oh, that was thirty years ago. This all you want to take in?

MRS. PETERS: She said she wanted an apron. Funny thing to want, for there isn't much to get you dirty in jail, goodness knows. But I suppose just to make her feel more natural. (*Crosses to cupboard.*) She said they was in the top drawer in this cupboard. Yes, here. And then her little shawl that always hung behind the door. (*Opens stair door and looks.*) Yes, here it is. (*Quickly shuts door leading upstairs.*)

MRS. HALE (*abruptly moving toward her*): Mrs. Peters?

MRS. PETERS: Yes, Mrs. Hale? (*At up right door.*)

MRS. HALE: Do you think she did it?

MRS. PETERS (*in a frightened voice*): Oh, I don't know.

MRS. HALE: Well, I don't think she did. Asking for an apron and her little shawl. Worrying about her fruit.

MRS. PETERS (*starts to speak, glances up, where footsteps are heard in the room above. In a low voice*): Mr. Peters says it looks bad for her. Mr. Henderson is awful sarcastic in a speech and he'll make fun of her sayin' she didn't wake up.

MRS. HALE: Well, I guess John Wright didn't wake when they was slipping that rope under his neck.

MRS. PETERS (*crossing slowly to table and placing shawl and apron on table with other clothing*): No, it's strange. It must have been done awful crafty and still. They say it was such a — funny way to kill a man, rigging it all up like that.

MRS. HALE (*crossing to left of Mrs. Peters at table*): That's just what Mr. Hale said. There was a gun in the house. He says that's what he can't understand.

MRS. PETERS: Mr. Henderson said coming out that what was needed for the case was a motive; something to show anger, or — sudden feeling.

MRS. HALE (*who is standing by the table*): Well, I don't see any signs of anger around here. (*She puts her hand on the dish towel, which lies on the table, stands looking down at table, one-half of which is clean, the other half messy.*) It's wiped to here. (*Makes a move as if to finish work, then turns and looks at loaf of bread outside the breadbox. Drops towel. In that voice of coming back to familiar things.*) Wonder how they are finding things upstairs. (*Crossing below table to down right.*) I hope she had it a little more redd up° up there. You know, it seems kind of *sneaking*. Locking her up in town and then coming out here and trying to get her own house to turn against her!

MRS. PETERS: But, Mrs. Hale, the law is the law.

MRS. HALE: I s'pose 'tis. (*Unbuttoning her coat.*) Better loosen up your things, Mrs. Peters. You won't feel them when you go out. (*Mrs. Peters takes off her fur tippet, goes to hang it on chair back left of table, stands looking at the work basket on floor near down left window.*)

MRS. PETERS: She was piecing a quilt. (*She brings the large sewing basket to the center table and they look at the bright pieces, Mrs. Hale above the table and Mrs. Peters left of it.*)

MRS. HALE: It's a log cabin pattern. Pretty, isn't it? I wonder if she was goin' to quilt it or just knot it? (*Footsteps have been heard coming down the stairs. The Sheriff enters followed by Hale and the County Attorney.*)

SHERIFF: They wonder if she was going to quilt it or just knot it! (*The men laugh, the women look abashed.*)

COUNTY ATTORNEY (*rubbing his hands over the stove*): Frank's fire didn't do much up there, did it? Well, let's go out to the barn and get that cleared up. (*The men go outside by up left door.*)

MRS. HALE (*resentfully*): I don't know as there's anything so strange, our takin' up our time with little things while we're waiting for them to get the evidence. (*She sits in chair right of table smoothing out a block with decision.*) I don't see as it's anything to laugh about.

MRS. PETERS (*apologetically*): Of course they've got awful important things on their minds. (*Pulls up a chair and joins Mrs. Hale at the left of the table.*)

MRS. HALE (*examining another block*): Mrs. Peters, look at this one. Here, this is the one she was working on, and look at the sewing! All the rest of it has been so nice and even. And look at this! It's all over the place! Why, it looks as if she didn't know what she was about! (*After she has said this they look at each other, then start to glance back at the door. After an instant Mrs. Hale has pulled at a knot and ripped the sewing.*)

MRS. PETERS: Oh, what are you doing, Mrs. Hale?

MRS. HALE (*mildly*): Just pulling out a stitch or two that's not sewed very good. (*Threading a needle.*) Bad sewing always made me fidgety.

MRS. PETERS (*with a glance at door, nervously*): I don't think we ought to touch things.

MRS. HALE: I'll just finish up this end. (*Suddenly stopping and leaning forward.*) Mrs. Peters?

MRS. PETERS: Yes, Mrs. Hale?

MRS. HALE: What do you suppose she was so nervous about?

MRS. PETERS: Oh — I don't know. I don't know as she was nervous. I sometimes sew awful queer when I'm just tired. (*Mrs. Hale starts to say something, looks at Mrs. Peters, then goes on sewing.*) Well, I must get these things wrapped up. They may be through sooner than we think. (*Putting*

---

redd up: Neat.

apron and other things together.) I wonder where I can find a piece of paper, and string. (*Rises.*)

MRS. HALE: In that cupboard, maybe.

MRS. PETERS (*crosses right looking in cupboard*): Why, here's a bird-cage. (*Holds it up.*) Did she have a bird, Mrs. Hale?

MRS. HALE: Why, I don't know whether she did or not — I've not been here for so long. There was a man around last year selling canaries cheap, but I don't know as she took one; maybe she did. She used to sing real pretty herself.

MRS. PETERS (*glancing around*): Seems funny to think of a bird here. But she must have had one, or why would she have a cage? I wonder what happened to it?

MRS. HALE: I s'pose maybe the cat got it.

MRS. PETERS: No, she didn't have a cat. She's got that feeling some people have about cats — being afraid of them. My cat got in her room and she was real upset and asked me to take it out.

MRS. HALE: My sister Bessie was like that. Queer, ain't it?

MRS. PETERS (*examining the cage*): Why, look at this door. It's broke. One hinge is pulled apart. (*Takes a step down to Mrs. Hale's right.*)

MRS. HALE (*looking too*): Looks as if someone must have been rough with it.

MRS. PETERS: Why, yes. (*She brings the cage forward and puts it on the table.*)

MRS. HALE (*glancing toward up left door*): I wish if they're going to find any evidence they'd be about it. I don't like this place.

MRS. PETERS: But I'm awful glad you came with me, Mrs. Hale. It would be lonesome for me sitting here alone.

MRS. HALE: It would, wouldn't it? (*Dropping her sewing.*) But I tell you what I do wish, Mrs. Peters. I wish I had come over sometimes when *she* was here. I — (*looking around the room*) — wish I had.

MRS. PETERS: But of course you were awful busy, Mrs. Hale — your house and your children.

MRS. HALE (*rises and crosses left*): I could've come. I stayed away because it weren't cheerful — and that's why I ought to have come. I — (*looking out left window*) — I've never liked this place. Maybe because it's down in a hollow and you don't see the road. I dunno what it is, but it's a lonesome place and always was. I wish I had come over to see Minnie Foster sometimes. I can see now — (*Shakes her head.*)

MRS. PETERS (*left of table and above it*): Well, you mustn't reproach yourself, Mrs. Hale. Somehow we just don't see how it is with other folks until — something turns up.

MRS. HALE: Not having children makes less work — but it makes a quiet house, and Wright out to work all day, and no company when he did come in. (*Turning from window.*) Did you know John Wright, Mrs. Peters?

MRS. PETERS: Not to know him; I've seen him in town. They say he was a good man.

MRS. HALE: Yes — good; he didn't drink, and kept his word as well as most, I guess, and paid his debts. But he was a hard man, Mrs. Peters. Just to pass the time of day with him — (*Shivers.*) Like a raw wind that gets to the bone. (*Pauses, her eye falling on the cage.*) I should think she would 'a' wanted a bird. But what do you suppose went with it?

MRS. PETERS: I don't know, unless it got sick and died. (*She reaches over and swings the broken door, swings it again, both women watch it.*)

MRS. HALE: You weren't raised round here, were you? (*Mrs. Peters shakes her head.*) You didn't know — her?

MRS. PETERS: Not till they brought her yesterday.

MRS. HALE: She — come to think of it, she was kind of like a bird herself — real sweet and pretty, but kind of timid and — fluttery. How — she — did — change. (*Silence: then as if struck by a happy thought and relieved to get back to everyday things. Crosses right above Mrs. Peters to cupboard, replaces small chair used to stand on to its original place down right.*) Tell you what, Mrs. Peters, why don't you take the quilt in with you? It might take up her mind.

MRS. PETERS: Why, I think that's a real nice idea, Mrs. Hale. There couldn't possibly be any objection to it could there? Now, just what would I take? I wonder if her patches are in here — and her things. (*They look in the sewing basket.*)

MRS. HALE (*crosses to right of table*): Here's some red. I expect this has got sewing things in it. (*Brings out a fancy box.*) What a pretty box. Looks like something somebody would give you. Maybe her scissors are in here. (*Opens box. Suddenly puts her hand to her nose.*) Why —— (*Mrs. Peters bends nearer, then turns her face away.*) There's something wrapped up in this piece of silk.

MRS. PETERS: Why, this isn't her scissors.

MRS. HALE (*lifting the silk*): Oh, Mrs. Peters — it's —— (*Mrs. Peters bends closer.*)

MRS. PETERS: It's the bird.

MRS. HALE: But, Mrs. Peters — look at it! Its neck! Look at its neck! It's all — other side *to.*

MRS. PETERS: Somebody — wrung — its — neck. (*Their eyes meet. A look of growing comprehension, of horror. Steps are heard outside. Mrs. Hale slips box under quilt pieces, and sinks into her chair. Enter Sheriff and County Attorney. Mrs. Peters steps down left and stands looking out of window.*)

COUNTY ATTORNEY (*as one turning from serious things to little pleasantries*): Well, ladies, have you decided whether she was going to quilt it or knot it? (*Crosses to center above table.*)

MRS. PETERS: We think she was going to — knot it. (*Sheriff crosses to right of stove, lifts stove lid, and glances at fire, then stands warming hands at stove.*)

COUNTY ATTORNEY: Well, that's interesting, I'm sure. (*Seeing the bird-cage.*) Has the bird flown?

MRS. HALE (*putting more quilt pieces over the box*): We think the — cat got it.

COUNTY ATTORNEY (*preoccupied*): Is there a cat? (*Mrs. Hale glances in a quick covert way at Mrs. Peters.*)

MRS. PETERS (*turning from window takes a step in*): Well, not *now.* They're superstitious, you know. They leave.

COUNTY ATTORNEY (*to Sheriff Peters, continuing an interrupted conversation*): No sign at all of anyone having come from the outside. Their own rope.

Now let's go up again and go over it piece by piece. (*They start upstairs.*) It would have to have been someone who knew just the ——— (*Mrs. Peters sits down left of table. The two women sit there not looking at one another, but as if peering into something and at the same time holding back. When they talk now it is in the manner of feeling their way over strange ground, as if afraid of what they are saying, but as if they cannot help saying it.*)

MRS. HALE (*hesitatively and in hushed voice*): She liked the bird. She was going to bury it in that pretty box.

MRS. PETERS (*in a whisper*): When I was a girl — my kitten — there was a boy took a hatchet, and before my eyes — and before I could get there ——— (*Covers her face an instant.*) If they hadn't held me back I would have — (*catches herself, looks upstairs where steps are heard, falters weakly*) — hurt him.

MRS. HALE (*with a slow look around her*): I wonder how it would seem never to have had any children around. (*Pause.*) No, Wright wouldn't like the bird — a thing that sang. She used to sing. He killed that, too.

MRS. PETERS (*moving uneasily*): We don't know who killed the bird.

MRS. HALE: I knew John Wright.

MRS. PETERS: It was an awful thing was done in this house that night, Mrs. Hale. Killing a man while he slept, slipping a rope around his neck that choked the life out of him.

MRS. HALE: His neck. Choked the life out of him. (*Her hand goes out and rests on the bird-cage.*)

MRS. PETERS (*with rising voice*): We don't know who killed him. We don't *know.*

MRS. HALE (*her own feeling not interrupted*): If there'd been years and years of nothing, then a bird to sing to you, it would be awful — still, after the bird was still.

MRS. PETERS (*something within her speaking*): I know what stillness is. When we homesteaded in Dakota, and my first baby died — after he was two years old, and me with no other then ———

MRS. HALE (*moving*): How soon do you suppose they'll be through looking for the evidence?

MRS. PETERS: I know what stillness is. (*Pulling herself back.*) The law has got to punish crime, Mrs. Hale.

MRS. HALE (*not as if answering that*): I wish you'd seen Minnie Foster when she wore a white dress with blue ribbons and stood up there in the choir and sang. (*A look around the room.*) Oh, I *wish* I'd come over here once in a while! That was a crime! That was a crime! Who's going to punish that?

MRS. PETERS (*looking upstairs*): We mustn't — take on.

MRS. HALE: I might have known she needed help! I know how things can be — for women. I tell you, it's queer, Mrs. Peters. We live close together and we live far apart. We all go through the same things — it's all just a different kind of the same thing. (*Brushes her eyes, noticing the jar of fruit, reaches out for it.*) If I was you I wouldn't tell her her fruit was gone. Tell her it *ain't.* Tell her it's all right. Take this in to prove it to her. She — she may never know whether it was broke or not.

MRS. PETERS (*takes the jar, looks about for something to wrap it in; takes petticoat from the clothes brought from the other room, very nervously begins winding this around the jar. In a false voice*): My, it's a good thing the men couldn't hear us. Wouldn't they just laugh! Getting all stirred up over a little thing like a — dead canary. As if that could have anything to do with — with — wouldn't they *laugh!* (*The men are heard coming downstairs.*)

MRS. HALE (*under her breath*): Maybe they would — maybe they wouldn't.

COUNTY ATTORNEY: No, Peters, it's all perfectly clear except a reason for doing it. But you know juries when it comes to women. If there was some definite thing. (*Crosses slowly to above table. Sheriff crosses down right. Mrs. Hale and Mrs. Peters remain seated at either side of table.*) Something to show — something to make a story about — a thing that would connect up with this strange way of doing it —— (*The women's eyes meet for an instant. Enter Hale from outer door.*)

HALE (*remaining by door*): Well, I've got the team around. Pretty cold out there.

COUNTY ATTORNEY: I'm going to stay awhile by myself. (*To the Sheriff.*) You can send Frank out for me, can't you? I want to go over everything. I'm not satisfied that we can't do better.

SHERIFF: Do you want to see what Mrs. Peters is going to take in? (*The Lawyer picks up the apron, laughs.*)

COUNTY ATTORNEY: Oh, I guess they're not very dangerous things the ladies have picked out. (*Moves a few things about, disturbing the quilt pieces which cover the box. Steps back.*) No, Mrs. Peters doesn't need supervising. For that matter a sheriff's wife is married to the law. Ever think of it that way, Mrs. Peters?

MRS. PETERS: Not — just that way.

SHERIFF (*chuckling*): Married to the law. (*Moves to down right door to the other room.*) I just want you to come in here a minute, George. We ought to take a look at these windows.

COUNTY ATTORNEY (*scoffingly*): Oh, windows!

SHERIFF: We'll be right out, Mr. Hale. (*Hale goes outside. The Sheriff follows the County Attorney into the room. Then Mrs. Hale rises, hands tight together, looking intensely at Mrs. Peters, whose eyes make a slow turn, finally meeting Mrs. Hale's. A moment Mrs. Hale holds her, then her own eyes point the way to where the box is concealed. Suddenly Mrs. Peters throws back quilt pieces and tries to put the box in the bag she is carrying. It is too big. She opens box, starts to take bird out, cannot touch it, goes to pieces, stands there helpless. Sound of a knob turning in the other room. Mrs. Hale snatches the box and puts it in the pocket of her big coat. Enter County Attorney and Sheriff, who remains down right.*)

COUNTY ATTORNEY (*crosses to up left door facetiously*): Well, Henry, at least we found out that she was not going to quilt it. She was going to — what is it you call it, ladies?

MRS. HALE (*standing center below table facing front, her hand against her pocket*): We call it — knot it, Mr. Henderson.

Curtain.

TENNESSEE WILLIAMS *(1911–1983) was born Thomas Lanier Williams in Columbus, Mississippi, the second child of Edwina Dakin Williams, the daughter of an Episcopal clergyman, and Cornelius Coffin Williams, a traveling salesman. Williams spent the first fifteen years of his life living with his mother and older sister, Rose, in more than sixteen homes until his father took a permanent job in St. Louis. Williams was an indifferent high school student, but he began to publish stories in school newspapers as a teenager. An English major in college, his favorite authors were dramatists — Chekhov, Ibsen, and Strindberg — and he decided to become a playwright. After attending two other universities, he enrolled at the University of Iowa in 1937, where he saw his first full-length plays produced onstage. After graduation he held different jobs to support himself while he worked on his plays, poetry, and short fiction.*

Williams wrote the story "Portrait of a Girl in Glass" in 1943. He turned the story into a play, The Gentleman Caller, *while he was under contract with M-G-M to write a script for a movie starring Lana Turner. (Williams had a cataract in one eye, so he was exempt from military service during World War II.) The script was turned down, and Williams left Hollywood soon after. He then rewrote the script as* The Glass Menagerie, *which opened in Chicago in December 1944. After a shaky start, the play ran for 561 performances in New York City and won the Drama Critics' Circle Award as the best American play of the year.*

In the introduction to Williams's Collected Stories, *the writer Gore Vidal analyzed how Williams used his life as the basis of his art:*

> *Like most natural writers, Tennessee could not possess his own life until he had written about it. This is common. But what is not common was the way that he went about not only recapturing lost time but then regaining it in a way that far surpassed the original experience. . . . [First he turned his memories into stories, then] he would make a play of the story and then — and this is why he was so compulsive a working playwright — he would have the play produced so that he could, like God, rearrange his original experience into something that was no longer God's and unpossessable but* his. *The frantic lifelong desire for play-productions was not just ambition or a need to be busy, it was the only way that he ever had of being entirely alive.*

In Williams's production notes to The Glass Menagerie, *he calls it a "memory play" and describes his vision of a revitalized, lyrical theater of feelings. Both the play and "Portrait of a Girl in Glass" are based on Williams's memories of his close relationship with his sister, Rose, who was institutionalized after a lobotomy authorized by Williams's parents while he was a student at the University of Iowa. In his autobiographical play, he portrayed his sister and himself as victims and outsiders in the family. He used his own name for himself as the character Tom and called his sister Laura, as well as punning on her name in the phrase "Blue Roses" later in her dialogue with the gentleman caller.*

When Williams turned the original short story into a play, he gave a much larger role to the figure of the mother Amanda, who tries to dominate the lives of her son and daughter. The young playwright William Inge, who met Williams just before The Glass Menagerie *was produced, recalled that the play was exciting because "it enabled me to see the true dynamics between life and art. . . . I don't think any of his plays is quite as personal as the* Menagerie, *although* Menagerie, *when you see it, does not strike you as a too personal play in any way at all. It's a real work of art . . .*

it's not self-indulgent, is what I'm trying to say. It is out of self, but it is conceived in terms of universality."

The Glass Menagerie *introduces several themes that reoccur in later Williams plays, including the fear of isolation and the need for understanding by the dispossessed. The most successful American playwright of his generation; Williams wrote several other prize-winning plays, including* A Streetcar Named Desire *(1948),* The Rose Tattoo *(1951),* Cat on a Hot Tin Roof *(1955),* Suddenly Last Summer *(1958),* Sweet Bird of Youth *(1959), and* The Night of the Iguana *(1961). All of them, like* The Glass Menagerie, *were made into motion pictures.*

RELATED COMMENTARIES: *Benjamin Nelson, "Problems in* The Glass Menagerie," *page 1987; Tennessee Williams, "Production Notes to* The Glass Menagerie," *page 2002; Tennessee Williams, "Portrait of a Girl in Glass," page 2004.*

TENNESSEE WILLIAMS

The Glass Menagerie

1945

nobody,not even the rain,has such small hands
– E. E. CUMMINGS

LIST OF CHARACTERS

AMANDA WINGFIELD, *the mother. A little woman of great but confused vitality clinging frantically to another time and place. Her characterization must be carefully created, not copied from type. She is not paranoiac, but her life is paranoia. There is much to admire in Amanda, and as much to love and pity as there is to laugh at. Certainly she has endurance and a kind of heroism, and though her foolishness makes her unwittingly cruel at times, there is tenderness in her slight person.*

LAURA WINGFIELD, *her daughter. Amanda, having failed to establish contact with reality, continues to live vitally in her illusions, but Laura's situation is even graver. A childhood illness has left her crippled, one leg slightly shorter than the other, and held in a brace. This defect need not be more than suggested on the stage. Stemming from this, Laura's separation increases till she is like a piece of her own glass collection, too exquisitely fragile to move from the shelf.*

TOM WINGFIELD, *her son. And the narrator of the play. A poet with a job in a warehouse. His nature is not remorseless, but to escape from a trap he has to act without pity.*

JIM O'CONNOR, *the gentleman caller. A nice, ordinary, young man.*

SCENE: *An alley in St. Louis.*

PART I: *Preparation for a Gentleman Caller.*

PART II: *The Gentleman Calls.*

TIME: *Now and the Past.*

SCENE I

The Wingfield apartment is in the rear of the building, one of those vast hivelike conglomerations of cellular living-units that flower as warty growths in overcrowded urban centers of lower middle-class population and are symptomatic of the impulse of this largest and fundamentally enslaved section of American society to avoid fluidity and differentiation and to exist and function as one interfused mass of automatism.

The apartment faces an alley and is entered by a fire-escape, a structure whose name is a touch of accidental poetic truth, for all of these huge buildings are always burning with the slow and implacable fires of human desperation. The fire-escape is included in the set — that is, the landing of it and steps descending from it.

The scene is memory and is therefore nonrealistic. Memory takes a lot of poetic license. It omits some details; others are exaggerated, according to the emotional value of the articles it touches, for memory is seated predominantly in the heart. The interior is therefore rather dim and poetic.

At the rise of the curtain, the audience is faced with the dark, grim rear wall of the Wingfield tenement. This building, which runs parallel to the footlights, is flanked on both sides by dark, narrow alleys which run into murky canyons of tangled clotheslines, garbage cans, and the sinister latticework of neighboring fire-escapes. It is up and down these side alleys that exterior entrances and exits are made, during the play. At the end of Tom's opening commentary, the dark tenement wall slowly reveals (by means of a transparency) the interior of the ground floor Wingfield apartment.

Downstage is the living room, which also serves as a sleeping room for Laura, the sofa unfolding to make her bed. Upstage, center, and divided by a wide arch or second proscenium with transparent faded portieres (or second curtain), is the dining room. In an old-fashioned what-not in the living room are seen scores of transparent glass animals. A blown-up photograph of the father hangs on the wall of the living room, facing the audience, to the left of the archway. It is the face of a very handsome young man in a doughboy's First World War cap. He is gallantly smiling, ineluctably smiling, as if to say, "I will be smiling forever."

The audience hears and sees the opening scene in the dining room through both the transparent fourth wall of the building and the transparent gauze portieres of the dining-room arch. It is during this revealing scene that the fourth wall slowly ascends, out of sight. This transparent exterior wall is not brought down again until the very end of the play, during Tom's final speech.

The narrator is an undisguised convention of the play. He takes whatever license with dramatic convention as is convenient to his purposes.

Tom enters dressed as a merchant sailor from alley, stage left, and strolls across the front of the stage to the fire-escape. There he stops and lights a cigarette. He addresses the audience.

TOM: Yes, I have tricks in my pocket, I have things up my sleeve. But I am the opposite of a stage magician. He gives you illusion that has the appearance of truth. I give you truth in the pleasant disguise of illusion. To begin with, I turn back time. I reverse it to that quaint period, the thirties, when the huge middle class of America was matriculating in a school for the blind. Their eyes had failed them, or they had failed their eyes, and so they were having their fingers pressed forcibly down on the fiery Braille alphabet of a dissolving economy. In Spain there was revolution. Here there was only shouting and confusion. In Spain there was Guernica.° Here there were disturbances of labor, sometimes pretty vio-

---

Guernica: A town in Spain annihilated by German bombers in 1937.

lent, in otherwise peaceful cities such as Chicago, Cleveland, Saint Louis. . . . This is the social background of the play.

(*Music.*)

The play is memory. Being a memory play, it is dimly lighted, it is sentimental, it is not realistic. In memory everything seems to happen to music. That explains the fiddle in the wings. I am the narrator of the play, and also a character in it. The other characters are my mother, Amanda, my sister, Laura, and a gentleman caller who appears in the final scenes. He is the most realistic character in the play, being an emissary from a world of reality that we were somehow set apart from. But since I have a poet's weakness for symbols, I am using this character also as a symbol; he is the long delayed but always expected something that we live for. There is a fifth character in the play who doesn't appear except in this larger-than-life photograph over the mantel. This is our father who left us a long time ago. He was a telephone man who fell in love with long distances; he gave up his job with the telephone company and skipped the light fantastic out of town. . . . The last we heard of him was a picture post-card from Mazatlán, on the Pacific coast of Mexico, containing a message of two words — "Hello — Good-bye!" and no address. I think the rest of the play will explain itself. . . .

Amanda's voice becomes audible through the portieres.

(*Legend on screen: "Où sont les neiges."*°)

He divides the portieres and enters the upstage area.

Amanda and Laura are seated at a drop-leaf table. Eating is indicated by gestures without food or utensils. Amanda faces the audience.

Tom and Laura are seated in profile.

The interior has lit up softly and through the scrim we see Amanda and Laura seated at the table in the upstage area.

AMANDA (*calling*): Tom?

TOM: Yes, Mother.

AMANDA: We can't say grace until you come to the table!

TOM: Coming, Mother. (*He bows slightly and withdraws, reappearing a few moments later in his place at the table.*)

AMANDA (*to her son*): Honey, don't *push* with your *fingers.* If you have to push with something, the thing to push with is a crust of bread. And chew — chew! Animals have sections in their stomachs which enable them to digest food without mastication, but human beings are supposed to chew their food before they swallow it down. Eat food leisurely, son, and really enjoy it. A well-cooked meal has lots of delicate flavors that have to be held in the mouth for appreciation. So chew your food and give your salivary glands a chance to function!

Tom deliberately lays his imaginary fork down and pushes his chair back from the table.

Où sont les neiges: Part of a line by the French poet François Villon; the complete line translates, "But where are the snows of Yesteryear?"

TOM: I haven't enjoyed one bite of this dinner because of your constant directions on how to eat it. It's you that makes me rush through meals with your hawklike attention to every bite I take. Sickening — spoils my appetite — all this discussion of animals' secretion — salivary glands — mastication!

AMANDA (*lightly*): Temperament like a Metropolitan star! (*He rises and crosses downstage.*) You're not excused from the table.

TOM: I am getting a cigarette.

AMANDA: You smoke too much.

Laura rises.

LAURA: I'll bring in the blanc mange.

He remains standing with his cigarette by the portieres during the following.

AMANDA (*rising*): No, sister, no, sister — you be the lady this time and I'll be the darky.

LAURA: I'm already up.

AMANDA: Resume your seat, little sister — I want you to stay fresh and pretty — for gentlemen callers!

LAURA: I'm not expecting any gentlemen callers.

AMANDA (*crossing out to kitchenette. Airily*): Sometimes they come when they are least expected! Why, I remember one Sunday afternoon in Blue Mountain — (*Enters kitchenette.*)

TOM: I know what's coming!

LAURA: Yes. But let her tell it.

TOM: Again?

LAURA: She loves to tell it.

Amanda returns with bowl of dessert.

AMANDA: One Sunday afternoon in Blue Mountain — your mother received — *seventeen!* — gentlemen callers! Why, sometimes there weren't chairs enough to accommodate them all. We had to send the nigger over to bring in folding chairs from the parish house.

TOM (*remaining at portieres*): How did you entertain those gentlemen callers?

AMANDA: I understood the art of conversation!

TOM: I bet you could talk.

AMANDA: Girls in those days *knew* how to talk, I can tell you.

TOM: Yes?

(*Image: Amanda as a girl on a porch greeting callers.*)

AMANDA: They knew how to entertain their gentlemen callers. It wasn't enough for a girl to be possessed of a pretty face and a graceful figure — although I wasn't slighted in either respect. She also needed to have a nimble wit and a tongue to meet all occasions.

TOM: What did you talk about?

AMANDA: Things of importance going on in the world! Never anything coarse or common or vulgar. (*She addresses Tom as though he were seated in the vacant chair at the table though he remains by portieres. He plays this scene as though he held the book.*) My callers were gentlemen — all! Among my callers were some of the most prominent young planters of the Mississippi Delta — planters and sons of planters!

Tom motions for music and a spot of light on Amanda.

Her eyes lift, her face glows, her voice becomes rich and elegiac.

(*Screen legend: "Où sont les neiges."*)

There was young Champ Laughlin who later became vice-president of the Delta Planters Bank. Hadley Stevenson who was drowned in Moon Lake and left his widow one hundred and fifty thousand in Government bonds. There were the Cutrere brothers, Wesley and Bates. Bates was one of my bright particular beaux! He got in a quarrel with that wild Wainright boy. They shot it out on the floor of Moon Lake Casino. Bates was shot through the stomach. Died in the ambulance on his way to Memphis. His widow was also well-provided for, came into eight or ten thousand acres, that's all. She married him on the rebound — never loved her — carried my picture on him the night he died! And there was that boy that every girl in the Delta had set her cap for! That beautiful, brilliant young Fitzhugh boy from Green County!

TOM: What did he leave his widow?

AMANDA: He never married! Gracious, you talk as though all of my old admirers had turned up their toes to the daisies!

TOM: Isn't this the first you mentioned that still survives?

AMANDA: That Fitzhugh boy went North and made a fortune — came to be known as the Wolf of Wall Street! He had the Midas touch, whatever he touched turned to gold! And I could have been Mrs. Duncan J. Fitzhugh, mind you! But — I picked your *father!*

LAURA (*rising*): Mother, let me clear the table.

AMANDA: No dear, you go in front and study your typewriter chart. Or practice your shorthand a little. Stay fresh and pretty! — It's almost time for our gentlemen callers to start arriving. (*She flounces girlishly toward the kitchenette.*) How many do you suppose we're going to entertain this afternoon?

Tom throws down the paper and jumps up with a groan.

LAURA (*alone in the dining room*): I don't believe we're going to receive any, Mother.

AMANDA (*reappearing, airily*): What? No one — not one? You must be joking! (*Laura nervously echoes her laugh. She slips in a fugitive manner through the half-open portieres and draws them gently behind her. A shaft of very clear light is thrown on her face against the faded tapestry of the curtains.*) (*Music: "The Glass Menagerie" under faintly.*) (*Lightly.*) Not one gentleman caller? It can't be true! There must be a flood, there must have been a tornado!

LAURA: It isn't a flood, it's not a tornado, Mother. I'm just not popular like you were in Blue Mountain. . . . (*Tom utters another groan. Laura glances at him with a faint, apologetic smile. Her voice catching a little.*) Mother's afraid I'm going to be an old maid.

(*The scene dims out with "Glass Menagerie" music.*)

SCENE II

"Laura, Haven't You Ever Liked Some Boy?"

On the dark stage the screen is lighted with the image of blue roses.

Gradually Laura's figure becomes apparent and the screen goes out.

The music subsides.

Laura is seated in the delicate ivory chair at the small clawfoot table.

She wears a dress of soft violet material for a kimono — her hair tied back from her forehead with a ribbon.

She is washing and polishing her collection of glass.

Amanda appears on the fire-escape steps. At the sound of her ascent, Laura catches her breath, thrusts the bowl of ornaments away, and seats herself stiffly before the diagram of the typewriter keyboard as though it held her spellbound. Something has happened to Amanda. It is written in her face as she climbs to the landing: a look that is grim and hopeless and a little absurd.

She has on one of those cheap or imitation velvety-looking cloth coats with imitation fur collar. Her hat is five or six years old, one of those dreadful cloche hats that were worn in the late twenties, and she is clasping an enormous black patent-leather pocketbook with nickel clasp and initials. This is her full-dress outfit, the one she usually wears to the D.A.R.°

Before entering she looks through the door.

She purses her lips, opens her eyes wide, rolls them upward, and shakes her head.

Then she slowly lets herself in the door. Seeing her mother's expression Laura touches her lips with a nervous gesture.

LAURA: Hello, Mother, I was — (*She makes a nervous gesture toward the chart on the wall. Amanda leans against the shut door and stares at Laura with a martyred look.*)

AMANDA: Deception? Deception? (*She slowly removes her hat and gloves, continuing the swift suffering stare. She lets the hat and gloves fall on the floor — a bit of acting.*)

LAURA (*shakily*): How was the D.A.R. meeting? (*Amanda slowly opens her purse and removes a dainty white handkerchief, which she shakes out delicately and delicately touches to her lips and nostrils.*) Didn't you go to the D.A.R. meeting, Mother?

AMANDA (*faintly, almost inaudibly*): — No. — No. (*Then more forcibly.*) I did not have the strength — to go to the D.A.R. In fact, I did not have the courage! I wanted to find a hole in the ground and hide myself in it forever! (*She crosses slowly to the wall and removes the diagram of the typewriter keyboard. She holds it in front of her for a second, staring at it sweetly and sorrowfully — then bites her lips and tears it in two pieces.*)

LAURA (*faintly*): Why did you do that, Mother? (*Amanda repeats the same procedure with the chart of the Gregg Alphabet.*°) Why are you —

D.A.R.: Daughters of the American Revolution, whose ancestors served the patriots' cause in the Revolutionary War. **Gregg Alphabet:** Shorthand system invented by John Robert Gregg.

AMANDA: Why? Why? How old are you, Laura?

LAURA: Mother, you know my age.

AMANDA: I thought that you were an adult; it seems that I was mistaken. (*She crosses slowly to the sofa and sinks down and stares at Laura.*)

LAURA: Please don't stare at me, Mother.

Amanda closes her eyes and lowers her head. Count ten.

AMANDA: What are we going to do, what is going to become of us, what is the future?

Count ten.

LAURA: Has something happened, Mother? (*Amanda draws a long breath and takes out the handkerchief again. Dabbing process.*) Mother, has — something happened?

AMANDA: I'll be all right in a minute. I'm just bewildered — (*count five*) — by life. . . .

LAURA: Mother, I wish that you would tell me what's happened.

AMANDA: As you know, I was supposed to be inducted into my office at the D.A.R. this afternoon. (*Image: A swarm of typewriters.*) But I stopped off at Rubicam's Business College to speak to your teachers about your having a cold and ask them what progress they thought you were making down there.

LAURA: Oh. . . .

AMANDA: I went to the typing instructor and introduced myself as your mother. She didn't know who you were. Wingfield, she said. We don't have any such student enrolled at the school! I assured her she did, that you had been going to classes since early in January. "I wonder," she said, "if you could be talking about that terribly shy little girl who dropped out of school after only a few days' attendance?" "No," I said, "Laura, my daughter, has been going to school every day for the past six weeks!" "Excuse me," she said. She took the attendance book out and there was your name, unmistakably printed, and all the dates you were absent until they decided that you had dropped out of school. I still said, "No, there must have been some mistake! There must have been some mix-up in the records!" And she said, "No — I remember her perfectly now. Her hand shook so that she couldn't hit the right keys! The first time we gave a speed-test, she broke down completely — was sick at the stomach and almost had to be carried into the wash-room! After that morning she never showed up any more. We phoned the house but never got any answer" — while I was working at Famous and Barr, I suppose, demonstrating those — Oh! I felt so weak I could barely keep on my feet. I had to sit down while they got me a glass of water! Fifty dollars' tuition, all of our plans — my hopes and ambitions for you — just gone up the spout, just gone up the spout like that. (*Laura draws a long breath and gets awkwardly to her feet. She crosses to the Victrola, and winds it up.*) What are you doing?

LAURA: Oh! (*She releases the handle and returns to her seat.*)

AMANDA: Laura, where have you been going when you've gone out pretending that you were going to business college?

LAURA: I've just been going out walking.

AMANDA: That's not true.

LAURA: It is. I just went walking.

AMANDA: Walking? Walking? In winter? Deliberately courting pneumonia in that light coat? Where did you walk to, Laura?

LAURA: It was the lesser of two evils, Mother. (*Image: Winter scene in park.*) I couldn't go back up. I — threw up — on the floor!

AMANDA: From half past seven till after five every day you mean to tell me you walked around in the park, because you wanted to make me think that you were still going to Rubicam's Business College?

LAURA: It wasn't as bad as it sounds. I went inside places to get warmed up.

AMANDA: Inside where?

LAURA: I went in the art museum and the bird-houses at the Zoo. I visited the penguins every day! Sometimes I did without lunch and went to the movies. Lately I've been spending most of my afternoons in the Jewel-box, that big glass house where they raise the tropical flowers.

AMANDA: You did all this to deceive me, just for the deception? (*Laura looks down.*) Why?

LAURA: Mother, when you're disappointed, you get that awful suffering look on your face, like the picture of Jesus' mother in the museum!

AMANDA: Hush!

LAURA: I couldn't face it.

Pause. A whisper of strings.

(*Legend: "The Crust of Humility."*)

AMANDA (*hopelessly fingering the huge pocketbook*): So what are we going to do the rest of our lives? Stay home and watch the parades go by? Amuse ourselves with the glass menagerie, darling? Eternally play those worn-out phonograph records your father left as a painful reminder of him? We won't have a business career — we've given that up because it gave us nervous indigestion! (*Laughs wearily.*) What is there left but dependency all our lives? I know so well what becomes of unmarried women who aren't prepared to occupy a position. I've seen such pitiful cases in the South — barely tolerated spinsters living upon the grudging patronage of sister's husband or brother's wife! — stuck away in some little mousetrap of a room — encouraged by one in-law to visit another — little birdlike women without any nest — eating the crust of humility all their life! Is that the future that we've mapped out for ourselves? I swear it's the only alternative I can think of! It isn't a very pleasant alternative, is it? Of course — some girls *do marry.* (*Laura twists her hands nervously.*) Haven't you ever liked some boy?

LAURA: Yes. I liked one once. (*Rises.*) I came across his picture a while ago.

AMANDA (*with some interest*): He gave you his picture?

LAURA: No, it's in the year-book.

AMANDA (*disappointed*): Oh — a high-school boy.

(*Screen image: Jim as a high-school hero bearing a silver cup.*)

LAURA: Yes. His name was Jim. (*Laura lifts the heavy annual from the clawfoot table.*) Here he is in *The Pirates of Penzance.*

AMANDA (*absently*): The what?

LAURA: The operetta the senior class put on. He had a wonderful voice and we sat across the aisle from each other Mondays, Wednesdays, and Fridays in the Aud. Here he is with the silver cup for debating! See his grin?

AMANDA (*absently*): He must have had a jolly disposition.

LAURA: He used to call me — Blue Roses.

(*Image: Blue roses.*)

AMANDA: Why did he call you such a name as that?

LAURA: When I had that attack of pleurosis — he asked me what was the matter when I came back. I said pleurosis — he thought that I said Blue Roses! So that's what he always called me after that. Whenever he saw me, he'd holler, "Hello, Blue Roses!" I didn't care for the girl that he went out with. Emily Meisenbach. Emily was the best-dressed girl at Soldan. She never struck me, though, as being sincere. . . . It says in the Personal Section — they're engaged. That's — six years ago! They must be married by now.

AMANDA: Girls that aren't cut out for business careers usually wind up married to some nice man. (*Gets up with a spark of revival.*) Sister, that's what you'll do!

Laura utters a startled, doubtful laugh. She reaches quickly for a piece of glass.

LAURA: But, Mother —

AMANDA: Yes? (*Crossing to photograph.*)

LAURA (*in a tone of frightened apology*): I'm — crippled!

(*Image: Screen.*)

AMANDA: Nonsense! Laura, I've told you never, never to use that word. Why, you're not crippled, you just have a little defect — hardly noticeable, even! When people have some slight disadvantage like that, they cultivate other things to make up for it — develop charm — and vivacity — and — *charm!* That's all you have to do! (*She turns again to the photograph.*) One thing your father had *plenty* of — was *charm!*

Tom motions to the fiddle in the wings.

(*The scene fades out with music.*)

SCENE III

(*Legend on the screen: "After the Fiasco — "*)

Tom speaks from the fire-escape landing.

TOM: After the fiasco at Rubicam's Business College, the idea of getting a gentleman caller for Laura began to play a more important part in Mother's calculations. It became an obsession. Like some archetype of the universal unconscious, the image of the gentleman caller haunted our small apartment. . . . (*Image: Young man at door with flowers.*) An evening at home rarely passed without some allusion to this image, this specter, this hope. . . . Even when he wasn't mentioned, his presence hung in Mother's preoccupied look and in my sister's frightened, apologetic manner — hung like a sentence passed upon the Wingfields! Mother was a woman of action as well as words. She began to take logical steps in the planned direction. Late that winter and in the early spring — realizing that extra money would be needed to properly feather the nest and plume the bird — she conducted a vigorous campaign on the telephone, roping in subscribers to one of those magazines for matrons called *The Home-maker's Companion,* the type of journal that features the serialized sublimations of ladies of letters who think in terms of delicate cuplike breasts, slim, tapering waists, rich, creamy thighs, eyes like wood-smoke in autumn, fingers that soothe and caress like strains of music, bodies as powerful as Etruscan sculpture.

(*Screen image:* Glamour *magazine cover.*)

Amanda enters with phone on long extension cord. She is spotted in the dim stage.

AMANDA: Ida Scott? This is Amanda Wingfield! We *missed* you at the D.A.R. last Monday! I said to myself: She's probably suffering with that sinus condition! How is that sinus condition? Horrors! Heaven have mercy! — You're a Christian martyr, yes, that's what you are, a Christian martyr! Well, I just now happened to notice that your subscription to the *Companion*'s about to expire! Yes, it expires with the next issue, honey! — just when that wonderful new serial by Bessie Mae Hopper is getting off to such an exciting start. Oh, honey, it's something that you can't miss! You remember how *Gone with the Wind* took everybody by storm? You simply couldn't go out if you hadn't read it. All everybody *talked* was Scarlett O'Hara. Well, this is a book that critics already compare to *Gone with the Wind.* It's the *Gone with the Wind* of the post–World War generation! — What? — Burning? — Oh, honey, don't let them burn, go take a look in the oven and I'll hold the wire! Heavens — I think she's hung up!

(*Dim out.*)

(*Legend on screen: "You think I'm in love with Continental Shoemakers?"*)

Before the stage is lighted, the violent voices of Tom and Amanda are heard. They are quarreling behind the portieres. In front of them stands Laura with clenched hands and panicky expression.

A clear pool of light on her figure throughout this scene.

TOM: What in Christ's name am I —

AMANDA (*shrilly*): Don't you use that —

TOM: Supposed to do!

AMANDA: Expression! Not in my —

TOM: Ohhh!

AMANDA: Presence! Have you gone out of your senses?

TOM: I have, that's true, *driven* out!

AMANDA: What is the matter with you, you — big — big — IDIOT!

TOM: Look — I've got *no thing,* no single thing —

AMANDA: Lower your voice!

TOM: In my life here that I can call my own! Everything is —

AMANDA: Stop that shouting!

TOM: Yesterday you confiscated my books! You had the nerve to —

AMANDA: I took that horrible novel back to the library — yes! That hideous book by that insane Mr. Lawrence.° (*Tom laughs wildly.*) I cannot control the output of diseased minds or people who cater to them — (*Tom laughs still more wildly.*) BUT I WON'T ALLOW SUCH FILTH BROUGHT INTO MY HOUSE! No, no, no, no, no!

TOM: House, house! Who pays rent on it, who makes a slave of himself to —

AMANDA (*fairly screeching*): Don't you DARE to —

TOM: No, no, *I* mustn't say things! *I've* got to just —

AMANDA: Let me tell you —

TOM: I don't want to hear any more! (*He tears the portieres open. The upstage area is lit with a turgid smoky red glow.*)

Amanda's hair is in metal curlers and she wears a very old bathrobe, much too large for her slight figure, a relic of the faithless Mr. Wingfield.

An upright typewriter and a wild disarray of manuscripts are on the drop-leaf table. The quarrel was probably precipitated by Amanda's interruption of his creative labor. A chair lying overthrown on the floor.

Their gesticulating shadows are cast on the ceiling by the fiery glow.

AMANDA: You *will* hear more, you —

TOM: No, I won't hear more, I'm going out!

AMANDA: You come right back in —

TOM: Out, out, out! Because I'm —

AMANDA: Come back here, Tom Wingfield! I'm not through talking to you!

TOM: Oh, go —

LAURA (*desperately*): Tom!

AMANDA: You're going to listen, and no more insolence from you! I'm at the end of my patience! (*He comes back toward her.*)

TOM: What do you think I'm at? Aren't I supposed to have any patience to reach the end of, Mother? I know, I know. It seems unimportant to you, what I'm *doing* — what I *want* to do — having a little *difference* between them! You don't think that —

AMANDA: I think you've been doing things that you're ashamed of. That's why you act like this. I don't believe that you go every night to the movies. Nobody goes to the movies night after night. Nobody in their right minds goes to the movies as often as you pretend to. People don't go to the movies at nearly midnight, and movies don't let out at two A.M. Come in stumbling. Muttering to yourself like a maniac! You get three hours' sleep and then go to work. Oh, I can picture the way you're doing down there. Moping, doping, because you're in no condition.

TOM (*wildly*): No, I'm in no condition!

Mr. Lawrence: D. H. Lawrence (1885–1930), English writer who propounded free sexuality.

AMANDA: What right have you got to jeopardize your job? Jeopardize the security of us all? How do you think we'd manage if you were —

TOM: Listen! You think I'm crazy *about* the *warehouse!* (*He bends fiercely toward her slight figure.*) You think I'm in love with the Continental Shoemakers? You think I want to spend fifty-five *years* down there in that — *celotex interior!* with — *fluorescent* — *tubes!* Look! I'd rather somebody picked up a crowbar and battered out my brains — than go back mornings! I *go!* Every time you come in yelling that God damn *"Rise and Shine!" "Rise and Shine!"* I say to myself "How *lucky dead* people are!" But I get up. I *go!* For sixty-five dollars a month I give up all that I dream of doing and being *ever!* And you say self — *self*'s all I ever think of. Why, listen, if self is what I thought of, Mother, I'd be where he is — ! (*Pointing to father's picture.*) As far as the system of transportation reaches! (*He starts past her. She grabs his arm.*) Don't grab at me, Mother!

AMANDA: Where are you going?

TOM: I'm going to the *movies!*

AMANDA: I don't believe that lie!

TOM (*crouching toward her, overtowering her tiny figure. She backs away, gasping*): I'm going to opium dens! Yes, opium dens, dens of vice and criminals' hang-outs, Mother. I've joined the Hogan gang, I'm a hired assassin, I carry a tommy-gun in a violin case! I run a string of cat-houses in the Valley! They call me Killer, Killer Wingfield, I'm leading a double-life, a simple, honest warehouse worker by day, by night a dynamic *czar* of the *underworld, Mother.* I go to gambling casinos, I spin away fortunes on the roulette table! I wear a patch over one eye and a false mustache, sometimes I put on green whiskers. On those occasions they call me — *El Diablo!*° Oh, I could tell you things to make you sleepless! My enemies plan to dynamite this place. They're going to blow us all sky-high some night! I'll be glad, very happy, and so will you! You'll go up, up on a broomstick, over Blue Mountain with seventeen gentlemen callers! You ugly — babbling old — *witch. . . .* (*He goes through a series of violent, clumsy movements, seizing his overcoat, lunging to the door, pulling it fiercely open. The women watch him, aghast. His arm catches in the sleeve of the coat as he struggles to pull it on. For a moment he is pinioned by the bulky garment. With an outraged groan he tears the coat off again, splitting the shoulders of it, and hurls it across the room. It strikes against the shelf of Laura's glass collection, there is a tinkle of shattering glass. Laura cries out as if wounded.*)

(*Music legend: "The Glass Menagerie."*)

LAURA (*shrilly*): *My glass!* — menagerie. . . . (*She covers her face and turns away.*)

But Amanda is still stunned and stupefied by the "ugly witch" so that she barely notices this occurrence. Now she recovers her speech.

AMANDA (*in an awful voice*): I won't speak to you — until you apologize! (*She crosses through portieres and draws them together behind her. Tom is left with*

El Diablo: The devil (Spanish).

Laura. Laura clings weakly to the mantel with her face averted. Tom stares at her stupidly for a moment. Then he crosses to shelf. Drops awkwardly to his knees to collect the fallen glass, glancing at Laura as if he would speak but couldn't.)

"The Glass Menagerie" steals in as

(*The scene dims out.*)

SCENE IV

The interior is dark. Faint light in the alley.

A deep-voiced bell in a church is tolling the hour of five as the scene commences.

Tom appears at the top of the alley. After each solemn boom of the bell in the tower, he shakes a little noise-maker or rattle as if to express the tiny spasm of man in contrast to the sustained power and dignity of the Almighty. This and the unsteadiness of his advance make it evident that he has been drinking.

As he climbs the few steps to the fire-escape landing light steals up inside. Laura appears in night-dress, observing Tom's empty bed in the front room.

Tom fishes in his pockets for the door-key, removing a motley assortment of articles in the search, including a perfect shower of movie-ticket stubs and an empty bottle. At last he finds the key, but just as he is about to insert it, it slips from his fingers. He strikes a match and crouches below the door.

TOM (*bitterly*): One crack — and it falls through!

Laura opens the door.

LAURA: Tom! Tom, what are you doing?

TOM: Looking for a door-key.

LAURA: Where have you been all this time?

TOM: I have been to the movies.

LAURA: All this time at the movies?

TOM: There was a very long program. There was a Garbo picture and a Mickey Mouse and a travelogue and a newsreel and a preview of coming attractions. And there was an organ solo and a collection for the milk-fund — simultaneously — which ended up in a terrible fight between a fat lady and an usher!

LAURA (*innocently*): Did you have to stay through everything?

TOM: Of course! And, oh, I forgot! There was a big stage show! The headliner on this stage show was Malvolio the Magician. He performed wonderful tricks, many of them, such as pouring water back and forth between pitchers. First it turned to wine and then it turned to beer and then it turned to whiskey. I know it was whiskey it finally turned into because he needed somebody to come up out of the audience to help him, and I came up — both shows! It was Kentucky Straight Bourbon. A very generous fellow, he gave souvenirs. (*He pulls from his back pocket a shimmering rainbow-colored scarf.*) He gave me this. This is his magic scarf. You can have it, Laura. You wave it over a canary cage and you get a bowl of gold-fish. You wave it over the gold-fish bowl and they fly away canaries. . . . But the wonderfullest trick of all was the coffin trick. We nailed him into a coffin and he got out of the coffin without removing one nail. (*He has come inside.*) There is a trick that would come in handy for me — get me out of this 2 by 4 situation! (*Flops onto bed and starts removing shoes.*)

LAURA: Tom — Shhh!

TOM: What you shushing me for?

LAURA: You'll wake up Mother.

TOM: Goody, goody! Pay 'er back for all those "Rise an' Shines." (*Lies down, groaning.*) You know it don't take much intelligence to get yourself into a nailed-up coffin, Laura. But who in hell ever got himself out of one without removing one nail?

As if in answer, the father's grinning photograph lights up.

(*Scene dims out.*)

Immediately following: The church bell is heard striking six. At the sixth stroke the alarm clock goes off in Amanda's room, and after a few moments we hear her calling: "Rise and Shine! Rise and Shine! Laura, go tell your brother to rise and shine!"

TOM (*sitting up slowly*): I'll rise — but I won't shine.

The light increases.

AMANDA: Laura, tell your brother his coffee is ready.

Laura slips into front room.

LAURA: Tom! it's nearly seven. Don't make Mother nervous. (*He stares at her stupidly. Beseechingly.*) Tom, speak to Mother this morning. Make up with her, apologize, speak to her!

TOM: She won't to me. It's her that started not speaking.

LAURA: If you just say you're sorry she'll start speaking.

TOM: Her not speaking — is that such a tragedy?

LAURA: Please — please!

AMANDA (*calling from kitchenette*): Laura, are you going to do what I asked you to do, or do I have to get dressed and go out myself?

LAURA: Going, going — soon as I get on my coat! (*She pulls on a shapeless felt hat with nervous, jerky movement, pleadingly glancing at Tom. Rushes awkwardly for coat. The coat is one of Amanda's, inaccurately made-over, the sleeves too short for Laura.*) Butter and what else?

AMANDA (*entering upstage*): Just butter. Tell them to charge it.

LAURA: Mother, they make such faces when I do that.

AMANDA: Sticks and stones may break my bones, but the expression on Mr. Garfinkel's face won't harm us! Tell your brother his coffee is getting cold.

LAURA (*at door*): Do what I asked you, will you, will you, Tom?

He looks sullenly away.

AMANDA: Laura, go now or just don't go at all!

LAURA (*rushing out*): Going — going! (*A second later she cries out. Tom springs up and crosses to the door. Amanda rushes anxiously in. Tom opens the door.*)

TOM: Laura?

LAURA: I'm all right. I slipped, but I'm all right.

AMANDA (*peering anxiously after her*): If anyone breaks a leg on those fire-escape steps, the landlord ought to be sued for every cent he possesses! (*She shuts door. Remembers she isn't speaking and returns to other room.*)

As Tom enters listlessly for his coffee, she turns her back to him and stands rigidly facing the window on the gloomy gray vault of the areaway. Its light on her face with its aged but childish features is cruelly sharp, satirical as a Daumier° print.

(*Music under: "Ave Maria."*)

Tom glances sheepishly but sullenly at her averted figure and slumps at the table. The coffee is scalding hot; he sips it and gasps and spits it back in the cup. At his gasp, Amanda catches her breath and half turns. Then catches herself and turns back to window.

Tom blows on his coffee, glancing sidewise at his mother. She clears her throat. Tom clears his. He starts to rise. Sinks back down again, scratches his head, clears his throat again. Amanda coughs. Tom raises his cup in both hands to blow on it, his eyes staring over the rim of it at his mother for several moments. Then he slowly sets the cup down and awkwardly and hesitantly rises from the chair.

TOM (*hoarsely*): Mother. I — I apologize. Mother. (*Amanda draws a quick, shuddering breath. Her face works grotesquely. She breaks into childlike tears.*) I'm sorry for what I said, for everything that I said, I didn't mean it.

AMANDA (*sobbingly*): My devotion has made me a witch and so I make myself hateful to my children!

TOM: No, you *don't*.

AMANDA: I worry so much, don't sleep, it makes me nervous!

TOM (*gently*): I understand that.

AMANDA: I've had to put up a solitary battle all these years. But you're my right-hand bower! Don't fall down, don't fail!

TOM (*gently*): I try, Mother.

AMANDA (*with great enthusiasm*): Try and you will SUCCEED! (*The notion makes her breathless.*) Why, you — you're just *full* of natural endowments! Both of my children — they're *unusual* children! Don't you think I know it? I'm so — *proud!* Happy and — feel I've — so much to be thankful for but — Promise me one thing, son!

TOM: What, Mother?

AMANDA: Promise, son, you'll — never be a drunkard!

TOM (*turns to her grinning*): I will never be a drunkard, Mother.

AMANDA: That's what frightened me so, that you'd be drinking! Eat a bowl of Purina!

TOM: Just coffee, Mother.

AMANDA: Shredded wheat biscuit?

TOM: No. No, Mother, just coffee.

AMANDA: You can't put in a day's work on an empty stomach. You've got ten minutes — don't gulp! Drinking too-hot liquids makes cancer of the stomach. . . . Put cream in.

Daumier: Honoré Daumier (1808–1879) was a French caricaturist, lithographer, and painter.

TOM: No, thank you.

AMANDA: To cool it.

TOM: No! No, thank you, I want it black.

AMANDA: I know, but it's not good for you. We have to do all that we can to build ourselves up. In these trying times we live in, all that we have to cling to is — each other. . . . That's why it's so important to — Tom, I — I sent out your sister so I could discuss something with you. If you hadn't spoken I would have spoken to you. (*Sits down.*)

TOM (*gently*): What is it, Mother, that you want to discuss?

AMANDA: Laura!

Tom puts his cup down slowly.

(*Legend on screen: "Laura."*)

(*Music: "The Glass Menagerie."*)

TOM: — Oh. — Laura . . .

AMANDA (*touching his sleeve*): You know how Laura is. So quiet but — still water runs deep! She notices things and I think she — broods about them. (*Tom looks up.*) A few days ago I came in and she was crying.

TOM: What about?

AMANDA: You.

TOM: Me?

AMANDA: She has an idea that you're not happy here.

TOM: What gave her that idea?

AMANDA: What gives her any idea? However, you do act strangely. I — I'm not criticizing, understand *that!* I know your ambitions do not lie in the warehouse, that like everybody in the whole wide world — you've had to — make sacrifices, but — Tom — Tom — life's not easy, it calls for — Spartan endurance! There's so many things in my heart that I cannot describe to you! I've never told you but I — *loved* your father. . . .

TOM (*gently*): I know that, Mother.

AMANDA: And you — when I see you taking after his ways! Staying out late — and — well, you *had* been drinking the night you were in that — terrifying condition! Laura says that you hate the apartment and that you go out nights to get away from it! Is that true, Tom?

TOM: No. You say there's so much in your heart that you can't describe to me. That's true of me, too. There's so much in my heart that I can't describe to *you!* So let's respect each other's —

AMANDA: But, why — *why,* Tom — are you always so *restless?* Where do you go to, nights?

TOM: I — go to the movies.

AMANDA: Why do you go to the movies so much, Tom?

TOM: I go to the movies because — I like adventure. Adventure is something I don't have much of at work, so I go to the movies.

AMANDA: But, Tom, you go to the movies *entirely too much!*

TOM: I like a lot of adventure.

Amanda looks baffled, then hurt. As the familiar inquisition resumes he becomes hard and impatient again. Amanda slips back into her querulous attitude toward him.

(*Image on screen: Sailing vessel with Jolly Roger.*)

AMANDA: Most young men find adventure in their careers.

TOM: Then most young men are not employed in a warehouse.

AMANDA: The world is full of young men employed in warehouses and offices and factories.

TOM: Do all of them find adventure in their careers?

AMANDA: They do or they do without it! Not everybody has a craze for adventure.

TOM: Man is by instinct a lover, a hunter, a fighter, and none of those instincts are given much play at the warehouse!

AMANDA: Man is by instinct! Don't quote instinct to me! Instinct is something that people have got away from! It belongs to animals! Christian adults don't want it!

TOM: What do Christian adults want, then, Mother?

AMANDA: Superior things! Things of the mind and the spirit! Only animals have to satisfy instincts! Surely your aims are somewhat higher than theirs! Than monkeys — pigs —

TOM: I reckon they're not.

AMANDA: You're joking. However, that isn't what I wanted to discuss.

TOM (*rising*): I haven't much time.

AMANDA (*pushing his shoulders*): Sit down.

TOM: You want me to punch in red° at the warehouse, Mother?

AMANDA: You have five minutes. I want to talk about Laura.

(*Legend: "Plans and Provisions."*)

TOM: All right! What about Laura?

AMANDA: We have to be making plans and provisions for her. She's older than you, two years, and nothing has happened. She just drifts along doing nothing. It frightens me terribly how she just drifts along.

TOM: I guess she's the type that people call home girls.

AMANDA: There's no such type, and if there is, it's a pity! That is unless the home is hers, with a husband!

TOM: What?

AMANDA: Oh, I can see the handwriting on the wall as plain as I see the nose in front of my face! It's terrifying! More and more you remind me of your father! He was out all hours without explanation — Then *left! Good-bye!* And me with the bag to hold. I saw that letter you got from the Merchant Marine. I know what you're dreaming of. I'm not standing here blindfolded. Very well, then. Then *do* it! But not till there's somebody to take your place.

TOM: What do you mean?

AMANDA: I mean that as soon as Laura has got somebody to take care of her, married, a home of her own, independent — why, then you'll be free to

---

punch in red: Show up late for work.

go wherever you please, on land, on sea, whichever way the wind blows! But until that time you've got to look out for your sister. I don't say me because I'm old and don't matter! I say for your sister because she's young and dependent. I put her in business college — a dismal failure! Frightened her so it made her sick to her stomach. I took her over to the Young People's League at the church. Another fiasco. She spoke to nobody, nobody spoke to her. Now all she does is fool with those pieces of glass and play those worn-out records. What kind of a life is that for a girl to lead!

TOM: What can I do about it?

AMANDA: Overcome selfishness! Self, self, self is all that you ever think of! (*Tom springs up and crosses to get his coat. It is ugly and bulky. He pulls on a cap with earmuffs.*) Where is your muffler? Put your wool muffler on! (*He snatches it angrily from the closet and tosses it around his neck and pulls both ends tight.*) Tom! I haven't said what I had in mind to ask you.

TOM: I'm too late to —

AMANDA (*catching his arms — very importunately. Then shyly.*): Down at the warehouse, aren't there some — nice young men?

TOM: No!

AMANDA: There *must* be — *some.*

TOM: Mother —

Gesture.

AMANDA: Find out one that's clean-living — doesn't drink and — ask him out for sister!

TOM: What?

AMANDA: For *sister!* To *meet!* Get *acquainted!*

TOM (*stamping to door*): Oh, my *go-osh!*

AMANDA: Will you? (*He opens door. Imploringly.*) Will you? (*He starts down.*) Will you? *Will* you, dear?

TOM (*calling back*): YES!

Amanda closes the door hesitantly and with a troubled but faintly hopeful expression.
(*Screen image:* Glamour *magazine cover.*)
Spot Amanda at phone.

AMANDA: Ella Cartwright? This is Amanda Wingfield! How are you, honey? How is that kidney condition? (*Count five.*) *Horrors!* (*Count five.*) You're a Christian martyr, yes, honey, that's what you are, a Christian martyr! Well, I just happened to notice in my little red book that your subscription to the *Companion* has just run out! I knew that you wouldn't want to miss out on the wonderful serial starting in this new issue. It's by Bessie Mae Hopper, the first thing she's written since *Honeymoon for Three.* Wasn't that a strange and interesting story? Well, this one is even lovelier, I believe. It has a sophisticated society background. It's all about the horsey set on Long Island!

(*Fade out.*)

SCENE V

(*Legend on screen: "Annunciation."*) *Fade with music.*

It is early dusk of a spring evening. Supper has just been finished in the Wingfield apartment. Amanda and Laura in light-colored dresses are removing dishes from the table, in the upstage area, which is shadowy, their movements formalized almost as a dance or ritual, their moving forms as pale and silent as moths.

Tom, in white shirt and trousers, rises from the table and crosses toward the fire-escape.

AMANDA (*as he passes her*): Son, will you do me a favor?

TOM: What?

AMANDA: Comb your hair! You look so pretty when your hair is combed! (*Tom slouches on sofa with evening paper. Enormous caption "Franco Triumphs."*°) There is only one respect in which I would like you to emulate your father.

TOM: What respect is that?

AMANDA: The care he always took of his appearance. He never allowed himself to look untidy. (*He throws down the paper and crosses to fire-escape.*) Where are you going?

TOM: I'm going out to smoke.

AMANDA: You smoke too much. A pack a day at fifteen cents a pack. How much would that amount to in a month? Thirty times fifteen is how much, Tom? Figure it out and you will be astounded at what you could save. Enough to give you a night-school course in accounting at Washington U! Just think what a wonderful thing that would be for you, son!

Tom is unmoved by the thought.

TOM: I'd rather smoke. (*He steps out on landing, letting the screen door slam.*)

AMANDA (*sharply*): I know! That's the tragedy of it. . . . (*Alone, she turns to look at her husband's picture.*)

(*Dance music: "All the World Is Waiting for the Sunrise!"*)

TOM (*to the audience*): Across the alley from us was the Paradise Dance Hall. On evenings in spring the windows and doors were open and the music came outdoors. Sometimes the lights were turned out except for a large glass sphere that hung from the ceiling. It would turn slowly about and filter the dusk with delicate rainbow colors. Then the orchestra played a waltz or a tango, something that had a slow and sensuous rhythm. Couples would come outside, to the relative privacy of the alley. You could see them kissing behind ash-pits and telephone poles. This was the compensation for lives that passed like mine, without any change or adventure. Adventure and change were imminent in this year. They were waiting around the corner for all these kids. Suspended in the mist over the Berchtesgaden,° caught in the folds of Chamberlain's° umbrella —

"Franco Triumphs": In January 1939 Francisco Franco's (1892–1975) victory over the Loyalists ended the Spanish Civil War. **Berchtesgaden:** A resort in the German Alps where Adolf Hitler had a heavily protected villa. **Chamberlain:** Neville Chamberlain (1869–1940) was the British prime minister who sought to avoid war with Hitler through a policy of appeasement.

In Spain there was Guernica! But here there was only hot swing music and liquor, dance halls, bars, and movies, and sex that hung in the gloom like a chandelier and flooded the world with brief, deceptive rainbows. . . . All the world was waiting for bombardments!

Amanda turns from the picture and comes outside.

AMANDA (*sighing*): A fire-escape landing's a poor excuse for a porch. (*She spreads a newspaper on a step and sits down, gracefully and demurely as if she were settling into a swing on a Mississippi veranda.*) What are you looking at?

TOM: The moon.

AMANDA: Is there a moon this evening?

TOM: It's rising over Garfinkel's Delicatessen.

AMANDA: So it is! A little silver slipper of a moon. Have you made a wish on it yet?

TOM: Um-hum.

AMANDA: What did you wish for?

TOM: That's a secret.

AMANDA: A secret, huh? Well, I won't tell mine either. I will be just as mysterious as you.

TOM: I bet I can guess what yours is.

AMANDA: Is my head so transparent?

TOM: You're not a sphinx.

AMANDA: No, I don't have secrets. I'll tell you what I wished for on the moon. Success and happiness for my precious children! I wish for that whenever there's a moon, and when there isn't a moon, I wish for it, too.

TOM: I thought perhaps you wished for a gentleman caller.

AMANDA: Why do you say that?

TOM: Don't you remember asking me to fetch one?

AMANDA: I remember suggesting that it would be nice for your sister if you brought home some nice young man from the warehouse. I think I've made that suggestion more than once.

TOM: Yes, you have made it repeatedly.

AMANDA: Well?

TOM: We are going to have one.

AMANDA: *What?*

TOM: A gentleman caller!

(*The Annunciation is celebrated with music.*)

Amanda rises.

(*Image on screen: Caller with bouquet.*)

AMANDA: You mean you have asked some nice young man to come over?

TOM: Yep. I've asked him to dinner.

AMANDA: You really did?

TOM: I did!

AMANDA: You did, and did he — *accept?*

TOM: He did!

AMANDA: Well, well — well, well! That's — lovely!

TOM: I thought that you would be pleased.

AMANDA: It's definite, then?

TOM: Very definite.

AMANDA: Soon?

TOM: Very soon.

AMANDA: For heaven's sake, stop putting on and tell me some things, will you?

TOM: What things do you want me to tell you?

AMANDA: Naturally I would like to know when he's *coming!*

TOM: He's coming tomorrow.

AMANDA: *Tomorrow?*

TOM: Yep. Tomorrow.

AMANDA: But, Tom!

TOM: Yes, Mother?

AMANDA: Tomorrow gives me no time!

TOM: Time for what?

AMANDA: Preparations! Why didn't you phone me at once, as soon as you asked him, the minute that he accepted? Then, don't you see, I could have been getting ready!

TOM: You don't have to make any fuss.

AMANDA: Oh, Tom, Tom, Tom, of course I have to make a fuss! I want things nice, not sloppy! Not thrown together. I'll certainly have to do some fast thinking, won't I?

TOM: I don't see why you have to think at all.

AMANDA: You just don't know. We can't have a gentleman caller in a pig-sty! All my wedding silver has to be polished, the monogrammed table linen ought to be laundered! The windows have to be washed and fresh curtains put up. And how about clothes? We have to *wear* something, don't we?

TOM: Mother, this boy is no one to make a fuss over!

AMANDA: Do you realize he's the first young man we've introduced to your sister? It's terrible, dreadful, disgraceful that poor little sister has never received a single gentleman caller! Tom, come inside! (*She opens the screen door.*)

TOM: What for?

AMANDA: I want to ask you some things.

TOM: If you're going to make such a fuss, I'll call it off, I'll tell him not to come.

AMANDA: You certainly won't do anything of the kind. Nothing offends people worse than broken engagements. It simply means I'll have to work like a Turk! We won't be brilliant, but we'll pass inspection. Come on inside. (*Tom follows, groaning.*) Sit down.

TOM: Any particular place you would like me to sit?

AMANDA: Thank heavens I've got that new sofa! I'm also making payments on a floor lamp I'll have sent out! And put the chintz covers on, they'll brighten things up! Of course I'd hoped to have these walls re-papered. . . . What is the young man's name?

TOM: His name is O'Connor.

AMANDA: That, of course, means fish — tomorrow is Friday! I'll have that salmon loaf — with Durkee's dressing! What does he do? He works at the warehouse?

TOM: Of course! How else would I —

AMANDA: Tom, he — doesn't drink?

TOM: Why do you ask me that?

AMANDA: Your father *did!*

TOM: Don't get started on that!

AMANDA: He *does* drink, then?

TOM: Not that I know of!

AMANDA: Make sure, be certain! The last thing I want for my daughter's a boy who drinks!

TOM: Aren't you being a little premature? Mr. O'Connor has not yet appeared on the scene!

AMANDA: But will tomorrow. To meet your sister, and what do I know about his character? Nothing! Old maids are better off than wives of drunkards!

TOM: Oh, my God!

AMANDA: Be still!

TOM (*leaning forward to whisper*): Lots of fellows meet girls whom they don't marry!

AMANDA: Oh, talk sensibly, Tom — and don't be sarcastic! (*She has gotten a hairbrush.*)

TOM: What are you doing?

AMANDA: I'm brushing that cow-lick down! What is this young man's position at the warehouse?

TOM (*submitting grimly to the brush and the interrogation*): This young man's position is that of a shipping clerk, Mother.

AMANDA: Sounds to me like a fairly responsible job, the sort of a job *you* would be in if you just had more *get-up.* What is his salary? Have you got any idea?

TOM: I would judge it to be approximately eighty-five dollars a month.

AMANDA: Well — not princely, but —

TOM: Twenty more than I make.

AMANDA: Yes, how well I know! But for a family man, eighty-five dollars a month is not much more than you can just get by on. . . .

TOM: Yes, but Mr. O'Connor is not a family man.

AMANDA: He might be, mightn't he? Some time in the future?

TOM: I see. Plans and provisions.

AMANDA: You are the only young man that I know of who ignores the fact that the future becomes the present, the present the past, and the past turns into everlasting regret if you don't plan for it!

TOM: I will think that over and see what I can make of it.

AMANDA: Don't be supercilious with your mother! Tell me some more about this — what do you call him?

TOM: James D. O'Connor. The D. is for Delaney.

AMANDA: Irish on *both* sides! *Gracious!* And doesn't drink?

TOM: Shall I call him up and ask him right this minute?

AMANDA: The only way to find out about those things is to make discreet inquiries at the proper moment. When I was a girl in Blue Mountain and it was suspected that a young man drank, the girl whose attentions he had been receiving, if any girl *was,* would sometimes speak to the minister of his church, or rather her father would if her father was living, and sort of feel him out on the young man's character. That is the way such things are discreetly handled to keep a young woman from making a tragic mistake!

TOM: Then how did you happen to make a tragic mistake?

AMANDA: That innocent look of your father's had everyone fooled! He *smiled* — the world was *enchanted!* No girl can do worse than put herself at the mercy of a handsome appearance! I hope that Mr. O'Connor is not too good-looking.

TOM: No, he's not too good-looking. He's covered with freckles and hasn't too much of a nose.

AMANDA: He's not right-down homely, though?

TOM: Not right-down homely. Just medium homely, I'd say.

AMANDA: Character's what to look for in a man.

TOM: That's what I've always said, Mother.

AMANDA: You've never said anything of the kind and I suspect you would never give it a thought.

TOM: Don't be suspicious of me.

AMANDA: At least I hope he's the type that's up and coming.

TOM: I think he really goes in for self-improvement.

AMANDA: What reason have you to think so?

TOM: He goes to night school.

AMANDA (*beaming*): Splendid! What does he do, I mean study?

TOM: Radio engineering and public speaking!

AMANDA: Then he has visions of being advanced in the world! Any young man who studies public speaking is aiming to have an executive job some day! And radio engineering? A thing for the future! Both of these facts are very illuminating. Those are the sort of things that a mother should know concerning any young man who comes to call on her daughter. Seriously or — not.

TOM: One little warning. He doesn't know about Laura. I didn't let on that we had dark ulterior motives. I just said, why don't you come have dinner with us? He said okay and that was the whole conversation.

AMANDA: I bet it was! You're eloquent as an oyster. However, he'll know about Laura when he gets here. When he sees how lovely and sweet and pretty she is, he'll thank his lucky stars he was asked to dinner.

TOM: Mother, you mustn't expect too much of Laura.

AMANDA: What do you mean?

TOM: Laura seems all those things to you and me because she's ours and we love her. We don't even notice she's crippled any more.

AMANDA: Don't say crippled! You know that I never allow that word to be used!

TOM: But face facts, Mother. She is and — that's not all —

AMANDA: What do you mean "not all"?

TOM: Laura is very different from other girls.

AMANDA: I think the difference is all to her advantage.

TOM: Not quite all — in the eyes of others — strangers — she's terribly shy and lives in a world of her own and those things make her seem a little peculiar to people outside the house.

AMANDA: Don't say peculiar.

TOM: Face the facts. She is.

(*The dance-hall music changes to a tango that has a minor and somewhat ominous tone.*)

AMANDA: In what way is she peculiar — may I ask?

TOM (*gently*): She lives in a world of her own — a world of — little glass ornaments, Mother. . . . (*Gets up. Amanda remains holding brush, looking at him, troubled.*) She plays old phonograph records and — that's about all — (*He glances at himself in the mirror and crosses to door.*)

AMANDA (*sharply*): Where are you going?

TOM: I'm going to the movies. (*Out screen door.*)

AMANDA: Not to the movies, every night to the movies! (*Follows quickly to screen door.*) I don't believe you always go to the movies! (*He is gone. Amanda looks worriedly after him for a moment. Then vitality and optimism return and she turns from the door. Crossing to portieres.*) Laura! Laura! (*Laura answers from kitchenette.*)

LAURA: Yes, Mother.

AMANDA: Let those dishes go and come in front! (*Laura appears with dish towel. Gaily.*) Laura, come here and make a wish on the moon!

LAURA (*entering*): Moon — moon?

AMANDA: A little silver slipper of a moon. Look over your left shoulder, Laura, and make a wish! (*Laura looks faintly puzzled as if called out of sleep. Amanda seizes her shoulders and turns her at angle by the door.*) Now! Now, darling, *wish!*

LAURA: What shall I wish for, Mother?

AMANDA (*her voice trembling and her eyes suddenly filling with tears*): Happiness! Good Fortune!

The violin rises and the stage dims out.

SCENE VI

(*Image: High-school hero.*)

TOM: And so the following evening I brought Jim home to dinner. I had known Jim slightly in high school. In high school Jim was a hero. He had tremendous Irish good nature and vitality with the scrubbed and polished look of white chinaware. He seemed to move in a continual spotlight. He was a star in basketball, captain of the debating club, president of the senior class and the glee club and he sang the male lead in the annual light operas. He was always running or bounding, never just walking. He seemed always at the point of defeating the law of gravity. He was shooting with such velocity through his adolescence that you would logically expect him to arrive at nothing short of the White House by the time he was thirty. But Jim apparently ran into more interference after his graduation from Soldan. His speed had definitely slowed. Six years after he left high school he was holding a job that wasn't much better than mine.

(*Image: Clerk.*)

He was the only one at the warehouse with whom I was on friendly terms. I was valuable to him as someone who could remember his former glory, who had seen him win basketball games and the silver cup in debating. He knew of my secret practice of retiring to a cabinet of the washroom to work on poems when business was slack in the warehouse. He called me Shakespeare. And while the other boys in the warehouse regarded me with suspicious hostility, Jim took a humorous attitude toward me. Gradually his attitude affected the others, their hostility wore off, and they also began to smile at me as people smile at an oddly fashioned dog who trots across their paths at some distance.

I knew that Jim and Laura had known each other at Soldan, and I had heard Laura speak admiringly of his voice. I didn't know if Jim remembered her or not. In high school Laura had been as unobtrusive as Jim had been astonishing. If he did remember Laura, it was not as my sister, for when I asked him to dinner, he grinned and said, "You know, Shakespeare, I never thought of you as having folks!"

He was about to discover that I did. . . .

(*Light upstage.*)

(*Legend on screen: "The Accent of a Coming Foot."*)

Friday evening. It is about five o'clock of a late spring evening which comes "scattering poems in the sky."

A delicate lemony light is in the Wingfield apartment.

Amanda has worked like a Turk in preparation for the gentleman caller. The results are astonishing. The new floor lamp with its rose-silk shade is in place, a colored paper lantern conceals the broken light fixture in the ceiling, new billowing white curtains are at the windows, chintz covers are on chairs and sofa, a pair of new sofa pillows make their initial appearance.

Open boxes and tissue paper are scattered on the floor.

Laura stands in the middle with lifted arms while Amanda crouches before her, adjusting the hem of the new dress, devout and ritualistic. The dress is colored and designed by memory. The arrangement of Laura's hair is changed; it is softer and more becoming. A fragile, unearthly prettiness has come out in Laura: she is like a piece of translucent glass touched by light, given a momentary radiance, not actual, not lasting.

AMANDA (*impatiently*): Why are you trembling?

LAURA: Mother, you've made me so nervous!

AMANDA: How have I made you nervous?

LAURA: By all this fuss! You make it seem so important!

AMANDA: I don't understand you, Laura. You couldn't be satisfied with just sitting home, and yet whenever I try to arrange something for you, you seem to resist it. (*She gets up.*) Now take a look at yourself. No, wait! Wait just a moment — I have an idea!

LAURA: What is it now?

Amanda produces two powder puffs which she wraps in handkerchiefs and stuffs in Laura's bosom.

LAURA: Mother, what are you doing?

AMANDA: They call them "Gay Deceivers"!

LAURA: I won't wear them!

AMANDA: You will!

LAURA: Why should I?

AMANDA: Because, to be painfully honest, your chest is flat.

LAURA: You make it seem like we were setting a trap.

AMANDA: All pretty girls are a trap, a pretty trap, and men expect them to be. (*Legend: "A Pretty Trap."*) Now look at yourself, young lady. This is the prettiest you will ever be! I've got to fix myself now! You're going to be surprised by your mother's appearance! (*She crosses through portieres, humming gaily.*)

Laura moves slowly to the long mirror and stares solemnly at herself.

A wind blows the white curtains inward in a slow, graceful motion and with a faint, sorrowful sighing.

AMANDA (*offstage*): It isn't dark enough yet. (*She turns slowly before the mirror with a troubled look*).

(*Legend on screen: "This Is My Sister: Celebrate Her with Strings!" Music.*)

AMANDA (*laughing, off*): I'm going to show you something. I'm going to make a spectacular appearance!

LAURA: What is it, Mother?

AMANDA: Possess your soul in patience — you will see! Something I've resurrected from that old trunk! Styles haven't changed so terribly much after all. . . . (*She parts the portieres.*) Now just look at your mother! (*She wears a girlish frock of yellowed voile with a blue silk sash. She carries a bunch of jonquils — the legend of her youth is nearly revived. Feverishly.*) This is the dress in which I led the cotillion. Won the cakewalk twice at Sunset Hill, wore one spring to the Governor's ball in Jackson! See how I sashayed around the ballroom, Laura? (*She raises her skirt and does a mincing step around the room.*) I wore it on Sundays for my gentlemen callers! I had it on the day I met your father — I had malaria fever all that spring. The change of climate from East Tennessee to the Delta — weakened resistance — I had a little temperature all the time — not enough to be serious — just enough to make me restless and giddy! Invitations poured in — parties all over the Delta! — "Stay in bed," said Mother, "you have fever!" — but I just wouldn't. — I took quinine but kept on going, going! — Evenings, dances! — Afternoons, long, long rides! Picnics — lovely! — So lovely, that country in May. — All lacy with dogwood, literally flooded with jonquils! — That was the spring I had the craze for jonquils. Jonquils became an absolute obsession. Mother said, "Honey, there's no more room for jonquils." And still I kept bringing in more jonquils. Whenever, wherever I saw them, I'd say, "Stop! Stop! I see jonquils!" I made the young men help me gather the jonquils! It was a joke, Amanda and her jonquils! Finally there were no more vases to hold them, every available space was filled with jonquils. No vases to hold them? All right, I'll hold them myself! And then I — (*She stops in front of the picture.*) (*Music.*) met your father! Malaria fever and jonquils and then — this — boy. . . . (*She switches on the rose-colored lamp.*) I hope they get here before it starts to rain. (*She crosses upstage and places the jonquils in bowl on table.*) I gave your brother a little extra change so he and Mr. O'Connor could take the service car home.

LAURA (*with altered look*): What did you say his name was?

AMANDA: O'Connor.

LAURA: What is his first name?

AMANDA: I don't remember. Oh, yes, I do. It was — Jim!

Laura sways slightly and catches hold of a chair.

(*Legend on screen: "Not Jim!"*)

LAURA (*faintly*): Not — Jim!

AMANDA: Yes, that was it, it was Jim! I've never known a Jim that wasn't nice!

(*Music: Ominous.*)

LAURA: Are you sure his name is Jim O'Connor?

AMANDA: Yes. Why?

LAURA: Is he the one that Tom used to know in high school?

AMANDA: He didn't say so. I think he just got to know him at the warehouse.

LAURA: There was a Jim O'Connor we both knew in high school — (*Then, with effort.*) If that is the one that Tom is bringing to dinner — you'll have to excuse me, I won't come to the table.

AMANDA: What sort of nonsense is this?

LAURA: You asked me once if I'd ever liked a boy. Don't you remember I showed you this boy's picture?

AMANDA: You mean the boy you showed me in the year-book?

LAURA: Yes, that boy.

AMANDA: Laura, Laura, were you in love with that boy?

LAURA: I don't know, Mother. All I know is I couldn't sit at the table if it was him!

AMANDA: It won't be him! It isn't the least bit likely. But whether it is or not, you will come to the table. You will not be excused.

LAURA: I'll have to be, Mother.

AMANDA: I don't intend to humor your silliness, Laura. I've had too much from you and your brother, both! So just sit down and compose yourself till they come. Tom has forgotten his key so you'll have to let them in, when they arrive.

LAURA (*panicky*): Oh, Mother — *you* answer the door!

AMANDA (*lightly*): I'll be in the kitchen — busy!

LAURA: Oh, Mother, please answer the door, don't make me do it!

AMANDA (*crossing into kitchenette*): I've got to fix the dressing for the salmon. Fuss, fuss — silliness! — over a gentleman caller!

Door swings shut. Laura is left alone.

(*Legend: "Terror!"*)

She utters a low moan and turns off the lamp — sits stiffly on the edge of the sofa, knotting her fingers together.

(*Legend on screen: "The Opening of a Door!"*)

Tom and Jim appear on the fire-escape steps and climb to landing. Hearing their approach, Laura rises with a panicky gesture. She retreats to the portieres.

The doorbell. Laura catches her breath and touches her throat. Low drums.

AMANDA (*calling*): Laura, sweetheart! The door!

Laura stares at it without moving.

JIM: I think we just beat the rain.

TOM: Uh-huh. (*He rings again, nervously. Jim whistles and fishes for a cigarette.*)

AMANDA (*very, very gaily*): Laura, that is your brother and Mr. O'Connor! Will you let them in, darling?

Laura crosses toward kitchenette door.

LAURA (*breathlessly*): Mother — you go to the door!

Amanda steps out of kitchenette and stares furiously at Laura. She points imperiously at the door.

LAURA: Please, please!

AMANDA (*in a fierce whisper*): What is the matter with you, you silly thing?

LAURA (*desperately*): Please, you answer it, *please!*

AMANDA: I told you I wasn't going to humor you, Laura. Why have you chosen this moment to lose your mind?

LAURA: Please, please, please, you go!

AMANDA: You'll have to go to the door because I can't!

LAURA (*despairingly*): I can't either!

AMANDA: Why?

LAURA: I'm *sick!*

AMANDA: I'm sick, too — of your nonsense! Why can't you and your brother be normal people? Fantastic whims and behavior! (*Tom gives a long ring.*) Preposterous goings on! Can you give me one reason — (*Calls out lyrically.*) COMING! JUST ONE SECOND! — why should you be afraid to open a door? Now you answer it, Laura!

LAURA: Oh, oh, oh . . . (*She returns through the portieres. Darts to the Victrola and winds it frantically and turns it on.*)

AMANDA: Laura Wingfield, you march right to that door!

LAURA: Yes — yes, Mother!

A faraway, scratchy rendition of "Dardanella" softens the air and gives her strength to move through it. She slips to the door and draws it cautiously open.

Tom enters with the caller, Jim O'Connor.

TOM: Laura, this is Jim. Jim, this is my sister, Laura.

JIM (*stepping inside*): I didn't know that Shakespeare had a sister!

LAURA (*retreating stiff and trembling from the door*): How — how do you do?

JIM (*heartily extending his hand*): Okay!

Laura touches it hesitantly with hers.

JIM: Your hand's *cold,* Laura!

LAURA: Yes, well — I've been playing the Victrola . . .

JIM: Must have been playing classical music on it! You ought to play a little hot swing music to warm you up!

LAURA: Excuse me — I haven't finished playing the Victrola . . .

She turns awkwardly and hurries into the front room. She pauses a second by the Victrola. Then catches her breath and darts through the portieres like a frightened deer.

JIM (*grinning*): What was the matter?

TOM: Oh — with Laura? Laura is — terribly shy.

JIM: Shy, huh? It's unusual to meet a shy girl nowadays. I don't believe you ever mentioned you had a sister.

TOM: Well, now you know. I have one. Here is the *Post Dispatch.* You want a piece of it?

JIM: Uh-huh.

TOM: What piece? The comics?

JIM: Sports! (*Glances at it.*) Ole Dizzy Dean is on his bad behavior.

TOM (*disinterest*): Yeah? (*Lights cigarette and crosses back to fire-escape door.*)

JIM: Where are *you* going?

TOM: I'm going out on the terrace.

JIM (*goes after him*): You know, Shakespeare — I'm going to sell you a bill of goods!

TOM: What goods?

JIM: A course I'm taking.

TOM: Huh?

JIM: In public speaking! You and me, we're not the warehouse type.

TOM: Thanks — that's good news. But what has public speaking got to do with it?

JIM: It fits you for — executive positions!

TOM: Awww.

JIM: I tell you it's done a helluva lot for me.

(*Image: Executive at desk.*)

TOM: In what respect?

JIM: In every! Ask yourself what is the difference between you an' me and men in the office down front? Brains? — No! — Ability? — No! Then what? Just one little thing —

TOM: What is that one little thing?

JIM: Primarily it amounts to — social poise! Being able to square up to people and hold your own on any social level!

AMANDA (*offstage*): Tom?

TOM: Yes, Mother?

AMANDA: Is that you and Mr. O'Connor?

TOM: Yes, Mother.

AMANDA: Well, you just make yourselves comfortable in there.

TOM: Yes, Mother.

AMANDA: Ask Mr. O'Connor if he would like to wash his hands.

JIM: Aw — no — no — thank you — I took care of that at the warehouse. Tom —
TOM: Yes?
JIM: Mr. Mendoza was speaking to me about you.
TOM: Favorably?
JIM: What do you think?
TOM: Well —
JIM: You're going to be out of a job if you don't wake up.
TOM: I am waking up —
JIM: You show no signs.
TOM: The signs are interior.

(*Image on screen: The sailing vessel with Jolly Roger again.*)

TOM: I'm planning to change. (*He leans over the rail speaking with quiet exhilaration. The incandescent marquees and signs of the first-run movie houses light his face from across the alley. He looks like a voyager.*) I'm right at the point of committing myself to a future that doesn't include the warehouse and Mr. Mendoza or even a night-school course in public speaking.
JIM: What are you gassing about?
TOM: I'm tired of the movies.
JIM: Movies!
TOM: Yes, movies! Look at them — (*A wave toward the marvels of Grand Avenue.*) All of those glamorous people — having adventures — hogging it all, gobbling the whole thing up! You know what happens? People go to the *movies* instead of *moving!* Hollywood characters are supposed to have all the adventures for everybody in America, while everybody in America sits in a dark room and watches them have them! Yes, until there's a war. That's when adventure becomes available to the masses! *Everyone's* dish, not only Gable's! Then the people in the dark room come out of the dark room to have some adventures themselves — Goody, goody — It's our turn now, to go to the South Sea Island — to make a safari — to be exotic, far-off — But I'm not patient. I don't want to wait till then. I'm tired of the *movies* and I am *about* to *move!*
JIM (*incredulously*): Move?
TOM: Yes.
JIM: When?
TOM: Soon!
JIM: Where? Where?

(*Theme three: Music seems to answer the question, while Tom thinks it over. He searches among his pockets.*)

TOM: I'm starting to boil inside. I know I seem dreamy, but inside — well, I'm boiling! Whenever I pick up a shoe, I shudder a little thinking how short life is and what I am doing! — Whatever that means. I know it doesn't mean shoes — except as something to wear on a traveler's feet! (*Finds paper.*) Look —
JIM: What?
TOM: I'm a member.

JIM (*reading*): The Union of Merchant Seamen.

TOM: I paid my dues this month, instead of the light bill.

JIM: You will regret it when they turn the lights off.

TOM: I won't be here.

JIM: How about your mother?

TOM: I'm like my father. The bastard son of a bastard! See how he grins? And he's been absent going on sixteen years!

JIM: You're just talking, you drip. How does your mother feel about it?

TOM: Shhh — Here comes Mother! Mother is not acquainted with my plans!

AMANDA (*enters portieres*): Where are you all?

TOM: On the terrace, Mother.

They start inside. She advances to them. Tom is distinctly shocked at her appearance. Even Jim blinks a little. He is making his first contact with girlish Southern vivacity and in spite of the night-school course in public speaking is somewhat thrown off the beam by the unexpected outlay of social charm.

Certain responses are attempted by Jim but are swept aside by Amanda's gay laughter and chatter. Tom is embarrassed but after the first shock Jim reacts very warmly. Grins and chuckles, is altogether won over.

(Image: Amanda as a girl.)

AMANDA (*coyly smiling, shaking her girlish ringlets*): Well, well, well, so this is Mr. O'Connor. Introductions entirely unnecessary. I've heard so much about you from my boy. I finally said to him, Tom — good gracious! — why don't you bring this paragon to supper? I'd like to meet this nice young man at the warehouse! — Instead of just hearing him sing your praises so much! I don't know why my son is so stand-offish — that's not Southern behavior! Let's sit down and — I think we could stand a little more air in here! Tom, leave the door open. I felt a nice fresh breeze a moment ago. Where has it gone? Mmm, so warm already! And not quite summer, even. We're going to burn up when summer really gets started. However, we're having — we're having a very light supper. I think light things are better fo' this time of year. The same as light clothes are. Light clothes an' light food are what warm weather calls fo'. You know our blood gets so thick during th' winter — it takes a while fo' us to *adjust* ou'selves! — when the season changes. . . . It's come so quick this year. I wasn't prepared. All of a sudden — heavens! Already summer! — I ran to the trunk an' pulled out this light dress — Terribly old! Historical almost! But feels so good — so good an' co-ol, y'know. . . .

TOM: Mother —

AMANDA: Yes, honey?

TOM: How about — supper?

AMANDA: Honey, you go ask Sister if supper is ready! You know that Sister is in full charge of supper! Tell her you hungry boys are waiting for it. (*To Jim.*) Have you met Laura?

JIM: She —

AMANDA: Let you in? Oh, good, you've met already! It's rare for a girl as sweet an' pretty as Laura to be domestic! But Laura is, thank heavens, not only pretty but also very domestic. I'm not at all. I never was a bit. I never could make a thing but angel-food cake. Well, in the South we had so many servants. Gone, gone, gone. All vestiges of gracious living! Gone completely! I wasn't prepared for what the future brought me. All of my gentlemen callers were sons of planters and so of course I assumed that I would be married to one and raise my family on a large piece of land with plenty of servants. But man proposes — and woman accepts the proposal! — To vary that old, old saying a little bit — I married no planter! I married a man who worked for the telephone company! — that gallantly smiling gentleman over there! (*Points to the picture.*) A telephone man who — fell in love with long distance! — Now he travels and I don't even know where! — But what am I going on for about my — tribulations! Tell me yours — I hope you don't have any! Tom?

TOM (*returning*): Yes, Mother?

AMANDA: Is supper nearly ready?

TOM: It looks to me like supper is on the table.

AMANDA: Let me look — (*She rises prettily and looks through portieres.*) Oh, lovely — But where is Sister?

TOM: Laura is not feeling well and she says that she thinks she'd better not come to the table.

AMANDA: What? — Nonsense! — Laura? Oh, Laura!

LAURA (*offstage, faintly*): Yes, Mother.

AMANDA: You really must come to the table. We won't be seated until you come to the table! Come in, Mr. O'Connor. You sit over there and I'll — Laura? Laura Wingfield! You're keeping us waiting, honey! We can't say grace until you come to the table!

The back door is pushed weakly open and Laura comes in. She is obviously quite faint, her lips trembling, her eyes wide and staring. She moves unsteadily toward the table.

(*Legend: "Terror!"*)

Outside a summer storm is coming abruptly. The white curtains billow inward at the windows and there is a sorrowful murmur and deep blue dusk.

Laura suddenly stumbles — She catches at a chair with a faint moan.

TOM: Laura!

AMANDA: Laura! (*There is a clap of thunder.*) (*Legend: "Ah!"*) (*Despairingly.*) Why, Laura, you *are* sick, darling! Tom, help your sister into the living room, dear! Sit in the living room, Laura — rest on the sofa. Well! (*To the gentleman caller.*) Standing over the hot stove made her ill! — I told her that it was just too warm this evening, but — (*Tom comes back in. Laura is on the sofa.*) Is Laura all right now?

TOM: Yes.

AMANDA: What *is* that? Rain? A nice cool rain has come up! (*She gives the gentleman caller a frightened look.*) I think we may — have grace — now . . . (*Tom looks at her stupidly.*) Tom, honey — you say grace!

TOM: Oh . . . "For these and all thy mercies — " (*They bow their heads, Amanda stealing a nervous glance at Jim. In the living room Laura, stretched on the sofa, clenches her hand to her lips, to hold back a shuddering sob.*) God's Holy Name be praised —

(*The scene dims out.*)

SCENE VII

A Souvenir

Half an hour later. Dinner is just being finished in the upstage area, which is concealed by the drawn portieres.

As the curtain rises Laura is still huddled upon the sofa, her feet drawn under her, her head resting on a pale blue pillow, her eyes wide and mysteriously watchful. The new floor lamp with its shade of rose-colored silk gives a soft, becoming light to her face, bringing out the fragile, unearthly prettiness which usually escapes attention. There is a steady murmur of rain, but it is slackening and stops soon after the scene begins; the air outside becomes pale and luminous as the moon breaks out.

A moment after the curtain rises, the lights in both rooms flicker and go out.

JIM: Hey, there, Mr. Light Bulb!

Amanda laughs nervously.

(*Legend: "Suspension of a Public Service."*)

AMANDA: Where was Moses when the lights went out? Ha-ha. Do you know the answer to that one, Mr. O'Connor?

JIM: No, Ma'am, what's the answer?

AMANDA: In the dark! (*Jim laughs appreciatively.*) Everybody sit still. I'll light the candles. Isn't it lucky we have them on the table? Where's a match? Which of you gentlemen can provide a match?

JIM: Here.

AMANDA: Thank you, sir.

JIM: Not at all, Ma'am!

AMANDA: I guess the fuse has burnt out. Mr. O'Connor, can you tell a burnt-out fuse? I know I can't and Tom is a total loss when it comes to mechanics. (*Sound: Getting up: Voices recede a little to kitchenette.*) Oh, be careful you don't bump into something. We don't want our gentleman caller to break his neck. Now wouldn't that be a fine howdy-do?

JIM: Ha-ha! Where is the fuse-box?

AMANDA: Right here next to the stove. Can you see anything?

JIM: Just a minute.

AMANDA: Isn't electricity a mysterious thing? Wasn't it Benjamin Franklin who tied a key to a kite? We live in such a mysterious universe, don't we? Some people say that science clears up all the mysteries for us. In my opinion it only creates more! Have you found it yet?

JIM: No, Ma'am. All these fuses look okay to me.

AMANDA: Tom!

TOM: Yes, Mother?

AMANDA: That light bill I gave you several days ago. The one I told you we got the notices about?

TOM: Oh. — Yeah.

(Legend: "Ha!")

AMANDA: You didn't neglect to pay it by any chance?

TOM: Why, I —

AMANDA: Didn't! I might have known it!

JIM: Shakespeare probably wrote a poem on that light bill, Mrs. Wingfield.

AMANDA: I might have known better than to trust him with it! There's such a high price for negligence in this world!

JIM: Maybe the poem will win a ten-dollar prize.

AMANDA: We'll just have to spend the remainder of the evening in the nineteenth century, before Mr. Edison made the Mazda lamp!

JIM: Candlelight is my favorite kind of light.

AMANDA: That shows you're romantic! But that's no excuse for Tom. Well, we got through dinner. Very considerate of them to let us get through dinner before they plunged us into everlasting darkness, wasn't it, Mr. O'Connor?

JIM: Ha-ha!

AMANDA: Tom, as a penalty for your carelessness you can help me with the dishes.

JIM: Let me give you a hand.

AMANDA: Indeed you will not!

JIM: I ought to be good for something.

AMANDA: Good for something? *(Her tone is rhapsodic.)* *You?* Why, Mr. O'Connor, nobody, *nobody's* given me this much entertainment in years — as you have!

JIM: Aw, now, Mrs. Wingfield!

AMANDA: I'm not exaggerating, not one bit! But Sister is all by her lonesome. You go keep her company in the parlor! I'll give you this lovely old candelabrum that used to be on the altar at the church of the Heavenly Rest. It was melted a little out of shape when the church burnt down. Lightning struck it one spring. Gypsy Jones was holding a revival at the time and he intimated that the church was destroyed because the Episcopalians gave card parties.

JIM: Ha-ha.

AMANDA: And how about coaxing Sister to drink a little wine? I think it would be good for her! Can you carry both at once?

JIM: Sure. I'm Superman!

AMANDA: Now, Thomas, get into this apron!

The door of kitchenette swings closed on Amanda's gay laughter; the flickering light approaches the portieres.

Laura sits up nervously as he enters. Her speech at first is low and breathless from the almost intolerable strain of being alone with a stranger.

(Legend: "I Don't Suppose You Remember Me at All!")

In her first speeches in this scene, before Jim's warmth overcomes her paralyzing shyness, Laura's voice is thin and breathless as though she has run up a steep flight of stairs.

Jim's attitude is gently humorous. In playing this scene it should be stressed that while the incident is apparently unimportant, it is to Laura the climax of her secret life.

JIM: Hello, there, Laura.
LAURA (*faintly*): Hello. (*She clears her throat.*)
JIM: How are you feeling now? Better?
LAURA: Yes. Yes, thank you.
JIM: This is for you. A little dandelion wine. (*He extends it toward her with extravagant gallantry.*)
LAURA: Thank you.
JIM: Drink it — but don't get drunk! (*He laughs heartily. Laura takes the glass uncertainly; laughs shyly.*) Where shall I set the candles?
LAURA: Oh — oh, anywhere . . .
JIM: How about here on the floor? Any objections?
LAURA: No.
JIM: I'll spread a newspaper under to catch the drippings. I like to sit on the floor. Mind if I do?
LAURA: Oh, no.
JIM: Give me a pillow?
LAURA: What?
JIM: A pillow!
LAURA: *Oh* . . . (*Hands him one quickly.*)
JIM: How about you? Don't you like to sit on the floor?
LAURA: Oh — yes.
JIM: Why don't you, then?
LAURA: I — will.
JIM: Take a pillow! (*Laura does. Sits on the other side of the candelabrum. Jim crosses his legs and smiles engagingly at her.*) I can't hardly see you sitting way over there.
LAURA: I can — see you.
JIM: I know, but that's not fair, I'm in the limelight. (*Laura moves her pillow closer.*) Good! Now I can see you! Comfortable?
LAURA: Yes.
JIM: So am I. Comfortable as a cow. Will you have some gum?
LAURA: No, thank you.
JIM: I think that I will indulge, with your permission. (*Musingly unwraps it and holds it up.*) Think of the fortune made by the guy that invented the first piece of chewing gum. Amazing, huh? The Wrigley Building is one of the sights of Chicago. — I saw it summer before last when I went up to the Century of Progress. Did you take in the Century of Progress?
LAURA: No, I didn't.
JIM: Well, it was quite a wonderful exposition. What impressed me most was the Hall of Science. Gives you an idea of what the future will be in America, even more wonderful than the present time is! (*Pause. Smiling at her.*) Your brother tells me you're shy. Is that right, Laura?
LAURA: I — don't know.

JIM: I judge you to be an old-fashioned type of girl. Well, I think that's a pretty good type to be. Hope you don't think I'm being too personal — do you?

LAURA (*hastily, out of embarrassment*): I believe I *will* take a piece of gum, if you — don't mind. (*Clearing her throat.*) Mr. O'Connor, have you — kept up with your singing?

JIM: Singing? Me?

LAURA: Yes. I remember what a beautiful voice you had.

JIM: When did you hear me sing?

(*Voice offstage in the pause.*)

VOICE (*offstage*): O blow, ye winds, heigh-ho,
A-roving I will go!
I'm off to my love
With a boxing glove —
Ten thousand miles away!

JIM: You say you've heard me sing?

LAURA: Oh, yes! Yes, very often . . . I — don't suppose you remember me — at all?

JIM (*smiling doubtfully*): You know I have an idea I've seen you before. I had that idea soon as you opened the door. It seemed almost like I was about to remember your name. But the name that I started to call you — wasn't a name! And so I stopped myself before I said it.

LAURA: Wasn't it — Blue Roses?

JIM (*springs up, grinning*): Blue Roses! My gosh, yes — Blue Roses! That's what I had on my tongue when you opened the door! Isn't it funny what tricks your memory plays? I didn't connect you with the high school somehow or other. But that's where it was; it was high school. I didn't even know you were Shakespeare's sister! Gosh, I'm sorry.

LAURA: I didn't expect you to. You — barely knew me!

JIM: But we did have a speaking acquaintance, huh?

LAURA: Yes, we — spoke to each other.

JIM: When did you recognize me?

LAURA: Oh, right away!

JIM: Soon as I came in the door?

LAURA: When I heard your name I thought it was probably you. I knew that Tom used to know you a little in high school. So when you came in the door — Well, then I was — sure.

JIM: Why didn't you *say* something, then?

LAURA (*breathlessly*): I didn't know what to say, I was — too surprised!

JIM: For goodness' sakes! You know, this sure is funny!

LAURA: Yes! Yes, isn't it, though . . .

JIM: Didn't we have a class in something together?

LAURA: Yes, we did.

JIM: What class was that?

LAURA: It was — singing — Chorus!

JIM: Aw!

LAURA: I sat across the aisle from you in the Aud.

JIM: Aw.

LAURA: Mondays, Wednesdays, and Fridays.

JIM: Now I remember — you always came in late.

LAURA: Yes, it was so hard for me, getting upstairs. I had that brace on my leg — it clumped so loud!

JIM: I never heard any clumping.

LAURA (*wincing in the recollection*): To me it sounded like — thunder!

JIM: Well, well, well. I never even noticed.

LAURA: And everybody was seated before I came in. I had to walk in front of all those people. My seat was in the back row. I had to go clumping all the way up the aisle with everyone watching!

JIM: You shouldn't have been self-conscious.

LAURA: I know, but I was. It was always such a relief when the singing started.

JIM: Aw, yes, I've placed you now! I used to call you Blue Roses. How was it that I got started calling you that?

LAURA: I was out of school a little while with pleurosis. When I came back you asked me what was the matter. I said I had pleurosis — you thought I said Blue Roses. That's what you always called me after that!

JIM: I hope you didn't mind.

LAURA: Oh, no — I liked it. You see, I wasn't acquainted with many — people. . . .

JIM: As I remember you sort of stuck by yourself.

LAURA: I — I — never had much luck at — making friends.

JIM: I don't see why you wouldn't.

LAURA: Well, I — started out badly.

JIM: You mean being —

LAURA: Yes, it sort of — stood between me —

JIM: You shouldn't have let it!

LAURA: I know, but it did, and —

JIM: You were shy with people!

LAURA: I tried not to be but never could —

JIM: Overcome it?

LAURA: No, I — I never could!

JIM: I guess being shy is something you have to work out of kind of gradually.

LAURA (*sorrowfully*): Yes — I guess it —

JIM: Takes time!

LAURA: Yes —

JIM: People are not so dreadful when you know them. That's what you have to remember! And everybody has problems, not just you, but practically everybody has got some problems. You think of yourself as having the only problems, as being the only one who is disappointed. But just look around you and you will see lots of people as disappointed as you are. For instance, I hoped when I was going to high school that I would be further along at this time, six years later, than I am now — You remember that wonderful write-up I had in *The Torch*?

LAURA: Yes! (*She rises and crosses to table.*)

JIM: It said I was bound to succeed in anything I went into! (*Laura returns with the annual.*) Holy Jeez! *The Torch!* (*He accepts it reverently. They smile across it with mutual wonder. Laura crouches beside him and they begin to turn through it. Laura's shyness is dissolving in his warmth.*)

LAURA: Here you are in *Pirates of Penzance!*

JIM (*wistfully*): I sang the baritone lead in that operetta.

LAURA (*rapidly*): So — *beautifully!*

JIM (*protesting*): Aw —

LAURA: Yes, yes — beautifully — beautifully!

JIM: You heard me?

LAURA: All three times!

JIM: No!

LAURA: Yes!

JIM: All three performances?

LAURA (*looking down*): Yes.

JIM: Why?

LAURA: I — wanted to ask you to — autograph my program.

JIM: Why didn't you ask me to?

LAURA: You were always surrounded by your own friends so much that I never had a chance to.

JIM: You should have just —

LAURA: Well, I — thought you might think I was —

JIM: Thought I might think you was — what?

LAURA: Oh —

JIM (*with reflective relish*): I was beleaguered by females in those days.

LAURA: You were terribly popular!

JIM: Yeah —

LAURA: You had such a — friendly way —

JIM: I was spoiled in high school.

LAURA: Everybody — liked you!

JIM: Including you?

LAURA: I — yes, I — I did, too — (*She gently closes the book in her lap.*)

JIM: Well, well, well! — Give me that program, Laura. (*She hands it to him. He signs it with a flourish.*) There you are — better late than never!

LAURA: Oh, I — what a — surprise!

JIM: My signature isn't worth very much right now. But some day — maybe — it will increase in value! Being disappointed is one thing and being discouraged is something else. I am disappointed but I'm not discouraged. I'm twenty-three years old. How old are you?

LAURA: I'll be twenty-four in June.

JIM: That's not old age.

LAURA: No, but —

JIM: You finished high school?

LAURA (*with difficulty*): I didn't go back.

JIM: You mean you dropped out?

LAURA: I made bad grades in my final examinations. (*She rises and replaces the book and the program. Her voice strained.*) How is — Emily Meisenbach getting along?

JIM: Oh, that kraut-head!

LAURA: Why do you call her that?

JIM: That's what she was.

LAURA: You're not still — going with her?

JIM: I never see her.

LAURA: It said in the Personal Section that you were — engaged!

JIM: I know, but I wasn't impressed by that — propaganda!

LAURA: It wasn't — the truth?

JIM: Only in Emily's optimistic opinion!

LAURA: Oh —

(*Legend: "What Have You Done since High School?"*)

Jim lights a cigarette and leans indolently back on his elbows smiling at Laura with a warmth and charm which light her inwardly with altar candles. She remains by the table and turns in her hands a piece of glass to cover her tumult.

JIM (*after several reflective puffs on a cigarette*): What have you done since high school? (*She seems not to hear him.*) Huh? (*Laura looks up.*) I said what have you done since high school, Laura?

LAURA: Nothing much.

JIM: You must have been doing something these six long years.

LAURA: Yes.

JIM: Well, then, such as what?

LAURA: I took a business course at business college —

JIM: How did that work out?

LAURA: Well, not very — well — I had to drop out, it gave me — indigestion —

Jim laughs gently.

JIM: What are you doing now?

LAURA: I don't do anything — much. Oh, please don't think I sit around doing nothing! My glass collection takes up a good deal of my time. Glass is something you have to take good care of.

JIM: What did you say — about glass?

LAURA: Collection I said — I have one — (*She clears her throat and turns away again, acutely shy.*)

JIM (*abruptly*): You know what I judge to be the trouble with you? Inferiority complex! Know what that is? That's what they call it when someone low-rates himself! I understand it because I had it, too. Although my case was not so aggravated as yours seems to be. I had it until I took up public speaking, developed my voice, and learned that I had an aptitude for science. Before that time I never thought of myself as being outstanding in any way whatsoever! Now I've never made a regular study of it, but I have a friend who says I can analyze people better than doctors that make a profession of it. I don't claim that to be necessarily true, but I can sure guess a person's psychology, Laura! (*Takes out his gum.*) Excuse me, Laura. I always take it out when the flavor is gone. I'll use this scrap of paper to wrap it in. I know how it is to get it stuck on a shoe. Yep — that's what I judge to be your principal trouble. A lack of confidence in yourself as a person. You don't have the proper amount of faith in yourself. I'm basing that fact on a number of your remarks and also on certain observations I've made. For instance that clumping you thought was so awful in high school. You say that you even dreaded to walk into class. You see what you did? You dropped out of school, you gave up an education because of a clump, which as far as I know was practically nonexistent! A little physical defect is what you have. Hardly noticeable even! Magnified thousands of times by imagination! You know what my strong advice to you is? Think of yourself as *superior* in some way!

LAURA: In what way would I think?

JIM: Why, man alive, Laura! Just look about you a little. What do you see? A world full of common people! All of 'em born and all of 'em going to die! Which of them has one-tenth of your good points! Or mine! Or anyone else's, as far as that goes — Gosh! Everybody excels in some one thing. Some in many! (*Unconsciously glances at himself in the mirror.*) All you've got to do is discover in *what!* Take me, for instance. (*He adjusts his tie at the mirror.*) My interest happened to lie in electrodynamics. I'm taking a course in radio engineering at night school, Laura, on top of a fairly responsible job at the warehouse. I'm taking that course and studying public speaking.

LAURA: Ohhhh.

JIM: Because I believe in the future of television! (*Turning back to her.*) I wish to be ready to go up right along with it. Therefore I'm planning to get in on the ground floor. In fact, I've already made the right connections and all that remains is for the industry itself to get under way! Full steam — (*His eyes are starry.*) *Knowledge* — Zzzzzp! *Money* — Zzzzzzp! — *Power!* That's the cycle democracy is built on! (*His attitude is convincingly dynamic. Laura stares at him, even her shyness eclipsed in her absolute wonder. He suddenly grins.*) I guess you think I think a lot of myself!

LAURA: No — o-o-o, I —

JIM: Now how about you? Isn't there something you take more interest in than anything else?

LAURA: Well, I do — as I said — have my — glass collection —

A peal of girlish laughter from the kitchen.

JIM: I'm not right sure I know what you're talking about. What kind of glass is it?

LAURA: Little articles of it, they're ornaments mostly! Most of them are little animals made out of glass, the tiniest little animals in the world. Mother calls them a glass menagerie! Here's an example of one, if you'd like to see it! This one is one of the oldest. It's nearly thirteen. (*He stretches out his hand.*) (*Music: "The Glass Menagerie."*) Oh, be careful — if you breathe, it breaks!

JIM: I'd better not take it. I'm pretty clumsy with things.

LAURA: Go on, I trust you with him! (*Places it in his palm.*) There now — you're holding him gently! Hold him over the light, he loves the light! You see how the light shines through him?

JIM: It sure does shine!

LAURA: I shouldn't be partial, but he is my favorite one.

JIM: What kind of thing is this one supposed to be?

LAURA: Haven't you noticed the single horn on his forehead?

JIM: A unicorn, huh?

LAURA: Mmm-hmmm!

JIM: Unicorns, aren't they extinct in the modern world?

LAURA: I know!

JIM: Poor little fellow, he must feel sort of lonesome.

LAURA (*smiling*): Well, if he does he doesn't complain about it. He stays on a shelf with some horses that don't have horns and all of them seem to get along nicely together.

JIM: How do you know?

LAURA (*lightly*): I haven't heard any arguments among them!

JIM (*grinning*): No arguments, huh? Well, that's a pretty good sign! Where shall I set him?

LAURA: Put him on the table. They all like a change of scenery once in a while!

JIM (*stretching*): Well, well, well, well — Look how big my shadow is when I stretch!

LAURA: Oh, oh, yes — it stretches across the ceiling!

JIM (*crossing to door*): I think it's stopped raining. (*Opens fire-escape door.*) Where does the music come from?

LAURA: From the Paradise Dance Hall across the alley.

JIM: How about cutting the rug a little, Miss Wingfield?

LAURA: Oh, I —

JIM: Or is your program filled up? Let me have a look at it. (*Grasps imaginary card.*) Why, every dance is taken! I'll have to scratch some out. (*Waltz music: "La Golondrina."*) Ahhh, a waltz! (*He executes some sweeping turns by himself then holds his arms toward Laura.*)

LAURA (*breathlessly*): I — can't dance!

JIM: There you go, that inferiority stuff!

LAURA: I've never danced in my life!

JIM: Come on, try!

LAURA: Oh, but I'd step on you!

JIM: I'm not made out of glass.

LAURA: How — how — how do we start?

JIM: Just leave it to me. You hold your arms out a little.

LAURA: Like this?

JIM: A little bit higher. Right. Now don't tighten up, that's the main thing about it — relax.

LAURA (*laughing breathlessly*): It's hard not to.

JIM: Okay.

LAURA: I'm afraid you can't budge me.

JIM: What do you bet I can't? (*He swings her into motion.*)

LAURA: Goodness, yes, you can!

JIM: Let yourself go, now, Laura, just let yourself go.

LAURA: I'm —

JIM: Come on!

LAURA: Trying.

JIM: Not so stiff — Easy does it!

LAURA: I know but I'm —

JIM: Loosen th' backbone! There now, that's a lot better.

LAURA: Am I?

JIM: Lots, lots better! (*He moves her about the room in a clumsy waltz.*)

LAURA: Oh, my!

JIM: Ha-ha!

LAURA: Goodness, yes you can!

JIM: Ha-ha-ha! (*They suddenly bump into the table. Jim stops.*) What did we hit on?

LAURA: Table.

JIM: Did something fall off it? I think —

LAURA: Yes.

JIM: I hope it wasn't the little glass horse with the horn!

LAURA: Yes.

JIM: Aw, aw, aw. Is it broken?

LAURA: Now it is just like all the other horses.

JIM: It's lost its —

LAURA: Horn! It doesn't matter. Maybe it's a blessing in disguise.

JIM: You'll never forgive me. I bet that that was your favorite piece of glass.

LAURA: I don't have favorites much. It's no tragedy, Freckles. Glass breaks so easily. No matter how careful you are. The traffic jars the shelves and things fall off them.

JIM: Still I'm awfully sorry that I was the cause.

LAURA (*smiling*): I'll just imagine he had an operation. The horn was removed to make him feel less — freakish! (*They both laugh.*) Now he will feel more at home with the other horses, the ones that don't have horns . . .

JIM: Ha-ha, that's very funny! (*Suddenly serious.*) I'm glad to see that you have a sense of humor. You know — you're — well — very different! Surprisingly different from anyone else I know! (*His voice becomes soft and hesitant with a genuine feeling.*) Do you mind me telling you that? (*Laura is abashed beyond speech.*) You make me feel sort of — I don't know how to put it! I'm usually pretty good at expressing things, but — This is something that I don't know how to say! (*Laura touches her throat and clears it — turns the broken unicorn in her hands.*) (*Even softer.*) Has anyone ever told you that you were pretty?

Pause: Music.

(*Laura looks up slowly, with wonder, and shakes her head.*) Well, you are! In a very different way from anyone else. And all the nicer because of the difference, too. (*His voice becomes low and husky. Laura turns away, nearly faint with the novelty of her emotions.*) I wish that you were my sister. I'd teach you to have some confidence in yourself. The different people are not like other people, but being different is nothing to be ashamed of. Because other people are not such wonderful people. They're one hundred times one thousand. You're one times one! They walk all over the earth. You just stay here. They're common as — weeds, but — you — well, you're — *Blue Roses!*

(*Image on screen: Blue Roses.*)

(*Music changes.*)

LAURA: But blue is wrong for — roses . . .

JIM: It's right for you — You're — pretty!

LAURA: In what respect am I pretty?

JIM: In all respects — believe me! Your eyes — your hair — are pretty! Your hands are pretty! (*He catches hold of her hand.*) You think I'm making this up because I'm invited to dinner and have to be nice. Oh, I could do that! I could put on an act for you, Laura, and say lots of things without being very sincere. But this time I am. I'm talking to you sincerely. I happened to notice you had this inferiority complex that keeps you from feeling comfortable with people. Somebody needs to build your confidence up and make you proud instead of shy and turning away and — blushing — Somebody ought to — ought to — *kiss* you, Laura! (*His hand slips slowly up her arm to her shoulder.*) (*Music swells tumultuously.*) (*He suddenly turns her about and kisses her on the lips. When he releases her Laura sinks on the sofa with a bright, dazed look. Jim backs away and fishes in his pocket for a cigarette.*) (*Legend on screen: "Souvenir."*) Stumble-john! (*He lights the cigarette, avoiding her look. There is a peal of girlish laughter from Amanda in the kitchen. Laura slowly raises and opens her hand. It still contains the little broken glass animal. She looks at it with a tender, bewildered expression.*) Stumble-john! I shouldn't have done that — That was way off the beam. You don't smoke, do you? (*She looks up, smiling, not hearing the question. He sits beside her a little gingerly. She looks at him speechlessly — waiting. He coughs decorously and moves a little farther aside as he considers the situation and senses her feelings, dimly, with perturbation. Gently.*) Would you — care for a — mint? (*She doesn't seem to hear him but her look grows brighter even.*) Peppermint — Life Saver? My pocket's a regular drug store — wherever I go . . . (*He pops a mint in his mouth. Then gulps and decides to make a clean breast of it. He speaks slowly and gingerly.*) Laura, you know, if I had a sister like you, I'd do the same thing as Tom. I'd bring out fellows — introduce her to them. The right type of boys of a type to — appreciate her. Only — well — he made a mistake about me. Maybe I've got no call to be saying this. That may not have been the idea in having me over. But what if it was? There's nothing wrong about that. The only trouble is that in my case — I'm not in a situation to — do the right thing. I can't take down your number and say I'll phone. I can't call up next week and — ask for a date. I thought I had better explain the situation in case you misunderstood it and — hurt your feelings. . . .

(*Pause. Slowly, very slowly, Laura's look changes, her eyes returning slowly from his to the ornament in her palm.*)

Amanda utters another gay laugh in the kitchen.

LAURA (*faintly*): You — won't — call again?

JIM: No, Laura, I can't. (*He rises from the sofa.*) As I was just explaining, I've — got strings on me, Laura, I've — been going steady! I go out all the time with a girl named Betty. She's a home-girl like you, and Catholic, and Irish, and in a great many ways we — get along fine. I met her last summer on a moonlight boat trip up the river to Alton, on the *Majestic.* Well — right away from the start it was — love! (*Legend: Love!*) (*Laura sways slightly forward and grips the arm of the sofa. He fails to notice, now enrapt in his own comfortable being.*) Being in love has made a new man of me! (*Leaning stiffly forward, clutching the arm of the sofa, Laura struggles visibly with her storm. But Jim is oblivious, she is a long way off.*) The power of love is really pretty tremendous! Love is something that — changes the whole world, Laura! (*The storm abates a little and Laura leans back. He notices her again.*) It happened that Betty's aunt took sick, she got a wire and had to go to Centralia. So Tom — when he asked me to dinner — I naturally just accepted the invitation, not knowing that you — that he — that I — (*He stops awkwardly.*) Huh — I'm a stumble-john! (*He flops back on the sofa. The holy candles in the altar of Laura's face have been snuffed out! There is a look of almost infinite desolation. Jim glances at her uneasily.*) I wish that you would — say something. (*She bites her lip which was trembling and then bravely smiles. She opens her hand again on the broken glass ornament. Then she gently takes his hand and raises it level with her own. She carefully places the unicorn in the palm of his hand, then pushes his fingers closed upon it.*) What are you — doing that for? You want me to have him? — Laura? (*She nods.*) What for?

LAURA: A — souvenir . . .

She rises unsteadily and crouches beside the Victrola to wind it up.

(*Legend on screen: "Things Have a Way of Turning Out So Badly."*)

(*Or image: "Gentleman caller waving good-bye! — Gaily."*)

At this moment Amanda rushes brightly back in the front room. She bears a pitcher of fruit punch in an old-fashioned cut-glass pitcher and a plate of macaroons. The plate has a gold border and poppies painted on it.

AMANDA: Well, well, well! Isn't the air delightful after the shower? I've made you children a little liquid refreshment. (*Turns gaily to the gentleman caller.*) Jim, do you know that song about lemonade?

"Lemonade, lemonade
Made in the shade and stirred with a spade —
Good enough for any old maid!"

JIM (*uneasily*): Ha-ha! No — I never heard it.

AMANDA: Why, Laura! You look so serious!

JIM: We were having a serious conversation.

AMANDA: Good! Now you're better acquainted!

JIM (*uncertainly*): Ha-ha! Yes.

AMANDA: You modern young people are much more serious-minded than my generation. I was so gay as a girl!

JIM: You haven't changed, Mrs. Wingfield.

AMANDA: Tonight I'm rejuvenated! The gaiety of the occasion, Mr. O'Connor! (*She tosses her head with a peal of laughter. Spills lemonade.*) Oooo! I'm baptizing myself!

JIM: Here — let me —

AMANDA (*setting the pitcher down*): There now. I discovered we had some maraschino cherries. I dumped them in, juice and all!

JIM: You shouldn't have gone to that trouble, Mrs. Wingfield.

AMANDA: Trouble, trouble? Why it was loads of fun! Didn't you hear me cutting up in the kitchen? I bet your ears were burning! I told Tom how outdone with him I was for keeping you to himself so long a time! He should have brought you over much, much sooner! Well, now that you've found your way, I want you to be a very frequent caller! Not just occasional but all the time. Oh, we're going to have a lot of gay times together! I see them coming! Mmm, just breathe that air! So fresh, and the moon's so pretty! I'll skip back out — I know where my place is when young folks are having a — serious conversation!

JIM: Oh, don't go out, Mrs. Wingfield. The fact of the matter is I've got to be going.

AMANDA: Going, now? You're joking! Why, it's only the shank of the evening, Mr. O'Connor!

JIM: Well, you know how it is.

AMANDA: You mean you're a young workingman and have to keep workingmen's hours. We'll let you off early tonight. But only on the condition that next time you stay later. What's the best night for you? Isn't Saturday night the best night for you workingmen?

JIM: I have a couple of time-clocks to punch, Mrs. Wingfield. One at morning, another one at night!

AMANDA: My, but you *are* ambitious! You work at night, too?

JIM: No, Ma'am, not work but — Betty! (*He crosses deliberately to pick up his hat. The band at the Paradise Dance Hall goes into a tender waltz.*)

AMANDA: Betty? Betty? Who's — Betty! (*There is an ominous cracking sound in the sky.*)

JIM: Oh, just a girl. The girl I go steady with! (*He smiles charmingly. The sky falls.*)

(*Legend: "The Sky Falls."*)

AMANDA (*a long-drawn exhalation*): Ohhhh . . . Is it a serious romance, Mr. O'Connor?

JIM: We're going to be married the second Sunday in June.

AMANDA: Ohhhh — how nice! Tom didn't mention that you were engaged to be married.

JIM: The cat's not out of the bag at the warehouse yet. You know how they are. They call you Romeo and stuff like that. (*He stops at the oval mirror to put *on his hat. He carefully shapes the brim and the crown to give a discreetly dashing effect.*) It's been a wonderful evening, Mrs. Wingfield. I guess this is what they mean by Southern hospitality.

AMANDA: It really wasn't anything at all.

JIM: I hope it don't seem like I'm rushing off. But I promised Betty I'd pick her up at the Wabash depot, an' by the time I get my jalopy down there her train'll be in. Some women are pretty upset if you keep 'em waiting.

AMANDA: Yes, I know — The tyranny of women! (*Extends her hand.*) Good-bye, Mr. O'Connor. I wish you luck — and happiness — and success! All three of them, and so does Laura — Don't you, Laura?

LAURA: Yes!

JIM (*taking her hand*): Good-bye, Laura. I'm certainly going to treasure that souvenir. And don't you forget the good advice I gave you. (*Raises his voice to a cheery shout.*) So long, Shakespeare! Thanks again, ladies — Good night!

He grins and ducks jauntily out.

Still bravely grimacing, Amanda closes the door on the gentleman caller. Then she turns back to the room with a puzzled expression. She and Laura don't dare to face each other. Laura crouches beside the Victrola to wind it.

AMANDA (*faintly*): Things have a way of turning out so badly. I don't believe that I would play the Victrola. Well, well — well — Our gentleman caller was engaged to be married! Tom!

TOM (*from back*): Yes, Mother?

AMANDA: Come in here a minute. I want to tell you something awfully funny.

TOM (*enters with macaroon and a glass of the lemonade*): Has the gentleman caller gotten away already?

AMANDA: The gentleman caller has made an early departure. What a wonderful joke you played on us!

TOM: How do you mean?

AMANDA: You didn't mention that he was engaged to be married.

TOM: Jim? Engaged?

AMANDA: That's what he just informed us.

TOM: I'll be jiggered! I didn't know about that.

AMANDA: That seems very peculiar.

TOM: What's peculiar about it?

AMANDA: Didn't you call him your best friend down at the warehouse?

TOM: He is, but how did I know?

AMANDA: It seems extremely peculiar that you wouldn't know your best friend was going to be married!

TOM: The warehouse is where I work, not where I know things about people!

AMANDA: You don't know things anywhere! You live in a dream; you manufacture illusions! (*He crosses to door.*) Where are you going?

TOM: I'm going to the movies.

AMANDA: That's right, now that you've had us make such fools of ourselves. The effort, the preparations, all the expense! The new floor lamp, the rug, the clothes for Laura! All for what? To entertain some other girl's fiancé! Go to the movies, go! Don't think about us, a mother deserted, an unmarried sister who's crippled and has no job! Don't let anything interfere with your selfish pleasure! Just go, go, go — to the movies!

TOM: All right, I will! The more you shout about my selfishness to me the quicker I'll go, and I won't go to the movies!

AMANDA: Go, then! Then go to the moon — you selfish dreamer!

Tom smashes his glass on the floor. He plunges out on the fire-escape, slamming the door. Laura screams — cut by door.

Dance-hall music up. Tom goes to the rail and grips it desperately, lifting his face in the chill white moonlight penetrating the narrow abyss of the alley.

(*Legend on screen: "And So Good-Bye . . ."*)

Tom's closing speech is timed with the interior pantomime. The interior scene is played as though viewed through sound-proof glass. Amanda appears to be making a comforting speech to Laura who is huddled upon the sofa. Now that we cannot hear the mother's speech, her silliness is gone and she has dignity and tragic beauty. Laura's dark hair hides her face until at the end of the speech she lifts it to smile at her mother. Amanda's gestures are slow and graceful, almost dancelike, as she comforts the daughter. At the end of her speech she glances a moment at the father's picture — then withdraws through the portieres. At close of Tom's speech, Laura blows out the candles, ending the play.

TOM: I didn't go to the moon, I went much further — for time is the longest distance between two places — Not long after that I was fired for writing a poem on the lid of a shoe-box. I left Saint Louis. I descended the steps of this fire-escape for a last time and followed, from then on, in my father's footsteps, attempting to find in motion what was lost in space — I traveled around a great deal. The cities swept about me like dead leaves, leaves that were brightly colored but torn away from the branches. I would have stopped, but I was pursued by something. It always came upon me unawares, taking me altogether by surprise. Perhaps it was a familiar bit of music. Perhaps it was only a piece of transparent glass — Perhaps I am walking along a street at night, in some strange city, before I have found companions. I pass the lighted window of a shop where perfume is sold. The window is filled with pieces of colored glass, tiny transparent bottles in delicate colors, like bits of a shattered rainbow. Then all at once my sister touches my shoulder. I turn around and look into her eyes. . . . Oh, Laura, Laura, I tried to leave you behind me, but I am more faithful than I intended to be! I reach for a cigarette, I cross the street, I run into the movies or a bar, I buy a drink, I speak to the nearest stranger — anything that can blow your candles out! (*Laura bends over the candles*) — for nowadays the world is lit by lightning! Blow out your candles, Laura — and so good-bye . . .

She blows the candles out.

(*The Scene Dissolves.*)

ARTHUR MILLER *(b. 1915), the son of a clothing manufacturer, was born in Manhattan but moved to Brooklyn as a teenager when his father's business collapsed during the Depression. After high school he worked for two years in an automobile parts warehouse to save money for his college tuition. He wrote his first play in 1935 as a journalism student at the University of Michigan, later recalling for a* Paris Review *interviewer that*

> *it was written on a spring vacation in six days. I was so young that I dared do such things, begin it and finish it in a week. I'd seen about two plays in my life, so I didn't know how long an act was supposed to be, but across the hall there was a fellow who did the costumes for the University theater and he said, "Well, it's roughly forty minutes." I had written an enormous amount of material and I got an alarm clock. It was all a lark to me, and not to be taken too seriously . . . that's what I told myself. As it turned out, the acts were longer than that, but the sense of timing was in me even from the beginning, and the play had a form right from the start.*

Miller's early plays won prizes at the University of Michigan, and he went on after graduation to write plays for radio and work for the Federal Theater Project. After failing with The Man Who Had All the Luck *in 1944, Miller had his first successful play in 1947 with* All My Sons.

In Boston during the pre-Broadway preview of this play, Miller had a chance meeting outside the Colonial Theater with his uncle Manny Newman, a traveling salesman. Their encounter suggested the idea of Death of a Salesman *to Miller a short time later. Miller recalled, "I could see his grim hotel room behind him, the long trip up from New York in his little car, the hopeless hope of the day's business. Without so much as acknowledging my greeting, he said, 'Buddy is doing very well.'" Miller understood that his uncle was a competitor at all times, and that he had taken the Colonial Theater marquee advertising Miller's new play as an irresistible challenge to assert that his own son, Buddy, was also a success. To Miller, his uncle was an absurd yet unforgettable figure, "so completely isolated from the ordinary laws of gravity, so elaborate in his fantastic inventions, and despite his ugliness so lyrically in love with fame and fortune and their inevitable descent on his family, that he possessed my imagination until I knew more or less precisely how he would react to any sign or word or idea."*

*Yet Miller was also aware that his uncle's unexpected appearance outside the Boston theater had another effect on him, cutting "through time like a knife through a layer cake." In the encounter Miller had felt himself reduced from an accomplished thirty-year-old playwright (*All My Sons *went on to win the year's Pulitzer Prize and a Drama Critics Circle Award) to an emotionally vulnerable adolescent. He decided to write a play about his uncle "without any transitions at all, dialogue that would simply leap from bone to bone of a skeleton that would not for an instant cease being added to, an organism as strictly economic as a leaf, as trim as an ant."*

In six weeks during the spring of 1948, Miller wrote the first draft of Death of a Salesman. *He credits a production of Tennessee Williams's* A Streetcar Named Desire *the previous November as another important influence that shaped his play: Williams's "words and their liberation, the joy of the writer in writing them, the radiant eloquence of its composition." The theater historian Brenda Murphy sees a link between Williams's poetic language in that play and "the poetry of the mundane that infuses* Salesman.*" Elia Kazan, who directed both* Streetcar *and* Salesman, *recalled that Miller was also greatly impressed with the staging of Williams's play, appearing to be "full of wonder at the theatre's expressive possibilities. [Miller] told me he was amazed at how simply and successfully the non-realistic elements in the play . . . blended with the realistic ones."*

Collaborating with Kazan and set designer Jo Mielziner, Miller extensively revised his preproduction script of Death of a Salesman. *It was the hit of the 1948–49 Broadway season, running for 742 performances and winning the Pulitzer Prize, the Drama Critics Circle Award, the Donaldson Award, and Tony Awards for best play, best direction, best scene design, and best supporting actor. Published as a script, the play became a best-seller, and it was the only play ever to be a Book-of-the-Month Club selection. Perhaps the drama critic Brooks Atkinson summarized its appeal for audiences in his* New York Times *review after the premier of the play: "Mr. Miller has looked with compassion into the hearts of some ordinary Americans and quietly transferred their hope and anguish to the theatre." In the essay "Tragedy and the Common Man," Miller interpreted Willy Loman's tragedy as that of Everyman: "The Chinese reaction to my Beijing production of* Salesman *would confirm what had become more and more obvious over the decades in the play's hundreds of productions throughout the world: Willy was representative everywhere, in every kind of system, of ourselves in this time."*

Miller has continued to write plays, most notably in The Crucible *(1953) and* A View from the Bridge *(1956). He also wrote the screenplay of the film* The Misfits *for his second wife, Marilyn Monroe, from whom he was divorced in 1961. Among his later plays are* After the Fall *(1964),* The Archbishop's Ceiling *(1977),* Danger: Memory! *(1986), and* The Last Yankee *(1993). Miller has also written a memoir,* Timebends *(1987), and excellent essays on the theater and the craft of playwriting, many of them collected in 1978 in* The Theatre Essays of Arthur Miller, *edited by Robert A. Martin.*

RELATED CASEBOOK: *See pages 2030–2048, including Arthur Miller, "On* Death of a Salesman *as an American Tragedy," page 2032; Arthur Miller, "From the* Paris Review *Interview," page 2035; Helge Normann Nilsen, "Marxism and the Early Plays of Arthur Miller," page 2037; John Beaufort, "Review of* Death of a Salesman,*" page 2041; John Lahr, "Making Willy Loman," page 2043.*

ARTHUR MILLER

Death of a Salesman

1949

Certain Private Conversations in Two Acts and a Requiem

CAST

WILLY LOMAN
LINDA
BIFF
HAPPY
BERNARD
THE WOMAN
CHARLEY
UNCLE BEN
HOWARD WAGNER
JENNY
STANLEY
MISS FORSYTHE
LETTA

SCENE: *The action takes place in Willy Loman's house and yard and in various places he visits in the New York and Boston of today.*

Throughout the play, in the stage directions, left and right mean stage left and stage right.

ACT I

A melody is heard, played upon a flute. It is small and fine, telling of grass and trees and the horizon. The curtain rises.

Before us is the Salesman's house. We are aware of towering, angular shapes behind it, surrounding it on all sides. Only the blue light of the sky falls upon the house and forestage; the surrounding area shows an angry glow of orange. As more light appears, we see a solid vault of apartment houses around the small, fragile-seeming home. An air of the dream clings to the place, a dream rising out of reality. The kitchen at center seems actual enough, for there is a kitchen table with three chairs, and a refrigerator. But no other fixtures are seen. At the back of the kitchen there is a draped entrance, which leads to the living-room. To the right of the kitchen, on a level raised two feet, is a bedroom furnished only with a brass bedstead and a straight chair. On a shelf over the bed a silver athletic trophy stands. A window opens onto the apartment house at the side.

Behind the kitchen, on a level raised six and a half feet, is the boys' bedroom, at present barely visible. Two beds are dimly seen, and at the back of the room a dormer window. (This bedroom is above the unseen living-room.) At the left a stairway curves up to it from the kitchen.

The entire setting is wholly or, in some places, partially transparent. The roof-line of the house is one-dimensional; under and over it we see the apartment buildings. Before the house lies an apron, curving beyond the forestage into the orchestra. This forward area serves as the back yard as well as the locale of all Willy's imaginings and of his city scenes. Whenever the action is in the present the actors observe the imaginary wall-lines, entering the house only through its door at the left. But in the scenes of the past these boundaries are broken, and characters enter or leave a room by stepping "through" a wall onto the forestage.

From the right, Willy Loman, the Salesman, enters, carrying two large sample cases. The flute plays on. He hears but is not aware of it. He is past sixty years of age, dressed quietly. Even as he crosses the stage to the doorway of the house, his exhaustion is apparent. He unlocks the door, comes into the kitchen, and thankfully lets his burden down, feeling the soreness of his palms. A word-sigh escapes his lips — it might be "Oh, boy, oh, boy." He closes the door, then carries his cases out into the living-room, through the draped kitchen doorway.

Linda, his wife, has stirred in her bed at the right. She gets out and puts on a robe, listening. Most often jovial, she has developed an iron repression of her exceptions to Willy's behavior — she more than loves him, she admires him, as though his mercurial nature, his temper, his massive dreams and little cruelties, served her only as sharp reminders of the turbulent longings within him, longings which she shares but lacks the temperament to utter and follow to their end.

LINDA (*hearing Willy outside the bedroom, calls with some trepidation*): Willy!

WILLY: It's all right. I came back.

LINDA: Why? What happened? (*Slight pause.*) Did something happen, Willy?

WILLY: No, nothing happened.

LINDA: You didn't smash the car, did you?

WILLY (*with casual irritation*): I said nothing happened. Didn't you hear me?

LINDA: Don't you feel well?

WILLY: I'm tired to the death. (*The flute has faded away. He sits on the bed beside her, a little numb.*) I couldn't make it. I just couldn't make it, Linda.

LINDA (*very carefully, delicately*): Where were you all day? You look terrible.

WILLY: I got as far as a little above Yonkers. I stopped for a cup of coffee. Maybe it was the coffee.

LINDA: What?

WILLY (*after a pause*): I suddenly couldn't drive any more. The car kept going off onto the shoulder, y'know?

LINDA (*helpfully*): Oh. Maybe it was the steering again. I don't think Angelo knows the Studebaker.

WILLY: No, it's me, it's me. Suddenly I realize I'm goin' sixty miles an hour and I don't remember the last five minutes. I'm — I can't seem to — keep my mind to it.

LINDA: Maybe it's your glasses. You never went for your new glasses.

WILLY: No, I see everything. I came back ten miles an hour. It took me nearly four hours from Yonkers.

LINDA (*resigned*): Well, you'll just have to take a rest, Willy, you can't continue this way.

WILLY: I just got back from Florida.

LINDA: But you didn't rest your mind. Your mind is overactive, and the mind is what counts, dear.

WILLY: I'll start out in the morning. Maybe I'll feel better in the morning. (*She is taking off his shoes.*) These goddam arch supports are killing me.

LINDA: Take an aspirin. Should I get you an aspirin? It'll soothe you.

WILLY (*with wonder*): I was driving along, you understand? And I was fine. I was even observing the scenery. You can imagine, me looking at scenery, on the road every week of my life. But it's so beautiful up there, Linda, the trees are so thick, and the sun is warm. I opened the windshield and just let the warm air bathe over me. And then all of a sudden I'm goin' off the road! I'm tellin' ya, I absolutely forgot I was driving. If I'd've gone the other way over the white line I might've killed somebody. So I went on again — and five minutes later I'm dreamin' again, and I nearly — (*He presses two fingers against his eyes.*) I have such thoughts, I have such strange thoughts.

LINDA: Willy, dear. Talk to them again. There's no reason why you can't work in New York.

WILLY: They don't need me in New York. I'm the New England man. I'm vital in New England.

LINDA: But you're sixty years old. They can't expect you to keep traveling every week.

WILLY: I'll have to send a wire to Portland. I'm supposed to see Brown and Morrison tomorrow morning at ten o'clock to show the line. Goddammit, I could sell them! (*He starts putting on his jacket.*)

LINDA (*taking the jacket from him*): Why don't you go down to the place tomorrow and tell Howard you've simply got to work in New York? You're too accommodating, dear.

WILLY: If old man Wagner was alive I'd a been in charge of New York now! That man was a prince, he was a masterful man. But that boy of his, that Howard, he don't appreciate. When I went north the first time, the Wagner Company didn't know where New England was!

LINDA: Why don't you tell those things to Howard, dear?

WILLY (*encouraged*): I will, I definitely will. Is there any cheese?

LINDA: I'll make you a sandwich.

WILLY: No, go to sleep. I'll take some milk. I'll be up right away. The boys in?

LINDA: They're sleeping. Happy took Biff on a date tonight.

WILLY (*interested*): That so?

LINDA: It was so nice to see them shaving together, one behind the other, in the bathroom. And going out together. You notice? The whole house smells of shaving lotion.

WILLY: Figure it out. Work a lifetime to pay off a house. You finally own it, and there's nobody to live in it.

LINDA: Well, dear, life is a casting off. It's always that way.

WILLY: No, no, some people — some people accomplish something. Did Biff say anything after I went this morning?

LINDA: You shouldn't have criticized him, Willy, especially after he just got off the train. You mustn't lose your temper with him.

WILLY: When the hell did I lose my temper? I simply asked him if he was making any money. Is that a criticism?

LINDA: But, dear, how could he make any money?

WILLY (*worried and angered*): There's such an undercurrent in him. He became a moody man. Did he apologize when I left this morning?

LINDA: He was crestfallen, Willy. You know how he admires you. I think if he finds himself, then you'll both be happier and not fight any more.

WILLY: How can he find himself on a farm? Is that a life? A farmhand? In the beginning, when he was young, I thought, well, a young man, it's good for him to tramp around, take a lot of different jobs. But it's more than ten years now and he has yet to make thirty-five dollars a week!

LINDA: He's finding himself, Willy.

WILLY: Not finding yourself at the age of thirty-four is a disgrace!

LINDA: Shh!

WILLY: The trouble is he's lazy, goddammit!

LINDA: Willy, please!

WILLY: Biff is a lazy bum!

LINDA: They're sleeping. Get something to eat. Go on down.

WILLY: Why did he come home? I would like to know what brought him home.

LINDA: I don't know. I think he's still lost, Willy. I think he's very lost.

WILLY: Biff Loman is lost. In the greatest country in the world a young man with such — personal attractiveness, gets lost. And such a hard worker. There's one thing about Biff — he's not lazy.

LINDA: Never.

WILLY (*with pity and resolve*): I'll see him in the morning; I'll have a nice talk with him. I'll get him a job selling. He could be big in no time. My God! Remember how they used to follow him around in high school? When he smiled at one of them their faces lit up. When he walked down the street . . . (*He loses himself in reminiscences.*)

LINDA (*trying to bring him out of it*): Willy, dear, I got a new kind of American-type cheese today. It's whipped.

WILLY: Why do you get American when I like Swiss?

LINDA: I just thought you'd like a change —

WILLY: I don't want a change! I want Swiss cheese. Why am I always being contradicted?

LINDA (*with a covering laugh*): I thought it would be a surprise.

WILLY: Why don't you open a window in here, for God's sake?

LINDA (*with infinite patience*): They're all open, dear.

WILLY: The way they boxed us in here. Bricks and windows, windows and bricks.

LINDA: We should've bought the land next door.

WILLY: The street is lined with cars. There's not a breath of fresh air in the neighborhood. The grass don't grow any more, you can't raise a carrot in the back yard. They should've had a law against apartment houses. Remember those two beautiful elm trees out there? When I and Biff hung the swing between them?

LINDA: Yeah, like being a million miles from the city.

WILLY: They should've arrested the builder for cutting those down. They massacred the neighborhood. (*Lost.*) More and more I think of those days, Linda. This time of year it was lilac and wisteria. And then the peonies would come out, and the daffodils. What fragrance in this room!

LINDA: Well, after all, people had to move somewhere.

WILLY: No, there's more people now.

LINDA: I don't think there's more people. I think —

WILLY: There's more people! That's what's ruining this country! Population is getting out of control. The competition is maddening! Smell the stink from that apartment house! And another one on the other side . . . How can they whip cheese?

On Willy's last line, Biff and Happy raise themselves up in their beds, listening.

LINDA: Go down, try it. And be quiet.

WILLY (*turning to Linda, guiltily*): You're not worried about me, are you, sweetheart?

BIFF: What's the matter?

HAPPY: Listen!

LINDA: You've got too much on the ball to worry about.

WILLY: You're my foundation and my support, Linda.

LINDA: Just try to relax, dear. You make mountains out of molehills.

WILLY: I won't fight with him any more. If he wants to go back to Texas, let him go.

LINDA: He'll find his way.

WILLY: Sure. Certain men just don't get started till later in life. Like Thomas Edison, I think. Or B. F. Goodrich. One of them was deaf. (*He starts for the bedroom doorway.*) I'll put my money on Biff.

LINDA: And Willy — if it's warm Sunday we'll drive in the country. And we'll open the windshield, and take lunch.

WILLY: No, the windshields don't open on the new cars.

LINDA: But you opened it today.

WILLY: Me? I didn't. (*He stops.*) Now isn't that peculiar! Isn't that a remarkable — (*He breaks off in amazement and fright as the flute is heard distantly.*)

LINDA: What, darling?

WILLY: That is the most remarkable thing.

LINDA: What, dear?

WILLY: I was thinking of the Chevy. (*Slight pause.*) Nineteen twenty-eight . . . when I had that red Chevy — (*Breaks off.*) That funny? I coulda sworn I was driving that Chevy today.

LINDA: Well, that's nothing. Something must've reminded you.

WILLY: Remarkable. Ts. Remember those days? The way Biff used to simonize that car? The dealer refused to believe there was eighty thousand miles on it. (*He shakes his head.*) Heh! (*To Linda.*) Close your eyes, I'll be right up. (*He walks out of the bedroom.*)

HAPPY (*to Biff*): Jesus, maybe he smashed up the car again!

LINDA (*calling after Willy*): Be careful on the stairs, dear! The cheese is on the middle shelf! (*She turns, goes over to the bed, takes his jacket, and goes out of the bedroom.*)

Light has risen on the boys' room. Unseen, Willy is heard talking to himself, "Eighty thousand miles," and a little laugh. Biff gets out of bed, comes downstage a bit, and stands attentively. Biff is two years older than his brother Happy, well built, but in these days bears a worn air and seems less self-assured. He has succeeded less, and his dreams are stronger and less acceptable than Happy's. Happy is tall, powerfully made. Sexuality is like a visible color on him, or a scent that many women have discovered. He, like his brother, is lost, but in a different way, for he has never allowed himself to turn his face toward defeat and is thus more confused and hard-skinned, although seemingly more content.

HAPPY (*getting out of bed*): He's going to get his license taken away if he keeps that up. I'm getting nervous about him, y'know, Biff?

BIFF: His eyes are going.

HAPPY: No, I've driven with him. He sees all right. He just doesn't keep his mind on it. I drove into the city with him last week. He stops at a green light and then it turns red and he goes. (*He laughs.*)

BIFF: Maybe he's color-blind.

HAPPY: Pop? Why he's got the finest eye for color in the business. You know that.

BIFF (*sitting down on his bed*): I'm going to sleep.

HAPPY: You're not still sour on Dad, are you, Biff?

BIFF: He's all right, I guess.

WILLY (*underneath them, in the living-room*): Yes, sir, eighty thousand miles — eighty-two thousand!

BIFF: You smoking?

HAPPY (*holding out a pack of cigarettes*): Want one?

BIFF (*taking a cigarette*): I can never sleep when I smell it.

WILLY: What a simonizing job, heh!

HAPPY (*with deep sentiment*): Funny, Biff, y'know? Us sleeping in here again? The old beds. (*He pats his bed affectionately.*) All the talk that went across those two beds, huh? Our whole lives.

BIFF: Yeah. Lotta dreams and plans.

HAPPY (*with a deep and masculine laugh*): About five hundred women would like to know what was said in this room.

They share a soft laugh.

BIFF: Remember that big Betsy something — what the hell was her name — over on Bushwick Avenue?

HAPPY (*combing his hair*): With the collie dog!

BIFF: That's the one. I got you in there, remember?

HAPPY: Yeah, that was my first time — I think. Boy, there was a pig! (*They laugh, almost crudely.*) You taught me everything I know about women. Don't forget that.

BIFF: I bet you forgot how bashful you used to be. Especially with girls.

HAPPY: Oh, I still am, Biff.

BIFF: Oh, go on.

HAPPY: I just control it, that's all. I think I got less bashful and you got more so. What happened, Biff? Where's the old humor, the old confidence? (*He shakes Biff's knee. Biff gets up and moves restlessly about the room.*) What's the matter?

BIFF: Why does Dad mock me all the time?

HAPPY: He's not mocking you, he —

BIFF: Everything I say there's a twist of mockery on his face. I can't get near him.

HAPPY: He just wants you to make good, that's all. I wanted to talk to you about Dad for a long time, Biff. Something's — happening to him. He — talks to himself.

BIFF: I noticed that this morning. But he always mumbled.

HAPPY: But not so noticeable. It got so embarrassing I sent him to Florida. And you know something? Most of the time he's talking to you.

BIFF: What's he say about me?

HAPPY: I can't make it out.

BIFF: What's he say about me?

HAPPY: I think the fact that you're not settled, that you're still kind of up in the air . . .

BIFF: There's one or two other things depressing him, Happy.

HAPPY: What do you mean?

BIFF: Never mind. Just don't lay it all to me.

HAPPY: But I think if you just got started — I mean — is there any future for you out there?

BIFF: I tell ya, Hap, I don't know what the future is. I don't know — what I'm supposed to want.

HAPPY: What do you mean?

BIFF: Well, I spent six or seven years after high school trying to work myself up. Shipping clerk, salesman, business of one kind or another. And it's a measly manner of existence. To get on that subway on the hot mornings in summer. To devote your whole life to keeping stock, or making phone calls, or selling or buying. To suffer fifty weeks of the year for the sake of a two-week vacation, when all you really desire is to be outdoors, with your shirt off. And always to have to get ahead of the next fella. And still — that's how you build a future.

HAPPY: Well, you really enjoy it on a farm? Are you content out there?

BIFF (*with rising agitation*): Hap, I've had twenty or thirty different kinds of jobs since I left home before the war, and it always turns out the same. I just realized it lately. In Nebraska when I herded cattle, and the Dakotas, and Arizona, and now in Texas. It's why I came home now, I guess, because I realized it. This farm I work on, it's spring there now, see? And they've got about fifteen new colts. There's nothing more inspiring or — beautiful than the sight of a mare and a new colt. And it's cool there now, see? Texas is cool now, and it's spring. And whenever spring comes to where I am, I suddenly get the feeling, my God, I'm not gettin' anywhere! What the hell am I doing, playing around with horses, twenty-eight dollars a week! I'm thirty-four years old, I oughta be makin' my future. That's when I come running home. And now, I get here, and I don't know what to do with myself. (*After a pause.*) I've always made a point of not wasting my life, and everytime I come back here I know that all I've done is to waste my life.

HAPPY: You're a poet, you know that, Biff? You're a — you're an idealist!

BIFF: No, I'm mixed up very bad. Maybe I oughta get married. Maybe I oughta get stuck into something. Maybe that's my trouble. I'm like a boy. I'm not married. I'm not in business, I just — I'm like a boy. Are you content, Hap? You're a success, aren't you? Are you content?

HAPPY: Hell, no!

BIFF: Why? You're making money, aren't you?

HAPPY (*moving about with energy, expressiveness*): All I can do now is wait for the merchandise manager to die. And suppose I get to be merchandise manager? He's a good friend of mine, and he just built a terrific estate on Long Island. And he lived there about two months and sold it, and now he's building another one. He can't enjoy it once it's finished. And I know that's just what I would do. I don't know what the hell I'm workin' for. Sometimes I sit in my apartment — all alone. And I think of the rent I'm paying. And it's crazy. But then, it's what I always wanted. My own apartment, a car, and plenty of women. And still, goddammit, I'm lonely.

BIFF (*with enthusiasm*): Listen, why don't you come out West with me?

HAPPY: You and I, heh?

BIFF: Sure, maybe we could buy a ranch. Raise cattle, use our muscles. Men built like we are should be working out in the open.

HAPPY (*avidly*): The Loman Brothers, heh?

BIFF (*with vast affection*): Sure, we'd be known all over the counties!

HAPPY (*enthralled*): That's what I dream about, Biff. Sometimes I want to just rip my clothes off in the middle of the store and outbox that goddam merchandise manager. I mean I can outbox, outrun, and outlift anybody in that store, and I have to take orders from those common, petty sons-of-bitches till I can't stand it any more.

BIFF: I'm tellin' you, kid, if you were with me I'd be happy out there.

HAPPY (*enthused*): See, Biff, everybody around me is so false that I'm constantly lowering my ideals . . .

BIFF: Baby, together we'd stand up for one another, we'd have someone to trust.

HAPPY: If I were around you —

BIFF: Hap, the trouble is we weren't brought up to grub for money. I don't know how to do it.

HAPPY: Neither can I!

BIFF: Then let's go!

HAPPY: The only thing is — what can you make out there?

BIFF: But look at your friend. Builds an estate and then hasn't the peace of mind to live in it.

HAPPY: Yeah, but when he walks into the store the waves part in front of him. That's fifty-two thousand dollars a year coming through the revolving door, and I got more in my pinky finger than he's got in his head.

BIFF: Yeah, but you just said —

HAPPY: I gotta show some of those pompous, self-important executives over there that Hap Loman can make the grade. I want to walk into the store the way he walks in. Then I'll go with you, Biff. We'll be together yet, I swear. But take those two we had tonight. Now weren't they gorgeous creatures?

BIFF: Yeah, yeah, most gorgeous I've had in years.

HAPPY: I get that any time I want, Biff. Whenever I feel disgusted. The trouble is, it gets like bowling or something. I just keep knockin' them over and it doesn't mean anything. You still run around a lot?

BIFF: Naa. I'd like to find a girl — steady, somebody with substance.

HAPPY: That's what I long for.

BIFF: Go on! You'd never come home.

HAPPY: I would! Somebody with character, with resistance! Like Mom, y'know? You're gonna call me a bastard when I tell you this. That girl Charlotte I was with tonight is engaged to be married in five weeks. (*He tries on his new hat.*)

BIFF: No kiddin'!

HAPPY: Sure, the guy's in line for the vice-presidency of the store. I don't know what gets into me, maybe I just have an overdeveloped sense of competition or something, but I went and ruined her, and furthermore I can't get rid of her. And he's the third executive I've done that to. Isn't that a crummy characteristic? And to top it all, I go to their weddings! (*Indignantly, but laughing.*) Like I'm not supposed to take bribes. Manufacturers offer me a hundred-dollar bill now and then to throw an order their way. You know how honest I am, but it's like this girl, see. I hate myself for it. Because I don't want the girl, and, still, I take it and — I love it!

BIFF: Let's go to sleep.

HAPPY: I guess we didn't settle anything, heh?

BIFF: I just got one idea that I think I'm going to try.

HAPPY: What's that?

BIFF: Remember Bill Oliver?

HAPPY: Sure, Oliver is very big now. You want to work for him again?

BIFF: No, but when I quit he said something to me. He put his arm on my shoulder, and he said, "Biff, if you ever need anything, come to me."

HAPPY: I remember that. That sounds good.

BIFF: I think I'll go to see him. If I could get ten thousand or even seven or eight thousand dollars I could buy a beautiful ranch.

HAPPY: I bet he'd back you. 'Cause he thought highly of you, Biff. I mean, they all do. You're well liked, Biff. That's why I say to come back here, and we both have the apartment. And I'm tellin' you, Biff, any babe you want . . .

BIFF: No, with a ranch I could do the work I like and still be something. I just wonder though. I wonder if Oliver still thinks I stole that carton of basketballs.

HAPPY: Oh, he probably forgot that long ago. It's almost ten years. You're too sensitive. Anyway, he didn't really fire you.

BIFF: Well, I think he was going to. I think that's why I quit. I was never sure whether he knew or not. I know he thought the world of me, though. I was the only one he'd let lock up the place.

WILLY (*below*): You gonna wash the engine, Biff?

HAPPY: Shh!

Biff looks at Happy, who is gazing down, listening. Willy is mumbling in the parlor.

HAPPY: You hear that?

They listen. Willy laughs warmly.

BIFF (*growing angry*): Doesn't he know Mom can hear that?

WILLY: Don't get your sweater dirty, Biff!

A look of pain crosses Biff's face.

HAPPY: Isn't that terrible? Don't leave again, will you? You'll find a job here. You gotta stick around. I don't know what to do about him, it's getting embarrassing.

WILLY: What a simonizing job!

BIFF: Mom's hearing that!

WILLY: No kiddin', Biff, you got a date? Wonderful!

HAPPY: Go on to sleep. But talk to him in the morning, will you?

BIFF (*reluctantly getting into bed*): With her in the house. Brother!

HAPPY (*getting into bed*): I wish you'd have a good talk with him.

The light on their room begins to fade.

BIFF (*to himself in bed*): That selfish, stupid . . .

HAPPY: Sh . . . Sleep, Biff.

Their light is out. Well before they have finished speaking, Willy's form is dimly seen below in the darkened kitchen. He opens the refrigerator, searches in there, and takes out a bottle of milk. The apartment houses are fading out, and the entire house and surroundings become covered with leaves. Music insinuates itself as the leaves appear.

WILLY: Just wanna be careful with those girls, Biff, that's all. Don't make any promises. No promises of any kind. Because a girl, y'know, they always believe what you tell 'em, and you're very young, Biff, you're too young to be talking seriously to girls.

Light rises on the kitchen. Willy, talking, shuts the refrigerator door and comes downstage to the kitchen table. He pours milk into a glass. He is totally immersed in himself, smiling faintly.

WILLY: Too young entirely, Biff. You want to watch your schooling first. Then when you're all set, there'll be plenty of girls for a boy like you. (*He smiles broadly at a kitchen chair.*) That so? The girls pay for you? (*He laughs.*) Boy, you must really be makin' a hit.

Willy is gradually addressing — physically — a point offstage, speaking through the wall of the kitchen, and his voice has been rising in volume to that of a normal conversation.

WILLY: I been wondering why you polish the car so careful. Ha! Don't leave the hubcaps, boys. Get the chamois to the hubcaps. Happy, use newspaper on the windows, it's the easiest thing. Show him how to do it, Biff! You see, Happy? Pad it up, use it like a pad. That's it, that's it, good work. You're doin' all right, Hap. (*He pauses, then nods in approbation for a few seconds, then looks upward.*) Biff, first thing we gotta do when we get time is clip that big branch over the house. Afraid it's gonna fall in a storm and hit the roof. Tell you what. We get a rope and sling her around, and then we climb up there with a couple of saws and take her down. Soon as you finish the car, boys, I wanna see ya. I got a surprise for you, boys.

BIFF (*offstage*): Whatta ya got, Dad?

WILLY: No, you finish first. Never leave a job till you're finished — remember that. (*Looking toward the "big trees."*) Biff, up in Albany I saw a beautiful hammock. I think I'll buy it next trip, and we'll hang it right between those two elms. Wouldn't that be something? Just swingin' there under those branches. Boy, that would be . . .

Young Biff and Young Happy appear from the direction Willy was addressing. Happy carries rags and a pail of water. Biff, wearing a sweater with a block "S," carries a football.

BIFF (*pointing in the direction of the car offstage*): How's that, Pop, professional?

WILLY: Terrific. Terrific job, boys. Good work, Biff.

HAPPY: Where's the surprise, Pop?

WILLY: In the back seat of the car.

HAPPY: Boy! (*He runs off.*)

BIFF: What is it, Dad? Tell me, what'd you buy?

WILLY (*laughing, cuffs him*): Never mind, something I want you to have.

BIFF (*turns and starts off*): What is it, Hap?

HAPPY (*offstage*): It's a punching bag!

BIFF: Oh, Pop!

WILLY: It's got Gene Tunney's signature on it!

Happy runs onstage with a punching bag.

BIFF: Gee, how'd you know we wanted a punching bag?

WILLY: Well, it's the finest thing for the timing.

HAPPY (*lies down on his back and pedals with his feet*): I'm losing weight, you notice, Pop?

WILLY (*to Happy*): Jumping rope is good too.

BIFF: Did you see the new football I got?

WILLY (*examining the ball*): Where'd you get a new ball?

BIFF: The coach told me to practice my passing.

WILLY: That so? And he gave you the ball, heh?

BIFF: Well, I borrowed it from the locker room. (*He laughs confidentially.*)

WILLY (*laughing with him at the theft*): I want you to return that.

HAPPY: I told you he wouldn't like it!

BIFF (*angrily*): Well, I'm bringing it back!

WILLY (*stopping the incipient argument, to Happy*): Sure, he's gotta practice with a regulation ball, doesn't he? (*To Biff.*) Coach'll probably congratulate you on your initiative!

BIFF: Oh, he keeps congratulating my initiative all the time, Pop.

WILLY: That's because he likes you. If somebody else took that ball there'd be an uproar. So what's the report, boys, what's the report?

BIFF: Where'd you go this time, Dad? Gee we were lonesome for you.

WILLY (*pleased, puts an arm around each boy and they come down to the apron*): Lonesome, heh?

BIFF: Missed you every minute.

WILLY: Don't say? Tell you a secret, boys. Don't breathe it to a soul. Someday I'll have my own business, and I'll never have to leave home any more.

HAPPY: Like Uncle Charley, heh?

WILLY: Bigger than Uncle Charley! Because Charley is not — liked. He's liked, but he's not — well liked.

BIFF: Where'd you go this time, Dad?

WILLY: Well, I got on the road, and I went north to Providence. Met the Mayor.

BIFF: The Mayor of Providence!

WILLY: He was sitting in the hotel lobby.

BIFF: What'd he say?

WILLY: He said, "Morning!" And I said, "You got a fine city here, Mayor." And then he had coffee with me. And then I went to Waterbury. Waterbury is a fine city. Big clock city, the famous Waterbury clock. Sold a nice bill there. And then Boston — Boston is the cradle of the Revolution. A fine city. And a couple of other towns in Mass., and on to Portland and Bangor and straight home!

BIFF: Gee, I'd love to go with you sometime, Dad.

WILLY: Soon as summer comes.

HAPPY: Promise?

WILLY: You and Hap and I, and I'll show you all the towns. America is full of beautiful towns and fine, upstanding people. And they know me, boys, they know me up and down New England. The finest people. And when I bring you fellas up, there'll be open sesame for all of us, 'cause one thing, boys: I have friends. I can park my car in any street in New England, and the cops protect it like their own. This summer, heh?

BIFF AND HAPPY (*together*): Yeah! You bet!

WILLY: We'll take our bathing suits.

HAPPY: We'll carry your bags, Pop!

WILLY: Oh, won't that be something! Me comin' into the Boston stores with you boys carryin' my bags. What a sensation!

Biff is prancing around, practicing passing the ball.

WILLY: You nervous, Biff, about the game?

BIFF: Not if you're gonna be there.

WILLY: What do they say about you in school, now that they made you captain?

HAPPY: There's a crowd of girls behind him everytime the classes change.

BIFF (*taking Willy's hand*): This Saturday, Pop, this Saturday — just for you, I'm going to break through for a touchdown.

HAPPY: You're supposed to pass.

BIFF: I'm takin' one play for Pop. You watch me, Pop, and when I take off my helmet, that means I'm breakin' out. Then you watch me crash through that line!

WILLY (*kisses Biff*): Oh, wait'll I tell this in Boston!

Bernard enters in knickers. He is younger than Biff, earnest and loyal, a worried boy.

BERNARD: Biff, where are you? You're supposed to study with me today.

WILLY: Hey, looka Bernard. What're you lookin' so anemic about, Bernard?

BERNARD: He's gotta study, Uncle Willy. He's got Regents next week.

HAPPY (*tauntingly, spinning Bernard around*): Let's box, Bernard!

BERNARD: Biff! (*He gets away from Happy.*) Listen, Biff, I heard Mr. Birnbaum say that if you don't start studyin' math, he's gonna flunk you, and you won't graduate. I heard him!

WILLY: You better study with him, Biff. Go ahead now.

BERNARD: I heard him!

BIFF: Oh, Pop, you didn't see my sneakers! (*He holds up a foot for Willy to look at.*)

WILLY: Hey, that's a beautiful job of printing!

BERNARD (*wiping his glasses*): Just because he printed University of Virginia on his sneakers doesn't mean they've got to graduate him, Uncle Willy!

WILLY (*angrily*): What're you talking about? With scholarships to three universities they're gonna flunk him?

BERNARD: But I heard Mr. Birnbaum say —

WILLY: Don't be a pest, Bernard! (*To his boys.*) What an anemic!

BERNARD: Okay, I'm waiting for you in my house, Biff.

Bernard goes off. The Lomans laugh.

WILLY: Bernard is not well liked, is he?

BIFF: He's liked, but he's not well liked.

HAPPY: That's right, Pop.

WILLY: That's just what I mean. Bernard can get the best marks in school, y'understand, but when he gets out in the business world, y'understand, you are going to be five times ahead of him. That's why I thank Almighty God you're both built like Adonises.° Because the man who makes an appearance in the business world, the man who creates personal interest, is the man who gets ahead. Be liked and you will never want. You take me, for instance. I never have to wait in line to see a buyer. "Willy Loman is here!" That's all they have to know, and I go right through.

BIFF: Did you knock them dead, Pop?

WILLY: Knocked 'em cold in Providence, slaughtered 'em in Boston.

HAPPY (*on his back, pedaling again*): I'm losing weight, you notice, Pop?

Linda enters, as of old, a ribbon in her hair, carrying a basket of washing.

LINDA (*with youthful energy*): Hello, dear!

WILLY: Sweetheart!

LINDA: How'd the Chevy run?

WILLY: Chevrolet, Linda, is the greatest car ever built. (*To the boys.*) Since when do you let your mother carry wash up the stairs?

BIFF: Grab hold there, boy!

HAPPY: Where to, Mom?

LINDA: Hang them up on the line. And you better go down to your friends, Biff. The cellar is full of boys. They don't know what to do with themselves.

BIFF: Ah, when Pop comes home they can wait!

WILLY (*laughs appreciatively*): You better go down and tell them what to do, Biff.

BIFF: I think I'll have them sweep out the furnace room.

WILLY: Good work, Biff.

BIFF (*goes through wall-line of kitchen to doorway at back and calls down*): Fellas! Everybody sweep out the furnace room! I'll be right down!

VOICES: All right! Okay, Biff.

BIFF: George and Sam and Frank, come out back! We're hangin' up the wash! Come on, Hap, on the double! (*He and Happy carry out the basket.*)

Adonises: In Greek Mythology Adonis is a youth known for his good looks and favored by Aphrodite, the goddess of love and beauty.

LINDA: The way they obey him!

WILLY: Well, that's training, the training. I'm tellin' you, I was sellin' thousands and thousands, but I had to come home.

LINDA: Oh, the whole block'll be at that game. Did you sell anything?

WILLY: I did five hundred gross in Providence and seven hundred gross in Boston.

LINDA: No! Wait a minute, I've got a pencil. (*She pulls pencil and paper out of her apron pocket.*) That makes your commission . . . Two hundred — my God! Two hundred and twelve dollars!

WILLY: Well, I didn't figure it yet, but . . .

LINDA: How much did you do?

WILLY: Well, I — I did — about a hundred and eighty gross in Providence. Well, no — it came to — roughly two hundred gross on the whole trip.

LINDA (*without hesitation*): Two hundred gross. That's . . . (*She figures.*)

WILLY: The trouble was that three of the stores were half closed for inventory in Boston. Otherwise I woulda broke records.

LINDA: Well, it makes seventy dollars and some pennies. That's very good.

WILLY: What do we owe?

LINDA: Well, on the first there's sixteen dollars on the refrigerator —

WILLY: Why sixteen?

LINDA: Well, the fan belt broke, so it was a dollar eighty.

WILLY: But it's brand new.

LINDA: Well, the man said that's the way it is. Till they work themselves in, y'know.

They move through the wall-line into the kitchen.

WILLY: I hope we didn't get stuck on that machine.

LINDA: They got the biggest ads of any of them!

WILLY: I know, it's a fine machine. What else?

LINDA: Well, there's nine-sixty for the washing machine. And for the vacuum cleaner there's three and a half due on the fifteenth. Then the roof, you got twenty-one dollars remaining.

WILLY: It don't leak, does it?

LINDA: No, they did a wonderful job. Then you owe Frank for the carburetor.

WILLY: I'm not going to pay that man! That goddam Chevrolet, they ought to prohibit the manufacture of that car!

LINDA: Well, you owe him three and a half. And odds and ends, comes to around a hundred and twenty dollars by the fifteenth.

WILLY: A hundred and twenty dollars! My God, if business don't pick up I don't know what I'm gonna do!

LINDA: Well, next week you'll do better.

WILLY: Oh, I'll knock 'em dead next week. I'll go to Hartford. I'm very well liked in Hartford. You know, the trouble is, Linda, people don't seem to take to me.

They move onto the forestage.

LINDA: Oh, don't be foolish.

WILLY: I know it when I walk in. They seem to laugh at me.

LINDA: Why? Why would they laugh at you? Don't talk that way, Willy.

Willy moves to the edge of the stage. Linda goes into the kitchen and starts to darn stockings.

WILLY: I don't know the reason for it, but they just pass me by. I'm not noticed.

LINDA: But you're doing wonderful, dear. You're making seventy to a hundred dollars a week.

WILLY: But I gotta be at it ten, twelve hours a day. Other men — I don't know — they do it easier. I don't know why — I can't stop myself — I talk too much. A man oughta come in with a few words. One thing about Charley. He's a man of few words, and they respect him.

LINDA: You don't talk too much, you're just lively.

WILLY (*smiling*): Well, I figure, what the hell, life is short, a couple of jokes. (*To himself.*) I joke too much! (*The smile goes.*)

LINDA: Why? You're —

WILLY: I'm fat. I'm very — foolish to look at, Linda. I didn't tell you, but Christmas time I happened to be calling on F. H. Stewarts, and a salesman I know, as I was going in to see the buyer I heard him say something about — walrus. And I — I cracked him right across the face. I won't take that. I simply will not take that. But they do laugh at me. I know that.

LINDA: Darling . . .

WILLY: I gotta overcome it. I know I gotta overcome it. I'm not dressing to advantage, maybe.

LINDA: Willy, darling, you're the handsomest man in the world —

WILLY: Oh, no, Linda.

LINDA: To me you are. (*Slight pause.*) The handsomest.

From the darkness is heard the laughter of a woman. Willy doesn't turn to it, but it continues through Linda's lines.

LINDA: And the boys, Willy. Few men are idolized by their children the way you are.

Music is heard as behind a scrim, to the left of the house, The Woman, dimly seen, is dressing.

WILLY (*with great feeling*): You're the best there is, Linda, you're a pal, you know that? On the road — on the road I want to grab you sometimes and just kiss the life outa you.

The laughter is loud now, and he moves into a brightening area at the left, where The Woman has come from behind the scrim and is standing, putting on her hat, looking into a "mirror" and laughing.

WILLY: 'Cause I get so lonely — especially when business is bad and there's nobody to talk to. I get the feeling that I'll never sell anything again, that I won't make a living for you, or a business, a business for the boys. (*He talks through The Woman's subsiding laughter; The Woman primps at the "mirror."*) There's so much I want to make for —

THE WOMAN: Me? You didn't make me, Willy. I picked you.

WILLY (*pleased*): You picked me?

THE WOMAN (*who is quite proper-looking, Willy's age*): I did. I've been sitting at that desk watching all the salesmen go by, day in, day out. But you've got such a sense of humor, and we do have such a good time together, don't we?

WILLY: Sure, sure. (*He takes her in his arms.*) Why do you have to go now?

THE WOMAN: It's two o'clock . . .

WILLY: No, come on in! (*He pulls her.*)

THE WOMAN: . . . my sisters'll be scandalized. When'll you be back?

WILLY: Oh, two weeks about. Will you come up again?

THE WOMAN: Sure thing. You do make me laugh. It's good for me. (*She squeezes his arm, kisses him.*) And I think you're a wonderful man.

WILLY: You picked me, heh?

THE WOMAN: Sure. Because you're so sweet. And such a kidder.

WILLY: Well, I'll see you next time I'm in Boston.

THE WOMAN: I'll put you right through to the buyers.

WILLY (*slapping her bottom*): Right. Well, bottoms up!

THE WOMAN (*slaps him gently and laughs*): You just kill me, Willy. (*He suddenly grabs her and kisses her roughly.*) You kill me. And thanks for the stockings. I love a lot of stockings. Well, good night.

WILLY: Good night. And keep your pores open!

THE WOMAN: Oh, Willy!

The Woman bursts out laughing, and Linda's laughter blends in. The Woman disappears into the dark. Now the area at the kitchen table brightens. Linda is sitting where she was at the kitchen table, but now is mending a pair of her silk stockings.

LINDA: You are, Willy. The handsomest man. You've got no reason to feel that —

WILLY (*coming out of The Woman's dimming area and going over to Linda*): I'll make it all up to you, Linda, I'll —

LINDA: There's nothing to make up, dear. You're doing fine, better than —

WILLY (*noticing her mending*): What's that?

LINDA: Just mending my stockings. They're so expensive —

WILLY (*angrily, taking them from her*): I won't have you mending stockings in this house! Now throw them out!

Linda puts the stockings in her pocket.

BERNARD (*entering on the run*): Where is he? If he doesn't study!

WILLY (*moving to the forestage, with great agitation*): You'll give him the answers!

BERNARD: I do, but I can't on a Regents! That's a state exam! They're liable to arrest me!

WILLY: Where is he? I'll whip him, I'll whip him!

LINDA: And he'd better give back that football, Willy, it's not nice.

WILLY: Biff! Where is he? Why is he taking everything?

LINDA: He's too rough with the girls, Willy. All the mothers are afraid of him!

WILLY: I'll whip him!

BERNARD: He's driving the car without a license!

The Woman's laugh is heard.

WILLY: Shut up!

LINDA: All the mothers —

WILLY: Shut up!

BERNARD (*backing quietly away and out*): Mr. Birnbaum says he's stuck up.

WILLY: Get outa here!

BERNARD: If he doesn't buckle down he'll flunk math! (*He goes off.*)

LINDA: He's right, Willy, you've gotta —

WILLY (*exploding at her*): There's nothing the matter with him! You want him to be a worm like Bernard? He's got spirit, personality . . .

As he speaks, Linda, almost in tears, exits into the living-room. Willy is alone in the kitchen, wilting and staring. The leaves are gone. It is night again, and the apartment houses look down from behind.

WILLY: Loaded with it. Loaded! What is he stealing? He's giving it back, isn't he? Why is he stealing? What did I tell him? I never in my life told him anything but decent things.

Happy in pajamas has come down the stairs; Willy suddenly becomes aware of Happy's presence.

HAPPY: Let's go now, come on.

WILLY (*sitting down at the kitchen table*): Huh! Why did she have to wax the floors herself? Everytime she waxes the floors she keels over. She knows that!

HAPPY: Shh! Take it easy. What brought you back tonight?

WILLY: I got an awful scare. Nearly hit a kid in Yonkers. God! Why didn't I go to Alaska with my brother Ben that time! Ben! That man was a genius, that man was success incarnate! What a mistake! He begged me to go.

HAPPY: Well, there's no use in —

WILLY: You guys! There was a man started with the clothes on his back and ended up with diamond mines!

HAPPY: Boy, someday I'd like to know how he did it.

WILLY: What's the mystery? The man knew what he wanted and went out and got it! Walked into a jungle, and comes out, the age of twenty-one, and he's rich! The world is an oyster, but you don't crack it open on a mattress!

HAPPY: Pop, I told you I'm gonna retire you for life.

WILLY: You'll retire me for life on seventy goddam dollars a week? And your women and your car and your apartment, and you'll retire me for life! Christ's sake, I couldn't get past Yonkers today! Where are you guys, where are you? The woods are burning! I can't drive a car!

Charley has appeared in the doorway. He is a large man, slow of speech, laconic, immovable. In all he says, despite what he says, there is pity, and, now, trepidation. He has a robe over pajamas, slippers on his feet. He enters the kitchen.

CHARLEY: Everything all right?

HAPPY: Yeah, Charley, everything's . . .

WILLY: What's the matter?

CHARLEY: I heard some noise. I thought something happened. Can't we do something about the walls? You sneeze in here, and in my house hats blow off.

HAPPY: Let's go to bed, Dad. Come on.

Charley signals to Happy to go.

WILLY: You go ahead, I'm not tired at the moment.

HAPPY (*to Willy*): Take it easy, huh? (*He exits.*)

WILLY: What're you doin' up?

CHARLEY (*sitting down at the kitchen table opposite Willy*): Couldn't sleep good. I had a heartburn.

WILLY: Well, you don't know how to eat.

CHARLEY: I eat with my mouth.

WILLY: No, you're ignorant. You gotta know about vitamins and things like that.

CHARLEY: Come on, let's shoot. Tire you out a little.

WILLY (*hesitantly*): All right. You got cards?

CHARLEY (*taking a deck from his pocket*): Yeah, I got them. Someplace. What is it with those vitamins?

WILLY (*dealing*): They build up your bones. Chemistry.

CHARLEY: Yeah, but there's no bones in a heartburn.

WILLY: What are you talkin' about? Do you know the first thing about it?

CHARLEY: Don't get insulted.

WILLY: Don't talk about something you don't know anything about.

They are playing. Pause.

CHARLEY: What're you doin' home?

WILLY: A little trouble with the car.

CHARLEY: Oh. (*Pause.*) I'd like to take a trip to California.

WILLY: Don't say.

CHARLEY: You want a job?

WILLY: I got a job, I told you that. (*After a slight pause.*) What the hell are you offering me a job for?

CHARLEY: Don't get insulted.

WILLY: Don't insult me.

CHARLEY: I don't see no sense in it. You don't have to go on this way.

WILLY: I got a good job. (*Slight pause.*) What do you keep comin' in here for?

CHARLEY: You want me to go?

WILLY (*after a pause, withering*): I can't understand it. He's going back to Texas again. What the hell is that?

CHARLEY: Let him go.

WILLY: I got nothin' to give him, Charley, I'm clean, I'm clean.

CHARLEY: He won't starve. None a them starve. Forget about him.

WILLY: Then what have I got to remember?

CHARLEY: You take it too hard. To hell with it. When a deposit bottle is broken you don't get your nickel back.

WILLY: That's easy enough for you to say.

CHARLEY: That ain't easy for me to say.

WILLY: Did you see the ceiling I put up in the living-room?

CHARLEY: Yeah, that's a piece of work. To put up a ceiling is a mystery to me. How do you do it?

WILLY: What's the difference?

CHARLEY: Well, talk about it.

WILLY: You gonna put up a ceiling?

CHARLEY: How could I put up a ceiling?

WILLY: Then what the hell are you bothering me for?

CHARLEY: You're insulted again.

WILLY: A man who can't handle tools is not a man. You're disgusting.

CHARLEY: Don't call me disgusting, Willy.

Uncle Ben, carrying a valise and an umbrella, enters the forestage from around the right corner of the house. He is a stolid man, in his sixties, with a mustache and an authoritative air. He is utterly certain of his destiny, and there is an aura of far places about him. He enters exactly as Willy speaks.

WILLY: I'm getting awfully tired, Ben.

Ben's music is heard. Ben looks around at everything.

CHARLEY: Good, keep playing; you'll sleep better. Did you call me Ben?

Ben looks at his watch.

WILLY: That's funny. For a second there you reminded me of my brother Ben.

BEN: I only have a few minutes. (*He strolls, inspecting the place. Willy and Charley continue playing.*)

CHARLEY: You never heard from him again, heh? Since that time?

WILLY: Didn't Linda tell you? Couple of weeks ago we got a letter from his wife in Africa. He died.

CHARLEY: That so.

BEN (*chuckling*): So this is Brooklyn, eh?

CHARLEY: Maybe you're in for some of his money.

WILLY: Naa, he had seven sons. There's just one opportunity I had with that man . . .

BEN: I must make a train, William. There are several properties I'm looking at in Alaska.

WILLY: Sure, sure! If I'd gone with him to Alaska that time, everything would've been totally different.

CHARLEY: Go on, you'd froze to death up there.

WILLY: What're you talking about?

BEN: Opportunity is tremendous in Alaska, William. Surprised you're not up there.

WILLY: Sure, tremendous.

CHARLEY: Heh?

WILLY: There was the only man I ever met who knew the answers.

CHARLEY: Who?

BEN: How are you all?

WILLY (*taking a pot, smiling*): Fine, fine.

CHARLEY: Pretty sharp tonight.

BEN: Is mother living with you?

WILLY: No, she died a long time ago.

CHARLEY: Who?

BEN: That's too bad. Fine specimen of a lady, Mother.

WILLY (*to Charley*): Heh?

BEN: I'd hoped to see the old girl.

CHARLEY: Who died?

BEN: Heard anything from Father, have you?

WILLY (*unnerved*): What do you mean, who died?

CHARLEY (*taking a pot*): What're you talkin' about?

BEN (*looking at his watch*): William, it's half-past eight!

WILLY (*as though to dispel his confusion he angrily stops Charley's hand*): That's my build!

CHARLEY: I put the ace —

WILLY: If you don't know how to play the game I'm not gonna throw my money away on you!

CHARLEY (*rising*): It was my ace, for God's sake!

WILLY: I'm through, I'm through!

BEN: When did Mother die?

WILLY: Long ago. Since the beginning you never knew how to play cards.

CHARLEY (*picks up the cards and goes to the door*): All right! Next time I'll bring a deck with five aces.

WILLY: I don't play that kind of game!

CHARLEY (*turning to him*): You ought to be ashamed of yourself!

WILLY: Yeah?

CHARLEY: Yeah! (*He goes out.*)

WILLY (*slamming the door after him*): Ignoramus!

BEN (*as Willy comes toward him through the wall-line of the kitchen*): So you're William.

WILLY (*shaking Ben's hand*): Ben! I've been waiting for you so long! What's the answer? How did you do it?

BEN: Oh, there's a story in that.

Linda enters the forestage, as of old, carrying the wash basket.

LINDA: Is this Ben?

BEN (*gallantly*): How do you do, my dear.

LINDA: Where've you been all these years? Willy's always wondered why you —

WILLY (*pulling Ben away from her impatiently*): Where is Dad? Didn't you follow him? How did you get started?

BEN: Well, I don't know how much you remember.

WILLY: Well, I was just a baby, of course, only three or four years old —

BEN: Three years and eleven months.

WILLY: What a memory, Ben!

BEN: I have many enterprises, William, and I have never kept books.

WILLY: I remember I was sitting under the wagon in — was it Nebraska?

BEN: It was South Dakota, and I gave you a bunch of wild flowers.

WILLY: I remember you walking away down some open road.

BEN (*laughing*): I was going to find Father in Alaska.

WILLY: Where is he?

BEN: At that age I had a very faulty view of geography, William. I discovered after a few days that I was heading due south, so instead of Alaska, I ended up in Africa.

LINDA: Africa!

WILLY: The Gold Coast!

BEN: Principally diamond mines.

LINDA: Diamond mines!

BEN: Yes, my dear. But I've only a few minutes —

WILLY: No! Boys! Boys! (*Young Biff and Happy appear.*) Listen to this. This is your Uncle Ben, a great man! Tell my boys, Ben!

BEN: Why, boys, when I was seventeen I walked into the jungle, and when I was twenty-one I walked out. (*He laughs.*) And by God I was rich.

WILLY (*to the boys*): You see what I been talking about? The greatest things can happen!

BEN (*glancing at his watch*): I have an appointment in Ketchikan Tuesday week.

WILLY: No, Ben! Please tell about Dad. I want my boys to hear. I want them to know the kind of stock they spring from. All I remember is a man with a big beard, and I was in Mamma's lap, sitting around a fire, and some kind of high music.

BEN: His flute. He played the flute.

WILLY: Sure, the flute, that's right!

New music is heard, a high, rollicking tune.

BEN: Father was a very great and a very wild-hearted man. We would start in Boston, and he'd toss the whole family into the wagon, and then he'd drive the team right across the country; through Ohio, and Indiana, Michigan, Illinois, and all the Western states. And we'd stop in the towns and sell the flutes that he'd made on the way. Great inventor, Father. With one gadget he made more in a week than a man like you could make in a lifetime.

WILLY: That's just the way I'm bringing them up, Ben — rugged, well liked, all-around.

BEN: Yeah? (*To Biff.*) Hit that, boy — hard as you can. (*He pounds his stomach.*)

BIFF: Oh, no, sir!

BEN (*taking boxing stance*): Come on, get to me. (*He laughs.*)

WILLY: Go to it, Biff! Go ahead, show him!

BIFF: Okay! (*He cocks his fists and starts in.*)

LINDA (*to Willy*): Why must he fight, dear?

BEN (*sparring with Biff*): Good boy! Good boy!

WILLY: How's that, Ben, heh?

HAPPY: Give him the left, Biff!

LINDA: Why are you fighting?

BEN: Good boy! (*Suddenly comes in, trips Biff, and stands over him, the point of his umbrella poised over Biff's eye.*)

LINDA: Look out, Biff!

BIFF: Gee!

BEN (*patting Biff's knee*): Never fight fair with a stranger, boy. You'll never get out of the jungle that way. (*Taking Linda's hand and bowing*): It was an honor and a pleasure to meet you, Linda.

LINDA (*withdrawing her hand coldly, frightened*): Have a nice — trip.

BEN (*to Willy*): And good luck with your — what do you do?

WILLY: Selling.

BEN: Yes. Well . . . (*He raises his hand in farewell to all.*)

WILLY: No, Ben, I don't want you to think . . . (*He takes Ben's arm to show him.*) It's Brooklyn, I know, but we hunt too.

BEN: Really, now.

WILLY: Oh, sure, there's snakes and rabbits and — that's why I moved out here. Why, Biff can fell any one of these trees in no time! Boys! Go right over to where they're building the apartment house and get some sand. We're gonna rebuild the entire front stoop now! Watch this, Ben!

BIFF: Yes, sir! On the double, Hap!

HAPPY (*as he and Biff run off*): I lost weight, Pop, you notice?

Charley enters in knickers, even before the boys are gone.

CHARLEY: Listen, if they steal any more from that building the watchman'll put the cops on them!

LINDA (*to Willy*): Don't let Biff . . .

Ben laughs lustily.

WILLY: You shoulda seen the lumber they brought home last week. At least a dozen six-by-tens worth all kinds a money.

CHARLEY: Listen, if that watchman —

WILLY: I gave them hell, understand. But I got a couple of fearless characters there.

CHARLEY: Willy, the jails are full of fearless characters.

BEN (*clapping Willy on the back, with a laugh at Charley*): And the stock exchange, friend!

WILLY (*joining in Ben's laughter*): Where are the rest of your pants?

CHARLEY: My wife bought them.

WILLY: Now all you need is a golf club and you can go upstairs and go to sleep. (*To Ben*). Great athlete! Between him and his son Bernard they can't hammer a nail!

BERNARD (*rushing in*): The watchman's chasing Biff!

WILLY (*angrily*): Shut up! He's not stealing anything!

LINDA (*alarmed, hurrying off left*): Where is he? Biff, dear! (*She exits.*)

WILLY (*moving toward the left, away from Ben*): There's nothing wrong. What's the matter with you?

BEN: Nervy boy. Good!

WILLY (*laughing*): Oh, nerves of iron, that Biff!

CHARLEY: Don't know what it is. My New England man comes back and he's bleedin', they murdered him up there.

WILLY: It's contacts, Charley, I got important contacts!

CHARLEY (*sarcastically*): Glad to hear it, Willy. Come in later, we'll shoot a little casino. I'll take some of your Portland money. (*He laughs at Willy and exits.*)

WILLY (*turning to Ben*): Business is bad, it's murderous. But not for me, of course.

BEN: I'll stop by on my way back to Africa.

WILLY (*longingly*): Can't you stay a few days? You're just what I need, Ben, because I — I have a fine position here, but I — well, Dad left when I was such a baby and I never had a chance to talk to him and I still feel — kind of temporary about myself.

BEN: I'll be late for my train.

They are at opposite ends of the stage.

WILLY: Ben, my boys — can't we talk? They'd go into the jaws of hell for me, see, but I —

BEN: William, you're being first-rate with your boys. Outstanding, manly chaps!

WILLY (*hanging on to his words*): Oh, Ben, that's good to hear! Because sometimes I'm afraid that I'm not teaching them the right kind of — Ben, how should I teach them?

BEN (*giving great weight to each word, and with a certain vicious audacity*): William, when I walked into the jungle, I was seventeen. When I walked out I was twenty-one. And, by God, I was rich! (*He goes off into darkness around the right corner of the house.*)

WILLY: . . . was rich! That's just the spirit I want to imbue them with! To walk into a jungle! I was right! I was right! I was right!

Ben is gone, but Willy is still speaking to him as Linda, in nightgown and robe, enters the kitchen, glances around for Willy, then goes to the door of the house, looks out, and sees him. Comes down to his left. He looks at her.

LINDA: Willy, dear? Willy?

WILLY: I was right!

LINDA: Did you have some cheese? (*He can't answer.*) It's very late, darling. Come to bed, heh?

WILLY (*looking straight up*): Gotta break your neck to see a star in this yard.

LINDA: You coming in?

WILLY: Whatever happened to that diamond watch fob? Remember? When Ben came from Africa that time? Didn't he give me a watch fob with a diamond in it?

LINDA: You pawned it, dear. Twelve, thirteen years ago. For Biff's radio correspondence course.

WILLY: Gee, that was a beautiful thing. I'll take a walk.

LINDA: But you're in your slippers.

WILLY (*starting to go around the house at the left*): I was right! I was! (*Half to Linda, as he goes, shaking his head.*) What a man! There was a man worth talking to. I was right!

LINDA (*calling after Willy*): But in your slippers, Willy!

Willy is almost gone when Biff, in his pajamas, comes down the stairs and enters the kitchen.

BIFF: What is he doing out there?

LINDA: Sh!

BIFF: God Almighty, Mom, how long has he been doing this?

LINDA: Don't, he'll hear you.

BIFF: What the hell is the matter with him?

LINDA: It'll pass by morning.

BIFF: Shouldn't we do anything?

LINDA: Oh, my dear, you should do a lot of things, but there's nothing to do, so go to sleep.

Happy comes down the stairs and sits on the steps.

HAPPY: I never heard him so loud, Mom.

LINDA: Well, come around more often; you'll hear him. (*She sits down at the table and mends the lining of Willy's jacket.*)

BIFF: Why didn't you ever write me about this, Mom?

LINDA: How would I write to you? For over three months you had no address.

BIFF: I was on the move. But you know I thought of you all the time. You know that, don't you, pal?

LINDA: I know, dear, I know. But he likes to have a letter. Just to know that there's still a possibility for better things.

BIFF: He's not like this all the time, is he?

LINDA: It's when you come home he's always the worst.

BIFF: When I come home?

LINDA: When you write you're coming, he's all smiles, and talks about the future, and — he's just wonderful. And then the closer you seem to come, the more shaky he gets, and then, by the time you get here, he's arguing, and he seems angry at you. I think it's just that maybe he can't bring himself to — to open up to you. Why are you so hateful to each other? Why is that?

BIFF (*evasively*): I'm not hateful, Mom.

LINDA: But you no sooner come in the door than you're fighting!

BIFF: I don't know why. I mean to change. I'm tryin', Mom, you understand?

LINDA: Are you home to stay now?

BIFF: I don't know. I want to look around, see what's doin'.

LINDA: Biff, you can't look around all your life, can you?

BIFF: I just can't take hold, Mom. I can't take hold of some kind of a life.

LINDA: Biff, a man is not a bird, to come and go with the springtime.

BIFF: Your hair . . . (*He touches her hair.*) Your hair got so gray.

LINDA: Oh, it's been gray since you were in high school. I just stopped dyeing it, that's all.

BIFF: Dye it again, will ya? I don't want my pal looking old. (*He smiles.*)

LINDA: You're such a boy! You think you can go away for a year and . . . You've got to get it into your head now that one day you'll knock on this door and there'll be strange people here —

BIFF: What are you talking about? You're not even sixty, Mom.

LINDA: But what about your father?

BIFF (*lamely*): Well, I meant him too.

HAPPY: He admires Pop.

LINDA: Biff, dear, if you don't have any feeling for him, then you can't have any feeling for me.

BIFF: Sure I can, Mom.

LINDA: No. You can't just come to see me, because I love him. (*With a threat, but only a threat, of tears.*) He's the dearest man in the world to me, and I won't have anyone making him feel unwanted and low and blue. You've got to make up your mind now, darling, there's no leeway any more. Either he's your father and you pay him that respect, or else you're not to come here. I know he's not easy to get along with — nobody knows that better than me — but . . .

WILLY (*from the left, with a laugh*): Hey, hey, Biffo!

BIFF (*starting to go out after Willy*): What the hell is the matter with him? (*Happy stops him.*)

LINDA: Don't — don't go near him!

BIFF: Stop making excuses for him! He always, always wiped the floor with you. Never had an ounce of respect for you.

HAPPY: He's always had respect for —

BIFF: What the hell do you know about it?

HAPPY (*surlily*): Just don't call him crazy!

BIFF: He's got no character — Charley wouldn't do this. Not in his own house — spewing out that vomit from his mind.

HAPPY: Charley never had to cope with what he's got to.

BIFF: People are worse off than Willy Loman. Believe me, I've seen them!

LINDA: Then make Charley your father, Biff. You can't do that, can you? I don't say he's a great man. Willy Loman never made a lot of money. His name was never in the paper. He's not the finest character that ever lived. But he's a human being, and a terrible thing is happening to him. So attention must be paid. He's not to be allowed to fall into his grave like an old dog. Attention, attention must be finally paid to such a person. You called him crazy —

BIFF: I didn't mean —

LINDA: No, a lot of people think he's lost his — balance. But you don't have to be very smart to know what his trouble is. The man is exhausted.

HAPPY: Sure!

LINDA: A small man can be just as exhausted as a great man. He works for a company thirty-six years this March, opens up unheard-of territories to their trademark, and now in his old age they take his salary away.

HAPPY (*indignantly*): I didn't know that, Mom.

LINDA: You never asked, my dear! Now that you get your spending money someplace else you don't trouble your mind with him.

HAPPY: But I gave you money last —

LINDA: Christmas time, fifty dollars! To fix the hot water it cost ninety-seven fifty! For five weeks he's been on straight commission, like a beginner, an unknown!

BIFF: Those ungrateful bastards!

LINDA: Are they any worse than his sons? When he brought them business, when he was young, they were glad to see him. But now his old friends, the old buyers that loved him so and always found some order to hand him in a pinch — they're all dead, retired. He used to be able to make six, seven calls a day in Boston. Now he takes his valises out of the car and puts them back and takes them out again and he's exhausted. Instead of walking he talks now. He drives seven hundred miles, and when he gets there no one knows him any more, no one welcomes him. And what goes through a man's mind, driving seven hundred miles home without having earned a cent? Why shouldn't he talk to himself? Why? When he has to go to Charley and borrow fifty dollars a week and pretend to me that it's his pay? How long can that go on? How long? You see what I'm sitting here and waiting for? And you tell me he has no character? The man who never worked a day but for your benefit? When does he get the medal for that? Is this his reward — to turn around at the age of sixty-three and find his sons, who he loved better than his life, one a philandering bum —

HAPPY: Mom!

LINDA: That's all you are, my baby! (*To Biff.*) And you! What happened to the love you had for him? You were such pals! How you used to talk to him on the phone every night! How lonely he was till he could come home to you!

BIFF: All right, Mom. I'll live here in my room, and I'll get a job. I'll keep away from him, that's all.

LINDA: No, Biff. You can't stay here and fight all the time.

BIFF: He threw me out of this house, remember that.

LINDA: Why did he do that? I never knew why.

BIFF: Because I know he's a fake and he doesn't like anybody around who knows!

LINDA: Why a fake? In what way? What do you mean?

BIFF: Just don't lay it all at my feet. It's between me and him — that's all I have to say. I'll chip in from now on. He'll settle for half my pay check. He'll be all right. I'm going to bed. (*He starts for the stairs.*)

LINDA: He won't be all right.

BIFF (*turning on the stairs, furiously*): I hate this city and I'll stay here. Now what do you want?

LINDA: He's dying, Biff.

Happy turns quickly to her, shocked.

BIFF (*after a pause*): Why is he dying?

LINDA: He's been trying to kill himself.

BIFF (*with great horror*): How?

LINDA: I live from day to day.

BIFF: What're you talking about?

LINDA: Remember I wrote you that he smashed up the car again? In February?

BIFF: Well?

LINDA: The insurance inspector came. He said that they have evidence. That all these accidents in the last year — weren't — weren't — accidents.

HAPPY: How can they tell that? That's a lie.

LINDA: It seems there's a woman . . . (*She takes a breath as*):

BIFF (*sharply but contained*): What woman?
LINDA (*simultaneously*): . . . and this woman . . .

LINDA: What?

BIFF: Nothing. Go ahead.

LINDA: What did you say?

BIFF: Nothing. I just said what woman?

HAPPY: What about her?

LINDA: Well, it seems she was walking down the road and saw his car. She says that he wasn't driving fast at all, and that he didn't skid. She says he came to that little bridge, and then deliberately smashed into the railing, and it was only the shallowness of the water that saved him.

BIFF: Oh, no, he probably just fell asleep again.

LINDA: I don't think he fell asleep.

BIFF: Why not?

LINDA: Last month . . . (*With great difficulty.*) Oh, boys, it's so hard to say a thing like this! He's just a big stupid man to you, but I tell you there's more good in him than in many other people. (*She chokes, wipes her eyes.*) I was looking for a fuse. The lights blew out, and I went down the cellar. And behind the fuse box — it happened to fall out — was a length of rubber pipe — just short.

HAPPY: No kidding?

LINDA: There's a little attachment on the end of it. I knew right away. And sure enough, on the bottom of the water heater there's a new little nipple on the gas pipe.

HAPPY (*angrily*): That — jerk.

BIFF: Did you have it taken off?

LINDA: I'm — I'm ashamed to. How can I mention it to him? Every day I go down and take away that little rubber pipe. But, when he comes home, I put it back where it was. How can I insult him that way? I don't know what to do. I live from day to day, boys. I tell you, I know every thought in his mind. It sounds so old-fashioned and silly, but I tell you he put his whole life into you and you've turned your backs on him. (*She is bent over in chair, weeping, her face in her hands.*) Biff, I swear to God! Biff, his life is in your hands!

HAPPY (*to Biff*): How do you like that damned fool!

BIFF (*kissing her*): All right, pal, all right. It's all settled now. I've been remiss. I know that, Mom. But now I'll stay, and I swear to you, I'll apply myself. (*Kneeling in front of her, in a fever of self-reproach.*) It's just — you see, Mom, I don't fit in business. Not that I won't try. I'll try, and I'll make good.

HAPPY: Sure you will. The trouble with you in business was you never tried to please people.

BIFF: I know, I —

HAPPY: Like when you worked for Harrison's. Bob Harrison said you were tops, and then you go and do some damn fool thing like whistling whole songs in the elevator like a comedian.

BIFF (*against Happy*): So what? I like to whistle sometimes.

HAPPY: You don't raise a guy to a responsible job who whistles in the elevator!

LINDA: Well, don't argue about it now.

HAPPY: Like when you'd go off and swim in the middle of the day instead of taking the line around.

BIFF (*his resentment rising*): Well, don't you run off? You take off sometimes, don't you? On a nice summer day?

HAPPY: Yeah, but I cover myself!

LINDA: Boys!

HAPPY: If I'm going to take a fade the boss can call any number where I'm supposed to be and they'll swear to him that I just left. I'll tell you something that I hate to say, Biff, but in the business world some of them think you're crazy.

BIFF (*angered*): Screw the business world!

HAPPY: All right, screw it! Great, but cover yourself!

LINDA: Hap, Hap!

BIFF: I don't care what they think! They've laughed at Dad for years, and you know why? Because we don't belong in this nuthouse of a city! We should be mixing cement on some open plain, or — or carpenters. A carpenter is allowed to whistle!

Willy walks in from the entrance of the house, at left.

WILLY: Even your grandfather was better than a carpenter. (*Pause. They watch him.*) You never grew up. Bernard does not whistle in the elevator, I assure you.

BIFF (*as though to laugh Willy out of it*): Yeah, but you do, Pop.

WILLY: I never in my life whistled in an elevator! And who in the business world thinks I'm crazy?

BIFF: I didn't mean it like that, Pop. Now don't make a whole thing out of it, will ya?

WILLY: Go back to the West! Be a carpenter, a cowboy, enjoy yourself!

LINDA: Willy, he was just saying —

WILLY: I heard what he said!

HAPPY (*trying to quiet Willy*): Hey, Pop, come on now . . .

WILLY (*continuing over Happy's line*): They laugh at me, heh? Go to Filene's, go to the Hub, go to Slattery's, Boston. Call out the name Willy Loman and see what happens! Big shot!

BIFF: All right, Pop.

WILLY: Big!

BIFF: All right!

WILLY: Why do you always insult me?

BIFF: I didn't say a word. (*To Linda.*) Did I say a word?

LINDA: He didn't say anything, Willy.

WILLY (*going to the doorway of the living-room*): All right, good night, good night.

LINDA: Willy, dear, he just decided . . .

WILLY (*to Biff*): If you get tired hanging around tomorrow, paint the ceiling I put up in the living-room.

BIFF: I'm leaving early tomorrow.

HAPPY: He's going to see Bill Oliver, Pop.

WILLY (*interestedly*): Oliver? For what?

BIFF (*with reserve, but trying, trying*): He always said he'd stake me. I'd like to go into business, so maybe I can take him up on it.

LINDA: Isn't that wonderful?

WILLY: Don't interrupt. What's wonderful about it? There's fifty men in the City of New York who'd stake him. (*To Biff.*) Sporting goods?

BIFF: I guess so. I know something about it and —

WILLY: He knows something about it! You know sporting goods better than Spalding, for God's sake! How much is he giving you?

BIFF: I don't know, I didn't even see him yet, but —

WILLY: Then what're you talkin' about?

BIFF (*getting angry*): Well, all I said was I'm gonna see him, that's all!

WILLY (*turning away*): Ah, you're counting your chickens again.

BIFF (*starting left for the stairs*): Oh, Jesus, I'm going to sleep!

WILLY (*calling after him*): Don't curse in this house!

BIFF (*turning*): Since when did you get so clean?

HAPPY (*trying to stop them*): Wait a . . .

WILLY: Don't use that language to me! I won't have it!

HAPPY (*grabbing Biff, shouts*): Wait a minute! I got an idea. I got a feasible idea. Come here, Biff, let's talk this over now, let's talk some sense here. When I was down in Florida last time, I thought of a great idea to sell sporting goods. It just came back to me. You and I, Biff — we have a line, the Loman Line. We train a couple of weeks, and put on a couple of exhibitions, see?

WILLY: That's an idea!

HAPPY: Wait! We form two basketball teams, see? Two water-polo teams. We play each other. It's a million dollars' worth of publicity. Two brothers, see? The Loman Brothers. Displays in the Royal Palms — all the hotels. And banners over the ring and the basketball court: "Loman Brothers." Baby, we could sell sporting goods!

WILLY: That is a one-million-dollar idea!

LINDA: Marvelous!

BIFF: I'm in great shape as far as that's concerned.

HAPPY: And the beauty of it is, Biff, it wouldn't be like a business. We'd be out playin' ball again . . .

BIFF (*enthused*): Yeah, that's . . .

WILLY: Million-dollar . . .

HAPPY: And you wouldn't get fed up with it, Biff. It'd be the family again. There'd be the old honor, and comradeship, and if you wanted to go off for a swim or somethin' — well, you'd do it! Without some smart cooky gettin' up ahead of you!

WILLY: Lick the world! You guys together could absolutely lick the civilized world.

BIFF: I'll see Oliver tomorrow. Hap, if we could work that out . . .

LINDA: Maybe things are beginning to —

WILLY (*wildly enthused, to Linda*): Stop interrupting! (*To Biff.*) But don't wear sport jacket and slacks when you see Oliver.

BIFF: No, I'll —

WILLY: A business suit, and talk as little as possible, and don't crack any jokes.

BIFF: He did like me. Always liked me.

LINDA: He loved you!

WILLY (*to Linda*): Will you stop! (*To Biff.*) Walk in very serious. You are not applying for a boy's job. Money is to pass. Be quiet, fine, and serious. Everybody likes a kidder, but nobody lends him money.

HAPPY: I'll try to get some myself, Biff. I'm sure I can.

WILLY: I see great things for you kids, I think your troubles are over. But remember, start big and you'll end big. Ask for fifteen. How much you gonna ask for?

BIFF: Gee, I don't know —

WILLY: And don't say "Gee." "Gee" is a boy's word. A man walking in for fifteen thousand dollars does not say "Gee!"

BIFF: Ten, I think, would be top though.

WILLY: Don't be so modest. You always started too low. Walk in with a big laugh. Don't look worried. Start off with a couple of your good stories to lighten things up. It's not what you say, it's how you say it — because personality always wins the day.

LINDA: Oliver always thought the highest of him —

WILLY: Will you let me talk?

BIFF: Don't yell at her, Pop, will ya?

WILLY (*angrily*): I was talking, wasn't I?

BIFF: I don't like you yelling at her all the time, and I'm tellin' you, that's all.

WILLY: What're you, takin' over this house?

LINDA: Willy —

WILLY (*turning on her*): Don't take his side all the time, goddammit!

BIFF (*furiously*): Stop yelling at her!

WILLY (*suddenly pulling on his cheek, beaten down, guilt ridden*): Give my best to Bill Oliver — he may remember me. (*He exits through the living-room doorway.*)

LINDA (*her voice subdued*): What'd you have to start that for? (*Biff turns away.*) You see how sweet he was as soon as you talked hopefully? (*She goes over to Biff.*) Come up and say good night to him. Don't let him go to bed that way.

HAPPY: Come on, Biff, let's buck him up.

LINDA: Please, dear. Just say good night. It takes so little to make him happy. Come. (*She goes through the living-room doorway, calling upstairs from within the living-room.*) Your pajamas are hanging in the bathroom, Willy!

HAPPY (*looking toward where Linda went out*): What a woman! They broke the mold when they made her. You know that, Biff?

BIFF: He's off salary. My God, working on commission!

HAPPY: Well, let's face it: he's no hot-shot selling man. Except that sometimes, you have to admit, he's a sweet personality.

BIFF (*deciding*): Lend me ten bucks, will ya? I want to buy some new ties.

HAPPY: I'll take you to a place I know. Beautiful stuff. Wear one of my striped shirts tomorrow.

BIFF: She got gray. Mom got awful old. Gee, I'm gonna go in to Oliver tomorrow and knock him for a —

HAPPY: Come on up. Tell that to Dad. Let's give him a whirl. Come on.

BIFF (*steamed up*): You know, with ten thousand bucks, boy!

HAPPY (*as they go into the living-room*): That's the talk, Biff, that's the first time I've heard the old confidence out of you! (*From within the living-room, fading off.*) You're gonna live with me, kid, and any babe you want just say the word . . . (*The last lines are hardly heard. They are mounting the stairs to their parents' bedroom.*)

LINDA (*entering her bedroom and addressing Willy, who is in the bathroom. She is straightening the bed for him*): Can you do anything about the shower? It drips.

WILLY (*from the bathroom*): All of a sudden everything falls to pieces! Goddam plumbing, oughta be sued, those people. I hardly finished putting it in and the thing . . . (*His words rumble off.*)

LINDA: I'm just wondering if Oliver will remember him. You think he might?

WILLY (*coming out of the bathroom in his pajamas*): Remember him? What's the matter with you, you crazy? If he'd've stayed with Oliver he'd be on top by now! Wait'll Oliver gets a look at him. You don't know the average caliber any more. The average young man today — (*he is getting into bed*) — is got a caliber of zero. Greatest thing in the world for him was to bum around.

Biff and Happy enter the bedroom. Slight pause.

WILLY (*stops short, looking at Biff*): Glad to hear it, boy.

HAPPY: He wanted to say good night to you, sport.

WILLY (*to Biff*): Yeah. Knock him dead, boy. What'd you want to tell me?

BIFF: Just take it easy, Pop. Good night. (*He turns to go.*)

WILLY (*unable to resist*): And if anything falls off the desk while you're talking to him — like a package or something — don't you pick it up. They have office boys for that.

LINDA: I'll make a big breakfast —

WILLY: Will you let me finish? (*To Biff.*) Tell him you were in the business in the West. Not farm work.

BIFF: All right, Dad.

LINDA: I think everything —

WILLY (*going right through her speech*): And don't undersell yourself. No less than fifteen thousand dollars.

BIFF (*unable to bear him*): Okay. Good night, Mom. (*He starts moving.*)

WILLY: Because you got a greatness in you, Biff, remember that. You got all kinds a greatness . . . (*He lies back, exhausted. Biff walks out.*)

LINDA (*calling after Biff*): Sleep well, darling!

HAPPY: I'm gonna get married, Mom. I wanted to tell you.

LINDA: Go to sleep, dear.

HAPPY (*going*): I just wanted to tell you.

WILLY: Keep up the good work. (*Happy exits.*) God . . . remember that Ebbets Field game? The championship of the city?

LINDA: Just rest. Should I sing to you?

WILLY: Yeah. Sing to me. (*Linda hums a soft lullaby.*) When that team came out — he was the tallest, remember?

LINDA: Oh, yes. And in gold.

Biff enters the darkened kitchen, takes a cigarette, and leaves the house. He comes downstage into a golden pool of light. He smokes, staring at the night.

WILLY: Like a young god. Hercules — something like that. And the sun, the sun all around him. Remember how he waved to me? Right up from the field, with the representatives of three colleges standing by? And the buyers I brought, and the cheers when he came out — Loman, Loman, Loman! God Almighty, he'll be great yet. A star like that, magnificent, can never really fade away!

The light on Willy is fading. The gas heater begins to glow through the kitchen wall, near the stairs, a blue flame beneath red coils.

LINDA (*timidly*): Willy dear, what has he got against you?

WILLY: I'm so tired. Don't talk any more.

Biff slowly returns to the kitchen. He stops, stares toward the heater.

LINDA: Will you ask Howard to let you work in New York?

WILLY: First thing in the morning. Everything'll be all right.

Biff reaches behind the heater and draws out a length of rubber tubing. He is horrified and turns his head toward Willy's room, still dimly lit, from which the strains of Linda's desperate but monotonous humming rise.

WILLY (*staring through the window into the moonlight*): Gee, look at the moon moving between the buildings!

Biff wraps the tubing around his hand and quickly goes up the stairs.

Curtain

ACT II

Music is heard, gay and bright. The curtain rises as the music fades away. Willy, in shirt sleeves, is sitting at the kitchen table, sipping coffee, his hat in his lap. Linda is filling his cup when she can.

WILLY: Wonderful coffee. Meal in itself.

LINDA: Can I make you some eggs?

WILLY: No. Take a breath.

LINDA: You look so rested, dear.

WILLY: I slept like a dead one. First time in months. Imagine, sleeping till ten on a Tuesday morning. Boys left nice and early, heh?

LINDA: They were out of here by eight o'clock.

WILLY: Good work!

LINDA: It was so thrilling to see them leaving together. I can't get over the shaving lotion in this house!

WILLY (*smiling*): Mmm —

LINDA: Biff was very changed this morning. His whole attitude seemed to be hopeful. He couldn't wait to get downtown to see Oliver.

WILLY: He's heading for a change. There's no question, there simply are certain men that take longer to get — solidified. How did he dress?

LINDA: His blue suit. He's so handsome in that suit. He could be a — anything in that suit!

Willy gets up from the table. Linda holds his jacket for him.

WILLY: There's no question, no question at all. Gee, on the way home tonight I'd like to buy some seeds.

LINDA (*laughing*): That'd be wonderful. But not enough sun gets back there. Nothing'll grow any more.

WILLY: You wait, kid, before it's all over we're gonna get a little place out in the country, and I'll raise some vegetables, a couple of chickens . . .

LINDA: You'll do it yet, dear.

Willy walks out of his jacket. Linda follows him.

WILLY: And they'll get married, and come for a weekend. I'd build a little guest house. 'Cause I got so many fine tools, all I'd need would be a little lumber and some peace of mind.

LINDA (*joyfully*): I sewed the lining . . .

WILLY: I could build two guest houses, so they'd both come. Did he decide how much he's going to ask Oliver for?

LINDA (*getting him into the jacket*): He didn't mention it, but I imagine ten or fifteen thousand. You going to talk to Howard today?

WILLY: Yeah. I'll put it to him straight and simple. He'll just have to take me off the road.

LINDA: And Willy, don't forget to ask for a little advance, because we've got the insurance premium. It's the grace period now.

WILLY: That's a hundred . . . ?

LINDA: A hundred and eight, sixty-eight. Because we're a little short again.

WILLY: Why are we short?

LINDA: Well, you had the motor job on the car . . .

WILLY: That goddam Studebaker!

LINDA: And you got one more payment on the refrigerator . . .

WILLY: But it just broke again!

LINDA: Well, it's old, dear.

WILLY: I told you we should've bought a well-advertised machine. Charley bought a General Electric and it's twenty years old and it's still good, that son-of-a-bitch.

LINDA: But, Willy —

WILLY: Whoever heard of a Hastings refrigerator? Once in my life I would like to own something outright before it's broken! I'm always in a race with the junkyard! I just finished paying for the car and it's on its last legs. The refrigerator consumes belts like a goddam maniac. They time those things. They time them so when you finally paid for them, they're used up.

LINDA (*buttoning up his jacket as he unbuttons it*): All told, about two hundred dollars would carry us, dear. But that includes the last payment on the mortgage. After this payment, Willy, the house belongs to us.

WILLY: It's twenty-five years!

LINDA: Biff was nine years old when we bought it.

WILLY: Well, that's a great thing. To weather a twenty-five year mortgage is —

LINDA: It's an accomplishment.

WILLY: All the cement, the lumber, the reconstruction I put in this house! There ain't a crack to be found in it any more.

LINDA: Well, it served its purpose.

WILLY: What purpose? Some stranger'll come along, move in, and that's that. If only Biff would take this house, and raise a family . . . (*He starts to go.*) Good-by, I'm late.

LINDA (*suddenly remembering*): Oh, I forgot! You're supposed to meet them for dinner.

WILLY: Me?

LINDA: At Frank's Chop House on Forty-eighth near Sixth Avenue.

WILLY: Is that so! How about you?

LINDA: No, just the three of you. They're gonna blow you to a big meal!

WILLY: Don't say! Who thought of that?

LINDA: Biff came to me this morning, Willy, and he said, "Tell Dad, we want to blow him to a big meal." Be there six o'clock. You and your two boys are going to have dinner.

WILLY: Gee whiz! That's really somethin'. I'm gonna knock Howard for a loop, kid. I'll get an advance, and I'll come home with a New York job. Goddammit, now I'm gonna do it!

LINDA: Oh, that's the spirit, Willy!

WILLY: I will never get behind a wheel the rest of my life!

LINDA: It's changing, Willy, I can feel it changing!

WILLY: Beyond a question. G'by, I'm late. (*He starts to go again.*)

LINDA (*calling after him as she runs to the kitchen table for a handkerchief*): You got your glasses?

WILLY (*feels for them, then comes back in*): Yeah, yeah, got my glasses.

LINDA (*giving him the handkerchief*): And a handkerchief.

WILLY: Yeah, handkerchief.

LINDA: And your saccharine?

WILLY: Yeah, my saccharine.

LINDA: Be careful on the subway stairs.

She kisses him, and a silk stocking is seen hanging from her hand. Willy notices it.

WILLY: Will you stop mending stockings? At least while I'm in the house. It gets me nervous. I can't tell you. Please.

Linda hides the stocking in her hand as she follows Willy across the forestage in front of the house.

LINDA: Remember, Frank's Chop House.

WILLY (*passing the apron*): Maybe beets would grow out there.

LINDA (*laughing*): But you tried so many times.

WILLY: Yeah. Well, don't work hard today. (*He disappears around the right corner of the house.*)

LINDA: Be careful!

As Willy vanishes, Linda waves to him. Suddenly the phone rings. She runs across the stage and into the kitchen and lifts it.

LINDA: Hello? Oh, Biff! I'm so glad you called, I just . . . Yes, sure, I just told him. Yes, he'll be there for dinner at six o'clock, I didn't forget. Listen, I was just dying to tell you. You know that little rubber pipe I told you about? That he connected to the gas heater? I finally decided to go down the cellar this morning and take it away and destroy it. But it's gone! Imagine? He took it away himself, it isn't there! (*She listens.*) When? Oh, then you took it. Oh — nothing, it's just that I'd hoped he'd taken it away himself. Oh, I'm not worried, darling, because this morning he left in such high spirits, it was like the old days! I'm not afraid any more. Did Mr. Oliver see you? . . . Well, you wait there then. And make a nice impression on him, darling. Just don't perspire too much before you see him. And have a nice time with Dad. He may have big news too! . . . That's right, a New York job. And be sweet to him tonight, dear. Be loving to him. Because he's only a little boat looking for a harbor. (*She is trembling with sorrow and joy.*) Oh, that's wonderful, Biff, you'll save his life. Thanks, darling. Just put your arm around him when he comes into the restaurant. Give him a smile. That's the boy . . . Good-by, dear . . . You got your comb? . . . That's fine. Good-by, Biff dear.

In the middle of her speech, Howard Wagner, thirty-six, wheels in a small typewriter table on which is a wire-recording machine and proceeds to plug it in. This is on the left forestage. Light slowly fades on Linda as it rises on Howard. Howard is intent on threading the machine and only glances over his shoulder as Willy appears.

WILLY: Pst! Pst!

HOWARD: Hello, Willy, come in.

WILLY: Like to have a little talk with you, Howard.

HOWARD: Sorry to keep you waiting. I'll be with you in a minute.

WILLY: What's that, Howard?

HOWARD: Didn't you ever see one of these? Wire recorder.

WILLY: Oh. Can we talk a minute?

HOWARD: Records things. Just got delivery yesterday. Been driving me crazy, the most terrific machine I ever saw in my life. I was up all night with it.

WILLY: What do you do with it?

HOWARD: I bought it for dictation, but you can do anything with it. Listen to this. I had it home last night. Listen to what I picked up. The first one is my daughter. Get this. (*He flicks the switch and "Roll Out the Barrel" is heard being whistled.*) Listen to that kid whistle.

WILLY: That is lifelike, isn't it?

HOWARD: Seven years old. Get that tone.

Willy: Ts, ts. Like to ask a little favor if you . . .

The whistling breaks off, and the voice of Howard's daughter is heard.

HIS DAUGHTER: "Now you, Daddy."

HOWARD: She's crazy for me! (*Again the same song is whistled.*) That's me! Ha! (*He winks.*)

WILLY: You're very good!

The whistling breaks off again. The machine runs silent for a moment.

HOWARD: Sh! Get this now, this is my son.

HIS SON: "The capital of Alabama is Montgomery; the capital of Arizona is Phoenix; the capital of Arkansas is Little Rock; the capital of California is Sacramento . . ." (*and on, and on*).

HOWARD (*holding up five fingers*): Five years old, Willy!

WILLY: He'll make an announcer some day!

HIS SON (*continuing*): "The capital . . ."

HOWARD: Get that — alphabetical order! (*The machine breaks off suddenly.*) Wait a minute. The maid kicked the plug out.

WILLY: It certainly is a —

HOWARD: Sh, for God's sake!

HIS SON: "It's nine o'clock, Bulova watch time. So I have to go to sleep."

WILLY: That really is —

HOWARD: Wait a minute! The next is my wife.

They wait.

HOWARD'S VOICE: "Go on, say something." (*Pause.*) "Well, you gonna talk?"

HIS WIFE: "I can't think of anything."

HOWARD'S VOICE: "Well, talk — it's turning."

HIS WIFE (*shyly, beaten*): "Hello." (*Silence.*) "Oh, Howard, I can't talk into this . . ."

HOWARD (*snapping the machine off*): That was my wife.

WILLY: That is a wonderful machine. Can we —

HOWARD: I tell you, Willy, I'm gonna take my camera, and my bandsaw, and all my hobbies, and out they go. This is the most fascinating relaxation I ever found.

WILLY: I think I'll get one myself.

HOWARD: Sure, they're only a hundred and a half. You can't do without it. Supposing you wanna hear Jack Benny, see? But you can't be at home at that hour. So you tell the maid to turn the radio on when Jack Benny comes on, and this automatically goes on with the radio . . .

WILLY: And when you come home you . . .

HOWARD: You can come home twelve o'clock, one o'clock, any time you like, and you get yourself a Coke and sit yourself down, throw the switch, and there's Jack Benny's program in the middle of the night!

WILLY: I'm definitely going to get one. Because lots of time I'm on the road, and I think to myself, what I must be missing on the radio!

HOWARD: Don't you have a radio in the car?

WILLY: Well, yeah, but who ever thinks of turning it on?

HOWARD: Say, aren't you supposed to be in Boston?

WILLY: That's what I want to talk to you about, Howard. You got a minute? (*He draws a chair in from the wing.*)

HOWARD: What happened? What're you doing here?

WILLY: Well . . .

HOWARD: You didn't crack up again, did you?

WILLY: Oh, no. No . . .

HOWARD: Geez, you had me worried there for a minute. What's the trouble?

WILLY: Well, tell you the truth, Howard. I've come to the decision that I'd rather not travel any more.

HOWARD: Not travel! Well, what'll you do?

WILLY: Remember, Christmas time, when you had the party here? You said you'd try to think of some spot for me here in town.

HOWARD: With us?

WILLY: Well, sure.

HOWARD: Oh, yeah, yeah. I remember. Well, I couldn't think of anything for you, Willy.

WILLY: I tell ya, Howard. The kids are all grown up, y'know. I don't need much any more. If I could take home — well, sixty-five dollars a week, I could swing it.

HOWARD: Yeah, but Willy, see I —

WILLY: I tell ya why, Howard. Speaking frankly and between the two of us, y'know — I'm just a little tired.

HOWARD: Oh, I could understand that, Willy. But you're a road man, Willy, and we do a road business. We've only got a half-dozen salesmen on the floor here.

WILLY: God knows, Howard, I never asked a favor of any man. But I was with the firm when your father used to carry you in here in his arms.

HOWARD: I know that, Willy, but —

WILLY: Your father came to me the day you were born and asked me what I thought of the name of Howard, may he rest in peace.

HOWARD: I appreciate that, Willy, but there just is no spot here for you. If I had a spot I'd slam you right in, but I just don't have a single solitary spot.

He looks for his lighter. Willy has picked it up and gives it to him. Pause.

WILLY (*with increasing anger*): Howard, all I need to set my table is fifty dollars a week.

HOWARD: But where am I going to put you, kid?

WILLY: Look, it isn't a question of whether I can sell merchandise, is it?

HOWARD: No, but it's a business, kid, and everybody's gotta pull his own weight.

WILLY (*desperately*): Just let me tell you a story, Howard —

HOWARD: 'Cause you gotta admit, business is business.

WILLY (*angrily*): Business is definitely business, but just listen for a minute. You don't understand this. When I was a boy — eighteen, nineteen — I was already on the road. And there was a question in my mind as to whether selling had a future for me. Because in those days I had a yearning to go to Alaska. See, there were three gold strikes in one month in Alaska, and I felt like going out. Just for the ride, you might say.

HOWARD (*barely interested*): Don't say.

WILLY: Oh, yeah, my father lived many years in Alaska. He was an adventurous man. We've got quite a little streak of self-reliance in our family. I thought I'd go out with my older brother and try to locate him, and maybe settle in the North with the old man. And I was almost decided to go, when I met a salesman in the Parker House. His name was Dave Singleman. And he was eighty-four years old, and he'd drummed merchandise in thirty-one states. And old Dave, he'd go up to his room, y'understand, put on his green velvet slippers — I'll never forget — and pick up his phone and call the buyers, and without ever leaving his room, at the age of eighty-four, he made his living. And when I saw that, I realized that selling was the greatest career a man could want. 'Cause what could be more satisfying than to be able to go, at the age of eighty-four, into twenty or thirty different cities, and pick up a phone, and be remembered and loved and helped by so many different people? Do you know? when he died — and by the way he died the death of a salesman, in his green velvet slippers in the smoker of the New York, New Haven, and Hartford, going into Boston — when he died, hundreds of salesmen and buyers were at his funeral. Things were sad on a lotta trains for months after that. (*He stands up. Howard has not looked at him.*) In those days there was personality in it, Howard. There was respect, and comradeship, and gratitude in it. Today, it's all cut and dried, and there's no chance for bringing friendship to bear — or personality. You see what I mean? They don't know me any more.

HOWARD (*moving away, to the right*): That's just the thing, Willy.

WILLY: If I had forty dollars a week — that's all I'd need. Forty dollars, Howard.

HOWARD: Kid, I can't take blood from a stone, I —

WILLY (*desperation is on him now*): Howard, the year Al Smith° was nominated, your father came to me and —

HOWARD (*starting to go off*): I've got to see some people, kid.

WILLY (*stopping him*): I'm talking about your father! There were promises made across this desk! You mustn't tell me you've got people to see — I put thirty-four years into this firm, Howard, and now I can't pay my insurance! You can't eat the orange and throw the peel away — a man is not a piece of fruit! (*After a pause.*) Now pay attention. Your father — in 1928 I had a big year. I averaged a hundred and seventy dollars a week in commissions.

HOWARD (*impatiently*): Now, Willy, you never averaged —

WILLY (*banging his hand on the desk*): I averaged a hundred and seventy dollars a week in the year of 1928! And your father came to me — or rather, I was in the office here — it was right over this desk — and he put his hand on my shoulder —

HOWARD (*getting up*): You'll have to excuse me, Willy, I gotta see some people. Pull yourself together. (*Going out.*) I'll be back in a little while.

On Howard's exit, the light on his chair grows very bright and strange.

Al Smith: The Democratic candidate for president of the United States in 1928, Smith lost the election to Herbert Hoover.

WILLY: Pull myself together! What the hell did I say to him? My God, I was yelling at him! How could I! (*Willy breaks off, staring at the light, which occupies the chair, animating it. He approaches this chair, standing across the desk from it.*) Frank, Frank, don't you remember what you told me that time? How you put your hand on my shoulder, and Frank . . . (*He leans on the desk and as he speaks the dead man's name he accidentally switches on the recorder, and instantly:*)

HOWARD'S SON: ". . . of New York is Albany. The capital of Ohio is Cincinnati, the capital of Rhode Island is . . . " (*The recitation continues.*)

WILLY (*leaping away with fright, shouting*): Ha! Howard! Howard! Howard!

HOWARD (*rushing in*): What happened?

WILLY (*pointing at the machine, which continues nasally, childishly, with the capital cities*): Shut it off! Shut it off!

HOWARD (*pulling the plug out*): Look, Willy . . .

WILLY (*pressing his hands to his eyes*): I gotta get myself some coffee. I'll get some coffee . . .

Willy starts to walk out. Howard stops him.

HOWARD (*rolling up the cord*): Willy, look . . .

WILLY: I'll go to Boston.

HOWARD: Willy, you can't go to Boston for us.

WILLY: Why can't I go?

HOWARD: I don't want you to represent us. I've been meaning to tell you for a long time now.

WILLY: Howard, are you firing me?

HOWARD: I think you need a good long rest, Willy.

WILLY: Howard —

HOWARD: And when you feel better, come back, and we'll see if we can work something out.

WILLY: But I gotta earn money, Howard. I'm in no position to —

HOWARD: Where are your sons? Why don't your sons give you a hand?

WILLY: They're working on a very big deal.

HOWARD: This is no time for false pride, Willy. You go to your sons and you tell them that you're tired. You've got two great boys, haven't you?

WILLY: Oh, no question, no question, but in the meantime . . .

HOWARD: Then that's that, heh?

WILLY: All right, I'll go to Boston tomorrow.

HOWARD: No, no.

WILLY: I can't throw myself on my sons. I'm not a cripple!

HOWARD: Look, kid, I'm busy this morning.

WILLY (*grasping Howard's arm*): Howard, you've got to let me go to Boston!

HOWARD (*hard, keeping himself under control*): I've got a line of people to see this morning. Sit down, take five minutes, and pull yourself together, and then go home, will ya? I need the office, Willy. (*He starts to go, turns, remembering the recorder, starts to push off the table holding the recorder.*) Oh, yeah. Whenever you can this week, stop by and drop off the samples.

You'll feel better, Willy, and then come back and we'll talk. Pull yourself together, kid, there's people outside.

Howard exits, pushing the table off left. Willy stares into space, exhausted. Now the music is heard — Ben's music — first distantly, then closer, closer. As Willy speaks, Ben enters from the right. He carries valise and umbrella.

WILLY: Oh, Ben, how did you do it? What is the answer? Did you wind up the Alaska deal already?

BEN: Doesn't take much time if you know what you're doing. Just a short business trip. Boarding ship in an hour. Wanted to say good-by.

WILLY: Ben, I've got to talk to you.

BEN (*glancing at his watch*): Haven't the time, William.

WILLY (*crossing the apron to Ben*): Ben, nothing's working out. I don't know what to do.

BEN: Now, look here, William. I've bought timberland in Alaska and I need a man to look after things for me.

WILLY: God, timberland! Me and my boys in those grand outdoors!

BEN: You've a new continent at your doorstep, William. Get out of these cities, they're full of talk and time payments and courts of law. Screw on your fists and you can fight for a fortune up there.

WILLY: Yes, yes! Linda, Linda!

Linda enters as of old, with the wash.

LINDA: Oh, you're back?

BEN: I haven't much time.

WILLY: No, wait! Linda, he's got a proposition for me in Alaska.

LINDA: But you've got — (*To Ben.*) He's got a beautiful job here.

WILLY: But in Alaska, kid, I could —

LINDA: You're doing well enough, Willy!

BEN (*to Linda*): Enough for what, my dear?

LINDA (*frightened of Ben and angry at him*): Don't say those things to him! Enough to be happy right here, right now. (*To Willy, while Ben laughs.*) Why must everybody conquer the world? You're well liked, and the boys love you, and someday — (*to Ben*) — why, old man Wagner told him just the other day that if he keeps it up he'll be a member of the firm, didn't he, Willy?

WILLY: Sure, sure. I am building something with this firm, Ben, and if a man is building something he must be on the right track, mustn't he?

BEN: What are you building? Lay your hand on it. Where is it?

WILLY (*hesitantly*): That's true, Linda, there's nothing.

LINDA: Why? (*To Ben.*) There's a man eighty-four years old —

WILLY: That's right, Ben, that's right. When I look at that man I say, what is there to worry about?

BEN: Bah!

WILLY: It's true, Ben. All he has to do is go into any city, pick up the phone, and he's making his living and you know why?

BEN (*picking up his valise*): I've got to go.

WILLY (*holding Ben back*): Look at this boy!

Biff, in his high school sweater, enters carrying suitcase. Happy carries Biff's shoulder guards, gold helmet, and football pants.

WILLY: Without a penny to his name, three great universities are begging for him, and from there the sky's the limit, because it's not what you do, Ben. It's who you know and the smile on your face! It's contacts, Ben, contacts! The whole wealth of Alaska passes over the lunch table at the Commodore Hotel, and that's the wonder, the wonder of this country, that a man can end with diamonds here on the basis of being liked! (*He turns to Biff.*) And that's why when you get out on that field today it's important. Because thousands of people will be rooting for you and loving you. (*To Ben, who has again begun to leave.*) And Ben! when he walks into a business office his name will sound out like a bell and all the doors will open to him! I've seen it, Ben, I've seen it a thousand times! You can't feel it with your hand like timber, but it's there!

BEN: Good-by, William.

WILLY: Ben, am I right? Don't you think I'm right? I value your advice.

BEN: There's a new continent at your doorstep, William. You could walk out rich. Rich! (*He is gone.*)

WILLY: We'll do it here, Ben! You hear me? We're gonna do it here!

Young Bernard rushes in. The gay music of the Boys is heard.

BERNARD: Oh, gee, I was afraid you left already!

WILLY: Why? What time is it?

BERNARD: It's half-past one!

WILLY: Well, come on, everybody! Ebbets Field next stop! Where's the pennants? (*He rushes through the wall-line of the kitchen and out into the living-room.*)

LINDA (*to Biff*): Did you pack fresh underwear?

BIFF (*who has been limbering up*): I want to go!

BERNARD: Biff, I'm carrying your helmet, ain't I?

HAPPY: I'm carrying the helmet.

BERNARD: How am I going to get in the locker room?

LINDA: Let him carry the shoulder guards. (*She puts her coat and hat on in the kitchen.*)

BERNARD: Can I, Biff? 'Cause I told everybody I'm going to be in the locker room.

HAPPY: In Ebbets Field it's the clubhouse.

BERNARD: I meant the clubhouse. Biff!

HAPPY: Biff!

BIFF (*grandly, after a slight pause*): Let him carry the shoulder guards.

HAPPY (*as he gives Bernard the shoulder guards*): Stay close to us now.

Willy rushes in with the pennants.

WILLY (*handing them out*): Everybody wave when Biff comes out on the field. (*Happy and Bernard run off.*) You set now, boy?

The music has died away.

BIFF: Ready to go, Pop. Every muscle is ready.

WILLY (*at the edge of the apron*): You realize what this means?

BIFF: That's right, Pop.

WILLY (*feeling Biff's muscles*): You're comin' home this afternoon captain of the All-Scholastic Championship Team of the City of New York.

BIFF: I got it, Pop. And remember, pal, when I take off my helmet, that touchdown is for you.

WILLY: Let's go! (*He is starting out, with his arm around Biff, when Charley enters, as of old, in knickers.*) I got no room for you, Charley.

CHARLEY: Room? For what?

WILLY: In the car.

CHARLEY: You goin' for a ride? I wanted to shoot some casino.

WILLY (*furiously*): Casino! (*Incredulously.*) Don't you realize what today is?

LINDA: Oh, he knows, Willy. He's just kidding you.

WILLY: That's nothing to kid about!

CHARLEY: No, Linda, what's goin' on?

LINDA: He's playing in Ebbets Field.

CHARLEY: Baseball in this weather?

WILLY: Don't talk to him. Come on, come on! (*He is pushing them out.*)

CHARLEY: Wait a minute, didn't you hear the news?

WILLY: What?

CHARLEY: Don't you listen to the radio? Ebbets Field just blew up.

WILLY: You go to hell! (*Charley laughs. Pushing them out.*) Come on, come on! We're late.

CHARLEY (*as they go*): Knock a homer, Biff, knock a homer!

WILLY (*the last to leave, turning to Charley*): I don't think that was funny, Charley. This is the greatest day of his life.

CHARLEY: Willy, when are you going to grow up?

WILLY: Yeah, heh? When this game is over, Charley, you'll be laughing out of the other side of your face. They'll be calling him another Red Grange. Twenty-five thousand a year.

CHARLEY (*kidding*): Is that so?

WILLY: Yeah, that's so.

CHARLEY: Well, then, I'm sorry, Willy. But tell me something.

WILLY: What?

CHARLEY: Who is Red Grange?

WILLY: Put up your hands. Goddam you, put up your hands!

Charley, chuckling, shakes his head and walks away, around the left corner of the stage. Willy follows him. The music rises to a mocking frenzy.

WILLY: Who the hell do you think you are, better than everybody else? You don't know everything, you big, ignorant, stupid . . . Put up your hands!

Light rises, on the right side of the forestage, on a small table in the reception room of Charley's office. Traffic sounds are heard. Bernard, now mature, sits whistling to himself. A pair of tennis rackets and an overnight bag are on the floor beside him.

WILLY (*offstage*): What are you walking away for? Don't walk away! If you're going to say something say it to my face! I know you laugh at me behind my back. You'll laugh out of the other side of your goddam face after this game. Touchdown! Touchdown! Eighty thousand people! Touchdown! Right between the goal posts.

Bernard is a quiet, earnest, but self-assured young man. Willy's voice is coming from right upstage now. Bernard lowers his feet off the table and listens. Jenny, his father's secretary, enters.

JENNY (*distressed*): Say, Bernard, will you go out in the hall?

BERNARD: What is that noise? Who is it?

JENNY: Mr. Loman. He just got off the elevator.

BERNARD (*getting up*): Who's he arguing with?

JENNY: Nobody. There's nobody with him. I can't deal with him any more, and your father gets all upset everytime he comes. I've got a lot of typing to do, and your father's waiting to sign it. Will you see him?

WILLY (*entering*): Touchdown! Touch — (*He sees Jenny.*) Jenny, Jenny, good to see you. How're ya? Workin'? Or still honest?

JENNY: Fine. How've you been feeling?

WILLY: Not much any more, Jenny. Ha, ha! (*He is surprised to see the rackets.*)

BERNARD: Hello, Uncle Willy.

WILLY (*almost shocked*): Bernard! Well, look who's here! (*He comes quickly, guiltily, to Bernard and warmly shakes his hand.*)

BERNARD: How are you? Good to see you.

WILLY: What are you doing here?

BERNARD: Oh, just stopped by to see Pop. Get off my feet till my train leaves. I'm going to Washington in a few minutes.

WILLY: Is he in?

BERNARD: Yes, he's in his office with the accountant. Sit down.

WILLY (*sitting down*): What're you going to do in Washington?

BERNARD: Oh, just a case I've got there, Willy.

WILLY: That so? (*Indicating the rackets.*) You going to play tennis there?

BERNARD: I'm staying with a friend who's got a court.

WILLY: Don't say. His own tennis court. Must be fine people, I bet.

BERNARD: They are, very nice. Dad tells me Biff's in town.

WILLY (*with a big smile*): Yeah, Biff's in. Working on a very big deal, Bernard.

BERNARD: What's Biff doing?

WILLY: Well, he's been doing very big things in the West. But he decided to establish himself here. Very big. We're having dinner. Did I hear your wife had a boy?

BERNARD: That's right. Our second.

WILLY: Two boys! What do you know!

BERNARD: What kind of a deal has Biff got?

WILLY: Well, Bill Oliver — very big sporting-goods man — he wants Biff very badly. Called him in from the West. Long distance, carte blanche, special deliveries. Your friends have their own private tennis court?

BERNARD: You still with the old firm, Willy?

WILLY (*after a pause*): I'm — I'm overjoyed to see how you made the grade, Bernard, overjoyed. It's an encouraging thing to see a young man really — really — Looks very good for Biff — very — (*He breaks off, then.*) Bernard — (*He is so full of emotion, he breaks off again.*)

BERNARD: What is it, Willy?

WILLY (*small and alone*): What — what's the secret?

BERNARD: What secret?

WILLY: How — how did you? Why didn't he ever catch on?

BERNARD: I wouldn't know that, Willy.

WILLY (*confidentially, desperately*): You were his friend, his boyhood friend. There's something I don't understand about it. His life ended after that Ebbets Field game. From the age of seventeen nothing good ever happened to him.

BERNARD: He never trained himself for anything.

WILLY: But he did, he did. After high school he took so many correspondence courses. Radio mechanics; television; God knows what, and never made the slightest mark.

BERNARD (*taking off his glasses*): Willy, do you want to talk candidly?

WILLY (*rising, faces Bernard*): I regard you as a very brilliant man, Bernard. I value your advice.

BERNARD: Oh, the hell with the advice, Willy. I couldn't advise you. There's just one thing I've always wanted to ask you. When he was supposed to graduate, and the math teacher flunked him —

WILLY: Oh, that son-of-a-bitch ruined his life.

BERNARD: Yeah, but, Willy, all he had to do was go to summer school and make up that subject.

WILLY: That's right, that's right.

BERNARD: Did you tell him not to go to summer school?

WILLY: Me? I begged him to go. I ordered him to go!

BERNARD: Then why wouldn't he go?

WILLY: Why? Why! Bernard, that question has been trailing me like a ghost for the last fifteen years. He flunked the subject, and laid down and died like a hammer hit him!

BERNARD: Take it easy, kid.

WILLY: Let me talk to you — I got nobody to talk to. Bernard, Bernard, was it my fault? Y'see? It keeps going around in my mind, maybe I did something to him. I got nothing to give him.

BERNARD: Don't take it so hard.

WILLY: Why did he lay down? What is the story there? You were his friend!

BERNARD: Willy, I remember, it was June, and our grades came out. And he'd flunked math.

WILLY: That son-of-a-bitch!

BERNARD: No, it wasn't right then. Biff just got very angry, I remember, and he was ready to enroll in summer school.

WILLY (*surprised*): He was?

BERNARD: He wasn't beaten by it at all. But then, Willy, he disappeared from the block for almost a month. And I got the idea that he'd gone up to New England to see you. Did he have a talk with you then?

Willy stares in silence.

BERNARD: Willy?

WILLY (*with a strong edge of resentment in his voice*): Yeah, he came to Boston. What about it?

BERNARD: Well, just that when he came back — I'll never forget this, it always mystifies me. Because I'd thought so well of Biff, even though he'd always taken advantage of me. I loved him, Willy, y'know? And he came back after that month and took his sneakers — remember those sneakers with "University of Virginia" printed on them? He was so proud of those, wore them every day. And he took them down in the cellar, and burned them up in the furnace. We had a fist fight. It lasted at least half an hour. Just the two of us, punching each other down the cellar, and crying right through it. I've often thought of how strange it was that I knew he'd given up his life. What happened in Boston, Willy?

Willy looks at him as at an intruder.

BERNARD: I just bring it up because you asked me.

WILLY (*angrily*): Nothing. What do you mean, "What happened?" What's that got to do with anything?

BERNARD: Well, don't get sore.

WILLY: What are you trying to do, blame it on me? If a boy lays down is that my fault?

BERNARD: Now, Willy, don't get —

WILLY: Well, don't — don't talk to me that way! What does that mean, "What happened?"

Charley enters. He is in his vest, and he carries a bottle of bourbon.

CHARLEY: Hey, you're going to miss that train. (*He waves the bottle.*)

BERNARD: Yeah, I'm going. (*He takes the bottle.*) Thanks, Pop. (*He picks up his rackets and bag.*) Good-by, Willy, and don't worry about it. You know. "If at first you don't succeed . . ."

WILLY: Yes, I believe in that.

BERNARD: But sometimes, Willy, it's better for a man just to walk away.

WILLY: Walk away?

BERNARD: That's right.

WILLY: But if you can't walk away?

BERNARD (*after a slight pause*): I guess that's when it's tough. (*Extending his hand.*) Good-by, Willy.

WILLY (*shaking Bernard's hand*): Good-by, boy.

CHARLEY (*an arm on Bernard's shoulder*): How do you like this kid? Gonna argue a case in front of the Supreme Court.

BERNARD (*protesting*): Pop!

WILLY (*genuinely shocked, pained, and happy*): No! The Supreme Court!

BERNARD: I gotta run. 'By, Dad!

CHARLEY: Knock 'em dead, Bernard!

Bernard goes off.

WILLY (*as Charley takes out his wallet*): The Supreme Court! And he didn't even mention it!

CHARLEY (*counting out money on the desk*): He don't have to — he's gonna do it.

WILLY: And you never told him what to do, did you? You never took any interest in him.

CHARLEY: My salvation is that I never took any interest in any thing. There's some money — fifty dollars. I got an accountant inside.

WILLY: Charley, look . . . (*With difficulty.*) I got my insurance to pay. If you can manage it — I need a hundred and ten dollars.

Charley doesn't reply for a moment; merely stops moving.

WILLY: I'd draw it from my bank but Linda would know, and I . . .

CHARLEY: Sit down, Willy.

WILLY (*moving toward the chair*): I'm keeping an account of everything, remember. I'll pay every penny back. (*He sits.*)

CHARLEY: Now listen to me, Willy.

WILLY: I want you to know I appreciate . . .

CHARLEY (*sitting down on the table*): Willy, what're you doin'? What the hell is goin' on in your head?

WILLY: Why? I'm simply . . .

CHARLEY: I offered you a job. You can make fifty dollars a week. And I won't send you on the road.

WILLY: I've got a job.

CHARLEY: Without pay? What kind of a job is a job without pay? (*He rises.*) Now, look, kid, enough is enough. I'm no genius but I know when I'm being insulted.

WILLY: Insulted!

CHARLEY: Why don't you want to work for me?

WILLY: What's the matter with you? I've got a job.

CHARLEY: Then what're you walkin' in here every week for?

WILLY (*getting up*): Well, if you don't want me to walk in here —

CHARLEY: I am offering you a job.

WILLY: I don't want your goddam job!

CHARLEY: When the hell are you going to grow up?

WILLY (*furiously*): You big ignoramus, if you say that to me again I'll rap you one! I don't care how big you are! (*He's ready to fight.*)

Pause.

CHARLEY (*kindly, going to him*): How much do you need, Willy?

WILLY: Charley, I'm strapped. I'm strapped. I don't know what to do. I was just fired.

CHARLEY: Howard fired you?

WILLY: That snotnose. Imagine that? I named him. I named him Howard.

CHARLEY: Willy, when're you gonna realize that them things don't mean anything? You named him Howard, but you can't sell that. The only thing you got in this world is what you can sell. And the funny thing is that you're a salesman, and you don't know that.

WILLY: I've always tried to think otherwise, I guess. I always felt that if a man was impressive, and well liked, that nothing —

CHARLEY: Why must everybody like you? Who liked J. P. Morgan? Was he impressive? In a Turkish bath he'd look like a butcher. But with his pockets on he was very well liked. Now listen, Willy, I know you don't like me, and nobody can say I'm in love with you, but I'll give you a job because — just for the hell of it, put it that way. Now what do you say?

WILLY: I — I just can't work for you, Charley.

CHARLEY: What're you, jealous of me?

WILLY: I can't work for you, that's all, don't ask me why.

CHARLEY (*angered, takes out more bills*): You been jealous of me all your life, you damned fool! Here, pay your insurance. (*He puts the money in Willy's hand.*)

WILLY: I'm keeping strict accounts.

CHARLEY: I've got some work to do. Take care of yourself. And pay your insurance.

WILLY (*moving to the right*): Funny, y'know? After all the highways, and the trains, and the appointments, and the years, you end up worth more dead than alive.

CHARLEY: Willy, nobody's worth nothin' dead. (*After a slight pause.*) Did you hear what I said?

Willy stands still, dreaming.

CHARLEY: Willy!

WILLY: Apologize to Bernard for me when you see him. I didn't mean to argue with him. He's a fine boy. They're all fine boys, and they'll end up big — all of them. Someday they'll all play tennis together. Wish me luck, Charley. He saw Bill Oliver today.

CHARLEY: Good luck.

WILLY (*on the verge of tears*): Charley, you're the only friend I got. Isn't that a remarkable thing? (*He goes out.*)

CHARLEY: Jesus!

Charley stares after him a moment and follows. All light blacks out. Suddenly raucous music is heard, and a red glow rises behind the screen at right. Stanley, a young waiter, appears, carrying a table, followed by Happy, who is carrying two chairs.

STANLEY (*putting the table down*): That's all right, Mr. Loman, I can handle it myself. (*He turns and takes the chairs from Happy and places them at the table.*)

HAPPY (*glancing around*): Oh, this is better.

STANLEY: Sure, in the front there you're in the middle of all kinds a noise. Whenever you got a party, Mr. Loman, you just tell me and I'll put you back here. Y'know, there's a lotta people they don't like it private, because when they go out they like to see a lotta action around them because they're sick and tired to stay in the house by theirself. But I know you, you ain't from Hackensack. You know what I mean?

HAPPY (*sitting down*): So how's it coming, Stanley?

STANLEY: Ah, it's a dog's life. I only wish during the war they'd a took me in the Army. I coulda been dead by now.

HAPPY: My brother's back, Stanley.

STANLEY: Oh, he come back, heh? From the Far West.

HAPPY: Yeah, big cattle man, my brother, so treat him right. And my father's coming too.

STANLEY: Oh, your father too!

HAPPY: You got a couple of nice lobsters?

STANLEY: Hundred per cent, big.

HAPPY: I want them with the claws.

STANLEY: Don't worry, I don't give you no mice. (*Happy laughs.*) How about some wine? It'll put a head on the meal.

HAPPY: No. You remember, Stanley, that recipe I brought you from overseas? With the champagne in it?

STANLEY: Oh, yeah, sure. I still got it tacked up yet in the kitchen. But that'll have to cost a buck apiece anyways.

HAPPY: That's all right.

STANLEY: What'd you, hit a number or somethin'?

HAPPY: No, it's a little celebration. My brother is — I think he pulled off a big deal today. I think we're going into business together.

STANLEY: Great! That's the best for you. Because a family business, you know what I mean? — that's the best.

HAPPY: That's what I think.

STANLEY: 'Cause what's the difference? Somebody steals? It's in the family. Know what I mean? (*Sotto voce.*°) Like this bartender here. The boss is goin' crazy what kinda leak he's got in the cash register. You put it in but it don't come out.

HAPPY (*raising his head*): Sh!

STANLEY: What?

HAPPY: You notice I wasn't lookin' right or left, was I?

STANLEY: No.

HAPPY: And my eyes are closed.

STANLEY: So what's the — ?

HAPPY: Strudel's comin'.

STANLEY (*catching on, looks around*): Ah, no, there's no —

He breaks off as a furred, lavishly dressed girl enters and sits at the next table. Both follow her with their eyes.

STANLEY: Geez, how'd ya know?

HAPPY: I got radar or something. (*Staring directly at her profile.*) Oooooooo . . . Stanley.

STANLEY: I think that's for you, Mr. Loman.

HAPPY: Look at that mouth. Oh, God. And the binoculars.

STANLEY: Geez, you got a life, Mr. Loman.

Sotto voce: Softly, "under the breath" (Italian).

HAPPY: Wait on her.

STANLEY (*going to the girl's table*): Would you like a menu, ma'am?

GIRL: I'm expecting someone, but I'd like a —

HAPPY: Why don't you bring her — excuse me, miss, do you mind? I sell champagne, and I'd like you to try my brand. Bring her a champagne, Stanley.

GIRL: That's awfully nice of you.

HAPPY: Don't mention it. It's all company money. (*He laughs.*)

GIRL: That's a charming product to be selling, isn't it?

HAPPY: Oh, gets to be like everything else. Selling is selling, y'know.

GIRL: I suppose.

HAPPY: You don't happen to sell, do you?

GIRL: No, I don't sell.

HAPPY: Would you object to a compliment from a stranger? You ought to be on a magazine cover.

GIRL (*looking at him a little archly*): I have been.

Stanley comes in with a glass of champagne.

HAPPY: What'd I say before, Stanley? You see? She's a cover girl.

STANLEY: Oh, I could see, I could see.

HAPPY (*to the Girl*): What magazine?

GIRL: Oh, a lot of them. (*She takes the drink.*) Thank you.

HAPPY: You know what they say in France, don't you? "Champagne is the drink of the complexion" — Hya, Biff!

Biff has entered and sits with Happy.

BIFF: Hello, kid. Sorry I'm late.

HAPPY: I just got here. Uh, Miss — ?

GIRL: Forsythe.

HAPPY: Miss Forsythe, this is my brother.

BIFF: Is Dad here?

HAPPY: His name is Biff. You might've heard of him. Great football player.

GIRL: Really? What team?

HAPPY: Are you familiar with football?

GIRL: No, I'm afraid I'm not.

HAPPY: Biff is quarterback with the New York Giants.

GIRL: Well, that is nice, isn't it? (*She drinks.*)

HAPPY: Good health.

GIRL: I'm happy to meet you.

HAPPY: That's my name. Hap. It's really Harold, but at West Point they called me Happy.

GIRL (*now really impressed*): Oh, I see. How do you do? (*She turns her profile.*)

BIFF: Isn't Dad coming?

HAPPY: You want her?

BIFF: Oh, I could never make that.

HAPPY: I remember the time that idea would never come into your head. Where's the old confidence, Biff?

BIFF: I just saw Oliver —

HAPPY: Wait a minute. I've got to see that old confidence again. Do you want her? She's on call.

BIFF: Oh, no. (*He turns to look at the Girl.*)

HAPPY: I'm telling you. Watch this. (*Turning to the Girl.*) Honey? (*She turns to him.*) Are you busy?

GIRL: Well, I am . . . but I could make a phone call.

HAPPY: Do that, will you, honey? And see if you can get a friend. We'll be here for a while. Biff is one of the greatest football players in the country.

GIRL (*standing up*): Well, I'm certainly happy to meet you.

HAPPY: Come back soon.

GIRL: I'll try.

HAPPY: Don't try, honey, try hard.

The Girl exits. Stanley follows, shaking his head in bewildered admiration.

HAPPY: Isn't that a shame now? A beautiful girl like that? That's why I can't get married. There's not a good woman in a thousand. New York is loaded with them, kid!

BIFF: Hap, look —

HAPPY: I told you she was on call!

BIFF (*strangely unnerved*): Cut it out, will ya? I want to say something to you.

HAPPY: Did you see Oliver?

BIFF: I saw him all right. Now look, I want to tell Dad a couple of things and I want you to help me.

HAPPY: What? Is he going to back you?

BIFF: Are you crazy? You're out of your goddam head, you know that?

HAPPY: Why? What happened?

BIFF (*breathlessly*): I did a terrible thing today, Hap. It's been the strangest day I ever went through. I'm all numb, I swear.

HAPPY: You mean he wouldn't see you?

BIFF: Well, I waited six hours for him, see? All day. Kept sending my name in. Even tried to date his secretary so she'd get me to him, but no soap.

HAPPY: Because you're not showin' the old confidence, Biff. He remembered you, didn't he?

BIFF (*stopping Happy with a gesture*): Finally, about five o'clock, he comes out. Didn't remember who I was or anything. I felt like such an idiot, Hap.

HAPPY: Did you tell him my Florida idea?

BIFF: He walked away. I saw him for one minute. I got so mad I could've torn the walls down! How the hell did I ever get the idea I was a salesman there? I even believed myself that I'd been a salesman for him! And then he gave me one look and — I realized what a ridiculous lie my whole life has been! We've been talking in a dream for fifteen years. I was a shipping clerk.

HAPPY: What'd you do?

BIFF (*with great tension and wonder*): Well, he left, see. And the secretary went out. I was all alone in the waiting-room. I don't know what came over me, Hap. The next thing I know I'm in his office — paneled walls, everything. I can't explain it. I — Hap, I took his fountain pen.

HAPPY: Geez, did he catch you?

BIFF: I ran out. I ran down all eleven flights. I ran and ran and ran.

HAPPY: That was an awful dumb — what'd you do that for?

BIFF (*agonized*): I don't know, I just — wanted to take something, I don't know. You gotta help me, Hap, I'm gonna tell Pop.

HAPPY: You crazy? What for?

BIFF: Hap, he's got to understand that I'm not the man somebody lends that kind of money to. He thinks I've been spiting him all these years and it's eating him up.

HAPPY: That's just it. You tell him something nice.

BIFF: I can't.

HAPPY: Say you got a lunch date with Oliver tomorrow.

BIFF: So what do I do tomorrow?

HAPPY: You leave the house tomorrow and come back at night and say Oliver is thinking it over. And he thinks it over for a couple of weeks, and gradually it fades away and nobody's the worse.

BIFF: But it'll go on forever!

HAPPY: Dad is never so happy as when he's looking forward to something!

Willy enters.

HAPPY: Hello, scout!

WILLY: Gee, I haven't been here in years!

Stanley has followed Willy in and sets a chair for him. Stanley starts off but Happy stops him.

HAPPY: Stanley!

Stanley stands by, waiting for an order.

BIFF (*going to Willy with guilt, as to an invalid*): Sit down, Pop. You want a drink?

WILLY: Sure, I don't mind.

BIFF: Let's get a load on.

WILLY: You look worried.

BIFF: N-no. (*To Stanley.*) Scotch all around. Make it doubles.

STANLEY: Doubles, right. (*He goes.*)

WILLY: You had a couple already, didn't you?

BIFF: Just a couple, yeah.

WILLY: Well, what happened, boy? (*Nodding affirmatively, with a smile.*) Everything go all right?

BIFF (*takes a breath, then reaches out and grasps Willy's hand.*) Pal . . . (*He is smiling bravely, and Willy is smiling too.*) I had an experience today.

HAPPY: Terrific, Pop.

WILLY: That so? What happened?

BIFF (*high, slightly alcoholic, above the earth*): I'm going to tell you everything from first to last. It's been a strange day. (*Silence. He looks around, composes himself as best he can, but his breath keeps breaking the rhythm of his voice.*) I had to wait quite a while for him, and —

WILLY: Oliver.

BIFF: Yeah, Oliver. All day, as a matter of cold fact. And a lot of — instances — facts, Pop, facts about my life came back to me. Who was it, Pop? Who ever said I was a salesman with Oliver?
WILLY: Well, you were.
BIFF: No, Dad, I was a shipping clerk.
WILLY: But you were practically —
BIFF (*with determination*): Dad, I don't know who said it first, but I was never a salesman for Bill Oliver.
WILLY: What're you talking about?
BIFF: Let's hold on to the facts tonight, Pop. We're not going to get anywhere bullin' around. I was a shipping clerk.
WILLY (*angrily*): All right, now listen to me —
BIFF: Why don't you let me finish?
WILLY: I'm not interested in stories about the past or any crap of that kind because the woods are burning, boys, you understand? There's a big blaze going on all around. I was fired today.
BIFF (*shocked*): How could you be?
WILLY: I was fired, and I'm looking for a little good news to tell your mother, because the woman has waited and the woman has suffered. The gist of it is that I haven't got a story left in my head, Biff. So don't give me a lecture about facts and aspects. I am not interested. Now what've you got to say to me?

Stanley enters with three drinks. They wait until he leaves.

WILLY: Did you see Oliver?
BIFF: Jesus, Dad!
WILLY: You mean you didn't go up there?
HAPPY: Sure he went up there.
BIFF: I did. I — saw him. How could they fire you?
WILLY (*on the edge of his chair*): What kind of a welcome did he give you?
BIFF: He won't even let you work on commission?
WILLY: I'm out! (*Driving.*) So tell me, he gave you a warm welcome?
HAPPY: Sure, Pop, sure!
BIFF (*driven*): Well, it was kind of —
WILLY: I was wondering if he'd remember you. (*To Happy.*) Imagine, man doesn't see him for ten, twelve years and gives him that kind of a welcome!
HAPPY: Damn right!
BIFF (*trying to return to the offensive*): Pop, look —
WILLY: You know why he remembered you, don't you? Because you impressed him in those days.
BIFF: Let's talk quietly and get this down to the facts, huh?
WILLY (*as though Biff had been interrupting*): Well, what happened? It's great news, Biff. Did he take you into his office or'd you talk in the waiting-room?
BIFF: Well, he came in, see, and —
WILLY (*with a big smile*): What'd he say? Betcha he threw his arm around you.
BIFF: Well, he kinda —

WILLY: He's a fine man. (*To Happy.*) Very hard man to see, y'know.

HAPPY (*agreeing*): Oh, I know.

WILLY (*to Biff*): Is that where you had the drinks?

BIFF: Yeah, he gave me a couple of — no, no!

HAPPY (*cutting in*): He told him my Florida idea.

WILLY: Don't interrupt. (*To Biff.*) How'd he react to the Florida idea?

BIFF: Dad, will you give me a minute to explain?

WILLY: I've been waiting for you to explain since I sat down here! What happened? He took you into his office and what?

BIFF: Well — I talked. And — and he listened, see.

WILLY: Famous for the way he listens, y'know. What was his answer?

BIFF: His answer was — (*He breaks off, suddenly angry.*) Dad, you're not letting me tell you what I want to tell you!

WILLY (*accusing, angered*): You didn't see him, did you?

BIFF: I did see him!

WILLY: What'd you insult him or something? You insulted him, didn't you?

BIFF: Listen, will you let me out of it, will you just let me out of it!

HAPPY: What the hell!

WILLY: Tell me what happened!

BIFF (*to Happy*): I can't talk to him!

A single trumpet note jars the ear. The light of green leaves stains the house, which holds the air of night and a dream. Young Bernard enters and knocks on the door of the house.

YOUNG BERNARD (*frantically*): Mrs. Loman, Mrs. Loman!

HAPPY: Tell him what happened!

BIFF (*to Happy*): Shut up and leave me alone!

WILLY: No, no! You had to go and flunk math!

BIFF: What math? What're you talking about?

YOUNG BERNARD: Mrs. Loman, Mrs. Loman!

Linda appears in the house, as of old.

WILLY (*wildly*): Math, math, math!

BIFF: Take it easy, Pop!

YOUNG BERNARD: Mrs. Loman!

WILLY (*furiously*): If you hadn't flunked you'd've been set by now!

BIFF: Now, look, I'm gonna tell you what happened, and you're going to listen to me.

YOUNG BERNARD: Mrs. Loman!

BIFF: I waited six hours —

HAPPY: What the hell are you saying?

BIFF: I kept sending in my name but he wouldn't see me. So finally he . . . (*He continues unheard as light fades low on the restaurant.*)

YOUNG BERNARD: Biff flunked math!

LINDA: No!

YOUNG BERNARD: Birnbaum flunked him! They won't graduate him!

LINDA: But they have to. He's gotta go to the university. Where is he? Biff! Biff!

YOUNG BERNARD: No, he left. He went to Grand Central.

LINDA: Grand — You mean he went to Boston!

YOUNG BERNARD: Is Uncle Willy in Boston?

LINDA: Oh, maybe Willy can talk to the teacher. Oh, the poor, poor boy!

Light on house area snaps out.

BIFF (*at the table, now audible, holding up a gold fountain pen*): . . . so I'm washed up with Oliver, you understand? Are you listening to me?

WILLY (*at a loss*): Yeah, sure. If you hadn't flunked —

BIFF: Flunked what? What're you talking about?

WILLY: Don't blame everything on me! I didn't flunk math — you did! What pen?

HAPPY: That was awful dumb, Biff, a pen like that is worth —

WILLY (*seeing the pen for the first time*): You took Oliver's pen?

BIFF (*weakening*): Dad, I just explained it to you.

WILLY: You stole Bill Oliver's fountain pen!

BIFF: I didn't exactly steal it! That's just what I've been explaining to you!

HAPPY: He had it in his hand and just then Oliver walked in, so he got nervous and stuck it in his pocket!

WILLY: My God, Biff!

BIFF: I never intended to do it, Dad!

OPERATOR'S VOICE: Standish Arms, good evening!

WILLY (*shouting*): I'm not in my room!

BIFF (*frightened*): Dad, what's the matter? (*He and Happy stand up.*)

OPERATOR: Ringing Mr. Loman for you!

WILLY: I'm not there, stop it!

BIFF (*horrified, gets down on one knee before Willy*): Dad, I'll make good, I'll make good. (*Willy tries to get to his feet. Biff holds him down.*) Sit down now.

WILLY: No, you're no good, you're no good for anything.

BIFF: I am, Dad, I'll find something else, you understand? Now don't worry about anything. (*He holds up Willy's face.*) Talk to me, Dad.

OPERATOR: Mr. Loman does not answer. Shall I page him?

WILLY (*attempting to stand, as though to rush and silence the Operator*): No, no, no!

HAPPY: He'll strike something, Pop.

WILLY: No, no . . .

BIFF (*desperately, standing over Willy*): Pop, listen! Listen to me! I'm telling you something good. Oliver talked to his partner about the Florida idea. You listening? He — he talked to his partner, and he came to me . . . I'm going to be all right, you hear? Dad, listen to me, he said it was just a question of the amount!

WILLY: Then you . . . got it?

HAPPY: He's gonna be terrific, Pop!

WILLY (*trying to stand*): Then you got it, haven't you? You got it! You got it!

BIFF (*agonized, holds Willy down*): No, no. Look, Pop. I'm supposed to have lunch with them tomorrow. I'm just telling you this so you'll know that I can still make an impression, Pop. And I'll make good somewhere, but I can't go tomorrow, see?

WILLY: Why not? You simply —

BIFF: But the pen, Pop!

WILLY: You give it to him and tell him it was an oversight!

HAPPY: Sure, have lunch tomorrow!

BIFF: I can't say that —

WILLY: You were doing a crossword puzzle and accidentally used his pen!

BIFF: Listen, kid, I took those balls years ago, now I walk in with his fountain pen? That clinches it, don't you see? I can't face him like that! I'll try elsewhere.

PAGE'S VOICE: Paging Mr. Loman!

WILLY: Don't you want to be anything?

BIFF: Pop, how can I go back?

WILLY: You don't want to be anything, is that what's behind it?

BIFF (*now angry at Willy for not crediting his sympathy*): Don't take it that way! You think it was easy walking into that office after what I'd done to him? A team of horses couldn't have dragged me back to Bill Oliver!

WILLY: Then why'd you go?

BIFF: Why did I go? Why did I go! Look at you! Look at what's become of you!

Off left, The Woman laughs.

WILLY: Biff, you're going to lunch tomorrow, or —

BIFF: I can't go. I've got no appointment!

HAPPY: Biff, for . . . !

WILLY: Are you spiting me?

BIFF: Don't take it that way! Goddammit!

WILLY (*strikes Biff and falters away from the table*): You rotten little louse! Are you spiting me?

THE WOMAN: Someone's at the door, Willy!

BIFF: I'm no good, can't you see what I am?

HAPPY (*separating them*): Hey, you're in a restaurant! Now cut it out, both of you! (*The girls enter.*) Hello, girls, sit down.

The Woman laughs, off left.

MISS FORSYTHE: I guess we might as well. This is Letta.

THE WOMAN: Willy, are you going to wake up?

BIFF (*ignoring Willy*): How're ya, miss, sit down. What do you drink?

MISS FORSYTHE: Letta might not be able to stay long.

LETTA: I gotta get up very early tomorrow. I got jury duty. I'm so excited! Were you fellows ever on a jury?

BIFF: No, but I been in front of them! (*The girls laugh.*) This is my father.

LETTA: Isn't he cute? Sit down with us, Pop.

HAPPY: Sit him down, Biff!

BIFF (*going to him*): Come on, slugger, drink us under the table. To hell with it! Come on, sit down, pal.

On Biff's last insistence, Willy is about to sit.

THE WOMAN (*now urgently*): Willy, are you going to answer the door!

The Woman's call pulls Willy back. He starts right, befuddled.

BIFF: Hey, where are you going?
WILLY: Open the door.
BIFF: The door?
WILLY: The washroom . . . the door . . . where's the door?
BIFF (*leading Willy to the left*): Just go straight down.

Willy moves left.

THE WOMAN: Willy, Willy, are you going to get up, get up, get up, get up?

Willy exits left.

LETTA: I think it's sweet you bring your daddy along.
MISS FORSYTHE: Oh, he isn't really your father!
BIFF (*at left, turning to her resentfully*): Miss Forsythe, you've just seen a prince walk by. A fine, troubled prince. A hard-working, unappreciated prince. A pal, you understand? A good companion. Always for his boys.
LETTA: That's so sweet.
HAPPY: Well, girls, what's the program? We're wasting time. Come on, Biff. Gather round. Where would you like to go?
BIFF: Why don't you do something for him?
HAPPY: Me!
BIFF: Don't you give a damn for him, Hap?
HAPPY: What're you talking about? I'm the one who —
BIFF: I sense it, you don't give a good goddamn about him. (*He takes the rolled-up hose from his pocket and puts it on the table in front of Happy.*) Look what I found in the cellar, for Christ's sake. How can you bear to let it go on?
HAPPY: Me? Who goes away? Who runs off and —
BIFF: Yeah, but he doesn't mean anything to you. You could help him — I can't! Don't you understand what I'm talking about? He's going to kill himself, don't you know that?
HAPPY: Don't I know it! Me!
BIFF: Hap, help him! Jesus . . . help him . . . Help me, help me, I can't bear to look at his face! (*Ready to weep, he hurries out, up right.*)
HAPPY (*starting after him*): Where are you going?
MISS FORSYTHE: What's he so mad about?
HAPPY: Come on, girls, we'll catch up with him.
MISS FORSYTHE (*as Happy pushes her out*): Say, I don't like that temper of his!
HAPPY: He's just a little overstrung, he'll be all right!
WILLY (*off left, as The Woman laughs*): Don't answer! Don't answer!
Letta: Don't you want to tell your father —
HAPPY: No, that's not my father. He's just a guy. Come on, we'll catch Biff, and, honey, we're going to paint this town! Stanley, where's the check! Hey, Stanley!

They exit. Stanley looks toward left.

STANLEY (*calling to Happy indignantly*): Mr. Loman! Mr. Loman!

Stanley picks up a chair and follows them off. Knocking is heard off left. The Woman enters, laughing. Willy follows her. She is in a black slip; he is buttoning his shirt. Raw, sensuous music accompanies their speech.

WILLY: Will you stop laughing? Will you stop?

THE WOMAN: Aren't you going to answer the door? He'll wake the whole hotel.

WILLY: I'm not expecting anybody.

THE WOMAN: Whyn't you have another drink, honey, and stop being so damn self-centered?

WILLY: I'm so lonely.

THE WOMAN: You know you ruined me, Willy? From now on, whenever you come to the office, I'll see that you go right through to the buyers. No waiting at my desk any more, Willy. You ruined me.

WILLY: That's nice of you to say that.

THE WOMAN: Gee, you are self-centered! Why so sad? You are the saddest, self-centeredest soul I ever did see-saw. (*She laughs. He kisses her.*) Come on inside, drummer boy. It's silly to be dressing in the middle of the night. (*As knocking is heard.*) Aren't you going to answer the door?

WILLY: They're knocking on the wrong door.

THE WOMAN: But I felt the knocking. And he heard us talking in here. Maybe the hotel's on fire!

WILLY (*his terror rising*): It's a mistake.

THE WOMAN: Then tell him to go away!

WILLY: There's nobody there.

THE WOMAN: It's getting on my nerves, Willy. There's somebody standing out there and it's getting on my nerves!

WILLY (*pushing her away from him*): All right, stay in the bathroom here, and don't come out. I think there's a law in Massachusetts about it, so don't come out. It may be that new room clerk. He looked very mean. So don't come out. It's a mistake, there's no fire.

The knocking is heard again. He takes a few steps away from her, and she vanishes into the wing. The light follows him, and now he is facing Young Biff, who carries a suitcase. Biff steps toward him. The music is gone.

BIFF: Why didn't you answer?

WILLY: Biff! What are you doing in Boston?

BIFF: Why didn't you answer? I've been knocking for five minutes, I called you on the phone —

WILLY: I just heard you. I was in the bathroom and had the door shut. Did anything happen home?

BIFF: Dad — I let you down.

WILLY: What do you mean?

BIFF: Dad . . .

WILLY: Biffo, what's this about? (*Putting his arm around Biff.*) Come on, let's go downstairs and get you a malted.

BIFF: Dad, I flunked math.

WILLY: Not for the term?

BIFF: The term. I haven't got enough credits to graduate.

WILLY: You mean to say Bernard wouldn't give you the answers?

BIFF: He did, he tried, but I only got a sixty-one.

WILLY: And they wouldn't give you four points?

BIFF: Birnbaum refused absolutely. I begged him, Pop, but he won't give me those points. You gotta talk to him before they close the school. Because if he saw the kind of man you are, and you just talked to him in your way, I'm sure he'd come through for me. The class came right before practice, see, and I didn't go enough. Would you talk to him? He'd like you, Pop. You know the way you could talk.

WILLY: You're on. We'll drive right back.

BIFF: Oh, Dad, good work! I'm sure he'll change it for you!

WILLY: Go downstairs and tell the clerk I'm checkin' out. Go right down.

BIFF: Yes, sir! See, the reason he hates me, Pop — one day he was late for class so I got up at the blackboard and imitated him. I crossed my eyes and talked with a lithp.

WILLY (*laughing*): You did? The kids like it?

BIFF: They nearly died laughing!

WILLY: Yeah? What'd you do?

BIFF: The thquare root of thixthy twee is . . . (*Willy bursts out laughing; Biff joins him.*) And in the middle of it he walked in!

Willy laughs and The Woman joins in offstage.

WILLY (*without hesitation*): Hurry downstairs and —

BIFF: Somebody in there?

WILLY: No, that was next door.

The Woman laughs offstage.

BIFF: Somebody got in your bathroom!

WILLY: No, it's the next room, there's a party —

THE WOMAN (*enters, laughing. She lisps this*): Can I come in? There's something in the bathtub, Willy, and it's moving!

Willy looks at Biff, who is staring open-mouthed and horrified at The Woman.

WILLY: Ah — you better go back to your room. They must be finished painting by now. They're painting her room so I let her take a shower here. Go back, go back . . . (*He pushes her.*)

THE WOMAN (*resisting*): But I've got to get dressed, Willy, I can't —

WILLY: Get out of here! Go back, go back . . . (*Suddenly striving for the ordinary*): This is Miss Francis, Biff, she's a buyer. They're painting her room. Go back, Miss Francis, go back . . .

THE WOMAN: But my clothes, I can't go out naked in the hall!

WILLY (*pushing her offstage*): Get outa here! Go back, go back!

Biff slowly sits down on his suitcase as the argument continues offstage.

THE WOMAN: Where's my stockings? You promised me stockings, Willy!

WILLY: I have no stockings here!

THE WOMAN: You had two boxes of size nine sheers for me, and I want them!

WILLY: Here, for God's sake, will you get outa here!

THE WOMAN (*enters holding a box of stockings*): I just hope there's nobody in the hall. That's all I hope. (*To Biff.*) Are you football or baseball?

BIFF: Football.

THE WOMAN (*angry, humiliated*): That's me too. G'night. (*She snatches her clothes from Willy, and walks out.*)

WILLY (*after a pause*): Well, better get going. I want to get to the school first thing in the morning. Get my suits out of the closet. I'll get my valise. (*Biff doesn't move.*) What's the matter? (*Biff remains motionless, tears falling.*) She's a buyer. Buys for J. H. Simmons. She lives down the hall — they're painting. You don't imagine — (*He breaks off. After a pause.*) Now listen, pal, she's just a buyer. She sees merchandise in her room and they have to keep it looking just so . . . (*Pause. Assuming command.*) All right, get my suits. (*Biff doesn't move.*) Now stop crying and do as I say. I gave you an order. Biff, I gave you an order! Is that what you do when I give you an order? How dare you cry! (*Putting his arm around Biff.*) Now look, Biff, when you grow up you'll understand about these things. You mustn't — you mustn't overemphasize a thing like this. I'll see Birnbaum first thing in the morning.

BIFF: Never mind.

WILLY (*getting down beside Biff*): Never mind! He's going to give you those points. I'll see to it.

BIFF: He wouldn't listen to you.

WILLY: He certainly will listen to me. You need those points for the U. of Virginia.

BIFF: I'm not going there.

WILLY: Heh? If I can't get him to change that mark you'll make it up in summer school. You've got all summer to —

BIFF (*his weeping breaking from him*): Dad . . .

WILLY (*infected by it*): Oh, my boy . . .

BIFF: Dad . . .

WILLY: She's nothing to me, Biff. I was lonely, I was terribly lonely.

BIFF: You — you gave her Mama's stockings! (*His tears break through and he rises to go.*)

WILLY (*grabbing for Biff*): I gave you an order!

BIFF: Don't touch me, you — liar!

WILLY: Apologize for that!

BIFF: You fake! You phony little fake! You fake! (*Overcome, he turns quickly and weeping fully goes out with his suitcase. Willy is left on the floor on his knees.*)

WILLY: I gave you an order! Biff, come back here or I'll beat you! Come back here! I'll whip you!

Stanley comes quickly in from the right and stands in front of Willy.

WILLY (*shouts at Stanley*): I gave you an order . . .

STANLEY: Hey, let's pick it up, pick it up, Mr. Loman. (*He helps Willy to his feet.*) Your boys left with the chippies. They said they'll see you home.

A second waiter watches some distance away.

WILLY: But we were supposed to have dinner together.

Music is heard, Willy's theme.

STANLEY: Can you make it?

WILLY: I'll — sure, I can make it. (*Suddenly concerned about his clothes.*) Do I — I look all right?

STANLEY: Sure, you look all right. (*He flicks a speck off Willy's lapel.*)

WILLY: Here — here's a dollar.

STANLEY: Oh, your son paid me. It's all right.

WILLY (*putting it in Stanley's hand*): No, take it. You're a good boy.

STANLEY: Oh, no, you don't have to . . .

WILLY: Here — here's some more, I don't need it any more. (*After a slight pause.*) Tell me — is there a seed store in the neighborhood?

STANLEY: Seeds? You mean like to plant?

As Willy turns, Stanley slips the money back into his jacket pocket.

WILLY: Yes. Carrots, peas . . .

STANLEY: Well, there's hardware stores on Sixth Avenue, but it may be too late now.

WILLY (*anxiously*): Oh, I'd better hurry. I've got to get some seeds. (*He starts off to the right.*) I've got to get some seeds, right away. Nothing's planted. I don't have a thing in the ground.

Willy hurries out as the light goes down. Stanley moves over to the right after him, watches him off. The other waiter has been staring at Willy.

STANLEY (*to the waiter*): Well, whatta you looking at?

The waiter picks up the chairs and moves off right. Stanley takes the table and follows him. The light fades on this area. There is a long pause, the sound of the flute coming over. The light gradually rises on the kitchen, which is empty. Happy appears at the door of the house, followed by Biff. Happy is carrying a large bunch of long-stemmed roses. He enters the kitchen, looks around for Linda. Not seeing her, he turns to Biff, who is just outside the house door, and makes a gesture with his hands, indicating "Not here, I guess." He looks into the living-room and freezes. Inside, Linda, unseen, is seated, Willy's coat on her lap. She rises ominously and quietly and moves toward Happy, who backs up into the kitchen, afraid.

HAPPY: Hey, what're you doing up? (*Linda says nothing but moves toward him implacably.*) Where's Pop? (*He keeps backing to the right, and now Linda is in full view in the doorway to the living-room.*) Is he sleeping?

LINDA: Where were you?

HAPPY (*trying to laugh it off*): We met two girls, Mom, very fine types. Here, we brought you some flowers. (*Offering them to her.*) Put them in your room, Ma.

She knocks them to the floor at Biff's feet. He has now come inside and closed the door behind him. She stares at Biff, silent.

HAPPY: Now what'd you do that for? Mom, I want you to have some flowers —

LINDA (*cutting Happy off, violently to Biff*): Don't you care whether he lives or dies?

HAPPY (*going to the stairs*): Come upstairs, Biff.

BIFF (*with a flare of disgust, to Happy*): Go away from me! (*To Linda.*) What do you mean, lives or dies? Nobody's dying around here, pal.

LINDA: Get out of my sight! Get out of here!

BIFF: I wanna see the boss.

LINDA: You're not going near him!

BIFF: Where is he? (*He moves into the living-room and Linda follows.*)

LINDA (*shouting after Biff*): You invite him for dinner. He looks forward to it all day — (*Biff appears in his parents' bedroom, looks around, and exits.*) — and then you desert him there. There's no stranger you'd do that to!

HAPPY: Why? He had a swell time with us. Listen, when I — (*Linda comes back into the kitchen*) — desert him I hope I don't outlive the day!

LINDA: Get out of here!

HAPPY: Now look, Mom . . .

LINDA: Did you have to go to women tonight? You and your lousy rotten whores!

Biff re-enters the kitchen.

HAPPY: Mom, all we did was follow Biff around trying to cheer him up! (*To Biff.*) Boy, what a night you gave me!

LINDA: Get out of here, both of you, and don't come back! I don't want you tormenting him any more. Go on now, get your things together! (*To Biff.*) You can sleep in his apartment. (*She starts to pick up the flowers and stops herself.*) Pick up this stuff, I'm not your maid any more. Pick it up, you bum, you!

Happy turns his back to her in refusal. Biff slowly moves over and gets down on his knees, picking up the flowers.

LINDA: You're a pair of animals! Not one, not another living soul would have had the cruelty to walk out on that man in a restaurant!

BIFF (*not looking at her*): Is that what he said?

LINDA: He didn't have to say anything. He was so humiliated he nearly limped when he came in.

HAPPY: But, Mom, he had a great time with us —

BIFF (*cutting him off violently*): Shut up!

Without another word, Happy goes upstairs.

LINDA: You! You didn't even go in to see if he was all right!

BIFF (*still on the floor in front of Linda, the flowers in his hand; with self-loathing*): No. Didn't. Didn't do a damned thing. How do you like that, heh? Left him babbling in a toilet.

LINDA: You louse. You . . .

BIFF: Now you hit it on the nose! (*He gets up, throws the flowers in the wastebasket.*) The scum of the earth, and you're looking at him!

LINDA: Get out of here!

BIFF: I gotta talk to the boss, Mom. Where is he?

LINDA: You're not going near him. Get out of this house!

BIFF (*with absolute assurance, determination*): No. We're gonna have an abrupt conversation, him and me.

LINDA: You're not talking to him!

Hammering is heard from outside the house, off right. Biff turns toward the noise.

LINDA (*suddenly pleading*): Will you please leave him alone?

BIFF: What's he doing out there?

LINDA: He's planting the garden!

BIFF (*quietly*): Now? Oh, my God!

Biff moves outside, Linda following. The light dies down on them and comes up on the center of the apron as Willy walks into it. He is carrying a flashlight, a hoe, and handful of seed packets. He raps the top of the hoe sharply to fix it firmly, and then moves to the left, measuring off the distance with his foot. He holds the flashlight to look at the seed packets, reading off the instructions. He is in the blue of night.

WILLY: Carrots . . . quarter-inch apart. Rows . . . one-foot rows. (*He measures it off.*) One foot. (*He puts down a package and measures off.*) Beets. (*He puts down another package and measures again.*) Lettuce. (*He reads the package, puts it down.*) One foot — (*He breaks off as Ben appears at the right and moves slowly down to him.*) What a proposition, ts, ts. Terrific, terrific. 'Cause she's suffered, Ben, the woman has suffered. You understand me? A man can't go out the way he came in, Ben, a man has got to add up to something. You can't, you can't — (*Ben moves toward him as though to interrupt.*) You gotta consider, now. Don't answer so quick. Remember, it's a guaranteed twenty-thousand-dollar proposition. Now look, Ben, I want you to go through the ins and outs of this thing with me. I've got nobody to talk to, Ben, and the woman has suffered, you hear me?

BEN (*standing still, considering*): What's the proposition?

WILLY: It's twenty thousand dollars on the barrelhead. Guaranteed, gilt-edged, you understand?

BEN: You don't want to make a fool of yourself. They might not honor the policy.

WILLY: How can they dare refuse? Didn't I work like a coolie to meet every premium on the nose? And now they don't pay off? Impossible!

BEN: It's called a cowardly thing, William.

WILLY: Why? Does it take more guts to stand here the rest of my life ringing up a zero?

BEN (*yielding*): That's a point, William. (*He moves, thinking, turns.*) And twenty thousand — that *is* something one can feel with the hand, it is there.

WILLY (*now assured, with rising power*): Oh, Ben, that's the whole beauty of it! I see it like a diamond, shining in the dark, hard and rough, that I can pick up and touch in my hand. Not like — like an appointment! This would not be another damned-fool appointment, Ben, and it changes all the aspects. Because he thinks I'm nothing, see, and so he spites me. But the funeral — (*Straightening up.*) Ben, that funeral will be massive! They'll come from Maine, Massachusetts, Vermont, New Hampshire! All the old-timers with the strange license plates — that boy will be thunderstruck, Ben, because he never realized — I am known! Rhode Island, New York, New Jersey — I am known, Ben, and he'll see it with his eyes once and for all. He'll see what I am, Ben! He's in for a shock, that boy!

BEN (*coming to the edge of the garden*): He'll call you a coward.

WILLY (*suddenly fearful*): No, that would be terrible.

BEN: Yes. And a damned fool.

WILLY: No, no, he mustn't, I won't have that! (*He is broken and desperate.*)

BEN: He'll hate you William.

The gay music of the Boys is heard.

WILLY: Oh, Ben, how do we get back to all the great times? Used to be so full of light, and comradeship, the sleigh-riding in winter, and the ruddiness on his cheeks. And always some kind of good news coming up, always something nice coming up ahead. And never even let me carry the valises in the house, and simonizing, simonizing that little red car! Why, why can't I give him something and not have him hate me?

BEN: Let me think about it. (*He glances at his watch.*) I still have a little time. Remarkable proposition, but you've got to be sure you're not making a fool of yourself.

Ben drifts off upstage and goes out of sight. Biff comes down from the left.

WILLY (*suddenly conscious of Biff, turns and looks up at him, then begins picking up the packages of seeds in confusion*): Where the hell is that seed? (*Indignantly.*) You can't see nothing out here! They boxed in the whole goddamn neighborhood!

BIFF: There are people all around here. Don't you realize that?

WILLY: I'm busy. Don't bother me.

BIFF (*taking the hoe from Willy*): I'm saying good-by to you, Pop. (*Willy looks at him, silent, unable to move.*) I'm not coming back any more.

WILLY: You're not going to see Oliver tomorrow?

BIFF: I've got no appointment, Dad.

WILLY: He put his arm around you, and you've got no appointment?

BIFF: Pop, get this now, will you? Everytime I've left it's been a fight that sent me out of here. Today I realized something about myself and I tried to explain it to you and I — I think I'm just not smart enough to make any sense out of it for you. To hell with whose fault it is or anything like that. (*He takes Willy's arm.*) Let's just wrap it up, heh? Come on in, we'll tell Mom. (*He gently tries to pull Willy to left.*)

WILLY (*frozen, immobile, with guilt in his voice*): No, I don't want to see her.

BIFF: Come on! (*He pulls again, and Willy tries to pull away.*)

WILLY (*highly nervous*): No, no, I don't want to see her.

BIFF (*tries to look into Willy's face, as if to find the answer there*): Why don't you want to see her?

WILLY (*more harshly now*): Don't bother me, will you?

BIFF: What do you mean, you don't want to see her? You don't want them calling you yellow, do you? This isn't your fault; it's me, I'm a bum. Now come inside! (*Willy strains to get away.*) Did you hear what I said to you?

Willy pulls away and quickly goes by himself into the house. Biff follows.

LINDA (*to Willy*): Did you plant, dear?

BIFF (*at the door, to Linda*): All right, we had it out. I'm going and I'm not writing any more.

LINDA (*going to Willy in the kitchen*): I think that's the best way, dear. 'Cause there's no use drawing it out, you'll just never get along.

Willy doesn't respond.

BIFF: People ask where I am and what I'm doing, you don't know, and you don't care. That way it'll be off your mind and you can start brightening up again. All right? That clears it, doesn't it? (*Willy is silent, and Biff goes to him.*) You gonna wish me luck, scout? (*He extends his hand.*) What do you say?

LINDA: Shake his hand, Willy.

WILLY (*turning to her, seething with hurt*): There's no necessity to mention the pen at all, y'know.

BIFF (*gently*): I've got no appointment, Dad.

WILLY (*erupting fiercely*): He put his arm around . . . ?

BIFF: Dad, you're never going to see what I am, so what's the use of arguing? If I strike oil I'll send you a check. Meantime forget I'm alive.

WILLY (*to Linda*): Spite, see?

BIFF: Shake hands, Dad.

WILLY: Not my hand.

BIFF: I was hoping not to go this way.

WILLY: Well, this is the way you're going. Good-by.

Biff looks at him a moment, then turns sharply and goes to the stairs.

WILLY (*stops him with*): May you rot in hell if you leave this house!

BIFF (*turning*): Exactly what is it that you want from me?

WILLY: I want you to know, on the train, in the mountains, in the valleys, wherever you go, that you cut down your life for spite!

BIFF: No, no.

WILLY: Spite, spite, is the word of your undoing! And when you're down and out, remember what did it. When you're rotting somewhere beside the railroad tracks, remember, and don't you dare blame it on me!

BIFF: I'm not blaming it on you!

WILLY: I won't take the rap for this, you hear?

Happy comes down the stairs and stands on the bottom step, watching.

BIFF: That's just what I'm telling you!

WILLY (*sinking into a chair at the table, with full accusation*): You're trying to put a knife in me — don't think I don't know what you're doing!

BIFF: All right, phony! Then let's lay it on the line. (*He whips the rubber tube out of his pocket and puts it on the table.*)

HAPPY: You crazy —

LINDA: Biff! (*She moves to grab the hose, but Biff holds it down with his hand.*)

BIFF: Leave it there! Don't move it!

WILLY (*not looking at it*): What is that?

BIFF: You know goddam well what that is.

WILLY (*caged, wanting to escape*): I never saw that.

BIFF: You saw it. The mice didn't bring it into the cellar! What is this supposed to do, make a hero out of you? This supposed to make me sorry for you?

WILLY: Never heard of it.

BIFF: There'll be no pity for you, you hear it? No pity!

WILLY (*to Linda*): You hear the spite!

BIFF: No, you're going to hear the truth — what you are and what I am!

LINDA: Stop it!

WILLY: Spite!

HAPPY (*coming down toward Biff*): You cut it now!

BIFF (*to Happy*): The man don't know who we are! The man is gonna know! (*To Willy.*) We never told the truth for ten minutes in this house!

HAPPY: We always told the truth!

BIFF (*turning on him*): You big blow, are you the assistant buyer? You're one of the two assistants to the assistant, aren't you?

HAPPY: Well, I'm practically —

BIFF: You're practically full of it! We all are! And I'm through with it. (*To Willy.*) Now hear this, Willy, this is me.

WILLY: I know you!

BIFF: You know why I had no address for three months? I stole a suit in Kansas City and I was in jail. (*To Linda, who is sobbing.*) Stop crying. I'm through with it.

Linda turns away from them, her hands covering her face.

WILLY: I suppose that's my fault!

BIFF: I stole myself out of every good job since high school!

WILLY: And whose fault is that?

BIFF: And I never got anywhere because you blew me so full of hot air I could never stand taking orders from anybody! That's whose fault it is!

WILLY: I hear that!

LINDA: Don't, Biff!

BIFF: It's goddam time you heard that! I had to be boss big shot in two weeks, and I'm through with it!

WILLY: Then hang yourself! For spite, hang yourself!

BIFF: No! Nobody's hanging himself, Willy! I ran down eleven flights with a pen in my hand today. And suddenly I stopped, you hear me? And in the middle of that office building, do you hear this? I stopped in the middle of that building and I saw — the sky. I saw the things that I love in this world. The work and the food and time to sit and smoke. And I looked at the pen and said to myself, what the hell am I grabbing this for? Why am I trying to become what I don't want to be? What am I doing in an office, making a contemptuous, begging fool of myself, when all I want is out there, waiting for me the minute I say I know who I am! Why can't I say that, Willy? (*He tries to make Willy face him, but Willy pulls away and moves to the left.*)

WILLY (*with hatred, threateningly*): The door of your life is wide open!

BIFF: Pop! I'm a dime a dozen, and so are you!

WILLY (*turning on him now in an uncontrolled outburst*): I am not a dime a dozen! I am Willy Loman, and you are Biff Loman!

Biff starts for Willy, but is blocked by Happy. In his fury, Biff seems on the verge of attacking his father.

BIFF: I am not a leader of men, Willy, and neither are you. You were never anything but a hard-working drummer who landed in the ash can like all the rest of them! I'm one dollar an hour, Willy! I tried seven states and couldn't raise it. A buck an hour! Do you gather my meaning? I'm not bringing home any prizes any more, and you're going to stop waiting for me to bring them home!

WILLY (*directly to Biff*): You vengeful, spiteful mutt!

Biff breaks from Happy. Willy, in fright, starts up the stairs. Biff grabs him.

BIFF (*at the peak of his fury*): Pop, I'm nothing! I'm nothing, Pop. Can't you understand that? There's no spite in it any more. I'm just what I am, that's all.

Biff's fury has spent itself, and he breaks down, sobbing, holding on to Willy, who dumbly fumbles for Biff's face.

WILLY (*astonished*): What're you doing? What're you doing? (*To Linda.*) Why is he crying?

BIFF (*crying, broken*): Will you let me go, for Christ's sake? Will you take that phony dream and burn it before something happens? (*Struggling to contain himself, he pulls away and moves to the stairs.*) I'll go in the morning. Put him — put him to bed. (*Exhausted, Biff moves up the stairs to his room.*)

WILLY (*after a long pause, astonished, elevated*): Isn't that — isn't that remarkable? Biff — he likes me!

LINDA: He loves you, Willy!

HAPPY (*deeply moved*): Always did, Pop.

WILLY: Oh, Biff! (*Staring wildly.*) He cried! Cried to me. (*He is choking with his love, and now cries out his promise.*) That boy — that boy is going to be magnificent!

Ben appears in the light just outside the kitchen.

BEN: Yes, outstanding, with twenty thousand behind him.

LINDA (*sensing the racing of his mind, fearfully, carefully*): Now come to bed, Willy. It's all settled now.

WILLY (*finding it difficult not to rush out of the house*): Yes, we'll sleep. Come on. Go to sleep, Hap.

BEN: And it does take a great kind of a man to crack the jungle.

In accents of dread, Ben's idyllic music starts up.

HAPPY (*his arm around Linda*): I'm getting married, Pop, don't forget it. I'm changing everything. I'm gonna run that department before the year is up. You'll see, Mom. (*He kisses her.*)

BEN: The jungle is dark but full of diamonds, Willy.

Willy turns, moves, listening to Ben.

LINDA: Be good. You're both good boys, just act that way, that's all.

HAPPY: 'Night, Pop. (*He goes upstairs.*)

LINDA (*to Willy*): Come, dear.

BEN (*with greater force*): One must go in to fetch a diamond out.

WILLY (*to Linda, as he moves slowly along the edge of the kitchen, toward the door*): I just want to get settled down, Linda. Let me sit alone for a little.

LINDA (*almost uttering her fear*): I want you upstairs.

WILLY (*taking her in his arms*): In a few minutes, Linda. I couldn't sleep right now. Go on, you look awful tired. (*He kisses her.*)

BEN: Not like an appointment at all. A diamond is rough and hard to the touch.

WILLY: Go on now. I'll be right up.

LINDA: I think this is the only way, Willy.

WILLY: Sure, it's the best thing.

BEN: Best thing!

WILLY: The only way. Everything is gonna be — go on, kid, get to bed. You look so tired.

LINDA: Come right up.

WILLY: Two minutes.

Linda goes into the living-room, then reappears in her bedroom. Willy moves just outside the kitchen door.

WILLY: Loves me. (*Wonderingly.*) Always loved me. Isn't that a remarkable thing? Ben, he'll worship me for it!

BEN (*with promise*): It's dark there, but full of diamonds.

WILLY: Can you imagine that magnificence with twenty thousand dollars in his pocket?

LINDA (*calling from her room*): Willy! Come up!

WILLY (*calling into the kitchen*): Yes! Yes. Coming! It's very smart, you realize that, don't you, sweetheart? Even Ben sees it. I gotta go, baby. 'By! 'By! (*Going over to Ben, almost dancing.*) Imagine? When the mail comes he'll be ahead of Bernard again!

BEN: A perfect proposition all around.

WILLY: Did you see how he cried to me? Oh, if I could kiss him, Ben!

BEN: Time, William, time!

WILLY: Oh, Ben, I always knew one way or another we were gonna make it, Biff and I!

BEN (*looking at his watch*): The boat. We'll be late. (*He moves slowly off into the darkness.*)

WILLY (*elegiacally, turning to the house*): Now when you kick off, boy, I want a seventy-yard boot, and get right down the field under the ball, and when you hit, hit low and hit hard, because it's important, boy. (*He swings around and faces the audience.*) There's all kinds of important people in the stands, and the first thing you know . . . (*Suddenly realizing he is alone.*) Ben! Ben, where do I . . . ? (*He makes a sudden movement of search.*) Ben, how do I . . . ?

LINDA (*calling*): Willy, you coming up?

WILLY (*uttering a gasp of fear, whirling about as if to quiet her*): Sh! (*He turns around as if to find his way; sounds, faces, voices, seem to be swarming in upon him and *he flicks at them, crying.*) Sh! Sh! (*Suddenly music, faint and high, stops him. It rises in intensity, almost to an unbearable scream. He goes up and down on his toes, and rushes off around the house.*) Shhh!

LINDA: Willy?

There is no answer. Linda waits. Biff gets up off his bed. He is still in his clothes. Happy sits up. Biff stands listening.

LINDA (*with real fear*): Willy, answer me! Willy!

There is the sound of a car starting and moving away at full speed.

LINDA: No!

BIFF (*rushing down the stairs*): Pop!

As the car speeds off, the music crashes down in a frenzy of sound, which becomes the soft pulsation of a single cello string. Biff slowly returns to his bedroom. He and Happy gravely don their jackets. Linda slowly walks out of her room. The music has developed into a dead march. The leaves of day are appearing over everything. Charley and Bernard, somberly dressed, appear and knock on the kitchen door. Biff and Happy slowly descend the stairs to the kitchen as Charley and Bernard enter. All stop a moment when Linda, in clothes of mourning, bearing a little bunch of roses, comes through the draped doorway into the kitchen. She goes to Charley and takes his arm. Now all move toward the audience, through the wall-line of the kitchen. At the limit of the apron, Linda lays down the flowers, kneels, and sits back on her heels. All stare down at the grave.

REQUIEM

CHARLEY: It's getting dark, Linda.

Linda doesn't react. She stares at the grave.

BIFF: How about it, Mom? Better get some rest, heh? They'll be closing the gate soon.

Linda makes no move. Pause.

HAPPY (*deeply angered*): He had no right to do that. There was no necessity for it. We would've helped him.

CHARLEY (*grunting*): Hmmm.

BIFF: Come along, Mom.

LINDA: Why didn't anybody come?

CHARLEY: It was a very nice funeral.

LINDA: But where are all the people he knew? Maybe they blame him.

CHARLEY: Naa. It's a rough world, Linda. They wouldn't blame him.

LINDA: I can't understand it. At this time especially. First time in thirty-five years we were just about free and clear. He only needed a little salary. He was even finished with the dentist.

CHARLEY: No man only needs a little salary.

LINDA: I can't understand it.

BIFF: There were a lot of nice days. When he'd come home from a trip; or on Sundays, making the stoop; finishing the cellar; putting on the new porch; when he built the extra bathroom; and put up the garage. You know something, Charley, there's more of him in that front stoop than in all the sales he ever made.

CHARLEY: Yeah. He was a happy man with a batch of cement.

LINDA: He was so wonderful with his hands.

BIFF: He had the wrong dreams. All, all, wrong.

HAPPY (*almost ready to fight Biff*): Don't say that!

BIFF: He never knew who he was.

CHARLEY (*stopping Happy's movement and reply. To Biff*): Nobody dast blame this man. You don't understand: Willy was a salesman. And for a salesman, there is no rock bottom to the life. He don't put a bolt to a nut, he don't tell you the law or give you medicine. He's a man way out there in the blue, riding on a smile and a shoeshine. And when they start not smiling back — that's an earthquake. And then you get yourself a couple of spots on your hat, and you're finished. Nobody dast blame this man. A salesman is got to dream, boy. It comes with the territory.

BIFF: Charley, the man didn't know who he was.

HAPPY (*infuriated*): Don't say that!

BIFF: Why don't you come with me, Happy?

HAPPY: I'm not licked that easily. I'm staying right in this city, and I'm gonna beat this racket! (*He looks at Biff, his chin set.*) The Loman Brothers!

BIFF: I know who I am, kid.

HAPPY: All right, boy. I'm gonna show you and everybody else that Willy Loman did not die in vain. He had a good dream. It's the only dream you can have — to come out number-one man. He fought it out here, and this is where I'm gonna win it for him.

BIFF (*with a hopeless glance at Happy, bends toward his mother*): Let's go, Mom.

LINDA: I'll be with you in a minute. Go on, Charley. (*He hesitates.*) I want to, just for a minute. I never had a chance to say good-by.

Charley moves away, followed by Happy. Biff remains a slight distance up and left of Linda. She sits there, summoning herself. The flute begins, not far away, playing behind her speech.

LINDA: Forgive me, dear. I can't cry. I don't know what it is, but I can't cry. I don't understand it. Why did you ever do that? Help me, Willy, I can't cry. It seems to me that you're just on another trip. I keep expecting you. Willy, dear, I can't cry. Why did you do it? I search and search and I search, and I can't understand it, Willy. I made the last payment on the house today. Today, dear. And there'll be nobody home. (*A sob rises in her throat.*) We're free and clear. (*Sobbing more fully, released.*) We're free. (*Biff comes slowly toward her.*) We're free . . . We're free . . .

Biff lifts her to her feet and moves out up right with her in his arms. Linda sobs quietly. Bernard and Charley come together and follow them, followed by Happy. Only the music of the flute is left on the darkening stage as over the house the hard towers of the apartment buildings rise into sharp focus, and

The Curtain Falls

EDWARD ALBEE *(b. 1928) was born in Washington, D.C. When he was two weeks old he was adopted by Reed and Frances Albee, a wealthy couple in Larchmont, New York, and named after his adopted grandfather, Edward Franklin Albee, part owner of the Keith-Albee Theater Circuit, a coast-to-coast chain of vaudeville theaters. Albee's family life was unhappy, and by the time he applied for Choate preparatory school, he knew he wanted to become a playwright. At Choate he published a one-act melodrama in the literary magazine. When Albee turned twenty-one, he received from his grandmother a $100,000 trust fund, which enabled him to drop out of Trinity College in Hartford and move to New York City to write plays. Albee supplemented the income from his inheritance by working a series of odd jobs, including that of a Western Union messenger. For nearly a decade he shared a floor-through apartment in Chelsea with William Flanagan, who recalled that Albee "adored the theatre from the beginning and there can't have been anything of even mild importance that we didn't see together." As an aspiring playwright, Albee admired the plays of Tennessee Williams, but when he discovered his own voice in the theater he said he recognized he was one of the "children of [Samuel] Beckett."*

Shortly before Albee's thirtieth birthday, when it looked as if he might have no talent for playwriting, he sat down at the kitchen table and wrote The Zoo Story. *Flanagan sent it to friends in Europe, and it was given a workshop production in German translation in Berlin in 1959, on a double bill with Beckett's one-act play* Krapp's Last Tape. *The following year both plays were produced in English in the off-Broadway Provincetown Playhouse. In 1960 Albee wrote a trilogy of one-act plays —* The Sandbox, The Death of Bessie Smith, *and* Fam and Yam *— which he followed in 1961 with* The American Dream *and* Bartleby, *an operatic adaptation of Herman Melville's story.* The Sandbox *and* The American Dream *were often produced on college campuses, and they made Albee's reputation until he scored his first success on Broadway with the full-length play* Who's Afraid of Virginia Woolf? *This won the Drama Critics Circle Award in 1962 and launched Albee's career as a major American playwright even before it was made into a successful film starring Elizabeth Taylor and Richard Burton. During the last thirty-five years Albee has won many prizes for his plays, including Pulitzer prizes for* Seascape *(1975) and* Three Tall Women *(1994).*

Albee has said that The Sandbox, *a fourteen-minute comedy that premiered at the Jazz Gallery in New York City, is one of his favorite works. Written in memory of his maternal grandmother and benefactor, who died in 1959 at the age of eighty-three, it is a satiric caricature of relationships within a dysfunctional family. Albee believes that playwrights have an important obligation beyond making a statement about the human condition; they must also attempt to change both their society and the theatrical forms within which their predecessors have worked. He has often been abrasive to critics who questioned the dark vision and experimental structure of his plays, as in his essay "Which Theater Is the Absurd One?":*

> *What of this theater? Is it, as it has been accused of being, obscure, sordid, destructive, anti-theater, perverse, and absurd (in the sense of foolish)? Or is it merely, as I have so often heard it put, that "This sort of stuff is too depressing, too . . . too mixed up; I go to the theater to relax and have a good time"?*
>
> *I would submit that it is this latter attitude — that the theater is a*

place to relax and have a good time — in conflict with the purpose of the Theater of the Absurd — which is to make a man face up to the human condition as it really is — that has produced all the brouhaha and the dissent. I would submit that the Theater of the Absurd, in the sense that it is truly the contemporary theater, facing as it does man's condition as it is, is the Realistic theater of our time; and that the supposed Realistic theater — the term used here to mean most of what is done on Broadway — in the sense that it panders to the public need for self-congratulation and reassurance and presents a false picture of ourselves to ourselves, is, with an occasional very lovely exception, really and truly the Theater of the Absurd.

RELATED COMMENTARIES: *Edward Albee, "On Playwriting," page 1949; Richard Amacher, "On* The Sandbox,*" page 1953.*

EDWARD ALBEE

The Sandbox

1960

THE PLAYERS

THE YOUNG MAN, *twenty-five, a good-looking, well-built boy in a bathing suit.*
MOMMY, *fifty-five, a well-dressed, imposing woman.*
DADDY, *sixty, a small man; gray, thin.*
GRANDMA, *eighty-six, a tiny, wizened woman with bright eyes.*
THE MUSICIAN, *no particular age, but young would be nice.*

NOTE: *When, in the course of the play, Mommy and Daddy call each other by these names, there should be no suggestion of regionalism. These names are of empty affection and point up the pre-senility and vacuity of their characters.*

THE SCENE: *A bare stage, with only the following: Near the footlights, far stage-right, two simple chairs set side by side, facing the audience; near the footlights, far stage-left, a chair facing stage-right with a music stand before it; farther back, and stage-center, slightly elevated and raked, a large child's sandbox with a toy pail and shovel; the background is the sky, which alters from brightest day to deepest night.*

At the beginning, it is brightest day; the Young Man is alone on stage, to the rear of the sandbox, and to one side. He is doing calisthenics; he does calisthenics until quite at the very end of the play. These calisthenics, employing the arms only, should suggest the beating and fluttering of wings. The Young Man is, after all, the Angel of Death.

Mommy and Daddy enter from stage-left, Mommy first.

MOMMY (*motioning to Daddy*): Well, here we are; this is the beach.
DADDY (*whining*): I'm cold.
MOMMY (*dismissing him with a little laugh*): Don't be silly; it's as warm as toast. Look at that nice young man over there: *he* doesn't think it's cold. (*Waves to the Young Man.*) Hello.

YOUNG MAN (*with an endearing smile*): Hi!

MOMMY (*looking about*): This will do perfectly . . . don't you think so, Daddy? There's sand there . . . and the water beyond. What do you think, Daddy?

DADDY (*vaguely*): Whatever you say, Mommy.

MOMMY (*with the same little laugh*): Well, of course . . . whatever I say. Then, it's settled, is it?

DADDY (*shrugs*): She's *your* mother, not mine.

MOMMY: *I* know she's my mother. What do you take me for? (*A pause.*) All right, now; let's get on with it. (*She shouts into the wings, stage-left.*) You! Out there! You can come in now.

The Musician enters, seats himself in the chair, stage-left, places music on the music stand, is ready to play. Mommy nods approvingly.

MOMMY: Very nice; very nice. Are you ready, Daddy? Let's go get Grandma.

DADDY: Whatever you say, Mommy.

MOMMY (*leading the way out, stage-left*): Of course, whatever I say. (*To the Musician.*) You can begin now.

The Musician begins playing; Mommy and Daddy exit; the Musician, all the while playing, nods to the Young Man.

YOUNG MAN (*with the same endearing smile*): Hi!

After a moment, Mommy and Daddy re-enter, carrying Grandma. She is borne in by their hands under her armpits; she is quite rigid; her legs are drawn up; her feet do not touch the ground; the expression on her ancient face is that of puzzlement and fear.

DADDY: Where do we put her?

MOMMY (*the same little laugh*): Wherever I say, of course. Let me see . . . well . . . all right, over there . . . in the sandbox. (*Pause.*) Well, what are you waiting for, Daddy? . . . The sandbox!

Together they carry Grandma over to the sandbox and more or less dump her in.

GRANDMA (*righting herself to a sitting position; her voice a cross between a baby's laugh and cry*): Ahhhhhh! Graaaaa!

DADDY (*dusting himself*): What do we do now?

MOMMY (*to the Musician*): You can stop now.

The Musician stops.

(*Back to Daddy.*) What do you mean, what do we do now? We go over there and sit down, of course. (*To the Young Man.*) Hello there.

YOUNG MAN (*again smiling*): Hi!

Mommy and Daddy move to the chairs, stage-right, and sit down. A pause.

GRANDMA (*same as before*): Ahhhhhh! Ah-haaaaaa! Graaaaaa!

DADDY: Do you think . . . do you think she's . . . comfortable?

MOMMY (*impatiently*): How would I know?

DADDY (*pause*): What do we do now?

MOMMY (*as if remembering*): We . . . wait. We . . . sit here . . . and we wait . . . that's what we do.

DADDY (*after a pause*): Shall we talk to each other?

MOMMY (*with that little laugh; picking something off her dress*): Well, *you* can talk, if you want to . . . if you can think of anything to *say* . . . if you can think of anything *new*.

DADDY (*thinks*): No . . . I suppose not.

MOMMY (*with a triumphant laugh*): Of course not!

GRANDMA (*banging the toy shovel against the pail*): Haaaaaa! Ah-haaaaaa!

MOMMY (*out over the audience*): Be quiet, Grandma . . . just be quiet, and wait.

Grandma throws a shovelful of sand at Mommy.

MOMMY (*still out over the audience*): She's throwing sand at me! You stop that, Grandma; you stop throwing sand at Mommy! (*To Daddy.*) She's throwing sand at me.

Daddy looks around at Grandma, who screams at him.

GRANDMA: GRAAAAA!

MOMMY: Don't look at her. Just . . . sit here . . . be very still . . . and wait. (*To the Musician.*) You . . . uh . . . you go ahead and do whatever it is you do.

The Musician plays.

Mommy and Daddy are fixed, staring out beyond the audience. Grandma looks at them, looks at the Musician, looks at the sandbox, throws down the shovel.

GRANDMA: Ah-haaaaaa! Graaaaaa! (*Looks for reaction; gets none. Now . . . directly to the audience.*) Honestly! What a way to treat an old woman! Drag her out of the house . . . stick her in a car . . . bring her out here from the city . . . dump her in a pile of sand . . . and leave her here to set. I'm eighty-six years old! I was married when I was seventeen. To a farmer. He died when I was thirty. (*To the Musician.*) Will you stop that, please?

The Musician stops playing.

I'm a feeble old woman . . . how do you expect anybody to hear me over that peep! peep! peep! (*To herself.*) There's no respect around here. (*To the Young Man.*) There's no respect around here!

YOUNG MAN (*same smile*): Hi!

GRANDMA (*after a pause, a mild double-take, continues, to the audience*): My husband died when I was thirty (*indicates Mommy*), and I had to raise that big cow over there all by my lonesome. You can imagine what *that* was like. Lordy! (*To the Young Man.*) Where'd they get *you?*

YOUNG MAN: Oh . . . I've been around for a while.

GRANDMA: I'll bet you have! Heh, heh, heh. Will you look at you!

YOUNG MAN (*flexing his muscles*): Isn't that something? (*Continues his calisthenics.*)

GRANDMA: Boy, oh boy; I'll say. Pretty good.

YOUNG MAN (*sweetly*): I'll say.

GRANDMA: Where ya from?

YOUNG MAN: Southern California.

GRANDMA (*nodding*): Figgers; figgers. What's your name, honey?

YOUNG MAN: I don't know. . . .

GRANDMA (*to the audience*): Bright, too!

YOUNG MAN: I mean . . . I mean, they haven't given me one yet . . . the studio . . .

GRANDMA (*giving him the once-over*): You don't say . . . you don't say. Well . . . uh, I've got to talk some more . . . don't you go 'way.

YOUNG MAN: Oh, no.

GRANDMA (*turning her attention back to the audience*): Fine; fine. (*Then, once more, back to the Young Man.*) You're . . . you're an actor, hunh?

YOUNG MAN (*beaming*): Yes. I am.

GRANDMA (*to the audience again; shrugs*): I'm smart that way. *Anyhow,* I had to raise . . . *that* over there all by my lonesome; and what's next to her there . . . that's what she married. Rich? I tell you . . . money, money, money. They took me off the *farm* . . . which was real decent of them . . . and they moved me into the big town house with *them* . . . fixed a nice place for me under the stove . . . gave me an army blanket . . . and my own dish . . . my very own dish! So, what have I got to complain about? Nothing, of course. I'm not complaining. (*She looks up at the sky, shouts to someone off stage.*) Shouldn't it be getting dark now, dear?

The lights dim; night comes on. The Musician begins to play; it becomes deepest night. There are spots on all the players, including the Young Man, who is, of course, continuing his calisthenics.

DADDY (*stirring*): It's nighttime.

MOMMY: Shhhh. Be still . . . wait.

DADDY (*whining*): It's so hot.

MOMMY: Shhhhhh. Be still . . . wait.

GRANDMA (*to herself*): That's better. Night. (*To the Musician.*) Honey, do you play all through this part?

The Musician nods.

Well, keep it nice and soft; that's a good boy.

The Musician nods again; plays softly.

That's nice.

There is an off-stage rumble.

DADDY (*starting*): What was that?

MOMMY (*beginning to weep*): It was nothing.

DADDY: It was . . . it was . . . thunder . . . or a wave breaking . . . or something.

MOMMY (*whispering, through her tears*): It was an off-stage rumble . . . and you know what *that* means. . . .

DADDY: I forget. . . .

MOMMY (*barely able to talk*): It means the time has come for poor Grandma . . . and I can't bear it!

DADDY (*vacantly*): I . . . I suppose you've got to be brave.

GRANDMA (*mocking*): That's right, kid; be brave. You'll bear up; you'll get over it.

Another off-stage rumble . . . louder.

MOMMY: Ohhhhhhhhhh . . . poor Grandma . . . poor Grandma. . . .

GRANDMA (*to Mommy*): I'm fine! I'm all right! It hasn't happened yet!

A violent off-stage rumble. All the lights go out, save the spot on the Young Man; the Musician stops playing.

MOMMY: Ohhhhhhhhhh. . . . Ohhhhhhhhhh. . . .

Silence.

GRANDMA: Don't put the lights up yet . . . I'm not ready; I'm not quite ready. (*Silence.*) All right, dear . . . I'm about done.

The lights come up again, to brightest day; the Musician begins to play. Grandma is discovered, still in the sandbox, lying on her side, propped up on an elbow, half covered, busily shoveling sand over herself.

GRANDMA (*muttering*): I don't know how I'm supposed to do anything with this goddam toy shovel. . . .

DADDY: Mommy! It's daylight!

MOMMY (*brightly*): So it is! Well! Our long night is over. We must put away our tears, take off our mourning . . . and face the future. It's our duty.

GRANDMA (*still shoveling; mimicking*): . . . take off our mourning . . . face the future. . . . Lordy!

Mommy and Daddy rise, stretch. Mommy waves to the Young Man.

YOUNG MAN (*with that smile*): Hi!

Grandma plays dead. (!) Mommy and Daddy go over to look at her; she is a little more than half buried in the sand; the toy shovel is in her hands, which are crossed on her breast.

MOMMY (*before the sandbox; shaking her head*): Lovely! It's . . . it's hard to be sad . . . she looks . . . so happy. (*With pride and conviction.*) It pays to do things well. (*To the Musician.*) All right, you can stop now, if you want to. I mean, stay around for a swim, or something; it's all right with us. (*She sighs heavily.*) Well, Daddy . . . off we go.

DADDY: Brave Mommy!

MOMMY: Brave Daddy!

They exit, stage-left.

GRANDMA (*after they leave; lying quite still*): It pays to do things well. . . . Boy, oh boy! (*She tries to sit up.*) . . . well, kids . . . (*but she finds she can't*) . . . I . . . I can't get up. I . . . I can't move. . . .

The Young Man stops his calisthenics, nods to the Musician, walks over to Grandma, kneels down by the sandbox.

GRANDMA: I . . . can't move. . . .

YOUNG MAN: Shhhhh . . . be very still. . . .

GRANDMA: I . . . I can't move. . . .

YOUNG MAN: Uh . . . ma'am; I . . . I have a line here.

GRANDMA: Oh, I'm sorry, sweetie; you go right ahead.

YOUNG MAN: I am . . . uh . . .

GRANDMA: Take your time, dear.

YOUNG MAN (*prepares; delivers the line like a real amateur*): I am the Angel of Death. I am . . . uh . . . I am come for you.

GRANDMA: What . . . wha . . . (*Then, with resignation.*) . . . ohhhh . . . ohhhh, I see.

The Young Man bends over, kisses Grandma gently on the forehead.

GRANDMA (*her eyes closed, her hands folded on her breast again, the shovel between her hands, a sweet smile on her face*): Well . . . that was very nice, dear. . . .

YOUNG MAN (*still kneeling*): Shhhhhh . . . be still. . . .

GRANDMA: What I meant was . . . you did that very well, dear. . . .

YOUNG MAN (*blushing*): . . . oh . . .

GRANDMA: No; I mean it. You've got that . . . you've got a quality.

YOUNG MAN (*with his endearing smile*): Oh . . . thank you; thank you very much . . . ma'am.

GRANDMA (*slowly; softly — as the Young Man puts his hands on top of Grandma's*): You're . . . you're welcome . . . dear.

Tableau. The Musician continues to play as the curtain slowly comes down.

Curtain

LORRAINE HANSBERRY *(1930–1965) was born in Chicago, the youngest of four children of Carl Hansberry, a successful real estate agent who founded one of the first African American banks in that city. Despite her parents' wealth, the family was forced by Chicago law to live in the ghetto on the South Side. When Hansberry was eight years old, her father bought a home in a white neighborhood. After the family moved into their new house, a mob threw a brick through the window, barely missing her. Carl Hansberry decided to stay in the house, although he had not been given clear title to it, and he began a civil rights suit to test the restrictive law. After he lost his case in the Illinois courts, he was supported by the National Association for the Advancement of Colored People (NAACP) to appeal the decision in the United States Supreme Court. The ruling was reversed, and the family continued to live in the house.*

In To Be Young, Gifted and Black *(1971), a posthumous collection of Hansberry's writing, she described how she became involved in a race riot in high school that radicalized her still further when she was seventeen. She attended officially integrated Englewood High School, but in 1947 the white students went on a strike against the blacks. Hansberry described how "the well-dressed, colored students like herself had stood amusedly around the parapet, staring, simply staring at the mob of several hundred striking whites, trading taunts and insults — but showing not the least inclination to further assert racial pride." Word about the riot at the high school spread from the affluent neighborhood to the South Side ghetto schools: "The ofays [whites] are out on strike and beating up and raping colored girls under the viaduct." Carloads of poor black students, "waving baseball bats and shouting slogans of the charge," drove up to Englewood High School. Hansberry watched them "come, pouring out of the bowels of the ghetto, the children of the unqualified oppressed: the black working class in their costumes of pegged pants and conked heads and tight skirts and almost knee-length sweaters and — worst of all —* colored *anklets, held up by rubber bands! Yes, they had come and they had fought . . . She never could forget one thing:* They had fought back!*"*

Hansberry's ambition in high school was to become a journalist. After two years at the University of Wisconsin, she transferred to the New School for Social Research in New York City. In New York she began working as a reporter and editor for Freedom, *a monthly magazine owned by the black actor Paul Robeson. After her marriage to the playwright Robert Nemiroff in 1953, she began to write plays full-time.* A Raisin in the Sun, *her first completed work, was produced on Broadway in 1959 with money raised by her friends, since Broadway audiences had never seen a commercially produced drama about black life. Hansberry became the first black playwright to win the New York Drama Critics Circle Award, a landmark achievement in American theater in view of both her gender and race.*

Hansberry took the title of A Raisin in the Sun *from a poem by Langston Hughes, "Harlem (A Dream Deferred)." In her play she looked beneath what Hughes called "the* surface *of Negro color" to dramatize the human situation of her characters, fulfilling Hughes's vision in his essay "Writers: Black and White" that an African American writer would succeed by becoming a "*writer *first,* colored *second. This means losing nothing of your racial identity. It is just that in the great sense of the word, anytime, any place, good art transcends land, race, or nationality, and color drops away. If you are a good writer, in the end neither blackness nor whiteness makes a difference to readers."*

In the early 1960s Hansberry used her prominence as a successful playwright to champion civil rights causes, as in The Movement: Documentary of a Struggle for Equality *(1964), a book of photographs in support of the Student Nonviolent Coordinating Committee (SNCC). Suffering from cancer, she completed only one other full-length play,* The Sign in Sidney Brustein's Window, *produced in 1964, three months before her death. In 1972 Nemiroff edited a volume of her short plays,* Les Blancs: The Collected Last Plays of Lorraine Hansberry, *and produced a musical version of* A Raisin in the Sun *that won a Tony Award.*

RELATED CASEBOOK: *See pages 2049–2067, including Lorraine Hansberry, "An Author's Reflections: Willy Loman, Walter Younger, and He Who Must Live," page 2050; Lorraine Hansberry, "My Shakespearean Experience," page 2054; James Baldwin, "Sweet Lorraine," page 2056; Julius Lester, "The Heroic Dimension in* A Raisin in the Sun,*" page 2058; Anne Cheney, "The African Heritage in* A Raisin in the Sun,*" page 2061; and Margaret B. Wilkerson, "Hansberry's Awareness of Culture and Gender," page 2064.*

LORRAINE HANSBERRY

A Raisin in the Sun

1959

Harlem (A Dream Deferred)

What happens to a dream deferred?

Does it dry up
Like a raisin in the sun?
Or fester like a sore —
And then run?
Does it stink like rotten meat?

Or crust and sugar over —
Like a syrupy sweet?

Maybe it just sags
Like a heavy load.

Or does it explode?
– LANGSTON HUGHES

CHARACTERS (IN ORDER OF APPEARANCE)

RUTH YOUNGER
TRAVIS YOUNGER
WALTER LEE YOUNGER, *brother*
BENEATHA YOUNGER
LENA YOUNGER, *Mama*
JOSEPH ASAGAI
GEORGE MURCHISON
MRS. JOHNSON
KARL LINDNER
BOBO
MOVING MEN

The action of the play is set in Chicago's Southside, sometime between World War II and the present.

ACT I

SCENE I. [*Friday morning.*]

The Younger living room would be a comfortable and well-ordered room if it were not for a number of indestructible contradictions to this state of being. Its furnishings are typical and undistinguished and their primary feature now is that they have clearly had to accommodate the living of too many people for too many years — and they are tired. Still, we can see that at some time, a time probably no longer remembered by the family (except perhaps for Mama), the furnishings of this room were actually selected with care and love and even hope — and brought to this apartment and arranged with taste and pride.

That was a long time ago. Now the once loved pattern of the couch upholstery has to fight to show itself from under acres of crocheted doilies and couch covers which have themselves finally come to be more important than the upholstery. And here a table or a chair has been moved to disguise the worn places in the carpet; but the carpet has fought back by showing its weariness, with depressing uniformity, elsewhere on its surface.

Weariness has, in fact, won in this room. Everything has been polished, washed, sat on, used, scrubbed too often. All pretenses but living itself have long since vanished from the very atmosphere of this room.

Moreover, a section of this room, for it is not really a room unto itself, though the landlord's lease would make it seem so, slopes backward to provide a small kitchen area, where the family prepares the meals that are eaten in the living room proper, which must also serve as dining room. The single window that has been provided for these "two" rooms is located in this kitchen area. The sole natural light the family may enjoy in the course of a day is only that which fights its way through this little window.

At left, a door leads to a bedroom which is shared by Mama and her daughter, Beneatha. At right, opposite, is a second room (which in the beginning of the life of this apartment was probably a breakfast room) which serves as a bedroom for Walter and his wife, Ruth.

Time: Sometime between World War II and the present.

Place: Chicago's Southside.

At Rise: It is morning dark in the living room. Travis is asleep on the make-down bed at center. An alarm clock sounds from within the bedroom at right, and presently Ruth enters from that room and closes the door behind her. She crosses sleepily toward the window. As she passes her sleeping son she reaches down and shakes him a little. At the window she raises the shade and a dusky Southside morning light comes in feebly. She fills a pot with water and puts it on to boil. She calls to the boy, between yawns, in a slightly muffled voice.

Ruth is about thirty. We can see that she was a pretty girl, even exceptionally so, but now it is apparent that life has been little that she expected, and disappointment has already begun to hang in her face. In a few years, before thirty-five even, she will be known among her people as a "settled woman."

She crosses to her son and gives him a good, final, rousing shake.

RUTH: Come on now, boy, it's seven thirty! (*Her son sits up at last, in a stupor of sleepiness.*) I say hurry up, Travis! You ain't the only person in the world got to use a bathroom! (*The child, a sturdy, handsome little boy of ten or eleven, drags himself out of the bed and almost blindly takes his towels and "today's clothes" from drawers and a closet and goes out to the bathroom, which is in an outside hall and which is shared by another family or families on the same floor. Ruth crosses to the bedroom door at right and opens it and calls in to her husband.*) Walter Lee! . . . It's after seven thirty! Lemme see you do some waking up in there now! (*She waits.*) You better get up from there, man! It's after seven thirty I tell you. (*She waits again.*) All right, you just go ahead and lay there and next thing you know Travis be finished and Mr. Johnson'll be in there and you'll be fussing and cussing round here like a madman! And be late too! (*She waits, at the end of patience.*) Walter Lee — it's time for you to GET UP!

She waits another second and then starts to go into the bedroom, but is apparently satisfied that her husband has begun to get up. She stops, pulls the door to, and returns to the kitchen area. She wipes her face with a moist cloth and runs her fingers through her sleep-disheveled hair in a vain effort and ties an apron around her housecoat. The bedroom door at right opens and her husband stands in the doorway in his pajamas, which are rumpled and mismated. He is a lean, intense young man in his middle thirties, inclined to quick nervous movements and erratic speech habits — and always in his voice there is a quality of indictment.

WALTER: Is he out yet?

RUTH: What you mean *out*? He ain't hardly got in there good yet.

WALTER (*wandering in, still more oriented to sleep than to a new day*): Well, what was you doing all that yelling for if I can't even get in there yet? (*Stopping and thinking.*) Check coming today?

RUTH: They *said* Saturday and this is just Friday and I hopes to God you ain't going to get up here first thing this morning and start talking to me 'bout no money — 'cause I 'bout don't want to hear it.

WALTER: Something the matter with you this morning?

RUTH: No — I'm just sleepy as the devil. What kind of eggs you want?

WALTER: Not scrambled. (*Ruth starts to scramble eggs.*) Paper come? (*Ruth points impatiently to the rolled up* Tribune *on the table, and he gets it and spreads it out and vaguely reads the front page.*) Set off another bomb yesterday.

RUTH (*maximum indifference*): Did they?

WALTER (*looking up*): What's the matter with you?

RUTH: Ain't nothing the matter with me. And don't keep asking me that this morning.

WALTER: Ain't nobody bothering you. (*Reading the news of the day absently again.*) Say Colonel McCormick is sick.

RUTH (*affecting tea-party interest*): Is he now? Poor thing.

WALTER (*sighing and looking at his watch*): Oh, me. (*He waits.*) Now what is that boy doing in that bathroom all this time? He just going to have to start getting up earlier. I can't be being late to work on account of him fooling around in there.

RUTH (*turning on him*): Oh, no he ain't going to be getting up no earlier no such thing! It ain't his fault that he can't get to bed no earlier nights 'cause he got a bunch of crazy good-for-nothing clowns sitting up running their mouths in what is supposed to be his bedroom after ten o'clock at night . . .

WALTER: That's what you mad about, ain't it? The things I want to talk about with my friends just couldn't be important in your mind, could they?

He rises and finds a cigarette in her handbag on the table and crosses to the little window and looks out, smoking and deeply enjoying this first one.

RUTH (*almost matter of factly, a complaint too automatic to deserve emphasis*): Why you always got to smoke before you eat in the morning?

WALTER (*at the window*): Just look at 'em down there . . . Running and racing to work . . . (*He turns and faces his wife and watches her a moment at the stove, and then, suddenly.*) You look young this morning, baby.

RUTH (*indifferently*): Yeah?

WALTER: Just for a second — stirring them eggs. Just for a second it was — you looked real young again. (*He reaches for her; she crosses away. Then, drily.*) It's gone now — you look like yourself again!

RUTH: Man, if you don't shut up and leave me alone.

WALTER (*looking out to the street again*): First thing a man ought to learn in life is not to make love to no colored woman first thing in the morning. You all some eeeevil people at eight o'clock in the morning.

Travis appears in the hall doorway, almost fully dressed and quite wide awake now, his towels and pajamas across his shoulders. He opens the door and signals for his father to make the bathroom in a hurry.

TRAVIS (*watching the bathroom*): Daddy, come on!

Walter gets his bathroom utensils and flies out to the bathroom.

RUTH: Sit down and have your breakfast, Travis.

TRAVIS: Mama, this is Friday. (*Gleefully.*) Check coming tomorrow, huh?

RUTH: You get your mind off money and eat your breakfast.

TRAVIS (*eating*): This is the morning we supposed to bring the fifty cents to school.

RUTH: Well, I ain't got no fifty cents this morning.

TRAVIS: Teacher say we have to.

RUTH: I don't care what teacher say. I ain't got it. Eat your breakfast, Travis.

TRAVIS: I *am* eating.

RUTH: Hush up now and just eat!

The boy gives her an exasperated look for her lack of understanding, and eats grudgingly.

TRAVIS: You think Grandmama would have it?

RUTH: No! And I want you to stop asking your grandmother for money, you hear me?

TRAVIS (*outraged*): Gaaaleee! I don't ask her, she just gimme it sometimes!

RUTH: Travis Willard Younger — I got too much on me this morning to be —

TRAVIS: Maybe Daddy —

RUTH: *Travis!*

The boy hushes abruptly. They are both quiet and tense for several seconds.

TRAVIS (*presently*): Could I maybe go carry some groceries in front of the supermarket for a little while after school then?

RUTH: Just hush, I said. (*Travis jabs his spoon into his cereal bowl viciously, and rests his head in anger upon his fists.*) If you through eating, you can get over there and make up your bed.

The boy obeys stiffly and crosses the room, almost mechanically, to the bed and more or less folds the bedding into a heap, then angrily gets his books and cap.

TRAVIS (*sulking and standing apart from her unnaturally*): I'm gone.

RUTH (*looking up from the stove to inspect him automatically*): Come here. (*He crosses to her and she studies his head.*) If you don't take this comb and fix this here head, you better! (*Travis puts down his books with a great sigh of oppression, and crosses to the mirror. His mother mutters under her breath about his "slubbornness."*) 'Bout to march out of here with that head looking just like chickens slept in it! I just don't know where you get your slubborn ways . . . And get your jacket, too. Looks chilly out this morning.

TRAVIS (*with conspicuously brushed hair and jacket*): I'm gone.

RUTH: Get carfare and milk money — (*Waving one finger.*) — and not a single penny for no caps, you hear me?

TRAVIS (*with sullen politeness*): Yes'm.

He turns in outrage to leave. His mother watches after him as in his frustration he approaches the door almost comically. When she speaks to him, her voice has become a very gentle tease.

RUTH (*mocking; as she thinks he would say it*): Oh, Mama makes me so mad sometimes, I don't know what to do! (*She waits and continues to his back as *he stands stock-still in front of the door.*) I wouldn't kiss that woman good-bye for nothing in this world this morning! (*The boy finally turns around and rolls his eyes at her, knowing the mood has changed and he is vindicated; he does not, however, move toward her yet.*) Not for nothing in this world! (*She finally laughs aloud at him and holds out her arms to him and we see that it is a way between them, very old and practiced. He crosses to her and allows her to embrace him warmly but keeps his face fixed with masculine rigidity. She holds him back from her presently and looks at him and runs her fingers over the features of his face. With utter gentleness —.*) Now — whose little old angry man are you?

TRAVIS (*the masculinity and gruffness start to fade at last*): Aw gaalee — Mama . . .

RUTH (*mimicking*): Aw — gaaaaalleeeee, Mama! (*She pushes him, with rough playfulness and finality, toward the door.*) Get on out of here or you going to be late.

TRAVIS (*in the face of love, new aggressiveness*): Mama, could I *please* go carry groceries?

RUTH: Honey, it's starting to get so cold evenings.

WALTER (*coming in from the bathroom and drawing a make-believe gun from a make-believe holster and shooting at his son*): What is it he wants to do?

RUTH: Go carry groceries after school at the supermarket.

WALTER: Well, let him go . . .

TRAVIS (*quickly, to the ally*): I *have* to — she won't gimme the fifty cents . . .

WALTER (*to his wife only*): Why not?

RUTH (*simply, and with flavor*): 'Cause we don't have it.

WALTER (*to Ruth only*): What you tell the boy things like that for? (*Reaching down into his pants with a rather important gesture.*) Here, son —

He hands the boy the coin, but his eyes are directed to his wife's. Travis takes the money happily.

TRAVIS: Thanks, Daddy.

He starts out. Ruth watches both of them with murder in her eyes. Walter stands and stares back at her with defiance, and suddenly reaches into his pocket again on an afterthought.

WALTER (*without even looking at his son, still staring hard at his wife*): In fact, here's another fifty cents . . . Buy yourself some fruit today — or take a taxicab to school or something!

TRAVIS: Whoopee —

He leaps up and clasps his father around the middle with his legs, and they face each other in mutual appreciation; slowly Walter Lee peeks around the boy to catch the violent rays from his wife's eyes and draws his head back as if shot.

WALTER: You better get down now — and get to school, man.

TRAVIS (*at the door*): O.K. Good-bye.

He exits.

WALTER (*after him, pointing with pride*): That's *my* boy. (*She looks at him in disgust and turns back to her work.*) You know what I was thinking 'bout in the bathroom this morning?

RUTH: No.

WALTER: How come you always try to be so pleasant!

RUTH: What is there to be pleasant 'bout!

WALTER: You want to know what I was thinking 'bout in the bathroom or not!

RUTH: I know what you thinking 'bout.

WALTER (*ignoring her*): 'Bout what me and Willy Harris was talking about last night.

RUTH (*immediately — a refrain*): Willy Harris is a good-for-nothing loudmouth.

WALTER: Anybody who talks to me has got to be a good-for-nothing loudmouth, ain't he? And what you know about who is just a good-for-nothing loudmouth? Charlie Atkins was just a "good-for-nothing loudmouth" too, wasn't he! When he wanted me to go in the dry-cleaning business with him. And now — he's grossing a hundred thousand a year. A hundred thousand dollars a year! You still call *him* a loudmouth!

RUTH (*bitterly*): Oh, Walter Lee . . .

She folds her head on her arms over the table.

WALTER (*rising and coming to her and standing over her*): You tired, ain't you? Tired of everything. Me, the boy, the way we live — this beat-up hole — everything. Ain't you? (*She doesn't look up, doesn't answer.*) So tired — moaning and groaning all the time, but you wouldn't do nothing to help, would you? You couldn't be on my side that long for nothing, could you?

RUTH: Walter, please leave me alone.

WALTER: A man needs for a woman to back him up . . .

RUTH: Walter —

WALTER: Mama would listen to you. You know she listen to you more than she do me and Bennie. She think more of you. All you have to do is just sit down with her when you drinking your coffee one morning and talking 'bout things like you do and — (*He sits down beside her and demonstrates graphically what he thinks her methods and tone should be.*) — you just sip your coffee, see, and say easy like that you been thinking 'bout that deal Walter Lee is so interested in, 'bout the store and all, and sip some more coffee, like what you saying ain't really that important to you — And the next thing you know, she be listening good and asking you questions and when I come home — I can tell her the details. This ain't no fly-by-night proposition, baby. I mean we figured it out, me and Willy and Bobo.

RUTH (*with a frown*): Bobo?

WALTER: Yeah. You see, this little liquor store we got in mind cost seventy-five thousand and we figured the initial investment on the place be 'bout thirty thousand, see. That be ten thousand each. Course, there's a couple of hundred you got to pay so's you don't spend your life just waiting for them clowns to let your license get approved —

RUTH: You mean graft?

WALTER (*frowning impatiently*): Don't call it that. See there, that just goes to show you what women understand about the world. Baby, don't *nothing* happen for you in the world 'less you pay *somebody* off!

RUTH: Walter, leave me alone! (*She raises her head and stares at him vigorously — then says, more quietly.*) *Eat* your eggs, they gonna be cold.

WALTER (*straightening up from her and looking off*): That's it. There you are. Man say to his woman: I got me a dream. His woman say: Eat your eggs. (*Sadly, but gaining in power.*) Man say: I got to take hold of this here world, baby! And a woman will say: Eat your eggs and go to work. (*Passionately now.*) Man say: I got to change my life, I'm choking to death, baby! And his woman say — (*In utter anguish as he brings his fists down on his thighs.*) — Your eggs is getting cold!

RUTH (*softly*): Walter, that ain't none of our money.

WALTER (*not listening at all or even looking at her*): This morning, I was lookin' in the mirror and thinking about it . . . I'm thirty-five years old; I been married eleven years and I got a boy who sleeps in the living room — (*Very, very quietly.*) — and all I got to give him is stories about how rich white people live . . .

RUTH: Eat your eggs, Walter.

WALTER (*slams the table and jumps up*): — DAMN MY EGGS — DAMN ALL THE EGGS THAT EVER WAS!

RUTH: Then go to work.

WALTER (*looking up at her*): See — I'm trying to talk to you 'bout myself — (*Shaking his head with the repetition.*) — and all you can say is eat them eggs and go to work.

RUTH (*wearily*): Honey, you never say nothing new. I listen to you every day, every night and every morning, and you never say nothing new. (*Shrugging.*) So you would rather *be* Mr. Arnold than be his chauffeur. So — I would *rather* be living in Buckingham Palace.

WALTER: That is just what is wrong with the colored woman in this world . . . Don't understand about building their men up and making 'em feel like they somebody. Like they can do something.

RUTH (*drily, but to hurt*): There *are* colored men who do things.

WALTER: No thanks to the colored woman.

RUTH: Well, being a colored woman, I guess I can't help myself none.

She rises and gets the ironing board and sets it up and attacks a huge pile of rough-dried clothes, sprinkling them in preparation for the ironing and then rolling them into tight fat balls.

WALTER (*mumbling*): We one group of men tied to a race of women with small minds!

His sister Beneatha enters. She is about twenty, as slim and intense as her brother. She is not as pretty as her sister-in-law, but her lean, almost intellectual face has a handsomeness of its own. She wears a bright-red flannel nightie, and her thick hair stands wildly about her head. Her speech is a mixture of many things; it is different from the rest of the family's insofar as education has permeated her sense of English — and perhaps the Midwest rather than the South has finally — at last — won out in her inflection; but not altogether, because over all of it is a soft slurring and transformed use of vowels which is the decided influence of the Southside. She passes through the room without looking at either Ruth or Walter and goes to the outside door and looks, a little blindly, out to the bathroom. She sees that it has been lost to the Johnsons. She closes the door with a sleepy vengeance and crosses to the table and sits down a little defeated.

BENEATHA: I am going to start timing those people.

WALTER: You should get up earlier.

BENEATHA (*her face in her hands. She is still fighting the urge to go back to bed*): Really — would you suggest dawn? Where's the paper?

WALTER (*pushing the paper across the table to her as he studies her almost clinically, as though he has never seen her before*): You a horrible-looking chick at this hour.

BENEATHA (*drily*): Good morning, everybody.

WALTER (*senselessly*): How is school coming?

BENEATHA (*in the same spirit*): Lovely. Lovely. And you know, biology is the greatest. (*Looking up at him.*) I dissected something that looked just like you yesterday.

WALTER: I just wondered if you've made up your mind and everything.

BENEATHA (*gaining in sharpness and impatience*): And what did I answer yesterday morning — and the day before that?

RUTH (*from the ironing board, like someone disinterested and old*): Don't be so nasty, Bennie.

BENEATHA (*still to her brother*): And the day before that and the day before that!

WALTER (*defensively*): I'm interested in you. Something wrong with that? Ain't many girls who decide —

WALTER AND BENEATHA (*in unison*): — "to be a doctor."

Silence.

WALTER: Have we figured out yet just exactly how much medical school is going to cost?

RUTH: Walter Lee, why don't you leave that girl alone and get out of here to work?

BENEATHA (*exits to the bathroom and bangs on the door*): Come on out of there, please!

She comes back into the room.

WALTER (*looking at his sister intently*): You know the check is coming tomorrow.

BENEATHA (*turning on him with a sharpness all her own*): That money belongs to Mama, Walter, and it's for her to decide how she wants to use it. I don't care if she wants to buy a house or a rocket ship or just nail it up somewhere and look at it. It's hers. Not ours — *hers.*

WALTER (*bitterly*): Now ain't that fine! You just got your mother's interest at heart, ain't you, girl? You such a nice girl — but if Mama got that money she can always take a few thousand and help you through school too — can't she?

BENEATHA: I have never asked anyone around here to do anything for me!

WALTER: No! And the line between asking and just accepting when the time comes is big and wide — ain't it!

BENEATHA (*with fury*): What do you want from me, Brother — that I quit school or just drop dead, which!

WALTER: I don't want nothing but for you to stop acting holy 'round here. Me and Ruth done made some sacrifices for you — why can't you do something for the family?

RUTH: Walter, don't be dragging me in it.

WALTER: You are in it — Don't you get up and go work in somebody's kitchen for the last three years to help put clothes on her back?

RUTH: Oh, Walter — that's not fair . . .

WALTER: It ain't that nobody expects you to get on your knees and say thank you, Brother; thank you, Ruth; thank you, Mama — and thank you, Travis, for wearing the same pair of shoes for two semesters —

BENEATHA (*dropping to her knees*): Well — I *do* — all right? — thank everybody! And forgive me for ever wanting to be anything at all! (*Pursuing him on her knees across the floor.*) FORGIVE ME, FORGIVE ME, FORGIVE ME!

RUTH: Please stop it! Your mama'll hear you.

WALTER: Who the hell told you you had to be a doctor? If you so crazy 'bout messing 'round with sick people — then go be a nurse like other women — or just get married and be quiet . . .

BENEATHA: Well — you finally got it said . . . It took you three years but you finally got it said. Walter, give up; leave me alone — it's Mama's money.

WALTER: *He was my father, too!*

BENEATHA: So what? He was mine, too — and Travis' grandfather — but the insurance money belongs to Mama. Picking on me is not going to make her give it to you to invest in any liquor stores — (*Under breath, dropping into a chair.*) — and I for one say, God bless Mama for that!

WALTER (*to Ruth*): See — did you hear? Did you hear!

RUTH: Honey, please go to work.

WALTER: Nobody in this house is ever going to understand me.

BENEATHA: Because you're a nut.

WALTER: Who's a nut?

BENEATHA: You — you are a nut. Thee is mad, boy.

WALTER (*looking at his wife and his sister from the door, very sadly*): The world's most backward race of people, and that's a fact.

BENEATHA (*turning slowly in her chair*): And then there are all those prophets who would lead us out of the wilderness — (*Walter slams out of the house.*) — into the swamps!

RUTH: Bennie, why you always gotta be pickin' on your brother? Can't you be a little sweeter sometimes? (*Door opens. Walter walks in. He fumbles with his cap, starts to speak, clears throat, looks everywhere but at Ruth. Finally:*)

WALTER (*to Ruth*): I need some money for carfare.

RUTH (*looks at him, then warms; teasing, but tenderly*): Fifty cents? (*She goes to her bag and gets money.*) Here — take a taxi!

Walter exits. Mama enters. She is a woman in her early sixties, full-bodied and strong. She is one of those women of a certain grace and beauty who wear it so unobtrusively that it takes a while to notice. Her dark-brown face is surrounded by the total whiteness of her hair, and, being a woman who has adjusted to many things in life and overcome many more, her face is full of strength. She has, we can see, wit and faith of a kind that keep her eyes lit and full of interest and expectancy. She is, in a word, a beautiful woman. Her bearing is perhaps most like the noble bearing of the women of the Hereros of Southwest Africa — rather as if she imagines that as she walks she still bears a basket or a vessel upon her head. Her speech, on the other hand, is as careless as her carriage is precise — she is inclined to slur everything — but her voice is perhaps not so much quiet as simply soft.

MAMA: Who that 'round here slamming doors at this hour?

She crosses through the room, goes to the window, opens it, and brings in a feeble little plant growing doggedly in a small pot on the window sill. She feels the dirt and puts it back out.

RUTH: That was Walter Lee. He and Bennie was at it again.

MAMA: My children and they tempers. Lord, if this little old plant don't get more sun than it's been getting it ain't never going to see spring again. (*She turns from the window.*) What's the matter with you this morning, Ruth? You looks right peaked. You aiming to iron all them things? Leave some for me. I'll get to 'em this afternoon. Bennie honey, it's too drafty for you to be sitting 'round half dressed. Where's your robe?

BENEATHA: In the cleaners.

MAMA: Well, go get mine and put it on.

BENEATHA: I'm not cold, Mama, honest.

MAMA: I know — but you so thin . . .

BENEATHA (*irritably*): Mama, I'm not cold.

MAMA (*seeing the make-down bed as Travis has left it*): Lord have mercy, look at that poor bed. Bless his heart — he tries, don't he?

She moves to the bed Travis has sloppily made up.

RUTH: No — he don't half try at all 'cause he knows you going to come along behind him and fix everything. That's just how come he don't know how to do nothing right now — you done spoiled that boy so.

MAMA (*folding bedding*): Well — he's a little boy. Ain't supposed to know 'bout housekeeping. My baby, that's what he is. What you fix for his breakfast this morning?

RUTH (*angrily*): I feed my son, Lena!

MAMA: I ain't meddling — (*Under breath; busy-bodyish.*) I just noticed all last week he had cold cereal, and when it starts getting this chilly in the fall a child ought to have some hot grits or something when he goes out in the cold —

RUTH (*furious*): I gave him hot oats — is that all right!

MAMA: I ain't meddling. (*Pause.*) Put a lot of nice butter on it? (*Ruth shoots her an angry look and does not reply.*) He likes lots of butter.

RUTH (*exasperated*): Lena —

MAMA (*to Beneatha. Mama is inclined to wander conversationally sometimes*): What was you and your brother fussing 'bout this morning?

BENEATHA: It's not important, Mama.

She gets up and goes to look out at the bathroom, which is apparently free, and she picks up her towels and rushes out.

MAMA: What was they fighting about?

RUTH: Now you know as well as I do.

MAMA (*shaking her head*): Brother still worrying hisself sick about that money?

RUTH: You know he is.

MAMA: You had breakfast?

RUTH: Some coffee.

MAMA: Girl, you better start eating and looking after yourself better. You almost thin as Travis.

RUTH: Lena —

MAMA: Un-hunh?

RUTH: What are you going to do with it?

MAMA: Now don't you start, child. It's too early in the morning to be talking about money. It ain't Christian.

RUTH: It's just that he got his heart set on that store —

MAMA: You mean that liquor store that Willy Harris want him to invest in?

RUTH: Yes —

MAMA: We ain't no business people, Ruth. We just plain working folks.

RUTH: Ain't nobody business people till they go into business. Walter Lee say colored people ain't never going to start getting ahead till they start gambling on some different kinds of things in the world — investments and things.

MAMA: What done got into you, girl? Walter Lee done finally sold you on investing.

RUTH: No. Mama, something is happening between Walter and me. I don't know what it is — but he needs something — something I can't give him any more. He needs this chance, Lena.

MAMA (*frowning deeply*): But liquor, honey —

RUTH: Well — like Walter say — I spec people going to always be drinking themselves some liquor.

MAMA: Well — whether they drinks it or not ain't none of my business. But whether I go into business selling it to 'em *is,* and I don't want that on my ledger this late in life. (*Stopping suddenly and studying her daughter-in-law.*) Ruth Younger, what's the matter with you today? You look like you could fall over right there.

RUTH: I'm tired.

MAMA: Then you better stay home from work today.

RUTH: I can't stay home. She'd be calling up the agency and screaming at them, "My girl didn't come in today — send me somebody! My girl didn't come in!" Oh, she just have a fit . . .

MAMA: Well, let her have it. I'll just call her up and say you got the flu —

RUTH (*laughing*): Why the flu?

MAMA: 'Cause it sounds respectable to 'em. Something white people get, too. They know 'bout the flu. Otherwise they think you been cut up or something when you tell 'em you sick.

RUTH: I got to go in. We need the money.

MAMA: Somebody would of thought my children done all but starved to death the way they talk about money here late. Child, we got a great big old check coming tomorrow.

RUTH (*sincerely, but also self-righteously*): Now that's your money. It ain't got nothing to do with me. We all feel like that — Walter and Bennie and me — even Travis.

MAMA (*thoughtfully, and suddenly very far away*): Ten thousand dollars —

RUTH: Sure is wonderful.

MAMA: Ten thousand dollars.

RUTH: You know what you should do, Miss Lena? You should take yourself a trip somewhere. To Europe or South America or someplace —

MAMA (*throwing up her hands at the thought*): Oh, child!

RUTH: I'm serious. Just pack up and leave! Go on away and enjoy yourself some. Forget about the family and have yourself a ball for once in your life —

MAMA (*drily*): You sound like I'm just about ready to die. Who'd go with me? What I look like wandering 'round Europe by myself?

RUTH: Shoot — these here rich white women do it all the time. They don't think nothing of packing up they suitcases and piling on one of them big steamships and — swoosh! — they gone, child.

MAMA: Something always told me I wasn't no rich white woman.

RUTH: Well — what are you going to do with it then?

MAMA: I ain't rightly decided. (*Thinking. She speaks now with emphasis.*) Some of it got to be put away for Beneatha and her schoolin' — and ain't nothing going to touch that part of it. Nothing. (*She waits several seconds, trying to make up her mind about something, and looks at Ruth a little tentatively before going on.*) Been thinking that we maybe could meet the notes on a little old two-story somewhere, with a yard where Travis could play in the summertime, if we use part of the insurance for a down payment and everybody kind of pitch in. I could maybe take on a little day work again, few days a week —

RUTH (*studying her mother-in-law furtively and concentrating on her ironing, anxious to encourage without seeming to*): Well, Lord knows, we've put enough rent into this here rat trap to pay for four houses by now . . .

MAMA (*looking up at the words "rat trap" and then looking around and leaning back and sighing — in a suddenly reflective mood —*): "Rat trap" — yes, that's all it is. (*Smiling.*) I remember just as well the day me and Big Walter moved in here. Hadn't been married but two weeks and wasn't planning on living here no more than a year. (*She shakes her head at the dissolved dream.*) We was going to set away, little by little, don't you know, and buy a little place out in Morgan Park. We had even picked out the house. (*Chuckling a little.*) Looks right dumpy today. But Lord, child, you should know all the dreams I had 'bout buying that house and fixing it up and making me a little garden in the back — (*She waits and stops smiling.*) And didn't none of it happen.

Dropping her hands in a futile gesture.

RUTH (*keeps her head down, ironing*): Yes, life can be a barrel of disappointments, sometimes.

MAMA: Honey, Big Walter would come in here some nights back then and slump down on that couch there and just look at the rug, and look at me and look at the rug and then back at me — and I'd know he was down then . . . really down. (*After a second very long and thoughtful pause; she is seeing back to times that only she can see.*) And then, Lord, when I lost that baby — little Claude — I almost thought I was going to lose Big Walter too. Oh, that man grieved hisself! He was one man to love his children.

RUTH: Ain't nothin' can tear at you like losin' your baby.

MAMA: I guess that's how come that man finally worked hisself to death like he done. Like he was fighting his own war with this here world that took his baby from him.

RUTH: He sure was a fine man, all right. I always liked Mr. Younger.

MAMA: Crazy 'bout his children! God knows there was plenty wrong with Walter Younger — hard-headed, mean, kind of wild with women — plenty wrong with him. But he sure loved his children. Always wanted them to have something — be something. That's where Brother gets all these notions, I reckon. Big Walter used to say, he'd get right wet in the eyes sometimes, lean his head back with the water standing in his eyes and say, "Seem like God didn't see fit to give the black man nothing but dreams — but He did give us children to make them dreams seem worthwhile." (*She smiles.*) He could talk like that, don't you know.

RUTH: Yes, he sure could. He was a good man, Mr. Younger.

MAMA: Yes, a fine man — just couldn't never catch up with his dreams, that's all.

Beneatha comes in, brushing her hair and looking up to the ceiling, where the sound of a vacuum cleaner has started up.

BENEATHA: What could be so dirty on that woman's rugs that she has to vacuum them every single day?

RUTH: I wish certain young women 'round here who I could name would take inspiration about certain rugs in a certain apartment I could also mention.

BENEATHA (*shrugging*): How much cleaning can a house need, for Christ's sakes.

MAMA (*not liking the Lord's name used thus*): Bennie!

RUTH: Just listen to her — just listen!

BENEATHA: Oh, God!

MAMA: If you use the Lord's name just one more time —

BENEATHA (*a bit of a whine*): Oh, Mama —

RUTH: Fresh — just fresh as salt, this girl!

BENEATHA (*drily*): Well — if the salt loses its savor —

MAMA: Now that will do. I just ain't going to have you 'round here reciting the scriptures in vain — you hear me?

BENEATHA: How did I manage to get on everybody's wrong side by just walking into a room?

RUTH: If you weren't so fresh —

BENEATHA: Ruth, I'm twenty years old.

MAMA: What time you be home from school today?

BENEATHA: Kind of late. (*With enthusiasm.*) Madeline is going to start my guitar lessons today.

Mama and Ruth look up with the same expression.

MAMA: Your *what* kind of lessons?

BENEATHA: Guitar.

RUTH: Oh, Father!

MAMA: How come you done taken it in your mind to learn to play the guitar?

BENEATHA: I just want to, that's all.

MAMA (*smiling*): Lord, child, don't you know what to do with yourself? How long it going to be before you get tired of this now — like you got tired of that little play-acting group you joined last year? (*Looking at Ruth.*) And what was it the year before that?

RUTH: The horseback-riding club for which she bought that fifty-five-dollar riding habit that's been hanging in the closet ever since!

MAMA (*to Beneatha*): Why you got to flit so from one thing to another, baby?

BENEATHA (*sharply*): I just want to learn to play the guitar. Is there anything wrong with that?

MAMA: Ain't nobody trying to stop you. I just wonders sometimes why you has to flit so from one thing to another all the time. You ain't never done nothing with all that camera equipment you brought home —

BENEATHA: I don't flit! I — I experiment with different forms of expression —

RUTH: Like riding a horse?

BENEATHA: — People have to express themselves one way or another.

MAMA: What is it you want to express?

BENEATHA (*angrily*): Me! (*Mama and Ruth look at each other and burst into raucous laughter.*) Don't worry — I don't expect you to understand.

MAMA (*to change the subject*): Who you going out with tomorrow night?

BENEATHA (*with displeasure*): George Murchison again.

MAMA (*pleased*): Oh — you getting a little sweet on him?

RUTH: You ask me, this child ain't sweet on nobody but herself — (*Under breath.*) Express herself!

They laugh.

BENEATHA: Oh — I like George all right, Mama. I mean I like him enough to go out with him and stuff, but —

RUTH (*for devilment*): What does *and stuff* mean?

BENEATHA: Mind your own business.

MAMA: Stop picking at her now, Ruth. (*She chuckles — then a suspicious sudden look at her daughter as she turns in her chair for emphasis.*) What DOES it mean?

BENEATHA (*wearily*): Oh, I just mean I couldn't ever really be serious about George. He's — he's so shallow.

RUTH: Shallow — what do you mean he's shallow? He's *Rich!*

MAMA: Hush, Ruth.

BENEATHA: I know he's rich. He knows he's rich, too.

RUTH: Well — what other qualities a man got to have to satisfy you, little girl?

BENEATHA: You wouldn't even begin to understand. Anybody who married Walter could not possibly understand.

MAMA (*outraged*): What kind of way is that to talk about your brother?

BENEATHA: Brother is a flip — let's face it.

MAMA (*to Ruth, helplessly*): What's a flip?

RUTH (*glad to add kindling*): She's saying he's crazy.

BENEATHA: Not crazy. Brother isn't really crazy yet — he — he's an elaborate neurotic.

MAMA: Hush your mouth!

BENEATHA: As for George. Well. George looks good — he's got a beautiful car and he takes me to nice places and, as my sister-in-law says, he is probably the richest boy I will ever get to know and I even like him sometimes — but if the Youngers are sitting around waiting to see if their little Bennie is going to tie up the family with the Murchisons, they are wasting their time.

RUTH: You mean you wouldn't marry George Murchison if he asked you someday? That pretty, rich thing? Honey, I knew you was odd —

BENEATHA: No I would not marry him if all I felt for him was what I feel now. Besides, George's family wouldn't really like it.

MAMA: Why not?

BENEATHA: Oh, Mama — The Murchisons are honest-to-God-real-*live*-rich colored people, and the only people in the world who are more snobbish than rich white people are rich colored people. I thought everybody knew that. I've met Mrs. Murchison. She's a scene!

MAMA: You must not dislike people 'cause they well off, honey.

BENEATHA: Why not? It makes just as much sense as disliking people 'cause they are poor, and lots of people do that.

RUTH (*a wisdom-of-the-ages manner. To Mama*): Well, she'll get over some of this —

BENEATHA: Get over it? What are you talking about, Ruth? Listen, I'm going to be a doctor. I'm not worried about who I'm going to marry yet — if I ever get married.

MAMA AND RUTH: *If!*

MAMA: Now, Bennie —

BENEATHA: Oh, I probably will . . . but first I'm going to be a doctor, and George, for one, still thinks that's pretty funny. I couldn't be bothered with that. I am going to be a doctor and everybody around here better understand that!

MAMA (*kindly*): 'Course you going to be a doctor, honey, God willing.

BENEATHA (*drily*): God hasn't got a thing to do with it.

MAMA: Beneatha — that just wasn't necessary.

BENEATHA: Well — neither is God. I get sick of hearing about God.

MAMA: Beneatha!

BENEATHA: I mean it! I'm just tired of hearing about God all the time. What has He got to do with anything? Does He pay tuition?

MAMA: You 'bout to get your fresh little jaw slapped!

RUTH: That's just what she needs, all right!

BENEATHA: Why? Why can't I say what I want to around here, like everybody else?

MAMA: It don't sound nice for a young girl to say things like that — you wasn't brought up that way. Me and your father went to trouble to get you and Brother to church every Sunday.

BENEATHA: Mama, you don't understand. It's all a matter of ideas, and God is just one idea I don't accept. It's not important. I am not going out and be immoral or commit crimes because I don't believe in God. I don't even think about it. It's just that I get tired of Him getting credit for all the things the human race achieves through its own stubborn effort. There simply is no blasted God — there is only man and it is *He* who makes miracles!

Mama absorbs this speech, studies her daughter, and rises slowly and crosses to Beneatha and slaps her powerfully across the face. After, there is only silence and the daughter drops her eyes from her mother's face, and Mama is very tall before her.

MAMA: Now — you say after me, in my mother's house there is still God. (*There is a long pause and Beneatha stares at the floor wordlessly. Mama repeats the phrase with precision and cool emotion.*) In my mother's house there is still God.

BENEATHA: In my mother's house there is still God.

A long pause.

MAMA (*walking away from Beneatha, too disturbed for triumphant posture. Stopping and turning back to her daughter*): There are some ideas we ain't going to have in this house. Not long as I am at the head of this family.

BENEATHA: Yes, ma'am.

Mama walks out of the room.

RUTH (*almost gently, with profound understanding*): You think you a woman, Bennie — but you still a little girl. What you did was childish — so you got treated like a child.

BENEATHA: I see. (*Quietly.*) I also see that everybody thinks it's all right for Mama to be a tyrant. But all the tyranny in the world will never put a God in the heavens!

She picks up her books and goes out. Pause.

RUTH (*goes to Mama's door*): She said she was sorry.

MAMA (*coming out, going to her plant*): They frightens me, Ruth. My children.

RUTH: You got good children, Lena. They just a little off sometimes — but they're good.

MAMA: No — there's something come down between me and them that don't let us understand each other and I don't know what it is. One done almost lost his mind thinking 'bout money all the time and the other done commence to talk about things I can't seem to understand in no form or fashion. What is it that's changing, Ruth.

RUTH (*soothingly, older than her years*): Now . . . you taking it all too seriously. You just got strong-willed children and it takes a strong woman like you to keep 'em in hand.

MAMA (*looking at her plant and sprinkling a little water on it*): They spirited all right, my children. Got to admit they got spirit — Bennie and Walter. Like this little old plant that ain't never had enough sunshine or nothing — and look at it . . .

She has her back to Ruth, who has had to stop ironing and lean against something and put the back of her hand to her forehead.

RUTH (*trying to keep Mama from noticing*): You . . . sure . . . loves that little old thing, don't you? . . .

MAMA: Well, I always wanted me a garden like I used to see sometimes at the back of the houses down home. This plant is close as I ever got to having one. (*She looks out of the window as she replaces the plant.*) Lord, ain't nothing as dreary as the view from this window on a dreary day, is there? Why ain't you singing this morning, Ruth? Sing that "No Ways Tired." That song always lifts me up so — (*She turns at last to see that Ruth has slipped quietly to the floor, in a state of semiconsciousness.*) Ruth! Ruth honey — what's the matter with you . . . Ruth!

Curtain.

SCENE II: [*The following morning.*]

It is the following morning; a Saturday morning, and house cleaning is in progress at the Youngers'. Furniture has been shoved hither and yon and Mama is giving the kitchen-area walls a washing down. Beneatha, in dungarees, with a handkerchief tied around her face, is spraying insecticide into the cracks in the walls. As they work, the radio is on and a Southside disk-jockey program is inappropriately filling the house with a rather exotic saxophone blues. Travis, the sole idle one, is leaning on his arms, looking out of the window.

TRAVIS: Grandmama, that stuff Bennie is using smells awful. Can I go downstairs, please?

MAMA: Did you get all them chores done already? I ain't seen you doing much.

TRAVIS: Yes'm — finished early. Where did Mama go this morning?

MAMA (*looking at Beneatha*): She had to go on a little errand.

The phone rings. Beneatha runs to answer it and reaches it before Walter, who has entered from bedroom.

TRAVIS: Where?

MAMA: To tend to her business.

BENEATHA: Haylo . . . (*Disappointed.*) Yes, he is. (*She tosses the phone to Walter, who barely catches it.*) It's Willy Harris again.

WALTER (*as privately as possible under Mama's gaze*): Hello, Willy. Did you get the papers from the lawyer? . . . No, not yet. I told you the mailman doesn't get here till ten-thirty . . . No, I'll come there . . . Yeah! Right away. (*He hangs up and goes for his coat.*)

BENEATHA: Brother, where did Ruth go?

WALTER (*as he exits*): How should I know!

TRAVIS: Aw come on, Grandma. Can I go outside?

MAMA: Oh, I guess so. You stay right in front of the house, though, and keep a good lookout for the postman.

TRAVIS: Yes'm. (*He darts into bedroom for stickball and bat, reenters, and sees Beneatha on her knees spraying under sofa with behind upraised. He edges closer to the target, takes aim, and lets her have it. She screams.*) Leave them poor little cockroaches alone, they ain't bothering you none! (*He runs as she swings the spraygun at him viciously and playfully.*) Grandma! Grandma!

MAMA: Look out there, girl, before you be spilling some of that stuff on that child!

TRAVIS (*safely behind the bastion of Mama*): That's right — look out, now! (*He exits.*)

BENEATHA (*drily*): I can't imagine that it would hurt him — it has never hurt the roaches.

MAMA: Well, little boys' hides ain't as tough as Southside roaches. You better get over there behind the bureau. I seen one marching out of there like Napoleon yesterday.

BENEATHA: There's really only one way to get rid of them, Mama —

MAMA: How?

BENEATHA: Set fire to this building! Mama, where did Ruth go?

MAMA (*looking at her with meaning*): To the doctor, I think.

BENEATHA: The doctor? What's the matter? (*They exchange glances.*) You don't think —

MAMA (*with her sense of drama*): Now I ain't saying what I think. But I ain't never been wrong 'bout a woman neither.

The phone rings.

BENEATHA (*at the phone*): Hay-lo . . . (*Pause, and a moment of recognition.*) Well — when did you get back! . . . And how was it? . . . Of course I've missed you — in my way . . . This morning? No . . . house cleaning and all that and Mama hates it if I let people come over when the house is like this . . . You *have?* Well, that's different . . . What is it — Oh, what the hell, come on over . . . Right, see you then. *Arrividerci.*

She hangs up.

MAMA (*who has listened vigorously, as is her habit*): Who is that you inviting over here with this house looking like this? You ain't got the pride you was born with!

BENEATHA: Asagai doesn't care how houses look, Mama — he's an intellectual.

MAMA: *Who?*

BENEATHA: Asagai — Joseph Asagai. He's an African boy I met on campus. He's been studying in Canada all summer.

MAMA: What's his name?

BENEATHA: Asagai, Joseph. Ah-sah-guy . . . He's from Nigeria.

MAMA: Oh, that's the little country that was founded by slaves way back . . .

BENEATHA: No, Mama — that's Liberia.

MAMA: I don't think I never met no African before.

BENEATHA: Well, do me a favor and don't ask him a whole lot of ignorant questions about Africans. I mean, do they wear clothes and all that —

MAMA: Well, now, I guess if you think we so ignorant 'round here maybe you shouldn't bring your friends here —

BENEATHA: It's just that people ask such crazy things. All anyone seems to know about when it comes to Africa is Tarzan —

MAMA (*indignantly*): Why should I know anything about Africa?

BENEATHA: Why do you give money at church for the missionary work?

MAMA: Well, that's to help save people.

BENEATHA: You mean save them from *heathenism* —

MAMA (*innocently*): Yes.

BENEATHA: I'm afraid they need more salvation from the British and the French.

Ruth comes in forlornly and pulls off her coat with dejection. They both turn to look at her.

RUTH (*dispiritedly*): Well, I guess from all the happy faces — everybody knows.

BENEATHA: You pregnant?

MAMA: Lord have mercy, I sure hope it's a little old girl. Travis ought to have a sister.

Beneatha and Ruth give her a hopeless look for this grandmotherly enthusiasm.

BENEATHA: How far along are you?

RUTH: Two months.

BENEATHA: Did you mean to? I mean did you plan it or was it an accident?

MAMA: What do you know about planning or not planning?

BENEATHA: Oh, Mama.

RUTH (*wearily*): She's twenty years old, Lena.

BENEATHA: Did you plan it, Ruth?

RUTH: Mind your own business.

BENEATHA: It is my business — where is he going to live, on the *roof?* (*There is silence following the remark as the three women react to the sense of it.*) Gee — I didn't mean that, Ruth, honest. Gee, I don't feel like that at all. I — I think it is wonderful.

RUTH (*dully*): Wonderful.

BENEATHA: Yes — really.

MAMA (*looking at Ruth, worried*): Doctor say everything going to be all right?

RUTH (*far away*): Yes — she says everything is going to be fine . . .

MAMA (*immediately suspicious*): "She" — What doctor you went to?

Ruth folds over, near hysteria.

MAMA (*worriedly hovering over Ruth*): Ruth honey — what's the matter with you — you sick?

Ruth has her fists clenched on her thighs and is fighting hard to suppress a scream that seems to be rising in her.

BENEATHA: What's the matter with her, Mama?

MAMA (*working her fingers in Ruth's shoulders to relax her*): She be all right. Women gets right depressed sometimes when they get her way. (*Speaking softly, expertly, rapidly.*) Now you just relax. That's right . . . just lean back, don't think 'bout nothing at all . . . nothing at all —

RUTH: I'm all right . . .

The glassy-eyed look melts and then she collapses into a fit of heavy sobbing. The bell rings.

BENEATHA: Oh, my God — that must be Asagai.

MAMA (*to Ruth*): Come on now, honey. You need to lie down and rest awhile . . . then have some nice hot food.

They exit, Ruth's weight on her mother-in-law. Beneatha, herself profoundly disturbed, opens the door to admit a rather dramatic-looking young man with a large package.

ASAGAI: Hello, Alaiyo —

BENEATHA (*holding the door open and regarding him with pleasure*): Hello . . . (*Long pause.*) Well — come in. And please excuse everything. My mother was very upset about my letting anyone come here with the place like this.

ASAGAI (*coming into the room*): You look disturbed too . . . Is something wrong?

BENEATHA (*still at the door, absently*): Yes . . . we've all got acute ghetto-itus. (*She smiles and comes toward him, finding a cigarette and sitting.*) So — sit down! No! Wait! (*She whips the spraygun off sofa where she had left it and puts the cushions back. At last perches on arm of sofa. He sits.*) So, how was Canada?

ASAGAI (*a sophisticate*): Canadian.

BENEATHA (*looking at him*): Asagai, I'm very glad you are back.

ASAGAI (*looking back at her in turn*): Are you really?

BENEATHA: Yes — very.

ASAGAI: Why? — you were quite glad when I went away. What happened?

BENEATHA: You went away.

ASAGAI: Ahhhhhhhh.

BENEATHA: Before — you wanted to be so serious before there was time.

ASAGAI: How much time must there be before one knows what one feels?

BENEATHA (*stalling this particular conversation. Her hands pressed together, in a deliberately childish gesture*): What did you bring me?

ASAGAI (*handing her the package*): Open it and see.

BENEATHA (*eagerly opening the package and drawing out some records and the colorful robes of a Nigerian woman*): Oh Asagai! . . . You got them for me! . . . How beautiful . . . and the records too! (*She lifts out the robes and runs to the mirror with them and holds the drapery up in front of herself.*)

ASAGAI (*coming to her at the mirror*): I shall have to teach you how to drape it properly. (*He flings the material about her for the moment and stands back to look at her.*) Ah — *Oh-pay-gay-day, oh-gbah-mu-shay.* (*A Yoruba exclamation for admiration.*) You wear it well . . . very well . . . mutilated hair and all.

BENEATHA (*turning suddenly*): My hair — what's wrong with my hair?

ASAGAI (*shrugging*): Were you born with it like that?

BENEATHA (*reaching up to touch it*): No . . . of course not.

She looks back to the mirror, disturbed.

ASAGAI (*smiling*): How then?

BENEATHA: You know perfectly well how . . . as crinkly as yours . . . that's how.

ASAGAI: And it is ugly to you that way?

BENEATHA (*quickly*): Oh, no — not ugly . . . (*More slowly, apologetically.*) But it's so hard to manage when it's, well — raw.

ASAGAI: And so to accommodate that — you mutilate it every week?

BENEATHA: It's not mutilation!

ASAGAI (*laughing aloud at her seriousness*): Oh . . . please! I am only teasing you because you are so very serious about these things. (*He stands back from her and folds his arms across his chest as he watches her pulling at her hair and frowning in the mirror.*) Do you remember the first time you met me at school? . . . (*He laughs.*) You came up to me and you said — and I thought you were the most serious little thing I had ever seen — you said: (*He imitates her.*) "Mr. Asagai — I want very much to talk with you. About Africa. You see, Mr. Asagai, I am looking for my *identity!*"

He laughs.

BENEATHA (*turning to him, not laughing*): Yes —

Her face is quizzical, profoundly disturbed.

ASAGAI (*still teasing and reaching out and taking her face in his hands and turning her profile to him*): Well . . . it is true that this is not so much a profile of a Hollywood queen as perhaps a queen of the Nile — (*A mock dismissal of the importance of the question.*) But what does it matter? Assimilationism is so popular in your country.

BENEATHA (*wheeling, passionately, sharply*): I am not an assimilationist!

ASAGAI (*the protest hangs in the room for a moment and Asagai studies her, his laughter fading*): Such a serious one. (*There is a pause.*) So — you like the robes? You must take excellent care of them — they are from my sister's personal wardrobe.

BENEATHA (*with incredulity*): You — you sent all the way home — for me?

ASAGAI (*with charm*): For you — I would do much more . . . Well, that is what I came for. I must go.

BENEATHA: Will you call me Monday?

ASAGAI: Yes . . . We have a great deal to talk about. I mean about identity and time and all that.

BENEATHA: Time?

ASAGAI: Yes. About how much time one needs to know what one feels.

BENEATHA: You see! You never understood that there is more than one kind of feeling which can exist between a man and a woman — or, at least, there should be.

ASAGAI (*shaking his head negatively but gently*): No. Between a man and a woman there need be only one kind of feeling. I have that for you . . . Now even . . . right this moment . . .

BENEATHA: I know — and by itself — it won't do. I can find that anywhere.

ASAGAI: For a woman it should be enough.

BENEATHA: I know — because that's what it says in all the novels that men write. But it isn't. Go ahead and laugh — but I'm not interested in being someone's little episode in America or — (*With feminine vengeance.*) — one of them! (*Asagai has burst into laughter again.*) That's funny as hell, huh!

ASAGAI: It's just that every American girl I have known has said that to me. White — black — in this you are all the same. And the same speech, too!

BENEATHA (*angrily*): Yuk, yuk, yuk!

ASAGAI: It's how you can be sure that the world's most liberated women are not liberated at all. You all talk about it too much!

Mama enters and is immediately all social charm because of the presence of a guest.

BENEATHA: Oh — Mama — this is Mr. Asagai.

MAMA: How do you do?

ASAGAI (*total politeness to an elder*): How do you do, Mrs. Younger. Please forgive me for coming at such an outrageous hour on a Saturday.

MAMA: Well, you are quite welcome. I just hope you understand that our house don't always look like this. (*Chatterish.*) You must come again. I would love to hear all about — (*Not sure of the name.*) — your country. I think it's so sad the way our American Negroes don't know nothing about Africa 'cept Tarzan and all that. And all that money they pour into these churches when they ought to be helping you people over there drive out them French and Englishmen done taken away your land.

The mother flashes a slightly superior look at her daughter upon completion of the recitation.

ASAGAI (*taken aback by this sudden and acutely unrelated expression of sympathy*): Yes . . . yes . . .

MAMA (*smiling at him suddenly and relaxing and looking him over*): How many miles is it from here to where you come from?

ASAGAI: Many thousands.

MAMA (*looking at him as she would Walter*): I bet you don't half look after yourself, being away from your mama either. I spec you better come 'round here from time to time to get yourself some decent homecooked meals . . .

ASAGAI (*moved*): Thank you. Thank you very much. (*They are all quiet, then —*) Well . . . I must go. I will call you Monday, Alaiyo.

MAMA: What's that he call you?

ASAGAI: Oh — "Alaiyo." I hope you don't mind. It is what you would call a nickname, I think. It is a Yoruba word. I am a Yoruba.

MAMA (*looking at Beneatha*): I — I thought he was from — (*Uncertain.*)

ASAGAI (*understanding*): Nigeria is my country. Yoruba is my tribal origin —

BENEATHA: You didn't tell us what Alaiyo means . . . for all I know, you might be calling me Little Idiot or something . . .

ASAGAI: Well . . . let me see . . . I do not know how just to explain it . . . The sense of a thing can be so different when it changes languages.

BENEATHA: You're evading.

ASAGAI: No — really it is difficult . . . (*Thinking.*) It means . . . it means One for Whom Bread — Food — Is Not Enough. (*He looks at her.*) Is that all right?

BENEATHA (*understanding, softly*): Thank you.

MAMA (*looking from one to the other and not understanding any of it*): Well . . . that's nice . . . You must come see us again — Mr. —

ASAGAI: Ah-sah-guy . . .

MAMA: Yes . . . Do come again.

ASAGAI: Good-bye.

He exits.

MAMA (*after him*): Lord, that's a pretty thing just went out here! (*Insinuatingly, to her daughter.*) Yes, I guess I see why we done commence to get so interested in Africa 'round here. Missionaries my aunt Jenny!

She exits.

BENEATHA: Oh, Mama! . . .

She picks up the Nigerian dress and holds it up to her in front of the mirror again. She sets the headdress on haphazardly and then notices her hair again and clutches at it and then replaces the headdress and frowns at herself. Then she starts to wriggle in front of the mirror as she thinks a Nigerian woman might. Travis enters and stands regarding her.

TRAVIS: What's the matter, girl, you cracking up?

BENEATHA: Shut up.

She pulls the headdress off and looks at herself in the mirror and clutches at her hair again and squinches her eyes as if trying to imagine something. Then, suddenly, she gets her raincoat and kerchief and hurriedly prepares for going out.

MAMA (*coming back into the room*): She's resting now. Travis, baby, run next door and ask Miss Johnson to please let me have a little kitchen cleanser. This here can is empty as Jacob's kettle.

TRAVIS: I just came in.

MAMA: Do as you told. (*He exits and she looks at her daughter.*) Where you going?

BENEATHA (*halting at the door*): To become a queen of the Nile!

She exits in a breathless blaze of glory. Ruth appears in the bedroom doorway.

MAMA: Who told you to get up?

RUTH: Ain't nothing wrong with me to be lying in no bed for. Where did Bennie go?

MAMA (*drumming her fingers*): Far as I could make out — to Egypt. (*Ruth just looks at her.*) What time is it getting to?

RUTH: Ten twenty. And the mailman going to ring that bell this morning just like he done every morning for the last umpteen years.

Travis comes in with the cleanser can.

TRAVIS: She say to tell you that she don't have much.

MAMA (*angrily*): Lord, some people I could name sure is tight-fisted! (*Directing her grandson.*) Mark two cans of cleanser on the list there. If she that hard up for kitchen cleanser, I sure don't want to forget to get her none!

RUTH: Lena — maybe the woman is just short on cleanser —

MAMA (*not listening*): — Much baking powder as she done borrowed from me all these years, she could of done gone into the baking business!

The bell sounds suddenly and sharply and all three are stunned — serious and silent — midspeech. In spite of all the other conversations and distractions of the morning, this is what they have been waiting for, even Travis, who looks helplessly from his mother to his grandmother. Ruth is the first to come to life again.

RUTH (*to Travis*): Get down them steps, boy!

Travis snaps to life and flies out to get the mail.

MAMA (*her eyes wide, her hand to her breast*): You mean it done really come?

RUTH (*excited*): Oh, Miss Lena!

MAMA (*collecting herself*): Well . . . I don't know what we all so excited about 'round here for. We known it was coming for months.

RUTH: That's a whole lot different from having it come and being able to hold it in your hands . . . a piece of paper worth ten thousand dollars . . . (*Travis bursts back into the room. He holds the envelope high above his head, like a little dancer, his face is radiant and he is breathless. He moves to his grandmother with sudden slow ceremony and puts the envelope into her hands. She accepts it, and then merely holds it and looks at it.*) Come on! Open it . . . Lord have mercy, I wish Walter Lee was here!

TRAVIS: Open it, Grandmama!

MAMA (*staring at it*): Now you all be quiet. It's just a check.

RUTH: Open it . . .

MAMA (*still staring at it*): Now don't act silly . . . We ain't never been no people to act silly 'bout no money —

RUTH (*swiftly*): We ain't never had none before — OPEN IT!

Mama finally makes a good strong tear and pulls out the thin blue slice of paper and inspects it closely. The boy and his mother study it raptly over Mama's shoulders.

MAMA: Travis! (*She is counting off with doubt.*) Is that the right number of zeros?

TRAVIS: Yes'm . . . ten thousand dollars. Gaalee, grandmama, you rich.

MAMA (*She holds the check away from her, still looking at it. Slowly her face sobers into a mask of unhappiness*): Ten thousand dollars. (*She hands it to Ruth.*) Put it away somewhere, Ruth. (*She does not look at Ruth; her eyes seem to be seeing something somewhere very far off.*) Ten thousand dollars they give you. Ten thousand dollars.

TRAVIS (*to his mother, sincerely*): What's the matter with Grandmama — don't she want to be rich?

RUTH (*distractedly*): You go on out and play now, baby. (*Travis exits. Mama starts wiping dishes absently, humming intently to herself. Ruth turns to her, with kind exasperation.*) You've gone and got yourself upset.

MAMA (*not looking at her*): I spec if it wasn't for you all . . . I would just put that money away or give it to the church or something.

RUTH: Now what kind of talk is that. Mr. Younger would just be plain mad if he could hear you talking foolish like that.

MAMA (*stopping and staring off*): Yes . . . he sure would. (*Sighing.*) We got enough to do with that money, all right. (*She halts then, and turns and looks at her daughter-in-law hard; Ruth avoids her eyes and Mama wipes her hands with finality and starts to speak firmly to Ruth.*) Where did you go today, girl?

RUTH: To the doctor.

MAMA (*impatiently*): Now, Ruth . . . you know better than that. Old Doctor Jones is strange enough in his way but there ain't nothing 'bout him make somebody slip and call him "she" — like you done this morning.

RUTH: Well, that's what happened — my tongue slipped.

MAMA: You went to see that woman, didn't you?

RUTH (*defensively, giving herself away*): What woman you talking about?

MAMA (*angrily*): That woman who —

Walter enters in great excitement.

WALTER: Did it come?

MAMA (*quietly*): Can't you give people a Christian greeting before you start asking about money?

WALTER (*to Ruth*): Did it come? (*Ruth unfolds the check and lays it quietly before him, watching him intently with thoughts of her own. Walter sits down and grasps it close and counts off the zeros.*) Ten thousand dollars — (*He turns suddenly, frantically to his mother and draws some papers out of his breast pocket.*) Mama — look. Old Willy Harris put everything on paper —

MAMA: Son — I think you ought to talk to your wife . . . I'll go on out and leave you alone if you want —

WALTER: I can talk to her later — Mama, look —

MAMA: Son —

WALTER: WILL SOMEBODY PLEASE LISTEN TO ME TODAY!

MAMA (*quietly*): I don't 'low no yellin' in this house, Walter Lee, and you know it — (*Walter stares at them in frustration and starts to speak several times.*) And there ain't going to be no investing in no liquor stores.

WALTER: But, Mama, you ain't even looked at it.

MAMA: I don't aim to have to speak on that again.

A long pause.

WALTER: You ain't looked at it and you don't aim to have to speak on that again? You ain't even looked at it and *you* have decided — (*Crumpling his papers.*) Well, *you* tell that to my boy tonight when you put him to sleep on the living-room couch . . . (*Turning to Mama and speaking directly to her.*) Yeah — and tell it to my wife, Mama, tomorrow when she has to go out of here to look after somebody else's kids. And tell it to *me*, Mama, every time we need a new pair of curtains and I have to watch *you* go out and work in somebody's kitchen. Yeah, you tell me then!

Walter starts out.

RUTH: Where you going?

WALTER: I'm going out!

RUTH: Where?

WALTER: Just out of this house somewhere —

RUTH (*getting her coat*): I'll come too.

WALTER: I don't want you to come!

RUTH: I got something to talk to you about, Walter.

WALTER: That's too bad.

MAMA (*still quietly*): Walter Lee — (*She waits and he finally turns and looks at her.*) Sit down.

WALTER: I'm a grown man, Mama.

MAMA: Ain't nobody said you wasn't grown. But you still in my house and my presence. And as long as you are — you'll talk to your wife civil. Now sit down.

RUTH (*suddenly*): Oh, let him go on out and drink himself to death! He makes me sick to my stomach! (*She flings her coat against him and exits to bedroom.*)

WALTER (*violently flinging the coat after her*): And you turn mine too, baby! (*The door slams behind her.*) That was my biggest mistake —

MAMA (*still quietly*): Walter, what is the matter with you?

WALTER: Matter with me? Ain't nothing the matter with *me!*

MAMA: Yes there is. Something eating you up like a crazy man. Something more than me not giving you this money. The past few years I been watching it happen to you. You get all nervous acting and kind of wild in the eyes — (*Walter jumps up impatiently at her words.*) I said sit there now, I'm talking to you!

WALTER: Mama — I don't need no nagging at me today.

MAMA: Seem like you getting to a place where you always tied up in some kind of knot about something. But if anybody ask you 'bout it you just yell at 'em and bust out the house and go out and drink somewheres. Walter Lee, people can't live with that. Ruth's a good, patient girl in her way — but you getting to be too much. Boy, don't make the mistake of driving that girl away from you.

WALTER: Why — what she do for me?

MAMA: She loves you.

WALTER: Mama — I'm going out. I want to go off somewhere and be by myself for a while.

MAMA: I'm sorry 'bout your liquor store, son. It just wasn't the thing for us to do. That's what I want to tell you about —

WALTER: I got to go out, Mama —

He rises.

MAMA: It's dangerous, son.

WALTER: What's dangerous?

MAMA: When a man goes outside his home to look for peace.

WALTER (*beseechingly*): Then why can't there never be no peace in this house then?

MAMA: You done found it in some other house?

WALTER: No — there ain't no woman! Why do women always think there's a woman somewhere when a man gets restless. (*Picks up the check.*) Do you know what this money means to me? Do you know what this money can do for us? (*Puts it back.*) Mama — Mama — I want so many things . . .

MAMA: Yes, son —

WALTER: I want so many things that they are driving me kind of crazy . . . Mama — look at me.

MAMA: I'm looking at you. You a good-looking boy. You got a job, a nice wife, a fine boy, and —

WALTER: A job. (*Looks at her.*) Mama, a job? I open and close car doors all day long. I drive a man around in his limousine and I say, "Yes, sir; no, sir; very good, sir; shall I take the Drive, sir?" Mama, that ain't no kind of job . . . that ain't nothing at all. (*Very quietly.*) Mama, I don't know if I can make you understand.

MAMA: Understand what, baby?

WALTER (*quietly*): Sometimes it's like I can see the future stretched out in front of me — just plain as day. The future, Mama. Hanging over there at the edge of my days. Just waiting for me — a big, looming blank space — full of *nothing.* Just waiting for *me.* But it don't have to be. (*Pause. Kneeling beside her chair.*) Mama — sometimes when I'm downtown and I pass them cool, quiet-looking restaurants where them white boys are sitting back and talking 'bout things . . . sitting there turning deals worth millions of dollars . . . sometimes I see guys don't look much older than me —

MAMA: Son — how come you talk so much 'bout money?

WALTER (*with immense passion*): Because it is life, Mama!

MAMA (*quietly*): Oh — (*Very quietly.*) So now it's life. Money is life. Once upon a time freedom used to be life — now it's money. I guess the world really do change . . .

WALTER: No — it was always money, Mama. We just didn't know about it.

MAMA: No . . . something has changed. (*She looks at him.*) You something new, boy. In my time we was worried about not being lynched and getting to the North if we could and how to stay alive and still have a pinch of dignity too . . . Now here come you and Beneatha — talking 'bout things we ain't never even thought about hardly, me and your daddy. You ain't satisfied or proud of nothing we done. I mean that you had a home; that we kept you out of trouble till you was grown; that you don't have to ride to work on the back of nobody's streetcar — You my children — but how different we done become.

WALTER (*a long beat. He pats her hand and gets up*): You just don't understand, Mama, you just don't understand.

MAMA: Son — do you know your wife is expecting another baby? (*Walter stands, stunned, and absorbs what his mother has said.*) That's what she wanted to talk to you about. (*Walter sinks down into a chair.*) This ain't for me to be telling — but you ought to know. (*She waits.*) I think Ruth is thinking 'bout getting rid of that child.

WALTER (*slowly understanding*): — No — no — Ruth wouldn't do that.

MAMA: When the world gets ugly enough — a woman will do anything for her family. *The part that's already living.*

WALTER: You don't know Ruth, Mama, if you think she would do that.

Ruth opens the bedroom door and stands there a little limp.

RUTH (*beaten*): Yes I would too, Walter. (*Pause.*) I gave her a five-dollar down payment.

There is total silence as the man stares at his wife and the mother stares at her son.

MAMA (*presently*): Well — (*Tightly.*) Well — son, I'm waiting to hear you say something . . . (*She waits.*) I'm waiting to hear how you be your father's son. Be the man he was . . . (*Pause. The silence shouts.*) Your wife say she going to destroy your child. And I'm waiting to hear you talk like him and say we a people who give children life, not who destroys them — (*She rises.*) I'm waiting to see you stand up and look like your daddy and say we done give up one baby to poverty and that we ain't going to give up nary another one . . . I'm waiting.

WALTER: Ruth — (*He can say nothing.*)

MAMA: If you a son of mine, tell her! (*Walter picks up his keys and his coat and walks out. She continues, bitterly.*) You . . . you are a disgrace to your father's memory. Somebody get me my hat!

Curtain.

ACT II

SCENE I

Time: Later the same day.

At rise: Ruth is ironing again. She has the radio going. Presently Beneatha's bedroom door opens and Ruth's mouth falls and she puts down the iron in fascination.

RUTH: What have we got on tonight!

BENEATHA (*emerging grandly from the doorway so that we can see her thoroughly robed in the costume Asagai brought*): You are looking at what a well-dressed Nigerian woman wears — (*She parades for Ruth, her hair completely hidden by the headdress; she is coquettishly fanning herself with an ornate oriental fan, mistakenly more like Butterfly than any Nigerian that ever was.*) Isn't it beautiful? (*She promenades to the radio and, with an arrogant flourish, turns off the good loud blues that is playing.*) Enough of this assimilationist junk! (*Ruth follows her with her eyes as she goes to the phonograph and puts on a record and turns and waits ceremoniously for the music to come up. Then, with a shout —*) OCOMOGOSIAY!

Ruth jumps. The music comes up, a lovely Nigerian melody. Beneatha listens, enraptured, her eyes far way — "back to the past." She begins to dance. Ruth is dumfounded.

RUTH: What kind of dance is that?

BENEATHA: A folk dance.

RUTH (*Pearl Bailey*°): What kind of folks do that, honey?

BENEATHA: It's from Nigeria. It's a dance of welcome.

RUTH: Who you welcoming?

BENEATHA: The men back to the village.

RUTH: Where they been?

BENEATHA: How should I know — out hunting or something. Anyway, they are coming back now . . .

RUTH: Well, that's good.

BENEATHA (*with the record*):

Alundi, alundi
Alundi alunya
Jop pu a jeepua
Ang gu sooooooooo

Pearl Bailey: A popular African American singer (1918–1990).

Ai yai yae . . .
Ayehaye — alundi . . .

Walter comes in during this performance; he has obviously been drinking. He leans against the door heavily and watches his sister, at first with distaste. Then his eyes look off — "back to the past" — as he lifts both his fists to the roof, screaming.

WALTER: YEAH . . . AND ETHIOPIA STRETCH FORTH HER HANDS AGAIN! . . .

RUTH (*drily, looking at him*): Yes — and Africa sure is claiming her own tonight. (*She gives them both up and starts ironing again.*)

WALTER (*all in a drunken, dramatic shout*): Shut up! . . . I'm diggin them drums . . . them drums move me! . . . (*He makes his weaving way to his wife's face and leans in close to her.*) In my *heart of hearts* — (*He thumps his chest.*) — I am much warrior!

RUTH (*without even looking up*): In your heart of hearts you are much drunkard.

WALTER (*coming away from her and starting to wander around the room, shouting*): Me and Jomo . . . (*Intently, in his sister's face. She has stopped dancing to watch him in this unknown mood.*) That's my man, Kenyatta.° (*Shouting and thumping his chest.*) FLAMING SPEAR! HOT DAMN! (*He is suddenly in possession of an imaginary spear and actively spearing enemies all over the room.*) OCOMOGOSIAY . . .

BENEATHA (*to encourage Walter, thoroughly caught up with this side of him*): *OCOMOGOSIAY,* FLAMING SPEAR!

WALTER: THE LION IS WAKING . . . OWIMOWEH!

He pulls his shirt open and leaps up on the table and gestures with his spear.

BENEATHA: OWIMOWEH!

WALTER (*on the table, very far gone, his eyes pure glass sheets. He sees what we cannot, that he is a leader of his people, a great chief, a descendant of Chaka,° and that the hour to march has come*): Listen, my black brothers —

BENEATHA: OCOMOGOSIAY!

WALTER: — Do you hear the waters rushing against the shores of the coastlands —

BENEATHA: OCOMOGOSIAY!

WALTER: — Do you hear the screeching of the cocks in yonder hills beyond where the chiefs meet in council for the coming of the mighty war —

BENEATHA: OCOMOGOSIAY!

And now the lighting shifts subtly to suggest the world of Walter's imagination, and the mood shifts from pure comedy. It is the inner Walter speaking: the Southside chauffeur has assumed an unexpected majesty.

WALTER: — Do you hear the beating of the wings of the birds flying low over the mountains and the low places of our land —

Kenyatta: Jomo Kenyatta (c. 1894–1978), a Kenyan politician involved in the country's nationalist movement. **Chaka:** Also spelled Shaka (c. 1787–1828), he became chief of the Zulu clan in 1816 and founded the great Zulu empire by conquering most of southern Africa.

BENEATHA: OCOMOGOSIAY!

WALTER: — Do you hear the singing of the women, singing the war songs of our fathers to the babies in the great houses? Singing the sweet war songs! (*The doorbell rings.*) OH, DO YOU HEAR, MY *BLACK* BROTHERS!

BENEATHA (*completely gone*): We hear you, Flaming Spear —

Ruth shuts off the phonograph and opens the door. George Murchison enters.

WALTER: Telling us to prepare for the GREATNESS OF THE TIME! (*Lights back to normal. He turns and sees George.*) Black Brother!

He extends his hand for the fraternal clasp.

GEORGE: Black Brother, hell!

RUTH (*having had enough, and embarrassed for the family*): Beneatha, you got company — what's the matter with you? Walter Lee Younger, get down off that table and stop acting like a fool . . .

Walter comes down off the table suddenly and makes a quick exit to the bathroom.

RUTH: He's had a little to drink . . . I don't know what her excuse is.

GEORGE (*to Beneatha*): Look honey, we're going to the theater — we're not going to be *in* it . . . so go change, huh?

Beneatha looks at him and slowly, ceremoniously, lifts her hands and pulls off the headdress. Her hair is close-cropped and unstraightened. George freezes midsentence and Ruth's eyes all but fall out of her head.

GEORGE: What in the name of —

RUTH (*touching Beneatha's hair*): Girl, you done lost your natural mind? Look at your head!

GEORGE: What have you done to your head — I mean your hair!

BENEATHA: Nothing — except cut it off.

RUTH: Now that's the truth — it's what ain't been done to it! You expect this boy to go out with you with your head all nappy like that?

BENEATHA (*looking at George*): That's up to George. If he's ashamed of his heritage —

GEORGE: Oh, don't be so proud of yourself, Bennie — just because you look eccentric.

BENEATHA: How can something that's natural be eccentric?

GEORGE: That's what being eccentric means — being natural. Get dressed.

BENEATHA: I don't like that, George.

RUTH: Why must you and your brother make an argument out of everything people say?

BENEATHA: Because I hate assimilationist Negroes!

RUTH: Will somebody please tell me what assimila-whoever means!

GEORGE: Oh, it's just a college girl's way of calling people Uncle Toms — but that isn't what it means at all.

RUTH: Well, what does it mean?

BENEATHA (*cutting George off and staring at him as she replies to Ruth*): It means someone who is willing to give up his own culture and submerge himself completely in the dominant, and in this case *oppressive* culture!

GEORGE: Oh, dear, dear, dear! Here we go! A lecture on the African past! On our Great West African Heritage! In one second we will hear all about the great Ashanti empires; the great Songhay civilizations; and the great sculpture of Bénin — and then some poetry in the Bantu — and the whole monologue will end with the word *heritage!* (*Nastily.*) Let's face it, baby, your heritage is nothing but a bunch of raggedy-assed spirituals and some grass huts!

BENEATHA: GRASS HUTS! (*Ruth crosses to her and forcibly pushes her toward the bedroom.*) See there . . . you are standing there in your splendid ignorance talking about people who were the first to smelt iron on the face of the earth! (*Ruth is pushing her through the door.*) The Ashanti were performing surgical operations when the English — (*Ruth pulls the door to, with Beneatha on the other side, and smiles graciously at George. Beneatha opens the door and shouts the end of the sentence defiantly at George.*) — were still tatooing themselves with blue dragons! (*She goes back inside.*)

RUTH: Have a seat, George. (*They both sit. Ruth folds her hands rather primly on her lap, determined to demonstrate the civilization of the family.*) Warm, ain't it? I mean for September. (*Pause.*) Just like they always say about Chicago weather: if it's too hot or cold for you, just wait a minute and it'll change. (*She smiles happily at this cliché of clichés.*) Everybody say it's got to do with them bombs and things they keep setting off. (*Pause.*) Would you like a nice cold beer?

GEORGE: No, thank you. I don't care for beer. (*He looks at his watch.*) I hope she hurries up.

RUTH: What time is the show?

GEORGE: It's an eight-thirty curtain. That's just Chicago, though. In New York standard curtain time is eight forty.

He is rather proud of this knowledge.

RUTH (*properly appreciating it*): You get to New York a lot?

GEORGE (*offhand*): Few times a year.

RUTH: Oh — that's nice. I've never been to New York.

Walter enters. We feel he has relieved himself, but the edge of unreality is still with him.

WALTER: New York ain't got nothing Chicago ain't. Just a bunch of hustling people all squeezed up together — being "Eastern."

He turns his face into a screw of displeasure.

GEORGE: Oh — you've been?

WALTER: *Plenty* of times.

RUTH (*shocked at the lie*): Walter Lee Younger!

WALTER (*staring her down*): Plenty! (*Pause.*) What we got to drink in this house? Why don't you offer this man some refreshment. (*To George.*) They don't know how to entertain people in this house, man.

GEORGE: Thank you — I don't really care for anything.

WALTER (*feeling his head; sobriety coming*): Where's Mama?

RUTH: She ain't come back yet.

WALTER (*looking Murchison over from head to toe, scrutinizing his carefully casual tweed sports jacket over cashmere V-neck sweater over soft eyelet shirt and tie, and soft slacks, finished off with white buckskin shoes*): Why all you college boys wear them faggoty-looking white shoes?

RUTH: Walter Lee!

George Murchison ignores the remark.

WALTER (*to Ruth*): Well, they look crazy as hell — white shoes, cold as it is.

RUTH (*crushed*): You have to excuse him —

WALTER: No he don't! Excuse me for what? What you always excusing me for! I'll excuse myself when I needs to be excused! (*A pause.*) They look as funny as them black knee socks Beneatha wears out of here all the time.

RUTH: It's the college *style,* Walter.

WALTER: Style, hell. She looks like she got burnt legs or something!

RUTH: Oh, Walter —

WALTER (*an irritable mimic*): Oh, Walter! Oh, Walter! (*To Murchison.*) How's your old man making out? I understand you all going to buy that big hotel on the Drive? (*He finds a beer in the refrigerator, wanders over to Murchison, sipping and wiping his lips with the back of his hand, and straddling a chair backwards to talk to the other man.*) Shrewd move. Your old man is all right, man. (*Tapping his head and half winking for emphasis.*) I mean he knows how to operate. I mean he thinks *big,* you know what I mean, I mean for a *home,* you know? But I think he's kind of running out of ideas now. I'd like to talk to him. Listen, man, I got some plans that could turn this city upside down. I mean think like he does. *Big.* Invest big, gamble big, hell, lose *big* if you have to, you know what I mean. It's hard to find a man on this whole Southside who understands my kind of thinking — you dig? (*He scrutinizes Murchison again, drinks his beer, squints his eyes and leans in close, confidential, man to man.*) Me and you ought to sit down and talk sometimes, man. Man, I got me some ideas . . .

MURCHISON (*with boredom*): Yeah — sometimes we'll have to do that, Walter.

WALTER (*understanding the indifference, and offended*): Yeah — well, when you get the time, man. I know you a busy little boy.

RUTH: Walter, please —

WALTER (*bitterly, hurt*): I know ain't nothing in this world as busy as you colored college boys with your fraternity pins and white shoes . . .

RUTH (*covering her face with humiliation*): Oh, Walter Lee —

WALTER: I see you all all the time — with the books tucked under your arms — going to your (*British A — a mimic.*) "clahsses." And for what! What the hell you learning over there? Filling up your heads — (*Counting off on his fingers.*) — with the sociology and the psychology — but they teaching you how to be a man? How to take over and run the world? They teaching you how to run a rubber plantation or a steel mill? Naw — just to talk proper and read books and wear them faggoty-looking white shoes . . .

GEORGE (*looking at him with distaste, a little above it all*): You're all wacked up with bitterness, man.

WALTER (*intently, almost quietly, between the teeth, glaring at the boy*): And you — ain't you bitter, man? Ain't you just about had it yet? Don't you see no stars gleaming that you can't reach out and grab? You happy? — You contented son-of-a-bitch — you happy? You got it made? Bitter? Man, I'm a volcano. Bitter? Here I am a giant — surrounded by ants! Ants who can't even understand what it is the giant is talking about.

RUTH (*passionately and suddenly*): Oh, Walter — ain't you with nobody!

WALTER (*violently*): No! 'Cause ain't nobody with me! Not even my own mother!

RUTH: Walter, that's a terrible thing to say!

Beneatha enters, dressed for the evening in a cocktail dress and earrings, hair natural.

GEORGE: Well — hey — (*Crosses to Beneatha; thoughtful, with emphasis, since this is a reversal.*) You look great!

WALTER (*seeing his sister's hair for the first time*): What's the matter with your head?

BENEATHA (*tired of the jokes now*): I cut it off, Brother.

WALTER (*coming close to inspect it and walking around her*): Well, I'll be damned. So that's what they mean by the African bush . . .

BENEATHA: Ha ha. Let's go, George.

GEORGE (*looking at her*): You know something? I like it. It's sharp. I mean it really is. (*Helps her into her wrap.*)

RUTH: Yes — I think so, too. (*She goes to the mirror and starts to clutch at her hair.*)

WALTER: Oh no! You leave yours alone, baby. You might turn out to have a pin-shaped head or something!

BENEATHA: See you all later.

RUTH: Have a nice time.

GEORGE: Thanks. Good night. (*Half out the door, he reopens it. To Walter.*) Good night, Prometheus!°

Beneatha and George exit.

WALTER (*to Ruth*): Who is Prometheus?

RUTH: I don't know. Don't worry about it.

WALTER (*in fury, pointing after George*): See there — they get to a point where they can't insult you man to man — they got to go talk about something ain't nobody never heard of!

RUTH: How do you know it was an insult? (*To humor him.*) Maybe Prometheus is a nice fellow.

WALTER: Prometheus! I bet there ain't even no such thing! I bet that simple-minded clown —

RUTH: Walter —

She stops what she is doing and looks at him.

WALTER (*yelling*): Don't start!

RUTH: Start what?

WALTER: Your nagging! Where was I? Who was I with? How much money did I spend?

RUTH (*plaintively*): Walter Lee — why don't we just try to talk about it . . .

Prometheus: In Greek myth, a Titan who was punished by Zeus for stealing fire from the gods and giving it to humankind.

WALTER (*not listening*): I been out talking with people who understand me. People who care about the things I got on my mind.

RUTH (*wearily*): I guess that means people like Willy Harris.

WALTER: Yes, people like Willy Harris.

RUTH (*with a sudden flash of impatience*): Why don't you all just hurry up and go into the banking business and stop talking about it!

WALTER: Why? You want to know why? 'Cause we all tied up in a race of people that don't know how to do nothing but moan, pray, and have babies!

The line is too bitter even for him and he looks at her and sits down.

RUTH: Oh, Walter . . . (*Softly.*) Honey, why can't you stop fighting me?

WALTER (*without thinking*): Who's fighting you? Who even cares about you?

This line begins the retardation of his mood.

RUTH: Well — (*She waits a long time, and then with resignation starts to put away her things.*) I guess I might as well go on to bed . . . (*More or less to herself.*) I don't know where we lost it . . . but we have . . . (*Then, to him.*) I — I'm sorry about this new baby, Walter. I guess maybe I better go on and do what I started . . . I guess I just didn't realize how bad things was with us . . . I guess I just didn't really realize — (*She starts out to the bedroom and stops.*) You want some hot milk?

WALTER: Hot milk?

RUTH: Yes — hot milk.

WALTER: Why hot milk?

RUTH: 'Cause after all that liquor you come home with you ought to have something hot in your stomach.

WALTER: I don't want no milk.

RUTH: You want some coffee then?

WALTER: No, I don't want no coffee. I don't want nothing hot to drink. (*Almost plaintively.*) Why you always trying to give me something to eat?

RUTH (*standing and looking at him helplessly*): What *else* can I give you, Walter Lee Younger?

She stands and looks at him and presently turns to go out again. He lifts his head and watches her going away from him in a new mood which began to emerge when he asked her "Who cares about you?"

WALTER: It's been rough, ain't it, baby? (*She hears and stops but does not turn around and he continues to her back.*) I guess between two people there ain't never as much understood as folks generally thinks there is. I mean like between me and you — (*She turns to face him.*) How we gets to the place where we scared to talk softness to each other. (*He waits, thinking hard himself.*) Why you think it got to be like that? (*He is thoughtful, almost as a child would be.*) Ruth, what is it gets into people ought to be close?

RUTH: I don't know, honey. I think about it a lot.

WALTER: On account of you and me, you mean? The way things are with us. The way something done come down between us.

RUTH: There ain't so much between us, Walter . . . Not when you come to me and try to talk to me. Try to be with me . . . a little even.

WALTER (*total honesty*): Sometimes . . . sometimes . . . I don't even know how to try.

RUTH: Walter —

WALTER: Yes?

RUTH (*coming to him, gently and with misgiving, but coming to him*): Honey . . . life don't have to be like this. I mean sometimes people can do things so that things are better . . . You remember how we used to talk when Travis was born . . . about the way we were going to live . . . the kind of house . . . (*She is stroking his head.*) Well, it's all starting to slip away from us . . .

He turns her to him and they look at each other and kiss, tenderly and hungrily. The door opens and Mama enters — Walter breaks away and jumps up. A beat.

WALTER: Mama, where have you been?

MAMA: My — them steps is longer than they used to be. Whew! (*She sits down and ignores him.*) How you feeling this evening, Ruth?

Ruth shrugs, disturbed at having been interrupted and watching her husband knowingly.

WALTER: Mama, where have you been all day?

MAMA (*still ignoring him and leaning on the table and changing to more comfortable shoes*): Where's Travis?

RUTH: I let him go out earlier and he ain't come back yet. Boy, is he going to get it!

WALTER: Mama!

MAMA (*as if she has heard him for the first time*): Yes, son?

WALTER: Where did you go this afternoon?

MAMA: I went downtown to tend to some business that I had to tend to.

WALTER: What kind of business?

MAMA: You know better than to question me like a child, Brother.

WALTER (*rising and bending over the table*): Where were you, Mama? (*Bringing his fists down and shouting.*) Mama, you didn't go do something with that insurance money, something crazy?

The front door opens slowly, interrupting him, and Travis peeks his head in, less than hopefully.

TRAVIS (*to his mother*): Mama, I —

RUTH: "Mama I" nothing! You're going to get it, boy! Get on in that bedroom and get yourself ready!

TRAVIS: But I —

MAMA: Why don't you all never let the child explain hisself.

RUTH: Keep out of it now, Lena.

Mama clamps her lips together, and Ruth advances toward her son menacingly.

RUTH: A thousand times I have told you not to go off like that —

MAMA (*holding out her arms to her grandson*): Well — at least let me tell him something. I want him to be the first one to hear . . . Come here, Travis (*The boy obeys, gladly.*) Travis — (*She takes him by the shoulder and looks into his face.*) — you know that money we got in the mail this morning?

TRAVIS: Yes'm —

MAMA: Well — what you think your grandmama gone and done with that money?

TRAVIS: I don't know, Grandmama.

MAMA (*putting her finger on his nose for emphasis*): She went out and she bought you a house! (*The explosion comes from Walter at the end of the revelation and he jumps up and turns away from all of them in a fury. Mama continues, to Travis.*) You glad about the house? It's going to be yours when you get to be a man.

TRAVIS: Yeah — I always wanted to live in a house.

MAMA: All right, gimme some sugar then — (*Travis puts his arms around her neck as she watches her son over the boy's shoulder. Then, to Travis, after the embrace.*) Now when you say your prayers tonight, you thank God and your grandfather — 'cause it was him who give you the house — in his way.

RUTH (*taking the boy from Mama and pushing him toward the bedroom*): Now you get out of here and get ready for your beating.

TRAVIS: Aw, Mama —

RUTH: Get on in there — (*Closing the door behind him and turning radiantly to her mother-in-law.*) So you went and did it!

MAMA (*quietly, looking at her son with pain*): Yes, I did.

RUTH (*raising both arms classically*): PRAISE GOD! (*Looks at Walter a moment, who says nothing. She crosses rapidly to her husband.*) Please, honey — let me be glad . . . you be glad too. (*She has laid her hands on his shoulders, but he shakes himself free of her roughly, without turning to face her.*) Oh, Walter . . . a home . . . *a home.* (*She comes back to Mama.*) Well — where is it? How big is it? How much it going to cost?

MAMA: Well —

RUTH: When we moving?

MAMA (*smiling at her*): First of the month.

RUTH (*throwing back her head with jubilance*): *Praise God!*

MAMA (*tentatively, still looking at her son's back turned against her and Ruth*): It's — it's a nice house too . . . (*She cannot help speaking directly to him. An imploring quality in her voice, her manner, makes her almost like a girl now.*) Three bedrooms — nice big one for you and Ruth . . . Me and Beneatha still have to share our room, but Travis have one of his own — and (*With difficulty.*) I figure if the — new baby — is a boy, we could get one of them double-decker outfits . . . And there's a yard with a little patch of dirt where I could maybe get to grow me a few flowers . . . And a nice big basement . . .

RUTH: Walter honey, be glad —

MAMA (*still to his back, fingering things on the table*): 'Course I don't want to make it sound fancier than it is . . . It's just a plain little old house — but it's made good and solid — and it will be *ours.* Walter Lee — it makes a difference in a man when he can walk on floors that belong to *him* . . .

RUTH: Where is it?

MAMA (*frightened at this telling*): Well — well — it's out there in Clybourne Park —

Ruth's radiance fades abruptly, and Walter finally turns slowly to face his mother with incredulity and hostility.

RUTH: Where?

MAMA (*matter-of-factly*): Four o six Clybourne Street, Clybourne Park.

RUTH: Clybourne Park? Mama, there ain't no colored people living in Clybourne Park.

MAMA (*almost idiotically*): Well, I guess there's going to be some now.

WALTER (*bitterly*): So that's the peace and comfort you went out and bought for us today!

MAMA (*raising her eyes to meet his finally*): Son — I just tried to find the nicest place for the least amount of money for my family.

RUTH (*trying to recover from the shock*): Well — well — 'course I ain't one never been 'fraid of no crackers, mind you — but — well, wasn't there no other houses nowhere?

MAMA: Them houses they put up for colored in them areas way out all seem to cost twice as much as other houses. I did the best I could.

RUTH (*struck senseless with the news, in its various degrees of goodness and trouble, she sits a moment, her fists propping her chin in thought, and then she starts to rise, bringing her fists down with vigor, the radiance spreading from cheek to cheek again*): Well — well — All I can say is — if this is my time in life — *MY* TIME — to say good-bye — (*And she builds with momentum as she starts to circle the room with an exuberant, almost tearfully happy release.*) — to these Goddamned cracking walls! — (*She pounds the walls.*) — and these marching roaches! — (*She wipes at an imaginary army of marching roaches.*) — and this cramped little closet which ain't now or never was no kitchen! . . . then I say it loud and good, HALLELUJAH! AND GOOD-BYE MISERY . . . I DON'T NEVER WANT TO SEE YOUR UGLY FACE AGAIN! (*She laughs joyously, having practically destroyed the apartment, and flings her arms up and lets them come down happily, slowly, reflectively, over her abdomen, aware for the first time perhaps that the life therein pulses with happiness and not despair.*) Lena?

MAMA (*moved, watching her happiness*): Yes, honey?

RUTH (*looking off*): Is there — is there a whole lot of sunlight?

MAMA (*understanding*): Yes, child, there's a whole lot of sunlight.

Long pause.

RUTH (*collecting herself and going to the door of the room Travis is in*): Well — I guess I better see 'bout Travis. (*To Mama.*) Lord, I sure don't feel like whipping nobody today!

She exits.

MAMA (*the mother and son are left alone now and the mother waits a long time, considering deeply, before she speaks*): Son — you — you understand what I done, don't you? (*Walter is silent and sullen.*) I — I just seen my family falling apart today . . . just falling to pieces in front of my eyes . . . We couldn't of gone on like we was today. We was going backwards 'stead of forwards — talking 'bout killing babies and wishing each other was dead . . . When it gets like that in life — you just got to do something different, push on out and do something bigger . . . (*She waits.*) I wish you say something, son . . . I wish you'd say how deep inside you you think I done the right thing —

WALTER (*crossing slowly to his bedroom door and finally turning there and speaking measuredly*): What you need me to say you done right for? *You* the head of this family. You run our lives like you want to. It was your money and you did what you wanted with it. So what you need for me to say it was all right for? (*Bitterly, to hurt her as deeply as he knows is possible.*) So you butchered up a dream of mine — you — who always talking 'bout your children's dreams . . .

MAMA: Walter Lee —

He just closes the door behind him. Mama sits alone, thinking heavily.

Curtain.

SCENE II

Time: Friday night, a few weeks later.

At rise: Packing crates mark the intention of the family to move. Beneatha and George come in, presumably from an evening out again.

GEORGE: O.K. . . . O.K., whatever you say . . . (*They both sit on the couch. He tries to kiss her. She moves away.*) Look, we've had a nice evening; let's not spoil it, huh? . . .

He again turns her head and tries to nuzzle in and she turns away from him, not with distaste but with momentary lack of interest; in a mood to pursue what they were talking about.

BENEATHA: I'm *trying* to talk to you.

GEORGE: We always talk.

BENEATHA: Yes — and I love to talk.

GEORGE (*exasperated; rising*): I know it and I don't mind it sometimes . . . I want you to cut it out, see — The moody stuff, I mean. I don't like it. You're a nice-looking girl . . . all over. That's all you need, honey, forget the atmosphere. Guys aren't going to go for the atmosphere — they're going to go for what they see. Be glad for that. Drop the Garbo routine. It doesn't go with you. As for myself, I want a nice — (*Groping.*) — simple (*Thoughtfully.*) — sophisticated girl . . . not a poet — O.K.?

He starts to kiss her, she rebuffs him again and he jumps up.

BENEATHA: Why are you angry, George?

GEORGE: Because this is stupid! I don't go out with you to discuss the nature of "quiet desperation" or to hear all about your thoughts — because the world will go on thinking what it thinks regardless —

BENEATHA: Then why read books? Why go to school?

GEORGE (*with artificial patience, counting on his fingers*): It's simple. You read books — to learn facts — to get grades — to pass the course — to get a degree. That's all — it has nothing to do with thoughts.

A long pause.

BENEATHA: I see. (*He starts to sit.*) Good night, George.

George looks at her a little oddly, and starts to exit. He meets Mama coming in.

GEORGE: Oh — hello, Mrs. Younger.
MAMA: Hello, George, how you feeling?
GEORGE: Fine — fine, how are you?
MAMA: Oh, a little tired. You know them steps can get you after a day's work. You all have a nice time tonight?
GEORGE: Yes — a fine time. A fine time.
MAMA: Well, good night.
GEORGE: Good night. (*He exits. Mama closes the door behind her.*)
MAMA: Hello, honey. What you sitting like that for?
BENEATHA: I'm just sitting.
MAMA: Didn't you have a nice time?
BENEATHA: No.
MAMA: No? What's the matter?
BENEATHA: Mama, George is a fool — honest. (*She rises.*)
MAMA (*hustling around unloading the packages she has entered with. She stops*): Is he, baby?
BENEATHA: Yes.

Beneatha makes up Travis's bed as she talks.

MAMA: You sure?
BENEATHA: Yes.
MAMA: Well — I guess you better not waste your time with no fools.

Beneatha looks up at her mother, watching her put groceries in the refrigerator. Finally she gathers up her things and starts into the bedroom. At the door she stops and looks back at her mother.

BENEATHA: Mama —
MAMA: Yes, baby —
BENEATHA: Thank you.
MAMA: For what?
BENEATHA: For understanding me this time.

She exits quickly and the mother stands, smiling a little, looking at the place where Beneatha just stood. Ruth enters.

RUTH: Now don't you fool with any of this stuff, Lena —
MAMA: Oh, I just thought I'd sort a few things out. Is Brother here?
RUTH: Yes.
MAMA (*with concern*): Is he —
RUTH (*reading her eyes*): Yes.

Mama is silent and someone knocks on the door. Mama and Ruth exchange weary and knowing glances and Ruth opens it to admit the neighbor, Mrs. Johnson,° who is a rather squeaky wide-eyed lady of no particular age, with a newspaper under her arm.

Mrs. Johnson: This character and the scene of her visit were cut from the original production and early editions of the play.

MAMA (*changing her expression to acute delight and a ringing cheerful greeting*): Oh — hello there, Johnson.

JOHNSON (*this is a woman who decided long ago to be enthusiastic about EVERYTHING in life and she is inclined to wave her wrist vigorously at the height of her exclamatory comments*): Hello there, yourself! H'you this evening, Ruth?

RUTH (*not much of a deceptive type*): Fine, Mis' Johnson, h'you?

JOHNSON: Fine. (*Reaching out quickly, playfully, and patting Ruth's stomach.*) Ain't you starting to poke out none yet! (*She mugs with delight at the over familiar remark and her eyes dart around looking at the crates and packing preparation; Mama's face is a cold sheet of endurance.*) Oh, ain't we getting ready round here, though! Yessir! Lookathere! I'm telling you the Youngers is really getting ready to "move on up a little higher!" — Bless God!

MAMA (*a little drily, doubting the total sincerity of the Blesser*): Bless God.

JOHNSON: He's good, ain't He?

MAMA: Oh yes, He's good.

JOHNSON: I mean sometimes He works in mysterious ways . . . but He works, don't He!

MAMA (*the same*): Yes, he does.

JOHNSON: I'm just soooooo happy for y'all. And this here child — (*about Ruth*) looks like she could just pop open with happiness, don't she. Where's all the rest of the family?

MAMA: Bennie's gone to bed —

JOHNSON: Ain't no . . . (*the implication is pregnancy*) sickness done hit you — I hope . . . ?

MAMA: No — she just tired. She was out this evening.

JOHNSON (*all is a coo, an emphatic coo*): Aw — ain't that lovely. She still going out with the little Murchison boy?

MAMA (*drily*): Ummmm huh.

JOHNSON: That's lovely. You sure got lovely children, Younger. Me and Isaiah talks all the time 'bout what fine children you was blessed with. We sure do.

MAMA: Ruth, give Mis' Johnson a piece of sweet potato pie and some milk.

JOHNSON: Oh honey, I can't stay hardly a minute — I just dropped in to see if there was anything I could do. (*Accepting the food easily.*) I guess y'all seen the news what's all over the colored paper this week . . .

MAMA: No — didn't get mine yet this week.

JOHNSON (*lifting her head and blinking with the spirit of catastrophe*): You mean you ain't read 'bout them colored people that was bombed out their place out there?

Ruth straightens with concern and takes the paper and reads it. Johnson notices her and feeds commentary.

JOHNSON: Ain't it something how bad these here white folks is getting here in Chicago! Lord, getting so you think you right down in Mississippi! (*With a tremendous and rather insincere sense of melodrama.*) 'Course I thinks it's wonderful how our folk keeps on pushing out. You hear some of these

Negroes round here talking 'bout how they don't go where they ain't wanted and all that — but not me, honey! (*This is a lie.*) Wilhemenia Othella Johnson goes anywhere, any time she feels like it! (*With head movement for emphasis.*) Yes I do! Why if we left it up to these here crackers, the poor niggers wouldn't have nothing — (*She clasps her hand over her mouth.*) Oh, I always forgets you don't 'low that word in your house.

MAMA (*quietly, looking at her*): No — I don't 'low it.

JOHNSON (*vigorously again*): Me neither! I was just telling Isaiah yesterday when he come using it in front of me — I said, "Isaiah, it's just like Mis' Younger says all the time —"

MAMA: Don't you want some more pie?

JOHNSON: No — no thank you; this was lovely. I got to get on over home and have my midnight coffee. I hear some people say it don't let them sleep but I finds I can't close my eyes right lessen I done had that laaaast cup of coffee . . . (*She waits. A beat. Undaunted.*) My Goodnight coffee, I calls it!

MAMA (*with much eye-rolling and communication between herself and Ruth*): Ruth, why don't you give Mis' Johnson some coffee.

Ruth gives Mama an unpleasant look for her kindness.

JOHNSON (*accepting the coffee*): Where's Brother tonight?

MAMA: He's lying down.

JOHNSON: MMmmmmmm, he sure gets his beauty rest, don't he? Good-looking man. Sure is a good-looking man! (*Reaching out to pat Ruth's stomach again.*) I guess that's how come we keep on having babies around here. (*She winks at Mama.*) One thing 'bout Brother, he always know how to have a *good* time. And soooooo ambitious! I bet it was his idea y'all moving out to Clybourne Park. Lord — I bet this time next month y'all's names will have been in the papers plenty — (*Holding up her hands to mark off each word of the headline she can see in front of her.*) "NEGROES INVADE CLYBOURNE PARK — BOMBED!"

MAMA (*she and Ruth look at the woman in amazement*): We ain't exactly moving out there to get bombed.

JOHNSON: Oh honey — you know I'm praying to God every day that don't nothing like that happen! But you have to think of life like it is — and these here Chicago peckerwoods is some baaaad peckerwoods.

MAMA (*wearily*): We done thought about all that Mis' Johnson.

Beneatha comes out of the bedroom in her robe and passes through to the bathroom. Mrs. Johnson turns.

JOHNSON: Hello there, Bennie!

BENEATHA (*crisply*): Hello, Mrs. Johnson.

JOHNSON: How is school?

BENEATHA (*crisply*): Fine, thank you. (*She goes out.*)

JOHNSON (*insulted*): Getting so she don't have much to say to nobody.

MAMA: The child was on her way to the bathroom.

JOHNSON: I know — but sometimes she act like ain't got time to pass the time of day with nobody ain't been to college. Oh — I ain't criticizing her none. It's just — you know how some of our young people gets when they get a little education. (*Mama and Ruth say nothing, just look at her.*) Yes — well. Well, I guess I better get on home. (*Unmoving.*) 'Course I can understand how she must be proud and everything — being the only one in the family to make something of herself. I know just being a chauffeur ain't never satisfied Brother none. He shouldn't feel like that, though. Ain't nothing wrong with being a chauffeur.

MAMA: There's plenty wrong with it.

JOHNSON: What?

MAMA: Plenty. My husband always said being any kind of a servant wasn't a fit thing for a man to have to be. He always said a man's hands was made to make things, or to turn the earth with — not to drive nobody's car for 'em — or — (*she looks at her own hands*) carry they slop jars. And my boy is just like him — he wasn't meant to wait on nobody.

JOHNSON (*rising, somewhat offended*): Mmmmmmmmm. The Youngers is too much for me! (*She looks around.*) You sure one proud-acting bunch of colored folks. Well — I always thinks like Booker T. Washington said that time — "Education has spoiled many a good plow hand" —

MAMA: Is that what old Booker T. said?

JOHNSON: He sure did.

MAMA: Well, it sounds just like him. The fool.

JOHNSON (*indignantly*): Well — he was one of our great men.

MAMA: Who said so?

JOHNSON (*nonplussed*): You know, me and you ain't never agreed about some things, Lena Younger. I guess I better be going —

RUTH (*quickly*): Good night.

JOHNSON: Good night. Oh — (*Thrusting it at her.*) You can keep the paper! (*With a trill.*) 'Night.

MAMA: Good night, Mis' Johnson.

Mrs. Johnson exits.

RUTH: If ignorance was gold . . .

MAMA: Shush. Don't talk about folks behind their backs.

RUTH: You do.

MAMA: I'm old and corrupted. (*Beneatha enters.*) You was rude to Mis' Johnson, Beneatha, and I don't like it at all.

BENEATHA (*at her door*): Mama, if there are two things we, as a people, have got to overcome, one is the Klu Klux Klan — and the other is Mrs. Johnson. (*She exits.*)

MAMA: Smart aleck.

The phone rings.

RUTH: I'll get it.

MAMA: Lord, ain't this a popular place tonight.

RUTH (*at the phone*): Hello — Just a minute. (*Goes to door.*) Walter, it's Mrs. Arnold. (*Waits. Goes back to the phone. Tense.*) Hello. Yes, this is his wife speaking . . . He's lying down now. Yes . . . well, he'll be in tomorrow. He's been very sick. Yes — I know we should have called, but we were so sure he'd be able to come in today. Yes — yes, I'm very sorry. Yes . . . Thank you very much. (*She hangs up. Walter is standing in the doorway of the bedroom behind her.*) That was Mrs. Arnold.

WALTER (*indifferently*): Was it?

RUTH: She said if you don't come in tomorrow that they are getting a new man . . .

WALTER: Ain't that sad — ain't that crying sad.

RUTH: She said Mr. Arnold has had to take a cab for three days . . . Walter, you ain't been to work for three days! (*This is a revelation to her.*) Where you been, Walter Lee Younger? (*Walter looks at her and starts to laugh.*) You're going to lose your job.

WALTER: That's right . . . (*He turns on the radio.*)

RUTH: Oh, Walter, and with your mother working like a dog every day —

A steamy, deep blues pours into the room.

WALTER: That's sad too — Everything is sad.

MAMA: What you been doing for these three days, son?

WALTER: Mama — you don't know all the things a man what got leisure can find to do in this city . . . What's this — Friday night? Well — Wednesday I borrowed Willy Harris' car and I went for a drive . . . just me and myself and I drove and drove . . . Way out . . . way past South Chicago, and I parked the car and I sat and looked at the steel mills all day long. I just sat in the car and looked at them big black chimneys for hours. Then I drove back and I went to the Green Hat. (*Pause.*) And Thursday — Thursday I borrowed the car again and I got in it and I pointed it the other way and I drove the other way — for hours — way, way up to Wisconsin, and I looked at the farms. I just drove and looked at the farms. Then I drove back and I went to the Green Hat. (*Pause.*) And today — today I didn't get the car. Today I just walked. All over the Southside. And I looked at the Negroes and they looked at me and finally I just sat down on the curb at Thirty-ninth and South Parkway and I just sat there and watched the Negroes go by. And then I went to the Green Hat. You all sad? You all depressed? And you know where I am going right now —

Ruth goes out quietly.

MAMA: Oh, Big Walter, is this the harvest of our days?

WALTER: You know what I like about the Green Hat? I like this little cat they got there who blows a sax . . . He blows. He talks to me. He ain't but 'bout five feet tall and he's got a conked head and his eyes is always closed and he's all music —

MAMA (*rising and getting some papers out of her handbag*): Walter —

WALTER: And there's this other guy who plays the piano . . . and they got a sound. I mean they can work on some music . . . They got the best little combo in the world in the Green Hat . . . You can just sit there and drink and listen to them three men play and you realize that don't nothing matter worth a damn, but just being there —

MAMA: I've helped do it to you, haven't I, son? Walter, I been wrong.

WALTER: Naw — you ain't never been wrong about nothing, Mama.

MAMA: Listen to me, now. I say I been wrong, son. That I been doing to you what the rest of the world been doing to you. (*She turns off the radio.*) Walter — (*She stops and he looks up slowly at her and she meets his eyes pleadingly.*) What you ain't never understood is that I ain't got nothing, don't own nothing, ain't never really wanted nothing that wasn't for you. There ain't nothing as precious to me . . . There ain't nothing worth holding on to, money, dreams, nothing else — if it means — if it means it's going to destroy my boy. (*She takes an envelope out of her handbag and puts it in front of him and he watches her without speaking or moving.*) I paid the man thirty-five hundred dollars down on the house. That leaves sixty-five hundred dollars. Monday morning I want you to take this money and take three thousand dollars and put it in a savings account for Beneatha's medical schooling. The rest you put in a checking account — with your name on it. And from now on any penny that come out of it or that go in it is for you to look after. For you to decide. (*She drops her hands a little helplessly.*) It ain't much, but it's all I got in the world and I'm putting it in your hands. I'm telling you to be the head of this family from now on like you supposed to be.

WALTER (*stares at the money*): You trust me like that, Mama?

MAMA: I ain't never stop trusting you. Like I ain't never stop loving you.

She goes out, and Walter sits looking at the money on the table. Finally, in a decisive gesture, he gets up, and, in mingled joy and desperation, picks up the money. At the same moment, Travis enters for bed.

TRAVIS: What's the matter, Daddy? You drunk?

WALTER (*sweetly, more sweetly than we have ever known him*): No, Daddy ain't drunk. Daddy ain't going to never be drunk again . . .

TRAVIS: Well, good night, Daddy.

The father has come from behind the couch and leans over, embracing his son.

WALTER: Son, I feel like talking to you tonight.

TRAVIS: About what?

WALTER: Oh, about a lot of things. About you and what kind of man you going to be when you grow up . . . Son — son, what do you want to be when you grow up?

TRAVIS: A bus driver.

WALTER (*laughing a little*): A what? Man, that ain't nothing to want to be!

TRAVIS: Why not?

WALTER: 'Cause, man — it ain't big enough — you know what I mean.

TRAVIS: I don't know then. I can't make up my mind. Sometimes Mama asks me that too. And sometimes when I tell her I just want to be like you — she says she don't want me to be like that and sometimes she says she does. . . .

WALTER (*gathering him up in his arms*): You know what, Travis? In seven years you going to be seventeen years old. And things is going to be very different with us in seven years, Travis. . . . One day when you are seventeen I'll come home — home from my office downtown somewhere —

TRAVIS: You don't work in no office, Daddy.

WALTER: No — but after tonight. After what your daddy gonna do tonight, there's going to be offices — a whole lot of offices. . . .

TRAVIS: What you gonna do tonight, Daddy?

WALTER: You wouldn't understand yet, son, but your daddy's gonna make a transaction . . . a business transaction that's going to change our lives. . . . That's how come one day when you 'bout seventeen years old I'll come home and I'll be pretty tired, you know what I mean, after a day of conferences and secretaries getting things wrong the way they do . . . 'cause an executive's life is hell, man — (*The more he talks the farther away he gets.*) And I'll pull the car up on the driveway . . . just a plain black Chrysler, I think, with white walls — no — black tires. More elegant. Rich people don't have to be flashy . . . though I'll have to get something a little sportier for Ruth — maybe a Cadillac convertible to do her shopping in. . . . And I'll come up the steps to the house and the gardener will be clipping away at the hedges and he'll say, "Good evening, Mr. Younger." And I'll say, "Hello, Jefferson, how are you this evening?" And I'll go inside and Ruth will come downstairs and meet me at the door and we'll kiss each other and she'll take my arm and we'll go up to your room to see you sitting on the floor with the catalogues of all the great schools in America around you. . . . All the great schools in the world! And — and I'll say, all right son — it's your seventeenth birthday, what is it you've decided? . . . Just tell me where you want to go to school and you'll *go.* Just tell me, what it is you want to be — and you'll *be* it. . . . Whatever you want to be — Yessir! (*He holds his arms open for Travis.*) You just name it, son . . . (*Travis leaps into them.*) and I hand you the world!

Walter's voice has risen in pitch and hysterical promise and on the last line he lifts Travis high.

Blackout.

SCENE III

Time: Saturday, moving day, one week later.

Before the curtain rises, Ruth's voice, a strident, dramatic church alto, cuts through the silence.

It is, in the darkness, a triumphant surge, a penetrating statement of expectation: "Oh, Lord, I don't feel no ways tired! Children, oh, glory hallelujah!"

As the curtain rises we see that Ruth is alone in the living room, finishing up the family's packing. It is moving day. She is nailing crates and tying cartons. Beneatha enters, carrying a guitar case, and watches her exuberant sister-in-law.

RUTH: Hey!

BENEATHA (*putting away the case*): Hi.

RUTH (*pointing at a package*): Honey — look in that package there and see what I found on sale this morning at the South Center. (*Ruth gets up and moves to the package and draws out some curtains.*) Lookahere — hand-turned hems!

BENEATHA: How do you know the window size out there?

RUTH (*who hadn't thought of that*): Oh — Well, they bound to fit something in the whole house. Anyhow, they was too good a bargain to pass up. (*Ruth slaps her head, suddenly remembering something.*) Oh, Bennie — I meant to put a special note on that carton over there. That's your mama's good china and she wants 'em to be very careful with it.

BENEATHA: I'll do it.

Beneatha finds a piece of paper and starts to draw large letters on it.

RUTH: You know what I'm going to do soon as I get in that new house?

BENEATHA: What?

RUTH: Honey — I'm going to run me a tub of water up to here . . . (*With her fingers practically up to her nostrils.*) And I'm going to get in it — and I am going to sit . . . and sit . . . and sit in that hot water and the first person who knocks to tell *me* to hurry up and come out —

BENEATHA: Gets shot at sunrise.

RUTH (*laughing happily*): You said it, sister! (*Noticing how large Beneatha is absent-mindedly making the note*): Honey, they ain't going to read that from no airplane.

BENEATHA (*laughing herself*): I guess I always think things have more emphasis if they are big, somehow.

RUTH (*looking up at her and smiling*): You and your brother seem to have that as a philosophy of life. Lord, that man — done changed so 'round here. You know — you know what we did last night? Me and Walter Lee?

BENEATHA: What?

RUTH (*smiling to herself*): We went to the movies. (*Looking at Beneatha to see if she understands.*) We went to the movies. You know the last time me and Walter went to the movies together?

BENEATHA: No.

RUTH: Me neither. That's how long it been. (*Smiling again.*) But we went last night. The picture wasn't much good, but that didn't seem to matter. We went — and we held hands.

BENEATHA: Oh, Lord!

RUTH: We held hands — and you know what?

BENEATHA: What?

RUTH: When we come out of the show it was late and dark and all the stores and things was closed up . . . and it was kind of chilly and there wasn't many people on the streets . . . and we was still holding hands, me and Walter.

BENEATHA: You're killing me.

Walter enters with a large package. His happiness is deep in him; he cannot keep still with his newfound exuberance. He is singing and wiggling and snapping his fingers. He puts his package in a corner and puts a phonograph record, which he has brought in with him, on the record player. As the music, soulful and sensuous, comes up he dances over to Ruth and tries to get her to dance with him. She gives in at last to his raunchiness and in a fit of giggling allows herself to be drawn into his mood. They dip and she melts into his arms in a classic, body-melting "slow drag."

BENEATHA (*regarding them a long time as they dance, then drawing in her breath for a deeply exaggerated comment which she does not particularly mean*): Talk about — olddddddddd-fashionedddddd — Negroes!

WALTER (*stopping momentarily*): What kind of Negroes?

He says this in fun. He is not angry with her today, nor with anyone. He starts to dance with his wife again.

BENEATHA: Old-fashioned.

WALTER (*as he dances with Ruth*): You know, when these *New Negroes* have their convention — (*Pointing at his sister.*) — that is going to be the chairman of the Committee on Unending Agitation. (*He goes on dancing, then stops.*) Race, race, race! . . . Girl, I do believe you are the first person in the history of the entire human race to successfully brainwash yourself. (*Beneatha breaks up and he goes on dancing. He stops again, enjoying his tease.*) Damn, even the N double A C P takes a holiday sometimes! (*Beneatha and Ruth laugh. He dances with Ruth some more and starts to laugh and stops and pantomimes someone over an operating table.*) I can just see that chick someday looking down at some poor cat on an operating table and before she starts to slice him, she says . . . (*Pulling his sleeves back maliciously.*) "By the way, what are your views on civil rights down there? . . ."

He laughs at her again and starts to dance happily. The bell sounds.

BENEATHA: Sticks and stones may break my bones but . . . words will never hurt me!

Beneatha goes to the door and opens it as Walter and Ruth go on with the clowning. Beneatha is somewhat surprised to see a quiet-looking middle-aged white man in a business suit holding his hat and a briefcase in his hand and consulting a small piece of paper.

MAN: Uh — how do you do, miss. I am looking for a Mrs. — (*He looks at the slip of paper.*) Mrs. Lena Younger? (*He stops short, struck dumb at the sight of the oblivious Walter and Ruth.*)

BENEATHA (*smoothing her hair with slight embarrassment*): Oh — yes, that's my mother. Excuse me. (*She closes the door and turns to quiet the other two.*) Ruth! Brother! (*Enunciating precisely but soundlessly: "There's a white man at the door!" They stop dancing, Ruth cuts off the phonograph, Beneatha opens the door. The man casts a curious quick glance at all of them.*) Uh — come in please.

MAN (*coming in*): Thank you.

BENEATHA: My mother isn't here just now. Is it business?

MAN: Yes . . . well, of a sort.

WALTER (*freely, the Man of the House*): Have a seat. I'm Mrs. Younger's son. I look after most of her business matters.

Ruth and Beneatha exchange amused glances.

MAN (*regarding Walter, and sitting*): Well — My name is Karl Lindner . . .

WALTER (*stretching out his hand*): Walter Younger. This is my wife — (*Ruth nods politely.*) — and my sister.

LINDNER: How do you do.

WALTER (*amiably, as he sits himself easily on a chair, leaning forward on his knees with interest and looking expectantly into the newcomer's face*): What can we do for you, Mr. Lindner!

LINDNER (*some minor shuffling of the hat and briefcase on his knees*): Well — I am a representative of the Clybourne Park Improvement Association —

WALTER (*pointing*): Why don't you sit your things on the floor?

LINDNER: Oh — yes. Thank you. (*He slides the briefcase and hat under the chair.*) And as I was saying — I am from the Clybourne Park Improvement Association and we have had it brought to our attention at the last meeting that you people — or at least your mother — has bought a piece of residential property at — (*He digs for the slip of paper again.*) — four o six Clybourne Street . . .

WALTER: That's right. Care for something to drink? Ruth, get Mr. Lindner a beer.

LINDNER (*upset for some reason*): Oh — no, really. I mean thank you very much, but no thank you.

RUTH (*innocently*): Some coffee?

LINDNER: Thank you, nothing at all.

Beneatha is watching the man carefully.

LINDNER: Well, I don't know how much you folks know about our organization. (*He is a gentle man; thoughtful and somewhat labored in his manner.*) It is one of these community organizations set up to look after — oh, you know, things like block upkeep and special projects and we also have what we call our New Neighbors Orientation Committee . . .

BENEATHA (*drily*): Yes — and what do they do?

LINDNER (*turning a little to her and then returning the main force to Walter*): Well — it's what you might call a sort of welcoming committee, I guess. I mean they, we — I'm the chairman of the committee — go around and see the new people who move into the neighborhood and sort of give them the lowdown on the way we do things out in Clybourne Park.

BENEATHA (*with appreciation of the two meanings, which escape Ruth and Walter*): Un-huh.

LINDNER: And we also have the category of what the association calls — (*he looks elsewhere*) — uh — special community problems . . .

BENEATHA: Yes — and what are some of those?

WALTER: Girl, let the man talk.

LINDNER (*with understated relief*): Thank you. I would sort of like to explain this thing in my own way. I mean I want to explain to you in a certain way.

WALTER: Go ahead.

LINDNER: Yes. Well. I'm going to try to get right to the point. I'm sure we'll all appreciate that in the long run.

BENEATHA: Yes.

WALTER: Be still now!

LINDNER: Well —

RUTH (*still innocently*): Would you like another chair — you don't look comfortable.

LINDNER (*more frustrated than annoyed*): No, thank you very much. Please. Well — to get right to the point, I — (*A great breath, and he is off at last.*) I am sure you people must be aware of some of the incidents which have happened in various parts of the city when colored people have moved into certain areas — (*Beneatha exhales heavily and starts tossing a piece of fruit up and down in the air.*) Well — because we have what I think is going to be a unique type of organization in American community life — not only do we deplore that kind of thing — but we are trying to do something about it. (*Beneatha stops tossing and turns with a new and quizzical interest to the man.*) We feel — (*gaining confidence in his mission because of the interest in the faces of the people he is talking to*) — we feel that most of the trouble in this world, when you come right down to it — (*he hits his knee for emphasis*) — most of the trouble exists because people just don't sit down and talk to each other.

RUTH (*nodding as she might in church, pleased with the remark*): You can say that again, mister.

LINDNER (*more encouraged by such affirmation*): That we don't try hard enough in this world to understand the other fellow's problem. The other guy's point of view.

RUTH: Now that's right.

Beneatha and Walter merely watch and listen with genuine interest.

LINDNER: Yes — that's the way we feel out in Clybourne Park. And that's why I was elected to come here this afternoon and talk to you people. Friendly like, you know, the way people should talk to each other and see if we couldn't find some way to work this thing out. As I say, the whole business is a matter of *caring* about the other fellow. Anybody can see that you are a nice family of folks, hard working and honest I'm sure. (*Beneatha frowns slightly, quizzically, her head tilted regarding him.*) Today everybody knows what it means to be on the outside of *something*. And of course, there is always somebody who is out to take advantage of people who don't always understand.

WALTER: What do you mean?

LINDNER: Well — you see our community is made up of people who've worked hard as the dickens for years to build up that little community. They're not rich and fancy people; just hard-working, honest people who don't really have much but those little homes and a dream of the kind of community they want to raise their children in. Now, I don't say we are perfect and there is a lot wrong in some of the things they want. But you've got to admit that a man, right or wrong, has the right to want to have the neighborhood he lives in a certain kind of way. And at the moment the overwhelming majority of our people out there feel that people get along better, take more of a common interest in the life of the community, when they share a common background. I want you to believe me when I tell you that race prejudice simply doesn't enter into it. It is a matter of the people of Clybourne Park believing, rightly or wrongly, as I say, that for the happiness of all concerned that our Negro families are happier when they live in their *own* communities.

BENEATHA (*with a grand and bitter gesture*): This, friends, is the Welcoming Committee!

WALTER (*dumfounded, looking at Lindner*): Is this what you came marching all the way over here to tell us?

LINDNER: Well, now we've been having a fine conversation. I hope you'll hear me all the way through.

WALTER (*tightly*): Go ahead, man.

LINDNER: You see — in the face of all the things I have said, we are prepared to make your family a very generous offer . . .

BENEATHA: Thirty pieces and not a coin less!

WALTER: Yeah?

LINDNER (*putting on his glasses and drawing a form out of the briefcase*): Our association is prepared, through the collective effort of our people, to buy the house from you at a financial gain to your family.

RUTH: Lord have mercy, ain't this the living gall!

WALTER: All right, you through?

LINDNER: Well, I want to give you the exact terms of the financial arrangement —

WALTER: We don't want to hear no exact terms of no arrangements. I want to know if you got any more to tell us 'bout getting together?

LINDNER (*taking off his glasses*): Well — I don't suppose that you feel . . .

WALTER: Never mind how I feel — you got any more to say 'bout how people ought to sit down and talk to each other? . . . Get out of my house, man.

He turns his back and walks to the door.

LINDNER (*looking around at the hostile faces and reaching and assembling his hat and briefcase*): Well — I don't understand why you people are reacting this way. What do you think you are going to gain by moving into a neighborhood where you just aren't wanted and where some elements — well — people can get awful worked up when they feel that their whole way of life and everything they've ever worked for is threatened.

WALTER: Get out.

LINDNER (*at the door, holding a small card*): Well — I'm sorry it went like this.

WALTER: Get out.

LINDNER (*almost sadly regarding Walter*): You just can't force people to change their hearts, son.

He turns and puts his card on a table and exits. Walter pushes the door to with stinging hatred, and stands looking at it. Ruth just sits and Beneatha just stands. They say nothing. Mama and Travis enter.

MAMA: Well — this all the packing got done since I left out of here this morning. I testify before God that my children got all the energy of the *dead!* What time the moving men due?

BENEATHA: Four o'clock. You had a caller, Mama.

She is smiling, teasingly.

MAMA: Sure enough — who?

BENEATHA (*her arms folded saucily*): The Welcoming Committee.

Walter and Ruth giggle.

MAMA (*innocently*): Who?

BENEATHA: The Welcoming Committee. They said they're sure going to be glad to see you when you get there.

WALTER (*devilishly*): Yeah, they said they can't hardly wait to see your face.

Laughter.

MAMA (*sensing their facetiousness*): What's the matter with you all?

WALTER: Ain't nothing the matter with us. We just telling you 'bout the gentleman who came to see you this afternoon. From the Clybourne Park Improvement Association.

MAMA: What he want?

RUTH (*in the same mood as Beneatha and Walter*): To welcome you, honey.

WALTER: He said they can't hardly wait. He said the one thing they don't have, that they just *dying* to have out there is a fine family of fine colored people! (*To Ruth and Beneatha.*) Ain't that right!

RUTH (*mockingly*): Yeah! He left his card —

BENEATHA (*handing card to Mama*): In case.

Mama reads and throws it on the floor — understanding and looking off as she draws her chair up to the table on which she has put her plant and some sticks and some cord.

MAMA: Father, give us strength. (*Knowingly — and without fun.*) Did he threaten us?

BENEATHA: Oh — Mama — they don't do it like that any more. He talked Brotherhood. He said everybody ought to learn how to sit down and hate each other with good Christian fellowship.

She and Walter shake hands to ridicule the remark.

MAMA (*sadly*): Lord, protect us . . .

RUTH: You should hear the money those folks raised to buy the house from us. All we paid and then some.

BENEATHA: What they think we going to do — eat 'em?

RUTH: No, honey, marry 'em.

MAMA (*shaking her head*): Lord, Lord, Lord . . .

RUTH: Well — that's the way the crackers crumble. (*A beat.*) Joke.

BENEATHA (*laughingly noticing what her mother is doing*): Mama, what are you doing?

MAMA: Fixing my plant so it won't get hurt none on the way . . .

BENEATHA: Mama, you going to take *that* to the new house?

MAMA: Un-huh —

BENEATHA: That raggedy-looking old thing?

MAMA (*stopping and looking at her*): It expresses ME!

RUTH (*with delight, to Beneatha*): So there, Miss Thing!

Walter comes to Mama suddenly and bends down behind her and squeezes her in his arms with all his strength. She is overwhelmed by the suddenness of it and, though delighted, her manner is like that of Ruth and Travis.

MAMA: Look out now, boy! You make me mess up my thing here!

WALTER (*his face lit, he slips down on his knees beside her, his arms still about her*): Mama . . . you know what it means to climb up in the chariot?

MAMA (*gruffly, very happy*): Get on away from me now . . .

RUTH (*near the gift-wrapped package, trying to catch Walter's eye*): Psst —

WALTER: What the old song say, Mama . . .

RUTH: Walter — Now?

She is pointing at the package.

WALTER (*speaking the lines, sweetly, playfully, in his mother's face*):

I got wings . . . you got wings . . .
All God's Children got wings . . .

MAMA: Boy — get out of my face and do some work . . .

WALTER:

When I get to heaven gonna put on my wings,
Gonna fly all over God's heaven . . .

BENEATHA (*teasingly, from across the room*): Everybody talking 'bout heaven ain't going there!

WALTER (*to Ruth, who is carrying the box across to them*): I don't know, you think we ought to give her that . . . Seems to me she ain't been very appreciative around here.

MAMA (*eying the box, which is obviously a gift*): What is that?

WALTER (*taking it from Ruth and putting it on the table in front of Mama*): Well — what you all think? Should we give it to her?

RUTH: Oh — she was pretty good today.

MAMA: I'll good you —

She turns her eyes to the box again.

BENEATHA: Open it, Mama.

She stands up, looks at it, turns and looks at all of them, and then presses her hands together and does not open the package.

WALTER (*sweetly*): Open it, Mama. It's for you. (*Mama looks in his eyes. It is the first present in her life without its being Christmas. Slowly she opens her package and lifts out, one by one, a brand-new sparkling set of gardening tools. Walter continues, prodding.*) Ruth made up the note — read it . . .

MAMA (*picking up the card and adjusting her glasses*): "To our own Mrs. Miniver° — Love from Brother, Ruth, and Beneatha." Ain't that lovely . . .

TRAVIS (*tugging at his father's sleeve*): Daddy, can I give her mine now?

WALTER: All right, son. (*Travis flies to get his gift.*)

MAMA: Now I don't have to use my knives and forks no more . . .

WALTER: Travis didn't want to go in with the rest of us, Mama. He got his own. (*Somewhat amused.*) We don't know what it is . . .

TRAVIS (*racing back in the room with a large hatbox and putting it in front of his grandmother*): Here!

MAMA: Lord have mercy, baby. You done gone and bought your grandmother a hat?

TRAVIS (*very proud*): Open it!

Mrs. Miniver: Title character of the 1942 film about a middle-class family's struggle to survive in wartorn Britain.

She does and lifts out an elaborate, but very elaborate, wide gardening hat, and all the adults break up at the sight of it.

RUTH: Travis, honey, what is that?

TRAVIS (*who thinks it is beautiful and appropriate*): It's a gardening hat! Like the ladies always have on in the magazines when they work in their gardens.

BENEATHA (*giggling fiercely*): Travis — we were trying to make Mama Mrs. Miniver — not Scarlett O'Hara!

MAMA (*indignantly*): What's the matter with you all! This here is a beautiful hat! (*Absurdly.*) I always wanted me one just like it!

She pops it on her head to prove it to her grandson, and the hat is ludicrous and considerably oversized.

RUTH: Hot dog! Go, Mama!

WALTER (*doubled over with laughter*): I'm sorry, Mama — but you look like you ready to go out and chop you some cotton sure enough!

They all laugh except Mama, out of deference to Travis's feelings.

MAMA (*gathering the boy up to her*): Bless your heart — this is the prettiest hat I ever owned — (*Walter, Ruth, and Beneatha chime in — noisily, festively, and insincerely congratulating Travis on his gift.*) What are we all standing around here for? We ain't finished packin' yet. Bennie, you ain't packed one book.

The bell rings.

BENEATHA: That couldn't be the movers . . . it's not hardly two good yet —

Beneatha goes into her room. Mama starts for door.

WALTER (*turning, stiffening*): Wait — wait — I'll get it.

He stands and looks at the door.

MAMA: You expecting company, son?

WALTER (*just looking at the door*): Yeah — yeah . . .

Mama looks at Ruth, and they exchange innocent and unfrightened glances.

MAMA (*not understanding*): Well, let them in, son.

BENEATHA (*from her room*): We need some more string.

MAMA: Travis — you run to the hardware and get me some string cord.

Mama goes out and Walter turns and looks at Ruth. Travis goes to a dish for money.

RUTH: Why don't you answer the door, man?

WALTER (*suddenly bounding across the floor to embrace her*): 'Cause sometimes it hard to let the future begin! (*Stooping down in her face.*)

I got wings! You got wings!
All God's children got wings!

He crosses to the door and throws it open. Standing there is a very slight little man in a not-too-prosperous business suit and with haunted frightened eyes and a hat pulled down tightly, brim up, around his forehead. Travis passes between the men and exits. Walter leans deep in the man's face, still in his jubilance.

When I get to heaven gonna put on my wings,
Gonna fly all over God's heaven . . .

The little man just stares at him.

Heaven —

Suddenly he stops and looks past the little man into the empty hallway.

Where's Willy, man?

BOBO: He ain't with me.

WALTER (*not disturbed*): Oh — come on in. You know my wife.

BOBO (*dumbly, taking off his hat*): Yes — h'you, Miss Ruth.

RUTH (*quietly, a mood apart from her husband already, seeing Bobo*): Hello, Bobo.

WALTER: You right on time today . . . Right on time. That's the way! (*He slaps Bobo on his back.*) Sit down . . . lemme hear.

Ruth stands stiffly and quietly in back of them, as though somehow she senses death, her eyes fixed on her husband.

BOBO (*his frightened eyes on the floor, his hat in his hands*): Could I please get a drink of water, before I tell you about it, Walter Lee?

Walter does not take his eyes off the man. Ruth goes blindly to the tap and gets a glass of water and brings it to Bobo.

WALTER: There ain't nothing wrong, is there?

BOBO: Lemme tell you —

WALTER: Man — didn't nothing go wrong?

BOBO: Lemme tell you — Walter Lee. (*Looking at Ruth and talking to her more than to Walter.*) You know how it was. I got to tell you how it was. I mean first I got to tell you how it was all the way . . . I mean about the money I put in, Walter Lee . . .

WALTER (*with taut agitation now*): What about the money you put in?

BOBO: Well — it wasn't much as we told you — me and Willy — (*He stops.*) I'm sorry, Walter. I got a bad feeling about it. I got a real bad feeling about it . . .

WALTER: Man, what you telling me about all this for? . . . Tell me what happened in Springfield . . .

BOBO: Springfield.

RUTH (*like a dead woman*): What was supposed to happen in Springfield?

BOBO (*to her*): This deal that me and Walter went into with Willy — Me and Willy was going to go down to Springfield and spread some money 'round so's we wouldn't have to wait so long for the liquor license . . . That's what we were going to do. Everybody said that was the way you had to do, you understand, Miss Ruth?

WALTER: Man — what happened down there?

BOBO (*a pitiful man, near tears*): I'm trying to tell you, Walter.

WALTER (*screaming at him suddenly*): THEN TELL ME, GODDAMMIT . . . WHAT'S THE MATTER WITH YOU?

BOBO: Man . . . I didn't go to no Springfield, yesterday.

WALTER (*halted, life hanging in the moment*): Why not?

BOBO (*the long way, the hard way to tell*): 'Cause I didn't have no reasons to . . .

WALTER: Man, what are you talking about!

BOBO: I'm talking about the fact that when I got to the train station yesterday morning — eight o'clock like we planned . . . Man — *Willy didn't never show up.*

WALTER: Why . . . where was he . . . where is he?

BOBO: That's what I'm trying to tell you . . . I don't know . . . I waited six hours . . . I called his house . . . and I waited . . . six hours . . . I waited in that train station six hours . . . (*Breaking into tears.*) That was all the extra money I had in the world . . . (*Looking up at Walter with the tears running down his face.*) Man, *Willy is gone.*

WALTER: Gone, what you mean Willy is gone? Gone where? You mean he went by himself. You mean he went off to Springfield by himself — to take care of getting the license — (*Turns and looks anxiously at Ruth.*) You mean maybe he didn't want too many people in on the business down there? (*Looks to Ruth again, as before.*) You know Willy got his own ways. (*Looks back to Bobo.*) Maybe you was late yesterday and he just went on down there without you. Maybe — maybe — he's been callin' you at home tryin' to tell you what happened or something. Maybe — maybe — he just got sick. He's somewhere — he's got to be somewhere. We just got to find him — me and you got to find him. (*Grabs Bobo senselessly by the collar and starts to shake him.*) We got to!

BOBO (*in sudden angry, frightened agony*): What's the matter with you, Walter! *When a cat take off with your money he don't leave you no road maps!*

WALTER (*turning madly, as though he is looking for Willy in the very room*): Willy! . . . Willy . . . don't do it . . . Please don't do it . . . Man, not with that money . . . Man, please, not with that money . . . Oh, God . . . Don't let it be true . . . (*He is wandering around, crying out for Willy and looking for him or perhaps for help from God.*) Man . . . I trusted you . . . Man, I put my life in your hands . . . (*He starts to crumple down on the floor as Ruth just covers her face in horror. Mama opens the door and comes into the room, with Beneatha behind her.*) Man . . . (*He starts to pound the floor with his fists, sobbing wildly.*) THAT MONEY IS MADE OUT OF MY FATHER'S FLESH —

BOBO (*standing over him helplessly*): I'm sorry, Walter . . . (*Only Walter's sobs reply. Bobo puts on his hat.*) I had my life staked on this deal, too . . .

He exits.

MAMA (*to Walter*): Son — (*She goes to him, bends down to him, talks to his bent head.*) Son . . . Is it gone? Son, I gave you sixty-five hundred dollars. Is it gone? All of it? Beneatha's money too?

WALTER (*lifting his head slowly*): Mama . . . I never . . . went to the bank at all . . .

MAMA (*not wanting to believe him*): You mean . . . your sister's school money . . . you used that too . . . Walter? . . .

WALTER: Yessss! All of it . . . It's all gone . . .

There is total silence. Ruth stands with her face covered with her hands; Beneatha leans forlornly against a wall, fingering a piece of red ribbon from the mother's gift. Mama stops and looks at her son without recognition and then, quite without thinking about it, starts to beat him senselessly in the face. Beneatha goes to them and stops it.

BENEATHA: Mama!

Mama stops and looks at both of her children and rises slowly and wanders vaguely, aimlessly away from them.

MAMA: I seen . . . him . . . night after night . . . come in . . . and look at that rug . . . and then look at me . . . the red showing in his eyes . . . the veins moving in his head . . . I seen him grow thin and old before he was forty . . . working and working and working like somebody's old horse . . . killing himself . . . and you — you give it all away in a day — (*She raises her arms to strike him again.*)

BENEATHA: Mama —

MAMA: Oh, God . . . (*She looks up to Him.*) Look down here — and show me the strength.

BENEATHA: Mama —

MAMA (*folding over*): Strength . . .

BENEATHA (*plaintively*): Mama . . .

MAMA: Strength!

Curtain.

ACT III

Time: An hour later.

At curtain, there is a sullen light of gloom in the living room, gray light not unlike that which began the first scene of Act I. At left we can see Walter within his room, alone with himself. He is stretched out on the bed, his shirt out and open, his arms under his head. He does not smoke, he does not cry out, he merely lies there, looking up at the ceiling, much as if he were alone in the world.

In the living room Beneatha sits at the table, still surrounded by the now almost ominous packing crates. She sits looking off. We feel that this is a mood struck perhaps an hour before, and it lingers now, full of the empty sound of profound disappointment. We see on a line from her brother's bedroom the sameness of their attitudes. Presently the bell rings and Beneatha rises without ambition or interest in answering. It is Asagai, smiling broadly, striding into the room with energy and happy expectation and conversation.

ASAGAI: I came over . . . I had some free time. I thought I might help with the packing. Ah, I like the look of packing crates! A household in preparation for a journey! It depresses some people . . . but for me . . . it is another feeling. Something full of the flow of life, do you understand? Movement, progress . . . It makes me think of Africa.

BENEATHA: Africa!

ASAGAI: What kind of a mood is this? Have I told you how deeply you move me?

BENEATHA: He gave away the money, Asagai . . .

ASAGAI: Who gave away what money?

BENEATHA: The insurance money. My brother gave it away.

ASAGAI: Gave it away?

BENEATHA: He made an investment! With a man even Travis wouldn't have trusted with his most worn-out marbles.

ASAGAI: And it's gone?

BENEATHA: Gone!

ASAGAI: I'm very sorry . . . And you, now?

BENEATHA: Me? . . . Me? . . . Me, I'm nothing . . . Me. When I was very small . . . we used to take our sleds out in the wintertime and the only hills we had were the ice-covered stone steps of some houses down the street. And we used to fill them in with snow and make them smooth and slide down them all day . . . and it was very dangerous, you know . . . far too steep . . . and sure enough one day a kid named Rufus came down too fast and hit the sidewalk and we saw his face just split open right there in front of us . . . And I remember standing there looking at his bloody open face thinking that was the end of Rufus. But the ambulance came and they took him to the hospital and they fixed the broken bones and they sewed it all up . . . and the next time I saw Rufus he just had a little line down the middle of his face . . . I never got over that . . .

ASAGAI: What?

BENEATHA: That that was what one person could do for another, fix him up — sew up the problem, make him all right again. That was the most marvelous thing in the world . . . I wanted to do that. I always thought it was the one concrete thing in the world that a human being could do. Fix up the sick, you know — and make them whole again. This was truly being God . . .

ASAGAI: You wanted to be God?

BENEATHA: No — I wanted to cure. It used to be so important to me. I wanted to cure. It used to matter. I used to care. I mean about people and how their bodies hurt . . .

ASAGAI: And you've stopped caring?

BENEATHA: Yes — I think so.

ASAGAI: Why?

BENEATHA (*bitterly*): Because it doesn't seem deep enough, close enough to what ails mankind! It was a child's way of seeing things — or an idealist's.

ASAGAI: Children see things very well sometimes — and idealists even better.

BENEATHA: I know that's what you think. Because you are still where I left off. You with all your talk and dreams about Africa! You still think you can patch up the world. Cure the Great Sore of Colonialism — (*loftily, mocking it*) with the Penicillin of Independence — !

ASAGAI: Yes!

BENEATHA: Independence *and then what?* What about all the crooks and thieves and just plain idiots who will come into power and steal and plunder the same as before — only now they will be black and do it in the name of the new Independence — WHAT ABOUT THEM?!

ASAGAI: That will be the problem for another time. First we must get there.

BENEATHA: And where does it end?

ASAGAI: End? Who even spoke of an end? To life? To living?

BENEATHA: An end to misery! To stupidity! Don't you see there isn't any real progress, Asagai, there is only one large circle that we march in, around and around, each of us with our own little picture in front of us — our own little mirage that we think is the future.

ASAGAI: That is the mistake.

BENEATHA: What?

ASAGAI: What you just said — about the circle. It isn't a circle—it is simply a long line — as in geometry, you know, one that reaches into infinity. And because we cannot see the end — we also cannot see how it changes. And it is very odd but those who see the changes — who dream, who will not give up — are called idealists . . . and those who see only the circle — we call *them* the "realists"!

BENEATHA: Asagai, while I was sleeping in that bed in there, people went out and took the future right out of my hands! And nobody asked me, nobody consulted me — they just went out and changed my life!

ASAGAI: Was it your money?

BENEATHA: What?

ASAGAI: Was it your money he gave away?

BENEATHA: It belonged to all of us.

ASAGAI: But did you earn it? Would you have had it at all if your father had not died?

BENEATHA: No.

ASAGAI: Then isn't there something wrong in a house — in a world — where all dreams, good or bad, must depend on the death of a man? I never thought to see *you* like this, Alaiyo. You! Your brother made a mistake and you are grateful to him so that now you can give up the ailing human race on account of it! You talk about what good is struggle, what good is anything! Where are we all going and why are we bothering!

BENEATHA: AND YOU CANNOT ANSWER IT!

ASAGAI (*shouting over her*): I LIVE THE ANSWER! (*Pause.*) In my village at home it is the exceptional man who can even read a newspaper . . . or who ever sees a book at all. I will go home and much of what I will have to say will seem strange to the people of my village. But I will teach and work and things will happen, slowly and swiftly. At times it will seem that nothing changes at all . . . and then again the sudden dramatic events which make history leap into the future. And then quiet again. Retrogression even. Guns, murder, revolution. And I even will have moments when I wonder if the quiet was not better than all that death and hatred. But I will look about my village at the illiteracy and disease and ignorance and I will not wonder long. And perhaps . . . perhaps I will be a great man . . . I mean perhaps I will hold on to the substance of truth and find my way always with the right course . . . and perhaps for it I will be butchered in my bed some night by the servants of empire . . .

BENEATHA: *The martyr!*

ASAGAI (*he smiles*): . . . or perhaps I shall live to be a very old man, respected and esteemed in my new nation . . . And perhaps I shall hold office and this is what I'm trying to tell you, Alaiyo: perhaps the things I believe now for my country will be wrong and outmoded, and I will not understand and do terrible things to have things my way or merely to keep my power. Don't you see that there will be young men and women — not British soldiers then, but my own black countrymen — to step out of the shadows some evening and slit my then useless throat? Don't you see they have always been there . . . that they always will be. And that such a thing as my own death will be an advance? They who might kill me even . . . actually replenish all that I was.

BENEATHA: Oh, Asagai, I know all that.

ASAGAI: Good! Then stop moaning and groaning and tell me what you plan to do.

BENEATHA: Do?

ASAGAI: I have a bit of a suggestion.

BENEATHA: What?

ASAGAI (*rather quietly for him*): That when it is all over — that you come home with me —

BENEATHA (*staring at him and crossing away with exasperation*): Oh — Asagai — at this moment you decide to be romantic!

ASAGAI (*quickly understanding the misunderstanding*): My dear, young creature of the New World — I do not mean across the city — I mean across the ocean: home — to Africa.

BENEATHA (*slowly understanding and turning to him with murmured amazement*): To Africa?

ASAGAI: Yes! . . . (*Smiling and lifting his arms playfully.*) Three hundred years later the African Prince rose up out of the seas and swept the maiden back across the middle passage over which her ancestors had come —

BENEATHA (*unable to play*): To — to Nigeria?

ASAGAI: Nigeria. Home. (*Coming to her with genuine romantic flippancy.*) I will show you our mountains and our stars; and give you cool drinks from gourds and teach you the old songs and the ways of our people — and, in time, we will pretend that — (*very softly*) — you have only been away for a day. Say that you'll come — (*He swings her around and takes her full in his arms in a kiss which proceeds to passion.*)

BENEATHA (*pulling away suddenly*): You're getting me all mixed up —

ASAGAI: Why?

BENEATHA: Too many things — too many things have happened today. I must sit down and think. I don't know what I feel about anything right this minute.

She promptly sits down and props her chin on her fist.

ASAGAI (*charmed*): All right, I shall leave you. No — don't get up. (*Touching her, gently, sweetly.*) Just sit awhile and think . . . Never be afraid to sit awhile and think. (*He goes to door and looks at her.*) How often I have looked at you and said, "Ah — so this is what the New World hath finally wrought . . ."

He exits. Beneatha sits on alone. Presently Walter enters from his room and starts to rummage through things, feverishly looking for something. She looks up and turns in her seat.

BENEATHA (*hissingly*): Yes — just look at what the New World hath wrought! . . . Just look! (*She gestures with bitter disgust.*) There he is! *Monsieur le petit bour-*

geois noir — himself! There he is — Symbol of a Rising Class! Entrepreneur! Titan of the system! (*Walter ignores her completely and continues frantically and destructively looking for something and hurling things to floor and tearing things out of their place in his search. Beneatha ignores the eccentricity of his actions and goes on with the monologue of insult.*) Did you dream of yachts on Lake Michigan, Brother? Did you see yourself on that Great Day sitting down at the Conference Table, surrounded by all the mighty bald-headed men in America? All halted, waiting, breathless, waiting for your pronouncements on industry? Waiting for you — Chairman of the Board! (*Walter finds what he is looking for — a small piece of white paper — and pushes it in his pocket and puts on his coat and rushes out without ever having looked at her. She shouts after him.*) I look at you and I see the final triumph of stupidity in the world!

The door slams and she returns to just sitting again. Ruth comes quickly out of Mama's room.

RUTH: Who was that?

BENEATHA: Your husband.

RUTH: Where did he go?

BENEATHA: Who knows — maybe he has an appointment at U.S. Steel.

RUTH (*anxiously, with frightened eyes*): You didn't say nothing bad to him, did you?

BENEATHA: Bad? Say anything bad to him? No — I told him he was a sweet boy and full of dreams and everything is strictly peachy keen, as the ofay kids say!

Mama enters from her bedroom. She is lost, vague, trying to catch hold, to make some sense of her former command of the world, but it still eludes her. A sense of waste overwhelms her gait; a measure of apology rides on her shoulders. She goes to her plant, which has remained on the table, looks at it, picks it up and takes it to the window sill and sits it outside, and she stands and looks at it a long moment. Then she closes the window, straightens her body with effort and turns around to her children.

MAMA: Well — ain't it a mess in here, though? (*A false cheerfulness, a beginning of something.*) I guess we all better stop moping around and get some work done. All this unpacking and everything we got to do. (*Ruth raises her head slowly in response to the sense of the line; and Beneatha in similar manner turns very slowly to look at her mother.*) One of you all better call the moving people and tell 'em not to come.

RUTH: Tell 'em not to come?

MAMA: Of course, baby. Ain't no need in 'em coming all the way here and having to go back. They charges for that too. (*She sits down, fingers to her brow, thinking.*) Lord, ever since I was a little girl, I always remembers people saying, "Lena — Lena Eggleston, you aims too high all the time. You needs to slow down and see life a little more like it is. Just slow down some." That's what they always used to say down home — "Lord, that Lena Eggleston is a high-minded thing. She'll get her due one day!"

RUTH: No, Lena . . .

MAMA: Me and Big Walter just didn't never learn right.

RUTH: Lena, no! We gotta go. Bennie — tell her . . .

She rises and crosses to Beneatha with her arms outstretched. Beneatha doesn't respond.

Tell her we can still move . . . the notes ain't but a hundred and twenty-five a month. We got four grown people in this house — we can work . . .

MAMA (*to herself*): Just aimed too high all the time —

RUTH (*turning and going to Mama fast — the words pouring out with urgency and desperation*): Lena — I'll work . . . I'll work twenty hours a day in all the kitchens in Chicago . . . I'll strap my baby on my back if I have to and scrub all the floors in America and wash all the sheets in America if I have to — but we got to MOVE! We got to get OUT OF HERE!!

Mama reaches out absently and pats Ruth's hand.

MAMA: No — I sees things differently now. Been thinking 'bout some of the things we could do to fix this place up some. I seen a second-hand bureau over on Maxwell Street just the other day that could fit right there. (*She points to where the new furniture might go. Ruth wanders away from her.*) Would need some new handles on it and then a little varnish and it look like something brand-new. And — we can put up them new curtains in the kitchen . . . Why this place be looking fine. Cheer us all up so that we forget trouble ever come . . . (*To Ruth.*) And you could get some nice screens to put up in your room round the baby's bassinet . . . (*She looks at both of them pleadingly.*) Sometimes you just got to know when to give up some things . . . and hold on to what you got . . .

Walter enters from the outside, looking spent and leaning against the door, his coat hanging from him.

MAMA: Where you been, son?

WALTER (*breathing hard*): Made a call.

MAMA: To who, son?

WALTER: To The Man. (*He heads for his room.*)

MAMA: What man, baby?

WALTER (*stops in the door*): The Man, Mama. Don't you know who The Man is?

RUTH: Walter Lee?

WALTER: *The Man.* Like the guys in the streets say — The Man. Captain Boss — Mistuh Charley . . . Old Cap'n Please Mr. Bossman . . .

BENEATHA (*suddenly*): Lindner!

WALTER: That's right! That's good. I told him to come right over.

BENEATHA (*fiercely, understanding*): For what? What do you want to see him for!

WALTER (*looking at his sister*): We going to do business with him.

MAMA: What you talking 'bout, son?

WALTER: Talking 'bout life, Mama. You all always telling me to see life like it is. Well — I laid in there on my back today . . . and I figured it out. Life just like it is. Who gets and who don't get. (*He sits down with his coat on and laughs.*) Mama, you know it's all divided up. Life is. Sure enough. Between the takers and the "tooken." (*He laughs.*) I've figured it out finally. (*He looks around at them.*) Yeah. Some of us always getting "tooken." (*He laughs.*) People like Willy Harris, they don't never get "tooken." And you know why the rest of us do? 'Cause we all mixed up. Mixed up bad. We get to looking 'round for the right and the wrong; and we worry about it and cry about it and stay up nights trying to figure out 'bout the wrong and the right of things all the time . . . And all the time, man, them takers is out there operating, just taking and taking. Willy Harris? Shoot — Willy Harris don't even count. He don't even count in the big scheme of things. But I'll say one thing for old Willy Harris . . . he's taught me something. He's taught me to keep my eye on what counts in this world. Yeah — (*Shouting out a little.*) Thanks, Willy!

RUTH: What did you call that man for, Walter Lee?

WALTER: Called him to tell him to come on over to the show. Gonna put on a show for the man. Just what he wants to see. You see, Mama, the man came here today and he told us that them people out there where you want us to move — well they so upset they willing to pay us *not* to move! (*He laughs again.*) And — and oh, Mama — you would of been proud of the way me and Ruth and Bennie acted. We told him to get out . . . Lord have mercy! We told the man to get out! Oh, we was some proud folks this afternoon, yeah. (*He lights a cigarette.*) We were still full of that old-time stuff . . .

RUTH (*coming toward him slowly*): You talking 'bout taking them people's money to keep us from moving in that house?

WALTER: I ain't just talking 'bout it, baby — I'm telling you that's what's going to happen!

BENEATHA: Oh, God! Where is the bottom! Where is the real honest-to-God bottom so he can't go any farther!

WALTER: See — that's the old stuff. You and that boy that was here today. You all want everybody to carry a flag and a spear and sing some marching songs, huh? You wanna spend your life looking into things and trying to find the right and the wrong part, huh? Yeah. You know what's going to happen to that boy someday — he'll find himself sitting in a dungeon, locked in forever — and the takers will have the key! Forget it, baby! There ain't no causes — there ain't nothing but taking in this world, and he who takes most is smartest — and it don't make a damn bit of difference *how.*

MAMA: You making something inside me cry, son. Some awful pain inside me.

WALTER: Don't cry, Mama. Understand. That white man is going to walk in that door able to write checks for more money than we ever had. It's important to him and I'm going to help him . . . I'm going to put on the show, Mama.

MAMA: Son — I come from five generations of people who was slaves and sharecroppers — but ain't nobody in my family never let nobody pay 'em no money that was a way of telling us we wasn't fit to walk the earth. We ain't never been that poor. (*Raising her eyes and looking at him.*) We ain't never been that — dead inside.

BENEATHA: Well — we are dead now. All the talk about dreams and sunlight that goes on in this house. It's all dead now.

WALTER: What's the matter with you all! I didn't make this world! It was give to me this way! Hell, yes, I want me some yachts someday! Yes, I want to hang some real pearls 'round my wife's neck. Ain't she supposed to wear no pearls? Somebody tell me — tell me, who decides which women is suppose to wear pearls in this world. I tell you I am a *man* — and I think my wife should wear some pearls in this world!

This last line hangs a good while and Walter begins to move about the room. The word "Man" has penetrated his consciousness; he mumbles it to himself repeatedly between strange agitated pauses as he moves about.

MAMA: Baby, how you going to feel on the inside?

WALTER: Fine! . . . Going to feel fine . . . a man . . .

MAMA: You won't have nothing left then, Walter Lee.

WALTER (*coming to her*): I'm going to feel fine, Mama. I'm going to look that son-of-a-bitch in the eyes and say — (*he falters*) — and say, "All right, Mr. Lindner — (*he falters even more*) — that's *your* neighborhood out there! You got the right to keep it like you want! You got the right to have it like you want! Just write the check and — the house is yours." And — and I am going to say — (*his voice almost breaks*) "And you — you people just put the money in my hand and you won't have to live next to this bunch of stinking niggers! . . ." (*He straightens up and moves away from his mother, walking around the room.*) And maybe — maybe I'll just get down on my black knees . . . (*He does so; Ruth and Bennie and Mama watch him in frozen horror.*) "Captain, Mistuh, Bossman — (*Groveling and grinning and wringing his hands in profoundly anguished imitation of the slow-witted movie stereotype.*) A-hee-hee-hee! Oh, yassuh boss! Yasssssuh! Great white — (*voice breaking, he forces himself to go on*) — Father, just gi' ussen de money, fo' God's sake, and we's — we's ain't gwine come out deh and dirty up yo' white folks neighborhood . . ." (*He breaks down completely.*) And I'll feel fine! Fine! FINE! (*He gets up and goes into the bedroom.*)

BENEATHA: That is not a man. That is nothing but a toothless rat.

MAMA: Yes — death done come in this here house. (*She is nodding, slowly, reflectively.*) Done come walking in my house on the lips of my children. You what supposed to be my beginning again. You — what supposed to be my harvest. (*To Beneatha.*) You — you mourning your brother?

BENEATHA: He's no brother of mine.

MAMA: What you say?

BENEATHA: I said that that individual in that room is no brother of mine.

MAMA: That's what I thought you said. You feeling like you better than he is today? (*Beneatha does not answer.*) Yes? What you tell him a minute ago? That he wasn't a man? Yes? You give him up for me? You done wrote his epitaph too — like the rest of the world? Well, who give you the privilege?

BENEATHA: Be on my side for once! You saw what he just did, Mama! You saw him — down on his knees. Wasn't it you who taught me to despise any man who would do that? Do what he's going to do?

MAMA: Yes — I taught you that. Me and your daddy. But I thought I taught you something else too . . . I thought I taught you to love him.

BENEATHA: Love him? There is nothing left to love.

MAMA: There is *always* something left to love. And if you ain't learned that, you ain't learned nothing. (*Looking at her.*) Have you cried for that boy today? I don't mean for yourself and for the family 'cause we lost the money. I mean for him: what he been through and what it done to him. Child, when do you think is the time to love somebody the most? When they done good and made things easy for everybody? Well then, you ain't through learning — because that ain't the time at all. It's when he's at his lowest and can't believe in hisself 'cause the world done whipped him so! When you starts measuring somebody, measure him right, child, measure him right. Make sure you done taken into account what hills and valleys he come through before he got to wherever he is.

Travis bursts into the room at the end of the speech, leaving the door open.

TRAVIS: Grandmama — the moving men are downstairs! The truck just pulled up.

MAMA (*turning and looking at him*): Are they, baby? They downstairs?

She sighs and sits. Lindner appears in the doorway. He peers in and knocks lightly, to gain attention, and comes in. All turn to look at him.

LINDNER (*hat and briefcase in hand*): Uh — hello . . .

Ruth crosses mechanically to the bedroom door and opens it and lets it swing open freely and slowly as the lights come up on Walter within, still in his coat, sitting at the far corner of the room. He looks up and out through the room to Lindner.

RUTH: He's here.

A long minute passes and Walter slowly gets up.

LINDNER (*coming to the table with efficiency, putting his briefcase on the table and starting to unfold papers and unscrew fountain pens*): Well, I certainly was glad to hear from you people. (*Walter has begun the trek out of the room, slowly and awkwardly, rather like a small boy, passing the back of his sleeve across his mouth from time to time.*) Life can really be so much simpler than people let it be most of the time. Well — with whom do I negotiate? You, Mrs. Younger, or your son here? (*Mama sits with her hands folded on her lap and her eyes closed as Walter advances. Travis goes closer to Lindner and looks at the papers curiously.*) Just some official papers, sonny.

RUTH: Travis, you go downstairs —

MAMA (*opening her eyes and looking into Walter's*): No. Travis, you stay right here. And you make him understand what you doing, Walter Lee. You teach him good. Like Willy Harris taught you. You show where our five generations done come to. (*Walter looks from her to the boy, who grins at him innocently.*) Go ahead, son — (*She folds her hands and closes her eyes.*) Go ahead.

WALTER (*at last crosses to Lindner, who is reviewing the contract*): Well, Mr. Lindner. (*Beneatha turns away.*) We called you — (*there is a profound, simple groping quality in his speech*) — because, well, me and my family (*He looks around and shifts from one foot to the other.*) Well — we are very plain people . . .

LINDNER: Yes —

WALTER: I mean — I have worked as a chauffeur most of my life — and my wife here, she does domestic work in people's kitchens. So does my mother. I mean — we are plain people . . .

LINDNER: Yes, Mr. Younger —

WALTER (*really like a small boy, looking down at his shoes and then up at the man*): And — uh — well, my father, well, he was a laborer most of his life. . . .

LINDNER (*absolutely confused*): Uh, yes — yes, I understand. (*He turns back to the contract.*)

WALTER (*a beat; staring at him*): And my father — (*With sudden intensity.*) My father almost *beat a man to death* once because this man called him a bad name or something, you know what I mean?

LINDNER (*looking up, frozen*): No, no, I'm afraid I don't —

WALTER (*a beat. The tension hangs; then Walter steps back from it*): Yeah. Well — what I mean is that we come from people who had a lot of *pride.* I mean — we are very proud people. And that's my sister over there and she's going to be a doctor — and we are very proud —

LINDNER: Well — I am sure that is very nice, but —

WALTER: What I am telling you is that we called you over here to tell you that we are very proud and that this — (*Signaling to Travis.*) Travis, come here. (*Travis crosses and Walter draws him before him facing the man.*) This is my son, and he makes the sixth generation our family in this country. And we have all thought about your offer —

LINDNER: Well, good . . . good —

WALTER: And we have decided to move into our house because my father — my father — he earned it for us brick by brick. (*Mama has her eyes closed and is rocking back and forth as though she were in church, with her head nodding the Amen yes.*) We don't want to make no trouble for nobody or fight no causes, and we will try to be good neighbors. And that's *all* we got to say about that. (*He looks the man absolutely in the eyes.*) We don't want your money. (*He turns and walks away.*)

LINDNER (*looking around at all of them*): I take it then — that you have decided to occupy . . .

BENEATHA: That's what the man said.

LINDNER (*to Mama in her reverie*): Then I would like to appeal to you, Mrs. Younger. You are older and wiser and understand things better I am sure . . .

MAMA: I am afraid you don't understand. My son said we was going to move and there ain't nothing left for me to say. (*Briskly.*) You know how these young folks is nowadays, mister. Can't do a thing with 'em! (*As he opens his mouth, she rises.*) Good-bye.

LINDNER (*folding up his materials*): Well — if you are that final about it . . . there is nothing left for me to say. (*He finishes, almost ignored by the family, who are concentrating on Walter Lee. At the door Lindner halts and looks around.*) I sure hope you people know what you're getting into.

He shakes his head and exits.

RUTH (*looking around and coming to life*): Well, for God's sake — if the moving men are here — LET'S GET THE HELL OUT OF HERE!

MAMA (*into action*): Ain't it the truth! Look at all this here mess. Ruth, put Travis' good jacket on him . . . Walter Lee, fix your tie and tuck your shirt in, you look like somebody's hoodlum! Lord have mercy, where is my plant? (*She flies to get it amid the general bustling of the family, who are deliberately trying to ignore the nobility of the past moment.*) You all start on down . . . Travis child, don't go empty-handed . . . Ruth, where did I put that box with my skillets in it? I want to be in charge of it myself . . . I'm going to make us the biggest dinner we ever ate tonight . . . Beneatha, what's the matter with them stockings? Pull them things up, girl . . .

The family starts to file out as two moving men appear and begin to carry out the heavier pieces of furniture, bumping into the family as they move about.

BENEATHA: Mama, Asagai asked me to marry him today and go to Africa —

MAMA (*in the middle of her getting-ready activity*): He did? You ain't old enough to marry nobody — (*Seeing the moving men lifting one of her chairs precariously.*) Darling, that ain't no bale of cotton, please handle it so we can sit in it again! I had that chair twenty-five years . . .

The movers sigh with exasperation and go on with their work.

BENEATHA (*girlishly and unreasonably trying to pursue the conversation*): To go to Africa, Mama — be a doctor in Africa . . .

MAMA (*distracted*): Yes, baby —

WALTER: *Africa!* What he want you to go to Africa for?

BENEATHA: To practice there . . .

WALTER: Girl, if you don't get all them silly ideas out your head! You better marry yourself a man with some loot . . .

BENEATHA (*angrily, precisely as in the first scene of the play*): What have you got to do with who I marry!

WALTER: Plenty. Now I think George Murchison —

BENEATHA: *George Murchison!* I wouldn't marry him if he was Adam and I was Eve!

Walter and Beneatha go out yelling at each other vigorously and the anger is loud and real till their voices diminish. Ruth stands at the door and turns to Mama and smiles knowingly.

MAMA (*fixing her hat at last*): Yeah — they something all right, my children . . .

RUTH: Yeah — they're something. Let's go, Lena.

MAMA (*stalling, starting to look around at the house*): Yes — I'm coming. Ruth —

RUTH: Yes?

MAMA (*quietly, woman to woman*): He finally come into his manhood today, didn't he? Kind of like a rainbow after the rain . . .

RUTH (*biting her lip lest her own pride explode in front of Mama*): Yes, Lena.

Walter's voice calls for them raucously.

WALTER (*off stage*): Y'all come on! These people charges by the hour, you know!

MAMA (*waving Ruth out vaguely*): All right, honey — go on down. I be down directly.

Ruth hesitates, then exits. Mama stands, at last alone in the living room, her plant on the table before her as the lights start to come down. She looks around at all the walls and ceilings and suddenly, despite herself, while the children call below, a great heaving thing rises in her and she puts her fist to her mouth to stifle it, takes a final desperate look, pulls her coat about her, pats her hat, and goes out. The lights dim down. The door opens and she comes back in, grabs her plant, and goes out for the last time.

Curtain.

ꕤ

AUGUST WILSON *(b. 1945) was born in a slum in Pittsburgh and raised with his five brothers and sisters by his African American mother, Daisy Wilson, who supported her children by working as a janitor downtown in the county courthouse. His father, a white man, abandoned the family; Wilson remembered that he was "a sporadic presence in our house." Wilson was also nurtured by his stepfather, David Bedford, who worked in the city sewer department. Bedford had been a football star in high school but spent twenty-three years in prison after killing a man in a robbery attempt. Wilson credits his mother for teaching him about black pride. He tells a story about the time she won a brand-new Speed Queen washing machine in a radio competition. When the station discovered she was black, they substituted a certificate for a secondhand washer. Wilson's mother was doing her family's laundry at the sink in her home on a scrub board, but she refused the radio's offer rather than be treated so unfairly.*

At age fifteen, Wilson dropped out of school, took a job running a freight elevator, and began to spend hours in the "Negro Section" of the Pittsburgh Public Library, where he read Ralph Ellison, Langston Hughes, and James Baldwin. Back in Pittsburgh after three years in the army, he bought his first typewriter for twenty dollars and began to write poetry before gradually shifting over, on the advice of a friend, to writing plays.

Wilson later told interviewer Will Haygood that what "pained" him enough to start his writing was the idea of African Americans streaming out of the South, trying to forget their past: "My mother came from North Carolina. And all my friends were always from someplace: Alabama, Georgia. And this is what happened invariably: One of my classmates would come to school and say, 'My grandmother died. And we got some land.' I'd say, 'When you gonna move?' They'd say, 'We gonna sell it.'" It was Wilson's belief that "we should have stayed in the South. We attempted to plant what in essence was an emerging culture, a culture that had grown out of our experience of two hundred years as slaves in the South. The cities of the urban North have not been hospitable. If we had stayed in the South, we could have strengthened the culture." In Fences, *Wilson dramatizes the continuing struggle of African Americans to find good jobs and hold together families forty years after leaving the South in the "Great Migration" from 1910 to 1930, when the black population doubled and tripled in Pittsburgh, Chicago, and New York City.*

In 1981 and 1982, the first professional productions of Wilson's plays were staged in little theaters in St. Paul and Pittsburgh. He also began sending his manuscripts to the Eugene O'Neill Playwrights Conference, which ran workshops to develop the talent of young American playwrights. The conference rejected his first plays but accepted his work-in-progress, Ma Rainey's Black Bottom. *"To this day," recalls Wilson, "that's about the highlight of my career."*

With Ma Rainey, *Wilson began his collaboration with the African American director of the Yale Repertory Theatre, Lloyd Richards, to whom he dedicated* Fences: *"For Lloyd Richards, who adds to whatever he touches." Wilson embarked on an ambitious ten-play cycle dramatizing different decades in the history of African Americans in the twentieth century. To date, the cycle consists of* Joe Turner's Come and Gone *(1983), set in 1911;* Ma Rainey's Black Bottom *(1981), set in 1927;* The Piano Lesson *(1986), set in 1936;* Seven Guitars *(1995), set in 1938;* Fences *(1983), set in 1957; and* Two Trains Running *(1989), set in 1969. As critic John Lahr acknowledges, "No other theatrical testament to African American life has been so popular or so poetic or so penetrating." Wilson's plays have earned him two Pulitzer Prizes, three New York Drama Critics Circle Awards, one Tony Award, and one American Theater Critics' Association Award.*

Wilson has dedicated himself as a playwright to writing a new history of black America, celebrating his people's African roots and humble beginnings instead of denying them. Such plays as Fences *are well-crafted dramas in the tradition of the European realistic theater, but Wilson also introduces elements of spontaneity into the stage action to express what he regards as the creative genius for improvisation in black culture. In the final scene of* Fences, *for example, Troy's brother Gabriel blows his trumpet and dances to open the gates of heaven so that Troy's spirit can enter, in an act Wilson describes as "a dance of atavistic signature and ritual." Wilson's inspiration for* Fences *was a collage by the African-American painter Romare Bearden called "Continuities," which depicts a man standing in his yard with a baby in his arms. When asked by television personality Bill Moyers if he ever grew "weary of thinking black, writing black, being asked questions about blacks," Wilson patiently replied, "How can one grow weary of that? Whites don't get tired of thinking white or being who they are. . . . Black is not limiting. There's no idea in the world that is not contained by black life. I could write forever about the black experience in America."*

RELATED COMMENTARIES: *Frank Rich, "Review of* Fences,*" page 1990; August Wilson, "Interview with David Savran," page 2012.*

AUGUST WILSON

Fences

1987

CHARACTERS

TROY MAXSON
JIM BONO, *Troy's friend*
ROSE, *Troy's wife*
LYONS, *Troy's oldest son by previous marriage*
GABRIEL, *Troy's brother*
CORY, *Troy and Rose's son*
RAYNELL, *Troy's daughter*

SETTING: *The setting is the yard which fronts the only entrance to the Maxson household, an ancient two-story brick house set back off a small alley in a big-city neighborhood.*

The entrance to the house is gained by two or three steps leading to a wooden porch badly in need of paint.

A relatively recent addition to the house and running its full width, the porch lacks congruence. It is a sturdy porch with a flat roof. One or two chairs of dubious value sit at one end where the kitchen window opens onto the porch. An old-fashioned icebox stands silent guard at the opposite end.

The yard is a small dirt yard, partially fenced, except for the last scene, with a wooden sawhorse, a pile of lumber, and other fence-building equipment set off to the side. Opposite is a tree from which hangs a ball made of rags. A baseball bat leans against the tree. Two oil drums serve as garbage receptacles and sit near the house at right to complete the setting.

THE PLAY: *Near the turn of the century, the destitute of Europe sprang on the city with tenacious claws and an honest and solid dream. The city devoured them. They swelled its belly until it burst into a thousand furnaces and sewing machines, a thousand butcher shops and bakers' ovens, a thousand churches and hospitals and funeral parlors and money-lenders. The city grew. It nourished itself and offered each man a partnership limited only by his talent, his guile, and his willingness and capacity for hard work. For the immigrants of Europe, a dream dared and won true.*

The descendants of African slaves were offered no such welcome or participation. They came from places called the Carolinas and the Virginias, Georgia, Alabama, Mississippi, and Tennessee. They came strong, eager, searching. The city rejected them and they fled and settled along the riverbanks and under bridges in shallow, ramshackle houses made of sticks and tarpaper. They collected rags and wood. They sold the use of their muscles and their bodies. They cleaned houses and washed clothes, they shined shoes, and in quiet desperation and vengeful pride, they stole, and lived in pursuit of their own dream. That they could breathe free, finally, and stand to meet life with the force of dignity and whatever eloquence the heart could call upon.

By 1957, the hard-won victories of the European immigrants had solidified the industrial might of America. War had been confronted and won with new energies that used loyalty and patriotism as its fuel. Life was rich, full, and flourishing. The Milwaukee Braves won the World Series, and the hot winds of change that would make the sixties a turbulent, racing, dangerous, and provocative decade had not yet begun to blow full.

ACT I

SCENE I: *It is 1957. Troy and Bono enter the yard, engaged in conversation. Troy is fifty-three years old, a large man with thick, heavy hands; it is this largeness that he strives to fill out and make an accommodation with. Together with his blackness, his largeness informs his sensibilities and the choices he has made in his life.*

Of the two men, Bono is obviously the follower. His commitment to their friendship of thirty-odd years is rooted in his admiration of Troy's honesty, capacity for hard work, and his strength, which Bono seeks to emulate.

It is Friday night, payday, and the one night of the week the two men engage in a ritual of talk and drink. Troy is usually the most talkative and at times he can be crude and almost vulgar, though he is capable of rising to profound heights of expression. The men carry lunch buckets and wear or carry burlap aprons and are dressed in clothes suitable to their jobs as garbage collectors.

BONO: Troy, you ought to stop that lying!

TROY: I ain't lying! The nigger had a watermelon this big. (*He indicates with his hands.*) Talking about . . . "What watermelon, Mr. Rand?" I liked to fell out! "What watermelon, Mr. Rand?" . . . And it sitting there big as life.

BONO: What did Mr. Rand say?

TROY: Ain't said nothing. Figure if the nigger too dumb to know he carrying a watermelon, he wasn't gonna get much sense out of him. Trying to hide that great big old watermelon under his coat. Afraid to let the white man see him carry it home.

BONO: I'm like you . . . I ain't got no time for them kind of people.

TROY: Now what he look like getting mad cause he see the man from the union talking to Mr. Rand?

BONO: He come to me talking about . . . "Maxson gonna get us fired." I told him to get away from me with that. He walked away from me calling you a troublemaker. What Mr. Rand say?

TROY: Ain't said nothing. He told me to go down the Commissioner's office next Friday. They called me down there to see them.

BONO: Well, as long as you got your complaint filed, they can't fire you. That's what one of them white fellows tell me.

TROY: I ain't worried about them firing me. They gonna fire me cause I asked a question? That's all I did. I went to Mr. Rand and asked him, "Why? Why you got the white mens driving and the colored lifting?" Told him "what's the matter, don't I count? You think only white fellows got sense enough to drive a truck. That ain't no paper job! Hell, anybody can drive a truck. How come you got all whites driving and the colored lifting?" He told me "take it to the union." Well, hell, that's what I done! Now they wanna come up with this pack of lies.

BONO: I told Brownie if the man come and ask him any questions . . . just tell the truth! It ain't nothing but something they done trumped up on you cause you filed a complaint on them.

TROY: Brownie don't understand nothing. All I want them to do is change the job description. Give everybody a chance to drive the truck. Brownie can't see that. He ain't got that much sense.

BONO: How you figure he be making out with that gal be up at Taylors' all the time . . . that Alberta gal?

TROY: Same as you and me. Getting just as much as we is. Which is to say nothing.

BONO: It is, huh? I figure you doing a little better than me . . . and I ain't saying what I'm doing.

TROY: Aw, nigger, took here . . . I know you. If you had got anywhere near that gal, twenty minutes later you be looking to tell somebody. And the first one you gonna tell . . . that you gonna want to brag to . . . is gonna be me.

BONO: I ain't saying that. I see where you be eyeing her.

TROY: I eye all the women. I don't miss nothing. Don't never let nobody tell you Troy Maxson don't eye the women.

BONO: You been doing more than eyeing her. You done bought her a drink or two.

TROY: Hell yeah, I bought her a drink! What that mean? I bought you one, too. What that mean cause I buy her a drink? I'm just being polite.

BONO: It's all right to buy her one drink. That's what you call being polite. But when you wanna be buying two or three . . . that's what you call eyeing her.

TROY: Look here, as long as you known me . . . you ever known me to chase after women?

BONO: Hell yeah! Long as I done known you. You forgetting I knew you when.

TROY: Naw, I'm talking about since I been married to Rose?

BONO: Oh, not since you been married to Rose. Now, that's the truth, there. I can say that.

TROY: All right then! Case closed.

BONO: I see you be walking up around Alberta's house. You supposed to be at Taylors' and you be walking up around there.

TROY: What you watching where I'm walking for? I ain't watching after you.

BONO: I seen you walking around there more than once.

TROY: Hell, you liable to see me walking anywhere! That don't mean nothing cause you see me walking around there.

BONO: Where she come from anyway? She just kinda showed up one day.

TROY: Tallahassee. You can look at her and tell she one of them Florida gals. They got some big healthy women down there. Grow them right up out the ground. Got a little bit of Indian in her. Most of them niggers down in Florida got some Indian in them.

BONO: I don't know about that Indian part. But she damn sure big and healthy. Woman wear some big stockings. Got them great big old legs and hips as wide as the Mississippi River.

TROY: Legs don't mean nothing. You don't do nothing but push them out of the way. But them hips cushion the ride!

BONO: Troy, you ain't got no sense.

TROY: It's the truth! Like you riding on Goodyears!

Rose enters from the house. She is ten years younger than Troy, her devotion to him stems from her recognition of the possibilities of her life without him: a succession of abusive men and their babies, a life of partying and running the streets, the Church, or aloneness with its attendant pain and frustration. She recognizes Troy's spirit as a fine and illuminating one and she either ignores or forgives his faults, only some of which she recognizes. Though she doesn't drink, her presence is an integral part of the Friday night rituals. She alternates between the porch and the kitchen, where supper preparations are under way.

ROSE: What you all out here getting into?

TROY: What you worried about what we getting into for? This is men talk, woman.

ROSE: What I care what you all talking about? Bono, you gonna stay for supper?

BONO: No, I thank you, Rose. But Lucille say she cooking up a pot of pigfeet.

TROY: Pigfeet! Hell, I'm going home with you! Might even stay the night if you got some pigfeet. You got something in there to top them pigfeet, Rose?

ROSE: I'm cooking up some chicken. I got some chicken and collard greens.

TROY: Well, go on back in the house and let me and Bono finish what we was talking about. This is men talk. I got some talk for you later. You know what kind of talk I mean. You go on and powder it up.

ROSE: Troy Maxson, don't you start that now!

TROY (*puts his arm around her*): Aw, woman . . . come here. Look here, Bono . . . when I met this woman . . . I got out that place, say, "Hitch up my pony, saddle up my mare . . . there's a woman out there for me somewhere. I looked here. Looked there. Saw Rose and latched on to her." I latched on to her and told her — I'm gonna tell you the truth — I told her, "Baby, I don't wanna marry, I just wanna be your man." Rose told me . . . tell him what you told me, Rose.

ROSE: I told him if he wasn't the marrying kind, then move out the way so the marrying kind could find me.

TROY: That's what she told me. "Nigger, you in my way. You blocking the view! Move out the way so I can find me a husband." I thought it over two or three days. Come back —

ROSE: Ain't no two or three days nothing. You was back the same night.

TROY: Come back, told her . . . "Okay, baby . . . but I'm gonna buy me a banty rooster and put him out there in the backyard . . . and when he see a stranger come, he'll flap his wings and crow . . ." Look here, Bono, I could watch the front door by myself . . . it was that back door I was worried about.

ROSE: Troy, you ought not talk like that. Troy ain't doing nothing but telling a lie.

TROY: Only thing is . . . when we first got married . . . forget the rooster . . . we ain't had no yard!

BONO: I hear you tell it. Me and Lucille was staying down there on Logan Street. Had two rooms with the outhouse in the back. I ain't mind the outhouse none. But when that goddamn wind blow through there in the winter . . . that's what I'm talking about! To this day I wonder why in the hell I ever stayed down there for six long years. But see, I didn't know I could do no better. I thought only white folks had inside toilets and things.

ROSE: There's a lot of people don't know they can do no better than they doing now. That's just something you got to learn. A lot of folks still shop at Bella's.

TROY: Ain't nothing wrong with shopping at Bella's. She got fresh food.

ROSE: I ain't said nothing about if she got fresh food. I'm talking about what she charge. She charge ten cents more than the A&P.

TROY: The A&P ain't never done nothing for me. I spends my money where I'm treated right. I go down to Bella, say, "I need a loaf of bread, I'll pay you Friday." She give it to me. What sense that make when I got money to go and spend it somewhere else and ignore the person who done right by me? That ain't in the Bible.

ROSE: We ain't talking about what's in the Bible. What sense it make to shop there when she overcharge?

TROY: You shop where you want to. I'll do my shopping where the people been good to me.

ROSE: Well, I don't think it's right for her to overcharge. That's all I was saying.

BONO: Look here . . . I got to get on. Lucille going be raising all kind of hell.

TROY: Where you going, nigger? We ain't finished this pint. Come here, finish this pint.

BONO: Well, hell, I am . . . if you ever turn the bottle loose.

TROY (*hands him the bottle*): The only thing I say about the A&P is I'm glad Cory got that job down there. Help him take care of his school clothes and things. Gabe done moved out and things getting tight around here. He got that job. . . . He can start to look out for himself.

ROSE: Cory done went and got recruited by a college football team.

TROY: I told that boy about that football stuff. The white man ain't gonna let him get nowhere with that football. I told him when he first come to me with it. Now you come telling me he done went and got more tied up in it. He ought to go and get recruited in how to fix cars or something where he can make a living.

ROSE: He ain't talking about making no living playing football. It's just something the boys in school do. They gonna send a recruiter by to talk to you. He'll tell you he ain't talking about making no living playing football. It's a honor to be recruited.

TROY: It ain't gonna get him nowhere. Bono'll tell you that.

BONO: If he be like you in the sports . . . he's gonna be all right. Ain't but two men ever played baseball as good as you. That's Babe Ruth and Josh Gibson.° Them's the only two men ever hit more home runs than you.

TROY: What it ever get me? Ain't got a pot to piss in or a window to throw it out of.

ROSE: Times have changed since you was playing baseball, Troy. That was before the war. Times have changed a lot since then.

TROY: How in hell they done changed?

ROSE: They got lots of colored boys playing ball now. Baseball and football.

BONO: You right about that, Rose. Times have changed, Troy. You just come along too early.

TROY: There ought not never have been no time called too early! Now you take that fellow . . . what's that fellow they had playing right field for the Yankees back then? You know who I'm talking about, Bono. Used to play right field for the Yankees.

ROSE: Selkirk?

TROY: Selkirk! That's it! Man batting .269, understand? .269. What kind of sense that make? I was hitting .432 with thirty-seven home runs! Man batting .269 and playing right field for the Yankees! I saw Josh Gibson's daughter yesterday. She walking around with raggedy shoes on her feet. Now I bet you Selkirk's daughter ain't walking around with raggedy shoes on her feet! I bet you that!

Josh Gibson: Powerful black baseball player (1911–1947), known in the 1930s as the Babe Ruth of the Negro leagues.

ROSE: They got a lot of colored baseball players now. Jackie Robinson was the first. Folks had to wait for Jackie Robinson.

TROY: I done seen a hundred niggers play baseball better than Jackie Robinson. Hell, I know some teams Jackie Robinson couldn't even make! What you talking about Jackie Robinson. Jackie Robinson wasn't nobody. I'm talking about if you could play ball then they ought to have let you play. Don't care what color you were. Come telling me I come along too early. If you could play . . . then they ought to have let you play.

Troy takes a long drink from the bottle.

ROSE: You gonna drink yourself to death. You don't need to be drinking like that.

TROY: Death ain't nothing. I done seen him. Done wrassled with him. You can't tell me nothing about death. Death ain't nothing but a fastball on the outside corner. And you know what I'll do to that! Lookee here, Bono . . . am I lying? You get one of them fastballs, about waist high, over the outside corner of the plate where you can get the meat of the bat on it . . . and good god! You can kiss it goodbye. Now, am I lying?

BONO: Naw, you telling the truth there. I seen you do it.

TROY: If I'm lying . . . that 450 feet worth of lying! (*Pause.*) That's all death is to me. A fastball on the outside corner.

ROSE: I don't know why you want to get on talking about death.

TROY: Ain't nothing wrong with talking about death. That's part of life. Everybody gonna die. You gonna die, I'm gonna die. Bono's gonna die. Hell, we all gonna die.

ROSE: But you ain't got to talk about it. I don't like to talk about it.

TROY: You the one brought it up. Me and Bono was talking about baseball . . . you tell me I'm gonna drink myself to death. Ain't that right, Bono? You know I don't drink this but one night out of the week. That's Friday night. I'm gonna drink just enough to where I can handle it. Then I cuts it loose. I leave it alone. So don't you worry about me drinking myself to death. 'Cause I ain't worried about Death. I done seen him. I done wrestled with him.

Look here, Bono . . . I looked up one day and Death was marching straight at me. Like Soldiers on Parade! The Army of Death was marching straight at me. The middle of July, 1941. It got real cold just like it be winter. It seem like Death himself reached out and touched me on the shoulder. He touch me just like I touch you. I got cold as ice and Death standing there grinning at me.

ROSE: Troy, why don't you hush that talk.

TROY: I say . . . What you want, Mr. Death? You be wanting me? You done brought your army to be getting me? I looked him dead in the eye. I wasn't fearing nothing. I was ready to tangle. Just like I'm ready to tangle now. The Bible say be ever vigilant. That's why I don't get but so drunk. I got to keep watch.

ROSE: Troy was right down there in Mercy Hospital. You remember he had pneumonia? Laying there with a fever talking plumb out of his head.

TROY: Death standing there staring at me . . . carrying that sickle in his hand. Finally he say, "You want bound over for another year?" See, just like that . . . "You want bound over for another year?" I told him, "Bound over hell! Let's settle this now!"

It seem like he kinda fell back when I said that, and all the cold went out of me. I reached down and grabbed that sickle and threw it just as far as I could throw it . . . and me and him commenced to wrestling.

We wrestled for three days and three nights. I can't say where I found the strength from. Every time it seemed like he was gonna get the best of me, I'd reach way down deep inside myself and find the strength to do him one better.

ROSE: Every time Troy tell that story he find different ways to tell it. Different things to make up about it.

TROY: I ain't making up nothing. I'm telling you the facts of what happened. I wrestled with Death for three days and three nights and I'm standing here to tell you about it. (*Pause.*) All right. At the end of the third night we done weakened each other to where we can't hardly move. Death stood up, throwed on his robe . . . had him a white robe with a hood on it. He throwed on that robe and went off to look for his sickle. Say, "I'll be back." Just like that. "I'll be back." I told him, say, "Yeah, but . . . you gonna have to find me!" I wasn't no fool. I wan't going looking for him. Death ain't nothing to play with. And I know he's gonna get me. I know I got to join his army . . . his camp followers. But as long as I keep my strength and see him coming . . . as long as I keep up my vigilance . . . he's gonna have to fight to get me. I ain't going easy.

BONO: Well, look here, since you got to keep up your vigilance . . . let me have the bottle.

TROY: Aw hell, I shouldn't have told you that part. I should have left out that part.

ROSE: Troy be talking that stuff and half the time don't even know what he be talking about.

TROY: Bono know me better than that.

BONO: That's right. I know you. I know you got some Uncle Remus° in your blood. You got more stories than the devil got sinners.

TROY: Aw hell, I done seen him too! Done talked with the devil.

ROSE: Troy, don't nobody wanna be hearing all that stuff.

Lyons enters the yard from the street. Thirty-four years old, Troy's son by a previous marriage, he sports a neatly trimmed goatee, sport coat, white shirt, tieless and buttoned at the collar. Though he fancies himself a musician, he is more caught up in the rituals and "idea" of being a musician than in the actual practice of the music. He has come to borrow money from Troy, and while he knows he will be successful, he is uncertain as to what extent his lifestyle will be held up to scrutiny and ridicule.

Uncle Remus: Created by Joel Chandler Harris (1848–1908), Uncle Remus is a fictional character who recounts traditional black folktales.

LYONS: Hey, Pop.

TROY: What you come "Hey, Popping" me for?

LYONS: How you doing, Rose? (*He kisses her.*) Mr. Bono. How you doing?

BONO: Hey, Lyons . . . how you been?

TROY: He must have been doing all right. I ain't seen him around here last week.

ROSE: Troy, leave your boy alone. He come by to see you and you wanna start all that nonsense.

TROY: I ain't bothering Lyons. (*Offers him the bottle.*) Here . . . get you a drink. We got an understanding. I know why he come by to see me and he know I know.

LYONS: Come on, Pop . . . I just stopped by to say hi . . . see how you was doing.

TROY: You ain't stopped by yesterday.

ROSE: You gonna stay for supper, Lyons? I got some chicken cooking in the oven.

LYONS: No, Rose . . . thanks. I was just in the neighborhood and thought I'd stop by for a minute.

TROY: You was in the neighborhood all right, nigger. You telling the truth there. You was in the neighborhood cause it's my payday.

LYONS: Well, hell, since you mentioned it . . . let me have ten dollars.

TROY: I'll be damned! I'll die and go to hell and play blackjack with the devil before I give you ten dollars.

BONO: That's what I wanna know about . . . that devil you done seen.

LYONS: What . . . Pop done seen the devil? You too much, Pops.

TROY: Yeah, I done seen him. Talked to him too!

ROSE: You ain't seen no devil. I done told you that man ain't had nothing to do with the devil. Anything you can't understand, you want to call it the devil.

TROY: Look here, Bono . . . I went down to see Hertzberger about some furniture. Got three rooms for two-ninety-eight. That what it say on the radio. "Three rooms . . . two-ninety-eight." Even made up a little song about it. Go down there . . . man tell me I can't get no credit. I'm working every day and can't get no credit. What to do? I got an empty house with some raggedy furniture in it. Cory ain't got no bed. He's sleeping on a pile of rags on the floor. Working every day and can't get no credit. Come back here — Rose'll tell you — madder than hell. Sit down . . . try to figure what I'm gonna do. Come a knock on the door. Ain't been living here but three days. Who know I'm here? Open the door . . . devil standing there bigger than life. White fellow . . . got on good clothes and everything. Standing there with a clipboard in his hand. I ain't had to say nothing. First words come out of his mouth was . . . "I understand you need some furniture and can't get no credit." I liked to fell over. He say, "I'll give you all the credit you want, but you got to pay the interest on it." I told him, "Give me three rooms worth and charge whatever you want." Next day a truck pulled up here and two men unloaded them three rooms. Man what drove the truck give me a book. Say send ten dollars, first of every month to the address in the book and everything will be all right. Say if I miss a payment the devil was coming back and it'll be hell to pay. That was fifteen years ago. To this day . . . the first of the month I send my ten dollars, Rose'll tell you.

ROSE: Troy lying.

TROY: I ain't never seen that man since. Now you tell me who else that could have been but the devil? I ain't sold my soul or nothing like that, you understand. Naw, I wouldn't have truck with the devil about nothing like that. I got my furniture and pays my ten dollars the first of the month just like clockwork.

BONO: How long you say you been paying this ten dollars a month?

TROY: Fifteen years!

BONO: Hell, ain't you finished paying for it yet? How much the man done charged you?

TROY: Ah hell, I done paid for it. I done paid for it ten times over! The fact is I'm scared to stop paying it.

ROSE: Troy lying. We got that furniture from Mr. Glickman. He ain't paying no ten dollars a month to nobody.

TROY: Aw hell, woman. Bono know I ain't that big a fool.

LYONS: I was just getting ready to say . . . I know where there's a bridge for sale.

TROY: Look here, I'll tell you this . . . it don't matter to me if he was the devil. It don't matter if the devil give credit. Somebody has got to give it.

ROSE: It ought to matter. You going around talking about having truck with the devil . . . God's the one you gonna have to answer to. He's the one gonna be at the Judgment.

LYONS: Yeah, well, look here, Pop . . . let me have that ten dollars. I'll give it back to you. Bonnie got a job working at the hospital.

TROY: What I tell you, Bono? The only time I see this nigger is when he wants something. That's the only time I see him.

LYONS: Come on, Pop, Mr. Bono don't want to hear all that. Let me have the ten dollars. I told you Bonnie working.

TROY: What that mean to me? "Bonnie working." I don't care if she working. Go ask her for the ten dollars if she working. Talking about "Bonnie working." Why ain't you working?

LYONS: Aw, Pop, you know I can't find no decent job. Where am I gonna get a job at? You know I can't get no job.

TROY: I told you I know some people down there. I can get you on the rubbish if you want to work. I told you that the last time you came by here asking me for something.

LYONS: Naw, Pop . . . thanks. That ain't for me. I don't wanna be carrying nobody's rubbish. I don't wanna be punching nobody's time clock.

TROY: What's the matter, you too good to carry people's rubbish? Where you think that ten dollars you talking about come from? I'm just supposed to haul people's rubbish and give my money to you cause you too lazy to work. You too lazy to work and wanna know why you ain't got what I got.

ROSE: What hospital Bonnie working at? Mercy?

LYONS: She's down at Passavant working in the laundry.

TROY: I ain't got nothing as it is. I give you that ten dollars and I got to eat beans the rest of the week. Naw . . . you ain't getting no ten dollars here.

LYONS: You ain't got to be eating no beans. I don't know why you wanna say that.

TROY: I ain't got no extra money. Gabe done moved over to Miss Pearl's paying her the rent and things done got tight around here. I can't afford to be giving you every payday.

LYONS: I ain't asked you to give me nothing. I asked you to loan me ten dollars. I know you got ten dollars.

TROY: Yeah, I got it. You know why I got it? Cause I don't throw my money away out there in the streets. You living the fast life . . . wanna be a musician . . . running around in them clubs and things . . . then, you learn to take care of yourself. You ain't gonna find me going and asking nobody for nothing. I done spent too many years without.

LYONS: You and me is two different people, Pop.

TROY: I done learned my mistake and learned to do what's right by it. You still trying to get something for nothing. Life don't owe you nothing. You owe it to yourself. Ask Bono. He'll tell you I'm right.

LYONS: You got your way of dealing with the world . . . I got mine. The only thing that matters to me is music.

TROY: Yeah, I can see that! It don't matter how you gonna eat . . . where your next dollar is coming from. You telling the truth there.

LYONS: I know I got to eat. But I got to live too. I need something that gonna help me to get out of the bed in the morning. Make me feel like I belong in the world. I don't bother nobody. I just stay with my music cause that's the only way I can find to live in the world. Otherwise there ain't no telling what I might do. Now I don't come criticizing you and how you live. I just come by to ask you for ten dollars. I don't wanna hear all that about how I live.

TROY: Boy, your mamma did a hell of a job raising you.

LYONS: You can't change me, Pop. I'm thirty-four years old. If you wanted to change me, you should have been there when I was growing up. I come by to see you . . . ask for ten dollars and you want to talk about how I was raised. You don't know nothing about how I was raised.

ROSE: Let the boy have ten dollars, Troy.

TROY (*to Lyons*): What the hell you looking at me for? I ain't got no ten dollars. You know what I do with my money. (*To Rose.*) Give him ten dollars if you want him to have it.

ROSE: I will. Just as soon as you turn it loose.

TROY (*handing Rose the money*): There it is. Seventy-six dollars and forty-two cents. You see this, Bono? Now, I ain't gonna get but six of that back.

ROSE: You ought to stop telling that lie. Here, Lyons. (*She hands him the money.*)

LYONS: Thanks, Rose. Look . . . I got to run . . . I'll see you later.

TROY: Wait a minute. You gonna say, "thanks, Rose" and ain't gonna look to see where she got that ten dollars from? See how they do me, Bono?

LYONS: I know she got it from you, Pop. Thanks. I'll give it back to you.

TROY: There he go telling another lie. Time I see that ten dollars . . . he'll be owing me thirty more.

LYONS: See you, Mr. Bono.

BONO: Take care, Lyons!

LYONS: Thanks, Pop. I'll see you again.

Lyons exits the yard.

TROY: I don't know why he don't go and get him a decent job and take care of that woman he got.

BONO: He'll be all right, Troy. The boy is still young.

TROY: The *boy* is thirty-four years old.

ROSE: Let's not get off into all that.

BONO: Look here . . . I got to be going. I got to be getting on. Lucille gonna be waiting.

TROY (*puts his arm around Rose*): See this woman, Bono? I love this woman. I love this woman so much it hurts. I love her so much . . . I done run out of ways of loving her. So I got to go back to basics. Don't you come by my house Monday morning talking about time to go to work . . . 'cause I'm still gonna be stroking!

ROSE: Troy! Stop it now!

BONO: I ain't paying him no mind, Rose. That ain't nothing but gin-talk. Go on, Troy. I'll see you Monday.

TROY: Don't you come by my house, nigger! I done told you what I'm gonna be doing.

The lights go down to black.

SCENE II: *The lights come up on Rose hanging up clothes. She hums and sings softly to herself. It is the following morning.*

ROSE (*sings*): Jesus, be a fence all around me every day
Jesus, I want you to protect me as I travel on my way.
Jesus, be a fence all around me every day.

Troy enters from the house.

Jesus, I want you to protect me
As I travel on my way.
(*To Troy.*) 'Morning. You ready for breakfast? I can fix it soon as I finish hanging up these clothes.

TROY: I got the coffee on. That'll be all right. I'll just drink some of that this morning.

ROSE: That 651 hit yesterday. That's the second time this month. Miss Pearl hit for a dollar . . . seem like those that need the least always get lucky. Poor folks can't get nothing.

TROY: Them numbers don't know nobody. I don't know why you fool with them. You and Lyons both.

ROSE: It's something to do.

TROY: You ain't doing nothing but throwing your money away.

ROSE: Troy, you know I don't play foolishly. I just play a nickel here and a nickel there.

TROY: That's two nickels you done thrown away.

ROSE: Now I hit sometimes . . . that makes up for it. It always comes in handy when I do hit. I don't hear you complaining then.

TROY: I ain't complaining now. I just say it's foolish. Trying to guess out of six hundred ways which way the number gonna come. If I had all the money niggers, these Negroes, throw away on numbers for one week — just one week — I'd be a rich man.

ROSE: Well, you wishing and calling it foolish ain't gonna stop folks from playing numbers. That's one thing for sure. Besides . . . some good things come from playing numbers. Look where Pope done bought him that restaurant off of numbers.

TROY: I can't stand niggers like that. Man ain't had two dimes to rub together. He walking around with his shoes all run over bumming money for cigarettes. All right. Got lucky there and hit the numbers . . .

ROSE: Troy, I know all about it.

TROY: Had good sense, I'll say that for him. He ain't throwed his money away. I seen niggers hit the numbers and go through two thousand dollars in four days. Man bought him that restaurant down there . . . fixed it up real nice . . . and then didn't want nobody to come in it! A Negro go in there and can't get no kind of service. I seen a white fellow come in there and order a bowl of stew. Pope picked all the meat out the pot for him. Man ain't had nothing but a bowl of meat! Negro come behind him and ain't got nothing but the potatoes and carrots. Talking about what numbers do for people, you picked a wrong example. Ain't done nothing but make a worser fool out of him than he was before.

ROSE: Troy, you ought to stop worrying about what happened at work yesterday.

TROY: I ain't worried. Just told me to be down there at the Commissioner's office on Friday. Everybody think they gonna fire me. I ain't worried about them firing me. You ain't got to worry about that. (*Pause.*) Where's Cory? Cory in the house? (*Calls.*) Cory?

ROSE: He gone out.

TROY: Out, huh? He gone out 'cause he know I want him to help me with this fence. I know how he is. That boy scared of work.

Gabriel enters. He comes halfway down the alley and, hearing Troy's voice, stops.

TROY (*continues*): He ain't done a lick of work in his life.

ROSE: He had to go to football practice. Coach wanted them to get in a little extra practice before the season start.

TROY: I got his practice . . . running out of here before he get his chores done.

ROSE: Troy, what is wrong with you this morning? Don't nothing set right with you. Go on back in there and go to bed . . . get up on the other side.

TROY: Why something got to be wrong with me? I ain't said nothing wrong with me.

ROSE: You got something to say about everything. First it's the numbers . . . then it's the way the man runs his restaurant . . . then you done got on Cory. What's it gonna be next? Take a look up there and see if the weather suits you . . . or is it gonna be how you gonna put up the fence with the clothes hanging in the yard.

TROY: You hit the nail on the head then.

ROSE: I know you like I know the back of my hand. Go on in there and get you some coffee . . . see if that straighten you up. 'Cause you ain't right this morning.

Troy starts into the house and sees Gabriel. Gabriel starts singing. Troy's brother, he is seven years younger than Troy. Injured in World War II, he has a metal plate in his head. He carries an old trumpet tied around his waist and believes with every fiber of his being that he is the Archangel Gabriel. He carries a chipped basket with an assortment of discarded fruits and vegetables he has picked up in the strip district and which be attempts to sell.

GABRIEL (*singing*): Yes, ma'am, I got plums
You ask me how I sell them
Oh ten cents apiece
Three for a quarter
Come and buy now
'Cause I'm here today
And tomorrow I'll be gone

Gabriel enters.

Hey, Rose!

ROSE: How you doing, Gabe?

GABRIEL: There's Troy . . . Hey, Troy!

TROY: Hey, Gabe.

Exit into kitchen.

ROSE (*to Gabriel*): What you got there?

GABRIEL: You know what I got, Rose. I got fruits and vegetables.

ROSE (*looking in basket*): Where's all these plums you talking about?

GABRIEL: I ain't got no plums today, Rose. I was just singing that. Have some tomorrow. Put me in a big order for plums. Have enough plums tomorrow for St. Peter and everybody.

Troy reenters from kitchen, crosses to steps.

(*To Rose.*) Troy's mad at me.

TROY: I ain't mad at you. What I got to be mad at you about? You ain't done nothing to me.

GABRIEL: I just moved over to Miss Pearl's to keep out from in your way. I ain't mean no harm by it.

TROY: Who said anything about that? I ain't said anything about that.

GABRIEL: You ain't mad at me, is you?

TROY: Naw . . . I ain't mad at you, Gabe. If I was mad at you I'd tell you about it.

GABRIEL: Got me two rooms. In the basement. Got my own door too. Wanna see my key? (*He holds up a key.*) That's my own key! Ain't nobody else got a key like that. That's my key! My two rooms!

TROY: Well, that's good, Gabe. You got your own key . . . that's good.

ROSE: You hungry, Gabe? I was just fixing to cook Troy his breakfast.

GABRIEL: I'll take some biscuits. You got some biscuits? Did you know when I was in heaven . . . every morning me and St. Peter would sit down by the gate and eat some big fat biscuits? Oh, yeah! We had us a good time. We'd sit there and eat us them biscuits and then St. Peter would go off to sleep and tell me to wake him up when it's time to open the gates for the judgment.

ROSE: Well, come on . . . I'll make up a batch of biscuits.

Rose exits into the house.

GABRIEL: Troy . . . St. Peter got your name in the book. I seen it. It say . . . Troy Maxson. I say . . . I know him! He got the same name like what I got. That's my brother!

TROY: How many times you gonna tell me that, Gabe?

GABRIEL: Ain't got my name in the book. Don't have to have my name. I done died and went to heaven. He got your name though. One morning St. Peter was looking at his book . . . marking it up for the judgment . . . and he let me see your name. Got it in there under M. Got Rose's name . . . I ain't seen it like I seen yours . . . but I know it's in there. He got a great big book. Got everybody's name what was ever been born. That's what he told me. But I seen your name. Seen it with my own eyes.

TROY: Go on in the house there. Rose going to fix you something to eat.

GABRIEL: Oh, I ain't hungry. I done had breakfast with Aunt Jemimah. She come by and cooked me up a whole mess of flapjacks. Remember how we used to eat them flapjacks?

TROY: Go on in the house and get you something to eat now.

GABRIEL: I got to go sell my plums. I done sold some tomatoes. Got me two quarters. Wanna see? (*He shows Troy his quarters.*) I'm gonna save them and buy me a new horn so St. Peter can hear me when it's time to open the gates. (*Gabriel stops suddenly. Listens.*) Hear that? That's the hellhounds. I got to chase them out of here. Go on get out of here! Get out! (*Gabriel exits singing.*)
Better get ready for the judgment
Better get ready for the judgment
My Lord is coming down

Rose enters from the house.

TROY: He gone off somewhere.

GABRIEL (*offstage*): Better get ready for the judgment
Better get ready for the judgment morning
Better get ready for the judgment
My God is coming down

ROSE: He ain't eating right. Miss Pearl say she can't get him to eat nothing.

TROY: What you want me to do about it, Rose? I done did everything I can for the man. I can't make him get well. Man got half his head blown away . . . what you expect?

ROSE: Seem like something ought to be done to help him.

TROY: Man don't bother nobody. He just mixed up from that metal plate he got in his head. Ain't no sense for him to go back into the hospital.

ROSE: Least he be eating right. They can help him take care of himself.

TROY: Don't nobody wanna be locked up, Rose. What you wanna lock him up for? Man go over there and fight the war . . . messin' around with them Japs, get half his head blown off . . . and they give him a lousy three thousand dollars. And I had to swoop down on that.

ROSE: Is you fixing to go into that again?

TROY: That's the only way I got a roof over my head . . . cause of that metal plate.

ROSE: Ain't no sense you blaming yourself for nothing. Gabe wasn't in no condition to manage that money. You done what was right by him. Can't nobody say you ain't done what was right by him. Look how long you took care of him . . . till he wanted to have his own place and move over there with Miss Pearl.

TROY: That ain't what I'm saying, woman! I'm just stating the facts. If my brother didn't have that metal plate in his head . . . I wouldn't have a pot to piss in or a window to throw it out of. And I'm fifty-three years old. Now see if you can understand that!

Troy gets up from the porch and starts to exit the yard.

ROSE: Where you going off to? You been running out of here every Saturday for weeks. I thought you was gonna work on this fence?

TROY: I'm gonna walk down to Taylors'. Listen to the ball game. I'll be back in a bit. I'll work on it when I get back.

He exits the yard. The lights go to black.

SCENE III: *The lights come up on the yard. It is four hours later. Rose is taking down the clothes from the line. Cory enters carrying his football equipment.*

ROSE: Your daddy like to had a fit with you running out of here this morning without doing your chores.

CORY: I told you I had to go to practice.

ROSE: He say you were supposed to help him with this fence.

CORY: He been saying that the last four or five Saturdays, and then he don't never do nothing but go down to Taylors'. Did you tell him about the recruiter?

ROSE: Yeah, I told him.

CORY: What he say?

ROSE: He ain't said nothing too much. You get in there and get started on your chores before he gets back. Go on and scrub down them steps before he gets back here hollering and carrying on.

CORY: I'm hungry. What you got to eat, Mama?

ROSE: Go on and get started on your chores. I got some meat loaf in there. Go on and make you a sandwich . . . and don't leave no mess in there.

Cory exits into the house. Rose continues to take down the clothes. Troy enters the yard and sneaks up and grabs her from behind.

Troy! Go on, now. You liked to scared me to death. What was the score of the game? Lucille had me on the phone and I couldn't keep up with it.

TROY: What I care about the game? Come here, woman. (*He tries to kiss her.*)

ROSE: I thought you went down Taylors' to listen to the game. Go on, Troy! You supposed to be putting up this fence.

TROY (*attempting to kiss her again*): I'll put it up when I finish with what is at hand.

ROSE: Go on, Troy. I ain't studying you.

TROY (*chasing after her*): I'm studying you . . . fixing to do my homework!

ROSE: Troy, you better leave me alone.

TROY: Where's Cory? That boy brought his butt home yet?

ROSE: He's in the house doing his chores.

TROY (*calling*): Cory! Get your butt out here, boy!

Rose exits into the house with the laundry. Troy goes over to the pile of wood, picks up a board, and starts sawing. Cory enters from the house.

TROY: You just now coming in here from leaving this morning?

CORY: Yeah, I had to go to football practice.

TROY: Yeah, what?

CORY: Yessir.

TROY: I ain't but two seconds off you noway. The garbage sitting in there overflowing . . . you ain't done none of your chores . . . and you come in here talking about "Yeah."

CORY: I was just getting ready to do my chores now, Pop . . .

TROY: Your first chore is to help me with this fence on Saturday. Everything else come after that. Now get that saw and cut them boards.

Cory takes the saw and begins cutting the boards. Troy continues working. There is a long pause.

CORY: Hey, Pop . . . why don't you buy a TV?

TROY: What I want with a TV? What I want one of them for?

CORY: Everybody got one. Earl, Ba Bra . . . Jesse!

TROY: I ain't asked you who had one. I say what I want with one?

CORY: So you can watch it. They got lots of things on TV. Baseball games and everything. We could watch the World Series.

TROY: Yeah . . . and how much this TV cost?

CORY: I don't know. They got them on sale for around two hundred dollars.

TROY: Two hundred dollars, huh?

CORY: That ain't that much, Pop.

TROY: Naw, it's just two hundred dollars. See that roof you got over your head at night? Let me tell you something about that roof. It's been over ten years since that roof was last tarred. See now . . . the snow come this winter and sit up there on that roof like it is . . . and it's gonna seep inside. It's just gonna be a little bit . . . ain't gonna hardly notice it. Then the next thing you know, it's gonna be leaking all over the house. Then the wood rot from all that water and you gonna need a whole new roof. Now, how much you think it cost to get that roof tarred?

CORY: I don't know.

TROY: Two hundred and sixty-four dollars . . . cash money. While you thinking about a TV, I got to be thinking about the roof . . . and whatever else go wrong around here. Now if you had two hundred dollars, what would you do . . . fix the roof or buy a TV?

CORY: I'd buy a TV. Then when the roof started to leak . . . when it needed fixing . . . I'd fix it.

TROY: Where you gonna get the money from? You done spent it for a TV. You gonna sit up and watch the water run all over your brand new TV.

CORY: Aw, Pop. You got money. I know you do.

TROY: Where I got it at, huh?

CORY: You got it in the bank.

TROY: You wanna see my bankbook? You wanna see that seventy-three dollars and twenty-two cents I got sitting up in there.

CORY: You ain't got to pay for it all at one time. You can put a down payment on it and carry it on home with you.

TROY: Not me. I ain't gonna owe nobody nothing if I can help it. Miss a payment and they come and snatch it right out your house. Then what you got? Now, soon as I get two hundred dollars clear, then I'll buy a TV. Right now, as soon as I get two hundred and sixty-four dollars, I'm gonna have this roof tarred.

CORY: Aw . . . Pop!

TROY: You go on and get you two hundred dollars and buy one if ya want it. I got better things to do with my money.

CORY: I can't get no two hundred dollars. I ain't never seen two hundred dollars.

TROY: I'll tell you what . . . you get you a hundred dollars and I'll put the other hundred with it.

CORY: All right, I'm gonna show you.

TROY: You gonna show me how you can cut them boards right now.

Cory begins to cut the boards. There is a long pause.

CORY: The Pirates won today. That makes five in a row.

TROY: I ain't thinking about the Pirates. Got an all-white team. Got that boy . . . that Puerto Rican boy . . . Clemente. Don't even half-play him. That boy could be something if they give him a chance. Play him one day and sit him on the bench the next.

CORY: He gets a lot of chances to play.

TROY: I'm talking about playing regular. Playing every day so you can get your timing. That's what I'm talking about.

CORY: They got some white guys on the team that don't play every day. You can't play everybody at the same time.

TROY: If they got a white fellow sitting on the bench . . . you can bet your last dollar he can't play! The colored guy got to be twice as good before he get on the team. That's why I don't want you to get all tied up in them sports. Man on the team and what it get him? They got colored on the team and don't use them. Same as not having them. All them teams the same.

CORY: The Braves got Hank Aaron and Wes Covington. Hank Aaron hit two home runs today. That makes forty-three.

TROY: Hank Aaron ain't nobody. That's what you supposed to do. That's how you supposed to play the game. Ain't nothing to it. It's just a matter of timing . . . getting the right follow-through. Hell, I can hit forty-three home runs right now!

CORY: Not off no major-league pitching, you couldn't.

TROY: We had better pitching in the Negro leagues. I hit seven home runs off of Satchel Paige.° You can't get no better than that!

CORY: Sandy Koufax. He's leading the league in strikeouts.

TROY: I ain't thinking of no Sandy Koufax.

CORY: You got Warren Spahn and Lew Burdette. I bet you couldn't hit no home runs off of Warren Spahn.

TROY: I'm through with it now. You go on and cut them boards. (*Pause.*) Your mama tell me you done got recruited by a college football team? Is that right?

CORY: Yeah. Coach Zellman say the recruiter gonna be coming by to talk to you. Get you to sign the permission papers.

TROY: I thought you supposed to be working down there at the A&P. Ain't you suppose to be working down there after school?

CORY: Mr. Stawicki say he gonna hold my job for me until after the football season. Say starting next week I can work weekends.

TROY: I thought we had an understanding about this football stuff? You suppose to keep up with your chores and hold that job down at the A&P. Ain't been around here all day on a Saturday. Ain't none of your chores done . . . and now you telling me you done quit your job.

CORY: I'm gonna be working weekends.

TROY: You damn right you are! And ain't no need for nobody coming around here to talk to me about signing nothing.

CORY: Hey, Pop . . . you can't do that. He's coming all the way from North Carolina.

TROY: I don't care where he coming from. The white man ain't gonna let you get nowhere with that football noway. You go on and get your book-learning so you can work yourself up in that A&P or learn how to fix cars or build houses or something, get you a trade. That way you have something can't nobody take away from you. You go on and learn how to put your hands to some good use. Besides hauling people's garbage.

CORY: I get good grades, Pop. That's why the recruiter wants to talk with you. You got to keep up your grades to get recruited. This way I'll be going to college. I'll get a chance . . .

TROY: First you gonna get your butt down there to the A&P and get your job back.

CORY: Mr. Stawicki done already hired somebody else 'cause I told him I was playing football.

TROY: You a bigger fool than I thought . . . to let somebody take away your job so you can play some football. Where you gonna get your money to take out your girlfriend and whatnot? What kind of foolishness is that to let somebody take away your job?

CORY: I'm still gonna be working weekends.

Satchel Paige: Legendary black pitcher (1906–1982) in the Negro leagues.

TROY: Naw . . . naw. You getting your butt out of here and finding you another job.

CORY: Come on, Pop! I got to practice. I can't work after school and play football too. The team needs me. That's what Coach Zellman say . . .

TROY: I don't care what nobody else say. I'm the boss . . . you understand? I'm the boss around here. I do the only saying what counts.

CORY: Come on, Pop!

TROY: I asked you . . . did you understand?

CORY: Yeah . . .

TROY: What?!

CORY: Yessir.

TROY: You go on down there to that A&P and see if you can get your job back. If you can't do both . . . then you quit the football team. You've got to take the crookeds with the straights.

CORY: Yessir. (*Pause.*) Can I ask you a question?

TROY: What the hell you wanna ask me? Mr. Stawicki the one you got the questions for.

CORY: How come you ain't never liked me?

TROY: Liked you? Who the hell say I got to like you? What law is there say I got to like you? Wanna stand up in my face and ask a damn fool-ass question like that. Talking about liking somebody. Come here, boy, when I talk to you.

Cory comes over to where Troy is working. He stands slouched over and Troy shoves him on his shoulder.

Straighten up, goddammit! I asked you a question . . . what law is there say I got to like you?

CORY: None.

TROY: Well, all right then! Don't you eat every day? (*Pause.*) Answer me when I talk to you! Don't you eat every day?

CORY: Yeah.

TROY: Nigger, as long as you in my house, you put that sir on the end of it when you talk to me!

CORY: Yes . . . sir.

TROY: You eat every day.

CORY: Yessir!

TROY: Got a roof over your head.

CORY: Yessir!

TROY: Got clothes on your back.

CORY: Yessir.

TROY: Why you think that is?

CORY: Cause of you.

TROY: Ah, hell I know it's 'cause of me . . . but why do you think that is?

CORY (*hesitant*): Cause you like me.

TROY: Like you? I go out of here every morning . . . bust my butt . . . putting up with them crackers° every day . . . cause I like you? You about the biggest

---

crackers: White people, often used to refer disparagingly to poor whites.

fool I ever saw. (*Pause.*) It's my job. It's my responsibility! You understand that? A man got to take care of his family. You live in my house . . . sleep you behind on my bedclothes . . . fill you belly up with my food . . . cause you my son. You my flesh and blood. Not 'cause I like you! Cause it's my duty to take care of you. I owe a responsibility to you! Let's get this straight right here . . . before it go along any further . . . I ain't got to like you. Mr. Rand don't give me my money come payday cause he likes me. He gives me cause he owe me. I done give you everything I had to give you. I gave you your life! Me and your mama worked that out between us. And liking your black ass wasn't part of the bargain. Don't you try and go through life worrying about if somebody like you or not. You best be making sure they doing right by you. You understand what I'm saying, boy?

CORY: Yessir.

TROY: Then get the hell out of my face, and get on down to that A&P.

Rose has been standing behind the screen door for much of the scene. She enters as Cory exits.

ROSE: Why don't you let the boy go ahead and play football, Troy? Ain't no harm in that. He's just trying to be like you with the sports.

TROY: I don't want him to be like me! I want him to move as far away from my life as he can get. You the only decent thing that ever happened to me. I wish him that. But I don't wish him a thing else from my life. I decided seventeen years ago that boy wasn't getting involved in no sports. Not after what they did to me in the sports.

ROSE: Troy, why don't you admit you was too old to play in the major leagues? For once . . . why don't you admit that?

TROY: What do you mean too old? Don't come telling me I was too old. I just wasn't the right color. Hell, I'm fifty-three years old and can do better than Selkirk's .269 right now!

ROSE: How's was you gonna play ball when you were over forty? Sometimes I can't get no sense out of you.

TROY: I got good sense, woman. I got sense enough not to let my boy get hurt over playing no sports. You been mothering that boy too much. Worried about if people like him.

ROSE: Everything that boy do . . . he do for you. He wants you to say "Good job, son." That's all.

TROY: Rose, I ain't got time for that. He's alive. He's healthy. He's got to make his own way. I made mine. Ain't nobody gonna hold his hand when he get out there in that world.

ROSE: Times have changed from when you was young, Troy. People change. The world's changing around you and you can't even see it.

TROY (*slow, methodical*): Woman . . . I do the best I can do. I come in here every Friday. I carry a sack of potatoes and a bucket of lard. You all line up at the door with your hands out. I give you the lint from my pockets. I give you my sweat and my blood. I ain't got no tears. I done spent them. We go upstairs in that room at night . . . and I fall down on you and try to blast a hole into forever. I get up Monday morning . . . find my lunch on the table. I go out. Make my way. Find my strength to carry me through to the next Friday. (*Pause.*) That's all I got, Rose. That's all I got to give. I can't give nothing else.

Troy exits into the house. The lights go down to black.

SCENE IV: *It is Friday. Two weeks later. Cory starts out of the house with his football equipment. The phone rings.*

CORY (*calling*): I got it! (*He answers the phone and stands in the screen door talking.*) Hello? Hey, Jesse. Naw . . . I was just getting ready to leave now.

ROSE (*calling*): Cory!

CORY: I told you, man, them spikes is all tore up. You can use them if you want, but they ain't no good. Earl got some spikes.

ROSE (*calling*): Cory!

CORY (*calling to Rose*): Mam? I'm talking to Jesse. (*Into phone.*) When she say that? (*Pause.*) Aw, you lying, man. I'm gonna tell her you said that.

ROSE (*calling*): Cory, don't you go nowhere!

CORY: I got to go to the game, Ma! (*Into the phone.*) Yeah, hey, look, I'll talk to you later. Yeah, I'll meet you over Earl's house. Later. Bye, Ma.

Cory exits the house and starts out the yard.

ROSE: Cory, where you going off to? You got that stuff all pulled out and thrown all over your room.

CORY (*in the yard*): I was looking for my spikes. Jesse wanted to borrow my spikes.

ROSE: Get up there and get that cleaned up before your daddy get back in here.

CORY: I got to go to the game! I'll clean it up *when I get back.*

Cory exits.

ROSE: That's all he need to do is see that room all messed up.

Rose exits into the house. Troy and Bono enter the yard. Troy is dressed in clothes other than his work clothes.

BONO: He told him the same thing he told you. Take it to the union.

TROY: Brownie ain't got that much sense. Man wasn't thinking about nothing. He wait until I confront them on it . . . then he wanna come crying seniority. (*Calls.*) Hey, Rose!

BONO: I wish I could have seen Mr. Rand's face when he told you.

TROY: He couldn't get it out of his mouth! Liked to bit his tongue! When they called me down there to the Commissioner's office . . . he thought they was gonna fire me. Like everybody else.

BONO: I didn't think they was gonna fire you. I thought they was gonna put you on the warning paper.

TROY: Hey, Rose! (*To Bono.*) Yeah, Mr. Rand like to bit his tongue.

Troy breaks the seal on the bottle, takes a drink, and hands it to Bono.

BONO: I see you run right down to Taylors' and told that Alberta gal.

TROY (*calling*): Hey, Rose! (*To Bono.*) I told everybody. Hey, Rose! I went down there to cash my check.

ROSE (*entering from the house*): Hush all that hollering, man! I know you out here. What they say down there at the Commissioner's office?

TROY: You supposed to come when I call you, woman. Bono'll tell you that. (*To Bono.*) Don't Lucille come when you call her?

ROSE: Man, hush your mouth. I ain't no dog . . . talk about "come when you call me."

TROY (*puts his arm around Rose*): You hear this Bono? I had me an old dog used to get uppity like that. You say, "C'mere, Blue!" . . . and he just lay there and look at you. End up getting a stick and chasing him away trying to make him come.

ROSE: I ain't studying you and your dog. I remember you used to sing that old song.

TROY (*he sings*): Hear it ring! Hear it ring!
I had a dog his name was Blue.

ROSE: Don't nobody wanna hear you sing that old song.

TROY (*sings*): You know Blue was mighty true.

ROSE: Used to have Cory running around here singing that song.

BONO: Hell, I remember that song myself.

TROY (*sings*): You know Blue was a good old dog.
Blue treed a possum in a hollow log.
That was my daddy's song. My daddy made up that song.

ROSE: I don't care who made it up. Don't nobody wanna hear you sing it.

TROY (*makes a song like calling a dog*): Come here, woman.

ROSE: You come in here carrying on, I reckon they ain't fired you. What they say down there at the Commissioner's office?

TROY: Look here, Rose . . . Mr. Rand called me into his office today when I got back from talking to them people down there . . . it come from up top . . . he called me in and told me they was making me a driver.

ROSE: Troy, you kidding!

TROY: No I ain't. Ask Bono.

ROSE: Well, that's great, Troy. Now you don't have to hassle them people no more.

Lyons enters from the street.

TROY: Aw hell, I wasn't looking to see you today. I thought you was in jail. Got it all over the front page of the *Courier* about them raiding Sefus' place . . . where you be hanging out with all them thugs.

LYONS: Hey, Pop . . . that ain't got nothing to do with me. I don't go down there gambling. I go down there to sit in with the band. I ain't got nothing to do with the gambling part. They got some good music down there.

TROY: They got some rogues . . . is what they got.

LYONS: How you been, Mr. Bono? Hi, Rose.

BONO: I see where you playing down at the Crawford Grill tonight.

ROSE: How come you ain't brought Bonnie like I told you. You should have brought Bonnie with you, she ain't been over in a month of Sundays.

LYONS: I was just in the neighborhood . . . thought I'd stop by.

TROY: Here he come . . .

BONO: Your daddy got a promotion on the rubbish. He's gonna be the first colored driver. Ain't got to do nothing but sit up there and read the paper like them white fellows.

LYONS: Hey, Pop . . . if you knew how to read you'd be all right.

BONO: Naw . . . naw . . . you mean if the nigger knew how to *drive* he'd be all right. Been fighting with them people about driving and ain't even got a license. Mr. Rand know you ain't got no driver's license?

TROY: Driving ain't nothing. All you do is point the truck where you want it to go. Driving ain't nothing.

BONO: Do Mr. Rand know you ain't got no driver's license? That's what I'm talking about. I ain't asked if driving was easy. I asked if Mr. Rand know you ain't got no driver's license.

TROY: He ain't got to know. The man ain't got to know my business. Time he find out, I have two or three driver's licenses.

LYONS (*going into his pocket*): Say, look here, Pop . . .

TROY: I knew it was coming. Didn't I tell you, Bono? I know what kind of "Look here, Pop" that was. The nigger fixing to ask me for some money. It's Friday night. It's my payday. All them rogues down there on the avenue . . . the ones that ain't in jail . . . and Lyons is hopping in his shoes to get down there with them.

LYONS: See, Pop . . . if you give somebody else a chance to talk sometime, you'd see that I was fixing to pay you back your ten dollars like I told you. Here . . . I told you I'd pay you when Bonnie got paid.

TROY: Naw . . . you go ahead and keep that ten dollars. Put it in the bank. The next time you feel like you wanna come by here and ask me for something . . . you go on down there and get that.

LYONS: Here's your ten dollars, Pop. I told you I don't want you to give me nothing. I just wanted to borrow ten dollars.

TROY: Naw . . . you go on and keep that for the next time you want to ask me.

LYONS: Come on, Pop . . . here go your ten dollars.

ROSE: Why don't you go on and let the boy pay you back, Troy?

LYONS: Here you go, Rose. If you don't take it I'm gonna have to hear about it for the next six months. (*He hands her the money.*)

ROSE: You can hand yours over here too, Troy.

TROY: You see this, Bono. You see how they do me.

BONO: Yeah, Lucille do me the same way.

Gabriel is heard singing offstage. He enters.

GABRIEL: Better get ready for the Judgment! Better get ready for . . . Hey! . . . Hey! . . . There's Troy's boy!

LYONS: How are you doing, Uncle Gabe?

GABRIEL: Lyons . . . The King of the jungle! Rose . . . hey, Rose. Got a flower for you. (*He takes a rose from his pocket.*) Picked it myself. That's the same rose like you is!

ROSE: That's right nice of you, Gabe.

LYONS: What you been doing, Uncle Gabe?

GABRIEL: Oh, I been chasing hellhounds and waiting on the time to tell St. Peter to open the gates.

LYONS: You been chasing hellhounds, huh? Well . . . you doing the right thing, Uncle Gabe. Somebody got to chase them.

GABRIEL: Oh, yeah . . . I know it. The devil's strong. The devil ain't no pushover. Hellhounds snipping at everybody's heels. But I got my trumpet waiting on the judgment time.

LYONS: Waiting on the Battle of Armageddon, huh?

GABRIEL: Ain't gonna be too much of a battle when God get to waving that Judgment sword. But the people's gonna have a hell of a time trying to get into heaven if them gates ain't open.

LYONS (*putting his arm around Gabriel*): You hear this, Pop. Uncle Gabe, you all right!

GABRIEL (*laughing with Lyons*): Lyons! King of the jungle.

ROSE: You gonna stay for supper, Gabe. Want me to fix you a plate?

GABRIEL: I'll take a sandwich, Rose. Don't want no plate. Just wanna eat with my hands. I'll take a sandwich.

ROSE: How about you, Lyons? You staying? Got some short ribs cooking.

LYONS: Naw, I won't eat nothing till after we finished playing. (*Pause.*) You ought to come down and listen to me play, Pop.

TROY: I don't like that Chinese music. All that noise.

ROSE: Go on in the house and wash up, Gabe . . . I'll fix you a sandwich.

GABRIEL (*to Lyons, as he exits*): Troy's mad at me.

LYONS: What you mad at Uncle Gabe for, Pop.

ROSE: He thinks Troy's mad at him cause he moved over to Miss Pearl's.

TROY: I ain't mad at the man. He can live where he want to live at.

LYONS: What he move over there for? Miss Pearl don't like nobody.

ROSE: She don't mind him none. She treats him real nice. She just don't allow all that singing.

TROY: She don't mind that rent he be paying . . . that's what she don't mind.

ROSE: Troy, I ain't going through that with you no more. He's over there cause he want to have his own place. He can come and go as he please.

TROY: Hell, he could come and go as he please here. I wasn't stopping him. I ain't put no rules on him.

ROSE: It ain't the same thing, Troy. And you know it.

Gabriel comes to the door.

Now, that's the last I wanna hear about that. I don't wanna hear nothing else about Gabe and Miss Pearl. And next week . . .

GABRIEL: I'm ready for my sandwich, Rose.

ROSE: And next week . . . when that recruiter come from that school . . . I want you to sign that paper and go on and let Cory play football. Then that'll be the last I have to hear about that.

TROY (*to Rose as she exits into the house*): I ain't thinking about Cory nothing.

LYONS: What . . . Cory got recruited? What school he going to?

TROY: That boy walking around here smelling his piss . . . thinking he's grown. Thinking he's gonna do what he want, irrespective of what I say. Look here, Bono . . . I left the Commissioner's office and went down to the A&P . . . that boy ain't working down there. He lying to me. Telling me he got his job back . . . telling me he working weekends . . . telling me he working after school . . . Mr. Stawicki tell me he ain't working down there at all!

LYONS: Cory just growing up. He's just busting at the seams trying to fill out your shoes.

TROY: I don't care what he's doing. When he get to the point where he wanna disobey me . . . then it's time for him to move on. Bono'll tell you that. I bet he ain't never disobeyed his daddy without paying the consequences.

BONO: I ain't never had a chance. My daddy came on through . . . but I ain't never knew him to see him . . . or what he had on his mind or where he went. Just moving on through. Searching out the New Land. That's what the old folks used to call it. See a fellow moving around from place to place . . . woman to woman . . . called it searching out the New Land. I can't say if he ever found it. I come along, didn't want no kids. Didn't know if I was gonna be in one place long enough to fix on them right as their daddy. I figured I was going searching too. As it turned out I been hooked up with Lucille near about as long as your daddy been with Rose. Going on sixteen years.

TROY: Sometimes I wish I hadn't known my daddy. He ain't cared nothing about no kids. A kid to him wasn't nothing. All he wanted was for you to learn how to walk so he could start you to working. When it come time for eating . . . he ate first. If there was anything left over, that's what you got. Man would sit down and eat two chickens and give you the wing.

LYONS: You ought to stop that, Pop. Everybody feed their kids. No matter how hard times is . . . everybody care about their kids. Make sure they have something to eat.

TROY: The only thing my daddy cared about was getting them bales of cotton in to Mr. Lubin. That's the only thing that mattered to him. Sometimes I used to wonder why he was living. Wonder why the devil hadn't come and got him. "Get them bales of cotton in to Mr. Lubin" and find out he owe him money . . .

LYONS: He should have just went on and left when he saw he couldn't get nowhere. That's what I would have done.

TROY: How he gonna leave with eleven kids? And where he gonna go? He ain't knew how to do nothing but farm. No, he was trapped and I think he knew it. But I'll say this for him . . . he felt a responsibility toward us. Maybe he ain't treated us the way I felt he should have . . . but without that responsibility he could have walked off and left us . . . made his own way.

BONO: A lot of them did. Back in those days what you talking about . . . they walk out their front door and just take on down one road or another and keep on walking.

LYONS: There you go! That's what I'm talking about.

BONO: Just keep on walking till you come to something else. Ain't you never heard of nobody having the walking blues? Well, that's what you call it when you just take off like that.

TROY: My daddy ain't had them walking blues! What you talking about? He stayed right there with his family. But he was just as evil as he could be. My mama couldn't stand him. Couldn't stand that evilness. She run off when I was about eight. She sneaked off one night after he had gone to sleep. Told me she was coming back for me. I ain't never seen her no more. All his women run off and left him. He wasn't good for nobody.

When my turn come to head out, I was fourteen and got to sniffing around Joe Canewell's daughter. Had us an old mule we called Greyboy. My daddy sent me out to do some plowing and I tied up Greyboy and went to fooling around with Joe Canewell's daughter. We done found us a nice little spot, got real cozy with each other. She about thirteen and we done figured we was grown anyway . . . so we down there enjoying ourselves . . . ain't thinking about nothing. We didn't know Greyboy had got loose and wandered back to the house and my daddy was looking for me. We down there by the creek enjoying ourselves when my daddy come up on us. Surprised us. He had them leather straps off the mule and commenced to whupping me like there was no tomorrow. I jumped up, mad and embarrassed. I was scared of my daddy. When he commenced to whupping on me . . . quite naturally I run to get out of the way. (*Pause.*)

Now I thought he was mad cause I ain't done my work. But I see where he was chasing me off so he could have the gal for himself. When I see what the matter of it was, I lost all fear of my daddy. Right there is where I become a man . . . at fourteen years of age. (*Pause.*)

Now it was my turn to run him off. I picked up them same reins that he had used on me. I picked up them reins and commenced to whupping on him. The gal jumped up and run off . . . and when my daddy turned to face me, I could see why the devil had never come to get him . . . cause he was the devil himself. I don't know what happened. When I woke up, I was laying right there by the creek, and Blue . . . this old dog we had . . . was licking my face. I thought I was blind. I couldn't see nothing. Both my eyes were swollen shut. I layed there and cried. I didn't know what I was gonna do. The only thing I knew was the time had come for me to leave my daddy's house. And right there the world suddenly got big. And it was a long time before I could cut it down to where I could handle it.

Part of that cutting down was when I got to the place where I could feel him kicking in my blood and knew that the only thing that separated us was the matter of a few years.

Gabriel enters from the house with a sandwich.

LYONS: What you got there, Uncle Gabe?

GABRIEL: Got me a ham sandwich. Rose gave me a ham sandwich.

TROY: I don't know what happened to him. I done lost touch with everybody except Gabriel. But I hope he's dead. I hope he found some peace.

LYONS: That's a heavy story, Pop. I didn't know you left home when you was fourteen.

TROY: And didn't know nothing. The only part of the world I knew was the forty-two acres of Mr. Lubin's land. That's all I knew about life.

LYONS: Fourteen's kinda young to be out on your own. (*Phone rings.*) I don't even think I was ready to be out on my own at fourteen. I don't know what I would have done.

TROY: I got up from the creek and walked on down to Mobile. I was through with farming. Figured I could do better in the city. So I walked the two hundred miles to Mobile.

LYONS: Wait a minute . . . you ain't walked no two hundred miles, Pop. Ain't nobody gonna walk no two hundred miles. You talking about some walking there.

BONO: That's the only way you got anywhere back in them days.

LYONS: Shhh. Damn if I wouldn't have hitched a ride with somebody!

TROY: Who you gonna hitch it with? They ain't had no cars and things like they got now. We talking about 1918.

ROSE (*entering*): What you all out here getting into?

TROY (*to Rose*): I'm telling Lyons how good he got it. He don't know nothing about this I'm talking.

ROSE: Lyons, that was Bonnie on the phone. She say you supposed to pick her up.

LYONS: Yeah, okay, Rose.

TROY: I walked on down to Mobile and hitched up with some of them fellows that was heading this way. Got up here and found out . . . not only couldn't you get a job . . . you couldn't find no place to live. I thought I was in freedom. Shhh. Colored folks living down there on the riverbanks in whatever kind of shelter they could find for themselves. Right down there under the Brady Street Bridge. Living in shacks made of sticks and tarpaper. Messed around there and went from bad to worse. Started stealing. First it was food. Then I figured, hell, if I steal money I can buy me some food. Buy me some shoes too! One thing led to another. Met your mama. I was young and anxious to be a man. Met your mama and had you. What I do that for? Now I got to worry about feeding you and her. Got to steal three times as much. Went out one day looking for somebody to rob . . . that's what I was, a robber. I'll tell you the truth. I'm ashamed of it today. But it's the truth. Went to rob this fellow . . . pulled out my knife . . . and he pulled out a gun. Shot me in the chest. It felt just like somebody had taken a hot branding iron and laid it on me. When he shot me I jumped at him with my knife. They told me I killed him and they put me in the penitentiary and locked me up for fifteen years. That's where I met Bono. That's where I learned how to play baseball. Got out that place and your mama had taken you and went on to make life without me. Fifteen years was a long time for her to wait. But that fifteen years cured me of that robbing stuff. Rose'll tell you. She asked me when I met her if I had gotten all that foolishness out of my system. And

I told her, "Baby, it's you and baseball all what count with me." You hear me, Bono? I meant it too. She say "Which one comes first?" I told her, "Baby, ain't no doubt it's baseball . . . but you stick and get old with me and we'll both outlive this baseball." Am I right, Rose? And it's true.

ROSE: Man, hush your mouth. You ain't said no such thing. Talking about, "Baby, you know you'll always be number one with me." That's what you was talking.

TROY: You hear that, Bono. That's why I love her.

BONO: Rose'll keep you straight. You get off the track, she'll straighten you up.

ROSE: Lyons, you better get on up and get Bonnie. She waiting on you.

LYONS (*gets up to go*): Hey, Pop, why don't you come on down to the Grill and hear me play?

TROY: I ain't going down there. I'm too old to be sitting around in them clubs.

BONO: You got to be good to play down at the Grill.

LYONS: Come on, Pop . . .

TROY: I got to get up in the morning.

LYONS: You ain't got to stay long.

TROY: Naw, I'm gonna get my supper and go on to bed.

LYONS: Well, I got to go. I'll see you again.

TROY: Don't you come around my house on my payday.

ROSE: Pick up the phone and let somebody know you coming. And bring Bonnie with you. You know I'm always glad to see her.

LYONS: Yeah, I'll do that, Rose. You take care now. See you, Pop. See you, Mr. Bono. See you, Uncle Gabe.

GABRIEL: Lyons! King of the jungle!

Lyons exits.

TROY: Is supper ready, woman? Me and you got some business to take care of. I'm gonna tear it up too.

ROSE: Troy, I done told you now!

TROY (*puts his arm around Bono*). Aw hell, woman . . . this is Bono. Bono like family. I done known this nigger since . . . how long I done know you?

BONO: It's been a long time.

TROY: I done known this nigger since Skippy was a pup. Me and him done been through some times.

BONO: You sure right about that.

TROY: Hell, I done know him longer than I known you. And we still standing shoulder to shoulder. Hey, look here, Bono . . . a man can't ask for no more than that. (*Drinks to him.*) I love you, nigger.

BONO: Hell, I love you too . . . but I got to get home see my woman. You got yours in hand. I got to go get mine.

Bono starts to exit as Cory enters the yard, dressed in his football uniform. He gives Troy a hard, uncompromising look.

CORY: What you do that for, Pop?

He throws his helmet down in the direction of Troy.

ROSE: What's the matter? Cory . . . what's the matter?

CORY: Papa done went up to the school and told Coach Zellman I can't play football no more. Wouldn't even let me play the game. Told him to tell the recruiter not to come.

ROSE: Troy . . .

TROY: What you Troying me for. Yeah, I did it. And the boy know why I did it.

CORY: Why you wanna do that to me? That was the one chance I had.

ROSE: Ain't nothing wrong with Cory playing football, Troy.

TROY: The boy lied to me. I told the nigger if he wanna play football . . . to keep up his chores and hold down that job at the A&P. That was the conditions. Stopped down there to see Mr. Stawicki . . .

CORY: I can't work after school during the football season, Pop! I tried to tell you that Mr. Stawicki's holding my job for me. You don't never want to listen to nobody. And then you wanna go and do this to me!

TROY: I ain't done nothing to you. You done it to yourself.

CORY: Just cause you didn't have a chance! You just scared I'm gonna be better than you, that's all.

TROY: Come here.

ROSE: Troy . . .

Cory reluctantly crosses over to Troy.

TROY: All right! See. You done made a mistake.

CORY: I didn't even do nothing!

TROY: I'm gonna tell you what your mistake was. See . . . you swung at the ball and didn't hit it. That's strike one. See, you in the batter's box now. You swung and you missed. That's strike one. Don't you strike out!

Lights fade to black.

ACT II

SCENE I: *The following morning. Cory is at the tree hitting the ball with the bat. He tries to mimic Troy, but his swing is awkward, less sure. Rose enters from the house.*

ROSE: Cory, I want you to help me with this cupboard.

CORY: I ain't quitting the team. I don't care what Poppa say.

ROSE: I'll talk to him when he gets back. He had to go see about your Uncle Gabe. The police done arrested him. Say he was disturbing the peace. He'll be back directly. Come on in here and help me clean out the top of this cupboard.

Cory exits into the house. Rose sees Troy and Bono coming down the alley.

Troy . . . what they say down there?

TROY: Ain't said nothing. I give them fifty dollars and they let him go. I'll talk to you about it. Where's Cory.

ROSE: He's in there helping me clean out these cupboards.

TROY: Tell him to get his butt out here.

Troy and Bono go over to the pile of wood. Bono picks up the saw and begins sawing.

TROY (*to Bono*): All they want is the money. That makes six or seven times I done went down there and got him. See me coming they stick out their *hands.*

BONO: Yeah. I know what you mean. That's all they care about . . . that money. They don't care about what's right. (*Pause.*) Nigger, why you got to go and get some hard wood? You ain't doing nothing but building a little old fence. Get you some soft pine wood. That's all you need.

TROY: I know what I'm doing. This is outside wood. You put pine wood inside the house. Pine wood is inside wood. This here is outside wood. Now you tell me where the fence is gonna be?

BONO: You don't need this wood. You can put it up with pine wood and it'll stand as long as you gonna be here looking at it.

TROY: How you know how long I'm gonna be here, nigger? Hell, I might just live forever. Live longer than old man Horsely.

BONO: That's what Magee used to say.

TROY: Magee's a damn fool. Now you tell me who you ever heard of gonna pull their own teeth with a pair of rusty pliers.

BONO: The old folks . . . my granddaddy used to pull his teeth with pliers. They ain't had no dentists for the colored folks back then.

TROY: Get clean pliers! You understand? Clean pliers! Sterilize them! Besides we ain't living back then. All Magee had to do was walk over to Doc Goldblum's.

BONO: I see where you and that Tallahassee gal . . . that Alberta . . . I see where you all done got tight.

TROY: What you mean "got tight"?

BONO: I see where you be laughing and joking with her all the time.

TROY: I laughs and jokes with all of them, Bono. You know me.

BONO: That ain't the kind of laughing and joking I'm talking about.

Cory enters from the house.

CORY: How you doing, Mr. Bono?

TROY: Cory? Get that saw from Bono and cut some wood. He talking about the wood's too hard to cut. Stand back there, Jim, and let that young boy show you how it's done.

BONO: He's sure welcome to it.

Cory takes the saw and begins to cut the wood.

Whew-e-e! Look at that. Big old strong boy. Look like Joe Louis. Hell, must be getting old the way I'm watching that boy whip through that wood.

CORY: I don't see why Mama want a fence around the yard noways.

TROY: Damn if I know either. What the hell she keeping out with it? She ain't got nothing nobody want.

BONO: Some people build fences to keep people out . . . and other people build fences to keep people in. Rose wants to hold on to you all. She loves you.

TROY: Hell, nigger, I don't need nobody to tell me my wife loves me, Cory . . . go on in the house and see if you can find that other saw.

CORY: Where's it at?

TROY: I said find it! Look for it till you find it!

Cory exits into the house.

What's that supposed to mean? Wanna keep us in?

BONO: Troy . . . I done known you seem like damn near my whole life. You and Rose both. I done know both of you all for a long time. I remember when you met Rose. When you was hitting them baseball out the park. A lot of them old gals was after you then. You had the pick of the litter. When you picked Rose, I was happy for you. That was the first time I knew you had any sense. I said . . . My man Troy knows what he's doing . . . I'm gonna follow this nigger . . . he might take me somewhere. I been following you too. I done learned a whole heap of things about life watching you. I done learned how to tell where the shit lies. How to tell it from the alfalfa. You done learned me a lot of things. You showed me how to not make the same mistakes . . . to take life as it comes along and keep putting one foot in front of the other. (*Pause.*) Rose a good woman, Troy.

TROY: Hell, nigger, I know she a good woman. I been married to her for eighteen years. What you got on your mind, Bono?

BONO: I just say she a good woman. Just like I say anything. I ain't got to have nothing on my mind.

TROY: You just gonna say she a good woman and leave it hanging out there like that? Why you telling me she a good woman?

BONO: She loves you, Troy. Rose loves you.

TROY: You saying I don't measure up. That's what you trying to say. I don't measure up cause I'm seeing this other gal. I know what you trying to say.

BONO: I know what Rose means to you, Troy. I'm just trying to say I don't want to see you mess up.

TROY: Yeah, I appreciate that, Bono. If you was messing around on Lucille I'd be telling you the same thing.

BONO: Well, that's all I got to say. I just say that because I love you both.

TROY: Hell, you know me . . . I wasn't out there looking for nothing. You can't find a better woman than Rose. I know that. But seems like this woman just stuck onto me where I can't shake her loose. I done wrestled with it, tried to throw her off me . . . but she just stuck on tighter. Now she's stuck on for good.

BONO: You's in control . . . that's what you tell me all the time. You responsible for what you do.

TROY: I ain't ducking the responsibility of it. As long as it sets right in my heart . . . then I'm okay. Cause that's all I listen to. It'll tell me right from wrong every time. And I ain't talking about doing Rose no bad turn. I love Rose. She done carried me a long ways and I love and respect her for that.

BONO: I know you do. That's why I don't want to see you hurt her. But what you gonna do when she find out? What you got then? If you try and juggle both of them . . . sooner or later you gonna drop one of them. That's common sense.

TROY: Yeah, I hear what you saying, Bono. I been trying to figure a way to work it out.

BONO: Work it out right, Troy. I don't want to be getting all up between you and Rose's business . . . but work it so it come out right.

TROY: Ah hell, I get all up between you and Lucille's business. When you gonna get that woman that refrigerator she been wanting? Don't tell me you ain't got no money now. I know who your banker is. Mellon don't need that money bad as Lucille want that refrigerator. I'll tell you that.

BONO: Tell you what I'll do . . . when you finish building this fence for Rose . . . I'll buy Lucille that refrigerator.

TROY: You done stuck your foot in your mouth now!

Troy grabs up a board and begins to saw. Bono starts to walk out the yard.

Hey, nigger . . . where you going?

BONO: I'm going home. I know you don't expect me to help you now. I'm protecting my money. I wanna see you put that fence up by yourself. That's what I want to see. You'll be here another six months without me.

TROY: Nigger, you ain't right.

BONO: When it comes to my money . . . I'm right as fireworks on the Fourth of July.

TROY: All right, we gonna see now. You better get out your bankbook.

Bono exits, and Troy continues to work. Rose enters from the house.

ROSE: What they say down there? What's happening with Gabe?

TROY: I went down there and got him out. Cost me fifty dollars. Say he was disturbing the peace. Judge set up a hearing for him in three weeks. Say to show cause why he shouldn't be recommitted.

ROSE: What was he doing that cause them to arrest him?

TROY: Some kids was teasing him and he run them off home. Say he was howling and carrying on. Some folks seen him and called the police. That's all it was.

ROSE: Well, what's you say? What'd you tell the judge?

TROY: Told him I'd look after him. It didn't make no sense to recommit the man. He stuck out his big greasy palm and told me to give him fifty dollars and take him on home.

ROSE: Where's he at now? Where'd he go off to?

TROY: He's gone on about his business. He don't need nobody to hold his hand.

ROSE: Well, I don't know. Seem like that would be the best place for him if they did put him into the hospital. I know what you're gonna say. But that's what I think would be best.

TROY: The man done had his life ruined fighting for what? And they wanna take and lock him up. Let him be free. He don't bother nobody.

ROSE: Well, everybody got their own way of looking at it I guess. Come on and get your lunch. I got a bowl of lima beans and some cornbread in the oven. Come on get something to eat. Ain't no sense you fretting over Gabe.

Rose turns to go into the house.

TROY: Rose . . . got something to tell you.

ROSE: Well, come on . . . wait till I get this food on the table.

TROY: Rose!

She stops and turns around.

I don't know how to say this. (*Pause.*) I can't explain it none. It just sort of grows on you till it gets out of hand. It starts out like a little bush . . . and the next thing you know it's a whole forest.

ROSE: Troy . . . what is you talking about?

TROY: I'm talking, woman, let me talk. I'm trying to find a way to tell you . . . I'm gonna be a daddy. I'm gonna be somebody's daddy.

ROSE: Troy . . . you're not telling me this? You're gonna be . . . what?

TROY: Rose . . . now . . . see . . .

ROSE: You telling me you gonna be somebody's daddy? You telling your *wife* this?

Gabriel enters from the street. He carries a rose in his hand.

GABRIEL: Hey, Troy! Hey, Rose!

ROSE: I have to wait eighteen years to hear something like this.

GABRIEL: Hey, Rose . . . I got a flower for you. (*He hands it to her*). That's a rose. Same rose like you is.

ROSE: Thanks, Gabe.

GABRIEL: Troy, you ain't mad at me is you? Them bad mens come and put me away. You ain't mad at me is you?

TROY: Naw, Gabe, I ain't mad at you.

ROSE: Eighteen years and you wanna come with this.

GABRIEL (*takes a quarter out of his pocket*): See what I got? Got a brand new quarter.

TROY: Rose . . . it's just . . .

ROSE: Ain't nothing you can say, Troy. Ain't no way of explaining that.

GABRIEL: Fellow that give me this quarter had a whole mess of them. I'm gonna keep this quarter till it stop shining.

ROSE: Gabe, go on in the house there. I got some watermelon in the frigidaire. Go on and get you a piece.

GABRIEL: Say, Rose . . . you know I was chasing hellhounds and them bad mens come and get me and take me away. Troy helped me. He come down there and told them they better let me go before he beat them up. Yeah, he did!

ROSE: You go on and get you a piece of watermelon, Gabe. Them bad mens is gone now.

GABRIEL: Okay, Rose . . . gonna get me some watermelon. The kind with the stripes on it.

Gabriel exits into the house.

ROSE: Why, Troy? Why? After all these years to come dragging this in to me now. It don't make no sense at your age. I could have expected this ten or fifteen years ago, but not now.

TROY: Age ain't got nothing to do with it, Rose.

ROSE: I done tried to be everything a wife should be. Everything a wife could be. Been married eighteen years and I got to live to see the day you tell me you been seeing another woman and done fathered a child by her. And you know I ain't never wanted no half nothing in my family. My whole family is half. Everybody got different fathers and mothers . . .

my two sisters and my brother. Can't hardly tell who's who. Can't never sit down and talk about Papa and Mama. It's your papa and your mama and my papa and my mama . . .

TROY: Rose . . . stop it now.

ROSE: I ain't never wanted that for none of my children. And now you wanna drag your behind in here and tell me something like this.

TROY: You ought to know. It's time for you to know.

ROSE: Well, I don't want to know, goddamn it!

TROY: I can't just make it go away. It's done now. I can't wish the circumstance of the thing away.

ROSE: And you don't want to either. Maybe you want to wish me and my boy away. Maybe that's what you want? Well, you can't wish us away. I've got eighteen years of my life invested in you. You ought to have stayed upstairs in my bed where you belong.

TROY: Rose . . . now listen to me . . . we can get a handle on this thing. We can talk this out . . . come to an understanding.

ROSE: All of a sudden it's "we." Where was "we" at when you was down there rolling around with some godforsaken woman? "We" should have come to an understanding before you started making a damn fool of yourself. You're a day late and a dollar short when it comes to an understanding with me.

TROY: It's just . . . She gives me a different idea . . . a different understanding about myself. I can step out of this house and get away from the pressures and problems . . . be a different man. I ain't got to wonder how I'm gonna pay the bills or get the roof fixed. I can just be a part of myself that I ain't never been.

ROSE: What I want to know . . . is do you plan to continue seeing her. That's all you can say to me.

TROY: I can sit up in her house and laugh. Do you understand what I'm saying. I can laugh out loud . . . and it feels good. It reaches all the way down to the bottom of my shoes. (*Pause.*) Rose, I can't give that up.

ROSE: Maybe you ought to go on and stay down there with her . . . if she's a better woman than me.

TROY: It ain't about nobody being a better woman or nothing. Rose, you ain't the blame. A man couldn't ask for no woman to be a better wife than you've been. I'm responsible for it. I done locked myself into a pattern trying to take care of you all that I forgot about myself.

ROSE: What the hell was I there for? That was my job, not somebody else's.

TROY: Rose, I done tried all my life to live decent . . . to live a clean . . . hard . . . useful life. I tried to be a good husband to you. In every way I knew how. Maybe I come into the world backwards, I don't know. But . . . you born with two strikes on you before you come to the plate. You got to guard it closely . . . always looking for the curve ball on the inside corner. You can't afford to let none get past you. You can't afford a call strike. If you going down . . . you going down swinging. Everything lined up against you. What you gonna do. I fooled them, Rose. I bunted. When I found you and Cory and a halfway decent job . . . I was safe. Couldn't nothing touch me. I wasn't gonna strike out no more. I wasn't going back to the penitentiary. I wasn't gonna lay in the street with a bottle of wine. I was safe. I had me a family. A job. I wasn't gonna get that last strike. I was on first looking for one of them boys to knock me in. To get me home.

ROSE: You should have stayed in my bed, Troy.

TROY: Then when I saw that gal . . . she firmed up my backbone. And I got to thinking that if I tried . . . I just might be able to steal second. Do you understand after eighteen years I wanted to steal second.

ROSE: You should have held me tight. You should have grabbed me and held on.

TROY: I stood on first base for eighteen years and I thought . . . well, goddamn it . . . go on for it!

ROSE: We're not talking about baseball! We're talking about you going off to lay in bed with another woman . . . and then bring it home to me. That's what we're talking about. We ain't talking about no baseball.

TROY: Rose, you're not listening to me. I'm trying the best I can to explain it to you. It's not easy for me to admit that I been standing in the same place for eighteen years.

ROSE: I been standing with you! I been right here with you, Troy. I got a life too. I gave eighteen years of my life to stand in the same spot with you. Don't you think I ever wanted other things? Don't you think I had dreams and hopes? What about my life? What about me? Don't you think it ever crossed my mind to want to know other men? That I wanted to lay up somewhere and forget about my responsibilities? That I wanted someone to make me laugh so I could feel good? You not the only one who's got wants and needs. But I held on to you, Troy. I took all my feelings, my wants and needs, my dreams . . . and I buried them inside you. I planted a seed and watched and prayed over it. I planted myself inside you and waited to bloom. And it didn't take me no eighteen years to find out the soil was hard and rocky and it wasn't never gonna bloom.

But I held on to you, Troy. I held you tighter. You was my husband. I owed you everything I had. Every part of me I could find to give you. And upstairs in that room . . . with the darkness falling in on me . . . I gave everything I had to try and erase the doubt that you wasn't the finest man in the world. And wherever you was going . . . I wanted to be there with you. Cause you was my husband. Cause that's the only way I was gonna survive as your wife. You always talking about what you give . . . and what you don't have to give. But you take too. You take . . . and don't even know nobody's giving!

Rose turns to exit into the house; Troy grabs her arm.

TROY: You say I take and don't give!

ROSE: Troy! You're hurting me!

TROY: You say I take and don't give.

ROSE: Troy . . . you're hurting my arm! Let go!

TROY: I done give you everything I got. Don't you tell that lie on me.

ROSE: Troy!

TROY: Don't you tell that lie on me!

Cory enters from the house.

CORY: Mama!

ROSE: Troy. You're hurting me.

TROY: Don't you tell me about no taking and giving.

Cory comes up behind Troy and grabs him. Troy, surprised, is thrown off balance just as Cory throws a glancing blow that catches him on the chest and knocks him down. Troy is stunned, as is Cory.

ROSE: Troy. Troy. No!

Troy gets to his feet and starts at Cory.

Troy . . . no. Please! Troy!

Rose pulls on Troy to hold him back. Troy stops himself.

TROY (*to Cory*): All right. That's strike two. You stay away from around me, boy. Don't you strike out. You living with a full count. Don't you strike out.

Troy exits out the yard as the lights go down.

SCENE II: *It is six months later, early afternoon. Troy enters from the house and starts to exit the yard. Rose enters from the house.*

ROSE: Troy, I want to talk to you.

TROY: All of a sudden, after all this time, you want to talk to me, huh? You ain't wanted to talk to me for months. You ain't wanted to talk to me last night. You ain't wanted no part of me then. What you wanna talk to me about now?

ROSE: Tomorrow's Friday.

TROY: I know what day tomorrow is. You think I don't know tomorrow's Friday? My whole life I ain't done nothing but look to see Friday coming and you got to tell me it's Friday.

ROSE: I want to know if you're coming home.

TROY: I always come home, Rose. You know that. There ain't never been a night I ain't come home.

ROSE: That ain't what I mean . . . and you know it. I want to know if you're coming straight home after work.

TROY: I figure I'd cash my check . . . hang out at Taylors' with the boys . . . maybe play a game of checkers . . .

ROSE: Troy, I can't live like this. I won't live like this. You livin' on borrowed time with me. It's been going on six months now you ain't been coming home.

TROY: I be here every night. Every night of the year. That's 365 days.

ROSE: I want you to come home tomorrow after work.

TROY: Rose . . . I don't mess up my pay. You know that now. I take my pay and I give it to you. I don't have no money but what you give me back. I just want to have a little time to myself . . . a little time to enjoy life.

ROSE: What about me? When's my time to enjoy life?

TROY: I don't know what to tell you, Rose. I'm doing the best I can.

ROSE: You ain't been home from work but time enough to change your clothes and run out . . . and you wanna call that the best you can do?

TROY: I'm going over to the hospital to see Alberta. She went into the hospital this afternoon. Look like she might have the baby early. I won't be gone long.

ROSE: Well, you ought to know. They went over to Miss Pearl's and got Gabe today. She said you told them to go ahead and lock him up.

TROY: I ain't said no such thing. Whoever told you that is telling a lie. Pearl ain't doing nothing but telling a big fat lie.

ROSE: She ain't had to tell me. I read it on the papers.

TROY: I ain't told them nothing of the kind.

ROSE:. I saw it right there on the papers.

TROY: What it say, huh?

ROSE: It said you told them to take him.

TROY: Then they screwed that up, just the way they screw up everything. I ain't worried about what they got on the paper.

ROSE: Say the government send part of his check to the hospital and the other part to you.

TROY: I ain't got nothing to do with that if that's the way it works. I ain't made up the rules about how it work.

ROSE: You did Gabe just like you did Cory. You wouldn't sign the paper for Cory . . . but you signed for Gabe. You signed that paper.

The telephone is heard ringing inside the house.

TROY: I told you I ain't signed nothing, woman! The only thing I signed was the release form. Hell, I can't read, I don't know what they had on that paper! I ain't signed nothing about sending Gabe away.

ROSE: I said send him to the hospital . . . you said let him be free . . . now you done went down there and signed him to the hospital for half his money. You went back on yourself, Troy. You gonna have to answer for that.

TROY: See now . . . you been over there talking to Miss Pearl. She done got mad cause she ain't getting Gabe's rent money. That's all it is. She's liable to say anything.

ROSE: Troy, I seen where you signed the paper.

TROY: You ain't seen nothing I signed. What she doing got papers on my brother anyway? Miss Pearl telling a big fat lie. And I'm gonna tell her about it too! You ain't seen nothing I signed. Say . . . you ain't seen nothing I signed.

Rose exits into the house to answer the telephone. Presently she returns.

ROSE: Troy . . . that was the hospital. Alberta had the baby.

TROY: What she have? What is it?

ROSE: It's a girl.

TROY: I better get on down to the hospital to see her.

ROSE: Troy . . .

TROY: Rose . . . I got to go see her now. That's only right . . . what's the matter . . . the baby's all right, ain't it?

ROSE: Alberta died having the baby.

TROY: Died . . . you say she's dead? Alberta's dead?

ROSE: They said they done all they could. They couldn't do nothing for her.

TROY: The baby? How's the baby?

ROSE: They say it's healthy. I wonder who's gonna bury her.

TROY: She had family, Rose. She wasn't living in the world by herself.

ROSE: I know she wasn't living in the world by herself.

TROY: Next thing you gonna want to know if she had any insurance.

ROSE: Troy, you ain't got to talk like that.

TROY: That's the first thing that jumped out your mouth. "Who's gonna bury her?" Like I'm fixing to take on that task for myself.

ROSE: I am your wife. Don't push me away.

TROY: I ain't pushing nobody away. Just give me some space. That's all. Just give me some room to breathe.

Rose exits into the house. Troy walks about the yard.

TROY (*with a quiet rage that threatens to consume him*): All right . . . Mr. Death. See now . . . I'm gonna tell you what I'm gonna do. I'm gonna take and build me a fence around this yard. See? I'm gonna build me a fence around what belongs to me. And then I want you to stay on the other side. See? You stay over there until you're ready for me. Then you come on. Bring your army. Bring your sickle. Bring your wrestling clothes. I ain't gonna fall down on my vigilance this time. You ain't gonna sneak up on me no more. When you ready for me . . . when the top of your list say Troy Maxson . . . that's when you come around here. You come up and knock on the front door. Ain't nobody else got nothing to do with this. This is between you and me. Man to man. You stay on the other side of that fence until you ready for me. Then you come up and knock on the front door. Anytime you want. I'll be ready for you.

The lights go down to black.

SCENE III: *The lights come up on the porch. It is late evening three days later. Rose sits listening to the ball game waiting for Troy. The final out of the game is made and Rose switches off the radio. Troy enters the yard carrying an infant wrapped in blankets. He stands back from the house and calls.*

Rose enters and stands on the porch. There is a long, awkward silence, the weight of which grows heavier with each passing second.

TROY: Rose . . . I'm standing here with my daughter in my arms. She ain't but a wee bittie little old thing. She don't know nothing about grownups' business. She innocent . . . and she ain't got no mama.

ROSE: What you telling me for, Troy?

She turns and exits into the house.

TROY: Well . . . I guess we'll just sit out here on the porch. (*He sits down on the porch. There is an awkward indelicateness about the way he handles the baby. His largeness engulfs and seems to swallow it. He speaks loud enough for Rose to hear.*) A man's got to do what's right for him. I ain't sorry for nothing I done. It felt right in my heart. (*To the baby.*) What you smiling at? Your daddy's a big man. Got these great big old hands. But sometimes he's scared. And right now your daddy's scared cause we sitting out here and ain't got no home. Oh, I been homeless before. I ain't had no little baby with me. But I been homeless. You just be out on the road by your lonesome and you see one of them trains coming and you just kinda go like this . . . (*He sings as a lullaby.*)

Please, Mr. Engineer let a man ride the line
Please, Mr. Engineer let a man ride the line
I ain't got no ticket please let me ride the blinds

(*Rose enters from the house. Troy hearing her steps behind him, stands and faces her.*)

She's my daughter, Rose. My own flesh and blood. I can't deny her no more than I can deny them boys. (*Pause.*) You and them boys is my family. You and them and this child is all I got in the world. So I guess what I'm saying is . . . I'd appreciate it if you'd help me take care of her.

ROSE: Okay, Troy . . . you're right. I'll take care of your baby for you . . . cause . . . like you say . . . she's innocent . . . and you can't visit the sins of the father upon the child. A motherless child has got a hard time. (*She takes the baby from him.*) From right now . . . this child got a mother. But you a womanless man.

Rose turns and exits into the house with the baby. Lights go down to black.

SCENE IV: *It is two months later. Lyons enters from the street. He knocks on the door and calls.*

LYONS: Hey, Rose! (*Pause.*) Rose!

ROSE (*from inside the house*): Stop that yelling. You gonna wake up Raynell. I just got her to sleep.

LYONS: I just stopped by to pay Papa this twenty dollars I owe him. Where's Papa at?

ROSE: He should be here in a minute. I'm getting ready to go down to the church. Sit down and wait on him.

LYONS: I got to go pick up Bonnie over her mother's house.

ROSE: Well, sit it down there on the table. He'll get it.

LYONS (*enters the house and sets the money on the table*): Tell Papa I said thanks. I'll see you again.

ROSE: All right, Lyons. We'll see you.

Lyons starts to exit as Cory enters.

CORY: Hey, Lyons.

LYONS: What's happening, Cory. Say man, I'm sorry I missed your graduation. You know I had a gig and couldn't get away. Otherwise, I would have been there, man. So what you doing?

CORY: I'm trying to find a job.

LYONS: Yeah I know how that go, man. It's rough out here. Jobs are scarce.

CORY: Yeah, I know.

LYONS: Look here, I got to run. Talk to Papa . . . he know some people. He'll be able to help get you a job. Talk to him . . . see what he say.

CORY: Yeah . . . all right, Lyons.

LYONS: You take care. I'll talk to you soon. We'll find some time to talk.

Lyons exits the yard. Cory wanders over to the tree, picks up the bat, and assumes a batting stance. He studies an imaginary pitcher and swings. Dissatisfied with the result, he tries again. Troy enters. They eye each other for a beat. Cory puts the bat down and exits the yard. Troy starts into the house as Rose exits with Raynell. She is carrying a cake.

TROY: I'm coming in and everybody's going out.

ROSE: I'm taking this cake down to the church for the bake sale. Lyons was by to see you. He stopped by to pay you your twenty dollars. It's laying in there on the table.

TROY (*going into his pocket*): Well . . . here go this money.

ROSE: Put it in there on the table, Troy. I'll get it.

TROY: What time you coming back?

ROSE: Ain't no use in you studying me. It don't matter what time I come back.

TROY: I just asked you a question, woman. What's the matter . . . can't I ask you a question?

ROSE: Troy, I don't want to go into it. Your dinner's in there on the stove. All you got to do is heat it up. And don't you be eating the rest of them cakes in there. I'm coming back for them. We having a bake sale at the church tomorrow.

Rose exits the yard. Troy sits down on the steps, takes a pint bottle from his pocket, opens it, and drinks. He begins to sing.

TROY: Hear it ring! Hear it ring!
Had an old dog his name was Blue
You know Blue was mighty true
You know Blue as a good old dog
Blue trees a possum in a hollow log
You know from that he was a good old dog

Bono enters the yard.

BONO: Hey, Troy.

TROY: Hey, what's happening, Bono?

BONO: I just thought I'd stop by to see you.

TROY: What you stop by and see me for? You ain't stopped by in a month of Sundays. Hell, I must owe you money or something.

BONO: Since you got your promotion I can't keep up with you. Used to see you every day. Now I don't even know what route you working.

TROY: They keep switching me around. Got me out in Greentree now . . . hauling white folks' garbage.

BONO: Greentree, huh? You lucky, at least you ain't got to be lifting them barrels. Damn if they ain't getting heavier. I'm gonna put in my two years and call it quits.

TROY: I'm thinking about retiring myself.

BONO: You got it easy. You can *drive* for another five years.

TROY: It ain't the same, Bono. It ain't like working the back of the truck. Ain't got nobody to talk to . . . feel like you working by yourself. Naw, I'm thinking about retiring. How's Lucille?

BONO: She all right. Her arthritis get to acting up on her sometime. Saw Rose on my way in. She going down to the church, huh?

TROY: Yeah, she took up going down there. All them preachers looking for somebody to fatten their pockets. (*Pause.*) Got some gin here.

BONO: Naw, thanks. I just stopped by to say hello.

TROY: Hell, nigger . . . you can take a drink. I ain't never known you to say no to a drink. You ain't got to work tomorrow.

BONO: I just stopped by. I'm fixing to go over to Skinner's. We got us a domino game going over his house every Friday.

TROY: Nigger, you can't play no dominoes. I used to whup you four games out of five.

BONO: Well, that learned me. I'm getting better.

TROY: Yeah? Well, that's all right.

BONO: Look here . . . I got to be getting on. Stop by sometime, huh?

TROY: Yeah, I'll do that, Bono. Lucille told Rose you bought her a new refrigerator.

BONO: Yeah, Rose told Lucille you had finally built your fence . . . so I figured we'd call it even.

TROY: I knew you would.

BONO:Yeah . . . okay. I'll be talking to you.

TROY: Yeah, take care, Bono. Good to see you. I'm gonna stop over.

BONO: Yeah. Okay, Troy.

Bono exits. Troy drinks from the bottle.

TROY: Old Blue died and I dig his grave
Let him down with a golden chain
Every night when I hear old Blue bark
I know Blue treed a possum in Noah's Ark.
Hear it ring! Hear it ring!

Cory enters the yard. They eye each other for a beat. Troy is sitting in the middle of the steps. Cory walks over.

CORY: I got to get by.

TROY: Say what? What's you say?

CORY: You in my way. I got to get by.

TROY: You got to get by where? This is my house. Bought and paid for. In full. Took me fifteen years. And if you wanna go in my house and I'm sitting on the steps . . . you say excuse me. Like your mama taught you.

CORY: Come on, Pop . . . I got to get by.

Cory starts to maneuver his way past Troy. Troy grabs his leg and shoves him back.

TROY: You just gonna walk over top of me?

CORY: I live here too!

TROY (*advancing toward him*): You just gonna walk over top of me in my own house?

CORY: I ain't scared of you.

TROY: I ain't asked if you was scared of me. I asked you if you was fixing to walk over top of me in my own house? That's the question. You ain't gonna say excuse me? You just gonna walk over top of me?

CORY: If you wanna put it like that.

TROY: How else am I gonna put it?

CORY: I was walking by you to go into the house cause you sitting on the steps drunk, singing to yourself. You can put it like that.

TROY: Without saying excuse me???

Cory doesn't respond.

I asked you a question. Without saying excuse me???

CORY: I ain't got to say excuse me to you. You don't count around here no more.

TROY: Oh, I see . . . I don't count around here no more. You ain't got to say excuse me to your daddy. All of a sudden you done got so grown that your daddy don't count around here no more . . . Around here in his own house and yard that he done paid for with the sweat of his brow. You done got so grown to where you gonna take over. You gonna take over my house. Is that right? You gonna wear my pants. You gonna go in there and stretch out on my bed. You ain't got to say excuse me cause I don't count around here no more. Is that right?

CORY: That's right. You always talking this dumb stuff. Now, why don't you just get out my way.

TROY: I guess you got someplace to sleep and something to put in your belly. You got that, huh? You got that? That's what you need. You got that, huh?

CORY: You don't know what I got. You ain't got to worry about what I got.

TROY: You right! You one hundred percent right! I done spent the last seventeen years worrying about what you got. Now it's your turn, see? I'll tell you what to do. You grown . . . we done established that. You a man. Now, let's see you act like one. Turn your behind around and walk out this yard. And when you get out there in the alley . . . you can forget about this house. See? 'Cause this is my house. You go on and be a man and get your own house. You can forget about this. 'Cause this is mine. You go on and get yours 'cause I'm through with doing for you.

CORY: You talking about what you did for me . . . what'd you ever give me?

TROY: Them feet and bones! That pumping heart, nigger! I give you more than anybody else is ever gonna give you.

CORY: You ain't never gave me nothing! You ain't never done nothing but hold me back. Afraid I was gonna be better than you. All you ever did was try and make me scared of you. I used to tremble every time you called my name. Every time I heard your footsteps in the house. Wondering all the time . . . what's Papa gonna say if I do this? . . . What's he gonna say if I do that? . . . What's Papa gonna say if I turn on the radio? And Mama, too . . . she tries . . . but she's scared of you.

TROY: You leave your mama out of this. She ain't got nothing to do with this.

CORY: I don't know how she stand you . . . after what you did to her.

TROY: I told you to leave your mama out of this!

He advances toward Cory.

CORY: What you gonna do . . . give me a whupping? You can't whup me no more. You're too old. You just an old man.

TROY (*shoves him on his shoulder*): Nigger! That's what you are. You just another nigger on the street to me!

CORY: You crazy! You know that?

TROY: Go on now! You got the devil in you. Get on away from me!

CORY: You just a crazy old man . . . talking about I got the devil in me.

TROY: Yeah, I'm crazy! If you don't get on the other side of that yard . . . I'm gonna show you how crazy I am! Go on . . . get the hell out of my yard.

CORY: It ain't your yard. You took Uncle Gabe's money he got from the army to buy this house and then you put him out.

TROY (*Troy advances on Cory*): Get your black ass out of my yard!

Troy's advance backs Cory up against the tree. Cory grabs up the bat.

CORY: I ain't going nowhere! Come on . . . put me out! I ain't scared of you.

TROY: That's my bat!

CORY: Come on!

TROY: Put my bat down!

CORY: Come on, put me out.

Cory swings at Troy, who backs across the yard.

What's the matter? You so bad . . . put me out!

Troy advances toward Cory.

CORY (*backing up*): Come on! Come on!

TROY: You're gonna have to use it! You wanna draw that bat back on me . . . you're gonna have to use it.

CORY: Come on! . . . Come on!

Cory swings the bat at Troy a second time. He misses. Troy continues to advance toward him.

TROY: You're gonna have to kill me! You wanna draw that bat back on me. You're gonna have to kill me.

Cory, backed up against the tree, can go no farther. Troy taunts him. He sticks out his head and offers him a target.

Come on! Come on!

Cory is unable to swing the bat. Troy grabs it.

TROY: Then I'll show you.

Cory and Troy struggle over the bat. The struggle is fierce and fully engaged. Troy ultimately is the stronger and takes the bat from Cory and stands over him ready to swing. He stops himself.

Go on and get away from around my house.

Cory, stung by his defeat, picks himself up, walks slowly out of the yard and up the alley.

CORY: Tell Mama I'll be back for my things.

TROY: They'll be on the other side of that fence.

Cory exits.

TROY: I can't taste nothing. Helluljah! I can't taste nothing no more. (*Troy assumes a batting posture and begins to taunt Death, the fastball on the outside corner.*) Come on! It's between you and me now! Come on! Anytime you want! Come on! I be ready for you . . . but I ain't gonna be easy.

The lights go down on the scene.

SCENE V: *The time is 1965. The lights come up in the yard. It is the morning of Troy's funeral. A funeral plaque with a light hangs beside the door. There is a small garden plot off to the side. There is noise and activity in the house as Rose, Gabriel, and Bono have gathered. The door opens and Raynell, seven years old, enters dressed in a flannel nightgown. She crosses to the garden and pokes around with a stick. Rose calls from the house.*

ROSE: Raynell!

RAYNELL: Mam?

ROSE: What you doing out there?

RAYNELL: Nothing.

Rose comes to the door.

ROSE: Girl, get in here and get dressed. What you doing?

RAYNELL: Seeing if my garden growed.

ROSE: I told you it ain't gonna grow overnight. You got to wait.

RAYNELL: It don't look like it never gonna grow. Dag!

ROSE: I told you a watched pot never boils. Get in here and get dressed.

RAYNELL: This ain't even no pot, Mama.

ROSE: You just have to give it a chance. It'll grow. Now you come on and do what I told you. We got to be getting ready. This ain't no morning to be playing around. You hear me?

RAYNELL: Yes, mam.

Rose exits into the house. Raynell continues to poke at her garden with a stick. Cory enters. He is dressed in a Marine corporal's uniform, and carries a duffel bag. His posture is that of a military man, and his speech has a clipped sternness.

CORY (*to Raynell*): Hi. (*Pause*). I bet your name is Raynell.

RAYNELL: Uh huh.

CORY: Is your mama home?

Raynell runs up on the porch and calls through the screen door.

RAYNELL: Mama . . . there's some man out here. Mama?

Rose comes to the door.

ROSE: Cory? Lord have mercy! Look here, you all!

Rose and Cory embrace in a tearful reunion as Bono and Lyons enter from the house dressed in funeral clothes.

BONO: Aw, looka here . . .

ROSE: Done got all grown up!

CORY: Don't cry, Mama. What you crying about?

ROSE: I'm just so glad you made it.

CORY: Hey Lyons. How you doing, Mr. Bono.

Lyons goes to embrace Cory.

LYONS: Look at you, man. Look at you. Don't he look good, Rose. Got them Corporal stripes.

ROSE: What took you so long.

CORY: You know how the Marines are, Mama. They got to get all their paperwork straight before they let you do anything.

ROSE: Well, I'm sure glad you made it. They let Lyons come. Your Uncle Gabe's still in the hospital. They don't know if they gonna let him out or not. I just talked to them a little while ago.

LYONS: A Corporal in the United States Marines.

BONO: Your daddy knew you had it in you. He used to tell me all the time.

LYONS: Don't he look good, Mr. Bono?

BONO: Yeah, he remind me of Troy when I first met him. (*Pause.*) Say, Rose, Lucille's down at the church with the choir. I'm gonna go down and get the pallbearers lined up. I'll be back to get you all.

ROSE: Thanks, Jim.

CORY: See you, Mr. Bono.

LYONS (*with his arm around Raynell*): Cory . . . look at Raynell. Ain't she precious? She gonna break a whole lot of hearts.

ROSE: Raynell, come and say hello to your brother. This is your brother, Cory. You remember Cory.

RAYNELL: No, Mam.

CORY: She don't remember me, Mama.

ROSE: Well, we talk about you. She heard us talk about you. (*To Raynell.*) This is your brother, Cory. Come on and say hello.

RAYNELL: Hi.

CORY: Hi. So you're Raynell. Mama told me a lot about you.

ROSE: You all come on into the house and let me fix you some breakfast. Keep up your strength.

CORY: I ain't hungry, Mama.

LYONS: You can fix me something, Rose. I'll be in there in a minute.

ROSE: Cory, you sure you don't want nothing. I know they ain't feeding you right.

CORY: No, Mama . . . thanks. I don't feel like eating. I'll get something later.

ROSE: Raynell . . . get on upstairs and get that dress on like I told you.

Rose and Raynell exit into the house.

LYONS: So . . . I hear you thinking about getting married.

CORY: Yeah, I done found the right one, Lyons. It's about time.

LYONS: Me and Bonnie been split up about four years now. About the time Papa retired. I guess she just got tired of all them changes I was putting her through. (*Pause.*) I always knew you was gonna make something out yourself. Your head was always in the right direction. So . . . you gonna stay in . . . make it a career . . . put in your twenty years?

CORY: I don't know. I got six already, I think that's enough.

LYONS: Stick with Uncle Sam and retire early. Ain't nothing out here. I guess Rose told you what happened with me. They got me down the workhouse. I thought I was being slick cashing other people's checks.

CORY: How much time you doing?

LYONS: They give me three years. I got that beat now. I ain't got but nine more months. It ain't so bad. You learn to deal with it like anything else. You got to take the crookeds with the straights. That's what Papa used to say. He used to say that when he struck out. I seen him strike out three times in a row . . . and the next time up he hit the ball over the grandstand. Right out there in Homestead Field. He wasn't satisfied hitting in the seats . . . he want to hit it over everything! After the game he had two hundred people standing around waiting to shake his hand. You got to take the crookeds with the straights. Yeah, Papa was something else.

CORY: You still playing?

LYONS: Cory . . . you know I'm gonna do that. There's some fellows down there we got us a band . . . we gonna try and stay together when we get out . . . but yeah, I'm still playing. It still helps me to get out of bed in the morning. As long as it do that I'm gonna be right there playing and trying to make some sense out of it.

ROSE (*calling*): Lyons, I got these eggs in the pan.

LYONS: Let me go on and get these eggs, man. Get ready to go bury Papa. (*Pause.*) How you doing? You doing all right?

Cory nods. Lyons touches him on the shoulder and they share a moment of silent grief. Lyons exits into the house. Cory wanders about the yard. Raynell enters.

RAYNELL: Hi.

CORY: Hi.

RAYNELL: Did you used to sleep in my room?

CORY: Yeah . . . that used to be my room.

RAYNELL: That's what Papa call it. "Cory's room." It got your football in the closet.

Rose comes to the door.

ROSE: Raynell, get in there and get them good shoes on.

RAYNELL: Mama, can't I wear these. Them other one hurt my feet.

ROSE: Well, they just gonna have to hurt your feet for a while. You ain't said they hurt your feet when you went down to the store and got them.

RAYNELL: They didn't hurt then. My feet done got bigger.

ROSE: Don't you give me no backtalk now. You get in there and get them shoes on.

Raynell exits into the house.

Ain't too much changed. He still got that piece of rag tied to that tree. He was out here swinging that bat. I was just ready to go back in the house. He swung that bat and then he just fell over. Seem like he swung it and stood there with this grin on his face . . . and then he just fell over. They carried him on down to the hospital, but I knew there wasn't no need . . . why don't you come on in the house?

CORY: Mama . . . I got something to tell you. I don't know how to tell you this . . . but I've got to tell you . . . I'm not going to Papa s funeral.

ROSE: Boy, hush your mouth. That's your daddy you talking about. I don't want hear that kind of talk this morning. I done raised you to come to this? You standing there all healthy and grown talking about you ain't going to your daddy's funeral?

CORY: Mama . . . listen . . .

ROSE: I don't want to hear it, Cory. You just get that thought out of your head.

CORY: I can't drag Papa with me everywhere I go. I've got to say no to him. One time in my life I've got to say no.

ROSE: Don't nobody have to listen to nothing like that. I know you and your daddy ain't seen eye to eye, but I ain't got to listen to that kind of talk this morning. Whatever was between you and your daddy . . . the time has come to put it aside. Just take it and set it over there on the shelf and forget about it. Disrespecting your daddy ain't gonna make you a man, Cory. You got to find a way to come to that on your own. Not going to your daddy's funeral ain't gonna make you a man.

CORY: The whole time I was growing up . . . living in his house . . . Papa was like a shadow that followed you everywhere. It weighed on you and sunk into your flesh. It would wrap around you and lay there until you couldn't tell which one was you anymore. That shadow digging in your flesh. Trying to crawl in. Trying to live through you. Everywhere I looked, Troy Maxson was staring back at me . . . hiding under the bed . . . in the closet. I'm just saying I've got to find a way to get rid of that shadow, Mama.

ROSE: You just like him. You got him in you good.

CORY: Don't tell me that, Mama.

ROSE: You Troy Maxson all over again.

CORY: I don't want to be Troy Maxson. I want to be me.

ROSE: You can't be nobody but who you are, Cory. That shadow wasn't nothing but you growing into yourself. You either got to grow into it or cut it down to fit you. But that's all you got to make life with. That's all you got to measure yourself against that world out there. Your daddy wanted you to be everything he wasn't . . . and at the same time he tried to make you into everything he was. I don't know if he was right or wrong . . . but I do know he meant to do more good than he meant to do harm. He wasn't always right. Sometimes when he touched he bruised. And sometimes when he took me in his arms he cut.

When I first met your daddy I thought . . . Here is a man I can lay down with and make a baby. That's the first thing I thought when I seen him. I was thirty years old and had done seen my share of men. But when he walked up to me and said "I can dance a waltz that'll make you dizzy," I thought, Rose Lee, here is a man that you can open yourself up to and be filled to bursting. Here is a man that can fill all them empty spaces you been tipping around the edges of. One of them empty spaces was being somebody's mother.

I married your daddy and settled down to cooking his supper and keeping clean sheets on the bed. When your daddy walked through the house he was so big he filled it up. That was my first mistake. Not to make him leave some room for me. For my part in the matter. But at that time I wanted that. I wanted a house that I could sing in. And that's what your daddy gave me. I didn't know to keep up his strength I had to give up little pieces of mine. I did that. I took on his life as mine and mixed up the pieces so that you couldn't hardly tell which was which anymore. It was my choice. It was my life and I didn't have to live it like that. But that's what life offered me in the way of being a woman and I took it. I grabbed hold of it with both hands.

By the time Raynell came into the house, me and your daddy had done lost touch with one another. I didn't want to make my blessing off of nobody's misfortune . . . but I took on to Raynell like she was all them babies I had wanted and never had. (*The phone rings.*) Like I'd been blessed to relive a part of my life. And if the Lord see fit to keep up my strength . . . I'm gonna do her just like your daddy did you . . . I'm gonna give her the best of what's in me.

RAYNELL (*entering, still with her old shoes*): Mama . . . Reverend Tollivier on the phone.

Rose exits into the house.

RAYNELL: Hi.

CORY: Hi.

RAYNELL: You in the Army or the Marines?

CORY: Marines.

RAYNELL: Papa said it was the Army. Did you know Blue?

CORY: Blue? Who's Blue?

RAYNELL: Papa's dog what he sing about all the time.

CORY (*singing*): Hear it ring! Hear it ring!
I had a dog his name was Blue
You know Blue was mighty true
You know Blue was a good old dog
Blue treed a possum in a hollow log
You know from that he was a good old dog.
Hear it ring! Hear it ring!

Raynell joins in singing.

CORY AND RAYNELL: Blue treed a possum out on a limb
Blue looked at me and I looked at him
Grabbed that possum and put him in a sack
Blue stayed there till I came back
Old Blue's feets was big and round
Never allowed a possum to touch the ground.

Old Blue died and I dug his grave
I dug his grave with a silver spade
Let him down with a golden chain
And every night I call his name
Go on Blue, you good dog you
Go on Blue, you good dog you

RAYNELL: Blue laid down and died like a man
Blue laid down and died . . .

BOTH: Blue laid down and died like a man
Now he's treeing possums in the Promised Land
I'm gonna tell you this to let you know
Blue's gone where the good dogs go
When I hear old Blue bark
When I hear old Blue bark
Blue treed a possum in Noah's Ark
Blue treed a possum in Noah's Ark.

Rose comes to the screen door.

ROSE: Cory, we gonna be ready to go in a minute.

CORY (*to Raynell*): You go on in the house and change them shoes like Mama told you so we can go to Papa's funeral.

RAYNELL: Okay, I'll be back.

Raynell exits into the house. Cory gets up and crosses over to the tree. Rose stands in the screen door watching him. Gabriel enters from the alley.

GABRIEL (*calling*): Hey, Rose!

ROSE: Gabe?

GABRIEL: I'm here, Rose. Hey Rose, I'm here!

Rose enters from the house.

ROSE: Lord . . . Look here, Lyons!

LYONS: See, told you, Rose . . . I told you they'd let him come.

CORY: How you doing, Uncle Gabe?

LYONS: How you doing, Uncle Gabe?

GABRIEL: Hey, Rose. It's time. It's time to tell St. Peter to open the gates. Troy, you ready? You ready, Troy. I'm gonna tell St. Peter to open the gates. You get ready now.

(*Gabriel, with great fanfare, braces himself to blow. The trumpet is without a mouthpiece. He puts the end of it into his mouth and blows with great force, like a man who has been waiting some twenty-odd years for this single moment. No sound comes out of the trumpet. He braces himself and blows again with the same result. A third time he blows. There is a weight of impossible description that falls away and leaves him bare and exposed to a frightful realization. It is a trauma that a sane and normal mind would be unable to withstand. He begins to dance. A slow, strange dance, eerie and life-giving. A dance of atavistic signature and ritual. Lyons attempts to embrace him. Gabriel pushes Lyons away. He begins to howl in what is an attempt at song, or perhaps a song turning back into itself in an attempt at speech. He finishes his dance and the gates of heaven stand open as wide as God's closet.*)

That's the way that go!

❧

MILCHA SANCHEZ-SCOTT *was born in 1955 in Bali, the daughter of a Colombian father who was an agronomist and a mother with Chinese, Indonesian, and Dutch ancestry. Educated as a young girl at a convent boarding school near London, where she learned English, Sanchez-Scott spent her vacations with her parents in San Marta, Colombia, on a ranch that had belonged to the family for four generations. In 1969 her family moved to California, where Sanchez-Scott attended high school and the University of San Diego, majoring in literature and philosophy. A series of jobs followed, including one at an employment agency in Los Angeles where she met recent immigrants who told her their stories. Sanchez-Scott became so interested in their experiences that she began taking notes. Shortly afterwards she found a job as an actress in an L.A. Theatre Works' project at the women's prison in Chino. There she* *worked with the writer Doris Baizley and was persuaded to use her notes as material for a play. This resulted in Sanchez-Scott's first play,* Latina, *which was commissioned by Susan Loewenberg of L.A. Theatre Works and premiered in 1980.*

In On New Ground, *Sanchez-Scott described her pleasure in finding her vocation as a playwright:*

> *I'd found a channel to get all sorts of things flowing out. I liked controlling my own time, and* making *things — I've always admired architects. Acting seemed very airy to me because I could never take it home and show it to anybody. I had trouble being alone for long periods, but then I would go to the airport or someplace else busy to write. . . .*
>
> *L.A. Theatre Works got a grant and we toured* Latina *up and down the state with ten Latin actresses who were always feuding. We had one who was illegal, and wouldn't perform anyplace she thought Immigration might come, so I had to go on in her place. Then Susan commissioned me to write something else, which turned out to be* Dog Lady *and* Cuban Swimmer. *I saw the long-distance swimmer Diana Nyad on TV and I saw [Alberto] Salazar — the Cuban runner — and started thinking. I wanted to set a play in the water. So I put a family on a boat and a swimmer in the water and said, "Now,* what?" *I happened to be in a church and saw the most beautiful Stations of the Cross. It struck me as a good outline for anybody undertaking an endeavor — there's all of this tripping and falling and rising. So that's what I used.*

Dog Lady *and* The Cuban Swimmer *were first produced in 1984. They were so successful —* The Cuban Swimmer *won a Le Compte de Nouy Foundation Award — that Sanchez-Scott went to New York City to participate in the theater workshop of playwright Irene Fornés. There Sanchez-Scott developed* Roosters *(1988). Currently she lives in Southern California. Her more recent plays include* Evening Star, City of Angels, *and* The Architect Piece.

MILCHA SANCHEZ-SCOTT

The Cuban Swimmer

1984

CHARACTERS

MARGARITA SUÁREZ, *the swimmer*
EDUARDO SUÁREZ, *her father, the coach*
SIMÓN SUÁREZ, *her brother*
AÍDA SUÁREZ, *the mother*
ABUELA, *her grandmother*
VOICE OF MEL MUNSON
VOICE OF MARY BETH WHITE
VOICE OF RADIO OPERATOR

SETTING: *The Pacific Ocean between San Pedro and Catalina Island.*

TIME: *Summer.*

Live conga drums can be used to punctuate the action of the play.

SCENE 1

Pacific Ocean. Midday. On the horizon, in perspective, a small boat enters upstage left, crosses to upstage right, and exits. Pause. Lower on the horizon, the same boat, in larger perspective, enters upstage right, crosses, and exits upstage left. Blackout.

SCENE 2

Pacific Ocean. Midday. The swimmer, Margarita Suárez, is swimming. On the boat following behind her are her father, Eduardo Suárez, holding a megaphone, and Simón, her brother, sitting on top of the cabin with his shirt off, punk sunglasses on, binoculars hanging on his chest.

EDUARDO (*leaning forward, shouting in time to Margarita's swimming*): *Uno, dos, uno, dos. Y uno, dos . . .* keep your shoulders parallel to the water.

SIMÓN: I'm gonna take these glasses off and look straight into the sun.

EDUARDO (*through megaphone*): *Muy bien, muy bien*° . . . but punch those arms in, baby.

SIMÓN (*looking directly at the sun through binoculars*): Come on, come on, zap me. Show me something. (*He looks behind at the shoreline and ahead at the sea.*) Stop! Stop, *Papi!* Stop!

Aída Suárez and Abuela, the swimmer's mother and grandmother, enter running from the back of the boat.

AÍDA AND ABUELA: *Qué? Qué es?*°

AÍDA: *Es un* shark?°

EDUARDO: Eh?

ABUELA: *Que es un* shark *dicen?*°

Eduardo blows whistle. Margarita looks up at the boat.

SIMÓN: No, *Papi*, no shark, no shark. We've reached the halfway mark.

ABUELA (*looking into the water*): *A dónde está?*°

AÍDA: It's not in the water.

ABUELA: Oh, no? Oh, no?

AÍDA: No! *A poco* do you think they're gonna have signs in the water to say you are halfway to Santa Catalina? No. It's done very scientific. *A ver, hijo,*° explain it to your grandma.

SIMÓN: Well, you see, Abuela — (*He points behind.*) There's San Pedro. (*He points ahead.*) And there's Santa Catalina. Looks halfway to me.

Abuela shakes her head and is looking back and forth, trying to make the decision, when suddenly the sound of a helicopter is heard.

ABUELA (*looking up*): *Virgencita de la Caridad del Cobre. Qué es eso?*°

Sound of helicopter gets closer. Margarita looks up.

MARGARITA: *Papi, Papi!*

Muy bien, muy bien: Very good, very good (Spanish). ***Qué? Qué es?:*** What? What is it? ***Es un shark?:*** Is it a shark? ***Que es un shark dicen?:*** Did they say a shark? ***A dónde está?:*** Where is it? ***A ver, hijo:*** Look here, son. ***Virgencita . . . es eso?:*** Virgin of Charity! What is that?

A small commotion on the boat, with everybody pointing at the helicopter above. Shadows of the helicopter fall on the boat. Simón looks up at it through binoculars.

Papi — qué es? What is it?

EDUARDO (*through megaphone*): Uh . . . uh . . . uh, *un momentico . . . mi hija.*° . . . Your *papi*'s got everything under control, understand? Uh . . . you just keep stroking. And stay . . . uh . . . close to the boat.

SIMÓN: Wow, *Papi!* We're on TV, man! Holy Christ, we're all over the fucking U.S.A.! It's Mel Munson and Mary Beth White!

AÍDA: *Por Dios!*° Simón, don't swear. And put on your shirt.

Aída fluffs her hair, puts on her sunglasses, and waves to the helicopter. Simón leans over the side of the boat and yells to Margarita.

SIMÓN: Yo, Margo! You're on TV, man.

EDUARDO: Leave your sister alone. Turn on the radio.

MARGARITA: *Papi! Qué está pasando?*°

ABUELA: *Que es la televisión dicen?* (*She shakes her head.*) *Porque como yo no puedo ver nada sin mis espejuelos.*°

Abuela rummages through the boat, looking for her glasses. Voices of Mel Munson and Mary Beth White are heard over the boat's radio.

MEL'S VOICE: As we take a closer look at the gallant crew of *La Havana* . . . and there . . . yes, there she is . . . the little Cuban swimmer from Long Beach, California, nineteen-year-old Margarita Suárez. The unknown swimmer is our Cinderella entry . . . a bundle of tenacity, battling her way through the choppy, murky waters of the cold Pacific to reach the Island of Romance . . . Santa Catalina . . . where should she be the first to arrive, two thousand dollars and a gold cup will be waiting for her.

AÍDA: Doesn't even cover our expenses.

ABUELA: *Qué dice?*

EDUARDO: Shhhh!

MARY BETH'S VOICE: This is really a family effort, Mel, and —

MEL'S VOICE: Indeed it is. Her trainer, her coach, her mentor, is her father, Eduardo Suárez. Not a swimmer himself, it says here, Mr. Suárez is head usher of the Holy Name Society and the owner-operator of Suárez Treasures of the Sea and Salvage Yard. I guess it's one of those places —

MARY BETH'S VOICE: If I might interject a fact here, Mel, assisting in this swim is Mrs. Suárez, who is a former Miss Cuba.

MEL'S VOICE: And a beautiful woman in her own right. Let's try and get a closer look.

Helicopter sound gets louder. Margarita, frightened, looks up again.

MARGARITA: *Papi!*

EDUARDO (*through megaphone*): *Mi hija,* don't get nervous . . . it's the press. I'm handling it.

---

un momentico . . . mi hija: Just a moment . . . my daughter. ***Por Dios!:*** For God's sake! ***Papi! . . . pasando?:*** Dad! What's happening? ***Que es la televisión . . . mis espejuelos:*** Did they say television? Because I can't see without my glasses.

AÍDA: I see how you're handling it.

EDUARDO (*through megaphone*): Do you hear? Everything is under control. Get back into your rhythm. Keep your elbows high and kick and kick and kick and kick . . .

ABUELA (*finds her glasses and puts them on*): *Ay sí, es la televisión* . . . (*She points to helicopter.*) *Qué lindo mira*° . . . (*She fluffs her hair, gives a big wave.*) *Aló América! Viva mi Margarita, viva todo los Cubanos en los Estados Unidos!*°

AÍDA: *Ay por Dios,* Cecilia, the man didn't come all this way in his helicopter to look at you jumping up and down, making a fool of yourself.

ABUELA: I don't care. I'm proud.

AÍDA: He can't understand you anyway.

ABUELA: *Viva* . . . (*She stops.*) *Simón, comó se dice viva?*°

SIMÓN: Hurray.

ABUELA: Hurray for *mi Margarita y* for all the Cubans living *en* the United States, *y un abrazo . . . Simón, abrazo . . .*

SIMÓN: A big hug.

ABUELA: *Sí,* a big hug to all my friends in Miami, Long Beach, Union City, except for my son Carlos, who lives in New York in sin! He lives . . . (*She crosses herself.*) in Brooklyn with a Puerto Rican woman in sin! *No decente . . .*

SIMÓN: Decent.

ABUELA: Carlos, *no decente.* This family, *decente.*

AÍDA: Cecilia, *por Dios.*

MEL'S VOICE: Look at that enthusiasm. The whole family has turned out to cheer little Margarita on to victory! I hope they won't be too disappointed.

MARY BETH'S VOICE: She seems to be making good time, Mel.

MEL'S VOICE: Yes, it takes all kinds to make a race. And it's a testimonial to the all-encompassing fairness . . . the greatness of this, the Wrigley Invitational Women's Swim to Catalina, where among all the professionals there is still room for the amateurs . . . like these, the simple people we see below us on the ragtag *La Havana,* taking their long-shot chance to victory. *Vaya con Dios!*°

Helicopter sound fading as family, including Margarita, watch silently. Static as Simón turns radio off. Eduardo walks to bow of boat, looks out on the horizon.

EDUARDO (*to himself*): Amateurs.

AÍDA: Eduardo, that person insulted us. Did you hear, Eduardo? That he called us a simple people in a ragtag boat? Did you hear . . . ?

ABUELA (*clenching her fist at departing helicopter*): *Mal-Rayo los parta!*°

SIMÓN (*same gesture*): Asshole!

Aída follows Eduardo as he goes to side of boat and stares at Margarita.

Qué lindo mira: Does it look nice? ***Aló América! . . . Estados Unidos!:*** Hello America! Hurray for my Margarita, hurray for all the Cubans in the United States! ***comó se dice viva?:*** How do you say "viva" (i.e., in English)? ***Vaya con Dios!:*** Bless You! ***Mal-Rayo los parta!:*** To hell with you!

AÍDA: This person comes in his helicopter to insult your wife, your family, your daughter . . .

MARGARITA (*pops her head out of the water*): *Papi?*

AÍDA: Do you hear me, Eduardo? I am not simple.

ABUELA: *Sí.*

AÍDA: I am complicated.

ABUELA: *Sí, demasiada complicada.*

AÍDA: Me and my family are not so simple.

SIMÓN: Mom, the guy's an asshole.

ABUELA (*shaking her fist at helicopter*): Asshole!

AÍDA: If my daughter was simple, she would not be in that water swimming.

MARGARITA: Simple? *Papi . . . ?*

AÍDA: *Ahora,*° Eduardo, this is what I want you to do. When we get to Santa Catalina, I want you to call the TV station and demand an apology.

EDUARDO: *Cállete mujer! Aquí mando yo.*° I will decide what is to be done.

MARGARITA: *Papi,* tell me what's going on.

EDUARDO: Do you understand what I am saying to you, Aída?

SIMÓN (*leaning over side of boat, to Margarita*): Yo Margo! You know that Mel Munson guy on TV? He called you a simple amateur and said you didn't have a chance.

ABUELA (*leaning directly behind Simón*): *Mi hija, insultó a la familia. Desgraciado!*

AÍDA (*leaning in behind Abuela*): He called us peasants! And your father is not doing anything about it. He just knows how to yell at me.

EDUARDO (*through megaphone*): Shut up! All of you! Do you want to break her concentration? Is that what you are after? Eh?

Abuela, Aída, and Simón shrink back. Eduardo paces before them.

Swimming is rhythm and concentration. You win a race *aquí.* (*Pointing to his head.*) Now . . . (*To Simón.*) you, take care of the boat, Aída *y Mama* . . . do something. Anything. Something practical.

Abuela and Aída get on knees and pray in Spanish.

Hija, give it everything, eh? . . . *por la familia. Uno . . . dos. . . .* You must win.

Simón goes into cabin. The prayers continue as lights change to indicate bright sunlight, later in the afternoon.

SCENE 3

Tableau for a couple of beats. Eduardo on bow with timer in one hand as he counts strokes per minute. Simón is in the cabin steering, wearing his sunglasses, baseball cap on backward. Abuela and Aída are at the side of the boat, heads down, hands folded, still muttering prayers in Spanish.

AÍDA AND ABUELA (*crossing themselves*): *En el nombre del Padre, del Hijo y del Espíritu Santo amén.*°

EDUARDO (*through megaphone*): You're stroking seventy-two!

Ahora: Now. ***Cállete mujer! . . . yo:*** Quiet, woman! I'm in charge here. ***En el nombre . . . amén:*** In the name of the Father, the Son, and the Holy Ghost, amen.

SIMÓN (*singing*): Mama's stroking, Mama's stroking seventy-two. . . .

EDUARDO (*through megaphone*): You comfortable with it?

SIMÓN (*singing*): Seventy-two, seventy-two, seventy-two for you.

AÍDA (*looking at the heavens*): *Ay*, Eduardo, *ven acá*,° we should be grateful that *Nuestro Señor*° gave us such a beautiful day.

ABUELA (*crosses herself*): *Sí, gracias a Dios*.°

EDUARDO: She's stroking seventy-two, with no problem. (*He throws a kiss to the sky.*) It's a beautiful day to win.

AÍDA: *Qué hermoso!*° So clear and bright. Not a cloud in the sky. *Mira!*° *Mira!* Even rainbows on the water . . . a sign from God.

SIMÓN (*singing*): Rainbows on the water . . . you in my arms . . .

ABUELA AND EDUARDO (*looking the wrong way*): *Dónde?*

AÍDA (*pointing toward Margarita*): There, dancing in front of Margarita, leading her on . . .

EDUARDO: Rainbows on . . . *Ay coño!* It's an oil slick! You . . . you . . . (*To Simón.*) Stop the boat. (*Runs to bow, yelling.*) Margarita! Margarita!

On the next stroke, Margarita comes up all covered in black oil.

MARGARITA: *Papi! Papi . . . !*

Everybody goes to the side and stares at Margarita, who stares back. Eduardo freezes.

AÍDA: *Apúrate*, Eduardo, move . . . what's wrong with you . . . *no me oíste*,° get my daughter out of the water.

EDUARDO (*softly*): We can't touch her. If we touch her, she's disqualified.

AÍDA: But I'm her mother.

EDUARDO: Not even by her own mother. Especially by her own mother. . . . You always want the rules to be different for you, you always want to be the exception. (*To Simón.*) And you . . . you didn't see it, eh? You were playing again?

SIMÓN: *Papi*, I was watching . . .

AÍDA (*interrupting*): *Pues*, do something Eduardo. You are the big coach, the monitor.

SIMÓN: Mentor! Mentor!

EDUARDO: How can a person think around you? (*He walks off to bow, puts head in hands.*)

ABUELA (*looking over side*): *Mira como todos los* little birds are dead. (*She crosses herself.*)

AÍDA: Their little wings are glued to their sides.

SIMÓN: Christ, this is like the La Brea tar pits.

AÍDA: They can't move their little wings.

ABUELA: *Esa niña tiene que moverse*.°

SIMÓN: Yeah, Margo, you gotta move, man.

Abuela and Simón gesture for Margarita to move. Aída gestures for her to swim.

---

ven acá: Look here. ***Nuestro Señor:*** Our Father (i.e., God). ***Sí, gracias a Dios:*** Yes, thanks be to God. ***Qué hermoso!:*** How beautiful! ***Mira!:*** Look! ***Apúrate . . . oíste:*** Finish this . . . didn't you hear me! ***Esa niña . . . moverse:*** That girl has to move.

ABUELA: *Anda niña, muévete.*°

AÍDA: Swim, *hija,* swim or the *aceite*° will stick to your wings.

MARGARITA: *Papi?*

ABUELA (*taking megaphone*): Your *papi* says "move it!"

Margarita with difficulty starts moving.

ABUELA, AÍDA, AND SIMÓN (*laboriously counting*): *Uno, dos . . . uno, dos . . . anda . . . uno, dos.*

EDUARDO (*running to take megaphone from Abuela*): *Uno, dos . . .*

Simón races into cabin and starts the engine. Abuela, Aída, and Eduardo count together.

SIMÓN (*looking ahead*): *Papi,* it's over there!

EDUARDO: Eh?

SIMÓN (*pointing ahead and to the right*): It's getting clearer over there.

EDUARDO (*through megaphone*): Now pay attention to me. Go to the right.

Simón, Abuela, Aída, and Eduardo all lean over side. They point ahead and to the right, except Abuela, who points to the left.

FAMILY (*shouting together*): *Para yá!*° *Para yá!*

Lights go down on boat. A special light on Margarita, swimming through the oil, and on Abuela, watching her.

ABUELA: *Sangre de mi sangre,*° you will be another to save us. En Bolondron, where your great-grandmother Luz Suárez was born, they say one day it rained blood. All the people, they run into their houses. They cry, they pray, *pero* your great-grandmother Luz she had *cojones* like a man. She run outside. She look straight at the sky. She shake her fist. And she say to the evil one, "*Mira . . .* (*Beating her chest.*) *coño, Diablo, aquí estoy si me quieres.*"° And she open her mouth, and she drunk the blood.

Blackout.

SCENE 4

Lights up on boat. Aída and Eduardo are on deck watching Margarita swim. We hear the gentle, rhythmic lap, lap, lap of the water, then the sound of inhaling and exhaling as Margarita's breathing becomes louder. Then Margarita's heartbeat is heard, with the lapping of the water and the breathing under it. These sounds continue beneath the dialogue to the end of the scene.

AÍDA: *Dios mío.* Look how she moves through the water . . .

EDUARDO: You see, it's very simple. It is a matter of concentration.

AÍDA: The first time I put her in water she came to life, she grew before my eyes. She moved, she smiled, she loved it more than me. She didn't want my breast any longer. She wanted the water.

EDUARDO: And of course, the rhythm. The rhythm takes away the pain and helps the concentration.

Anda niña, muévete: Come on, girl, move. ***aceite:*** Oil. ***Para yá!:*** Over there. ***Sangre de . . . sangre:*** Blood of my blood. ***Mira . . . me quieres:*** Look . . . damn it, Devil, here I am if you want me.

Pause. Aída and Eduardo watch Margarita.

AÍDA: Is that my child or a seal . . .

EDUARDO: Ah, a seal, the reason for that is that she's keeping her arms very close to her body. She cups her hands, and then she reaches and digs, reaches and digs.

AÍDA: To think that a daughter of mine . . .

EDUARDO: It's the training, the hours in the water. I used to tie weights around her little wrists and ankles.

AÍDA: A spirit, an ocean spirit, must have entered my body when I was carrying her.

EDUARDO (*to Margarita*): Your stroke is slowing down.

Pause. We hear Margarita's heartbeat with the breathing under, faster now.

AÍDA: Eduardo, that night, the night on the boat . . .

EDUARDO: Ah, the night on the boat again . . . the moon was . . .

AÍDA: The moon was full. We were coming to America. . . . *Qué romantico.*

Heartbeat and breathing continue.

EDUARDO: We were cold, afraid, with no money, and on top of everything, you were hysterical, yelling at me, tearing at me with your nails. (*Opens his shirt, points to the base of his neck.*) Look, I still bear the scars . . . telling me that I didn't know what I was doing . . . saying that we were going to die. . . .

AÍDA: You took me, you stole me from my home . . . you didn't give me a chance to prepare. You just said we have to go now, now! Now, you said. You didn't let me take anything. I left everything behind. . . . I left everything behind.

EDUARDO: Saying that I wasn't good enough, that your father didn't raise you so that I could drown you in the sea.

AÍDA: You didn't let me say even a good-bye. You took me, you stole me, you tore me from my home.

EDUARDO: I took you so we could be married.

AÍDA: That was in Miami. But that night on the boat, Eduardo. . . . We were not married, that night on the boat.

EDUARDO: *No pasó nada!*° Once and for all get it out of your head, it was cold, you hated me, and we were afraid. . . .

AÍDA: *Mentiroso!*°

EDUARDO: A man can't do it when he is afraid.

AÍDA: Liar! You did it very well.

EDUARDO: I did?

AÍDA: *Sí.* Gentle. You were so gentle and then strong . . . my passion for you so deep. Standing next to you . . . I would ache . . . looking at your hands I would forget to breathe, you were irresistible.

EDUARDO: I was?

No pasó nada!: Nothing happened! ***Mentiroso!:*** Liar!

AÍDA: You took me into your arms, you touched my face with your fingertips . . . you kissed my eyes . . . *la esquina de la boca y*° . . .

EDUARDO: *Sí, sí,* and then . . .

AÍDA: I look at your face on top of mine, and I see the lights of Havana in your eyes. That's when you seduced me.

EDUARDO: Shhh, they're gonna hear you.

Lights go down. Special on Aída.

AÍDA: That was the night. A woman doesn't forget those things . . . and later that night was the dream . . . the dream of a big country with fields of fertile land and big, giant things growing. And there by a green, slimy pond I found a giant pea pod and when I opened it, it was full of little, tiny baby frogs.

Aída crosses herself as she watches Margarita. We hear louder breathing and heartbeat.

MARGARITA: Santa Teresa. Little Flower of God, pray for me. San Martín de Porres, pray for me. Santa Rosa de Lima, *Virgencita de la Caridad del Cobre,* pray for me. . . . Mother pray for me.

SCENE 5

Loud howling of wind is heard, as lights change to indicate unstable weather, fog, and mist. Family on deck, braced and huddled against the wind. Simón is at the helm.

AÍDA: *Ay Dios mío, qué viento.*

EDUARDO (*through megaphone*): Don't drift out . . . that wind is pushing you out. (*To Simón.*) You! Slow down. Can't you see your sister is drifting out?

SIMÓN: It's the wind, *Papi.*

AÍDA: Baby, don't go so far. . . .

ABUELA (*to heaven*): *Ay Gran Poder de Dios, quita este maldito viento.*°

SIMÓN: Margo! Margo! Stay close to the boat.

EDUARDO: Dig in. Dig in hard. . . . Reach down from your guts and dig in.

ABUELA (*to heaven*): *Ay Virgen de la Caridad del Cobre, por lo más tú quieres a pararla.*

AÍDA (*putting her hand out, reaching for Margarita*): Baby, don't go far.

Abuela crosses herself. Action freezes. Lights get dimmer, special on Margarita. She keeps swimming, stops, starts again, stops, then, finally exhausted, stops altogether. The boat stops moving.

EDUARDO: What's going on here? Why are we stopping?

SIMÓN: *Papi,* she's not moving! Yo Margo!

The family all run to the side.

EDUARDO: *Hija!* . . . *Hijita!* You're tired, eh?

AÍDA: *Por supuesto*° she's tired. I like to see you get in the water, waving your arms and legs from San Pedro to Santa Catalina. A person isn't a machine, a person has to rest.

---

la esquina de la boca y . . . : The corner of the mouth and . . . ***Ay Gran . . . viento:*** By the great power of God, keep the cursed winds away. ***Por supuesto:*** Of course.

SIMÓN: Yo, Mama! Cool out, it ain't fucking brain surgery.

EDUARDO (*to Simón*): Shut up, you. (*Louder to Margarita.*) I guess your mother's right for once, huh? . . . I guess you had to stop, eh? . . . Give your brother, the idiot . . . a chance to catch up with you.

SIMÓN (*clowning like Mortimer Snerd*°): Dum dee dum dee dum ooops, ah shucks . . .

EDUARDO: I don't think he's Cuban.

SIMÓN (*like Ricky Ricardo*°): *Oye,* Lucy! I'm home! Ba ba lu!

EDUARDO (*joins in clowning, grabbing Simón in a headlock*): What am I gonna do with this idiot, eh? I don't understand this idiot. He's not like us, Margarita. (*Laughing.*) You think if we put him into your bathing suit with a cap on his head . . . (*He laughs hysterically.*) You think anyone would know . . . huh? Do you think anyone would know? (*Laughs.*)

SIMÓN (*vamping*): *Ay, mi amor.* Anybody looking for tits would know.

Eduardo slaps Simón across the face, knocking him down. Aída runs to Simón's aid. Abuela holds Eduardo back.

MARGARITA: *Mía culpa!*° *Mía culpa!*

ABUELA: *Qué dices hija?*

MARGARITA: *Papi,* it's my fault, it's all my fault. . . . I'm so cold, I can't move. . . . I put my face in the water . . . and I hear them whispering . . . laughing at me. . . .

AÍDA: Who is laughing at you?

MARGARITA: The fish are all biting me . . . they hate me . . . they whisper about me. She can't swim, they say. She can't glide. She has no grace. . . . Yellowtails, bonita, tuna, man-o'-war, snug-nose sharks, *los baracudas* . . . they all hate me . . . only the dolphins care . . . and sometimes I hear the whales crying . . . she is lost, she is dead. I'm so numb, I can't feel. *Papi! Papi!* Am I dead?

EDUARDO: *Vamos,* baby, punch those arms in. Come on . . . do you hear me?

MARGARITA: *Papi* . . . *Papi* . . . forgive me. . . .

All is silent on the boat. Eduardo drops his megaphone, his head bent down in dejection. Abuela, Aída, Simón, all leaning over the side of the boat. Simón slowly walks away.

AÍDA: *Mi hija, qué tienes?*°

SIMÓN: Oh, Christ, don't make her say it. Please don't make her say it.

ABUELA: Say what? *Qué cosa?*

SIMÓN: She wants to quit, can't you see she's had enough?

ABUELA: *Mira, para eso. Esta niña* is turning blue.

AÍDA: *Oyeme, hi mija.* Do you want to come out of the water?

MARGARITA: *Papi?*

SIMÓN (*to Eduardo*): She won't come out until *you* tell her.

AÍDA: Eduardo . . . answer your daughter.

Mortimer Snerd: A popular ventriloquist doll. **Ricky Ricardo:** The husband of Lucy on the 1950s television show *I Love Lucy;* the role was played by Desi Arnaz. ***Mía culpa!:*** It's my fault! ***qué tienes?:*** What do you need?

EDUARDO: *Le dije* to concentrate . . . concentrate on your rhythm. Then the rhythm would carry her . . . ay, it's a beautiful thing, Aída. It's like yoga, like meditation, the mind over matter . . . the mind controlling the body . . . that's how the great things in the world have been done. I wish you . . . I wish my wife could understand.

MARGARITA: *Papi?*

SIMÓN (*to Margarita*): Forget him.

AÍDA (*imploring*): Eduardo, *por favor.*

EDUARDO (*walking in circles*): Why didn't you let her concentrate? Don't you understand, the concentration, the rhythm is everything. But no, you wouldn't listen. (*Screaming to the ocean.*) Goddamn Cubans, why, God, why do you make us go everywhere with our families? (*He goes to back of boat.*)

AÍDA (*opening her arms*): *Mi hija, ven,* come to *Mami.* (*Rocking.*) Your *mami* knows.

Abuela has taken the training bottle, puts it in a net. She and Simón lower it to Margarita.

SIMÓN: Take this. Drink it. (*As Margarita drinks, Abuela crosses herself.*)

AÍDA: *Sangre de mi sangre.*

Music comes up softly. Margarita drinks, gives the bottle back, stretches out her arms, as if on a cross. Floats on her back. She begins a graceful backstroke. Lights fade on boat as special lights come up on Margarita. She stops. Slowly turns over and starts to swim, gradually picking up speed. Suddenly as if in pain she stops, tries again, then stops in pain again. She becomes disoriented and falls to the bottom of the sea. Special on Margarita at the bottom of the sea.

MARGARITA: *Ya no puedo* . . . I can't. . . . A person isn't a machine . . . *es mi culpa* . . . Father forgive me . . . *Papi! Papi!* One, two. *Uno, dos.* (*Pause.*) *Papi! A dónde estás?* (*Pause.*) One, two, one, two. *Papi! Ay, Papi!* Where are you . . . ? Don't leave me. . . . Why don't you answer me? (*Pause. She starts to swim, slowly.*) *Uno, dos, uno dos.* Dig in, dig in. (*Stops swimming.*) *Por favor, Papi!* (*Starts to swim again.*) One, two, one, two. Kick from your hip, kick from your hip. (*Stops swimming. Starts to cry.*) Oh God, please. . . . (*Pause.*) Hail Mary, full of grace . . . dig in, dig in . . . the Lord is with thee. . . . (*She swims to the rhythm of her Hail Mary.*) Hail Mary, full of grace . . . dig in, dig in . . . the Lord is with thee . . . dig in, dig in. . . . Blessed art thou among women. . . . *Mami,* it hurts. You let go of my hand. I'm lost. . . . And blessed is the fruit of thy womb, now and at the hour of our death. Amen. I don't want to die, I don't want to die.

Margarita is still swimming. Blackout. She is gone.

SCENE 6

Lights up on boat, we hear radio static. There is a heavy mist. On deck we see only black outline of Abuela with shawl over her head. We hear the voices of Eduardo, Aída, and radio operator.

EDUARDO'S VOICE: La Havana! Coming from San Pedro. Over.

RADIO OPERATOR'S VOICE: Right, DT6-6, you say you've lost a swimmer.

AÍDA'S VOICE: Our child, our only daughter . . . listen to me. Her name is Margarita Inez Suárez, she is wearing a black one-piece bathing suit cut high in the legs with a white racing stripe down the sides, a white bathing cap with goggles and her whole body covered with a . . . with a . . .

EDUARDO'S VOICE: With lanolin and paraffin.

AÍDA'S VOICE: *Sí . . . con lanolin and paraffin.*

More radio static. Special on Simón, on the edge of the boat.

SIMÓN: Margo! Yo Margo! (*Pause.*) Man don't do this. (*Pause.*) Come on. . . . Come on. . . . (*Pause.*) God, why does everything have to be so hard? (*Pause.*) Stupid. You know you're not supposed to die for this. Stupid. It's his dream and he can't even swim. (*Pause.*) Punch those arms in. Come home. Come home. I'm your little brother. Don't forget what Mama said. You're not supposed to leave me behind. *Vamos,* Margarita, take your little brother, hold his hand tight when you cross the street. He's so little. (*Pause.*) Oh, Christ, give us a sign. . . . I know! I know! Margo, I'll send you a message . . . like mental telepathy. I'll hold my breath, close my eyes, and I'll bring you home. (*He takes a deep breath; a few beats.*) This time I'll beep . . . I'll send out sonar signals like a dolphin. (*He imitates dolphin sounds.*)

The sound of real dolphins takes over from Simón, then fades into sound of Abuela saying the Hail Mary in Spanish, as full lights come up slowly.

SCENE 7

Eduardo coming out of cabin, sobbing, Aída holding him. Simón anxiously scanning the horizon. Abuela looking calmly ahead.

EDUARDO: *Es mi culpa, sí, es mi culpa.* (*He hits his chest.*)

AÍDA: *Ya, ya viejo*° . . . it was my sin . . . I left my home.

EDUARDO: Forgive me, forgive me. I've lost our daughter, our sister, our granddaughter, *mi carne, mi sangre, mis ilusiones.*° (*To heaven.*) *Dios mío,* take me . . . take me, I say . . . Goddammit, take me!

SIMÓN: I'm going in.

AÍDA AND EDUARDO: No!

EDUARDO (*grabbing and holding Simón, speaking to heaven*): God, take me, not my children. They are my dreams, my illusions . . . and not this one, this one is my mystery . . . he has my secret dreams. In him are the parts of me I cannot see.

Eduardo embraces Simón. Radio static becomes louder.

AÍDA: I . . . I think I see her.

SIMÓN: No, it's just a seal.

ABUELA (*looking out with binoculars*): *Mi nietacita,*° *dónde estás?* (*She feels her heart.*) I don't feel the knife in my heart . . . my little fish is not lost.

Radio crackles with static. As lights dim on boat, voices of Mel and Mary Beth are heard over the radio.

Ya, ya viejo: Yes, yes, old man. ***mi carne, mi sangre, mis ilusiones:*** My flesh, my blood, my dreams. ***nietacita:*** Little granddaughter.

MEL'S VOICE: Tragedy has marred the face of the Wrigley International Women's Race to Catalina. The Cuban swimmer, little Margarita Suárez, has reportedly been lost at sea. Coast Guard and divers are looking for her as we speak. Yet in spite of this tragedy the race must go on because . . .

MARY BETH'S VOICE (*interrupting loudly*): Mel!

MEL'S VOICE (*startled*): What!

MARY BETH'S VOICE: Ah . . . excuse me, Mel . . . we have a winner. We've just received word from Catalina that one of the swimmers is just fifty yards from the breakers . . . it's, oh, it's . . . Margarita Suárez!

Special on family in cabin listening to radio.

MEL'S VOICE: What? I thought she died!

Special on Margarita, taking off bathing cap, trophy in hand, walking on the water.

MARY BETH'S VOICE: Ahh . . . unless . . . unless this is a tragic . . . No . . . there she is, Mel. Margarita Suárez! The only one in the race wearing a black bathing suit cut high in the legs with a racing stripe down the side.

Family cheering, embracing.

SIMÓN (*screaming*): Way to go, Margo!

MEL'S VOICE: This is indeed a miracle! It's a resurrection! Margarita Suárez, with a flotilla of boats to meet her, is now walking on the waters, through the breakers . . . onto the beach, with crowds of people cheering her on. What a jubilation! This is a miracle!

Sounds of crowds cheering. Lights and cheering sounds fade.

Blackout.

ꕤ

PHILIP KAN GOTANDA *(b. 1951) is the third son of a second-generation Japanese American doctor who was interred in a camp for Japanese Americans in Arkansas during World War II. After the war, his father resumed his medical practice in Stockton, California, where he met and married a schoolteacher and began a family. As a teenager, Gotanda was passionately interested in music and spent hours practicing the guitar, playing in bands, and composing songs. Enrolling at the University of California at Santa Cruz in 1969, he studied psychology for a year, but he left college to travel in Japan. There he discovered what he called "racial anonymity." He later said,*

> *I didn't go to Japan, I left America. Here, I felt that I just couldn't find my niche. In Japan, I had a somewhat mystical experience. For the first time in my life, I experienced a sense of racial anonymity. I was living without the burden of racism, I didn't have to work at constantly deflecting it. The mantle of racism lifted off my shoulders and drifted away. What an extraordinary feeling.*

Yet, even in his ancestral homeland, Gotanda found that he still experienced minority status and identity, since he was regarded there as a sansei, a Japanese American, not as a Japanese. Returning to the United States, Gotanda enrolled at the University of California at Santa Barbara, graduating in 1973, and he completed a degree at Hastings College of Law five years later.

While he worked at the North Beach–Chinatown Legal Aid Society in San Francisco, Gotanda wrote his first play, a musical titled The Avocado Kid or Zen in the Art of Guacamole, *based on a classic Japanese children's tale. Gotanda's debut as a playwright coincided with the development of several Asian American theater companies, including the East West Players in Los Angeles, the Asian American Theatre Workshop in San Francisco, and the Pan-Asian Repertory Theatre in New York. In the 1960s these theater companies dramatized the work of Asian writers like Yukio Mishima and featured Asian American actors in classic American and European plays. By the late 1970s the companies were eager to develop a uniquely Asian American cultural aesthetic. Gotanda began to write plays for the Asian American theater companies in 1979. His work evolved from early musicals such as* Bullet Headed Birds *to straight dramas such as* The Wash *(1987), which is part of a family trilogy along with the plays* Fish Head Soup *and* A Song for a Nisei Fisherman. *As the critic Michael Omi understood,*

> *The result of Gotanda's leap from the "margins" to the mainstream of the theater world has been a broadening of his audience without a dramatic shift in subject or tone on his part. In several plays, Japanese American references and vernacular are treated as "natural" elements of the dialogue, with little effort expended to make it accessible or intelligible to non-Japanese American audiences. His cultural specificity, however, is strategically utilized as a way of affording his audience a more expansive look at who and what America really is. . . . He depicts the rituals, the relationships, the conversations, and, in essence, the sight, sounds, and smells of Japanese America.*

The initial idea for The Wash *evolved from two real-life stories. The first was the middle-aged nisei mother of a friend of Gotanda who had separated from her husband and begun a love affair — something rare in Japanese American communities, where a nisei woman usually submerges her own dreams in order to nurture the dreams of her husband and children. The second source was a divorced writer whose ex-husband continued to mow her lawn regularly. When Gotanda conceived* The Wash, *the lawn became laundry.*

Participating in a panel of playwrights discussing the future of American theater in 1999, August Wilson eloquently called for more diversity in our national theater:

> *The question that comes to my mind is what is American about the American theater? We have an art form that is based on European dramatic values, an age-old dramaturgy that is handed down from the Greeks. That is the art form that I work in and one that I embrace.*
>
> *America is a society that is multiracial and multicultural. Yet the values of the American theater are based on European-American values. Values of other cultures are not seen as valid. . . . If we're going to have something that is called an American theater, then we have to allow room for the esthetic values of Hispanics, for Asians, African-Americans, for all the racial and cultural groups that make up this society, as well as for the age-old tried-and-true values of the European-American.*

Philip Gotanda is firmly committed to writing plays like The Wash *for Asian American theater companies, which he calls "the one place you can truly define what this thing called an Asian-American theatrical aesthetic is. It's the place where you can develop it in its purest form." His plays reflect a blend of elements from his own life experiences and the history of Japanese American society, dramatizing the intimate mixture of the two.*

PHILIP KAN GOTANDA

The Wash

1987

PLACE: *Center stage is Nobu's place, the old family home. Stage right is Kiyoko's restaurant. Stage left is Masi's small apartment. The clothesline is in the upstage area. The downstage area is used to play several scenes that take place elsewhere.*

The set should be realistic but elemental, allowing for an underlying abstract feeling. Nobu's place is the most complete, with Masi's and Kiyoko's places more minimal.

TIME: *The play takes place in the present over a period of six months — July to January. Clothing that reflects the seasonal changes might assist in showing the passage of time.*

CHARACTERS

NOBU MATSUMOTO, *Nisei (second-generation Japanese American). Sixty-eight years old. Retired produce man. Separated from wife, Masi. Lives alone in the family house.*

MASI MATSUMOTO, *Nisei. Sixty-seven years old. Left Nobu. Does housework for a living. Lives in a small apartment by herself.*

KIYOKO HASEGAWA, *in her mid-fifties. Originally from Japan. Previously married to an American soldier, now a widow. Seeing Nobu. Owns and runs a small Japanese restaurant.*

SADAO NAKASATO, *Nisei. Sixty-five years old. Widower. Seeing Masi. Retired pharmacist.*

MARSHA MATSUMOTO, *Sansei (third-generation Japanese American). Thirty-three years old. Single. Older daughter of Nobu and Masi. Works as a dental hygienist in a nearby big city.*

JUDY ADAMS, *Sansei. Twenty-nine years old. Married to James, and has a baby. Younger daughter of Nobu and Masi. Fifth-grade teacher. Not working at present.*

TIMOTHY, *Judy's baby.*

CHIYO FROELICH, *originally from Japan, but has lived most of her adult life in the United States. Late forties. Divorced. Friend of Kiyoko. Owns and runs small beauty salon next door to Kiyoko's restaurant.*

CURLEY SAKATA, *Hawaiian Nisei in his mid-fifties. Speaks with a thick pidgin that comes and goes at his convenience. Works as the cook at Kiyoko's restaurant.*

ACT ONE

SCENE ONE: *Nobu's place, the old family home. Along the upstage area is the kitchen. Stage left is a door that leads to the outside, the proverbial side-door entrance into the kitchen that everyone uses. Stage right of the kitchen, along the upstage side, is a door leading to the hallway and bedrooms, a sink, refrigerator, stove. There is a kitchen table with a pile of dirty clothes on it. On the stove, a pot of water is boiling.*

In the dish rack there are a teapot, some dishes, chopsticks, etc. Down right a TV is on quietly. A long couch is angled facing the TV, with a long coffee table in front of it. On the table sits the yet undeveloped skeleton of a large kite Nobu is building. Throughout the course of the play, the kite becomes more and more pronounced in its construction.

The pile of dirty clothes is lit in a shaft of light. Lights come up to half on Nobu's place. Nobu asleep, lengthwise on the couch, facing the TV. Newspaper is sprawled over his chest. Mouth open, snoring loudly. TV lights come up. Nobu can be seen in the flickering light of the television screen. Lights come full up. Nobu awakens with a start, newspaper falling to the floor. Pulls himself upright and just sits and stares into space for a moment, trying to awaken.

Then he picks up the newspaper, tosses it in a heap on the couch. Checks to examine the progress he's making on the kite. Carefully sets the kite back on the table and shuffles over to the stove to shut the boiling water off. He gets a plate and a pair of chopsticks from the dish rack, puts the two hot dogs that had been boiling onto the plate. Then he gets some tea out and puts it into the teapot which he has taken from the rack. About to throw out the hot-dog water to boil some new water, then stops, thinks. Proceeds just to pour the hot-dog water into the teapot and use it to make tea.

Nobu reaches into the refrigerator and pulls out a bowl of cold rice, covered over in cellophane, and a small bottle of French's mustard. He uncovers the rice, scoops some of it into a rice bowl using his chopsticks, pours hot tea over it. The tea starts to spill, and he quickly bends down and slurps up the excess. He opens the mustard and, using his chopsticks again, shovels a healthy portion of mustard onto his hot dogs. Licks the mustard off his chopsticks. Then he carefully makes his way back to the couch with the plate of hot dogs and bowl of rice. Sets the food down on the coffee table and begins to eat while working on the kite and watching television.

While he is eating, Masi enters through the side door with two large brown paper bags. She's struggling to open and close the door with both bands so full. Nobu turns around and notices her but gives no greeting and makes no effort to help her. Instead, goes back to eating, working on the kite, and watching TV. She is not upset by his actions. She has no expectation of assistance from him. Business as usual. Masi sets both bags on the kitchen table and catches her breath. She proceeds to put vegetables from one of the bags into the refrigerator. Tomatoes and Japanese eggplant.

MASI (*putting vegetables into refrigerator*): If you have any more dirty clothes I can take them now. Nobu? Is this everything?

NOBU (*not turning, eating*): Want some hot dog?

MASI: No, I ate before. Got these from Mr. Rossi. The tomatoes are soft, so eat them right away. (*Folds bag and puts it into drawer. She knows this place well. Walks over and checks his shirt collar from behind.*) No more clothes?

NOBU (*brushing her hand away*): No, already.

Masi goes over to the other bag and begins unpacking the freshly washed clothes in neat piles on the kitchen table.

MASI (*unpacking*): I just finished cleaning Dr. Harrison's place. You should see the bathrooms. If you see the family walk down the street, they look so clean and neat. But the toilets, kitanai.°

---

kitanai: Dirty. [All notes are Gotanda's unless otherwise indicated.]

Finished unpacking, Masi takes a cup out of the rack and pours herself a cup of tea. She walks over to the couch and sits down next to Nobu and watches TV. She takes a sip of tea and makes a face. Nobu notices.

NOBU: Hot-dog water.

Masi decides not to drink. She looks at the unfinished kite frame.

MASI: You gonna fly this one? (*Picking up the kite.*) Nobu, why don't you at least try a different design this . . .

NOBU: My old man did it this way. (*Mutters.*) Jesus Christ . . .

MASI (*gathering clothes*): Have you talked to the kids? (*No response.*) Marsha said she stopped by. (*Beat.*) You know if you don't see Judy's baby soon he's going to be all grown up. Nobu?

NOBU: No.

Masi gives up trying to talk to him at all.

MASI: No more dirty clothes, Nobu?

Nobu shakes his head without turning away from the TV.

MASI: All right, then I'm going.

Masi leaves with the bag of old clothes. Nobu continues to watch TV for a few moments. Then, turns and stares at the door. Dim to half, with the TV light illuminating Nobu. Marsha lit in pool of light looking towards Nobu.

MARSHA: Dad?

Nobu turns to look at Marsha momentarily, then back to the television. Judy is lit in a pool of light, holding Timothy.

JUDY: Mom?

Masi moves away. Masi turns to look at Judy momentarily, then exits. Marsha and Judy dim to darkness. Nobu and Masi dim to darkness. We hear Japanese restaurant Muzak.

End of scene.

SCENE TWO: *Kiyoko's restaurant. Afternoon, next day. Lights come up. Kiyoko struggling to move Chiyo's Karaoke° equipment out of the way.*

KIYOKO (*calling*): Curley! Curley! Can you help me with this!

Curley Sakata enters, wiping face with towel and holding beer. Speaks in a Hawaiian pidgin. He can lose it if he wants to.

CURLEY: Easy, easy, no go break da speaker. Bumbai° Curley's sweet sounds no can come out. (*Helping her move the equipment.*)

KIYOKO (*struggling*): Why can't Chiyo keep this at her place?

CURLEY: Hey, cannot sing Karaoke at a beauty shop. Has to be nightclub place like dis.

KIYOKO: This is a restaurant . . .

As they finish moving the equipment, Kiyoko notices Curley's beer. Stares at him.

Karaoke: Japanese singing accompaniment machine. **Bumbai:** Hawaiian slang for "by and by."

CURLEY (*feigning innocence*): What'sa matta?

KIYOKO: Curley.

CURLEY: It makes my cooking mo' betta.

Kiyoko continues to stare.

CURLEY: I'm thirsty, I wanted a beer.

KIYOKO (*taking his beer*): No more drinking on the job, I told you.

CURLEY: But it makes my cooking mo' betta. If I feel betta, my cooking mo' betta. No bull lie yo.

KIYOKO (*scooting Curley back to the kitchen*): Your face turns red like a tomato and everything tastes like shoyu.°

CURLEY (*exiting into the back, scratching his behind*): This place no fun no mo'.

KIYOKO: And don't scratch your oshiri,° you're the cook, remember?

As Kiyoko goes back to wiping, Nobu enters and walks up to Kiyoko. She notices.

KIYOKO: Irasshaii, welcome.

NOBU (*holds out his hand to her*): Excuse me. Here.

Kiyoko doesn't know what's going on. Nobu takes Kiyoko's hand and gives her money.

NOBU: Here, here, you gave me too much. You gave me too much change. When I paid my bill. I was emptying out my pockets at my house when I noticed.

KIYOKO (*looking at the money*): Twenty-five cents?

NOBU (*nodding*): Un-huh. It cost six seventy-five, I gave you seven bucks, and you gave me back fifty cents. So . . .

Nobu nods toward the money. He's not sure what to do next. Awkward beat. Then turns to leave.

KIYOKO: Wait, wait.

Nobu stops. Beat. For a moment Kiyoko doesn't know what to say.

KIYOKO: You walked all the way back here to give me twenty-five cents?

NOBU: You gave me too much. So I . . .

Kiyoko doesn't know what to say.

NOBU: All right then.

Nobu turns to leave again.

KIYOKO: No, wait, wait. Sit, sit, please sit. I'll get you some tea.

Kiyoko guides him to a seat and goes to get his tea. Curley has been watching the action. Sipping on a new beer.

CURLEY: Eh, Mr. Abe Lincoln? You come in a lot, huh. For lunch.

NOBU: Almost every day.

CURLEY (*approaching*): And dat's your seat, huh? All da time you gotta sit in dat same seat. Last week Mr. Koyama was sitting dere — I saw you come in — you left and came back later when dat seat was open. What'sa matta, your butt got a magnet for dat seat?

KIYOKO (*bringing tea, shooing Curley away*): Curley. Go, go . . .

---

shoyu: Soy sauce. **oshiri:** Backside.

CURLEY (*moving away, to Nobu*): And you always order da same thing.
NOBU: The combo plate.
KIYOKO: And you like the eggplant pickle.
NOBU: Un-huh.
KIYOKO: Kagoshima style.
NOBU: Kagoshima ka? My family's from there.
KIYOKO: Ara, Kagoshima? Honto, yo?° Doko kara, where?
NOBU: The, uh, southern part.
KIYOKO: Ahhh. Watashi no, north part, Yokokawa. (*Awkward beat. Motioning to his tea.*) Dozo.° (*Nobu sips the tea.*)
KIYOKO: What is your name?
NOBU (*getting up*): Nobu. Nobu Matsumoto.
KIYOKO: Ah, Matsumoto-san. Kiyoko. Kiyoko Hasegawa. Dozo yoroshiku?°

As Nobu starts to bow awkwardly, Kiyoko extends her hand to shake. He's caught off guard and both are slightly embarrassed. Nobu recovers and reaches out to shake Kiyoko's hand. Curley watches, amused. Dim to darkness.

End of scene.

SCENE THREE: *Masi's place. Three weeks later. Small apartment with bedroom downstage from main room. Sadao is lit seated on sofa in a pool of light. Masi is in half-light at counter fixing coffee.*

SADAO: We were all sitting around in somebody's living room, when someone said, "How come you still wear your wedding ring?" They weren't being mean. That's why we were there. To ask those kinds of things. I didn't know what to say. Speechless. Then someone else said, "Sadao, you always complain about not meeting people, not being able to start a new life — how come you still wear your ring?" I began to cry. Like a little boy. I remember thinking, "How strange. I am crying in front of all these people that I don't know. And yet I feel no shame." The room was so still. All you could hear was my crying. Then I heard a tapping sound. I looked up and noticed a woman sitting across from me, slapping the sandals she was wearing against the bottom of her feet. Tap, tap, tap . . . I said I didn't know why. It just never crossed my mind to take it off. "Why should I take the ring off?" Then one of the widows, the one who formed the group, said, "Because you're not married anymore."

Lights come up on the rest of the apartment area. Masi is at the small kitchen counter fixing two cups of Sanka coffee. She wasn't quite prepared for him sharing such personal details of his life and is a bit unsure how to respond. Sadao in turn fears he may have gotten a bit carried away.

MASI (*bringing coffee over*): Cream? It's nondairy creamer.

Sadao shakes head.

MASI: If you want tea?
SADAO: No, this is fine. I ran on a bit, didn't I?
MASI: No, no, it's all right. (*Pause.*) It's just Sanka.

Ara . . . yo?: From Kagoshima? Really? **Dozo:** Please. **Dozo yoroshiku?:** How do you do?

SADAO: Good. Otherwise the caffeine keeps me up all night. Have you tried decaffeinated coffee?

Masi motions to the Sanka, unsure of what he means.

SADAO: No, the bean. They actually make a decaffeinated bean.

MASI: No, we never did anything like that. Just instant. Yuban makes a good instant coffee. That's what I usually drink, but I don't have any since I moved over here.

SADAO: No, I've never tried it.

MASI: I'll have to get some next time I go shopping.

SADAO: They have this process they use. On the bean. I mean they don't grow a decaffeinated bean. I don't know what's worse. The caffeine in it or the chemicals they use to get the caffeine out. (*Laughing at his own joke. Gathering momentum.*) I have a little grinder. Braun? You know a Braun?

Masi doesn't know what it is. Awkward pause.

MASI: We never did anything like that. We just drink instant.

SADAO: I like Sanka. I have to drink it all the time. Doctor's orders. (*Imitating.*) "If you drink coffee, Sadao, drink Sanka!" (*Laughs valiantly at his attempt at humor. Masi stares at her cup. Sadao notices and offers a feeble explanation.*) Blood pressure . . .

They both drink in silence. Suddenly, Sadao remembers something.

SADAO: Oh. I forgot. (*Sadao reaches down and picks up a fishing pole and reel wrapped up like presents.*)

MASI (*surprised*): Sadao, what's this?

Sadao holds out pole.

MASI: I can't.

Nobu lit in half-light at his place watching TV. His face illuminated by the flickering screen's glow.

SADAO: No, no, it's for you.

MASI: But Sadao . . .

SADAO: No, no, it's for *you*.

MASI (*one hand on it*): Sadao, you shouldn't have.

SADAO: Go 'head. Open it up.

MASI (*takes it and begins unwrapping it*): No, I can't accept this. I don't have anything for you.

Masi unwraps pole, which is broken down into pieces. Sadao sets reel on table and takes pole from Masi and proceeds to put it together.

SADAO: See, it goes like this. And then you're all set to catch fish. (*Hands it back to Masi.*) I told you I was going to take you. Now you can't refuse.

MASI: Yeah, but . . .

SADAO: Thought I was kidding, huh?

MASI: But this is so expensive. I know how much these things cost, 'cause of Nobu. I don't know anything about fishing. He's the fisherman. I just pack the lunch and off he goes.

SADAO: Well, this time you're going and it's lots of fun. Economical, too. You get to eat what you catch.

MASI: But you have to do all that walking.

SADAO: No, who said that? We sit on the bank and fish from there. We'll pack a good lunch — I'll make it — you bring the cards so we can play blackjack. We have to practice.

MASI: I don't play.

SADAO: That's why we have to practice, so we can go to Tahoe. If there's a good game on we'll have to watch it. I'll bring my portable TV. I love the Giants.

MASI: What about fishing?

SADAO: Only if we have time. See, this is how you cast out. (*Demonstrating.*) You hook your index finger around the line here. Turn the bail and . . . (*Casts.*)

Nobu, still lit in half-light, gets up to phone Masi. Phone rings. Masi goes over and answers it. It's Nobu. Slowly lights dim on Sadao and rest of apartment. Masi and Nobu are lit.

MASI: Hello.

NOBU (*lit in small pool of light*): You coming to pick up the clothes?

MASI: Nobu? I was just there. You mean next week? Don't worry, I'll be there. I do it every week, don't I? Nobu?

NOBU: I'm not worried. You all right?

MASI: Yes, I'm all right. Did you want something? (*No response.*) I got more vegetables. Do you need some more?

NOBU: No. (*Pause.*) Can you bring more eggplant?

MASI: I don't have any more.

NOBU: All right then.

MASI: I'll ask Mr. Rossi. He can always get lots more. (*Pause.*) Nobu, I have to go now.

NOBU: I went fishing so I got a lot of dirty clothes.

MASI: All right. Don't worry, I'll be by.

NOBU: I'm not worried.

MASI: Bye.

NOBU: Bye.

Dim to darkness.

End of scene.

SCENE FOUR: *Poker game. Curley is setting up Karaoke machine. Chiyo and Kiyoko are at the table. Chiyo is dealing out cards. Wears a poker visor. They are playing five-card stud, one card down and one up.*

CHIYO: Kiyoko, I never said I didn't like him.

CURLEY (*fiddling with the machine*): Test, test.

KIYOKO: Curley, you in this game or not?

CURLEY (*singing into microphone*): "Tiny bubbles . . ."

CHIYO: I just don't think he's right for you, that's all. He's too old.

KIYOKO: Curley, we're waiting.

CURLEY: Okay, okay . . .

CHIYO: Dealer's high, I bet a nickel.

KIYOKO: I see you.

Curley moves to table, guzzling a beer and carrying a six-pack in his other hand. They both notice Curley chugging down the rest of his beer, making loud gurgling sounds. Curley notices them staring.

CURLEY: You gotta drink beer when you're playing poker or you aren't playing poker. You're just playing cards. I don't like cards. Hate cards. (*Holds up another beer.*) I *love* poker.

KIYOKO (*to Curley*): Ante, ante . . .

CHIYO: Go dancing with Eddie and me. Yeah come, come . . .

KIYOKO: Chiyo, how can I do that? Who's gonna run this place, huh?

CHIYO: Come on, Kiyoko, you work too hard.

KIYOKO: The refrigeration unit's breaking down, Mr. Sato says we can't fix it anymore . . .

CHIYO: Kiyoko, I met one of Eddie's friends, Ray Jensen. He's good-looking, yo. Tall, lotsa fun to be with . . .

KIYOKO: Chiyo, Chiyo, I'm too busy. I'm not looking for that kind of thing anymore.

CHIYO: What do you mean, "that kind of thing"?

KIYOKO: That kind of thing, thinking about men and getting all . . .

CURLEY: I like it when da wahinis talk dirt.

Kiyoko and Chiyo shoot Curley a dirty look.

CURLEY: Geez, don't lose your coconut.

KIYOKO: I like Nobu, he's a nice man, Chiyo. He comes in here, we sit down and eat together and then he goes home. I like that.

CHIYO (*to Kiyoko*): Okay, okay. Two sixes, a pair of saxophones. (*To Curley.*) A three of diamonds gives you . . . nothing. (*To self.*) Eight of puppy toes to the dealer, working on a possible club flush. (*To Kiyoko.*) Pair of saxes high. He's married, Kiyoko.

KIYOKO: Ten cents. They're separated.

CHIYO: But did he tell you? Huh? I call.

KIYOKO: Curley, you in or not?

CURLEY: Don't rush me, don't rush me.

CHIYO: No, you had to hear it from me. Eighty-year-old Mrs. Nakamura with the blue hair comes to my beauty shop, "I want my perm and a blue rinse," yak-yakking away. I decide to do some snooping for my good friend. "Nakamura-san? Oh, Nakamura-san? You know this Nobu guy?"

CURLEY: Old magnet butt?

CHIYO: I know his kind, Kiyoko, old Japanese-type guys. She left him, he can't get over that. He's still thinking about her. He only wants you for one thing — your tempura. Yeah. He's over here every day, desho?° You're feeding him. He's eating up all your profits.

KIYOKO: Chiyo.

---

desho: Isn't he?

CHIYO (*to Kiyoko*): Nine of spades. No help there. (*To Curley.*) A trois. Oh, a pair of threes. (*To self.*) And for the dealer . . . another club. Flush looking very possible. (*To Kiyoko.*) Pair of saxes still high.

KIYOKO: Check.

CHIYO: Check. He checks, too.

CURLEY: I'm thinking, I'm thinking . . .

CHIYO: I try looking out for you and what do you do? You get mad at me.

KIYOKO: Nobu is an honest man. That's all I know. One time I gave him too much change, he walked all the way . . .

CURLEY (*overlapping, mimicking Kiyoko*): . . . He walked all the way back to return it. Twenty-five cents.

CHIYO (*overlapping Curley, mimicking Kiyoko, too*): . . . return it. Twenty-five cents.

Curley and Chiyo laugh.

CHIYO: Good investment. He gets a $4.50 combo plate free now. Last card, down and dirty.

Chiyo starts dealing as she and Curley calm down.

KIYOKO: Look, he's just a friend. That's all he is. I don't see why you're all making such a fuss.

CHIYO (*showing her card*): Another puppy toes — flush, flush, flush.

KIYOKO: Fifty cents.

CURLEY (*surprised*): Fifty cents.

CHIYO (*confidently*): I see you and I bump you one dollar.

CURLEY (*in disbelief*): One dollar . . .

KIYOKO (*eyes Chiyo's cards and tries to decide whether to stay in or not*): I call you.

CHIYO: You got the three-of-a-kind?

KIYOKO: Pair of sixes, that's all. You got the flush?

CHIYO: Pair of eights! Hah!

Chiyo's about to grab the pot when Curley puts down his cards.

CURLEY: Excusez-moi's, but I got three trois's.

CHIYO: Curley . . .

KIYOKO: Oh, Curley . . .

CURLEY (*holding up beer*): Hate cards. *Love* poker.

Dim to darkness.

End of scene.

SCENE FIVE: *Nobu's place. Marsha's dinner party scene. Marsha busy at stove. Nobu seated in his chair.*

NOBU: What do you mean, "be nice to Mama"?

MARSHA: All I'm saying is just try to be nice to her when she gets here. Say something nice about the way she looks or about the way she dresses . . .

NOBU: I'm always nice to Mama. I'm always good to her.

MARSHA (*moving over to Nobu and adjusting his clothes*): Dad, Dad, I just want us to have a good time tonight, okay? All of us, together. And besides, I made you your favorite. (*Marsha moves back to stove.*)

NOBU: Yeah, but how come Mama has to live over there, huh? She should be at home here. How come Mama has to live way in the hell over there?

Masi enters carrying a small paper bag.

MARSHA: Hi, Mom. (*Taking bag.*) Here, let me take that.

MASI (*to Nobu*): Just some leftover fruit that was in the icebox. Starting to rot so eat it right away. And this is for you.

Masi hands package to Marsha. Masi and Nobu acknowledge each other awkwardly.

MARSHA: Thanks, Mom. (*Takes package.*) Judy and the baby couldn't make it.

MASI: She called me.

NOBU: Eh? (*Nobu's expression reveals he didn't know they had been going to come.*)

MARSHA (*offering explanation to Nobu*): Jimmy wasn't going to come. (*Pause.*) Sit down, sit down. Dinner's almost ready in a minute. Roast beef. Dad, coffee? Tea for you, Mom? (*Marsha goes to kitchen. Silence.*)

NOBU: She wanted to eat at her place. I told her to cook dinner here.

Pause.

MASI: Her place is cozy, neh.

NOBU: Marsha's? Looks like the rooms back in camp.°

MASI: At least she's clean. Not like the younger one.

Pause.

NOBU: How you been?

MASI: All right.

NOBU: Isogashii no?°

MASI: No. The usual.

NOBU: I called the other night, no one answered.

Masi doesn't offer an explanation.

NOBU: How you been?

Marsha interrupts, carrying an ashtray.

MARSHA: Dad, look what Mom gave me. She's taking a ceramics class. Judy got her to go. (*Hands him the ashtray.*) She made it. (*Nobu stares at it.*)

MASI: It's an ashtray.

NOBU: You don't smoke.

MASI: I'll get Daddy's coffee. (*Masi exits with cup.*)

MARSHA: Dad, just say you like it. That's all you have to say. Just say it's nice.

NOBU: Yeah, but you don't smoke. Why give an ashtray if you don't smoke?

Masi returns with a cup of coffee for Nobu and tea for herself. Marsha gives Nobu an encouraging nudge and exits into kitchen.

NOBU (*holding ashtray*): It's a nice ashtray. Is this where you go all the time? I call in the evening. I guess that's where you must be. (*Pause.*) Remember those dances they used to have in the camps? You were a good dancer. You were. Best in the camps.

MASI: You couldn't dance at all. You were awful.

NOBU: Remember that fellow Chester Yoshikawa? That friend of yours?

---

in camp: Refers to the United States government's forced relocation and isolation of 120,000 Japanese Americans in internment camps following the Japanese attack on Pearl Harbor in 1941 and lasting until the end of World War II. [Editors' note.] **Isogashii no?:** Busy?

MASI: He could dance so good.

NOBU: Remember that dance you were supposed to meet me out front of the canteen? We were all going to meet there and then go to the dance together. Shig, Chester, and a couple others. Everybody else, they went on ahead. I waited and waited . . .

MASI: Nobu, that was forty years ago.

NOBU: Yeah, I know, but remember you were supposed to meet . . .

MASI (*interrupts*): That's over forty years ago. How can I remember something like that?

NOBU: You didn't show up. Chester didn't show up either.

Masi puts cream and sugar into Nobu's coffee.

MASI: Nobu, didn't we talk about this? I'm sure we did. Probably something came up and I had to help Mama and Papa.

NOBU: Where were you, huh?

MASI: How am I supposed to remember that far back? Chester died in Italy with the rest of the 442° boys.

NOBU: Where the hell were you?

MASI: How in the hell am I supposed to remember that far back!

NOBU (*notices his coffee*): *You* put the cream and sugar in. That's not mine.

Pushes coffee away. Masi realizes what she's done.

MASI: That's right. You like to put the cream and sugar in yourself.

NOBU: I like to put it in myself.

MASI (*pushing cup towards him*): It's the way you like it, the same thing.

NOBU (*pushes it back*): No, it's not the same thing.

Marsha puts her head in and watches.

MASI: All right, all right, I'll drink it myself. Here, you can drink mine.

Masi shoves her tea to Nobu and grabs the coffee cup.

NOBU: What are you doing?

MASI: I don't mind.

Masi starts to raise cup, but Nobu reaches for it.

NOBU: It's no good for you, Mama. Your blood pressure. Remember what Doc Takei . . .

MASI (*interrupts, clinging to cup*): Who gives a damn? You make such a fuss about it. Monku, monku, monku.° I'll drink it.

NOBU (*struggling with Masi*): It's no good for you, Mama. (*Coffee spills on the table. To Masi.*) Clean it up.

MASI: I'm not going to clean it up.

MARSHA (*entering*): I'll clean it up.

While Marsha starts to wipe the table, Masi grabs Nobu's coffee cup and exits into the kitchen.

442: World War II all–Japanese American U.S. Army combat unit. **Monku, . . . monku:** Kvetch, kvetch, kvetch.

MASI (*exiting*): I'll get him more coffee.
MARSHA: Dad.
NOBU: That's the way she is.

Masi returns with Nobu's coffee and sets it down in front of him. Then, she turns and quickly exits.

MARSHA (*chasing after Masi*): Mom . . .

Nobu is left alone with his cup of coffee. Marsha reenters and watches him. He slowly puts in the cream and sugar himself. Raises his cup to his lips but cannot drink. Sets it back down and stares at it. Marsha continues to watch. Dim to darkness.

End of scene.

SCENE SIX: *That same night. After hours at the restaurant. Chiyo and Curley with microphones singing a song like "Sukiyaki" to the accompaniment of the Karaoke machine. Curley begins to do the hula. Kiyoko laughing and clapping along. They're all having a good time. Nobu enters. He wasn't expecting this and is not sure what to do. As Chiyo continues to sing, Curley notices him.*

CURLEY (*calling*): Nobu! Nobu!

Kiyoko goes up to Nobu, who is turning to leave.

KIYOKO (*catching him and trying to make him enter*): Nobu, come in, come in — Chiyo and Curley set up the machine and we're all singing . . . (*Nobu doesn't budge. Kiyoko notices that he is upset about something. Gently*) Nobu? Sit down. Come in for a while. Sit, sit. I'll get you a beer.

Kiyoko leads the reluctant Nobu to his seat as Chiyo and Curley continue to sing. Kiyoko clears the table and goes back up to the counter for his beer. Chiyo and Curley have just finished their song and are now teasing Nobu to also join in.

CURLEY: Come on, your turn, Nobu.
CHIYO: Sing, sing.
CURLEY: It's Karaoke night at Hasegawa's!
CHIYO: Ojiisan, dozo!°
CHIYO AND CURLEY (*chanting*): Nobu, Nobu, Nobu . . .
KIYOKO (*returning with his beer*): Chiyo, Curley, leave him alone, leave him alone . . .

They stop, move back to the Karaoke machine

CURLEY (*muttering*): What a bugga.
KIYOKO (*to Nobu*): Tsukemono?°

Nobu nods and Kiyoko exits. Nobu is left alone. Then he begins to sing, first softly, then growing in volume.

NOBU: Nen, nen kororiyo okororiyo,
Bōya wa yoi ko da nen ne shina.
Bōya yo mari wa doko e itta?
Ano yama koete sato e itta.°

Ojiisan, dozo!: Old man, please! **Tsukemono:** Japanese pickled vegetable. **Nen, . . . itta:** Sleep, sleep, hushabye, / Little boy, good boy, go to sleep now. / Little boy, where has your ball gone? / Way over the mountains to the distant fields.

CURLEY: What's he singing?
CHIYO: I don't know.
KIYOKO (*reentering*): It's a lullaby.

Chiyo and Curley start to laugh at Nobu singing a baby's song.

KIYOKO: Shh! Shh!

Hearing them, Nobu stops. Kiyoko walks to Nobu's table. Kiyoko starts to sing to help Nobu out. Nobu joins back in. Nobu's voice is not pretty. But it is earnest and straightforward, filling the traditional song with a gutsy soulfulness. Kiyoko and Nobu finish the song together.

NOBU (*quietly*): My papa used to sing it to me.

Dim to darkness.

End of scene.

SCENE SEVEN: *Masi's place, three weeks later. Afternoon. Masi at clothesline. Judy visiting with Timothy.*

JUDY: I don't see how you had two of us, Mom. I need sleep. Large doses of it. Jimmy's so lazy sometimes. I even kick him "accidentally" when Timothy starts crying. Think he gets up to feed the baby?
MASI: Daddy used to.
JUDY: Used to what?
MASI: Get up at night and feed you kids.
JUDY: Dad? You're kidding.
MASI: He used to sing to you. No wonder you kids would cry.

They laugh.

JUDY: I saw your new phone-answering machine.
MASI (*proud*): Yeah. For messages.
JUDY (*kidding*): What? You got a new boyfriend?
MASI: Judy.
JUDY: Well, why not, Mom? You moved out. It's about time you started meeting new people. Once you get a divorce you're going to have to do that any . . .
MASI (*interrupts*): I'm not getting a divorce.
JUDY: What are you going to do? You live here, Dad's over there . . . (*No response.*) You can't do that forever.
MASI: I just do his wash. That's all I do. Just his wash. (*Pause. Masi hanging clothes.*) I think you should call Dad.
JUDY: Mom, what can I say to him? I can't talk about my husband, I can't talk about my baby.
MASI: Judy, you know how Dad is.
JUDY: All he can talk about is how he can't show his face at Tak's barbershop because I married a kurochan.°
MASI: He's not going to call you.
JUDY: Of course not — we'd have to talk.

---

kurochan: A black.

Silence. Judy goes back to the baby. Masi watches her.

MASI: Judy.
JUDY: What?
MASI: He needs you.
JUDY: Why can't he accept it? Why can't he just say, "It's okay, it's okay, Judy"? I just need him to say that much.
MASI: He can't. Papa can't.
JUDY: Why? Why the hell not?

Masi and Judy look at each other. Dim to darkness.

End of scene.

SCENE EIGHT: *Kiyoko's restaurant, that same evening. We hear the rhythmic pounding of fists on flesh. As lights come up, Nobu and Kiyoko are lit in a pool of light. Kiyoko is standing in back of Nobu pounding his back with fists in a punching manner. She is massaging Nobu. This is a supreme joy for him. Kiyoko likes doing it for him.*

KIYOKO (*not stopping*): Enough?
NOBU (*voice vibrating from the steady blows*): Nooo . . .

They continue in silence, both enjoying the activity.

KIYOKO: Enough?
NOBU: Nooo . . . (*Kiyoko's arms are just too tired.*)
KIYOKO (*stopping*): Ahh . . .
NOBU (*stretching*): Oisho!° Masi used to do it. Sometimes Marsha does it now.
KIYOKO (*pouring tea*): You're lucky you have children, Nobu. Especially daughters. Harry and I wanted children. They're good, neh.

Awkward silence. Nobu abruptly pulls out a small gift-wrapped box and holds it out to Kiyoko.

NOBU: Here.

Kiyoko's too surprised to take it. From here, spoken in Japanese, except where otherwise indicated.

NOBU: Anata no birthday present. Hayo akenesai.°
KIYOKO (*taking it*): Ara! Nobu . . . (*Opens it and holds up the earrings.*) Nobu-chan.
NOBU: Earrings. Inamasu Jewelry Store no mae o totara me ni tsuitanda ne.°
KIYOKO: Mah, kirei, Nobu-chan. Tsukete miru.°

Kiyoko exits. Nobu lit in pool of light.

MEMORY SEQUENCE. *Masi lit in pool of light.*

MASI: Why don't you want me anymore? (*No response.*) We don't sleep . . . You know what I mean and don't give me that kind of look. Is it me? The way my body . . . I've seen those magazines you keep in the back closet with your fishing and hunting gear. I mean, it's all right. I'm just trying to know about us. What happened.

Oisho!: Ahh! **Anata . . . akenesai:** Your birthday present. Hurry, open it. **Inamasu . . . ne:** I was walking by Inamasu's store when I spotted them. **Mah, . . . miru:** They're pretty, Nobu. Let me try them on.

NOBU: Nothing. Nothing happened. What's the matter with you?
MASI: Then why don't you . . . sleep with me?
NOBU: By the time I get home from work I'm tired. Shig all day long, ordering me around, do this, do that. I even had to get up at five o'clock this morning to pick up the produce 'cause his damn son-in-law is a lazy son of a bitch. I'm tired, I'm tired, Masi.
MASI: What about those magazines?
NOBU: I'll throw 'em out, okay? First thing tomorrow I'll throw 'em in the trash and burn 'em. That make you feel better?

Masi is hurt by his angry response.

NOBU: Masi? (*No response.*) Masi. You're pretty. You are.

Memory ends. Masi withdraws into shadows.

Kiyoko returns to Nobu with the earrings on. Lights come up.

KIYOKO (*posing*): Nobu-chan?
NOBU: Suteki da nah.°

Kiyoko attempts to embrace Nobu. It's too uncomfortable for Nobu and he gently pushes her away. Kiyoko is quite embarrassed. From now on they speak in English again.

KIYOKO: How come you do that to me? (*No response.*) Don't you like it?
NOBU: I like it. But I don't like it, too.

Dim to darkness.

End of scene.

SCENE NINE: *Masi's apartment, four or five days later. Couch has rumpled blanket on it. Morning. Sadao is standing holding the door open for a surprised Marsha. Sadao is dressed only in pants and an undershirt. Marsha is holding a box of manju (Japanese pastry). They have never met.*

SADAO: Good morning.
MARSHA: Is my mother . . . Is Mrs. Matsumoto here?
MASI (*off*): Who is it?
SADAO: Come on in, please come in.

Masi enters in a bathrobe with her hair tied up in a towel as if just washed.

MASI (*momentarily caught off guard*): Oh, hi, Marsha. Come in.
MARSHA (*entering hesitantly*): Hello, Mom.
MASI: This is Sadao Nakasato. (*To Sadao.*) My eldest one, Marsha.
SADAO: Hello, Marsha.
MARSHA: Hello. (*Awkward pause. Marsha remembers her package.*) Oh, I just thought I'd bring some manju by. (*Handing it to Masi.*) I didn't think it was that early. Next time I guess I'll call first.
SADAO: Hmm, love manju. Some of my favorites. Especially the ones with the kinako on top. The brown powdery stuff?
MARSHA: I meant to drop it off last night but I called and no one was here.
MASI: Oh, we got in late from fishing.
SADAO: We caught the limit.

Suteki da nah: Looks beautiful.

MASI (*looking at phone-answering machine*): I have to remember to turn this machine on.

SADAO: In fact, Masi caught more than me.

MASI: Teamwork. I catch them and Sadao takes them off the hook. Sit down and have breakfast with us. Sit, sit.

MARSHA: That's okay, Mom.

MASI: It was so late last night I told Sadao to sleep on the couch. So he did. He said he would cook breakfast for me in the morning. Right over there on the couch.

Masi and Sadao are nodding to each other in agreement. Marsha doesn't move.

SADAO: Waffles.

MASI: You sure you know how?

SADAO: I can make them, good ones. From scratch.

MASI: Sit down, sit down.

MARSHA: No, no, Mom. I really should be going. I'm going to stop over at the house. To see Dad, too.

MASI: No, wait, wait . . . I have some fish for you.

Masi is wrapping up two packages of fish with newspaper. Marsha notices.

MARSHA: Mom, I don't want any fish.

MASI (*handing her a package*): Then give it to Brad.

MARSHA: Mom, I'm not seeing him anymore.

MASI: Oh. Then give it to Dad.

MARSHA: What do I tell him?

MASI (*momentary pause*): Just give it to him. No use wasting it. He can eat fish morning, noon, and night.

Masi hustles Marsha towards the door.

SADAO: No waffles? They're low cholesterol.

MARSHA: Uh, no thanks. Nice to meet you, Mr. Nakasato. (*Marsha pauses at door. They exchange glances.*) Bye, Mom. (*Marsha exits.*)

MASI (*calling after*): Tell Daddy I'll bring his clothes by, that I've been busy. And tell him to put his old clothes in a pile where I can see it. Last time I couldn't find one of his underwear and he got mad at me. (*Closes door.*) It was under the icebox.

As Sadao rambles on, Masi seems lost in her thoughts.

SADAO (*caught up in his cooking*): Everything's low cholesterol. Except for the Cool Whip. But that doesn't count because that's optional. Where's the MSG? That's my secret. My daughter gets so mad at me. "Dad, you're a pharmacist, you should know better than to use MSG." She's a health food nut . . .

Sadao is bending down to look in a lower cabinet for the MSG. As he disappears, Masi moves into a pool of light.

MEMORY SEQUENCE. *Nobu lit in pool of light.*

NOBU: No, Masi, I said size eight, size eight hooks.

MASI: You told me to buy size six, not size eight. That's not what you told me.

NOBU: I get home from the store I expect you to . . . Jesus Christ . . . (*Starting to pace.*)

MASI: Nobu, Nobu, you didn't tell me to get size eight hooks. You told me size . . .

NOBU (*interrupts*): I said size eight. I said size eight hooks. (*Pause.*) This is my house. Masi? After I come home from that damn store — here . . . This is *my* house.

Silence.

MASI (*quietly*): I'm sorry. I'm wrong. You said size eight hooks.

Nobu withdraws. Lights up. End of memory.

Sadao gets up from behind the cabinet with the MSG.

SADAO: You don't mind, do you? Masi? The ajinomoto, the MSG. Is it OK with you?

MASI: Yes, yes, it's fine.

Sadao is aware of Masi's pensiveness.

SADAO: Sometimes I add prune juice, but then you have to go easy on the MSG. The prune juice really does add a nice hint of flavor to the waffles if you don't overdo it.

Nobu lit in half-light looking at his unfinished kite frame.

SADAO: Everything in moderation. I think these people got a little carried away with this MSG thing. Of course, I'm not running a Chinese restaurant, either. I'm just talking about a tiny pinch of the stuff . . .

As lights go to half on Sadao and Masi, Nobu is lit in a pool of light. He lifts the kite above his head and begins to move it as if it were flying. For a moment Nobu seems to be a child making believe that his kite is soaring high above in the clouds. Nobu goes to half-light.

End of scene.

SCENE TEN: *Neighborhood streets. Kiyoko and Chiyo enter, checking the addresses on houses.*

CHIYO: Kiyoko, what's the address? What's the number?

KIYOKO (*looking at a piece of paper*): 2158 A Street.

CHIYO (*looking*): 2152, 2154 . . . There it is.

Judy hurries in, wiping her hands.

JUDY: Just a minute, I'm coming! (*Judy stops when she sees the two strangers at her door.*) Yes?

KIYOKO: I am a friend of your father. My name is Kiyoko Hasegawa.

CHIYO: Chiyo Froelich.

JUDY: Hi.

KIYOKO: I run a restaurant. Hasegawa's?

CHIYO: Chiyo's Hair Salon, right next door.

JUDY: Oh . . . Yeah, yeah.

KIYOKO: We are having a small get-together at my place for your father.

CHIYO: A birthday party.

They hear the baby crying.

KIYOKO: Oh, that must be Timothy.

CHIYO: Nobu should see him.

Awkward pause.

JUDY (*starting to withdraw*): I really should . . . Excuse me . . .

CHIYO (*to Kiyoko*): Show Judy your earrings. Kiyoko, show her.

KIYOKO: Chiyo.

CHIYO: He gave them to her. Your father. For her birthday.

KIYOKO: For my birthday. He comes to my restaurant almost every day. He likes my cooking. That's how come I know him so good.

CHIYO (*kidding*): He's so mendokusai.° I don't like cucumber pickle, I like eggplant. Monku, monku all the time.

KIYOKO: Oh, it's no trouble at all. I like to do things like that. I like to cook for Nobu. (*Timothy starts to cry in the back.*)

JUDY (*starting to leave*): I really need to get back to the baby . . .

KIYOKO: So can you come?

CHIYO: To the birthday?

JUDY (*exiting*): I'm not sure. I'm really busy these days. Nice meeting you.

Dim to darkness.

End of scene.

SCENE ELEVEN: *Lights up on Nobu with his kite. Masi in half-light moves away from Sadao. She's holding the fishing pole. Nobu puts down the kite frame. Thinking. Picks up the phone and dials Masi's place.*

Masi's place in half-light. Sadao at the counter making waffles. He hears the phone machine click on but does not answer it. Masi is off to the side studying her rod and reel.

NOBU: Masi? You got any . . . Masi?

Masi's phone machine kicks in. Nobu doesn't know how to deal with it.

MASI'S RECORDED VOICE: Hello. This is Masi Matsumoto. I'm not in right now, so please wait for the tone and leave your name, your number, and a short message. Thank you. Bye-bye.

Nobu listens to the message end. The beep sounds. He's panicked, not quite sure what to do.

NOBU: I am Nobu Matsumoto. My telephone number is 751 . . . damn. (*Checks the number.*) 751-8263. (*Not sure if he has said his name.*) I am Nobu Matsumoto.

Nobu hangs up. Picks up his kite and stares at it. Masi lit in pool of light. Casting. She is working on perfecting her technique, putting together all the little things that Sadao has taught her. She goes through one complete cycle without a hitch. Very smooth. Having done the whole thing without a mistake gives her great satisfaction. She smiles to herself. It feels good. She begins again. Dim to darkness on Masi and Nobu.

End of act one.

---

mendokusai: Troublesome.

ACT TWO

SCENE ONE: *Kiyoko's restaurant, four weeks later. Surprise birthday party for Nobu. Judy stands by herself out front, picking at the food. Curley and Marsha are in the kitchen and Kiyoko and Chiyo scurry about with last-minute preparations. Over the restaurant speakers we hear a forties tune like "String of Pearls."*

KIYOKO (*calling*): Curley! Hurry up with the chicken teri! (*Checking the food items.*) Ara! I forgot the dip. Chiyo, go talk, go talk.

Kiyoko pushes Chiyo towards Judy, then hurries back into the kitchen as Curley and Marsha enter, carrying more food. Marsha is holding her nose.

CHIYO (*to Judy, in passing*): Nobu's favorite song. (*Stops momentarily, touching Judy's hair.*) You come see me, I know what to do with it.

Chiyo heads back to the kitchen as Marsha and Curley are setting their dishes down.

CURLEY: If you think this stink, wait 'til you try my famous homyu.

MARSHA (*attempting to be polite*): No, really, it wasn't that bad.

CURLEY: All orientals gotta have stink food. It's part of our culture. Chinese, Japanese, Koreans, Filipinos — we all got one dish that is so stink. Filipinos got fish-gut paste, bagaoong. Koreans, kim chee. Whew! Chinese got this thing called hamha, shrimp paste. My mudda used to cook with it. Whew! Stink like something went die.

Chiyo enters.

CHIYO (*admonishing*): Curley.

CURLEY (*ignoring Chiyo*): And us Buddhaheads eat takuan, the pickled horseradish. When you open up the bottle, the neighbors call to see if your toilet went explode!

CHIYO (*poking head into the kitchen*): Kiyoko! He's at it again!

CURLEY: Next time you come I make you my homyu.

JUDY: Homyu? (*To Marsha.*) You know homyu?

MARSHA: It's some kind of vegetable dish or something? . . .

CURLEY: No, no, no . . . What's a matta? You guys live on Mars? You never heard of homyu? Homyu. Steamed pork hash. It's my specialty. Gotta have the stinky fish on top. That's the secret. Lotsa pake° places don't use that fish anymore. Know why? Too stink! Chase all the haole° customers away. Take pork butt, chop it into small pieces. Little pig snout, huh? Throw it in. Tastes so ono.° Four water chestnuts, chopped. Teaspoon of cornstarch . . .

Kiyoko enters with dip, Chiyo trailing.

KIYOKO (*interrupts*): Curley! Curley! Go do the cake!

MARSHA (*to Curley*): I'll help you.

CHIYO: Kiyoko, when is he coming?

KIYOKO (*to Chiyo*): He should be on his way . . . (*To Marsha.*) You shouldn't help anymore. Eat, eat. Talk to Chiyo. (*Continues.*)

MARSHA (*overlapping*): We met already . . .

---

pake: Chinese. **haole:** White **ono:** Tasty.

KIYOKO (*continues. To Curley*): Go, go, put the candles on the cake. No beer, either.

CURLEY (*exiting, calling back to Marsha while scratching his butt*): Stinky fish. Don't forget the stinky fish . . .

KIYOKO (*following him out*): Don't scratch your . . .

Kiyoko remembers the guests. As they exit, Chiyo approaches Judy and Marsha.

CHIYO: I've never seen her like this. She's acting like a kid back there. (*Catching her breath and looking the two daughters over.*) You're Judy, neh, the fifth-grade teacher?

JUDY: I am the fifth-grade teacher.

CHIYO: And you're the dental . . . (*Continues.*)

MARSHA (*overlapping*): . . . Hygienist, I told you earlier . . .

CHIYO (*continues*): . . . hygienist — yeah, yeah, you told me before. (*Quietly laughs about her mistake. Calms down.*) So. What do you think of the both of them? Nobu and Kiyoko?

Awkward pause.

MARSHA: I think it's . . . good. I think it's good.

Chiyo looks to Judy, who is silent.

CHIYO (*touching her hair gently*): You come see me. I know what to do with it.

Chiyo turns and walks back towards the kitchen.

MARSHA: Judy.

JUDY: This is stupid — what am I doing here?

MARSHA: We're doing this for Dad.

JUDY: You really think he's going to want us here?

MARSHA: Judy . . .

JUDY: Do you?

Kiyoko hurries in, followed by Chiyo.

KIYOKO: Curley called — Nobu's not home, so he's coming. (*To Marsha, feigning enthusiasm.*) I'm so glad you could make it. Judy said you weren't sure whether you could all come or not.

MARSHA: Oh no, no. We wouldn't have missed it.

KIYOKO: Nobu-chan will be so happy you are here.

MARSHA: It was very kind of you to invite us.

KIYOKO: Oh no, no, no. I wanted all of you here.

CHIYO: Yeah, yeah, we wanted all of you here.

KIYOKO (*to Judy*): Where is the baby?

JUDY: Jimmy's home baby-sitting him.

CHIYO: Next time you bring him. We got plenty of room here.

KIYOKO: Yes, please, please. Next time you bring the baby and Jimmy, too. I want to get to know all of Nobu-chan's family.

Curley rushes in with his ukelele.

CURLEY: HAYO! HAYO!° THE BUGGA'S COMING! THE BUGGA'S COMING!

HAYO! HAYO!: Hurry! hurry!

CHIYO: I'll get the cake. Hide! Hide!
CURLEY: I got the lights.
KIYOKO (*to Marsha and Judy*): In here, in here . . . (*Darkness. Nobu enters cautiously.*)
NOBU: Kiyoko! Kiyoko!

The lights come up abruptly, then begin a slow fade through the rest of the scene.

ALL: SURPRISE!

Nobu is first happy. Then he sees Judy and Marsha. He is in shock. Chiyo and Curley lead everyone in a rousing, celebratory birthday song as Kiyoko enters with a birthday cake decorated with burning candles. Nobu is attempting to appear happy, but he is becoming more and more upset that his daughters are there. Lights continue their slow fade through the song, which is beginning to fall apart. Kiyoko is now standing next to Nobu holding the cake out in front of him. She senses something is wrong. The song ends with Curley and Kiyoko mumbling the last few lyrics. Silence. Nobu's face is illuminated by the glowing candles. Nobu makes no move to blow out the candles. The moment is now uncomfortable. Kiyoko is very upset.

KIYOKO: Nobu-chan, please.
JUDY (*irritated*): Dad.

Nobu still refuses to blow out the candles. Moment is now extremely awkward. No one knows what to do.

MARSHA (*gently*): Daddy.

Slowly Nobu leans forward and with a forceful breath extinguishes the candles.

End of scene.

SCENE TWO: *Masi's place, the same night. Sadao and Masi on couch. Both are propped up, Sadao intently watching TV and Masi peering at the TV over the magazine she holds in front of her. Sadao keeps switching the channel with his remote control. Each time Masi starts to settle into a program, Sadao switches the channel, causing her to jerk her head from the shock.*

MASI: Sadao?

Sado is busy switching channels.

MASI: Sadao?
SADAO: Hmm?
MASI: Could you please keep it on one?
SADAO (*realizing what he's been doing*): Oh. I'm sorry. (*Starts switching channels again.*) Which one? This one? How's this?
MASI: Fine, fine. That's fine.

They settle into watching TV.

MASI: Sadao?
SADAO: Hmm?
MASI: I don't feel good. (*Pause.*) I think something's wrong with me.
SADAO: What, what? Want me to call Doc Takei?
MASI: No, no . . .
SADAO: You have a fever? Headache? What's wrong?

MASI: No, no, nothing like that. (*Pause. Thinking.*) I'm too happy.
SADAO: What?
MASI: I feel . . . too happy.

Sadao stares at her, uncomprehending.

MASI: I used to feel like this as a kid, I think. But it was . . . different.

Pause.

SADAO: You feel too happy?
MASI: When you're a kid you get ice cream and 'member how you used to feel? Happy, right? But then you eat it all up and it's gone, or you eat too much of it and you throw up. But this just goes on and on.
SADAO: You mean us?

Masi nods.

SADAO: Yeah, but this is a little different from ice cream, don't you . . .
MASI (*interrupts*): Of course, of course, Sadao.
SADAO: What about with Nobu? Didn't you go through this with him?

Masi shakes her head.

SADAO: I mean in the beginning when you first met? When you got married?
MASI: No, it wasn't like that. (*Pause.*) I think something's wrong with me. You know how they say there's no such thing as an accident? That you really wanted it to happen and so it did? I don't think I ever really cared for Nobu. Not the way he cared for me. There was someone else who liked me in camp. I liked him, too. I married Nobu. Something's wrong with me, huh? Now you make me feel too happy. I don't like it. It makes me . . . unhappy.

They both laugh. Sadao reaches out and places his hand on top of hers.

MASI: Was she in a lot of pain?

Sadao doesn't follow her comment.

MASI: Your wife. Towards the end. In the hospital.
SADAO (*realizes she's talking about his first wife, Mary*): She just slept all the time. No, not too much. After about two weeks she went into a coma and that was it. You can't tell. Cancer's like that. Mary was pretty lucky, I guess. (*Pause. Thinking.*) There's nothing wrong with you. Really, there isn't. (*Pause. Trying to decide whether to say something or not.*) You scare me. You know that? Sometimes you scare me half to death. I don't want to go through that again. I told myself, "Never, ever again." Dead is better than feeling that kind of pain. But this . . . this is . . . I don't know . . . To get a second chance . . . (*Pause.*) There's nothing good about growing old. You spend most of your time taking medicine and going to the doctor so you won't die. The rest of the time you spend going to the funerals of your friends who did die, and they were taking the same medicine and seeing the same doctors, so what's the use, anyway? Huh? (*Sarcastically.*) The golden years . . . Look at us. Here we are. At our age. Not even married. Can you imagine what the kids are thinking?
MASI: We're not doing anything wrong.

SADAO: Of course, I know, I know.

MASI: We're not doing anything wrong, Sadao. We're not.

SADAO: I know. But when I really think about what we're doing . . . it embarrasses the hell out of me!

They look at each other, then suddenly burst out laughing. They gradually calm down.

MASI: I scare you half to death. And you . . . you make me feel so good I feel awful.

They look at each other for a moment, then slowly reach out and embrace. Dim to darkness.

End of scene.

SCENE THREE: *Kiyoko's restaurant, one week later. Nobu is sitting at counter sipping sake and eating eggplant pickles. Curley is watching him from the service window. He comes out, sipping on a beer.*

CURLEY (*takes a big gulp*): Know why I like to drink beer? Know why? (*As Nobu looks up, Curley answers his own question with a loud, satisfying burp.*) Ahh. I like to let things out. Makes me feel good. Don't like to keep things bottled up inside. Not good for you. Give you an ulcer. Cancer. Maybe you just blow up and disappear altogether, huh. (*Laughs at his own joke. Notices Nobu isn't laughing.*) That's the problem with you kotonks. You buggas from the mainland all the time too serious.

Nobu glances back towards the door.

CURLEY: No worry, no worry. Kiyoko going be back soon. Chiyo's place — yak, yak, yak. Hey, you had lots of girl friends when you was small kid time?

Nobu shrugs.

CURLEY: Strong silent type, huh? Me? Lotsa wahinis. All the time like to play with Curley. (*Mimicking the girls.*) "Curley, darling, you're so cute . . . you're so funny" . . . But I not all the time cute. I not all the time funny. How come you all the time come around here and you still got one wife?

NOBU: We're separated.

CURLEY: So when you gonna get the divorce?

NOBU: No.

Curley doesn't understand.

NOBU: *No.*

CURLEY: What about Kiyoko?

No response. Nobu keeps drinking.

CURLEY: I don't like you. I like you. I don't like you 'cause you make Kiyoko feel lousy. I like you 'cause you make her happy. Hey, she's my boss — who you think catch hell if she not feeling good? Hey, I don't like catching hell for what you do . . .

NOBU (*interrupts*): It's none of your business — Kiyoko and me.

CURLEY: None of my business? Hey, brudda, Kiyoko may be feeding your face but I'm the guy who's cooking the meals.

Nobu stares down at his pickles.

CURLEY: Nobu?

NOBU: What?

CURLEY: You like Kiyoko? (*No response.*) Well, do you?

NOBU (*under his breath*): Yeah, I guess so.

CURLEY: "Yeah, I guess so" what?

NOBU (*mumbling*): I like Kiyoko.

CURLEY: Jesus. Talking to you kotonks is like pulling teeth.

NOBU: I LIKE KIYOKO! (*Pause.*) I like Kiyoko.

Curley leans forward towards Nobu and burps loudly.

CURLEY: Feels good, huh?

Nobu is disgusted. Curley smiles. Dim to darkness.

End of scene.

SCENE FOUR: *Nobu's place, one week later. Masi enters, carrying the wash in a brown paper bag. She unpacks the clothes and stacks them neatly on the kitchen table. She picks up the old clothes off the floor, folds them, and puts them in the bag. As she looks up, one gets the sense that she is trying to decide whether to say hello to Nobu or just leave. She looks for a moment towards the hallway, then decides otherwise. Just as she turns and starts to make her way towards the door with the bag, Nobu enters from the hallway.*

NOBU: Masi, is that you?

Nobu realizes that she's leaving without bothering to say hello. Masi senses this and feels guilty.

MASI: I was going. I'm a little late. I was just going to leave the clothes and go. (*As she speaks, she notices the dirty dishes on the coffee table. She puts down the bag and proceeds to clean up the mess as she continues to talk.*) I didn't know you were in the back . . . (*Masi points to the dishes in the sink, while Nobu just watches.*) Nobu, why don't you wash the dishes once in a while? Clean up.

NOBU: Place is a dump anyway.

Masi stops and looks at him. Nobu presses the point.

NOBU: Place is a dump, Mama. Neighborhood's no good. Full of colored people. Mexicans . . .

MASI (*putting dishes in sink*): Well, move then. Move to the north side like me. I kept saying that all along. For the kids — better schools, better neighborhood . . . Think you listen to me? (*Mimicking Nobu.*) "I don't like hakujin — white people make me nervous." So you don't like white people, you don't like black people, you don't like Mexicans . . . So who do you like? Huh? Monku, monku, monku.

NOBU (*muttering*): I don't mind Mexicans. (*Pause.*) I told Shig you can't keep stocking all that Japanese things when the Nihonjins° are moving out of the neighborhood. You gotta sell to the Mexicans and not all that cheap crap too, 'cause they can tell. Think Shig listens to me? He's the big store

---

Nihonjins: Japanese.

owner. The big man. If I was running the store it woulda been different. Different. (*Pause.*) And your old man said he'd get me that store.

MASI: It wasn't his fault. He didn't plan on the war, Nobu.

NOBU: He promised he could set me . . . (*Continues.*)

MASI (*overlapping*): It wasn't his fault.

NOBU (*continuing*): . . . up in business or anything else I wanted to do.

MASI: IT WASN'T HIS FAULT! (*Silence.*) Who wanted to be in the relocation camps? Did you? Do you think he wanted to be in there? It broke Papa's heart. He spent his entire life building up that farm. Papa was a proud man. A very proud man. It broke his heart when he lost it. And how come you didn't go to the bank like I told you? I told you to go to the bank and ask for . . .

NOBU: I'm just saying I'd run the business different. Shig is a baka, a fool. That's all I'm saying.

MASI: You're retired. Shig passed away eight years ago. The store's not even . . . (*Continues.*)

NOBU (*overlapping*): If all the Japanese move out you can't keep selling all those Japanese things, you can't. That's all I'm saying.

MASI (*continuing*): . . . there any more. It's a cleaner's.

Silence. Masi picks up the paper bag of old clothes and starts to move towards the door. She's had enough.

NOBU: Masi?

MASI (*stops*): What?

NOBU: Mr. Rossi give you any more fish?

MASI (*uncomfortable lying*): No. Not lately.

Pause.

NOBU: Mama?

MASI: Is your back bothering you, Nobu? (*No response.*) Want me to momo° it for you?

Nobu nods. As Masi moves to put the bag down, Nobu removes his undershirt so he is bare chested. He seats himself. Masi begins to massage his shoulders from behind. They continue in silence. Nobu is enjoying the moment. He begins to laugh quietly to himself.

MASI: What?

NOBU: When I started work at your papa's farm, he wanted to put me in the packing shed. I said, "No, I want to work in the fields." It was so hot, 110 degrees out there. He thought I was nuts. But I knew every day at eight in the morning and twelve noon you and your sister would bring the water out to us.

MASI (*laughing as she recalls*): Nobu.

NOBU: I wanted to watch you.

MASI: You would just stand there with your cup, staring at me.

NOBU: Hell, I didn't know what to say.

MASI: You drank so much water, Lila and I thought maybe you had rabies. We used to call you "Nobu, the Mad Dog." (*Both laughing.*) Papa liked you.

---

momo: Massage.

NOBU: Boy, he was a tough son of a bitch.

MASI: I didn't think anyone could keep up with Papa. But you could work like a horse. You and Papa. Proud. Stubborn.

Masi massages Nobu in silence.

NOBU: Masi? Why don't you cook me breakfast?

MASI: What?

NOBU: Cook me breakfast. I miss my hot rice and raw egg in the morning.

MASI: It's late, Nobu. You have your wash. I'm not going to come all the way back over here just to cook you . . .

NOBU (*interrupts*): Just breakfast. Then in the morning when we get up you can go back to your place.

Masi stops, realizing he is asking her to spend the night. Masi does not move. Nobu stares ahead. More silence. Then, tentatively, she moves her hands forward and begins to massage him. A faint smile appears on Nobu's face. Dim to darkness.

End of scene.

SCENE FIVE: *Kiyoko's restaurant, one week later. Curley, after hours, seated in semi-darkness. Feet up on table, accompanying himself on the ukelele and singing a sad Hawaiian folk song, like "Manuela Boy."*

As he sings, Masi's place lit in pool of light. Sadao stands before the door Masi has just opened. In Sadao's right hand he holds a suitcase and in his left several fishing poles. On his head sits a fishing hat. Sadao has come to move in with Masi. For a moment they look at each other in silence. Then Masi invites him in. Sadao enters. Dim to darkness.

Dim to darkness on Curley as he finishes the song.

End of scene.

SCENE SIX: *Nobu's place, three days later. Late afternoon. Judy has stopped by with Timothy. Judy sets the baby down on the kitchen table upstage of Nobu. Nobu turns to look at Judy, then returns to working on the kite and watching TV. This is the first time Judy has visited Nobu since their breakup over her marriage. He has never seen Timothy.*

JUDY (*moving down towards Nobu*): I was just driving by and I thought I'd stop in. (*No response.*) You doing okay, Dad? (*Silence.*) You know, Mom? I just wanted to say . . .

NOBU (*interrupts*): Did he come?

JUDY (*exasperated*): No, he did not.

NOBU: He can come to the house now.

JUDY: "He can come to the house now"? Jesus Christ. Dad, he isn't one of your children. He doesn't need your permission. He's a . . . (*Continues.*)

NOBU (*overlapping*): This is my house. He needs my permission.

JUDY (*continues*): . . . grown man. I don't want to fight. I didn't come here to fight with you, Dad.

NOBU: I *said* he can come . . .

JUDY (*interrupts*): He won't come, he doesn't like you!

Silence.

NOBU: Damn kurochan . . .

JUDY: He's black, not kurochan. It's "African American." (*Pause.*) Everybody marries out, okay? Sanseis don't like Sanseis.

NOBU: Tak's son married a Nihonjin, Shig's daughter did, your cousin Patsy . . . (*Continues.*)

JUDY (*overlapping*): Okay, okay, I didn't, I didn't, all right.

NOBU (*continues*): . . . did, Marsha's going to. (*Pause. Looks back to Timothy.*)

JUDY: But is that any reason not to see my baby? He's a part of you, too.

NOBU: No, no. Japanese marry other Japanese, their kids are Yonsei° — not these damn ainoko.°

Silence.

JUDY: You're gonna die out, you know that. You're gonna be extinct and nobody's gonna give a goddamn.

Timothy has begun to cry softly. She goes over and picks the baby up, trying to soothe him. Judy, composing herself, decides to try one last time to say what she came to tell her father. Judy walks back to Nobu, this time carrying Timothy with her.

JUDY: Dad? (*No response.*) Dad, you know Mom's moving out of the house? I didn't put her up to it. Honest. (*Silence. Nobu stares straight ahead. Judy begins to cry.*) If I did . . . I'm sorry.

NOBU: Judy . . .

More silence from Nobu. Judy gives up trying to talk to this man. As she turns to leave, she notices Nobu. He is looking towards her, at Timothy. Something in his expression makes Judy bring the baby over to Nobu.

JUDY (*holding the baby out*): Timothy. Your grandson.

For a moment there is hesitation. We are not sure whether Nobu is going to take the baby. Then, Nobu reaches out and takes Timothy. Judy watches as Nobu awkwardly holds his grandson for the first time. As Judy begins to withdraw from the scene upstage into a pool of light, Marsha is also lit upstage in her own separate pool of light. Nobu remains lit holding Timothy. He begins to hum the traditional Japanese lullaby "Donguri." Marsha and Judy watch Nobu and Timothy as they speak.

MARSHA: You didn't tell Dad, did you?

JUDY: No. I just brought the baby by.

MARSHA: It's going to kill him when he finds out.

JUDY: He's got that other woman.

MARSHA: Judy. (*Pause.*) Maybe he already knows about Mom and Mr. Nakasato.

JUDY: I don't think so. I really don't think so.

They continue to watch as Nobu begins to sing the "Donguri" song to Timothy.

NOBU (*singing*):

> Donguri koro koro, donguri ko
> Oike ni hamatte, saa taihen
> Dojō ga dette kite, "konnichiwa"
> Timothy isshoni, asobimashō . . .°

Yonsei: Fourth-generation Japanese American. **ainoko:** Biracial person.
Donguri . . . asobimashō:
Acorn, acorn, rolling along
Fell into a pond, what will we do?
Up comes a loach fish, says, "Good afternoon."
Timothy, let's go play together.

Repeat.

Marsha and Judy dim to darkness first. Nobu is left alone in a pool of light singing to Timothy. As he dims to darkness, we hear the whir of a coffee grinder.

End of scene.

SCENE SEVEN: *Masi's place, two days later. Masi has asked Judy and Marsha over for a talk. She has just told them she is going over to see Nobu. She is going to tell him that she wants to divorce him and to marry again.*

The two daughters sit uneasily while Masi is at the counter preparing coffee. Masi is trying to get the Braun grinder to work. She's getting the feel of it by pushing the button. We hear the whir of the spinning rotor blade.

She's ready. Takes the plastic top off and pours the beans in. Then, presses the start button. Just as the grinder picks up top speed Masi accidentally pulls the plastic top off. Beans go flying every which way! Pelting her face, bouncing off the cabinets. Quiet. Masi peeks from behind her hands. A couple of beans embedded in her hair fall to the counter. Masi is upset. The daughters are embarrassed. Normally, this would be a funny situation for them.

Marsha starts to pick up the beans scattered on the floor. Judy starts to giggle — it's all too ridiculous.

JUDY (*trying to suppress her laughter*): I'm sorry, I'm sorry . . .
MARSHA: I'll clean it up.

Masi begins to laugh.

JUDY: God, what a mess.
MASI (*to Marsha*): Let it go, don't bother. I'll take care of it later.

Judy finds a man's sock.

JUDY (*teasing*): What's this? This belong to Mr. Nakasato?
MASI (*grabbing it*): Judy.
MARSHA: Why didn't you just leave sooner? You didn't have to stick around for us.
MASI: I didn't. I was . . . I was scared.
MARSHA: Of Dad?
MASI: I don't know. Everything.
JUDY: Was it 'cause I kept harping on you to move out on him all those years? Is that why you left?
MARSHA: What's the difference now?
JUDY: Marsha.

Pause.

MASI: There are things you kids don't know. I didn't want to talk about them to you but . . . Daddy and I, we didn't sleep . . . (*Continues.*)
JUDY (*overlapping*): That's okay, Mom. Really, it's okay . . .
MASI (*continues*): . . . together. Every time I wanted to, he would push me away. Ten, fifteen years he didn't want me. (*Pause.*) We were having one of our arguments, just like always. And he was going on and on about how it was my fault this and my fault that. And I was trying to explain

my side of it, when he turned on me, "Shut up, Mama. You don't know anything. You're stupid." Stupid. After forty-two years of letting him be right he called me that. And I understood. He didn't even need me to make him be right anymore. He just needed me to be stupid. I was tired. I couldn't fight him anymore. He won. He finally made me feel like shit. (*Shocking Judy and Marsha with her strong language.*) That was the night I left him and came over to your place. (*Nodding towards Judy.*) I like Sadao. (*Turns to Marsha.*) I like Sadao very much.

Marsha turns away, then gets up and exits. Masi sends Judy after Marsha to comfort her. Dim to darkness.

End of scene.

SCENE EIGHT: *Nobu's place, the same day. "String of Pearls" can be heard playing faintly in the background. He's flexing himself in front of a small wall mirror. He adjusts the collar of his shirt and tugs at his sweater until it looks right. Nobu checks his watch. As he begins to pick up some of the scattered clothes on the floor, Masi enters. Music cue ends.*

Nobu quickly gets up and moves to the sofa. Masi goes over to the kitchen area and takes clothes out of the bag, setting them neatly on the table. She picks up the dirty clothes off the floor, folds them, and puts them into the bag. As she's doing this, Nobu gets up, shuffles over to the stove, and turn on the flame to heat some water. Stands there and watches the water heat up.

MASI (*sits down on sofa*): I want to talk, Nobu.

No response. Nobu gets the tea out and pours some into the pot.

MASI: I have something I want to tell you.
NOBU (*moving back to couch*): Want some tea?

As Nobu sits, Masi gets up and moves towards the sink area. She gets a sponge and wipes off the tea leaves he has spilled on the counter. Nobu turns on the TV and stares at it.

MASI: You know Dorothy and Henry's son, George?
NOBU: The pharmacist or something?
MASI: No, the lawyer one. He's the lawyer one. I went to see him. I went to see about a divorce. About getting one. (*No response.*) I want to get married again. So I went to George to see about a divorce. I wanted to tell you first so you'd know. I didn't want you to hear from someone else. I know how you hate that kind of thing. Thinking something's going on behind your back.
NOBU: Wait, wait, wait a second. You want to get . . . What? What's all this?
MASI: It's the best thing, Nobu. We've been separated how long now? How long have we been living different places?
NOBU: I don't know. I never thought about it. Not too long.
MASI: Thirteen months.
NOBU: Thirteen months, who cares? I never thought about it.
MASI: It's the same as being divorced, isn't it?
NOBU: It doesn't seem that long. You moved out of this house. It wasn't my idea. It was your idea. I never liked it.

MASI: It doesn't matter whose idea it was. It's been over a year since we . . .
NOBU (*interrupts*): You want to get married? Yeah, I know it's been over a year but I always thought . . . You know, that we'd . . .
MASI (*interrupts*): It's been over a year, Nobu.
NOBU: I know! I said I know.

Pause.

MASI: I've been seeing someone. It wasn't planned or anything. It just happened.
NOBU: What do you mean, "seeing someone"? What do you mean?
MASI: He's very nice. A widower. He takes me fishing. He has a nice vegetable garden that he . . .
NOBU (*interrupts*): Who is he? Do I know him? Is it someone I know?
MASI: His name is Sadao Nakasato. His wife died about two years ago. He's related to Dorothy and Henry. Nobu, it's the best thing for both of us.
NOBU: You keep saying it's the best thing, the best thing. (*Pause.*) Masi, why did you sleep with me that night?

Silence.

MASI: Aren't you seeing somebody?
NOBU: No. Not like that.
MASI: But the kids said she's very nice. That she invited . . .
NOBU (*interrupts*): It's totally different! I'm not seeing anyone! (*Pause.*) How long have you been seeing this guy? How long?
MASI: Please, Nobu. You always get what *you* want. I always let you have your way. For once just let . . .
NOBU (*interrupts*): HOW LONG!
MASI: About five months.
NOBU: FIVE MONTHS! How come you never told me? Do the girls know, too? The girls know! Everybody knows? Five months. FIVE GODDAMN MONTHS AND I DON'T KNOW!!

Nobu breaks the kite.

MASI: I asked them not to tell you.
NOBU: Why? Why the hell not? Don't I have a right to know?
MASI: Because I knew you'd react this way. Just like this. Yelling and screaming just like you always do.
NOBU: Everybody in this whole goddamn town knows except me! How could you do this to me! Masi! HOW COULD YOU DO THIS TO ME??

Nobu has her by the shoulders and is shaking her violently.

MASI: Are you going to hit me?

Pause. Nobu slowly composes himself and lets her go.

MASI: Because I want to be happy, Nobu. I want to be happy.

Masi exits. Nobu left standing alone. Dim to darkness.

End of scene.

SCENE NINE: *Kiyoko's restaurant, evening of the same day. Chiyo and Kiyoko seated at table, lit in pool of light.*

KIYOKO: Nine years. That's how long it has been. Nine years since Harry passed away. He never treated me like this. I call, I go over there. Harry never treated me like this.

CHIYO: Kiyoko. Maybe you have to stop thinking about Nobu. Hmm? Maybe . . . maybe you should give him up. (*Silence.*) Kiyoko. Lots more fish in the ocean. Lots more. Go out with us. Come on.

KIYOKO: I don't do those kinds of things.

CHIYO: I'll introduce you to some new guys. Remember Ray — you met him? I've been telling him about . . .

KIYOKO (*interrupts*): I don't do those kinds of things. (*Pause.*) It's not easy for me, Chiyo. (*Silence.*) When Harry died, right after? I started taking the bus to work. I had a car, I could drive. It was easier to drive. I took the bus. For twenty-five years you go to sleep with him, wake up next to him, he shaves while you shower, comes in from the yard all sweaty. Then he's gone. No more Harry in bed. No more smell of aftershave in the towel you're drying off with. No more sweaty Harry coming up and hugging me. I had a car. I took the bus. I missed men's smells. I missed the smell of men. Every morning I would get up and walk to the corner to take the bus. It would be full of all these men going to work. And it would be full of all these men coming home from work. I would sit there pretending to read my magazine . . . (*Inhales. Discovering the different smells.*) Soap . . . just washed skin . . . aftershave lotion . . . sweat . . .

Lights come up to half in the restaurant. Curley bursts through the kitchen doors holding a plate of his famous homyu. Brings it over and sets it down on the table, which is now lit in a full pool of light.

CURLEY: Homyu! Homyu!

CHIYO: Curley, kusai yo!

CURLEY: I know stink, but stink GOOD!

KIYOKO: Curley!

CURLEY (*motioning*): Hayo, hayo — all dis good food back dere going to waste. Gonna need a gas mask for all da stinky stuff back dere. Come on, come on. I been cooking all day. Hayo, hayo, Kau Kau time.°

As lights dim, Curley ushers Kiyoko and Chiyo offstage into the kitchen.

End of scene.

SCENE TEN: *Nobu's place, two days later. Knock at the door, and Marsha enters carrying a brown paper bag. Nobu is watching TV.*

MARSHA: Mom asked me to drop these by and to pick up the dirty clothes.

No response. Marsha unpacks the newly washed clothes.

MARSHA: Kiyoko's been calling me. She's worried about you. She says you won't see anybody. Why don't you just talk to her, Dad?

NOBU: How come you didn't tell me? All the time you come here and you never mention it once. You. I feel so goddamn ashamed. All the time right under my nose. Everyone laughing at me behind my . . .

Kau Kau time: Time to eat.

MARSHA (*interrupts*): Dad, Dad, it's not like that at all. I just didn't think it was all that important to tell . . .

NOBU (*interrupts*): Oh, come on! Mom told you not to tell me so she could go sneaking 'round with that son of a bitch!

MARSHA: All right, all right, but it's not like that at all. No one's trying to hide anything from you and no one's laughing at you.

NOBU (*moving her towards the couch and pushing her down while speaking*): Sit down, sit down over here. Who is he? What does he do? Tell me 'bout him! Tell me!

MARSHA (*seated*): What do you want me to say? Huh, Dad? They're happy. He's a nice man.

NOBU (*repeating*): "He's a nice man." What the hell's that supposed to mean?

MARSHA: He treats her like a very special person.

NOBU: Well, everyone does that in the beginning. In the beginning it's so easy to be . . .

MARSHA (*interrupts*): She laughs. All the time she's laughing. They're like two little kids. They hold hands. Did you ever do that? I'm embarrassed to be around them. He takes her fishing. He has a little camper and they drive up to Lake Berryessa and camp overnight . . . (*Continues right through.*)

NOBU: All right, all right . . .

MARSHA (*continues*): . . . He teaches her how to bait the hook and cast it out.

NOBU (*overlapping*): She doesn't like fishing.

MARSHA (*continues*): I mean you never even took her fishing.

NOBU: I tried to take her lots of times. She wouldn't go.

MARSHA (*continues*): They even dig up worms in his garden at his house. I saw them. Side by side . . . (*Continues.*)

NOBU: All right, I said.

MARSHA (*continues*): . . . sitting on the ground digging up worms and . . . (*Continues.*)

NOBU (*overlapping*): ALL RIGHT! ALL RIGHT!

MARSHA (*continues*): . . . putting them in a coffee can! I MEAN DID YOU EVER DO THAT FOR MOM!! (*Pause. Quieter.*) Did you? (*Getting worked up again.*) You're so . . . so stupid. You are. You're stupid. All you had to say was "Come back. Please come back." You didn't even have to say, "I'm sorry." (*Continues.*)

NOBU (*overlapping*): I'm your father . . .

MARSHA (*continues*): . . . Mom would've come back. She would've. That's all you had to say. Three lousy words: "Please come back." (*Continues.*)

NOBU (*overlapping*): I'm your father . . .

MARSHA (*continues*): . . . You ruined everything. It's all too late! YOU WRECKED EVERYTHING! (*Pause. Composing herself.*) I'm so mixed up. When I look at Mom I'm happy for her. When I think about you . . . I don't know. You have Kiyoko.

NOBU: That's not the same. I'm talking about your Mama.

MARSHA: Dad, Kiyoko cares a great deal about you. She's been calling Judy and me day and night.

NOBU: She knocks on the door but I don't let her in. She's not Mama.

MARSHA: Dad. What do you want me to say? That's the way it is. I used to keep thinking you two would get back together. I couldn't imagine life any other way. But slowly I just got used to it. Mom over there, and you here. Then all this happened. I mean, sometimes I can't recognize Mom anymore. What do you want me to say? You'll get used to it.

NOBU (*pause, upset, then stubbornly*): No.

Marsha looks at her father sadly.

MARSHA: You'll get used to it.

Dim to darkness on Marsha and Nobu.

End of scene.

SCENE ELEVEN: *Masi and Judy at the clothesline. Judy holds Timothy while Masi hangs clothes. An agitated Nobu enters and begins to pull Masi home.*

JUDY: Dad . . .

MASI: Nobu . . .

NOBU: I won't yell, Mama, I won't yell at you anymore. I won't monku about . . . (*Continues.*)

MASI (*overlapping*): Nobu? Nobu, what are you . . .

Continues.

JUDY (*overlapping*): Dad, Dad . . .

MASI (*continuing*): . . . doing? Let go, Nobu . . .

NOBU (*continuing*): . . . the store or about your papa — I won't monku, I won't do any of that stuff . . .

MASI: Let go of my arm!

Silence.

NOBU: I tried, I tried, Masi. After the war, after we got out of camp? After . . . (*Continues.*)

MASI (*overlapping*): Nobu, camp? What are you . . .

NOBU (*continuing*): . . . we got out I went to the bank like you told me. So your papa can't give me money, that's all right . . . (*Continues.*)

MASI (*overlapping*): Nobu, what's this — you never told me . . .

NOBU (*continuing*): . . . I'll do it on my own. I got there and ask the man how do I sign up to get money. He says, "Sit there and wait." I wait, I wait, I wait five whole goddamn hours. I go up, "How come nobody sees me?" He says, "Sorry, but the person to see you is sick, come back tomorrow." I get so pissed off I throw the magazines all over the place. Everyone is looking. I don't give a damn, I'm shaking I'm so pissed off. And then, and then . . . I'm filled with shame. Shame. Because I threw their magazines all over. After what they did to me, *I'm* ashamed, me, *me.* When I get home I feel something getting so tight inside of me. In my guts, tighter and tighter, getting all balled up. How come I feel like this? Huh? How come I feel like this? I'm scared, Masi. I'm scared. Please. I need . . . (*Continues.*)

MASI (*overlapping*): You don't understand, you don't . . .

NOBU (*continuing*): . . . you. I need you. *You.* You know. You understand how it is now. Please, please, you come home, you come . . . (*Continues. Nobu begins to pull Masi home.*)

MASI (*overlapping*): Nobu, Nobu, I can't, I . . .

NOBU (*continuing*): . . . home now, Mama. Just like always. You come home . . . (*Continues.*)

MASI (*overlapping*): . . . can't, Nobu.

NOBU: . . . just like always . . .

MASI: I can't.

Nobu begins to break down, letting go of Masi. Begins to plead.

NOBU: I'm sorry, I'm sorry, Masi. It's no good, it's no good, Masi. Please come home. Please come home. Please . . .

Judy pulls Masi away and they withdraw from the scene. Nobu is left alone in a pool of light. Slowly he pulls himself upright, staring into the darkness. He turns and crosses back to his room. He reaches behind his chair and pulls out a long, narrow object wrapped in cloth. As he unwraps it, we see what it is, a shotgun. We hear the mournful wail of a shakuhachi *flute. Nobu sits down on the chair with the gun across his lap. Dim to darkness on Nobu.*

End of scene.

SCENE TWELVE: *Kiyoko's restaurant. Chiyo at the phone dialing Nobu's number. A concerned Curley stands guard next to her. Kiyoko has told them not to bother with him anymore. Kiyoko appears and watches them. She makes no attempt to stop them. Chiyo lets the phone ring.*

Nobu, seated in his chair, stares at the phone ringing next to him. He gets up, still holding the gun, and exits.

No one is answering. Chiyo and Curley exchange disappointed looks. Only then does Kiyoko burst in on them.

KIYOKO: How come you keep doing that? Huh? Don't phone him anymore. I told you, didn't I?

Kiyoko exits.

CURLEY (*to Chiyo*): Hey, maybe it's none of our business.

Dim to darkness on the restaurant.

End of scene.

SCENE THIRTEEN: *Masi's place, one week later. Nobu standing inside with a shotgun. Sadao asleep offstage in the bedroom.*

NOBU: Where is he?

Masi stares at the gun.

MASI: He went to buy the newspaper.

NOBU (*notices Masi watching him cautiously*): It's not loaded. (*Beat.*) I thought about it all week, all week. Coming over here, shooting the son of a bitch. I coulda. I coulda done it. (*Pause.*) I just wanted to show you. Both of you. That's why I brought it. Don't worry. It's not loaded. (*Nobu cracks the gun and shows her that it is not loaded.*) I just wanted to show both of you how it was, how I was feeling. But it's all right. You two. It's all right now.

Nobu sets the gun against the wall. Masi watches him, trying to decide if it is indeed safe.

MASI: Nobu.

NOBU: Yeah?

MASI: He's taking a nap. In the bedroom. He likes to do that after dinner.

NOBU: What is he? An old man or something?

MASI: He just likes to take naps. You do, too.

NOBU: In front of the TV. But I don't go into the bedroom and lie down. Well, where is he? Bring him out. Don't I get to meet him?

MASI: You sure? (*Masi looks at him for a long while. She believes him. She turns to go wake Sadao up, then stops.*) Chester Yoshikawa? That night in the camps when I didn't show up for the dance? Chester Yoshikawa? We just talked. That's all.

Masi leaves for the bedroom to awaken Sadao. Nobu looks slowly around the apartment. It's Masi and yet it isn't. Nobu suddenly has no desire to meet Sadao. He doesn't want to see them together in this apartment. Nobu exits abruptly. Masi appears cautiously leading out a yawning Sadao. They look around. No Nobu. All they see is his shotgun leaning against the wall.

As Masi and Sadao dim to darkness, Marsha and Judy are lit in a pool of light extreme downstage. Marsha is holding a small kite and slowly moving it above Timothy who is held by Judy. They sit in silence as Marsha moves the kite.

JUDY: I can't believe he gave the kite to Timothy. He gets so mad if you even touch them. And he never flies them.

Pause.

MARSHA (*moving the kite*): No. He never flies them.

They dim to half. They turn to watch the action taking place center stage.

End of scene.

SCENE FOURTEEN: *Darkness. Two days later. Onstage, the TV light comes on. Nobu's face lit by the screen's light. Lights come up and Nobu is now lit in a pool of light, seated at sofa watching TV. No kite on the coffee table. The rest of the place is in darkness. Masi is lit in a pool of light. She stands, staring pensively downstage into space. In her arms she is holding the brown paper bag of newly washed clothes. She turns and moves towards Nobu's place.*

As she enters the lights come up full on the house.

Nobu is still sitting on the sofa watching TV. Masi goes over to the kitchen table and takes out the newly washed clothes, stacking them in neat piles on the table. She then proceeds to pick up the clothes scattered on the floor and to put them in the bag. She is ready to leave. Masi takes the bag of dirty clothes and moves towards the door, then stops. She makes up her mind about something she has been struggling with for a while. Masi returns to the kitchen and leaves the bag of Nobu's dirty clothes on the table. As she opens the door to leave, Masi looks back at Nobu and watches him for a brief moment.

During this whole time, Nobu has never turned around to look at Masi though he is very aware of what is going on. Masi sadly turns and exits through the door. Lights dim with Nobu silently watching TV. Briefly, Nobu's face is lit by the dancing light of the television screen. At the same instant, the brown paper bag of wash on the table is illuminated by a shaft of light. His phone begins to ring. Nobu turns to look at it. Blackout on Nobu. The wash fades into darkness. The phone continues to ring for a few moments. Then, silence.

End of play.

CARYL CHURCHILL, *author of over twenty plays, was born in London in 1938 and earned a B.A. in English from Oxford University in 1960. The following year she married the barrister David Harter, with whom she had three sons. Churchill saw her first play,* Downstairs, *produced at Oxford by the Oriel College Dramatic Society, but during the decade after her graduation she mostly wrote plays for radio and television broadcast while she looked after her young children.*

In 1972 Churchill's play Owners *was produced by the Royal Court Theatre in London. It dramatized issues of social class and power structures that Churchill would develop during the 1970s in plays like* Vinegar Tom, *written for the feminist theater collective Monstrous Regiment in 1976. By the time she wrote her biggest success* Top Girls *in 1982, Churchill was recognized as a major presence in British theater. This play questioned the social rise of ambitious women and examined the price that women pay for success in the world of business and government. In 1982–83 Churchill won an Obie Award for* Top Girls, *followed by the Susan Smith Blackburn Prize in 1984 for* Fen *and the Olivier Award in 1987 for* Serious Money.

In the 1990s Churchill began to write more experimental plays, like Heart's Desire, *which was first produced in 1997 with another one-act play* Blue Kettle *under the title* Blue Heart *by Out of Joint and the Royal Court Theatre. Instead of following the realistic theatrical tradition in* Heart's Desire, *the playwright emphasized what critic Amelia Kritzer called "the full range of inconsistency, contradiction, and ambiguity available in a dramatic situation."* Heart's Desire *questions the conventions of theater, challenging linear patterns of plot development to make unfamiliar the familiar family drama of a father, mother, and aunt who are anxiously waiting for a daughter to arrive home after many years in Australia. There is no coherent narrative developed in the play and no resolution of the conflict between the characters. Instead, the audience gets a range of perspectives on the situation as Churchill disrupts the narrative with manic repetition of dialogue and unexpected comic effects. Characterized by theater critics as a "socialist-feminist" play,* Heart's Desire *is an open-ended, fresh way of examining an emotionally complex, unresolved family situation.*

RELATED COMMENTARY: *Caryl Churchill, "Interview with Kathleen Betsko and Rachel Koenig," page 1967.*

CARYL CHURCHILL

Heart's Desire

1997

CHARACTERS

BRIAN
ALICE
MAISIE

SUSY
LEWIS
LOTS OF CHILDREN
TWO GUNMEN
YOUNG AUSTRALIAN WOMAN
OFFICIAL
BIRD

Brian and Alice are married. Maisie is Brian's sister. They are all about sixty. Susy, their daughter, is thirty-five; Lewis, their son, is younger.

The scene is Brian and Alice's kitchen.

Alice and Maisie. Alice setting knives and forks on table, Maisie fidgets about the room. Brian enters putting on a red sweater.

BRIAN: She's taking her time.
ALICE: Not really.

They all stop, Brian goes out. Others reset to beginning and do exactly what they did before as Brian enters putting on a tweed jacket.

BRIAN: She's taking her time.
ALICE: Not really.

They all stop, Brian goes out, others reset and Brian enters putting on an old cardigan.

BRIAN: She's taking her time.
ALICE: Not really.
BRIAN: We should have met the plane.
ALICE: We should not.
MAISIE: What I really envy her for is the fauna because it's down a completely separate branch of evolution and I would love I would really love to see a platypus, not in a zoo but in its natural habitat. Imagine going to feed the ducks and there is something that is not a duck and nor is it a water-rat or a mole, it's the paws make me think of a mole, but imagine this furry creature with its ducky face, it makes you think what else could have existed, tigers with trunks, anyway the platypus has always been my favourite animal, it doesn't lay eggs like a duck, it's a marsupial like a kangaroo so the baby's born like a thread like a speck and has to crawl into the pouch, is that right, is a platypus a marsupial or not actually I'm not sure about that, maybe it does lay eggs like a duck, I'll look it up or I'll ask her when she comes and I wonder if she's ever seen one, maybe she went swimming in a river and there was this little furry —

Reset to top. Brian comes in putting on old cardigan.

BRIAN: She's taking her time.
ALICE: Not really.
BRIAN: We should have met the plane.
ALICE: We should not.
BRIAN: She'll be exhausted.
ALICE: She's a woman of thirty-five.
BRIAN: How can you speak of your daughter?
ALICE: She's a woman of thirty-five.
BRIAN: You're so right of course.

ALICE: She can travel round the world, she can travel the last few miles.
BRIAN: It's so delightful for you always being so right.
ALICE: That's it.
BRIAN: It's what?
ALICE: I'm leaving.
BRIAN: Oh ha ha we're all supposed to be frantic and beg you to stay and say very sorry.
ALICE: I wouldn't bother.
BRIAN: I'm not going to bother don't worry.

Exit Alice.

MAISIE: Alice?

Brian and Maisie wait.

BRIAN: She'll just have a cry.

Alice enters in coat with bag.

ALICE: Tell her I'm sorry and I'll phone later to tell her where I am.

Exit Alice.

BRIAN: Was that the front door? Alice? Alice.
MAISIE: I don't think you —

Reset to top, Alice in room as before, Maisie as before, Brian enters putting on old cardigan.

BRIAN: She's taking her time.
ALICE: Not really.
BRIAN: We should have met the plane.
ALICE: We should not.
BRIAN: She'll be exhausted.
ALICE: She's a woman of thirty-five.
BRIAN: How can you speak of your daughter?
ALICE: She's a woman of thirty-five.
BRIAN: You're so right of course.
ALICE: She can travel round the world, she can travel the last few miles.
BRIAN: It's so delightful for you always being so right.
ALICE: She didn't want to be met.
MAISIE: She'll be here in a few minutes.
BRIAN: I'm talking about spontaneity.
ALICE: She doesn't want fuss.
BRIAN: She says that but it wouldn't be if she didn't know she was being met and there we just were or there I was —

Phone rings.

Hello? speaking. Ah. Right. Yes. Thank you.

MAISIE: What?
BRIAN: There's been an accident.
ALICE: The plane?
BRIAN: The tube.° Didn't I say we should have met her?

---

tube: British nickname for "subway."

ALICE: Is she — ?

Set back to top as before. Brian enters putting on old cardigan.

BRIAN: She's taking her time.
ALICE: Not really.
BRIAN: We should have met the plane.
ALICE: We should not.
BRIAN: She'll be exhausted.
ALICE: She's a woman of thirty-five.
BRIAN: How can you speak of your daughter?
ALICE: She's a woman of thirty-five.
BRIAN: You're so right of course.
ALICE: She can travel round the world, she can travel the last few miles.
BRIAN: It's so delightful for you always being so right.
ALICE: She didn't want to be met.
MAISIE: She'll be here in a few minutes.
BRIAN: I'm talking about spontaneity.
ALICE: She doesn't want fuss.
BRIAN: She says that but it wouldn't be if she didn't know she was being met and there we just were or there I was if you insisted on not coming, she'd like it when it happened, the moment she caught sight she'd be delighted.
ALICE: Well we didn't so I don't see the point of worrying about it now.
BRIAN: She'll never come home from Australia again.
ALICE: What do you mean?

Maisie trips over.

ALICE: Oh, what?
BRIAN: What the hell?
MAISIE: Sorry, all right, I'm all right.
ALICE: You haven't hurt yourself?
MAISIE: No. Yes. Not really.
ALICE: Can you get up?
MAISIE: Yes of course. Well. It's just my ankle. Oh dear.
BRIAN: How did you do that?
ALICE: Sit down and let's have a look at it.
MAISIE: Oh ow. No no it's nothing. Ow.

Set back. Brian enters putting on cardigan.

BRIAN: She's taking her time.
ALICE: Not really.
BRIAN: We should have met the plane.
ALICE: We should not.
BRIAN: She'll be exhausted.
ALICE: She's a woman of thirty-five.
BRIAN: How can you speak of your daughter?
ALICE: She's a woman of thirty-five.
BRIAN: You're so right of course.
ALICE: She can travel round the world, she can travel the last few miles.
BRIAN: It's so delightful for you always being so right.

ALICE: She didn't want to be met.
MAISIE: She'll be here in a few minutes.
BRIAN: I'm talking about spontaneity.
ALICE: She doesn't want fuss.
BRIAN: She says that but it wouldn't be if she didn't know she was being met and there we just were or there I was if you insisted on not coming, she'd like it when it happened, the moment she caught sight she'd be delighted.
ALICE: Well we didn't so I don't see the point of worrying about it now.
BRIAN: She'll never come home from Australia again.
ALICE: What do you mean? of course she'll come again.
BRIAN: In the event she goes back of course she'll come again but she'll never come back for the first time again.

Enter Lewis, drunk.

LEWIS: Where is she?
BRIAN: You're not coming in here in that condition.
LEWIS: Where's my big sister? I want to give her a kiss.
BRIAN: You'll see her when you're sober.
ALICE: Now it's all right, Brian. Susy isn't here yet, Lewis.
LEWIS: You've probably got her hidden under the table. Dad knows where she is, don't you Dad? Daddy always knows where Susy is. Hello Aunty Maisie, want a drink? Let's go to the pub, Maisie, and get away from this load of —

Lewis goes, setback as before. This time do the repeat at double speed, all movements accurate though fast.

BRIAN: She's taking her time.
ALICE: Not really.
BRIAN: We should have met the plane.
ALICE: We should not.
BRIAN: She'll be exhausted.
ALICE: She's a woman of thirty-five.
BRIAN: How can you speak of your daughter?
ALICE: She's a woman of thirty-five.
BRIAN: You're so right of course.
ALICE: She can travel round the world, she can travel the last few miles.
BRIAN: It's so delightful for you always being so right.
ALICE: She didn't want to be met.
MAISIE: She'll be here in a few minutes.
BRIAN: I'm talking about spontaneity.
ALICE: She doesn't want fuss.
BRIAN: She says that but it wouldn't be if she didn't know she was being met and there we just were or there I was if you insisted on not coming, she'd like it when it happened, the moment she caught sight she'd be delighted.
ALICE: Well we didn't so I don't see the point of worrying about it now.
BRIAN: She'll never come home from Australia again.
ALICE: What do you mean? of course she'll come again.
BRIAN: In the event she goes back of course she'll come again but she'll never come back for the first time again.

Resume normal speed.

MAISIE: It's all this waiting.
ALICE: I hope she does come soon because I'm getting hungry.
BRIAN: You don't have to wait to eat.
ALICE: No it's her special lunch.
MAISIE: Are you going to tell her straight away?
BRIAN: That's not something for you to worry about, Maisie.
ALICE: We're all in it together.
MAISIE: We've all got perfectly good alibis.
BRIAN: But they don't believe alibis any more. It's all forensic, it's all genetic.
ALICE: But there can't be any forensic if none of us did anything, I don't know why you have to act like a guilty person when it's nothing to do with any of us except that the body was found in our garden, it was dumped in our garden as everybody knows.
MAISIE: I keep telling the police about the postman but they haven't taken it in.
BRIAN: I happen to know that a great many people are wrongfully convicted and I don't live in a dream that suggests that terrible things only befall people in newspapers.
MAISIE: So I'll just say nothing and leave it to you.

Reset to just after "all this waiting."

ALICE: I hope she does come soon because I'm getting hungry.
BRIAN: You don't have to wait to eat.
ALICE: No it's her special lunch.
BRIAN: I should just go ahead and eat since you've clearly no sense of occasion anyway. She's not going to care if there's lunch, she'll be exhausted, she'll go to bed.
ALICE: That's all right if that's what she wants to do.
BRIAN: You make yourself a doormat to that girl, you always did, she won't be grateful for lunch she'll be on a diet.
MAISIE: Now the one diet that is a good diet is the Hay diet which is to do with not combining —

Reset to just after "wants to do."

BRIAN: You make yourself a doormat to that girl, you always did, she won't be grateful for lunch she'll be on a diet.
ALICE: Are you pleased she's coming back?
BRIAN: What's the matter with you now?
ALICE: You don't sleem peased — you don't pleem seased —

Reset to after "coming back."

BRIAN: What's the matter with you now?
ALICE: You don't seem pleased, you seem cross.
MAISIE: The tube's very quick, she'll be here in no time I'm sure.

A horde of small children rush in, round the room and out again.

Reset to "of course she'll come again."

BRIAN: In the event she goes back of course she'll come again but she'll never come back for the first time again.

MAISIE: It's all this waiting.

ALICE: I hope she does come soon because I'm getting hungry.

BRIAN: You don't have to wait to eat.

ALICE: No it's her special lunch.

BRIAN: I should just go ahead and eat since you've clearly no sense of occasion anyway. She's not going to care if there's lunch, she'll be exhausted, she'll go to bed.

ALICE: That's all right if that's what she wants to do.

BRIAN: You make yourself a doormat to that girl, you always did, she won't be grateful for lunch she'll be on a diet.

ALICE: Are you pleased she's coming back?

BRIAN: What's the matter with you now?

ALICE: You don't seem pleased, you seem cross.

MAISIE: The tube's very quick, she'll be here in no time I'm sure.

BRIAN: You're the thing makes me cross, drive me insane with your wittering.

ALICE: This should be a lovely day. You spoil everything.

BRIAN: You've done it now, it was a lovely day, you've spoilt it.

Enter Lewis, drunk.

LEWIS: I'm unhappy. What are you going to do about it?

ALICE: You know you have to help yourself, Lewis.

LEWIS: But it never stops.

BRIAN: Lewis, I wish you'd died at birth. If I'd known what you'd grow up like I'd have killed either you or myself the day you were born.

LEWIS: You see this is where I get it from. Is it any wonder?

Reset to after "doesn't want fuss."

BRIAN: She says that but it wouldn't be if she didn't know she was being met and there we just were or there I was if you insisted on not coming, she'd like it when it happened, the moment she caught sight she'd be delighted.

ALICE: Well we didn't so I don't see the point of worrying about it now.

BRIAN: She'll never come home from Australia again.

ALICE: What do you mean? of course she'll come again.

BRIAN: In the event she goes back of course she'll come again but she'll never come back for the first time again.

MAISIE: It's all this waiting.

ALICE: I hope she does come soon because I'm getting hungry.

BRIAN: You don't have to wait to eat.

ALICE: No it's her special lunch.

BRIAN: I should just go ahead and eat since you've clearly no sense of occasion anyway. She's not going to care if there's lunch, she'll be exhausted, she'll go to bed.

ALICE: That's all right if that's what she wants to do.

BRIAN: You make yourself a doormat to that girl, you always did, she won't be grateful for lunch she'll be on a diet.

ALICE: Are you pleased she's coming back?
BRIAN: What's the matter with you now?
ALICE: You don't seem pleased, you seem cross.
MAISIE: The tube's very quick, she'll be here in no time I'm sure.
BRIAN: You're the thing makes me cross, drive me insane with your wittering.
ALICE: This should be a lovely day. You spoil everything.
BRIAN: You've done it now, it was a lovely day, you've spoilt it.
ALICE: All I'm saying is be nice to her.
BRIAN: Be nice to her?
ALICE: Yes I'm just saying be nice to her.

Two Gunmen burst in and kill them all, then leave.

Reset to top. As far as possible keep the movements that go with the part lines.

BRIAN: She's taking
ALICE: Not
BRIAN: We should have
ALICE: We should not
BRIAN: She'll be
ALICE: She's a woman
BRIAN: How can you speak
ALICE: She's a
BRIAN: You're so
ALICE: She can travel
BRIAN: It's so delightful
ALICE: She didn't want
MAISIE: She'll be here
BRIAN: I'm talking about
ALICE: She doesn't
BRIAN: She says that but
ALICE: Well we didn't
BRIAN: She'll never
ALICE: What do you
BRIAN: In the event
MAISIE: It's all this
ALICE: I hope she
BRIAN: You don't have to
ALICE: No it's
BRIAN: I should just
ALICE: That's all right if
BRIAN: You make yourself a
ALICE: Are you pleased
BRIAN: What's the matter
ALICE: You don't seem
MAISIE: The tube's very
BRIAN: You're the thing
ALICE: This should be a lovely

BRIAN: You've done it
ALICE: All I'm saying is
BRIAN: Be nice
ALICE: Yes I'm just saying be nice to her.
BRIAN: When am I not nice to her? am I not a good father is that what you're going to say? do you want to say that? say it.
ALICE: I'm just —
BRIAN: Say it say it.
ALICE: Just be nice to her that's all.
BRIAN: Nice.
ALICE: Fine, you're going to be nice that's all I'm saying.
BRIAN: I should leave you. I'm the one should have gone to Australia.
ALICE: I wish you had.
BRIAN: Snipsnap, sharp tongue.
ALICE: No I do wish you had. Because I'd have stayed here and been happy. Because I'm afraid I haven't been faithful to you.
BRIAN: What are you saying? An affair?
ALICE: Fifteen years.
BRIAN: Did you know about this, Maisie?
ALICE: Don't bring Maisie into it.
BRIAN: Don't tell me what not to do. Has everyone been deceiving me?
MAISIE: I did know a little bit.
BRIAN: Fifteen . . . ? you mean when we were on holiday in Portugal you were already . . . ?

Reset to after "spoilt it."

ALICE: All I'm saying is be nice to her.
BRIAN: Be nice to her?
ALICE: Yes I'm just saying be nice to her.
BRIAN: When am I not nice to her? am I not a good father is that what you're going to say? do you want to say that? say it.
ALICE: I'm just —
BRIAN: Say it say it.
ALICE: Just be nice to her that's all.
BRIAN: Nice.
ALICE: Fine, you're going to be nice that's all I'm saying.
BRIAN: I should leave you. I'm the one should have gone to Australia.
ALICE: Go back with her I should.
BRIAN: Maybe I'll do that.
ALICE: Though mind you she wouldn't stay in Australia in that case would she? She'd have to move on to New Zealand. Or Hawaii, I think she'd move to Tonga probably.
MAISIE: I do think waiting is one of the hardest things.
BRIAN: Waiting isn't the problem.
MAISIE: Is something else?
BRIAN: Of course not.

ALICE: Something is.

BRIAN: I'm terribly hungry.

MAISIE: We're all getting a bit peckish. Why don't I cut up some little cubes of cheese?

BRIAN: No, I'm hungry — I'll tell you.

ALICE: What?

BRIAN: I'm telling you. I have this terrible urge to eat myself.

ALICE: To bite your skin?

BRIAN: Yes to bite but to eat — never mind.

ALICE: No it's all right, you can tell us.

BRIAN: Starting with my fingernails like this —

MAISIE: Yes you always have bitten your fingernails.

BRIAN: But the whole finger, if I hold it with my other hand it won't happen but what I want to do is chew up my finger, I want my whole hand in my mouth. Don't despise me.

ALICE: Of course not, dear. I'm sure plenty of people —

BRIAN: My whole arm, swallow it right up to the shoulder, then the other arm gobble gobble up to the shoulder, and big bite left big bite right that's both the shoulders in.

MAISIE: Is this something you've always wanted to do or — ?

BRIAN: And the shoulders bring the rest of my body, eat my heart, eat my lungs, down my ribs I go, munch my belly, crunch my prick, and oh my whole body's in my mouth now so there's just my legs sticking out, I've eaten it all up.

ALICE: Have you thought of seeing someone about —

BRIAN: Then snap snap up my legs to the knees the calves the ankles just the feet sticking out of my mouth now gollop gollop I've swallowed my feet, there's only my head and my big mouth wants it, my big mouth turns round and ahh there goes my head into my mouth I've swallowed my head I've swallowed my whole self up I'm all mouth can my mouth swallow my mouth yes yes my mouth's taking a big bite ahh.

Reset to after "Tonga probably."

MAISIE: I do think waiting is one of the hardest things.
(*Sings.*) Oh for the wings for the wings of a dove etc.

Reset to after "just saying be nice to her."

BRIAN: When am I not nice to her? am I not a good father is that what you're going to say? do you want to say that? say it.

ALICE: I'm just —

BRIAN: Say it say it.

ALICE: Just be nice to her that's all.

BRIAN: Nice.

ALICE: Fine, you're going to be nice that's all I'm saying.

BRIAN: I should leave you. I'm the one should have gone to Australia.

ALICE: Go back with her I should.

BRIAN: Maybe I'll do that.

ALICE: Though mind you she wouldn't stay in Australia in that case would she? She'd have to move on to New Zealand. Or Hawaii, I think she'd move to Tonga probably.

MAISIE: I do think waiting is one of the hardest things. Waiting for arrivals and also waiting to say goodbye, that's even worse when you're waiting on a station platform or a quayside or the airport or just at home the day someone's going waiting for the time when they go I think that's far worse than when they've gone though of course when they've gone you think why didn't I make better use of them when they were still there, you can't do right in those situations.

BRIAN: It's not that you don't have a sense of occasion. You know exactly what an occasion is and you deliberately set out to ruin it. I've thought for forty years you were a stupid woman, now I know you're simply nasty.

Lewis comes in, drunk.

LEWIS: It's time we had it out. It's time we spoke the truth.

MAISIE: Lewis, you're always speaking the truth and where does it get you?

LEWIS: I want my life to begin.

ALICE: Lewis, there is one little rule in this house and what is it? it is that you don't come into this room when you've been drinking. Do we stop you drinking? no because we can't stop you drinking. Do we throw you out in the street? no because for some reason we are too tenderhearted and that is probably wrong of us. But there is one little rule and if you keep breaking it —

BRIAN: Out. Out.

LEWIS: No more. No more. No more.

BRIAN: Out.

Reset to top. This time it is only last words that are said; mark gestures and positions at those points as far as possible.

BRIAN: time.

ALICE: really.

BRIAN: the plane.

ALICE: not.

BRIAN: exhausted.

ALICE: thirty-five.

BRIAN: your daughter.

ALICE: thirty-five.

BRIAN: of course.

ALICE: last few miles.

BRIAN: so right.

ALICE: to be met.

MAISIE: few minutes.

BRIAN: spontaneity.

ALICE: fuss.

BRIAN: she'd be delighted.

ALICE: now.

BRIAN: again.
ALICE: again.
BRIAN: again.
MAISIE: waiting.
ALICE: getting hungry.
BRIAN: eat.
ALICE: lunch.
BRIAN: bed.
ALICE: wants to do.
BRIAN: on a diet.
ALICE: coming back?
BRIAN: now?
ALICE: cross.
MAISIE: in no time I'm sure.
BRIAN: insane with your wittering.
ALICE: spoil everything.
BRIAN: spoilt it.
ALICE: nice to her.
BRIAN: nice to her?
ALICE: nice to her.
BRIAN: say it.
ALICE: just.
BRIAN: say it.
ALICE: that's all.
BRIAN: Nice.
ALICE: all I'm saying.
BRIAN: Australia.
ALICE: I should.
BRIAN: do that.
ALICE: Tonga probably.
MAISIE: in those situations.
BRIAN: nasty.

Doorbell rings.

Maisie goes off. Alice and Brian embrace. Cries of welcome off.

Enter Susy with Maisie behind her.

SUSY: Mummy. Daddy. How wonderful to be home.

Reset to after "maybe I'll do that."

ALICE: Though mind you she wouldn't stay in Australia in that case would she? She'd have to move on to New Zealand. Or Hawaii, I think she'd move to Tonga probably.

MAISIE: I do think waiting is one of the hardest things. Waiting for arrivals and also waiting to say goodbye, that's even worse when you're waiting on a station platform or a quayside or the airport or just at home the day someone's going waiting for the time when they go I think that's far worse than when they've gone though of course when they've gone you think why didn't I make better use of them when they were still there, you can't do right in those situations.

BRIAN: It's not that you don't have a sense of occasion. You know exactly what an occasion is and you deliberately set out to ruin it. I've thought for forty years you were a stupid woman, now I know you're simply nasty.

Doorbell rings.

MAISIE: That'll be her.

Brian goes out.

MAISIE: We'll see a change in her.

Brian returns followed by a young Australian woman.

ALICE: Oh.

BRIAN: This is a friend, you said a friend of Susy's, I don't quite . . .

ALICE: Hello do come in. How lovely. Did you travel together?

YOUNG WOMAN: It's great to be here. Susy's told me so much about you. She said to be sure to look you up.

BRIAN: And she's just behind you is she?

ALICE: Did you travel in separately from the airport? Did you come on the tube?

YOUNG WOMAN: I came on a bus.

ALICE: That's a good way.

YOUNG WOMAN: But what's this about Susy? Susy's not here.

MAISIE: She hasn't arrived yet.

YOUNG WOMAN: Susy's coming too? that's amazing. She saw me off on the plane.

BRIAN: Of course Susy's coming.

MAISIE: Do you know Susy very well? is she an old friend?

YOUNG WOMAN: I live with Susy. Hasn't she told you about me? I thought she wrote to tell you to expect me.

ALICE: I'm terribly sorry, I don't think . . .

MAISIE: Is Susy not coming home?

YOUNG WOMAN: I thought that was something she didn't want to do but of course I could be wrong. She said she was coming?

Reset to after "those situations."

BRIAN: It's not that you don't have a sense of occasion. You know exactly what an occasion is and you deliberately set out to ruin it. I've thought for forty years you were a stupid woman, now I know you're simply nasty.

Doorbell rings.

MAISIE: That'll be her.

ALICE: Do you want to go?

Brian goes off and comes back almost at once jostled by a man in uniform.

OFFICIAL: Papers.

ALICE: What?

BRIAN: Papers, he has to see our papers. Passport. Driving licence. Birth certificate. Season ticket. Our papers are all in order. I'm sure you'll find everything in order.

MAISIE: Don't let them take me away.

Reset to after "getting hungry," go as fast as possible. Precision matters, intelligibility doesn't.

ALICE: I hope she does come soon because I'm getting hungry.

BRIAN: You don't have to wait to eat.

ALICE: No it's her special lunch.

BRIAN: I should just go ahead and eat since you've clearly no sense of occasion anyway. She's not going to care if there's lunch, she'll be exhausted, she'll go to bed.

ALICE: That's all right if that's what she wants to do.

BRIAN: You make yourself a doormat to that girl, you always did, she won't be grateful for lunch she'll be on a diet

ALICE: Are you pleased she's coming back?

BRIAN: What's the matter with you now?

ALICE: You don't seem pleased, you seem cross.

MAISIE: The tube's very quick, she'll be here in no time I'm sure.

BRIAN: You're the thing makes me cross, drive me insane with your wittering.

ALICE: This should be a lovely day. You spoil everything.

BRIAN: You've done it now, it was a lovely day, you've spoilt it.

ALICE: All I'm saying is be nice to her.

BRIAN: Be nice to her?

ALICE: Yes I'm just saying be nice to her.

BRIAN: When am I not nice to her? am I not a good father is that what you're going to say? do you want to say that? say it.

ALICE: I'm just —

BRIAN: Say it say it.

ALICE: Just be nice to her that's all.

BRIAN: Nice.

ALICE: Fine, you're going to be nice that's all I'm saying.

BRIAN: I should leave you. I'm the one should have gone to Australia.

ALICE: Go back with her I should.

BRIAN: Maybe I'll do that.

ALICE: Though mind you she wouldn't stay in Australia in that case would she? She'd have to move on to New Zealand. Or Hawaii, I think she'd move to Tonga probably.

MAISIE: I do think waiting is one of the hardest things. Waiting for arrivals and also waiting to say goodbye, that's even worse when you're waiting on a station platform or a quayside or the airport or just at home the day someone's going waiting for the time when they go I think that's far worse than when they've gone though of course when they've gone you think why didn't I make better use of them when they were still there, you can't do right on those occasions.

Set back to after "worse than when they've gone." Continue at speed.

MAISIE: though of course when they've gone you think why didn't I make better use of them when they were still there, you can't do right in those situations.

BRIAN: It's not that you don't have a sense of occasion. You know exactly what an occasion is and you deliberately set out to ruin it. I've thought for forty years you were a stupid woman, now I know you're simply nasty.

Doorbell rings. Return to normal speed.

MAISIE: That'll be her.
ALICE: Do you want to go?
Brian goes off. A ten-foot-tall bird enters.
Reset to after "situations."

BRIAN: It's not occasion occasion deliberately ruin it forty years stupid nasty.

Doorbell rings.

MAISIE: That'll be her.
BRIAN: Do you want to go?

Silence. They don't answer the door and they wait in silence a longer time than you think you can get away with.

Reset to after "nasty."

Doorbell rings.

MAISIE: That'll be her.
ALICE: Do you want to go?

Brian doesn't move. Alice goes off.

MAISIE: Do you ever wake up in the night and be frightened of dying? I'm not at all bothered in the daytime. We've all got to do it after all. Think what a lot of people have done it already. Even the young will have to, even the ones who haven't been born yet will have to, it's not a problem theoretically is it, it's the condition of life. I'm not afraid of an afterlife well maybe a little, I'd rather there wasn't one wouldn't you, imagine finding you were dead that would be frightening but of course maybe it wouldn't we don't know, but really I think we just stop, I think either we're alive or we know nothing so death never really happens to us, but still sometimes in the night there's a chill in my blood and I think what is it what am I frightened of and then I think oh death that's what it is again and I—

Reset to after "that'll be her."
ALICE: Do you want to go?
Brian doesn't move. Alice goes out. Cries of welcome off. Alice and Susy enter.

SUSY: Here I am.
BRIAN: You are my heart's desire.

Reset to top. Brian enters putting on cardigan.

BRIAN: She's taking her time.
ALICE: Not really.
BRIAN: We should have met the plane.
ALICE: We should not.
BRIAN: She'll be exhausted.

ALICE: She's a woman of thirty-five.
BRIAN: How can you speak of your daughter?
ALICE: She's a woman of thirty-five.
BRIAN: You're so right of course.
ALICE: She can travel round the world, she can travel the last few miles.
BRIAN: It's so delightful for you always being so right.
ALICE: She didn't want to be met.
MAISIE: She'll be here in a few minutes.
BRIAN: I'm talking about spontaneity.
ALICE: She doesn't want fuss.
BRIAN: She says that but it wouldn't be if she didn't know she was being met and there we just were or there I was if you insisted on not coming, she'd like it when it happened, the moment she caught sight she'd be delighted.
ALICE: Well we didn't so I don't see the point of worrying about it now.
BRIAN: She'll never come home from Australia again.
ALICE: What do you mean? of course she'll come again.
BRIAN: In the event she goes back of course she'll come again but she'll never come back for the first time again.
MAISIE: It's all this waiting.
ALICE: I hope she does come soon because I'm getting hungry.
BRIAN: You don't have to wait to eat.
ALICE: No it's her special lunch.
BRIAN: I should just go ahead and eat since you've clearly no sense of occasion anyway. She's not going to care if there's lunch, she'll be exhausted, she'll go to bed.
ALICE: That's all right if that's what she wants to do.
BRIAN: You make yourself a doormat to that girl, you always did, she won't be grateful for lunch she'll be on a diet.
ALICE: Are you pleased she's coming back?
BRIAN: What's the matter with you now?
ALICE: You don't seem pleased, you seem cross.
MAISIE: The tube's very quick; she'll be here in no time I'm sure.
BRIAN: You're the thing makes me cross, drive me insane with your wittering.
ALICE: This should be a lovely day. You spoil everything.
BRIAN: You've done it now, it was a lovely day, you've spoilt it.
ALICE: All I'm saying is be nice to her.
BRIAN: Be nice to her?
ALICE: Yes I'm just saying be nice to her.
BRIAN: When am I not nice to her? am I not a good father is that what you're going to say? do you want to say that? say it.
ALICE: I'm just —
BRIAN: Say it say it.
ALICE: Just be nice to her that's all.
BRIAN: Nice.
ALICE: Fine, you're going to be nice that's all I'm saying.
BRIAN: I should leave you. I'm the one should have gone to Australia.

ALICE: Go back with her I should.

BRIAN: Maybe I'll do that.

ALICE: Though mind you she wouldn't stay in Australia in that case would she? She'd have to move on to New Zealand. Or Hawaii, I think she'd move to Tonga probably.

MAISIE: I do think waiting is one of the hardest things. Waiting for arrivals and also waiting to say goodbye, that's even worse when you're waiting on a station platform or a quayside or the airport or just at home the day someone's going waiting for the time when they go I think that's far worse than when they've gone though of course when they've gone you think why didn't I make better use of them when they were still there, you can't do right in those situations.

BRIAN: It's not that you don't have a sense of occasion. You know exactly what an occasion is and you deliberately set out to ruin it. I've thought for forty years you were a stupid woman, now I know you're simply nasty.

Doorbell rings.

MAISIE: That'll be her.

ALICE: Do you want to go?

Brian doesn't move. Alice goes out. Cries of welcome off. Alice and Susy enter.

SUSY: Here I am.

BRIAN: Here you are.

ALICE: Yes here she is.

SUSY: Hello aunty.

BRIAN: You are my heart's —

Reset to top. Brian enters putting on old cardigan.

BRIAN: She's taking her time.

End.

ꕥ

22

COMMENTARIES ON PLAYS AND PLAYWRIGHTS

EDWARD ALBEE *often discusses various topics relating to his work as a playwright. This commentary was originally published in* Dramatics *magazine.*

EDWARD ALBEE

On Playwriting

1989

There are a couple of things you should know. I am a playwright. I've written twenty-six plays, I think, in the past thirty-three years, which makes me a little less lazy than I sometimes think I am. Some of them have been very popular, which means people have come to see them. Some have been very unpopular.

Sometimes, being a little protective of the least popular, sometimes I think the least popular ones are superior to the more popular ones. One of the things you learn very quickly in our society is that there is not necessarily much relationship between popularity and excellence. Quite often the very best stuff is participated in by the fewest people. But you mustn't fall into the trap, either, of assuming that because nobody likes what you have done it is very good. Sometimes people don't like what you've done because it is terrible. We'll talk about that possibility, too.

It is a tough racket. It can be pretty heartbreaking, and you really have to, deep down, have a toughness to yourself, or you're not going to be able to survive in the theatre.

ON WHERE THE IDEAS FOR PLAYS COME FROM

Damned if I know. All of a sudden one day I'll be going about my own business, walking around or something, and I'll suddenly realize that I must have been thinking about a play for quite a while, even though I didn't know I was thinking about it. Because by the time I become aware that I have been thinking about a play, it's coming along quite nicely. The characters are there, the situation has begun to create itself.

I'm sure the creativity, where the ideas come from, comes from the unconscious part of the mind, which as you know makes up 90 percent of the mind. I'm convinced that is where the ideas originate, they evolve and eventually enter into the conscious mind. You keep working on them, and then eventually you write them down.

ON HIS METHOD OF WORKING

When I sit down I don't know what the first line of the play is going to be. I know what the destination is, but I don't have any idea necessarily how I am going to get there. I believe in letting the characters determine that in their situation. How they behave determines where it goes.

I try to stand back and sort of push them and guide them so the thing won't go off in all sorts of directions that it shouldn't go off in. I believe that when the characters do that it's really me doing that, since the characters can't do anything unless I tell them what to do. They don't exist. They really do exist, but they don't. They can't say anything unless I write it down for them. It is a trick you play on yourself, thinking that the characters are doing your work when really you're doing it and assigning it to the various characters.

I'm not one of these playwrights — and I'm not saying you shouldn't be this kind of playwright — I'm not one of these playwrights who writes a twenty-five-page synopsis of what the play is going to be about. I don't write down histories of the natures of the characters. I don't plot out each scene before I write it.

The only thing I do is when it is ready, when it is time to start writing something down, I wait longer than most playwrights do. Sometimes I keep an idea in my head five or six years before I'll write it down. I start at the beginning and write straight through to the end. That's the way I write. It's nice that way. You have lots of surprises. You discover all sorts of things that you were planning to do that you didn't know you were going to do.

ON THE IDEAL CONDITIONS FOR WRITING

I think it is probably better to be awake, sober, and drug-free. I suspect those three conditions are probably helpful. But beyond that, I just have to feel like writing. I'm not one of these people who goes to the desk every single day and writes. I wait until my head gets filled with stuff and I have to get it out of my head.

I used to drink occasionally and take a little grass now and again back when I was real young. And I thought that I could write an awful lot better if I did. But it wasn't very good. It seemed wonderful at the time. Marvelous. I'd look at it the next day and say, "What the hell was that all about?"

ON THE IMPORTANCE OF CONFLICT IN DRAMA

Plays are basically about something that is wrong. Plays are about people that are not getting along with each other terribly well. Situations that are wrong. Most serious plays, good plays, are about something that's wrong that should be corrected. You can't write a very good play about a bunch of people getting along with each other very, very well and there is absolutely no argument. You can't do it. It's not going to be a play. There has to be conflict. And until the conflict is resolved there is tension, because of the conflict. People in conflict with each other, people in conflict with society, their government, philosophically, politically, socially. There is conflict and conflict produces tension. And the solution to the problem releases tension and that is probably when the play should end.

ON A PLAYWRIGHT'S SOURCES OF THE DETAILS OF CHARACTER

You keep your eyes and ears open and store it away until you need it. Part of it comes from yourself. You can't write a character unless you can get inside the character and imagine the way the character thinks.

And the rest you make up. You invent. That's why you're able to write men, women, young people, old people, black, white, no matter who or what you are. It's your responsibility and your ability to be able to do all that. You have to be able to put yourself into whatever character you are writing. So you look and listen and make things up.

ON STUDYING THE WORK OF OTHER PLAYWRIGHTS

There are some twentieth-century playwrights that I think it is very important for anybody who wants to be a playwright to know about. You start with Chekhov, one of the first great playwrights of the twentieth century. Then you have Pirandello, an extraordinary playwright that not enough people know about. And there is Brecht, a real interesting playwright, and Samuel Beckett, who may be the best of the bunch. He and Chekhov may be the best of the bunch. You have those four. That's a pretty good group to study.

But let me tell you one thing, if you are going to learn from other writers, don't only read the great ones, because if you do that you'll get so filled with despair and the fear that you'll never be able to do anywhere near as well as they did that you'll stop writing. I recommend that you read a lot of bad stuff, too. It's very encouraging. "Hey, I can do so much better than this." Read the greatest stuff but read the stuff that isn't so great, too. Great stuff is very discouraging. If you read only Beckett and Chekhov you'll go away and only deliver telegrams at Western Union.

ON BEING TRUE TO ONE'S OWN VISION

They tell you that commercial plays should be a little over two hours long. A play should be as long as it needs to be. It can be ten minutes, it can be seven hours. What should the play be about? It should be about whatever you can make a stage experience, only that. Whatever you can make valid. What style should it be written in? Whatever style is right for the play.

There are no limits, you see, except succeeding at what you do. In the commercial theatre they want certain things. They want happy problems. They want the plays to be a certain length. They want everybody to be able to walk out of the theatre fairly happy. If it can be a musical, so much the better. That's what the commercial theatre is all about. If you're that kind of a writer, okay. But if you're the kind of writer who wants to write a very grim, seven-hour play, then that's what you should write. If you want to write a play so angry, so filled with rage, that it practically takes the audience and hits them in the head or slaps them in the face, then that's the kind of play you should write.

You should write exactly what the play needs to be and pay no attention to anything else. That's all that matters. The rest is commerce, the rest is compromise. You'll be asked to do a lot of that, but hold off. One of the lovely things about being a playwright is that you can do whatever you want to do. While a lot of people would rather you do something else, they can't stop you.

ON COLLABORATION

Now, if you're in rehearsal for the first time with your play and the director says to you, maybe that scene is a little long, you may want to think about cutting it. Pay a little attention; maybe the director is right.

You go back and you look at the scene and say yes, that scene seems long. Then you have to say to yourself, does this scene seem long because I wrote it too long or because of the way it is being directed? If the director directed it differently would it still seem too long? So maybe you will ask that the scene be directed differently.

If you realize the scene is too long no matter how it is directed, then you realize, gee, I wrote this scene too long, maybe I better cut it a little bit. Then you make your own cuts. You have to be very careful because sometimes suggestions are not made to help the play but to help actors or to make things easier. You have the right to not change anything, but don't be a fool. Change things if somebody else is right.

But if you do change something because somebody else is right, you must instantly take credit for it yourself. That's very important.

RICHARD AMACHER *analyzed Albee's short experimental plays in the chapter titled "Pity and Fear in Miniature" in his study* Edward Albee *(1982). Before discussing the characters in* The Sandbox, *Amacher dissected the plot of the drama. According to his scheme, Scene 1 (exposition) introduces the characters and Mommy's scheme to get rid of Grandma. Scenes 2 through 5 (rising action) show the* *failure of her plan. Scene 6 (climax and conclusion) brings an unexpected turn of events that ultimately satisfies our expectations.*

Richard Amacher

On *The Sandbox*

1982

THE CHARACTERS IN CONFLICT

The five characters in the play have obviously been selected with great care and in accord with the artistic principle of economy of means. Grandma, for example, is not only the leading character, or *protagonist,* but also the *chorus.* Her mimicking of Mommy and her mocking of Daddy, as well as her early cries, some of which are like screams of antagonism or growls of disgust, reinforce the self-revealing speeches of these two unsympathetic characters, just as the chanted explanations of the Greek chorus in ancient tragedies underlined similar aspects of the characterization and the action. In one or two places Grandma also functions as the stage manager or director, for she calls out directions to the stage hand about dimming the lights and she tells the musician how to play his music — "Keep it nice and soft" — in the night scene signifying the approach of death.

Study of the conflicting forces in *The Sandbox* shows us how central the character of Grandma is. On the surface, it appears that we have two pairs of characters struggling against each other — Mommy and Daddy in the antagonist group (who are really trying to bury Grandma, as we see by their symbolic action of heartlessly dumping her into the sandbox); and Grandma and the Young Man in the protagonist group. This ostensible pairing of unsympathetic and sympathetic characters overshadows a less obvious conflict — that between Grandma, an admirable old lady full of spiritual vitality, and the Young Man, the Angel of Death. Despite the Young Man's modesty and politeness, he is, after all, the Angel of Death; and while Grandma recognizes that her life cannot go on forever, she nevertheless still has a certain spark of spunky rebelliousness and fight left in her — enough, as a matter of fact, so that the manner of her final encounter with death becomes a suspenseful question: Will she fight to the end? Or will she resign herself to the inevitable — the superior power of the Angel of Death?

Grandma struggles against the injustice of her daughter's and her son-in-law's treatment of her more than she does against the Young Man, whom she finds attractive, pleasant, sympathetic. Although his approach is gradual, he, when the time comes, accomplishes his work quickly and efficiently — even apologetically, so polite is he — with a kiss and a laying on of hands that resembles a benediction. This kind of treatment Grandma will accept. But in resentment of her daughter's and son-in-law's standing around and not only waiting for her to die but even hastening the process, she throws sand and yells at them menacingly.

In the course of the action, Grandma moves from *"puzzlement and fear"* to acceptance. When she says "You're welcome . . . dear" to the Angel of Death at the end of the play, we see her conquer her fear of the unknown and admire her all the more. We begin to sense her heroic nature, for it is death and dying she struggles against, sympathetic as the Young Man, to her surprise, and relief, finally turns out to be after her discovery of his essential nature.

Grandma is just as sensitive to the Young Man's physical power and beauty as Mommy — in fact, more so. When he flexes his muscles for her and asks, "Isn't that something?," she answers, "Boy, oh boy; I'll say. Pretty good." Her conversation with and admiration of the Young Man is interspersed with the story of her life and hard times, which arouses sympathy for her, particularly as she stresses the fact that she is neither complaining nor feeling sorry for herself.

PITY AND FEAR: AROUSAL AND PURGATION

Grandma effectively arouses pity and fear in the audience. We *pity* her because she deserves better than she has received. After the early death of her husband, after a hard life spent in sacrificing to her undeserving daughter, after being uprooted from her natural setting on the farm (her husband having been a farmer) and transported to the city, where she was treated like a dog, she deserves something more than merely dying. But it would be unrealistic for her not to die, for the expectation of her dying has been established from almost the beginning of this play when she is carried in and dumped in the sandbox.

We *fear* for Grandma because in Aristotelian terms she is a person like ourselves — neither entirely good nor bad. In addition, her fragility, because of her great age as well as because of the great powers arrayed against her — Mommy with her "imposing" vigor, Daddy with his wealth, the Young Man with his immense power as the Angel of Death — makes us sense that her position is indeed precarious. The four off-stage rumbles especially arouse in the audience a feeling of the Young Man's power; and, since we tend to identify ourselves with Grandma, fear is aroused in us. The arousal of this fear continues until the point where the Young Man kisses her; then we are fearful that he may severely hurt her. After all, there are various ways of suffering in the death of the body.

Purgation of fear and pity in *The Sandbox* results from the demonstration that Grandma is not going to suffer more — from our comprehension that death, contrary to our usual expectations, is, for her, a sweet, welcome experience. If pity and fear are not only effectively aroused but also competently purged in this play, if these are the distinctive and characteristic emotions making up the effect of the play, we must conclude that the play is a *tragedy.* And so it is — a serious tragedy — well flavored with irony and absurdity — from Grandma's juvenile antics in the sandbox and her reference to her daughter as a "big cow" to the awkward embarrassment of the Young Man. Touches like these may not exhale the high seriousness of tone that critics like [Joseph] Krutch might like to find in modern tragedy, but we must remember that we are living in the age of the "absurd."

There are, quite naturally, different kinds of tragedy. Aristotle lists two general directions that the turn of fortune may take — either from good to bad or from bad to good. In *The Sandbox* the turn seems to be the second kind, and Grandma goes from a state of querulousness and rebellion, mostly against her daughter, to one of insight, acceptance, and peace. Beyond the essential brevity of the action imitated in the play, the use of music, an equivalent of "Song" in Aristotle's list of the essential parts of tragedy (see *Poetics*), gives *The Sandbox* a certain Grecian lyrical quality.

As mentioned earlier, Grandma acts as chorus in talking directly to the audience, as she provides the exposition about her past and complains about her daughter's treatment of her. In at least two speeches Mommy also plays this role of chorus, but Albee has her talk superciliously *"out over the audience,"* when she complains about Grandma's throwing sand at her. But more important than this incidental use of the characters for chorus effects is the way both the music and the Musician, as an actual character in the play, function as chorus.

The Sandbox, Albee's second one-act tragedy, was well received. And although it may be argued that its frequent revivals have resulted from its relative ease and cheapness of production, its popularity, in our opinion, is also due to its enduring merits as a work of art.

❧

ARISTOTLE *(384–322 B.C.), the Greek philosopher, included an analysis of tragedy in his* Poetics *a century after Sophocles' plays were performed during the Great Dionysia in Athens. A student of Plato, Aristotle founded his own school, called the Lyceum, where he lectured on philosophy, science, and the arts. His lectures or treatises were so insightful that they were preserved by his students, and nearly two thousand years later, they form the basis of literary criticism. As the critic Lee Jacobus points out, Aristotle's work not only provides insight into the theoretical basis of the work of the Greek playwrights, but it also "helps us see that the drama was significant enough in Greek intellectual life to warrant an examination by the most influential Greek minds."*

ARISTOTLE

On the Elements and General Principles of Tragedy

c. 340 B.C.

TRANSLATED BY GERALD F. ELSE

TRAGEDY AND ITS SIX CONSTITUENT ELEMENTS

. . . At present let us deal with tragedy, recovering from what has been said so far the definition of its essential nature, as it was in development. Tragedy, then, is a process of imitating an action which has serious implications, is complete, and possesses magnitude; by means of language which has been made sensuously attractive, with each of its varieties found separately in the parts; enacted by the persons themselves and not presented through narrative; through a course of pity and fear completing the purification of tragic acts which have those emotional characteristics. By "language made sensuously attractive" I mean language that has rhythm and melody, and by "its varieties found separately" I mean the fact that certain parts of the play are carried on through spoken verses alone and others the other way around, through song.

Now first of all, since they perform the imitation through action (by acting it), the adornment of their visual appearance will perforce constitute some part of the making of tragedy; and song-composition and verbal expression also, for those are the media in which they perform the imitation. By "verbal expression" I mean the actual composition of the verses, and by "song-composition" something whose meaning is entirely clear.

Next, since it is an imitation of an action and is enacted by certain people who are performing the action, and since those people must necessarily have certain traits both of character and thought (for it is thanks to these two factors that we speak of people's actions also as having a defined character, and it is in accordance with their actions that all either succeed or fail); and since the imitation of the action is the plot, for by "plot" I mean here the structuring of the events, and by the "characters" that in accordance with which we say that the persons who are acting have a defined moral character, and by "thought" all the passages in which they attempt to prove some thesis or set forth an opinion — it follows of necessity, then, that tragedy as a whole has just six constituent elements, in relation to the essence that makes it a distinct species; and they are plot, characters, verbal expression, thought, visual adornment, and song-composition. For the elements by which they imitate are two (i.e., verbal expression and song-composition), the manner in which they imitate is one (visual adornment), the things they imitate are three (plot, characters, thought), and there is nothing more beyond these. These then are the constituent forms they use.

THE RELATIVE IMPORTANCE OF THE SIX ELEMENTS

The greatest of these elements is the structuring of the incidents. For tragedy is an imitation not of men but of a life, an action, and they have moral quality in accordance with their characters but are happy or unhappy in accordance with their actions; hence they are not active in order to imitate their characters, but they include the characters along with the actions for the sake of the latter. Thus the structure of events, the plot, is the goal of tragedy, and the goal is the greatest thing of all. . . .

Again: if one strings end to end speeches that are expressive of character and carefully worked in thought and expression, he still will not achieve the result which we said was the aim of tragedy; the job will be done much better by a tragedy that is more deficient in these other respects but has a plot, a structure of events. It is much the same case as with painting: the most beautiful pigments smeared on at random will not give as much pleasure as a black-and-white outline picture. Besides, the most powerful means tragedy has for swaying our feelings, namely the peripeties and recognitions,° are elements of plot.

---

peripeties and recognitions: The turning-about of fortune and the recognition on the part of the tragic hero of the truth. This is, for Aristotle, a critical moment in the drama, especially if both events happen simultaneously, as they do in *Oedipus the King*. It is quite possible for these moments to happen apart from one another. [All notes are the translator's.]

Again: an indicative sign is that those who are beginning a poetic career manage to hit the mark in verbal expression and character portrayal sooner than they do in plot construction; and the same is true of practically all the earliest poets.

So plot is the basic principle, the heart and soul, as it were, of tragedy, and the characters come second: . . . it is the imitation of an action and imitates the persons primarily for the sake of their action.

Third in rank is thought. This is the ability to state the issues and appropriate points pertaining to a given topic, an ability which springs from the arts of politics and rhetoric; in fact the earliest poets made their characters talk "politically," the present-day poets rhetorically. But "character" is that kind of utterance which clearly reveals the bent of a man's moral choice (hence there is no character in that class of utterances in which there is nothing at all that the speaker is choosing or rejecting), while "thought" is the passages in which they try to prove that something is so or not so, or state some general principle.

Fourth is the verbal expression of the speeches. I mean by this the same thing that was said earlier, that the "verbal expression" is the conveyance of thought through language: a statement which has the same meaning whether one says "verses" or "speeches."

The song-composition of the remaining parts is the greatest of the sensuous attractions, and the visual adornment of the dramatic persons can have a strong emotional effect but is the least artistic element, the least connected with the poetic art; in fact the force of tragedy can be felt even without benefit of public performance and actors, while for the production of the visual effect the property man's art is even more decisive than that of the poets.

GENERAL PRINCIPLES OF THE TRAGIC PLOT

With these distinctions out of the way, let us next discuss what the structuring of the events should be like, since this is both the basic and the most important element in the tragic art. We have established, then, that tragedy is an imitation of an action which is complete and whole and has some magnitude (for there is also such a thing as a whole that has no magnitude). "Whole" is that which has beginning, middle, and end. "Beginning" is that which does not necessarily follow on something else, but after it something else naturally is or happens; "end," the other way around, is that which naturally follows on something else, either necessarily or for the most part, but nothing else after it; and "middle" that which naturally follows on something else and something else on it. So, then, well-constructed plots should neither begin nor end at any chance point but follow the guidelines just laid down.

Furthermore, since the beautiful, whether a living creature or anything that is composed of parts, should not only have these in a fixed order to one another but also possess a definite size which does not depend on chance — for beauty depends on size and order; hence neither can a very tiny creature turn out to be beautiful (since our perception of it grows blurred as it approaches the period of imperceptibility) nor an excessively huge one (for then it cannot all be perceived at once and so its unity and wholeness are lost), if for example there were a creature a thousand miles long — so, just as in the case of living creatures they must have some size, but one that can be taken in a single view, so with plots: they should have length, but such that they are easy to remember. As to a limit of the length, the one is determined by the tragic competitions and the ordinary span of attention. (If they had to compete with a hundred tragedies they would compete by the water clock, as they say used to be done [?].) But the limit fixed by the very nature of the case is: the longer the plot, up to the point of still being perspicuous as a whole, the finer it is so far as size is concerned; or to put it in general terms, the length in which, with things happening in unbroken sequence, a shift takes place either probably or necessarily from bad to good fortune or from good to bad — that is an acceptable norm of length.

But a plot is not unified, as some people think, simply because it has to do with a single person. A large, indeed an indefinite number of things can happen to a given individual, some of which go to constitute no unified event; and in the same way there can be many acts of a given individual from which no single action emerges. Hence it seems clear that those poets are wrong who have composed *Heracleïds, Theseïds,* and the like. They think that since Heracles was a single person it follows that the plot will be single too. But Homer, superior as he is in all other respects, appears to have grasped this point well also, thanks either to art or nature, for in composing an *Odyssey* he did not incorporate into it everything that happened to the hero, for example how he was wounded on Mt. Parnassus° or how he feigned madness at the muster, neither of which events, by happening, made it at all necessary or probable that the other should happen. Instead, he composed the *Odyssey* — and the *Iliad* similarly — around a unified action of the kind we have been talking about.

A poetic imitation, then, ought to be unified in the same way as a single imitation in any other mimetic field, by having a single object: since the plot is an imitation of an action, the latter ought to be both unified and complete, and the component events ought to be so firmly compacted that if any one of them is shifted to another place, or removed, the whole is loosened up and dislocated; for an element whose addition or subtraction makes no perceptible extra difference is not really a part of the whole.

From what has been said it is also clear that the poet's job is not to report what has happened but what is likely to happen: that is, what is capable of happening according to the rule of probability or necessity. Thus the difference between the historian and the poet is not in their utterances being in verse or prose (it would be quite possible for Herodotus' work to be translated into verse, and it would not be any the less a history with verse than it is without it); the difference lies in the fact that the historian speaks of what has happened, the poet of the kind of thing that *can* happen. Hence also poetry is a more philosophical and serious business than history; for poetry speaks more of universals, history of particulars. "Universal" in this case is what kind of person is likely

---

Mt. Parnassus: A mountain in central Greece traditionally sacred to Apollo. In legend, Odysseus was wounded there, but the point Aristotle is making is that the writer of epics need not include every detail of his hero's life in a given work. Homer, in writing the *Odyssey,* was working with a hero, Odysseus, whose story had been legendary long before he began writing.

to do or say certain kinds of things, according to probability or necessity; that is what poetry aims at, although it gives its persons particular names afterward; while the "particular" is what Alcibiades did or what happened to him.

In the field of comedy this point has been grasped: our comic poets construct their plots on the basis of general probabilities and then assign names to the persons quite arbitrarily, instead of dealing with individuals as the old iambic poets° did. But in tragedy they still cling to the historically given names. The reason is that what is possible is persuasive; so what has not happened we are not yet ready to believe is possible, while what has happened is, we feel, obviously possible: for it would not have happened if it were impossible. Nevertheless, it is a fact that even in our tragedies, in some cases only one or two of the names are traditional, the rest being invented, and in some others none at all. It is so, for example, in Agathon's *Antheus* — the names in it are as fictional as the events — and it gives no less pleasure because of that. Hence the poets ought not to cling at all costs to the traditional plots, around which our tragedies are constructed. And in fact it is absurd to go searching for this kind of authentication, since even the familiar names are familiar to only a few in the audience and yet give the same kind of pleasure to all.

So from these considerations it is evident that the poet should be a maker of his plots more than of his verses, insofar as he is a poet by virtue of his imitations and what he imitates is actions. Hence even if it happens that he puts something that has actually taken place into poetry, he is none the less a poet; for there is nothing to prevent some of the things that have happened from being the kind of things that can happen, and that is the sense in which he is their maker.

SIMPLE AND COMPLEX PLOTS

Among simple plots and actions the episodic are the worst. By "episodic" plot I mean one in which there is no probability or necessity for the order in which the episodes follow one another. Such structures are composed by the bad poets because they are bad poets, but by the good poets because of the actors: in composing contest pieces for them, and stretching out the plot beyond its capacity, they are forced frequently to dislocate the sequence.

Furthermore, since the tragic imitation is not only of a complete action but also of events that are fearful and pathetic,° and these come about best when they come about contrary to one's expectation yet logically, one following from the other; that way they will be more productive of wonder than if they happen merely at random, by chance — because even among chance occurrences the ones people consider most marvelous are those that seem to

---

old iambic poets: Aristotle may be referring to Archilochus (fl. 650 B.C.) and the iambic style he developed. The iamb is a metrical foot of two syllables, a short and a long syllable, and was the most popular metrical style before the time of Aristotle. "Dealing with individuals" implies using figures already known to the audience rather than figures whose names can be arbitrarily assigned because no one knows who they are.
fearful and pathetic: Aristotle said that tragedy should evoke two emotions: terror and pity. The terror results from our realizing that what is happening to the hero might just as easily happen to us; the pity results from our human sympathy with a fellow sufferer. Therefore, the fearful and pathetic represent significant emotions appropriate to our witnessing drama.

have come about as if on purpose: for example the way the statue of Mitys at Argos killed the man who had been the cause of Mitys' death, by falling on him while he was attending the festival; it stands to reason, people think, that such things don't happen by chance — so plots of that sort cannot fail to be artistically superior.

Some plots are simple, others are complex; indeed the actions of which the plots are imitations already fall into these two categories. By "simple" action I mean one the development of which being continuous and unified in the manner stated above, the reversal comes without peripety or recognition, and by "complex" action one in which the reversal is continuous but with recognition or peripety or both. And these developments must grow out of the very structure of the plot itself, in such a way that on the basis of what has happened previously this particular outcome follows either by necessity or in accordance with probability; for there is a greater difference in whether these events happen because of those or merely after them.

"Peripety" is a shift of what is being undertaken to the opposite in the way previously stated, and that in accordance with probability or necessity as we have just been saying; as for example in the *Oedipus* the man who has come, thinking that he will reassure Oedipus, that is, relieve him of his fear with respect to his mother, by revealing who he once was, brings about the opposite; and in the *Lynceus,* as he (Lynceus) is being led away with every prospect of being executed, and Danaus pursuing him with every prospect of doing the executing, it comes about as a result of the other things that have happened in the play that *he* is executed and Lynceus is saved. And "recognition" is, as indeed the name indicates, a shift from ignorance to awareness, pointing in the direction either of close blood ties or of hostility, of people who have previously been in a clearly marked state of happiness or unhappiness.

The finest recognition is one that happens at the same time as a peripety, as is the case with the one in the *Oedipus.* Naturally, there are also other kinds of recognition: it is possible for one to take place in the prescribed manner in relation to inanimate objects and chance occurrences, and it is possible to recognize whether a person has acted or not acted. But the form that is most integrally a part of the plot, the action, is the one aforesaid; for that kind of recognition combined with peripety will excite either pity or fear (and these are the kinds of action of which tragedy is an imitation according to our definition), because both good and bad fortune will also be most likely to follow that kind of event. Since, further, the recognition is a recognition of persons, some are of one person by the other one only (when it is already known who the "other one" is), but sometimes it is necessary for both persons to go through a recognition, as for example Iphigenia is recognized by her brother through the sending of the letter, but of him by Iphigenia another recognition is required.

These then are two elements of plot: peripety and recognition; third is the *pathos.* Of these, peripety and recognition have been discussed; a *pathos* is a destructive or painful act, such as deaths on stage, paroxysms of pain, woundings, and all that sort of thing.

MARY WHITLOCK BLUNDELL *discussed the differences in Sophocles' play between the characters of Creon and Antigone in the literary study* Helping Friends and Harming Enemies: A Study in Sophocles and Greek Ethics, *published by Cambridge University Press in 1989.*

MARY WHITLOCK BLUNDELL

From *Helping Friends and Harming Enemies: A Study in Sophocles and Greek Ethics*

1989

Creon and Antigone are alike in several ways, especially the inconsistency of their values and the way they are driven by passion below a surface of rational argument. Both are also one-sided in their commitments. The poet could have given the champion of the *polis*° a much stronger case. But he could also have let Antigone meet and conquer Creon on his own ground (for example by arguing that her two brothers were equally responsible for the war). The narrowness of both is revealed by their failure really to engage in argument. Creon's two main statements of principle actually occur in Antigone's absence. When they do confront each other, in the brief passage of stichomythia° with which we began, they argue at cross purposes, repeatedly missing each other's point.

This does not mean, however, that they are equally limited in the values to which they adhere. Antigone is sometimes accused of being as narrowly one-sided as Creon in her allegiance to the family and disregard for the interests and *nomoi*° of the *polis.* "If one listened only to Antigone, one would not know that a war had taken place or that anything called 'city' was ever in danger."[1] Nor can it be denied that she ignores competing concepts of *nomos* and justice which have their claims, no matter how shoddily Creon may represent them. Creon's misapplication of his principles does not undermine their claim to consideration, and the rightness of Antigone's cause does not of itself justify the passionate narrowness with which she pursues it. But although she does not acknowledge the authority of the *polis,* she never explicitly rejects it, as Creon does the family. Moreover she acts ultimately to the city's advantage. As Creon himself so ironically puts it, "the man who is worthwhile in family matters will also turn out to be just in the *polis.*" It is Creon's own scorn not just for the family but for public opinion which finally brings the *polis* "doom instead of *soteria.*"° He who began by saving Thebes from its enemies ends by stirring up other cities with enmity. He tells Antigone she is alone in her views, but she retorts that, on the contrary, all those present (namely the chorus of the city's elders) are on her side. Moreover she foresees great glory from

[1]Martha C. Nussbaum, *The Fragility of Goodness: Luck and Ethics in Greek Tragedy and Philosophy* (New York: Cambridge UP, 1986), p. 63.

polis: City-state (Greek). **stichomythia:** Dialogue delivered in alternating lines; often used to show vigorous dispute. ***nomoi:*** Laws, standards (singular, *nomos*) (Greek). ***soteria:*** Salvation; the root, *soter,* means "savior."

her deed, which the context suggests is to derive from none other than her fellow citizens. Creon can make no such claims for himself. Indeed Haemon will hint that his father's behaviour may be destroying a glorious reputation. With the loss of his son's loyalty, Creon also loses the last shreds of his claim to represent the *polis.* But Antigone's words are vindicated when Haemon reports the admiration of the ordinary citizens, echoing her own evaluation of her deed. Even the chorus, while withholding direct approval of Antigone's actions, promise her praise and glory for the manner of her death.

Antigone does once suggest that she is violating the will of the *polis* as represented by its citizens. But she does so only in the extremity of her isolation, lamenting that she is "friendless" and even questioning her divine support. She has cut herself off from her sister and quarrelled with the chorus, and has not, of course, heard Haemon's report of public sympathy for her fate. Under the circumstances it is not unreasonable that she should now believe she is defying the will of the citizens. But she claims that she would do so under the most extreme provocation, implying respect for the *polis* if not its present king. She restricts her defiance to the drastic circumstances of the present crisis, acknowledging the potential conflict between her own priorities and the demands of civic life.

As Antigone goes to her death, she emphatically calls the city itself, its gods and its most prominent citizens, the chorus, to bear witness to her fate. Does this tell us that she has learned the limitations of her own narrow principles? Or is it a reproach to the apathetic chorus? Surely the latter. She shows no sign of regret or newfound insight into the civic value of obedience. But she addresses the chorus in ways suggesting their special responsibility not just as citizens, but as Theban aristocrats who might be expected to play a role in public life. She calls them "citizens of the fatherland," "wealthy men of the *polis,*" "leading men of Thebes." When she refers to herself as "the last remaining daughter of the royal house," she is reasserting her status as a member of the ruling family, to which the chorus are supposedly loyal, and to which Creon is tied only by marriage. This royal status is linked with her reverence for the gods, especially her ancestral gods. Her obligations to the *polis* and her dead family are not mutually exclusive. She has not failed the citizens, for the burial was both in their best interest and called for by their "established laws." But they, intimidated by Creon, have abandoned her. She therefore accuses the chorus of mockery and *hubris,*° the same hostile laughter that she inflicted on her sister and (in his view) on Creon.

One-sided and "autonomous" though she may be, Antigone's obsession is less sterile and destructive than Creon's. He, as he so much likes to remind us, is the sole ruler of the *polis.* In order to achieve a just and stable social order, such a ruler must acknowledge and balance competing claims and values. If these are ultimately incommensurable, he must attempt a compromise, however uneasy. As Haemon eloquently insists, he must know how to bend with the storm. He must respect the ties of natural *philia,*° and at the same time pro-

---

hubris: A complex term in Greek ethical thought that implies an impious overreaching of human limits. ***philia:*** Love, affinity (Greek).

mote political *philia* by adopting policies that meet the citizens' approval. Antigone abides heroically by the first variety of *philia* as she interprets it, and can make some claim to the second, but Creon is a failure at both.

AIMÉ CÉSAIRE *was born in 1913 on the West Indian island of Martinique. From 1913 to 1939 he lived in France, where he launched the literary movement he called "negritude," which called for black writers to champion their racial identity in their work. Césaire first coined the word* negritude *in his poem* Return to My Native Land *(1939), just before he moved back to Martinique to write poetry and serve as mayor of his home town. In the 1950s Césaire began writing plays that he hoped would revolutionize the theater. He adapted Shakespeare's* The Tempest *"for a Black Theatre" into the French political drama* A Tempest *in 1969; it was translated into English by Richard Miller in 1986. Here is Cesaire's new ending of the play.*

AIMÉ CÉSAIRE

Final Scene from A Tempest *(Act 3, Scene 5)*

1969, 1986

[*Prospero's Cave — present are: Prospero, Caliban, Antonio, Gonzalo, Nobles.*]

PROSPERO: Come here, Caliban. Have you got anything to say in your own defence? Take advantage of my good humor. I'm in a forgiving mood today.

CALIBAN: I'm not interested in defending myself. My only regret is that I've failed.

PROSPERO: What were you hoping for?

CALIBAN: To get back my island and regain my freedom.

PROSPERO: And what would you do all alone here on this island, haunted by the devil, tempest-tossed?

CALIBAN: First of all, I'd get rid of you! I'd spit you out, all your works and pomps! Your "white" magic!

PROSPERO: That's a fairly negative program . . .

CALIBAN: You don't understand it . . . I say I'm going to spit you out, and that's very positive . . .

PROSPERO: Well, the world is really upside down . . . We've seen everything now: Caliban as a dialectician! However, in spite of everything I'm fond of you, Caliban. Come, let's make peace. We've lived together for ten years and worked side by side! Ten years count for something, after all! We've ended up by becoming compatriots!

CALIBAN: You know very well that I'm not interested in peace. I'm interested in being free! Free, you hear?

PROSPERO: It's odd . . . no matter what you do, you won't succeed in making me believe that I'm a tyrant!

CALIBAN: Understand what I say, Prospero:
For years I bowed my head
for years I took it, all of it —
your insults, your ingratitude . . .
and worst of all, more degrading than all the rest,
your condescension.
But now, it's over!
Over, do you hear?
Of course, at the moment
You're still stronger than I am.
But I don't give a damn for your power
or for your dogs or your police or your inventions!
And do you know why?
It's because I know I'll get you.
I'll impale you! And on a stake that you've sharpened yourself!
You'll have impaled yourself!
Prospero, you're a great magician:
you're an old hand at deception.
And you lied to me so much,
about the world, about myself,
that you ended up by imposing on me
an image of myself:
underdeveloped, in your words, undercompetent
that's how you made me see myself!
And I hate that image . . . and it's false!
But now I know you, you old cancer,
And I also know myself!
And I know that one day
my bare fist, just that,
will be enough to crush your world!
The old world is crumbling down!

Isn't it true? Just look!
It even bores you to death.
And by the way . . . you have a chance to get it over with:
You can pick up and leave.
You can go back to Europe.
But the hell you will!
I'm sure you won't leave.
You make me laugh with your "mission"!
Your "vocation"!
Your vocation is to hassle me.
And that's why you'll stay,
just like those guys who founded the colonies
and who now can't live anywhere else.
You're just an old addict, that's what you are!

PROSPERO: Poor Caliban! You know that you're headed towards your own ruin. You're sliding towards suicide! You know I will be the stronger, and stronger all the time. I pity you!

CALIBAN: And I hate you!

PROSPERO: Beware! My generosity has its limits.

CALIBAN (*shouting*):

Shango marches with strength
along his path, the sky!
Shango is a fire-bearer,
his steps shake the heavens
and the earth
Shango, Shango, ho!

PROSPERO: I have uprooted the oak and raised the sea,
I have caused the mountain to tremble and have bared my chest to adversity.
With Jove I have traded thunderbolt for thunderbolt.
Better yet — from a brutish monster I have made man!
But ah! To have failed to find the path to man's heart . . .
if that be where man is.

(*to Caliban*)

Well, I hate you as well!
For it is you who have made me
doubt myself for the first time.

(*to the Nobles*)

. . . My friends, come near. We must say farewell . . . I shall not be going with you. My fate is here: I shall not run from it.

ANTONIO: What, Sire?

PROSPERO: Hear me well.
I am not in any ordinary sense a master,
as this savage thinks,
but rather the conductor of a boundless score:
this isle,
summoning voices, I alone,
and mingling them at my pleasure,
arranging out of confusion
one intelligible line.
Without me, who would be able to draw music from all that?
This isle is mute without me.
My duty, thus, is here,
and here I shall stay.

GONZALO: Oh day full rich in miracles!

PROSPERO: Do not be distressed, Antonio, be you the lieutenant of my goods and make use of them as procurator until that time when Ferdinand and Miranda may take effective possession of them, joining them with the Kingdom of Naples. Nothing of that which has been set for them must be postponed: Let their marriage be celebrated at Naples with all royal splendor. Honest Gonzalo, I place my trust in your word. You shall stand as father to our princess at this ceremony.

GONZALO: Count on me, Sire.

PROSPERO: Gentlemen, farewell.

They exit.

And now, Caliban, it's you and me!
What I have to tell you will be brief
Ten times, a hundred times, I've tried to save you,
above all from yourself
But you have always answered me with wrath
and venom,
like the opossum that pulls itself up by its own tail
the better to bite the hand that tears it from the darkness.
Well, my boy, I shall set aside my indulgent nature
and henceforth I will answer your violence
with violence!

Time passes, symbolized by the curtain's being lowered halfway and reraised. In semi-darkness Prospero appears, aged and weary. His gestures are jerky and automatic, his speech weak, toneless, trite.

PROSPERO: Odd, but for some time now we seem to be overrun with opossums. They're everywhere. Peccaries, wild boar, all this unclean nature! But mainly opossums. Those eyes! The vile grins they have! It's as though the jungle was laying siege to the cave . . . But I shall stand firm . . . I shall not let my work perish! (*Shouting*) I shall protect civilization! (*He fires in all directions.*) They're done for! Now, this way I'll be able to have some peace and quiet for a while. But it's cold. Odd how the climate's changed. Cold on this island . . . Have to think about making a fire . . . Well, Caliban, old fellow, it's just us two now, here on the island . . . only you and me. You and me. You-me . . . me-you! What in the hell is he up to? (*Shouting*) Caliban!

In the distance, above the sound of the surf and the chirping of birds, we hear snatches of Caliban's song:

FREEDOM HI-DAY, FREEDOM HI-DAY!

CARYL CHURCHILL *was interviewed on February 25, 1984, by Kathleen Betsko and Rachel Koenig while the playwright was in New York City for a production of her play* Fen *at the Public Theater. At first Churchill was reluctant to be interviewed, but she became so inquisitive about her interviewers' research into the status of American women playwrights that she began to ask them what they later called a series of "rapid and incisive questions" about their work, which they answered in considerable detail. When they played back the tapes of their meeting with Churchill, they discovered that "the interviewers had become the interviewees." Betsko and Koenig's* *conversation with Churchill was included in their book* Interviews with Contemporary Women Playwrights *(1987).*

Caryl Churchill

Interview with Kathleen Betsko and Rachel Koenig

1984

Interviewer: Is there a female aesthetic? And we'd like you to wrap this question up once and for all. [Laughter]

Churchill: I don't see how you can tell until there are so many plays by women that you can begin to see what they have in common that's different from the way men have written, and there are still relatively so few. And we have things in common with male playwrights who are worried about similar things in their particular country and who have worked in the same theaters with the same directors. So it's hard to separate out and think of "women playwrights" rather than just "playwrights." Though I do remember before I wrote *Top Girls* thinking about women barristers° — how they were in a minority and had to imitate men to succeed — and I was thinking of them as different from me. And then I thought, "Wait a minute, my whole concept of what plays might be is from plays written by men. I don't have to put on a wig, speak in a special voice, but how far do I assume things that have been defined by men?" There isn't a simple answer to that. And I remember long before that thinking of the "maleness" of the traditional structure of plays, with conflict and building in a certain way to a climax. But it's not something I think about very often. Playwriting will change not just because more women are doing it but because more women are doing other things as well. And of course men will be influenced by that too. So maybe you'll still be no nearer to defining a female aesthetic.

Interviewer: Some of the playwrights we've interviewed suggest there are no "lost masterpieces" and that "the cream will rise to the top" in terms of women's writing for the stage.

Churchill: Most theaters are still controlled by men and people do tend to be able to see promise in people who are like themselves. Women directors have pointed out to me how established men tend to take a young male director under their wing, and seem to feel more uncomfortable with a woman director because they can't quite see where she is, because they weren't like that at her age. I think the same thing can happen with writers: If you're at the stage where you are promising but not doing it all that well yet, it's perhaps easier for a man choosing plays to see the potential in a man writer. I don't know about "lost masterpieces" but people don't usually start out writing masterpieces and women may have less chance of getting started. Having productions does seem to make people write better.

---

barristers: Courtroom lawyers in Britain. The traditional court attire for a barrister includes a wig — usually of long white curly hair.

Interviewer: Has the political climate for women dramatists changed drastically since you began writing plays?

Churchill: I began writing plays in 1958, and I don't think I knew of any other women playwrights then. Luckily, I didn't think about it. Do you know Tillie Olsen's book *Silences*? She says that at different times, whole categories of people are enabled to write. You tend to think of your own development only having to do with yourself and it's exciting to discover it in a historical context. When I began it was quite hard for any playwrights to get started in London. The English Stage Company had just started a policy of doing new writing at the Royal Court, but that was almost the only place. I had student productions at first, and then wrote for radio. In the late sixties and early seventies there was a surge of fringe theaters and interest in new writing, starting with the Theatre Upstairs and the Royal Court, and that was the first place to do a professional stage production of one of my plays, *Owners*, in 1972. For a while, a lot of writers were getting produced for the first time, though far fewer women than men. Gradually during the seventies the number of women increased, coming partly through fringe theaters and partly through women's theater groups. In the last five years there seem to be far more women playwrights and some theaters are more open to them, though others still aren't. At the moment, because of the financial cuts, it's again become quite hard for all playwrights. Theaters are having to do co-productions with other theaters because they haven't enough money to do a whole year's work on their grants, so it means one new play gets done instead of two. The Royal Court, for instance, can now only afford to do four new plays in the main house instead of eight. But I get the impression life is even harder for playwrights in the United States than in England because of there not being a subsidized theater.

Interviewer: In Laurie Stone's *Village Voice* interview [March 1, 1983], you talked about women becoming executives and you said, "Well, that's not what I mean by feminism." What exactly do you mean by feminism?

Churchill: When I was in the States in '79 I talked to some women who were saying how well things were going for women in America now with far more top executives being women, and I was struck by the difference between that and the feminism I was used to in England, which is far more closely connected with socialism. And that was one of the ideas behind writing *Top Girls*, that achieving things isn't necessarily good, it matters *what* you achieve.

Thatcher had just become prime minister; there was talk about whether it was an advance to have a woman prime minister if it was someone with policies like hers: She may be a woman but she isn't a sister, she may be a sister but she isn't a comrade. And, in fact, things have got much worse for women under Thatcher. So that's the context of that remark. I do find it hard to conceive of a right-wing feminism. Of course, socialism and feminism aren't synonymous, but I feel strongly about both and wouldn't be interested in a form of one that didn't include the other.

Interviewer: Do you think it's odd, given the fact that there is at best indifference, at worst hostility, [toward] political plays in America, that your works are so popular here?

Churchill: Is it true that on the whole plays here tend to be more family-centered, personal, individual-centered?

Interviewer: Yes, more psychological.

Churchill: Whereas I've been quite heavily exposed to a tradition of looking at the larger context of groups of people. It doesn't mean you don't look at families or individuals within that, but you are also looking at bigger things. Like with the kind of work Joint Stock Theatre Group has done, where you go and research a subject and where you have a lot of characters, even if played by only a few people. It tends to open things out.

Interviewer: The critics do ask, "Where are the American plays with the larger social issues?" Unfortunately, when one comes along our own critics usually turn thumbs down if the politics are overt. An overt political position is considered poor craft or preaching.

Churchill: When I was in San Francisco I was talking to the people at the Eureka Theatre [where Richard Seyd directed a production of *Cloud Nine* in 1983] and they were talking about developing a school of playwriting which would break away from family-centered plays, and write about other issues. . . .

Interviewer: Does the playwright have an obligation to take a moral political stance?

Churchill: It's almost impossible not to take one, whether you intend to or not. Most plays can be looked at from a political perspective and have said something, even if it isn't what you set out to say. If you wrote a West End comedy relying on conventional sexist jokes, that's taking a moral and political stance, though the person who wrote it might say, "I was just writing an entertaining show." Whatever you do your point of view is going to show somewhere. It usually only gets noticed and called "political" if it's against the status quo. There are times when I feel I want to deal with immediate issues and times when I don't. I do like the stuff of theater, in the same way people who are painting like paint; and of course when you say "moral and political" that doesn't have to imply reaching people logically or overtly, because theater can reach people on all kinds of other levels too. Sometimes one side or the other is going to have more weight. Sometimes it's going to be about images, more like a dream to people, and sometimes it's going to be more like reading an article. And there's room for all that. But either way, the issues you feel strongly about are going to come through, and they're going to be a moral and political stance in some form. Sometimes more explicitly, sometimes less.

ꕥ

FRANCIS FERGUSSON, *the eminent theater critic, discussed the way Sophocles reimagined his source of the traditional myth of Oedipus in this essay from* The Idea of a Theater *(1949). Fergusson also analyzed how Sophocles developed the important role of the chorus to help the spectators of this drama form "a new perception of the immediate situation."*

Francis Fergusson

Oedipus, Myth and Play 1949

When Sophocles came to write his play he had the myth of Oedipus to start with. Laius and Jocasta, King and Queen of Thebes, are told by the oracle that their son will grow up to kill his father and marry his mother. The infant, his feet pierced, is left on Mount Kitharon to die. But a shepherd finds him and takes care of him; at last gives him to another shepherd, who takes him to Corinth, and there the King and Queen bring him up as their own son. But Oedipus — "Clubfoot" — is plagued in his turn by the oracle; he hears that he is fated to kill his father and marry his mother; and to escape that fate he leaves Corinth never to return. On his journey he meets an old man with his servants; gets into a dispute with him, and kills him and all his followers. He comes to Thebes at the time when the Sphinx is preying upon that City; solves the riddle which the Sphinx propounds, and saves the City. He marries the widowed Queen, Jocasta; has several children by her; rules prosperously for many years. But, when Thebes is suffering under a plague and a drought, the oracle reports that the gods are angry because Laius' slayer is unpunished. Oedipus, as King, undertakes to find him; discovers that he is himself the culprit and that Jocasta is his own mother. He blinds himself and goes into exile. From this time forth he becomes a sort of sacred relic, like the bones of a saint; perilous, but "good medicine" for the community that possesses him. He dies, at last, at Athens, in a grove sacred to the Eumenides, female spirits of fertility and night.

It is obvious, even from this sketch, that the myth, which covers several generations, has as much narrative material as *Gone with the Wind.* We do not know what versions of the story Sophocles used. It is the way of myths that they generate whole progenies of elaborations and varying versions. They are so suggestive, seem to say so much, yet so mysteriously, that the mind cannot rest content with any single form, but must add, or interpret, or simplify — reduce to terms which the reason can accept. Mr. William Troy suggests that "what is possibly most in order at the moment is a thoroughgoing refurbishment of the medieval fourfold method of interpretation, which was first developed, it will be recalled, for just such a purpose — to make at least partially available to the reason that complex of human problems which are embedded, deep and imponderable, in the Myth."[1] It appears that Sophocles, in his play, succeeded in preserving the suggestive mystery of the Oedipus myth, while presenting it in a wonderfully unified dramatic form; and this drama has all the dimensions which the fourfold method was intended to explore.

Everyone knows that when Sophocles planned the plot of the play itself, he started almost at the end of the story, when the plague descends upon the City of Thebes which Oedipus and Jocasta had been ruling with great success for a number of years. The action of the play takes less than a day, and consists of Oedipus' quest for Laius' slayer — his consulting the Oracle of Apollo, his

[1]"Myth, Method and the Future," by William Troy. *Chimera,* Spring 1946.

examination of the Prophet, Tiresias, and of a series of witnesses, ending with the old Shepherd who gave him to the King and Queen of Corinth. The play ends when Oedipus is unmistakably revealed as himself the culprit.

At this literal level, the play is intelligible as a murder mystery. Oedipus takes the role of District Attorney; and when he at last convicts himself, we have a twist, a *coup de théâtre,* of unparalleled excitement. But no one who sees or reads the play can rest content with its literal coherence. Questions as to its meaning arise at once: Is Oedipus really guilty, or simply a victim of the gods, or his famous complex, of fate, of original sin? How much did he know, all along? How much did Jocasta know? The first, and most deeply instinctive effort of the mind, when confronted with this play, is to endeavor to reduce its meanings to some set of rational categories.

The critics of the Age of Reason tried to understand it as a fable of the enlightened moral will, in accordance with the philosophy of that time. Voltaire's version of the play, following Corneille, and his comments upon it, may be taken as typical. He sees it as essentially a struggle between a strong and righteous Oedipus, and the malicious and very human gods, aided and abetted by the corrupt priest Tiresias; he makes it an antireligious tract, with an unmistakable moral to satisfy the needs of the discursive intellect. In order to make Oedipus "sympathetic" to his audience, he elides, as much as possible, the incest motif; and he adds an irrelevant love story. He was aware that his version and interpretation were not those of Sophocles but, with the complacent provinciality of his period, he attributes the difference to the darkness of the age in which *Sophocles* lived.

Other attempts to rationalize *Oedipus Rex* are subtler than Voltaire's, and take us further toward an understanding of the play. Freud's reduction of the play to the concepts of his psychology reveals a great deal, opens up perspectives which we are still exploring. If one reads *Oedipus* in the light of Fustel de Coulanges's *The Ancient City,* one may see it as the expression of the ancient patriarchal religion of the Greeks. And other interpretations of the play, theological, philosophical, historical, are available, none of them wrong, but all partial, all reductions of Sophocles' masterpiece to an alien set of categories. For the peculiar virtue of Sophocles' presentation of the myth is that it preserves the ultimate mystery by focusing upon the tragic human at a level beneath, or prior to any rationalization whatever. The plot is so arranged that we see the action, as it were, illumined from many sides at once.

By starting the play at the end of the story, and showing on stage only the last crucial episode in Oedipus' life, the past and present action of the protagonist are revealed together; and, in each other's light, are at last felt as one. Oedipus' quest for the slayer of Laius becomes a quest for the hidden reality of his own past; and as that slowly comes into focus, like repressed material under psychoanalysis — with sensory and emotional immediacy, yet in the light of acceptance and understanding — his immediate quest also reaches its end: he comes to see himself (the Savior of the City) and the guilty one, the plague of Thebes, at once and at one.

This presentation of the myth of Oedipus constitutes, in one sense, an "interpretation" of it. What Sophocles saw as the essence of Oedipus' nature and destiny is not what Seneca or Dryden or Cocteau saw; and one may grant that even Sophocles did not exhaust the possibilities in the materials of the myth. But Sophocles' version of the myth does not constitute a "reduction" in the same sense as the rest.

I have said that the action which Sophocles shows is a quest, the quest for Laius' slayer; and that as Oedipus' past is unrolled before us his whole life is seen as a kind of quest for his true nature and destiny. But since the object of this quest is not clear until the end, the seeking action takes many forms, as its object appears in different lights. The object, indeed, the final perception, the "truth," looks so different at the end from what it did at the beginning that Oedipus' action itself may seem not a quest, but its opposite, a flight. Thus it would be hard to say, simply, that Oedipus either succeeds or fails. He succeeds; but his success is his undoing. He fails to find what, in one way, he sought; yet from another point of view his search is brilliantly successful. The same ambiguities surround his effort to discover who and what he is. He seems to find that he is nothing; yet thereby finds himself. And what of his relation to the gods? His quest may be regarded as a heroic attempt to escape their decrees, or as an attempt, based upon some deep natural faith, to discover what their wishes are, and what true obedience would be. In one sense Oedipus suffers forces he can neither control nor understand, the puppet of fate; yet at the same time he wills and intelligently intends his every move.

The meaning, or spiritual content of the play, is not to be sought by trying to resolve such ambiguities as these. The spiritual content of the play is the tragic action which Sophocles directly presents; and this action is in its essence *zweideutig:* triumph and destruction, darkness and enlightenment, mourning and rejoicing, at any moment we care to consider it. But this action has also a shape: a beginning, middle, and end, in time. It starts with the reasoned purpose of finding Laius' slayer. But this aim meets unforeseen difficulties, evidences which do not fit, and therefore shake the purpose as it was first understood; and so the characters suffer the piteous and terrible sense of the mystery of the human situation. From this suffering or passion, with its shifting visions, a new perception of the situation emerges; and on that basis the purpose of the action is redefined, and a new movement starts. This movement, or *tragic rhythm of action,* constitutes the shape of the play as a whole; it is also the shape of each episode, each discussion between principals with the chorus following. Mr. Kenneth Burke has studied the tragic rhythm in his *Philosophy of Literary Form,* and also in *A Grammar of Motives,* where he gives the three moments traditional designations which are very suggestive: *Poiema, Pathema, Mathema.* They may also be called, for convenience, Purpose, Passion (or Suffering) and Perception. It is this tragic rhythm of action which is the substance or spiritual content of the play, and the clue to its extraordinarily comprehensive form.

In order to illustrate these points in more detail, it is convenient to examine the scene between Oedipus and Tiresias with the chorus following it. This episode, being early in the play (the first big agon), presents, as it were, a preview of the whole action and constitutes a clear and complete example of action in the tragic rhythm. . . .

■ ■ ■

The Cambridge School of Classical Anthropologists has shown in great detail that the form of Greek tragedy follows the form of a very ancient ritual, that of the *Enniautos-Daimon,* or seasonal god.[2] This was one of the most influential discoveries of the last few generations, and it gives us new insights into *Oedipus* which I think are not yet completely explored. The clue to Sophocles' dramatizing of the myth of Oedipus is to be found in this ancient ritual, which had a similar form and meaning — that is, it also moved in the "tragic rhythm."

Experts in classical anthropology, like experts in other fields, dispute innumerable questions of fact and of interpretation which the layman can only pass over in respectful silence. One of the thornier questions seems to be whether myth or ritual came first. Is the ancient ceremony merely an enactment of the Ur-Myth of the year-god — Attis, or Adonis, or Osiris, or the "Fisher-King" — in any case that Hero-King-Father-High-Priest who fights with his rival, is slain and dismembered, then rises anew with the spring season? Or did the innumerable myths of this kind arise to "explain" a ritual which was perhaps mimed or danced or sung to celebrate the annual change of seasons?

For the purpose of understanding the form and meaning of *Oedipus,* it is not necessary to worry about the answer to this question of historic fact. The figure of Oedipus himself fulfills all the requirements of the scapegoat, the dismembered king or god-figure. The situation in which Thebes is presented at the beginning of the play — in peril of its life; its crops, its herds, its women mysteriously infertile, signs of a mortal disease of the City, and the disfavor of the gods — is like the withering which winter brings, and calls, in the same way, for struggle, dismemberment, death, and renewal. And this tragic sequence is the substance of the play. It is enough to know that myth and ritual are close together in their genesis, two direct imitations of the perennial experience of the race.

But when one considers *Oedipus* as a ritual one understands it in ways which one cannot by thinking of it merely as a dramatization of a story, even that story. Harrison has shown that the Festival of Dionysos, based ultimately upon the yearly vegetation ceremonies, included *rites de passage,* like that celebrating the assumption of adulthood — celebrations of the mystery of individual growth and development. At the same time, it was a prayer for the welfare of the whole City; and this welfare was understood not only as material prosperity, but also as the natural order of the family, the ancestors, the present members, and the generations still to come, and, by the same token, obedience to the gods who were jealous, each in his own province, of this natural and divinely sanctioned order and proportion.

We must suppose that Sophocles' audience (the whole population of the City) came early, prepared to spend the day in the bleachers. At their feet was the semicircular dancing-ground for the chorus, and the thrones for the

---

[2]See especially Jane Ellen Harrison's *Ancient Art and Ritual,* and her *Themis* which contains an "Excursus on the ritual forms preserved in Greek Tragedy" by Professor Gilbert Murray.

priests, and the altar. Behind that was the raised platform for the principal actors, backed by the all-purpose, emblematic façade, which would presently be taken to represent Oedipus' palace in Thebes. The actors were not professionals in our sense, but citizens selected for a religious office, and Sophocles himself had trained them and the chorus.

This crowd must have had as much appetite for thrills and diversion as the crowds who assemble in our day for football games and musical comedies, and Sophocles certainly holds the attention with an exciting show. At the same time his audience must have been alert for the fine points of poetry and dramaturgy, for *Oedipus* is being offered in competition with other plays on the same bill. But the element which distinguishes this theater, giving it its unique directness and depth, is the *ritual expectancy* which Sophocles assumed in his audience. The nearest thing we have to this ritual sense of theater is, I suppose, to be found at an Easter performance of the *Mattias Passion.* We also can observe something similar in the dances and ritual mummery of the Pueblo Indians. Sophocles' audience must have been prepared, like the Indians standing around their plaza, to consider the playing, the make-believe it was about to see — the choral invocations, with dancing and chanting; the reasoned discourses and the terrible combats of the protagonists; the mourning, the rejoicing, and the contemplation of the final stage-picture of epiphany — as imitating and celebrating the mystery of human nature and destiny. And this mystery was at once that of individual growth and development, and that of the precarious life of the human City.

I have indicated how Sophocles presents the life of the mythic Oedipus in the tragic rhythm, the mysterious quest of life. Oedipus is shown seeking his own true being; but at the same time and by the same token, the welfare of the City. When one considers the ritual form of the whole play, it becomes evident that it presents the tragic but perennial, even normal, quest of the whole City for its well-being. In this larger action, Oedipus is only the protagonist, the first and most important champion. This tragic quest is realized by all the characters in their various ways; but in the development of the action as a whole it is the chorus alone that plays a part as important as that of Oedipus; its counterpart, in fact. The chorus holds the balance between Oedipus and his antagonists, marks the progress of their struggles, and restates the main theme, and its new variation, after each dialogue or agon. The ancient ritual was probably performed by a chorus alone without individual developments and variations, and the chorus, in *Oedipus,* is still the element that throws most light on the ritual form of the play as a whole.

The chorus consists of twelve or fifteen "Elders of Thebes." This group is not intended to represent literally all of the citizens either of Thebes or of Athens. The play opens with a large delegation of Theban citizens before Oedipus' palace, and the chorus proper does not enter until after the prologue. Nor does the chorus speak directly for the Athenian audience; we are asked throughout to make-believe that the theater is the agora at Thebes; and at the same time Sophocles' audience is witnessing a ritual. It would, I think, be more accurate to say that the chorus represents the point of view and the faith of Thebes as a whole, and, by analogy, of the Athenian audience. Their errand before Oedipus' palace is like that of Sophocles' audience in the theater: they are watching a sacred combat, in the issue of which they have an all-important and official stake. Thus they represent the audience and the citizens in a particular way — not as a mob formed in response to some momentary feeling, but rather as an organ of a highly self-conscious community: something closer to the "conscience of the race" than to the overheated affectivity of a mob.

According to Aristotle, a Sophoclean chorus is a character that takes an important role in the action of the play, instead of merely making incidental music between the scenes, as in the plays of Euripides. The chorus may be described as a group personality, like an old Parliament. It has its own traditions, habits of thought and feeling, and mode of being. It exists, in a sense, as a living entity, but not with the sharp actuality of an individual. It perceives; but its perception is at once wider and vaguer than that of a single man. It shares, in its way, the seeking action of the play as a whole; but it cannot act in all the modes; it depends upon the chief agonists to invent and try out the detail of policy, just as a rather helpless but critical Parliament depends upon the Prime Minister to act but, in its less specific form of life, survives his destruction.

When the chorus enters after the prologue, with its questions, its invocation of the various gods, and its focus upon the hidden and jeopardized welfare of the City — Athens or Thebes — the list of essential *dramatis personae,* as well as the elements needed to celebrate the ritual, is complete, and the main action can begin. It is the function of the chorus to mark the stages of this action, and to perform the suffering and perceiving part of the tragic rhythm. The protagonist and his antagonists develop the "purpose" with which the tragic sequence begins; the chorus, with its less than individual being, broods over the agons, marks their stages with a word (like that of the chorus leader in the middle of the Tiresias scene), and (expressing its emotions and visions in song and dance) suffers the results, and the new perception at the end of the fight.

The choral odes are lyrics but they are not to be understood as poetry, the art of words, only, for they are intended also to be danced and sung. And though each chorus has its own shape, like that of a discrete lyric — its beginning, middle, and end — it represents also one passion or pathos in the changing action of the whole. This passion, like the other moments in the tragic rhythm, is felt at so general or, rather, so deep a level that it seems to contain both the mob ferocity that Nietzsche felt in it and, at the other extreme, the patience of prayer. It is informed by faith in the unseen order of nature and the gods, and moves through a sequence of modes of suffering. This may be illustrated from the chorus I have quoted at the end of the Tiresias scene.

It begins (close to the savage emotion of the end of the fight) with images suggesting that cruel "Bacchic frenzy" which is supposed to be the common root of tragedy and of the "old" comedy: "In panoply of fire and lightning / The son of Zeus now springs upon him." In the first antistrophe these images come together more clearly as we relish the chase; and the fleeing culprit, as we imagine him, begins to resemble Oedipus, who is lame, and always associated with the rough wilderness of Kitharon. But in the second strophe, as though appalled by its ambivalent feelings and the imagined possibilities, the chorus sinks back into a more dark and patient posture of suffering, "in awe," "hovering in hope." In the second antistrophe this is developed into something like the orthodox Christian attitude of prayer, based on faith, and assuming the possibility of a hitherto unimaginable truth and answer: "Zeus and Apollo are wise," etc. The whole chorus then ends with a new vision of Oedipus, of the culprit, and of the direction in which the welfare of the City is to be sought. This vision is still colored by the chorus's human love of Oedipus as Hero, for the chorus has still its own purgation to complete, cannot as yet accept completely either the suffering in store for it, or Oedipus as scapegoat. But it marks the end of the first complete "purpose-passion-perception" unit, and lays the basis for the new purpose which will begin the next unit.

It is also to be noted that the chorus changes the scene which we, as audience, are to imagine. During the agon between Oedipus and Tiresias, our attention is fixed upon their clash, and the scene is literal, close, and immediate: before Oedipus' palace. When the fighters depart and the choral music starts, the focus suddenly widens, as though we had been removed to a distance. We become aware of the interested City around the bright arena; and beyond that, still more dimly, of Nature, sacred to the hidden gods. Mr. Burke has expounded the fertile notion that human action may be understood in terms of the scene in which it occurs, and vice versa: the scene is defined by the mode of action. The chorus's action is not limited by the sharp, rationalized purposes of the protagonist; its mode of action, more patient, less sharply realized, is cognate with a wider, if less accurate, awareness of the scene of human life. But the chorus's action, as I have remarked, is not that of passion itself (Nietzsche's cosmic void of night) but suffering informed by the faith of the tribe in a human and a divinely sanctioned natural order: "If such deeds as these are honored," the chorus asks after Jocasta's impiety, "why should I dance and sing?" Thus it is one of the most important functions of the chorus to reveal, in its widest and most mysterious extent, the theater of human life which the play, and indeed the whole Festival of Dionysos, assumed. Even when the chorus does not speak, but only watches, it maintains this theme and this perspective — ready to take the whole stage when the fighters depart.

If one thinks of the movements of the play, it appears that the tragic rhythm analyzes human action temporally into successive modes, as a crystal analyzes a white beam of light spatially into the colored bands of the spectrum. The chorus, always present, represents one of these modes, and at the recurrent moments when reasoned purpose is gone, it takes the stage with its faith-informed passion, moving through an ordered succession of modes of suffering, to a new perception of the immediate situation.

ꙮ

SIGMUND FREUD *(1856–1939) used Sophocles' play in* The Interpretation of Dreams *(1900) to derive the term* Oedipus complex, *which is central to his explanation of neurosis in his theory of psychoanalysis. Freud sought to explain the drama's enduring psychological appeal for audiences despite its lack of a contemporary religious context. He hypothesized that audiences respond to Sophocles' tragedy* *because they recognize that Oedipus's relationship to his parents "might have been ours" as children. According to Freud's interpretation, the incest theme is dramatized so forcefully in* Oedipus the King *that it enables us to recognize our own "primeval wishes," suppressed in our later psychological development as individuals.*

SIGMUND FREUD

The Oedipus Complex

1900

In my experience, which is already extensive, the chief part in the mental lives of all children who later become psychoneurotics is played by their parents. Being in love with the one parent and hating the other are among the essential constituents of the stock of psychical impulses which is formed at that time and which is of such importance in determining the symptoms of the later neurosis. It is not my belief, however, that psychoneurotics differ sharply in this respect from other human beings who remain normal — that they are able, that is, to create something absolutely new and peculiar to themselves. It is far more probable — and this is confirmed by occasional observations on normal children — that they are only distinguished by exhibiting on a magnified scale feelings of love and hatred to their parents which occur less obviously and less intensely in the minds of most children.

This discovery is confirmed by a legend that has come down to us from classical antiquity: a legend whose profound and universal power to move can only be understood if the hypothesis I have put forward in regard to the psychology of children has an equally universal validity. What I have in mind is the legend of King Oedipus and Sophocles' drama which bears his name.

Oedipus, son of Laius, King of Thebes, and of Jocasta, was exposed as an infant because an oracle had warned Laius that the still unborn child would be his father's murderer. The child was rescued and grew up as a prince in an alien court, until, in doubts as to his origin, he too questioned the oracle and was warned to avoid his home since he was destined to murder his father and take his mother in marriage. On the road leading away from what he believed was his home, he met King Laius and slew him in a sudden quarrel. He came next to Thebes and solved the riddle set him by the Sphinx who barred his way. Out of gratitude the Thebans made him their king and gave him Jocasta's hand in marriage. He reigned long in peace and honor, and she who, unknown to him, was his mother bore him two sons and two daughters. Then at last a plague broke out and the Thebans made inquiry once more of the oracle. It is at this point that Sophocles' tragedy opens. The messengers bring back the reply that the plague will cease when the murderer of Laius has been driven from the land.

> But he, where is he? Where shall now be read
> The fading record of this ancient guilt?[1]

---

[1]Lewis Campbell's translation (1883), lines 108ff. [Cf. lines 123–124 of the Fagles translation in this volume. — Editors' note]

The action of the play consists in nothing other than the process of revealing, with cunning delays and ever-mounting excitement — a process that can be likened to the work of a psychoanalysis — that Oedipus himself is the murderer of Laius, but further that he is the son of the murdered man and of Jocasta. Appalled at the abomination which he has unwittingly perpetrated, Oedipus blinds himself and forsakes his home. The oracle has been fulfilled.

Oedipus Rex is what is known as a tragedy of destiny. Its tragic effect is said to lie in the contrast between the supreme will of the gods and the vain attempts of mankind to escape the evil that threatens them. The lesson which, it is said, the deeply moved spectator should learn from the tragedy is submission to the divine will and realization of his own impotence. Modern dramatists have accordingly tried to achieve a similar tragic effect by weaving the same contrast into a plot invented by themselves. But the spectators have looked on unmoved while a curse or an oracle was fulfilled in spite of all the efforts of some innocent man: later tragedies of destiny have failed in their effect.

If *Oedipus Rex* moves a modern audience no less than it did the contemporary Greek one, the explanation can only be that its effect does not lie in the contrast between destiny and human will, but is to be looked for in the particular nature of the material on which that contrast is exemplified. There must be something which makes a voice within us ready to recognize the compelling force of destiny in the *Oedipus*, while we can dismiss as merely arbitrary such dispositions as are laid down in [Grillparzer's] *Die Ahnfrau* or other modern tragedies of destiny. And a factor of this kind is in fact involved in the story of King Oedipus. His destiny moves us only because it might have been ours — because the oracle laid the same curse upon us before our birth as upon him. It is the fate of all of us, perhaps, to direct our first sexual impulse toward our mother and our first hatred and our first murderous wish against our father. Our dreams convince us that that is so. King Oedipus, who slew his father Laius and married his mother Jocasta, merely shows us the fulfillment of our own childhood wishes. But, more fortunate than he, we have meanwhile succeeded, in so far as we have not become psychoneurotics, in detaching our sexual impulses from our mothers and in forgetting our jealousy of our fathers. Here is one in whom these primeval wishes of our childhood have been fulfilled, and we shrink back from him with the whole force of the repression by which those wishes have since that time been held down within us. While the poet, as he unravels the past, brings to light the guilt of Oedipus, he is at the same time compelling us to recognize our own inner minds, in which those same impulses, though suppressed, are still to be found. The contrast with which the closing Chorus leaves us confronted —

> . . . Fix on Oedipus your eyes,
> Who resolved the dark enigma, noblest champion and most wise.
> Like a star his envied fortune mounted beaming far and wide:
> Now he sinks in seas of anguish, whelmed beneath a raging tide . . .[2]

---

[2]Lewis Campbell's translation, lines 1524ff. [Cf. lines 1678–1682 in the Fagles translation in this volume. — Editors' note]

— strikes as a warning at ourselves and our pride, at us who since our childhood have grown so wise and so mighty in our own eyes. Like Oedipus, we live in ignorance of these wishes, repugnant to morality, which have been forced upon us by Nature, and after their revelation we may all of us well seek to close our eyes to the scenes of our childhood.[3]

There is an unmistakable indication in the text of Sophocles' tragedy itself that the legend of Oedipus sprang from some primeval dream material which had as its content the distressing disturbance of a child's relation to his parents owing to the first stirrings of sexuality. At a point when Oedipus, though he is not yet enlightened, has begun to feel troubled by his recollection of the oracle, Jocasta consoles him by referring to a dream which many people dream, though, as she thinks, it has no meaning:

> Many a man ere now in dreams hath lain
> With her who bare him. He hath least annoy
> Who with such omens troubleth not his mind.[4]

Today, just as then, many men dream of having sexual relations with their mothers, and speak of the fact with indignation and astonishment. It is clearly the key to the tragedy and the complement to the dream of the dreamer's father being dead. The story of Oedipus is the reaction of the imagination to these two typical dreams. And just as these dreams, when dreamt by adults, are accompanied by feelings of repulsion, so too the legend must include horror and self-punishment. Its further modification originates once again in a misconceived secondary revision of the material, which has sought to exploit it for theological purposes. . . . The attempt to harmonize divine omnipotence with human responsibility must naturally fail in connection with this subject matter just as with any other.

❧

HENRIK IBSEN *wrote his first notes for the play that would become* A Doll House *on October 19, 1878. At first he conceived of the drama essentially as a marital conflict that would lead to Nora's destruction because of what he saw as her entrapment in a patriarchal society. This excerpt from Ibsen's notes is from the translator A. G. Chater's* From Ibsen's Workshop *(1978).*

---

[3][*Footnote added by Freud in 1914 edition.*] None of the findings of psychoanalytic research has provoked such embittered denials, such fierce opposition — or such amusing contortions — on the part of critics as this indication of the childhood impulses toward incest which persist in the unconscious. An attempt has even been made recently to make out, in the face of all experience, that the incest should only be taken as "symbolic." — Ferenczi (1912) has proposed an ingenious "overinterpretation" of the Oedipus myth, based on a passage in one of Schopenhauer's letters. [*Added 1919.*] Later studies have shown that the "Oedipus complex," which was touched upon for the first time in the above paragraphs in the *Interpretation of Dreams,* throws a light of undreamt-of importance on the history of the human race and the evolution of religion and morality.

[4]Lewis Campbell's translation, lines 982ff. [Cf. lines 1074–1078 in the Fagles translation in this volume. — Editors' note]

Henrik Ibsen

Notes for A Doll House

1878

There are two kinds of spiritual law, two kinds of conscience, one in man and another, altogether different, in woman. They do not understand each other; but in practical life the woman is judged by man's law, as though she were not a woman but a man.

The wife in the play ends by having no idea of what is right or wrong; natural feeling on the one hand and belief in authority on the other have altogether bewildered her.

A woman cannot be herself in the society of the present day, which is an exclusively masculine society, with laws framed by men and with a judicial system that judges feminine conduct from a masculine point of view.

She has committed forgery, and she is proud of it; for she did it out of love for her husband, to save his life. But this husband with his commonplace principles of honor is on the side of the law and looks at the question from the masculine point of view.

Spiritual conflicts. Oppressed and bewildered by the belief in authority, she loses faith in her moral right and ability to bring up her children. Bitterness. A mother in modern society, like certain insects who go away and die when she has done her duty in the propagation of the race. Love of life, of home, of husband and children and family. Now and then a womanly shaking off of her thoughts. Sudden return of anxiety and terror. She must bear it all alone. The catastrophe approaches, inexorably, inevitably. Despair, conflict, and destruction.

Leonard Mustazza *considers the similarities and differences between Glaspell's play and short story. This essay was published in the literary journal* Studies in Short Fiction.

Leonard Mustazza

Generic Translation and Thematic Shift in Glaspell's Trifles *and "A Jury of Her Peers"*

1989

Commentators on Susan Glaspell's classic feminist short story, "A Jury of Her Peers" (1917), and the one-act play from which it derives, *Trifles* (1916), have tended to regard the two works as essentially alike. And even those few who have noticed the changes that Glaspell made in the process of generic translation have done so only in passing. In his monograph on Glaspell, Arthur Waterman, who seems to have a higher regard for the story than for the play, suggests that the story is a "moving fictional experience" because of the progressive honing of the author's skills, the story's vivid realism owing to her work as a local-color writer for the *Des Moines Daily News,* and its unified plot due to its dramatic origin.[1] More specifically, Elaine Hedges appropriately notes the significance of Glaspell's change in titles from *Trifles,* which emphasizes the supposedly trivial household items with which the women "acquit" their accused peer, to "A Jury of Her Peers," which emphasizes the question of legality. In 1917, Hedges observes, women were engaged in the final years of their fight for the vote, and Glaspell's change in titles thus "emphasizes the story's contemporaneity, by calling attention to its references to the issue of women's legal place in American society."[2] Apart from these and a few other passing remarks, however, critics have chosen to focus on one work or the other. Indeed, thematic criticisms of the respective pieces are virtually indistinguishable, most of these commentaries focusing on the question of assumed "roles" in the works.[3]

On one level, there is good reason for this lack of differentiation. Not only is the overall narrative movement of the works similar, but Glaspell incorporated in the short story virtually every single line of the dialogue from *Trifles.*[4] By the same token, though, she also added much to the short story,

---

[1]Arthur E. Waterman, *Susan Glaspell* (New York: Twayne, 1966), pp. 29–30.

[2]Elaine Hedges, "Small Things Reconsidered: Susan Glaspell's 'A Jury of Her Peers,'" *Women's Studies,* 12, No. 1 (1986), 106.

[3]Rachel France notes that *Trifles* reveals "the dichotomy between men and women in rural life," an important feature of that dichotomy being the men's "proclivity for the letter of the law" as opposed to the women's more humane understanding of justice ("Apropos of Women and the Folk Play," in *Women in American Theatre: Careers, Images, Movements,* ed. Helen Krich Chinoy and Linda Walsh Jenkins [New York: Crown, 1981], p. 151). Karen Alkalay-Gut observes three polarities in "Jury": the opposition between the large external male world and the women's more circumscribed place within the home; the attitudes of men and women generally; and the distinction between *law,* which is identified with "the imposition of abstractions on individual circumstances," and *justice,* "the extrapolation of judgment from individual circumstances" ("Jury of Her Peers: The Importance of *Trifles,*" *Studies in Short Fiction,* 21 [Winter 1984], 2). Karen Stein calls the play "an anomaly in the murder mystery genre, which is predominantly a male tour de force." By bonding together, she goes on, the women act in a manner that is "diametrically opposed to the solo virtuosity usually displayed by male detectives" ("The Women's World of Glaspell's *Trifles,*" in *Women in American Theatre,* ed. Helen Krich Chinoy and Linda Walsh Jenkins [New York: Crown, 1981], p. 254). Judith Fetterly also advances an interesting and imaginative interpretation. She sees the characters in "Jury" as readers and the trivial household items as their text. The men fail to read the same meanings in that text that the women do because they are committed to "the equation of textuality with masculine subject matter and masculine point of view" ("Reading about Reading: 'A Jury of Her Peers,' 'The Murders in the Rue Morge,' and 'The Yellow Wallpaper,'" in *Gender and Reading: Essays on Readers, Texts and Contexts,* ed. Elizabeth A. Flynn and Patrocinio P. Schweickart [Baltimore: Johns Hopkins Univ. Press, 1986], pp. 147–48).

[4]Elaine Hedges notes that one reference included in the play but omitted from "Jury" is Mrs. Hale's lament that, because of Mr. Wright's parsimony, Minnie could not join the Ladies' Aid, a society in which women cooperated with the local church to make items like carpets and quilts. These items were then sold to support ministers' salaries and to aid foreign missions. Minnie is thus denied not only the company of other women but also one of the few public roles that farm women were allowed to play ("Small Things Reconsidered," p. 102). In this regard, the story reveals, as Jeannie McKnight suggests, "a kind of classic 'cabin fever' as motivation for the homicide . . ." ("American Dream, Nightmare Underside: Diaries, Letters, and Fiction of Women on the American Frontier," in *Women, Women Writers, and the West,* ed. L. L. Lee and Merrill Lewis [Troy, NY: Whitson, 1979], p. 31).

which is about twice as long as the play. The nature of these additions is twofold, the first and most obvious being her descriptions of locales, modes of utterance, characters, props, and so on — the kinds of descriptions that the prose writer's form will allow but the dramatist's will not. The other type of alteration is more subtle, and it involves the revisions, embellishments, and redirections that occur when an existent story is retold. When, for instance, a novel is turned into a film or a play, the best that can be said about the generic translation is that it is "faithful," but never is it identical. So it is with "Jury." It is certainly faithful to the play, but it is also different in a variety of ways, and it is these differences, which took place in the act of generic translation, that I would like to consider here.

In her article on *Trifles*, Beverly Smith makes an interesting observation. Noting that the women in the play, Mrs. Hale and Mrs. Peters, function as defense counsel for and jury of their accused peer, Minnie Foster Wright, she goes on to suggest that the men's role, their official capacities notwithstanding, are comparable to that of a Greek Chorus, "the voice of the community's conscience," entering at various points to reiterate their major themes — Minnie's guilt and the triviality of the women's occupations, avocations, and preoccupations.[5] This equation is, I think, quite useful, for the periodic entries, commentaries, and exits of the male characters in both Glaspell works do in fact mark the progressive stages of the narrative, which primarily concerns the women, including the absent Minnie Foster.[6] Though not on stage for the entire drama, as is the Greek Chorus, the men nevertheless function in much the same way, providing commentary and separating the major movements of the narrative. What is more, if we regard the men's exits from the stage as marking these movements, we will recognize the first principal difference between the play and the story — namely, that the latter contains twice as many movements as the former and is therefore necessarily a more developed and complex work.

Trifles opens with Mr. Hale's account of what he found when he arrived at the Wright farm the day before. Of the women themselves, we know almost nothing beyond their general appearances as described in the opening stage directions — that Mrs. Peters, the sheriff's wife, is "a slight wiry woman [with] a thin nervous face"; and that Mrs. Hale, the witness's wife, is larger than Mrs. Peters and "comfortable looking," though now appearing fearful and disturbed as she enters the scene of the crime. Standing close together as they enter the Wrights' home, the women remain almost completely undifferentiated until, some time later, they begin to speak. Thus, Glaspell underscores here the male/female polarities that she will explore in the course of the play.

---

[5]Beverly A. Smith, "Women's Work — Trifles? The Skill and Insight of Playwright Susan Glaspell," *International Journal of Women's Studies*, 5 (March–April 1982), 175.

[6]Cynthia Sutherland aptly observes that the story's effect depends to a large extent upon the removal of Minnie from the sight of the audience, thus focusing our attention on the facts of her plight rather than on her appearance and mannerisms ("American Women Playwrights as Mediators of the 'Woman Problem,'" *Modern Drama*, 21 [September 1978], 323).

Her entire narrative technique is different in the prose version. That story begins in Mrs. Hale's disordered kitchen, which will later serve as a point of comparison with the major scene of the story, Mrs. Wright's kitchen. Annoyed at being called away from her housework, she nevertheless agrees to Sheriff Peters's request that she come along to accompany Mrs. Peters, who is there to fetch some personal effects for the jailed woman. Quite unlike the play's opening, which emphasizes the physical closeness of and the attitudinal similarities between the women, "Jury," taking us as it does into Mrs. Hale's thoughts, emphasizes the women's apartness:

> She had met Mrs. Peters the year before at the county fair, and the thing she remembered about her was that *she didn't seem to like the sheriff's wife.* She was small and thin and didn't have a strong voice. Mrs. Gorman, the sheriff's wife before Gorman went out and Peters came in, had a voice that somehow seemed to be backing up the law with every word. But if Mrs. Peters didn't look like a sheriff's wife, Peters made up for it in looking like a sheriff. . . . a heavy man with a big voice, who was particularly genial with the law-abiding, as if to make it plain that he knew the difference between criminals and non-criminals. (emphasis added)

Interestingly, for all the added material here, Glaspell omits mention of what the women look like. In fact, we will get no explicit statements on their appearance.

On the other hand, what we do get in this revised opening is much that sharply differentiates the story from the play. In the latter, we are provided with no indication of Mrs. Hale's bad feelings about the sheriff's wife, and, if anything, their close physical proximity leads us to conclude the opposite. Although the women in the story will later assume this same protective stance when they enter the accused's kitchen and then again when the county attorney criticizes Mrs. Wright's kitchen, the movement together there is little more than reflexive. Elaine Hedges has argued that the latter movement together begins the process of establishing "their common bonds with each other and with Minnie."[7] This may be so of their physical proximity in the play, where no distance is established between the women at the outset, but the story presents a different situation altogether, for any emotional closeness we might infer from their act is undercut by our knowledge of Mrs. Hale's lack of respect for Mrs. Peters, particularly by comparison with her predecessor, Mrs. Gorman.

Ironically, however, despite her seeming mismatch with her husband, her lack of corporal "presence," Mrs. Peters turns out to be more suited to her assumed public role than Mrs. Hale had suspected — all too suited, in fact, since she perfectly assumes her male-approved role. "Of course Mrs. Peters is one of us," the county attorney asserts prior to getting on with his investigation of the house, and that statement turns out to be laden with meaning in the story. In *Trifles,* when the men leave to go about their investigative business, the women, we are told, "listen to the men's steps, then look about the

---

[7]"Small Things Reconsidered," p. 98.

kitchen." In "Jury," however, we get much more. Again here, the women stand motionless, listening to the men's footsteps, but this momentary stasis is followed by a significant gesture: "Then, *as if releasing herself from something strange,* Mrs. Hale began to arrange the dirty pans under the sink, which the county attorney's disdainful push of the foot had deranged" (emphasis added). One is prompted here to ask: what is this "something strange" from which she releases herself? Though the actions described in the play and the story are the same, why does Glaspell not include in the stage directions to the play an indication of Mrs. Hale's facial expression?

The answer, I think, lies again in the expanded and altered context of "Jury," where the author continually stresses the distance between the women. If Mrs. Peters is, as the county attorney has suggested, one of "them," Mrs. Hale certainly is not, and she distances herself from her male-approved peer in word and deed. The something strange from which she releases herself is, in this context, her reflexive movement towards Mrs. Peters. Mrs. Hale is, in fact, both extricating herself from the male strictures placed upon all of the women and asserting her intellectual independence. Karen Alkalay-Gut has correctly observed that, to the men, the disorder of Mrs. Wright's kitchen implies her "potential homicidal tendencies, inconceivable in a good wife."[8] For her part, Mrs. Hale is rejecting the men's specious reasoning, complaining about the lawyer's disdainful treatment of the kitchen things and asserting, "I'd hate to have men comin' into my kitchen, snoopin' round and criticizin'," obviously recalling the disorder in her kitchen and resenting the conclusions about her that could be drawn. Lacking that opening scene, the play simply does not resonate so profoundly.

Even more telling is a subtle but important change that Glaspell made following Mrs. Hale's testy assertion. In both the play and the story, Mrs. Peters offers the meek defense, "Of course it's no more than their duty," and then the two works diverge. In *Trifles,* Mrs. Peters manages to change the subject. Noticing some dough that Mrs. Wright had been preparing the day before, she says flatly, "she had set bread," and that statement directs Mrs. Hale's attention to the half-done and ruined kitchen chores. In effect, the flow of conversation is mutually directed in the play, and the distance between the women is thus minimized. When she wrote the play, however, Glaspell omitted mention of the bread and instead took us into Mrs. Hale's thoughts, as she does at the beginning of the story:

> She thought of the flour in her kitchen at home — half sifted, half not sifted. She had been interrupted, and had left things half done. What had interrupted Minnie Foster? Why had that work been left half done? She made a move as if to finish it, — unfinished things always bothered her, — and then she glanced around and saw that Mrs. Peters was watching her — and she didn't want Mrs. Peters to get that feeling she got of work begun and then — for some reason — not finished.
>
> "It's a shame about her fruit," she said. . . .

---

[8]"Jury of Her Peers: The Importance of *Trifles,*" p. 3.

Although mention of the ruined fruit preserves is included in the play as well, two significant additions are made in the above passage. First, there is the continual comparison between Mrs. Hale's life and Mrs. Wright's. Second, and more important, we get the clear sense here of Mrs. Hale's suspicion of Mrs. Peters, her not wanting to call attention to the unfinished job for fear that the sheriff's wife will get the wrong idea — or, in this case, the right idea, for the evidence of disturbance, however circumstantial, is something the men may be able to use against Mrs. Wright. In other words, unlike the play, the story posits a different set of polarities, with Mrs. Peters presumably occupying a place within the official party and Mrs. Hale taking the side of the accused against all of them.

We come at this point to a crossroads in the story. Mrs. Hale can leave things as they are and keep information to herself, or she can recruit Mrs. Peters as a fellow "juror" in the case, moving the sheriff's wife away from her sympathy for her husband's position and towards identification with the accused woman. Mrs. Hale chooses the latter course and sets about persuading Mrs. Peters to emerge, in Alkalay-Gut's words, "as an individual distinct from her role as sheriff's wife." Once that happens, "her identification with Minnie is rapid and becomes complete."[9]

The persuasive process begins easily but effectively, with Mrs. Hale reflecting upon the change in Minnie Foster Wright over the thirty or so years she has known her — the change, to use the metaphor that Glaspell will develop, from singing bird to muted caged bird. She follows this reminiscence with a direct question to Mrs. Peters about whether the latter thinks that Minnie killed her husband. "Oh, I don't know," is the frightened response in both works, but, as always, the story provides more insight and tension than does the drama. Still emphasizing in her revision the distance between the women, Glaspell has Mrs. Hale believe that her talk of the youthful Minnie has fallen on deaf ears: "Much difference it makes to her whether Minnie Foster had pretty clothes when she was a girl." This sense of the other woman's indifference to such irrelevant trivialities is occasioned not only by Mrs. Hale's persistent belief in the other woman's official role but also by an odd look that crosses Mrs. Peters's face. At second glance, however, Mrs. Hale notices something else that melts her annoyance and undercuts her suspicions about the sheriff's wife: "Then she looked again, and she wasn't so sure; in fact, she hadn't at any time been perfectly sure about Mrs. Peters. She had that shrinking manner, and yet her eyes looked as if they could see a long way into things." Whereas the play shows the women meandering towards concurrence, the short story is here seen to evolve — and part of that evolution, we must conclude, is due to Mrs. Hale's ability to persuade her peer to regard the case from her perspective. The look that she sees in Mrs. Peters's eyes suggests to her that she might be able to persuade her, that the potential for identification is there. Hence, when she asks whether Mrs. Peters thinks Minnie is guilty, the question resonates here in ways the play does not.

---

[9]"Jury of Her Peers: The Importance of *Trifles*," p. 6.

Accordingly, Mrs. Hale will become much more aggressive in her arguments hereafter, taking on something of the persuader's hopeful hostility, which, in the case of the story, stands in marked contrast to the hostility she felt for Mrs. Peters's official role earlier. Thus, when Mrs. Peters tries to retreat into a male argument, weakly asserting that "the law is the law," the Mrs. Hale of the short story does not let the remark pass, as the one in *Trifles* does: "the law is the law — and a bad stove is a bad stove. How'd you like to cook on this?" Even she, however, is startled by Mrs. Peters's immediate response to her homey analogy and *ad hominem* attack: "A person gets discouraged — and loses heart," Mrs. Peters says — "That look of seeing . . . through a thing to something else" back on her face.

As far as I am concerned, the addition of this passage is the most important change that Glaspell made in her generic translation. Having used this direct personal attack and having noted the ambivalence that Mrs. Peters feels for her role as sheriff's wife, Mrs. Hale will now proceed to effect closure of the gap between them — again, a gap that is never this widely opened in *Trifles.* Now Mrs. Hale will change her entire mode of attack, pushing the limits, doing things she hesitated doing earlier, assailing Mrs. Peters whenever she lapses into her easy conventional attitudes. For instance, when Mrs. Peters objects to Mrs. Hale's repair of a badly knitted quilt block — in effect, tampering with circumstantial evidence of Minnie's mental disturbance of the day before — Mrs. Hale proceeds to do it anyway. As a measure of how much she has changed, we have only to compare this act with her earlier hesitation to finish another chore for fear of what Mrs. Peters might think. She has no reason to be distrustful of Mrs. Peters any longer, for the process of identification is now well underway.

That identification becomes quite evident by the time the women find the most compelling piece of circumstantial evidence against Mrs. Wright — the broken bird cage and the dead bird, its neck wrung and its body placed in a pretty box in Mrs. Wright's sewing basket. When the men notice the cage and Mrs. Hale misleadingly speculates that a cat may have been at it, it is Mrs. Peters who confirms the matter. Asked by the county attorney whether a cat was on the premises, Mrs. Peters — fully aware that there is no cat and never has been — quickly and evasively replies, "Well, not *now*. . . . They're superstitious, you know; they leave." Not only is Mrs. Peters deliberately lying here, but, more important, she is assuming quite another role from the one she played earlier. Uttering a banality, she plays at being the shallow woman who believes in superstitions, thus consciously playing one of the roles the men expect her to assume and concealing her keen intellect from them, her ability to extrapolate facts from small details.

From this point forward, the play and the short story are essentially the same. Mrs. Hale will continue her persuasive assault, and Mrs. Peters will continue to struggle inwardly. The culmination of this struggle occurs when, late in the story, the county attorney says that "a sheriff's wife is married to the law," and she responds, "Not — just that way." In "Jury," however, this protest carries much greater force than it does in *Trifles* for the simple reason that it is a measure of how far Mrs. Peters has come in the course of the short story.

Appropriately enough, too, Mrs. Hale has the final word in both narratives. Asked derisively by the county attorney what stitch Mrs. Wright had been using to make her quilt, Mrs. Hale responds with false sincerity, "We call it — knot it, Mr. Henderson." Most critics have read this line as an ironic reference to the women's solidarity at this point.[10] That is quite true, but, as I have been suggesting here, the progress towards this solidarity varies subtly but unmistakably in the two narratives. Whereas *Trifles*, opening as it does with the women's close physical proximity, reveals the dichotomy between male and female concepts of justice and social roles, "A Jury of Her Peers" is much more concerned with the separateness of the women themselves and their self-injurious acquiescence in male-defined roles. Hence, in her reworking of the narrative, Glaspell did much more than translate the material from one genre to another. Rather, she subtly changed its theme, and, in so doing, she wrote a story that is much more interesting, resonant, and disturbing than the slighter drama from which it derives.

BENJAMIN NELSON *discussed what he considered the strengths and weaknesses of* The Glass Menagerie *in his critical study* Tennessee Williams: The Man and His Work *(1961). Nelson asked himself whether or not the play can be defined as a tragedy, and drew his conclusion after referring to Williams's short fiction.*

BENJAMIN NELSON

Problems in The Glass Menagerie

1961

The Glass Menagerie exhibits several of Williams's weaknesses as well as his strengths as a playwright. The great strength of the play is of course the delicate, sympathetic, yet objective creation of meaningful people in a meaningful situation. Williams has caught a decisive and desperate moment in the lives of four individuals and given it illumination and a sense of deep meaning — no small feat for any writer.

His characterizations are not equally realized. He has been unable to create Laura on more than a single dimension, while Amanda is overwhelming in her multi-faceted delineation. On a more technical level the play manifests a doubt on the part of its author toward the power of the written word. As a backdrop for *The Glass Menagerie,* Williams originally wished to use a screen to

[10]Beverly Smith sees "the bond among women [as] the essential knot" ("Women's Work," p. 179). Cynthia Sutherland regards the reference to knotting as "a subdued, ironic, and grisly reminder of the manner in which a stifled wife has enacted her desperate retaliation" ("American Women Playwrights," p. 323). And Elaine Hedges argues that the reference has three meanings: the rope that Minnie knotted around her husband's neck; the bond among the women; and the fact that the women have tied the men in knots ("Small Things Reconsidered," p. 107).

register emotions and present images from the past, present, and future. For example, when Jim O'Connor confesses to the family that he is going steady with another girl, the legend on the screen is to read, "The Sky Falls." Fortunately, [actor-director] Eddie Dowling deleted these touches of the poet from his production, but the play still abounds with a number of pretentious statements on the part of Tom as Narrator.

I assume that the final scene between Amanda and Laura is played in pantomime because Williams wished to portray Amanda's dignity through her gestures and her daughter's reaction, rather than through the mother's speech, which during the course of the drama has been either shrill, simpering, or saucy. But in relegating this scene to background silence while Tom makes a self-conscious statement about drifting like a dead leaf "attempting to find in motion what was lost in space," he has substituted a painfully pretentious narration for what could have been an intense and luminous moment between the two women.

Again, on the credit side of the author, his play presents genuine situation, motivation, and, as Joseph Wood Krutch has noted, "a hard substantial core of shrewd observation and deft, economical characterization." But Mr. Krutch also noted that "this hard core is enveloped in a fuzzy haze of pretentious, sentimental, pseudo-poetic verbiage."[1] In *The Glass Menagerie,* the strained lyricism runs parallel with dialogue that is fresh, alive, and highly characteristic, particularly in the speech of Amanda. This dialogue fortunately dominates the proceedings, but the excess of self-conscious "poetical" passages is quite apparent and is a fault of which Williams is to be guilty in much of his later work.

But the great weakness of *The Glass Menagerie* does not lie in its author's artistic or technical deficiencies. The weakness lies at the core of the play and evolves out of what is to become the playwright's hardening philosophical commitment. We can begin to comprehend this when we ask ourselves whether or not *The Glass Menagerie* is a tragedy. It presents a tragic situation and characters who, despite their moodiness and foolishness and self-deception, possess a sense of the tragic. With the possible exception of Laura, they are intensely genuine and the destruction of their dreams and aspirations bears the illusion of great importance. But the play is not a tragedy. The universe of *The Glass Menagerie* does not allow tragedy.

Everyone in the play is a failure and in the course of their drama they all perish a little. Amanda, the most heroic of the quartet, is pitiful but not tragic because from the outset she is doomed to failure despite her desperate struggle to right things. None of these people are given the opportunity to triumph against a fate which is as malignant as it is implacable. Their struggle is a rearguard action against life, a continuous retreat. This retreat may be moving, pathetic, melodramatic, or boisterous, but it is always a withdrawal. After all, what is the world outside the glass menagerie?

> There was only hot swing music and liquor, dance halls, bars, and movies, and sex that hung in the gloom like a chandelier and flooded

---

[1] Joseph Wood Krutch, *The Nation* 14 April 1945: 24.

> the world with brief, deceptive rainbows. . . . All the world was waiting for bombardments!

The world outside the Wingfield apartment is a world of illusions, also, even more deceptive and destructive than those held by Amanda and Laura. It is the world of *Stairs to the Roof* and this time the escape is not to a new star but into the individual and personal illusions fostered by each of the characters as his private defense against destruction. Jim waits for the day when his "zzzzzp!" will at last disperse his fear and uncertainty; Laura creates her own sparkling, cold world which gives the illusion of warmth but is as eternal in its unreality as the glass from which it is composed; Amanda strikes out with all her power against her fate by clinging to the past as to a shield; and Tom, recognizing the plight of his family, can do no more than drift away from them, rudderless, frightened, and never really as far from Amanda and Laura as he knows he should be.

Not one of these individuals can cope with his situation. They struggle and their hopes and the destruction of these hopes possess a sense of great importance because Williams has created genuine people in an intensely genuine situation, but they lack the completeness to truly cope with their dilemma. They are not responsible for what has happened to them and they are much too helpless to do more than delay the inevitable. And destruction is inevitable because it is implicit in the universe of Tennessee Williams.

> For the sins of the world are really only its partialities, and these are what sufferings must atone for. . . . The nature of man is full of such makeshift arrangements, devised by himself to cover his incompletion. He feels a part of himself to be like a missing wall or a room left unfurnished and he tries as well as he can to make up for it. The use of imagination, resorting to dreams or the loftier purpose of art, is a mask he devises to cover his incompletion. Or violence such as a war, between two men or among a number of nations, is also a blind and senseless compensation for that which is not yet formed in human nature. Then there is still another compensation. This one is found in the principle of atonement, the surrender of self to violent treatment by others with the idea of thereby cleansing one's self of his guilt.[2]

This statement emanates from the core of Williams's thought and is perhaps his most illuminating commentary about himself and his work. It represents a philosophy, or let us say an attitude toward man in his universe, which is to manifest itself in all his work. It is taken from his short story, "Desire and the Black Masseur," which deals with the final compensation cited in the above quotation: purification through violence. In this tale, a man atones for what the author feels is cosmic fragmentation and guilt by allowing — and actually furthering — his destruction by a cannibal. In *Battle of Angels* and *The Purification*, we find this same kind of violent cleansing.

---

[2]Tennessee Williams, "Desire and the Black Masseur," *One Arm and Other Stories* (New York, 1948), 85.

The Glass Menagerie is a far cry from any of these works; it is the most nonviolent drama written by Williams. Nevertheless it adheres to the belief set forth in the short story. The underlying belief in *The Glass Menagerie* is that there is very little, if any, reason for living. Man is by nature incomplete because his universe is fragmented. There is nothing to be done about this condition because nothing *can* be done about it. Human guilt becomes a corollary of universal guilt and man's life is an atonement for the human condition. In each character in *The Glass Menagerie* there is a part "like a missing wall or a room left unfurnished and he tries as well as he can to make up for it." The mask devised by Laura and Amanda and Tom and Jim is "the use of imagination, resorting to dreams." The Wingfields are broken, fragmented people because "the sins of the world are really only its partialities." They are really not at all responsible for their condition, and thus are in no way able to cope with it. They are trapped in a determined universe. Without some kind of responsibility on the part of the protagonist there is opportunity neither for tragic elevation nor tragic fall. The Wingfields were doomed the moment they were born. At best their struggles will allow them to survive . . . for a time. They will never be allowed to triumph. Thus their struggles, their hopes, and even their eventual destruction can never move far beyond pathos. The beauty and magic of *The Glass Menagerie* is that this pathos is genuine, objective, and deeply moving.

*

FRANK RICH *was the* New York Times *drama and music critic in 1987, when he reviewed August Wilson's new play* Fences. *While Rich admired the play, especially James Earl Jones's magnetic performance as Troy, the critic found fault with the drama's "clunky" old-fashioned plot structure. Assisted by director Lloyd Richards and the audience responses at the out-of-town tryouts of* Fences, *Wilson had already completely rewritten it several times in an attempt to solve what he recognized as the play's structural problems.*

FRANK RICH

Review of Fences

1987

To hear his wife tell it, Troy Maxson, the middle-aged Pittsburgh sanitation worker at the center of *Fences*, is "so big" that he fills up his tenement house just by walking through it. Needless to say, that description could also apply to James Earl Jones, the actor who has found what may be the best role of his career in August Wilson's new play, at the 46th Street Theater. But the remarkable stature of the character — and of the performance — is not a matter of sheer size. If Mr. Jones's Troy is a mountainous man prone to tyrannical eruptions of rage, he is also a dignified, delicate figure capable of cradling a tiny baby, of pleading gravely to his wife for understanding, of standing still to stare death unflinchingly in the eye. A black man, a free man, a descendant of slaves, a menial laborer, a father, a husband, a lover — Mr. Jones's Troy embraces all the contradictions of being black and male and American in his time.

That time is 1957 — three decades after the period of Mr. Wilson's previous and extraordinary *Ma Rainey's Black Bottom.* For blacks like Troy in the industrial North of *Fences,* social and economic equality is more a legal principle than a reality: the Maxson's slum neighborhood, a panorama of grimy brick and smokestack-blighted sky in James D. Sandefur's eloquent design, is a cauldron of busted promises, waiting to boil over. The conflagration is still a decade away — the streetlights burn like the first sparks of distant insurrection — so Mr. Wilson writes about the pain of an extended family lost in the wilderness of de facto segregation and barren hope.

It speaks of the power of the play — and of the cast assembled by the director, Lloyd Richards — that Mr. Jones's patriarch doesn't devour the rest of *Fences* so much as become the life force that at once nurtures and stunts the characters who share his blood. The strongest countervailing player is his wife, Rose, luminously acted by Mary Alice. Rose is a quiet woman who, as she says, "planted herself" in the "hard and rocky" soil of her husband. But she never bloomed: marriage brought frustration and betrayal in equal measure with affection.

Even so, Ms. Alice's performance emphasizes strength over self-pity, open anger over festering bitterness. The actress finds the spiritual quotient in the acceptance that accompanies Rose's love for a scarred, profoundly complicated man. It's rare to find a marriage of any sort presented on stage with such balance — let alone one in which the husband has fathered children by three different women. Mr. Wilson grants both partners the right to want to escape the responsibilities of their domestic drudgery while affirming their respective claims to forgiveness.

The other primary relationship of *Fences* is that of Troy to his son Cory (Courtney B. Vance) — a promising seventeen-year-old football player being courted by a college recruiter. Troy himself was once a baseball player in the Negro Leagues — early enough to hit homers off Satchel Paige, too early to benefit from Jackie Robinson's breakthrough — and his bitter, long-ago disappointment leads him to decree a different future for his son. But while Troy wants Cory to settle for a workhorse trade guaranteeing a weekly paycheck, the boy resists. The younger Maxson is somehow convinced that the dreams of his black generation need not end in the city's mean alleys with the carting of white men's garbage.

The struggle between father and son over conflicting visions of black identity, aspirations, and values is the play's narrative fulcrum, and a paradigm of violent divisions that would later tear apart a society. As written, the conflict is also a didactic one, reminiscent of old-fashioned plays, black and white, about disputes between first-generation American parents and their rebellious children.

In *Ma Rainey* — set at a blues recording session — Mr. Wilson's characters were firecrackers exploding in a bottle, pursuing jagged theatrical riffs reflective of their music and of their intimacy with the Afro-American experience that gave birth to that music. The relative tameness of *Fences* — with its laboriously worked-out titular metaphor, its slow-fused Act I exposition — is as much an expression of its period as its predecessor was of the hotter 20s. Intentionally or not — and perhaps to the satisfaction of those who found the more esthetically daring *Ma Rainey* too "plotless" — Mr. Wilson invokes the clunkier dramaturgy of Odets, Miller, and Hansberry on this occasion.

Such formulaic theatrical tidiness, while exasperating at times, proves a minor price for the gripping second act (strengthened since the play's Yale debut in 1985) and for the scattered virtuoso passages throughout. Like *Ma Rainey* and the latest Wilson work seen at Yale (*Joe Turner's Come and Gone*, also promised for New York), *Fences* leaves no doubt that Mr. Wilson is a major writer, combining a poet's ear for vernacular with a robust sense of humor (political and sexual), a sure instinct for crackling dramatic incident, and a passionate commitment to a great subject.

Mr. Wilson continues to see history as fully as he sees his characters. In one scene, Troy and his oldest friend (played with brimming warmth by Ray Aranha) weave an autobiographical "talking blues" — a front-porch storytelling jaunt from the antebellum plantation through the pre-industrial urban South, jail, and northward migration. *Fences* is pointedly bracketed by two disparate wars that swallowed up black manhood, and, as always with Mr. Wilson, is as keenly cognizant of its characters' bonds to Africa, however muted here, as their bondage to white America. One hears the cadences of a centuries-old heritage in Mr. Jones's efforts to shout down the devil. It is a frayed scrap of timeless blues singing, unpretty but unquenchable, that proves the over-powering cathartic link among the disparate branches of the Maxson family tree.

Under the exemplary guidance of Mr. Richards — whose staging falters only in the awkward scene transitions — the entire cast is impressive, including Frankie R. Faison in the problematic (but finally devastating) role of a brain-damaged, horn-playing uncle named Gabriel, and Charles Brown, as a Maxson son who falls into the sociological crack separating the play's two principal generations. As Cory, Courtney B. Vance is not only formidable in challenging Mr. Jones to a psychological (and sometimes physical) kill-or-be-killed battle for supremacy but also seems to grow into Troy's vocal timbre and visage by the final scene. Like most sons, Mr. Vance just can't elude "the shadow" of his father, no matter how hard he tries. Such is the long shadow Mr. Jones's father casts in *Fences* that theatergoers from all kinds of families may find him impossible to escape.

ꙮ

MURIEL RUKEYSER *(1913–1980) was an outspoken feminist in her poetry, plays, and novels. Her wryly humorous prose poem "Myth" about Oedipus's meeting with the Sphinx, included in her book* Breaking Open *(1973), imagines a second encounter between them. Rukeyser offers a new perspective on the meaning of their exchange and suggests that Oedipus's tactless answer to the winged female monster when he first answers her riddle (and not Freud's hypothesis of the incest taboo) is the explanation of the Greek king's tragic fate.*

MURIEL RUKEYSER

Myth

1973

Long afterward, Oedipus, old and blinded, walked the
roads.   He smelled a familiar smell.   It was
the Sphinx.   Oedipus said, "I want to ask one question.
Why didn't I recognize my mother?" "You gave the
wrong answer," said the Sphinx.   "But that was what
made everything possible," said Oedipus.   "No," she said.
"When I asked, What walks on four legs in the morning,
two at noon, and three in the evening, you answered,
Man.   You didn't say anything about woman."
"When you say Man," said Oedipus, "you include women
too. Everyone knows that."   She said, "That's what
you think."

SANDRA SAARI, *a Norwegian critic, has compared the first draft of Ibsen's* A Doll House *with the published version and concluded that the playwright significantly changed the conflict between Nora and Torvald in his revision of his play. In the "Final Copy" of* A Doll House, *Ibsen transformed Nora into a mature person who becomes capable of defining reality for herself by the end of the drama. Saari's close reading of the two versions helps us understand Ibsen's refusal to say that he had deliberately worked for the cause of women's rights in* A Doll House. *In Saari's explanation, Ibsen believed "that the essential definition of a person is humanness, not gender, and that what causes things to appear otherwise are social constructs." Saari's article appeared in volume six of* Contemporary Approaches to Ibsen, *published in Oslo by Norwegian University Press in 1988.*

SANDRA SAARI

Female Becomes Human: Nora Transformed in A Doll House

1988

In his first notes for the play, Ibsen conceived of the conflict leading to complete confusion and finally to destruction. In the Final Copy, the conflict leads to Nora's clear, rational perception of reality and consequently to her rejection of the child-wife role. When the miracle doesn't happen, Nora is no longer willing to base her actions toward Torvald on the ideal of love. From the beginning of the play, Nora perceives that Torvald has faults such as egotism and jealousy, but, understanding that "miracles don't happen every day," she discounts these faults as being superficial, not essential. There is good reason for her to interpret them thus. Torvald describes himself as having great inner strength in a crisis, and he explicitly espouses love as his highest value.

In the Draft, Nora says Torvald forfeited her love when she saw that he wasn't better than she was. In the Final Copy, she says he forfeited her love when the miracle didn't happen. "The miracle," the approach of which Nora had already announced to an uncomprehending Mrs. Linde in Act 2, has the ring of unrealistic fantasy. But it is, in fact, a further development in the Final Copy, of Nora's ability to see things in a rational and ordered manner. What she means by "miracle" is: an action in the real world that confirms beyond all doubt her belief that their marriage is based on the shared ideal of love, in particular, that Torvald loves her, as she loves him, above all else, above even life itself. When the miracle doesn't happen, when what happens is instead a disconfirmation of her belief, then she relinquishes her belief.

The disconfirmation is unarguable. Upon receiving Krogstad's first letter, revealing the forgery and blackmail, Torvald responds with unmistakable self-centeredness. He dismisses Nora's protestations of having done it because "I have loved you above all else in the world," as mere "idiotic alibis." He berates Nora as "a hypocrite, a liar, and, even worse, a criminal," the social offense being for him the worst. He blames her father for her lack of proper upbringing, and her, for destroying all his own happiness, after all he has done for her. And it virtually goes without saying that he capitulates immediately to the blackmail and focuses all his concern on how to preserve appearances in the eyes of the world. There is never the slightest hint of any self-sacrifice to protect Nora. At Torvald's core is more of the petty egotism whose manifestations Nora had inaccurately interpreted as merely superficial.

But, it is not this evidence Nora cites in describing what makes Torvald a stranger to her. He is someone with whom she is no longer able to associate herself because of his hypocrisy. "After your terror was over," she says, "and when all danger was past, then for you, it was as though nothing at all had happened. I was, precisely as before, your little songbird, your doll, about whom you had to be twice as protective from now on." If Torvald can complacently return to their former relationship, if his actions don't strike him as highly anomalous in view of his professed ideals, then all along his professed ideals were a form of hypocrisy, were mere superficial rhetoric and not the description of his essential self that Nora had taken them to be. If that which would make them equal in essence — the mutuality of ideal love — doesn't inform the husband-wife relationship, then the form — male-dominated, hierarchical — in fact turns out to be the essence of the marriage. If Torvald's first duty isn't to her, then Nora's first duty is to herself.

At the end of Act 2, Nora had "danced herself free," to use Daniel Haakonsen's felicitous phrase, in response to a reality that didn't conform to Torvald's instruction. At the end of Act 3, Nora has rationally thought herself into freedom from Torvald's interpretation of reality. She then sets out to define reality for herself.

ꕥ

George Bernard Shaw *(1856–1950), the British playwright, was one of the first authors to recognize the importance of Ibsen's work in the theater. In* The Quintessence of Ibsenism *(1891; rev. ed. 1913) Shaw summarized the plot of the play and analyzed Nora's character with great sensitivity to the social issues that Ibsen had raised in the drama.*

George Bernard Shaw

On A Doll House

1891

In the famous [*Doll*] *House,* the pillar of society who owns the doll is a model husband, father, and citizen. In his little household, with the three darling children and the affectionate little wife, all on the most loving terms with one another, we have the sweet home, the womanly woman, the happy family life of the idealist's dream. Mrs. Nora Helmer is happy in the belief that she has attained a valid realization of all these illusions; that she is an ideal wife and mother; and that Helmer is an ideal husband who would, if the necessity arose, give his life to save her reputation. A few simply contrived incidents disabuse her effectually on all these points. One of her earliest acts of devotion to her husband has been the secret raising of a sum of money to enable him to make a tour which was necessary to restore his health. As he would have broken down sooner than go into debt, she has had to persuade him that the money was a gift from her father. It was really obtained from a moneylender, who refused to make her the loan unless she induced her father to endorse the promissory note. This being impossible, as her father was dying at the time, she took the shortest way out of the difficulty by writing the name herself, to the entire satisfaction of the moneylender, who, though not at all duped, knew that forged bills are often the surest to be paid. Since then she has slaved in secret at scrivener's work until she has nearly paid off the debt.

At this point Helmer is made manager of the bank in which he is employed; and the moneylender, wishing to obtain a post there, uses the forged bill to force Nora to exert her influence with Helmer on his behalf. But she, having a hearty contempt for the man, cannot be persuaded by him that there was any harm in putting her father's name on the bill, and ridicules the suggestion that the law would not recognize that she was right under the circumstances. It is her husband's own contemptuous denunciation of a forgery formerly committed by the moneylender himself that destroys her self-satisfaction and opens her eyes to her ignorance of the serious business of the world to which her husband belongs: the world outside the home he shares with her. When he goes on to tell her that commercial dishonesty is generally to be traced to the influence of bad mothers, she begins to perceive that the happy way in which she plays with the children, and the care she takes to dress them nicely, are not sufficient to constitute her a fit person to train them. To redeem the forged bill, she resolves to borrow the balance due upon it from an intimate friend of the family. She has learnt to coax her husband into giving her what she asks by appealing to his affection for her: that is, by playing all sorts of pretty tricks until he is wheedled into an amorous humor. This plan she has adopted without thinking about it, instinctively taking the line of least resistance with him. And now she naturally takes the same line with her husband's friend. An unexpected declaration of love from him is the result; and it at once explains to her the real nature of the domestic influence she has been so proud of.

All her illusions about herself are now shatterd. She sees herself as an ignorant and silly woman, a dangerous mother, and a wife kept for her husband's pleasure merely; but she clings all the harder to her illusion about him: He is still the ideal husband who would make any sacrifice to rescue her from ruin. She resolves to kill herself rather than allow him to destroy his own career by taking the forgery on himself to save her reputation. The final disillusion comes when he, instead of at once proposing to pursue this ideal line of conduct when he hears of the forgery, naturally enough flies into a vulgar rage and heaps invective on her for disgracing him. Then she sees that their whole family life has been a fiction: their home a mere doll's house in which they have been playing at ideal husband and father, wife and mother. So she leaves him then and there and goes out into the real world to find out its reality for herself, and to gain some position not fundamentally false, refusing to see her children again until she is fit to be in charge of them, or to live with him until she and he become capable of a more honorable relation to one another. He at first cannot understand what has happened, and flourishes the shattered ideals over her as if they were as potent as ever. He presents the course most agreeable to him — that of her staying at home and avoiding a scandal — as her duty to her husband, to her children, and to her religion; but the magic of these disguises is gone; and at last even he understands what has really happened, and sits down alone to wonder whether that more honorable relation can ever come to pass between them.

WILLIAM STRACHEY *wrote a letter describing the storm that caused Captain George Somers to run ashore with his ship and crew on the then-unknown island of Bermuda in 1610. This letter is considered to be one of the main sources influencing Shakespeare when he created* The Tempest *a short time afterwards.*

WILLIAM STRACHEY

From True Repertory of the Wrack

1610

A dreadful storm and hideous began to blow from out the northeast, which swelling and roaring as it were by fits, some hours with more violence than others, at length did beat all light from heaven; which like an hell of darkness turned black upon us, so much the more fuller of horror, as in such cases horror and fear use to overrun the troubled and overmastered senses of all, which (taken up with amazement) the ears lay so sensible to the terrible cries and murmurs of the winds, and distraction of our company, as who was most armed and best prepared was not a little shaken.

For four and twenty hours the storm in a restless tumult had blown so exceedingly, as we could not apprehend in our imaginations any possibility of greater violence, yet did we still find it, not only more terrible, but more constant, fury added to fury, and one storm urging a second more outrageous than the former; whether it so wrought upon our fears or indeed met with new forces. Sometimes strikes [shrieks?] in our ship amongst women and passengers not used to such hurly and discomforts made us look one upon the other with troubled hearts and panting bosoms; our clamors drowned in the winds, and the winds in thunder. Prayers might well be in the heart and lips, but drowned in the outcries of the officers. Nothing heard that could give comfort, nothing seen that might encourage hope. . . . It could not be said to rain, the waters like whole rivers did flood in the air. . . . Here the glut of water (as if throttling the wind erewhile) was no sooner a little emptied and qualified, but instantly the winds (as having gotten their mouths now free and at liberty) spake more loud and grew tumultuous and malignant. . . . There was not a moment in which the sudden splitting or instant oversetting of the ship was not expected.

Howbeit this was not all. It pleased God to bring a greater affliction yet upon us; for in the beginning of the storm we had received likewise a mighty leak. And the ship . . . was grown five foot suddenly deep with water above her ballast, and we almost drowned within whilst we sat looking when to perish from above. This, imparting no less terror than danger, ran through the whole ship with much fright and amazement, startled and turned the blood, and took down the braves of the most hardy mariner of them all, insomuch as he that before happily felt not the sorrow of others, now began to sorrow for himself when he saw such a pond of water so suddenly broken in, and which he knew could not (without present avoiding) but instantly sink him. . . .

Once, so huge a sea brake upon the poop and quarter° upon us, as it covered our ship from stern to stem, like a garment or a vast cloud, it filled her brim full for a while within, from the hatches up to the spar deck . . . with much clamor encouraged and called upon others; who gave her now up, rent in pieces and absolutely lost.

During all this time, the heavens looked so black upon us that it was not possible the elevation of the pole might be observed; nor a star by night, not sunbeam by day was to be seen. Only upon the Thursday night, Sir George Somers, being upon the watch, had an apparition of a little round light, like a faint star, trembling, and streaming along with a sparkling blaze, half the height upon the mainmast, and shooting sometimes from shroud to shroud, tempting to settle as it were upon any of the four shrouds. And for three or four hours together, or rather more, half the night it kept with us; running

---

poop and quarter: *Poop* is the enclosed superstructure of the stern of a ship; *quarter* refers to the quarter deck, the stern area of a ship's upper deck.

sometimes along the mainyard to the very end, and then returning. At which, Sir George Somers called divers° about him and showed them the same, who observed it with much wonder and carefulness. But upon a sudden, toward the morning watch, they lost the sight of it and knew not what way it made. The superstitious seamen make many constructions of this sea fire, which nevertheless is usual in storms: the same (it may be) which the Grecians were wont in the Mediterranean to call Castor and Pollux, of which, if one only appeared without the other, they took it for an evil sign of great tempest. The Italians, and such, who lie open to the Adriatic and Tyrrhene Sea, call it (a sacred Body) *Corpo sancto;* The Spaniards call it Saint Elmo,° and have an authentic and miraculous legend for it. Be it what it will, we laid other foundations of safety or ruin, then in the rising or falling of it, could it have served us now miraculously to have taken our height by, it might have struck amazement, and a reverence in our devotions, according to the due of a miracle. But it did not light us any whit the more to our known way, who ran now (as do hoodwinked men) at all adventures, sometimes north, and northeast, then north and by west, and sometimes half the compass.

. . . Sir George Somers, when no man dreamed of such happiness, had discovered and cried land. . . . We were enforced to run her ashore as near the land as we could, which brought us within three-quarters of a mile of shore. . . .

We found it to be the dangerous and dreaded island, or rather islands of the Bermuda. . . . And that the rather, because they be so terrible to all that ever touched on them, and such tempests, thunders, and other fearful objects are seen and heard about them, that they be called commonly the Devil's Islands, and are feared and avoided of all sea travelers alive above any other place in the world. Yet it pleased our merciful God to make even this hideous and hated place both the place of our safety and means of our deliverance.

And hereby also, I hope to deliver the world from a foul and general error: it being counted of most that they can be no habitation for men, but rather given over to devils and wicked spirits. Whereas indeed we find them now by experience to be as habitable and commodious as most countries of the same climate and situation; insomuch as if the entrance into them were as easy as the place itself is contenting, it had long ere this been inhabited as well as other islands. Thus shall we make it appear that Truth is the daughter of Time, and that men ought not to deny everything which is not subject to their own sense.

Sure it is that there are no rivers nor running springs of fresh water to be found upon any of them. When we came first, we digged and found certain gushings and soft bubblings which, being either in bottoms or on the side of hanging ground, were only fed with rain water which nevertheless soon sinketh into the earth and vanisheth away, or emptieth itself out of sight into the sea without any channel above or upon the superficies of the earth. For according as their rains fell, we had wells and pits (which we digged) either half full, or absolute exhausted and dry, howbeit some low bottoms (which

---

divers: Various — referring to members of the crew in this text. **Saint Elmo:** Named for the patron saint of sailors, St. Elmo's fire is a flaming phenomenon seen in stormy weather at prominent points on a ship; it is caused by a discharge of electricity.

the continual descent from the hills filled full, and in those flats could have no passage away) we found to continue as fishing ponds, standing pools, continually summer and winter full of fresh water.

A kind of webfooted fowl there is, of the bigness of an English green plover, or seamew, which all the summer we saw not, and in the darkest nights of November and December (for in the night they only feed) they would come forth, but not fly far from home, and hovering in the air, and over the sea, made a strange hollow and harsh howling . . . which birds with a light bough in a dark night (as in our lowbelling) we caught. I have been at the taking of three hundred in an hour, and we might have laden our boats. Our men found a pretty way to take them, which was by standing on the rocks or sands by the seaside, and hollowing, laughing, and making the strangest outcry that possibly they could. With the noise whereof the birds would come flocking to that place, and settle upon the very arms and head of him that so cried, and still creep nearer and nearer, answering the noise themselves; by which our men would weigh them with their hand, and which weighed heaviest they took for the best and let the others alone, and so our men would take twenty dozen in two hours of the chiefest of them; and they were a good and well-relished fowl, fat and full as a partridge . . . which birds for their blindness (for they see weakly in the day) and for their cry and hooting, we called the sea owl.

In these dangers and devilish disquiets (whilst the almighty God wrought for us and sent us, miraculously delivered from the calamities of the sea, all blessings upon the shore to content and bind us to gratefulness) thus enraged amongst ourselves, to the destruction each of other, into what a mischief and misery had we been given up, had we not had a governor with his authority to have suppressed the same? Yet was there a worse practice, faction, and conjuration afoot, deadly and bloody, in which the life of our governor with many others were threatened and could not but miscarry in his fall. But such is ever the will of God (who in the execution of His judgments, breaketh the firebrands upon the head of him who first kindleth them) there were, who conceived that our governor indeed neither durst, nor had authority to put in execution, or pass the act of justice upon anyone, how treacherous or impious so ever. . . . They persevered therefore not only to draw unto them such a number and associates as they could work in to the abandoning of our governor and to the inhabiting of this island. They had now purposed to have made a surprise of the storehouse. . . .

But as all giddy and lawless attempts have always something of imperfection, and that as well by the property of the action, which holdeth of disobedience and rebellion (both full of fear) as through the ignorance of the devisers themselves; so in this (besides those defects) there were some of the association, who not strong enough fortified in their own conceits, brake from the plot itself, and (before the time was ripe for the execution thereof) discovered the whole order, and every agent and actor thereof, who nevertheless were not suddenly apprehended, by reason the confederates were divided and separated in place, some with us, and the chief with Sir George Somers. . . .

JOAN TEMPLETON *prepared her ironic summary of the responses of a dozen critics writing about Ibsen's theme in his famous play for the* Publication of the Modern Language Association. *After reading the critics, you may find Templeton's conclusion surprises you in its uncompromising statement of uncommon sense.*

JOAN TEMPLETON

Is A Doll House *a Feminist Text?* *1989*

> A Doll House *is no more about women's rights than Shakespeare's* Richard II *is about the divine right of kings, or* Ghosts *about syphilis. . . . Its theme is the need of every individual to find out the kind of person he or she is and to strive to become that person.*[1]

Ibsen has been resoundingly saved from feminism, or, as it was called in his day, "the woman question." His rescuers customarily cite a statement the dramatist made on 26 May 1898 at a seventieth-birthday banquet given in his honor by the Norwegian Women's Rights League:

> I thank you for the toast, but must disclaim the honor of having consciously worked for the women's rights movement. . . . True enough, it is desirable to solve the woman problem, along with all the others; but that has not been the whole purpose. My task has been the description of humanity.[2]

Ibsen's champions like to take this disavowal as a precise reference to his purpose in writing *A Doll House* twenty years earlier, his "original intention," according to Maurice Valency.[3] Ibsen's biographer Michael Meyer urges all reviewers of *Doll House* revivals to learn Ibsen's speech by heart,[4] and James McFarlane, editor of *The Oxford Ibsen*, includes it in his explanatory material on *A Doll House*, under "Some Pronouncements of the Author," as though Ibsen had been speaking of the play.[5] Whatever propaganda feminists may have made of *A Doll House*, Ibsen, it is argued, never meant to write a play about the highly topical subject of women's rights; Nora's conflict represents something other than, or something more than, woman's. In an article commemorating the half century of Ibsen's death, R. M. Adams explains, "*A Doll House* represents a woman imbued with the idea of becoming a person, but it proposes nothing categorical about women becoming people; in fact, its real theme has nothing to do with the sexes."[6] Over twenty years later, after feminism had resurfaced as an international movement, Einar Haugen, the doyen

---

[1]Michael Meyer, *Ibsen* (Garden City: Doubleday, 1971), 457.

[2]Henrik Ibsen, *Letters and Speeches*, ed. and trans. Evert Sprinchorn (New York: Hill, 1964), 337.

[3]Maurice Valency, *The Flower and the Castle: An Introduction to Modern Drama* (New York: Schocken, 1982), 151.

[4]Meyer, 774.

[5]James McFarlane, "*A Doll's House:* Commentary" in *The Oxford Ibsen*, ed. McFarlane (Oxford UP, 1961), V, 456.

[6]R. M. Adams, "The Fifty-First Anniversary," *Hudson Review* 10 (1957), 416.

of American Scandinavian studies, insisted that "Ibsen's Nora is not just a woman arguing for female liberation; she is much more. She embodies the comedy as well as the tragedy of modern life."[7] In the Modern Language Association's *Approaches to Teaching* A Doll House, the editor speaks disparagingly of "reductionist views of [*A Doll House*] as a feminist drama." Summarizing a "major theme" in the volume as "the need for a broad view of the play and a condemnation of a static approach," she warns that discussions of the play's "connection with feminism" have value only if they are monitored, "properly channeled and kept firmly linked to Ibsen's text."[8]

Removing the woman question from *A Doll House* is presented as part of a corrective effort to free Ibsen from his erroneous reputation as a writer of thesis plays, a wrongheaded notion usually blamed on Shaw, who, it is claimed, mistakenly saw Ibsen as the nineteenth century's greatest iconoclast and offered that misreading to the public as *The Quintessence of Ibsenism.* Ibsen, it is now de rigueur to explain, did not stoop to "issues." He was a poet of the truth of the human soul. That Nora's exit from her dollhouse has long been the principal international symbol for women's issues, including many that far exceed the confines of her small world, is irrelevant to the essential meaning of *A Doll House,* a play, in Richard Gilman's phrase, "pitched beyond sexual difference."[9] Ibsen, explains Robert Brustein, "was completely indifferent to (the woman question) except as a metaphor for individual freedom."[10] Discussing the relation of *A Doll House* to feminism, Halvdan Koht, author of the definitive Norwegian Ibsen life, says in summary, "Little by little the topical controversy died away; what remained was the work of art, with its demand for truth in every human relation."[11]

Thus, it turns out, the *Uncle Tom's Cabin* of the women's rights movement is not really about women at all. "Fiddle-faddle," pronounced R. M. Adams, dismissing feminist claims for the play.[12] Like angels, Nora has no sex. Ibsen meant her to be Everyman.

TENNESSEE WILLIAMS *published his notes describing how he envisioned an ideal production of* The Glass Menagerie *on the stage in 1945, soon after the play had survived its shaky premiere at the Civic Theatre in Chicago. Jo Mielziner designed the sets and Paul Bowles composed the music for the original production. The play caught on with audiences because in the first three weeks of its run it was championed*

[7]Einar Haugen, *Ibsen's Drama: Author to Audience* (Minneapolis: U of Minnesota P, 1979), vii.

[8]Yvonne Shafer, ed., *Approaches to Teaching Ibsen's* A Doll House (New York: MLA, 1985), 32.

[9]Richard Gilman, *The Making of Modern Drama* (New York: Farrar, 1972), 65.

[10]Robert Brustein, *The Theatre of Revolt* (New York: Little, 1962), 105.

[11]Halvdan Koht, *Life of Ibsen* (New York: Blom, 1971), 323.

[12]Adams, 416.

almost daily in laudatory articles by the Chicago Tribune *theater critic Claudia Cassidy. As Donald Spoto wrote in* The Kindness of Strangers: The Life of Tennessee Williams *(1985), "In an unusual example of journalistic salvation, a play was for once not lost but kept alive because of critical support."*

TENNESSEE WILLIAMS

Production Notes to The Glass Menagerie

1945

Being a "memory play," *The Glass Menagerie* can be presented with unusual freedom of convention. Because of its considerably delicate or tenuous material, atmospheric touches and subtleties of direction play a particularly important part. Expressionism and all other unconventional techniques in drama have only one valid aim, and that is a closer approach to truth. When a play employs unconventional techniques, it is not, or certainly shouldn't be, trying to escape its responsibility of dealing with reality, or interpreting experience, but is actually or should be attempting to find a closer approach, a more penetrating and vivid expression of things as they are. The straight realistic play with its genuine Frigidaire and authentic ice cubes, its characters that speak exactly as its audience speaks, corresponds to the academic landscape and has the same virtue of a photographic likeness. Everyone should know nowadays the unimportance of the photographic in art: that truth, life, or reality is an organic thing which the poetic imagination can represent or suggest, in essence, only through transformation, through changing into other forms than those which were merely present in appearance.

These remarks are not meant as a preface only to this particular play. They have to do with a conception of a new, plastic theater which must take the place of the exhausted theater of realistic conventions if the theater is to resume vitality as a part of our culture.

The Screen Device. There is *only one important difference between the original and acting version of the play* and that is the *omission* in the latter of the device which I tentatively included in my *original* script. This device was the use of a screen on which were projected magic-lantern slides bearing images or titles. I do not regret the omission of this device from the present Broadway production. The extraordinary power of Miss Taylor's° performance made it suitable to have the utmost simplicity in the physical production. But I think it may be interesting to some readers to see how this device was conceived. So I am putting it into the published manuscript. These images and legends, projected from behind, were cast on a section of wall between the front-room and dining-room areas, which should be indistinguishable from the rest when not in use.

Miss Taylor's: Laurette Taylor (1884–1946) played the role of Amanda in the original Broadway production.

The purpose of this will probably be apparent. It is to give accent to certain values in each scene. Each scene contains a particular point (or several) which is structurally the most important. In an episodic play, such as this, the basic structure or narrative line may be obscured from the audience; the effect may seem fragmentary rather than architectural. This may not be the fault of the play so much as a lack of attention in the audience. The legend or image upon the screen will strengthen the effect of what is merely allusion in the writing and allow the primary point to be made more simply and lightly than if the entire responsibility were on the spoken lines. Aside from this structural value, I think the screen will have a definite emotional appeal, less definable but just as important. An imaginative producer or director may invent many other uses for this device than those indicated in the present script. In fact the possibilities of the device seem much larger to me than the instance of this play can possibly utilize.

The Music. Another extra-literary accent in this play is provided by the use of music. A single recurring tune, "The Glass Menagerie," is used to give emotional emphasis to suitable passages. This tune is like circus music, not when you are on the grounds or in the immediate vicinity of the parade, but when you are at some distance and very likely thinking of something else. It seems under those circumstances to continue almost interminably and it weaves in and out of your preoccupied consciousness; then it is the lightest, most delicate music in the world and perhaps the saddest. It expresses the surface vivacity of life with the underlying strain of immutable and inexpressible sorrow. When you look at a piece of delicately spun glass you think of two things: how beautiful it is and how easily it can be broken. Both of those ideas should be woven into the recurring tune, which dips in and out of the play as if it were carried on a wind that changes. It serves as a thread of connection and allusion between the narrator with his separate point in time and space and the subject of his story. Between each episode it returns as reference to the emotion, nostalgia, which is the first condition of the play. It is primarily Laura's music and therefore comes out most clearly when the play focuses upon her and the lovely fragility of glass which is her image.

The Lighting. The lighting in the play is not realistic. In keeping with the atmosphere of memory, the stage is dim. Shafts of light are focused on selected areas or actors, sometimes in contradistinction to what is the apparent center. For instance, in the quarrel scene between Tom and Amanda, in which Laura has no active part, the clearest pool of light is on her figure. This is also true of the supper scene, when her silent figure on the sofa should remain the visual center. The light upon Laura should be distinct from the others, having a peculiar pristine clarity such as light used in early religious portraits of female saints or madonnas. A certain correspondence to light in religious paintings, such as El Greco's,° where the figures are radiant in atmosphere that is relatively dusky,

---

El Greco: Painter (1541–1614) known for the uncanny lighting in his large canvases.

could be effectively used throughout the play. (It will also permit a more effective use of the screen.) A free, imaginative use of light can be of enormous value in giving a mobile, plastic quality to plays of a more or less static nature.

Tennessee Williams *wrote the story "Portrait of a Girl in Glass" in 1943. He turned the story into a play,* The Gentleman Caller, *while he was under contract with M-G-M and then rewrote the script as* The Glass Menagerie, *which opened in Chicago in December 1944.*

Williams continued writing short stories in addition to plays for most of his life. "Portrait of a Girl in Glass" was published in 1948 in his first collection of short fiction, One Arm and Other Stories. *An autobiographical story, it is based on Williams's close relationship with his sister, Rose, who was institutionalized after her prefrontal lobotomy in 1937. Williams used his own name Tom for himself as one of the characters in the story, and he called the character based on his sister Laura. The story takes place in St. Louis in the early 1930s, during the Depression, at a time when Williams had been taken out of college by his father to work at the International Shoe Company, where his father had found a job fifteen years before.*

Tennessee Williams

Portrait of a Girl in Glass 1948

We lived in a third floor apartment on Maple Street in Saint Louis, on a block which also contained the Ever-ready Garage, a Chinese laundry, and a bookie shop disguised as a cigar store.

Mine was an anomalous character, one that appeared to be slated for radical change or disaster, for I was a poet who had a job in a warehouse. As for my sister Laura, she could be classified even less readily than I. She made no positive motion toward the world but stood at the edge of the water, so to speak, with feet that anticipated too much cold to move. She'd never have budged an inch, I'm pretty sure, if my mother who was a relatively aggressive sort of woman had not shoved her roughly forward, when Laura was twenty years old, by enrolling her as a student in a nearby business college. Out of her "magazine money" (she sold subscriptions to women's magazines), Mother had paid my sister's tuition for a term of six months. It did not work out. Laura tried to memorize the typewriter keyboard, she had a chart at home, she used to sit silently in front of it for hours, staring at it while she cleaned and polished her infinite number of little glass ornaments. She did this every evening after dinner. Mother would caution me to be very quiet. "Sister is looking at her typewriter chart!" I felt somehow that it would do her no good, and I was right. She would seem to know the positions of the keys until the weekly speed drill got underway, and then they would fly from her mind like a bunch of startled birds.

At last she couldn't bring herself to enter the school any more. She kept this failure a secret for a while. She left the house each morning as before and spent six hours walking around the park. This was in February, and all the walking outdoors regardless of weather brought on influenza. She was in bed for a couple of weeks with a curiously happy little smile on her face. Of course Mother phoned the business college to let them know she was ill. Whoever was talking on the other end of the line had some trouble, it seems, in remembering who Laura was, which annoyed my mother and she spoke up pretty sharply. "Laura has been attending that school of yours for two months, you certainly ought to recognize her name!" Then came the stunning disclosure. The person sharply retorted, after a moment or two, that now she *did* remember the Wingfield girl, and that she had not been at the business college *once* in about a month. Mother's voice became strident. Another person was brought to the phone to verify the statement of the first. Mother hung up and went to Laura's bedroom where she lay with a tense and frightened look in place of the faint little smile. Yes, admitted my sister, what they said was true. "I couldn't go any longer, it scared me too much, it made me sick at the stomach!"

After this fiasco, my sister stayed at home and kept in her bedroom mostly. This was a narrow room that had two windows on a dusky areaway between two wings of the building. We called this areaway Death Valley for a reason that seems worth telling. There were a great many alley cats in the neighborhood and one particularly vicious dirty white Chow who stalked them continually. In the open or on the fire escapes they could usually elude him but now and again he cleverly contrived to run some youngster among them into the cul-de-sac of this narrow areaway at the far end of which, directly beneath my sister's bedroom windows, they made the blinding discovery that what had appeared to be an avenue of escape was really a locked arena, a gloomy vault of concrete and brick with walls too high for any cat to spring, in which they must suddenly turn to spit at their death until it was hurled upon them. Hardly a week went by without a repetition of this violent drama. The areaway had grown to be hateful to Laura because she could not look out on it without recalling the screams and the snarls of killing. She kept the shades drawn down, and as Mother would not permit the use of electric current except when needed, her days were spent almost in perpetual twilight. There were three pieces of dingy ivory furniture in the room, a bed, a bureau, a chair. Over the bed was a remarkably bad religious painting, a very effeminate head of Christ with teardrops visible just below the eyes. The charm of the room was produced by my sister's collection of glass. She loved colored glass and had covered the walls with shelves of little glass articles, all of them light and delicate in color. These she washed and polished with endless care. When you entered the room there was always this soft, transparent radiance in it which came from the glass absorbing whatever faint light came through the shades on Death Valley. I have no idea how many articles there were of this delicate glass. There must have been hundreds of them. But Laura could tell you exactly. She loved each one.

She lived in a world of glass and also a world of music. The music came from a 1920 victrola and a bunch of records that dated from about the same period, pieces such as "Whispering" or "The Love Nest" or "Dardanella." These records were souvenirs of our father, a man whom we barely remembered, whose name was spoken rarely. Before his sudden and unexplained disappearance from our lives, he had made this gift to the household, the phonograph and the records, whose music remained as a sort of apology for him. Once in a while, on payday at the warehouse, I would bring home a new record. But Laura seldom cared for these new records, maybe because they reminded her too much of the noisy tragedies in Death Valley or the speed drills at the business college. The tunes she loved were the ones she had always heard. Often she sang to herself at night in her bedroom. Her voice was thin, it usually wandered off-key. Yet it had a curious child-like sweetness. At eight o'clock in the evening I sat down to write in my own mousetrap of a room. Through the closed doors, through the walls, I would hear my sister singing to herself, a piece like "Whispering" or "I Love You" or "Sleepy Time Gal," losing the tune now and then but always preserving the minor atmosphere of the music. I think that was why I always wrote such strange and sorrowful poems in those days. Because I had in my ears the wispy sound of my sister serenading her pieces of colored glass, washing them while she sang or merely looking down at them with her vague blue eyes until the points of gem-like radiance in them gently drew the arching particles of reality from her mind and finally produced a state of hypnotic calm in which she even stopped singing or washing the glass and merely sat without motion until my mother knocked at the door and warned her against the waste of electric current.

I don't believe that my sister was actually foolish. I think the petals of her mind had simply closed through fear, and it's no telling how much they had closed upon in the way of secret wisdom. She never talked very much, not even to me, but once in a while she did pop out with something that took you by surprise.

After work at the warehouse or after I'd finished my writing in the evening, I'd drop in her room for a little visit because she had a restful and soothing effect on nerves that were worn rather thin from trying to ride two horses simultaneously in two opposite directions.

I usually found her seated in the straight-back ivory chair with a piece of glass cupped tenderly in her palm.

"What are you doing? Talking to it?" I asked.

"No," she answered gravely, "I was just looking at it."

On the bureau were two pieces of fiction which she had received as Christmas or birthday presents. One was a novel called the *Rose-Garden Husband* by someone whose name escapes me. The other was *Freckles* by Gene Stratton Porter. I never saw her reading the *Rose-Garden Husband,* but the other book was one that she actually lived with. It had probably never occurred to Laura that a book was something you read straight through and then laid aside as finished. The character Freckles, a one-armed orphan youth who worked in a lumber camp, was someone that she invited into her bedroom now and then for a friendly visit just as she did me. When I came in and found this novel open upon her lap, she would gravely remark that Freckles was having some trouble with the foreman of the lumber camp or that he had just received an injury to his spine when a tree fell on him. She frowned with genuine sorrow when she reported these misadventures of her story-book hero, possibly not recalling how successfully he came through them all, that the injury to the spine fortuitously resulted in the discovery of rich parents and that the bad-tempered foreman had a heart of gold at the end of the book. Freckles became involved in romance with a girl he called The Angel, but my sister usually stopped reading when this girl became too prominent in the story. She closed the book or turned back to the lonelier periods in the orphan's story. I only remember her making one reference to this heroine of the novel. "The Angel is nice," she said, "but seems to be kind of conceited about her looks."

Then one time at Christmas, while she was trimming the artificial tree, she picked up the Star of Bethlehem that went on the topmost branch and held it gravely toward the chandelier.

"Do stars have five points really?" she enquired.

This was the sort of thing that you didn't believe and that made you stare at Laura with sorrow and confusion.

"No," I told her, seeing she really meant it, "they're round like the earth and most of them much bigger."

She was gently surprised by this new information. She went to the window to look up at the sky which was, as usual during Saint Louis winters, completely shrouded by smoke.

"It's hard to tell," she said, and returned to the tree.

So time passed on till my sister was twenty-three. Old enough to be married, but the fact of the matter was she had never even had a date with a boy. I don't believe this seemed as awful to her as it did to Mother.

At breakfast one morning Mother said to me, "Why don't you cultivate some nice young friends? How about down at the warehouse? Aren't there some young men down there you could ask to dinner?"

This suggestion surprised me because there was seldom quite enough food on her table to satisfy three people. My mother was a terribly stringent housekeeper, God knows we were poor enough in actuality, but my mother had an almost obsessive dread of becoming even poorer. A not unreasonable fear since the man of the house was a poet who worked in a warehouse, but one which I thought played too important a part in all her calculations.

Almost immediately Mother explained herself.

"I think it might be nice," she said, "for your sister."

I brought Jim home to dinner a few nights later. Jim was a big red-haired Irishman who had the scrubbed and polished look of well-kept chinaware. His big square hands seemed to have a direct and very innocent hunger for touching his friends. He was always clapping them on your arms or shoulders and they burned through the cloth of your shirt like plates taken out of an oven. He was the best-liked man in the warehouse and oddly enough he was the only one that I was on good terms with. He found me agreeably ridiculous, I think. He knew of my secret practice of retiring to a cabinet in the lavatory and working on rhyme schemes when work was slack in the warehouse, and of sneaking up on the roof now and then to smoke my cigarette with a view across the river at the undulant open country of Illinois. No doubt I was classified as screwy in Jim's mind as much as in the others', but while their attitude was suspicious and hostile when they first knew me, Jim's was warmly tolerant from the beginning. He called me Slim, and gradually his cordial acceptance drew the others around, and while he remained the only one who actually had anything to do with me, the others had now begun to smile when they saw me as people smile at an oddly fashioned dog who crosses their path at some distance.

Nevertheless it took some courage for me to invite Jim to dinner. I thought about it all week and delayed the action till Friday noon, the last possible moment, as the dinner was set for that evening.

"What are you doing tonight?" I finally asked him.

"Not a God damn thing," said Jim. "I had a date but her Aunt took sick and she's hauled her freight to Centralia!"

"Well," I said, "why don't you come over for dinner?"

"Sure!" said Jim. He grinned with astonishing brightness.

I went outside to phone the news to Mother.

Her voice that was never tired responded with an energy that made the wires crackle.

"I suppose he's Catholic?" she said.

"Yes," I told her, remembering the tiny silver cross on his freckled chest.

"Good!" she said. "I'll bake a salmon loaf!"

And so we rode home together in his jalopy.

I had a curious feeling of guilt and apprehension as I led the lamb-like Irishman up three flights of cracked marble steps to the door of Apartment F, which was not thick enough to hold inside it the odor of baking salmon.

Never having a key, I pressed the bell.

"Laura!" came Mother's voice. "That's Tom and Mr. Delaney! Let them in!"

There was a long, long pause.

"Laura?" she called again. "I'm busy in the kitchen, you answer the door!"

Then at last I heard my sister's footsteps. They went right past the door at which we were standing and into the parlor. I heard the creaking noise of the phonograph crank. Music commenced. One of the oldest records, a march of Sousa's, put on to give her the courage to let in a stranger.

The door came timidly open and there she stood in a dress from Mother's wardrobe, a black chiffon ankle-length and high-heeled slippers on which she balanced uncertainly like a tipsy crane of melancholy plumage. Her eyes stared back at us with a glassy brightness and her delicate wing-like shoulders were hunched with nervousness.

"Hello!" said Jim, before I could introduce him.

He stretched out his hand. My sister touched it only for a second.

"Excuse me!" she whispered, and turned with a breathless rustle back to her bedroom door, the sanctuary beyond it briefly revealing itself with the tinkling, muted radiance of glass before the door closed rapidly but gently on her wraith-like figure.

Jim seemed to be incapable of surprise.

"Your sister?" he asked.

"Yes, that was her," I admitted. "She's terribly shy with strangers."

"She looks like you," said Jim, "except she's pretty."

Laura did not reappear till called to dinner. Her place was next to Jim at the drop-leaf table and all through the meal her figure was slightly tilted away from his. Her face was feverishly bright and one eyelid, the one on the side toward Jim, had developed a nervous wink. Three times in the course of the dinner she dropped her fork on her plate with a terrible clatter and she was continually raising the water glass to her lips for hasty little gulps. She went on doing this even after the water was gone from the glass. And her handling of the silver became more awkward and hurried all the time.

I thought of nothing to say.

To Mother belonged the conversational honors, such as they were. She asked the caller about his home and family. She was delighted to learn that his father had a business of his own, a retail shoe store somewhere in Wyoming. The news that he went to night school to study accounting was still more edifying. What was his heart set on beside the warehouse? Radio-engineering? My, my, my! It was easy to see that here was a very up-and-coming young man who was certainly going to make his place in the world!

Then she started to talk about her children. Laura, she said, was not cut out for business. She was domestic, however, and making a home was really a girl's best bet.

Jim agreed with all this and seemed not to sense the ghost of an implication. I suffered through it dumbly, trying not to see Laura trembling more and more beneath the incredible unawareness of Mother.

And bad as it was, excruciating in fact, I thought with dread of the moment when dinner was going to be over, for then the diversion of food would be taken away, we would have to go into the little steam-heated parlor. I fancied the four of us having run out of talk, even Mother's seemingly endless store of questions about Jim's home and his job all used up finally — the four of us, then, just sitting there in the parlor, listening to the hiss of the radiator and nervously clearing our throats in the kind of self-consciousness that gets to be suffocating.

But when the blancmange was finished, a miracle happened.

Mother got up to clear the dishes away. Jim gave me a clap on the shoulders and said, "Hey, Slim, let's go have a look at those old records in there!"

He sauntered carelessly into the front room and flopped down on the floor beside the victrola. He began sorting through the collection of worn-out records and reading their titles aloud in a voice so hearty that it shot like beams of sunlight through the vapors of self-consciousness engulfing my sister and me.

He was sitting directly under the floor-lamp and all at once my sister jumped up and said to him, "Oh — you have freckles!"

Jim grinned. "Sure that's what my folks call me — Freckles!"

"Freckles?" Laura repeated. She looked toward me as if for the confirmation of some too wonderful hope. I looked away quickly, not knowing whether to feel relieved or alarmed at the turn that things were taking.

Jim had wound the victrola and put on *Dardanella*.

He grinned at Laura.

"How about you an' me cutting the rug a little?"

"What?" said Laura breathlessly, smiling and smiling.

"Dance!" he said, drawing her into his arms.

As far as I knew she had never danced in her life. But to my everlasting wonder she slipped quite naturally into those huge arms of Jim's, and they danced round and around the small steam-heated parlor, bumping against the sofa and chairs and laughing loudly and happily together. Something opened up in my sister's face. To say it was love is not too hasty a judgment, for after all he had freckles and that was what his folks called him. Yes, he had undoubtedly assumed the identity — for all practical purposes — of the one-armed orphan youth who lived in the Limberlost, that tall and misty region to which she retreated whenever the walls of Apartment F became too close to endure.

Mother came back in with some lemonade. She stopped short as she entered the portieres.

"Good heavens! Laura? Dancing?"

Her look was absurdly grateful as well as startled.

"But isn't she stepping all over you, Mr. Delaney?"

"What if she does?" said Jim, with bearish gallantry. "I'm not made of eggs!"

"Well, well, well!" said Mother, senselessly beaming.

"She's light as a feather!" said Jim. "With a little more practice she'd dance as good as Betty!"

There was a little pause of silence.

"Betty?" said Mother.

"The girl I go out with!" said Jim.

"Oh!" said Mother.

She set the pitcher of lemonade carefully down and with her back to the caller and her eyes on me, she asked him just how often he and the lucky young lady went out together.

"Steady!" said Jim.

Mother's look, remaining on my face, turned into a glare of fury.

"Tom didn't mention that you went out with a girl!"

"Nope," said Jim. "I didn't mean to let the cat out of the bag. The boys at the warehouse'll kid me to death when Slim gives the news away."

He laughed heartily but his laughter dropped heavily and awkwardly away as even his dull senses were gradually penetrated by the unpleasant sensation the news of Betty had made.

"Are you thinking of getting married?" said Mother.

"First of next month!" he told her.

It took her several moments to pull herself together. Then she said in a dismal tone, "How nice! If Tom had only told us we could have asked you *both*!"

Jim had picked up his coat.

"Must you be going?" said Mother.

"I hope it don't seem like I'm rushing off," said Jim, "but Betty's gonna get back on the eight o'clock train an' by the time I get my jalopy down to the Wabash depot —"

"Oh, then, we mustn't keep you."

Soon as he'd left, we all sat down, looking dazed.

Laura was the first to speak.

"Wasn't he nice?" she asked. "And all those freckles!"

"Yes," said Mother. Then she turned to me.

"You didn't mention that he was engaged to be married!"

"Well, how did I know that he was engaged to be married?"

"I thought you called him your best friend down at the warehouse?"

"Yes, but I didn't know he was going to be married!"

"How peculiar!" said Mother. "How very peculiar!"

"No," said Laura gently, getting up from the sofa. "There's nothing peculiar about it."

She picked up one of the records and blew on its surface a little as if it were dusty, then set it softly back down.

"People in love," she said, "take everything for granted."

What did she mean by that? I never knew.

She slipped quietly back to her room and closed the door.

Not very long after that I lost my job at the warehouse. I was fired for writing a poem on the lid of a shoe-box. I left Saint Louis and took to moving around. The cities swept about me like dead leaves, leaves that were brightly colored but torn away from the branches. My nature changed. I grew to be firm and sufficient.

In five years' time I had nearly forgotten home. I had to forget it, I couldn't carry it with me. But once in a while, usually in a strange town before I have found companions, the shell of deliberate hardness is broken through. A door comes softly and irresistibly open. I hear the tired old music my unknown father left in the place he abandoned as faithlessly as I. I see the faint and sorrowful radiance of the glass, hundreds of little transparent pieces of it in very delicate colors. I hold my breath, for if my sister's face appears among them — the night is hers!

ꕥ

AUGUST WILSON *was interviewed by David Savran about the father-son relationship in* Fences *between Troy Maxson and his son Cory. The interview was published in Savran's book* In Their Own Voices *(1987).*

August Wilson

Interview with David Savran 1987

Savran: In reading *Fences,* I came to view Troy more and more critically as the play progressed, sharing Rose's point of view. We see that Troy has been crippled by his father. That's being replayed in Troy's relationship with Cory. Do you think there's a way out of that cycle?

Wilson: Surely. First of all, we're all like our parents. The things we are taught early in life, how to respond to the world, our sense of morality — everything, we get from them. Now you can take that legacy and do with it anything you want to do. It's in your hands. Cory is Troy's son. How can he be Troy's son without sharing Troy's values? I was trying to get at why Troy made the choices he made, how they have influenced his values and how he attempts to pass those along to his son. Each generation gives the succeeding generation what they think they need. One question in the play is "Are the tools we are given sufficient to compete in a world that is different from the one our parents knew?" I think they are — it's just that we have to do different things with the tools. That's all Troy has to give. Troy's flaw is that he does not recognize that the world was changing. That's because he spent fifteen years in a penitentiary.

As African-Americans, we should demand to participate in society as Africans. That's the way out of the vicious cycle of poverty and neglect that exists in 1987 in America, where you have a huge percentage of blacks living in the equivalent of South African townships, in housing projects. No one is inviting these people to participate in society. Look at the poverty levels — $8,500 for a family of four, if you have $8,501 you're not counted. Those statistics would go up enormously if we had an honest assessment of the cost of living in America. I don't know how anybody can support a family of four on $8,500. What I'm saying is that 85 or 90 percent of blacks in America are living in abject poverty and, for the most part, are crowded into what amount to concentration camps. The situation for blacks in America is worse than it was forty years ago. Some sociologists will tell you about the tremendous progress we've made. They didn't put me out when I walked in the door. And you can always point to someone who works on Wall Street, or is a doctor. But they don't count in the larger scheme of things.

Savran: Do you have any idea how these political changes could take place?

Wilson: I'm not sure. I know that blacks must be allowed their cultural differences. I think the process of assimilation to white American society was a big mistake. We don't want to be like you. Blacks living in housing projects are isolated from the society, for the most part — living as they choose, as Africans. Only they don't realize the value in what they're doing because they have accepted their victimization. They've marked themselves as victims. Once they recognize that, they can begin to move through society in a different manner, from a stronger position, and claim what is theirs.

Savran: A project of yours is to point up what happens when oppression is internalized.

Wilson: Yes, transfer of aggression to the wrong target. I think it's interesting that the two roads open to blacks for "full participation" are entertainment and sports. *Ma Rainey* and *Fences,* and I didn't plan it that way. I don't think that they're the correct roads. I think Troy's right. Now with the benefit of historical perspective, I can say that the athletic scholarship was actually a way of exploiting. Now you've got two million kids who think they're going to play in the NBA. In the sixties the universities made a lot of money off of athletics. You had kids playing for free who, by and large, were not getting educated, were taking courses in basketweaving. Some of them could barely read.

Savran: Troy may be right about that issue, but it seems that he has passed on certain destructive traits in spite of himself. Take the hostility between father and son.

Wilson: I think every generation says to the previous generation: you're in my way, I've got to get by. The father-son conflict is actually a normal generational conflict that happens all the time.

Savran: So it's a healthy and a good thing?

Wilson: Oh, sure. Troy is seeing this boy walk around, smelling his piss. Two men cannot live in the same household. Troy would have been tremendously disappointed if Cory had not challenged him. Troy knows that this boy has to go out and do battle with that world: "So I had best prepare him because I know that's a harsh, cruel place out there. But that's going to be easy compared to what he's getting here. Ain't nobody gonna whip your ass like I'm gonna whip it." He has a tremendous love for the kid. But he's not going to say, "I love you," he's going to demonstrate it. He's carrying garbage for seventeen years just for the kid. The only world Troy knows is the one that he made. Cory's going to go on to find another one, he's going to arrive at the same place as Troy. I think one of the most important lines in the play is when Troy is talking about his father: "I got to the place where I could feel him kicking in my blood and knew that the only thing that separated us was the matter of a few years."

Hopefully, Cory will do things a bit differently with his son. For Troy, sports was not the way to go, the white man wouldn't let him get away with that. "Get you a job, with your hands, something that nobody can take away from you." The idea of school — he doesn't know what that is. That's for white folks. Very few blacks had paperwork jobs. But if you knew how to fix cars, you could always make some money. That's what Troy wants for Cory. There aren't many people who ever jumped up in Troy's face. So he's proud of the kid at the same time that he expresses a hurt that all men feel. You got to cut your kid loose at some point. There's that sense of loss and separation. You find out how Troy left his father's house and you see how Cory leaves his house. I suspect with Cory it will repeat with some differences and maybe, after five or six generations, they'll find a different way to do it.

Savran: Where Cory ends up is very ambiguous, as a marine in 1965.

Wilson: Yes. For the average black kid on the street, that was an alternative. You went into the army because you could learn how to do something. I can remember my parents talking about the son of some friends: "He's in the navy. He *did* something" — as opposed to standing on the street corner, shooting drugs, drinking wine, and robbing stores. Lyons says to Cory, "I always knew you were going to make something out of yourself." It really wounds me. He's a corporal in the marines. For blacks, that is a sense of accomplishment. Therein lies one of the tragedies of blacks in America. Cory says, "I don't know. I put in six years. That's enough." Anyone who goes into the army and makes a career out of it is a loser. They sit there and are nurtured by the army and they don't have to confront life. Then they get out of the army and find there's nothing to do. They didn't learn any skills. And if they did, they can't find a job. Four months later, they're shooting dope. In the sixties a whole bunch of blacks went over, fought and died in the Vietnam War. The survivors came back to the same street corners and found out nothing had changed. They still couldn't get a job.

At the end of *Fences* every person, with the exception of Raynell, is institutionalized. Rose is in a church. Lyons is in a penitentiary. Gabriel's in a mental hospital, and Cory's in the marines. The only free person is the girl, Troy's daughter, the hope for the future. That was conscious on my part because in '57 that's what I saw. Blacks have relied on institutions which are really foreign — except for the black church, which has been our saving grace. I have some problems with it but I recognize it as a central social organization and sometimes an economic organization for the black community. I would like to see blacks develop their own institutions that respond to their needs.

23

CASEBOOKS ON PLAYS AND PLAYWRIGHTS

WILLIAM SHAKESPEARE

LORRAINE HANSBERRY

ARTHUR MILLER

CASEBOOK ON WILLIAM SHAKESPEARE'S *HAMLET*

This Casebook on Shakespeare's Hamlet *contains seven items to help you understand the play. The section begins with a commentary by Geoffrey Bullough, who discusses other treatments of this basic plot closer to Shakespeare's time, one by the French historian François de Belleforest (1530–1583) and the other by the Elizabethan playwright Thomas Kyd (1558–1594), whose play* The Spanish Tragedy *was the most popular revenge tragedy in the London theater before Shakespeare's* Hamlet. *Bullough speculates that one of the plays Kyd wrote shortly before Shakespeare created his version of the popular story might have been the original* Hamlet. *The text of this play (nicknamed "the* Ur-Hamlet*" by modern historians) unfortunately has not survived. Bullough's discussion of the role of the ghost in* Hamlet *is continued by the critic H. D. F. Kitto, whose reading analyzes the similarities between Shakespeare's play and Sophocles'* Oedipus the King.

Next, the excerpt from the letter by the English Romantic poet John Keats to his brothers on December 21, 1817, contains his comments on what he calls Shakespeare's "negative capability." This term has been widely discussed by generations of critics since the publication of Keats's letter. Some interpret it as Shakespeare's ability as a dramatist to lose his identity in the creation of a wide range of characters. Others believe that Keats meant that as a poet Shakespeare was able to deal with uncertainty, that he did not adhere (as did Milton in Paradise Lost, *for example) to the strict tenets of religion or moral philosophy, trusting his "sense of Beauty" instead. In a 1906 commentary, Russian writer Leo Tolstoy offers another point of view when he attacks Shakespeare for having what he considered an "immoral frame of mind."*

Virginia Woolf's speculation about what would have happened if Shakespeare had a sister is from her book A Room of One's Own *(1929). Woolf's description of how a woman's life differed from a man's life in Elizabethan England helps us understand how this brilliant playwright, possibly the most articulate person ever to create works of literature in English, could be the father of two daughters who signed legal documents with an "X" and probably were illiterate. (See historian S. Schoenbaum's* William Shakespeare: A Compact Documentary Life *[1977].)*

T. S. Eliot's controversial analysis of "Hamlet and His Problems" was published in 1934. In this essay Eliot introduced his term objective correlative, *often used by later critics. Eliot defines the term as referring to a specific "set of objects, a situation, a chain of events" in a literary work that suggests to the reader a particular emotion the writer wishes to evoke. Then Eliot goes on to criticize the play for lacking sufficient physical events in the plot to motivate Hamlet's deep feelings.*

The final commentary is a contemporary response to Hamlet *by the English playwright Tom Stoppard. In his two-part play* Dogg's Hamlet, Cahoot's Macbeth *(1979), Stoppard included this farcical version of Shakespeare's* Hamlet *to be performed as an "encore."*

An image of William Shakespeare included on the First Folio, a collected edition of Shakespeare plays published seven years after his death. (Reprinted by permission of The Folger Shakespeare Library.)

GEOFFREY BULLOUGH

Sources of Shakespeare's Hamlet

1973

There was no Ghost in Saxo [Grammaticus] or [François de] Belleforest, but it was the feature of the *Ur-Hamlet* which most affected spectators and lingered on in public memory, so that in 1596 Thomas Lodge (in *Wits Miserie*) described a devil looking "as pale as the Visard of the ghost which cried so miserably at the Theatre, like an oister-wife, Hamlet, revenge."

When [Thomas] Kyd, or whoever else wrote it, adapted Belleforest's tale in terms of Senecan drama,° he dealt only with the first part of Amleth's life until his triumph over Feng, and changed the climax of that to make it tragic and (no doubt) easier to stage. The main factors shaping the altered plot were the secrecy of Amleth's father's murder and the introduction of his Ghost to incite the hero to revenge. Whereas in *The Spanish Tragedy* the Ghost of Andrea (killed before the play opens) accompanies Revenge to watch the action and "serve for Chorus in this tragedie," taking no part in the action save to express impatience at the slowness with which punishment falls on the wicked, in the *Ur-Hamlet* the father's Ghost really had some reason for demanding vengeance, and presumably started off the action by revealing it. This was a new departure in ghostly behaviour,[1] and it makes me believe that *Hamlet* was written after *The Spanish Tragedy.*

Seneca's dramas lacked the religious attitude of Greek tragedy and the theme of personal revenge superseded divine retribution; horror became a dominant effect, and the Senecan Chorus contributed to this.[2] Thus at the beginning of *Agamemnon,* Thyestes' Ghost rises from Hell to describe his own adultery with his brother Atreus' wife, and how Atreus took revenge by feasting him on the flesh of his own son; tells too how he raped his own daughter Pelopea (who later married Atreus) and had by her a son, Aegysthus, who is now Clytemnestra's paramour and will shortly help her murder Thyestes' nephew, her husband Agamemnon. The Ghost does not interfere in the action; it expounds the past and prepares the atmosphere of horror. The *Agamemnon* also has a scene in which Electra accuses her mother of adultery and murder — a striking anticipation of the closet-scene in *Hamlet.* The Amleth saga was in this tradition of fraternal hate and incest; hence no doubt its appeal to Elizabethan Senecan playwrights.

In *Troades* Talthybius tells how the Ghost of Achilles demanded the sacrifice of Polyxena (whom he had loved while living) before the Greek fleet could sail from Troy. In the Latin play this ghost did not appear in person, but Jasper Heywood introduced it in Act II of his translation, craving revenge on the Trojans.[3] Ignoring this proof of survival after death, Seneca's Chorus later doubts whether the soul lives on. There is a resemblance here to the apparent inconsistency in *Hamlet* where, soon after accepting the Ghost as his "father's spirit," the hero speaks of "the undiscover'd country from whose bourn / No traveller returns."

Professor Eleanor Prosser's study of the ghosts in Elizabethan drama shows that many act as Chorus or Prologue, or as the retributory voices of conscience, and that these are almost all pagan ghosts risen from Hades.[4] Few

---

Senecan drama: Tragedies by the Roman playwright and Stoic philosopher Seneca (4 B.C.–A.D. 65).

[1]Cf. F. T. Bowers, *Elizabethan Revenge Tragedy,* Gloucester, Mass., 1940; E. Prosser, *Hamlet and Revenge,* Stanford, 1967.

[2]H. B. Charlton, *The Senecan Tradition in Renaissance Tragedy,* 1946.

[3]Cf. G. Ll. Evans, "Shakespeare, Seneca and the Kingdom of Violence," in *Roman Drama,* ed. T. A. Dorey and D. R. Dudley, 1965.

[4]E. Prosser, *op. cit.* Appendix A.

ghosts show Christian characteristics. After *Hamlet* three or four mingle Christian and pagan qualities. Only Andrugio in *Antonio's Revenge* (probably derived from the *Ur-Hamlet*) and the Ghost in *Hamlet* "appear to a protagonist to command blood revenge." (This occasionally occurred in Italian Senecan tragedies.) Andrugio's Ghost comes from his coffin to demand that his son

> Invent some stratagem of vengeance
> Which, but to think on, may like lightning glide
> With horror through thy breast.

He combines delight in the most awful tortures with assurances that he is in league with Heaven. But the play is so confused in tone that some critics have regarded it as a parody. Old Hamlet's Ghost is unique in the problems it posits, and "Shakespeare may well have intended to jolt his audience into a fresh response to what had become a hackneyed convention."[5] It is extremely unlikely that the inventor of Andrea in *The Spanish Tragedy* also created a spirit so complex as that in *Hamlet* Q2.

This is not a suitable place in which to enter the debate about the nature of this ghost. W. W. Greg's suggestion that it is a figment of Hamlet's imagination was countered by E. Stoll who thought it an objectivation of Elizabethan popular lore. For J. D. Wilson it was an occasion for Shakespeare to present three different attitudes to ghosts: the Catholic view (of Marcellus and Bernardo) that a soul could come from Purgatory; the sceptical view of Horatio (like Reginald Scot's) but soon changed to belief; and Hamlet's Protestant view (held by L. Lavater and James VI) that ghosts were probably devils but might be angels, never the souls of men. Another school of thought, including Roy W. Battenhouse and Miss Prosser, argues that the Ghost is a damned spirit come to mislead Hamlet into offending against the divine injunction against revenge.

My own view is nearer to that of I. J. Semper who saw the Ghost as a visitant from Purgatory and that of Sister Miriam who sees Hamlet as justifiably doubting and testing it. But we should not exaggerate the doctrinal strictness of Shakespeare's approach or assume that he was a Catholic because he used the idea of Purgatory. P. N. Siegel was right to insist: "The Hamlet Ghost is a compound of the Senecan revenge ghost, the Catholic purgatorial spirit and the popular graveyard spook, created for an audience prepared by theatrical tradition, by what Cardinal Newman called "floating religious opinions" (as against official dogma) and by current folklore to give it dramatic credence."[6] The pagan element appears in the Ghost's insistence on quasi-physical horrors unspeakable and the reference to "Lethe wharf"; its purgatorial quality in [act 1, scene 5]. It has an almost Miltonic apprehension of virtue and vice; it loves the Sacraments and deeply regrets having died. "Unhousel'd, disappointed, unaneal'd." Its folklore features include the hour when it walks and when it disappears, and its knocking underground.

---

[5]Prosser, *op. cit.* pp. 101–102.

[6]P. N. Siegel, "Discerning the Ghost in *Hamlet*," *PMLA*, lxxviii, 1963, p. 148.

H. D. F. Kitto

Hamlet *and the* Oedipus

1956

The *Oedipus Tyrannus*° begins by describing twice, once in dialogue and once in lyrics, the plague which is afflicting Thebes. The cause of the plague is the presence in the city of a man who has done two things foul and unnatural above all others: he has killed his own father, and he is living incestuously with his own mother. The details of the plague are so described that we can see how its nature is strictly proportioned to its cause: to death is added sterility; the soil of Thebes, the animals, and the human kind are all barren. The meaning is obvious — unless we make it invisible by reducing the play to the stature of Tragedy of Character: what Oedipus has done is an affront to what we should call Nature, to what Sophocles calls Dikê; and since it is the first law of Nature, or Dikê, that she cannot indefinitely tolerate what is . . . contrary to Nature, she rises at last against these unpurged affronts. The plague of sterility is the outcome of the unnatural things which Oedipus has done to his parents.

Hamlet begins in the same way. The two soldiers Marcellus and Bernardo, and Horatio, who is both a soldier and a scholar, are almost terrified out of their wits by something so clean contrary to the natural order that

I might not this believe
Without the sensible and true avouch
Of mine own eyes.

Professor Dover Wilson, learned in sixteenth-century demonology, has explained that the eschatology of Horatio and Hamlet is Protestant, that the Ghost is a Catholic ghost, and that Bernardo and Marcellus are plain untheological Elizabethans. On this it would be impertinent for an ignoramus to express an opinion, but it does seem that if the "statists" in Shakespeare's audience, and scholars from the Inns of Court, saw and savoured theological *expertise* in this scene, they would be in danger of missing the main point: that the repeated appearances of the Ghost are something quite outside ordinary experience. Horatio the scholar has heard of something similar, in ancient history, "a little ere the mightiest Julius fell." So perhaps this present unnatural terror "bodes some strange eruption to our state"; or — a less disturbing thought — perhaps the ghost is concerned for some uphoarded treasure hidden in the womb of the Earth.

But at this point Shakespeare decides to write some poetry — and he is never so dangerous as when he is writing poetry:

It faded on the crowing of the cock.
Some say that ever 'gainst that season comes
Wherein our Saviour's birth is celebrated,
The bird of dawning singeth all night long:
And then, they say, no spirit dare stir abroad,

Oedipus Tyrannus: "Oedipus the Tyrant," another name for Sophocles' play.

> The nights are wholesome; then no planets strike,
> No fairy takes, nor witch hath power to charm,
> So hallowed and so gracious is the time.

Pretty good, for a simple soldier. The intense and solemn beauty of these verses lifts us, and was designed to lift us, high above the level of Horatio's conjectures. The night "wherein our Saviour's birth is celebrated" is holy and pure beyond all others; therefore these nights which the Ghost makes hideous by rising so incredibly from the grave, are impure beyond most. Unless Greek Tragedy has bemused me, this passage does more than "give a religious background to the supernatural happenings" of the scene;[1] they give the "background," that is, the logical and dynamic centre, of the whole play. We are in the presence of evil. Hamlet's own prophetic soul recognises this as soon as he hears of the Ghost:

> Foul deeds will rise,
> Though all the earth o'erwhelm them, to men's eyes.

If we may assume that Shakespeare had not read Sophocles — and that Hamlet had not read him, at Wittenberg, behind Shakespeare's back — the parallel with the *Oedipus* becomes the more interesting; for when Oedipus has at last discovered the truth the Chorus observes:

> Time sees all, and it has found you out, in your own despite. It exacts
> Dikê from you for that unnatural marriage that united mother with son.

"Foul deeds will rise": there are evils so great that Nature will not allow them to lie unpurged. So, returning to the battlements with Hamlet, and enquiring with him

> Why thy canonized bones, hearsed in death,
> Have burst their cerements; why the sepulchre
> Wherein we saw thee quietly inurned
> Hath o'ped his ponderous and marble jaws
> To cast thee up again —

we learn the cause: fratricide, incest, "Murder most foul, strange and unnatural."

Here, most emphatically stated, are the very foundations and framework of the tragedy. We can, of course, neglect these, and erect a framework of our own which we find more interesting or more congenial to us. We can say, with Dr. Gregg, that the Ghost is all my eye; or, with Professor Dover Wilson, that the first act, "a little play of itself," is "an epitome of the ghost-lore of the age" — in which case it becomes something of a learned Prologue to the real play;[2] or, like Dr. de Madariaga, we can neglect this encircling presence of evil, and substitute what we know of sixteenth-century Court manners; or, again

---

[1]Dover Wilson, *What Happens in "Hamlet,"* p. 67.

[2]Or, if it is not this, let it be shown what its organic function is. Shakespeare, having a capacious mind, may well have been keenly interested in contemporary ghost-lore, but our first question is: what has he done with it as a creative artist? Or has he done nothing with it?

without constant reference to the background which Shakespeare himself erected, we can subtly anatomise the soul and mind of Hamlet, on the assumption that Hamlet is the whole play. But if we do these things, let us not then complain that Shakespeare attempted a task too difficult for him, or conclude that the play is an ineffable mystery. Turning it into "secular" tragedy we shall be using the wrong focus. The correct focus is one which will set the whole action against a background of Nature and Heaven; for this is the background which the dramatist himself has provided.

JOHN KEATS

From a Letter to George and Thomas Keats, 21 December 1817

Hampstead Sunday

My dear Brothers,

I must crave your pardon for not having written ere this. . . .

. . . Brown and Dilke walked with me and back from the Christmas pantomime. I had not a dispute but a disquisition, with Dilke on various subjects; several things dove-tailed in my mind, and at once it struck me what quality went to form a Man of Achievement, especially in Literature and which Shakespeare possessed so enormously — I mean *Negative Capability,* that is, when a man is capable of being in uncertainties, mysteries, doubts, without any irritable reaching after fact and reason — [Samuel Taylor] Coleridge, for instance, would let go by a fine isolated verisimilitude caught from the Penetralium of mystery, from being incapable of remaining content with half-knowledge. This pursued through volumes would perhaps take us no further than this, that with a great poet the sense of Beauty overcomes every other consideration, or rather obliterates all consideration.

[Percy Bysshe] Shelley's poem is out, and there are words about its being objected to as much as "Queen Mab" was. Poor Shelley, I think he has his Quota of good qualities, in sooth la!! Write soon to your most sincere friend and affectionate Brother

John.

LEO TOLSTOY

Shakespeare's Immoral Frame of Mind *1906*

I remember the astonishment I felt when I first read Shakespeare. I expected to receive a powerful aesthetic pleasure, but having read, one after the other, works regarded as his best, *King Lear, Romeo and Juliet, Hamlet,* and *Macbeth,* not only did I feel no delight, but I felt an irresistible repulsion and tedium, and doubted as to whether I was senseless in feeling works regarded as the summit of perfection by the whole of the civilized world to be trivial and positively bad, or whether the significance which this civilized world attributes to the works of Shakespeare was itself senseless. My consternation was increased by the fact that I always keenly felt the beauties of poetry in every form; then why should artistic works recognized by the whole world as those of a genius — the works of Shakespeare — not only fail to please me, but be disagreeable to me? . . .

All his characters speak, not their own, but always one and the same Shakespearean pretentious and unnatural language, in which not only they could not speak, but in which no living man ever has spoken or does speak. . . . From his first words, exaggeration is seen: the exaggeration of events, the exaggeration of emotion, and the exaggeration of effects. One sees at once that he does not believe in what he says, that it is of no necessity to him, that he invents the events he describes and is indifferent to his characters — that he has conceived them only for the stage and therefore makes them do and say only what may strike his public, and so we do not believe either in the events or in the actions or in the sufferings of the characters.

He alone can write a drama who has got something to say to men, and that something of the greatest importance for them: about man's relation to God, to the Universe, to the All, the Eternal, the Infinite. But when, thanks to the German theories about objective art, the idea was established that for the drama this was quite unnecessary, then it became obvious how a writer like Shakespeare — who had not got developed in his mind the religious convictions proper to his time, who, in fact, had no convictions at all, but heaped up in his drama all possible events, horrors, fooleries, discussions, and effects — could appear to be a dramatic writer of the greatest genius.

But these are all external reasons. The fundamental inner cause of Shakespeare's fame was and is this — that his dramas . . . corresponded to the irreligious and immoral frame of mind of the upper classes of his time and ours.

VIRGINIA WOOLF

What If Shakespeare Had Had a Sister? *1929*

Let me imagine, since facts are so hard to come by, what would have happened had Shakespeare had a wonderfully gifted sister, called Judith, let us say. Shakespeare himself went, very probably — his mother was an heiress — to the grammar school, where he may have learnt Latin — Ovid, Virgil and Horace — and the elements of grammar and logic. He was, it is well known, a wild boy who poached rabbits, perhaps shot a deer, and had, rather sooner than he should have done, to marry a woman in the neighborhood, who bore him a child rather quicker than was right. That escapade sent him to seek his fortune in London. He had, it seemed, a taste for the theater; he began by holding horses at the stage door. Very soon he got work in the theater, became a successful actor, and lived at the hub of the universe, meeting everybody, knowing everybody, practicing his art on the boards, exercising his wits in the streets, and even getting access to the palace of the queen. Meanwhile his extraordinarily gifted sister, let us suppose, remained at home. She was as adventurous, as imaginative, as agog to see the world as he was. But she was not sent to school. She had no chance of learning grammar and logic, let alone of reading Horace and Virgil. She picked up a book now and then, one of her brother's perhaps, and read a few pages. But then her parents came in and told her to mend the stockings or mind the stew and not moon about with books and papers. They would have spoken sharply but kindly, for they were substantial people who knew the conditions of life for a woman and loved their daughter — indeed, more likely than not she was the apple of her father's eye. Perhaps she scribbled some pages up in an apple loft on the sly, but was careful to hide them or set fire to them. Soon, however, before she was out of her teens, she was to be betrothed to the son of a neighboring wool-stapler. She cried out that marriage was hateful to her, and for that she was severely beaten by her father. Then he ceased to scold her. He begged her instead not to hurt him, not to shame him in this matter of her marriage. He would give her a chain of beads or a fine petticoat, he said; and there were tears in his eyes. How could she disobey him? How could she break his heart? The force of her own gift alone drove her to it. She made up a small parcel of her belongings, let herself down by a rope one summer's night, and took the road to London. She was not seventeen. The birds that sang in the hedge were not more musical than she was. She had the quickest fancy, a gift like her brother's, for the tune of words. Like him, she had a taste for the theater. She stood at the stage door; she wanted to act, she said. Men laughed in her face. The manager — a fat, loose-lipped man — guffawed. He bellowed something about poodles dancing and women acting — no woman, he said, could possibly be an actress. He hinted — you can imagine what. She could get no training in her craft. Could she even seek her dinner in a tavern or roam the streets at midnight? Yet her genius was for fiction and lusted to feed abundantly upon the lives of men and women and the study of their ways. At last — for she was very young, oddly like Shakespeare the poet in her face, with the same grey eyes and rounded brows — at last Nick Greene the actor-manager took pity on her; she found herself with child by that gentleman and so — who shall measure the heat and violence of the poet's heart when caught and tangled in a woman's body? — killed herself one winter's night and lies buried at some cross-roads where the omnibuses now stop outside the Elephant and Castle.

That, more or less, is how the story would run, I think, if a woman in Shakespeare's day had had Shakespeare's genius. . . . Any woman born with a great gift in the sixteenth century would certainly have gone crazed, shot herself, or ended her days in some lonely cottage outside the village, half witch, half wizard, feared and mocked at. . . . To have lived a free life in London in the sixteenth century would have meant for a woman who was poet and playwright a nervous stress and dilemma which might well have killed her. Had she survived, whatever she had written would have been twisted and deformed, issuing from a strained and morbid imagination. And undoubtedly, I thought, looking at the shelf where there are no plays by women, her work would have gone unsigned.

T. S. Eliot

Hamlet and His Problems

1934

Few critics have ever admitted that *Hamlet* the play is the primary problem, and Hamlet the character only secondary. And Hamlet the character has had an especial temptation for that most dangerous type of critic: the critic with a mind which is naturally of the creative order, but which through some weakness in creative power exercises itself in criticism instead. These minds often find in Hamlet a vicarious existence for their own artistic realization. Such a mind had Goethe, who made of Hamlet a Werther; and such had [Samuel Taylor] Coleridge who made of Hamlet a Coleridge; and probably neither of these men in writing about Hamlet remembered that his first business was to study a work of art. The kind of criticism that Goethe and Coleridge produced, in writing of Hamlet, is the most misleading kind possible. For they both possessed unquestionable critical insight, and both make their critical aberrations the more plausible by the substitution — of their own Hamlet for Shakespeare's — which their creative gift effects. We should be thankful that Walter Pater° did not fix his attention on this play.

Two writers of our time, Mr. J. M. Robertson and Professor Stoll of the University of Minnesota, have issued small books which can be praised for moving in the other direction. Mr. Stoll performs a service in recalling to our attention the labors of the critics of the seventeenth and eighteenth centuries, observing that

> they knew less about psychology than more recent Hamlet critics, but they were nearer in spirit to Shakespeare's art; and as they insisted on the importance of the effect of the whole rather than on the importance of the leading character, they were nearer, in their old-fashioned way, to the secret of dramatic art in general.

Qua work of art, the work of art cannot be interpreted; there is nothing to interpret; we can only criticize it according to standards, in comparison to other works of art; and for "interpretation" the chief task is the presentation of relevant historical facts which the reader is not assumed to know. Mr. Robertson points out, very pertinently, how critics have failed in their "interpretation" of *Hamlet* by ignoring what ought to be very obvious: that *Hamlet* is a stratification, that it represents the efforts of a series of men, each making what he could out of the work of his predecessors. The *Hamlet* of Shakespeare will appear to us very differently if, instead of treating the whole action of the play as due to Shakespeare's design, we perceive his *Hamlet* to be superposed upon much cruder material which persists even in the final form.

We know that there was an older play by Thomas Kyd, that extraordinary dramatic (if not poetic) genius who was in all probability the author of two plays so dissimilar as the *Spanish Tragedy* and *Arden of Feversham;* and

---

Walter Pater: English writer and critic (1839–1894) known for his complex, ornate style.

what this play was like we can guess from three clues: from the *Spanish Tragedy* itself, from the tale of Belleforest upon which Kyd's *Hamlet* must have been based, and from a version acted in Germany in Shakespeare's lifetime which bears strong evidence of having been adapted from the earlier, not from the later, play. From these three sources it is clear that in the earlier play the motive was a revenge motive simply; that the action or delay is caused, as in the *Spanish Tragedy,* solely by the difficulty of assassinating a monarch surrounded by guards; and that the "madness" of Hamlet was feigned in order to escape suspicion, and successfully. In the final play of Shakespeare, on the other hand, there is a motive which is more important than that of revenge, and which explicitly "blunts" the latter; the delay in revenge is unexplained on grounds of necessity or expediency; and the effect of the "madness" is not to lull but to arouse the king's suspicion. The alteration is not complete enough, however, to be convincing. Furthermore, there are verbal parallels so close to the *Spanish Tragedy* as to leave no doubt that in places Shakespeare was merely *revising* the text of Kyd. And finally there are unexplained scenes — the Polonius-Laertes and the Polonius-Reynaldo scenes — for which there is little excuse; these scenes are not in the verse style of Kyd, and not beyond doubt in the style of Shakespeare. These Mr. Robertson believes to be scenes in the original play of Kyd reworked by a third hand, perhaps Chapman,° before Shakespeare touched the play. And he concludes, with very strong show of reason, that the original play of Kyd was, like certain other revenge plays, in two parts of five acts each. The upshot of Mr. Robertson's examination is, we believe, irrefragable: that Shakespeare's *Hamlet,* so far as it is Shakespeare's, is a play dealing with the effect of a mother's guilt upon her son, and that Shakespeare was unable to impose this motive successfully upon the "intractable" material of the old play.

Of the intractibility there can be no doubt. So far from being Shakespeare's masterpiece, the play is most certainly an artistic failure. In several ways the play is puzzling, and disquieting as is none of the others. Of all the plays it is the longest and is possibly the one on which Shakespeare spent most pains; and yet he has left in it superfluous and inconsistent scenes which even hasty revision should have noticed. The versification is variable. Lines like

> Look, the morn, in russet mantle clad,
> Walks o'er the dew of yon high eastern hill,

are of the Shakespeare of *Romeo and Juliet*. The lines in act V, scene II,

> Sir, in my heart there was a kind of fighting
> That would not let me sleep . . .
> Up from my cabin,
> My sea-grown scarf'd about me, in the dark
> Grop'd I to find out them: had my desire;
> finger'd their packet;

Chapman: George Chapman (1559?–1634), Renaissance poet and playwright.

are of his quite mature. Both workmanship and thought are in an unstable position. We are surely justified in attributing the play, with that other profoundly interesting play of "intractable" material and astonishing versification, *Measure for Measure,* to a period of crisis, after which follow the tragic successes which culminate in *Coriolanus. Coriolanus* may be not as "interesting" as *Hamlet,* but it is, with *Antony and Cleopatra,* Shakespeare's most assured artistic success. And probably more people have thought *Hamlet* a work of art because they found it interesting, than have found it interesting because it is a work of art. It is the *Mona Lisa* of literature.

The grounds of *Hamlet*'s failure are not immediately obvious. Mr. Robertson is undoubtedly correct in concluding that the essential emotion of the play is the feeling of a son toward a guilty mother:

> [Hamlet's] tone is that of one who has suffered tortures on the score of his mother's degradation. . . . The guilt of a mother is an almost intolerable motive for drama, but it had to be maintained and emphasized to supply a psychological solution, or rather a hint of one.

This, however, is by no means the whole story. It is not merely the "guilt of a mother" that cannot be handled as Shakespeare handled the suspicion of Othello, the infatuation of Antony, or the pride of Coriolanus. The subject might conceivably have expanded into a tragedy like these, intelligible, self-complete, in the sunlight. *Hamlet,* like the sonnets, is full of some stuff that the writer could not drag to light, contemplate, or manipulate into art. And when we search for this feeling, we find it, as in the sonnets, very difficult to localize. You cannot point to it in the speeches; indeed, if you examine the two famous soliloquies you see the versification of Shakespeare, but a content which might be claimed by another, perhaps by the author of the *Revenge of Bussy d'Ambois,*° act V, scene I. We find Shakespeare's *Hamlet* not in the action, not in any quotations that we might select, so much as in an unmistakable tone which is unmistakably not in the earlier play.

The only way of expressing emotion in the form of art is by finding an "objective correlative"; in other words, a set of objects, a situation, a chain of events which shall be the formula of that *particular* emotion; such that when the external facts, which must terminate in sensory experience, are given, the emotion is immediately evoked. If you examine any of Shakespeare's more successful tragedies, you will find this exact equivalence; you will find that the state of mind of Lady Macbeth walking in her sleep has been communicated to you by a skillful accumulation of imagined sensory impressions; the words of Macbeth on hearing of his wife's death strike us as if, given the sequence of events, these words were automatically released by the last event in the series. The artistic "inevitability" lies in this complete adequacy of the external to the emotion; and this is precisely what is deficient in *Hamlet.* Hamlet (the man) is dominated by an emotion which is inexpressible, because it is

---

Revenge of Bussy d'Ambois: Tragedy (1610–11) by George Chapman.

in *excess* of the facts as they appear. And the supposed identity of Hamlet with his author is genuine to this point: that Hamlet's bafflement at the absence of objective equivalent to his feelings is a prolongation of the bafflement of his creator in the face of his artistic problem. Hamlet is up against the difficulty that his disgust is occasioned by his mother, but that his mother is not an adequate equivalent for it; his disgust envelops and exceeds her. It is thus a feeling which he cannot understand; he cannot objectify it, and it therefore remains to poison life and obstruct action. None of the possible actions can satisfy it; and nothing that Shakespeare can do with the plot can express Hamlet for him. And it must be noticed that the very nature of the *données*° of the problem precludes objective equivalence. To have heightened the criminality of Gertrude would have been to provide the formula for a totally different emotion in Hamlet; it is just *because* her character is so negative and insignificant that she arouses in Hamlet the feeling which she is incapable of representing.

The "madness" of Hamlet lay to Shakespeare's hand; in the earlier play a simple ruse, and to the end, we may presume, understood as a ruse by the audience. For Shakespeare it is less than madness and more than feigned. The levity of Hamlet, his repetition of phrase, his puns, are not part of a deliberate plan of dissimulation, but a form of emotional relief. In the character Hamlet it is the buffoonery of an emotion which can find no outlet in action; in the dramatist it is the buffoonery of an emotion which he cannot express in art. The intense feeling, ecstatic or terrible, without an object or exceeding its object, is something which every person of sensibility has known; it is doubtless a subject of study for pathologists. It often occurs in adolescence: the ordinary person puts these feelings to sleep, or trims down his feelings to fit the business world; the artist keeps them alive by his ability to intensify the world to his emotions. The Hamlet of Laforgue° is an adolescent; the Hamlet of Shakespeare is not, he has not that explanation and excuse. We must simply admit that here Shakespeare tackled a problem which proved too much for him. Why he attempted it at all is an insoluble puzzle; under compulsion of what experience he attempted to express the inexpressibly horrible, we cannot ever know. We need a great many facts in his biography; and we should like to know whether, and when, and after or at the same time as what personal experience, he read Montaigne's *Apologie de Raimond Sebond.*° We should have, finally, to know something which is by hypothesis unknowable, for we assume it to be an experience which, in the manner indicated, exceeded the facts. We should have to understand things which Shakespeare did not understand himself.

---

données: Term employed by the American novelist Henry James to refer to the "givens" about a narrative — the assumptions and motifs from which it proceeds. **Laforgue:** Jules Laforgue (1860–1887), French poet. **Montaigne's *Apologie de Raimond Sebond:*** Michel de Montaigne (1533–1592), whose "apology" for the fifteenth-century Spaniard served as Montaigne's own defense of his opinion on the futility of reason.

Tom Stoppard

Dogg's Hamlet: The Encore

1979

SCENE: *Staging the play on a double-decker London bus, Stoppard gave directions for two folding screens to be placed left and right at the back of the playing area. The screen on the left had a bolt through the top for a cut-out sun, moon, and crown on hinges to be swung in and out of sight. The other screen had a two-dimensional grave for Ophelia.*

Flourish of trumpets, crown hinges up. Enter Claudius and Gertrude.

CLAUDIUS: Our sometime sister, now our Queen,
(Enter Hamlet.)
Have we taken to wife.
(Crown hinges down.)

HAMLET: That it should come to this!
(Exit Claudius and Gertrude. Wind noise. Moon hinges up. Enter Horatio above.)

HORATIO: My lord, I saw him yesternight —
The King, your father.

HAMLET: Angels and ministers of grace defend us!
(Exit, running, through rest of speech.)
Something is rotten in the state of Denmark.
(Enter Ghost above.)

GHOST: I am thy father's spirit.
The serpent that did sting thy father's life
(Enter Hamlet above.)
Now wears his crown.

HAMLET: O my prophetic soul!
Hereafter I shall think meet
To put an antic disposition on.
(Moon hinges down. Exeunt. Short flourish of trumpets. Enter Polonius below, running. Crown hinges up.)

POLONIUS: Look where sadly the poor wretch comes.
(Exit Polonius, running, Enter Hamlet.)

HAMLET: I have heard that guilty creatures sitting at a play
Have by the very cunning of the scene been struck.
(Enter Claudius, Gertrude, Ophelia, Marcellus, and Horatio joking. All sit to watch imaginary play, puppets appear above screen.)
If he but blench, I know my course.
(Masque music. Claudius rises.)
The King rises!

ALL: Give o'er the play!
(Exeunt all except Gertrude and Hamlet. Crown hinges down.)

HAMLET: I'll take the ghost's word for a thousand pounds.
(Enter Polonius, goes behind arras. Short flourish of trumpets.)
Mother, you have my father much offended.

GERTRUDE: Help!
POLONIUS: Help, Ho!
HAMLET: (*Stabs Polonius.*) Dead for a ducat, dead!
(Polonius falls dead offstage. Exit Gertrude and Hamlet. Short flourish of trumpets. Enter Claudius followed by Hamlet.)
CLAUDIUS: Hamlet, this deed must send thee hence.
(Exit Hamlet.)
Do it, England.
(Exit Claudius. Enter Ophelia, falls to ground. Rises and pulls gravestone to cover herself. Bell tolls twice. Enter Gravedigger and Hamlet.)
HAMLET: A pirate gave us chase. I alone became their prisoner.
(Takes skull from Gravedigger.)
Alas poor Yorick — but soft (*Returns skull to Gravedigger.*)
— This is I,
Hamlet the Dane!
(Exit Gravedigger. Enter Laertes.)
LAERTES: The devil take thy soul!
(They grapple, then break. Enter Osric between them with swords. They draw. Crown hinges up. Enter Claudius and Gertrude with goblets.)
HAMLET: Come on, Sir!
(Laertes and Hamlet fight.)
OSRIC: A hit, a very palpable hit!
CLAUDIUS: Give him the cup. Gertrude, do not drink!
GERTRUDE: I am poisoned! (*Dies.*)
LAERTES: Hamlet, thou art slain! (*Dies.*)
HAMLET: Then venom to thy work! (*Kills Claudius. Crown hinges down.*)
The rest is silence. (*Dies.*)
(*Two shots offstage. End.*)

CASEBOOK ON ARTHUR MILLER'S *DEATH OF A SALESMAN*

Arthur Miller analyzed what he considered the tragic dimension in Willy Loman's character when Death of a Salesman *was published by Viking Press in 1957. In his introduction to the play, Miller discussed how his view of a tragic hero differed from Aristotle's formulation in the* Poetics. *Miller then went on to describe his dramatic method of calling Willy Loman's values into question by presenting what Miller called "an opposing system" of love within the family to counter American society's false ideals of power and success. As Miller remarked during a symposium on his play the following year, "The trouble with Willy Loman is that he has tremendously powerful ideals. . . . [If] Willy Loman, for instance, had not had a very profound sense that his life as lived had left him hollow, he would have died contentedly polishing his car on some Sunday afternoon at a ripe old age. The fact is he has values.*

The fact that they cannot be realized is what is driving him mad." In Miller's 1966 interview in the Paris Review, *he discussed his plays in the context of the radical political theater of the 1930s, the absurd theater of the 1960s, and the then-recent play* Cat on a Hot Tin Roof *by his contemporary Tennessee Williams.*

Helge Normann Nilsen examined the influence of Marxist theory on Death of a Salesman *in an essay that appeared in the journal* English Studies *in 1994. Her essay is followed by John Beaufort's review of* Death of a Salesman, *which appeared under the heading "Arthur Miller's New Play an Absorbing Experience" in the* Christian Science Monitor *on February 19, 1949. John Lahr described the compositional process of* Death of a Salesman *in a* New Yorker *profile on January 25, 1999.*

Arthur Miller in 1961. (Reprinted from the collections of the Library of Congress.)

Arthur Miller

On Death of a Salesman *as an American Tragedy*

1957

I set out not to "write a tragedy" in this play, but to show the truth as I saw it. However, some of the attacks upon it as a pseudo-tragedy contain ideas so misleading, and in some cases so laughable, that it might be in place here to deal with a few of them.

Aristotle having spoken of a fall from the heights, it goes without saying that someone of the common mold cannot be a fit tragic hero. It is now many centuries since Aristotle lived. There is no more reason for falling down in a faint before his *Poetics* than before Euclid's geometry, which has been amended numerous times by men with new insights; nor, for that matter, would I choose to have my illness diagnosed by Hippocrates rather than the most ordinary graduate of an American medical school, despite the Greek's genius. Things do change, and even a genius is limited by his time and the nature of his society.

I would deny, on grounds of simple logic, this one of Aristotle's contentions if only because he lived in a slave society. When a vast number of people are divested of alternatives, as slaves are, it is rather inevitable that one will not be able to imagine drama, let alone tragedy, as being possible for any but the higher ranks of society. There is a legitimate question of stature here, but none of rank, which is so often confused with it. So long as the hero may be said to have had alternatives of a magnitude to have materially changed the course of his life, it seems to me that in this respect at least, he cannot be debarred from the heroic role.

The question of rank is significant to me only as it reflects the question of the social application of the hero's career. There is no doubt that if a character is shown on the stage who goes through the most ordinary actions, and is suddenly revealed to be the President of the United States, his actions immediately assume a much greater magnitude, and pose the possibilities of much greater meaning, than if he is the corner grocer. But at the same time, his stature as a hero is not so utterly dependent upon his rank that the corner grocer cannot outdistance him as a tragic figure — providing, of course, that the grocer's career engages the issues of, for instance, the survival of the race, the relationships of man to God — the questions, in short, whose answers define humanity and the right way to live so that the world is a home, instead of a battleground or a fog in which disembodied spirits pass each other in an endless twilight.

In this respect *Death of a Salesman* is a slippery play to categorize because nobody in it stops to make a speech objectively stating the great issues which I believe it embodies. If it were a worse play, less closely articulating its meanings with its actions, I think it would have more quickly satisfied a certain kind of criticism. But it was meant to be less a play than a fact; it refused admission to its author's opinions and opened itself to a revelation of process and the operations of an ethic, of social laws of action no less powerful in their effects upon individuals than any tribal law administered by gods with names. I need not claim that this play is a genuine solid gold tragedy for my opinions on tragedy to be held valid. My purpose here is simply to point out a historical fact which must be taken into account in any consideration of tragedy, and it is the sharp alteration in the meaning of rank in society between the present time and the distant past. More important to me is the fact that this particular kind of argument obscures much more relevant considerations.

One of these is the question of intensity. It matters not at all whether a modern play concerns itself with a grocer or a president if the intensity of the hero's commitment to his course is less than the maximum possible. It matters not at all whether the hero falls from a great height or a small one, whether he is highly conscious or only dimly aware of what is happening, whether his pride brings the fall or an unseen pattern written behind clouds; if the intensity, the human passion to surpass his given bounds, the fanatic insistence upon his self-conceived role — if these are not present there can only be an outline of tragedy but no living thing. I believe, for myself, that the lasting appeal of tragedy is due to our need to face the fact of death in order to strengthen ourselves for life, and that over and above this function of the tragic viewpoint there are and will be a great number of formal variations which no single definition will ever embrace.

Another issue worth considering is the so-called tragic victory, a question closely related to the consciousness of the hero. One makes nonsense of this if a "victory" means that the hero makes us feel some certain joy when, for instance, he sacrifices himself for a "cause," and unhappy and morose because he dies without one. To begin at the bottom, a man's death is and ought to be an essentially terrifying thing and ought to make nobody happy. But in a great variety of ways even death, the ultimate negative, can be, and appear to be, an assertion of bravery, and can serve to separate the death of man from the death of animals; and I think it is this distinction which underlies any conceptions of a victory in death. For a society of faith, the nature of the death can prove the existence of the spirit, and posit its immortality. For a secular society it is perhaps more difficult for such a victory to document itself and to make itself felt, but, conversely, the need to offer greater proofs of the humanity of man can make that victory more real. It goes without saying that in a society where there is basic disagreement as to the right way to live, there can hardly be agreement as to the right way to die, and both life and death must be heavily weighted with meaningless futility.

It was not out of any deference to a tragic definition that Willy Loman is filled with a joy, however broken-hearted, as he approaches his end, but simply that my sense of his character dictated his joy, and even what I felt was an exultation. In terms of his character, he has achieved a very powerful piece of knowledge, which is that he is loved by his son and has been embraced by him and forgiven. In this he is given his existence, so to speak — his fatherhood, for which he has always striven and which until now he could not achieve. That he is unable to take this victory thoroughly to his heart, that it closes the circle for him and propels him to his death, is the wage of his sin, which was to have committed himself so completely to the counterfeits of dignity and the false coinage embodied in his idea of success that he can prove his existence only by bestowing "power" on his posterity, a power deriving from the sale of his last asset, himself, for the price of his insurance policy.

I must confess here to a miscalculation, however. I did not realize while writing the play that so many people in the world do not see as clearly, or would not admit, as I thought they must, how futile most lives are; so there could be no hope of consoling the audience for the death of this man. I did not realize either how few would be impressed by the fact that this man is actually a very brave spirit who cannot settle for half but must pursue his dream of himself to the end. Finally, I thought it must be clear, even obvious, that this was no dumb brute heading mindlessly to his catastrophe.

I have no need to be Willy's advocate before the jury which decides who is and who is not a tragic hero. I am merely noting that the lingering ponderousness of so many ancient definitions has blinded students and critics to the facts before them, and not only in regard to this play. Had Willy been unaware of his separation from values that endure he would have died contentedly while polishing his car, probably on a Sunday afternoon with the ball game coming over the radio. But he was agonized by his awareness of being in a false position, so constantly haunted by the hollowness of all he had placed his faith in, so aware, in short, that he must somehow be filled in his spirit or fly apart, that he staked his very life on the ultimate assertion. That he had not the intellectual fluency to verbalize his situation is not the same thing as saying that he lacked awareness, even an overly intensified consciousness that the life he had made was without form and inner meaning.

To be sure, had he been able to know that he was as much the victim of his beliefs as their defeated exemplar, had he known how much of guilt he ought to bear and how much to shed from his soul, he would be more conscious. But it seems to me that there is of necessity a severe limitation of self-awareness in any character, even the most knowing, which serves to define him as a character, and more, that this very limit serves to complete the tragedy and, indeed, to make it at all possible. Complete consciousness is possible only in a play about forces, like *Prometheus,*° but not in a play about people. I think that the point is whether there is a sufficient awareness in the hero's career to make the audience supply the rest. Had Oedipus, for instance, been more conscious and more aware of the forces at work upon him he must surely have said that he was not really to blame for having cohabited with his mother since neither he nor anyone else knew she was his mother. He must surely decide to divorce her, provide for their children, firmly resolve to investigate the family background of his next wife, and thus deprive us of a very fine play and the name for a famous neurosis. But he is conscious only up to a point, the point at which guilt begins. Now he is inconsolable and must tear out his eyes. What is tragic about this? Why is it not even ridiculous? How can we respect a man who goes to such extremities over something he could in no way help or prevent? The answer, I think, is not that we respect the man, but

Prometheus: *Prometheus Bound* by the Greek tragedian Aeschylus (c. 525–456 B.C.).

that we respect the Law he has so completely broken, wittingly or not, for it is that Law which, we believe, defines us as men. The confusion of some critics viewing *Death of a Salesman* in this regard is that they do not see that Willy Loman has broken a law without whose protection life is insupportable if not incomprehensible to him and to many others; it is the law which says that a failure in society and in business has no right to live. Unlike the law against incest, the law of success is not administered by statute or church, but it is very nearly as powerful in its grip upon men. The confusion increases because, while it is a law, it is by no means a wholly agreeable one even as it is slavishly obeyed, for to fail is no longer to belong to society, in his estimate. Therefore, the path is opened for those who wish to call Willy merely a foolish man even as they themselves are living in obedience to the same law that killed him. Equally, the fact that Willy's law — the belief, in other words, which administers guilt to him — is not a civilizing statute whose destruction menaces us all; it is, rather, a deeply believed and deeply suspect "good" which, when questioned as to its value, as it is in this play, serves more to raise our anxieties than to reassure us of the existence of an unseen but humane metaphysical system in the world. My attempt in the play was to counter this anxiety with an opposing system which, so to speak, is in a race for Willy's faith, and it is the system of love which is the opposite of the law of success. It is embodied in Biff Loman, but by the time Willy can perceive his love it can serve only as an ironic comment upon the life he sacrificed for power and for success and its tokens.

ARTHUR MILLER

From the Paris Review *Interview*

1967

Interviewer: Many of your plays have that father-son relationship as the dominant theme. Were you very close to your father?

Miller: I was. I still am, but I think, actually, that my plays don't reflect directly my relationship to him. It's a very primitive thing in my plays. That is, the father was really a figure who incorporated both power and some kind of a moral law which he had either broken himself or had fallen prey to. He figures as an immense shadow. . . . I didn't expect that of my own father, literally, but of his position, apparently I did. The reason that I was able to write about the relationship, I think now, was because it had a mythical quality to me. If I had ever thought that I was writing about my father, I suppose I never could have done it. My father is, literally, a much more realistic guy than Willy Loman, and much more successful as a personality. And he'd be the last man in the world to ever commit suicide. Willy is based on an individual whom I knew very little, who was a salesman; it was years later that I realized I had only seen that man about a total of four hours in twenty years. He gave one of those impressions that is basic, evidently. When I thought of him, he would simply be a mute man: he said no more than two hundred words to me. I was a kid. Later on, I had another of that kind of contact, with a man whose fantasy was always overreaching his real outline. I've always been aware of that kind of an agony, of someone who has some driving, implacable wish in him which never goes away, which he can never block out. And it broods over him, it makes him happy sometimes or it makes him suicidal, but it never leaves him. Any hero whom we even begin to think of as tragic is obsessed, whether it's Lear or Hamlet or the women in the Greek plays.

Interviewer: Do any of the younger playwrights create heroes — in your opinion?

Miller: I tell you, I may be working on a different wave length, but I don't think they are looking at character any more, at the documentation of facts about people. All experience is looked at now from a schematic point of view. These playwrights won't let the characters escape for a moment from their preconceived scheme of how dreadful the world is. It is very much like the old strike plays. The scheme then was that someone began a play with a bourgeois ideology and got involved in some area of experience which had a connection to the labor movement — either it was actually a strike or, in a larger sense, it was the collapse of capitalism — and he ended the play with some new positioning vis-à-vis that collapse. He started without an enlightenment and he ended with some kind of enlightenment. And you could predict that in the first five minutes. Very few of those plays could be done any more, because they're absurd now. I've found over the years that a similar thing has happened with the so-called absurd theater. Predictable.

Interviewer: In other words, the notion of tragedy about which you were talking earlier is absent from this preconceived view of the world.

Miller: Absolutely. The tragic hero was supposed to join the scheme of things by his sacrifice. It's a religious thing, I've always thought. He threw some sharp light upon the hidden scheme of existence, either by breaking one of its profoundest laws, as Oedipus breaks a taboo, and therefore proves the existence of the taboo, or by proving a moral world at the cost of his own life. And that's the victory. We need him, as the vanguard of the race. We need his crime. That crime is a civilizing crime. Well, *now* the view is that it's an inconsolable universe. Nothing is proved by a crime excepting that some people are freer to produce crime than others, and usually they are more honest than the others. There is no final reassertion of a community at all. There isn't the kind of communication that a child demands. The best you could say is that it is intelligent.

Interviewer: Then it's aware —

Miller: It's aware, but it will not admit into itself any moral universe at all. Another thing that's missing is the positioning of the author in relation to power. I always assumed that underlying any story is the question of who should wield power. See, in *Death of a Salesman* you have two viewpoints. They show what would happen if we all took Willy's viewpoint toward the world, or if we all took Biff's. And took it seriously, as almost a political fact. I'm debating really which way the world ought to be run; I'm speaking of psychology and the spirit, too. For example, a play that isn't usually linked with this kind of problem is Tennessee Williams's *Cat on a Hot Tin Roof.* It struck me sharply that what is at stake there is the father's great power. He's the owner, literally, of an empire of land and farms. And he wants to immortalize that power, he wants to hand it on, because he's dying. The son has a much finer appreciation of justice and human relations than the father. The father is rougher, more Philistine; he's cruder; and when we speak of the fineness of emotions, we would probably say the son has them and the father lacks them. When I saw the play I thought, This is going to be simply marvelous because the person with the sensitivity will be presented with power and what is he going to do about it? But it never gets to that. It gets deflected onto a question of personal neurosis. It comes to a dead end. If we're talking about tragedy, the Greeks would have done something miraculous with that idea. They would have stuck the son with the power, and faced him with the racking conflicts of the sensitive man having to rule. And then you would throw light on what the tragedy of power is.

Interviewer: Which is what you were getting at in *Incident at Vichy*.

Miller: That's exactly what I was after. But I feel today's stage turns away from any consideration of power, which always lies at the heart of tragedy. I use Williams's play as an example because he's that excellent that his problems are symptomatic of the time — *Cat* ultimately came down to the mendacity of human relations. It was a most accurate personalization but it bypasses the issue which the play seems to me to raise, namely the mendacity in social relations. I still believe that when a play questions, even threatens, our social arrangement, that is when it really shakes us profoundly and dangerously, and that is when you've got to be great; good isn't enough.

Interviewer: Do you think that people in general now rationalize so, and have so many euphemisms for death, that they can't face tragedy?

Miller: I wonder whether there isn't a certain — I'm speaking now of all classes of people — you could call it a softness, or else a genuine inability to face the tough decisions and the dreadful results of error.

HELGE NORMANN NILSEN

Marxism and the Early Plays of Arthur Miller

1994

During the period from the nineteen-thirties through the forties Marxism exercised a controlling influence on Arthur Miller's work. This is evident in several of his earliest, unpublished plays, propaganda pieces advocating the overthrow of capitalism and the establishment of a socialist system.[1] The political tendency of these plays is too obvious to be ignored, but it has escaped the attention of most readers that the same message is embodied in the first three plays that Miller published. These are *The Man Who Had All the Luck* (1944), *All My Sons* (1947) and *Death of a Salesman* (1949), his most famous work.

[1]Miller has described his own and his friends' early adoption of Marxism in his autobiography: "We enjoyed a certain unity within ourselves by virtue of a higher consciousness bestowed by our expectation of a socialist evolution of the planet," *Timebends: A Life* (New York, 1987), p. 70.

If one compares the unpublished plays with the published ones, the common features emerge. American capitalism is criticized and rejected, and an alternative, socialist community and system of values are pointed to. The message is implicit rather than explicit in the printed works, but the political agenda remains the same. The most important reason behind Miller's commitment to radicalism is that the Great Depression created in him a lasting and traumatic impression of the devastating power of economic forces in the shaping of people's lives. This also meant that, in the early plays, he portrayed and analyzed his major characters as products of the American capitalist society and its influence.[2] At the same time he managed to give them individuality and persuasiveness as characters.

Miller's political attitudes at the time emerge mainly in the plays in question, but are also described in his autobiography. They fall within the tradition of analysis and criticism of capitalism established by Marx and the movements building on his theories. Miller's critique can be summed up as follows: capitalism is inhuman in its glorification of private property and its exclusive orientation toward profitmaking. Human beings are sacrificed to economic interests in ways that are not only immoral, but even criminal in nature. In business, ruthless competition is the norm. People's moral character is threatened. They may become scoundrels, or rendered insane and suicidal. Egocentric individualism reigns supreme, and society fosters no sense of responsibility to anyone beyond self and family. There is an unjust concentration of financial power into a few hands, making all others powerless and bereft of economic security. The capitalists also control most of the cultural life of society and the media, spreading their conservative political views. No institution or aspect of society can escape this influence. The false values of materialism and the cult of success threaten to extinguish human love and caring. Conformism rules, turning people into mere cogs in the machine of production, and genuine individualism and even enjoyment of life become hard to obtain. The coming socialist society, on the other hand, will be built on solidarity, human brotherhood, and the ownership of the workers and citizens of the means of production.[3] . . .

Death of a Salesman is . . . rooted in the playwright's early, agonized reactions to the Depression. Marxism had taught him that this disaster was one of the vagaries of capitalism, and his early, militant stance is suggested in an observation recorded in a notebook containing an early version of the play: "The restrictions, like all tyrannies, exist by default of revolutionary resis-

[2]In the early forties Miller attended a Marxist study group and was proposed for membership in the American Communist Party. In *The New York Times,* May 25, 1947, his name appeared on a list of sponsors of the World Youth Festival, organized by the communist World Federation of Democratic Youth. See J. Schlueter and J. K. Flanagan, *Arthur Miller* (New York, 1987), pp. 6, 146.

[3]Interpreting Marx, R. W. Miller states that: "under socialism and communism, most people are less dominated, more in possession of their lives, since they are better able to develop their capacities in light of their own assessments of their needs. Moreover, their interactions will be governed to a greater extent than now by mutual well-wishing and concern," "Marx and Morality," in *Marxism,* ed. J. R. Pennock and J. W. Chapman (New York, 1983), p. 60.

tance."[4] The reference is to formal conventions in drama, but the choice of words reveals a political radicalism also.

As in the other plays, victimization by the free play of economic forces is the main theme of *Death of a Salesman.* It is suggested in the initial stage direction: "A melody is heard, played upon a flute. It is small and fine, telling of grass and trees and the horizon. Before us is the salesman's house. We are aware of towering, angular shapes behind it, surrounding it on all sides." The people in the house are threatened and overwhelmed by the tall buildings, symbols of the crushing power of those who win out in a capitalist struggle that has no room for failures and losers.

Willy Loman, the aging salesman, is worn out to the point of breakdown by his many years on the road. But he remains a firm believer in capitalist values and has transferred his hope of success to his son Biff. Willy is a dreamer, and the play contrasts his dreams with the harsh realities of failure and mediocrity that he tries to shut out of his mind. Corrupted, or brainwashed by the system, Willy is blind to its destructiveness and is obsessed by his plans for Biff.

Biff, however, has begun to rebel against his father's ideas and to feel his way towards different standards, meaning those that Miller associates with the socialist society. Unlike his brother Happy, he has "allowed himself to turn his face toward defeat," and even this becomes a possible source of strength for him. His lack of conventional success is slowly teaching him, not that he is worthless, but that he may not be cut out for a business career and may actually be better off without it. He is trying to understand himself and discover his real identity, this also being an aim of socialism as Miller understood it. But Biff is not yet sure of himself, in the first part of the play, and still feels guilty for not being a success. He has returned to his parents in a last attempt to fulfill his father's dreams.

Happy, who has a good job and wants to get further ahead, also has doubts about his own careerism but cannot find anything to put in its place. Biff struggles with this issue, searching for and finally finding another path for himself. However, his father remains a man whose self-respect depends entirely on his role as a breadwinner and useful cog in the production machine. He worships the memory of Ben, the youth who walked into the jungle of Africa at the age of seventeen and came out rich at twenty-one, a powerful *entrepreneur.* What Willy fails to realize is that only a very few can hope to be that successful. His greatest illusion is his belief in the capitalist myth that every man can succeed in business if he only uses his opportunities. Willy is also haunted by the equally superhuman success ideal embodied in his grandfather, a heroic pioneer figure who drove across America with his family, supporting them all by selling flutes that he made himself.

The scene in which Willy is fired by his young boss Howard is a perfect illustration of the logic of the capitalist economic mechanism. Willy has been with the firm since before Howard was born, but the almost familiar relationship between these two still counts for nothing. Mortally afraid of ruin, like

---

[4]Notebook, in longhand, undated, in the Harry Ransom Humanities Research Center.

Keller, Willy appeals to Howard's conscience, reminding him how long and faithfully he has worked for the company, but to no avail. Howard is not evil, however; he is even able to sympathize with Willy's plight, but this in no way interferes with his decision to fire an aging employee who can no longer ring up any sales. Howard, like Ben or Charley, a businessman who is Willy's friend and neighbor, abides by the law of profitability first that is supreme in the world of capitalist business. He is impersonal about it, again like Charley or Ben, regarding it as a law of nature.[5]

Wanting to help Willy, Charley offers him a job, but the former refuses to take it, feeling that it would be a kind of charity and would violate the image he has of himself as a self-reliant, honorable individual who does not depend on others. Rugged individualism is the ideology of the *laissez-faire* capitalism that he believes in so deeply. But the facts are that Willy's failure is destroying him and that Biff's similar fate makes his father reject him. The all-important success ideal prevents Willy from perceiving Biff as a person and an individual. Capitalist values distort and destroy what should have been a rewarding human relationship between father and son.

The horrifying consequences of a blind adherence to these values emerge in Willy's decision to commit suicide so that his life insurance payment will enable Biff to rise in the world. But Biff, like Chris Keller, instead becomes the vehicle through which Miller subtly introduces his alternative socialist perceptions and values into his work. Biff thus becomes the only character in the drama who really understands the destructive nature of capitalist priorities and feels pity and concern for his father, exclaiming: "I can't bear to look at his face!" He tries to make Willy understand the realities of their situation, which is that their lives have been dominated by a dream that is no better than a lie. Biff has realized that the whole family are victims, in various ways and like most people, of capitalist oppression and false standards. They are basically downtrodden people, "a dime a dozen." But this, of course, is the very thing that Willy refuses to admit, and he denies it furiously. Biff tries to impress upon him that they ought to lower their expectations and rely on the comforts of love and human caring. Willy, however, is not willing to correct his capitalist hierarchy of values and accuses Biff of betrayal. His son, he says, is "vengeful" and "spiteful." But Biff continues his attempt to break through to his father's feelings and establish a genuine connection and respect between them. Hence his plaintive cry: "Pop, I'm nothing . . . I'm just what I am, that's all."

In this central scene, Willy does perceive that his son wants to show him his love, but is unable to respond to this in a simple way. Instead, and in keeping with his blinkered vision, he grotesquely interprets Biff's love as yet another sign of his potentially glorious future, or as a part of the fine personality that

---

[5]Brian Parker argues that because Howard and Charley, both capitalists, are ordinary men and not evil, *Death of a Salesman* cannot be an anti-capitalist play. But the fact that these are not bad men does not change the workings of the system that they represent. See "Point of View in Arthur Miller's *Death of a Salesman,*" *Arthur Miller: A Collection of Critical Essays* (Englewood Cliffs, 1969), p. 99.

will help making him rich: "That boy — that boy is going to be magnificent!" The insurance money will yet secure Biff's success, he thinks, and is deluded enough to assume that his son will be thankful for the sacrifice he is making.

But at Willy Loman's grave it is capitalism and the dreams it is responsible for that are indicted. Looking back on his father's life, Biff firmly declares: "He had the wrong dreams. All, all wrong." *Death of a Salesman* suggests that the right dreams are opposed to rapacious capitalism and that they are about justice, love, and genuine selfhood as envisaged by Marxism.

. . . In *Death of a Salesman* the jobless Willy Loman has become mentally disturbed, his suicide for the sake of money an eloquent testimony to the corrosive effects of the tyrannical success ideal extolled by his society. Willy is a victim, both directly and indirectly, of the logic of a capitalism which says that human worth is proportional to economic achievement. Taken as a whole, these dramas build a powerful indictment against the American capitalist system that Miller knew, but they do not stop at that point. Whether openly or more discreetly, they suggest the possibility of another, just and humane society. This new, socialist world will be built on the principles of love, mutual concern, and sharing rather than competition.

JOHN BEAUFORT

Review of Death of a Salesman

1949

Arthur Miller's *Death of a Salesman* is a profoundly absorbing theater experience. With his new drama, Mr. Miller amply fulfills the promise of his earlier work, *All My Sons,* which won a Critics Circle Award in 1947.

Mr. Miller has now diagnosed in dramatic terms the desperate case of a certain Willy Loman, stocking salesman, who suddenly discovers that his small world of hopes and loves and aspirations has been built on a terrible self-deception. His values have played him false. His life's goal has turned out to be a retreating mirage at the edge of a wasteland.

The stunned awakening carries with it no sense of why the dream of Success for himself and his sons has turned into a nightmare. Willy Loman possesses little more than the capacity to experience the awful realization, to grope for answers that do not come, and to destroy himself in a gesture of sacrifice which he yearningly hopes will regain the respect of his family, particularly of his son Biff.

In *Death of a Salesman,* which opened recently at the Morosco Theater, Mr. Miller covers the final day or two in Willy Loman's life. By projecting the drama from the standpoint of Willy's distraught condition, the playwright moves back and forth, in terms of time, between the happy days when Willy's two sons were high school youngsters and the present disintegrating state of the Loman household. To say that Mr. Miller uses the "flashback" technique scarcely suggests the virtuosity of his achievement. No adjustment is required of the spectator to follow the constant stream-of-consciousness movement. Past and present are fused into one immediate drama.

DIRECTION SKILLFUL

Mr. Miller's playwrighting talent is admirably complemented by the direction of Elia Kazan. Here are all the force and skill of the characteristic Kazan performance, together with perhaps a greater degree of compassion and tender concern with humanity than Mr. Kazan has heretofore achieved. It may be that *Death of a Salesman* makes greater demands upon him in this respect than previous plays.

As in *All My Sons,* Mr. Miller is again writing primarily about a father-and-son relationship. Again, the author presents a case of close relationship without mutual understanding of a man and his son whose natural affection is blighted by what emerge as two divergent concepts of life. As in any such separation, the growing estrangement is marked by an increasing inability to communicate and, finally, in a violent conflict.

As a salesman suddenly reaching the end of the road, Willy regards Biff, his golden-haired hope, as a failure. Biff, at thirty-four, is a sometimes ranch hand without tangible assets or discernible prospects. Notwithstanding his inclination for an outdoor life, he has come home to try settling down and resuming the business career from which he fled. In the course of the rising dramatic action, a flashback reveals that Biff, who adored his father, once discovered Willy in a hotel room with a woman. The disintegration of their relationship began at that crisis.

TEMPESTUOUS SCENES

In the tempestuous scenes with his now mature son, Willy insists that Biff's adult antagonism and his actions result from spite. Biff insists that he is simply unable to conform to the pattern of a businessman's life, that only in working outdoors and with his hands does he find any real satisfaction. Willy, it develops, also was never happier than when building something around his house.

In this context, the salesman's actual suicide appears to be only the final act in a kind of living death. Willy has turned his back on a way of life which might have satisfied him and engaged instead in a futile race for the symbols of material success. Since he lacks the aggressive imagination and initiative of his adventurous brother, Willy Loman's existence has been an endless battle to meet the next installment, pay off the mortgage, keep up with his life insurance. The final obligations to mortgage and insurance are met just before Willy ends his life. Thus *Death of a Salesman* makes its final, ironically tragic thrust.

I hope to see the play again for a number of reasons, not the least of which is the excellent performances. Lee J. Cobb moves through the final hours of Willy's life with a growing, numbing weariness. A rough, shambling kind of man, Mr. Cobb's Willy suggests the good heart, the simple faith, the complacent confidence in slogans and advertisements which survive only so long as an illusion lasts. Nothing is finer in Mr. Cobb's performance than his fondling of a gold cigarette case near the end of the play — a gesture of wistful admiration for the material success which has eluded all his hustling.

As Willy's wife, Mildred Dunnock portrays the devotion, the sharp, fierce loyalty, the sensitivity to a human being's need for decent treatment which perhaps go as far as it is humanly possible to go in ameliorating the plight of the Willy Lomans of the world. I have not seen a finer performance than Miss Dunnock's this season. . . .

Jo Mielziner has devised an ingenious skeletonized set in which the Loman household is dwarfed and crushed under the weight of the stone and brick of the apartment buildings which have sprung up around it. It was presumably from such buildings that the Loman boys — with their father's indulgent approval — stole the lumber which went into Willy's improvements. Here again Mr. Miller points to the moral flaw in Willy's system of values.

For in *Death of a Salesman,* Miller is writing once more about moral responsibility and the misconception of what constitutes moral responsibility. He is writing about the conflict in people and between people. It remains for Biff, who alone perceives the significance of the conflict, to claim his ultimate freedom. Therein lies the catharsis of the play, the journey through "pity and fear" to a heightened sense of what the individual must mean to himself and to others, a repudiation of the false measurements of success. This is not the whole answer. But it is more than Willy Loman perceived.

JOHN LAHR

Making Willy Loman

1999

On a crisp April weekend in 1948, Arthur Miller, then only thirty-three and enjoying the first flush of fame after the Broadway success the previous year of *All My Sons,* waved goodbye to his first wife, Mary, and their two young kids, in Brooklyn, and set off for Roxbury, Connecticut, where he intended to build a cabin on a hillock just behind a Colonial house he had recently purchased for the family, which stood at the aptly named crossroads of Tophet (another name for Hell) and Gold Mine. "It was a purely instinctive act," Miller, who long ago traded up from that first forty-four-acre property to a four-hundred-acre spread on Painter Hill, a few miles down the road, told me recently. "I had never built a building in my life."

Miller had a play in mind, too; his impulse for the cabin was "to sit in the middle of it, and shut the door, and let things happen." All Miller knew about his new play was that it would be centered on a travelling salesman who would die at the end and that two of the lines were "Willy?" "It's all right. I came back" — words that to Miller spoke "the whole disaster in a nutshell." He says, "I mean, imagine a salesman who can't get past Yonkers. It's the end of the world. It's like an actor saying 'It's all right. I can't speak.'" As he worked away on his cabin, he repeated the play's two lines like a kind of mantra. "I kept saying, 'As soon as I get the roof on and the windows in, I'm gonna start this thing,'" he recalls. "And indeed I started on a morning in spring. Everything was starting to bud. Beautiful weather."

Miller had fashioned a desk out of an old door. As he sat down to it his tools and nails were still stashed in a corner of the studio, which was as yet unpainted and smelled of raw wood. "I started in the morning, went through the day, then had dinner, and then I went back there and worked till — I don't know — one or two o'clock in the morning," he says. "It sort of unveiled itself, I was the stenographer. I could hear them. I could hear them, literally." When Miller finally lay down to sleep that first night, he realized he'd been crying. "My eyes still burned and my throat was sore from talking it all out and shouting and laughing," he later wrote in his autobiography, *Timebends.* In one day, he had produced, almost intact, the first act of *Death of a Salesman,* which has since sold about eleven million copies, making it probably the most successful modern play ever published. The show, which is being put on somewhere in the world almost every day of the year, celebrates its fiftieth anniversary next month with a Broadway revival from Chicago's Goodman Theatre, directed by Robert Falls and starring Brian Dennehey as the fanatical and frazzled drummer Willy Loman.

"He didn't write *Death of a Salesman;* he *released* it," the play's original director, Elia Kazan, said in his autobiography, *A Life.* "It was there inside him, stored up waiting to be turned loose." To Miller, there was a "dream's quality in my memory of the writing and the day or two that followed its completion." In his notebook for *Death of a Salesman* — a sixty-six-page document chronicling the play's creation, which is kept with his papers at the University of Texas at Austin — he wrote, "He who understands everything about his subject cannot write it. I write as much to discover as to explain." After that first day of inspiration, it took Miller six weeks to call forth the second act and to make Willy remember enough "so he would kill himself." The form of the play — where past and present coalesce in a lyrical dramatic arc — was one that Miller felt he'd been "searching for since the beginning of my writing life." *Death of a Salesman* seems to spill out of Willy's panic-stricken, protean imagination, and not out of a playwright's detached viewpoint. "The play is written from the sidewalk instead of from a skyscraper," Miller says of its first-person urgency. But, ironically, it was from the deck of a skyscraper that Miller contemplated beginning his drama, in a kind of Shakespearean foreshadowing of Willy's suicidal delirium. The notebook's first entry reads:

> Scene 1 — Atop Empire State. 2 guards. "Who will die today? It's that kind of day . . . fog, and poor visibility. They like to jump into a cloud. Who will it be today?"

As Miller navigated his way through the rush of characters and plot ideas, the notebook acted as ballast. "In every scene remember his size, ugliness," Miller reminds himself about Loman on its second page. "Remember his own attitude. Remember *pity.*" He analyzes his characters' motives. "Willy wants his sons to destroy his failure," he writes, and on a later page, "Willy resents Linda's unbroken, patient forgiveness (knowing there must be great hidden hatred for him in her heart)." In Miller's notebook, characters emerge sound and fully formed. For instance, of Willy's idealized elder son, Biff, who is a lost soul fallen from his high-school glory and full of hate for his father, he writes, "Biff is travelled, oppressed by guilt of failure, of not making money although a kind of indolence pleases him: an easygoing way of life. . . . Truthfully, Biff is not really bright enough to make a businessman. *Wants everything too fast."* Miller also talks to himself about the emotional stakes and the trajectory of scenes:

> Have it happen that Willy's life is in Biff's hands — aside from Biff succeeding. There is Willy's guilt to Biff re: The Woman. But is that retrievable? There is Biff's disdain for Willy's character, his false aims, his pretense and these Biff cannot finally give up or alter. Discover the link between Biff's work views and his antiwork feelings.

Although the notebook begins with a series of choppy asides and outlines, it soon becomes an expansive, exact handwritten log of Miller's contact with his inner voices. For instance, it reveals the development of Charley, Loman's benevolent next-door neighbor, whose laconic evenhandedness was, in Miller's eyes, partly a projection of his own father. Charley speaks poignantly to Biff at Willy's graveside ("Nobody dast blame this man"); what appears in the last scene as a taut and memorable nine-line speech, a kind of eulogy, was mined from words (here indicated in italics) that were part of a much longer improvisation in the notebook

> A salesman doesn't build anything, *he don't put a bolt to a nut* or a seed in the ground. A man who doesn't build anything must be liked. He must be cheerful on bad days. Even calamities mustn't break through. Cause one thing, he has got to be liked. *He don't tell you the law or give you medicine.* So there's no rock bottom to your life. All you know is that on good days or bad, you gotta come in cheerful. No calamity must be permitted to break through, Cause one thing, always, you're a man who's gotta be believed. You're way out there *riding on a smile and a shoeshine. And when they start not smilin' back,* the sky falls in. *And then get a couple of spots on your hat, and you're finished. Cause there's no rock bottom to your life.*

Here, as in all his notes for the play, Miller's passion and his flow are apparent in the surprising absence of cross-outs; the pages exude a startling alertness. He is listening not just to the voices of his characters but to the charmed country silence around him, which seems to define his creative state of grace:

> Roxbury — At night the insects softly thumping the screens like a blind man pushing with his fingers in the dark. . . . The crickets, frogs, whippoorwills altogether, a scream from the breast of the earth when everyone is gone. The evening sky, faded gray, like the sea pressing up against the windows, or an opaque gray screen. (Through which someone is looking in at me?)

. . . Willy Loman's particular terror goes to the core of American individualism, in which the reputable self and the issue of wealth are hopelessly tangled. "A man can't go out the way he came in," Willy says to Ben. "A man has got to add up to something." Willy, who, at sixty, has no job, no money, no loyalty from his boys, is sensationally lacking in assets and in their social corollary — a sense of blessing. "He envies those who are blessed; he feels unblessed, but he's striving for it," Miller says. Although Willy's wife, Linda, famously says of him that "attention must be paid," he feels invisible to the world. "I'm not noticed," he says. Later, Linda confides to the boys, "For five weeks he's been on straight commission, like a beginner, an unknown!" As Miller puts it now, "The whole idea of people failing with us is that they can no longer be loved. You haven't created a persona which people will pay for, see, experience, or come close to. It's almost like death. You have a deathly touch. People who succeed are loved because they exude some magical formula for fending off destruction, fending off death." He continues, "It's the most brutal way of looking at life that one can imagine, because it discards anyone who does not measure up. It wants to destroy them. It's been going on since the Puritan times. You are beyond the blessing of God. You're beyond the reach of God. That God rewards those who deserve it. It's a moral condemnation that goes on. You don't want to be near this failure."

Death of a Salesman was the first play to dramatize this punishing — and particularly American — interplay of panic and achievement. Before *Salesman,* Eugene O'Neill's *The Iceman Cometh* (1946) raised the issue in the eerie calm of Harry Hope's bar, whose sodden habitués have retreated from competitiveness into a perverse contentment; as one of the characters says, "No one here has to worry about where they're going next, because there is no farther they can go." But in Willy Loman, Miller was able to bring both the desperation and the aspiration of American life together in one character.

Willy is afflicted by the notion of winning — what Brecht called "the black addiction of the brain." He cheats at cards; he encourages his boys to seek every advantage. Victory haunts him and his feckless sons. In a scene from the notebook, Biff and Happy tell Willy of their plan to go into business. "Step on it, boys, there ain't a minute to lose," Willy tells them, but their souls are strangled by their father's heroic dreams, which hang over them like some sort of spiritual kudzu. In another notebook entry, Biff rounds fiercely on Willy: "I don't care if you live or die. You think I'm mad at you because of the Woman, don't you? I am, but I'm madder because you botched up my life, because I can't tear you out of my heart, because I keep trying to make good, be something for you, to succeed for you."

In dramatizing the fantasy of competition, Miller's play was the first to dissect cultural envy in action — that process of invidious comparison which drives society forward but also drives it crazy. "You lose your life to it!" Miller says of the envy that feeds Willy's restlessness. "It's the ultimate outer-directional emotion. In other words, I am doing this not because it's flowing from me but because it's flowing against him." He goes on, "You're living in a mirror. It's a life of reflections. Emptiness. Emptiness. Emptiness. Hard to go to sleep at night. And hard to wake up." In his mind, Willy is competing with his brother Ben; with Dave Singleman, a successful old salesman who could make a living "without ever leaving his room" and who died a placid, accomplished death on a train to Boston; with his neighbor Charley, who owns his own business; and with Charley's successful lawyer son, Bernard. "Where's Willy in all this?" Miller asks. "He's competed himself to death. He's not existing anymore, or hardly."

In his notebook Miller wrote, "It is the combination of guilt (of failure), hate, and love — all in conflict that he resolves by 'accomplishing' a 20,000 dollar death." In death, Willy is worth more than in life. His suicide is the ultimate expression of his confusion of success with love and also of his belief in winning at all costs. As a father, he overlooked Biff's small childhood acts of larceny — taking sand from a building site, stealing basketballs, getting the answers for tests from the nerdy, studious Bernard — and Biff has continued his habit into adulthood, out of a combination of envy and revenge. A notebook citation reads, "It is necessary to (1) reveal to Willy that Biff stole to queer himself, and did it to hurt Willy," and "(2) And that he did it because of the Woman and all the disillusionment it implied." In the final version of the play, Biff, admitting in passing that he spent three months in a Kansas City jail for lifting a suit, tells Willy, "I stole myself out of every good job since high school!" At first, Miller saw the twenty thousand dollars of insurance money as cash to put Biff on the straight and narrow. "'My boy's a thief — with 20,000 he'd stop it,'" he wrote in the notebook. Instead, Willy's suicide — the final show of force and fraud, in keeping with his demented competitive fantasies — is pitched on a more grandiose and perverse note. In an early draft of the terrific penultimate scene, where Biff exposes Willy and calls it quits with him and his dream, there is this exchange:

> BIFF (*to him*): What the hell do you want from me? What do you want from me?
> WILLY: — Greatness —
> BIFF: No —

In Miller's final draft, Willy, who will not accept his son's confession of thievery, takes Biff's greatness as a given as he visualizes his own suicide. "Can you imagine that magnificence with twenty thousand dollars in his pocket?" he says to Ben. He adds, "Imagine? When the mail comes he'll be ahead of Bernard again." When he goes to his death, Willy, in his mind, is on a football field with Biff, and full of vindictive triumph ("When you hit, hit low and hit hard, because it's important, boy"). "He dies sending his son through the goalposts," Miller says. "He dies moving." Miller pauses. "I think now that Kazan had it right from the beginning. He said, 'It's a love story.'"

On the last page of his notebook, Miller scribbled a short speech to give to the original cast after its members had read the play in galleys: "I want you all to know now that the cannons are quiet that this production has been the most gratifying I have known. I believe you are the finest ever gathered for any play and I am exceedingly proud and gratified not only for myself but for the American theatre." (The original cast included Lee J. Cobb as Willy, with Mildred Dunnock, Arthur Kennedy, and Cameron Mitchell.) In its passage to greatness, *Death of a Salesman* was enhanced enormously by the poetic set design of Jo Mielziner, who created a series of platforms, with Willy's house as a haunting omnipresent background. However, as Elia Kazan pointed out in his autobiography, "The stage direction in the original manuscript that Art gave me to read directly after he'd finished it does not mention a home as a scenic element. It reads, 'A pinpoint travelling spot lights a small area on stage left. The Salesman is revealed. He takes out his keys and opens an invisible door.'" Kazan continues, "It was a play waiting for a directorial solution." It got it. *Death of a Salesman* also got its share of bad suggestions. Kazan's then wife, Molly Day Thacher, who was a playreader for the Group Theatre and had some influence over Kazan, tried to get Miller, as he remembers it, "to cut out Uncle Ben, all the memory scenes, and simply make it a realistic little narrative." And the coproducer, Kermit Bloomgarden, nervous of a play with *Death* in its title, took a poll among theatregoers which asked, "Would you go to see a play called *Death of a Salesman*?" Nobody would. "They had a list of about fifteen titles," Miller says. "One was *Free and Clear.* I'll never forget that."

In the intervening half century, the surface of American life has changed, but its mad competitiveness hasn't. "I'm not aware of any change in the way people look at this play," Miller says, but he admits that Willy's complaints about loyalty from the head office ring strange to contemporary ears. "Workers now — not just workers but management — know that nobody will have much pity for them." Last year, in a poll taken by the Royal National Theatre of eight hundred English theatre professionals, Miller was voted the greatest contemporary playwright; but in America, where in some quarters he's seen as a kind of Jeremiah, Miller is not accorded quite the same honor. He ascribes his decline in popularity to the erosion of the "unified audience" that came with the rise of the avant-garde in the early sixties. "The only theatre available to a playwright in the late forties was Broadway," Miller writes in the fiftieth-anniversary edition of *Salesman.* "That theatre had one single audience . . . catering to very different levels of age, culture, education, and intellectual sophistication." He continues, "One result of this mix was the ideal, if not frequent fulfillment, of a kind of play that would be complete rather than fragmentary, an emotional rather than an intellectual experience, a play basically of heart with its ulterior moral gesture integrated with action rather than rhetoric. In fact, it was a Shakespearean ideal, a theatre for anyone with an understanding of English and perhaps some common sense."

But there was nothing Shakespearean in the response to "that damned disturbing play," as Kazan called it, on the night of its debut, February 10, 1949, in Philadelphia. "The curtain came down and nothing happened," Miller says. "People sat there a good two or three minutes, then somebody stood up with his coat. Several men — I didn't see women doing this — were helpless. They were sitting there with handkerchiefs over their faces. It was like a funeral." He continues, "I didn't know whether the show was dead or alive. The cast was back there wondering what had happened. Nobody'd pulled the curtain up. Finally, someone thought to applaud, and then the house came apart."

ꟹ

CASEBOOK ON LORRAINE HANSBERRY'S *A RAISIN IN THE SUN*

Lorraine Hansberry reflected on the relationship between Walter Lee in A Raisin in the Sun *and Willy Loman in* Death of a Salesman *in an article published in* The Village Voice Reader *in 1962. She wrote about her "Shakespearean Experience" in high school in* To Be Young, Gifted and Black, *which was published four years after*

Lorraine Hansberry. (Reprinted by permission of Jewell Gresham Nemiroff.)

her death in 1965. In this piece, Hansberry began to shape her memoir of her high-school English teacher nicknamed "Pale Hecate" as an essay, but within a few paragraphs she was so deeply involved in her memories of adolescence that she dramatized them in dialogue form as a series of imaginary exchanges between the teacher and her students.

James Baldwin described his impressions of Hansberry in "Sweet Lorraine," his introduction to the 1969 edition of To Be Young, Gifted and Black. *Julius Lester analyzed "the heroic dimension" of* A Raisin in the Sun *in his introduction to an early edition of Hansberry's* Les Blancs: The Collected Last Plays *(1972).*

Anne Cheney discussed the African heritage in A Raisin in the Sun *in her 1984 critical study of Hansberry for Twayne's United States Authors Series. Margaret B. Wilkerson considered Hansberry's "awareness of culture and gender" in a new introduction to* Les Blancs *published in 1994.*

LORRAINE HANSBERRY

An Author's Reflections: Willy Loman, Walter Younger, and He Who Must Live

1962

> A man can't go out the way he came in . . . Ben, that funeral will be massive!
>
> – WILLY LOMAN, 1946

> We have all thought about your offer and we have decided to move into our house.
>
> – WALTER LEE YOUNGER, 1958

Some of the acute partisanship revolving around *A Raisin in the Sun* is amusing. Those who announce that they find the piece less than fine are regarded in some quarters with dramatic hostility, as though such admission automatically implied the meanest of racist reservations. On the other hand, the ultra-sophisticates have hardly acquitted themselves less ludicrously, gazing coolly down their noses at those who are moved by the play, and going on at length about "melodrama" and/or "soap opera" as if these were not completely definable terms which cannot simply be tacked onto any play and all plays we do not like.

Personally, I find no pain whatever — at least of the traditional ego type — in saying that *Raisin* is a play which contains dramaturgical incompletions. Fine plays tend to utilize one big fat character who runs right through the middle of the structure, by action or implication, with whom we rise or fall. A central character as such is certainly lacking from *Raisin.* I should be delighted to pretend that it was *inventiveness,* as some suggest for me, but it is, also, craft inadequacy and creative indecision. The result is that neither Walter Lee nor Mama Younger loom large enough to monumentally command the play. I consider it an enormous dramatic fault if no one else does. (Nor am I less critical of the production which, by and large, performance and direction alike, is splendid. Yet I should have preferred that the second-act curtain, for instance, be performed with quiet assertion rather than the apparently popular declamatory opulence which prevails.)

All in all, however, I believe that, for the most part, the play has been magnificently understood. In some cases it was not only thematically absorbed but attention was actually paid to the tender treacherousness of its craft-imposed "simplicity." Some, it is true, quite missed that part of the overt intent and went on to harangue the bones of the play with rather useless observations of the terribly clear fact that they are old bones indeed. More meaningful discussions tended to delve into the flesh which hangs from those bones and its implications in mid-century American drama and life.

In that connection it is interesting to note that while the names of Chekhov, O'Casey, and the early Odets were introduced for comparative purposes in some of the reviews, almost no one — with the exception of Gerald Weales in *Commentary* — discovered a simple line of descent between Walter Lee Younger and the last great hero in American drama to also *accept* the values of his culture, Willy Loman. I am sure that the already mentioned primary fault of the play must account in part for this. The family so overwhelms the play that Walter Lee necessarily fails as the true symbol he should be, even though *his* ambitions, *his* frustrations, and *his* decisions are those which decisively drive the play on. But however recognizable he proves to be, he fails to dominate our imagination and finally emerges as a reasonably interesting study, but not, like Arthur Miller's great character — and like Hamlet, of course — a summation of an immense (though not crucial) portion of his culture.

Then too, in fairness to the author and to Sidney Poitier's basically brilliant portrayal of Walter Lee, we must not completely omit reference to some of the prior attitudes which were brought into the theatre from the world outside. For in the minds of many, Walter remains, despite the play, despite performance, what American radical traditions *wish* him to be: an exotic. Some writers have been astonishingly incapable of discussing his purely *class* aspirations and have persistently confounded them with what they consider to be an exotic being's longing to "wheel and deal" in what they further consider to be (and what Walter never can) "the white man's world." Very few people today must consider the ownership of a liquor store as an expression of extraordinary affluence, and yet, as joined to a dream of Walter Younger, it takes on, for some, aspects of the fantastic. We have grown accustomed to the dynamics of "Negro" personality as expressed by white authors. Thus, de Emperor, de Lawd, and, of course, Porgy still haunt our frame of reference when a new character emerges. We have become romantically jealous of the great image of a prototype whom we believe is summarized by the wishfulness of a self-assumed opposite. Presumably there is a quality in human beings that makes us *wish* that we *were* capable of primitive contentments; the *universality* of ambition and its anguish can escape us only if we construct elaborate legends about the rudimentary simplicity of *other* men.

America, for this reason, long ago fell in love with the image of the simple, lovable, and glandular "Negro." We all know that Catfish Row was never intended to slander anyone; it was intended as a mental haven for readers and audiences who could bask in the unleashed passions of those "lucky ones" for whom abandonment was apparently permissible. In an almost paradoxical fashion, it disturbs the soul of man to truly understand what he invariably senses: that *nobody* really finds oppression and/or poverty tolerable. If we ever destroy the image of the black people who supposedly do find those things tolerable in America, then that much-touted "guilt" which allegedly haunts most middle-class white Americans with regard to the Negro question would really become unendurable. It would also mean the death of a dubious literary tradition, but it would undoubtedly and more significantly help toward the more rapid transformation of the status of a people who have never found their imposed misery very charming.

My colleagues and I were reduced to mirth and tears by that gentleman writing his review of our play in a Connecticut paper who remarked of his pleasure at seeing how "our dusky brethren" could "come up with a song and hum their troubles away." It did not disturb the writer in the least that there is no such implication in the entire three acts. He did not need it in the play; he had it in his head.

For all these reasons, then, I imagine that the ordinary impulse to compare Willy Loman and Walter Younger was remote. Walter Lee Younger jumped out at us from a play about a largely unknown world. We knew who Willy Loman was instantaneously; we recognized his milieu. We also knew at once that he represented that curious paradox in what the *English* character in that *English* play could call, though dismally, "The American Age." Willy Loman was a product of a nation of great military strength, indescribable material wealth, and incredible mastery of the physical realm, which nonetheless was unable, in 1946, to produce a *typical* hero who was capable of an affirmative view of life.

I believe it is a testament to Miller's brilliance that it is hardly a misstatement of the case, as some preferred to believe. Something has indeed gone wrong with at least part of the American dream, and Willy Loman is the victim of the detour. Willy had to be overwhelmed on the stage as, in fact, his prototypes are in everyday life. Coming out of his section of our great sprawling middle class, preoccupied with its own restlessness and displaying its obsession for the possession of trivia, Willy was indeed trapped. His predicament in a New World where there just aren't any more forests to clear or virgin railroads to lay or native American empires to first steal and then build upon left him with nothing but some left-over values which had forgotten how to prize industriousness over cunning, usefulness over mere acquisition, and, above all, humanism over "success." The potency of the great tale of a salesman's death was in our familiar recognition of his entrapment which, suicide or no, is *deathly*.

What then of this new figure who appears in American drama in 1958; from what source is he drawn so that, upon inspection, and despite class differences, so much of his encirclement must still remind us of that of Willy Loman? Why, finally, is it possible that when his third-act will is brought to bear, *his* typicality is capable of a choice which *affirms* life? After all, Walter Younger is an American more than he is anything else. His ordeal, give or take his personal expression of it, is not extraordinary but intensely familiar like Willy's. The two of them have virtually no values which have not come out of their culture, and to a significant point, no view of the possible solutions to their problems which do not also come out of the self-same culture. Walter can find no peace with that part of society which seems to permit him entry and no entry into that which has willfully excluded him. He shares with Willy Loman the acute awareness that *something* is obstructing some abstract progress that he feels he *should* be making; that *something* is in the way of his ascendancy. It does not occur to either of them to question the nature of this desired "ascendancy." Walter accepts, he believes in the "world" as it has been presented to him. When we first meet him, he does not wish to alter *it;* merely to change *his* position in it. His mentors and his associates all take the view that the institutions which frustrate him are somehow impeccable, or, at best, "unfortunate." "Things being as they are," he must look to *himself* as the only source of any rewards he may expect. Within himself, he is encouraged to believe, are the only seeds of defeat or victory within the universe. And Walter believes this and when opportunity, haphazard and rooted in death, prevails, he acts.

But the obstacles which are introduced are gigantic; the weight of the loss of the money is in fact the weight of death. In Walter Lee Younger's life, somebody *has* to die for ten thousand bucks to pile up — if then. Elsewhere in the world, in the face of catastrophe, he might be tempted to don the saffron robes of acceptance and sit on a mountain top all day contemplating the divine justice of his misery. Or, history being what it is turning out to be, he might wander down to his first Communist Party meeting. But here in the dynamic and confusing post-war years on the South Side of Chicago, his choices of action are equal to those gestures only in symbolic terms. The American ghetto hero may give up and contemplate his misery in rose-colored bars to the melodies of hypnotic saxophones, but revolution seems alien to him in his circumstances (America), and it is easier to dream of personal wealth than of a communal state wherein universal dignity is supposed to be a corollary. Yet his position in time and space does allow for one other alternative: he may take his place on any one of a number of frontiers of challenge. Challenges (such as helping to break down restricted neighborhoods) which are admittedly limited because they most certainly do not threaten the basic social order.

But why is even this final choice possible, considering the ever-present (and ever-so-popular) vogue of despair? Well, that is where Walter departs from Willy Loman; there is a second pulse in his still dual culture. His people have had "somewhere" they have been trying to get for so long that more sophisticated confusions do not yet bind them. *Thus the weight and power of their current social temperament intrudes and affects him, and it is, at the moment, at least, gloriously and rigidly affirmative.* In the course of *their* brutally difficult ascent, they have dismissed the ostrich and still sing, *"Went to the rock to hide my face, but the rock cried out: 'No hidin' place down here!'"* Walter is, despite his lack of consciousness of it, inextricably as much wedded to his special mass as Willy was to his, and the moods of each are able to decisively determine the dramatic typicality. Furthermore, the very nature of the situation of American Negroes can force their representative hero to recognize that for his *true* ascendancy he must ultimately be at cross-purposes with at least certain of his culture's values. It is to the pathos of Willy Loman that his section of American life seems to have momentarily lost that urgency; that he cannot, like Walter, draw on the strength of an incredible people who, historically, have simply refused to give up.

In other words, the symbolism of moving into the new house is quite as small as it seems and quite as significant. For if there are no waving flags and marching songs at the barricades as Walter marches out with his little battalion, it is not because the battle lacks nobility. On the contrary, he has picked up in his way, still imperfect and wobbly in his small view of human destiny, what I believe Arthur Miller once called "the golden thread of history." He becomes, in spite of those who are too intrigued with despair and hatred of man to see it, King Oedipus refusing to tear out his eyes, but attacking the Oracle instead. He is that last Jewish patriot manning his rifle in the burning ghetto at Warsaw; he is that young girl who swam into sharks to save a friend a few weeks ago; he is Anne Frank,° still believing in people; he is the nine small heroes of Little Rock;° he is Michelangelo creating David and Beethoven bursting forth with the Ninth Symphony. He is all those things because he has finally reached out in his tiny moment and caught that sweet essence which is human dignity, and it shines like the old star-touched dream that it is in his eyes. We see, in the moment, I think, what becomes, and not for Negroes alone, but for Willy and all of us, entirely an American responsibility.

Out in the darkness where we watch, most of us are not afraid to cry.

LORRAINE HANSBERRY

My Shakespearean Experience — 1969

1

My High School Yearbook bears the dedication: "Englewood High trains for citizenship in a world of many different peoples. Who could better

---

Anne Frank: A German Jewish teenager (1929–1945) who, during World War II, hid from the Nazis with her family for twenty-five months in an annex of rooms in Amsterdam. She recorded the experience in her diary which was published in 1947, two years after her death from typhus in a Nazi concentration camp.

nine small heroes of Little Rock: Following the U.S. Supreme Court's ruling that racial segregation in U.S. schools was unconstitutional, nine black teenagers defied white mobs and a hostile governor and marched into Little Rock, Arkansas's Central High School on September 25, 1957. They were supported by the federal government.

appreciate this wonderful country than our forefathers who traveled hundreds of miles from every known nation, seeking a land of freedom from discrimination of race, color, or creed." And in illustration, there is this:

> *The Great Branches of Man at Englewood High:* in front, Mangolia Ali of East Indian Mohammedan descent; second couple, Nancy Diagre and Harold Bradley, Negroid; middle couple, Rosalind Sherr and William Krugman, Jewish religion, not a racial stock; next, Eleanor Trester and Theodore Flood, Caucasoid; extreme right, Lois Lee and Barbara Nomura, Mongoloid; rear, left, Mr. Thompson, principal.

2

I was reminded of Englewood by a questionnaire which came from *Show* magazine the other day. . . .

THE SHAKESPEAREAN EXPERIENCE
SHOW POLL #5, February 1964

Some Questions Answered by: Robert Bolt, Jean Cocteau, T. S. Eliot, Tyrone Guthrie, Lorraine Hansberry, Joan Littlewood, Harold Pinter, Alain Robbe-Grillet, Igor Stravinsky, Harry S Truman

QUESTION: *What was your first contact with Shakespeare?*

High School. English literature classwork. We had to read and memorize speeches from *Macbeth* and *Julius Caesar* all under the auspices of a strange and bewigged teacher who we, after this induction, naturally and cruelly christened "Pale Hecate" — God rest her gentle, enraptured, and igniting soul!

Pale Hecate enters, ruler in hand, and takes her place in the classroom. She surveys the class. They come to attention as her eye falls on each in turn.

PALE HECATE: Y'do not read, nor speak, nor write the English language! I suspect that y'do not even *think* in it! God only knows in what language y'do think, or if you think at all. 'Tis true the *English* have done little enough with the tongue, but being the English I expect it was the best they could do. (*They giggle.*) In any case, I'll have it learned properly before a living one of y'll pass out of this class. That I will! (*Waving a composition book and indicating the grade marked in red at the top.*) As for *you*, Miss — as for you, indeed, surely you will recognize the third letter of the alphabet when y'have seen it?

STUDENT: "C."

PALE HECATE: Aye, a "C" it 'tis! You're a bright and clever one now after all, aren't y'lass? (*The class snickers.*) And now, my brilliance, would you also be informing us as to what a grade signifies when it is thus put upon the page?

STUDENT: Average.

PALE HECATE: "Average." Yes, yes — and what else in your case, my iridescence? Well then, I'll be tellin' you in fine order. It stands for "cheat," my luminous one! (*The class sobers.*) For them that will do *half* when *all* is called for; for them that will slip and slide through life at the edge of their minds, never once pushing into the interior to see what wonders are hiding there — content to drift along on whatever gets them by, *cheating* themselves, *cheating* the world, *cheating* Nature! That is what the "C" means, my dear child — (*she smiles*) — my pet (*they giggle; in rapid order she raps each on the head with her ruler*) — my laziest *Queen of the Ethiopes!*

She exits or dims out.

QUESTION: *Which is your favorite Shakespeare play and why?*

Favorite? It is like choosing the "superiority" of autumn days; mingling titles permits a reply: *Othello* and *Hamlet*. Why? There is a sweetness in the former that lingers long after the tragedy is done. A kind of possibility that we suspect in man wherein even its flaw is a tribute. The latter because there remains a depth in the Prince that, as we all know, constantly re-engages as we mature. And it does seem that the wit remains the brightest and most instructive in all dramatic literature.

QUESTION: *What is the most important result of your familiarity with Shakespeare? What has he given you?*

Comfort and agitation so bound together that they are inseparable. Man, as set down in the plays, is large. Enormous. Capable of anything at all. And yet fragile, too, this view of the human spirit; one feels it ought be respected and protected and loved rather fiercely.

Rollicking times, Shakespeare has given me. I love to laugh and his humor is that of everyday; of every man's foible at no man's expense. Language. At thirteen a difficult and alien tedium, those Elizabethan cadences; but soon a balm, a thrilling source of contact with life.

JAMES BALDWIN

Sweet Lorraine

1969

That's the way I always felt about her, and so I won't apologize for calling her that now. *She* understood it: in that far too brief a time when we walked and talked and laughed and drank together, sometimes in the streets and bars and restaurants of the Village, sometimes at her house, sometimes at my house, sometimes gracelessly fleeing the houses of others; and sometimes seeming, for anyone who didn't know us, to be having a knockdown, drag-out battle. We spent a lot of time arguing about history and tremendously related subjects in her Bleecker Street and, later, Waverly Place flat. And often, just when I was certain that she was about to throw me out, as being altogether too rowdy a type, she would stand up, her hands on her hips (for these down-home sessions she always wore slacks) and pick up my empty glass as though she intended to throw it at me. Then she would walk into the kitchen, saying, with a haughty toss of her head, "Really, Jimmy. You ain't *right*, child!" With which stern put-down, she would hand me another drink and launch into a brilliant analysis of just why I wasn't "right." I would often stagger down her stairs as the sun came up, usually in the middle of a paragraph and always in the middle of a laugh. That marvelous laugh. That marvelous face. I loved her, she was my sister and my comrade. Her going did not so much make me lonely as make me realize how lonely we were. We had that respect for each other which perhaps is only felt by people on the same side of the barricades, listening to the accumulating thunder of the hooves of horses and the treads of tanks.

The first time I ever saw Lorraine was at the Actors' Studio, in the winter of '57–58. She was there as an observer of the Workshop Production of *Giovanni's Room.*° She sat way up in the bleachers, taking on some of the biggest names in the American theater because she had liked the play and they, in the main, hadn't. I was enormously grateful to her, she seemed to speak for me; and afterwards she talked to me with a gentleness and generosity never to be forgotten. A small, shy, determined person, with that strength dictated by absolutely impersonal ambition: she was not trying to "make it" — she was trying to keep the faith.

We really met, however, in Philadelphia, in 1959, when *A Raisin in the Sun* was at the beginning of its amazing career. Much has been written about this play; I personally feel that it will demand a far less guilty and constricted people than the present-day Americans to be able to assess it at all; as an historical achievement, anyway, no one can gainsay its importance. What is relevant here is that I had never in my life seen so many black people in the theater. And the reason was that never before, in the entire history of the American theater, had so much of the truth of black people's lives been seen on the stage. Black people ignored the theater because the theater had always ignored them.

But, in *Raisin,* black people recognized that house and all the people in it — the mother, the son, the daughter, and the daughter-in-law, and supplied the play with an interpretative element which could not be present in the minds of white people: a kind of claustrophobic terror, created not only by their knowledge of the house but by their knowledge of the streets. And when the curtain came down, Lorraine and I found ourselves in the backstage alley, where she was immediately mobbed. I produced a pen and Lorraine handed me her handbag and began signing autographs. "It only happens once," she said. I stood there and watched. I watched the people, who loved Lorraine for what she had brought to them; and watched Lorraine, who loved the people for what they brought to *her.* It was not, for her, a matter of being admired. She was being corroborated and confirmed. She was wise enough and honest enough to recognize that black American artists are a very special case. One is not merely an artist and one is not judged merely as an artist: the black people crowding around Lorraine, whether or not they considered her an artist, assuredly considered her a witness. This country's concept of art and artists has the effect, scarcely worth mentioning by now, of isolating the artist from the people. One can see the effect of this in the irrelevance of so much of the work produced by celebrated white artists; but the effect of this isolation on a

---

Giovanni's Room: Baldwin's 1956 novel about a young American in Paris dealing with issues of his sexual identity.

black artist is absolutely fatal. He *is,* already, as a black American citizen, isolated from most of his white countrymen. At the crucial hour, he can hardly look to his artistic peers for help, for they do not know enough about him to be able to correct him. To continue to grow, to remain in touch with himself, he needs the support of that community from which, however, all of the pressures of American life incessantly conspire to remove him. And when he is effectively removed, he falls silent — and the people have lost another hope.

Much of the strain under which Lorraine worked was produced by her knowledge of this reality, and her determined refusal to be destroyed by it. She was a very young woman, with an overpowering vision, and fame had come to her early — she must certainly have wished, often enough, that fame had seen fit to drag its feet a little. For fame and recognition are not synonymous, especially not here, and her fame was to cause her to be criticized very harshly, very loudly, and very often by both black and white people who were unable to believe, apparently, that a really serious intention could be contained in so glamorous a frame. She took it all with a kind of astringent good humor, refusing, for example, even to consider defending herself when she was being accused of being a "slum-lord" because of her family's real-estate holdings in Chicago. I called her during that time, and all she said — with a wry laugh — was, "My God, Jimmy, do you realize you're only the second person who's called me today? And you know how my phone kept ringing *before!*" She was not surprised. She was devoted to the human race, but she was not romantic about it.

Julius Lester

The Heroic Dimension in A Raisin in the Sun

1972

A Raisin in the Sun is no intellectual abstraction about upward mobility and conspicuous consumption. It goes right to the core of practically every black family in the ghettos of Chicago, New York, Los Angeles, and elsewhere. Whether they have a picture of Jesus, Martin Luther King, or Malcolm X on the lead-painted walls of their rat-infested tenement, all of them want to get the hell out of there as quickly as they can. Maybe black militants don't know it, or don't want to admit it, but Malcolm X made a down payment on a house in a suburban community a few weeks before he was murdered. And one surely can't accuse Malcolm of bourgeois aspirations. He merely wanted what every black wants — a home of his own adequate to his needs, at a minimum, and the fulfillment of his desires, at the most. . . . *A Raisin in the Sun* is most definitely about "human dignity" because Lorraine Hansberry is concerned with the attitude we must have toward material things if we are to be their master and not their slave. Is that attitude to be Mama's? Or is it to be Walter's? And, for blacks, locked out from these things for so long, the question is a crucial one. As blacks acquire more and more of America's material offerings, are they, too, going to be transformed by their acquisitions into mindless consumers like the majority of whites? Or are they going to continue to walk in the path of righteousness like their forebears? Lorraine Hansberry summarized it well when, in a letter, she wrote of the play:

> . . . we cannot . . . very well succumb to monetary values and know the survival of certain interior aspects of man which . . . must remain if we are to loom larger than other creatures on this planet. . . . Our people fight daily and magnificently for a more comfortable material base for their lives; they desperately need and hourly sacrifice for clean homes, decent food, personal and group dignity and the abolition of terroristic violence as their children's heritage. So, in that sense, I am certainly a materialist in the first order.
>
> However, the distortion of this aspiration surrounds us in the form of an almost maniacal lusting for "acquisitions." It seems to have absorbed the national mentality and Negroes, to be sure, have certainly been affected by it. The young man in the play, Walter Lee, is meant to symbolize their number. Consequently, in the beginning, he dreams not so much of being comfortable and imparting the most meaningful gifts to his son (education in depth, humanist values, a worship of dignity) but merely of being what it seems to him the "successful" portion of humankind is — "rich." Toward this end he is willing to make an old trade; urgently willing. On the fact that some aspect of his society has brought him to this point, the core of the drama hangs.

Walter blames himself, his wife, and his mother for what he sees as his personal failure. And only at the end of the play does it become possible for him to realize that there is a puppeteer manipulating him, a puppeteer who brought him dangerously close to destroying his family and himself.

The climax of the play comes after Walter's deal to get a liquor license falls through. Mama Younger has made a $3500 down payment on a house and gives the remaining money to Walter to do with as he wishes after he deposits $2500 in a savings account for Beneatha's education. Walter, however, takes the entire $6500 and gives it to one of his two future "partners." One of the "partners" absconds with the money. A Mr. Lindner, a white man from the neighborhood into which they are to move, comes and offers to buy the house from them for more than they would eventually pay. The whites in the neighborhood do not want a black family moving in. Previously, Walter had scornfully turned the man down. However, when he learns that his money has been stolen, he calls Mr. Lindner on the phone and tells him that they will sell the house. Mr. Lindner comes over and Walter finds that he is unable to go through with it. There is something in him — a little bit of self-respect is still left; he tells Mr. Lindner that they are going to move in. And with Walter making his first step toward being a man, a *black* man, the play ends.

Few see the heroism in Walter's simple act of assertion. Indeed, how many who have seen the play or the movie have not thought that Walter was a fool for *not* accepting the money? How one views Walter's act is a direct reflection of how much one accepts the American dream. And there is the significance of the fact that the play ends with the Youngers moving into a "white" neighborhood. To see this as a confirmation of the American dream is to accept the myth that blacks have wanted nothing more than to be integrated with whites. In actuality, the fact that the neighborhood is white is the least important thing about it. It merely happened to be the neighborhood in which Mama Younger could find a nice house she could afford. And it is this simple, practical element which has always been mistaken by whites as a desire on the part of blacks to be "integrated." But why, the question could be raised, would the Youngers persist in moving into a neighborhood where they are not wanted, where they may be subjected to harassment or even physical violence? They persist, as all blacks persist, not because it is any great honor to live among whites, but because one cannot consider himself a human being as long as he acquiesces to restrictions placed upon him by others, particularly if those restrictions are based solely on race or religion. If Walter had accepted the money, he would have been saying, in graphic language, You are right, we are niggers and don't have the right to live where we can afford to. But, with that earthy eloquence of a black still close to his roots, Walter says, "We have decided to move into our house because my father — my father — he earned it." And, in that realization, Walter learns also that it was not a black woman who castrated him. It was America and his own acceptance of America's values. No woman can make him a man. He has to do it himself.

He is a hero, a twentieth-century hero. We still long, of course, for the heroes who seemed to ride history as if it were a bronco and they were champion rodeo riders. But those heroes — if they were ever real — come from a time when life, perhaps, was somewhat less complex. But the problems that face man in the latter twentieth century are large, larger than any one of us, and the sword of a knight in armor is laughable to the dragons roaming our countryside. Our heroes are more difficult to recognize only because they appear so small beside the overwhelming enemies they must slay. But because they appear small does not mean that they are, and it does not make their acts less heroic. Walter Lee Younger has his contemporary historic counterpart in the person of a small, quiet black woman named Rosa Parks who refused to get out of a seat on a bus in Montgomery, Alabama. It would have been so easy for her to have relinquished her seat to a white person that day — as it would have been easy for Walter to have taken the money. But something in her, as in him, said No. And in that quiet dissent, both of them said Yes to human dignity. They said No to those who would define them and thereby deny their existence, and by saying No, they began to define themselves. There have been many Rosa Parks, but few of them have mysteriously set in motion a whole movement for social change. Walter Lee Younger is one of those whose act probably set nothing in motion. And that only increases its heroic dimension. In an article in *The Village Voice,* which compared Walter to Willy Loman, Lorraine Hansberry described the hero she saw in Walter Younger:

> For if there are no waving flags and marching songs at the barricades as Walter marches out with his little battalion, it is not because the battle lacks nobility. On the contrary, he has picked up in his way, still imper-

fect and wobbly in his small view of human destiny, what I believe Arthur Miller once called "the golden thread of history." He becomes, in spite of those who are too intrigued with despair and hatred of man to see it, King Oedipus refusing to tear out his eyes, but attacking the Oracle instead. He is that last Jewish patriot manning his rifle in the burning ghetto at Warsaw; he is that young girl who swam into sharks to save a friend a few weeks ago; he is Anne Frank, still believing in people; he is the nine small heroes of Little Rock; he is Michelangelo creating David, and Beethoven bursting forth with the Ninth Symphony. He is all those things because he has finally reached out in his tiny moment and caught that sweet essence which is human dignity, and it shines like the old star-touched dream that is in his eyes.

ANNE CHENEY

The African Heritage in A Raisin in the Sun

1984

A moving testament to the strength and endurance of the human spirit, *A Raisin in the Sun* is a quiet celebration of the black family, the importance of African roots, the equality of women, the vulnerability of marriage, the true value of money, the survival of the individual, and the nature of man's dreams. A well-made play, *Raisin* at first seems a plea for racial tolerance or a fable of man's overcoming an insensitive society, but the simple eloquence of the characters elevates the play into a universal representation of all people's hopes, fears, and dreams.

On January 19, 1959, a timid Lorraine Hansberry wrote her mother about *Raisin:* "Mama, it is a play that tells the truth about people, Negroes and life and I think it will help a lot of people to understand how we are just as complicated as they are . . . people who are the very essence of human dignity. . . . I hope it will make you very proud."[1] Indeed, *A Raisin in the Sun* made not only Nannie Perry Hansberry proud but also artists — both black and white. *Raisin* was the first play by a black writer ever to win the prestigious New York Drama Critics' Circle Award. The play would become "an American classic, published and produced in some thirty languages abroad and in thousands of productions across the country." . . . James Baldwin [said]: "Never before in the entire history of the American theatre had so much of the truth of Black people's lives been seen on the stage."[2] Despite the earlier contributions of Langston Hughes, David Littlejohn wrote, "It would not be unfair in dating the emergence of a serious and mature Negro theater in America from 1959, the date of Lorraine Hansberry's *A Raisin in the Sun.*"[3]. . .

[1]Lorraine Hansberry, *To Be Young, Gifted and Black: Lorraine Hansberry in Her Own Words,* adapted by Robert Nemiroff (New York: New American Library, 1970), p. 109.

[2]Robert Nemiroff, "Lorraine Hansberry Biography," unpublished paper.

[3]David Littlejohn, *Black on White: A Critical Survey of Writings by American Negroes* (New York: Grossman Publishers, 1966), p. 79.

Today some black critics feel that *A Raisin in the Sun* is a play whose time has passed — a simplistic, halting treatment of race relations. Some are confused by Hansberry's professed nationalism, when she seems to favor integration. Harold Cruse even calls *Raisin* a "cleverly written piece of glorified soap opera." Hansberry used the traditional form of the well-made play in *Raisin,* especially observing the unities of action, place, and time. The action of the play is carefully delineated: act 1 serves as the beginning, act 2 as the middle, and act 3 as the tightly knit end. Furthermore, all action is carefully and causally related. Hansberry strictly abides by the unity of place: all action transpires in one room of the Youngers' South Side Chicago apartment. Stretching the unity of time from one day to one month (not unusual for a modern dramatist), Hansberry still maintains unity of impression with the central emotional concerns of the Younger family: Walter's search for a dream, Lena's faith in God and the family, Beneatha's hope for a new world.

Hansberry needed this rather traditional form to control the innovative ideas and themes of *Raisin.* Far from being a stereotyped or romanticized treatment of black life, the play embodies ideas that have been uncommon on the Broadway stage in any period. Resurrecting the ideas of the Harlem Renaissance and anticipating the new thinking of the 1960s, Hansberry examines the importance of African roots, traditional versus innovative women, the nature of marriage, the real meaning of money, the search for human dignity. Most significantly, she addresses the sensitive question of to what extent people, in liberating themselves from the burdens of discrimination, should aspire to a white middle-class way of life.

During her *Freedom* years, Lorraine Hansberry continued to study African history with encouragement from Paul Robeson, W. E. B. Du Bois, and Louis Burnham.° "She had spent hours of her younger years poring over maps of the African continent. . . . She was at one, texture, blood . . . with the sound of a mighty Congo drum."[4] She imaginatively knew the lions, drumbeats, quiet sandy nights, respected the antiquity of Ethiopia founded in 1000 B.C. Stirred by Kenya and Ghana wresting control from Europe and England, Hansberry inevitably incorporated her knowledge of Africa in her first play. More than earlier playwrights, Hansberry made Africa a serious, yet natural, issue on Broadway.

In *Raisin* even George Murchison, Beneatha's beau, has an awareness of his African past. In the fever of Walter Lee's and Beneatha's mock African dance in act 2, George remarks sarcastically: "In one second we will hear all about the great Ashanti empires; the great Songhay civilizations; and the great sculpture of Benin — and then some poetry in the Bantu." George had probably learned in a college atmosphere that the Songhai empire was a powerful western African kingdom, which garnered wealth from its export of ivory and gold between 850

Robeson . . . Burnham: African American authors and intellectuals associated with the Harlem Renaissance.

[4]*Young, Gifted and Black,* p. 75.

and 1500 A.D. (Mali and Ghana — not to be confused with the modern state of Ghana — were equally old and powerful empires.) Along the coast of Nigeria, Benin was another expansive empire, noted for its bronze and gold art objects, that came to power around 1500. Coming to power about 1700, Ashanti was still another western kingdom famous for its heroic warriors.[5]

In the stage directions, Hansberry writes that Lena has "the noble bearing of the women of the Hereros of Southwest Africa," who were essentially a pastoral people. Thus Hansberry identifies Lena as an "earth mother," one who nurtures both her family and her plant as well as she can. But Lena reveals her total ignorance of African history by a parroting of Beneatha's earlier remarks in her politely naive, unwittingly humorous speech to Joseph Asagai, the young Nigerian visitor: "I think it's so sad the way our American Negroes don't know nothing about Africa 'cept Tarzan and all that. And all that money they pour into these churches when they ought to be helping you people over there drive out them French and Englishmen done taken away your Land."

Most of the African material in *A Raisin in the Sun,* however, surfaces in conversations between Beneatha and Joseph Asagai. Touched by Beneatha's beauty and idealism, Asagai lovingly nicknames her Alaiyo — a Yoruban word for "One for Whom Bread — Food — Is Not Enough." In act 3, after Walter Lee has been duped out of his $6,500, Asagai visits an embittered, distraught Beneatha. Speaking of his beloved Nigeria, Asagai reveals his basic philosophy of life, of Africa: "A household in preparation for a journey . . . it is another feeling. Something full of the flow of life. . . . Movement, progress. . . . It makes me think of Africa." Perhaps he sees in Beneatha a microcosmic America — one struggling to overthrow the limitations imposed on her by an alien culture.

Asagai's village in Nigeria is one where most people cannot read, where many have not even seen a book. In the village, there are mountains and stars, cool drinks from gourds at the well, old songs, people who move slowly, anciently. But Nigeria also has guns, murder, revolution, illiteracy, disease, ignorance. Asagai understands the inevitability of change and progress in Africa; he imagines for a moment the consequences should he betray the movement. "Don't you see that . . . young men and women . . . my own black countrymen . . . [may] . . . step out of the shadows some evening and slit my then useless throat?" Rebuking Beneatha for becoming discouraged over one small frustration (Walter's losing the money), Asagai views his possible death as an advance toward freedom for himself and his people. "They who might kill me even . . . actually replenish me." Asagai's beliefs certainly contribute to Beneatha's transition from brittle idealist to a more tolerant human being.

In an interview with Studs Terkel (Chicago, May 2, 1959), Lorraine Hansberry referred to Joseph Asagai as her "favorite character" in *Raisin.* He represents the "true intellectual" with no pretense, no illusions. A revolutionary and nationalist, he realizes that initially black African leaders may be as

---

[5]A. Adu Boahen, "Kingdoms of West Africa," in *History of Africa* (New York: McGraw-Hill, 1971), pp. 177–88.

corrupt as their white predecessors (Idi Amin of Uganda bore out this theory in the 1970s). Nevertheless, he shares Hansberry's conviction that "before you can start talking about what's wrong with independence, get it." More the idealist than the practical, effective leader — compared to Kenyatta and Nkrumah° — Asagai is willing to die at the hands of his countrymen for the general good and freedom. (Harold Issacs suggests that his name derives from the Zulu word *asegai,* "sawed-off spear.")[6] On a more obvious level, Asagai certainly refutes the stage stereotype of the African with "a bone through his nose, or his ears."[7]

In *A Raisin in the Sun,* then, Africa becomes a symbol of a proud heritage and a troublesome but hopeful future. To Hansberry's great credit, Africa is a natural, at times humorous, element in the Younger family — as Walter Lee shouts "HOT DAMN! FLAMING SPEAR," as Beneatha dresses in Nigerian robes, as Mama speaks of Tarzan, churches, and Englishmen.

MARGARET B. WILKERSON

Hansberry's Awareness of Culture and Gender

1994

As a black writer, Hansberry was caught in a paradox of expectations. She was expected to write about that which she "knew best," the black experience, and yet that expression was doomed to be called parochial and narrow. Hansberry, however, challenged these facile categories and forced a redefinition of the term "universality," one which would include the dissonant voice of an oppressed American minority. As a young college student, she had wandered into a rehearsal of Sean O'Casey's *Juno and the Paycock.* Hearing in the wails and moans of the Irish characters a universal cry of human misery, she determined to capture that sound in the idiom of her own people — so that it could be heard by all. "One of the most sound ideas in dramatic writing," she would later conclude, "is that in order to create the universal, you must pay very great attention to the specific. Universality, I think, emerges from truthful identity of what is. . . . In other words, I think people, to the extent we accept them and believe them as who they're supposed to be, to that extent they can become everybody."[1] Such a choice by a black writer posed an unusual challenge to the literary establishment and a divided society ill-prepared to comprehend its meaning.

Kenyatta and Nkrumah: Jomo Kenyatta (1894–1978) and Kwame Nkrumah (1909–1972), respectively, former presidents of Kenya and Ghana.

[6]Harold Issacs, "Five Writers and Their African Ancestors, Part II," *Phylon* 21 (Winter 1960):330.

[7]Lorraine Hansberry in interview with Studs Terkel, Chicago, May 2, 1959.

[1]Lorraine Hansberry, *To Be Young, Gifted and Black: Lorraine Hansberry in Her Own Words.* Adapted by Robert Nemiroff (New York: New American Library, 1970), p. 128.

"All art is ultimately social: that which agitates and that which prepares the mind for slumber," Hansberry argued, attacking another basic tenet held by traditional critics. One of the most fundamental illusions of her time and culture, she believed, is the idea that art is not and should not make a social statement. The belief in "l'art pour l'art" permeates literary and theatrical criticism, denying the integral relationship between society and art. "The writer is deceived who thinks he has some other choice. The question is not whether one will make a social statement in one's work — but only *what* the statement will say, for if it says anything at all, it will be social."[2]

It would have been impossible for a person of her background and sensitivity to divorce herself from the momentous social and political events of the 1950s and 1960s. This period witnessed the beginning of a Cold War between the U.S. and Soviet superpowers, a rising demand by blacks for civil rights at home, and a growing intransigence by colonized peoples throughout the world. Isolation is the enemy of black writers, Hansberry believed; they are obligated to participate in the intellectual and social affairs of humankind everywhere.

This abhorrence for narrowness and parochialism led her to examine the hidden alliance between racism and sexism long before it was popular to do so, and to shape a vision cognizant of the many dimensions of colonialism and oppression. Anticipating the women's movement of the 1970s, Hansberry was already aware of the peculiar oppression under which women lived and the particular devastation visited upon women of color.

With the statement "I was born black and a female,"[3] Hansberry immediately established the basis for a tension that informed her world view. Her consciousness, of both ethnicity and gender from the very beginning, brought awareness of two key forces of conflict and oppression in the contemporary world. Because she embraced these dual truths despite their implicit competition for her attention (a competition exacerbated by external pressures), her vision was expansive enough to contain and even synthesize what to others would be contradictions. Thus, she was amused in 1955 at progressive friends who protested whenever she posed "so much as an itsy-bitsy analogy between the situation, say, of the Negro people in the U.S. — and women." She was astonished to be accused by a woman of being bitter and of thinking that men are beasts simply because she expressed the view that women are oppressed. "Must I hate 'men' any more than I hate 'white people' — because some of them are savage and others commit savage acts," she asked herself. "Of course not!" she answered vehemently.[4]

This recognition of the tension implicit in her blackness and femaleness was the starting point for her philosophical journey from the South Side of

---

[2]Lorraine Hansberry, "The Negro Writer and His Roots: Toward a New Romanticism," *The Black Scholar,* Volume 12, Number 2, March/April, 1981, p. 5.

[3]Ibid., p. 11.

[4]Excerpted from Lorraine Hansberry's unpublished, untitled notes. New York City, November 16, 1955.

Chicago to the world community. The following quote charts that journey and the expansion of Hansberry's consciousness, which is unconstrained by culture and gender, but which at the same time refuses to diminish the importance of either.

> I was born on the South Side of Chicago. I was born black and a female. I was born in a depression after one world war, and came into my adolescence during another. While I was still in my teens the first atom bombs were dropped on human beings at Nagasaki and Hiroshima. And by the time I was twenty-three years old, my government and that of the Soviet Union had entered actively into the worst conflict of nerves in human history — the Cold War.
>
> I have lost friends and relatives through cancer, lynching, and war. I have been personally the victim of physical attack which was the offspring of racial and political hysteria. I have worked with the handicapped and seen the ravages of congenital diseases that we have not yet conquered, because we spend our time and ingenuity in far less purposeful wars; I have known persons afflicted with drug addiction and alcoholism and mental illness. I see daily on the streets of New York, street gangs and prostitutes and beggars. I have, like all of you, on a thousand occasions seen indescribable displays of man's very real inhumanity to man, and I have come to maturity, as we all must, knowing that greed and malice and indifference to human misery and bigotry and corruption, brutality, and perhaps above all else, ignorance — the prime ancient and persistent enemy of man — abound in this world.
>
> I say all of this to say that one cannot live with sighted eyes and feeling heart and not know and react to the miseries which afflict this world.[5]

Her "sighted eyes and feeling heart" were what enabled her to hear the wail of her own people in O'Casey's *Juno and the Paycock*, a play steeped in Irish history and tradition. And those eloquent moans sent her forth to capture that collective cry in a black idiom.

Hansberry's cognizance of being black and female formed the basis for her comprehensive world-view. Just as she could accept fully the implications and responsibility of both blackness and femaleness, so was she also aware of the many other competing and equally legitimate causes which grow out of humankind's misery. The one issue that deeply concerned her but that she did not address publicly was homosexuality. The repressive atmosphere of the 1950s, coupled with the homophobia of the general society, including politically left organizations, caused her to suppress her writings that explored issues of sexuality and gender relations. Nevertheless, she pushed and teased these boundaries by probing the nature of the individual within the specifics of culture, ethnicity, and gender. In the midst of her expansiveness, she refused to diminish the pain, suffering, or truths of any one group in order to benefit another, a factor which made her plays particularly rich and her char-

---

[5]Ibid., pp. 11–12.

acters thoroughly complex. Hence, she could write authentically about a black family in *A Raisin in the Sun* and yet produce, in the same instance, a play which appealed to both blacks and whites, bridging for a moment the historical and cultural gaps between them.

Her universalism, which redefines that much abused term, grew out of a deep, complex encounter with the specific terms of human experience as it occurs for blacks, women, whites, and many other groups of people. Her universalism was not facile, nor did it gloss over the things that divide people. She engaged those issues, worked through them to find whatever may be, *a priori,* the human commonality that lies beneath. It was as if she believed that one can understand and embrace the human family (with all its familial warfare) only to the extent that one can engage the truths (however partisan they may seem) of a social, cultural individual. "We must turn our eyes outward," she wrote, "but to do so we must also turn them inward toward our people and their complex and still transitory culture."[6] When she turned inward, she saw not only color but gender as well — a prism of humanity.

[6]Ibid., p. 7.

PART FIVE

DEVELOPING YOUR IDEAS ABOUT LITERATURE

- *Hostility to [literary] theory usually means an opposition to other people's theories and an oblivion of one's own.*

  – TERRY EAGLETON

- *The natural and sensible starting point for work in literary scholarship is the interpretation and analysis of the works of literature themselves.*

  – RENÉ WELLEK AND AUSTIN WARREN

- *Art is not created in a vacuum; it is the work not simply of a person, but of an author fixed in time and space, answering a community of which he is an important, because articulate, part.*

  – WILBUR SCOTT

24

CRITICAL PERSPECTIVES AND LITERARY THEORY

Literature is what gets taught.
– ROLAND BARTHES

In the opening pages of his book *Literary Theory,* the contemporary English critic Terry Eagleton wrote that "Hostility to theory usually means an opposition to other people's theories and an oblivion of one's own." You may feel that literary theory is formidable, but as you begin to explore the various commentaries by short story writers, poets, dramatists, and critics in this anthology, you will discover that they make available many different approaches to the study of literature. In the Commentaries on Stories and Storytellers, for example, Sandra M. Gilbert and Susan Gubar give a feminist reading of Charlotte Perkins Gilman's "The Yellow Wallpaper" and J. Hillis Miller develops a deconstructive reading of Herman Melville's "Bartleby, the Scrivener," to list only two selections in the anthology. You may also have read student essays adapting a reader-response perspective (the paper on Eudora Welty's "A Worn Path" in Part One) and a formalist approach (the paper on characterization in "Peter Klaus the Goatherd" and "Rip Van Winkle" in Part Three). Reading different critical interpretations may also make you become more aware of the assumptions that underlie your own thoughts about literature.

Literary theory is the term used in academic criticism to characterize particular methods of inquiry into the nature and value of literature. Formulating general critical principles — rather than analyzing particular literary texts — is the job of theorists like Terry Eagleton, whereas your assignment is usually to analyze a specific story, poem, or play. The following ten critical approaches to literary texts are the ones you will encounter most frequently in your reading of the commentaries, or secondary sources. They offer some useful perspectives to consider in your critical thinking and writing about literature.

FORMALIST CRITICISM

Formalist criticism is probably the most basic approach to the analysis of literature. Along with other theoretical perspectives, critics often use it to develop their interpretation of literary texts. René Wellek and Austin Warren, the pioneering practitioners of formalism in the United States, wrote in their *Theory of Literature* (1942) that "the natural and sensible starting point for work in literary scholarship is the interpretation and analysis of the works of literature themselves."

Formalists regard a work of fiction, poetry, or drama as a world in itself that can be understood by its intrinsic nature — focusing on form over content. There is an implicit formalist approach inherent in the organization of this textbook into chapters featuring a discussion of the elements of the short story, the poem, and the play. However, a pure formalist would not include headnotes about the authors, considering facts about the author's life and historical times irrelevant to the appreciation of a text. Instead, a formalist would concentrate on analyzing how the various elements of a literary work are integrated into the complex and unique structure of a self-contained aesthetic work.

For example, the academic critic Cleanth Brooks Jr. and the poet Robert Penn Warren give a formalist analysis of T. S. Eliot's "The Love Song of J. Alfred Prufrock" on page 1156 of this anthology. Their discussion was included in *Understanding Poetry* (1938), a college textbook which introduced generations of teachers and students to the formalist techniques of what was then called "New Criticism" based on a close reading of the text. In Brooks and Warren's discussion of Eliot's poem, they emphasize the irony implicit in its tone. They compare Prufrock's character to that of Hamlet, but for the most part their references remain inside the text, explicating the poem line by line to unravel the complexity of Eliot's linguistic and cultural erudition.

BIOGRAPHICAL CRITICISM

In "The Formalist Critic," Cleanth Brooks Jr. stated that

> the formalist critic is concerned primarily with the work itself. Speculation on the mental processes of the author takes the critic away from the work into biography and psychology. There is no reason, of course, why he should not turn away into biography and psychology. Such explorations are very much worth making. But they should not be confused with an account of the work. Such studies describe the process of composition, not the structure of the thing composed. . . .

Unlike formalist criticism, **biographical criticism** starts with the premise that stories, poems, and plays are written by human beings, and that important facts about the life of an author can shed light on literary texts. Usually this kind of critical approach develops the thesis of an essay by suggesting the connection of *cause and effect*. That is, you maintain that the imaginative world of the text has characteristics that originate from causes or sources in the author's background.

You have probably written papers about literature in a biographical context. A favorite high-school English term paper project is to assign an author as a topic, requiring research into the details about his or her life. If you ever wrote this kind of paper, you may have organized your material chronologically, tracing the life of your author and listing his or her most important literary works, often with no clearly defined thesis in mind. In writing essays for college English classes based on a unified central idea, on the other hand, you must ask yourself how knowing the facts of an author's life can help you to understand a specific text. Usually you do not attempt to survey an author's complete works in a short paper.

A biographical approach to literature requires at least as much care as formalist criticism — care in presenting only the relevant facts of an author's life and in using a sensitive interpretation of them to show clear connections between the writer's experience or personality and the work. Brett C. Millier's discussion of Elizabeth Bishop's poem "One Art" (p. 1198) is an exemplary use of the biographical approach to literature. Millier has focused this account of Bishop's revision of the poem through a careful examination of the seventeen drafts of the manuscript. In the long middle paragraph of the analysis, Millier introduces Bishop's biographical information, a summary of the poet's losses beginning with the disappearance and death of her parents when she was still a child. The biographical critic then concludes that the list of these personal losses encoded into the poem is an example of Bishop's method of "reticence" as a confessional poet, part of her lifelong process of acquiring self-discipline.

PSYCHOLOGICAL CRITICISM

Psychological criticism is indebted to modern psychology, which began with the psychoanalytic theories of its founder, the Austrian psychoanalyst Sigmund Freud (1856–1939). Freud wrote that he learned nearly as much about psychology from reading authors such as Sophocles and Shakespeare as he did from his clinical work with his patients in Vienna as an analyst and physician. Freud's writing about psychology, along with books by his disciples including Carl Jung, Marie Bonaparte, and Bruno Bettelheim, modified our understanding of human behavior, introducing such concepts as the unconscious forces of the id and the superego active within every individual.

Three approaches are most often taken by critics interested in exploring the psychological aspect of literature. First is the investigation of the creative process and the nature of literary genius. This field of investigation can also include other forms of genius — musical, mathematical, and so forth. The second is the study of an individual writer (or artist or musician or scientist), particularly appropriate if, like the American poets Anne Sexton, Sylvia Plath, and Robert Lowell, the individual was deeply involved in psychological therapy or analysis. The third is the analysis of fictional characters, which began with Freud's study of the character of Oedipus when he analyzed Sophocles' play in his book *The Interpretation of Dreams* (1900).

An excerpt from Freud's discussion of "The Oedipus Complex" is on page 1977 of this anthology. Freud begins his analysis by referring to the childhood of his neurotic patients, many of whom he observed possessing on "a magnified scale feelings of love and hatred to their parents." The psychoanalyst then summarizes the plot of *Oedipus the King,* observing that Sophocles has dramatized "a legend whose profound and universal power to move can only be understood if the hypothesis I have put forward in regard to the psychology of children has an equally universal validity." Freud argues that the destiny of the fictional king of Thebes "moves us only because it might have been ours — because the oracle laid the same curse upon us before our birth as upon him." Moving from literary analysis to psychological generalizations, Freud used literature to formulate universal theories about human psychology that have continued to influence our ideas for over a century.

MYTHOLOGICAL CRITICISM

Mythological criticism developed out of psychoanalytic theory in the work of Freud's younger disciple, the Swiss psychiatrist Carl G. Jung. A man of vast reading in anthropology and comparative religion as well as literature, Jung formulated the theory of the archetype. Derived from the experience of the human race in different cultures, archetypes consist of images present in the unconscious mind of every individual, which Jung called the "collective unconscious." Archetypal images of the sun, for example, are inherent in every culture and give rise to storytelling that results in tribal myths. The critic Northrop Frye defined the archetype in strictly literary terms as "a symbol, usually an image, which recurs often enough in literature to be recognizable as an element of one's literary experience as a whole."

When critics characterize archetypal images in specific works of literature, they usually refer to several texts beyond the one being scrutinized in order to establish an underlying pattern of similarity. On page 1970 the theater critic Francis Fergusson's discussion of "Oedipus, Myth and Play" from *The Idea of a Theater* (1949) moves from a summary of the plot of the play to a paragraph speculating on the different versions of the Oedipus myth possibly known by the playwright. Fergusson then suggests how later authors like Pierre Corneille, Voltaire, and Fustel de Coulanges interpreted Oedipus after Sophocles. The erudition of this mythological approach to reading Oedipus as a universal scapegoat figure leads Fergusson to conclude his analysis with a lively description of what he calls "the ritual expectancy" of the rowdy crowd in the Greek theater assembled to watch Sophocles' play.

HISTORICAL CRITICISM

Historical criticism approaches a literary work through its historical context, the events that were occurring in the world during the time the author wrote a particular story, poem, or play. This method is often combined with the biographical approach, if the historical events contributed to the author's thought process and resulted in the creation of a work of literature. Historical critics may also explain the meaning that the work had for its original readers, especially if the text includes words that had different connotations in the past.

The critic Sally Fitzgerald, who was a close friend of the writer Flannery O'Connor, takes a historical approach in her discussion of the 1953 short story "A Good Man Is Hard to Find" (p. 787). During the years of their friendship, O'Connor sent Fitzgerald clippings of articles with "lurid headlines" from local newspapers of her hometown, Milledgeville, Georgia. Although O'Connor was merely trying to amuse Fitzgerald, the critic saved the clippings and used them in an article about O'Connor titled "Happy Endings," published in *Image* in 1997. The newspaper clippings from the early 1950s included accounts of a prize-winning child singer "decked out in ribbons and tutu and sausage curls," whose winning song was titled "A Good Man Is Hard to Find," as well as a series of articles about a criminal "aloose" in the region who totaled up a record of twenty-six kidnappings and ten car thefts, among other high jinks, in what Fitzgerald described in her essay as "two fun-filled weeks." The critic suggests how these documents may have influenced O'Connor when she created the fictional character of The Misfit. Fitzgerald concludes by using the newspaper articles to shed light on the theme of redemption which ends the story.

SOCIOLOGICAL CRITICISM

Sociological criticism is written by critics interested in exploring the economic, racial, and political context in which works of literature are created and read. Examining the relationships between writers and their society, these critics focus on the ideological aspects inherent in stories, poems, and plays. As the critic Wilbur Scott understood, "Art is not created in a vacuum; it is the work not simply of a person, but of an author fixed in time and space, answering a community of which he is an important, because articulate, part." The novelist Joseph Conrad went even further in making a connection between literature and society when he wrote in *Notes on Life and Letters* that

> Fiction is history, human history, or it is nothing. But it is also more than that; it stands on firmer ground, being based on the reality of forms and the observation of social phenomena, whereas history is based on documents, and the reading of print and handwriting — on second-hand impression. Thus fiction is nearer truth.

Perhaps the most controversial type of sociological criticism is **Marxist criticism**. Marxist critics, including the Hungarian philosopher Georg Lukács, believe that all art is political. This approach can become highly theoretical, as in Mikhail Bakhtin and V. N. Voloshinov's 1929 study *Marxism and the Philosophy of Language,* which argues that language is fundamentally "dialogic," a focus of social struggle and contradiction. As Eagleton explained in *Literary Theory,* for these critics, "It was not simply a matter of asking 'what the sign [word] meant,' but of investigating its varied history, as conflicting social groups, classes, individuals, and discourses sought to appropriate it and imbue it with their own meanings. Language, in short, was a field of ideological contention, not a monolithic system."

In this anthology, Helge Normann Nilsen examines the influence of Marxist theory on *Death of a Salesman* in her essay "Marxism and the Early Plays of Arthur Miller" on page 2037. Nilsen bases her analysis of Miller's political attitudes on his statements about the destructive aspects of capitalism in his autobiography, bolstering her argument with footnotes from the playwright's *Timebends: A Life* (1987).

READER-RESPONSE CRITICISM

For much of the twentieth century, the formalist approach to "close reading" of stories, poems, and plays was the most popular method of analysis in American college classrooms. After the turbulent social changes of the 1960s, literary critics in the United States became receptive to many new approaches to the text. The critic Ross Murfin has summarized the reaction against the "New Critical" practices:

> About 1970, the New Criticism came under attack by reader-response critics (who believe that the meaning of a work is not inherent in its internal form but rather is cooperatively produced by the reader and the text) and poststructuralists (who, following the philosophy of Jacques Derrida, argue that texts are inevitably self-contradictory and that we can find form in them only by ignoring or suppressing conflicting details or elements). In retrospect it is clear that, in their outspoken opposition to the New Criticism notwithstanding, the reader-response critics and poststructuralists of the 1970s were very much *like* their formalist predecessors in two important respects: for the most part, they ignored the world beyond the text and its reader, and, for the most part, they ignored the historical contexts within which literary works are written and read.

Reader-response criticism postulates that reading is as much a creative act as the writing of a text, because both involve the play of imagination and intelligence. Some reader-response critics even go so far as to say that a literary text has no existence outside of a reader's mind. Recognizing that different readers can find different meaning in works of literature, reader-response critics also emphasize the fact that the same reader can, at different periods of his or her life, find the experience of reading a book changes with maturity. If you keep the notes you take on reading *Hamlet* as a college freshman, for example, you will probably find that in twenty years or so, your interpretation of the play will change if you read it again or see a new production in the theater.

On page 729 of this anthology, the literary critic Cheryl B. Torsney gives a reader-response interpretation of Alice Walker's "Everyday Use" based on an experience at Parchman Farm, the Mississippi state penitentiary, meeting a prisoner who was a skilled quilter. This encounter taught Torsney a great deal about the life of many poverty-stricken southern blacks, and caused her to revise her reading of Walker's short story.

POSTSTRUCTURALIST AND DECONSTRUCTIONIST CRITICISM

Poststructuralist and **deconstructionist criticism** are two modern approaches to critical theory that, like reader-response criticism, focus on the multiple, sometimes self-contradictory meanings that exist in a literary work — meanings that resist a final interpretation. Critics who practice these approaches believe in a basic logical syllogism:

A. Human language is fundamentally unstable, as its meaning is dependent on changing but omnipresent social and historical factors.
B. Literary texts are composed of human language.
C. Therefore, literary texts are fundamentally unstable. Q.E.D.

Arguing that the literary text is unstable, deconstructionist critics like the French authorities Roland Barthes and Michel Foucault have called for "the death of literature" and "the death of the author." In 1968 Barthes explained in his essay "The Death of the Author" that

> Once the Author is removed, the claim to decipher a text becomes quite futile. To give a text an Author is to impose a limit on that text, to furnish it with a final signified, to close the writing. Such a conception suits criticism very well, the latter then allotting itself the important task of discovering the Author (or its hypostases: society, history, psyche, liberty) beneath the work: when the Author has been found, the text is "explained" — victory to the critic. . . . In the multiplicity of writing, everything is to be *disentangled,* nothing *deciphered;* the structure can be followed, "run" (like the thread of a stocking) at every point and at every level, but there is nothing beneath. . . . writing ceaselessly posits meaning ceaselessly to evaporate it, carrying out a systematic exemption of meaning.

While formalists find coherence in the different elements of a text, deconstructionists show how the author's language can be broken or "deconstructed" into irreconcilable meanings. Their efforts have influenced many contemporary critics, and their theories are worth investigating if you continue your study of literature in upper-division courses and graduate school.

You can sample their approach in the list of books at the end of this section, as well as in J. Hillis Miller's deconstructive reading of Herman Melville's "Bartleby, the Scrivener" on page 695 of this anthology. Miller takes a mythological approach (analyzing versions of the Pygmalion myth) in his deconstruction of Melville's text. The critic illuminates how Melville "disables reading" any one particular interpretation into the story by selecting the lawyer, Bartleby's employer, as his narrator.

GENDER CRITICISM

Gender criticism emerged in the wake of the development of feminist criticism on American college campuses in the 1970s, gradually evolving into gender criticism with the inclusion of gay and lesbian critics. This branch of critical theory is indebted to early works such as the French critic Simone de

Beauvoir's *The Second Sex* (1949) as well as the American feminists Betty Friedan's *The Feminine Mystique* (1963) and Kate Millett's *Sexual Politics* (1970).

Gender critics are concerned with the gender and sexual orientation of both writers and readers of literature. They argue that our patriarchal culture is so imbued with assumptions of heterosexual male superiority that we must continuously correct the imbalance by identifying and analyzing its components and negative influences. Explaining how gender has influenced both an author's work and a reader's response to a literary text, this approach often contains aspects of reader-response criticism.

On page 681 of this anthology you can read the feminist commentary of the eminent critics Sandra M. Gilbert and Susan Gubar on Charlotte Perkins Gilman's "The Yellow Wallpaper." This excerpt is taken from their book *The Madwoman in the Attic: The Woman Writer and the Nineteenth-Century Literary Imagination* (1979). Gilbert and Gubar place the story within the context of what they call the "literature of confinement," where a woman trapped by the patriarchal society attempts to free herself "through strategic re-definitions of self, art, and society."

CULTURAL CRITICISM

Cultural criticism, like gender criticism, can be viewed as an important contemporary development in literary studies erected upon the sturdy but limited foundation of formalist practice. Cultural critics, including New Historicists, do not advocate any one particular approach to literary study. Frequently they participate in interdisciplinary approaches, combining more than one field of academic study due to their assumption that individual works of literature should be approached as part of a larger cultural context. For example, if you investigated the changes in 1960s popular music as reflected in Joyce Carol Oates's "Where Are You Going, Where Have You Been?," incorporating musical history into your essay, you have been practicing cultural criticism.

As the poet X. J. Kennedy realizes,

> In theory, a cultural studies critic might employ any methodology. In practice, however, he or she will most often borrow concepts from deconstruction, Marxism analysis, gender criticism, race theory, and psychology. . . . Whereas traditional critical approaches often sought to demonstrate the unity of a literary work, cultural studies often seeks to portray social, political, and psychological conflicts it masks.

Leslie Marmon Silko uses the methodology of a cultural critic in her essay analyzing "Language and Literature from a Pueblo Indian Perspective" on page 711 of this anthology.

SELECTED BIBLIOGRAPHY

GENERAL OVERVIEW

Eagleton, Terry. *Literary Theory: An Introduction.* 2nd ed. Minneapolis: U of Minnesota P, 1996.

Selden, Raman. *Theory of Criticism.* New York: Addison Wesley, 1988.

THE CHANGING LITERARY CANON

Lauter, Paul. *Canons and Contexts.* New York: Oxford UP, 1991.

FORMALIST CRITICISM

Brooks, Cleanth. *The Well Wrought Urn: Studies in the Structure of Poetry.* New York: Reynal and Hitchcock, 1947.

Eliot, T. S. *The Sacred Wood: Essays in Poetty and Criticism.* London: Methuen, 1920.

Ransom, John Crowe. *The New Criticism.* Norfolk, CT: New Directions, 1941.

Wellek, René, and Austin Warren. *Theory of Literature.* New York: Harcourt, Brace and World, 1949.

BIOGRAPHICAL AND PSYCHOLOGICAL CRITICISM

Bloom, Harold. *The Anxiety of Influence.* New York: Oxford UP, 1978.

Crews, Frederick. *Out of My System: Psychoanalysis, Ideology, and Critical Method.* New York: Oxford UP, 1975.

Freud, Sigmund. *The Standard Edition of the Complete Psychological Works.* 24 vols. Ed. James Strachey. London: Hogarth Press and the Institute of Psychoanalysis, 1940–68.

Lesser, Simon O. *Fiction and the Unconscious.* Chicago: U of Chicago P, 1957.

Skura, Meredith Anne. *The Literary Use of the Psychoanalytic Process.* New Haven: Yale UP, 1981.

MYTHOLOGICAL CRITICISM

Bodkin, Maud. *Archetypal Patterns in Poetry.* London: Oxford UP, 1934.

Frye, Northrop. *Anatomy of Criticism: Four Essays.* Princeton: Princeton UP, 1957.

Jung, Carl Gustav. *Collected Works.* Ed. Herbert Read, Michael Fordham, and Gerhard Adler. 17 vols. New York: Pantheon, 1953.

HISTORICAL AND SOCIOLOGICAL CRITICISM

Escarpit, Robert. *Sociology of Literature.* Painesville, OH: Lake Erie College P, 1965.

Frow, John. *Marxist and Literary History.* Cambridge: Harvard UP, 1986.

Lindenberger, Herbert. *Historical Drama: The Relation of Literature and Reality.* Chicago: U of Chicago P, 1985.

Williams, Raymond. *Marxism and Literature.* Oxford: Oxford UP, 1977.

READER-RESPONSE CRITICISM

Booth, Wayne C. *The Rhetoric of Fiction.* Chicago: U of Chicago P, 1983.

Eco, Umberto. *The Role of the Reader: Explorations in the Semiotics of Texts.* Bloomington: Indiana UP, 1979.

Fish, Stanley. *Is There a Text in This Class? The Authority of Interpretive Communities.* Cambridge: Harvard UP, 1980.

Freund, Elizabeth. *The Return of the Reader: Reader-Response Criticism.* London: Methuen, 1987.

Tompkins, Jane P., ed. *Reader-Response Criticism: From Formalism to Post-Structuralism.* Baltimore: Johns Hopkins UP, 1980.

POSTSTRUCTURALIST AND DECONSTRUCTIONIST CRITICISM

Barthes, Roland. *The Rustle of Language.* New York: Hill and Wang, 1986.

Culler, Jonathan. *On Deconstruction: Theory and Criticism after Structuralism.* Ithaca: Cornell UP, 1982.

Derrida, Jacques. *Of Grammatology.* Baltimore: Johns Hopkins UP, 1976.

Foucault, Michel. *Language, Counter-Memory, Practice.* Ithaca: Cornell UP, 1977.

Smith, Barbara Herrnstein. *On the Margins of Discourse: The Relation of Literature to Language.* Chicago: U of Chicago P, 1979.

GENDER CRITICISM

Baym, Nina. *Feminism and American Literary History.* New Brunswick: Rutgers UP, 1992.

Edelman, Lee. *Homographesis: Essays in Gay Literary and Cultural Theory.* New York: Routledge, 1994.

Fetterley, Judith. *The Resisting Reader: A Feminist Approach to American Fiction.* Bloomington: Indiana UP, 1978.

Jagose, Annamarie. *Queer Theory.* Victoria: Melbourne UP, 1996.

Sedgwick, Eve Kosofsky. *Between Men: English Literature and Male Homosocial Desire.* New York: Columbia UP, 1985.

Showalter, Elaine. *A Literature of Their Own.* Princeton: Princeton UP, 1977.

Smith, Barbara. *Toward a Black Feminist Criticism.* New York: Out and Out, 1977.

CULTURAL CRITICISM

Clayton, Jay, and Eric Rothstein, eds. *Influence and Intertextuality in Literary History.* Madison: U of Wisconsin P, 1991.

Cox, Jeffrey N., and Larry J. Reynolds. *New Historical Literary Study: Essays on Reproducing Texts, Representing History.* Princeton: Princeton UP, 1993.

Geertz, Clifford. *The Interpretation of Cultures.* New York: Basic Books, 1973.

Storey, John, ed. *What Is Cultural Studies?* New York: St. Martin's, 1996.

White, Hayden. *Tropics of Discourse: Essays in Cultural Criticism.* Baltimore: Johns Hopkins UP, 1978.

25

BASIC TYPES OF LITERARY PAPERS

Regardless of your choice of a critical perspective to formulate your ideas about literature, you will probably be using one of the three basic ways to develop your critical thinking in your essays. Here are examples of these useful rhetorical strategies along with student essays incorporating them.

EXPLICATION

The word **explication** is derived from a Latin word that means "unfolding." When you explicate a text, you unfold its meaning in an essay, proceeding carefully to interpret it passage by passage, sometimes even line by line or word by word. A good explication concentrates on details, quoting the text of the story, poem, or play to bring the details to the attention of a reader who might have missed them approaching the text from a different perspective.

An entire story, poem, or play is usually too long to explicate completely — the explication would be far longer than the original work. You usually select a short passage or section that relates to the idea you are developing. If a poem is brief, you can explicate all of it, as in the following student essay on Langston Hughes's poem "The Negro Speaks of Rivers" (p. 1056). In a play, you could choose to explicate a key scene or a crucial dialogue. In a story, you could concentrate on the opening or closing paragraph, where you might suggest the implications of the text to develop the central idea of your essay.

Explication does not usually concern itself with the author's life or times, but his or her historical period may determine the definitions of words or the meaning of concepts that appear in the passage you are interpreting. If the literary work is a century or more old, the meanings of some words may have changed. The explication is supposed to reveal what the author might have meant when he or she wrote the poem, story, or play (not assuming conscious intentions but explicating possibilities).

For older literature, you will have to do a little research if the passage you choose for explication contains words whose meanings have changed. The *Oxford English Dictionary,* available in the reference section of your college library, will give you the meaning of a word in a particular era. The philosophical, religious, scientific, or political beliefs of the author or of his or her historical time may also enter into your interpretation of the text. The main emphasis in explication, however, is on the meaning of the words — both *denotative* and *connotative* — and the way those words affect you.

STUDENT ESSAY

An Interpretation of Langston Hughes's

"The Negro Speaks of Rivers"

In the poem "The Negro Speaks of Rivers," Langston Hughes uses elements of the blues to suggest the history of blacks from ancient Egypt to the twentieth century through the extended metaphor of the river. He explores the cultural identity and endurance of his people, emphasizing his racial uniqueness by his rejection of traditional European writing styles.

At the beginning of "The Negro Speaks of Rivers," Hughes is searching for his cultural identity. The poem is written in plain-spoken free verse, with an emphasis on spoken rhythm and an intimate, blues-like tone as opposed to a structured rhyme and formal rhythmic scheme. A statement of his situation in the first line ("I've known rivers") is repeated in the second, as in a blues lyric, but extended so it can be followed with a third line that stands alone as well as comments on the first two. With this third line ("My soul has grown deep like the rivers"), Hughes begins a brief historical account as the voice of the African American race.

This history celebrates the transition from slavery to freedom, suggesting the strength of his race by connecting it to the image of the river. The representation of rivers and pyramids in the next lines of the poem suggests the endurance of the human spirit through time, mystically connecting his heritage to something "older than the flow of human blood in human veins." As the rivers continue to flow, so do his people continue to thrive through the changing times and the slow acceptance of racial differences.

Hughes then moves from this portrayal of his race in the bondage of slavery from the old world to the new, where Abraham Lincoln symbolizes the progressive movement from slavery to freedom. Hughes's pride and love for his race can be seen as the water of the Mississippi turns "all golden in the sunset." The last three lines of the poem suggest the sadness and complexity of the racial situation in Hughes's somber conclusion. As in a blues lyric, he ends by repeating the line that introduced his historical panorama of African American history: "My soul has grown deep like the rivers."

ANALYSIS

An **analysis** of a literary work is the result of the process of separating it into its parts in order to study the whole. Analysis is commonly applied in thinking about almost any complex subject. When you are asked to analyze literature, you must break it down into various parts and then usually select a single aspect for close study. Often what you are analyzing is one of the elements of fiction, poetry, or drama — an aspect of style, characterization, dialogue, setting, or symbolism, for example.

Whereas explication deals with a specific section of the text, analysis can range further, discussing details through the story, poem, or play that are related to your thesis. You cannot possibly analyze every word of a literary work any more than you would attempt to explicate all of it. You might begin with a general idea, or arrive at one by thinking about some smaller detail that catches your attention, as the student did by analyzing the storyteller's voice in "A Worn Path" (see pp. 22–23).

Most students find that when they are asked to write an essay analyzing a poem, they can come closer to the poem by copying it out double-spaced into a computer or writing it in longhand on paper. Then you can scribble your observations about the poem in the margins of your paper, brainstorming alongside the text itself. To analyze Robert Frost's poem "Mending Wall" (p. 1027), for example, you could write a list of adjectives and uses for a wall — *to hide, block out, a barrier, protection, a blockade, safety, security, separation,* and so on — to familiarize yourself with the "walled" metaphor of the poem. You could also annotate Frost's use of language and the technical means of poetry. You could consider the title, weighing its various connotations in your mind after you've studied the poem. When one student tried freewriting about her response to the poem, she was reminded of a photograph of Ireland on a travel poster. This memory inspired her opening paragraph in the following essay, "Nature and Neighbors in Robert Frost's 'Mending Wall.'"

STUDENT ESSAY

Nature and Neighbors
in Robert Frost's "Mending Wall"

Funnel paragraph, narrows down to focus on assigned topic of paper.

Ireland is known for its rolling green countryside. Without forests, the land appears to be a sea of green stretching to a sea of blue. The land, however, is not uninterrupted; there are a few roads and homes floating in that green sea, and they are even further outnumbered by Ireland's stone walls. They streak across every grazing field, surround the family farmhouses, and never seem to be in need of repair. The reason these walls remain has little to do with the skill of their original builders. Years of maintenance keeps them strong. Why the walls are maintained, despite the fact that few sheep graze within their boundaries, can be explained by examining Robert Frost's poem "Mending Wall."

Summary of poem's subject.

The wall is in need of repair as the narrator and his neighbor meet to fill in the gaps a cold winter has made. As the two walk along the wall at "spring mending time" one on each side, they replace the fallen stones and rebuild the tumbled-down boundaries. As the stones are restored to their places in the wall, the chaos of nature is replaced by a man-made sense of order.

Summary of poem's theme.

The neighbors "set the wall between [them] once again," and in doing so, they strengthen the order a year of freedom has weakened. As they repair the wall, they are restoring order to the natural world in which they live and work and to their emotional worlds, where the relationships they have with one another reside. In both cases, the wall symbolizes the control the two men wish to possess over unpredictable forces in their lives.

Beginning of analysis — ritual as a sense of control over nature.

As a control over nature, the wall has many weaknesses. When nature does not work against the wall in New England, sending "the frozen ground swell under it," hunters come through, leaving "not one stone on a stone." Each year in an annual ritual, the two neighbors must meet again to repair the damage not because they enjoy the endless process of rebuilding the wall, but because the wall's presence gives them some sense of control over the chaos of nature. The wall divides the wilderness into manageable segments that are far easier to maintain than an endless expanse of farmland. In a visible and tangible way, the wall reminds the two that, despite nature's awesome power, they can in some, though impermanent, way check that power.

The borders the wall forms also indicate where the responsibility of one person ends and the duty of another begins. It is in this way that the wall crosses from control over nature to a controlling factor in the neighbors' relationship. Despite the fact that the wall separates two plots of trees, and the "apple trees will never get across and eat the cones under [the] pines," the wall is necessary in maintaining their friendly and mutually beneficial relationship. As the neighbor states, in the most memorable line of the poem, "Good fences make good neighbors." And in answer to the narrator's question of "Why do they make good neighbors?," one can look to the final image of the poem, a comparison of the neighbor to "an old stone savage armed."

Ritual as a statement of the neighbors' relationship — use of quotations.

In addition to illustrating the idea of ancient property rights, this image turns the neighbor into a threatening creature; revealing anything to him could prove dangerous. "He moves in darkness"--not the darkness caused by the shade a tree casts on a sunny day but a deeper darkness that holds the power to damage emotions that the wall symbolically protects. Therefore, the wall is a wise protection against a potentially hostile invader. It is for this reason that a wall, in this case a mental wall or symbolic sense of limits, is essential in the relationship.

Analysis of poetic imagery as it relates to the theme of the poem.

Below the surface of any human being is the potential to do harm, just as in the distance, on a clear day, a storm may be brewing. Though it is not the trusting thing to do, both neighbors understand the necessity of the wall in separating their properties and respecting personal space. The narrator begins to question his faith in the wall and the distrust it perpetuates, but in the end, as is evident by his repetition of the line "Good fences make good neighbors," he realizes the truth in such a motto. For the symbolic protection it affords and its ability to give some order to chaos, the wall has become a part of their lives.

Fresh comparison to a natural phenomenon.

Beginning of conclusion.

In Ireland, as in New England, the old stone walls remain, climbing to the tops of mountains and disappearing over the ridge. They seem to hold the green sea of grasses down as a

Conclusion refers back to opening paragraph and restates thesis sentence.

row of stones might hold down a blanket on a breezy day. In the walls the neighbors find a sense of control over their wild land, restraining the endless landscape in manageable squares and rectangles, keeping each neighbor's overgrown field of nettles within the walls and allowing responsibility to begin and end with the stone borders. In a way the good relations between neighbors are maintained with as much devotion as the walls have been maintained over the years.

COMPARISON AND CONTRAST

If you were to write about two works of literature in this anthology, you would probably use the technique of **comparison and contrast**. When making a comparison, you place the two works side by side and comment on their similarities. When contrasting them, you point out their differences. It is always more meaningful to compare and contrast two literary works that have something in common than two that are unrelated. As you work on your essay you will find that if there are not important similarities between the two works, your discussion will be as strained and pointless as an attempt to link closely any two dissimilar objects, like elephants and oranges.

If you decide to use the method of comparison and contrast to develop the ideas in your essay, it is usually smoother to mingle them as you go along, rather than using contrast in the first half of your paper and comparison in the second half. The result of such a fifty-fifty split is rarely a unified essay. Rather, it tends to give the impression of two separate analyses linked together at the last minute.

The following student paper uses the method of comparison and contrast in developing an idea about two stories by Edgar Allan Poe and Nathaniel Hawthorne.

In his essay, the student shaped the first paragraph as a funnel leading to his central idea. Next he compared the ways in which the two stories were similar. Then he went on in the rest of his paper to analyze the differences between them. Throughout, elements of both stories were compared and contrasted side by side, sometimes with general analytic comments, at other times with explication and interpretation of the text.

STUDENT ESSAY

The Single Effect in Nathaniel Hawthorne's "Young Goodman Brown" and Edgar Allan Poe's "The Cask of Amontillado"

General backgrouund information on topic.

In addition to writing short fiction, Edgar Allan Poe published literary criticism, in which he explained his own standards for prose tales. Poe stated that the primary goal in creating works in this literary genre should be the development of a "certain . . . single effect." According to Poe, an author invents such incidents in the story as will establish this "preconceived effect." Poe introduced this theory in one of his reviews of a collection of Nathaniel Hawthorne's tales. The theory was conceived by Poe and based on the work of Hawthorne, so the stories of both men emphasize the creation of such a "single effect."

Summary of most important facts about topic.

Topic narrowed to thesis sentence.

Hawthorne's "Young Goodman Brown" and Poe's "The Cask of Amontillado" show each author's use of the method of "single effect." Poe's story examines the psychological processes in a madman's plot for revenge, and Hawthorne's story describes a man's fall from innocence, but both tales are constructed similarly. The action of both stories features a single character. Both stories are unified by a central theme. Every word, phrase, and image used by the author moves the theme closer to complete development. Neither story is realistic--that is, the events described are not plausible as real-life experiences. When Goodman Brown walks with a flesh-and-blood devil, for example, it is immediately clear that the story is a fantasy, because flesh-and-blood devils did not exist in Puritan Salem. A similar world of fantasy operates in "The Cask of Amontillado." The ease with which the narrator is able to lead Fortunato to his death is not true to life as we know it.

Important similarities.

Single protagonist.

Central theme.

Not realistic.

Specific examples.

Begin analyzing differences.

Both stories feature a single character, and both emphasize a unity of single effect in developing their themes, but there are some fundamental differences between the stories. The first is created by the nature of the two literary forms the authors use. Hawthorne was writing a moral allegory. Every aspect of the story symbolizes something else. Goodman Brown's wife, for example, is the embodiment of morality and simple faith; even her name, "Faith," contributes to this symbolic meaning. The story would have a different effect if she were named "Gertrude." Poe was writing a psychological fantasy. Fortunato is shown dressed in a cap similar to one that would be worn by a court jester. By calling attention to his outfit, the narrator, Montresor, adds to the degradation of Fortunato, which is part of the aim of his plan for revenge. Poe's fantasy is based on human emotions, while Hawthorne's allegory is based on intellect.

Hawthorne's form.

Good example.

Contrast with Poe's form.

Summarize differences.

There is another major difference in the style of the two stories. Poe said that the first sentence of any tale should bring out the effect on which the rest depends. Although Poe set up the rules, Hawthorne did not keep to them. The opening sentence of "Young Goodman Brown" is in no hurry: "Young Goodman Brown came forth at sunset into the street at Salem village; but put his head back, after crossing the threshold, to exchange a parting kiss with his young wife." Goodman Brown is going on a journey, but the nature of the journey--which is central to the theme--is not clear. The concise opening of Poe's tale, however, reveals the theme: "The thousand injuries of Fortunato I had borne as I best could; but when he ventured upon insult, I vowed revenge." This sentence leaves no doubt in the reader's mind about the meaning of the story. The narrator declares that revenge is foremost in his mind, and the action that follows develops the idea of a character obsessed by the desire for revenge.

Another feature of Poe's theory related to another difference in the stories.

Quote to give evidence of difference.

Contrast with Hawthorne.

Both Poe and Hawthorne were artists deeply interested in creating works of fiction. Despite their differences of form and literary style, both created unified stories based on a "single effect," as shown in the two classic tales "Young Goodman Brown" and "The Cask of Amontillado."

Concluding summary clear, but a little brief.

The method of comparison and contrast works especially well when you are thinking about two or more works by a single writer. You can also use this method when you analyze two works that are closely related, as in the student paper on "Peter Klaus the Goatherd" and "Rip Van Winkle" in Chapter 3 (p. 51), and the paper on the differences between *Trifles* and "A Jury of Her Peers" in Chapter 20 (p. 1313).

WRITING ABOUT THE CONTEXT OF LITERATURE

In addition to developing an idea by explication, analysis, or comparison and contrast — all methods primarily involving a close reading of the text — there are other ways to write about literature. The *context* of stories, poems, and plays is important to our understanding and appreciation of the text, as you have learned from reading the headnotes to each author's work in this anthology. The context of literature is usually defined as the biographical and historical background of the work. Literature does not exist in a vacuum. Created by a human being at some particular time in history, it is intended to speak to other human beings about ideas that have human relevance. Any critical method that clarifies the meaning and the pattern of literature is valuable, and often literary critics use more than one method in their approach to a text.

A paper on the context of literature is also an expository essay based on the development of a central idea or thesis statement. A critic creating this kind of essay, as for example in biographical criticism, develops the thesis of the paper by suggesting the connection of *cause and effect*. That is, you maintain that the story, poem, or play has characteristics that originate from causes or sources in the author's background — personal life, historical period, or literary influences. For example, you can use Kate Chopin's statement on her discovery of Maupassant's stories (p. 670) to show something about her own method of writing short fiction. To establish this connection between the life and work of a writer, you could also analyze or explicate a Chopin story, or compare one of her stories with one of Maupassant's.

Material from other classes can also be used in papers about literature. If you major in history or psychology, for example, you can investigate the way stories, poems, or plays are sometimes read to give valuable historical or psychological information about the world they describe. You are not limited to writing about remote times when considering essays that take this approach. Joyce Carol Oates's story "Where Are You Going, Where Have You Been?" is about modern teenage life. A paper about it could investigate the connection between Oates's fantasy and psychological theories about adolescence in contemporary America. Characters in literature are often used in psychological and sociological textbooks to illustrate pathological symptoms or complexes. Sociology textbooks, for example, cite Oates's fictional characters as representing current tendencies toward *anomie*, a condition in which normative standards of conduct have weakened or disappeared. It is possible in writing about literature to illustrate philosophical, historical, sociological, or psychological material you are familiar with through your work in other college courses.

At times the background of the author can suggest an ideological approach: Richard Wright was a communist, Tillie Olsen is a feminist, Flannery O'Connor was a Catholic, and so forth. At other times an ideology held by the student but not necessarily by the author can lead to a fresh reading of a story. Depending on what you as a reader bring to "The Metamorphosis," for example, there is a "Freudian Kafka, an existentialist Kafka, a Catholic Kafka, a Marxist Kafka, a Zionist Kafka," and so forth, as suggested by the critic Hans Eichner.

Proceed with your literary analysis according to your ideology with great care, realizing that you might become insensitive to nuances of meaning other than those you are predisposed to find in a doctrinaire interpretation of the text. At the same time an ideological approach can illuminate aspects of literature that are particularly valid and relevant for contemporary readers. A feminist interpretation of "Young Goodman Brown," for example, must not take the story literally, because Hawthorne wrote it as a moral allegory, but a feminist could use the story to argue provocatively about implied sexual stereotyping in Hawthorne's characterization of women.

If you possess fluency in a foreign language, you can also bring your own special knowledge to your papers about literature. In the Commentaries on Stories and Storytellers, Leo Tolstoy's attempt to read his own philosophy into Anton Chekhov's "The Darling" (p. 726) led one student who could read Russian back to the original version of Chekhov's story. She read "The Darling" in Russian and compared the English translation in this anthology with the original text. In the opening paragraph of her essay, she wrote personally as a reader-response critic, but in the next paragraph she gave a detailed analysis of the Russian words she found in the story.

STUDENT ESSAY

Anton Chekhov's "The Darling"

in Russian and English Translation

The Russian version of Anton Chekhov's "The Darling" was clearer to me than the translated version. Because I grew up in Russia before emigrating to the United States, I could relate to the description of the streets and the house in the provincial town where Olenka lived. This was clear in both the English and the Russian versions of the story. But the original version gave me a better understanding of the character of Olenka. She appeared as a genuinely religious person in the Russian version, not only because she went to church and used expressions like "May the Mother of God give you health," but also because Chekhov's choice of words for the title of the story made you understand how religious Olenka truly is.

In the Russian version, the title of the story is "Duschechka," a word that comes from the word soul--duscha. The direct translation would be "the dear little soul," meaning a spiritual person with a good heart. This description perfectly suits Olenka. She is affectionate but naive in her relationships with men, falling in love with each of her two husbands out of pity. Introducing her in the first paragraph, Chekhov calls her by her nickname "Olenka" instead of her Christian name "Olga" to suggest that her character is childish and foolish: "Olenka, the daughter of the retired collegiate assessor, Plemyanniakov, was sitting in her back porch, lost in thought."

Later in the story we learn that Olenka completely identifies with all of the men in her life, including her lover the veterinary surgeon and his young son, Sasha. She thinks like each of them and talks about what they talk about. She does not have her own opinion about anything; just like a child she needs to depend upon someone. Chekhov successfully emphasized her complete emotional dependency on others throughout the story. Just as the soul needs the body for completion, so Olenka needs to be in love to be alive. Chekhov wrote realistic stories, not religious parables, but perhaps Tolstoy's instinct that there might be a religious subtext here isn't so far from the truth. I believe I came closer to understanding

Chekhov's story about "The Dear Little Soul" when I read it in Russian.

You misread literature if you think of it as absolute, perfect, final statements far removed from the commonplaces of life. It needs the reader's involvement to come alive. Through their aesthetic patterns, stories, poems, and plays show us what life is like. What they are ultimately saying, in their affirmation of life and human creativity, is — in the words of Henry James — "Live! Live!"

26

WRITING RESEARCH PAPERS

THREE KEYS TO LITERARY RESEARCH

The first key to doing good research is to understand its purpose. In a literature class using this anthology, research writing is really an extension of the other sorts of writing you will do, such as explication, analysis, or comparison and contrast. As with these other sorts of writing, the purpose is for you to learn more about one or more pieces of literature, and perhaps about the context in which it was written, and to pass what you learn on to a reader.

The second key to doing effective literary research is understanding that a good research paper is not a dull collection of facts and quotations. Rather, a research paper is a type of essay. As with any other essay, a research paper should have a strong and compelling thesis, maintain a focus on a particular question or issue, and clearly be a product of serious, original thinking on the part of its author.

The third key to literary research is simple and practical: Do not wait. Get moving with the process of your paper as soon as you get the assignment, and never put off working on it under the assumption that you'll have plenty of time later. Sometimes the best research materials may be difficult to find, and they may take longer to read and understand than you anticipate. Organizing thoughts provoked by many sources and presenting them in a clear manner may take quite a bit of time too. Finally, you will probably need extra editing and proofreading time to make sure you get the details of citation and documentation just right.

FINDING AND FOCUSING A TOPIC

The topic of your research paper may be assigned by your teacher, or you may have free choice as to what you will write about. Either way, you will need to do some thinking and focusing before you dive into the research. Regardless of the form of your assignment, try to bring something of yourself, your personality and interests, to your research.

Once you have chosen a topic or found an approach to an assigned topic, try to stick with it. It can be tempting to drop your topic or change directions if the first stages of the research don't go as smoothly as you had hoped. Students cause themselves many wasted hours and a great deal of anguish by changing topics before giving their original ideas the real chance they deserve.

Assigned Topics

Even if the topic is assigned, it is still your job to make it your own and to find an angle which will allow you to write an original essay on the subject. Consider for example the two following topics:

1. What is the function of the literary allusions in Eliot's "The Love Song of J. Alfred Prufrock"?
2. The nineteenth century was a time of great upheaval in norms regarding marriage and family. How does Ibsen's *A Doll House* reflect this upheaval?

In both of these topics, the questions are broad, and given enough time and energy you would probably end up with far more to say than you could comfortably fit into a single, well-focused paper. In other words, you need to narrow and focus the topics so that your paper takes on a clear purpose and you have the chance to develop fully whatever ideas you choose to pursue.

For the first question, you would probably need to begin by doing some library research in literary criticism and history in order to develop a sense of what the possibilities are and how these might fit in with your own initial response to Eliot's poem. Only after this stage could you proceed to narrowing the topic and focusing your research on those aspects of the poem most interesting to you. For the second question, you might be able to find an initial direction for your research right away and frame some questions you would like to answer. You could then proceed with your research knowing from the start what to look for.

Choosing Your Own Topic

If you are given free, or relatively free, choice of a topic for your paper, your initial job is both harder and easier than if you are given a specific assignment. It can be difficult, when faced with the almost limitless possibilities of such a project, to focus your thoughts and get down to work. Still, you have the opportunity to begin with a writer or a piece of literature that you find especially exciting and choose to investigate an issue in which you have some personal investment.

The best place to begin finding your topic is by choosing a piece of literature which had a strong effect on you. Read through the work and its headnote again, making note of those things you find most worth thinking more about, especially any unanswered questions you may have.

Then take some time to brainstorm a list of questions about the work, the author, and the context. Write down all your questions, even those which you think you won't be pursuing. Try to move quickly beyond the sorts of questions which can be answered with a *yes* or *no* or which can be answered by a simple piece of information — *who, when,* and *where* questions. Think instead of meaty *how, what,* and *why* questions. What are the major themes and issues in the literature? How does the literature relate to other writings (by the same author or others)? What impact did the author's life have on his or her work? How did social and historical conditions shape the literature? What did previous critics and researchers — experts on this author, perhaps — have to say about the work?

Once you have a substantial list, check it for the two or three questions that most interest you. Would one of these make a good focus for your paper? If you can find enough information about the issues the question raises, could you write a paper of the appropriate length and type? Is the question narrow enough in its scope that you can investigate it thoroughly? If so, you are just about ready to begin researching. If not, look over your list again and try talking to your instructor or fellow students to see if they can offer some further refinements of your ideas. If you are concerned that the information you need will not be out there, have a backup question ready. In any case, it's important to be flexible in the early stages of your research and allow your questions to evolve and grow more complex as you become more of an expert on the topic you have chosen.

FINDING AND USING SOURCES

There are as many ways of proceeding with research as there are researchers. In working on previous projects, you may have developed your own perfect method for keeping track of sources, taking notes, and organizing your ideas. If, on the other hand, you haven't done a great deal of research (or if you have had less than satisfactory experiences with research), you might benefit from trying out the method outlined in the next section, which has worked for many researchers over the years. The system involves taking two different kinds of notes: bibliographic notes to find and acknowledge your sources, and content notes to keep track of the information you find in these sources. As you become a more practiced researcher, you will probably find yourself adapting the method to fit your own working style. The only solid rule is to be precise with your notes and references. Nothing is more frustrating than finding a gap or mistake in your notes and having to go back to the library to check a page number or the spelling of a name.

Begin your research by thinking about what sources you will need to complete your project. Plan a strategy to find those sources — the section on library research will suggest some approaches — and start a working bibliography of the books, articles, and other resources that will help you answer your research questions.

Library Research

Once you have reread the primary source (the literature about which you are writing), the headnote on the writer, and any related information in the commentaries or casebook sections of this textbook, continue your search in the college or university library. How you proceed will depend upon your topic and focus, so consider some questions before you start your search. Is your topic primarily literary, leading you to books and articles that focus on a writer's life and works? Or will you be delving into questions about history or religion or philosophy or other fields outside literary criticism? Are you researching a well-established author or one who has recently emerged and hasn't yet attracted much attention? Do you have some specific questions in mind at this point, or do you want to browse around and see how other researchers have approached your primary source? At any time during your research, you can ask a reference librarian for help, either while using one of the tools described below or simply to discuss where to look next.

The most complete listing of publications in the field of literature is the Modern Language Association's *MLA International Bibliography.* Published annually and available in some libraries in electronic format, this bibliography can provide the most thorough list of sources if what you are looking for is scholarly books and articles about writers and their work. It also covers linguistics, folklore, and to some extent, film criticism.

The print version of this bibliography covers a year at a time and is in two volumes, one that lists works by nationality, period, author, and work and another volume that is an alphabetical subject index. If, for example, you wanted to see what had been published recently on D. H. Lawrence's story "The Rocking-Horse Winner," you could look in the first volume of the most recent year, find the section for English literature, then the subsection for the twentieth century (labeled *1900–99*), and then the listing for Lawrence, which would be further subdivided for general studies and for each of his major works. If you are using an electronic version, which may be available through your library's Web site or at a CD-ROM station in the library, you can type in the name of an author or the title of a work to see what has been published on that topic. You can also search by a theme or subject or combine a topic and author (such as *Lawrence and childhood*). As with all unfamiliar electronic databases, spending ten minutes skimming through the help screens or asking a librarian how to get started is a wise investment of time.

The *MLA International Bibliography* is a good place to get a sense of how literary scholars have approached a primary source. However, because it strives for completeness, it can provide an overwhelming amount of sources when the work is well known and frequently analyzed by critics. On the other hand, you may not find enough information. If you are researching a contemporary writer, you may find few sources because there usually is a time lag before a writer gains scholarly attention. And the *MLA International Bibliography* doesn't cover publications in other fields, such as history. If, for example, you are writing about a story by Sandra Cisneros, you may have questions about the Chicana experience in Texas in the middle decades of the twentieth century. For these needs, most libraries provide access to an interdisciplinary database of articles covering the major journals in various fields, including history, urban affairs, and ethnic studies. Many also index some popular publications that may include book reviews of contemporary fiction or interviews with writers. Ask your reference librarians which interdisciplinary databases are available locally and whether they might work for your topic.

Your library's online catalog is another resource. An excellent first step is to find a basic critical study of a writer and his or her works. Look for recently published, general studies that will give you background knowledge of your author's life and work to ground your research. As with all scholarly writing, these texts will provide useful bibliographies that will point you to the most significant books and articles about your topic.

The reference section of your library is a rich source of background and factual information. A series such as *Contemporary Literary Criticism* or *American Writers* can provide a quick and thorough overview of a writer's life and work. The *Encyclopedia of the American Religious Experience* might give you insight into the spiritual world of Emily Dickinson; the *Encyclopedia of African American History and Culture* may answer questions raised in reading a play by Lorraine Hansberry. The reference section is full of such specialized resources. A librarian will be able to take you straight to the sources that will provide answers.

Finally, don't expect to gather all of your sources in one or two visits to the library. As you find resources, scan through them to evaluate how they might be useful, what issues they raise, and what publications they cite as critical evidence. Read as you research and let that reading help you refine the questions you are asking.

Using the Web for Research

The World Wide Web is an increasingly popular place to conduct research. For some topics, such as public affairs, politics, and popular culture, it is an excellent source of information; for others, including many topics in literature, it is less useful. Most literary scholars are more likely to publish their work in the form of journal articles and books than they are to put it on the Web to mingle indiscriminately with a sixth grader's term paper or a hobbyist's fan page. However, you might find interesting sites devoted to the culture of a period or digitized primary-source collections at sites such as the *Electronic Text Center* at the University of Virginia or the *American Memory* project at the Library of Congress, where you can find old film clips, recordings of speeches, and such treasures as Orson Welles's hand-annotated working script for a production of *Macbeth* that he directed in Harlem in 1936.

General search engines are of limited use for the literary scholar. Search engines work by mining the Web mechanically, pulling together sites based on words used on pages and in URLs, regardless of quality or depth. Relevance ratings are assigned not by actually reading the sites but by counting the number of uses of a word or by some other automated mechanism. And even the most thorough search engines currently index less than 20 percent of the Web. If you use a search engine, try to focus your search. For example, a search for "Shakespeare" will retrieve tens of thousands of sites, many of them of limited usefulness. But a search that uses the terms *Hamlet, Branagh,* and *film* will narrow your search to sites about the 1996 Kenneth Branagh film version of *Hamlet.* An alternative to using general search engines is to use subject-oriented selective Web directories such as the Argus Clearinghouse or Scout Signpost. These have been compiled by researchers who have attempted to find and organize by subject the best sites on the Web. Another option is to seek out valuable digital collections such as the *American Memory* project and use the search capabilities of that site to find useful resources. Finally, reference librarians pay attention to quality Web sites and may be able to point you to helpful sites.

In addition to sites available to anyone on the Web, many subscription information sources are now being made available by libraries through the Web. Library catalogs and indexes are frequently accessible through Web browsers. If your library has an electronic version of the *MLA International Bibliography,* it may be Web-based. Your library may also subscribe to full-text journal collections such as Project Muse or JSTOR, which reproduce the contents of hundreds of scholarly journals in Web format. And they may have access to general resources such as Lexis/Nexis Universe, which provides newspaper and magazine coverage as well as political and legal information. These sites are not part of the "free" Web and are not indexed by general search engines. They are generally available to a campus community either through the campus network or by modem, but may not be accessible if you connect to the Internet through a service provider other than your college or university.

Your research will most likely require you to use a combination of electronic and print resources. Above all, bear in mind that you want to find the best sources you can, regardless of how they are packaged.

Evaluating Your Sources

Not all information is created equal, and just because an item has found its way into print (or has a place on a flashy Web site), you should not necessarily believe it. You should evaluate every potential source you identify in at least two ways before you include it in your paper, first to determine if the source is respectable (that is, likely to be accurate) and second to find out if it is really appropriate to your purpose.

The first and most obvious question to ask is, Who wrote and published the information? For an academic paper, the best and most reliable sources are usually scholarly journals and books published by university presses. This is not to say that a paperback book, an article from a popular magazine, or a Web site can never be an appropriate source in an academic paper. Depending on the topic of your paper, these may prove to be valuable and even vital sources. But don't forget in compiling your bibliography that in general your paper will carry more weight if it derives its substance from scholarly sources.

Dates are also worth being aware of. Not all literary research needs to be absolutely up to date; sometimes historical research is the key to a successful paper. But if you have a choice between two critical studies, one written in 1954 and one written in 1994, use the more recent one unless you have a compelling reason to choose the other. Not only will the recent work be based on more up-to-date theories and utilize recently discovered information, but it is also likely to incorporate the ideas of earlier researchers as well.

Special caution is needed when evaluating online sources. The Internet is a vast and largely uncensored place, and much of the information available on it is incomplete, misleading, or just plain wrong. If you can't tell whether a Robert Frost Web page was posted by a professor of American literature or a middle-school student doing a project for English class, be sure to confirm any doubtful information. Sometimes the author of a Web site will include a link to a personal home page at the bottom of the page, where you might learn more about the author's credentials. If an organization has sponsored a Web project, look for links to information about the purpose and nature of the organization. URLs can offer clues as to whether the site is running on a university server (*.edu*), a commercial server (*.com*), a federal government server (*.gov*), a school (*.k12*), or the site of a nonprofit organization (*.org*). Country abbreviations such as *.ca* for Canada or *.uk* for United Kingdom may also be useful clues. If you delete the part of the URL after the first slash, you can sometimes learn something useful. It may reveal that your author has posted a page at a particular university (which doesn't necessarily tell you about its academic quality — most universities allow the members of its community to post just about anything on their sites) or at a federal government agency such as the Library of Congress (which is particular about its content). Apply to Web sites the same criteria of accuracy and relevance that you use in evaluating printed information.

Once you have established the general respectability of your sources, you need to be sure that they are actually pertinent to your research question. Including information tangential to your point just because it is interesting or comes from a strong source will not improve your paper. Your first priority should be to make the paper as sharp and well focused as possible, even if it means leaving out some fascinating ideas or facts you encounter.

Your Working Bibliography

Each time you identify a potential source of information, you will add a reference to your **working bibliography**. More and more these days, researchers keep bibliographies as computer files that can later be adapted into a list of works cited. If you like to work on a computer, and especially if you have a notebook model you can take to the library with you, by all means keep your working bibliography this way. The traditional way of keeping bibliographic notes, however, is on 3″ × 5″ note cards, one reference to a card, and even many computer-literate researchers still prefer this method because they can take notes anywhere without worrying about booting up a computer.

Complete instructions on the information you will need to turn your working bibliography into a list of works cited can be found in the section on MLA format (p. 2107). The rule of thumb: If you think there is any chance the information may be needed, write it down. Copy source information from the title and copyright pages of a book (or the pages of an article or other short work).

It will save you time and trouble in preparing your list of works cited if you put the correct format for capitalization and punctuation in your bibliographic references. All titles and publication information should appear in capital and lowercase letters, even when the original is in all capitals. Subtitles are separated from titles by a colon. The titles of long works should be either underlined or italicized (not both); these works include books, plays, newspapers, magazines, journals, CDs, films, and radio and television programs. Titles of short works are put in quotation marks, not underlined or italicized; these works include stories, poems, essays, articles, chapters of books, songs, and single episodes of radio or television programs.

For a book, your bibliographic references should always present the full name of the author or editor; the full title of the book (underlined or italicized); the city, publisher, and date of publication. In addition, if the book is an edition other than the first, a volume in a series, a translation, or a work in more than one volume, provide that information too. The example shows a useful format for writing down this information and one easily adaptable for your list of works cited.

BIBLIOGRAPHY ENTRY FOR A BOOK

Morrison, Toni. Beloved. New York: Knopf, 1987.

If your source is an article in a journal, magazine, or newspaper, the information will be slightly different. You will still begin with the name of the author and the title of the article (in quotation marks), followed by the title of the periodical in which the article appeared (underlined or italicized). For an academic journal, next comes the volume number and year of publication. For a magazine or newspaper, note the date (or month for a monthly publication) and year and the edition if one is given. For all types of periodicals, be sure to note the inclusive pages on which the article appeared.

BIBLIOGRAPHY ENTRY FOR A PERIODICAL

Kaplan, Amy. "Imperial Triangles: Mark Twain's Foreign Affairs." Modern Fiction Studies 43 (1997): 237-48.

Many academic books are collections of short works or essays written by a number of different authors on a certain topic. If you include such sources, make note of the author of the essay or chapter, the title of the chapter, the title and editor of the book, and the same publication information as for a book by a single author. The same format is used for works (including poems, stories, plays, and nonfiction essays and articles) in anthologies.

WORK IN A COLLECTION OR ANTHOLOGY

Davis, Tracy C. "Shotgun Wedlock: Annie Oakley's Power Politics in the Wild West." Gender in Performance: The Presentation of Difference in the Performing Arts. Ed. Laurence Senelick. Hanover, NH: UP of New England, 1992. 141-57.

If you intend to use online or other electronic sources, you will need to collect bibliographic information similar to that for traditional print sources, with a few notable additions. Full citation formats to use in your list of works cited are shown in the section on MLA format (p. 2107), but the following brief guidelines should help you proceed at the information-gathering stage of your research. It is not always possible to find all of the information called for, especially for Internet sources. If any of the information you need from any source — electronic or traditional — is missing, simply skip it and keep the format of the rest of your citation exactly the same.

For full-text articles published in both print and electronic formats, give the print source (if there is one) followed by the date of access and the electronic address.

Mohammed, Patricia. "Midnight's Children and the Legacy of Nationalism." Callaloo 20.4 (1997): 737-52. 14 Nov. 1999 <http://muse.jhu.edu/journals/callaloo/v020/20.4mohammed.html>.

Some electronic addresses for articles retrieved through a database can be extremely long. In such a case, provide the name of the database and its electronic address.

Vonnegut, Kurt. "Despite Tough Guys, Life Is Not the Only School for Real Novelists." New York Times 24 May 1999, El. 14 Nov. 1999 Lexis/Nexis Universe. <http://web.lexis-nexis.com/universe>.

There are several kinds of Internet sources you might use in your research beyond the Web-accessible databases your library provides. These include Web sites, e-mail messages, and postings to newsgroups and e-mail lists. Full documentation styles for each may be found in the section on MLA format. For Web sites, give as much of the following information as you can find: author, title of the section of the site (in quotation marks), title of the site itself (underlined), the name of any institution or organization associated with the site, the date of access, and (in angle brackets) the URL.

"The New Deal Stage: Selections from the Federal Theatre Project, 1935-1939." American Memory. Library of Congress. 14 Nov. 1999 <http://memory.loc.gov/ammem/fedtp/fthome.html>.

When citing communications through e-mail, newsgroups, or e-mail discussion lists, include the author of the message; the subject line (in quotation marks); the description *Online posting;* the date; the name of the forum, if relevant; the date of access; and the URL in angle brackets or, if no URL is available, the e-mail address of the list's moderator.

> Austin, David. "Re: Hoff Summer's Critique." Online posting. 9 July 1999. 14 Nov. 1999 <news:soc.feminism>.

When is your working bibliography complete? There is no easy answer to that question because the number and types of sources you need will depend upon the sort of paper you are writing. Also, as your research proceeds, you will likely come across additional references you will want to follow up, so in theory the bibliography is in flux until the paper is completed. Realistically, though, at some point you need to stop looking for leads and begin working with the sources themselves.

WORKING WITH SOURCES AND TAKING NOTES

So far, we have discussed how to find the information sources you will need for your research. This detective work is what many people think of when they hear the word "research." But it is only now — when the sources are in your hands — that the real research begins, as you start the intellectual work of reading, assimilating, and working with your sources.

Careful note taking is crucial to this phase of the process. No matter how sharp your memory or your organizational skills, as you work with a growing number of sources, it is easy to forget who wrote what, or even if an idea was original to you or came from another author. So it is especially important to keep yourself well organized at this point. You should have a stack of cards or a computer file with your bibliographic notes, but now you will begin to take the second kind of notes for your project — content notes. Most researchers prefer to take content notes on larger (generally 4″ × 6″) cards, that serve the dual purpose of making them instantly distinguishable from bibliographic cards and allow more room to make comments on the notes. Once again, if you work with a computer, you can take notes directly into a word-processing file.

As you begin to read each source, start a new note card with a heading indicating the author's last name and perhaps a shortened version of the source's title. If you are using more than one source by the same author, noting the source on each card will save you a lot of trouble should your cards get shuffled later on. Also be sure to include on all notes the page numbers from which the note is taken. When the time comes to write your paper and document your sources, you will need to provide page references for every fact, opinion, or idea you get from an outside source, whether you use the author's words or your own to record the idea.

A good way to begin note taking is with a brief summary (perhaps a few sentences) of the author's main point or idea. Try to phrase this summary in your own words. This will not only help you to be sure that you have understood your reading, it will also help you compose your essay later on because you will already have had to think through the ideas and produce some prose of your own. Remember that just changing the order of the author's words or substituting a few words of your own is not the same as writing notes in your own voice.

After you have the main idea down, your notes can grow more specific, homing in on those elements of your reading that most relate to the research question you have set for yourself. If a section of one of your sources seems especially important or speaks directly to your question, devote a separate card to it. Remember that you might disagree with an author and still find his or her ideas important, if only as points to argue against in your paper. When you are comfortably familiar with your authors and their arguments, you will almost certainly want to pull out some direct quotations from your sources. It is best to reserve quoting for times when the author has written something in memorable and effective language or when he or she expresses an idea so succinctly and clearly that you really can't imagine saying it any better. If you find yourself wanting to note more than a few short quotations from each source, you may not be focusing on what's important. When you transcribe a quotation, put the material in quotation marks; always double check to make sure that your transcription is scrupulously accurate. Remember to note the page number from which the quotation was taken. If the quotation spans two pages in the original, mark the spot in your note at which the new page begins.

Imagine, for example, you were focusing your research on the ways gender roles are portrayed in Charlotte Perkins Gilman's "The Yellow Wallpaper." Sandra M. Gilbert and Susan Gubar's commentary on the story, reprinted in this anthology, directly relates to this issue and would be a good place to start your research. Here are examples of how you might write three note cards — a summary, a paraphrase, and a quotation — from this source. The numbers in parentheses are page numbers in the original. These cards would, of course, be keyed to bibliographic cards giving the authors' full names, the article's complete title, and the necessary publication information.

SUMMARY

The authors focus on the ways in which women--in literature and in real life--are made to feel trapped and imprisoned, in actual rooms and houses as well as in social roles. The wallpaper symbolically imprisons the narrator, and her madness allows her a sort of freedom.

PARAPHRASE

The woman trapped behind the wallpaper represents how the narrator herself is trapped in circumstances beyond her control. In freeing the woman, she frees herself through her madness. (682)

QUOTATION

"[. . .] even when a supposedly 'mad' woman has been sentenced to imprisonment in the 'infected' house of her own body, she may discover that, as Sylvia Plath was to put it seventy years later, she 'has a self to recover, a queen.'" (683)

Of course, as you work with your sources and take notes from them, don't let yourself be so swept up in other people's words and arguments that you forget your own purpose and ideas in writing the paper. Write your own responses and opinions directly on your note cards — but be sure to distinguish them from the author's ideas, perhaps by using a different color ink. If your reading sparks any major new ideas from you (which ideally it will), make note of these on separate cards, indicating your own name as a heading and treating these cards for now as you would the material from outside sources.

DRAFTING YOUR RESEARCH PAPER

By the time you have read and assimilated your preliminary research materials, you should basically know the direction of your paper and what you want it to say. Now is the time to write a tentative thesis statement and to begin drafting your paper. A thesis statement does not just name your topic or state a fact; it asserts what the rest of your paper will argue. It should be clearly focused and guide the reader as to the general direction of your paper. Consider these two potential theses:

1. Kate Chopin's writing was very controversial in its day.
2. By developing characters like Mrs. Mallard from "The Story of an Hour," Kate Chopin proved that she was interested more in portraying emotional truth than in the social norms of her day.

The first of these is too vague, merely stating a fact that can be easily verified. The second is more specific, more interesting, and gives its writer a real assertion to defend. The tentative thesis as you initially draft it may or may not find its way into your final paper, but it should help you set a single, manageable task for yourself and keep you on track as you begin organizing your notes and ideas.

After you have drafted your tentative thesis, you must impose some order on the pile of notes and ideas you have amassed. (If you have taken your notes on a computer, this is a good time to print out a hard copy. You may wish to cut the printout into individual notes so that you can shuffle them around.) Whatever method you normally use to begin writing can probably be adapted to deal with including outside sources as well. But if you are having trouble getting all your thoughts in order, one way to start is by arranging smaller stacks of related notes on subtopics. Don't worry if the stacks are very uneven or if some notes seem to be unrelated to the others; you can deal with these anomalies later. And don't forget to include the notes that contain your own original ideas; they are the most important notes you have.

Now look over the cards again and put aside any that no longer seem relevant to your thesis. At this point you may discover that ideas are represented in your research about which you do not have enough information, and you will want to follow these up with more reading. You can continue with your research now, or you can proceed with writing the paper, leaving a space to be filled in later.

Start drafting your paper by whatever process has worked for you in the past for other types of writing. Some students find it helpful to begin with an outline (formal or not) or a list of key points. Others prefer to jump right into the writing itself, knowing that they will probably have to substantially reorganize the draft work at a later stage. Part One of this anthology provides several ideas, beginning on page 14, for how to use brainstorming, freewriting, listing, and questioning to start drafting.

The following sections suggest how to develop your research materials as you write. Don't forget, though, that this is *your* paper, not a mere presentation of other people's ideas, however compelling they may be. Each time you mention an idea from an outside source, comment on it thoroughly. You may agree, dispute, analyze, or explain, but never let a quote or thought from someone else stand on its own.

Summarizing, Paraphrasing, and Quoting

You can integrate the material you have found in your research sources into your paper in three ways — as summaries, paraphrases, or quotations. Each of these techniques is useful, and you will probably end up using all three in your paper. Each time you write from a source, consider your purpose in using this source.

Integrating summaries. To help your readers understand the background and the important questions within your topic, you will sometimes want to provide a quick overview of an author's main ideas or major contributions to scholarship. In these cases, rather than give an exhaustive account of all an author has to say, you should provide brief summaries. In some cases, the summary may be as simple as rephrasing a part of your summary note card for a source. For instance, the example of a summary note from the feminist reading of "The Yellow Wallpaper" (p. 2102) might appear in your paper as follows.

> Gilbert and Gubar focus on the ways in which women--in literature and in real life--are made to feel trapped and imprisoned, in actual rooms and houses as well as in social roles.

Note that such a summary gives direct credit to the authors whose ideas you are discussing and presents those ideas succinctly, without getting bogged down in the article's supporting details.

Integrating paraphrases. You will sometimes want to focus on a more specific point made by one of your sources, and in these cases you will need either to paraphrase or to quote. As a general rule, think about paraphrasing first and save quoting for especially important points. As it did at the note-taking stage, paraphrasing makes clear that you understand the material with which you are working. It also keeps the ideas in your own words so that they fit in better with your own prose style. The example shows a paraphrase of part of the Gilbert and Gubar essay just summarized.

> Gilbert and Gubar consider the narrator's madness--and women's madness in general--a sort of triumph which allows her to be free of her oppressive surroundings.

Although the words of this paraphrase do not appear in the original essay, the idea it expresses is Gilbert and Gubar's. A paraphrase of this sort acknowledges the source of the idea while setting up the expectation that you will offer further comment on the critics' reading.

Integrating quotations. When you want your readers to pay special attention to the material you are using, the time has come for quoting. Many students worry about how to integrate quotations into their research papers, but with practice it eventually becomes much easier and more natural. Keep in mind a few formatting features and helpful tips as you begin working with quotations from both primary and secondary sources. First, quotations should be short, using as few words as you can while conveying what you need to. Long quotations are distracting, can be difficult to integrate with your own prose, and may suggest (unjustifiably or not) that you are trying to pad your paper.

Quotations of four lines of prose (from a literary or a critical source) or three lines of poetry should be integrated into your paragraph and enclosed within quotation marks. For longer quotations, set off the quoted material from your paragraph by beginning a new line and indenting an inch from the left margin only. It will be clear to your readers that any material thus set off is a quotation, so do not use quotation marks and do not switch to single spacing. The examples show the formats for integrating a short and a long quotation.

> Melville begins "Bartleby, the Scrivener" with the narrator's description of himself as "a rather elderly man" (458). Melville's narrator begins by telling us the following information about himself:
>
> > I am a rather elderly man. The nature of my avocations, for the last thirty years, has brought me into more than ordinary contact with what would seem an interesting and somewhat singular set of men, of whom, as yet, nothing, that I know of, has ever been written--I mean, the law-copyists, or scriveners. (458)

Indicate deletions with an ellipsis. A few special situations deserve note. In some cases, you might wish to change a quotation slightly to make it fit the grammar of your sentence, or you may choose to delete part of a quotation in the interest of being succinct. Any additions or changes in wording that you make should be placed within brackets. Short deletions that you make should be indicated with an ellipsis within brackets. For deletions of more than a sentence, use four periods for the ellipsis (the first period is closed up; a space then follows each one). The example shows changes and a short deletion from the Melville passage quoted.

> The narrator says that "the nature of [his] avocations [. . .] has brought [him] into more than ordinary contact with what would seem an interesting and somewhat singular set of men" (458).

Of course, it is dishonest to put words into someone else's mouth, so it is important that any changes you make do not affect the basic content or meaning of the passage you quote.

Indicate line breaks in a short quotation from a poem. When a short quotation is from a poem, you need to indicate any line breaks that occur within the quotation. This is done with a slash mark, with single spaces before and after.

> Gary Snyder asks, "What use, Milton, a silly story / Of our lost general parents, / eaters of fruit?" (10-12).

Indicate a quotation within a quotation. When part of the material you need to put in quotation marks is already in quotation marks in the original use single quotation marks to indicate the marks which appear in the original and double quotation marks to indicate what you are quoting.

> The narrator calls, "'Bartleby! quick, I am waiting'" (465).

> In his essay "The Origin of 'Cathedral,'" Tom Jenks recalls the first time he met Raymond Carver.

In addition to understanding the correct format for presenting and punctuating quotations, you will need to integrate them smoothly into your paper so that they do not interrupt or distract from your original prose. Three ways of integrating quotations are explained, from the least to the most effective.

Avoid the floating quotation. First, try to avoid the *floating quotation,* which is simply a sentence or phrase lifted out of the original and put in quotation marks with the attribution of the source and any commentary coming in another sentence (if at all).

> "Rage, rage against the dying of the light" (3). These words show Dylan Thomas's passionate sorrow at his father's impending death.

This method creates two problems. First, because the quotation is self-contained, it leaves a reader (albeit momentarily) to ponder its source and wonder why it has been presented at this point. Also, it makes for choppy reading; it presents an awkward transition from the poet's voice to that of the commentator.

Use an attributed quotation. When possible, then, you should always use at least an *attributed quotation,* which identifies the author with a lead-in to the quotation.

> Thomas writes, "Rage, rage against the dying of the light" (3). In doing so he demonstrates his passionate sorrow at his father's impending death.

With this type of quotation, the reader sees immediately where the quoted text comes from and knows (or at least expects) that your commentary will follow.

Use an integrated quotation. Even more effective is the *integrated quotation;* it not only attributes the quoted material to its author but smoothly makes the quotation a part of your own sentence.

> Thomas demonstrates his passionate sorrow when he begs his father to "rage against the dying of the light" (3).

This is the hardest sort of integration to achieve because you have to make the quotation fit in grammatically with your own sentence. Usually, though, the payoff in sharp prose is well worth a little time spent in revising.

DOCUMENTING YOUR SOURCES

Beginning researchers often find frustrating the precise format they must follow in giving credit to sources. Once again, understanding why documentation format exists as it does will help you to learn how to do it right. Documentation serves two purposes: It protects you from charges of plagiarism, and it allows your readers to find the source of any quoted or cited material.

Nearly all students know that copying the words of an author and turning them in as their own work is plagiarism. What many do not realize, however, is that plagiarism can take more subtle forms. In fact, because they don't fully understand the concept, students often plagiarize unintentionally. Plagiarism occurs any time a writer uses another person's words or *ideas* without giving full credit to the original source. So even if you paraphrase another writer's thoughts entirely in your own words, you must document fully where those thoughts originated. Your readers will assume that everything not credited in your paper is either your original idea or that you are trying to take credit for it. The only exception to the rule on crediting sources is that you need not document common knowledge, which might be defined as anything that a reasonably well-educated person should be expected to know. The name of the U.S. president or the fact that William Shakespeare was an English playwright, for instance, would not need to be attributed. If you are unsure whether or not something counts as common knowledge, document it.

MLA Format

Several systems of documentation are used in academic disciplines, and while these systems vary, they all serve the same purpose. For papers in literature and some of the humanities, the format is the one developed by the Modern Language Association, or MLA. The system breaks down into two parts.

First are brief in-text parenthetical citations that occur in the body of a paper to indicate an author and page number for each summary, paraphrase, or quotation. Second is a works cited list (a bibliography) that provides complete information about the sources for those citations. When readers come across a reference to an author in the body of your paper, they can then turn to the list of works cited, look up the name, and find out more about the source. Check the *MLA Handbook* for complete instructions on citing all types of sources.

In-Text or Parenthetical Citations

MLA style presents two types of in-text citations: when the author's name appears in a signal phrase, or when the name is not included or there is no signal phrase. In the first, you signal the author's name in the lead-in to your citation (see instructions for attributed and integrated quotations, p. 2106) and provide a page reference in parentheses following the citation. The examples demonstrate the method using both a short and long quotation from literature.

SHORT QUOTATION WITH AUTHOR'S NAME IN TEXT

In Lorraine Hansberry's A Raisin in the Sun, Walter says, "Rich people don't have to be flashy" (1810).

LONG QUOTATION WITH AUTHOR'S NAME IN TEXT

In his poem "Mexicans Begin Jogging," Gary Soto asks,

> What could I do but yell vivas
> To baseball, milkshakes, and those sociologists
> Who would clock me
> As I jog into the next century
> On the power of a great, silly grin. (17-21)

For circumstances such as works by more than one author, multiple works by the same author, anonymous works, and works by corporate authors, the system for in-text citations is essentially the same, with a few notable differences.

WORK WITH TWO OR THREE AUTHORS

According to Gates and Appiah, . . .

WORK WITH MORE THAN THREE AUTHORS

Berger et al. claim . . .

If your paper refers to more than one work by the same author or to an anonymous work, it is especially important to include the name of the work in your signal phrase.

MORE THAN ONE WORK BY THE SAME AUTHOR

In "Technique in Writing the Short Story," Chekhov argues . . .

ANONYMOUS WORK

A U.S. News and World Report article titled "Barbour Gets a Comeuppance" states that . . .

If the author is an organization rather than an individual, use the organization name.

ORGANIZATION AS AUTHOR

The American Psychological Association reports that . . .

The second type of MLA in-text citation is used when the author is not named in a signal phrase. In this case, both the author's last name and the page number appear in the parentheses.

CITATION WITH AUTHOR'S NAME IN REFERENCE

The authors explain that "a setting may be either a simple backdrop to the action or it may be crucial in itself" (DeMarr and Bekerman 109).

The citation consists of only the last name (or names) and page number with no additional punctuation or information. The exception to this is when your paper cites more than one work by the same author; in this case your citation should include the author's name followed by a comma, the title (or a shortened version of it) of the work being cited, and the page number.

CITATION WITH AUTHOR'S NAME AND TITLE OF WORK IN REFERENCE

The author feels that words must mean what they say (Welty, "Is Phoenix Jackson's Grandson Really Dead?" 12).

List of Works Cited

Start your list of works cited on a new page in your paper, with the words "Works Cited" centered at the top. Continue double-spacing throughout, but do not add additional spaces between entries. Use hanging indentation in your list of works cited; this means that all lines *except* the first of each entry are indented. All entries are alphabetized by author's last name (or in the event of an anonymous work, by the first word of the title, disregarding *a, an,* or *the*).

Citing information from books. An entry for a book should contain as much of the following information as is applicable, in the following order and format, with periods between groups of elements. For most books you will use, details on editor, translator, volume, or series will not be needed.

1. The name of the author (or editor, if no author is listed), last name first
2. The title (underlined or in italics), including any subtitle (separate the title from subtitle by a colon)
3. The name of the editor (for a book with both author and editor), translator, or compiler (with the abbreviation "ed.," "trans.," or "comp.")

4. The edition, if it is not the first
5. Volume used if the book is part of a multivolume set
6. Series name if the book is part of a series
7. City of publication (followed by a colon), name of the publisher (comma), and year of publication

The most basic entry would be for a book by a single author or editor.

BOOK BY A SINGLE AUTHOR OR EDITOR

Moody, Anthony David. Thomas Stearns Eliot, Poet. 2nd ed. Cambridge: Cambridge UP, 1994.

Adams, Hazard, ed. Critical Essays on William Blake. Boston: Hall, 1991.

Citing works in anthologies. When you are citing an article, story, poem, or other shorter work that appears as a part of a book, include as much of the following information as you can.

1. The name of the author of the short work
2. The title of the short work, enclosed in quotation marks
3. The name of the anthology's editor
4. All relevant publication information just as it would appear in a book citation
5. The inclusive page numbers for the shorter work

To cite a work of literature in an anthology or an article or chapter in a compilation:

WORK IN AN ANTHOLOGY

Ellison, Ralph. "Battle Royal." Literature and Its Writers: An Introduction to Fiction, Poetry, and Drama. 2nd ed. Ed. Ann Charters and Samuel Charters. Boston: Bedford, 2001. 220-30.

Citing works in periodicals. When you cite sources from journals, magazines, or newspapers, include the following information.

1. The name of the author of the short work
2. The title of the short work, enclosed in quotation marks
3. The title of the periodical, underlined or italicized
4. All relevant publication information (specified in the examples)
5. The inclusive page numbers for the shorter work

For a work in a scholarly journal with continuous pagination (that is, a journal that numbers the pages straight through a volume year, as if each issue were a part of a single work), publication information should include the volume number and the year of publication (in parentheses), followed by a colon and the page numbers.

ARTICLE IN A SCHOLARLY JOURNAL

Montgomery, Thomas. "The Presence of a Text: The Poema de Cid." MLN 108 (1993): 199-213.

Citing newspaper articles. To cite an article in a newspaper, include the date (day, month, then year) and an edition if one is listed on the masthead, followed by a colon and the page number. Remember that many papers paginate each section separately, so you may need to include a section number or letter as part of the page number.

ARTICLE IN A NEWSPAPER

Smith, Roberta. "Drawing That Pushes Beyond the Boundaries." New York Times 12 Mar. 1997, late ed.: C25.

Citing other sources. You may want to cite a review, a television or radio program, a video or sound recording, a letter, e-mail communication, or interview. The following models demonstrate the basic format to follow.

REVIEW

Brantley, Ben. "A Pedophile Even a Mother Could Love." Rev. of How I Learned to Drive by Paula Vogel. New York Times 17 Mar. 1997, late ed.: C11.

TELEVISION OR RADIO PROGRAM

"The Living Language." The Power of the Word. Narr. Bill Moyers. PBS. WGBH, Boston. 12 Mar. 1994.

VIDEO OR SOUND RECORDING

Brook, Peter, dir. William Shakespeare's King Lear. Orion, 1970.

Kinnell, Galway. "In the Hotel of Lost Light." The Poetry and Voice of Galway Kinnell. Caedmon Cassette, 1971.

LETTER, E-MAIL COMMUNICATION, OR INTERVIEW

Crane, Carolyn. Letter to the author. 8 Feb. 1997.

Higgins, Andrew J. E-mail to the author. 4 June 1997.

Smith, Melanie. Personal interview [or Telephone interview]. 12 Apr. 1997.

Citing CD-ROMs, the Internet, and other electronic sources. Cite information from a CD-ROM, the Internet, and other electronic sources using these formats. If any of the required information is missing from an electronic source, skip it and keep the format for the rest of the citation exactly the same.

NONPERIODICAL PUBLICATION ON CD-ROM

"Brontë, Emily." Discovering Authors. Vers. 1.0. CD-ROM. Detroit: Gale, 1992.

PERIODICALLY PUBLISHED DATABASE ON CD-ROM

Gauch, Patricia Lee. "A Quest for the Heart of Fantasy." New Advocate 7.3 (1994): 159-67. Abstract. ERIC. CD-ROM. Silverplatter, 1999.

WEB SITE

"Native American Authors." Internet Public Library. 14 Nov. 1999 <http://www.ipl.org/ref/native/>.

NEWSGROUP POSTING

Karg, Moritz. "New Web Directory for Human Rights." Online posting. 11 Oct. 1999. 14 Nov. 1999 <news:soc.rights.human>.

The instructions and examples above will cover the vast majority of the sources you encounter. Complete information for how to cite these and any other type of source as well as additional information on conducting research and the mechanics of writing and formatting a research paper can be found in:

Gibaldi, Joseph. *MLA Handbook for Writers of Research Papers.* 5th ed. New York: MLA, 1999.

Footnotes and Endnotes

You will have noticed that the MLA format, with its in-text citations and list of works cited, does not require footnotes or endnotes to refer to sources. However, the format does allow for the use of notes in two specific circumstances. The first instance is for *bibliographic notes* in which the writer of the research paper, in addition to referring the reader to one or more sources, makes specific comment on the sources themselves. The second is for *content notes,* in which the writer makes a comment that is related to the research topic but does not fit easily within the text of the paper itself. Both types of notes should be used only when you cannot find another way to integrate the information, and for most research papers such notes will probably not be necessary.

Unless your instructor specifically asks for footnotes, always use endnotes instead. As the name implies, endnotes appear at the end of the paper — on a separate page, after the text but before the Works Cited list. To signal a note in your paper, use a superscript numeral in the text matching the numeral that precedes the note. Notes should be in the same type font and size as the rest of your paper and should maintain double spacing. For examples of both sorts of notes, see the sample research paper that begins on page 2114.

REVISING YOUR RESEARCH PAPER

Once your research paper is completely drafted, with all sources fully integrated and documented, the time has come to revise it, just as you would any other paper. The following six-part checklist provides a systematic method for approaching revision. You might also ask a classmate, or even your instructor, to look over the draft and offer advice.

1. First, look again at your tentative thesis statement. Now that you have written the paper, does the thesis still seem exactly right? It is possible, even likely, that in the process of writing you may have refined or changed your ideas about your topic. If so, reword the thesis to accurately reflect your new thinking.

2. Now look again at the supporting evidence you offer in each body paragraph. Do all of the ideas directly relate to and uphold the thesis? If any of them do not, you should cut these sections from your paper, regardless of the intrinsic interest of the ideas or the strength of the writing.
3. Are there any portions of the paper where you worry that the argument may be thin or underdeveloped or where the connection to your thesis may not be entirely clear? If so, you should try to explain your ideas more fully. You may even need to do some additional research to fill in the gaps.
4. After any necessary cuts and additions have been made, you may need to slightly reorganize the paper. Is your argument presented in the most logical order and are all related ideas kept together? Rearrange and revise any awkwardly placed paragraphs or sentences.
5. Does the style and voice sound at all like your usual writing? It is easy when reading the thoughts and words of other authors to begin adopting the style of these authors and losing your own voice. Check to make sure that the vocabulary and tone reflects your personality and your attitude toward the subject. By writing in your own voice, you make the material and the project your own.
6. Finally, carefully review the assignment and make sure that your essay conforms to your instructor's guidelines in all respects. In the event of disagreement, his or her guidelines should always take precedence over those offered here or anywhere else.

Your essay should now be ready for the final polish before you turn it in. Print out a clean copy and review it twice more. The first time, edit and proofread for word choice, grammar, spelling, and punctuation as well as any other small changes that will improve style and readability. If you are in doubt about anything, look it up. Even small mistakes can have a large negative effect on a reader. The second time, go over the format of all quotations, parenthetical references, and your works cited page to make sure that they are consistent and conform exactly to guidelines. You are now ready to make your last changes, print out a final copy, and turn in a research paper you can be proud of.

STUDENT RESEARCH PAPER

The student research paper that follows puts into practice the instructions and suggestions we have been discussing. You can also use it as a guide to proper manuscript format. Unless your teacher calls for some other format (such as a cover page), you should begin in the upper left corner of page 1 with your name, your instructor's name, the course for which you are writing the paper, and the date you turn it in. Double-space and center the title of your paper in capitals and lowercase letters without underlining or quotation marks (unless, of course, a quotation or title appears within your own title). Then begin the paper itself, with regular one-inch margins and double-spacing throughout (including for quotations and the list of works cited). A running head with your last name and the page number should appear in the upper right corner of each page. All word-processing programs make it easy to include such headings.

Silva 1 *Writer's name typed before page number.*

Jennifer Silva

Professor Gardner

English 102

7 November ----

Format for paper without a title page.

Emily Dickinson and Religion

Title centered and double-spaced.

Upon a cursory examination of her biography, it could be easy to dismiss religion as playing an insignificant role in Emily Dickinson's life and work. At the time of the Second Great Awakening, when most of New England was swept along by the fervent religious revival movement, Dickinson resisted. Even after the rest of her family formally joined the church, she refused since she just could not accept all aspects of church doctrine (Benet 19). Even in her poems, because "most have predictable rhyme schemes" and are "easy to memorize," it is easy to overlook the religious value (Schmidt 31). Many readers and critics have, in fact, drawn attention to her unconventional views, claiming that "she was deprived of an orthodox and steady religious faith" (Wilbur 1248) or that "she fought against God" (Tanter). But in overlooking or dismissing the important role that religion played in her life, we miss an important element of Emily Dickinson's poetry.

In-text citation for paraphrase.

In-text citation for Internet source; no page number.

Even though she never felt able to fully accept all aspects of Christian doctrine, it would be wrong to assume that religion did not influence Dickinson's life and work. In fact, religion and her faith in God seems to have played a large role. Emily Dickinson was raised in a deeply religious household. As a child, she was discouraged from reading anything except the Bible (Higginson 1242). In her childhood, adolescence, and early twenties, she attended church with her family twice every Sunday, hearing at least 1,500 sermons during this period. From the letters she wrote, it is clear that she was "capable of being transported by a good sermon" and "the effect on her of these weekly [. . .] invasions of her spirit [. . .] was profound" (Doriani 45). While she still didn't accept all of the conventions of the church, Dickinson wrote to her brother Austin that the preachings of Professor Edwards Amasa Park of Andover Theological Seminary, Reverend Edward S. Dwight, and especially Reverend Charles Wadsworth, among others, greatly inspired her (Doriani 46).

Ellipses in brackets indicate omitted text.

Silva 2

The influence of religion on her life spills over into her poetry, which reveals her strong belief in God and heaven. Dickinson discloses her great faith, her ability to believe without the assurance of concrete proof, in the poem "I never saw a Moor--." She writes,

> I never spoke with God
> Nor visited in Heaven--
> Yet certain am I of the spot
> As if the Checks were given-- (5-8)

Indent quotation of three or more lines of poetry, four or more lines of prose.

She does not have to see God or heaven to know that they exist, just as she has never seen "a Moor" or "the Sea" but still knows "how the Heather looks / And what a Billow be" (3-4). For her, the existence of heaven is as real and certain as the existence of the heather and billow. How can she be so sure of the existence of these things she cannot see? Presumably, she has learned about the heather and billows through the written and spoken accounts of others. In the same way, she accepts the existence of God and heaven probably as a result of the influence of the Bible, the words of the many preachers she has heard in her life, and the teachings of her family. Surrounded by these testimonies since early childhood, Dickinson feels she can faithfully commit herself to believing in God and heaven's existence. Many avid readers of her poetry agree that "she never forsook her strong beliefs in God" (Nelson).

Page number only; author cited in text.

Her faith and religion are such a significant part of her life that words with religious connotations even appear in her poems about other subjects, as if her immersion in religion is so great that she cannot separate it from other parts of her life. Even in her poetry about secular subjects, Dickinson's "Puritan heritage persistently provided her with a vocabulary, with metaphors, for experience that she and her world understood" (Juhasz 124). In poems about love and death (such as "Love--thou art high--," "If you were coming in the Fall," and "Because I could not stop for Death--") appear the words "eternity" and "Eden," words with significant religious meaning and implications which affect the connotations of the poems. "I taste a liquor never brewed--" includes the religious words "seraphs" and "saints": "[. . .] Seraphs swing their snowy Hats-- / And

Slash indicates line break in poetry.

Silva 3

Saints--to windows run--" (13-14). Religion has a place in all parts of her life, and consequently in all of her poetry. We can read these poems without focusing on their religious content, but to do so deprives us of an important layer of their meaning.

Even the formal style of her poetry reflects the influence of religion, for the hymns she learned in church and psalms she read in the Bible shaped her work. Many of her poems, "written in simple quatrains, generally in iambic tetrameter [. . .] with only the second and fourth lines rhyming," follow the same basic pattern as church hymns (Charters and Charters 1002).[1] Poems written in this hymn-like form--with approximate rhyme of the second and fourth lines, written in primarily iambic tetrameter and trimeter in simple quatrains--include "Because I could not stop for Death--," "If you were coming in the Fall," and "I heard a Fly buzz--when I died--." Once again, while these poems do not focus on explicitly religious subjects, the impact of religion on their form and content is evident.

Superscript numeral for endnote.

Because of the hymn-like quality of Dickinson's poetry, readers can be swept along quickly by the rhythm and miss some of the meaning of a poem. To alleviate this problem, Dickinson uses dashes as pauses to slow fast-moving lines, similar to the pausing technique she observed preachers using to emphasize a thought or hold the audience's attention (Doriani 48). For example, to place emphasis on the word "Nobody" in line 2 of the poem "I'm Nobody! Who are you?," she surrounds the word with dashes: "Are you--Nobody--Too?" Similarly, in "I died for Beauty--but was scarce" Dickinson uses dashes to slow down the reading of line 7 and emphasize the word "Truth": "And I--for Truth--Themself are One--." By adopting a convention used by the preachers who impressed her, Dickinson not only indicates the influence of religion in her life but also enhances the quality of her poetry for readers.

Another preaching technique that Dickinson adopted for her poetry concerns the use of natural speech. In addition to pausing for emphasis, "the practice of the preachers of the Puritan legacy [. . . was] to reject an affected style or an eloquence not characteristic of ordinary speech" (Doriani 16). This style is mirrored in much of Dickinson's poetry. Even

Brackets for addition or change to citation.

when attempting to capture a complex concept like hope in her poetry, she skillfully expresses her thoughts with refreshingly simple, yet elegant language without compromising the elevated content. In " 'Hope' is the thing with feathers--" she describes the complicated feeling of hope with very simple words and metaphors: "the thing with feathers-- / That perches in the soul-- / [. . .] sweetest--in the Gale [. . .]" (1-2, 5). At times, Dickinson even seems to be conversing with the reader through her poems. The poem "I'm Nobody! Who are you?" addresses the reader directly in a conversational tone. The many preachers that she heard using this type of language in speeches and sermons must surely have influenced her poetry style.

Much has been made of the fact that the young Emily Dickinson "found that she must refuse to become a professing Christian" (Wilbur 1248).[2] But even though Dickinson's religion has no church, her faith in God should not be doubted. A distinction must be made between nonconformist religious views and an outright rejection of God or religious values. Throughout her life, Dickinson strongly believed, "God's residence is next to mine, / His furniture is love" ("Who has" 197). Her God resides with her always--a guiding force touching all aspects of her life. Her faith is strong and unwavering. And if we read her work carefully and with an open mind, we can see that Dickinson's religious faith did not die with her in her Amherst house in 1886. Its fervor and vitality are still alive in her elegant poetry, preserved in simple verse to inspire generations for all time.

Silva 5

Notes

[1] A number of interesting studies--including Morris and Wolosky--discuss the ways in which Dickinson adapted and reshaped the hymn form in her poems.

Bibliographic endnote commenting on sources.

[2] Nearly all biographies of the poet stress her resistance to the doctrine preached during her brief time at Mount Holyoke Seminary.

Content endnote.

Silva 6

Works Cited

Benet, Laura. The Mystery of Emily Dickinson. New York: Dodd, 1974.

Book by a single author.

Charters, Ann, and Samuel Charters, eds. Literature and Its Writers: An Introduction to Fiction, Poetry, and Drama. 2nd ed. Boston: Bedford/St. Martin's, 2001.

Anthology cited by editors' names.

Dickinson, Emily. "'Hope' is the thing with feathers--." Charters and Charters 1006.

---. "I died for Beauty--but was scarce." Charters and Charters 1008.

More than one work by an author.

---. "I'm Nobody! Who are you?" Charters and Charters 1007.

---. "I never saw a Moor--." Charters and Charters 1013.

---. "I taste a liquor never brewed--." Charters and Charters 1005.

---. "Who has not found the heaven below." Selected Poems and Letters of Emily Dickinson. Ed. Robert N. Linscott. Garden City, NY: Anchor, 1959. 197.

Doriani, Beth Maclay. Emily Dickinson, Daughter of Prophecy. Amherst: U of Massachusetts P, 1996.

Higginson, Thomas Wentworth. "Emily Dickinson's Letters." Charters and Charters 1235-44.

Cross-reference to another citation in an anthology.

Juhasz, Suzanne. The Undiscovered Continent: Emily Dickinson and the Space of the Mind. Bloomington: Indiana UP, 1983.

Morris, Timothy. "The Development of Dickinson's Style." American Literature 60 (1988): 226-41. 14 Nov. 1999. JSTOR. <http://wwwjstor.org>.

Article in a scholarly journal.

Nelson, Perry L. "Re: Dashes and Meter." Online posting. 29 July 1996. EMWEB. 14 Nov. 1999 <http://lal.cs.byu.edu/mlists/emweb/199607/19960729-12.html>.

Internet source.

Schmidt, Elizabeth. "Imagining Emily." New York Times Book Review 2 Mar. 1997: 31.

Article in a newspaper.

Tanter, Marcy. "ED as War Poet." Online posting. 9 Jan. 1997. EMWEB. 14 Nov. 1999 <http://lal.cs.byu.edu/mlists/emweb/199701/19970109-1.html>.

Wilbur, Richard. "On Emily Dickinson." Charters and Charters 1248-49.

Wolosky, Shira. "Rhetoric or Not: Hymnal Tropes in Emily Dickinson and Isaac Watts." New England Quarterly 61 (1988): 214-32.

Acknowledgments (continued from p. iv)

Margaret Atwood. "Gertrude Talks Back" from *Good Bones and Simple Murders*. Copyright © 1983, 1992, 1994 by O. W. Toad Ltd. A Nan A. Talese Book. Reprinted by permission of Doubleday, a division of Random House, Inc., and McClelland & Stewart Ltd.

James Baldwin. "Sonny's Blues," copyright © 1965 by James Baldwin, was originally published in the *Partisan Review*. Copyright renewed. Collected into *Going to Meet the Man*, published by Vintage Books. Reprinted by arrangement with the James Baldwin Estate.

Toni Cade Bambara. "The Lesson" from *Gorilla, My Love*. Copyright © 1972 by Toni Cade Bambara. Reprinted by permission of Random House, Inc.

Raymond Carver. "The Bath" from *What We Talk About When We Talk About Love*. Copyright © 1981 by Raymond Carver. "Cathedral" and "A Small, Good Thing" from *Cathedral*. Copyright © 1983 by Raymond Carver. Reprinted by permission of Alfred A. Knopf, a division of Random House, Inc.

John Cheever. "The Swimmer" from *The Stories of John Cheever*. Copyright © 1964 by John Cheever. Reprinted by permission of Alfred A. Knopf, a division of Random House, Inc.

Anton Chekhov. "The Lady with the Pet Dog" from *The Portable Chekhov*, ed. Avrahm Yarmolinsky. Copyright 1947, © 1968 by Viking Penguin, Inc. Renewed © 1975 by Avrahm Yarmolinsky. Reprinted by permission of Viking Penguin, a division of Penguin Putnam, Inc.

Sandra Cisneros. "Little Miracles, Kept Promises" from *Woman Hollering Creek*. Copyright © 1991 by Sandra Cisneros, published by Vintage Books. Reprinted by permission of Susan Bergholz Literary Services, NY.

Edwidge Danticat. "New York Day Woman" from *Krik? Krak!* Copyright © 1995 by Edwidge Danticat. Reprinted by permission of Soho Press.

Ralph Ellison. "Battle Royal" from *Invisible Man*. Copyright © 1948 by Ralph Ellison. Reprinted by permission of Random House, Inc.

Louise Erdrich. "The Red Convertible" from *Love Medicine, New and Expanded Version*. Copyright © 1984, 1993 by Louise Erdrich. Reprinted by permission of Henry Holt and Company.

William Faulkner. "A Rose for Emily." Copyright 1930 and renewed 1958 by William Faulkner. "That Evening Sun." Copyright 1931 and renewed 1959 by William Faulkner. Reprinted by permission of Random House, Inc.

Mary Gaitskill. "Tiny, Smiling Daddy" from *Because They Wanted To*. Copyright © 1997 by Mary Gaitskill. Reprinted by permission of Simon & Schuster, Inc.

Gabriel García Márquez. "A Very Old Man with Enormous Wings" from *Leaf Storm and Other Stories*. Copyright © 1971 by Gabriel García Márquez. Reprinted by permission of HarperCollins Publishers, Inc.

Nadine Gordimer. "The Diamond Mine" from the May 10, 1999, issue of *The New Yorker*. Copyright © 1999 by Nadine Gordimer. Reprinted by permission of Russell & Volkening, Inc.

Bessie Head. "The Prisoner Who Wore Glasses" from *Under African Skies: Modern African Stories*, ed. Charles R. Larson. Copyright © 1997 by C. R. Larson. Reprinted by permission of Farrar, Straus & Giroux, Inc.

Ernest Hemingway. "Hills Like White Elephants" from *The Short Stories of Ernest Hemingway*. Copyright 1927 by Charles Scribner's Sons, renewed © 1955 by Ernest Hemingway. Reprinted by permission of Scribner, a division of Simon & Schuster, Inc.

Amy Hempel. "In the Cemetery Where Al Jolson Was Born" from *Reasons to Live*. Copyright © 1985 by Amy Hempel. Reprinted by permission of Darhansoff/Verrill Agency.

Zora Neale Hurston. "Sweat" from *Spunk: The Selected Stories* (Berkeley: Turtle Island Foundation, 1985). First published in 1926 as part of "The Eatonville Anthology." Copyright 1926 by Zora Neale Hurston. Reprinted by permission of the Zora Neale Hurston Estate. "The Gilded Six-Bits" from *Spunk: The Selected Stories* (Berkeley: Turtle Island Foundation, 1985). Reprinted by permission of HarperCollins Publishers. "How It Feels to Be Colored Me" from *I Love Myself When I Am Laughing*. "Story in Harlem Slang" from the July 1942 issue of the *American Mercury* and from *Zora Neale Hurston: Novels and Stories*, published by Library of America. Reprinted by permission of the Zora Neale Hurston Estate and the Victoria Sanders Agency.

Shirley Jackson. "The Lottery" from *The Lottery and Other Stories*. Copyright 1948, 1949 by Shirley Jackson, renewed © 1976, 1977 by Laurence Hyman, Barry Hyman, Mrs. Sarah Webster, and Mrs. Joanne Schnurer. Reprinted by permission of Farrar, Straus & Giroux, Inc.

Gish Jen. "Chin" from *Who's Irish?* Copyright © 1999 by Gish Jen. Reprinted by permission of Alfred A. Knopf, a division of Random House, Inc.

Franz Kafka. "The Metamorphosis" from *Franz Kafka: The Complete Stories*, ed. Nahum N. Glatzer and trans. Willa and Edwin Muir. Copyright 1946, 1947, 1948, 1949, © 1954, 1958,

1971 by Schocken Books. Reprinted by permission of Schocken Books, a division of Random House, Inc.

Jamaica Kincaid. "Girl" from *At the Bottom of the River*. Copyright © 1978, 1983 by Jamaica Kincaid. Reprinted by permission of Farrar, Straus & Giroux, Inc.

Guy de Maupassant. "The Necklace" from *Short Stories of Guy de Maupassant*, trans. Marjorie Laurie (New York: Dutton, 1934). Reprinted by permission of Everyman's Library / David Campbell Publishers.

Alice Munro. "How I Met My Husband" from *Something I've Been Meaning to Tell*. Copyright © 1974 by Alice Munro. Originally published by McGraw-Hill Ryerson. Reprinted by permission of Virginia Barber Literary Agency. All rights reserved.

Joyce Carol Oates. "Where Are You Going, Where Have You Been?" from *The Wheel of Love and Other Stories* (New York: Vanguard, 1970). Copyright © 1970 by Joyce Carol Oates. Reprinted by permission of John Hawkins Associates, Inc.

Tim O'Brien. "The Things They Carried" from *The Things They Carried*. Originally published in the August 1986 issue of *Esquire*. Copyright © 1989 by Tim O'Brien. Reprinted by permission of the Houghton Mifflin Company.

Flannery O'Connor. "Everything That Rises Must Converge" from *The Complete Stories*. Copyright © 1971 by the Estate of Mary Flannery O'Connor. Reprinted by permission of Farrar, Straus and Giroux, LLC. "A Good Man Is Hard to Find" and "Good Country People" from *A Good Man Is Hard to Find and Other Stories*. Copyright 1953 by Flannery O'Connor and renewed © 1981 by Regina O'Connor. Reprinted by permission of Harcourt, Inc.

Frank O'Connor. "Guests of the Nation" from *Collected Stories*. Originally appeared in *The Atlantic Monthly* (1931). Copyright 1931 by Frank O'Connor. Reprinted by permission of Alfred A. Knopf, a division of Random House, Inc., and the Joan Daves Agency.

Tillie Olsen. "I Stand Here Ironing" from *Tell Me a Riddle*. Copyright © 1956, 1957, 1960, 1961 by Tillie Olsen. Reprinted by permission of Dell Publishing, a division of Random House, Inc.

Cynthia Ozick. "The Shawl" from *The Shawl*. Copyright © 1980, 1983 by Cynthia Ozick. Reprinted by permission of Alfred A. Knopf, a division of Random House, Inc.

Grace Paley. "A Conversation with My Father" from *Enormous Changes at the Last Minute*. Copyright © 1971, 1974 by Grace Paley. Reprinted by permission of Farrar, Straus & Giroux, Inc.

Leslie Marmon Silko. "The Man to Send Rain Clouds" from *Storyteller*. Copyright © 1981 by Leslie Marmon Silko. Reprinted by permission of Seaver Books, New York, NY.

John Steinbeck. "The Chrysanthemums" from *The Long Valley*. Copyright 1937, renewed © 1965 by John Steinbeck. Reprinted by permission of Viking Penguin, a division of Penguin Putnam, Inc.

Amy Tan. "Two Kinds" from *The Joy Luck Club*. Copyright © 1989 by Amy Tan. Reprinted by permission of Penguin Putnam, Inc.

John Updike. "A & P" from *Pigeon Feathers and Other Stories*. Copyright © 1962 by John Updike. Reprinted by permission of Alfred A. Knopf, a division of Random House, Inc.

Helena María Viramontes. "Miss Clairol" from *Chicana Creativity and Criticism: Charting New Frontiers in American Literature*, Second Edition, ed. Maria Herrera-Sobek and Helena María Viramontes. Copyright © 1988 by Helena María Viramontes and Maria Herrera-Sobek. Copyright © 1996 by University of New Mexico Press. Reprinted by permission of the publisher.

Alice Walker. "Everyday Use" from *In Love and Trouble: Stories of Black Women*. Copyright © 1973 by Alice Walker. Reprinted by permission of Harcourt, Inc.

John Edgar Wideman. "newborn thrown in trash and dies" from *All Stories Are True*. Copyright © 1992 by John Edgar Wideman. Reprinted by permission of Pantheon Books, a division of Random House, Inc.

Tobias Wolff. "Say Yes" from *Back in the World*. Copyright © 1981 by Tobias Wolff. Reprinted by permission of International Creative Management, Inc.

Richard Wright. "The Man Who Was Almost a Man" from *Eight Men*. Copyright 1940, © 1961 by Richard Wright, renewed © 1989 by Ellen Wright. Originally published in *Harper's Bazaar* (1939), titled "Almos' a Man." Reprinted by permission of HarperCollins Publishers, Inc.

FICTION COMMENTARIES

Sherwood Anderson. "Form, Not Plot, in the Short Story" from *A Story Teller's Life* (New York: B. W. Huebsch, 1924). Copyright 1924 by B. W. Huebsch, renewed 1952 by Eleanor Copenhaver Anderson. Reprinted by permission of Harold Ober Associates, Inc.

James Baldwin. Excerpt from *Notes of a Native Son*. Copyright © 1955, renewed 1983 by James Baldwin. Reprinted by permission of Beacon Press, Boston.

Rosalie Murphy Baum. "The Shape of Hurston's Fiction" from *Zora in Florida,* ed. Steve Glassman and Kathryn L. Seidel. Copyright © 1991 by Rosalie Murphy Baum. Reprinted by permission of the University Press of Florida.
Wayne C. Booth. "A Rhetorical Reading of O'Connor's 'Everything That Rises Must Converge'" from *A Rhetoric of Irony*. Copyright © 1974 by The University of Chicago Press. Reprinted by permission of the author and the University of Chicago Press.
Robert H. Brinkmeyer Jr. "Flannery O'Connor and Her Readers" from *The Art and Vision of Flannery O'Connor*. Copyright © 1989 by Louisiana State University Press. Reprinted by permission of Louisiana State University Press.
John Cheever. "Why I Write Short Stories" from the October 30, 1978, issue of *Newsweek*. Copyright © 1978 by John Cheever. Reprinted by permission of The Wylie Agency, Inc.
Kate Chopin. "How I Stumbled upon Maupassant" from *The Complete Works of Kate Chopin,* ed. Per Seyersted. Copyright © 1969 by Louisiana State University Press. Reprinted by permission of Louisiana State University Press.
Ralph Ellison. "The Influence of Folklore on 'Battle Royal'" from *Shadow and Act*. Copyright © 1953, 1964 and renewed 1981, 1992 by Ralph Ellison. Reprinted by permission of Random House, Inc.
William Faulkner. "The Meaning of 'A Rose for Emily'" from *Faulkner in the University,* ed. Frederick Gwynn and Joseph Blotner (Charlottesville: Virginia, 1959). Reprinted by permission of University Press of Virginia.
Sally Fitzgerald. "Southern Sources of 'A Good Man Is Hard to Find'" excerpted from "Happy Endings" in the Summer 1997 issue of *Image*. Reprinted by permission of Image.
Sandra M. Gilbert and Susan Gubar. "A Feminist Reading of 'The Yellow Wallpaper'" from *Madwoman in the Attic*. Copyright © 1979 by Yale University. Reprinted by permission of Yale University Press.
Janice H. Harris. "Levels of Meaning in Lawrence's 'The Rocking-Horse Winner'" from *The Short Fiction of D. H. Lawrence*. Copyright © 1984 by Rutgers, the State University. Reprinted by permission of Rutgers University Press.
Robert E. Hemenway. "On 'Story in Harlem Slang'" from *Zora Neale Hurston: A Literary Biography*. Copyright © 1977 by the Board of Trustees of the University of Illinois. Reprinted by permission of University of Illinois Press.
Langston Hughes. "Democracy, Negroes, and Writers" excerpted from a speech to the League of American Writers for the Fourth American Writers' Congress, June 6–8, 1941, from The Langston Hughes Papers, James Weldon Johnson Collection, Beinecke Rare Book and Manuscript Library, Yale University Library. Published in *Good Morning Revolution: Uncollected Writing of Social Protest,* ed. Faith Berry (Citadel Press, 1973). Reprinted by permission of Harold Ober Associates, Inc.
Shirley Jackson. "The Morning of June 28, 1948, and 'The Lottery'" (editors' title; originally titled "Biography of a Story") from *Come Along with Me,* ed. Stanley Edgar Hyman. Copyright 1948, 1952, © 1960 by Shirley Jackson. Reprinted by permission of Viking Penguin, a division of Penguin Putnam, Inc.
Tom Jenks. "The Origin of 'Cathedral'" from *Remembering Ray: A Composite Biography of Raymond Carver,* ed. William L. Stull and Maureen P. Carroll. Copyright © 1993 by William L. Stull and Maureen P. Carroll. Reprinted by permission of Capra Press, Santa Barbara, CA.
Bobbie Ann Mason. "On Tim O'Brien's 'The Things They Carried'" from the August 1986 issue of *Esquire*. Reprinted by permission of International Creative Management, Inc.
Dorothy Tuck McFarland. "On 'Good Country People'" from *Flannery O'Connor*. Copyright © 1976 by Frederick Unger. Reprinted by permission of The Continuum Publishing Group.
J. Hillis Miller. "Who Is He? Melville's 'Bartleby, the Scrivener'" from *Versions of Pygmalion*. Copyright © 1990 by the President and Fellows of Harvard College. Reprinted by permission of Harvard University Press.
Vladimir Nabokov. "A Reading of Chekhov's 'The Lady with the Little Dog'" from *Lectures on Literature*. Copyright © 1981 by The Estate of Vladimir Nabokov. Reprinted by permission of Harcourt, Inc.
Jim Naughton. "As Raymond Carver Muses, His Stature Grows" from the November 23, 1982, issue of the *Post-Standard* (Syracuse, NY). Reprinted by permission of the author.
Flannery O'Connor. "From Letters, 1954–55" excerpted from *The Habit of Being,* sel. and ed. Sally Fitzgerald. Copyright © 1979 by Regina O'Connor. "Writing Short Stories" and "The Element of Surprise in 'A Good Man Is Hard to Find'" (excerpted from "On Her Own Work") from *Mystery and Manners: Occasional Prose,* sel. and ed. Sally Fitzgerald and Robert Fitzgerald. Copyright © 1969 by The Estate of Mary Flannery O'Connor. All reprinted by permission of Farrar, Straus & Giroux, Inc.
A. O. Scott. "Looking for Raymond Carver" from the August 12, 1999, issue of *The New York*

Review. Copyright © 1999 NYREV, Inc. Reprinted by permission of The New York Review of Books.

Kathleen Westfall Shute. "On 'The Bath' and 'A Small, Good Thing'" from "Finding the Words: The Struggle for Salvation in the Fiction of Raymond Carver," *Hollins Critic* 24.5 (1987). Reprinted by permission of the publisher.

Leslie Marmon Silko. "Language and Literature from a Pueblo Indian Perspective" from *English Literature: Opening Up the Canon,* ed. Leslie A. Fiedler and Houston A. Baker Jr. Copyright © 1979 by Leslie Marmon Silko. Reprinted by permission of Johns Hopkins University Press.

Harry Stone. "'Araby' and the Writings of James Joyce" from the Fall 1965 issue of *Antioch Review*. Copyright © 1965. Reprinted by permission of Antioch Review.

Amy Tan. "In the Canon, For All the Wrong Reasons" from the Fall 1996 issue of *The Threepenny Review*. Copyright © 1996. Reprinted by permission of the Sandra Dijkstra Agency.

Cheryl B. Torsney. "'Everyday Use': My Sojourn at Parchman Farm" from *The Intimate Critique: Autobiographical Literary Criticism,* ed. Diane P. Freedman, Olivia Frey, and Frances Murphy Zauhar. Copyright © 1993. Reprinted by permission of Duke University Press.

John Updike. "Kafka and the Metamorphosis" from *Odd Jobs*. Copyright © 1991 by John Updike. Reprinted by permission of Alfred A. Knopf, a division of Random House, Inc.

Alice Walker. "Zora Neale Hurston: A Cautionary Tale and a Partisan View," Foreword from *Zora Neale Hurston: A Literary Biography* by Robert E. Hemenway. Copyright © 1977 by the Board of Trustees of the University of Illinois. Reprinted by permission of the University of Illinois Press.

Eudora Welty. "Plot and Character in Chekhov's 'The Darling'" (editors' title; originally titled "Reality in Chekhov's Stories") from *The Eye of the Story: Selected Essays and Reviews*. Copyright © 1978 by Eudora Welty. Reprinted by permission of Random House, Inc.

POETRY

Diane Ackerman. "Sweep Me through Your Many-Chambered Heart" from *Jaguar of Sweet Laughter*. Copyright © 1991 by Diane Ackerman. Reprinted by permission of Random House, Inc.

Rolf Aggestam. "Lightning Bolt," trans. Samuel Charters from *Att Fla En Blixt (To Skin a Bolt of Lightning),* published by Wahlstrom and Wistrand (Sweden). Reprinted by permission of the author.

Anna Akhmatova. "Instead of a Preface" from *Selected Poems,* trans. Richard McKane. Copyright © 1967 by Richard McKane. Reprinted by permission of Bloodaxe Books Ltd.

Margaret Atwood. "Siren Song" from *You Are Happy, Selected Poems 1965–1975*. Copyright © 1976 by Margaret Atwood. Reprinted by permission of Houghton Mifflin Co. and Oxford University Press, Canada. All rights reserved.

W. H. Auden. "On the Circuit" and "Musée des Beaux Arts" from *Collected Poems*. Copyright © 1976 by Edward Mendelson, William Meredith, and Monroe K. Spears, Executors of the Estate of W. H. Auden. Reprinted by permission of Random House, Inc.

Amiri Baraka. "For Hettie" from *Preface to a Twenty Volume Suicide Note*. Copyright by Amiri Baraka. Reprinted by permission of Sterling Lord Literistic, Inc.

Bashō. "Day by day," "Having no talent," and "Ripening barley —" from *The Essential Haiku: Versions of Bashō, Buson, and Issa,* ed. with an introduction by Robert Hass. Introduction and Selection copyright © 1994 by Robert Hass. Unless otherwise noted, all translations copyright © 1994 by Robert Hass. Reprinted by permission of HarperCollins Publishers, Inc.

Michael Benedikt. "The Meat Epitaph" from *Night Cries*. Copyright © 1975. (Wesleyan University Press). Reprinted by permission of the University Press of New England.

John Berryman. "A Professor's Song" from *John Berryman: Collected Poems, 1937–1971,* ed. Charles Thornbury. Copyright © 1989 by Kate Donahue Berryman. Reprinted by permission of Farrar, Straus & Giroux, Inc.

Elizabeth Bishop. "One Art," "The Bight," "Sestina," "The Armadillo," and "The Fish" from *The Complete Poems, 1927–1979*. Copyright © 1979, 1983 by Alice Helen Methfessel. Reprinted by permission of Farrar, Straus & Giroux, Inc.

Robert Bly. "August Rain" from *Selected Poems*. Copyright © 1986 by Robert Bly. Reprinted by permission of HarperCollins Publishers.

Gwendolyn Brooks. "We Real Cool" and "The Mother" from *Blacks* (Chicago: Third World, 1987). Copyright © 1987 by Gwendolyn Brooks Blakely. Reprinted by permission of the author.

Lorna Dee Cervantes. "For Virginia Chavez," "Poem for the Young White Man Who Asked Me How I, an Intelligent, Well-Read Person Could Believe in the War between Races," and "Barco de Refugiados" are from *Emplumada,* © 1981. Reprinted by permission of the University of Pittsburgh Press. "Refugee Ship" from *A Decade of Hispanic Literature: An Anniversary Anthology,* ed. Nicolás Kanellos (Houston: Arte Publico–University of Houston, 1982). Reprinted by permission of the publisher.

Marilyn Chin. "How I Got That Name" and "Sad Guitar" from *The Phoenix Gone, The Terrace Empty*. Copyright © 1994 by Marilyn Chin. Reprinted by permission of Milkweed Editions, www.milkweed.org.

A. Cinna. "Did Ophelia ask Hamlet to bed?" from *The Penguin Book of Limericks,* ed. E. O. Parrott (New York: Viking Penguin, 1983). Reprinted by permission.

Amy Clampitt. "Fog" and "The Dakota" from *The Kingfisher*. Copyright © 1983 by Amy Clampitt. Reprinted by permission of Alfred A. Knopf, a division of Random House, Inc.

Wendy Cope. "Two Cures for Love" from *Serious Concerns*. Copyright © 1992. Reprinted by permission of Faber & Faber Ltd. "The fine English poet, John Donne" from *The Penguin Book of Limericks,* ed. E. O. Parrott (New York: Viking Penguin, 1983). Reprinted by permission of the author.

Countee Cullen. "Yet Do I Marvel" from *Color*. Copyright 1925 by Harper & Brothers, renewed 1953 by Ida M. Cullen. Reprinted by permission of Thompson & Thompson, New York.

E. E. Cummings. "when god lets my body be"; "since feeling is first"; "somewhere i have never travelled,gladly beyond"; "Buffalo Bill 's"; "goodby Betty, don't remember me"; and "in Just-" from *Complete Poems: 1904–1962,* ed. George J. Firmage. Copyright 1923, 1925, 1926, 1931, 1935, 1938, 1939, 1940, 1944, 1945, 1946, 1947, 1948, 1949, 1950, 1951, 1952, 1953, 1954, © 1955, 1956, 1957, 1958, 1959, 1960, 1961, 1962, 1963, 1966, 1967, 1968, 1972, 1973, 1974, 1975, 1976, 1977, 1978, 1979, 1980, 1981, 1982, 1983, 1984, 1985, 1986, 1987, 1988, 1989, 1990, 1991 by the Trustees for the E. E. Cummings Trust. Copyright © 1973, 1976, 1978, 1979, 1981, 1983, 1985, 1991 by George James Firmage. Reprinted by permission of Liveright Publishing Corporation.

H.D. [Hilda Doolittle]. "May 1943" (Part IV), "Mid-day," "Oread," and "Orchard" from *Collected Poems, 1912–1944*. Copyright © 1982 by The Estate of Hilda Doolittle. Reprinted by permission of New Directions Publishing Corporation.

Emily Dickinson. #156 / "You love me — you are sure —"; #199/ "I'm 'wife' — I've finished that —"; #214 / "I taste a liquor never brewed —"; #224 / "I've nothing else — to bring, You know —"; #249 / "Wild Nights — Wild Nights!"; #254 / "'Hope' is the thing with feathers"; #258 / "There's a certain Slant of light,"; #288 / "I'm Nobody! Who are you?"; #341 / "After great pain, a formal feeling comes —"; #435 / "Much Madness is divinest Sense"; #449 / "I died for Beauty — but was scarce"; #453 / "Love — thou art high —"; #465 / "I heard a Fly buzz — when I died —"; #511 / "If you were coming in the Fall"; #528 / "Mine — by the Right of the White Election!"; #712 / "Because I could not stop for Death —"; #827 / "The Only News I know"; #861 / "Split the Lark — and you'll find the Music —"; #875 / "I stepped from Plank to Plank"; #986 / "A narrow Fellow in the Grass"; and #1052 / "I never saw a Moor —" from *The Poems of Emily Dickinson,* ed. Thomas H. Johnson (Cambridge, MA: The Belknap Press of Harvard University Press). Copyright © 1951, 1955, 1979, 1983 by the President and Fellows of Harvard College.

Rita Dove. "Sonnet in Primary Colors" from *Mother Love*. Copyright © 1995 by Rita Dove. Reprinted by permission of the author and W. W. Norton & Company, Inc.

Helen Dunmore. "Wild Strawberries" from *Short Days, Long Nights*. Copyright © 1991. Reprinted by permission of Bloodaxe Books Ltd.

Richard Eberhart. "The Groundhog" from *Collected Poems, 1930–1986*. Copyright © 1960, 1976, 1987 by Richard Eberhart. Reprinted by permission of Oxford University Press, Inc.

Ed O.G. "Be a Father to Your Child." Copyright © 1988 by Pariken Music (BMI). Reprinted by permission of Pariken Music.

T. S. Eliot. "The Love Song of J. Alfred Prufrock" from *T. S. Eliot: The Complete Poems And Plays, 1909–1950*. Copyright 1917 by T. S. Eliot. Reprinted by permission of Faber & Faber Ltd.

Louise Erdrich. "Indian Boarding School: The Runaways" from *Jacklight*. Copyright © 1984 by Louise Erdrich. Reprinted by permission of Henry Holt and Company, LLC.

Lawrence Ferlinghetti. "Constantly Risking Absurdity," "In Goya's greatest scenes we seem to see," and "Dog" from *A Coney Island of the Mind*. Copyright © 1958 by Lawrence Ferlinghetti. Reprinted by permission of New Directions Publishing Corporation.

Carolyn Forché. "The Colonel" from *The Country Between Us*. Copyright © 1981 by Carolyn Forché. Originally appeared in Women's International Resource Exchange. Reprinted by permission of HarperCollins Publishers, Inc.

Robert Frost. "The Pasture," "Fire and Ice," "To Earthward," "Stopping by Woods on a Snowy Evening," and "For travelers going sidereal" from *The Poetry of Robert Frost,* ed. Edward Connery Lathem. Copyright 1923, 1939, © 1967, 1969 by Henry Holt and Company. Copyright 1951 by Robert Frost. All reprinted by permission of Henry Holt and Company, LLC.

Allen Ginsberg. "Mugging," copyright © 1974 by Allen Ginsberg; "A Supermarket in California," copyright © 1955 by Allen Ginsberg; *Howl* (Part I), copyright © 1955 by Allen Ginsberg; and "America," copyright © 1956, 1959 by Allen Ginsberg, copyright renewed, from *Collected Poems, 1947–1980.* Reprinted by permission of HarperCollins Publishers, Inc.

Louise Glück. "Windows," "Terminal Resemblance," and "First Memory" from *Ararat* (Ecco Press). Copyright © 1990 by Louise Glück. Reprinted by permission of HarperCollins Publishers, Inc.

Richard Leighton Green. "(Apropos Coleridge's 'Kubla Khan') When approached by a person from Porlock" from *The Penguin Book of Limericks,* ed. E. O. Parrott (New York: Viking Penguin, 1984).

Linda Gregg. "Not Understanding Emily Dickinson" from *Nineteen New American Poets of the Golden Gate,* ed. Philip Dow (New York: Harcourt Brace, 1984). Copyright © 1984 by Linda Gregg. Reprinted by permission of the author.

Robert Hass. "A Story about the Body" from *Human Wishes.* Copyright © 1989 by Robert Hass. First published by the Ecco Press in 1989. Reprinted by permission of HarperCollins Publishers, Inc.

Robert Hayden. "Those Winter Sundays," copyright © 1966 by Robert Hayden; "A Letter from Phillis Wheatley," ed. by Frederick Glaysher, copyright © 1966 by Robert Hayden; and "Frederick Douglass," ed. by Frederick Glaysher, copyright © 1978 by Robert Hayden, from *Collected Poems of Robert Hayden,* ed. Frederick Glaysher. Reprinted by permission of Liveright Publishing Corporation.

Seamus Heaney. "Digging" from *Selected Poems 1966–1987.* Copyright © 1990 by Seamus Heaney. Reprinted by permission of Farrar, Straus & Giroux, Inc., and Faber & Faber Ltd. "The Gutteral Muse" from *Field Work.* Copyright © 1981 by Seamus Heaney. Reprinted by permission of Farrar, Straus and Giroux, LLC, and Faber & Faber Ltd.

Zbigniew Herbert. "On Translating Poetry" from *Zbigniew Herbert: Selected Poems,* trans. John and Bogdana Carpenter. Copyright © 1997 by John Carpenter. Reprinted by permission of Oxford University Press.

Tobey Hiller. "The Poem (or Alice's Remarks on Reading the Fine Print on the Bottle's Label)" from *Certain Weathers* (Berkeley, CA: Oyez, 1987). Copyright © 1987 by Tobey Hiller. Excerpt from "the closing of the south park road" by Tobey Hiller. Both poems are reprinted by permission of the author.

Langston Hughes. "Mother to Son," "Bound No'th Blues," "Song for a Dark Girl," "House in the World," "Florida Road Workers," "I, Too," "The Negro Speaks of Rivers," "Down Where I Am," "Personal," "Little Lyric (*Of Great Importance*)," "Merry-Go-Round," "Dream Deferred," and "Theme for English B" from *Collected Poems.* Copyright © 1994 by the Estate of Langston Hughes. Reprinted by permission of Alfred A. Knopf, a division of Random House, Inc.

Ted Hughes. "Pike" from *Lupercal.* Copyright © 1960 by Ted Hughes. "Wind" from *New Selected Poems.* Copyright © 1995 by Ted Hughes. "Fulbright Scholars" from *Birthday Letters.* Copyright © 1998 by Ted Hughes. Reprinted by permission of Faber & Faber Ltd. and HarperCollins Publishers, Inc.

Randall Jarrell. "The Death of the Ball Turret Gunner" and "Next Day" from *The Complete Poems.* Copyright © 1969, renewed 1997 by Mary von S. Jarrell. Reprinted by permission of Farrar, Straus & Giroux, Inc.

Louis Jenkins. "How to Tell a Wolf from a Dog" from *Nice Fish: New and Selected Prose Poems.* Copyright © 1995 by Louis Jenkins. Reprinted by permission of the author and Holy Cow! Press.

Elizabeth Jennings. "My Grandmother" from *Collected Poems of Elizabeth Jennings* (Carcanet Press). Reprinted by permission of David Higham Associates.

Jackie Kay. "Brendon Gallacher" from *Two's Company.* Copyright © 1992. Reprinted by permission of Penguin Books U.K.

X. J. Kennedy. "Andrew Marvell's 'To His Coy Mistress'" from *Touchstones: American Poets on a Favorite Poem,* ed. Robert Pack and Jay Parini (Hanover, NH: Middlebury College P, 1996). Copyright © 1996 by the President and Fellows of Middlebury College. Reprinted by permission of the University Press of New England.

Jane Kenyon. "Winter Lambs," "Otherwise," and "Catching Frogs" from *Otherwise: New & Selected Poems.* Copyright © 1996 by the Estate of Jane Kenyon. Reprinted with the permission of Graywolf Press, Saint Paul, MN.

Jack Kerouac. "The nightingale is singing," "Birds singing," "The summer chair," and "In my medicine cabinet" from *Scattered Poems,* comp. Ann Charters (San Francisco: City Lights

Books, 1971). Copyright © 1971 by the Estate of Jack Kerouac. Reprinted by permission of Sterling Lord Literistic, Inc.

Hugh Kingsmill. "What, Still Alive at Twenty-Two?" from *The Best of Hugh Kingsmill.* Copyright © 1970 by Brook Kingsmill-Lunn. Reprinted by permission of The Rev. Brook Kingsmill-Lunn.

Galway Kinnell. "Oatmeal" from *When One Has Lived a Long Time Alone.* Copyright © 1990 by Galway Kinnell. Reprinted by permission of Alfred A. Knopf, a division of Random House, Inc. "The Man Splitting Wood in the Daybreak" from *Three Books.* Copyright © 1993 by Galway Kinnell. Previously published in *The Past* (1985). Reprinted by permission of Houghton Mifflin Company. All rights reserved.

Yusef Komunyakaa. "Facing It" from *Dien Cai Dau* (Middletown, CT: Wesleyan University Press, 1988). Copyright © 1988 by Yusef Komunyakaa. Reprinted by permission of the University Press of New England.

D. H. Lawrence. "Mountain Lion" from *The Complete Poems of D. H. Lawrence,* edited by V. de Sola Pinto & F. W. Roberts. Copyright © 1964, 1971 by Angelo Ravagli and C. M. Weekley, Executors of the Estate of Frieda Lawrence Ravagli. Reprinted by permission of Viking Penguin, a division of Penguin Putnam, Inc.

Irving Layton. "Don't Blame the Apple" from *The Tightrope Dancer.* Reprinted by permission of the author.

Annie Lennox. "Why?" Copyright © 1992 BMG Music Publishing Ltd. (PRS) and La Lennoxa (PRS). All rights for the U.S. administered by BMG Songs, Inc. (ASCAP). All rights reserved. Used by permission.

Denise Levertov. "Grey Sparrow Addresses the Mind's Ear" from *Poems 1960–1967.* Copyright © 1966 by Denise Levertov. "July 1968" and "The Day the Audience Walked Out on Me, and Why" from *Poems 1968–1972.* Copyright © 1970 by Denise Levertov. All reprinted by permission of New Directions Publishing Corporation.

Philip Levine. "Starlight" from *Ashes.* Copyright © 1971, 1979 by Philip Levine. "The Fox" from *One for the Rose.* Copyright © 1982 by Philip Levine. (Atheneum) Reprinted by permission of Simon & Schuster, Inc.

Audre Lorde. "Hanging Fire" from *The Black Unicorn.* Copyright © 1978 by Audre Lorde. "Now That I Am Forever with Child" from *Collected Poems.* Copyright © 1997 by the Estate of Audre Lorde. Reprinted by permission of W. W. Norton & Co. "Teacher" from *A Land Where Other People Lived.* Copyright © 1973. Reprinted by permission of Broadside Press.

Robert Lowell. "Skunk Hour" from *Life Studies.* Copyright © 1959 by Robert Lowell, renewed © 1987 by Harriet W. Lowell, Sheridan Lowell, and Caroline Lowell. Reprinted with the permission of Farrar, Straus & Giroux, Inc. "For the Union Dead" from *For the Union Dead.* Copyright © 1959 by Robert Lowell, renewed © 1987 by Harriet W. Lowell, Sheridan Lowell, and Caroline Lowell. Reprinted with the permission of Farrar, Straus & Giroux, Inc. "Epilogue" from *Day by Day.* Copyright © 1977 by Robert Lowell. Reprinted with the permission of Farrar, Straus & Giroux, Inc.

Archibald MacLeish. "Ars Poetica" from *Collected Poems, 1917–1982.* Copyright © 1985 by The Estate of Archibald MacLeish. Reprinted by permission of Houghton Mifflin Company. All rights reserved.

W. S. Merwin. "Birds Waking" from *The First Four Books of Poems: A Mask for Janus, The Dancing Bears, Green with Beasts, The Drunk in the Furnace.* Copyright © 1975. (Atheneum) Reprinted by permission of Simon & Schuster, Inc.

Edna St.Vincent Millay. Sonnets I, II, III, IV, IX, and XI of *Sonnets from an Ungrafted Tree;* "Childhood Is the Kingdom Where Nobody Dies"; and "The courage that my mother had" from *Collected Poems* (HarperCollins). Copyright © 1923, 1934, 1951, 1954, 1962, 1982 by Edna St. Vincent Millay and Norma Millay Ellis. All rights reserved. Reprinted by permission of Elizabeth Barnett, Literary Executor.

Janice Mirikitani. "Recipe" from *Shedding Silence.* Copyright © 1987 by Janice Mirikitani. Reprinted by permission of Celestial Arts, P.O. Box 7123, Berkeley, CA 94707.

Adrian Mitchell. "Celia Celia" from *Hearts on the Left: Poems 1953–1984.* Copyright © 1997. Reprinted by permission of Peters Fraser & Dunlop.

Marianne Moore. "Critics and Connoisseurs," "The Fish," and "I May, I Might, I Must" from *The Complete Poems of Marianne Moore.* Copyright 1935, 1941, 1944 by Marianne Moore, renewed © 1963 by Marianne Moore and T. S. Eliot, 1969, 1972 by Marianne Moore. Reprinted by permission of Simon & Schuster, Inc.

Pat Mora. "Elena" from *Chants* (Houston: Arte Publico–University of Houston, 1984). Reprinted with permission from the publisher.

Andrew Motion. "Anne Frank Huis" from *The Pleasure Steamers.* Copyright © 1974. Reprinted by permission of Carcanet Press Ltd.

Ogden Nash. "Reflections on Ice Breaking" from *Verses from 1929 On*. Copyright © 1930 by Ogden Nash. First appeared in *The New Yorker*. Reprinted by permission of Little, Brown and Company.

Frank O'Hara. "The Day Lady Died" from *Lunch Poems*. Copyright © 1964 by Frank O'Hara. Reprinted by permission of City Light Books.

Sharon Olds. "At the Bay" from *Blood, Tin, Straw*. Copyright © 1999 by Sharon Olds. "The Race" from *The Father*. Copyright © 1992 by Sharon Olds. "Sex without Love," "The Death of Marilyn Monroe," "The One Girl at the Boys' Party," and "The Elder Sister" from *The Dead and the Living*. Copyright © 1983 by Sharon Olds. "The Planned Child" from *The Wellspring*. Copyright © 1996 by Sharon Olds. "Summer Solstice, New York City" from *The Gold Cell*. Copyright © 1987 by Sharon Olds. All reprinted by permission of Alfred A. Knopf, a division of Random House, Inc.

Mary Oliver. "Picking Blueberries, Austerlitz, New York, 1957" from *New and Selected Poems*. Copyright © 1992 by Mary Oliver. Reprinted by permission of Beacon Press, Boston.

Wilfred Owen. "Dulce et Decorum Est" from *The Collected Poems of Wilfred Owen*. Copyright © 1963 by Chatto & Windus, Ltd. Reprinted by permission of New Directions Publishing Corporation.

Dorothy Parker. "Indian Summer" from *The Portable Dorothy Parker*. Copyright 1926, renewed © 1954 by Dorothy Parker. Reprinted by permission of Viking Penguin, a division of Penguin Putnam, Inc.

Linda Pastan. "To a Daughter Leaving Home" from *The Imperfect Paradise*. Copyright © 1988 by Linda Pastan. Reprinted by permission of W. W. Norton & Company, Inc.

Marge Piercy. "In which she begs (like everybody else) that love may last" from *Stone, Paper, Knife*. Copyright © 1983 by Marge Piercy. "The woman in the ordinary" from *Circles on the Water*. Copyright © 1982 by Marge Piercy. "It ain't heavy, it's my purse" from *Mars and Her Children*. Copyright © 1992 by Middlemarsh, Inc. All are reprinted by permission of Alfred A. Knopf, a division of Random House, Inc.

Sylvia Plath. "Mirror" from *Crossing the Water*. Copyright © 1960, 1963 by Ted Hughes. "Morning Song," "Daddy," and "Lady Lazarus" from *Ariel*. Copyright © 1961, 1963, 1966 by Ted Hughes. All reprinted by permission of HarperCollins Publishers and Faber & Faber Ltd.

Ezra Pound. "A Pact" from *Personae*. Copyright 1926 by Ezra Pound. Reprinted by permission of New Directions Publishing Corporation.

Dudley Randall. "Ballad of Birmingham" from *Cities Burning*, ed. Doughtry Long (Broadside Press). Reprinted by permission of the author.

John Crowe Ransom. "Bells for John Whiteside's Daughter" from *Selected Poems*. Copyright 1924 by Alfred A. Knopf, Inc., and renewed 1952 by John Crowe Ransom. Reprinted by permission of Alfred A. Knopf, Inc., a division of Random House, Inc.

Irina Ratushinskaya. "I Will Live and Survive" from *No, I'm Not Afraid*, trans. David McDuff. Copyright © 1986. Reprinted by permission of Bloodaxe Books Ltd.

Adrienne Rich. "Diving into the Wreck" from *Diving into the Wreck: Poems 1971–1972*. Copyright © 1973 by W. W. Norton & Company, Inc. Reprinted by permission of W. W. Norton & Company, Inc.

Theodore Roethke. "My Papa's Waltz," copyright 1942 by Hearst Magazines, Inc. "Elegy for Jane" copyright 1950 by Theodore Roethke. "I Knew a Woman," copyright 1954 by Theodore Roethke. "The Waking," copyright 1953 by Theodore Roethke. All from *Collected Poems of Theodore Roethke*. Reprinted by permission of Doubleday, a division of Random House, Inc.

Tadeusz Rozewicz. "Pigtail" from *They Came to See a Poet*, trans. Adam Czerniawski. Copyright © 1976 by Princeton University Press. Reprinted by permission of Princeton University Press.

Mary Jo Salter. "Welcome to Hiroshima" from *Henry Purcell in Japan*. Copyright © 1984 by Mary Jo Salter. Reprinted by permission of Alfred A. Knopf, a division of Random House, Inc.

Anne Sexton. "Little Girl, My String Bean, My Lovely Woman" from *Live or Die*. Copyright © 1966 by Anne Sexton. "The Starry Night" from *All My Pretty Ones*. Copyright © 1962 by Anne Sexton, renewed 1990 by Linda Sexton. Reprinted by permission of Houghton Mifflin Company.

Stevie Smith. "Not Waving but Drowning" from *The Collected Poems of Stevie Smith*. Copyright © 1972 by Stevie Smith. Reprinted by permission of New Directions Publishing Corporation.

Gary Snyder "Ripples on the Surface" and "Milton by Firelight" from *No Nature*. Copyright © 1992 by Gary Snyder. Reprinted by permission of North Point Press, a division of Farrar, Straus & Giroux, Inc. "Four Poems for Robin" from *The Back Country*. Copyright © 1968 by Gary Snyder. Reprinted by permission of New Directions Publishing Corporation.

Cathy Song. "The White Porch" from *Picture Bride*. Copyright © 1983. Reprinted by permission of Yale University Press. "Heaven" from *Frameless Windows, Squares of Light*. Copyright © 1988 by Cathy Song. Reprinted by permission of W. W. Norton & Company, Inc.

Gary Soto."Mexicans Begin Jogging" from *New and Selected Poems*. Copyright © 1995. Published by Chronicle Books, San Francisco. Reprinted by permission.

Wole Soyinka. "Telephone Conversation" from *Ibadan* 10 (November 1960): 34.

Wallace Stevens. "The Emperor of Ice-Cream" and "Thirteen Ways of Looking at a Blackbird" from *Collected Poems*. Copyright 1923 and renewed 1951 by Wallace Stevens. Reprinted by permission of Alfred A. Knopf, a division of Random House, Inc.

Anne Stevenson. "The Fish Are All Sick" from *Collected Poems, 1955–1995*. Copyright © by Anne Stevenson. Reprinted by permission of the author.

Wislawa Szymborska. "Bodybuilders' Contest" and "True Love" from *View with a Grain of Sand*. Copyright © 1993 by Wislawa Szymborska. English translation by Stanislaw Baránczak and Clare Cavanagh. Copyright © 1995 by Harcourt, Inc. Reprinted by permission of the publisher.

Genevieve Taggard. "With Child" from *Collected Poems, 1918–1938*. Copyright 1938 by Harper & Row Publishers, Inc. renewed © 1966. Reprinted by permission of Marcia T. Liles.

Dylan Thomas. "The Last Time I Slept with the Queen" from *The Silver Treasury of Light Verse*. Reprinted by permission of Harold Ober Associates, Inc. Copyright © 1956 by New American Library. "Do Not Go Gentle into That Good Night" from *The Poems of Dylan Thomas*. Copyright © 1952 by Dylan Thomas. Reprinted by permission of New Directions Publishing Corporation and David Higham Associates.

Tomas Tranströmer. "Allegro," trans. Samuel Charters. Reprinted by permission of the author.

Anne Waldman. "To the Censorious Ones" from *Kill or Cure*. Copyright © 1994 by Anne Waldman. Reprinted by permission of Viking Penguin, a division of Penguin Putnam, Inc.

Alice Walker. "I Said to Poetry" from *Horses Make a Landscape Look More Beautiful*. Copyright © 1984 by Alice Walker. Reprinted by permission of Harcourt, Inc.

Big Joe Williams. "Levee Break Blues" is reprinted by permission of Stainless Music Corporation.

Miller Williams. "Thinking about Bill, Dead of AIDS" from *Living on the Surface: New and Selected Poems*. Copyright © 1989 by Miller Williams. Reprinted by permission of Louisiana State University Press.

William Carlos Williams. "Danse Russe," "The Widow's Lament in Springtime," "The Red Wheelbarrow," "Spring and All" (section I), and "Night" from *Collected Poems: 1909–1939*, Volume I. Copyright © 1938 by New Directions Publishing Corporation. Reprinted by permission of New Directions Publishing Corporation.

Richard Wright. "I would like a bell," "An empty sickbed," "A freezing morning," and "A soft wind at dawn" from *The Richard Wright Reader*, ed. Ellen Wright and Michel Fabre. Copyright © 1978 by Richard Wright. Reprinted by permission of Arcade Publishing.

James Wright. "Lying in a Hammock at William Duffy's Farm in Pine Island, Minnesota," "To Flood Stage Again," "Milkweed," and "A Blessing" from *Collected Poems*. Copyright © 1971 by James Wright. Wesleyan University Press. Reprinted by permission of University Press of New England.

W. B. Yeats. "Leda and the Swan" copyright 1928 by Macmillan Publishing Company; copyright renewed © 1956 by Georgie Yeats. Reprinted with the permission of Simon & Schuster from *The Poems of W. B. Yeats: A New Edition*, ed. Richard J. Finneran.

POETRY COMMENTARIES

Harold Bloom. "On Frost at Midnight" from *The Visionary Company* by Harold Bloom. Copyright © 1961 by Harold Bloom. Reprinted by permission of the author.

Joseph Brodsky. "On Grief and Reason" excerpted from the September 26, 1994, issue of *The New Yorker*. Copyright © 1995 by Joseph Brodsky. Reprinted by permission of the Estate of Joseph Brodsky and Farrar, Straus & Giroux, Inc.

Cleanth Brooks Jr. and Robert Penn Warren. "On Eliot's 'The Love Song of J. Alfred Prufrock'" (editors' title) from *Understanding Poetry: An Anthology for College Students*. Copyright 1938. Reprinted by permission of Henry Holt and Company, LLC.

Ann Charters. "'Working the Room': Sharon Olds Reads Her Poetry at the Miami International Book Fair" (November 20, 1999). Reprinted by permission of the author.

Marilyn Chin. "On the Canon," copyright © 1995, from *June Jordan's Poetry for the People*, ed.

Lauren Mullen and the Blueprint Collective. Reprinted by permission of Taylor and Francis, Inc./Routledge, Inc., http://www.routledge-ny.com.

Robert Creeley. "On Whitman's Poetry" (editors' title) from *Whitman,* ed. Robert Creeley. Copyright © 1973 by Robert Creeley. Reprinted by permission of Viking Penguin, a division of Penguin Putnam, Inc.

Rita Dove. "An Intact World" from *Mother Love*. Originally in *Hungry Mind Review* 58. Copyright © 1995 by Rita Dove. Reprinted by permission of the author and W. W. Norton & Company.

T. S. Eliot. "William Blake" from *Selected Essays 1917–1932*. Copyright 1930 and renewed © 1958 by T. S. Eliot. Reprinted by permission of Harcourt, Inc., and Faber & Faber Ltd. "Tradition and Individual Talent" (excerpt) from *Selected Prose of T. S. Eliot,* ed. Frank Kermode (London: Faber & Faber, 1975). Originally published in *Egoist* (September and December 1919). Copyright 1919 and renewed 1947 by T. S. Eliot. Reprinted by permission of Faber & Faber Ltd.

Jessie Fauset. "Meeting Langston Hughes" (editors' title, originally an untitled review of *The Weary Blues*) from the March 1926 issue of *The Crisis*. Copyright 1926 by the National Urban League, Inc. Reprinted by permission of The Crisis Publishing Company.

Rose C. Feld. "An Interview with Robert Frost" from the October 21, 1923, issue of *The New York Times Book Review*. Copyright 1923 by The New York Times Company. Reprinted by permission.

Robert Frost. "The Figure a Poem Makes" from *Complete Poems of Robert Frost*. Copyright 1949 by Henry Holt and Company. Reprinted by permission of Henry Holt and Company, LLC.

Philip L. Gerber. "On 'After Apple-Picking'" (editors' title) from *Robert Frost*. Copyright © 1966 by Twayne Publishers, Inc. Copyright © 1982 by G. K. Hall, Inc. Reprinted by permission of Twayne Publishers, an imprint of Simon & Schuster, Inc.

Allen Ginsberg. "On His Poetic Craft" (interview) from *The Poet's Craft: Interviews from The New York Quarterly,* ed. William Packard (New York: Paragon House, 1987). Originally published in *The New York Quarterly,* issue 6. Reprinted by permission of The New York Quarterly.

Louise Glück. "Poems *Are* Autobiography" (editors' title) excerpted from *Proofs and Theories: Essays on Poetry*. Copyright © 1994 by Louise Glück. Reprinted by permission of HarperCollins Publishers, Inc.

Robert Hayden. "On Negro Poetry" excerpted from the Introduction to *Kaleidoscope: Poems by American Negro Poets,* ed. Robert Hayden. Copyright © 1967 by Harcourt Brace & Company, renewed 1995 by Maia Patillo. Reprinted by permission of Harcourt, Inc.

Anthony Hecht. "The Dover Bitch" from *Collected Earlier Poems*. Copyright © 1990 by Anthony Hecht. Reprinted by permission of Alfred A. Knopf, a division of Random House, Inc.

Jonathan Holden. "The Dichotomy between Men's and Women's Writing" from *A Profile of Twentieth-Century American Poetry,* ed. Jack Myers and David Wojahn. Copyright © 1991. Reprinted by permission of Southern Illinois University Press.

Richard Howard. "'Some Tribal Female Who Is Known but Forbidden': Anne Sexton" (editors' title) from *Alone with America* by Richard Howard (New York: Atheneum Publishers, 1980). Copyright © 1980 by Richard Howard. Reprinted by permission of the author.

David Huddle. "The 'Banked Fire' of Robert Hayden's 'Those Winter Sundays'" from *Touchstones: American Poets on a Favorite Poem,* ed. Robert Pack and Jay Parini. Copyright © 1992 by the President and Fellows of Middlebury College. Reprinted by permission of the University Press of New England.

Langston Hughes. "Langston Hughes as Folk Poet" from *Collected Poems*. Copyright © 1994 by the Estate of Langston Hughes. Reprinted by permission of Alfred A. Knopf, a division of Random House, Inc. "A Toast to Harlem" from *The Best of Simple*. Copyright © 1961 by Langston Hughes, renewed 1989 by George Houston Bass. Reprinted by permission of Hill & Wang, a division of Farrar, Straus & Giroux, Inc.

Thomas H. Johnson. "The Text of Emily Dickinson's Poetry" (editors' title) from the Introduction to *The Complete Poems of Emily Dickinson,* ed. Thomas H. Johnson. Copyright © 1960 by Thomas H. Johnson, renewed 1988 by Catherine R. Johnson. Reprinted by permission of Harvard University Press.

Erica Jong. "Devouring Time: Shakespeare's Sonnets" from *Touchstones: American Poets on a Favorite Poem,* ed. Robert Pack and Jay Parini. Copyright © 1996 by the President and Fellows of Middlebury College. Reprinted by permission of the University Press of New England.

X. J. Kennedy. "Andrew Marvell's 'To His Coy Mistress'" (editors' title) from *Touchstones: American Poets on a Favorite Poem,* ed. Robert Pack and Jay Parini. Copyright © 1996 by the President and Fellows of Middlebury College. Reprinted by permission of the University Press of New England.

Galway Kinnell. "The Deconstruction of Emily Dickinson" from *Imperfect Thirst* by Galway

Kinnell. Originally published in *The American Poetry Review*. Copyright © 1994 by Galway Kinnell. Reprinted by permission of the Houghton Mifflin Company. All rights reserved.

Philip Levine. Excerpt from *Keats in Detroit* by Philip Levine. Copyright © 1995 by The New York Times Company. Reprinted by permission.

Robert Lowell. "An Explanation of 'Skunk Hour'" (editors' title) from *The Contemporary Poet as Artist and Critic*, ed. Anthony Ostroff. Copyright © 1964 by Little, Brown and Company. Reprinted by permission of the publishers. "Foreword to Sylvia Plath's *Ariel*." Copyright © 1963 and renewed 1991 by Ted Hughes. Reprinted by permission of HarperCollins Publishers, Inc. "On Robert Frost" from *Notebook*, rev. and expanded ed. Copyright © 1967, 1968, 1969, 1970 by Robert Lowell, copyright renewed 1998 by Harriet Lowell. Reprinted by permission of Farrar, Straus and Giroux, LLC.

Christopher Merrill. "Wyatt's 'They Flee from Me'" (editors' title) from *Touchstones: American Poets on a Favorite Poem*, ed. Robert Pack and Jay Parini. Copyright © 1996 by the President and Fellows of Middlebury College. Reprinted by permission of the University Press of New England.

Brett C. Millier. "On Elizabeth Bishop's 'One Art'" Copyright © 1993 by Brett C. Millier. Reprinted by permission of the author. A fuller treatment of the subject appears in *Elizabeth Bishop: Life and the Memory of It* by Brett C. Millier. Lines from the first draft of "One Art" by Elizabeth Bishop [Elizabeth Bishop Papers, 60.2] are quoted by permission of the Special Collections of the Vassar College Libraries and Elizabeth Bishop's literary executor, Alice H. Methfessel.

Marianne Moore. "Some Answers to Questions Posed by Howard Nemerov" from *Poets on Poetry*, ed. Howard Nemerov. Copyright © 1966 by Basic Books, Inc., renewed 1994 by Margaret Nemerov. Reprinted by permission of Basic Books, Inc.

Sharon Olds. Excerpt from the *Salon* interview. *Salon*, interview by Dwight Garner. www.salon1999.com/weekly/interview.html. Reprinted by permission.

Alicia Ostriker. "The Poet as Heroine: H.D." from *Writing Like a Woman*. Copyright © 1983 by University of Michigan. Reprinted by permission of the University of Michigan Press.

Marge Piercy. "Imagery Can't Really Be Taught" (editors' title) quoted in *Fooling with Words* by Bill Morrow. Copyright © 1999. Reprinted by permission of William Morrow.

Plato. "On Banishing Poets from the State" (editors' title) from *The Republic*, trans. G. M. A. Grube. Copyright © 1974. Reprinted by permission of Hackett Publishing Company, Inc.

Robert Potts. "Rock 'n' Roll Is the New Poetry" from "Beat Surrender" by Robert Potts in *The Guardian* (U.K., Sunday Edition), October 6, 1999. Reprinted by permission.

Ezra Pound. "On the Principles of Imagism" (editors' title) excerpted from "A Retrospect" in *Literary Essays of Ezra Pound*, ed. T. S. Eliot. Copyright 1935 by Ezra Pound. "What I Feel about Walt Whitman" from *Selected Prose 1909–1965*, ed. William Cookson. Copyright © 1955 by Ezra Pound. Copyright © 1973 by The Estate of Ezra Pound. Reprinted by permission of New Directions Publishing Corporation.

Sherod Santos. "Shelley in Ruins: The Appeal of 'Ozymandias'" from *Touchstones: American Poets on a Favorite Poem*, ed. Robert Pack and Jay Parini. Copyright © 1996 by the President and Fellows of Middlebury College. Reprinted by permission of the University Press of New England.

Peter Schmitt. "Sad Heart at the Supermarket: Randall Jarrell's 'Next Day'" from *Touchstones: American Poets on a Favorite Poem*, ed. Robert Pack and Jay Parini. Copyright © 1996 by the President and Fellows of Middlebury College. Reprinted by permission of the University Press of New England.

Louis Simpson. "On Lowell's 'Skunk Hour'" (editors' title) from *A Revolution in Taste: Studies of W. H. Auden, Dylan Thomas, Allen Ginsberg, Sylvia Plath, and Robert Lowell*. Copyright © 1978 by Louis Simpson. Reprinted by permission of Simon & Schuster, Inc.

Dinitia Smith. "The Creative Mind; The Examined Life, without Punctuation." Copyright © 1999 by The New York Times Company. Reprinted by permission.

Gary Smith. "On Gwendolyn Brooks's *A Street in Bronzeville*" from *MELUS* 10.3 (Fall 1983). Copyright © 1983 by The Society for the Study of Multi-Ethnic Literature in the United States. Reprinted by permission of the author.

Eric Trethewey. "The Virtue of Arnold's 'Dover Beach'" from *Touchstones: American Poets on a Favorite Poem*, ed. Robert Pack and Jay Parini. Copyright © 1996 by the President and Fellows of Middlebury College. Reprinted by permission of the University Press of New England.

Helen Vendler. "On Louise Glück" (editors' title) from *The Music of What Happens: Poems, Poets, Critics* by Helen Vendler. Copyright © 1988 by the President and Fellows of Harvard College. Reprinted by permission of Harvard University Press.

Richard Wilbur. "On Emily Dickinson" (editors' title) excerpted from "Sumptuous Destitution" in *Emily Dickinson: Three Views* by Richard Wilbur, Louise Bogan, and Archibald

MacLeish (Amherst, MA: Amherst College P, 1960). This piece was later reprinted in *Responses* (New York: Harcourt Brace, 1976). Copyright © 1960 by Richard Wilbur. Reprinted by permission of the author.

William Carlos Williams. "Introduction to *Howl*" from the Introduction to *Howl* by Allen Ginsberg. Copyright © 1956. Reprinted by permission of HarperCollins Publishers, Inc.

Richard Wright. "A Review of *The Big Sea*" from *Langston Hughes: Critical Perspectives* (Gates & Appiah) and the October 18, 1940, issue of *The New Republic*. Copyright © 1940 by Richard Wright. Reprinted by permission of John Hawkins Associates, Inc.

DRAMA

Edward Albee. *The Sandbox* from *The Zoo Story, The Death of Bessie Smith, and The Sandbox: Three Plays* (New York: Coward McCann, 1960). Copyright © 1959 and renewed 1987 by Edward Albee. Reprinted by permission of William Morris Agency, Inc., on behalf of the author. CAUTION: Professionals and amateurs are hereby warned that *The Sandbox* is subject to a royalty. It is fully protected under the copyright laws of the United States of America and of all countries covered by the International Copyright Union (including the Dominion of Canada and the rest of the British Commonwealth), the Berne Convention, the Pan-American Copyright Convention and the Universal Copyright Convention as well as all countries with which the United States has reciprocal copyright relations. All rights, including professional/amateur state rights, motion picture, recitation, lecturing, public reading, radio broadcasting, television, video or sound recording, all other forms of mechanical or electronic reproduction, such as CD-ROM, CD-I, information storage and retrieval systems and photocopying, and the rights of translation into foreign languages, are strictly reserved. Particular emphasis is laid upon the matter of readings, permission for which must be secured from the author's agent in writing. Inquiries concerning rights should be addressed to: William Morris Agency, Inc., 1325 Avenue of the Americas, New York, NY 10019, Attn: Owen Laster.

Caryl Churchill. *Heart's Desire* from *Blue Heart* (London: Nick Hern Books). Copyright © 1997 by Caryl Churchill Limited. Reprinted by permission of Nick Hern Books.

Lorraine Hansberry. *A Raisin in the Sun*. Copyright © 1958 by Robert Nemiroff as an unpublished work. Copyright © 1959, 1966, 1984, by Robert Nemiroff. Reprinted by permission of Random House, Inc.

Henrik Ibsen. *A Doll House* from *The Complete Major Prose Plays of Henrik Ibsen*, trans. Rolf Fjelde. Copyright © 1965, 1970, 1978 by Rolf Fjelde. Reprinted by permission of Dutton Signet, a division of Penguin Putnam, Inc.

Philip Kan Gotanda. *The Wash*. Copyright © 1991 by Philip Kan Gotanda. CAUTION: The play *The Wash* included in this volume is reprinted by permission of the author and Dramatists Play Service, Inc. The stage performance rights in this Play are controlled exclusively by Dramatists Play Service, Inc., 440 Park Avenue South, New York, NY 10016. No professional or nonprofessional performance of the Play may be given without obtaining, in advance, the written permission of Dramatists Play Service, Inc., and paying the requisite fee. Inquiries concerning all other rights should be addressed to Helen Merrill Ltd., 295 Lafayette Street, Suite 915, New York, NY 10012.

Arthur Miller. *Death of a Salesman*. Copyright 1949, renewed © 1977 by Arthur Miller. Reprinted by permission of Viking Penguin, a division of Penguin Putnam, Inc.

Molière [Jean-Baptiste Poquelin]. Excerpt from *The Misanthrope, Comedy in Five Acts, 1666*. Copyright © 1955 and renewed 1983 by Richard Wilbur. Reprinted by permission of Harcourt, Inc.

Willy Russell. Excerpt from Act 1, Scene 6, of *Educating Rita* (New York: Samuel French, 1981). Copyright © 1981 by Willy Russell. Reprinted by permission of Methuen Publishing Ltd.

Milcha Sanchez-Scott. *The Cuban Swimmer*. Copyright © 1994 by Milcha Sanchez-Scott. Originally produced in New York City by INTAR Hispanic American Arts Center. All rights reserved. CAUTION: Professionals and amateurs are hereby warned that *The Cuban Swimmer* is subject to a royalty. It is fully protected under the copyright laws of the United States of America and of all countries covered by the International Copyright Union (including the Dominion of Canada and the rest of the British Commonwealth), the Berne Convention, the Pan-American Copyright Convention and the Universal Copyright Convention as well as all countries with which the United States has reciprocal copyright relations. All rights, including professional/amateur state rights, motion picture, recitation, lecturing, public reading, radio broadcasting, television, video or sound recording, all other forms of mechanical or electronic reproduction, such as CD-ROM, CD-I, information storage and retrieval systems and photocopying and the rights of translation into foreign languages, are strictly reserved. Particular emphasis is laid upon the matter of readings, permission for which must be secured from the author's agent in writing. Inquiries concerning rights should be addressed to: William Morris Agency, Inc., 1325 Avenue of the Americas, New York, NY 10019.

William Shakespeare. *The Tempest* from *The Complete Works of Shakespeare,* Fourth Edition, ed. David Bevington. Copyright © 1997 by Addison-Wesley Educational Publishers, Inc. Reprinted by permission. *Hamlet, Prince of Denmark* from *An Introduction to Shakespeare,* Revised Edition, ed. Craig & Bevington. Reprinted by permission of Addison-Wesley Educational Publishers, Inc.

Sophocles. *Antigone* and *Oedipus the King* from *Three Theban Plays,* trans. Robert Fagles. Copyright © 1982 by Robert Fagles. Reprinted by permission of Viking Penguin, a division of Penguin Putnam, Inc.

Wendy Wasserstein. *Tender Offer*. Copyright © 1991 by Wendy Wasserstein. First published in *Antaeus* 66 (Spring 1991). No part of this material may be reproduced in whole or in part without the express written permission of the author or her agent. Reprinted by permission of Rosenstone/Wender.

Tennessee Williams. *The Glass Menagerie*. Copyright © 1945 by Tennessee Williams and Edwina D. Williams, and renewed 1973 by Tennessee Williams. Reprinted by permission of Random House, Inc.

August Wilson. *Fences*. Copyright © 1986 by August Wilson. Reprinted by permission of Dutton Signet, a division of Penguin Putnam, Inc.

DRAMA COMMENTARIES

Edward Albee. "On Playwriting" from *Dramatics*. Copyright © by Edward Albee. Reprinted by permission of William Morris Agency, Inc.

Richard Amacher. "On *The Sandbox*" (editors' title) from *Edward Albee*. Copyright © 1969 by Twayne Publishers, Inc. Reprinted by permission of Twayne Publishers, an imprint of Simon & Schuster Macmillan.

Aristotle. "On the Elements and General Principles of Tragedy" (editors' title) from *Poetics,* trans. Gerald F. Else. Copyright © 1967. Reprinted by permission of the University of Michigan Press.

James Baldwin. "Sweet Lorraine" Copyright © 1969 by James Baldwin. "Sweet Lorraine" was originally published in *Esquire*. Collected in *The Price of the Ticket* (New York: St. Martin's, 1985). Reprinted by arrangement with the James Baldwin Estate.

John Beaufort. "*Death of a Salesman*: Arthur Miller's New Play an Absorbing Experience." Copyright © 1949 by The Christian Science Publishing Society. This review first appeared in the February 19, 1949, issue of *The Christian Science Monitor* and is reproduced with permission. All rights reserved.

Mary Whitlock Blundell. Excerpt from *Helping Friends and Harming Enemies: A Study in Sophocles and Greek Ethics*. Copyright © 1989. Reprinted by permission of Cambridge University Press.

Geoffrey Bullough. "Sources of Shakespeare's *Hamlet*" (editors' title) from *Narrative and Dramatic Sources of Shakespeare,* 8 vols. Copyright © 1964 and renewed 1992 by Geoffrey Bullough. Reprinted by permission of Columbia University Press.

Aimé Césaire. Final scene from *A Tempest,* trans. Richard Miller. Copyright © 1992 by Richard Miller. Originally published in French as *Une Tempeste* by Editions du Seuil, Paris. Copyright © 1969 by Editions du Seuil. Reprinted by permission of David Campbell Publishers Ltd.

Anne Cheney. "The African Heritage in *A Raisin in the Sun*" (editors' title) from *Lorraine Hansberry*. Copyright © 1984 by G. K. Hall & Company. Reprinted by permission of Twayne Publishers, an imprint of Simon & Schuster Macmillan.

Caryl Churchill. "Interview with Kathleen Betsko and Rachel Koenig" from *Interviews with Contemporary Women Playwrights* by Kathleen Betsko and Rachel Koenig. Copyright © 1987 by Kathleen Betsko and Rachel Koenig. Reprinted by permission of HarperCollins Publishers, Inc.

T. S. Eliot. "Hamlet and His Problems" from *Selected Prose of T. S. Eliot,* ed. Frank Kermode. Originally published in *Athenaeum* (September 26, 1919). Copyright 1919 and renewed 1947 by T. S. Eliot. Reprinted by permission of Faber & Faber Ltd.

Francis Fergusson. "Oedipus, Myth and Play" from *The Idea of a Theater*. Copyright 1949 by Princeton University Press. Reprinted by permission of the publisher.

Sigmund Freud. "The Oedipus Complex" (editors' title) from *The Interpretation of Dreams,* trans. James Strachey. Published in the United States by Basic Books, Inc., 1956, by arrangement with George Allen & Unwin, Ltd. and the Hogarth Press, Ltd. Reprinted by permission of Basic Books, Inc.

Lorraine Hansberry. "An Author's Reflections: Willy Loman, Walter Younger and He Who Must Live" from *The Village Voice Reader,* ed. Daniel Wolf and Edwin Fancher (New York: Doubleday, 1962). Reprinted by permission of The Village Voice.

H. D. F. Kitto. "*Hamlet* and the *Oedipus*" from *Form and Meaning in Drama*. Copyright © 1956. Reprinted by permission of Methuen Publishing Ltd.

John Lahr. "Making Willy Loman" from the January 25, 1999, issue of *The New Yorker*. Copyright © 1999 by John Lahr. Reprinted by permission of the author.

Julius Lester. "The Heroic Dimension in *A Raisin in the Sun*" (editors' title) from *Les Blancs: The Collected Last Plays of Lorraine Hansberry,* ed. Robert Nemiroff. Copyright © 1972 by Julius Lester. Reprinted by permission of the author, in care of Claudia Menza, Literary Agent.

Arthur Miller. Excerpt from an interview in *Paris Review* 38. Copyright © 1967 by The Paris Review, Inc. Reprinted by permission of The Paris Review.

Leonard Mustazza. "Generic Translation and Thematic Shift in Susan Glaspell's *Trifles* and 'A Jury of Her Peers'" from *Studies in Short Fiction* 26 (1989): 489–96. Copyright © 1989 by Newbury College. Reprinted by permission of Studies in Short Fiction, Newbury College, Newbury, SC.

Benjamin Nelson. "Problems in *The Glass Menagerie*" from *Tennessee Williams: The Man and His Work* (New York: I. Obolensky, 1961). Copyright © 1961 by Benjamin Nelson. Reprinted by permission of the author.

Helge Normann Nilsen. "Marxism and the Early Plays of Arthur Miller" originally titled "From *Honors at Dawn* to *Death of a Salesman*: Marxism and the Early Plays of Arthur Miller" in *English Studies* 75.2 (1994). Copyright © 1994 by Swets & Zeitlinger. Reprinted by permission of Swets Publishing Service, Lisse, The Netherlands.

Frank Rich. "A Review of *Fences*." Originally titled "Theatre Family Ties in Wilson's *Fences*." Copyright © 1987 by The New York Times Company. Reprinted by permission.

Muriel Rukeyser. "Myth" from *A Muriel Rukeyser Reader,* ed. Jan Heller Levi (New York: Norton, 1994). Originally collected in *Breaking Open* (New York: Random, 1973). Copyright © 1973 by Muriel Rukeyser. Reprinted by permission of William L. Rukeyser.

Sandra Saari. "Female Becomes Human: Nora Transformed in *A Doll House*" from *Contemporary Approaches to Ibsen: Reports from the Fourth International Ibsen Seminar* (Skien, 1988). Reprinted by permission of Norwegian University Press.

Bernard Shaw. "On *A Doll House*" from *The Quintessence of Ibsenism, Now Completed to the Death of Ibsen* (New York: Brentano, 1919). Originally published (London: W. Scott, 1891). Reprinted by permission of the Society of Authors.

Tom Stoppard. *Dogg's Hamlet: The Encore* excerpted from *Dogg's Hamlet, Cahoot's Macbeth*. Copyright © 1979 by Tom Stoppard. Reprinted by permission of Peters, Fraser & Dunlop Group and Faber & Faber Ltd.

Joan Templeton. "Is *A Doll House* a Feminist Text?" excerpted from "The *Doll House* Backlash: Criticism, Feminism, and Ibsen" in *Proceedings of the Modern Language Association* (January 1989). Copyright © 1989 by The Modern Language Association. Reprinted by permission of The Modern Language Association.

Leo Tolstoy. "Shakespeare's Immoral Frame of Mind" from *Shakespeare: Court, Crowd, and Playhouse,* ed. François Laroque (London: Thames & Hudson, 1993). Copyright © 1993 by François Laroque. Reprinted by permission of Editions Gallimard, Paris.

Margaret B. Wilkerson. "Hansberry's Awareness of Culture and Gender" excerpted from *Les Blancs: The Collected Last Plays of Lorraine Hansberry,* ed. Robert Nemiroff. Copyright © 1972 by Robert Nemiroff. Reprinted by permission of Random House, Inc.

Tennessee Williams. "Production Notes to *The Glass Menagerie*" from *The Theatre of Tennessee Williams,* Volume 1. Copyright © 1945 by Tennessee Williams and Edwina D. Williams. "Portrait of a Girl in Glass" from *Collected Stories*. Copyright © 1948 by Tennessee Williams. Reprinted by permission of New Directions Publishing Corporation.

August Wilson. "Interview with David Savran" from *In Their Own Voices* by David Savran. Copyright © 1987. Reprinted by permission of Theatre Communications Group.

Virginia Woolf. "What If Shakespeare Had Had a Sister?" (editors' title) excerpted from *A Room of One's Own* by Virginia Woolf. Copyright 1929 by Harcourt, Inc., and renewed 1957 by Leonard Woolf. Reprinted by permission of the publisher.

INDEX OF FIRST LINES

INDEX OF AUTHORS AND TITLES

INDEX OF TERMS

The boldfaced page references indicate where a key term is highlighted in the text.

Fine plays tend to utilize the one big fat character who runs right through the middle of the structure, by action or implication, with whom we rise or fall.
■ **LORRAINE HANSBERRY**

General rules in art are useful chiefly as a lamp in a mine, or a handrail down a black stairway: they are necessary for the sake of the guidance they give, but it is a mistake, once they are formulated, to be too much in awe of them.
■ **EDITH WHARTON**

A poem is the very image of life expressed in its eternal truth.
■ **PERCY BYSSHE SHELLEY**

To learn to write is to learn to have ideas.
■ **ROBERT FROST**

A major writer combines these three — storyteller, teacher, enchanter — but it is the enchanter in him that predominates and makes him a major writer.
■ **VLADIMIR NABOKOV**

Fiction is history, human history, or it is nothing. But it is also more than that; it stands on firmer ground, being based on the reality of forms and the observation of social phenomena, whereas history is based on documents, and the reading of print and handwriting — on second-hand impression. Thus fiction is nearer truth.
■ **JOSEPH CONRAD**